30 YEARS OF
NEW MUSICAL EXPRESS
NME
ALBUM CHARTS

BOXTREE

Z 827838

Thirty Years Of NME Album Charts is designed and produced by:

Osborne Books, 70 High Street, Snainton, North Yorkshire YO13 9AJ

The compilers and authors would like to thank the following people who have helped in various and invaluable ways: Eileen Buss, Michael Randolfi, Alan Lewis, Fiona Foulgar, Steve Sutherland, Dick Whincup, Sarah Beattie, Nigel Hinton, Phil Hardy, Andy Lineham, J Blackmore Reed, Arthur Berman, Bryan Hodgson.

Cover design by Phil Clark
Photo research by Cate Jago

781.66 0942

First published in the UK 1993 by:
BOXTREE Ltd
Broadwall House
21 Broadwall
London SE1 9PL

10 9 8 7 6 5 4 3 2 1

NME Album Charts June 1962 to May 1988, Copyright IPC Magazines Ltd.
NME Album Charts June 1988 to July 1993, Copyright MRIB Ltd.

Linotron output by Adverset, Scarborough
Printed and bound in Great Britain by
BPCC Hazell Books Ltd
Member of BPCC Ltd

ISBN: 1 85283 889 2

A catalogue record for this book is available from the British Library.

The NME Album Charts

The charts that follow differ in some important respects from those printed weekly in the NME. As in the sister volume to this book, *Forty Years Of NME Charts,* the date at the head of each chart is the Saturday at the end of the week in which the chart was published. In order to fit the space available we have very occasionally abbreviated the titles of records. The full title of the record can be found in the indexes. Under intense pressure of producing the best music weekly in Britain, mistakes were sometimes made in compiling the chart. These have been corrected wherever possible.

Along with most other papers and magazines the NME usually misses one or two issues over the Christmas and New Year period. We have not duplicated the previous week's chart for these missing weeks, but gone on to the next published chart.

The Title Index and Artist Index are both a guide to locating records in the charts, and a complete guide to the chart career of every artist that has appeared in the NME Album Chart. A full explanation of how the indexes should be used is given on page 412.

*The NME album charts
started on the right note –
with Elvis at Number 1*

9 June 1962

- 1 BLUE HAWAII
  Elvis Presley (RCA)
- 2 WEST SIDE STORY
  Soundtrack (Philips)
- 3 IT'S TRAD DAD
  Soundtrack (Columbia)
- 4 SOUTH PACIFIC
  Soundtrack (RCA)
- 5 THE YOUNG ONES
  Cliff Richard & the Shadows (Columbia)
- 6 I REMEMBER TOMMY
  Frank Sinatra (Reprise)
- 7 SINATRA AND STRINGS
  Frank Sinatra (Reprise)
- 8 THE BLACK AND WHITE MINSTREL SHOW
  George Mitchell Minstrels (HMV)
- 9 THE SOUND OF MUSIC
  London Cast (HMV)
- 10 HONEY HIT PARADE
  Various Artists (Golden Guinea)

16 June 1962

- 1 1 BLUE HAWAII
  Elvis Presley (RCA)
- 2 2 WEST SIDE STORY
  Soundtrack (Philips)
- 3 3 IT'S TRAD DAD
  Soundtrack (Columbia)
- 5 4 THE YOUNG ONES
  Cliff Richard & the Shadows (Columbia)
- 4 5 SOUTH PACIFIC
  Soundtrack (RCA)
- 8 6 THE BLACK AND WHITE MINSTREL SHOW
  George Mitchell Minstrels (HMV)
- 7 7 SINATRA AND STRINGS
  Frank Sinatra (Reprise)
- - 8 THE ROARING TWENTIES - SONGS FROM THE TV SERIES
  Dorothy Provine (Warner Bros.)
- 6 9 I REMEMBER TOMMY
  Frank Sinatra (Reprise)
- - 10 THE SHADOWS
  Shadows (Columbia)

23 June 1962

- 2 1 WEST SIDE STORY
  Soundtrack (Philips)
- 1 2 BLUE HAWAII
  Elvis Presley (RCA)
- 7 3 SINATRA AND STRINGS
  Frank Sinatra (Reprise)
- 6 4 THE BLACK AND WHITE MINSTREL SHOW
  George Mitchell Minstrels (HMV)
- 4 5 THE YOUNG ONES
  Cliff Richard & the Shadows (Columbia)
- 5 6 SOUTH PACIFIC
  Soundtrack (RCA)
- 3 6 IT'S TRAD DAD
  Soundtrack (Columbia)
- 10 8 THE SHADOWS
  Shadows (Columbia)
- 6 9 I REMEMBER TOMMY
  Frank Sinatra (Reprise)
- 8 10 THE ROARING TWENTIES - SONGS FROM THE TV SERIES
  Dorothy Provine (Warner Bros.)

30 June 1962

- 1 1 WEST SIDE STORY
  Soundtrack (Philips)
- 2 2 BLUE HAWAII
  Elvis Presley (RCA)
- 6 3 SOUTH PACIFIC
  Soundtrack (RCA)
- 4 4 THE BLACK AND WHITE MINSTREL SHOW
  George Mitchell Minstrels (HMV)
- 6 5 IT'S TRAD DAD
  Soundtrack (Columbia)
- 3 6 SINATRA AND STRINGS
  Frank Sinatra (Reprise)
- 5 7 THE YOUNG ONES
  Cliff Richard & the Shadows (Columbia)
- 10 8 THE ROARING TWENTIES - SONGS FROM THE TV SERIES
  Dorothy Provine (Warner Bros.)
- - 9 ANOTHER BLACK AND WHITE MINSTREL SHOW
  George Mitchell Minstrels (HMV)
- - 10 WIMOWEH
  Karl Denver (Ace of Clubs)
- 9 10 I REMEMBER TOMMY
  Frank Sinatra (Reprise)

7 July 1962

- - 1 POT LUCK Elvis Presley (RCA)
- 1 2 WEST SIDE STORY
  Soundtrack (Philips)
- 2 3 BLUE HAWAII
  Elvis Presley (RCA)
- 4 4 THE BLACK AND WHITE MINSTREL SHOW
  George Mitchell Minstrels (HMV)
- 6 5 SINATRA AND STRINGS
  Frank Sinatra (Reprise)
- 5 6 IT'S TRAD DAD
  Soundtrack (Columbia)
- 8 7 THE ROARING TWENTIES - SONGS FROM THE TV SERIES
  Dorothy Provine (Warner Bros.)
- 3 8 SOUTH PACIFIC
  Soundtrack (RCA)
- 9 9 ANOTHER BLACK AND WHITE MINSTREL SHOW
  George Mitchell Minstrels (HMV)
- - 10 STRANGER ON THE SHORE
  Mr. Acker Bilk (Columbia)

14 July 1962

- 1 1 POT LUCK Elvis Presley (RCA)
- 2 2 WEST SIDE STORY
  Soundtrack (Philips)
- 3 3 BLUE HAWAII
  Elvis Presley (RCA)
- 8 4 SOUTH PACIFIC
  Soundtrack (RCA)
- 4 5 THE BLACK AND WHITE MINSTREL SHOW
  George Mitchell Minstrels (HMV)
- 6 6 IT'S TRAD DAD
  Soundtrack (Columbia)
- 5 7 SINATRA AND STRINGS
  Frank Sinatra (Reprise)
- - 8 BLITZ! Original Cast (HMV)
- 7 9 THE ROARING TWENTIES - SONGS FROM THE TV SERIES
  Dorothy Provine (Warner Bros.)
- - 10 THE YOUNG ONES
  Cliff Richard & the Shadows (Columbia)
- - 10 TWISTIN' 'N' TWANGIN'
  Duane Eddy (London)

21 July 1962

- 1 1 POT LUCK Elvis Presley (RCA)
- 2 2 WEST SIDE STORY
  Soundtrack (Philips)
- 3 3 BLUE HAWAII
  Elvis Presley (RCA)
- 5 4 THE BLACK AND WHITE MINSTREL SHOW
  George Mitchell Minstrels (HMV)
- 4 5 SOUTH PACIFIC
  Soundtrack (RCA)
- 6 6 IT'S TRAD DAD
  Soundtrack (Columbia)
- 8 7 BLITZ! Original Cast (HMV)
- 7 7 SINATRA AND STRINGS
  Frank Sinatra (Reprise)
- 10 9 THE YOUNG ONES
  Cliff Richard & the Shadows (Columbia)
- 9 10 THE ROARING TWENTIES - SONGS FROM THE TV SERIES
  Dorothy Provine (Warner Bros.)

28 July 1962

- 1 1 POT LUCK Elvis Presley (RCA)
- 2 2 WEST SIDE STORY
  Soundtrack (Philips)
- 4 3 THE BLACK AND WHITE MINSTREL SHOW
  George Mitchell Minstrels (HMV)
- 5 4 SOUTH PACIFIC
  Soundtrack (RCA)
- 3 5 BLUE HAWAII
  Elvis Presley (RCA)
- 7 6 BLITZ! Original Cast (HMV)
- 6 7 IT'S TRAD DAD
  Soundtrack (Columbia)
- - 8 MODERN SOUNDS IN COUNTRY AND WESTERN MUSIC Ray Charles (HMV)
- 7 8 SINATRA AND STRINGS
  Frank Sinatra (Reprise)
- - 10 THE SOUND OF MUSIC
  London Cast (HMV)

The album chart was born - but the single still ruled. Most LPs were greatest hits compilations, film soundtracks or spin-offs from TV. Aside from "sophisticated artistes" (Frank Sinatra) only the very biggest-sellers in pop made LPs of new material at all, and even these offered potential singles plus filler tracks. Exceptions were Ray Charles' *Modern Sounds In Country And Western* (a prototype Concept Album: a radical fusion of country and soul) and *Honey Hit Parade*, a spin-off from a Radio Luxembourg show.

August – September 1962

last this
week

4 August 1962

2	1	WEST SIDE STORY Soundtrack (Philips)
1	2	POT LUCK Elvis Presley (RCA)
5	3	BLUE HAWAII Elvis Presley (RCA)
3	4	THE BLACK AND WHITE MINSTREL SHOW George Mitchell Minstrels (HMV)
4	5	SOUTH PACIFIC Soundtrack (RCA)
8	6	MODERN SOUNDS IN COUNTRY AND WESTERN MUSIC Ray Charles (HMV)
-	7	THE SHADOWS Shadows (Columbia)
8	8	SINATRA AND STRINGS Frank Sinatra (Reprise)
-	9	THE BUDDY HOLLY STORY VOL. 1 Buddy Holly (Coral)
7	10	IT'S TRAD DAD Soundtrack (Columbia)

11 August 1962

2	1	POT LUCK Elvis Presley (RCA)
1	2	WEST SIDE STORY Soundtrack (Philips)
5	3	SOUTH PACIFIC Soundtrack (RCA)
4	4	THE BLACK AND WHITE MINSTREL SHOW George Mitchell Minstrels (HMV)
-	5	BLITZ! Original Cast (HMV)
3	6	BLUE HAWAII Elvis Presley (RCA)
6	7	MODERN SOUNDS IN COUNTRY AND WESTERN MUSIC Ray Charles (HMV)
-	8	TWISTIN' 'N' TWANGIN' Duane Eddy (London)
-	9	THE YOUNG ONES Cliff Richard & the Shadows (Columbia)
8	10	SINATRA AND STRINGS Frank Sinatra (Reprise)

18 August 1962

1	1	POT LUCK Elvis Presley (RCA)
2	2	WEST SIDE STORY Soundtrack (Philips)
4	3	THE BLACK AND WHITE MINSTREL SHOW George Mitchell Minstrels (HMV)
5	4	BLITZ! Original Cast (HMV)
3	5	SOUTH PACIFIC Soundtrack (RCA)
6	6	BLUE HAWAII Elvis Presley (RCA)
8	7	TWISTIN' 'N' TWANGIN' Duane Eddy (London)
7	8	MODERN SOUNDS IN COUNTRY AND WESTERN MUSIC Ray Charles (HMV)
-	9	LONDON BY NIGHT Frank Sinatra (Reprise)
10	10	SINATRA AND STRINGS Frank Sinatra (Reprise)

25 August 1962

2	1	WEST SIDE STORY Soundtrack (Philips)
1	2	POT LUCK Elvis Presley (RCA)
3	3	THE BLACK AND WHITE MINSTREL SHOW George Mitchell Minstrels (HMV)
6	4	BLUE HAWAII Elvis Presley (RCA)
4	5	SOUTH PACIFIC Soundtrack (RCA)
4	6	BLITZ! Original Cast (HMV)
8	7	MODERN SOUNDS IN COUNTRY AND WESTERN MUSIC Ray Charles (HMV)
7	8	TWISTIN' 'N' TWANGIN' Duane Eddy (London)
-	9	THE SHADOWS Shadows (Columbia)
-	10	A PICTURE OF YOU Joe Brown (Golden Guinea)
-	10	STRANGER ON THE SHORE Mr. Acker Bilk (Columbia)

1 September 1962

1	1	WEST SIDE STORY Soundtrack (Philips)
2	2	POT LUCK Elvis Presley (RCA)
-	3	THE BEST OF BALL, BARBER AND BILK Kenny Ball, Chris Barber & Acker Bilk (Golden Guinea)
-	4	A GOLDEN AGE OF DONEGAN Lonnie Donegan (Golden Guinea)
3	5	THE BLACK AND WHITE MINSTREL SHOW George Mitchell Minstrels (HMV)
5	5	SOUTH PACIFIC Soundtrack (RCA)
4	7	BLUE HAWAII Elvis Presley (RCA)
10	7	A PICTURE OF YOU Joe Brown (Golden Guinea)
6	9	BLITZ! Original Cast (HMV)
7	10	MODERN SOUNDS IN COUNTRY AND WESTERN MUSIC Ray Charles (HMV)

8 September 1962

1	1	WEST SIDE STORY Soundtrack (Philips)
4	2	A GOLDEN AGE OF DONEGAN Lonnie Donegan (Golden Guinea)
2	3	POT LUCK Elvis Presley (RCA)
3	4	THE BEST OF BALL, BARBER AND BILK Kenny Ball, Chris Barber & Acker Bilk (Golden Guinea)
5	5	THE BLACK AND WHITE MINSTREL SHOW George Mitchell Minstrels (HMV)
5	6	SOUTH PACIFIC Soundtrack (RCA)
7	7	A PICTURE OF YOU Joe Brown (Golden Guinea)
7	8	BLUE HAWAII Elvis Presley (RCA)
9	9	BLITZ! Original Cast (HMV)
-	10	THE MUSIC MAN Soundtrack (Warner Bros.)

15 September 1962

1	1	WEST SIDE STORY Soundtrack (Philips)
2	2	A GOLDEN AGE OF DONEGAN Lonnie Donegan (Golden Guinea)
4	3	THE BEST OF BALL, BARBER AND BILK Kenny Ball, Chris Barber & Acker Bilk (Golden Guinea)
3	4	POT LUCK Elvis Presley (RCA)
7	5	A PICTURE OF YOU Joe Brown (Golden Guinea)
5	6	THE BLACK AND WHITE MINSTREL SHOW George Mitchell Minstrels (HMV)
6	7	SOUTH PACIFIC Soundtrack (RCA)
8	8	BLUE HAWAII Elvis Presley (RCA)
-	9	MODERN SOUNDS IN COUNTRY AND WESTERN MUSIC Ray Charles (HMV)
-	10	THE SOUND OF MUSIC London Cast (HMV)
-	10	'S WONDERFUL 'S MARVELLOUS Ray Conniff (CBS)

22 September 1962

1	1	WEST SIDE STORY Soundtrack (Philips)
2	2	A GOLDEN AGE OF DONEGAN Lonnie Donegan (Golden Guinea)
3	3	THE BEST OF BALL, BARBER AND BILK Kenny Ball, Chris Barber & Acker Bilk (Golden Guinea)
4	4	POT LUCK Elvis Presley (RCA)
6	5	THE BLACK AND WHITE MINSTREL SHOW George Mitchell Minstrels (HMV)
5	6	A PICTURE OF YOU Joe Brown (Golden Guinea)
7	7	SOUTH PACIFIC Soundtrack (RCA)
8	8	BLUE HAWAII Elvis Presley (RCA)
9	9	MODERN SOUNDS IN COUNTRY AND WESTERN MUSIC Ray Charles (HMV)
-	10	32 MINUTES AND 17 SECONDS Cliff Richard (Columbia)

Radio Luxembourg was the only respite from the BBC Light Programme: it actually played lots of records, because it sold airtime to record companies. The big ones (EMI and Decca, embracing exciting American-music labels: London, Coral, RCA) had half-hour shows, like Jimmy Savile's Teen And 20 Disc Club (Elvis was member no. 11321). Smaller companies (Pye, Philips) had quarter-hours they struggled to fill with Britishers – note the hits on Pye's cheap label Golden Guinea.

6

29 September 1962

last week	this week	
1	1	WEST SIDE STORY Soundtrack (Philips)
2	2	A GOLDEN AGE OF DONEGAN Lonnie Donegan (Golden Guinea)
3	3	THE BEST OF BALL, BARBER AND BILK Kenny Ball, Chris Barber & Acker Bilk (Golden Guinea)
6	4	A PICTURE OF YOU Joe Brown (Golden Guinea)
4	5	POT LUCK Elvis Presley (RCA)
10	6	32 MINUTES AND 17 SECONDS Cliff Richard (Columbia)
5	7	THE BLACK AND WHITE MINSTREL SHOW George Mitchell Minstrels (HMV)
8	8	BLUE HAWAII Elvis Presley (RCA)
7	9	SOUTH PACIFIC Soundtrack (RCA)
9	10	MODERN SOUNDS IN COUNTRY AND WESTERN MUSIC Ray Charles (HMV)

6 October 1962

1	1	WEST SIDE STORY Soundtrack (Philips)
3	2	THE BEST OF BALL, BARBER AND BILK Kenny Ball, Chris Barber & Acker Bilk (Golden Guinea)
2	3	A GOLDEN AGE OF DONEGAN Lonnie Donegan (Golden Guinea)
4	4	A PICTURE OF YOU Joe Brown (Golden Guinea)
7	5	THE BLACK AND WHITE MINSTREL SHOW George Mitchell Minstrels (HMV)
5	6	POT LUCK Elvis Presley (RCA)
6	7	32 MINUTES AND 17 SECONDS Cliff Richard (Columbia)
10	8	MODERN SOUNDS IN COUNTRY AND WESTERN MUSIC Ray Charles (HMV)
-	9	'S WONDERFUL 'S MARVELLOUS Ray Conniff (CBS)
-	9	RAY CONNIFF HI-FI COMPANION Ray Conniff (Philips)
-	9	A PICTURE OF JOE BROWN Joe Brown (Ace of Clubs)

13 October 1962

1	1	WEST SIDE STORY Soundtrack (Philips)
3	2	A GOLDEN AGE OF DONEGAN Lonnie Donegan (Golden Guinea)
2	3	THE BEST OF BALL, BARBER AND BILK Kenny Ball, Chris Barber & Acker Bilk (Golden Guinea)
-	4	OUT OF THE SHADOWS Shadows (Columbia)
5	5	THE BLACK AND WHITE MINSTREL SHOW George Mitchell Minstrels (HMV)
4	6	A PICTURE OF YOU Joe Brown (Golden Guinea)
7	7	32 MINUTES AND 17 SECONDS Cliff Richard (Columbia)
-	8	SOUTH PACIFIC Soundtrack (RCA)
-	9	THE SOUND OF MUSIC London Cast (HMV)
-	10	BLITZ! Original Cast (HMV)

20 October 1962

1	1	WEST SIDE STORY Soundtrack (Philips)
4	2	OUT OF THE SHADOWS Shadows (Columbia)
3	3	THE BEST OF BALL, BARBER AND BILK Kenny Ball, Chris Barber & Acker Bilk (Golden Guinea)
2	4	A GOLDEN AGE OF DONEGAN Lonnie Donegan (Golden Guinea)
6	5	A PICTURE OF YOU Joe Brown (Golden Guinea)
5	6	THE BLACK AND WHITE MINSTREL SHOW George Mitchell Minstrels (HMV)
7	7	32 MINUTES AND 17 SECONDS Cliff Richard (Columbia)
-	8	POT LUCK Elvis Presley (RCA)
-	9	MODERN SOUNDS IN COUNTRY AND WESTERN MUSIC Ray Charles (HMV)
-	9	PORGY AND BESS Soundtrack (Philips)

27 October 1962

2	1	OUT OF THE SHADOWS Shadows (Columbia)
1	2	WEST SIDE STORY Soundtrack (CBS)
3	3	THE BEST OF BALL, BARBER AND BILK Kenny Ball, Chris Barber & Acker Bilk (Golden Guinea)
4	4	A GOLDEN AGE OF DONEGAN Lonnie Donegan (Golden Guinea)
-	5	ON STAGE WITH THE GEORGE MITCHELL MINSTRELS George Mitchell Minstrels (HMV)
7	6	32 MINUTES & 17 SECONDS Cliff Richard (Columbia)
5	7	A PICTURE OF YOU Joe Brown (Golden Guinea)
-	8	SOUTH PACIFIC Soundtrack (RCA)
8	9	POT LUCK Elvis Presley (RCA)
6	10	THE BLACK AND WHITE MINSTREL SHOW George Mitchell Minstrels (HMV)
-	10	NAT 'KING' COLE SINGS, THE GEORGE SHEARING QUINTET PLAYS Nat 'King' Cole & George Shearing (Capitol)

3 November 1962

2	1	WEST SIDE STORY Soundtrack (CBS)
1	2	OUT OF THE SHADOWS Shadows (Columbia)
5	3	ON STAGE WITH THE GEORGE MITCHELL MINSTRELS George Mitchell Minstrels (HMV)
3	4	THE BEST OF BALL, BARBER AND BILK Kenny Ball, Chris Barber & Acker Bilk (Golden Guinea)
4	5	A GOLDEN AGE OF DONEGAN Lonnie Donegan (Golden Guinea)
8	6	SOUTH PACIFIC Soundtrack (RCA)
9	6	POT LUCK Elvis Presley (RCA)
10	8	THE BLACK AND WHITE MINSTREL SHOW George Mitchell Minstrels (HMV)
-	9	MODERN SOUNDS IN COUNTRY AND WESTERN MUSIC Ray Charles (HMV)
7	10	A PICTURE OF YOU Joe Brown (Golden Guinea)

10 November 1962

1	1	WEST SIDE STORY Soundtrack (CBS)
2	2	OUT OF THE SHADOWS Shadows (Columbia)
3	3	ON STAGE WITH THE GEORGE MITCHELL MINSTRELS George Mitchell Minstrels (HMV)
4	4	THE BEST OF BALL, BARBER AND BILK Kenny Ball, Chris Barber & Acker Bilk (Golden Guinea)
5	5	A GOLDEN AGE OF DONEGAN Lonnie Donegan (Golden Guinea)
6	6	SOUTH PACIFIC Soundtrack (RCA)
-	7	NAT 'KING' COLE SINGS, THE GEORGE SHEARING QUINTET PLAYS Nat 'King' Cole & George Shearing (Capitol)
8	8	THE BLACK AND WHITE MINSTREL SHOW George Mitchell Minstrels (HMV)
10	8	A PICTURE OF YOU Joe Brown (Golden Guinea)
6	10	POT LUCK Elvis Presley (RCA)

17 November 1962

1	1	WEST SIDE STORY Soundtrack (CBS)
3	2	ON STAGE WITH THE GEORGE MITCHELL MINSTRELS George Mitchell Minstrels (HMV)
2	3	OUT OF THE SHADOWS Shadows (Columbia)
8	4	THE BLACK AND WHITE MINSTREL SHOW George Mitchell Minstrels (HMV)
5	5	A GOLDEN AGE OF DONEGAN Lonnie Donegan (Golden Guinea)
4	6	THE BEST OF BALL, BARBER AND BILK Kenny Ball, Chris Barber & Acker Bilk (Golden Guinea)
6	7	SOUTH PACIFIC Soundtrack (RCA)
8	8	A PICTURE OF YOU Joe Brown (Golden Guinea)
-	9	BOBBY VEE MEETS THE CRICKETS Bobby Vee & the Crickets (Liberty)
7	10	NAT 'KING' COLE SINGS, THE GEORGE SHEARING QUINTET PLAYS Nat 'King' Cole & George Shearing (Capitol)

BBC DJ Brian Matthew wrote in his book *Trad Mad* that "the sixties may well come to be labelled the ten years of Trad..." Mercifully he was mistaken. Trad was to prove a short-lived craze, though this autumn was its zenith. Not content with pastiches of pre-war jazz for people alarmed by anything more modern, adults also bought huge numbers of Black And White Minstrel records, stimulated by TV series in which white Britons parodied Dixieland. In the real Deep South segregation remained.

November – December 1962

24 November 1962

last	this	
2	1	ON STAGE WITH THE GEORGE MITCHELL MINSTRELS George Mitchell Minstrels (HMV)
1	2	WEST SIDE STORY Soundtrack (CBS)
3	3	OUT OF THE SHADOWS Shadows (Columbia)
6	4	THE BEST OF BALL, BARBER AND BILK Kenny Ball, Chris Barber & Acker Bilk (Golden Guinea)
4	5	THE BLACK AND WHITE MINSTREL SHOW George Mitchell Minstrels (HMV)
5	5	A GOLDEN AGE OF DONEGAN Lonnie Donegan (Golden Guinea)
-	7	POT LUCK Elvis Presley (RCA)
8	8	A PICTURE OF YOU Joe Brown (Golden Guinea)
7	9	SOUTH PACIFIC Soundtrack (RCA)
9	9	BOBBY VEE MEETS THE CRICKETS Bobby Vee & the Crickets (Liberty)

1 December 1962

last	this	
1	1	ON STAGE WITH THE GEORGE MITCHELL MINSTRELS George Mitchell Minstrels (HMV)
2	2	WEST SIDE STORY Soundtrack (CBS)
4	3	THE BEST OF BALL, BARBER AND BILK Kenny Ball, Chris Barber & Acker Bilk (Golden Guinea)
3	4	OUT OF THE SHADOWS Shadows (Columbia)
5	5	THE BLACK AND WHITE MINSTREL SHOW George Mitchell Minstrels (HMV)
5	6	A GOLDEN AGE OF DONEGAN Lonnie Donegan (Golden Guinea)
9	7	BOBBY VEE MEETS THE CRICKETS Bobby Vee & the Crickets (Liberty)
8	8	A PICTURE OF YOU Joe Brown (Golden Guinea)
9	9	SOUTH PACIFIC Soundtrack (RCA)
7	10	POT LUCK Elvis Presley (RCA)

8 December 1962

last	this	
1	1	ON STAGE WITH THE GEORGE MITCHELL MINSTRELS George Mitchell Minstrels (HMV)
2	2	WEST SIDE STORY Soundtrack (CBS)
5	3	THE BLACK AND WHITE MINSTREL SHOW George Mitchell Minstrels (HMV)
4	4	OUT OF THE SHADOWS Shadows (Columbia)
3	5	THE BEST OF BALL, BARBER AND BILK Kenny Ball, Chris Barber & Acker Bilk (Golden Guinea)
6	6	A GOLDEN AGE OF DONEGAN Lonnie Donegan (Golden Guinea)
7	7	BOBBY VEE MEETS THE CRICKETS Bobby Vee & the Crickets (Liberty)
-	8	ROCK 'N' ROLL NO. 2 Elvis Presley (RCA)
9	9	SOUTH PACIFIC Soundtrack (RCA)
10	10	POT LUCK Elvis Presley (RCA)

15 December 1962

last	this	
1	1	ON STAGE WITH THE GEORGE MITCHELL MINSTRELS George Mitchell Minstrels (HMV)
2	2	WEST SIDE STORY Soundtrack (CBS)
8	3	ROCK 'N' ROLL NO. 2 Elvis Presley (RCA)
3	4	THE BLACK AND WHITE MINSTREL SHOW George Mitchell Minstrels (HMV)
7	5	BOBBY VEE MEETS THE CRICKETS Bobby Vee & the Crickets (Liberty)
4	6	OUT OF THE SHADOWS Shadows (Columbia)
9	7	SOUTH PACIFIC Soundtrack (RCA)
-	8	ANOTHER BLACK AND WHITE MINSTREL SHOW George Mitchell Minstrels (HMV)
-	9	32 MINUTES AND 17 SECONDS Cliff Richard (Columbia)
5	10	THE BEST OF BALL, BARBER AND BILK Kenny Ball, Chris Barber & Acker Bilk (Golden Guinea)

22 December 1962

last	this	
1	1	ON STAGE WITH THE GEORGE MITCHELL MINSTRELS George Mitchell Minstrels (HMV)
4	2	THE BLACK AND WHITE MINSTREL SHOW George Mitchell Minstrels (HMV)
2	3	WEST SIDE STORY Soundtrack (CBS)
3	4	ROCK 'N' ROLL NO. 2 Elvis Presley (RCA)
8	5	ANOTHER BLACK AND WHITE MINSTREL SHOW George Mitchell Minstrels (HMV)
5	6	BOBBY VEE MEETS THE CRICKETS Bobby Vee & the Crickets (Liberty)
6	6	OUT OF THE SHADOWS Shadows (Columbia)
7	8	SOUTH PACIFIC Soundtrack (RCA)
10	9	THE BEST OF BALL, BARBER AND BILK Kenny Ball, Chris Barber & Acker Bilk (Golden Guinea)
-	10	SINATRA AND SWINGING BRASS Frank Sinatra (Reprise)

29 December 1962

last	this	
1	1	ON STAGE WITH THE GEORGE MITCHELL MINSTRELS George Mitchell Minstrels (HMV)
2	2	THE BLACK AND WHITE MINSTREL SHOW George Mitchell Minstrels (HMV)
4	3	ROCK 'N' ROLL NO. 2 Elvis Presley (RCA)
3	4	WEST SIDE STORY Soundtrack (CBS)
6	5	OUT OF THE SHADOWS Shadows (Columbia)
5	6	ANOTHER BLACK AND WHITE MINSTREL SHOW George Mitchell Minstrels (HMV)
9	7	THE BEST OF BALL, BARBER AND BILK Kenny Ball, Chris Barber & Acker Bilk (Golden Guinea)
10	8	SINATRA AND SWINGING BRASS Frank Sinatra (Reprise)
6	8	BOBBY VEE MEETS THE CRICKETS Bobby Vee & the Crickets (Liberty)
8	10	SOUTH PACIFIC Soundtrack (RCA)

The grown-ups dreamed of a white Christmas with the Black And White Minstrels at Nos 1,2 and 5. While parents also bought each other soundtracks of musicals, trad, Sinatra and swinging brass, there was room in the charts for just three pop acts: Bobby Vee meeting the Crickets, the Shadows and Elvis. Vee personified the legendary clean-cut Bobbies of post-rock'n'roll; the Shadows were big because they had headed another craze of the day: for guitar-based instrumental hit singles.

5 January 1963

last this
week

1	1	ON STAGE WITH THE GEORGE MITCHELL MINSTRELS George Mitchell Minstrels (HMV)
4	2	WEST SIDE STORY Soundtrack (CBS)
2	3	THE BLACK AND WHITE MINSTREL SHOW George Mitchell Minstrels (HMV)
5	4	OUT OF THE SHADOWS Shadows (Columbia)
3	5	ROCK 'N' ROLL NO. 2 Elvis Presley (RCA)
8	6	BOBBY VEE MEETS THE CRICKETS Bobby Vee & the Crickets (Liberty)
6	7	ANOTHER BLACK AND WHITE MINSTREL SHOW George Mitchell Minstrels (HMV)
10	7	SOUTH PACIFIC Soundtrack (RCA)
7	9	THE BEST OF BALL, BARBER AND BILK Kenny Ball, Chris Barber & Acker Bilk (Golden Guinea)
8	9	SINATRA AND SWINGING BRASS Frank Sinatra (Reprise)

12 January 1963

2	1	WEST SIDE STORY Soundtrack (CBS)
1	2	ON STAGE WITH THE GEORGE MITCHELL MINSTRELS George Mitchell Minstrels (HMV)
4	3	OUT OF THE SHADOWS Shadows (Columbia)
6	4	BOBBY VEE MEETS THE CRICKETS Bobby Vee & the Crickets (Liberty)
5	5	ROCK 'N' ROLL NO. 2 Elvis Presley (RCA)
3	6	THE BLACK AND WHITE MINSTREL SHOW George Mitchell Minstrels (HMV)
7	7	SOUTH PACIFIC Soundtrack (RCA)
-	8	A PICTURE OF YOU Joe Brown (Golden Guinea)
7	9	ANOTHER BLACK AND WHITE MINSTREL SHOW George Mitchell Minstrels (HMV)
9	9	SINATRA AND SWINGING BRASS Frank Sinatra (Reprise)

19 January 1963

1	1	WEST SIDE STORY Soundtrack (CBS)
4	2	BOBBY VEE MEETS THE CRICKETS Bobby Vee & the Crickets (Liberty)
3	3	OUT OF THE SHADOWS Shadows (Columbia)
5	4	ROCK 'N' ROLL NO. 2 Elvis Presley (RCA)
2	5	ON STAGE WITH THE GEORGE MITCHELL MINSTRELS George Mitchell Minstrels (HMV)
6	6	THE BLACK AND WHITE MINSTREL SHOW George Mitchell Minstrels (HMV)
7	7	SOUTH PACIFIC Soundtrack (RCA)
-	8	32 MINUTES AND 17 SECONDS Cliff Richard (Columbia)
9	9	SINATRA AND SWINGING BRASS Frank Sinatra (Reprise)
-	10	A BOBBY VEE RECORDING SESSION Bobby Vee (Liberty)

26 January 1963

1	1	WEST SIDE STORY Soundtrack (CBS)
-	2	SUMMER HOLIDAY Cliff Richard & the Shadows (Columbia)
-	3	GIRLS! GIRLS! GIRLS! Elvis Presley (RCA)
3	4	OUT OF THE SHADOWS Shadows (Columbia)
5	5	ON STAGE WITH THE GEORGE MITCHELL MINSTRELS George Mitchell Minstrels (HMV)
2	6	BOBBY VEE MEETS THE CRICKETS Bobby Vee & the Crickets (Liberty)
4	7	ROCK 'N' ROLL NO. 2 Elvis Presley (RCA)
6	8	THE BLACK AND WHITE MINSTREL SHOW George Mitchell Minstrels (HMV)
7	9	SOUTH PACIFIC Soundtrack (RCA)
-	10	THE BEST OF BALL, BARBER AND BILK Kenny Ball, Chris Barber & Acker Bilk (Golden Guinea)

2 February 1963

2	1	SUMMER HOLIDAY Cliff Richard & the Shadows (Columbia)
3	2	GIRLS! GIRLS! GIRLS! Elvis Presley (RCA)
1	3	WEST SIDE STORY Soundtrack (CBS)
4	4	OUT OF THE SHADOWS Shadows (Columbia)
9	5	SOUTH PACIFIC Soundtrack (RCA)
6	6	BOBBY VEE MEETS THE CRICKETS Bobby Vee & the Crickets (Liberty)
7	6	ROCK 'N' ROLL NO. 2 Elvis Presley (RCA)
5	8	ON STAGE WITH THE GEORGE MITCHELL MINSTRELS George Mitchell Minstrels (HMV)
8	9	THE BLACK AND WHITE MINSTREL SHOW George Mitchell Minstrels (HMV)
-	10	A GOLDEN AGE OF DONEGAN VOL 2 Lonnie Donegan (Golden Guinea)

9 February 1963

1	1	SUMMER HOLIDAY Cliff Richard & the Shadows (Columbia)
2	2	GIRLS! GIRLS! GIRLS! Elvis Presley (RCA)
3	3	WEST SIDE STORY Soundtrack (CBS)
4	4	OUT OF THE SHADOWS Shadows (Columbia)
5	5	SOUTH PACIFIC Soundtrack (RCA)
9	6	THE BLACK AND WHITE MINSTREL SHOW George Mitchell Minstrels (HMV)
10	7	A GOLDEN AGE OF DONEGAN VOL 2 Lonnie Donegan (Golden Guinea)
8	8	ON STAGE WITH THE GEORGE MITCHELL MINSTRELS George Mitchell Minstrels (HMV)
6	9	BOBBY VEE MEETS THE CRICKETS Bobby Vee & the Crickets (Liberty)
-	10	A BOBBY VEE RECORDING SESSION Bobby Vee (Liberty)
-	10	GYPSY Soundtrack (Warner Bros.)

16 February 1963

1	1	SUMMER HOLIDAY Cliff Richard & the Shadows (Columbia)
2	2	GIRLS! GIRLS! GIRLS! Elvis Presley (RCA)
3	3	WEST SIDE STORY Soundtrack (CBS)
-	4	I'LL REMEMBER YOU Frank Ifield (Columbia)
4	5	OUT OF THE SHADOWS Shadows (Columbia)
5	6	SOUTH PACIFIC Soundtrack (RCA)
6	7	THE BLACK AND WHITE MINSTREL SHOW George Mitchell Minstrels (HMV)
9	8	BOBBY VEE MEETS THE CRICKETS Bobby Vee & the Crickets (Liberty)
-	9	MODERN SOUNDS IN COUNTRY AND WESTERN MUSIC, VOL. 2 Ray Charles (HMV)
-	10	THE BUDDY HOLLY STORY VOL 1 Buddy Holly (Coral)

23 February 1963

1	1	SUMMER HOLIDAY Cliff Richard & the Shadows (Columbia)
2	2	GIRLS! GIRLS! GIRLS! Elvis Presley (RCA)
4	3	I'LL REMEMBER YOU Frank Ifield (Columbia)
3	4	WEST SIDE STORY Soundtrack (CBS)
-	5	SINATRA/BASIE Frank Sinatra & Count Basie (Reprise)
7	6	THE BLACK AND WHITE MINSTREL SHOW George Mitchell Minstrels (HMV)
5	7	OUT OF THE SHADOWS Shadows (Columbia)
6	7	SOUTH PACIFIC Soundtrack (RCA)
8	9	BOBBY VEE MEETS THE CRICKETS Bobby Vee & the Crickets (Liberty)
-	10	ON STAGE WITH THE GEORGE MITCHELL MINSTRELS George Mitchell Minstrels (HMV)

Shads boss Cliff Richard leapt straight in at No.2 with the LP of his film about taking a London double-decker for a *Summer Holiday* in Europe. This cheer reached the top slot in freezing February (it was the coldest winter in living memory; Sylvia Plath killed herself in London that month). Cliff held the latest Presley movie-soundtrack at bay and was to remain at No.1 right through till May, when The Beatles would introduce themselves to the LP top spot and hold on to it for five months straight.

March – April 1963

2 March 1963

last	this	
1	1	SUMMER HOLIDAY Cliff Richard & the Shadows (Columbia)
3	2	I'LL REMEMBER YOU Frank Ifield (Columbia)
2	3	GIRLS! GIRLS! GIRLS! Elvis Presley (RCA)
5	4	SINATRA/BASIE Frank Sinatra & Count Basie (Reprise)
4	5	WEST SIDE STORY Soundtrack (CBS)
7	6	OUT OF THE SHADOWS Shadows (Columbia)
10	7	ON STAGE WITH THE GEORGE MITCHELL MINSTRELS George Mitchell Minstrels (HMV)
7	8	SOUTH PACIFIC Soundtrack (RCA)
6	9	THE BLACK AND WHITE MINSTREL SHOW George Mitchell Minstrels (HMV)
9	10	BOBBY VEE MEETS THE CRICKETS Bobby Vee & the Crickets (Liberty)

9 March 1963

1	1	SUMMER HOLIDAY Cliff Richard & the Shadows (Columbia)
4	2	SINATRA/BASIE Frank Sinatra & Count Basie (Reprise)
3	3	GIRLS! GIRLS! GIRLS! Elvis Presley (RCA)
2	4	I'LL REMEMBER YOU Frank Ifield (Columbia)
5	5	WEST SIDE STORY Soundtrack (CBS)
-	6	ALL STAR FESTIVAL Various Artists (United Nations)
6	7	OUT OF THE SHADOWS Shadows (Columbia)
-	7	STEPTOE AND SON TV Cast (Pye)
8	9	SOUTH PACIFIC Soundtrack (RCA)
7	10	ON STAGE WITH THE GEORGE MITCHELL MINSTRELS George Mitchell Minstrels (HMV)
9	10	THE BLACK AND WHITE MINSTREL SHOW George Mitchell Minstrels (HMV)

16 March 1963

1	1	SUMMER HOLIDAY Cliff Richard & the Shadows (Columbia)
2	2	SINATRA/BASIE Frank Sinatra & Count Basie (Reprise)
4	3	I'LL REMEMBER YOU Frank Ifield (Columbia)
3	4	GIRLS! GIRLS! GIRLS! Elvis Presley (RCA)
6	5	ALL STAR FESTIVAL Various Artists (United Nations)
5	6	WEST SIDE STORY Soundtrack (CBS)
9	7	SOUTH PACIFIC Soundtrack (RCA)
7	8	STEPTOE AND SON TV Cast (Pye)
7	9	OUT OF THE SHADOWS Shadows (Columbia)
10	10	THE BLACK AND WHITE MINSTREL SHOW George Mitchell Minstrels (HMV)

23 March 1963

1	1	SUMMER HOLIDAY Cliff Richard & the Shadows (Columbia)
2	2	SINATRA/BASIE Frank Sinatra & Count Basie (Reprise)
3	3	I'LL REMEMBER YOU Frank Ifield (Columbia)
4	4	GIRLS! GIRLS! GIRLS! Elvis Presley (RCA)
5	5	ALL STAR FESTIVAL Various Artists (United Nations)
6	6	WEST SIDE STORY Soundtrack (CBS)
7	7	SOUTH PACIFIC Soundtrack (RCA)
9	7	OUT OF THE SHADOWS Shadows (Columbia)
8	9	STEPTOE AND SON TV Cast (Pye)
-	10	RICHARD CHAMBERLAIN SINGS Richard Chamberlain (MGM)

30 March 1963

1	1	SUMMER HOLIDAY Cliff Richard & the Shadows (Columbia)
2	2	SINATRA/BASIE Frank Sinatra & Count Basie (Reprise)
3	3	I'LL REMEMBER YOU Frank Ifield (Columbia)
5	4	ALL STAR FESTIVAL Various Artists (United Nations)
4	5	GIRLS! GIRLS! GIRLS! Elvis Presley (RCA)
-	6	REMINISCING Buddy Holly (Coral)
6	7	WEST SIDE STORY Soundtrack (CBS)
7	8	SOUTH PACIFIC Soundtrack (RCA)
-	9	PLEASE PLEASE ME Beatles (Parlophone)
7	10	OUT OF THE SHADOWS Shadows (Columbia)

6 April 1963

1	1	SUMMER HOLIDAY Cliff Richard & the Shadows (Columbia)
6	2	REMINISCING Buddy Holly (Coral)
2	3	SINATRA/BASIE Frank Sinatra & Count Basie (Reprise)
3	3	I'LL REMEMBER YOU Frank Ifield (Columbia)
5	5	GIRLS! GIRLS! GIRLS! Elvis Presley (RCA)
9	6	PLEASE PLEASE ME Beatles (Parlophone)
4	7	ALL STAR FESTIVAL Various Artists (United Nations)
7	8	WEST SIDE STORY Soundtrack (CBS)
10	9	OUT OF THE SHADOWS Shadows (Columbia)
8	10	SOUTH PACIFIC Soundtrack (RCA)

13 April 1963

1	1	SUMMER HOLIDAY Cliff Richard & the Shadows (Columbia)
2	2	REMINISCING Buddy Holly (Coral)
7	3	ALL STAR FESTIVAL Various Artists (United Nations)
3	4	SINATRA/BASIE Frank Sinatra & Count Basie (Reprise)
6	5	PLEASE PLEASE ME Beatles (Parlophone)
3	6	I'LL REMEMBER YOU Frank Ifield (Columbia)
5	7	GIRLS! GIRLS! GIRLS! Elvis Presley (RCA)
8	8	WEST SIDE STORY Soundtrack (CBS)
9	9	OUT OF THE SHADOWS Shadows (Columbia)
-	10	THE EDDIE COCHRAN MEMORIAL ALBUM Eddie Cochran (Liberty)

20 April 1963

1	1	SUMMER HOLIDAY Cliff Richard & the Shadows (Columbia)
2	2	REMINISCING Buddy Holly (Coral)
5	3	PLEASE PLEASE ME Beatles (Parlophone)
3	4	ALL STAR FESTIVAL Various Artists (United Nations)
6	5	I'LL REMEMBER YOU Frank Ifield (Columbia)
8	6	WEST SIDE STORY Soundtrack (CBS)
4	7	SINATRA/BASIE Frank Sinatra & Count Basie (Reprise)
9	8	OUT OF THE SHADOWS Shadows (Columbia)
-	9	SOUTH PACIFIC Soundtrack (RCA)
-	9	ON STAGE WITH THE GEORGE MITCHELL MINSTRELS George Mitchell Minstrels (HMV)
-	9	BOBBY VEE'S GOLDEN GREATS Bobby Vee (Liberty)

The Beatles' LP chart arrival came at No.9 that March, three places below a curious posthumous album by Buddy Holly. *Reminiscing* offered some previously-unissued Holly overdubbed by The Fireballs at the behest of producer Norman Petty, whose studio in Clovis New Mexico was almost as famous as Sam Phillips' Sun studio in Memphis. At this time record-buyers knew nothing of such matters as outtakes; each time "new" Holly material emerged, they were surprised there was any left.

April – June 1963

27 April 1963

last week	this week	Title	Artist
1	1	SUMMER HOLIDAY	Cliff Richard & the Shadows (Columbia)
3	2	PLEASE PLEASE ME	Beatles (Parlophone)
2	3	REMINISCING	Buddy Holly (Coral)
6	4	WEST SIDE STORY	Soundtrack (CBS)
4	5	ALL STAR FESTIVAL	Various Artists (United Nations)
5	6	I'LL REMEMBER YOU	Frank Ifield (Columbia)
-	7	GIRLS! GIRLS! GIRLS!	Elvis Presley (RCA)
7	8	SINATRA/BASIE	Frank Sinatra & Count Basie (Reprise)
9	9	SOUTH PACIFIC	Soundtrack (RCA)
-	10	HATS OFF TO DEL SHANNON	Del Shannon (London)

4 May 1963

last week	this week	Title	Artist
1	1	SUMMER HOLIDAY	Cliff Richard & the Shadows (Columbia)
2	2	PLEASE PLEASE ME	Beatles (Parlophone)
3	3	REMINISCING	Buddy Holly (Coral)
4	4	WEST SIDE STORY	Soundtrack (CBS)
6	5	I'LL REMEMBER YOU	Frank Ifield (Columbia)
7	6	GIRLS! GIRLS! GIRLS!	Elvis Presley (RCA)
5	7	ALL STAR FESTIVAL	Various Artists (United Nations)
8	7	SINATRA/BASIE	Frank Sinatra & Count Basie (Reprise)
-	9	ALL ALONE AM I	Brenda Lee (Brunswick)
-	9	STEPTOE AND SON	TV Cast (Pye)

11 May 1963

last week	this week	Title	Artist
2	1	PLEASE PLEASE ME	Beatles (Parlophone)
1	2	SUMMER HOLIDAY	Cliff Richard & the Shadows (Columbia)
3	3	REMINISCING	Buddy Holly (Coral)
-	4	IT HAPPENED AT THE WORLD'S FAIR	Elvis Presley (RCA)
5	5	I'LL REMEMBER YOU	Frank Ifield (Columbia)
4	6	WEST SIDE STORY	Soundtrack (CBS)
-	7	JUST FOR FUN	Soundtrack (Decca)
6	8	GIRLS! GIRLS! GIRLS!	Elvis Presley (RCA)
7	8	ALL STAR FESTIVAL	Various Artists (United Nations)
7	10	SINATRA/BASIE	Frank Sinatra & Count Basie (Reprise)

18 May 1963

last week	this week	Title	Artist
1	1	PLEASE PLEASE ME	Beatles (Parlophone)
2	2	SUMMER HOLIDAY	Cliff Richard & the Shadows (Columbia)
4	3	IT HAPPENED AT THE WORLD'S FAIR	Elvis Presley (RCA)
3	4	REMINISCING	Buddy Holly (Coral)
6	5	WEST SIDE STORY	Soundtrack (CBS)
5	6	I'LL REMEMBER YOU	Frank Ifield (Columbia)
7	7	JUST FOR FUN	Soundtrack (Decca)
8	7	GIRLS! GIRLS! GIRLS!	Elvis Presley (RCA)
10	7	SINATRA/BASIE	Frank Sinatra & Count Basie (Reprise)
-	10	ALL ALONE AM I	Brenda Lee (Brunswick)

25 May 1963

last week	this week	Title	Artist
1	1	PLEASE PLEASE ME	Beatles (Parlophone)
3	2	IT HAPPENED AT THE WORLD'S FAIR	Elvis Presley (RCA)
2	3	SUMMER HOLIDAY	Cliff Richard & the Shadows (Columbia)
4	4	REMINISCING	Buddy Holly (Coral)
5	5	WEST SIDE STORY	Soundtrack (CBS)
-	6	BILLY	Billy Fury (Decca)
-	7	ALL STAR FESTIVAL	Various Artists (United Nations)
6	8	I'LL REMEMBER YOU	Frank Ifield (Columbia)
-	9	SAMMY DAVIS JR. AT THE COCONUT GROVE	Sammy Davis Jnr. (Reprise)
7	10	SINATRA/BASIE	Frank Sinatra & Count Basie (Reprise)

1 June 1963

last week	this week	Title	Artist
1	1	PLEASE PLEASE ME	Beatles (Parlophone)
3	2	SUMMER HOLIDAY	Cliff Richard & the Shadows (Columbia)
2	3	IT HAPPENED AT THE WORLD'S FAIR	Elvis Presley (RCA)
5	4	WEST SIDE STORY	Soundtrack (CBS)
4	5	REMINISCING	Buddy Holly (Coral)
6	6	BILLY	Billy Fury (Decca)
10	7	SINATRA/BASIE	Frank Sinatra & Count Basie (Reprise)
7	8	ALL STAR FESTIVAL	Various Artists (United Nations)
8	9	I'LL REMEMBER YOU	Frank Ifield (Columbia)
-	10	HATS OFF TO DEL SHANNON	Del Shannon (London)

8 June 1963

last week	this week	Title	Artist
1	1	PLEASE PLEASE ME	Beatles (Parlophone)
2	2	SUMMER HOLIDAY	Cliff Richard & the Shadows (Columbia)
3	3	IT HAPPENED AT THE WORLD'S FAIR	Elvis Presley (RCA)
4	4	WEST SIDE STORY	Soundtrack (CBS)
6	5	BILLY	Billy Fury (Decca)
5	5	REMINISCING	Buddy Holly (Coral)
9	7	I'LL REMEMBER YOU	Frank Ifield (Columbia)
-	8	SOUTH PACIFIC	Soundtrack (RCA)
-	9	ALL ALONE AM I	Brenda Lee (Brunswick)
-	9	RAY CHARLES' GREATEST HITS	Ray Charles (HMV)

15 June 1963

last week	this week	Title	Artist
1	1	PLEASE PLEASE ME	Beatles (Parlophone)
2	2	SUMMER HOLIDAY	Cliff Richard & the Shadows (Columbia)
3	3	IT HAPPENED AT THE WORLD'S FAIR	Elvis Presley (RCA)
5	4	REMINISCING	Buddy Holly (Coral)
-	5	THE SHADOWS' GREATEST HITS	Shadows (Columbia)
5	6	BILLY	Billy Fury (Decca)
4	7	WEST SIDE STORY	Soundtrack (CBS)
7	8	I'LL REMEMBER YOU	Frank Ifield (Columbia)
-	9	THE EDDIE COCHRAN MEMORIAL ALBUM	Eddie Cochran (Liberty)
-	10	HATS OFF TO DEL SHANNON	Del Shannon (London)

Eddie Cochran had died in 1960, Holly in 1959. Here they were charting three and four years on. This gave the lie to the prevalent notion that pop was ephemeral rubbish by nine-day wonders without the staying-power of "real entertainers". Yet to look back on this first year's LP chart is to ask whatever happened to the George Mitchell Minstrels, the Ray Conniff Singers, Dorothy Provine? What Sammy Davis Jnr record remains even an "easy listening" favourite? 30 years on, Holly, Presley and Cliff are the survivors.

June – August 1963

22 June 1963

last	this		
1	1	PLEASE PLEASE ME	Beatles (Parlophone)
2	2	SUMMER HOLIDAY	Cliff Richard & the Shadows (Columbia)
5	3	THE SHADOWS' GREATEST HITS	Shadows (Columbia)
3	4	IT HAPPENED AT THE WORLD'S FAIR	Elvis Presley (RCA)
7	5	WEST SIDE STORY	Soundtrack (CBS)
4	6	REMINISCING	Buddy Holly (Coral)
6	7	BILLY	Billy Fury (Decca)
8	8	I'LL REMEMBER YOU	Frank Ifield (Columbia)
-	9	SOUTH PACIFIC	Soundtrack (RCA)
-	10	BOBBY VEE'S GOLDEN GREATS	Bobby Vee (Liberty)

29 June 1963

1	1	PLEASE PLEASE ME	Beatles (Parlophone)
3	2	THE SHADOWS' GREATEST HITS	Shadows (Columbia)
2	3	SUMMER HOLIDAY	Cliff Richard & the Shadows (Columbia)
5	4	WEST SIDE STORY	Soundtrack (CBS)
4	5	IT HAPPENED AT THE WORLD'S FAIR	Elvis Presley (RCA)
8	6	I'LL REMEMBER YOU	Frank Ifield (Columbia)
6	7	REMINISCING	Buddy Holly (Coral)
7	8	BILLY	Billy Fury (Decca)
9	9	SOUTH PACIFIC	Soundtrack (RCA)
-	10	GIRLS! GIRLS! GIRLS!	Elvis Presley (RCA)

6 July 1963

1	1	PLEASE PLEASE ME	Beatles (Parlophone)
2	2	THE SHADOWS' GREATEST HITS	Shadows (Columbia)
5	3	IT HAPPENED AT THE WORLD'S FAIR	Elvis Presley (RCA)
4	4	WEST SIDE STORY	Soundtrack (CBS)
3	5	SUMMER HOLIDAY	Cliff Richard & the Shadows (Columbia)
7	6	REMINISCING	Buddy Holly (Coral)
8	7	BILLY	Billy Fury (Decca)
9	8	SOUTH PACIFIC	Soundtrack (RCA)
6	9	I'LL REMEMBER YOU	Frank Ifield (Columbia)
-	9	SINATRA/BASIE	Frank Sinatra & Count Basie (Reprise)

13 July 1963

1	1	PLEASE PLEASE ME	Beatles (Parlophone)
2	2	THE SHADOWS' GREATEST HITS	Shadows (Columbia)
5	3	SUMMER HOLIDAY	Cliff Richard & the Shadows (Columbia)
4	4	WEST SIDE STORY	Soundtrack (CBS)
3	5	IT HAPPENED AT THE WORLD'S FAIR	Elvis Presley (RCA)
9	6	I'LL REMEMBER YOU	Frank Ifield (Columbia)
-	7	CLIFF'S HIT ALBUM	Cliff Richard (Columbia)
6	8	REMINISCING	Buddy Holly (Coral)
-	9	BASSEY SPECTACULAR	Shirley Bassey (Philips)
7	10	BILLY	Billy Fury (Decca)

20 July 1963

1	1	PLEASE PLEASE ME	Beatles (Parlophone)
2	2	THE SHADOWS' GREATEST HITS	Shadows (Columbia)
7	3	CLIFF'S HIT ALBUM	Cliff Richard (Columbia)
5	4	IT HAPPENED AT THE WORLD'S FAIR	Elvis Presley (RCA)
4	5	WEST SIDE STORY	Soundtrack (CBS)
3	6	SUMMER HOLIDAY	Cliff Richard & the Shadows (Columbia)
9	7	BASSEY SPECTACULAR	Shirley Bassey (Philips)
6	8	I'LL REMEMBER YOU	Frank Ifield (Columbia)
8	9	REMINISCING	Buddy Holly (Coral)
-	10	SOUTH PACIFIC	Soundtrack (RCA)

27 July 1963

1	1	PLEASE PLEASE ME	Beatles (Parlophone)
2	2	THE SHADOWS' GREATEST HITS	Shadows (Columbia)
3	3	CLIFF'S HIT ALBUM	Cliff Richard (Columbia)
4	4	IT HAPPENED AT THE WORLD'S FAIR	Elvis Presley (RCA)
5	5	WEST SIDE STORY	Soundtrack (CBS)
6	6	SUMMER HOLIDAY	Cliff Richard & the Shadows (Columbia)
9	7	REMINISCING	Buddy Holly (Coral)
8	8	I'LL REMEMBER YOU	Frank Ifield (Columbia)
-	8	THE CONCERT SINATRA	Frank Sinatra (Reprise)
7	10	BASSEY SPECTACULAR	Shirley Bassey (Philips)

3 August 1963

1	1	PLEASE PLEASE ME	Beatles (Parlophone)
2	2	THE SHADOWS' GREATEST HITS	Shadows (Columbia)
3	3	CLIFF'S HIT ALBUM	Cliff Richard (Columbia)
5	4	WEST SIDE STORY	Soundtrack (CBS)
4	5	IT HAPPENED AT THE WORLD'S FAIR	Elvis Presley (RCA)
6	6	SUMMER HOLIDAY	Cliff Richard & the Shadows (Columbia)
8	7	I'LL REMEMBER YOU	Frank Ifield (Columbia)
7	8	REMINISCING	Buddy Holly (Coral)
8	9	THE CONCERT SINATRA	Frank Sinatra (Reprise)
10	10	BASSEY SPECTACULAR	Shirley Bassey (Philips)
-	10	BILLY	Billy Fury (Decca)

10 August 1963

1	1	PLEASE PLEASE ME	Beatles (Parlophone)
2	2	THE SHADOWS' GREATEST HITS	Shadows (Columbia)
3	3	CLIFF'S HIT ALBUM	Cliff Richard (Columbia)
4	4	WEST SIDE STORY	Soundtrack (CBS)
5	5	IT HAPPENED AT THE WORLD'S FAIR	Elvis Presley (RCA)
7	6	I'LL REMEMBER YOU	Frank Ifield (Columbia)
8	7	REMINISCING	Buddy Holly (Coral)
-	8	MEET THE SEARCHERS	Searchers (Pye)
9	9	THE CONCERT SINATRA	Frank Sinatra (Reprise)
6	10	SUMMER HOLIDAY	Cliff Richard & the Shadows (Columbia)

Many other enduring pop artists were around, but most were in the singles charts. Hit 45ers of 1962-1963 included the Everlys, Shirelles, Crystals, Drifters, Rick Nelson, Jerry Lee Lewis, Sam Cooke and Roy Orbison. Now, however, with the Beatles topping the LP chart, it was the Mersey Sound that threatened them. Merseybeat was the punk of its day: grassroots music anyone could play, it was (to begin with) rough stuff. It was now big enough for another Liverpool group, the Searchers, to chart with an LP.

17 August 1963

last / this week

1	1	PLEASE PLEASE ME	Beatles (Parlophone)
2	2	THE SHADOWS' GREATEST HITS	Shadows (Columbia)
3	3	CLIFF'S HIT ALBUM	Cliff Richard (Columbia)
8	4	MEET THE SEARCHERS	Searchers (Pye)
4	5	WEST SIDE STORY	Soundtrack (CBS)
5	6	IT HAPPENED AT THE WORLD'S FAIR	Elvis Presley (RCA)
9	7	THE CONCERT SINATRA	Frank Sinatra (Reprise)
-	8	BILLY	Billy Fury (Decca)
-	9	SOUTH PACIFIC	Soundtrack (RCA)
-	10	THE BUDDY HOLLY STORY VOL 1	Buddy Holly (Coral)

24 August 1963

1	1	PLEASE PLEASE ME	Beatles (Parlophone)
4	2	MEET THE SEARCHERS	Searchers (Pye)
2	3	THE SHADOWS' GREATEST HITS	Shadows (Columbia)
3	3	CLIFF'S HIT ALBUM	Cliff Richard (Columbia)
5	5	WEST SIDE STORY	Soundtrack (CBS)
6	6	IT HAPPENED AT THE WORLD'S FAIR	Elvis Presley (RCA)
7	7	THE CONCERT SINATRA	Frank Sinatra (Reprise)
-	8	SUMMER HOLIDAY	Cliff Richard & the Shadows (Columbia)
-	9	I'LL REMEMBER YOU	Frank Ifield (Columbia)
10	10	THE BUDDY HOLLY STORY VOL 1	Buddy Holly (Coral)
-	10	STEPTOE AND SON	TV Cast (Pye)
-	10	PICKWICK	London Cast (Philips)

31 August 1963

1	1	PLEASE PLEASE ME	Beatles (Parlophone)
3	2	THE SHADOWS' GREATEST HITS	Shadows (Columbia)
3	3	CLIFF'S HIT ALBUM	Cliff Richard (Columbia)
2	4	MEET THE SEARCHERS	Searchers (Pye)
5	5	WEST SIDE STORY	Soundtrack (CBS)
-	6	KENNY BALL'S GOLDEN HITS	Kenny Ball (Golden Guinea)
10	7	STEPTOE AND SON	TV Cast (Pye)
6	8	IT HAPPENED AT THE WORLD'S FAIR	Elvis Presley (RCA)
7	8	THE CONCERT SINATRA	Frank Sinatra (Reprise)
-	10	SOUTH PACIFIC	Soundtrack (RCA)

7 September 1963

1	1	PLEASE PLEASE ME	Beatles (Parlophone)
2	2	THE SHADOWS' GREATEST HITS	Shadows (Columbia)
3	3	CLIFF'S HIT ALBUM	Cliff Richard (Columbia)
4	4	MEET THE SEARCHERS	Searchers (Pye)
6	5	KENNY BALL'S GOLDEN HITS	Kenny Ball (Golden Guinea)
5	6	WEST SIDE STORY	Soundtrack (CBS)
7	7	STEPTOE AND SON	TV Cast (Pye)
8	8	THE CONCERT SINATRA	Frank Sinatra (Reprise)
-	9	RAY CHARLES' GREATEST HITS	Ray Charles (HMV)
-	10	I'LL REMEMBER YOU	Frank Ifield (Columbia)

14 September 1963

1	1	PLEASE PLEASE ME	Beatles (Parlophone)
2	2	THE SHADOWS' GREATEST HITS	Shadows (Columbia)
4	3	MEET THE SEARCHERS	Searchers (Pye)
3	4	CLIFF'S HIT ALBUM	Cliff Richard (Columbia)
5	5	KENNY BALL'S GOLDEN HITS	Kenny Ball (Golden Guinea)
7	6	STEPTOE AND SON	TV Cast (Pye)
6	7	WEST SIDE STORY	Soundtrack (CBS)
10	8	I'LL REMEMBER YOU	Frank Ifield (Columbia)
-	9	REMINISCING	Buddy Holly (Coral)
8	10	THE CONCERT SINATRA	Frank Sinatra (Reprise)

21 September 1963

1	1	PLEASE PLEASE ME	Beatles (Parlophone)
2	2	THE SHADOWS' GREATEST HITS	Shadows (Columbia)
3	3	MEET THE SEARCHERS	Searchers (Pye)
4	4	CLIFF'S HIT ALBUM	Cliff Richard (Columbia)
5	5	KENNY BALL'S GOLDEN HITS	Kenny Ball (Golden Guinea)
7	6	WEST SIDE STORY	Soundtrack (CBS)
-	7	BORN FREE	Frank Ifield (Columbia)
6	8	STEPTOE AND SON	TV Cast (Pye)
10	9	THE CONCERT SINATRA	Frank Sinatra (Reprise)
8	10	I'LL REMEMBER YOU	Frank Ifield (Columbia)

28 September 1963

1	1	PLEASE PLEASE ME	Beatles (Parlophone)
3	2	MEET THE SEARCHERS	Searchers (Pye)
7	3	BORN FREE	Frank Ifield (Columbia)
2	4	THE SHADOWS' GREATEST HITS	Shadows (Columbia)
5	5	KENNY BALL'S GOLDEN HITS	Kenny Ball (Golden Guinea)
4	6	CLIFF'S HIT ALBUM	Cliff Richard (Columbia)
6	7	WEST SIDE STORY	Soundtrack (CBS)
-	8	WHEN IN SPAIN	Cliff Richard (Columbia)
8	9	STEPTOE AND SON	TV Cast (Pye)
-	10	HITSVILLE	Various Artists (Golden Guinea)

5 October 1963

1	1	PLEASE PLEASE ME	Beatles (Parlophone)
2	2	MEET THE SEARCHERS	Searchers (Pye)
3	3	BORN FREE	Frank Ifield (Columbia)
4	4	THE SHADOWS' GREATEST HITS	Shadows (Columbia)
8	5	WHEN IN SPAIN	Cliff Richard (Columbia)
5	6	KENNY BALL'S GOLDEN HITS	Kenny Ball (Golden Guinea)
-	7	SINATRA'S SINATRA	Frank Sinatra (Reprise)
-	8	CHUCK BERRY ON STAGE	Chuck Berry (Pye International)
7	9	WEST SIDE STORY	Soundtrack (CBS)
6	10	CLIFF'S HIT ALBUM	Cliff Richard (Columbia)

The LP chart said less about the new beat groups' success than about the medium. Cheap and ideal for the short guitar-bass-drum number, the single and Merseybeat seemed made for each other, even while the music really thrived live in small venues for the young working-class. So the LP chart showed only the tip of the tip of this sweaty iceberg; the real tip remained the singles chart, topped August-October by the Searchers, Billy J. Kramer (his second No.1), the Beatles and counterfeit-Merseysiders the Tremeloes.

October – November 1963

12 October 1963

last	this		
1	1	PLEASE PLEASE ME	Beatles (Parlophone)
2	2	MEET THE SEARCHERS	Searchers (Pye)
3	3	BORN FREE	Frank Ifield (Columbia)
6	4	KENNY BALL'S GOLDEN HITS	Kenny Ball (Golden Guinea)
5	5	WHEN IN SPAIN	Cliff Richard (Columbia)
4	6	THE SHADOWS' GREATEST HITS	Shadows (Columbia)
7	7	SINATRA'S SINATRA	Frank Sinatra (Reprise)
8	8	CHUCK BERRY ON STAGE	Chuck Berry (Pye International)
9	9	WEST SIDE STORY	Soundtrack (CBS)
-	9	STEPTOE AND SON	TV Cast (Pye)

19 October 1963

1	1 PLEASE PLEASE ME	Beatles (Parlophone)
2	2 MEET THE SEARCHERS	Searchers (Pye)
3	3 BORN FREE	Frank Ifield (Columbia)
4	4 KENNY BALL'S GOLDEN HITS	Kenny Ball (Golden Guinea)
6	5 THE SHADOWS' GREATEST HITS	Shadows (Columbia)
5	6 WHEN IN SPAIN	Cliff Richard (Columbia)
8	7 CHUCK BERRY ON STAGE	Chuck Berry (Pye International)
9	8 WEST SIDE STORY	Soundtrack (CBS)
-	9 HOW DO YOU LIKE IT	Gerry & the Pacemakers (Columbia)
7	10 SINATRA'S SINATRA	Frank Sinatra (Reprise)
-	10 FOOL BRITANNIA	Original Cast (Ember)

26 October 1963

1	1 PLEASE PLEASE ME	Beatles (Parlophone)
3	2 BORN FREE	Frank Ifield (Columbia)
2	3 MEET THE SEARCHERS	Searchers (Pye)
9	4 HOW DO YOU LIKE IT	Gerry & the Pacemakers (Columbia)
4	5 KENNY BALL'S GOLDEN HITS	Kenny Ball (Golden Guinea)
5	6 THE SHADOWS' GREATEST HITS	Shadows (Columbia)
6	7 WHEN IN SPAIN	Cliff Richard (Columbia)
10	8 SINATRA'S SINATRA	Frank Sinatra (Reprise)
8	9 WEST SIDE STORY	Soundtrack (CBS)
-	10 TRINI LOPEZ AT P.J.'S	Trini Lopez (Reprise)

2 November 1963

1	1 PLEASE PLEASE ME	Beatles (Parlophone)
3	2 MEET THE SEARCHERS	Searchers (Pye)
2	3 BORN FREE	Frank Ifield (Columbia)
4	4 HOW DO YOU LIKE IT	Gerry & the Pacemakers (Columbia)
6	5 THE SHADOWS' GREATEST HITS	Shadows (Columbia)
8	6 SINATRA'S SINATRA	Frank Sinatra (Reprise)
10	7 TRINI LOPEZ AT P.J.'S	Trini Lopez (Reprise)
9	8 WEST SIDE STORY	Soundtrack (CBS)
-	9 CHUCK BERRY ON STAGE	Chuck Berry (Pye International)
5	10 KENNY BALL'S GOLDEN HITS	Kenny Ball (Golden Guinea)

9 November 1963

1	1 PLEASE PLEASE ME	Beatles (Parlophone)
4	2 HOW DO YOU LIKE IT	Gerry & the Pacemakers (Columbia)
2	3 MEET THE SEARCHERS	Searchers (Pye)
5	4 THE SHADOWS' GREATEST HITS	Shadows (Columbia)
7	5 TRINI LOPEZ AT P.J.'S	Trini Lopez (Reprise)
3	6 BORN FREE	Frank Ifield (Columbia)
6	7 SINATRA'S SINATRA	Frank Sinatra (Reprise)
8	8 WEST SIDE STORY	Soundtrack (CBS)
-	9 FREDDIE AND THE DREAMERS	Freddie & the Dreamers (Columbia)
10	10 KENNY BALL'S GOLDEN HITS	Kenny Ball (Golden Guinea)

16 November 1963

1	1 PLEASE PLEASE ME	Beatles (Parlophone)
2	2 HOW DO YOU LIKE IT	Gerry & the Pacemakers (Columbia)
3	3 MEET THE SEARCHERS	Searchers (Pye)
10	4 KENNY BALL'S GOLDEN HITS	Kenny Ball (Golden Guinea)
-	5 SUGAR AND SPICE	Searchers (Pye)
9	6 FREDDIE AND THE DREAMERS	Freddie & the Dreamers (Columbia)
6	7 BORN FREE	Frank Ifield (Columbia)
4	8 THE SHADOWS' GREATEST HITS	Shadows (Columbia)
8	9 WEST SIDE STORY	Soundtrack (CBS)
-	10 ON TOUR WITH THE GEORGE MITCHELL MINSTRELS	George Mitchell Minstrels (HMV)

23 November 1963

1	1 PLEASE PLEASE ME	Beatles (Parlophone)
2	2 HOW DO YOU LIKE IT	Gerry & the Pacemakers (Columbia)
3	3 MEET THE SEARCHERS	Searchers (Pye)
6	4 FREDDIE AND THE DREAMERS	Freddie & the Dreamers (Columbia)
9	5 WEST SIDE STORY	Soundtrack (CBS)
-	6 TRINI LOPEZ AT P.J.'S	Trini Lopez (Reprise)
10	7 ON TOUR WITH THE GEORGE MITCHELL MINSTRELS	George Mitchell Minstrels (HMV)
8	8 THE SHADOWS' GREATEST HITS	Shadows (Columbia)
5	9 SUGAR AND SPICE	Searchers (Pye)
7	10 BORN FREE	Frank Ifield (Columbia)

30 November 1963

-	1 WITH THE BEATLES	Beatles (Parlophone)
1	2 PLEASE PLEASE ME	Beatles (Parlophone)
2	3 HOW DO YOU LIKE IT	Gerry & the Pacemakers (Columbia)
9	4 SUGAR AND SPICE	Searchers (Pye)
5	5 WEST SIDE STORY	Soundtrack (CBS)
3	6 MEET THE SEARCHERS	Searchers (Pye)
7	7 ON TOUR WITH THE GEORGE MITCHELL MINSTRELS	George Mitchell Minstrels (HMV)
6	8 TRINI LOPEZ AT P.J.'S	Trini Lopez (Reprise)
-	9 SINATRA'S SINATRA	Frank Sinatra (Reprise)
4	10 FREDDIE AND THE DREAMERS	Freddie & the Dreamers (Columbia)

As Billy J. Kramer and Brian Poole made clear, the raw excitement of the new beat groups was to remain largely uncaptured on record, while vinyl success met those who made the music chirpy, clean and sweet. So the LP chart opened up also to Merseyside's Gerry & the Pacemakers, whose hit singles were written by Tin Pan Alley's Mitch Murray, and Manchester's gruesome Freddie & the Dreamers, more novelty act than beat group, whose first hit had been a limp cover of an inspired, weird R&B classic by James Ray.

last week	this week	7 December 1963
1	1	WITH THE BEATLES Beatles (Parlophone)
2	2	PLEASE PLEASE ME Beatles (Parlophone)
4	3	SUGAR AND SPICE Searchers (Pye)
3	4	HOW DO YOU LIKE IT Gerry & the Pacemakers (Columbia)
5	5	WEST SIDE STORY Soundtrack (CBS)
6	6	MEET THE SEARCHERS Searchers (Pye)
10	7	FREDDIE AND THE DREAMERS Freddie & the Dreamers (Columbia)
9	8	SINATRA'S SINATRA Frank Sinatra (Reprise)
7	9	ON TOUR WITH THE GEORGE MITCHELL MINSTRELS George Mitchell Minstrels (HMV)
-	10	KENNY BALL'S GOLDEN HITS Kenny Ball (Golden Guinea)
-	10	THE SHADOWS' GREATEST HITS Shadows (Columbia)

14 December 1963

1	1	WITH THE BEATLES Beatles (Parlophone)
2	2	PLEASE PLEASE ME Beatles (Parlophone)
4	3	HOW DO YOU LIKE IT Gerry & the Pacemakers (Columbia)
5	4	WEST SIDE STORY Soundtrack (CBS)
7	5	FREDDIE AND THE DREAMERS Freddie & the Dreamers (Columbia)
3	6	SUGAR AND SPICE Searchers (Pye)
6	7	MEET THE SEARCHERS Searchers (Pye)
9	7	ON TOUR WITH THE GEORGE MITCHELL MINSTRELS George Mitchell Minstrels (HMV)
-	9	BORN FREE Frank Ifield (Columbia)
-	9	SOUTH PACIFIC Soundtrack (RCA)

21 December 1963

1	1	WITH THE BEATLES Beatles (Parlophone)
2	2	PLEASE PLEASE ME Beatles (Parlophone)
3	3	HOW DO YOU LIKE IT Gerry & the Pacemakers (Columbia)
4	4	WEST SIDE STORY Soundtrack (CBS)
7	5	MEET THE SEARCHERS Searchers (Pye)
5	6	FREDDIE AND THE DREAMERS Freddie & the Dreamers (Columbia)
-	7	KENNY BALL'S GOLDEN HITS Kenny Ball (Golden Guinea)
6	8	SUGAR AND SPICE Searchers (Pye)
7	9	ON TOUR WITH THE GEORGE MITCHELL MINSTRELS George Mitchell Minstrels (HMV)
9	9	BORN FREE Frank Ifield (Columbia)

28 December 1963

1	1	WITH THE BEATLES Beatles (Parlophone)
2	2	PLEASE PLEASE ME Beatles (Parlophone)
4	3	WEST SIDE STORY Soundtrack (CBS)
9	4	ON TOUR WITH THE GEORGE MITCHELL MINSTRELS George Mitchell Minstrels (HMV)
-	5	KATHY KIRBY SINGS 16 HITS FROM STARS AND GARTERS Kathy Kirby (Decca)
3	6	HOW DO YOU LIKE IT Gerry & the Pacemakers (Columbia)
6	7	FREDDIE AND THE DREAMERS Freddie & the Dreamers (Columbia)
-	7	MRS. MILLS' PARTY Mrs. Mills (Parlophone)
-	7	SINATRA'S SINATRA Frank Sinatra (Reprise)
7	10	KENNY BALL'S GOLDEN HITS Kenny Ball (Golden Guinea)

It was a tradition for DJs to play US originals once and their "home-grown" covers interminably. This obtained both before Merseybeat (Marty Wilde vastly outsold Richie Valens with *Donna*, despite Valens dying in the Holly plane-crash as his disc was released) and after it. In 1965 the TV show *Thank Your Lucky Stars* claimed that the Righteous Brothers' *You've Lost That Loving Feeling* was too dull to hit and that Cilla Black's was superior. For beat groups, though, it was different: they covered obscure R&B because they loved it. This Christmas, beat groups occupied four of the top five LP slots.

From the sublime to the ridiculous.
Roy Orbison (left) has charted in every decade, as have the Shadows (below left).
The heyday of the Black and White Minstrels has thankfully passed, but they are still playing at a theatre somewhere...

January – February 1964

4 January 1964

last week	this		
1	1	WITH THE BEATLES	Beatles (Parlophone)
2	2	PLEASE PLEASE ME	Beatles (Parlophone)
6	3	HOW DO YOU LIKE IT	Gerry & the Pacemakers (Columbia)
4	4	ON TOUR WITH THE GEORGE MITCHELL MINSTRELS	George Mitchell Minstrels (HMV)
7	4	FREDDIE AND THE DREAMERS	Freddie & the Dreamers (Columbia)
3	6	WEST SIDE STORY	Soundtrack (CBS)
5	7	KATHY KIRBY SINGS 16 HITS FROM STARS AND GARTERS	Kathy Kirby (Decca)
10	8	KENNY BALL'S GOLDEN HITS	Kenny Ball (Golden Guinea)
7	9	MRS. MILLS' PARTY	Mrs. Mills (Parlophone)
7	10	SINATRA'S SINATRA	Frank Sinatra (Reprise)
-	10	MEET THE SEARCHERS	Searchers (Pye)

11 January 1964

1	1	WITH THE BEATLES	Beatles (Parlophone)
2	2	PLEASE PLEASE ME	Beatles (Parlophone)
3	3	HOW DO YOU LIKE IT	Gerry & the Pacemakers (Columbia)
-	4	FUN IN ACAPULCO	Elvis Presley (RCA)
6	5	WEST SIDE STORY	Soundtrack (CBS)
4	6	FREDDIE AND THE DREAMERS	Freddie & the Dreamers (Columbia)
7	7	KATHY KIRBY SINGS 16 HITS FROM STARS AND GARTERS	Kathy Kirby (Decca)
4	8	ON TOUR WITH THE GEORGE MITCHELL MINSTRELS	George Mitchell Minstrels (HMV)
8	9	KENNY BALL'S GOLDEN HITS	Kenny Ball (Golden Guinea)
-	10	TRINI LOPEZ AT P.J.'S	Trini Lopez (Reprise)

18 January 1964

1	1	WITH THE BEATLES	Beatles (Parlophone)
2	2	PLEASE PLEASE ME	Beatles (Parlophone)
4	3	FUN IN ACAPULCO	Elvis Presley (RCA)
3	4	HOW DO YOU LIKE IT	Gerry & the Pacemakers (Columbia)
5	5	WEST SIDE STORY	Soundtrack (CBS)
7	6	KATHY KIRBY SINGS 16 HITS FROM STARS AND GARTERS	Kathy Kirby (Decca)
-	7	BORN FREE	Frank Ifield (Columbia)
8	8	ON TOUR WITH THE GEORGE MITCHELL MINSTRELS	George Mitchell Minstrels (HMV)
6	9	FREDDIE AND THE DREAMERS	Freddie & the Dreamers (Columbia)
10	9	TRINI LOPEZ AT P.J.'S	Trini Lopez (Reprise)

25 January 1964

1	1	WITH THE BEATLES	Beatles (Parlophone)
2	2	PLEASE PLEASE ME	Beatles (Parlophone)
4	3	HOW DO YOU LIKE IT	Gerry & the Pacemakers (Columbia)
5	4	WEST SIDE STORY	Soundtrack (CBS)
3	5	FUN IN ACAPULCO	Elvis Presley (RCA)
6	6	KATHY KIRBY SINGS 16 HITS FROM STARS AND GARTERS	Kathy Kirby (Decca)
7	7	BORN FREE	Frank Ifield (Columbia)
9	7	FREDDIE AND THE DREAMERS	Freddie & the Dreamers (Columbia)
8	9	ON TOUR WITH THE GEORGE MITCHELL MINSTRELS	George Mitchell Minstrels (HMV)
-	10	PICKWICK	London Cast (Philips)

1 February 1964

1	1	WITH THE BEATLES	Beatles (Parlophone)
2	2	PLEASE PLEASE ME	Beatles (Parlophone)
4	3	WEST SIDE STORY	Soundtrack (CBS)
3	4	HOW DO YOU LIKE IT	Gerry & the Pacemakers (Columbia)
-	5	MEET THE SEARCHERS	Searchers (Pye)
6	6	KATHY KIRBY SINGS 16 HITS FROM STARS AND GARTERS	Kathy Kirby (Decca)
9	7	ON TOUR WITH THE GEORGE MITCHELL MINSTRELS	George Mitchell Minstrels (HMV)
7	8	BORN FREE	Frank Ifield (Columbia)
7	9	FREDDIE AND THE DREAMERS	Freddie & the Dreamers (Columbia)
-	9	SUGAR AND SPICE	Searchers (Pye)
-	9	I LEFT MY HEART IN SAN FRANCISCO	Tony Bennett (CBS)

8 February 1964

1	1	WITH THE BEATLES	Beatles (Parlophone)
2	2	PLEASE PLEASE ME	Beatles (Parlophone)
3	3	WEST SIDE STORY	Soundtrack (CBS)
4	4	HOW DO YOU LIKE IT	Gerry & the Pacemakers (Columbia)
9	5	SUGAR AND SPICE	Searchers (Pye)
6	6	KATHY KIRBY SINGS 16 HITS FROM STARS AND GARTERS	Kathy Kirby (Decca)
8	6	BORN FREE	Frank Ifield (Columbia)
5	8	MEET THE SEARCHERS	Searchers (Pye)
-	8	READY STEADY GO!	Various Artists (Decca)
9	10	I LEFT MY HEART IN SAN FRANCISCO	Tony Bennett (CBS)

15 February 1964

1	1	WITH THE BEATLES	Beatles (Parlophone)
2	2	PLEASE PLEASE ME	Beatles (Parlophone)
3	3	WEST SIDE STORY	Soundtrack (CBS)
4	4	HOW DO YOU LIKE IT	Gerry & the Pacemakers (Columbia)
8	5	MEET THE SEARCHERS	Searchers (Pye)
8	5	READY STEADY GO!	Various Artists (Decca)
-	7	STAY WITH THE HOLLIES	Hollies (Parlophone)
5	8	SUGAR AND SPICE	Searchers (Pye)
6	8	BORN FREE	Frank Ifield (Columbia)
-	10	KENNY BALL'S GOLDEN HITS	Kenny Ball (Golden Guinea)

22 February 1964

1	1	WITH THE BEATLES	Beatles (Parlophone)
2	2	PLEASE PLEASE ME	Beatles (Parlophone)
3	3	WEST SIDE STORY	Soundtrack (CBS)
4	4	HOW DO YOU LIKE IT	Gerry & the Pacemakers (Columbia)
7	5	STAY WITH THE HOLLIES	Hollies (Parlophone)
-	6	KATHY KIRBY SINGS 16 HITS FROM STARS AND GARTERS	Kathy Kirby (Decca)
5	7	MEET THE SEARCHERS	Searchers (Pye)
-	8	ON TOUR WITH THE GEORGE MITCHELL MINSTRELS	George Mitchell Minstrels (HMV)
-	9	JAZZ SEBASTIAN BACH	Les Swingle Singers (Philips)
8	10	SUGAR AND SPICE	Searchers (Pye)
8	10	BORN FREE	Frank Ifield (Columbia)

By now the real 1960s had begun, but the old guard fought on. The cash for LP-buying still belonged to adults whose ideas of "good music" pre-dated rock'n'roll. Despite the civil rights struggle in the USA (summer 1963 had seen Martin Luther King's "I have a dream" speech) the Minstrels were back. So was Kathy Kirby, a young dance-band-era revivalist with glossy red lipstick and black-seamed nylons. Mrs Mills' image was more cleaning-lady than star; she tinkled singalongable medleys on her joanna.

February – April 1964

last this week

29 February 1964

last	this		
1	1	WITH THE BEATLES	Beatles (Parlophone)
2	2	PLEASE PLEASE ME	Beatles (Parlophone)
3	3	WEST SIDE STORY	Soundtrack (CBS)
4	4	HOW DO YOU LIKE IT	Gerry & the Pacemakers (Columbia)
5	5	STAY WITH THE HOLLIES	Hollies (Parlophone)
7	6	MEET THE SEARCHERS	Searchers (Pye)
-	7	READY STEADY GO!	Various Artists (Decca)
8	8	ON TOUR WITH THE GEORGE MITCHELL MINSTRELS	George Mitchell Minstrels (HMV)
-	8	IN DREAMS	Roy Orbison (London)
10	10	BORN FREE	Frank Ifield (Columbia)

7 March 1964

last	this		
1	1	WITH THE BEATLES	Beatles (Parlophone)
2	2	PLEASE PLEASE ME	Beatles (Parlophone)
3	3	WEST SIDE STORY	Soundtrack (CBS)
5	4	STAY WITH THE HOLLIES	Hollies (Parlophone)
4	5	HOW DO YOU LIKE IT	Gerry & the Pacemakers (Columbia)
7	6	READY STEADY GO!	Various Artists (Decca)
-	7	FUN IN ACAPULCO	Elvis Presley (RCA)
8	8	IN DREAMS	Roy Orbison (London)
10	9	BORN FREE	Frank Ifield (Columbia)
-	10	SUGAR AND SPICE	Searchers (Pye)
-	10	TEEN SCENE	Chet Atkins (RCA)

14 March 1964

last	this		
1	1	WITH THE BEATLES	Beatles (Parlophone)
2	2	PLEASE PLEASE ME	Beatles (Parlophone)
3	3	WEST SIDE STORY	Soundtrack (CBS)
4	4	STAY WITH THE HOLLIES	Hollies (Parlophone)
9	5	BORN FREE	Frank Ifield (Columbia)
5	6	HOW DO YOU LIKE IT	Gerry & the Pacemakers (Columbia)
-	7	KATHY KIRBY SINGS 16 HITS FROM STARS AND GARTERS	Kathy Kirby (Decca)
-	7	RHYTHM AND BLUES AT THE FLAMINGO	Georgie Fame (Columbia)
9	9	TRINI LOPEZ AT P.J.'S	Trini Lopez (Reprise)
-	10	SOUTH PACIFIC	Soundtrack (RCA)

21 March 1964

last	this		
1	1	WITH THE BEATLES	Beatles (Parlophone)
4	2	STAY WITH THE HOLLIES	Hollies (Parlophone)
3	3	WEST SIDE STORY	Soundtrack (CBS)
2	4	PLEASE PLEASE ME	Beatles (Parlophone)
6	5	HOW DO YOU LIKE IT	Gerry & the Pacemakers (Columbia)
10	6	SOUTH PACIFIC	Soundtrack (RCA)
-	7	ON TOUR WITH THE GEORGE MITCHELL MINSTRELS	George Mitchell Minstrels (HMV)
-	7	MORE TRINI LOPEZ AT P.J.'S	Trini Lopez (Reprise)
9	9	BLUE SKIES	Frank Ifield (Columbia)
-	9	FREDDIE AND THE DREAMERS	Freddie & the Dreamers (Columbia)

28 March 1964

last	this		
1	1	WITH THE BEATLES	Beatles (Parlophone)
4	2	PLEASE PLEASE ME	Beatles (Parlophone)
3	3	WEST SIDE STORY	Soundtrack (CBS)
2	4	STAY WITH THE HOLLIES	Hollies (Parlophone)
5	5	HOW DO YOU LIKE IT	Gerry & the Pacemakers (Columbia)
-	6	THE SHADOWS' GREATEST HITS	Shadows (Columbia)
-	7	KATHY KIRBY SINGS 16 HITS FROM STARS AND GARTERS	Kathy Kirby (Decca)
6	8	SOUTH PACIFIC	Soundtrack (RCA)
7	8	MORE TRINI LOPEZ AT P.J.'S	Trini Lopez (Reprise)
-	10	SUGAR AND SPICE	Searchers (Pye)

4 April 1964

last	this		
1	1	WITH THE BEATLES	Beatles (Parlophone)
2	2	PLEASE PLEASE ME	Beatles (Parlophone)
3	3	WEST SIDE STORY	Soundtrack (CBS)
4	4	STAY WITH THE HOLLIES	Hollies (Parlophone)
-	5	ELVIS' GOLDEN RECORDS VOL 3	Elvis Presley (RCA)
8	6	SOUTH PACIFIC	Soundtrack (RCA)
6	7	THE SHADOWS' GREATEST HITS	Shadows (Columbia)
-	7	GOOD 'N' COUNTRY	Jim Reeves (RCA)
5	9	HOW DO YOU LIKE IT	Gerry & the Pacemakers (Columbia)
7	9	KATHY KIRBY SINGS 16 HITS FROM STARS AND GARTERS	Kathy Kirby (Decca)

11 April 1964

last	this		
1	1	WITH THE BEATLES	Beatles (Parlophone)
2	2	PLEASE PLEASE ME	Beatles (Parlophone)
4	3	STAY WITH THE HOLLIES	Hollies (Parlophone)
3	4	WEST SIDE STORY	Soundtrack (CBS)
5	5	ELVIS' GOLDEN RECORDS VOL 3	Elvis Presley (RCA)
9	6	HOW DO YOU LIKE IT	Gerry & the Pacemakers (Columbia)
7	7	GOOD 'N' COUNTRY	Jim Reeves (RCA)
-	8	AT THE DROP OF ANOTHER HAT	Michael Flanders & Donald Swann (Parlophone)
-	9	BLUE SKIES	Frank Ifield (Columbia)
-	10	FREDDIE AND THE DREAMERS	Freddie & the Dreamers (Columbia)

18 April 1964

last	this		
1	1	WITH THE BEATLES	Beatles (Parlophone)
4	2	WEST SIDE STORY	Soundtrack (CBS)
2	3	PLEASE PLEASE ME	Beatles (Parlophone)
3	4	STAY WITH THE HOLLIES	Hollies (Parlophone)
-	5	A GIRL CALLED DUSTY	Dusty Springfield (Philips)
-	6	A SESSION WITH THE DAVE CLARK FIVE	Dave Clark Five (Columbia)
5	7	ELVIS' GOLDEN RECORDS VOL 3	Elvis Presley (RCA)
8	8	AT THE DROP OF ANOTHER HAT	Michael Flanders & Donald Swann (Parlophone)
-	9	JAZZ SEBASTIAN BACH	Les Swingle Singers (Philips)
-	9	IN THE WIND	Peter, Paul & Mary (Warner Bros.)

Beatlemania was such that the sleevenotes of the Fab Four's LP *Please Please Me* already sounded quaint: "Possibly," these had dared boast, "the most exciting British group since the Shadows." The LP sold in such huge numbers that it had reached No.11 in the singles chart the previous December, while on 28 March 1964 the American Top 5 was all Beatles. Australian Frank Ifield, meanwhile, was nearing the end as a big star in Britain, with four No.1 singles behind him, plus many smaller hits, 4 in 1964 alone.

25 April 1964

last week / this week

last	this	Title
-	1	THE ROLLING STONES — Rolling Stones (Decca)
1	2	WITH THE BEATLES — Beatles (Parlophone)
2	3	WEST SIDE STORY — Soundtrack (CBS)
6	4	A SESSION WITH THE DAVE CLARK FIVE — Dave Clark Five (Columbia)
3	5	PLEASE PLEASE ME — Beatles (Parlophone)
4	6	STAY WITH THE HOLLIES — Hollies (Parlophone)
5	7	A GIRL CALLED DUSTY — Dusty Springfield (Philips)
9	8	IN THE WIND — Peter, Paul & Mary (Warner Bros.)
-	8	SOUTH PACIFIC — Soundtrack (RCA)
7	10	ELVIS' GOLDEN RECORDS VOL 3 — Elvis Presley (RCA)

2 May 1964

last	this	Title
1	1	THE ROLLING STONES — Rolling Stones (Decca)
2	2	WITH THE BEATLES — Beatles (Parlophone)
3	3	WEST SIDE STORY — Soundtrack (CBS)
4	4	A SESSION WITH THE DAVE CLARK FIVE — Dave Clark Five (Columbia)
6	5	STAY WITH THE HOLLIES — Hollies (Parlophone)
5	6	PLEASE PLEASE ME — Beatles (Parlophone)
7	7	A GIRL CALLED DUSTY — Dusty Springfield (Philips)
10	8	ELVIS' GOLDEN RECORDS VOL 3 — Elvis Presley (RCA)
8	9	IN THE WIND — Peter, Paul & Mary (Warner Bros.)
-	10	BLUE SKIES — Frank Ifield (Columbia)
-	10	TRIBUTE TO EDDIE — Heinz (Decca)

9 May 1964

last	this	Title
1	1	THE ROLLING STONES — Rolling Stones (Decca)
2	2	WITH THE BEATLES — Beatles (Parlophone)
3	3	WEST SIDE STORY — Soundtrack (CBS)
4	4	A SESSION WITH THE DAVE CLARK FIVE — Dave Clark Five (Columbia)
7	5	A GIRL CALLED DUSTY — Dusty Springfield (Philips)
-	6	DANCE WITH THE SHADOWS — Shadows (Columbia)
5	7	STAY WITH THE HOLLIES — Hollies (Parlophone)
6	8	PLEASE PLEASE ME — Beatles (Parlophone)
-	9	SOUTH PACIFIC — Soundtrack (RCA)
-	10	ON TOUR WITH THE GEORGE MITCHELL MINSTRELS — George Mitchell Minstrels (HMV)

16 May 1964

last	this	Title
1	1	THE ROLLING STONES — Rolling Stones (Decca)
2	2	WITH THE BEATLES — Beatles (Parlophone)
4	3	A SESSION WITH THE DAVE CLARK FIVE — Dave Clark Five (Columbia)
6	4	DANCE WITH THE SHADOWS — Shadows (Columbia)
3	5	WEST SIDE STORY — Soundtrack (CBS)
5	6	A GIRL CALLED DUSTY — Dusty Springfield (Philips)
7	7	STAY WITH THE HOLLIES — Hollies (Parlophone)
-	8	JAZZ SEBASTIAN BACH — Les Swingle Singers (Philips)
8	9	PLEASE PLEASE ME — Beatles (Parlophone)
10	10	ON TOUR WITH THE GEORGE MITCHELL MINSTRELS — George Mitchell Minstrels (HMV)

23 May 1964

last	this	Title
1	1	THE ROLLING STONES — Rolling Stones (Decca)
2	2	WITH THE BEATLES — Beatles (Parlophone)
4	3	DANCE WITH THE SHADOWS — Shadows (Columbia)
5	4	WEST SIDE STORY — Soundtrack (CBS)
3	5	A SESSION WITH THE DAVE CLARK FIVE — Dave Clark Five (Columbia)
6	6	A GIRL CALLED DUSTY — Dusty Springfield (Philips)
-	7	SOUTH PACIFIC — Soundtrack (RCA)
-	8	IN DREAMS — Roy Orbison (London)
-	8	THE LATEST AND THE GREATEST — Chuck Berry (Pye International)
8	10	JAZZ SEBASTIAN BACH — Les Swingle Singers (Philips)
9	10	PLEASE PLEASE ME — Beatles (Parlophone)

30 May 1964

last	this	Title
1	1	THE ROLLING STONES — Rolling Stones (Decca)
2	2	WITH THE BEATLES — Beatles (Parlophone)
3	3	DANCE WITH THE SHADOWS — Shadows (Columbia)
5	4	A SESSION WITH THE DAVE CLARK FIVE — Dave Clark Five (Columbia)
-	5	IT'S THE SEARCHERS — Searchers (Pye)
4	6	WEST SIDE STORY — Soundtrack (CBS)
8	7	THE LATEST AND THE GREATEST — Chuck Berry (Pye International)
-	8	STAY WITH THE HOLLIES — Hollies (Parlophone)
-	9	ELVIS' GOLDEN RECORDS VOL 3 — Elvis Presley (RCA)
8	10	IN DREAMS — Roy Orbison (London)

6 June 1964

last	this	Title
1	1	THE ROLLING STONES — Rolling Stones (Decca)
2	2	WITH THE BEATLES — Beatles (Parlophone)
5	3	IT'S THE SEARCHERS — Searchers (Pye)
3	4	DANCE WITH THE SHADOWS — Shadows (Columbia)
7	4	THE LATEST AND THE GREATEST — Chuck Berry (Pye International)
4	6	A SESSION WITH THE DAVE CLARK FIVE — Dave Clark Five (Columbia)
6	7	WEST SIDE STORY — Soundtrack (CBS)
9	8	ELVIS' GOLDEN RECORDS VOL 3 — Elvis Presley (RCA)
-	8	MORE CHUCK BERRY — Chuck Berry (Pye International)
8	10	STAY WITH THE HOLLIES — Hollies (Parlophone)

13 June 1964

last	this	Title
1	1	THE ROLLING STONES — Rolling Stones (Decca)
4	2	DANCE WITH THE SHADOWS — Shadows (Columbia)
3	3	IT'S THE SEARCHERS — Searchers (Pye)
2	4	WITH THE BEATLES — Beatles (Parlophone)
4	5	THE LATEST AND THE GREATEST — Chuck Berry (Pye International)
6	5	A SESSION WITH THE DAVE CLARK FIVE — Dave Clark Five (Columbia)
7	5	WEST SIDE STORY — Soundtrack (CBS)
-	8	SHOWCASE — Buddy Holly (Coral)
-	8	PRESENTING DIONNE WARWICK — Dionne Warwick (Pye International)
10	10	STAY WITH THE HOLLIES — Hollies (Parlophone)

The Rolling Stones' debut LP also sold strongly enough to enter the singles chart, jumping straight to No.1 in the LPs. They managed this despite ignoring co-manager Eric Easton's advice to Andrew Loog Oldham in 1963: "The singer," said Easton, "will have to go. The BBC won't like him." The Folk Revival, a major US trend since 1961, brushed the LP chart via Peter, Paul & Mary. Bob Dylan's LP chart debut was as their sleevenote-writer, and composer of *Blowin' In The Wind*,

June – August 1964

20 June 1964

1	1	THE ROLLING STONES — Rolling Stones (Decca)
3	2	IT'S THE SEARCHERS — Searchers (Pye)
4	3	WITH THE BEATLES — Beatles (Parlophone)
8	4	SHOWCASE — Buddy Holly (Coral)
2	5	DANCE WITH THE SHADOWS — Shadows (Columbia)
5	6	WEST SIDE STORY — Soundtrack (CBS)
5	7	A SESSION WITH THE DAVE CLARK FIVE — Dave Clark Five (Columbia)
10	8	STAY WITH THE HOLLIES — Hollies (Parlophone)
-	8	IN DREAMS — Roy Orbison (London)
5	10	THE LATEST AND THE GREATEST — Chuck Berry (Pye International)

27 June 1964

1	1 THE ROLLING STONES — Rolling Stones (Decca)
4	2 SHOWCASE — Buddy Holly (Coral)
3	3 WITH THE BEATLES — Beatles (Parlophone)
5	4 DANCE WITH THE SHADOWS — Shadows (Columbia)
2	5 IT'S THE SEARCHERS — Searchers (Pye)
-	6 KISSIN' COUSINS — Elvis Presley (RCA)
6	7 WEST SIDE STORY — Soundtrack (CBS)
-	7 THE BACHELORS PLUS 16 GREAT SONGS — Bachelors (Decca)
-	7 THE MERSEYBEATS — Merseybeats (Fontana)
8	10 IN DREAMS — Roy Orbison (London)

4 July 1964

1	1 THE ROLLING STONES — Rolling Stones (Decca)
7	2 THE BACHELORS PLUS 16 GREAT SONGS — Bachelors (Decca)
2	3 SHOWCASE — Buddy Holly (Coral)
3	4 WITH THE BEATLES — Beatles (Parlophone)
6	5 KISSIN' COUSINS — Elvis Presley (RCA)
10	6 IN DREAMS — Roy Orbison (London)
4	7 DANCE WITH THE SHADOWS — Shadows (Columbia)
5	8 IT'S THE SEARCHERS — Searchers (Pye)
7	9 WEST SIDE STORY — Soundtrack (CBS)
7	10 THE MERSEYBEATS — Merseybeats (Fontana)

11 July 1964

1	1 THE ROLLING STONES — Rolling Stones (Decca)
5	2 KISSIN' COUSINS — Elvis Presley (RCA)
-	3 WONDERFUL LIFE — Cliff Richard & the Shadows (Columbia)
2	4 THE BACHELORS PLUS 16 GREAT SONGS — Bachelors (Decca)
8	5 IT'S THE SEARCHERS — Searchers (Pye)
3	6 SHOWCASE — Buddy Holly (Coral)
7	7 DANCE WITH THE SHADOWS — Shadows (Columbia)
4	8 WITH THE BEATLES — Beatles (Parlophone)
9	9 WEST SIDE STORY — Soundtrack (CBS)
-	10 THE LATEST AND THE GREATEST — Chuck Berry (Pye International)

18 July 1964

-	1 A HARD DAY'S NIGHT — Beatles (Parlophone)
1	2 THE ROLLING STONES — Rolling Stones (Decca)
3	3 WONDERFUL LIFE — Cliff Richard & the Shadows (Columbia)
4	4 THE BACHELORS PLUS 16 GREAT SONGS — Bachelors (Decca)
2	5 KISSIN' COUSINS — Elvis Presley (RCA)
9	6 WEST SIDE STORY — Soundtrack (CBS)
5	7 IT'S THE SEARCHERS — Searchers (Pye)
7	8 DANCE WITH THE SHADOWS — Shadows (Columbia)
8	9 WITH THE BEATLES — Beatles (Parlophone)
6	10 SHOWCASE — Buddy Holly (Coral)

25 July 1964

1	1 A HARD DAY'S NIGHT — Beatles (Parlophone)
2	2 THE ROLLING STONES — Rolling Stones (Decca)
3	3 WONDERFUL LIFE — Cliff Richard & the Shadows (Columbia)
5	4 KISSIN' COUSINS — Elvis Presley (RCA)
9	5 WITH THE BEATLES — Beatles (Parlophone)
6	6 WEST SIDE STORY — Soundtrack (CBS)
4	7 THE BACHELORS PLUS 16 GREAT SONGS — Bachelors (Decca)
7	8 IT'S THE SEARCHERS — Searchers (Pye)
8	9 DANCE WITH THE SHADOWS — Shadows (Columbia)
10	10 SHOWCASE — Buddy Holly (Coral)

1 August 1964

1	1 A HARD DAY'S NIGHT — Beatles (Parlophone)
2	2 THE ROLLING STONES — Rolling Stones (Decca)
3	3 WONDERFUL LIFE — Cliff Richard & the Shadows (Columbia)
7	4 THE BACHELORS PLUS 16 GREAT SONGS — Bachelors (Decca)
4	5 KISSIN' COUSINS — Elvis Presley (RCA)
6	6 WEST SIDE STORY — Soundtrack (CBS)
5	7 WITH THE BEATLES — Beatles (Parlophone)
-	8 A GIRL CALLED DUSTY — Dusty Springfield (Philips)
8	9 IT'S THE SEARCHERS — Searchers (Pye)
9	10 DANCE WITH THE SHADOWS — Shadows (Columbia)

8 August 1964

1	1 A HARD DAY'S NIGHT — Beatles (Parlophone)
2	2 THE ROLLING STONES — Rolling Stones (Decca)
3	3 WONDERFUL LIFE — Cliff Richard & the Shadows (Columbia)
4	4 THE BACHELORS PLUS 16 GREAT SONGS — Bachelors (Decca)
8	5 A GIRL CALLED DUSTY — Dusty Springfield (Philips)
5	6 KISSIN' COUSINS — Elvis Presley (RCA)
6	7 WEST SIDE STORY — Soundtrack (CBS)
9	8 IT'S THE SEARCHERS — Searchers (Pye)
-	9 PRESENTING DIONNE WARWICK — Dionne Warwick (Pye International)
7	10 WITH THE BEATLES — Beatles (Parlophone)

The title *Stay With The Hollies* referred to their revival of an 88-second masterpiece by Maurice Williams & the Zodiacs, *Stay* (to re-chart in 1978 by Jackson Browne), which they followed up with Doris Troy's *Just One Look*. Chuck Berry was surprised to be charting (he was also riding high with the 45 *No Particular Place To Go*), for despite his legendary status he had gone from 1958 till 1963 with no UK hit. (His only No.1 was to be 1972's *My Ding-A-Ling*, a ponderous novelty-item.)

August – October 1964

15 August 1964

last	this		
1	1	A HARD DAY'S NIGHT	Beatles (Parlophone)
2	2	THE ROLLING STONES	Rolling Stones (Decca)
3	3	WONDERFUL LIFE	Cliff Richard & the Shadows (Columbia)
4	4	THE BACHELORS PLUS 16 GREAT SONGS	Bachelors (Decca)
6	5	KISSIN' COUSINS	Elvis Presley (RCA)
-	6	A TOUCH OF VELVET	Jim Reeves (RCA)
10	7	WITH THE BEATLES	Beatles (Parlophone)
-	8	GENTLEMAN JIM	Jim Reeves (RCA)
7	9	WEST SIDE STORY	Soundtrack (CBS)
-	9	HELLO DOLLY	Louis Armstrong (London)

22 August 1964

1	1	A HARD DAY'S NIGHT	Beatles (Parlophone)
2	2	THE ROLLING STONES	Rolling Stones (Decca)
3	3	WONDERFUL LIFE	Cliff Richard & the Shadows (Columbia)
4	4	THE BACHELORS PLUS 16 GREAT SONGS	Bachelors (Decca)
8	5	GENTLEMAN JIM	Jim Reeves (RCA)
6	6	A TOUCH OF VELVET	Jim Reeves (RCA)
9	7	WEST SIDE STORY	Soundtrack (CBS)
5	8	KISSIN' COUSINS	Elvis Presley (RCA)
7	9	WITH THE BEATLES	Beatles (Parlophone)
-	10	IT'S THE SEARCHERS	Searchers (Pye)

29 August 1964

1	1	A HARD DAY'S NIGHT	Beatles (Parlophone)
2	2	THE ROLLING STONES	Rolling Stones (Decca)
3	3	WONDERFUL LIFE	Cliff Richard & the Shadows (Columbia)
4	4	THE BACHELORS PLUS 16 GREAT SONGS	Bachelors (Decca)
5	5	GENTLEMAN JIM	Jim Reeves (RCA)
7	6	WEST SIDE STORY	Soundtrack (CBS)
8	7	KISSIN' COUSINS	Elvis Presley (RCA)
-	8	GOOD 'N' COUNTRY	Jim Reeves (RCA)
6	9	A TOUCH OF VELVET	Jim Reeves (RCA)
-	10	HE'LL HAVE TO GO	Jim Reeves (RCA)

5 September 1964

1	1	A HARD DAY'S NIGHT	Beatles (Parlophone)
2	2	THE ROLLING STONES	Rolling Stones (Decca)
-	3	MOONLIGHT AND ROSES	Jim Reeves (RCA)
3	4	WONDERFUL LIFE	Cliff Richard & the Shadows (Columbia)
4	5	THE BACHELORS PLUS 16 GREAT SONGS	Bachelors (Decca)
5	5	GENTLEMAN JIM	Jim Reeves (RCA)
6	7	WEST SIDE STORY	Soundtrack (CBS)
9	8	A TOUCH OF VELVET	Jim Reeves (RCA)
8	9	GOOD 'N' COUNTRY	Jim Reeves (RCA)
7	10	KISSIN' COUSINS	Elvis Presley (RCA)

12 September 1964

1	1	A HARD DAY'S NIGHT	Beatles (Parlophone)
3	2	MOONLIGHT AND ROSES	Jim Reeves (RCA)
2	3	THE ROLLING STONES	Rolling Stones (Decca)
-	4	FIVE FACES OF MANFRED MANN	Manfred Mann (HMV)
5	5	GENTLEMAN JIM	Jim Reeves (RCA)
4	6	WONDERFUL LIFE	Cliff Richard & the Shadows (Columbia)
5	7	THE BACHELORS PLUS 16 GREAT SONGS	Bachelors (Decca)
8	7	A TOUCH OF VELVET	Jim Reeves (RCA)
-	9	A GIRL CALLED DUSTY	Dusty Springfield (Philips)
7	10	WEST SIDE STORY	Soundtrack (CBS)

19 September 1964

1	1	A HARD DAY'S NIGHT	Beatles (Parlophone)
3	2	THE ROLLING STONES	Rolling Stones (Decca)
2	3	MOONLIGHT AND ROSES	Jim Reeves (RCA)
4	4	FIVE FACES OF MANFRED MANN	Manfred Mann (HMV)
6	5	WONDERFUL LIFE	Cliff Richard & the Shadows (Columbia)
7	6	THE BACHELORS PLUS 16 GREAT SONGS	Bachelors (Decca)
5	7	GENTLEMAN JIM	Jim Reeves (RCA)
10	8	WEST SIDE STORY	Soundtrack (CBS)
-	9	GOD BE WITH YOU	Jim Reeves (RCA)
7	10	A TOUCH OF VELVET	Jim Reeves (RCA)

26 September 1964

1	1	A HARD DAY'S NIGHT	Beatles (Parlophone)
3	2	MOONLIGHT AND ROSES	Jim Reeves (RCA)
2	3	THE ROLLING STONES	Rolling Stones (Decca)
4	3	FIVE FACES OF MANFRED MANN	Manfred Mann (HMV)
7	5	GENTLEMAN JIM	Jim Reeves (RCA)
6	6	THE BACHELORS PLUS 16 GREAT SONGS	Bachelors (Decca)
5	7	WONDERFUL LIFE	Cliff Richard & the Shadows (Columbia)
9	8	GOD BE WITH YOU	Jim Reeves (RCA)
8	9	WEST SIDE STORY	Soundtrack (CBS)
10	9	A TOUCH OF VELVET	Jim Reeves (RCA)
-	9	GOOD 'N' COUNTRY	Jim Reeves (RCA)

3 October 1964

1	1	A HARD DAY'S NIGHT	Beatles (Parlophone)
3	2	THE ROLLING STONES	Rolling Stones (Decca)
3	3	FIVE FACES OF MANFRED MANN	Manfred Mann (HMV)
2	4	MOONLIGHT AND ROSES	Jim Reeves (RCA)
6	5	THE BACHELORS PLUS 16 GREAT SONGS	Bachelors (Decca)
7	6	WONDERFUL LIFE	Cliff Richard & the Shadows (Columbia)
5	7	GENTLEMAN JIM	Jim Reeves (RCA)
9	8	A TOUCH OF VELVET	Jim Reeves (RCA)
9	9	WEST SIDE STORY	Soundtrack (CBS)
-	10	IT MIGHT AS WELL BE SWING	Frank Sinatra/Count Basie (Reprise)

If Chuck Berry was a relative chart stranger, rock and blues classics remained in the public ear. Berry's *Johnny B. Goode*, Little Richard songs and Muddy Waters' *Got My Mojo Working* were core repertoire for every beat group, and now they were on vinyl.

The Swinging Blue Jeans had hit with *Good Golly Miss Molly*, the Beatles with their *Long Tall Sally* EP, and in November the Stones would be No.1 with *Little Red Rooster*, learnt from Howlin' Wolf. Oldest originator with a hit was Louis Armstrong.

October – November 1964

10 October 1964

last	this	
1	1	A HARD DAY'S NIGHT Beatles (Parlophone)
2	2	THE ROLLING STONES Rolling Stones (Decca)
3	3	FIVE FACES OF MANFRED MANN Manfred Mann (HMV)
4	4	MOONLIGHT AND ROSES Jim Reeves (RCA)
5	5	THE BACHELORS PLUS 16 GREAT SONGS Bachelors (Decca)
6	6	WONDERFUL LIFE Cliff Richard & the Shadows (Columbia)
-	6	THE KINKS Kinks (Pye)
7	8	GENTLEMAN JIM Jim Reeves (RCA)
9	9	WEST SIDE STORY Soundtrack (CBS)
-	10	FAME AT LAST Georgie Fame (Columbia)

17 October 1964

1	1	A HARD DAY'S NIGHT Beatles (Parlophone)
2	2	THE ROLLING STONES Rolling Stones (Decca)
3	3	FIVE FACES OF MANFRED MANN Manfred Mann (HMV)
4	4	MOONLIGHT AND ROSES Jim Reeves (RCA)
6	5	THE KINKS Kinks (Pye)
6	6	WONDERFUL LIFE Cliff Richard & the Shadows (Columbia)
5	6	THE BACHELORS PLUS 16 GREAT SONGS Bachelors (Decca)
9	8	WEST SIDE STORY Soundtrack (CBS)
8	9	GENTLEMAN JIM Jim Reeves (RCA)
-	10	IN DREAMS Roy Orbison (London)

24 October 1964

1	1	A HARD DAY'S NIGHT Beatles (Parlophone)
3	2	FIVE FACES OF MANFRED MANN Manfred Mann (HMV)
2	3	THE ROLLING STONES Rolling Stones (Decca)
5	4	THE KINKS Kinks (Pye)
4	5	MOONLIGHT AND ROSES Jim Reeves (RCA)
6	6	THE BACHELORS PLUS 16 GREAT SONGS Bachelors (Decca)
-	7	IN THE HOLLIES STYLE Hollies (Parlophone)
8	8	WEST SIDE STORY Soundtrack (CBS)
-	9	GOLDFINGER Soundtrack (United Artists)
9	10	GENTLEMAN JIM Jim Reeves (RCA)
6	10	WONDERFUL LIFE Cliff Richard & the Shadows (Columbia)

31 October 1964

1	1	A HARD DAY'S NIGHT Beatles (Parlophone)
3	2	THE ROLLING STONES Rolling Stones (Decca)
4	3	THE KINKS Kinks (Pye)
2	4	FIVE FACES OF MANFRED MANN Manfred Mann (HMV)
5	5	MOONLIGHT AND ROSES Jim Reeves (RCA)
6	6	THE BACHELORS PLUS 16 GREAT SONGS Bachelors (Decca)
-	7	IN DREAMS Roy Orbison (London)
10	8	GENTLEMAN JIM Jim Reeves (RCA)
7	9	IN THE HOLLIES STYLE Hollies (Parlophone)
10	10	WONDERFUL LIFE Cliff Richard & the Shadows (Columbia)

7 November 1964

1	1	A HARD DAY'S NIGHT Beatles (Parlophone)
2	2	THE ROLLING STONES Rolling Stones (Decca)
4	3	FIVE FACES OF MANFRED MANN Manfred Mann (HMV)
3	4	THE KINKS Kinks (Pye)
5	5	MOONLIGHT AND ROSES Jim Reeves (RCA)
7	6	IN DREAMS Roy Orbison (London)
6	7	THE BACHELORS PLUS 16 GREAT SONGS Bachelors (Decca)
10	8	WONDERFUL LIFE Cliff Richard & the Shadows (Columbia)
9	9	IN THE HOLLIES STYLE Hollies (Parlophone)
-	10	FRANK IFIELD'S GREATEST HITS Frank Ifield (Columbia)
8	10	GENTLEMAN JIM Jim Reeves (RCA)

14 November 1964

1	1	A HARD DAY'S NIGHT Beatles (Parlophone)
4	2	THE KINKS Kinks (Pye)
2	3	THE ROLLING STONES Rolling Stones (Decca)
-	4	THE ANIMALS Animals (Columbia)
3	5	FIVE FACES OF MANFRED MANN Manfred Mann (HMV)
-	6	THE FREEWHEELIN' BOB DYLAN Bob Dylan (CBS)
5	7	MOONLIGHT AND ROSES Jim Reeves (RCA)
6	8	IN DREAMS Roy Orbison (London)
8	9	WONDERFUL LIFE Cliff Richard & the Shadows (Columbia)
9	10	IN THE HOLLIES STYLE Hollies (Parlophone)

21 November 1964

1	1	A HARD DAY'S NIGHT Beatles (Parlophone)
4	2	THE ANIMALS Animals (Columbia)
3	3	THE ROLLING STONES Rolling Stones (Decca)
2	3	THE KINKS Kinks (Pye)
5	5	FIVE FACES OF MANFRED MANN Manfred Mann (HMV)
10	6	IN THE HOLLIES STYLE Hollies (Parlophone)
6	7	THE FREEWHEELIN' BOB DYLAN Bob Dylan (CBS)
7	8	MOONLIGHT AND ROSES Jim Reeves (RCA)
-	9	THE BACHELORS PLUS 16 GREAT SONGS Bachelors (Decca)
9	10	WONDERFUL LIFE Cliff Richard & the Shadows (Columbia)

28 November 1964

1	1	A HARD DAY'S NIGHT Beatles (Parlophone)
3	2	THE ROLLING STONES Rolling Stones (Decca)
2	3	THE ANIMALS Animals (Columbia)
3	4	THE KINKS Kinks (Pye)
8	5	MOONLIGHT AND ROSES Jim Reeves (RCA)
5	6	FIVE FACES OF MANFRED MANN Manfred Mann (HMV)
9	7	THE BACHELORS PLUS 16 GREAT SONGS Bachelors (Decca)
-	8	MEET THE SUPREMES Supremes (Stateside)
-	9	ANOTHER SIDE OF BOB DYLAN Bob Dylan (CBS)
-	10	IN DREAMS Roy Orbison (London)

Plane-crash victim Jim Reeves enjoyed phenomenal success in 1964. By October he had only two LPs in the Top 10, but there had been six of them since mid-August. In the last week of September, five of the Top 10 were Jim Reeves LPs. Another would arrive for Christmas. By year's end, he was the artist with the most chart weeks to his credit, Beatles notwithstanding. Meanwhile November saw Bob Dylan's first entry to the chart in his own right, with (oddly) both his second LP and his fourth.

last week	this week	5 December 1964		12 December 1964		19 December 1964		26 December 1964
1	1	A HARD DAY'S NIGHT Beatles (Parlophone)	- 1	BEATLES FOR SALE Beatles (Parlophone)	1 1	BEATLES FOR SALE Beatles (Parlophone)	1 1	BEATLES FOR SALE Beatles (Parlophone)
2	2	THE ROLLING STONES Rolling Stones (Decca)	1 2	A HARD DAY'S NIGHT Beatles (Parlophone)	4 2	12 SONGS OF CHRISTMAS Jim Reeves (RCA)	4 2	THE BACHELORS PLUS 16 GREAT SONGS Bachelors (Decca)
3	3	THE ANIMALS Animals (Columbia)	2 3	THE ROLLING STONES Rolling Stones (Decca)	2 3	A HARD DAY'S NIGHT Beatles (Parlophone)	10 3	LUCKY 13 SHADES OF VAL DOONICAN Val Doonican (Decca)
5	4	MOONLIGHT AND ROSES Jim Reeves (RCA)	7 4	12 SONGS OF CHRISTMAS Jim Reeves (RCA)	9 4	THE BACHELORS PLUS 16 GREAT SONGS Bachelors (Decca)	2 4	12 SONGS OF CHRISTMAS Jim Reeves (RCA)
4	5	THE KINKS Kinks (Pye)	5 5	THE KINKS Kinks (Pye)	6 5	OH, PRETTY WOMAN Roy Orbison (London)	3 5	A HARD DAY'S NIGHT Beatles (Parlophone)
7	6	THE BACHELORS PLUS 16 GREAT SONGS Bachelors (Decca)	8 6	OH, PRETTY WOMAN Roy Orbison (London)	3 6	THE ROLLING STONES Rolling Stones (Decca)	6 6	THE ROLLING STONES Rolling Stones (Decca)
-	7	12 SONGS OF CHRISTMAS Jim Reeves (RCA)	4 7	MOONLIGHT AND ROSES Jim Reeves (RCA)	7 7	MOONLIGHT AND ROSES Jim Reeves (RCA)	5 6	OH, PRETTY WOMAN Roy Orbison (London)
-	8	OH, PRETTY WOMAN Roy Orbison (London)	3 8	THE ANIMALS Animals (Columbia)	5 8	THE KINKS Kinks (Pye)	7 8	MOONLIGHT AND ROSES Jim Reeves (RCA)
6	9	FIVE FACES OF MANFRED MANN Manfred Mann (HMV)	9 9	FIVE FACES OF MANFRED MANN Manfred Mann (HMV)	9 9	ALADDIN AND HIS WONDERFUL LAMP Cliff Richard & the Shadows (Columbia)	9 9	ALADDIN AND HIS WONDERFUL LAMP Cliff Richard & the Shadows (Columbia)
-	10	ALADDIN AND HIS WONDERFUL LAMP Cliff Richard & the Shadows (Columbia)	6 9	THE BACHELORS PLUS 16 GREAT SONGS Bachelors (Decca)	- 10	LUCKY 13 SHADES OF VAL DOONICAN Val Doonican (Decca)	- 10	THE ANIMALS Animals (Columbia)
8	10	MEET THE SUPREMES Supremes (Stateside)	10 9	ALADDIN AND HIS WONDERFUL LAMP Cliff Richard & the Shadows (Columbia)				

Both Dylan LPs dropped out of the Top 10 after only a week but the wonder is that they had made it at all, with no chart single to stimulate sales. Every other act in the LP Top 10 at the time had big hit singles behind them. The Beatles, the Animals, the Kinks and Manfred Mann had all had recent No.1s; the Bachelors had scored a No.1 and three other Top 5 singles this year; the Supremes had had a No.2 in September and a No.1 earlier in November; Cliff Richard was about to get his fourth Top 10 of the year; the Hollies had already had four Top 10s in the last twelve months; Roy Orbison had just enjoyed his second No.1 of the year; and the Stones were at No.1 now. In contrast, Bob Dylan was not to enter the Top 10 singles chart until the following year. His success with two unsupported LPs, therefore, was something special - and hinted at the changes he was almost singlehandedly to bring about in the near future. Even as Beatlemania raged on both sides of the Atlantic, Dylan was to be the catalyst for the imminent split between "pop" and "rock", revolutionising what songs could say, calling radio's bluff in demanding the 3-minute single, deposing the 45 from its pre-eminent position, and empowering the LP as a medium in its own right. Thus the LP became the album. Dylan was to change the language of the industry as well as of the song. He would even change the Beatles.

January – February 1965

last this
week

2 January 1965

1	1	BEATLES FOR SALE — Beatles (Parlophone)
4	2	12 SONGS OF CHRISTMAS — Jim Reeves (RCA)
2	3	THE BACHELORS PLUS 16 GREAT SONGS — Bachelors (Decca)
5	4	A HARD DAY'S NIGHT — Beatles (Parlophone)
3	5	LUCKY 13 SHADES OF VAL DOONICAN — Val Doonican (Decca)
8	6	MOONLIGHT AND ROSES — Jim Reeves (RCA)
6	7	OH, PRETTY WOMAN — Roy Orbison (London)
9	8	ALADDIN AND HIS WONDERFUL LAMP — Cliff Richard & the Shadows (Columbia)
-	9	SPOTLIGHT ON THE MINSTRELS — George Mitchell Minstrels (HMV)
6	10	THE ROLLING STONES — Rolling Stones (Decca)

9 January 1965

1	1	BEATLES FOR SALE — Beatles (Parlophone)
5	2	LUCKY 13 SHADES OF VAL DOONICAN — Val Doonican (Decca)
3	3	THE BACHELORS PLUS 16 GREAT SONGS — Bachelors (Decca)
4	4	A HARD DAY'S NIGHT — Beatles (Parlophone)
10	5	THE ROLLING STONES — Rolling Stones (Decca)
7	6	OH, PRETTY WOMAN — Roy Orbison (London)
8	7	ALADDIN AND HIS WONDERFUL LAMP — Cliff Richard & the Shadows (Columbia)
6	8	MOONLIGHT AND ROSES — Jim Reeves (RCA)
-	9	THE ANIMALS — Animals (Columbia)
-	10	FAME AT LAST — Georgie Fame (Columbia)

16 January 1965

1	1	BEATLES FOR SALE — Beatles (Parlophone)
3	2	THE BACHELORS PLUS 16 GREAT SONGS — Bachelors (Decca)
2	3	LUCKY 13 SHADES OF VAL DOONICAN — Val Doonican (Decca)
4	4	A HARD DAY'S NIGHT — Beatles (Parlophone)
6	5	OH, PRETTY WOMAN — Roy Orbison (London)
5	6	THE ROLLING STONES — Rolling Stones (Decca)
7	7	ALADDIN AND HIS WONDERFUL LAMP — Cliff Richard & the Shadows (Columbia)
-	8	THE KINKS — Kinks (Pye)
9	9	THE ANIMALS — Animals (Columbia)
10	10	FAME AT LAST — Georgie Fame (Columbia)

23 January 1965

-	1	THE ROLLING STONES NO 2 — Rolling Stones (Decca)
1	2	BEATLES FOR SALE — Beatles (Parlophone)
3	3	LUCKY 13 SHADES OF VAL DOONICAN — Val Doonican (Decca)
2	4	THE BACHELORS PLUS 16 GREAT SONGS — Bachelors (Decca)
4	5	A HARD DAY'S NIGHT — Beatles (Parlophone)
8	6	THE KINKS — Kinks (Pye)
5	7	OH, PRETTY WOMAN — Roy Orbison (London)
7	8	ALADDIN AND HIS WONDERFUL LAMP — Cliff Richard & the Shadows (Columbia)
6	9	THE ROLLING STONES — Rolling Stones (Decca)
-	10	GENE PITNEY'S BIG SIXTEEN — Gene Pitney (Stateside)

30 January 1965

1	1	THE ROLLING STONES NO 2 — Rolling Stones (Decca)
2	2	BEATLES FOR SALE — Beatles (Parlophone)
3	3	LUCKY 13 SHADES OF VAL DOONICAN — Val Doonican (Decca)
-	4	THE BEST OF JIM REEVES — Jim Reeves (RCA)
4	5	THE BACHELORS PLUS 16 GREAT SONGS — Bachelors (Decca)
6	6	THE KINKS — Kinks (Pye)
5	7	A HARD DAY'S NIGHT — Beatles (Parlophone)
-	8	THE LENNON-McCARTNEY SONGBOOK — Keely Smith (Reprise)
10	9	GENE PITNEY'S BIG SIXTEEN — Gene Pitney (Stateside)
8	10	ALADDIN AND HIS WONDERFUL LAMP — Cliff Richard & the Shadows (Columbia)

6 February 1965

1	1	THE ROLLING STONES NO 2 — Rolling Stones (Decca)
2	2	BEATLES FOR SALE — Beatles (Parlophone)
4	3	THE BEST OF JIM REEVES — Jim Reeves (RCA)
3	4	LUCKY 13 SHADES OF VAL DOONICAN — Val Doonican (Decca)
6	5	THE KINKS — Kinks (Pye)
5	6	THE BACHELORS PLUS 16 GREAT SONGS — Bachelors (Decca)
8	7	THE LENNON-McCARTNEY SONGBOOK — Keely Smith (Reprise)
7	8	A HARD DAY'S NIGHT — Beatles (Parlophone)
-	9	THE VOICE OF WINSTON CHURCHILL — Winston Churchill (Decca)
-	10	ANOTHER SIDE OF BOB DYLAN — Bob Dylan (CBS)

13 February 1965

1	1	THE ROLLING STONES NO 2 — Rolling Stones (Decca)
2	2	BEATLES FOR SALE — Beatles (Parlophone)
3	3	THE BEST OF JIM REEVES — Jim Reeves (RCA)
4	4	LUCKY 13 SHADES OF VAL DOONICAN — Val Doonican (Decca)
-	5	CILLA — Cilla Black (Parlophone)
9	6	THE VOICE OF WINSTON CHURCHILL — Winston Churchill (Decca)
5	7	THE KINKS — Kinks (Pye)
6	8	THE BACHELORS PLUS 16 GREAT SONGS — Bachelors (Decca)
10	9	ANOTHER SIDE OF BOB DYLAN — Bob Dylan (CBS)
-	10	THE ANIMALS — Animals (Columbia)

20 February 1965

1	1	THE ROLLING STONES NO 2 — Rolling Stones (Decca)
2	2	BEATLES FOR SALE — Beatles (Parlophone)
3	3	THE BEST OF JIM REEVES — Jim Reeves (RCA)
5	4	CILLA — Cilla Black (Parlophone)
4	5	LUCKY 13 SHADES OF VAL DOONICAN — Val Doonican (Decca)
6	6	THE VOICE OF WINSTON CHURCHILL — Winston Churchill (Decca)
-	7	I'M GONNA BE STRONG — Gene Pitney (Stateside)
9	8	ANOTHER SIDE OF BOB DYLAN — Bob Dylan (CBS)
7	9	THE KINKS — Kinks (Pye)
10	10	THE ANIMALS — Animals (Columbia)

Winston Churchill, born 1874, took the Jim Reeves chart-route. Like Dylan, he had no supporting 45. The LP emphasised wartime speech extracts. More curious was The Keely Smith *Lennon-McCartney Songbook*. (This US female vocalist didn't really co-write the Beatles' songs). One of chart history's least-remembered entries, its success was due partly to the magic label "Lennon-McCartney", and partly to Frank Sinatra's label Reprise – it had already achieved chart placings for eleven albums.

27 February 1965

last week / this week

last	this		
1	1	THE ROLLING STONES NO 2	Rolling Stones (Decca)
2	2	BEATLES FOR SALE	Beatles (Parlophone)
3	3	THE BEST OF JIM REEVES	Jim Reeves (RCA)
4	4	CILLA Cilla Black (Parlophone)	
6	5	THE VOICE OF WINSTON CHURCHILL	Winston Churchill (Decca)
5	6	LUCKY 13 SHADES OF VAL DOONICAN	Val Doonican (Decca)
8	7	ANOTHER SIDE OF BOB DYLAN	Bob Dylan (CBS)
9	8	THE KINKS Kinks (Pye)	
7	9	I'M GONNA BE STRONG	Gene Pitney (Stateside)
-	10	SANDIE Sandie Shaw (Pye)	

6 March 1965

1	1	THE ROLLING STONES NO 2 Rolling Stones (Decca)
2	2	BEATLES FOR SALE Beatles (Parlophone)
10	3	SANDIE Sandie Shaw (Pye)
3	4	THE BEST OF JIM REEVES Jim Reeves (RCA)
5	5	THE VOICE OF WINSTON CHURCHILL Winston Churchill (Decca)
6	6	LUCKY 13 SHADES OF VAL DOONICAN Val Doonican (Decca)
8	7	THE KINKS Kinks (Pye)
9	8	I'M GONNA BE STRONG Gene Pitney (Stateside)
4	9	CILLA Cilla Black (Parlophone)
-	10	THE BACHELORS PLUS 16 GREAT SONGS Bachelors (Decca)

13 March 1965

1	1	THE ROLLING STONES NO 2 Rolling Stones (Decca)
2	2	BEATLES FOR SALE Beatles (Parlophone)
4	3	THE BEST OF JIM REEVES Jim Reeves (RCA)
3	4	SANDIE Sandie Shaw (Pye)
-	5	KINDA KINKS Kinks (Pye)
6	6	LUCKY 13 SHADES OF VAL DOONICAN Val Doonican (Decca)
9	7	CILLA Cilla Black (Parlophone)
5	8	THE VOICE OF WINSTON CHURCHILL Winston Churchill (Decca)
-	9	THE FREEWHEELIN' BOB DYLAN Bob Dylan (CBS)
-	10	MARY POPPINS Soundtrack (HMV)

20 March 1965

1	1	THE ROLLING STONES NO 2 Rolling Stones (Decca)
5	2	KINDA KINKS Kinks (Pye)
2	3	BEATLES FOR SALE Beatles (Parlophone)
4	4	SANDIE Sandie Shaw (Pye)
-	5	THE PRETTY THINGS Pretty Things (Fontana)
7	6	CILLA Cilla Black (Parlophone)
9	7	THE FREEWHEELIN' BOB DYLAN Bob Dylan (CBS)
-	8	ANOTHER SIDE OF BOB DYLAN Bob Dylan (CBS)
-	9	THE UNFORGETTABLE NAT 'KING' COLE Nat 'King' Cole (Capitol)
6	10	LUCKY 13 SHADES OF VAL DOONICAN Val Doonican (Decca)

27 March 1965

1	1	THE ROLLING STONES NO 2 Rolling Stones (Decca)
2	2	KINDA KINKS Kinks (Pye)
3	3	BEATLES FOR SALE Beatles (Parlophone)
4	4	SANDIE Sandie Shaw (Pye)
7	5	THE FREEWHEELIN' BOB DYLAN Bob Dylan (CBS)
5	6	THE PRETTY THINGS Pretty Things (Fontana)
-	7	THE BEST OF JIM REEVES Jim Reeves (RCA)
-	8	THE TIMES THEY ARE A-CHANGIN' Bob Dylan (CBS)
8	9	ANOTHER SIDE OF BOB DYLAN Bob Dylan (CBS)
6	10	CILLA Cilla Black (Parlophone)

3 April 1965

1	1	THE ROLLING STONES NO 2 Rolling Stones (Decca)
3	2	BEATLES FOR SALE Beatles (Parlophone)
5	3	THE FREEWHEELIN' BOB DYLAN Bob Dylan (CBS)
2	4	KINDA KINKS Kinks (Pye)
8	5	THE TIMES THEY ARE A-CHANGIN' Bob Dylan (CBS)
6	6	THE PRETTY THINGS Pretty Things (Fontana)
4	6	SANDIE Sandie Shaw (Pye)
7	8	THE BEST OF JIM REEVES Jim Reeves (RCA)
-	9	LUCKY 13 SHADES OF VAL DOONICAN Val Doonican (Decca)
-	10	A COLLECTION OF 16 TAMLA MOTOWN HITS Various Artists (Tamla Motown)

10 April 1965

1	1	THE ROLLING STONES NO 2 Rolling Stones (Decca)
3	2	THE FREEWHEELIN' BOB DYLAN Bob Dylan (CBS)
2	3	BEATLES FOR SALE Beatles (Parlophone)
4	3	KINDA KINKS Kinks (Pye)
5	5	THE TIMES THEY ARE A-CHANGIN' Bob Dylan (CBS)
6	6	THE PRETTY THINGS Pretty Things (Fontana)
-	6	CLIFF RICHARD Cliff Richard (Columbia)
-	8	SOUNDS LIKE THE SEARCHERS Searchers (Pye)
-	9	HAVE I TOLD YOU LATELY THAT I LOVE YOU Jim Reeves (RCA)
-	10	THE UNFORGETTABLE NAT 'KING' COLE Nat 'King' Cole (Capitol)

17 April 1965

1	1	THE ROLLING STONES NO 2 Rolling Stones (Decca)
3	2	BEATLES FOR SALE Beatles (Parlophone)
2	3	THE FREEWHEELIN' BOB DYLAN Bob Dylan (CBS)
5	4	THE TIMES THEY ARE A-CHANGIN' Bob Dylan (CBS)
9	5	HAVE I TOLD YOU LATELY THAT I LOVE YOU Jim Reeves (RCA)
6	6	THE PRETTY THINGS Pretty Things (Fontana)
3	7	KINDA KINKS Kinks (Pye)
6	8	CLIFF RICHARD Cliff Richard (Columbia)
-	9	MARY POPPINS Soundtrack (HMV)
-	10	THE SOUND OF MUSIC Soundtrack (RCA)

February saw *Another Side Of Bob Dylan*, his fourth LP, back in the Top 10, and by the end of March he was in the lists with a vengeance, with his second album, *Freewheelin'*, re-entering alongside his newly-arrived third LP, while its title-track, aptly named *The Times They Are A-Changin'*, finally took him into the singles chart. In April this went Top 10, as he came to Britain for what would prove his last solo-acoustic tour, captured on D.A. Pennebaker's pioneering rock-doc *Don't Look Back*.

April – June 1965

24 April 1965

last week	this week		
2	1	BEATLES FOR SALE	Beatles (Parlophone)
1	2	THE ROLLING STONES NO 2	Rolling Stones (Decca)
3	3	THE FREEWHEELIN' BOB DYLAN	Bob Dylan (CBS)
9	4	MARY POPPINS	Soundtrack (HMV)
10	5	THE SOUND OF MUSIC	Soundtrack (RCA)
4	5	THE TIMES THEY ARE A-CHANGIN'	Bob Dylan (CBS)
-	7	ANOTHER SIDE OF BOB DYLAN	Bob Dylan (CBS)
7	8	KINDA KINKS	Kinks (Pye)
6	9	THE PRETTY THINGS	Pretty Things (Fontana)
8	10	CLIFF RICHARD	Cliff Richard (Columbia)

1 May 1965

last week	this week		
1	1	BEATLES FOR SALE	Beatles (Parlophone)
2	2	THE ROLLING STONES NO 2	Rolling Stones (Decca)
3	3	THE FREEWHEELIN' BOB DYLAN	Bob Dylan (CBS)
4	4	MARY POPPINS	Soundtrack (HMV)
10	5	CLIFF RICHARD	Cliff Richard (Columbia)
-	6	GIRL HAPPY	Elvis Presley (RCA)
5	7	THE SOUND OF MUSIC	Soundtrack (RCA)
5	8	THE TIMES THEY ARE A-CHANGIN'	Bob Dylan (CBS)
9	9	THE PRETTY THINGS	Pretty Things (Fontana)
8	10	KINDA KINKS	Kinks (Pye)

8 May 1965

last week	this week		
1	1	BEATLES FOR SALE	Beatles (Parlophone)
3	2	THE FREEWHEELIN' BOB DYLAN	Bob Dylan (CBS)
2	3	THE ROLLING STONES NO 2	Rolling Stones (Decca)
6	4	GIRL HAPPY	Elvis Presley (RCA)
4	5	MARY POPPINS	Soundtrack (HMV)
7	6	THE SOUND OF MUSIC	Soundtrack (RCA)
8	7	THE TIMES THEY ARE A-CHANGIN'	Bob Dylan (CBS)
-	8	ANOTHER SIDE OF BOB DYLAN	Bob Dylan (CBS)
-	9	THE JIM REEVES WAY	Jim Reeves (RCA)
9	10	THE PRETTY THINGS	Pretty Things (Fontana)
-	10	MARIANNE FAITHFULL	Marianne Faithfull (Decca)

15 May 1965

last week	this week		
2	1	THE FREEWHEELIN' BOB DYLAN	Bob Dylan (CBS)
1	2	BEATLES FOR SALE	Beatles (Parlophone)
4	3	GIRL HAPPY	Elvis Presley (RCA)
5	3	MARY POPPINS	Soundtrack (HMV)
7	5	THE TIMES THEY ARE A-CHANGIN'	Bob Dylan (CBS)
6	6	THE SOUND OF MUSIC	Soundtrack (RCA)
-	7	ANIMAL TRACKS	Animals (Columbia)
3	8	THE ROLLING STONES NO 2	Rolling Stones (Decca)
9	9	THE JIM REEVES WAY	Jim Reeves (RCA)
-	10	BRINGING IT ALL BACK HOME	Bob Dylan (CBS)
-	10	CLIFF RICHARD	Cliff Richard (Columbia)

22 May 1965

last week	this week		
10	1	BRINGING IT ALL BACK HOME	Bob Dylan (CBS)
7	2	ANIMAL TRACKS	Animals (Columbia)
-	3	HIT MAKER	Burt Bacharach (London)
2	4	BEATLES FOR SALE	Beatles (Parlophone)
1	5	THE FREEWHEELIN' BOB DYLAN	Bob Dylan (CBS)
3	6	MARY POPPINS	Soundtrack (HMV)
5	7	THE TIMES THEY ARE A-CHANGIN'	Bob Dylan (CBS)
9	7	THE JIM REEVES WAY	Jim Reeves (RCA)
6	9	THE SOUND OF MUSIC	Soundtrack (RCA)
-	10	WHAT'S BIN DID AND WHAT'S BIN HID	Donovan (Pye)

29 May 1965

last week	this week		
1	1	BRINGING IT ALL BACK HOME	Bob Dylan (CBS)
3	2	HIT MAKER	Burt Bacharach (London)
5	3	THE FREEWHEELIN' BOB DYLAN	Bob Dylan (CBS)
9	4	THE SOUND OF MUSIC	Soundtrack (RCA)
4	5	BEATLES FOR SALE	Beatles (Parlophone)
10	6	WHAT'S BIN DID AND WHAT'S BIN HID	Donovan (Pye)
6	7	MARY POPPINS	Soundtrack (HMV)
7	8	THE JIM REEVES WAY	Jim Reeves (RCA)
2	9	ANIMAL TRACKS	Animals (Columbia)
-	10	THE ROLLING STONES NO 2	Rolling Stones (Decca)

5 June 1965

last week	this week		
1	1	BRINGING IT ALL BACK HOME	Bob Dylan (CBS)
4	2	THE SOUND OF MUSIC	Soundtrack (RCA)
2	3	HIT MAKER	Burt Bacharach (London)
7	4	MARY POPPINS	Soundtrack (HMV)
5	5	BEATLES FOR SALE	Beatles (Parlophone)
6	6	WHAT'S BIN DID AND WHAT'S BIN HID	Donovan (Pye)
9	6	ANIMAL TRACKS	Animals (Columbia)
3	8	THE FREEWHEELIN' BOB DYLAN	Bob Dylan (CBS)
10	9	THE ROLLING STONES NO 2	Rolling Stones (Decca)
8	10	THE JIM REEVES WAY	Jim Reeves (RCA)

12 June 1965

last week	this week		
1	1	BRINGING IT ALL BACK HOME	Bob Dylan (CBS)
2	2	THE SOUND OF MUSIC	Soundtrack (RCA)
3	3	HIT MAKER	Burt Bacharach (London)
8	4	THE FREEWHEELIN' BOB DYLAN	Bob Dylan (CBS)
6	5	ANIMAL TRACKS	Animals (Columbia)
6	6	WHAT'S BIN DID AND WHAT'S BIN HID	Donovan (Pye)
4	7	MARY POPPINS	Soundtrack (HMV)
5	7	BEATLES FOR SALE	Beatles (Parlophone)
9	9	THE SEEKERS	Seekers (Decca)
-	10	'14'	Various Artists (Decca)

In mid-tour, Dylan was told by the Sheriff of Nottingham's wife: "everybody loves you... I think the songs are very wonderful. And you write them yourself, too, don't you, sometimes?" By May Day, Dylan's "electric" single, *Subterranean Homesick Blues,* was in the Top 20 alongside his two-year-old "protest" song; soon after, his new album, with one acoustic and one electric side, topped the LP chart. The Sheriff's wife surely preferred the LPs just below it in early June: *The Sound of Music* and *Hit Maker.*

last this week **19 June 1965**

last	this	
1	1	BRINGING IT ALL BACK HOME Bob Dylan (CBS)
2	2	THE SOUND OF MUSIC Soundtrack (RCA)
3	3	HIT MAKER Burt Bacharach (London)
6	4	WHAT'S BIN DID AND WHAT'S BIN HID Donovan (Pye)
7	5	MARY POPPINS Soundtrack (HMV)
7	6	BEATLES FOR SALE Beatles (Parlophone)
4	7	THE FREEWHEELIN' BOB DYLAN Bob Dylan (CBS)
9	8	THE SEEKERS Seekers (Decca)
-	9	ALONG CAME JONES Tom Jones (Decca)
-	10	JOAN BAEZ/5 Joan Baez (Fontana)

26 June 1965

2	1	THE SOUND OF MUSIC Soundtrack (RCA)
1	2	BRINGING IT ALL BACK HOME Bob Dylan (CBS)
4	3	WHAT'S BIN DID AND WHAT'S BIN HID Donovan (Pye)
3	4	HIT MAKER Burt Bacharach (London)
5	5	MARY POPPINS Soundtrack (HMV)
10	6	JOAN BAEZ/5 Joan Baez (Fontana)
7	7	THE FREEWHEELIN' BOB DYLAN Bob Dylan (CBS)
6	8	BEATLES FOR SALE Beatles (Parlophone)
-	9	HOLLY IN THE HILLS Buddy Holly (Coral)
8	10	THE SEEKERS Seekers (Decca)

3 July 1965

2	1	BRINGING IT ALL BACK HOME Bob Dylan (CBS)
1	2	THE SOUND OF MUSIC Soundtrack (RCA)
6	3	JOAN BAEZ/5 Joan Baez (Fontana)
3	4	WHAT'S BIN DID AND WHAT'S BIN HID Donovan (Pye)
5	5	MARY POPPINS Soundtrack (HMV)
4	6	HIT MAKER Burt Bacharach (London)
-	7	A WORLD OF OUR OWN Seekers (Columbia)
9	8	HOLLY IN THE HILLS Buddy Holly (Coral)
8	9	BEATLES FOR SALE Beatles (Parlophone)
-	9	THE ROLLING STONES NO 2 Rolling Stones (Decca)

10 July 1965

1	1	BRINGING IT ALL BACK HOME Bob Dylan (CBS)
2	2	THE SOUND OF MUSIC Soundtrack (RCA)
3	3	JOAN BAEZ/5 Joan Baez (Fontana)
7	4	A WORLD OF OUR OWN Seekers (Columbia)
4	5	WHAT'S BIN DID AND WHAT'S BIN HID Donovan (Pye)
5	6	MARY POPPINS Soundtrack (HMV)
6	7	HIT MAKER Burt Bacharach (London)
-	8	THE FREEWHEELIN' BOB DYLAN Bob Dylan (CBS)
-	9	JOAN BAEZ Joan Baez (Fontana)
8	10	HOLLY IN THE HILLS Buddy Holly (Coral)

17 July 1965

1	1	BRINGING IT ALL BACK HOME Bob Dylan (CBS)
2	2	THE SOUND OF MUSIC Soundtrack (RCA)
3	3	JOAN BAEZ/5 Joan Baez (Fontana)
4	4	A WORLD OF OUR OWN Seekers (Columbia)
6	5	MARY POPPINS Soundtrack (HMV)
-	6	THE SOUND OF THE SHADOWS Shadows (Columbia)
7	7	HIT MAKER Burt Bacharach (London)
5	8	WHAT'S BIN DID AND WHAT'S BIN HID Donovan (Pye)
8	9	THE FREEWHEELIN' BOB DYLAN Bob Dylan (CBS)
10	9	HOLLY IN THE HILLS Buddy Holly (Coral)

24 July 1965

2	1	THE SOUND OF MUSIC Soundtrack (RCA)
1	2	BRINGING IT ALL BACK HOME Bob Dylan (CBS)
3	3	JOAN BAEZ/5 Joan Baez (Fontana)
6	4	THE SOUND OF THE SHADOWS Shadows (Columbia)
5	5	MARY POPPINS Soundtrack (HMV)
7	6	HIT MAKER Burt Bacharach (London)
9	7	HOLLY IN THE HILLS Buddy Holly (Coral)
9	8	THE FREEWHEELIN' BOB DYLAN Bob Dylan (CBS)
8	9	WHAT'S BIN DID AND WHAT'S BIN HID Donovan (Pye)
-	10	JOAN BAEZ IN CONCERT, VOL. 2 Joan Baez (Fontana)
-	10	ALMOST THERE Andy Williams (CBS)

31 July 1965

1	1	THE SOUND OF MUSIC Soundtrack (RCA)
2	2	BRINGING IT ALL BACK HOME Bob Dylan (CBS)
3	3	JOAN BAEZ/5 Joan Baez (Fontana)
5	4	MARY POPPINS Soundtrack (HMV)
4	5	THE SOUND OF THE SHADOWS Shadows (Columbia)
10	6	ALMOST THERE Andy Williams (CBS)
10	7	JOAN BAEZ IN CONCERT, VOL. 2 Joan Baez (Fontana)
9	8	WHAT'S BIN DID AND WHAT'S BIN HID Donovan (Pye)
-	9	A WORLD OF OUR OWN Seekers (Columbia)
8	10	THE FREEWHEELIN' BOB DYLAN Bob Dylan (CBS)

7 August 1965

1	1	THE SOUND OF MUSIC Soundtrack (RCA)
4	2	MARY POPPINS Soundtrack (HMV)
2	3	BRINGING IT ALL BACK HOME Bob Dylan (CBS)
3	4	JOAN BAEZ/5 Joan Baez (Fontana)
-	5	THE MAGNIFICENT MOODIES Moody Blues (Decca)
6	5	ALMOST THERE Andy Williams (CBS)
5	7	THE SOUND OF THE SHADOWS Shadows (Columbia)
7	8	JOAN BAEZ IN CONCERT, VOL. 2 Joan Baez (Fontana)
9	9	A WORLD OF OUR OWN Seekers (Columbia)
-	10	BEATLES FOR SALE Beatles (Parlophone)

Burt Bacharach and Hal David were a "sophisticat" Goffin-King: a series of their songs became unfailing hits for whoever recorded them, while being instantly recognisable as Bacharach-Davids. There was *Walk On By* and *You'll Never Get To Heaven* by Dionne Warwick - the former would chart again for the Stranglers in 1978 - *Anyone Who Had A Heart* by Dionne Warwick and by Cilla Black. *Trains And Boats And Planes* was a 1965 hit by Billy J. Kramer and by Bacharach himself.

August – October 1965

14 August 1965

-	1	HELP! Beatles (Parlophone)
1	2	THE SOUND OF MUSIC Soundtrack (RCA)
2	3	MARY POPPINS Soundtrack (HMV)
4	4	JOAN BAEZ/5 Joan Baez (Fontana)
3	5	BRINGING IT ALL BACK HOME Bob Dylan (CBS)
5	6	THE MAGNIFICENT MOODIES Moody Blues (Decca)
5	7	ALMOST THERE Andy Williams (CBS)
7	8	THE SOUND OF THE SHADOWS Shadows (Columbia)
8	9	JOAN BAEZ IN CONCERT, VOL. 2 Joan Baez (Fontana)
9	10	A WORLD OF OUR OWN Seekers (Columbia)

21 August 1965

1	1	HELP! Beatles (Parlophone)
2	2	THE SOUND OF MUSIC Soundtrack (RCA)
3	3	MARY POPPINS Soundtrack (HMV)
4	4	JOAN BAEZ/5 Joan Baez (Fontana)
6	5	THE MAGNIFICENT MOODIES Moody Blues (Decca)
5	5	BRINGING IT ALL BACK HOME Bob Dylan (CBS)
7	7	ALMOST THERE Andy Williams (CBS)
8	8	THE SOUND OF THE SHADOWS Shadows (Columbia)
-	9	MR. TAMBOURINE MAN Byrds (CBS)
9	10	JOAN BAEZ IN CONCERT, VOL. 2 Joan Baez (Fontana)

28 August 1965

1	1	HELP! Beatles (Parlophone)
2	2	THE SOUND OF MUSIC Soundtrack (RCA)
3	3	MARY POPPINS Soundtrack (HMV)
4	4	JOAN BAEZ/ 5 Joan Baez (Fontana)
9	5	MR. TAMBOURINE MAN Byrds (CBS)
7	6	ALMOST THERE Andy Williams (CBS)
5	7	BRINGING IT ALL BACK HOME Bob Dylan (CBS)
8	8	THE SOUND OF THE SHADOWS Shadows (Columbia)
-	8	CATCH US IF YOU CAN Dave Clark Five (Columbia)
-	10	THE TIMES THEY ARE A-CHANGIN' Bob Dylan (CBS)

4 September 1965

1	1	HELP! Beatles (Parlophone)
2	2	THE SOUND OF MUSIC Soundtrack (RCA)
3	3	MARY POPPINS Soundtrack (HMV)
4	4	JOAN BAEZ/5 Joan Baez (Fontana)
7	5	BRINGING IT ALL BACK HOME Bob Dylan (CBS)
6	6	ALMOST THERE Andy Williams (CBS)
5	7	MR. TAMBOURINE MAN Byrds (CBS)
8	8	THE SOUND OF THE SHADOWS Shadows (Columbia)
-	9	THE FREEWHEELIN' BOB DYLAN Bob Dylan (CBS)
-	10	FLAMING STAR AND SUMMER KISSES Elvis Presley (RCA)

11 September 1965

1	1	HELP! Beatles (Parlophone)
2	2	THE SOUND OF MUSIC Soundtrack (RCA)
3	3	MARY POPPINS Soundtrack (HMV)
5	4	BRINGING IT ALL BACK HOME Bob Dylan (CBS)
6	5	ALMOST THERE Andy Williams (CBS)
4	6	JOAN BAEZ/5 Joan Baez (Fontana)
10	7	FLAMING STAR AND SUMMER KISSES Elvis Presley (RCA)
-	8	JOAN BAEZ IN CONCERT, VOL. 2 Joan Baez (Fontana)
-	9	CATCH US IF YOU CAN Dave Clark Five (Columbia)
-	10	THE ROLLING STONES NO 2 Rolling Stones (Decca)

18 September 1965

1	1	HELP! Beatles (Parlophone)
2	2	THE SOUND OF MUSIC Soundtrack (RCA)
3	3	MARY POPPINS Soundtrack (HMV)
5	4	ALMOST THERE Andy Williams (CBS)
6	5	JOAN BAEZ/5 Joan Baez (Fontana)
4	6	BRINGING IT ALL BACK HOME Bob Dylan (CBS)
7	7	FLAMING STAR AND SUMMER KISSES Elvis Presley (RCA)
-	8	MORE GREAT SONG HITS Bachelors (Decca)
-	9	THERE IS ONLY ONE ROY ORBISON Roy Orbison (London)
8	10	JOAN BAEZ IN CONCERT, VOL. 2 Joan Baez (Fontana)
-	10	MY FAIR LADY Soundtrack (CBS)

25 September 1965

1	1	HELP! Beatles (Parlophone)
2	2	THE SOUND OF MUSIC Soundtrack (RCA)
3	3	MARY POPPINS Soundtrack (HMV)
4	4	ALMOST THERE Andy Williams (CBS)
6	5	BRINGING IT ALL BACK HOME Bob Dylan (CBS)
5	6	JOAN BAEZ/5 Joan Baez (Fontana)
9	7	THERE IS ONLY ONE ROY ORBISON Roy Orbison (London)
7	8	FLAMING STAR AND SUMMER KISSES Elvis Presley (RCA)
-	9	ALL I REALLY WANT TO DO Cher (Liberty)
10	10	JOAN BAEZ IN CONCERT, VOL. 2 Joan Baez (Fontana)

2 October 1965

1	1	HELP! Beatles (Parlophone)
2	2	THE SOUND OF MUSIC Soundtrack (RCA)
-	3	OUT OF OUR HEADS Rolling Stones (Decca)
3	4	MARY POPPINS Soundtrack (HMV)
4	5	ALMOST THERE Andy Williams (CBS)
9	6	ALL I REALLY WANT TO DO Cher (Liberty)
5	7	BRINGING IT ALL BACK HOME Bob Dylan (CBS)
6	8	JOAN BAEZ/5 Joan Baez (Fontana)
-	9	HOLLIES Hollies (Parlophone)
8	10	FLAMING STAR AND SUMMER KISSES Elvis Presley (RCA)

And then came Joan Baez. Since mid-June she'd been quietly storming the chart (in parallel with the single *There But For Fortune*), with her exciting LP titles *Joan Baez In Concert No.5*, *Joan Baez*, and *Joan Baez In Concert No.2* (in that order). The first and last of these were to stay in and around the Top 10 all through August and September, by which time she had another hit single with Dylan's *It's All Over Now Baby Blue*, while he rode the charts with the 6-minute long single *Like A Rolling Stone*.

9 October 1965

last week	this week
1	1 HELP! Beatles (Parlophone)
3	2 OUT OF OUR HEADS Rolling Stones (Decca)
2	3 THE SOUND OF MUSIC Soundtrack (RCA)
4	4 MARY POPPINS Soundtrack (HMV)
5	5 ALMOST THERE Andy Williams (CBS)
-	6 HIGHWAY 61 REVISITED Bob Dylan (CBS)
-	7 LOOK AT US Sonny & Cher (Atlantic)
9	8 HOLLIES Hollies (Parlophone)
6	9 ALL I REALLY WANT TO DO Cher (Liberty)
7	9 BRINGING IT ALL BACK HOME Bob Dylan (CBS)

16 October 1965

last week	this week
1	1 HELP! Beatles (Parlophone)
3	2 THE SOUND OF MUSIC Soundtrack (RCA)
2	3 OUT OF OUR HEADS Rolling Stones (Decca)
4	4 MARY POPPINS Soundtrack (HMV)
6	5 HIGHWAY 61 REVISITED Bob Dylan (CBS)
5	6 ALMOST THERE Andy Williams (CBS)
7	7 LOOK AT US Sonny & Cher (Atlantic)
-	8 EVERYTHING'S COMING UP DUSTY Dusty Springfield (Philips)
8	9 HOLLIES Hollies (Parlophone)
-	10 FLAMING STAR AND SUMMER KISSES Elvis Presley (RCA)

23 October 1965

last week	this week
1	1 HELP! Beatles (Parlophone)
2	2 THE SOUND OF MUSIC Soundtrack (RCA)
3	3 OUT OF OUR HEADS Rolling Stones (Decca)
4	3 MARY POPPINS Soundtrack (HMV)
5	5 HIGHWAY 61 REVISITED Bob Dylan (CBS)
6	6 ALMOST THERE Andy Williams (CBS)
8	7 EVERYTHING'S COMING UP DUSTY Dusty Springfield (Philips)
7	8 LOOK AT US Sonny & Cher (Atlantic)
-	9 MANN MADE Manfred Mann (HMV)
-	10 MORE GREAT SONG HITS Bachelors (Decca)

30 October 1965

last week	this week
2	1 THE SOUND OF MUSIC Soundtrack (RCA)
1	2 HELP! Beatles (Parlophone)
3	3 OUT OF OUR HEADS Rolling Stones (Decca)
3	4 MARY POPPINS Soundtrack (HMV)
6	5 ALMOST THERE Andy Williams (CBS)
5	6 HIGHWAY 61 REVISITED Bob Dylan (CBS)
7	7 EVERYTHING'S COMING UP DUSTY Dusty Springfield (Philips)
8	8 LOOK AT US Sonny & Cher (Atlantic)
9	9 MANN MADE Manfred Mann (HMV)
-	10 ALL I REALLY WANT TO DO Cher (Liberty)

6 November 1965

last week	this week
1	1 THE SOUND OF MUSIC Soundtrack (RCA)
3	2 OUT OF OUR HEADS Rolling Stones (Decca)
2	3 HELP! Beatles (Parlophone)
4	4 MARY POPPINS Soundtrack (HMV)
5	5 ALMOST THERE Andy Williams (CBS)
6	6 HIGHWAY 61 REVISITED Bob Dylan (CBS)
7	7 EVERYTHING'S COMING UP DUSTY Dusty Springfield (Philips)
8	8 LOOK AT US Sonny & Cher (Atlantic)
9	9 MANN MADE Manfred Mann (HMV)
-	10 FAIRYTALE Donovan (Pye)

13 November 1965

last week	this week
1	1 THE SOUND OF MUSIC Soundtrack (RCA)
3	2 HELP! Beatles (Parlophone)
4	3 MARY POPPINS Soundtrack (HMV)
2	4 OUT OF OUR HEADS Rolling Stones (Decca)
7	5 EVERYTHING'S COMING UP DUSTY Dusty Springfield (Philips)
5	6 ALMOST THERE Andy Williams (CBS)
6	7 HIGHWAY 61 REVISITED Bob Dylan (CBS)
8	8 LOOK AT US Sonny & Cher (Atlantic)
9	9 MANN MADE Manfred Mann (HMV)
10	10 FAIRYTALE Donovan (Pye)
-	10 FAREWELL ANGELINA Joan Baez (Fontana)

20 November 1965

last week	this week
1	1 THE SOUND OF MUSIC Soundtrack (RCA)
2	2 HELP! Beatles (Parlophone)
4	3 OUT OF OUR HEADS Rolling Stones (Decca)
3	4 MARY POPPINS Soundtrack (HMV)
6	5 ALMOST THERE Andy Williams (CBS)
7	6 HIGHWAY 61 REVISITED Bob Dylan (CBS)
5	7 EVERYTHING'S COMING UP DUSTY Dusty Springfield (Philips)
10	8 FAREWELL ANGELINA Joan Baez (Fontana)
8	9 LOOK AT US Sonny & Cher (Atlantic)
9	10 MANN MADE Manfred Mann (HMV)

27 November 1965

last week	this week
1	1 THE SOUND OF MUSIC Soundtrack (RCA)
2	2 HELP! Beatles (Parlophone)
4	3 MARY POPPINS Soundtrack (HMV)
3	4 OUT OF OUR HEADS Rolling Stones (Decca)
5	5 ALMOST THERE Andy Williams (CBS)
6	6 HIGHWAY 61 REVISITED Bob Dylan (CBS)
10	7 MANN MADE Manfred Mann (HMV)
8	8 FAREWELL ANGELINA Joan Baez (Fontana)
-	9 MY FAIR LADY Soundtrack (CBS)
9	10 LOOK AT US Sonny & Cher (Atlantic)

Baez wasn't the only Dylan-associated artist straddling both charts. The Byrds' *Mr Tambourine Man* had been a No.1 single and a No.5 album; now Dylan's *All I Really Want To Do* went Top 10 for them and Cher, giving her a hit album too. Manfred Mann, after a hit EP featuring *God On Our Side*, went Top 3 with the Dylan song, *If You Gotta Go Go Now*, and LP-charted in October. Donovan, "Britain's Dylan", now had a hit album too, while Baez had yet another in *Farewell Angelina* - again a Dylan title.

December 1965

On the other hand *The Sound Of Music, Mary Poppins*, Andy Williams, Tony Bennett, Dudley Moore and *My Fair Lady* told a different Christmas story. That Elvis' album couldn't sustain its place in the Top 10 on the big day reflected two trends: first, it was a ragbag collection of tracks, typifying his label's disrepect for his catalogue; second, it mirrored his falling status, both because of all the awful formula-movies he'd been making and because, since the birth of the Beatles, he was yesterday's man. The Beatles still ruled – they had a new No.1 LP and the No.1 single (*Day Tripper/We Can Work It Out*). If Mary and Tony and Andy (and even Elvis) suggested Christmas past, and the Beatles the Christmas present, one future was surely hinted at by the puns lurking unsubtlely in both the Beatles' single title *Day Tripper* and the title of the Stones' latest LP *Out Of Our Heads*.

January – February 1966

last week	this week	**1 January 1966**
1	1	RUBBER SOUL — Beatles (Parlophone)
2	2	THE SOUND OF MUSIC — Soundtrack (RCA)
3	3	MARY POPPINS — Soundtrack (HMV)
6	4	MY GENERATION — Who (Brunswick)
7	5	MY FAIR LADY — Soundtrack (CBS)
4	6	TAKE IT EASY WITH THE WALKER BROTHERS — Walker Brothers (Philips)
-	7	ALMOST THERE — Andy Williams (CBS)
-	7	TEARS OF HAPPINESS — Ken Dodd (Columbia)
7	9	HELP! — Beatles (Parlophone)
4	9	FAREWELL ANGELINA — Joan Baez (Fontana)

8 January 1966

1	1	RUBBER SOUL — Beatles (Parlophone)
2	2	THE SOUND OF MUSIC — Soundtrack (RCA)
3	3	MARY POPPINS — Soundtrack (HMV)
9	4	HELP! — Beatles (Parlophone)
4	5	MY GENERATION — Who (Brunswick)
7	6	TEARS OF HAPPINESS — Ken Dodd (Columbia)
6	7	TAKE IT EASY WITH THE WALKER BROTHERS — Walker Brothers (Philips)
-	8	OUT OF OUR HEADS — Rolling Stones (Decca)
-	9	I LEFT MY HEART IN SAN FRANCISCO — Tony Bennett (CBS)
-	10	HAREM HOLIDAY — Elvis Presley (RCA)

15 January 1966

1	1	RUBBER SOUL — Beatles (Parlophone)
2	2	THE SOUND OF MUSIC — Soundtrack (RCA)
3	3	MARY POPPINS — Soundtrack (HMV)
4	4	HELP! — Beatles (Parlophone)
5	4	MY GENERATION — Who (Brunswick)
6	6	TEARS OF HAPPINESS — Ken Dodd (Columbia)
7	7	TAKE IT EASY WITH THE WALKER BROTHERS — Walker Brothers (Philips)
8	7	OUT OF OUR HEADS — Rolling Stones (Decca)
-	9	GOING PLACES — Herb Alpert & the Tijuana Brass (Pye International)
-	10	MY FAIR LADY — Soundtrack (CBS)
-	10	THE OTHER SIDE OF DUDLEY MOORE — Dudley Moore (Decca)

22 January 1966

1	1	RUBBER SOUL — Beatles (Parlophone)
2	2	THE SOUND OF MUSIC — Soundtrack (RCA)
3	3	MARY POPPINS — Soundtrack (HMV)
-	4	SECOND ALBUM — Spencer Davis Group (Fontana)
4	5	MY GENERATION — Who (Brunswick)
7	6	TAKE IT EASY WITH THE WALKER BROTHERS — Walker Brothers (Philips)
6	7	TEARS OF HAPPINESS — Ken Dodd (Columbia)
4	8	HELP! — Beatles (Parlophone)
-	9	MY NAME IS BARBRA, TWO — Barbra Streisand (CBS)
-	10	THEIR FIRST LP — Spencer Davis Group (Fontana)

29 January 1966

1	1	RUBBER SOUL — Beatles (Parlophone)
2	2	THE SOUND OF MUSIC — Soundtrack (RCA)
4	3	SECOND ALBUM — Spencer Davis Group (Fontana)
3	4	MARY POPPINS — Soundtrack (HMV)
-	5	A MAN AND HIS MUSIC — Frank Sinatra (Reprise)
6	6	TAKE IT EASY WITH THE WALKER BROTHERS — Walker Brothers (Philips)
5	7	MY GENERATION — Who (Brunswick)
10	8	THEIR FIRST LP — Spencer Davis Group (Fontana)
7	9	TEARS OF HAPPINESS — Ken Dodd (Columbia)
-	10	GOING PLACES — Herb Alpert & the Tijuana Brass (Pye International)
-	10	A WORLD OF OUR OWN — Seekers (Columbia)

5 February 1966

1	1	RUBBER SOUL — Beatles (Parlophone)
3	2	SECOND ALBUM — Spencer Davis Group (Fontana)
2	3	THE SOUND OF MUSIC — Soundtrack (RCA)
5	4	A MAN AND HIS MUSIC — Frank Sinatra (Reprise)
4	5	MARY POPPINS — Soundtrack (HMV)
6	6	TAKE IT EASY WITH THE WALKER BROTHERS — Walker Brothers (Philips)
-	7	OTIS BLUE — Otis Redding (Atlantic)
-	8	MY NAME IS BARBRA, TWO — Barbra Streisand (CBS)
-	9	OUT OF OUR HEADS — Rolling Stones (Decca)
-	10	HAREM HOLIDAY — Elvis Presley (RCA)

12 February 1966

1	1	RUBBER SOUL — Beatles (Parlophone)
3	2	THE SOUND OF MUSIC — Soundtrack (RCA)
2	3	SECOND ALBUM — Spencer Davis Group (Fontana)
4	4	A MAN AND HIS MUSIC — Frank Sinatra (Reprise)
6	5	TAKE IT EASY WITH THE WALKER BROTHERS — Walker Brothers (Philips)
5	6	MARY POPPINS — Soundtrack (HMV)
8	7	MY NAME IS BARBRA, TWO — Barbra Streisand (CBS)
7	8	OTIS BLUE — Otis Redding (Atlantic)
9	8	OUT OF OUR HEADS — Rolling Stones (Decca)
-	10	HELP! — Beatles (Parlophone)

19 February 1966

1	1	RUBBER SOUL — Beatles (Parlophone)
2	2	THE SOUND OF MUSIC — Soundtrack (RCA)
3	3	SECOND ALBUM — Spencer Davis Group (Fontana)
4	4	A MAN AND HIS MUSIC — Frank Sinatra (Reprise)
5	5	TAKE IT EASY WITH THE WALKER BROTHERS — Walker Brothers (Philips)
6	5	MARY POPPINS — Soundtrack (HMV)
-	7	BEACH BOYS' PARTY! — Beach Boys (Capitol)
8	8	OTIS BLUE — Otis Redding (Atlantic)
10	9	HELP! — Beatles (Parlophone)
7	10	MY NAME IS BARBRA, TWO — Barbra Streisand (CBS)

Crispian St. Peters, with three 1966 hit 45s (*You Were On My Mind, Pied Piper and Changes*), claimed in the music press: "My songs are better than the Beatles' songs. You just wait. People will be singing my songs when they've forgotten who the Beatles were." He never reached the LP chart. In contrast, *The Sound Of Music*, in there since the chart began, would still be selling enough to stay in the Top 10 as the 1970s dawned, and still in the chart when the Beatles broke up.

February – April 1966

last week	this week	26 February 1966
1	1	RUBBER SOUL Beatles (Parlophone)
2	2	THE SOUND OF MUSIC Soundtrack (RCA)
3	3	SECOND ALBUM Spencer Davis Group (Fontana)
7	4	BEACH BOYS' PARTY! Beach Boys (Capitol)
8	4	OTIS BLUE Otis Redding (Atlantic)
5	6	MARY POPPINS Soundtrack (HMV)
-	6	GOING PLACES Herb Alpert & the Tijuana Brass (Pye International)
-	8	BYE BYE BLUES Bert Kaempfert (Polydor)
-	9	OUT OF OUR HEADS Rolling Stones (Decca)
4	10	A MAN AND HIS MUSIC Frank Sinatra (Reprise)
-	10	IN TOWN P.J. Proby (Liberty)

last week	this week	5 March 1966
2	1	THE SOUND OF MUSIC Soundtrack (RCA)
1	2	RUBBER SOUL Beatles (Parlophone)
8	3	BYE BYE BLUES Bert Kaempfert (Polydor)
4	4	BEACH BOYS' PARTY! Beach Boys (Capitol)
6	5	MARY POPPINS Soundtrack (HMV)
3	6	SECOND ALBUM Spencer Davis Group (Fontana)
4	7	OTIS BLUE Otis Redding (Atlantic)
10	8	IN TOWN P.J. Proby (Liberty)
6	9	GOING PLACES Herb Alpert & the Tijuana Brass (Pye International)
-	10	TAKE IT EASY WITH THE WALKER BROTHERS Walker Brothers (Philips)

last week	this week	12 March 1966
1	1	THE SOUND OF MUSIC Soundtrack (RCA)
2	2	RUBBER SOUL Beatles (Parlophone)
4	3	BEACH BOYS' PARTY! Beach Boys (Capitol)
10	4	TAKE IT EASY WITH THE WALKER BROTHERS Walker Brothers (Philips)
6	5	SECOND ALBUM Spencer Davis Group (Fontana)
5	6	MARY POPPINS Soundtrack (HMV)
7	7	OTIS BLUE Otis Redding (Atlantic)
9	7	GOING PLACES Herb Alpert & the Tijuana Brass (Pye International)
-	9	A-TOM-IC JONES Tom Jones (Decca)
-	10	A STRING OF TONY'S HITS Tony Bennett (CBS)
3	10	BYE BYE BLUES Bert Kaempfert (Polydor)
8	10	IN TOWN P.J. Proby (Liberty)

last week	this week	19 March 1966
1	1	THE SOUND OF MUSIC Soundtrack (RCA)
2	2	RUBBER SOUL Beatles (Parlophone)
3	3	BEACH BOYS' PARTY! Beach Boys (Capitol)
10	4	BYE BYE BLUES Bert Kaempfert (Polydor)
4	5	TAKE IT EASY WITH THE WALKER BROTHERS Walker Brothers (Philips)
6	5	MARY POPPINS Soundtrack (HMV)
-	7	A MAN AND HIS MUSIC Frank Sinatra (Reprise)
7	8	OTIS BLUE Otis Redding (Atlantic)
-	9	MAY EACH DAY Andy Williams (CBS)
5	10	SECOND ALBUM Spencer Davis Group (Fontana)
7	10	GOING PLACES Herb Alpert & the Tijuana Brass (Pye International)

last week	this week	26 March 1966
1	1	THE SOUND OF MUSIC Soundtrack (RCA)
2	2	RUBBER SOUL Beatles (Parlophone)
3	3	BEACH BOYS' PARTY! Beach Boys (Capitol)
5	4	TAKE IT EASY WITH THE WALKER BROTHERS Walker Brothers (Philips)
4	5	BYE BYE BLUES Bert Kaempfert (Polydor)
10	5	GOING PLACES Herb Alpert & the Tijuana Brass (Pye International)
10	7	SECOND ALBUM Spencer Davis Group (Fontana)
5	8	MARY POPPINS Soundtrack (HMV)
8	9	OTIS BLUE Otis Redding (Atlantic)
9	10	MAY EACH DAY Andy Williams (CBS)

last week	this week	2 April 1966
1	1	THE SOUND OF MUSIC Soundtrack (RCA)
2	2	RUBBER SOUL Beatles (Parlophone)
4	3	TAKE IT EASY WITH THE WALKER BROTHERS Walker Brothers (Philips)
5	4	GOING PLACES Herb Alpert & the Tijuana Brass (Pye International)
8	5	MARY POPPINS Soundtrack (HMV)
5	6	BYE BYE BLUES Bert Kaempfert (Polydor)
3	7	BEACH BOYS' PARTY! Beach Boys (Capitol)
10	8	MAY EACH DAY Andy Williams (CBS)
9	9	OTIS BLUE Otis Redding (Atlantic)
-	10	MY NAME IS BARBRA, TWO Barbra Streisand (CBS)

last week	this week	9 April 1966
1	1	THE SOUND OF MUSIC Soundtrack (RCA)
2	2	RUBBER SOUL Beatles (Parlophone)
3	3	TAKE IT EASY WITH THE WALKER BROTHERS Walker Brothers (Philips)
4	4	GOING PLACES Herb Alpert & the Tijuana Brass (Pye International)
5	5	MARY POPPINS Soundtrack (HMV)
6	6	BYE BYE BLUES Bert Kaempfert (Polydor)
-	7	SECOND ALBUM Spencer Davis Group (Fontana)
9	8	OTIS BLUE Otis Redding (Atlantic)
10	8	MY NAME IS BARBRA, TWO Barbra Streisand (CBS)
-	10	SOLID GOLD SOUL Various Artists (Atlantic)

last week	this week	16 April 1966
1	1	THE SOUND OF MUSIC Soundtrack (RCA)
2	2	RUBBER SOUL Beatles (Parlophone)
3	3	TAKE IT EASY WITH THE WALKER BROTHERS Walker Brothers (Philips)
7	4	SECOND ALBUM Spencer Davis Group (Fontana)
4	5	GOING PLACES Herb Alpert & the Tijuana Brass (Pye International)
5	6	MARY POPPINS Soundtrack (HMV)
6	7	BYE BYE BLUES Bert Kaempfert (Polydor)
8	8	MY NAME IS BARBRA, TWO Barbra Streisand (CBS)
8	9	OTIS BLUE Otis Redding (Atlantic)
10	10	SOLID GOLD SOUL Various Artists (Atlantic)

P.J. Proby was another whose chart profile shortchanges his talent. Blessed with an immense vocal range, his Top 10 hits on Decca in 1964, *Hold Me* and *Together*, upbeat white R&B using a high, near-demented voice flailing in the mix, were instantly followed by ballads on Liberty with a deep, rich, voice, starting with an inspired *Somewhere*, from *West Side Story*, and, later, the same show's *Maria*, on which a post-climactic falsetto swooped down to operatic full-throated declamation. Great.

23 April 1966

last week / this week

1	1	THE SOUND OF MUSIC Soundtrack (RCA)
-	2	AFTERMATH Rolling Stones (Decca)
2	3	RUBBER SOUL Beatles (Parlophone)
3	4	TAKE IT EASY WITH THE WALKER BROTHERS Walker Brothers (Philips)
6	5	MARY POPPINS Soundtrack (HMV)
7	6	BYE BYE BLUES Bert Kaempfert (Polydor)
4	7	SECOND ALBUM Spencer Davis Group (Fontana)
5	8	GOING PLACES Herb Alpert & the Tijuana Brass (Pye International)
10	9	SOLID GOLD SOUL Various Artists (Atlantic)
-	10	BEACH BOYS' PARTY! Beach Boys (Capitol)
-	10	MANTOVANI MAGIC Mantovani (Decca)

30 April 1966

2	1	AFTERMATH Rolling Stones (Decca)
1	2	THE SOUND OF MUSIC Soundtrack (RCA)
3	3	RUBBER SOUL Beatles (Parlophone)
4	4	TAKE IT EASY WITH THE WALKER BROTHERS Walker Brothers (Philips)
10	5	MANTOVANI MAGIC Mantovani (Decca)
5	6	MARY POPPINS Soundtrack (HMV)
8	7	GOING PLACES Herb Alpert & the Tijuana Brass (Pye International)
-	8	FRANKIE AND JOHNNY Elvis Presley (RCA)
6	9	BYE BYE BLUES Bert Kaempfert (Polydor)
9	10	SOLID GOLD SOUL Various Artists (Atlantic)

7 May 1966

1	1	AFTERMATH Rolling Stones (Decca)
2	2	THE SOUND OF MUSIC Soundtrack (RCA)
3	3	RUBBER SOUL Beatles (Parlophone)
4	4	TAKE IT EASY WITH THE WALKER BROTHERS Walker Brothers (Philips)
5	5	MANTOVANI MAGIC Mantovani (Decca)
8	6	FRANKIE AND JOHNNY Elvis Presley (RCA)
-	7	THE MOST OF THE ANIMALS Animals (Columbia)
7	8	GOING PLACES Herb Alpert & the Tijuana Brass (Pye International)
-	9	SECOND ALBUM Spencer Davis Group (Fontana)
10	10	SOLID GOLD SOUL Various Artists (Atlantic)

14 May 1966

1	1	AFTERMATH Rolling Stones (Decca)
2	2	SOUND OF MUSIC Soundtrack (RCA)
3	3	RUBBER SOUL Beatles (Parlophone)
5	4	MANTOVANI MAGIC Mantovani (Decca)
7	5	THE MOST OF THE ANIMALS Animals (Columbia)
4	6	TAKE IT EASY WITH THE WALKER BROTHERS Walker Brothers (Philips)
6	7	FRANKIE AND JOHNNY Elvis Presley (RCA)
-	8	CILLA SINGS A RAINBOW Cilla Black (Parlophone)
8	9	GOING PLACES Herb Alpert & the Tijuana Brass (Pye International)
-	10	SHADOW MUSIC Shadows (Columbia)

21 May 1966

1	1	AFTERMATH Rolling Stones (Decca)
2	2	THE SOUND OF MUSIC Soundtrack (RCA)
-	3	SMALL FACES Small Faces (Decca)
3	4	RUBBER SOUL Beatles (Parlophone)
8	5	CILLA SINGS A RAINBOW Cilla Black (Parlophone)
-	5	SWEET THINGS Georgie Fame (Columbia)
5	7	THE MOST OF THE ANIMALS Animals (Columbia)
10	8	SHADOW MUSIC Shadows (Columbia)
4	9	MANTOVANI MAGIC Mantovani (Decca)
-	10	DAYDREAM Lovin' Spoonful (Pye)
6	10	TAKE IT EASY WITH THE WALKER BROTHERS Walker Brothers (Philips)

28 May 1966

1	1	AFTERMATH Rolling Stones (Decca)
2	2	THE SOUND OF MUSIC Soundtrack (RCA)
3	3	SMALL FACES Small Faces (Decca)
4	4	RUBBER SOUL Beatles (Parlophone)
7	5	THE MOST OF THE ANIMALS Animals (Columbia)
8	6	SHADOW MUSIC Shadows (Columbia)
5	7	SWEET THINGS Georgie Fame (Columbia)
10	8	TAKE IT EASY WITH THE WALKER BROTHERS Walker Brothers (Philips)
-	9	ANIMALISMS Animals (Columbia)
9	10	MANTOVANI MAGIC Mantovani (Decca)
-	10	THE SONNY SIDE OF CHER Cher (Liberty)

4 June 1966

1	1	AFTERMATH Rolling Stones (Decca)
2	2	THE SOUND OF MUSIC Soundtrack (RCA)
3	3	SMALL FACES Small Faces (Decca)
7	4	SWEET THINGS Georgie Fame (Columbia)
9	5	ANIMALISMS Animals (Columbia)
4	6	RUBBER SOUL Beatles (Parlophone)
-	7	CILLA SINGS A RAINBOW Cilla Black (Parlophone)
5	8	THE MOST OF THE ANIMALS Animals (Columbia)
8	9	TAKE IT EASY WITH THE WALKER BROTHERS Walker Brothers (Philips)
10	10	MANTOVANI MAGIC Mantovani (Decca)

11 June 1966

1	1	AFTERMATH Rolling Stones (Decca)
2	2	THE SOUND OF MUSIC Soundtrack (RCA)
3	3	SMALL FACES Small Faces (Decca)
5	4	ANIMALISMS Animals (Columbia)
4	5	SWEET THINGS Georgie Fame (Columbia)
7	6	CILLA SINGS A RAINBOW Cilla Black (Parlophone)
6	7	RUBBER SOUL Beatles (Parlophone)
8	8	THE MOST OF THE ANIMALS Animals (Columbia)
-	8	SHADOW MUSIC Shadows (Columbia)
9	10	TAKE IT EASY WITH THE WALKER BROTHERS Walker Brothers (Philips)

Without ruffling the LP chart, Dusty Springfield, Manfred Mann and Frank Sinatra all scored No.1 singles in this period. *You Don't Have To Say You Love Me* was Dusty's first, *Pretty Flamingo* Manfred Mann's second. Meanwhile Bob Dylan toured Britain again, now backed by rocker Ronnie Hawkins' ex-musos The Hawks (later The Band). Led by guitarist Robbie Robertson, they and Bob got booed nightly. The famous audience cry of "Judas!", long attributed to London, actually happened in Manchester.

June – August 1966

18 June 1966

last week	this week	
1	1	AFTERMATH — Rolling Stones (Decca)
2	2	THE SOUND OF MUSIC — Soundtrack (RCA)
3	3	SMALL FACES — Small Faces (Decca)
4	4	ANIMALISMS — Animals (Columbia)
7	5	RUBBER SOUL — Beatles (Parlophone)
5	6	SWEET THINGS — Georgie Fame (Columbia)
6	7	CILLA SINGS A RAINBOW — Cilla Black (Parlophone)
8	8	SHADOW MUSIC — Shadows (Columbia)
10	9	TAKE IT EASY WITH THE WALKER BROTHERS — Walker Brothers (Philips)
8	10	THE MOST OF THE ANIMALS — Animals (Columbia)

25 June 1966

last week	this week	
1	1	AFTERMATH — Rolling Stones (Decca)
2	2	THE SOUND OF MUSIC — Soundtrack (RCA)
3	3	SMALL FACES — Small Faces (Decca)
6	4	SWEET THINGS — Georgie Fame (Columbia)
7	5	CILLA SINGS A RAINBOW — Cilla Black (Parlophone)
4	6	ANIMALISMS — Animals (Columbia)
-	7	THE MAMAS & THE PAPAS — Mamas & Papas (RCA)
5	8	RUBBER SOUL — Beatles (Parlophone)
10	9	THE MOST OF THE ANIMALS — Animals (Columbia)
8	10	SHADOW MUSIC — Shadows (Columbia)

2 July 1966

last week	this week	
2	1	THE SOUND OF MUSIC — Soundtrack (RCA)
1	2	AFTERMATH — Rolling Stones (Decca)
3	3	SMALL FACES — Small Faces (Decca)
7	4	THE MAMAS & THE PAPAS — Mamas & Papas (RCA)
4	5	SWEET THINGS — Georgie Fame (Columbia)
5	6	CILLA SINGS A RAINBOW — Cilla Black (Parlophone)
-	7	TAKE IT EASY WITH THE WALKER BROTHERS — Walker Brothers (Philips)
6	8	ANIMALISMS — Animals (Columbia)
-	9	STRANGERS IN THE NIGHT — Frank Sinatra (Reprise)
9	10	THE MOST OF THE ANIMALS — Animals (Columbia)

9 July 1966

last week	this week	
1	1	THE SOUND OF MUSIC — Soundtrack (RCA)
2	2	AFTERMATH — Rolling Stones (Decca)
4	3	THE MAMAS & THE PAPAS — Mamas & Papas (RCA)
9	4	STRANGERS IN THE NIGHT — Frank Sinatra (Reprise)
5	5	SWEET THINGS — Georgie Fame (Columbia)
-	6	PET SOUNDS — Beach Boys (Capitol)
3	7	SMALL FACES — Small Faces (Decca)
6	8	CILLA SINGS A RAINBOW — Cilla Black (Parlophone)
7	9	TAKE IT EASY WITH THE WALKER BROTHERS — Walker Brothers (Philips)
-	9	DAVE DEE, DOZY, BEAKY, MICK & TICH — Dave Dee, Dozy, Beaky, Mick & Tich (Fontana)

16 July 1966

last week	this week	
1	1	THE SOUND OF MUSIC — Soundtrack (RCA)
2	2	AFTERMATH — Rolling Stones (Decca)
6	3	PET SOUNDS — Beach Boys (Capitol)
5	4	SWEET THINGS — Georgie Fame (Columbia)
4	5	STRANGERS IN THE NIGHT — Frank Sinatra (Reprise)
3	6	THE MAMAS & THE PAPAS — Mamas & Papas (RCA)
9	7	DAVE DEE, DOZY, BEAKY, MICK & TICH — Dave Dee, Dozy, Beaky, Mick & Tich (Fontana)
-	8	SUMMER DAYS (AND SUMMER NIGHTS!!) — Beach Boys (Capitol)
7	9	SMALL FACES — Small Faces (Decca)
-	9	WOULD YOU BELIEVE — Hollies (Parlophone)

23 July 1966

last week	this week	
1	1	THE SOUND OF MUSIC — Soundtrack (RCA)
2	2	AFTERMATH — Rolling Stones (Decca)
3	3	PET SOUNDS — Beach Boys (Capitol)
6	4	THE MAMAS & THE PAPAS — Mamas & Papas (RCA)
8	5	SUMMER DAYS (AND SUMMER NIGHTS!!) — Beach Boys (Capitol)
5	6	STRANGERS IN THE NIGHT — Frank Sinatra (Reprise)
4	7	SWEET THINGS — Georgie Fame (Columbia)
9	8	WOULD YOU BELIEVE — Hollies (Parlophone)
9	9	SMALL FACES — Small Faces (Decca)
7	10	DAVE DEE, DOZY, BEAKY, MICK & TICH — Dave Dee, Dozy, Beaky, Mick & Tich (Fontana)
-	10	YARDBIRDS — Yardbirds (Columbia)

30 July 1966

last week	this week	
1	1	THE SOUND OF MUSIC — Soundtrack (RCA)
3	2	PET SOUNDS — Beach Boys (Capitol)
2	3	AFTERMATH — Rolling Stones (Decca)
5	4	SUMMER DAYS (AND SUMMER NIGHTS!!) — Beach Boys (Capitol)
6	5	STRANGERS IN THE NIGHT — Frank Sinatra (Reprise)
7	5	SWEET THINGS — Georgie Fame (Columbia)
10	7	YARDBIRDS — Yardbirds (Columbia)
4	8	THE MAMAS & THE PAPAS — Mamas & Papas (RCA)
-	9	BLUES BREAKERS — John Mayall with Eric Clapton (Decca)
8	10	WOULD YOU BELIEVE — Hollies (Parlophone)

6 August 1966

last week	this week	
1	1	THE SOUND OF MUSIC — Soundtrack (RCA)
2	2	PET SOUNDS — Beach Boys (Capitol)
3	3	AFTERMATH — Rolling Stones (Decca)
4	4	SUMMER DAYS (AND SUMMER NIGHTS!!) — Beach Boys (Capitol)
5	5	STRANGERS IN THE NIGHT — Frank Sinatra (Reprise)
5	6	SWEET THINGS — Georgie Fame (Columbia)
-	7	PARADISE HAWAIIAN STYLE — Elvis Presley (RCA)
8	8	THE MAMAS & THE PAPAS — Mamas & Papas (RCA)
7	9	YARDBIRDS — Yardbirds (Columbia)
10	9	WOULD YOU BELIEVE — Hollies (Parlophone)

While the Stones suffered the ignominy of being knocked off the top slot by *The Sound Of Music* instead of by the Beatles, the Beach Boys turned from muscle-bound WASPs (recent charting album *Beach Boys' Party!*) into serious artists of radical musical complexity with their new LP entry, the limpid *Pet Sounds*, and its single, *Good Vibrations*, which alone had taken the same gestation period as a human baby. It was the peak of writer/producer Brian Wilson's career, and hung the term "genius" around his neck.

13 August 1966

last week / this week

last	this		
-	1	REVOLVER	Beatles (Parlophone)
1	2	THE SOUND OF MUSIC	Soundtrack (RCA)
2	3	PET SOUNDS	Beach Boys (Capitol)
3	4	AFTERMATH	Rolling Stones (Decca)
4	5	SUMMER DAYS (AND SUMMER NIGHTS!!)	Beach Boys (Capitol)
-	6	BLUES BREAKERS	John Mayall with Eric Clapton (Decca)
-	6	FROM NOWHERE ... THE TROGGS	Troggs (Fontana)
7	8	PARADISE HAWAIIAN STYLE	Elvis Presley (RCA)
-	9	STRANGERS IN THE NIGHT	Bert Kaempfert (Polydor)
-	10	I COULDN'T LIVE WITHOUT YOUR LOVE	Petula Clark (Pye)

20 August 1966

1	1	REVOLVER	Beatles (Parlophone)
2	2	THE SOUND OF MUSIC	Soundtrack (RCA)
3	3	PET SOUNDS	Beach Boys (Capitol)
4	4	AFTERMATH	Rolling Stones (Decca)
-	5	BLONDE ON BLONDE	Bob Dylan (CBS)
5	6	SUMMER DAYS (AND SUMMER NIGHTS!!)	Beach Boys (Capitol)
6	7	BLUES BREAKERS	John Mayall with Eric Clapton (Decca)
6	8	FROM NOWHERE ... THE TROGGS	Troggs (Fontana)
8	9	PARADISE HAWAIIAN STYLE	Elvis Presley (RCA)
9	10	STRANGERS IN THE NIGHT	Bert Kaempfert (Polydor)

27 August 1966

1	1	REVOLVER	Beatles (Parlophone)
2	2	THE SOUND OF MUSIC	Soundtrack (RCA)
3	3	PET SOUNDS	Beach Boys (Capitol)
5	4	BLONDE ON BLONDE	Bob Dylan (CBS)
8	5	FROM NOWHERE ... THE TROGGS	Troggs (Fontana)
6	6	SUMMER DAYS (AND SUMMER NIGHTS!!)	Beach Boys (Capitol)
4	7	AFTERMATH	Rolling Stones (Decca)
7	8	BLUES BREAKERS	John Mayall with Eric Clapton (Decca)
9	9	PARADISE HAWAIIAN STYLE	Elvis Presley (RCA)
-	10	SMALL FACES	Small Faces (Decca)

3 September 1966

1	1	REVOLVER	Beatles (Parlophone)
2	2	THE SOUND OF MUSIC	Soundtrack (RCA)
3	3	PET SOUNDS	Beach Boys (Capitol)
4	4	BLONDE ON BLONDE	Bob Dylan (CBS)
6	5	SUMMER DAYS (AND SUMMER NIGHTS!!)	Beach Boys (Capitol)
8	5	BLUES BREAKERS	John Mayall with Eric Clapton (Decca)
-	7	GOING PLACES	Herb Alpert & the Tijuana Brass (Pye International)
5	8	FROM NOWHERE ... THE TROGGS	Troggs (Fontana)
7	8	AFTERMATH	Rolling Stones (Decca)
10	10	SMALL FACES	Small Faces (Decca)

10 September 1966

1	1	REVOLVER	Beatles (Parlophone)
2	2	THE SOUND OF MUSIC	Soundtrack (RCA)
3	3	PET SOUNDS	Beach Boys (Capitol)
-	4	PORTRAIT	Walker Brothers (Philips)
4	5	BLONDE ON BLONDE	Bob Dylan (CBS)
5	6	BLUES BREAKERS	John Mayall with Eric Clapton (Decca)
5	7	SUMMER DAYS (AND SUMMER NIGHTS!!)	Beach Boys (Capitol)
10	8	SMALL FACES	Small Faces (Decca)
8	9	FROM NOWHERE ... THE TROGGS	Troggs (Fontana)
8	10	AFTERMATH	Rolling Stones (Decca)

17 September 1966

1	1	REVOLVER	Beatles (Parlophone)
2	2	THE SOUND OF MUSIC	Soundtrack (RCA)
4	3	PORTRAIT	Walker Brothers (Philips)
3	4	PET SOUNDS	Beach Boys (Capitol)
-	5	WELL RESPECTED KINKS	Kinks (Marble Arch)
5	6	BLONDE ON BLONDE	Bob Dylan (CBS)
6	7	BLUES BREAKERS	John Mayall with Eric Clapton (Decca)
-	8	AUTUMN '66	Spencer Davis Group (Fontana)
-	9	STARS CHARITY FANTASIA	Various Artists (Philips)
9	10	FROM NOWHERE ... THE TROGGS	Troggs (Fontana)

24 September 1966

1	1	REVOLVER	Beatles (Parlophone)
2	2	THE SOUND OF MUSIC	Soundtrack (RCA)
3	3	PORTRAIT	Walker Brothers (Philips)
4	4	PET SOUNDS	Beach Boys (Capitol)
8	5	AUTUMN '66	Spencer Davis Group (Fontana)
6	6	BLONDE ON BLONDE	Bob Dylan (CBS)
7	7	BLUES BREAKERS	John Mayall with Eric Clapton (Decca)
5	8	WELL RESPECTED KINKS	Kinks (Marble Arch)
-	9	THE CLASSIC ROY ORBISON	Roy Orbison (London)
9	10	STARS CHARITY FANTASIA	Various Artists (Philips)

1 October 1966

2	1	THE SOUND OF MUSIC	Soundtrack (RCA)
1	2	REVOLVER	Beatles (Parlophone)
3	3	PORTRAIT	Walker Brothers (Philips)
4	4	PET SOUNDS	Beach Boys (Capitol)
8	5	WELL RESPECTED KINKS	Kinks (Marble Arch)
6	6	BLONDE ON BLONDE	Bob Dylan (CBS)
5	7	AUTUMN '66	Spencer Davis Group (Fontana)
10	8	STARS CHARITY FANTASIA	Various Artists (Philips)
-	9	GOING PLACES	Herb Alpert & the Tijuana Brass (Pye International)
7	10	BLUES BREAKERS	John Mayall with Eric Clapton (Decca)

In the Beach Boys' *Pet Sounds* and the newly-arrived *Blonde On Blonde*, a double-album, the LP chart had two classics. They heralded the age of Progressive Rock. From now until about 1973, when the real 1970s began, this movement would prove a force for good, producing some of the most creative, richly diverse, musically fresh and longest-lasting work in popular music history. Only later would its decay into self-indulgent elitism and murky torpor make the very term Progressive Rock one of abuse.

October – November 1966

8 October 1966

last	this		
1	1	THE SOUND OF MUSIC	Soundtrack (RCA)
2	2	REVOLVER	Beatles (Parlophone)
3	3	PORTRAIT	Walker Brothers (Philips)
4	4	PET SOUNDS	Beach Boys (Capitol)
7	5	AUTUMN '66	Spencer Davis Group (Fontana)
5	6	WELL RESPECTED KINKS	Kinks (Marble Arch)
8	7	STARS CHARITY FANTASIA	Various Artists (Philips)
9	8	GOING PLACES	Herb Alpert & the Tijuana Brass (Pye International)
6	9	BLONDE ON BLONDE	Bob Dylan (CBS)
-	9	SINATRA AT THE SANDS	Frank Sinatra (Reprise)

15 October 1966

1	1	THE SOUND OF MUSIC	Soundtrack (RCA)
2	2	REVOLVER	Beatles (Parlophone)
3	3	PORTRAIT	Walker Brothers (Philips)
4	4	PET SOUNDS	Beach Boys (Capitol)
9	5	BLONDE ON BLONDE	Bob Dylan (CBS)
6	6	WELL RESPECTED KINKS	Kinks (Marble Arch)
5	7	AUTUMN '66	Spencer Davis Group (Fontana)
8	8	GOING PLACES	Herb Alpert & the Tijuana Brass (Pye International)
9	9	SINATRA AT THE SANDS	Frank Sinatra (Reprise)
-	10	BLUES BREAKERS	John Mayall with Eric Clapton (Decca)

22 October 1966

1	1	THE SOUND OF MUSIC	Soundtrack (RCA)
2	2	REVOLVER	Beatles (Parlophone)
3	3	PORTRAIT	Walker Brothers (Philips)
6	4	WELL RESPECTED KINKS	Kinks (Marble Arch)
4	5	PET SOUNDS	Beach Boys (Capitol)
-	6	SOUND VENTURE	Georgie Fame (Columbia)
5	7	BLONDE ON BLONDE	Bob Dylan (CBS)
-	8	STARS CHARITY FANTASIA	Various Artists (Philips)
8	9	GOING PLACES	Herb Alpert & the Tijuana Brass (Pye International)
7	10	AUTUMN '66	Spencer Davis Group (Fontana)

29 October 1966

1	1	THE SOUND OF MUSIC	Soundtrack (RCA)
2	2	REVOLVER	Beatles (Parlophone)
-	3	GOLDEN HITS	Dusty Springfield (Philips)
3	4	PORTRAIT	Walker Brothers (Philips)
5	5	PET SOUNDS	Beach Boys (Capitol)
4	6	WELL RESPECTED KINKS	Kinks (Marble Arch)
6	7	SOUND VENTURE	Georgie Fame (Columbia)
9	8	GOING PLACES	Herb Alpert & the Tijuana Brass (Pye International)
10	9	AUTUMN '66	Spencer Davis Group (Fontana)
8	10	STARS CHARITY FANTASIA	Various Artists (Philips)

5 November 1966

1	1	THE SOUND OF MUSIC	Soundtrack (RCA)
2	2	REVOLVER	Beatles (Parlophone)
3	3	GOLDEN HITS	Dusty Springfield (Philips)
-	4	DISTANT DRUMS	Jim Reeves (RCA)
5	5	PET SOUNDS	Beach Boys (Capitol)
4	6	PORTRAIT	Walker Brothers (Philips)
7	7	SOUND VENTURE	Georgie Fame (Columbia)
8	8	GOING PLACES	Herb Alpert & the Tijuana Brass (Pye International)
6	9	WELL RESPECTED KINKS	Kinks (Marble Arch)
-	10	DRIVIN' YOU WILD	Cliff Bennett (Music for Pleasure)

12 November 1966

1	1	THE SOUND OF MUSIC	Soundtrack (RCA)
2	2	REVOLVER	Beatles (Parlophone)
4	3	DISTANT DRUMS	Jim Reeves (RCA)
3	4	GOLDEN HITS	Dusty Springfield (Philips)
-	5	BEST OF THE BEACH BOYS	Beach Boys (Capitol)
-	6	BIG HITS (HIGH TIDE AND GREEN GRASS)	Rolling Stones (Decca)
5	7	PET SOUNDS	Beach Boys (Capitol)
6	8	PORTRAIT	Walker Brothers (Philips)
8	9	GOING PLACES	Herb Alpert & the Tijuana Brass (Pye International)
9	9	WELL RESPECTED KINKS	Kinks (Marble Arch)

19 November 1966

1	1	THE SOUND OF MUSIC	Soundtrack (RCA)
5	2	BEST OF THE BEACH BOYS	Beach Boys (Capitol)
3	3	DISTANT DRUMS	Jim Reeves (RCA)
6	4	BIG HITS (HIGH TIDE AND GREEN GRASS)	Rolling Stones (Decca)
2	5	REVOLVER	Beatles (Parlophone)
4	6	GOLDEN HITS	Dusty Springfield (Philips)
7	7	PET SOUNDS	Beach Boys (Capitol)
-	8	COME THE DAY	Seekers (Columbia)
9	9	GOING PLACES	Herb Alpert & the Tijuana Brass (Pye International)
-	10	SOUND VENTURE	Georgie Fame (Columbia)

26 November 1966

1	1	THE SOUND OF MUSIC	Soundtrack (RCA)
2	2	BEST OF THE BEACH BOYS	Beach Boys (Capitol)
3	3	DISTANT DRUMS	Jim Reeves (RCA)
4	4	BIG HITS (HIGH TIDE AND GREEN GRASS)	Rolling Stones (Decca)
6	5	GOLDEN HITS	Dusty Springfield (Philips)
8	6	COME THE DAY	Seekers (Columbia)
-	7	CALIFORNIA HOLIDAY	Elvis Presley (RCA)
5	8	REVOLVER	Beatles (Parlophone)
7	9	PET SOUNDS	Beach Boys (Capitol)
-	10	FOUR TOPS ON TOP	Four Tops (Tamla Motown)

Matching those *Well Respected Kinks*, which was on Pye's cheap-LP label Marble Arch (successor to Golden Guinea), Cliff Bennett & The Rebel Rousers' November chart-entry marked the debut of EMI's cheap label Music for Pleasure. While the group's name commemorated a venerable (1958) Duane Eddy hit, they played, extremely well for British copyists, Drifters-style mid-60s soul. Their third and final hit single, *Got To Get You Into My Life* (revisited in 1978 by Earth Wind & Fire), had peaked in September.

December 1966

last week	this week	3 December 1966
1	1	THE SOUND OF MUSIC — Soundtrack (RCA)
2	2	BEST OF THE BEACH BOYS — Beach Boys (Capitol)
3	3	DISTANT DRUMS — Jim Reeves (RCA)
6	4	COME THE DAY — Seekers (Columbia)
4	5	BIG HITS (HIGH TIDE AND GREEN GRASS) — Rolling Stones (Decca)
5	6	GOLDEN HITS — Dusty Springfield (Philips)
8	7	REVOLVER — Beatles (Parlophone)
10	7	FOUR TOPS ON TOP — Four Tops (Tamla Motown)
9	9	PET SOUNDS — Beach Boys (Capitol)
7	10	CALIFORNIA HOLIDAY — Elvis Presley (RCA)

10 December 1966

1	1	THE SOUND OF MUSIC — Soundtrack (RCA)
2	2	BEST OF THE BEACH BOYS — Beach Boys (Capitol)
3	3	DISTANT DRUMS — Jim Reeves (RCA)
4	4	COME THE DAY — Seekers (Columbia)
5	5	BIG HITS (HIGH TIDE AND GREEN GRASS) — Rolling Stones (Decca)
6	6	GOLDEN HITS — Dusty Springfield (Philips)
-	7	GOING PLACES — Herb Alpert & the Tijuana Brass (Pye International)
-	8	GENTLE SHADES OF VAL DOONICAN — Val Doonican (Decca)
9	9	PET SOUNDS — Beach Boys (Capitol)
-	10	HERE COME THE MINSTRELS — George Mitchell Minstrels (HMV)

17 December 1966

1	1	THE SOUND OF MUSIC — Soundtrack (RCA)
2	2	BEST OF THE BEACH BOYS — Beach Boys (Capitol)
4	3	COME THE DAY — Seekers (Columbia)
3	4	DISTANT DRUMS — Jim Reeves (RCA)
8	5	GENTLE SHADES OF VAL DOONICAN — Val Doonican (Decca)
6	6	GOLDEN HITS — Dusty Springfield (Philips)
-	7	A COLLECTION OF BEATLES OLDIES (BUT GOLDIES) — Beatles (Parlophone)
-	8	REVOLVER — Beatles (Parlophone)
-	8	HAND CLAPPIN' - FOOT STOMPIN' - FUNKY BUTT - LIVE! Geno Washington (Pye)
-	10	COME TO MY PARTY — Mrs. Mills (Parlophone)
7	11	GOING PLACES — Herb Alpert & the Tijuana Brass (Pye International)
-	12	SUPREMES A-GO-GO — Supremes (Tamla Motown)
-	13	THE BEST OF JIM REEVES — Jim Reeves (RCA)
5	14	BIG HITS (HIGH TIDE AND GREEN GRASS) — Rolling Stones (Decca)
-	14	12 SONGS OF CHRISTMAS — Jim Reeves (RCA)

24 December 1966

1	1	THE SOUND OF MUSIC — Soundtrack (RCA)
2	2	BEST OF THE BEACH BOYS — Beach Boys (Capitol)
4	3	DISTANT DRUMS — Jim Reeves (RCA)
3	4	COME THE DAY — Seekers (Columbia)
5	5	GENTLE SHADES OF VAL DOONICAN — Val Doonican (Decca)
8	6	HAND CLAPPIN' - FOOT STOMPIN' - FUNKY BUTT - LIVE! Geno Washington (Pye)
7	7	A COLLECTION OF BEATLES OLDIES (BUT GOLDIES) — Beatles (Parlophone)
-	8	A QUICK ONE Who (Reaction)
14	9	12 SONGS OF CHRISTMAS — Jim Reeves (RCA)
-	10	FRESH CREAM — Cream (Reaction)
14	11	BIG HITS (HIGH TIDE AND GREEN GRASS) — Rolling Stones (Decca)
-	12	STARS CHARITY FANTASIA — Various Artists (Philips)
11	13	GOING PLACES — Herb Alpert & the Tijuana Brass (Pye International)
-	14	HERE COME THE MINSTRELS — George Mitchell Minstrels (HMV)
-	15	BACHELORS' GIRLS — Bachelors (Decca)

31 December 1966

1	1	THE SOUND OF MUSIC — Soundtrack (RCA)
2	2	BEST OF THE BEACH BOYS — Beach Boys (Capitol)
5	3	GENTLE SHADES OF VAL DOONICAN — Val Doonican (Decca)
3	4	DISTANT DRUMS — Jim Reeves (RCA)
-	5	FINDERS KEEPERS — Cliff Richard & the Shadows (Columbia)
4	6	COME THE DAY — Seekers (Columbia)
7	6	A COLLECTION OF BEATLES OLDIES (BUT GOLDIES) — Beatles (Parlophone)
6	8	HAND CLAPPIN' - FOOT STOMPIN' - FUNKY BUTT - LIVE! Geno Washington (Pye)
8	8	A QUICK ONE Who (Reaction)
11	10	BIG HITS (HIGH TIDE AND GREEN GRASS) — Rolling Stones (Decca)
9	11	12 SONGS OF CHRISTMAS — Jim Reeves (RCA)
10	12	FRESH CREAM — Cream (Reaction)
12	13	STARS CHARITY FANTASIA — Various Artists (Philips)
13	14	GOING PLACES — Herb Alpert & the Tijuana Brass (Pye International)
14	15	HERE COME THE MINSTRELS — George Mitchell Minstrels (HMV)

The NME now began to publish the Top 15 albums rather than the Top 10. While this acknowledged the growing importance of the album as a medium for artists and listeners, and thus of LP sales to the industry, no surprises or delights were immediately revealed by the records making it into the extra published places. If this is Christmas it has to be time for more of Mrs Mills, Jim Reeves, the Bachelors, Herb Alpert & the Tijuana Brass, and oh dear, here come the Black & White Minstrels.

Sgt Pepper was to be the album to have in 1967. By the end of the year Otis Redding was dead and Dylan had gone to the country.
Andy Williams kept on smiling.

January – February 1967

7 January 1967

last week	this week	
1	1	THE SOUND OF MUSIC Soundtrack (RCA)
2	2	BEST OF THE BEACH BOYS Beach Boys (Capitol)
6	3	COME THE DAY Seekers (Columbia)
3	4	GENTLE SHADES OF VAL DOONICAN Val Doonican (Decca)
8	5	A QUICK ONE Who (Reaction)
4	6	DISTANT DRUMS Jim Reeves (RCA)
8	7	HAND CLAPPIN'–FOOT STOMPIN'–FUNKY BUTT–LIVE Geno Washington (Piccadilly)
12	8	FRESH CREAM Cream (Reaction)
5	9	FINDERS KEEPERS Cliff Richard & the Shadows (Columbia)
6	10	A COLLECTION OF BEATLES OLDIES (BUT GOLDIES) Beatles (Parlophone)
10	11	BIG HITS (HIGH TIDE & GREEN GRASS) Rolling Stones (Decca)
15	12	HERE COME THE MINSTRELS George Mitchell Minstrels (HMV)
-	13	REVOLVER Beatles (Parlophone)
-	14	GOLDEN HITS Dusty Springfield (Philips)
-	15	THE BEST OF JIM REEVES Jim Reeves (RCA)

14 January 1967

1	1	THE SOUND OF MUSIC Soundtrack (RCA)
2	2	BEST OF THE BEACH BOYS Beach Boys (Capitol)
3	3	COME THE DAY Seekers (Columbia)
5	4	A QUICK ONE Who (Reaction)
6	5	DISTANT DRUMS Jim Reeves (RCA)
4	6	GENTLE SHADES OF VAL DOONICAN Val Doonican (Decca)
8	7	FRESH CREAM Cream (Reaction)
14	8	GOLDEN HITS Dusty Springfield (Philips)
10	9	A COLLECTION OF BEATLES OLDIES (BUT GOLDIES) Beatles (Parlophone)
7	10	HAND CLAPPIN'–FOOT STOMPIN'–FUNKY BUTT–LIVE Geno Washington (Piccadilly)
-	10	GOING PLACES Herb Alpert & the Tijuana Brass (Pye International)
9	12	FINDERS KEEPERS Cliff Richard & the Shadows (Columbia)
-	13	PET SOUNDS Beach Boys (Capitol)
11	14	BIG HITS (HIGH TIDE & GREEN GRASS) Rolling Stones (Decca)
13	15	REVOLVER Beatles (Parlophone)

21 January 1967

1	1	THE SOUND OF MUSIC Soundtrack (RCA)
2	2	BEST OF THE BEACH BOYS Beach Boys (Capitol)
3	3	COME THE DAY Seekers (Columbia)
4	4	A QUICK ONE Who (Reaction)
5	5	DISTANT DRUMS Jim Reeves (RCA)
12	6	FINDERS KEEPERS Cliff Richard & the Shadows (Columbia)
7	7	FRESH CREAM Cream (Reaction)
10	8	GOING PLACES Herb Alpert & the Tijuana Brass (Pye International)
6	9	GENTLE SHADES OF VAL DOONICAN Val Doonican (Decca)
9	10	A COLLECTION OF BEATLES OLDIES (BUT GOLDIES) Beatles (Parlophone)
10	11	HAND CLAPPIN'–FOOT STOMPIN'–FUNKY BUTT–LIVE Geno Washington (Piccadilly)
-	12	BOB DYLAN'S GREATEST HITS Bob Dylan (CBS)
8	13	GOLDEN HITS Dusty Springfield (Philips)
14	14	BIG HITS (HIGH TIDE & GREEN GRASS) Rolling Stones (Decca)
13	15	PET SOUNDS Beach Boys (Capitol)

28 January 1967

1	1	THE SOUND OF MUSIC Soundtrack (RCA)
-	2	THE MONKEES Monkees (RCA)
2	3	BEST OF THE BEACH BOYS Beach Boys (Capitol)
-	4	BETWEEN THE BUTTONS Rolling Stones (Decca)
7	5	FRESH CREAM Cream (Reaction)
3	6	COME THE DAY Seekers (Columbia)
4	7	A QUICK ONE Who (Reaction)
6	8	FINDERS KEEPERS Cliff Richard & the Shadows (Columbia)
5	8	DISTANT DRUMS Jim Reeves (RCA)
11	10	HAND CLAPPIN'–FOOT STOMPIN'–FUNKY BUTT–LIVE Geno Washington (Piccadilly)
9	11	GENTLE SHADES OF VAL DOONICAN Val Doonican (Decca)
10	12	A COLLECTION OF BEATLES OLDIES (BUT GOLDIES) Beatles (Parlophone)
14	13	BIG HITS (HIGH TIDE & GREEN GRASS) Rolling Stones (Decca)
8	13	GOING PLACES Herb Alpert & the Tijuana Brass (Pye International)
-	15	REVOLVER Beatles (Parlophone)

4 February 1967

2	1	THE MONKEES Monkees (RCA)
1	2	THE SOUND OF MUSIC Soundtrack (RCA)
4	3	BETWEEN THE BUTTONS Rolling Stones (Decca)
3	4	BEST OF THE BEACH BOYS Beach Boys (Capitol)
6	5	COME THE DAY Seekers (Columbia)
5	6	FRESH CREAM Cream (Reaction)
7	7	A QUICK ONE Who (Reaction)
8	8	FINDERS KEEPERS Cliff Richard & the Shadows (Columbia)
11	9	GENTLE SHADES OF VAL DOONICAN Val Doonican (Decca)
10	10	HAND CLAPPIN'–FOOT STOMPIN'–FUNKY BUTT–LIVE Geno Washington (Piccadilly)
8	11	DISTANT DRUMS Jim Reeves (RCA)
12	12	A COLLECTION OF BEATLES OLDIES (BUT GOLDIES) Beatles (Parlophone)
13	13	GOING PLACES Herb Alpert & the Tijuana Brass (Pye International)
-	14	FOUR TOPS ON TOP Four Tops (Tamla Motown)
-	15	FROM THE HEART Tom Jones (Decca)

11 February 1967

1	1	THE MONKEES Monkees (RCA)
2	2	THE SOUND OF MUSIC Soundtrack (RCA)
3	3	BETWEEN THE BUTTONS Rolling Stones (Decca)
4	4	BEST OF THE BEACH BOYS Beach Boys (Capitol)
7	5	A QUICK ONE Who (Reaction)
5	6	COME THE DAY Seekers (Columbia)
11	7	DISTANT DRUMS Jim Reeves (RCA)
8	8	FINDERS KEEPERS Cliff Richard & the Shadows (Columbia)
6	9	FRESH CREAM Cream (Reaction)
10	10	HAND CLAPPIN'–FOOT STOMPIN'–FUNKY BUTT–LIVE Geno Washington (Piccadilly)
-	11	FOUR TOPS LIVE Four Tops (Tamla Motown)
13	12	GOING PLACES Herb Alpert & the Tijuana Brass (Pye International)
9	13	GENTLE SHADES OF VAL DOONICAN Val Doonican (Decca)
12	14	A COLLECTION OF BEATLES OLDIES (BUT GOLDIES) Beatles (Parlophone)
-	15	SRO Herb Alpert & the Tijuana Brass (Pye International)

18 February 1967

1	1	THE MONKEES Monkees (RCA)
2	2	THE SOUND OF MUSIC Soundtrack (RCA)
3	3	BETWEEN THE BUTTONS Rolling Stones (Decca)
4	4	BEST OF THE BEACH BOYS Beach Boys (Capitol)
6	5	COME THE DAY Seekers (Columbia)
11	6	FOUR TOPS LIVE Four Tops (Tamla Motown)
7	7	DISTANT DRUMS Jim Reeves (RCA)
8	8	FINDERS KEEPERS Cliff Richard & the Shadows (Columbia)
12	9	GOING PLACES Herb Alpert & the Tijuana Brass (Pye International)
9	10	FRESH CREAM Cream (Reaction)
5	11	A QUICK ONE Who (Reaction)
10	12	HAND CLAPPIN'–FOOT STOMPIN'–FUNKY BUTT–LIVE Geno Washington (Piccadilly)
15	13	SRO Herb Alpert & the Tijuana Brass (Pye International)
14	14	A COLLECTION OF BEATLES OLDIES (BUT GOLDIES) Beatles (Parlophone)
13	15	GENTLE SHADES OF VAL DOONICAN Val Doonican (Decca)

25 February 1967

1	1	THE MONKEES Monkees (RCA)
2	2	THE SOUND OF MUSIC Soundtrack (RCA)
3	3	BETWEEN THE BUTTONS Rolling Stones (Decca)
4	4	BEST OF THE BEACH BOYS Beach Boys (Capitol)
5	5	COME THE DAY Seekers (Columbia)
6	6	FOUR TOPS LIVE Four Tops (Tamla Motown)
13	7	SRO Herb Alpert & the Tijuana Brass (Pye International)
12	8	HAND CLAPPIN'–FOOT STOMPIN'–FUNKY BUTT–LIVE Geno Washington (Piccadilly)
9	9	GOING PLACES Herb Alpert & the Tijuana Brass (Pye International)
-	10	TROGGLODYNAMITE Troggs (Page One)
7	11	DISTANT DRUMS Jim Reeves (RCA)
8	12	FINDERS KEEPERS Cliff Richard & the Shadows (Columbia)
-	13	BOB DYLAN'S GREATEST HITS Bob Dylan (CBS)
15	13	GENTLE SHADES OF VAL DOONICAN Val Doonican (Decca)
10	15	FRESH CREAM Cream (Reaction)

Geno Washington & the Ram Jam Band were surely thrilled to find themselves high in the chart, and for so long, with *Hand Clappin'-Footstompin'-Funky Butt Live*. As this ponderously wacky title hints, Geno was felt to be great live but unreproduceable on disc. On February 18, his album at No.12, he achieved his highest-ever singles placing: the forgettable *Michael (The Lover)* made No.30 for one week. Yet he was an institution for many years, seemingly second on the bill at every student ball ever held.

March – April 1967

4 March 1967

1	1	THE MONKEES Monkees (RCA)
2	2	THE SOUND OF MUSIC Soundtrack (RCA)
3	3	BETWEEN THE BUTTONS Rolling Stones (Decca)
4	4	BEST OF THE BEACH BOYS Beach Boys (Capitol)
8	5	HAND CLAPPIN'–FOOT STOMPIN' –FUNKY BUTT–LIVE Geno Washington (Piccadilly)
5	6	COME THE DAY Seekers (Columbia)
6	6	FOUR TOPS LIVE Four Tops (Tamla Motown)
9	8	GOING PLACES Herb Alpert & the Tijuana Brass (Pye International)
7	9	SRO Herb Alpert & the Tijuana Brass (Pye International)
-	10	MANTOVANI'S GOLDEN HITS Mantovani (Decca)
10	11	TROGGLODYNAMITE Troggs (Page One)
13	12	BOB DYLAN'S GREATEST HITS Bob Dylan (CBS)
15	13	FRESH CREAM Cream (Reaction)
11	14	DISTANT DRUMS Jim Reeves (RCA)
12	15	FINDERS KEEPERS Cliff Richard & the Shadows (Columbia)

11 March 1967

1	1	THE MONKEES Monkees (RCA)
2	2	THE SOUND OF MUSIC Soundtrack (RCA)
4	3	BEST OF THE BEACH BOYS Beach Boys (Capitol)
3	4	BETWEEN THE BUTTONS Rolling Stones (Decca)
6	5	COME THE DAY Seekers (Columbia)
5	6	HAND CLAPPIN'–FOOT STOMPIN' –FUNKY BUTT–LIVE Geno Washington (Piccadilly)
11	7	TROGGLODYNAMITE Troggs (Page One)
6	8	FOUR TOPS LIVE Four Tops (Tamla Motown)
8	9	GOING PLACES Herb Alpert & the Tijuana Brass (Pye International)
9	10	SRO Herb Alpert & the Tijuana Brass (Pye International)
14	11	DISTANT DRUMS Jim Reeves (RCA)
-	12	COLOUR MY WORLD Petula Clark (Pye)
10	13	MANTOVANI'S GOLDEN HITS Mantovani (Decca)
15	14	FINDERS KEEPERS Cliff Richard & the Shadows (Columbia)
12	15	BOB DYLAN'S GREATEST HITS Bob Dylan (CBS)

18 March 1967

1	1	THE MONKEES Monkees (RCA)
2	2	THE SOUND OF MUSIC Soundtrack (RCA)
4	3	BETWEEN THE BUTTONS Rolling Stones (Decca)
3	4	BEST OF THE BEACH BOYS Beach Boys (Capitol)
8	5	FOUR TOPS LIVE Four Tops (Tamla Motown)
10	6	SRO Herb Alpert & the Tijuana Brass (Pye International)
9	7	GOING PLACES Herb Alpert & the Tijuana Brass (Pye International)
6	8	HAND CLAPPIN'–FOOT STOMPIN' –FUNKY BUTT–LIVE Geno Washington (Piccadilly)
7	9	TROGGLODYNAMITE Troggs (Page One)
5	10	COME THE DAY Seekers (Columbia)
11	11	DISTANT DRUMS Jim Reeves (RCA)
13	12	MANTOVANI'S GOLDEN HITS Mantovani (Decca)
-	13	THE TEMPTATIONS' GREATEST HITS Temptations (Tamla Motown)
-	14	HALL OF FAME Georgie Fame (Columbia)
-	15	A HARD ROAD John Mayall's Bluesbreakers (Decca)

25 March 1967

2	1	THE SOUND OF MUSIC Soundtrack (RCA)
1	2	THE MONKEES Monkees (RCA)
3	3	BETWEEN THE BUTTONS Rolling Stones (Decca)
4	4	BEST OF THE BEACH BOYS Beach Boys (Capitol)
-	5	IMAGES Walker Brothers (Philips)
8	6	HAND CLAPPIN'–FOOT STOMPIN' –FUNKY BUTT–LIVE Geno Washington (Piccadilly)
5	7	FOUR TOPS LIVE Four Tops (Tamla Motown)
9	8	TROGGLODYNAMITE Troggs (Page One)
10	9	COME THE DAY Seekers (Columbia)
7	10	GOING PLACES Herb Alpert & the Tijuana Brass (Pye Internationall)
6	11	SRO Herb Alpert & the Tijuana Brass (Pye International)
12	11	MANTOVANI'S GOLDEN HITS Mantovani (Decca)
14	13	HALL OF FAME Georgie Fame (Columbia)
15	14	A HARD ROAD John Mayall's Bluesbreakers (Decca)
11	15	DISTANT DRUMS Jim Reeves (RCA)

1 April 1967

2	1	THE MONKEES Monkees (RCA)
1	2	THE SOUND OF MUSIC Soundtrack (RCA)
4	3	BEST OF THE BEACH BOYS Beach Boys (Capitol)
9	4	COME THE DAY Seekers (Columbia)
5	5	IMAGES Walker Brothers (Philips)
7	6	FOUR TOPS LIVE Four Tops (Tamla Motown)
3	7	BETWEEN THE BUTTONS Rolling Stones (Decca)
11	8	SRO Herb Alpert & the Tijuana Brass (Pye International)
13	9	HALL OF FAME Georgie Fame (Columbia)
10	10	GOING PLACES Herb Alpert & the Tijuana Brass (Pye International)
-	11	SURFER GIRL Beach Boys (Capitol)
14	12	A HARD ROAD John Mayall's Bluesbreakers (Decca)
6	13	HAND CLAPPIN'–FOOT STOMPIN' –FUNKY BUTT–LIVE Geno Washington (Piccadilly)
11	14	MANTOVANI'S GOLDEN HITS Mantovani (Decca)
8	15	TROGGLODYNAMITE Troggs (Page One)

8 April 1967

2	1	THE SOUND OF MUSIC Soundtrack (RCA)
1	2	THE MONKEES Monkees (RCA)
3	3	BEST OF THE BEACH BOYS Beach Boys (Capitol)
5	4	IMAGES Walker Brothers (Philips)
4	5	COME THE DAY Seekers (Columbia)
-	6	GREEN GREEN GRASS OF HOME Tom Jones (Decca)
7	7	BETWEEN THE BUTTONS Rolling Stones (Decca)
6	8	FOUR TOPS LIVE Four Tops (Tamla Motown)
13	9	HAND CLAPPIN'–FOOTSTOMPIN' –FUNKY BUTT–LIVE Geno Washington (Piccadilly)
9	10	HALL OF FAME Georgie Fame (Columbia)
12	10	A HARD ROAD John Mayall's Bluesbreakers (Decca)
10	12	GOING PLACES Herb Alpert & the Tijuana Brass (Pye International)
11	13	SURFER GIRL Beach Boys (Capitol)
14	14	MANTOVANI'S GOLDEN HITS Mantovani (Decca)
-	15	TRINI LOPEZ IN LONDON Trini Lopez (Reprise)

15 April 1967

1	1	THE SOUND OF MUSIC Soundtrack (RCA)
-	2	MORE OF THE MONKEES Monkees (RCA)
2	3	THE MONKEES Monkees (RCA)
3	4	BEST OF THE BEACH BOYS Beach Boys (Capitol)
6	5	GREEN GREEN GRASS OF HOME Tom Jones (Decca)
4	6	IMAGES Walker Brothers (Philips)
5	7	COME THE DAY Seekers (Columbia)
8	8	FOUR TOPS LIVE Four Tops (Tamla Motown)
10	9	HALL OF FAME Georgie Fame (Columbia)
15	10	TRINI LOPEZ IN LONDON Trini Lopez (Reprise)
9	11	HAND CLAPPIN'–FOOT STOMPIN' –FUNKY BUTT–LIVE Geno Washington (Piccadilly)
-	12	MATTHEW AND SON Cat Stevens (Deram)
12	13	GOING PLACES Herb Alpert & the Tijuana Brass (Pye International)
-	13	DR. ZHIVAGO Soundtrack (MGM)
-	15	FIDDLER ON THE ROOF London Cast (CBS)

22 April 1967

2	1	MORE OF THE MONKEES Monkees (RCA)
1	2	THE SOUND OF MUSIC Soundtrack (RCA)
3	3	THE MONKEES Monkees (RCA)
5	4	GREEN GREEN GRASS OF HOME Tom Jones (Decca)
4	5	BEST OF THE BEACH BOYS Beach Boys (Capitol)
6	6	IMAGES Walker Brothers (Philips)
8	7	FOUR TOPS LIVE Four Tops (Tamla Motown)
7	8	COME THE DAY Seekers (Columbia)
15	9	FIDDLER ON THE ROOF London Cast (CBS)
13	10	DR. ZHIVAGO Soundtrack (MGM)
12	11	MATTHEW AND SON Cat Stevens (Deram)
10	12	TRINI LOPEZ IN LONDON Trini Lopez (Reprise)
9	13	HALL OF FAME Georgie Fame (Columbia)
-	14	THIS IS JAMES LAST James Last (Polydor)
11	15	HAND CLAPPIN'–FOOT STOMPIN' –FUNKY BUTT–LIVE Geno Washington (Piccadilly)

An extra-good couple of months for Easy Listening music. Why is it called this? Do you know anyone who finds it easy to listen to? Imagine, after two Herb Alpert albums and *Distant Drums*, rushing to listen easily to these new entries: *Mantovani's Golden Hits*, the soundtracks of *Dr Zhivago* and *Fiddler On The Roof* and, Last but not least, *This Is James L.* Not the sounds we generally think of as vintage Early 1967. *Fresh Cream* did manage to get in there too – now that was more like it.

29 April 1967

last	this	Title / Artist (Label)
2	1	THE SOUND OF MUSIC — Soundtrack (RCA)
1	2	MORE OF THE MONKEES — Monkees (RCA)
3	3	THE MONKEES — Monkees (RCA)
4	4	GREEN GREEN GRASS OF HOME — Tom Jones (Decca)
5	5	BEST OF THE BEACH BOYS — Beach Boys (Capitol)
9	6	FIDDLER ON THE ROOF — London Cast (CBS)
6	7	IMAGES — Walker Brothers (Philips)
14	8	THIS IS JAMES LAST — James Last (Polydor)
7	9	FOUR TOPS LIVE — Four Tops (Tamla Motown)
11	10	MATTHEW AND SON — Cat Stevens (Deram)
8	11	COME THE DAY — Seekers (Columbia)
10	11	DR. ZHIVAGO Soundtrack (MGM)
12	13	TRINI LOPEZ IN LONDON — Trini Lopez (Reprise)
15	14	HAND CLAPPIN'–FOOT STOMPIN'–FUNKY BUTT–LIVE — Geno Washington (Piccadilly)
-	15	SECOMBE'S PERSONAL CHOICE — Harry Secombe (Philips)

6 May 1967

last	this	Title / Artist (Label)
1	1	THE SOUND OF MUSIC — Soundtrack (RCA)
2	2	MORE OF THE MONKEES — Monkees (RCA)
3	3	THE MONKEES — Monkees (RCA)
4	4	GREEN GREEN GRASS OF HOME — Tom Jones (Decca)
5	5	BEST OF THE BEACH BOYS — Beach Boys (Capitol)
6	6	FIDDLER ON THE ROOF — London Cast (CBS)
8	7	THIS IS JAMES LAST — James Last (Polydor)
10	8	MATTHEW AND SON — Cat Stevens (Deram)
11	9	COME THE DAY — Seekers (Columbia)
7	10	IMAGES — Walker Brothers (Philips)
-	11	HALL OF FAME — Georgie Fame (Columbia)
14	12	HAND CLAPPIN'–FOOT STOMPIN' –FUNKY BUTT–LIVE — Geno Washington (Piccadilly)
9	13	FOUR TOPS LIVE — Four Tops (Tamla Motown)
-	14	HIT THE ROAD STAX — Various Artists (Stax)
11	15	DR. ZHIVAGO Soundtrack (MGM)

13 May 1967

last	this	Title / Artist (Label)
1	1	THE SOUND OF MUSIC — Soundtrack (RCA)
2	2	MORE OF THE MONKEES — Monkees (RCA)
3	3	THE MONKEES — Monkees (RCA)
4	4	GREEN GREEN GRASS OF HOME — Tom Jones (Decca)
5	5	BEST OF THE BEACH BOYS — Beach Boys (Capitol)
6	6	FIDDLER ON THE ROOF — London Cast (CBS)
7	7	THIS IS JAMES LAST — James Last (Polydor)
10	8	IMAGES — Walker Brothers (Philips)
9	9	COME THE DAY — Seekers (Columbia)
13	10	FOUR TOPS LIVE — Four Tops (Tamla Motown)
8	11	MATTHEW AND SON — Cat Stevens (Deram)
11	12	HALL OF FAME — Georgie Fame (Columbia)
-	13	SECOMBE'S PERSONAL CHOICE — Harry Secombe (Philips)
15	14	DR. ZHIVAGO Soundtrack (MGM)
12	15	HAND CLAPPIN'–FOOT STOMPIN'–FUNKY BUTT–LIVE — Geno Washington (Piccadilly)

20 May 1967

last	this	Title / Artist (Label)
1	1	THE SOUND OF MUSIC — Soundtrack (RCA)
2	2	MORE OF THE MONKEES — Monkees (RCA)
4	3	GREEN GREEN GRASS OF HOME — Tom Jones (Decca)
3	4	THE MONKEES — Monkees (RCA)
5	5	BEST OF THE BEACH BOYS — Beach Boys (Capitol)
6	6	FIDDLER ON THE ROOF — London Cast (CBS)
7	7	THIS IS JAMES LAST — James Last (Polydor)
-	8	A DROP OF THE HARD STUFF — Dubliners (Major Minor)
13	9	SECOMBE'S PERSONAL CHOICE — Harry Secombe (Philips)
11	10	MATTHEW AND SON — Cat Stevens (Deram)
8	11	IMAGES — Walker Brothers (Philips)
-	12	GOING PLACES — Herb Alpert & the Tijuana Brass (Pye International)
9	13	COME THE DAY — Seekers (Columbia)
15	14	HAND CLAPPIN'–FOOT STOMPIN' –FUNKY BUTT–LIVE — Geno Washington (Piccadilly)
14	15	DR. ZHIVAGO Soundtrack (MGM)

27 May 1967

last	this	Title / Artist (Label)
1	1	THE SOUND OF MUSIC — Soundtrack (RCA)
2	2	MORE OF THE MONKEES — Monkees (RCA)
-	3	ARE YOU EXPERIENCED — Jimi Hendrix Experience (Track)
3	4	GREEN GREEN GRASS OF HOME — Tom Jones (Decca)
8	5	A DROP OF THE HARD STUFF — Dubliners (Major Minor)
4	6	THE MONKEES — Monkees (RCA)
6	7	FIDDLER ON THE ROOF — London Cast (CBS)
5	8	BEST OF THE BEACH BOYS — Beach Boys (Capitol)
7	9	THIS IS JAMES LAST — James Last (Polydor)
9	10	SECOMBE'S PERSONAL CHOICE — Harry Secombe (Philips)
12	11	GOING PLACES — Herb Alpert & the Tijuana Brass (Pye International)
14	12	HAND CLAPPIN'–FOOT STOMPIN' –FUNKY BUTT–LIVE — Geno Washington (Piccadilly)
-	13	RELEASE ME — Engelbert Humperdinck (Decca)
15	14	DR. ZHIVAGO Soundtrack (MGM)
10	15	MATTHEW AND SON — Cat Stevens (Deram)
13	15	COME THE DAY — Seekers (Columbia)

3 June 1967

last	this	Title / Artist (Label)
-	1	SGT. PEPPER'S LONELY HEARTS CLUB BAND — Beatles (Parlophone)
1	2	THE SOUND OF MUSIC — Soundtrack (RCA)
3	3	ARE YOU EXPERIENCED — Jimi Hendrix Experience (Track)
2	4	MORE OF THE MONKEES — Monkees (RCA)
5	5	A DROP OF THE HARD STUFF — Dubliners (Major Minor)
4	6	GREEN GREEN GRASS OF HOME — Tom Jones (Decca)
7	7	FIDDLER ON THE ROOF — London Cast (CBS)
8	8	BEST OF THE BEACH BOYS — Beach Boys (Capitol)
9	9	THIS IS JAMES LAST — James Last (Polydor)
6	10	THE MONKEES — Monkees (RCA)
13	11	RELEASE ME — Engelbert Humperdinck (Decca)
11	12	GOING PLACES — Herb Alpert & the Tijuana Brass (Pye International)
14	13	DR. ZHIVAGO Soundtrack (MGM)
15	14	MATTHEW AND SON — Cat Stevens (Deram)
10	15	SECOMBE'S PERSONAL CHOICE — Harry Secombe (Philips)

10 June 1967

last	this	Title / Artist (Label)
1	1	SGT. PEPPER'S LONELY HEARTS CLUB BAND — Beatles (Parlophone)
2	2	THE SOUND OF MUSIC — Soundtrack (RCA)
3	3	ARE YOU EXPERIENCED — Jimi Hendrix Experience (Track)
4	4	MORE OF THE MONKEES — Monkees (RCA)
5	5	A DROP OF THE HARD STUFF — Dubliners (Major Minor)
8	6	BEST OF THE BEACH BOYS — Beach Boys (Capitol)
6	7	GREEN GREEN GRASS OF HOME — Tom Jones (Decca)
7	8	FIDDLER ON THE ROOF — London Cast (CBS)
11	9	RELEASE ME — Engelbert Humperdinck (Decca)
9	10	THIS IS JAMES LAST — James Last (Polydor)
10	11	THE MONKEES — Monkees (RCA)
12	12	GOING PLACES — Herb Alpert & the Tijuana Brass (Pye International)
13	13	DR. ZHIVAGO Soundtrack (MGM)
-	14	HERE COME THE TREMELOES — Tremeloes (CBS)
15	15	SECOMBE'S PERSONAL CHOICE — Harry Secombe (Philips)

17 June 1967

last	this	Title / Artist (Label)
1	1	SGT. PEPPER'S LONELY HEARTS CLUB BAND — Beatles (Parlophone)
2	2	THE SOUND OF MUSIC — Soundtrack (RCA)
3	3	ARE YOU EXPERIENCED — Jimi Hendrix Experience (Track)
4	4	MORE OF THE MONKEES — Monkees (RCA)
8	5	FIDDLER ON THE ROOF — London Cast (CBS)
7	6	GREEN GREEN GRASS OF HOME — Tom Jones (Decca)
9	7	RELEASE ME — Engelbert Humperdinck (Decca)
6	8	BEST OF THE BEACH BOYS — Beach Boys (Capitol)
5	9	A DROP OF THE HARD STUFF — Dubliners (Major Minor)
10	10	THIS IS JAMES LAST — James Last (Polydor)
12	11	GOING PLACES — Herb Alpert & the Tijuana Brass (Pye International)
11	12	THE MONKEES — Monkees (RCA)
-	13	EVOLUTION — Hollies (Parlophone)
13	14	DR. ZHIVAGO Soundtrack (MGM)
14	15	HERE COME THE TREMELOES — Tremeloes (CBS)

It was the age of Motown (Detroit) and Stax (Memphis). The Four Tops had just been No.1 with their fourth hit since '65; other Motowners included the Supremes (five Top 10s since 1964), Temptations (five hits already) and Martha & the Vandellas (four). Stax couldn't quite compete but had Otis Redding, Sam & Dave, Carla Thomas, Rufus Thomas, Booker T. and more. Between them they created not just hits but instant classics. *Hit The Road Stax* captured perhaps the most exciting, soul tour package ever.

June – August 1967

last this
week

24 June 1967

1	1	SGT. PEPPER'S LONELY HEARTS CLUB BAND — Beatles (Parlophone)
2	2	THE SOUND OF MUSIC — Soundtrack (RCA)
3	3	ARE YOU EXPERIENCED — Jimi Hendrix Experience (Track)
4	4	MORE OF THE MONKEES — Monkees (RCA)
5	5	FIDDLER ON THE ROOF — London Cast (CBS)
7	6	RELEASE ME — Engelbert Humperdinck (Decca)
6	7	GREEN GREEN GRASS OF HOME — Tom Jones (Decca)
8	8	BEST OF THE BEACH BOYS — Beach Boys (Capitol)
9	9	A DROP OF THE HARD STUFF — Dubliners (Major Minor)
11	10	GOING PLACES — Herb Alpert & the Tijuana Brass (Pye International)
10	11	THIS IS JAMES LAST — James Last (Polydor)
13	12	EVOLUTION Hollies (Parlophone)
12	13	THE MONKEES Monkees (RCA)
15	14	HERE COME THE TREMELOES — Tremeloes (CBS)
14	15	DR. ZHIVAGO Soundtrack (MGM)

1 July 1967

1	1	SGT. PEPPER'S LONELY HEARTS CLUB BAND — Beatles (Parlophone)
2	2	THE SOUND OF MUSIC — Soundtrack (RCA)
3	3	ARE YOU EXPERIENCED — Jimi Hendrix Experience (Track)
4	4	MORE OF THE MONKEES — Monkees (RCA)
5	5	FIDDLER ON THE ROOF — London Cast (CBS)
9	6	A DROP OF THE HARD STUFF — Dubliners (Major Minor)
7	7	GREEN GREEN GRASS OF HOME — Tom Jones (Decca)
8	8	BEST OF THE BEACH BOYS — Beach Boys (Capitol)
6	9	RELEASE ME — Engelbert Humperdinck (Decca)
13	10	THE MONKEES Monkees (RCA)
12	11	EVOLUTION Hollies (Parlophone)
11	12	THIS IS JAMES LAST — James Last (Polydor)
10	13	GOING PLACES — Herb Alpert & the Tijuana Brass (Pye International)
-	14	TOM JONES LIVE AT THE TALK OF THE TOWN — Tom Jones (Decca)
-	15	THE MAMAS AND PAPAS DELIVER Mamas & Papas (RCA)

8 July 1967

1	1	SGT. PEPPER'S LONELY HEARTS CLUB BAND — Beatles (Parlophone)
2	2	THE SOUND OF MUSIC — Soundtrack (RCA)
-	3	HEADQUARTERS — Monkees (RCA)
3	4	ARE YOU EXPERIENCED — Jimi Hendrix Experience (Track)
4	5	MORE OF THE MONKEES — Monkees (RCA)
5	6	FIDDLER ON THE ROOF — London Cast (CBS)
6	7	A DROP OF THE HARD STUFF — Dubliners (Major Minor)
9	8	RELEASE ME — Engelbert Humperdinck (Decca)
11	9	EVOLUTION Hollies (Parlophone)
8	10	BEST OF THE BEACH BOYS — Beach Boys (Capitol)
7	11	GREEN GREEN GRASS OF HOME — Tom Jones (Decca)
14	12	TOM JONES LIVE AT THE TALK OF THE TOWN — Tom Jones (Decca)
13	13	GOING PLACES — Herb Alpert & the Tijuana Brass (Pye International)
12	14	THIS IS JAMES LAST — James Last (Polydor)
15	15	THE MAMAS AND PAPAS DELIVER Mamas & Papas (RCA)

15 July 1967

1	1	SGT. PEPPER'S LONELY HEARTS CLUB BAND — Beatles (Parlophone)
3	2	HEADQUARTERS — Monkees (RCA)
2	3	THE SOUND OF MUSIC — Soundtrack (RCA)
4	4	ARE YOU EXPERIENCED — Jimi Hendrix Experience (Track)
6	5	FIDDLER ON THE ROOF — London Cast (CBS)
5	6	MORE OF THE MONKEES — Monkees (RCA)
8	7	RELEASE ME — Engelbert Humperdinck (Decca)
10	8	BEST OF THE BEACH BOYS — Beach Boys (Capitol)
12	9	TOM JONES LIVE AT THE TALK OF THE TOWN — Tom Jones (Decca)
9	10	EVOLUTION Hollies (Parlophone)
15	11	THE MAMAS AND PAPAS DELIVER Mamas & Papas (RCA)
-	11	DR. ZHIVAGO Soundtrack (MGM)
-	13	SMALL FACES — Small Faces (Immediate)
13	14	GOING PLACES — Herb Alpert & the Tijuana Brass (Pye International)
7	15	A DROP OF THE HARD STUFF — Dubliners (Major Minor)

22 July 1967

1	1	SGT. PEPPER'S LONELY HEARTS CLUB BAND — Beatles (Parlophone)
2	2	HEADQUARTERS — Monkees (RCA)
3	3	THE SOUND OF MUSIC — Soundtrack (RCA)
4	4	ARE YOU EXPERIENCED — Jimi Hendrix Experience (Track)
5	5	FIDDLER ON THE ROOF — London Cast (CBS)
8	6	BEST OF THE BEACH BOYS — Beach Boys (Capitol)
6	7	MORE OF THE MONKEES — Monkees (RCA)
10	8	EVOLUTION Hollies (Parlophone)
11	8	THE MAMAS AND PAPAS DELIVER Mamas & Papas (RCA)
7	10	RELEASE ME — Engelbert Humperdinck (Decca)
-	11	SOUNDS LIKE Herb Alpert & the Tijuana Brass (A&M)
11	12	DR. ZHIVAGO Soundtrack (MGM)
15	13	A DROP OF THE HARD STUFF — Dubliners (Major Minor)
13	14	SMALL FACES — Small Faces (Immediate)
9	15	TOM JONES LIVE AT THE TALK OF THE TOWN — Tom Jones (Decca)

29 July 1967

1	1	SGT. PEPPER'S LONELY HEARTS CLUB BAND — Beatles (Parlophone)
2	2	HEADQUARTERS — Monkees (RCA)
3	3	THE SOUND OF MUSIC — Soundtrack (RCA)
4	4	ARE YOU EXPERIENCED — Jimi Hendrix Experience (Track)
5	5	FIDDLER ON THE ROOF — London Cast (CBS)
6	6	BEST OF THE BEACH BOYS — Beach Boys (Capitol)
8	7	THE MAMAS AND PAPAS DELIVER Mamas & Papas (RCA)
7	8	MORE OF THE MONKEES — Monkees (RCA)
15	9	TOM JONES LIVE AT THE TALK OF THE TOWN — Tom Jones (Decca)
12	10	DR. ZHIVAGO Soundtrack (MGM)
-	11	THIS IS JAMES LAST — James Last (Polydor)
11	12	SOUNDS LIKE Herb Alpert & the Tijuana Brass (A&M)
-	13	JIGSAW Shadows (Columbia)
10	14	RELEASE ME — Engelbert Humperdinck (Decca)
-	15	GOING PLACES — Herb Alpert & the Tijuana Brass (Pye International)

5 August 1967

1	1	SGT. PEPPER'S LONELY HEARTS CLUB BAND — Beatles (Parlophone)
2	2	HEADQUARTERS — Monkees (RCA)
3	3	THE SOUND OF MUSIC — Soundtrack (RCA)
4	4	ARE YOU EXPERIENCED — Jimi Hendrix Experience (Track)
9	5	TOM JONES LIVE AT THE TALK OF THE TOWN — Tom Jones (Decca)
5	6	FIDDLER ON THE ROOF — London Cast (CBS)
6	7	BEST OF THE BEACH BOYS — Beach Boys (Capitol)
13	8	JIGSAW Shadows (Columbia)
7	9	THE MAMAS AND PAPAS DELIVER Mamas & Papas (RCA)
8	10	MORE OF THE MONKEES — Monkees (RCA)
10	10	DR. ZHIVAGO Soundtrack (MGM)
14	12	RELEASE ME — Engelbert Humperdinck (Decca)
12	13	SOUNDS LIKE Herb Alpert & the Tijuana Brass (A&M)
11	14	THIS IS JAMES LAST — James Last (Polydor)
-	15	SMALL FACES — Small Faces (Immediate)

12 August 1967

1	1	SGT. PEPPER'S LONELY HEARTS CLUB BAND — Beatles (Parlophone)
2	2	HEADQUARTERS — Monkees (RCA)
3	3	THE SOUND OF MUSIC — Soundtrack (RCA)
4	4	ARE YOU EXPERIENCED — Jimi Hendrix Experience (Track)
-	5	THE PIPER AT THE GATES OF DAWN Pink Floyd (Columbia)
7	6	BEST OF THE BEACH BOYS — Beach Boys (Capitol)
5	7	TOM JONES LIVE AT THE TALK OF THE TOWN — Tom Jones (Decca)
6	8	FIDDLER ON THE ROOF — London Cast (CBS)
8	9	JIGSAW Shadows (Columbia)
10	9	DR. ZHIVAGO Soundtrack (MGM)
9	11	THE MAMAS AND PAPAS DELIVER Mamas & Papas (RCA)
14	12	THIS IS JAMES LAST — James Last (Polydor)
12	13	RELEASE ME — Engelbert Humperdinck (Decca)
10	14	MORE OF THE MONKEES — Monkees (RCA)
15	15	SMALL FACES — Small Faces (Immediate)

By now the chart was enriched by Jimi Hendrix's *Are You Experienced?*, which had crashed straight into May's Top 3. Seattle's James Marshall Hendrix, brought to Britain by the Animals' Chas Chandler, had been feted by the guitar-gods of Swinging London, the Who's Pete Townshend and ex-Yardbird Cream-member Eric Clapton. The Jimi Henrix Experience had charted with *Hey Joe* in January, *Purple Haze* in April and *The Wind Cries Mary* in May. *Burning of the Midnight Lamp* followed.

19 August 1967

last	this	
1	1	SGT. PEPPER'S LONELY HEARTS CLUB BAND Beatles (Parlophone)
3	2	THE SOUND OF MUSIC Soundtrack (RCA)
2	3	HEADQUARTERS Monkees (RCA)
5	4	THE PIPER AT THE GATES OF DAWN Pink Floyd (Columbia)
4	5	ARE YOU EXPERIENCED Jimi Hendrix Experience (Track)
6	6	BEST OF THE BEACH BOYS Beach Boys (Capitol)
9	7	JIGSAW Shadows (Columbia)
7	8	TOM JONES LIVE AT THE TALK OF THE TOWN Tom Jones (Decca)
8	9	FIDDLER ON THE ROOF London Cast (CBS)
11	10	THE MAMAS AND PAPAS DELIVER Mamas & Papas (RCA)
9	11	DR. ZHIVAGO Soundtrack (MGM)
12	12	THIS IS JAMES LAST James Last (Polydor)
15	13	SMALL FACES Small Faces (Immediate)
14	14	MORE OF THE MONKEES Monkees (RCA)
-	15	GOING PLACES Herb Alpert & the Tijuana Brass (Pye International)

26 August 1967

1	1	SGT. PEPPER'S LONELY HEARTS CLUB BAND Beatles (Parlophone)
2	2	THE SOUND OF MUSIC Soundtrack (RCA)
3	3	HEADQUARTERS Monkees (RCA)
4	4	THE PIPER AT THE GATES OF DAWN Pink Floyd (Columbia)
6	5	BEST OF THE BEACH BOYS Beach Boys (Capitol)
8	6	TOM JONES LIVE AT THE TALK OF THE TOWN Tom Jones (Decca)
5	7	ARE YOU EXPERIENCED Jimi Hendrix Experience (Track)
11	8	DR. ZHIVAGO Soundtrack (MGM)
7	9	JIGSAW Shadows (Columbia)
9	10	FIDDLER ON THE ROOF London Cast (CBS)
13	11	SMALL FACES Small Faces (Immediate)
12	12	THIS IS JAMES LAST James Last (Polydor)
15	13	GOING PLACES Herb Alpert & the Tijuana Brass (Pye International)
10	14	THE MAMAS AND PAPAS DELIVER Mamas & Papas (RCA)
-	15	A DROP OF THE HARD STUFF Dubliners (Major Minor)

2 September 1967

1	1	SGT. PEPPER'S LONELY HEARTS CLUB BAND Beatles (Parlophone)
2	2	THE SOUND OF MUSIC Soundtrack (RCA)
3	3	HEADQUARTERS Monkees (RCA)
4	4	THE PIPER AT THE GATES OF DAWN Pink Floyd (Columbia)
5	5	BEST OF THE BEACH BOYS Beach Boys (Capitol)
8	6	DR. ZHIVAGO Soundtrack (MGM)
6	7	TOM JONES LIVE AT THE TALK OF THE TOWN Tom Jones (Decca)
7	8	ARE YOU EXPERIENCED Jimi Hendrix Experience (Track)
14	9	THE MAMAS AND PAPAS DELIVER Mamas & Papas (RCA)
9	10	JIGSAW Shadows (Columbia)
12	11	THIS IS JAMES LAST James Last (Polydor)
15	11	A DROP OF THE HARD STUFF Dubliners (Major Minor)
10	13	FIDDLER ON THE ROOF London Cast (CBS)
13	14	GOING PLACES Herb Alpert & the Tijuana Brass (Pye International)
11	15	SMALL FACES Small Faces (Immediate)

9 September 1967

1	1	SGT. PEPPER'S LONELY HEARTS CLUB BAND Beatles (Parlophone)
2	2	THE SOUND OF MUSIC Soundtrack (RCA)
4	3	PIPER AT THE GATES OF DAWN Pink Floyd (Columbia)
3	4	HEADQUARTERS Monkees (RCA)
5	5	BEST OF THE BEACH BOYS Beach Boys (Capitol)
-	6	SCOTT Scott Walker (Philips)
8	7	ARE YOU EXPERIENCED Jimi Hendrix Experience (Track)
6	8	DR ZHIVAGO Soundtrack (MGM)
9	9	THE MAMAS AND PAPAS DELIVER Mamas & Papas (RCA)
13	10	FIDDLER ON THE ROOF London Cast (CBS)
10	11	JIGSAW Shadows (Columbia)
7	12	TOM JONES LIVE AT THE TALK OF THE TOWN Tom Jones (Decca)
14	13	GOING PLACES Herb Alpert & the Tijuana Brass (Pye International)
-	13	RELEASE ME Engelbert Humperdinck (Decca)
15	15	SMALL FACES Small Faces (Immediate)

16 September 1967

1	1	SGT. PEPPER'S LONELY HEARTS CLUB BAND Beatles (Parlophone)
2	2	THE SOUND OF MUSIC Soundtrack (RCA)
5	3	BEST OF THE BEACH BOYS Beach Boys (Capitol)
4	4	HEADQUARTERS Monkees (RCA)
6	5	SCOTT Scott Walker (Philips)
3	6	THE PIPER AT THE GATES OF DAWN Pink Floyd (Columbia)
8	7	DR. ZHIVAGO Soundtrack (MGM)
12	8	TOM JONES LIVE AT THE TALK OF THE TOWN Tom Jones (Decca)
13	9	RELEASE ME Engelbert Humperdinck (Decca)
7	10	ARE YOU EXPERIENCED Jimi Hendrix Experience (Track)
10	11	FIDDLER ON THE ROOF London Cast (CBS)
11	12	JIGSAW Shadows (Columbia)
15	13	SMALL FACES Small Faces (Immediate)
9	14	THE MAMAS AND PAPAS DELIVER Mamas & Papas (RCA)
13	15	GOING PLACES Herb Alpert & the Tijuana Brass (Pye International)

23 September 1967

1	1	SGT. PEPPER'S LONELY HEARTS CLUB BAND Beatles (Parlophone)
2	2	THE SOUND OF MUSIC Soundtrack (RCA)
5	3	SCOTT Scott Walker (Philips)
3	4	BEST OF THE BEACH BOYS Beach Boys (Capitol)
4	5	HEADQUARTERS Monkees (RCA)
7	6	DR. ZHIVAGO Soundtrack (MGM)
6	7	THE PIPER AT THE GATES OF DAWN Pink Floyd (Columbia)
8	8	TOM JONES LIVE AT THE TALK OF THE TOWN Tom Jones (Decca)
10	9	ARE YOU EXPERIENCED Jimi Hendrix Experience (Track)
9	10	RELEASE ME Engelbert Humperdinck (Decca)
-	11	THE WALKER BROTHERS STORY Walker Brothers (Philips)
-	12	CRUSADE John Mayall (Decca)
11	13	FIDDLER ON THE ROOF London Cast (CBS)
14	14	THE MAMAS AND PAPAS DELIVER Mamas & Papas (RCA)
-	15	BUDDY HOLLY'S GREATEST HITS Buddy Holly (Ace of Hearts)

30 September 1967

1	1	SGT. PEPPER'S LONELY HEARTS CLUB BAND Beatles (Parlophone)
2	2	THE SOUND OF MUSIC Soundtrack (RCA)
3	3	SCOTT Scott Walker (Philips)
4	4	BEST OF THE BEACH BOYS Beach Boys (Capitol)
6	5	DR. ZHIVAGO Soundtrack (MGM)
5	6	HEADQUARTERS Monkees (RCA)
7	7	THE PIPER AT THE GATES OF DAWN Pink Floyd (Columbia)
8	8	TOM JONES LIVE AT THE TALK OF THE TOWN Tom Jones (Decca)
-	9	HIPSTERS, FLIPSTERS, FINGER-POPPIN' DADDIES Geno Washington (Piccadilly)
-	10	RAYMOND LEFEVRE Raymond Lefevre (Major Minor)
11	11	THE WALKER BROTHERS STORY Walker Brothers (Philips)
12	11	CRUSADE John Mayall (Decca)
10	13	RELEASE ME Engelbert Humperdinck (Decca)
9	14	ARE YOU EXPERIENCED Jimi Hendrix Experience (Track)
13	15	FIDDLER ON THE ROOF London Cast (CBS)

7 October 1967

1	1	SGT. PEPPER'S LONELY HEARTS CLUB BAND Beatles (Parlophone)
2	2	THE SOUND OF MUSIC Soundtrack (RCA)
3	3	SCOTT Scott Walker (Philips)
4	4	BEST OF THE BEACH BOYS Beach Boys (Capitol)
5	5	DR. ZHIVAGO Soundtrack (MGM)
13	6	RELEASE ME Engelbert Humperdinck (Decca)
9	7	HIPSTERS, FLIPSTERS, FINGER-POPPIN' DADDIES Geno Washington (Piccadilly)
6	8	HEADQUARTERS Monkees (RCA)
11	9	CRUSADE John Mayall (Decca)
11	10	THE WALKER BROTHERS STORY Walker Brothers (Philips)
7	11	THE PIPER AT THE GATES OF DAWN Pink Floyd (Columbia)
10	12	RAYMOND LEFEVRE Raymond Lefevre (Major Minor)
8	13	TOM JONES LIVE AT THE TALK OF THE TOWN Tom Jones (Decca)
15	14	FIDDLER ON THE ROOF Topol & London Cast (CBS)
-	15	MORE OF THE HARD STUFF Dubliners (Major Minor)

Watch out, Geno's back. *Hipsters, Flipsters, Fingerpoppin' Daddies* indeed. But loopy titles, becoming de rigeur, seemed more drugster than funkster. It wasn't fingers these people were poppin'. With the singles topped by Scott McKenzie's *San Francisco*, bottomed by Procol Harum's ex-No.1 *Whiter Shade of Pale* and embracing Pink Floyd, Flowerpot Men, *All You Need Is Love* and even the Stones claiming *We Love You*, the LP chart had *Sgt Pepper* and *Piper At The Gates of Dawn*.

October – December 1967

last this
week

14 October 1967

1	1	SGT. PEPPER'S LONELY HEARTS CLUB BAND	Beatles (Parlophone)
2	2	THE SOUND OF MUSIC	Soundtrack (RCA)
3	3	SCOTT	Scott Walker (Philips)
5	4	DR. ZHIVAGO	Soundtrack (MGM)
4	5	BEST OF THE BEACH BOYS	Beach Boys (Capitol)
7	6	HIPSTERS, FLIPSTERS, FINGER-POPPIN' DADDIES	Geno Washington (Piccadilly)
12	7	RAYMOND LEFEVRE	Raymond Lefevre (Major Minor)
15	8	MORE OF THE HARD STUFF	Dubliners (Major Minor)
6	9	RELEASE ME	Engelbert Humperdinck (Decca)
10	10	THE WALKER BROTHERS STORY	Walker Brothers (Philips)
-	11	BEST OF THE BEACH BOYS VOL 2	Beach Boys (Capitol)
9	12	CRUSADE	John Mayall (Decca)
8	13	HEADQUARTERS	Monkees (RCA)
11	14	THE PIPER AT THE GATES OF DAWN	Pink Floyd (Columbia)
13	15	TOM JONES LIVE AT THE TALK OF THE TOWN	Tom Jones (Decca)

21 October 1967

2	1	THE SOUND OF MUSIC	Soundtrack (RCA)
1	2	SGT. PEPPER'S LONELY HEARTS CLUB BAND	Beatles (Parlophone)
3	3	SCOTT	Scott Walker (Philips)
4	4	DR. ZHIVAGO	Soundtrack (MGM)
-	5	BREAKTHROUGH	Various Artists (Studio 2)
11	6	BEST OF THE BEACH BOYS VOL 2	Beach Boys (Capitol)
5	7	BEST OF THE BEACH BOYS	Beach Boys (Capitol)
8	8	MORE OF THE HARD STUFF	Dubliners (Major Minor)
7	9	RAYMOND LEFEVRE	Raymond Lefevre (Major Minor)
6	9	HIPSTERS, FLIPSTERS, FINGER-POPPIN' DADDIES	Geno Washington (Piccadilly)
9	11	RELEASE ME	Engelbert Humperdinck (Decca)
12	12	CRUSADE	John Mayall (Decca)
-	13	UNIVERSAL SOLDIER	Donovan (Marble Arch)
-	14	BRITISH MOTOWN CHARTBUSTERS	Various Artists (Tamla Motown)
14	15	THE PIPER AT THE GATES OF DAWN	Pink Floyd (Columbia)

28 October 1967

1	1	THE SOUND OF MUSIC	Soundtrack (RCA)
2	2	SGT. PEPPER'S LONELY HEARTS CLUB BAND	Beatles (Parlophone)
5	3	BREAKTHROUGH	Various Artists (Studio 2)
6	4	BEST OF THE BEACH BOYS VOL 2	Beach Boys (Capitol)
4	5	DR. ZHIVAGO	Soundtrack (MGM)
14	6	BRITISH MOTOWN CHARTBUSTERS	Various Artists (Tamla Motown)
13	7	UNIVERSAL SOLDIER	Donovan (Marble Arch)
3	8	SCOTT	Scott Walker (Philips)
9	9	RAYMOND LEFEVRE	Raymond Lefevre (Major Minor)
8	10	MORE OF THE HARD STUFF	Dubliners (Major Minor)
7	11	BEST OF THE BEACH BOYS	Beach Boys (Capitol)
11	12	RELEASE ME	Engelbert Humperdinck (Decca)
-	13	VANILLA FUDGE	Vanilla Fudge (Atlantic)
9	14	HIPSTERS, FLIPSTERS, FINGER-POPPIN' DADDIES	Geno Washington (Piccadilly)
-	15	THOROUGHLY MODERN MILLIE	Soundtrack (Brunswick)

4 November 1967

1	1	THE SOUND OF MUSIC	Soundtrack (RCA)
2	2	SGT. PEPPER'S LONELY HEARTS CLUB BAND	Beatles (Parlophone)
3	3	BREAKTHROUGH	Various Artists (Studio 2)
4	4	BEST OF THE BEACH BOYS VOL 2	Beach Boys (Capitol)
6	5	BRITISH MOTOWN CHARTBUSTERS	Various Artists (Tamla Motown)
5	6	DR. ZHIVAGO	Soundtrack (MGM)
7	7	UNIVERSAL SOLDIER	Donovan (Marble Arch)
8	8	SCOTT	Scott Walker (Philips)
11	9	BEST OF THE BEACH BOYS	Beach Boys (Capitol)
12	10	RELEASE ME	Engelbert Humperdinck (Decca)
10	11	MORE OF THE HARD STUFF	Dubliners (Major Minor)
9	12	RAYMOND LEFEVRE	Raymond Lefevre (Major Minor)
-	13	THE BEE GEES' FIRST	Bee Gees (Polydor)
15	14	THOROUGHLY MODERN MILLIE	Soundtrack (Brunswick)
14	15	HIPSTERS, FLIPSTERS, FINGER-POPPIN' DADDIES	Geno Washington (Piccadilly)

11 November 1967

1	1	THE SOUND OF MUSIC	Soundtrack (RCA)
2	2	SGT. PEPPER'S LONELY HEARTS CLUB BAND	Beatles (Parlophone)
3	3	BREAKTHROUGH	Various Artists (Studio 2)
5	4	BRITISH MOTOWN CHARTBUSTERS	Various Artists (Tamla Motown)
4	5	BEST OF THE BEACH BOYS VOL 2	Beach Boys (Capitol)
-	6	SMILEY SMILE	Beach Boys (Capitol)
7	7	UNIVERSAL SOLDIER	Donovan (Marble Arch)
6	8	DR. ZHIVAGO	Soundtrack (MGM)
8	9	SCOTT	Scott Walker (Philips)
-	10	DISRAELI GEARS	Cream (Reaction)
11	11	MORE OF THE HARD STUFF	Dubliners (Major Minor)
9	12	BEST OF THE BEACH BOYS	Beach Boys (Capitol)
10	13	RELEASE ME	Engelbert Humperdinck (Decca)
12	14	RAYMOND LEFEVRE	Raymond Lefevre (Major Minor)
13	15	THE BEE GEES' FIRST	Bee Gees (Polydor)

18 November 1967

1	1	THE SOUND OF MUSIC	Soundtrack (RCA)
2	2	SGT. PEPPER'S LONELY HEARTS CLUB BAND	Beatles (Parlophone)
4	3	BRITISH MOTOWN CHARTBUSTERS	Various Artists (Tamla Motown)
3	4	BREAKTHROUGH	Various Artists (Studio 2)
10	5	DISRAELI GEARS	Cream (Reaction)
5	6	BEST OF THE BEACH BOYS VOL 2	Beach Boys (Capitol)
7	7	UNIVERSAL SOLDIER	Donovan (Marble Arch)
6	8	SMILEY SMILE	Beach Boys (Capitol)
8	9	DR. ZHIVAGO	Soundtrack (MGM)
-	10	THE LAST WALTZ	Engelbert Humperdinck (Decca)
-	11	THOROUGHLY MODERN MILLIE	Soundtrack (Brunswick)
11	12	MORE OF THE HARD STUFF	Dubliners (Major Minor)
12	13	BEST OF THE BEACH BOYS	Beach Boys (Capitol)
15	14	THE BEE GEES' FIRST	Bee Gees (Polydor)
13	15	RELEASE ME	Engelbert Humperdinck (Decca)

25 November 1967

1	1	THE SOUND OF MUSIC	Soundtrack (RCA)
2	2	SGT. PEPPER'S LONELY HEARTS CLUB BAND	Beatles (Parlophone)
4	3	BREAKTHROUGH	Various Artists (Studio 2)
5	4	DISRAELI GEARS	Cream (Reaction)
3	5	BRITISH MOTOWN CHARTBUSTERS	Various Artists (Tamla Motown)
10	6	THE LAST WALTZ	Engelbert Humperdinck (Decca)
6	7	BEST OF THE BEACH BOYS VOL 2	Beach Boys (Capitol)
7	8	UNIVERSAL SOLDIER	Donovan (Marble Arch)
8	9	SMILEY SMILE	Beach Boys (Capitol)
-	10	UNEQUALLED Equals (President)	
15	11	RELEASE ME	Engelbert Humperdinck (Decca)
-	12	REACH OUT	Four Tops (Tamla Motown)
13	13	BEST OF THE BEACH BOYS	Beach Boys (Capitol)
9	14	DR. ZHIVAGO	Soundtrack (MGM)
11	15	THOROUGHLY MODERN MILLIE	Soundtrack (Brunswick)

2 December 1967

1	1	THE SOUND OF MUSIC	Soundtrack (RCA)
4	2	DISRAELI GEARS	Cream (Reaction)
2	3	SGT. PEPPER'S LONELY HEARTS CLUB BAND	Beatles (Parlophone)
5	4	BRITISH MOTOWN CHARTBUSTERS	Various Artists (Tamla Motown)
6	5	THE LAST WALTZ	Engelbert Humperdinck (Decca)
3	6	BREAKTHROUGH	Various Artists (Studio 2)
7	7	BEST OF THE BEACH BOYS VOL 2	Beach Boys (Capitol)
10	8	UNEQUALLED Equals (President)	
8	9	UNIVERSAL SOLDIER	Donovan (Marble Arch)
9	10	SMILEY SMILE	Beach Boys (Capitol)
14	11	DR. ZHIVAGO	Soundtrack (MGM)
-	12	TOM JONES LIVE AT THE TALK OF THE TOWN	Tom Jones (Decca)
12	13	REACH OUT	Four Tops (Tamla Motown)
-	14	SUNNY AFTERNOON	Kinks (Marble Arch)
13	15	BEST OF THE BEACH BOYS	Beach Boys (Capitol)

Bringing in *Disraeli Gears* and *Smiley Smile*, this was the Indian summer of love. Donovan, with a hit LP named after a Buffy St. Marie protest song, had said on TV: "When you are aware, there are no such things as hate and envy: there is only love... My job is writing beautiful things about beauty. You see, my life is beautiful." Paul McCartney had declared that "God is in everything. People who are hungry, who are sick and dying, should try to show love." Too much.

9 December 1967

last	this		
1	1	THE SOUND OF MUSIC	Soundtrack (RCA)
3	2	SGT. PEPPER'S LONELY HEARTS CLUB BAND	Beatles (Parlophone)
6	3	BREAKTHROUGH	Various Artists (Studio 2)
4	4	BRITISH MOTOWN CHARTBUSTERS	Various Artists (Tamla Motown)
2	5	DISRAELI GEARS	Cream (Reaction)
5	6	THE LAST WALTZ	Engelbert Humperdinck (Decca)
-	7	VAL DOONICAN ROCKS, BUT GENTLY	Val Doonican (Pye)
7	8	BEST OF THE BEACH BOYS VOL 2	Beach Boys (Capitol)
11	9	DR. ZHIVAGO Soundtrack (MGM)	
14	10	SUNNY AFTERNOON	Kinks (Marble Arch)
12	11	TOM JONES LIVE AT THE TALK OF THE TOWN	Tom Jones (Decca)
9	12	UNIVERSAL SOLDIER	Donovan (Marble Arch)
10	13	SMILEY SMILE	Beach Boys (Capitol)
13	14	REACH OUT	Four Tops (Tamla Motown)
15	15	BEST OF THE BEACH BOYS	Beach Boys (Capitol)
8	15	UNEQUALLED	Equals (President)

16 December 1967

1	1	THE SOUND OF MUSIC	Soundtrack (RCA)
2	2	SGT. PEPPER'S LONELY HEARTS CLUB BAND	Beatles (Parlophone)
7	3	VAL DOONICAN ROCKS, BUT GENTLY	Val Doonican (Pye)
4	4	BRITISH MOTOWN CHARTBUSTERS	Various Artists (Tamla Motown)
3	5	BREAKTHROUGH	Various Artists (Studio 2)
6	6	THE LAST WALTZ	Engelbert Humperdinck (Decca)
5	7	DISRAELI GEARS	Cream (Reaction)
-	8	AXIS: BOLD AS LOVE	Jimi Hendrix Experience (Track)
9	9	DR. ZHIVAGO Soundtrack (MGM)	
8	10	BEST OF THE BEACH BOYS VOL 2	Beach Boys (Capitol)
14	11	REACH OUT	Four Tops (Tamla Motown)
-	12	GREAT WALTZES	Roberto Mann (Deram)
11	13	TOM JONES LIVE AT THE TALK OF THE TOWN	Tom Jones (Decca)
15	14	BEST OF THE BEACH BOYS	Beach Boys (Capitol)
15	15	UNEQUALLED	Equals (President)

23 December 1967

1	1	THE SOUND OF MUSIC	Soundtrack (RCA)
2	2	SGT. PEPPER'S LONELY HEARTS CLUB BAND	Beatles (Parlophone)
3	3	VAL DOONICAN ROCKS, BUT GENTLY	Val Doonican (Pye)
6	3	THE LAST WALTZ	Engelbert Humperdinck (Decca)
4	5	BRITISH MOTOWN CHARTBUSTERS	Various Artists (Tamla Motown)
7	6	DISRAELI GEARS	Cream (Reaction)
13	7	TOM JONES LIVE AT THE TALK OF THE TOWN	Tom Jones (Decca)
5	8	BREAKTHROUGH	Various Artists (Studio 2)
8	9	AXIS: BOLD AS LOVE	Jimi Hendrix Experience (Track)
-	10	THEIR SATANIC MAJESTIES REQUEST	Rolling Stones (Decca)
11	11	REACH OUT	Four Tops (Tamla Motown)
9	12	DR. ZHIVAGO Soundtrack (MGM)	
10	13	BEST OF THE BEACH BOYS VOL 2	Beach Boys (Capitol)
14	14	BEST OF THE BEACH BOYS	Beach Boys (Capitol)
12	15	GREAT WALTZES	Roberto Mann (Deram)

30 December 1967

1	1	THE SOUND OF MUSIC	Soundtrack (RCA)
2	2	SGT. PEPPER'S LONELY HEARTS CLUB BAND	Beatles (Parlophone)
3	3	VAL DOONICAN ROCKS, BUT GENTLY	Val Doonican (Pye)
3	4	THE LAST WALTZ	Engelbert Humperdinck (Decca)
5	5	BRITISH MOTOWN CHARTBUSTERS	Various Artists (Tamla Motown)
6	6	DISRAELI GEARS	Cream (Reaction)
10	7	THEIR SATANIC MAJESTIES REQUEST	Rolling Stones (Decca)
7	8	TOM JONES LIVE AT THE TALK OF THE TOWN	Tom Jones (Decca)
8	9	BREAKTHROUGH	Various Artists (Studio 2)
11	10	REACH OUT	Four Tops (Tamla Motown)
9	11	AXIS: BOLD AS LOVE	Jimi Hendrix Experience (Track)
12	12	DR. ZHIVAGO Soundtrack (MGM)	
13	13	BEST OF THE BEACH BOYS VOL 2	Beach Boys (Capitol)
15	14	GREAT WALTZES	Roberto Mann (Deram)
14	15	BEST OF THE BEACH BOYS	Beach Boys (Capitol)

The late David Widgery, one radical journalist not beguiled by the heady smell of flower power, offered this rejoinder in OZ magazine: "We believe a lot of lies... The world's turned on... it's the psychedelic storming of the Winter Palace... Which is a pity. Because at the moment the hippies in England represent about as powerful a challenge to the power of the state as the people who put foreign coins in their gas meters." But, armed with *Sgt. Pepper's Lonely Hearts Club Band*, *Their Satanic Majesties Request* and *Axis: Bold As Love*, at least they had deposed the Minstrels.

January – February 1968

6 January 1968

last	this		
2	1	SGT. PEPPER'S LONELY HEARTS CLUB BAND	Beatles (Parlophone)
3	2	VAL DOONICAN ROCKS, BUT GENTLY	Val Doonican (Pye)
1	3	THE SOUND OF MUSIC	Soundtrack (RCA)
7	4	THEIR SATANIC MAJESTIES REQUEST	Rolling Stones (Decca)
4	5	THE LAST WALTZ	Engelbert Humperdinck (Decca)
5	6	BRITISH MOTOWN CHARTBUSTERS	Various Artists (Tamla Motown)
10	7	REACH OUT	Four Tops (Tamla Motown)
11	8	AXIS: BOLD AS LOVE	Jimi Hendrix Experience (Track)
-	9	13 SMASH HITS	Tom Jones (Decca)
6	10	DISRAELI GEARS	Cream (Reaction)
9	10	BREAKTHROUGH	Various Artists (Studio 2)
8	12	TOM JONES LIVE AT THE TALK OF THE TOWN	Tom Jones (Decca)
-	13	PISCES, AQUARIUS, CAPRICORN & JONES LTD	Monkees (RCA Victor)
15	14	BEST OF THE BEACH BOYS	Beach Boys (Capitol)
-	15	MR. FANTASY	Traffic (Island)

13 January 1968

1	1	SGT. PEPPER'S LONELY HEARTS CLUB BAND	Beatles (Parlophone)
3	2	THE SOUND OF MUSIC	Soundtrack (RCA)
2	3	VAL DOONICAN ROCKS, BUT GENTLY	Val Doonican (Pye)
7	4	REACH OUT	Four Tops (Tamla Motown)
6	5	BRITISH MOTOWN CHARTBUSTERS	Various Artists (Tamla Motown)
4	6	THEIR SATANIC MAJESTIES REQUEST	Rolling Stones (Decca)
5	7	THE LAST WALTZ	Engelbert Humperdinck (Decca)
9	8	13 SMASH HITS	Tom Jones (Decca)
8	9	AXIS: BOLD AS LOVE	Jimi Hendrix Experience (Track)
13	9	PISCES, AQUARIUS, CAPRICORN & JONES LTD	Monkees (RCA Victor)
10	11	DISRAELI GEARS	Cream (Reaction)
15	12	MR. FANTASY	Traffic (Island)
10	13	BREAKTHROUGH	Various Artists (Studio 2)
12	14	TOM JONES LIVE AT THE TALK OF THE TOWN	Tom Jones (Decca)
-	15	DR. ZHIVAGO	Soundtrack (MGM)

20 January 1968

3	1	VAL DOONICAN ROCKS, BUT GENTLY	Val Doonican (Pye)
1	2	SGT. PEPPER'S LONELY HEARTS CLUB BAND	Beatles (Parlophone)
2	3	THE SOUND OF MUSIC	Soundtrack (RCA)
6	4	THEIR SATANIC MAJESTIES REQUEST	Rolling Stones (Decca)
4	5	REACH OUT	Four Tops (Tamla Motown)
5	6	BRITISH MOTOWN CHARTBUSTERS	Various Artists (Tamla Motown)
7	7	THE LAST WALTZ	Engelbert Humperdinck (Decca)
-	8	SUPREMES' GREATEST HITS	Supremes (Tamla Motown)
8	9	13 SMASH HITS	Tom Jones (Decca)
9	10	PISCES, AQUARIUS, CAPRICORN & JONES LTD	Monkees (RCA Victor)
-	11	FOUR TOPS' GREATEST HITS	Four Tops (Tamla Motown)
9	12	AXIS: BOLD AS LOVE	Jimi Hendrix Experience (Track)
-	13	THE WHO SELL OUT	Who (Reaction)
12	14	MR. FANTASY	Traffic (Island)
11	15	DISRAELI GEARS	Cream (Reaction)

27 January 1968

3	1	THE SOUND OF MUSIC	Soundtrack (RCA)
5	2	REACH OUT	Four Tops (Tamla Motown)
1	3	VAL DOONICAN ROCKS, BUT GENTLY	Val Doonican (Pye)
8	4	SUPREMES' GREATEST HITS	Supremes (Tamla Motown)
2	5	SGT. PEPPER'S LONELY HEARTS CLUB BAND	Beatles (Parlophone)
11	6	FOUR TOPS' GREATEST HITS	Four Tops (Tamla Motown)
4	7	THEIR SATANIC MAJESTIES REQUEST	Rolling Stones (Decca)
6	8	BRITISH MOTOWN CHARTBUSTERS	Various Artists (Tamla Motown)
9	9	13 SMASH HITS	Tom Jones (Decca)
12	10	AXIS: BOLD AS LOVE	Jimi Hendrix Experience (Track)
10	11	PISCES, AQUARIUS, CAPRICORN & JONES LTD	Monkees (RCA Victor)
7	12	THE LAST WALTZ	Engelbert Humperdinck (Decca)
13	13	THE WHO SELL OUT	Who (Reaction)
15	14	DISRAELI GEARS	Cream (Reaction)
14	15	MR. FANTASY	Traffic (Island)

3 February 1968

4	1	SUPREMES' GREATEST HITS	Supremes (Tamla Motown)
1	2	THE SOUND OF MUSIC	Soundtrack (RCA)
6	3	FOUR TOPS' GREATEST HITS	Four Tops (Tamla Motown)
2	4	REACH OUT	Four Tops (Tamla Motown)
3	4	VAL DOONICAN ROCKS, BUT GENTLY	Val Doonican (Pye)
5	6	SGT. PEPPER'S LONELY HEARTS CLUB BAND	Beatles (Parlophone)
8	7	BRITISH MOTOWN CHARTBUSTERS	Various Artists (Tamla Motown)
9	8	13 SMASH HITS	Tom Jones (Decca)
11	9	PISCES, AQUARIUS, CAPRICORN & JONES LTD	Monkees (RCA Victor)
12	10	THE LAST WALTZ	Engelbert Humperdinck (Decca)
7	11	THEIR SATANIC MAJESTIES REQUEST	Rolling Stones (Decca)
-	12	BREAKTHROUGH	Various Artists (Studio 2)
10	13	AXIS: BOLD AS LOVE	Jimi Hendrix Experience (Track)
13	14	THE WHO SELL OUT	Who (Reaction)
15	15	MR. FANTASY	Traffic (Island)

10 February 1968

1	1	SUPREMES' GREATEST HITS	Supremes (Tamla Motown)
2	2	THE SOUND OF MUSIC	Soundtrack (RCA)
3	3	FOUR TOPS' GREATEST HITS	Four Tops (Tamla Motown)
6	4	SGT. PEPPER'S LONELY HEARTS CLUB BAND	Beatles (Parlophone)
4	5	VAL DOONICAN ROCKS, BUT GENTLY	Val Doonican (Pye)
4	6	REACH OUT	Four Tops (Tamla Motown)
8	7	13 SMASH HITS	Tom Jones (Decca)
7	8	BRITISH MOTOWN CHARTBUSTERS	Various Artists (Tamla Motown)
10	9	THE LAST WALTZ	Engelbert Humperdinck (Decca)
11	10	THEIR SATANIC MAJESTIES REQUEST	Rolling Stones (Decca)
-	11	OTIS BLUE	Otis Redding (Atlantic)
14	12	THE WHO SELL OUT	Who (Reaction)
9	13	PISCES, AQUARIUS, CAPRICORN & JONES LTD	Monkees (RCA Victor)
12	14	BREAKTHROUGH	Various Artists (Studio 2)
-	15	PARADISE LOST	Herd (Fontana)

17 February 1968

1	1	SUPREMES' GREATEST HITS	Supremes (Tamla Motown)
2	2	THE SOUND OF MUSIC	Soundtrack (RCA)
3	3	FOUR TOPS' GREATEST HITS	Four Tops (Tamla Motown)
7	4	13 SMASH HITS	Tom Jones (Decca)
4	5	SGT. PEPPER'S LONELY HEARTS CLUB BAND	Beatles (Parlophone)
5	6	VAL DOONICAN ROCKS, BUT GENTLY	Val Doonican (Pye)
8	7	BRITISH MOTOWN CHARTBUSTERS	Various Artists (Tamla Motown)
14	8	BREAKTHROUGH	Various Artists (Studio 2)
6	9	REACH OUT	Four Tops (Tamla Motown)
9	10	THE LAST WALTZ	Engelbert Humperdinck (Decca)
13	11	PISCES, AQUARIUS, CAPRICORN & JONES LTD	Monkees (RCA Victor)
-	12	THIS IS CHAQUITO AND QUEDO BRASS	Chaquito & Quedo Brass (Fontana)
11	13	OTIS BLUE	Otis Redding (Atlantic)
12	14	THE WHO SELL OUT	Who (Reaction)
10	15	THEIR SATANIC MAJESTIES REQUEST	Rolling Stones (Decca)

24 February 1968

1	1	SUPREMES' GREATEST HITS	Supremes (Tamla Motown)
3	2	FOUR TOPS' GREATEST HITS	Four Tops (Tamla Motown)
2	3	THE SOUND OF MUSIC	Soundtrack (RCA)
4	4	13 SMASH HITS	Tom Jones (Decca)
5	5	SGT. PEPPER'S LONELY HEARTS CLUB BAND	Beatles (Parlophone)
8	6	BREAKTHROUGH	Various Artists (Studio 2)
6	7	VAL DOONICAN ROCKS, BUT GENTLY	Val Doonican (Pye)
7	8	BRITISH MOTOWN CHARTBUSTERS	Various Artists (Tamla Motown)
11	9	PISCES, AQUARIUS, CAPRICORN & JONES LTD	Monkees (RCA Victor)
10	10	THE LAST WALTZ	Engelbert Humperdinck (Decca)
13	11	OTIS BLUE	Otis Redding (Atlantic)
9	12	REACH OUT	Four Tops (Tamla Motown)
12	13	THIS IS CHAQUITO AND QUEDO BRASS	Chaquito & Quedo Brass (Fontana)
-	14	HORIZONTAL	Bee Gees (Polydor)
14	15	THE WHO SELL OUT	Who (Reaction)

Statistics say the Beatles' new year began well. Pepper was top again; in the singles chart they were No.1 with *Hello Goodbye* and No.2 with the *Magical Mystery Tour* double-EP (an album in the USA). Yet the TV-film behind this lead-ballooned. It was the first thumb's down for the Fab Four. Famously thumbs-up Paul commented: "If everything Beethoven had written had been great it would have been one grey sludge, but... There were good bits and bad bits, and that's the way we are."

2 March 1968

last this
week

1	1	SUPREMES' GREATEST HITS	Supremes (Tamla Motown)
-	2	JOHN WESLEY HARDING	Bob Dylan (CBS)
2	3	FOUR TOPS' GREATEST HITS	Four Tops (Tamla Motown)
3	4	THE SOUND OF MUSIC	Soundtrack (RCA)
4	5	13 SMASH HITS	Tom Jones (Decca)
6	6	BREAKTHROUGH	Various Artists (Studio 2)
5	7	SGT. PEPPER'S LONELY HEARTS CLUB BAND	Beatles (Parlophone)
8	8	BRITISH MOTOWN CHARTBUSTERS	Various Artists (Tamla Motown)
-	9	THIS IS BERT KAEMPFERT	Bert Kaempfert (Polydor)
-	10	HISTORY OF OTIS REDDING	Otis Redding (Volt)
11	11	OTIS BLUE	Otis Redding (Atlantic)
13	12	THIS IS CHAQUITO AND QUEDO BRASS	Chaquito & Quedo Brass (Fontana)
9	13	PISCES, AQUARIUS, CAPRICORN & JONES LTD	Monkees (RCA Victor)
14	14	HORIZONTAL	Bee Gees (Polydor)
10	15	THE LAST WALTZ	Engelbert Humperdinck (Decca)

9 March 1968

1	1	SUPREMES' GREATEST HITS	Supremes (Tamla Motown)
2	2	JOHN WESLEY HARDING	Bob Dylan (CBS)
3	3	FOUR TOPS' GREATEST HITS	Four Tops (Tamla Motown)
4	4	THE SOUND OF MUSIC	Soundtrack (RCA)
10	5	HISTORY OF OTIS REDDING	Otis Redding (Volt)
5	6	13 SMASH HITS	Tom Jones (Decca)
8	7	BRITISH MOTOWN CHARTBUSTERS	Various Artists (Tamla Motown)
9	8	THIS IS BERT KAEMPFERT	Bert Kaempfert (Polydor)
14	9	HORIZONTAL	Bee Gees (Polydor)
6	10	BREAKTHROUGH	Various Artists (Studio 2)
-	11	WILD HONEY	Beach Boys (Capitol)
-	12	2 IN 3	Esther & Abi Ofarim (Philips)
7	13	SGT. PEPPER'S LONELY HEARTS CLUB BAND	Beatles (Parlophone)
-	14	PETER GREEN'S FLEETWOOD MAC	Fleetwood Mac (Blue Horizon)
-	15	VAL DOONICAN ROCKS, BUT GENTLY	Val Doonican (Pye)

16 March 1968

2	1	JOHN WESLEY HARDING	Bob Dylan (CBS)
1	2	SUPREMES' GREATEST HITS	Supremes (Tamla Motown)
4	3	THE SOUND OF MUSIC	Soundtrack (RCA)
5	4	HISTORY OF OTIS REDDING	Otis Redding (Volt)
3	5	FOUR TOPS' GREATEST HITS	Four Tops (Tamla Motown)
12	6	2 IN 3	Esther & Abi Ofarim (Philips)
8	7	THIS IS BERT KAEMPFERT	Bert Kaempfert (Polydor)
6	8	13 SMASH HITS	Tom Jones (Decca)
11	9	WILD HONEY	Beach Boys (Capitol)
14	10	PETER GREEN'S FLEETWOOD MAC	Fleetwood Mac (Blue Horizon)
9	11	HORIZONTAL	Bee Gees (Polydor)
7	12	BRITISH MOTOWN CHARTBUSTERS	Various Artists (Tamla Motown)
13	13	SGT. PEPPER'S LONELY HEARTS CLUB BAND	Beatles (Parlophone)
15	14	VAL DOONICAN ROCKS, BUT GENTLY	Val Doonican (Pye)
-	15	OTIS BLUE	Otis Redding (Atlantic)

23 March 1968

1	1	JOHN WESLEY HARDING	Bob Dylan (CBS)
2	2	SUPREMES' GREATEST HITS	Supremes (Tamla Motown)
4	3	HISTORY OF OTIS REDDING	Otis Redding (Volt)
3	4	THE SOUND OF MUSIC	Soundtrack (RCA)
-	5	THIS IS SOUL	Various Artists (Atlantic)
5	6	FOUR TOPS' GREATEST HITS	Four Tops (Tamla Motown)
6	7	2 IN 3	Esther & Abi Ofarim (Philips)
9	8	WILD HONEY	Beach Boys (Capitol)
8	9	13 SMASH HITS	Tom Jones (Decca)
10	10	PETER GREEN'S FLEETWOOD MAC	Fleetwood Mac (Blue Horizon)
13	11	SGT. PEPPER'S LONELY HEARTS CLUB BAND	Beatles (Parlophone)
12	12	BRITISH MOTOWN CHARTBUSTERS	Various Artists (Tamla Motown)
7	13	THIS IS BERT KAEMPFERT	Bert Kaempfert (Polydor)
11	14	HORIZONTAL	Bee Gees (Polydor)
14	15	VAL DOONICAN ROCKS, BUT GENTLY	Val Doonican (Pye)

30 March 1968

1	1	JOHN WESLEY HARDING	Bob Dylan (CBS)
5	2	THIS IS SOUL	Various Artists (Atlantic)
3	3	HISTORY OF OTIS REDDING	Otis Redding (Volt)
2	4	SUPREMES' GREATEST HITS	Supremes (Tamla Motown)
4	5	THE SOUND OF MUSIC	Soundtrack (RCA)
6	6	FOUR TOPS' GREATEST HITS	Four Tops (Tamla Motown)
8	7	WILD HONEY	Beach Boys (Capitol)
10	8	PETER GREEN'S FLEETWOOD MAC	Fleetwood Mac (Blue Horizon)
7	9	2 IN 3	Esther & Abi Ofarim (Philips)
9	10	13 SMASH HITS	Tom Jones (Decca)
12	11	BRITISH MOTOWN CHARTBUSTERS	Various Artists (Tamla Motown)
-	12	LIVE AT THE TALK OF THE TOWN	Diana Ross & the Supremes (Tamla Motown)
-	13	OTIS BLUE	Otis Redding (Atlantic)
11	14	SGT. PEPPER'S LONELY HEARTS CLUB BAND	Beatles (Parlophone)
13	15	THIS IS BERT KAEMPFERT	Bert Kaempfert (Polydor)

6 April 1968

1	1	JOHN WESLEY HARDING	Bob Dylan (CBS)
2	2	THIS IS SOUL	Various Artists (Atlantic)
3	3	HISTORY OF OTIS REDDING	Otis Redding (Volt)
5	4	THE SOUND OF MUSIC	Soundtrack (RCA)
4	5	SUPREMES' GREATEST HITS	Supremes (Tamla Motown)
6	6	FOUR TOPS' GREATEST HITS	Four Tops (Tamla Motown)
7	7	WILD HONEY	Beach Boys (Capitol)
8	8	PETER GREEN'S FLEETWOOD MAC	Fleetwood Mac (Blue Horizon)
9	9	2 IN 3	Esther & Abi Ofarim (Philips)
12	10	LIVE AT THE TALK OF THE TOWN	Diana Ross & the Supremes (Tamla Motown)
10	11	13 SMASH HITS	Tom Jones (Decca)
14	12	SGT. PEPPER'S LONELY HEARTS CLUB BAND	Beatles (Parlophone)
-	13	THE HANGMAN'S BEAUTIFUL DAUGHTER	Incredible String Band (Elektra)
-	14	OTIS REDDING IN EUROPE	Otis Redding (Stax)
-	15	MOVE	Move (Regal Zonophone)

13 April 1968

1	1	JOHN WESLEY HARDING	Bob Dylan (CBS)
2	2	THIS IS SOUL	Various Artists (Atlantic)
3	3	HISTORY OF OTIS REDDING	Otis Redding (Volt)
4	4	THE SOUND OF MUSIC	Soundtrack (RCA)
8	5	PETER GREEN'S FLEETWOOD MAC	Fleetwood Mac (Blue Horizon)
5	6	SUPREMES' GREATEST HITS	Supremes (Tamla Motown)
6	7	FOUR TOPS' GREATEST HITS	Four Tops (Tamla Motown)
13	8	THE HANGMAN'S BEAUTIFUL DAUGHTER	Incredible String Band (Elektra)
7	9	WILD HONEY	Beach Boys (Capitol)
9	10	2 IN 3	Esther & Abi Ofarim (Philips)
10	11	LIVE AT THE TALK OF THE TOWN	Diana Ross & the Supremes (Tamla Motown)
-	12	SCOTT 2	Scott Walker (Philips)
15	13	MOVE	Move (Regal Zonophone)
-	14	ROUND AMEN CORNER	Amen Corner (Deram)
14	15	OTIS REDDING IN EUROPE	Otis Redding (Stax)

20 April 1968

1	1	JOHN WESLEY HARDING	Bob Dylan (CBS)
2	2	THIS IS SOUL	Various Artists (Atlantic)
4	3	THE SOUND OF MUSIC	Soundtrack (RCA)
6	4	SUPREMES' GREATEST HITS	Supremes (Tamla Motown)
3	5	HISTORY OF OTIS REDDING	Otis Redding (Volt)
7	6	FOUR TOPS' GREATEST HITS	Four Tops (Tamla Motown)
5	7	PETER GREEN'S FLEETWOOD MAC	Fleetwood Mac (Blue Horizon)
8	8	THE HANGMAN'S BEAUTIFUL DAUGHTER	Incredible String Band (Elektra)
9	9	WILD HONEY	Beach Boys (Capitol)
10	10	2 IN 3	Esther & Abi Ofarim (Philips)
12	11	SCOTT 2	Scott Walker (Philips)
11	12	LIVE AT THE TALK OF THE TOWN	Diana Ross & the Supremes (Tamla Motown)
15	13	OTIS REDDING IN EUROPE	Otis Redding (Stax)
-	14	13 SMASH HITS	Tom Jones (Decca)
13	15	MOVE	Move (Regal Zonophone)

Back came Bob Dylan, after motorcycle-crashing from the public eye in 1966, on the eve of *Blonde On Blonde*'s release. CBS concocted a *Bob Dylan's Greatest Hits* - which seemed, at the time, a vulgar title - but there had been no new release in eighteen months. In a period when pop acts averaged two albums a year, it felt like aeons. John Wesley Harding proved spare, demanding, countrified: and as fierce a stance as possible against psychedelic overkill. The public sent it to No.1 for seven weeks.

April – June 1968

27 April 1968

1	1	JOHN WESLEY HARDING Bob Dylan (CBS)
2	2	THIS IS SOUL Various Artists (Atlantic)
5	3	HISTORY OF OTIS REDDING Otis Redding (Volt)
3	4	THE SOUND OF MUSIC Soundtrack (RCA)
6	5	FOUR TOPS' GREATEST HITS Four Tops (Tamla Motown)
11	6	SCOTT 2 Scott Walker (Philips)
4	7	SUPREMES' GREATEST HITS Supremes (Tamla Motown)
7	8	PETER GREEN'S FLEETWOOD MAC Fleetwood Mac (Blue Horizon)
8	8	THE HANGMAN'S BEAUTIFUL DAUGHTER Incredible String Band (Elektra)
10	10	2 IN 3 Esther & Abi Ofarim (Philips)
13	11	OTIS REDDING IN EUROPE Otis Redding (Stax)
12	12	LIVE AT THE TALK OF THE TOWN Diana Ross & the Supremes (Tamla Motown)
15	13	MOVE Move (Regal Zonophone)
9	14	WILD HONEY Beach Boys (Capitol)
-	15	SHER-OO! Cilla Black (Parlophone)

4 May 1968

2	1	THIS IS SOUL Various Artists (Atlantic)
1	2	JOHN WESLEY HARDING Bob Dylan (CBS)
3	3	HISTORY OF OTIS REDDING Otis Redding (Volt)
4	4	THE SOUND OF MUSIC Soundtrack (RCA)
7	5	SUPREMES' GREATEST HITS Supremes (Tamla Motown)
6	6	SCOTT 2 Scott Walker (Philips)
8	7	PETER GREEN'S FLEETWOOD MAC Fleetwood Mac (Blue Horizon)
8	8	THE HANGMAN'S BEAUTIFUL DAUGHTER Incredible String Band (Elektra)
-	9	SMASH HITS Jimi Hendrix Experience (Track)
5	10	FOUR TOPS' GREATEST HITS Four Tops (Tamla Motown)
15	11	SHER-OO! Cilla Black (Parlophone)
-	12	THE JUNGLE BOOK Soundtrack (Disneyland)
13	13	MOVE Move (Regal Zonophone)
-	14	A GIFT FROM A FLOWER TO A GARDEN Donovan (Pye)
14	15	WILD HONEY Beach Boys (Capitol)

11 May 1968

1	1	THIS IS SOUL Various Artists (Atlantic)
2	2	JOHN WESLEY HARDING Bob Dylan (CBS)
6	3	SCOTT 2 Scott Walker (Philips)
3	4	HISTORY OF OTIS REDDING Otis Redding (Volt)
4	5	THE SOUND OF MUSIC Soundtrack (RCA)
9	6	SMASH HITS Jimi Hendrix Experience (Track)
5	7	SUPREMES' GREATEST HITS Supremes (Tamla Motown)
7	8	PETER GREEN'S FLEETWOOD MAC Fleetwood Mac (Blue Horizon)
-	9	LIVE AT THE TALK OF THE TOWN Diana Ross & the Supremes (Tamla Motown)
8	10	THE HANGMAN'S BEAUTIFUL DAUGHTER Incredible String Band (Elektra)
10	11	FOUR TOPS' GREATEST HITS Four Tops (Tamla Motown)
14	12	A GIFT FROM A FLOWER TO A GARDEN Donovan (Pye)
12	13	THE JUNGLE BOOK Soundtrack (Disneyland)
11	14	SHER-OO! Cilla Black (Parlophone)
-	15	2 IN 3 Esther & Abi Ofarim (Philips)

18 May 1968

1	1	THIS IS SOUL Various Artists (Atlantic)
2	2	JOHN WESLEY HARDING Bob Dylan (CBS)
3	3	SCOTT 2 Scott Walker (Philips)
4	4	HISTORY OF OTIS REDDING Otis Redding (Volt)
5	5	THE SOUND OF MUSIC Soundtrack (RCA)
6	6	SMASH HITS Jimi Hendrix Experience (Track)
7	7	SUPREMES' GREATEST HITS Supremes (Tamla Motown)
10	8	THE HANGMAN'S BEAUTIFUL DAUGHTER Incredible String Band (Elektra)
13	9	THE JUNGLE BOOK Soundtrack (Disneyland)
8	10	PETER GREEN'S FLEETWOOD MAC Fleetwood Mac (Blue Horizon)
11	11	FOUR TOPS' GREATEST HITS Four Tops (Tamla Motown)
12	12	A GIFT FROM A FLOWER TO A GARDEN Donovan (Pye)
9	13	LIVE AT THE TALK OF THE TOWN Diana Ross & the Supremes (Tamla Motown)
14	14	SHER-OO! Cilla Black (Parlophone)
-	15	13 SMASH HITS Tom Jones (Decca)

25 May 1968

1	1	THIS IS SOUL Various Artists (Atlantic)
2	2	JOHN WESLEY HARDING Bob Dylan (CBS)
3	3	SCOTT 2 Scott Walker (Philips)
4	4	HISTORY OF OTIS REDDING Otis Redding (Volt)
6	5	SMASH HITS Jimi Hendrix Experience (Track)
5	6	THE SOUND OF MUSIC Soundtrack (RCA)
7	7	SUPREMES' GREATEST HITS Supremes (Tamla Motown)
10	8	PETER GREEN'S FLEETWOOD MAC Fleetwood Mac (Blue Horizon)
-	9	THE DOCK OF THE BAY Otis Redding (Stax)
9	10	THE JUNGLE BOOK Soundtrack (Disneyland)
8	11	THE HANGMAN'S BEAUTIFUL DAUGHTER Incredible String Band (Elektra)
12	12	A GIFT FROM A FLOWER TO A GARDEN Donovan (Pye)
11	13	FOUR TOPS' GREATEST HITS Four Tops (Tamla Motown)
-	13	LOVE ANDY Andy Williams (CBS)
-	15	BUDDY HOLLY'S GREATEST HITS Buddy Holly (Ace of Hearts)

1 June 1968

1	1	THIS IS SOUL Various Artists (Atlantic)
3	2	SCOTT 2 Scott Walker (Philips)
2	3	JOHN WESLEY HARDING Bob Dylan (CBS)
6	4	THE SOUND OF MUSIC Soundtrack (RCA)
4	5	HISTORY OF OTIS REDDING Otis Redding (Volt)
5	6	SMASH HITS Jimi Hendrix Experience (Track)
9	7	THE DOCK OF THE BAY Otis Redding (Stax)
8	8	PETER GREEN'S FLEETWOOD MAC Fleetwood Mac (Blue Horizon)
13	9	LOVE ANDY Andy Williams (CBS)
10	10	THE JUNGLE BOOK Soundtrack (Disneyland)
11	11	THE HANGMAN'S BEAUTIFUL DAUGHTER Incredible String Band (Elektra)
7	12	SUPREMES' GREATEST HITS Supremes (Tamla Motown)
13	13	FOUR TOPS' GREATEST HITS Four Tops (Tamla Motown)
-	14	VALLEY OF THE DOLLS Dionne Warwick (Pye)
12	15	A GIFT FROM A FLOWER TO A GARDEN Donovan (Pye)

8 June 1968

1	1	THIS IS SOUL Various Artists (Atlantic)
2	2	SCOTT 2 Scott Walker (Philips)
3	3	JOHN WESLEY HARDING Bob Dylan (CBS)
7	4	THE DOCK OF THE BAY Otis Redding (Stax)
9	5	LOVE ANDY Andy Williams (CBS)
4	6	THE SOUND OF MUSIC Soundtrack (RCA)
5	7	HISTORY OF OTIS REDDING Otis Redding (Volt)
6	8	SMASH HITS Jimi Hendrix Experience (Track)
8	8	PETER GREEN'S FLEETWOOD MAC Fleetwood Mac (Blue Horizon)
-	10	TOM JONES LIVE AT THE TALK OF THE TOWN Tom Jones (Decca)
11	11	THE HANGMAN'S BEAUTIFUL DAUGHTER Incredible String Band (Elektra)
10	12	THE JUNGLE BOOK Soundtrack (Disneyland)
12	13	SUPREMES' GREATEST HITS Supremes (Tamla Motown)
14	14	VALLEY OF THE DOLLS Dionne Warwick (Pye)
15	15	A GIFT FROM A FLOWER TO A GARDEN Donovan (Pye)

15 June 1968

1	1	THIS IS SOUL Various Artists (Atlantic)
3	2	JOHN WESLEY HARDING Bob Dylan (CBS)
2	3	SCOTT 2 Scott Walker (Philips)
5	4	LOVE ANDY Andy Williams (CBS)
6	5	THE SOUND OF MUSIC Soundtrack (RCA)
8	6	SMASH HITS Jimi Hendrix Experience (Track)
7	7	HISTORY OF OTIS REDDING Otis Redding (Volt)
4	8	THE DOCK OF THE BAY Otis Redding (Stax)
-	9	OGDENS NUT GONE FLAKE Small Faces (Immediate)
13	10	SUPREMES' GREATEST HITS Supremes (Tamla Motown)
8	11	PETER GREEN'S FLEETWOOD MAC Fleetwood Mac (Blue Horizon)
12	12	THE JUNGLE BOOK Soundtrack (Disneyland)
14	13	VALLEY OF THE DOLLS Dionne Warwick (Pye)
11	14	THE HANGMAN'S BEAUTIFUL DAUGHTER Incredible String Band (Elektra)
10	15	TOM JONES LIVE AT THE TALK OF THE TOWN Tom Jones (Decca)

Otis Redding died in December 1967, his plane crashing into a lake. He'd had a British mod following since 1965, with hit singles and an album; for whites his 1967 Monterey Pop Festival performance (besuited, while all around him wore kaftans and bells) had clinched his status as Mr Soul. Now *Otis Blue* had re-entered the charts in February, followed by *History Of Otis Redding*, *Otis Redding In Europe*, and *Dock of the Bay* in May. The posthumous single of that title proved his biggest hit.

22 June 1968

last this week

last	this		
1	1	THIS IS SOUL	Various Artists (Atlantic)
9	2	OGDENS NUT GONE FLAKE	Small Faces (Immediate)
4	3	LOVE ANDY	Andy Williams (CBS)
5	4	THE SOUND OF MUSIC	Soundtrack (RCA)
2	5	JOHN WESLEY HARDING	Bob Dylan (CBS)
11	6	PETER GREEN'S FLEETWOOD MAC	Fleetwood Mac (Blue Horizon)
6	7	SMASH HITS	Jimi Hendrix Experience (Track)
3	8	SCOTT 2 Scott Walker (Philips)	
8	9	THE DOCK OF THE BAY	Otis Redding (Stax)
13	10	VALLEY OF THE DOLLS	Dionne Warwick (Pye)
-	11	OPEN Julie Driscoll & the	Brian Auger Trinity (Marmalade)
7	12	HISTORY OF OTIS REDDING	Otis Redding (Volt)
10	13	SUPREMES' GREATEST HITS	Supremes (Tamla Motown)
12	14	THE JUNGLE BOOK	Soundtrack (Disneyland)
14	15	THE HANGMAN'S BEAUTIFUL DAUGHTER	Incredible String Band (Elektra)

29 June 1968

last	this		
1	1	THIS IS SOUL	Various Artists (Atlantic)
2	2	OGDENS NUT GONE FLAKE	Small Faces (Immediate)
3	3	LOVE ANDY Andy Williams (CBS)	
5	4	JOHN WESLEY HARDING	Bob Dylan (CBS)
8	5	SCOTT 2 Scott Walker (Philips)	
7	6	SMASH HITS	Jimi Hendrix Experience (Track)
12	7	HISTORY OF OTIS REDDING	Otis Redding (Volt)
4	8	THE SOUND OF MUSIC	Soundtrack (RCA)
11	9	OPEN Julie Driscoll & the	Brian Auger Trinity (Marmalade)
6	10	PETER GREEN'S FLEETWOOD MAC	Fleetwood Mac (Blue Horizon)
9	10	THE DOCK OF THE BAY	Otis Redding (Stax)
10	12	VALLEY OF THE DOLLS	Dionne Warwick (Pye)
-	13	40 BLUE FINGERS FRESHLY PACKED AND READY TO SERVE	Chicken Shack (Blue Horizon)
14	14	THE JUNGLE BOOK	Soundtrack (Disneyland)
-	15	CRAZY WORLD OF ARTHUR BROWN	Crazy World Of Arthur Brown (Track)

6 July 1968

last	this		
2	1	OGDENS NUT GONE FLAKE	Small Faces (Immediate)
1	2	THIS IS SOUL	Various Artists (Atlantic)
3	3	LOVE ANDY Andy Williams (CBS)	
8	4	THE SOUND OF MUSIC	Soundtrack (RCA)
10	5	THE DOCK OF THE BAY	Otis Redding (Stax)
5	6	SCOTT 2 Scott Walker (Philips)	
7	7	HONEY Andy Williams (CBS)	
4	8	JOHN WESLEY HARDING	Bob Dylan (CBS)
6	9	SMASH HITS	Jimi Hendrix Experience (Track)
14	10	THE JUNGLE BOOK	Soundtrack (Disneyland)
9	11	OPEN Julie Driscoll & the	Brian Auger Trinity (Marmalade)
15	12	CRAZY WORLD OF ARTHUR BROWN	Crazy World Of Arthur Brown (Track)
13	13	40 BLUE FINGERS FRESHLY PACKED AND READY TO SERVE	Chicken Shack (Blue Horizon)
7	14	HISTORY OF OTIS REDDING	Otis Redding (Volt)
10	15	PETER GREEN'S FLEETWOOD MAC	Fleetwood Mac (Blue Horizon)

13 July 1968

last	this		
1	1	OGDENS NUT GONE FLAKE	Small Faces (Immediate)
2	2	THIS IS SOUL	Various Artists (Atlantic)
4	3	THE SOUND OF MUSIC	Soundtrack (RCA)
7	4	HONEY Andy Williams (CBS)	
5	5	THE DOCK OF THE BAY	Otis Redding (Stax)
3	6	LOVE ANDY Andy Williams (CBS)	
12	7	CRAZY WORLD OF ARTHUR BROWN	Crazy World Of Arthur Brown (Track)
8	8	JOHN WESLEY HARDING	Bob Dylan (CBS)
11	9	OPEN Julie Driscoll & the	Brian Auger Trinity (Marmalade)
10	10	THE JUNGLE BOOK	Soundtrack (Disneyland)
-	11	BARE WIRES	John Mayall (Decca)
15	12	PETER GREEN'S FLEETWOOD MAC	Fleetwood Mac (Blue Horizon)
-	13	THE BIRDS, THE BEES AND THE MONKEES	Monkees (RCA)
9	14	SMASH HITS	Jimi Hendrix Experience (Track)
6	15	SCOTT 2 Scott Walker (Philips)	

20 July 1968

last	this		
1	1	OGDENS NUT GONE FLAKE	Small Faces (Immediate)
3	2	THE SOUND OF MUSIC	Soundtrack (RCA)
2	3	THIS IS SOUL	Various Artists (Atlantic)
4	4	HONEY Andy Williams (CBS)	
7	5	CRAZY WORLD OF ARTHUR BROWN	Crazy World Of Arthur Brown (Track)
10	6	THE JUNGLE BOOK	Soundtrack (Disneyland)
13	7	THE BIRDS, THE BEES AND THE MONKEES	Monkees (RCA)
14	8	SMASH HITS	Jimi Hendrix Experience (Track)
9	9	OPEN Julie Driscoll & the	Brian Auger Trinity (Marmalade)
6	10	LOVE ANDY Andy Williams (CBS)	
12	11	PETER GREEN'S FLEETWOOD MAC	Fleetwood Mac (Blue Horizon)
-	12	40 BLUE FINGERS FRESHLY PACKED AND READY TO SERVE	Chicken Shack (Blue Horizon)
5	13	THE DOCK OF THE BAY	Otis Redding (Stax)
-	14	A SAUCERFUL OF SECRETS	Pink Floyd (Columbia)
8	15	JOHN WESLEY HARDING	Bob Dylan (CBS)

27 July 1968

last	this		
1	1	OGDENS NUT GONE FLAKE	Small Faces (Immediate)
3	2	THIS IS SOUL	Various Artists (Atlantic)
5	3	CRAZY WORLD OF ARTHUR BROWN	Crazy World Of Arthur Brown (Track)
-	4	DELILAH Tom Jones (Decca)	
-	5	BOOKENDS	Simon & Garfunkel (CBS)
2	6	THE SOUND OF MUSIC	Soundtrack (RCA)
-	7	A MAN WITHOUT LOVE	Engelbert Humperdinck (Decca)
4	8	HONEY Andy Williams (CBS)	
7	9	THE BIRDS, THE BEES AND THE MONKEES	Monkees (RCA)
-	10	BARE WIRES John Mayall (Decca)	
14	11	A SAUCERFUL OF SECRETS	Pink Floyd (Columbia)
6	12	THE JUNGLE BOOK	Soundtrack (Disneyland)
11	12	PETER GREEN'S FLEETWOOD MAC	Fleetwood Mac (Blue Horizon)
10	14	LOVE ANDY Andy Williams (CBS)	
8	15	SMASH HITS	Jimi Hendrix Experience (Track)
-	15	TYRANNOSAURUS REX	Tyrannosaurus Rex (Regal Zonophone)

3 August 1968

last	this		
5	1	BOOKENDS	Simon & Garfunkel (CBS)
4	2	DELILAH Tom Jones (Decca)	
1	3	OGDENS NUT GONE FLAKE	Small Faces (Immediate)
3	4	CRAZY WORLD OF ARTHUR BROWN	Crazy World Of Arthur Brown (Track)
7	5	A MAN WITHOUT LOVE	Engelbert Humperdinck (Decca)
10	6	BARE WIRES John Mayall (Decca)	
2	7	THIS IS SOUL	Various Artists (Atlantic)
6	8	THE SOUND OF MUSIC	Soundtrack (RCA)
8	9	HONEY Andy Williams (CBS)	
11	10	A SAUCERFUL OF SECRETS	Pink Floyd (Columbia)
15	11	SMASH HITS	Jimi Hendrix Experience (Track)
-	12	THE ROCK MACHINE TURNS YOU ON Various Artists (CBS)	
12	13	THE JUNGLE BOOK	Soundtrack (Disneyland)
-	14	IN SEARCH OF THE LOST CHORD Moody Blues (Deram)	
12	15	PETER GREEN'S FLEETWOOD MAC	Fleetwood Mac (Blue Horizon)
15	15	TYRANNOSAURUS REX	Tyrannosaurus Rex (Regal Zonophone)

10 August 1968

last	this		
2	1	DELILAH Tom Jones (Decca)	
1	2	BOOKENDS	Simon & Garfunkel (CBS)
5	3	A MAN WITHOUT LOVE	Engelbert Humperdinck (Decca)
4	4	CRAZY WORLD OF ARTHUR BROWN	Crazy World Of Arthur Brown (Track)
3	5	OGDENS NUT GONE FLAKE	Small Faces (Immediate)
7	6	THIS IS SOUL	Various Artists (Atlantic)
8	7	THE SOUND OF MUSIC	Soundtrack (RCA)
6	8	BARE WIRES	John Mayall (Decca)
12	9	THE ROCK MACHINE TURNS YOU ON Various Artists (CBS)	
13	10	THE JUNGLE BOOK	Soundtrack (Disneyland)
10	11	A SAUCERFUL OF SECRETS	Pink Floyd (Columbia)
11	12	SMASH HITS	Jimi Hendrix Experience (Track)
14	13	IN SEARCH OF THE LOST CHORD Moody Blues (Deram)	
15	14	PETER GREEN'S FLEETWOOD MAC	Fleetwood Mac (Blue Horizon)
9	15	HONEY Andy Williams (CBS)	

The Incredible String Band, whose third (and classic) album was ending its chart run, were THE British hippy band; led by Celtic folkie Robin Williamson and ex-R&B guitarist Mike Heron, they patented the alternative life: love, peace and rural communality.

Their wonderfully wiffly songs, on exotic instruments, wriggled between the charming, the mystical and the twee. It's taken 25 years to restore them from unpersondom to history - and to learn that Mike and Robin loathed each other all along.

August – October 1968

last this
week

17 August 1968

last	this		
2	1	BOOKENDS	Simon & Garfunkel (CBS)
1	2	DELILAH	Tom Jones (Decca)
3	3	A MAN WITHOUT LOVE	Engelbert Humperdinck (Decca)
7	4	THE SOUND OF MUSIC	Soundtrack (RCA)
4	5	CRAZY WORLD OF ARTHUR BROWN	Crazy World Of Arthur Brown (Track)
8	6	BARE WIRES	John Mayall (Decca)
5	7	OGDENS NUT GONE FLAKE	Small Faces (Immediate)
-	8	HOLLIES' GREATEST HITS	Hollies (Parlophone)
6	9	THIS IS SOUL	Various Artists (Atlantic)
13	9	IN SEARCH OF THE LOST CHORD	Moody Blues (Deram)
11	11	A SAUCERFUL OF SECRETS	Pink Floyd (Columbia)
10	12	THE JUNGLE BOOK	Soundtrack (Disneyland)
-	12	BOOGIE WITH CANNED HEAT	Canned Heat (Liberty)
-	14	WHEELS OF FIRE	Cream (Polydor)
9	15	THE ROCK MACHINE TURNS YOU ON	Various Artists (CBS)

24 August 1968

last	this		
1	1	BOOKENDS	Simon & Garfunkel (CBS)
2	2	DELILAH	Tom Jones (Decca)
8	3	HOLLIES' GREATEST HITS	Hollies (Parlophone)
3	4	A MAN WITHOUT LOVE	Engelbert Humperdinck (Decca)
5	4	CRAZY WORLD OF ARTHUR BROWN	Crazy World Of Arthur Brown (Track)
6	6	BARE WIRES	John Mayall (Decca)
14	7	WHEELS OF FIRE	Cream (Polydor)
9	8	IN SEARCH OF THE LOST CHORD	Moody Blues (Deram)
9	9	THIS IS SOUL	Various Artists (Atlantic)
7	10	OGDENS NUT GONE FLAKE	Small Faces (Immediate)
12	11	THE JUNGLE BOOK	Soundtrack (Disneyland)
12	12	BOOGIE WITH CANNED HEAT	Canned Heat (Liberty)
4	13	THE SOUND OF MUSIC	Soundtrack (RCA)
11	14	A SAUCERFUL OF SECRETS	Pink Floyd (Columbia)
-	15	WHEELS OF FIRE IN THE STUDIO	Cream (Polydor)

31 August 1968

last	this		
1	1	BOOKENDS	Simon & Garfunkel (CBS)
2	2	DELILAH	Tom Jones (Decca)
3	3	HOLLIES' GREATEST HITS	Hollies (Parlophone)
7	4	WHEELS OF FIRE	Cream (Polydor)
8	5	IN SEARCH OF THE LOST CHORD	Moody Blues (Deram)
4	6	A MAN WITHOUT LOVE	Engelbert Humperdinck (Decca)
6	6	BARE WIRES	John Mayall (Decca)
4	8	CRAZY WORLD OF ARTHUR BROWN	Crazy World Of Arthur Brown (Track)
13	9	THE SOUND OF MUSIC	Soundtrack (RCA)
12	10	BOOGIE WITH CANNED HEAT	Canned Heat (Liberty)
11	11	THE JUNGLE BOOK	Soundtrack (Disneyland)
15	11	WHEELS OF FIRE IN THE STUDIO	Cream (Polydor)
9	13	THIS IS SOUL	Various Artists (Atlantic)
10	14	OGDENS NUT GONE FLAKE	Small Faces (Immediate)
-	15	MR. WONDERFUL	Fleetwood Mac (Blue Horizon)

7 September 1968

last	this		
1	1	BOOKENDS	Simon & Garfunkel (CBS)
3	2	HOLLIES' GREATEST HITS	Hollies (Parlophone)
2	3	DELILAH	Tom Jones (Decca)
4	4	WHEELS OF FIRE	Cream (Polydor)
5	5	IN SEARCH OF THE LOST CHORD	Moody Blues (Deram)
6	6	A MAN WITHOUT LOVE	Engelbert Humperdinck (Decca)
9	7	THE SOUND OF MUSIC	Soundtrack (RCA)
8	8	CRAZY WORLD OF ARTHUR BROWN	Crazy World Of Arthur Brown (Track)
6	9	BARE WIRES	John Mayall (Decca)
10	10	BOOGIE WITH CANNED HEAT	Canned Heat (Liberty)
15	10	MR WONDERFUL	Fleetwood Mac (Blue Horizon)
13	12	THIS IS SOUL	Various Artists (Atlantic)
11	13	WHEELS OF FIRE IN THE STUDIO	Cream (Polydor)
11	14	THE JUNGLE BOOK	Soundtrack (Disneyland)
14	15	OGDENS NUT GONE FLAKE	Small Faces (Immediate)

14 September 1968

last	this		
1	1	BOOKENDS	Simon & Garfunkel (CBS)
2	2	HOLLIES' GREATEST HITS	Hollies (Parlophone)
3	3	DELILAH	Tom Jones (Decca)
4	4	WHEELS OF FIRE	Cream (Polydor)
10	5	MR. WONDERFUL	Fleetwood Mac (Blue Horizon)
5	6	IN SEARCH OF THE LOST CHORD	Moody Blues (Deram)
7	7	THE SOUND OF MUSIC	Soundtrack (RCA)
10	8	BOOGIE WITH CANNED HEAT	Canned Heat (Liberty)
6	9	A MAN WITHOUT LOVE	Engelbert Humperdinck (Decca)
12	10	THIS IS SOUL	Various Artists (Atlantic)
-	11	THE SEEKERS AT THE TALK OF THE TOWN	Seekers (Columbia)
14	12	THE JUNGLE BOOK	Soundtrack (Disneyland)
8	13	CRAZY WORLD OF ARTHUR BROWN	Crazy World Of Arthur Brown (Track)
9	14	BARE WIRES	John Mayall (Decca)
-	15	JOHNNY CASH AT FOLSOM PRISON	Johnny Cash (CBS)

21 September 1968

last	this		
2	1	HOLLIES' GREATEST HITS	Hollies (Parlophone)
1	2	BOOKENDS	Simon & Garfunkel (CBS)
3	3	DELILAH	Tom Jones (Decca)
5	4	MR. WONDERFUL	Fleetwood Mac (Blue Horizon)
4	5	WHEELS OF FIRE	Cream (Polydor)
11	5	THE SEEKERS AT THE TALK OF THE TOWN	Seekers (Columbia)
8	7	BOOGIE WITH CANNED HEAT	Canned Heat (Liberty)
6	8	IN SEARCH OF THE LOST CHORD	Moody Blues (Deram)
9	9	A MAN WITHOUT LOVE	Engelbert Humperdinck (Decca)
-	10	WAITING FOR THE SUN	Doors (Elektra)
7	11	THE SOUND OF MUSIC	Soundtrack (RCA)
10	12	THIS IS SOUL	Various Artists (Atlantic)
-	13	ARETHA NOW	Aretha Franklin (Atlantic)
12	14	THE JUNGLE BOOK	Soundtrack (Disneyland)
14	15	BARE WIRES	John Mayall (Decca)

28 September 1968

last	this		
1	1	HOLLIES' GREATEST HITS	Hollies (Parlophone)
3	2	DELILAH	Tom Jones (Decca)
2	3	BOOKENDS	Simon & Garfunkel (CBS)
5	4	THE SEEKERS AT THE TALK OF THE TOWN	Seekers (Columbia)
5	5	WHEELS OF FIRE	Cream (Polydor)
9	6	A MAN WITHOUT LOVE	Engelbert Humperdinck (Decca)
7	7	BOOGIE WITH CANNED HEAT	Canned Heat (Liberty)
11	7	THE SOUND OF MUSIC	Soundtrack (RCA)
4	9	MR. WONDERFUL	Fleetwood Mac (Blue Horizon)
10	10	WAITING FOR THE SUN	Doors (Elektra)
8	11	IN SEARCH OF THE LOST CHORD	Moody Blues (Deram)
13	12	ARETHA NOW	Aretha Franklin (Atlantic)
14	13	THE JUNGLE BOOK	Soundtrack (Disneyland)
-	14	IDEA	Bee Gees (Polydor)
-	15	JOHNNY CASH AT FOLSOM PRISON	Johnny Cash (CBS)

5 October 1968

last	this		
1	1	HOLLIES' GREATEST HITS	Hollies (Parlophone)
4	2	THE SEEKERS AT THE TALK OF THE TOWN	Seekers (Columbia)
3	3	BOOKENDS	Simon & Garfunkel (CBS)
2	4	DELILAH	Tom Jones (Decca)
7	5	BOOGIE WITH CANNED HEAT	Canned Heat (Liberty)
5	6	WHEELS OF FIRE	Cream (Polydor)
7	7	THE SOUND OF MUSIC	Soundtrack (RCA)
11	8	IN SEARCH OF THE LOST CHORD	Moody Blues (Deram)
10	9	WAITING FOR THE SUN	Doors (Elektra)
6	10	A MAN WITHOUT LOVE	Engelbert Humperdinck (Decca)
14	11	IDEA	Bee Gees (Polydor)
9	12	MR. WONDERFUL	Fleetwood Mac (Blue Horizon)
12	13	ARETHA NOW	Aretha Franklin (Atlantic)
13	13	THE JUNGLE BOOK	Soundtrack (Disneyland)
15	15	JOHNNY CASH AT FOLSOM PRISON	Johnny Cash (CBS)

Most unusual was the charting of both a single-LP and a double of Cream's *Wheels Of Fire* - the double far more successfully. September saw the launch of the Beatles' Apple label. CBS' prog-rock compilation *Rock Machine Turns You On* was an interesting title.

The previous year the BBC had banned the Beatles' Day In The Life because it included "I'd love to turn you on." Now it was already a hip marketing phrase. Later the BBC would adapt it for their jingle "Radio 1 really turns you on".

12 October 1968

last week	this week	Entry
1	1	HOLLIES' GREATEST HITS — Hollies (Parlophone)
2	2	THE SEEKERS AT THE TALK OF THE TOWN — Seekers (Columbia)
3	3	BOOKENDS — Simon & Garfunkel (CBS)
11	4	IDEA — Bee Gees (Polydor)
7	5	THE SOUND OF MUSIC — Soundtrack (RCA)
5	6	BOOGIE WITH CANNED HEAT — Canned Heat (Liberty)
4	7	DELILAH — Tom Jones (Decca)
9	8	WAITING FOR THE SUN — Doors (Elektra)
8	9	IN SEARCH OF THE LOST CHORD — Moody Blues (Deram)
6	10	WHEELS OF FIRE — Cream (Polydor)
10	11	A MAN WITHOUT LOVE — Engelbert Humperdinck (Decca)
15	12	JOHNNY CASH AT FOLSOM PRISON — Johnny Cash (CBS)
12	13	MR. WONDERFUL — Fleetwood Mac (Blue Horizon)
13	14	ARETHA NOW — Aretha Franklin (Atlantic)
13	15	THE JUNGLE BOOK — Soundtrack (Disneyland)

19 October 1968

last	this	Entry
1	1	HOLLIES' GREATEST HITS — Hollies (Parlophone)
2	2	THE SEEKERS AT THE TALK OF THE TOWN — Seekers (Columbia)
3	3	BOOKENDS — Simon & Garfunkel (CBS)
5	4	THE SOUND OF MUSIC — Soundtrack (RCA)
4	5	IDEA — Bee Gees (Polydor)
7	6	DELILAH — Tom Jones (Decca)
10	7	WHEELS OF FIRE — Cream (Polydor)
11	8	A MAN WITHOUT LOVE — Engelbert Humperdinck (Decca)
6	9	BOOGIE WITH CANNED HEAT — Canned Heat (Liberty)
8	10	WAITING FOR THE SUN — Doors (Elektra)
9	11	IN SEARCH OF THE LOST CHORD — Moody Blues (Deram)
14	12	ARETHA NOW — Aretha Franklin (Atlantic)
12	13	JOHNNY CASH AT FOLSOM PRISON — Johnny Cash (CBS)
-	14	THE WORLD OF MANTOVANI — Mantovani (Decca)
-	15	TRAFFIC — Traffic (Island)

26 October 1968

last	this	Entry
1	1	HOLLIES' GREATEST HITS — Hollies (Parlophone)
2	2	THE SEEKERS AT THE TALK OF THE TOWN — Seekers (Columbia)
5	3	IDEA — Bee Gees (Polydor)
3	4	BOOKENDS — Simon & Garfunkel (CBS)
4	5	THE SOUND OF MUSIC — Soundtrack (RCA)
6	6	DELILAH — Tom Jones (Decca)
15	7	TRAFFIC — Traffic (Island)
-	8	THIS WAS — Jethro Tull (Island)
14	9	THE WORLD OF MANTOVANI — Mantovani (Decca)
7	10	WHEELS OF FIRE — Cream (Polydor)
8	11	A MAN WITHOUT LOVE — Engelbert Humperdinck (Decca)
11	12	IN SEARCH OF THE LOST CHORD — Moody Blues (Deram)
9	13	BOOGIE WITH CANNED HEAT — Canned Heat (Liberty)
10	14	WAITING FOR THE SUN — Doors (Elektra)
13	15	JOHNNY CASH AT FOLSOM PRISON — Johnny Cash (CBS)

2 November 1968

last	this	Entry
1	1	HOLLIES' GREATEST HITS — Hollies (Parlophone)
2	2	THE SEEKERS AT THE TALK OF THE TOWN — Seekers (Columbia)
3	3	IDEA — Bee Gees (Polydor)
5	4	THE SOUND OF MUSIC — Soundtrack (RCA)
8	5	THIS WAS — Jethro Tull (Island)
4	6	BOOKENDS — Simon & Garfunkel (CBS)
7	7	TRAFFIC — Traffic (Island)
6	8	DELILAH — Tom Jones (Decca)
-	9	THE GOOD, THE BAD & THE UGLY — Soundtrack (United Artists)
-	10	ELECTRIC LADYLAND — Jimi Hendrix Experience (Track)
11	11	A MAN WITHOUT LOVE — Engelbert Humperdinck (Decca)
14	12	WAITING FOR THE SUN — Doors (Elektra)
10	13	WHEELS OF FIRE — Cream (Polydor)
-	14	THE JUNGLE BOOK — Soundtrack (Disneyland)
13	15	BOOGIE WITH CANNED HEAT — Canned Heat (Liberty)

9 November 1968

last	this	Entry
1	1	HOLLIES' GREATEST HITS — Hollies (Parlophone)
2	2	THE SEEKERS AT THE TALK OF THE TOWN — Seekers (Columbia)
3	3	IDEA — Bee Gees (Polydor)
4	4	THE SOUND OF MUSIC — Soundtrack (RCA)
10	5	ELECTRIC LADYLAND — Jimi Hendrix Experience (Track)
6	6	BOOKENDS — Simon & Garfunkel (CBS)
5	7	THIS WAS — Jethro Tull (Island)
9	8	THE GOOD, THE BAD & THE UGLY — Soundtrack (United Artists)
8	9	DELILAH — Tom Jones (Decca)
7	10	TRAFFIC — Traffic (Island)
11	11	A MAN WITHOUT LOVE — Engelbert Humperdinck (Decca)
-	12	FELICIANO — Jose Feliciano (RCA)
-	13	JOHNNY CASH AT FOLSOM PRISON — Johnny Cash (CBS)
13	14	WHEELS OF FIRE — Cream (Polydor)
-	15	THE WORLD OF MANTOVANI — Mantovani (Decca)

16 November 1968

last	this	Entry
1	1	HOLLIES' GREATEST HITS — Hollies (Parlophone)
2	2	THE SEEKERS AT THE TALK OF THE TOWN — Seekers (Columbia)
8	3	THE GOOD, THE BAD & THE UGLY — Soundtrack (United Artists)
5	4	ELECTRIC LADYLAND — Jimi Hendrix Experience (Track)
4	5	THE SOUND OF MUSIC — Soundtrack (RCA)
7	6	THIS WAS — Jethro Tull (Island)
3	7	IDEA — Bee Gees (Polydor)
6	8	BOOKENDS — Simon & Garfunkel (CBS)
-	9	THE GRADUATE — Soundtrack (CBS)
12	10	FELICIANO — Jose Feliciano (RCA)
15	11	THE WORLD OF MANTOVANI — Mantovani (Decca)
-	12	BEST OF THE SEEKERS — Seekers (Columbia)
-	13	THE JUNGLE BOOK — Soundtrack (Disneyland)
9	14	DELILAH — Tom Jones (Decca)
11	15	A MAN WITHOUT LOVE — Engelbert Humperdinck (Decca)

23 November 1968

last	this	Entry
1	1	HOLLIES' GREATEST HITS — Hollies (Parlophone)
4	2	ELECTRIC LADYLAND — Jimi Hendrix Experience (Track)
2	3	THE SEEKERS AT THE TALK OF THE TOWN — Seekers (Columbia)
3	4	THE GOOD, THE BAD & THE UGLY — Soundtrack (United Artists)
9	5	THE GRADUATE — Soundtrack (CBS)
12	6	BEST OF THE SEEKERS — Seekers (Columbia)
5	7	THE SOUND OF MUSIC — Soundtrack (RCA)
10	8	FELICIANO — Jose Feliciano (RCA)
6	9	THIS WAS — Jethro Tull (Island)
11	10	THE WORLD OF MANTOVANI — Mantovani (Decca)
-	11	BEST OF THE BEACH BOYS VOL 3 — Beach Boys (Capitol)
14	12	DELILAH — Tom Jones (Decca)
7	13	IDEA — Bee Gees (Polydor)
8	13	BOOKENDS — Simon & Garfunkel (CBS)
15	15	A MAN WITHOUT LOVE — Engelbert Humperdinck (Decca)

30 November 1968

last	this	Entry
-	1	THE BEATLES — Beatles (Apple)
6	2	BEST OF THE SEEKERS — Seekers (Columbia)
2	3	ELECTRIC LADYLAND — Jimi Hendrix Experience (Track)
1	4	HOLLIES' GREATEST HITS — Hollies (Parlophone)
7	5	THE SOUND OF MUSIC — Soundtrack (RCA)
4	6	THE GOOD, THE BAD & THE UGLY — Soundtrack (United Artists)
5	7	THE GRADUATE — Soundtrack (CBS)
3	8	THE SEEKERS AT THE TALK OF THE TOWN — Seekers (Columbia)
10	9	THE WORLD OF MANTOVANI — Mantovani (Decca)
8	10	FELICIANO — Jose Feliciano (RCA)
11	11	BEST OF THE BEACH BOYS VOL 3 — Beach Boys (Capitol)
9	12	THIS WAS — Jethro Tull (Island)
13	13	IDEA — Bee Gees (Polydor)
-	14	VAL — Val Doonican (Pye)
12	15	DELILAH — Tom Jones (Decca)

This period starts with an Apple single topping the chart, Mary Hopkins' *Those Were The Days*; it ends with an Apple album topping it, the Beatles' White Album. This displaced *Hollies' Greatest Hits*, top for ten weeks. By now the Hollies had racked up eighteen hit singles, starting with minor 1963 hit *Just Like Me*, running through thirteen Top 10s to *Listen To Me*, peaking at 7 this October/November. And you never met anyone who admitted to liking them: not even their own Graham Nash.

December 1968

December is the gruellest month. The spirit of the Black & White Minstrels conjured up a chart embracing not just Mantovani (and of course *The Sound Of Music*) but TWO Val Doonicans and TWO Seekers albums. Perhaps after all those psychedelic epic records called *Piper At The Gates of Dawn* and *In Search of the Lost Chord* (Pink Floyd and Moody Blues), some people's aunties bought them *The Seekers At The Talk Of The Town* by mistake. NME staff certainly made a mistake. No doubt too busy seeking that lost chord at the gates of dawn, they couldn't quite get it together to sort out the year-end's chart, man. Those were the days, my friend.

4 January 1969

last week / this week

last	this		
1	1	THE BEATLES	Beatles (Apple)
2	2	BEST OF THE SEEKERS	Seekers (Columbia)
3	3	BEGGARS BANQUET	Rolling Stones (Decca)
4	4	THE WORLD OF VAL DOONICAN	Val Doonican (Decca)
5	5	THE SOUND OF MUSIC	Soundtrack (RCA)
6	6	THE GRADUATE	Soundtrack (CBS)
7	7	HELP YOURSELF	Tom Jones (Decca)
12	8	THE GOOD, THE BAD & THE UGLY	Soundtrack (United Artists)
10	9	HOLLIES' GREATEST HITS	Hollies (Parlophone)
14	10	THE WORLD OF THE BACHELORS	Bachelors (Decca)
11	11	VAL	Val Doonican (Pye)
8	12	THE WORLD OF MANTOVANI	Mantovani (Decca)
13	12	I PRETEND	Des O'Connor (Columbia)
9	14	ELECTRIC LADYLAND	Jimi Hendrix (Track)
-	15	A TOUCH OF SADNESS	Jim Reeves (RCA)

11 January 1969

1	1 THE BEATLES	Beatles (Apple)
2	2 BEST OF THE SEEKERS	Seekers (Columbia)
3	3 BEGGARS BANQUET	Rolling Stones (Decca)
4	4 THE WORLD OF VAL DOONICAN	Val Doonican (Decca)
5	5 THE SOUND OF MUSIC	Soundtrack (RCA)
6	6 THE GRADUATE	Soundtrack (CBS)
9	7 HOLLIES' GREATEST HITS	Hollies (Parlophone)
7	8 HELP YOURSELF	Tom Jones (Decca)
12	9 THE WORLD OF MANTOVANI	Mantovani (Decca)
-	10 FELICIANO Jose Feliciano (RCA)	
14	11 ELECTRIC LADYLAND	Jimi Hendrix (Track)
11	12 VAL	Val Doonican (Pye)
-	13 BOOKENDS	Simon & Garfunkel (CBS)
14	14 THIS WAS Jethro Tull (Island)	
8	15 THE GOOD, THE BAD & THE UGLY	Soundtrack (United Artists)

18 January 1969

1	1 THE BEATLES	Beatles (Apple)
2	2 BEST OF THE SEEKERS	Seekers (Columbia)
5	3 THE SOUND OF MUSIC	Soundtrack (RCA)
3	4 BEGGARS BANQUET	Rolling Stones (Decca)
4	4 THE WORLD OF VAL DOONICAN	Val Doonican (Decca)
8	6 HELP YOURSELF	Tom Jones (Decca)
9	7 THE WORLD OF MANTOVANI	Mantovani (Decca)
6	8 THE GRADUATE	Soundtrack (CBS)
7	9 HOLLIES' GREATEST HITS	Hollies (Parlophone)
-	10 DIANA ROSS & THE SUPREMES' GREATEST HITS	Diana Ross & the Supremes (Tamla Motown)
-	11 BEST OF NAT 'KING' COLE	Nat 'King' Cole (Capitol)
11	11 BEST OF THE BEACH BOYS VOL 3	Beach Boys (Capitol)
12	13 VAL	Val Doonican (Pye)
10	14 FELICIANO Jose Feliciano (RCA)	
-	15 FOUR TOPS' GREATEST HITS	Four Tops (Tamla Motown)

25 January 1969

1	1 THE BEATLES	Beatles (Apple)
2	2 BEST OF THE SEEKERS	Seekers (Columbia)
8	3 THE GRADUATE	Soundtrack (CBS)
4	4 BEGGARS BANQUET	Rolling Stones (Decca)
4	5 THE WORLD OF VAL DOONICAN	Val Doonican (Decca)
3	6 THE SOUND OF MUSIC	Soundtrack (RCA)
6	7 HELP YOURSELF	Tom Jones (Decca)
-	8 DIANA ROSS AND THE SUPREMES JOIN THE TEMPTATIONS	Diana Ross & the Supremes with the Temptations (Tamla Motown)
9	9 YELLOW SUBMARINE	Beatles (Apple)
11	10 BEST OF THE BEACH BOYS VOL 3	Beach Boys (Capitol)
9	11 HOLLIES' GREATEST HITS	Hollies (Parlophone)
-	12 HAIR	London Cast (Polydor)
13	13 VAL	Val Doonican (Pye)
7	13 THE WORLD OF MANTOVANI	Mantovani (Decca)
10	15 DIANA ROSS & THE SUPREMES' GREATEST HITS	Diana Ross &the Supremes (Tamla Motown)

1 February 1969

2	1 BEST OF THE SEEKERS	Seekers (Columbia)
1	2 THE BEATLES	Beatles (Apple)
9	3 YELLOW SUBMARINE	Beatles (Apple)
8	4 DIANA ROSS AND THE SUPREMES JOIN THE TEMPTATIONS	Diana Ross & the Supremes with the Temptations (Tamla Motown)
3	5 THE GRADUATE	Soundtrack (CBS)
6	6 THE SOUND OF MUSIC	Soundtrack (RCA)
4	7 BEGGARS BANQUET	Rolling Stones (Decca)
5	8 THE WORLD OF VAL DOONICAN	Val Doonican (Decca)
7	9 HELP YOURSELF	Tom Jones (Decca)
12	10 HAIR	London Cast (Polydor)
-	11 FELICIANO Jose Feliciano (RCA)	
-	12 SOUNDS OF SILENCE	Simon & Garfunkel (CBS)
12	12 LOVE CHILD	Diana Ross & the Supremes (Tamla Motown)
13	14 WORLD OF MANTOVANI	Mantovani (Decca)
10	14 BEST OF THE BEACH BOYS VOL 3	Beach Boys (Capitol)

8 February 1969

4	1 DIANA ROSS AND THE SUPREMES JOIN THE TEMPTATIONS	Diana Ross & the Supremes with the Temptations (Tamla Motown)
2	2 THE BEATLES	Beatles (Apple)
1	3 BEST OF THE SEEKERS	Seekers (Columbia)
5	4 THE GRADUATE Soundtrack (CBS)	
3	5 YELLOW SUBMARINE	Beatles (Apple)
6	6 THE SOUND OF MUSIC	Soundtrack (RCA)
8	7 THE WORLD OF VAL DOONICAN	Val Doonican (Decca)
7	8 BEGGARS BANQUET	Rolling Stones (Decca)
10	9 HAIR London Cast (Polydor)	
11	10 FELICIANO Jose Feliciano (RCA)	
12	11 LOVE CHILD Diana Ross & the Supremes (Tamla Motown)	
-	12 HOLLIES' GREATEST HITS	Hollies (Parlophone)
9	13 HELP YOURSELF	Tom Jones (Decca)
-	13 BEST OF NAT 'KING' COLE	Nat 'King' Cole (Capitol)
-	15 BRITISH MOTOWN CHARTBUSTERS VOL 2	Various Artists (Tamla Motown)

Week 1's only real new entrant was Jim Reeves. In May, a rather different country would top the charts, Dylan's *Nashville Skyline*, with his 1962 song *Girl Of The North Country* as a duet with Johnny Cash, whose own *Johnny Cash At Folsom Prison* had hit in 1968. But the new country rock owed more to a highly influential LP that hadn't made the charts at all, *Sweetheart Of The Rodeo* by the Byrds.

February – April 1969

15 February 1969

last	this	
1	1	DIANA ROSS AND THE SUPREMES JOIN THE TEMPTATIONS — Diana Ross & the Supremes with the Temptations (Tamla Motown)
3	2	BEST OF THE SEEKERS — Seekers (Columbia)
5	3	YELLOW SUBMARINE — Beatles (Apple)
2	4	THE BEATLES — Beatles (Apple)
4	5	THE GRADUATE — Soundtrack (CBS)
6	6	THE SOUND OF MUSIC — Soundtrack (RCA)
9	7	HAIR — London Cast (Polydor)
8	8	BEGGARS BANQUET — Rolling Stones (Decca)
11	8	LOVE CHILD — Diana Ross & the Supremes (Tamla Motown)
7	10	THE WORLD OF VAL DOONICAN — Val Doonican (Decca)
10	11	FELICIANO — Jose Feliciano (RCA)
-	12	THE GOOD, THE BAD & THE UGLY — Soundtrack (United Artists)
13	13	HELP YOURSELF — Tom Jones (Decca)
12	13	HOLLIES' GREATEST HITS — Hollies (Parlophone)
15	15	BRITISH MOTOWN CHARTBUSTERS VOL 2 — Various Artists (Tamla Motown)

22 February 1969

last	this	
1	1	DIANA ROSS AND THE SUPREMES JOIN THE TEMPTATIONS — Diana Ross & the Supremes with the Temptations (Tamla Motown)
2	2	BEST OF THE SEEKERS — Seekers (Columbia)
4	3	THE BEATLES — Beatles (Apple)
3	4	YELLOW SUBMARINE — Beatles (Apple)
6	5	THE SOUND OF MUSIC — Soundtrack (RCA)
5	6	THE GRADUATE — Soundtrack (CBS)
7	7	HAIR — London Cast (Polydor)
10	8	THE WORLD OF VAL DOONICAN — Val Doonican (Decca)
8	9	BEGGARS BANQUET — Rolling Stones (Decca)
13	9	HELP YOURSELF — Tom Jones (Decca)
11	11	FELICIANO — Jose Feliciano (RCA)
-	12	THE WORLD OF MANTOVANI — Mantovani (Decca)
8	13	LOVE CHILD — Diana Ross & the Supremes (Tamla Motown)
-	14	EARLY ALPERT — Herb Alpert (Marble Arch)
-	15	'NUFF SAID — Nina Simone (RCA)

1 March 1969

last	this	
1	1	DIANA ROSS AND THE SUPREMES JOIN THE TEMPTATIONS — Diana Ross & the Supremes with the Temptations (Tamla Motown)
2	2	BEST OF THE SEEKERS — Seekers (Columbia)
3	3	THE BEATLES — Beatles (Apple)
4	4	YELLOW SUBMARINE — Beatles (Apple)
7	4	HAIR — London Cast (Polydor)
6	6	THE GRADUATE — Soundtrack (CBS)
5	7	THE SOUND OF MUSIC — Soundtrack (RCA)
8	8	THE WORLD OF VAL DOONICAN — Val Doonican (Decca)
-	9	ENGELBERT — Engelbert Humperdinck (Decca)
-	10	DISRAELI GEARS — Cream (Reaction)
9	11	BEGGARS BANQUET — Rolling Stones (Decca)
-	12	STONEDHENGE — Ten Years After (Deram)
12	13	THE WORLD OF MANTOVANI — Mantovani (Decca)
9	14	HELP YOURSELF — Tom Jones (Decca)
11	15	FELICIANO — Jose Feliciano (RCA)

8 March 1969

last	this	
1	1	DIANA ROSS AND THE SUPREMES JOIN THE TEMPTATIONS — Diana Ross & the Supremes with the Temptations (Tamla Motown)
2	2	BEST OF THE SEEKERS — Seekers (Columbia)
-	3	GOODBYE — Cream (Polydor)
9	4	ENGELBERT — Engelbert Humperdinck (Decca)
-	5	POSTCARD — Mary Hopkin (Apple)
3	6	THE BEATLES — Beatles (Apple)
7	7	THE SOUND OF MUSIC — Soundtrack (RCA)
6	8	THE GRADUATE — Soundtrack (CBS)
12	9	STONEDHENGE — Ten Years After (Deram)
4	10	HAIR — London Cast (Polydor)
4	11	YELLOW SUBMARINE — Beatles (Apple)
8	12	THE WORLD OF VAL DOONICAN — Val Doonican (Decca)
-	13	BEST OF CILLA BLACK — Cilla Black (Parlophone)
13	14	THE WORLD OF MANTOVANI — Mantovani (Decca)
11	15	BEGGARS BANQUET — Rolling Stones (Decca)

15 March 1969

last	this	
1	1	DIANA ROSS AND THE SUPREMES JOIN THE TEMPTATIONS — Diana Ross & the Supremes with the Temptations (Tamla Motown)
3	2	GOODBYE — Cream (Polydor)
2	3	BEST OF THE SEEKERS — Seekers (Columbia)
4	4	ENGELBERT — Engelbert Humperdinck (Decca)
12	5	THE WORLD OF VAL DOONICAN — Val Doonican (Decca)
5	6	POSTCARD — Mary Hopkin (Apple)
6	7	THE BEATLES — Beatles (Apple)
7	8	THE SOUND OF MUSIC — Soundtrack (RCA)
-	9	ROCK MACHINE I LOVE YOU — Various Artists (CBS)
9	10	STONEDHENGE — Ten Years After (Deram)
10	11	HAIR — London Cast (Polydor)
-	12	YOU CAN ALL JOIN IN — Various Artists (Island)
14	13	THE WORLD OF MANTOVANI — Mantovani (Decca)
11	14	YELLOW SUBMARINE — Beatles (Apple)
-	15	20/20 — Beach Boys (Capitol)

22 March 1969

last	this	
2	1	GOODBYE — Cream (Polydor)
3	2	BEST OF THE SEEKERS — Seekers (Columbia)
1	3	DIANA ROSS AND THE SUPREMES JOIN THE TEMPTATIONS — Diana Ross & the Supremes with the Temptations (Tamla Motown)
4	4	ENGELBERT — Engelbert Humperdinck (Decca)
6	5	POSTCARD — Mary Hopkin (Apple)
8	6	THE SOUND OF MUSIC — Soundtrack (RCA)
11	7	HAIR — London Cast (Polydor)
9	8	ROCK MACHINE I LOVE YOU — Various Artists (CBS)
-	9	PETER SARSTEDT — Peter Sarstedt (United Artists)
7	10	THE BEATLES — Beatles (Apple)
10	11	STONEDHENGE — Ten Years After (Deram)
13	12	THE WORLD OF MANTOVANI — Mantovani (Decca)
5	13	THE WORLD OF VAL DOONICAN — Val Doonican (Decca)
-	14	THE FOUR AND ONLY SEEKERS — Seekers (Music for Pleasure)
-	15	GENTLE ON MY MIND — Dean Martin (Reprise)

29 March 1969

last	this	
1	1	GOODBYE — Cream (Polydor)
2	2	BEST OF THE SEEKERS — Seekers (Columbia)
3	3	DIANA ROSS AND THE SUPREMES JOIN THE TEMPTATIONS — Diana Ross & the Supremes with the Temptations (Tamla Motown)
4	4	ENGELBERT — Engelbert Humperdinck (Decca)
6	5	THE SOUND OF MUSIC — Soundtrack (RCA)
8	6	ROCK MACHINE I LOVE YOU — Various Artists (CBS)
5	7	POSTCARD — Mary Hopkin (Apple)
-	8	ODESSA — Bee Gees (Polydor)
11	9	STONEDHENGE — Ten Years After (Deram)
10	10	THE BEATLES — Beatles (Apple)
9	11	PETER SARSTEDT — Peter Sarstedt (United Artists)
13	12	THE WORLD OF VAL DOONICAN — Val Doonican (Decca)
7	13	HAIR — London Cast (Polydor)
14	14	THE FOUR AND ONLY SEEKERS — Seekers (Music for Pleasure)
-	15	YOU CAN ALL JOIN IN — Various Artists (Island)

5 April 1969

last	this	
1	1	GOODBYE — Cream (Polydor)
2	2	BEST OF THE SEEKERS — Seekers (Columbia)
3	3	DIANA ROSS AND THE SUPREMES JOIN THE TEMPTATIONS — Diana Ross & the Supremes with the Temptations (Tamla Motown)
6	4	ROCK MACHINE I LOVE YOU — Various Artists (CBS)
4	5	ENGELBERT — Engelbert Humperdinck (Decca)
11	6	PETER SARSTEDT — Peter Sarstedt (United Artists)
5	7	THE SOUND OF MUSIC — Soundtrack (RCA)
15	8	YOU CAN ALL JOIN IN — Various Artists (Island)
-	8	20/20 — Beach Boys (Capitol)
10	10	THE BEATLES — Beatles (Apple)
12	11	THE WORLD OF VAL DOONICAN — Val Doonican (Decca)
-	12	GENTLE ON MY MIND — Dean Martin (Reprise)
8	13	ODESSA — Bee Gees (Polydor)
-	14	SCOTT 3 — Scott Walker (Philips)
-	15	FAMILY ENTERTAINMENT — Family (Reprise)

Cream returned, straight in at No.3 with the apt *Goodbye*. Cream was disbanding, becoming so-called supergroup Blind Faith, which was so ego-unwieldy it would manage only two gigs and one LP. Another sign of the times was the entry of Nina Simone, long a favourite of those who said Ray Charles was too pop. An accomplished pianist, Simone responded to the new Black Power politics, her rich voice articulating this anger on a 1968 single still in the charts in February, *Ain't Got No - I Got Life*.

12 April 1969

last week / this week

- 1 1 GOODBYE — Cream (Polydor)
- 2 2 BEST OF THE SEEKERS — Seekers (Columbia)
- 5 3 ENGELBERT — Engelbert Humperdinck (Decca)
- 7 4 THE SOUND OF MUSIC — Soundtrack (RCA)
- 14 5 SCOTT 3 — Scott Walker (Philips)
- 3 6 DIANA ROSS AND THE SUPREMES JOIN THE TEMPTATIONS — Diana Ross & the Supremes with the Temptations (Tamla Motown)
- 12 7 GENTLE ON MY MIND — Dean Martin (Reprise)
- 8 8 20/20 — Beach Boys (Capitol)
- - 9 POSTCARD — Mary Hopkin (Apple)
- - 10 WORLD STAR FESTIVAL — Various Artists (Philips)
- 11 11 THE WORLD OF VAL DOONICAN — Val Doonican (Decca)
- 13 12 ODESSA — Bee Gees (Polydor)
- 4 13 ROCK MACHINE I LOVE YOU — Various Artists (CBS)
- 10 14 THE BEATLES — Beatles (Apple)
- 15 15 FAMILY ENTERTAINMENT — Family (Reprise)

19 April 1969

- 2 1 BEST OF THE SEEKERS — Seekers (Columbia)
- 1 2 GOODBYE — Cream (Polydor)
- 5 3 SCOTT 3 — Scott Walker (Philips)
- 4 4 THE SOUND OF MUSIC — Soundtrack (RCA)
- 6 5 DIANA ROSS AND THE SUPREMES JOIN THE TEMPTATIONS — Diana Ross & the Supremes with the Temptations (Tamla Motown)
- 9 6 POSTCARD — Mary Hopkin (Apple)
- - 7 OLIVER! — Soundtrack (RCA)
- - 8 LED ZEPPELIN — Led Zeppelin (Atlantic)
- - 9 HAIR — London Cast (Polydor)
- 3 10 ENGELBERT — Engelbert Humperdinck (Decca)
- 8 11 20/20 — Beach Boys (Capitol)
- 7 12 GENTLE ON MY MIND — Dean Martin (Reprise)
- 13 13 ROCK MACHINE I LOVE YOU — Various Artists (CBS)
- 14 14 THE BEATLES — Beatles (Apple)
- 11 15 THE WORLD OF VAL DOONICAN — Val Doonican (Decca)

26 April 1969

- 1 1 GOODBYE — Cream (Polydor)
- 1 2 BEST OF THE SEEKERS — Seekers (Columbia)
- 3 3 SCOTT 3 — Scott Walker (Philips)
- 7 4 OLIVER! — Soundtrack (RCA)
- 4 5 THE SOUND OF MUSIC — Soundtrack (RCA)
- - 6 ELVIS: NBC TV SPECIAL — Elvis Presley (RCA)
- 9 7 HAIR — London Cast (Polydor)
- 6 8 POSTCARD — Mary Hopkin (Apple)
- 8 9 LED ZEPPELIN — Led Zeppelin (Atlantic)
- - 10 ON THE THRESHOLD OF A DREAM — Moody Blues (Deram)
- 12 11 GENTLE ON MY MIND — Dean Martin (Reprise)
- 11 12 20/20 — Beach Boys (Capitol)
- 5 13 DIANA ROSS AND THE SUPREMES JOIN THE TEMPTATIONS — Diana Ross & the Supremes with the Temptations (Tamla Motown)
- - 14 THE WORLD OF BLUES POWER — Various Artists (Decca)
- 15 15 THE WORLD OF VAL DOONICAN — Val Doonican (Decca)

3 May 1969

- 1 1 GOODBYE — Cream (Polydor)
- 2 2 BEST OF THE SEEKERS — Seekers (Columbia)
- 9 3 ON THE THRESHOLD OF A DREAM — Moody Blues (Deram)
- 7 4 HAIR — London Cast (Polydor)
- 9 5 LED ZEPPELIN — Led Zeppelin (Atlantic)
- 11 6 GENTLE ON MY MIND — Dean Martin (Reprise)
- 4 7 OLIVER! — Soundtrack (RCA)
- 5 8 THE SOUND OF MUSIC — Soundtrack (RCA)
- 3 9 SCOTT 3 — Scott Walker (Philips)
- 8 10 POSTCARD — Mary Hopkin (Apple)
- 6 11 ELVIS: NBC TV SPECIAL — Elvis Presley (RCA)
- 12 12 20/20 — Beach Boys (Capitol)
- - 13 SONGS FROM A ROOM — Leonard Cohen (CBS)
- 13 14 DIANA ROSS AND THE SUPREMES JOIN THE TEMPTATIONS — Diana Ross & the Supremes with the Temptations (Tamla Motown)
- 14 15 THE WORLD OF BLUES POWER — Various Artists (Decca)

10 May 1969

- 3 1 ON THE THRESHOLD OF A DREAM — Moody Blues (Deram)
- 2 2 BEST OF THE SEEKERS — Seekers (Columbia)
- 1 3 GOODBYE — Cream (Polydor)
- 11 4 ELVIS: NBC TV SPECIAL — Elvis Presley (RCA)
- 13 5 SONGS FROM A ROOM — Leonard Cohen (CBS)
- 7 6 OLIVER! — Soundtrack (RCA)
- 6 7 GENTLE ON MY MIND — Dean Martin (Reprise)
- 5 8 LED ZEPPELIN — Led Zeppelin (Atlantic)
- 4 9 HAIR — London Cast (Polydor)
- 8 10 THE SOUND OF MUSIC — Soundtrack (RCA)
- 10 11 POSTCARD — Mary Hopkin (Apple)
- 9 12 SCOTT 3 — Scott Walker (Philips)
- - 13 NASHVILLE SKYLINE — Bob Dylan (CBS)
- - 14 HOLLIES SING DYLAN — Hollies (Parlophone)
- - 15 DUSTY IN MEMPHIS — Dusty Springfield (Philips)

17 May 1969

- 1 1 ON THE THRESHOLD OF A DREAM — Moody Blues (Deram)
- 13 2 NASHVILLE SKYLINE — Bob Dylan (CBS)
- 2 3 BEST OF THE SEEKERS — Seekers (Columbia)
- 4 4 ELVIS: NBC TV SPECIAL — Elvis Presley (RCA)
- 3 5 GOODBYE — Cream (Polydor)
- 5 6 SONGS FROM A ROOM — Leonard Cohen (CBS)
- 6 7 OLIVER! — Soundtrack (RCA)
- 14 8 HOLLIES SING DYLAN — Hollies (Parlophone)
- 9 9 HAIR — London Cast (Polydor)
- 8 10 LED ZEPPELIN — Led Zeppelin (Atlantic)
- 7 11 GENTLE ON MY MIND — Dean Martin (Reprise)
- 10 12 THE SOUND OF MUSIC — Soundtrack (RCA)
- - 13 20/20 — Beach Boys (Capitol)
- 11 14 POSTCARD — Mary Hopkin (Apple)
- 15 15 DUSTY IN MEMPHIS — Dusty Springfield (Philips)

24 May 1969

- 2 1 NASHVILLE SKYLINE — Bob Dylan (CBS)
- 1 2 ON THE THRESHOLD OF A DREAM — Moody Blues (Deram)
- 3 3 BEST OF THE SEEKERS — Seekers (Columbia)
- 8 4 HOLLIES SING DYLAN — Hollies (Parlophone)
- 5 5 GOODBYE — Cream (Polydor)
- 4 6 ELVIS: NBC TV SPECIAL — Elvis Presley (RCA)
- 6 7 SONGS FROM A ROOM — Leonard Cohen (CBS)
- 7 8 OLIVER! — Soundtrack (RCA)
- 9 9 HAIR — London Cast (Polydor)
- 10 10 LED ZEPPELIN — Led Zeppelin (Atlantic)
- 12 11 THE SOUND OF MUSIC — Soundtrack (RCA)
- 11 12 GENTLE ON MY MIND — Dean Martin (Reprise)
- - 13 THE BEATLES — Beatles (Apple)
- - 14 THE WORLD OF MANTOVANI — Mantovani (Decca)
- - 15 THE FOUR AND ONLY SEEKERS — Seekers (Music for Pleasure)

31 May 1969

- 1 1 NASHVILLE SKYLINE — Bob Dylan (CBS)
- 2 2 ON THE THRESHOLD OF A DREAM — Moody Blues (Deram)
- 4 3 HOLLIES SING DYLAN — Hollies (Parlophone)
- 3 4 BEST OF THE SEEKERS — Seekers (Columbia)
- 6 5 ELVIS: NBC TV SPECIAL — Elvis Presley (RCA)
- 9 6 HAIR — London Cast (Polydor)
- 5 7 GOODBYE — Cream (Polydor)
- 8 8 SONGS FROM A ROOM — Leonard Cohen (CBS)
- - 9 TOMMY — Who (Track)
- 10 10 LED ZEPPELIN — Led Zeppelin (Atlantic)
- 8 11 OLIVER! — Soundtrack (RCA)
- 11 12 THE SOUND OF MUSIC — Soundtrack (RCA)
- 14 13 THE WORLD OF MANTOVANI — Mantovani (Decca)
- - 14 SURROUND YOURSELF WITH CILLA — Cilla Black (Parlophone)
- 12 15 GENTLE ON MY MIND — Dean Martin (Reprise)

Pop journalist, and later film-maker Tony Palmer, at this time the Observer's pop critic, paid this tribute to the disbanding group Cream (Eric Clapton, Jack Bruce and Ginger Baker): "Cream have almost single-handedly given pop a musical authority which only the deaf cannot acknowledge and only the ignorant cannot hear." Which was odd because he also said that the Beatles had given us "a deluge of joyful music-making which only the ignorant will not hear and only the deaf will not acknowledge."

June – July 1969

7 June 1969

last week	this week		
1	1	NASHVILLE SKYLINE	Bob Dylan (CBS)
2	2	ON THE THRESHOLD OF A DREAM	Moody Blues (Deram)
3	3	HOLLIES SING DYLAN	Hollies (Parlophone)
7	4	GOODBYE	Cream (Polydor)
4	5	BEST OF THE SEEKERS	Seekers (Columbia)
6	6	HAIR	London Cast (Polydor)
8	7	SONGS FROM A ROOM	Leonard Cohen (CBS)
11	8	OLIVER!	Soundtrack (RCA)
5	9	ELVIS: NBC TV SPECIAL	Elvis Presley (RCA)
9	10	TOMMY	Who (Track)
-	11	MY WAY	Frank Sinatra (Reprise)
12	12	THE SOUND OF MUSIC	Soundtrack (RCA)
10	13	LED ZEPPELIN	Led Zeppelin (Atlantic)
-	13	2001: A SPACE ODYSSEY	Soundtrack (MGM)
13	15	THE WORLD OF MANTOVANI	Mantovani (Decca)
14	16	SURROUND YOURSELF WITH CILLA	Cilla Black (Parlophone)
15	17	GENTLE ON MY MIND	Dean Martin (Reprise)
-	18	OVER AND OVER	Nana Mouskouri (Fontana)
-	19	THE WORLD OF VAL DOONICAN	Val Doonican (Decca)
-	19	SOUNDS OF SILENCE	Simon & Garfunkel (CBS)

14 June 1969

last week	this week		
1	1	NASHVILLE SKYLINE	Bob Dylan (CBS)
2	2	ON THE THRESHOLD OF A DREAM	Moody Blues (Deram)
6	3	HAIR	London Cast (Polydor)
11	4	MY WAY	Frank Sinatra (Reprise)
5	5	BEST OF THE SEEKERS	Seekers (Columbia)
8	6	OLIVER!	Soundtrack (RCA)
10	7	TOMMY	Who (Track)
3	8	HOLLIES SING DYLAN	Hollies (Parlophone)
4	9	GOODBYE	Cream (Polydor)
13	10	2001: A SPACE ODYSSEY	Soundtrack (MGM)
7	11	SONGS FROM A ROOM	Leonard Cohen (CBS)
9	12	ELVIS: NBC TV SPECIAL	Elvis Presley (RCA)
12	13	THE SOUND OF MUSIC	Soundtrack (RCA)
17	14	GENTLE ON MY MIND	Dean Martin (Reprise)
-	15	20/20	Beach Boys (Capitol)
15	16	THE WORLD OF MANTOVANI	Mantovani (Decca)
13	17	LED ZEPPELIN	Led Zeppelin (Atlantic)
-	18	THE BEATLES	Beatles (Apple)
19	19	THE WORLD OF VAL DOONICAN	Val Doonican (Decca)
-	19	UNICORN	Tyrannosaurus Rex (Regal Zonophone)

21 June 1969

last week	this week		
4	1	MY WAY	Frank Sinatra (Reprise)
1	2	NASHVILLE SKYLINE	Bob Dylan (CBS)
2	3	ON THE THRESHOLD OF A DREAM	Moody Blues (Deram)
10	4	2001: A SPACE ODYSSEY	Soundtrack (MGM)
6	5	OLIVER!	Soundtrack (RCA)
3	6	HAIR	London Cast (Polydor)
5	7	BEST OF THE SEEKERS	Seekers (Columbia)
9	8	GOODBYE	Cream (Polydor)
7	9	TOMMY	Who (Track)
8	10	HOLLIES SING DYLAN	Hollies (Parlophone)
-	11	THIS IS TOM JONES	Tom Jones (Decca)
19	12	THE WORLD OF VAL DOONICAN	Val Doonican (Decca)
14	13	GENTLE ON MY MIND	Dean Martin (Reprise)
12	14	ELVIS: NBC TV SPECIAL	Elvis Presley (RCA)
17	15	LED ZEPPELIN	Led Zeppelin (Atlantic)
13	16	THE SOUND OF MUSIC	Soundtrack (RCA)
11	16	SONGS FROM A ROOM	Leonard Cohen (CBS)
16	18	THE WORLD OF MANTOVANI	Mantovani (Decca)
-	19	RAY CONNIFF, HIS ORCHESTRA, HIS CHORUS, HIS SINGERS, HIS SOUND	Ray Conniff (CBS)
19	20	UNICORN	Tyrannosaurus Rex (Regal Zonophone)

28 June 1969

last week	this week		
1	1	MY WAY	Frank Sinatra (Reprise)
11	2	THIS IS TOM JONES	Tom Jones (Decca)
2	3	NASHVILLE SKYLINE	Bob Dylan (CBS)
9	4	TOMMY	Who (Track)
6	5	HAIR	London Cast (Polydor)
4	6	2001: A SPACE ODYSSEY	Soundtrack (MGM)
3	7	ON THE THRESHOLD OF A DREAM	Moody Blues (Deram)
5	8	OLIVER!	Soundtrack (RCA)
19	9	RAY CONNIFF, HIS ORCHESTRA, HIS CHORUS, HIS SINGERS, HIS SOUND	Ray Conniff (CBS)
-	10	OVER AND OVER	Nana Mouskouri (Fontana)
7	11	BEST OF THE SEEKERS	Seekers (Columbia)
-	12	FLAMING STAR	Elvis Presley (RCA International)
-	13	ACCORDING TO MY HEART	Jim Reeves (RCA International)
18	14	THE WORLD OF MANTOVANI	Mantovani (Decca)
13	15	GENTLE ON MY MIND	Dean Martin (Reprise)
10	16	HOLLIES SING DYLAN	Hollies (Parlophone)
14	17	ELVIS: NBC TV SPECIAL	Elvis Presley (RCA)
12	18	THE WORLD OF VAL DOONICAN	Val Doonican (Decca)
15	19	LED ZEPPELIN	Led Zeppelin (Atlantic)
-	19	THE WORLD OF CHARLIE KUNZ	Charlie Kunz (Decca)

5 July 1969

last week	this week		
2	1	THIS IS TOM JONES	Tom Jones (Decca)
1	2	MY WAY	Frank Sinatra (Reprise)
3	3	NASHVILLE SKYLINE	Bob Dylan (CBS)
7	4	ON THE THRESHOLD OF A DREAM	Moody Blues (Deram)
12	5	FLAMING STAR	Elvis Presley (RCA International)
13	6	ACCORDING TO MY HEART	Jim Reeves (RCA International)
5	7	HAIR	London Cast (Polydor)
9	8	RAY CONNIFF, HIS ORCHESTRA, HIS CHORUS, HIS SINGERS, HIS SOUND	Ray Conniff (CBS)
6	9	2001: A SPACE ODYSSEY	Soundtrack (MGM)
4	10	TOMMY	Who (Track)
8	11	OLIVER!	Soundtrack (RCA)
11	12	BEST OF THE SEEKERS	Seekers (Columbia)
17	13	ELVIS: NBC TV SPECIAL	Elvis Presley (RCA)
-	14	SOUNDTRACK FROM THE FILM 'MORE'	Pink Floyd (Columbia)
16	15	HOLLIES SING DYLAN	Hollies (Parlophone)
-	16	TCB	Diana Ross & the Supremes & the Temptations (Tamla Motown)
16	16	SCOTT WALKER SINGS SONGS FROM HIS TV SERIES	Scott Walker (Philips)
18	18	THE WORLD OF VAL DOONICAN	Val Doonican (Decca)
-	19	THE SOUND OF MUSIC	Soundtrack (RCA)
15	20	GENTLE ON MY MIND	Dean Martin (Reprise)

12 July 1969

last week	this week		
1	1	THIS IS TOM JONES	Tom Jones (Decca)
5	2	FLAMING STAR	Elvis Presley (RCA International)
6	3	ACCORDING TO MY HEART	Jim Reeves (RCA International)
2	4	MY WAY	Frank Sinatra (Reprise)
3	5	NASHVILLE SKYLINE	Bob Dylan (CBS)
4	6	ON THE THRESHOLD OF A DREAM	Moody Blues (Deram)
16	7	SCOTT WALKER SINGS SONGS FROM HIS TV SERIES	Scott Walker (Philips)
8	8	RAY CONNIFF, HIS ORCHESTRA, HIS CHORUS, HIS SINGERS, HIS SOUND	Ray Conniff (CBS)
7	9	HAIR	London Cast (Polydor)
11	10	OLIVER!	Soundtrack (RCA)
9	11	2001: A SPACE ODYSSEY	Soundtrack (MGM)
10	12	TOMMY	Who (Track)
16	13	TCB	Diana Ross & the Supremes & the Temptations (Tamla Motown)
-	14	LED ZEPPELIN	Led Zeppelin (Atlantic)
13	15	ELVIS: NBC TV SPECIAL	Elvis Presley (RCA)
12	16	BEST OF THE SEEKERS	Seekers (Columbia)
14	16	SOUNDTRACK FROM THE FILM 'MORE'	Pink Floyd (Columbia)
-	18	THE BEST OF CLIFF	Cliff Richard (Columbia)
15	19	HOLLIES SING DYLAN	Hollies (Parlophone)
18	20	THE WORLD OF VAL DOONICAN	Val Doonican (Decca)

The Top 15 became the Top 20; mad titles abounded. The Moody Blues, a competent beat group with an excellent debut single, *Go Now*, copied from Bessie Banks, had metamorphosed rapidly into mystical-twaddle concept-album makers, their latest being *On The Threshold Of A Dream*, temporarily on the threshold of the top. Listening to the Moody Blues, a reviewer was later to suggest, was "like mainlining yoghurt". Preferable, surely, to the practice urged by June 7's No.16: *Surround Yourself With Cilla*.

July – August 1969

19 July 1969

last	this		
1	1	THIS IS TOM JONES	Tom Jones (Decca)
3	2	ACCORDING TO MY HEART	Jim Reeves (RCA International)
2	3	FLAMING STAR	Elvis Presley (RCA International)
4	4	MY WAY	Frank Sinatra (Reprise)
6	5	ON THE THRESHOLD OF A DREAM	Moody Blues (Deram)
5	6	NASHVILLE SKYLINE	Bob Dylan (CBS)
7	7	SCOTT WALKER SINGS SONGS FROM HIS TV SERIES	Scott Walker (Philips)
11	8	2001: A SPACE ODYSSEY	Soundtrack (MGM)
10	9	OLIVER!	Soundtrack (RCA)
16	10	SOUNDTRACK FROM THE FILM 'MORE'	Pink Floyd (Columbia)
9	11	HAIR	London Cast (Polydor)
8	12	RAY CONNIFF, HIS ORCHESTRA, HIS CHORUS, HIS SINGERS, HIS SOUND	Ray Conniff (CBS)
13	13	TCB	Diana Ross & the Supremes & the Temptations (Tamla Motown)
18	14	THE BEST OF CLIFF	Cliff Richard (Columbia)
20	15	THE WORLD OF VAL DOONICAN	Val Doonican (Decca)
-	16	THE BEATLES	Beatles (Apple)
14	17	LED ZEPPELIN	Led Zeppelin (Atlantic)
16	18	BEST OF THE SEEKERS	Seekers (Columbia)
15	19	ELVIS: NBC TV SPECIAL	Elvis Presley (RCA)
12	20	TOMMY	Who (Track)

26 July 1969

last	this		
1	1	THIS IS TOM JONES	Tom Jones (Decca)
3	2	FLAMING STAR	Elvis Presley (RCA International)
2	3	ACCORDING TO MY HEART	Jim Reeves (RCA International)
4	4	MY WAY	Frank Sinatra (Reprise)
8	5	2001: A SPACE ODYSSEY	Soundtrack (MGM)
14	6	THE BEST OF CLIFF	Cliff Richard (Columbia)
13	7	TCB	Diana Ross & the Supremes & the Temptations (Tamla Motown)
6	8	NASHVILLE SKYLINE	Bob Dylan (CBS)
11	9	HAIR	London Cast (Polydor)
9	10	OLIVER!	Soundtrack (RCA)
17	11	LED ZEPPELIN	Led Zeppelin (Atlantic)
5	12	ON THE THRESHOLD OF A DREAM	Moody Blues (Deram)
7	13	SCOTT WALKER SINGS SONGS FROM HIS TV SERIES	Scott Walker (Philips)
10	14	SOUNDTRACK FROM THE FILM 'MORE'	Pink Floyd (Columbia)
-	15	THE WORLD OF MANTOVANI	Mantovani (Decca)
12	16	RAY CONNIFF, HIS ORCHESTRA, HIS CHORUS, HIS SINGERS, HIS SOUND	Ray Conniff (CBS)
15	17	THE WORLD OF VAL DOONICAN	Val Doonican (Decca)
-	18	THE SOUND OF MUSIC	Soundtrack (RCA)
-	19	GOODBYE	Cream (Polydor)
-	20	THE WORLD OF THE BACHELORS	Bachelors (Decca)

2 August 1969

last	this		
2	1	FLAMING STAR	Elvis Presley (RCA International)
3	2	ACCORDING TO MY HEART	Jim Reeves (RCA International)
5	3	2001: A SPACE ODYSSEY	Soundtrack (MGM)
1	4	THIS IS TOM JONES	Tom Jones (Decca)
6	5	THE BEST OF CLIFF	Cliff Richard (Columbia)
10	6	OLIVER!	Soundtrack (RCA)
9	7	HAIR	London Cast (Polydor)
8	8	NASHVILLE SKYLINE	Bob Dylan (CBS)
-	8	STAND UP	Jethro Tull (Island)
4	10	MY WAY	Frank Sinatra (Reprise)
17	11	THE WORLD OF VAL DOONICAN	Val Doonican (Decca)
-	12	UNHALFBRICKING	Fairport Convention (Island)
-	13	BEST OF THE SEEKERS	Seekers (Columbia)
11	14	LED ZEPPELIN	Led Zeppelin (Atlantic)
20	15	THE WORLD OF THE BACHELORS	Bachelors (Decca)
16	16	RAY CONNIFF, HIS ORCHESTRA, HIS CHORUS, HIS SINGERS, HIS SOUND	Ray Conniff (CBS)
7	17	TCB	Diana Ross & the Supremes & the Temptations (Tamla Motown)
18	18	THE SOUND OF MUSIC	Soundtrack (RCA)
12	18	ON THE THRESHOLD OF A DREAM	Moody Blues (Deram)
-	20	WARM	Herb Alpert & the Tijuana Brass (A&M)

9 August 1969

last	this		
8	1	STAND UP	Jethro Tull (Island)
1	2	FLAMING STAR	Elvis Presley (RCA International)
2	3	ACCORDING TO MY HEART	Jim Reeves (RCA International)
3	4	2001: A SPACE ODYSSEY	Soundtrack (MGM)
4	5	THIS IS TOM JONES	Tom Jones (Decca)
7	6	HAIR	London Cast (Polydor)
10	7	MY WAY	Frank Sinatra (Reprise)
8	8	NASHVILLE SKYLINE	Bob Dylan (CBS)
12	9	UNHALFBRICKING	Fairport Convention (Island)
5	10	THE BEST OF CLIFF	Cliff Richard (Columbia)
16	11	RAY CONNIFF, HIS ORCHESTRA, HIS CHORUS, HIS SINGERS, HIS SOUND	Ray Conniff (CBS)
14	12	LED ZEPPELIN	Led Zeppelin (Atlantic)
11	13	THE WORLD OF VAL DOONICAN	Val Doonican (Decca)
17	14	TCB	Diana Ross & the Supremes & the Temptations (Tamla Motown)
-	15	AHEAD RINGS OUT	Blodwyn Pig (Island)
18	16	ON THE THRESHOLD OF A DREAM	Moody Blues (Deram)
13	17	BEST OF THE SEEKERS	Seekers (Columbia)
6	18	OLIVER!	Soundtrack (RCA)
-	19	THE BEST OF GLENN MILLER	Glenn Miller (RCA International)
20	20	WARM	Herb Alpert & the Tijuana Brass (A&M)

16 August 1969

last	this		
1	1	STAND UP	Jethro Tull (Island)
4	2	2001: A SPACE ODYSSEY	Soundtrack (MGM)
3	3	ACCORDING TO MY HEART	Jim Reeves (RCA International)
2	4	FLAMING STAR	Elvis Presley (RCA International)
6	5	HAIR	London Cast (Polydor)
5	6	THIS IS TOM JONES	Tom Jones (Decca)
18	7	OLIVER!	Soundtrack (RCA)
-	8	FROM ELVIS IN MEMPHIS	Elvis Presley (RCA)
8	9	UNHALFBRICKING	Fairport Convention (Island)
10	10	THE BEST OF CLIFF	Cliff Richard (Columbia)
16	11	ON THE THRESHOLD OF A DREAM	Moody Blues (Deram)
17	12	BEST OF THE SEEKERS	Seekers (Columbia)
15	12	AHEAD RINGS OUT	Blodwyn Pig (Island)
12	14	LED ZEPPELIN	Led Zeppelin (Atlantic)
7	15	MY WAY	Frank Sinatra (Reprise)
-	15	JOHNNY CASH AT SAN QUENTIN	Johnny Cash (CBS)
19	17	THE BEST OF GLENN MILLER	Glenn Miller (RCA International)
11	18	RAY CONNIFF, HIS ORCHESTRA, HIS CHORUS, HIS SINGERS, HIS SOUND	Ray Conniff (CBS)
8	19	NASHVILLE SKYLINE	Bob Dylan (CBS)
13	20	THE WORLD OF VAL DOONICAN	Val Doonican (Decca)

23 August 1969

last	this		
1	1	STAND UP	Jethro Tull (Island)
2	2	2001: A SPACE ODYSSEY	Soundtrack (MGM)
3	3	ACCORDING TO MY HEART	Jim Reeves (RCA International)
8	4	FROM ELVIS IN MEMPHIS	Elvis Presley (RCA)
4	5	FLAMING STAR	Elvis Presley (RCA International)
7	6	OLIVER!	Soundtrack (RCA)
9	7	UNHALFBRICKING	Fairport Convention (Island)
5	8	HAIR	London Cast (Polydor)
6	9	THIS IS TOM JONES	Tom Jones (Decca)
12	10	AHEAD RINGS OUT	Blodwyn Pig (Island)
15	11	JOHNNY CASH AT SAN QUENTIN	Johnny Cash (CBS)
10	12	THE BEST OF CLIFF	Cliff Richard (Columbia)
14	13	LED ZEPPELIN	Led Zeppelin (Atlantic)
20	14	THE WORLD OF VAL DOONICAN	Val Doonican (Decca)
-	15	AS SAFE AS YESTERDAY IS	Humble Pie (Immediate)
11	16	ON THE THRESHOLD OF A DREAM	Moody Blues (Deram)
18	16	RAY CONNIFF, HIS ORCHESTRA, HIS CHORUS, HIS SINGERS, HIS SOUND	Ray Conniff (CBS)
15	18	MY WAY	Frank Sinatra (Reprise)
-	19	THE PIOUS BIRD OF GOOD OMEN	Fleetwood Mac (Blue Horizon)
17	20	THE BEST OF GLENN MILLER	Glenn Miller (RCA International)

In 1968, signalling the end of his run of abysmal movies, Elvis made his momentous TV "comeback": but this didn't get shown on TV in Britain till 1969, so a renewal of interest in Presley was only now reflected in healthy chart returns. Even now, one of the charting albums was *Flaming Star*, a typically careless compilation and named after an old film, 1960's *Flaming Star*. Meanwhile on July 3, aged 25, the most genuinely sinister of the Rolling Stones, Brian Jones, died in his swimming pool.

August – October 1969

30 August 1969

last	this	Title	Artist (Label)
1	1	STAND UP	Jethro Tull (Island)
4	2	FROM ELVIS IN MEMPHIS	Elvis Presley (RCA)
2	3	2001: A SPACE ODYSSEY	Soundtrack (MGM)
3	4	ACCORDING TO MY HEART	Jim Reeves (RCA International)
11	5	JOHNNY CASH AT SAN QUENTIN	Johnny Cash (CBS)
7	6	UNHALFBRICKING	Fairport Convention (Island)
8	7	HAIR	London Cast (Polydor)
5	8	FLAMING STAR	Elvis Presley (RCA International)
6	9	OLIVER!	Soundtrack (RCA)
13	10	LED ZEPPELIN	Led Zeppelin (Atlantic)
10	11	AHEAD RINGS OUT	Blodwyn Pig (Island)
-	12	LOOKING BACK	John Mayall (Decca)
9	13	THIS IS TOM JONES	Tom Jones (Decca)
16	14	RAY CONNIFF, HIS ORCHESTRA, HIS CHORUS, HIS SINGERS, HIS SOUND	Ray Conniff (CBS)
12	15	THE BEST OF CLIFF	Cliff Richard (Columbia)
15	16	AS SAFE AS YESTERDAY IS	Humble Pie (Immediate)
-	17	THE SOUND OF MUSIC	Soundtrack (RCA)
14	18	THE WORLD OF VAL DOONICAN	Val Doonican (Decca)
-	19	CROSBY, STILLS & NASH	Crosby, Stills & Nash (Atlantic)
-	20	JIM REEVES AND SOME FRIENDS	Jim Reeves (RCA)

6 September 1969

last	this	Title	Artist (Label)
1	1	STAND UP	Jethro Tull (Island)
2	2	FROM ELVIS IN MEMPHIS	Elvis Presley (RCA)
5	3	JOHNNY CASH AT SAN QUENTIN	Johnny Cash (CBS)
7	4	HAIR	London Cast (Polydor)
3	5	2001: A SPACE ODYSSEY	Soundtrack (MGM)
9	6	OLIVER!	Soundtrack (RCA)
4	7	ACCORDING TO MY HEART	Jim Reeves (RCA)
6	8	UNHALFBRICKING	Fairport Convention (Island)
11	9	AHEAD RINGS OUT	Blodwyn Pig (Island)
12	10	LOOKING BACK	John Mayall (Decca)
8	11	FLAMING STAR	Elvis Presley (RCA International)
-	12	THE PIOUS BIRD OF GOOD OMEN	Fleetwood Mac (Blue Horizon)
17	13	THE SOUND OF MUSIC	Soundtrack (RCA)
-	13	NICE	Nice (Immediate)
-	15	ON THE THRESHOLD OF A DREAM	Moody Blues (Deram)
-	16	THE WORLD OF MANTOVANI	Mantovani (Decca)
10	17	LED ZEPPELIN	Led Zeppelin (Atlantic)
16	17	AS SAFE AS YESTERDAY IS	Humble Pie (Immediate)
13	19	THIS IS TOM JONES	Tom Jones (Decca)
14	20	RAY CONNIFF, HIS ORCHESTRA, HIS CHORUS, HIS SINGERS, HIS SOUND	Ray Conniff (CBS)

13 September 1969

last	this	Title	Artist (Label)
1	1	STAND UP	Jethro Tull (Island)
-	2	BLIND FAITH	Blind Faith (Polydor)
3	3	JOHNNY CASH AT SAN QUENTIN	Johnny Cash (CBS)
2	4	FROM ELVIS IN MEMPHIS	Elvis Presley (RCA)
6	5	OLIVER!	Soundtrack (RCA)
13	6	NICE	Nice (Immediate)
4	7	HAIR	London Cast (Polydor)
7	8	ACCORDING TO MY HEART	Jim Reeves (RCA)
5	9	2001: A SPACE ODYSSEY	Soundtrack (MGM)
9	10	AHEAD RINGS OUT	Blodwyn Pig (Island)
8	11	UNHALFBRICKING	Fairport Convention (Island)
10	12	LOOKING BACK	John Mayall (Decca)
11	13	FLAMING STAR	Elvis Presley (RCA International)
-	14	THE BEST OF CLIFF	Cliff Richard (Columbia)
17	15	LED ZEPPELIN	Led Zeppelin (Atlantic)
17	16	AS SAFE AS YESTERDAY IS	Humble Pie (Immediate)
-	17	NASHVILLE SKYLINE	Bob Dylan (CBS)
-	18	BEST OF THE SEEKERS	Seekers (Columbia)
20	19	RAY CONNIFF, HIS ORCHESTRA, HIS CHORUS, HIS SINGERS, HIS SOUND	Ray Conniff (CBS)
-	20	CROSBY, STILLS & NASH	Crosby, Stills & Nash (Atlantic)

20 September 1969

last	this	Title	Artist (Label)
3	1	JOHNNY CASH AT SAN QUENTIN	Johnny Cash (CBS)
2	2	BLIND FAITH	Blind Faith (Polydor)
1	3	STAND UP	Jethro Tull (Island)
6	4	NICE	Nice (Immediate)
4	5	FROM ELVIS IN MEMPHIS	Elvis Presley (RCA)
7	6	HAIR	London Cast (Polydor)
8	7	ACCORDING TO MY HEART	Jim Reeves (RCA International)
5	8	OLIVER!	Soundtrack (RCA)
11	8	UNHALFBRICKING	Fairport Convention (Island)
17	10	NASHVILLE SKYLINE	Bob Dylan (CBS)
9	11	2001: A SPACE ODYSSEY	Soundtrack (MGM)
-	12	THE SOUND OF MUSIC	Soundtrack (RCA)
12	13	LOOKING BACK	John Mayall (Decca)
-	14	THROUGH THE PAST DARKLY (BIG HITS VOL 2)	Rolling Stones (Decca)
15	15	LED ZEPPELIN	Led Zeppelin (Atlantic)
-	16	THE WORLD OF VAL DOONICAN	Val Doonican (Decca)
10	17	AHEAD RINGS OUT	Blodwyn Pig (Island)
13	18	FLAMING STAR	Elvis Presley (RCA International)
20	19	CROSBY, STILLS & NASH	Crosby, Stills & Nash (Atlantic)
16	20	AS SAFE AS YESTERDAY IS	Humble Pie (Immediate)

27 September 1969

last	this	Title	Artist (Label)
1	1	JOHNNY CASH AT SAN QUENTIN	Johnny Cash (CBS)
2	2	BLIND FAITH	Blind Faith (Polydor)
3	3	STAND UP	Jethro Tull (Island)
14	4	THROUGH THE PAST DARKLY (BIG HITS VOL 2)	Rolling Stones (Decca)
10	5	NASHVILLE SKYLINE	Bob Dylan (CBS)
4	6	NICE	Nice (Immediate)
6	7	HAIR	London Cast (Polydor)
11	7	2001: A SPACE ODYSSEY	Soundtrack (MGM)
5	9	FROM ELVIS IN MEMPHIS	Elvis Presley (RCA)
-	10	BEST OF GENE PITNEY	Gene Pitney (Stateside)
8	11	OLIVER!	Soundtrack (RCA)
7	11	ACCORDING TO MY HEART	Jim Reeves (RCA International)
13	13	LOOKING BACK	John Mayall (Decca)
-	14	CLOUD NINE	Temptations (Tamla Motown)
-	15	SONGS FOR A TAILOR	Jack Bruce (Polydor)
-	16	THIS IS TOM JONES	Tom Jones (Decca)
-	17	FUNNY GIRL	Soundtrack (CBS)
-	18	BEST OF THE SEEKERS	Seekers (Columbia)
16	18	THE WORLD OF VAL DOONICAN	Val Doonican (Decca)
-	18	THE BEST OF CLIFF	Cliff Richard (Columbia)

4 October 1969

last	this	Title	Artist (Label)
-	1	ABBEY ROAD	Beatles (Apple)
1	2	JOHNNY CASH AT SAN QUENTIN	Johnny Cash (CBS)
4	3	THROUGH THE PAST DARKLY (BIG HITS VOL 2)	Rolling Stones (Decca)
2	4	BLIND FAITH	Blind Faith (Polydor)
3	5	STAND UP	Jethro Tull (Island)
7	6	HAIR	London Cast (Polydor)
11	7	ACCORDING TO MY HEART	Jim Reeves (RCA International)
6	8	NICE	Nice (Immediate)
9	9	FROM ELVIS IN MEMPHIS	Elvis Presley (RCA)
-	9	THE WORLD OF MANTOVANI VOL 2	Mantovani (Decca)
5	11	NASHVILLE SKYLINE	Bob Dylan (CBS)
11	12	OLIVER!	Soundtrack (RCA)
18	13	THE WORLD OF VAL DOONICAN	Val Doonican (Decca)
15	14	SONGS FOR A TAILOR	Jack Bruce (Polydor)
-	15	SSSSH	Ten Years After (Deram)
7	16	2001: A SPACE ODYSSEY	Soundtrack (MGM)
-	17	RAY CONNIFF, HIS ORCHESTRA, HIS CHORUS, HIS SINGERS, HIS SOUND	Ray Conniff (CBS)
-	18	THE SOUND OF MUSIC	Soundtrack (RCA)
-	19	AHEAD RINGS OUT	Blodwyn Pig (Island)
-	20	LED ZEPPELIN	Led Zeppelin (Atlantic)

More classics in the chart: Fairport Convention's *Unhalfbricking*, a highpoint of English folk-rock, and *Led Zeppelin*, the epoch-making debut album by the biggest white group on Atlantic Records, a group famous for refusing to issue singles. Meanwhile supergroup Blind Faith had played their debut gig in Hyde Park in June, the USA had gone to Woodstock and now 250,000 here went to the 2nd Isle of Wight Festival, at the end of August, for The Who, Marsha Hunt, Richie Havens and Bob Dylan and The Band.

11 October 1969

last week	this week	title	artist
1	1	ABBEY ROAD	Beatles (Apple)
2	2	JOHNNY CASH AT SAN QUENTIN	Johnny Cash (CBS)
3	3	THROUGH THE PAST DARKLY (BIG HITS VOL 2)	Rolling Stones (Decca)
4	4	BLIND FAITH	Blind Faith (Polydor)
15	5	SSSSH	Ten Years After (Deram)
6	6	HAIR	London Cast (Polydor)
11	7	NASHVILLE SKYLINE	Bob Dylan (CBS)
9	8	THE WORLD OF MANTOVANI VOL 2	Mantovani (Decca)
5	9	STAND UP	Jethro Tull (Island)
-	10	THEN PLAY ON	Fleetwood Mac (Reprise)
14	11	SONGS FOR A TAILOR	Jack Bruce (Polydor)
8	12	NICE	Nice (Immediate)
-	13	BEST OF GENE PITNEY	Gene Pitney (Stateside)
12	14	OLIVER!	Soundtrack (RCA)
7	15	ACCORDING TO MY HEART	Jim Reeves (RCA International)
9	16	FROM ELVIS IN MEMPHIS	Elvis Presley (RCA)
13	17	THE WORLD OF VAL DOONICAN	Val Doonican (Decca)
20	18	LED ZEPPELIN	Led Zeppelin (Atlantic)
-	19	THE WORLD OF VAL DOONICAN VOL 2	Val Doonican (Decca)
16	20	2001: A SPACE ODYSSEY	Soundtrack (MGM)

18 October 1969

last week	this week	title	artist
1	1	ABBEY ROAD	Beatles (Apple)
2	2	JOHNNY CASH AT SAN QUENTIN	Johnny Cash (CBS)
3	3	THROUGH THE PAST DARKLY (BIG HITS VOL 2)	Rolling Stones (Decca)
5	4	SSSSH	Ten Years After (Deram)
10	5	THEN PLAY ON	Fleetwood Mac (Reprise)
4	6	BLIND FAITH	Blind Faith (Polydor)
6	7	HAIR	London Cast (Polydor)
7	8	NASHVILLE SKYLINE	Bob Dylan (CBS)
11	8	SONGS FOR A TAILOR	Jack Bruce (Polydor)
8	10	THE WORLD OF MANTOVANI VOL 2	Mantovani (Decca)
14	11	OLIVER!	Soundtrack (RCA)
9	12	STAND UP	Jethro Tull (Island)
12	13	NICE	Nice (Immediate)
13	14	BEST OF GENE PITNEY	Gene Pitney (Stateside)
-	15	THE COUNTRY SIDE OF JIM REEVES	Jim Reeves (RCA Camden)
-	16	BEST OF THE SEEKERS	Seekers (Columbia)
18	17	LED ZEPPELIN	Led Zeppelin (Atlantic)
19	18	THE WORLD OF VAL DOONICAN	Val Doonican (Decca)
16	19	FROM ELVIS IN MEMPHIS	Elvis Presley (RCA)
-	20	A MAN ALONE	Frank Sinatra (Reprise)

25 October 1969

last week	this week	title	artist
1	1	ABBEY ROAD	Beatles (Apple)
2	2	JOHNNY CASH AT SAN QUENTIN	Johnny Cash (CBS)
3	3	THROUGH THE PAST DARKLY (BIG HITS VOL 2)	Rolling Stones (Decca)
-	4	MOTOWN CHARTBUSTERS VOL 3	Various Artists (Tamla Motown)
4	5	SSSSH	Ten Years After (Deram)
5	6	THEN PLAY ON	Fleetwood Mac (Reprise)
8	7	NASHVILLE SKYLINE	Bob Dylan (CBS)
8	8	SONGS FOR A TAILOR	Jack Bruce (Polydor)
6	9	BLIND FAITH	Blind Faith (Polydor)
10	10	THE WORLD OF MANTOVANI VOL 2	Mantovani (Decca)
7	11	HAIR	London Cast (Polydor)
11	12	OLIVER!	Soundtrack (RCA)
-	13	IN THE COURT OF THE CRIMSON KING	King Crimson (Island)
-	14	THE SOUND OF MUSIC	Soundtrack (RCA)
15	15	THE COUNTRY SIDE OF JIM REEVES	Jim Reeves (RCA Camden)
12	16	STAND UP	Jethro Tull (Island)
-	17	2001: A SPACE ODYSSEY	Soundtrack (MGM)
16	18	BEST OF THE SEEKERS	Seekers (Columbia)
13	19	NICE	Nice (Immediate)
14	20	BEST OF GENE PITNEY	Gene Pitney (Stateside)

1 November 1969

last week	this week	title	artist
1	1	ABBEY ROAD	Beatles (Apple)
2	2	JOHNNY CASH AT SAN QUENTIN	Johnny Cash (CBS)
4	3	MOTOWN CHARTBUSTERS VOL 3	Various Artists (Tamla Motown)
3	4	THROUGH THE PAST DARKLY (BIG HITS VOL 2)	Rolling Stones (Decca)
13	5	IN THE COURT OF THE CRIMSON KING	King Crimson (Island)
6	6	THEN PLAY ON	Fleetwood Mac (Reprise)
5	7	SSSSH	Ten Years After (Deram)
7	8	NASHVILLE SKYLINE	Bob Dylan (CBS)
11	9	HAIR	London Cast (Polydor)
8	10	SONGS FOR A TAILOR	Jack Bruce (Polydor)
-	11	BEST OF CREAM	Cream (Polydor)
15	12	THE COUNTRY SIDE OF JIM REEVES	Jim Reeves (RCA Camden)
20	13	BEST OF GENE PITNEY	Gene Pitney (Stateside)
10	13	THE WORLD OF MANTOVANI VOL 2	Mantovani (Decca)
14	15	THE SOUND OF MUSIC	Soundtrack (RCA)
-	16	A MAN ALONE	Frank Sinatra (Reprise)
9	17	BLIND FAITH	Blind Faith (Polydor)
12	18	OLIVER!	Soundtrack (RCA)
-	19	BEST OF THE BEE GEES	Bee Gees (Polydor)
16	20	STAND UP	Jethro Tull (Island)

8 November 1969

last week	this week	title	artist
1	1	ABBEY ROAD	Beatles (Apple)
2	2	JOHNNY CASH AT SAN QUENTIN	Johnny Cash (CBS)
3	3	MOTOWN CHARTBUSTERS VOL 3	Various Artists (Tamla Motown)
5	4	IN THE COURT OF THE CRIMSON KING	King Crimson (Island)
4	5	THROUGH THE PAST DARKLY (BIG HITS VOL 2)	Rolling Stones (Decca)
6	6	THEN PLAY ON	Fleetwood Mac (Reprise)
-	7	LED ZEPPELIN II	Led Zeppelin (Atlantic)
19	8	BEST OF THE BEE GEES	Bee Gees (Polydor)
11	9	BEST OF CREAM	Cream (Polydor)
7	10	SSSSH	Ten Years After (Deram)
-	11	TOM JONES LIVE IN LAS VEGAS	Tom Jones (Decca)
15	12	THE SOUND OF MUSIC	Soundtrack (RCA)
9	13	HAIR	London Cast (Polydor)
8	14	NASHVILLE SKYLINE	Bob Dylan (CBS)
-	15	UMMAGUMMA	Pink Floyd (Harvest)
-	15	NICE ENOUGH TO EAT	Various Artists (Island)
13	17	BEST OF GENE PITNEY	Gene Pitney (Stateside)
16	18	A MAN ALONE	Frank Sinatra (Reprise)
13	19	THE WORLD OF MANTOVANI VOL 2	Mantovani (Decca)
-	20	NICE	Nice (Immediate)
17	20	BLIND FAITH	Blind Faith (Polydor)

15 November 1969

last week	this week	title	artist
1	1	ABBEY ROAD	Beatles (Apple)
3	2	MOTOWN CHARTBUSTERS VOL 3	Various Artists (Tamla Motown)
2	3	JOHNNY CASH AT SAN QUENTIN	Johnny Cash (CBS)
7	4	LED ZEPPELIN II	Led Zeppelin (Atlantic)
4	5	IN THE COURT OF THE CRIMSON KING	King Crimson (Island)
8	6	BEST OF THE BEE GEES	Bee Gees (Polydor)
11	7	TOM JONES LIVE IN LAS VEGAS	Tom Jones (Decca)
9	8	BEST OF CREAM	Cream (Polydor)
5	9	THROUGH THE PAST DARKLY (BIG HITS VOL 2)	Rolling Stones (Decca)
6	10	THEN PLAY ON	Fleetwood Mac (Reprise)
15	11	UMMAGUMMA	Pink Floyd (Harvest)
10	12	SSSSH	Ten Years After (Deram)
13	13	HAIR	London Cast (Polydor)
-	14	OLIVER!	Soundtrack (RCA)
14	14	NASHVILLE SKYLINE	Bob Dylan (CBS)
-	16	BEST OF THE SEEKERS	Seekers (Columbia)
15	17	NICE ENOUGH TO EAT	Various Artists (Island)
-	18	THE COUNTRY SIDE OF JIM REEVES	Jim Reeves (RCA Camden)
-	19	STAND UP	Jethro Tull (Island)
19	20	THE WORLD OF MANTOVANI VOL 2	Mantovani (Decca)
18	20	A MAN ALONE	Frank Sinatra (Reprise)

Yet more classics: *Abbey Road*, the avant-garde *In The Court Of The Crimson King* and *Ummagumma*. Geoffrey Cannon was still remembering summer: "Like love, or a child's face, some events keep an unanalysable beautify and vivacity... and what they are depends upon the thoughts directed to and contained in them... so with the Blind Faith concert... I'd no need to telephone friends; everyone I knew would be in the park... thinking the same thoughts as me." This man became editor of *Radio Times*.

22 November 1969

last week	this week	Title	Artist
1	1	ABBEY ROAD	Beatles (Apple)
2	2	MOTOWN CHARTBUSTERS VOL 3	Various Artists (Tamla Motown)
3	3	JOHNNY CASH AT SAN QUENTIN	Johnny Cash (CBS)
4	4	LED ZEPPELIN II	Led Zeppelin (Atlantic)
7	5	TOM JONES LIVE IN LAS VEGAS	Tom Jones (Decca)
11	6	UMMAGUMMA	Pink Floyd (Harvest)
5	7	IN THE COURT OF THE CRIMSON KING	King Crimson (Island)
6	8	BEST OF THE BEE GEES	Bee Gees (Polydor)
8	9	BEST OF CREAM	Cream (Polydor)
10	10	THEN PLAY ON	Fleetwood Mac (Reprise)
9	11	THROUGH THE PAST DARKLY (BIG HITS VOL 2)	Rolling Stones (Decca)
-	12	THE SOUND OF MUSIC	Soundtrack (RCA)
14	13	NASHVILLE SKYLINE	Bob Dylan (CBS)
12	14	SSSSH	Ten Years After (Deram)
17	15	NICE ENOUGH TO EAT	Various Artists (Island)
14	16	OLIVER!	Soundtrack (RCA)
18	17	THE COUNTRY SIDE OF JIM REEVES	Jim Reeves (RCA Camden)
19	18	STAND UP	Jethro Tull (Island)
20	19	THE WORLD OF MANTOVANI VOL 2	Mantovani (Decca)
13	20	HAIR	London Cast (Polydor)

29 November 1969

last week	this week	Title	Artist
1	1	ABBEY ROAD	Beatles (Apple)
3	2	JOHNNY CASH AT SAN QUENTIN	Johnny Cash (CBS)
2	3	MOTOWN CHARTBUSTERS VOL 3	Various Artists (Tamla Motown)
4	4	LED ZEPPELIN II	Led Zeppelin (Atlantic)
5	5	TOM JONES LIVE IN LAS VEGAS	Tom Jones (Decca)
8	6	BEST OF THE BEE GEES	Bee Gees (Polydor)
-	7	TO OUR CHILDREN'S CHILDREN'S CHILDREN	Moody Blues (Threshold)
9	8	BEST OF CREAM	Cream (Polydor)
6	8	UMMAGUMMA	Pink Floyd (Harvest)
7	10	IN THE COURT OF THE CRIMSON KING	King Crimson (Island)
11	11	THROUGH THE PAST DARKLY (BIG HITS VOL 2)	Rolling Stones (Decca)
19	12	THE WORLD OF MANTOVANI VOL 2	Mantovani (Decca)
-	13	ENGELBERT HUMPERDINCK	Engelbert Humperdinck (Decca)
16	14	OLIVER!	Soundtrack (RCA)
-	15	BEST OF THE SEEKERS	Seekers (Columbia)
10	16	THEN PLAY ON	Fleetwood Mac (Reprise)
12	17	THE SOUND OF MUSIC	Soundtrack (RCA)
17	18	THE COUNTRY SIDE OF JIM REEVES	Jim Reeves (RCA/Camden)
-	19	TURNING POINT	John Mayall (Polydor)
15	20	NICE ENOUGH TO EAT	Various Artists (Island)

6 December 1969

last week	this week	Title	Artist
1	1	ABBEY ROAD	Beatles (Apple)
3	2	MOTOWN CHARTBUSTERS VOL 3	Various Artists (Tamla Motown)
2	3	JOHNNY CASH AT SAN QUENTIN	Johnny Cash (CBS)
5	4	TOM JONES LIVE IN LAS VEGAS	Tom Jones (Decca)
4	5	LED ZEPPELIN II	Led Zeppelin (Atlantic)
7	6	TO OUR CHILDREN'S CHILDREN'S CHILDREN	Moody Blues (Threshold)
8	7	BEST OF CREAM	Cream (Polydor)
6	8	BEST OF THE BEE GEES	Bee Gees (Polydor)
8	9	UMMAGUMMA	Pink Floyd (Harvest)
13	10	ENGELBERT HUMPERDINCK	Engelbert Humperdinck (Decca)
17	11	THE SOUND OF MUSIC	Soundtrack (RCA)
10	12	IN THE COURT OF THE CRIMSON KING	King Crimson (Island)
15	13	BEST OF THE SEEKERS	Seekers (Columbia)
11	14	THROUGH THE PAST DARKLY (BIG HITS VOL 2)	Rolling Stones (Decca)
14	15	OLIVER!	Soundtrack (RCA)
12	15	THE WORLD OF MANTOVANI VOL 2	Mantovani (Decca)
16	17	THEN PLAY ON	Fleetwood Mac (Reprise)
-	18	STAND UP	Jethro Tull (Island)
20	19	NICE ENOUGH TO EAT	Various Artists (Island)
18	20	THE COUNTRY SIDE OF JIM REEVES	Jim Reeves (RCA Camden)

13 December 1969

last week	this week	Title	Artist
1	1	ABBEY ROAD	Beatles (Apple)
2	2	MOTOWN CHARTBUSTERS VOL 3	Various Artists (Tamla Motown)
4	3	TOM JONES LIVE IN LAS VEGAS	Tom Jones (Decca)
-	4	LET IT BLEED	Rolling Stones (Decca)
6	5	TO OUR CHILDREN'S CHILDREN'S CHILDREN	Moody Blues (Threshold)
3	6	JOHNNY CASH AT SAN QUENTIN	Johnny Cash (CBS)
5	7	LED ZEPPELIN II	Led Zeppelin (Atlantic)
10	8	ENGELBERT HUMPERDINCK	Engelbert Humperdinck (Decca)
19	9	NICE ENOUGH TO EAT	Various Artists (Island)
11	10	THE SOUND OF MUSIC	Soundtrack (RCA)
8	11	BEST OF THE BEE GEES	Bee Gees (Polydor)
7	12	BEST OF CREAM	Cream (Polydor)
15	13	OLIVER!	Soundtrack (RCA)
9	14	UMMAGUMMA	Pink Floyd (Harvest)
15	15	THE WORLD OF MANTOVANI VOL 2	Mantovani (Decca)
14	16	THROUGH THE PAST DARKLY (BIG HITS VOL 2)	Rolling Stones (Decca)
18	17	STAND UP	Jethro Tull (Island)
12	17	IN THE COURT OF THE CRIMSON KING	Crimson King (Island)
-	19	AMERICA	Herb Alpert & the Tijuana Brass (A&M)
-	20	HAIR	London Cast (Polydor)

20 December 1969

last week	this week	Title	Artist
1	1	ABBEY ROAD	Beatles (Apple)
2	2	MOTOWN CHARTBUSTERS VOL 3	Various Artists (Tamla Motown)
3	3	TOM JONES LIVE IN LAS VEGAS	Tom Jones (Decca)
4	4	LET IT BLEED	Rolling Stones (Decca)
6	5	JOHNNY CASH AT SAN QUENTIN	Johnny Cash (CBS)
5	6	TO OUR CHILDREN'S CHILDREN'S CHILDREN	Moody Blues (Threshold)
8	7	ENGELBERT HUMPERDINCK	Engelbert Humperdinck (Decca)
10	8	THE SOUND OF MUSIC	Soundtrack (RCA)
7	9	LED ZEPPELIN II	Led Zeppelin (Atlantic)
15	10	THE WORLD OF MANTOVANI VOL 2	Mantovani (Decca)
-	11	BEST OF THE SEEKERS	Seekers (Columbia)
13	12	OLIVER!	Soundtrack (RCA)
-	13	TIGHTEN UP VOL 2	Various Artists (Trojan)
12	14	BEST OF CREAM	Cream (Polydor)
-	15	MY CHERIE AMOUR	Stevie Wonder (Tamla Motown)
17	16	STAND UP	Jethro Tull (Island)
11	16	BEST OF THE BEE GEES	Bee Gees (Polydor)
20	17	HAIR	London Cast (Polydor)
-	17	GET TOGETHER WITH ANDY WILLIAMS	Andy Williams (CBS)
14	19	UMMAGUMMA	Pink Floyd (Harvest)
17	20	IN THE COURT OF THE CRIMSON KING	King Crimson (Island)

27 December 1969

last week	this week	Title	Artist
1	1	ABBEY ROAD	Beatles (Apple)
3	2	TOM JONES LIVE IN LAS VEGAS	Tom Jones (Decca)
4	3	LET IT BLEED	Rolling Stones (Decca)
2	4	MOTOWN CHARTBUSTERS VOL 3	Various Artists (Tamla Motown)
5	5	JOHNNY CASH AT SAN QUENTIN	Johnny Cash (CBS)
6	6	TO OUR CHILDREN'S CHILDREN'S CHILDREN	Moody Blues (Threshold)
7	7	ENGELBERT HUMPERDINCK	Engelbert Humperdinck (Decca)
9	8	LED ZEPPELIN II	Led Zeppelin (Atlantic)
12	9	OLIVER!	Soundtrack (RCA)
8	10	THE SOUND OF MUSIC	Soundtrack (RCA)
13	11	TIGHTEN UP VOL 2	Various Artists (Trojan)
11	12	BEST OF THE SEEKERS	Seekers (Columbia)
14	13	BEST OF CREAM	Cream (Polydor)
-	14	EASY RIDER	Soundtrack (Stateside)
16	15	BEST OF THE BEE GEES	Bee Gees (Polydor)
10	17	THE WORLD OF MANTOVANI VOL 2	Mantovani (Decca)
17	18	GET TOGETHER WITH ANDY WILLIAMS	Andy Williams (CBS)
	20	SYD LAWRENCE PLAYS GLENN MILLER	Syd Lawrence (Fontana)

The years that technically ended the 1960s had been spectacularly eventful. 1968 had seen the zenith of student radicalism, a period in which it had been possible not only to bring down President Johnson but to believe that, via socialism, anarchy and/or dropping out, tuning in and turning on, the revolution was coming. In 1969 Woodstock was talked of in America as Woodstock Nation, a coming-together of tribes. In Britain, people were torn between International Socialism and International Times. The old folks at home were shamelessly tuning in and dropping out to *Sid Lawrence Plays Glen Miller*.

Decadence and facial hair at the end of the 60s. From the top: Jethro Tull, Jimi Hendrix, the Faces, Pink Floyd

January – February 1970

3 January 1970

last	this		
1	1	ABBEY ROAD	Beatles (Apple)
3	2	LET IT BLEED	Rolling Stones (Decca)
2	3	TOM JONES LIVE IN LAS VEGAS	Tom Jones (Decca)
4	4	MOTOWN CHARTBUSTERS VOL 3	Various Artists (Tamla Motown)
5	5	JOHNNY CASH AT SAN QUENTIN	Johnny Cash (CBS)
6	6	TO OUR CHILDREN'S CHILDREN'S CHILDREN	Moody Blues (Threshold)
7	7	ENGELBERT HUMPERDINCK	Engelbert Humperdinck (Decca)
8	8	LED ZEPPELIN II	Led Zeppelin (Atlantic)
-	9	AMERICA	Herb Alpert & the Tijuana Brass (A&M)
10	10	THE SOUND OF MUSIC	Soundtrack (RCA)
9	11	OLIVER!	Soundtrack (RCA)
11	12	TIGHTEN UP VOL 2	Various Artists (Trojan)
12	13	BEST OF THE SEEKERS	Seekers (Columbia)
14	14	EASY RIDER	Soundtrack (Stateside)
13	15	BEST OF CREAM	Cream (Polydor)
17	16	THE WORLD OF MANTOVANI VOL 2	Mantovani (Decca)
15	17	BEST OF THE BEE GEES	Bee Gees (Polydor)
18	18	GET TOGETHER WITH ANDY WILLIAMS	Andy Williams (CBS)
20	19	SYD LAWRENCE PLAYS GLENN MILLER	Syd Lawrence (Fontana)
-	20	HAIR	London Cast (Polydor)

10 January 1970

last	this		
1	1	ABBEY ROAD	Beatles (Apple)
4	2	MOTOWN CHARTBUSTERS VOL 3	Various Artists (Tamla Motown)
2	3	LET IT BLEED	Rolling Stones (Decca)
3	4	TOM JONES LIVE IN LAS VEGAS	Tom Jones (Decca)
8	5	LED ZEPPELIN II	Led Zeppelin (Atlantic)
6	6	TO OUR CHILDREN'S CHILDREN'S CHILDREN	Moody Blues (Threshold)
5	7	JOHNNY CASH AT SAN QUENTIN	Johnny Cash (CBS)
7	8	ENGELBERT HUMPERDINCK	Engelbert Humperdinck (Decca)
9	9	AMERICA	Herb Alpert & the Tijuana Brass (A&M)
12	10	TIGHTEN UP VOL 2	Various Artists (Trojan)
11	11	OLIVER!	Soundtrack (RCA)
15	12	BEST OF CREAM	Cream (Polydor)
10	13	THE SOUND OF MUSIC	Soundtrack (RCA)
20	14	HAIR	London Cast (Polydor)
16	15	THE WORLD OF MANTOVANI VOL 2	Mantovani (Decca)
-	16	MY CHERIE AMOUR	Stevie Wonder (Tamla Motown)
14	17	EASY RIDER	Soundtrack (Stateside)
18	18	GET TOGETHER WITH ANDY WILLIAMS	Andy Williams (CBS)
-	19	IN THE COURT OF THE CRIMSON KING	King Crimson (Island)
-	20	NICE ENOUGH TO EAT	Various Artists (Island)

17 January 1970

last	this		
1	1	ABBEY ROAD	Beatles (Apple)
2	2	MOTOWN CHARTBUSTERS VOL 3	Various Artists (Tamla Motown)
5	3	LED ZEPPELIN II	Led Zeppelin (Atlantic)
3	4	LET IT BLEED	Rolling Stones (Decca)
4	5	TOM JONES LIVE IN LAS VEGAS	Tom Jones (Decca)
6	6	TO OUR CHILDREN'S CHILDREN'S CHILDREN	Moody Blues (Threshold)
7	7	JOHNNY CASH AT SAN QUENTIN	Johnny Cash (CBS)
10	8	TIGHTEN UP VOL 2	Various Artists (Trojan)
17	9	EASY RIDER	Soundtrack (Stateside)
8	10	ENGELBERT HUMPERDINCK	Engelbert Humperdinck (Decca)
9	11	AMERICA	Herb Alpert & the Tijuana Brass (A&M)
-	12	BASKET OF LIGHT	Pentangle (Transatlantic)
13	13	THE SOUND OF MUSIC	Soundtrack (RCA)
12	14	BEST OF CREAM	Cream (Polydor)
11	15	OLIVER!	Soundtrack (RCA)
20	16	NICE ENOUGH TO EAT	Various Artists (Island)
19	17	IN THE COURT OF THE CRIMSON KING	King Crimson (Island)
-	18	BEST OF THE SEEKERS	Seekers (Columbia)
16	19	MY CHERIE AMOUR	Stevie Wonder (Tamla Motown)
-	20	THE GLENN MILLER STORY	Glenn Miller (RCA)

24 January 1970

last	this		
1	1	ABBEY ROAD	Beatles (Apple)
2	2	MOTOWN CHARTBUSTERS VOL 3	Various Artists (Tamla Motown)
3	3	LED ZEPPELIN II	Led Zeppelin (Atlantic)
4	4	LET IT BLEED	Rolling Stones (Decca)
6	5	TO OUR CHILDREN'S CHILDREN'S CHILDREN	Moody Blues (Threshold)
5	6	TOM JONES LIVE IN LAS VEGAS	Tom Jones (Decca)
7	7	JOHNNY CASH AT SAN QUENTIN	Johnny Cash (CBS)
8	8	TIGHTEN UP VOL 2	Various Artists (Trojan)
9	9	EASY RIDER	Soundtrack (Stateside)
11	10	AMERICA	Herb Alpert & the Tijuana Brass (A&M)
13	11	THE SOUND OF MUSIC	Soundtrack (RCA)
14	12	BEST OF CREAM	Cream (Polydor)
12	13	BASKET OF LIGHT	Pentangle (Transatlantic)
17	14	IN THE COURT OF THE CRIMSON KING	King Crimson (Island)
-	15	LIEGE AND LIEF	Fairport Convention (Island)
-	16	THE WORLD OF JOHN MAYALL	John Mayall (Decca)
18	17	BEST OF THE SEEKERS	Seekers (Columbia)
-	18	THE WORLD OF MANTOVANI VOL 2	Mantovani (Decca)
15	19	OLIVER!	Soundtrack (RCA)
10	20	ENGELBERT HUMPERDINCK	Engelbert Humperdinck (Decca)

31 January 1970

last	this		
1	1	ABBEY ROAD	Beatles (Apple)
2	1	MOTOWN CHARTBUSTERS VOL 3	Various Artists (Tamla Motown)
3	3	LED ZEPPELIN II	Led Zeppelin (Atlantic)
4	4	LET IT BLEED	Rolling Stones (Decca)
6	5	TOM JONES LIVE IN LAS VEGAS	Tom Jones (Decca)
9	6	EASY RIDER	Soundtrack (Stateside)
5	7	TO OUR CHILDREN'S CHILDREN'S CHILDREN	Moody Blues (Threshold)
7	8	JOHNNY CASH AT SAN QUENTIN	Johnny Cash (CBS)
8	9	TIGHTEN UP VOL 2	Various Artists (Trojan)
13	10	BASKET OF LIGHT	Pentangle (Transatlantic)
10	11	AMERICA	Herb Alpert & the Tijuana Brass (A&M)
12	12	BEST OF CREAM	Cream (Polydor)
16	13	THE WORLD OF JOHN MAYALL	John Mayall (Decca)
14	14	IN THE COURT OF THE CRIMSON KING	King Crimson (Island)
20	15	ENGELBERT HUMPERDINCK	Engelbert Humperdinck (Decca)
-	16	CHICAGO TRANSIT AUTHORITY	Chicago (CBS)
11	17	THE SOUND OF MUSIC	Soundtrack (RCA)
17	18	BEST OF THE SEEKERS	Seekers (Columbia)
15	19	LIEGE AND LIEF	Fairport Convention (Island)
19	20	OLIVER!	Soundtrack (RCA)

7 February 1970

last	this		
3	1	LED ZEPPELIN II	Led Zeppelin (Atlantic)
1	2	MOTOWN CHARTBUSTERS VOL 3	Various Artists (Tamla Motown)
1	3	ABBEY ROAD	Beatles (Apple)
4	4	LET IT BLEED	Rolling Stones (Decca)
6	5	EASY RIDER	Soundtrack (Stateside)
5	6	TOM JONES LIVE IN LAS VEGAS	Tom Jones (Decca)
10	7	BASKET OF LIGHT	Pentangle (Transatlantic)
8	8	JOHNNY CASH AT SAN QUENTIN	Johnny Cash (CBS)
9	9	TIGHTEN UP VOL 2	Various Artists (Trojan)
11	10	AMERICA	Herb Alpert & the Tijuana Brass (A&M)
19	11	LIEGE AND LIEF	Fairport Convention (Island)
7	12	TO OUR CHILDREN'S CHILDREN'S CHILDREN	Moody Blues (Threshold)
-	13	FUNNY GIRL	Soundtrack (CBS)
-	14	A SONG FOR ME	Family (Reprise)
16	15	CHICAGO TRANSIT AUTHORITY	Chicago (CBS)
13	16	THE WORLD OF JOHN MAYALL	John Mayall (Decca)
17	17	THE SOUND OF MUSIC	Soundtrack (RCA)
12	18	BEST OF CREAM	Cream (Polydor)
-	19	PAINT YOUR WAGON	Soundtrack (Paramount)
18	20	BEST OF THE SEEKERS	Seekers (Columbia)

1970: but first, let it be remembered that some who contributed crucially to the music of the late 1960s never showed up in the chart at all, despite making seminal albums of the period. Van Morrison was one of these. He had disbanded his Northern Ireland beat group, Them, recorded some tentative material in New York, and then, out of nowhere, in 1968, made *Astral Weeks*: way ahead of its time, visionary and bright, celebratory, youthful, timeless. It would be hard to name a more important 1960s album.

14 February 1970

last week	this week		
1	1	LED ZEPPELIN II	Led Zeppelin (Atlantic)
2	2	MOTOWN CHARTBUSTERS VOL 3	Various Artists (Tamla Motown)
3	3	ABBEY ROAD	Beatles (Apple)
5	4	EASY RIDER	Soundtrack (Stateside)
4	5	LET IT BLEED	Rolling Stones (Decca)
14	6	A SONG FOR ME	Family (Reprise)
7	7	BASKET OF LIGHT	Pentangle (Transatlantic)
-	8	BRIDGE OVER TROUBLED WATER	Simon & Garfunkel (CBS)
6	9	TOM JONES LIVE IN LAS VEGAS	Tom Jones (Decca)
9	10	TIGHTEN UP VOL 2	Various Artists (Trojan)
8	11	JOHNNY CASH AT SAN QUENTIN	Johnny Cash (CBS)
19	12	PAINT YOUR WAGON	Soundtrack (Paramount)
15	13	CHICAGO TRANSIT AUTHORITY	Chicago (CBS)
10	14	AMERICA	Herb Alpert & the Tijuana Brass (A&M)
12	15	TO OUR CHILDREN'S CHILDREN'S CHILDREN	Moody Blues (Threshold)
16	16	THE WORLD OF JOHN MAYALL	John Mayall (Decca)
-	17	CREAM OF THE CROP	Diana Ross & the Supremes (Tamla Motown)
13	18	FUNNY GIRL	Soundtrack (CBS)
18	19	BEST OF CREAM	Cream (Polydor)
-	20	PUZZLE PEOPLE	Temptations (Tamla Motown)

21 February 1970

8	1	BRIDGE OVER TROUBLED WATER	Simon & Garfunkel (CBS)
1	2	LED ZEPPELIN II	Led Zeppelin (Atlantic)
2	3	MOTOWN CHARTBUSTERS VOL 3	Various Artists (Tamla Motown)
3	4	ABBEY ROAD	Beatles (Apple)
4	5	EASY RIDER	Soundtrack (Stateside)
6	6	A SONG FOR ME	Family (Reprise)
11	7	JOHNNY CASH AT SAN QUENTIN	Johnny Cash (CBS)
7	8	BASKET OF LIGHT	Pentangle (Transatlantic)
12	9	PAINT YOUR WAGON	Soundtrack (Paramount)
9	10	TOM JONES LIVE IN LAS VEGAS	Tom Jones (Decca)
10	11	TIGHTEN UP VOL 2	Various Artists (Trojan)
13	12	CHICAGO TRANSIT AUTHORITY	Chicago (CBS)
5	13	LET IT BLEED	Rolling Stones (Decca)
14	14	AMERICA	Herb Alpert & the Tijuana Brass (A&M)
20	15	PUZZLE PEOPLE	Temptations (Tamla Motown)
18	16	FUNNY GIRL	Soundtrack (CBS)
16	17	THE WORLD OF JOHN MAYALL	John Mayall (Decca)
15	18	TO OUR CHILDREN'S CHILDREN'S CHILDREN	Moody Blues (Threshold)
-	19	TOGETHER	Diana Ross & the Supremes (Tamla Motown)
-	20	ON THE BOARDS	Taste (Polydor)

28 February 1970

1	1	BRIDGE OVER TROUBLED WATER	Simon & Garfunkel (CBS)
3	2	MOTOWN CHARTBUSTERS VOL 3	Various Artists (Tamla Motown)
2	3	LED ZEPPELIN II	Led Zeppelin (Atlantic)
4	4	ABBEY ROAD	Beatles (Apple)
9	5	PAINT YOUR WAGON	Soundtrack (Paramount)
5	6	EASY RIDER	Soundtrack (Stateside)
6	7	A SONG FOR ME	Family (Reprise)
8	8	BASKET OF LIGHT	Pentangle (Transatlantic)
13	9	LET IT BLEED	Rolling Stones (Decca)
11	10	TIGHTEN UP VOL 2	Various Artists (Trojan)
7	11	JOHNNY CASH AT SAN QUENTIN	Johnny Cash (CBS)
14	12	AMERICA	Herb Alpert & the Tijuana Brass (A&M)
10	13	TOM JONES LIVE IN LAS VEGAS	Tom Jones (Decca)
12	14	CHICAGO TRANSIT AUTHORITY	Chicago (CBS)
-	15	CANNED HEAT COOKBOOK	Canned Heat (Liberty)
16	16	FUNNY GIRL	Soundtrack (CBS)
20	17	ON THE BOARDS	Taste (Polydor)
-	18	HELLO DOLLY	Soundtrack (Stateside)
-	19	CREAM OF THE CROP	Diana Ross & the Supremes (Tamla Motown)
-	20	THE WORLD OF MANTOVANI VOL 2	Mantovani (Decca)

7 March 1970

1	1	BRIDGE OVER TROUBLED WATER	Simon & Garfunkel (CBS)
-	2	FROM MEMPHIS TO VEGAS - FROM VEGAS TO MEMPHIS	Elvis Presley (RCA)
3	2	LED ZEPPELIN II	Led Zeppelin (Atlantic)
5	3	PAINT YOUR WAGON	Soundtrack (Paramount)
2	4	MOTOWN CHARTBUSTERS VOL 3	Various Artists (Tamla Motown)
6	5	EASY RIDER	Soundtrack (Stateside)
4	6	ABBEY ROAD	Beatles (Apple)
16	7	FUNNY GIRL	Soundtrack (CBS)
-	8	HELLO I'M JOHNNY CASH	Johnny Cash (CBS)
7	9	A SONG FOR ME	Family (Reprise)
8	10	BASKET OF LIGHT	Pentangle (Transatlantic)
9	11	LET IT BLEED	Rolling Stones (Decca)
11	13	JOHNNY CASH AT SAN QUENTIN	Johnny Cash (CBS)
15	14	CANNED HEAT COOKBOOK	Canned Heat (Liberty)
10	15	TIGHTEN UP VOL 2	Various Artists (Trojan)
-	16	BEST OF CREAM	Cream (Polydor)
13	17	TOM JONES LIVE IN LAS VEGAS	Tom Jones (Decca)
14	18	CHICAGO TRANSIT AUTHORITY	Chicago (CBS)
-	19	THE SOUND OF MUSIC	Soundtrack (RCA)
12	20	AMERICA	Herb Alpert & the Tijuana Brass (A&M)

14 March 1970

1	1	BRIDGE OVER TROUBLED WATER	Simon & Garfunkel (CBS)
3	2	PAINT YOUR WAGON	Soundtrack (Paramount)
2	3	LED ZEPPELIN II	Led Zeppelin (Atlantic)
5	4	EASY RIDER	Soundtrack (Stateside)
4	5	MOTOWN CHARTBUSTERS VOL 3	Various Artists (Tamla Motown)
6	6	ABBEY ROAD	Beatles (Apple)
8	7	HELLO I'M JOHNNY CASH	Johnny Cash (CBS)
2	8	FROM MEMPHIS TO VEGAS - FROM VEGAS TO MEMPHIS	Elvis Presley (RCA)
15	9	TIGHTEN UP VOL 2	Various Artists (Trojan)
10	10	BASKET OF LIGHT	Pentangle (Transatlantic)
14	11	CANNED HEAT COOKBOOK	Canned Heat (Liberty)
7	12	FUNNY GIRL	Soundtrack (CBS)
-	13	HOT RATS	Frank Zappa (Reprise)
20	14	AMERICA	Herb Alpert & the Tijuana Brass (A&M)
9	15	A SONG FOR ME	Family (Reprise)
17	16	TOM JONES LIVE IN LAS VEGAS	Tom Jones (Decca)
11	17	LET IT BLEED	Rolling Stones (Decca)
-	18	DIANA ROSS PRESENTS THE JACKSON FIVE	Jackson Five (Tamla Motown)
18	19	CHICAGO TRANSIT AUTHORITY	Chicago (CBS)
19	20	THE SOUND OF MUSIC	Soundtrack (RCA)

21 March 1970

1	1	BRIDGE OVER TROUBLED WATER	Simon & Garfunkel (CBS)
2	2	PAINT YOUR WAGON	Soundtrack (Paramount)
3	3	LED ZEPPELIN II	Led Zeppelin (Atlantic)
4	4	EASY RIDER	Soundtrack (Stateside)
5	5	MOTOWN CHARTBUSTERS VOL 3	Various Artists (Tamla Motown)
8	6	FROM MEMPHIS TO VEGAS - FROM VEGAS TO MEMPHIS	Elvis Presley (RCA)
7	7	HELLO I'M JOHNNY CASH	Johnny Cash (CBS)
6	8	ABBEY ROAD	Beatles (Apple)
11	9	CANNED HEAT COOKBOOK	Canned Heat (Liberty)
-	10	FILL YOUR HEAD WITH ROCK	Various Artists (CBS)
12	11	FUNNY GIRL	Soundtrack (CBS)
10	12	BASKET OF LIGHT	Pentangle (Transatlantic)
9	13	TIGHTEN UP VOL 2	Various Artists (Trojan)
13	14	HOT RATS	Frank Zappa (Reprise)
14	15	AMERICA	Herb Alpert & the Tijuana Brass (A&M)
-	16	WILLY AND THE POOR BOYS	Creedence Clearwater Revival (Liberty)
-	17	BLACK SABBATH	Black Sabbath (Vertigo)
-	18	JOHNNY CASH AT SAN QUENTIN	Johnny Cash (CBS)
15	19	A SONG FOR ME	Family (Reprise)
20	20	THE SOUND OF MUSIC	Soundtrack (RCA)

Another whose influential, innovative albums had never charted was Frank Zappa. His Mothers of Invention had made their recording debut with a double-album (at first a single LP in Britain). 1966's *Freak Out!* had been followed by *Absolutely Free* and, its cover splendidly parodying Sgt Pepper's, *We're Only In It For The Money*, a title that mocked hippies as much as their parents. Zappa finally charted with 1969's *Hot Rats*, showcasing his fierce proficiency as guitarist, composer and producer.

March – May 1970

28 March 1970

last	this		
1	1	BRIDGE OVER TROUBLED WATER	Simon & Garfunkel (CBS)
2	2	PAINT YOUR WAGON	Soundtrack (Paramount)
3	3	LED ZEPPELIN II	Led Zeppelin (Atlantic)
4	4	EASY RIDER	Soundtrack (Stateside)
5	5	MOTOWN CHARTBUSTERS VOL 3	Various Artists (Tamla Motown)
10	5	FILL YOUR HEAD WITH ROCK	Various Artists (CBS)
7	7	HELLO I'M JOHNNY CASH	Johnny Cash (CBS)
6	8	FROM MEMPHIS TO VEGAS - FROM VEGAS TO MEMPHIS	Elvis Presley (RCA)
-	9	JIM REEVES' GOLDEN RECORDS	Jim Reeves (RCA International)
8	10	ABBEY ROAD	Beatles (Apple)
11	11	FUNNY GIRL	Soundtrack (CBS)
9	12	CANNED HEAT COOKBOOK	Canned Heat (Liberty)
-	13	DIANA ROSS PRESENTS THE JACKSON FIVE	Jackson Five (Tamla Motown)
-	14	BUDDY HOLLY'S GREATEST HITS	Buddy Holly (Coral)
12	15	BASKET OF LIGHT	Pentangle (Transatlantic)
16	16	WILLY AND THE POOR BOYS	Creedence Clearwater Revival (Liberty)
-	17	CHICAGO TRANSIT AUTHORITY	Chicago (CBS)
-	18	BEST OF THE SEEKERS	Seekers (Columbia)
13	19	TIGHTEN UP VOL 2	Various Artists (Trojan)
20	20	THE SOUND OF MUSIC	Soundtrack (RCA)

4 April 1970

last	this		
1	1	BRIDGE OVER TROUBLED WATER	Simon & Garfunkel (CBS)
4	2	EASY RIDER	Soundtrack (Stateside)
2	3	PAINT YOUR WAGON	Soundtrack (Paramount)
3	4	LED ZEPPELIN II	Led Zeppelin (Atlantic)
5	5	FILL YOUR HEAD WITH ROCK	Various Artists (CBS)
5	6	MOTOWN CHARTBUSTERS VOL 3	Various Artists (Tamla Motown)
7	7	HELLO I'M JOHNNY CASH	Johnny Cash (CBS)
8	8	FROM MEMPHIS TO VEGAS - FROM VEGAS TO MEMPHIS	Elvis Presley (RCA)
10	9	ABBEY ROAD	Beatles (Apple)
16	10	WILLY AND THE POOR BOYS	Creedence Clearwater Revival (Liberty)
17	11	CHICAGO TRANSIT AUTHORITY	Chicago (CBS)
9	12	JIM REEVES' GOLDEN RECORDS	Jim Reeves (RCA International)
-	13	ANDY WILLIAMS' GREATEST HITS	Andy Williams (CBS)
-	14	BLACK SABBATH	Black Sabbath (Vertigo)
-	15	JOHNNY CASH AT SAN QUENTIN	Johnny Cash (CBS)
12	16	CANNED HEAT COOKBOOK	Canned Heat (Liberty)
15	17	BASKET OF LIGHT	Pentangle (Transatlantic)
-	18	LIVE AT THE TALK OF THE TOWN	Temptations (Tamla Motown)
19	19	HOT RATS	Frank Zappa (Reprise)
14	20	BUDDY HOLLY'S GREATEST HITS	Buddy Holly (Coral)

11 April 1970

last	this		
1	1	BRIDGE OVER TROUBLED WATER	Simon & Garfunkel (CBS)
2	2	EASY RIDER	Soundtrack (Stateside)
3	3	PAINT YOUR WAGON	Soundtrack (Paramount)
5	4	FILL YOUR HEAD WITH ROCK	Various Artists (CBS)
4	5	LED ZEPPELIN II	Led Zeppelin (Atlantic)
13	6	ANDY WILLIAMS' GREATEST HITS	Andy Williams (CBS)
6	7	MOTOWN CHARTBUSTERS VOL 3	Various Artists (Tamla Motown)
-	8	CHICAGO	Chicago (CBS)
8	9	FROM MEMPHIS TO VEGAS - FROM VEGAS TO MEMPHIS	Elvis Presley (RCA)
12	10	JIM REEVES' GOLDEN RECORDS	Jim Reeves (RCA International)
9	11	ABBEY ROAD	Beatles (Apple)
-	12	THE EXQUISITE NANA MOUSKOURI	Nana Mouskouri (Fontana)
10	13	WILLY AND THE POOR BOYS	Creedence Clearwater Revival (Liberty)
7	14	HELLO I'M JOHNNY CASH	Johnny Cash (CBS)
19	15	HOT RATS	Frank Zappa (Reprise)
11	16	CHICAGO TRANSIT AUTHORITY	Chicago (CBS)
-	17	HAIR	London Cast (Polydor)
-	18	FUNNY GIRL	Soundtrack (CBS)
-	19	TIGHTEN UP VOL 2	Various Artists (Trojan)
16	20	CANNED HEAT COOKBOOK	Canned Heat (Liberty)

18 April 1970

last	this		
1	1	BRIDGE OVER TROUBLED WATER	Simon & Garfunkel (CBS)
6	2	ANDY WILLIAMS' GREATEST HITS	Andy Williams (CBS)
2	3	EASY RIDER	Soundtrack (Stateside)
3	4	PAINT YOUR WAGON	Soundtrack (Paramount)
5	5	LED ZEPPELIN II	Led Zeppelin (Atlantic)
4	6	FILL YOUR HEAD WITH ROCK	Various Artists (CBS)
8	7	CHICAGO	Chicago (CBS)
7	8	MOTOWN CHARTBUSTERS VOL 3	Various Artists (Tamla Motown)
-	9	BLACK SABBATH	Black Sabbath (Vertigo)
-	10	TOM	Tom Jones (Decca)
11	11	ABBEY ROAD	Beatles (Apple)
12	12	THE EXQUISITE NANA MOUSKOURI	Nana Mouskouri (Fontana)
10	13	JIM REEVES' GOLDEN RECORDS	Jim Reeves (RCA International)
9	14	FROM MEMPHIS TO VEGAS - FROM VEGAS TO MEMPHIS	Elvis Presley (RCA)
15	14	HOT RATS	Frank Zappa (Reprise)
-	16	EMPTY ROOMS	John Mayall (Polydor)
14	17	HELLO I'M JOHNNY CASH	Johnny Cash (CBS)
-	18	BASKET OF LIGHT	Pentangle (Transatlantic)
18	19	FUNNY GIRL	Soundtrack (CBS)
19	20	TIGHTEN UP VOL 2	Various Artists (Trojan)

25 April 1970

last	this		
1	1	BRIDGE OVER TROUBLED WATER	Simon & Garfunkel (CBS)
2	2	ANDY WILLIAMS' GREATEST HITS	Andy Williams (CBS)
5	3	LED ZEPPELIN II	Led Zeppelin (Atlantic)
3	4	EASY RIDER	Soundtrack (Stateside)
6	5	FILL YOUR HEAD WITH ROCK	Various Artists (CBS)
-	6	McCARTNEY	Paul McCartney (Apple)
4	7	PAINT YOUR WAGON	Soundtrack (Paramount)
9	8	BLACK SABBATH	Black Sabbath (Vertigo)
7	9	CHICAGO	Chicago (CBS)
14	10	HOT RATS	Frank Zappa (Reprise)
11	11	ABBEY ROAD	Beatles (Apple)
8	12	MOTOWN CHARTBUSTERS VOL 3	Various Artists (Tamla Motown)
10	13	TOM	Tom Jones (Decca)
18	14	BASKET OF LIGHT	Pentangle (Transatlantic)
13	15	JIM REEVES' GOLDEN RECORDS	Jim Reeves (RCA International)
-	16	SENTIMENTAL JOURNEY	Ringo Starr (Apple)
-	17	WILLY AND THE POOR BOYS	Creedence Clearwater Revival (Liberty)
14	18	FROM MEMPHIS TO VEGAS - FROM VEGAS TO MEMPHIS	Elvis Presley (RCA)
12	19	THE EXQUISITE NANA MOUSKOURI	Nana Mouskouri (Fontana)
20	19	TIGHTEN UP VOL 2	Various Artists (Trojan)

2 May 1970

last	this		
1	1	BRIDGE OVER TROUBLED WATER	Simon & Garfunkel (CBS)
6	2	McCARTNEY	Paul McCartney (Apple)
2	3	ANDY WILLIAMS' GREATEST HITS	Andy Williams (CBS)
3	4	LED ZEPPELIN II	Led Zeppelin (Atlantic)
4	5	EASY RIDER	Soundtrack (Stateside)
7	6	PAINT YOUR WAGON	Soundtrack (Paramount)
5	7	FILL YOUR HEAD WITH ROCK	Various Artists (CBS)
13	8	TOM	Tom Jones (Decca)
9	9	CHICAGO	Chicago (CBS)
8	10	BLACK SABBATH	Black Sabbath (Vertigo)
-	11	GETTING TO THIS	Blodwyn Pig (Island)
11	12	ABBEY ROAD	Beatles (Apple)
12	13	MOTOWN CHARTBUSTERS VOL 3	Various Artists (Tamla Motown)
17	14	WILLY AND THE POOR BOYS	Creedence Clearwater Revival (Liberty)
16	15	SENTIMENTAL JOURNEY	Ringo Starr (Apple)
-	16	REGGAE CHARTBUSTERS	Various Artists (Trojan)
-	17	CRICKLEWOOD GREEN	Ten Years After (Deram)
15	18	JIM REEVES' GOLDEN RECORDS	Jim Reeves (RCA International)
-	19	A MEMORIAL 1944-1969	Glenn Miller (RCA)
-	20	LET'S BE FRIENDS	Elvis Presley (RCA Camden)

Unlike Morrison and Zappa, Simon & Garfunkel never had problems charting. *Bridge Over Troubled Water* leapt to No.1 and would remain there till June, when the Beatles would temporarily dislodge it. By mid-August *Bridge* would be top again, and remain so, but for a brief disruption from the Moodies, till October. Never leaving the Top 5, it would return to No.1 in March 1971, and again that July-August. It would still be in the Top 10 in September 1972, more than 2 AND A HARRRRRRF years after entering it.

9 May 1970

last week	this week		
1	1	BRIDGE OVER TROUBLED WATER	Simon & Garfunkel (CBS)
2	2	McCARTNEY	Paul McCartney (Apple)
3	3	ANDY WILLIAMS' GREATEST HITS	Andy Williams (CBS)
4	4	LED ZEPPELIN II	Led Zeppelin (Atlantic)
5	5	EASY RIDER	Soundtrack (Stateside)
8	6	TOM	Tom Jones (Decca)
6	7	PAINT YOUR WAGON	Soundtrack (Paramount)
10	8	BLACK SABBATH	Black Sabbath (Vertigo)
-	8	BENEFIT	Jethro Tull (Chrysalis)
11	10	GETTING TO THIS	Blodwyn Pig (Island)
12	11	ABBEY ROAD	Beatles (Apple)
17	12	CRICKLEWOOD GREEN	Ten Years After (Deram)
7	13	FILL YOUR HEAD WITH ROCK	Various Artists (CBS)
13	14	MOTOWN CHARTBUSTERS VOL 3	Various Artists (Tamla Motown)
-	15	BEST OF THE SEEKERS	Seekers (Columbia)
9	16	CHICAGO	Chicago (CBS)
14	17	WILLY AND THE POOR BOYS	Creedence Clearwater Revival (Liberty)
-	18	SACHA	Sacha Distel (Warner Bros.)
15	19	SENTIMENTAL JOURNEY	Ringo Starr (Apple)
-	20	MORRISON HOTEL	Doors (Elektra)

16 May 1970

last week	this week		
1	1	BRIDGE OVER TROUBLED WATER	Simon & Garfunkel (CBS)
2	2	McCARTNEY	Paul McCartney (Apple)
-	3	LET IT BE	Beatles (Apple)
3	4	ANDY WILLIAMS' GREATEST HITS	Andy Williams (CBS)
8	5	BENEFIT	Jethro Tull (Chrysalis)
5	6	EASY RIDER	Soundtrack (Stateside)
4	7	LED ZEPPELIN II	Led Zeppelin (Atlantic)
6	8	TOM	Tom Jones (Decca)
12	9	CRICKLEWOOD GREEN	Ten Years After (Deram)
17	10	WILLY AND THE POOR BOYS	Creedence Clearwater Revival (Liberty)
13	10	FILL YOUR HEAD WITH ROCK	Various Artists (CBS)
7	12	PAINT YOUR WAGON	Soundtrack (Paramount)
-	13	THE WORLD BEATERS SING THE WORLD BEATERS	England Football World Cup Squad (Pye)
8	14	BLACK SABBATH	Black Sabbath (Vertigo)
14	15	MOTOWN CHARTBUSTERS VOL 3	Various Artists (Tamla Motown)
-	16	REGGAE CHARTBUSTERS	Various Artists (Trojan)
-	17	LET'S BE FRIENDS	Elvis Presley (RCA Camden)
10	18	GETTING TO THIS	Blodwyn Pig (Island)
19	19	SENTIMENTAL JOURNEY	Ringo Starr (Apple)
11	20	ABBEY ROAD	Beatles (Apple)

23 May 1970

last week	this week		
1	1	BRIDGE OVER TROUBLED WATER	Simon & Garfunkel (CBS)
3	2	LET IT BE	Beatles (Apple)
2	3	McCARTNEY	Paul McCartney (Apple)
4	4	ANDY WILLIAMS' GREATEST HITS	Andy Williams (CBS)
5	5	BENEFIT	Jethro Tull (Chrysalis)
6	6	EASY RIDER	Soundtrack (Stateside)
12	6	PAINT YOUR WAGON	Soundtrack (Paramount)
9	8	CRICKLEWOOD GREEN	Ten Years After (Deram)
13	9	THE WORLD BEATERS SING THE WORLD BEATERS	England Football World Cup Squad (Pye)
8	9	TOM	Tom Jones (Decca)
14	11	BLACK SABBATH	Black Sabbath (Vertigo)
17	12	LET'S BE FRIENDS	Elvis Presley (RCA Camden)
7	13	LED ZEPPELIN II	Led Zeppelin (Atlantic)
-	14	IN THE WAKE OF POSEIDON	King Crimson (Island)
20	15	ABBEY ROAD	Beatles (Apple)
10	16	WILLY AND THE POOR BOYS	Creedence Clearwater Revival (Liberty)
10	16	FILL YOUR HEAD WITH ROCK	Various Artists (CBS)
15	18	MOTOWN CHARTBUSTERS VOL 3	Various Artists (Tamla Motown)
-	19	DIANA ROSS AND THE SUPREMES' GREATEST HITS VOL 2	Diana Ross & the Supremes (Tamla Motown)
-	19	BEST OF THE SEEKERS	Seekers (Columbia)

30 May 1970

last week	this week		
1	1	BRIDGE OVER TROUBLED WATER	Simon & Garfunkel (CBS)
2	2	LET IT BE	Beatles (Apple)
3	3	McCARTNEY	Paul McCartney (Apple)
4	4	ANDY WILLIAMS' GREATEST HITS	Andy Williams (CBS)
5	4	BENEFIT	Jethro Tull (Chrysalis)
9	6	TOM	Tom Jones (Decca)
13	7	LED ZEPPELIN II	Led Zeppelin (Atlantic)
9	8	THE WORLD BEATERS SING THE WORLD BEATERS	England Football World Cup Squad (Pye)
6	9	EASY RIDER	Soundtrack (Stateside)
11	10	BLACK SABBATH	Black Sabbath (Vertigo)
6	11	PAINT YOUR WAGON	Soundtrack (Paramount)
16	12	FILL YOUR HEAD WITH ROCK	Various Artists (CBS)
8	13	CRICKLEWOOD GREEN	Ten Years After (Deram)
-	14	WATERTOWN	Frank Sinatra (Reprise)
-	15	DEJA VU	Crosby, Stills, Nash & Young (Atlantic)
16	16	WILLY AND THE POOR BOYS	Creedence Clearwater Revival (Liberty)
12	17	LET'S BE FRIENDS	Elvis Presley (RCA Camden)
15	18	ABBEY ROAD	Beatles (Apple)
14	19	IN THE WAKE OF POSEIDON	King Crimson (Island)
18	20	MOTOWN CHARTBUSTERS VOL 3	Various Artists (Tamla Motown)

6 June 1970

last week	this week		
2	1	LET IT BE	Beatles (Apple)
1	2	BRIDGE OVER TROUBLED WATER	Simon & Garfunkel (CBS)
3	3	McCARTNEY	Paul McCartney (Apple)
4	4	ANDY WILLIAMS' GREATEST HITS	Andy Williams (CBS)
9	5	EASY RIDER	Soundtrack (Stateside)
4	6	BENEFIT	Jethro Tull (Chrysalis)
15	7	DEJA VU	Crosby, Stills, Nash & Young (Atlantic)
7	8	LED ZEPPELIN II	Led Zeppelin (Atlantic)
-	9	LIVE AT LEEDS	Who (Track)
11	10	PAINT YOUR WAGON	Soundtrack (Paramount)
8	11	THE WORLD BEATERS SING THE WORLD BEATERS	England Football World Cup Squad (Pye)
19	12	IN THE WAKE OF POSEIDON	King Crimson (Island)
10	13	BLACK SABBATH	Black Sabbath (Vertigo)
6	14	TOM	Tom Jones (Decca)
13	15	CRICKLEWOOD GREEN	Ten Years After (Deram)
12	16	FILL YOUR HEAD WITH ROCK	Various Artists (CBS)
17	17	LET'S BE FRIENDS	Elvis Presley (RCA Camden)
16	18	WILLY AND THE POOR BOYS	Creedence Clearwater Revival (Liberty)
20	19	MOTOWN CHARTBUSTERS VOL 3	Various Artists (Tamla Motown)
18	20	ABBEY ROAD	Beatles (Apple)

13 June 1970

last week	this week		
1	1	LET IT BE	Beatles (Apple)
2	2	BRIDGE OVER TROUBLED WATER	Simon & Garfunkel (CBS)
3	3	McCARTNEY	Paul McCartney (Apple)
9	4	LIVE AT LEEDS	Who (Track)
5	5	EASY RIDER	Soundtrack (Stateside)
4	6	ANDY WILLIAMS' GREATEST HITS	Andy Williams (CBS)
7	7	DEJA VU	Crosby, Stills, Nash & Young (Atlantic)
11	8	THE WORLD BEATERS SING THE WORLD BEATERS	England Football World Cup Squad (Pye)
10	9	PAINT YOUR WAGON	Soundtrack (Paramount)
8	10	LED ZEPPELIN II	Led Zeppelin (Atlantic)
14	11	TOM	Tom Jones (Decca)
6	12	BENEFIT	Jethro Tull (Chrysalis)
15	13	CRICKLEWOOD GREEN	Ten Years After (Deram)
12	14	IN THE WAKE OF POSEIDON	King Crimson (Island)
18	15	WILLY AND THE POOR BOYS	Creedence Clearwater Revival (Liberty)
-	16	DIANA ROSS AND THE SUPREMES' GREATEST HITS VOL 2	Diana Ross & the Supremes (Tamla Motown)
-	17	HOT RATS	Frank Zappa (Reprise)
-	18	REGGAE CHARTBUSTERS	Various Artists (Trojan)
13	19	BLACK SABBATH	Black Sabbath (Vertigo)
17	20	LET'S BE FRIENDS	Elvis Presley (RCA Camden)

The Beatles were disintegrating, but they were spilling all over the charts in the process. May 16 shows McCartney at No.2 with *Let It Be* at No.3, and, echoing that pattern lower down, Ringo Starr's album at No.19, immediately above *Abbey Road*. Allen Klein plus John George and Ringo had tried to delay McCartney's album so as to not to detract from sales of *Let It Be*. Ringo was sent to Paul's house to tell him. Paul flew into such a fearful bate that they all backed down.

June – July 1970

20 June 1970

last	this		
1	1	LET IT BE	Beatles (Apple)
2	2	BRIDGE OVER TROUBLED WATER	
			Simon & Garfunkel (CBS)
3	3	McCARTNEY	Paul McCartney (Apple)
4	4	LIVE AT LEEDS	Who (Track)
5	5	EASY RIDER	Soundtrack (Stateside)
7	6	DEJA VU Crosby, Stills, Nash & Young (Atlantic)
6	7	ANDY WILLIAMS' GREATEST HITS	
			Andy Williams (CBS)
10	8	LED ZEPPELIN II	Led Zeppelin (Atlantic)
8	9	THE WORLD BEATERS SING THE WORLD BEATERS	
			England Football World Cup Squad (Pye)
14	10	IN THE WAKE OF POSEIDON	
			King Crimson (Island)
9	11	PAINT YOUR WAGON	Soundtrack (Paramount)
12	12	BENEFIT	Jethro Tull (Chrysalis)
-	13	LADIES OF THE CANYON Joni Mitchell (Reprise)
19	14	BLACK SABBATH	Black Sabbath (Vertigo)
11	15	TOM	Tom Jones (Decca)
-	16	BUMPERS	Various Artists (Island)
-	17	FILL YOUR HEAD WITH ROCK	
			Various Artists (CBS)
17	18	HOT RATS	Frank Zappa (Reprise)
18	19	REGGAE CHARTBUSTERS	
			Various Artists (Trojan)
15	20	WILLY AND THE POOR BOYS	
			Creedence Clearwater Revival (Liberty)

27 June 1970

last	this		
2	1	BRIDGE OVER TROUBLED WATER	
			Simon & Garfunkel (CBS)
1	2	LET IT BE	Beatles (Apple)
4	3	LIVE AT LEEDS	Who (Track)
3	4	McCARTNEY	Paul McCartney (Apple)
5	5	EASY RIDER	Soundtrack (Stateside)
7	6	ANDY WILLIAMS' GREATEST HITS	
			Andy Williams (CBS)
6	7	DEJA VU Crosby, Stills, Nash & Young (Atlantic)
8	8	LED ZEPPELIN II	Led Zeppelin (Atlantic)
-	9	CAN'T HELP FALLING IN LOVE	
			Andy Williams (CBS)
9	10	THE WORLD BEATERS SING THE WORLD BEATERS	
			England Football World Cup Squad (Pye)
16	11	BUMPERS	Various Artists (Island)
-	12	LIVE CREAM	Cream (Polydor)
-	13	DEEP PURPLE IN ROCK	Deep Purple (Harvest)
12	14	BENEFIT	Jethro Tull (Chrysalis)
-	15	FIVE BRIDGES	Nice (Charisma)
-	16	HERB ALPERT'S GREATEST HITS	
			Herb Alpert & the Tijuana Brass (A&M)
10	17	IN THE WAKE OF POSEIDON	
			King Crimson (Island)
11	18	PAINT YOUR WAGON	Soundtrack (Paramount)
13	19	LADIES OF THE CANYON	
			Joni Mitchell (Reprise)
-	20	THE SOUND OF MUSIC	Soundtrack (RCA)

4 July 1970

last	this		
1	1	BRIDGE OVER TROUBLED WATER	
			Simon & Garfunkel (CBS)
2	2	LET IT BE	Beatles (Apple)
5	3	EASY RIDER	Soundtrack (Stateside)
3	4	LIVE AT LEEDS	Who (Track)
13	5	DEEP PURPLE IN ROCK	Deep Purple (Harvest)
4	6	McCARTNEY	Paul McCartney (Apple)
11	7	BUMPERS	Various Artists (Island)
-	8	SELF PORTRAIT	Bob Dylan (CBS)
12	9	LIVE CREAM	Cream (Polydor)
7	10	DEJA VU Crosby, Stills, Nash & Young (Atlantic)
9	11	CAN'T HELP FALLING IN LOVE	
			Andy Williams (CBS)
8	12	LED ZEPPELIN II	Led Zeppelin (Atlantic)
15	13	FIVE BRIDGES	Nice (Charisma)
6	14	ANDY WILLIAMS' GREATEST HITS	
			Andy Williams (CBS)
18	15	PAINT YOUR WAGON	Soundtrack (Paramount)
-	16	BAND OF GYPSIES	Jimi Hendrix (Track)
17	17	IN THE WAKE OF POSEIDON	
			King Crimson (Island)
19	18	LADIES OF THE CANYON	
			Joni Mitchell (Reprise)
14	19	BENEFIT	Jethro Tull (Chrysalis)
-	20	PICNIC - A BREATH OF FRESH AIR	
			Various Artists (Harvest)

11 July 1970

last	this		
1	1	BRIDGE OVER TROUBLED WATER	
			Simon & Garfunkel (CBS)
2	2	LET IT BE	Beatles (Apple)
4	3	LIVE AT LEEDS	Who (Track)
8	4	SELF PORTRAIT	Bob Dylan (CBS)
7	5	BUMPERS	Various Artists (Island)
3	6	EASY RIDER	Soundtrack (Stateside)
5	7	DEEP PURPLE IN ROCK	Deep Purple (Harvest)
13	8	FIVE BRIDGES	Nice (Charisma)
6	9	McCARTNEY	Paul McCartney (Apple)
-	10	FIRE AND WATER	Free (Island)
9	11	LIVE CREAM	Cream (Polydor)
12	12	LED ZEPPELIN II	Led Zeppelin (Atlantic)
16	13	BAND OF GYPSIES	Jimi Hendrix (Track)
10	14	DEJA VU Crosby, Stills, Nash & Young (Atlantic)
11	15	CAN'T HELP FALLING IN LOVE	
			Andy Williams (CBS)
15	16	PAINT YOUR WAGON	Soundtrack (Paramount)
14	17	ANDY WILLIAMS' GREATEST HITS	
			Andy Williams (CBS)
20	18	PICNIC - A BREATH OF FRESH AIR	
			Various Artists (Harvest)
-	19	THIRD	Soft Machine (CBS)
-	20	WE MADE IT HAPPEN	
			Engelbert Humperdinck (Decca)

18 July 1970

last	this		
2	1	LET IT BE	Beatles (Apple)
1	2	BRIDGE OVER TROUBLED WATER	
			Simon & Garfunkel (CBS)
4	3	SELF PORTRAIT	Bob Dylan (CBS)
10	4	FIRE AND WATER	Free (Island)
5	5	BUMPERS	Various Artists (Island)
9	6	McCARTNEY	Paul McCartney (Apple)
11	7	LIVE CREAM	Cream (Polydor)
6	8	EASY RIDER	Soundtrack (Stateside)
14	9	DEJA VU Crosby, Stills, Nash & Young (Atlantic)
7	10	DEEP PURPLE IN ROCK	Deep Purple (Harvest)
8	11	FIVE BRIDGES	Nice (Charisma)
13	12	BAND OF GYPSIES	Jimi Hendrix (Track)
12	13	LED ZEPPELIN II	Led Zeppelin (Atlantic)
3	14	LIVE AT LEEDS	Who (Track)
16	15	PAINT YOUR WAGON	Soundtrack (Paramount)
15	16	CAN'T HELP FALLING IN LOVE	
			Andy Williams (CBS)
17	17	ANDY WILLIAMS' GREATEST HITS	
			Andy Williams (CBS)
18	18	PICNIC - A BREATH OF FRESH AIR	
			Various Artists (Harvest)
20	19	WE MADE IT HAPPEN	
			Engelbert Humperdinck (Decca)
-	20	FILL YOUR HEAD WITH ROCK	
			Various Artists (CBS)

25 July 1970

last	this		
2	1	BRIDGE OVER TROUBLED WATER	
			Simon & Garfunkel (CBS)
4	2	FIRE AND WATER	Free (Island)
1	3	LET IT BE	Beatles (Apple)
3	4	SELF PORTRAIT	Bob Dylan (CBS)
5	5	BUMPERS	Various Artists (Island)
10	6	DEEP PURPLE IN ROCK	Deep Purple (Harvest)
11	7	FIVE BRIDGES	Nice (Charisma)
7	8	LIVE CREAM	Cream (Polydor)
6	9	McCARTNEY	Paul McCartney (Apple)
8	10	EASY RIDER	Soundtrack (Stateside)
15	11	PAINT YOUR WAGON	Soundtrack (Paramount)
-	12	ON STAGE: FEBRUARY 1970	
			Elvis Presley (RCA)
14	13	LIVE AT LEEDS	Who (Track)
9	14	DEJA VU Crosby, Stills, Nash & Young (Atlantic)
13	15	LED ZEPPELIN II	Led Zeppelin (Atlantic)
12	16	BAND OF GYPSIES	Jimi Hendrix (Track)
-	17	FULL HOUSE	Fairport Convention (Island)
18	18	PICNIC - A BREATH OF FRESH AIR	
			Various Artists (Harvest)
17	19	ANDY WILLIAMS' GREATEST HITS	
			Andy Williams (CBS)
-	20	STEPPENWOLF LIVE	Steppenwolf (Dunhill)

The Who's vivid *Live At Leeds* (their first album since *Tommy*) had charted earlier in June. Now it rose to 3 before suddenly plunging, from 3 to 14 in one week. Pete Townshend, interviewed this spring, had said of his work: "If you look at any form of art, you can find something in the best of pop which completely eliminates the old form... If you think Mahler's 9th Symphony is overwhelming, I can play you a tape I made in my studio at home which is MORE overwhelming."

August – September 1970

1 August 1970

last week	this week		
3	1	LET IT BE	Beatles (Apple)
4	2	SELF PORTRAIT	Bob Dylan (CBS)
1	3	BRIDGE OVER TROUBLED WATER	Simon & Garfunkel (CBS)
2	4	FIRE AND WATER	Free (Island)
9	5	McCARTNEY	Paul McCartney (Apple)
6	6	DEEP PURPLE IN ROCK	Deep Purple (Harvest)
15	7	LED ZEPPELIN II	Led Zeppelin (Atlantic)
10	8	EASY RIDER	Soundtrack (Stateside)
7	9	FIVE BRIDGES	Nice (Charisma)
11	10	PAINT YOUR WAGON	Soundtrack (Paramount)
8	11	LIVE CREAM	Cream (Polydor)
12	12	ON STAGE: FEBRUARY 1970	Elvis Presley (RCA)
19	13	ANDY WILLIAMS' GREATEST HITS	Andy Williams (CBS)
5	14	BUMPERS	Various Artists (Island)
13	15	LIVE AT LEEDS	Who (Track)
14	16	DEJA VU Crosby, Stills, Nash & Young (Atlantic)	
-	17	MOTOWN CHARTBUSTERS VOL 3	Various Artists (Tamla Motown)
16	18	BAND OF GYPSIES	Jimi Hendrix (Track)
-	19	WOODSTOCK	Soundtrack (Atlantic)
-	20	CRICKLEWOOD GREEN Ten Years After (Deram)	

8 August 1970

1	1	LET IT BE	Beatles (Apple)
3	2	BRIDGE OVER TROUBLED WATER	Simon & Garfunkel (CBS)
4	3	FIRE AND WATER	Free (Island)
12	4	ON STAGE: FEBRUARY 1970	Elvis Presley (RCA)
2	5	SELF PORTRAIT	Bob Dylan (CBS)
6	6	DEEP PURPLE IN ROCK	Deep Purple (Harvest)
5	7	McCARTNEY	Paul McCartney (Apple)
7	8	PAINT YOUR WAGON	Soundtrack (Paramount)
9	9	LED ZEPPELIN II	Led Zeppelin (Atlantic)
14	10	BUMPERS	Various Artists (Island)
8	11	EASY RIDER	Soundtrack (Stateside)
9	12	FIVE BRIDGES	Nice (Charisma)
13	13	ANDY WILLIAMS' GREATEST HITS	Andy Williams (CBS)
16	14	DEJA VU Crosby, Stills, Nash & Young (Atlantic)	
11	15	LIVE CREAM	Cream (Polydor)
15	16	LIVE AT LEEDS	Who (Track)
17	17	A QUESTION OF BALANCE	Moody Blues (Threshold)
19	18	WOODSTOCK	Soundtrack (Atlantic)
-	19	FULL HOUSE	Fairport Convention (Island)
-	20	JOHN BARLEYCORN MUST DIE Traffic (Island)	

15 August 1970

2	1	BRIDGE OVER TROUBLED WATER	Simon & Garfunkel (CBS)
1	2	LET IT BE	Beatles (Apple)
3	3	FIRE AND WATER	Free (Island)
4	4	ON STAGE: FEBRUARY 1970	Elvis Presley (RCA)
17	5	A QUESTION OF BALANCE	Moody Blues (Threshold)
5	6	SELF PORTRAIT	Bob Dylan (CBS)
6	7	DEEP PURPLE IN ROCK	Deep Purple (Harvest)
9	8	LED ZEPPELIN II	Led Zeppelin (Atlantic)
8	9	PAINT YOUR WAGON	Soundtrack (Paramount)
11	10	EASY RIDER	Soundtrack (Stateside)
7	11	McCARTNEY	Paul McCartney (Apple)
10	12	BUMPERS	Various Artists (Island)
13	13	ANDY WILLIAMS' GREATEST HITS	Andy Williams (CBS)
16	14	LIVE AT LEEDS	Who (Track)
-	15	THE WORLD OF JOHNNY CASH	Johnny Cash (CBS)
-	16	STEPPENWOLF LIVE	Steppenwolf (Dunhill)
20	17	JOHN BARLEYCORN MUST DIE Traffic (Island)	
14	18	DEJA VU Crosby, Stills, Nash & Young (Atlantic)	
12	19	FIVE BRIDGES	Nice (Charisma)
15	20	LIVE CREAM	Cream (Polydor)

22 August 1970

1	1	BRIDGE OVER TROUBLED WATER	Simon & Garfunkel (CBS)
5	2	A QUESTION OF BALANCE	Moody Blues (Threshold)
4	3	ON STAGE: FEBRUARY 1970	Elvis Presley (RCA)
2	4	LET IT BE	Beatles (Apple)
3	5	FIRE AND WATER	Free (Island)
6	6	SELF PORTRAIT	Bob Dylan (CBS)
9	7	PAINT YOUR WAGON	Soundtrack (Paramount)
7	8	DEEP PURPLE IN ROCK	Deep Purple (Harvest)
8	9	LED ZEPPELIN II	Led Zeppelin (Atlantic)
10	10	EASY RIDER	Soundtrack (Stateside)
13	11	ANDY WILLIAMS' GREATEST HITS	Andy Williams (CBS)
11	12	McCARTNEY	Paul McCartney (Apple)
-	13	BLOOD SWEAT AND TEARS	Blood Sweat & Tears (CBS)
15	14	THE WORLD OF JOHNNY CASH	Johnny Cash (CBS)
17	15	JOHN BARLEYCORN MUST DIE Traffic (Island)	
12	16	BUMPERS	Various Artists (Island)
-	17	MUNGO JERRY	Mungo Jerry (Dawn)
20	18	LIVE CREAM	Cream (Polydor)
19	19	FIVE BRIDGES	Nice (Charisma)
18	20	DEJA VU Crosby, Stills, Nash & Young (Atlantic)	

29 August 1970

1	1	BRIDGE OVER TROUBLED WATER	Simon & Garfunkel (CBS)
2	2	A QUESTION OF BALANCE	Moody Blues (Threshold)
4	3	LET IT BE	Beatles (Apple)
3	4	ON STAGE: FEBRUARY 1970	Elvis Presley (RCA)
5	5	FIRE AND WATER	Free (Island)
8	6	DEEP PURPLE IN ROCK	Deep Purple (Harvest)
9	7	LED ZEPPELIN II	Led Zeppelin (Atlantic)
7	8	PAINT YOUR WAGON	Soundtrack (Paramount)
6	9	SELF PORTRAIT	Bob Dylan (CBS)
16	10	BUMPERS	Various Artists (Island)
10	11	EASY RIDER	Soundtrack (Stateside)
14	12	THE WORLD OF JOHNNY CASH	Johnny Cash (CBS)
12	13	McCARTNEY	Paul McCartney (Apple)
13	14	BLOOD SWEAT AND TEARS	Blood Sweat & Tears (CBS)
11	15	ANDY WILLIAMS' GREATEST HITS	Andy Williams (CBS)
15	16	JOHN BARLEYCORN MUST DIE Traffic (Island)	
-	17	LIVE AT LEEDS	Who (Track)
-	18	WOODSTOCK	Soundtrack (Atlantic)
18	19	LIVE CREAM	Cream (Polydor)
20	20	DEJA VU Crosby, Stills, Nash & Young (Atlantic)	

5 September 1970

2	1	A QUESTION OF BALANCE	Moody Blues (Threshold)
1	2	BRIDGE OVER TROUBLED WATER	Simon & Garfunkel (CBS)
3	3	LET IT BE	Beatles (Apple)
4	4	ON STAGE: FEBRUARY 1970	Elvis Presley (RCA)
5	5	FIRE AND WATER	Free (Island)
7	6	LED ZEPPELIN II	Led Zeppelin (Atlantic)
-	7	SOMETHING	Shirley Bassey (United Artists)
6	8	DEEP PURPLE IN ROCK	Deep Purple (Harvest)
11	9	EASY RIDER	Soundtrack (Stateside)
-	10	COSMO'S FACTORY	Creedence Clearwater Revival (Liberty)
8	11	PAINT YOUR WAGON	Soundtrack (Paramount)
15	12	ANDY WILLIAMS' GREATEST HITS	Andy Williams (CBS)
13	13	McCARTNEY	Paul McCartney (Apple)
9	14	SELF PORTRAIT	Bob Dylan (CBS)
10	15	BUMPERS	Various Artists (Island)
12	16	THE WORLD OF JOHNNY CASH	Johnny Cash (CBS)
18	17	WOODSTOCK	Soundtrack (Atlantic)
14	18	BLOOD SWEAT AND TEARS	Blood Sweat & Tears (CBS)
19	19	LIVE CREAM	Cream (Polydor)
16	20	JOHN BARLEYCORN MUST DIE Traffic (Island)	

Dylan had issued *Self Portrait*, a double album of other people's songs and far too many musicians, and although it was in the charts, suddenly Bob Dylan wasn't hip any more. Still very hip were the stars of this August's Isle Of Wight Music Festival, Jimi Hendrix and the Doors. Yet while 1970's Doors' album, *Morrison Hotel*, was up to standard, Jim Morrison himself was by this point giving bleary performances verging on self-parody. Hendrix gave a great performance. It was, in the event, his last.

67

September – October 1970

12 September 1970

last this
week

last	this		
1	1	A QUESTION OF BALANCE	Moody Blues (Threshold)
2	2	BRIDGE OVER TROUBLED WATER	Simon & Garfunkel (CBS)
4	3	ON STAGE: FEBRUARY 1970	Elvis Presley (RCA)
3	4	LET IT BE	Beatles (Apple)
-	5	'GET YOUR YA-YA'S OUT!'	Rolling Stones (Decca)
5	6	FIRE AND WATER	Free (Island)
11	7	PAINT YOUR WAGON	Soundtrack (Paramount)
10	8	COSMO'S FACTORY	Creedence Clearwater Revival (Liberty)
9	9	EASY RIDER	Soundtrack (Stateside)
16	10	THE WORLD OF JOHNNY CASH	Johnny Cash (CBS)
7	11	SOMETHING	Shirley Bassey (United Artists)
8	12	DEEP PURPLE IN ROCK	Deep Purple (Harvest)
6	13	LED ZEPPELIN II	Led Zeppelin (Atlantic)
13	14	McCARTNEY	Paul McCartney (Apple)
15	15	BUMPERS	Various Artists (Island)
14	16	SELF PORTRAIT	Bob Dylan (CBS)
12	17	ANDY WILLIAMS' GREATEST HITS	Andy Williams (CBS)
18	18	BLOOD SWEAT AND TEARS	Blood Sweat & Tears (CBS)
20	19	JOHN BARLEYCORN MUST DIE	Traffic (Island)
-	20	CAN'T HELP FALLING IN LOVE	Andy Williams (CBS)

19 September 1970

1	1	A QUESTION OF BALANCE	Moody Blues (Threshold)
2	2	BRIDGE OVER TROUBLED WATER	Simon & Garfunkel (CBS)
8	3	COSMO'S FACTORY	Creedence Clearwater Revival (Liberty)
3	4	ON STAGE: FEBRUARY 1970	Elvis Presley (RCA)
5	5	'GET YOUR YA-YA'S OUT!'	Rolling Stones (Decca)
4	6	LET IT BE	Beatles (Apple)
11	7	SOMETHING	Shirley Bassey (United Artists)
7	8	PAINT YOUR WAGON	Soundtrack (Paramount)
12	9	DEEP PURPLE IN ROCK	Deep Purple (Harvest)
10	10	LED ZEPPELIN II	Led Zeppelin (Atlantic)
13	11	THE WORLD OF JOHNNY CASH	Johnny Cash (CBS)
6	12	FIRE AND WATER	Free (Island)
9	13	EASY RIDER	Soundtrack (Stateside)
20	14	CAN'T HELP FALLING IN LOVE	Andy Williams (CBS)
-	15	ERIC CLAPTON	Eric Clapton (Polydor)
14	16	McCARTNEY	Paul McCartney (Apple)
16	17	SELF PORTRAIT	Bob Dylan (CBS)
-	18	MAD DOGS AND ENGLISHMEN	Joe Cocker (A&M)
17	19	ANDY WILLIAMS' GREATEST HITS	Andy Williams (CBS)
-	19	THE SPINNERS ARE IN TOWN	Spinners (Fontana)

26 September 1970

2	1	BRIDGE OVER TROUBLED WATER	Simon & Garfunkel (CBS)
3	2	COSMO'S FACTORY	Creedence Clearwater Revival (Liberty)
5	3	'GET YOUR YA-YA'S OUT!'	Rolling Stones (Decca)
1	4	A QUESTION OF BALANCE	Moody Blues (Threshold)
4	5	ON STAGE: FEBRUARY 1970	Elvis Presley (RCA)
10	6	LED ZEPPELIN II	Led Zeppelin (Atlantic)
8	7	PAINT YOUR WAGON	Soundtrack (Paramount)
7	8	SOMETHING	Shirley Bassey (United Artists)
6	9	LET IT BE	Beatles (Apple)
9	10	DEEP PURPLE IN ROCK	Deep Purple (Harvest)
-	11	MOTOWN CHARTBUSTERS VOL 3	Various Artists (Tamla Motown)
-	12	THE BEACH BOYS' GREATEST HITS	Beach Boys (Capitol)
14	13	CAN'T HELP FALLING IN LOVE	Andy Williams (CBS)
12	14	FIRE AND WATER	Free (Island)
19	15	ANDY WILLIAMS' GREATEST HITS	Andy Williams (CBS)
-	15	THE EVERLY BROTHERS' ORIGINAL GREATEST HITS	Everly Brothers (CBS)
-	17	PARANOID	Black Sabbath (Vertigo)
18	18	MAD DOGS AND ENGLISHMEN	Joe Cocker (A&M)
-	19	OVER AND OVER	Nana Mouskouri (Fontana)
13	20	EASY RIDER	Soundtrack (Stateside)

3 October 1970

1	1	BRIDGE OVER TROUBLED WATER	Simon & Garfunkel (CBS)
3	2	'GET YOUR YA-YA'S OUT!'	Rolling Stones (Decca)
2	3	COSMO'S FACTORY	Creedence Clearwater Revival (Liberty)
4	4	A QUESTION OF BALANCE	Moody Blues (Threshold)
10	5	DEEP PURPLE IN ROCK	Deep Purple (Harvest)
17	6	PARANOID	Black Sabbath (Vertigo)
5	7	ON STAGE: FEBRUARY 1970	Elvis Presley (RCA)
6	8	LED ZEPPELIN II	Led Zeppelin (Atlantic)
7	9	PAINT YOUR WAGON	Soundtrack (Paramount)
12	10	THE BEACH BOYS' GREATEST HITS	Beach Boys (Capitol)
8	11	SOMETHING	Shirley Bassey (United Artists)
13	12	CAN'T HELP FALLING IN LOVE	Andy Williams (CBS)
9	13	LET IT BE	Beatles (Apple)
15	14	THE EVERLY BROTHERS' ORIGINAL GREATEST HITS	Everly Brothers (CBS)
11	15	MOTOWN CHARTBUSTERS VOL 3	Various Artists (Tamla Motown)
18	16	MAD DOGS AND ENGLISHMEN	Joe Cocker (A&M)
20	17	EASY RIDER	Soundtrack (Stateside)
15	18	ANDY WILLIAMS' GREATEST HITS	Andy Williams (CBS)
-	19	THE WORLD OF JOHNNY CASH	Johnny Cash (CBS)
-	20	CANDLES IN THE RAIN	Melanie (Buddah)

10 October 1970

1	1	BRIDGE OVER TROUBLED WATER	Simon & Garfunkel (CBS)
2	2	'GET YOUR YA-YA'S OUT!'	Rolling Stones (Decca)
4	3	A QUESTION OF BALANCE	Moody Blues (Threshold)
6	4	PARANOID	Black Sabbath (Vertigo)
8	5	LED ZEPPELIN II	Led Zeppelin (Atlantic)
3	6	COSMO'S FACTORY	Creedence Clearwater Revival (Liberty)
5	7	DEEP PURPLE IN ROCK	Deep Purple (Harvest)
11	8	SOMETHING	Shirley Bassey (United Artists)
20	9	CANDLES IN THE RAIN	Melanie (Buddah)
14	10	THE EVERLY BROTHERS' ORIGINAL GREATEST HITS	Everly Brothers (CBS)
13	11	LET IT BE	Beatles (Apple)
9	12	PAINT YOUR WAGON	Soundtrack (Paramount)
17	13	EASY RIDER	Soundtrack (Stateside)
10	14	THE BEACH BOYS' GREATEST HITS	Beach Boys (Capitol)
7	15	ON STAGE: FEBRUARY 1970	Elvis Presley (RCA)
12	16	CAN'T HELP FALLING IN LOVE	Andy Williams (CBS)
19	17	WORLD OF JOHNNY CASH	Johnny Cash (CBS)
15	18	MOTOWN CHARTBUSTERS VOL 3	Various Artists (Tamla Motown)
-	19	BAND OF GYPSIES	Jimi Hendrix (Track)
18	20	ANDY WILLIAMS' GREATEST HITS	Andy Williams (CBS)

17 October 1970

4	1	PARANOID	Black Sabbath (Vertigo)
1	2	BRIDGE OVER TROUBLED WATER	Simon & Garfunkel (CBS)
2	3	'GET YOUR YA-YA'S OUT!'	Rolling Stones (Decca)
3	4	A QUESTION OF BALANCE	Moody Blues (Threshold)
9	5	CANDLES IN THE RAIN	Melanie (Buddah)
5	6	LED ZEPPELIN II	Led Zeppelin (Atlantic)
6	7	COSMO'S FACTORY	Creedence Clearwater Revival (Liberty)
7	8	DEEP PURPLE IN ROCK	Deep Purple (Harvest)
-	9	ROCK BUSTER	Various Artists (CBS)
12	10	PAINT YOUR WAGON	Soundtrack (Paramount)
-	11	ATOM HEART MOTHER	Pink Floyd (Harvest)
-	12	MOTOWN CHARTBUSTERS VOL 4	Various Artists (Tamla Motown)
8	13	SOMETHING	Shirley Bassey (United Artists)
11	14	LET IT BE	Beatles (Apple)
14	15	THE BEACH BOYS' GREATEST HITS	Beach Boys (Capitol)
15	16	ON STAGE: FEBRUARY 1970	Elvis Presley (RCA)
10	17	THE EVERLY BROTHERS' ORIGINAL GREATEST HITS	Everly Brothers (CBS)
-	18	FUTURE BLUES	Canned Heat (Liberty)
-	19	STAGE FRIGHT	Band (Capitol)
19	20	BAND OF GYPSIES	Jimi Hendrix (Track)

James Marshall Hendrix died on September 18. Sixteen days later, on October 4, Janis Joplin died of a heroin overdose. Hendrix had once said: "It's funny the way most people love the dead. Once you are dead you are made for life." Yet Hendrix's *Band Of Gypsies*, entering the chart on October 10, dropped out again only two weeks later. The posthumous release of Hendrix albums - many times more than ever issued in his lifetime - was slow to happen. Nor did death deliver Janis Joplin to the charts.

October – November 1970

24 October 1970

last week	this week		
1	1	PARANOID	Black Sabbath (Vertigo)
2	2	BRIDGE OVER TROUBLED WATER	Simon & Garfunkel (CBS)
3	3	'GET YOUR YA-YA'S OUT!'	Rolling Stones (Decca)
12	4	MOTOWN CHARTBUSTERS VOL 4	Various Artists (Tamla Motown)
8	5	DEEP PURPLE IN ROCK	Deep Purple (Harvest)
4	6	A QUESTION OF BALANCE	Moody Blues (Threshold)
6	7	LED ZEPPELIN II	Led Zeppelin (Atlantic)
7	8	COSMO'S FACTORY	Creedence Clearwater Revival (Liberty)
11	9	ATOM HEART MOTHER	Pink Floyd (Harvest)
5	10	CANDLES IN THE RAIN	Melanie (Buddah)
9	11	ROCK BUSTER	Various Artists (CBS)
19	12	STAGE FRIGHT	Band (Capitol)
13	13	SOMETHING	Shirley Bassey (United Artists)
15	14	THE BEACH BOYS' GREATEST HITS	Beach Boys (Capitol)
-	15	TIGHTEN UP VOL 3	Various Artists (Trojan)
10	16	PAINT YOUR WAGON	Soundtrack (Paramount)
16	17	ON STAGE	Elvis Presley (RCA)
-	18	THIS GUY'S IN LOVE WITH YOU	Herb Alpert & the Tijuana Brass (A&M)
17	19	THE EVERLY BROTHERS' ORIGINAL GREATEST HITS	Everly Brothers (CBS)
14	20	LET IT BE	Beatles (Apple)

31 October 1970

-	1	LED ZEPPELIN III	Led Zeppelin (Atlantic)
4	2	MOTOWN CHARTBUSTERS VOL 4	Various Artists (Tamla Motown)
1	3	PARANOID	Black Sabbath (Vertigo)
9	4	ATOM HEART MOTHER	Pink Floyd (Harvest)
2	5	BRIDGE OVER TROUBLED WATER	Simon & Garfunkel (CBS)
5	6	DEEP PURPLE IN ROCK	Deep Purple (Harvest)
3	7	'GET YOUR YA-YA'S OUT!'	Rolling Stones (Decca)
10	8	CANDLES IN THE RAIN	Melanie (Buddah)
8	9	COSMO'S FACTORY	Creedence Clearwater Revival (Liberty)
11	10	ROCK BUSTER	Various Artists (CBS)
7	11	LED ZEPPELIN II	Led Zeppelin (Atlantic)
6	12	A QUESTION OF BALANCE	Moody Blues (Threshold)
16	13	PAINT YOUR WAGON	Soundtrack (Paramount)
-	14	EASY LISTENING	Various Artists (Polydor)
14	15	THE BEACH BOYS' GREATEST HITS	Beach Boys (Capitol)
15	16	TIGHTEN UP VOL 3	Various Artists (Trojan)
19	17	THE EVERLY BROTHERS' ORIGINAL GREATEST HITS	Everly Brothers (CBS)
18	18	THIS GUY'S IN LOVE WITH YOU	Herb Alpert & the Tijuana Brass (A&M)
-	19	DEJA VU	Crosby, Stills, Nash & Young (Atlantic)
-	20	TOTAL SOUND	Various Artists (Studio Two)

7 November 1970

2	1	MOTOWN CHARTBUSTERS VOL 4	Various Artists (Tamla Motown)
1	2	LED ZEPPELIN III	Led Zeppelin (Atlantic)
8	3	CANDLES IN THE RAIN	Melanie (Buddah)
5	4	BRIDGE OVER TROUBLED WATER	Simon & Garfunkel (CBS)
3	5	PARANOID	Black Sabbath (Vertigo)
4	6	ATOM HEART MOTHER	Pink Floyd (Harvest)
6	7	DEEP PURPLE IN ROCK	Deep Purple (Harvest)
11	8	LED ZEPPELIN II	Led Zeppelin (Atlantic)
7	9	'GET YOUR YA-YA'S OUT!'	Rolling Stones (Decca)
9	10	COSMO'S FACTORY	Creedence Clearwater Revival (Liberty)
10	11	ROCK BUSTER	Various Artists (CBS)
13	12	PAINT YOUR WAGON	Soundtrack (Paramount)
14	13	EASY LISTENING	Various Artists (Polydor)
-	14	AFTER THE GOLD RUSH	Neil Young (Reprise)
16	15	TIGHTEN UP VOL 3	Various Artists (Trojan)
17	16	THE EVERLY BROTHERS' ORIGINAL GREATEST HITS	Everly Brothers (CBS)
15	17	THE BEACH BOYS' GREATEST HITS	Beach Boys (Capitol)
20	18	TOTAL SOUND	Various Artists (Studio Two)
-	19	OVER AND OVER	Nana Mouskouri (Fontana)
12	20	A QUESTION OF BALANCE	Moody Blues (Threshold)

14 November 1970

2	1	LED ZEPPELIN III	Led Zeppelin (Atlantic)
1	2	MOTOWN CHARTBUSTERS VOL 4	Various Artists (Tamla Motown)
4	3	BRIDGE OVER TROUBLED WATER	Simon & Garfunkel (CBS)
5	4	PARANOID	Black Sabbath (Vertigo)
3	5	CANDLES IN THE RAIN	Melanie (Buddah)
6	6	ATOM HEART MOTHER	Pink Floyd (Harvest)
7	7	DEEP PURPLE IN ROCK	Deep Purple (Harvest)
14	8	AFTER THE GOLD RUSH	Neil Young (Reprise)
13	9	EASY LISTENING	Various Artists (Polydor)
9	10	'GET YOUR YA-YA'S OUT!'	Rolling Stones (Decca)
12	11	PAINT YOUR WAGON	Soundtrack (Paramount)
8	12	LED ZEPPELIN II	Led Zeppelin (Atlantic)
10	13	COSMO'S FACTORY	Creedence Clearwater Revival (Liberty)
11	14	ROCK BUSTER	Various Artists (CBS)
18	15	TOTAL SOUND	Various Artists (Studio Two)
-	16	I WHO HAVE NOTHING	Tom Jones (Decca)
16	17	THE EVERLY BROTHERS' ORIGINAL GREATEST HITS	Everly Brothers (CBS)
15	18	TIGHTEN UP VOL 3	Various Artists (Trojan)
-	19	FULL CREAM	Cream (Polydor)
17	20	THE BEACH BOYS' GREATEST HITS	Beach Boys (Capitol)

21 November 1970

1	1	LED ZEPPELIN III	Led Zeppelin (Atlantic)
2	2	MOTOWN CHARTBUSTERS VOL 4	Various Artists (Tamla Motown)
4	3	PARANOID	Black Sabbath (Vertigo)
3	4	BRIDGE OVER TROUBLED WATER	Simon & Garfunkel (CBS)
7	5	DEEP PURPLE IN ROCK	Deep Purple (Harvest)
6	6	ATOM HEART MOTHER	Pink Floyd (Harvest)
5	7	CANDLES IN THE RAIN	Melanie (Buddah)
-	8	NEW MORNING	Bob Dylan (CBS)
9	9	EASY LISTENING	Various Artists (Polydor)
8	10	AFTER THE GOLD RUSH	Neil Young (Reprise)
16	11	I WHO HAVE NOTHING	Tom Jones (Decca)
12	12	LED ZEPPELIN II	Led Zeppelin (Atlantic)
11	13	PAINT YOUR WAGON	Soundtrack (Paramount)
14	14	ROCK BUSTER	Various Artists (CBS)
10	15	'GET YOUR YA-YA'S OUT!'	Rolling Stones (Decca)
13	16	COSMO'S FACTORY	Creedence Clearwater Revival (Liberty)
15	17	TOTAL SOUND	Various Artists (Studio Two)
-	18	JOHNNY CASH AT SAN QUENTIN	Johnny Cash (CBS)
20	19	THE BEACH BOYS' GREATEST HITS	Beach Boys (Capitol)
-	20	ANYWAY	Family (Reprise)

28 November 1970

1	1	LED ZEPPELIN III	Led Zeppelin (Atlantic)
2	2	MOTOWN CHARTBUSTERS VOL 4	Various Artists (Tamla Motown)
4	3	BRIDGE OVER TROUBLED WATER	Simon & Garfunkel (CBS)
7	4	CANDLES IN THE RAIN	Melanie (Buddah)
5	5	DEEP PURPLE IN ROCK	Deep Purple (Harvest)
3	6	PARANOID	Black Sabbath (Vertigo)
10	7	AFTER THE GOLD RUSH	Neil Young (Reprise)
9	8	EASY LISTENING	Various Artists (Polydor)
8	9	NEW MORNING	Bob Dylan (CBS)
6	10	ATOM HEART MOTHER	Pink Floyd (Harvest)
-	11	EMERSON LAKE AND PALMER	Emerson Lake & Palmer (Island)
-	12	ANDY WILLIAMS' GREATEST HITS	Andy Williams (CBS)
12	13	LED ZEPPELIN II	Led Zeppelin (Atlantic)
11	14	I WHO HAVE NOTHING	Tom Jones (Decca)
18	15	JOHNNY CASH AT SAN QUENTIN	Johnny Cash (CBS)
-	16	SWEET BABY JAMES	James Taylor (Warner Bros.)
20	17	ANYWAY	Family (Reprise)
13	18	PAINT YOUR WAGON	Soundtrack (Paramount)
19	19	THE BEACH BOYS' GREATEST HITS	Beach Boys (Capitol)
15	20	'GET YOUR YA-YA'S OUT!'	Rolling Stones (Decca)
17	21	TOTAL SOUND	Various Artists (Studio Two)
-	22	ABRAXAS	Santana (CBS)
-	23	EASY RIDER	Soundtrack (Stateside)
16	24	COSMO'S FACTORY	Creedence Clearwater Revival (Liberty)
-	25	CAN'T HELP FALLING IN LOVE	Andy Williams (CBS)
-	26	ELVIS' CHRISTMAS ALBUM	Elvis Presley (RCA)
14	27	ROCK BUSTER	Various Artists (CBS)
-	28	SOMETHING	Shirley Bassey (United Artists)
-	29	THE SOUND OF MUSIC	Soundtrack (RCA)
-	30	THIS GUY'S IN LOVE WITH YOU	Herb Alpert & the Tijuana Brass (A&M)

The genre later called Heavy Metal was spreading fast. Led Zeppelin II was joined by Led Zeppelin III, making a dramatic entrance straight in at No.1, and in the process knocking one of the Zeppelin wannabe groups off the top spot, Black Sabbath and Paranoid, while a few rungs down lurked *Deep Purple In Rock*. (The term wannabe hadn't arrived yet either.) Meanwhile, as from November 28, the NME chart expanded again, this time to offer the Top 30.

December 1970

5 December 1970

last week	this week	
1	1	LED ZEPPELIN III — Led Zeppelin (Atlantic)
2	2	MOTOWN CHARTBUSTERS VOL 4 — Various Artists (Tamla Motown)
9	3	NEW MORNING — Bob Dylan (CBS)
3	4	BRIDGE OVER TROUBLED WATER — Simon & Garfunkel (CBS)
5	5	DEEP PURPLE IN ROCK — Deep Purple (Harvest)
4	6	CANDLES IN THE RAIN — Melanie (Buddah)
8	7	EASY LISTENING — Various Artists (Polydor)
12	8	ANDY WILLIAMS' GREATEST HITS — Andy Williams (CBS)
17	9	ANYWAY — Family (Reprise)
10	10	ATOM HEART MOTHER — Pink Floyd (Harvest)
7	11	AFTER THE GOLD RUSH — Neil Young (Reprise)
18	12	PAINT YOUR WAGON — Soundtrack (Paramount)
13	13	LED ZEPPELIN II — Led Zeppelin (Atlantic)
6	14	PARANOID — Black Sabbath (Vertigo)
22	15	ABRAXAS — Santana (CBS)
11	16	EMERSON LAKE AND PALMER — Emerson Lake & Palmer (Island)
-	17	(UNTITLED) — Byrds (CBS)
15	18	JOHNNY CASH AT SAN QUENTIN — Johnny Cash (CBS)
29	19	THE SOUND OF MUSIC — Soundtrack (RCA)
21	20	TOTAL SOUND — Various Artists (Studio Two)
16	21	SWEET BABY JAMES — James Taylor (Warner Bros.)
28	22	SOMETHING — Shirley Bassey (United Artists)
20	23	'GET YOUR YA-YA'S OUT!' — Rolling Stones (Decca)
24	24	COSMO'S FACTORY — Creedence Clearwater Revival (Liberty)
-	25	THE WORLD OF JOHNNY CASH — Johnny Cash (CBS)
14	26	I WHO HAVE NOTHING — Tom Jones (Decca)
-	27	THE EVERLY BROTHERS' ORIGINAL GREATEST HITS — Everly Brothers (CBS)
-	28	THE ANDY WILLIAMS SHOW — Andy Williams (CBS)
26	29	ELVIS' CHRISTMAS ALBUM — Elvis Presley (RCA)
27	30	ROCK BUSTER — Various Artists (CBS)

12 December 1970

last week	this week	
1	1	LED ZEPPELIN III — Led Zeppelin (Atlantic)
2	2	MOTOWN CHARTBUSTERS VOL 4 — Various Artists (Tamla Motown)
4	3	BRIDGE OVER TROUBLED WATER — Simon & Garfunkel (CBS)
8	4	ANDY WILLIAMS' GREATEST HITS — Andy Williams (CBS)
3	5	NEW MORNING — Bob Dylan (CBS)
16	6	EMERSON LAKE AND PALMER — Emerson Lake & Palmer (Island)
6	7	CANDLES IN THE RAIN — Melanie (Buddah)
5	8	DEEP PURPLE IN ROCK — Deep Purple (Harvest)
11	9	AFTER THE GOLD RUSH — Neil Young (Reprise)
15	10	ABRAXAS — Santana (CBS)
14	11	PARANOID — Black Sabbath (Vertigo)
10	12	ATOM HEART MOTHER — Pink Floyd (Harvest)
7	13	EASY LISTENING — Various Artists (Polydor)
18	14	JOHNNY CASH AT SAN QUENTIN — Johnny Cash (CBS)
13	15	LED ZEPPELIN II — Led Zeppelin (Atlantic)
29	16	ELVIS' CHRISTMAS ALBUM — Elvis Presley (RCA)
12	17	PAINT YOUR WAGON — Soundtrack (Paramount)
26	18	I WHO HAVE NOTHING — Tom Jones (Decca)
9	19	ANYWAY — Family (Reprise)
19	20	THE SOUND OF MUSIC — Soundtrack (RCA)
-	21	STEPHEN STILLS — Stephen Stills (Atlantic)
28	22	THE ANDY WILLIAMS SHOW — Andy Williams (CBS)
21	23	SWEET BABY JAMES — James Taylor (Warner Bros.)
-	24	CAN'T HELP FALLING IN LOVE — Andy Williams (CBS)
-	25	SUNFLOWER — Beach Boys (Stateside)
-	26	LET IT BE — Beatles (Apple)
20	27	TOTAL SOUND — Various Artists (Studio Two)
23	28	'GET YOUR YA-YA'S OUT!' — Rolling Stones (Decca)
22	29	SOMETHING — Shirley Bassey (United Artists)
-	30	THE BEACH BOYS' GREATEST HITS — Beach Boys (Capitol)

19 December 1970

last week	this week	
2	1	MOTOWN CHARTBUSTERS VOL 4 — Various Artists (Tamla Motown)
1	2	LED ZEPPELIN III — Led Zeppelin (Atlantic)
4	3	ANDY WILLIAMS' GREATEST HITS — Andy Williams (CBS)
5	4	NEW MORNING — Bob Dylan (CBS)
6	5	EMERSON LAKE AND PALMER — Emerson Lake & Palmer (Island)
3	6	BRIDGE OVER TROUBLED WATER — Simon & Garfunkel (CBS)
13	7	EASY LISTENING — Various Artists (Polydor)
8	8	DEEP PURPLE IN ROCK — Deep Purple (Harvest)
23	9	SWEET BABY JAMES — James Taylor (Warner Bros.)
17	10	PAINT YOUR WAGON — Soundtrack (Paramount)
9	11	AFTER THE GOLD RUSH — Neil Young (Reprise)
12	12	ATOM HEART MOTHER — Pink Floyd (Harvest)
24	13	CAN'T HELP FALLING IN LOVE — Andy Williams (CBS)
7	14	CANDLES IN THE RAIN — Melanie (Buddah)
10	15	ABRAXAS — Santana (CBS)
19	16	ANYWAY — Family (Reprise)
-	17	12 SONGS FOR CHRISTMAS — Jim Reeves (RCA International)
21	18	STEPHEN STILLS — Stephen Stills (Atlantic)
27	19	TOTAL SOUND — Various Artists (Studio Two)
15	20	LED ZEPPELIN II — Led Zeppelin (Atlantic)
-	21	OVER AND OVER — Nana Mouskouri (Fontana)
20	22	THE SOUND OF MUSIC — Soundtrack (RCA)
11	23	PARANOID — Black Sabbath (Vertigo)
16	24	ELVIS' CHRISTMAS ALBUM — Elvis Presley (RCA)
18	25	I WHO HAVE NOTHING — Tom Jones (Decca)
-	26	AIR CONDITIONING — Curved Air (Warner Bros.)
30	27	THE BEACH BOYS' GREATEST HITS — Beach Boys (Capitol)
25	28	SUNFLOWER — Beach Boys (Stateside)
29	29	THE GLEN CAMPBELL ALBUM — Glen Campbell (Capitol)
-	30	(UNTITLED) — Byrds (CBS)

26 December 1970

last week	this week	
2	1	LED ZEPPELIN III — Led Zeppelin (Atlantic)
3	2	ANDY WILLIAMS' GREATEST HITS — Andy Williams (CBS)
6	3	BRIDGE OVER TROUBLED WATER — Simon & Garfunkel (CBS)
4	4	NEW MORNING — Bob Dylan (CBS)
1	5	MOTOWN CHARTBUSTERS VOL 4 — Various Artists (Tamla Motown)
5	6	EMERSON LAKE AND PALMER — Emerson Lake & Palmer (Island)
-	7	FRANK SINATRA'S GREATEST HITS VOL 2 — Frank Sinatra (Reprise)
9	8	SWEET BABY JAMES — James Taylor (Warner Bros.)
8	9	DEEP PURPLE IN ROCK — Deep Purple (Harvest)
7	10	EASY LISTENING — Various Artists (Polydor)
-	11	ALL THINGS MUST PASS — George Harrison (Apple)
-	12	JOHNNY CASH AT SAN QUENTIN — Johnny Cash (CBS)
-	13	THE ANDY WILLIAMS SHOW — Andy Williams (CBS)
20	14	LED ZEPPELIN II — Led Zeppelin (Atlantic)
10	15	PAINT YOUR WAGON — Soundtrack (Paramount)
13	16	CAN'T HELP FALLING IN LOVE — Andy Williams (CBS)
22	17	THE SOUND OF MUSIC — Soundtrack (RCA)
29	18	THE GLEN CAMPBELL ALBUM — Glen Campbell (Capitol)
11	19	AFTER THE GOLD RUSH — Neil Young (Reprise)
15	20	ABRAXAS — Santana (CBS)
14	21	CANDLES IN THE RAIN — Melanie (Buddah)
16	22	ANYWAY — Family (Reprise)
21	23	OVER AND OVER — Nana Mouskouri (Fontana)
17	24	12 SONGS FOR CHRISTMAS — Jim Reeves (RCA International)
26	25	AIR CONDITIONING — Curved Air (Warner Bros.)
-	26	LET IT BE — Beatles (Apple)
-	27	THE JOHNNY CASH SHOW — Johnny Cash (CBS)
23	28	PARANOID — Black Sabbath (Vertigo)
18	29	STEPHEN STILLS — Stephen Stills (Atlantic)
24	30	ELVIS' CHRISTMAS ALBUM — Elvis Presley (RCA)

It's that Jim Reeves time of year again, and a great encouragement to the public, apparently, to buy Andy Williams records. Andy, a replacement Perry Como, was born wearing a cardigan. This yuletide saw him with three Top 20 albums. Shirley Bassey reached the charts with *Something*, titled after the song that had given her a Top 5 single earlier in the year and that, along with *Here Comes The Sun*, had been proving to an embattled Lennon and McCartney that George Harrison really could write songs. The year ended with the entry of George's own (triple) solo album *All Things Must Pass*, destined for immense success.

2 January 1971

last week	this week	title	artist
2	1	ANDY WILLIAMS' GREATEST HITS	Andy Williams (CBS)
1	2	LED ZEPPELIN III	Led Zeppelin (Atlantic)
3	3	BRIDGE OVER TROUBLED WATER	Simon & Garfunkel (CBS)
5	4	MOTOWN CHARTBUSTERS VOL 4	Various Artist (Tamla Motown)
7	5	FRANK SINATRA'S GREATEST HITS VOL 2	Frank Sinatra (Reprise)
11	6	ALL THINGS MUST PASS	George Harrison (Apple)
6	7	EMERSON LAKE & PALMER	Emerson, Lake & Palmer (Island)
15	8	PAINT YOUR WAGON	Soundtrack (Paramount)
12	9	JOHNNY CASH AT SAN QUENTIN	Johnny Cash (CBS)
16	10	CAN'T HELP FALLING IN LOVE	Andy Williams (CBS)
9	11	DEEP PURPLE IN ROCK	Deep Purple (Harvest)
17	12	THE SOUND OF MUSIC	Soundtrack (RCA)
8	13	SWEET BABY JAMES	James Taylor (Warner Bros.)
24	14	12 SONGS OF CHRISTMAS	Jim Reeves (RCA International)
4	15	NEW MORNING	Bob Dylan (CBS)
18	16	THE GLEN CAMPBELL ALBUM	Glen Campbell (Capitol)
10	17	EASY LISTENING	Various Artists (Polydor)
25	18	AIR CONDITIONING	Curved Air (Warner Bros.)
20	19	ABRAXAS	Santana (CBS)
26	20	LET IT BE	Beatles (Apple)
13	21	ANDY WILLIAMS SHOW	Andy Williams (CBS)
27	22	JOHNNY CASH SHOW	Johnny Cash (CBS)
21	23	CANDLES IN THE RAIN	Melanie (Buddah)
-	24	THE BEACH BOYS' GREATEST HITS	Beach Boys (Capitol)
19	25	AFTER THE GOLD RUSH	Neil Young (Reprise)
23	26	OVER AND OVER	Nana Mouskouri (Fontana)
22	27	ANYWAY	Family (Reprise)
28	28	PARANOID	Black Sabbath (Vertigo)
30	29	ELVIS' CHRISTMAS ALBUM	Elvis Presley (RCA)
-	30	ATOM HEART MOTHER	Pink Floyd (Harvest)

9 January 1971

last week	this week	title	artist
1	1	ANDY WILLIAMS' GREATEST HITS	Andy Williams (CBS)
4	2	MOTOWN CHARTBUSTERS VOL 4	Various Artists (Tamla Motown)
3	3	BRIDGE OVER TROUBLED WATER	Simon & Garfunkel (CBS)
2	4	LED ZEPPELIN III	Led Zeppelin (Atlantic)
6	5	ALL THINGS MUST PASS	George Harrison (Apple)
11	6	DEEP PURPLE IN ROCK	Deep Purple (Harvest)
9	7	JOHNNY CASH AT SAN QUENTIN	Johnny Cash (CBS)
7	8	EMERSON LAKE & PALMER	Emerson, Lake & Palmer (Island)
8	9	PAINT YOUR WAGON	Soundtrack (Paramount)
5	10	FRANK SINATRA'S GREATEST HITS VOL 2	Frank Sinatra (Reprise)
10	11	CAN'T HELP FALLING IN LOVE	Andy Williams (CBS)
18	12	AIR CONDITIONING	Curved Air (Warner Bros.)
23	13	CANDLES IN THE RAIN	Melanie (Buddah)
26	14	OVER AND OVER	Nana Mouskouri (Fontana)
12	15	THE SOUND OF MUSIC	Soundtrack (RCA)
16	16	THE GLEN CAMPBELL ALBUM	Glen Campbell (Capitol)
20	17	LET IT BE	Beatles (Apple)
13	18	SWEET BABY JAMES	James Taylor (Warner Bros.)
15	19	NEW MORNING	Bob Dylan (CBS)
17	20	EASY LISTENING	Various Artists (Polydor)
21	21	ANDY WILLIAMS SHOW	Andy Williams (CBS)
24	22	THE BEACH BOYS' GREATEST HITS	Beach Boys (Capitol)
-	23	TOTAL SOUND	Various Artists (Studio Two)
-	24	STEPHEN STILLS	Stephen Stills (Atlantic)
30	25	ATOM HEART MOTHER	Pink Floyd (Harvest)
-	26	LED ZEPPELIN II	Led Zeppelin (Atlantic)
27	27	ANYWAY	Family (Reprise)
22	28	JOHNNY CASH SHOW	Johnny Cash (CBS)
19	29	ABRAXAS	Santana (CBS)
28	30	PARANOID	Black Sabbath (Vertigo)

16 January 1971

last week	this week	title	artist
3	1	BRIDGE OVER TROUBLED WATER	Simon & Garfunkel (CBS)
1	2	ANDY WILLIAMS' GREATEST HITS	Andy Williams (CBS)
2	3	MOTOWN CHARTBUSTERS VOL 4	Various Artists (Tamla Motown)
4	4	LED ZEPPELIN III	Led Zeppelin (Atlantic)
5	5	ALL THINGS MUST PASS	George Harrison (Apple)
8	6	EMERSON LAKE & PALMER	Emerson, Lake & Palmer (Island)
18	7	SWEET BABY JAMES	James Taylor (Warner Bros.)
6	8	DEEP PURPLE IN ROCK	Deep Purple (Harvest)
13	9	CANDLES IN THE RAIN	Melanie (Buddah)
9	10	PAINT YOUR WAGON	Soundtrack (Paramount)
10	11	FRANK SINATRA'S GREATEST HITS VOL 2	Frank Sinatra (Reprise)
7	12	JOHNNY CASH AT SAN QUENTIN	Johnny Cash (CBS)
25	13	ATOM HEART MOTHER	Pink Floyd (Harvest)
19	14	NEW MORNING	Bob Dylan (CBS)
11	15	CAN'T HELP FALLING IN LOVE	Andy Williams (CBS)
20	16	EASY LISTENING	Various Artists (Polydor)
-	17	JOHN LENNON/PLASTIC ONO BAND	John Lennon & the Plastic Ono Band (Apple)
-	18	AFTER THE GOLD RUSH	Neil Young (Reprise)
16	19	THE GLEN CAMPBELL ALBUM	Glen Campbell (Capitol)
22	20	THE BEACH BOYS' GREATEST HITS	Beach Boys (Capitol)
-	21	T. REX	T. Rex (Fly)
26	22	LED ZEPPELIN II	Led Zeppelin (Atlantic)
14	23	OVER AND OVER	Nana Mouskouri (Fontana)
15	24	THE SOUND OF MUSIC	Soundtrack (RCA)
29	25	ABRAXAS	Santana (CBS)
12	26	AIR CONDITIONING	Curved Air (Warner Bros.)
-	27	WATT	Ten Years After (Deram)
17	28	LET IT BE	Beatles (Apple)
-	29	SOMETHING	Shirley Bassey (United Artists)
-	30	LEFTOVER WINE	Melanie (Buddah)

23 January 1971

last week	this week	title	artist
2	1	ANDY WILLIAMS' GREATEST HITS	Andy Williams (CBS)
1	2	BRIDGE OVER TROUBLED WATER	Simon & Garfunkel (CBS)
4	3	LED ZEPPELIN III	Led Zeppelin (Atlantic)
3	4	MOTOWN CHARTBUSTERS VOL 4	Various Artists (Tamla Motown)
5	5	ALL THINGS MUST PASS	George Harrison (Apple)
6	6	EMERSON LAKE & PALMER	Emerson, Lake & Palmer (Island)
7	7	SWEET BABY JAMES	James Taylor (Warner Bros.)
8	8	DEEP PURPLE IN ROCK	Deep Purple (Harvest)
11	9	FRANK SINATRA'S GREATEST HITS VOL 2	Frank Sinatra (Reprise)
18	10	AFTER THE GOLD RUSH	Neil Young (Reprise)
-	11	TUMBLEWEED CONNECTION	Elton John (DJM)
21	12	T. REX	T. Rex (Fly)
27	13	WATT	Ten Years After (Deram)
13	14	ATOM HEART MOTHER	Pink Floyd (Harvest)
10	15	PAINT YOUR WAGON	Soundtrack (Paramount)
25	16	ABRAXAS	Santana (CBS)
16	17	EASY LISTENING	Various Artists (Polydor)
12	18	JOHNNY CASH AT SAN QUENTIN	Johnny Cash (CBS)
26	19	AIR CONDITIONING	Curved Air (Warner Bros.)
28	20	LET IT BE	Beatles (Apple)
15	21	CAN'T HELP FALLING IN LOVE	Andy Williams (CBS)
9	22	CANDLES IN THE RAIN	Melanie (Buddah)
17	23	JOHN LENNON/PLASTIC ONO BAND	John Lennon & the Plastic Ono Band (Apple)
24	24	THE SOUND OF MUSIC	Soundtrack (RCA)
22	25	LED ZEPPELIN II	Led Zeppelin (Atlantic)
19	26	THE GLEN CAMPBELL ALBUM	Glen Campbell (Capitol)
14	27	NEW MORNING	Bob Dylan (CBS)
-	28	STEPHEN STILLS	Stephen Stills (Atlantic)
30	29	LEFTOVER WINE	Melanie (Buddah)
23	30	OVER AND OVER	Nana Mouskouri (Fontana)

No wonder people were grateful when George Harrison jumped up the January singles chart from No.14 to No.1 with *My Sweet Lord*: it displaced *Grandad* by Clive Dunn, which T. Rex's *Ride A White Swan* had failed to do. Others currently with hit singles were the Jackson Five, Neil Diamond, Glen Campbell, Gilbert O'Sullivan, Ken Dodd, White Plains, Ann Murray, Chairmen of the Board, Dorothy Squires (a querulous *My Way*) and Roger Whittaker. All things must pass.

January – February 1971

last week	this week				

30 January 1971

last	this	
5	1	ALL THINGS MUST PASS George Harrison (Apple)
2	2	BRIDGE OVER TROUBLED WATER Simon & Garfunkel (CBS)
1	3	ANDY WILLIAMS' GREATEST HITS Andy Williams (CBS)
4	4	MOTOWN CHARTBUSTERS VOL 4 Various Artists (Tamla Motown)
3	5	LED ZEPPELIN III Led Zeppelin (Atlantic)
7	6	SWEET BABY JAMES James Taylor (Warner Bros.)
6	7	EMERSON LAKE & PALMER Emerson, Lake & Palmer (Island)
9	8	FRANK SINATRA'S GREATEST HITS VOL 2 Frank Sinatra (Reprise)
13	9	WATT Ten Years After (Deram)
10	10	AFTER THE GOLD RUSH Neil Young (Reprise)
11	11	TUMBLEWEED CONNECTION Elton John (DJM)
12	12	T. REX T. Rex (Fly)
15	13	PAINT YOUR WAGON Soundtrack (Paramount)
17	14	EASY LISTENING Various Artists (Polydor)
19	15	AIR CONDITIONING Curved Air (Warner Bros.)
8	16	DEEP PURPLE IN ROCK Deep Purple (Harvest)
23	17	JOHN LENNON/PLASTIC ONO BAND John Lennon & the Plastic Ono Band (Apple)
25	18	LED ZEPPELIN II Led Zeppelin (Atlantic)
22	19	CANDLES IN THE RAIN Melanie (Buddah)
16	20	ABRAXAS Santana (CBS)
18	21	JOHNNY CASH AT SAN QUENTIN Johnny Cash (CBS)
-	22	ELVIS: THAT'S THE WAY IT IS Elvis Presley (RCA)
28	23	STEPHEN STILLS Stephen Stills (Atlantic)
-	24	PENDULUM Creedence Clearwater Revival (Liberty)
29	25	LEFTOVER WINE Melanie (Buddah)
-	26	ELTON JOHN Elton John (DJM)
14	27	ATOM HEART MOTHER Pink Floyd (Harvest)
26	28	THE GLEN CAMPBELL ALBUM Glen Campbell (Capitol)
-	29	GOLD Neil Diamond (UNI)
20	30	LET IT BE Beatles (Apple)

6 February 1971

last	this	
1	1	ALL THINGS MUST PASS George Harrison (Apple)
2	2	BRIDGE OVER TROUBLED WATER Simon & Garfunkel (CBS)
3	3	ANDY WILLIAMS' GREATEST HITS Andy Williams (CBS)
4	4	MOTOWN CHARTBUSTERS VOL 4 Various Artists (Tamla Motown)
5	5	LED ZEPPELIN III Led Zeppelin (Atlantic)
11	6	TUMBLEWEED CONNECTION Elton John (DJM)
6	7	SWEET BABY JAMES James Taylor (Warner Bros.)
7	8	EMERSON LAKE & PALMER Emerson, Lake & Palmer (Island)
8	9	FRANK SINATRA'S GREATEST HITS VOL 2 Frank Sinatra (Reprise)
16	10	DEEP PURPLE IN ROCK Deep Purple (Harvest)
30	11	LET IT BE Beatles (Apple)
9	12	WATT Ten Years After (Deram)
17	13	JOHN LENNON/PLASTIC ONO BAND John Lennon & the Plastic Ono Band (Apple)
18	14	LED ZEPPELIN II Led Zeppelin (Atlantic)
-	15	CAN'T HELP FALLING IN LOVE Andy Williams (CBS)
19	16	CANDLES IN THE RAIN Melanie (Buddah)
15	17	AIR CONDITIONING Curved Air (Warner Bros.)
22	18	ELVIS: THAT'S THE WAY IT IS Elvis Presley (RCA)
12	19	T. REX T. Rex (Fly)
24	20	PENDULUM Creedence Clearwater Revival (Liberty)
21	21	JOHNNY CASH AT SAN QUENTIN Johnny Cash (CBS)
23	22	STEPHEN STILLS Stephen Stills (Atlantic)
10	23	AFTER THE GOLD RUSH Neil Young (Reprise)
14	24	EASY LISTENING Various Artists (Polydor)
13	25	PAINT YOUR WAGON Soundtrack (Paramount)
-	26	OVER AND OVER Nana Mouskouri (Fontana)
-	27	McGUINNESS FLINT McGuinness Flint (Capitol)
26	28	ELTON JOHN Elton John (DJM)
25	29	LEFTOVER WINE Melanie (Buddah)
20	30	ABRAXAS Santana (CBS)

13 February 1971

last	this	
1	1	ALL THINGS MUST PASS George Harrison (Apple)
2	2	BRIDGE OVER TROUBLED WATER Simon & Garfunkel (CBS)
6	3	TUMBLEWEED CONNECTION Elton John (DJM)
3	4	ANDY WILLIAMS' GREATEST HITS Andy Williams (CBS)
4	5	MOTOWN CHARTBUSTERS VOL 4 Various Artists (Tamla Motown)
7	6	SWEET BABY JAMES James Taylor (Warner Bros.)
5	7	LED ZEPPELIN III Led Zeppelin (Atlantic)
17	8	AIR CONDITIONING Curved Air (Warner Bros.)
8	9	EMERSON LAKE & PALMER Emerson, Lake & Palmer (Island)
10	10	DEEP PURPLE IN ROCK Deep Purple (Harvest)
9	11	FRANK SINATRA'S GREATEST HITS VOL 2 Frank Sinatra (Reprise)
23	12	AFTER THE GOLD RUSH Neil Young (Reprise)
13	13	JOHN LENNON/PLASTIC ONO BAND John Lennon & the Plastic Ono Band (Apple)
24	14	EASY LISTENING Various Artists (Polydor)
18	15	ELVIS: THAT'S THE WAY IT IS Elvis Presley (RCA)
20	16	PENDULUM Creedence Clearwater Revival (Liberty)
19	17	T. REX T. Rex (Fly)
27	18	McGUINNESS FLINT McGuinness Flint (Capitol)
-	19	DEJA VU Crosby Stills Nash & Young (Atlantic)
15	20	CAN'T HELP FALLING IN LOVE Andy Williams (CBS)
12	21	WATT Ten Years After (Deram)
22	22	STEPHEN STILLS Stephen Stills (Atlantic)
21	23	JOHNNY CASH AT SAN QUENTIN Johnny Cash (CBS)
16	24	CANDLES IN THE RAIN Melanie (Buddah)
14	25	LED ZEPPELIN II Led Zeppelin (Atlantic)
26	26	OVER AND OVER Nana Mouskouri (Fontana)
25	27	PAINT YOUR WAGON Soundtrack (Paramount)
29	28	LEFTOVER WINE Melanie (Buddah)
-	29	WISHBONE ASH Wishbone Ash (MCA)
28	30	ELTON JOHN Elton John (DJM)

20 February 1971

last	this	
1	1	ALL THINGS MUST PASS George Harrison (Apple)
2	2	BRIDGE OVER TROUBLED WATER Simon & Garfunkel (CBS)
3	3	TUMBLEWEED CONNECTION Elton John (DJM)
4	4	ANDY WILLIAMS' GREATEST HITS Andy Williams (CBS)
5	5	MOTOWN CHARTBUSTERS VOL 4 Various Artists (Tamla Motown)
30	5	ELTON JOHN Elton John (DJM)
7	6	LED ZEPPELIN III Led Zeppelin (Atlantic)
12	6	AFTER THE GOLD RUSH Neil Young (Reprise)
8	7	AIR CONDITIONING Curved Air (Warner Bros.)
11	8	FRANK SINATRA'S GREATEST HITS VOL 2 Frank Sinatra (Reprise)
6	9	SWEET BABY JAMES James Taylor (Warner Bros.)
10	10	DEEP PURPLE IN ROCK Deep Purple (Harvest)
9	11	EMERSON LAKE & PALMER Emerson, Lake & Palmer (Island)
14	12	EASY LISTENING Various Artists (Polydor)
13	13	JOHN LENNON/PLASTIC ONO BAND John Lennon & the Plastic Ono Band (Apple)
21	14	WATT Ten Years After (Deram)
16	17	PENDULUM Creedence Clearwater Revival (Liberty)
15	18	ELVIS: THAT'S THE WAY IT IS Elvis Presley (RCA)
17	19	T. REX T. Rex (Fly)
20	20	CAN'T HELP FALLING IN LOVE Andy Williams (CBS)
25	21	LED ZEPPELIN II Led Zeppelin (Atlantic)
24	22	CANDLES IN THE RAIN Melanie (Buddah)
19	23	DEJA VU Crosby Stills Nash & Young (Atlantic)
29	24	WISHBONE ASH Wishbone Ash (MCA)
28	25	LEFTOVER WINE Melanie (Buddah)
23	26	JOHNNY CASH AT SAN QUENTIN Johnny Cash (CBS)
18	27	McGUINNESS FLINT McGuinness Flint (Capitol)
-	28	CLOSE TO YOU Carpenters (A&M)
-	29	MY WAY Frank Sinatra (Reprise)
-	30	LET IT BE Beatles (Apple)

John Lennon & The Plastic Ono Band was not an album that much pleased the public. However, a new superstar did: Elton John, at first perceived as an "authentic-sounding" Brit R&B singer good at southern fried ballads with soulful piano. An English Leon Russell, almost. Signed to little DJM - it stood for Dick James Music, and had once had the Beatles' song-publishing - suddenly in February Elton had two Top 5 albums at once, (his 2nd and 3rd LPs) helped by just one hit single, *Your Song*.

February – March 1971

27 February 1971

last	this	
1	1	ALL THINGS MUST PASS George Harrison (Apple)
2	2	BRIDGE OVER TROUBLED WATER Simon & Garfunkel (CBS)
3	3	TUMBLEWEED CONNECTION Elton John (DJM)
9	4	SWEET BABY JAMES James Taylor (Warner Bros.)
4	5	ANDY WILLIAMS' GREATEST HITS Andy Williams (CBS)
5	6	MOTOWN CHARTBUSTERS VOL 4 Various Artists (Tamla Motown)
6	7	LED ZEPPELIN III Led Zeppelin (Atlantic)
8	8	FRANK SINATRA'S GREATEST HITS VOL 2 Frank Sinatra (Reprise)
7	9	AIR CONDITIONING Curved Air (Warner Bros.)
11	10	EMERSON LAKE & PALMER Emerson, Lake & Palmer (Island)
10	11	DEEP PURPLE IN ROCK Deep Purple (Harvest)
18	12	ELVIS: THAT'S THE WAY IT IS Elvis Presley (RCA)
17	13	PENDULUM Creedence Clearwater Revival (Liberty)
-	14	CHICAGO 3 Chicago (CBS)
19	15	T. REX T. Rex (Fly)
6	16	AFTER THE GOLD RUSH Neil Young (Reprise)
12	17	EASY LISTENING Various Artists (Polydor)
-	18	STEPHEN STILLS Stephen Stills (Atlantic)
14	19	WATT Ten Years After (Deram)
-	20	THE SOUND OF MUSIC Soundtrack (RCA)
5	21	ELTON JOHN Elton John (DJM)
-	22	PAINT YOUR WAGON Soundtrack (Paramount)
13	23	JOHN LENNON/PLASTIC ONO BAND John Lennon & the Plastic Ono Band (Apple)
22	24	CANDLES IN THE RAIN Melanie (Buddah)
-	25	GOLD Neil Diamond (UNI)
20	26	CAN'T HELP FALLING IN LOVE Andy Williams (CBS)
25	27	LEFTOVER WINE Melanie (Buddah)
29	28	MY WAY Frank Sinatra (Reprise)
23	29	DEJA VU Crosby Stills Nash & Young (Atlantic)
24	30	WISHBONE ASH Wishbone Ash (MCA)

6 March 1971

last	this	
1	1	ALL THINGS MUST PASS George Harrison (Apple)
2	2	BRIDGE OVER TROUBLED WATER Simon & Garfunkel (CBS)
3	3	TUMBLEWEED CONNECTION Elton John (DJM)
5	4	ANDY WILLIAMS' GREATEST HITS Andy Williams (CBS)
4	5	SWEET BABY JAMES James Taylor (Warner Bros.)
6	6	MOTOWN CHARTBUSTERS VOL 4 Various Artists (Tamla Motown)
7	7	LED ZEPPELIN III Led Zeppelin (Atlantic)
9	8	AIR CONDITIONING Curved Air (Warner Bros.)
13	9	PENDULUM Creedence Clearwater Revival (Liberty)
11	10	DEEP PURPLE IN ROCK Deep Purple (Harvest)
8	11	FRANK SINATRA'S GREATEST HITS VOL 2 Frank Sinatra (Reprise)
19	12	WATT Ten Years After (Deram)
23	13	JOHN LENNON/PLASTIC ONO BAND John Lennon & the Plastic Ono Band (Apple)
21	14	ELTON JOHN Elton John (DJM)
15	15	CHICAGO 3 Chicago (CBS)
16	16	AFTER THE GOLD RUSH Neil Young (Reprise)
10	17	EMERSON LAKE & PALMER Emerson, Lake & Palmer (Island)
12	18	ELVIS: THAT'S THE WAY IT IS Elvis Presley (RCA)
18	19	STEPHEN STILLS Stephen Stills (Atlantic)
17	20	EASY LISTENING Various Artists (Polydor)
-	21	LED ZEPPELIN II Led Zeppelin (Atlantic)
24	22	CANDLES IN THE RAIN Melanie (Buddah)
25	23	GOLD Neil Diamond (UNI)
-	24	ABRAXAS Santana (CBS)
15	25	T. REX T. Rex (Fly)
-	26	TAP ROOT MANUSCRIPT Neil Diamond (UNI)
20	27	THE SOUND OF MUSIC Soundtrack (RCA)
-	28	THE YES ALBUM Yes (Atlantic)
-	29	LET IT BE Beatles (Apple)
27	30	LEFTOVER WINE Melanie (Buddah)

13 March 1971

last	this	
1	1	ALL THINGS MUST PASS George Harrison (Apple)
2	2	BRIDGE OVER TROUBLED WATER Simon & Garfunkel (CBS)
3	3	TUMBLEWEED CONNECTION Elton John (DJM)
4	4	ANDY WILLIAMS' GREATEST HITS Andy Williams (CBS)
5	5	SWEET BABY JAMES James Taylor (Warner Bros.)
7	6	LED ZEPPELIN III Led Zeppelin (Atlantic)
14	7	ELTON JOHN Elton John (DJM)
9	8	PENDULUM Creedence Clearwater Revival (Liberty)
11	9	FRANK SINATRA'S GREATEST HITS VOL 2 Frank Sinatra (Reprise)
28	10	THE YES ALBUM Yes (Atlantic)
8	11	AIR CONDITIONING Curved Air (Warner Bros.)
10	12	DEEP PURPLE IN ROCK Deep Purple (Harvest)
17	13	EMERSON LAKE & PALMER Emerson, Lake & Palmer (Island)
6	14	MOTOWN CHARTBUSTERS VOL 4 Various Artists (Tamla Motown)
-	15	THE BEST OF T. REX T. Rex (Fly)
19	16	STEPHEN STILLS Stephen Stills (Atlantic)
26	17	TAP ROOT MANUSCRIPT Neil Diamond (UNI)
-	18	WHALES AND NIGHTINGALES Judy Collins (Elektra)
23	19	GOLD Neil Diamond (UNI)
16	20	AFTER THE GOLD RUSH Neil Young (Reprise)
15	21	CHICAGO 3 Chicago (CBS)
-	22	STONE AGE Rolling Stones (Decca)
-	23	HOME LOVIN' MAN Andy Williams (CBS)
21	24	LED ZEPPELIN II Led Zeppelin (Atlantic)
18	25	ELVIS: THAT'S THE WAY IT IS Elvis Presley (RCA)
20	26	EASY LISTENING Various Artists (Polydor)
13	27	JOHN LENNON/ PLASTIC ONO BAND John Lennon & the Plastic Ono Band (Apple)
-	28	LIVE TASTE Taste (Polydor)
12	29	WATT Ten Years After (Deram)
29	30	LET IT BE Beatles (Apple)

20 March 1971

last	this	
2	1	BRIDGE OVER TROUBLED WATER Simon & Garfunkel (CBS)
1	2	ALL THINGS MUST PASS George Harrison (Apple)
3	3	TUMBLEWEED CONNECTION Elton John (DJM)
23	4	HOME LOVIN' MAN Andy Williams (CBS)
4	5	ANDY WILLIAMS' GREATEST HITS Andy Williams (CBS)
15	6	THE BEST OF T. REX T. Rex (Fly)
6	7	LED ZEPPELIN III Led Zeppelin (Atlantic)
9	8	FRANK SINATRA'S GREATEST HITS VOL 2 Frank Sinatra (Reprise)
12	9	DEEP PURPLE IN ROCK Deep Purple (Harvest)
10	10	THE YES ALBUM Yes (Atlantic)
22	11	STONE AGE Rolling Stones (Decca)
26	12	EASY LISTENING Various Artists (Polydor)
5	13	SWEET BABY JAMES James Taylor (Warner Bros.)
7	14	ELTON JOHN Elton John (DJM)
14	15	MOTOWN CHARTBUSTERS VOL 4 Various Artists (Tamla Motown)
13	16	EMERSON LAKE & PALMER Emerson, Lake & Palmer (Island)
8	17	PENDULUM Creedence Clearwater Revival (Liberty)
11	18	AIR CONDITIONING Curved Air (Warner Bros.)
19	19	GOLD Neil Diamond (UNI)
21	20	CHICAGO 3 Chicago (CBS)
27	21	JOHN LENNON/PLASTIC ONO BAND John Lennon & the Plastic Ono Band (Apple)
24	22	LED ZEPPELIN II Led Zeppelin (Atlantic)
-	23	THE WORLD OF YOUR 100 BEST TUNES Various Artists (Decca)
-	24	THE SOUND OF MUSIC Soundtrack (RCA)
	25	PORTRAIT IN MUSIC Burt Bacharach (A&M)
17	26	TAP ROOT MANUSCRIPT Neil Diamond (UNI)
18	27	WHALES AND NIGHTINGALES Judy Collins (Elektra)
16	28	STEPHEN STILLS Stephen Stills (Atlantic)
28	29	LIVE TASTE Taste (Polydor)
20	30	AFTER THE GOLD RUSH Neil Young (Reprise)

Symptomatic of the age was a chart that included *Deja Vu* by supplemented supergroup Crosby Stills Nash & Young (Young was the supplement), plus Wishbone Ash, Yes, Judy Collins' *Whales And Nightingales*, two Melanie albums and Ten Years After. Ten Years After, fronted by Alvin Lee, a faster-than-thou guitarist, had been one of the unexpected popular successes at Woodstock. While their one hit single, *Love Like A Man*, had reached No.7 the previous August, *Watt* was not their first hit album.

March – April 1971

last week	this week	27 March 1971
1	1	BRIDGE OVER TROUBLED WATER Simon & Garfunkel (CBS)
4	2	HOME LOVIN' MAN Andy Williams (CBS)
2	3	ALL THINGS MUST PASS George Harrison (Apple)
5	4	ANDY WILLIAMS' GREATEST HITS Andy Williams (CBS)
-	5	CRY OF LOVE Jimi Hendrix (Track)
3	6	TUMBLEWEED CONNECTION Elton John (DJM)
10	7	THE YES ALBUM Yes (Atlantic)
7	8	LED ZEPPELIN III Led Zeppelin (Atlantic)
8	9	FRANK SINATRA'S GREATEST HITS VOL 2 Frank Sinatra (Reprise)
9	10	DEEP PURPLE IN ROCK Deep Purple (Harvest)
11	11	STONE AGE Rolling Stones (Decca)
20	12	CHICAGO 3 Chicago (CBS)
15	13	MOTOWN CHARTBUSTERS VOL 4 Various Artists (Tamla Motown)
12	14	EASY LISTENING Various Artists (Polydor)
16	15	EMERSON LAKE & PALMER Emerson, Lake & Palmer (Island)
6	16	THE BEST OF T. REX T. Rex (Fly)
19	17	GOLD Neil Diamond (UNI)
-	18	AQUALUNG Jethro Tull (Chrysalis)
-	19	T. REX T. Rex (Fly)
13	20	SWEET BABY JAMES James Taylor (Warner Bros.)
14	21	ELTON JOHN Elton John (DJM)
17	22	PENDULUM Creedence Clearwater Revival (Liberty)
18	23	AIR CONDITIONING Curved Air (Warner Bros.)
-	24	ABRAXAS Santana (CBS)
-	25	WATT Ten Years After (Deram)
26	26	TAP ROOT MANUSCRIPT Neil Diamond (UNI)
-	27	PAINT YOUR WAGON Soundtrack (Paramount)
24	28	THE SOUND OF MUSIC Soundtrack (RCA)
28	29	STEPHEN STILLS Stephen Stills (Atlantic)
29	30	LIVE TASTE Taste (Polydor)

		3 April 1971
1	1	BRIDGE OVER TROUBLED WATER Simon & Garfunkel (CBS)
2	2	HOME LOVIN' MAN Andy Williams (CBS)
3	3	ALL THINGS MUST PASS George Harrison (Apple)
5	4	CRY OF LOVE Jimi Hendrix (Track)
4	5	ANDY WILLIAMS' GREATEST HITS Andy Williams (CBS)
6	6	TUMBLEWEED CONNECTION Elton John (DJM)
8	7	LED ZEPPELIN III Led Zeppelin (Atlantic)
16	8	THE BEST OF T. REX T. Rex (Fly)
13	9	MOTOWN CHARTBUSTERS VOL 4 Various Artists (Tamla Motown)
9	10	FRANK SINATRA'S GREATEST HITS VOL 2 Frank Sinatra (Reprise)
7	11	THE YES ALBUM Yes (Atlantic)
14	12	EASY LISTENING Various Artists (Polydor)
11	13	STONE AGE Rolling Stones (Decca)
22	14	PENDULUM Creedence Clearwater Revival (Liberty)
10	15	DEEP PURPLE IN ROCK Deep Purple (Harvest)
24	16	ABRAXAS Santana (CBS)
15	17	EMERSON LAKE & PALMER Emerson, Lake & Palmer (Island)
18	18	AQUALUNG Jethro Tull (Chrysalis)
17	19	GOLD Neil Diamond (UNI)
21	20	ELTON JOHN Elton John (DJM)
23	21	AIR CONDITIONING Curved Air (Warner Bros.)
12	22	CHICAGO 3 Chicago (CBS)
20	23	SWEET BABY JAMES James Taylor (Warner Bros.)
28	24	THE SOUND OF MUSIC Soundtrack (RCA)
29	25	STEPHEN STILLS Stephen Stills (Atlantic)
-	26	LED ZEPPELIN II Led Zeppelin (Atlantic)
26	27	TAP ROOT MANUSCRIPT Neil Diamond (UNI)
-	28	ELVIS COUNTRY Elvis Presley (RCA)
25	29	WATT Ten Years After (Deram)
30	30	LIVE TASTE Taste (Polydor)

		10 April 1971
2	1	HOME LOVIN' MAN Andy Williams (CBS)
1	2	BRIDGE OVER TROUBLED WATER Simon & Garfunkel (CBS)
3	3	ALL THINGS MUST PASS George Harrison (Apple)
4	4	CRY OF LOVE Jimi Hendrix (Track)
13	5	STONE AGE Rolling Stones (Decca)
6	6	TUMBLEWEED CONNECTION Elton John (DJM)
5	7	ANDY WILLIAMS' GREATEST HITS Andy Williams (CBS)
-	8	MOTOWN CHARTBUSTERS VOL 5 Various Artists (Tamla Motown)
10	9	FRANK SINATRA'S GREATEST HITS VOL 2 Frank Sinatra (Reprise)
12	10	EASY LISTENING Various Artists (Polydor)
9	11	MOTOWN CHARTBUSTERS VOL 4 Various Artists (Tamla Motown)
28	12	ELVIS COUNTRY Elvis Presley (RCA)
7	13	LED ZEPPELIN III Led Zeppelin (Atlantic)
8	14	THE BEST OF T. REX T. Rex (Fly)
11	15	THE YES ALBUM Yes (Atlantic)
18	16	AQUALUNG Jethro Tull (Chrysalis)
-	17	PORTRAIT IN MUSIC Burt Bacharach (A&M)
14	18	PENDULUM Creedence Clearwater Revival (Liberty)
17	19	EMERSON LAKE & PALMER Emerson, Lake & Palmer (Island)
15	20	DEEP PURPLE IN ROCK Deep Purple (Harvest)
20	21	ELTON JOHN Elton John (DJM)
19	22	GOLD Neil Diamond (UNI)
16	23	ABRAXAS Santana (CBS)
23	24	SWEET BABY JAMES James Taylor (Warner Bros.)
21	25	AIR CONDITIONING Curved Air (Warner Bros.)
27	26	TAP ROOT MANUSCRIPT Neil Diamond (UNI)
22	27	CHICAGO 3 Chicago (CBS)
30	28	LIVE TASTE Taste (Polydor)
24	29	THE SOUND OF MUSIC Soundtrack (RCA)
26	30	LED ZEPPELIN II Led Zeppelin (Atlantic)

		17 April 1971
2	1	BRIDGE OVER TROUBLED WATER Simon & Garfunkel (CBS)
1	2	HOME LOVIN' MAN Andy Williams (CBS)
4	3	CRY OF LOVE Jimi Hendrix (Track)
6	4	TUMBLEWEED CONNECTION Elton John (DJM)
8	5	MOTOWN CHARTBUSTERS VOL 5 Various Artists (Tamla Motown)
3	6	ALL THINGS MUST PASS George Harrison (Apple)
16	7	AQUALUNG Jethro Tull (Chrysalis)
9	8	FRANK SINATRA'S GREATEST HITS VOL 2 Frank Sinatra (Reprise)
14	9	THE BEST OF T. REX T. Rex (Fly)
12	10	ELVIS COUNTRY Elvis Presley (RCA)
7	11	ANDY WILLIAMS' GREATEST HITS Andy Williams (CBS)
15	12	THE YES ALBUM Yes (Atlantic)
19	13	EMERSON LAKE & PALMER Emerson, Lake & Palmer (Island)
10	14	EASY LISTENING Various Artists (Polydor)
5	15	STONE AGE Rolling Stones (Decca)
11	16	MOTOWN CHARTBUSTERS VOL 4 Various Artists (Tamla Motown)
13	17	LED ZEPPELIN III Led Zeppelin (Atlantic)
27	18	CHICAGO 3 Chicago (CBS)
25	19	AIR CONDITIONING Curved Air (Warner Bros.)
18	20	PENDULUM Creedence Clearwater Revival (Liberty)
20	21	DEEP PURPLE IN ROCK Deep Purple (Harvest)
23	22	ABRAXAS Santana (CBS)
21	23	ELTON JOHN Elton John (DJM)
24	24	SWEET BABY JAMES James Taylor (Warner Bros.)
30	25	LED ZEPPELIN II Led Zeppelin (Atlantic)
28	26	LIVE TASTE Taste (Polydor)
22	27	GOLD Neil Diamond (UNI)
26	28	TAP ROOT MANUSCRIPT Neil Diamond (UNI)
29	29	THE SOUND OF MUSIC Soundtrack (RCA)
17	30	PORTRAIT IN MUSIC Burt Bacharach (A&M)

Jimi Hendrix's first posthumous hit LP arrived, but unlike Andy Williams' *Home Lovin' Man*, it couldn't displace *Bridge Over Troubled Water* from the top slot. While Andy was leering down over the LP charts, his prototype, Perry Como himself, was enjoying a revival. He was drifting down from the No.2 slot in the singles chart (his first time in this Top 20 since 1960) with *It's Impossible*; the album of the same name would chart in June. His last Top 20 album had been *Como's Golden Records*, in 1958-59.

24 April 1971

last	this	title	artist
2	1	HOME LOVIN' MAN	Andy Williams (CBS)
5	2	MOTOWN CHARTBUSTERS VOL 5	Various Artists (Tamla Motown)
1	3	BRIDGE OVER TROUBLED WATER	Simon & Garfunkel (CBS)
7	4	AQUALUNG	Jethro Tull (Chrysalis)
3	5	CRY OF LOVE	Jimi Hendrix (Track)
12	6	THE YES ALBUM	Yes (Atlantic)
-	7	ELEGY	Nice (Chrisma)
11	8	ANDY WILLIAMS' GREATEST HITS	Andy Williams (CBS)
30	9	PORTRAIT IN MUSIC	Burt Bacharach (A&M)
15	10	STONE AGE	Rolling Stones (Decca)
-	11	SONGS OF LOVE & HATE	Leonard Cohen (CBS)
4	12	TUMBLEWEED CONNECTION	Elton John (DJM)
8	13	FRANK SINATRA'S GREATEST HITS VOL 2	Frank Sinatra (Reprise)
6	14	ALL THINGS MUST PASS	George Harrison (Apple)
-	15	IF I COULD ONLY REMEMBER MY NAME	David Crosby (Atlantic)
14	16	EASY LISTENING	Various Artists (Polydor)
-	17	SPLIT	Groundhogs (Liberty)
-	18	DEATH WALKS BEHIND YOU	Atomic Rooster (Charisma)
21	19	DEEP PURPLE IN ROCK	Deep Purple (Harvest)
9	20	THE BEST OF T. REX	T. Rex (Fly)
-	21	2001: A SPACE ODYSSEY	Soundtrack (MGM)
10	22	ELVIS COUNTRY	Elvis Presley (RCA)
23	23	ELTON JOHN	Elton John (DJM)
25	24	LED ZEPPELIN II	Led Zeppelin (Atlantic)
-	25	T. REX	T. Rex (Fly)
17	26	LED ZEPPELIN III	Led Zeppelin (Atlantic)
19	27	AIR CONDITIONING	Curved Air (Warner Bros.)
13	28	EMERSON LAKE & PALMER	Emerson, Lake & Palmer (Island)
22	29	ABRAXAS	Santana (CBS)
24	30	SWEET BABY JAMES	James Taylor (Warner Bros.)

1 May 1971

last	this	title	artist
2	1	MOTOWN CHARTBUSTERS VOL 5	Various Artists (Tamla Motown)
1	2	HOME LOVIN' MAN	Andy Williams (CBS)
-	3	STICKY FINGERS	Rolling Stones (Rolling Stones)
3	4	BRIDGE OVER TROUBLED WATER	Simon & Garfunkel (CBS)
11	5	SONGS OF LOVE & HATE	Leonard Cohen (CBS)
4	6	AQUALUNG	Jethro Tull (Chrysalis)
6	7	THE YES ALBUM	Yes (Atlantic)
5	8	CRY OF LOVE	Jimi Hendrix (Track)
7	9	ELEGY	Nice (Chrisma)
23	10	ELTON JOHN	Elton John (DJM)
17	11	SPLIT	Groundhogs (Liberty)
15	12	IF I COULD ONLY REMEMBER MY NAME	David Crosby (Atlantic)
13	13	FRANK SINATRA'S GREATEST HITS VOL 2	Frank Sinatra (Reprise)
22	14	ELVIS COUNTRY	Elvis Presley (RCA)
8	15	ANDY WILLIAMS' GREATEST HITS	Andy Williams (CBS)
-	16	IT'S IMPOSSIBLE	Perry Como (RCA)
12	17	TUMBLEWEED CONNECTION	Elton John (DJM)
14	18	ALL THINGS MUST PASS	George Harrison (Apple)
9	19	PORTRAIT IN MUSIC	Burt Bacharach (A&M)
16	20	EASY LISTENING	Various Artists (Polydor)
19	21	DEEP PURPLE IN ROCK	Deep Purple (Harvest)
24	22	LED ZEPPELIN II	Led Zeppelin (Atlantic)
-	23	PAINT YOUR WAGON	Soundtrack (Paramount)
25	24	T. REX	T. Rex (Fly)
26	25	LED ZEPPELIN III	Led Zeppelin (Atlantic)
-	26	ELECTRONICALLY TESTED	Mungo Jerry (Dawn)
21	27	2001: A SPACE ODYSSEY	Soundtrack (MGM)
28	28	EMERSON LAKE & PALMER	Emerson, Lake & Palmer (Island)
-	29	THE COMPLEAT TOM PAXTON	Tom Paxton (Elektra)
27	30	AIR CONDITIONING	Curved Air (Warner Bros.)

8 May 1971

last	this	title	artist
3	1	STICKY FINGERS	Rolling Stones (Rolling Stones)
1	2	MOTOWN CHARTBUSTERS VOL 5	Various Artists (Tamla Motown)
2	3	HOME LOVIN' MAN	Andy Williams (CBS)
4	4	BRIDGE OVER TROUBLED WATER	Simon & Garfunkel (CBS)
5	5	SONGS OF LOVE & HATE	Leonard Cohen (CBS)
7	6	THE YES ALBUM	Yes (Atlantic)
9	7	ELEGY	Nice (Chrisma)
12	8	IF I COULD ONLY REMEMBER MY NAME	David Crosby (Atlantic)
8	9	CRY OF LOVE	Jimi Hendrix (Track)
15	10	ANDY WILLIAMS' GREATEST HITS	Andy Williams (CBS)
11	11	SPLIT	Groundhogs (Liberty)
6	12	AQUALUNG	Jethro Tull (Chrysalis)
20	13	EASY LISTENING	Various Artists (Polydor)
14	14	ELVIS COUNTRY	Elvis Presley (RCA)
10	15	ELTON JOHN	Elton John (DJM)
-	16	SYMPHONIES FOR THE 70s	Waldo de los Rios (A&M)
18	17	ALL THINGS MUST PASS	George Harrison (Apple)
22	18	LED ZEPPELIN II	Led Zeppelin (Atlantic)
19	19	PORTRAIT IN MUSIC	Burt Bacharach (A&M)
-	20	17.11.70	Elton John (DJM)
-	21	FRIENDS	Soundtrack (Paramount)
-	22	SOMETHING ELSE	Shirley Bassey (United Artists)
13	23	FRANK SINATRA'S GREATEST HITS VOL 2	Frank Sinatra (Reprise)
23	24	PAINT YOUR WAGON	Soundtrack (Paramount)
26	25	ELECTRONICALLY TESTED	Mungo Jerry (Dawn)
-21	26	DEEP PURPLE IN ROCK	Deep Purple (Harvest)
-	27	AFTER THE GOLD RUSH	Neil Young (Reprise)
16	28	IT'S IMPOSSIBLE	Perry Como (RCA)
17	29	TUMBLEWEED CONNECTION	Elton John (DJM)
-	30	DEATH WALKS BEHIND YOU	Atomic Rooster (Charisma)

15 May 1971

last	this	title	artist
1	1	STICKY FINGERS	Rolling Stones (Rolling Stones)
2	2	MOTOWN CHARTBUSTERS VOL 5	Various Artists (Tamla Motown)
3	3	HOME LOVIN' MAN	Andy Williams (CBS)
5	4	SONGS OF LOVE & HATE	Leonard Cohen (CBS)
4	5	BRIDGE OVER TROUBLED WATER	Simon & Garfunkel (CBS)
9	6	CRY OF LOVE	Jimi Hendrix (Track)
-	7	FOUR WAY STREET	Crosby Stills Nash & Young (Atlantic)
6	8	THE YES ALBUM	Yes (Atlantic)
14	9	ELVIS COUNTRY	Elvis Presley (RCA)
23	10	FRANK SINATRA'S GREATEST HITS VOL 2	Frank Sinatra (Reprise)
10	11	ANDY WILLIAMS' GREATEST HITS	Andy Williams (CBS)
12	12	AQUALUNG	Jethro Tull (Chrysalis)
11	13	SPLIT	Groundhogs (Liberty)
7	14	ELEGY	Nice (Chrisma)
16	15	SYMPHONIES FOR THE 70s	Waldo de los Rios (A&M)
13	16	EASY LISTENING	Various Artists (Polydor)
18	17	LED ZEPPELIN II	Led Zeppelin (Atlantic)
26	18	DEEP PURPLE IN ROCK	Deep Purple (Harvest)
22	19	SOMETHING ELSE	Shirley Bassey (United Artists)
8	20	IF I COULD ONLY REMEMBER MY NAME	David Crosby (Atlantic)
24	21	PAINT YOUR WAGON	Soundtrack (Paramount)
15	22	ELTON JOHN	Elton John (DJM)
19	23	PORTRAIT IN MUSIC	Burt Bacharach (A&M)
17	24	ALL THINGS MUST PASS	George Harrison (Apple)
20	25	17.11.70	Elton John (DJM)
25	26	ELECTRONICALLY TESTED	Mungo Jerry (Dawn)
-	27	SWEET BABY JAMES	James Taylor (Warner Bros.)
-	28	OVER AND OVER	Nana Mouskouri (Fontana)
-	29	CLUB REGGAE	Various Artists (Trojan)
-	30	ABRAXAS	Santana (CBS)

A curious error arose in these charts (now corrected). April 24 showed *Elvis Country* plummet to No.26, and *I'm 10,000 Years Old* arrive at 22. This then disappeared and *Elvis Country* regained the Top 20. In fact *I'm 10,000 Years Old* was *Elvis Country*'s sub-title, not another album. It's the name of a song used on the LP only in short extracts, in place of the gaps between the proper tracks. This daft attempt to make Elvis "modern" marred an LP rightly popular as his best in ages.

May – June 1971

22 May 1971

last	this	Album / Artist
1	1	STICKY FINGERS — Rolling Stones (Rolling Stones)
3	2	HOME LOVIN' MAN — Andy Williams (CBS)
2	3	MOTOWN CHARTBUSTERS VOL 5 — Various Artists (Tamla Motown)
4	4	SONGS OF LOVE & HATE — Leonard Cohen (CBS)
5	5	BRIDGE OVER TROUBLED WATER — Simon & Garfunkel (CBS)
7	6	FOUR WAY STREET — Crosby Stills Nash & Young (Atlantic)
15	7	SYMPHONIES FOR THE 70s — Waldo de los Rios (A&M)
6	8	CRY OF LOVE — Jimi Hendrix (Track)
8	9	THE YES ALBUM — Yes (Atlantic)
13	10	SPLIT — Groundhogs (Liberty)
10	11	FRANK SINATRA'S GREATEST HITS VOL 2 — Frank Sinatra (Reprise)
14	12	ELEGY — Nice (Chrisma)
12	13	AQUALUNG — Jethro Tull (Chrysalis)
11	14	ANDY WILLIAMS' GREATEST HITS — Andy Williams (CBS)
-	15	MUD SLIDE SLIM AND THE BLUE HORIZON — James Taylor (Warner Bros.)
9	16	ELVIS COUNTRY — Elvis Presley (RCA)
19	17	SOMETHING ELSE — Shirley Bassey (United Artists)
20	18	IF I COULD ONLY REMEMBER MY NAME — David Crosby (Atlantic)
16	19	EASY LISTENING — Various Artists (Polydor)
18	20	DEEP PURPLE IN ROCK — Deep Purple (Harvest)
30	21	ABRAXAS — Santana (CBS)
28	22	OVER AND OVER — Nana Mouskouri (Fontana)
17	23	LED ZEPPELIN II — Led Zeppelin (Atlantic)
21	24	PAINT YOUR WAGON — Soundtrack (Paramount)
-	25	IT'S IMPOSSIBLE — Perry Como (RCA)
-	26	THE BEST OF T. REX — T. Rex (Fly)
22	27	ELTON JOHN — Elton John (DJM)
25	28	17.11.70 — Elton John (DJM)
27	29	SWEET BABY JAMES — James Taylor (Warner Bros.)
23	30	PORTRAIT IN MUSIC — Burt Bacharach (A&M)

29 May 1971

last	this	Album / Artist
1	1	STICKY FINGERS — Rolling Stones (Rolling Stones)
2	2	HOME LOVIN' MAN — Andy Williams (CBS)
3	3	MOTOWN CHARTBUSTERS VOL 5 — Various Artists (Tamla Motown)
5	4	BRIDGE OVER TROUBLED WATER — Simon & Garfunkel (CBS)
4	5	SONGS OF LOVE & HATE — Leonard Cohen (CBS)
7	6	SYMPHONIES FOR THE 70s — Waldo de los Rios (A&M)
10	7	SPLIT — Groundhogs (Liberty)
6	8	FOUR WAY STREET — Crosby Stills Nash & Young (Atlantic)
25	9	IT'S IMPOSSIBLE — Perry Como (RCA)
-	10	RAM — Paul McCartney (Apple)
13	11	AQUALUNG — Jethro Tull (Chrysalis)
14	12	ANDY WILLIAMS' GREATEST HITS — Andy Williams (CBS)
15	13	MUD SLIDE SLIM AND THE BLUE HORIZON — James Taylor (Warner Bros.)
11	14	FRANK SINATRA'S GREATEST HITS VOL 2 — Frank Sinatra (Reprise)
8	15	CRY OF LOVE — Jimi Hendrix (Track)
9	16	THE YES ALBUM — Yes (Atlantic)
30	17	PORTRAIT IN MUSIC — Burt Bacharach (A&M)
23	18	LED ZEPPELIN II — Led Zeppelin (Atlantic)
-	19	ALL THINGS MUST PASS — George Harrison (Apple)
12	20	ELEGY — Nice (Chrisma)
20	21	DEEP PURPLE IN ROCK — Deep Purple (Harvest)
17	22	SOMETHING ELSE — Shirley Bassey (United Artists)
19	23	EASY LISTENING — Various Artists (Polydor)
29	24	SWEET BABY JAMES — James Taylor (Warner Bros.)
-	25	THE GOOD BOOK — Melanie (Buddah)
-	26	AFTER THE GOLD RUSH — Neil Young (Reprise)
21	27	ABRAXAS — Santana (CBS)
-	28	SHE'S A LADY — Tom Jones (Decca)
22	29	OVER AND OVER — Nana Mouskouri (Fontana)
24	30	PAINT YOUR WAGON — Soundtrack (Paramount)

5 June 1971

last	this	Album / Artist
1	1	STICKY FINGERS — Rolling Stones (Rolling Stones)
3	2	MOTOWN CHARTBUSTERS VOL 5 — Various Artists (Tamla Motown)
2	3	HOME LOVIN' MAN — Andy Williams (CBS)
4	4	BRIDGE OVER TROUBLED WATER — Simon & Garfunkel (CBS)
10	5	RAM — Paul McCartney (Apple)
5	6	SONGS OF LOVE & HATE — Leonard Cohen (CBS)
6	7	SYMPHONIES FOR THE 70s — Waldo de los Rios (A&M)
7	8	SPLIT — Groundhogs (Liberty)
13	9	MUD SLIDE SLIM AND THE BLUE HORIZON — James Taylor (Warner Bros.)
8	10	FOUR WAY STREET — Crosby Stills Nash & Young (Atlantic)
12	11	ANDY WILLIAMS' GREATEST HITS — Andy Williams (CBS)
25	12	THE GOOD BOOK — Melanie (Buddah)
15	13	CRY OF LOVE — Jimi Hendrix (Track)
9	14	IT'S IMPOSSIBLE — Perry Como (RCA)
27	15	ABRAXAS — Santana (CBS)
29	16	OVER AND OVER — Nana Mouskouri (Fontana)
28	17	SHE'S A LADY — Tom Jones (Decca)
16	18	THE YES ALBUM — Yes (Atlantic)
24	19	SWEET BABY JAMES — James Taylor (Warner Bros.)
-	20	RELICS — Pink Floyd (Starline)
14	21	FRANK SINATRA'S GREATEST HITS VOL 2 — Frank Sinatra (Reprise)
-	22	OSIBISA — Osibisa (Decca)
11	23	AQUALUNG — Jethro Tull (Chrysalis)
20	24	ELEGY — Nice (Chrisma)
19	25	ALL THINGS MUST PASS — George Harrison (Apple)
21	26	DEEP PURPLE IN ROCK — Deep Purple (Harvest)
17	27	PORTRAIT IN MUSIC — Burt Bacharach (A&M)
22	28	SOMETHING ELSE — Shirley Bassey (United Artists)
18	29	LED ZEPPELIN II — Led Zeppelin (Atlantic)
26	30	AFTER THE GOLD RUSH — Neil Young (Reprise)

12 June 1971

last	this	Album / Artist
1	1	STICKY FINGERS — Rolling Stones (Rolling Stones)
2	2	MOTOWN CHARTBUSTERS VOL 5 — Various Artists (Tamla Motown)
4	3	BRIDGE OVER TROUBLED WATER — Simon & Garfunkel (CBS)
5	4	RAM — Paul McCartney (Apple)
8	5	SPLIT — Groundhogs (Liberty)
7	6	SYMPHONIES FOR THE 70s — Waldo de los Rios (A&M)
3	7	HOME LOVIN' MAN — Andy Williams (CBS)
9	8	MUD SLIDE SLIM AND THE BLUE HORIZON — James Taylor (Warner Bros.)
10	9	FOUR WAY STREET — Crosby Stills Nash & Young (Atlantic)
6	10	SONGS OF LOVE & HATE — Leonard Cohen (CBS)
11	11	ANDY WILLIAMS' GREATEST HITS — Andy Williams (CBS)
17	12	SHE'S A LADY — Tom Jones (Decca)
28	13	SOMETHING ELSE — Shirley Bassey (United Artists)
18	14	THE YES ALBUM — Yes (Atlantic)
21	15	FRANK SINATRA'S GREATEST HITS VOL 2 — Frank Sinatra (Reprise)
-	16	SINATRA & COMPANY — Frank Sinatra (Reprise)
12	17	THE GOOD BOOK — Melanie (Buddah)
26	18	DEEP PURPLE IN ROCK — Deep Purple (Harvest)
29	19	LED ZEPPELIN II — Led Zeppelin (Atlantic)
16	20	OVER AND OVER — Nana Mouskouri (Fontana)
-	21	TARKUS — Emerson Lake & Palmer (Island)
-	22	DEJA VU — Crosby Stills Nash & Young (Atlantic)
13	23	CRY OF LOVE — Jimi Hendrix (Track)
-	24	ELVIS: THAT'S THE WAY IT IS — Elvis Presley (RCA)
30	25	AFTER THE GOLD RUSH — Neil Young (Reprise)
19	26	SWEET BABY JAMES — James Taylor (Warner Bros.)
14	27	IT'S IMPOSSIBLE — Perry Como (RCA)
15	28	ABRAXAS — Santana (CBS)
27	29	PORTRAIT IN MUSIC — Burt Bacharach (A&M)
20	30	RELICS — Pink Floyd (Starline)

Sticky Fingers, the Stones' 13th album (counting hits packages), was the first on their own label, and free of Decca. It introduced the famous lolling-tongue-and-lips design. Rock groups had long been keen on these corporate logos; oddly, the Stones chose one that used the personality cult of Mick Jagger, well-known owner of said lips, to symbolise the world's greatest rock band. *Sticky Fingers* was their fourth No.1 album (some charts said their sixth), and perhaps their best. Ultimate highlight: *Moonlight Mile*.

19 June 1971

last week	this week		
1	1	STICKY FINGERS	Rolling Stones (Rolling Stones)
4	2	RAM	Paul McCartney (Apple)
3	3	BRIDGE OVER TROUBLED WATER	Simon & Garfunkel (CBS)
2	4	MOTOWN CHARTBUSTERS VOL 5	Various Artists (Tamla Motown)
8	5	MUD SLIDE SLIM AND THE BLUE HORIZON	James Taylor (Warner Bros.)
5	6	SPLIT	Groundhogs (Liberty)
7	7	HOME LOVIN' MAN	Andy Williams (CBS)
21	8	TARKUS	Emerson Lake & Palmer (Island)
6	9	SYMPHONIES FOR THE 70s	Waldo de los Rios (A&M)
9	10	FOUR WAY STREET	Crosby Stills Nash & Young (Atlantic)
10	11	SONGS OF LOVE & HATE	Leonard Cohen (CBS)
17	12	THE GOOD BOOK	Melanie (Buddah)
11	13	ANDY WILLIAMS' GREATEST HITS	Andy Williams (CBS)
14	14	THE YES ALBUM	Yes (Atlantic)
20	15	OVER AND OVER	Nana Mouskouri (Fontana)
30	16	RELICS	Pink Floyd (Starline)
13	17	SOMETHING ELSE	Shirley Bassey (United Artists)
16	18	SINATRA & COMPANY	Frank Sinatra (Reprise)
15	19	FRANK SINATRA'S GREATEST HITS VOL 2	Frank Sinatra (Reprise)
26	20	SWEET BABY JAMES	James Taylor (Warner Bros.)
19	21	LED ZEPPELIN II	Led Zeppelin (Atlantic)
12	22	SHE'S A LADY	Tom Jones (Decca)
27	23	IT'S IMPOSSIBLE	Perry Como (RCA)
18	24	DEEP PURPLE IN ROCK	Deep Purple (Harvest)
-	25	THE MAGNIFICENT SEVEN	Supremes & Four Tops (Tamla Motown)
22	26	DEJA VU	Crosby Stills Nash & Young (Atlantic)
25	27	AFTER THE GOLD RUSH	Neil Young (Reprise)
29	28	PORTRAIT IN MUSIC	Burt Bacharach (A&M)
-	29	THIS IS MANUEL	Manuel & His Music of the Mountains (Studio Two)
-	30	AQUALUNG	Jethro Tull (Chrysalis)

26 June 1971

1	1	STICKY FINGERS	Rolling Stones (Rolling Stones)
2	2	RAM	Paul McCartney (Apple)
8	3	TARKUS	Emerson Lake & Palmer (Island)
3	4	BRIDGE OVER TROUBLED WATER	Simon & Garfunkel (CBS)
4	5	MOTOWN CHARTBUSTERS VOL 5	Various Artists (Tamla Motown)
6	6	SPLIT	Groundhogs (Liberty)
5	7	MUD SLIDE SLIM AND THE BLUE HORIZON	James Taylor (Warner Bros.)
7	8	HOME LOVIN' MAN	Andy Williams (CBS)
10	9	FOUR WAY STREET	Crosby Stills Nash & Young (Atlantic)
9	10	SYMPHONIES FOR THE 70s	Waldo de los Rios (A&M)
11	11	SONGS OF LOVE & HATE	Leonard Cohen (CBS)
18	12	SINATRA & COMPANY	Frank Sinatra (Reprise)
13	13	ANDY WILLIAMS' GREATEST HITS	Andy Williams (CBS)
-	14	FREE LIVE	Free (Island)
-	15	SONGS FOR BEGINNERS	Graham Nash (Atlantic)
16	16	RELICS	Pink Floyd (Starline)
12	17	THE GOOD BOOK	Melanie (Buddah)
-	18	ABRAXAS	Santana (CBS)
19	19	FRANK SINATRA'S GREATEST HITS VOL 2	Frank Sinatra (Reprise)
-	20	COLOSSEUM LIVE	Colosseum (Bronze)
27	21	AFTER THE GOLD RUSH	Neil Young (Reprise)
22	22	SHE'S A LADY	Tom Jones (Decca)
15	23	OVER AND OVER	Nana Mouskouri (Fontana)
30	24	AQUALUNG	Jethro Tull (Chrysalis)
14	25	THE YES ALBUM	Yes (Atlantic)
-	26	TAP ROOT MANUSCRIPT	Neil Diamond (UNI)
25	27	THE MAGNIFICENT SEVEN	Supremes & Four Tops (Tamla Motown)
20	28	SWEET BABY JAMES	James Taylor (Warner Bros.)
23	29	IT'S IMPOSSIBLE	Perry Como (RCA)
28	30	PORTRAIT IN MUSIC	Burt Bacharach (A&M)

3 July 1971

4	1	BRIDGE OVER TROUBLED WATER	Simon & Garfunkel (CBS)
2	2	RAM	Paul McCartney (Apple)
1	3	STICKY FINGERS	Rolling Stones (Rolling Stones)
3	4	TARKUS	Emerson Lake & Palmer (Island)
5	5	MOTOWN CHARTBUSTERS VOL 5	Various Artists (Tamla Motown)
14	6	FREE LIVE	Free (Island)
8	7	HOME LOVIN' MAN	Andy Williams (CBS)
6	8	SPLIT	Groundhogs (Liberty)
7	9	MUD SLIDE SLIM AND THE BLUE HORIZON	James Taylor (Warner Bros.)
10	10	SYMPHONIES FOR THE 70s	Waldo de los Rios (A&M)
12	11	SINATRA & COMPANY	Frank Sinatra (Reprise)
15	12	SONGS FOR BEGINNERS	Graham Nash (Atlantic)
-	13	THIS IS MANUEL	Manuel & His Music of the Mountains (Studio Two)
-	14	THE SOUND OF MUSIC	Soundtrack (RCA)
13	15	ANDY WILLIAMS' GREATEST HITS	Andy Williams (CBS)
9	16	FOUR WAY STREET	Crosby Stills Nash & Young (Atlantic)
16	17	RELICS	Pink Floyd (Starline)
11	18	SONGS OF LOVE & HATE	Leonard Cohen (CBS)
-	19	LED ZEPPELIN II	Led Zeppelin (Atlantic)
-	20	DEJA VU	Crosby Stills Nash & Young (Atlantic)
19	21	FRANK SINATRA'S GREATEST HITS VOL 2	Frank Sinatra (Reprise)
-	22	BACK TO THE ROOTS	John Mayall (Polydor)
20	23	COLOSSEUM LIVE	Colosseum (Bronze)
-	24	OSIBISA	Osibisa (Decca)
25	25	THE YES ALBUM	Yes (Atlantic)
-	26	TURN ON THE SUN	Nana Mouskouri (Fontana)
23	27	OVER AND OVER	Nana Mouskouri (Fontana)
21	28	AFTER THE GOLD RUSH	Neil Young (Reprise)
30	29	PORTRAIT IN MUSIC	Burt Bacharach (A&M)
18	30	ABRAXAS	Santana (CBS)
27	30	THE MAGNIFICENT SEVEN	Supremes & Four Tops (Tamla Motown)

10 July 1971

2	1	RAM	Paul McCartney (Apple)
1	2	BRIDGE OVER TROUBLED WATER	Simon & Garfunkel (CBS)
4	3	TARKUS	Emerson Lake & Palmer (Island)
5	4	MOTOWN CHARTBUSTERS VOL 5	Various Artists (Tamla Motown)
6	5	FREE LIVE	Free (Island)
3	6	STICKY FINGERS	Rolling Stones (Rolling Stones)
10	7	SYMPHONIES FOR THE 70s	Waldo de los Rios (A&M)
9	8	MUD SLIDE SLIM AND THE BLUE HORIZON	James Taylor (Warner Bros.)
7	9	HOME LOVIN' MAN	Andy Williams (CBS)
8	10	SPLIT	Groundhogs (Liberty)
-	11	ANGEL DELIGHT	Fairport Convention (Island)
11	12	SINATRA & COMPANY	Frank Sinatra (Reprise)
15	13	ANDY WILLIAMS' GREATEST HITS	Andy Williams (CBS)
13	14	THIS IS MANUEL	Manuel & His Music of the Mountains (Studio Two)
21	15	FRANK SINATRA'S GREATEST HITS VOL 2	Frank Sinatra (Reprise)
19	16	LED ZEPPELIN II	Led Zeppelin (Atlantic)
-	17	THE GOOD BOOK	Melanie (Buddah)
16	18	FOUR WAY STREET	Crosby Stills Nash & Young (Atlantic)
25	19	THE YES ALBUM	Yes (Atlantic)
17	20	RELICS	Pink Floyd (Starline)
14	21	THE SOUND OF MUSIC	Soundtrack (RCA)
18	22	SONGS OF LOVE & HATE	Leonard Cohen (CBS)
27	23	OVER AND OVER	Nana Mouskouri (Fontana)
-	24	THE WORLD OF YOUR 100 BEST TUNES	Various Artists (Decca)
12	25	SONGS FOR BEGINNERS	Graham Nash (Atlantic)
30	26	THE MAGNIFICENT SEVEN	Supremes & Four Tops (Tamla Motown)
28	27	AFTER THE GOLD RUSH	Neil Young (Reprise)
30	28	ABRAXAS	Santana (CBS)
22	29	BACK TO THE ROOTS	John Mayall (Polydor)
26	30	TURN ON THE SUN	Nana Mouskouri (Fontana)

This Is Manuel was an album that would yo-yo in and out of the charts over the coming weeks (in at 29, out again, in at 13, then 14, then out, back in at 18, back out again). It was not a comedy album by the Spanish waiter character from Fawlty Towers, but an "easy listening" LP by Manuel & His Music Of The Mountains. In turn, these happy peasants from the foothills of the Andes were not forerunners of World Music; they were British bandleader Geoff Love and His Orchestra.

July – August 1971

Geoff Love was having a busy year. Under his own name he would soon make the chart with the LP *Big War Movie Themes*, and then the parts too low for NME to reach, with *Big Western Movie Themes* and *Big Love Movie Themes*. In July, Jim Morrison died in his bath in Paris, and in August, sax maestro King Curtis was murdered back in the USA. August also saw George Harrison organise and star in the Concert For Bangla Desh in New York City – a Live Aid before its time.

14 August 1971

last week	this week		
4	1	EVERY GOOD BOY DESERVES FAVOUR	Moody Blues (Threshold)
1	2	BRIDGE OVER TROUBLED WATER	Simon & Garfunkel (CBS)
7	3	BLUE	Joni Mitchell (Reprise)
2	4	RAM	Paul McCartney (Apple)
3	5	MOTOWN CHARTBUSTERS VOL 5	Various Artists (Tamla Motown)
5	6	STICKY FINGERS	Rolling Stones (Rolling Stones)
8	7	TARKUS	Emerson Lake & Palmer (Island)
9	8	MUD SLIDE SLIM AND THE BLUE HORIZON	James Taylor (Warner Bros.)
11	9	EVERY PICTURE TELLS A STORY	Rod Stewart (Mercury)
10	10	LOVE STORY	Andy Williams (CBS)
-	11	TAPESTRY	Carole King (A&M)
-	12	HOT HITS SIX	Various Artists (Music for Pleasure)
-	13	STEPHEN STILLS 2	Stephen Stills (Atlantic)
-	14	MASTER OF REALITY	Black Sabbath (Vertigo)
20	15	AFTER THE GOLD RUSH	Neil Young (Reprise)
19	16	JIM REEVES' GOLDEN RECORDS	Jim Reeves (RCA)
24	17	THE YES ALBUM	Yes (Atlantic)
13	18	SWEET BABY JAMES	James Taylor (Warner Bros.)
29	19	LED ZEPPELIN II	Led Zeppelin (Atlantic)
-	20	HOME LOVIN' MAN	Andy Williams (CBS)
12	21	LOVE LETTERS FROM ELVIS	Elvis Presley (RCA)
23	22	L.A. WOMAN	Doors (Elektra)
-	23	B S & T 4	Blood Sweat & Tears (CBS)
26	24	RELICS	Pink Floyd (Starline)
16	25	SPLIT	Groundhogs (Liberty)
15	26	THE MAGNIFICENT SEVEN	Supremes & Four Tops (Tamla Motown)
17	27	ANDY WILLIAMS' GREATEST HITS	Andy Williams (CBS)
21	28	C'MON EVERYBODY	Elvis Presley (RCA International)
22	29	PAINT YOUR WAGON	Soundtrack (Paramount)
28	30	SONGS OF LOVE & HATE	Leonard Cohen (CBS)

21 August 1971

1	1	EVERY GOOD BOY DESERVES FAVOUR	Moody Blues (Threshold)
2	2	BRIDGE OVER TROUBLED WATER	Simon & Garfunkel (CBS)
4	3	RAM	Paul McCartney (Apple)
5	4	MOTOWN CHARTBUSTERS VOL 5	Various Artists (Tamla Motown)
8	5	MUD SLIDE SLIM AND THE BLUE HORIZON	James Taylor (Warner Bros.)
3	6	BLUE	Joni Mitchell (Reprise)
6	7	STICKY FINGERS	Rolling Stones (Rolling Stones)
11	8	TAPESTRY	Carole King (A&M)
7	9	TARKUS	Emerson Lake & Palmer (Island)
10	10	LOVE STORY	Andy Williams (CBS)
28	11	C'MON EVERYBODY	Elvis Presley (RCA International)
18	12	SWEET BABY JAMES	James Taylor (Warner Bros.)
14	13	MASTER OF REALITY	Black Sabbath (Vertigo)
-	14	TOP OF THE POPS 18	Various Artists (Hallmark)
27	15	ANDY WILLIAMS' GREATEST HITS	Andy Williams (CBS)
15	16	AFTER THE GOLD RUSH	Neil Young (Reprise)
9	17	EVERY PICTURE TELLS A STORY	Rod Stewart (Mercury)
12	18	HOT HITS SIX	Various Artists (Music for Pleasure)
13	19	STEPHEN STILLS 2	Stephen Stills (Atlantic)
25	20	SPLIT	Groundhogs (Liberty)
-	21	FREE LIVE	Free (Island)
29	22	PAINT YOUR WAGON	Soundtrack (Paramount)
26	23	THE MAGNIFICENT SEVEN	Supremes & Four Tops (Tamla Motown)
24	24	RELICS	Pink Floyd (Starline)
19	25	LED ZEPPELIN II	Led Zeppelin (Atlantic)
17	26	THE YES ALBUM	Yes (Atlantic)
-	27	DEEP PURPLE IN ROCK	Deep Purple (Harvest)
20	28	HOME LOVIN' MAN	Andy Williams (CBS)
-	29	SYMPHONIES FOR THE 70s	Waldo de los Rios (A&M)
30	30	SONGS OF LOVE & HATE	Leonard Cohen (CBS)

28 August 1971

1	1	EVERY GOOD BOY DESERVES FAVOUR	Moody Blues (Threshold)
2	2	BRIDGE OVER TROUBLED WATER	Simon & Garfunkel (CBS)
6	3	BLUE	Joni Mitchell (Reprise)
3	4	RAM	Paul McCartney (Apple)
5	5	MUD SLIDE SLIM AND THE BLUE HORIZON	James Taylor (Warner Bros.)
9	6	TARKUS	Emerson Lake & Palmer (Island)
17	7	EVERY PICTURE TELLS A STORY	Rod Stewart (Mercury)
8	8	TAPESTRY	Carole King (A&M)
4	9	MOTOWN CHARTBUSTERS VOL 5	Various Artists (Tamla Motown)
7	10	STICKY FINGERS	Rolling Stones (Rolling Stones)
13	11	MASTER OF REALITY	Black Sabbath (Vertigo)
14	12	TOP OF THE POPS 18	Various Artists (Hallmark)
10	13	LOVE STORY	Andy Williams (CBS)
11	14	C'MON EVERYBODY	Elvis Presley (RCA International)
18	15	HOT HITS SIX	Various Artists (Music for Pleasure)
15	16	ANDY WILLIAMS' GREATEST HITS	Andy Williams (CBS)
12	17	SWEET BABY JAMES	James Taylor (Warner Bros.)
-	18	EXPERIENCE	Jimi Hendrix Experience (Ember)
-	19	THE INTIMATE JIM REEVES	Jim Reeves (RCA International)
16	20	AFTER THE GOLD RUSH	Neil Young (Reprise)
22	21	PAINT YOUR WAGON	Soundtrack (Paramount)
21	22	FREE LIVE	Free (Island)
-	23	LIVE PERFORMANCE	Spinners (Fontana)
24	24	RELICS	Pink Floyd (Starline)
20	25	SPLIT	Groundhogs (Liberty)
19	26	STEPHEN STILLS 2	Stephen Stills (Atlantic)
-	27	LOVE STORY	Soundtrack (Paramount)
25	28	LED ZEPPELIN II	Led Zeppelin (Atlantic)
27	29	DEEP PURPLE IN ROCK	Deep Purple (Harvest)
28	30	HOME LOVIN' MAN	Andy Williams (CBS)

4 September 1971

1	1	EVERY GOOD BOY DESERVES FAVOUR	Moody Blues (Threshold)
2	2	BRIDGE OVER TROUBLED WATER	Simon & Garfunkel (CBS)
5	3	MUD SLIDE SLIM AND THE BLUE HORIZON	James Taylor (Warner Bros.)
8	4	TAPESTRY	Carole King (A&M)
4	5	RAM	Paul McCartney (Apple)
3	6	BLUE	Joni Mitchell (Reprise)
11	7	MASTER OF REALITY	Black Sabbath (Vertigo)
9	8	MOTOWN CHARTBUSTERS VOL 5	Various Artists (Tamla Motown)
10	9	STICKY FINGERS	Rolling Stones (Rolling Stones)
12	10	TOP OF THE POPS 18	Various Artists (Hallmark)
14	11	C'MON EVERYBODY	Elvis Presley (RCA International)
7	12	EVERY PICTURE TELLS A STORY	Rod Stewart (Mercury)
13	13	LOVE STORY	Andy Williams (CBS)
17	14	SWEET BABY JAMES	James Taylor (Warner Bros.)
6	15	TARKUS	Emerson Lake & Palmer (Island)
15	16	HOT HITS SIX	Various Artists (Music for Pleasure)
-	17	WHO'S NEXT	Who (Polydor)
-	18	EVERYTHING IS EVERYTHING	Diana Ross (Tamla Motown)
21	19	PAINT YOUR WAGON	Soundtrack (Paramount)
25	20	SPLIT	Groundhogs (Liberty)
18	21	EXPERIENCE	Jimi Hendrix Experience (Ember)
22	22	FREE LIVE	Free (Island)
20	23	AFTER THE GOLD RUSH	Neil Young (Reprise)
23	24	LIVE PERFORMANCE	Spinners (Fontana)
30	25	HOME LOVIN' MAN	Andy Williams (CBS)
24	26	RELICS	Pink Floyd (Starline)
16	27	ANDY WILLIAMS' GREATEST HITS	Andy Williams (CBS)
19	28	THE INTIMATE JIM REEVES	Jim Reeves (RCA International)
-	29	IN HEARING OF	Atomic Rooster (Pegasus)
28	30	LED ZEPPELIN II	Led Zeppelin (Atlantic)

Every Picture Tells A Story was not Rod Stewart's first album since leaving the Faces. *Gasoline Alley* had come first; but *Every Picture Tells A Story* was to prove the huge turning-point in Rod the Mod's career: the first of six consecutive No.1 albums, issued at the rate of one a year from now till 1976's *Night On The Town*, by which time Rod was the tabloids' Richard Burton of rock, street cred blown, while back in gasoline alley the punks were baying at the garage door.

11 September 1971

last week	this week	
1	1	EVERY GOOD BOY DESERVES FAVOUR — Moody Blues (Threshold)
2	2	BRIDGE OVER TROUBLED WATER — Simon & Garfunkel (CBS)
5	3	RAM — Paul McCartney (Apple)
3	4	MUD SLIDE SLIM AND THE BLUE HORIZON — James Taylor (Warner Bros.)
4	5	TAPESTRY — Carole King (A&M)
12	6	EVERY PICTURE TELLS A STORY — Rod Stewart (Mercury)
6	7	BLUE — Joni Mitchell (Reprise)
7	8	MASTER OF REALITY — Black Sabbath (Vertigo)
9	9	STICKY FINGERS — Rolling Stones (Rolling Stones)
8	10	MOTOWN CHARTBUSTERS VOL 5 — Various Artists (Tamla Motown)
-	11	FIREBALL — Deep Purple (Harvest)
15	12	TARKUS — Emerson Lake & Palmer (Island)
17	13	WHO'S NEXT — Who (Polydor)
14	14	SWEET BABY JAMES — James Taylor (Warner Bros.)
27	15	ANDY WILLIAMS' GREATEST HITS — Andy Williams (CBS)
21	16	EXPERIENCE — Jimi Hendrix Wxperience (Ember)
11	17	C'MON EVERYBODY — Elvis Presley (RCA International)
13	18	LOVE STORY — Andy Williams (CBS)
-	19	BIG WAR MOVIE THEMES — Geoff Love & His Orchestra (Music for Pleasure)
22	20	FREE LIVE — Free (Island)
-	21	SYMPHONIES FOR THE 70s — Waldo de los Rios (A&M)
-	22	DEJA VU — Crosby Stills Nash & Young (Atlantic)
20	23	SPLIT — Groundhogs (Liberty)
16	24	HOT HITS SIX — Various Artists (Music for Pleasure)
25	25	HOME LOVIN' MAN — Andy Williams (CBS)
10	26	TOP OF THE POPS 18 — Various Artists (Hallmark)
-	27	LOVE STORY — Soundtrack (Paramount)
19	28	PAINT YOUR WAGON — Soundtrack (Paramount)
23	29	AFTER THE GOLD RUSH — Neil Young (Reprise)
24	30	LIVE PERFORMANCE — Spinners (Fontana)

18 September 1971

5	1	TAPESTRY — Carole King (A&M)
1	2	EVERY GOOD BOY DESERVES FAVOUR — Moody Blues (Threshold)
2	3	BRIDGE OVER TROUBLED WATER — Simon & Garfunkel (CBS)
4	4	MUD SLIDE SLIM AND THE BLUE HORIZON — James Taylor (Warner Bros.)
13	5	WHO'S NEXT — Who (Polydor)
6	6	EVERY PICTURE TELLS A STORY — Rod Stewart (Mercury)
3	7	RAM — Paul McCartney (Apple)
11	8	FIREBALL — Deep Purple (Harvest)
8	9	MASTER OF REALITY — Black Sabbath (Vertigo)
14	10	SWEET BABY JAMES — James Taylor (Warner Bros.)
7	11	BLUE — Joni Mitchell (Reprise)
12	12	TARKUS — Emerson Lake & Palmer (Island)
16	13	EXPERIENCE — Jimi Hendrix Experience (Ember)
9	14	STICKY FINGERS — Rolling Stones (Rolling Stones)
15	15	ANDY WILLIAMS' GREATEST HITS — Andy Williams (CBS)
18	16	LOVE STORY — Andy Williams (CBS)
27	17	LOVE STORY — Soundtrack (Paramount)
10	18	MOTOWN CHARTBUSTERS VOL 5 — Various Artists (Tamla Motown)
30	19	LIVE PERFORMANCE — Spinners (Fontana)
26	20	TOP OF THE POPS 18 — Various Artists (Hallmark)
25	21	HOME LOVIN' MAN — Andy Williams (CBS)
17	22	C'MON EVERYBODY — Elvis Presley (RCA International)
28	23	PAINT YOUR WAGON — Soundtrack (Paramount)
-	24	OVER AND OVER — Nana Mouskouri (Fontana)
-	25	THE BEST OF T. REX — T. Rex (Fly)
20	26	FREE LIVE — Free (Island)
-	27	IN HEARING OF — Atomic Rooster (Pegasus)
23	28	SPLIT — Groundhogs (Liberty)
24	29	HOT HITS SIX — Various Artists (Music for Pleasure)
21	30	SYMPHONIES FOR THE 70s — Waldo de los Rios (A&M)

25 September 1971

6	1	EVERY PICTURE TELLS A STORY — Rod Stewart (Mercury)
3	2	BRIDGE OVER TROUBLED WATER — Simon & Garfunkel (CBS)
5	3	WHO'S NEXT — Who (Polydor)
2	4	EVERY GOOD BOY DESERVES FAVOUR — Moody Blues (Threshold)
1	5	TAPESTRY — Carole King (A&M)
4	6	MUD SLIDE SLIM AND THE BLUE HORIZON — James Taylor (Warner Bros.)
8	7	FIREBALL — Deep Purple (Harvest)
11	8	BLUE — Joni Mitchell (Reprise)
7	9	RAM — Paul McCartney (Apple)
10	10	SWEET BABY JAMES — James Taylor (Warner Bros.)
15	11	ANDY WILLIAMS' GREATEST HITS — Andy Williams (CBS)
18	12	MOTOWN CHARTBUSTERS VOL 5 — Various Artists (Tamla Motown)
9	13	MASTER OF REALITY — Black Sabbath (Vertigo)
16	14	LOVE STORY — Andy Williams (CBS)
12	15	TARKUS — Emerson Lake & Palmer (Island)
20	16	TOP OF THE POPS 18 — Various Artists (Hallmark)
17	17	LOVE STORY — Soundtrack (Paramount)
22	18	C'MON EVERYBODY — Elvis Presley (RCA International)
14	19	STICKY FINGERS — Rolling Stones (Rolling Stones)
-	20	MAN IN BLACK — Johnny Cash (CBS)
13	21	EXPERIENCE — Jimi Hendrix Experience (Ember)
21	22	HOME LOVIN' MAN — Andy Williams (CBS)
30	23	SYMPHONIES FOR THE 70s — Waldo de los Rios (A&M)
-	24	GIMME SHELTER — Rolling Stones (Decca)
23	25	PAINT YOUR WAGON — Soundtrack (Paramount)
19	26	LIVE PERFORMANCE — Spinners (Fontana)
29	27	HOT HITS SIX — Various Artists (Music for Pleasure)
24	28	OVER AND OVER — Nana Mouskouri (Fontana)
25	29	THE BEST OF T. REX — T. Rex (Fly)
-	30	THE INTIMATE JIM REEVES — Jim Reeves (RCA International)

2 October 1971

1	1	EVERY PICTURE TELLS A STORY — Rod Stewart (Mercury)
5	2	TAPESTRY — Carole King (A&M)
3	3	WHO'S NEXT — Who (Polydor)
7	4	FIREBALL — Deep Purple (Harvest)
6	5	MUD SLIDE SLIM AND THE BLUE HORIZON — James Taylor (Warner Bros.)
2	6	BRIDGE OVER TROUBLED WATER — Simon & Garfunkel (CBS)
4	7	EVERY GOOD BOY DESERVES FAVOUR — Moody Blues (Threshold)
9	8	RAM — Paul McCartney (Apple)
8	9	BLUE — Joni Mitchell (Reprise)
10	10	SWEET BABY JAMES — James Taylor (Warner Bros.)
12	11	MOTOWN CHARTBUSTERS VOL 5 — Various Artists (Tamla Motown)
-	12	ELECTRIC WARRIOR — T. Rex (Fly)
13	13	MASTER OF REALITY — Black Sabbath (Vertigo)
-	14	DIANA! — Diana Ross (Tamla Motown)
-	15	TEASER & THE FIRECAT — Cat Stevens (Island)
11	16	ANDY WILLIAMS' GREATEST HITS — Andy Williams (CBS)
-	17	I'M STILL WAITING — Diana Ross (Tamla Motown)
16	18	TOP OF THE POPS 18 — Various Artists (Hallmark)
14	19	LOVE STORY — Andy Williams (CBS)
-	20	EVERYTHING IS EVERYTHING — Diana Ross (Tamla Motown)
24	21	GIMME SHELTER — Rolling Stones (Decca)
19	22	STICKY FINGERS — Rolling Stones (Rolling Stones)
20	23	MAN IN BLACK — Johnny Cash (CBS)
-	24	CURVED AIR — Curved Air (Warner Bros.)
15	25	TARKUS — Emerson Lake & Palmer (Island)
18	26	C'MON EVERYBODY — Elvis Presley (RCA International)
23	27	SYMPHONIES FOR THE 70s — Waldo de los Rios (A&M)
29	28	THE BEST OF T. REX — T. Rex (Fly)
-	29	THIS IS MANUEL — Manuel & His Music of the Mountains (Studio Two)
-	30	TOUCH — Supremes (Tamla Motown)

Carole King's *Tapestry* typified a movement whereby those who had made ultra-successful pop hits now apologised for this sordid and vulgar attainment, and sought to prove themselves serious artists with albums of deliberately uncommercial songs of great length and wiffliness. As producer and writer, Carole King and her ex-partner Jerry Goffin had been pop hit factories, even making their babysitter, Little Eva, a star. Shocking. *Tapestry* was King's penance; it would enjoy some 90 weeks in the chart.

9 October 1971

last week	this week	
1	1	EVERY PICTURE TELLS A STORY Rod Stewart (Mercury)
2	2	TAPESTRY Carole King (A&M)
6	3	BRIDGE OVER TROUBLED WATER Simon & Garfunkel (CBS)
5	4	MUD SLIDE SLIM AND THE BLUE HORIZON James Taylor (Warner Bros.)
4	5	FIREBALL Deep Purple (Harvest)
7	6	EVERY GOOD BOY DESERVES FAVOUR Moody Blues (Threshold)
15	7	TEASER & THE FIRECAT Cat Stevens (Island)
3	8	WHO'S NEXT Who (Polydor)
9	9	BLUE Joni Mitchell (Reprise)
10	10	SWEET BABY JAMES James Taylor (Warner Bros.)
8	11	RAM Paul McCartney (Apple)
12	12	ELECTRIC WARRIOR T. Rex (Fly)
11	13	MOTOWN CHARTBUSTERS VOL 5 Various Artists (Tamla Motown)
13	14	MASTER OF REALITY Black Sabbath (Vertigo)
17	15	I'M STILL WAITING Diana Ross (Tamla Motown)
16	16	ANDY WILLIAMS' GREATEST HITS Andy Williams (CBS)
-	17	TOP OF THE POPS 19 Various Artists (Hallmark)
23	18	MAN IN BLACK Johnny Cash (CBS)
19	19	LOVE STORY Andy Williams (CBS)
14	20	DIANA! Diana Ross (Tamla Motown)
24	21	CURVED AIR Curved Air (Warner Bros.)
25	22	TARKUS Emerson Lake & Palmer (Island)
26	23	C'MON EVERYBODY Elvis Presley (RCA International)
27	24	SYMPHONIES FOR THE 70s Waldo de los Rios (A&M)
-	25	PAINT YOUR WAGON Soundtrack (Paramount)
-	26	EXPERIENCE Jimi Hendrix Experience (Ember)
-	27	LOVE STORY Soundtrack (Paramount)
-	28	CARPENTERS Carpenters (A&M)
-	29	LOVELACE WATKINS LIVE AT THE TALK OF THE TOWN Lovelace Watkins (York)
29	30	THIS IS MANUEL Manuel & His Music of the Mountains (Studio Two)

16 October 1971

1	1	EVERY PICTURE TELLS A STORY Rod Stewart (Mercury)
2	2	TAPESTRY Carole King (A&M)
12	3	ELECTRIC WARRIOR T. Rex (Fly)
5	4	FIREBALL Deep Purple (Harvest)
3	5	BRIDGE OVER TROUBLED WATER Simon & Garfunkel (CBS)
4	6	MUD SLIDE SLIM AND THE BLUE HORIZON James Taylor (Warner Bros.)
8	7	WHO'S NEXT Who (Polydor)
6	8	EVERY GOOD BOY DESERVES FAVOUR Moody Blues (Threshold)
10	9	SWEET BABY JAMES James Taylor (Warner Bros.)
7	10	TEASER & THE FIRECAT Cat Stevens (Island)
15	11	I'M STILL WAITING Diana Ross (Tamla Motown)
9	12	BLUE Joni Mitchell (Reprise)
17	13	TOP OF THE POPS 19 Various Artists (Hallmark)
-	14	MOTOWN CHARTBUSTERS VOL 6 Various Artists (Tamla Motown)
-	15	PILGRIMAGE Wishbone Ash (MCA)
21	16	CURVED AIR Curved Air (Warner Bros.)
18	17	MAN IN BLACK Johnny Cash (CBS)
14	18	MASTER OF REALITY Black Sabbath (Vertigo)
23	19	C'MON EVERYBODY Elvis Presley (RCA International)
20	20	DIANA! Diana Ross (Tamla Motown)
11	21	RAM Paul McCartney (Apple)
19	22	LOVE STORY Andy Williams (CBS)
16	23	ANDY WILLIAMS' GREATEST HITS Andy Williams (CBS)
13	24	MOTOWN CHARTBUSTERS VOL 5 Various Artists (Tamla Motown)
24	25	SYMPHONIES FOR THE 70s Waldo de los Rios (A&M)
25	26	PAINT YOUR WAGON Soundtrack (Paramount)
27	27	LOVE STORY Soundtrack (Paramount)
28	28	THE CARPENTERS Carpenters (A&M)
22	29	TARKUS Emerson Lake & Palmer (Island)
-	30	THE WORLD OF YOUR 100 BEST TUNES VOL. 2 Various Artists (Decca)

23 October 1971

1	1	EVERY PICTURE TELLS A STORY Rod Stewart (Mercury)
2	2	TAPESTRY Carole King (A&M)
4	3	FIREBALL Deep Purple (Harvest)
3	4	ELECTRIC WARRIOR T. Rex (Fly)
5	5	BRIDGE OVER TROUBLED WATER Simon & Garfunkel (CBS)
6	6	MUD SLIDE SLIM AND THE BLUE HORIZON James Taylor (Warner Bros.)
10	7	TEASER & THE FIRECAT Cat Stevens (Island)
7	8	WHO'S NEXT Who (Polydor)
8	9	EVERY GOOD BOY DESERVES FAVOUR Moody Blues (Threshold)
14	10	MOTOWN CHARTBUSTERS VOL 6 Various Artists (Tamla Motown)
-	11	IMAGINE John Lennon (Apple)
15	12	PILGRIMAGE Wishbone Ash (MCA)
11	13	I'M STILL WAITING Diana Ross (Tamla Motown)
16	14	CURVED AIR Curved Air (Warner Bros.)
9	15	SWEET BABY JAMES James Taylor (Warner Bros.)
21	16	RAM Paul McCartney (Apple)
30	17	THE WORLD OF YOUR 100 BEST TUNES VOL. 2 Various Artists (Decca)
12	18	BLUE Joni Mitchell (Reprise)
13	19	TOP OF THE POPS 19 Various Artists (Hallmark)
28	20	THE CARPENTERS Carpenters (A&M)
18	21	MASTER OF REALITY Black Sabbath (Vertigo)
-	22	BIG WAR MOVIE THEMES Geoff Love & His Orchestra (Music for Pleasure)
24	23	MOTOWN CHARTBUSTERS VOL 5 Various Artists (Tamla Motown)
27	24	LOVE STORY Soundtrack (Paramount)
26	25	PAINT YOUR WAGON Soundtrack (Paramount)
29	26	TARKUS Emerson Lake & Palmer (Island)
19	27	C'MON EVERYBODY Elvis Presley (RCA International)
22	28	LOVE STORY Andy Williams (CBS)
17	29	MAN IN BLACK Johnny Cash (CBS)
-	30	THE INTIMATE JIM REEVES Jim Reeves (RCA International)

30 October 1971

1	1	EVERY PICTURE TELLS A STORY Rod Stewart (Mercury)
10	2	MOTOWN CHARTBUSTERS VOL 6 Various Artists (Tamla Motown)
4	3	ELECTRIC WARRIOR T. Rex (Fly)
2	4	TAPESTRY Carole King (A&M)
5	5	BRIDGE OVER TROUBLED WATER Simon & Garfunkel (CBS)
11	6	IMAGINE John Lennon (Apple)
6	7	MUD SLIDE SLIM AND THE BLUE HORIZON James Taylor (Warner Bros.)
7	8	TEASER & THE FIRECAT Cat Stevens (Island)
8	9	WHO'S NEXT Who (Polydor)
3	10	FIREBALL Deep Purple (Harvest)
13	11	I'M STILL WAITING Diana Ross (Tamla Motown)
-	12	HOT HITS SEVEN Various Artists (Music for Pleasure)
12	13	PILGRIMAGE Wishbone Ash (MCA)
9	14	EVERY GOOD BOY DESERVES FAVOUR Moody Blues (Threshold)
15	15	SWEET BABY JAMES James Taylor (Warner Bros.)
14	16	CURVED AIR Curved Air (Warner Bros.)
-	17	THE WORLD OF YOUR 100 BEST TUNES Various Artists (Decca)
17	18	THE WORLD OF YOUR 100 BEST TUNES VOL. 2 Various Artists (Decca)
24	19	LOVE STORY Soundtrack (Paramount)
20	20	THE CARPENTERS Carpenters (A&M)
16	21	RAM Paul McCartney (Apple)
18	22	BLUE Joni Mitchell (Reprise)
19	23	TOP OF THE POPS 19 Various Artists (Hallmark)
23	24	MOTOWN CHARTBUSTERS VOL 5 Various Artists (Tamla Motown)
-	25	ANDY WILLIAMS' GREATEST HITS Andy Williams (CBS)
29	26	MAN IN BLACK Johnny Cash (CBS)
21	27	MASTER OF REALITY Black Sabbath (Vertigo)
-	28	LED ZEPPELIN II Led Zeppelin (Atlantic)
22	29	BIG WAR MOVIE THEMES Geoff Love & His Orchestra (Music for Pleasure)
25	30	PAINT YOUR WAGON Soundtrack (Paramount)

On October 29, gifted lead guitarist Duane Allman died in a motorcycle crash in Macon, Georgia: his hometown and that of his record-company, Capricorn. Duane would soon ride the charts on Clapton's Derek & The Dominoes LP *Layla* (duelling with Eric/Derek on the title track). The Allmans had never made the British charts in Duane's lifetime, and wouldn't do so till 1973. Nor would Van Morrison, though his first albums were his most influential. Jerry Lee Lewis has never been in the NME chart.

November 1971

6 November 1971

last	this		
1	1	EVERY PICTURE TELLS A STORY	Rod Stewart (Mercury)
2	2	MOTOWN CHARTBUSTERS VOL 6	Various Artists (Tamla Motown)
6	3	IMAGINE	John Lennon (Apple)
3	4	ELECTRIC WARRIOR	T. Rex (Fly)
4	5	TAPESTRY	Carole King (A&M)
5	6	BRIDGE OVER TROUBLED WATER	Simon & Garfunkel (CBS)
8	7	TEASER & THE FIRECAT	Cat Stevens (Island)
7	8	MUD SLIDE SLIM AND THE BLUE HORIZON	James Taylor (Warner Bros.)
9	9	WHO'S NEXT	Who (Polydor)
11	10	I'M STILL WAITING	Diana Ross (Tamla Motown)
10	11	FIREBALL	Deep Purple (Harvest)
16	12	CURVED AIR	Curved Air (Warner Bros.)
12	13	HOT HITS SEVEN	Various Artists (Music for Pleasure)
13	14	PILGRIMAGE	Wishbone Ash (MCA)
-	15	SANTANA 3	Santana (CBS)
20	16	THE CARPENTERS	Carpenters (A&M)
22	17	BLUE	Joni Mitchell (Reprise)
-	18	FOG ON THE TYNE	Lindisfarne (Charisma)
18	19	THE WORLD OF YOUR 100 BEST TUNES VOL. 2	Various Artists (Decca)
15	20	SWEET BABY JAMES	James Taylor (Warner Bros.)
14	21	EVERY GOOD BOY DESERVES FAVOUR	Moody Blues (Threshold)
24	22	MOTOWN CHARTBUSTERS VOL 5	Various Artists (Tamla Motown)
-	23	SPACE IN TIME	Ten Years After (Chrysalis)
-	24	AFTER THE GOLD RUSH	Neil Young (Reprise)
25	25	ANDY WILLIAMS' GREATEST HITS	Andy Williams (CBS)
26	26	MAN IN BLACK	Johnny Cash (CBS)
29	27	BIG WAR MOVIE THEMES	Geoff Love & His Orchestra (Music for Pleasure)
27	28	MASTER OF REALITY	Black Sabbath (Vertigo)
-	29	NANCY & LEE	Nancy Sinatra & Lee Hazlewood (Reprise)
30	30	PAINT YOUR WAGON	Soundtrack (Paramount)

13 November 1971

last	this		
1	1	EVERY PICTURE TELLS A STORY	Rod Stewart (Mercury)
3	2	IMAGINE	John Lennon (Apple)
5	3	TAPESTRY	Carole King (A&M)
2	4	MOTOWN CHARTBUSTERS VOL 6	Various Artists (Tamla Motown)
4	5	ELECTRIC WARRIOR	T. Rex (Fly)
7	6	TEASER & THE FIRECAT	Cat Stevens (Island)
6	7	BRIDGE OVER TROUBLED WATER	Simon & Garfunkel (CBS)
8	8	MUD SLIDE SLIM AND THE BLUE HORIZON	James Taylor (Warner Bros.)
9	9	WHO'S NEXT	Who (Polydor)
15	10	SANTANA 3	Santana (CBS)
16	11	THE CARPENTERS	Carpenters (A&M)
18	12	FOG ON THE TYNE	Lindisfarne (Charisma)
10	13	I'M STILL WAITING	Diana Ross (Tamla Motown)
11	14	FIREBALL	Deep Purple (Harvest)
14	15	PILGRIMAGE	Wishbone Ash (MCA)
13	16	HOT HITS SEVEN	Various Artists (Music for Pleasure)
-	17	MEDDLE	Pink Floyd (Harvest)
20	18	SWEET BABY JAMES	James Taylor (Warner Bros.)
-	19	FEARLESS	Family (Reprise)
-	20	TOP OF THE POPS 20	Various Artists (Hallmark)
-	21	JIMI HENDRIX AT THE ISLE OF WIGHT, 1970	Jimi Hendrix (Polydor)
12	22	CURVED AIR	Curved Air (Warner Bros.)
17	23	BLUE	Joni Mitchell (Reprise)
25	24	ANDY WILLIAMS' GREATEST HITS	Andy Williams (CBS)
21	25	EVERY GOOD BOY DESERVES FAVOUR	Moody Blues (Threshold)
-	26	IN SEARCH OF SPACE	Hawkwind (United Artists)
24	27	AFTER THE GOLD RUSH	Neil Young (Reprise)
-	28	RAM	Paul McCartney (Apple)
19	29	THE WORLD OF YOUR 100 BEST TUNES VOL. 2	Various Artists (Decca)
-	30	ANOTHER MONTY PYTHON RECORD	Monty Python's Flying Circus (Charisma)

20 November 1971

last	this		
1	1	EVERY PICTURE TELLS A STORY	Rod Stewart (Mercury)
2	2	IMAGINE	John Lennon (Apple)
4	3	MOTOWN CHARTBUSTERS VOL 6	Various Artists (Tamla Motown)
3	4	TAPESTRY	Carole King (A&M)
5	5	ELECTRIC WARRIOR	T. Rex (Fly)
6	6	TEASER & THE FIRECAT	Cat Stevens (Island)
7	7	BRIDGE OVER TROUBLED WATER	Simon & Garfunkel (CBS)
10	8	SANTANA 3	Santana (CBS)
8	9	MUD SLIDE SLIM AND THE BLUE HORIZON	James Taylor (Warner Bros.)
9	10	WHO'S NEXT	Who (Polydor)
12	11	FOG ON THE TYNE	Lindisfarne (Charisma)
17	12	MEDDLE	Pink Floyd (Harvest)
11	13	THE CARPENTERS	Carpenters (A&M)
-	14	LED ZEPPELIN IV	Led Zeppelin (Atlantic)
14	15	FIREBALL	Deep Purple (Harvest)
29	16	THE WORLD OF YOUR 100 BEST TUNES VOL. 2	Various Artists (Decca)
15	17	PILGRIMAGE	Wishbone Ash (MCA)
16	18	HOT HITS SEVEN	Various Artists (Music for Pleasure)
-	19	FRAGILE	Yes (Atlantic)
21	20	JIMI HENDRIX AT THE ISLE OF WIGHT, 1970	Jimi Hendrix (Polydor)
25	21	EVERY GOOD BOY DESERVES FAVOUR	Moody Blues (Threshold)
20	22	TOP OF THE POPS 20	Various Artists (Hallmark)
26	23	IN SEARCH OF SPACE	Hawkwind (United Artists)
-	24	TOM JONES AT CAESAR'S PALACE LAS VEGAS	Tom Jones (Decca)
-	25	SPACE IN TIME	Ten Years After (Chrysalis)
19	26	FEARLESS	Family (Reprise)
-	27	THE WORLD OF YOUR 100 BEST TUNES	Various Artists (Decca)
18	28	SWEET BABY JAMES	James Taylor (Warner Bros.)
13	29	I'M STILL WAITING	Diana Ross (Tamla Motown)
22	30	CURVED AIR	Curved Air (Warner Bros.)

27 November 1971

last	this		
2	1	IMAGINE	John Lennon (Apple)
1	2	EVERY PICTURE TELLS A STORY	Rod Stewart (Mercury)
5	3	ELECTRIC WARRIOR	T. Rex (Fly)
4	4	TAPESTRY	Carole King (A&M)
12	5	MEDDLE	Pink Floyd (Harvest)
8	6	SANTANA 3	Santana (CBS)
14	7	LED ZEPPELIN IV	Led Zeppelin (Atlantic)
3	8	MOTOWN CHARTBUSTERS VOL 6	Various Artists (Tamla Motown)
7	9	BRIDGE OVER TROUBLED WATER	Simon & Garfunkel (CBS)
6	10	TEASER & THE FIRECAT	Cat Stevens (Island)
20	11	JIMI HENDRIX AT THE ISLE OF WIGHT, 1970	Jimi Hendrix (Polydor)
22	12	TOP OF THE POPS 20	Various Artists (Hallmark)
-	13	PICTURES AT AN EXHIBITION	Emerson, Lake & Palmer (Island)
26	14	FEARLESS	Family (Reprise)
19	15	FRAGILE	Yes (Atlantic)
11	16	FOG ON THE TYNE	Lindisfarne (Charisma)
10	17	WHO'S NEXT	Who (Polydor)
15	18	FIREBALL	Deep Purple (Harvest)
9	19	MUD SLIDE SLIM AND THE BLUE HORIZON	James Taylor (Warner Bros.)
13	20	THE CARPENTERS	Carpenters (A&M)
-	21	THIS IS POURCEL	Franck Pourcel (Studio Two)
-	22	SURF'S UP	Beach Boys (Stateside)
16	23	THE WORLD OF YOUR 100 BEST TUNES VOL. 2	Various Artists (Decca)
29	24	I'M STILL WAITING	Diana Ross (Tamla Motown)
24	25	TOM JONES AT CAESAR'S PALACE LAS VEGAS	Tom Jones (Decca)
23	26	IN SEARCH OF SPACE	Hawkwind (United Artists)
18	27	HOT HITS SEVEN	Various Artists (Music for Pleasure)
27	28	THE WORLD OF YOUR 100 BEST TUNES	Various Artists (Decca)
17	29	PILGRIMAGE	Wishbone Ash (MCA)
30	30	CURVED AIR	Curved Air (Warner Bros.)

Imagine had entered the charts on October 23, and took its time to reach the top. McCartney's album *Ram*, released hard on its heels, jumped in at No.28 on November 13 and then dropped out again. *Imagine* there's no gloating. It was to be Lennon's longest-lingering chart album, not least because its title-track was so sumptuous. Only much later was it issued as a single: it first entered in November 1975 (without especial success), and was a hit again when reissued after Lennon's death in 1980.

4 December 1971

last week	this week		
1	1	IMAGINE	John Lennon (Apple)
2	2	EVERY PICTURE TELLS A STORY	Rod Stewart (Mercury)
3	3	ELECTRIC WARRIOR	T. Rex (Fly)
7	4	LED ZEPPELIN IV	Led Zeppelin (Atlantic)
8	5	MOTOWN CHARTBUSTERS VOL 6	Various Artists (Tamla Motown)
4	6	TAPESTRY	Carole King (A&M)
13	7	PICTURES AT AN EXHIBITION	Emerson, Lake & Palmer (Island)
6	8	SANTANA 3	Santana (CBS)
9	9	BRIDGE OVER TROUBLED WATER	Simon & Garfunkel (CBS)
10	10	TEASER & THE FIRECAT	Cat Stevens (Island)
5	11	MEDDLE	Pink Floyd (Harvest)
15	12	FRAGILE	Yes (Atlantic)
20	13	THE CARPENTERS	Carpenters (A&M)
19	14	MUD SLIDE SLIM AND THE BLUE HORIZON	James Taylor (Warner Bros.)
16	15	FOG ON THE TYNE	Lindisfarne (Charisma)
-	16	FOUR TOPS GREATEST HITS VOL. 2	Four Tops (Tamla Motown)
22	17	SURF'S UP	Beach Boys (Stateside)
11	18	JIMI HENDRIX AT THE ISLE OF WIGHT, 1970	Jimi Hendrix (Polydor)
17	19	WHO'S NEXT	Who (Polydor)
21	20	THIS IS POURCEL	Franck Pourcel (Studio Two)
25	21	TOM JONES AT CAESAR'S PALACE LAS VEGAS	Tom Jones (Decca)
-	22	PERFORMANCE-ROCKIN' AT THE FILLMORE	Humble Pie (A&M)
-	23	SHAFT	Isaac Hayes (Stax)
12	24	TOP OF THE POPS 20	Various Artists (Hallmark)
23	25	THE WORLD OF YOUR 100 BEST TUNES VOL. 2	Various Artists (Decca)
14	26	FEARLESS	Family (Reprise)
24	27	I'M STILL WAITING	Diana Ross (Tamla Motown)
26	28	IN SEARCH OF SPACE	Hawkwind (United Artists)
28	29	THE WORLD OF YOUR 100 BEST TUNES	Various Artists (Decca)
27	30	HOT HITS SEVEN	Various Artists (Music for Pleasure)

11 December 1971

1	1	IMAGINE	John Lennon (Apple)
4	2	LED ZEPPELIN IV	Led Zeppelin (Atlantic)
3	3	ELECTRIC WARRIOR	T. Rex (Fly)
2	4	EVERY PICTURE TELLS A STORY	Rod Stewart (Mercury)
7	5	PICTURES AT AN EXHIBITION	Emerson, Lake & Palmer (Island)
6	6	TAPESTRY	Carole King (A&M)
5	7	MOTOWN CHARTBUSTERS VOL 6	Various Artists (Tamla Motown)
12	8	FRAGILE	Yes (Atlantic)
11	9	MEDDLE	Pink Floyd (Harvest)
13	10	THE CARPENTERS	Carpenters (A&M)
10	11	TEASER & THE FIRECAT	Cat Stevens (Island)
8	12	SANTANA 3	Santana (CBS)
9	13	BRIDGE OVER TROUBLED WATER	Simon & Garfunkel (CBS)
23	14	SHAFT	Isaac Hayes (Stax)
14	15	MUD SLIDE SLIM AND THE BLUE HORIZON	James Taylor (Warner Bros.)
17	16	SURF'S UP	Beach Boys (Stateside)
24	17	TOP OF THE POPS 20	Various Artists (Hallmark)
-	18	MEATY BEATY BIG AND BOUNCY	Who (Track)
-	19	RAINBOW BRIDGE	Jimi Hendrix (Reprise)
-	20	12 SONGS OF CHRISTMAS	Jim Reeves (RCA International)
19	21	WHO'S NEXT	Who (Polydor)
21	22	TOM JONES AT CAESAR'S PALACE LAS VEGAS	Tom Jones (Decca)
-	23	GLEN CAMPBELL'S GREATEST HITS	Glen Campbell (Capitol)
15	24	FOG ON THE TYNE	Lindisfarne (Charisma)
22	25	PERFORMANCE-ROCKIN' AT THE FILLMORE	Humble Pie (A&M)
20	26	THIS IS POURCEL	Franck Pourcel (Studio Two)
-	27	CLOSE TO YOU	Carpenters (A&M)
-	28	HOT HITS EIGHT	Various Artists (Music for Pleasure)
26	29	FEARLESS	Family (Reprise)
18	30	JIMI HENDRIX AT THE ISLE OF WIGHT, 1970	Jimi Hendrix (Polydor)

18 December 1971

2	1	LED ZEPPELIN IV	Led Zeppelin (Atlantic)
1	2	IMAGINE	John Lennon (Apple)
3	3	ELECTRIC WARRIOR	T. Rex (Fly)
4	4	EVERY PICTURE TELLS A STORY	Rod Stewart (Mercury)
7	5	MOTOWN CHARTBUSTERS VOL 6	Various Artists (Tamla Motown)
5	6	PICTURES AT AN EXHIBITION	Emerson, Lake & Palmer (Island)
13	7	BRIDGE OVER TROUBLED WATER	Simon & Garfunkel (CBS)
6	8	TAPESTRY	Carole King (A&M)
8	9	FRAGILE	Yes (Atlantic)
11	10	TEASER & THE FIRECAT	Cat Stevens (Island)
10	11	THE CARPENTERS	Carpenters (A&M)
9	12	MEDDLE	Pink Floyd (Harvest)
-	13	WILD LIFE	Wings (Parlophone)
20	14	12 SONGS OF CHRISTMAS	Jim Reeves (RCA International)
14	15	SHAFT	Isaac Hayes (Stax)
17	16	TOP OF THE POPS 20	Various Artists (Hallmark)
18	17	MEATY BEATY BIG AND BOUNCY	Who (Track)
28	18	HOT HITS EIGHT	Various Artists (Music for Pleasure)
-	19	A NOD'S AS GOOD AS A WINK ... TO A BLIND HORSE	Faces (Warner Bros.)
26	20	THIS IS POURCEL	Franck Pourcel (Studio Two)
19	21	RAINBOW BRIDGE	Jimi Hendrix (Reprise)
15	22	MUD SLIDE SLIM AND THE BLUE HORIZON	James Taylor (Warner Bros.)
23	23	GLEN CAMPBELL'S GREATEST HITS	Glen Campbell (Capitol)
-	24	THE SOUND OF MUSIC	Soundtrack (RCA)
16	25	SURF'S UP	Beach Boys (Stateside)
21	26	WHO'S NEXT	Who (Polydor)
-	27	WORDS AND MUSIC	Benny Hill (Columbia)
12	28	SANTANA 3	Santana (CBS)
-	29	THE WORLD OF YOUR 100 BEST TUNES VOL. 2	Various Artists (Decca)
-	30	ELVIS' CHRISTMAS ALBUM	Elvis Presley (RCA International)

25 December 1971

1	1	LED ZEPPELIN IV	Led Zeppelin (Atlantic)
3	2	ELECTRIC WARRIOR	T. Rex (Fly)
2	3	IMAGINE	John Lennon (Apple)
4	4	EVERY PICTURE TELLS A STORY	Rod Stewart (Mercury)
19	5	A NOD'S AS GOOD AS A WINK ... TO A BLIND HORSE	Faces (Warner Bros.)
5	6	MOTOWN CHARTBUSTERS VOL 6	Various Artists (Tamla Motown)
10	7	TEASER & THE FIRECAT	Cat Stevens (Island)
7	8	BRIDGE OVER TROUBLED WATER	Simon & Garfunkel (CBS)
6	9	PICTURES AT AN EXHIBITION	Emerson, Lake & Palmer (Island)
15	10	SHAFT	Isaac Hayes (Stax)
13	11	WILD LIFE	Wings (Parlophone)
17	12	MEATY BEATY BIG AND BOUNCY	Who (Track)
8	13	TAPESTRY	Carole King (A&M)
14	14	12 SONGS OF CHRISTMAS	Jim Reeves (RCA International)
11	15	THE CARPENTERS	Carpenters (A&M)
28	16	SANTANA 3	Santana (CBS)
30	17	ELVIS' CHRISTMAS ALBUM	Elvis Presley (RCA International)
22	18	MUD SLIDE SLIM AND THE BLUE HORIZON	James Taylor (Warner Bros.)
9	19	FRAGILE	Yes (Atlantic)
12	20	MEDDLE	Pink Floyd (Harvest)
-	21	FIREBALL	Deep Purple (Harvest)
-	22	TOP OF THE POPS 21	Various Artists (Hallmark)
-	23	A SONG FOR YOU	Andy Williams (CBS)
21	24	RAINBOW BRIDGE	Jimi Hendrix (Reprise)
16	25	TOP OF THE POPS 20	Various Artists (Hallmark)
26	26	WHO'S NEXT	Who (Polydor)
20	27	THIS IS POURCEL	Franck Pourcel (Studio Two)
27	28	WORDS AND MUSIC	Benny Hill (Columbia)
18	29	HOT HITS EIGHT	Various Artists (Music for Pleasure)
25	30	SURF'S UP	Beach Boys (Stateside)

Emerson Lake & Palmer were overblowing Modest Petrovich Mussorgsky in the Top 10. John Peel on their London debut gig: "a tragic waste of talent and electricity." Other 1971 quotes by album chart entrants: When John and Yoko wanted a New York apartment, and Yoko found one on the Bowery, John said: "Oh no, luv, no there. I don't want to walk out me door and see people dying in the gutter - really I don't." And from the rehearsals for the Concert For Bangla Desh at Madison Square Garden: George Harrison asked Bob Dylan if he planned to sing his early hit Blowin' In The Wind; Dylan replied, "Well George, are you gonna sing I Want To Hold Your Hand?"

January 1972

1 January 1972

last week	this week	Title	Artist
2	1	ELECTRIC WARRIOR	T. Rex (Fly)
3	2	IMAGINE	John Lennon (Apple)
1	3	LED ZEPPELIN IV	Led Zeppelin (Atlantic)
7	4	TEASER AND THE FIRECAT	Cat Stevens (Island)
4	5	EVERY PICTURE TELLS A STORY	Rod Stewart (Philips)
8	6	BRIDGE OVER TROUBLED WATER	Simon & Garfunkel (CBS)
5	7	A NOD'S AS GOOD AS A WINK ... TO A BLIND HORSE	Faces (Warner Bros.)
9	8	PICTURES AT AN EXHIBITION	Emerson Lake & Palmer (Island)
6	9	MOTOWN CHARTBUSTERS VOL 6	Various Artists (Tamla Motown)
13	10	TAPESTRY	Carole King (A&M)
12	11	MEATY BEATY BIG AND BOUNCY	Who (Track)
19	12	FRAGILE	Yes (Atlantic)
10	13	SHAFT	Isaac Hayes (Stax)
16	14	SANTANA 3	Santana (CBS)
15	15	CARPENTERS	Carpenters (A&M)
11	16	WILD LIFE	Wings (Parlophone)
17	17	ELVIS' CHRISTMAS ALBUM	Elvis Presley (RCA Intenational)
-	18	FOUR TOPS' GREATEST HITS, VOLS. 1 AND 2	Four Tops (Tamla Motown)
27	19	THIS IS POURCEL	Franck Pourcel (Studio Two)
28	20	WORDS AND MUSIC	Benny Hill (Columbia)
24	21	RAINBOW BRIDGE	Jimi Hendrix (Reprise)
-	22	MUSIC	Carole King (A&M)
21	23	FIREBALL	Deep Purple (Harvest)
18	24	MUD SLIDE SLIM AND THE BLUE HORIZON	James Taylor (Warner Bros.)
14	25	12 SONGS OF CHRISTMAS	Jim Reeves (RCA International)
-	26	JIM REEVES' GOLDEN RECORDS	Jim Reeves (RCA International)
-	27	HIMSELF	Gilbert O'Sullivan (MAM)
29	28	HOT HITS EIGHT	Various Artists (Music for Pleasure)
20	29	MEDDLE	Pink Floyd (Harvest)
26	30	WHO'S NEXT	Who (Polydor)

8 January 1972

last week	this week	Title	Artist
1	1	ELECTRIC WARRIOR	T. Rex (Fly)
2	2	IMAGINE	John Lennon (Apple)
3	3	LED ZEPPELIN IV	Led Zeppelin (Atlantic)
4	4	TEASER AND THE FIRECAT	Cat Stevens (Island)
6	5	BRIDGE OVER TROUBLED WATER	Simon & Garfunkel (CBS)
5	6	EVERY PICTURE TELLS A STORY	Rod Stewart (Philips)
7	7	A NOD'S AS GOOD AS A WINK ... TO A BLIND HORSE	Faces (Warner Bros.)
10	8	TAPESTRY	Carole King (A&M)
13	9	SHAFT	Isaac Hayes (Stax)
9	10	MOTOWN CHARTBUSTERS VOL 6	Various Artists (Tamla Motown)
8	11	PICTURES AT AN EXHIBITION	Emerson Lake & Palmer (Island)
15	12	CARPENTERS	Carpenters (A&M)
22	13	MUSIC	Carole King (A&M)
16	14	WILD LIFE	Wings (Parlophone)
29	15	MEDDLE	Pink Floyd (Harvest)
24	16	MUD SLIDE SLIM AND THE BLUE HORIZON	James Taylor (Warner Bros.)
21	17	RAINBOW BRIDGE	Jimi Hendrix (Reprise)
23	18	FIREBALL	Deep Purple (Harvest)
27	19	HIMSELF	Gilbert O'Sullivan (MAM)
30	20	WHO'S NEXT	Who (Polydor)
11	21	MEATY BEATY BIG AND BOUNCY	Who (Track)
12	22	FRAGILE	Yes (Atlantic)
14	23	SANTANA 3	Santana (CBS)
-	24	STONES	Neil Diamond (Uni)
18	25	FOUR TOPS' GREATEST HITS, VOLS. 1 AND 2	Four Tops (Tamla Motown)
19	26	THIS IS POURCEL	Franck Pourcel (Studio Two)
20	27	WORDS AND MUSIC	Benny Hill (Columbia)
25	28	12 SONGS OF CHRISTMAS	Jim Reeves (RCA International)
-	29	MORE BOB DYLAN GREATEST HITS	Bob Dylan (CBS)
-	30	FOG ON THE TYNE	Lindisfarne (Charisma)

15 January 1972

last week	this week	Title	Artist
1	1	ELECTRIC WARRIOR	T. Rex (Fly)
7	2	A NOD'S AS GOOD AS A WINK ... TO A BLIND HORSE	Faces (Warner Bros.)
4	3	TEASER AND THE FIRECAT	Cat Stevens (Island)
2	4	IMAGINE	John Lennon (Apple)
3	5	LED ZEPPELIN IV	Led Zeppelin (Atlantic)
5	6	BRIDGE OVER TROUBLED WATER	Simon & Garfunkel (CBS)
9	7	SHAFT	Isaac Hayes (Stax)
6	8	EVERY PICTURE TELLS A STORY	Rod Stewart (Philips)
11	9	PICTURES AT AN EXHIBITION	Emerson Lake & Palmer (Island)
10	10	MOTOWN CHARTBUSTERS VOL 6	Various Artists (Tamla Motown)
-	11	JESUS CHRIST SUPERSTAR	Various Artists (MCA)
8	12	TAPESTRY	Carole King (A&M)
29	13	MORE BOB DYLAN GREATEST HITS	Bob Dylan (CBS)
12	14	CARPENTERS	Carpenters (A&M)
18	15	FIREBALL	Deep Purple (Harvest)
21	16	MEATY BEATY BIG AND BOUNCY	Who (Track)
19	17	HIMSELF	Gilbert O'Sullivan (MAM)
15	18	MEDDLE	Pink Floyd (Harvest)
16	19	MUD SLIDE SLIM AND THE BLUE HORIZON	James Taylor (Warner Bros.)
-	20	ANDY WILLIAMS' GREATEST HITS	Andy Williams (CBS)
-	21	CLOSE TO YOU	Carpenters (A&M)
27	22	WORDS AND MUSIC	Benny Hill (Columbia)
-	23	GATHER ME	Melanie (Buddah)
17	24	RAINBOW BRIDGE	Jimi Hendrix (Reprise)
13	25	MUSIC	Carole King (A&M)
20	26	WHO'S NEXT	Who (Polydor)
26	27	THIS IS POURCEL	Franck Pourcel (Studio Two)
22	28	FRAGILE	Yes (Atlantic)
14	29	WILD LIFE	Wings (Parlophone)
23	30	SANTANA 3	Santana (CBS)

22 January 1972

last week	this week	Title	Artist
3	1	TEASER AND THE FIRECAT	Cat Stevens (Island)
2	2	A NOD'S AS GOOD AS A WINK ... TO A BLIND HORSE	Faces (Warner Bros.)
1	3	ELECTRIC WARRIOR	T. Rex (Fly)
4	4	IMAGINE	John Lennon (Apple)
5	5	LED ZEPPELIN IV	Led Zeppelin (Atlantic)
-	6	THE CONCERT FOR BANGLA DESH	Various Artists (Apple)
6	7	BRIDGE OVER TROUBLED WATER	Simon & Garfunkel (CBS)
17	8	HIMSELF	Gilbert O'Sullivan (MAM)
10	9	MOTOWN CHARTBUSTERS VOL 6	Various Artists (Tamla Motown)
12	10	TAPESTRY	Carole King (A&M)
8	11	EVERY PICTURE TELLS A STORY	Rod Stewart (Philips)
15	12	FIREBALL	Deep Purple (Harvest)
16	13	MEATY BEATY BIG AND BOUNCY	Who (Track)
11	14	JESUS CHRIST SUPERSTAR	Various Artists (MCA)
25	15	MUSIC	Carole King (A&M)
14	16	THE CARPENTERS	Carpenters (A&M)
19	17	MUD SLIDE SLIM AND THE BLUE HORIZON	James Taylor (Warner Bros.)
18	18	MEDDLE	Pink Floyd (Harvest)
20	19	ANDY WILLIAMS' GREATEST HITS	Andy Williams (CBS)
23	20	GATHER ME	Melanie (Buddah)
9	21	PICTURES AT AN EXHIBITION	Emerson Lake & Palmer (Island)
-	22	FOG ON THE TYNE	Lindisfarne (Charisma)
21	23	CLOSE TO YOU	Carpenters (A&M)
28	24	FRAGILE	Yes (Atlantic)
13	25	MORE BOB DYLAN GREATEST HITS	Bob Dylan (CBS)
-	26	HOT HITS NINE	Various Artists (Music for Pleasure)
-	27	AMERICA	America (Warner Bros.)
7	28	SHAFT	Isaac Hayes (Stax)
-	29	STONES	Neil Diamond (Uni)
24	30	RAINBOW BRIDGE	Jimi Hendrix (Reprise)

The double-album called (here) *More Bob Dylan Greatest Hits*, released some months after its American issue, was in its way oddly titled, since Dylan fans rushed to buy it because it offered a number of tracks never previously released, including a 1963 concert recording of *Tomorrow Is A Long Time*, one of the two Dylan songs that Elvis Presley recorded. This, and *Don't Think Twice It's Alright*, were "bonus tracks" used to pad out one of Elvis' mid-60s film soundtrack albums.

January – February 1972

last week	this week	29 January 1972
1	1	TEASER AND THE FIRECAT Cat Stevens (Island)
2	2	A NOD'S AS GOOD AS A WINK ... TO A BLIND HORSE Faces (Warner Bros.)
3	3	ELECTRIC WARRIOR T. Rex (Fly)
6	4	THE CONCERT FOR BANGLA DESH Various Artists (Apple)
4	5	IMAGINE John Lennon (Apple)
7	6	BRIDGE OVER TROUBLED WATER Simon & Garfunkel (CBS)
8	7	HIMSELF Gilbert O'Sullivan (MAM)
5	8	LED ZEPPELIN IV Led Zeppelin (Atlantic)
14	9	JESUS CHRIST SUPERSTAR Various Artists (MCA)
10	10	TAPESTRY Carole King (A&M)
11	11	EVERY PICTURE TELLS A STORY Rod Stewart (Philips)
20	12	GATHER ME Melanie (Buddah)
12	13	FIREBALL Deep Purple (Harvest)
21	14	PICTURES AT AN EXHIBITION Emerson Lake & Palmer (Island)
15	15	MUSIC Carole King (A&M)
9	16	MOTOWN CHARTBUSTERS VOL 6 Various Artists (Tamla Motown)
25	17	MORE BOB DYLAN GREATEST HITS Bob Dylan (CBS)
26	18	HOT HITS NINE Various Artists (Music for Pleasure)
24	19	FRAGILE Yes (Atlantic)
13	20	MEATY BEATY BIG AND BOUNCY Who (Track)
27	21	AMERICA America (Warner Bros.)
29	22	STONES Neil Diamond (Uni)
16	23	THE CARPENTERS Carpenters (A&M)
17	24	MUD SLIDE SLIM AND THE BLUE HORIZON James Taylor (Warner Bros.)
28	25	SHAFT Isaac Hayes (Stax)
-	26	HENDRIX IN THE WEST Jimi Hendrix (Polydor)
18	27	MEDDLE Pink Floyd (Harvest)
22	28	FOG ON THE TYNE Lindisfarne (Charisma)
-	29	WILD LIFE Wings (Parlophone)
19	30	ANDY WILLIAMS' GREATEST HITS Andy Williams (CBS)

		5 February 1972
1	1	TEASER AND THE FIRECAT Cat Stevens (Island)
2	2	A NOD'S AS GOOD AS A WINK ... TO A BLIND HORSE Faces (Warner Bros.)
3	3	ELECTRIC WARRIOR T. Rex (Fly)
4	4	THE CONCERT FOR BANGLA DESH Various Artists (Apple)
5	5	IMAGINE John Lennon (Apple)
6	6	BRIDGE OVER TROUBLED WATER Simon & Garfunkel (CBS)
8	7	LED ZEPPELIN IV Led Zeppelin (Atlantic)
9	8	JESUS CHRIST SUPERSTAR Various Artists (MCA)
11	9	EVERY PICTURE TELLS A STORY Rod Stewart (Philips)
26	10	HENDRIX IN THE WEST Jimi Hendrix (Polydor)
12	11	GATHER ME Melanie (Buddah)
7	12	HIMSELF Gilbert O'Sullivan (MAM)
17	13	MORE BOB DYLAN GREATEST HITS Bob Dylan (CBS)
-	14	NEIL REID Neil Reid (Decca)
23	15	THE CARPENTERS Carpenters (A&M)
21	16	AMERICA America (Warner Bros.)
14	17	PICTURES AT AN EXHIBITION Emerson Lake & Palmer (Island)
19	18	FRAGILE Yes (Atlantic)
25	19	SHAFT Isaac Hayes (Stax)
15	20	MUSIC Carole King (A&M)
13	21	FIREBALL Deep Purple (Harvest)
16	22	MOTOWN CHARTBUSTERS VOL 6 Various Artists (Tamla Motown)
10	23	TAPESTRY Carole King (A&M)
24	24	MUD SLIDE SLIM AND THE BLUE HORIZON James Taylor (Warner Bros.)
30	25	ANDY WILLIAMS' GREATEST HITS Andy Williams (CBS)
20	26	MEATY BEATY BIG AND BOUNCY Who (Track)
18	27	HOT HITS NINE Various Artists (Music for Pleasure)
22	28	STONES Neil Diamond (Uni)
-	29	TEA FOR THE TILLERMAN Cat Stevens (Island)
-	30	RAINBOW BRIDGE Jimi Hendrix (Reprise)

		12 February 1972
1	1	TEASER AND THE FIRECAT Cat Stevens (Island)
3	2	ELECTRIC WARRIOR T. Rex (Fly)
2	3	A NOD'S AS GOOD AS A WINK ... TO A BLIND HORSE Faces (Warner Bros.)
6	4	BRIDGE OVER TROUBLED WATER Simon & Garfunkel (CBS)
7	5	LED ZEPPELIN IV Led Zeppelin (Atlantic)
5	6	IMAGINE John Lennon (Apple)
4	7	THE CONCERT FOR BANGLA DESH Various Artists (Apple)
14	8	NEIL REID Neil Reid (Decca)
12	9	HIMSELF Gilbert O'Sullivan (MAM)
9	10	EVERY PICTURE TELLS A STORY Rod Stewart (Philips)
10	11	HENDRIX IN THE WEST Jimi Hendrix (Polydor)
16	12	AMERICA America (Warner Bros.)
11	13	GATHER ME Melanie (Buddah)
20	14	MUSIC Carole King (A&M)
13	15	MORE BOB DYLAN GREATEST HITS Bob Dylan (CBS)
22	16	MOTOWN CHARTBUSTERS VOL 6 Various Artists (Tamla Motown)
19	17	SHAFT Isaac Hayes (Stax)
23	18	TAPESTRY Carole King (A&M)
17	19	PICTURES AT AN EXHIBITION Emerson Lake & Palmer (Island)
-	20	MEDDLE Pink Floyd (Harvest)
26	21	MEATY BEATY BIG AND BOUNCY Who (Track)
-	22	GLEN CAMPBELL'S GREATEST HITS Glen Campbell (Capitol)
-	23	THERE'S A RIOT GOIN' ON Sly & the Family Stone (Epic)
28	24	STONES Neil Diamond (Uni)
18	25	FRAGILE Yes (Atlantic)
-	26	FOG ON THE TYNE Lindisfarne (Charisma)
-	27	WILD LIFE Wings (Parlophone)
27	28	HOT HITS NINE Various Artists (Music for Pleasure)
21	29	FIREBALL Deep Purple (Harvest)
-	30	NILSSON SCHMILSSON Nilsson (RCA)

		19 February 1972
1	1	TEASER AND THE FIRECAT Cat Stevens (Island)
2	2	ELECTRIC WARRIOR T. Rex (Fly)
3	3	A NOD'S AS GOOD AS A WINK ... TO A BLIND HORSE Faces (Warner Bros.)
8	4	NEIL REID Neil Reid (Decca)
7	5	THE CONCERT FOR BANGLA DESH Various Artists (Apple)
11	6	HENDRIX IN THE WEST Jimi Hendrix (Polydor)
4	7	BRIDGE OVER TROUBLED WATER Simon & Garfunkel (CBS)
6	8	IMAGINE John Lennon (Apple)
-	9	PAUL SIMON Paul Simon (CBS)
5	10	LED ZEPPELIN IV Led Zeppelin (Atlantic)
13	11	GATHER ME Melanie (Buddah)
-	12	JESUS CHRIST SUPERSTAR Various Artists (MCA)
14	13	MUSIC Carole King (A&M)
25	14	FRAGILE Yes (Atlantic)
18	15	TAPESTRY Carole King (A&M)
9	16	HIMSELF Gilbert O'Sullivan (MAM)
12	17	AMERICA America (Warner Bros.)
-	18	WOYAYA Osibisa (MCA)
19	19	PICTURES AT AN EXHIBITION Emerson Lake & Palmer (Island)
15	20	MORE BOB DYLAN GREATEST HITS Bob Dylan (CBS)
16	21	MOTOWN CHARTBUSTERS VOL 6 Various Artists (Tamla Motown)
10	22	EVERY PICTURE TELLS A STORY Rod Stewart (Philips)
-	23	TEA FOR THE TILLERMAN Cat Stevens (Island)
22	24	GLEN CAMPBELL'S GREATEST HITS Glen Campbell (Capitol)
21	25	MEATY BEATY BIG AND BOUNCY Who (Track)
30	26	NILSSON SCHMILSSON Nilsson (RCA)
26	27	FOG ON THE TYNE Lindisfarne (Charisma)
24	28	STONES Neil Diamond (UNI)
27	29	WILD LIFE Wings (Parlophone)
20	30	MEDDLE Pink Floyd (Harvest)

Teaser And The Firecat was not only Cat Stevens' No.1 album (his fourth LP, his third for Chris Blackwell's Island label and to prove his longest-lasting chart contender). *Teaser And The Firecat* was also the title of Stevens' children's book. The story is told in Chinese, English, French, German, Italian, Greek, Hebrew, Japanese, Russian, Spanish and Welsh. Stevens' previous album, *Tea For The Tillerman*, was sufficiently boosted by the great success of *Firecat* to re-enter the chart in February.

February – March 1972

26 February 1972

last	this		
4	1	NEIL REID	Neil Reid (Decca)
2	2	ELECTRIC WARRIOR	T. Rex (Fly)
1	3	TEASER AND THE FIRECAT	Cat Stevens (Island)
9	4	PAUL SIMON	Paul Simon (CBS)
3	5	A NOD'S AS GOOD AS A WINK ... TO A BLIND HORSE	Faces (Warner Bros.)
7	6	BRIDGE OVER TROUBLED WATER	Simon & Garfunkel (CBS)
8	7	IMAGINE	John Lennon (Apple)
5	8	THE CONCERT FOR BANGLA DESH	Various Artists (Apple)
10	9	LED ZEPPELIN IV	Led Zeppelin (Atlantic)
-	10	HARVEST	Neil Young (Reprise)
17	11	AMERICA	America (Warner Bros.)
26	12	NILSSON SCHMILSSON	Nilsson (RCA)
16	13	HIMSELF	Gilbert O'Sullivan (MAM)
12	14	JESUS CHRIST SUPERSTAR	Various Artists (MCA)
6	15	HENDRIX IN THE WEST	Jimi Hendrix (Polydor)
15	16	TAPESTRY	Carole King (A&M)
18	17	WOYAYA	Osibisa (MCA)
22	18	EVERY PICTURE TELLS A STORY	Rod Stewart (Philips)
21	19	MOTOWN CHARTBUSTERS VOL 6	Various Artists (Tamla Motown)
-	20	THE PERSUADERS	John Barry Orchestra (CBS)
27	21	FOG ON THE TYNE	Lindisfarne (Charisma)
-	22	TOP OF THE POPS 22	Various Artists (Hallmark)
14	23	FRAGILE	Yes (Atlantic)
30	24	MEDDLE	Pink Floyd (Harvest)
11	25	GATHER ME	Melanie (Buddah)
25	26	MEATY BEATY BIG AND BOUNCY	Who (Track)
13	27	MUSIC	Carole King (A&M)
20	28	MORE BOB DYLAN GREATEST HITS	Bob Dylan (CBS)
23	29	TEA FOR THE TILLERMAN	Cat Stevens (Island)
24	30	GLEN CAMPBELL'S GREATEST HITS	Glen Campbell (Capitol)

4 March 1972

last	this		
4	1	PAUL SIMON	Paul Simon (CBS)
3	2	TEASER AND THE FIRECAT	Cat Stevens (Island)
1	3	NEIL REID	Neil Reid (Decca)
2	4	ELECTRIC WARRIOR	T. Rex (Fly)
5	5	A NOD'S AS GOOD AS A WINK ... TO A BLIND HORSE	Faces (Warner Bros.)
6	6	BRIDGE OVER TROUBLED WATER	Simon & Garfunkel (CBS)
10	7	HARVEST	Neil Young (Reprise)
13	8	HIMSELF	Gilbert O'Sullivan (MAM)
12	9	NILSSON SCHMILSSON	Nilsson (RCA)
7	10	IMAGINE	John Lennon (Apple)
21	11	FOG ON THE TYNE	Lindisfarne (Charisma)
19	12	MOTOWN CHARTBUSTERS VOL 6	Various Artists (Tamla Motown)
15	13	HENDRIX IN THE WEST	Jimi Hendrix (Polydor)
8	14	THE CONCERT FOR BANGLA DESH	Various Artists (Apple)
22	15	TOP OF THE POPS 22	Various Artists (Hallmark)
11	16	AMERICA	America (Warner Bros.)
9	17	LED ZEPPELIN IV	Led Zeppelin (Atlantic)
18	18	EVERY PICTURE TELLS A STORY	Rod Stewart (Philips)
25	19	GATHER ME	Melanie (Buddah)
-	20	GRAVE NEW WORLD	Strawbs (A&M)
16	21	TAPESTRY	Carole King (A&M)
14	22	JESUS CHRIST SUPERSTAR	Various Artists (MCA)
-	23	I CAPRICORN	Shirley Bassey (United Artists)
23	24	FRAGILE	Yes (Atlantic)
27	25	MUSIC	Carole King (A&M)
24	26	MEDDLE	Pink Floyd (Harvest)
-	27	ELVIS: THAT'S THE WAY IT IS	Elvis Presley (RCA)
20	28	THE PERSUADERS	John Barry Orchestra (CBS)
-	29	ANDY WILLIAMS' GREATEST HITS	Andy Williams (CBS)
-	30	FLEETWOOD MAC'S GREATEST HITS	Fleetwood Mac (CBS)

11 March 1972

last	this		
1	1	PAUL SIMON	Paul Simon (CBS)
7	2	HARVEST	Neil Young (Reprise)
2	3	TEASER AND THE FIRECAT	Cat Stevens (Island)
3	4	NEIL REID	Neil Reid (Decca)
4	5	ELECTRIC WARRIOR	T. Rex (Fly)
6	6	BRIDGE OVER TROUBLED WATER	Simon & Garfunkel (CBS)
5	7	A NOD'S AS GOOD AS A WINK ... TO A BLIND HORSE	Faces (Warner Bros.)
8	8	HIMSELF	Gilbert O'Sullivan (MAM)
9	9	NILSSON SCHMILSSON	Nilsson (RCA)
11	10	FOG ON THE TYNE	Lindisfarne (Charisma)
20	11	GRAVE NEW WORLD	Strawbs (A&M)
13	12	HENDRIX IN THE WEST	Jimi Hendrix (Polydor)
10	13	IMAGINE	John Lennon (Apple)
17	14	LED ZEPPELIN IV	Led Zeppelin (Atlantic)
14	15	THE CONCERT FOR BANGLA DESH	Various Artists (Apple)
-	16	AMERICAN PIE	Don McLean (United Artists)
15	17	TOP OF THE POPS 22	Various Artists (Hallmark)
12	18	MOTOWN CHARTBUSTERS VOL 6	Various Artists (Tamla Motown)
22	19	JESUS CHRIST SUPERSTAR	Various Artists (MCA)
24	20	FRAGILE	Yes (Atlantic)
-	21	TEA FOR THE TILLERMAN	Cat Stevens (Island)
-	22	THE CARPENTERS	Carpenters (A&M)
-	23	THICK AS A BRICK	Jethro Tull (Chrysalis)
21	24	TAPESTRY	Carole King (A&M)
29	25	ANDY WILLIAMS' GREATEST HITS	Andy Williams (CBS)
-	26	PICTURES AT AN EXHIBITION	Emerson Lake & Palmer (Island)
26	27	MEDDLE	Pink Floyd (Harvest)
-	28	MILESTONES	Rolling Stones (Decca)
18	29	EVERY PICTURE TELLS A STORY	Rod Stewart (Philips)
19	30	GATHER ME	Melanie (Buddah)

18 March 1972

last	this		
1	1	PAUL SIMON	Paul Simon (CBS)
2	2	HARVEST	Neil Young (Reprise)
3	3	TEASER AND THE FIRECAT	Cat Stevens (Island)
9	4	NILSSON SCHMILSSON	Nilsson (RCA)
6	5	BRIDGE OVER TROUBLED WATER	Simon & Garfunkel (CBS)
4	6	NEIL REID	Neil Reid (Decca)
8	7	HIMSELF	Gilbert O'Sullivan (MAM)
10	8	FOG ON THE TYNE	Lindisfarne (Charisma)
16	9	AMERICAN PIE	Don McLean (United Artists)
5	10	ELECTRIC WARRIOR	T. Rex (Fly)
23	11	THICK AS A BRICK	Jethro Tull (Chrysalis)
7	12	A NOD'S AS GOOD AS A WINK ... TO A BLIND HORSE	Faces (Warner Bros.)
11	13	GRAVE NEW WORLD	Strawbs (A&M)
13	14	IMAGINE	John Lennon (Apple)
12	15	HENDRIX IN THE WEST	Jimi Hendrix (Polydor)
14	16	LED ZEPPELIN IV	Led Zeppelin (Atlantic)
-	17	BABY I'M A WANT-YOU	Bread (Elektra)
22	18	THE CARPENTERS	Carpenters (A&M)
-	19	WHO WILL SAVE THE WORLD?	Groundhogs (United Artists)
21	20	TEA FOR THE TILLERMAN	Cat Stevens (Island)
24	21	TAPESTRY	Carole King (A&M)
15	22	THE CONCERT FOR BANGLA DESH	Various Artists (Apple)
27	23	MEDDLE	Pink Floyd (Harvest)
20	24	FRAGILE	Yes (Atlantic)
17	25	TOP OF THE POPS 22	Various Artists (Hallmark)
19	26	JESUS CHRIST SUPERSTAR	Various Artists (MCA)
30	27	GATHER ME	Melanie (Buddah)
18	28	MOTOWN CHARTBUSTERS VOL 6	Various Artists (Tamla Motown)
-	29	TOP TV THEMES	Johnny Keating (Studio Two)
29	30	EVERY PICTURE TELLS A STORY	Rod Stewart (Philips)

The "modern" musical had shifted from *West Side Story* to *Hair* to *Jesus Christ Superstar*. The cast of the latter included Yvonne Elliman and Murray Head, and a one-week hit maxi-single taken from the show featured *I Don't Know How To Love Him* by Elliman and *Superstar* by Head. Elliman would sing with Eric Clapton on his *461 Ocean Boulevard* (1974) and have Top 10 singles in 1976-7 (*Love Me*) and 1978 (*If I Can't Have You*); Murray Head would have a 1984 hit with *One Night In Bangkok*.

last week	this week	25 March 1972
1	1	PAUL SIMON Paul Simon (CBS)
2	2	HARVEST Neil Young (Reprise)
4	3	NILSSON SCHMILSSON Nilsson (RCA)
7	4	HIMSELF Gilbert O'Sullivan (MAM)
6	5	NEIL REID Neil Reid (Decca)
3	6	TEASER AND THE FIRECAT Cat Stevens (Island)
5	7	BRIDGE OVER TROUBLED WATER Simon & Garfunkel (CBS)
11	8	THICK AS A BRICK Jethro Tull (Chrysalis)
8	9	FOG ON THE TYNE Lindisfarne (Charisma)
10	10	ELECTRIC WARRIOR T. Rex (Fly)
9	11	AMERICAN PIE Don McLean (United Artists)
13	12	GRAVE NEW WORLD Strawbs (A&M)
12	13	A NOD'S AS GOOD AS A WINK ... TO A BLIND HORSE Faces (Warner Bros.)
19	14	WHO WILL SAVE THE WORLD? Groundhogs (United Artists)
14	15	IMAGINE John Lennon (Apple)
15	16	HENDRIX IN THE WEST Jimi Hendrix (Polydor)
-	17	MILESTONES Rolling Stones (Decca)
25	18	TOP OF THE POPS 22 Various Artists (Hallmark)
18	19	THE CARPENTERS Carpenters (A&M)
21	20	TAPESTRY Carole King (A&M)
26	21	JESUS CHRIST SUPERSTAR Various Artists (MCA)
29	22	TOP TV THEMES Johnny Keating (Studio Two)
-	23	WE'D LIKE TO TEACH THE WORLD TO SING New Seekers (Polydor)
20	24	TEA FOR THE TILLERMAN Cat Stevens (Island)
22	25	THE CONCERT FOR BANGLA DESH Various Artists (Apple)
16	26	LED ZEPPELIN IV Led Zeppelin (Atlantic)
28	27	MOTOWN CHARTBUSTERS VOL 6 Various Artists (Tamla Motown)
30	28	EVERY PICTURE TELLS A STORY Rod Stewart (Philips)
17	29	BABY I'M A WANT-YOU Bread (Elektra)
23	30	MEDDLE Pink Floyd (Harvest)

1 April 1972

1	1	PAUL SIMON Paul Simon (CBS)
3	2	NILSSON SCHMILSSON Nilsson (RCA)
2	3	HARVEST Neil Young (Reprise)
4	4	HIMSELF Gilbert O'Sullivan (MAM)
9	5	FOG ON THE TYNE Lindisfarne (Charisma)
11	6	AMERICAN PIE Don McLean (United Artists)
6	7	TEASER AND THE FIRECAT Cat Stevens (Island)
8	8	THICK AS A BRICK Jethro Tull (Chrysalis)
5	9	NEIL REID Neil Reid (Decca)
7	10	BRIDGE OVER TROUBLED WATER Simon & Garfunkel (CBS)
10	11	ELECTRIC WARRIOR T. Rex (Fly)
23	12	WE'D LIKE TO TEACH THE WORLD TO SING New Seekers (Polydor)
14	13	WHO WILL SAVE THE WORLD? Groundhogs (United Artists)
12	14	GRAVE NEW WORLD Strawbs (A&M)
15	15	IMAGINE John Lennon (Apple)
26	16	LED ZEPPELIN IV Led Zeppelin (Atlantic)
16	17	HENDRIX IN THE WEST Jimi Hendrix (Polydor)
-	18	FAREWELL TO THE GREYS Band of the Royal Scots Guards (RCA)
13	19	A NOD'S AS GOOD AS A WINK ... TO A BLIND HORSE Faces (Warner Bros.)
29	20	BABY I'M A WANT-YOU Bread (Elektra)
19	21	THE CARPENTERS Carpenters (A&M)
-	22	SLADE ALIVE Slade (Polydor)
17	23	MILESTONES Rolling Stones (Decca)
22	24	TOP TV THEMES Johnny Keating (Studio Two)
-	25	NEW AGE OF ATLANTIC Various Artists (Atlantic)
-	26	HOT HITS TEN Various Artists (Music for Pleasure)
-	27	WOYAYA Osibisa (MCA)
28	28	EVERY PICTURE TELLS A STORY Rod Stewart (Philips)
20	29	TAPESTRY Carole King (A&M)
21	30	JESUS CHRIST SUPERSTAR Various Artists (MCA)

8 April 1972

5	1	FOG ON THE TYNE Lindisfarne (Charisma)
3	2	HARVEST Neil Young (Reprise)
2	3	NILSSON SCHMILSSON Nilsson (RCA)
4	4	HIMSELF Gilbert O'Sullivan (MAM)
10	5	BRIDGE OVER TROUBLED WATER Simon & Garfunkel (CBS)
1	6	PAUL SIMON Paul Simon (CBS)
7	7	TEASER AND THE FIRECAT Cat Stevens (Island)
12	8	WE'D LIKE TO TEACH THE WORLD TO SING New Seekers (Polydor)
6	9	AMERICAN PIE Don McLean (United Artists)
8	10	THICK AS A BRICK Jethro Tull (Chrysalis)
9	11	NEIL REID Neil Reid (Decca)
11	12	ELECTRIC WARRIOR T. Rex (Fly)
-	13	MACHINE HEAD Deep Purple (Purple)
-	14	GARDEN IN THE CITY Melanie (Buddah)
15	15	IMAGINE John Lennon (Apple)
19	16	A NOD'S AS GOOD AS A WINK ... TO A BLIND HORSE Faces (Warner Bros.)
26	17	HOT HITS TEN Various Artists (Music for Pleasure)
30	18	JESUS CHRIST SUPERSTAR Various Artists (MCA)
23	19	MILESTONES Rolling Stones (Decca)
14	20	GRAVE NEW WORLD Strawbs (A&M)
13	21	WHO WILL SAVE THE WORLD? Groundhogs (United Artists)
29	22	TAPESTRY Carole King (A&M)
20	23	BABY I'M A WANT-YOU Bread (Elektra)
22	24	SLADE ALIVE Slade (Polydor)
-	24	MOTOWN CHARTBUSTERS VOL 6 Various Artists (Tamla Motown)
-	26	GLEN CAMPBELL'S GREATEST HITS Glen Campbell (Capitol)
18	27	FAREWELL TO THE GREYS Band of the Royal Scots Guards (RCA)
-	28	FRAGILE Yes (Atlantic)
17	29	HENDRIX IN THE WEST Jimi Hendrix (Polydor)
16	30	LED ZEPPELIN IV Led Zeppelin (Atlantic)

15 April 1972

2	1	HARVEST Neil Young (Reprise)
1	2	FOG ON THE TYNE Lindisfarne (Charisma)
4	3	HIMSELF Gilbert O'Sullivan (MAM)
3	4	NILSSON SCHMILSSON Nilsson (RCA)
6	5	PAUL SIMON Paul Simon (CBS)
8	6	WE'D LIKE TO TEACH THE WORLD TO SING New Seekers (Polydor)
10	7	THICK AS A BRICK Jethro Tull (Chrysalis)
5	8	BRIDGE OVER TROUBLED WATER Simon & Garfunkel (CBS)
9	9	AMERICAN PIE Don McLean (United Artists)
7	10	TEASER AND THE FIRECAT Cat Stevens (Island)
24	11	SLADE ALIVE Slade (Polydor)
13	12	MACHINE HEAD Deep Purple (Purple)
20	13	GRAVE NEW WORLD Strawbs (A&M)
12	14	ELECTRIC WARRIOR T. Rex (Fly)
15	15	IMAGINE John Lennon (Apple)
16	16	A NOD'S AS GOOD AS A WINK ... TO A BLIND HORSE Faces (Warner Bros.)
27	17	FAREWELL TO THE GREYS Band of the Royal Scots Guards (RCA)
17	18	HOT HITS TEN Various Artists (Music for Pleasure)
11	19	NEIL REID Neil Reid (Decca)
-	20	C.C.S. C.C.S. (RAK)
14	21	GARDEN IN THE CITY Melanie (Buddah)
22	22	TAPESTRY Carole King (A&M)
28	23	FRAGILE Yes (Atlantic)
21	24	WHO WILL SAVE THE WORLD? Groundhogs (United Artists)
23	25	BABY I'M A WANT-YOU Bread (Elektra)
-	26	NEW AGE OF ATLANTIC Various Artists (Atlantic)
29	27	HENDRIX IN THE WEST Jimi Hendrix (Polydor)
30	28	LED ZEPPELIN IV Led Zeppelin (Atlantic)
18	29	JESUS CHRIST SUPERSTAR Various Artists (MCA)
24	30	MOTOWN CHARTBUSTERS VOL 6 Various Artists (Tamla Motown)

Neil Reid's excitingly-titled ex-No.1 album *Neil Reid*, now slipping down the Top 10, must be one of the least-remembered No.1 albums of the post-war years, by one of the least-remembered artists. Reid, a television talent-show find, had entered the singles chart on Christmas Day 1971 with *Mother Of Mine*, which peaked at No.4 in February. His follow-up single would barely scrape the bottom of the Top 50; his second album, *Smile*, would do no better, later in the year.

22 April 1972

last week	this week	Title / Artist (Label)
1	1	HARVEST Neil Young (Reprise)
2	2	FOG ON THE TYNE Lindisfarne (Charisma)
12	3	MACHINE HEAD Deep Purple (Purple)
5	4	PAUL SIMON Paul Simon (CBS)
6	5	WE'D LIKE TO TEACH THE WORLD TO SING New Seekers (Polydor)
4	6	NILSSON SCHMILSSON Nilsson (RCA)
3	7	HIMSELF Gilbert O'Sullivan (MAM)
8	8	BRIDGE OVER TROUBLED WATER Simon & Garfunkel (CBS)
17	9	FAREWELL TO THE GREYS Band of the Royal Scots Guards (RCA)
7	10	THICK AS A BRICK Jethro Tull (Chrysalis)
11	11	SLADE ALIVE Slade (Polydor)
10	12	TEASER AND THE FIRECAT Cat Stevens (Island)
14	13	ELECTRIC WARRIOR T. Rex (Fly)
-	14	PROPHETS, SEERS AND SAGES THE ANGELS OF THE AGES/MY PEOPLE WERE FAIR AND HAD SKY IN THEIR HAIR, BUT NOW THEY'RE CONTENT TO WEAR STARS ON THEIR BROWS Tyrannosaurus Rex (Fly)
9	15	AMERICAN PIE Don McLean (United Artists)
25	16	BABY I'M A WANT-YOU Bread (Elektra)
13	17	GRAVE NEW WORLD Strawbs (A&M)
15	18	IMAGINE John Lennon (Apple)
21	19	GARDEN IN THE CITY Melanie (Buddah)
18	20	HOT HITS TEN Various Artists (Music for Pleasure)
16	21	A NOD'S AS GOOD AS A WINK ... TO A BLIND HORSE Faces (Warner Bros.)
22	22	TAPESTRY Carole King (A&M)
-	23	TOP OF THE POPS 23 Various Artists (Hallmark)
-	24	SMOKIN' Humble Pie (A&M)
30	25	MOTOWN CHARTBUSTERS VOL 6 Various Artists (Tamla Motown)
27	26	HENDRIX IN THE WEST Jimi Hendrix (Polydor)
-	27	THE CARPENTERS Carpenters (A&M)
24	28	WHO WILL SAVE THE WORLD? Groundhogs (United Artists)
23	29	FRAGILE Yes (Atlantic)
20	30	C.C.S. C.C.S. (RAK)

29 April 1972

last week	this week	Title / Artist (Label)
1	1	HARVEST Neil Young (Reprise)
3	2	MACHINE HEAD Deep Purple (Purple)
2	3	FOG ON THE TYNE Lindisfarne (Charisma)
6	4	NILSSON SCHMILSSON Nilsson (RCA)
7	5	HIMSELF Gilbert O'Sullivan (MAM)
5	6	WE'D LIKE TO TEACH THE WORLD TO SING New Seekers (Polydor)
8	7	BRIDGE OVER TROUBLED WATER Simon & Garfunkel (CBS)
4	8	PAUL SIMON Paul Simon (CBS)
10	9	THICK AS A BRICK Jethro Tull (Chrysalis)
9	10	FAREWELL TO THE GREYS Band of the Royal Scots Guards (RCA)
14	11	PROPHETS, SEERS AND SAGES THE ANGELS OF THE AGES/MY PEOPLE WERE FAIR AND HAD SKY IN THEIR HAIR, BUT NOW THEY'RE CONTENT TO WEAR STARS ON THEIR BROWS Tyrannosaurus Rex (Fly)
13	12	ELECTRIC WARRIOR T. Rex (Fly)
11	13	SLADE ALIVE Slade (Polydor)
12	14	TEASER AND THE FIRECAT Cat Stevens (Island)
15	15	AMERICAN PIE Don McLean (United Artists)
16	16	BABY I'M A WANT-YOU Bread (Elektra)
17	17	GRAVE NEW WORLD Strawbs (A&M)
-	18	GODSPELL London Cast (Bell)
19	19	GARDEN IN THE CITY Melanie (Buddah)
23	20	TOP OF THE POPS 23 Various Artists (Hallmark)
18	21	IMAGINE John Lennon (Apple)
21	22	A NOD'S AS GOOD AS A WINK ... TO A BLIND HORSE Faces (Warner Bros.)
28	23	WHO WILL SAVE THE WORLD? Groundhogs (United Artists)
-	24	NEIL REID Neil Reid (Decca)
25	25	MOTOWN CHARTBUSTERS VOL 6 Various Artists (Tamla Motown)
-	26	THE PARTRIDGE FAMILY ... SOUND MAGAZINE Partridge Family (Bell)
24	27	SMOKIN' Humble Pie (A&M)
-	28	ALL TOGETHER NOW Argent (Epic)
22	29	TAPESTRY Carole King (A&M)
-	30	LED ZEPPELIN IV Led Zeppelin (Atlantic)

6 May 1972

last week	this week	Title / Artist (Label)
2	1	MACHINE HEAD Deep Purple (Purple)
1	2	HARVEST Neil Young (Reprise)
11	3	PROPHETS, SEERS AND SAGES THE ANGELS OF THE AGES/MY PEOPLE WERE FAIR AND HAD SKY IN THEIR HAIR, BUT NOW THEY'RE CONTENT TO WEAR STARS ON THEIR BROWS Tyrannosaurus Rex (Fly)
3	4	FOG ON THE TYNE Lindisfarne (Charisma)
8	5	PAUL SIMON Paul Simon (CBS)
7	6	BRIDGE OVER TROUBLED WATER Simon & Garfunkel (CBS)
5	7	HIMSELF Gilbert O'Sullivan (MAM)
13	8	SLADE ALIVE Slade (Polydor)
4	9	NILSSON SCHMILSSON Nilsson (RCA)
9	10	THICK AS A BRICK Jethro Tull (Chrysalis)
10	11	FAREWELL TO THE GREYS Band of the Royal Scots Guards (RCA)
6	12	WE'D LIKE TO TEACH THE WORLD TO SING New Seekers (Polydor)
12	13	ELECTRIC WARRIOR T. Rex (Fly)
21	14	IMAGINE John Lennon (Apple)
14	15	TEASER AND THE FIRECAT Cat Stevens (Island)
16	16	BABY I'M A WANT-YOU Bread (Elektra)
15	17	AMERICAN PIE Don McLean (United Artists)
18	18	GODSPELL London Cast (Bell)
29	19	TAPESTRY Carole King (A&M)
26	20	THE PARTRIDGE FAMILY ... SOUND MAGAZINE Partridge Family (Bell)
-	21	GLEN CAMPBELL'S GREATEST HITS Glen Campbell (Capitol)
-	22	JESUS CHRIST SUPERSTAR Various Artists (MCA)
28	23	ALL TOGETHER NOW Argent (Epic)
20	24	TOP OF THE POPS 23 Various Artists (Hallmark)
22	25	A NOD'S AS GOOD AS A WINK ... TO A BLIND HORSE Faces (Warner Bros.)
19	26	GARDEN IN THE CITY Melanie (Buddah)
-	27	TICKET TO RIDE Carpenters (A&M)
17	28	GRAVE NEW WORLD Strawbs (A&M)
24	29	NEIL REID Neil Reid (Decca)
-	30	TEA FOR THE TILLERMAN Cat Stevens (Island)

13 May 1972

last week	this week	Title / Artist (Label)
1	1	MACHINE HEAD Deep Purple (Purple)
2	2	HARVEST Neil Young (Reprise)
4	3	FOG ON THE TYNE Lindisfarne (Charisma)
3	4	PROPHETS, SEERS AND SAGES THE ANGELS OF THE AGES/MY PEOPLE WERE FAIR AND HAD SKY IN THEIR HAIR, BUT NOW THEY'RE CONTENT TO WEAR STARS ON THEIR BROWS Tyrannosaurus Rex (Fly)
11	5	FAREWELL TO THE GREYS Band of the Royal Scots Guards (RCA)
6	6	BRIDGE OVER TROUBLED WATER Simon & Garfunkel (CBS)
12	7	WE'D LIKE TO TEACH THE WORLD TO SING New Seekers (Polydor)
5	8	PAUL SIMON Paul Simon (CBS)
-	9	BOLAN BOOGIE T. Rex (Fly)
7	10	HIMSELF Gilbert O'Sullivan (MAM)
9	11	NILSSON SCHMILSSON Nilsson (RCA)
15	12	TEASER AND THE FIRECAT Cat Stevens (Island)
13	13	ELECTRIC WARRIOR T. Rex (Fly)
8	14	SLADE ALIVE Slade (Polydor)
16	15	BABY I'M A WANT-YOU Bread (Elektra)
17	16	AMERICAN PIE Don McLean (United Artists)
23	17	ALL TOGETHER NOW Argent (Epic)
28	18	GRAVE NEW WORLD Strawbs (A&M)
24	19	TOP OF THE POPS 23 Various Artists (Hallmark)
19	20	TAPESTRY Carole King (A&M)
-	21	HOT HITS ELEVEN Various Artists (Music for Pleasure)
26	22	GARDEN IN THE CITY Melanie (Buddah)
-	23	DAVID CROSBY AND GRAHAM NASH David Crosby & Graham Nash (Atlantic)
-	24	MANASSAS Stephen Stills' Manassas (Atlantic)
10	25	THICK AS A BRICK Jethro Tull (Chrysalis)
21	26	GLEN CAMPBELL'S GREATEST HITS Glen Campbell (Capitol)
18	27	GODSPELL London Cast (Bell)
-	28	CHERISH David Cassidy (Bell)
-	29	NICELY OUT OF TIME Lindisfarne (Charisma)
-	30	A THING CALLED LOVE Johnny Cash (CBS)

Neil Young was top with his great album *Harvest*, and the other members of CSN&Y charted too, David Crosby & Graham Nash with an LP so-titled, and Stephen Stills with his band and LP *Manassas* (a re-entry). NB.: it was beyond the pale for anyone at this time to use the term "LP"; this was as prohibited by hipness and cool as saying "group". Part of punk's war on the old hip would be the defiant use of these long-scorned labels, not only by punters but by the younger, shorter-haired people in the music industry.

20 May 1972

last week	this week		
3	1	FOG ON THE TYNE	Lindisfarne (Charisma)
1	2	MACHINE HEAD	Deep Purple (Purple)
2	3	HARVEST Neil Young (Reprise)	
9	4	BOLAN BOOGIE T. Rex (Fly)	
5	5	FAREWELL TO THE GREYS	Band of the Royal Scots Guards (RCA)
6	6	BRIDGE OVER TROUBLED WATER	Simon & Garfunkel (CBS)
8	7	PAUL SIMON Paul Simon (CBS)	
4	8	PROPHETS, SEERS AND SAGES THE ANGELS OF THE AGES/MY PEOPLE WERE FAIR AND HAD SKY IN THEIR HAIR, BUT NOW THEY'RE CONTENT TO WEAR STARS ON THEIR BROWS	Tyrannosaurus Rex (Fly)
10	9	HIMSELF	Gilbert O'Sullivan (MAM)
14	10	SLADE ALIVE Slade (Polydor)	
7	11	WE'D LIKE TO TEACH THE WORLD TO SING	New Seekers (Polydor)
13	12	ELECTRIC WARRIOR	T. Rex (Fly)
12	13	TEASER AND THE FIRECAT	Cat Stevens (Island)
15	13	BABY I'M A WANT-YOU	Bread (Elektra)
25	15	THICK AS A BRICK	Jethro Tull (Chrysalis)
28	16	CHERISH David Cassidy (Bell)	
11	17	NILSSON SCHMILSSON	Nilsson (RCA)
30	18	A THING CALLED LOVE	Johnny Cash (CBS)
21	19	HOT HITS ELEVEN Various	Artists (Music for Pleasure)
16	20	AMERICAN PIE	Don McLean (United Artists)
24	21	MANASSAS	Stephen Stills' Manassas (Atlantic)
20	22	TAPESTRY Carole King (A&M)	
26	23	GLEN CAMPBELL'S GREATEST HITS Glen Campbell (Capitol)	
-	24	ARGUS Wishbone Ash (MCA)	
-	25	A SONG FOR YOU	Jack Jones (RCA)
-	26	IMAGINE John Lennon (Apple)	
23	27	DAVID CROSBY AND GRAHAM NASH	David Crosby & Graham Nash (Atlantic)
27	28	GODSPELL London Cast (Bell)	
18	29	GRAVE NEW WORLD	Strawbs (A&M)
-	30	THE PARTRIDGE FAMILY ... SOUND MAGAZINE	Partridge Family (Bell)

27 May 1972

4	1	BOLAN BOOGIE T. Rex (Fly)	
1	2	FOG ON THE TYNE	Lindisfarne (Charisma)
3	3	HARVEST Neil Young (Reprise)	
7	4	PAUL SIMON Paul Simon (CBS)	
2	5	MACHINE HEAD	Deep Purple (Purple)
16	6	CHERISH David Cassidy (Bell)	
6	7	BRIDGE OVER TROUBLED WATER	Simon & Garfunkel (CBS)
5	8	FAREWELL TO THE GREYS	Band of the Royal Scots Guards (RCA)
24	9	ARGUS Wishbone Ash (MCA)	
20	10	AMERICAN PIE	Don McLean (United Artists)
12	11	ELECTRIC WARRIOR	T. Rex (Fly)
9	12	HIMSELF	Gilbert O'Sullivan (MAM)
18	13	A THING CALLED LOVE	Johnny Cash (CBS)
-	14	HONKY CHATEAU	Elton John (DJM)
26	15	IMAGINE John Lennon (Apple)	
17	16	NILSSON SCHMILSSON	Nilsson (RCA)
11	17	WE'D LIKE TO TEACH THE WORLD TO SING	New Seekers (Polydor)
13	18	BABY I'M A WANT-YOU	Bread (Elektra)
8	19	PROPHETS, SEERS AND SAGES THE ANGELS OF THE AGES/MY PEOPLE WERE FAIR AND HAD SKY IN THEIR HAIR, BUT NOW THEY'RE CONTENT TO WEAR STARS ON THEIR BROWS	Tyrannosaurus Rex (Fly)
10	20	SLADE ALIVE Slade (Polydor)	
13	21	TEASER AND THE FIRECAT	Cat Stevens (Island)
-	22	LIVE IN EUROPE	Rory Gallagher (Polydor)
-	23	THE MUSIC PEOPLE	Various Artists (CBS)
27	24	DAVID CROSBY AND GRAHAM NASH	David Crosby & Graham Nash (Atlantic)
19	25	HOT HITS ELEVEN Various	Artists (Music for Pleasure)
-	26	BREADWINNERS	Jack Jones (RCA)
22	27	TAPESTRY Carole King (A&M)	
21	28	MANASSAS	Stephen Stills' Manassas (Atlantic)
-	29	NICELY OUT OF TIME	Lindisfarne (Charisma)
25	30	A SONG FOR YOU	Jack Jones (RCA)

3 June 1972

1	1	BOLAN BOOGIE T. Rex (Fly)	
-	2	EXILE ON MAIN STREET	Rolling Stones (Rolling Stones)
14	3	HONKY CHATEAU	Elton John (DJM)
6	4	CHERISH David Cassidy (Bell)	
-	5	20 DYNAMIC HITS	Various Artists (K-Tel)
7	6	BRIDGE OVER TROUBLED WATER	Simon & Garfunkel (CBS)
2	7	FOG ON THE TYNE	Lindisfarne (Charisma)
5	8	MACHINE HEAD	Deep Purple (Purple)
22	9	LIVE IN EUROPE	Rory Gallagher (Polydor)
9	10	ARGUS Wishbone Ash (MCA)	
26	11	BREADWINNERS	Jack Jones (RCA)
3	12	HARVEST Neil Young (Reprise)	
8	13	FAREWELL TO THE GREYS	Band of the Royal Scots Guards (RCA)
19	14	PROPHETS, SEERS AND SAGES THE ANGELS OF THE AGES/MY PEOPLE WERE FAIR AND HAD SKY IN THEIR HAIR, BUT NOW THEY'RE CONTENT TO WEAR STARS ON THEIR BROWS	Tyrannosaurus Rex (Fly)
10	15	AMERICAN PIE	Don McLean (United Artists)
4	16	PAUL SIMON Paul Simon (CBS)	
18	17	BABY I'M A WANT-YOU	Bread (Elektra)
23	18	THE MUSIC PEOPLE	Various Artists (CBS)
25	19	HOT HITS ELEVEN Various	Artists (Music for Pleasure)
11	20	ELECTRIC WARRIOR	T. Rex (Fly)
21	21	TEASER AND THE FIRECAT	Cat Stevens (Island)
-	22	ELVIS NOW Elvis Presley (RCA)	
-	23	MOONLIGHT AND ROSES	Jim Reeves (RCA International)
12	24	HIMSELF	Gilbert O'Sullivan (MAM)
15	25	IMAGINE John Lennon (Apple)	
16	26	NILSSON SCHMILSSON	Nilsson (RCA)
27	27	TAPESTRY Carole King (A&M)	
28	28	MANASSAS	Stephen Stills' Manassas (Atlantic)
13	29	A THING CALLED LOVE	Johnny Cash (CBS)
20	30	SLADE ALIVE Slade (Polydor)	

10 June 1972

1	1	BOLAN BOOGIE T. Rex (Fly)	
3	2	HONKY CHATEAU	Elton John (DJM)
2	3	EXILE ON MAIN STREET	Rolling Stones (Rolling Stones)
4	4	CHERISH David Cassidy (Bell)	
15	5	AMERICAN PIE	Don McLean (United Artists)
6	6	BRIDGE OVER TROUBLED WATER	Simon & Garfunkel (CBS)
8	7	MACHINE HEAD	Deep Purple (Purple)
7	8	FOG ON THE TYNE	Lindisfarne (Charisma)
11	9	BREADWINNERS	Jack Jones (RCA)
5	10	20 DYNAMIC HITS	Various Artists (K-Tel)
12	11	HARVEST Neil Young (Reprise)	
10	12	ARGUS Wishbone Ash (MCA)	
16	13	PAUL SIMON Paul Simon (CBS)	
9	14	LIVE IN EUROPE	Rory Gallagher (Polydor)
13	15	FAREWELL TO THE GREYS	Band of the Royal Scots Guards (RCA)
29	16	A THING CALLED LOVE	Johnny Cash (CBS)
21	17	TEASER AND THE FIRECAT	Cat Stevens (Island)
24	18	HIMSELF	Gilbert O'Sullivan (MAM)
30	19	SLADE ALIVE Slade (Polydor)	
17	20	BABY I'M A WANT-YOU	Bread (Elektra)
18	21	THE MUSIC PEOPLE	Various Artists (CBS)
-	22	NICELY OUT OF TIME	Lindisfarne (Charisma)
22	23	ELVIS NOW Elvis Presley (RCA)	
27	24	TAPESTRY Carole King (A&M)	
14	25	PROPHETS, SEERS AND SAGES THE ANGELS OF THE AGES/MY PEOPLE WERE FAIR AND HAD SKY IN THEIR HAIR, BUT NOW THEY'RE CONTENT TO WEAR STARS ON THEIR BROWS	Tyrannosaurus Rex (Fly)
-	26	THE WORLD OF 100 BEST TUNES VOL 3	Various Artists (Decca)
20	27	ELECTRIC WARRIOR	T. Rex (Fly)
28	28	MANASSAS	Stephen Stills' Manassas (Atlantic)
-	29	GODSPELL London Cast (Bell)	
-	30	FREE AT LAST Free (Island)	

Tynesiders Lindisfarne made No.1 again. The title track was not the band's big hit: *Meet Me On The Corner* and *Lady Eleanor* reached No.5 and No.7. Others in the singles chart the same week included *Vincent* (Don MacLean), *Sister Jane* (New World), *Rockin' Robin* (Michael Jackson) *Mary Had A Little Lamb* (Wings) and *Me And Julio Down By The School Yard* (Paul Simon) Meanwhile album entrant *Godspell* was by the London cast, among whom were David Essex and Jeremy Irons.

June – July 1972

17 June 1972

last	this		
3	1	EXILE ON MAIN STREET	Rolling Stones (Rolling Stones)
1	2	BOLAN BOOGIE	T. Rex (Fly)
5	3	AMERICAN PIE	Don McLean (United Artists)
2	4	HONKY CHATEAU	Elton John (DJM)
8	5	FOG ON THE TYNE	Lindisfarne (Charisma)
9	6	BREADWINNERS	Jack Jones (RCA)
4	7	CHERISH	David Cassidy (Bell)
6	8	BRIDGE OVER TROUBLED WATER	Simon & Garfunkel (CBS)
10	9	20 DYNAMIC HITS	Various Artists (K-Tel)
12	10	ARGUS	Wishbone Ash (MCA)
7	11	MACHINE HEAD	Deep Purple (Purple)
11	12	HARVEST	Neil Young (Reprise)
19	13	SLADE ALIVE	Slade (Polydor)
13	14	PAUL SIMON	Paul Simon (CBS)
15	15	FAREWELL TO THE GREYS	Band of the Royal Scots Guards (RCA)
20	16	BABY I'M A WANT-YOU	Bread (Elektra)
-	17	OBSCURED BY CLOUDS	Pink Floyd (Harvest)
18	18	HIMSELF	Gilbert O'Sullivan (MAM)
17	19	TEASER AND THE FIRECAT	Cat Stevens (Island)
24	20	TAPESTRY	Carole King (A&M)
27	21	ELECTRIC WARRIOR	T. Rex (Fly)
-	22	GLEN CAMPBELL'S GREATEST HITS	Glen Campbell (Capitol)
25	23	PROPHETS, SEERS AND SAGES THE ANGELS OF THE AGES/MY PEOPLE WERE FAIR AND HAD SKY IN THEIR HAIR, BUT NOW THEY'RE CONTENT TO WEAR STARS ON THEIR BROWS	Tyrannosaurus Rex (Fly)
14	24	LIVE IN EUROPE	Rory Gallagher (Polydor)
21	25	THE MUSIC PEOPLE	Various Artists (CBS)
16	26	A THING CALLED LOVE	Johnny Cash (CBS)
22	27	NICELY OUT OF TIME	Lindisfarne (Charisma)
28	28	MANASSAS	Stephen Stills' Manassas (Atlantic)
23	29	ELVIS NOW	Elvis Presley (RCA)
-	30	DEMONS AND WIZARDS	Uriah Heep (Bronze)

24 June 1972

	this		
1	1	EXILE ON MAIN STREET	Rolling Stones (Rolling Stones)
2	2	BOLAN BOOGIE	T. Rex (Fly)
3	3	AMERICAN PIE	Don McLean (United Artists)
4	4	HONKY CHATEAU	Elton John (DJM)
5	5	FOG ON THE TYNE	Lindisfarne (Charisma)
9	6	20 DYNAMIC HITS	Various Artists (K-Tel)
7	7	CHERISH	David Cassidy (Bell)
10	8	ARGUS	Wishbone Ash (MCA)
17	9	OBSCURED BY CLOUDS	Pink Floyd (Harvest)
13	10	SLADE ALIVE	Slade (Polydor)
6	11	BREADWINNERS	Jack Jones (RCA)
11	12	MACHINE HEAD	Deep Purple (Purple)
8	13	BRIDGE OVER TROUBLED WATER	Simon & Garfunkel (CBS)
-	14	FREE AT LAST	Free (Island)
12	15	HARVEST	Neil Young (Reprise)
21	16	ELECTRIC WARRIOR	T. Rex (Fly)
30	16	DEMONS AND WIZARDS	Uriah Heep (Bronze)
24	18	LIVE IN EUROPE	Rory Gallagher (Polydor)
14	19	PAUL SIMON	Paul Simon (CBS)
16	20	BABY I'M A WANT-YOU	Bread (Elektra)
27	21	NICELY OUT OF TIME	Lindisfarne (Charisma)
-	22	THE RISE AND FALL OF ZIGGY STARDUST AND THE SPIDERS FROM MARS	David Bowie (RCA)
15	23	FAREWELL TO THE GREYS	Band of the Royal Scots Guards (RCA)
20	24	TAPESTRY	Carole King (A&M)
26	25	A THING CALLED LOVE	Johnny Cash (CBS)
29	26	ELVIS NOW	Elvis Presley (RCA)
-	27	THE DRIFTERS' GREATEST HITS	Drifters (Atlantic)
19	28	TEASER AND THE FIRECAT	Cat Stevens (Island)
-	29	NILSSON SCHMILSSON	Nilsson (RCA)
22	30	GLEN CAMPBELL'S GREATEST HITS	Glen Campbell (Capitol)

1 July 1972

	this		
3	1	AMERICAN PIE	Don McLean (United Artists)
1	2	EXILE ON MAIN STREET	Rolling Stones (Rolling Stones)
4	3	HONKY CHATEAU	Elton John (DJM)
6	4	20 DYNAMIC HITS	Various Artists (K-Tel)
2	5	BOLAN BOOGIE	T. Rex (Fly)
13	6	BRIDGE OVER TROUBLED WATER	Simon & Garfunkel (CBS)
9	7	OBSCURED BY CLOUDS	Pink Floyd (Harvest)
10	8	SLADE ALIVE	Slade (Polydor)
5	9	FOG ON THE TYNE	Lindisfarne (Charisma)
7	10	CHERISH	David Cassidy (Bell)
14	11	FREE AT LAST	Free (Island)
11	12	BREADWINNERS	Jack Jones (RCA)
27	13	THE DRIFTERS' GREATEST HITS	Drifters (Atlantic)
-	14	TAPESTRY	Don McLean (United Artists)
8	15	ARGUS	Wishbone Ash (MCA)
-	16	CLOSE UP	Tom Jones (Decca)
12	17	MACHINE HEAD	Deep Purple (Purple)
16	17	ELECTRIC WARRIOR	T. Rex (Fly)
22	19	THE RISE AND FALL OF ZIGGY STARDUST AND THE SPIDERS FROM MARS	David Bowie (RCA)
21	20	NICELY OUT OF TIME	Lindisfarne (Charisma)
18	21	LIVE IN EUROPE	Rory Gallagher (Polydor)
-	22	GOLD	Neil Diamond (Uni)
-	23	LIVING IN THE PAST	Jethro Tull (Chrysalis)
15	24	HARVEST	Neil Young (Reprise)
20	25	BABY I'M A WANT-YOU	Bread (Elektra)
25	26	A THING CALLED LOVE	Johnny Cash (CBS)
-	27	IMAGINE	John Lennon (Apple)
-	28	HIMSELF	Gilbert O'Sullivan (MAM)
28	29	TEASER AND THE FIRECAT	Cat Stevens (Island)
19	30	PAUL SIMON	Paul Simon (CBS)

8 July 1972

	this		
1	1	AMERICAN PIE	Don McLean (United Artists)
4	2	20 DYNAMIC HITS	Various Artists (K-Tel)
5	3	BOLAN BOOGIE	T. Rex (Fly)
2	4	EXILE ON MAIN STREET	Rolling Stones (Rolling Stones)
3	5	HONKY CHATEAU	Elton John (DJM)
6	6	BRIDGE OVER TROUBLED WATER	Simon & Garfunkel (CBS)
7	7	OBSCURED BY CLOUDS	Pink Floyd (Harvest)
8	7	SLADE ALIVE	Slade (Polydor)
-	9	TRILOGY	Emerson Lake & Palmer (Island)
12	10	BREADWINNERS	Jack Jones (RCA)
19	11	THE RISE AND FALL OF ZIGGY STARDUST AND THE SPIDERS FROM MARS	David Bowie (RCA)
9	12	FOG ON THE TYNE	Lindisfarne (Charisma)
10	13	CHERISH	David Cassidy (Bell)
24	14	HARVEST	Neil Young (Reprise)
21	15	LIVE IN EUROPE	Rory Gallagher (Polydor)
23	16	LIVING IN THE PAST	Jethro Tull (Chrysalis)
11	17	FREE AT LAST	Free (Island)
15	18	ARGUS	Wishbone Ash (MCA)
28	19	HIMSELF	Gilbert O'Sullivan (MAM)
30	19	PAUL SIMON	Paul Simon (CBS)
-	21	DEMONS AND WIZARDS	Uriah Heep (Bronze)
29	22	TEASER AND THE FIRECAT	Cat Stevens (Island)
17	23	MACHINE HEAD	Deep Purple (Purple)
16	24	CLOSE UP	Tom Jones (Decca)
26	25	A THING CALLED LOVE	Johnny Cash (CBS)
22	26	GOLD	Neil Diamond (Uni)
17	27	ELECTRIC WARRIOR	T. Rex (Fly)
14	28	TAPESTRY	Don McLean (United Artists)
20	29	NICELY OUT OF TIME	Lindisfarne (Charisma)
-	30	ELVIS NOW	Elvis Presley (RCA)

The rise of *The Rise And Fall Of Ziggy Stardust And The Spiders From Mars* marked the album chart arrival of David Bowie, that ex-One Hit Wonder c/o 1969's *Space Oddity*. Bowie's first record was *Liza Jane*, by Davie Jones With The King Bees, 1964.

Others included two 1966 Pye singles produced by Tony Hatch. His debut LP was 1967's *David Bowie*, his next 1969's, um, *David Bowie*. *The Man Who Sold The World* and *Hunky Dory*, both 1971, would chart AFTER Ziggy Stardust.

July – August 1972

It had surely been an odd decision by Don MacLean and his record company to call his post-*American Pie* album *Tapestry*, when Carole King's LP of the same name had been one of the most prominent records of the previous couple of years. There were now signs that the 1970s were beginning properly to emerge: a new emphasis on glam, and on a knowing, detached manipulation of style, was beginning to be evident in a chart that now included not only Bowie but Roxy Music and Alice Cooper.

August – September 1972

12 August 1972

last week	this week	
1	1	SIMON AND GARFUNKEL'S GREATEST HITS — Simon & Garfunkel (CBS)
4	2	NEVER A DULL MOMENT — Rod Stewart (Mercury)
2	3	THE SLIDER — T. Rex (T. Rex Wax Co)
3	4	SCHOOL'S OUT — Alice Cooper (Warner Bros.)
5	5	20 DYNAMIC HITS — Various Artists (K-Tel)
7	6	SLADE ALIVE — Slade (Polydor)
7	7	THE RISE AND FALL OF ZIGGY STARDUST AND THE SPIDERS FROM MARS — David Bowie (RCA)
6	8	AMERICAN PIE — Don McLean (United Artists)
13	9	MOODS — Neil Diamond (Uni)
12	10	BRIDGE OVER TROUBLED WATER — Simon & Garfunkel (CBS)
11	11	ELVIS AS RECORDED LIVE AT MADISON SQUARE GARDEN — Elvis Presley (RCA)
9	12	TRILOGY — Emerson Lake & Palmer (Island)
21	13	HIMSELF — Gilbert O'Sullivan (MAM)
10	14	TWENTY FANTASTIC HITS — Various Artists (Arcade)
18	15	LOVE THEME FROM THE GODFATHER — Andy Williams (CBS)
16	16	LIVING IN THE PAST — Jethro Tull (Chrysalis)
14	17	CHERISH — David Cassidy (Bell)
19	18	EXILE ON MAIN STREET — Rolling Stones (Rolling Stones)
27	19	TAPESTRY — Don McLean (United Artists)
15	20	HONKY CHATEAU — Elton John (DJM)
25	21	FOG ON THE TYNE — Lindisfarne (Charisma)
-	22	JANIS JOPLIN IN CONCERT — Janis Joplin (CBS)
20	23	BOLAN BOOGIE — T. Rex (Fly)
-	24	ARGUS — Wishbone Ash (MCA)
-	25	MACHINE HEAD — Deep Purple (Purple)
24	26	BREADWINNERS — Jack Jones (RCA)
17	27	ROXY MUSIC — Roxy Music (Island)
26	28	OBSCURED BY CLOUDS — Pink Floyd (Harvest)
29	29	SON OF SCHMILSSON — Nilsson (RCA)
28	30	RIDE A WHITE SWAN — T. Rex (Music for Pleasure)

19 August 1972

last week	this week	
2	1	NEVER A DULL MOMENT — Rod Stewart (Mercury)
1	2	SIMON AND GARFUNKEL'S GREATEST HITS — Simon & Garfunkel (CBS)
3	3	THE SLIDER — T. Rex (T. Rex Wax Co)
4	4	SCHOOL'S OUT — Alice Cooper (Warner Bros.)
9	5	MOODS — Neil Diamond (Uni)
14	6	TWENTY FANTASTIC HITS — Various Artists (Arcade)
7	7	THE RISE AND FALL OF ZIGGY STARDUST AND THE SPIDERS FROM MARS — David Bowie (RCA)
5	8	20 DYNAMIC HITS — Various Artists (K-Tel)
6	9	SLADE ALIVE — Slade (Polydor)
8	10	AMERICAN PIE — Don McLean (United Artists)
11	11	ELVIS AS RECORDED LIVE AT MADISON SQUARE GARDEN — Elvis Presley (RCA)
12	12	TRILOGY — Emerson Lake & Palmer (Island)
-	13	SIMPLY — Jack Jones (Coral)
10	14	BRIDGE OVER TROUBLED WATER — Simon & Garfunkel (CBS)
13	15	HIMSELF — Gilbert O'Sullivan (MAM)
20	16	HONKY CHATEAU — Elton John (DJM)
15	17	LOVE THEME FROM THE GODFATHER — Andy Williams (CBS)
27	18	ROXY MUSIC — Roxy Music (Island)
-	19	IN SEARCH OF SPACE — Hawkwind (United Artists)
26	20	BREADWINNERS — Jack Jones (RCA)
17	21	CHERISH — David Cassidy (Bell)
19	22	TAPESTRY — Don McLean (United Artists)
24	23	ARGUS — Wishbone Ash (MCA)
28	24	OBSCURED BY CLOUDS — Pink Floyd (Harvest)
16	25	LIVING IN THE PAST — Jethro Tull (Chrysalis)
18	26	EXILE ON MAIN STREET — Rolling Stones (Rolling Stones)
-	27	HARVEST — Neil Young (Reprise)
21	28	FOG ON THE TYNE — Lindisfarne (Charisma)
22	29	JANIS JOPLIN IN CONCERT — Janis Joplin (CBS)
25	30	MACHINE HEAD — Deep Purple (Purple)

26 August 1972

last week	this week	
1	1	NEVER A DULL MOMENT — Rod Stewart (Mercury)
2	2	SIMON AND GARFUNKEL'S GREATEST HITS — Simon & Garfunkel (CBS)
4	3	SCHOOL'S OUT — Alice Cooper (Warner Bros.)
3	4	THE SLIDER — T. Rex (T. Rex Wax Co)
5	5	MOODS — Neil Diamond (Uni)
6	6	TWENTY FANTASTIC HITS — Various Artists (Arcade)
9	7	SLADE ALIVE — Slade (Polydor)
10	8	AMERICAN PIE — Don McLean (United Artists)
8	9	20 DYNAMIC HITS — Various Artists (K-Tel)
7	10	THE RISE AND FALL OF ZIGGY STARDUST AND THE SPIDERS FROM MARS — David Bowie (RCA)
14	11	BRIDGE OVER TROUBLED WATER — Simon & Garfunkel (CBS)
12	12	TRILOGY — Emerson Lake & Palmer (Island)
15	13	HIMSELF — Gilbert O'Sullivan (MAM)
11	14	ELVIS AS RECORDED LIVE AT MADISON SQUARE GARDEN — Elvis Presley (RCA)
19	15	IN SEARCH OF SPACE — Hawkwind (United Artists)
18	16	ROXY MUSIC — Roxy Music (Island)
-	17	THE EDWARD WOODWARD ALBUM — Edward Woodward (Jam)
17	18	LOVE THEME FROM THE GODFATHER — Andy Williams (CBS)
13	19	SIMPLY — Jack Jones (Coral)
20	20	BREADWINNERS — Jack Jones (RCA)
27	21	HARVEST — Neil Young (Reprise)
16	22	HONKY CHATEAU — Elton John (DJM)
21	23	CHERISH — David Cassidy (Bell)
26	24	EXILE ON MAIN STREET — Rolling Stones (Rolling Stones)
22	25	TAPESTRY — Don McLean (United Artists)
28	26	FOG ON THE TYNE — Lindisfarne (Charisma)
24	27	OBSCURED BY CLOUDS — Pink Floyd (Harvest)
25	28	LIVING IN THE PAST — Jethro Tull (Chrysalis)
-	29	CARLOS SANTANA AND BUDDY MILES LIVE! — Carlos Santana & Buddy Miles (CBS)
-	30	BOLAN BOOGIE — T. Rex (Fly)

2 September 1972

last week	this week	
1	1	NEVER A DULL MOMENT — Rod Stewart (Mercury)
2	2	SIMON AND GARFUNKEL'S GREATEST HITS — Simon & Garfunkel (CBS)
3	3	SCHOOL'S OUT — Alice Cooper (Warner Bros.)
6	4	TWENTY FANTASTIC HITS — Various Artists (Arcade)
5	5	MOODS — Neil Diamond (Uni)
7	6	SLADE ALIVE — Slade (Polydor)
4	7	THE SLIDER — T. Rex (T. Rex Wax Co)
8	8	AMERICAN PIE — Don McLean (United Artists)
10	9	THE RISE AND FALL OF ZIGGY STARDUST AND THE SPIDERS FROM MARS — David Bowie (RCA)
11	10	BRIDGE OVER TROUBLED WATER — Simon & Garfunkel (CBS)
12	11	TRILOGY — Emerson Lake & Palmer (Island)
13	12	HIMSELF — Gilbert O'Sullivan (MAM)
9	13	20 DYNAMIC HITS — Various Artists (K-Tel)
18	14	LOVE THEME FROM THE GODFATHER — Andy Williams (CBS)
20	15	BREADWINNERS — Jack Jones (RCA)
23	16	CHERISH — David Cassidy (Bell)
28	17	LIVING IN THE PAST — Jethro Tull (Chrysalis)
14	18	ELVIS AS RECORDED LIVE AT MADISON SQUARE GARDEN — Elvis Presley (RCA)
16	19	ROXY MUSIC — Roxy Music (Island)
26	20	FOG ON THE TYNE — Lindisfarne (Charisma)
17	21	THE EDWARD WOODWARD ALBUM — Edward Woodward (Jam)
21	22	HARVEST — Neil Young (Reprise)
15	23	IN SEARCH OF SPACE — Hawkwind (United Artists)
-	24	JACKSON FIVE'S GREATEST HITS — Jackson Five (Tamla Motown)
22	25	HONKY CHATEAU — Elton John (DJM)
27	26	OBSCURED BY CLOUDS — Pink Floyd (Harvest)
29	27	CARLOS SANTANA AND BUDDY MILES LIVE! — Santana & Buddy Miles (CBS)
19	28	SIMPLY — Jack Jones (Coral)
25	29	TAPESTRY — Don McLean (United Artists)
24	30	EXILE ON MAIN STREET — Rolling Stones (Rolling Stones)

It was a year since British singer-songwriter-pianist Gilbert O'Sullivan's *Himself* had first charted; a quiet success, it was re-climbing the Top 20. In November, its follow-up, *Back To Front*, would jump in at No.9 and top the chart two weeks later. O'Sullivan had first appeared dressed as a Dickensian urchin to plug his successful single *Nothing Rhymed* (No.7 in December 1990); a year and several minor hits later came *No Matter How I Try* (a No.5) and then this year his "classic", *Alone Again (Naturally)*.

September 1972

last this week   **9 September 1972**

last	this	title
1	1	NEVER A DULL MOMENT Rod Stewart (Mercury)
2	2	SIMON AND GARFUNKEL'S GREATEST HITS Simon & Garfunkel (CBS)
3	3	SCHOOL'S OUT Alice Cooper (Warner Bros.)
6	4	SLADE ALIVE Slade (Polydor)
7	5	THE SLIDER T. Rex (T. Rex Wax Co)
4	6	TWENTY FANTASTIC HITS Various Artists (Arcade)
5	7	MOODS Neil Diamond (Uni)
8	8	AMERICAN PIE Don McLean (United Artists)
9	9	THE RISE AND FALL OF ZIGGY STARDUST AND THE SPIDERS FROM MARS David Bowie (RCA)
10	10	BRIDGE OVER TROUBLED WATER Simon & Garfunkel (CBS)
19	11	ROXY MUSIC Roxy Music (Island)
11	12	TRILOGY Emerson Lake & Palmer (Island)
13	13	20 DYNAMIC HITS Various Artists (K-Tel)
23	14	IN SEARCH OF SPACE Hawkwind (United Artists)
	15	
14	16	LOVE THEME FROM THE GODFATHER Andy Williams (CBS)
15	17	BREADWINNERS Jack Jones (RCA)
26	18	OBSCURED BY CLOUDS Pink Floyd (Harvest)
17	19	LIVING IN THE PAST Jethro Tull (Chrysalis)
27	20	CARLOS SANTANA AND BUDDY MILES LIVE! Carlos Santana & Buddy Miles (CBS)
-	21	MACHINE HEAD Deep Purple (Purple)
-	22	EVERY PICTURE TELLS A STORY Rod Stewart (Philips)
	23	
25	24	HONKY CHATEAU Elton John (DJM)
20	25	FOG ON THE TYNE Lindisfarne (Charisma)
16	26	CHERISH David Cassidy (Bell)
-	27	HISTORY OF ERIC CLAPTON Eric Clapton (Polydor)
	28	
	29	
-	30	KILLER Alice Cooper (Warner Bros.)

16 September 1972

last	this	title
1	1	NEVER A DULL MOMENT Rod Stewart (Mercury)
2	2	SIMON AND GARFUNKEL'S GREATEST HITS Simon & Garfunkel (CBS)
6	3	TWENTY FANTASTIC HITS Various Artists (Arcade)
3	4	SCHOOL'S OUT Alice Cooper (Warner Bros.)
5	5	THE SLIDER T. Rex (T. Rex Wax Co)
4	6	SLADE ALIVE Slade (Polydor)
11	7	ROXY MUSIC Roxy Music (Island)
9	8	THE RISE AND FALL OF ZIGGY STARDUST AND THE SPIDERS FROM MARS David Bowie (RCA)
10	9	BRIDGE OVER TROUBLED WATER Simon & Garfunkel (CBS)
26	10	CHERISH David Cassidy (Bell)
7	11	MOODS Neil Diamond (Uni)
16	12	LOVE THEME FROM THE GODFATHER Andy Williams (CBS)
13	13	20 DYNAMIC HITS Various Artists (K-Tel)
8	14	AMERICAN PIE Don McLean (United Artists)
17	15	BREADWINNERS Jack Jones (RCA)
24	16	HONKY CHATEAU Elton John (DJM)
12	17	TRILOGY Emerson Lake & Palmer (Island)
14	18	IN SEARCH OF SPACE Hawkwind (United Artists)
30	19	KILLER Alice Cooper (Warner Bros.)
25	20	FOG ON THE TYNE Lindisfarne (Charisma)
-	21	LOVE IT TO DEATH Alice Cooper (Warner Bros.)
-	22	CLOSE TO THE EDGE Yes (Atlantic)
-	23	TEASER AND THE FIRECAT Cat Stevens (Island)
27	24	HISTORY OF ERIC CLAPTON Eric Clapton (Polydor)
-	25	THE EDWARD WOODWARD ALBUM Edward Woodward (Jam)
20	26	CARLOS SANTANA AND BUDDY MILES LIVE! Carlos Santana & Buddy Miles (CBS)
22	27	EVERY PICTURE TELLS A STORY Rod Stewart (Philips)
18	28	OBSCURED BY CLOUDS Pink Floyd (Harvest)
19	29	LIVING IN THE PAST Jethro Tull (Chrysalis)
21	30	MACHINE HEAD Deep Purple (Purple)

23 September 1972

last	this	title
2	1	SIMON AND GARFUNKEL'S GREATEST HITS Simon & Garfunkel (CBS)
1	2	NEVER A DULL MOMENT Rod Stewart (Mercury)
5	3	THE SLIDER T. Rex (T. Rex Wax Co)
6	4	SLADE ALIVE Slade (Polydor)
3	5	TWENTY FANTASTIC HITS Various Artists (Arcade)
7	6	ROXY MUSIC Roxy Music (Island)
4	7	SCHOOL'S OUT Alice Cooper (Warner Bros.)
11	8	MOODS Neil Diamond (Uni)
9	9	BRIDGE OVER TROUBLED WATER Simon & Garfunkel (CBS)
10	10	CHERISH David Cassidy (Bell)
14	11	AMERICAN PIE Don McLean (United Artists)
8	12	THE RISE AND FALL OF ZIGGY STARDUST AND THE SPIDERS FROM MARS David Bowie (RCA)
17	13	TRILOGY Emerson Lake & Palmer (Island)
22	14	CLOSE TO THE EDGE Yes (Atlantic)
-	15	20 ALL TIME GREATS OF THE 50s Various Artists (K-Tel)
16	16	HONKY CHATEAU Elton John (DJM)
18	17	IN SEARCH OF SPACE Hawkwind (United Artists)
12	18	LOVE THEME FROM THE GODFATHER Andy Williams (CBS)
25	19	THE EDWARD WOODWARD ALBUM Edward Woodward (Jam)
23	20	TEASER AND THE FIRECAT Cat Stevens (Island)
-	21	HIMSELF Gilbert O'Sullivan (MAM)
27	22	EVERY PICTURE TELLS A STORY Rod Stewart (Philips)
21	23	LOVE IT TO DEATH Alice Cooper (Warner Bros.)
13	24	20 DYNAMIC HITS Various Artists (K-Tel)
20	25	FOG ON THE TYNE Lindisfarne (Charisma)
24	26	HISTORY OF ERIC CLAPTON Eric Clapton (Polydor)
15	27	BREADWINNERS Jack Jones (RCA)
-	28	BLACK SABBATH VOL 4 Black Sabbath (Vertigo)
-	29	HARVEST Neil Young (Reprise)
-	30	NICELY OUT OF TIME Lindisfarne (Charisma)

30 September 1972

last	this	title
2	1	NEVER A DULL MOMENT Rod Stewart (Mercury)
1	2	SIMON AND GARFUNKEL'S GREATEST HITS Simon & Garfunkel (CBS)
14	3	CLOSE TO THE EDGE Yes (Atlantic)
4	4	SLADE ALIVE Slade (Polydor)
-	5	CATCH BULL AT FOUR Cat Stevens (Island)
15	6	20 ALL TIME GREATS OF THE 50s Various Artists (K-Tel)
6	7	ROXY MUSIC Roxy Music (Island)
3	8	THE SLIDER T. Rex (T. Rex Wax Co)
8	9	MOODS Neil Diamond (Uni)
28	10	BLACK SABBATH VOL 4 Black Sabbath (Vertigo)
-	11	DINGLY DELL Lindisfarne (Charisma)
7	12	SCHOOL'S OUT Alice Cooper (Warner Bros.)
5	13	TWENTY FANTASTIC HITS Various Artists (Arcade)
9	14	BRIDGE OVER TROUBLED WATER Simon & Garfunkel (CBS)
11	15	AMERICAN PIE Don McLean (United Artists)
10	16	CHERISH David Cassidy (Bell)
19	17	THE EDWARD WOODWARD ALBUM Edward Woodward (Jam)
16	18	HONKY CHATEAU Elton John (DJM)
-	19	SING ALONG WITH MAX Max Bygraves (Pye)
12	20	THE RISE AND FALL OF ZIGGY STARDUST AND THE SPIDERS FROM MARS David Bowie (RCA)
13	21	TRILOGY Emerson Lake & Palmer (Island)
-	22	CHICAGO V Chicago (CBS)
22	23	EVERY PICTURE TELLS A STORY Rod Stewart (Philips)
29	24	HARVEST Neil Young (Reprise)
-	25	KILLER Alice Cooper (Warner Bros.)
18	26	LOVE THEME FROM THE GODFATHER Andy Williams (CBS)
25	27	FOG ON THE TYNE Lindisfarne (Charisma)
21	28	HIMSELF Gilbert O'Sullivan (MAM)
24	29	20 DYNAMIC HITS Various Artists (K-Tel)
-	30	ALL THE YOUNG DUDES Mott the Hoople (CBS)

Yes, 21 years ago people were already buying retrospective Clapton albums: *History of Eric Clapton* was in fact only the second LP under Eric's own name. Three Alice Cooper chart LPs reflected the popularity of *School's Out*, a No.1 single. Similarly Rod Stewart's second No.1 album, *Never A Dull Moment*, coincided with his topping the singles chart with *You Wear It Well*, soon displaced by Slade's *Mama Weer All Crazee Now*. This singalonga-noddyholda group also boasted a Top 5 album.

October 1972

last week	this week		last week	this week		last week	this week		last week	this week	

7 October 1972

last	this	
1	1	NEVER A DULL MOMENT — Rod Stewart (Mercury)
2	2	SIMON AND GARFUNKEL'S GREATEST HITS — Simon & Garfunkel (CBS)
3	3	CLOSE TO THE EDGE — Yes (Atlantic)
4	4	SLADE ALIVE — Slade (Polydor)
5	5	CATCH BULL AT FOUR — Cat Stevens (Island)
11	6	DINGLY DELL — Lindisfarne (Charisma)
7	7	ROXY MUSIC — Roxy Music (Island)
10	8	BLACK SABBATH VOL 4 — Black Sabbath (Vertigo)
9	9	MOODS — Neil Diamond (Uni)
20	10	THE RISE AND FALL OF ZIGGY STARDUST AND THE SPIDERS FROM MARS — David Bowie (RCA)
6	11	20 ALL TIME GREATS OF THE 50s — Various Artists (K-Tel)
8	12	THE SLIDER — T. Rex (T. Rex Wax Co)
13	13	TWENTY FANTASTIC HITS — Various Artists (Arcade)
14	14	BRIDGE OVER TROUBLED WATER — Simon & Garfunkel (CBS)
19	15	SING ALONG WITH MAX — Max Bygraves (Pye)
21	16	TRILOGY — Emerson Lake & Palmer (Island)
23	16	EVERY PICTURE TELLS A STORY — Rod Stewart (Philips)
22	18	CHICAGO V — Chicago (CBS)
30	19	ALL THE YOUNG DUDES — Mott the Hoople (CBS)
16	20	CHERISH — David Cassidy (Bell)
12	21	SCHOOL'S OUT — Alice Cooper (Warner Bros.)
-	22	BANDSTAND — Family (Reprise)
25	23	KILLER — Alice Cooper (Warner Bros.)
-	24	TEASER AND THE FIRECAT — Cat Stevens (Island)
-	25	LAYLA AND OTHER ASSORTED LOVE SONGS — Derek & the Dominoes (Polydor)
-	26	PORTRAIT OF DONNY — Donny Osmond (MGM)
-	27	LOVE IT TO DEATH — Alice Cooper (Warner Bros.)
17	28	THE EDWARD WOODWARD ALBUM — Edward Woodward (Jam)
-	29	IN SEARCH OF SPACE — Hawkwind (United Artists)
28	30	HIMSELF — Gilbert O'Sullivan (MAM)

14 October 1972

last	this	
1	1	NEVER A DULL MOMENT — Rod Stewart (Mercury)
5	2	CATCH BULL AT FOUR — Cat Stevens (Island)
2	3	SIMON AND GARFUNKEL'S GREATEST HITS — Simon & Garfunkel (CBS)
3	4	CLOSE TO THE EDGE — Yes (Atlantic)
4	5	SLADE ALIVE — Slade (Polydor)
8	6	BLACK SABBATH VOL 4 — Black Sabbath (Vertigo)
7	7	ROXY MUSIC — Roxy Music (Island)
6	8	DINGLY DELL — Lindisfarne (Charisma)
10	9	THE RISE AND FALL OF ZIGGY STARDUST AND THE SPIDERS FROM MARS — David Bowie (RCA)
11	10	20 ALL TIME GREATS OF THE 50s — Various Artists (K-Tel)
20	11	CHERISH — David Cassidy (Bell)
13	12	TWENTY FANTASTIC HITS — Various Artists (Arcade)
9	13	MOODS — Neil Diamond (Uni)
21	14	SCHOOL'S OUT — Alice Cooper (Warner Bros.)
15	15	SING ALONG WITH MAX — Max Bygraves (Pye)
18	16	CHICAGO V — Chicago (CBS)
14	17	BRIDGE OVER TROUBLED WATER — Simon & Garfunkel (CBS)
-	18	AMERICAN PIE — Don McLean (United Artists)
16	19	TRILOGY — Emerson Lake & Palmer (Island)
29	20	IN SEARCH OF SPACE — Hawkwind (United Artists)
22	21	BANDSTAND — Family (Reprise)
-	22	SOMETIME IN NEW YORK CITY — John & Yoko Lennon (Apple)
12	23	THE SLIDER — T. Rex (T. Rex Wax Co)
-	24	THE FOUR SIDES OF MELANIE — Melanie (Buddah)
24	25	TEASER AND THE FIRECAT — Cat Stevens (Island)
-	26	HONKY CHATEAU — Elton John (DJM)
-	27	ELVIS AS RECORDED LIVE AT MADISON SQUARE GARDEN — Elvis Presley (RCA)
23	28	KILLER — Alice Cooper (Warner Bros.)
26	29	PORTRAIT OF DONNY — Donny Osmond (MGM)
16	30	EVERY PICTURE TELLS A STORY — Rod Stewart (Philips)

21 October 1972

last	this	
3	1	SIMON AND GARFUNKEL'S GREATEST HITS — Simon & Garfunkel (CBS)
1	2	NEVER A DULL MOMENT — Rod Stewart (Mercury)
2	3	CATCH BULL AT FOUR — Cat Stevens (Island)
6	4	BLACK SABBATH VOL 4 — Black Sabbath (Vertigo)
4	5	CLOSE TO THE EDGE — Yes (Atlantic)
5	6	SLADE ALIVE — Slade (Polydor)
10	7	20 ALL TIME GREATS OF THE 50s — Various Artists (K-Tel)
8	8	DINGLY DELL — Lindisfarne (Charisma)
15	9	SING ALONG WITH MAX — Max Bygraves (Pye)
11	10	CHERISH — David Cassidy (Bell)
13	11	MOODS — Neil Diamond (Uni)
9	12	THE RISE AND FALL OF ZIGGY STARDUST AND THE SPIDERS FROM MARS — David Bowie (RCA)
-	13	20 STAR TRACKS — Various Artists (Ronco)
7	14	ROXY MUSIC — Roxy Music (Island)
21	15	BANDSTAND — Family (Reprise)
17	16	BRIDGE OVER TROUBLED WATER — Simon & Garfunkel (CBS)
19	17	TRILOGY — Emerson Lake & Palmer (Island)
14	18	SCHOOL'S OUT — Alice Cooper (Warner Bros.)
12	19	TWENTY FANTASTIC HITS — Various Artists (Arcade)
-	20	STAR PORTRAIT — Johnny Cash (CBS)
28	21	KILLER — Alice Cooper (Warner Bros.)
24	22	THE FOUR SIDES OF MELANIE — Melanie (Buddah)
29	23	PORTRAIT OF DONNY — Donny Osmond (MGM)
20	24	IN SEARCH OF SPACE — Hawkwind (United Artists)
22	25	SOMETIME IN NEW YORK CITY — John & Yoko Lennon (Apple)
-	26	CIRCLES — New Seekers (Polydor)
-	27	NICE 'N' EASY — Various Artists (Philips)
-	28	WHO CAME FIRST — Pete Townshend (Track)
30	29	EVERY PICTURE TELLS A STORY — Rod Stewart (Philips)
18	30	AMERICAN PIE — Don McLean (United Artists)

28 October 1972

last	this	
1	1	SIMON AND GARFUNKEL'S GREATEST HITS — Simon & Garfunkel (CBS)
3	2	CATCH BULL AT FOUR — Cat Stevens (Island)
2	3	NEVER A DULL MOMENT — Rod Stewart (Mercury)
7	4	20 ALL TIME GREATS OF THE 50s — Various Artists (K-Tel)
5	5	CLOSE TO THE EDGE — Yes (Atlantic)
9	6	SING ALONG WITH MAX — Max Bygraves (Pye)
4	7	BLACK SABBATH VOL 4 — Black Sabbath (Vertigo)
8	8	DINGLY DELL — Lindisfarne (Charisma)
6	9	SLADE ALIVE — Slade (Polydor)
10	10	CHERISH — David Cassidy (Bell)
13	11	20 STAR TRACKS — Various Artists (Ronco)
12	12	THE RISE AND FALL OF ZIGGY STARDUST AND THE SPIDERS FROM MARS — David Bowie (RCA)
17	13	TRILOGY — Emerson Lake & Palmer (Island)
19	14	TWENTY FANTASTIC HITS — Various Artists (Arcade)
29	15	EVERY PICTURE TELLS A STORY — Rod Stewart (Philips)
16	16	BRIDGE OVER TROUBLED WATER — Simon & Garfunkel (CBS)
-	17	A SONG FOR YOU — Carpenters (A&M)
11	18	MOODS — Neil Diamond (Uni)
18	19	SCHOOL'S OUT — Alice Cooper (Warner Bros.)
20	20	STAR PORTRAIT — Johnny Cash (CBS)
25	21	SOMETIME IN NEW YORK CITY — John & Yoko Lennon (Apple)
23	22	PORTRAIT OF DONNY — Donny Osmond (MGM)
-	23	GLITTER — Gary Glitter (Bell)
30	24	AMERICAN PIE — Don McLean (United Artists)
15	25	BANDSTAND — Family (Reprise)
26	26	CIRCLES — New Seekers (Polydor)
28	27	WHO CAME FIRST — Pete Townshend (Track)
-	28	HIMSELF — Gilbert O'Sullivan (MAM)
14	29	ROXY MUSIC — Roxy Music (Island)
-	30	THE SLIDER — T. Rex (T. Rex Wax Co)

From now until year's end, the No.1 singles would be David Cassidy's *How Can I Be Sure*, Lieutenant Pidgeon's *Mouldy Old Dough*, Gilbert O'Sullivan's *Clair*, Chuck Berry's *My Ding-A-Ling*, Slade's *Gudbuy T'Jane* and Little Jimmy Osmond's *Long-Haired Lover From Liverpool*. In this climate, an albums chart that embraced *Sing Along With Max* and *Portrait Of Donny* (Osmond), might be said to make sense. John & Yoko Lennon, now so billed, seemed under-appreciated with *Sometime In New York City*.

4 November 1972

last week	this week	
1	1	SIMON AND GARFUNKEL'S GREATEST HITS — Simon & Garfunkel (CBS)
2	2	CATCH BULL AT FOUR — Cat Stevens (Island)
3	3	NEVER A DULL MOMENT — Rod Stewart (Mercury)
4	4	20 ALL TIME GREATS OF THE 50s — Various Artists (K-Tel)
23	5	GLITTER — Gary Glitter (Bell)
9	6	SLADE ALIVE — Slade (Polydor)
6	7	SING ALONG WITH MAX — Max Bygraves (Pye)
5	8	CLOSE TO THE EDGE — Yes (Atlantic)
7	9	BLACK SABBATH VOL 4 — Black Sabbath (Vertigo)
11	10	20 STAR TRACKS — Various Artists (Ronco)
12	11	THE RISE AND FALL OF ZIGGY STARDUST AND THE SPIDERS FROM MARS — David Bowie (RCA)
8	12	DINGLY DELL — Lindisfarne (Charisma)
-	13	BEST OF BREAD — Bread (Elektra)
16	14	BRIDGE OVER TROUBLED WATER — Simon & Garfunkel (CBS)
10	15	CHERISH — David Cassidy (Bell)
14	16	TWENTY FANTASTIC HITS — Various Artists (Arcade)
25	17	BANDSTAND — Family (Reprise)
18	18	MOODS — Neil Diamond (Uni)
29	19	ROXY MUSIC — Roxy Music (Island)
21	20	SOMETIME IN NEW YORK CITY — John & Yoko Lennon (Apple)
-	21	HOT HITS 14 — Various Artists (Music for Pleasure)
28	22	HIMSELF — Gilbert O'Sullivan (MAM)
13	23	TRILOGY — Emerson Lake & Palmer (Island)
24	24	AMERICAN PIE — Don McLean (United Artists)
19	25	SCHOOL'S OUT — Alice Cooper (Warner Bros.)
17	26	A SONG FOR YOU — Carpenters (A&M)
15	27	EVERY PICTURE TELLS A STORY — Rod Stewart (Philips)
-	28	BREADWINNERS — Jack Jones (RCA)
20	29	STAR PORTRAIT — Johnny Cash (CBS)
22	30	PORTRAIT OF DONNY — Donny Osmond (MGM)

11 November 1972

1	1	SIMON AND GARFUNKEL'S GREATEST HITS — Simon & Garfunkel (CBS)
2	2	CATCH BULL AT FOUR — Cat Stevens (Island)
3	3	NEVER A DULL MOMENT — Rod Stewart (Mercury)
4	4	20 ALL TIME GREATS OF THE 50s — Various Artists (K-Tel)
9	5	BLACK SABBATH VOL 4 — Black Sabbath (Vertigo)
5	6	GLITTER — Gary Glitter (Bell)
10	7	20 STAR TRACKS — Various Artists (Ronco)
7	8	SING ALONG WITH MAX — Max Bygraves (Pye)
-	9	BACK TO FRONT — Gilbert O'Sullivan (MAM)
15	10	CHERISH — David Cassidy (Bell)
6	11	SLADE ALIVE — Slade (Polydor)
13	12	BEST OF BREAD — Bread (Elektra)
8	13	CLOSE TO THE EDGE — Yes (Atlantic)
17	14	BANDSTAND — Family (Reprise)
11	15	THE RISE AND FALL OF ZIGGY STARDUST AND THE SPIDERS FROM MARS — David Bowie (RCA)
30	16	PORTRAIT OF DONNY — Donny Osmond (MGM)
14	17	BRIDGE OVER TROUBLED WATER — Simon & Garfunkel (CBS)
18	18	MOODS — Neil Diamond (Uni)
20	19	SOMETIME IN NEW YORK CITY — John & Yoko Lennon (Apple)
12	20	DINGLY DELL — Lindisfarne (Charisma)
26	21	A SONG FOR YOU — Carpenters (A&M)
27	22	EVERY PICTURE TELLS A STORY — Rod Stewart (Philips)
22	23	HIMSELF — Gilbert O'Sullivan (MAM)
16	24	TWENTY FANTASTIC HITS — Various Artists (Arcade)
-	25	FOXTROT — Genesis (Charisma)
-	26	KILLER — Alice Cooper (Warner Bros.)
29	27	STAR PORTRAIT — Johnny Cash (CBS)
25	28	SCHOOL'S OUT — Alice Cooper (Warner Bros.)
-	29	DIANA ROSS' GREATEST HITS — Diana Ross (Tamla Motown)
24	30	AMERICAN PIE — Don McLean (United Artists)

18 November 1972

1	1	SIMON AND GARFUNKEL'S GREATEST HITS — Simon & Garfunkel (CBS)
4	2	20 ALL TIME GREATS OF THE 50s — Various Artists (K-Tel)
2	3	CATCH BULL AT FOUR — Cat Stevens (Island)
9	4	BACK TO FRONT — Gilbert O'Sullivan (MAM)
3	5	NEVER A DULL MOMENT — Rod Stewart (Mercury)
12	6	BEST OF BREAD — Bread (Elektra)
8	7	SING ALONG WITH MAX — Max Bygraves (Pye)
7	8	20 STAR TRACKS — Various Artists (Ronco)
6	9	GLITTER — Gary Glitter (Bell)
10	10	CHERISH — David Cassidy (Bell)
5	11	BLACK SABBATH VOL 4 — Black Sabbath (Vertigo)
11	12	SLADE ALIVE — Slade (Polydor)
-	13	22 DYNAMIC HITS — Various Artists (K-Tel)
13	14	CLOSE TO THE EDGE — Yes (Atlantic)
16	15	PORTRAIT OF DONNY — Donny Osmond (MGM)
17	16	BRIDGE OVER TROUBLED WATER — Simon & Garfunkel (CBS)
21	17	A SONG FOR YOU — Carpenters (A&M)
-	18	WAR HEROES — Jimi Hendrix (Polydor)
15	19	THE RISE AND FALL OF ZIGGY STARDUST AND THE SPIDERS FROM MARS — David Bowie (RCA)
-	20	20 FANTASTIC HITS VOL 2 — Various Artists (Arcade)
20	21	DINGLY DELL — Lindisfarne (Charisma)
-	22	CARAVANSERAI — Santana (CBS)
29	23	DIANA ROSS' GREATEST HITS — Diana Ross (Tamla Motown)
-	24	TRILOGY — Emerson Lake & Palmer (Island)
14	25	BANDSTAND — Family (Reprise)
28	26	SCHOOL'S OUT — Alice Cooper (Warner Bros.)
-	27	THE LAST GOON SHOW OF ALL — Goons (BBC)
22	28	EVERY PICTURE TELLS A STORY — Rod Stewart (Philips)
-	29	JACKSON FIVE'S GREATEST HITS — Jackson Five (Tamla Motown)
-	30	I CAN SEE CLEARLY NOW — Johnny Nash (CBS)

25 November 1972

4	1	BACK TO FRONT — Gilbert O'Sullivan (MAM)
1	2	SIMON AND GARFUNKEL'S GREATEST HITS — Simon & Garfunkel (CBS)
3	3	CATCH BULL AT FOUR — Cat Stevens (Island)
5	4	NEVER A DULL MOMENT — Rod Stewart (Mercury)
2	5	20 ALL TIME GREATS OF THE 50s — Various Artists (K-Tel)
13	6	22 DYNAMIC HITS — Various Artists (K-Tel)
7	7	SING ALONG WITH MAX — Max Bygraves (Pye)
12	8	SLADE ALIVE — Slade (Polydor)
-	9	SEVENTH SOJOURN — Moody Blues (Threshold)
6	10	BEST OF BREAD — Bread (Elektra)
8	11	20 STAR TRACKS — Various Artists (Ronco)
9	12	GLITTER — Gary Glitter (Bell)
11	13	BLACK SABBATH VOL 4 — Black Sabbath (Vertigo)
20	14	20 FANTASTIC HITS VOL 2 — Various Artists (Arcade)
22	15	CARAVANSERAI — Santana (CBS)
15	16	PORTRAIT OF DONNY — Donny Osmond (MGM)
27	17	THE LAST GOON SHOW OF ALL — Goons (BBC)
14	18	CLOSE TO THE EDGE — Yes (Atlantic)
17	19	A SONG FOR YOU — Carpenters (A&M)
21	20	DINGLY DELL — Lindisfarne (Charisma)
26	21	SCHOOL'S OUT — Alice Cooper (Warner Bros.)
28	22	EVERY PICTURE TELLS A STORY — Rod Stewart (Philips)
10	23	CHERISH — David Cassidy (Bell)
16	24	BRIDGE OVER TROUBLED WATER — Simon & Garfunkel (CBS)
19	25	THE RISE AND FALL OF ZIGGY STARDUST AND THE SPIDERS FROM MARS — David Bowie (RCA)
24	26	TRILOGY — Emerson Lake & Palmer (Island)
18	27	WAR HEROES — Jimi Hendrix (Polydor)
-	28	MOODS — Neil Diamond (Uni)
29	29	JACKSON FIVE'S GREATEST HITS — Jackson Five (Tamla Motown)
25	30	BANDSTAND — Family (Reprise)

Much of the chart was now hits compilations, both of the *Jackson Five's Greatest Hits* sort and the *20 All Time Greats Of The 50s* by Various Artists sort: the latter thrown together by specialist companies, like K-Tel, Arcade and Ronco, which signed no acts themselves but repackaged others' back-catalogues. So dominant were these becoming that the industry discussed changing the rules of chart-entry to exclude them. Current hit singles included the Shangri-Las' *Leader Of The Pack* and Neil Sedaka's *Oh Carol*.

December 1972

2 December 1972

last	this	
2	1	SIMON AND GARFUNKEL'S GREATEST HITS Simon & Garfunkel (CBS)
3	2	CATCH BULL AT FOUR Cat Stevens (Island)
1	3	BACK TO FRONT Gilbert O'Sullivan (MAM)
5	4	20 ALL TIME GREATS OF THE 50s Various Artists (K-Tel)
4	5	NEVER A DULL MOMENT Rod Stewart (Mercury)
-	6	SLAYED Slade (Polydor)
6	7	22 DYNAMIC HITS Various Artists (K-Tel)
9	8	SEVENTH SOJOURN Moody Blues (Threshold)
-	9	25 ROCKIN' AND ROLLIN' GREATS Various Artists (K-Tel)
12	10	GLITTER Gary Glitter (Bell)
15	11	CARAVANSERAI Santana (CBS)
16	12	PORTRAIT OF DONNY Donny Osmond (MGM)
7	13	SING ALONG WITH MAX Max Bygraves (Pye)
11	14	20 STAR TRACKS Various Artists (Ronco)
14	15	20 FANTASTIC HITS VOL 2 Various Artists (Arcade)
10	16	BEST OF BREAD Bread (Elektra)
-	17	MOTOWN CHARTBUSTERS VOL 7 Various Artists (Tamla Motown)
24	18	BRIDGE OVER TROUBLED WATER Simon & Garfunkel (CBS)
27	19	WAR HEROES Jimi Hendrix (Polydor)
17	20	THE LAST GOON SHOW OF ALL Goons (BBC)
-	21	BOBBY CRUSH Bobby Crush (Philips)
13	22	BLACK SABBATH VOL 4 Black Sabbath (Vertigo)
-	23	LOOKIN' THROUGH THE WINDOWS Jackson Five (Tamla Motown)
23	24	CHERISH David Cassidy (Bell)
8	25	SLADE ALIVE Slade (Polydor)
26	26	TRILOGY Emerson Lake & Palmer (Island)
-	27	BREADWINNERS Jack Jones (RCA)
19	28	A SONG FOR YOU Carpenters (A&M)
18	29	CLOSE TO THE EDGE Yes (Atlantic)
20	30	DINGLY DELL Lindisfarne (Charisma)

9 December 1972

last	this	
3	1	BACK TO FRONT Gilbert O'Sullivan (MAM)
2	2	CATCH BULL AT FOUR Cat Stevens (Island)
9	3	25 ROCKIN' AND ROLLIN' GREATS Various Artists (K-Tel)
6	4	SLAYED Slade (Polydor)
8	5	SEVENTH SOJOURN Moody Blues (Threshold)
1	6	SIMON AND GARFUNKEL'S GREATEST HITS Simon & Garfunkel (CBS)
5	7	NEVER A DULL MOMENT Rod Stewart (Mercury)
7	8	22 DYNAMIC HITS Various Artists (K-Tel)
12	9	PORTRAIT OF DONNY Donny Osmond (MGM)
15	10	20 FANTASTIC HITS VOL 2 Various Artists (Arcade)
4	11	20 ALL TIME GREATS OF THE 50s Various Artists (K-Tel)
13	12	SING ALONG WITH MAX Max Bygraves (Pye)
11	13	CARAVANSERAI Santana (CBS)
17	14	MOTOWN CHARTBUSTERS VOL 7 Various Artists (Tamla Motown)
24	15	CHERISH David Cassidy (Bell)
25	16	SLADE ALIVE Slade (Polydor)
16	17	BEST OF BREAD Bread (Elektra)
28	18	A SONG FOR YOU Carpenters (A&M)
-	19	THE MAGICIAN'S BIRTHDAY Uriah Heep (Island)
19	20	WAR HEROES Jimi Hendrix (Polydor)
20	21	THE LAST GOON SHOW OF ALL Goons (BBC)
14	22	20 STAR TRACKS Various Artists (Ronco)
18	23	BRIDGE OVER TROUBLED WATER Simon & Garfunkel (CBS)
10	24	GLITTER Gary Glitter (Bell)
23	25	LOOKIN' THROUGH THE WINDOWS Jackson Five (Tamla Motown)
22	26	BLACK SABBATH VOL 4 Black Sabbath (Vertigo)
30	27	DINGLY DELL Lindisfarne (Charisma)
26	28	TRILOGY Emerson Lake & Palmer (Island)
-	29	TOO YOUNG Donny Osmond (MGM)
-	30	MOODS Neil Diamond (Uni)

16 December 1972

last	this	
1	1	BACK TO FRONT Gilbert O'Sullivan (MAM)
4	2	SLAYED Slade (Polydor)
6	3	SIMON AND GARFUNKEL'S GREATEST HITS Simon & Garfunkel (CBS)
3	4	25 ROCKIN' AND ROLLIN' GREATS Various Artists (K-Tel)
11	5	20 ALL TIME GREATS OF THE 50s Various Artists (K-Tel)
2	6	CATCH BULL AT FOUR Cat Stevens (Island)
7	7	NEVER A DULL MOMENT Rod Stewart (Mercury)
9	8	PORTRAIT OF DONNY Donny Osmond (MGM)
5	9	SEVENTH SOJOURN Moody Blues (Threshold)
13	10	CARAVANSERAI Santana (CBS)
12	11	SING ALONG WITH MAX Max Bygraves (Pye)
8	12	22 DYNAMIC HITS Various Artists (K-Tel)
17	13	BEST OF BREAD Bread (Elektra)
-	14	SING ALONG WITH MAX VOL 2 Max Bygraves (Pye)
14	15	MOTOWN CHARTBUSTERS VOL 7 Various Artists (Tamla Motown)
-	16	DOREMI FASOL LATIDO Hawkwind (United Artists)
21	17	THE LAST GOON SHOW OF ALL Goons (BBC)
10	18	20 FANTASTIC HITS VOL 2 Various Artists (Arcade)
29	19	TOO YOUNG Donny Osmond (MGM)
-	20	JACKSON FIVE'S GREATEST HITS Jackson Five (Tamla Motown)
-	21	OSMONDS LIVE Osmonds (MGM)
15	22	CHERISH David Cassidy (Bell)
-	23	ANDY WILLIAMS' GREATEST HITS VOL 2 Andy Williams (CBS)
16	24	SLADE ALIVE Slade (Polydor)
23	25	BRIDGE OVER TROUBLED WATER Simon & Garfunkel (CBS)
25	26	LOOKIN' THROUGH THE WINDOWS Jackson Five (Tamla Motown)
24	27	GLITTER Gary Glitter (Bell)
22	28	20 STAR TRACKS Various Artists (Ronco)
26	29	BLACK SABBATH VOL 4 Black Sabbath (Vertigo)
27	30	DINGLY DELL Lindisfarne (Charisma)

23 December 1972

last	this	
1	1	BACK TO FRONT Gilbert O'Sullivan (MAM)
2	2	SLAYED Slade (Polydor)
4	3	25 ROCKIN' AND ROLLIN' GREATS Various Artists (K-Tel)
3	4	SIMON AND GARFUNKEL'S GREATEST HITS Simon & Garfunkel (CBS)
8	5	PORTRAIT OF DONNY Donny Osmond (MGM)
12	6	22 DYNAMIC HITS Various Artists (K-Tel)
5	7	20 ALL TIME GREATS OF THE 50s Various Artists (K-Tel)
9	8	SEVENTH SOJOURN Moody Blues (Threshold)
7	9	NEVER A DULL MOMENT Rod Stewart (Mercury)
11	10	SING ALONG WITH MAX Max Bygraves (Pye)
19	11	TOO YOUNG Donny Osmond (MGM)
22	12	CHERISH David Cassidy (Bell)
18	13	20 FANTASTIC HITS VOL 2 Various Artists (Arcade)
15	14	MOTOWN CHARTBUSTERS VOL 7 Various Artists (Tamla Motown)
-	15	CRAZY HORSES Osmonds (MGM)
6	16	CATCH BULL AT FOUR Cat Stevens (Island)
16	17	DOREMI FASOL LATIDO Hawkwind (United Artists)
14	18	SING ALONG WITH MAX VOL 2 Max Bygraves (Pye)
10	19	CARAVANSERAI Santana (CBS)
-	20	MADE IN JAPAN Deep Purple (Purple)
26	21	LOOKIN' THROUGH THE WINDOWS Jackson Five (Tamla Motown)
20	22	JACKSON FIVE'S GREATEST HITS Jackson Five (Tamla Motown)
-	23	BOBBY CRUSH Bobby Crush (Philips)
-	24	A SONG FOR YOU Carpenters (A&M)
17	25	THE LAST GOON SHOW OF ALL Goons (BBC)
13	26	BEST OF BREAD Bread (Elektra)
28	27	20 STAR TRACKS Various Artists (Ronco)
23	28	ANDY WILLIAMS' GREATEST HITS VOL 2 Andy Williams (CBS)
-	29	IMAGINE John Lennon (Apple)
25	30	BRIDGE OVER TROUBLED WATER Simon & Garfunkel (CBS)

With everything from the Goons onwards in the charts, David Widgery wrote in this month's Socialist Worker that "on the principle that almost anything would be better than the 1970s, the pioneering pop singles of the late 1950s and 1960s are being remorselessly re-released to swamp any originality which might be struggling to the surface. This has reached such a point that half the record-buying public appears to be awash with nostalgia over experiences they never had in the first place."

last week	this week	30 December 1972
2	1	SLAYED Slade (Polydor)
7	2	20 ALL TIME GREATS OF THE 50s Various Artists (K-Tel)
1	3	BACK TO FRONT Gilbert O'Sullivan (MAM)
3	4	25 ROCKIN' AND ROLLIN' GREATS Various Artists (K-Tel)
5	5	PORTRAIT OF DONNY Donny Osmond (MGM)
4	6	SIMON AND GARFUNKEL'S GREATEST HITS Simon & Garfunkel (CBS)
6	7	22 DYNAMIC HITS Various Artists (K-Tel)
11	8	TOO YOUNG Donny Osmond (MGM)
16	9	CATCH BULL AT FOUR Cat Stevens (Island)
9	10	NEVER A DULL MOMENT Rod Stewart (Mercury)
8	11	SEVENTH SOJOURN Moody Blues (Threshold)
13	12	20 FANTASTIC HITS VOL 2 Various Artists (Arcade)
10	13	SING ALONG WITH MAX Max Bygraves (Pye)
15	14	CRAZY HORSES Osmonds (MGM)
12	15	CHERISH David Cassidy (Bell)
20	16	MADE IN JAPAN Deep Purple (Purple)
-	17	PHIL SPECTOR'S CHRISTMAS ALBUM Various Artists (Apple)
30	18	BRIDGE OVER TROUBLED WATER Simon & Garfunkel (CBS)
29	19	IMAGINE John Lennon (Apple)
27	20	20 STAR TRACKS Various Artists (Ronco)
14	21	MOTOWN CHARTBUSTERS VOL 7 Various Artists (Tamla Motown)
21	22	LOOKIN' THROUGH THE WINDOWS Jackson Five (Tamla Motown)
19	23	CARAVANSERAI Santana (CBS)
17	24	DOREMI FASOL LATIDO Hawkwind (United Artists)
26	25	BEST OF BREAD Bread (Elektra)
23	26	BOBBY CRUSH Bobby Crush (Philips)
28	27	ANDY WILLIAMS' GREATEST HITS VOL 2 Andy Williams (CBS)
18	28	SING ALONG WITH MAX VOL 2 Max Bygraves (Pye)
-	29	SLADE ALIVE Slade (Polydor)
24	30	A SONG FOR YOU Carpenters (A&M)

The new and the old: Slade (top) and The Who

January 1973

6 January 1973

last	this		
1	1	SLAYED	Slade (Polydor)
3	2	BACK TO FRONT	Gilbert O'Sullivan (MAM)
6	3	SIMON & GARFUNKEL'S GREATEST HITS	Simon & Garfunkel (CBS)
5	4	PORTRAIT OF DONNY	Donny Osmond (MGM)
2	5	20 ALL TIME GREATS OF THE 50s	Various Artists (K-Tel)
4	6	25 ROCKIN' & ROLLIN' GREATS	Various Artists (K-Tel)
9	7	CATCH BULL AT FOUR	Cat Stevens (Island)
7	8	22 DYNAMIC HITS	Various Artists (K-Tel)
10	9	NEVER A DULL MOMENT	Rod Stewart (Mercury)
14	10	CRAZY HORSES	Osmonds (MGM)
12	11	20 FANTASTIC HITS VOL 2	Various Artists (Arcade)
15	12	CHERISH	David Cassidy (Bell)
8	13	TOO YOUNG	Donny Osmond (MGM)
11	14	SEVENTH SOJOURN	Moody Blues (Threshold)
13	15	SING ALONG WITH MAX	Max Bygraves (Pye)
16	16	MADE IN JAPAN	Deep Purple (Purple)
-	17	THE STRAUSS FAMILY	Cyril Ornadel & the London Symphony Orchestra (Polydor)
21	18	MOTOWN CHARTBUSTERS VOL 7	Various Artists (Tamla Motown)
29	19	SLADE ALIVE	Slade (Polydor)
20	20	20 STAR TRACKS	Various Artists (Ronco)
24	21	DOREMI FASOL LATIDO	Hawkwind (United Artists)
23	22	CARAVANSERAI	Santana (CBS)
-	23	BEN	Michael Jackson (Tamla Motown)
-	24	HIMSELF	Gilbert O'Sullivan (MAM)
28	25	SING ALONG WITH MAX VOL 2	Max Bygraves (Pye)
18	26	BRIDGE OVER TROUBLED WATER	Simon & Garfunkel (CBS)
22	27	LOOKIN' THROUGH THE WINDOWS	Jackson Five (Tamla Motown)
19	28	IMAGINE	John Lennon (Apple)
25	29	BEST OF BREAD	Bread (Elektra)
30	30	A SONG FOR YOU	Carpenters (A&M)

13 January 1973

last	this		
1	1	SLAYED	Slade (Polydor)
2	2	BACK TO FRONT	Gilbert O'Sullivan (MAM)
4	3	PORTRAIT OF DONNY	Donny Osmond (MGM)
3	4	SIMON & GARFUNKEL'S GREATEST HITS	Simon & Garfunkel (CBS)
9	5	NEVER A DULL MOMENT	Rod Stewart (Mercury)
7	6	CATCH BULL AT FOUR	Cat Stevens (Island)
10	7	CRAZY HORSES	Osmonds (MGM)
14	8	SEVENTH SOJOURN	Moody Blues (Threshold)
16	9	MADE IN JAPAN	Deep Purple (Purple)
5	10	20 ALL TIME GREATS OF THE 50s	Various Artists (K-Tel)
13	11	TOO YOUNG	Donny Osmond (MGM)
-	12	NO SECRETS	Carly Simon (Elektra)
18	13	MOTOWN CHARTBUSTERS VOL 7	Various Artists (Tamla Motown)
17	14	THE STRAUSS FAMILY	Cyril Ornadel & the London Symphony Orchestra (Polydor)
21	15	DOREMI FASOL LATIDO	Hawkwind (United Artists)
6	16	25 ROCKIN' & ROLLIN' GREATS	Various Artists (K-Tel)
23	17	BEN	Michael Jackson (Tamla Motown)
11	18	20 FANTASTIC HITS VOL 2	Various Artists (Arcade)
12	19	CHERISH	David Cassidy (Bell)
8	20	22 DYNAMIC HITS	Various Artists (K-Tel)
15	21	SING ALONG WITH MAX	Max Bygraves (Pye)
19	22	SLADE ALIVE	Slade (Polydor)
-	23	TOMMY	London Symphony Orchestra & Chamber Choir with Guest Soloists (A&M)
26	24	BRIDGE OVER TROUBLED WATER	Simon & Garfunkel (CBS)
29	25	BEST OF BREAD	Bread (Elektra)
-	26	OSMONDS LIVE	Osmonds (MGM)
24	27	HIMSELF	Gilbert O'Sullivan (MAM)
-	28	MOVING WAVES	Focus (Polydor)
-	29	ALL DIRECTIONS	Temptations (Tamla Motown)
22	30	CARAVANSERAI	Santana (CBS)

20 January 1973

last	this		
1	1	SLAYED	Slade (Polydor)
2	2	BACK TO FRONT	Gilbert O'Sullivan (MAM)
4	3	SIMON & GARFUNKEL'S GREATEST HITS	Simon & Garfunkel (CBS)
6	4	CATCH BULL AT FOUR	Cat Stevens (Island)
7	5	CRAZY HORSES	Osmonds (MGM)
5	6	NEVER A DULL MOMENT	Rod Stewart (Mercury)
3	7	PORTRAIT OF DONNY	Donny Osmond (MGM)
9	8	MADE IN JAPAN	Deep Purple (Purple)
-	9	THE RISE AND FALL OF ZIGGY STARDUST AND THE SPIDERS FROM MARS	David Bowie (RCA)
12	10	NO SECRETS	Carly Simon (Elektra)
8	11	SEVENTH SOJOURN	Moody Blues (Threshold)
30	12	CARAVANSERAI	Santana (CBS)
17	13	BEN	Michael Jackson (Tamla Motown)
13	14	MOTOWN CHARTBUSTERS VOL 7	Various Artists (Tamla Motown)
14	15	THE STRAUSS FAMILY	Cyril Ornadel & the London Symphony Orchestra (Polydor)
11	16	TOO YOUNG	Donny Osmond (MGM)
16	17	25 ROCKIN' & ROLLIN' GREATS	Various Artists (K-Tel)
20	18	22 DYNAMIC HITS	Various Artists (K-Tel)
18	19	20 FANTASTIC HITS VOL 2	Various Artists (Arcade)
24	20	BRIDGE OVER TROUBLED WATER	Simon & Garfunkel (CBS)
22	21	SLADE ALIVE	Slade (Polydor)
26	22	OSMONDS LIVE	Osmonds (MGM)
21	23	SING ALONG WITH MAX	Max Bygraves (Pye)
23	24	TOMMY	London Symphony Orchestra & Chamber Choir with Guest Soloists (A&M)
10	25	20 ALL TIME GREATS OF THE 50s	Various Artists (K-Tel)
15	26	DOREMI FASOL LATIDO	Hawkwind (United Artists)
19	27	CHERISH	David Cassidy (Bell)
-	28	BREADWINNERS	Jack Jones (RCA)
-	29	FOR THE ROSES	Joni Mitchell (Asylum)
28	30	MOVING WAVES	Focus (Polydor)

27 January 1973

last	this		
1	1	SLAYED	Slade (Polydor)
2	2	BACK TO FRONT	Gilbert O'Sullivan (MAM)
10	3	NO SECRETS	Carly Simon (Elektra)
3	4	SIMON & GARFUNKEL'S GREATEST HITS	Simon & Garfunkel (CBS)
7	5	PORTRAIT OF DONNY	Donny Osmond (MGM)
4	6	CATCH BULL AT FOUR	Cat Stevens (Island)
6	7	NEVER A DULL MOMENT	Rod Stewart (Mercury)
9	8	THE RISE AND FALL OF ZIGGY STARDUST AND THE SPIDERS FROM MARS	David Bowie (RCA)
16	9	TOO YOUNG	Donny Osmond (MGM)
8	10	MADE IN JAPAN	Deep Purple (Purple)
11	11	SEVENTH SOJOURN	Moody Blues (Threshold)
15	12	THE STRAUSS FAMILY	Cyril Ornadel & the London Symphony Orchestra (Polydor)
30	13	MOVING WAVES	Focus (Polydor)
5	14	CRAZY HORSES	Osmonds (MGM)
-	15	PILEDRIVER	Status Quo (Vertigo)
17	16	25 ROCKIN' & ROLLIN' GREATS	Various Artists (K-Tel)
13	17	BEN	Michael Jackson (Tamla Motown)
19	18	20 FANTASTIC HITS VOL 2	Various Artists (Arcade)
-	19	ALL DIRECTIONS	Temptations (Tamla Motown)
20	20	BRIDGE OVER TROUBLED WATER	Simon & Garfunkel (CBS)
27	21	CHERISH	David Cassidy (Bell)
14	22	MOTOWN CHARTBUSTERS VOL 7	Various Artists (Tamla Motown)
-	23	TRILOGY	Emerson Lake & Palmer (Island)
-	24	BEST OF BREAD	Bread (Elektra)
29	25	FOR THE ROSES	Joni Mitchell (Asylum)
12	26	CARAVANSERAI	Santana (CBS)
24	27	TOMMY	London Symphony Orchestra & Chamber Choir with Guest Soloists (A&M)
-	28	IMAGINE	John Lennon (Apple)
21	29	SLADE ALIVE	Slade (Polydor)
23	30	SING ALONG WITH MAX	Max Bygraves (Pye)

Carly Simon, of America's wealthy elite, one of the Simons of the Simon & Schuster publishing empire, was doing very nicely with her album *No Secrets* and the hit single *You're So Vain*. Its punch-line "You're so vain you prob'ly think this song is about you, don't you?" made the song a self-reflexive text, though since this post-structuralist term was not yet available, people had to content themselves with surmising that Carly had aimed it at Warren Beatty, the well-known film-star and womaniser.

3 February 1973

last / this week

last	this		
1	1	SLAYED	Slade (Polydor)
2	2	BACK TO FRONT	
			Gilbert O'Sullivan (MAM)
4	3	SIMON & GARFUNKEL'S GREATEST HITS	
			Simon & Garfunkel (CBS)
3	4	NO SECRETS	
			Carly Simon (Elektra)
6	5	CATCH BULL AT FOUR	
			Cat Stevens (Island)
-	6	DON'T SHOOT ME I'M ONLY THE PIANO PLAYER	
			Elton John (DJM)
12	7	THE STRAUSS FAMILY	
			Cyril Ornadel & the London Symphony Orchestra (Polydor)
8	8	THE RISE AND FALL OF ZIGGY STARDUST AND THE SPIDERS FROM MARS	
			David Bowie (RCA)
11	9	SEVENTH SOJOURN	
			Moody Blues (Threshold)
5	10	PORTRAIT OF DONNY	
			Donny Osmond (MGM)
7	11	NEVER A DULL MOMENT	
			Rod Stewart (Mercury)
15	12	PILEDRIVER	
			Status Quo (Vertigo)
13	13	MOVING WAVES	
			Focus (Polydor)
14	14	CRAZY HORSES	
			Osmonds (MGM)
10	15	MADE IN JAPAN	
			Deep Purple (Purple)
19	16	ALL DIRECTIONS	
			Temptations (Tamla Motown)
9	17	TOO YOUNG	
			Donny Osmond (MGM)
-	18	FOCUS 3	Focus (Polydor)
20	19	BRIDGE OVER TROUBLED WATER	
			Simon & Garfunkel (CBS)
-	20	TALKING BOOK	
			Stevie Wonder (Tamla Motown)
18	21	20 FANTASTIC HITS VOL 2	
			Various Artists (Arcade)
-	22	BREADWINNERS	
			Jack Jones (RCA)
17	23	BEN	Michael Jackson (Tamla Motown)
-	24	HEARTBREAKER	Free (Island)
22	25	MOTOWN CHARTBUSTERS VOL 7	
			Various Artists (Tamla Motown)
16	26	25 ROCKIN' & ROLLIN' GREATS	
			Various Artists (K-Tel)
-	27	HIMSELF	
			Gilbert O'Sullivan (MAM)
29	28	SLADE ALIVE	Slade (Polydor)
23	29	TRILOGY	
			Emerson Lake & Palmer (Island)
28	30	IMAGINE	
			John Lennon (Apple)

10 February 1973

6	1	DON'T SHOOT ME I'M ONLY THE PIANO PLAYER	
			Elton John (DJM)
4	2	NO SECRETS	
			Carly Simon (Elektra)
2	3	BACK TO FRONT	
			Gilbert O'Sullivan (MAM)
1	4	SLAYED	Slade (Polydor)
5	5	CATCH BULL AT FOUR	
			Cat Stevens (Island)
3	6	SIMON & GARFUNKEL'S GREATEST HITS	
			Simon & Garfunkel (CBS)
13	7	MOVING WAVES	
			Focus (Polydor)
12	8	PILEDRIVER	
			Status Quo (Vertigo)
7	9	THE STRAUSS FAMILY	
			Cyril Ornadel & the London Symphony Orchestra (Polydor)
8	10	THE RISE AND FALL OF ZIGGY STARDUST AND THE SPIDERS FROM MARS	
			David Bowie (RCA)
24	11	HEARTBREAKER	Free (Island)
18	12	FOCUS 3	Focus (Polydor)
11	13	NEVER A DULL MOMENT	
			Rod Stewart (Mercury)
15	14	MADE IN JAPAN	
			Deep Purple (Purple)
14	15	CRAZY HORSES	
			Osmonds (MGM)
-	16	WHO DO YOU THINK WE ARE	
			Deep Purple (Purple)
10	17	PORTRAIT OF DONNY	
			Donny Osmond (MGM)
17	18	TOO YOUNG	
			Donny Osmond (MGM)
9	19	SEVENTH SOJOURN	
			Moody Blues (Threshold)
20	20	TALKING BOOK	
			Stevie Wonder (Tamla Motown)
19	21	BRIDGE OVER TROUBLED WATER	
			Simon & Garfunkel (CBS)
26	22	25 ROCKIN' & ROLLIN' GREATS	
			Various Artists (K-Tel)
-	23	BEST OF BREAD	
			Bread (Elektra)
16	24	ALL DIRECTIONS	
			Temptations (Tamla Motown)
23	25	BEN	Michael Jackson (Tamla Motown)
22	26	BREADWINNERS	
			Jack Jones (RCA)
29	27	TRILOGY	
			Emerson Lake & Palmer (Island)
-	28	KILLER JOE	
			Little Jimmy Osmond (MGM)
-	29	A SONG FOR YOU	
			Carpenters (A&M)
-	30	OSMONDS LIVE	Osmonds (MGM)

17 February 1973

1	1	DON'T SHOOT ME I'M ONLY THE PIANO PLAYER	
			Elton John (DJM)
2	2	NO SECRETS	
			Carly Simon (Elektra)
4	3	SLAYED	Slade (Polydor)
3	4	BACK TO FRONT	
			Gilbert O'Sullivan (MAM)
6	5	SIMON & GARFUNKEL'S GREATEST HITS	
			Simon & Garfunkel (CBS)
11	6	HEARTBREAKER	Free (Island)
12	7	FOCUS 3	Focus (Polydor)
9	8	THE STRAUSS FAMILY	
			Cyril Ornadel & the London Symphony Orchestra (Polydor)
7	9	MOVING WAVES	
			Focus (Polydor)
8	10	PILEDRIVER	
			Status Quo (Vertigo)
5	11	CATCH BULL AT FOUR	
			Cat Stevens (Island)
10	12	THE RISE AND FALL OF ZIGGY STARDUST AND THE SPIDERS FROM MARS	
			David Bowie (RCA)
19	13	SEVENTH SOJOURN	
			Moody Blues (Threshold)
17	14	PORTRAIT OF DONNY	
			Donny Osmond (MGM)
16	15	WHO DO YOU THINK WE ARE	
			Deep Purple (Purple)
13	16	NEVER A DULL MOMENT	
			Rod Stewart (Mercury)
26	17	BREADWINNERS	
			Jack Jones (RCA)
15	18	CRAZY HORSES	
			Osmonds (MGM)
-	19	THE SIX WIVES OF HENRY VIII	
			Rick Wakeman (A&M)
14	20	MADE IN JAPAN	
			Deep Purple (Purple)
18	21	TOO YOUNG	
			Donny Osmond (MGM)
21	22	BRIDGE OVER TROUBLED WATER	
			Simon & Garfunkel (CBS)
23	23	BEST OF BREAD	
			Bread (Elektra)
20	24	TALKING BOOK	
			Stevie Wonder (Tamla Motown)
-	25	SING ALONG WITH MAX	
			Max Bygraves (Pye)
-	26	HOT AUGUST NIGHT	
			Neil Diamond (Uni)
-	27	GLITTER	Gary Glitter (Bell)
28	28	KILLER JOE	
			Little Jimmy Osmond (MGM)
-	29	MOTOWN CHARTBUSTERS VOL 7	
			Various Artists (Tamla Motown)
-	30	SLADE ALIVE	
			Slade (Polydor)

24 February 1973

1	1	DON'T SHOOT ME I'M ONLY THE PIANO PLAYER	
			Elton John (DJM)
2	2	NO SECRETS	
			Carly Simon (Elektra)
3	3	SLAYED	Slade (Polydor)
9	4	MOVING WAVES	
			Focus (Polydor)
4	5	BACK TO FRONT	
			Gilbert O'Sullivan (MAM)
10	6	PILEDRIVER	
			Status Quo (Vertigo)
15	7	WHO DO YOU THINK WE ARE	
			Deep Purple (Purple)
7	8	FOCUS 3	Focus (Polydor)
8	9	THE STRAUSS FAMILY	
			Cyril Ornadel & the London Symphony Orchestra (Polydor)
11	10	CATCH BULL AT FOUR	
			Cat Stevens (Island)
5	11	SIMON & GARFUNKEL'S GREATEST HITS	
			Simon & Garfunkel (CBS)
19	12	THE SIX WIVES OF HENRY VIII	
			Rick Wakeman (A&M)
6	13	HEARTBREAKER	Free (Island)
13	14	SEVENTH SOJOURN	
			Moody Blues (Threshold)
24	15	TALKING BOOK	
			Stevie Wonder (Tamla Motown)
12	16	THE RISE AND FALL OF ZIGGY STARDUST AND THE SPIDERS FROM MARS	
			David Bowie (RCA)
-	17	ROCK ME BABY	
			David Cassidy (Bell)
20	18	MADE IN JAPAN	
			Deep Purple (Purple)
-	19	BURSTING AT THE SEAMS	
			Strawbs (A&M)
16	20	NEVER A DULL MOMENT	
			Rod Stewart (Mercury)
28	21	KILLER JOE	
			Little Jimmy Osmond (MGM)
26	22	HOT AUGUST NIGHT	
			Neil Diamond (Uni)
-	23	HOLLAND	Beach Boys (Reprise)
14	24	PORTRAIT OF DONNY	
			Donny Osmond (MGM)
23	25	BEST OF BREAD	
			Bread (Elektra)
22	26	BRIDGE OVER TROUBLED WATER	
			Simon & Garfunkel (CBS)
25	27	SING ALONG WITH MAX	
			Max Bygraves (Pye)
21	28	TOO YOUNG	
			Donny Osmond (MGM)
18	29	CRAZY HORSES	
			Osmonds (MGM)
-	30	TRILOGY	
			Emerson Lake & Palmer (Island)

Canadian Joni Mitchell's minor hit album *For The Roses* had just left the Top 30 after peaking at 25. Mitchell, singer-songwriter of several anthemic 1960s songs, was slowly acquiring gravitas, through the dexterity of her very personal writing and perform- ance (on piano as well as guitar). About to move among the rock superstar elite, she would soon make more heavily promoted albums and go off at many jazzy tangents, but *For The Roses* was a true classic; its warm, intelligent appeal is undiminished today.

3 March 1973

Last	This	Title / Artist (Label)
1	1	DON'T SHOOT ME I'M ONLY THE PIANO PLAYER — Elton John (DJM)
2	2	NO SECRETS — Carly Simon (Elektra)
5	3	BACK TO FRONT — Gilbert O'Sullivan (MAM)
3	4	SLAYED — Slade (Polydor)
7	5	WHO DO YOU THINK WE ARE — Deep Purple (Purple)
4	6	MOVING WAVES — Focus (Polydor)
8	7	FOCUS 3 — Focus (Polydor)
11	8	SIMON & GARFUNKEL'S GREATEST HITS — Simon & Garfunkel (CBS)
9	9	THE STRAUSS FAMILY — Cyril Ornadel & the London Symphony Orchestra (Polydor)
6	10	PILEDRIVER — Status Quo (Vertigo)
10	11	CATCH BULL AT FOUR — Cat Stevens (Island)
17	12	ROCK ME BABY — David Cassidy (Bell)
12	13	THE SIX WIVES OF HENRY VIII — Rick Wakeman (A&M)
19	14	BURSTING AT THE SEAMS — Strawbs (A&M)
13	15	HEARTBREAKER — Free (Island)
-	16	ALOHA FROM HAWAII VIA SATELLITE — Elvis Presley (RCA)
-	17	BLUEPRINT — Rory Gallagher (Polydor)
26	18	BRIDGE OVER TROUBLED WATER — Simon & Garfunkel (CBS)
16	19	THE RISE AND FALL OF ZIGGY STARDUST AND THE SPIDERS FROM MARS — David Bowie (RCA)
-	20	A CLOCKWORK ORANGE — Soundtrack (Warner Bros.)
14	21	SEVENTH SOJOURN — Moody Blues (Threshold)
-	22	JAMES LAST IN RUSSIA — James Last (Polydor)
23	23	HOLLAND — Beach Boys (Reprise)
20	24	NEVER A DULL MOMENT — Rod Stewart (Mercury)
15	25	TALKING BOOK — Stevie Wonder (Tamla Motown)
22	26	HOT AUGUST NIGHT — Neil Diamond (Uni)
-	27	MOTOWN CHARTBUSTERS VOL 7 — Various Artists (Tamla Motown)
24	28	PORTRAIT OF DONNY — Donny Osmond (MGM)
-	29	GLITTER — Gary Glitter (Bell)
28	30	TOO YOUNG — Donny Osmond (MGM)

10 March 1973

Last	This	Title / Artist (Label)
1	1	DON'T SHOOT ME I'M ONLY THE PIANO PLAYER — Elton John (DJM)
6	2	MOVING WAVES — Focus (Polydor)
14	3	BURSTING AT THE SEAMS — Strawbs (A&M)
2	4	NO SECRETS — Carly Simon (Elektra)
4	5	SLAYED — Slade (Polydor)
12	6	ROCK ME BABY — David Cassidy (Bell)
3	7	BACK TO FRONT — Gilbert O'Sullivan (MAM)
13	8	THE SIX WIVES OF HENRY VIII — Rick Wakeman (A&M)
5	9	WHO DO YOU THINK WE ARE — Deep Purple (Purple)
8	10	SIMON & GARFUNKEL'S GREATEST HITS — Simon & Garfunkel (CBS)
10	11	PILEDRIVER — Status Quo (Vertigo)
7	12	FOCUS 3 — Focus (Polydor)
9	13	THE STRAUSS FAMILY — Cyril Ornadel & the London Symphony Orchestra (Polydor)
17	14	BLUEPRINT — Rory Gallagher (Polydor)
20	15	A CLOCKWORK ORANGE — Soundtrack (Warner Bros.)
25	16	TALKING BOOK — Stevie Wonder (Tamla Motown)
11	17	CATCH BULL AT FOUR — Cat Stevens (Island)
26	18	HOT AUGUST NIGHT — Neil Diamond (Uni)
19	19	THE RISE AND FALL OF ZIGGY STARDUST AND THE SPIDERS FROM MARS — David Bowie (RCA)
30	20	TOO YOUNG — Donny Osmond (MGM)
23	21	HOLLAND — Beach Boys (Reprise)
16	22	ALOHA FROM HAWAII VIA SATELLITE — Elvis Presley (RCA)
15	23	HEARTBREAKER — Free (Island)
22	24	JAMES LAST IN RUSSIA — James Last (Polydor)
18	25	BRIDGE OVER TROUBLED WATER — Simon & Garfunkel (CBS)
28	26	PORTRAIT OF DONNY — Donny Osmond (MGM)
24	27	NEVER A DULL MOMENT — Rod Stewart (Mercury)
-	28	KILLER JOE — Little Jimmy Osmond (MGM)
29	29	GLITTER — Gary Glitter (Bell)
21	30	SEVENTH SOJOURN — Moody Blues (Threshold)

17 March 1973

Last	This	Title / Artist (Label)
1	1	DON'T SHOOT ME I'M ONLY THE PIANO PLAYER — Elton John (DJM)
2	2	MOVING WAVES — Focus (Polydor)
-	3	BILLION DOLLAR BABIES — Alice Cooper (Warner Bros.)
4	4	NO SECRETS — Carly Simon (Elektra)
3	5	BURSTING AT THE SEAMS — Strawbs (A&M)
8	6	THE SIX WIVES OF HENRY VIII — Rick Wakeman (A&M)
5	7	SLAYED — Slade (Polydor)
6	8	ROCK ME BABY — David Cassidy (Bell)
12	9	FOCUS 3 — Focus (Polydor)
7	10	BACK TO FRONT — Gilbert O'Sullivan (MAM)
15	11	A CLOCKWORK ORANGE — Soundtrack (Warner Bros.)
9	12	WHO DO YOU THINK WE ARE — Deep Purple (Purple)
11	13	PILEDRIVER — Status Quo (Vertigo)
14	14	BLUEPRINT — Rory Gallagher (Polydor)
10	15	SIMON & GARFUNKEL'S GREATEST HITS — Simon & Garfunkel (CBS)
22	16	ALOHA FROM HAWAII VIA SATELLITE — Elvis Presley (RCA)
26	17	PORTRAIT OF DONNY — Donny Osmond (MGM)
16	18	TALKING BOOK — Stevie Wonder (Tamla Motown)
19	19	THE RISE AND FALL OF ZIGGY STARDUST AND THE SPIDERS FROM MARS — David Bowie (RCA)
13	20	THE STRAUSS FAMILY — Cyril Ornadel & the London Symphony Orchestra (Polydor)
18	21	HOT AUGUST NIGHT — Neil Diamond (Uni)
17	22	CATCH BULL AT FOUR — Cat Stevens (Island)
21	23	HOLLAND — Beach Boys (Reprise)
-	24	20 FLASHBACK GREATS OF THE 60s — Various Artists (K-Tel)
27	25	NEVER A DULL MOMENT — Rod Stewart (Mercury)
25	26	BRIDGE OVER TROUBLED WATER — Simon & Garfunkel (CBS)
-	26	COSMIC WHEELS — Donovan (Epic)
-	28	CRAZY HORSES — Osmonds (MGM)
24	29	JAMES LAST IN RUSSIA — James Last (Polydor)
23	30	HEARTBREAKER — Free (Island)

24 March 1973

Last	This	Title / Artist (Label)
1	1	DON'T SHOOT ME I'M ONLY THE PIANO PLAYER — Elton John (DJM)
2	2	MOVING WAVES — Focus (Polydor)
3	3	BILLION DOLLAR BABIES — Alice Cooper (Warner Bros.)
-	4	THE DARK SIDE OF THE MOON — Pink Floyd (Harvest)
7	5	SLAYED — Slade (Polydor)
5	6	BURSTING AT THE SEAMS — Strawbs (A&M)
-	7	TANX — T. Rex (T. Rex)
15	8	SIMON & GARFUNKEL'S GREATEST HITS — Simon & Garfunkel (CBS)
10	9	BACK TO FRONT — Gilbert O'Sullivan (MAM)
8	10	ROCK ME BABY — David Cassidy (Bell)
12	11	WHO DO YOU THINK WE ARE — Deep Purple (Purple)
24	20	FLASHBACK GREATS OF THE 60s — Various Artists (K-Tel)
11	13	A CLOCKWORK ORANGE — Soundtrack (Warner Bros.)
9	14	FOCUS 3 — Focus (Polydor)
6	15	THE SIX WIVES OF HENRY VIII — Rick Wakeman (A&M)
4	16	NO SECRETS — Carly Simon (Elektra)
13	17	PILEDRIVER — Status Quo (Vertigo)
20	18	THE STRAUSS FAMILY — Cyril Ornadel & the London Symphony Orchestra (Polydor)
14	19	BLUEPRINT — Rory Gallagher (Polydor)
17	20	PORTRAIT OF DONNY — Donny Osmond (MGM)
16	21	ALOHA FROM HAWAII VIA SATELLITE — Elvis Presley (RCA)
-	22	TOO YOUNG — Donny Osmond (MGM)
26	23	BRIDGE OVER TROUBLED WATER — Simon & Garfunkel (CBS)
25	24	NEVER A DULL MOMENT — Rod Stewart (Mercury)
21	25	HOT AUGUST NIGHT — Neil Diamond (Uni)
22	26	CATCH BULL AT FOUR — Cat Stevens (Island)
23	27	HOLLAND — Beach Boys (Reprise)
-	27	SEVENTH SOJOURN — Moody Blues (Threshold)
29	29	JAMES LAST IN RUSSIA — James Last (Polydor)
30	30	HEARTBREAKER — Free (Island)

Elvis' *Aloha From Hawaii* was in the 9-day wonder of quadrophonic sound. Elton John's No.1 was his eighth LP, and his last before the bloating effects of superstardom disfigured his work. Though it offered the fatuous *Crocodile Rock*, there was also *Daniel* and *High Flying Bird*. Next would come double-LP *Goodbye Yellowbrick Road*, *Caribou* and the desperately-titled, lavish *Captain Fantastic And The Brown Dirt Cowboy*. By 1976 John's sales would account for 2% of all record sales worldwide.

last week	this week	31 March 1973
3	1	BILLION DOLLAR BABIES — Alice Cooper (Warner Bros.)
1	2	DON'T SHOOT ME I'M ONLY THE PIANO PLAYER — Elton John (DJM)
4	3	THE DARK SIDE OF THE MOON — Pink Floyd (Harvest)
7	4	TANX — T. Rex (T. Rex)
10	5	ROCK ME BABY — David Cassidy (Bell)
12	6	20 FLASHBACK GREATS OF THE 60s — Various Artists (K-Tel)
2	7	MOVING WAVES — Focus (Polydor)
6	8	BURSTING AT THE SEAMS — Strawbs (A&M)
5	9	SLAYED — Slade (Polydor)
8	10	SIMON & GARFUNKEL'S GREATEST HITS — Simon & Garfunkel (CBS)
9	11	BACK TO FRONT — Gilbert O'Sullivan (MAM)
13	12	A CLOCKWORK ORANGE — Soundtrack (Warner Bros.)
-	13	40 FANTASTIC HITS OF THE 50s AND 60s — Various Artists (Arcade)
11	14	WHO DO YOU THINK WE ARE — Deep Purple (Purple)
15	15	THE SIX WIVES OF HENRY VIII — Rick Wakeman (A&M)
-	15	FOR YOUR PLEASURE — Roxy Music (Island)
19	17	BLUEPRINT — Rory Gallagher (Polydor)
16	18	NO SECRETS — Carly Simon (Elektra)
14	19	FOCUS 3 — Focus (Polydor)
-	20	COSMIC WHEELS — Donovan (Epic)
17	21	PILEDRIVER — Status Quo (Vertigo)
27	22	HOLLAND — Beach Boys (Reprise)
20	23	PORTRAIT OF DONNY — Donny Osmond (MGM)
24	24	NEVER A DULL MOMENT — Rod Stewart (Mercury)
25	25	HOT AUGUST NIGHT — Neil Diamond (Uni)
-	26	THE RISE AND FALL OF ZIGGY STARDUST AND THE SPIDERS FROM MARS — David Bowie (RCA)
-	27	ELO 2 — Electric Light Orchestra (Harvest)
29	28	JAMES LAST IN RUSSIA — James Last (Polydor)
23	29	BRIDGE OVER TROUBLED WATER — Simon & Garfunkel (CBS)
26	29	CATCH BULL AT FOUR — Cat Stevens (Island)

		7 April 1973
3	1	THE DARK SIDE OF THE MOON — Pink Floyd (Harvest)
4	2	TANX — T. Rex (T. Rex)
2	3	DON'T SHOOT ME I'M ONLY THE PIANO PLAYER — Elton John (DJM)
1	4	BILLION DOLLAR BABIES — Alice Cooper (Warner Bros.)
-	5	HOUSES OF THE HOLY — Led Zeppelin (Atlantic)
6	6	20 FLASHBACK GREATS OF THE 60s — Various Artists (K-Tel)
15	7	FOR YOUR PLEASURE — Roxy Music (Island)
18	8	NO SECRETS — Carly Simon (Elektra)
11	9	BACK TO FRONT — Gilbert O'Sullivan (MAM)
13	10	40 FANTASTIC HITS OF THE 50s AND 60s — Various Artists (Arcade)
9	11	SLAYED — Slade (Polydor)
12	12	A CLOCKWORK ORANGE — Soundtrack (Warner Bros.)
10	13	SIMON & GARFUNKEL'S GREATEST HITS — Simon & Garfunkel (CBS)
7	14	MOVING WAVES — Focus (Polydor)
8	15	BURSTING AT THE SEAMS — Strawbs (A&M)
5	16	ROCK ME BABY — David Cassidy (Bell)
17	17	BLUEPRINT — Rory Gallagher (Polydor)
14	18	WHO DO YOU THINK WE ARE — Deep Purple (Purple)
23	19	PORTRAIT OF DONNY — Donny Osmond (MGM)
24	20	NEVER A DULL MOMENT — Rod Stewart (Mercury)
29	21	BRIDGE OVER TROUBLED WATER — Simon & Garfunkel (CBS)
26	22	THE RISE AND FALL OF ZIGGY STARDUST AND THE SPIDERS FROM MARS — David Bowie (RCA)
15	23	THE SIX WIVES OF HENRY VIII — Rick Wakeman (A&M)
20	23	COSMIC WHEELS — Donovan (Epic)
25	25	HOT AUGUST NIGHT — Neil Diamond (Uni)
-	26	EAT IT — Humble Pie (A&M)
-	27	HARVEST — Neil Young (Reprise)
-	28	HOT HITS SEVENTEEN — Various Artists (Music for Pleasure)
-	29	ALOHA FROM HAWAII VIA SATELLITE — Elvis Presley (RCA)
21	30	PILEDRIVER — Status Quo (Vertigo)

		14 April 1973
3	1	DON'T SHOOT ME I'M ONLY THE PIANO PLAYER — Elton John (DJM)
4	2	BILLION DOLLAR BABIES — Alice Cooper (Warner Bros.)
7	3	FOR YOUR PLEASURE — Roxy Music (Island)
1	4	THE DARK SIDE OF THE MOON — Pink Floyd (Harvest)
5	5	HOUSES OF THE HOLY — Led Zeppelin (Atlantic)
2	6	TANX — T. Rex (T. Rex)
6	7	20 FLASHBACK GREATS OF THE 60s — Various Artists (K-Tel)
9	8	BACK TO FRONT — Gilbert O'Sullivan (MAM)
-	9	OOH LA LA — Faces (Warner Bros.)
12	10	A CLOCKWORK ORANGE — Soundtrack (Warner Bros.)
10	11	40 FANTASTIC HITS OF THE 50s AND 60s — Various Artists (Arcade)
16	12	ROCK ME BABY — David Cassidy (Bell)
11	13	SLAYED — Slade (Polydor)
13	14	SIMON & GARFUNKEL'S GREATEST HITS — Simon & Garfunkel (CBS)
14	14	MOVING WAVES — Focus (Polydor)
8	16	NO SECRETS — Carly Simon (Elektra)
-	17	TOGETHER — Jack Jones (RCA)
15	18	BURSTING AT THE SEAMS — Strawbs (A&M)
30	19	PILEDRIVER — Status Quo (Vertigo)
19	20	PORTRAIT OF DONNY — Donny Osmond (MGM)
-	21	LIZA WITH A Z — Liza Minnelli (CBS)
23	22	THE SIX WIVES OF HENRY VIII — Rick Wakeman (A&M)
-	23	FOCUS 3 — Focus (Polydor)
18	24	WHO DO YOU THINK WE ARE — Deep Purple (Purple)
23	25	COSMIC WHEELS — Donovan (Epic)
-	26	BIRDS OF FIRE — Mahavishnu Orchestra (CBS)
-	27	TOO YOUNG — Donny Osmond (MGM)
17	28	BLUEPRINT — Rory Gallagher (Polydor)
25	29	HOT AUGUST NIGHT — Neil Diamond (Uni)
-	30	TALKING BOOK — Stevie Wonder (Tamla Motown)

		21 April 1973
5	1	HOUSES OF THE HOLY — Led Zeppelin (Atlantic)
3	2	FOR YOUR PLEASURE — Roxy Music (Island)
2	3	BILLION DOLLAR BABIES — Alice Cooper (Warner Bros.)
1	4	DON'T SHOOT ME I'M ONLY THE PIANO PLAYER — Elton John (DJM)
9	5	OOH LA LA — Faces (Warner Bros.)
4	6	THE DARK SIDE OF THE MOON — Pink Floyd (Harvest)
10	7	A CLOCKWORK ORANGE — Soundtrack (Warner Bros.)
6	8	TANX — T. Rex (T. Rex)
8	9	BACK TO FRONT — Gilbert O'Sullivan (MAM)
11	10	40 FANTASTIC HITS OF THE 50s AND 60s — Various Artists (Arcade)
7	11	20 FLASHBACK GREATS OF THE 60s — Various Artists (K-Tel)
13	12	SLAYED — Slade (Polydor)
-	13	BELIEVE IN MUSIC — Various Artists (K-Tel)
12	14	ROCK ME BABY — David Cassidy (Bell)
14	15	SIMON & GARFUNKEL'S GREATEST HITS — Simon & Garfunkel (CBS)
16	16	NO SECRETS — Carly Simon (Elektra)
21	17	LIZA WITH A Z — Liza Minnelli (CBS)
14	18	MOVING WAVES — Focus (Polydor)
17	19	TOGETHER — Jack Jones (RCA)
18	20	BURSTING AT THE SEAMS — Strawbs (A&M)
29	21	HOT AUGUST NIGHT — Neil Diamond (Uni)
22	22	THE SIX WIVES OF HENRY VIII — Rick Wakeman (A&M)
-	23	LARKS' TONGUES IN ASPIC — King Crimson (Island)
25	24	COSMIC WHEELS — Donovan (Epic)
19	25	PILEDRIVER — Status Quo (Vertigo)
-	26	HIMSELF — Gilbert O'Sullivan (MAM)
30	27	TALKING BOOK — Stevie Wonder (Tamla Motown)
23	28	FOCUS 3 — Focus (Polydor)
-	28	BECK, BOGERT & APPICE — Jeff Beck, Tim Bogert & Carmine Appice (Epic)
27	30	TOO YOUNG — Donny Osmond (MGM)

Atlantic Records held a 25th Anniversary weekend in Paris – a lavish get-together of 500 salesmen and their wives from across the USA ("rack-jobbers from Kansas", as the music-writers sniffily said) plus execs, PR and press. Everyone was given a pink sampler-cassette of Atlantic's forthcoming "product". The music-press muttered darkly about how white the label had become. As the UK chart of the time shows, Atlantic acts included Led Zeppelin, whose *Houses Of The Holy* reached No.1 the next weekend.

last week	this week	28 April 1973
5	1	OOH LA LA — Faces (Warner Bros.)
1	2	HOUSES OF THE HOLY — Led Zeppelin (Atlantic)
3	3	BILLION DOLLAR BABIES — Alice Cooper (Warner Bros.)
2	4	FOR YOUR PLEASURE — Roxy Music (Island)
6	5	THE DARK SIDE OF THE MOON — Pink Floyd (Harvest)
-	6	ALADDIN SANE — David Bowie (RCA)
9	7	BACK TO FRONT — Gilbert O'Sullivan (MAM)
4	8	DON'T SHOOT ME I'M ONLY THE PIANO PLAYER — Elton John (DJM)
7	9	A CLOCKWORK ORANGE — Soundtrack (Warner Bros.)
8	10	TANX — T. Rex (T. Rex)
11	11	20 FLASHBACK GREATS OF THE 60s — Various Artists (K-Tel)
10	12	40 FANTASTIC HITS OF THE 50s AND 60s — Various Artists (Arcade)
13	13	BELIEVE IN MUSIC — Various Artists (K-Tel)
14	14	ROCK ME BABY — David Cassidy (Bell)
15	15	SIMON & GARFUNKEL'S GREATEST HITS — Simon & Garfunkel (CBS)
16	16	NO SECRETS — Carly Simon (Elektra)
-	17	THE BEATLES 1962-1966 — Beatles (Apple)
24	18	COSMIC WHEELS — Donovan (Epic)
22	19	THE SIX WIVES OF HENRY VIII — Rick Wakeman (A&M)
12	20	SLAYED — Slade (Polydor)
17	21	LIZA WITH A Z — Liza Minnelli (CBS)
-	21	20 FANTASTIC HITS VOL 3 — Various Artists (Arcade)
26	23	HIMSELF — Gilbert O'Sullivan (MAM)
21	24	HOT AUGUST NIGHT — Neil Diamond (Uni)
18	25	MOVING WAVES — Focus (Polydor)
27	26	TALKING BOOK — Stevie Wonder (Tamla Motown)
-	27	THE BEATLES 1967-1970 — Beatles (Apple)
28	28	FOCUS 3 — Focus (Polydor)
-	29	BLUEPRINT — Rory Gallagher (Polydor)
-	30	BRIDGE OVER TROUBLED WATER — Simon & Garfunkel (CBS)

last week	this week	5 May 1973
6	1	ALADDIN SANE — David Bowie (RCA)
1	2	OOH LA LA — Faces (Warner Bros.)
3	3	BILLION DOLLAR BABIES — Alice Cooper (Warner Bros.)
2	4	HOUSES OF THE HOLY — Led Zeppelin (Atlantic)
5	5	THE DARK SIDE OF THE MOON — Pink Floyd (Harvest)
7	6	BACK TO FRONT — Gilbert O'Sullivan (MAM)
12	7	40 FANTASTIC HITS OF THE 50s AND 60s — Various Artists (Arcade)
4	8	FOR YOUR PLEASURE — Roxy Music (Island)
8	9	DON'T SHOOT ME I'M ONLY THE PIANO PLAYER — Elton John (DJM)
21	10	20 FANTASTIC HITS VOL 3 — Various Artists (Arcade)
10	11	TANX — T. Rex (T. Rex)
11	12	20 FLASHBACK GREATS OF THE 60s — Various Artists (K-Tel)
13	13	BELIEVE IN MUSIC — Various Artists (K-Tel)
14	14	ROCK ME BABY — David Cassidy (Bell)
17	15	THE BEATLES 1962-1966 — Beatles (Apple)
27	16	THE BEATLES 1967-1970 — Beatles (Apple)
20	17	SLAYED — Slade (Polydor)
-	18	TOGETHER — Jack Jones (RCA)
9	19	A CLOCKWORK ORANGE — Soundtrack (Warner Bros.)
-	20	PORTRAIT OF DONNY — Donny Osmond (MGM)
-	21	PILEDRIVER — Status Quo (Vertigo)
15	22	SIMON & GARFUNKEL'S GREATEST HITS — Simon & Garfunkel (CBS)
18	23	COSMIC WHEELS — Donovan (Epic)
25	24	MOVING WAVES — Focus (Polydor)
26	25	TALKING BOOK — Stevie Wonder (Tamla Motown)
16	26	NO SECRETS — Carly Simon (Elektra)
28	27	FOCUS 3 — Focus (Polydor)
23	28	HIMSELF — Gilbert O'Sullivan (MAM)
30	29	BRIDGE OVER TROUBLED WATER — Simon & Garfunkel (CBS)
21	30	LIZA WITH A Z — Liza Minnelli (CBS)

last week	this week	12 May 1973
1	1	ALADDIN SANE — David Bowie (RCA)
16	2	THE BEATLES 1967-1970 — Beatles (Apple)
15	3	THE BEATLES 1962-1966 — Beatles (Apple)
2	4	OOH LA LA — Faces (Warner Bros.)
3	5	BILLION DOLLAR BABIES — Alice Cooper (Warner Bros.)
4	6	HOUSES OF THE HOLY — Led Zeppelin (Atlantic)
5	7	THE DARK SIDE OF THE MOON — Pink Floyd (Harvest)
6	8	BACK TO FRONT — Gilbert O'Sullivan (MAM)
8	9	FOR YOUR PLEASURE — Roxy Music (Island)
9	10	DON'T SHOOT ME I'M ONLY THE PIANO PLAYER — Elton John (DJM)
13	11	BELIEVE IN MUSIC — Various Artists (K-Tel)
26	12	NO SECRETS — Carly Simon (Elektra)
7	13	40 FANTASTIC HITS OF THE 50s AND 60s — Various Artists (Arcade)
-	14	SINGALONGAMAX — Max Bygraves (Pye)
10	15	20 FANTASTIC HITS VOL 3 — Various Artists (Arcade)
-	16	CABARET — Soundtrack (Probe)
-	17	RED ROSE SPEEDWAY — Paul McCartney & Wings (Apple)
22	18	SIMON & GARFUNKEL'S GREATEST HITS — Simon & Garfunkel (CBS)
12	19	20 FLASHBACK GREATS OF THE 60s — Various Artists (K-Tel)
11	20	TANX — T. Rex (T. Rex)
19	21	A CLOCKWORK ORANGE — Soundtrack (Warner Bros.)
14	22	ROCK ME BABY — David Cassidy (Bell)
20	23	PORTRAIT OF DONNY — Donny Osmond (MGM)
30	24	LIZA WITH A Z — Liza Minnelli (CBS)
17	25	SLAYED — Slade (Polydor)
29	26	BRIDGE OVER TROUBLED WATER — Simon & Garfunkel (CBS)
-	27	CATCH BULL AT FOUR — Cat Stevens (Island)
21	28	PILEDRIVER — Status Quo (Vertigo)
-	29	TRANSFORMER — Lou Reed (RCA)
-	30	THE SIX WIVES OF HENRY VIII — Rick Wakeman (A&M)

last week	this week	19 May 1973
2	1	THE BEATLES 1967-1970 — Beatles (Apple)
1	2	ALADDIN SANE — David Bowie (RCA)
3	3	THE BEATLES 1962-1966 — Beatles (Apple)
6	4	HOUSES OF THE HOLY — Led Zeppelin (Atlantic)
4	5	OOH LA LA — Faces (Warner Bros.)
5	6	BILLION DOLLAR BABIES — Alice Cooper (Warner Bros.)
7	7	THE DARK SIDE OF THE MOON — Pink Floyd (Harvest)
9	8	FOR YOUR PLEASURE — Roxy Music (Island)
17	9	RED ROSE SPEEDWAY — Paul McCartney & Wings (Apple)
8	10	BACK TO FRONT — Gilbert O'Sullivan (MAM)
-	11	YESSONGS — Yes (Atlantic)
24	12	LIZA WITH A Z — Liza Minnelli (CBS)
14	13	SINGALONGAMAX — Max Bygraves (Pye)
16	14	CABARET — Soundtrack (Probe)
-	15	DALTREY — Roger Daltrey (Track)
12	16	NO SECRETS — Carly Simon (Elektra)
11	17	BELIEVE IN MUSIC — Various Artists (K-Tel)
18	18	SIMON & GARFUNKEL'S GREATEST HITS — Simon & Garfunkel (CBS)
15	19	20 FANTASTIC HITS VOL 3 — Various Artists (Arcade)
10	20	DON'T SHOOT ME I'M ONLY THE PIANO PLAYER — Elton John (DJM)
-	21	ALONE TOGETHER — Donny Osmond (MGM)
13	22	40 FANTASTIC HITS OF THE 50s AND 60s — Various Artists (Arcade)
21	23	A CLOCKWORK ORANGE — Soundtrack (Warner Bros.)
20	24	TANX — T. Rex (T. Rex)
29	25	TRANSFORMER — Lou Reed (RCA)
22	26	ROCK ME BABY — David Cassidy (Bell)
-	27	FOCUS 3 — Focus (Polydor)
-	28	URIAH HEEP LIVE — Uriah Heep (Bronze)
28	29	PILEDRIVER — Status Quo (Vertigo)
-	30	COSMIC WHEELS — Donovan (Epic)

Bowie's *Aladdin Sane* would twice be knocked off the No.1 slot in the coming weeks, and would twice regain it. The records that displaced him were *The Beatles 1967-1970* and *The Beatles 1962-1966*. These simultaneous releases leapt up the chart in parallel (27 and 17, 16 and 15, 2 and 3, 1 and 3, 2 and 3, 2 and 3, 2 and 1) and each topped the chart during May and June. Containing singles and other selected tracks, they would each remain in the Top 50 for more than two years.

26 May 1973

last week	this week	
2	1	ALADDIN SANE — David Bowie (RCA)
1	2	THE BEATLES 1967-1970 — Beatles (Apple)
3	3	THE BEATLES 1962-1966 — Beatles (Apple)
9	4	RED ROSE SPEEDWAY — Paul McCartney & Wings (Apple)
7	5	THE DARK SIDE OF THE MOON — Pink Floyd (Harvest)
5	6	OOH LA LA — Faces (Warner Bros.)
11	7	YESSONGS — Yes (Atlantic)
8	8	FOR YOUR PLEASURE — Roxy Music (Island)
4	9	HOUSES OF THE HOLY — Led Zeppelin (Atlantic)
6	10	BILLION DOLLAR BABIES — Alice Cooper (Warner Bros.)
10	11	BACK TO FRONT — Gilbert O'Sullivan (MAM)
14	12	CABARET — Soundtrack (Probe)
13	13	SINGALONGAMAX — Max Bygraves (Pye)
12	14	LIZA WITH A Z — Liza Minnelli (CBS)
15	15	DALTREY — Roger Daltrey (Track)
25	16	TRANSFORMER — Lou Reed (RCA)
17	17	BELIEVE IN MUSIC — Various Artists (K-Tel)
16	18	NO SECRETS — Carly Simon (Elektra)
23	19	A CLOCKWORK ORANGE — Soundtrack (Warner Bros.)
18	20	SIMON & GARFUNKEL'S GREATEST HITS — Simon & Garfunkel (CBS)
22	21	40 FANTASTIC HITS OF THE 50s AND 60s — Various Artists (Arcade)
-	22	THERE GOES RHYMIN' SIMON — Paul Simon (CBS)
20	23	DON'T SHOOT ME I'M ONLY THE PIANO PLAYER — Elton John (DJM)
21	24	ALONE TOGETHER — Donny Osmond (MGM)
28	25	URIAH HEEP LIVE — Uriah Heep (Bronze)
-	26	NEVER NEVER NEVER — Shirley Bassey (United Artists)
26	27	ROCK ME BABY — David Cassidy (Bell)
-	28	SLAYED — Slade (Polydor)
30	29	COSMIC WHEELS — Donovan (Epic)
-	30	SONGS FROM HER TV SERIES — Nana Mouskouri (Philips)

2 June 1973

1	1	ALADDIN SANE — David Bowie (RCA)
2	2	THE BEATLES 1967-1970 — Beatles (Apple)
3	3	THE BEATLES 1962-1966 — Beatles (Apple)
5	4	THE DARK SIDE OF THE MOON — Pink Floyd (Harvest)
4	5	RED ROSE SPEEDWAY — Paul McCartney & Wings (Apple)
-	6	20 FANTASTIC HITS VOL 3 — Various Artists (Arcade)
7	7	YESSONGS — Yes (Atlantic)
-	8	PURE GOLD — Various Artists (EMI)
14	9	LIZA WITH A Z — Liza Minnelli (CBS)
10	10	BILLION DOLLAR BABIES — Alice Cooper (Warner Bros.)
15	11	DALTREY — Roger Daltrey (Track)
12	12	CABARET — Soundtrack (Probe)
11	13	BACK TO FRONT — Gilbert O'Sullivan (MAM)
-	14	20 ORIGINAL CHART HITS — Various Artists (Philips)
-	15	WISHBONE 4 — Wishbone Ash (MCA)
19	16	A CLOCKWORK ORANGE — Soundtrack (Warner Bros.)
-	17	THAT'LL BE THE DAY - SOUNDTRACK — Various Artists (Ronco)
9	18	HOUSES OF THE HOLY — Led Zeppelin (Atlantic)
16	19	TRANSFORMER — Lou Reed (RCA)
17	20	BELIEVE IN MUSIC — Various Artists (K-Tel)
18	21	NO SECRETS — Carly Simon (Elektra)
8	22	FOR YOUR PLEASURE — Roxy Music (Island)
6	23	OOH LA LA — Faces (Warner Bros.)
21	24	40 FANTASTIC HITS OF THE 50s AND 60s — Various Artists (Arcade)
24	25	ALONE TOGETHER — Donny Osmond (MGM)
-	26	ROCKY MOUNTAIN HIGH — John Denver (RCA)
22	27	THERE GOES RHYMIN' SIMON — Paul Simon (CBS)
13	28	SINGALONGAMAX — Max Bygraves (Pye)
29	29	COSMIC WHEELS — Donovan (Epic)
25	30	URIAH HEEP LIVE — Uriah Heep (Bronze)

9 June 1973

3	1	THE BEATLES 1962-1966 — Beatles (Apple)
2	2	THE BEATLES 1967-1970 — Beatles (Apple)
1	3	ALADDIN SANE — David Bowie (RCA)
5	4	RED ROSE SPEEDWAY — Paul McCartney & Wings (Apple)
8	5	PURE GOLD — Various Artists (EMI)
4	6	THE DARK SIDE OF THE MOON — Pink Floyd (Harvest)
-	7	TOUCH ME — Gary Glitter (Bell)
15	8	WISHBONE 4 — Wishbone Ash (MCA)
7	9	YESSONGS — Yes (Atlantic)
27	10	THERE GOES RHYMIN' SIMON — Paul Simon (CBS)
6	11	20 FANTASTIC HITS VOL 3 — Various Artists (Arcade)
9	12	LIZA WITH A Z — Liza Minnelli (CBS)
11	13	DALTREY — Roger Daltrey (Track)
16	14	A CLOCKWORK ORANGE — Soundtrack (Warner Bros.)
13	15	BACK TO FRONT — Gilbert O'Sullivan (MAM)
17	16	THAT'LL BE THE DAY - SOUNDTRACK — Various Artists (Ronco)
10	17	BILLION DOLLAR BABIES — Alice Cooper (Warner Bros.)
25	18	ALONE TOGETHER — Donny Osmond (MGM)
-	19	SIMON & GARFUNKEL'S GREATEST HITS — Simon & Garfunkel (CBS)
23	20	OOH LA LA — Faces (Warner Bros.)
19	21	TRANSFORMER — Lou Reed (RCA)
-	22	NEVER NEVER NEVER — Shirley Bassey (United Artists)
18	23	HOUSES OF THE HOLY — Led Zeppelin (Atlantic)
26	24	ROCKY MOUNTAIN HIGH — John Denver (RCA)
30	25	URIAH HEEP LIVE — Uriah Heep (Bronze)
-	26	SPACE RITUAL ALIVE — Hawkwind (United Artists)
21	27	NO SECRETS — Carly Simon (Elektra)
12	28	CABARET — Soundtrack (Probe)
22	29	FOR YOUR PLEASURE — Roxy Music (Island)
-	30	FAUST TAPES — Faust (Virgin)

16 June 1973

3	1	ALADDIN SANE — David Bowie (RCA)
5	2	PURE GOLD — Various Artists (EMI)
2	3	THE BEATLES 1967-1970 — Beatles (Apple)
1	4	THE BEATLES 1962-1966 — Beatles (Apple)
4	5	RED ROSE SPEEDWAY — Paul McCartney & Wings (Apple)
6	6	THE DARK SIDE OF THE MOON — Pink Floyd (Harvest)
10	7	THERE GOES RHYMIN' SIMON — Paul Simon (CBS)
9	8	YESSONGS — Yes (Atlantic)
7	9	TOUCH ME — Gary Glitter (Bell)
16	10	THAT'LL BE THE DAY - SOUNDTRACK — Various Artists (Ronco)
8	11	WISHBONE 4 — Wishbone Ash (MCA)
18	12	ALONE TOGETHER — Donny Osmond (MGM)
21	13	TRANSFORMER — Lou Reed (RCA)
11	14	20 FANTASTIC HITS VOL 3 — Various Artists (Arcade)
12	15	LIZA WITH A Z — Liza Minnelli (CBS)
13	16	DALTREY — Roger Daltrey (Track)
26	17	SPACE RITUAL ALIVE — Hawkwind (United Artists)
14	18	A CLOCKWORK ORANGE — Soundtrack (Warner Bros.)
-	19	20 ORIGINAL CHART HITS — Various Artists (Philips)
24	20	ROCKY MOUNTAIN HIGH — John Denver (RCA)
22	21	NEVER NEVER NEVER — Shirley Bassey (United Artists)
15	22	BACK TO FRONT — Gilbert O'Sullivan (MAM)
28	23	CABARET — Soundtrack (Probe)
30	24	FAUST TAPES — Faust (Virgin)
19	25	SIMON & GARFUNKEL'S GREATEST HITS — Simon & Garfunkel (CBS)
29	26	FOR YOUR PLEASURE — Roxy Music (Island)
17	27	BILLION DOLLAR BABIES — Alice Cooper (Warner Bros.)
25	28	URIAH HEEP LIVE — Uriah Heep (Bronze)
23	29	HOUSES OF THE HOLY — Led Zeppelin (Atlantic)
-	30	TALKING BOOK — Stevie Wonder (Tamla Motown)

The top rungs of the chart had The Beatles at No.2 and No.3, with Paul McCartney at No.4. In the concurrent singles charts, Paul & Wings were dropping down the Top 20 with *My Love* while George was jumping in with *Give Me Love (Give Me Peace On Earth)*. He would soon rejoin the album chart too, with *Living In The Material World*. Other typically 1973ish acts in the chart included Faust, Uriah Heep, Hawkwind, Lou Reed and John Denver. Donny Osmond and David Cassidy were still there.

June – July 1973

With *Aladdin Sane* back on top, Bowie's earlier album *Hunky Dory* began a climb up the chart. Mid-August would find both in the Top 5. *That'll Be The Day* was the soundtrack album from a surprisingly successful film starring ex-Godspell actor David Essex as a fairground lad, and featuring Rosemary Leach and Ringo Starr. A follow-up, *Stardust*, more lavish but less convincing, starred David Essex again. His debut in the singles chart would be in August, with *Rock On*, a No.1 for a week in September.

21 July 1973

28 July 1973

4 August 1973

11 August 1973

Mike Oldfield's *Tubular Bells* arrived in the chart. It had been a long journey for Oldfield to get it there. Turned down by every record label in Britain, it became the bedrock big seller of Richard Branson's young Virgin label. Another historic entry was the debut, at last, by Van Morrison, whose *Hard Nose The Highway* now succeeded where such albums as *Moondance* (1970) and the great *St.Dominic's Preview* (1972) had failed. Even now, No.23 was as high as Van the Man could manage.

August – September 1973

last week	this week	17 August 1973
1	1	WE CAN MAKE IT — Peters & Lee (Philips)
3	2	ALADDIN SANE — David Bowie (RCA)
4	3	NOW AND THEN — Carpenters (A&M)
5	4	HUNKY DORY — David Bowie (RCA)
2	5	THAT'LL BE THE DAY - SOUNDTRACK — Various Artists (Ronco)
6	6	FOREIGNER — Cat Stevens (Island)
7	7	THE BEATLES 1967-1970 — Beatles (Apple)
9	8	THE DARK SIDE OF THE MOON — Pink Floyd (Harvest)
11	9	THE BEATLES 1962-1966 — Beatles (Apple)
-	10	SING IT AGAIN ROD — Rod Stewart (Mercury)
8	11	AND I LOVE YOU SO — Perry Como (RCA)
13	12	LOVE DEVOTION SURRENDER — Carlos Santana & Mahavishnu John McLaughlin (CBS)
10	13	TOUCH ME — Gary Glitter (Bell)
12	14	THERE GOES RHYMIN' SIMON — Paul Simon (CBS)
-	15	MOTT — Mott The Hoople (CBS)
18	16	LIVING IN THE MATERIAL WORLD — George Harrison (Apple)
20	17	SCHOOL DAYS — Alice Cooper (Warner Bros.)
24	18	THE RISE AND FALL OF ZIGGY STARDUST AND THE SPIDERS FROM MARS — David Bowie (RCA)
15	19	TUBULAR BELLS — Mike Oldfield (Virgin)
17	20	A PASSION PLAY — Jethro Tull (Chrysalis)
14	21	SIMON & GARFUNKEL'S GREATEST HITS — Simon & Garfunkel (CBS)
16	22	A CLOCKWORK ORANGE — Soundtrack (Warner Bros.)
26	23	HARD NOSE THE HIGHWAY — Van Morrison (Warner Bros.)
23	24	A LITTLE TOUCH OF SCHMILSSON IN THE NIGHT — Nilsson (RCA)
19	25	RAZAMANAZ — Nazareth (Mooncrest)
-	26	THE PLAN — Osmonds (MGM)
29	27	GENESIS LIVE — Genesis (Charisma)
-	28	SPACE ODDITY — David Bowie (RCA)
22	29	BACK TO FRONT — Gilbert O'Sullivan (MAM)
-	30	CABARET — Soundtrack (Probe)

last week	this week	25 August 1973
3	1	NOW AND THEN — Carpenters (A&M)
1	2	WE CAN MAKE IT — Peters & Lee (Philips)
2	3	ALADDIN SANE — David Bowie (RCA)
4	4	HUNKY DORY — David Bowie (RCA)
6	5	FOREIGNER — Cat Stevens (Island)
10	6	SING IT AGAIN ROD — Rod Stewart (Mercury)
11	7	AND I LOVE YOU SO — Perry Como (RCA)
13	8	TOUCH ME — Gary Glitter (Bell)
5	9	THAT'LL BE THE DAY - SOUNDTRACK — Various Artists (Ronco)
7	10	THE BEATLES 1967-1970 — Beatles (Apple)
12	11	LOVE DEVOTION SURRENDER — Carlos Santana & Mahavishnu John McLaughlin (CBS)
15	12	MOTT — Mott The Hoople (CBS)
8	13	THE DARK SIDE OF THE MOON — Pink Floyd (Harvest)
19	14	TUBULAR BELLS — Mike Oldfield (Virgin)
26	15	THE PLAN — Osmonds (MGM)
18	16	THE RISE AND FALL OF ZIGGY STARDUST AND THE SPIDERS FROM MARS — David Bowie (RCA)
21	17	SIMON & GARFUNKEL'S GREATEST HITS — Simon & Garfunkel (CBS)
-	18	BOULDERS — Roy Wood (Harvest)
27	19	GENESIS LIVE — Genesis (Charisma)
25	20	RAZAMANAZ — Nazareth (Mooncrest)
9	21	THE BEATLES 1962-1966 — Beatles (Apple)
-	22	INNERVISIONS — Stevie Wonder (Tamla Motown)
17	23	SCHOOL DAYS — Alice Cooper (Warner Bros.)
20	24	A PASSION PLAY — Jethro Tull (Chrysalis)
29	25	BACK TO FRONT — Gilbert O'Sullivan (MAM)
28	26	SPACE ODDITY — David Bowie (RCA)
22	27	A CLOCKWORK ORANGE — Soundtrack (Warner Bros.)
-	28	20 EXPLOSIVE HITS — Various Artists (K-Tel)
24	29	A LITTLE TOUCH OF SCHMILSSON IN THE NIGHT — Nilsson (RCA)
-	30	LINDISFARNE LIVE — Lindisfarne (Charisma)

last week	this week	1 September 1973
1	1	NOW AND THEN — Carpenters (A&M)
3	2	ALADDIN SANE — David Bowie (RCA)
6	3	SING IT AGAIN ROD — Rod Stewart (Mercury)
2	4	WE CAN MAKE IT — Peters & Lee (Philips)
4	5	HUNKY DORY — David Bowie (RCA)
15	6	THE PLAN — Osmonds (MGM)
9	7	THAT'LL BE THE DAY - SOUNDTRACK — Various Artists (Ronco)
7	8	AND I LOVE YOU SO — Perry Como (RCA)
16	9	THE RISE AND FALL OF ZIGGY STARDUST AND THE SPIDERS FROM MARS — David Bowie (RCA)
10	10	THE BEATLES 1967-1970 — Beatles (Apple)
8	11	TOUCH ME — Gary Glitter (Bell)
17	12	SIMON & GARFUNKEL'S GREATEST HITS — Simon & Garfunkel (CBS)
13	13	THE DARK SIDE OF THE MOON — Pink Floyd (Harvest)
19	14	GENESIS LIVE — Genesis (Charisma)
12	15	MOTT — Mott the Hoople (CBS)
5	16	FOREIGNER — Cat Stevens (Island)
21	17	THE BEATLES 1962-1966 — Beatles (Apple)
27	18	A CLOCKWORK ORANGE — Soundtrack (Warner Bros.)
20	19	RAZAMANAZ — Nazareth (Mooncrest)
14	20	TUBULAR BELLS — Mike Oldfield (Virgin)
18	21	BOULDERS — Roy Wood (Harvest)
-	22	TOUCH ME IN THE MORNING — Diana Ross (Tamla Motown)
22	23	INNERVISIONS — Stevie Wonder (Tamla Motown)
24	24	PASSION PLAY — Jethro Tull (Chrysalis)
-	25	24 GOLDEN GREATS OF THE 60s — Various Artists (K-Tel)
28	26	20 EXPLOSIVE HITS — Various Artists (K-Tel)
29	27	A LITTLE TOUCH OF SCHMILSSON IN THE NIGHT — Nilsson (RCA)
-	28	THERE GOES RHYMIN' SIMON — Paul Simon (CBS)
-	29	BRIDGE OVER TROUBLED WATER — Simon & Garfunkel (CBS)
11	30	LOVE DEVOTION SURRENDER — Carlos Santana & Mahavishnu John McLaughlin (CBS)

last week	this week	8 September 1973
3	1	SING IT AGAIN ROD — Rod Stewart (Mercury)
1	2	NOW AND THEN — Carpenters (A&M)
4	3	WE CAN MAKE IT — Peters & Lee (Philips)
5	4	HUNKY DORY — David Bowie (RCA)
2	5	ALADDIN SANE — David Bowie (RCA)
6	6	THE PLAN — Osmonds (MGM)
7	7	THAT'LL BE THE DAY — Various Artists (Ronco)
16	8	FOREIGNER — Cat Stevens (Island)
13	9	DARK SIDE OF THE MOON — Pink Floyd (Harvest)
22	10	TOUCH ME IN THE MORNING — Diana Ross (Tamla Motown)
15	11	MOTT — Mott the Hoople (CBS)
21	12	BOULDERS — Roy Wood (Harvest)
20	13	TUBULAR BELLS — Mike Oldfield (Virgin)
8	14	AND I LOVE YOU SO — Perry Como (RCA)
10	15	THE BEATLES 1967-1970 — Beatles (Apple)
11	16	TOUCH ME — Gary Glitter (Bell)
12	17	SIMON & GARFUNKEL'S GREATEST HITS — Simon & Garfunkel (CBS)
23	18	INNERVISIONS — Stevie Wonder (Tamla Motown)
9	19	THE RISE AND FALL OF ZIGGY STARDUST AND THE SPIDERS FROM MARS — David Bowie (RCA)
25	20	24 GOLDEN GREATS OF THE 60s — Various Artists (K-Tel)
14	21	GENESIS LIVE — Genesis (Charisma)
17	22	THE BEATLES 1962-1966 — Beatles (Apple)
26	23	20 EXPLOSIVE HITS — Various Artists (K-Tel)
24	24	PASSION PLAY — Jethro Tull (Chrysalis)
30	25	LOVE DEVOTION SURRENDER — Carlos Santana & Mahavishnu John McLaughlin (CBS)
-	26	SCHOOL DAYS — Alice Cooper (Warner Bros.)
19	27	RAZAMANAZ — Nazareth (Mooncrest)
27	28	A LITTLE TOUCH OF SCHMILSSON IN THE NIGHT — Nilsson (RCA)
-	29	LINDISFARNE LIVE — Lindisfarne (Charisma)
28	30	THERE GOES RHYMIN' SIMON — Paul Simon (CBS)

Glam-rock's ugliest star, Gary Glitter, loitered around the Top 10 with his uninvitingly-titled album *Touch Me*, and scored a No.1 single with *I'm The Leader Of The Gang*, though this soon gave way to Donny Osmond's *Young Love* and Wizzard's *Angel Fingers*.

Talking of which, Mr Glitter had declared in May: "There's a scene in Last Tango In Paris where Brando says 'I don't need to talk but we can still communicate.' And he grunts and groans. That's pretty similar to what I achieve."

last week	this week	15 September 1973
1	1	SING IT AGAIN ROD Rod Stewart (Mercury)
2	2	NOW AND THEN Carpenters (A&M)
5	3	ALADDIN SANE David Bowie (RCA)
3	4	WE CAN MAKE IT Peters & Lee (Philips)
4	5	HUNKY DORY David Bowie (RCA)
6	6	THE PLAN Osmonds (MGM)
-	7	GOAT'S HEAD SOUP Rolling Stones (Rolling Stones)
10	8	TOUCH ME IN THE MORNING Diana Ross (Tamla Motown)
18	9	INNERVISIONS Stevie Wonder (Tamla Motown)
14	10	AND I LOVE YOU SO Perry Como (RCA)
7	11	THAT'LL BE THE DAY - SOUNDTRACK Various Artists (Ronco)
17	12	SIMON & GARFUNKEL'S GREATEST HITS Simon & Garfunkel (CBS)
15	13	THE BEATLES 1967-1970 Beatles (Apple)
11	14	MOTT Mott The Hoople (CBS)
20	15	24 GOLDEN GREATS OF THE 60s Various Artists (K-Tel)
23	16	20 EXPLOSIVE HITS Various Artists (K-Tel)
16	17	TOUCH ME Gary Glitter (Bell)
12	18	BOULDERS Roy Wood (Harvest)
19	19	THE RISE AND FALL OF ZIGGY STARDUST AND THE SPIDERS FROM MARS David Bowie (RCA)
13	20	TUBULAR BELLS Mike Oldfield (Virgin)
9	21	THE DARK SIDE OF THE MOON Pink Floyd (Harvest)
21	22	GENESIS LIVE Genesis (Charisma)
25	23	LOVE DEVOTION SURRENDER Carlos Santana & Mahavishnu John McLaughlin (CBS)
-	24	TRANSFORMER Lou Reed (RCA)
8	25	FOREIGNER Cat Stevens (Island)
30	26	THERE GOES RHYMIN' SIMON Paul Simon (CBS)
22	27	THE BEATLES 1962-1966 Beatles (Apple)
-	28	SINGALONGAMAX Max Bygraves (Pye)
27	29	RAZAMANAZ Nazareth (Mooncrest)
-	30	THE TRA-LA DAYS ARE OVER Neil Sedaka (MGM)

		22 September 1973
1	1	SING IT AGAIN ROD Rod Stewart (Mercury)
7	2	GOAT'S HEAD SOUP Rolling Stones (Rolling Stones)
3	3	ALADDIN SANE David Bowie (RCA)
2	4	NOW AND THEN Carpenters (A&M)
4	5	WE CAN MAKE IT Peters & Lee (Philips)
5	6	HUNKY DORY David Bowie (RCA)
13	7	THE BEATLES 1967-1970 Beatles (Apple)
9	8	INNERVISIONS Stevie Wonder (Tamla Motown)
8	9	TOUCH ME IN THE MORNING Diana Ross (Tamla Motown)
6	10	THE PLAN Osmonds (MGM)
14	11	MOTT Mott The Hoople (CBS)
10	12	AND I LOVE YOU SO Perry Como (RCA)
12	13	SIMON & GARFUNKEL'S GREATEST HITS Simon & Garfunkel (CBS)
15	14	24 GOLDEN GREATS OF THE 60s Various Artists (K-Tel)
23	15	LOVE DEVOTION SURRENDER Carlos Santana & Mahavishnu John McLaughlin (CBS)
18	16	BOULDERS Roy Wood (Harvest)
11	17	THAT'LL BE THE DAY - SOUNDTRACK Various Artists (Ronco)
27	18	THE BEATLES 1962-1966 Beatles (Apple)
20	19	TUBULAR BELLS Mike Oldfield (Virgin)
19	20	THE RISE AND FALL OF ZIGGY STARDUST AND THE SPIDERS FROM MARS David Bowie (RCA)
16	21	20 EXPLOSIVE HITS Various Artists (K-Tel)
17	22	TOUCH ME Gary Glitter (Bell)
21	23	THE DARK SIDE OF THE MOON Pink Floyd (Harvest)
22	24	GENESIS LIVE Genesis (Charisma)
26	25	THERE GOES RHYMIN' SIMON Paul Simon (CBS)
29	26	RAZAMANAZ Nazareth (Mooncrest)
25	27	FOREIGNER Cat Stevens (Island)
24	28	TRANSFORMER Lou Reed (RCA)
-	29	ELVIS Elvis Presley (RCA)
-	30	BRIDGE OVER TROUBLED WATER Simon & Garfunkel (CBS)

		29 September 1973
2	1	GOAT'S HEAD SOUP Rolling Stones (Rolling Stones)
1	2	SING IT AGAIN ROD Rod Stewart (Mercury)
4	3	NOW AND THEN Carpenters (A&M)
3	4	ALADDIN SANE David Bowie (RCA)
5	5	WE CAN MAKE IT Peters & Lee (Philips)
6	6	HUNKY DORY David Bowie (RCA)
7	7	THE BEATLES 1967-1970 Beatles (Apple)
13	8	SIMON & GARFUNKEL'S GREATEST HITS Simon & Garfunkel (CBS)
12	9	AND I LOVE YOU SO Perry Como (RCA)
-	10	SINGALONGAMAX VOL 4 Max Bygraves (Pye)
-	11	SLADEST Slade (Polydor)
19	12	TUBULAR BELLS Mike Oldfield (Virgin)
8	13	INNERVISIONS Stevie Wonder (Tamla Motown)
10	14	THE PLAN Osmonds (MGM)
21	15	20 EXPLOSIVE HITS Various Artists (K-Tel)
11	16	MOTT Mott The Hoople (CBS)
16	17	BOULDERS Roy Wood (Harvest)
20	18	THE RISE AND FALL OF ZIGGY STARDUST AND THE SPIDERS FROM MARS David Bowie (RCA)
-	19	A LITTLE TOUCH OF SCHMILSSON IN THE NIGHT Nilsson (RCA)
-	20	HELLO Status Quo (Vertigo)
-	21	GOOD VIBRATIONS Various Artists (Ronco)
24	22	GENESIS LIVE Genesis (Charisma)
23	23	THE DARK SIDE OF THE MOON Pink Floyd (Harvest)
-	24	I'M A WRITER NOT A FIGHTER Gilbert O'Sullivan (MAM)
18	25	THE BEATLES 1962-1966 Beatles (Apple)
9	26	TOUCH ME IN THE MORNING Diana Ross (Tamla Motown)
25	27	THERE GOES RHYMIN' SIMON Paul Simon (CBS)
29	28	ELVIS Elvis Presley (RCA)
17	29	THAT'LL BE THE DAY - SOUNDTRACK Various Artists (Ronco)
28	30	TRANSFORMER Lou Reed (RCA)'

		6 October 1973
1	1	GOATS HEAD SOUP Rolling Stones (Rolling Stones)
2	2	SING IT AGAIN ROD Rod Stewart (Mercury)
11	3	SLADEST Slade (Polydor)
3	4	NOW AND THEN Carpenters (A&M)
4	5	ALADDIN SANE David Bowie (RCA)
24	6	I'M A WRITER NOT A FIGHTER Gilbert O'Sullivan (MAM)
9	7	AND I LOVE YOU SO Perry Como (RCA)
6	8	HUNKY DORY David Bowie (RCA)
10	9	SINGALONGAMAX VOL 4 Max Bygraves (Pye)
5	10	WE CAN MAKE IT Peters & Lee (Philips)
16	11	MOTT Mott The Hoople (CBS)
15	12	20 EXPLOSIVE HITS Various Artists (K-Tel)
20	13	HELLO Status Quo (Vertigo)
21	14	GOOD VIBRATIONS Various Artists (Ronco)
7	15	THE BEATLES 1967-1970 Beatles (Apple)
-	16	CLASSICS 100 Various Orchestras (K-Tel)
8	17	SIMON & GARFUNKEL'S GREATEST HITS Simon & Garfunkel (CBS)
14	18	THE PLAN Osmonds (MGM)
13	19	INNERVISIONS Stevie Wonder (Tamla Motown)
12	20	TUBULAR BELLS Mike Oldfield (Virgin)
26	21	TOUCH ME IN THE MORNING Diana Ross (Tamla Motown)
22	22	GENESIS LIVE Genesis (Charisma)
-	23	ALL TIME CLASSICS London Symphony Orchestra (Arcade)
-	24	SWEET FREEDOM Uriah Heep (Island)
17	25	BOULDERS Roy Wood (Harvest)
25	26	THE BEATLES 1962-1966 Beatles (Apple)
18	27	THE RISE AND FALL OF ZIGGY STARDUST AND THE SPIDERS FROM MARS David Bowie (RCA)
23	28	THE DARK SIDE OF THE MOON Pink Floyd (Harvest)
-	29	A CLOCKWORK ORANGE Soundtrack (Warner Bros.)
19	30	A LITTLE TOUCH OF SCHMILSSON IN THE NIGHT Nilsson (RCA)

On September 19, Gram Parsons died of an overdose. As suggested already, Parsons had shitkick-started country rock with the Byrds on their 1968 *Sweetheart Of The Rodeo* album. Then he formed the *Flying Burrito Brothers* but quit this excellent non-charting band in 1970. Later Parsons made two solo albums, in the course of which he helped his old friend Emmylou Harris head for stardom. He was also a friend of Keith Richards, whose new Stones album now topped the chart.

October – November 1973

Revisiting other people's old songs was a trend of the day. The Band's 1973 album *Moondog Matinee* was entirely covers of oldies, such as Clarence Frogman Henry's *Ain't Got No Home*, Junior Parker's *Mystery Train* and Chuck Berry's *Promised Land*. The album didn't chart, but two similar projects did: Bryan Ferry's LP *These Foolish Things* (in at No.26) was similarly, if less affectionately, retro – and so was Bowie's *Pin Ups*, a collection of his British 1960s favourites, including the Merseybeats' song *Sorrow*.

10 November 1973

Last	This	Title	Artist (Label)
1	1	BOWIE PIN-UPS	David Bowie (RCA)
2	2	HELLO	Status Quo (Vertigo)
12	3	GOODBYE YELLOW BRICK ROAD	Elton John (DJM)
7	4	AND I LOVE YOU SO	Perry Como (RCA)
4	5	SLADEST	Slade (Polydor)
3	6	NOW AND THEN	Carpenters (A&M)
13	7	THESE FOOLISH THINGS	Bryan Ferry (Island)
5	8	I'M A WRITER NOT A FIGHTER	Gilbert O'Sullivan (MAM)
6	9	SELLING ENGLAND BY THE POUND	Genesis (Charisma)
14	10	ALADDIN SANE	David Bowie (RCA)
8	11	GOAT'S HEAD SOUP	Rolling Stones (Rolling Stones)
10	12	THE DARK SIDE OF THE MOON	Pink Floyd (Harvest)
11	13	SING IT AGAIN ROD	Rod Stewart (Mercury)
-	14	20 POWER HITS	Various Artists (K-Tel)
9	15	SINGALONGAMAX VOL 4	Max Bygraves (Pye)
-	16	MOTOWN CHARTBUSTERS VOL 8	Various Artists (Tamla Motown)
25	17	HUNKY DORY	David Bowie (RCA)
15	18	CLASSICS 100	Various Orchestras (K-Tel)
18	19	TOUCH ME IN THE MORNING	Diana Ross (Tamla Motown)
29	20	ANGEL CLARE	Art Garfunkel (CBS)
23	21	THE PLAN	Osmonds (MGM)
16	22	ALL TIME CLASSICS	London Symphony Orchestra (Arcade)
21	23	GOOD VIBRATIONS	Various Artists (Ronco)
22	24	SIMON & GARFUNKEL'S GREATEST HITS	Simon & Garfunkel (CBS)
-	25	THE RISE AND FALL OF ZIGGY STARDUST AND THE SPIDERS FROM MARS	David Bowie (RCA)
-	26	SING ALONG WITH MAX VOL 2	Max Bygraves (Pye)
-	27	ERIC CLAPTON'S RAINBOW CONCERT	Eric Clapton (RSO)
20	28	THE BEATLES 1967-1970	Beatles (Apple)
26	29	THE BEATLES 1962-1966	Beatles (Apple)
28	30	FOCUS AT THE RAINBOW	Focus (Polydor)

17 November 1973

Last	This	Title	Artist (Label)
1	1	BOWIE PIN-UPS	David Bowie (RCA)
3	2	GOODBYE YELLOW BRICK ROAD	Elton John (DJM)
2	3	HELLO	Status Quo (Vertigo)
4	4	AND I LOVE YOU SO	Perry Como (RCA)
5	5	SLADEST	Slade (Polydor)
7	6	THESE FOOLISH THINGS	Bryan Ferry (Island)
8	7	I'M A WRITER NOT A FIGHTER	Gilbert O'Sullivan (MAM)
6	8	NOW AND THEN	Carpenters (A&M)
12	9	THE DARK SIDE OF THE MOON	Pink Floyd (Harvest)
-	10	QUADROPHENIA	Who (Track)
13	11	SING IT AGAIN ROD	Rod Stewart (Mercury)
15	12	SINGALONGAMAX VOL 4	Max Bygraves (Pye)
9	13	SELLING ENGLAND BY THE POUND	Genesis (Charisma)
14	14	20 POWER HITS	Various Artists (K-Tel)
17	15	HUNKY DORY	David Bowie (RCA)
16	16	MOTOWN CHARTBUSTERS VOL 8	Various Artists (Tamla Motown)
11	17	GOAT'S HEAD SOUP	Rolling Stones (Rolling Stones)
21	18	THE PLAN	Osmonds (MGM)
10	19	ALADDIN SANE	David Bowie (RCA)
27	20	ERIC CLAPTON'S RAINBOW CONCERT	Eric Clapton (RSO)
-	21	SINGALONGAMAX	Max Bygraves (Pye)
30	22	FOCUS AT THE RAINBOW	Focus (Polydor)
28	23	THE BEATLES 1967-1970	Beatles (Apple)
18	24	CLASSICS 100	Various Orchestras (K-Tel)
24	25	SIMON & GARFUNKEL'S GREATEST HITS	Simon & Garfunkel (CBS)
25	26	THE RISE AND FALL OF ZIGGY STARDUST AND THE SPIDERS FROM MARS	David Bowie (RCA)
23	27	GOOD VIBRATIONS	Various Artists (Ronco)
-	28	TUBULAR BELLS	Mike Oldfield (Virgin)
-	29	INNERVISIONS	Stevie Wonder (Tamla Motown)
-	30	WE CAN MAKE IT	Peters & Lee (Philips)

24 November 1973

Last	This	Title	Artist (Label)
1	1	BOWIE PIN-UPS	David Bowie (RCA)
2	2	GOODBYE YELLOW BRICK ROAD	Elton John (DJM)
10	3	QUADROPHENIA	Who (Track)
3	4	HELLO	Status Quo (Vertigo)
8	5	NOW AND THEN	Carpenters (A&M)
7	6	I'M A WRITER NOT A FIGHTER	Gilbert O'Sullivan (MAM)
4	7	AND I LOVE YOU SO	Perry Como (RCA)
6	8	THESE FOOLISH THINGS	Bryan Ferry (Island)
5	9	SLADEST	Slade (Polydor)
9	10	THE DARK SIDE OF THE MOON	Pink Floyd (Harvest)
14	11	20 POWER HITS	Various Artists (K-Tel)
11	12	SING IT AGAIN ROD	Rod Stewart (Mercury)
13	13	SELLING ENGLAND BY THE POUND	Genesis (Charisma)
19	14	ALADDIN SANE	David Bowie (RCA)
18	15	THE PLAN	Osmonds (MGM)
17	16	GOATS HEAD SOUP	Rolling Stones (Rolling Stones)
16	17	MOTOWN CHARTBUSTERS VOL 8	Various Artists (Tamla Motown)
12	18	SINGALONGAMAX VOL 4	Max Bygraves (Pye)
15	19	HUNKY DORY	David Bowie (RCA)
-	20	DREAMS ARE NOTHIN' MORE THAN WISHES	David Cassidy (Bell)
-	21	ROCK ON	David Essex (CBS)
23	22	THE BEATLES 1967-1970	Beatles (Apple)
27	23	GOOD VIBRATIONS	Various Artists (Ronco)
25	24	SIMON & GARFUNKEL'S GREATEST HITS	Simon & Garfunkel (CBS)
-	25	THE BEATLES 1962-1966	Beatles (Apple)
-	26	STRANDED	Roxy Music (Island)
24	27	CLASSICS 100	Various Orchestras (K-Tel)
28	28	TUBULAR BELLS	Mike Oldfield (Virgin)
-	29	JESUS CHRIST SUPERSTAR	Soundtrack (MCA)
20	30	ERIC CLAPTON'S RAINBOW CONCERT	Eric Clapton (RSO)

1 December 1973

Last	This	Title	Artist (Label)
1	1	BOWIE PIN-UPS	David Bowie (RCA)
2	2	GOODBYE YELLOW BRICK ROAD	Elton John (DJM)
3	3	QUADROPHENIA	Who (Track)
6	4	I'M A WRITER NOT A FIGHTER	Gilbert O'Sullivan (MAM)
7	5	AND I LOVE YOU SO	Perry Como (RCA)
5	6	NOW AND THEN	Carpenters (A&M)
11	7	20 POWER HITS	Various Artists (K-Tel)
8	8	THESE FOOLISH THINGS	Bryan Ferry (Island)
4	9	HELLO	Status Quo (Vertigo)
9	10	SLADEST	Slade (Polydor)
26	11	STRANDED	Roxy Music (Island)
15	12	THE PLAN	Osmonds (MGM)
10	13	THE DARK SIDE OF THE MOON	Pink Floyd (Harvest)
21	14	ROCK ON	David Essex (CBS)
-	15	LOUD 'N' PROUD	Nazareth (Mooncrest)
20	16	DREAMS ARE NOTHIN' MORE THAN WISHES	David Cassidy (Bell)
14	17	ALADDIN SANE	David Bowie (RCA)
13	18	SELLING ENGLAND BY THE POUND	Genesis (Charisma)
18	19	SINGALONGAMAX VOL 4	Max Bygraves (Pye)
12	20	SING IT AGAIN ROD	Rod Stewart (Mercury)
-	21	RINGO	Ringo Starr (Apple)
16	22	GOAT'S HEAD SOUP	Rolling Stones (Rolling Stones)
17	23	MOTOWN CHARTBUSTERS VOL 8	Various Artists (Tamla Motown)
23	24	GOOD VIBRATIONS	Various Artists (Ronco)
-	25	A SONG FOR YOU	Carpenters (A&M)
22	26	THE BEATLES 1967-1970	Beatles (Apple)
19	27	HUNKY DORY	David Bowie (RCA)
-	28	TATTOO	Rory Gallagher (Polydor)
24	29	SIMON & GARFUNKEL'S GREATEST HITS	Simon & Garfunkel (CBS)
-	30	SINGALONGAMAX	Max Bygraves (Pye)

Frank Zappa hadn't charted since 1970's *Weasels Ripped My Flesh*, but his *Grand Wazoo* sleevenotes summed up the current chart: "The enemy... has 5000 dynamic male vocalists in tuxedos who stand in the middle of the road, loosen their bowties and arch one eyebrow... 5000 dynamic (but carefully understated) male vocalists in old Levi clothes who cry, sulk, whimper and play harmonica, plus 5000 more... of indeterminate sex who can't sing at all but dance good and do hot moves with the mike wire."

December 1973

8 December 1973

last	this		
1	1	BOWIE PIN-UPS	David Bowie (RCA)
3	2	QUADROPHENIA	Who (Track)
11	3	STRANDED	Roxy Music (Island)
4	4	I'M A WRITER NOT A FIGHTER	Gilbert O'Sullivan (MAM)
5	5	AND I LOVE YOU SO	Perry Como (RCA)
2	6	GOODBYE YELLOW BRICK ROAD	Elton John (DJM)
16	7	DREAMS ARE NOTHIN' MORE THAN WISHES	David Cassidy (Bell)
7	8	20 POWER HITS	Various Artists (K-Tel)
9	9	HELLO	Status Quo (Vertigo)
6	10	NOW AND THEN	Carpenters (A&M)
8	11	THESE FOOLISH THINGS	Bryan Ferry (Island)
10	12	SLADEST	Slade (Polydor)
13	13	THE DARK SIDE OF THE MOON	Pink Floyd (Harvest)
26	14	THE BEATLES 1967-1970	Beatles (Apple)
12	15	THE PLAN	Osmonds (MGM)
15	16	LOUD 'N' PROUD	Nazareth (Mooncrest)
-	17	WELCOME	Santana (CBS)
21	18	RINGO	Ringo Starr (Apple)
-	19	CLASSICS 100	Various Orchestras (K-Tel)
29	20	SIMON & GARFUNKEL'S GREATEST HITS	Simon & Garfunkel (CBS)
-	21	MIND GAMES	John Lennon (Apple)
14	22	ROCK ON	David Essex (CBS)
23	23	MOTOWN CHARTBUSTERS VOL 8	Various Artists (Tamla Motown)
17	24	ALADDIN SANE	David Bowie (RCA)
18	25	SELLING ENGLAND BY THE POUND	Genesis (Charisma)
20	26	SING IT AGAIN ROD	Rod Stewart (Mercury)
-	27	THE BEATLES 1962-1966	Beatles (Apple)
-	28	SABBATH BLOODY SABBATH	Black Sabbath (WWA)
27	29	HUNKY DORY	David Bowie (RCA)
24	30	GOOD VIBRATIONS	Various Artists (Ronco)

15 December 1973

1	1	BOWIE PIN-UPS	David Bowie (RCA)
6	2	GOODBYE YELLOW BRICK ROAD	Elton John (DJM)
3	3	STRANDED	Roxy Music (Island)
2	4	QUADROPHENIA	Who (Track)
4	5	I'M A WRITER NOT A FIGHTER	Gilbert O'Sullivan (MAM)
10	6	NOW AND THEN	Carpenters (A&M)
18	7	RINGO	Ringo Starr (Apple)
5	8	AND I LOVE YOU SO	Perry Como (RCA)
7	9	DREAMS ARE NOTHIN' MORE THAN WISHES	David Cassidy (Bell)
21	10	MIND GAMES	John Lennon (Apple)
-	11	BRAIN SALAD SURGERY	Emerson, Lake & Palmer (Manticore)
28	12	SABBATH BLOODY SABBATH	Black Sabbath (WWA)
13	13	THE DARK SIDE OF THE MOON	Pink Floyd (Harvest)
-	14	TALES FROM TOPOGRAPHIC OCEANS	Yes (Atlantic)
12	15	SLADEST	Slade (Polydor)
9	16	HELLO	Status Quo (Vertigo)
22	17	ROCK ON	David Essex (CBS)
8	18	20 POWER HITS	Various Artists (K-Tel)
-	19	OL' BLUE EYES IS BACK	Frank Sinatra (Reprise)
20	20	SIMON & GARFUNKEL'S GREATEST HITS	Simon & Garfunkel (CBS)
17	21	WELCOME	Santana (CBS)
14	22	THE BEATLES 1967-1970	Beatles (Apple)
-	23	BAND ON THE RUN	Paul McCartney & Wings (Parlophone)
16	24	LOUD 'N' PROUD	Nazareth (Mooncrest)
24	25	ALADDIN SANE	David Bowie (RCA)
15	26	THE PLAN	Osmonds (MGM)
11	27	THESE FOOLISH THINGS	Bryan Ferry (Island)
25	28	SELLING ENGLAND BY THE POUND	Genesis (Charisma)
-	29	SINGALONGAPARTY SONG	Max Bygraves (Pye)
-	30	COMMAND PERFORMANCE	Various Artists (Ronco)

22 December 1973

3	1	STRANDED	Roxy Music (Island)
1	2	BOWIE PIN-UPS	David Bowie (RCA)
9	3	DREAMS ARE NOTHIN' MORE THAN WISHES	David Cassidy (Bell)
2	4	GOODBYE YELLOW BRICK ROAD	Elton John (DJM)
5	5	I'M A WRITER NOT A FIGHTER	Gilbert O'Sullivan (MAM)
4	6	QUADROPHENIA	Who (Track)
7	7	RINGO	Ringo Starr (Apple)
6	8	NOW AND THEN	Carpenters (A&M)
8	9	AND I LOVE YOU SO	Perry Como (RCA)
14	10	TALES FROM TOPOGRAPHIC OCEANS	Yes (Atlantic)
10	11	MIND GAMES	John Lennon (Apple)
29	12	SINGALONGAPARTY SONG	Max Bygraves (Pye)
-	13	20 EVERLASTING MEMORIES OF THE 50s	Various Artists (K-Tel)
18	14	20 POWER HITS	Various Artists (K-Tel)
11	15	BRAIN SALAD SURGERY	Emerson, Lake & Palmer (Manticore)
16	16	HELLO	Status Quo (Vertigo)
12	17	SABBATH BLOODY SABBATH	Black Sabbath (WWA)
13	18	THE DARK SIDE OF THE MOON	Pink Floyd (Harvest)
17	19	ROCK ON	David Essex (CBS)
30	20	COMMAND PERFORMANCE	Various Artists (Ronco)
21	21	WELCOME	Santana (CBS)
23	22	BAND ON THE RUN	Paul McCartney & Wings (Parlophone)
15	23	SLADEST	Slade (Polydor)
19	24	OL' BLUE EYES IS BACK	Frank Sinatra (Reprise)
-	25	CLASSICS 100	Various Orchestras (K-Tel)
-	26	A TIME FOR US	Donny Osmond (MGM)
-	27	TUBULAR BELLS	Mike Oldfield (Virgin)
-	28	TOUCH ME	Gary Glitter (Bell)
24	29	LOUD 'N' PROUD	Nazareth (Mooncrest)
-	30	MOTOWN CHARTBUSTERS VOL 8	Various Artists (Tamla Motown)

This month's chart included John, Paul and Ringo as well as two Beatles LPs. In fact Ringo's album was notable for featuring all four ex-Beatles on it, though never all at once. He was also enjoying a hit single with *Photograph*, which had peaked at No.4, while Paul's *Helen Wheels* only reached No.12 and John's single of *Mind Games* couldn't better No.19. Deep Purple ended the year officially acclaimed as the world's Loudest Performing Rock Band (117 decibels) in the Guinness Book of Records.

5 January 1974

last this week

Last	This	Title	Artist
4	1	GOODBYE YELLOW BRICK ROAD	Elton John (DJM)
2	2	BOWIE PIN-UPS	David Bowie (RCA)
23	3	SLADEST	Slade (Polydor)
1	4	STRANDED	Roxy Music (Island)
5	5	I'M A WRITER NOT A FIGHTER	Gilbert O'Sullivan (MGM)
7	6	RINGO	Ringo Starr (Apple)
15	7	BRAIN SALAD SURGERY	Emerson, Lake & Palmer (Manticore)
3	8	DREAMS ARE NOTHIN' MORE THAN WISHES	David Cassidy (Bell)
11	9	MIND GAMES	John Lennon (Apple)
10	10	TALES FROM TOPOGRAPHIC OCEANS	Yes (Atlantic)
22	11	BAND ON THE RUN	Paul McCartney & Wings (Parlophone)
-	12	SING IT AGAIN ROD	Rod Stewart (Mercury)
9	13	AND I LOVE YOU SO	Perry Como (RCA)
8	14	NOW AND THEN	Carpenters (A&M)
20	15	COMMAND PERFORMANCE	Various Artists (Ronco)
18	16	THE DARK SIDE OF THE MOON	Pink Floyd (Harvest)
17	17	SABBATH BLOODY SABBATH	Black Sabbath (WWA)
26	18	A TIME FOR US	Donny Osmond (MGM)
19	19	ROCK ON	David Essex (CBS)
-	20	THE PLAN	Osmonds (MGM)
28	21	TOUCH ME	Gary Glitter (Bell)
-	22	SILVERBIRD	Leo Sayer (Chrysalis)
-	23	SIMON AND GARFUNKEL'S GREATEST HITS	Simon & Garfunkel (CBS)
-	24	THE BEATLES 1967-1970	Beatles (Apple)
16	25	HELLO	Status Quo (Vertigo)
-	26	THE BEATLES 1962-1966	Beatles (Apple)
6	27	QUADROPHENIA	Who (Track)
-	28	TWENTY NO. 1s	Various Artists (Arcade)
14	29	20 POWER HITS	Various Artists (K-Tel)
27	30	TUBULAR BELLS	Mike Oldfield (Virgin)

12 January 1974

This		Title	Artist
1	1	GOODBYE YELLOW BRICK ROAD	Elton John (DJM)
2	2	BOWIE PIN-UPS	David Bowie (RCA)
5	3	I'M A WRITER NOT A FIGHTER	Gilbert O'Sullivan (MGM)
7	4	BRAIN SALAD SURGERY	Emerson, Lake & Palmer (Manticore)
10	5	TALES FROM TOPOGRAPHIC OCEANS	Yes (Atlantic)
3	6	SLADEST	Slade (Polydor)
11	7	BAND ON THE RUN	Paul McCartney & Wings (Parlophone)
18	8	A TIME FOR US	Donny Osmond (MGM)
22	9	SILVERBIRD	Leo Sayer (Chrysalis)
8	10	DREAMS ARE NOTHIN' MORE THAN WISHES	David Cassidy (Bell)
13	11	AND I LOVE YOU SO	Perry Como (RCA)
21	12	TOUCH ME	Gary Glitter (Bell)
4	13	STRANDED	Roxy Music (Island)
14	14	NOW AND THEN	Carpenters (A&M)
6	15	RINGO	Ringo Starr (Apple)
9	16	MIND GAMES	John Lennon (Apple)
27	17	QUADROPHENIA	Who (Track)
24	18	THE BEATLES 1967-1970	Beatles (Apple)
-	19	BACK TO FRONT	Gilbert O'Sullivan (MGM)
19	20	ROCK ON	David Essex (CBS)
-	21	OL' BLUE EYES IS BACK	Frank Sinatra (Reprise)
23	22	SIMON AND GARFUNKEL'S GREATEST HITS	Simon & Garfunkel (CBS)
20	23	THE PLAN	Osmonds (MGM)
16	24	THE DARK SIDE OF THE MOON	Pink Floyd (Harvest)
26	25	THE BEATLES 1962-1966	Beatles (Apple)
-	26	20 EVERLASTING MEMORIES OF THE 50s	Various Artists (K-Tel)
-	27	THE RISE AND FALL OF ZIGGY STARDUST AND THE SPIDERS FROM MARS	David Bowie (RCA)
25	28	HELLO	Status Quo (Vertigo)
-	29	DIANA AND MARVIN	Diana Ross & Marvin Gaye (Tamla Motown)
-	30	WELCOME	Santana (CBS)

19 January 1974

	This	Title	Artist
4	1	BRAIN SALAD SURGERY	Emerson, Lake & Palmer (Manticore)
1	2	GOODBYE YELLOW BRICK ROAD	Elton John (DJM)
2	3	BOWIE PIN-UPS	David Bowie (RCA)
5	4	TALES FROM TOPOGRAPHIC OCEANS	Yes (Atlantic)
3	5	I'M A WRITER NOT A FIGHTER	Gilbert O'Sullivan (MGM)
10	6	DREAMS ARE NOTHIN' MORE THAN WISHES	David Cassidy (Bell)
13	7	STRANDED	Roxy Music (Island)
11	8	AND I LOVE YOU SO	Perry Como (RCA)
6	9	SLADEST	Slade (Polydor)
-	10	OVERTURE AND BEGINNERS	Rod Stewart & the Faces (Mercury)
12	11	TOUCH ME	Gary Glitter (Bell)
24	12	THE DARK SIDE OF THE MOON	Pink Floyd (Harvest)
21	13	OL' BLUE EYES IS BACK	Frank Sinatra (Reprise)
8	14	A TIME FOR US	Donny Osmond (MGM)
-	15	THE SINGLES 1969-1973	Carpenters (A&M)
9	16	SILVERBIRD	Leo Sayer (Chrysalis)
15	17	RINGO	Ringo Starr (Apple)
17	18	QUADROPHENIA	Who (Track)
14	19	NOW AND THEN	Carpenters (A&M)
7	20	BAND ON THE RUN	Paul McCartney & Wings (Parlophone)
-	21	TUBULAR BELLS	Mike Oldfield (Virgin)
20	22	ROCK ON	David Essex (CBS)
18	23	THE BEATLES 1967-1970	Beatles (Apple)
-	24	SABBATH BLOODY SABBATH	Black Sabbath (WWA)
28	25	HELLO	Status Quo (Vertigo)
-	26	BRIDGE OVER TROUBLED WATER	Simon & Garfunkel (CBS)
23	27	THE PLAN	Osmonds (MGM)
16	28	MIND GAMES	John Lennon (Apple)
-	29	MUSCLE OF LOVE	Alice Cooper (Warner Bros.)
22	30	SIMON AND GARFUNKEL'S GREATEST HITS	Simon & Garfunkel (CBS)

26 January 1974

	This	Title	Artist
1	1	BRAIN SALAD SURGERY	Emerson, Lake & Palmer (Manticore)
3	2	BOWIE PIN-UPS	David Bowie (RCA)
2	3	GOODBYE YELLOW BRICK ROAD	Elton John (DJM)
4	4	TALES FROM TOPOGRAPHIC OCEANS	Yes (Atlantic)
9	5	SLADEST	Slade (Polydor)
20	6	BAND ON THE RUN	Paul McCartney & Wings (Parlophone)
5	7	I'M A WRITER NOT A FIGHTER	Gilbert O'Sullivan (MGM)
15	8	THE SINGLES 1969-1973	Carpenters (A&M)
7	9	STRANDED	Roxy Music (Island)
12	10	THE DARK SIDE OF THE MOON	Pink Floyd (Harvest)
16	11	SILVERBIRD	Leo Sayer (Chrysalis)
8	12	AND I LOVE YOU SO	Perry Como (RCA)
22	13	ROCK ON	David Essex (CBS)
14	14	A TIME FOR US	Donny Osmond (MGM)
10	15	OVERTURE AND BEGINNERS	Rod Stewart & the Faces (Mercury)
6	16	DREAMS ARE NOTHIN' MORE THAN WISHES	David Cassidy (Bell)
21	17	TUBULAR BELLS	Mike Oldfield (Virgin)
-	18	GLITTER	Gary Glitter (Bell)
18	19	QUADROPHENIA	Who (Track)
29	20	MUSCLE OF LOVE	Alice Cooper (Warner Bros.)
19	21	NOW AND THEN	Carpenters (A&M)
11	22	TOUCH ME	Gary Glitter (Bell)
30	23	SIMON AND GARFUNKEL'S GREATEST HITS	Simon & Garfunkel (CBS)
13	24	OL' BLUE EYES IS BACK	Frank Sinatra (Reprise)
-	25	THESE FOOLISH THINGS	Bryan Ferry (Island)
-	26	ALADDIN SANE	David Bowie (RCA)
25	27	HELLO	Status Quo (Vertigo)
-	28	DIANA AND MARVIN	Diana Ross & Marvin Gaye (Tamla Motown)
28	29	MIND GAMES	John Lennon (Apple)
17	30	RINGO	Ringo Starr (Apple)

Silverbird (No.22) marked the debut of Adam Faith protege Leo Sayer, whose debut single *The Show Must Go On* would top the charts this month. Leo Sayer looked and sounded like a Gilbert O'Sullivan without the image problem. John Lennon seemed to have an image problem too. He turned up this month at the LA Troubadour club with a Kotex [sanitary towel] on his head. Glared at by a waitress, he asked "D'you know who I am?" "Yes, you're some asshole with a Kotex on your head."

February 1974

2 February 1974

last	this		
8	1	THE SINGLES 1969-1973	Carpenters (A&M)
11	2	SILVERBIRD	Leo Sayer (Chrysalis)
12	3	AND I LOVE YOU SO	Perry Como (RCA)
1	4	BRAIN SALAD SURGERY	Emerson, Lake & Palmer (Manticore)
6	5	BAND ON THE RUN	Paul McCartney & Wings (Parlophone)
15	6	OVERTURE AND BEGINNERS	Rod Stewart & the Faces (Mercury)
2	7	BOWIE PIN-UPS	David Bowie (RCA)
10	8	THE DARK SIDE OF THE MOON	Pink Floyd (Harvest)
4	9	TALES FROM TOPOGRAPHIC OCEANS	Yes (Atlantic)
9	10	STRANDED	Roxy Music (Island)
7	11	I'M A WRITER NOT A FIGHTER	Gilbert O'Sullivan (MGM)
5	12	SLADEST	Slade (Polydor)
3	13	GOODBYE YELLOW BRICK ROAD	Elton John (DJM)
13	14	ROCK ON	David Essex (CBS)
17	15	TUBULAR BELLS	Mike Oldfield (Virgin)
-	16	SOLITAIRE	Andy Williams (CBS)
28	17	DIANA AND MARVIN	Diana Ross & Marvin Gaye (Tamla Motown)
23	18	SIMON AND GARFUNKEL'S GREATEST HITS	Simon & Garfunkel (CBS)
18	19	GLITTER	Gary Glitter (Bell)
24	20	OL' BLUE EYES IS BACK	Frank Sinatra (Reprise)
19	21	QUADROPHENIA	Who (Track)
-	22	HUNKY DORY	David Bowie (RCA)
-	23	THE BEATLES 1967-1970	Beatles (Apple)
27	24	HELLO	Status Quo (Vertigo)
30	25	RINGO	Ringo Starr (Apple)
21	26	NOW AND THEN	Carpenters (A&M)
20	27	MUSCLE OF LOVE	Alice Cooper (Warner Bros.)
22	28	TOUCH ME	Gary Glitter (Bell)
-	29	THE BEATLES 1962-1966	Beatles (Apple)
-	30	BRIDGE OVER TROUBLED WATER	Simon & Garfunkel (CBS)

9 February 1974

last	this		
1	1	THE SINGLES 1969-1973	Carpenters (A&M)
2	2	SILVERBIRD	Leo Sayer (Chrysalis)
3	3	AND I LOVE YOU SO	Perry Como (RCA)
5	4	BAND ON THE RUN	Paul McCartney & Wings (Parlophone)
6	5	OVERTURE AND BEGINNERS	Rod Stewart & the Faces (Mercury)
7	6	BOWIE PIN-UPS	David Bowie (RCA)
4	7	BRAIN SALAD SURGERY	Emerson, Lake & Palmer (Manticore)
8	8	THE DARK SIDE OF THE MOON	Pink Floyd (Harvest)
9	9	TALES FROM TOPOGRAPHIC OCEANS	Yes (Atlantic)
11	10	I'M A WRITER NOT A FIGHTER	Gilbert O'Sullivan (MGM)
12	11	SLADEST	Slade (Polydor)
15	12	TUBULAR BELLS	Mike Oldfield (Virgin)
13	13	GOODBYE YELLOW BRICK ROAD	Elton John (DJM)
10	14	STRANDED	Roxy Music (Island)
16	15	SOLITAIRE	Andy Williams (CBS)
-	16	TOUCH ME IN THE MORNING	Diana Ross (Tamla Motown)
18	17	SIMON AND GARFUNKEL'S GREATEST HITS	Simon & Garfunkel (CBS)
-	18	TOM JONES' GREATEST HITS	Tom Jones (Decca)
14	19	ROCK ON	David Essex (CBS)
23	20	THE BEATLES 1967-1970	Beatles (Apple)
-	21	TWENTY NO. 1s	Various Artists (Arcade)
26	22	NOW AND THEN	Carpenters (A&M)
17	23	DIANA AND MARVIN	Diana Ross & Marvin Gaye (Tamla Motown)
20	24	OL' BLUE EYES IS BACK	Frank Sinatra (Reprise)
-	25	MOONTAN	Golden Earring (Track)
-	26	ALADDIN SANE	David Bowie (RCA)
25	27	RINGO	Ringo Starr (Apple)
30	28	BRIDGE OVER TROUBLED WATER	Simon & Garfunkel (CBS)
29	29	THE BEATLES 1962-1966	Beatles (Apple)
22	30	HUNKY DORY	David Bowie (RCA)

16 February 1974

last	this		
1	1	THE SINGLES 1969-1973	Carpenters (A&M)
2	2	SILVERBIRD	Leo Sayer (Chrysalis)
3	3	AND I LOVE YOU SO	Perry Como (RCA)
-	4	OLD NEW BORROWED AND BLUE	Slade (Polydor)
4	5	BAND ON THE RUN	Paul McCartney & Wings (Parlophone)
15	6	SOLITAIRE	Andy Williams (CBS)
8	7	THE DARK SIDE OF THE MOON	Pink Floyd (Harvest)
5	8	OVERTURE AND BEGINNERS	Rod Stewart & the Faces (Mercury)
12	9	TUBULAR BELLS	Mike Oldfield (Virgin)
7	10	BRAIN SALAD SURGERY	Emerson, Lake & Palmer (Manticore)
21	11	TWENTY NO. 1s	Various Artists (Arcade)
10	12	I'M A WRITER NOT A FIGHTER	Gilbert O'Sullivan (MGM)
14	13	STRANDED	Roxy Music (Island)
9	14	TALES FROM TOPOGRAPHIC OCEANS	Yes (Atlantic)
-	15	PLANET WAVES	Bob Dylan (Island)
6	16	BOWIE PIN-UPS	David Bowie (RCA)
17	17	SIMON AND GARFUNKEL'S GREATEST HITS	Simon & Garfunkel (CBS)
-	18	HARBOUR	Jack Jones (RCA)
13	19	GOODBYE YELLOW BRICK ROAD	Elton John (DJM)
23	20	DIANA AND MARVIN	Diana Ross & Marvin Gaye (Tamla Motown)
22	21	NOW AND THEN	Carpenters (A&M)
18	22	TOM JONES' GREATEST HITS	Tom Jones (Decca)
16	23	TOUCH ME IN THE MORNING	Diana Ross (Tamla Motown)
25	24	MOONTAN	Golden Earring (Track)
26	25	ALADDIN SANE	David Bowie (RCA)
19	26	ROCK ON	David Essex (CBS)
-	27	INNERVISIONS	Stevie Wonder (Tamla Motown)
-	28	LET'S GET IT ON	Marvin Gaye (Tamla Motown)
29	29	THE BEATLES 1962-1966	Beatles (Apple)
27	30	RINGO	Ringo Starr (Apple)

23 February 1974

last	this		
1	1	THE SINGLES 1969-1973	Carpenters (A&M)
4	2	OLD NEW BORROWED AND BLUE	Slade (Polydor)
2	3	SILVERBIRD	Leo Sayer (Chrysalis)
3	4	AND I LOVE YOU SO	Perry Como (RCA)
5	5	BAND ON THE RUN	Paul McCartney & Wings (Parlophone)
6	6	SOLITAIRE	Andy Williams (CBS)
8	7	OVERTURE AND BEGINNERS	Rod Stewart & the Faces (Mercury)
12	8	I'M A WRITER NOT A FIGHTER	Gilbert O'Sullivan (MGM)
11	9	TWENTY NO. 1s	Various Artists (Arcade)
15	10	PLANET WAVES	Bob Dylan (Island)
7	11	THE DARK SIDE OF THE MOON	Pink Floyd (Harvest)
9	12	TUBULAR BELLS	Mike Oldfield (Virgin)
19	13	GOODBYE YELLOW BRICK ROAD	Elton John (DJM)
10	14	BRAIN SALAD SURGERY	Emerson, Lake & Palmer (Manticore)
17	15	SIMON AND GARFUNKEL'S GREATEST HITS	Simon & Garfunkel (CBS)
16	16	BOWIE PIN-UPS	David Bowie (RCA)
14	17	TALES FROM TOPOGRAPHIC OCEANS	Yes (Atlantic)
23	18	TOUCH ME IN THE MORNING	Diana Ross (Tamla Motown)
20	19	DIANA AND MARVIN	Diana Ross & Marvin Gaye (Tamla Motown)
21	20	NOW AND THEN	Carpenters (A&M)
-	21	THE BEATLES 1967-1970	Beatles (Apple)
30	22	RINGO	Ringo Starr (Apple)
13	23	STRANDED	Roxy Music (Island)
-	24	OL' BLUE EYES IS BACK	Frank Sinatra (Reprise)
18	25	HARBOUR	Jack Jones (RCA)
22	26	TOM JONES' GREATEST HITS	Tom Jones (Decca)
-	27	A NICE PAIR	Pink Floyd (Harvest)
29	28	THE BEATLES 1962-1966	Beatles (Apple)
-	29	BURN	Deep Purple (Purple)
24	30	MOONTAN	Golden Earring (Track)

Emerson Lake & Palmer's *Brain Salad Surgery* would be their last No.1 album; it had now been displaced by the Carpenters' *The Singles 1969-1973*, which was to manage more weeks at No.1 than anything since Simon & Garfunkel's *Bridge Over Troubled Water*. It would sit there for 19 weeks... which was odd, because they'd only had four Top 10 hits. *Tom Jones' Greatest Hits*, which jumped into the Top 20 on February 9, were selected from his nineteen Top 20 singles and five minor hits.

March 1974

It was odd to see Dylan on Island instead of CBS. His Columbia contract had expired in 1972; for *Planet Waves*, cut with The Band in five days in November 1973, Dylan did a one-off US deal with David Geffen's Elektra/Asylum company (part of WEA, Columbia's chief rival); here, Chris Blackwell's Island label was used. The forthcoming live album from Dylan's mega-successful 1974 "come-back" tour would also go to Asylum and Island. CBS, forced to renegotiate with Dylan, would then re-sign him.

113

March – April 1974

Charlie Rich's *Behind Closed Doors* album made a shaky start, entering but then dropping from the Top 20 for two weeks before re-climbing, eventually to No.5. The album arrived as Rich's *The Most Beautiful Girl In The World* was peaking at No.2 in the singles chart. The follow-up single would be the album's title track, which would prove his second huge crossover country hit. Rich, a fine singer and excellent pianist, had been one of the early stars of Sun Records subsidiary Phillips International in Memphis.

27 April 1974

last week	this week	
1	1	THE SINGLES 1969-1973 Carpenters (A&M)
3	2	GOODBYE YELLOW BRICK ROAD Elton John (DJM)
2	3	BAND ON THE RUN Paul McCartney & Wings (Parlophone)
5	4	BUDDAH AND THE CHOCOLATE BOX Cat Stevens (Island)
8	5	TUBULAR BELLS Mike Oldfield (Virgin)
6	6	DIANA AND MARVIN Diana Ross & Marvin Gaye (Tamla Motown)
4	7	QUEEN II Queen (EMI)
12	8	THE STING Soundtrack (MCA)
14	9	THE HOOPLE Mott The Hoople (CBS)
19	10	BEHIND CLOSED DOORS Charlie Rich (Epic)
18	11	THE DARK SIDE OF THE MOON Pink Floyd (Harvest)
13	12	NOW AND THEN Carpenters (A&M)
9	13	MILLICAN AND NESBIT Millican & Nesbit (Pye)
15	14	BURN Deep Purple (Purple)
7	15	OLD NEW BORROWED AND BLUE Slade (Polydor)
11	16	ALAN FREEMAN'S HISTORY OF POP Various Artists (Arcade)
25	17	PHAEDRA Tangerine Dream (Virgin)
28	18	INNERVISIONS Stevie Wonder (Tamla Motown)
10	19	GLEN CAMPBELL'S GREATEST HITS Glen Campbell (Capitol)
-	20	THE STORY OF POP Various Artists (K-Tel)
21	21	NOW WE ARE SIX Steeleye Span (Chrysalis)
23	22	THE UNTOUCHABLE Alvin Stardust (Magnet)
16	23	AND I LOVE YOU SO Perry Como (RCA)
-	24	THE BEATLES 1967-1970 Beatles (Apple)
22	25	TOGETHER New Seekers (Polydor)
20	26	SOLITAIRE Andy Williams (CBS)
29	27	BY YOUR SIDE Peters & Lee (Philips)
-	28	SELLING ENGLAND BY THE POUND Genesis (Charisma)
-	29	JOURNEY THROUGH THE '60S Various Artists (Ronco)
26	30	HOT CAKES Carly Simon (Elektra)

4 May 1974

last week	this week	
1	1	THE SINGLES 1969-1973 Carpenters (A&M)
2	2	GOODBYE YELLOW BRICK ROAD Elton John (DJM)
3	3	BAND ON THE RUN Paul McCartney & Wings (Parlophone)
4	4	BUDDAH AND THE CHOCOLATE BOX Cat Stevens (Island)
6	5	DIANA AND MARVIN Diana Ross & Marvin Gaye (Tamla Motown)
5	6	TUBULAR BELLS Mike Oldfield (Virgin)
7	7	QUEEN II Queen (EMI)
15	8	OLD NEW BORROWED AND BLUE Slade (Polydor)
8	9	THE STING Soundtrack (MCA)
10	10	BEHIND CLOSED DOORS Charlie Rich (Epic)
18	11	INNERVISIONS Stevie Wonder (Tamla Motown)
13	12	MILLICAN AND NESBIT Millican & Nesbit (Pye)
11	13	THE DARK SIDE OF THE MOON Pink Floyd (Harvest)
12	14	NOW AND THEN Carpenters (A&M)
17	15	PHAEDRA Tangerine Dream (Virgin)
19	16	GLEN CAMPBELL'S GREATEST HITS Glen Campbell (Capitol)
9	17	THE HOOPLE Mott The Hoople (CBS)
14	18	BURN Deep Purple (Purple)
22	19	THE UNTOUCHABLE Alvin Stardust (Magnet)
16	20	ALAN FREEMAN'S HISTORY OF POP Various Artists (Arcade)
23	21	AND I LOVE YOU SO Perry Como (RCA)
24	22	THE BEATLES 1967-1970 Beatles (Apple)
27	23	BY YOUR SIDE Peters & Lee (Philips)
-	24	SIMON AND GARFUNKEL'S GREATEST HITS Simon & Garfunkel (CBS)
21	25	NOW WE ARE SIX Steeleye Span (Chrysalis)
25	26	TOGETHER New Seekers (Polydor)
29	27	JOURNEY THROUGH THE '60S Various Artists (Ronco)
-	28	COURT AND SPARK Joni Mitchell (Asylum)
28	29	SELLING ENGLAND BY THE POUND Genesis (Charisma)
-	30	AMERICAN GRAFFITI Soundtrack (MCA)

11 May 1974

last week	this week	
1	1	THE SINGLES 1969-1973 Carpenters (A&M)
2	2	GOODBYE YELLOW BRICK ROAD Elton John (DJM)
3	3	BAND ON THE RUN Paul McCartney & Wings (Parlophone)
4	4	BUDDAH AND THE CHOCOLATE BOX Cat Stevens (Island)
10	5	BEHIND CLOSED DOORS Charlie Rich (Epic)
6	6	TUBULAR BELLS Mike Oldfield (Virgin)
5	7	DIANA AND MARVIN Diana Ross & Marvin Gaye (Tamla Motown)
7	8	QUEEN II Queen (EMI)
11	9	INNERVISIONS Stevie Wonder (Tamla Motown)
8	10	OLD NEW BORROWED AND BLUE Slade (Polydor)
17	11	THE HOOPLE Mott The Hoople (CBS)
12	12	MILLICAN AND NESBIT Millican & Nesbit (Pye)
14	13	NOW AND THEN Carpenters (A&M)
13	14	THE DARK SIDE OF THE MOON Pink Floyd (Harvest)
9	15	THE STING Soundtrack (MCA)
21	16	AND I LOVE YOU SO Perry Como (RCA)
-	17	SUPER BAD Various Artists (K-Tel)
15	18	PHAEDRA Tangerine Dream (Virgin)
-	19	QUO Status Quo (Vertigo)
25	20	NOW WE ARE SIX Steeleye Span (Chrysalis)
18	21	BURN Deep Purple (Purple)
22	22	THE BEATLES 1967-1970 Beatles (Apple)
29	23	SELLING ENGLAND BY THE POUND Genesis (Charisma)
-	24	JOURNEY TO THE CENTRE OF THE EARTH Rick Wakeman (A&M)
24	25	SIMON AND GARFUNKEL'S GREATEST HITS Simon & Garfunkel (CBS)
28	26	COURT AND SPARK Joni Mitchell (Asylum)
-	27	SWEET FANNY ADAMS Sweet (RCA)
16	28	GLEN CAMPBELL'S GREATEST HITS Glen Campbell (Capitol)
27	29	JOURNEY THROUGH THE '60S Various Artists (Ronco)
19	30	THE UNTOUCHABLE Alvin Stardust (Magnet)

18 May 1974

last week	this week	
1	1	THE SINGLES 1969-1973 Carpenters (A&M)
2	2	GOODBYE YELLOW BRICK ROAD Elton John (DJM)
4	3	BUDDAH AND THE CHOCOLATE BOX Cat Stevens (Island)
3	4	BAND ON THE RUN Paul McCartney & Wings (Parlophone)
6	5	TUBULAR BELLS Mike Oldfield (Virgin)
7	6	DIANA AND MARVIN Diana Ross & Marvin Gaye (Tamla Motown)
5	7	BEHIND CLOSED DOORS Charlie Rich (Epic)
15	8	THE STING Soundtrack (MCA)
19	9	QUO Status Quo (Vertigo)
8	10	QUEEN II Queen (EMI)
17	11	SUPER BAD Various Artists (K-Tel)
12	12	MILLICAN AND NESBIT Millican & Nesbit (Pye)
14	13	THE DARK SIDE OF THE MOON Pink Floyd (Harvest)
24	14	JOURNEY TO THE CENTRE OF THE EARTH Rick Wakeman (A&M)
9	15	INNERVISIONS Stevie Wonder (Tamla Motown)
10	16	OLD NEW BORROWED AND BLUE Slade (Polydor)
11	17	THE HOOPLE Mott The Hoople (CBS)
13	18	NOW AND THEN Carpenters (A&M)
18	19	PHAEDRA Tangerine Dream (Virgin)
21	20	BURN Deep Purple (Purple)
29	21	JOURNEY THROUGH THE '60S Various Artists (Ronco)
16	22	AND I LOVE YOU SO Perry Como (RCA)
22	23	THE BEATLES 1967-1970 Beatles (Apple)
25	24	SIMON AND GARFUNKEL'S GREATEST HITS Simon & Garfunkel (CBS)
-	25	RAMPANT Nazareth (Mooncrest)
28	26	GLEN CAMPBELL'S GREATEST HITS Glen Campbell (Capitol)
-	27	WOMBLING SONGS Wombles (CBS)
-	28	SGT PEPPER'S LONELY HEARTS CLUB BAND Beatles (Parlophone)
-	28	THE BEATLES 1962-1966 Beatles (Apple)
23	30	SELLING ENGLAND BY THE POUND Genesis (Charisma)

Who were Millican And Nesbit? Their next album would be called *Everybody Knows Millican And Nesbit*, but this was a large claim then, let alone now. Although this UK male vocal duo had reached No.2 with the LP now hovering around the No.12 slot, their only previous celebrity had been via the very minor hit single *Vaya Con Dios*, which had reached No.21 and promptly vanished again. That follow-up album would make the lower reaches of the chart, for three weeks only, in 1975. Who were they? Coalminers.

May – June 1974

---

last this
week

25 May 1974

last week	this week	
1	1	THE SINGLES 1969-1973 Carpenters (A&M)
2	2	GOODBYE YELLOW BRICK ROAD Elton John (DJM)
9	3	QUO Status Quo (Vertigo)
14	4	JOURNEY TO THE CENTRE OF THE EARTH Rick Wakeman (A&M)
5	5	TUBULAR BELLS Mike Oldfield (Virgin)
4	6	BAND ON THE RUN Paul McCartney & Wings (Parlophone)
7	7	BEHIND CLOSED DOORS Charlie Rich (Epic)
8	8	THE STING Soundtrack (MCA)
6	9	DIANA AND MARVIN Diana Ross & Marvin Gaye (Tamla Motown)
3	10	BUDDAH AND THE CHOCOLATE BOX Cat Stevens (Island)
18	11	NOW AND THEN Carpenters (A&M)
12	12	MILLICAN AND NESBIT Millican & Nesbit (Pye)
15	13	INNERVISIONS Stevie Wonder (Tamla Motown)
13	14	THE DARK SIDE OF THE MOON Pink Floyd (Harvest)
11	15	SUPER BAD Various Artists (K-Tel)
22	16	AND I LOVE YOU SO Perry Como (RCA)
25	17	RAMPANT Nazareth (Mooncrest)
-	18	SWEET FANNY ADAMS Sweet (RCA)
20	19	BURN Deep Purple (Purple)
10	20	QUEEN II Queen (EMI)
19	21	PHAEDRA Tangerine Dream (Virgin)
27	22	WOMBLING SONGS Wombles (CBS)
-	23	BY YOUR SIDE Peters & Lee (Philips)
24	24	SIMON AND GARFUNKEL'S GREATEST HITS Simon & Garfunkel (CBS)
30	25	SELLING ENGLAND BY THE POUND Genesis (Charisma)
17	26	THE HOOPLE Mott The Hoople (CBS)
26	27	GLEN CAMPBELL'S GREATEST HITS Glen Campbell (Capitol)
16	28	OLD NEW BORROWED AND BLUE Slade (Polydor)
-	29	SOLITAIRE Andy Williams (CBS)
-	30	BEST OF BREAD Bread (Elektra)

1 June 1974

last week	this week	
1	1	THE SINGLES 1969-1973 Carpenters (A&M)
4	2	JOURNEY TO THE CENTRE OF THE EARTH Rick Wakeman (A&M)
-	3	DIAMOND DOGS David Bowie (RCA)
6	4	BAND ON THE RUN Paul McCartney & Wings (Parlophone)
3	5	QUO Status Quo (Vertigo)
5	6	TUBULAR BELLS Mike Oldfield (Virgin)
2	7	GOODBYE YELLOW BRICK ROAD Elton John (DJM)
8	8	THE STING Soundtrack (MCA)
7	9	BEHIND CLOSED DOORS Charlie Rich (Epic)
10	10	BUDDAH AND THE CHOCOLATE BOX Cat Stevens (Island)
9	11	DIANA AND MARVIN Diana Ross & Marvin Gaye (Tamla Motown)
11	12	NOW AND THEN Carpenters (A&M)
21	13	PHAEDRA Tangerine Dream (Virgin)
14	14	THE DARK SIDE OF THE MOON Pink Floyd (Harvest)
15	15	SUPER BAD Various Artists (K-Tel)
24	16	SIMON AND GARFUNKEL'S GREATEST HITS Simon & Garfunkel (CBS)
25	17	SELLING ENGLAND BY THE POUND Genesis (Charisma)
16	18	AND I LOVE YOU SO Perry Como (RCA)
-	19	KIMONO MY HOUSE Sparks (Island)
13	20	INNERVISIONS Stevie Wonder (Tamla Motown)
27	21	GLEN CAMPBELL'S GREATEST HITS Glen Campbell (Capitol)
18	22	SWEET FANNY ADAMS Sweet (RCA)
-	23	RHINOS WINOS AND LUNATICS Man (United Artists)
-	24	EASY EASY Scotland World Cup Squad (Polydor)
23	25	BY YOUR SIDE Peters & Lee (Philips)
22	26	WOMBLING SONGS Wombles (CBS)
-	27	THE BEATLES 1967-1970 Beatles (Apple)
12	28	MILLICAN AND NESBIT Millican & Nesbit (Pye)
19	29	BURN Deep Purple (Purple)
-	30	SCOTT JOPLIN/PIANO RAGS Joshua Rifkin (Nonesuch)

8 June 1974

last week	this week	
1	1	THE SINGLES 1969-1973 Carpenters (A&M)
2	2	JOURNEY TO THE CENTRE OF THE EARTH Rick Wakeman (A&M)
3	3	DIAMOND DOGS David Bowie (RCA)
6	4	TUBULAR BELLS Mike Oldfield (Virgin)
5	5	QUO Status Quo (Vertigo)
4	6	BAND ON THE RUN Paul McCartney & Wings (Parlophone)
7	7	GOODBYE YELLOW BRICK ROAD Elton John (DJM)
9	8	BEHIND CLOSED DOORS Charlie Rich (Epic)
8	9	THE STING Soundtrack (MCA)
15	10	SUPER BAD Various Artists (K-Tel)
19	11	KIMONO MY HOUSE Sparks (Island)
25	12	BY YOUR SIDE Peters & Lee (Philips)
14	13	THE DARK SIDE OF THE MOON Pink Floyd (Harvest)
11	14	DIANA AND MARVIN Diana Ross & Marvin Gaye (Tamla Motown)
18	15	AND I LOVE YOU SO Perry Como (RCA)
20	16	INNERVISIONS Stevie Wonder (Tamla Motown)
21	17	GLEN CAMPBELL'S GREATEST HITS Glen Campbell (Capitol)
10	18	BUDDAH AND THE CHOCOLATE BOX Cat Stevens (Island)
-	19	HAMBURGER CONCERTO Focus (Polydor)
12	20	NOW AND THEN Carpenters (A&M)
16	21	SIMON AND GARFUNKEL'S GREATEST HITS Simon & Garfunkel (CBS)
23	22	RHINOS WINOS AND LUNATICS Man (United Artists)
13	23	PHAEDRA Tangerine Dream (Virgin)
24	24	EASY EASY Scotland World Cup Squad (Polydor)
28	25	MILLICAN AND NESBIT Millican & Nesbit (Pye)
-	26	BAD COMPANY Bad Company (Island)
26	27	WOMBLING SONGS Wombles (CBS)
-	28	WE CAN MAKE IT Peters & Lee (Philips)
22	29	SWEET FANNY ADAMS Sweet (RCA)
-	30	SOLITAIRE Andy Williams (CBS)

15 June 1974

last week	this week	
3	1	DIAMOND DOGS David Bowie (RCA)
1	2	THE SINGLES 1969-1973 Carpenters (A&M)
5	3	QUO Status Quo (Vertigo)
2	4	JOURNEY TO THE CENTRE OF THE EARTH Rick Wakeman (A&M)
4	5	TUBULAR BELLS Mike Oldfield (Virgin)
11	6	KIMONO MY HOUSE Sparks (Island)
7	7	GOODBYE YELLOW BRICK ROAD Elton John (DJM)
6	8	BAND ON THE RUN Paul McCartney & Wings (Parlophone)
10	9	SUPER BAD Various Artists (K-Tel)
13	10	THE DARK SIDE OF THE MOON Pink Floyd (Harvest)
9	11	THE STING Soundtrack (MCA)
8	12	BEHIND CLOSED DOORS Charlie Rich (Epic)
14	13	DIANA AND MARVIN Diana Ross & Marvin Gaye (Tamla Motown)
12	14	BY YOUR SIDE Peters & Lee (Philips)
26	15	BAD COMPANY Bad Company (Island)
15	16	AND I LOVE YOU SO Perry Como (RCA)
23	17	PHAEDRA Tangerine Dream (Virgin)
17	18	GLEN CAMPBELL'S GREATEST HITS Glen Campbell (Capitol)
16	19	INNERVISIONS Stevie Wonder (Tamla Motown)
24	20	EASY EASY Scotland World Cup Squad (Polydor)
18	21	BUDDAH AND THE CHOCOLATE BOX Cat Stevens (Island)
21	22	SIMON AND GARFUNKEL'S GREATEST HITS Simon & Garfunkel (CBS)
-	23	BETWEEN TODAY AND YESTERDAY Alan Price (Warner Bros.)
-	24	RAMPANT Nazareth (Mooncrest)
20	25	NOW AND THEN Carpenters (A&M)
19	26	HAMBURGER CONCERTO Focus (Polydor)
-	27	MONKEY GRIP Bill Wyman (Rolling Stones)
-	28	IN FOR THE KILL Budgie (MCA)
-	29	THESE FOOLISH THINGS Bryan Ferry (Island)
27	30	WOMBLING SONGS Wombles (CBS)

Rhinos Winos And Lunatics was Welsh band Man's second minor hit album; *Back Into The Future* had made some charts, though not NME's. Fronted by Deke Leonard, who had a cult following, Man was a self-deprecating guitar band. A later, cut-priced LP would have the splendid title *Man Live At The Paget Rooms, Penarth*. Also Welsh were Budgie, a self-deprecating name in itself. *In For The Kill*, their first and biggest LP, entered the chart at No.28. It was downhill all the way after that.

116

22 June 1974

last week / this week

last	this		
1	1	DIAMOND DOGS	David Bowie (RCA)
2	2	THE SINGLES 1969-1973	Carpenters (A&M)
4	3	JOURNEY TO THE CENTRE OF THE EARTH	Rick Wakeman (A&M)
3	4	QUO	Status Quo (Vertigo)
6	5	KIMONO MY HOUSE	Sparks (Island)
15	6	BAD COMPANY	Bad Company (Island)
8	7	BAND ON THE RUN	Paul McCartney & Wings (Parlophone)
5	8	TUBULAR BELLS	Mike Oldfield (Virgin)
7	9	GOODBYE YELLOW BRICK ROAD	Elton John (DJM)
12	10	BEHIND CLOSED DOORS	Charlie Rich (Epic)
14	11	BY YOUR SIDE	Peters & Lee (Philips)
9	12	SUPER BAD	Various Artists (K-Tel)
16	13	AND I LOVE YOU SO	Perry Como (RCA)
-	14	SHEET MUSIC	10 C.C. (UK)
13	15	DIANA AND MARVIN	Diana Ross & Marvin Gaye (Tamla Motown)
11	16	THE STING	Soundtrack (MCA)
18	17	GLEN CAMPBELL'S GREATEST HITS	Glen Campbell (Capitol)
20	18	EASY EASY	Scotland World Cup Squad (Polydor)
-	19	REMEMBER ME THIS WAY	Gary Glitter (Bell)
-	20	THE WAY WE WERE	Andy Williams (CBS)
10	21	THE DARK SIDE OF THE MOON	Pink Floyd (Harvest)
22	22	SIMON AND GARFUNKEL'S GREATEST HITS	Simon & Garfunkel (CBS)
25	23	NOW AND THEN	Carpenters (A&M)
-	24	DIANA ROSS LIVE	Diana Ross (Tamla Motown)
21	25	BUDDAH AND THE CHOCOLATE BOX	Cat Stevens (Island)
19	26	INNERVISIONS	Stevie Wonder (Tamla Motown)
-	27	QUEEN II	Queen (EMI)
-	28	SCOTT JOPLIN/PIANO RAGS	Joshua Rifkin (Nonesuch)
-	29	CAMEMBERT ELECTRIQUE	Gong (Virgin)
28	30	IN FOR THE KILL	Budgie (MCA)

29 June 1974

1	1	DIAMOND DOGS	David Bowie (RCA)
2	2	THE SINGLES 1969-1973	Carpenters (A&M)
6	3	BAD COMPANY	Bad Company (Island)
5	4	KIMONO MY HOUSE	Sparks (Island)
3	5	JOURNEY TO THE CENTRE OF THE EARTH	Rick Wakeman (A&M)
8	6	TUBULAR BELLS	Mike Oldfield (Virgin)
7	7	BAND ON THE RUN	Paul McCartney & Wings (Parlophone)
9	8	GOODBYE YELLOW BRICK ROAD	Elton John (DJM)
4	9	QUO	Status Quo (Vertigo)
14	10	SHEET MUSIC	10 C.C. (UK)
10	11	BEHIND CLOSED DOORS	Charlie Rich (Epic)
19	12	REMEMBER ME THIS WAY	Gary Glitter (Bell)
16	13	THE STING	Soundtrack (MCA)
12	14	SUPER BAD	Various Artists (K-Tel)
21	15	THE DARK SIDE OF THE MOON	Pink Floyd (Harvest)
13	16	AND I LOVE YOU SO	Perry Como (RCA)
17	17	GLEN CAMPBELL'S GREATEST HITS	Glen Campbell (Capitol)
20	18	THE WAY WE WERE	Andy Williams (CBS)
15	19	DIANA AND MARVIN	Diana Ross & Marvin Gaye (Tamla Motown)
18	20	EASY EASY	Scotland World Cup Squad (Polydor)
11	21	BY YOUR SIDE	Peters & Lee (Philips)
-	22	ATLANTIC BLACK GOLD	Various Artists (Atlantic)
-	23	PHAEDRA	Tangerine Dream (Virgin)
23	24	NOW AND THEN	Carpenters (A&M)
-	25	THE PSYCHOMODO	Cockney Rebel (EMI)
26	26	INNERVISIONS	Stevie Wonder (Tamla Motown)
-	27	HAMBURGER CONCERTO	Focus (Polydor)
-	28	WOMBLING SONGS	Wombles (CBS)
-	29	BETWEEN TODAY AND YESTERDAY	Alan Price (Warner Bros.)
-	30	BEST OF BREAD	Bread (Elektra)

6 July 1974

1	1	DIAMOND DOGS	David Bowie (RCA)
2	2	THE SINGLES 1969-1973	Carpenters (A&M)
6	3	TUBULAR BELLS	Mike Oldfield (Virgin)
7	4	BAND ON THE RUN	Paul McCartney & Wings (Parlophone)
-	5	CARIBOU	Elton John (DJM)
12	6	REMEMBER ME THIS WAY	Gary Glitter (Bell)
4	7	KIMONO MY HOUSE	Sparks (Island)
3	8	BAD COMPANY	Bad Company (Island)
5	9	JOURNEY TO THE CENTRE OF THE EARTH	Rick Wakeman (A&M)
9	10	QUO	Status Quo (Vertigo)
8	11	GOODBYE YELLOW BRICK ROAD	Elton John (DJM)
-	12	AZNAVOUR SINGS AZNAVOUR VOL 3	Charles Aznavour (Barclay)
10	13	SHEET MUSIC	10 C.C. (UK)
-	14	22 ELECTRIFYING HITS	Various Artists (K-Tel)
15	15	THE DARK SIDE OF THE MOON	Pink Floyd (Harvest)
25	16	THE PSYCHOMODO	Cockney Rebel (EMI)
11	17	BEHIND CLOSED DOORS	Charlie Rich (Epic)
19	18	DIANA AND MARVIN	Diana Ross & Marvin Gaye (Tamla Motown)
16	19	AND I LOVE YOU SO	Perry Como (RCA)
18	20	THE WAY WE WERE	Andy Williams (CBS)
14	21	SUPER BAD	Various Artists (K-Tel)
24	22	NOW AND THEN	Carpenters (A&M)
20	23	EASY EASY	Scotland World Cup Squad (Polydor)
-	24	HIS 12 GREATEST HITS	Neil Diamond (MCA)
13	25	THE STING	Soundtrack (MCA)
-	26	LAUGHTER IN THE RAIN	Neil Sedaka (Polydor)
-	27	DIANA ROSS LIVE	Diana Ross (Tamla Motown)
21	28	BY YOUR SIDE	Peters & Lee (Philips)
28	29	WOMBLING SONGS	Wombles (CBS)
23	30	PHAEDRA	Tangerine Dream (Virgin)

13 July 1974

4	1	BAND ON THE RUN	Paul McCartney & Wings (Parlophone)
2	2	THE SINGLES 1969-1973	Carpenters (A&M)
5	3	CARIBOU	Elton John (DJM)
3	4	TUBULAR BELLS	Mike Oldfield (Virgin)
1	5	DIAMOND DOGS	David Bowie (RCA)
6	6	REMEMBER ME THIS WAY	Gary Glitter (Bell)
9	7	JOURNEY TO THE CENTRE OF THE EARTH	Rick Wakeman (A&M)
8	8	BAD COMPANY	Bad Company (Island)
7	9	KIMONO MY HOUSE	Sparks (Island)
11	10	GOODBYE YELLOW BRICK ROAD	Elton John (DJM)
13	11	SHEET MUSIC	10 C.C. (UK)
15	12	THE DARK SIDE OF THE MOON	Pink Floyd (Harvest)
20	13	THE WAY WE WERE	Andy Williams (CBS)
17	14	BEHIND CLOSED DOORS	Charlie Rich (Epic)
25	15	THE STING	Soundtrack (MCA)
12	16	AZNAVOUR SINGS AZNAVOUR VOL 3	Charles Aznavour (Barclay)
19	17	AND I LOVE YOU SO	Perry Como (RCA)
-	18	BETWEEN TODAY AND YESTERDAY	Alan Price (Warner Bros.)
-	19	ANOTHER TIME, ANOTHER PLACE	Bryan Ferry (Island)
16	20	THE PSYCHOMODO	Cockney Rebel (EMI)
14	21	22 ELECTRIFYING HITS	Various Artists (K-Tel)
24	22	HIS 12 GREATEST HITS	Neil Diamond (MCA)
18	23	DIANA AND MARVIN	Diana Ross & Marvin Gaye (Tamla Motown)
21	24	SUPER BAD	Various Artists (K-Tel)
-	25	CAMEMBERT ELECTRIQUE	Gong (Virgin)
30	26	PHAEDRA	Tangerine Dream (Virgin)
-	27	ATLANTIC BLACK GOLD	Various Artists (Atlantic)
-	28	GLEN CAMPBELL'S GREATEST HITS	Glen Campbell (Capitol)
10	29	QUO	Status Quo (Vertigo)
-	30	SIMON AND GARFUNKEL'S GREATEST HITS	Simon & Garfunkel (CBS)

This period ends with a Top 5 of real mega-sellers. McCartney's *Band On The Run* had been a slow riser (first charting the previous December) but would end up the second best-selling LP of the year, in Britain and the USA. The Carpenters' *The Singles 1969-1973* would beat it in the UK, with Mike Oldfield's *Tubular Bells* third (17th in the USA). Elton John's *Caribou* would be 1974's 15th best-seller here and its 12th in the USA. Bowie's *Diamond Dogs* would be Britain's 14th best-seller.

July – August 1974

Bob Dylan and the Band's live double-album *Before The Flood* charted. Dylan's first live album, it set a precedent in failing to capture anything remotely close to the highlights of the tour it tried to represent. Later, the triple-LP *Bob Dylan At Budokan* would offer no hint at all of the rigorous splendours of the 1978 tours; nor would *Real Live*, 1984, illuminate that year's march through Europe.

In a London hotel-room on July 29, 1974, Mama Cass Elliott died, aged 31.

August – September 1974

17 August 1974

last	this		
1	1	BAND ON THE RUN	Paul McCartney & Wings (Parlophone)
2	2	TUBULAR BELLS	Mike Oldfield (Virgin)
5	3	THE SINGLES 1969-1973	Carpenters (A&M)
3	4	CARIBOU	Elton John (DJM)
4	5	ANOTHER TIME, ANOTHER PLACE	Bryan Ferry (Island)
6	6	KIMONO MY HOUSE	Sparks (Island)
8	7	THE DARK SIDE OF THE MOON	Pink Floyd (Harvest)
7	8	JOURNEY TO THE CENTRE OF THE EARTH	Rick Wakeman (A&M)
9	9	AND I LOVE YOU SO	Perry Como (RCA)
11	10	DIAMOND DOGS	David Bowie (RCA)
12	11	SHEET MUSIC	10 C.C. (UK)
21	12	DAVID CASSIDY LIVE	David Cassidy (Bell)
14	13	FULFILLINGNESS' FIRST FINALE	Stevie Wonder (Tamla Motown)
15	14	HIS 12 GREATEST HITS	Neil Diamond (MCA)
-	15	WELCOME BACK MY FRIENDS TO THE SHOW THAT NEVER ENDS	Emerson, Lake & Palmer (Manticore)
10	16	GOODBYE YELLOW BRICK ROAD	Elton John (DJM)
13	17	REMEMBER ME THIS WAY	Gary Glitter (Bell)
-	18	ROCK YOUR BABY	George McCrae (Jay Boy)
19	19	BEFORE THE FLOOD	Bob Dylan (Island)
27	20	DIANA AND MARVIN	Diana Ross & Marvin Gaye (Tamla Motown)
-	21	461 OCEAN BOULEVARD	Eric Clapton (RSO)
23	22	SOLO CONCERT	Billy Connolly (Transatlantic)
22	23	20 SMASH HITS	Various Artists (Arcade)
17	24	SIMON AND GARFUNKEL'S GREATEST HITS	Simon & Garfunkel (CBS)
18	25	LAUGHTER IN THE RAIN	Neil Sedaka (Polydor)
16	26	BAD COMPANY	Bad Company (Island)
-	27	GLEN CAMPBELL'S GREATEST HITS	Glen Campbell (Capitol)
-	28	PERRY	Perry Como (RCA)
29	29	INNERVISIONS	Stevie Wonder (Tamla Motown)
-	30	THE THREE DEGREES	Three Degrees (Philadelphia International)

24 August 1974

last	this		
1	1	BAND ON THE RUN	Paul McCartney & Wings (Parlophone)
2	2	TUBULAR BELLS	Mike Oldfield (Virgin)
6	3	KIMONO MY HOUSE	Sparks (Island)
5	4	ANOTHER TIME, ANOTHER PLACE	Bryan Ferry (Island)
3	5	THE SINGLES 1969-1973	Carpenters (A&M)
4	6	CARIBOU	Elton John (DJM)
7	7	THE DARK SIDE OF THE MOON	Pink Floyd (Harvest)
8	8	JOURNEY TO THE CENTRE OF THE EARTH	Rick Wakeman (A&M)
13	9	FULFILLINGNESS' FIRST FINALE	Stevie Wonder (Tamla Motown)
18	10	ROCK YOUR BABY	George McCrae (Jay Boy)
14	11	HIS 12 GREATEST HITS	Neil Diamond (MCA)
9	12	AND I LOVE YOU SO	Perry Como (RCA)
21	13	461 OCEAN BOULEVARD	Eric Clapton (RSO)
17	14	REMEMBER ME THIS WAY	Gary Glitter (Bell)
16	15	GOODBYE YELLOW BRICK ROAD	Elton John (DJM)
11	16	SHEET MUSIC	10 C.C. (UK)
20	17	DIANA AND MARVIN	Diana Ross & Marvin Gaye (Tamla Motown)
15	18	WELCOME BACK MY FRIENDS TO THE SHOW THAT NEVER ENDS	Emerson, Lake & Palmer (Manticore)
-	19	THE PSYCHOMODO	Cockney Rebel (EMI)
10	20	DIAMOND DOGS	David Bowie (RCA)
28	21	PERRY	Perry Como (RCA)
26	22	BAD COMPANY	Bad Company (Island)
22	23	SOLO CONCERT	Billy Connolly (Transatlantic)
19	24	BEFORE THE FLOOD	Bob Dylan (Island)
30	25	THE THREE DEGREES	Three Degrees (Philadelphia International)
29	26	INNERVISIONS	Stevie Wonder (Tamla Motown)
24	27	SIMON AND GARFUNKEL'S GREATEST HITS	Simon & Garfunkel (CBS)
-	28	LIVE AT DRURY LANE	Monty Python's Flying Circus (Charisma)
-	29	OUR BEST TO YOU	Osmonds (MGM)
-	30	EDDY AND THE FALCONS	Wizzard (Warner Bros.)

31 August 1974

last	this		
1	1	BAND ON THE RUN	Paul McCartney & Wings (Parlophone)
2	2	TUBULAR BELLS	Mike Oldfield (Virgin)
5	3	THE SINGLES 1969-1973	Carpenters (A&M)
4	4	ANOTHER TIME, ANOTHER PLACE	Bryan Ferry (Island)
18	5	WELCOME BACK MY FRIENDS TO THE SHOW THAT NEVER ENDS	Emerson, Lake & Palmer (Manticore)
3	6	KIMONO MY HOUSE	Sparks (Island)
7	7	THE DARK SIDE OF THE MOON	Pink Floyd (Harvest)
6	8	CARIBOU	Elton John (DJM)
13	9	461 OCEAN BOULEVARD	Eric Clapton (RSO)
9	10	FULFILLINGNESS' FIRST FINALE	Stevie Wonder (Tamla Motown)
19	11	THE PSYCHOMODO	Cockney Rebel (EMI)
11	12	HIS 12 GREATEST HITS	Neil Diamond (MCA)
8	13	JOURNEY TO THE CENTRE OF THE EARTH	Rick Wakeman (A&M)
25	14	THE THREE DEGREES	Three Degrees (Philadelphia International)
16	15	SHEET MUSIC	10 C.C. (UK)
27	16	SIMON AND GARFUNKEL'S GREATEST HITS	Simon & Garfunkel (CBS)
21	17	PERRY	Perry Como (RCA)
14	18	REMEMBER ME THIS WAY	Gary Glitter (Bell)
23	19	SOLO CONCERT	Billy Connolly (Transatlantic)
12	20	AND I LOVE YOU SO	Perry Como (RCA)
29	21	OUR BEST TO YOU	Osmonds (MGM)
-	22	DAVID CASSIDY LIVE	David Cassidy (Bell)
10	23	ROCK YOUR BABY	George McCrae (Jay Boy)
28	24	LIVE AT DRURY LANE	Monty Python's Flying Circus (Charisma)
17	25	DIANA AND MARVIN	Diana Ross & Marvin Gaye (Tamla Motown)
22	26	BAD COMPANY	Bad Company (Island)
24	27	BEFORE THE FLOOD	Bob Dylan (Island)
15	28	GOODBYE YELLOW BRICK ROAD	Elton John (DJM)
26	29	INNERVISIONS	Stevie Wonder (Tamla Motown)
-	30	BLACK EXPLOSION	Various Artists (Ronco)

7 September 1974

last	this		
1	1	BAND ON THE RUN	Paul McCartney & Wings (Parlophone)
2	2	TUBULAR BELLS	Mike Oldfield (Virgin)
3	3	THE SINGLES 1969-1973	Carpenters (A&M)
9	4	461 OCEAN BOULEVARD	Eric Clapton (RSO)
4	5	ANOTHER TIME, ANOTHER PLACE	Bryan Ferry (Island)
6	6	KIMONO MY HOUSE	Sparks (Island)
-	7	HERGEST RIDGE	Mike Oldfield (Virgin)
21	8	OUR BEST TO YOU	Osmonds (MGM)
10	9	FULFILLINGNESS' FIRST FINALE	Stevie Wonder (Tamla Motown)
5	10	WELCOME BACK MY FRIENDS TO THE SHOW THAT NEVER ENDS	Emerson, Lake & Palmer (Manticore)
8	11	CARIBOU	Elton John (DJM)
7	12	THE DARK SIDE OF THE MOON	Pink Floyd (Harvest)
13	13	JOURNEY TO THE CENTRE OF THE EARTH	Rick Wakeman (A&M)
11	14	THE PSYCHOMODO	Cockney Rebel (EMI)
23	15	ROCK YOUR BABY	George McCrae (Jay Boy)
20	16	AND I LOVE YOU SO	Perry Como (RCA)
14	17	THE THREE DEGREES	Three Degrees (Philadelphia International)
15	18	SHEET MUSIC	10 C.C. (UK)
28	19	GOODBYE YELLOW BRICK ROAD	Elton John (DJM)
12	20	HIS 12 GREATEST HITS	Neil Diamond (MCA)
24	21	LIVE AT DRURY LANE	Monty Python's Flying Circus (Charisma)
-	22	BACK HOME AGAIN	John Denver (RCA)
16	23	SIMON AND GARFUNKEL'S GREATEST HITS	Simon & Garfunkel (CBS)
22	24	DAVID CASSIDY LIVE	David Cassidy (Bell)
30	25	BLACK EXPLOSION	Various Artists (Ronco)
19	26	SOLO CONCERT	Billy Connolly (Transatlantic)
-	27	REMEMBER YOU'RE A WOMBLE	Wombles (CBS)
17	28	PERRY	Perry Como (RCA)
-	29	GLEN CAMPBELL'S GREATEST HITS	Glen Campbell (Capitol)
-	30	EDDY AND THE FALCONS	Wizzard (Warner Bros.)

Billy Connolly's *Solo Concert* was the first of several hit albums by Scotland's great comic. The title *Solo Concert* referred to the fact that he'd been half of the Humblebums, along with singer-songwriter Gerry Rafferty, who had made a well-regarded but non-charting LP of his own, *Can I Have My Money Back?* (also on the British indie label Transatlantic), before forming Stealer's Wheel, which had had a big 1973 hit with *Stuck In The Middle With You* and the more modest *Star* earlier in 1974.

September – October 1974

14 September 1974

last	this	Album	Artist (Label)
1	1	BAND ON THE RUN	Paul McCartney & Wings (Parlophone)
2	2	TUBULAR BELLS	Mike Oldfield (Virgin)
3	3	THE SINGLES 1969-1973	Carpenters (A&M)
4	4	461 OCEAN BOULEVARD	Eric Clapton (RSO)
8	5	OUR BEST TO YOU	Osmonds (MGM)
7	6	HERGEST RIDGE	Mike Oldfield (Virgin)
5	7	ANOTHER TIME, ANOTHER PLACE	Bryan Ferry (Island)
14	8	THE PSYCHOMODO	Cockney Rebel (EMI)
22	9	BACK HOME AGAIN	John Denver (RCA)
12	10	THE DARK SIDE OF THE MOON	Pink Floyd (Harvest)
11	11	CARIBOU	Elton John (DJM)
9	12	FULFILLINGNESS' FIRST FINALE	Stevie Wonder (Tamla Motown)
13	13	JOURNEY TO THE CENTRE OF THE EARTH	Rick Wakeman (A&M)
16	14	AND I LOVE YOU SO	Perry Como (RCA)
17	15	THE THREE DEGREES	Three Degrees (Philadelphia International)
10	16	WELCOME BACK MY FRIENDS TO THE SHOW THAT NEVER ENDS	Emerson, Lake & Palmer (Manticore)
6	17	KIMONO MY HOUSE	Sparks (Island)
-	18	TAPESTRY OF DREAMS	Charles Aznavour (Barclay)
26	19	SOLO CONCERT	Billy Connolly (Transatlantic)
19	20	GOODBYE YELLOW BRICK ROAD	Elton John (DJM)
15	21	ROCK YOUR BABY	George McCrae (Jay Boy)
28	22	PERRY	Perry Como (RCA)
23	23	SIMON AND GARFUNKEL'S GREATEST HITS	Simon & Garfunkel (CBS)
-	24	THE STING	Soundtrack (MCA)
-	25	THE BEATLES 1967-1970	Beatles (Apple)
20	26	HIS 12 GREATEST HITS	Neil Diamond (MCA)
27	27	REMEMBER YOU'RE A WOMBLE	Wombles (CBS)
18	28	SHEET MUSIC	10 C.C. (UK)
-	29	DIAMOND DOGS	David Bowie (RCA)
-	30	BEST OF BREAD	Bread (Elektra)

21 September 1974

last	this	Album	Artist (Label)
6	1	HERGEST RIDGE	Mike Oldfield (Virgin)
2	2	TUBULAR BELLS	Mike Oldfield (Virgin)
1	3	BAND ON THE RUN	Paul McCartney & Wings (Parlophone)
7	4	ANOTHER TIME, ANOTHER PLACE	Bryan Ferry (Island)
9	5	BACK HOME AGAIN	John Denver (RCA)
3	6	THE SINGLES 1969-1973	Carpenters (A&M)
4	7	461 OCEAN BOULEVARD	Eric Clapton (RSO)
10	8	THE DARK SIDE OF THE MOON	Pink Floyd (Harvest)
12	9	FULFILLINGNESS' FIRST FINALE	Stevie Wonder (Tamla Motown)
8	10	THE PSYCHOMODO	Cockney Rebel (EMI)
5	11	OUR BEST TO YOU	Osmonds (MGM)
-	12	HEY!	Glitter Band (Bell)
17	13	KIMONO MY HOUSE	Sparks (Island)
-	14	BLACK EXPLOSION	Various Artists (Ronco)
11	15	CARIBOU	Elton John (DJM)
-	16	RAINBOW	Peters & Lee (Philips)
23	17	SIMON AND GARFUNKEL'S GREATEST HITS	Simon & Garfunkel (CBS)
16	18	WELCOME BACK MY FRIENDS TO THE SHOW THAT NEVER ENDS	Emerson, Lake & Palmer (Manticore)
26	19	HIS 12 GREATEST HITS	Neil Diamond (MCA)
13	20	JOURNEY TO THE CENTRE OF THE EARTH	Rick Wakeman (A&M)
15	21	THE THREE DEGREES	Three Degrees (Philadelphia International)
14	22	AND I LOVE YOU SO	Perry Como (RCA)
28	23	SHEET MUSIC	10 C.C. (UK)
-	24	IN THE HALL OF THE MOUNTAIN GRILL	Hawkwind (United Artists)
-	25	DIANA AND MARVIN	Diana Ross & Marvin Gaye (Tamla Motown)
-	26	BY YOUR SIDE	Peters & Lee (Philips)
-	27	THE BEST OF JOHN DENVER	John Denver (RCA)
-	28	SANTANA'S GREATEST HITS	Santana (CBS)
29	29	DIAMOND DOGS	David Bowie (RCA)
22	30	PERRY	Perry Como (RCA)

28 September 1974

last	this	Album	Artist (Label)
1	1	HERGEST RIDGE	Mike Oldfield (Virgin)
2	2	TUBULAR BELLS	Mike Oldfield (Virgin)
3	3	BAND ON THE RUN	Paul McCartney & Wings (Parlophone)
5	4	BACK HOME AGAIN	John Denver (RCA)
4	5	ANOTHER TIME, ANOTHER PLACE	Bryan Ferry (Island)
6	6	THE SINGLES 1969-1973	Carpenters (A&M)
11	7	OUR BEST TO YOU	Osmonds (MGM)
15	8	CARIBOU	Elton John (DJM)
7	9	461 OCEAN BOULEVARD	Eric Clapton (RSO)
9	10	FULFILLINGNESS' FIRST FINALE	Stevie Wonder (Tamla Motown)
10	11	THE PSYCHOMODO	Cockney Rebel (EMI)
16	12	RAINBOW	Peters & Lee (Philips)
8	13	THE DARK SIDE OF THE MOON	Pink Floyd (Harvest)
28	14	SANTANA'S GREATEST HITS	Santana (CBS)
21	15	THE THREE DEGREES	Three Degrees (Philadelphia International)
12	16	HEY!	Glitter Band (Bell)
23	17	SHEET MUSIC	10 C.C. (UK)
14	18	BLACK EXPLOSION	Various Artists (Ronco)
13	19	KIMONO MY HOUSE	Sparks (Island)
17	20	SIMON AND GARFUNKEL'S GREATEST HITS	Simon & Garfunkel (CBS)
20	21	JOURNEY TO THE CENTRE OF THE EARTH	Rick Wakeman (A&M)
24	22	IN THE HALL OF THE MOUNTAIN GRILL	Hawkwind (United Artists)
-	23	MUD ROCK	Mud (RAK)
-	24	TAPESTRY OF DREAMS	Charles Aznavour (Barclay)
27	25	THE BEST OF JOHN DENVER	John Denver (RCA)
19	26	HIS 12 GREATEST HITS	Neil Diamond (MCA)
-	27	ROCK YOUR BABY	George McCrae (Jay Boy)
-	28	INNERVISIONS	Stevie Wonder (Tamla Motown)
25	29	DIANA AND MARVIN	Diana Ross & Marvin Gaye (Tamla Motown)
18	30	WELCOME BACK MY FRIENDS TO THE SHOW THAT NEVER ENDS	Emerson, Lake & Palmer (Manticore)

5 October 1974

last	this	Album	Artist (Label)
2	1	TUBULAR BELLS	Mike Oldfield (Virgin)
1	2	HERGEST RIDGE	Mike Oldfield (Virgin)
4	3	BACK HOME AGAIN	John Denver (RCA)
3	4	BAND ON THE RUN	Paul McCartney & Wings (Parlophone)
5	5	ANOTHER TIME, ANOTHER PLACE	Bryan Ferry (Island)
6	6	THE SINGLES 1969-1973	Carpenters (A&M)
12	7	RAINBOW	Peters & Lee (Philips)
13	8	THE DARK SIDE OF THE MOON	Pink Floyd (Harvest)
8	9	CARIBOU	Elton John (DJM)
-	10	ROLLIN'	Bay City Rollers (Bell)
9	11	461 OCEAN BOULEVARD	Eric Clapton (RSO)
7	12	OUR BEST TO YOU	Osmonds (MGM)
10	13	FULFILLINGNESS' FIRST FINALE	Stevie Wonder (Tamla Motown)
14	14	SANTANA'S GREATEST HITS	Santana (CBS)
23	15	MUD ROCK	Mud (RAK)
17	16	SHEET MUSIC	10 C.C. (UK)
11	17	THE PSYCHOMODO	Cockney Rebel (EMI)
24	18	TAPESTRY OF DREAMS	Charles Aznavour (Barclay)
18	19	BLACK EXPLOSION	Various Artists (Ronco)
15	20	THE THREE DEGREES	Three Degrees (Philadelphia International)
21	21	JOURNEY TO THE CENTRE OF THE EARTH	Rick Wakeman (A&M)
16	22	HEY!	Glitter Band (Bell)
22	23	IN THE HALL OF THE MOUNTAIN GRILL	Hawkwind (United Artists)
19	24	KIMONO MY HOUSE	Sparks (Island)
-	25	GOODBYE YELLOW BRICK ROAD	Elton John (DJM)
25	26	THE BEST OF JOHN DENVER	John Denver (RCA)
26	27	HIS 12 GREATEST HITS	Neil Diamond (MCA)
27	28	ROCK YOUR BABY	George McCrae (Jay Boy)
28	29	INNERVISIONS	Stevie Wonder (Tamla Motown)
-	30	SOLO CONCERT	Billy Connolly (Transatlantic)

Mike Oldfield's second album, *Hergest Ridge*, was named after a real place on the Welsh border. Another second album, *Remember You're A Womble*, referred to a set of children's TV characters. The Wombles picked up litter on Wimbledon Common. The creator of their jolly, whimsical, and insufferably twee music, Mike Batt, picked up a fortune. The year would end not with a bang but a Womble: the No.3 single for the last week of 1974 was to be *A Wombling Merry Christmas*, their fifth Top 20 hit.

12 October 1974

last week / this week

1	1	TUBULAR BELLS — Mike Oldfield (Virgin)
2	2	HERGEST RIDGE — Mike Oldfield (Virgin)
3	3	BACK HOME AGAIN — John Denver (RCA)
-	4	SMILER — Rod Stewart (Mercury)
4	5	BAND ON THE RUN — Paul McCartney & Wings (Parlophone)
5	6	ANOTHER TIME, ANOTHER PLACE — Bryan Ferry (Island)
11	7	461 OCEAN BOULEVARD — Eric Clapton (RSO)
16	8	SHEET MUSIC — 10 C.C. (UK)
10	9	ROLLIN' — Bay City Rollers (Bell)
6	10	THE SINGLES 1969-1973 — Carpenters (A&M)
15	11	MUD ROCK — Mud (RAK)
9	12	CARIBOU — Elton John (DJM)
14	13	SANTANA'S GREATEST HITS — Santana (CBS)
8	14	THE DARK SIDE OF THE MOON — Pink Floyd (Harvest)
7	15	RAINBOW — Peters & Lee (Philips)
19	16	BLACK EXPLOSION — Various Artists (Ronco)
-	17	HANG ON IN THERE BABY — Johnny Bristol (MGM)
20	18	THE THREE DEGREES (Philadelphia International)
12	19	OUR BEST TO YOU — Osmonds (MGM)
22	20	HEY! — Glitter Band (Bell)
18	21	TAPESTRY OF DREAMS — Charles Aznavour (Barclay)
13	22	FULFILLINGNESS' FIRST FINALE — Stevie Wonder (Tamla Motown)
-	23	WALLS AND BRIDGES — John Lennon (Apple)
26	24	THE BEST OF JOHN DENVER — John Denver (RCA)
21	25	JOURNEY TO THE CENTRE OF THE EARTH — Rick Wakeman (A&M)
23	26	IN THE HALL OF THE MOUNTAIN GRILL — Hawkwind (United Artists)
-	27	SIMON AND GARFUNKEL'S GREATEST HITS — Simon & Garfunkel (CBS)
17	28	THE PSYCHOMODO — Cockney Rebel (EMI)
-	29	THESE FOOLISH THINGS — Bryan Ferry (Island)
-	30	DAVID ESSEX — David Essex (CBS)
-	30	NEW SKIN FOR THE OLD CEREMONY — Leonard Cohen (CBS)

19 October 1974

3	1	BACK HOME AGAIN — John Denver (RCA)
9	2	ROLLIN' — Bay City Rollers (Bell)
5	3	BAND ON THE RUN — Paul McCartney & Wings (Parlophone)
1	4	TUBULAR BELLS — Mike Oldfield (Virgin)
4	5	SMILER — Rod Stewart (Mercury)
2	6	HERGEST RIDGE — Mike Oldfield (Virgin)
6	7	ANOTHER TIME, ANOTHER PLACE — Bryan Ferry (Island)
8	8	SHEET MUSIC — 10 C.C. (UK)
13	9	SANTANA'S GREATEST HITS — Santana (CBS)
23	10	WALLS AND BRIDGES — John Lennon (Apple)
10	11	THE SINGLES 1969-1973 — Carpenters (A&M)
11	12	MUD ROCK — Mud (RAK)
17	13	HANG ON IN THERE BABY — Johnny Bristol (MGM)
15	14	RAINBOW — Peters & Lee (Philips)
24	15	THE BEST OF JOHN DENVER — John Denver (RCA)
22	16	FULFILLINGNESS' FIRST FINALE — Stevie Wonder (Tamla Motown)
16	17	BLACK EXPLOSION — Various Artists (Ronco)
20	18	HEY! — Glitter Band (Bell)
-	19	JUST A BOY — Leo Sayer (Chrysalis)
18	20	THE THREE DEGREES — Three Degrees (Philadelphia International)
7	21	461 OCEAN BOULEVARD — Eric Clapton (RSO)
12	22	CARIBOU — Elton John (DJM)
-	23	MOTOWN CHARTBUSTERS VOL 9 — Various Artists (Tamla Motown)
14	24	THE DARK SIDE OF THE MOON — Pink Floyd (Harvest)
-	25	ODDS 'N' SODS — Who (Track)
-	26	A STRANGER IN MY OWN BACK YARD — Gilbert O'Sullivan (MAM)
-	27	SO FAR — Crosby Stills Nash & Young (Atlantic)
19	28	OUR BEST TO YOU — Osmonds (MGM)
-	29	ROCK YOUR BABY — George McCrae (Jay Boy)
30	30	DAVID ESSEX — David Essex (CBS)

26 October 1974

5	1	SMILER — Rod Stewart (Mercury)
4	2	TUBULAR BELLS — Mike Oldfield (Virgin)
2	3	ROLLIN' — Bay City Rollers (Bell)
1	4	BACK HOME AGAIN — John Denver (RCA)
6	5	HERGEST RIDGE — Mike Oldfield (Virgin)
3	6	BAND ON THE RUN — Paul McCartney & Wings (Parlophone)
10	7	WALLS AND BRIDGES — John Lennon (Apple)
9	8	SANTANA'S GREATEST HITS — Santana (CBS)
11	9	THE SINGLES 1969-1973 — Carpenters (A&M)
7	10	ANOTHER TIME, ANOTHER PLACE — Bryan Ferry (Island)
19	11	JUST A BOY — Leo Sayer (Chrysalis)
30	12	DAVID ESSEX — David Essex (CBS)
8	13	SHEET MUSIC — 10 C.C. (UK)
-	14	IT'S ONLY ROCK 'N' ROLL — Rolling Stones (Rolling Stones)
26	15	A STRANGER IN MY OWN BACK YARD — Gilbert O'Sullivan (MAM)
12	16	MUD ROCK — Mud (RAK)
24	17	THE DARK SIDE OF THE MOON — Pink Floyd (Harvest)
14	18	RAINBOW — Peters & Lee (Philips)
13	19	HANG ON IN THERE BABY — Johnny Bristol (MGM)
22	20	CARIBOU — Elton John (DJM)
25	20	ODDS 'N' SODS — Who (Track)
15	22	THE BEST OF JOHN DENVER — John Denver (RCA)
17	23	BLACK EXPLOSION — Various Artists (Ronco)
29	24	ROCK YOUR BABY — George McCrae (Jay Boy)
-	25	TAPESTRY OF DREAMS — Charles Aznavour (Barclay)
18	26	HEY! — Glitter Band (Bell)
28	27	OUR BEST TO YOU — Osmonds (MGM)
21	28	461 OCEAN BOULEVARD — Eric Clapton (RSO)
23	29	MOTOWN CHARTBUSTERS VOL 9 — Various Artists (Tamla Motown)
16	30	FULFILLINGNESS' FIRST FINALE — Stevie Wonder (Tamla Motown)

2 November 1974

1	1	SMILER — Rod Stewart (Mercury)
3	2	ROLLIN' — Bay City Rollers (Bell)
2	3	TUBULAR BELLS — Mike Oldfield (Virgin)
14	4	IT'S ONLY ROCK 'N' ROLL — Rolling Stones (Rolling Stones)
7	5	WALLS AND BRIDGES — John Lennon (Apple)
6	6	BAND ON THE RUN — Paul McCartney & Wings (Parlophone)
5	7	HERGEST RIDGE — Mike Oldfield (Virgin)
11	8	JUST A BOY — Leo Sayer (Chrysalis)
4	9	BACK HOME AGAIN — John Denver (RCA)
12	10	DAVID ESSEX — David Essex (CBS)
10	11	ANOTHER TIME, ANOTHER PLACE — Bryan Ferry (Island)
20	12	ODDS 'N' SODS — Who (Track)
9	13	THE SINGLES 1969-1973 — Carpenters (A&M)
8	14	SANTANA'S GREATEST HITS — Santana (CBS)
15	15	A STRANGER IN MY OWN BACK YARD — Gilbert O'Sullivan (MAM)
17	16	THE DARK SIDE OF THE MOON — Pink Floyd (Harvest)
29	17	MOTOWN CHARTBUSTERS VOL 9 — Various Artists (Tamla Motown)
16	18	MUD ROCK — Mud (RAK)
13	19	SHEET MUSIC — 10 C.C. (UK)
-	20	THE IMPOSSIBLE DREAM — Sensational Alex Harvey Band (Vertigo)
-	21	CAN'T GET ENOUGH OF YOUR LOVE BABE — Barry White (20th Century)
24	22	ROCK YOUR BABY — George McCrae (Jay Boy)
19	23	HANG ON IN THERE BABY — Johnny Bristol (MGM)
23	24	BLACK EXPLOSION — Various Artists (Ronco)
-	25	STARDUST - SOUNDTRACK — Various Artists (Ronco)
22	26	THE BEST OF JOHN DENVER — John Denver (RCA)
26	27	HEY! — Glitter Band (Bell)
-	28	STONE GON' — Barry White (Pye)
27	29	OUR BEST TO YOU — Osmonds (MGM)
18	30	RAINBOW — Peters & Lee (Philips)

October 12 was the last of four remarkable weeks in which Mike Oldfield had held both the No.1 and the No.2 positions in the album chart. He had no concurrent hit single. The top singles in this four-week period were Carl Douglas' *Kung Fu Fighting*, Peter Shelley's *Gee Baby* (not the Buzzcocks' future lead singer) and Ken Boothe's *Everything I Own*, a cover of an old Bread song done again later by Boy George. None of these 1974 No.1 single-makers would ever have a hit album.

November 1974

last week	this week	9 November 1974
2	1	ROLLIN' Bay City Rollers (Bell)
1	2	SMILER Rod Stewart (Mercury)
8	3	JUST A BOY Leo Sayer (Chrysalis)
4	4	IT'S ONLY ROCK 'N' ROLL Rolling Stones (Rolling Stones)
3	5	TUBULAR BELLS Mike Oldfield (Virgin)
6	6	BAND ON THE RUN Paul McCartney & Wings (Parlophone)
5	7	WALLS AND BRIDGES John Lennon (Apple)
10	8	DAVID ESSEX David Essex (CBS)
13	9	THE SINGLES 1969-1973 Carpenters (A&M)
7	10	HERGEST RIDGE Mike Oldfield (Virgin)
-	11	DAVID LIVE David Bowie (RCA)
15	12	A STRANGER IN MY OWN BACK YARD Gilbert O'Sullivan (MAM)
9	13	BACK HOME AGAIN John Denver (RCA)
21	14	CAN'T GET ENOUGH OF YOUR LOVE BABE Barry White (20th Century)
16	15	THE DARK SIDE OF THE MOON Pink Floyd (Harvest)
25	16	STARDUST - SOUNDTRACK Various (Ronco)
11	17	ANOTHER TIME, ANOTHER PLACE Bryan Ferry (Island)
12	18	ODDS 'N' SODS Who (Track)
14	18	SANTANA'S GREATEST HITS Santana (CBS)
18	20	MUD ROCK Mud (RAK)
-	21	WAR CHILD Jethro Tull (Chrysalis)
-	22	I'M LEAVING IT ALL UP TO YOU Donny & Marie Osmond (MGM)
22	23	ROCK YOUR BABY George McCrae (Jay Boy)
30	24	RAINBOW Peters & Lee (Philips)
17	25	MOTOWN CHARTBUSTERS VOL 9 Various Artists (Tamla Motown)
20	26	THE IMPOSSIBLE DREAM Sensational Alex Harvey Band (Vertigo)
28	27	STONE GON' Barry White (Pye)
26	28	THE BEST OF JOHN DENVER John Denver (RCA)
19	29	SHEET MUSIC 10 C.C. (UK)
23	30	HANG ON IN THERE BABY Johnny Bristol (MGM)

last week	this week	16 November 1974
1	1	ROLLIN' Bay City Rollers (Bell)
2	2	SMILER Rod Stewart (Mercury)
5	3	TUBULAR BELLS Mike Oldfield (Virgin)
3	4	JUST A BOY Leo Sayer (Chrysalis)
4	5	IT'S ONLY ROCK 'N' ROLL Rolling Stones (Rolling Stones)
8	6	DAVID ESSEX David Essex (CBS)
6	7	BAND ON THE RUN Paul McCartney & Wings (Parlophone)
14	8	CAN'T GET ENOUGH OF YOUR LOVE BABE Barry White (20th Century)
13	9	BACK HOME AGAIN John Denver (RCA)
11	10	DAVID LIVE David Bowie (RCA)
15	11	THE DARK SIDE OF THE MOON Pink Floyd (Harvest)
-	12	ELVIS PRESLEY'S 40 GREATEST HITS Elvis Presley (Arcade)
7	13	WALLS AND BRIDGES John Lennon (Apple)
9	14	THE SINGLES 1969-1973 Carpenters (A&M)
-	15	ELTON JOHN'S GREATEST HITS Elton John (DJM)
12	16	A STRANGER IN MY OWN BACK YARD Gilbert O'Sullivan (MAM)
10	17	HERGEST RIDGE Mike Oldfield (Virgin)
-	18	SHEER HEART ATTACK Queen (EMI)
18	19	ODDS 'N' SODS Who (Track)
16	20	STARDUST - SOUNDTRACK Various Artists (Ronco)
-	21	PROPAGANDA Sparks (Island)
21	22	WAR CHILD Jethro Tull (Chrysalis)
18	23	SANTANA'S GREATEST HITS Santana (CBS)
17	24	ANOTHER TIME, ANOTHER PLACE Bryan Ferry (Island)
-	25	BLACK EXPLOSION Various Artists (Ronco)
22	26	I'M LEAVING IT ALL UP TO YOU Donny & Marie Osmond (MGM)
-	27	MEDDLE Pink Floyd (Harvest)
-	28	STORMBRINGER Deep Purple (Purple)
29	29	SHEET MUSIC 10 C.C. (UK)
-	30	HEY! Glitter Band (Bell)

last week	this week	23 November 1974
6	1	DAVID ESSEX David Essex (CBS)
1	2	ROLLIN' Bay City Rollers (Bell)
2	3	SMILER Rod Stewart (Mercury)
12	4	ELVIS PRESLEY'S 40 GREATEST HITS Elvis Presley (Arcade)
15	5	ELTON JOHN'S GREATEST HITS Elton John (DJM)
3	6	TUBULAR BELLS Mike Oldfield (Virgin)
10	7	DAVID LIVE David Bowie (RCA)
8	8	CAN'T GET ENOUGH OF YOUR LOVE BABE Barry White (20th Century)
4	9	JUST A BOY Leo Sayer (Chrysalis)
7	10	BAND ON THE RUN Paul McCartney & Wings (Parlophone)
5	11	IT'S ONLY ROCK 'N' ROLL Rolling Stones (Rolling Stones)
21	12	PROPAGANDA Sparks (Island)
-	13	THIS IS THE MOODY BLUES Moody Blues (Threshold)
18	14	SHEER HEART ATTACK Queen (EMI)
14	15	THE SINGLES 1969-1973 Carpenters (A&M)
-	16	COUNTRY LIFE Roxy Music (Island)
11	17	THE DARK SIDE OF THE MOON Pink Floyd (Harvest)
-	18	SERENADE Neil Diamond (CBS)
13	19	WALLS AND BRIDGES John Lennon (Apple)
16	20	A STRANGER IN MY OWN BACK YARD Gilbert O'Sullivan (MAM)
20	21	STARDUST - SOUNDTRACK Various (Ronco)
9	22	BACK HOME AGAIN John Denver (RCA)
28	23	STORMBRINGER Deep Purple (Purple)
-	24	MOTOWN CHARTBUSTERS VOL 9 Various Artists (Tamla Motown)
-	25	MUSIC EXPLOSION Various Artists (K-Tel)
17	26	HERGEST RIDGE Mike Oldfield (Virgin)
-	27	MUD ROCK Mud (RAK)
22	28	WAR CHILD Jethro Tull (Chrysalis)
-	29	THE BEST OF JOHN DENVER John Denver (RCA)
24	30	ANOTHER TIME, ANOTHER PLACE Bryan Ferry (Island)

last week	this week	30 November 1974
5	1	ELTON JOHN'S GREATEST HITS Elton John (DJM)
2	2	ROLLIN' Bay City Rollers (Bell)
8	3	CAN'T GET ENOUGH OF YOUR LOVE BABE Barry White (20th Century)
4	4	ELVIS PRESLEY'S 40 GREATEST HITS Elvis Presley (Arcade)
1	5	DAVID ESSEX David Essex (CBS)
14	6	SHEER HEART ATTACK Queen (EMI)
6	7	TUBULAR BELLS Mike Oldfield (Virgin)
7	8	DAVID LIVE David Bowie (RCA)
3	9	SMILER Rod Stewart (Mercury)
23	10	STORMBRINGER Deep Purple (Purple)
12	11	PROPAGANDA Sparks (Island)
10	12	BAND ON THE RUN Paul McCartney & Wings (Parlophone)
13	13	THIS IS THE MOODY BLUES Moody Blues (Threshold)
15	14	THE SINGLES 1969-1973 Carpenters (A&M)
16	15	COUNTRY LIFE Roxy Music (Island)
21	16	STARDUST - SOUNDTRACK Various (Ronco)
17	17	THE DARK SIDE OF THE MOON Pink Floyd (Harvest)
11	18	IT'S ONLY ROCK 'N' ROLL Rolling Stones (Rolling Stones)
9	19	JUST A BOY Leo Sayer (Chrysalis)
24	20	MOTOWN CHARTBUSTERS VOL 9 Various Artists (Tamla Motown)
25	21	MUSIC EXPLOSION Various Artists (K-Tel)
19	22	WALLS AND BRIDGES John Lennon (Apple)
27	23	MUD ROCK Mud (RAK)
18	24	SERENADE Neil Diamond (CBS)
22	25	BACK HOME AGAIN John Denver (RCA)
-	26	30 SMASH HITS OF THE WAR YEARS Concert Band & Chorus of the RAF (Crest)
28	27	WAR CHILD Jethro Tull (Chrysalis)
-	28	I'M LEAVING IT ALL UP TO YOU Donny & Marie Osmond (MGM)
-	29	40 ALL TIME HONKY TONK HITS Warren Carr (Robin)
20	30	A STRANGER IN MY OWN BACK YARD Gilbert O'Sullivan (MAM)

Topping both charts was David Essex (single: *Gonna Make You A Star*) above the Rollers (No.5 in the singles). Despite these successes, the LP chart little indicated the prevalence of teenybop acts. Arty albums by people like Yes and Rick Wakeman wearied the grown-ups, let alone teenagers. Grown-ups could opt for pub-rock; the pubescent only had *Top Of The Pops* and puppy-faced idols: Essex, the Rollers, Rubettes, Pilot, Donny, Shawaddywaddy and at a push on the airbrush, Glitter and Suzi Quatro.

December 1974

7 December 1974

last week	this week	
1	1	ELTON JOHN'S GREATEST HITS Elton John (DJM)
4	2	ELVIS PRESLEY'S 40 GREATEST HITS Elvis Presley (Arcade)
2	3	ROLLIN' Bay City Rollers (Bell)
6	4	SHEER HEART ATTACK Queen (EMI)
15	5	COUNTRY LIFE Roxy Music (Island)
5	6	DAVID ESSEX David Essex (CBS)
3	7	CAN'T GET ENOUGH OF YOUR LOVE BABE Barry White (20th Century)
7	8	TUBULAR BELLS Mike Oldfield (Virgin)
10	9	STORMBRINGER Deep Purple (Purple)
11	10	PROPAGANDA Sparks (Island)
9	11	SMILER Rod Stewart (Mercury)
14	12	THE SINGLES 1969-1973 Carpenters (A&M)
13	13	THIS IS THE MOODY BLUES Moody Blues (Threshold)
8	14	DAVID LIVE David Bowie (RCA)
-	15	THERE'S THE RUB Wishbone Ash (EMI)
16	16	STARDUST - SOUNDTRACK Various (Ronco)
17	17	THE DARK SIDE OF THE MOON Pink Floyd (Harvest)
19	18	JUST A BOY Leo Sayer (Chrysalis)
12	19	BAND ON THE RUN Paul McCartney & Wings (Parlophone)
23	20	MUD ROCK Mud (RAK)
24	21	SERENADE Neil Diamond (CBS)
21	22	MUSIC EXPLOSION Various Artists (K-Tel)
-	23	SLADE IN FLAME Slade (Polydor)
25	24	BACK HOME AGAIN John Denver (RCA)
18	25	IT'S ONLY ROCK 'N' ROLL Rolling Stones (Rolling Stones)
-	26	BARBOLETTA Santana (CBS)
26	27	30 SMASH HITS OF THE WAR YEARS Concert Band & Chorus of the RAF (Crest)
-	28	CRIME OF THE CENTURY Supertramp (A&M)
-	29	AND I LOVE YOU SO Perry Como (RCA)
20	30	MOTOWN CHARTBUSTERS VOL 9 Various Artists (Tamla Motown)

14 December 1974

last week	this week	
1	1	ELTON JOHN'S GREATEST HITS Elton John (DJM)
2	2	ELVIS PRESLEY'S 40 GREATEST HITS Elvis Presley (Arcade)
6	3	DAVID ESSEX David Essex (CBS)
7	4	CAN'T GET ENOUGH OF YOUR LOVE BABE Barry White (20th Century)
3	5	ROLLIN' Bay City Rollers (Bell)
4	6	SHEER HEART ATTACK Queen (EMI)
5	7	COUNTRY LIFE Roxy Music (Island)
9	8	STORMBRINGER Deep Purple (Purple)
11	9	SMILER Rod Stewart (Mercury)
8	10	TUBULAR BELLS Mike Oldfield (Virgin)
17	11	THE DARK SIDE OF THE MOON Pink Floyd (Harvest)
10	12	PROPAGANDA Sparks (Island)
-	13	SHOWADDYWADDY Showaddywaddy (Bell)
13	14	THIS IS THE MOODY BLUES Moody Blues (Threshold)
19	15	BAND ON THE RUN Paul McCartney & Wings (Parlophone)
-	16	THE LAMB LIES DOWN ON BROADWAY Genesis (Charisma)
12	17	THE SINGLES 1969-1973 Carpenters (A&M)
20	18	MUD ROCK Mud (RAK)
-	19	RELAYER Yes (Atlantic)
22	20	MUSIC EXPLOSION Various Artists (K-Tel)
14	21	DAVID LIVE David Bowie (RCA)
24	22	BACK HOME AGAIN John Denver (RCA)
15	23	THERE'S THE RUB Wishbone Ash (EMI)
-	24	GOODNIGHT VIENNA Ringo Starr (Apple)
16	25	STARDUST - SOUNDTRACK Various (Ronco)
23	26	SLADE IN FLAME Slade (Polydor)
-	27	SANTANA'S GREATEST HITS Santana (CBS)
-	28	A STRANGER IN MY OWN BACK YARD Gilbert O'Sullivan (MAM)
29	29	AND I LOVE YOU SO Perry Como (RCA)
30	30	MOTOWN CHARTBUSTERS VOL 9 Various Artists (Tamla Motown)

21 December 1974

last week	this week	
1	1	ELTON JOHN'S GREATEST HITS Elton John (DJM)
3	2	DAVID ESSEX David Essex (CBS)
4	3	CAN'T GET ENOUGH OF YOUR LOVE BABE Barry White (20th Century)
2	4	ELVIS PRESLEY'S 40 GREATEST HITS Elvis Presley (Arcade)
5	5	ROLLIN' Bay City Rollers (Bell)
6	6	SHEER HEART ATTACK Queen (EMI)
10	7	TUBULAR BELLS Mike Oldfield (Virgin)
9	8	SMILER Rod Stewart (Mercury)
17	9	THE SINGLES 1969-1973 Carpenters (A&M)
15	10	BAND ON THE RUN Paul McCartney & Wings (Parlophone)
26	11	SLADE IN FLAME Slade (Polydor)
11	12	THE DARK SIDE OF THE MOON Pink Floyd (Harvest)
7	13	COUNTRY LIFE Roxy Music (Island)
13	14	SHOWADDYWADDY Showaddywaddy (Bell)
20	15	MUSIC EXPLOSION Various Artists (K-Tel)
8	16	STORMBRINGER Deep Purple (Purple)
18	17	MUD ROCK Mud (RAK)
29	18	AND I LOVE YOU SO Perry Como (RCA)
21	19	DAVID LIVE David Bowie (RCA)
19	20	RELAYER Yes (Atlantic)
14	21	THIS IS THE MOODY BLUES Moody Blues (Threshold)
22	22	BACK HOME AGAIN John Denver (RCA)
25	23	STARDUST - SOUNDTRACK Soundtrack (Ronco)
-	24	LOVE ME FOR A REASON Osmonds (MGM)
12	25	PROPAGANDA Sparks (Island)
-	26	JUST A BOY Leo Sayer (Chrysalis)
-	27	ENGELBERT HUMPERDINCK'S GREATEST HITS Engelbert Humperdinck (Decca)
27	28	SANTANA'S GREATEST HITS Santana (CBS)
-	29	COP YER WHACK OF THIS Billy Connolly (Transatlantic)
-	30	GOODBYE YELLOW BRICK ROAD Elton John (DJM)

28 December 1974

last week	this week	
1	1	ELTON JOHN'S GREATEST HITS Elton John (DJM)
2	2	DAVID ESSEX David Essex (CBS)
5	3	ROLLIN' Bay City Rollers (Bell)
3	4	CAN'T GET ENOUGH OF YOUR LOVE BABE Barry White (20th Century)
4	5	ELVIS PRESLEY'S 40 GREATEST HITS Elvis Presley (Arcade)
7	6	TUBULAR BELLS Mike Oldfield (Virgin)
12	7	THE DARK SIDE OF THE MOON Pink Floyd (Harvest)
14	8	SHOWADDYWADDY Showaddywaddy (Bell)
6	9	SHEER HEART ATTACK Queen (EMI)
11	10	SLADE IN FLAME Slade (Polydor)
13	11	COUNTRY LIFE Roxy Music (Island)
8	12	SMILER Rod Stewart (Mercury)
20	13	RELAYER Yes (Atlantic)
27	14	ENGELBERT HUMPERDINCK'S GREATEST HITS Engelbert Humperdinck (Decca)
9	15	THE SINGLES 1969-1973 Carpenters (A&M)
16	16	STORMBRINGER Deep Purple (Purple)
24	17	LOVE ME FOR A REASON Osmonds (MGM)
17	18	MUD ROCK Mud (RAK)
10	19	BAND ON THE RUN Paul McCartney & Wings (Parlophone)
18	20	AND I LOVE YOU SO Perry Como (RCA)
15	21	MUSIC EXPLOSION Various Artists (K-Tel)
29	22	COP YER WHACK OF THIS Billy Connolly (Transatlantic)
21	23	THIS IS THE MOODY BLUES Moody Blues (Threshold)
19	24	DAVID LIVE David Bowie (RCA)
-	25	OUR BEST TO YOU Osmonds (MGM)
23	26	STARDUST - SOUNDTRACK Various (Ronco)
-	27	SINGALONGAMAXMAS Max Bygraves (Pye)
-	28	SERENADE Neil Diamond (CBS)
25	29	PROPAGANDA Sparks (Island)
-	30	40 ALL TIME HONKY TONK HITS Warren Carr (Robin)

Typically, Elvis Presley's record-company had leased out the tracks for his 40 Greatest Hits collection to cheapo specialist Arcade. This didn't happen to the other artists with charting hits collections: not Elton John, holding Elvis off the top of the chart, not the Carpenters, Santana nor Engelbert Humperdinck, whose *Greatest Hits* jumped to No.14 over the Christmas period. Engelbert's hits had begun in 1967, with Release Me; his 12th and last Top 30 single had been 1972's *Too Beautiful To Last*.

All sorts charting in the mid 70s:
Tom Jones (top)
Left to right at bottom:
Slim Whitman
Mike Oldfield
Marc Bolan

last this week

4 January 1975

last	this		
1	1	ELTON JOHN'S GREATEST HITS	Elton John (DJM)
2	2	DAVID ESSEX	David Essex (CBS)
4	3	CAN'T GET ENOUGH OF YOUR LOVE	Barry White (20th Century)
3	4	ROLLIN' Bay City Rollers (Bell)	
6	5	TUBULAR BELLS	Mike Oldfield (Virgin)
5	6	ELVIS PRESLEY'S 40 GREATEST HITS	Elvis Presley (Arcade)
13	7	RELAYER Yes (Atlantic)	
9	8	SHEER HEART ATTACK	Queen (EMI)
10	9	SLADE IN FLAME	Slade (Polydor)
18	10	MUD ROCK Mud (RAK)	
7	11	THE DARK SIDE OF THE MOON	Pink Floyd (Harvest)
8	12	SHOWADDYWADDY	Showaddywaddy (Bell)
11	13	COUNTRY LIFE	Roxy Music (Island)
12	14	SMILER Rod Stewart (Mercury)	
14	15	ENGELBERT HUMPERDINCK'S GREATEST HITS	Engelbert Humperdinck (Decca)
15	16	THE SINGLES 1969-1973	Carpenters (A&M)
16	17	STORMBRINGER	Deep Purple (Purple)
26	18	STARDUST - SOUNDTRACK	Various (Ronco)
24	19	DAVID LIVE	David Bowie (RCA)
20	20	AND I LOVE YOU SO	Perry Como (RCA)
19	21	BAND ON THE RUN	Paul McCartney & Wings (Parlophone)
17	22	LOVE ME FOR A REASON	Osmonds (MGM)
30	23	40 ALL TIME HONKY TONK HITS Various Artists (Robin)	
23	24	THIS IS THE MOODY BLUES	Moody Blues (Threshold)
-	25	KEEP ON WOMBLING	Wombles (CBS)
21	26	MUSIC EXPLOSION	Various Artists (K-Tel)
-	27	HERGEST RIDGE	Mike Oldfield (Virgin)
-	28	JUST A BOY	Leo Sayer (Chrysalis)
-	29	RAINBOW	Peters & Lee (Philips)
-	30	SIMON & GARFUNKEL'S GREATEST HITS	Simon & Garfunkel (CBS)

11 January 1975

last	this		
1	1	ELTON JOHN'S GREATEST HITS Elton John (DJM)	
2	2	DAVID ESSEX	David Essex (CBS)
3	3	CAN'T GET ENOUGH OF YOUR LOVE	Barry White (20th Century)
5	4	TUBULAR BELLS	Mike Oldfield (Virgin)
4	5	ROLLIN' Bay City Rollers (Bell)	
11	6	THE DARK SIDE OF THE MOON	Pink Floyd (Harvest)
8	7	SHEER HEART ATTACK	Queen (EMI)
10	8	MUD ROCK Mud (RAK)	
7	9	RELAYER Yes (Atlantic)	
6	10	ELVIS PRESLEY'S 40 GREATEST HITS	Elvis Presley (Arcade)
15	11	ENGELBERT HUMPERDINCK'S GREATEST HITS	Engelbert Humperdinck (Decca)
14	12	SMILER Rod Stewart (Mercury)	
12	13	SHOWADDYWADDY	Showaddywaddy (Bell)
9	14	SLADE IN FLAME	Slade (Polydor)
21	15	BAND ON THE RUN	Paul McCartney & Wings (Parlophone)
16	16	THE SINGLES 1969-1973	Carpenters (A&M)
22	17	LOVE ME FOR A REASON	Osmonds (MGM)
13	18	COUNTRY LIFE	Roxy Music (Island)
20	19	AND I LOVE YOU SO	Perry Como (RCA)
30	20	SIMON & GARFUNKEL'S GREATEST HITS	Simon & Garfunkel (CBS)
19	21	DAVID LIVE David Bowie (RCA)	
18	22	STARDUST - SOUNDTRACK	Various (Ronco)
24	23	THIS IS THE MOODY BLUES	Moody Blues (Threshold)
17	24	STORMBRINGER	Deep Purple (Purple)
-	25	MEDDLE Pink Floyd (Harvest)	
-	26	MOTOWN CHARTBUSTERS VOL 9	Various Artists (Tamla Motown)
-	27	NOT FRAGILE	Bachman Turner Overdrive (Mercury)
-	28	REMEMBER YOU'RE A WOMBLE Wombles (CBS)	
26	29	MUSIC EXPLOSION	Various Artists (K-Tel)
-	30	COP YER WHACK OF THIS	Billy Connolly (Polydor)

18 January 1975

last	this		
1	1	ELTON JOHN'S GREATEST HITS Elton John (DJM)	
2	2	DAVID ESSEX	David Essex (CBS)
3	3	CAN'T GET ENOUGH OF YOUR LOVE	Barry White (20th Century)
5	4	ROLLIN' Bay City Rollers (Bell)	
4	5	TUBULAR BELLS	Mike Oldfield (Virgin)
11	6	ENGELBERT HUMPERDINCK'S GREATEST HITS	Engelbert Humperdinck (Decca)
6	7	THE DARK SIDE OF THE MOON	Pink Floyd (Harvest)
7	8	SHEER HEART ATTACK	Queen (EMI)
9	9	RELAYER Yes (Atlantic)	
8	10	MUD ROCK Mud (RAK)	
19	11	AND I LOVE YOU SO	Perry Como (RCA)
16	12	THE SINGLES 1969-1973	Carpenters (A&M)
10	13	ELVIS PRESLEY'S 40 GREATEST HITS	Elvis Presley (Arcade)
12	14	SMILER Rod Stewart (Mercury)	
15	15	BAND ON THE RUN	Paul McCartney & Wings (Parlophone)
17	16	LOVE ME FOR A REASON	Osmonds (MGM)
14	17	SLADE IN FLAME	Slade (Polydor)
13	18	SHOWADDYWADDY	Showaddywaddy (Bell)
18	19	COUNTRY LIFE	Roxy Music (Island)
27	20	NOT FRAGILE	Bachman Turner Overdrive (Mercury)
20	21	SIMON & GARFUNKEL'S GREATEST HITS	Simon & Garfunkel (CBS)
-	22	CRIME OF THE CENTURY	Supertramp (A&M)
-	23	ROCK YOUR BABY	George McCrae (Jayboy)
24	24	STORMBRINGER	Deep Purple (Purple)
29	25	MUSIC EXPLOSION	Various Artists (K-Tel)
23	26	THIS IS THE MOODY BLUES	Moody Blues (Threshold)
21	27	DAVID LIVE	David Bowie (RCA)
-	28	KEEP ON WOMBLING	Wombles (CBS)
-	29	PROPAGANDA	Sparks (Island)
22	30	STARDUST - SOUNDTRACK	Various (Ronco)

25 January 1975

last	this		
1	1	ELTON JOHN'S GREATEST HITS Elton John (DJM)	
5	2	TUBULAR BELLS	Mike Oldfield (Virgin)
2	3	DAVID ESSEX	David Essex (CBS)
8	4	SHEER HEART ATTACK	Queen (EMI)
6	5	ENGELBERT HUMPERDINCK'S GREATEST HITS	Engelbert Humperdinck (Decca)
4	6	ROLLIN' Bay City Rollers (Bell)	
3	7	CAN'T GET ENOUGH OF YOUR LOVE	Barry White (20th Century)
7	8	THE DARK SIDE OF THE MOON	Pink Floyd (Harvest)
10	9	MUD ROCK Mud (RAK)	
15	10	BAND ON THE RUN	Paul McCartney & Wings (Parlophone)
12	11	THE SINGLES 1969-1973	Carpenters (A&M)
11	12	AND I LOVE YOU SO	Perry Como (RCA)
13	13	ELVIS PRESLEY'S 40 GREATEST HITS	Elvis Presley (Arcade)
21	14	SIMON & GARFUNKEL GREATEST HITS	Simon & Garfunkel (CBS)
9	15	RELAYER Yes (Atlantic)	
22	16	CRIME OF THE CENTURY	Supertramp (A&M)
14	17	SMILER Rod Stewart (Mercury)	
20	18	NOT FRAGILE	Bachman Turner Overdrive (Mercury)
30	19	STARDUST - SOUNDTRACK	Various (Ronco)
19	20	COUNTRY LIFE	Roxy Music (Island)
-	21	SERENADE	Neil Diamond (CBS)
-	22	GOODBYE YELLOW BRICK ROAD Elton John (DJM)	
17	23	SLADE IN FLAME	Slade (Polydor)
16	24	LOVE ME FOR A REASON	Osmonds (MGM)
-	25	MEDDLE Pink Floyd (Harvest)	
-	26	HIS 12 GREATEST HITS	Neil Diamond (MCA)
-	27	COP YER WHACK OF THIS	Billy Connolly (Polydor)
18	28	SHOWADDYWADDY	Showaddywaddy (Bell)
-	29	MOTOWN CHARTBUSTERS VOL 9	Various Artists (Tamla Motown)
-	30	THE THREE DEGREES	Three Degrees (Philadelphia International)

The year began with *Mud Rock* at No.10, while Mud were top of the singles chart with *Lonely This Christmas*, their seventh hit and their third No.1. (The first had been the immortal dance-hall favourite *Tiger Feet*, and the second the less memorable *The Cat Crept In*, top for one week, both in 1974.) Mud, fronted by the decidedly post-adolescent Les Gray, was one of the most successful of the retro-pop bands. *Mud Rock* was the first and most successful of their three Top 30 albums.

February 1975

1 February 1975

last week	this week		
1	1	ELTON JOHN'S GREATEST HITS	Elton John (DJM)
5	2	ENGELBERT HUMPERDINCK'S GREATEST HITS	Engelbert Humperdinck (Decca)
3	3	DAVID ESSEX	David Essex (CBS)
2	4	TUBULAR BELLS	Mike Oldfield (Virgin)
4	5	SHEER HEART ATTACK	Queen (EMI)
11	6	THE SINGLES 1969-1973	Carpenters (A&M)
6	7	ROLLIN' Bay City Rollers (Bell)	
10	8	BAND ON THE RUN	Paul McCartney & Wings (Parlophone)
7	9	CAN'T GET ENOUGH OF YOUR LOVE Barry White (20th Century)	
8	10	THE DARK SIDE OF THE MOON	Pink Floyd (Harvest)
9	11	MUD ROCK	Mud (RAK)
16	12	CRIME OF THE CENTURY	Supertramp (A&M)
13	13	ELVIS PRESLEY'S 40 GREATEST HITS	Elvis Presley (Arcade)
14	14	SIMON & GARFUNKEL'S GREATEST HITS	Simon & Garfunkel (CBS)
18	15	NOT FRAGILE	Bachman Turner Overdrive (Mercury)
15	16	RELAYER	Yes (Atlantic)
17	17	SMILER Rod Stewart (Mercury)	
20	18	COUNTRY LIFE	Roxy Music (Island)
12	19	AND I LOVE YOU SO	Perry Como (RCA)
27	20	COP YER WHACK OF THIS	Billy Connolly (Polydor)
19	21	STARDUST - SOUNDTRACK	Various (Ronco)
26	22	HIS 12 GREATEST HITS	Neil Diamond (MCA)
-	23	STORMBRINGER	Deep Purple (Purple)
-	24	PROPAGANDA Sparks (Island)	
-	25	GET DANCING	Various Artists (K-Tel)
-	26	BRIDGE OVER TROUBLED WATER	Simon & Garfunkel (CBS)
28	27	SHOWADDYWADDY	Showaddywaddy (Bell)
21	28	SERENADE	Neil Diamond (CBS)
-	29	BACK HOME AGAIN	John Denver (RCA)
-	30	ROCK YOUR BABY	George McCrae (Jayboy)

8 February 1975

last week	this week		
1	1	ELTON JOHN'S GREATEST HITS	Elton John (DJM)
2	2	ENGELBERT HUMPERDINCK'S GREATEST HITS	Engelbert Humperdinck (Decca)
4	3	TUBULAR BELLS	Mike Oldfield (Virgin)
5	4	SHEER HEART ATTACK	Queen (EMI)
9	5	CAN'T GET ENOUGH OF YOUR LOVE Barry White (20th Century)	
3	6	DAVID ESSEX	David Essex (CBS)
7	7	ROLLIN' Bay City Rollers (Bell)	
10	8	THE DARK SIDE OF THE MOON	Pink Floyd (Harvest)
12	9	CRIME OF THE CENTURY	Supertramp (A&M)
6	10	THE SINGLES 1969-1973	Carpenters (A&M)
8	11	BAND ON THE RUN	Paul McCartney & Wings (Parlophone)
11	12	MUD ROCK	Mud (RAK)
13	13	ELVIS PRESLEY'S 40 GREATEST HITS	Elvis Presley (Arcade)
15	14	NOT FRAGILE	Bachman Turner Overdrive (Mercury)
14	15	SIMON & GARFUNKEL GREATEST HITS	Simon & Garfunkel (CBS)
21	16	STARDUST - SOUNDTRACK	Various (Ronco)
27	17	SHOWADDYWADDY	Showaddywaddy (Bell)
25	18	GET DANCING	Various Artists (K-Tel)
16	19	RELAYER	Yes (Atlantic)
22	20	HIS 12 GREATEST HITS	Neil Diamond (MCA)
19	21	AND I LOVE YOU SO	Perry Como (RCA)
17	22	SMILER Rod Stewart (Mercury)	
24	23	PROPAGANDA Sparks (Island)	
30	24	ROCK YOUR BABY	George McCrae (Jayboy)
-	25	BLOOD ON THE TRACKS	Bob Dylan (CBS)
-	26	THE BEST OF JOHN DENVER	John Denver (RCA)
-	27	DAVID LIVE	David Bowie (RCA)
-	28	FREE AND EASY	Helen Reddy (Capitol)
28	29	SERENADE	Neil Diamond (CBS)
20	30	COP YER WHACK OF THIS	Billy Connolly (Polydor)

15 February 1975

last week	this week		
2	1	ENGELBERT HUMPERDINCK'S GREATEST HITS	Engelbert Humperdinck (Decca)
1	2	ELTON JOHN'S GREATEST HITS	Elton John (DJM)
3	3	TUBULAR BELLS	Mike Oldfield (Virgin)
4	4	SHEER HEART ATTACK	Queen (EMI)
10	5	THE SINGLES 1969-1973	Carpenters (A&M)
18	6	GET DANCING	Various Artists (K-Tel)
5	7	CAN'T GET ENOUGH OF YOUR LOVE Barry White (20th Century)	
6	8	DAVID ESSEX	David Essex (CBS)
8	9	THE DARK SIDE OF THE MOON	Pink Floyd (Harvest)
7	10	ROLLIN' Bay City Rollers (Bell)	
12	11	MUD ROCK	Mud (RAK)
11	12	BAND ON THE RUN	Paul McCartney & Wings (Parlophone)
9	13	CRIME OF THE CENTURY	Supertramp (A&M)
15	14	SIMON & GARFUNKEL'S GREATEST HITS	Simon & Garfunkel (CBS)
13	15	ELVIS PRESLEY'S 40 GREATEST HITS	Elvis Presley (Arcade)
16	16	STARDUST - SOUNDTRACK	Various (Ronco)
28	17	FREE AND EASY	Helen Reddy (Capitol)
17	18	SHOWADDYWADDY	Showaddywaddy (Bell)
-	19	THE ORCHESTRAL TUBULAR BELLS	Royal Philharmonic Orchestra & Mike Oldfield (Virgin)
-	20	DONNY Donny Osmond (MGM)	
20	21	HIS 12 GREATEST HITS	Neil Diamond (MCA)
21	22	AND I LOVE YOU SO	Perry Como (RCA)
25	23	BLOOD ON THE TRACKS	Bob Dylan (CBS)
14	24	NOT FRAGILE	Bachman Turner Overdrive (Mercury)
30	25	COP YER WHACK OF THIS	Billy Connolly (Polydor)
19	26	RELAYER	Yes (Atlantic)
-	27	SLADE IN FLAME	Slade (Polydor)
-	28	COUNTRY LIFE	Roxy Music (Island)
-	29	BRIDGE OVER TROUBLED WATER	Simon & Garfunkel (CBS)
23	30	PROPAGANDA Sparks (Island)	

22 February 1975

last week	this week		
1	1	ENGELBERT HUMPERDINCK'S GREATEST HITS	Engelbert Humperdinck (Decca)
2	2	ELTON JOHN'S GREATEST HITS	Elton John (DJM)
4	3	SHEER HEART ATTACK	Queen (EMI)
3	4	TUBULAR BELLS	Mike Oldfield (Virgin)
23	5	BLOOD ON THE TRACKS	Bob Dylan (CBS)
9	6	THE DARK SIDE OF THE MOON	Pink Floyd (Harvest)
7	7	CAN'T GET ENOUGH OF YOUR LOVE Barry White (20th Century)	
5	8	THE SINGLES 1969-1973	Carpenters (A&M)
8	9	DAVID ESSEX	David Essex (CBS)
10	10	ROLLIN' Bay City Rollers (Bell)	
13	11	CRIME OF THE CENTURY	Supertramp (A&M)
6	12	GET DANCING	Various Artists (K-Tel)
-	13	ON THE LEVEL	Status Quo (Vertigo)
14	14	SIMON & GARFUNKEL'S GREATEST HITS	Simon & Garfunkel (CBS)
12	15	BAND ON THE RUN	Paul McCartney & Wings (Parlophone)
11	16	MUD ROCK	Mud (RAK)
22	17	AND I LOVE YOU SO	Perry Como (RCA)
-	18	STREETS	Ralph McTell (Warner Bros.)
15	19	ELVIS PRESLEY'S 40 GREATEST HITS	Elvis Presley (Arcade)
16	20	STARDUST - SOUNDTRACK	Various (Ronco)
20	21	DONNY Donny Osmond (MGM)	
24	22	NOT FRAGILE	Bachman Turner Overdrive (Mercury)
18	23	SHOWADDYWADDY	Showaddywaddy (Bell)
25	24	COP YER WHACK OF THIS	Billy Connolly (Polydor)
21	25	HIS 12 GREATEST HITS	Neil Diamond (MCA)
19	26	THE ORCHESTRAL TUBULAR BELLS	Royal Philharmonic Orchestra & Mike Oldfield (Virgin)
-	27	RAINBOW Peters & Lee (Philips)	
-	28	THE MAIN EVENT	Frank Sinatra (Reprise)
-	29	COMMONER'S CROWN	Steeleye Span (Chrysalis)
-	30	MEDDLE Pink Floyd (Harvest)	

Bob Dylan, unhip for years, now charted with *Blood On The Tracks*, which would never go beyond a briefly-held No.5, yet would prove arguably the decade's best "rock" album; even NME made it Album of the Year. Charting the same week was a singer much bigger in America than in Britain, Helen Reddy. *Angie Baby*, her one significant UK single, was about to peak at No.5. Her records claimed a feminist alignment; but British writer Nigel Fountain commented: "I know an Auntie Tom when I see one."

1 March 1975

last week	this week	
2	1	ELTON JOHN'S GREATEST HITS Elton John (DJM)
3	2	SHEER HEART ATTACK Queen (EMI)
4	3	TUBULAR BELLS Mike Oldfield (Virgin)
1	4	ENGELBERT HUMPERDINCK'S GREATEST HITS Engelbert Humperdinck (Decca)
13	5	ON THE LEVEL Status Quo (Vertigo)
5	6	BLOOD ON THE TRACKS Bob Dylan (CBS)
11	7	CRIME OF THE CENTURY Supertramp (A&M)
8	8	THE SINGLES 1969-1973 Carpenters (A&M)
20	9	STARDUST - SOUNDTRACK Various (Ronco)
6	10	THE DARK SIDE OF THE MOON Pink Floyd (Harvest)
12	11	GET DANCING Various Artists (K-Tel)
10	12	ROLLIN' Bay City Rollers (Bell)
14	13	SIMON & GARFUNKEL'S GREATEST HITS Simon & Garfunkel (CBS)
9	14	DAVID ESSEX David Essex (CBS)
7	15	CAN'T GET ENOUGH OF YOUR LOVE Barry White (20th Century)
22	16	NOT FRAGILE Bachman Turner Overdrive (Mercury)
15	17	BAND ON THE RUN Paul McCartney & Wings (Parlophone)
19	18	ELVIS PRESLEY'S 40 GREATEST HITS Elvis Presley (Arcade)
25	19	HIS 12 GREATEST HITS Neil Diamond (MCA)
17	20	AND I LOVE YOU SO Perry Como (RCA)
18	21	STREETS Ralph McTell (Warner Bros.)
23	22	SHOWADDYWADDY Showaddywaddy (Bell)
26	23	THE ORCHESTRAL TUBULAR BELLS Royal Philharmonic Orchestra & Mike Oldfield (Virgin)
24	24	COP YER WHACK OF THIS Billy Connolly (Polydor)
-	25	PROMISED LAND Elvis Presley (RCA)
-	26	THE BEST OF JOHN DENVER John Denver (RCA)
-	27	BRIDGE OVER TROUBLED WATER Simon & Garfunkel (CBS)
-	28	AVERAGE WHITE BAND Average White Band (Atlantic)
-	29	BEST OF BREAD Bread (Elektra)
-	30	MUSIC EXPLOSION Various Artists (K-Tel)

8 March 1975

5	1	ON THE LEVEL Status Quo (Vertigo)
1	2	ELTON JOHN'S GREATEST HITS Elton John (DJM)
3	3	TUBULAR BELLS Mike Oldfield (Virgin)
7	4	CRIME OF THE CENTURY Supertramp (A&M)
2	5	SHEER HEART ATTACK Queen (EMI)
4	6	ENGELBERT HUMPERDINCK'S GREATEST HITS Engelbert Humperdinck (Decca)
6	7	BLOOD ON THE TRACKS Bob Dylan (CBS)
-	8	PHYSICAL GRAFFITI Led Zeppelin (Swansong)
8	9	THE SINGLES 1969-1973 Carpenters (A&M)
15	10	CAN'T GET ENOUGH OF YOUR LOVE Barry White (20th Century)
10	11	THE DARK SIDE OF THE MOON Pink Floyd (Harvest)
13	12	SIMON & GARFUNKEL'S GREATEST HITS Simon & Garfunkel (CBS)
11	13	GET DANCING Various Artists (K-Tel)
12	14	ROLLIN' Bay City Rollers (Bell)
19	15	HIS 12 GREATEST HITS Neil Diamond (MCA)
21	16	STREETS Ralph McTell (Warner Bros.)
18	17	ELVIS PRESLEY'S 40 GREATEST HITS Elvis Presley (Arcade)
14	18	DAVID ESSEX David Essex (CBS)
16	19	NOT FRAGILE Bachman Turner Overdrive (Mercury)
17	20	BAND ON THE RUN Paul McCartney & Wings (Parlophone)
-	21	THE 10TH ANNIVERSARY ALBUM/20 GREATEST HITS Tom Jones (Decca)
9	22	STARDUST - SOUNDTRACK Various (Ronco)
-	23	ROCK 'N' ROLL John Lennon (Apple)
-	24	FOR EARTH BELOW Robin Trower (Chrysalis)
-	25	MUD ROCK Mud (RAK)
20	26	AND I LOVE YOU SO Perry Como (RCA)
-	27	SLADE IN FLAME Slade (Polydor)
-	28	FREE AND EASY Helen Reddy (Capitol)
28	29	AVERAGE WHITE BAND Average White Band (Atlantic)
24	30	COP YER WHACK OF THIS Billy Connolly (Polydor)

15 March 1975

1	1	ON THE LEVEL Status Quo (Vertigo)
2	2	ELTON JOHN'S GREATEST HITS Elton John (DJM)
8	3	PHYSICAL GRAFFITI Led Zeppelin (Swansong)
3	4	TUBULAR BELLS Mike Oldfield (Virgin)
7	5	BLOOD ON THE TRACKS Bob Dylan (CBS)
4	6	CRIME OF THE CENTURY Supertramp (A&M)
21	7	THE 10TH ANNIVERSARY ALBUM/20 GREATEST HITS Tom Jones (Decca)
5	8	SHEER HEART ATTACK Queen (EMI)
6	9	ENGELBERT HUMPERDINCK'S GREATEST HITS Engelbert Humperdinck (Decca)
9	10	THE SINGLES 1969-1973 Carpenters (A&M)
29	11	AVERAGE WHITE BAND Average White Band (Atlantic)
13	12	GET DANCING Various Artists (K-Tel)
23	13	ROCK 'N' ROLL John Lennon (Apple)
11	14	THE DARK SIDE OF THE MOON Pink Floyd (Harvest)
12	15	SIMON & GARFUNKEL'S GREATEST HITS Simon & Garfunkel (CBS)
10	16	CAN'T GET ENOUGH OF YOUR LOVE Barry White (20th Century)
14	17	ROLLIN' Bay City Rollers (Bell)
-	18	THE BEST YEARS OF OUR LIVES Steve Harley & Cockney Rebel (EMI)
-	19	SOULED OUT Various Artists (K-Tel)
16	20	STREETS Ralph McTell (Warner Bros.)
20	21	BAND ON THE RUN Paul McCartney & Wings (Parlophone)
-	22	THE SHIRLEY BASSEY SINGLES ALBUM Shirley Bassey (United Artists)
28	23	FREE AND EASY Helen Reddy (Capitol)
30	24	COP YER WHACK OF THIS Billy Connolly (Polydor)
19	25	NOT FRAGILE Bachman Turner Overdrive (Mercury)
15	26	HIS 12 GREATEST HITS Neil Diamond (MCA)
25	27	MUD ROCK Mud (RAK)
17	28	ELVIS PRESLEY'S 40 GREATEST HITS Elvis Presley (Arcade)
-	29	THE ORCHESTRAL TUBULAR BELLS Royal Philharmonic Orchestra & Mike Oldfield (Virgin)
22	30	STARDUST - SOUNDTRACK Various (Ronco)

22 March 1975

1	1	ON THE LEVEL Status Quo (Vertigo)
3	2	PHYSICAL GRAFFITI Led Zeppelin (Swansong)
6	3	CRIME OF THE CENTURY Supertramp (A&M)
7	4	THE 10TH ANNIVERSARY ALBUM/20 GREATEST HITS Tom Jones (Decca)
2	5	ELTON JOHN'S GREATEST HITS Elton John (DJM)
4	6	TUBULAR BELLS Mike Oldfield (Virgin)
11	7	AVERAGE WHITE BAND Average White Band (Atlantic)
9	8	ENGELBERT HUMPERDINCK'S GREATEST HITS Engelbert Humperdinck (Decca)
22	9	THE SHIRLEY BASSEY SINGLES ALBUM Shirley Bassey (United Artists)
13	10	ROCK 'N' ROLL John Lennon (Apple)
18	11	THE BEST YEARS OF OUR LIVES Steve Harley & Cockney Rebel (EMI)
10	12	THE SINGLES 1969-1973 Carpenters (A&M)
5	13	BLOOD ON THE TRACKS Bob Dylan (CBS)
16	14	CAN'T GET ENOUGH OF THIS LOVE Barry White (20th Century)
15	15	SIMON & GARFUNKEL GREATEST HITS Simon & Garfunkel (CBS)
8	16	SHEER HEART ATTACK Queen (EMI)
19	17	SOULED OUT Various Artists (K-Tel)
14	18	THE DARK SIDE OF THE MOON Pink Floyd (Harvest)
26	19	HIS 12 GREATEST HITS Neil Diamond (MCA)
-	20	WELCOME TO MY NIGHTMARE Alice Cooper (Anchor)
17	21	ROLLIN' Bay City Rollers (Bell)
21	22	BAND ON THE RUN Wings (Parlophone)
12	23	GET DANCING Various Artists (K-Tel)
-	24	BLACK MUSIC Various Artists (Arcade)
-	25	BRIDGE OVER TROUBLED WATER Simon & Garfunkel (CBS)
-	26	YESTERDAYS Yes (Atlantic)
-	27	BLUE JAYS Justin Hayward & John Lodge (Threshold)
20	28	STREETS Ralph McTell (Warner Bros.)
-	29	SLADE IN FLAME Slade (Polydor)
-	30	BEST OF BREAD Bread (Elektra)

Folkie Ralph McTell had charted in late February with *Streets*, and now spent March on the lower rungs before slipping off again. This must have disappointed Warners, who, in the tradition of the day, had tried to take a modest artist and, by pouring money into a heavily-marketed album, transform the scale of his career. The title *Streets* referred to McTell's song *Streets Of London*, which, in his repertoire for years, had topped January's singles chart for a fortnight. It would be his only Top 30 hit.

March – April 1975

29 March 1975

last week	this week	Album	Artist (Label)
2	1	PHYSICAL GRAFFITI	Led Zeppelin (Swansong)
1	2	ON THE LEVEL	Status Quo (Vertigo)
3	3	CRIME OF THE CENTURY	Supertramp (A&M)
4	4	THE 10TH ANNIVERSARY ALBUM/20 GREATEST HITS	Tom Jones (Decca)
5	5	ELTON JOHN'S GREATEST HITS	Elton John (DJM)
11	6	THE BEST YEARS OF OUR LIVES	Steve Harley & Cockney Rebel (EMI)
6	7	TUBULAR BELLS	Mike Oldfield (Virgin)
9	8	THE SHIRLEY BASSEY SINGLES ALBUM	Shirley Bassey (United Artists)
7	9	AVERAGE WHITE BAND	Average White Band (Atlantic)
-	10	THE ORIGINAL SOUNDTRACK	10 C.C. (Mercury)
13	11	BLOOD ON THE TRACKS	Bob Dylan (CBS)
12	12	THE SINGLES 1969-1973	Carpenters (A&M)
14	13	CAN'T GET ENOUGH OF YOUR LOVE	Barry White (20th Century)
27	14	BLUE JAYS	Justin Hayward & John Lodge (Threshold)
8	15	ENGELBERT HUMPERDINCK'S GREATEST HITS	Engelbert Humperdinck (Decca)
15	16	SIMON & GARFUNKEL'S GREATEST HITS	Simon & Garfunkel (CBS)
10	17	ROCK 'N' ROLL	John Lennon (Apple)
-	18	TOMMY	Soundtrack (Polydor)
-	19	I'M COMING HOME	Johnny Mathis (CBS)
18	20	THE DARK SIDE OF THE MOON	Pink Floyd (Harvest)
16	21	SHEER HEART ATTACK	Queen (EMI)
23	22	GET DANCING	Various Artists (K-Tel)
-	23	YOUNG AMERICANS	David Bowie (RCA)
21	24	ROLLIN'	Bay City Rollers (Bell)
-	25	COP YER WHACK OF THIS	Billy Connolly (Polydor)
20	26	WELCOME TO MY NIGHTMARE	Alice Cooper (Anchor)
-	27	TELLY	Telly Savalas (MCA)
22	28	BAND ON THE RUN	Paul McCartney & Wings (Parlophone)
17	29	SOULED OUT	Various Artists (K-Tel)
-	30	AN EVENING WITH JOHN DENVER	John Denver (RCA)

5 April 1975

LW	TW	Album	Artist (Label)
1	1	PHYSICAL GRAFFITI	Led Zeppelin (Swansong)
4	2	THE 10TH ANNIVERSARY ALBUM/20 GREATEST HITS	Tom Jones (Decca)
2	3	ON THE LEVEL	Status Quo (Vertigo)
3	4	CRIME OF THE CENTURY	Supertramp (A&M)
6	5	THE BEST YEARS OF OUR LIVES	Steve Harley & Cockney Rebel (EMI)
5	6	ELTON JOHN'S GREATEST HITS	Elton John (DJM)
9	7	AVERAGE WHITE BAND	Average White Band (Atlantic)
16	8	SIMON & GARFUNKEL'S GREATEST HITS	Simon & Garfunkel (CBS)
10	9	THE ORIGINAL SOUNDTRACK	10 C.C. (Mercury)
8	10	THE SHIRLEY BASSEY SINGLES ALBUM	Shirley Bassey (United Artists)
17	11	ROCK 'N' ROLL	John Lennon (Apple)
7	12	TUBULAR BELLS	Mike Oldfield (Virgin)
23	13	YOUNG AMERICANS	David Bowie (RCA)
14	14	BLUE JAYS	Justin Hayward & John Lodge (Threshold)
-	15	STRAIGHT SHOOTER	Bad Company (Island)
-	16	YESTERDAYS	Yes (Atlantic)
-	17	THERE'S ONE IN EVERY CROWD	Eric Clapton (RSO)
21	18	SHEER HEART ATTACK	Queen (EMI)
-	19	THE MYTHS AND LEGENDS OF KING ARTHUR AND THE KNIGHTS OF THE ROUND TABLE	Rick Wakeman & the English Rock Ensemble (A&M)
15	20	ENGELBERT HUMPERDINCK'S GREATEST HITS	Engelbert Humperdinck (Decca)
12	21	THE SINGLES 1969-1973	Carpenters (A&M)
20	22	THE DARK SIDE OF THE MOON	Pink Floyd (Harvest)
27	23	TELLY	Telly Savalas (MCA)
24	24	ROLLIN'	Bay City Rollers (Bell)
11	25	BLOOD ON THE TRACKS	Bob Dylan (CBS)
29	26	SOULED OUT	Various Artists (K-Tel)
-	27	BEST OF BREAD	Bread (Elektra)
13	28	CAN'T GET ENOUGH OF YOUR LOVE	Barry White (20th Century)
-	29	BLACK MUSIC	Various Artists (Arcade)
28	30	BAND ON THE RUN	Paul McCartney & Wings (Parlophone)

12 April 1975

LW	TW	Album	Artist (Label)
1	1	PHYSICAL GRAFFITI	Led Zeppelin (Swansong)
13	2	YOUNG AMERICANS	David Bowie (RCA)
10	3	THE SHIRLEY BASSEY SINGLES ALBUM	Shirley Bassey (United Artists)
14	4	BLUE JAYS	Justin Hayward & John Lodge (Threshold)
2	5	THE 10TH ANNIVERSARY ALBUM/20 GREATEST HITS	Tom Jones (Decca)
9	6	THE ORIGINAL SOUNDTRACK	10 C.C. (Mercury)
4	7	CRIME OF THE CENTURY	Supertramp (A&M)
5	8	THE BEST YEARS OF OUR LIVES	Steve Harley & Cockney Rebel (EMI)
3	9	ON THE LEVEL	Status Quo (Vertigo)
19	10	THE MYTHS AND LEGENDS OF KING ARTHUR AND THE KNIGHTS OF THE ROUND TABLE	Rick Wakeman & the English Rock Ensemble (A&M)
15	11	STRAIGHT SHOOTER	Bad Company (Island)
6	12	ELTON JOHN'S GREATEST HITS	Elton John (DJM)
-	13	THE BEST OF THE STYLISTICS	Stylistics (Avco)
26	14	SOULED OUT	Various Artists (K-Tel)
12	15	TUBULAR BELLS	Mike Oldfield (Virgin)
7	16	AVERAGE WHITE BAND	Average White Band (Atlantic)
24	17	ROLLIN'	Bay City Rollers (Bell)
25	18	BLOOD ON THE TRACKS	Bob Dylan (CBS)
23	19	TELLY	Telly Savalas (MCA)
11	20	ROCK 'N' ROLL	John Lennon (Apple)
28	21	CAN'T GET ENOUGH OF YOUR LOVE	Barry White (20th Century)
17	22	THERE'S ONE IN EVERY CROWD	Eric Clapton (RSO)
16	23	YESTERDAYS	Yes (Atlantic)
-	24	TOMMY	Soundtrack (Polydor)
18	25	SHEER HEART ATTACK	Queen (EMI)
21	26	THE SINGLES 1969-1973	Carpenters (A&M)
22	27	THE DARK SIDE OF THE MOON	Pink Floyd (Harvest)
30	28	BLACK MUSIC	Various Artists (Arcade)
8	29	SIMON & GARFUNKEL'S GREATEST HITS	Simon & Garfunkel (CBS)
30	30	BAND ON THE RUN	Paul McCartney & Wings (Parlophone)

19 April 1975

LW	TW	Album	Artist (Label)
2	1	YOUNG AMERICANS	David Bowie (RCA)
10	2	THE MYTHS AND LEGENDS OF KING ARTHUR AND THE KNIGHTS OF THE ROUND TABLE	Rick Wakeman & the English Rock Ensemble (A&M)
3	3	THE SHIRLEY BASSEY SINGLES ALBUM	Shirley Bassey (United Artists)
6	4	THE ORIGINAL SOUNDTRACK	10 C.C. (Mercury)
1	5	PHYSICAL GRAFFITI	Led Zeppelin (Swansong)
13	6	THE BEST OF THE STYLISTICS	Stylistics (Avco)
4	7	BLUE JAYS	Justin Hayward & John Lodge (Threshold)
11	8	STRAIGHT SHOOTER	Bad Company (Island)
5	9	THE 10TH ANNIVERSARY ALBUM/20 GREATEST HITS	Tom Jones (Decca)
12	10	ELTON JOHN'S GREATEST HITS	Elton John (DJM)
15	11	TUBULAR BELLS	Mike Oldfield (Virgin)
8	12	THE BEST YEARS OF OUR LIVES	Steve Harley & Cockney Rebel (EMI)
9	13	ON THE LEVEL	Status Quo (Vertigo)
24	14	TOMMY	Soundtrack (Polydor)
7	15	CRIME OF THE CENTURY	Supertramp (A&M)
17	16	ROLLIN'	Bay City Rollers (Bell)
22	17	THERE'S ONE IN EVERY CROWD	Eric Clapton (RSO)
14	18	SOULED OUT	Various Artists (K-Tel)
16	19	AVERAGE WHITE BAND	Average White Band (Atlantic)
26	20	THE SINGLES 1969-1973	Carpenters (A&M)
19	21	TELLY	Telly Savalas (MCA)
18	22	BLOOD ON THE TRACKS	Bob Dylan (CBS)
29	23	SIMON & GARFUNKEL'S GREATEST HITS	Simon & Garfunkel (CBS)
23	24	YESTERDAYS	Yes (Atlantic)
-	25	JUST ANOTHER WAY TO SAY I LOVE YOU	Barry White (20th Century)
-	26	RUBYCON	Tangerine Dream (Virgin)
-	27	ENGELBERT HUMPERDINCK'S GREATEST HITS	Engelbert Humperdinck (Decca)
-	28	IAN HUNTER	Ian Hunter (CBS)
20	29	ROCK 'N' ROLL	John Lennon (Apple)
-	30	COP YER WHACK OF THIS	Billy Connolly (Polydor)

The Average White Band had entered the chart on March 1, and was now peaking at No.7. They were a modest British group, very 1975: they played quiet funk - as if for themselves, rather than an audience - that somehow managed to sound wholly unrelated in spirit to the black music it was based upon. Their first and biggest hit single, *Pick Up The Pieces*, had peaked at No.6 in March. Founding member Robbie McIntosh had died of a drugs overdose the previous September.

26 April 1975

last week	this week	
-	1	ONCE UPON A STAR Bay City Rollers (Bell)
2	2	THE MYTHS AND LEGENDS OF KING ARTHUR AND THE KNIGHTS OF THE ROUND TABLE Rick Wakeman & the English Rock Ensemble (A&M)
6	3	THE BEST OF THE STYLISTICS Stylistics (Avco)
4	4	THE ORIGINAL SOUNDTRACK 10 C.C. (Mercury)
3	5	THE SHIRLEY BASSEY SINGLES ALBUM Shirley Bassey (United Artists)
7	6	BLUE JAYS Justin Hayward & John Lodge (Threshold)
8	7	STRAIGHT SHOOTER Bad Company (Island)
5	8	PHYSICAL GRAFFITI Led Zeppelin (Swansong)
1	9	YOUNG AMERICANS David Bowie (RCA)
14	10	TOMMY Soundtrack (Polydor)
9	11	THE 10TH ANNIVERSARY ALBUM/20 GREATEST HITS Tom Jones (Decca)
16	12	ROLLIN' Bay City Rollers (Bell)
10	13	ELTON JOHN'S GREATEST HITS Elton John (DJM)
12	14	THE BEST YEARS OF OUR LIVES Steve Harley & Cockney Rebel (EMI)
15	15	CRIME OF THE CENTURY Supertramp (A&M)
11	16	TUBULAR BELLS Mike Oldfield (Virgin)
17	17	THERE'S ONE IN EVERY CROWD Eric Clapton (RSO)
13	18	ON THE LEVEL Status Quo (Vertigo)
26	19	RUBYCON Tangerine Dream (Virgin)
18	20	SOULED OUT Various (K-Tel)
19	21	AVERAGE WHITE BAND Average White Band (Atlantic)
-	22	ROCK 'N' ROLL DUDES Glitter Band (Bell)
-	23	MEMORIES ARE MADE OF HITS Perry Como (RCA)
20	24	THE SINGLES 1969-1973 Carpenters (A&M)
21	25	TELLY Telly Savalas (MCA)
27	26	ENGELBERT HUMPERDINCK'S GREATEST HITS Engelbert Humperdinck (Decca)
25	27	JUST ANOTHER WAY TO SAY I LOVE YOU Barry White (20th Century)
-	28	THE DARK SIDE OF THE MOON Pink Floyd (Harvest)
22	29	BLOOD ON THE TRACKS Bob Dylan (CBS)
23	30	SIMON & GARFUNKEL GREATEST HITS Simon & Garfunkel (CBS)

3 May 1975

last	this	
1	1	ONCE UPON A STAR Bay City Rollers (Bell)
3	2	THE BEST OF THE STYLISTICS Stylistics (Avco)
2	3	THE MYTHS AND LEGENDS OF KING ARTHUR AND THE KNIGHTS OF THE ROUND TABLE Rick Wakeman & the English Rock Ensemble (A&M)
6	4	BLUE JAYS Justin Hayward & John Lodge (Threshold)
5	5	THE SHIRLEY BASSEY SINGLES ALBUM Shirley Bassey (United Artists)
4	6	THE ORIGINAL SOUNDTRACK 10 C.C. (Mercury)
7	7	STRAIGHT SHOOTER Bad Company (Island)
16	8	TUBULAR BELLS Mike Oldfield (Virgin)
8	9	PHYSICAL GRAFFITI Led Zeppelin (Swansong)
11	10	THE 10TH ANNIVERSARY ALBUM/20 GREATEST HITS Tom Jones (Decca)
12	11	ROLLIN' Bay City Rollers (Bell)
9	12	YOUNG AMERICANS David Bowie (RCA)
13	13	ELTON JOHN'S GREATEST HITS Elton John (DJM)
27	14	JUST ANOTHER WAY TO SAY I LOVE YOU Barry White (20th Century)
10	15	TOMMY Soundtrack (Polydor)
17	16	THERE'S ONE IN EVERY CROWD Eric Clapton (RSO)
18	17	ON THE LEVEL Status Quo (Vertigo)
14	18	THE BEST YEARS OF OUR LIVES Steve Harley & Cockney Rebel (EMI)
23	19	MEMORIES ARE MADE OF HITS Perry Como (RCA)
24	20	THE SINGLES 1969-1973 Carpenters (A&M)
19	21	RUBYCON Tangerine Dream (Virgin)
21	22	AVERAGE WHITE BAND Average White Band (Atlantic)
20	23	SOULED OUT Various Artists (K-Tel)
15	24	CRIME OF THE CENTURY Supertramp (A&M)
29	25	BLOOD ON THE TRACKS Bob Dylan (CBS)
22	26	ROCK 'N' ROLL DUDES Glitter Band (Bell)
30	27	SIMON & GARFUNKEL GREATEST HITS Simon & Garfunkel (CBS)
28	28	THE DARK SIDE OF THE MOON Pink Floyd (Harvest)
25	29	TELLY Telly Savalas (MCA)
-	30	YESTERDAYS Yes (Atlantic)

10 May 1975

last	this	
1.	1	ONCE UPON A STAR Bay City Rollers (Bell)
2	2	THE BEST OF THE STYLISTICS Stylistics (Avco)
3	3	THE MYTHS AND LEGENDS OF KING ARTHUR AND THE KNIGHTS OF THE ROUND TABLE Rick Wakeman & the English Rock Ensemble (A&M)
4	4	BLUE JAYS Justin Hayward & John Lodge (Threshold)
7	5	STRAIGHT SHOOTER Bad Company (Island)
5	6	THE SHIRLEY BASSEY SINGLES ALBUM Shirley Bassey (United Artists)
6	7	THE ORIGINAL SOUNDTRACK 10 C.C. (Mercury)
8	8	TUBULAR BELLS Mike Oldfield (Virgin)
13	9	ELTON JOHN'S GREATEST HITS Elton John (DJM)
26	10	ROCK 'N' ROLL DUDES Glitter Band (Bell)
10	11	THE 10TH ANNIVERSARY ALBUM/20 GREATEST HITS Tom Jones (Decca)
21	12	RUBYCON Tangerine Dream (Virgin)
11	13	ROLLIN' Bay City Rollers (Bell)
14	14	JUST ANOTHER WAY TO SAY I LOVE YOU Barry White (20th Century)
9	15	PHYSICAL GRAFFITI Led Zeppelin (Swansong)
28	16	THE DARK SIDE OF THE MOON Pink Floyd (Harvest)
-	17	KATY LIED Steely Dan (ABC)
19	18	MEMORIES ARE MADE OF HITS Perry Como (RCA)
17	19	ON THE LEVEL Status Quo (Vertigo)
25	20	BLOOD ON THE TRACKS Bob Dylan (CBS)
20	21	THE SINGLES 1969-1973 Carpenters (A&M)
12	22	YOUNG AMERICANS David Bowie (RCA)
15	23	TOMMY Soundtrack (Polydor)
16	24	THERE'S ONE IN EVERY CROWD Eric Clapton (RSO)
23	25	SOULED OUT Various Artists (K-Tel)
27	26	SIMON & GARFUNKEL GREATEST HITS Simon & Garfunkel (CBS)
-	27	ROCK 'N' ROLL John Lennon (Apple)
22	28	AVERAGE WHITE BAND Average White Band (Atlantic)
-	29	AL GREEN'S GREATEST HITS Al Green (London)
18	30	THE BEST YEARS OF OUR LIVES Steve Harley & Cockney Rebel (EMI)

17 May 1975

last	this	
1	1	ONCE UPON A STAR Bay City Rollers (Bell)
2	2	THE BEST OF THE STYLISTICS Stylistics (Avco)
6	3	THE SHIRLEY BASSEY SINGLES ALBUM Shirley Bassey (United Artists)
13	4	ROLLIN' Bay City Rollers (Bell)
3	5	THE MYTHS AND LEGENDS OF KING ARTHUR AND THE KNIGHTS OF THE ROUND TABLE Rick Wakeman & the English RocK Ensemble (A&M)
5	6	STRAIGHT SHOOTER Bad Company (Island)
7	7	THE ORIGINAL SOUNDTRACK 10 C.C. (Mercury)
8	8	TUBULAR BELLS Mike Oldfield (Virgin)
4	9	BLUE JAYS Justin Hayward & John Lodge (Threshold)
21	10	THE SINGLES 1969-1973 Carpenters (A&M)
14	11	JUST ANOTHER WAY TO SAY I LOVE YOU Barry White (20th Century)
9	12	ELTON JOHN'S GREATEST HITS Elton John (DJM)
11	13	THE 10TH ANNIVERSARY ALBUM/20 GREATEST HITS Tom Jones (Decca)
27	14	ROCK 'N' ROLL John Lennon (Apple)
10	15	ROCK 'N' ROLL DUDES Glitter Band (Bell)
12	16	RUBYCON Tangerine Dream (Virgin)
15	17	PHYSICAL GRAFFITI Led Zeppelin (Swansong)
26	18	SIMON & GARFUNKEL GREATEST HITS Simon & Garfunkel (CBS)
18	19	MEMORIES ARE MADE OF HITS Perry Como (RCA)
16	20	THE DARK SIDE OF THE MOON Pink Floyd (Harvest)
-	21	IAN HUNTER Ian Hunter (CBS)
24	22	THERE'S ONE IN EVERY CROWD Eric Clapton (RSO)
-	23	THE BEST OF TAMMY WYNETTE Tammy Wynette (Epic)
-	24	GLEN CAMPBELL'S GREATEST HITS Glen Campbell (Capitol)
25	25	SOULED OUT Various Artists (K-Tel)
29	26	AL GREEN'S GREATEST HITS Al Green (London)
-	27	TOMORROW BELONGS TO ME Sensational Alex Harvey Band (Phonogram)
23	28	TOMMY Soundtrack (Polydor)
-	29	STAMPEDE Doobie Brothers (Warner Bros.)
-	30	CRIME OF THE CENTURY Supertramp (A&M)

Once Upon A Star leapt in at No.1, above the Stylistics, a group no-one seemed to notice was always charting. Their hit 45s had started in 1972, with *Betcha By Golly Wow* and *I'm Stone In Love With You*; they regained the Top 10 with 1974's *Rockin' Roll Baby, You Make Me Feel Brand New* and *Let's Put It All Together. Star On A TV Show* had made No.13; *Sing Baby Sing* would soon reach No.3; in August *I Can't Give You Anything (But My Love)* would be No.1.

May – June 1975

24 May 1975

last week	this week	
1	1	ONCE UPON A STAR Bay City Rollers (Bell)
2	2	THE BEST OF THE STYLISTICS Stylistics (Avco)
5	3	THE MYTHS AND LEGENDS OF KING ARTHUR AND THE KNIGHTS OF THE ROUND TABLE Rick Wakeman & The English Rock Ensemble (A&M)
7	4	THE ORIGINAL SOUNDTRACK 10 C.C. (Mercury)
9	5	BLUE JAYS Justin Hayward & John Lodge (Threshold)
3	6	THE SHIRLEY BASSEY SINGLES ALBUM Shirley Bassey (United Artists)
13	7	THE 10TH ANNIVERSARY ALBUM/20 GREATEST HITS Tom Jones (Decca)
11	8	JUST ANOTHER WAY TO SAY I LOVE YOU Barry White (20th Century)
4	9	ROLLIN' Bay City Rollers (Bell)
12	10	ELTON JOHN'S GREATEST HITS Elton John (DJM)
-	11	TAKE GOOD CARE OF YOURSELF Three Degrees (Philadelphia International)
-	12	AUTOBAHN Kraftwerk (Vertigo)
10	13	THE SINGLES 1969-1973 Carpenters (A&M)
8	14	TUBULAR BELLS Mike Oldfield (Virgin)
6	15	STRAIGHT SHOOTER Bad Company (Island)
16	16	RUBYCON Tangerine Dream (Virgin)
23	17	THE BEST OF TAMMY WYNETTE Tammy Wynette (Epic)
-	18	FOX Fox (GTO)
14	19	ROCK 'N' ROLL John Lennon (Apple)
27	20	TOMORROW BELONGS TO ME Sensational Alex Harvey Band (Phonogram)
20	21	THE DARK SIDE OF THE MOON Pink Floyd (Harvest)
-	22	CAN'T GET ENOUGH OF YOUR LOVE Barry White (20th Century)
17	23	PHYSICAL GRAFFITI Led Zeppelin (Swansong)
25	24	SOULED OUT Various (K-Tel)
26	25	AL GREEN'S GREATEST HITS Al Green (London)
-	26	24 CARAT PURPLE Deep Purple (Purple)
18	27	SIMON & GARFUNKEL'S GREATEST HITS Simon & Garfunkel (CBS)
-	28	ON THE LEVEL Status Quo (Vertigo)
-	29	ENGELBERT HUMPERDINCK'S GREATEST HITS Engelbert Humperdinck (Decca)
24	30	GLEN CAMPBELL'S GREATEST HITS Glen Campbell (Capitol)

31 May 1975

last week	this week	
1	1	ONCE UPON A STAR Bay City Rollers (Bell)
2	2	THE BEST OF THE STYLISTICS Stylistics (Avco)
17	3	THE BEST OF TAMMY WYNETTE Tammy Wynette (Epic)
-	4	CAPTAIN FANTASTIC AND THE BROWN DIRT COWBOY Elton John (DJM)
12	5	AUTOBAHN Kraftwerk (Vertigo)
4	6	THE ORIGINAL SOUNDTRACK 10 C.C. (Mercury)
18	7	FOX Fox (GTO)
14	8	TUBULAR BELLS Mike Oldfield (Virgin)
13	9	THE SINGLES 1969-1973 Carpenters (A&M)
6	10	THE SHIRLEY BASSEY SINGLES ALBUM Shirley Bassey (United Artists)
10	11	ELTON JOHN'S GREATEST HITS Elton John (DJM)
9	12	ROLLIN' Bay City Rollers (Bell)
11	13	TAKE GOOD CARE OF YOURSELF Three Degrees (Philadelphia International)
7	14	THE 10TH ANNIVERSARY ALBUM/20 GREATEST HITS Tom Jones (Decca)
8	15	JUST ANOTHER WAY TO SAY I LOVE YOU Barry White (20th Century)
26	16	24 CARAT PURPLE Deep Purple (Purple)
5	17	BLUE JAYS Justin Hayward & John Lodge (Threshold)
-	18	STAMPEDE Doobie Brothers (Warner Bros.)
15	19	STRAIGHT SHOOTER Bad Company (Island)
23	20	PHYSICAL GRAFFITI Led Zeppelin (Swansong)
16	21	RUBYCON Tangerine Dream (Virgin)
3	22	THE MYTHS AND LEGENDS OF KING ARTHUR AND THE KNIGHTS OF THE ROUND TABLE Rick Wakeman & the English Rock Ensemble (A&M)
19	23	ROCK 'N' ROLL John Lennon (Apple)
25	24	AL GREEN'S GREATEST HITS Al Green (London)
-	25	ROCKET Various Artists (Arcade)
-	26	IAN HUNTER Ian Hunter (CBS)
21	27	THE DARK SIDE OF THE MOON Pink Floyd (Harvest)
-	28	JUDITH Judy Collins (Elektra)
27	29	SIMON & GARFUNKEL GREATEST HITS Simon & Garfunkel (CBS)
20	30	TOMORROW BELONGS TO ME Sensational Alex Harvey Band (Phonogram)

7 June 1975

last week	this week	
1	1	ONCE UPON A STAR Bay City Rollers (Bell)
2	2	THE BEST OF THE STYLISTICS Stylistics (Avco)
4	3	CAPTAIN FANTASTIC AND THE BROWN DIRT COWBOY Elton John (DJM)
3	4	THE BEST OF TAMMY WYNETTE Tammy Wynette (Epic)
6	5	THE ORIGINAL SOUNDTRACK 10 C.C. (Mercury)
5	6	AUTOBAHN Kraftwerk (Vertigo)
7	7	FOX Fox (GTO)
9	8	THE SINGLES 1969-1973 Carpenters (A&M)
15	9	JUST ANOTHER WAY TO SAY I LOVE YOU Barry White (20th Century)
8	10	TUBULAR BELLS Mike Oldfield (Virgin)
12	11	ROLLIN' Bay City Rollers (Bell)
28	12	JUDITH Judy Collins (Elektra)
10	13	THE SHIRLEY BASSEY SINGLES ALBUM Shirley Bassey (United Artists)
13	14	TAKE GOOD CARE OF YOURSELF Three Degrees (Philadelphia International)
17	15	BLUE JAYS Justin Hayward & John Lodge (Threshold)
11	16	ELTON JOHN'S GREATEST HITS Elton John (DJM)
14	17	THE 10TH ANNIVERSARY ALBUM/20 GREATEST HITS Tom Jones (Decca)
19	18	STRAIGHT SHOOTER Bad Company (Island)
22	19	THE MYTHS AND LEGENDS OF KING ARTHUR AND THE KNIGHTS OF THE ROUND TABLE Rick Wakeman & the English Rock Ensemble (A&M)
20	20	PHYSICAL GRAFFITI Led Zeppelin (Swansong)
21	21	RUBYCON Tangerine Dream (Virgin)
29	22	SIMON & GARFUNKEL GREATEST HITS Simon & Garfunkel (CBS)
16	23	24 CARAT PURPLE Deep Purple (Purple)
27	24	THE DARK SIDE OF THE MOON Pink Floyd (Harvest)
24	25	AL GREEN'S GREATEST HITS Al Green (London)
18	26	STAMPEDE Doobie Brothers (Warner Bros.)
25	27	ROCKET Various Artists (Arcade)
-	28	MUSIC POWER Various Artists (K-Tel)
23	29	ROCK 'N' ROLL John Lennon (Apple)
-	30	KATY LIED Steely Dan (ABC)

14 June 1975

last week	this week	
3	1	CAPTAIN FANTASTIC AND THE BROWN DIRT COWBOY Elton John (DJM)
2	2	THE BEST OF THE STYLISTICS Stylistics (Avco)
1	3	ONCE UPON A STAR Bay City Rollers (Bell)
5	4	THE ORIGINAL SOUNDTRACK 10 C.C. (Mercury)
4	5	THE BEST OF TAMMY WYNETTE Tammy Wynette (Epic)
6	6	AUTOBAHN Kraftwerk (Vertigo)
12	7	JUDITH Judy Collins (Elektra)
-	8	VENUS AND MARS Wings (Apple)
7	9	FOX Fox (GTO)
10	10	TUBULAR BELLS Mike Oldfield (Virgin)
14	11	TAKE GOOD CARE OF YOURSELF Three Degrees (Philadelphia International)
20	12	PHYSICAL GRAFFITI Led Zeppelin (Swansong)
8	13	THE SINGLES 1969-1973 Carpenters (A&M)
9	14	JUST ANOTHER WAY TO SAY I LOVE YOU Barry White (20th Century)
16	15	ELTON JOHN'S GREATEST HITS Elton John (DJM)
11	16	ROLLIN' Bay City Rollers (Bell)
23	17	24 CARAT PURPLE Deep Purple (Purple)
19	18	THE MYTHS AND LEGENDS OF KING ARTHUR AND THE KNIGHTS OF THE ROUND TABLE Rick Wakeman & the English Rock Ensemble (A&M)
-	19	I FEEL A SONG Gladys Knight & the Pips (Buddah)
17	20	THE 10TH ANNIVERSARY ALBUM/20 GREATEST HITS Tom Jones (Decca)
15	21	BLUE JAYS Justin Hayward & John Lodge (Threshold)
18	22	STRAIGHT SHOOTER Bad Company (Island)
22	23	SIMON & GARFUNKEL GREATEST HITS Simon & Garfunkel (CBS)
26	24	STAMPEDE Doobie Brothers (Warner Bros.)
-	25	WARRIOR ON THE EDGE OF TIME Hawkwind (United Artists)
-	26	GREATEST HITS OF 10 C.C. 10 C.C. (UK)
28	27	MUSIC POWER Various Artists (K-Tel)
21	28	RUBYCON Tangerine Dream (Virgin)
24	29	THE DARK SIDE OF THE MOON Pink Floyd (Harvest)
13	30	THE SHIRLEY BASSEY SINGLES ALBUM Shirley Bassey (United Artists)

John Lennon's retro-album *Rock'N'Roll*, produced by Phil Spector, was not reviving his chart fortunes. Entering at No.27 in mid-May, it had jumped to No.14 only to fall back to No.19, then 23, 29, out. The week it left, Paul McCartney's Wings jumped straight into the Top 10 at No.8 with *Venus And Mars*. Barry White, a large man with a curiously tuneless voice and a certain sexual *je ne sais quoi* for Medallion Woman, was enjoying, briefly, two hit albums.

21 June 1975

last week	this week	
1	1	CAPTAIN FANTASTIC AND THE BROWN DIRT COWBOY Elton John (DJM)
2	2	THE BEST OF THE STYLISTICS Stylistics (Avco)
3	3	ONCE UPON A STAR Bay City Rollers (Bell)
4	4	THE ORIGINAL SOUNDTRACK 10 C.C. (Mercury)
5	5	THE BEST OF TAMMY WYNETTE Tammy Wynette (Epic)
8	6	VENUS AND MARS Wings (Apple)
6	7	AUTOBAHN Kraftwerk (Vertigo)
11	8	TAKE GOOD CARE OF YOURSELF Three Degrees (Philadelphia International)
10	9	TUBULAR BELLS Mike Oldfield (Virgin)
9	10	FOX Fox (GTO)
7	11	JUDITH Judy Collins (Elektra)
26	12	GREATEST HITS OF 10 C.C. 10 C.C. (UK)
29	13	THE DARK SIDE OF THE MOON Pink Floyd (Harvest)
15	14	ELTON JOHN'S GREATEST HITS Elton John (DJM)
-	15	HORIZON Carpenters (A&M)
16	16	ROLLIN' Bay City Rollers (Bell)
-	17	I'M STILL GONNA NEED YOU Osmonds (MGM)
13	18	THE SINGLES 1969-1973 Carpenters (A&M)
19	19	I FEEL A SONG Gladys Knight & the Pips (Buddah)
18	20	THE MYTHS AND LEGENDS OF KING ARTHUR AND THE KNIGHTS OF THE ROUND TABLE Rick Wakeman & the English Rock Ensemble (A&M)
24	21	STAMPEDE Doobie Brothers (Warner Bros.)
23	22	SIMON & GARFUNKEL'S GREATEST HITS Simon & Garfunkel (CBS)
17	23	24 CARAT PURPLE Deep Purple (Purple)
14	24	JUST ANOTHER WAY TO SAY I LOVE YOU Barry White (20th Century)
12	25	PHYSICAL GRAFFITI Led Zeppelin (Swansong)
20	26	THE 10TH ANNIVERSARY ALBUM/20 GREATEST HITS Tom Jones (Decca)
30	27	THE SHIRLEY BASSEY SINGLES ALBUM Shirley Bassey (United Artists)
-	28	GLEN CAMPBELL'S GREATEST HITS Glen Campbell (Capitol)
-	29	ROCK 'N' ROLL John Lennon (Apple)
22	30	STRAIGHT SHOOTER Bad Company (Island)

28 June 1975

1	1	CAPTAIN FANTASTIC AND THE BROWN DIRT COWBOY Elton John (DJM)
6	2	VENUS AND MARS Wings (Apple)
4	3	THE ORIGINAL SOUNDTRACK 10 C.C. (Mercury)
2	4	THE BEST OF THE STYLISTICS Stylistics (Avco)
3	5	ONCE UPON A STAR Bay City Rollers (Bell)
15	6	HORIZON Carpenters (A&M)
7	7	AUTOBAHN Kraftwerk (Vertigo)
8	8	TAKE GOOD CARE OF YOURSELF Three Degrees (Philadelphia International)
5	9	THE BEST OF TAMMY WYNETTE Tammy Wynette (Epic)
14	10	ELTON JOHN'S GREATEST HITS Elton John (DJM)
9	11	TUBULAR BELLS Mike Oldfield (Virgin)
12	12	GREATEST HITS OF 10 C.C. 10 C.C. (UK)
11	13	JUDITH Judy Collins (Elektra)
10	14	FOX Fox (GTO)
18	15	THE SINGLES 1969-1973 Carpenters (A&M)
16	16	ROLLIN' Bay City Rollers (Bell)
19	17	I FEEL A SONG Gladys Knight & the Pips (Buddah)
17	18	I'M STILL GONNA NEED YOU Osmonds (MGM)
13	19	THE DARK SIDE OF THE MOON Pink Floyd (Harvest)
-	20	STAND BY YOUR MAN Tammy Wynette (Epic)
25	21	PHYSICAL GRAFFITI Led Zeppelin (Swansong)
20	22	THE MYTHS AND LEGENDS OF KING ARTHUR AND THE KNIGHTS OF THE ROUND TABLE Rick Wakeman & the English Rock Ensemble (A&M)
22	23	SIMON & GARFUNKEL'S GREATEST HITS Simon & Garfunkel (CBS)
-	24	BEST OF BREAD Bread (Elektra)
30	25	STRAIGHT SHOOTER Bad Company (Island)
21	26	STAMPEDE Doobie Brothers (Warner Bros.)
23	27	24 CARAT PURPLE Deep Purple (Purple)
-	28	ON THE LEVEL Status Quo (Vertigo)
24	29	JUST ANOTHER WAY TO SAY I LOVE YOU Barry White (20th Century)
27	30	THE SHIRLEY BASSEY SINGLES ALBUM Shirley Bassey (United Artists)

5 July 1975

2	1	VENUS AND MARS Wings (Apple)
1	2	CAPTAIN FANTASTIC AND THE BROWN DIRT COWBOY Elton John (DJM)
6	3	HORIZON Carpenters (A&M)
3	4	THE ORIGINAL SOUNDTRACK 10 C.C. (Mercury)
4	5	THE BEST OF THE STYLISTICS Stylistics (Avco)
5	6	ONCE UPON A STAR Bay City Rollers (Bell)
12	7	GREATEST HITS OF 10 C.C. 10 C.C. (UK)
7	8	AUTOBAHN Kraftwerk (Vertigo)
8	9	TAKE GOOD CARE OF YOURSELF Three Degrees (Philadelphia International)
16	10	ROLLIN' Bay City Rollers (Bell)
13	11	JUDITH Judy Collins (Elektra)
11	12	TUBULAR BELLS Mike Oldfield (Virgin)
9	13	THE BEST OF TAMMY WYNETTE Tammy Wynette (Epic)
15	14	THE SINGLES 1969-1973 Carpenters (A&M)
19	15	THE DARK SIDE OF THE MOON Pink Floyd (Harvest)
14	16	FOX Fox (GTO)
-	17	MADE IN THE SHADE Rolling Stones (Atlantic)
24	18	BEST OF BREAD Bread (Elektra)
10	19	ELTON JOHN'S GREATEST HITS Elton John (DJM)
20	20	STAND BY YOUR MAN Tammy Wynette (Epic)
-	21	ONE OF THESE NIGHTS Eagles (Asylum)
17	22	I FEEL A SONG Gladys Knight & the Pips (Buddah)
27	23	24 CARAT PURPLE Deep Purple (Purple)
22	24	THE MYTHS AND LEGENDS OF KING ARTHUR AND THE KNIGHTS OF THE ROUND TABLE Rick Wakeman & the English Rock Ensemble (A&M)
-	25	SNOWFLAKES ARE DANCING Tomita (Red Seal)
18	26	I'M STILL GONNA NEED YOU Osmonds (MGM)
-	27	RUBYCON Tangerine Dream (Virgin)
-	28	BAND ON THE RUN Paul McCartney & Wings (Parlophone)
23	29	SIMON & GARFUNKEL GREATEST HITS Simon & Garfunkel (CBS)
-	30	CUT THE CAKE Average White Band (Atlantic)

12 July 1975

1	1	VENUS AND MARS Wings (Apple)
3	2	HORIZON Carpenters (A&M)
2	3	CAPTAIN FANTASTIC AND THE BROWN DIRT COWBOY Elton John (DJM)
4	4	THE ORIGINAL SOUNDTRACK 10 C.C. (Mercury)
6	5	ONCE UPON A STAR Bay City Rollers (Bell)
5	6	THE BEST OF THE STYLISTICS Stylistics (Avco)
13	7	THE BEST OF TAMMY WYNETTE Tammy Wynette (Epic)
7	8	GREATEST HITS OF 10 C.C. 10 C.C. (UK)
12	9	TUBULAR BELLS Mike Oldfield (Virgin)
14	10	THE SINGLES 1969-1973 Carpenters (A&M)
8	11	AUTOBAHN Kraftwerk (Vertigo)
9	12	TAKE GOOD CARE OF YOURSELF Three Degrees (Philadelphia International)
23	13	24 CARAT PURPLE Deep Purple (Purple)
19	14	ELTON JOHN'S GREATEST HITS Elton John (DJM)
17	15	MADE IN THE SHADE Rolling Stones (Atlantic)
10	16	ROLLIN' Bay City Rollers (Bell)
11	17	JUDITH Judy Collins (Elektra)
-	18	PHYSICAL GRAFFITI Led Zeppelin (Swansong)
25	19	SNOWFLAKES ARE DANCING Tomita (Red Seal)
-	20	RETURN TO FANTASY Uriah Heep (Bronze)
20	21	STAND BY YOUR MAN Tammy Wynette (Epic)
22	22	I FEEL A SONG Gladys Knight & the Pips (Buddah)
-	23	THANK YOU BABY Stylistics (Avco)
15	24	THE DARK SIDE OF THE MOON Pink Floyd (Harvest)
-	25	STEP TWO Showaddywaddy (Bell)
29	26	SIMON & GARFUNKEL GREATEST HITS Simon & Garfunkel (CBS)
28	27	BAND ON THE RUN Paul McCartney & Wings (Parlophone)
16	28	FOX Fox (GTO)
21	29	ONE OF THESE NIGHTS Eagles (Asylum)
18	30	BEST OF BREAD Bread (Elektra)

Lennon's *Rock' N' Roll* resurfaced briefly at No.29 and then left again. Two weeks later, McCartney had the satisfaction of seeing Wings replace the mega-selling *Captain Fantastic And The Brown Dirt Cowboy* at No.1, where *Venus And Mars* would stay for six weeks. Rick Wakeman was recovering from the shock of the May 31 chart, which had seen the humiliating plummet from No.3 to No.22 of his *Myths And Legends Of King Arthur And The Knights Of The Round Table* (to give it its full if uninteresting title).

July – August 1975

The singles chart was, even by 1970s standards, now oldie-mad. To the old songs revisited were added old records reissued: The Chi-Lites were No.5 with *Have You Seen Her* (their 1972 hit); Brian Hyland was about to peak at No.6 with *Sealed With A Kiss* (one of his 1962 hits); Desmond Dekker was just leaving with *The Israelites* (his 1969 hit). The LP chart oldies collections were joined by Dylan's double-album *The Basement Tapes*, recorded on a home tape machine with the Band in 1967.

16 August 1975

last week	this week		
9	1	THE BEST OF THE STYLISTICS	Stylistics (Avco)
1	2	VENUS AND MARS	Wings (Apple)
2	3	HORIZON	Carpenters (A&M)
4	4	ONCE UPON A STAR	Bay City Rollers (Bell)
3	5	CAPTAIN FANTASTIC AND THE BROWN DIRT COWBOY	Elton John (DJM)
13	6	THANK YOU BABY	Stylistics (Avco)
5	7	MUD ROCK II	Mud (RAK)
7	8	ONE OF THESE NIGHTS	Eagles (Asylum)
11	9	CAT STEVENS' GREATEST HITS	Cat Stevens (Island)
8	10	THE BASEMENT TAPES	Bob Dylan (CBS)
6	11	THE ORIGINAL SOUNDTRACK	10 C.C. (Mercury)
21	12	TEN YEARS NON STOP JUBILEE	James Last (Polydor)
15	13	THE SINGLES 1969-1973	Carpenters (A&M)
20	14	ROLLIN'	Bay City Rollers (Bell)
10	15	STEP TWO	Showaddywaddy (Bell)
29	16	WHEN WILL I SEE YOU AGAIN	Johnny Mathis (CBS)
12	17	TUBULAR BELLS	Mike Oldfield (Virgin)
17	18	THE DARK SIDE OF THE MOON	Pink Floyd (Harvest)
18	19	SNOWFLAKES ARE DANCING	Tomita (Red Seal)
16	20	THE BEST OF TAMMY WYNETTE	Tammy Wynette (Epic)
19	21	ELTON JOHN'S GREATEST HITS	Elton John (DJM)
25	22	RIDE A ROCK HORSE	Roger Daltrey (Polydor)
23	23	24 CARAT PURPLE	Deep Purple (Purple)
24	24	SIMON & GARFUNKEL'S GREATEST HITS	Simon & Garfunkel (CBS)
-	25	FROM MIGHTY OAKS	Ray Thomas (Threshold)
-	26	THE HIGHER THEY CLIMB	David Cassidy (RCA)
22	27	GREATEST HITS OF 10 C.C.	10 C.C. (UK)
-	28	BAND ON THE RUN	Paul McCartney & Wings (Parlophone)
14	29	THE SNOW GOOSE	Camel (Decca)
-	30	TAKE TWO	Diane Solomon (Philips)

23 August 1975

1	1	THE BEST OF THE STYLISTICS	Stylistics (Avco)
2	2	VENUS AND MARS	Wings (Apple)
3	3	HORIZON	Carpenters (A&M)
6	4	THANK YOU BABY	Stylistics (Avco)
4	5	ONCE UPON A STAR	Bay City Rollers (Bell)
8	6	ONE OF THESE NIGHTS	Eagles (Asylum)
5	7	CAPTAIN FANTASTIC AND THE BROWN DIRT COWBOY	Elton John (DJM)
9	8	CAT STEVENS' GREATEST HITS	Cat Stevens (Island)
11	9	THE ORIGINAL SOUNDTRACK	10 C.C. (Mercury)
7	10	MUD ROCK II	Mud (RAK)
20	11	THE BEST OF TAMMY WYNETTE	Tammy Wynette (Epic)
12	12	TEN YEARS NON STOP JUBILEE	James Last (Polydor)
16	13	WHEN WILL I SEE YOU AGAIN	Johnny Mathis (CBS)
-	14	ATLANTIC CROSSING	Rod Stewart (Warner Bros.)
10	15	THE BASEMENT TAPES	Bob Dylan (CBS)
18	16	THE DARK SIDE OF THE MOON	Pink Floyd (Harvest)
13	17	THE SINGLES 1969-1973	Carpenters (A&M)
24	18	SIMON & GARFUNKEL'S GREATEST HITS	Simon & Garfunkel (CBS)
17	19	TUBULAR BELLS	Mike Oldfield (Virgin)
22	20	RIDE A ROCK HORSE	Roger Daltrey (Polydor)
15	21	STEP TWO	Showaddywaddy (Bell)
14	22	ROLLIN'	Bay City Rollers (Bell)
21	23	ELTON JOHN'S GREATEST HITS	Elton John (DJM)
23	24	24 CARAT PURPLE	Deep Purple (Purple)
19	25	SNOWFLAKES ARE DANCING	Tomita (Red Seal)
29	26	THE SNOW GOOSE	Camel (Decca)
26	27	THE HIGHER THEY CLIMB	David Cassidy (RCA)
27	28	GREATEST HITS OF 10 C.C.	10 C.C. (UK)
-	29	DISCO BABY	Van McCoy (Avco)
-	30	MADE IN THE SHADE	Rolling Stones (Atlantic)

30 August 1975

1	1	THE BEST OF THE STYLISTICS	Stylistics (Avco)
3	2	HORIZON	Carpenters (A&M)
5	3	ONCE UPON A STAR	Bay City Rollers (Bell)
2	4	VENUS AND MARS	Wings (Apple)
14	5	ATLANTIC CROSSING	Rod Stewart (Warner Bros.)
4	6	THANK YOU BABY	Stylistics (Avco)
6	7	ONE OF THESE NIGHTS	Eagles (Asylum)
7	8	CAPTAIN FANTASTIC AND THE BROWN DIRT COWBOY	Elton John (DJM)
8	9	CAT STEVENS' GREATEST HITS	Cat Stevens (Island)
10	10	MUD ROCK II	Mud (RAK)
19	11	TUBULAR BELLS	Mike Oldfield (Virgin)
12	12	TEN YEARS NON STOP JUBILEE	James Last (Polydor)
20	13	RIDE A ROCK HORSE	Roger Daltrey (Polydor)
9	14	THE ORIGINAL SOUNDTRACK	10 C.C. (Mercury)
16	15	THE DARK SIDE OF THE MOON	Pink Floyd (Harvest)
17	16	THE SINGLES 1969-1973	Carpenters (A&M)
15	17	THE BASEMENT TAPES	Bob Dylan (CBS)
13	18	WHEN WILL I SEE YOU AGAIN	Johnny Mathis (CBS)
22	19	ROLLIN'	Bay City Rollers (Bell)
25	20	SNOWFLAKES ARE DANCING	Tomita (Red Seal)
28	21	GREATEST HITS OF 10 C.C.	10 C.C. (UK)
27	22	THE HIGHER THEY CLIMB	David Cassidy (RCA)
24	23	24 CARAT PURPLE	Deep Purple (Purple)
30	24	MADE IN THE SHADE	Rolling Stones (Atlantic)
18	25	SIMON & GARFUNKEL'S GREATEST HITS	Simon & Garfunkel (CBS)
26	26	THE SNOW GOOSE	Camel (Decca)
-	27	NEXT	Sensational Alex Harvey Band (Vertigo)
11	28	THE BEST OF TAMMY WYNETTE	Tammy Wynette (Epic)
21	29	STEP TWO	Showaddywaddy (Bell)
-	30	PICTURES AT AN EXHIBITION	Tomita (Red Seal)

6 September 1975

5	1	ATLANTIC CROSSING	Rod Stewart (Warner Bros.)
1	2	THE BEST OF THE STYLISTICS	Stylistics (Avco)
6	3	THANK YOU BABY	Stylistics (Avco)
2	4	HORIZON	Carpenters (A&M)
4	5	VENUS AND MARS	Wings (Apple)
7	6	ONE OF THESE NIGHTS	Eagles (Asylum)
3	7	ONCE UPON A STAR	Bay City Rollers (Bell)
9	8	CAT STEVENS' GREATEST HITS	Cat Stevens (Island)
10	9	MUD ROCK II	Mud (RAK)
11	10	TUBULAR BELLS	Mike Oldfield (Virgin)
8	11	CAPTAIN FANTASTIC AND THE BROWN DIRT COWBOY	Elton John (DJM)
14	12	THE ORIGINAL SOUNDTRACK	10 C.C. (Mercury)
15	13	THE DARK SIDE OF THE MOON	Pink Floyd (Harvest)
12	14	TEN YEARS NON STOP JUBILEE	James Last (Polydor)
13	15	RIDE A ROCK HORSE	Roger Daltrey (Polydor)
16	16	THE SINGLES 1969-1973	Carpenters (A&M)
23	17	24 CARAT PURPLE	Deep Purple (Purple)
19	18	ROLLIN'	Bay City Rollers (Bell)
29	19	STEP TWO	Showaddywaddy (Bell)
-	20	E.C. WAS HERE	Eric Clapton (Polydor)
-	21	THE VERY BEST OF ROGER WHITTAKER	Roger Whittaker (EMI)
-	22	RAINBOW	Ritchie Blackmore (Oyster)
17	23	THE BASEMENT TAPES	Bob Dylan (CBS)
20	24	SNOWFLAKES ARE DANCING	Tomita (Red Seal)
26	25	THE SNOW GOOSE	Camel (Decca)
28	26	THE BEST OF TAMMY WYNETTE	Tammy Wynette (Epic)
18	27	WHEN WILL I SEE YOU AGAIN	Johnny Mathis (CBS)
-	28	TOMMY	Soundtrack (Polydor)
27	29	NEXT	Sensational Alex Harvey Band (Vertigo)
-	30	ELTON JOHN'S GREATEST HITS	Elton John (DJM)

Stylistics time again, with their long-serving *Best Of* album now jumping right back up, this time to No.1, while *Thank You Baby* rose so high that the week the group lost the top spot, September 6, they found themselves at Nos.2 and 3 instead. Their single *I Can't Give You Anything (But My Love)* was knocked off the No.1 slot by Rod Stewart's *Sailing* the week before his album *Atlantic Crossing* knocked *Best Of The Stylistics* from the No.1 LP slot. It was Stewart's fifth consecutive No.1 LP.

September – October 1975

13 September 1975

last	this	Title / Artist (Label)
1	1	ATLANTIC CROSSING Rod Stewart (Warner Bros.)
2	2	THE BEST OF THE STYLISTICS Stylistics (Avco)
4	3	HORIZON Carpenters (A&M)
6	4	ONE OF THESE NIGHTS Eagles (Asylum)
3	5	THANK YOU BABY Stylistics (Avco)
5	6	VENUS AND MARS Wings (Apple)
8	7	CAT STEVENS' GREATEST HITS Cat Stevens (Island)
21	8	THE VERY BEST OF ROG ER WHITTAKER Roger Whittaker (EMI)
7	9	ONCE UPON A STAR Bay City Rollers (Bell)
11	10	CAPTAIN FANTASTIC AND THE BROWN DIRT COWBOY Elton John (DJM)
10	11	TUBULAR BELLS Mike Oldfield (Virgin)
13	12	THE DARK SIDE OF THE MOON Pink Floyd (Harvest)
12	13	THE ORIGINAL SOUNDTRACK 10 C.C. (Mercury)
9	14	MUD ROCK II Mud (RAK)
16	15	THE SINGLES 1969-1973 Carpenters (A&M)
20	16	E.C. WAS HERE Eric Clapton (Polydor)
17	17	24 CARAT PURPLE Deep Purple (Purple)
-	18	STRAIGHT SHOOTER Bad Company (Island)
-	19	ANOTHER YEAR Leo Sayer (Chrysalis)
22	20	RAINBOW Ritchie Blackmore (Oyster)
15	21	RIDE A ROCK HORSE Roger Daltrey (Polydor)
19	22	STEP TWO Showaddywaddy (Bell)
26	23	THE BEST OF TAMMY WYNETTE Tammy Wynette (Epic)
-	24	THE SUN COLLECTION Elvis Presley (RCA)
24	25	SNOWFLAKES ARE DANCING Tomita (Red Seal)
14	26	TEN YEARS NON STOP JUBILEE James Last (Polydor)
28	27	TOMMY Soundtrack (Polydor)
18	28	ROLLIN' Bay City Rollers (Bell)
-	29	SIMON & GARFUNKEL'S GREATEST HITS Simon & Garfunkel (CBS)
-	30	MRS. 'ARDIN'S KID Mike Harding (Transatlantic)

20 September 1975

last	this	Title / Artist (Label)
1	1	ATLANTIC CROSSING Rod Stewart (Warner Bros.)
2	2	THE BEST OF THE STYLISTICS Stylistics (Avco)
3	3	HORIZON Carpenters (A&M)
8	4	THE VERY BEST OF ROG ER WHITTAKER Roger Whittaker (EMI)
7	5	CAT STEVENS' GREATEST HITS Cat Stevens (Island)
4	6	ONE OF THESE NIGHTS Eagles (Asylum)
5	7	THANK YOU BABY Stylistics (Avco)
6	8	VENUS AND MARS Wings (Apple)
9	9	ONCE UPON A STAR Bay City Rollers (Bell)
20	10	RAINBOW Ritchie Blackmore (Oyster)
19	11	ANOTHER YEAR Leo Sayer (Chrysalis)
11	12	TUBULAR BELLS Mike Oldfield (Virgin)
12	13	THE DARK SIDE OF THE MOON Pink Floyd (Harvest)
10	14	CAPTAIN FANTASTIC AND THE BROWN DIRT COWBOY Elton John (DJM)
16	15	E.C. WAS HERE Eric Clapton (Polydor)
-	16	WISH YOU WERE HERE Pink Floyd (Harvest)
13	17	THE ORIGINAL SOUNDTRACK 10 C.C. (Mercury)
15	18	THE SINGLES 1969-1973 Carpenters (A&M)
26	19	TEN YEARS NON STOP JUBILEE James Last (Polydor)
18	20	STRAIGHT SHOOTER Bad Company (Island)
-	21	SABOTAGE Black Sabbath (Vertigo)
21	22	RIDE A ROCK HORSE Roger Daltrey (Polydor)
-	23	ALL THE FUN OF THE FAIR David Essex (CBS)
17	24	24 CARAT PURPLE Deep Purple (Purple)
29	25	SIMON & GARFUNKEL'S GREATEST HITS Simon & Garfunkel (CBS)
14	26	MUD ROCK II Mud (RAK)
24	27	THE SUN COLLECTION Elvis Presley (RCA)
-	28	LIVE Sensational Alex Harvey Band (Vertigo)
22	29	STEP TWO Showaddywaddy (Bell)
-	30	ELTON JOHN'S GREATEST HITS Elton John (DJM)

27 September 1975

last	this	Title / Artist (Label)
1	1	ATLANTIC CROSSING Rod Stewart (Warner Bros.)
2	2	THE BEST OF THE STYLISTICS Stylistics (Avco)
16	3	WISH YOU WERE HERE Pink Floyd (Harvest)
5	4	CAT STEVENS' GREATEST HITS Cat Stevens (Island)
4	5	THE VERY BEST OF ROG ER WHITTAKER Roger Whittaker (EMI)
3	6	HORIZON Carpenters (A&M)
8	7	VENUS AND MARS Wings (Apple)
6	8	ONE OF THESE NIGHTS Eagles (Asylum)
7	9	THANK YOU BABY Stylistics (Avco)
9	10	ONCE UPON A STAR Bay City Rollers (Bell)
12	11	TUBULAR BELLS Mike Oldfield (Virgin)
11	12	ANOTHER YEAR Leo Sayer (Chrysalis)
23	13	ALL THE FUN OF THE FAIR David Essex (CBS)
10	14	RAINBOW Ritchie Blackmore (Oyster)
15	15	E.C. WAS HERE Eric Clapton (Polydor)
14	16	CAPTAIN FANTASTIC AND THE BROWN DIRT COWBOY Elton John (DJM)
25	17	SIMON & GARFUNKEL'S GREATEST HITS Simon & Garfunkel (CBS)
13	18	THE DARK SIDE OF THE MOON Pink Floyd (Harvest)
18	19	THE SINGLES 1969-1973 Carpenters (A&M)
21	20	SABOTAGE Black Sabbath (Vertigo)
28	21	LIVE Sensational Alex Harvey Band (Vertigo)
20	22	STRAIGHT SHOOTER Bad Company (Island)
17	23	THE ORIGINAL SOUNDTRACK 10 C.C. (Mercury)
27	24	THE SUN COLLECTION Elvis Presley (RCA)
19	25	TEN YEARS NON STOP JUBILEE James Last (Polydor)
-	26	THE MYTHS AND LEGENDS OF KING ARTHUR AND THE KNIGHTS OF THE ROUND TABLE Rick Wakeman & the English Rock Ensemble (A&M)
-	27	TOMMY Soundtrack (Polydor)
-	28	MRS. 'ARDIN'S KID Mike Harding (Transatlantic)
-	29	ROLLIN' Bay City Rollers (Bell)
-	30	40 SINGALONG PUB SONGS Various Artists (K-Tel)

4 October 1975

last	this	Title / Artist (Label)
1	1	ATLANTIC CROSSING Rod Stewart (Warner Bros.)
3	2	WISH YOU WERE HERE Pink Floyd (Harvest)
2	3	THE BEST OF THE STYLISTICS Stylistics (Avco)
5	4	THE VERY BEST OF ROG ER WHITTAKER Roger Whittaker (EMI)
4	5	CAT STEVENS' GREATEST HITS Cat Stevens (Island)
6	6	HORIZON Carpenters (A&M)
13	7	ALL THE FUN OF THE FAIR David Essex (CBS)
20	8	SABOTAGE Black Sabbath (Vertigo)
7	9	VENUS AND MARS Wings (Apple)
12	10	ANOTHER YEAR Leo Sayer (Chrysalis)
21	11	LIVE Sensational Alex Harvey Band (Vertigo)
9	12	THANK YOU BABY Stylistics (Avco)
11	13	TUBULAR BELLS Mike Oldfield (Virgin)
8	14	ONE OF THESE NIGHTS Eagles (Asylum)
10	15	ONCE UPON A STAR Bay City Rollers (Bell)
19	16	THE SINGLES 1969-1973 Carpenters (A&M)
17	17	SIMON & GARFUNKEL'S GREATEST HITS Simon & Garfunkel (CBS)
16	18	CAPTAIN FANTASTIC AND THE BROWN DIRT COWBOY Elton John (DJM)
15	19	E.C. WAS HERE Eric Clapton (Polydor)
-	20	ELTON JOHN'S GREATEST HITS Elton John (DJM)
25	21	TEN YEARS NON STOP JUBILEE James Last (Polydor)
18	22	THE DARK SIDE OF THE MOON Pink Floyd (Harvest)
-	23	MISTY Ray Stevens (Janus)
23	24	THE ORIGINAL SOUNDTRACK 10 C.C. (Mercury)
14	25	RAINBOW Ritchie Blackmore (Oyster)
-	26	JIM REEVES' 40 GOLDEN GREATS Jim Reeves (Arcade)
26	27	THE MYTHS AND LEGENDS OF KING ARTHUR AND THE KNIGHTS OF THE ROUND TABLE Rick Wakeman & the English Rock Ensemble (A&M)
-	28	MINSTREL IN THE GALLERY Jethro Tull (Chrysalis)
24	29	THE SUN COLLECTION Elvis Presley (RCA)
-	30	FAVOURITES Peters & Lee (Philips)

Several of those now charting had done so in a previous life. The crucial part of Wings had emerged from the Beatles; Bad Company, now with its second chart album beginning an erratic climb, had been formed around Paul Rodgers and Simon Kirke of Free; Ritchie Blackmore, ex-Deep Purple, was in the chart with Rainbow, which would become the name of his new band; Rick Wakeman was ex-Yes; and Roger Daltrey, though he hadn't quit the Who, was making his solo album debut.

October – November 1975

The god of MOR was ready for Christmas: hence we found chart homage offered to James Last; the re-entry of Perry Como's *40 Greatest Hits* (he'd never had 40 hits); Peters & Lee; the newly-devised *40 Singalong Pub Songs* torture; the Carpenters twice over; the predictable ascent of Jim Reeves again (his 22nd posthumous Top 30 album); the arrival of the *Good Bad But Beautiful* (not necessarily in that order) Shirley Bassey; and, Top 10, the circumspectly-titled *Very Best Of Roger Whittaker*.

November 1975

8 November 1975

last week	this week	
2	1	JIM REEVES' 40 GOLDEN GREATS Jim Reeves (Arcade)
3	2	WISH YOU WERE HERE Pink Floyd (Harvest)
4	3	FAVOURITES Peters & Lee (Philips)
1	4	ATLANTIC CROSSING Rod Stewart (Warner Bros.)
5	5	ALL THE FUN OF THE FAIR David Essex (CBS)
9	6	BREAKAWAY Art Garfunkel (CBS)
17	7	PERRY COMO'S 40 GREATEST HITS Perry Como (K-Tel)
6	8	THE VERY BEST OF ROGER WHITTAKER Roger Whittaker (EMI)
12	9	ROCK OF THE WESTIES Elton John (DJM)
11	10	SIREN Roxy Music (Island)
7	11	THE BEST OF THE STYLISTICS Stylistics (Avco)
8	12	THE WHO BY NUMBERS Who (Polydor)
18	13	GOOD BAD BUT BEAUTIFUL Shirley Bassey (United Artists)
21	14	STILL CRAZY AFTER ALL THESE YEARS Paul Simon (CBS)
-	15	ALL AROUND MY HAT Steeleye Span (Chrysalis)
19	16	ONE OF THESE NIGHTS Eagles (Asylum)
10	17	CAT STEVENS' GREATEST HITS Cat Stevens (Island)
20	18	WINDSONG John Denver (RCA)
-	19	MUD'S GREATEST HITS Mud (RAK)
-	20	WE ALL HAD DOCTOR'S PAPERS Max Boyce (EMI)`
-	21	OMMADAWN Mike Oldfield (Virgin)
24	22	SIMON & GARFUNKEL'S GREATEST HITS Simon & Garfunkel (CBS)
13	23	VENUS AND MARS Wings (Apple)
15	24	ANOTHER YEAR Leo Sayer (Chrysalis)
16	25	HORIZON Carpenters (A&M)
25	26	MALPRACTICE Dr. Feelgood (United Artists)
26	27	TUBULAR BELLS Mike Oldfield (Virgin)
-	28	CHANGING ALL THE TIME Smokie (RAK)
14	29	INDISCREET Sparks (Island)
27	30	RABBITS ON AND ON Jasper Carrott (DJM)

15 November 1975

last week	this week	
1	1	JIM REEVES' 40 GOLDEN GREATS Jim Reeves (Arcade)
10	2	SIREN Roxy Music (Island)
7	3	PERRY COMO'S 40 GREATEST HITS Perry Como (K-Tel)
9	4	ROCK OF THE WESTIES Elton John (DJM)
3	5	FAVOURITES Peters & Lee (Philips)
6	6	BREAKAWAY Art Garfunkel (CBS)
4	7	ATLANTIC CROSSING Rod Stewart (Warner Bros.)
2	8	WISH YOU WERE HERE Pink Floyd (Harvest)
5	9	ALL THE FUN OF THE FAIR David Essex (CBS)
21	10	OMMADAWN Mike Oldfield (Virgin)
8	11	THE VERY BEST OF ROGER WHITTAKER Roger Whittaker (EMI)
11	12	THE BEST OF THE STYLISTICS Stylistics (Avco)
20	13	WE ALL HAD DOCTOR'S PAPERS Max Boyce (EMI)`
14	14	STILL CRAZY AFTER ALL THESE YEARS Paul Simon (CBS)
15	15	ALL AROUND MY HAT Steeleye Span (Chrysalis)
12	16	THE WHO BY NUMBERS Who (Polydor)
16	17	ONE OF THESE NIGHTS Eagles (Asylum)
13	18	GOOD BAD BUT BEAUTIFUL Shirley Bassey (United Artists)
-	19	SHAVED FISH John Lennon (Apple)
18	20	WINDSONG John Denver (RCA)
28	21	CHANGING ALL THE TIME Smokie (RAK)
-	22	BLAZING BULLETS Various Artists (Ronco)
19	23	MUD'S GREATEST HITS Mud (RAK)
17	24	CAT STEVENS' GREATEST HITS Cat Stevens (Island)
-	25	SABOTAGE Black Sabbath (Vertigo)
-	26	RHINESTONE COWBOY Glen Campbell (Capitol)
-	27	DOWN THE DUST PIPE Status Quo (Golden Hour)
30	28	RABBITS ON AND ON Jasper Carrott (DJM)
22	29	SIMON & GARFUNKEL'S GREATEST HITS Simon & Garfunkel (CBS)
24	30	ANOTHER YEAR Leo Sayer (Chrysalis)

22 November 1975

last week	this week	
1	1	JIM REEVES' 40 GOLDEN GREATS Jim Reeves (Arcade)
3	2	PERRY COMO'S 40 GREATEST HITS Perry Como (K-Tel)
4	3	ROCK OF THE WESTIES Elton John (DJM)
2	4	SIREN Roxy Music (Island)
5	5	FAVOURITES Peters & Lee (Philips)
7	6	ATLANTIC CROSSING Rod Stewart (Warner Bros.)
10	7	OMMADAWN Mike Oldfield (Virgin)
8	8	WISH YOU WERE HERE Pink Floyd (Harvest)
6	9	BREAKAWAY Art Garfunkel (CBS)
19	10	SHAVED FISH John Lennon (Apple)
15	11	ALL AROUND MY HAT Steeleye Span (Chrysalis)
9	12	ALL THE FUN OF THE FAIR David Essex (CBS)
13	13	WE ALL HAD DOCTOR'S PAPERS Max Boyce (EMI)`
11	14	THE VERY BEST OF ROGER WHITTAKER Roger Whittaker (EMI)
17	15	ONE OF THESE NIGHTS Eagles (Asylum)
12	16	THE BEST OF THE STYLISTICS Stylistics (Avco)
18	17	GOOD BAD BUT BEAUTIFUL Shirley Bassey (United Artists)
-	18	MOTOWN GOLD Various Artists (Tamla Motown)
-	19	BEGINNINGS Steve Howe (Atlantic)
-	20	GOOFY GREATS Various Artists (K-Tel)
14	21	STILL CRAZY AFTER ALL THESE YEARS Paul Simon (CBS)
20	22	WINDSONG John Denver (RCA)
-	23	COME TASTE THE BAND Deep Purple (Purple)
16	24	THE WHO BY NUMBERS Who (Polydor)
24	25	CAT STEVENS' GREATEST HITS Cat Stevens (Island)
23	26	MUD'S GREATEST HITS Mud (RAK)
29	27	SIMON & GARFUNKEL GREATEST HITS Simon & Garfunkel (CBS)
-	28	TUBULAR BELLS Mike Oldfield (Virgin)
-	29	MAKE THE PARTY LAST James Last (Polydor)
-	30	DISCO HITS '75 Various Artists (Arcade)

29 November 1975

last week	this week	
2	1	PERRY COMO'S 40 GREATEST HITS Perry Como (K-Tel)
1	2	JIM REEVES' 40 GOLDEN GREATS Jim Reeves (Arcade)
5	3	FAVOURITES Peters & Lee (Philips)
7	4	OMMADAWN Mike Oldfield (Virgin)
6	5	ATLANTIC CROSSING Rod Stewart (Warner Bros.)
11	6	ALL AROUND MY HAT Steeleye Span (Chrysalis)
10	7	SHAVED FISH John Lennon (Apple)
4	8	SIREN Roxy Music (Island)
3	9	ROCK OF THE WESTIES Elton John (DJM)
15	10	ONE OF THESE NIGHTS Eagles (Asylum)
8	11	WISH YOU WERE HERE Pink Floyd (Harvest)
12	12	ALL THE FUN OF THE FAIR David Essex (CBS)
9	13	BREAKAWAY Art Garfunkel (CBS)
14	14	THE VERY BEST OF ROGER WHITTAKER Roger Whittaker (EMI)
16	15	THE BEST OF THE STYLISTICS Stylistics (Avco)
29	16	MAKE THE PARTY LAST James Last (Polydor)
13	17	WE ALL HAD DOCTOR'S PAPERS Max Boyce (EMI)`
18	18	MOTOWN GOLD Various Artists (Tamla Motown)
17	19	GOOD BAD BUT BEAUTIFUL Shirley Bassey (United Artists)
-	20	BARRY WHITE'S GREATEST HITS Barry White (20th Century)
19	21	BEGINNINGS Steve Howe (Atlantic)
23	22	COME TASTE THE BAND Deep Purple (Purple)
27	23	SIMON & GARFUNKEL GREATEST HITS Simon & Garfunkel (CBS)
-	24	BORN TO RUN Bruce Springsteen (CBS)
24	25	THE WHO BY NUMBERS Who (Polydor)
-	26	HOT CHOCOLATE Hot Chocolate (RAK)
20	27	GOOFY GREATS Various Artists (K-Tel)
-	28	RHINESTONE COWBOY Glen Campbell (Capitol)
-	29	GET RIGHT INTAE HIM Billy Connolly (Polydor)
30	30	DISCO HITS '75 Various Artists (Arcade)

What year was it? Jim Reeves battled with Perry Como for top place (two more RCA artists leased to the cheapo labels). Meanwhile Art Garfunkel battled with Paul Simon and with Simon & Garfunkel, Max Boyce and Jasper Carrott battled with Billy Connolly (*Get Right Intae Him* was his third Top 30 album) and Mike Oldfield with Mike Oldfield. John Lennon's *Shaved Fish*, surprisingly, didn't have to battle it out with Paul McCartney's anything. A one-week-only chart debut by Bruce Springsteen proved it was 1975.

December 1975

last week	this week	6 December 1975
1	1	PERRY COMO'S 40 GREATEST HITS — Perry Como (K-Tel)
2	2	JIM REEVES' 40 GOLDEN GREATS — Jim Reeves (Arcade)
3	3	FAVOURITES — Peters & Lee (Philips)
-	4	A NIGHT AT THE OPERA — Queen (EMI)
4	5	OMMADAWN — Mike Oldfield (Virgin)
5	6	ATLANTIC CROSSING — Rod Stewart (Warner Bros.)
6	7	ALL AROUND MY HAT — Steeleye Span (Chrysalis)
8	8	SIREN — Roxy Music (Island)
7	9	SHAVED FISH — John Lennon (Apple)
9	10	ROCK OF THE WESTIES — Elton John (DJM)
16	11	MAKE THE PARTY LAST — James Last (Polydor)
10	12	ONE OF THESE NIGHTS — Eagles (Asylum)
11	13	WISH YOU WERE HERE — Pink Floyd (Harvest)
12	14	ALL THE FUN OF THE FAIR — David Essex (CBS)
-	15	CRISIS? WHAT CRISIS? — Supertramp (A&M)
-	16	WOULDN'T YOU LIKE IT? — Bay City Rollers (Bell)
15	17	THE BEST OF THE STYLISTICS — Stylistics (Avco)
30	18	DISCO HITS '75 — Various Artists (Arcade)
-	19	ROLLED GOLD — Rolling Stones (Decca)
13	20	BREAKAWAY — Art Garfunkel (CBS)
29	21	GET RIGHT INTAE HIM — Billy Connolly (Polydor)
14	22	THE VERY BEST OF ROGER WHITTAKER — Roger Whittaker (EMI)
20	23	BARRY WHITE'S GREATEST HITS — Barry White (20th Century)
17	24	WE ALL HAD DOCTOR'S PAPERS — Max Boyce (EMI)`
22	25	COME TASTE THE BAND — Deep Purple (Purple)
-	26	THE DARK SIDE OF THE MOON — Pink Floyd (Harvest)
-	27	SONGS OF JOY — Nigel Brooks Singers (K-Tel)
18	28	MOTOWN GOLD — Various Artists (Tamla Motown)
28	29	RHINESTONE COWBOY — Glen Campbell (Capitol)
25	30	THE WHO BY NUMBERS — Who (Polydor)

last	this	13 December 1975
1	1	PERRY COMO'S 40 GREATEST HITS — Perry Como (K-Tel)
4	2	A NIGHT AT THE OPERA — Queen (EMI)
3	3	FAVOURITES — Peters & Lee (Philips)
2	4	JIM REEVES' 40 GOLDEN GREATS — Jim Reeves (Arcade)
11	5	MAKE THE PARTY LAST — James Last (Polydor)
9	6	SHAVED FISH — John Lennon (Apple)
19	7	ROLLED GOLD — Rolling Stones (Decca)
7	8	ALL AROUND MY HAT — Steeleye Span (Chrysalis)
6	9	ATLANTIC CROSSING — Rod Stewart (Warner Bros.)
15	10	CRISIS? WHAT CRISIS? — Supertramp (A&M)
21	11	GET RIGHT INTAE HIM — Billy Connolly (Polydor)
5	12	OMMADAWN — Mike Oldfield (Virgin)
16	13	WOULDN'T YOU LIKE IT? — Bay City Rollers (Bell)
8	14	SIREN — Roxy Music (Island)
18	15	DISCO HITS '75 — Various Artists (Arcade)
14	16	ALL THE FUN OF THE FAIR — David Essex (CBS)
12	17	ONE OF THESE NIGHTS — Eagles (Asylum)
13	18	WISH YOU WERE HERE — Pink Floyd (Harvest)
10	19	ROCK OF THE WESTIES — Elton John (DJM)
-	20	24 ORIGINAL HITS — Drifters (Atlantic)
17	21	THE BEST OF THE STYLISTICS — Stylistics (Avco)
27	22	SONGS OF JOY — Nigel Brooks Singers (K-Tel)
24	23	WE ALL HAD DOCTOR'S PAPERS — Max Boyce (EMI)`
28	24	MOTOWN GOLD — Various Artists (Tamla Motown)
-	25	YOU ARE BEAUTIFUL — Stylistics (Avco)
23	26	BARRY WHITE'S GREATEST HITS — Barry White (20th Century)
-	27	ELVIS PRESLEY'S 40 GREATEST HITS — Elvis Presley (Arcade)
22	28	THE VERY BEST OF ROGER WHITTAKER — Roger Whittaker (EMI)
-	29	LIVE! — Bob Marley & the Wailers (Island)
-	30	BLAZING BULLETS — Various Artists (Ronco)

last	this	20 December 1975
1	1	PERRY COMO'S 40 GREATEST HITS — Perry Como (K-Tel)
2	2	A NIGHT AT THE OPERA — Queen (EMI)
4	3	JIM REEVES' 40 GOLDEN GREATS — Jim Reeves (Arcade)
5	4	MAKE THE PARTY LAST — James Last (Polydor)
13	5	WOULDN'T YOU LIKE IT? — Bay City Rollers (Bell)
8	6	ALL AROUND MY HAT — Steeleye Span (Chrysalis)
6	7	SHAVED FISH — John Lennon (Apple)
12	8	OMMADAWN — Mike Oldfield (Virgin)
9	9	ATLANTIC CROSSING — Rod Stewart (Warner Bros.)
7	10	ROLLED GOLD — Rolling Stones (Decca)
22	11	SONGS OF JOY — Nigel Brooks Singers (K-Tel)
3	12	FAVOURITES — Peters & Lee (Philips)
11	13	GET RIGHT INTAE HIM — Billy Connolly (Polydor)
21	14	THE BEST OF THE STYLISTICS — Stylistics (Avco)
10	15	CRISIS? WHAT CRISIS? — Supertramp (A&M)
18	16	WISH YOU WERE HERE — Pink Floyd (Harvest)
20	17	24 ORIGINAL HITS — Drifters (Atlantic)
16	18	ALL THE FUN OF THE FAIR — David Essex (CBS)
14	19	SIREN — Roxy Music (Island)
15	20	DISCO HITS '75 — Various Artists (Arcade)
17	21	ONE OF THESE NIGHTS — Eagles (Asylum)
26	22	BARRY WHITE'S GREATEST HITS — Barry White (20th Century)
24	23	MOTOWN GOLD — Various Artists (Tamla Motown)
27	24	ELVIS PRESLEY'S 40 GREATEST HITS — Elvis Presley (Arcade)
25	25	YOU ARE BEAUTIFUL — Stylistics (Avco)
23	26	WE ALL HAD DOCTOR'S PAPERS — Max Boyce (EMI)`
28	27	THE VERY BEST OF ROGER WHITTAKER — Roger Whittaker (EMI)
19	28	ROCK OF THE WESTIES — Elton John (DJM)
-	29	THE GREATEST HITS OF WALT DISNEY — Various Artists (Ronco)
-	30	40 SUPER GREATS — Various Artists (K-Tel)

last	this	27 December 1975
2	1	A NIGHT AT THE OPERA — Queen (EMI)
1	2	PERRY COMO'S 40 GREATEST HITS — Perry Como (K-Tel)
3	3	JIM REEVES' 40 GOLDEN GREATS — Jim Reeves (Arcade)
5	4	WOULDN'T YOU LIKE IT? — Bay City Rollers (Bell)
4	5	MAKE THE PARTY LAST — James Last (Polydor)
17	6	24 ORIGINAL HITS — Drifters (Atlantic)
12	7	FAVOURITES — Peters & Lee (Philips)
8	8	OMMADAWN — Mike Oldfield (Virgin)
9	9	ATLANTIC CROSSING — Rod Stewart (Warner Bros.)
7	10	SHAVED FISH — John Lennon (Apple)
11	11	SONGS OF JOY — Nigel Brooks Singers (K-Tel)
10	12	ROLLED GOLD — Rolling Stones (Decca)
6	13	ALL AROUND MY HAT — Steeleye Span (Chrysalis)
18	14	ALL THE FUN OF THE FAIR — David Essex (CBS)
24	15	ELVIS PRESLEY'S 40 GREATEST HITS — Elvis Presley (Arcade)
13	16	GET RIGHT INTAE HIM — Billy Connolly (Polydor)
15	17	CRISIS? WHAT CRISIS? — Supertramp (A&M)
16	18	WISH YOU WERE HERE — Pink Floyd (Harvest)
29	19	THE GREATEST HITS OF WALT DISNEY — Various Artists (Ronco)
20	20	DISCO HITS '75 — Various Artists (Arcade)
22	21	BARRY WHITE'S GREATEST HITS — Barry White (20th Century)
30	22	40 SUPER GREATS — Various Artists (K-Tel)
21	23	ONE OF THESE NIGHTS — Eagles (Asylum)
14	24	THE BEST OF THE STYLISTICS — Stylistics (Avco)
23	25	MOTOWN GOLD — Various Artists (Tamla Motown)
27	26	THE VERY BEST OF ROGER WHITTAKER — Roger Whittaker (EMI)
28	27	ROCK OF THE WESTIES — Elton John (DJM)
-	28	SIMON & GARFUNKEL'S GREATEST HITS — Simon & Garfunkel (CBS)
26	29	WE ALL HAD DOCTOR'S PAPERS — Max Boyce (EMI)`
-	30	THE NEW GOODIES LP — Goodies (Bradley's)

Queen's *A Night At The Opera* would be followed by *A Day At The Races*, both Marx Brothers film titles. Their first No.1 LP ran parallel with their first No.1 single, *Bohemian Rhapsody*, top throughout December. Supertramp, now largely forgotten, was hugely successful, very '70s, and lingered on in the charts as late as 1986. Our most commercial folk-rock group, Steeleye Span, built around Tim Hart and Maddy Prior, were having their biggest hit LP, while *All Around My Hat* was also a Top 10 single.

January 1976

3 January 1976

last	this	title / artist
1	1	A NIGHT AT THE OPERA Queen (EMI)
2	2	PERRY COMO'S 40 GREATEST HITS Perry Como (K-Tel)
5	3	MAKE THE PARTY LAST James Last (Polydor)
3	4	JIM REEVES' 40 GOLDEN GREATS Jim Reeves (Arcade)
4	5	WOULDN'T YOU LIKE IT? Bay City Rollers (Bell)
6	6	24 ORIGINAL HITS Drifters (Atlantic)
8	7	OMMADAWN Mike Oldfield (Virgin)
7	8	FAVOURITES Peters & Lee (Philips)
9	9	ATLANTIC CROSSING Rod Stewart (Warner Bros.)
14	10	ALL THE FUN OF THE FAIR David Essex (CBS)
22	11	40 SUPER GREATS Various Artists (K-Tel)
16	12	GET RIGHT INTAE HIM Billy Connolly (Polydor)
11	13	SONGS OF JOY Nigel Brooks Singers (K-Tel)
13	14	ALL AROUND MY HAT Steeleye Span (Chrysalis)
15	15	ELVIS PRESLEY'S 40 GREATEST HITS Elvis Presley (Arcade)
20	16	DISCO HITS '75 Various Artists (Arcade)
12	17	ROLLED GOLD Rolling Stones (Decca)
10	18	SHAVED FISH John Lennon (Apple)
24	19	BEST OF THE STYLISTICS Stylistics (Avco)
19	20	THE GREATEST HITS OF WALT DISNEY Various Artists (Ronco)
18	21	WISH YOU WERE HERE Pink Floyd (Harvest)
17	22	CRISIS? WHAT CRISIS? Supertramp (A&M)
23	23	ONE OF THESE NIGHTS Eagles (Asylum)
-	24	SUPERSONIC Various Artists (Stallion)
-	25	GOOFY GREATS Various Artists (K-Tel)
-	26	BREAKAWAY Art Garfunkel (CBS)
21	27	BARRY WHITE'S GREATEST HITS Barry White (20th Century)
26	28	THE VERY BEST OF ROGER WHITTAKER Roger Whittaker (EMI)
-	29	FISH OUT OF WATER Chris Squire (Atlantic)
28	30	SIMON & GARFUNKEL'S GREATEST HITS Simon & Garfunkel (CBS)

10 January 1976

last	this	title / artist
1	1	A NIGHT AT THE OPERA Queen (EMI)
2	2	PERRY COMO'S 40 GREATEST HITS Perry Como (K-Tel)
7	3	OMMADAWN Mike Oldfield (Virgin)
3	4	MAKE THE PARTY LAST James Last (Polydor)
6	5	24 ORIGINAL HITS Drifters (Atlantic)
9	6	ATLANTIC CROSSING Rod Stewart (Warner Bros.)
5	7	WOULDN'T YOU LIKE IT? Bay City Rollers (Bell)
14	8	ALL AROUND MY HAT Steeleye Span (Chrysalis)
4	9	JIM REEVES' 40 GOLDEN GREATS Jim Reeves (Arcade)
8	10	FAVOURITES Peters & Lee (Philips)
10	11	ALL THE FUN OF THE FAIR David Essex (CBS)
18	12	SHAVED FISH John Lennon (Apple)
22	13	CRISIS? WHAT CRISIS? Supertramp (A&M)
17	14	ROLLED GOLD Rolling Stones (Decca)
12	15	GET RIGHT INTAE HIM Billy Connolly (Polydor)
19	16	BEST OF THE STYLISTICS Stylistics (Avco)
23	17	ONE OF THESE NIGHTS Eagles (Asylum)
21	18	WISH YOU WERE HERE Pink Floyd (Harvest)
29	19	FISH OUT OF WATER Chris Squire (Atlantic)
11	20	40 SUPER GREATS Various Artists (K-Tel)
26	21	BREAKAWAY Art Garfunkel (CBS)
15	22	ELVIS PRESLEY'S 40 GREATEST HITS Elvis Presley (Arcade)
28	23	THE VERY BEST OF ROGER WHITTAKER Roger Whittaker (EMI)
13	24	SONGS OF JOY Nigel Brooks Singers (K-Tel)
16	25	DISCO HITS '75 Various Artists (Arcade)
20	26	THE GREATEST HITS OF WALT DISNEY Various Artists (Ronco)
-	27	THE TOP 25 FROM YOUR 100 BEST TUNES Various Artists (Decca)
-	28	THE HISSING OF SUMMER LAWNS Joni Mitchell (Asylum)
27	29	BARRY WHITE'S GREATEST HITS Barry White (20th Century)
-	30	TUBULAR BELLS Mike Oldfield (Virgin)

17 January 1976

last	this	title / artist
1	1	A NIGHT AT THE OPERA Queen (EMI)
2	2	PERRY COMO'S 40 GREATEST HITS Perry Como (K-Tel)
3	3	OMMADAWN Mike Oldfield (Virgin)
5	4	24 ORIGINAL HITS Drifters (Atlantic)
7	5	WOULDN'T YOU LIKE IT? Bay City Rollers (Bell)
4	6	MAKE THE PARTY LAST James Last (Polydor)
6	7	ATLANTIC CROSSING Rod Stewart (Warner Bros.)
9	8	JIM REEVES' 40 GOLDEN GREATS Jim Reeves (Arcade)
8	9	ALL AROUND MY HAT Steeleye Span (Chrysalis)
16	10	BEST OF THE STYLISTICS Stylistics (Avco)
15	11	GET RIGHT INTAE HIM Billy Connolly (Polydor)
14	12	ROLLED GOLD Rolling Stones (Decca)
10	13	FAVOURITES Peters & Lee (Philips)
11	14	ALL THE FUN OF THE FAIR David Essex (CBS)
12	15	SHAVED FISH John Lennon (Apple)
18	16	WISH YOU WERE HERE Pink Floyd (Harvest)
17	17	ONE OF THESE NIGHTS Eagles (Asylum)
13	18	CRISIS? WHAT CRISIS? Supertramp (A&M)
29	19	BARRY WHITE'S GREATEST HITS Barry White (20th Century)
-	20	THE BEST OF ROY ORBISON Roy Orbison (Arcade)
19	21	FISH OUT OF WATER Chris Squire (Atlantic)
-	22	STILL CRAZY AFTER ALL THESE YEARS Paul Simon (CBS)
24	23	SONGS OF JOY Nigel Brooks Singers (K-Tel)
22	24	ELVIS PRESLEY'S 40 GREATEST HITS Elvis Presley (Arcade)
28	25	THE HISSING OF SUMMER LAWNS Joni Mitchell (Asylum)
-	26	MOTOWN GOLD Various Artists (Tamla Motown)
21	27	BREAKAWAY Art Garfunkel (CBS)
25	28	DISCO HITS '75 Various Artists (Arcade)
30	29	TUBULAR BELLS Mike Oldfield (Virgin)
-	30	SIMON & GARFUNKEL'S GREATEST HITS Simon & Garfunkel (CBS)

24 January 1976

last	this	title / artist
1	1	A NIGHT AT THE OPERA Queen (EMI)
3	2	OMMADAWN Mike Oldfield (Virgin)
4	3	24 ORIGINAL HITS Drifters (Atlantic)
2	4	PERRY COMO'S 40 GREATEST HITS Perry Como (K-Tel)
20	5	THE BEST OF ROY ORBISON Roy Orbison (Arcade)
7	6	ATLANTIC CROSSING Rod Stewart (Warner Bros.)
5	7	WOULDN'T YOU LIKE IT? Bay City Rollers (Bell)
-	8	HOW DARE YOU 10 C.C. (Mercury)
22	9	STILL CRAZY AFTER ALL THESE YEARS Paul Simon (CBS)
6	10	MAKE THE PARTY LAST James Last (Polydor)
12	11	ROLLED GOLD Rolling Stones (Decca)
10	12	BEST OF THE STYLISTICS Stylistics (Avco)
16	13	WISH YOU WERE HERE Pink Floyd (Harvest)
8	14	JIM REEVES' 40 GOLDEN GREATS Jim Reeves (Arcade)
9	15	ALL AROUND MY HAT Steeleye Span (Chrysalis)
14	16	ALL THE FUN OF THE FAIR David Essex (CBS)
-	17	DESIRE Bob Dylan (CBS)
11	18	GET RIGHT INTAE HIM Billy Connolly (Polydor)
13	19	FAVOURITES Peters & Lee (Philips)
17	20	ONE OF THESE NIGHTS Eagles (Asylum)
25	21	THE HISSING OF SUMMER LAWNS Joni Mitchell (Asylum)
18	22	CRISIS? WHAT CRISIS? Supertramp (A&M)
15	23	SHAVED FISH John Lennon (Apple)
-	24	MUSIC EXPRESS Various Artists (K-Tel)
23	25	SONGS OF JOY Nigel Brooks Singers (K-Tel)
29	26	TUBULAR BELLS Mike Oldfield (Virgin)
27	27	BREAKAWAY Art Garfunkel (CBS)
-	28	40 SUPER GREATS Various Artists (K-Tel)
19	29	BARRY WHITE'S GREATEST HITS Barry White (20th Century)
-	30	SHEER HEART ATTACK Queen (EMI)

This was the first year since album charts began that Frank Sinatra didn't enter the Top 30 at least once. Britain's first LP chart, Melody Maker's, began in 1958; from then till the NME chart arrived, Sinatra had 16 Top 20 hit LPs. Then, from *I Remember Tommy* and *Sinatra And Strings*, both in the first NME chart (Top 10 only) back in June 1962, through to *Main Event* in February 1975, this remarkable singer (and convincing screen actor) had racked up some 26 further Top 30 album successes.

last week	this week	31 January 1976
1	1	A NIGHT AT THE OPERA — Queen (EMI)
3	2	24 ORIGINAL HITS — Drifters (Atlantic)
5	3	THE BEST OF ROY ORBISON — Roy Orbison (Arcade)
2	4	OMMADAWN — Mike Oldfield (Virgin)
9	5	STILL CRAZY AFTER ALL THESE YEARS — Paul Simon (CBS)
4	6	PERRY COMO'S 40 GREATEST HITS — Perry Como (K-Tel)
8	7	HOW DARE YOU — 10 C.C. (Mercury)
6	8	ATLANTIC CROSSING — Rod Stewart (Warner Bros.)
17	9	DESIRE — Bob Dylan (CBS)
13	10	WISH YOU WERE HERE — Pink Floyd (Harvest)
10	11	MAKE THE PARTY LAST — James Last (Polydor)
24	12	MUSIC EXPRESS — Various Artists (K-Tel)
7	13	WOULDN'T YOU LIKE IT? — Bay City Rollers (Bell)
22	14	CRISIS? WHAT CRISIS? — Supertramp (A&M)
11	15	ROLLED GOLD — Rolling Stones (Decca)
12	16	BEST OF THE STYLISTICS — Stylistics (Avco)
21	17	THE HISSING OF SUMMER LAWNS — Joni Mitchell (Asylum)
16	18	ALL THE FUN OF THE FAIR — David Essex (CBS)
20	19	ONE OF THESE NIGHTS — Eagles (Asylum)
-	20	THE VERY BEST OF SLIM WHITMAN — Slim Whitman (United Artists)
14	21	JIM REEVES' 40 GOLDEN GREATS — Jim Reeves (Arcade)
-	22	MOTOWN GOLD — Various Artists (Tamla Motown)
30	23	SHEER HEART ATTACK — Queen (EMI)
15	24	ALL AROUND MY HAT — Steeleye Span (Chrysalis)
25	25	SONGS OF JOY — Nigel Brooks Singers (K-Tel)
-	26	THE VERY BEST OF ROGER WHITTAKER — Roger Whittaker (EMI)
18	27	GET RIGHT INTAE HIM — Billy Connolly (Polydor)
26	28	TUBULAR BELLS — Mike Oldfield (Virgin)
23	29	SHAVED FISH — John Lennon (Apple)
-	30	STATION TO STATION — David Bowie (RCA)

last	this	7 February 1976
7	1	HOW DARE YOU — 10 C.C. (Mercury)
9	2	DESIRE — Bob Dylan (CBS)
1	3	A NIGHT AT THE OPERA — Queen (EMI)
3	4	THE BEST OF ROY ORBISON — Roy Orbison (Arcade)
2	5	24 ORIGINAL HITS — Drifters (Atlantic)
4	6	OMMADAWN — Mike Oldfield (Virgin)
5	7	STILL CRAZY AFTER ALL THESE YEARS — Paul Simon (CBS)
12	8	MUSIC EXPRESS — Various Artists (K-Tel)
6	9	PERRY COMO'S 40 GREATEST HITS — Perry Como (K-Tel)
8	10	ATLANTIC CROSSING — Rod Stewart (Warner Bros.)
20	11	THE VERY BEST OF SLIM WHITMAN — Slim Whitman (United Artists)
30	12	STATION TO STATION — David Bowie (RCA)
-	13	SING LOFTY — Don Estelle & Windsor Davies (EMI)
17	14	THE HISSING OF SUMMER LAWNS — Joni Mitchell (Asylum)
23	15	SHEER HEART ATTACK — Queen (EMI)
15	16	ROLLED GOLD — Rolling Stones (Decca)
-	17	STAR TRACKING '76 — Various Artists (Ronco)
13	18	WOULDN'T YOU LIKE IT? — Bay City Rollers (Bell)
-	19	ABBA — Abba (Epic)
-	20	SUNBURST FINISH — Be-Bop Deluxe (Harvest)
14	21	CRISIS? WHAT CRISIS? — Supertramp (A&M)
10	22	WISH YOU WERE HERE — Pink Floyd (Harvest)
19	23	ONE OF THESE NIGHTS — Eagles (Asylum)
22	24	MOTOWN GOLD — Various Artists (Tamla Motown)
16	25	BEST OF THE STYLISTICS — Stylistics (Avco)
-	26	BARRY WHITE'S GREATEST HITS — Barry White (20th Century)
21	27	JIM REEVES' 40 GOLDEN GREATS — Jim Reeves (Arcade)
11	28	MAKE THE PARTY LAST — James Last (Polydor)
28	29	TUBULAR BELLS — Mike Oldfield (Virgin)
-	30	SIMON & GARFUNKEL'S GREATEST HITS — Simon & Garfunkel (CBS)

last	this	14 February 1976
2	1	DESIRE — Bob Dylan (CBS)
1	2	HOW DARE YOU — 10 C.C. (Mercury)
3	3	A NIGHT AT THE OPERA — Queen (EMI)
4	4	THE BEST OF ROY ORBISON — Roy Orbison (Arcade)
11	5	THE VERY BEST OF SLIM WHITMAN — Slim Whitman (United Artists)
6	6	OMMADAWN — Mike Oldfield (Virgin)
5	7	24 ORIGINAL HITS — Drifters (Atlantic)
12	8	STATION TO STATION — David Bowie (RCA)
8	9	MUSIC EXPRESS — Various Artists (K-Tel)
24	10	MOTOWN GOLD — Various Artists (Tamla Motown)
7	11	STILL CRAZY AFTER ALL THESE YEARS — Paul Simon (CBS)
9	12	PERRY COMO'S 40 GREATEST HITS — Perry Como (K-Tel)
14	13	THE HISSING OF SUMMER LAWNS — Joni Mitchell (Asylum)
19	14	ABBA — Abba (Epic)
10	15	ATLANTIC CROSSING — Rod Stewart (Warner Bros.)
15	16	SHEER HEART ATTACK — Queen (EMI)
29	17	TUBULAR BELLS — Mike Oldfield (Virgin)
-	18	BREAKAWAY — Art Garfunkel (CBS)
13	19	SING LOFTY — Don Estelle & Windsor Davies (EMI)
-	20	RUN WITH THE PACK — Bad Company (Island)
21	21	CRISIS? WHAT CRISIS? — Supertramp (A&M)
20	22	SUNBURST FINISH — Be-Bop Deluxe (Harvest)
-	23	CARNIVAL — Manuel & His Music of the Mountains (Studio Two)
23	24	ONE OF THESE NIGHTS — Eagles (Asylum)
16	25	ROLLED GOLD — Rolling Stones (Decca)
-	26	LOVE TO LOVE YOU BABY — Donna Summer (GTO)
-	27	QUEEN II — Queen (EMI)
27	28	JIM REEVES' 40 GOLDEN GREATS — Jim Reeves (Arcade)
22	29	WISH YOU WERE HERE — Pink Floyd (Harvest)
25	30	BEST OF THE STYLISTICS — Stylistics (Avco)

last	this	21 February 1976
1	1	DESIRE — Bob Dylan (CBS)
5	2	THE VERY BEST OF SLIM WHITMAN — Slim Whitman (United Artists)
2	3	HOW DARE YOU — 10 C.C. (Mercury)
4	4	THE BEST OF ROY ORBISON — Roy Orbison (Arcade)
8	5	STATION TO STATION — David Bowie (RCA)
3	6	A NIGHT AT THE OPERA — Queen (EMI)
9	7	MUSIC EXPRESS — Various Artists (K-Tel)
7	8	24 ORIGINAL HITS — Drifters (Atlantic)
6	9	OMMADAWN — Mike Oldfield (Virgin)
11	10	STILL CRAZY AFTER ALL THESE YEARS — Paul Simon (CBS)
12	11	PERRY COMO'S 40 GREATEST HITS — Perry Como (K-Tel)
-	12	THE BEST OF HELEN REDDY — Helen Reddy (Capitol)
20	13	RUN WITH THE PACK — Bad Company (Island)
14	14	ABBA — Abba (Epic)
10	15	MOTOWN GOLD — Various Artists (Tamla Motown)
23	16	CARNIVAL — Manuel & His Music of the Mountains (Studio Two)
22	17	SUNBURST FINISH — Be-Bop Deluxe (Harvest)
18	18	BREAKAWAY — Art Garfunkel (CBS)
15	19	ATLANTIC CROSSING — Rod Stewart (Warner Bros.)
13	20	THE HISSING OF SUMMER LAWNS — Joni Mitchell (Asylum)
-	21	TIMELESS FLIGHT — Steve Harley & Cockney Rebel (EMI)
26	22	LOVE TO LOVE YOU BABY — Donna Summer (GTO)
17	23	TUBULAR BELLS — Mike Oldfield (Virgin)
25	24	ROLLED GOLD — Rolling Stones (Decca)
29	25	WISH YOU WERE HERE — Pink Floyd (Harvest)
19	26	SING LOFTY — Don Estelle & Windsor Davies (EMI)
21	27	CRISIS? WHAT CRISIS? — Supertramp (A&M)
24	28	ONE OF THESE NIGHTS — Eagles (Asylum)
16	29	SHEER HEART ATTACK — Queen (EMI)
-	30	SONGS OF JOY — Nigel Brooks Singers (K-Tel)

Roy Orbison hadn't been in the singles chart since 1969, and hadn't had a real hit since 1966; when *Roy Orbison's Greatest Hits* had been issued in 1967, and his *All-Time Greatest Hits* in 1973, they had barely sold. Now the power of TV-advertising proved itself for the cheapo Arcade label and *The Best Of Roy Orbison* reached the Top 3. Orbison himself spent the mid-70s playing cabaret circuits, unloved by most of those who would proclaim their eternal devotion to him when he died.

28 February 1976

last week	this week	Title	Artist
1	1	DESIRE	Bob Dylan (CBS)
2	2	THE VERY BEST OF SLIM WHITMAN	Slim Whitman (United Artists)
4	3	THE BEST OF ROY ORBISON	Roy Orbison (Arcade)
13	3	RUN WITH THE PACK	Bad Company (Island)
6	5	A NIGHT AT THE OPERA	Queen (EMI)
5	6	STATION TO STATION	David Bowie (RCA)
16	7	CARNIVAL	Manuel & His Music of the Mountains (Studio Two)
8	8	24 ORIGINAL HITS	Drifters (Atlantic)
15	9	MOTOWN GOLD	Various Artists (Tamla Motown)
9	10	OMMADAWN	Mike Oldfield (Virgin)
3	11	HOW DARE YOU	10 C.C. (Mercury)
12	12	THE BEST OF HELEN REDDY	Helen Reddy (Capitol)
7	13	MUSIC EXPRESS	Various Artists (K-Tel)
17	14	SUNBURST FINISH	Be-Bop Deluxe (Harvest)
11	15	PERRY COMO'S 40 GREATEST HITS	Perry Como (K-Tel)
21	16	TIMELESS FLIGHT	Steve Harley & Cockney Rebel (EMI)
14	17	ABBA	Abba (Epic)
22	18	LOVE TO LOVE YOU BABY	Donna Summer (GTO)
-	19	A TRICK OF THE TAIL	Genesis (Charisma)
10	20	STILL CRAZY AFTER ALL THESE YEARS	Paul Simon (CBS)
24	21	ROLLED GOLD	Rolling Stones (Decca)
29	22	SHEER HEART ATTACK	Queen (EMI)
27	23	CRISIS? WHAT CRISIS?	Supertramp (A&M)
18	24	BREAKAWAY	Art Garfunkel (CBS)
-	25	NO REGRETS	Walker Brothers (GTO)
23	26	TUBULAR BELLS	Mike Oldfield (Virgin)
25	27	WISH YOU WERE HERE	Pink Floyd (Harvest)
20	28	THE HISSING OF SUMMER LAWNS	Joni Mitchell (Asylum)
-	29	THE BEST OF THE STYLISTICS	Stylistics (Avco)
30	30	SONGS OF JOY	Nigel Brooks Singers (K-Tel)

6 March 1976

last week	this week	Title	Artist
2	1	THE VERY BEST OF SLIM WHITMAN	Slim Whitman (United Artists)
7	2	CARNIVAL	Manuel & His Music of the Mountains (Studio Two)
3	3	THE BEST OF ROY ORBISON	Roy Orbison (Arcade)
3	4	RUN WITH THE PACK	Bad Company (Island)
19	5	A TRICK OF THE TAIL	Genesis (Charisma)
5	6	A NIGHT AT THE OPERA	Queen (EMI)
1	7	DESIRE	Bob Dylan (CBS)
11	8	HOW DARE YOU	10 C.C. (Mercury)
10	9	OMMADAWN	Mike Oldfield (Virgin)
12	10	THE BEST OF HELEN REDDY	Helen Reddy (Capitol)
6	11	STATION TO STATION	David Bowie (RCA)
17	12	ABBA	Abba (Epic)
8	13	24 ORIGINAL HITS	Drifters (Atlantic)
13	14	MUSIC EXPRESS	Various Artists (K-Tel)
9	15	MOTOWN GOLD	Various Artists (Tamla Motown)
15	16	PERRY COMO'S 40 GREATEST HITS	Perry Como (K-Tel)
16	17	TIMELESS FLIGHT	Steve Harley & Cockney Rebel (EMI)
14	18	SUNBURST FINISH	Be-Bop Deluxe (Harvest)
20	19	STILL CRAZY AFTER ALL THESE YEARS	Paul Simon (CBS)
-	20	THE BEST OF GLADYS KNIGHT & THE PIPS	Gladys Knight & the Pips (Buddah)
22	21	SHEER HEART ATTACK	Queen (EMI)
-	22	ONE OF THESE NIGHTS	Eagles (Asylum)
30	23	SONGS OF JOY	Nigel Brooks Singers (K-Tel)
24	24	BREAKAWAY	Art Garfunkel (CBS)
-	25	BREAKAWAY	Gallagher & Lyle (A&M)
-	26	ELITE HOTEL	Emmylou Harris (Reprise)
21	27	ROLLED GOLD	Rolling Stones (Decca)
-	28	QUEEN II	Queen (EMI)
-	29	LET THE MUSIC PLAY	Barry White (20th Century)
27	30	WISH YOU WERE HERE	Pink Floyd (Harvest)

13 March 1976

last week	this week	Title	Artist
1	1	THE VERY BEST OF SLIM WHITMAN	Slim Whitman (United Artists)
2	2	CARNIVAL	Manuel & His Music of the Mountains (Studio Two)
3	3	THE BEST OF ROY ORBISON	Roy Orbison (Arcade)
4	4	RUN WITH THE PACK	Bad Company (Island)
5	5	A TRICK OF THE TAIL	Genesis (Charisma)
6	6	A NIGHT AT THE OPERA	Queen (EMI)
7	7	DESIRE	Bob Dylan (CBS)
8	8	HOW DARE YOU	10 C.C. (Mercury)
9	9	OMMADAWN	Mike Oldfield (Virgin)
10	10	THE BEST OF HELEN REDDY	Helen Reddy (Capitol)
11	11	STATION TO STATION	David Bowie (RCA)
12	12	ABBA	Abba (Epic)
13	13	24 ORIGINAL HITS	Drifters (Atlantic)
14	14	MUSIC EXPRESS	Various Artists (K-Tel)
15	15	MOTOWN GOLD	Various Artists (Tamla Motown)
16	16	PERRY COMO'S 40 GREATEST HITS	Perry Como (K-Tel)
17	17	TIMELESS FLIGHT	Steve Harley & Cockney Rebel (EMI)
18	18	SUNBURST FINISH	Be-Bop Deluxe (Harvest)
19	19	STILL CRAZY AFTER ALL THESE YEARS	Paul Simon (CBS)
20	20	THE BEST OF GLADYS KNIGHT & THE PIPS	Gladys Knight & the Pips (Buddah)
21	21	SHEER HEART ATTACK	Queen (EMI)
22	22	ONE OF THESE NIGHTS	Eagles (Asylum)
23	23	SONGS OF JOY	Nigel Brooks Singers (K-Tel)
24	24	BREAKAWAY	Art Garfunkel (CBS)
25	25	BREAKAWAY	Gallagher & Lyle (A&M)
26	26	ELITE HOTEL	Emmylou Harris (Reprise)
27	27	ROLLED GOLD	Rolling Stones (Decca)
28	28	QUEEN II	Queen (EMI)
29	29	LET THE MUSIC PLAY	Barry White (20th Century)
30	30	WISH YOU WERE HERE	Pink Floyd (Harvest)

20 March 1976

last week	this week	Title	Artist
7	1	DESIRE	Bob Dylan (CBS)
2	2	CARNIVAL	Manuel & His Music of the Mountains (Studio Two)
5	3	A TRICK OF THE TAIL	Genesis (Charisma)
1	4	THE VERY BEST OF SLIM WHITMAN	Slim Whitman (United Artists)
-	5	THEIR GREATEST HITS 1971–1975	Eagles (Asylum)
8	6	HOW DARE YOU	10 C.C. (Mercury)
4	7	RUN WITH THE PACK	Bad Company (Island)
10	8	THE BEST OF HELEN REDDY	Helen Reddy (Capitol)
3	9	THE BEST OF ROY ORBISON	Roy Orbison (Arcade)
-	10	BLUE FOR YOU	Status Quo (Vertigo)
6	11	A NIGHT AT THE OPERA	Queen (EMI)
25	12	BREAKAWAY	Gallagher & Lyle (A&M)
20	13	THE BEST OF GLADYS KNIGHT & THE PIPS	Gladys Knight & the Pips (Buddah)
13	14	24 ORIGINAL HITS	Drifters (Atlantic)
-	15	THE FOUR SEASONS STORY	Four Seasons (Private Stock)
11	16	STATION TO STATION	David Bowie (RCA)
15	17	MOTOWN GOLD	Various Artists (Tamla Motown)
9	18	OMMADAWN	Mike Oldfield (Virgin)
26	19	ELITE HOTEL	Emmylou Harris (Reprise)
18	20	SUNBURST FINISH	Be-Bop Deluxe (Harvest)
-	21	GLENN MILLER - A MEMORIAL 1944-1968	Glenn Miller (RCA)
12	22	ABBA	Abba (Epic)
29	23	LET THE MUSIC PLAY	Barry White (20th Century)
14	24	MUSIC EXPRESS	Various Artists (K-Tel)
-	25	THE BEST OF JOHN DENVER	John Denver (RCA)
27	26	ROLLED GOLD	Rolling Stones (Decca)
-	27	THE HISSING OF SUMMER LAWNS	Joni Mitchell (Asylum)
-	28	LIVE	Robin Trower (Chrysalis)
-	29	WHO LOVES YOU	Four Seasons (Warner Bros.)
-	30	CRISIS? WHAT CRISIS?	Supertramp (A&M)

In February, destitute ex-Supreme Florence Ballard died of a heart attack. On March 19, on a transatlantic flight, so did Paul Kossoff of Free; his second heart attack, both had been drug-induced. So was the death of Uriah Heep's Gary Thain, also in March. In April, US folk-singer Phil Ochs would commit suicide. Meanwhile February-March saw Ochs' old Greenwich Village rival Bob Dylan topping the LP charts (for four weeks), for the first time in years. He hasn't done it again since.

last week	this week	27 March 1976
10	1	BLUE FOR YOU — Status Quo (Vertigo)
5	2	THEIR GREATEST HITS 1971–1975 — Eagles (Asylum)
2	3	CARNIVAL — Manuel & the Music of the Mountains (Studio Two)
3	4	A TRICK OF THE TAIL — Genesis (Charisma)
1	5	DESIRE — Bob Dylan (CBS)
7	6	RUN WITH THE PACK — Bad Company (Island)
6	7	HOW DARE YOU — 10 C.C. (Mercury)
4	8	THE VERY BEST OF SLIM WHITMAN — Slim Whitman (United Artists)
8	9	THE BEST OF HELEN REDDY — Helen Reddy (Capitol)
12	10	BREAKAWAY — Gallagher & Lyle (A&M)
9	11	THE BEST OF ROY ORBISON — Roy Orbison (Arcade)
11	12	A NIGHT AT THE OPERA — Queen (EMI)
14	13	24 ORIGINAL HITS — Drifters (Atlantic)
13	14	THE BEST OF GLADYS KNIGHT & THE PIPS — Gladys Knight & the Pips (Buddah)
17	15	MOTOWN GOLD — Various Artists (Tamla Motown)
19	16	ELITE HOTEL — Emmylou Harris (Reprise)
15	17	THE FOUR SEASONS STORY — Four Seasons (Private Stock)
23	18	LET THE MUSIC PLAY — Barry White (20th Century)
18	19	OMMADAWN — Mike Oldfield (Virgin)
21	20	GLENN MILLER - A MEMORIAL 1944-1968 — Glenn Miller (RCA)
25	21	THE BEST OF JOHN DENVER — John Denver (RCA)
-	22	BRASS CONSTRUCTION — Brass Construction (United Artists)
-	23	WALK RIGHT BACK WITH THE EVERLYS — Everly Brothers (Warner Bros.)
20	24	SUNBURST FINISH — Be-Bop Deluxe (Harvest)
-	25	DIANA ROSS — Diana Ross (Tamla Motown)
-	26	RAISIN' HELL — Fatback Band (Polydor)
24	27	MUSIC EXPRESS — Various Artists (K-Tel)
-	28	RODRIGO: CONCIERTO DE ARANJUEZ — John Williams with the English Chamber Orchestra (CBS)
22	29	ABBA — Abba (Epic)
29	30	WHO LOVES YOU — Four Seasons (Warner Bros.)

last week	this week	3 April 1976
1	1	BLUE FOR YOU — Status Quo (Vertigo)
2	2	THEIR GREATEST HITS 1971–1975 — Eagles (Asylum)
4	3	A TRICK OF THE TAIL — Genesis (Charisma)
10	3	BREAKAWAY — Gallagher & Lyle (A&M)
3	5	CARNIVAL — Manuel & His Music of the Mountains (Studio Two)
8	6	THE VERY BEST OF SLIM WHITMAN — Slim Whitman (United Artists)
7	7	HOW DARE YOU — 10 C.C. (Mercury)
5	8	DESIRE — Bob Dylan (CBS)
25	9	DIANA ROSS — Diana Ross (Tamla Motown)
6	10	RUN WITH THE PACK — Bad Company (Island)
21	11	THE BEST OF JOHN DENVER — John Denver (RCA)
9	12	THE BEST OF HELEN REDDY — Helen Reddy (Capitol)
-	13	REBEL — John Miles (Decca)
17	14	THE FOUR SEASONS STORY — Four Seasons (Private Stock)
11	15	THE BEST OF ROY ORBISON — Roy Orbison (Arcade)
16	16	ELITE HOTEL — Emmylou Harris (Reprise)
-	17	NOBODY'S FOOL — Slade (Polydor)
12	18	A NIGHT AT THE OPERA — Queen (EMI)
14	19	THE BEST OF GLADYS KNIGHT & THE PIPS — Gladys Knight & the Pips (Buddah)
-	20	JUKE BOX JIVE — Various Artists (K-Tel)
-	21	LIVE — Robin Trower (Chrysalis)
22	22	BRASS CONSTRUCTION — Brass Construction (United Artists)
13	23	24 ORIGINAL HITS — Drifters (Atlantic)
-	24	GREATEST HITS — Abba (Epic)
24	25	SUNBURST FINISH — Be-Bop Deluxe (Harvest)
-	26	ROCK FOLLIES — Soundtrack (Island)
18	27	LET THE MUSIC PLAY — Barry White (20th Century)
19	28	OMMADAWN — Mike Oldfield (Virgin)
15	29	MOTOWN GOLD — Various Artists (Tamla Motown)
-	30	BY INVITATION ONLY — Various Artists (Atlantic)

last week	this week	10 April 1976
2	1	THEIR GREATEST HITS 1971–1975 — Eagles (Asylum)
1	2	BLUE FOR YOU — Status Quo (Vertigo)
26	3	ROCK FOLLIES — Soundtrack (Island)
13	4	REBEL — John Miles (Decca)
3	5	BREAKAWAY — Gallagher & Lyle (A&M)
9	5	DIANA ROSS — Diana Ross (Tamla Motown)
8	7	DESIRE — Bob Dylan (CBS)
3	8	A TRICK OF THE TAIL — Genesis (Charisma)
-	8	WINGS AT THE SPEED OF SOUND — Wings (EMI)
5	10	CARNIVAL — Manuel & the Music of the Mountains (Studio Two)
7	11	HOW DARE YOU — 10 C.C. (Mercury)
11	12	THE BEST OF JOHN DENVER — John Denver (RCA)
12	13	THE BEST OF HELEN REDDY — Helen Reddy (Capitol)
19	14	THE BEST OF GLADYS KNIGHT & THE PIPS — Gladys Knight & the Pips (Buddah)
24	15	GREATEST HITS — Abba (Epic)
20	16	JUKE BOX JIVE — Various Artists (K-Tel)
6	17	THE VERY BEST OF SLIM WHITMAN — Slim Whitman (United Artists)
-	18	WALK RIGHT BACK WITH THE EVERLYS — Everly Brothers (Warner Bros.)
10	19	RUN WITH THE PACK — Bad Company (Island)
27	20	LET THE MUSIC PLAY — Barry White (20th Century)
18	21	A NIGHT AT THE OPERA — Queen (EMI)
16	22	ELITE HOTEL — Emmylou Harris (Reprise)
-	23	PENTHOUSE TAPES — Sensational Alex Harvey Band (Vertigo)
15	24	THE BEST OF ROY ORBISON — Roy Orbison (Arcade)
22	25	BRASS CONSTRUCTION — Brass Construction (United Artists)
30	26	BY INVITATION ONLY — Various Artists (Atlantic)
28	27	OMMADAWN — Mike Oldfield (Virgin)
14	28	THE FOUR SEASONS STORY — Four Seasons (Private Stock)
23	29	24 ORIGINAL HITS — Drifters (Atlantic)
-	30	GARY GLITTER'S GREATEST HITS — Gary Glitter (Bell)

last week	this week	17 April 1976
3	1	ROCK FOLLIES — Soundtrack (Island)
1	2	THEIR GREATEST HITS 1971–1975 — Eagles (Asylum)
5	3	DIANA ROSS — Diana Ross (Tamla Motown)
4	4	REBEL — John Miles (Decca)
16	5	JUKE BOX JIVE — Various Artists (K-Tel)
7	6	DESIRE — Bob Dylan (CBS)
11	7	HOW DARE YOU — 10 C.C. (Mercury)
2	8	BLUE FOR YOU — Status Quo (Vertigo)
5	9	BREAKAWAY — Gallagher & Lyle (A&M)
8	10	WINGS AT THE SPEED OF SOUND — Wings (EMI)
23	11	PENTHOUSE TAPES — Sensational Alex Harvey Band (Vertigo)
10	12	CARNIVAL — Manuel & His Music of the Mountains (Studio Two)
15	13	GREATEST HITS — Abba (Epic)
12	14	THE BEST OF JOHN DENVER — John Denver (RCA)
-	15	PRESENCE — Led Zeppelin (Swansong)
17	16	THE VERY BEST OF SLIM WHITMAN — Slim Whitman (United Artists)
8	17	A TRICK OF THE TAIL — Genesis (Charisma)
24	18	THE BEST OF ROY ORBISON — Roy Orbison (Arcade)
-	19	AMIGOS — Santana (CBS)
13	20	THE BEST OF HELEN REDDY — Helen Reddy (Capitol)
21	21	A NIGHT AT THE OPERA — Queen (EMI)
25	22	BRASS CONSTRUCTION — Brass Construction (United Artists)
-	23	LIVE — Joe Walsh (ABC)
26	24	BY INVITATION ONLY — Various Artists (Atlantic)
19	25	RUN WITH THE PACK — Bad Company (Island)
-	26	JAILBREAK — Thin Lizzy (Vertigo)
20	27	LET THE MUSIC PLAY — Barry White (20th Century)
-	28	CRY TOUGH — Nils Lofgren (A&M)
14	29	THE BEST OF GLADYS KNIGHT & THE PIPS — Gladys Knight & the Pips (Buddah)
-	30	SUNBURST FINISH — Be-Bop Deluxe (Harvest)

Blue For You was the fifth mega-album by Britain's lowest common denominators of rock, Status Quo. The Eagles' *Greatest Hits*, their fourth LP, was their biggest: which was odd, because they were the classic 1970s American albums band and had only had three hit singles, *One Of These Nights*, *Lyin' Eyes* and, now, *Take It To The Limit*. Their least chart-successful LP had been their finest, *Desperado*. Soon would come *Hotel California*, an artifact held in special contempt by the newly-emerging punks.

April – May 1976

24 April 1976

last week	this week	Title
1	1	ROCK FOLLIES — Soundtrack (Island)
10	2	WINGS AT THE SPEED OF SOUND — Wings (EMI)
5	3	JUKE BOX JIVE — Various Artists (K-Tel)
13	4	GREATEST HITS — Abba (Epic)
3	5	DIANA ROSS — Diana Ross (Tamla Motown)
8	6	BLUE FOR YOU — Status Quo (Vertigo)
15	7	PRESENCE — Led Zeppelin (Swansong)
2	8	THEIR GREATEST HITS 1971–1975 — Eagles (Asylum)
4	9	REBEL — John Miles (Decca)
6	10	DESIRE — Bob Dylan (CBS)
17	11	A TRICK OF THE TAIL — Genesis (Charisma)
28	12	CRY TOUGH — Nils Lofgren (A&M)
7	13	HOW DARE YOU — 10 C.C. (Mercury)
-	14	MOONMADNESS — Camel (Decca)
22	15	BRASS CONSTRUCTION — Brass Construction (United Artists)
11	16	PENTHOUSE TAPES — Sensational Alex Harvey Band (Vertigo)
9	17	BREAKAWAY — Gallagher & Lyle (A&M)
-	18	NO EARTHLY CONNECTION — Rick Wakeman (A&M)
29	19	THE BEST OF GLADYS KNIGHT & THE PIPS — Gladys Knight & the Pips (Buddah)
19	20	AMIGOS — Santana (CBS)
14	21	THE BEST OF JOHN DENVER — John Denver (RCA)
27	22	LET THE MUSIC PLAY — Barry White (20th Century)
20	23	THE BEST OF HELEN REDDY — Helen Reddy (Capitol)
25	24	RUN WITH THE PACK — Bad Company (Island)
-	25	INSTRUMENTAL GOLD — Various Artists (Warwick)
-	26	PATRICK MORAZ — Patrick Moraz (Charisma)
-	27	TUBULAR BELLS — Mike Oldfield (Virgin)
-	28	THE FOUR SEASONS STORY — Four Seasons (Private Stock)
16	29	THE VERY BEST OF SLIM WHITMAN — Slim Whitman (United Artists)
18	30	THE BEST OF ROY ORBISON — Roy Orbison (Arcade)

1 May 1976

last week	this week	Title
1	1	ROCK FOLLIES — Soundtrack (Island)
7	2	PRESENCE — Led Zeppelin (Swansong)
2	3	WINGS AT THE SPEED OF SOUND — Wings (EMI)
4	4	GREATEST HITS — Abba (Epic)
3	5	JUKE BOX JIVE — Various Artists (K-Tel)
6	6	BLUE FOR YOU — Status Quo (Vertigo)
5	7	DIANA ROSS — Diana Ross (Tamla Motown)
8	8	THEIR GREATEST HITS 1971–1975 — Eagles (Asylum)
9	9	REBEL — John Miles (Decca)
18	10	NO EARTHLY CONNECTION — Rick Wakeman (A&M)
13	11	HOW DARE YOU — 10 C.C. (Mercury)
10	12	DESIRE — Bob Dylan (CBS)
14	13	MOONMADNESS — Camel (Decca)
11	14	A TRICK OF THE TAIL — Genesis (Charisma)
21	15	THE BEST OF JOHN DENVER — John Denver (RCA)
-	16	BLACK AND BLUE — Rolling Stones (Rolling Stones)
19	17	THE BEST OF GLADYS KNIGHT & THE PIPS — Gladys Knight & the Pips (Buddah)
12	18	CRY TOUGH — Nils Lofgren (A&M)
16	19	PENTHOUSE TAPES — Sensational Alex Harvey Band (Vertigo)
15	20	BRASS CONSTRUCTION — Brass Construction (United Artists)
20	21	AMIGOS — Santana (CBS)
25	22	INSTRUMENTAL GOLD — Various Artists (Warwick)
-	23	CARNIVAL — Manuel & His Music of the Mountains (Studio Two)
-	24	PAT BOONE ORIGINALS — Pat Boone (ABC)
-	25	LOVE AND KISSES FROM — Brotherhood of Man (Pye)
22	26	LET THE MUSIC PLAY — Barry White (20th Century)
-	27	HAPPY TO BE — Demis Roussos (Philips)
26	28	PATRICK MORAZ — Patrick Moraz (Charisma)
17	29	BREAKAWAY — Gallagher & Lyle (A&M)
29	30	THE VERY BEST OF SLIM WHITMAN — Slim Whitman (United Artists)

8 May 1976

last week	this week	Title
1	1	ROCK FOLLIES — Soundtrack (Island)
4	2	GREATEST HITS — Abba (Epic)
2	3	PRESENCE — Led Zeppelin (Swansong)
3	4	WINGS AT THE SPEED OF SOUND — Wings (EMI)
10	5	NO EARTHLY CONNECTION — Rick Wakeman (A&M)
8	6	THEIR GREATEST HITS 1971–1975 — Eagles (Asylum)
11	7	HOW DARE YOU — 10 C.C. (Mercury)
7	8	DIANA ROSS — Diana Ross (Tamla Motown)
5	9	JUKE BOX JIVE — Various Artists (K-Tel)
6	10	BLUE FOR YOU — Status Quo (Vertigo)
9	11	REBEL — John Miles (Decca)
12	12	DESIRE — Bob Dylan (CBS)
16	13	BLACK AND BLUE — Rolling Stones (Rolling Stones)
-	14	WHO LOVES YOU — Four Seasons (Warner Bros.)
25	15	LOVE AND KISSES FROM — Brotherhood of Man (Pye)
-	16	LIVE IN LONDON — John Denver (RCA)
15	17	THE BEST OF JOHN DENVER — John Denver (RCA)
22	18	INSTRUMENTAL GOLD — Various Artists (Warwick)
21	19	AMIGOS — Santana (CBS)
14	20	A TRICK OF THE TAIL — Genesis (Charisma)
24	21	PAT BOONE ORIGINALS — Pat Boone (ABC)
13	22	MOONMADNESS — Camel (Decca)
-	23	HERE AND THERE — Elton John (DJM)
-	24	DOUBLY DEVINE — Sydney Devine (Philips)
-	25	HIT MACHINE — Various Artists (K-Tel)
17	26	THE BEST OF GLADYS KNIGHT & THE PIPS — Gladys Knight & the Pips (Buddah)
30	27	THE VERY BEST OF SLIM WHITMAN — Slim Whitman (United Artists)
18	28	CRY TOUGH — Nils Lofgren (A&M)
-	29	24 ORIGINAL HITS — Drifters (Atlantic)
19	30	PENTHOUSE TAPES — Sensational Alex Harvey Band (Vertigo)

15 May 1976

last week	this week	Title
2	1	GREATEST HITS — Abba (Epic)
13	2	BLACK AND BLUE — Rolling Stones (Rolling Stones)
4	3	WINGS AT THE SPEED OF SOUND — Wings (EMI)
3	4	PRESENCE — Led Zeppelin (Swansong)
8	5	DIANA ROSS — Diana Ross (Tamla Motown)
1	6	ROCK FOLLIES — Soundtrack (Island)
7	7	HOW DARE YOU — 10 C.C. (Mercury)
9	8	JUKE BOX JIVE — Various Artists (K-Tel)
6	9	THEIR GREATEST HITS 1971–1975 — Eagles (Asylum)
18	10	INSTRUMENTAL GOLD — Various Artists (Warwick)
5	11	NO EARTHLY CONNECTION — Rick Wakeman (A&M)
10	12	BLUE FOR YOU — Status Quo (Vertigo)
11	13	REBEL — John Miles (Decca)
20	14	A TRICK OF THE TAIL — Genesis (Charisma)
12	15	DESIRE — Bob Dylan (CBS)
26	16	THE BEST OF GLADYS KNIGHT & THE PIPS — Gladys Knight & the Pips (Buddah)
14	17	WHO LOVES YOU — Four Seasons (Warner Bros.)
15	18	LOVE AND KISSES FROM — Brotherhood of Man (Pye)
16	19	LIVE IN LONDON — John Denver (RCA)
25	20	HIT MACHINE — Various Artists (K-Tel)
17	21	THE BEST OF JOHN DENVER — John Denver (RCA)
24	22	DOUBLY DEVINE — Sydney Devine (Philips)
19	23	AMIGOS — Santana (CBS)
-	24	THE BEATLES 1962-1966 — Beatles (Apple)
21	25	PAT BOONE ORIGINALS — Pat Boone (ABC)
30	26	PENTHOUSE TAPES — Sensational Alex Harvey Band (Vertigo)
23	27	HERE AND THERE — Elton John (DJM)
29	28	24 ORIGINAL HITS — Drifters (Atlantic)
-	29	BREAKAWAY — Gallagher & Lyle (A&M)
27	30	THE VERY BEST OF SLIM WHITMAN — Slim Whitman (United Artists)

Rock Follies came from TV series about a group of three female singers, one of whom was played by Rula Lenska, later an item with Dennis Waterman, another actor who imagined he could sing. Hello again to Manuel, Pat Boone (his first chart LP since 1960), and Demis Roussos (see description for Barry White, May-June 1975). But goodbye to ex-Yardbird Keith Relf: he was electrocuted in May. His only solo chart appearance had been at No.50 in the singles for one week in 1966 with *Mr Zero*.

last week	this week	22 May 1976
1	1	GREATEST HITS Abba (Epic)
3	2	WINGS AT THE SPEED OF SOUND Wings (EMI)
2	3	BLACK AND BLUE Rolling Stones (Rolling Stones)
4	4	PRESENCE Led Zeppelin (Swansong)
19	5	LIVE IN LONDON John Denver (RCA)
6	6	ROCK FOLLIES Soundtrack (Island)
5	7	DIANA ROSS Diana Ross (Tamla Motown)
7	8	HOW DARE YOU 10 C.C. (Mercury)
27	9	HERE AND THERE Elton John (DJM)
20	10	HIT MACHINE Various Artists (K-Tel)
9	11	THEIR GREATEST HITS 1971–1975 Eagles (Asylum)
11	12	NO EARTHLY CONNECTION Rick Wakeman (A&M)
10	13	INSTRUMENTAL GOLD Various Artists (Warwick)
16	14	THE BEST OF GLADYS KNIGHT & THE PIPS Gladys Knight & the Pips (Buddah)
15	15	DESIRE Bob Dylan (CBS)
18	16	LOVE AND KISSES FROM Brotherhood of Man (Pye)
12	17	BLUE FOR YOU Status Quo (Vertigo)
29	18	BREAKAWAY Gallagher & Lyle (A&M)
13	19	REBEL John Miles (Decca)
8	20	JUKE BOX JIVE Various Artists (K-Tel)
-	21	SOME OF ME POEMS AND SONGS Pam Ayres (Galaxy)
17	22	WHO LOVES YOU Four Seasons (Warner Bros.)
14	23	A TRICK OF THE TAIL Genesis (Charisma)
-	24	I'M NEARLY FAMOUS Cliff Richard (EMI)
-	25	THE ROYAL SCAM Steely Dan (ABC)
-	26	PATRICK MORAZ Patrick Moraz (Charisma)
-	27	RASTAMAN VIBRATION Bob Marley & the Wailers (Island)
23	28	AMIGOS Santana (CBS)
-	29	I WANT YOU Marvin Gaye (Tamla Motown)
25	30	PAT BOONE ORIGINALS Pat Boone (ABC)

last	this	29 May 1976
1	1	GREATEST HITS Abba (Epic)
3	2	BLACK AND BLUE Rolling Stones (Rolling Stones)
2	3	WINGS AT THE SPEED OF SOUND Wings (EMI)
5	4	LIVE IN LONDON John Denver (RCA)
4	5	PRESENCE Led Zeppelin (Swansong)
7	6	DIANA ROSS Diana Ross (Tamla Motown)
13	7	INSTRUMENTAL GOLD Various Artists (Warwick)
14	8	THE BEST OF GLADYS KNIGHT & THE PIPS Gladys Knight & the Pips (Buddah)
10	9	HIT MACHINE Various Artists (K-Tel)
6	10	ROCK FOLLIES Soundtrack (Island)
11	11	THEIR GREATEST HITS 1971–1975 Eagles (Asylum)
9	12	HERE AND THERE Elton John (DJM)
22	13	WHO LOVES YOU Four Seasons (Warner Bros.)
12	14	NO EARTHLY CONNECTION Rick Wakeman (A&M)
24	15	I'M NEARLY FAMOUS Cliff Richard (EMI)
20	16	JUKE BOX JIVE Various Artists (K-Tel)
8	17	HOW DARE YOU 10 C.C. (Mercury)
-	18	A TOUCH OF COUNTRY Various Artists (Topaz)
15	19	DESIRE Bob Dylan (CBS)
21	20	SOME OF ME POEMS AND SONGS Pam Ayres (Galaxy)
18	21	BREAKAWAY Gallagher & Lyle (A&M)
23	22	A TRICK OF THE TAIL Genesis (Charisma)
-	23	ON TOUR David Essex (CBS)
28	24	AMIGOS Santana (CBS)
-	25	WINDSONG John Denver (RCA)
19	26	REBEL John Miles (Decca)
16	27	LOVE AND KISSES FROM Brotherhood of Man (Pye)
-	28	LOVE, LIFE AND FEELINGS Shirley Bassey (United Artists)
-	29	TOO OLD TO ROCK 'N' ROLL, TOO YOUNG TO DIE Jethro Tull (Chrysalis)
25	30	THE ROYAL SCAM Steely Dan (ABC)

last	this	5 June 1976
1	1	GREATEST HITS Abba (Epic)
4	2	LIVE IN LONDON John Denver (RCA)
3	3	WINGS AT THE SPEED OF SOUND Wings (EMI)
2	4	BLACK AND BLUE Rolling Stones (Rolling Stones)
6	5	DIANA ROSS Diana Ross (Tamla Motown)
5	6	PRESENCE Led Zeppelin (Swansong)
15	7	I'M NEARLY FAMOUS Cliff Richard (EMI)
8	8	THE BEST OF GLADYS KNIGHT & THE PIPS Gladys Knight & the Pips (Buddah)
9	9	HIT MACHINE Various Artists (K-Tel)
-	10	FRAMPTON COMES ALIVE Peter Frampton (A&M)
10	11	ROCK FOLLIES Soundtrack (Island)
13	12	WHO LOVES YOU Four Seasons (Warner Bros.)
30	13	THE ROYAL SCAM Steely Dan (ABC)
11	14	THEIR GREATEST HITS 1971–1975 Eagles (Asylum)
7	15	INSTRUMENTAL GOLD Various Artists (Warwick)
21	16	BREAKAWAY Gallagher & Lyle (A&M)
18	17	A TOUCH OF COUNTRY Various Artists (Topaz)
16	18	JUKE BOX JIVE Various Artists (K-Tel)
12	19	HERE AND THERE Elton John (DJM)
17	20	HOW DARE YOU 10 C.C. (Mercury)
14	21	NO EARTHLY CONNECTION Rick Wakeman (A&M)
22	22	A TRICK OF THE TAIL Genesis (Charisma)
-	23	STATION TO STATION David Bowie (RCA)
19	24	DESIRE Bob Dylan (CBS)
-	25	SIMON & GARFUNKEL'S GREATEST HITS Simon & Garfunkel (CBS)
-	26	REACH FOR THE SKY Sutherland Brothers & Quiver (CBS)
27	27	LOVE AND KISSES FROM Brotherhood of Man (Pye)
-	28	CRY TOUGH Nils Lofgren (A&M)
-	29	BLUE FOR YOU Status Quo (Vertigo)
-	30	ROLLED GOLD Rolling Stones (Decca)

last	this	12 June 1976
1	1	GREATEST HITS Abba (Epic)
2	2	LIVE IN LONDON John Denver (RCA)
3	3	WINGS AT THE SPEED OF SOUND Wings (EMI)
4	4	BLACK AND BLUE Rolling Stones (Rolling Stones)
7	5	I'M NEARLY FAMOUS Cliff Richard (EMI)
8	6	THE BEST OF GLADYS KNIGHT & THE PIPS Gladys Knight & the Pips (Buddah)
15	7	INSTRUMENTAL GOLD Various Artists (Warwick)
10	8	FRAMPTON COMES ALIVE Peter Frampton (A&M)
5	9	DIANA ROSS Diana Ross (Tamla Motown)
6	10	PRESENCE Led Zeppelin (Swansong)
-	11	CHANGESONEBOWIE David Bowie (WEA)
9	12	HIT MACHINE Various Artists (K-Tel)
12	13	WHO LOVES YOU Four Seasons (Warner Bros.)
16	14	BREAKAWAY Gallagher & Lyle (A&M)
19	15	HERE AND THERE Elton John (DJM)
13	16	THE ROYAL SCAM Steely Dan (ABC)
17	17	A TOUCH OF COUNTRY Various Artists (Topaz)
20	18	HOW DARE YOU 10 C.C. (Mercury)
14	19	THEIR GREATEST HITS 1971–1975 Eagles (Asylum)
11	20	ROCK FOLLIES Soundtrack (Island)
26	21	REACH FOR THE SKY Sutherland Brothers & Quiver (CBS)
-	22	DESTROYER Kiss (Casablanca)
18	23	JUKE BOX JIVE Various Artists (K-Tel)
-	24	THE BEST OF JOHN DENVER John Denver (RCA)
-	25	JAILBREAK Thin Lizzy (Vertigo)
22	26	A TRICK OF THE TAIL Genesis (Charisma)
25	27	SIMON & GARFUNKEL'S GREATEST HITS Simon & Garfunkel (CBS)
21	28	NO EARTHLY CONNECTION Rick Wakeman (A&M)
-	29	LOVE, LIFE AND FEELINGS Shirley Bassey (United Artists)
28	30	CRY TOUGH Nils Lofgren (A&M)

Howlin' Wolf (Chester Burnett) had died in Chicago in January, so Keith Relf had just outlived one of the grandest old heroes of the beat-groups. Relf was the third British musician electrocuted in modern times, after Les Harvey of Stone the Crows (May 1972) and John Rostill of the Shadows (November 1973). Shads boss Cliff Richard now returned to the album chart with the gruesomely coy title *I'm Nearly Famous*; John Denvermania now returned the risible title *Windsong* to the chart, to join two other Denver LPs.

June – July 1976

19 June 1976

26 June 1976

3 July 1976

10 July 1976

Odd figures here. Bob Marley had entered the album chart at No.27 in May with *Rastaman Vibration*, but had promptly disappeared again. Yet in other charts, this album rose as high as No.15, consolidating Marley's position as reggae's international star, after 1975's *Natty Dread* and his celebrated London Lyceum concert that summer. Nonetheless, Marley's biggest LP hits were still to come, with *Exodus* (1977), *Kaya* (1978), *Uprising* (1980) and more albums after Marley's death from cancer in 1981.

July – August 1976

17 July 1976

last week	this week	Title / Artist (Label)
1	1	A NIGHT ON THE TOWN — Rod Stewart (Riva)
2	2	GREATEST HITS — Abba (Epic)
5	3	HAPPY TO BE — Demis Roussos (Philips)
7	4	20 GOLDEN GREATS — Beach Boys (Capitol)
4	5	WINGS AT THE SPEED OF SOUND — Wings (EMI)
3	6	LIVE IN LONDON — John Denver (RCA)
8	7	CHANGESONEBOWIE — David Bowie (WEA)
6	8	A KIND OF HUSH — Carpenters (A&M)
9	9	FOREVER AND EVER — Demis Roussos (Philips)
10	10	FRAMPTON COMES ALIVE — Peter Frampton (A&M)
29	11	PASSPORT — Nana Mouskouri (Philips)
19	12	A LITTLE BIT MORE — Dr. Hook (Capitol)
-	13	LAUGHTER AND TEARS - THE BEST OF NEIL SEDAKA TODAY — Neil Sedaka (Polydor)
15	14	THEIR GREATEST HITS 1971–1975 — Eagles (Asylum)
12	15	ROCK 'N' ROLL MUSIC — Beatles (Apple)
13	16	JAILBREAK — Thin Lizzy (Vertigo)
11	17	THE BEST OF GLADYS KNIGHT & THE PIPS — Gladys Knight & the Pips (Buddah)
16	18	RAINBOW RISING — Ritchie Blackmore (Polydor)
23	19	BREAKAWAY — Gallagher & Lyle (A&M)
21	20	I'M NEARLY FAMOUS — Cliff Richard (EMI)
-	21	DIANA ROSS — Diana Ross (Tamla Motown)
17	22	THE ROYAL SCAM — Steely Dan (ABC)
24	23	I ONLY HAVE EYES FOR YOU — Johnny Mathis (CBS)
-	24	BEAUTIFUL NOISE — Neil Diamond (CBS)
18	25	INSTRUMENTAL GOLD — Various Artists (Warwick)
22	26	FLY LIKE AN EAGLE — Steve Miller Band (Mercury)
25	27	KING COTTON — Fivepenny Piece (EMI)
28	28	HIT MACHINE — Various Artists (K-Tel)
27	29	RED CARD — Streetwalkers (Vertigo)
-	30	BELLAMY BROTHERS — Bellamy Brothers (Warner Bros.)

24 July 1976

last week	this week	Title / Artist (Label)
4	1	20 GOLDEN GREATS — Beach Boys (Capitol)
1	2	A NIGHT ON THE TOWN — Rod Stewart (Riva)
9	3	FOREVER AND EVER — Demis Roussos (Philips)
3	4	HAPPY TO BE — Demis Roussos (Philips)
2	5	GREATEST HITS — Abba (Epic)
13	6	LAUGHTER AND TEARS - THE BEST OF NEIL SEDAKA TODAY — Neil Sedaka (Polydor)
8	7	A KIND OF HUSH — Carpenters (A&M)
7	8	CHANGESONEBOWIE — David Bowie (WEA)
12	9	A LITTLE BIT MORE — Dr. Hook (Capitol)
11	10	PASSPORT — Nana Mouskouri (Philips)
6	11	LIVE IN LONDON — John Denver (RCA)
24	12	BEAUTIFUL NOISE — Neil Diamond (CBS)
5	13	WINGS AT THE SPEED OF SOUND — Wings (EMI)
14	14	THEIR GREATEST HITS 1971–1975 — Eagles (Asylum)
10	15	FRAMPTON COMES ALIVE — Peter Frampton (A&M)
16	16	JAILBREAK — Thin Lizzy (Vertigo)
15	17	ROCK 'N' ROLL MUSIC — Beatles (Apple)
17	18	THE BEST OF GLADYS KNIGHT & THE PIPS — Gladys Knight & the Pips (Buddah)
21	19	DIANA ROSS — Diana Ross (Tamla Motown)
-	20	VIVA! — Roxy Music (Island)
26	21	FLY LIKE AN EAGLE — Steve Miller Band (Mercury)
-	22	OLIAS OF SUNHILLOW — Jon Anderson (Atlantic)
-	23	BLACK AND BLUE — Rolling Stones (Rolling Stones)
19	24	BREAKAWAY — Gallagher & Lyle (A&M)
20	25	I'M NEARLY FAMOUS — Cliff Richard (EMI)
23	26	I ONLY HAVE EYES FOR YOU — Johnny Mathis (CBS)
-	27	ONE MAN SHOW — Mike Harding (Philips)
25	28	INSTRUMENTAL GOLD — Various Artists (Warwick)
-	29	COMBINE HARVESTER — Wurzels (One Up)
-	30	15 BIG ONES — Beach Boys (Reprise)

31 July 1976

last week	this week	Title / Artist (Label)
1	1	20 GOLDEN GREATS — Beach Boys (Capitol)
3	2	FOREVER AND EVER — Demis Roussos (Philips)
2	3	A NIGHT ON THE TOWN — Rod Stewart (Riva)
6	4	LAUGHTER AND TEARS - THE BEST OF NEIL SEDAKA TODAY — Neil Sedaka (Polydor)
7	5	A KIND OF HUSH — Carpenters (A&M)
10	6	PASSPORT — Nana Mouskouri (Philips)
5	7	GREATEST HITS — Abba (Epic)
4	8	HAPPY TO BE — Demis Roussos (Philips)
9	9	A LITTLE BIT MORE — Dr. Hook (Capitol)
8	10	CHANGESONEBOWIE — David Bowie (WEA)
12	11	BEAUTIFUL NOISE — Neil Diamond (CBS)
15	12	FRAMPTON COMES ALIVE — Peter Frampton (A&M)
13	13	WINGS AT THE SPEED OF SOUND — Wings (EMI)
11	14	LIVE IN LONDON — John Denver (RCA)
22	15	OLIAS OF SUNHILLOW — Jon Anderson (Atlantic)
17	16	ROCK 'N' ROLL MUSIC — Beatles (Apple)
16	17	JAILBREAK — Thin Lizzy (Vertigo)
20	18	VIVA! — Roxy Music (Island)
19	19	DIANA ROSS — Diana Ross (Tamla Motown)
14	20	THEIR GREATEST HITS 1971–1975 — Eagles (Asylum)
18	21	THE BEST OF GLADYS KNIGHT & THE PIPS — Gladys Knight & the Pips (Buddah)
27	22	ONE MAN SHOW — Mike Harding (Philips)
24	23	BREAKAWAY — Gallagher & Lyle (A&M)
-	24	ALICE COOPER GOES TO HELL — Alice Cooper (Warner Bros.)
-	25	HOW DARE YOU — 10 C.C. (Mercury)
30	26	15 BIG ONES — Beach Boys (Reprise)
25	27	I'M NEARLY FAMOUS — Cliff Richard (EMI)
23	28	BLACK AND BLUE — Rolling Stones (Rolling Stones)
-	29	SOUVENIRS — Demis Roussos (Philips)
-	30	WIRED — Jeff Beck (CBS)

7 August 1976

last week	this week	Title / Artist (Label)
1	1	20 GOLDEN GREATS — Beach Boys (Capitol)
2	2	FOREVER AND EVER — Demis Roussos (Philips)
6	3	PASSPORT — Nana Mouskouri (Philips)
4	4	LAUGHTER AND TEARS - THE BEST OF NEIL SEDAKA TODAY — Neil Sedaka (Polydor)
3	5	A NIGHT ON THE TOWN — Rod Stewart (Riva)
9	6	A LITTLE BIT MORE — Dr. Hook (Capitol)
7	7	GREATEST HITS — Abba (Epic)
8	8	HAPPY TO BE — Demis Roussos (Philips)
10	9	CHANGESONEBOWIE — David Bowie (WEA)
5	10	A KIND OF HUSH — Carpenters (A&M)
11	11	BEAUTIFUL NOISE — Neil Diamond (CBS)
14	12	LIVE IN LONDON — John Denver (RCA)
15	13	OLIAS OF SUNHILLOW — Jon Anderson (Atlantic)
13	14	WINGS AT THE SPEED OF SOUND — Wings (EMI)
18	15	VIVA! — Roxy Music (Island)
20	16	THEIR GREATEST HITS 1971–1975 — Eagles (Asylum)
12	17	FRAMPTON COMES ALIVE — Peter Frampton (A&M)
-	18	SAHB STORIES — Sensational Alex Harvey Band (Mountain)
17	19	JAILBREAK — Thin Lizzy (Vertigo)
16	20	ROCK 'N' ROLL MUSIC — Beatles (Apple)
24	21	ALICE COOPER GOES TO HELL — Alice Cooper (Warner Bros.)
22	22	ONE MAN SHOW — Mike Harding (Philips)
21	23	THE BEST OF GLADYS KNIGHT & THE PIPS — Gladys Knight & the Pips (Buddah)
-	24	DON WILLIAMS' GREATEST HITS VOL 1 — Don Williams (ABC)
19	25	DIANA ROSS — Diana Ross (Tamla Motown)
-	26	YOUNG HEARTS RUN FREE — Candi Staton (Warner Bros.)
-	27	SIMON & GARFUNKEL'S GREATEST HITS — Simon & Garfunkel (CBS)
26	28	15 BIG ONES — Beach Boys (Reprise)
23	29	BREAKAWAY — Gallagher & Lyle (A&M)
30	30	WIRED — Jeff Beck (CBS)

Rod Stewart's *Night On The Town* was the first on his own label, Riva. *Atlantic Crossing* should have been on Rod's own label but at the last moment had to appear on Warners. Rod's first name-choice had been Rampant Records but, after spending extravagantly on artwork, his management found that Rampant Records was a registered business name, owned by, well, me. Stewart, notoriously mean (he once got a Rembrandt for Christmas from Elton John, and gave an ice-bucket in return), declined to buy the name.

August – September 1976

Roussosmania, as Demis reposed twice over in the Top 10, with *Forever And Ever* titled after a single that had got nowhere when first released but was now also the selling-point of the extraordinary EP *The Roussos Phenomenon*, which had topped the singles chart in July. This was also a time of comedy hits: the Wurzels re-entry *Combine Harvester* had, weeks earlier, charted alongside Mike Harding and just after Pam Ayres. Of course, some said Demis Roussos was the biggest comic of them all.

11 September 1976

last week	this week		
1	1	20 GOLDEN GREATS	Beach Boys (Capitol)
3	2	LAUGHTER AND TEARS - THE BEST OF NEIL SEDAKA TODAY	Neil Sedaka (Polydor)
4	3	A NIGHT ON THE TOWN	Rod Stewart (Riva)
5	4	FOREVER AND EVER	Demis Roussos (Philips)
6	5	GREATEST HITS	Abba (Epic)
9	6	WINGS AT THE SPEED OF SOUND	Wings (EMI)
2	7	DIANA ROSS' GREATEST HITS II	Diana Ross (Tamla Motown)
8	8	A LITTLE BIT MORE	Dr. Hook (Capitol)
10	9	PASSPORT	Nana Mouskouri (Philips)
12	10	BEAUTIFUL NOISE	Neil Diamond (CBS)
7	11	VIVA!	Roxy Music (Island)
11	12	JAILBREAK	Thin Lizzy (Vertigo)
15	13	LIVE IN LONDON	John Denver (RCA)
25	14	BLUE FOR YOU	Status Quo (Vertigo)
17	15	HAPPY TO BE	Demis Roussos (Philips)
18	16	THEIR GREATEST HITS 1971–1975	Eagles (Asylum)
14	17	A KIND OF HUSH	Carpenters (A&M)
16	18	FRAMPTON COMES ALIVE	Peter Frampton (A&M)
13	19	CHANGESONEBOWIE	David Bowie (WEA)
26	20	TWIGGY	Twiggy (Mercury)
24	21	OLIAS OF SUNHILLOW	Jon Anderson (Atlantic)
-	22	THE BEST OF GLADYS KNIGHT & THE PIPS	Gladys Knight & the Pips (Buddah)
19	23	SAHB STORIES	Sensational Alex Harvey Band (Mountain)
22	24	ATLANTIC CROSSING	Rod Stewart (Warner Bros.)
21	25	SPIRIT	John Denver (RCA)
-	26	BREAKAWAY	Gallagher & Lyle (A&M)
20	27	THE DARK SIDE OF THE MOON	Pink Floyd (Harvest)
-	28	HASTEN DOWN THE WIND	Linda Ronstadt (Asylum)
-	29	ROCK 'N' ROLL MUSIC	Beatles (Apple)
27	30	I'M NEARLY FAMOUS	Cliff Richard (EMI)

18 September 1976

1	1	20 GOLDEN GREATS	Beach Boys (Capitol)
2	2	LAUGHTER AND TEARS - THE BEST OF NEIL SEDAKA TODAY	Neil Sedaka (Polydor)
5	3	GREATEST HITS	Abba (Epic)
3	4	A NIGHT ON THE TOWN	Rod Stewart (Riva)
6	5	WINGS AT THE SPEED OF SOUND	Wings (EMI)
7	6	DIANA ROSS' GREATEST HITS II	Diana Ross (Tamla Motown)
8	7	A LITTLE BIT MORE	Dr. Hook (Capitol)
4	8	FOREVER AND EVER	Demis Roussos (Philips)
9	9	PASSPORT	Nana Mouskouri (Philips)
25	10	SPIRIT	John Denver (RCA)
26	11	BREAKAWAY	Gallagher & Lyle (A&M)
18	12	FRAMPTON COMES ALIVE	Peter Frampton (A&M)
11	13	VIVA!	Roxy Music (Island)
10	14	BEAUTIFUL NOISE	Neil Diamond (CBS)
12	15	JAILBREAK	Thin Lizzy (Vertigo)
-	16	NO REASON TO CRY	Eric Clapton (RSO)
16	17	THEIR GREATEST HITS 1971–1975	Eagles (Asylum)
24	18	ATLANTIC CROSSING	Rod Stewart (Warner Bros.)
20	19	TWIGGY	Twiggy (Mercury)
19	20	CHANGESONEBOWIE	David Bowie (WEA)
14	21	BLUE FOR YOU	Status Quo (Vertigo)
23	22	SAHB STORIES	Sensational Alex Harvey Band (Mountain)
-	23	THE BEST OF THE STYLISTICS VOL.2	Stylistics (Avco)
27	24	THE DARK SIDE OF THE MOON	Pink Floyd (Harvest)
28	25	HASTEN DOWN THE WIND	Linda Ronstadt (Asylum)
13	26	LIVE IN LONDON	John Denver (RCA)
22	27	THE BEST OF GLADYS KNIGHT & THE PIPS	Gladys Knight & the Pips (Buddah)
30	28	I'M NEARLY FAMOUS	Cliff Richard (EMI)
21	29	OLIAS OF SUNHILLOW	Jon Anderson (Atlantic)
-	30	THE ROARING SILENCE	Manfred Mann Earthband (Bronze)

25 September 1976

4	1	A NIGHT ON THE TOWN	Rod Stewart (Riva)
3	2	GREATEST HITS	Abba (Epic)
10	3	SPIRIT	John Denver (RCA)
2	4	LAUGHTER AND TEARS - THE BEST OF NEIL SEDAKA TODAY	Neil Sedaka (Polydor)
6	5	DIANA ROSS' GREATEST HITS II	Diana Ross (Tamla Motown)
1	6	20 GOLDEN GREATS	Beach Boys (Capitol)
5	7	WINGS AT THE SPEED OF SOUND	Wings (EMI)
8	8	FOREVER AND EVER	Demis Roussos (Philips)
7	9	A LITTLE BIT MORE	Dr. Hook (Capitol)
16	10	NO REASON TO CRY	Eric Clapton (RSO)
15	11	JAILBREAK	Thin Lizzy (Vertigo)
11	12	BREAKAWAY	Gallagher & Lyle (A&M)
12	13	FRAMPTON COMES ALIVE	Peter Frampton (A&M)
14	14	BEAUTIFUL NOISE	Neil Diamond (CBS)
9	15	PASSPORT	Nana Mouskouri (Philips)
18	16	ATLANTIC CROSSING	Rod Stewart (Warner Bros.)
13	17	VIVA!	Roxy Music (Island)
23	18	THE BEST OF THE STYLISTICS VOL.2	Stylistics (Avco)
20	19	CHANGESONEBOWIE	David Bowie (WEA)
30	20	THE ROARING SILENCE	Manfred Mann Earthband (Bronze)
17	21	THEIR GREATEST HITS 1971–1975	Eagles (Asylum)
27	22	THE BEST OF GLADYS KNIGHT & THE PIPS	Gladys Knight & the Pips (Buddah)
29	23	OLIAS OF SUNHILLOW	Jon Anderson (Atlantic)
19	24	TWIGGY	Twiggy (Mercury)
-	25	JOAN ARMATRADING	Joan Armatrading (A&M)
-	26	BIGGER THAN BOTH OF US	Darryl Hall & John Oates (RCA)
-	27	MODERN MUSIC	Be-Bop Deluxe (Harvest)
21	28	BLUE FOR YOU	Status Quo (Vertigo)
-	29	HAPPY TO BE	Demis Roussos (Philips)
26	30	LIVE IN LONDON	John Denver (RCA)

2 October 1976

2	1	GREATEST HITS	Abba (Epic)
6	2	20 GOLDEN GREATS	Beach Boys (Capitol)
1	3	A NIGHT ON THE TOWN	Rod Stewart (Riva)
5	4	DIANA ROSS' GREATEST HITS II	Diana Ross (Tamla Motown)
4	5	LAUGHTER AND TEARS - THE BEST OF NEIL SEDAKA TODAY	Neil Sedaka (Polydor)
3	6	SPIRIT	John Denver (RCA)
8	7	FOREVER AND EVER	Demis Roussos (Philips)
7	8	WINGS AT THE SPEED OF SOUND	Wings (EMI)
18	9	THE BEST OF THE STYLISTICS VOL.2	Stylistics (Avco)
9	10	A LITTLE BIT MORE	Dr. Hook (Capitol)
12	11	BREAKAWAY	Gallagher & Lyle (A&M)
13	12	FRAMPTON COMES ALIVE	Peter Frampton (A&M)
14	13	BEAUTIFUL NOISE	Neil Diamond (CBS)
16	14	ATLANTIC CROSSING	Rod Stewart (Warner Bros.)
10	15	NO REASON TO CRY	Eric Clapton (RSO)
22	16	THE BEST OF GLADYS KNIGHT & THE PIPS	Gladys Knight & the Pips (Buddah)
11	17	JAILBREAK	Thin Lizzy (Vertigo)
15	18	PASSPORT	Nana Mouskouri (Philips)
-	19	DEDICATION	Bay City Rollers (Bell)
30	20	LIVE IN LONDON	John Denver (RCA)
20	21	THE ROARING SILENCE	Manfred Mann Earthband (Bronze)
21	22	THEIR GREATEST HITS 1971–1975	Eagles (Asylum)
17	23	VIVA!	Roxy Music (Island)
-	24	DEREK AND CLIVE LIVE	Peter Cook & Dudley Moore (Island)
-	25	HARD RAIN	Bob Dylan (CBS)
25	26	JOAN ARMATRADING	Joan Armatrading (A&M)
27	27	MODERN MUSIC	Be-Bop Deluxe (Harvest)
-	28	LET'S STICK TOGETHER	Bryan Ferry (Atlantic)
19	29	CHANGESONEBOWIE	David Bowie (WEA)
26	30	BIGGER THAN BOTH OF US	Darryl Hall & John Oates (RCA)

Joan Armatrading, born in St.Kitts but raised in Birmingham, can be said to be not only the UK's first black woman singer-songwriter but our most credible singer-songwriter full stop. *Joan Armatrading* was not her first album: that had been on Fly/Cube, a London music-publisher's small subsidiary label. However, now signed to A&M, she was starting to build a sustained career on her own quiet terms. She would be THE favourite of the British women's movement, yet remain a highly individual artist.

October 1976

9 October 1976

last	this	Title / Artist
1	1	GREATEST HITS Abba (Epic)
3	2	A NIGHT ON THE TOWN Rod Stewart (Riva)
9	3	THE BEST OF THE STYLISTICS VOL.2 Stylistics (Avco)
2	4	20 GOLDEN GREATS Beach Boys (Capitol)
8	5	WINGS AT THE SPEED OF SOUND Wings (EMI)
7	6	FOREVER AND EVER Demis Roussos (Philips)
4	7	DIANA ROSS' GREATEST HITS II Diana Ross (Tamla Motown)
5	8	LAUGHTER AND TEARS - THE BEST OF NEIL SEDAKA TODAY Neil Sedaka (Polydor)
-	9	STUPIDITY Dr. Feelgood (United Artists)
19	10	DEDICATION Bay City Rollers (Bell)
6	11	SPIRIT John Denver (RCA)
14	12	ATLANTIC CROSSING Rod Stewart (Warner Bros.)
24	13	DEREK AND CLIVE LIVE Peter Cook & Dudley Moore (Island)
26	14	JOAN ARMATRADING Joan Armatrading (A&M)
21	15	THE ROARING SILENCE Manfred Mann Earthband (Bronze)
12	16	FRAMPTON COMES ALIVE Peter Frampton (A&M)
10	17	A LITTLE BIT MORE Dr. Hook (Capitol)
22	18	THEIR GREATEST HITS 1971–1975 Eagles (Asylum)
13	19	BEAUTIFUL NOISE Neil Diamond (CBS)
-	20	20 ITALIAN LOVE SONGS Various Artists (K-Tel)
16	21	THE BEST OF GLADYS KNIGHT & THE PIPS Gladys Knight & the Pips (Buddah)
25	22	HARD RAIN Bob Dylan (CBS)
11	23	BREAKAWAY Gallagher & Lyle (A&M)
28	24	LET'S STICK TOGETHER Bryan Ferry (Atlantic)
27	25	MODERN MUSIC Be-Bop Deluxe (Harvest)
30	26	BIGGER THAN BOTH OF US Darryl Hall & John Oates (RCA)
15	27	NO REASON TO CRY Eric Clapton (RSO)
23	28	VIVA! Roxy Music (Island)
-	29	THE WHO STORY Who (Polydor)
18	30	PASSPORT Nana Mouskouri (Philips)

16 October 1976

last	this	Title / Artist
2	1	A NIGHT ON THE TOWN Rod Stewart (Riva)
1	2	GREATEST HITS Abba (Epic)
3	3	THE BEST OF THE STYLISTICS VOL.2 Stylistics (Avco)
4	4	20 GOLDEN GREATS Beach Boys (Capitol)
9	5	STUPIDITY Dr. Feelgood (United Artists)
8	6	LAUGHTER AND TEARS - THE BEST OF NEIL SEDAKA Neil Sedaka (Polydor)
12	7	ATLANTIC CROSSING Rod Stewart (Warner Bros.)
22	8	HARD RAIN Bob Dylan (CBS)
6	9	FOREVER AND EVER Demis Roussos (Philips)
7	10	DIANA ROSS' GREATEST HITS II Diana Ross (Tamla Motown)
10	11	DEDICATION Bay City Rollers (Bell)
29	12	THE WHO STORY Who (Polydor)
16	13	FRAMPTON COMES ALIVE Peter Frampton (A&M)
5	14	WINGS AT THE SPEED OF SOUND Wings (EMI)
-	15	SONGS IN THE KEY OF LIFE Stevie Wonder (Tamla Motown)
11	16	SPIRIT John Denver (RCA)
20	17	20 ITALIAN LOVE SONGS Various Artists (K-Tel)
15	18	THE ROARING SILENCE Manfred Mann Earthband (Bronze)
-	19	SOUL MOTION Various Artists (K-Tel)
14	20	JOAN ARMATRADING Joan Armatrading (A&M)
19	21	BEAUTIFUL NOISE Neil Diamond (CBS)
21	22	THE BEST OF GLADYS KNIGHT & THE PIPS Gladys Knight & the Pips (Buddah)
13	23	DEREK AND CLIVE LIVE Peter Cook & Dudley Moore (Island)
17	24	A LITTLE BIT MORE Dr. Hook (Capitol)
18	25	THEIR GREATEST HITS 1971–1975 Eagles (Asylum)
25	26	MODERN MUSIC Be-Bop Deluxe (Harvest)
24	27	LET'S STICK TOGETHER Bryan Ferry (Atlantic)
27	28	NO REASON TO CRY Eric Clapton (RSO)
-	29	GENE PITNEY'S GREATEST HITS Gene Pitney (Arcade)
23	30	BREAKAWAY Gallagher & Lyle (A&M)

23 October 1976

last	this	Title / Artist
2	1	GREATEST HITS Abba (Epic)
12	2	THE WHO STORY Who (Polydor)
1	3	A NIGHT ON THE TOWN Rod Stewart (Riva)
8	4	HARD RAIN Bob Dylan (CBS)
3	5	THE BEST OF THE STYLISTICS VOL.2 Stylistics (Avco)
15	6	SONGS IN THE KEY OF LIFE Stevie Wonder (Tamla Motown)
5	7	STUPIDITY Dr. Feelgood (United Artists)
6	8	LAUGHTER AND TEARS - THE BEST OF NEIL SEDAKA TODAY Neil Sedaka (Polydor)
11	9	DEDICATION Bay City Rollers (Bell)
4	10	20 GOLDEN GREATS Beach Boys (Capitol)
10	11	DIANA ROSS' GREATEST HITS II Diana Ross (Tamla Motown)
19	12	SOUL MOTION Various Artists (K-Tel)
7	13	ATLANTIC CROSSING Rod Stewart (Warner Bros.)
9	14	FOREVER AND EVER Demis Roussos (Philips)
20	15	JOAN ARMATRADING Joan Armatrading (A&M)
14	16	WINGS AT THE SPEED OF SOUND Wings (EMI)
-	17	COUNTRY COMFORT Various Artists (K-Tel)
23	18	DEREK AND CLIVE LIVE Peter Cook & Dudley Moore (Island)
13	19	FRAMPTON COMES ALIVE Peter Frampton (A&M)
16	20	SPIRIT John Denver (RCA)
17	21	20 ITALIAN LOVE SONGS Various Artists (K-Tel)
29	22	GENE PITNEY'S GREATEST HITS Gene Pitney (Arcade)
-	23	LONG MAY YOU RUN Stills-Young Band (Reprise)
-	24	ALBEDO 0.39 Vangelis (RCA)
21	25	BEAUTIFUL NOISE Neil Diamond (CBS)
18	26	THE ROARING SILENCE Manfred Mann Earthband (Bronze)
-	27	JAILBREAK Thin Lizzy (Vertigo)
-	28	"L" Steve Hillage (Virgin)
25	29	THEIR GREATEST HITS 1971–1975 Eagles (Asylum)
22	30	THE BEST OF GLADYS KNIGHT & THE PIPS Gladys Knight & the Pips (Buddah)

30 October 1976

last	this	Title / Artist
2	1	THE WHO STORY Who (Polydor)
1	2	GREATEST HITS Abba (Epic)
6	3	SONGS IN THE KEY OF LIFE Stevie Wonder (Tamla Motown)
3	4	A NIGHT ON THE TOWN Rod Stewart (Riva)
5	5	THE BEST OF THE STYLISTICS VOL.2 Stylistics (Avco)
12	6	SOUL MOTION Various Artists (K-Tel)
13	7	ATLANTIC CROSSING Rod Stewart (Warner Bros.)
7	8	STUPIDITY Dr. Feelgood (United Artists)
19	9	FRAMPTON COMES ALIVE Peter Frampton (A&M)
14	10	FOREVER AND EVER Demis Roussos (Philips)
10	11	20 GOLDEN GREATS Beach Boys (Capitol)
4	12	HARD RAIN Bob Dylan (CBS)
15	13	JOAN ARMATRADING Joan Armatrading (A&M)
8	14	LAUGHTER AND TEARS - THE BEST OF NEIL SEDAKA TODAY Neil Sedaka (Polydor)
-	15	THE SONG REMAINS THE SAME Led Zeppelin (Swansong)
11	16	DIANA ROSS' GREATEST HITS II Diana Ross (Tamla Motown)
22	17	GENE PITNEY'S GREATEST HITS Gene Pitney (Arcade)
17	18	COUNTRY COMFORT Various Artists (K-Tel)
9	19	DEDICATION Bay City Rollers (Bell)
16	20	WINGS AT THE SPEED OF SOUND Wings (EMI)
26	21	THE ROARING SILENCE Manfred Mann Earthband (Bronze)
20	22	SPIRIT John Denver (RCA)
29	23	THEIR GREATEST HITS 1971–1975 Eagles (Asylum)
25	24	BEAUTIFUL NOISE Neil Diamond (CBS)
-	25	BLUE MOVES Elton John (Rocket)
21	26	20 ITALIAN LOVE SONGS Various Artists (K-Tel)
18	27	DEREK AND CLIVE LIVE Peter Cook & Dudley Moore (Island)
-	28	OUT ON THE STREET David Essex (CBS)
30	29	THE BEST OF GLADYS KNIGHT & THE PIPS Gladys Knight & the Pips (Buddah)
28	30	"L" Steve Hillage (Virgin)

Enter the rude *Derek And Clive Live* by comedian and *Private Eye* owner Peter Cook and jazz-pianist turned comic Dudley Moore. It was the second of three LPs taken into the charts by Cook and Moore, each on a different label. *Once Moore With Cook* had been a minor hit in 1966; *Derek And Clive Come Again* would climax at No.22 in January 1978. "Cuddly" Dudley Moore would metamorphose into a 1980s Hollywood superstar, while Cook would make a US TV series that flopped.

6 November 1976

last week	this week	
3	1	SONGS IN THE KEY OF LIFE Stevie Wonder (Tamla Motown)
1	2	THE WHO STORY Who (Polydor)
2	3	GREATEST HITS Abba (Epic)
4	4	A NIGHT ON THE TOWN Rod Stewart (Riva)
6	5	SOUL MOTION Various Artists (K-Tel)
7	6	ATLANTIC CROSSING Rod Stewart (Warner Bros.)
8	7	STUPIDITY Dr. Feelgood (United Artists)
9	8	FRAMPTON COMES ALIVE Peter Frampton (A&M)
10	9	FOREVER AND EVER Demis Roussos (Philips)
25	10	BLUE MOVES Elton John (Rocket)
5	11	THE BEST OF THE STYLISTICS VOL.2 Stylistics (Avco)
13	12	JOAN ARMATRADING Joan Armatrading (A&M)
24	13	BEAUTIFUL NOISE Neil Diamond (CBS)
15	14	THE SONG REMAINS THE SAME Led Zeppelin (Swansong)
-	15	100 GOLDEN GREATS Max Bygraves (Ronco)
11	16	20 GOLDEN GREATS Beach Boys (Capitol)
18	17	COUNTRY COMFORT Various Artists (K-Tel)
12	18	HARD RAIN Bob Dylan (CBS)
30	19	"L" Steve Hillage (Virgin)
17	20	GENE PITNEY'S GREATEST HITS Gene Pitney (Arcade)
-	21	BERT WEEDON'S 22 GOLDEN GUITAR GREATS Bert Weedon (Warwick)
14	22	LAUGHTER AND TEARS - THE BEST OF NEIL SEDAKA TODAY Neil Sedaka (Polydor)
-	23	JOHNNY THE FOX Thin Lizzy (Vertigo)
28	24	OUT ON THE STREET David Essex (CBS)
-	25	OCTOBERON Barclay James Harvest (Polydor)
22	26	SPIRIT John Denver (RCA)
27	27	DEREK AND CLIVE LIVE Peter Cook & Dudley Moore (Island)
-	28	ALBEDO 0.39 Vangelis (RCA)
16	29	DIANA ROSS' GREATEST HITS II Diana Ross (Tamla Motown)
21	30	THE ROARING SILENCE Manfred Mann Earthband (Bronze)

13 November 1976

1	1	SONGS IN THE KEY OF LIFE Stevie Wonder (Tamla Motown)
5	2	SOUL MOTION Various Artists (K-Tel)
3	3	GREATEST HITS Abba (Epic)
2	4	THE WHO STORY Who (Polydor)
14	5	THE SONG REMAINS THE SAME Led Zeppelin (Swansong)
10	6	BLUE MOVES Elton John (Rocket)
8	7	FRAMPTON COMES ALIVE Peter Frampton (A&M)
9	8	FOREVER AND EVER Demis Roussos (Philips)
11	9	THE BEST OF THE STYLISTICS VOL.2 Stylistics (Avco)
23	10	JOHNNY THE FOX Thin Lizzy (Vertigo)
12	11	JOAN ARMATRADING Joan Armatrading (A&M)
4	12	A NIGHT ON THE TOWN Rod Stewart (Riva)
20	13	GENE PITNEY'S GREATEST HITS Gene Pitney (Arcade)
13	14	BEAUTIFUL NOISE Neil Diamond (CBS)
6	15	ATLANTIC CROSSING Rod Stewart (Warner Bros.)
-	16	20 GOLDEN GREATS Glen Campbell (Capitol)
17	17	COUNTRY COMFORT Various Artists (K-Tel)
-	18	A LITTLE BIT MORE Dr. Hook (Capitol)
7	19	STUPIDITY Dr. Feelgood (United Artists)
21	20	BERT WEEDON'S 22 GOLDEN GUITAR GREATS Bert Weedon (Warwick)
29	21	DIANA ROSS' GREATEST HITS II Diana Ross (Tamla Motown)
19	22	"L" Steve Hillage (Virgin)
-	23	TECHNICAL ECSTASY Black Sabbath (Vertigo)
15	24	100 GOLDEN GREATS Max Bygraves (Ronco)
-	25	ONE MORE FROM THE ROAD Lynyrd Skynyrd (MCA)
-	26	FRANKIE VALLI & THE FOUR SEASONS' GREATEST HITS Frankie Valli & the Four Seasons (K-Tel)
18	27	HARD RAIN Bob Dylan (CBS)
24	28	OUT ON THE STREET David Essex (CBS)
22	29	LAUGHTER AND TEARS - THE BEST OF NEIL SEDAKA TODAY Neil Sedaka (Polydor)
-	30	CHICAGO X Chicago (CBS)

20 November 1976

1	1	SONGS IN THE KEY OF LIFE Stevie Wonder (Tamla Motown)
2	2	SOUL MOTION Various Artists (K-Tel)
4	3	THE WHO STORY Who (Polydor)
6	4	BLUE MOVES Elton John (Rocket)
3	5	GREATEST HITS Abba (Epic)
5	6	THE SONG REMAINS THE SAME Led Zeppelin (Swansong)
8	7	FOREVER AND EVER Demis Roussos (Philips)
24	8	100 GOLDEN GREATS Max Bygraves (Ronco)
10	9	JOHNNY THE FOX Thin Lizzy (Vertigo)
20	10	BERT WEEDON'S 22 GOLDEN GUITAR GREATS Bert Weedon (Warwick)
11	11	JOAN ARMATRADING Joan Armatrading (A&M)
7	12	FRAMPTON COMES ALIVE Peter Frampton (A&M)
9	13	THE BEST OF THE STYLISTICS VOL.2 Stylistics (Avco)
15	14	ATLANTIC CROSSING Rod Stewart (Warner Bros.)
-	15	ARRIVAL Abba (Epic)
12	16	A NIGHT ON THE TOWN Rod Stewart (Riva)
16	17	20 GOLDEN GREATS Glen Campbell (Capitol)
18	18	A LITTLE BIT MORE Dr. Hook (Capitol)
-	19	HOT CHOCOLATE'S GREATEST HITS Hot Chocolate (RAK)
30	20	CHICAGO X Chicago (CBS)
13	21	GENE PITNEY'S GREATEST HITS Gene Pitney (Arcade)
14	22	BEAUTIFUL NOISE Neil Diamond (CBS)
23	23	TECHNICAL ECSTASY Black Sabbath (Vertigo)
26	24	FRANKIE VALLI & THE FOUR SEASONS' GREATEST HITS Frankie Valli & the Four Seasons (K-Tel)
-	25	DEREK AND CLIVE LIVE Peter Cook & Dudley Moore (Island)
22	26	"L" Steve Hillage (Virgin)
-	27	FLEETWOOD MAC Fleetwood Mac (Reprise)
-	28	20 ORIGINAL DEAN MARTIN HITS Dean Martin (Reprise)
28	29	OUT ON THE STREET David Essex (CBS)
21	30	DIANA ROSS' GREATEST HITS II Diana Ross (Tamla Motown)

27 November 1976

17	1	20 GOLDEN GREATS Glen Campbell (Capitol)
1	2	SONGS IN THE KEY OF LIFE Stevie Wonder (Tamla Motown)
10	3	BERT WEEDON'S 22 GOLDEN GUITAR GREATS Bert Weedon (Warwick)
8	4	100 GOLDEN GREATS Max Bygraves (Ronco)
6	5	THE SONG REMAINS THE SAME Led Zeppelin (Swansong)
4	6	BLUE MOVES Elton John (Rocket)
2	7	SOUL MOTION Various Artists (K-Tel)
3	8	THE WHO STORY Who (Polydor)
15	9	ARRIVAL Abba (Epic)
5	10	GREATEST HITS Abba (Epic)
7	11	FOREVER AND EVER Demis Roussos (Philips)
28	12	20 ORIGINAL DEAN MARTIN HITS Dean Martin (Reprise)
12	13	FRAMPTON COMES ALIVE Peter Frampton (A&M)
19	14	HOT CHOCOLATE'S GREATEST HITS Hot Chocolate (RAK)
16	15	A NIGHT ON THE TOWN Rod Stewart (Riva)
24	16	FRANKIE VALLI & THE FOUR SEASONS' GREATEST HITS Frankie Valli & the Four Seasons (K-Tel)
12	17	THE BEST OF THE STYLISTICS VOL.2 Stylistics (Avco)
18	18	A LITTLE BIT MORE Dr. Hook (Capitol)
9	19	JOHNNY THE FOX Thin Lizzy (Vertigo)
11	20	JOAN ARMATRADING Joan Armatrading (A&M)
20	21	CHICAGO X Chicago (CBS)
22	22	BEAUTIFUL NOISE Neil Diamond (CBS)
25	23	DEREK AND CLIVE LIVE Peter Cook & Dudley Moore (Island)
27	24	FLEETWOOD MAC Fleetwood Mac (Reprise)
14	25	ATLANTIC CROSSING Rod Stewart (Warner Bros.)
-	26	20 GOLDEN GREATS Beach Boys (Capitol)
-	27	ALL THIS AND WORLD WAR II Various Artists (Riva)
-	28	BOXED Mike Oldfield (Virgin)
-	29	THE INCREDIBLE PLAN Max Boyce (EMI)
-	30	HENRY MANCINI Henry Mancini (Arcade)

TV-advertised albums had brought many unlikely, even unwelcome, artists back into the charts, decades after their heyday: none so unexpectedly as Bert Weedon, Britain's first rock'n'roll guitar star. His very name had always made people guffaw (more so even than Conway Twitty's), and even as he was enjoying his hits - which were only in the period 1959-1961 - they were felt to be hopelessly feeble and, well, British. His real achievement, indeed, had been to make the Shadows sound exciting.

December 1976

4 December 1976

last week	this week	Title / Artist (Label)
1	1	20 GOLDEN GREATS — Glen Campbell (Capitol)
9	2	ARRIVAL — Abba (Epic)
2	3	SONGS IN THE KEY OF LIFE — Stevie Wonder (Tamla Motown)
3	4	BERT WEEDON'S 22 GOLDEN GUITAR GREATS — Bert Weedon (Warwick)
4	5	100 GOLDEN GREATS — Max Bygraves (Ronco)
5	6	THE SONG REMAINS THE SAME — Led Zeppelin (Swansong)
7	7	SOUL MOTION — Various Artists (K-Tel)
10	8	GREATEST HITS — Abba (Epic)
6	9	BLUE MOVES — Elton John (Rocket)
14	10	HOT CHOCOLATE'S GREATEST HITS — Hot Chocolate (RAK)
12	11	20 ORIGINAL DEAN MARTIN HITS — Dean Martin (Reprise)
16	12	FRANKIE VALLI & THE FOUR SEASONS' GREATEST HITS — Frankie Valli & the Four Seasons (K-Tel)
8	13	THE WHO STORY — Who (Polydor)
17	14	THE BEST OF THE STYLISTICS VOL.2 — Stylistics (Avco)
13	15	FRAMPTON COMES ALIVE — Peter Frampton (A&M)
-	16	LIVE IN EUROPE — Deep Purple (Purple)
11	17	FOREVER AND EVER — Demis Roussos (Philips)
21	18	CHICAGO X — Chicago (CBS)
-	19	SOUNDS OF GLORY — Various Artists (Arcade)
-	20	DISCO ROCKET — Various Artists (K-Tel)
27	21	ALL THIS AND WORLD WAR II — Various Artists (Riva)
18	22	A LITTLE BIT MORE — Dr. Hook (Capitol)
24	23	FLEETWOOD MAC — Fleetwood Mac (Reprise)
15	24	A NIGHT ON THE TOWN — Rod Stewart (Riva)
25	25	ATLANTIC CROSSING — Rod Stewart (Warner Bros.)
-	26	A NEW WORLD RECORD — Electric Light Orchestra (Jet)
-	27	GENE PITNEY'S GREATEST HITS — Gene Pitney (Arcade)
20	28	JOAN ARMATRADING — Joan Armatrading (A&M)
-	29	DAVID SOUL — David Soul (Private Stock)
29	30	THE INCREDIBLE PLAN — Max Boyce (EMI)

11 December 1976

last week	this week	Title / Artist (Label)
1	1	20 GOLDEN GREATS — Glen Campbell (Capitol)
2	2	ARRIVAL — Abba (Epic)
3	3	SONGS IN THE KEY OF LIFE — Stevie Wonder (Tamla Motown)
5	4	100 GOLDEN GREATS — Max Bygraves (Ronco)
4	5	BERT WEEDON'S 22 GOLDEN GUITAR GREATS — Bert Weedon (Warwick)
8	6	GREATEST HITS — Abba (Epic)
12	7	FRANKIE VALLI & THE FOUR SEASONS' GREATEST HITS — Frankie Valli & the Four Seasons (K-Tel)
10	8	HOT CHOCOLATE'S GREATEST HITS — Hot Chocolate (RAK)
9	9	BLUE MOVES — Elton John (Rocket)
11	10	20 ORIGINAL DEAN MARTIN HITS — Dean Martin (Reprise)
6	11	THE SONG REMAINS THE SAME — Led Zeppelin (Swansong)
20	12	DISCO ROCKET — Various Artists (K-Tel)
16	13	LIVE IN EUROPE — Deep Purple (Purple)
13	14	THE WHO STORY — Who (Polydor)
7	15	SOUL MOTION — Various Artists (K-Tel)
18	16	CHICAGO X — Chicago (CBS)
17	17	FOREVER AND EVER — Demis Roussos (Philips)
14	18	THE BEST OF THE STYLISTICS VOL.2 — Stylistics (Avco)
15	19	FRAMPTON COMES ALIVE — Peter Frampton (A&M)
29	20	DAVID SOUL — David Soul (Private Stock)
22	21	A LITTLE BIT MORE — Dr. Hook (Capitol)
-	22	THOUGHTS OF LOVE — Shirley Bassey (United Artists)
-	23	ENDLESS FLIGHT — Leo Sayer (Chrysalis)
19	24	SOUNDS OF GLORY — Various Artists (Arcade)
-	25	JOHNNY THE FOX — Thin Lizzy (Vertigo)
26	26	A NEW WORLD RECORD — Electric Light Orchestra (Jet)
24	27	A NIGHT ON THE TOWN — Rod Stewart (Riva)
21	28	ALL THIS AND WORLD WAR II — Various Artists (Riva)
25	29	ATLANTIC CROSSING — Rod Stewart (Warner Bros.)
23	30	FLEETWOOD MAC — Fleetwood Mac (Reprise)

18 December 1976

last week	this week	Title / Artist (Label)
1	1	20 GOLDEN GREATS — Glen Campbell (Capitol)
2	2	ARRIVAL — Abba (Epic)
5	3	BERT WEEDON'S 22 GOLDEN GUITAR GREATS — Bert Weedon (Warwick)
7	4	FRANKIE VALLI & THE FOUR SEASONS' GREATEST HITS — Frankie Valli & the Four Seasons (K-Tel)
4	5	100 GOLDEN GREATS — Max Bygraves (Ronco)
3	6	SONGS IN THE KEY OF LIFE — Stevie Wonder (Tamla Motown)
6	7	GREATEST HITS — Abba (Epic)
12	8	DISCO ROCKET — Various Artists (K-Tel)
26	9	A NEW WORLD RECORD — Electric Light Orchestra (Jet)
8	10	HOT CHOCOLATE'S GREATEST HITS — Hot Chocolate (RAK)
20	11	DAVID SOUL — David Soul (Private Stock)
-	12	A DAY AT THE RACES — Queen (EMI)
9	13	BLUE MOVES — Elton John (Rocket)
14	14	THE WHO STORY — Who (Polydor)
17	15	FOREVER AND EVER — Demis Roussos (Philips)
10	16	20 ORIGINAL DEAN MARTIN HITS — Dean Martin (Reprise)
22	17	THOUGHTS OF LOVE — Shirley Bassey (United Artists)
11	18	THE SONG REMAINS THE SAME — Led Zeppelin (Swansong)
18	19	THE BEST OF THE STYLISTICS VOL.2 — Stylistics (Avco)
15	20	SOUL MOTION — Various Artists (K-Tel)
21	21	A LITTLE BIT MORE — Dr. Hook (Capitol)
19	22	FRAMPTON COMES ALIVE — Peter Frampton (A&M)
-	23	DEREK AND CLIVE LIVE — Peter Cook & Dudley Moore (Island)
-	24	SHOWADDYWADDY'S GREATEST HITS — Showaddywaddy (Arista)
-	25	THE INCREDIBLE PLAN — Max Boyce (EMI)
16	26	CHICAGO X — Chicago (CBS)
28	27	ALL THIS AND WORLD WAR II — Various Artists (Riva)
24	28	SOUNDS OF GLORY — Various Artists (Arcade)
23	29	ENDLESS FLIGHT — Leo Sayer (Chrysalis)
27	30	A NIGHT ON THE TOWN — Rod Stewart (Riva)

25 December 1976

last week	this week	Title / Artist (Label)
2	1	ARRIVAL — Abba (Epic)
1	2	20 GOLDEN GREATS — Glen Campbell (Capitol)
6	3	SONGS IN THE KEY OF LIFE — Stevie Wonder (Tamla Motown)
5	4	100 GOLDEN GREATS — Max Bygraves (Ronco)
4	5	FRANKIE VALLI & THE FOUR SEASONS' GREATEST HITS — Frankie Valli & the Four Seasons (K-Tel)
12	6	A DAY AT THE RACES — Queen (EMI)
7	7	GREATEST HITS — Abba (Epic)
3	8	22 GOLDEN GUITAR GREATS — Bert Weedon (Warwick)
9	9	A NEW WORLD RECORD — Electric Light Orchestra (Jet)
11	10	DAVID SOUL — David Soul (Private Stock)
8	11	DISCO ROCKET — Various Artists (K-Tel)
10	12	HOT CHOCOLATE'S GREATEST HITS — Hot Chocolate (RAK)
13	13	BLUE MOVES — Elton John (Rocket)
24	14	SHOWADDYWADDY'S GREATEST HITS — Showaddywaddy (Arista)
14	15	THE WHO STORY — Who (Polydor)
16	16	20 ORIGINAL DEAN MARTIN HITS — Dean Martin (Reprise)
17	17	THOUGHTS OF LOVE — Shirley Bassey (United Artists)
15	18	FOREVER AND EVER — Demis Roussos (Philips)
-	19	HOTEL CALIFORNIA — Eagles (Asylum)
19	20	THE BEST OF THE STYLISTICS VOL.2 — Stylistics (Avco)
-	21	GILBERT O'SULLIVAN'S GREATEST HITS — Gilbert O'Sullivan (MAM)
18	22	THE SONG REMAINS THE SAME — Led Zeppelin (Swansong)
22	23	FRAMPTON COMES ALIVE — Peter Frampton (A&M)
-	24	SOME MORE OF ME POEMS AND SONGS — Pam Ayres (Galaxy)
21	25	A LITTLE BIT MORE — Dr. Hook (Capitol)
-	26	44 SUPERSTARS — Various Artists (K-Tel)
20	27	SOUL MOTION — Various Artists (K-Tel)
30	28	A NIGHT ON THE TOWN — Rod Stewart (Riva)
-	29	ATLANTIC BRIDGE — Billy Connolly (Polydor)
23	30	DEREK AND CLIVE LIVE — Peter Cook & Dudley Moore (Island)

Signs were abroad that rock's rococo period was doomed. Elton John's two latest albums, the live *Here And There* and the studio-cut *Blue Moves*, had done hopelessly badly by his sales standards, while a live album of crude pub-rock, *Stupidity* by Dr Feelgood (fronted by guitar-ace Wilko Johnson and vocalist Lee Brilleaux) had reached No.1 in every chart but the NME's. September had seen a two-day "punk" festival at London's 100 Club, with debuts by the Clash, Buzzcocks, Siouxsie & the Banshees (including Sid Vicious), the Damned, Vibrators and... the Sex Pistols. In December, TV's Bill Grundy made the Pistols national heroes of unwholesomeness, and they made their single *Anarchy In The UK*.

8 January 1977

last week / this week

last	this	
1	1	ARRIVAL Abba (Epic)
3	2	SONGS IN THE KEY OF LIFE Stevie Wonder (Tamla Motown)
2	3	20 GOLDEN GREATS Glen Campbell (Capitol)
14	4	SHOWADDYWADDY'S GREATEST HITS Showaddywaddy (Arista)
6	5	A DAY AT THE RACES Queen (EMI)
4	6	100 GOLDEN GREATS Max Bygraves (Ronco)
11	7	DISCO ROCKET Various Artists (K-Tel)
7	8	GREATEST HITS Abba (Epic)
5	9	FRANKIE VALLI & THE FOUR SEASONS' GREATEST HITS Frankie Valli & the Four Seasons (K-Tel)
9	10	A NEW WORLD RECORD Electric Light Orchestra (Jet)
10	11	DAVID SOUL David Soul (Private Stock)
19	12	HOTEL CALIFORNIA Eagles (Asylum)
8	13	BERT WEEDON'S 22 GOLDEN GUITAR GREATS Bert Weedon (Warwick)
13	14	BLUE MOVES Elton John (Rocket)
12	15	HOT CHOCOLATE'S GREATEST HITS Hot Chocolate (RAK)
17	16	THOUGHTS OF LOVE Shirley Bassey (United Artists)
15	17	THE WHO STORY Who (Polydor)
21	18	GILBERT O'SULLIVAN'S GREATEST HITS Gilbert O'Sullivan (MAM)
24	19	SOME MORE OF ME POEMS AND SONGS Pam Ayres (Galaxy)
16	20	20 ORIGINAL DEAN MARTIN HITS Dean Martin (Reprise)
-	21	WINGS OVER AMERICA Wings (EMI)
22	22	THE SONG REMAINS THE SAME Led Zeppelin (Swan Song)
18	23	FOREVER AND EVER Demis Roussos (Philips)
20	24	BEST OF THE STYLISTICS VOL 2 Stylistics (Avco)
-	25	THIRTY THREE AND A THIRD George Harrison (Dark Horse)
-	26	ATLANTIC CROSSING Rod Stewart (Warner Bros.)
-	27	SOUNDS OF GLORY Various Artists (Arcade)
26	28	44 SUPERSTARS Various Artists (K-Tel)
29	29	ATLANTIC BRIDGE Billy Connolly (Polydor)
-	30	BOXED Mike Oldfield (Virgin)

15 January 1977

last	this	
1	1	ARRIVAL Abba (Epic)
5	2	A DAY AT THE RACES Queen (EMI)
11	3	DAVID SOUL David Soul (Private Stock)
8	4	GREATEST HITS Abba (Epic)
2	5	SONGS IN THE KEY OF LIFE Stevie Wonder (Tamla Motown)
12	6	HOTEL CALIFORNIA Eagles (Asylum)
4	7	SHOWADDYWADDY'S GREATEST HITS Showaddywaddy (Arista)
10	8	A NEW WORLD RECORD Electric Light Orchestra (Jet)
3	9	20 GOLDEN GREATS Glen Campbell (Capitol)
-	10	RED RIVER VALLEY Slim Whitman (United Artists)
6	11	MAX BYGRAVES' 100 GOLDEN GREATS Max Bygraves (Ronco)
9	12	FRANKIE VALLI & THE FOUR SEASONS' GREATEST HITS Frankie Valli & the Four Seasons (K-Tel)
21	13	WINGS OVER AMERICA Wings (EMI)
7	14	DISCO ROCKET Various Artists (K-Tel)
16	15	THOUGHTS OF LOVE Shirley Bassey (United Artists)
15	16	HOT CHOCOLATE'S GREATEST HITS Hot Chocolate (RAK)
18	17	GILBERT O'SULLIVAN'S GREATEST HITS Gilbert O'Sullivan (MAM)
14	18	BLUE MOVES Elton John (Rocket)
30	19	BOXED Mike Oldfield (Virgin)
-	20	I ONLY HAVE EYES FOR YOU Johnny Mathis (CBS)
13	21	BERT WEEDON'S 22 GOLDEN GUITAR GREATS Bert Weedon (Warwick)
24	22	BEST OF THE STYLISTICS VOL 2 Stylistics (Avco)
17	23	THE WHO STORY Who (Polydor)
-	24	WIND AND WUTHERING Genesis (Charisma)
19	25	SOME MORE OF ME POEMS AND SONGS Pam Ayres (Galaxy)
23	26	FOREVER AND EVER Demis Roussos (Philips)
-	27	EVITA Various Artists (MCA)
28	28	44 SUPERSTARS Various Artists (K-Tel)
-	29	GREATEST HITS Linda Ronstadt (Asylum)
22	30	THE SONG REMAINS THE SAME Led Zeppelin (Swan Song)

22 January 1977

last	this	
10	1	RED RIVER VALLEY Slim Whitman (United Artists)
1	2	ARRIVAL Abba (Epic)
2	3	A DAY AT THE RACES Queen (EMI)
6	4	HOTEL CALIFORNIA Eagles (Asylum)
3	5	DAVID SOUL David Soul (Private Stock)
5	6	SONGS IN THE KEY OF LIFE Stevie Wonder (Tamla Motown)
4	7	GREATEST HITS Abba (Epic)
7	8	SHOWADDYWADDY'S GREATEST HITS Showaddywaddy (Arista)
13	9	WINGS OVER AMERICA Wings (EMI)
24	10	WIND AND WUTHERING Genesis (Charisma)
12	11	FRANKIE VALLI & THE FOUR SEASONS' GREATEST HITS Frankie Valli & the Four Seasons (K-Tel)
8	12	A NEW WORLD RECORD Electric Light Orchestra (Jet)
14	13	DISCO ROCKET Various Artists (K-Tel)
11	14	100 GOLDEN GREATS Max Bygraves (Ronco)
9	15	20 GOLDEN GREATS Glen Campbell (Capitol)
16	16	HOT CHOCOLATE'S GREATEST HITS Hot Chocolate (RAK)
27	17	EVITA Various Artists (MCA)
17	18	GILBERT O'SULLIVAN'S GREATEST HITS Gilbert O'Sullivan (MAM)
18	19	BLUE MOVES Elton John (Rocket)
28	20	44 SUPERSTARS Various Artists (K-Tel)
26	21	FOREVER AND EVER Demis Roussos (Philips)
-	22	THEIR GREATEST HITS 1971-1975 Eagles (Asylum)
19	23	BOXED Mike Oldfield (Virgin)
-	24	LOW David Bowie (RCA)
23	25	THE WHO STORY Who (Polydor)
-	26	DIANA ROSS GREATEST HITS 2 Diana Ross (Tamla Motown)
-	27	SOUL MOTION Various Artists (K-Tel)
22	28	BEST OF THE STYLISTICS VOL 2 Stylistics (Avco)
-	29	ATLANTIC CROSSING Rod Stewart (Warner Bros.)
21	30	BERT WEEDON'S 22 GOLDEN GUITAR GREATS Bert Weedon (Warwick)

29 January 1977

last	this	
1	1	RED RIVER VALLEY Slim Whitman (United Artists)
5	2	DAVID SOUL David Soul (Private Stock)
2	3	ARRIVAL Abba (Epic)
4	4	HOTEL CALIFORNIA Eagles (Asylum)
3	5	A DAY AT THE RACES Queen (EMI)
7	6	GREATEST HITS Abba (Epic)
6	7	SONGS IN THE KEY OF LIFE Stevie Wonder (Tamla Motown)
10	8	WIND AND WUTHERING Genesis (Charisma)
9	9	WINGS OVER AMERICA Wings (EMI)
8	10	SHOWADDYWADDY'S GREATEST HITS Showaddywaddy (Arista)
17	11	EVITA Various Artists (MCA)
12	12	A NEW WORLD RECORD Electric Light Orchestra (Jet)
15	13	20 GOLDEN GREATS Glen Campbell (Capitol)
13	14	DISCO ROCKET Various Artists (K-Tel)
24	15	LOW David Bowie (RCA)
11	16	FRANKIE VALLI & THE FOUR SEASONS' GREATEST HITS Frankie Valli & the Four Seasons (K-Tel)
16	17	HOT CHOCOLATE'S GREATEST HITS Hot Chocolate (RAK)
-	18	ENDLESS FLIGHT Leo Sayer (Chrysalis)
-	19	A NIGHT ON THE TOWN Rod Stewart (Riva)
14	20	100 GOLDEN GREATS Max Bygraves (Ronco)
18	21	GILBERT O'SULLIVAN'S GREATEST HITS Gilbert O'Sullivan (MAM)
-	22	THE SONG REMAINS THE SAME Led Zeppelin (Swan Song)
19	23	BLUE MOVES Elton John (Rocket)
-	24	I ONLY HAVE EYES FOR YOU Johnny Mathis (CBS)
29	25	ATLANTIC CROSSING Rod Stewart (Warner Bros.)
25	26	THE WHO STORY Who (Polydor)
-	27	THOUGHTS OF LOVE Shirley Bassey (United Artists)
21	28	FOREVER AND EVER Demis Roussos (Philips)
-	29	LOST WITHOUT YOUR LOVE Bread (Elektra)
27	30	SOUL MOTION Various Artists (K-Tel)

Bert Weedon had reached No.3! In 1976! So for everyone who remembered the guitar world of Britain 1959-1961, where was Max Harris' Greatest Hits? Where was The Best Of Wout Steenhuis? Rhet Stoller's 22 Golden Greats? The punters of 1977 could have charted them alongside Max Bygraves' *100 Golden Greats* - his last real hit (an aberrational 1973 *Deck Of Cards* aside) had been in 1960 - and Slim Whitman's *Red River Valley*; HIS last real hit (1974's *Happy Anniversary* aside) had been in 1957.

February 1977

David Soul, of TV cop series *Starsky & Hutch*, topped the singles chart with UK million-seller *Don't Give Up On Us*. Hence his Top 3 album. No surprise either to see the 7th Genesis album, *Wind And Wuthering*, in the Top 10, though it had charted only in January and was already falling. Their first hit LPs had been 1972's *Foxtrot* and 1973's *Genesis Live* and *Selling England By The Pound*. 1974's *Nursery Cryme* had flopped. Their biggest LPs were to be from 1978 onwards.

5 March 1977

last week	this week		
1	1	20 GOLDEN GREATS	Shadows (EMI)
2	2	ANIMALS	Pink Floyd (Harvest)
4	3	ENDLESS FLIGHT	Leo Sayer (Chrysalis)
3	4	EVITA	Various Artists (MCA)
11	5	ARRIVAL	Abba (Epic)
6	6	20 GREAT HEARTBREAKERS	Various Artists (K-Tel)
10	7	LOW	David Bowie (RCA)
5	8	DAVID SOUL	David Soul (Private Stock)
12	9	MOTORVATIN'	Chuck Berry (Chess)
7	10	SONGS IN THE KEY OF LIFE	Stevie Wonder (Tamla Motown)
9	11	RED RIVER VALLEY	Slim Whitman (United Artists)
16	12	BOSTON	Boston (Epic)
8	13	HOTEL CALIFORNIA	Eagles (Asylum)
20	14	WHITE ROCK	Rick Wakeman (A&M)
19	15	WIND AND WUTHERING	Genesis (Charisma)
13	16	GREATEST HITS	Abba (Epic)
14	17	WINGS OVER AMERICA	Wings (EMI)
15	18	A NEW WORLD RECORD	Electric Light Orchestra (Jet)
-	19	STATUS QUO LIVE	Status Quo (Vertigo)
17	20	DANCE TO THE MUSIC	Various Artists (K-Tel)
18	21	SONGS FROM THE WOOD	Jethro Tull (Chrysalis)
28	22	IN YOUR MIND	Bryan Ferry (Polydor)
30	23	RUMOURS	Fleetwood Mac (Warner Bros.)
21	24	JOHNNY THE FOX	Thin Lizzy (Vertigo)
22	25	A DAY AT THE RACES	Queen (EMI)
-	26	THEIR GREATEST HITS 1971–1975	Eagles (Asylum)
24	27	BERT WEEDON'S 22 GOLDEN GUITAR GREATS	Bert Weedon (Warwick)
-	28	FRANKIE VALLI & THE FOUR SEASONS' GREATEST HITS	Frankie Valli & the Four Seasons (K-Tel)
-	29	ELVIS IN DEMAND	Elvis Presley (RCA)
-	30	THE BEST OF LENA MARTELL	Lena Martell (Pye)

12 March 1977

1	1	20 GOLDEN GREATS	Shadows (EMI)
2	2	ANIMALS	Pink Floyd (Harvest)
3	3	ENDLESS FLIGHT	Leo Sayer (Chrysalis)
4	4	EVITA	Various Artists (MCA)
6	5	20 GREAT HEARTBREAKERS	Various Artists (K-Tel)
5	6	ARRIVAL	Abba (Epic)
7	7	LOW	David Bowie (RCA)
23	8	RUMOURS	Fleetwood Mac (Warner Bros.)
22	9	IN YOUR MIND	Bryan Ferry (Polydor)
8	10	DAVID SOUL	David Soul (Private Stock)
16	11	GREATEST HITS	Abba (Epic)
10	12	SONGS IN THE KEY OF LIFE	Stevie Wonder (Tamla Motown)
11	13	RED RIVER VALLEY	Slim Whitman (United Artists)
9	14	MOTORVATIN'	Chuck Berry (Chess)
-	15	VISIONS	Don Williams (ABC)
20	16	DANCE TO THE MUSIC	Various Artists (K-Tel)
13	17	HOTEL CALIFORNIA	Eagles (Asylum)
17	18	WINGS OVER AMERICA	Wings (EMI)
19	19	STATUS QUO LIVE	Status Quo (Vertigo)
12	20	BOSTON	Boston (Epic)
15	21	WIND AND WUTHERING	Genesis (Charisma)
-	22	PORTRAIT OF SINATRA	Frank Sinatra (Reprise)
21	23	SONGS FROM THE WOOD	Jethro Tull (Chrysalis)
14	24	WHITE ROCK	Rick Wakeman (A&M)
18	25	A NEW WORLD RECORD	Electric Light Orchestra (Jet)
30	26	THE BEST OF LENA MARTELL	Lena Martell (Pye)
25	27	A DAY AT THE RACES	Queen (EMI)
27	28	BERT WEEDON'S 22 GOLDEN GUITAR GREATS	Bert Weedon (Warwick)
-	29	SONGWRITER	Justin Hayward (Deram)
24	30	JOHNNY THE FOX	Thin Lizzy (Vertigo)

19 March 1977

1	1	20 GOLDEN GREATS	Shadows (EMI)
3	2	ENDLESS FLIGHT	Leo Sayer (Chrysalis)
5	3	20 GREAT HEARTBREAKERS	Various Artists (K-Tel)
2	4	ANIMALS	Pink Floyd (Harvest)
6	5	ARRIVAL	Abba (Epic)
4	6	EVITA	Various Artists (MCA)
19	7	STATUS QUO LIVE	Status Quo (Vertigo)
9	8	IN YOUR MIND	Bryan Ferry (Polydor)
8	9	RUMOURS	Fleetwood Mac (Warner Bros.)
7	10	LOW	David Bowie (RCA)
10	11	DAVID SOUL	David Soul (Private Stock)
11	12	GREATEST HITS	Abba (Epic)
17	13	HOTEL CALIFORNIA	Eagles (Asylum)
22	14	PORTRAIT OF SINATRA	Frank Sinatra (Reprise)
-	15	COMING OUT	Manhattan Transfer (Atlantic)
12	16	SONGS IN THE KEY OF LIFE	Stevie Wonder (Tamla Motown)
15	17	VISIONS	Don Williams (ABC)
-	18	PETER GABRIEL	Peter Gabriel (Charisma)
16	19	DANCE TO THE MUSIC	Various Artists (K-Tel)
20	20	BOSTON	Boston (Epic)
25	21	A NEW WORLD RECORD	Electric Light Orchestra (Jet)
23	22	SONGS FROM THE WOOD	Jethro Tull (Chrysalis)
14	23	MOTORVATIN'	Chuck Berry (Chess)
13	24	RED RIVER VALLEY	Slim Whitman (United Artists)
18	25	WINGS OVER AMERICA	Wings (EMI)
26	26	THE BEST OF LENA MARTELL	Lena Martell (Pye)
21	27	WIND AND WUTHERING	Genesis (Charisma)
-	28	THE BEST OF JOHN DENVER VOL.2	John Denver (RCA)
28	29	BERT WEEDON'S 22 GOLDEN GUITAR GREATS	Bert Weedon (Warwick)
-	30	EVERY FACE TELLS A STORY	Cliff Richard (EMI)

26 March 1977

1	1	20 GOLDEN GREATS	Shadows (EMI)
5	2	ARRIVAL	Abba (Epic)
14	3	PORTRAIT OF SINATRA	Frank Sinatra (Reprise)
4	4	ANIMALS	Pink Floyd (Harvest)
2	5	ENDLESS FLIGHT	Leo Sayer (Chrysalis)
3	6	20 GREAT HEARTBREAKERS	Various Artists (K-Tel)
7	7	STATUS QUO LIVE	Status Quo (Vertigo)
8	8	IN YOUR MIND	Bryan Ferry (Polydor)
6	9	EVITA	Various Artists (MCA)
10	10	LOW	David Bowie (RCA)
9	11	RUMOURS	Fleetwood Mac (Warner Bros.)
15	12	COMING OUT	Manhattan Transfer (Atlantic)
12	13	GREATEST HITS	Abba (Epic)
18	14	PETER GABRIEL	Peter Gabriel (Charisma)
21	15	A NEW WORLD RECORD	Electric Light Orchestra (Jet)
16	16	SONGS IN THE KEY OF LIFE	Stevie Wonder (Tamla Motown)
-	17	HOLLIES LIVE HITS	Hollies (Polydor)
17	18	VISIONS	Don Williams (ABC)
13	19	HOTEL CALIFORNIA	Eagles (Asylum)
11	20	DAVID SOUL	David Soul (Private Stock)
-	21	DAMNED DAMNED DAMNED	Damned (Stiff)
25	22	WINGS OVER AMERICA	Wings (EMI)
30	23	EVERY FACE TELLS A STORY	Cliff Richard (EMI)
28	24	THE BEST OF JOHN DENVER VOL.2	John Denver (RCA)
22	25	SONGS FROM THE WOOD	Jethro Tull (Chrysalis)
26	26	THE BEST OF LENA MARTELL	Lena Martell (Pye)
-	27	BURNIN' SKY	Bad Company (Island)
27	28	WIND AND WUTHERING	Genesis (Charisma)
20	29	BOSTON	Boston (Epic)
24	30	RED RIVER VALLEY	Slim Whitman (United Artists)

Chuck Berry *Motorvatin'* up into the Top 10 WAS a surprise: the album was on a real label, the legendary Chicago blues label Chess, no hit single fuelled Chuck's ride up the album chart, and he'd had no hit album since 1964's non-Top 10er *You Never Can Tell*. His endless fund of classic rock and roll songs, however, had never ceased to give others chart material, including on the Beatles' hit compilation album of 1976, *Rock'N'Roll Music*, itself a Chuck Berry song-title.

2 April 1977

last week	this week	
1	1	20 GOLDEN GREATS — Shadows (EMI)
3	2	PORTRAIT OF SINATRA — Frank Sinatra (Reprise)
2	3	ARRIVAL — Abba (Epic)
4	4	ANIMALS — Pink Floyd (Harvest)
5	5	ENDLESS FLIGHT — Leo Sayer (Chrysalis)
12	6	COMING OUT — Manhattan Transfer (Atlantic)
17	7	HOLLIES LIVE HITS — Hollies (Polydor)
7	8	STATUS QUO LIVE — Status Quo (Vertigo)
8	9	IN YOUR MIND — Bryan Ferry (Polydor)
6	10	20 GREAT HEARTBREAKERS — Various Artists (K-Tel)
9	11	EVITA — Various Artists (MCA)
13	12	GREATEST HITS — Abba (Epic)
11	13	RUMOURS — Fleetwood Mac (Warner Bros.)
10	14	LOW — David Bowie (RCA)
15	15	A NEW WORLD RECORD — Electric Light Orchestra (Jet)
14	16	PETER GABRIEL — Peter Gabriel (Charisma)
20	17	DAVID SOUL — David Soul (Private Stock)
23	18	EVERY FACE TELLS A STORY — Cliff Richard (EMI)
19	19	HOTEL CALIFORNIA — Eagles (Asylum)
27	20	BURNIN' SKY — Bad Company (Island)
26	21	THE BEST OF LENA MARTELL — Lena Martell (Pye)
16	22	SONGS IN THE KEY OF LIFE — Stevie Wonder (Tamla Motown)
30	23	RED RIVER VALLEY — Slim Whitman (United Artists)
24	24	THE BEST OF JOHN DENVER VOL.2 — John Denver (RCA)
25	25	SONGS FROM THE WOOD — Jethro Tull (Chrysalis)
29	26	BOSTON — Boston (Epic)
18	27	VISIONS — Don Williams (ABC)
-	28	WORKS — Emerson Lake & Palmer (Manticore)
-	29	KIKI DEE — Kiki Dee (Rocket)
-	30	MARQUEE MOON — Television (Elektra)

9 April 1977

last week	this week	
2	1	PORTRAIT OF SINATRA — Frank Sinatra (Reprise)
3	2	ARRIVAL — Abba (Epic)
1	3	20 GOLDEN GREATS — Shadows (EMI)
5	4	ENDLESS FLIGHT — Leo Sayer (Chrysalis)
8	5	STATUS QUO LIVE — Status Quo (Vertigo)
4	6	ANIMALS — Pink Floyd (Harvest)
7	7	HOLLIES LIVE HITS — Hollies (Polydor)
12	8	GREATEST HITS — Abba (Epic)
6	9	COMING OUT — Manhattan Transfer (Atlantic)
13	10	RUMOURS — Fleetwood Mac (Warner Bros.)
11	11	EVITA — Various Artists (MCA)
18	12	EVERY FACE TELLS A STORY — Cliff Richard (EMI)
10	13	20 GREAT HEARTBREAKERS — Various Artists (K-Tel)
15	14	A NEW WORLD RECORD — Electric Light Orchestra (Jet)
16	15	PETER GABRIEL — Peter Gabriel (Charisma)
9	16	IN YOUR MIND — Bryan Ferry (Polydor)
14	17	LOW — David Bowie (RCA)
24	18	THE BEST OF JOHN DENVER VOL.2 — John Denver (RCA)
19	19	HOTEL CALIFORNIA — Eagles (Asylum)
21	20	THE BEST OF LENA MARTELL — Lena Martell (Pye)
28	21	WORKS — Emerson Lake & Palmer (Manticore)
17	22	DAVID SOUL — David Soul (Private Stock)
22	23	SONGS IN THE KEY OF LIFE — Stevie Wonder (Tamla Motown)
20	24	BURNIN' SKY — Bad Company (Island)
-	25	THE UNFORGETTABLE GLENN MILLER — Glenn Miller (RCA)
30	26	MARQUEE MOON — Television (Elektra)
25	27	SONGS FROM THE WOOD — Jethro Tull (Chrysalis)
-	28	DAMNED DAMNED DAMNED — Damned (Stiff)
23	29	RED RIVER VALLEY — Slim Whitman (United Artists)
26	30	BOSTON — Boston (Epic)

16 April 1977

last week	this week	
2	1	ARRIVAL — Abba (Epic)
4	2	ENDLESS FLIGHT — Leo Sayer (Chrysalis)
1	3	PORTRAIT OF SINATRA — Frank Sinatra (Reprise)
3	4	20 GOLDEN GREATS — Shadows (EMI)
7	5	HOLLIES LIVE HITS — Hollies (Polydor)
6	6	ANIMALS — Pink Floyd (Harvest)
9	7	COMING OUT — Manhattan Transfer (Atlantic)
10	8	RUMOURS — Fleetwood Mac (Warner Bros.)
8	9	GREATEST HITS — Abba (Epic)
5	10	STATUS QUO LIVE — Status Quo (Vertigo)
12	11	EVERY FACE TELLS A STORY — Cliff Richard (EMI)
11	11	EVITA — Various Artists (MCA)
18	13	THE BEST OF JOHN DENVER VOL.2 — John Denver (RCA)
21	14	WORKS — Emerson Lake & Palmer (Manticore)
16	15	IN YOUR MIND — Bryan Ferry (Polydor)
15	16	PETER GABRIEL — Peter Gabriel (Charisma)
13	17	20 GREAT HEARTBREAKERS — Various Artists (K-Tel)
14	18	A NEW WORLD RECORD — Electric Light Orchestra (Jet)
22	19	DAVID SOUL — David Soul (Private Stock)
17	20	LOW — David Bowie (RCA)
25	21	THE UNFORGETTABLE GLENN MILLER — Glenn Miller (RCA)
-	22	A STAR IS BORN — Soundtrack (CBS)
19	23	HOTEL CALIFORNIA — Eagles (Asylum)
-	24	BARRY WHITE'S GREATEST HITS VOL 2 — Barry White (20th Century)
23	25	SONGS IN THE KEY OF LIFE — Stevie Wonder (Tamla Motown)
24	26	BURNIN' SKY — Bad Company (Island)
-	27	LIVING LEGENDS — Everly Brothers (Warwick)
30	28	BOSTON — Boston (Epic)
-	29	DANDY IN THE UNDERWORLD — T. Rex (EMI)
28	30	DAMNED DAMNED DAMNED — Damned (Stiff)

23 April 1977

last week	this week	
1	1	ARRIVAL — Abba (Epic)
2	2	ENDLESS FLIGHT — Leo Sayer (Chrysalis)
3	3	PORTRAIT OF SINATRA — Frank Sinatra (Reprise)
4	4	20 GOLDEN GREATS — Shadows (EMI)
5	5	HOLLIES LIVE HITS — Hollies (Polydor)
6	6	ANIMALS — Pink Floyd (Harvest)
14	7	WORKS — Emerson Lake & Palmer (Manticore)
9	8	GREATEST HITS — Abba (Epic)
8	9	RUMOURS — Fleetwood Mac (Warner Bros.)
10	10	STATUS QUO LIVE — Status Quo (Vertigo)
16	11	PETER GABRIEL — Peter Gabriel (Charisma)
23	12	HOTEL CALIFORNIA — Eagles (Asylum)
7	13	COMING OUT — Manhattan Transfer (Atlantic)
21	14	THE UNFORGETTABLE GLENN MILLER — Glenn Miller (RCA)
18	15	A NEW WORLD RECORD — Electric Light Orchestra (Jet)
11	16	EVERY FACE TELLS A STORY — Cliff Richard (EMI)
11	17	EVITA — Various Artists (MCA)
22	18	A STAR IS BORN — Soundtrack (CBS)
20	19	LOW — David Bowie (RCA)
13	20	THE BEST OF JOHN DENVER VOL.2 — John Denver (RCA)
25	21	SONGS IN THE KEY OF LIFE — Stevie Wonder (Tamla Motown)
24	22	BARRY WHITE'S GREATEST HITS VOL 2 — Barry White (20th Century)
15	23	IN YOUR MIND — Bryan Ferry (Polydor)
19	24	DAVID SOUL — David Soul (Private Stock)
-	25	THE CLASH — Clash (CBS)
26	26	BURNIN' SKY — Bad Company (Island)
-	27	SMOKIE'S GREATEST HITS — Smokie (RAK)
27	28	LIVING LEGENDS — Everly Brothers (Warwick)
17	29	20 GREAT HEARTBREAKERS — Various Artists (K-Tel)
-	30	THE MAGIC OF DEMIS ROUSSOS — Demis Roussos (Philips)

Fleetwood Mac's *Rumours* was making an unobrusive start to its long career: eventually 440-odd weeks in the Top 100, thus beating even *Dark Side Of The Moon* by Pink Floyd; their *Animals*, still in the Top 10 after peaking at No.2 in March, was their 11th hit LP. Floyd hadn't bothered with hit singles since *See Emily Play*, ten years earlier. Another huge UK band, Jethro Tull, were struggling with THEIR 11th Top 30 album, *Songs From The Wood*, but had recently had an EP in the singles chart.

30 April 1977

last week	this week	Title	Artist (Label)
1	1	ARRIVAL	Abba (Epic)
2	2	ENDLESS FLIGHT	Leo Sayer (Chrysalis)
3	3	PORTRAIT OF SINATRA	Frank Sinatra (Reprise)
4	4	20 GOLDEN GREATS	Shadows (EMI)
8	5	GREATEST HITS	Abba (Epic)
12	6	HOTEL CALIFORNIA	Eagles (Asylum)
6	7	ANIMALS	Pink Floyd (Harvest)
14	8	THE UNFORGETTABLE GLENN MILLER	Glenn Miller (RCA)
5	9	HOLLIES LIVE HITS	Hollies (Polydor)
7	10	WORKS	Emerson Lake & Palmer (Manticore)
18	11	A STAR IS BORN	Soundtrack (CBS)
9	12	RUMOURS	Fleetwood Mac (Warner Bros.)
11	13	PETER GABRIEL	Peter Gabriel (Charisma)
10	14	STATUS QUO LIVE	Status Quo (Vertigo)
21	15	SONGS IN THE KEY OF LIFE	Stevie Wonder (Tamla Motown)
17	16	EVITA	Various Artists (MCA)
15	17	A NEW WORLD RECORD	Electric Light Orchestra (Jet)
16	18	EVERY FACE TELLS A STORY	Cliff Richard (EMI)
30	19	THE MAGIC OF DEMIS ROUSSOS	Demis Roussos (Philips)
27	20	SMOKIE'S GREATEST HITS	Smokie (RAK)
28	21	LIVING LEGENDS	Everly Brothers (Warwick)
22	22	BARRY WHITE'S GREATEST HITS VOL 2	Barry White (20th Century)
20	23	THE BEST OF JOHN DENVER VOL.2	John Denver (RCA)
19	24	LOW	David Bowie (RCA)
-	25	EVEN IN THE QUIETEST MOMENTS	Supertramp (A&M)
13	26	COMING OUT	Manhattan Transfer (Atlantic)
-	27	SHOWADDYWADDY'S GREATEST HITS	Showaddywaddy (Arista)
25	28	THE CLASH	Clash (CBS)
24	29	DAVID SOUL	David Soul (Private Stock)
23	30	IN YOUR MIND	Bryan Ferry (Polydor)

7 May 1977

last week	this week	Title	Artist (Label)
1	1	ARRIVAL	Abba (Epic)
6	2	HOTEL CALIFORNIA	Eagles (Asylum)
3	3	PORTRAIT OF SINATRA	Frank Sinatra (Reprise)
2	4	ENDLESS FLIGHT	Leo Sayer (Chrysalis)
5	5	GREATEST HITS	Abba (Epic)
12	6	RUMOURS	Fleetwood Mac (Warner Bros.)
4	7	20 GOLDEN GREATS	Shadows (EMI)
9	8	HOLLIES LIVE HITS	Hollies (Polydor)
20	9	SMOKIE'S GREATEST HITS	Smokie (RAK)
7	10	ANIMALS	Pink Floyd (Harvest)
11	11	A STAR IS BORN	Soundtrack (CBS)
8	12	THE UNFORGETTABLE GLENN MILLER	Glenn Miller (RCA)
10	13	WORKS	Emerson Lake & Palmer (Manticore)
25	14	EVEN IN THE QUIETEST MOMENTS	Supertramp (A&M)
21	15	LIVING LEGENDS	Everly Brothers (Warwick)
15	16	SONGS IN THE KEY OF LIFE	Stevie Wonder (Tamla Motown)
13	17	PETER GABRIEL	Peter Gabriel (Charisma)
14	18	STATUS QUO LIVE	Status Quo (Vertigo)
17	19	A NEW WORLD RECORD	Electric Light Orchestra (Jet)
28	20	THE CLASH	Clash (CBS)
-	21	STRANGLERS IV (RATTUS NORVEGICUS)	Stranglers (United Artists)
18	22	EVERY FACE TELLS A STORY	Cliff Richard (EMI)
-	23	DECEPTIVE BENDS	10 C.C. (Philips)
22	24	BARRY WHITE'S GREATEST HITS VOL 2	Barry White (20th Century)
19	25	THE MAGIC OF DEMIS ROUSSOS	Demis Roussos (Philips)
23	26	THE BEST OF JOHN DENVER VOL.2	John Denver (RCA)
-	27	THEIR GREATEST HITS 1971–1975	Eagles (Asylum)
16	28	EVITA	Various Artists (MCA)
29	29	DAVID SOUL	David Soul (Private Stock)
26	30	COMING OUT	Manhattan Transfer (Atlantic)

14 May 1977

last week	this week	Title	Artist (Label)
1	1	ARRIVAL	Abba (Epic)
2	2	HOTEL CALIFORNIA	Eagles (Asylum)
4	3	ENDLESS FLIGHT	Leo Sayer (Chrysalis)
11	4	A STAR IS BORN	Soundtrack (CBS)
7	5	20 GOLDEN GREATS	Shadows (EMI)
6	6	RUMOURS	Fleetwood Mac (Warner Bros.)
5	7	GREATEST HITS	Abba (Epic)
3	7	PORTRAIT OF SINATRA	Frank Sinatra (Reprise)
9	9	SMOKIE'S GREATEST HITS	Smokie (RAK)
10	10	ANIMALS	Pink Floyd (Harvest)
17	11	PETER GABRIEL	Peter Gabriel (Charisma)
21	12	STRANGLERS IV (RATTUS NORVEGICUS)	Stranglers (United Artists)
8	13	HOLLIES LIVE HITS	Hollies (Polydor)
16	14	SONGS IN THE KEY OF LIFE	Stevie Wonder (Tamla Motown)
14	15	EVEN IN THE QUIETEST MOMENTS	Supertramp (A&M)
-	16	THE BEATLES AT THE HOLLYWOOD BOWL	Beatles (Parlophone)
27	17	THEIR GREATEST HITS 1971–1975	Eagles (Asylum)
15	18	LIVING LEGENDS	Everly Brothers (Warwick)
13	19	WORKS	Emerson Lake & Palmer (Manticore)
18	20	STATUS QUO LIVE	Status Quo (Vertigo)
19	21	A NEW WORLD RECORD	Electric Light Orchestra (Jet)
12	22	THE UNFORGETTABLE GLENN MILLER	Glenn Miller (RCA)
23	23	DECEPTIVE BENDS	10 C.C. (Philips)
20	24	THE CLASH	Clash (CBS)
-	25	HIT ACTION	Various Artists (K-Tel)
-	26	A PERIOD OF TRANSITION	Van Morrison (Warner Bros.)
28	27	EVITA	Various Artists (MCA)
25	28	THE MAGIC OF DEMIS ROUSSOS	Demis Roussos (Philips)
22	29	EVERY FACE TELLS A STORY	Cliff Richard (EMI)
-	30	ALL TO YOURSELF	Jack Jones (RCA)

21 May 1977

last week	this week	Title	Artist (Label)
1	1	ARRIVAL	Abba (Epic)
2	2	HOTEL CALIFORNIA	Eagles (Asylum)
4	3	A STAR IS BORN	Soundtrack (CBS)
23	4	DECEPTIVE BENDS	10 C.C. (Philips)
7	5	GREATEST HITS	Abba (Epic)
12	6	STRANGLERS IV (RATTUS NORVEGICUS)	Stranglers (United Artists)
3	7	ENDLESS FLIGHT	Leo Sayer (Chrysalis)
5	8	20 GOLDEN GREATS	Shadows (EMI)
6	9	RUMOURS	Fleetwood Mac (Warner Bros.)
16	10	THE BEATLES AT THE HOLLYWOOD BOWL	Beatles (Parlophone)
7	11	PORTRAIT OF SINATRA	Frank Sinatra (Reprise)
10	12	ANIMALS	Pink Floyd (Harvest)
9	13	SMOKIE'S GREATEST HITS	Smokie (RAK)
11	14	PETER GABRIEL	Peter Gabriel (Charisma)
14	15	SONGS IN THE KEY OF LIFE	Stevie Wonder (Tamla Motown)
17	16	THEIR GREATEST HITS 1971–1975	Eagles (Asylum)
15	17	EVEN IN THE QUIETEST MOMENTS	Supertramp (A&M)
19	18	WORKS	Emerson Lake & Palmer (Manticore)
13	19	HOLLIES LIVE HITS	Hollies (Polydor)
21	20	A NEW WORLD RECORD	Electric Light Orchestra (Jet)
20	21	STATUS QUO LIVE	Status Quo (Vertigo)
22	22	THE UNFORGETTABLE GLENN MILLER	Glenn Miller (RCA)
18	23	LIVING LEGENDS	Everly Brothers (Warwick)
24	24	THE CLASH	Clash (CBS)
30	25	ALL TO YOURSELF	Jack Jones (RCA)
-	26	IZITSO	Cat Stevens (Island)
-	27	ATLANTIC CROSSING	Rod Stewart (Warner Bros.)
-	28	DETROIT SPINNERS' SMASH HITS	Detroit Spinners (Atlantic)
-	29	THE BEST OF THE FACES	Faces (Riva)
-	30	TIME LOVES A HERO	Little Feat (Warner Bros.)

Damned Damned Damned was the first punk album to chart, on April 9, followed by *The Clash* and now *Stranglers IV (Rattus Norvegicus)*. The Stranglers were a band risen from the streets, and with the possible exception of boyish-looking Jean-Jacques Burnel (the Paul McCartney of the group) they were rather elderly to be fronting a youth movement. However, their 2nd hit single was imminent and they were cleverly marketed by United Artists, which had also signed Buzzcocks.

May – June 1977

28 May 1977

Last	This	Title	Artist (Label)
2	1	HOTEL CALIFORNIA	Eagles (Asylum)
1	2	ARRIVAL	Abba (Epic)
4	3	DECEPTIVE BENDS	10 C.C. (Philips)
3	4	A STAR IS BORN	Soundtrack (CBS)
10	5	THE BEATLES AT THE HOLLYWOOD BOWL	Beatles (Parlophone)
13	6	SMOKIE'S GREATEST HITS	Smokie (RAK)
5	7	GREATEST HITS	Abba (Epic)
8	8	20 GOLDEN GREATS	Shadows (EMI)
6	9	STRANGLERS IV (RATTUS NORVEGICUS)	Stranglers (United Artists)
7	10	ENDLESS FLIGHT	Leo Sayer (Chrysalis)
9	11	RUMOURS	Fleetwood Mac (Warner Bros.)
11	12	PORTRAIT OF SINATRA	Frank Sinatra (Reprise)
14	13	PETER GABRIEL	Peter Gabriel (Charisma)
12	14	ANIMALS	Pink Floyd (Harvest)
15	15	SONGS IN THE KEY OF LIFE	Stevie Wonder (Tamla Motown)
16	16	THEIR GREATEST HITS 1971–1975	Eagles (Asylum)
23	17	LIVING LEGENDS	Everly Brothers (Warwick)
24	18	THE CLASH	Clash (CBS)
25	19	ALL TO YOURSELF	Jack Jones (RCA)
20	20	A NEW WORLD RECORD	Electric Light Orchestra (Jet)
26	21	IZITSO	Cat Stevens (Island)
19	22	HOLLIES LIVE HITS	Hollies (Polydor)
17	23	EVEN IN THE QUIETEST MOMENTS	Supertramp (A&M)
-	24	HIT ACTION	Various Artists (K-Tel)
-	25	SIN AFTER SIN	Judas Priest (CBS)
-	26	IN THE CITY	Jam (Polydor)
27	27	ATLANTIC CROSSING	Rod Stewart (Warner Bros.)
-	28	MOROCCAN ROLL	Brand X (Charisma)
21	29	STATUS QUO LIVE	Status Quo (Vertigo)
30	30	TIME LOVES A HERO	Little Feat (Warner Bros.)

4 June 1977

Last	This	Title	Artist (Label)
1	1	HOTEL CALIFORNIA	Eagles (Asylum)
2	2	ARRIVAL	Abba (Epic)
3	3	DECEPTIVE BENDS	10 C.C. (Philips)
4	4	A STAR IS BORN	Soundtrack (CBS)
5	5	THE BEATLES AT THE HOLLYWOOD BOWL	Beatles (Parlophone)
10	6	ENDLESS FLIGHT	Leo Sayer (Chrysalis)
9	7	STRANGLERS IV (RATTUS NORVEGICUS)	Stranglers (United Artists)
11	8	RUMOURS	Fleetwood Mac (Warner Bros.)
7	9	GREATEST HITS	Abba (Epic)
16	10	THEIR GREATEST HITS 1971–1975	Eagles (Asylum)
8	11	20 GOLDEN GREATS	Shadows (EMI)
19	12	ALL TO YOURSELF	Jack Jones (RCA)
13	13	PETER GABRIEL	Peter Gabriel (Charisma)
14	14	ANIMALS	Pink Floyd (Harvest)
6	15	SMOKIE'S GREATEST HITS	Smokie (RAK)
12	16	PORTRAIT OF SINATRA	Frank Sinatra (Reprise)
20	17	A NEW WORLD RECORD	Electric Light Orchestra (Jet)
21	18	IZITSO	Cat Stevens (Island)
-	19	THE MUPPET SHOW	Muppets (Pye)
30	20	TIME LOVES A HERO	Little Feat (Warner Bros.)
-	21	A NIGHT ON THE TOWN	Rod Stewart (Riva)
24	22	HIT ACTION	Various Artists (K-Tel)
15	23	SONGS IN THE KEY OF LIFE	Stevie Wonder (Tamla Motown)
27	24	ATLANTIC CROSSING	Rod Stewart (Warner Bros.)
23	25	EVEN IN THE QUIETEST MOMENTS	Supertramp (A&M)
18	26	THE CLASH	Clash (CBS)
29	27	STATUS QUO LIVE	Status Quo (Vertigo)
-	28	BOOK OF DREAMS	Steve Miller Band (Mercury)
-	29	THE BEATLES LIVE AT THE STAR CLUB IN HAMBURG, GERMANY 1962	Beatles (Lingasong)
22	30	HOLLIES LIVE HITS	Hollies (Polydor)

11 June 1977

Last	This	Title	Artist (Label)
2	1	ARRIVAL	Abba (Epic)
3	2	DECEPTIVE BENDS	10 C.C. (Philips)
1	3	HOTEL CALIFORNIA	Eagles (Asylum)
4	4	A STAR IS BORN	Soundtrack (CBS)
5	5	THE BEATLES AT THE HOLLYWOOD BOWL	Beatles (Parlophone)
6	6	ENDLESS FLIGHT	Leo Sayer (Chrysalis)
10	7	THEIR GREATEST HITS 1971–1975	Eagles (Asylum)
8	8	RUMOURS	Fleetwood Mac (Warner Bros.)
12	9	ALL TO YOURSELF	Jack Jones (RCA)
7	10	STRANGLERS IV (RATTUS NORVEGICUS)	Stranglers (United Artists)
15	11	SMOKIE'S GREATEST HITS	Smokie (RAK)
28	12	BOOK OF DREAMS	Steve Miller Band (Mercury)
9	13	GREATEST HITS	Abba (Epic)
21	14	A NIGHT ON THE TOWN	Rod Stewart (Riva)
17	15	A NEW WORLD RECORD	Electric Light Orchestra (Jet)
19	16	THE MUPPET SHOW	Muppets (Pye)
24	17	ATLANTIC CROSSING	Rod Stewart (Warner Bros.)
25	18	EVEN IN THE QUIETEST MOMENTS	Supertramp (A&M)
14	19	ANIMALS	Pink Floyd (Harvest)
-	20	THE BEST OF THE FACES	Faces (Riva)
-	21	SNEAKIN' SUSPICION	Dr. Feelgood (United Artists)
23	22	SONGS IN THE KEY OF LIFE	Stevie Wonder (Tamla Motown)
13	23	PETER GABRIEL	Peter Gabriel (Charisma)
18	24	IZITSO	Cat Stevens (Island)
20	25	TIME LOVES A HERO	Little Feat (Warner Bros.)
16	26	PORTRAIT OF SINATRA	Frank Sinatra (Reprise)
29	27	THE BEATLES LIVE AT THE STAR CLUB IN HAMBURG, GERMANY 1962	Beatles (Lingasong)
-	28	THIS IS NIECY	Deniece Williams (CBS)
30	29	HOLLIES LIVE HITS	Hollies (Polydor)
11	30	20 GOLDEN GREATS	Shadows (EMI)

18 June 1977

Last	This	Title	Artist (Label)
1	1	ARRIVAL	Abba (Epic)
4	2	A STAR IS BORN	Soundtrack (CBS)
3	3	HOTEL CALIFORNIA	Eagles (Asylum)
5	4	THE BEATLES AT THE HOLLYWOOD BOWL	Beatles (Parlophone)
2	5	DECEPTIVE BENDS	10 C.C. (Philips)
16	6	THE MUPPET SHOW	Muppets (Pye)
10	7	STRANGLERS IV (RATTUS NORVEGICUS)	Stranglers (United Artists)
15	8	A NEW WORLD RECORD	Electric Light Orchestra (Jet)
8	9	RUMOURS	Fleetwood Mac (Warner Bros.)
13	10	GREATEST HITS	Abba (Epic)
7	11	THEIR GREATEST HITS 1971–1975	Eagles (Asylum)
6	12	ENDLESS FLIGHT	Leo Sayer (Chrysalis)
30	13	20 GOLDEN GREATS	Shadows (EMI)
-	14	EXODUS	Bob Marley & the Wailers (Island)
11	15	SMOKIE'S GREATEST HITS	Smokie (RAK)
19	16	ANIMALS	Pink Floyd (Harvest)
17	17	ATLANTIC CROSSING	Rod Stewart (Warner Bros.)
24	18	IZITSO	Cat Stevens (Island)
12	19	BOOK OF DREAMS	Steve Miller Band (Mercury)
-	20	IN FLIGHT	George Benson (Warner Bros.)
9	21	ALL TO YOURSELF	Jack Jones (RCA)
-	22	SHEER MAGIC	Acker Bilk (Warwick)
-	23	TOM PETTY & THE HEARTBREAKERS	Tom Petty & the Heartbreakers (Shelter)
-	24	THE CLASH	Clash (CBS)
-	25	WORKS	Emerson Lake & Palmer (Manticore)
21	26	SNEAKIN' SUSPICION	Dr. Feelgood (United Artists)
14	27	A NIGHT ON THE TOWN	Rod Stewart (Riva)
-	28	I'M IN YOU	Peter Frampton (A&M)
18	29	EVEN IN THE QUIETEST MOMENTS	Supertramp (A&M)
23	30	PETER GABRIEL	Peter Gabriel (Charisma)

The Jam joined the album chart, as the Stranglers held onto the Top 10 and the Clash faltered way below. The ideal medium for punk was of course live performance, and next best was the single. As with Merseybeat 15 years before, album charts couldn't reflect the scale of punk's penetration, but only hint at events in the singles market. The Clash had no big single; the Stranglers did. How appropriate to the spirit of the times that *The Beatles Live At The Star Club Hamburg* should now chart.

25 June 1977

last week	this week		
4	1	THE BEATLES AT THE HOLLYWOOD BOWL	Beatles (Parlophone)
1	2	ARRIVAL	Abba (Epic)
6	3	THE MUPPET SHOW	Muppets (Pye)
3	4	HOTEL CALIFORNIA	Eagles (Asylum)
2	5	A STAR IS BORN	Soundtrack (CBS)
5	6	DECEPTIVE BENDS	10 C.C. (Philips)
7	7	STRANGLERS IV (RATTUS NORVEGICUS)	Stranglers (United Artists)
8	8	A NEW WORLD RECORD	Electric Light Orchestra (Jet)
22	9	SHEER MAGIC	Acker Bilk (Warwick)
12	10	ENDLESS FLIGHT	Leo Sayer (Chrysalis)
9	11	RUMOURS	Fleetwood Mac (Warner Bros.)
-	12	ROCK FOLLIES 77	Various Artists (Polydor)
-	13	THE JOHNNY MATHIS COLLECTION	Johnny Mathis (CBS)
14	14	EXODUS	Bob Marley & the Wailers (Island)
10	15	GREATEST HITS	Abba (Epic)
11	16	THEIR GREATEST HITS 1971–1975	Eagles (Asylum)
17	17	ATLANTIC CROSSING	Rod Stewart (Warner Bros.)
27	18	A NIGHT ON THE TOWN	Rod Stewart (Riva)
16	19	ANIMALS	Pink Floyd (Harvest)
13	20	20 GOLDEN GREATS	Shadows (EMI)
20	21	IN FLIGHT	George Benson (Warner Bros.)
21	22	ALL TO YOURSELF	Jack Jones (RCA)
28	23	I'M IN YOU	Peter Frampton (A&M)
19	24	BOOK OF DREAMS	Steve Miller Band (Mercury)
-	25	SILK DEGREES	Boz Scaggs (CBS)
23	26	TOM PETTY & THE HEARTBREAKERS	Tom Petty & the Heartbreakers (Shelter)
30	27	PETER GABRIEL	Peter Gabriel (Charisma)
-	28	KENNY ROGERS	Kenny Rogers (United Artists)
15	29	SMOKIE'S GREATEST HITS	Smokie (RAK)
26	30	SNEAKIN' SUSPICION	Dr. Feelgood (United Artists)

2 July 1977

3	1	THE MUPPET SHOW	Muppets (Pye)
5	2	A STAR IS BORN	Soundtrack (CBS)
4	3	HOTEL CALIFORNIA	Eagles (Asylum)
2	4	ARRIVAL	Abba (Epic)
1	5	THE BEATLES AT THE HOLLYWOOD BOWL	Beatles (Parlophone)
7	6	STRANGLERS IV (RATTUS NORVEGICUS)	Stranglers (United Artists)
11	7	RUMOURS	Fleetwood Mac (Warner Bros.)
6	8	DECEPTIVE BENDS	10 C.C. (Philips)
8	9	A NEW WORLD RECORD	Electric Light Orchestra (Jet)
13	10	THE JOHNNY MATHIS COLLECTION	Johnny Mathis (CBS)
25	11	SILK DEGREES	Boz Scaggs (CBS)
14	12	EXODUS	Bob Marley & the Wailers (Island)
21	12	IN FLIGHT	George Benson (Warner Bros.)
15	14	GREATEST HITS	Abba (Epic)
9	15	SHEER MAGIC	Acker Bilk (Warwick)
16	16	THEIR GREATEST HITS 1971–1975	Eagles (Asylum)
12	16	ROCK FOLLIES 77	Various Artists (Polydor)
23	18	I'M IN YOU	Peter Frampton (A&M)
17	19	ATLANTIC CROSSING	Rod Stewart (Warner Bros.)
10	20	ENDLESS FLIGHT	Leo Sayer (Chrysalis)
-	21	I REMEMBER YESTERDAY	Donna Summer (GTO)
26	22	TOM PETTY & THE HEARTBREAKERS	Tom Petty & the Heartbreakers (Shelter)
-	23	LOVE AT THE GREEK	Neil Diamond (CBS)
28	24	KENNY ROGERS	Kenny Rogers (United Artists)
18	25	A NIGHT ON THE TOWN	Rod Stewart (Riva)
-	26	EVEN IN THE QUIETEST MOMENTS	Supertramp (A&M)
29	27	SMOKIE'S GREATEST HITS	Smokie (RAK)
-	28	WORKS	Emerson Lake & Palmer (Manticore)
-	29	CAT SCRATCH FEVER	Ted Nugent (Epic)
24	30	BOOK OF DREAMS	Steve Miller Band (Mercury)

9 July 1977

2	1	A STAR IS BORN	Soundtrack (CBS)
1	2	THE MUPPET SHOW	Muppets (Pye)
3	3	HOTEL CALIFORNIA	Eagles (Asylum)
4	4	ARRIVAL	Abba (Epic)
9	5	A NEW WORLD RECORD	Electric Light Orchestra (Jet)
10	6	THE JOHNNY MATHIS COLLECTION	Johnny Mathis (CBS)
8	7	DECEPTIVE BENDS	10 C.C. (Philips)
6	8	STRANGLERS IV (RATTUS NORVEGICUS)	Stranglers (United Artists)
5	9	THE BEATLES AT THE HOLLYWOOD BOWL	Beatles (Parlophone)
23	10	LOVE AT THE GREEK	Neil Diamond (CBS)
12	11	EXODUS	Bob Marley & the Wailers (Island)
7	12	RUMOURS	Fleetwood Mac (Warner Bros.)
28	13	WORKS	Emerson Lake & Palmer (Manticore)
14	14	GREATEST HITS	Abba (Epic)
18	15	I'M IN YOU	Peter Frampton (A&M)
20	16	ENDLESS FLIGHT	Leo Sayer (Chrysalis)
-	17	THE ROXY, LONDON WC2	Various Artists (Harvest)
21	18	I REMEMBER YESTERDAY	Donna Summer (GTO)
12	19	IN FLIGHT	George Benson (Warner Bros.)
24	20	KENNY ROGERS	Kenny Rogers (United Artists)
-	21	COMING OUT	Manhattan Transfer (Atlantic)
26	22	EVEN IN THE QUIETEST MOMENTS	Supertramp (A&M)
-	23	STEVE WINWOOD	Steve Winwood (Island)
15	24	SHEER MAGIC	Acker Bilk (Warwick)
-	25	AMERICAN STARS 'N' BARS	Neil Young (Reprise)
22	26	TOM PETTY & THE HEARTBREAKERS	Tom Petty & the Heartbreakers (Shelter)
29	27	CAT SCRATCH FEVER	Ted Nugent (Epic)
11	28	SILK DEGREES	Boz Scaggs (CBS)
16	29	ROCK FOLLIES 77	Various Artists (Polydor)
-	30	PURE MANIA	Vibrators (Epic)

16 July 1977

1	1	A STAR IS BORN	Soundtrack (CBS)
6	2	THE JOHNNY MATHIS COLLECTION	Johnny Mathis (CBS)
4	3	ARRIVAL	Abba (Epic)
2	4	THE MUPPET SHOW	Muppets (Pye)
3	5	HOTEL CALIFORNIA	Eagles (Asylum)
8	6	STRANGLERS IV (RATTUS NORVEGICUS)	Stranglers (United Artists)
18	7	I REMEMBER YESTERDAY	Donna Summer (GTO)
7	8	DECEPTIVE BENDS	10 C.C. (Philips)
11	9	EXODUS	Bob Marley & the Wailers (Island)
9	10	THE BEATLES AT THE HOLLYWOOD BOWL	Beatles (Parlophone)
10	11	LOVE AT THE GREEK	Neil Diamond (CBS)
12	12	RUMOURS	Fleetwood Mac (Warner Bros.)
5	13	A NEW WORLD RECORD	Electric Light Orchestra (Jet)
13	14	WORKS	Emerson Lake & Palmer (Manticore)
19	15	IN FLIGHT	George Benson (Warner Bros.)
-	16	THE BEST OF THE MAMAS AND THE PAPAS	Mamas & Papas (Arcade)
-	17	20 ALL TIME GREATS	Connie Francis (Polydor)
25	18	AMERICAN STARS 'N' BARS	Neil Young (Reprise)
15	19	I'M IN YOU	Peter Frampton (A&M)
16	20	ENDLESS FLIGHT	Leo Sayer (Chrysalis)
23	21	STEVE WINWOOD	Steve Winwood (Island)
26	22	TOM PETTY & THE HEARTBREAKERS	Tom Petty & the Heartbreakers (Shelter)
-	23	CSN	Crosby Stills & Nash (Atlantic)
20	24	KENNY ROGERS	Kenny Rogers (United Artists)
27	25	CAT SCRATCH FEVER	Ted Nugent (Epic)
17	26	THE ROXY, LONDON WC2	Various Artists (Harvest)
24	27	SHEER MAGIC	Acker Bilk (Warwick)
30	28	PURE MANIA	Vibrators (Epic)
22	29	EVEN IN THE QUIETEST MOMENTS	Supertramp (A&M)
28	30	SILK DEGREES	Boz Scaggs (CBS)

More punk charted: *The Roxy, London WC2* (a prinicipal venue for the music, pogo-ing and gobbing) and the Vibrators. Ranged against it was music from every previous era: 50s crooners Jack Jones and Johnny Mathis, the latter enjoying a career revival; 1961 Trad craze artist Acker Bilk; re-born '60s British blues-boom group Fleetwood Mac; hippies Crosby Stills & Nash and, at the top, *The Beatles At The Hollywood Bowl* and the soundtrack of a remake of an old Judy Garland film.

July – August 1977

Exodus gave Bob Marley a deserved substantial hit. No such hit for US punks Television (though punk was different there: more James Dean-Brando-early Elvis-to-Velvet Underground in look, more precise yet garage-band in sound). Television, led by guitarist Tom Verlaine, had recently had a minor hit, *Marquee Moon*, title song from their perfect debut album, and now reached the Top 20 with another single from it (*Prove It*): but the album had barely scraped the Top 30 for a fortnight in April.

last week	this week	20 August 1977
2	1	GOING FOR THE ONE — Yes (Atlantic)
3	2	I REMEMBER YESTERDAY — Donna Summer (GTO)
4	3	A STAR IS BORN — Soundtrack (CBS)
5	4	20 ALL TIME GREATS — Connie Francis (Polydor)
8	5	RUMOURS — Fleetwood Mac (Warner Bros.)
1	5	THE JOHNNY MATHIS COLLECTION — Johnny Mathis (CBS)
11	7	STRANGLERS IV (RATTUS NORVEGICUS) — Stranglers (United Artists)
7	8	HOTEL CALIFORNIA — Eagles (Asylum)
10	9	THE MUPPET SHOW — Muppets (Pye)
6	10	LOVE AT THE GREEK — Neil Diamond (CBS)
22	11	LOVE FOR SALE — Boney M (Atlantic)
9	12	ARRIVAL — Abba (Epic)
14	13	WORKS — Emerson Lake & Palmer (Manticore)
16	14	ON STAGE — Rainbow (Polydor)
18	15	THE BEST OF ROD STEWART — Rod Stewart (Mercury)
15	16	A NEW WORLD RECORD — Electric Light Orchestra (Jet)
-	17	NEW WAVE — Various Artists (Vertigo)
12	18	EXODUS — Bob Marley & the Wailers (Island)
21	19	SMOKIE'S GREATEST HITS — Smokie (RAK)
13	20	DECEPTIVE BENDS — 10 C.C. (Philips)
-	21	OXYGENE — Jean-Michel Jarre (Polydor)
17	22	LIVE! IN THE AIR AGE — Be Bop Deluxe (Harvest)
27	23	STREISAND SUPERMAN — Barbra Streisand (CBS)
-	24	MY AIM IS TRUE — Elvis Costello (Stiff)
26	25	COMING OUT — Manhattan Transfer (Atlantic)
-	26	IN THE CITY — Jam (Polydor)
30	27	ENDLESS FLIGHT — Leo Sayer (Chrysalis)
24	28	ANIMALS — Pink Floyd (Harvest)
19	29	THE BEST OF THE MAMAS AND THE PAPAS — Mamas & Papas (Arcade)
-	30	FLOATERS — Floaters (ABC)

		27 August 1977
1	1	GOING FOR THE ONE — Yes (Atlantic)
3	2	A STAR IS BORN — Soundtrack (CBS)
4	2	20 ALL TIME GREATS — Connie Francis (Polydor)
2	4	I REMEMBER YESTERDAY — Donna Summer (GTO)
5	5	RUMOURS — Fleetwood Mac (Warner Bros.)
5	6	THE JOHNNY MATHIS COLLECTION — Johnny Mathis (CBS)
21	7	OXYGENE — Jean-Michel Jarre (Polydor)
8	8	HOTEL CALIFORNIA — Eagles (Asylum)
12	9	ARRIVAL — Abba (Epic)
7	10	STRANGLERS IV (RATTUS NORVEGICUS) — Stranglers (United Artists)
-	11	MOODY BLUE — Elvis Presley (RCA)
11	12	LOVE FOR SALE — Boney M (Atlantic)
10	13	LOVE AT THE GREEK — Neil Diamond (CBS)
15	14	THE BEST OF ROD STEWART — Rod Stewart (Mercury)
13	15	WORKS — Emerson Lake & Palmer (Manticore)
-	16	40 GREATEST — Elvis Presley (RCA)
9	17	THE MUPPET SHOW — Muppets (Pye)
17	18	NEW WAVE — Various Artists (Vertigo)
14	19	ON STAGE — Rainbow (Polydor)
22	20	LIVE! IN THE AIR AGE — Be Bop Deluxe (Harvest)
-	21	WELCOME TO MY WORLD — Elvis Presley (RCA)
30	22	FLOATERS — Floaters (ABC)
18	23	EXODUS — Bob Marley & the Wailers (Island)
20	24	DECEPTIVE BENDS — 10 C.C. (Philips)
26	25	IN THE CITY — Jam (Polydor)
16	26	A NEW WORLD RECORD — Electric Light Orchestra (Jet)
19	27	SMOKIE'S GREATEST HITS — Smokie (RAK)
24	28	MY AIM IS TRUE — Elvis Costello (Stiff)
23	29	STREISAND SUPERMAN — Barbra Streisand (CBS)
29	30	THE BEST OF THE MAMAS AND THE PAPAS — Mamas & Papas (Arcade)

		3 September 1977
11	1	MOODY BLUE — Elvis Presley (RCA)
2	2	A STAR IS BORN — Soundtrack (CBS)
7	3	OXYGENE — Jean-Michel Jarre (Polydor)
2	4	20 ALL TIME GREATS — Connie Francis (Polydor)
4	5	I REMEMBER YESTERDAY — Donna Summer (GTO)
1	6	GOING FOR THE ONE — Yes (Atlantic)
5	7	RUMOURS — Fleetwood Mac (Warner Bros.)
6	8	THE JOHNNY MATHIS COLLECTION — Johnny Mathis (CBS)
10	9	STRANGLERS IV (RATTUS NORVEGICUS) — Stranglers (United Artists)
9	10	ARRIVAL — Abba (Epic)
8	11	HOTEL CALIFORNIA — Eagles (Asylum)
12	12	LOVE FOR SALE — Boney M (Atlantic)
23	13	EXODUS — Bob Marley & the Wailers (Island)
16	14	40 GREATEST — Elvis Presley (RCA)
18	15	NEW WAVE — Various Artists (Vertigo)
21	16	WELCOME TO MY WORLD — Elvis Presley (RCA)
17	17	THE MUPPET SHOW — Muppets (Pye)
22	18	FLOATERS — Floaters (ABC)
28	19	MY AIM IS TRUE — Elvis Costello (Stiff)
14	20	THE BEST OF ROD STEWART — Rod Stewart (Mercury)
13	21	LOVE AT THE GREEK — Neil Diamond (CBS)
24	21	DECEPTIVE BENDS — 10 C.C. (Philips)
27	23	SMOKIE'S GREATEST HITS — Smokie (RAK)
-	24	I, ROBOT — Alan Parsons Project (Arista)
-	25	STEVE WINWOOD — Steve Winwood (Island)
15	26	WORKS — Emerson Lake & Palmer (Manticore)
20	27	LIVE! IN THE AIR AGE — Be Bop Deluxe (Harvest)
-	28	THIS IS NIECY — Deniece Williams (CBS)
26	29	A NEW WORLD RECORD — Electric Light Orchestra (Jet)
19	30	ON STAGE — Rainbow (Polydor)

		10 September 1977
3	1	OXYGENE — Jean-Michel Jarre (Polydor)
1	2	MOODY BLUE — Elvis Presley (RCA)
7	3	RUMOURS — Fleetwood Mac (Warner Bros.)
2	4	A STAR IS BORN — Soundtrack (CBS)
4	4	20 ALL TIME GREATS — Connie Francis (Polydor)
16	6	WELCOME TO MY WORLD — Elvis Presley (RCA)
6	7	GOING FOR THE ONE — Yes (Atlantic)
5	8	I REMEMBER YESTERDAY — Donna Summer (GTO)
14	9	40 GREATEST — Elvis Presley (RCA)
9	10	STRANGLERS IV (RATTUS NORVEGICUS) — Stranglers (United Artists)
11	11	HOTEL CALIFORNIA — Eagles (Asylum)
15	12	NEW WAVE — Various Artists (Vertigo)
10	13	ARRIVAL — Abba (Epic)
8	14	THE JOHNNY MATHIS COLLECTION — Johnny Mathis (CBS)
12	15	LOVE FOR SALE — Boney M (Atlantic)
19	16	MY AIM IS TRUE — Elvis Costello (Stiff)
-	17	20 GOLDEN GREATS — Diana Ross & the Supremes (Motown)
20	18	THE BEST OF ROD STEWART — Rod Stewart (Mercury)
13	19	EXODUS — Bob Marley & the Wailers (Island)
-	20	G.I. BLUES — Elvis Presley (RCA)
29	21	A NEW WORLD RECORD — Electric Light Orchestra (Jet)
-	22	ELVIS IN DEMAND — Elvis Presley (RCA)
26	23	WORKS — Emerson Lake & Palmer (Manticore)
21	24	LOVE AT THE GREEK — Neil Diamond (CBS)
-	25	MAGIC FLY — Space (Pye)
-	26	BLUE HAWAII — Elvis Presley (RCA)
17	27	THE MUPPET SHOW — Muppets (Pye)
-	28	ROCK 'N' ROLL WITH THE MODERN LOVERS — Jonathan Richman & the Modern Lovers (Beserkeley)
-	29	CABRETTA — Mink De Ville (Capitol)
30	30	ON STAGE — Rainbow (Polydor)

Elvis Presley died on August 16. The dramatic impact on sales of his rich, randomly available catalogue began to show in the August 27 chart. *Moody Blue*, his most recent album, recorded live and at his Graceland home-studio, was not a wholly unworthy last testament. Its chilling 1977 live performance of *Unchained Melody* seemed to express Presley's lonely despair and yet to show that, whatever shape he was in, his bravery of voice, especially in hitting the high notes, was undiminished.

September – October 1977

By September 10, three Presley albums were Top 10 and another two were joining the 30. Now three more entered. Stocks ran out all over the world. People bought whatever was available: *GI Blues*, for example, the soundtrack album from his lacklustre first post-Army movie, made in 1960 but wholly lacking the genius evident on that year's *Elvis Is Back* LP. *Elvis In Demand* was a compilation supposedly requested by UK fanclub members. Marc Bolan died on September 16, to no immediate chart effect.

October – November 1977

15 October 1977

last week	this week		
1	1	**20 GOLDEN GREATS**	Diana Ross & the Supremes (Motown)
2	2	**OXYGENE**	Jean-Michel Jarre (Polydor)
8	3	**NO MORE HEROES**	Stranglers (United Artists)
7	4	**RUMOURS**	Fleetwood Mac (Warner Bros.)
3	5	**MOODY BLUE**	Elvis Presley (RCA)
16	6	**LOVE YOU LIVE**	Rolling Stones (Rolling Stones)
11	7	**BAD REPUTATION**	Thin Lizzy (Vertigo)
4	8	**A STAR IS BORN**	Soundtrack (CBS)
5	9	**MAGIC FLY**	Space (Pye)
9	10	**GOING FOR THE ONE**	Yes (Atlantic)
30	11	**AJA**	Steely Dan (ABC)
10	12	**PLAYING TO AN AUDIENCE OF ONE**	David Soul (Private Stock)
12	13	**SHOW SOME EMOTION**	Joan Armatrading (A&M)
15	14	**I REMEMBER YESTERDAY**	Donna Summer (GTO)
6	15	**20 ALL TIME GREATS**	Connie Francis (Polydor)
-	16	**40 GOLDEN GREATS**	Cliff Richard (EMI)
22	17	**BOOMTOWN RATS**	Boomtown Rats (Ensign)
19	18	**HOME ON THE RANGE**	Slim Whitman (United Artists)
29	19	**PASSAGE**	Carpenters (A&M)
17	20	**HOTEL CALIFORNIA**	Eagles (Asylum)
26	21	**TWO DAYS AWAY**	Elkie Brooks (A&M)
-	22	**THUNDER IN MY HEART**	Leo Sayer (Chrysalis)
18	23	**THE VERY BEST OF FRANKIE LAINE**	Frankie Laine (Warwick)
-	24	**RAIN DANCES**	Camel (Decca)
13	25	**EXODUS**	Bob Marley & the Wailers (Island)
14	26	**WELCOME TO MY WORLD**	Elvis Presley (RCA)
24	27	**THE BEST OF ROD STEWART**	Rod Stewart (Mercury)
23	28	**ARRIVAL**	Abba (Epic)
-	28	**FAREWELL TO KINGS**	Rush (Mercury)
-	30	**GOLD AND IVORY**	David Essex (CBS)

22 October 1977

1	1	**20 GOLDEN GREATS**	Diana Ross & the Supremes (Motown)
3	2	**NO MORE HEROES**	Stranglers (United Artists)
2	3	**OXYGENE**	Jean-Michel Jarre (Polydor)
4	4	**RUMOURS**	Fleetwood Mac (Warner Bros.)
5	5	**MOODY BLUE**	Elvis Presley (RCA)
10	6	**GOING FOR THE ONE**	Yes (Atlantic)
19	6	**PASSAGE**	Carpenters (A&M)
18	8	**HOME ON THE RANGE**	Slim Whitman (United Artists)
7	8	**BAD REPUTATION**	Thin Lizzy (Vertigo)
8	10	**A STAR IS BORN**	Soundtrack (CBS)
6	11	**LOVE YOU LIVE**	Rolling Stones (Rolling Stones)
12	12	**PLAYING TO AN AUDIENCE OF ONE**	David Soul (Private Stock)
11	13	**AJA**	Steely Dan (ABC)
16	14	**40 GOLDEN GREATS**	Cliff Richard (EMI)
9	15	**MAGIC FLY**	Space (Pye)
13	15	**SHOW SOME EMOTION**	Joan Armatrading (A&M)
14	17	**I REMEMBER YESTERDAY**	Donna Summer (GTO)
21	18	**TWO DAYS AWAY**	Elkie Brooks (A&M)
22	19	**THUNDER IN MY HEART**	Leo Sayer (Chrysalis)
-	20	**STRANGLERS IV (RATTUS NORVEGICUS)**	Stranglers (United Artists)
20	21	**HOTEL CALIFORNIA**	Eagles (Asylum)
-	22	**ELTON JOHN'S GREATEST HITS VOL 2**	Elton John (DJM)
-	23	**GREATEST HITS**	Abba (Epic)
-	24	**SECONDS OUT**	Genesis (Charisma)
15	24	**20 ALL TIME GREATS**	Connie Francis (Polydor)
17	26	**BOOMTOWN RATS**	Boomtown Rats (Ensign)
27	27	**THE BEST OF ROD STEWART**	Rod Stewart (Mercury)
24	28	**RAIN DANCES**	Camel (Decca)
25	29	**EXODUS**	Bob Marley & the Wailers (Island)
-	30	**GONE TO EARTH**	Barclay James Harvest (Polydor)

29 October 1977

1	1	**20 GOLDEN GREATS**	Diana Ross & the Supremes (Motown)
2	2	**NO MORE HEROES**	Stranglers (United Artists)
14	3	**40 GOLDEN GREATS**	Cliff Richard (EMI)
8	4	**HOME ON THE RANGE**	Slim Whitman (United Artists)
4	5	**RUMOURS**	Fleetwood Mac (Warner Bros.)
11	6	**LOVE YOU LIVE**	Rolling Stones (Rolling Stones)
3	7	**OXYGENE**	Jean-Michel Jarre (Polydor)
5	7	**MOODY BLUE**	Elvis Presley (RCA)
10	9	**A STAR IS BORN**	Soundtrack (CBS)
6	11	**PASSAGE**	Carpenters (A&M)
6	10	**GOING FOR THE ONE**	Yes (Atlantic)
8	12	**BAD REPUTATION**	Thin Lizzy (Vertigo)
-	13	**HEROES**	David Bowie (RCA)
12	14	**PLAYING TO AN AUDIENCE OF ONE**	David Soul (Private Stock)
17	14	**I REMEMBER YESTERDAY**	Donna Summer (GTO)
19	16	**THUNDER IN MY HEART**	Leo Sayer (Chrysalis)
18	17	**TWO DAYS AWAY**	Elkie Brooks (A&M)
22	18	**ELTON JOHN'S GREATEST HITS VOL 2**	Elton John (DJM)
15	19	**SHOW SOME EMOTION**	Joan Armatrading (A&M)
-	20	**SOUL CITY**	Various Artists (K-Tel)
15	21	**MAGIC FLY**	Space (Pye)
24	22	**SECONDS OUT**	Genesis (Charisma)
13	23	**AJA**	Steely Dan (ABC)
-	24	**COUNTRY BOY**	Don Williams (ABC)
24	25	**20 ALL TIME GREATS**	Connie Francis (Polydor)
-	26	**THE JOHNNY MATHIS COLLECTION**	Johnny Mathis (CBS)
21	27	**HOTEL CALIFORNIA**	Eagles (Asylum)
23	28	**GREATEST HITS**	Abba (Epic)
20	29	**STRANGLERS IV (RATTUS NORVEGICUS)**	Stranglers (United Artists)
27	30	**THE BEST OF ROD STEWART**	Rod Stewart (Mercury)

5 November 1977

1	1	**20 GOLDEN GREATS**	Diana Ross & the Supremes (Motown)
3	2	**40 GOLDEN GREATS**	Cliff Richard (EMI)
2	3	**NO MORE HEROES**	Stranglers (United Artists)
5	4	**RUMOURS**	Fleetwood Mac (Warner Bros.)
13	5	**HEROES**	David Bowie (RCA)
4	6	**HOME ON THE RANGE**	Slim Whitman (United Artists)
7	7	**OXYGENE**	Jean-Michel Jarre (Polydor)
22	8	**SECONDS OUT**	Genesis (Charisma)
16	9	**THUNDER IN MY HEART**	Leo Sayer (Chrysalis)
9	10	**A STAR IS BORN**	Soundtrack (CBS)
10	11	**GOING FOR THE ONE**	Yes (Atlantic)
6	12	**LOVE YOU LIVE**	Rolling Stones (Rolling Stones)
7	13	**MOODY BLUE**	Elvis Presley (RCA)
18	14	**ELTON JOHN'S GREATEST HITS VOL 2**	Elton John (DJM)
-	15	**THE SOUND OF BREAD**	Bread (Elektra)
11	16	**PASSAGE**	Carpenters (A&M)
28	17	**GREATEST HITS**	Abba (Epic)
14	18	**PLAYING TO AN AUDIENCE OF ONE**	David Soul (Private Stock)
23	19	**AJA**	Steely Dan (ABC)
20	20	**SOUL CITY**	Various Artists (K-Tel)
-	21	**NEVER MIND THE BOLLOCKS HERE'S THE SEX PISTOLS**	Sex Pistols (Virgin)
12	22	**BAD REPUTATION**	Thin Lizzy (Vertigo)
14	23	**I REMEMBER YESTERDAY**	Donna Summer (GTO)
-	23	**NEWS OF THE WORLD**	Queen (EMI)
21	25	**MAGIC FLY**	Space (Pye)
30	26	**THE BEST OF ROD STEWART**	Rod Stewart (Mercury)
-	27	**FRONT PAGE NEWS**	Wishbone Ash (MCA)
-	28	**THEIR GREATEST HITS 1971–1975**	Eagles (Asylum)
-	29	**ELVIS IN CONCERT**	Elvis Presley (RCA)
-	30	**OUT OF THE BLUE**	Electric Light Orchestra (Jet)

Electric Light Orchestra were fronted by Jeff Lynne, once Roy Wood's lesser half in the Move. Roy later had some slight success with Wizzard but Lynne's ELO was far bigger. The overblown double-album *Out Of The Blue* would be their longest-charting. Jet Records belonged to notorious former Small Faces manager Don Arden, who'd said in 1972: "In an industry riddled with drug addicts, homosexuals and hangers-on, I am one of the few real men left." But *Never Mind The Bollocks Here's The Sex Pistols*.

November 1977

12 November 1977

last	this		
15	1	THE SOUND OF BREAD	Bread (Elektra)
2	2	40 GOLDEN GREATS	Cliff Richard (EMI)
1	3	20 GOLDEN GREATS	Diana Ross & the Supremes (Motown)
21	4	NEVER MIND THE BOLLOCKS HERE'S THE SEX PISTOLS	Sex Pistols (Virgin)
3	5	NO MORE HEROES	Stranglers (United Artists)
4	6	RUMOURS	Fleetwood Mac (Warner Bros.)
-	7	FOOTLOOSE & FANCY FREE	Rod Stewart (Riva)
9	8	THUNDER IN MY HEART	Leo Sayer (Chrysalis)
8	9	SECONDS OUT	Genesis (Charisma)
5	10	HEROES	David Bowie (RCA)
11	11	GOING FOR THE ONE	Yes (Atlantic)
7	12	OXYGENE	Jean-Michel Jarre (Polydor)
10	13	A STAR IS BORN	Soundtrack (CBS)
16	13	PASSAGE	Carpenters (A&M)
6	15	HOME ON THE RANGE	Slim Whitman (United Artists)
-	16	MOONFLOWER	Santana (CBS)
14	16	ELTON JOHN'S GREATEST HITS VOL 2	Elton John (DJM)
23	18	NEWS OF THE WORLD	Queen (EMI)
30	19	OUT OF THE BLUE	Electric Light Orchestra (Jet)
20	20	SOUL CITY	Various Artists (K-Tel)
-	21	FEELINGS	Various Artists (K-Tel)
29	22	ELVIS IN CONCERT	Elvis Presley (RCA)
18	23	PLAYING TO AN AUDIENCE OF ONE	David Soul (Private Stock)
-	24	ONCE UPON A TIME	Donna Summer (GTO)
23	25	I REMEMBER YESTERDAY	Donna Summer (GTO)
12	26	LOVE YOU LIVE	Rolling Stones (Rolling Stones)
17	27	GREATEST HITS	Abba (Epic)
-	28	30 GREATEST	Gladys Knight & the Pips (K-Tel)
13	29	MOODY BLUE	Elvis Presley (RCA)
22	30	BAD REPUTATION	Thin Lizzy (Vertigo)

19 November 1977

last	this		
1	1	THE SOUND OF BREAD	Bread (Elektra)
4	2	NEVER MIND THE BOLLOCKS HERE'S THE SEX PISTOLS	Sex Pistols (Virgin)
3	3	20 GOLDEN GREATS	Diana Ross & the Supremes (Motown)
5	4	NO MORE HEROES	Stranglers (United Artists)
21	5	FEELINGS Various Artists (K-Tel)	
2	6	40 GOLDEN GREATS	Cliff Richard (EMI)
18	7	NEWS OF THE WORLD	Queen (EMI)
7	8	FOOTLOOSE & FANCY FREE	Rod Stewart (Riva)
16	9	MOONFLOWER	Santana (CBS)
6	10	RUMOURS	Fleetwood Mac (Warner Bros.)
16	11	ELTON JOHN'S GREATEST HITS VOL 2	Elton John (DJM)
9	11	SECONDS OUT	Genesis (Charisma)
10	13	HEROES	David Bowie (RCA)
19	14	OUT OF THE BLUE	Electric Light Orchestra (Jet)
8	15	THUNDER IN MY HEART	Leo Sayer (Chrysalis)
-	15	ROCKIN' ALL OVER THE WORLD	Status Quo (Vertigo)
12	17	OXYGENE	Jean-Michel Jarre (Polydor)
13	18	PASSAGE	Carpenters (A&M)
11	19	GOING FOR THE ONE	Yes (Atlantic)
22	20	ELVIS IN CONCERT	Elvis Presley (RCA)
28	20	30 GREATEST	Gladys Knight & the Pips (K-Tel)
20	22	SOUL CITY	Various Artists (K-Tel)
27	23	GREATEST HITS Abba (Epic)	
15	24	HOME ON THE RANGE	Slim Whitman (United Artists)
-	25	ECHOES OF THE 60s	Various Artists (Phil Spector International)
-	26	STREET SURVIVORS	Lynyrd Skynyrd (MCA)
-	27	30 GOLDEN GREATS	George Mitchell Minstrels (EMI)
13	28	A STAR IS BORN	Soundtrack (CBS)
-	29	GET STONED	Rolling Stones (Arcade)
29	30	MOODY BLUE	Elvis Presley (RCA)

26 November 1977

last	this		
1	1	THE SOUND OF BREAD	Bread (Elektra)
2	2	NEVER MIND THE BOLLOCKS HERE'S THE SEX PISTOLS	Sex Pistols (Virgin)
8	3	FOOTLOOSE & FANCY FREE	Rod Stewart (Riva)
7	4	NEWS OF THE WORLD	Queen (EMI)
14	5	OUT OF THE BLUE	Electric Light Orchestra (Jet)
9	6	MOONFLOWER Santana (CBS)	
10	7	RUMOURS	Fleetwood Mac (Warner Bros.)
5	8	FEELINGS	Various Artists (K-Tel)
6	9	40 GOLDEN GREATS	Cliff Richard (EMI)
11	10	SECONDS OUT	Genesis (Charisma)
3	11	20 GOLDEN GREATS	Diana Ross & the Supremes (Motown)
4	12	NO MORE HEROES	Stranglers (United Artists)
-	13	DISCO FEVER	Various Artists (K-Tel)
20	14	30 GREATEST	Gladys Knight & the Pips (K-Tel)
15	15	ROCKIN' ALL OVER THE WORLD	Status Quo (Vertigo)
29	16	GET STONED	Rolling Stones (Arcade)
20	17	ELVIS IN CONCERT	Elvis Presley (RCA)
13	18	HEROES David Bowie (RCA)	
23	19	GREATEST HITS Abba (Epic)	
11	20	ELTON JOHN'S GREATEST HITS VOL 2	Elton John (DJM)
15	20	THUNDER IN MY HEART	Leo Sayer (Chrysalis)
-	22	ROXY MUSIC'S GREATEST HITS	Roxy Music (Polydor)
18	23	PASSAGE Carpenters (A&M)	
27	24	30 GOLDEN GREATS	George Mitchell Minstrels (EMI)
-	25	STICK TO ME	Graham Parker & the Rumour (Vertigo)
19	26	GOING FOR THE ONE	Yes (Atlantic)
26	27	STREET SURVIVORS	Lynyrd Skynyrd (MCA)
-	28	LET THERE BE ROCK	AC/DC (Atlantic)
-	29	RED STAR	Showaddywaddy (Arista)
-	30	BLACK JOY Soundtrack (Ronco)	

3 December 1977

last	this		
1	1	THE SOUND OF BREAD	Bread (Elektra)
3	2	FOOTLOOSE & FANCY FREE	Rod Stewart (Riva)
2	3	NEVER MIND THE BOLLOCKS HERE'S THE SEX PISTOLS	Sex Pistols (Virgin)
15	4	ROCKIN' ALL OVER THE WORLD	Status Quo (Vertigo)
4	5	NEWS OF THE WORLD	Queen (EMI)
13	6	DISCO FEVER	Various Artists (K-Tel)
5	7	OUT OF THE BLUE	Electric Light Orchestra (Jet)
6	8	MOONFLOWER Santana (CBS)	
8	9	FEELINGS	Various Artists (K-Tel)
9	10	40 GOLDEN GREATS	Cliff Richard (EMI)
14	11	30 GREATEST	Gladys Knight & the Pips (K-Tel)
11	12	20 GOLDEN GREATS	Diana Ross & the Supremes (Motown)
7	13	RUMOURS	Fleetwood Mac (Warner Bros.)
16	13	GET STONED	Rolling Stones (Arcade)
24	15	30 GOLDEN GREATS	George Mitchell Minstrels (EMI)
12	16	NO MORE HEROES	Stranglers (United Artists)
17	17	ELVIS IN CONCERT	Elvis Presley (RCA)
20	18	ELTON JOHN'S GREATEST HITS VOL 2	Elton John (DJM)
10	19	SECONDS OUT	Genesis (Charisma)
19	20	GREATEST HITS Abba (Epic)	
18	21	HEROES David Bowie (RCA)	
-	22	ECHOES OF THE 60s	Various Artists (Phil Spector International)
-	23	WORKS VOL 2	Emerson Lake & Palmer (Manticore)
26	24	GOING FOR THE ONE	Yes (Atlantic)
-	25	HOME ON THE RANGE	Slim Whitman (United Artists)
-	26	SOUL CITY Various Artists (K-Tel)	
23	27	PASSAGE Carpenters (A&M)	
20	28	THUNDER IN MY HEART	Leo Sayer (Chrysalis)
22	29	ROXY MUSIC'S GREATEST HITS	Roxy Music (Polydor)
28	30	LET THERE BE ROCK	AC/DC (Atlantic)

Up from No.21 to No.4 for the Pistols, who then reached No.1 in most charts, though not the NME's, the music paper that had championed them first. It was almost a year after the first of their unarguable singles, *Anarchy In The UK* had charted on Christmas Day, 1976. *God Save The Queen*, a timely poke at British attitudes in Jubilee Year, had made No.1 in June, despite an airplay and W.H.Smith ban. *Pretty Vacant*, issued with *Queen* still Top 5, had peaked at 5 in July-August.

December 1977

10 December 1977

last	this	
1	1	THE SOUND OF BREAD — Bread (Elektra)
6	2	DISCO FEVER — Various Artists (K-Tel)
11	3	30 GREATEST — Gladys Knight & the Pips (K-Tel)
9	4	FEELINGS — Various Artists (K-Tel)
2	5	FOOTLOOSE & FANCY FREE — Rod Stewart (Riva)
4	6	ROCKIN' ALL OVER THE WORLD — Status Quo (Vertigo)
5	7	NEWS OF THE WORLD — Queen (EMI)
3	8	NEVER MIND THE BOLLOCKS HERE'S THE SEX PISTOLS — Sex Pistols (Virgin)
7	9	OUT OF THE BLUE — Electric Light Orchestra (Jet)
13	10	RUMOURS — Fleetwood Mac (Warner Bros.)
13	11	GET STONED — Rolling Stones (Arcade)
8	12	MOONFLOWER — Santana (CBS)
10	13	40 GOLDEN GREATS — Cliff Richard (EMI)
15	14	30 GOLDEN GREATS — George Mitchell Minstrels (EMI)
-	15	ONCE UPON A TIME — Donna Summer (GTO)
17	16	ELVIS IN CONCERT — Elvis Presley (RCA)
18	17	ELTON JOHN'S GREATEST HITS VOL 2 — Elton John (DJM)
20	18	GREATEST HITS — Abba (Epic)
16	19	NO MORE HEROES — Stranglers (United Artists)
-	20	ARRIVAL — Abba (Epic)
29	21	ROXY MUSIC'S GREATEST HITS — Roxy Music (Polydor)
24	22	GOING FOR THE ONE — Yes (Atlantic)
-	22	SLOWHAND — Eric Clapton (RSO)
21	24	HEROES — David Bowie (RCA)
12	25	20 GOLDEN GREATS — Diana Ross & the Supremes (Motown)
28	26	THUNDER IN MY HEART — Leo Sayer (Chrysalis)
-	27	GREATEST HITS, ETC. — Paul Simon (CBS)
-	28	CRIMINAL RECORD — Rick Wakeman (A&M)
-	29	A STAR IS BORN — Soundtrack (CBS)
-	30	RED STAR — Showaddywaddy (Arista)

17 December 1977

last	this	
2	1	DISCO FEVER — Various Artists (K-Tel)
1	2	THE SOUND OF BREAD — Bread (Elektra)
4	3	FEELINGS Various Artists (K-Tel)
8	4	NEVER MIND THE BOLLOCKS HERE'S THE SEX PISTOLS — Sex Pistols (Virgin)
3	5	30 GREATEST — Gladys Knight & the Pips (K-Tel)
5	6	FOOTLOOSE & FANCY FREE — Rod Stewart (Riva)
10	7	RUMOURS — Fleetwood Mac (Warner Bros.)
6	8	ROCKIN' ALL OVER THE WORLD — Status Quo (Vertigo)
7	8	NEWS OF THE WORLD — Queen (EMI)
11	10	GET STONED — Rolling Stones (Arcade)
12	11	MOONFLOWER Santana (CBS)
27	12	GREATEST HITS, ETC. — Paul Simon (CBS)
-	13	DEREK AND CLIVE COME AGAIN — Peter Cook & Dudley Moore (Virgin)
13	14	40 GOLDEN GREATS — Cliff Richard (EMI)
9	15	OUT OF THE BLUE — Electric Light Orchestra (Jet)
19	16	NO MORE HEROES — Stranglers (United Artists)
16	17	ELVIS IN CONCERT — Elvis Presley (RCA)
30	17	RED STAR — Showaddywaddy (Arista)
18	19	GREATEST HITS Abba (Epic)
14	20	30 GOLDEN GREATS — George Mitchell Minstrels (EMI)
-	21	I'M GLAD YOU'RE HERE WITH ME TONIGHT Neil Diamond (CBS)
-	22	WORKS VOL 2 — Emerson Lake & Palmer (Manticore)
17	23	ELTON JOHN'S GREATEST HITS VOL 2 Elton John (DJM)
25	24	20 GOLDEN GREATS — Diana Ross & the Supremes (Motown)
15	25	ONCE UPON A TIME — Donna Summer (GTO)
28	26	CRIMINAL RECORD — Rick Wakeman (A&M)
22	27	SLOWHAND Eric Clapton (RSO)
21	28	ROXY MUSIC'S GREATEST HITS — Roxy Music (Polydor)
-	29	SECONDS OUT — Genesis (Charisma)
20	30	ARRIVAL Abba (Epic)

24 December 1977

last	this	
1	1	DISCO FEVER — Various Artists (K-Tel)
2	2	THE SOUND OF BREAD — Bread (Elektra)
4	3	NEVER MIND THE BOLLOCKS HERE'S THE SEX PISTOLS — Sex Pistols (Virgin)
5	4	30 GREATEST — Gladys Knight & the Pips (K-Tel)
6	5	FOOTLOOSE & FANCY FREE — Rod Stewart (Riva)
7	6	RUMOURS — Fleetwood Mac (Warner Bros.)
8	6	NEWS OF THE WORLD — Queen (EMI)
12	6	GREATEST HITS, ETC. — Paul Simon (CBS)
3	9	FEELINGS Various Artists (K-Tel)
24	10	20 GOLDEN GREATS — Diana Ross & the Supremes (Motown)
11	11	MOONFLOWER Santana (CBS)
10	12	GET STONED — Rolling Stones (Arcade)
8	13	ROCKIN' ALL OVER THE WORLD — Status Quo (Vertigo)
15	14	OUT OF THE BLUE — Electric Light Orchestra (Jet)
-	15	20 COUNTRY CLASSICS — Tammy Wynette (CBS)
14	16	40 GOLDEN GREATS — Cliff Richard (EMI)
19	17	GREATEST HITS Abba (Epic)
21	18	I'M GLAD YOU'RE HERE WITH ME TONIGHT Neil Diamond (CBS)
20	19	30 GOLDEN GREATS — George Mitchell Minstrels (EMI)
13	20	DEREK AND CLIVE COME AGAIN — Peter Cook & Dudley Moore (Virgin)
16	21	NO MORE HEROES — Stranglers (United Artists)
30	22	ARRIVAL Abba (Epic)
23	23	ELTON JOHN'S GREATEST HITS VOL 2 Elton John (DJM)
-	24	THE MUPPET SHOW — Muppets (Pye)
25	25	ONCE UPON A TIME — Donna Summer (GTO)
27	26	SLOWHAND — Eric Clapton (RSO)
-	27	THE BEST OF BING — Bing Crosby (MCA)
-	28	LIVE AND LET LIVE — 10 C.C. (Mercury)
17	29	RED STAR — Showaddywaddy (Arista)
-	30	SEASONS Bing Crosby (Polydor)

After this year's *Izitso* no Cat Stevens album (aside from a 1990 *Very Best Of*) would chart again. Farewell too to November plane-crash fatalities Ronnie Van Zandt, lead singer, and other members of Lynyrd Skynyrd, a rootsier Allman Brothers whose LPs and chart placings never matched their live grandeur and popularity. Their 1974 UK tour as support to Dutch group Golden Earring, was their first time out of the American south. Their anthemic *Free Bird* would become a hit single in 1982.

*Punk offered no
worries to
Frank Sinatra
(top);
below:
Johnny Rotten
and the original
Bat Out Of Hell
– Meatloaf*

January 1978

7 January 1978

last week	this week	
1	1	DISCO FEVER Various Artists (K-Tel)
2	2	THE SOUND OF BREAD Bread (WEA)
9	3	FEELINGS Various Artists (K-Tel)
3	4	NEVER MIND THE BOLLOCKS HERE'S THE SEX PISTOLS Sex Pistols (Virgin)
4	5	30 GREATEST Gladys Knight & the Pips (K-Tel)
5	6	FOOTLOOSE & FANCY FREE Rod Stewart (Riva)
6	7	RUMOURS Fleetwood Mac (Warner Bros.)
6	8	NEWS OF THE WORLD Queen (EMI)
15	9	20 COUNTRY CLASSICS Tammy Wynette (CBS)
13	10	ROCKIN' ALL OVER THE WORLD Status Quo (Vertigo)
12	11	GET STONED Rolling Stones (Arcade)
11	12	MOONFLOWER Santana (CBS)
14	13	OUT OF THE BLUE Electric Light Orchestra (Jet)
18	14	I'M GLAD YOU'RE HERE WITH ME TONIGHT Neil Diamond (CBS)
10	15	20 GOLDEN GREATS Diana Ross & the Supremes (Tamla Motown)
-	16	ELVIS IN CONCERT Elvis Presley (RCA)
6	17	GREATEST HITS, ETC. Paul Simon (CBS)
16	18	40 GOLDEN GREATS Cliff Richard (EMI)
30	19	SEASONS Bing Crosby (Polydor)
27	20	THE BEST OF BING Bing Crosby (MCA)
17	21	GREATEST HITS Abba (Epic)
19	22	30 GOLDEN GREATS George Mitchell Minstrels (EMI)
-	23	THUNDER IN MY HEART Leo Sayer (Chrysalis)
-	24	ECHOES OF THE 60s Various Artists (Phil Spector International)
-	25	THE JOHNNY NASH COLLECTION Johnny Nash (Epic)
22	26	ARRIVAL Abba (Epic)
29	27	RED STAR Showaddywaddy (Arista)
21	28	NO MORE HEROES Stranglers (United Artists)
24	29	THE MUPPET SHOW Muppets (Pye)
23	30	ELTON JOHN'S GREATEST HITS VOL 2 Elton John (DJM)

14 January 1978

1	1	DISCO FEVER Various Artists (K-Tel)
2	2	THE SOUND OF BREAD Bread (WEA)
7	3	RUMOURS Fleetwood Mac (Warner Bros.)
6	4	FOOTLOOSE & FANCY FREE Rod Stewart (Riva)
9	5	20 COUNTRY CLASSICS Tammy Wynette (CBS)
5	6	30 GREATEST Gladys Knight & the Pips (K-Tel)
-	7	DONNA SUMMER'S GREATEST HITS Donna Summer (GTO)
8	8	NEWS OF THE WORLD Queen (EMI)
13	9	OUT OF THE BLUE Electric Light Orchestra (Jet)
17	10	GREATEST HITS, ETC. Paul Simon (CBS)
3	11	FEELINGS Various Artists (K-Tel)
10	12	ROCKIN' ALL OVER THE WORLD Status Quo (Vertigo)
30	13	ELTON JOHN'S GREATEST HITS VOL 2 Elton John (DJM)
4	13	NEVER MIND THE BOLLOCKS HERE'S THE SEX PISTOLS Sex Pistols (Virgin)
15	15	20 GOLDEN GREATS Diana Ross & the Supremes (Tamla Motown)
21	16	GREATEST HITS Abba (Epic)
11	17	GET STONED Rolling Stones (Arcade)
14	18	I'M GLAD YOU'RE HERE WITH ME TONIGHT Neil Diamond (CBS)
12	19	MOONFLOWER Santana (CBS)
27	20	RED STAR Showaddywaddy (Arista)
-	21	LIVE AND LET LIVE 10 c.c. (Mercury)
26	22	ARRIVAL Abba (Epic)
-	23	EXODUS Bob Marley & the Wailers (Island)
-	24	DEREK AND CLIVE COME AGAIN Peter Cook & Dudley Moore (Virgin)
16	25	ELVIS IN CONCERT Elvis Presley (RCA)
25	26	THE JOHNNY NASH COLLECTION Johnny Nash (Epic)
-	27	GOING FOR THE ONE Yes (Atlantic)
-	28	BY REQUEST Salvation Army (Warwick)
-	29	NEW BOOTS & PANTIES!! Ian Dury & the Blockheads (Stiff)
29	30	THE MUPPET SHOW Muppets (Pye)

21 January 1978

3	1	RUMOURS Fleetwood Mac (Warner Bros.)
2	2	THE SOUND OF BREAD Bread (WEA)
1	3	DISCO FEVER Various Artists (K-Tel)
7	4	DONNA SUMMER'S GREATEST HITS Donna Summer (GTO)
13	4	NEVER MIND THE BOLLOCKS HERE'S THE SEX PISTOLS Sex Pistols (Virgin)
5	6	20 COUNTRY CLASSICS Tammy Wynette (CBS)
11	7	FEELINGS Various Artists (K-Tel)
13	8	ELTON JOHN'S GREATEST HITS VOL 2 Elton John (DJM)
4	9	FOOTLOOSE & FANCY FREE Rod Stewart (Riva)
9	10	OUT OF THE BLUE Electric Light Orchestra (Jet)
15	11	20 GOLDEN GREATS Diana Ross & the Supremes (Tamla Motown)
10	12	GREATEST HITS, ETC. Paul Simon (CBS)
6	13	30 GREATEST Gladys Knight & the Pips (K-Tel)
8	13	NEWS OF THE WORLD Queen (EMI)
16	15	GREATEST HITS Abba (Epic)
19	15	MOONFLOWER Santana (CBS)
23	17	EXODUS Bob Marley & the Wailers (Island)
22	18	ARRIVAL Abba (Epic)
20	19	RED STAR Showaddywaddy (Arista)
17	20	GET STONED Rolling Stones (Arcade)
12	21	ROCKIN' ALL OVER THE WORLD Status Quo (Vertigo)
24	22	DEREK AND CLIVE COME AGAIN Peter Cook & Dudley Moore (Virgin)
29	23	NEW BOOTS & PANTIES!! Ian Dury & the Blockheads (Stiff)
-	24	ALL 'N' ALL Earth Wind & Fire (CBS)
28	25	BY REQUEST Salvation Army (Warwick)
-	26	LOVE SONGS Beatles (Parlophone)
25	27	ELVIS IN CONCERT Elvis Presley (RCA)
-	28	40 GOLDEN GREATS Cliff Richard (EMI)
-	29	SECONDS OUT Genesis (Charisma)
-	30	DARTS Darts (Magnet)

28 January 1978

1	1	RUMOURS Fleetwood Mac (Warner Bros.)
2	2	THE SOUND OF BREAD Bread (WEA)
3	3	DISCO FEVER Various Artists (K-Tel)
4	4	DONNA SUMMER'S GREATEST HITS Donna Summer (GTO)
4	5	NEVER MIND THE BOLLOCKS HERE'S THE SEX PISTOLS Sex Pistols (Virgin)
6	6	20 COUNTRY CLASSICS Tammy Wynette (CBS)
-	7	THE ALBUM Abba (Epic)
9	8	FOOTLOOSE & FANCY FREE Rod Stewart (Riva)
10	9	OUT OF THE BLUE Electric Light Orchestra (Jet)
8	9	ELTON JOHN'S GREATEST HITS VOL 2 Elton John (DJM)
13	11	30 GREATEST Gladys Knight & the Pips (K-Tel)
15	12	MOONFLOWER Santana (CBS)
26	13	LOVE SONGS Beatles (Parlophone)
7	14	FEELINGS Various Artists (K-Tel)
13	15	NEWS OF THE WORLD Queen (EMI)
18	16	ARRIVAL Abba (Epic)
17	17	EXODUS Bob Marley & the Wailers (Island)
21	18	ROCKIN' ALL OVER THE WORLD Status Quo (Vertigo)
12	19	GREATEST HITS, ETC. Paul Simon (CBS)
11	20	20 GOLDEN GREATS Diana Ross & the Supremes (Tamla Motown)
15	21	GREATEST HITS Abba (Epic)
22	22	DEREK AND CLIVE COME AGAIN Peter Cook & Dudley Moore (Virgin)
20	23	GET STONED Rolling Stones (Arcade)
-	24	I'M GLAD YOU'RE HERE WITH ME TONIGHT Neil Diamond (CBS)
-	25	OLIVIA NEWTON-JOHN'S GREATEST HITS Olivia Newton-John (EMI)
24	26	ALL 'N' ALL Earth Wind & Fire (CBS)
-	27	THE JOHNNY NASH COLLECTION Johnny Nash (Epic)
28	28	40 GOLDEN GREATS Cliff Richard (EMI)
-	29	DON JUAN'S RECKLESS DAUGHTER Joni Mitchell (Asylum)
-	30	RUNNING ON EMPTY Jackson Browne (Asylum)

Current disco was like Donna Summer music: it owed more to 1970s Bee Gees than to the late '60s disco funk of people like Isaac Hayes. By the end of January the ex-No.1 album *Disco Fever* and Donna were together in the Top 3. Ms Summer's current hit single, *Love's Unkind*, was also in the Top 3. She'd had other high-flyers like *Love To Love You Baby* (her 1976 chart debut) and August 1977's chart-topper *I Feel Love*, and many minor hits. More would follow.

February 1978

4 February 1978

last	this		
1	1	RUMOURS	
		Fleetwood Mac (Warner Bros.)	
7	2	THE ALBUM	Abba (Epic)
2	3	THE SOUND OF BREAD	
			Bread (WEA)
4	4	DONNA SUMMER'S GREATEST	
		HITS	Donna Summer (GTO)
8	5	FOOTLOOSE & FANCY FREE	
			Rod Stewart (Riva)
9	6	ELTON JOHN'S GREATEST HITS	
		VOL 2	Elton John (DJM)
6	7	20 COUNTRY CLASSICS	
			Tammy Wynette (CBS)
3	8	DISCO FEVER	
			Various Artists (K-Tel)
5	9	NEVER MIND THE BOLLOCKS	
		HERE'S THE SEX PISTOLS	
			Sex Pistols (Virgin)
9	10	OUT OF THE BLUE	
		Electric Light Orchestra (Jet)	
-	11	REFLECTIONS	
			Andy Williams (CBS)
13	12	LOVE SONGS	
			Beatles (Parlophone)
21	13	GREATEST HITS	Abba (Epic)
15	14	NEWS OF THE WORLD	
			Queen (EMI)
24	15	I'M GLAD YOU'RE HERE WITH	
		ME TONIGHT	
			Neil Diamond (CBS)
12	16	MOONFLOWER	Santana (CBS)
-	17	FLORAL DANCE	Brighouse &
		Rastrick Brass Band (Logo)	
17	18	EXODUS	Bob Marley
		& the Wailers (Island)	
19	19	GREATEST HITS, ETC.	
			Paul Simon (CBS)
26	20	ALL 'N' ALL	
		Earth Wind & Fire (CBS)	
20	21	20 GOLDEN GREATS	
		Diana Ross & the Supremes	
		(Tamla Motown)	
14	22	FEELINGS Various Artists (K-Tel)	
25	23	OLIVIA NEWTON-JOHN'S	
		GREATEST HITS	
		Olivia Newton-John (EMI)	
11	24	30 GREATEST	
		Gladys Knight & the Pips (K-Tel)	
-	25	NEW BOOTS & PANTIES!!	
		Ian Dury & the Blockheads (Stiff)	
18	26	ROCKIN' ALL OVER THE WORLD	
		Status Quo (Vertigo)	
16	27	ARRIVAL	Abba (Epic)
-	28	VARIATONS	
		Andrew Lloyd Webber (MCA)	
-	29	WE MUST BELIEVE IN MAGIC	
		Crystal Gayle (United Artists)	
29	29	DON JUAN'S RECKLESS	
		DAUGHTER Joni Mitchell (Asylum)	

11 February 1978

2	1	THE ALBUM	Abba (Epic)
1	2	RUMOURS	
		Fleetwood Mac (Warner Bros.)	
4	3	DONNA SUMMER'S GREATEST	
		HITS	Donna Summer (GTO)
5	4	FOOTLOOSE & FANCY FREE	
			Rod Stewart (Riva)
3	5	THE SOUND OF BREAD	
			Bread (WEA)
18	6	EXODUS	
		Bob Marley & the Wailers (Island)	
9	7	NEVER MIND THE BOLLOCKS	
		HERE'S THE SEX PISTOLS	
			Sex Pistols (Virgin)
8	8	DISCO FEVER	
			Various Artists (K-Tel)
10	9	OUT OF THE BLUE	
		Electric Light Orchestra (Jet)	
7	10	20 COUNTRY CLASSICS	
			Tammy Wynette (CBS)
25	11	NEW BOOTS & PANTIES!!	
		Ian Dury & the Blockheads (Stiff)	
12	12	LOVE SONGS	
			Beatles (Parlophone)
11	13	REFLECTIONS	
			Andy Williams (CBS)
6	14	ELTON JOHN'S GREATEST HITS	
		VOL 2	Elton John (DJM)
17	15	FLORAL DANCE	Brighouse &
		Rastrick Brass Band (Logo)	
20	16	ALL 'N' ALL	
		Earth Wind & Fire (CBS)	
22	16	FEELINGS Various Artists (K-Tel)	
28	18	VARIATONS	
		Andrew Lloyd Webber (MCA)	
16	19	MOONFLOWER	Santana (CBS)
24	20	30 GREATEST	
		Gladys Knight & the Pips (K-Tel)	
14	20	NEWS OF THE WORLD	
			Queen (EMI)
13	22	GREATEST HITS	Abba (Epic)
23	23	OLIVIA NEWTON-JOHN'S	
		GREATEST HITS	
		Olivia Newton-John (EMI)	
21	24	20 GOLDEN GREATS	
		Diana Ross & the Supremes	
		(Tamla Motown)	
15	25	I'M GLAD YOU'RE HERE WITH	
		ME TONIGHT Neil Diamond (CBS)	
27	26	ARRIVAL	Abba (Epic)
29	27	DON JUAN'S RECKLESS	
		DAUGHTER	
		Joni Mitchell (Asylum)	
-	28	BEST FRIENDS	Cleo Laine
		& John Williams (RCA)	
-	29	STAR WARS	
		Soundtrack (20th Century)	
19	30	GREATEST HITS, ETC.	
			Paul Simon (CBS)

18 February 1978

1	1	THE ALBUM	Abba (Epic)
2	2	RUMOURS	
		Fleetwood Mac (Warner Bros.)	
9	3	OUT OF THE BLUE	
		Electric Light Orchestra (Jet)	
3	4	DONNA SUMMER'S GREATEST	
		HITS	Donna Summer (GTO)
6	5	EXODUS	
		Bob Marley & the Wailers (Island)	
4	6	FOOTLOOSE & FANCY FREE	
			Rod Stewart (Riva)
5	7	THE SOUND OF BREAD	
			Bread (WEA)
18	8	VARIATONS	
		Andrew Lloyd Webber (MCA)	
11	9	NEW BOOTS & PANTIES!!	
		Ian Dury & the Blockheads (Stiff)	
13	10	REFLECTIONS	
			Andy Williams (CBS)
8	11	DISCO FEVER	
			Various Artists (K-Tel)
12	12	LOVE SONGS	
			Beatles (Parlophone)
14	13	ELTON JOHN'S GREATEST HITS	
		VOL 2	Elton John (DJM)
19	14	MOONFLOWER	Santana (CBS)
7	15	NEVER MIND THE BOLLOCKS	
		HERE'S THE SEX PISTOLS	
			Sex Pistols (Virgin)
15	16	FLORAL DANCE	
		Brighouse & Rastrick Brass Band	
		(Logo)	
16	17	ALL 'N' ALL	
		Earth Wind & Fire (CBS)	
10	18	20 COUNTRY CLASSICS	
			Tammy Wynette (CBS)
16	19	FEELINGS	
			Various Artists (K-Tel)
22	20	GREATEST HITS	Abba (Epic)
25	21	I'M GLAD YOU'RE HERE WITH	
		ME TONIGHT	
			Neil Diamond (CBS)
-	22	WHITE MUSIC	XTC (Virgin)
-	23	RUNNING ON EMPTY	
		Jackson Browne (Asylum)	
-	24	PLASTIC LETTERS	
			Blondie (Chrysalis)
29	25	STAR WARS	
		Soundtrack (20th Century)	
-	26	DARTS	Darts (Magnet)
-	27	THE MUPPET SHOW VOL. 2	
			Muppets (Pye)
-	28	DISCO STARS	
			Various Artists (K-Tel)
20	29	30 GREATEST	
		Gladys Knight & the Pips (K-Tel)	
27	30	DON JUAN'S RECKLESS	
		DAUGHTER	
		Joni Mitchell (Asylum)	

25 February 1978

1	1	THE ALBUM	Abba (Epic)
2	2	RUMOURS	
		Fleetwood Mac (Warner Bros.)	
8	3	VARIATONS	
		Andrew Lloyd Webber (MCA)	
6	4	FOOTLOOSE & FANCY FREE	
			Rod Stewart (Riva)
3	5	OUT OF THE BLUE	
		Electric Light Orchestra (Jet)	
4	6	DONNA SUMMER'S GREATEST	
		HITS	Donna Summer (GTO)
9	7	NEW BOOTS & PANTIES!!	
		Ian Dury & the Blockheads (Stiff)	
11	8	DISCO FEVER	
			Various Artists (K-Tel)
5	9	EXODUS	
		Bob Marley & the Wailers (Island)	
15	9	NEVER MIND THE BOLLOCKS	
		HERE'S THE SEX PISTOLS	
			Sex Pistols (Virgin)
10	11	REFLECTIONS	
			Andy Williams (CBS)
7	12	THE SOUND OF BREAD	
			Bread (WEA)
13	12	ELTON JOHN'S GREATEST HITS	
		VOL 2	Elton John (DJM)
16	14	FLORAL DANCE	
		Brighouse & Rastrick Brass Band	
		(Logo)	
17	15	ALL 'N' ALL	
		Earth Wind & Fire (CBS)	
12	16	LOVE SONGS	
			Beatles (Parlophone)
22	17	WHITE MUSIC	XTC (Virgin)
-	18	I WANT TO LIVE	
			John Denver (RCA)
19	19	ARRIVAL	Abba (Epic)
-	20	FEELINGS	
			Various Artists (K-Tel)
21	21	I'M GLAD YOU'RE HERE WITH	
		ME TONIGHT	
			Neil Diamond (CBS)
-	22	ROCKIN' ALL OVER THE WORLD	
			Status Quo (Vertigo)
27	23	THE MUPPET SHOW VOL. 2	
			Muppets (Pye)
20	24	GREATEST HITS	Abba (Epic)
-	25	BEST FRIENDS	Cleo Laine
		& John Williams (RCA)	
-	26	COUNTRY GIRL MEETS	
		COUNTRY BOY	
		Various Artists (CBS/Warwick)	
-	27	WE MUST BELIEVE IN MAGIC	
		Crystal Gayle (United Artists)	
28	28	DISCO STARS	
			Various Artists (K-Tel)
25	29	STAR WARS	
		Soundtrack (20th Century)	
-	30	OLIVIA NEWTON-JOHN'S	
		GREATEST HITS	
		Olivia Newton-John (EMI)	

Another Donna arose. Celebrations took place all over Britain, specially in Scotland, as an act destined never to make the album chart knocked Wings' *Mull Of Kintyre* off the top of the singles chart, where it had solidified for nine weeks. The further achievement of Althia and Donna's delightfully loopy *Uptown Top Ranking* was of course to give another meaning to the brand-name Rank other than as in the long-popular expression "having a J. Arthur". In the LP chart, solemn Swedish glam ruled.

4 March 1978

last week	this week		
1	1	THE ALBUM	Abba (Epic)
2	2	RUMOURS	Fleetwood Mac (Warner Bros.)
3	3	VARIATONS	Andrew Lloyd Webber (MCA)
6	4	DONNA SUMMER'S GREATEST HITS	Donna Summer (GTO)
5	5	OUT OF THE BLUE	Electric Light Orchestra (Jet)
11	6	REFLECTIONS	Andy Williams (CBS)
4	7	FOOTLOOSE & FANCY FREE	Rod Stewart (Riva)
7	8	NEW BOOTS & PANTIES!!	Ian Dury & the Blockheads (Stiff)
12	9	THE SOUND OF BREAD	Bread (WEA)
-	10	20 GOLDEN GREATS	Buddy Holly & the Crickets (MCA)
28	11	DISCO STARS	Various Artists (K-Tel)
24	12	GREATEST HITS	Abba (Epic)
-	13	DARTS	Darts (Magnet)
15	14	ALL 'N' ALL	Earth Wind & Fire (CBS)
9	15	EXODUS	Bob Marley & the Wailers (Island)
9	16	NEVER MIND THE BOLLOCKS HERE'S THE SEX PISTOLS	Sex Pistols (Virgin)
-	17	THE KICK INSIDE	Kate Bush (EMI)
-	18	DRASTIC PLASTIC	Be-Bop Deluxe (Harvest)
20	19	FEELINGS	Various Artists (K-Tel)
-	20	PASTICHE	Manhattan Transfer (Atlantic)
-	21	30 GREATEST	Gladys Knight & the Pips (K-Tel)
8	22	DISCO FEVER	Various Artists (K-Tel)
16	23	LOVE SONGS	Beatles (Parlophone)
-	24	IN FULL BLOOM	Rose Royce (Warner Bros.)
12	25	ELTON JOHN'S GREATEST HITS VOL 2	Elton John (DJM)
29	26	STAR WARS	Soundtrack (20th Century)
17	27	WHITE MUSIC	XTC (Virgin)
-	28	CITY TO CITY	Gerry Rafferty (United Artists)
23	29	THE MUPPET SHOW VOL. 2	Muppets (Pye)
25	30	BEST FRIENDS	Cleo Laine & John Williams (RCA)

11 March 1978

1	1	THE ALBUM	Abba (Epic)
2	2	RUMOURS	Fleetwood Mac (Warner Bros.)
3	3	VARIATONS	Andrew Lloyd Webber (MCA)
5	4	OUT OF THE BLUE	Electric Light Orchestra (Jet)
6	5	REFLECTIONS	Andy Williams (CBS)
10	6	20 GOLDEN GREATS	Buddy Holly & the Crickets (MCA)
7	7	FOOTLOOSE & FANCY FREE	Rod Stewart (Riva)
8	8	NEW BOOTS & PANTIES!!	Ian Dury & the Blockheads (Stiff)
13	9	DARTS	Darts (Magnet)
11	10	DISCO STARS	Various Artists (K-Tel)
17	11	THE KICK INSIDE	Kate Bush (EMI)
4	12	DONNA SUMMER'S GREATEST HITS	Donna Summer (GTO)
-	13	25 THUMPING GREAT HITS	Dave Clark Five (Polydor)
28	14	CITY TO CITY	Gerry Rafferty (United Artists)
9	15	THE SOUND OF BREAD	Bread (WEA)
-	16	BOOGIE NIGHTS	Various Artists (Ronco)
-	17	ARRIVAL	Abba (Epic)
15	18	EXODUS	Bob Marley & the Wailers (Island)
14	19	ALL 'N' ALL	Earth Wind & Fire (CBS)
12	20	GREATEST HITS	Abba (Epic)
29	21	THE MUPPET SHOW VOL. 2	Muppets (Pye)
24	22	IN FULL BLOOM	Rose Royce (Warner Bros.)
23	23	LOVE SONGS	Beatles (Parlophone)
-	24	PLASTIC LETTERS	Blondie (Chrysalis)
-	25	WAITING FOR COLUMBUS	Little Feat (Warner Bros.)
26	26	STAR WARS	Soundtrack (20th Century)
-	27	JESUS OF COOL	Nick Lowe (Radar)
30	28	BEST FRIENDS	Cleo Laine & John Williams (RCA)
18	29	DRASTIC PLASTIC	Be-Bop Deluxe (Harvest)
20	30	PASTICHE	Manhattan Transfer (Atlantic)

18 March 1978

1	1	THE ALBUM	Abba (Epic)
6	2	20 GOLDEN GREATS	Buddy Holly & the Crickets (MCA)
5	3	REFLECTIONS	Andy Williams (CBS)
11	4	THE KICK INSIDE	Kate Bush (EMI)
2	5	RUMOURS	Fleetwood Mac (Warner Bros.)
3	6	VARIATONS	Andrew Lloyd Webber (MCA)
4	7	OUT OF THE BLUE	Electric Light Orchestra (Jet)
9	8	DARTS	Darts (Magnet)
13	9	25 THUMPING GREAT HITS	Dave Clark Five (Polydor)
7	10	FOOTLOOSE & FANCY FREE	Rod Stewart (Riva)
15	11	THE SOUND OF BREAD	Bread (WEA)
19	12	ALL 'N' ALL	Earth Wind & Fire (CBS)
14	13	CITY TO CITY	Gerry Rafferty (United Artists)
8	14	NEW BOOTS & PANTIES!!	Ian Dury & the Blockheads (Stiff)
-	15	FONZIE'S FAVOURITES	Various Artists (Warwick)
12	16	DONNA SUMMER'S GREATEST HITS	Donna Summer (GTO)
24	17	PLASTIC LETTERS	Blondie (Chrysalis)
10	18	DISCO STARS	Various Artists (K-Tel)
17	19	ARRIVAL	Abba (Epic)
22	20	IN FULL BLOOM	Rose Royce (Warner Bros.)
20	21	GREATEST HITS	Abba (Epic)
30	21	PASTICHE	Manhattan Transfer (Atlantic)
-	23	SATURDAY NIGHT FEVER	Soundtrack (RSO)
16	24	BOOGIE NIGHTS	Various Artists (Ronco)
27	25	JESUS OF COOL	Nick Lowe (Radar)
18	26	EXODUS	Bob Marley & the Wailers (Island)
-	27	NEVER MIND THE BOLLOCKS HERE'S THE SEX PISTOLS	Sex Pistols (Virgin)
21	28	THE MUPPET SHOW VOL. 2	Muppets (Pye)
23	29	LOVE SONGS	Beatles (Parlophone)
28	30	BEST FRIENDS	Cleo Laine & John Williams (RCA)

25 March 1978

1	1	THE ALBUM	Abba (Epic)
2	2	20 GOLDEN GREATS	Buddy Holly & the Crickets (MCA)
4	3	THE KICK INSIDE	Kate Bush (EMI)
3	4	REFLECTIONS	Andy Williams (CBS)
7	5	OUT OF THE BLUE	Electric Light Orchestra (Jet)
5	6	RUMOURS	Fleetwood Mac (Warner Bros.)
6	7	VARIATONS	Andrew Lloyd Webber (MCA)
13	7	CITY TO CITY	Gerry Rafferty (United Artists)
17	9	PLASTIC LETTERS	Blondie (Chrysalis)
24	10	BOOGIE NIGHTS	Various Artists (Ronco)
18	11	DISCO STARS	Various Artists (K-Tel)
8	12	DARTS	Darts (Magnet)
14	13	NEW BOOTS & PANTIES!!	Ian Dury & the Blockheads (Stiff)
15	13	FONZIE'S FAVOURITES	Various Artists (Warwick)
21	15	PASTICHE	Manhattan Transfer (Atlantic)
26	16	EXODUS	Bob Marley & the Wailers (Island)
10	17	FOOTLOOSE & FANCY FREE	Rod Stewart (Riva)
9	18	25 THUMPING GREAT HITS	Dave Clark Five (Polydor)
-	19	KAYA	Bob Marley & the Wailers (Island)
11	20	THE SOUND OF BREAD	Bread (WEA)
-	21	THIS YEAR'S MODEL	Elvis Costello (Radar)
25	22	JESUS OF COOL	Nick Lowe (Radar)
21	23	GREATEST HITS	Abba (Epic)
16	24	DONNA SUMMER'S GREATEST HITS	Donna Summer (GTO)
12	25	ALL 'N' ALL	Earth Wind & Fire (CBS)
19	26	ARRIVAL	Abba (Epic)
-	27	THEIR GREATEST HITS 1971-1975	Eagles (Asylum)
-	28	ANOTHER MUSIC IN A DIFFERENT KITCHEN	Buzzcocks (United Artists)
-	29	BAT OUT OF HELL	Meatloaf (Epic)
23	30	SATURDAY NIGHT FEVER	Soundtrack (RSO)

"New" arrivals included old pub-rocker Ian Dury, on the punk indie label Stiff; *New Boots & Panties*, a sleeper that had first pottered into the chart basement the previous October, first made the 30 for a fortnight in January and then re-entered with more conviction in February. Kate Bush debuted with *The Kick Inside*, which kicked up high, as did Gerry Rafferty's first post-Stealers Wheel solo album *City To City*. Bush's *Wuthering Heights* single was No.1; Rafferty's *Baker Street* would peak at No.2 in early April.

April 1978

1 April 1978

last week	this week	title
3	1	THE KICK INSIDE — Kate Bush (EMI)
1	2	THE ALBUM — Abba (Epic)
2	3	20 GOLDEN GREATS — Buddy Holly & the Crickets (MCA)
6	4	RUMOURS — Fleetwood Mac (Warner Bros.)
4	5	REFLECTIONS — Andy Williams (CBS)
5	6	OUT OF THE BLUE — Electric Light Orchestra (Jet)
9	7	PLASTIC LETTERS — Blondie (Chrysalis)
7	8	CITY TO CITY — Gerry Rafferty (United Artists)
7	9	VARIATONS — Andrew Lloyd Webber (MCA)
13	10	FONZIE'S FAVOURITES — Various Artists (Warwick)
10	11	BOOGIE NIGHTS — Various Artists (Ronco)
18	12	25 THUMPING GREAT HITS — Dave Clark Five (Polydor)
12	13	DARTS — Darts (Magnet)
15	14	PASTICHE — Manhattan Transfer (Atlantic)
19	15	KAYA — Bob Marley & the Wailers (Island)
30	16	SATURDAY NIGHT FEVER — Soundtrack (RSO)
25	17	ALL 'N' ALL — Earth Wind & Fire (CBS)
21	18	THIS YEAR'S MODEL — Elvis Costello (Radar)
26	19	ARRIVAL — Abba (Epic)
-	20	IN FULL BLOOM — Rose Royce (Warner Bros.)
-	21	20 GOLDEN GREATS — Nat 'King' Cole (Capitol)
13	22	NEW BOOTS & PANTIES!! — Ian Dury & the Blockheads (Stiff)
16	23	EXODUS — Bob Marley & the Wailers (Island)
23	24	GREATEST HITS — Abba (Epic)
-	25	WATERMARK — Art Garfunkel (CBS)
17	26	FOOTLOOSE & FANCY FREE — Rod Stewart (Riva)
11	27	DISCO STARS — Various Artists (K-Tel)
22	28	JESUS OF COOL — Nick Lowe (Radar)
24	29	DONNA SUMMER'S GREATEST HITS — Donna Summer (GTO)
29	30	BAT OUT OF HELL — Meatloaf (Epic)

8 April 1978

last week	this week	title
1	1	THE KICK INSIDE — Kate Bush (EMI)
3	2	20 GOLDEN GREATS — Buddy Holly & the Crickets (MCA)
2	3	THE ALBUM — Abba (Epic)
8	4	CITY TO CITY — Gerry Rafferty (United Artists)
21	5	20 GOLDEN GREATS — Nat 'King' Cole (Capitol)
16	6	SATURDAY NIGHT FEVER — Soundtrack (RSO)
5	7	REFLECTIONS — Andy Williams (CBS)
6	8	OUT OF THE BLUE — Electric Light Orchestra (Jet)
4	9	RUMOURS — Fleetwood Mac (Warner Bros.)
15	10	KAYA — Bob Marley & the Wailers (Island)
7	11	PLASTIC LETTERS — Blondie (Chrysalis)
10	12	FONZIE'S FAVOURITES — Various Artists (Warwick)
-	13	LONDON TOWN — Wings (EMI)
18	14	THIS YEAR'S MODEL — Elvis Costello (Radar)
14	15	PASTICHE — Manhattan Transfer (Atlantic)
-	16	AND THEN THERE WERE THREE — Genesis (Charisma)
11	17	BOOGIE NIGHTS — Various Artists (Ronco)
12	18	25 THUMPING GREAT HITS — Dave Clark Five (Polydor)
27	19	DISCO STARS — Various Artists (K-Tel)
9	20	VARIATONS — Andrew Lloyd Webber (MCA)
-	21	THE SOUND OF BREAD — Bread (WEA)
13	22	DARTS — Darts (Magnet)
24	23	GREATEST HITS — Abba (Epic)
17	24	ALL 'N' ALL — Earth Wind & Fire (CBS)
-	25	ANOTHER MUSIC IN A DIFFERENT KITCHEN — Buzzcocks (United Artists)
-	26	THE STRANGER — Billy Joel (CBS)
30	27	BAT OUT OF HELL — Meatloaf (Epic)
22	28	NEW BOOTS & PANTIES!! — Ian Dury & the Blockheads (Stiff)
20	29	IN FULL BLOOM — Rose Royce (Warner Bros.)
25	30	WATERMARK — Art Garfunkel (CBS)

15 April 1978

last week	this week	title
5	1	20 GOLDEN GREATS — Nat 'King' Cole (Capitol)
3	2	THE ALBUM — Abba (Epic)
6	3	SATURDAY NIGHT FEVER — Soundtrack (RSO)
2	4	20 GOLDEN GREATS — Buddy Holly & the Crickets (MCA)
1	5	THE KICK INSIDE — Kate Bush (EMI)
10	6	KAYA — Bob Marley & the Wailers (Island)
4	7	CITY TO CITY — Gerry Rafferty (United Artists)
14	8	THIS YEAR'S MODEL — Elvis Costello (Radar)
13	9	LONDON TOWN — Wings (EMI)
11	10	PLASTIC LETTERS — Blondie (Chrysalis)
16	11	AND THEN THERE WERE THREE — Genesis (Charisma)
7	12	REFLECTIONS — Andy Williams (CBS)
8	13	OUT OF THE BLUE — Electric Light Orchestra (Jet)
15	14	PASTICHE — Manhattan Transfer (Atlantic)
8	15	RUMOURS — Fleetwood Mac (Warner Bros.)
25	16	ANOTHER MUSIC IN A DIFFERENT KITCHEN — Buzzcocks (United Artists)
12	17	FONZIE'S FAVOURITES — Various Artists (Warwick)
-	18	ARRIVAL — Abba (Epic)
17	19	BOOGIE NIGHTS — Various Artists (Ronco)
20	20	VARIATONS — Andrew Lloyd Webber (MCA)
-	21	EXODUS — Bob Marley & the Wailers (Island)
27	22	BAT OUT OF HELL — Meatloaf (Epic)
22	23	DARTS — Darts (Magnet)
18	24	25 THUMPING GREAT HITS — Dave Clark Five (Polydor)
21	25	THE SOUND OF BREAD — Bread (WEA)
28	26	NEW BOOTS & PANTIES!! — Ian Dury & the Blockheads (Stiff)
-	27	BEST FRIENDS — Cleo Laine & John Williams (RCA)
24	28	ALL 'N' ALL — Earth Wind & Fire (CBS)
-	29	TELL US THE TRUTH — Sham 69 (Phonogram)
-	30	THE RUTLES — Rutles (Warner Bros.)

22 April 1978

last week	this week	title
1	1	20 GOLDEN GREATS — Nat 'King' Cole (Capitol)
3	2	SATURDAY NIGHT FEVER — Soundtrack (RSO)
11	3	AND THEN THERE WERE THREE — Genesis (Charisma)
9	4	LONDON TOWN — Wings (EMI)
2	5	THE ALBUM — Abba (Epic)
6	6	KAYA — Bob Marley & the Wailers (Island)
4	7	20 GOLDEN GREATS — Buddy Holly & the Crickets (MCA)
7	8	CITY TO CITY — Gerry Rafferty (United Artists)
5	9	THE KICK INSIDE — Kate Bush (EMI)
8	10	THIS YEAR'S MODEL — Elvis Costello (Radar)
-	11	THE STUD - SOUNDTRACK — Various Artists (Ronco)
10	12	PLASTIC LETTERS — Blondie (Chrysalis)
15	13	RUMOURS — Fleetwood Mac (Warner Bros.)
13	14	OUT OF THE BLUE — Electric Light Orchestra (Jet)
30	15	THE RUTLES — Rutles (Warner Bros.)
14	16	PASTICHE — Manhattan Transfer (Atlantic)
26	17	NEW BOOTS & PANTIES!! — Ian Dury & the Blockheads (Stiff)
16	18	FONZIE'S FAVOURITES — Various Artists (Warwick)
12	19	REFLECTIONS — Andy Williams (CBS)
22	20	BAT OUT OF HELL — Meatloaf (Epic)
-	21	ANYTIME, ANYWHERE — Rita Coolidge (A&M)
-	22	PENNIES FROM HEAVEN — Various Artists (World Records)
-	23	YOU LIGHT UP MY LIFE — Johnny Mathis (CBS)
16	24	ANOTHER MUSIC IN A DIFFERENT KITCHEN — Buzzcocks (United Artists)
20	25	VARIATONS — Andrew Lloyd Webber (MCA)
-	26	DISCO STARS — Various Artists (K-Tel)
28	27	ALL 'N' ALL — Earth Wind & Fire (CBS)
27	28	BEST FRIENDS — Cleo Laine & John Williams (RCA)
24	29	25 THUMPING GREAT HITS — Dave Clark Five (Polydor)
-	30	20 CLASSIC HITS — Platters (Mercury)

Elvis Costello's second album, *This Year's Model*, followed 1977's model, *My Aim Is True*. New Wave rather than punk, Costello was an old folkie really, but his remarkable lyrics had indeed contributed to the abrasion of the moment. Buzzcocks charted with debut LP *Another Music In A Different Kitchen*, a title typical of their ex-artschool management's style. Meat Loaf's *Bat Out Of Hell* was starting a chart run of 400+ weeks: longer than every other LP between 1958 and 1992 except Fleetwood Mac's *Rumours*.

29 April 1978

last week	this week		
2	1	SATURDAY NIGHT FEVER	Soundtrack (RSO)
3	2	AND THEN THERE WERE THREE	Genesis (Charisma)
1	3	20 GOLDEN GREATS	Nat 'King' Cole (Capitol)
4	4	LONDON TOWN	Wings (EMI)
5	5	THE ALBUM	Abba (Epic)
6	6	KAYA	Bob Marley & the Wailers (Island)
8	7	CITY TO CITY	Gerry Rafferty (United Artists)
10	8	THIS YEAR'S MODEL	Elvis Costello (Radar)
7	9	20 GOLDEN GREATS	Buddy Holly & the Crickets (MCA)
9	10	THE KICK INSIDE	Kate Bush (EMI)
11	11	THE STUD - SOUNDTRACK	Various Artists (Ronco)
12	12	PLASTIC LETTERS	Blondie (Chrysalis)
16	13	PASTICHE	Manhattan Transfer (Atlantic)
15	14	THE RUTLES	Rutles (Warner Bros.)
13	15	RUMOURS	Fleetwood Mac (Warner Bros.)
-	16	LONG LIVE ROCK & ROLL	Rainbow (Polydor)
14	17	OUT OF THE BLUE	Electric Light Orchestra (Jet)
22	18	PENNIES FROM HEAVEN	Various Artists (World Records)
18	19	FONZIE'S FAVOURITES	Various Artists (Warwick)
17	20	NEW BOOTS & PANTIES!!	Ian Dury & the Blockheads (Stiff)
20	21	BAT OUT OF HELL	Meatloaf (Epic)
-	22	ADVENTURE	Television (Elektra)
23	23	YOU LIGHT UP MY LIFE	Johnny Mathis (CBS)
-	24	EASTER	Patti Smith (Arista)
30	25	20 CLASSIC HITS	Platters (Mercury)
-	26	GREEN	Steve Hillage (Virgin Records)
19	27	REFLECTIONS	Andy Williams (CBS)
-	28	THE STRANGER	Billy Joel (CBS)
-	29	GREATEST HITS	Abba (Epic)
21	30	ANYTIME, ANYWHERE	Rita Coolidge (A&M)

6 May 1978

1	SATURDAY NIGHT FEVER	Soundtrack (RSO)
2	AND THEN THERE WERE THREE	Genesis (Charisma)
3	20 GOLDEN GREATS	Nat 'King' Cole (Capitol)
4	LONDON TOWN	Wings (EMI)
5	THE ALBUM	Abba (Epic)
6	CITY TO CITY	Gerry Rafferty (United Artists)
7	THE STUD - SOUNDTRACK	Various Artists (Ronco)
8	KAYA	Bob Marley & the Wailers (Island)
9	20 GOLDEN GREATS	Buddy Holly & the Crickets (MCA)
10	THE RUTLES	Rutles (Warner Bros.)
11	THE KICK INSIDE	Kate Bush (EMI)
12	RUMOURS	Fleetwood Mac (Warner Bros.)
13	THIS YEAR'S MODEL	Elvis Costello (Radar)
13	YOU LIGHT UP MY LIFE	Johnny Mathis (CBS)
15	ADVENTURE	Television (Elektra)
16	PLASTIC LETTERS	Blondie (Chrysalis)
16	LONG LIVE ROCK & ROLL	Rainbow (Polydor)
18	PASTICHE	Manhattan Transfer (Atlantic)
19	BAT OUT OF HELL	Meatloaf (Epic)
20	FONZIE'S FAVOURITES	Various Artists (Warwick)
21	OUT OF THE BLUE	Electric Light Orchestra (Jet)
22	20 CLASSIC HITS	Platters (Mercury)
23	PENNIES FROM HEAVEN	Various Artists (World Records)
24	EASTER	Patti Smith (Arista)
25	NEW BOOTS & PANTIES!!	Ian Dury & the Blockheads (Stiff)
26	ANYTIME, ANYWHERE	Rita Coolidge (A&M)
27	ANOTHER MUSIC IN A DIFFERENT KITCHEN	Buzzcocks (United Artists)
28	HEAVY HORSES	Jethro Tull (Chrysalis)
29	GREEN	Steve Hillage (Virgin Records)
30	HERMIT OF MINK HOLLOW	Todd Rundgren (Bearsville)

(left-column week numbers for 6 May: 1, 2, 3, 4, 5, 7, 11, 6, 9, 14, 10, 15, 8, 23, 22, 12, 16, 13, 21, 19, 17, 25, 18, 24, 20, 30, -, -, 26, -)

13 May 1978

1	SATURDAY NIGHT FEVER	Soundtrack (RSO)
2	AND THEN THERE WERE THREE	Genesis (Charisma)
3	20 GOLDEN GREATS	Nat 'King' Cole (Capitol)
4	THE STUD - SOUNDTRACK	Various Artists (Ronco)
5	LONDON TOWN	Wings (EMI)
6	CITY TO CITY	Gerry Rafferty (United Artists)
7	THE ALBUM	Abba (Epic)
8	YOU LIGHT UP MY LIFE	Johnny Mathis (CBS)
9	RUMOURS	Fleetwood Mac (Warner Bros.)
10	LONG LIVE ROCK & ROLL	Rainbow (Polydor)
11	KAYA	Bob Marley & the Wailers (Island)
12	PENNIES FROM HEAVEN	Various Artists (World Records)
13	BAT OUT OF HELL	Meatloaf (Epic)
14	20 GOLDEN GREATS	Buddy Holly & the Crickets (MCA)
15	PLASTIC LETTERS	Blondie (Chrysalis)
16	20 GOLDEN GREATS	Frank Sinatra (EMI)
17	THIS YEAR'S MODEL	Elvis Costello (Radar)
18	EASTER	Patti Smith (Arista)
18	THE RUTLES	Rutles (Warner Bros.)
20	ANYTIME, ANYWHERE	Rita Coolidge (A&M)
21	NEW BOOTS & PANTIES!!	Ian Dury & the Blockheads (Stiff)
22	PASTICHE	Manhattan Transfer (Atlantic)
23	HEAVY HORSES	Jethro Tull (Chrysalis)
24	A LITTLE BIT MORE	Dr. Hook (Capitol)
25	THE KICK INSIDE	Kate Bush (EMI)
26	20 CLASSIC HITS	Platters (Mercury)
27	SHOOTING STAR	Elkie Brooks (A&M)
28	OUT OF THE BLUE	Electric Light Orchestra (Jet)
29	FONZIE'S FAVOURITES	Various Artists (Warwick)
30	GREEN	Steve Hillage (Virgin Records)

(left-column week numbers for 13 May: 1, 2, 3, 7, 4, 6, 5, 13, 12, 16, 8, 23, 19, 9, 16, -, 13, 24, 10, 26, 25, 18, 28, -, 11, 22, -, 21, 20, 29)

20 May 1978

1	SATURDAY NIGHT FEVER	Soundtrack (RSO)
2	AND THEN THERE WERE THREE	Genesis (Charisma)
3	THE STUD - SOUNDTRACK	Various Artists (Ronco)
4	20 GOLDEN GREATS	Nat 'King' Cole (Capitol)
5	YOU LIGHT UP MY LIFE	Johnny Mathis (CBS)
6	THE ALBUM	Abba (Epic)
7	20 GOLDEN GREATS	Frank Sinatra (EMI)
8	LONG LIVE ROCK & ROLL	Rainbow (Polydor)
9	LONDON TOWN	Wings (EMI)
10	RUMOURS	Fleetwood Mac (Warner Bros.)
10	CITY TO CITY	Gerry Rafferty (United Artists)
12	EASTER	Patti Smith (Arista)
13	ANYTIME, ANYWHERE	Rita Coolidge (A&M)
14	KAYA	Bob Marley & the Wailers (Island)
15	BAT OUT OF HELL	Meatloaf (Epic)
16	NEW BOOTS & PANTIES!!	Ian Dury & the Blockheads (Stiff)
17	HEAVY HORSES	Jethro Tull (Chrysalis)
18	PASTICHE	Manhattan Transfer (Atlantic)
19	PENNIES FROM HEAVEN	Various Artists (World Records)
20	THE RUTLES	Rutles (Warner Bros.)
21	20 CLASSIC HITS	Platters (Mercury)
22	PLASTIC LETTERS	Blondie (Chrysalis)
23	THIS YEAR'S MODEL	Elvis Costello (Radar)
24	THE KICK INSIDE	Kate Bush (EMI)
25	20 GOLDEN GREATS	Buddy Holly & the Crickets (MCA)
26	GREEN	Steve Hillage (Virgin Records)
27	ANOTHER MUSIC IN A DIFFERENT KITCHEN	Buzzcocks (United Artists)
28	A LITTLE BIT MORE	Dr. Hook (Capitol)
29	SHOOTING STAR	Elkie Brooks (A&M)
30	THE LAST WALTZ	Soundtrack (Warner Bros.)

(left-column week numbers for 20 May: 1, 2, 4, 3, 8, 7, 16, 10, 5, 9, 6, 18, 20, 11, 13, 21, 23, 22, 12, 18, 26, 15, 17, 25, 14, 30, -, 24, 27, -)

Easter was New York City punk poet Patti Smith's first, and only sizeable, hit LP. Credited to the Patti Smith Group, it featured her thumping great classic single *Because The Night*, written by Bruce Springsteen, which charted on May 6 and peaked at No.3 two weeks later. The Platters, 1950s giants still on every pub jukebox in Britain to this day with *Great Pretender/Only You*, had never had a hit LP and hadn't had a hit single since *Harbour Lights* dropped out of the Top 20 in April 1960.

May – June 1978

27 May 1978

last week	this week	title / artist
1	1	SATURDAY NIGHT FEVER — Soundtrack (RSO)
3	2	THE STUD - SOUNDTRACK — Various Artists (Ronco)
6	3	THE ALBUM — Abba (Epic)
5	4	YOU LIGHT UP MY LIFE — Johnny Mathis (CBS)
2	5	AND THEN THERE WERE THREE — Genesis (Charisma)
7	6	20 GOLDEN GREATS — Frank Sinatra (EMI)
4	7	20 GOLDEN GREATS — Nat 'King' Cole (Capitol)
8	8	LONG LIVE ROCK & ROLL — Rainbow (Polydor)
9	9	LONDON TOWN — Wings (EMI)
19	10	PENNIES FROM HEAVEN — Various Artists (World Records)
-	11	BLACK AND WHITE — Stranglers (United Artists)
10	12	RUMOURS — Fleetwood Mac (Warner Bros.)
18	13	PASTICHE — Manhattan Transfer (Atlantic)
12	14	EASTER — Patti Smith (Arista)
15	15	BAT OUT OF HELL — Meatloaf (Epic)
21	16	20 CLASSIC HITS — Platters (Mercury)
-	16	THANK GOD IT'S FRIDAY — Soundtrack (Casablanca)
16	18	NEW BOOTS & PANTIES!! — Ian Dury & the Blockheads (Stiff)
13	19	ANYTIME, ANYWHERE — Rita Coolidge (A&M)
-	20	POWER IN THE DARK — Tom Robinson Band (EMI)
-	21	EVERYONE PLAYS DARTS — Darts (Magnet)
25	22	20 GOLDEN GREATS — Buddy Holly & the Crickets (MCA)
10	23	CITY TO CITY — Gerry Rafferty (United Artists)
14	24	KAYA — Bob Marley & the Wailers (Island)
23	25	THIS YEAR'S MODEL — Elvis Costello (Radar)
-	26	OUT OF THE BLUE — Electric Light Orchestra (Jet)
24	27	THE KICK INSIDE — Kate Bush (EMI)
29	28	SHOOTING STAR — Elkie Brooks (A&M)
22	29	PLASTIC LETTERS — Blondie (Chrysalis)
-	30	POWERAGE — AC/DC (Atlantic)

3 June 1978

last week	this week	title / artist
1	1	SATURDAY NIGHT FEVER — Soundtrack (RSO)
3	2	THE ALBUM — Abba (Epic)
5	3	AND THEN THERE WERE THREE — Genesis (Charisma)
2	4	THE STUD - SOUNDTRACK — Various Artists (Ronco)
11	5	BLACK AND WHITE — Stranglers (United Artists)
14	6	EASTER — Patti Smith (Arista)
7	7	20 GOLDEN GREATS — Nat 'King' Cole (Capitol)
18	8	NEW BOOTS & PANTIES!! — Ian Dury & the Blockheads (Stiff)
6	9	20 GOLDEN GREATS — Frank Sinatra (EMI)
19	10	ANYTIME, ANYWHERE — Rita Coolidge (A&M)
15	11	BAT OUT OF HELL — Meatloaf (Epic)
12	12	RUMOURS — Fleetwood Mac (Warner Bros.)
4	13	YOU LIGHT UP MY LIFE — Johnny Mathis (CBS)
-	14	THE PARKERILLA — Graham Parker & the Rumour (Vertigo)
9	14	LONDON TOWN — Wings (EMI)
23	16	CITY TO CITY — Gerry Rafferty (United Artists)
13	17	PASTICHE — Manhattan Transfer (Atlantic)
8	18	LONG LIVE ROCK & ROLL — Rainbow (Polydor)
24	19	KAYA — Bob Marley & the Wailers (Island)
29	20	PLASTIC LETTERS — Blondie (Chrysalis)
20	21	POWER IN THE DARK — Tom Robinson Band (EMI)
16	22	20 CLASSIC HITS — Platters (Mercury)
21	23	EVERYONE PLAYS DARTS — Darts (Magnet)
22	24	20 GOLDEN GREATS — Buddy Holly & the Crickets (MCA)
10	25	PENNIES FROM HEAVEN — Various Artists (World Records)
-	26	I KNOW 'COS I WAS THERE — Max Boyce (EMI)
27	27	THE KICK INSIDE — Kate Bush (EMI)
30	28	POWERAGE — AC/DC (Atlantic)
-	29	BUT SERIOUSLY FOLKS — Joe Walsh (Asylum)
-	30	APPROVED BY THE MOTORS — Motors (Virgin)

10 June 1978

last week	this week	title / artist
1	1	SATURDAY NIGHT FEVER — Soundtrack (RSO)
5	2	BLACK AND WHITE — Stranglers (United Artists)
2	3	THE ALBUM — Abba (Epic)
4	4	THE STUD - SOUNDTRACK — Various Artists (Ronco)
3	5	AND THEN THERE WERE THREE — Genesis (Charisma)
10	6	ANYTIME, ANYWHERE — Rita Coolidge (A&M)
17	7	PASTICHE — Manhattan Transfer (Atlantic)
9	8	20 GOLDEN GREATS — Frank Sinatra (EMI)
7	9	20 GOLDEN GREATS — Nat 'King' Cole (Capitol)
23	10	EVERYONE PLAYS DARTS — Darts (Magnet)
8	11	NEW BOOTS & PANTIES!! — Ian Dury & the Blockheads (Stiff)
21	12	POWER IN THE DARK — Tom Robinson Band (EMI)
6	13	EASTER — Patti Smith (Arista)
11	14	BAT OUT OF HELL — Meatloaf (Epic)
13	15	YOU LIGHT UP MY LIFE — Johnny Mathis (CBS)
26	16	I KNOW 'COS I WAS THERE — Max Boyce (EMI)
14	17	THE PARKERILLA — Graham Parker & the Rumour (Vertigo)
14	18	LONDON TOWN — Wings (EMI)
12	19	RUMOURS — Fleetwood Mac (Warner Bros.)
19	20	KAYA — Bob Marley & the Wailers (Island)
-	21	THE LENA MARTELL COLLECTION — Lena Martell (Ronco)
20	22	PLASTIC LETTERS — Blondie (Chrysalis)
18	23	LONG LIVE ROCK & ROLL — Rainbow (Polydor)
-	24	SHOOTING STAR — Elkie Brooks (A&M)
28	25	POWERAGE — AC/DC (Atlantic)
25	26	PENNIES FROM HEAVEN — Various Artists (World Records)
-	27	THIS YEAR'S MODEL — Elvis Costello (Radar)
-	28	THE STRANGER — Billy Joel (CBS)
-	29	LIVE AND DANGEROUS — Thin Lizzy (Vertigo)
30	30	APPROVED BY THE MOTORS — Motors (Virgin)

17 June 1978

last week	this week	title / artist
2	1	BLACK AND WHITE — Stranglers (United Artists)
1	2	SATURDAY NIGHT FEVER — Soundtrack (RSO)
3	3	THE ALBUM — Abba (Epic)
4	4	THE STUD - SOUNDTRACK — Various Artists (Ronco)
10	5	EVERYONE PLAYS DARTS — Darts (Magnet)
5	6	AND THEN THERE WERE THREE — Genesis (Charisma)
6	7	ANYTIME, ANYWHERE — Rita Coolidge (A&M)
7	8	PASTICHE — Manhattan Transfer (Atlantic)
-	9	DISCO DOUBLE — Various Artists (K-Tel)
15	10	YOU LIGHT UP MY LIFE — Johnny Mathis (CBS)
-	11	SOME GIRLS — Rolling Stones (EMI)
11	12	NEW BOOTS & PANTIES!! — Ian Dury & the Blockheads (Stiff)
12	13	POWER IN THE DARK — Tom Robinson Band (EMI)
9	14	20 GOLDEN GREATS — Nat 'King' Cole (Capitol)
16	15	I KNOW 'COS I WAS THERE — Max Boyce (EMI)
29	16	LIVE AND DANGEROUS — Thin Lizzy (Vertigo)
13	17	EASTER — Patti Smith (Arista)
14	18	BAT OUT OF HELL — Meatloaf (Epic)
19	19	RUMOURS — Fleetwood Mac (Warner Bros.)
-	20	THE KICK INSIDE — Kate Bush (EMI)
-	21	NATURAL HIGH — Commodores (Motown)
-	22	DAVID GILMOUR — David Gilmour (Harvest)
24	23	SHOOTING STAR — Elkie Brooks (A&M)
8	24	20 GOLDEN GREATS — Frank Sinatra (EMI)
-	25	OUT OF THE BLUE — Electric Light Orchestra (Jet)
23	26	LONG LIVE ROCK & ROLL — Rainbow (Polydor)
-	27	OCTAVE — Moody Blues (Threshold)
28	28	THE STRANGER — Billy Joel (CBS)
27	29	THIS YEAR'S MODEL — Elvis Costello (Radar)
20	30	KAYA — Bob Marley & the Wailers (Island)

While the custard of the singles chart bubbled under the unyieldingly thick skin of John Travolta & Olivia Newton-John's *You're The One That I Want*, from the film (but not the stage-show) of *Grease*, the album chart shivered with *Saturday Night Fever*. These long occupancies of the top slots confirmed that both singles and albums were, after some doldrum years, enjoying huge sales again. Punk had re-activated the power of music in people's lives, as Beatlemania had done in days of yore.

24 June 1978

last week	this week		
2	1	SATURDAY NIGHT FEVER	Soundtrack (RSO)
16	2	LIVE AND DANGEROUS	Thin Lizzy (Vertigo)
1	3	BLACK AND WHITE	Stranglers (United Artists)
3	4	THE ALBUM	Abba (Epic)
12	5	NEW BOOTS & PANTIES!!	Ian Dury & the Blockheads (Stiff)
13	6	POWER IN THE DARK	Tom Robinson Band (EMI)
4	7	THE STUD - SOUNDTRACK	Various Artists (Ronco)
18	8	BAT OUT OF HELL	Meatloaf (Epic)
10	9	YOU LIGHT UP MY LIFE	Johnny Mathis (CBS)
11	10	SOME GIRLS	Rolling Stones (EMI)
5	11	EVERYONE PLAYS DARTS	Darts (Magnet)
14	12	20 GOLDEN GREATS	Nat 'King' Cole (Capitol)
-	13	PETER GABRIEL	Peter Gabriel (Charisma)
-	14	DARKNESS ON THE EDGE OF TOWN	Bruce Springsteen (CBS)
7	15	ANYTIME, ANYWHERE	Rita Coolidge (A&M)
15	16	I KNOW 'COS I WAS THERE	Max Boyce (EMI)
9	17	DISCO DOUBLE	Various Artists (K-Tel)
8	18	PASTICHE	Manhattan Transfer (Atlantic)
22	19	DAVID GILMOUR	David Gilmour (Harvest)
20	20	THE KICK INSIDE	Kate Bush (EMI)
-	21	STREET LEGAL	Bob Dylan (CBS)
6	22	AND THEN THERE WERE THREE	Genesis (Charisma)
19	23	RUMOURS	Fleetwood Mac (Warner Bros.)
24	24	20 GOLDEN GREATS	Frank Sinatra (EMI)
27	25	OCTAVE	Moody Blues (Threshold)
17	26	EASTER	Patti Smith (Arista)
-	27	PENNIES FROM HEAVEN	Various Artists (World Records)
28	28	THE STRANGER	Billy Joel (CBS)
30	29	KAYA	Bob Marley & the Wailers (Island)
21	30	NATURAL HIGH	Commodores (Motown)

1 July 1978

1	1	SATURDAY NIGHT FEVER	Soundtrack (RSO)
2	2	LIVE AND DANGEROUS	Thin Lizzy (Vertigo)
10	3	SOME GIRLS	Rolling Stones (EMI)
4	4	THE ALBUM	Abba (Epic)
3	5	BLACK AND WHITE	Stranglers (United Artists)
8	6	BAT OUT OF HELL	Meatloaf (Epic)
5	7	NEW BOOTS & PANTIES!!	Ian Dury & the Blockheads (Stiff)
9	7	YOU LIGHT UP MY LIFE	Johnny Mathis (CBS)
20	9	THE KICK INSIDE	Kate Bush (EMI)
7	10	THE STUD - SOUNDTRACK	Various Artists (Ronco)
25	11	OCTAVE	Moody Blues (Threshold)
11	12	EVERYONE PLAYS DARTS	Darts (Magnet)
21	13	STREET LEGAL	Bob Dylan (CBS)
16	14	I KNOW 'COS I WAS THERE	Max Boyce (EMI)
6	15	POWER IN THE DARK	Tom Robinson Band (EMI)
18	16	PASTICHE	Manhattan Transfer (Atlantic)
22	17	AND THEN THERE WERE THREE	Genesis (Charisma)
17	18	DISCO DOUBLE	Various Artists (K-Tel)
13	19	PETER GABRIEL	Peter Gabriel (Charisma)
14	20	DARKNESS ON THE EDGE OF TOWN	Bruce Springsteen (CBS)
23	21	RUMOURS	Fleetwood Mac (Warner Bros.)
24	22	20 GOLDEN GREATS	Frank Sinatra (EMI)
19	23	DAVID GILMOUR	David Gilmour (Harvest)
15	24	ANYTIME, ANYWHERE	Rita Coolidge (A&M)
-	25	OUT OF THE BLUE	Electric Light Orchestra (Jet)
12	26	20 GOLDEN GREATS	Nat 'King' Cole (Capitol)
-	27	REAL LIFE	Magazine (Virgin)
29	28	KAYA	Bob Marley & the Wailers (Island)
27	29	PENNIES FROM HEAVEN	Various Artists (World Records)
-	30	THE LENA MARTELL COLLECTION	Lena Martell (Ronco)

8 July 1978

1	1	SATURDAY NIGHT FEVER	Soundtrack (RSO)
2	2	LIVE AND DANGEROUS	Thin Lizzy (Vertigo)
3	3	SOME GIRLS	Rolling Stones (EMI)
11	4	OCTAVE	Moody Blues (Threshold)
13	5	STREET LEGAL	Bob Dylan (CBS)
4	6	THE ALBUM	Abba (Epic)
9	7	THE KICK INSIDE	Kate Bush (EMI)
7	8	NEW BOOTS & PANTIES!!	Ian Dury & the Blockheads (Stiff)
7	9	YOU LIGHT UP MY LIFE	Johnny Mathis (CBS)
6	10	BAT OUT OF HELL	Meatloaf (Epic)
5	11	BLACK AND WHITE	Stranglers (United Artists)
17	12	AND THEN THERE WERE THREE	Genesis (Charisma)
15	13	POWER IN THE DARK	Tom Robinson Band (EMI)
10	14	THE STUD - SOUNDTRACK	Various Artists (Ronco)
-	15	A TONIC FOR THE TROOPS	Boomtown Rats (Ensign)
14	16	I KNOW 'COS I WAS THERE	Max Boyce (EMI)
16	17	PASTICHE	Manhattan Transfer (Atlantic)
21	18	RUMOURS	Fleetwood Mac (Warner Bros.)
20	19	DARKNESS ON THE EDGE OF TOWN	Bruce Springsteen (CBS)
23	19	DAVID GILMOUR	David Gilmour (Harvest)
19	21	PETER GABRIEL	Peter Gabriel (Charisma)
22	22	20 GOLDEN GREATS	Frank Sinatra (EMI)
27	23	REAL LIFE	Magazine (Virgin)
18	24	DISCO DOUBLE	Various Artists (K-Tel)
25	25	OUT OF THE BLUE	Electric Light Orchestra (Jet)
-	26	WAR OF THE WORLDS	Jeff Wayne (CBS)
12	27	EVERYONE PLAYS DARTS	Darts (Magnet)
29	28	PENNIES FROM HEAVEN	Various Artists (World Records)
24	29	ANYTIME, ANYWHERE	Rita Coolidge (A&M)
-	30	CITY TO CITY	Gerry Rafferty (United Artists)

15 July 1978

1	1	SATURDAY NIGHT FEVER	Soundtrack (RSO)
5	2	STREET LEGAL	Bob Dylan (CBS)
3	3	SOME GIRLS	Rolling Stones (EMI)
2	4	LIVE AND DANGEROUS	Thin Lizzy (Vertigo)
4	5	OCTAVE	Moody Blues (Threshold)
7	6	THE KICK INSIDE	Kate Bush (EMI)
6	7	THE ALBUM	Abba (Epic)
15	8	A TONIC FOR THE TROOPS	Boomtown Rats (Ensign)
-	9	20 GOLDEN GREATS	Hollies (EMI)
8	10	NEW BOOTS & PANTIES!!	Ian Dury & the Blockheads (Stiff)
26	11	WAR OF THE WORLDS	Jeff Wayne (CBS)
12	12	AND THEN THERE WERE THREE	Genesis (Charisma)
10	13	BAT OUT OF HELL	Meatloaf (Epic)
-	14	GREASE	Soundtrack (RSO)
9	15	YOU LIGHT UP MY LIFE	Johnny Mathis (CBS)
17	16	PASTICHE	Manhattan Transfer (Atlantic)
14	17	THE STUD - SOUNDTRACK	Various Artists (Ronco)
21	18	PETER GABRIEL	Peter Gabriel (Charisma)
11	19	BLACK AND WHITE	Stranglers (United Artists)
-	20	ROCK RULES	Various Artists (K-Tel)
16	21	I KNOW 'COS I WAS THERE	Max Boyce (EMI)
23	22	REAL LIFE	Magazine (Virgin)
-	23	GOODBYE GIRL	David Gates (Elektra)
-	24	BACK & FOURTH	Lindisfarne (Mercury)
19	25	DARKNESS ON THE EDGE OF TOWN	Bruce Springsteen (CBS)
-	26	YOU'RE GONNA GET IT	Tom Petty & the Heartbreakers (Shelter)
-	27	THE LENA MARTELL COLLECTION	Lena Martell (Ronco)
-	28	20 GOLDEN GREATS	Nat 'King' Cole (Capitol)
13	29	POWER IN THE DARK	Tom Robinson Band (EMI)
19	30	DAVID GILMOUR	David Gilmour (Harvest)

Bob Dylan's six June nights at Earls Court, followed by July 15's Picnic at Blackbushe (his first UK tour for 12 years) gained him extraordinarily good press (especially considering that for many New Wavers, in and outside the industry, he was a useful symbol of the hated old order), and pulled in massive crowds. It wasn't quite enough to put his new studio album *Street Legal* to the No.1 slot. Nor could the Rolling Stones quite manage this with their best LP in years, *Some Girls*.

July – August 1978

Boney M's *Night Flight To Venus* was launched up the chart by their single *Rivers Of Babylon / Brown Girl In The Ring*, a June No.1 and a 2-million-seller in the UK alone. (Wonder how these West Indian girls and boys regarded the Stones' LP, with its title song's "Black girls just wanna get fucked all night".) Thin Lizzy's *Live And Dangerous* was their fourth hit album, and followed a concert at the Rainbow in March which had been televised in many countries (though not Britain).

August – September 1978

19 August 1978

last week	this week	Title	Artist
1	1	SATURDAY NIGHT FEVER	Soundtrack (RSO)
8	2	20 GIANT HITS	Nolan Sisters (Target)
2	3	20 GOLDEN GREATS	Hollies (EMI)
3	4	STREET LEGAL	Bob Dylan (CBS)
4	5	NIGHT FLIGHT TO VENUS	Boney M (Atlantic/Hansa)
5	6	GREASE	Soundtrack (RSO)
11	7	WAR OF THE WORLDS	Jeff Wayne (CBS)
6	8	LIVE AND DANGEROUS	Thin Lizzy (Vertigo)
14	9	A TONIC FOR THE TROOPS	Boomtown Rats (Ensign)
9	10	OUT OF THE BLUE	Electric Light Orchestra (Jet)
10	11	THE KICK INSIDE	Kate Bush (EMI)
-	11	STAR PARTY	Various Artists (K-Tel)
17	13	HANDSWORTH REVOLUTION	Steel Pulse (Island)
12	14	OCTAVE	Moody Blues (Threshold)
7	14	SOME GIRLS	Rolling Stones (EMI)
13	16	NATURAL HIGH	Commodores (Motown)
15	17	BUT SERIOUSLY FOLKS	Joe Walsh (Asylum)
26	18	BAT OUT OF HELL	Meatloaf (Epic)
22	19	RUMOURS	Fleetwood Mac (Warner Bros.)
23	20	THE ALBUM	Abba (Epic)
24	21	IMAGES	Don Williams (K-Tel)
16	22	NEW BOOTS & PANTIES!!	Ian Dury & the Blockheads (Stiff)
29	23	CLASSIC ROCK	London Symphony Orchestra (K-Tel)
28	24	AND THEN THERE WERE THREE	Genesis (Charisma)
19	25	CAN'T STAND THE REZILLOS	Rezillos (Sire)
-	26	BLAM!!	Brothers Johnson (A&M)
27	27	BLACK AND WHITE	Stranglers (United Artists)
-	28	LOVE ME AGAIN	Rita Coolidge (A&M)
20	29	ROCK RULES	Various Artists (K-Tel)
17	30	THANK GOD ITS FRIDAY	Soundtrack (Casablanca)

26 August 1978

last week	this week	Title	Artist
1	1	SATURDAY NIGHT FEVER	Soundtrack (RSO)
5	2	NIGHT FLIGHT TO VENUS	Boney M (Atlantic/Hansa)
4	3	STREET LEGAL	Bob Dylan (CBS)
7	4	WAR OF THE WORLDS	Jeff Wayne (CBS)
6	5	GREASE	Soundtrack (RSO)
2	6	20 GIANT HITS	Nolan Sisters (Target)
16	7	NATURAL HIGH	Commodores (Motown)
8	8	LIVE AND DANGEROUS	Thin Lizzy (Vertigo)
3	9	20 GOLDEN GREATS	Hollies (EMI)
14	10	SOME GIRLS	Rolling Stones (EMI)
23	11	CLASSIC ROCK	London Symphony Orchestra (K-Tel)
11	12	STAR PARTY	Various Artists (K-Tel)
14	13	OCTAVE	Moody Blues (Threshold)
10	14	OUT OF THE BLUE	Electric Light Orchestra (Jet)
11	15	THE KICK INSIDE	Kate Bush (EMI)
18	15	BAT OUT OF HELL	Meatloaf (Epic)
25	17	CAN'T STAND THE REZILLOS	Rezillos (Sire)
17	18	BUT SERIOUSLY FOLKS	Joe Walsh (Asylum)
22	19	NEW BOOTS & PANTIES!!	Ian Dury & the Blockheads (Stiff)
21	20	IMAGES	Don Williams (K-Tel)
20	21	THE ALBUM	Abba (Epic)
29	22	ROCK RULES	Various Artists (K-Tel)
13	23	HANDSWORTH REVOLUTION	Steel Pulse (Island)
9	24	A TONIC FOR THE TROOPS	Boomtown Rats (Ensign)
-	25	PASTICHE	Manhattan Transfer (Atlantic)
26	26	BLAM!!	Brothers Johnson (A&M)
24	27	AND THEN THERE WERE THREE	Genesis (Charisma)
-	28	SHADOW DANCING	Andy Gibb (RSO)
-	29	EVERYONE PLAYS DARTS	Darts (Magnet)
19	30	RUMOURS	Fleetwood Mac (Warner Bros.)

2 September 1978

last week	this week	Title	Artist
1	1	SATURDAY NIGHT FEVER	Soundtrack (RSO)
3	2	STREET LEGAL	Bob Dylan (CBS)
2	3	NIGHT FLIGHT TO VENUS	Boney M (Atlantic/Hansa)
4	4	WAR OF THE WORLDS	Jeff Wayne (CBS)
5	5	GREASE	Soundtrack (RSO)
6	6	20 GIANT HITS	Nolan Sisters (Target)
8	7	LIVE AND DANGEROUS	Thin Lizzy (Vertigo)
10	8	SOME GIRLS	Rolling Stones (EMI)
9	9	20 GOLDEN GREATS	Hollies (EMI)
7	10	NATURAL HIGH	Commodores (Motown)
13	11	OCTAVE	Moody Blues (Threshold)
11	12	CLASSIC ROCK	London Symphony Orchestra (K-Tel)
12	13	STAR PARTY	Various Artists (K-Tel)
14	14	OUT OF THE BLUE	Electric Light Orchestra (Jet)
-	15	WHO ARE YOU	Who (Polydor)
15	16	THE KICK INSIDE	Kate Bush (EMI)
17	17	CAN'T STAND THE REZILLOS	Rezillos (Sire)
20	18	IMAGES	Don Williams (K-Tel)
24	19	A TONIC FOR THE TROOPS	Boomtown Rats (Ensign)
18	20	BUT SERIOUSLY FOLKS	Joe Walsh (Asylum)
19	21	NEW BOOTS & PANTIES!!	Ian Dury & the Blockheads (Stiff)
15	22	BAT OUT OF HELL	Meatloaf (Epic)
-	23	DOUBLE VISION	Foreigner (Atlantic)
23	24	HANDSWORTH REVOLUTION	Steel Pulse (Island)
27	25	AND THEN THERE WERE THREE	Genesis (Charisma)
21	26	THE ALBUM	Abba (Epic)
-	27	JAMES GALWAY PLAYS SONGS FOR ANNIE	James Galway (RCA Red Seal)
22	28	ROCK RULES	Various Artists (K-Tel)
26	29	BLAM!!	Brothers Johnson (A&M)
29	30	EVERYONE PLAYS DARTS	Darts (Magnet)

9 September 1978

last week	this week	Title	Artist
3	1	NIGHT FLIGHT TO VENUS	Boney M (Atlantic/Hansa)
5	2	GREASE	Soundtrack (RSO)
4	3	WAR OF THE WORLDS	Jeff Wayne (CBS)
1	4	SATURDAY NIGHT FEVER	Soundtrack (RSO)
12	5	CLASSIC ROCK	London Symphony Orchestra (K-Tel)
6	5	20 GIANT HITS	Nolan Sisters (Target)
10	7	NATURAL HIGH	Commodores (Motown)
18	8	IMAGES	Don Williams (K-Tel)
2	9	STREET LEGAL	Bob Dylan (CBS)
13	10	STAR PARTY	Various Artists (K-Tel)
8	11	SOME GIRLS	Rolling Stones (EMI)
7	12	LIVE AND DANGEROUS	Thin Lizzy (Vertigo)
14	13	OUT OF THE BLUE	Electric Light Orchestra (Jet)
22	14	BAT OUT OF HELL	Meatloaf (Epic)
15	15	WHO ARE YOU	Who (Polydor)
11	16	OCTAVE	Moody Blues (Threshold)
9	17	20 GOLDEN GREATS	Hollies (EMI)
19	18	A TONIC FOR THE TROOPS	Boomtown Rats (Ensign)
17	19	CAN'T STAND THE REZILLOS	Rezillos (Sire)
26	20	THE ALBUM	Abba (Epic)
16	21	THE KICK INSIDE	Kate Bush (EMI)
-	22	THE LENA MARTELL COLLECTION	Lena Martell (Ronco)
21	23	NEW BOOTS & PANTIES!!	Ian Dury & the Blockheads (Stiff)
-	24	WHO PAYS THE FERRYMAN	Yannis Markopoulos (BBC)
25	25	AND THEN THERE WERE THREE	Genesis (Charisma)
-	26	RUMOURS	Fleetwood Mac (Warner Bros.)
29	27	BLAM!!	Brothers Johnson (A&M)
23	28	DOUBLE VISION	Foreigner (Atlantic)
24	29	HANDSWORTH REVOLUTION	Steel Pulse (Island)
-	30	REAL LIFE	Magazine (Virgin)

The Who's 13th Top 30 album, *Who Are You*, joined the chart at No.15 on September 2. Five days later, Keith Moon died of an overdose of sedatives used as a "treatment" for alcoholism. He had been the group's drummer since its inception in 1962, and had long been a well-loved British institution (for acting as if he should have been in one). Pete Townshend said of his death: "It's something we have been expecting for twenty years." He was eventually replaced by Kenny Jones, formerly of the Faces.

September – October 1978

16 September 1978

last	this		
1	1	NIGHT FLIGHT TO VENUS	Boney M (Atlantic/Hansa)
3	2	WAR OF THE WORLDS	Jeff Wayne (CBS)
5	3	CLASSIC ROCK	London Symphony Orchestra (K-Tel)
2	4	GREASE	Soundtrack (RSO)
15	5	WHO ARE YOU	Who (Polydor)
8	6	IMAGES	Don Williams (K-Tel)
9	7	STREET LEGAL	Bob Dylan (CBS)
4	8	SATURDAY NIGHT FEVER	Soundtrack (RSO)
7	9	NATURAL HIGH	Commodores (Motown)
10	10	STAR PARTY	Various Artists (K-Tel)
-	11	JAMES GALWAY PLAYS SONGS FOR ANNIE	James Galway (RCA Red Seal)
-	12	DON'T LOOK BACK	Boston (Epic)
17	12	20 GOLDEN GREATS	Hollies (EMI)
5	14	20 GIANT HITS	Nolan Sisters (Target)
19	15	CAN'T STAND THE REZILLOS	Rezillos (Sire)
13	16	OUT OF THE BLUE	Electric Light Orchestra (Jet)
16	17	OCTAVE	Moody Blues (Threshold)
20	18	THE ALBUM	Abba (Epic)
14	19	BAT OUT OF HELL	Meatloaf (Epic)
12	20	LIVE AND DANGEROUS	Thin Lizzy (Vertigo)
23	21	NEW BOOTS & PANTIES!!	Ian Dury & the Blockheads (Stiff)
25	22	AND THEN THERE WERE THREE	Genesis (Charisma)
-	23	SHADOW DANCING	Andy Gibb (RSO)
29	24	HANDSWORTH REVOLUTION	Steel Pulse (Island)
-	25	SUNLIGHT	Herbie Hancock (CBS)
-	26	EVERYONE PLAYS DARTS	Darts (Magnet)
11	27	SOME GIRLS	Rolling Stones (EMI)
26	28	RUMOURS	Fleetwood Mac (Warner Bros.)
-	29	Q: ARE WE NOT MEN? A: WE ARE DEVO!	Devo (Virgin)
-	30	LEO SAYER	Leo Sayer (Chrysalis)

23 September 1978

last	this		
1	1	NIGHT FLIGHT TO VENUS	Boney M (Atlantic/Hansa)
6	2	IMAGES	Don Williams (K-Tel)
4	3	GREASE	Soundtrack (RSO)
2	4	WAR OF THE WORLDS	Jeff Wayne (CBS)
3	5	CLASSIC ROCK	London Symphony Orchestra (K-Tel)
8	6	SATURDAY NIGHT FEVER	Soundtrack (RSO)
5	7	WHO ARE YOU	Who (Polydor)
11	8	JAMES GALWAY PLAYS SONGS FOR ANNIE	James Galway (RCA Red Seal)
9	9	NATURAL HIGH	Commodores (Motown)
12	10	DON'T LOOK BACK	Boston (Epic)
7	11	STREET LEGAL	Bob Dylan (CBS)
-	12	BLOODY TOURISTS	10 c.c. (Mercury)
10	13	STAR PARTY	Various Artists (K-Tel)
16	14	OUT OF THE BLUE	Electric Light Orchestra (Jet)
14	15	20 GIANT HITS	Nolan Sisters (Target)
12	16	20 GOLDEN GREATS	Hollies (EMI)
15	17	CAN'T STAND THE REZILLOS	Rezillos (Sire)
22	18	AND THEN THERE WERE THREE	Genesis (Charisma)
29	19	Q: ARE WE NOT MEN? A: WE ARE DEVO!	Devo (Virgin)
27	20	SOME GIRLS	Rolling Stones (EMI)
28	21	RUMOURS	Fleetwood Mac (Warner Bros.)
19	22	BAT OUT OF HELL	Meatloaf (Epic)
20	23	LIVE AND DANGEROUS	Thin Lizzy (Vertigo)
23	24	SHADOW DANCING	Andy Gibb (RSO)
-	25	PARALLEL LINES	Blondie (Chrysalis)
18	26	THE ALBUM	Abba (Epic)
-	27	DOUBLE VISION	Foreigner (Atlantic)
-	28	THE BRIDE STRIPPED BARE	Bryan Ferry (Polydor)
-	29	THE LENA MARTELL COLLECTION	Lena Martell (Ronco)
30	30	LEO SAYER	Leo Sayer (Chrysalis)

30 September 1978

last	this		
3	1	GREASE	Soundtrack (RSO)
1	2	NIGHT FLIGHT TO VENUS	Boney M (Atlantic/Hansa)
2	3	IMAGES	Don Williams (K-Tel)
4	4	WAR OF THE WORLDS	Jeff Wayne (CBS)
6	5	SATURDAY NIGHT FEVER	Soundtrack (RSO)
5	6	CLASSIC ROCK	London Symphony Orchestra (K-Tel)
25	7	PARALLEL LINES	Blondie (Chrysalis)
7	8	WHO ARE YOU	Who (Polydor)
12	9	BLOODY TOURISTS	10 c.c. (Mercury)
10	10	DON'T LOOK BACK	Boston (Epic)
9	11	NATURAL HIGH	Commodores (Motown)
11	12	STREET LEGAL	Bob Dylan (CBS)
8	13	JAMES GALWAY PLAYS SONGS FOR ANNIE	James Galway (RCA Red Seal)
14	14	OUT OF THE BLUE	Electric Light Orchestra (Jet)
23	15	LIVE AND DANGEROUS	Thin Lizzy (Vertigo)
19	16	Q: ARE WE NOT MEN? A: WE ARE DEVO!	Devo (Virgin)
-	17	BIG WHEELS OF MOTOWN	Various Artists (Motown)
-	18	NEW BOOTS & PANTIES!!	Ian Dury & the Blockheads (Stiff)
30	19	LEO SAYER	Leo Sayer (Chrysalis)
13	20	STAR PARTY	Various Artists (K-Tel)
21	21	RUMOURS	Fleetwood Mac (Warner Bros.)
-	22	OCTAVE	Moody Blues (Threshold)
-	23	SUNLIGHT	Herbie Hancock (CBS)
-	24	TORMATO	Yes (Atlantic)
22	25	BAT OUT OF HELL	Meatloaf (Epic)
28	26	THE BRIDE STRIPPED BARE	Bryan Ferry (Polydor)
27	27	DOUBLE VISION	Foreigner (Atlantic)
-	28	THE KICK INSIDE	Kate Bush (EMI)
17	29	CAN'T STAND THE REZILLOS	Rezillos (Sire)
26	30	THE ALBUM	Abba (Epic)

7 October 1978

last	this		
1	1	GREASE	Soundtrack (RSO)
2	2	NIGHT FLIGHT TO VENUS	Boney M (Atlantic/Hansa)
9	3	BLOODY TOURISTS	10 c.c. (Mercury)
3	4	IMAGES	Don Williams (K-Tel)
4	5	WAR OF THE WORLDS	Jeff Wayne (CBS)
5	5	SATURDAY NIGHT FEVER	Soundtrack (RSO)
7	7	PARALLEL LINES	Blondie (Chrysalis)
6	8	CLASSIC ROCK	London Symphony Orchestra (K-Tel)
10	9	DON'T LOOK BACK	Boston (Epic)
8	10	WHO ARE YOU	Who (Polydor)
-	11	ROSE ROYCE STRIKES AGAIN	Rose Royce (Whitfield)
17	12	BIG WHEELS OF MOTOWN	Various Artists (Motown)
12	13	STREET LEGAL	Bob Dylan (CBS)
19	14	LEO SAYER	Leo Sayer (Chrysalis)
24	15	TORMATO	Yes (Atlantic)
16	16	Q: ARE WE NOT MEN? A: WE ARE DEVO!	Devo (Virgin)
13	17	JAMES GALWAY PLAYS SONGS FOR ANNIE	James Galway (RCA Red Seal)
11	18	NATURAL HIGH	Commodores (Motown)
26	19	THE BRIDE STRIPPED BARE	Bryan Ferry (Polydor)
20	20	STAR PARTY	Various Artists (K-Tel)
14	21	OUT OF THE BLUE	Electric Light Orchestra (Jet)
-	22	ROAD TO RUIN	Ramones (Sire)
25	23	BAT OUT OF HELL	Meatloaf (Epic)
-	24	STAGE	David Bowie (RCA)
-	25	BREATHLESS	Camel (Decca)
15	26	LIVE AND DANGEROUS	Thin Lizzy (Vertigo)
21	27	RUMOURS	Fleetwood Mac (Warner Bros.)
-	28	LIVING IN THE USA	Linda Ronstadt (Asylum)
-	29	GHOSTS OF PRINCES IN TOWERS	Rich Kids (EMI)
22	30	OCTAVE	Moody Blues (Threshold)

The Ramones were an important iconic American punky group on Sire Records; the Rezillos were an unimportant British punky group on Sire, whose only hit single, the mistitled *Top Of The Pops*, had just peaked at No.13. For 1980 *Motorbike Beat*, they tried to improve their luck with a radical name-change... to the Revillos. *James Galway Plays Songs For Annie* referred to this flute-toting professional Irishman's recent revival (No.4 in June) of John Denver's mawkish *Annie's Song* (No.2 for Denver in 1974).

14 October 1978

last week	this week		
1	1	GREASE	Soundtrack (RSO)
4	2	IMAGES	Don Williams (K-Tel)
2	3	NIGHT FLIGHT TO VENUS	Boney M (Atlantic/Hansa)
3	4	BLOODY TOURISTS	10 c.c. (Mercury)
5	5	WAR OF THE WORLDS	Jeff Wayne (CBS)
12	6	BIG WHEELS OF MOTOWN	Various Artists (Motown)
5	7	SATURDAY NIGHT FEVER	Soundtrack (RSO)
7	8	PARALLEL LINES	Blondie (Chrysalis)
8	9	CLASSIC ROCK	London Symphony Orchestra (K-Tel)
15	10	TORMATO	Yes (Atlantic)
10	11	WHO ARE YOU	Who (Polydor)
19	12	THE BRIDE STRIPPED BARE	Bryan Ferry (Polydor)
11	13	ROSE ROYCE STRIKES AGAIN	Rose Royce (Whitfield)
9	14	DON'T LOOK BACK	Boston (Epic)
24	15	STAGE	David Bowie (RCA)
21	15	OUT OF THE BLUE	Electric Light Orchestra (Jet)
23	17	BAT OUT OF HELL	Meatloaf (Epic)
-	18	BROTHERHOOD OF MAN	Brotherhood of Man (K-Tel)
22	19	ROAD TO RUIN	Ramones (Sire)
13	20	STREET LEGAL	Bob Dylan (CBS)
18	21	NATURAL HIGH	Commodores (Motown)
26	22	LIVE AND DANGEROUS	Thin Lizzy (Vertigo)
27	23	RUMOURS	Fleetwood Mac (Warner Bros.)
16	24	Q: ARE WE NOT MEN? A: WE ARE DEVO!	Devo (Virgin)
17	25	JAMES GALWAY PLAYS SONGS FOR ANNIE	James Galway (RCA Red Seal)
14	26	LEO SAYER	Leo Sayer (Chrysalis)
-	27	LOVE BITES	Buzzcocks (United Artists)
-	28	NEVER SAY DIE	Black Sabbath (Vertigo)
-	29	THAT'S WHAT FRIENDS ARE FOR	Johnny Mathis & Deniece Williams (CBS)
-	30	20 GOLDEN GREATS	Kinks (Ronco)

21 October 1978

1	1	GREASE	Soundtrack (RSO)
6	2	BIG WHEELS OF MOTOWN	Various Artists (Motown)
3	3	NIGHT FLIGHT TO VENUS	Boney M (Atlantic/Hansa)
4	4	BLOODY TOURISTS	10 c.c. (Mercury)
5	5	WAR OF THE WORLDS	Jeff Wayne (CBS)
9	6	CLASSIC ROCK	London Symphony Orchestra (K-Tel)
2	7	IMAGES	Don Williams (K-Tel)
15	8	STAGE	David Bowie (RCA)
10	9	TORMATO	Yes (Atlantic)
13	10	ROSE ROYCE STRIKES AGAIN	Rose Royce (Whitfield)
8	11	PARALLEL LINES	Blondie (Chrysalis)
7	12	SATURDAY NIGHT FEVER	Soundtrack (RSO)
27	13	LOVE BITES	Buzzcocks (United Artists)
15	14	OUT OF THE BLUE	Electric Light Orchestra (Jet)
14	15	DON'T LOOK BACK	Boston (Epic)
18	16	BROTHERHOOD OF MAN	Brotherhood of Man (K-Tel)
28	17	NEVER SAY DIE	Black Sabbath (Vertigo)
21	18	NATURAL HIGH	Commodores (Motown)
-	19	LIVE & MORE	Donna Summer (Casablanca)
11	20	WHO ARE YOU	Who (Polydor)
26	21	LEO SAYER	Leo Sayer (Chrysalis)
-	22	LIVE BURSTING OUT	Jethro Tull (Chrysalis)
-	23	TO THE LIMIT	Joan Armatrading (A&M)
24	24	Q: ARE WE NOT MEN? A: WE ARE DEVO!	Devo (Virgin)
19	25	ROAD TO RUIN	Ramones (Sire)
30	26	20 GOLDEN GREATS	Kinks (Ronco)
12	27	THE BRIDE STRIPPED BARE	Bryan Ferry (Polydor)
-	28	BREATHLESS	Camel (Decca)
-	29	GREEN LIGHT	Cliff Richard (EMI)
-	30	JOURNEY TO ADDIS	Third World (Island)

28 October 1978

1	1	GREASE	Soundtrack (RSO)
5	2	WAR OF THE WORLDS	Jeff Wayne (CBS)
3	3	NIGHT FLIGHT TO VENUS	Boney M (Atlantic/Hansa)
2	3	BIG WHEELS OF MOTOWN	Various Artists (Motown)
7	5	IMAGES	Don Williams (K-Tel)
6	6	CLASSIC ROCK	London Symphony Orchestra (K-Tel)
4	7	BLOODY TOURISTS	10 c.c. (Mercury)
10	8	ROSE ROYCE STRIKES AGAIN	Rose Royce (Whitfield)
12	9	SATURDAY NIGHT FEVER	Soundtrack (RSO)
17	10	NEVER SAY DIE	Black Sabbath (Vertigo)
19	11	LIVE & MORE	Donna Summer (Casablanca)
13	12	LOVE BITES	Buzzcocks (United Artists)
8	13	STAGE	David Bowie (RCA)
16	14	BROTHERHOOD OF MAN	Brotherhood of Man (K-Tel)
14	15	OUT OF THE BLUE	Electric Light Orchestra (Jet)
-	16	SATIN CITY	Various Artists (CBS)
11	17	PARALLEL LINES	Blondie (Chrysalis)
22	18	LIVE BURSTING OUT	Jethro Tull (Chrysalis)
30	19	JOURNEY TO ADDIS	Third World (Island)
9	20	TORMATO	Yes (Atlantic)
-	21	WELL, WELL, SAID THE ROCKING CHAIR	Dean Friedman (Lifesong)
26	22	20 GOLDEN GREATS	Kinks (Ronco)
-	23	JAMES GALWAY PLAYS SONGS FOR ANNIE	James Galway (RCA Red Seal)
23	24	TO THE LIMIT	Joan Armatrading (A&M)
21	25	LEO SAYER	Leo Sayer (Chrysalis)
-	26	STREET LEGAL	Bob Dylan (CBS)
29	27	GREEN LIGHT	Cliff Richard (EMI)
-	28	ECSTASY	Various Artists (Lotus)
15	29	DON'T LOOK BACK	Boston (Epic)
-	30	A TONIC FOR THE TROOPS	Boomtown Rats (Ensign)

4 November 1978

1	1	GREASE	Soundtrack (RSO)
3	2	NIGHT FLIGHT TO VENUS	Boney M (Atlantic/Hansa)
3	3	BIG WHEELS OF MOTOWN	Various Artists (Motown)
2	4	WAR OF THE WORLDS	Jeff Wayne (CBS)
14	5	BROTHERHOOD OF MAN	Brotherhood of Man (K-Tel)
9	6	SATURDAY NIGHT FEVER	Soundtrack (RSO)
5	7	IMAGES	Don Williams (K-Tel)
17	8	PARALLEL LINES	Blondie (Chrysalis)
13	9	STAGE	David Bowie (RCA)
-	10	EMOTIONS	Various Artists (K-Tel)
8	11	ROSE ROYCE STRIKES AGAIN	Rose Royce (Whitfield)
15	12	OUT OF THE BLUE	Electric Light Orchestra (Jet)
6	13	CLASSIC ROCK	London Symphony Orchestra (K-Tel)
30	14	A TONIC FOR THE TROOPS	Boomtown Rats (Ensign)
25	15	LEO SAYER	Leo Sayer (Chrysalis)
7	16	BLOODY TOURISTS	10 c.c. (Mercury)
20	17	TORMATO	Yes (Atlantic)
18	18	LIVE BURSTING OUT	Jethro Tull (Chrysalis)
-	19	SOME ENCHANTED EVENING	Blue Oyster Cult (CBS)
12	20	LOVE BITES	Buzzcocks (United Artists)
24	21	TO THE LIMIT	Joan Armatrading (A&M)
-	22	GO 2	XTC (Virgin)
11	23	LIVE & MORE	Donna Summer (Casablanca)
-	24	25TH ANNIVERSARY ALBUM	Shirley Bassey (United Artists)
-	25	MANHATTAN TRANSFER LIVE	Manhattan Transfer (Atlantic)
-	26	MOVING TARGETS	Penetration (Virgin)
10	27	NEVER SAY DIE	Black Sabbath (Vertigo)
-	28	A SINGLE MAN	Elton John (Rocket)
-	29	EVEN NOW	Barry Manilow (Arista)
-	30	IF YOU CAN'T STAND THE HEAT	Status Quo (Vertigo)

The Buzzcocks' second LP, *Love Bites*, charted mid-October, peaked at 12 and would quit by mid-November. This also typified what happened with the classic singles of Manchester's finest. *What Do I Get* had peaked at 28; *I Don't Mind* never made the 30; *Love You More* had peaked at 22; *Ever Fallen In Love (With Someone You Shouldn't've)* was peaking at No.13 now. They never topped that. *Ever Fallen* would be a bigger hit for Fine Young Cannibals in 1987; Buzzcocks would re-form in the 1990s.

November – December 1978

11 November 1978

last	this		
1	1	GREASE	Soundtrack (RSO)
2	2	NIGHT FLIGHT TO VENUS	Boney M (Atlantic/Hansa)
4	3	WAR OF THE WORLDS	Jeff Wayne (CBS)
10	4	EMOTIONS	Various Artists (K-Tel)
7	5	IMAGES	Don Williams (K-Tel)
3	6	BIG WHEELS OF MOTOWN	Various Artists (Motown)
6	7	SATURDAY NIGHT FEVER	Soundtrack (RSO)
9	8	STAGE	David Bowie (RCA)
12	9	OUT OF THE BLUE	Electric Light Orchestra (Jet)
13	10	CLASSIC ROCK	London Symphony Orchestra (K-Tel)
8	11	PARALLEL LINES	Blondie (Chrysalis)
5	12	BROTHERHOOD OF MAN	Brotherhood of Man (K-Tel)
16	13	BLOODY TOURISTS	10 c.c. (Mercury)
28	14	A SINGLE MAN	Elton John (Rocket)
30	15	IF YOU CAN'T STAND THE HEAT	Status Quo (Vertigo)
-	16	ALL MOD CONS	Jam (Polydor)
-	17	I'M COMING HOME	Tom Jones (Lotus)
-	18	IF YOU WANT BLOOD YOU'VE GOT IT	AC/DC (Atlantic)
-	19	INNER SECRETS	Santana (CBS)
14	20	A TONIC FOR THE TROOPS	Boomtown Rats (Ensign)
-	21	WELL, WELL, SAID THE ROCKING CHAIR	Dean Friedman (Lifesong)
11	22	ROSE ROYCE STRIKES AGAIN	Rose Royce (Whitfield)
15	23	LEO SAYER	Leo Sayer (Chrysalis)
24	24	25TH ANNIVERSARY ALBUM	Shirley Bassey (United Artists)
25	25	MANHATTAN TRANSFER LIVE	Manhattan Transfer (Atlantic)
-	26	EXPRESSIONS	Don Williams (ABC)
17	27	TORMATO	Yes (Atlantic)
23	28	LIVE & MORE	Donna Summer (Casablanca)
-	29	THE AMAZING DARTS	Darts (K-Tel/Magnet)
-	30	ECSTASY	Various Artists (Lotus)

18 November 1978

1	1	GREASE	Soundtrack (RSO)
2	2	NIGHT FLIGHT TO VENUS	Boney M (Atlantic/Hansa)
15	3	IF YOU CAN'T STAND THE HEAT	Status Quo (Vertigo)
4	4	EMOTIONS	Various Artists (K-Tel)
14	5	A SINGLE MAN	Elton John (Rocket)
5	6	IMAGES	Don Williams (K-Tel)
20	7	A TONIC FOR THE TROOPS	Boomtown Rats (Ensign)
3	8	WAR OF THE WORLDS	Jeff Wayne (CBS)
6	9	BIG WHEELS OF MOTOWN	Various Artists (Motown)
7	10	SATURDAY NIGHT FEVER	Soundtrack (RSO)
16	11	ALL MOD CONS	Jam (Polydor)
12	12	BROTHERHOOD OF MAN	Brotherhood of Man (K-Tel)
9	13	OUT OF THE BLUE	Electric Light Orchestra (Jet)
11	14	PARALLEL LINES	Blondie (Chrysalis)
8	15	STAGE	David Bowie (RCA)
10	16	CLASSIC ROCK	London Symphony Orchestra (K-Tel)
28	17	LIVE & MORE	Donna Summer (Casablanca)
29	18	THE AMAZING DARTS	Darts (K-Tel/Magnet)
19	19	INNER SECRETS	Santana (CBS)
18	20	IF YOU WANT BLOOD YOU'VE GOT IT	AC/DC (Atlantic)
25	21	MANHATTAN TRANSFER LIVE	Manhattan Transfer (Atlantic)
23	22	LEO SAYER	Leo Sayer (Chrysalis)
27	23	TORMATO	Yes (Atlantic)
24	24	25TH ANNIVERSARY ALBUM	Shirley Bassey (United Artists)
-	25	JAZZ	Queen (EMI)
22	26	ROSE ROYCE STRIKES AGAIN	Rose Royce (Whitfield)
-	27	20 GOLDEN GREATS	Neil Diamond (MCA)
-	28	DON'T WALK BOOGIE	Various Artists (EMI)
13	29	BLOODY TOURISTS	10 c.c. (Mercury)
30	30	ECSTASY	Various Artists (Lotus)

25 November 1978

1	1	GREASE	Soundtrack (RSO)
4	2	EMOTIONS	Various Artists (K-Tel)
11	3	ALL MOD CONS	Jam (Polydor)
7	4	A TONIC FOR THE TROOPS	Boomtown Rats (Ensign)
5	5	A SINGLE MAN	Elton John (Rocket)
27	6	20 GOLDEN GREATS	Neil Diamond (MCA)
2	7	NIGHT FLIGHT TO VENUS	Boney M (Atlantic/Hansa)
3	8	IF YOU CAN'T STAND THE HEAT	Status Quo (Vertigo)
8	9	WAR OF THE WORLDS	Jeff Wayne (CBS)
13	10	OUT OF THE BLUE	Electric Light Orchestra (Jet)
21	10	MANHATTAN TRANSFER LIVE	Manhattan Transfer (Atlantic)
24	12	25TH ANNIVERSARY ALBUM	Shirley Bassey (United Artists)
25	13	JAZZ	Queen (EMI)
6	14	IMAGES	Don Williams (K-Tel)
-	15	EVERGREEN	Acker Bilk (Warwick)
17	16	LIVE & MORE	Donna Summer (Casablanca)
20	17	IF YOU WANT BLOOD YOU'VE GOT IT	AC/DC (Atlantic)
18	18	THE AMAZING DARTS	Darts (K-Tel/Magnet)
19	19	INNER SECRETS	Santana (CBS)
9	20	BIG WHEELS OF MOTOWN	Various Artists (Motown)
14	21	PARALLEL LINES	Blondie (Chrysalis)
-	22	GIVE 'EM ENOUGH ROPE	Clash (CBS)
23	23	TORMATO	Yes (Atlantic)
-	24	WELL, WELL, SAID THE ROCKING CHAIR	Dean Friedman (Lifesong)
12	25	BROTHERHOOD OF MAN	Brotherhood of Man (K-Tel)
-	26	40 GREATEST	Elvis Presley (RCA)
-	27	HEMISPHERES	Rush (Mercury)
-	28	LIONHEART	Kate Bush (EMI)
28	29	DON'T WALK BOOGIE	Various Artists (EMI)
-	30	EXPRESSIONS	Don Williams (ABC)

2 December 1978

1	1	GREASE	Soundtrack (RSO)
6	2	20 GOLDEN GREATS	Neil Diamond (MCA)
22	3	GIVE 'EM ENOUGH ROPE	Clash (CBS)
7	4	NIGHT FLIGHT TO VENUS	Boney M (Atlantic/Hansa)
2	5	EMOTIONS	Various Artists (K-Tel)
13	6	JAZZ	Queen (EMI)
-	7	MIDNIGHT HUSTLE	Various Artists (K-Tel)
8	8	IF YOU CAN'T STAND THE HEAT	Status Quo (Vertigo)
5	9	A SINGLE MAN	Elton John (Rocket)
9	10	WAR OF THE WORLDS	Jeff Wayne (CBS)
4	11	A TONIC FOR THE TROOPS	Boomtown Rats (Ensign)
14	11	IMAGES	Don Williams (K-Tel)
3	13	ALL MOD CONS	Jam (Polydor)
10	14	MANHATTAN TRANSFER LIVE	Manhattan Transfer (Atlantic)
12	15	25TH ANNIVERSARY ALBUM	Shirley Bassey (United Artists)
-	16	BLONDES HAVE MORE FUN	Rod Stewart (Riva)
-	17	BOOGIE FEVER	Various Artists (Ronco)
16	18	LIVE & MORE	Donna Summer (Casablanca)
15	19	EVERGREEN	Acker Bilk (Warwick)
18	20	THE AMAZING DARTS	Darts (K-Tel/Magnet)
28	21	LIONHEART	Kate Bush (EMI)
10	22	OUT OF THE BLUE	Electric Light Orchestra (Jet)
-	23	SATURDAY NIGHT FEVER	Soundtrack (RSO)
21	24	PARALLEL LINES	Blondie (Chrysalis)
-	25	THE SINGLES 1974-1978	Carpenters (A&M)
25	26	BROTHERHOOD OF MAN	Brotherhood of Man (K-Tel)
-	27	EVITA	London Cast (MCA)
-	28	THAT'S LIFE	Sham 69 (Polydor)
19	29	INNER SECRETS	Santana (CBS)
27	30	HEMISPHERES	Rush (Mercury)

Some disingenuous titles entered the charts. *All Mod Cons*, by the Jam, punned on the fact that this nifty and resourceful punk band had been founded on re-inventing the spirit of the early Who, Mod heroes supreme. *Ecstasy*, by Various Artists, did not refer with uncanny foresight to the designer-drug of the 1980s, and Queen's 6th hit album *Jazz* did not refer to its musical contents, which no more resembled jazz than *Classic Rock* resembled either rock or the classics (let alone classic rock).

December 1978

The second LP of Carpenters 45s leapt into the Top 3. Their 1974-78 hit singles had included revisits to perfectly harmless old songs like Hank Williams' *Jambalaya* and the Marvelettes' *Please Mr Postman*, plus songs that more readily deserved the Carpenter treatment – *Solitaire* and *There's A Kind Of Hush All Over The World* – plus something called *Calling Occupants Of Interplanetary Craft (The Recognized Anthem Of World Contact Day)* from 1977. Meanwhile enter Siouxsie & the Banshees and X Ray Spex.

January 1979

MOR ruled, most "new" entries were re-entries and the biggest new arrival, John Lydon's Public Image Ltd, was much less interesting than the Sex Pistols. The singles chart was almost as moribund: Village People's *Y.M.C.A.* was displaced at No.1 by Ian Dury's *Hit Me With Your Rhythm Stick* and other entrants included Buzzcocks' *Promises* (another re-entry) and *Hello This Is Joanie* by Paul Evans, his first appearance since *Seven Little Girls (Sitting In The Back Seat)*, No.25 for one week in 1959.

3 February 1979

last this
week

1	1	DON'T WALK, BOOGIE — Various Artists (EMI)
5	2	PARALLEL LINES — Blondie (Chrysalis)
4	3	GREATEST HITS 1976-1978 — Showaddywaddy (Arista)
7	4	ARMED FORCES — Elvis Costello (Radar)
2	5	THE SINGLES 1974-1978 — Carpenters (A&M)
6	6	ACTION REPLAY — Various Artists (K-Tel)
14	7	EQUINOXE — Jean-Michel Jarre (Polydor)
10	8	GREASE — Soundtrack (RSO)
19	9	NEW BOOTS AND PANTIES!! — Ian Dury & the Blockheads (Stiff)
8	10	A SINGLE MAN — Elton John (Rocket)
17	11	A TONIC FOR THE TROOPS — Boomtown Rats (Ensign)
12	12	NIGHT FLIGHT TO VENUS — Boney M (Atlantic/Hansa)
3	12	WINGS' GREATEST — Wings (Parlophone)
11	14	THE BEST OF EARTH WIND & FIRE, VOL. 1 — Earth Wind & Fire (CBS)
25	15	EVEN NOW — Barry Manilow (Arista)
8	16	BLONDES HAVE MORE FUN — Rod Stewart (Riva)
26	17	INCANTATIONS — Mike Oldfield (Virgin)
20	18	20 GOLDEN GREATS — Doris Day (Warwick)
16	19	WAR OF THE WORLDS — Jeff Wayne (CBS)
-	20	CRUISIN' — Village People (Mercury)
23	21	YOU DON'T BRING ME FLOWERS — Neil Diamond (CBS)
24	22	EMOTIONS — Various Artists (K-Tel)
15	23	20 GOLDEN GREATS — Neil Diamond (MCA)
-	24	52ND STREET — Billy Joel (CBS)
-	25	BAT OUT OF HELL — Meatloaf (Epic)
-	26	THE AMAZING DARTS — Darts (K-Tel/Magnet)
18	27	OUT OF THE BLUE — Electric Light Orchestra (Jet)
21	28	GIVE 'EM ENOUGH ROPE — Clash (CBS)
-	29	TOTALLY HOT — Olivia Newton-John (EMI)
13	30	MIDNIGHT HUSTLE — Various Artists (K-Tel)

10 February 1979

2	1	PARALLEL LINES — Blondie (Chrysalis)
6	2	ACTION REPLAY — Various Artists (K-Tel)
1	3	DON'T WALK, BOOGIE — Various Artists (EMI)
4	4	ARMED FORCES — Elvis Costello (Radar)
14	5	THE BEST OF EARTH WIND & FIRE, VOL. 1 — Earth Wind & Fire (CBS)
15	6	EVEN NOW — Barry Manilow (Arista)
9	7	NEW BOOTS AND PANTIES!! — Ian Dury & the Blockheads (Stiff)
3	8	GREATEST HITS 1976-1978 — Showaddywaddy (Arista)
10	9	A SINGLE MAN — Elton John (Rocket)
5	10	THE SINGLES 1974-1978 — Carpenters (A&M)
7	11	EQUINOXE — Jean-Michel Jarre (Polydor)
8	11	GREASE — Soundtrack (RSO)
12	13	WINGS' GREATEST — Wings (Parlophone)
16	14	BLONDES HAVE MORE FUN — Rod Stewart (Riva)
27	15	OUT OF THE BLUE — Electric Light Orchestra (Jet)
12	16	NIGHT FLIGHT TO VENUS — Boney M (Atlantic/Hansa)
11	17	A TONIC FOR THE TROOPS — Boomtown Rats (Ensign)
-	18	C'EST CHIC — Chic (Atlantic)
21	19	YOU DON'T BRING ME FLOWERS — Neil Diamond (CBS)
20	20	CRUISIN' — Village People (Mercury)
-	21	SPIRITS HAVING FLOWN — Bee Gees (RSO)
25	22	BAT OUT OF HELL — Meatloaf (Epic)
24	23	52ND STREET — Billy Joel (CBS)
23	24	20 GOLDEN GREATS — Neil Diamond (MCA)
17	25	INCANTATIONS — Mike Oldfield (Virgin)
-	26	COMMODORES' GREATEST HITS — Commodores (Motown)
-	27	THREE LIGHT YEARS — Electric Light Orchestra (Jet)
-	28	JAZZ — Queen (EMI)
19	29	WAR OF THE WORLDS — Jeff Wayne (CBS)
22	30	EMOTIONS — Various Artists (K-Tel)

17 February 1979

1	1	PARALLEL LINES — Blondie (Chrysalis)
2	2	ACTION REPLAY — Various Artists (K-Tel)
4	3	ARMED FORCES — Elvis Costello (Radar)
3	4	DON'T WALK, BOOGIE — Various Artists (EMI)
5	5	THE BEST OF EARTH WIND & FIRE, VOL. 1 — Earth Wind & Fire (CBS)
11	6	EQUINOXE — Jean-Michel Jarre (Polydor)
6	7	EVEN NOW — Barry Manilow (Arista)
13	8	WINGS' GREATEST — Wings (Parlophone)
7	9	NEW BOOTS AND PANTIES!! — Ian Dury & the Blockheads (Stiff)
11	10	GREASE — Soundtrack (RSO)
21	11	SPIRITS HAVING FLOWN — Bee Gees (RSO)
-	12	THE MARTY ROBBINS COLLECTION — Marty Robbins (Lotus)
14	12	BLONDES HAVE MORE FUN — Rod Stewart (Riva)
9	14	A SINGLE MAN — Elton John (Rocket)
-	15	STRANGERS IN THE NIGHT — UFO (Chrysalis)
18	16	C'EST CHIC — Chic (Atlantic)
25	17	INCANTATIONS — Mike Oldfield (Virgin)
23	18	52ND STREET — Billy Joel (CBS)
24	19	20 GOLDEN GREATS — Neil Diamond (MCA)
8	20	GREATEST HITS 1976-1978 — Showaddywaddy (Arista)
17	21	A TONIC FOR THE TROOPS — Boomtown Rats (Ensign)
28	22	JAZZ — Queen (EMI)
29	23	WAR OF THE WORLDS — Jeff Wayne (CBS)
10	24	THE SINGLES 1974-1978 — Carpenters (A&M)
15	25	OUT OF THE BLUE — Electric Light Orchestra (Jet)
-	26	TOTALLY HOT — Olivia Newton-John (EMI)
19	27	YOU DON'T BRING ME FLOWERS — Neil Diamond (CBS)
-	28	LIVE AND DANGEROUS — Thin Lizzy (Vertigo)
22	29	BAT OUT OF HELL — Meatloaf (Epic)
-	30	PLASTIC LETTERS — Blondie (Chrysalis)

24 February 1979

1	1	PARALLEL LINES — Blondie (Chrysalis)
11	2	SPIRITS HAVING FLOWN — Bee Gees (RSO)
2	3	ACTION REPLAY — Various Artists (K-Tel)
3	4	ARMED FORCES — Elvis Costello (Radar)
5	5	THE BEST OF EARTH WIND & FIRE, VOL. 1 — Earth Wind & Fire (CBS)
4	6	DON'T WALK, BOOGIE — Various Artists (EMI)
9	7	NEW BOOTS AND PANTIES!! — Ian Dury & the Blockheads (Stiff)
15	8	STRANGERS IN THE NIGHT — UFO (Chrysalis)
12	9	THE MARTY ROBBINS COLLECTION — Marty Robbins (Lotus)
6	10	EQUINOXE — Jean-Michel Jarre (Polydor)
8	11	WINGS' GREATEST — Wings (Parlophone)
-	12	THANK YOU VERY MUCH – REUNION CONCERT AT THE LONDON PALLADIUM — Cliff Richard & the Shadows (EMI)
16	13	C'EST CHIC — Chic (Atlantic)
12	14	BLONDES HAVE MORE FUN — Rod Stewart (Riva)
23	15	WAR OF THE WORLDS — Jeff Wayne (CBS)
7	16	EVEN NOW — Barry Manilow (Arista)
25	17	OUT OF THE BLUE — Electric Light Orchestra (Jet)
14	18	A SINGLE MAN — Elton John (Rocket)
19	19	20 GOLDEN GREATS — Neil Diamond (MCA)
-	20	NIGHT FLIGHT TO VENUS — Boney M (Atlantic/Hansa)
-	21	CRUISIN' — Village People (Mercury)
-	22	FORCE MAJEURE — Tangerine Dream (Virgin)
-	23	REFLECTIONS — George Hamilton IV (Lotus)
27	24	YOU DON'T BRING ME FLOWERS — Neil Diamond (CBS)
-	25	THE INCREDIBLE SHRINKING DICKIES — Dickies (A&M)
29	26	BAT OUT OF HELL — Meatloaf (Epic)
10	27	GREASE — Soundtrack (RSO)
18	28	52ND STREET — Billy Joel (CBS)
17	29	INCANTATIONS — Mike Oldfield (Virgin)
-	30	VALLEY OF THE DOLLS — Generation X (Chrysalis)

This month saw the death of Sid Vicious, whose solid contribution to music was his extraordinary filmed performance of *My Way*. He OD'd while on trial for the murder of girlfriend Nancy Spungen in New York's legendary Chelsea Hotel, where, among many other things, Bob Dylan said he'd written *Blonde On Blonde*'s *Sad-Eyed Lady Of The Lowlands*. Meanwhile Blondie, essentially Debbie Harry and guitarist Chris Stein, hit No.1. *Parallel Lines*, the group's third LP, would eventually sell 20 million worldwide.

March 1979

3 March 1979

last	this		
1	1	PARALLEL LINES	Blondie (Chrysalis)
4	2	ARMED FORCES	Elvis Costello (Radar)
2	3	SPIRITS HAVING FLOWN	Bee Gees (RSO)
3	4	ACTION REPLAY	Various Artists (K-Tel)
14	5	BLONDES HAVE MORE FUN	Rod Stewart (Riva)
9	6	THE MARTY ROBBINS COLLECTION	Marty Robbins (Lotus)
12	7	THANK YOU VERY MUCH – REUNION CONCERT AT THE LONDON PALLADIUM	Cliff Richard & the Shadows (EMI)
6	8	DON'T WALK, BOOGIE	Various Artists (EMI)
8	9	STRANGERS IN THE NIGHT	UFO (Chrysalis)
19	10	20 GOLDEN GREATS	Neil Diamond (MCA)
20	11	NIGHT FLIGHT TO VENUS	Boney M (Atlantic/Hansa)
5	12	THE BEST OF EARTH WIND & FIRE, VOL. 1	Earth Wind & Fire (CBS)
10	13	EQUINOXE	Jean-Michel Jarre (Polydor)
18	14	A SINGLE MAN	Elton John (Rocket)
7	15	NEW BOOTS AND PANTIES!!	Ian Dury & the Blockheads (Stiff)
17	16	OUT OF THE BLUE	Electric Light Orchestra (Jet)
26	17	BAT OUT OF HELL	Meatloaf (Epic)
11	17	WINGS' GREATEST	Wings (Parlophone)
13	19	C'EST CHIC	Chic (Atlantic)
27	20	GREASE	Soundtrack (RSO)
16	21	EVEN NOW	Barry Manilow (Arista)
21	22	CRUISIN'	Village People (Mercury)
22	23	FORCE MAJEURE	Tangerine Dream (Virgin)
15	24	WAR OF THE WORLDS	Jeff Wayne (CBS)
-	25	A COLLECTION OF THEIR 20 GREATEST HITS	Three Degrees (Epic)
25	26	THE INCREDIBLE SHRINKING DICKIES	Dickies (A&M)
-	27	THE CARS	Cars (Elektra)
-	28	LIVE HERALD	Steve Hillage (Virgin)
-	29	IMAGES	Don Williams (K-Tel)
28	30	52ND STREET	Billy Joel (CBS)

10 March 1979

last	this		
1	1	PARALLEL LINES	Blondie (Chrysalis)
3	2	SPIRITS HAVING FLOWN	Bee Gees (RSO)
2	3	ARMED FORCES	Elvis Costello (Radar)
4	4	ACTION REPLAY	Various Artists (K-Tel)
7	5	THANK YOU VERY MUCH – REUNION CONCERT AT THE LONDON PALLADIUM	Cliff Richard & the Shadows (EMI)
6	5	THE MARTY ROBBINS COLLECTION	Marty Robbins (Lotus)
5	7	BLONDES HAVE MORE FUN	Rod Stewart (Riva)
15	8	NEW BOOTS AND PANTIES!!	Ian Dury & the Blockheads (Stiff)
9	9	STRANGERS IN THE NIGHT	UFO (Chrysalis)
-	10	MANILOW MAGIC	Barry Manilow (Arista)
17	11	BAT OUT OF HELL	Meatloaf (Epic)
12	12	THE BEST OF EARTH WIND & FIRE, VOL. 1	Earth Wind & Fire (CBS)
17	13	WINGS' GREATEST HITS	Wings (Parlophone)
13	14	EQUINOXE	Jean-Michel Jarre (Polydor)
30	15	52ND STREET	Billy Joel (CBS)
19	16	C'EST CHIC	Chic (Atlantic)
-	17	DIRE STRAITS	Dire Straits (Vertigo)
10	17	20 GOLDEN GREATS	Neil Diamond (MCA)
26	19	THE INCREDIBLE SHRINKING DICKIES	Dickies (A&M)
16	20	OUT OF THE BLUE	Electric Light Orchestra (Jet)
-	21	THE GREAT ROCK'N'ROLL SWINDLE	Sex Pistols (Virgin)
20	22	GREASE	Soundtrack (RSO)
-	23	YOU DON'T BRING ME FLOWERS	Neil Diamond (CBS)
8	24	DON'T WALK, BOOGIE	Various Artists (EMI)
-	25	TURN THE MUSIC UP	Players Association (Vanguard)
21	26	EVEN NOW	Barry Manilow (Arista)
-	27	CLASSIC ROCK - THE SECOND MOVEMENT	London Symphony Orchestra (K-Tel)
24	28	WAR OF THE WORLDS	Jeff Wayne (CBS)
-	29	INFLAMMABLE MATERIAL	Stiff Little Fingers (Rough Trade)
25	30	A COLLECTION OF THEIR 20 GREATEST HITS	Three Degrees (Epic)

17 March 1979

last	this		
1	1	PARALLEL LINES	Blondie (Chrysalis)
2	2	SPIRITS HAVING FLOWN	Bee Gees (RSO)
10	3	MANILOW MAGIC	Barry Manilow (Arista)
3	4	ARMED FORCES	Elvis Costello (Radar)
16	5	C'EST CHIC	Chic (Atlantic)
5	6	THANK YOU VERY MUCH – REUNION CONCERT AT THE LONDON PALLADIUM	Cliff Richard & the Shadows (EMI)
5	7	THE MARTY ROBBINS COLLECTION	Marty Robbins (Lotus)
12	8	THE BEST OF EARTH WIND & FIRE, VOL. 1	Earth Wind & Fire (CBS)
7	9	BLONDES HAVE MORE FUN	Rod Stewart (Riva)
21	10	THE GREAT ROCK'N'ROLL SWINDLE	Sex Pistols (Virgin)
15	11	52ND STREET	Billy Joel (CBS)
-	12	LIVE (X CERT)	Stranglers (United Artists)
4	13	ACTION REPLAY	Various Artists (K-Tel)
9	14	STRANGERS IN THE NIGHT	UFO (Chrysalis)
8	15	NEW BOOTS AND PANTIES!!	Ian Dury & the Blockheads (Stiff)
11	16	BAT OUT OF HELL	Meatloaf (Epic)
14	17	EQUINOXE	Jean-Michel Jarre (Polydor)
17	18	DIRE STRAITS	Dire Straits (Vertigo)
22	19	GREASE	Soundtrack (RSO)
20	20	OUT OF THE BLUE	Electric Light Orchestra (Jet)
13	21	WINGS' GREATEST	Wings (Parlophone)
30	22	A COLLECTION OF THEIR 20 GREATEST HITS	Three Degrees (Epic)
-	23	CHEAP TRICK AT BUDOKAN	Cheap Trick (Epic)
19	24	THE INCREDIBLE SHRINKING DICKIES	Dickies (A&M)
28	25	WAR OF THE WORLDS	Jeff Wayne (CBS)
29	26	INFLAMMABLE MATERIAL	Stiff Little Fingers (Rough Trade)
25	27	TURN THE MUSIC UP	Players Association (Vanguard)
-	28	NEW DIMENSIONS	Three Degrees (Ariola)
-	29	FEETS DON'T FAIL ME NOW	Herbie Hancock (CBS)
17	30	20 GOLDEN GREATS	Neil Diamond (MCA)

24 March 1979

last	this		
2	1	SPIRITS HAVING FLOWN	Bee Gees (RSO)
1	2	PARALLEL LINES	Blondie (Chrysalis)
4	3	ARMED FORCES	Elvis Costello (Radar)
5	4	C'EST CHIC	Chic (Atlantic)
3	5	MANILOW MAGIC	Barry Manilow (Arista)
10	6	THE GREAT ROCK'N'ROLL SWINDLE	Sex Pistols (Virgin)
7	7	THE MARTY ROBBINS COLLECTION	Marty Robbins (Lotus)
18	8	DIRE STRAITS	Dire Straits (Vertigo)
22	9	A COLLECTION OF THEIR 20 GREATEST HITS	Three Degrees (Epic)
-	10	BARBRA STREISAND'S GREATEST HITS VOL 2	Barbra Streisand (CBS)
12	11	LIVE (X CERT)	Stranglers (United Artists)
6	12	THANK YOU VERY MUCH – REUNION CONCERT AT THE LONDON PALLADIUM	Cliff Richard & the Shadows (EMI)
8	13	THE BEST OF EARTH WIND & FIRE, VOL. 1	Earth Wind & Fire (CBS)
15	13	NEW BOOTS AND PANTIES!!	Ian Dury & the Blockheads (Stiff)
17	15	EQUINOXE	Jean-Michel Jarre (Polydor)
11	16	52ND STREET	Billy Joel (CBS)
-	17	DESOLATION ANGELS	Bad Company (Swan Song)
27	18	TURN THE MUSIC UP	Players Association (Vanguard)
-	19	SCARED TO DANCE	Skids (Virgin)
24	20	THE INCREDIBLE SHRINKING DICKIES	Dickies (A&M)
-	21	STATELESS	Lene Lovich (Stiff)
20	22	OUT OF THE BLUE	Electric Light Orchestra (Jet)
16	23	BAT OUT OF HELL	Meatloaf (Epic)
9	24	BLONDES HAVE MORE FUN	Rod Stewart (Riva)
-	25	SHEIK YERBOUTI	Frank Zappa (CBS)
23	26	CHEAP TRICK AT BUDOKAN	Cheap Trick (Epic)
-	27	FEEL NO FRET	Average White Band (RCA)
-	28	TRB 2	Tom Robinson Band (EMI)
-	29	NIGHT FLIGHT TO VENUS	Boney M (Atlantic/Hansa)
26	30	INFLAMMABLE MATERIAL	Stiff Little Fingers (Rough Trade)

March 10 saw the first arrival of a band so cosily 1970s-progressive-rock that it was surprising they'd secured a record deal at all in the prevailing climate: Dire Straits. *The Great Rock & Roll Swindle*, released after the Sex Pistols were no longer functioning, would peak at No.5. A Derek Jarman-style film of the same name was more interesting in prospect than reality. A single, coupling *Swindle* with *Rock Around The Clock*, would manage just three weeks in the Top 30 in October-November.

last week	this week	31 March 1979
4	1	C'EST CHIC Chic (Atlantic)
5	2	MANILOW MAGIC Barry Manilow (Arista)
1	3	SPIRITS HAVING FLOWN Bee Gees (RSO)
2	4	PARALLEL LINES Blondie (Chrysalis)
6	5	THE GREAT ROCK'N'ROLL SWINDLE Sex Pistols (Virgin)
10	6	BARBRA STREISAND'S GREATEST HITS VOL 2 Barbra Streisand (CBS)
3	7	ARMED FORCES Elvis Costello (Radar)
8	8	DIRE STRAITS Dire Straits (Vertigo)
9	9	A COLLECTION OF THEIR 20 GREATEST HITS Three Degrees (Epic)
16	10	52ND STREET Billy Joel (CBS)
23	11	BAT OUT OF HELL Meatloaf (Epic)
7	12	THE MARTY ROBBINS COLLECTION Marty Robbins (Lotus)
12	13	THANK YOU VERY MUCH – REUNION CONCERT AT THE LONDON PALLADIUM Cliff Richard & the Shadows (EMI)
11	14	LIVE (X CERT) Stranglers (United Artists)
15	15	EQUINOXE Jean-Michel Jarre (Polydor)
17	16	DESOLATION ANGELS Bad Company (Swan Song)
-	17	MANIFESTO Roxy Music (Polydor)
13	18	THE BEST OF EARTH WIND & FIRE, VOL. 1 Earth Wind & Fire (CBS)
27	19	FEEL NO FRET Average White Band (RCA)
28	20	TRB 2 Tom Robinson Band (EMI)
24	21	BLONDES HAVE MORE FUN Rod Stewart (Riva)
-	22	ACTION REPLAY Various Artists (K-Tel)
22	23	OUT OF THE BLUE Electric Light Orchestra (Jet)
-	24 20	GOLDEN GREATS Neil Diamond (MCA)
-	25	REFLECTIONS George Hamilton IV (Lotus)
19	26	SCARED TO DANCE Skids (Virgin)
25	27	SHEIK YERBOUTI Frank Zappa (CBS)
13	28	NEW BOOTS AND PANTIES!! Ian Dury & the Blockheads (Stiff)
29	29	NIGHT FLIGHT TO VENUS Boney M (Atlantic/Hansa)
-	30	BREAKFAST IN AMERICA Supertramp (A&M)

		7 April 1979
6	1	BARBRA STREISAND'S GREATEST HITS VOL 2 Barbra Streisand (CBS)
2	2	MANILOW MAGIC Barry Manilow (Arista)
4	3	PARALLEL LINES Blondie (Chrysalis)
3	4	SPIRITS HAVING FLOWN Bee Gees (RSO)
1	5	C'EST CHIC Chic (Atlantic)
5	6	THE GREAT ROCK'N'ROLL SWINDLE Sex Pistols (Virgin)
8	7	DIRE STRAITS Dire Straits (Vertigo)
7	8	ARMED FORCES Elvis Costello (Radar)
-	8	THE VERY BEST OF LEO SAYER Leo Sayer (Chrysalis)
9	10	A COLLECTION OF THEIR 20 GREATEST HITS Three Degrees (Epic)
30	11	BREAKFAST IN AMERICA Supertramp (A&M)
16	12	DESOLATION ANGELS Bad Company (Swan Song)
11	13	BAT OUT OF HELL Meatloaf (Epic)
12	14	THE MARTY ROBBINS COLLECTION Marty Robbins (Lotus)
18	15	THE BEST OF EARTH WIND & FIRE, VOL. 1 Earth Wind & Fire (CBS)
10	16	52ND STREET Billy Joel (CBS)
13	17	THANK YOU VERY MUCH – REUNION CONCERT AT THE LONDON PALLADIUM Cliff Richard & the Shadows (EMI)
19	18	FEEL NO FRET Average White Band (RCA)
-	19	TURN THE MUSIC UP Players Association (Vanguard)
28	20	NEW BOOTS AND PANTIES!! Ian Dury & the Blockheads (Stiff)
-	21	LIONHEART Kate Bush (EMI)
17	22	MANIFESTO Roxy Music (Polydor)
14	23	LIVE (X CERT) Stranglers (United Artists)
20	24	TRB 2 Tom Robinson Band (EMI)
15	25	EQUINOXE Jean-Michel Jarre (Polydor)
-	26	OVERKILL Motorhead (Bronze)
26	27	SCARED TO DANCE Skids (Virgin)
-	28	LOVE TRACK Gloria Gaynor (Polydor)
-	29	THE INCREDIBLE SHRINKING DICKIES Dickies (A&M)
-	30	STATELESS Lene Lovich (Stiff)

		14 April 1979
1	1	BARBRA STREISAND'S GREATEST HITS VOL 2 Barbra Streisand (CBS)
11	2	BREAKFAST IN AMERICA Supertramp (A&M)
5	3	C'EST CHIC Chic (Atlantic)
2	4	MANILOW MAGIC Barry Manilow (Arista)
7	5	DIRE STRAITS Dire Straits (Vertigo)
8	6	THE VERY BEST OF LEO SAYER Leo Sayer (Chrysalis)
3	7	PARALLEL LINES Blondie (Chrysalis)
4	8	SPIRITS HAVING FLOWN Bee Gees (RSO)
6	9	THE GREAT ROCK'N'ROLL SWINDLE Sex Pistols (Virgin)
8	10	ARMED FORCES Elvis Costello (Radar)
12	11	DESOLATION ANGELS Bad Company (Swan Song)
16	12	52ND STREET Billy Joel (CBS)
-	13	COUNTRY PORTRAITS Various Artists (Warwick)
22	14	MANIFESTO Roxy Music (Polydor)
21	15	LIONHEART Kate Bush (EMI)
10	16	A COLLECTION OF THEIR 20 GREATEST HITS Three Degrees (Epic)
14	17	THE MARTY ROBBINS COLLECTION Marty Robbins (Lotus)
18	18	FEEL NO FRET Average White Band (RCA)
13	19	BAT OUT OF HELL Meatloaf (Epic)
24	20	TRB 2 Tom Robinson Band (EMI)
27	21	SCARED TO DANCE Skids (Virgin)
-	22	YOU DON'T BRING ME FLOWERS Neil Diamond (CBS)
-	23	SQUEEZING OUT SPARKS Graham Parker & the Rumour (Vertigo)
25	24	EQUINOXE Jean-Michel Jarre (Polydor)
-	25	COUNTRY LIFE Various Artists (EMI)
15	26	THE BEST OF EARTH WIND & FIRE, VOL. 1 Earth Wind & Fire (CBS)
-	27	VAN HALEN II Van Halen (Warner Bros.)
19	28	TURN THE MUSIC UP Players Association (Vanguard)
-	29	IMPERIAL WIZARD David Essex (Mercury)
-	30	DISCO INFERNO Various Artists (K-Tel)

		21 April 1979
1	1	BARBRA STREISAND'S GREATEST HITS VOL 2 Barbra Streisand (CBS)
6	2	THE VERY BEST OF LEO SAYER Leo Sayer (Chrysalis)
3	3	C'EST CHIC Chic (Atlantic)
5	4	DIRE STRAITS Dire Straits (Vertigo)
4	5	MANILOW MAGIC Barry Manilow (Arista)
8	6	SPIRITS HAVING FLOWN Bee Gees (RSO)
7	7	PARALLEL LINES Blondie (Chrysalis)
9	8	THE GREAT ROCK'N'ROLL SWINDLE Sex Pistols (Virgin)
2	9	BREAKFAST IN AMERICA Supertramp (A&M)
15	10	LIONHEART Kate Bush (EMI)
13	11	COUNTRY PORTRAITS Various Artists (Warwick)
10	12	ARMED FORCES Elvis Costello (Radar)
30	13	DISCO INFERNO Various Artists (K-Tel)
17	14	THE MARTY ROBBINS COLLECTION Marty Robbins (Lotus)
14	15	MANIFESTO Roxy Music (Polydor)
18	16	FEEL NO FRET Average White Band (RCA)
26	17	THE BEST OF EARTH WIND & FIRE, VOL. 1 Earth Wind & Fire (CBS)
19	18	BAT OUT OF HELL Meatloaf (Epic)
16	19	A COLLECTION OF THEIR 20 GREATEST HITS Three Degrees (Epic)
29	20	IMPERIAL WIZARD David Essex (Mercury)
25	21	COUNTRY LIFE Various Artists (EMI)
28	22	TURN THE MUSIC UP Players Association (Vanguard)
-	23	SECOND HAND DAYLIGHT Magazine (Virgin)
11	24	DESOLATION ANGELS Bad Company (Swan Song)
27	25	VAN HALEN II Van Halen (Warner Bros.)
23	26	SQUEEZING OUT SPARKS Graham Parker & the Rumour (Vertigo)
-	27	THE CARS Cars (Elektra)
-	28	THE INCREDIBLE SHRINKING DICKIES Dickies (A&M)
12	29	52ND STREET Billy Joel (CBS)
20	30	TRB 2 Tom Robinson Band (EMI)

Frank Zappa had signed to Columbia, and *Sheik Yerbouti* (in at No.25 in March), the first LP of the partnership, thus got a special push, giving Zappa his biggest UK hit since 1969's *Hot Rats*. Motorhead's *Overkill* was their 2nd LP but their first Top 30 hit.

Likewise with Van Halen's *Van Halen II*. Neither had yet had a single. Original Buzzcock Howard Devoto's band Magazine had already a (minor) hit single with the beautfiully picture-sleeved *Shot By Both Sides*. *Secondhand Daylight* was their 2nd album.

April – May 1979

28 April 1979

Last	This	Album / Artist (Label)
2	1	THE VERY BEST OF LEO SAYER — Leo Sayer (Chrysalis)
1	2	BARBRA STREISAND'S GREATEST HITS VOL 2 — Barbra Streisand (CBS)
3	3	C'EST CHIC — Chic (Atlantic)
4	4	DIRE STRAITS — Dire Straits (Vertigo)
9	5	BREAKFAST IN AMERICA — Supertramp (A&M)
7	6	PARALLEL LINES — Blondie (Chrysalis)
6	7	SPIRITS HAVING FLOWN — Bee Gees (RSO)
8	8	THE GREAT ROCK'N'ROLL SWINDLE — Sex Pistols (Virgin)
19	9	A COLLECTION OF THEIR 20 GREATEST HITS — Three Degrees (Epic)
21	10	COUNTRY LIFE — Various Artists (EMI)
13	11	DISCO INFERNO — Various Artists (K-Tel)
25	12	VAN HALEN II — Van Halen (Warner Bros.)
10	13	LIONHEART — Kate Bush (EMI)
16	14	FEEL NO FRET — Average White Band (RCA)
11	15	COUNTRY PORTRAITS — Various Artists (Warwick)
5	16	MANILOW MAGIC — Barry Manilow (Arista)
-	17	FATE FOR BREAKFAST — Art Garfunkel (CBS)
18	18	BAT OUT OF HELL — Meatloaf (Epic)
-	19	LAST THE WHOLE NIGHT THROUGH — James Last (Polydor)
12	20	ARMED FORCES — Elvis Costello (Radar)
20	21	IMPERIAL WIZARD — David Essex (Mercury)
15	22	MANIFESTO — Roxy Music (Polydor)
-	23	LA (LIGHT ALBUM) — Beach Boys (Caribou)
-	24	THE MARK II PURPLE SINGLES — Deep Purple (Purple)
24	25	DESOLATION ANGELS — Bad Company (Swan Song)
29	26	52ND STREET — Billy Joel (CBS)
-	27	YOU DON'T BRING ME FLOWERS — Neil Diamond (CBS)
-	28	STRANGERS IN THE NIGHT — UFO (Chrysalis)
27	29	THE CARS — Cars (Elektra)
14	30	THE MARTY ROBBINS COLLECTION — Marty Robbins (Lotus)

5 May 1979

Last	This	Album / Artist (Label)
1	1	THE VERY BEST OF LEO SAYER — Leo Sayer (Chrysalis)
2	2	BARBRA STREISAND'S GREATEST HITS VOL 2 — Barbra Streisand (CBS)
5	3	BREAKFAST IN AMERICA — Supertramp (A&M)
3	4	C'EST CHIC — Chic (Atlantic)
10	4	COUNTRY LIFE — Various Artists (EMI)
4	6	DIRE STRAITS — Dire Straits (Vertigo)
6	7	PARALLEL LINES — Blondie (Chrysalis)
11	8	DISCO INFERNO — Various Artists (K-Tel)
17	9	FATE FOR BREAKFAST — Art Garfunkel (CBS)
7	10	SPIRITS HAVING FLOWN — Bee Gees (RSO)
13	11	LIONHEART — Kate Bush (EMI)
16	12	MANILOW MAGIC — Barry Manilow (Arista)
8	13	THE GREAT ROCK'N'ROLL SWINDLE — Sex Pistols (Virgin)
22	14	MANIFESTO — Roxy Music (Polydor)
15	15	COUNTRY PORTRAITS — Various Artists (Warwick)
20	16	ARMED FORCES — Elvis Costello (Radar)
14	17	FEEL NO FRET — Average White Band (RCA)
19	18	LAST THE WHOLE NIGHT THROUGH — James Last (Polydor)
21	19	IMPERIAL WIZARD — David Essex (Mercury)
9	20	A COLLECTION OF THEIR 20 GREATEST HITS — Three Degrees (Epic)
-	21	LIVIN' INSIDE YOUR LOVE — George Benson (Warner Bros.)
-	22	BLACK ROSE — Thin Lizzy (Phonogram)
23	23	LA (LIGHT ALBUM) — Beach Boys (Caribou)
-	24	WINGS' GREATEST — Wings (Parlophone)
12	25	VAN HALEN II — Van Halen (Warner Bros.)
17	26	BAT OUT OF HELL — Meatloaf (Epic)
24	27	THE MARK II PURPLE SINGLES — Deep Purple (Purple)
30	28	THE MARTY ROBBINS COLLECTION — Marty Robbins (Lotus)
-	29	WAR OF THE WORLDS — Jeff Wayne (CBS)
-	30	OVERKILL — Motorhead (Bronze)

12 May 1979

Last	This	Album / Artist (Label)
1	1	THE VERY BEST OF LEO SAYER — Leo Sayer (Chrysalis)
3	2	BREAKFAST IN AMERICA — Supertramp (A&M)
9	3	FATE FOR BREAKFAST — Art Garfunkel (CBS)
4	4	C'EST CHIC — Chic (Atlantic)
10	5	SPIRITS HAVING FLOWN — Bee Gees (RSO)
4	6	COUNTRY LIFE — Various Artists (EMI)
6	7	DIRE STRAITS — Dire Straits (Vertigo)
7	8	PARALLEL LINES — Blondie (Chrysalis)
2	9	BARBRA STREISAND'S GREATEST HITS VOL 2 — Barbra Streisand (CBS)
22	10	BLACK ROSE — Thin Lizzy (Phonogram)
18	11	LAST THE WHOLE NIGHT THROUGH — James Last (Polydor)
12	12	MANILOW MAGIC — Barry Manilow (Arista)
-	13	OUT OF THE BLUE — Electric Light Orchestra (Jet)
11	14	LIONHEART — Kate Bush (EMI)
20	15	A COLLECTION OF THEIR 20 GREATEST HITS — Three Degrees (Epic)
8	16	DISCO INFERNO — Various Artists (K-Tel)
13	17	THE GREAT ROCK'N'ROLL SWINDLE — Sex Pistols (Virgin)
-	18	VOULEZ VOUS — Abba (Epic)
14	19	MANIFESTO — Roxy Music (Polydor)
-	20	HI ENERGY — Various Artists (K-Tel)
-	21	OUTLANDOS D'AMOUR — Police (A&M)
26	22	BAT OUT OF HELL — Meatloaf (Epic)
27	23	THE MARK II PURPLE SINGLES — Deep Purple (Purple)
17	24	FEEL NO FRET — Average White Band (RCA)
16	25	ARMED FORCES — Elvis Costello (Radar)
21	26	LIVIN' INSIDE YOUR LOVE — George Benson (Warner Bros.)
19	27	IMPERIAL WIZARD — David Essex (Mercury)
29	28	WAR OF THE WORLDS — Jeff Wayne (CBS)
15	29	COUNTRY PORTRAITS — Various Artists (Warwick)
-	30	COOL FOR CATS — Squeeze (A&M)

19 May 1979

Last	This	Album / Artist (Label)
1	1	THE VERY BEST OF LEO SAYER — Leo Sayer (Chrysalis)
10	2	BLACK ROSE — Thin Lizzy (Phonogram)
3	3	FATE FOR BREAKFAST — Art Garfunkel (CBS)
2	4	BREAKFAST IN AMERICA — Supertramp (A&M)
7	5	DIRE STRAITS — Dire Straits (Vertigo)
6	6	COUNTRY LIFE — Various Artists (EMI)
8	7	PARALLEL LINES — Blondie (Chrysalis)
4	8	C'EST CHIC — Chic (Atlantic)
21	9	OUTLANDOS D'AMOUR — Police (A&M)
5	10	SPIRITS HAVING FLOWN — Bee Gees (RSO)
9	11	BARBRA STREISAND'S GREATEST HITS VOL 2 — Barbra Streisand (CBS)
18	12	VOULEZ VOUS — Abba (Epic)
11	13	LAST THE WHOLE NIGHT THROUGH — James Last (Polydor)
15	14	A COLLECTION OF THEIR 20 GREATEST HITS — Three Degrees (Epic)
19	15	MANIFESTO — Roxy Music (Polydor)
20	16	HI ENERGY — Various Artists (K-Tel)
14	17	LIONHEART — Kate Bush (EMI)
-	18	WE ARE FAMILY — Sister Sledge (Atlantic)
12	19	MANILOW MAGIC — Barry Manilow (Arista)
17	20	THE GREAT ROCK'N'ROLL SWINDLE — Sex Pistols (Virgin)
26	21	LIVIN' INSIDE YOUR LOVE — George Benson (Warner Bros.)
24	22	FEEL NO FRET — Average White Band (RCA)
27	23	IMPERIAL WIZARD — David Essex (Mercury)
16	24	DISCO INFERNO — Various Artists (K-Tel)
-	25	THE INCREDIBLE SHRINKING DICKIES — Dickies (A&M)
13	26	OUT OF THE BLUE — Electric Light Orchestra (Jet)
22	27	BAT OUT OF HELL — Meatloaf (Epic)
28	28	WAR OF THE WORLDS — Jeff Wayne (CBS)
23	29	THE MARK II PURPLE SINGLES — Deep Purple (Purple)
-	30	GO WEST — Village People (Mercury)

The chart of May 12 saw Police's Top 30 entry with debut album *Outlandos D'Amour*, a week after the single *Roxanne* (possibly their best) joined the other Top 30. *Roxanne* was not their first 45: *Can't Stand Losing You* had been issued in 1978 but would be released after the success of *Roxanne* and the band's album, and would peak at No.2 in August; October would see *Message In A Bottle* give them their first No.1 single and, with *Regatta de Blanc*, a No.1 album to go with it.

26 May 1979

last this week

last	this		
12	1	VOULEZ VOUS	Abba (Epic)
1	2	THE VERY BEST OF LEO SAYER	Leo Sayer (Chrysalis)
3	3	FATE FOR BREAKFAST	Art Garfunkel (CBS)
4	4	BREAKFAST IN AMERICA	Supertramp (A&M)
2	5	BLACK ROSE	Thin Lizzy (Phonogram)
7	6	PARALLEL LINES	Blondie (Chrysalis)
10	7	SPIRITS HAVING FLOWN	Bee Gees (RSO)
8	8	C'EST CHIC	Chic (Atlantic)
5	9	DIRE STRAITS	Dire Straits (Vertigo)
13	10	LAST THE WHOLE NIGHT THROUGH	James Last (Polydor)
15	11	MANIFESTO	Roxy Music (Polydor)
5	12	COUNTRY LIFE	Various Artists (EMI)
11	13	BARBRA STREISAND'S GREATEST HITS VOL 2	Barbra Streisand (CBS)
26	14	OUT OF THE BLUE	Electric Light Orchestra (Jet)
9	15	OUTLANDOS D'AMOUR	Police (A&M)
17	16	LIONHEART	Kate Bush (EMI)
19	17	MANILOW MAGIC	Barry Manilow (Arista)
16	18	HI ENERGY	Various Artists (K-Tel)
-	19	THE BILLIE JO SPEARS SINGLES ALBUM	Billie Jo Spears (United Artists)
14	20	A COLLECTION OF THEIR 20 GREATEST HITS	Three Degrees (Epic)
-	21	ARMED FORCES	Elvis Costello (Radar)
30	22	GO WEST	Village People (Mercury)
-	23	BOB DYLAN AT BUDOKAN	Bob Dylan (CBS)
21	24	LIVIN' INSIDE YOUR LOVE	George Benson (Warner Bros.)
-	25	THE UNDERTONES	Undertones (Sire)
-	26	BOOGIE BUS	Various Artists (Polystar)
18	27	WE ARE FAMILY	Sister Sledge (Atlantic)
20	28	THE GREAT ROCK'N'ROLL SWINDLE	Sex Pistols (Virgin)
28	29	WAR OF THE WORLDS	Jeff Wayne (CBS)
-	30	DO IT YOURSELF	Ian Dury & the Blockheads (Stiff)

2 June 1979

last	this		
1	1	VOULEZ VOUS	Abba (Epic)
2	2	THE VERY BEST OF LEO SAYER	Leo Sayer (Chrysalis)
3	3	FATE FOR BREAKFAST	Art Garfunkel (CBS)
4	4	BREAKFAST IN AMERICA	Supertramp (A&M)
6	5	PARALLEL LINES	Blondie (Chrysalis)
11	6	MANIFESTO	Roxy Music (Polydor)
5	7	BLACK ROSE	Thin Lizzy (Phonogram)
9	8	DIRE STRAITS	Dire Straits (Vertigo)
30	9	DO IT YOURSELF	Ian Dury & the Blockheads (Stiff)
19	10	THE BILLIE JO SPEARS SINGLES ALBUM	Billie Jo Spears (United Artists)
23	11	BOB DYLAN AT BUDOKAN	Bob Dylan (CBS)
7	12	SPIRITS HAVING FLOWN	Bee Gees (RSO)
10	13	LAST THE WHOLE NIGHT THROUGH	James Last (Polydor)
14	14	OUT OF THE BLUE	Electric Light Orchestra (Jet)
13	15	BARBRA STREISAND'S GREATEST HITS VOL 2	Barbra Streisand (CBS)
8	16	C'EST CHIC	Chic (Atlantic)
15	17	OUTLANDOS D'AMOUR	Police (A&M)
-	18	A MONUMENT TO BRITISH ROCK	Various Artists (Harvest)
25	19	THE UNDERTONES	Undertones (Sire)
12	20	COUNTRY LIFE	Various Artists (EMI)
17	21	MANILOW MAGIC	Barry Manilow (Arista)
16	22	LIONHEART	Kate Bush (EMI)
27	23	WE ARE FAMILY	Sister Sledge (Atlantic)
-	24	BAT OUT OF HELL	Meatloaf (Epic)
22	25	GO WEST	Village People (Mercury)
24	26	LIVIN' INSIDE YOUR LOVE	George Benson (Warner Bros.)
18	27	HI ENERGY	Various Artists (K-Tel)
28	28	THE GREAT ROCK'N'ROLL SWINDLE	Sex Pistols (Virgin)
-	29	SPECTRAL MORNINGS	Steve Hackett (Charisma)
-	30	ROCK LEGENDS	Various Artists (Ronco)

9 June 1979

last	this		
1	1	VOULEZ VOUS	Abba (Epic)
9	2	DO IT YOURSELF	Ian Dury & the Blockheads (Stiff)
5	3	PARALLEL LINES	Blondie (Chrysalis)
3	4	FATE FOR BREAKFAST	Art Garfunkel (CBS)
6	5	MANIFESTO	Roxy Music (Polydor)
2	6	THE VERY BEST OF LEO SAYER	Leo Sayer (Chrysalis)
4	7	BREAKFAST IN AMERICA	Supertramp (A&M)
11	8	CHEAP TRICK AT BUDOKAN	Bob Dylan (CBS)
7	9	BLACK ROSE	Thin Lizzy (Phonogram)
-	10	DISCOVERY	Electric Light Orchestra (Jet)
10	11	THE BILLIE JO SPEARS SINGLES ALBUM	Billie Jo Spears (United Artists)
8	12	DIRE STRAITS	Dire Straits (Vertigo)
17	13	OUTLANDOS D'AMOUR	Police (A&M)
13	14	LAST THE WHOLE NIGHT THROUGH	James Last (Polydor)
19	15	THE UNDERTONES	Undertones (Sire)
16	16	C'EST CHIC	Chic (Atlantic)
18	17	A MONUMENT TO BRITISH ROCK	Various Artists (Harvest)
12	18	SPIRITS HAVING FLOWN	Bee Gees (RSO)
20	19	COUNTRY LIFE	Various Artists (EMI)
23	20	WE ARE FAMILY	Sister Sledge (Atlantic)
25	21	GO WEST	Village People (Mercury)
14	22	OUT OF THE BLUE	Electric Light Orchestra (Jet)
15	23	BARBRA STREISAND'S GREATEST HITS VOL 2	Barbra Streisand (CBS)
-	24	LOVEDRIVE	Scorpions (Harvest)
29	25	SPECTRAL MORNINGS	Steve Hackett (Charisma)
-	26	KNUCKLE SANDWICH	Various Artists (EMI Int)
-	27	BOOGIE BUS	Various Artists (Polystar)
-	28	THIS IS IT	Various Artists (CBS)
26	29	LIVIN' INSIDE YOUR LOVE	George Benson (Warner Bros.)
21	30	MANILOW MAGIC	Barry Manilow (Arista)

16 June 1979

last	this		
1	1	VOULEZ VOUS	Abba (Epic)
2	2	DO IT YOURSELF	Ian Dury & the Blockheads (Stiff)
3	3	PARALLEL LINES	Blondie (Chrysalis)
10	4	DISCOVERY	Electric Light Orchestra (Jet)
5	5	MANIFESTO	Roxy Music (Polydor)
7	6	BREAKFAST IN AMERICA	Supertramp (A&M)
-	7	LODGER	David Bowie (RCA)
4	8	FATE FOR BREAKFAST	Art Garfunkel (CBS)
28	9	THIS IS IT	Various Artists (CBS)
14	10	LAST THE WHOLE NIGHT THROUGH	James Last (Polydor)
6	11	THE VERY BEST OF LEO SAYER	Leo Sayer (Chrysalis)
8	12	BOB DYLAN AT BUDOKAN	Bob Dylan (CBS)
9	13	BLACK ROSE	Thin Lizzy (Phonogram)
11	14	THE BILLIE JO SPEARS SINGLES ALBUM	Billie Jo Spears (United Artists)
-	15	NIGHT OWL	Gerry Rafferty (United Artists)
13	16	OUTLANDOS D'AMOUR	Police (A&M)
17	17	A MONUMENT TO BRITISH ROCK	Various Artists (Harvest)
12	18	DIRE STRAITS	Dire Straits (Vertigo)
26	19	KNUCKLE SANDWICH	Various Artists (EMI Int)
-	20	SKY	Sky (Ariola)
-	21	BAD GIRLS	Donna Summer (Casablanca)
27	22	BOOGIE BUS	Various Artists (Polystar)
-	23	COMMUNIQUE	Dire Straits (Phonogram)
15	24	THE UNDERTONES	Undertones (Sire)
18	25	SPIRITS HAVING FLOWN	Bee Gees (RSO)
-	26	I AM	Earth Wind & Fire (CBS)
-	27	ARMED FORCES	Elvis Costello (Radar)
16	28	C'EST CHIC	Chic (Atlantic)
-	29	CHEAP TRICK AT BUDOKAN	Cheap Trick (Epic)
-	30	RHAPSODIES	Rick Wakeman (A&M)

At the other No.10, the woman with the handbag entered. It would have seemed laughable if predicted in 1968 when posters declared "London Paris Rome Berlin, We Shall Fight And We Shall Win", the police attack on the Vietnam demo outside London's US Embassy politicised many hippies, and revolution was in the air. Now Margaret Thatcher was voted in, not least by thrusting young record-execs. Within months, huge musicbiz cutbacks meant that many found they'd voted themselves out of work.

June – July 1979

23 June 1979

last	this		
4	1	DISCOVERY	Electric Light Orchestra (Jet)
3	2	PARALLEL LINES	Blondie (Chrysalis)
1	3	VOULEZ VOUS	Abba (Epic)
5	4	MANIFESTO	Roxy Music (Polydor)
9	5	THIS IS IT	Various Artists (CBS)
7	6	LODGER	David Bowie (RCA)
2	7	DO IT YOURSELF	Ian Dury & the Blockheads (Stiff)
10	8	LAST THE WHOLE NIGHT THROUGH	James Last (Polydor)
20	9	SKY	Sky (Ariola)
6	10	BREAKFAST IN AMERICA	Supertramp (A&M)
11	11	THE VERY BEST OF LEO SAYER	Leo Sayer (Chrysalis)
15	12	NIGHT OWL	Gerry Rafferty (United Artists)
8	13	FATE FOR BREAKFAST	Art Garfunkel (CBS)
23	14	COMMUNIQUE	Dire Straits (Phonogram)
12	15	BOB DYLAN AT BUDOKAN	Bob Dylan (CBS)
-	16	REPLICAS	Tubeway Army (Beggars Banquet)
18	17	DIRE STRAITS	Dire Straits (Vertigo)
24	18	THE UNDERTONES	Undertones (Sire)
21	19	BAD GIRLS	Donna Summer (Casablanca)
13	20	BLACK ROSE	Thin Lizzy (Phonogram)
14	21	THE BILLIE JO SPEARS SINGLES ALBUM	Billie Jo Spears (United Artists)
26	22	I AM	Earth Wind & Fire (CBS)
17	23	A MONUMENT TO BRITISH ROCK	Various Artists (Harvest)
25	24	SPIRITS HAVING FLOWN	Bee Gees (RSO)
-	25	OUT OF THE BLUE	Electric Light Orchestra (Jet)
22	26	BOOGIE BUS	Various Artists (Polystar)
30	27	RHAPSODIES	Rick Wakeman (A&M)
28	28	C'EST CHIC	Chic (Atlantic)
-	29	GO WEST	Village People (Mercury)
-	30	WE ARE FAMILY	Sister Sledge (Atlantic)

30 June 1979

last	this		
1	1	DISCOVERY	Electric Light Orchestra (Jet)
2	2	PARALLEL LINES	Blondie (Chrysalis)
8	3	LAST THE WHOLE NIGHT THROUGH	James Last (Polydor)
14	4	COMMUNIQUE	Dire Straits (Phonogram)
3	5	VOULEZ VOUS	Abba (Epic)
7	6	DO IT YOURSELF	Ian Dury & the Blockheads (Stiff)
6	7	LODGER	David Bowie (RCA)
22	8	I AM	Earth Wind & Fire (CBS)
16	9	REPLICAS	Tubeway Army (Beggars Banquet)
12	10	NIGHT OWL	Gerry Rafferty (United Artists)
4	11	MANIFESTO	Roxy Music (Polydor)
11	12	THE VERY BEST OF LEO SAYER	Leo Sayer (Chrysalis)
9	13	SKY	Sky (Ariola)
10	14	BREAKFAST IN AMERICA	Supertramp (A&M)
-	15	BACK TO THE EGG	Wings (Parlophone)
19	16	BAD GIRLS	Donna Summer (Casablanca)
5	17	THIS IS IT	Various Artists (CBS)
13	18	FATE FOR BREAKFAST	Art Garfunkel (CBS)
26	19	BOOGIE BUS	Various Artists (Polystar)
20	20	BLACK ROSE	Thin Lizzy (Phonogram)
21	21	THE BILLIE JO SPEARS SINGLES ALBUM	Billie Jo Spears (United Artists)
15	22	BOB DYLAN AT BUDOKAN	Bob Dylan (CBS)
25	23	OUT OF THE BLUE	Electric Light Orchestra (Jet)
-	24	RICKIE LEE JONES	Rickie Lee Jones (Warner Bros.)
25	25	ARMED FORCES	Elvis Costello (Radar)
18	26	THE UNDERTONES	Undertones (Sire)
-	27	THAT SUMMER	Various Artists (Arista)
17	28	DIRE STRAITS	Dire Straits (Vertigo)
-	29	MANILOW MAGIC	Barry Manilow (Arista)
-	30	OUTLANDOS D'AMOUR	Police (A&M)

7 July 1979

last	this		
1	1	DISCOVERY	Electric Light Orchestra (Jet)
8	2	I AM	Earth Wind & Fire (CBS)
4	3	COMMUNIQUE	Dire Straits (Phonogram)
15	4	BACK TO THE EGG	Wings (Parlophone)
9	5	REPLICAS	Tubeway Army (Beggars Banquet)
3	6	LAST THE WHOLE NIGHT THROUGH	James Last (Polydor)
5	7	VOULEZ VOUS	Abba (Epic)
2	8	PARALLEL LINES	Blondie (Chrysalis)
6	9	DO IT YOURSELF	Ian Dury & the Blockheads (Stiff)
7	10	LODGER	David Bowie (RCA)
10	11	NIGHT OWL	Gerry Rafferty (United Artists)
11	12	MANIFESTO	Roxy Music (Polydor)
13	13	SKY	Sky (Ariola)
24	14	RICKIE LEE JONES	Rickie Lee Jones (Warner Bros.)
-	15	BRIDGES	John Williams (Lotus)
14	16	BREAKFAST IN AMERICA	Supertramp (A&M)
17	17	THIS IS IT	Various Artists (CBS)
20	18	BLACK ROSE	Thin Lizzy (Phonogram)
12	19	THE VERY BEST OF LEO SAYER	Leo Sayer (Chrysalis)
22	20	BOB DYLAN AT BUDOKAN	Bob Dylan (CBS)
21	21	THE BILLIE JO SPEARS SINGLES ALBUM	Billie Jo Spears (United Artists)
-	22	A MONUMENT TO BRITISH ROCK	Various Artists (Harvest)
30	23	OUTLANDOS D'AMOUR	Police (A&M)
29	24	MANILOW MAGIC	Barry Manilow (Arista)
18	25	FATE FOR BREAKFAST	Art Garfunkel (CBS)
-	26	THE KIDS ARE ALRIGHT	Who (Polydor)
28	27	DIRE STRAITS	Dire Straits (Vertigo)
-	28	BAT OUT OF HELL	Meatloaf (Epic)
19	29	BOOGIE BUS	Various Artists (Polystar)
-	30	REPEAT WHEN NECESSARY	Dave Edmunds (Swan Song)

14 July 1979

last	this		
8	1	PARALLEL LINES	Blondie (Chrysalis)
5	2	REPLICAS	Tubeway Army (Beggars Banquet)
1	3	DISCOVERY	Electric Light Orchestra (Jet)
2	4	I AM	Earth Wind & Fire (CBS)
6	5	LAST THE WHOLE NIGHT THROUGH	James Last (Polydor)
3	6	COMMUNIQUE	Dire Straits (Phonogram)
7	7	VOULEZ VOUS	Abba (Epic)
4	8	BACK TO THE EGG	Wings (Parlophone)
16	9	BREAKFAST IN AMERICA	Supertramp (A&M)
11	10	NIGHT OWL	Gerry Rafferty (United Artists)
15	11	BRIDGES	John Williams (Lotus)
13	12	SKY	Sky (Ariola)
12	13	MANIFESTO	Roxy Music (Polydor)
10	14	LODGER	David Bowie (RCA)
14	15	RICKIE LEE JONES	Rickie Lee Jones (Warner Bros.)
24	16	MANILOW MAGIC	Barry Manilow (Arista)
-	17	LIVE KILLERS	Queen (EMI)
19	18	THE VERY BEST OF LEO SAYER	Leo Sayer (Chrysalis)
9	19	DO IT YOURSELF	Ian Dury & the Blockheads (Stiff)
-	20	BAD GIRLS	Donna Summer (Casablanca)
20	21	BOB DYLAN AT BUDOKAN	Bob Dylan (CBS)
-	22	COOL FOR CATS	Squeeze (A&M)
18	23	BLACK ROSE	Thin Lizzy (Phonogram)
21	24	THE BILLIE JO SPEARS SINGLES ALBUM	Billie Jo Spears (United Artists)
17	25	THIS IS IT	Various Artists (CBS)
-	26	NEVER MIND THE BOLLOCKS HERE'S THE SEX PISTOLS	Sex Pistols (Virgin)
23	27	OUTLANDOS D'AMOUR	Police (A&M)
26	28	THE KIDS ARE ALRIGHT	Who (Polydor)
-	29	THE BEST DISCO ALBUM IN THE WORLD	Various Artists (Warner Bros.)
-	30	WE ARE FAMILY	Sister Sledge (Atlantic)

Tubeway Army's *Replicas* entered at No.16, and leapt on its way to the top of the album chart. Tubeway Army, not longhand for the Tubes, was actually Gary Numan, a small British wannabowie who would famously fly aeroplanes as a hobby. Tubeway Army had come from nowhere to top the singles chart of July 7 with *Are Friends Electric*. In their vapourtrails, debut album *Tubeway Army* would chart in August, and, credited to Numan, follow-up single *Cars* would be a second No.1 single in September.

last	this		
	week	**21 July 1979**	

21 July 1979

last	this		
2	1	REPLICAS	Tubeway Army
		(Beggars Banquet)	
4	2	I AM	Earth Wind & Fire (CBS)
3	3	DISCOVERY	
		Electric Light Orchestra (Jet)	
11	4	BRIDGES	
		John Williams (Lotus)	
7	5	VOULEZ VOUS	Abba (Epic)
17	6	LIVE KILLERS	Queen (EMI)
1	7	PARALLEL LINES	
		Blondie (Chrysalis)	
9	8	BREAKFAST IN AMERICA	
		Supertramp (A&M)	
5	9	LAST THE WHOLE NIGHT	
		THROUGH	
		James Last (Polydor)	
8	10	BACK TO THE EGG	
		Wings (Parlophone)	
6	11	COMMUNIQUE	
		Dire Straits (Phonogram)	
10	12	NIGHT OWL	
		Gerry Rafferty (United Artists)	
29	13	THE BEST DISCO ALBUM IN THE	
		WORLD	
		Various Artists (Warner Bros.)	
15	14	RICKIE LEE JONES	
		Rickie Lee Jones (Warner Bros.)	
12	15	SKY	Sky (Ariola)
14	16	LODGER	David Bowie (RCA)
13	17	MANIFESTO	
		Roxy Music (Polydor)	
19	18	DO IT YOURSELF	
		Ian Dury & the Blockheads (Stiff)	
16	19	MANILOW MAGIC	
		Barry Manilow (Arista)	
-	20	THE WORLD IS FULL OF	
		MARRIED MEN - SOUNDTRACK	
		Various Artists (Ronco)	
-	21	RUST NEVER SLEEPS	
		Neil Young (Reprise)	
20	22	BAD GIRLS	
		Donna Summer (Casablanca)	
-	23	THE BEST OF THE DOOLEYS	
		Dooleys (GTO)	
-	24	CANDY-O	Cars (Elektra)
25	25	THIS IS IT	
		Various Artists (CBS)	
27	26	OUTLANDOS D'AMOUR	
		Police (A&M)	
-	27	THE WARRIORS	
		Soundtrack (A&M)	
-	28	MORNING DANCE	
		Spyro Gyra (Infinity)	
-	29	REPEAT WHEN NECESSARY	
		Dave Edmunds (Swan Song)	
23	30	BLACK ROSE	
		Thin Lizzy (Phonogram)	

28 July 1979

1	1	REPLICAS	Tubeway Army
		(Beggars Banquet)	
3	2	DISCOVERY	
		Electric Light Orchestra (Jet)	
13	3	THE BEST DISCO ALBUM IN THE	
		WORLD	
		Various Artists (Warner Bros.)	
8	4	BREAKFAST IN AMERICA	
		Supertramp (A&M)	
7	5	PARALLEL LINES	
		Blondie (Chrysalis)	
4	6	BRIDGES	
		John Williams (Lotus)	
11	7	COMMUNIQUE	
		Dire Straits (Phonogram)	
2	8	I AM	Earth Wind & Fire (CBS)
5	9	VOULEZ VOUS	
		Abba (Epic)	
6	9	LIVE KILLERS	Queen (EMI)
12	11	NIGHT OWL	
		Gerry Rafferty (United Artists)	
9	12	LAST THE WHOLE NIGHT	
		THROUGH	
		James Last (Polydor)	
10	13	BACK TO THE EGG	
		Wings (Parlophone)	
21	14	RUST NEVER SLEEPS	
		Neil Young (Reprise)	
19	15	MANILOW MAGIC	
		Barry Manilow (Arista)	
18	15	DO IT YOURSELF	
		Ian Dury & the Blockheads (Stiff)	
26	17	OUTLANDOS D'AMOUR	
		Police (A&M)	
16	18	LODGER	David Bowie (RCA)
14	19	RICKIE LEE JONES	
		Rickie Lee Jones (Warner Bros.)	
22	20	BAD GIRLS	
		Donna Summer (Casablanca)	
23	21	THE BEST OF THE DOOLEYS	
		Dooleys (GTO)	
-	22	FATE FOR BREAKFAST	
		Art Garfunkel (CBS)	
15	23	SKY	Sky (Ariola)
17	24	MANIFESTO	
		Roxy Music (Polydor)	
-	25	THE VERY BEST OF LEO SAYER	
		Leo Sayer (Chrysalis)	
24	26	CANDY-O	Cars (Elektra)
28	27	MORNING DANCE	
		Spyro Gyra (Infinity)	
-	28	STREET LIFE	Crusaders (MCA)
-	29	DIRE STRAITS	
		Dire Straits (Vertigo)	
-	30	THE GREAT ROCK'N'ROLL	
		SWINDLE	Sex Pistols (Virgin)

4 August 1979

3	1	THE BEST DISCO ALBUM IN THE	
		WORLD	
		Various Artists (Warner Bros.)	
1	2	REPLICAS	Tubeway Army
		(Beggars Banquet)	
2	3	DISCOVERY	
		Electric Light Orchestra (Jet)	
9	4	VOULEZ VOUS	Abba (Epic)
7	5	COMMUNIQUE	
		Dire Straits (Phonogram)	
5	6	PARALLEL LINES	
		Blondie (Chrysalis)	
8	7	I AM	Earth Wind & Fire (CBS)
4	8	BREAKFAST IN AMERICA	
		Supertramp (A&M)	
6	9	BRIDGES	
		John Williams (Lotus)	
17	10	OUTLANDOS D'AMOUR	
		Police (A&M)	
11	11	NIGHT OWL	
		Gerry Rafferty (United Artists)	
9	11	LIVE KILLERS	Queen (EMI)
19	13	RICKIE LEE JONES	
		Rickie Lee Jones (Warner Bros.)	
18	14	LODGER	David Bowie (RCA)
12	15	LAST THE WHOLE NIGHT	
		THROUGH	
		James Last (Polydor)	
15	16	MANILOW MAGIC	
		Barry Manilow (Arista)	
13	17	BACK TO THE EGG	
		Wings (Parlophone)	
14	18	RUST NEVER SLEEPS	
		Neil Young (Reprise)	
15	19	DO IT YOURSELF	
		Ian Dury & the Blockheads (Stiff)	
21	20	THE BEST OF THE DOOLEYS	
		Dooleys (GTO)	
22	21	FATE FOR BREAKFAST	
		Art Garfunkel (CBS)	
20	22	BAD GIRLS	
		Donna Summer (Casablanca)	
25	23	THE VERY BEST OF LEO SAYER	
		Leo Sayer (Chrysalis)	
24	24	MANIFESTO	
		Roxy Music (Polydor)	
30	25	THE GREAT ROCK'N'ROLL	
		SWINDLE	Sex Pistols (Virgin)
27	26	MORNING DANCE	
		Spyro Gyra (Infinity)	
26	27	CANDY-O	Cars (Elektra)
28	28	STREET LIFE	Crusaders (MCA)
-	29	20 GOLDEN GREATS	
		Beach Boys (Capitol)	
-	30	SOME PRODUCT - CARRI ON	
		SEX PISTOLS	
		Sex Pistols (Virgin)	

11 August 1979

1	1	THE BEST DISCO ALBUM IN THE	
		WORLD	
		Various Artists (Warner Bros.)	
2	2	REPLICAS	Tubeway Army
		(Beggars Banquet)	
3	3	DISCOVERY	
		Electric Light Orchestra (Jet)	
7	4	I AM	Earth Wind & Fire (CBS)
8	5	BREAKFAST IN AMERICA	
		Supertramp (A&M)	
4	6	VOULEZ VOUS	Abba (Epic)
9	7	BRIDGES	
		John Williams (Lotus)	
6	8	PARALLEL LINES	
		Blondie (Chrysalis)	
5	9	COMMUNIQUE	
		Dire Straits (Phonogram)	
20	10	THE BEST OF THE DOOLEYS	
		Dooleys (GTO)	
10	11	OUTLANDOS D'AMOUR	
		Police (A&M)	
14	12	LODGER	David Bowie (RCA)
19	13	DO IT YOURSELF	
		Ian Dury & the Blockheads (Stiff)	
11	14	LIVE KILLERS	Queen (EMI)
17	15	BACK TO THE EGG	
		Wings (Parlophone)	
28	16	STREET LIFE	Crusaders (MCA)
11	17	NIGHT OWL	
		Gerry Rafferty (United Artists)	
26	18	MORNING DANCE	
		Spyro Gyra (Infinity)	
18	19	RUST NEVER SLEEPS	
		Neil Young (Reprise)	
30	20	SOME PRODUCT - CARRI ON	
		SEX PISTOLS	
		Sex Pistols (Virgin)	
22	21	BAD GIRLS	
		Donna Summer (Casablanca)	
29	22	20 GOLDEN GREATS	
		Beach Boys (Capitol)	
23	23	THE VERY BEST OF LEO SAYER	
		Leo Sayer (Chrysalis)	
-	24	THE KIDS ARE ALRIGHT	
		Who (Polydor)	
27	25	CANDY-O	Cars (Elektra)
-	26	GO WEST	
		Village People (Mercury)	
16	27	MANILOW MAGIC	
		Barry Manilow (Arista)	
13	28	RICKIE LEE JONES	
		Rickie Lee Jones (Warner Bros.)	
-	29	THE BOSS	
		Diana Ross (Motown)	
24	30	MANIFESTO	
		Roxy Music (Polydor)	

Jazz-funk outfit the Crusaders were jumping up the singles chart with the title track of their *Street Life* LP. The single, which featured Randy Crawford as uncredited vocalist, would peak at No.4, the album at 5, both on September 22. They would enjoy an extremely minor 1981 hit single, *I'm So Glad I'm Standing Here Today*, with "featured vocalist Joe Cocker". Veteran Neil Young shared the credits with his sometime band Crazy Horse on *Rust Never Sleeps*, his most successful album since 1972's *Harvest*.

August – September 1979

18 August 1979

last	this	
1	1	THE BEST DISCO ALBUM IN THE WORLD — Various Artists (Warner Bros.)
3	2	DISCOVERY — Electric Light Orchestra (Jet)
2	3	REPLICAS — Tubeway Army (Beggars Banquet)
4	4	I AM — Earth Wind & Fire (CBS)
5	4	BREAKFAST IN AMERICA — Supertramp (A&M)
6	5	VOULEZ VOUS — Abba (Epic)
11	7	OUTLANDOS D'AMOUR — Police (A&M)
20	8	SOME PRODUCT - CARRI ON SEX PISTOLS — Sex Pistols (Virgin)
10	9	THE BEST OF THE DOOLEYS — Dooleys (GTO)
8	10	PARALLEL LINES — Blondie (Chrysalis)
9	11	COMMUNIQUE — Dire Straits (Phonogram)
7	12	BRIDGES — John Williams (Lotus)
16	13	STREET LIFE — Crusaders (MCA)
17	14	NIGHT OWL — Gerry Rafferty (United Artists)
13	15	DO IT YOURSELF — Ian Dury & the Blockheads (Stiff)
18	16	MORNING DANCE — Spyro Gyra (Infinity)
19	17	RUST NEVER SLEEPS — Neil Young (Reprise)
14	18	LIVE KILLERS — Queen (EMI)
-	19	EXPOSED — Mike Oldfield (Virgin)
27	20	MANILOW MAGIC — Barry Manilow (Arista)
12	21	LODGER — David Bowie (RCA)
26	22	GO WEST — Village People (Mercury)
22	23	20 GOLDEN GREATS — Beach Boys (Capitol)
30	24	MANIFESTO — Roxy Music (Polydor)
-	25	OUT OF THE BLUE — Electric Light Orchestra (Jet)
23	26	THE VERY BEST OF LEO SAYER — Leo Sayer (Chrysalis)
-	27	WELCOME TO THE CRUISE — Judie Tzuke (Rocket)
-	28	DIRE STRAITS — Dire Straits (Vertigo)
-	29	B-52s — B-52s (Island)
15	30	BACK TO THE EGG — Wings (Parlophone)

25 August 1979

last	this	
2	1	DISCOVERY — Electric Light Orchestra (Jet)
1	2	THE BEST DISCO ALBUM IN THE WORLD — Various Artists (Warner Bros.)
3	3	REPLICAS — Tubeway Army (Beggars Banquet)
4	4	BREAKFAST IN AMERICA — Supertramp (A&M)
4	5	I AM — Earth Wind & Fire (CBS)
5	6	VOULEZ VOUS — Abba (Epic)
8	7	SOME PRODUCT - CARRI ON SEX PISTOLS — Sex Pistols (Virgin)
9	8	THE BEST OF THE DOOLEYS — Dooleys (GTO)
16	9	MORNING DANCE — Spyro Gyra (Infinity)
13	10	STREET LIFE — Crusaders (MCA)
7	11	OUTLANDOS D'AMOUR — Police (A&M)
19	12	EXPOSED — Mike Oldfield (Virgin)
10	13	PARALLEL LINES — Blondie (Chrysalis)
18	14	LIVE KILLERS — Queen (EMI)
-	15	HIGHWAY TO HELL — AC/DC (Atlantic)
12	16	BRIDGES — John Williams (Lotus)
14	17	NIGHT OWL — Gerry Rafferty (United Artists)
20	18	MANILOW MAGIC — Barry Manilow (Arista)
-	19	DOWN TO EARTH — Rainbow (Polydor)
23	20	20 GOLDEN GREATS — Beach Boys (Capitol)
11	21	COMMUNIQUE — Dire Straits (Phonogram)
26	22	THE VERY BEST OF LEO SAYER — Leo Sayer (Chrysalis)
15	23	DO IT YOURSELF — Ian Dury & the Blockheads (Stiff)
-	24	MIDNIGHT MAGIC — Commodores (Motown)
-	25	TEENAGE WARNING — Angelic Upstarts (Warner Bros.)
-	26	BAD GIRLS — Donna Summer (Casablanca)
27	27	RISQUE — Chic (Atlantic)
27	28	WELCOME TO THE CRUISE — Judie Tzuke (Rocket)
17	29	RUST NEVER SLEEPS — Neil Young (Reprise)
-	30	THE WARRIORS — Soundtrack (A&M)

1 September 1979

last	this	
2	1	THE BEST DISCO ALBUM IN THE WORLD — Various Artists (Warner Bros.)
1	2	DISCOVERY — Electric Light Orchestra (Jet)
3	3	REPLICAS — Tubeway Army (Beggars Banquet)
5	4	I AM — Earth Wind & Fire (CBS)
4	5	BREAKFAST IN AMERICA — Supertramp (A&M)
10	6	STREET LIFE — Crusaders (MCA)
19	7	DOWN TO EARTH — Rainbow (Polydor)
7	8	SOME PRODUCT - CARRI ON SEX PISTOLS — Sex Pistols (Virgin)
9	9	MORNING DANCE — Spyro Gyra (Infinity)
15	10	HIGHWAY TO HELL — AC/DC (Atlantic)
6	11	VOULEZ VOUS — Abba (Epic)
-	12	IN THROUGH THE OUT DOOR — Led Zeppelin (Swan Song)
13	13	PARALLEL LINES — Blondie (Chrysalis)
11	14	OUTLANDOS D'AMOUR — Police (A&M)
16	15	BRIDGES — John Williams (Lotus)
8	16	THE BEST OF THE DOOLEYS — Dooleys (GTO)
-	17	SLOW TRAIN COMING — Bob Dylan (CBS)
12	18	EXPOSED — Mike Oldfield (Virgin)
14	19	LIVE KILLERS — Queen (EMI)
21	20	COMMUNIQUE — Dire Straits (Phonogram)
17	21	NIGHT OWL — Gerry Rafferty (United Artists)
-	22	MANIFESTO — Roxy Music (Polydor)
-	23	TUBEWAY ARMY — Tubeway Army (Beggars Banquet)
23	24	DO IT YOURSELF — Ian Dury & the Blockheads (Stiff)
27	25	RISQUE — Chic (Atlantic)
28	26	WELCOME TO THE CRUISE — Judie Tzuke (Rocket)
18	27	MANILOW MAGIC — Barry Manilow (Arista)
29	28	RUST NEVER SLEEPS — Neil Young (Reprise)
25	29	TEENAGE WARNING — Angelic Upstarts (Warner Bros.)
26	30	BAD GIRLS — Donna Summer (Casablanca)

8 September 1979

last	this	
2	1	DISCOVERY — Electric Light Orchestra (Jet)
4	2	I AM — Earth Wind & Fire (CBS)
5	3	BREAKFAST IN AMERICA — Supertramp (A&M)
1	4	THE BEST DISCO ALBUM IN THE WORLD — Various Artists (Warner Bros.)
6	5	STREET LIFE — Crusaders (MCA)
13	6	PARALLEL LINES — Blondie (Chrysalis)
9	7	MORNING DANCE — Spyro Gyra (Infinity)
11	8	VOULEZ VOUS — Abba (Epic)
8	9	SOME PRODUCT - CARRI ON SEX PISTOLS — Sex Pistols (Virgin)
10	10	HIGHWAY TO HELL — AC/DC (Atlantic)
19	11	LIVE KILLERS — Queen (EMI)
14	12	OUTLANDOS D'AMOUR — Police (A&M)
3	12	REPLICAS — Tubeway Army (Beggars Banquet)
7	14	DOWN TO EARTH — Rainbow (Polydor)
12	15	IN THROUGH THE OUT DOOR — Led Zeppelin (Swan Song)
21	16	NIGHT OWL — Gerry Rafferty (United Artists)
25	17	RISQUE — Chic (Atlantic)
15	18	BRIDGES — John Williams (Lotus)
26	19	WELCOME TO THE CRUISE — Judie Tzuke (Rocket)
16	20	THE BEST OF THE DOOLEYS — Dooleys (GTO)
-	21	MIDNIGHT MAGIC — Commodores (Motown)
23	22	TUBEWAY ARMY — Tubeway Army (Beggars Banquet)
18	23	EXPOSED — Mike Oldfield (Virgin)
20	24	COMMUNIQUE — Dire Straits (Phonogram)
24	25	DO IT YOURSELF — Ian Dury & the Blockheads (Stiff)
17	26	SLOW TRAIN COMING — Bob Dylan (CBS)
28	27	RUST NEVER SLEEPS — Neil Young (Reprise)
-	28	RUMOURS — Fleetwood Mac (Warner Bros.)
29	29	TEENAGE WARNING — Angelic Upstarts (Warner Bros.)
22	30	MANIFESTO — Roxy Music (Polydor)

Bob Dylan's controversial *Slow Train Coming*, an evangelising Christian harangue that had the old New Leftie tagged as Born Again, came in at No.17, plummeted to No.26 and would leap straight up to No.2 the following week. This suggested supply or distribution problems on release, rather than a very wayward public response. The album, musically and lyrically rich, had been produced at Muscle Shoals studios in Sheffield Alabama using Atlantic Records veteran producer and atheist Jerry Wexler.

15 September 1979

last week	this week	Album
1	1	DISCOVERY — Electric Light Orchestra (Jet)
26	2	SLOW TRAIN COMING — Bob Dylan (CBS)
2	3	I AM — Earth Wind & Fire (CBS)
15	4	IN THROUGH THE OUT DOOR — Led Zeppelin (Swan Song)
8	5	VOULEZ VOUS — Abba (Epic)
12	6	REPLICAS — Tubeway Army (Beggars Banquet)
3	7	BREAKFAST IN AMERICA — Supertramp (A&M)
4	8	THE BEST DISCO ALBUM IN THE WORLD — Various Artists (Warner Bros.)
5	9	STREET LIFE — Crusaders (MCA)
14	10	DOWN TO EARTH — Rainbow (Polydor)
6	11	PARALLEL LINES — Blondie (Chrysalis)
30	12	MANIFESTO — Roxy Music (Polydor)
12	13	OUTLANDOS D'AMOUR — Police (A&M)
9	14	SOME PRODUCT - CARRI ON SEX PISTOLS — Sex Pistols (Virgin)
20	15	THE BEST OF THE DOOLEYS — Dooleys (GTO)
7	16	MORNING DANCE — Spyro Gyra (Infinity)
-	17	ROCK 'N' ROLL JUVENILE — Cliff Richard (EMI)
21	18	MIDNIGHT MAGIC — Commodores (Motown)
-	19	THE PLEASURE PRINCIPLE — Gary Numan (Beggars Banquet)
16	20	NIGHT OWL — Gerry Rafferty (United Artists)
10	21	HIGHWAY TO HELL — AC/DC (Atlantic)
22	22	TUBEWAY ARMY — Tubeway Army (Beggars Banquet)
19	23	WELCOME TO THE CRUISE — Judie Tzuke (Rocket)
-	24	STRING OF HITS — Shadows (EMI)
18	25	BRIDGES — John Williams (Lotus)
25	26	DO IT YOURSELF — Ian Dury & the Blockheads (Stiff)
11	27	LIVE KILLERS — Queen (EMI)
-	28	LOOK SHARP — Joe Jackson (A&M)
-	29	INTO THE MUSIC — Van Morrison (Vertigo)
-	30	DRUMS AND WIRES — XTC (Virgin)

22 September 1979

last week	this week	Album
1	1	DISCOVERY — Electric Light Orchestra (Jet)
4	2	IN THROUGH THE OUT DOOR — Led Zeppelin (Swan Song)
2	3	SLOW TRAIN COMING — Bob Dylan (CBS)
17	4	ROCK 'N' ROLL JUVENILE — Cliff Richard (EMI)
9	5	STREET LIFE — Crusaders (MCA)
3	6	I AM — Earth Wind & Fire (CBS)
8	7	THE BEST DISCO ALBUM IN THE WORLD — Various Artists (Warner Bros.)
7	8	BREAKFAST IN AMERICA — Supertramp (A&M)
19	9	THE PLEASURE PRINCIPLE — Gary Numan (Beggars Banquet)
24	10	STRING OF HITS — Shadows (EMI)
5	11	VOULEZ VOUS — Abba (Epic)
11	12	PARALLEL LINES — Blondie (Chrysalis)
18	13	MIDNIGHT MAGIC — Commodores (Motown)
13	14	OUTLANDOS D'AMOUR — Police (A&M)
20	15	NIGHT OWL — Gerry Rafferty (United Artists)
6	16	REPLICAS — Tubeway Army (Beggars Banquet)
-	17	MANILOW MAGIC — Barry Manilow (Arista)
-	18	OCEANS OF FANTASY — Boney M (Atlantic/Hansa)
16	19	MORNING DANCE — Spyro Gyra (Infinity)
10	20	DOWN TO EARTH — Rainbow (Polydor)
25	21	BRIDGES — John Williams (Lotus)
14	22	SOME PRODUCT - CARRI ON SEX PISTOLS — Sex Pistols (Virgin)
29	23	INTO THE MUSIC — Van Morrison (Vertigo)
21	24	HIGHWAY TO HELL — AC/DC (Atlantic)
-	25	THE SINGLES ALBUM — Eddie Cochran (United Artists)
15	26	THE BEST OF THE DOOLEYS — Dooleys (GTO)
-	27	WAR OF THE WORLDS — Jeff Wayne (CBS)
23	28	WELCOME TO THE CRUISE — Judie Tzuke (Rocket)
27	29	LIVE KILLERS — Queen (EMI)
12	30	MANIFESTO — Roxy Music (Polydor)

29 September 1979

last week	this week	Album
4	1	ROCK 'N' ROLL JUVENILE — Cliff Richard (EMI)
9	2	THE PLEASURE PRINCIPLE — Gary Numan (Beggars Banquet)
2	3	IN THROUGH THE OUT DOOR — Led Zeppelin (Swan Song)
1	4	DISCOVERY — Electric Light Orchestra (Jet)
3	5	SLOW TRAIN COMING — Bob Dylan (CBS)
10	6	STRING OF HITS — Shadows (EMI)
5	7	I AM — Earth Wind & Fire (CBS)
5	8	STREET LIFE — Crusaders (MCA)
16	9	REPLICAS — Tubeway Army (Beggars Banquet)
11	10	VOULEZ VOUS — Abba (Epic)
13	11	MIDNIGHT MAGIC — Commodores (Motown)
14	12	OUTLANDOS D'AMOUR — Police (A&M)
12	13	PARALLEL LINES — Blondie (Chrysalis)
8	14	BREAKFAST IN AMERICA — Supertramp (A&M)
20	15	DOWN TO EARTH — Rainbow (Polydor)
-	16	JOIN HANDS — Siouxsie & the Banshees (Polydor)
7	17	THE BEST DISCO ALBUM IN THE WORLD — Various Artists (Warner Bros.)
24	18	HIGHWAY TO HELL — AC/DC (Atlantic)
30	19	MANIFESTO — Roxy Music (Polydor)
15	20	NIGHT OWL — Gerry Rafferty (United Artists)
18	21	OCEANS OF FANTASY — Boney M (Atlantic/Hansa)
-	22	OFF THE WALL — Michael Jackson (Epic)
19	23	MORNING DANCE — Spyro Gyra (Infinity)
21	24	BRIDGES — John Williams (Lotus)
17	25	MANILOW MAGIC — Barry Manilow (Arista)
23	26	INTO THE MUSIC — Van Morrison (Vertigo)
-	27	HERE — Leo Sayer (Chrysalis)
28	28	WELCOME TO THE CRUISE — Judie Tzuke (Rocket)
-	29	CUT — Slits (Island)
25	30	THE SINGLES ALBUM — Eddie Cochran (United Artists)

6 October 1979

last week	this week	Album
2	1	THE PLEASURE PRINCIPLE — Gary Numan (Beggars Banquet)
21	2	OCEANS OF FANTASY — Boney M (Atlantic/Hansa)
1	3	ROCK 'N' ROLL JUVENILE — Cliff Richard (EMI)
6	4	STRING OF HITS — Shadows (EMI)
4	5	DISCOVERY — Electric Light Orchestra (Jet)
3	6	IN THROUGH THE OUT DOOR — Led Zeppelin (Swan Song)
5	7	SLOW TRAIN COMING — Bob Dylan (CBS)
-	8	THE ADVENTURES OF THE HERSHAM BOYS — Sham 69 (Polydor)
7	9	I AM — Earth Wind & Fire (CBS)
12	10	OUTLANDOS D'AMOUR — Police (A&M)
8	11	STREET LIFE — Crusaders (MCA)
14	12	BREAKFAST IN AMERICA — Supertramp (A&M)
11	13	MIDNIGHT MAGIC — Commodores (Motown)
10	14	VOULEZ VOUS — Abba (Epic)
22	15	OFF THE WALL — Michael Jackson (Epic)
-	16	EAT TO THE BEAT — Blondie (Chrysalis)
9	17	REPLICAS — Tubeway Army (Beggars Banquet)
13	18	PARALLEL LINES — Blondie (Chrysalis)
19	19	MANIFESTO — Roxy Music (Polydor)
16	20	JOIN HANDS — Siouxsie & the Banshees (Polydor)
17	21	THE BEST DISCO ALBUM IN THE WORLD — Various Artists (Warner Bros.)
15	22	DOWN TO EARTH — Rainbow (Polydor)
-	23	THE LONG RUN — Eagles (Asylum)
-	24	HOT TRACKS — Various Artists (K-Tel)
-	25	WAR OF THE WORLDS — Jeff Wayne (CBS)
20	26	NIGHT OWL — Gerry Rafferty (United Artists)
23	27	MORNING DANCE — Spyro Gyra (Infinity)
28	28	WELCOME TO THE CRUISE — Judie Tzuke (Rocket)
-	29	LIVE KILLERS — Queen (EMI)
29	30	CUT — Slits (Island)

Off The Wall was Michael Jackson's first solo album since quitting Motown and signing with Columbia subsidiary Epic. It would peak at No.3 and last in the chart for 170-odd weeks, slightly LONGER than 1982's *Thriller*. Sham 69's *Adventures Of The Hersham Boys* peaked as it entered. Its title plugged hit single *Hersham Boys*, a No.5 in August. Neither success would be repeated. The Eagles' *The Long Run* would be their last Top 5er too, though not such a long runner as 1985's *Best Of The Eagles*.

October – November 1979

last week	this week	13 October 1979
1	1	THE PLEASURE PRINCIPLE Gary Numan (Beggars Banquet)
3	2	ROCK 'N' ROLL JUVENILE Cliff Richard (EMI)
2	3	OCEANS OF FANTASY Boney M (Atlantic/Hansa)
4	4	STRING OF HITS Shadows (EMI)
5	5	DISCOVERY Electric Light Orchestra (Jet)
16	6	EAT TO THE BEAT Blondie (Chrysalis)
-	7	THE RAVEN Stranglers (United Artists)
14	8	OFF THE WALL Michael Jackson (Epic)
-	9	REGGATTA DE BLANC Police (A&M)
7	10	SLOW TRAIN COMING Bob Dylan (CBS)
10	11	OUTLANDOS D'AMOUR Police (A&M)
8	12	THE ADVENTURES OF THE HERSHAM BOYS Sham 69 (Polydor)
9	13	I AM Earth Wind & Fire (CBS)
13	14	MIDNIGHT MAGIC Commodores (Motown)
-	15	10 C.C.'s GREATEST HITS 10 C.C. (Mercury)
11	16	STREET LIFE Crusaders (MCA)
6	17	IN THROUGH THE OUT DOOR Led Zeppelin (Swan Song)
-	18	UNLEASHED IN THE EAST Judas Priest (CBS)
26	19	NIGHT OWL Gerry Rafferty (United Artists)
12	20	BREAKFAST IN AMERICA Supertramp (A&M)
22	21	DOWN TO EARTH Rainbow (Polydor)
17	22	REPLICAS Tubeway Army (Beggars Banquet)
14	23	VOULEZ VOUS Abba (Epic)
18	24	PARALLEL LINES Blondie (Chrysalis)
23	25	THE LONG RUN Eagles (Asylum)
21	26	THE BEST DISCO ALBUM IN THE WORLD Various Artists (Warner Bros.)
20	27	JOIN HANDS Siouxsie & the Banshees (Polydor)
25	28	WAR OF THE WORLDS Jeff Wayne (CBS)
-	29	SURVIVAL Bob Marley & the Wailers (Island)
-	30	A DIFFERENT KIND OF TENSION Buzzcocks (United Artists)

		20 October 1979
9	1	REGGATTA DE BLANC Police (A&M)
7	2	THE RAVEN Stranglers (United Artists)
6	3	EAT TO THE BEAT Blondie (Chrysalis)
25	4	THE LONG RUN Eagles (Asylum)
1	5	THE PLEASURE PRINCIPLE Gary Numan (Beggars Banquet)
5	6	DISCOVERY Electric Light Orchestra (Jet)
8	7	OFF THE WALL Michael Jackson (Epic)
3	8	OCEANS OF FANTASY Boney M (Atlantic/Hansa)
11	9	OUTLANDOS D'AMOUR Police (A&M)
4	10	STRING OF HITS Shadows (EMI)
2	11	ROCK 'N' ROLL JUVENILE Cliff Richard (EMI)
17	12	IN THROUGH THE OUT DOOR Led Zeppelin (Swan Song)
18	13	UNLEASHED IN THE EAST Judas Priest (CBS)
13	14	I AM Earth Wind & Fire (CBS)
20	15	BREAKFAST IN AMERICA Supertramp (A&M)
10	16	SLOW TRAIN COMING Bob Dylan (CBS)
21	17	DOWN TO EARTH Rainbow (Polydor)
14	18	MIDNIGHT MAGIC Commodores (Motown)
15	19	10 C.C.'s GREATEST HITS 10 C.C. (Mercury)
23	20	VOULEZ VOUS Abba (Epic)
24	21	PARALLEL LINES Blondie (Chrysalis)
12	22	THE ADVENTURES OF THE HERSHAM BOYS Sham 69 (Polydor)
16	23	STREET LIFE Crusaders (MCA)
-	24	I'M THE MAN Joe Jackson (A&M)
22	25	REPLICAS Tubeway Army (Beggars Banquet)
-	26	QUADROPHENIA Soundtrack (Polydor)
19	27	NIGHT OWL Gerry Rafferty (United Artists)
-	28	LOVE HUNTER Whitesnake (United Artists)
-	29	LENA'S MUSIC ALBUM Lena Martell (Pye)
29	30	SURVIVAL Bob Marley & the Wailers (Island)

		27 October 1979
1	1	REGGATTA DE BLANC Police (A&M)
3	2	EAT TO THE BEAT Blondie (Chrysalis)
7	3	OFF THE WALL Michael Jackson (Epic)
4	4	THE LONG RUN Eagles (Asylum)
-	5	WHATEVER YOU WANT Status Quo (Vertigo)
10	6	STRING OF HITS Shadows (EMI)
5	7	THE PLEASURE PRINCIPLE Gary Numan (Beggars Banquet)
6	8	DISCOVERY Electric Light Orchestra (Jet)
2	9	THE RAVEN Stranglers (United Artists)
8	10	OCEANS OF FANTASY Boney M (Atlantic/Hansa)
-	11	TUSK Fleetwood Mac (Warner Bros.)
29	12	LENA'S MUSIC ALBUM Lena Martell (Pye)
17	13	DOWN TO EARTH Rainbow (Polydor)
12	14	IN THROUGH THE OUT DOOR Led Zeppelin (Swan Song)
11	15	ROCK 'N' ROLL JUVENILE Cliff Richard (EMI)
14	16	I AM Earth Wind & Fire (CBS)
19	17	10 C.C.'s GREATEST HITS 10 C.C. (Mercury)
9	18	OUTLANDOS D'AMOUR Police (A&M)
15	19	BREAKFAST IN AMERICA Supertramp (A&M)
18	20	MIDNIGHT MAGIC Commodores (Motown)
-	21	ONE VOICE Barry Manilow (Arista)
25	22	REPLICAS Tubeway Army (Beggars Banquet)
-	23	THE CRACK Ruts (Virgin)
30	24	SURVIVAL Bob Marley & the Wailers (Island)
13	25	UNLEASHED IN THE EAST Judas Priest (CBS)
22	26	THE ADVENTURES OF THE HERSHAM BOYS Sham 69 (Polydor)
28	27	LOVE HUNTER Whitesnake (United Artists)
-	28	THE UNRECORDED JASPER CARROTT Jasper Carrott (DJM)
16	29	SLOW TRAIN COMING Bob Dylan (CBS)
24	30	I'M THE MAN Joe Jackson (A&M)

		3 November 1979
1	1	REGGATTA DE BLANC Police (A&M)
4	2	THE LONG RUN Eagles (Asylum)
2	3	EAT TO THE BEAT Blondie (Chrysalis)
11	4	TUSK Fleetwood Mac (Warner Bros.)
3	5	OFF THE WALL Michael Jackson (Epic)
12	6	LENA'S MUSIC ALBUM Lena Martell (Pye)
5	7	WHATEVER YOU WANT Status Quo (Vertigo)
7	8	THE PLEASURE PRINCIPLE Gary Numan (Beggars Banquet)
16	9	I AM Earth Wind & Fire (CBS)
21	10	ONE VOICE Barry Manilow (Arista)
8	11	DISCOVERY Electric Light Orchestra (Jet)
-	12	BOMBER Motorhead (Bronze)
-	13	MR. UNIVERSE Gillan (Acrobat)
13	14	DOWN TO EARTH Rainbow (Polydor)
6	15	STRING OF HITS Shadows (EMI)
10	16	OCEANS OF FANTASY Boney M (Atlantic/Hansa)
28	17	THE UNRECORDED JASPER CARROTT Jasper Carrott (DJM)
18	18	OUTLANDOS D'AMOUR Police (A&M)
9	19	THE RAVEN Stranglers (United Artists)
17	20	10 C.C.'s GREATEST HITS 10 C.C. (Mercury)
29	21	SLOW TRAIN COMING Bob Dylan (CBS)
24	22	SURVIVAL Bob Marley & the Wailers (Island)
-	23	SPECIALS Specials (2-Tone)
15	24	ROCK 'N' ROLL JUVENILE Cliff Richard (EMI)
-	25	WAR OF THE WORLDS Jeff Wayne (CBS)
-	26	MARATHON Santana (CBS)
14	27	IN THROUGH THE OUT DOOR Led Zeppelin (Swan Song)
19	28	BREAKFAST IN AMERICA Supertramp (A&M)
22	29	REPLICAS Tubeway Army (Beggars Banquet)
23	30	THE CRACK Ruts (Virgin)

Charting by 2 Tone Records' the Specials proved the presence of the punk-influenced Ska Revival. Heavy Metal had never gone away but was enjoying what seemed a revival. Ozzy Osbourne had quit Black Sabbath, but here were not only Led Zeppelin, Rainbow and Motorhead (led by ex-Hawkwind roadie Lemmie) but also Judas Priest's first Top 20 LP, the live *Unleashed In The East*, Whitesnake's first Top 30 LP, and ex-Deep Purple member Ian Gillan's band Gillan (previously the Ian Gillan Band).

10 November 1979

last week	this week		
1	1	REGGATTA DE BLANC	Police (A&M)
4	2	TUSK	Fleetwood Mac (Warner Bros.)
3	3	EAT TO THE BEAT	Blondie (Chrysalis)
6	4	LENA'S MUSIC ALBUM	Lena Martell (Pye)
2	5	THE LONG RUN	Eagles (Asylum)
7	6	WHATEVER YOU WANT	Status Quo (Vertigo)
5	7	OFF THE WALL	Michael Jackson (Epic)
-	8	ROCK 'N' ROLLER DISCO	Various Artists (Ronco)
23	9	SPECIALS	Specials (2-Tone)
20	10	10 C.C.'s GREATEST HITS	10 C.C. (Mercury)
15	11	STRING OF HITS	Shadows (EMI)
12	12	BOMBER	.Motorhead (Bronze)
11	13	DISCOVERY	Electric Light Orchestra (Jet)
19	14	THE RAVEN	Stranglers (United Artists)
16	15	OCEANS OF FANTASY	Boney M (Atlantic/Hansa)
13	16	MR UNIVERSE	Gillan (Acrobat)
9	17	I AM	Earth Wind & Fire (CBS)
-	18	GREATEST HITS VOL 2	Abba (Epic)
-	19	THE FINE ART OF SURFACING	Boomtown Rats (Ensign)
-	20	PARALLEL LINES	Blondie (Chrysalis)
-	21	JOURNEY THROUGH THE SECRET LIFE OF PLANTS	Stevie Wonder (Motown)
14	22	DOWN TO EARTH	Rainbow (Polydor)
-	23	MIDNIGHT MAGIC	Commodores (Motown)
22	24	SURVIVAL	Bob Marley & the Wailers (Island)
-	25	HOT TRACKS	Various Artists (K-Tel)
8	26	THE PLEASURE PRINCIPLE	Gary Numan (Beggars Banquet)
10	27	ONE VOICE	Barry Manilow (Arista)
-	28	ONE STEP BEYOND	Madness (Stiff)
24	29	ROCK 'N' ROLL JUVENILE	Cliff Richard (EMI)
-	30	A CURIOUS FEELING	Tony Banks (Charisma)

17 November 1979

1	1	REGGATTA DE BLANC	Police (A&M)
2	2	TUSK	Fleetwood Mac (Warner Bros.)
18	3	GREATEST HITS VOL 2	Abba (Epic)
8	4	ROCK 'N' ROLLER DISCO	Various Artists (Ronco)
10	5	10 C.C.'s GREATEST HITS	10 C.C. (Mercury)
4	6	LENA'S MUSIC ALBUM	Lena Martell (Pye)
19	7	THE FINE ART OF SURFACING	Boomtown Rats (Ensign)
-	8	ROD STEWART VOL. 1 GREATEST HITS	Rod Stewart (Riva)
9	9	SPECIALS	Specials (2-Tone)
5	10	THE LONG RUN	Eagles (Asylum)
21	11	JOURNEY THROUGH THE SECRET LIFE OF PLANTS	Stevie Wonder (Motown)
7	12	OFF THE WALL	Michael Jackson (Epic)
3	13	EAT TO THE BEAT	Blondie (Chrysalis)
6	13	WHATEVER YOU WANT	Status Quo (Vertigo)
23	15	MIDNIGHT MAGIC	Commodores (Motown)
-	16	MANTOVANI'S 20 GOLDEN GREATS	Mantovani (Warwick)
11	17	STRING OF HITS	Shadows (EMI)
28	18	ONE STEP BEYOND	Madness (Stiff)
-	19	OUT OF THIS WORLD	Moody Blues (K-Tel)
-	20	BREAKFAST IN AMERICA	Supertramp (A&M)
-	21	QUADROPHENIA	Soundtrack (Polydor)
-	22	ON THE RADIO – GREATEST HITS VOLS 1 & 2	Donna Summer (Casablanca)
-	23	PLEASURE AND PAIN	Dr Hook (Capitol)
20	24	PARALLEL LINES	Blondie (Chrysalis)
-	25	BAT OUT OF HELL	Meatloaf (Epic)
17	26	I AM	Earth Wind & Fire (CBS)
12	27	BOMBER	Motorhead (Bronze)
22	28	DOWN TO EARTH	Rainbow (Polydor)
-	29	BEE GEES' GREATEST HITS	Bee Gees (RSO)
14	30	THE RAVEN	Stranglers (United Artists)

24 November 1979

8	1	ROD STEWART VOL. 1 GREATEST HITS	Rod Stewart (Riva)
3	2	GREATEST HITS VOL 2	Abba (Epic)
1	3	REGGATTA DE BLANC	Police (A&M)
2	4	TUSK	Fleetwood Mac (Warner Bros.)
12	5	OFF THE WALL	Michael Jackson (Epic)
6	6	LENA'S MUSIC ALBUM	Lena Martell (Pye)
-	7	20 GOLDEN GREATS	Diana Ross (Motown)
5	8	10 C.C.'s GREATEST HITS	10 C.C. (Mercury)
9	8	SPECIALS	Specials (2-Tone)
4	10	ROCK 'N' ROLLER DISCO	Various Artists (Ronco)
11	11	JOURNEY THROUGH THE SECRET LIFE OF PLANTS	Stevie Wonder (Motown)
19	12	OUT OF THIS WORLD	Moody Blues (K-Tel)
10	13	THE LONG RUN	Eagles (Asylum)
7	14	THE FINE ART OF SURFACING	Boomtown Rats (Ensign)
16	15	MANTOVANI'S 20 GOLDEN GREATS	Mantovani (Warwick)
29	16	BEE GEES' GREATEST HITS	Bee Gees (RSO)
26	17	I AM	Earth Wind & Fire (CBS)
18	18	ONE STEP BEYOND	Madness (Stiff)
15	19	MIDNIGHT MAGIC	Commodores (Motown)
22	20	ON THE RADIO – GREATEST HITS VOLS 1 & 2	Donna Summer (Casablanca)
17	21	STRING OF HITS	Shadows (EMI)
-	22	OUTLANDOS D'AMOUR	Police (A&M)
13	23	EAT TO THE BEAT	Blondie (Chrysalis)
-	24	DISCOVERY	Electric Light Orchestra (Jet)
-	25	SOMETIMES YOU WIN	Dr Hook (Capitol)
-	26	RISE	Herb Alpert (A&M)
23	27	PLEASURE AND PAIN	Dr Hook (Capitol)
-	28	CREPES AND DRAPES	Showaddywaddy (Arista)
-	29	WET	Barbra Streisand (CBS)
-	30	SETTING SONS	Jam (Polydor)

1 December 1979

2	1	GREATEST HITS VOL 2	Abba (Epic)
7	2	20 GOLDEN GREATS	Diana Ross (Motown)
1	3	ROD STEWART VOL. 1 GREATEST HITS	Rod Stewart (Riva)
3	4	REGGATTA DE BLANC	Police (A&M)
10	5	ROCK 'N' ROLLER DISCO	Various Artists (Ronco)
15	6	MANTOVANI'S 20 GOLDEN GREATS	Mantovani (Warwick)
4	7	TUSK	Fleetwood Mac (Warner Bros.)
5	8	OFF THE WALL	Michael Jackson (Epic)
30	9	SETTING SONS	Jam (Polydor)
6	10	LENA'S MUSIC ALBUM	Lena Martell (Pye)
12	11	OUT OF THIS WORLD	Moody Blues (K-Tel)
-	12	LOVE SONGS	Elvis Presley (K-Tel)
8	13	SPECIALS	Specials (2-Tone)
8	14	10 C.C.'s GREATEST HITS	10 C.C. (Mercury)
24	15	DISCOVERY	Electric Light Orchestra (Jet)
18	16	ONE STEP BEYOND	Madness (Stiff)
23	17	EAT TO THE BEAT	Blondie (Chrysalis)
11	18	JOURNEY THROUGH THE SECRET LIFE OF PLANTS	Stevie Wonder (Motown)
25	19	SOMETIMES YOU WIN	Dr Hook (Capitol)
29	20	WET	Barbra Streisand (CBS)
17	21	I AM	Earth Wind & Fire (CBS)
16	22	BEE GEES' GREATEST HITS	Bee Gees (RSO)
13	23	THE LONG RUN	Eagles (Asylum)
21	24	STRING OF HITS	Shadows (EMI)
-	25	NIGHT MOVES	Various Artists (K-Tel)
14	26	THE FINE ART OF SURFACING	Boomtown Rats (Ensign)
20	27	ON THE RADIO – GREATEST HITS VOLS 1 & 2	Donna Summer (Casablanca)
26	28	RISE	Herb Alpert (A&M)
22	29	OUTLANDOS D'AMOUR	Police (A&M)
19	30	MIDNIGHT MAGIC	Commodores (Motown)

A double dose of Dr Hook reflected the success of *When You're In Love With A Beautiful Woman*, infinitely less memorable than their first big hit, 1972's *Sylvia's Mother*. Likewise the Stevie Wonder of *The Secret Life Of Plants* seemed far less engaging than the 12-year-old harmonica star of *Fingertips Part 2*, his live debut single from 1963, the only US No.1 ever made on which you hear a musician shout "What key?! What key?!" By December 1, the Top 3 was congealing for Christmas.

December 1979

8 December 1979

last	this	
1	1	GREATEST HITS VOL 2 — Abba (Epic)
3	2	ROD STEWART VOL. 1 GREATEST HITS — Rod Stewart (Riva)
2	3	20 GOLDEN GREATS — Diana Ross (Motown)
12	4	LOVE SONGS — Elvis Presley (K-Tel)
4	5	REGGATTA DE BLANC — Police (A&M)
9	6	SETTING SONS — Jam (Polydor)
5	7	ROCK 'N' ROLLER DISCO — Various Artists (Ronco)
10	8	LENA'S MUSIC ALBUM — Lena Martell (Pye)
6	9	MANTOVANI'S 20 GOLDEN GREATS — Mantovani (Warwick)
25	10	NIGHT MOVES — Various Artists (K-Tel)
-	11	ELO'S GREATEST HITS — Electric Light Orchestra (Jet)
8	12	OFF THE WALL — Michael Jackson (Epic)
14	13	10 C.C.'s GREATEST HITS — 10 C.C. (Mercury)
19	14	SOMETIMES YOU WIN — Dr Hook (Capitol)
7	15	TUSK — Fleetwood Mac (Warner Bros.)
13	16	SPECIALS — Specials (2-Tone)
11	17	OUT OF THIS WORLD — Moody Blues (K-Tel)
17	18	EAT TO THE BEAT — Blondie (Chrysalis)
24	19	STRING OF HITS — Shadows (EMI)
16	20	ONE STEP BEYOND — Madness (Stiff)
27	21	ON THE RADIO – GREATEST HITS VOLS 1 & 2 — Donna Summer (Casablanca)
-	22	ECHOES OF GOLD — Adrian Brett (Warwick)
20	23	WET — Barbra Streisand (CBS)
-	24	NEW HORIZONS — Don Williams (K-Tel)
23	25	THE LONG RUN — Eagles (Asylum)
15	26	DISCOVERY — Electric Light Orchestra (Jet)
22	27	BEE GEES' GREATEST HITS — Bee Gees (RSO)
-	28	THE WALL — Pink Floyd (Harvest)
-	29	GLORY BOYS — Secret Affair (I Spy)
29	30	OUTLANDOS D'AMOUR — Police (A&M)

15 December 1979

last	this	
1	1	GREATEST HITS VOL 2 — Abba (Epic)
2	2	ROD STEWART VOL. 1 GREATEST HITS — Rod Stewart (Riva)
4	3	LOVE SONGS — Elvis Presley (K-Tel)
5	4	REGGATTA DE BLANC — Police (A&M)
3	5	20 GOLDEN GREATS — Diana Ross (Motown)
7	6	ROCK 'N' ROLLER DISCO — Various Artists (Ronco)
28	7	THE WALL — Pink Floyd (Harvest)
10	8	NIGHT MOVES — Various Artists (K-Tel)
6	9	SETTING SONS — Jam (Polydor)
8	10	LENA'S MUSIC ALBUM — Lena Martell (Pye)
11	11	ELO'S GREATEST HITS — Electric Light Orchestra (Jet)
15	12	TUSK — Fleetwood Mac (Warner Bros.)
12	13	OFF THE WALL — Michael Jackson (Epic)
26	14	DISCOVERY — Electric Light Orchestra (Jet)
-	15	CREPES AND DRAPES — Showaddywaddy (Arista)
17	16	OUT OF THIS WORLD — Moody Blues (K-Tel)
13	17	10 C.C.'s GREATEST HITS — 10 C.C. (Mercury)
20	18	ONE STEP BEYOND — Madness (Stiff)
18	19	EAT TO THE BEAT — Blondie (Chrysalis)
9	20	MANTOVANI'S 20 GOLDEN GREATS — Mantovani (Warwick)
16	21	SPECIALS — Specials (2-Tone)
14	22	SOMETIMES YOU WIN — Dr Hook (Capitol)
19	23	STRING OF HITS — Shadows (EMI)
-	24	METAL BOX — Public Image Ltd. (Virgin)
23	25	WET — Barbra Streisand (CBS)
29	26	GLORY BOYS — Secret Affair (I Spy)
-	27	THE BEST OF CHIC — Chic (Atlantic)
22	28	ECHOES OF GOLD — Adrian Brett (Warwick)
-	29	ON PAROLE — Motorhead (Liberty)
-	30	JOURNEY THROUGH THE SECRET LIFE OF PLANTS — Stevie Wonder (Motown)

22 December 1979

last	this	
1	1	GREATEST HITS VOL 2 — Abba (Epic)
2	2	ROD STEWART VOL. 1 GREATEST HITS — Rod Stewart (Riva)
3	3	LOVE SONGS — Elvis Presley (K-Tel)
5	4	20 GOLDEN GREATS — Diana Ross (Motown)
4	5	REGGATTA DE BLANC — Police (A&M)
7	6	THE WALL — Pink Floyd (Harvest)
8	7	NIGHT MOVES — Various Artists (K-Tel)
11	8	ELO'S GREATEST HITS — Electric Light Orchestra (Jet)
6	9	ROCK 'N' ROLLER DISCO — Various Artists (Ronco)
19	10	EAT TO THE BEAT — Blondie (Chrysalis)
10	11	LENA'S MUSIC ALBUM — Lena Martell (Pye)
13	12	OFF THE WALL — Michael Jackson (Epic)
9	13	SETTING SONS — Jam (Polydor)
18	14	ONE STEP BEYOND — Madness (Stiff)
-	14	PEACE IN THE VALLEY — Various Artists (Ronco)
17	16	10 C.C.'s GREATEST HITS — 10 C.C. (Mercury)
12	17	TUSK — Fleetwood Mac (Warner Bros.)
21	18	SPECIALS — Specials (2-Tone)
-	19	20 HOTTEST HITS — Hot Chocolate (RAK)
20	20	MANTOVANI'S 20 GOLDEN GREATS — Mantovani (Warwick)
15	21	CREPES AND DRAPES — Showaddywaddy (Arista)
24	22	METAL BOX — Public Image Ltd. (Virgin)
-	23	TRANQUILITY — Mary O'Hara (Warwick)
16	24	OUT OF THIS WORLD — Moody Blues (K-Tel)
-	25	SID SINGS — Sid Vicious (Virgin)
25	26	WET — Barbra Streisand (CBS)
23	27	STRING OF HITS — Shadows (EMI)
-	28	BEE GEES' GREATEST HITS — Bee Gees (RSO)
-	29	OUTLANDOS D'AMOUR — Police (A&M)
28	30	ECHOES OF GOLD — Adrian Brett (Warwick)

Over a third of the chart comprised records called Greatest Hits or Golden Greats; others were similarly retrospective. Across three Top 10s, there were only four genuinely current albums: Police's *Regatta de Blanc*, the Jam's *Setting Sons*, Pink Floyd's *The Wall* and Blondie's *Eat To The Beat*. Meanwhile the singles chart revived old Dusty Springfield and Miracles songs, and included the Moody Blues' 1967/1972 hit *Nights In White Satin*. The decade was ending as it had begun, awash in recycled nostalgia.

12 January 1980

last week	this week	
2	1	ROD STEWART'S GREATEST HITS — Rod Stewart (Riva)
5	2	REGATTA DE BLANC — Police (A&M)
1	3	ABBA'S GREATEST HITS VOL 2 — Abba (Epic)
6	4	THE WALL — Pink Floyd (Harvest)
19	5	20 HOTTEST HITS — Hot Chocolate (RAK)
3	6	LOVE SONGS — Elvis Presley (K-Tel)
14	7	PEACE IN THE VALLEY — Various Artists (Ronco)
10	8	EAT TO THE BEAT — Blondie (Chrysalis)
12	8	OFF THE WALL — Michael Jackson (Epic)
28	10	BEE GEES' GREATEST HITS — Bee Gees (RSO)
8	11	ELO'S GREATEST HITS — Electric Light Orchestra (Jet)
14	12	ONE STEP BEYOND — Madness (Stiff)
4	13	20 GOLDEN GREATS — Diana Ross (Motown)
17	14	TUSK — Fleetwood Mac (Warner Bros.)
-	15	LONDON CALLING — Clash (CBS)
-	16	PARALLEL LINES — Blondie (Chrysalis)
26	17	WET — Barbra Streisand (CBS)
29	18	OUTLANDOS D'AMOUR — Police (A&M)
-	19	FAWLTY TOWERS — TV Soundtrack (BBC)
18	20	THE SPECIALS — Specials (2-Tone)
7	21	NIGHT MOVES — Various Artists (K-Tel)
-	22	DISCOVERY — Electric Light Orchestra (Jet)
21	23	CREPES AND DRAPES — Showaddywaddy (Arista)
23	24	TRANQUILITY — Mary O'Hara (Warwick)
-	25	THE KENNY ROGERS SINGLES ALBUM — Kenny Rogers (United Artists)
-	26	ASTAIRE — Peter Skellern (Mercury)
-	27	ALL ABOARD — Various Artists (EMI)
25	28	SID SINGS — Sid Vicious (Virgin)
-	29	SOMETIMES YOU WIN — Dr Hook (Capitol)
-	30	THE SECRET POLICEMAN'S BALL — Various Artists (Island)

19 January 1980

last week	this week	
3	1	ABBA'S GREATEST HITS VOL 2 — Abba (Epic)
2	2	REGATTA DE BLANC — Police (A&M)
1	3	ROD STEWART'S GREATEST HITS — Rod Stewart (Riva)
5	4	20 HOTTEST HITS — Hot Chocolate (RAK)
4	5	THE WALL — Pink Floyd (Harvest)
8	6	OFF THE WALL — Michael Jackson (Epic)
10	7	BEE GEES' GREATEST HITS — Bee Gees (RSO)
12	8	ONE STEP BEYOND — Madness (Stiff)
8	9	EAT TO THE BEAT — Blondie (Chrysalis)
13	10	20 GOLDEN GREATS — Diana Ross (Motown)
6	11	LOVE SONGS — Elvis Presley (K-Tel)
11	12	ELO'S GREATEST HITS — Electric Light Orchestra (Jet)
-	13	VIDEO STARS — Various Artists (K-Tel)
18	14	OUTLANDOS D'AMOUR — Police (A&M)
15	15	LONDON CALLING — Clash (CBS)
20	16	THE SPECIALS — Specials (2-Tone)
-	17	THE BEST OF CHIC — Chic (Atlantic)
14	18	TUSK — Fleetwood Mac (Warner Bros.)
-	19	20 GREAT LOVE SONGS — Slim Whitman (United Artists)
23	20	CREPES AND DRAPES — Showaddywaddy (Arista)
-	21	20 GOLDEN GREATS — Mantovani (Warwick)
16	22	PARALLEL LINES — Blondie (Chrysalis)
30	23	THE SECRET POLICEMAN'S BALL — Various Artists (Island)
7	24	PEACE IN THE VALLEY — Various Artists (Ronco)
-	25	PLATINUM — Mike Oldfield (Virgin)
-	26	LENA'S MUSIC ALBUM — Lena Martell (Pye)
-	27	SETTING SONS — Jam (Polydor)
-	28	WAR OF THE WORLDS — Jeff Wayne (CBS)
19	29	FAWLTY TOWERS — TV Soundtrack (BBC)
22	30	DISCOVERY — Electric Light Orchestra (Jet)

26 January 1980

last week	this week	
2	1	REGATTA DE BLANC — Police (A&M)
1	2	ABBA'S GREATEST HITS VOL 2 — Abba (Epic)
-	3	PRETENDERS — Pretenders (Real)
8	4	ONE STEP BEYOND — Madness (Stiff)
9	5	EAT TO THE BEAT — Blondie (Chrysalis)
5	6	THE WALL — Pink Floyd (Harvest)
7	7	BEE GEES' GREATEST HITS — Bee Gees (RSO)
3	8	ROD STEWART'S GREATEST HITS — Rod Stewart (Riva)
4	9	20 HOTTEST HITS — Hot Chocolate (RAK)
16	10	THE SPECIALS — Specials (2-Tone)
13	11	VIDEO STARS — Various Artists (K-Tel)
6	12	OFF THE WALL — Michael Jackson (Epic)
17	13	THE BEST OF CHIC — (Atlantic)
15	14	LONDON CALLING — Clash (CBS)
10	15	20 GOLDEN GREATS — Diana Ross (Motown)
12	16	ELO'S GREATEST HITS — Electric Light Orchestra (Jet)
-	17	NO PLACE TO RUN — UFO (Chrysalis)
-	18	SOMETIMES YOU WIN — Dr Hook (Capitol)
11	19	LOVE SONGS — Elvis Presley (K-Tel)
19	20	20 GREAT LOVE SONGS — Slim Whitman (United Artists)
-	21	SEMI DETACHED SUBURBAN — Manfred Mann (EMI)
24	22	PEACE IN THE VALLEY — Various Artists (Ronco)
29	23	FAWLTY TOWERS — TV Soundtrack (BBC)
18	24	TUSK — Fleetwood Mac (Warner Bros.)
14	25	OUTLANDOS D'AMOUR — Police (A&M)
27	26	SETTING SONS — Jam (Polydor)
22	27	PARALLEL LINES — Blondie (Chrysalis)
-	28	THE FINE ART OF SURFACING — Boomtown Rats (Ensign)
-	29	GREATEST HITS, 1972-1978 — 10 c.c (Mercury)
-	30	SID SINGS — Sid Vicious (Virgin)

2 February 1980

last week	this week	
3	1	PRETENDERS — Pretenders (Real)
4	2	ONE STEP BEYOND — Madness (Stiff)
1	3	REGATTA DE BLANC — Police (A&M)
11	4	VIDEO STARS — Various Artists (K-Tel)
2	5	ABBA'S GREATEST HITS VOL 2 — Abba (Epic)
6	6	THE WALL — Pink Floyd (Harvest)
9	7	20 HOTTEST HITS — Hot Chocolate (RAK)
12	8	OFF THE WALL — Michael Jackson (Epic)
5	9	EAT TO THE BEAT — Blondie (Chrysalis)
8	10	ROD STEWART'S GREATEST HITS — Rod Stewart (Riva)
10	11	THE SPECIALS — Specials (2-Tone)
7	12	BEE GEES' GREATEST HITS — Bee Gees (RSO)
17	13	NO PLACE TO RUN — UFO (Chrysalis)
15	14	20 GOLDEN GREATS — Diana Ross (Motown)
16	15	ELO'S GREATEST HITS — Electric Light Orchestra (Jet)
27	16	PARALLEL LINES — Blondie (Chrysalis)
24	17	TUSK — Fleetwood Mac (Warner Bros.)
-	18	PERMANENT WAVES — Rush (Mercury)
-	19	SEPTEMBER MORN — Neil Diamond (CBS)
23	20	FAWLTY TOWERS — TV Soundtrack (BBC)
14	21	LONDON CALLING — Clash (CBS)
21	22	SEMI DETACHED SUBURBAN — Manfred Mann (EMI)
-	23	THE SUMMIT — Various Artists (K-Tel)
18	24	SOMETIMES YOU WIN — Dr Hook (Capitol)
-	25	SHORT STORIES — Jon & Vangelis (Polydor)
-	26	ASTAIRE — Peter Skellern (Mercury)
25	27	OUTLANDOS D'AMOUR — Police (A&M)
28	28	THE FINE ART OF SURFACING — Boomtown Rats (Ensign)
-	29	THE PLEASURE PRINCIPLE — Gary Numan (Beggars Banquet)
26	30	SETTING SONS — Jam (Polydor)

Despite (or perhaps because of) the near-million-selling success of Pink Floyd's *Another Brick In The Wall* single, the band's double album *The Wall*, from which it was extracted, failed to top the chart, or even break the still-continuing Abba/Rod Stewart/Police stranglehold on the Top 3. More fortunate, though, were the Pretenders, whose eponymous debut album hit the top immediately on the heels of their *Brass In Pocket* single, while Madness finally made No.2 after an almost 3-month climb through the lower reaches.

February – March 1980

last this week

9 February 1980

1 1 PRETENDERS
Pretenders (Real)
2 2 ONE STEP BEYOND
Madness (Stiff)
3 3 REGATTA DE BLANC
Police (A&M)
4 4 VIDEO STARS
Various Artists (K-Tel)
25 5 SHORT STORIES
Jon & Vangelis (Polydor)
12 6 BEE GEES' GREATEST HITS
Bee Gees (RSO)
11 7 THE SPECIALS
Specials (2-Tone)
18 8 PERMANENT WAVES
Rush (Mercury)
5 9 ABBA'S GREATEST HITS VOL 2
Abba (Epic)
8 10 OFF THE WALL
Michael Jackson (Epic)
9 11 EAT TO THE BEAT
Blondie (Chrysalis)
- 12 THE KENNY ROGERS SINGLES ALBUM
Kenny Rogers (United Artists)
- 13 I'M THE MAN
Joe Jackson (A&M)
26 14 ASTAIRE
Peter Skellern (Mercury)
13 15 NO PLACE TO RUN
UFO (Chrysalis)
19 16 SEPTEMBER MORN
Neil Diamond (CBS)
16 17 PARALLEL LINES
Blondie (Chrysalis)
10 18 ROD STEWART'S GREATEST HITS
Rod Stewart (Riva)
23 19 THE SUMMIT
Various Artists (K-Tel)
17 20 TUSK
Fleetwood Mac (Warner Bros.)
14 21 20 GOLDEN GREATS
Diana Ross (Motown)
22 22 SEMI DETACHED SUBURBAN
Manfred Mann (EMI)
27 23 OUTLANDOS D'AMOUR
Police (A&M)
- 24 SID SINGS
Sid Vicious (Virgin)
20 25 FAWLTY TOWERS
TV Soundtrack (BBC)
7 26 20 HOTTEST HITS
Hot Chocolate (RAK)
30 27 SETTING SONS
Jam (Polydor)
24 28 SOMETIMES YOU WIN
Dr Hook (Capitol)
- 29 THE LAST DANCE
Various Artists (EMI)
- 30 GOLDEN COLLECTION
Charley Pride (K-Tel)

16 February 1980

1 1 PRETENDERS
Pretenders (Real)
29 2 THE LAST DANCE
Various Artists (EMI)
2 3 ONE STEP BEYOND
Madness (Stiff)
3 4 REGATTA DE BLANC
Police (A&M)
10 5 OFF THE WALL
Michael Jackson (Epic)
5 5 SHORT STORIES
Jon & Vangelis (Polydor)
7 7 THE SPECIALS
Specials (2-Tone)
8 8 PERMANENT WAVES
Rush (Mercury)
6 9 BEE GEES' GREATEST HITS
Bee Gees (RSO)
13 10 I'M THE MAN
Joe Jackson (A&M)
- 11 KENNY
Kenny Rogers (United Artists)
28 12 SOMETIMES YOU WIN
Dr Hook (Capitol)
16 12 SEPTEMBER MORN
Neil Diamond (CBS)
9 14 ABBA'S GREATEST HITS VOL 2
Abba (Epic)
- 15 METAMATIC
John Foxx (Metalbeat)
18 16 ROD STEWART'S GREATEST HITS
Rod Stewart (Riva)
4 17 VIDEO STARS
Various Artists (K-Tel)
- 18 THE WALL
Pink Floyd (Harvest)
17 19 PARALLEL LINES
Blondie (Chrysalis)
23 20 OUTLANDOS D'AMOUR
Police (A&M)
26 21 20 HOTTEST HITS
Hot Chocolate (RAK)
- 22 FLEX Lene Lovich (Stiff)
- 23 STRING OF HITS
Shadows (EMI)
11 24 EAT TO THE BEAT
Blondie (Chrysalis)
19 25 THE SUMMIT
Various Artists (K-Tel)
20 26 TUSK
Fleetwood Mac (Warner Bros.)
15 27 NO PLACE TO RUN
UFO (Chrysalis)
- 28 END OF THE CENTURY
Ramones (Sire)
- 29 SUNBURN - ORIGINAL SOUNDTRACK
Various Artists (Warwick)
21 30 20 GOLDEN GREATS
Diana Ross (Motown)

23 February 1980

2 1 THE LAST DANCE
Various Artists (EMI)
3 2 ONE STEP BEYOND
Madness (Stiff)
1 3 PRETENDERS
Pretenders (Real)
4 4 REGATTA DE BLANC
Police (A&M)
5 5 SHORT STORIES
Jon & Vangelis (Polydor)
11 6 KENNY
Kenny Rogers (United Artists)
7 7 THE SPECIALS
Specials (2-Tone)
15 8 METAMATIC
John Foxx (Metalbeat)
10 9 I'M THE MAN
Joe Jackson (A&M)
5 10 OFF THE WALL
Michael Jackson (Epic)
28 11 END OF THE CENTURY
Ramones (Sire)
- 12 THE NOLAN SISTERS
Nolans (Epic)
8 13 PERMANENT WAVES
Rush (Mercury)
- 14 JUST FOR YOU
Des O'Connor (Warwick)
- 15 GET HAPPY!
Elvis Costello (F Beat)
9 16 BEE GEES' GREATEST HITS
Bee Gees (RSO)
12 16 SEPTEMBER MORN
Neil Diamond (CBS)
14 18 ABBA'S GREATEST HITS VOL 2
Abba (Epic)
20 19 OUTLANDOS D'AMOUR
Police (A&M)
19 20 PARALLEL LINES
Blondie (Chrysalis)
- 21 LONDON CALLING
Clash (CBS)
- 22 GOLDEN COLLECTION
Charley Pride (K-Tel)
29 23 SUNBURN - ORIGINAL SOUNDTRACK
Various Artists (Warwick)
22 24 FLEX
Lene Lovich (Stiff)
24 25 EAT TO THE BEAT
Blondie (Chrysalis)
- 26 CAPTAIN BEAKY AND HIS BAND
Keith Michell (Polydor)
- 27 THE FINE ART OF SURFACING
Boomtown Rats (Ensign)
18 28 THE WALL
Pink Floyd (Harvest)
- 29 THE KENNY ROGERS SINGLES ALBUM
Kenny Rogers (United Artists)
17 30 VIDEO STARS
Various Artists (K-Tel)

1 March 1980

1 1 THE LAST DANCE
Various Artists (EMI)
15 2 GET HAPPY!
Elvis Costello (F Beat)
- 3 TOO MUCH PRESSURE
Selecter (2-Tone)
2 4 ONE STEP BEYOND
Madness (Stiff)
3 5 PRETENDERS
Pretenders (Real)
4 6 REGATTA DE BLANC
Police (A&M)
10 7 OFF THE WALL
Michael Jackson (Epic)
5 8 SHORT STORIES
Jon & Vangelis (Polydor)
6 9 KENNY
Kenny Rogers (United Artists)
7 10 THE SPECIALS
Specials (2-Tone)
- 11 TELL ME ON A SUNDAY
Marti Webb (Polydor)
- 12 STRING OF HITS
Shadows (EMI)
9 13 I'M THE MAN
Joe Jackson (A&M)
28 14 THE WALL
Pink Floyd (Harvest)
- 15 LIGHT UP THE NIGHT
Brothers Johnson (A&M)
14 16 JUST FOR YOU
Des O'Connor (Warwick)
16 16 SEPTEMBER MORN
Neil Diamond (CBS)
25 18 EAT TO THE BEAT
Blondie (Chrysalis)
12 19 THE NOLAN SISTERS
Nolans (Epic)
- 20 FLOGGING A DEAD HORSE
Sex Pistols (Virgin)
23 21 SUNBURN - ORIGINAL SOUNDTRACK
Various Artists (Warwick)
- 22 SOMETIMES YOU WIN
Dr Hook (Capitol)
16 23 BEE GEES' GREATEST HITS
Bee Gees (RSO)
26 24 CAPTAIN BEAKY AND HIS BAND
Keith Michell (Polydor)
13 25 PERMANENT WAVES
Rush (Mercury)
11 26 END OF THE CENTURY
Ramones (Sire)
- 27 CATCHING THE SUN
Spyro Gyra (MCA)
- 28 ROCK AND ROLL JUVENILE
Cliff Richard (EMI)
18 29 ABBA'S GREATEST HITS VOL 2
Abba (Epic)
22 30 GOLDEN COLLECTION
Charley Pride (K-Tel)

The big-selling *Last Dance* compilation was, though its title disguised the fact, part of EMI's "EMTV" series (the 20th such, in fact), usually devoted to an artist's 20 Golden Greats. This one was a collection of classic ballads from the Motown back-catalogue, and had a successful TV ad campaign, becoming the first chart-topping Various Artists compilation of the '80s. Former Ultravox vocalist John Foxx scored an unexpected top-tenner with *Metamatic*, though the album's sales (and chart) span was extremely limited.

March 1980

8 March 1980

last week / this week

last	this		
1	1	THE LAST DANCE	Various Artists (EMI)
6	2	REGATTA DE BLANC	Police (A&M)
5	3	PRETENDERS	Pretenders (Real)
9	4	KENNY	Kenny Rogers (United Artists)
2	5	GET HAPPY!	Elvis Costello (F Beat)
7	6	OFF THE WALL	Michael Jackson (Epic)
11	7	TELL ME ON A SUNDAY	Marti Webb (Polydor)
12	8	STRING OF HITS	Shadows (EMI)
8	9	SHORT STORIES	Jon & Vangelis (Polydor)
4	10	ONE STEP BEYOND	Madness (Stiff)
3	11	TOO MUCH PRESSURE	Selecter (2-Tone)
10	12	THE SPECIALS	Specials (2-Tone)
-	13	OUTLANDOS D'AMOUR	Police (A&M)
30	14	GOLDEN COLLECTION	Chareye Pride (K-Tel)
18	15	EAT TO THE BEAT	Blondie (Chrysalis)
15	16	LIGHT UP THE NIGHT	Brothers Johnson (A&M)
-	17	THE AGE OF PLASTIC	Buggles (Island)
-	18	THE KENNY ROGERS SINGLES ALBUM	Kenny Rogers (United Artists)
16	18	SEPTEMBER MORN	Neil Diamond (CBS)
20	20	FLOGGING A DEAD HORSE	Sex Pistols (Virgin)
16	21	JUST FOR YOU	Des O'Connor (Warwick)
13	22	I'M THE MAN	Joe Jackson (A&M)
14	23	THE WALL	Pink Floyd (Harvest)
29	24	ABBA'S GREATEST HITS VOL 2	Abba (Epic)
-	25	METAL FOR MUTHAS	Various Artists (EMI)
25	26	PERMANENT WAVES	Rush (Mercury)
19	27	THE NOLAN SISTERS	Nolans (Epic)
28	28	ROCK AND ROLL JUVENILE	Cliff Richard (EMI)
-	29	PARALLEL LINES	Blondie (Chrysalis)
22	30	SOMETIMES YOU WIN	Dr Hook (Capitol)

15 March 1980

8	1	STRING OF HITS	Shadows (EMI)
2	2	REGATTA DE BLANC	Police (A&M)
1	3	THE LAST DANCE	Various Artists (EMI)
3	4	PRETENDERS	Pretenders (Real)
15	5	EAT TO THE BEAT	Blondie (Chrysalis)
4	6	KENNY	Kenny Rogers (United Artists)
7	7	TELL ME ON A SUNDAY	Marti Webb (Polydor)
5	8	GET HAPPY!	Elvis Costello (F Beat)
-	9	ROSE ROYCE'S GREATEST HITS	Rose Royce (Whitfield)
14	10	GOLDEN COLLECTION	Charlie Pride (K-Tel)
11	11	TOO MUCH PRESSURE	Selecter (2-Tone)
10	12	ONE STEP BEYOND	Madness (Stiff)
13	13	OUTLANDOS D'AMOUR	Police (A&M)
9	13	SHORT STORIES	Jon & Vangelis (Polydor)
12	15	THE SPECIALS	Specials (2-Tone)
-	16	REALITY EFFECT	Tourists (Logo)
16	17	LIGHT UP THE NIGHT	Brothers Johnson (A&M)
25	18	METAL FOR MUTHAS	Various Artists (EMI)
6	19	OFF THE WALL	Michael Jackson (Epic)
27	20	THE NOLAN SISTERS	Nolans (Epic)
28	21	ROCK AND ROLL JUVENILE	Cliff Richard (EMI)
-	22	DOWN TO EARTH	Rainbow (Polydor)
-	23	K C & THE SUNSHINE BAND'S GREATEST HITS	K C & the Sunshine Band (TK)
23	24	THE WALL	Pink Floyd (Harvest)
26	25	PERMANENT WAVES	Rush (Mercury)
-	26	SMALLCREEP'S DAY	Mike Rutherford (Charisma)
20	27	FLOGGING A DEAD HORSE	Sex Pistols (Virgin)
-	28	ON THE RADIO: GREATEST HITS VOLS. 1 & 2	Donna Summer (Casablanca)
-	29	TEARS AND LAUGHTER	Johnny Mathis (CBS)
24	30	ABBA'S GREATEST HITS VOL 2	Abba (Epic)

22 March 1980

29	1	TEARS AND LAUGHTER	Johnny Mathis (CBS)
1	2	STRING OF HITS	Shadows (EMI)
7	3	TELL ME ON A SUNDAY	Marti Webb (Polydor)
3	4	THE LAST DANCE	Various Artists (EMI)
9	5	ROSE ROYCE'S GREATEST HITS	Rose Royce (Whitfield)
2	6	REGATTA DE BLANC	Police (A&M)
8	7	GET HAPPY!	Elvis Costello (F Beat)
5	8	EAT TO THE BEAT	Blondie (Chrysalis)
-	9	NOBODY'S HERO	Stiff Little Fingers (Chrysalis)
10	10	GOLDEN COLLECTION	Charlie Pride (K-Tel)
22	11	DOWN TO EARTH	Rainbow (Polydor)
-	12	HEARTBREAKERS	Matt Monro (EMI)
19	13	OFF THE WALL	Michael Jackson (Epic)
4	14	PRETENDERS	Pretenders (Real)
-	15	THE CRYSTAL GAYLE SINGLES ALBUM	Crystal Gayle (United Artists)
12	16	ONE STEP BEYOND	Madness (Stiff)
11	17	TOO MUCH PRESSURE	Selecter (2-Tone)
17	18	LIGHT UP THE NIGHT	Brothers Johnson (A&M)
15	19	THE SPECIALS	Specials (2-Tone)
6	20	KENNY	Kenny Rogers (United Artists)
13	21	OUTLANDOS D'AMOUR	Police (A&M)
-	22	THE WHISPERS	Whispers (Solar)
23	23	K C & THE SUNSHINE BAND'S GREATEST HITS	K C & the Sunshine Band (TK)
-	24	AGAINST THE WIND	Bob Seger (Capitol)
-	25	OFFICIAL BOOTLEG ALBUM	Blues Band (Arista)
16	26	REALITY EFFECT	Tourists (Logo)
25	27	PERMANENT WAVES	Rush (Mercury)
21	28	ROCK AND ROLL JUVENILE	Cliff Richard (EMI)
-	29	FREEDOM AT POINT ZERO	Jefferson Starship (Grunt)
-	30	METRO MUSIC	Martha & the Muffins (Dindisc)

29 March 1980

1	1	TEARS AND LAUGHTER	Johnny Mathis (CBS)
3	2	TELL ME ON A SUNDAY	Marti Webb (Polydor)
6	3	REGATTA DE BLANC	Police (A&M)
5	4	ROSE ROYCE'S GREATEST HITS	Rose Royce (Whitfield)
2	5	STRING OF HITS	Shadows (EMI)
-	6	GLASS HOUSES	Billy Joel (CBS)
7	7	GET HAPPY!	Elvis Costello (F Beat)
12	8	HEARTBREAKERS	Matt Monro (EMI)
21	9	OUTLANDOS D'AMOUR	Police (A&M)
9	10	NOBODY'S HERO	Stiff Little Fingers (Chrysalis)
4	11	THE LAST DANCE	Various Artists (EMI)
15	12	THE CRYSTAL GAYLE SINGLES ALBUM	Crystal Gayle (United Artists)
10	13	GOLDEN COLLECTION	Charlie Pride (K-Tel)
11	14	DOWN TO EARTH	Rainbow (Polydor)
19	15	THE SPECIALS	Specials (2-Tone)
-	16	12 GOLD BARS	Status Quo (Vertigo)
13	17	OFF THE WALL	Michael Jackson (Epic)
8	18	EAT TO THE BEAT	Blondie (Chrysalis)
18	19	LIGHT UP THE NIGHT	Brothers Johnson (A&M)
20	20	KENNY	Kenny Rogers (United Artists)
14	21	PRETENDERS	Pretenders (Real)
-	22	LOUD AND CLEAR	Sammy Hagar (Capitol)
16	23	ONE STEP BEYOND	Madness (Stiff)
17	24	TOO MUCH PRESSURE	Selecter (2-Tone)
24	25	AGAINST THE WIND	Bob Seger (Capitol)
-	26	MAKE YOUR MOVE	Captain & Tennille (Casablanca)
27	27	PERMANENT WAVES	Rush (Mercury)
-	28	PSYCHEDELIC FURS	Psychedelic Furs (CBS)
-	29	COCKNEY REJECTS' GREATEST HITS VOL 1	Cockney Rejects (Zonophone)
23	30	K C & THE SUNSHINE BAND'S GREATEST HITS	K C & the Sunshine Band (TK)

String Of Hits - a collection of interpretations of other people's hits, rather than their own successes - was to be one of the Shadows' biggest-selling albums of all-time, second only to their *20 Golden Greats* package. Its sudden resurrection to the top of the chart after months on the market was down to clever marketing - EMI ran a new TV ad campaign for it. Also heavily TV-featured was Johnny Mathis' *Tears And Laughter*, a 20-track compilation which included his recent hit singles.

April 1980

5 April 1980

It was a widely-accepted truism in the British record business of the late-1970s and early 1980s, when disco held sway in the singles charts, that disco or dance-based acts just couldn't sell albums in large quantities. Nobody had told Rose Royce about this, however, with the result that their hits compilation was the biggest LP seller of April 1980, outdoing not only the new Genesis album *Duke*, but also the more predictably big-selling hits package *12 Gold Bars* by Status Quo.

3 May 1980

last week	this week	
1	1	ROSE ROYCE'S GREATEST HITS — Rose Royce (Whitfield)
2	2	12 GOLD BARS — Status Quo (Vertigo)
18	3	SKY 2 — Sky (Ariola)
5	4	THE MAGIC OF BONEY M — Boney M (Atlantic/Hansa)
-	5	IRON MAIDEN — Iron Maiden (EMI)
11	6	THE BOBBY VEE SINGLES ALBUM — Bobby Vee (United Artists)
3	7	DUKE — Genesis (Charisma)
-	8	SUZI QUATRO'S GREATEST HITS — Suzi Quatro (RAK)
29	9	BY REQUEST — Lena Martell (Ronco)
-	10	HYPNOTISED — Undertones (Sire)
-	11	SNAKES AND LADDERS — Gerry Rafferty (United Artists)
7	12	THE BARBARA DICKSON ALBUM — Barbara Dickson (Epic)
-	13	HEAVEN AND HELL — Black Sabbath (Vertigo)
4	14	BRITISH STEEL — Judas Priest (CBS)
14	15	COUNTRY NUMBER ONE — Don Gibson (Warwick)
6	16	REGATTA DE BLANC — Police (A&M)
-	17	SOMETIMES YOU WIN — Dr Hook (Capitol)
15	18	TELL ME ON A SUNDAY — Marti Webb (Polydor)
16	19	FACADES — Sad Cafe (RCA)
21	20	PRETENDERS — Pretenders (Real)
8	21	WHEELS OF STEEL — Saxon (Carrere)
-	22	SNAP, CRACKLE AND BOP — John Cooper-Clark (Epic)
23	23	EAT TO THE BEAT — Blondie (Chrysalis)
9	24	TEARS AND LAUGHTER — Johnny Mathis (CBS)
19	25	HEARTBREAKERS — Matt Monro (EMI)
24	26	THE SPECIALS — Specials (2-Tone)
-	27	SKA 'N' B — Bad Manners (Magnet)
28	28	BRAND NEW AGE — U K Subs (Gem)
-	29	OFF THE WALL — Michael Jackson (Epic)
13	30	ONE STEP BEYOND — Madness (Stiff)

10 May 1980

last week	this week	
4	1	THE MAGIC OF BONEY M — Boney M (Atlantic/Hansa)
1	2	ROSE ROYCE'S GREATEST HITS — Rose Royce (Whitfield)
3	3	SKY 2 — Sky (Ariola)
8	4	SUZI QUATRO'S GREATEST HITS — Suzi Quatro (RAK)
7	5	DUKE — Genesis (Charisma)
2	6	12 GOLD BARS — Status Quo (Vertigo)
-	7	EMPTY GLASS — Pete Townshend (Atco)
10	8	HYPNOTISED — Undertones (Sire)
6	9	THE BOBBY VEE SINGLES ALBUM — Bobby Vee (United Artists)
9	10	BY REQUEST — Lena Martell (Ronco)
11	11	SNAKES AND LADDERS — Gerry Rafferty (United Artists)
12	12	THE BARBARA DICKSON ALBUM — Barbara Dickson (Epic)
5	13	IRON MAIDEN — Iron Maiden (EMI)
16	14	REGATTA DE BLANC — Police (A&M)
29	15	OFF THE WALL — Michael Jackson (Epic)
14	16	BRITISH STEEL — Judas Priest (CBS)
13	17	HEAVEN AND HELL — Black Sabbath (Vertigo)
21	18	WHEELS OF STEEL — Saxon (Carrere)
20	19	PRETENDERS — Pretenders (Real)
17	20	SOMETIMES YOU WIN — Dr Hook (Capitol)
-	21	WILD HORSES — Wild Horses (EMI)
19	22	FACADES — Sad Cafe (RCA)
30	23	ONE STEP BEYOND — Madness (Stiff)
27	24	SKA 'N' B — Bad Manners (Magnet)
24	25	TEARS AND LAUGHTER — Johnny Mathis (CBS)
-	26	17 SECONDS — Cure (Fiction)
-	27	GLASS HOUSES — Billy Joel (CBS)
15	28	COUNTRY NUMBER ONE — Don Gibson (Warwick)
23	29	EAT TO THE BEAT — Blondie (Chrysalis)
-	30	BRAND NEW AGE — UK Subs (Gem)

17 May 1980

last week	this week	
1	1	THE MAGIC OF BONEY M — Boney M (Atlantic/Hansa)
3	2	SKY 2 — Sky (Ariola)
2	3	ROSE ROYCE'S GREATEST HITS — Rose Royce (Whitfield)
4	4	SUZI QUATRO'S GREATEST HITS — Suzi Quatro (RAK)
9	5	THE BOBBY VEE SINGLES ALBUM — Bobby Vee (United Artists)
5	6	DUKE — Genesis (Charisma)
20	7	SOMETIMES YOU WIN — Dr Hook (Capitol)
8	8	HYPNOTISED — Undertones (Sire)
6	9	12 GOLD BARS — Status Quo (Vertigo)
10	10	BY REQUEST — Lena Martell (Ronco)
17	11	HEAVEN AND HELL — Black Sabbath (Vertigo)
15	12	OFF THE WALL — Michael Jackson (Epic)
7	13	EMPTY GLASS — Pete Townshend (Atco)
12	14	THE BARBARA DICKSON ALBUM — Barbara Dickson (Epic)
13	15	IRON MAIDEN — Iron Maiden (EMI)
11	16	SNAKES AND LADDERS — Gerry Rafferty (United Artists)
-	17	JUST ONE NIGHT — Eric Clapton (RSO)
14	18	REGATTA DE BLANC — Police (A&M)
-	19	SPORTS CAR — Judie Tzuke (Rocket)
18	20	WHEELS OF STEEL — Saxon (Carrere)
23	21	ONE STEP BEYOND — Madness (Stiff)
27	22	GLASS HOUSES — Billy Joel (CBS)
24	23	SKA 'N' B — Bad Manners (Magnet)
25	24	TEARS AND LAUGHTER — Johnny Mathis (CBS)
26	25	17 SECONDS — Cure (Fiction)
30	26	BRAND NEW AGE — UK Subs (Gem)
22	27	FACADES — Sad Cafe (RCA)
21	28	WILD HORSES — Wild Horses (EMI)
-	29	THE CORRECT USE OF SOAP — Magazine (Virgin)
-	30	ANIMAL MAGNETISM — Scorpions (Harvest)

24 May 1980

last week	this week	
1	1	THE MAGIC OF BONEY M — Boney M (Atlantic/Hansa)
2	2	SKY 2 — Sky (Ariola)
3	3	ROSE ROYCE'S GREATEST HITS — Rose Royce (Whitfield)
4	4	SUZI QUATRO'S GREATEST HITS — Suzi Quatro (RAK)
19	5	SPORTS CAR — Judie Tzuke (Rocket)
9	6	12 GOLD BARS — Status Quo (Vertigo)
17	7	JUST ONE NIGHT — Eric Clapton (RSO)
6	8	DUKE — Genesis (Charisma)
7	9	SOMETIMES YOU WIN — Dr Hook (Capitol)
5	10	THE BOBBY VEE SINGLES ALBUM — Bobby Vee (United Artists)
14	11	THE BARBARA DICKSON ALBUM — Barbara Dickson (Epic)
10	12	BY REQUEST — Lena Martell (Ronco)
12	13	OFF THE WALL — Michael Jackson (Epic)
12	14	EMPTY GLASS — Pete Townshend (Atco)
11	15	HEAVEN AND HELL — Black Sabbath (Vertigo)
8	16	HYPNOTISED — Undertones (Sire)
18	17	REGATTA DE BLANC — Police (A&M)
16	18	SNAKES AND LADDERS — Gerry Rafferty (United Artists)
15	19	IRON MAIDEN — Iron Maiden (EMI)
-	20	GOOD MORNING AMERICA — Various Artists (K-Tel)
-	21	EAT TO THE BEAT — Blondie (Chrysalis)
24	22	TEARS AND LAUGHTER — Johnny Mathis (CBS)
-	23	WAR OF THE WORLDS — Jeff Wayne (CBS)
-	24	HAPPY DAYS — Various Artists (K-Tel)
21	25	ONE STEP BEYOND — Madness (Stiff)
26	26	BRAND NEW AGE — UK Subs (Gem)
22	27	GLASS HOUSES — Billy Joel (CBS)
29	28	THE CORRECT USE OF SOAP — Magazine (Virgin)
20	29	WHEELS OF STEEL — Saxon (Carrere)
-	30	SOLO IN SOHO — Philip Lynott (Vertigo)

Boney M's *The Magic Of* compilation took the best part of a month to get into high gear, but once at the chart top it fended off *Sky 2*, the pop/classical instrumental group's biggest-selling album. The chart was heavy with greatest hits sets (on May 17, the whole Top Five except *Sky 2* were hits compilations), and particularly remarkable among them was *The Bobby Vee Singles album*, which was the former teen idol's first UK top twenty entry of any kind for 17 years.

May – June 1980

31 May 1980

last week	this week	title	artist
1	1	THE MAGIC OF BONEY M	Boney M (Atlantic/Hansa)
2	2	SKY 2	Sky (Ariola)
3	3	ROSE ROYCE'S GREATEST HITS	Rose Royce (Whitfield)
13	4	OFF THE WALL	Michael Jackson (Epic)
7	5	JUST ONE NIGHT	Eric Clapton (RSO)
8	6	DUKE	Genesis (Charisma)
5	7	SPORTS CAR	Judie Tzuke (Rocket)
15	8	HEAVEN AND HELL	Black Sabbath (Vertigo)
6	9	12 GOLD BARS	Status Quo (Vertigo)
-	10	ME MYSELF I	Joan Armatrading (A&M)
25	11	ONE STEP BEYOND	Madness (Stiff)
16	12	HYPNOTISED	Undertones (Sire)
18	13	SNAKES AND LADDERS	Gerry Rafferty (United Artists)
-	14	PRETENDERS	Pretenders (Real)
4	15	SUZI QUATRO'S GREATEST HITS	Suzi Quatro (RAK)
-	16	McCARTNEY 2	Paul McCartney (Parlophone)
10	17	THE BOBBY VEE SINGLES ALBUM	Bobby Vee (United Artists)
17	18	REGATTA DE BLANC	Police (A&M)
-	19	I JUST CAN'T STOP IT	Beat (Go Feet)
-	20	MAGIC REGGAE	Various Artists (K-Tel)
9	21	SOMETIMES YOU WIN	Dr Hook (Capitol)
-	22	LITTLE DREAMER	Peter Green (PVK)
20	23	GOOD MORNING AMERICA	Various Artists (K-Tel)
29	24	WHEELS OF STEEL	Saxon (Carrere)
-	25	SO FAR AWAY	Chords (Polydor)
11	26	THE BARBARA DICKSON ALBUM	Barbara Dickson (Epic)
14	27	EMPTY GLASS	Pete Townshend (Atco)
-	28	17 SECONDS	Cure (Fiction)
19	29	IRON MAIDEN	Iron Maiden (EMI)
23	30	WAR OF THE WORLDS	Jeff Wayne (CBS)

7 June 1980

last week	this week	title	artist
16	1	McCARTNEY 2	Paul McCartney (Parlophone)
2	2	SKY 2	Sky (Ariola)
19	3	I JUST CAN'T STOP IT	Beat (Go Feet)
1	4	THE MAGIC OF BONEY M	Boney M (Atlantic/Hansa)
-	5	FLESH AND BLOOD	Roxy Music (Polydor)
10	6	ME MYSELF I	Joan Armatrading (A&M)
3	7	ROSE ROYCE'S GREATEST HITS	Rose Royce (Whitfield)
-	8	CHAMPAGNE AND ROSES	Various Artists (Polydor)
5	9	JUST ONE NIGHT	Eric Clapton (RSO)
4	10	OFF THE WALL	Michael Jackson (Epic)
6	11	DUKE	Genesis (Charisma)
7	12	SPORTS CAR	Judie Tzuke (Rocket)
13	13	SNAKES AND LADDERS	Gerry Rafferty (United Artists)
-	14	TRAVELOGUE	Human League (Virgin)
8	15	HEAVEN AND HELL	Black Sabbath (Vertigo)
21	16	SOMETIMES YOU WIN	Dr Hook (Capitol)
9	17	12 GOLD BARS	Status Quo (Vertigo)
15	18	SUZI QUATRO'S GREATEST HITS	Suzi Quatro (RAK)
26	19	THE BARBARA DICKSON ALBUM	Barbara Dickson (Epic)
18	20	REGATTA DE BLANC	Police (A&M)
11	21	ONE STEP BEYOND	Madness (Stiff)
-	22	21 AT 33	Elton John (Rocket)
-	23	SHINE	Average White Band (RCA)
28	24	17 SECONDS	Cure (Fiction)
-	25	PETER GABRIEL	Peter Gabriel (Charisma)
-	26	FROM A TO B	New Musik (GTO)
-	27	LET'S GET SERIOUS	Jermaine Jackson (Motown)
29	28	IRON MAIDEN	Iron Maiden (EMI)
20	29	MAGIC REGGAE	Various Artists (K-Tel)
22	30	LITTLE DREAMER	Peter Green (PVK)

14 June 1980

last week	this week	title	artist
1	1	McCARTNEY 2	Paul McCartney (Parlophone)
5	2	FLESH AND BLOOD	Roxy Music (Polydor)
25	3	PETER GABRIEL	Peter Gabriel (Charisma)
6	4	ME MYSELF I	Joan Armatrading (A&M)
3	5	I JUST CAN'T STOP IT	Beat (Go Feet)
4	6	THE MAGIC OF BONEY M	Boney M (Atlantic/Hansa)
8	7	CHAMPAGNE AND ROSES	Various Artists (Polydor)
2	8	SKY 2	Sky (Ariola)
10	9	OFF THE WALL	Michael Jackson (Epic)
22	10	21 AT 33	Elton John (Rocket)
7	11	ROSE ROYCE'S GREATEST HITS	Rose Royce (Whitfield)
-	12	READY AND WILLING	Whitesnake (United Artists)
17	13	12 GOLD BARS	Status Quo (Vertigo)
9	14	JUST ONE NIGHT	Eric Clapton (RSO)
11	15	DUKE	Genesis (Charisma)
-	16	GOOD MORNING AMERICA	Various Artists (K-Tel)
-	17	THE UP ESCALATOR	Graham Parker & the Rumour (Stiff)
16	18	SOMETIMES YOU WIN	Dr Hook (Capitol)
20	19	REGATTA DE BLANC	Police (A&M)
27	20	LET'S GET SERIOUS	Jermaine Jackson (Motown)
28	21	IRON MAIDEN	Iron Maiden (EMI)
29	22	MAGIC REGGAE	Various Artists (K-Tel)
15	23	HEAVEN AND HELL	Black Sabbath (Vertigo)
14	24	TRAVELOGUE	Human League (Virgin)
18	25	SUZI QUATRO'S GREATEST HITS	Suzi Quatro (RAK)
13	26	SNAKES AND LADDERS	Gerry Rafferty (United Artists)
-	27	THEMES FOR DREAMS	Various Artists (K-Tel)
-	28	SOMETIMES WHEN WE TOUCH	Cleo Laine/James Galway (RCA)
23	29	SHINE	Average White Band (RCA)
21	30	ONE STEP BEYOND	Madness (Stiff)

21 June 1980

last week	this week	title	artist
2	1	FLESH AND BLOOD	Roxy Music (Polydor)
1	2	McCARTNEY 2	Paul McCartney (Parlophone)
3	3	PETER GABRIEL	Peter Gabriel (Charisma)
7	4	CHAMPAGNE AND ROSES	Various Artists (Polydor)
12	5	READY AND WILLING	Whitesnake (United Artists)
9	6	OFF THE WALL	Michael Jackson (Epic)
6	7	THE MAGIC OF BONEY M	Boney M (Atlantic/Hansa)
5	8	I JUST CAN'T STOP IT	Beat (Go Feet)
22	9	MAGIC REGGAE	Various Artists (K-Tel)
8	10	SKY 2	Sky (Ariola)
4	11	ME MYSELF I	Joan Armatrading (A&M)
10	12	21 AT 33	Elton John (Rocket)
15	13	DUKE	Genesis (Charisma)
11	14	ROSE ROYCE'S GREATEST HITS	Rose Royce (Whitfield)
-	15	HOT WAX	Various Artists (K-Tel)
19	16	REGATTA DE BLANC	Police (A&M)
14	17	JUST ONE NIGHT	Eric Clapton (RSO)
20	18	LET'S GET SERIOUS	Jermaine Jackson (Motown)
-	19	ORCHESTRAL MANOEUVRES IN THE DARK	Orchestral Manoeuvres in the Dark (Dindisc)
28	20	SOMETIMES WHEN WE TOUCH	Cleo Laine/James Galway (RCA)
-	21	THE GREAT ROCK AND ROLL SWINDLE	Soundtrack (Virgin)
13	22	12 GOLD BARS	Status Quo (Vertigo)
18	23	SOMETIMES YOU WIN	Dr Hook (Capitol)
16	24	GOOD MORNING AMERICA	Various Artists (K-Tel)
-	25	LADY T	Teena Marie (Motown)
-	26	TANGRAM	Tangerine Dream (Virgin)
29	27	SHINE	Average White Band (RCA)
17	28	THE UP ESCALATOR	Graham Parker & the Rumour (Stiff)
24	29	TRAVELOGUE	Human League (Virgin)
27	30	THEMES FOR DREAMS	Various Artists (K-Tel)

After a decade of billing himself and his ever-changing group as Wings, Paul McCartney finally issued an album credited to himself as a soloist once again - and emphasised the point by linking it, title-wise, to his first solo effort *McCartney* 10 years earlier in May 1970. Peter Gabriel, meanwhile, was taking the my-work-bears-my-name game to extraordinary lengths - *Peter Gabriel* was his third album to carry that title in just over three years, and would not be the last!

28 June 1980

last week	this week	Entry
3	1	PETER GABRIEL — Peter Gabriel (Charisma)
15	2	HOT WAX — Various Artists (K-Tel)
1	3	FLESH AND BLOOD — Roxy Music (Polydor)
2	4	McCARTNEY 2 — Paul McCartney (Parlophone)
11	5	ME MYSELF I — Joan Armatrading (A&M)
7	6	I JUST CAN'T STOP IT — Beat (Go Feet)
9	7	MAGIC REGGAE — Various Artists (K-Tel)
10	8	SKY 2 — Sky (Ariola)
4	9	CHAMPAGNE AND ROSES — Various Artists (Polydor)
5	10	READY AND WILLING — Whitesnake (United Artists)
6	11	OFF THE WALL — Michael Jackson (Epic)
7	12	THE MAGIC OF BONEY M — Boney M (Atlantic/Hansa)
27	13	SHINE — Average White Band (RCA)
14	14	ROSE ROYCE'S GREATEST HITS — Rose Royce (Whitfield)
21	15	THE GREAT ROCK AND ROLL SWINDLE — Soundtrack (Virgin)
-	16	DIANA — Diana Ross (Motown)
-	17	CHAIN LIGHTNING — Don McLean (EMI America)
13	18	DUKE — Genesis (Charisma)
16	19	REGATTA DE BLANC — Police (A&M)
-	20	THE PHOTOS — Photos (CBS)
-	21	DREAMS — Grace Slick (RCA)
12	22	21 AT 33 — Elton John (Rocket)
-	23	ROBERTA FLACK AND DONNY HATHAWAY — Roberta Flack & Donny Hathaway (Atlantic)
20	24	SOMETIMES WHEN WE TOUCH — Cleo Laine/James Galway (RCA)
-	25	DEFECTOR — Steve Hackett (Charisma)
28	26	THE UP ESCALATOR — Graham Parker & the Rumour (Stiff)
23	27	SOMETIMES YOU WIN — Dr Hook (Capitol)
19	28	ORCHESTRAL MANOEUVRES IN THE DARK — Orchestral Manoeuvres in the Dark (Dindisc)
17	29	JUST ONE NIGHT — Eric Clapton (RSO)
-	30	THE WANDERERS - ORIGINAL SOUNDTRACK — Various Artists (GEM)

5 July 1980

last week	this week	Entry
3	1	FLESH AND BLOOD — Roxy Music (Polydor)
2	2	HOT WAX — Various Artists (K-Tel)
4	3	McCARTNEY 2 — Paul McCartney (Parlophone)
7	4	MAGIC REGGAE — Various Artists (K-Tel)
1	5	PETER GABRIEL — Peter Gabriel (Charisma)
-	6	UPRISING — Bob Marley & the Wailers (Island)
8	7	SKY 2 — Sky (Ariola)
-	8	SAVED — Bob Dylan (CBS)
20	9	THE PHOTOS — Photos (CBS)
5	10	ME MYSELF I — Joan Armatrading (A&M)
9	11	CHAMPAGNE AND ROSES — Various Artists (Polydor)
6	12	I JUST CAN'T STOP IT — Beat (Go Feet)
19	13	REGATTA DE BLANC — Police (A&M)
16	14	DIANA — Diana Ross (Motown)
18	15	DUKE — Genesis (Charisma)
22	16	21 AT 33 — Elton John (Rocket)
10	17	READY AND WILLING — Whitesnake (United Artists)
-	18	EMOTIONAL RESCUE — Rolling Stones (Rolling Stones)
23	19	ROBERTA FLACK AND DONNY HATHAWAY — Roberta Flack & Donny Hathaway (Atlantic)
13	20	SHINE — Average White Band (RCA)
11	21	OFF THE WALL — Michael Jackson (Epic)
17	22	CHAIN LIGHTNING — Don McLean (EMI America)
12	23	THE MAGIC OF BONEY M — Boney M (Atlantic/Hansa)
14	24	ROSE ROYCE'S GREATEST HITS — Rose Royce (Whitfield)
15	25	THE GREAT ROCK AND ROLL SWINDLE — Soundtrack (Virgin)
25	26	DEFECTOR — Steve Hackett (Charisma)
26	27	THE UP ESCALATOR — Graham Parker & the Rumour (Stiff)
30	28	THE WANDERERS - ORIGINAL SOUNDTRACK — Various Artists (GEM)
28	29	ORCHESTRAL MANOEUVRES IN THE DARK — Orchestral Manoeuvres in the Dark (Dindisc)
29	30	JUST ONE NIGHT — Eric Clapton (RSO)

12 July 1980

last week	this week	Entry
1	1	FLESH AND BLOOD — Roxy Music (Polydor)
18	2	EMOTIONAL RESCUE — Rolling Stones (Rolling Stones)
3	3	McCARTNEY 2 — Paul McCartney (Parlophone)
2	4	HOT WAX — Various Artists (K-Tel)
10	5	ME MYSELF I — Joan Armatrading (A&M)
7	6	SKY 2 — Sky (Ariola)
6	7	UPRISING — Bob Marley & the Wailers (Island)
21	8	OFF THE WALL — Michael Jackson (Epic)
5	9	PETER GABRIEL — Peter Gabriel (Charisma)
8	10	SAVED — Bob Dylan (CBS)
15	11	DUKE — Genesis (Charisma)
12	12	I JUST CAN'T STOP IT — Beat (Go Feet)
11	13	CHAMPAGNE AND ROSES — Various Artists (Polydor)
23	14	THE MAGIC OF BONEY M — Boney M (Atlantic/Hansa)
13	15	REGATTA DE BLANC — Police (A&M)
22	16	CHAIN LIGHTNING — Don McLean (EMI America)
17	17	READY AND WILLING — Whitesnake (United Artists)
20	18	SHINE — Average White Band (RCA)
14	19	DIANA — Diana Ross (Motown)
9	20	THE PHOTOS — Photos (CBS)
26	21	DEFECTOR — Steve Hackett (Charisma)
-	22	BLACK SABBATH LIVE AT LAST — Black Sabbath (NEMS)
27	23	THE UP ESCALATOR — Graham Parker & the Rumour (Stiff)
4	24	MAGIC REGGAE — Various Artists (K-Tel)
-	25	KING OF THE ROAD — Boxcar Willie (Warwick)
-	26	SOUNDS SENSATIONAL — Bert Kaempfert (Polydor)
-	27	KILLER WATTS — Various Artists (Epic)
16	28	21 AT 33 — Elton John (Rocket)
24	29	ROSE ROYCE'S GREATEST HITS — Rose Royce (Whitfield)
28	30	THE WANDERERS — Soundtrack (GEM)

19 July 1980

last week	this week	Entry
2	1	EMOTIONAL RESCUE — Rolling Stones (Rolling Stones)
1	2	FLESH AND BLOOD — Roxy Music (Polydor)
-	3	THE GAME — Queen (EMI)
5	4	ME MYSELF I — Joan Armatrading (A&M)
3	5	McCARTNEY 2 — Paul McCartney (Parlophone)
6	6	SKY 2 — Sky (Ariola)
22	7	BLACK SABBATH LIVE AT LAST — Black Sabbath (NEMS)
7	8	UPRISING — Bob Marley & the Wailers (Island)
9	9	PETER GABRIEL — Peter Gabriel (Charisma)
12	10	I JUST CAN'T STOP IT — Beat (Go Feet)
8	11	OFF THE WALL — Michael Jackson (Epic)
11	12	DUKE — Genesis (Charisma)
17	13	READY AND WILLING — Whitesnake (United Artists)
16	14	CHAIN LIGHTNING — Don McLean (EMI America)
10	15	SAVED — Bob Dylan (CBS)
4	16	HOT WAX — Various Artists (K-Tel)
18	17	SHINE — Average White Band (RCA)
26	18	SOUNDS SENSATIONAL — Bert Kaempfert (Polydor)
25	19	KING OF THE ROAD — Boxcar Willie (Warwick)
19	20	DIANA — Diana Ross (Motown)
20	21	THE PHOTOS — Photos (CBS)
29	22	ROSE ROYCE'S GREATEST HITS — Rose Royce (Whitfield)
15	23	REGATTA DE BLANC — Police (A&M)
24	24	MAGIC REGGAE — Various Artists (K-Tel)
14	25	THE MAGIC OF BONEY M — Boney M (Atlantic/Hansa)
13	26	CHAMPAGNE AND ROSES — Various Artists (Polydor)
-	27	WHEELS OF STEEL — Saxon (Carrere)
-	28	XANADU — Soundtrack (Jet)
-	29	BEAT BOYS IN THE JET AGE — Lambrettas (Rocket)
21	30	DEFECTOR — Steve Hackett (Charisma)

The Photos, a UK group led by striking girl vocalist Wendy Wu, surprised many with the Top 10 success of their eponymous album, particularly since they never managed to have single success, at this or any other time (it must have been down to all that heavy music paper coverage focusing on the extremely photogenic Wendy). The Rolling Stones and Joan Armatrading, meanwhile, both charted albums of which they simultaneously issued the title song as a single - in both cases, the LP sold better.

July – August 1980

26 July 1980

last	this	Title / Artist (Label)
3	1	THE GAME — Queen (EMI)
1	2	EMOTIONAL RESCUE — Rolling Stones (Rolling Stones)
28	3	XANADU — Soundtrack (Jet)
8	4	UPRISING — Bob Marley & the Wailers (Island)
2	5	FLESH AND BLOOD — Roxy Music (Polydor)
11	6	OFF THE WALL — Michael Jackson (Epic)
5	7	McCARTNEY 2 — Paul McCartney (Parlophone)
19	8	KING OF THE ROAD — Boxcar Willie (Warwick)
6	9	SKY 2 — Sky (Ariola)
4	10	ME MYSELF I — Joan Armatrading (A&M)
-	11	DEEPEST PURPLE — Deep Purple (Harvest)
20	12	DIANA — Diana Ross (Motown)
16	13	HOT WAX — Various Artists (K-Tel)
23	14	REGATTA DE BLANC — Police (A&M)
9	15	PETER GABRIEL — Peter Gabriel (Charisma)
-	16	GIVE ME THE NIGHT — George Benson (Warner Bros.)
12	17	DUKE — Genesis (Charisma)
17	18	SHINE — Average White Band (RCA)
7	19	BLACK SABBATH LIVE AT LAST — Black Sabbath (NEMS)
13	20	READY AND WILLING — Whitesnake (United Artists)
-	21	VIENNA — Ultravox (Chrysalis)
25	22	THE MAGIC OF BONEY M — Boney M (Atlantic/Hansa)
14	23	CHAIN LIGHTNING — Don McLean (EMI America)
15	24	SAVED — Bob Dylan (CBS)
-	25	CULTOSAURUS ERECTUS — Blue Oyster Cult (CBS)
-	26	THEMES FOR DREAMS — Pierre Belmonde (K-Tel)
10	27	I JUST CAN'T STOP IT — Beat (Go Feet)
-	28	DEMOLITION — Girlschool (Bronze)
-	29	HOT LOVE — David Essex (Phonogram)
-	30	BAT OUT OF HELL — Meatloaf (Epic)

2 August 1980

last	this	Title / Artist (Label)
3	1	XANADU — Soundtrack (Jet)
2	2	EMOTIONAL RESCUE — Rolling Stones (Rolling Stones)
5	3	FLESH AND BLOOD — Roxy Music (Polydor)
4	4	UPRISING — Bob Marley & the Wailers (Island)
16	5	GIVE ME THE NIGHT — George Benson (Warner Bros.)
1	6	THE GAME — Queen (EMI)
11	7	DEEPEST PURPLE — Deep Purple (Harvest)
6	8	OFF THE WALL — Michael Jackson (Epic)
7	9	McCARTNEY 2 — Paul McCartney (Parlophone)
10	10	ME MYSELF I — Joan Armatrading (A&M)
9	11	SKY 2 — Sky (Ariola)
8	12	KING OF THE ROAD — Boxcar Willie (Warwick)
27	13	I JUST CAN'T STOP IT — Beat (Go Feet)
19	14	BLACK SABBATH LIVE AT LAST — Black Sabbath (NEMS)
-	15	SEARCHING FOR THE YOUNG SOUL REBELS — Dexy's Midnight Runners (Parlophone)
12	16	DIANA — Diana Ross (Motown)
24	17	SAVED — Bob Dylan (CBS)
-	18	ALL FOR YOU — Johnny Mathis (CBS)
-	19	MAGIC REGGAE — Various Artists (K-Tel)
15	20	PETER GABRIEL — Peter Gabriel (Charisma)
20	21	READY AND WILLING — Whitesnake (United Artists)
21	22	VIENNA — Ultravox (Chrysalis)
13	23	HOT WAX — Various Artists (K-Tel)
17	24	DUKE — Genesis (Charisma)
-	25	CLOSER — Joy Division (Factory)
-	26	SMALL FACES BIG HITS — Small Faces (Immediate/Virgin)
14	27	REGATTA DE BLANC — Police (A&M)
18	28	SHINE — Average White Band (RCA)
25	29	CULTOSAURUS ERECTUS — Blue Oyster Cult (CBS)
-	30	MANILOW MAGIC — Barry Manilow (Arista)

9 August 1980

last	this	Title / Artist (Label)
1	1	XANADU — Soundtrack (Jet)
7	2	DEEPEST PURPLE — Deep Purple (Harvest)
6	3	THE GAME — Queen (EMI)
3	4	FLESH AND BLOOD — Roxy Music (Polydor)
5	5	GIVE ME THE NIGHT — George Benson (Warner Bros.)
2	6	EMOTIONAL RESCUE — Rolling Stones (Rolling Stones)
4	7	UPRISING — Bob Marley & the Wailers (Island)
8	8	OFF THE WALL — Michael Jackson (Epic)
15	9	SEARCHING FOR THE YOUNG SOUL REBELS — Dexy's Midnight Runners (Parlophone)
-	10	ANOTHER STRING OF HOT HITS — Shadows (EMI)
10	11	ME MYSELF I — Joan Armatrading (A&M)
9	12	McCARTNEY 2 — Paul McCartney (Parlophone)
11	13	SKY 2 — Sky (Ariola)
13	14	I JUST CAN'T STOP IT — Beat (Go Feet)
25	15	CLOSER — Joy Division (Factory)
16	16	DIANA — Diana Ross (Motown)
22	17	VIENNA — Ultravox (Chrysalis)
30	18	MANILOW MAGIC — Barry Manilow (Arista)
19	19	MAGIC REGGAE — Various Artists (K-Tel)
12	20	KING OF THE ROAD — Boxcar Willie (Warwick)
-	21	RHAPSODY AND BLUES — Crusaders (MCA)
27	22	REGATTA DE BLANC — Police (A&M)
14	23	BLACK SABBATH LIVE AT LAST — Black Sabbath (NEMS)
20	24	PETER GABRIEL — Peter Gabriel (Charisma)
18	25	ALL FOR YOU — Johnny Mathis (CBS)
-	26	WHEELS OF STEEL — Saxon (Carrere)
17	27	SAVED — Bob Dylan (CBS)
-	28	BRAZILIAN LOVE AFFAIR — George Duke (Epic)
-	29	ROMANTIC GUITAR — Paul Brett (K-Tel)
-	30	CROCODILES — Echo & the Bunnymen (Korova)

16 August 1980

last	this	Title / Artist (Label)
4	1	FLESH AND BLOOD — Roxy Music (Polydor)
1	2	XANADU — Soundtrack (Jet)
-	3	BACK IN BLACK — AC/DC (Atlantic)
2	4	DEEPEST PURPLE — Deep Purple (Harvest)
7	5	UPRISING — Bob Marley & the Wailers (Island)
5	6	GIVE ME THE NIGHT — George Benson (Warner Bros.)
16	7	DIANA — Diana Ross (Motown)
6	8	EMOTIONAL RESCUE — Rolling Stones (Rolling Stones)
15	9	CLOSER — Joy Division (Factory)
8	10	OFF THE WALL — Michael Jackson (Epic)
9	11	SEARCHING FOR THE YOUNG SOUL REBELS — Dexy's Midnight Runners (Parlophone)
24	12	PETER GABRIEL — Peter Gabriel (Charisma)
14	13	I JUST CAN'T STOP IT — Beat (Go Feet)
3	14	THE GAME — Queen (EMI)
13	15	SKY 2 — Sky (Ariola)
10	16	ANOTHER STRING OF HOT HITS — Shadows (EMI)
17	17	VIENNA — Ultravox (Chrysalis)
22	18	REGATTA DE BLANC — Police (A&M)
20	19	KING OF THE ROAD — Boxcar Willie (Warwick)
18	20	MANILOW MAGIC — Barry Manilow (Arista)
19	21	MAGIC REGGAE — Various Artists (K-Tel)
-	22	BEAT BOYS IN THE JET AGE — Lambrettas (Rocket)
-	22	LIVE 1979 — Hawkwind (Bronze)
-	24	XOO MULTIPLIES — Yellow Magic Orchestra (A&M)
-	25	DO A RUNNER — Athletico Spizz '80 (A&M)
21	26	RHAPSODY AND BLUES — Crusaders (MCA)
12	27	McCARTNEY 2 — Paul McCartney (Parlophone)
11	28	ME MYSELF I — Joan Armatrading (A&M)
-	29	BREAKING GLASS — Hazel O'Connor (A&M)
-	30	SMALL FACES BIG HITS — Small Faces (Immediate/Virgin)

Xanadu, an extraordinarily inane film musical which Olivia Newton-John and Gene Kelly should have known better than to approach with a bargepole, nonetheless proved a big commercial success in terms of its spin-off recordings. In addition to the soundtrack album topping the chart, the title song by Olivia and ELO was a No.1 single, and there were *three* more hit singles from the movie - Olivia's *Magic*, ELO's *I'm Alive*, and the Newton-John/Cliff Richard duet *Suddenly*.

last this week

23 August 1980

last	this		
1	1	FLESH AND BLOOD	Roxy Music (Polydor)
6	2	GIVE ME THE NIGHT	George Benson (Warner Bros.)
2	3	XANADU	Soundtrack (Jet)
4	4	DEEPEST PURPLE	Deep Purple (Harvest)
3	5	BACK IN BLACK	AC/DC (Atlantic)
7	6	DIANA	Diana Ross (Motown)
8	7	EMOTIONAL RESCUE	Rolling Stones (Rolling Stones)
5	8	UPRISING	Bob Marley & the Wailers (Island)
15	9	SKY 2	Sky (Ariola)
9	10	CLOSER	Joy Division (Factory)
10	11	OFF THE WALL	Michael Jackson (Epic)
-	12	GLORY ROAD	Gillan (Virgin)
11	13	SEARCHING FOR THE YOUNG SOUL REBELS	Dexy's Midnight Runners (Parlophone)
20	14	MANILOW MAGIC	Barry Manilow (Arista)
14	15	THE GAME	Queen (EMI)
13	16	I JUST CAN'T STOP IT	Beat (Go Feet)
19	17	KING OF THE ROAD	Boxcar Willie (Warwick)
22	18	LIVE 1979	Hawkwind (Bronze)
17	19	VIENNA	Ultravox (Chrysalis)
18	20	REGATTA DE BLANC	Police (A&M)
-	21	KALEIDOSCOPE	Siouxsie & the Banshees (Polydor)
29	22	BREAKING GLASS	Hazel O'Connor (A&M)
-	23	BAT OUT OF HELL	Meatloaf (Epic)
-	24	THE WALL	Pink Floyd (Harvest)
-	25	WAR OF THE WORLDS	Jeff Wayne (CBS)
27	26	McCARTNEY 2	Paul McCartney (Parlophone)
-	27	CAN'T STOP THE MUSIC	Soundtrack (Mercury)
-	28	DUKE	Genesis (Charisma)
-	28	DUMB WAITERS	Korgis (Rialto)
-	30	SKA 'N' B	Bad Manners (Magnet)

30 August 1980

last	this		
2	1	GIVE ME THE NIGHT	George Benson (Warner Bros.)
1	2	FLESH AND BLOOD	Roxy Music (Polydor)
3	3	XANADU	Soundtrack (Jet)
5	4	BACK IN BLACK	AC/DC (Atlantic)
4	5	DEEPEST PURPLE	Deep Purple (Harvest)
6	6	DIANA	Diana Ross (Motown)
19	7	VIENNA	Ultravox (Chrysalis)
9	8	SKY 2	Sky (Ariola)
26	9	McCARTNEY 2	Paul McCartney (Parlophone)
11	10	OFF THE WALL	Michael Jackson (Epic)
16	11	I JUST CAN'T STOP IT	Beat (Go Feet)
13	12	SEARCHING FOR THE YOUNG SOUL REBELS	Dexy's Midnight Runners (Parlophone)
-	13	LIVING IN A FANTASY	Leo Sayer (Chrysalis)
7	14	EMOTIONAL RESCUE	Rolling Stones (Rolling Stones)
-	15	ELVIS ARON PRESLEY	Elvis Presley (RCA)
21	16	KALEIDOSCOPE	Siouxsie & the Banshees (Polydor)
14	17	MANILOW MAGIC	Barry Manilow (Arista)
20	18	REGATTA DE BLANC	Police (A&M)
17	19	KING OF THE ROAD	Boxcar Willie (Warwick)
30	20	SKA 'N' B	Bad Manners (Magnet)
25	21	WAR OF THE WORLDS	Jeff Wayne (CBS)
12	22	GLORY ROAD	Gillan (Virgin)
8	23	UPRISING	Bob Marley & the Wailers (Island)
23	24	BAT OUT OF HELL	Meatloaf (Epic)
15	25	THE GAME	Queen (EMI)
10	26	CLOSER	Joy Division (Factory)
27	27	CAN'T STOP THE MUSIC	Soundtrack (Mercury)
-	28	ME MYSELF I	Joan Armatrading (A&M)
18	29	LIVE 1979	Hawkwind (Bronze)
28	30	DUMB WAITERS	Korgis (Rialto)

6 September 1980

last	this		
1	1	GIVE ME THE NIGHT	George Benson (Warner Bros.)
2	2	FLESH AND BLOOD	Roxy Music (Polydor)
10	3	OFF THE WALL	Michael Jackson (Epic)
6	4	DIANA	Diana Ross (Motown)
4	5	BACK IN BLACK	AC/DC (Atlantic)
-	5	BREAKING GLASS	Hazel O'Connor (A&M)
8	7	SKY 2	Sky (Ariola)
3	8	XANADU	Soundtrack (Jet)
-	9	DRAMA	Yes (Atlantic)
23	10	UPRISING	Bob Marley & the Wailers (Island)
16	11	KALEIDOSCOPE	Siouxsie & the Banshees (Polydor)
17	12	MANILOW MAGIC	Barry Manilow (Arista)
5	13	DEEPEST PURPLE	Deep Purple (Harvest)
22	14	GLORY ROAD	Gillan (Virgin)
28	15	ME MYSELF I	Joan Armatrading (A&M)
7	16	VIENNA	Ultravox (Chrysalis)
13	17	LIVING IN A FANTASY	Leo Sayer (Chrysalis)
11	18	I JUST CAN'T STOP IT	Beat (Go Feet)
15	19	ELVIS ARON PRESLEY	Elvis Presley (RCA)
9	20	McCARTNEY 2	Paul McCartney (Parlophone)
26	21	CLOSER	Joy Division (Factory)
27	22	CAN'T STOP THE MUSIC	Soundtrack (Mercury)
14	23	EMOTIONAL RESCUE	Rolling Stones (Rolling Stones)
12	24	SEARCHING FOR THE YOUNG SOUL REBELS	Dexy's Midnight Runners (Parlophone)
25	25	THE GAME	Queen (EMI)
20	26	SKA 'N' B	Bad Manners (Magnet)
24	27	BAT OUT OF HELL	Meatloaf (Epic)
18	28	REGATTA DE BLANC	Police (A&M)
-	29	PETER GABRIEL	Peter Gabriel (Charisma)
30	30	DUMB WAITERS	Korgis (Rialto)

13 September 1980

last	this		
2	1	FLESH AND BLOOD	Roxy Music (Polydor)
1	2	GIVE ME THE NIGHT	George Benson (Warner Bros.)
8	3	XANADU	Soundtrack (Jet)
5	4	BREAKING GLASS	Hazel O'Connor (A&M)
5	5	BACK IN BLACK	AC/DC (Atlantic)
-	6	SIGNING OFF	UB40 (Graduate)
3	7	OFF THE WALL	Michael Jackson (Epic)
14	8	GLORY ROAD	Gillan (Virgin)
22	9	CAN'T STOP THE MUSIC	Soundtrack (Mercury)
9	10	DRAMA	Yes (Atlantic)
18	11	I JUST CAN'T STOP IT	Beat (Go Feet)
10	12	UPRISING	Bob Marley & the Wailers (Island)
7	13	SKY 2	Sky (Ariola)
3	14	DIANA	Diana Ross (Motown)
15	15	ME MYSELF I	Joan Armatrading (A&M)
11	16	KALEIDOSCOPE	Siouxsie & the Banshees (Polydor)
16	17	VIENNA	Ultravox (Chrysalis)
12	18	MANILOW MAGIC	Barry Manilow (Arista)
-	19	I'M NO HERO	Cliff Richard (EMI)
13	20	DEEPEST PURPLE	Deep Purple (Harvest)
-	21	TELEKON	Gary Newman (Beggars Banquet)
24	22	SEARCHING FOR THE YOUNG SOUL REBELS	Dexy's Midnight Runners (Parlophone)
17	23	LIVING IN A FANTASY	Leo Sayer (Chrysalis)
-	24	ONE TRICK PONY	Paul Simon (Warner Bros.)
19	25	ELVIS ARON PRESLEY	Elvis Presley (RCA)
21	26	CLOSER	Joy Division (Factory)
-	27	WARM LEATHERETTE	Grace Jones (Island)
-	28	CLUES	Robert Palmer (Island)
-	29	ON THE RIVIERA	Gibson Brothers (Island)
-	30	WILD CAT	Tygers Of Pan Tang (MCA)

Elvis Aron Presley was an 8-LP boxed set, issued to commemorate the third anniversary of Presley's death, and containing mostly rare or previously unreleased material by him. Retailing at over £30, it became both the most expensive and largest album package yet to reach the UK Top 20. Hazel O'Connor's *Breaking Glass* album, which gave her a Top 5 debut, contained the songs from the British film of the same title, in which the singer had a starring role as a manipulated punk vocalist.

September – October 1980

20 September 1980

Last	This	Album	Artist (Label)
6	1	SIGNING OFF	UB40 (Graduate)
21	2	TELEKON	Gary Newman (Beggars Banquet)
1	3	FLESH AND BLOOD	Roxy Music (Polydor)
2	4	GIVE ME THE NIGHT	George Benson (Warner Bros.)
4	5	BREAKING GLASS	Hazel O'Connor (A&M)
5	6	BACK IN BLACK	AC/DC (Atlantic)
19	7	I'M NO HERO	Cliff Richard (EMI)
10	8	DRAMA	Yes (Atlantic)
18	9	MANILOW MAGIC	Barry Manilow (Arista)
14	10	DIANA	Diana Ross (Motown)
-	11	FAME	Soundtrack (Jet)
3	12	XANADU	Soundtrack (Jet)
7	13	OFF THE WALL	Michael Jackson (Epic)
11	14	I JUST CAN'T STOP IT	Beat (Go Feet)
13	15	SKY 2	Sky (Ariola)
-	16	NEVER FOR EVER	Kate Bush (EMI)
24	17	ONE TRICK PONY	Paul Simon (Warner Bros.)
9	18	CAN'T STOP THE MUSIC	Soundtrack (Mercury)
-	19	WILD PLANET	B52s (Island)
8	20	GLORY ROAD	Gillan (Virgin)
-	21	NOW WE MAY BEGIN	Randy Crawford (Warner Bros.)
-	22	GLASS HOUSES	Billy Joel (CBS)
-	23	FRESH FRUIT FOR ROTTING VEGETABLES	Dead Kennedys (Cherry Red)
15	24	ME MYSELF I	Joan Armatrading (A&M)
-	25	CHANGE OF ADDRESS	Shadows (Polydor)
12	26	UPRISING	Bob Marley & the Wailers (Island)
16	27	KALEIDOSCOPE	Siouxsie & the Banshees (Polydor)
20	28	DEEPEST PURPLE	Deep Purple (Harvest)
23	29	LIVING IN A FANTASY	Leo Sayer (Chrysalis)
29	30	ON THE RIVIERA	Gibson Brothers (Island)

27 September 1980

Last	This	Album	Artist (Label)
2	1	TELEKON	Gary Newman (Beggars Banquet)
1	2	SIGNING OFF	UB40 (Graduate)
16	3	NEVER FOR EVER	Kate Bush (EMI)
7	4	I'M NO HERO	Cliff Richard (EMI)
9	5	MANILOW MAGIC	Barry Manilow (Arista)
21	6	NOW WE MAY BEGIN	Randy Crawford (Warner Bros.)
4	7	GIVE ME THE NIGHT	George Benson (Warner Bros.)
3	8	FLESH AND BLOOD	Roxy Music (Polydor)
-	9	OZZY OSBOURNE'S BLIZZARD OF OZ	Ozzy Osbourne (Jet)
25	10	CHANGE OF ADDRESS	Shadows (Polydor)
6	11	BACK IN BLACK	AC/DC (Atlantic)
5	12	BREAKING GLASS	Hazel O'Connor (A&M)
-	13	SCARY MONSTERS AND SUPER CREEPS	David Bowie (RCA)
10	14	DIANA	Diana Ross (Motown)
15	15	SKY 2	Sky (Ariola)
8	16	DRAMA	Yes (Atlantic)
17	17	ONE TRICK PONY	Paul Simon (Warner Bros.)
12	18	XANADU	Soundtrack (Jet)
-	19	HANX	Stiff Little Fingers (Chrysalis)
-	20	BLACK SEA	XTC (Virgin)
11	21	FAME	Soundtrack (Jet)
-	22	THE GAME	Queen (EMI)
18	23	CAN'T STOP THE MUSIC	Soundtrack (Mercury)
-	24	REGATTA DE BLANC	Police (A&M)
26	25	UPRISING	Bob Marley & the Wailers (Island)
29	26	LIVING IN A FANTASY	Leo Sayer (Chrysalis)
20	27	GLORY ROAD	Gillan (Virgin)
-	28	McVICAR	Roger Daltrey (Polydor)
22	29	GLASS HOUSES	Billy Joel (CBS)
13	30	OFF THE WALL	Michael Jackson (Epic)

4 October 1980

Last	This	Album	Artist (Label)
3	1	NEVER FOR EVER	Kate Bush (EMI)
13	2	SCARY MONSTERS AND SUPER CREEPS	David Bowie (RCA)
2	3	SIGNING OFF	UB40 (Graduate)
-	4	MOUNTING EXCITEMENT	Various Artists (K-Tel)
6	5	NOW WE MAY BEGIN	Randy Crawford (Warner Bros.)
1	6	TELEKON	Gary Newman (Beggars Banquet)
8	7	FLESH AND BLOOD	Roxy Music (Polydor)
-	8	THE ABSOLUTE GAME	Skids (Virgin)
4	9	I'M NO HERO	Cliff Richard (EMI)
-	10	THE VERY BEST OF DON McLEAN	Don McLean (United Artists)
5	11	MANILOW MAGIC	Barry Manilow (Arista)
7	12	GIVE ME THE NIGHT	George Benson (Warner Bros.)
19	13	HANX	Stiff Little Fingers (Chrysalis)
-	14	LIVE CRASH COURSE	UK Subs (Gem)
12	15	BREAKING GLASS	Hazel O'Connor (A&M)
22	16	THE GAME	Queen (EMI)
9	17	OZZY OSBOURNE'S BLIZZARD OF OZ	Ozzy Osbourne (Jet)
20	18	BLACK SEA	XTC (Virgin)
14	19	DIANA	Diana Ross (Motown)
-	20	GOLD	Three Degrees (Ariola)
-	21	I JUST CAN'T STOP IT	Beat (Go Feet)
15	22	SKY 2	Sky (Ariola)
30	23	OFF THE WALL	Michael Jackson (Epic)
-	24	I AM WOMAN	Various Artists (Polydor)
10	25	CHANGE OF ADDRESS	Shadows (Polydor)
18	26	XANADU	Soundtrack (Jet)
-	27	THE LOVE ALBUM	Various Artists (K-Tel)
-	28	FRESH FRUIT FOR ROTTING VEGETABLES	Dead Kennedys (Cherry Red)
29	29	GLASS HOUSES	Billy Joel (CBS)
-	30	ABSOLUTELY	Madness (Stiff)

11 October 1980

Last	This	Album	Artist (Label)
2	1	SCARY MONSTERS AND SUPER CREEPS	David Bowie (RCA)
1	2	NEVER FOR EVER	Kate Bush (EMI)
4	3	MOUNTING EXCITEMENT	Various Artists (K-Tel)
-	4	ZENYATTA MONDATTA	Police (A&M)
9	5	THE VERY BEST OF DON McLEAN	Don McLean (United Artists)
5	6	NOW WE MAY BEGIN	Randy Crawford (Warner Bros.)
9	7	I'M NO HERO	Cliff Richard (EMI)
30	8	ABSOLUTELY	Madness (Stiff)
3	9	SIGNING OFF	UB40 (Graduate)
-	10	MORE SPECIALS	Specials (2-Tone)
15	11	BREAKING GLASS	Hazel O'Connor (A&M)
11	12	MANILOW MAGIC	Barry Manilow (Arista)
12	13	GIVE ME THE NIGHT	George Benson (Warner Bros.)
-	14	PARIS	Supertramp (A&M)
7	15	FLESH AND BLOOD	Roxy Music (Polydor)
6	16	TELEKON	Gary Newman (Beggars Banquet)
7	17	THE ABSOLUTE GAME	Skids (Virgin)
20	18	GOLD	Three Degrees (Ariola)
13	19	HANX	Stiff Little Fingers (Chrysalis)
14	20	LIVE CRASH COURSE	UK Subs (Gem)
22	21	SKY 2	Sky (Ariola)
28	22	FRESH FRUIT FOR ROTTING VEGETABLES	Dead Kennedys (Cherry Red)
17	23	OZZY OSBOURNE'S BLIZZARD OF OZ	Ozzy Osbourne (Jet)
-	24	A TOUCH OF LOVE	Gladys Knight and the Pips (K-Tel)
23	25	OFF THE WALL	Michael Jackson (Epic)
-	26	MIDNITE DYNAMOS	Matchbox (Magnet)
-	27	BACK IN BLACK	AC/DC (Atlantic)
27	28	THE LOVE ALBUM	Various Artists (K-Tel)
16	29	THE GAME	Queen (EMI)
24	30	I AM WOMAN	Various Artists (Polydor)

With *Signing Off* (the title being a wry allusion to their own band name), UB40 joined the elite to have scored a chart-topper with their first album release, and also gave a rare Number 1 album to a small indie label - in this case, the West Midland-based Graduate Records. Kate Bush, meanwhile, made it two Number 1's from her first three releases, and Gary Numan three chart-toppers in a row. The Shadows' title appeared to note their label move from EMI to Polydor.

last week	this week	18 October 1980		
4	1	ZENYATTA MONDATTA		Police (A&M)
8	2	ABSOLUTELY		Madness (Stiff)
1	3	SCARY MONSTERS AND SUPER CREEPS		David Bowie (RCA)
2	4	NEVER FOR EVER		Kate Bush (EMI)
-	5	GUILTY		Barbra Streisand (CBS)
3	6	MOUNTING EXCITEMENT		Various Artists (K-Tel)
5	7	THE VERY BEST OF DON McLEAN		Don McLean (United Artists)
12	8	MANILOW MAGIC		Barry Manilow (Arista)
10	9	MORE SPECIALS		Specials (2-Tone)
11	10	BREAKING GLASS		Hazel O'Connor (A&M)
14	11	PARIS		Supertramp (A&M)
8	12	SIGNING OFF		UB40 (Graduate)
-	13	TRIUMPH		Jacksons (Epic)
26	14	MIDNITE DYNAMOS		Matchbox (Magnet)
6	15	NOW WE MAY BEGIN		Randy Crawford (Warner Bros.)
13	16	GIVE ME THE NIGHT		George Benson (Warner Bros.)
16	17	TELEKON		Gary Newman (Beggars Banquet)
15	18	FLESH AND BLOOD		Roxy Music (Polydor)
7	19	I'M NO HERO		Cliff Richard (EMI)
-	20	DIANA		Diana Ross (Motown)
30	21	I AM WOMAN		Various Artists (Polydor)
18	22	GOLD		Three Degrees (Ariola)
24	23	A TOUCH OF LOVE		Gladys Knight & the Pips (K-Tel)
-	24	PAULINE MURRAY & THE INVISIBLE GIRLS		Pauline Murray & the Invisible Girls (Elusive)
21	25	SKY 2		Sky (Ariola)
27	26	BACK IN BLACK		AC/DC (Atlantic)
17	27	THE ABSOLUTE GAME		Skids (Virgin)
28	28	THE LOVE ALBUM		Various Artists (K-Tel)
29	29	THE GAME		Queen (EMI)
-	30	BLACK SEA		XTC (Virgin)

last	this	25 October 1980		
1	1	ZENYATTA MONDATTA		Police (A&M)
5	2	GUILTY		Barbra Streisand (CBS)
2	3	ABSOLUTELY		Madness (Stiff)
6	4	MOUNTING EXCITEMENT		Various Artists (K-Tel)
4	5	NEVER FOR EVER		Kate Bush (EMI)
3	5	SCARY MONSTERS AND SUPER CREEPS		David Bowie (RCA)
11	7	PARIS		Supertramp (A&M)
9	8	MORE SPECIALS		Specials (2-Tone)
8	9	MANILOW MAGIC		Barry Manilow (Arista)
-	10	CHINATOWN		Thin Lizzy (Vertigo)
7	11	THE VERY BEST OF DON McLEAN		Don McLean (United Artists)
10	12	BREAKING GLASS		Hazel O'Connor (A&M)
13	13	TRIUMPH		Jacksons (Epic)
12	14	SIGNING OFF		UB40 (Graduate)
23	15	A TOUCH OF LOVE		Gladys Knight & the Pips (K-Tel)
18	16	FLESH AND BLOOD		Roxy Music (Polydor)
28	17	THE LOVE ALBUM		Various Artists (K-Tel)
16	18	GIVE ME THE NIGHT		George Benson (Warner Bros.)
22	19	GOLD		Three Degrees (Ariola)
21	20	I AM WOMAN		Various Artists (Polydor)
15	21	NOW WE MAY BEGIN		Randy Crawford (Warner Bros.)
14	22	MIDNITE DYNAMOS		Matchbox (Magnet)
-	23	REGATTA DE BLANC		Police (A&M)
19	24	I'M NO HERO		Cliff Richard (EMI)
17	25	TELEKON		Gary Newman (Beggars Banquet)
-	26	MONSTERS OF ROCK		Various Artists (Polydor)
24	27	PAULINE MURRAY & THE INVISIBLE GIRLS		Pauline Murray & the Invisible Girls (Elusive)
-	28	BEAT CRAZY		Joe Jackson (A&M)
-	29	CONTRACTUAL OBLIGATION ALBUM		Monty Python's Flying Circus (Charisma)
27	30	THE ABSOLUTE GAME		Skids (Virgin)

last	this	1 November 1980		
1	1	ZENYATTA MONDATTA		Police (A&M)
2	2	GUILTY		Barbra Streisand (CBS)
-	3	JUST SUPPOSIN'		Status Quo (Vertigo)
-	4	THE RIVER		Bruce Springsteen (CBS)
5	5	SCARY MONSTERS AND SUPER CREEPS		David Bowie (RCA)
3	6	ABSOLUTELY		Madness (Stiff)
29	7	CONTRACTUAL OBLIGATION ALBUM		Monty Python's Flying Circus (Charisma)
17	8	THE LOVE ALBUM		Various Artists (K-Tel)
7	9	PARIS		Supertramp (A&M)
4	10	MOUNTING EXCITEMENT		Various Artists (K-Tel)
5	10	NEVER FOR EVER		Kate Bush (EMI)
20	12	I AM WOMAN		Various Artists (Polydor)
13	13	TRIUMPH		Jacksons (Epic)
11	14	THE VERY BEST OF DON McLEAN		Don McLean (United Artists)
10	15	CHINATOWN		Thin Lizzy (Vertigo)
18	16	GIVE ME THE NIGHT		George Benson (Warner Bros.)
9	17	MANILOW MAGIC		Barry Manilow (Arista)
12	17	BREAKING GLASS		Hazel O'Connor (A&M)
-	19	MAKIN' MOVIES		Dire Straits (Vertigo)
24	20	I'M NO HERO		Cliff Richard (EMI)
19	21	GOLD		Three Degrees (Ariola)
-	22	MY GENERATION		Who (Virgin)
14	23	SIGNING OFF		UB40 (Graduate)
-	24	KILLING JOKE		Killing Joke (Polydor)
23	25	REGATTA DE BLANC		Police (A&M)
16	26	FLESH AND BLOOD		Roxy Music (Polydor)
-	27	FULL HOUSE		Dooleys (GTO)
22	28	MIDNITE DYNAMOS		Matchbox (Magnet)
21	29	NOW WE MAY BEGIN		Randy Crawford (Warner Bros.)
-	30	FACES		Earth, Wind & Fire (CBS)

last	this	8 November 1980		
1	1	ZENYATTA MONDATTA		Police (A&M)
2	2	GUILTY		Barbra Streisand (CBS)
-	3	ORGANISATION		Orchestral Manoeuvres in the Dark (Dindisc)
3	4	JUST SUPPOSIN'		Status Quo (Vertigo)
8	5	THE LOVE ALBUM		Various Artists (K-Tel)
4	6	THE RIVER		Bruce Springsteen (CBS)
21	7	GOLD		Three Degrees (Ariola)
30	8	FACES		Earth, Wind & Fire (CBS)
17	9	MANILOW MAGIC		Barry Manilow (Arista)
-	10	HOTTER THAN JULY		Stevie Wonder (Motown)
10	11	NEVER FOR EVER		Kate Bush (EMI)
13	12	TRIUMPH		Jacksons (Epic)
7	13	CONTRACTUAL OBLIGATION ALBUM		Monty Python's Flying Circus (Charisma)
6	14	ABSOLUTELY		Madness (Stiff)
5	15	SCARY MONSTERS AND SUPER CREEPS		David Bowie (RCA)
-	16	REMAIN IN LIGHT		Talking Heads (Sire)
12	17	I AM WOMAN		Various Artists (Polydor)
19	18	MAKIN' MOVIES		Dire Straits (Vertigo)
17	19	BREAKING GLASS		Hazel O'Connor (A&M)
-	20	THE VERY BEST OF ELTON JOHN		Elton John (K-Tel)
16	21	GIVE ME THE NIGHT		George Benson (Warner Bros.)
-	22	A TOUCH OF LOVE		Gladys Knight & the Pips (K-Tel)
15	23	CHINATOWN		Thin Lizzy (Vertigo)
25	24	REGATTA DE BLANC		Police (A&M)
-	25	LITTLE MISS DYNAMITE		Brenda Lee (Warwick)
9	26	PARIS		Supertramp (A&M)
-	27	INHERIT THE WIND		Wilton Felder (MCA)
14	28	THE VERY BEST OF DON McLEAN		Don McLean (United Artists)
22	29	MY GENERATION		Who (Virgin)
10	30	MOUNTING EXCITEMENT		Various Artists (K-Tel)

The Police dominated album sales for a full month with their third release (and second chart-topper) *Zenyatta Mondatta*, buoyed by the simultaneous Number 1 success of the extracted single *Don't Stand So Close To Me*. This consistent run denied chart-topping success both to Madness' second album *Absolutely*, and to Barbra Streisand with her Bee Gees-produced set *Guilty*, though the latter was to make the runner-up slot virtually its own for more than two months, up until the end of the year.

November – December 1980

In a familiar pattern, many of the big name acts started releasing albums as the lucrative year-end sales period drew near, and inevitably there was not room for all of them at the top of the chart, though Stevie Wonder leapt in early to give Motown a now not-too-frequent chart-topper with his long-awaited *Hotter Than July*. The return of Brenda Lee to the album chart after more 17 years was, inevitably, down to Warwick TV-marketing a compilation of her old hit singles.

December 1980

13 December 1980

1	1	SUPER TROUPER Abba (Epic)
3	2	GUILTY Barbra Streisand (CBS)
9	3	NOT THE 9 O'CLOCK NEWS TV Cast (BBC)
5	4	BARRY Barry Manilow (Arista)
6	5	ZENYATTA MONDATTA Police (A&M)
2	6	AUTOAMERICAN Blondie (Chrysalis)
-	7	SOUND AFFECTS Jam (Polydor)
4	8	FOOLISH BEHAVIOUR Rod Stewart (Riva)
9	9	INSPIRATIONS Elvis Presley (K-Tel)
-	10	DR HOOK'S GREATEST HITS Dr Hook (Capitol)
11	11	KINGS OF THE WILD FRONTIER Adam & the Ants (CBS)
12	12	THE JAZZ SINGER Neil Diamond (Capitol)
23	13	HOTTER THAN JULY Stevie Wonder (Motown)
7	14	CHART EXPLOSION Various Artists (K-Tel)
27	15	ABSOLUTELY Madness (Stiff)
14	16	COUNTRY LEGENDS Various Artists (Ronco)
8	17	DOUBLE FANTASY John Lennon & Yoko Ono (Warner Bros./Geffen)
25	18	MAKING WAVES Nolans (Epic)
-	19	MANILOW MAGIC Barry Manilow (Arista)
-	20	SIGNING OFF UB40 (Graduate)
20	21	ORGANISATION Orchestral Manoeuvres in the Dark (Dindisc)
15	22	LITTLE MISS DYNAMITE Brenda Lee (Warwick)
-	23	CLASSICS FOR DREAMING James Last (Polydor)
28	24	GOLD Three Degrees (Ariola)
-	25	SPACE INVADERS Various Artists (Ronco)
13	26	THE RIVER Bruce Springsteen (CBS)
18	27	THE LOVE ALBUM Various Artists (K-Tel)
19	28	ACE OF SPADES Motorhead (Bronze)
22	29	RADIOACTIVE Various Artists (Ronco)
16	30	LOONIE TUNES Bad Manners (Magnet)

20 December 1980

1	1	SUPER TROUPER Abba (Epic)
2	2	GUILTY Barbra Streisand (CBS)
6	3	AUTOAMERICAN Blondie (Chrysalis)
7	3	SOUND AFFECTS Jam (Polydor)
17	5	DOUBLE FANTASY John Lennon & Yoko Ono (Warner Bros./Geffen)
9	6	INSPIRATIONS Elvis Presley (K-Tel)
10	7	DR HOOK'S GREATEST HITS Dr Hook (Capitol)
5	8	ZENYATTA MONDATTA Police (A&M)
14	9	CHART EXPLOSION Various Artists (K-Tel)
3	10	NOT THE 9 O'CLOCK NEWS TV Cast (BBC)
23	11	CLASSICS FOR DREAMING James Last (Polydor)
12	12	THE JAZZ SINGER Neil Diamond (Capitol)
4	13	BARRY Barry Manilow (Arista)
19	14	MANILOW MAGIC Barry Manilow (Arista)
-	15	BEST OF BARRY MANILOW Barry Manilow (Arista)
11	16	KINGS OF THE WILD FRONTIER Adam & the Ants (CBS)
8	17	FOOLISH BEHAVIOUR Rod Stewart (Riva)
18	18	MAKING WAVES Nolans (Epic)
22	19	LITTLE MISS DYNAMITE Brenda Lee (Warwick)
-	20	SING 20 NUMBER ONE HITS Brotherhood Of Man (Warwick)
15	21	ABSOLUTELY Madness (Stiff)
20	22	SIGNING OFF UB40 (Graduate)
-	22	FLEETWOOD MAC LIVE Fleetwood Mac (Warner Bros.)
13	24	HOTTER THAN JULY Stevie Wonder (Motown)
-	25	SANDINISTA Clash (CBS)
28	26	ACE OF SPADES Motorhead (Bronze)
-	27	20 GOLDEN GREATS OF KEN DODD Ken Dodd (Warwick)
-	28	PLAY Magazine (Virgin)
29	28	RADIOACTIVE Various Artists (Ronco)
-	30	LAUGHTER Ian Dury & the Blockheads (Stiff)

Abba once again hugely outsold the competition at Christmas, as in 1979 – this time with a set of new material, *Super Trouper,* rather than a hits collection. Almost inevitably, the title song was simultaneously a Number 1 single.

January 1981

3 January 1981

last	this		
1	1	SUPER TROUPER	Abba (Epic)
5	2	DOUBLE FANTASY	John Lennon & Yoko Ono (Geffen)
7	3	DR HOOK'S GREATEST HITS	Dr Hook (Capitol)
13	4	BARRY Barry Manilow (Arista)	
2	5	GUILTY	Barbra Streisand (CBS)
9	6	CHART EXPLOSION	Various Artists (K-Tel)
-	6	FLASH GORDON	Queen (EMI)
6	8	INSPIRATIONS	Elvis Presley (K-Tel)
10	8	NOT THE NINE O'CLOCK NEWS	TV Cast (BBC)
8	10	ZENYATTA MONDATTA	Police (A&M)
3	11	AUTOAMERICAN	Blondie (Chrysalis)
27	12	20 GOLDEN GREATS OF KEN DODD	Ken Dodd (Warwick)
12	13	THE JAZZ SINGER	Neil Diamond (Capitol)
14	14	MANILOW MAGIC	Barry Manilow (Arista)
20	15	SING 20 NUMBER ONE HITS	Brotherhood Of Man (Warwick)
21	16	ABSOLUTELY	Madness (Stiff)
3	17	SOUND AFFECTS	Jam (Polydor)
11	18	CLASSICS FOR DREAMING	James Last (Polydor)
17	19	FOOLISH BEHAVIOUR	Rod Stewart (Riva)
26	20	ACE OF SPADES	Motorhead (Bronze)
-	21	BEATLES BALLADS	Beatles (Parlophone)
16	22	KINGS OF THE WILD FRONTIER	Adam & the Ants (CBS)
24	23	HOTTER THAN JULY	Stevie Wonder (Motown)
-	24	AXE ATTACK	Various Artists (K-Tel)
-	25	BRIGHT LIGHTS	Showaddywaddy (Arista)
22	26	SIGNING OFF	UB40 (Graduate)
25	27	SANDINISTA	Clash (CBS)
-	28	SCARY MONSTERS AND SUPER CREEPS	David Bowie (RCA)
-	29	SLADE SMASHES	Slade (Polydor)
15	30	BEST OF BARRY MANILOW	Barry Manilow (Arista)

10 January 1981

last	this		
2	1	DOUBLE FANTASY	John Lennon & Yoko Ono (Geffen)
1	1	SUPER TROUPER	Abba (Epic)
8	3	NOT THE NINE O'CLOCK NEWS	TV Cast (BBC)
3	4	DR HOOK'S GREATEST HITS	Dr Hook (Capitol)
11	5	AUTOAMERICAN	Blondie (Chrysalis)
22	6	KINGS OF THE WILD FRONTIER	Adam & the Ants (CBS)
10	7	ZENYATTA MONDATTA	Police (A&M)
4	8	BARRY	Barry Manilow (Arista)
5	9	GUILTY	Barbra Streisand (CBS)
16	10	ABSOLUTELY	Madness (Stiff)
6	11	FLASH GORDON	Queen (EMI)
14	12	MANILOW MAGIC	Barry Manilow (Arista)
13	13	THE JAZZ SINGER	Neil Diamond (Capitol)
12	14	20 GOLDEN GREATS OF KEN DODD	Ken Dodd (Warwick)
18	15	CLASSICS FOR DREAMING	James Last (Polydor)
19	16	FOOLISH BEHAVIOUR	Rod Stewart (Riva)
6	17	CHART EXPLOSION	Various Artists (K-Tel)
8	18	INSPIRATIONS	Elvis Presley (K-Tel)
28	19	SCARY MONSTERS AND SUPER CREEPS	David Bowie (RCA)
27	20	SANDINISTA	Clash (CBS)
26	21	SIGNING OFF	UB40 (Graduate)
29	22	SLADE SMASHES	Slade (Polydor)
23	23	HOTTER THAN JULY	Stevie Wonder (Motown)
24	24	AXE ATTACK	Various Artists (K-Tel)
30	25	BEST OF BARRY MANILOW	Barry Manilow (Arista)
-	26	YESSHOWS Yes (Atlantic)	
-	27	GAUCHO	Steely Dan (MCA)
-	28	NIGHT LIFE	Various Artists (K-Tel)
17	29	SOUND AFFECTS	Jam (Polydor)
25	30	BRIGHT LIGHTS	Showaddywaddy (Arista)

17 January 1981

last	this		
1	1	SUPER TROUPER	Abba (Epic)
4	2	DR HOOK'S GREATEST HITS	Dr Hook (Capitol)
1	3	DOUBLE FANTASY	John Lennon & Yoko Ono (Geffen)
-	4	IMAGINE	John Lennon (Apple)
12	5	MANILOW MAGIC	Barry Manilow (Arista)
7	6	ZENYATTA MONDATTA	Police (A&M)
11	7	FLASH GORDON	Queen (EMI)
6	8	KINGS OF THE WILD FRONTIER	Adam & the Ants (CBS)
3	9	NOT THE NINE O'CLOCK NEWS	TV Cast (BBC)
8	10	BARRY Barry Manilow (Arista)	
9	11	GUILTY	Barbra Streisand (CBS)
14	12	20 GOLDEN GREATS OF KEN DODD	Ken Dodd (Warwick)
10	13	ABSOLUTELY	Madness (Stiff)
23	14	HOTTER THAN JULY	Stevie Wonder (Motown)
-	15	THE VERY BEST OF DAVID BOWIE	David Bowie (K-Tel)
5	16	AUTOAMERICAN	Blondie (Chrysalis)
16	17	FOOLISH BEHAVIOUR	Rod Stewart (Riva)
15	18	CLASSICS FOR DREAMING	James Last (Polydor)
18	19	INSPIRATIONS	Elvis Presley (K-Tel)
17	20	CHART EXPLOSION	Various Artists (K-Tel)
29	21	SOUND AFFECTS	Jam (Polydor)
13	22	THE JAZZ SINGER	Neil Diamond (Capitol)
26	23	YESSHOWS	Yes (Atlantic)
19	24	SCARY MONSTERS AND SUPER CREEPS	David Bowie (RCA)
-	25	SHAVED FISH	John Lennon (Apple)
21	26	SIGNING OFF	UB40 (Graduate)
25	27	BEST OF BARRY MANILOW	Barry Manilow (Arista)
22	28	SLADE SMASHES	Slade (Polydor)
-	29	MAKIN' MOVIES	Dire Straits (Vertigo)
20	30	SANDINISTA	Clash (CBS)

24 January 1981

last	this		
3	1	DOUBLE FANTASY	John Lennon & Yoko Ono (Geffen)
15	2	THE VERY BEST OF DAVID BOWIE	David Bowie (K-Tel)
1	3	SUPER TROUPER	Abba (Epic)
2	4	DR HOOK'S GREATEST HITS	Dr Hook (Capitol)
8	5	KINGS OF THE WILD FRONTIER	Adam & the Ants (CBS)
6	6	ZENYATTA MONDATTA	Police (A&M)
11	7	GUILTY	Barbra Streisand (CBS)
9	8	NOT THE NINE O'CLOCK NEWS	TV Cast (BBC)
7	9	FLASH GORDON	Queen (EMI)
5	9	MANILOW MAGIC	Barry Manilow (Arista)
4	11	IMAGINE	John Lennon (Apple)
13	12	ABSOLUTELY	Madness (Stiff)
16	13	AUTOAMERICAN	Blondie (Chrysalis)
10	14	BARRY	Barry Manilow (Arista)
14	15	HOTTER THAN JULY	Stevie Wonder (Motown)
22	16	THE JAZZ SINGER	Neil Diamond (Capitol)
26	17	SIGNING OFF	UB40 (Graduate)
12	18	20 GOLDEN GREATS OF KEN DODD	Ken Dodd (Warwick)
-	19	SKY 2	Sky (Ariola)
-	20	ARC OF A DIVER	Steve Winwood (Island)
29	21	MAKIN' MOVIES	Dire Straits (Vertigo)
25	22	SHAVED FISH	John Lennon (Apple)
17	23	FOOLISH BEHAVIOUR	Rod Stewart (Riva)
23	24	YESSHOWS	Yes (Atlantic)
-	25	NIGHT LIFE	Various Artists (K-Tel)
-	26	MAKING WAVES	Nolans (Epic)
18	27	CLASSICS FOR DREAMING	James Last (Polydor)
19	28	INSPIRATIONS	Elvis Presley (K-Tel)
30	29	SANDINISTA	Clash (CBS)
-	30	DIRK WEARS WHITE SOX	Adam & the Ants (Do It)

The shocking assassination of John Lennon pushed his and Yoko's "comeback" *Double Fantasy* album, which had not exhibited chart-topping potential during its first weeks on sale, to No.1 in the New Year, while the Lennon tragedy was also responsible for returning his *Imagine* album (again, alongside a chart-topping single - the title track) and the *Shaved Fish* compilation of his earlier hits, to the chart. *Not The Nine O'Clock News* achieved the extraordinary feat for a comedy album of a Top 3 place.

last week	this week	31 January 1981
5	1	KINGS OF THE WILD FRONTIER — Adam & the Ants (CBS)
4	2	DR HOOK'S GREATEST HITS — Dr Hook (Capitol)
2	3	THE VERY BEST OF DAVID BOWIE — David Bowie (K-Tel)
1	4	DOUBLE FANTASY — John Lennon & Yoko Ono (Geffen)
3	5	SUPER TROUPER — Abba (Epic)
11	6	IMAGINE — John Lennon (Apple)
7	7	GUILTY — Barbra Streisand (CBS)
9	8	MANILOW MAGIC — Barry Manilow (Arista)
9	9	FLASH GORDON — Queen (EMI)
14	10	BARRY — Barry Manilow (Arista)
-	11	MONDO BONGO — Boomtown Rats (Mercury)
21	12	MAKIN' MOVIES — Dire Straits (Vertigo)
22	13	SHAVED FISH — John Lennon (Apple)
6	14	ZENYATTA MONDATTA — Police (A&M)
15	15	HOTTER THAN JULY — Stevie Wonder (Motown)
20	16	ARC OF A DIVER — Steve Winwood (Island)
8	17	NOT THE NINE O'CLOCK NEWS — TV Cast (BBC)
-	18	PARADISE THEATER — Styx (A&M)
12	19	ABSOLUTELY — Madness (Stiff)
-	20	THE WILD, THE WILLING & THE INNOCENT — UFO (Chrysalis)
17	21	SIGNING OFF — UB40 (Graduate)
13	22	AUTOAMERICAN — Blondie (Chrysalis)
29	23	SANDINISTA — Clash (CBS)
24	24	YESSHOWS — Yes (Atlantic)
19	25	SKY 2 — Sky (Ariola)
-	26	THE RIVER — Bruce Springsteen (CBS)
-	27	SCARY MONSTERS AND SUPER CREEPS — David Bowie (RCA)
26	28	MAKING WAVES — Nolans (Epic)
27	29	CLASSICS FOR DREAMING — James Last (Polydor)
16	30	THE JAZZ SINGER — Neil Diamond (Capitol)

		7 February 1981
1	1	KINGS OF THE WILD FRONTIER — Adam & the Ants (CBS)
3	2	THE VERY BEST OF DAVID BOWIE — David Bowie (K-Tel)
8	3	MANILOW MAGIC — Barry Manilow (Arista)
4	4	DOUBLE FANTASY — John Lennon & Yoko Ono (Geffen)
6	5	IMAGINE — John Lennon (Apple)
10	6	BARRY — Barry Manilow (Arista)
2	7	DR HOOK'S GREATEST HITS — Dr Hook (Capitol)
7	8	GUILTY — Barbra Streisand (CBS)
11	8	MONDO BONGO — Boomtown Rats (Mercury)
12	10	MAKIN' MOVIES — Dire Straits (Vertigo)
18	11	PARADISE THEATER — Styx (A&M)
21	12	SIGNING OFF — UB40 (Graduate)
15	13	HOTTER THAN JULY — Stevie Wonder (Motown)
-	13	TRUST — Elvis Costello & the Attractions (F-Beat)
-	15	TAKE MY TIME — Sheena Easton (EMI)
-	16	VIENNA — Ultravox (Chrysalis)
19	17	ABSOLUTELY — Madness (Stiff)
30	18	THE JAZZ SINGER — Neil Diamond (Capitol)
13	19	SHAVED FISH — John Lennon (Apple)
5	19	SUPER TROUPER — Abba (Epic)
16	21	ARC OF A DIVER — Steve Winwood (Island)
9	22	FLASH GORDON — Queen (EMI)
17	23	NOT THE NINE O'CLOCK NEWS — TV Cast (BBC)
-	23	VISAGE — Visage (Polydor)
22	25	AUTOAMERICAN — Blondie (Chrysalis)
-	26	LADY — Kenny Rogers (Liberty)
27	27	SCARY MONSTERS AND SUPER CREEPS — David Bowie (RCA)
-	28	GAP BAND 3 — Gap Band (Mercury)
-	29	BACK IN BLACK — AC/DC (Atlantic)
-	29	LOONEE TUNES — Bad Manners (Magnet)

		14 February 1981
4	1	DOUBLE FANTASY — John Lennon & Yoko Ono (Geffen)
1	2	KINGS OF THE WILD FRONTIER — Adam & the Ants (CBS)
2	3	THE VERY BEST OF DAVID BOWIE — David Bowie (K-Tel)
3	4	MANILOW MAGIC — Barry Manilow (Arista)
5	5	IMAGINE — John Lennon (Apple)
18	6	THE JAZZ SINGER — Neil Diamond (Capitol)
10	7	MAKIN' MOVIES — Dire Straits (Vertigo)
16	8	VIENNA — Ultravox (Chrysalis)
8	9	MONDO BONGO — Boomtown Rats (Mercury)
7	10	DR HOOK'S GREATEST HITS — Dr Hook (Capitol)
13	11	HOTTER THAN JULY — Stevie Wonder (Motown)
6	12	BARRY — Barry Manilow (Arista)
8	13	GUILTY — Barbra Streisand (CBS)
19	13	SHAVED FISH — John Lennon (Apple)
23	15	VISAGE — Visage (Polydor)
21	16	ARC OF A DIVER — Steve Winwood (Island)
15	17	TAKE MY TIME — Sheena Easton (EMI)
11	18	PARADISE THEATER — Styx (A&M)
19	18	SUPER TROUPER — Abba (Epic)
12	20	SIGNING OFF — UB40 (Graduate)
22	21	FLASH GORDON — Queen (EMI)
-	22	SOUTHERN FREEEZ — Freeez (Beggars Banquet)
25	23	AUTOAMERICAN — Blondie (Chrysalis)
17	24	ABSOLUTELY — Madness (Stiff)
13	25	TRUST — Elvis Costello & the Attractions (F-Beat)
-	26	DIRK WEARS WHITE SOX — Adam & the Ants (Do It)
-	27	SOUND AFFECTS — Jam (Polydor)
-	28	THE RIVER — Bruce Springsteen (CBS)
-	29	NIGHT LIFE — Various Artists (K-Tel)
27	30	SCARY MONSTERS AND SUPER CREEPS — David Bowie (RCA)

		21 February 1981
2	1	KINGS OF THE WILD FRONTIER — Adam & the Ants (CBS)
8	2	VIENNA — Ultravox (Chrysalis)
1	3	DOUBLE FANTASY — John Lennon & Yoko Ono (Geffen)
3	4	THE VERY BEST OF DAVID BOWIE — David Bowie (K-Tel)
7	5	MAKIN' MOVIES — Dire Straits (Vertigo)
5	6	IMAGINE — John Lennon (Apple)
13	7	SHAVED FISH — John Lennon (Apple)
-	8	DANCE CRAZE — Soundtrack (2-Tone)
6	9	THE JAZZ SINGER — Neil Diamond (Capitol)
4	10	MANILOW MAGIC — Barry Manilow (Arista)
-	11	FACE VALUE — Phil Collins (Virgin)
15	12	VISAGE — Visage (Polydor)
13	13	GUILTY — Barbra Streisand (CBS)
12	14	BARRY — Barry Manilow (Arista)
9	15	MONDO BONGO — Boomtown Rats (Mercury)
17	16	TAKE MY TIME — Sheena Easton (EMI)
10	17	DR HOOK'S GREATEST HITS — Dr Hook (Capitol)
24	18	ABSOLUTELY — Madness (Stiff)
16	19	ARC OF A DIVER — Steve Winwood (Island)
11	20	HOTTER THAN JULY — Stevie Wonder (Motown)
26	21	DIRK WEARS WHITE SOX — Adam & the Ants (Do It)
-	22	MOVING PICTURES — Rush (Mercury)
23	23	AUTOAMERICAN — Blondie (Chrysalis)
18	24	PARADISE THEATER — Styx (A&M)
20	25	SIGNING OFF — UB40 (Graduate)
18	26	SUPER TROUPER — Abba (Epic)
22	27	SOUTHERN FREEEZ — Freeez (Beggars Banquet)
-	28	REMAIN IN LIGHT — Talking Heads (Sire)
-	29	CANDLES — Heatwave (GTO)
25	30	TRUST — Elvis Costello & the Attractions (F-Beat)

Adam & The Ants' *King Of The Wild Frontier* had been hanging around the upper part of the chart for over two months when it was vaulted to the top by an explosion of what the press inevitably dubbd "Antmania", as the group suddenly emerged as the newest teen fad and put two singles, *Antmusic* and *Young Parisians*, simultaneously into the Top 10. The normally MOR/pop-orientated K-Tel, meanwhile, broke successful new ground by licensing a package of familiar David Bowie material from RCA.

February – March 1981

Phil Collins' first solo album *Face Value* emulated his group Genesis' *Duke* the previous year by giving him a week at Number 1, shortly after his *In The Air Tonight* had dropped from that position on the singles chart. The Number 1 slot was something of which Phil Collins was to see a great deal, particularly as a soloist, over the decade to come. Ultravox' *Vienna*, like its title track as a single, was the first big album success for the band, now led by Midge Ure.

A second Adam & the Ants album hit the charts.

28 March 1981

last week	this week		
1	1	KINGS OF THE WILD FRONTIER	Adam & the Ants (CBS)
2	2	FACE VALUE	Phil Collins (Virgin)
5	3	JOURNEYS TO GLORY	Spandau Ballet (Reformation)
6	4	THE JAZZ SINGER	Neil Diamond (Capitol)
3	5	VIENNA	Ultravox (Chrysalis)
10	6	MAKIN' MOVIES	Dire Straits (Vertigo)
7	7	DANCE CRAZE	Soundtrack (2-Tone)
9	7	DIFFICULT TO CURE	Rainbow (Polydor)
4	9	STRAY CATS	Stray Cats (Arista)
12	10	SOUTHERN FREEEZ	Freeez (Beggars Banquet)
11	11	MANILOW MAGIC	Barry Manilow (Arista)
17	12	VISAGE	Visage (Polydor)
-	13	FACE DANCES	Who (Polydor)
8	14	DOUBLE FANTASY	John Lennon & Yoko Ono (Geffen)
15	15	REMAIN IN LIGHT	Talking Heads (Sire)
16	16	VERY BEST OF RITA COOLIDGE	Rita Coolidge (A&M)
22	17	DIRK WEARS WHITE SOX	Adam & the Ants (Do It)
-	18	HOTTER THAN JULY	Stevie Wonder (Motown)
-	19	NEVER TOO LATE	Status Quo (Vertigo)
19	20	ANOTHER TICKET	Eric Clapton (RSO)
-	21	20 GOLDEN GREATS OF AL JOLSON	Al Jolson (MCA)
-	22	FROM THE TEAROOMS OF MARS TO THE HELLHOLES OF URANUS	Landscape (RCA)
-	23	SOUND AFFECTS	Jam (Polydor)
14	24	MOVING PICTURES	Rush (Mercury)
23	25	GUILTY	Barbra Streisand (CBS)
-	25	IMAGINATION	Whispers (Solar)
-	25	SOLID GOLD	Gang of Four (EMI)
21	28	KILLERS	Iron Maiden (EMI)
23	29	BARRY	Barry Manilow (Arista)
-	30	HE WHO DARES WINS	Theatre of Hate (SSSSS)

4 April 1981

1	1	KINGS OF THE WILD FRONTIER	Adam & the Ants (CBS)
2	2	FACE VALUE	Phil Collins (Virgin)
19	3	NEVER TOO LATE	Status Quo (Vertigo)
4	4	THE JAZZ SINGER	Neil Diamond (Capitol)
-	5	SKY 3	Sky (Ariola)
13	6	FACE DANCES	Who (Polydor)
3	7	JOURNEYS TO GLORY	Spandau Ballet (Reformation)
18	8	HOTTER THAN JULY	Stevie Wonder (Motown)
9	9	STRAY CATS	Stray Cats (Arista)
11	10	MANILOW MAGIC	Barry Manilow (Arista)
14	11	DOUBLE FANTASY	John Lennon & Yoko Ono (Geffen)
12	12	VISAGE	Visage (Polydor)
10	13	SOUTHERN FREEEZ	Freeez (Beggars Banquet)
5	14	VIENNA	Ultravox (Chrysalis)
30	15	HE WHO DARES WINS	Theatre of Hate (SSSSS)
25	16	SOLID GOLD	Gang of Four (EMI)
16	17	VERY BEST OF RITA COOLIDGE	Rita Coolidge (A&M)
21	18	20 GOLDEN GREATS OF AL JOLSON	Al Jolson (MCA)
6	19	MAKIN' MOVIES	Dire Straits (Vertigo)
7	20	DANCE CRAZE	Soundtrack (2-Tone)
24	21	MOVING PICTURES	Rush (Mercury)
17	22	DIRK WEARS WHITE SOX	Adam & the Ants (Do It)
15	23	REMAIN IN LIGHT	Talking Heads (Sire)
25	24	GUILTY	Barbra Streisand (CBS)
-	25	FLESH AND BLOOD	Roxy Music (Polydor)
-	25	MY LIFE IN THE BUSH OF GHOSTS	Brian Eno & David Byrne (Polydor)
20	27	ANOTHER TICKET	Eric Clapton (RSO)
-	28	TOYAH TOYAH TOYAH	Toyah (Safari)
-	29	LEAGUE OF GENTLEMEN	Robert Fripp (EG)
-	30	KILIMANJARO	Teardrop Explodes (Mercury)

11 April 1981

1	1	KINGS OF THE WILD FRONTIER	Adam & the Ants (CBS)
14	2	VIENNA	Ultravox (Chrysalis)
5	3	SKY 3	Sky (Ariola)
2	4	FACE VALUE	Phil Collins (Virgin)
6	5	FACE DANCES	Who (Polydor)
8	6	HOTTER THAN JULY	Stevie Wonder (Motown)
4	7	THE JAZZ SINGER	Neil Diamond (Capitol)
10	8	MANILOW MAGIC	Barry Manilow (Arista)
3	9	NEVER TOO LATE	Status Quo (Vertigo)
12	10	VISAGE	Visage (Polydor)
11	11	DOUBLE FANTASY	John Lennon & Yoko Ono (Geffen)
-	12	INTUITION	Linx (Chrysalis)
7	13	JOURNEYS TO GLORY	Spandau Ballet (Reformation)
-	14	BARRY	Barry Manilow (Arista)
19	15	MAKIN' MOVIES	Dire Straits (Vertigo)
-	16	THIS OLE HOUSE	Shakin' Stevens (Epic)
17	17	VERY BEST OF RITA COOLIDGE	Rita Coolidge (A&M)
9	18	STRAY CATS	Stray Cats (Arista)
24	19	GUILTY	Barbra Streisand (CBS)
25	20	FLESH AND BLOOD	Roxy Music (Polydor)
-	21	DIFFICULT TO CURE	Rainbow (Polydor)
-	22	TO LOVE AGAIN	Diana Ross (Motown)
-	23	THE RIVER	Bruce Springsteen (CBS)
22	24	DIRK WEARS WHITE SOX	Adam & the Ants (Do It)
28	24	TOYAH TOYAH TOYAH	Toyah (Safari)
-	26	THE ROGER WHITTAKER ALBUM	Roger Whittaker (K-Tel)
20	27	DANCE CRAZE	Soundtrack (2-Tone)
-	28	FROM THE TEAROOMS OF MARS TO THE HELLHOLES OF URANUS	Landscape (RCA)
30	29	KILIMANJARO	Teardrop Explodes (Mercury)
13	29	SOUTHERN FREEEZ	Freeez (Beggars Banquet)

18 April 1981

1	1	KINGS OF THE WILD FRONTIER	Adam & the Ants (CBS)
6	2	HOTTER THAN JULY	Stevie Wonder (Motown)
15	3	MAKIN' MOVIES	Dire Straits (Vertigo)
3	3	SKY 3	Sky (Ariola)
9	5	NEVER TOO LATE	Status Quo (Vertigo)
4	6	FACE VALUE	Phil Collins (Virgin)
5	7	FACE DANCES	Who (Polydor)
7	8	THE JAZZ SINGER	Neil Diamond (Capitol)
16	9	THIS OLE HOUSE	Shakin' Stevens (Epic)
2	10	VIENNA	Ultravox (Chrysalis)
10	11	VISAGE	Visage (Polydor)
13	12	JOURNEYS TO GLORY	Spandau Ballet (Reformation)
8	13	MANILOW MAGIC	Barry Manilow (Arista)
12	14	INTUITION	Linx (Chrysalis)
-	15	FLOWERS OF ROMANCE	Public Image Limited (Virgin)
-	16	CHRISTOPHER CROSS	Christopher Cross (Warner Bros.)
24	17	DIRK WEARS WHITE SOX	Adam & the Ants (Do It)
17	18	VERY BEST OF RITA COOLIDGE	Rita Coolidge (A&M)
29	19	KILIMANJARO	Teardrop Explodes (Mercury)
-	20	390 DEGREES OF SIMULATED STEREO	Pere Ubu (Rough Trade)
-	21	COME AN' GET IT	Whitesnake (Liberty)
11	22	DOUBLE FANTASY	John Lennon & Yoko Ono (Geffen)
28	23	FROM THE TEAROOMS OF MARS TO THE HELLHOLES OF URANUS	Landscape (RCA)
-	24	REMIXTURE	Various Artists (Champagne)
20	25	FLESH AND BLOOD	Roxy Music (Polydor)
18	26	STRAY CATS	Stray Cats (Arista)
-	27	THE ADVENTURES OF THIN LIZZY	Thin Lizzy (Vertigo)
-	28	HE WHO DARES WINS	Theatre of Hate (SSSSS)
-	29	AUTHOR! AUTHOR!	Scars (Pre)
-	30	FUN IN SPACE	Roger Taylor (EMI)

Adam & The Ants' *Kings Of The Wild Frontier* finally put down the opposition and settled down into an unchallenged period of 12 weeks - or virtually a quarter of the year - as the country's best-selling album, continually being given new impetus by successive hit singles like its title track and the Number 1 seller *Stand And Deliver*. Spandau Ballet made the Top 3 with their debut set, and the tiny independent SSSS label sold (albeit briefly) remarkably well with new-wavers Theatre Of Hate.

April – May 1981

25 April 1981

last	this		
1	1	KINGS OF THE WILD FRONTIER	Adam & the Ants (CBS)
2	2	HOTTER THAN JULY	Stevie Wonder (Motown)
15	3	FLOWERS OF ROMANCE	Public Image Limited (Virgin)
21	4	COME AN' GET IT	Whitesnake (Liberty)
9	5	THIS OLE HOUSE	Shakin' Stevens (Epic)
8	6	THE JAZZ SINGER	Neil Diamond (Capitol)
3	7	SKY 3	Sky (Ariola)
3	8	MAKIN' MOVIES	Dire Straits (Vertigo)
6	9	FACE VALUE	Phil Collins (Virgin)
14	10	INTUITION	Linx (Chrysalis)
30	11	FUN IN SPACE	Roger Taylor (EMI)
10	12	VIENNA	Ultravox (Chrysalis)
12	13	JOURNEYS TO GLORY	Spandau Ballet (Reformation)
5	14	NEVER TOO LATE	Status Quo (Vertigo)
13	15	MANILOW MAGIC	Barry Manilow (Arista)
-	16	FAITH	Cure (Fiction)
7	17	FACE DANCES	Who (Polydor)
11	18	VISAGE	Visage (Polydor)
-	19	HIT AND RUN	Girlschool (Bronze)
29	20	AUTHOR! AUTHOR!	Scars (Pre)
27	21	THE ADVENTURES OF THIN LIZZY	Thin Lizzy (Vertigo)
22	22	DOUBLE FANTASY	John Lennon & Yoko Ono (Geffen)
23	23	FROM THE TEAROOMS OF MARS TO THE HELLHOLES OF URANUS	Landscape (RCA)
-	24	FUTURE SHOCK	Gillan (Virgin)
16	25	CHRISTOPHER CROSS	Christopher Cross (Warner Bros.)
-	26	SPELLBOUND	Tygers of Pan Tang (MCA)
28	27	HE WHO DARES WINS	Theatre of Hate (SSSSS)
-	28	TO LOVE AGAIN	Diana Ross (Motown)
-	29	JAZZ FUNK	Incognito (Ensign)
20	30	390 DEGREES OF SIMULATED STEREO	Pere Ubu (Rough Trade)

2 May 1981

last	this		
1	1	KINGS OF THE WILD FRONTIER	Adam & the Ants (CBS)
2	2	HOTTER THAN JULY	Stevie Wonder (Motown)
24	3	FUTURE SHOCK	Gillan (Virgin)
4	4	COME AN' GET IT	Whitesnake (Liberty)
3	4	FLOWERS OF ROMANCE	Public Image Limited (Virgin)
8	6	MAKIN' MOVIES	Dire Straits (Vertigo)
7	6	SKY 3	Sky (Ariola)
16	8	FAITH	Cure (Fiction)
5	9	THIS OLE HOUSE	Shakin' Stevens (Epic)
6	10	THE JAZZ SINGER	Neil Diamond (Capitol)
13	11	JOURNEYS TO GLORY	Spandau Ballet (Reformation)
19	12	HIT AND RUN	Girlschool (Bronze)
9	13	FACE VALUE	Phil Collins (Virgin)
-	14	GO FOR IT	Stiff Little Fingers (Chrysalis)
10	15	INTUITION	Linx (Chrysalis)
-	16	LIVING ORNAMENTS 1979-1980	Gary Numan (Beggars Banquet)
15	17	MANILOW MAGIC	Barry Manilow (Arista)
23	18	FROM THE TEAROOMS OF MARS TO THE HELLHOLES OF URANUS	Landscape (RCA)
17	19	FACE DANCES	Who (Polydor)
12	20	VIENNA	Ultravox (Chrysalis)
-	21	TO EACH	A Certain Ratio (Factory)
14	22	NEVER TOO LATE	Status Quo (Vertigo)
-	23	PSYCHEDELIC JUNGLE	Cramps (IRS)
11	24	FUN IN SPACE	Roger Taylor (EMI)
-	25	BARRY	Barry Manilow (Arista)
-	26	THE ROGER WHITTAKER ALBUM	Roger Whittaker (K-Tel)
20	27	AUTHOR! AUTHOR!	Scars (Pre)
18	28	VISAGE	Visage (Polydor)
21	29	THE ADVENTURES OF THIN LIZZY	Thin Lizzy (Vertigo)
-	30	CHART BUSTERS '81	Various Artists (K-Tel)

9 May 1981

last	this		
1	1	KINGS OF THE WILD FRONTIER	Adam & the Ants (CBS)
2	2	HOTTER THAN JULY	Stevie Wonder (Motown)
16	3	LIVING ORNAMENTS 1979-1980	Gary Numan (Beggars Banquet)
10	4	THE JAZZ SINGER	Neil Diamond (Capitol)
3	5	FUTURE SHOCK	Gillan (Virgin)
30	6	CHART BUSTERS '81	Various Artists (K-Tel)
8	7	FAITH	Cure (Fiction)
4	8	COME AN' GET IT	Whitesnake (Liberty)
4	9	FLOWERS OF ROMANCE	Public Image Limited (Virgin)
12	10	HIT AND RUN	Girlschool (Bronze)
6	11	MAKIN' MOVIES	Dire Straits (Vertigo)
13	12	FACE VALUE	Phil Collins (Virgin)
11	13	JOURNEYS TO GLORY	Spandau Ballet (Reformation)
14	14	GO FOR IT	Stiff Little Fingers (Chrysalis)
20	15	VIENNA	Ultravox (Chrysalis)
6	16	SKY 3	Sky (Ariola)
21	17	TO EACH	A Certain Ratio (Factory)
-	18	DOUBLE FANTASY	John Lennon & Yoko Ono (Geffen)
-	19	CHARIOTS OF FIRE	Vangelis (Polydor)
17	20	MANILOW MAGIC	Barry Manilow (Arista)
15	21	INTUITION	Linx (Chrysalis)
-	22	CHRISTOPHER CROSS	Christopher Cross (Warner Bros.)
-	23	THE DUDE	Quincy Jones (A&M)
-	24	HI INFIDELITY	REO Speedwagon (Epic)
-	24	VERY BEST OF RITA COOLIDGE	Rita Coolidge (A&M)
19	26	FACE DANCES	Who (Polydor)
27	27	AUTHOR! AUTHOR!	Scars (Pre)
-	27	MAKING WAVES	Nolans (Epic)
18	29	FROM THE TEAROOMS OF MARS TO THE HELLHOLES OF URANUS	Landscape (RCA)
23	30	PSYCHEDELIC JUNGLE	Cramps (A&M)

16 May 1981

last	this		
1	1	KINGS OF THE WILD FRONTIER	Adam & the Ants (CBS)
3	2	LIVING ORNAMENTS 1979-1980	Gary Numan (Beggars Banquet)
2	3	HOTTER THAN JULY	Stevie Wonder (Motown)
13	4	JOURNEYS TO GLORY	Spandau Ballet (Reformation)
-	5	THIS OLE HOUSE	Shakin' Stevens (Epic)
4	6	THE JAZZ SINGER	Neil Diamond (Capitol)
6	7	CHART BUSTERS '81	Various Artists (K-Tel)
5	8	FUTURE SHOCK	Gillan (Virgin)
14	9	GO FOR IT	Stiff Little Fingers (Chrysalis)
11	10	MAKIN' MOVIES	Dire Straits (Vertigo)
-	11	ROLL ON	Various Artists (Polystar)
20	12	MANILOW MAGIC	Barry Manilow (Arista)
8	13	COME AN' GET IT	Whitesnake (Liberty)
16	14	SKY 3	Sky (Ariola)
12	15	FACE VALUE	Phil Collins (Virgin)
19	16	CHARIOTS OF FIRE	Vangelis (Polydor)
7	17	FAITH	Cure (Fiction)
10	18	HIT AND RUN	Girlschool (Bronze)
17	19	TO EACH	A Certain Ratio (Factory)
23	20	THE DUDE	Quincy Jones (A&M)
9	21	FLOWERS OF ROMANCE	Public Image Limited (Virgin)
-	22	WHA'PPEN?	Beat (Go Feet)
27	23	MAKING WAVES	Nolans (Epic)
-	24	PUNKS NOT DEAD	Exploited (Secret)
24	25	HI INFIDELITY	REO Speedwagon (Epic)
15	26	VIENNA	Ultravox (Chrysalis)
30	27	PSYCHEDELIC JUNGLE	Cramps (IRS)
18	28	DOUBLE FANTASY	John Lennon & Yoko Ono (Geffen)
-	29	POSITIVE TOUCH	Undertones (Ardeck)
-	30	BARRY	Barry Manilow (Arista)
-	30	THIS IS ENNIO MORICONE	Ennio Morricone (EMI)

The resurgence to Number 2 by Stevie Wonder's *Hotter Than July* had much to do with the huge succes of the latest single extracted from it, the ballad *Lately*. Meanwhile, there was a sudden bigger-than-usual presence by heavy rock bands in the Top 10, via albums by Gillan and Whitesnake (both led by former Deep Purple vocalists), and the all-girl metal quartet Girlschool, who had far bigger success with their *Hit And Run* set than they ever managed with any of their singles.

last week	this week	**23 May 1981**
1	1	KINGS OF THE WILD FRONTIER — Adam & the Ants (CBS)
22	2	WHA'PPEN? — Beat (Go Feet)
5	3	THIS OLE HOUSE — Shakin' Stevens (Epic)
-	4	STARS ON 45 — Starsound (CBS)
3	5	HOTTER THAN JULY — Stevie Wonder (Motown)
29	6	POSITIVE TOUCH — Undertones (Ardeck)
16	7	CHARIOTS OF FIRE — Vangelis (Polydor)
11	8	ROLL ON — Various Artists (Polystar)
2	9	LIVING ORNAMENTS 1979-1980 — Gary Numan (Beggars Banquet)
24	10	PUNKS NOT DEAD — Exploited (Secret)
25	11	HI INFIDELITY — REO Speedwagon (Epic)
4	12	JOURNEYS TO GLORY — Spandau Ballet (Reformation)
7	13	CHART BUSTERS '81 — Various Artists (K-Tel)
9	14	GO FOR IT — Stiff Little Fingers (Chrysalis)
6	15	THE JAZZ SINGER — Neil Diamond (Capitol)
8	16	FUTURE SHOCK — Gillan (Virgin)
13	17	COME AN' GET IT — Whitesnake (Liberty)
10	18	MAKIN' MOVIES — Dire Straits (Vertigo)
-	19	STRAY CATS — Stray Cats (Arista)
17	20	FAITH — Cure (Fiction)
19	21	TO EACH — A Certain Ratio (Factory)
30	22	BARRY — Barry Manilow (Arista)
14	23	SKY 3 — Sky (Ariola)
15	24	FACE VALUE — Phil Collins (Virgin)
-	25	COMPUTER WORLD — Kraftwerk (EMI)
-	26	NIGHTCLUBBING — Grace Jones (Island)
-	27	I AM THE PHOENIX — Judy Tzuke (Rocket)
18	28	HIT AND RUN — Girlschool (Bronze)
-	29	BAD FOR GOOD — Jim Steinman (Epic)
27	30	PSYCHEDELIC JUNGLE — Cramps (IRS)

last week	this week	**30 May 1981**
1	1	KINGS OF THE WILD FRONTIER — Adam & the Ants (CBS)
4	2	STARS ON 45 — Starsound (CBS)
2	3	WHA'PPEN? — Beat (Go Feet)
3	4	THIS OLE HOUSE — Shakin' Stevens (Epic)
-	5	QUIT DREAMING AND GET ON THE BEAM — Bill Nelson (Mercury)
5	6	HOTTER THAN JULY — Stevie Wonder (Motown)
25	7	COMPUTER WORLD — Kraftwerk (EMI)
-	8	TALK TALK TALK — Psychedelic Furs (CBS)
11	9	HI INFIDELITY — REO Speedwagon (Epic)
-	10	LONG DISTANCE VOYAGER — Moody Blues (Threshold)
7	11	CHARIOTS OF FIRE — Vangelis (Polydor)
29	12	BAD FOR GOOD — Jim Steinman (Epic)
10	13	PUNKS NOT DEAD — Exploited (Secret)
-	14	THE ADVENTURES OF THIN LIZZY — Thin Lizzy (Vertigo)
6	15	POSITIVE TOUCH — Undertones (Ardeck)
19	16	STRAY CATS — Stray Cats (Arista)
27	17	I AM THE PHOENIX — Judy Tzuke (Rocket)
-	18	PLAYING WITH A DIFFERENT SEX — Au Pairs (Human)
-	19	THE DUDE — Quincy Jones (A&M)
20	20	FAITH — Cure (Fiction)
8	21	ROLL ON — Various Artists (Polystar)
14	22	GO FOR IT — Stiff Little Fingers (Chrysalis)
-	23	EAST SIDE STORY — Squeeze (A&M)
-	24	DISCO DAZE AND DISCO NITES — Various Artists (Ronco)
18	25	MAKIN' MOVIES — Dire Straits (Vertigo)
12	26	JOURNEYS TO GLORY — Spandau Ballet (Reformation)
9	27	LIVING ORNAMENTS 1979-1980 — Gary Numan (Beggars Banquet)
13	28	CHART BUSTERS '81 — Various Artists (K-Tel)
22	29	BARRY — Barry Manilow (Arista)
-	30	FAIR WARNING — Van Halen (Warner Bros.)

last week	this week	**6 June 1981**
2	1	STARS ON 45 — Starsound (CBS)
1	2	KINGS OF THE WILD FRONTIER — Adam & the Ants (CBS)
-	3	ANTHEM — Toyah (Safari)
3	4	WHA'PPEN? — Beat (Go Feet)
4	5	THIS OLE HOUSE — Shakin' Stevens (Epic)
24	6	DISCO DAZE AND DISCO NITES — Various Artists (Ronco)
6	7	HOTTER THAN JULY — Stevie Wonder (Motown)
10	8	LONG DISTANCE VOYAGER — Moody Blues (Threshold)
-	9	THE JAZZ SINGER — Neil Diamond (Capitol)
14	10	THE ADVENTURES OF THIN LIZZY — Thin Lizzy (Vertigo)
-	11	SECRET COMBINATION — Randy Crawford (Warner Bros.)
5	12	QUIT DREAMING AND GET ON THE BEAM — Bill Nelson (Mercury)
9	13	HI INFIDELITY — REO Speedwagon (Epic)
15	14	POSITIVE TOUCH — Undertones (Ardeck)
11	15	CHARIOTS OF FIRE — Vangelis (Polydor)
16	16	STRAY CATS — Stray Cats (Arista)
12	17	BAD FOR GOOD — Jim Steinman (Epic)
23	18	EAST SIDE STORY — Squeeze (A&M)
18	19	PLAYING WITH A DIFFERENT SEX — Au Pairs (Human)
19	20	THE DUDE — Quincy Jones (A&M)
7	21	COMPUTER WORLD — Kraftwerk (EMI)
-	22	THEMES — Various Artists (K-Tel)
17	23	I AM THE PHOENIX — Judy Tzuke (Rocket)
13	24	PUNKS NOT DEAD — Exploited (Secret)
25	25	MAKIN' MOVIES — Dire Straits (Vertigo)
-	26	TO EACH — A Certain Ratio (Factory)
-	27	CAN'T GET ENOUGH — Eddy Grant (Ice)
20	28	FAITH — Cure (Fiction)
-	29	FUTURE SHOCK — Gillan (Virgin)
26	30	JOURNEYS TO GLORY — Spandau Ballet (Reformation)

last week	this week	**13 June 1981**
3	1	ANTHEM — Toyah (Safari)
1	2	STARS ON 45 — Starsound (CBS)
-	3	PRESENT ARMS — UB40 (DEP Int)
-	4	HEAVEN UP THERE — Echo & the Bunnymen (Korova)
2	5	KINGS OF THE WILD FRONTIER — Adam & the Ants (CBS)
5	6	THIS OLE HOUSE — Shakin' Stevens (Epic)
4	7	WHA'PPEN? — Beat (Go Feet)
15	8	CHARIOTS OF FIRE — Vangelis (Polydor)
17	9	BAD FOR GOOD — Jim Steinman (Epic)
19	10	PLAYING WITH A DIFFERENT SEX — Au Pairs (Human)
-	11	THE FOX — Elton John (Rocket)
22	12	THEMES — Various Artists (K-Tel)
6	13	DISCO DAZE AND DISCO NITES — Various Artists (Ronco)
7	14	HOTTER THAN JULY — Stevie Wonder (Motown)
21	15	COMPUTER WORLD — Kraftwerk (EMI)
8	16	LONG DISTANCE VOYAGER — Moody Blues (Threshold)
13	17	HI INFIDELITY — REO Speedwagon (Epic)
12	18	QUIT DREAMING AND GET ON THE BEAM — Bill Nelson (Mercury)
24	19	PUNKS NOT DEAD — Exploited (Secret)
17	20	EAST SIDE STORY — Squeeze (A&M)
11	21	SECRET COMBINATION — Randy Crawford (Warner Bros.)
25	22	MAKIN' MOVIES — Dire Straits (Vertigo)
-	23	MAGNETIC FIELDS — Jean Michael Jarre (Polydor)
-	24	NIGHT PEOPLE — Classix Nouveaux (Liberty)
14	25	POSITIVE TOUCH — Undertones (Ardeck)
-	26	NIGHTCLUBBING — Grace Jones (Island)
-	27	KILIMANJARO — Teardrop Explodes (Mercury)
-	28	SOMEWHERE IN ENGLAND — George Harrison (Dark Horse)
29	29	GO FOR IT — Stiff Little Fingers (Chrysalis)
-	30	THE RIVER — Bruce Springsteen (CBS)

The first album to break Adam & The Ants' stranglehold at Number 1 was the album-length version of the Continentally-recorded *Stars On 45* soundalike medley, credited to Starsound and actually the brainchild of Dutch producer Jaap Eggermont. The concept sparked a whole fad for such re-creations, and umpteen hit singles by assorted copyists, though only the Dutch original troubled the upper reaches of the album chart. Another surprise in the Top 10 were hardcore punk band the Exploited.

20 June 1981

last week	this week		
3	1	PRESENT ARMS	UB40 (DEP Int)
2	2	STARS ON 45	Starsound (CBS)
1	3	ANTHEM	Toyah (Safari)
13	4	DISCO DAZE AND DISCO NITES	Various Artists (Ronco)
5	5	KINGS OF THE WILD FRONTIER	Adam & the Ants (CBS)
7	6	WHA'PPEN?	Beat (Go Feet)
18	7	QUIT DREAMING AND GET ON THE BEAM	Bill Nelson (Mercury)
8	8	CHARIOTS OF FIRE	Vangelis (Polydor)
4	9	HEAVEN UP THERE	Echo & the Bunnymen (Korova)
10	10	THEMES	Various Artists (K-Tel)
23	11	MAGNETIC FIELDS	Jean Michael Jarre (Polydor)
6	12	THIS OLE HOUSE	Shakin' Stevens (Epic)
28	13	SOMEWHERE IN ENGLAND	George Harrison (Dark Horse)
16	14	LONG DISTANCE VOYAGER	Moody Blues (Threshold)
-	15	FACE VALUE	Phil Collins (Virgin)
10	16	PLAYING WITH A DIFFERENT SEX	Au Pairs (Human)
17	17	HI INFIDELITY	REO Speedwagon (Epic)
-	18	VIENNA	Ultravox (Chrysalis)
15	19	COMPUTER WORLD	Kraftwerk (EMI)
19	20	PUNKS NOT DEAD	Exploited (Secret)
21	21	SECRET COMBINATION	Randy Crawford (Warner Bros.)
30	22	THE RIVER	Bruce Springsteen (CBS)
10	23	THE FOX	Elton John (Rocket)
26	24	NIGHTCLUBBING	Grace Jones (Island)
27	25	KILIMANJARO	Teardrop Explodes (Mercury)
20	26	EAST SIDE STORY	Squeeze (A&M)
-	27	WHAT'S THIS FOR	Killing Joke (Malicious Damage)
-	28	I AM THE PHOENIX	Judy Tzuke (Rocket)
9	29	BAD FOR GOOD	Jim Steinman (Epic)
-	30	THE DUDE	Quincy Jones (A&M)

27 June 1981

last week	this week		
2	1	STARS ON 45	Starsound (CBS)
3	2	ANTHEM	Toyah (Safari)
4	3	DISCO DAZE AND DISCO NITES	Various Artists (Ronco)
5	4	KINGS OF THE WILD FRONTIER	Adam & the Ants (CBS)
1	5	PRESENT ARMS	UB40 (DEP Int)
8	6	CHARIOTS OF FIRE	Vangelis (Polydor)
12	7	THIS OLE HOUSE	Shakin' Stevens (Epic)
11	8	MAGNETIC FIELDS	Jean Michael Jarre (Polydor)
18	9	VIENNA	Ultravox (Chrysalis)
6	10	WHA'PPEN?	Beat (Go Feet)
15	11	FACE VALUE	Phil Collins (Virgin)
9	11	HEAVEN UP THERE	Echo & the Bunnymen (Korova)
-	13	NO SLEEP 'TIL HAMMERSMITH	Motorhead (Bronze)
14	14	LONG DISTANCE VOYAGER	Moody Blues (Threshold)
17	15	HI INFIDELITY	REO Speedwagon (Epic)
22	16	THE RIVER	Bruce Springsteen (CBS)
10	16	THEMES	Various Artists (K-Tel)
16	18	PLAYING WITH A DIFFERENT SEX	Au Pairs (Human)
-	19	JUJU	Siouxsie & the Banshees (Polydor)
20	20	PUNKS NOT DEAD	Exploited (Secret)
27	21	WHAT'S THIS FOR	Killing Joke (Malicious Damage)
21	22	SECRET COMBINATION	Randy Crawford (Warner Bros.)
-	23	BEING WITH YOU	Smokey Robinson (Motown)
-	24	MISTAKEN IDENTITY	Kim Carnes (EMI America)
13	25	SOMEWHERE IN ENGLAND	George Harrison (Dark Horse)
-	26	MAKIN' MOVIES	Dire Straits (Vertigo)
25	27	KILIMANJARO	Teardrop Explodes (Mercury)
-	28	HOTTER THAN JULY	Stevie Wonder (Motown)
-	29	TALK TALK TALK	Psychedelic Furs (CBS)
-	30	RED	Black Uhuru (Island)

4 July 1981

last week	this week		
5	1	PRESENT ARMS	UB40 (DEP Int)
13	2	NO SLEEP 'TIL HAMMERSMITH	Motorhead (Bronze)
1	3	STARS ON 45	Starsound (CBS)
3	4	DISCO DAZE AND DISCO NITES	Various Artists (Ronco)
2	5	ANTHEM	Toyah (Safari)
19	6	JUJU	Siouxsie & the Banshees (Polydor)
-	7	DURAN DURAN	Duran Duran (EMI)
11	8	FACE VALUE	Phil Collins (Virgin)
6	9	CHARIOTS OF FIRE	Vangelis (Polydor)
15	10	HI INFIDELITY	REO Speedwagon (Epic)
4	11	KINGS OF THE WILD FRONTIER	Adam & the Ants (CBS)
8	12	MAGNETIC FIELDS	Jean Michael Jarre (Polydor)
22	13	SECRET COMBINATION	Randy Crawford (Warner Bros.)
23	14	BEING WITH YOU	Smokey Robinson (Motown)
-	15	BAD FOR GOOD	Jim Steinman (Epic)
16	16	THEMES	Various Artists (K-Tel)
9	17	VIENNA	Ultravox (Chrysalis)
14	18	LONG DISTANCE VOYAGER	Moody Blues (Threshold)
7	19	THIS OLE HOUSE	Shakin' Stevens (Epic)
26	20	MAKIN' MOVIES	Dire Straits (Vertigo)
-	21	2,000,000 VOICES	Angelic Upstarts (Zonophone)
27	22	KILIMANJARO	Teardrop Explodes (Mercury)
29	22	TALK TALK TALK	Psychedelic Furs (CBS)
-	24	EAST SIDE STORY	Squeeze (A&M)
21	25	WHAT'S THIS FOR	Killing Joke (Malicious Damage)
10	26	WHA'PPEN?	Beat (Go Feet)
-	27	MADE IN AMERICA	Carpenters (A&M)
16	28	THE RIVER	Bruce Springsteen (CBS)
-	29	POLECATS ARE GO	Polecats (Mercury)
18	30	PLAYING WITH A DIFFERENT SEX	Au Pairs (Human)

11 July 1981

last week	this week		
2	1	NO SLEEP 'TIL HAMMERSMITH	Motorhead (Bronze)
1	2	PRESENT ARMS	UB40 (DEP Int)
3	3	STARS ON 45	Starsound (CBS)
4	4	DISCO DAZE AND DISCO NITES	Various Artists (Ronco)
5	5	ANTHEM	Toyah (Safari)
-	6	LOVE SONGS	Cliff Richard (EMI)
7	7	DURAN DURAN	Duran Duran (EMI)
11	8	KINGS OF THE WILD FRONTIER	Adam & the Ants (CBS)
9	9	CHARIOTS OF FIRE	Vangelis (Polydor)
6	10	JUJU	Siouxsie & the Banshees (Polydor)
12	11	MAGNETIC FIELDS	Jean Michael Jarre (Polydor)
13	12	SECRET COMBINATION	Randy Crawford (Warner Bros.)
8	13	FACE VALUE	Phil Collins (Virgin)
29	14	POLECATS ARE GO	Polecats (Mercury)
28	15	THE RIVER	Bruce Springsteen (CBS)
16	16	THEMES	Various Artists (K-Tel)
27	17	MADE IN AMERICA	Carpenters (A&M)
15	18	BAD FOR GOOD	Jim Steinman (Epic)
-	19	KIM WILDE	Kim Wilde (RAK)
19	19	THIS OLE HOUSE	Shakin' Stevens (Epic)
22	21	KILIMANJARO	Teardrop Explodes (Mercury)
-	22	JUMPIN' JIVE	Joe Jackson (A&M)
-	23	THE JAZZ SINGER	Neil Diamond (Capitol)
17	23	VIENNA	Ultravox (Chrysalis)
-	25	HOTTER THAN JULY	Stevie Wonder (Motown)
-	26	BAT OUT OF HELL	Meatloaf (Epic/Cleveland Int)
-	27	THE DUDE	Quincy Jones (A&M)
10	28	HI INFIDELITY	REO Speedwagon (Epic)
14	29	BEING WITH YOU	Smokey Robinson (Motown)
21	30	2,000,000 VOICES	Angelic Upstarts (Zonophone)

The successful *Disco Daze And Disco Nites* package was actually two separate dance compilation albums - *Disco Daze* and *Disco Nites*, the thrust of whose TV campaign was that you bought one and received the other free. Neither was available separately, but the set's Top 3 success suggests that the gimmick was a successful one. Toyah became one of the few female soloists to have a Number 1 album, while Vangelis' *Chariots Of Fire* contained his Oscar-winning music from the film of the same title.

18 July 1981

last week	this week	Title	Artist (Label)
1	1	NO SLEEP 'TIL HAMMERSMITH	Motorhead (Bronze)
4	2	DISCO DAZE AND DISCO NITES	Various Artists (Ronco)
6	3	LOVE SONGS	Cliff Richard (EMI)
2	4	PRESENT ARMS	UB40 (DEP Int)
19	5	KIM WILDE	Kim Wilde (RAK)
7	6	DURAN DURAN	Duran Duran (EMI)
3	7	STARS ON 45	Starsound (CBS)
12	8	SECRET COMBINATION	Randy Crawford (Warner Bros.)
5	9	ANTHEM	Toyah (Safari)
8	10	KINGS OF THE WILD FRONTIER	Adam & the Ants (CBS)
10	11	JUJU	Siouxsie & the Banshees (Polydor)
9	12	CHARIOTS OF FIRE	Vangelis (Polydor)
-	13	PENIS ENVY	Crass (Crass)
25	14	HOTTER THAN JULY	Stevie Wonder (Motown)
11	15	MAGNETIC FIELDS	Jean Michael Jarre (Polydor)
-	16	NAH POO THE ART OF BLUFF	Wah! (Eternal)
17	17	MADE IN AMERICA	Carpenters (A&M)
18	18	BAD FOR GOOD	Jim Steinman (Epic)
28	19	HI INFIDELITY	REO Speedwagon (Epic)
22	20	JUMPIN' JIVE	Joe Jackson (A&M)
19	21	THIS OLE HOUSE	Shakin' Stevens (Epic)
23	22	VIENNA	Ultravox (Chrysalis)
-	23	BEST OF MICHAEL JACKSON	Michael Jackson (Motown)
-	24	THE PARTY MIX ALBUM	B52's (Island)
-	25	HEAVEN UP THERE	Echo & the Bunnymen (Korova)
-	26	MAGIC, MURDER & THE WEATHER	Magazine (Virgin)
-	27	WHAT'S THIS FOR	Killing Joke (Malicious Damage)
26	28	BAT OUT OF HELL	Meatloaf (Epic)
16	29	THEMES	Various Artists (K-Tel)
15	30	THE RIVER	Bruce Springsteen (CBS)

25 July 1981

last week	this week	Title	Artist (Label)
3	1	LOVE SONGS	Cliff Richard (EMI)
1	2	NO SLEEP 'TIL HAMMERSMITH	Motorhead (Bronze)
5	3	KIM WILDE	Kim Wilde (RAK)
7	4	STARS ON 45	Starsound (CBS)
6	5	DURAN DURAN	Duran Duran (EMI)
9	6	ANTHEM	Toyah (Safari)
2	7	DISCO DAZE AND DISCO NITES	Various Artists (Ronco)
10	8	KINGS OF THE WILD FRONTIER	Adam & the Ants (CBS)
18	9	BAD FOR GOOD	Jim Steinman (Epic)
11	10	JUJU	Siouxsie & the Banshees (Polydor)
8	11	SECRET COMBINATION	Randy Crawford (Warner Bros.)
16	12	NAH POO THE ART OF BLUFF	Wah! (Eternal)
4	13	PRESENT ARMS	UB40 (DEP Int)
23	14	BEST OF MICHAEL JACKSON	Michael Jackson (Motown)
13	15	PENIS ENVY	Crass (Crass)
15	16	MAGNETIC FIELDS	Jean Michael Jarre (Polydor)
12	17	CHARIOTS OF FIRE	Vangelis (Polydor)
20	18	JUMPIN' JIVE	Joe Jackson (A&M)
19	19	HI INFIDELITY	REO Speedwagon (Epic)
14	20	HOTTER THAN JULY	Stevie Wonder (Motown)
-	21	I'VE GOT THE MELODY	Odyssey (RCA)
21	22	THIS OLE HOUSE	Shakin' Stevens (Epic)
17	23	MADE IN AMERICA	Carpenters (A&M)
-	24	TALK TALK TALK	Psychedelic Furs (CBS)
25	25	HEAVEN UP THERE	Echo & the Bunnymen (Korova)
-	26	EAST SIDE STORY	Squeeze (A&M)
28	27	BAT OUT OF HELL	Meatloaf (Epic)
-	28	PUNKS NOT DEAD	Exploited (Secret)
-	29	THE ONLY FUN IN TOWN	Josef K (Postcard)
30	30	THE RIVER	Bruce Springsteen (CBS)

1 August 1981

last week	this week	Title	Artist (Label)
1	1	LOVE SONGS	Cliff Richard (EMI)
3	2	KIM WILDE	Kim Wilde (RAK)
4	3	STARS ON 45	Starsound (CBS)
2	4	NO SLEEP 'TIL HAMMERSMITH	Motorhead (Bronze)
11	5	SECRET COMBINATION	Randy Crawford (Warner Bros.)
5	6	DURAN DURAN	Duran Duran (EMI)
8	7	KINGS OF THE WILD FRONTIER	Adam & the Ants (CBS)
9	8	BAD FOR GOOD	Jim Steinman (Epic)
20	9	HOTTER THAN JULY	Stevie Wonder (Motown)
13	10	PRESENT ARMS	UB40 (DEP Int)
7	11	DISCO DAZE AND DISCO NITES	Various Artists (Ronco)
6	12	ANTHEM	Toyah (Safari)
14	13	BEST OF MICHAEL JACKSON	Michael Jackson (Motown)
18	14	JUMPIN' JIVE	Joe Jackson (A&M)
19	15	HI INFIDELITY	REO Speedwagon (Epic)
10	16	JUJU	Siouxsie & the Banshees (Polydor)
16	17	MAGNETIC FIELDS	Jean Michael Jarre (Polydor)
12	18	NAH POO THE ART OF BLUFF	Wah! (Eternal)
-	19	PRECIOUS TIME	Pat Benatar (Chrysalis)
30	20	THE RIVER	Bruce Springsteen (CBS)
17	21	CHARIOTS OF FIRE	Vangelis (Polydor)
15	22	PENIS ENVY	Crass (Crass)
25	23	HEAVEN UP THERE	Echo & the Bunnymen (Korova)
-	24	FIRE OF UNKNOWN ORIGIN	Blue Oyster Cult (CBS)
27	25	BAT OUT OF HELL	Meatloaf (Epic)
-	26	HIGH & DRY	Def Leppard (Vertigo)
23	27	MADE IN AMERICA	Carpenters (A&M)
-	28	JOURNEYS TO GLORY	Spandau Ballet (Reformation)
22	29	THIS OLE HOUSE	Shakin' Stevens (Epic)
-	30	FACE VALUE	Phil Collins (Virgin)

8 August 1981

last week	this week	Title	Artist (Label)
1	1	LOVE SONGS	Cliff Richard (EMI)
2	2	KIM WILDE	Kim Wilde (RAK)
4	3	NO SLEEP 'TIL HAMMERSMITH	Motorhead (Bronze)
7	4	KINGS OF THE WILD FRONTIER	Adam & the Ants (CBS)
3	5	STARS ON 45	Starsound (CBS)
13	6	BEST OF MICHAEL JACKSON	Michael Jackson (Motown)
5	7	SECRET COMBINATION	Randy Crawford (Warner Bros.)
9	8	HOTTER THAN JULY	Stevie Wonder (Motown)
6	9	DURAN DURAN	Duran Duran (EMI)
15	10	HI INFIDELITY	REO Speedwagon (Epic)
10	11	PRESENT ARMS	UB40 (DEP Int)
8	12	BAD FOR GOOD	Jim Steinman (Epic)
16	13	JUJU	Siouxsie & the Banshees (Polydor)
12	14	ANTHEM	Toyah (Safari)
20	15	THE RIVER	Bruce Springsteen (CBS)
-	16	CATS	Various Artists (Polydor)
-	17	ROCK CLASSICS	London Symphony Orchestra & Royal Chorale Society (K-Tel)
30	18	FACE VALUE	Phil Collins (Virgin)
21	19	CHARIOTS OF FIRE	Vangelis (Polydor)
-	20	BELLA DONNA	Stevie Nicks (WEA)
29	21	THIS OLE HOUSE	Shakin' Stevens (Epic)
11	22	DISCO DAZE AND DISCO NITES	Various Artists (Ronco)
14	23	JUMPIN' JIVE	Joe Jackson (A&M)
-	24	4	Foreigner (Atlantic)
18	25	NAH POO THE ART OF BLUFF	Wah! (Eternal)
25	26	BAT OUT OF HELL	Meatloaf (Epic)
26	27	HIGH & DRY	Def Leppard (Vertigo)
23	28	HEAVEN UP THERE	Echo & the Bunnymen (Korova)
-	29	PUNKS NOT DEAD	Exploited (Secret)
-	30	ARC OF A DIVER	Steve Winwood (Island)
30		I'VE GOT THE MELODY	Odyssey (RCA)

Love Songs, which was to be one of Cliff Richard's all-time best-selling albums, was not a new set, but a collection of his most popular ballads, stretching from contemporary recordings right back to the early 1960s. Its success prevented the first album by Marty Wilde's daughter Kim from topping the chart (though it went a place higher than her debut single *Kids In America*). The Number 1 Cliff deposed was heavy metal trio Motorhead's biggest-ever seller, capturing their storming stage act.

August – September 1981

last this week

15 August 1981

1	1	LOVE SONGS — Cliff Richard (EMI)
-	2	TIME — Electric Light Orchestra (Jet)
9	3	DURAN DURAN — Duran Duran (EMI)
5	4	STARS ON 45 — Starsound (CBS)
7	5	SECRET COMBINATION — Randy Crawford (Warner Bros.)
2	6	KIM WILDE — Kim Wilde (RAK)
-	7	KOO KOO — Debbie Harry (Chrysalis)
8	8	HOTTER THAN JULY — Stevie Wonder (Motown)
17	9	ROCK CLASSICS — London Symphony Orchestra & Royal Chorale Society (K-Tel)
3	10	NO SLEEP 'TIL HAMMERSMITH — Motorhead (Bronze)
20	11	BELLA DONNA — Stevie Nicks (WEA)
10	12	HI INFIDELITY — REO Speedwagon (Epic)
4	13	KINGS OF THE WILD FRONTIER — Adam & the Ants (CBS)
11	14	PRESENT ARMS — UB40 (DEP Int)
-	15	THE OFFICIAL BBC ALBUM OF THE ROYAL WEDDING — BBC Recording (BBC)
16	16	CATS — Various Artists (Polydor)
21	17	THIS OLE HOUSE — Shakin' Stevens (Epic)
23	18	JUMPIN' JIVE — Joe Jackson (A&M)
14	19	ANTHEM — Toyah (Safari)
12	20	BAD FOR GOOD — Jim Steinman (Epic)
26	21	BAT OUT OF HELL — Meatloaf (Epic)
-	22	PRETENDERS II — Pretenders (Real)
15	23	THE RIVER — Bruce Springsteen (CBS)
-	24	STARTRAX CLUB DISCO — Various Artists (Picksy)
6	25	BEST OF MICHAEL JACKSON — Michael Jackson (Motown)
22	26	DISCO DAZE AND DISCO NITES — Various Artists (Ronco)
25	27	NAH POO THE ART OF BLUFF — Wah! (Eternal)
-	28	PIRATES — Rickie Lee Jones (Warner Bros.)
13	29	JUJU — Siouxsie & the Banshees (Polydor)
28	30	HEAVEN UP THERE — Echo & the Bunnymen (Korova)

22 August 1981

2	1	TIME — Electric Light Orchestra (Jet)
1	2	LOVE SONGS — Cliff Richard (EMI)
3	3	DURAN DURAN — Duran Duran (EMI)
12	4	HI INFIDELITY — REO Speedwagon (Epic)
7	5	KOO KOO — Debbie Harry (Chrysalis)
5	6	SECRET COMBINATION — Randy Crawford (Warner Bros.)
8	7	HOTTER THAN JULY — Stevie Wonder (Motown)
22	8	PRETENDERS II — Pretenders (Real)
6	9	KIM WILDE — Kim Wilde (RAK)
21	10	BAT OUT OF HELL — Meatloaf (Epic)
13	11	KINGS OF THE WILD FRONTIER — Adam & the Ants (CBS)
4	12	STARS ON 45 — Starsound (CBS)
15	13	THE OFFICIAL BBC ALBUM OF THE ROYAL WEDDING — BBC Recording (BBC)
16	14	CATS — Various Artists (Polydor)
10	15	NO SLEEP 'TIL HAMMERSMITH — Motorhead (Bronze)
11	16	BELLA DONNA — Stevie Nicks (WEA)
17	17	THIS OLE HOUSE — Shakin' Stevens (Epic)
20	18	BAD FOR GOOD — Jim Steinman (Epic)
14	19	PRESENT ARMS — UB40 (DEP Int)
-	20	BUCKS FIZZ — Bucks Fizz (RCA)
9	21	ROCK CLASSICS — London Symphony Orchestra & Royal Chorale Society (K-Tel)
25	22	BEST OF MICHAEL JACKSON — Michael Jackson (Motown)
18	23	JUMPIN' JIVE — Joe Jackson (A&M)
26	24	DISCO DAZE AND DISCO NITES — Various Artists (Ronco)
19	25	ANTHEM — Toyah (Safari)
-	26	JOURNEYS TO GLORY — Spandau Ballet (Reformation)
-	27	THE PARTY MIX ALBUM — B52's (Island)
-	28	THE JAZZ SINGER — Neil Diamond (Capitol)
23	29	THE RIVER — Bruce Springsteen (CBS)
-	30	FACE VALUE — Phil Collins (Virgin)

29 August 1981

1	1	TIME — Electric Light Orchestra (Jet)
3	2	DURAN DURAN — Duran Duran (EMI)
2	3	LOVE SONGS — Cliff Richard (EMI)
13	4	THE OFFICIAL BBC ALBUM OF THE ROYAL WEDDING — BBC Recording (BBC)
6	5	SECRET COMBINATION — Randy Crawford (Warner Bros.)
8	6	PRETENDERS II — Pretenders (Real)
9	7	KIM WILDE — Kim Wilde (RAK)
7	8	HOTTER THAN JULY — Stevie Wonder (Motown)
5	9	KOO KOO — Debbie Harry (Chrysalis)
10	10	BAT OUT OF HELL — Meatloaf (Epic)
12	11	STARS ON 45 — Starsound (CBS)
16	12	BELLA DONNA — Stevie Nicks (WEA)
11	13	KINGS OF THE WILD FRONTIER — Adam & the Ants (CBS)
17	14	THIS OLE HOUSE — Shakin' Stevens (Epic)
19	15	PRESENT ARMS — UB40 (DEP Int)
15	16	NO SLEEP 'TIL HAMMERSMITH — Motorhead (Bronze)
4	17	HI INFIDELITY — REO Speedwagon (Epic)
20	18	BUCKS FIZZ — Bucks Fizz (RCA)
21	19	ROCK CLASSICS — London Symphony Orchestra & Royal Chorale Society (K-Tel)
18	20	BAD FOR GOOD — Jim Steinman (Epic)
22	21	BEST OF MICHAEL JACKSON — Michael Jackson (Motown)
-	22	CURED — Steve Hackett (Charisma)
29	23	THE RIVER — Bruce Springsteen (CBS)
-	24	JUJU — Siouxsie & the Banshees (Polydor)
25	25	ANTHEM — Toyah (Safari)
14	26	CATS — Various Artists (Polydor)
-	27	THE LAST CALL — Anti-Pasti (Rondelet)
30	28	FACE VALUE — Phil Collins (Virgin)
-	29	MADE IN AMERICA — Carpenters (A&M)
-	30	20 GOLDEN GREATS — Beach Boys (Capitol)

5 September 1981

1	1	TIME — Electric Light Orchestra (Jet)
3	2	LOVE SONGS — Cliff Richard (EMI)
5	3	SECRET COMBINATION — Randy Crawford (Warner Bros.)
15	4	PRESENT ARMS — UB40 (DEP Int)
2	5	DURAN DURAN — Duran Duran (EMI)
-	6	SHOT OF LOVE — Bob Dylan (CBS)
14	7	THIS OLE HOUSE — Shakin' Stevens (Epic)
4	8	THE OFFICIAL BBC ALBUM OF THE ROYAL WEDDING — BBC Recording (BBC)
10	9	BAT OUT OF HELL — Meatloaf (Epic)
7	10	KIM WILDE — Kim Wilde (RAK)
6	11	PRETENDERS II — Pretenders (Real)
12	12	BELLA DONNA — Stevie Nicks (WEA)
22	13	CURED — Steve Hackett (Charisma)
8	14	HOTTER THAN JULY — Stevie Wonder (Motown)
-	15	TRAVELOGUE — Human League (Virgin)
17	16	HI INFIDELITY — REO Speedwagon (Epic)
13	17	KINGS OF THE WILD FRONTIER — Adam & the Ants (CBS)
21	18	BEST OF MICHAEL JACKSON — Michael Jackson (Motown)
25	19	ANTHEM — Toyah (Safari)
28	20	FACE VALUE — Phil Collins (Virgin)
20	21	BAD FOR GOOD — Jim Steinman (Epic)
18	22	BUCKS FIZZ — Bucks Fizz (RCA)
-	23	BOY — U2 (Island)
9	24	KOO KOO — Debbie Harry (Chrysalis)
-	25	LEVEL 42 — Level 42 (Polydor)
26	26	CATS — Various Artists (Polydor)
-	27	4 — Foreigner (Atlantic)
11	28	STARS ON 45 — Starsound (CBS)
19	29	ROCK CLASSICS — London Symphony Orchestra & Royal Chorale Society (K-Tel)
-	30	VIENNA — Ultravox (Chrysalis)

Time was ELO's first new album for over two years, but its almost immediate ascent to, and four-week stay at, the chart top underlined the Jeff Lynne-led group's continuing huge popularity - they were up to their 21st hit single at this time, with *Hold On Tight*, taken from *Time*. Meanwhile, BBC Records' souvenir album of the highlights of Charles and Diana's wedding became one of the very few documentary LPs ever to reach the Top 10. How many of those buyers still play it?

last week	this week	12 September 1981
1	1	TIME Electric Light Orchestra (Jet)
2	2	LOVE SONGS Cliff Richard (EMI)
5	3	DURAN DURAN Duran Duran (EMI)
3	4	SECRET COMBINATION Randy Crawford (Warner Bros.)
16	5	HI INFIDELITY REO Speedwagon (Epic)
4	6	PRESENT ARMS UB40 (DEP Int)
-	7	DEAD RINGER Meatloaf (Epic)
10	8	KIM WILDE Kim Wilde (RAK)
6	9	SHOT OF LOVE Bob Dylan (CBS)
11	10	PRETENDERS II Pretenders (Real)
22	11	BUCKS FIZZ Bucks Fizz (RCA)
8	12	THE OFFICIAL BBC ALBUM OF THE ROYAL WEDDING BBC Recording (BBC)
7	13	THIS OLE HOUSE Shakin' Stevens (Epic)
-	14	TATTOO YOU Rolling Stones (Rolling Stones)
9	15	BAT OUT OF HELL Meatloaf (Epic)
17	16	KINGS OF THE WILD FRONTIER Adam & the Ants (CBS)
14	17	HOTTER THAN JULY Stevie Wonder (Motown)
15	18	TRAVELOGUE Human League (Virgin)
12	19	BELLA DONNA Stevie Nicks (WEA)
19	20	ANTHEM Toyah (Safari)
24	21	KOO KOO Debbie Harry (Chrysalis)
-	22	NO SLEEP 'TIL HAMMERSMITH Motorhead (Bronze)
25	23	LEVEL 42 Level 42 (Polydor)
23	24	BOY U2 (Island)
13	25	CURED Steve Hackett (Charisma)
27	26	4 Foreigner (Atlantic)
21	27	BAD FOR GOOD Jim Steinman (Epic)
-	28	JUJU Siouxsie & the Banshees (Polydor)
28	29	STARS ON 45 Starsound (CBS)
-	30	CHRISTOPHER CROSS Christopher Cross (Warner Bros.)

		19 September 1981
7	1	DEAD RINGER Meatloaf (Epic)
14	2	TATTOO YOU Rolling Stones (Rolling Stones)
-	3	DANCE Gary Numan (Beggars Banquet)
2	4	LOVE SONGS Cliff Richard (EMI)
4	5	SECRET COMBINATION Randy Crawford (Warner Bros.)
-	6	SONS & FASCINATION/SISTERS FEELINGS CALL Simple Minds (Virgin)
1	7	TIME Electric Light Orchestra (Jet)
3	8	DURAN DURAN Duran Duran (EMI)
5	9	HI INFIDELITY REO Speedwagon (Epic)
-	10	WALK UNDER LADDERS Joan Armatrading (A&M)
15	11	BAT OUT OF HELL Meatloaf (Epic)
6	12	PRESENT ARMS UB40 (DEP Int)
-	13	RAGE IN EDEN Ultravox (Chrysalis)
10	14	PRETENDERS II Pretenders (Real)
20	15	ANTHEM Toyah (Safari)
9	16	SHOT OF LOVE Bob Dylan (CBS)
13	17	THIS OLE HOUSE Shakin' Stevens (Epic)
8	18	KIM WILDE Kim Wilde (RAK)
-	19	COVER PLUS Hazel O'Connor (Albion)
11	20	BUCKS FIZZ Bucks Fizz (RCA)
24	21	BOY U2 (Island)
17	22	HOTTER THAN JULY Stevie Wonder (Motown)
16	23	KINGS OF THE WILD FRONTIER Adam & the Ants (CBS)
18	24	TRAVELOGUE Human League (Virgin)
19	25	BELLA DONNA Stevie Nicks (WEA)
23	26	LEVEL 42 Level 42 (Polydor)
28	27	JUJU Siouxsie & the Banshees (Polydor)
-	28	20 GOLDEN GREATS Beach Boys (Capitol)
-	29	ROCK CLASSICS London Symphony Orchestra & Royal Chorale Society (K-Tel)
22	30	NO SLEEP 'TIL HAMMERSMITH Motorhead (Bronze)

		26 September 1981
1	1	DEAD RINGER Meatloaf (Epic)
2	2	TATTOO YOU Rolling Stones (Rolling Stones)
13	3	RAGE IN EDEN Ultravox (Chrysalis)
3	4	DANCE Gary Numan (Beggars Banquet)
7	5	TIME Electric Light Orchestra (Jet)
-	6	SHAKY Shakin' Stevens (Epic)
4	7	LOVE SONGS Cliff Richard (EMI)
-	8	STARS ON 45 VOL 2 Starsound (CBS)
-	9	WIRED FOR SOUND Cliff Richard (EMI)
8	10	DURAN DURAN Duran Duran (EMI)
5	11	SECRET COMBINATION Randy Crawford (Warner Bros.)
12	12	PRESENT ARMS UB40 (DEP Int)
11	13	BAT OUT OF HELL Meatloaf (Epic)
-	14	CELEBRATION Johnny Mathis (CBS)
10	15	WALK UNDER LADDERS Joan Armatrading (A&M)
6	16	SONS & FASCINATION/SISTERS FEELINGS CALL Simple Minds (Virgin)
-	17	ABACAB Genesis (Charisma)
-	18	HITS RIGHT UP YOUR STREET Shadows (Polydor)
-	19	HAPPY BIRTHDAY Altered Images (Epic)
-	20	DANCE DANCE DANCE Various Artists (K-Tel)
23	21	KINGS OF THE WILD FRONTIER Adam & the Ants (CBS)
-	22	SUPER HITS 1 & 2 Various Artists (Ronco)
-	23	MICHAEL SCHENKER GROUP Michael Schenker Group (Chrysalis)
-	24	PENTHOUSE AND PAVEMENT Heaven 17 (BEF/Virgin)
17	25	THIS OLE HOUSE Shakin' Stevens (Epic)
-	26	BLACK & WHITE Pointer Sisters (Planet)
24	27	TRAVELOGUE Human League (Virgin)
9	28	HI INFIDELITY REO Speedwagon (Epic)
16	29	SHOT OF LOVE Bob Dylan (CBS)
-	30	SLEEP NO MORE Comsat Angels (Polydor)

		3 October 1981
17	1	ABACAB Genesis (Charisma)
1	2	DEAD RINGER Meatloaf (Epic)
2	3	TATTOO YOU Rolling Stones (Rolling Stones)
3	4	RAGE IN EDEN Ultravox (Chrysalis)
6	5	SHAKY Shakin' Stevens (Epic)
5	6	TIME Electric Light Orchestra (Jet)
9	7	WIRED FOR SOUND Cliff Richard (EMI)
22	8	SUPER HITS 1 & 2 Various Artists (Ronco)
-	9	HOOKED ON CLASSICS Louis Clark & the Royal Philharmonic Orchestra (K-Tel)
14	10	CELEBRATION Johnny Mathis (CBS)
15	11	WALK UNDER LADDERS Joan Armatrading (A&M)
24	12	PENTHOUSE AND PAVEMENT Heaven 17 (BEF/Virgin)
11	13	SECRET COMBINATION Randy Crawford (Warner Bros.)
13	14	BAT OUT OF HELL Meatloaf (Epic)
12	15	PRESENT ARMS UB40 (DEP Int)
4	16	DANCE Gary Numan (Beggars Banquet)
21	17	KINGS OF THE WILD FRONTIER Adam & the Ants (CBS)
10	18	DURAN DURAN Duran Duran (EMI)
7	19	LOVE SONGS Cliff Richard (EMI)
-	20	ANGELIC UPSTARTS Angelic Upstarts (Zonophone)
19	21	HAPPY BIRTHDAY Altered Images (Epic)
8	22	STARS ON 45 VOL 2 Starsound (CBS)
-	23	LEVEL 42 Level 42 (Polydor)
18	24	HITS RIGHT UP YOUR STREET Shadows (Polydor)
23	25	MICHAEL SCHENKER GROUP Michael Schenker Group (Chrysalis)
-	26	BUCKS FIZZ Bucks Fizz (RCA)
26	27	BLACK & WHITE Pointer Sisters (Planet)
20	28	DANCE DANCE DANCE Various Artists (K-Tel)
-	29	DENIM AND LEATHER Saxon (Carrere)
-	30	THE GARDEN John Foxx (Virgin)

Meatloaf's *Dead Ringer* was the belated follow-up to his huge 1978 seller *Bat Out Of Hell*, and though it proved to have nothing like the chart staying power of its predecessor, it initially sold much more quickly, securing a Number 1 position which held the Rolling Stones' *Tattoo You* to runner-up status. With the release of *Wired For Sound* and continuing success of *Love Songs*, Cliff Richard had two albums in the Top Ten simultaneously for the first time since the heady days of 1963.

October 1981

10 October 1981

last	this		
2	1	DEAD RINGER	Meatloaf (Epic)
1	2	ABACAB	Genesis (Charisma)
9	3	HOOKED ON CLASSICS	Louis Clark & the Royal Philharmonic Orchestra (K-Tel)
8	4	SUPER HITS 1 & 2	Various Artists (Ronco)
-	5	IF I SHOULD LOVE AGAIN	Barry Manilow (Arista)
7	6	WIRED FOR SOUND	Cliff Richard (EMI)
5	7	SHAKY	Shakin' Stevens (Epic)
4	8	RAGE IN EDEN	Ultravox (Chrysalis)
-	9	GHOST IN THE MACHINE	Police (A&M)
3	10	TATTOO YOU	Rolling Stones (Rolling Stones)
10	11	CELEBRATION	Johnny Mathis (CBS)
15	12	PRESENT ARMS	UB40 (DEP Int)
6	13	TIME	Electric Light Orchestra (Jet)
12	14	PENTHOUSE AND PAVEMENT	Heaven 17 (BEF/Virgin)
13	15	SECRET COMBINATION	Randy Crawford (Warner Bros.)
29	16	DENIM AND LEATHER	Saxon (Carrere)
19	17	LOVE SONGS	Cliff Richard (EMI)
-	18	BEAT THE CARROTT	Jasper Carrott (DJM)
18	19	DURAN DURAN	Duran Duran (EMI)
-	20	SONS & FASCINATION/SISTERS FEELINGS CALL	Simple Minds (Virgin)
24	21	HITS RIGHT UP YOUR STREET	Shadows (Polydor)
-	22	YOU COULD HAVE BEEN WITH ME	Sheena Easton (EMI)
30	23	THE GARDEN	John Foxx (Virgin)
11	24	WALK UNDER LADDERS	Joan Armatrading (A&M)
-	25	ANTHEM	Toyah (Safari)
28	26	DANCE DANCE DANCE	Various Artists (K-Tel)
-	27	ASSEMBLAGE	Japan (Hansa)
16	28	DANCE	Gary Numan (Beggars Banquet)
-	29	DISCIPLINE	King Crimson (Polydor)
-	30	THE VERY BEST OF ANNE MURRAY	Anne Murray (Capitol)

17 October 1981

last	this		
9	1	GHOST IN THE MACHINE	Police (A&M)
-	2	7	Madness (Stiff)
4	3	SUPER HITS 1 & 2	Various Artists (Ronco)
2	4	ABACAB	Genesis (Charisma)
7	5	SHAKY	Shakin' Stevens (Epic)
5	6	IF I SHOULD LOVE AGAIN	Barry Manilow (Arista)
1	7	DEAD RINGER	Meatloaf (Epic)
10	8	TATTOO YOU	Rolling Stones (Rolling Stones)
6	9	WIRED FOR SOUND	Cliff Richard (EMI)
3	10	HOOKED ON CLASSICS	Louis Clark & the Royal Philharmonic Orchestra (K-Tel)
8	11	RAGE IN EDEN	Ultravox (Chrysalis)
11	12	CELEBRATION	Johnny Mathis (CBS)
15	13	SECRET COMBINATION	Randy Crawford (Warner Bros.)
16	14	DENIM AND LEATHER	Saxon (Carrere)
27	15	ASSEMBLAGE	Japan (Hansa)
14	16	PENTHOUSE AND PAVEMENT	Heaven 17 (BEF/Virgin)
17	17	LOVE SONGS	Cliff Richard (EMI)
20	18	SONS & FASCINATION/SISTERS FEELINGS CALL	Simple Minds (Virgin)
12	19	PRESENT ARMS	UB40 (DEP Int)
18	20	BEAT THE CARROTT	Jasper Carrott (DJM)
30	21	THE VERY BEST OF ANNE MURRAY	Anne Murray (Capitol)
13	22	TIME	Electric Light Orchestra (Jet)
22	23	YOU COULD HAVE BEEN WITH ME	Sheena Easton (EMI)
-	24	HAPPY BIRTHDAY	Altered Images (Epic)
-	25	NINE TONIGHT	Bob Seger & the Silver Bullet Band (Capitol)
23	26	THE GARDEN	John Foxx (Virgin)
-	27	20 GOLDEN GREATS	Diana Ross (Motown)
-	28	FRESH QUOTA	Status Quo (Phonogram)
-	29	BAT OUT OF HELL	Meatloaf (Epic)
-	30	BLACK & WHITE	Pointer Sisters (Planet)

24 October 1981

last	this		
1	1	GHOST IN THE MACHINE	Police (A&M)
5	2	SHAKY	Shakin' Stevens (Epic)
2	3	7	Madness (Stiff)
6	4	IF I SHOULD LOVE AGAIN	Barry Manilow (Arista)
7	5	DEAD RINGER	Meatloaf (Epic)
3	6	SUPER HITS 1 & 2	Various Artists (Ronco)
8	7	TATTOO YOU	Rolling Stones (Rolling Stones)
4	8	ABACAB	Genesis (Charisma)
10	9	HOOKED ON CLASSICS	Louis Clark & the Royal Philharmonic Orchestra (K-Tel)
-	10	STILL	Joy Division (Factory)
9	11	WIRED FOR SOUND	Cliff Richard (EMI)
11	12	RAGE IN EDEN	Ultravox (Chrysalis)
12	13	CELEBRATION	Johnny Mathis (CBS)
14	14	DENIM AND LEATHER	Saxon (Carrere)
19	14	PRESENT ARMS	UB40 (DEP Int)
-	16	DARE	Human League (Virgin)
16	16	PENTHOUSE AND PAVEMENT	Heaven 17 (BEF/Virgin)
24	18	HAPPY BIRTHDAY	Altered Images (Epic)
-	19	HITS RIGHT UP YOUR STREET	Shadows (Polydor)
13	20	SECRET COMBINATION	Randy Crawford (Warner Bros.)
-	20	OCTOBER	U2 (Island)
-	22	ROCK CLASSICS	London Symphony Orchestra & Royal Chorale Society (K-Tel)
26	23	THE GARDEN	John Foxx (Virgin)
-	24	ISMISM	Godley & Creme (Polydor)
21	25	THE VERY BEST OF ANNE MURRAY	Anne Murray (Capitol)
22	26	TIME	Electric Light Orchestra (Jet)
-	27	KINGS OF THE WILD FRONTIER	Adam & the Ants (CBS)
15	28	ASSEMBLAGE	Japan (Hansa)
-	29	DURAN DURAN	Duran Duran (EMI)
-	30	WALK UNDER LADDERS	Joan Armatrading (A&M)

31 October 1981

last	this		
1	1	GHOST IN THE MACHINE	Police (A&M)
16	2	DARE	Human League (Virgin)
4	3	IF I SHOULD LOVE AGAIN	Barry Manilow (Arista)
2	4	SHAKY	Shakin' Stevens (Epic)
3	5	7	Madness (Stiff)
9	6	HOOKED ON CLASSICS	Louis Clark & the Royal Philharmonic Orchestra (K-Tel)
6	7	SUPER HITS 1 & 2	Various Artists (Ronco)
8	8	ABACAB	Genesis (Charisma)
5	9	DEAD RINGER	Meatloaf (Epic)
-	10	HEDGEHOG SANDWICH	Not the Nine O'clock News (BBC)
20	11	OCTOBER	U2 (Island)
10	12	STILL	Joy Division (Factory)
-	12	BODY TALK	Imagination (R&B)
-	14	GOSH IT'S BAD MANNERS	Bad Manners (Magnet)
11	15	WIRED FOR SOUND	Cliff Richard (EMI)
7	16	TATTOO YOU	Rolling Stones (Rolling Stones)
13	17	CELEBRATION	Johnny Mathis (CBS)
12	18	RAGE IN EDEN	Ultravox (Chrysalis)
26	19	TIME	Electric Light Orchestra (Jet)
16	20	PENTHOUSE AND PAVEMENT	Heaven 17 (BEF/Virgin)
14	21	DENIM AND LEATHER	Saxon (Carrere)
22	22	ROCK CLASSICS	London Symphony Orchestra & Royal Chorale Society (K-Tel)
24	23	ISMISM	Godley & Creme (Polydor)
-	24	SONIC ATTACK	Hawkwind (RCA)
-	25	MASK	Bauhaus (Beggars Banquet)
20	26	SECRET COMBINATION	Randy Crawford (Warner Bros.)
25	27	THE VERY BEST OF ANNE MURRAY	Anne Murray (Capitol)
18	28	HAPPY BIRTHDAY	Altered Images (Epic)
-	29	TOM TOM CLUB	Tom Tom Club (Island)
28	30	ASSEMBLAGE	Japan (Hansa)

The Police proved their consistency by completing a hat-trick of Number 1 albums with *Ghost In The Machine*. Its three weeks atop the chart prevented likely contenders like Madness, Shakin' Stevens and Barry Manilow from making Number 1 - although the trio's current single *Invisible Sun* stalled at Number 2. *Hedgehog Sandwich* gave Not The Nine O'Clock News a second Top-Tenner, a unique achievement for a comedy team, while *Hooked On Classics* was a classical variation on the Stars On 45 formula.

7 November 1981

last week	this week	Title / Artist (Label)
2	1	DARE — Human League (Virgin)
4	2	SHAKY — Shakin' Stevens (Epic)
1	3	GHOST IN THE MACHINE — Police (A&M)
3	4	IF I SHOULD LOVE AGAIN — Barry Manilow (Arista)
5	5	7 — Madness (Stiff)
6	6	HOOKED ON CLASSICS — Louis Clark & the Royal Philharmonic Orchestra (K-Tel)
7	7	SUPER HITS 1 & 2 — Various Artists (Ronco)
-	8	ALMOST BLUE — Elvis Costello (F-Beat)
-	9	LOVE IS — Various Artists (K-Tel)
-	10	BEST OF BLONDIE — Blondie (Chrysalis)
11	11	OCTOBER — U2 (Island)
28	12	HAPPY BIRTHDAY — Altered Images (Epic)
12	13	STILL — Joy Division (Factory)
10	14	HEDGEHOG SANDWICH — Not the Nine O'clock News (BBC)
14	15	GOSH IT'S BAD MANNERS — Bad Manners (Magnet)
8	16	ABACAB — Genesis (Charisma)
17	17	CELEBRATION — Johnny Mathis (CBS)
21	18	DENIM AND LEATHER — Saxon (Carrere)
12	19	BODY TALK — Imagination (R&B)
16	20	TATTOO YOU — Rolling Stones (Rolling Stones)
26	21	SECRET COMBINATION — Randy Crawford (Warner Bros.)
24	22	SONIC ATTACK — Hawkwind (RCA)
-	23	CARRY ON OI! — Various Artists (Secret)
-	24	SEE JUNGLE! SEE JUNGLE! GO JOIN YOUR GANG YEAH CITY ALL OVER! GO APE CRAZY — Bow Wow Wow (RCA)
9	25	DEAD RINGER — Meatloaf (Epic)
18	25	RAGE IN EDEN — Ultravox (Chrysalis)
-	27	PHYSICAL — Olivia Newton-John (EMI)
25	28	MASK — Bauhaus (Beggars Banquet)
-	29	EXIT STAGE LEFT — Rush (Mercury)
-	29	NO CAUSE FOR CONCERN — Vice Squad (Zonophone)

14 November 1981

last week	this week	Title / Artist (Label)
1	1	DARE — Human League (Virgin)
-	2	QUEEN'S GREATEST HITS — Queen (EMI)
2	3	SHAKY — Shakin' Stevens (Epic)
10	4	BEST OF BLONDIE — Blondie (Chrysalis)
3	5	GHOST IN THE MACHINE — Police (A&M)
8	6	ALMOST BLUE — Elvis Costello (F-Beat)
29	7	EXIT STAGE LEFT — Rush (Mercury)
4	8	IF I SHOULD LOVE AGAIN — Barry Manilow (Arista)
-	9	PRINCE CHARMING — Adam & the Ants (CBS)
5	10	7 — Madness (Stiff)
-	11	DOUBLE TROUBLE — Gillan (Virgin)
13	12	STILL — Joy Division (Factory)
9	13	LOVE IS — Various Artists (K-Tel)
-	14	ARCHITECTURE AND MORALITY — Orchestral Manoeuvres in the Dark (Dindisc)
16	15	ABACAB — Genesis (Charisma)
-	16	DIARY OF A MADMAN — Ozzy Osbourne (Jet)
14	17	HEDGEHOG SANDWICH — Not the Nine O'clock News (BBC)
6	18	HOOKED ON CLASSICS — Louis Clark & the Royal Philharmonic Orchestra (K-Tel)
-	19	WIRED FOR SOUND — Cliff Richard (EMI)
7	20	SUPER HITS 1 & 2 — Various Artists (Ronco)
11	21	OCTOBER — U2 (Island)
12	22	HAPPY BIRTHDAY — Altered Images (Epic)
19	23	BODY TALK — Imagination (R&B)
-	24	MONSTER TRACKS — Various Artists (Polydor)
-	25	SPEAK AND SPELL — Depeche Mode (Mute)
-	26	WHY DO FOOLS FALL IN LOVE — Diana Ross (Capitol)
29	27	NO CAUSE FOR CONCERN — Vice Squad (Zonophone)
-	28	PLEASURE — Girls At Our Best (Happy Birthday)
27	29	PHYSICAL — Olivia Newton-John (EMI)
15	30	GOSH IT'S BAD MANNERS — Bad Manners (Magnet)

21 November 1981

last week	this week	Title / Artist (Label)
9	1	PRINCE CHARMING — Adam & the Ants (CBS)
1	2	DARE — Human League (Virgin)
14	3	ARCHITECTURE AND MORALITY — Orchestral Manoeuvres in the Dark (Dindisc)
2	4	QUEEN'S GREATEST HITS — Queen (EMI)
5	5	GHOST IN THE MACHINE — Police (A&M)
25	6	SPEAK AND SPELL — Depeche Mode (Mute)
3	7	SHAKY — Shakin' Stevens (Epic)
-	8	TONIGHT I'M YOURS — Rod Stewart (Riva)
4	9	BEST OF BLONDIE — Blondie (Chrysalis)
-	10	MOB RULES — Black Sabbath (Vertigo)
7	11	EXIT STAGE LEFT — Rush (Mercury)
6	12	ALMOST BLUE — Elvis Costello (F-Beat)
16	13	DIARY OF A MADMAN — Ozzy Osbourne (Jet)
13	14	LOVE IS — Various Artists (K-Tel)
-	15	RAISE! — Earth Wind & Fire (CBS)
17	16	HEDGEHOG SANDWICH — Not the Nine O'clock News (BBC)
12	17	STILL — Joy Division (Factory)
-	18	PUNKS NOT DEAD — Exploited (Secret)
-	19	PEARLS — Elkie Brooks (A&M)
10	20	7 — Madness (Stiff)
20	21	SUPER HITS 1 & 2 — Various Artists (Ronco)
11	22	DOUBLE TROUBLE — Gillan (Virgin)
8	23	IF I SHOULD LOVE AGAIN — Barry Manilow (Arista)
-	24	THE GEORGE BENSON COLLECTION — George Benson (Warner Bros.)
-	25	SECRET COMBINATION — Randy Crawford (Warner Bros.)
18	26	HOOKED ON CLASSICS — Louis Clark & the Royal Philharmonic Orchestra (K-Tel)
-	27	BEST OF RAINBOW — Rainbow (Polydor)
15	28	ABACAB — Genesis (Charisma)
-	28	SEE JUNGLE! SEE JUNGLE! GO JOIN YOUR GANG YEAH CITY ALL OVER! GO APE CRAZY — Bow Wow Wow (RCA)
21	30	OCTOBER — U2 (Island)

28 November 1981

last week	this week	Title / Artist (Label)
1	1	PRINCE CHARMING — Adam & the Ants (CBS)
4	2	QUEEN'S GREATEST HITS — Queen (EMI)
3	3	ARCHITECTURE AND MORALITY — Orchestral Manoeuvres in the Dark (Dindisc)
5	4	GHOST IN THE MACHINE — Police (A&M)
2	5	DARE — Human League (Virgin)
9	6	BEST OF BLONDIE — Blondie (Chrysalis)
7	7	SHAKY — Shakin' Stevens (Epic)
8	8	TONIGHT I'M YOURS — Rod Stewart (Riva)
12	9	ALMOST BLUE — Elvis Costello (F-Beat)
19	10	PEARLS — Elkie Brooks (A&M)
15	11	RAISE! — Earth Wind & Fire (CBS)
6	12	SPEAK AND SPELL — Depeche Mode (Mute)
-	13	CHART HITS '81 — Various Artists (K-Tel)
26	14	HOOKED ON CLASSICS — Louis Clark & the Royal Philharmonic Orchestra (K-Tel)
10	15	MOB RULES — Black Sabbath (Vertigo)
11	16	EXIT STAGE LEFT — Rush (Mercury)
-	17	TIN DRUM — Japan (Virgin)
28	18	ABACAB — Genesis (Charisma)
-	19	WIRED FOR SOUND — Cliff Richard (EMI)
14	20	LOVE IS — Various Artists (K-Tel)
23	21	IF I SHOULD LOVE AGAIN — Barry Manilow (Arista)
-	22	ALL THE GREAT HITS — Diana Ross (Motown)
-	23	DE NINA A MUJER — Julio Iglesias (CBS)
24	24	THE GEORGE BENSON COLLECTION — George Benson (Warner Bros.)
17	25	STILL — Joy Division (Factory)
21	26	SUPER HITS 1 & 2 — Various Artists (Ronco)
27	27	BEST OF RAINBOW — Rainbow (Polydor)
20	28	7 — Madness (Stiff)
16	29	HEDGEHOG SANDWICH — Not the Nine O'clock News (BBC)
-	30	BODY TALK — Imagination (R&B)

As always, the hot chart names came out to play for the pre-Christmas market. Human League's *Dare* initially gave way quite quickly at the top to Adam & The Ants' *Prince Charming*, though would get a second boost when the million-selling single *Don't You Want Me* was extracted from it. *Queen's Greatest Hits*, rounding up most of the quartet's major hit singles to date, would eventually become the best-selling compilation album of all time in the UK, remaining a steady seller throughout the decade.

December 1981

5 December 1981

last	this		
2	1	QUEEN'S GREATEST HITS	Queen (EMI)
13	2	CHART HITS '81	Various Artists (K-Tel)
5	3	DARE	Human League (Virgin)
6	4	BEST OF BLONDIE	Blondie (Chrysalis)
1	5	PRINCE CHARMING	Adam & the Ants (CBS)
3	6	ARCHITECTURE AND MORALITY	Orchestral Manoeuvres in the Dark (Dindisc)
23	7	DE NINA A MUJER	Julio Iglesias (CBS)
7	8	SHAKY	Shakin' Stevens (Epic)
17	9	TIN DRUM	Japan (Virgin)
10	10	PEARLS	Elkie Brooks (A&M)
4	11	GHOST IN THE MACHINE	Police (A&M)
8	12	TONIGHT I'M YOURS	Rod Stewart (Riva)
12	13	SPEAK AND SPELL	Depeche Mode (Mute)
-	14	THE SIMON & GARFUNKEL COLLECTION	Simon & Garfunkel (CBS)
11	15	RAISE!	Earth Wind & Fire (CBS)
16	16	EXIT STAGE LEFT	Rush (Mercury)
-	17	MOVEMENT	New Order (Factory)
9	18	ALMOST BLUE	Elvis Costello (F-Beat)
-	19	HANSIMANIA	James Last (Polydor)
22	20	ALL THE GREAT HITS	Diana Ross (Motown)
28	21	7	Madness (Stiff)
27	22	BEST OF RAINBOW	Rainbow (Polydor)
20	23	LOVE IS	Various Artists (K-Tel)
-	24	NON-STOP EROTIC CABARET	Soft Cell (Some Bizzare)
-	25	WHY DO FOOLS FALL IN LOVE	Diana Ross (Capitol)
14	26	HOOKED ON CLASSICS	Louis Clark & the Royal Philharmonic Orchestra (K-Tel)
21	27	IF I SHOULD LOVE AGAIN	Barry Manilow (Arista)
-	28	THE VERY BEST OF SHOWADDYWADDY	Showaddywaddy (Arista)
-	29	LA FOLIE	Stranglers (Liberty)
19	30	WIRED FOR SOUND	Cliff Richard (EMI)

12 December 1981

last	this		
2	1	CHART HITS '81	Various Artists (K-Tel)
1	2	QUEEN'S GREATEST HITS	Queen (EMI)
-	3	FOR THOSE ABOUT TO ROCK	AC/DC (Atlantic)
5	4	PRINCE CHARMING	Adam & the Ants (CBS)
10	5	PEARLS	Elkie Brooks (A&M)
3	6	DARE	Human League (Virgin)
4	7	BEST OF BLONDIE	Blondie (Chrysalis)
14	8	THE SIMON & GARFUNKEL COLLECTION	Simon & Garfunkel (CBS)
24	9	NON-STOP EROTIC CABARET	Soft Cell (Some Bizzare)
12	10	TONIGHT I'M YOURS	Rod Stewart (Riva)
6	11	ARCHITECTURE AND MORALITY	Orchestral Manoeuvres in Dark (Dindisc)
7	12	DE NINA A MUJER	Julio Iglesias (CBS)
8	13	SHAKY	Shakin' Stevens (Epic)
9	14	TIN DRUM	Japan (Virgin)
15	15	RAISE!	Earth Wind & Fire (CBS)
20	16	ALL THE GREAT HITS	Diana Ross (Motown)
30	17	WIRED FOR SOUND	Cliff Richard (EMI)
22	18	BEST OF RAINBOW	Rainbow (Polydor)
26	19	HOOKED ON CLASSICS	Louis Clark & Philharmonic Orchestra (K-Tel)
11	20	GHOST IN THE MACHINE	Police (A&M)
28	21	THE VERY BEST OF SHOWADDYWADDY	Showaddywaddy (Arista)
19	22	HANSIMANIA	James Last (Polydor)
18	23	ALMOST BLUE	Elvis Costello (F-Beat)
-	24	WILDER	Teardrop Explodes (Mercury)
-	25	BEGIN THE BEGUINE	Julio Iglesias (CBS)
13	26	SPEAK AND SPELL	Depeche Mode (Mute)
-	27	RENEGADE	Thin Lizzy (Vertigo)
-	28	PERHAPS LOVE	Placido Domingo & John Denver (CBS)
-	29	COUNTRY GIRL	Billy Jo Spears (Warwick)
-	30	THE PICK OF BILLY CONNOLLY	Billy Connolly (Polydor)

19 December 1981

last	this		
6	1	DARE	Human League (Virgin)
4	2	PRINCE CHARMING	Adam & the Ants (CBS)
1	3	CHART HITS '81	Various Artists (K-Tel)
2	4	QUEEN'S GREATEST HITS	Queen (EMI)
5	5	PEARLS	Elkie Brooks (A&M)
25	6	BEGIN THE BEGUINE	Julio Iglesias (CBS)
7	7	BEST OF BLONDIE	Blondie (Chrysalis)
8	8	THE SIMON & GARFUNKEL COLLECTION	Simon & Garfunkel (CBS)
3	9	FOR THOSE ABOUT TO ROCK	AC/DC (Atlantic)
20	10	GHOST IN THE MACHINE	Police (A&M)
13	11	SHAKY	Shakin' Stevens (Epic)
10	12	TONIGHT I'M YOURS	Rod Stewart (Riva)
9	13	NON-STOP EROTIC CABARET	Soft Cell (Some Bizzare)
11	14	ARCHITECTURE AND MORALITY	Orchestral Manoeuvres in the Dark (Dindisc)
-	15	THE VISITORS	Abba (Epic)
19	16	HOOKED ON CLASSICS	Louis Clark & Philharmonic Orchestra (K-Tel)
29	17	COUNTRY GIRL	Billy Jo Spears (Warwick)
15	18	RAISE!	Earth Wind & Fire (CBS)
14	19	TIN DRUM	Japan (Virgin)
16	20	ALL THE GREAT HITS	Diana Ross (Motown)
-	21	ONCE UPON A TIME	Siouxsie & the Banshees (Polydor)
22	22	HANSIMANIA	James Last (Polydor)
17	23	WIRED FOR SOUND	Cliff Richard (EMI)
12	24	DE NINA A MUJER	Julio Iglesias (CBS)
28	25	PERHAPS LOVE	Placido Domingo & John Denver (CBS)
-	26	MOVEMENT	New Order (Factory)
24	27	WILDER	Teardrop Explodes (Mercury)
23	28	ALMOST BLUE	Elvis Costello (F-Beat)
18	29	BEST OF RAINBOW	Rainbow (Polydor)
30	30	THE PICK OF BILLY CONNOLLY	Billy Connolly (Polydor)

Topping the pre-Christmas singles chart with *Begin The Beguine*, Latin hearthrob vocalist Julio Iglesias suddenly found the kind of success in the UK that he enjoyed elsewhere in the world, manifested in two albums in the Top 30 simultaneously. Elkie Brooks scored the biggest-selling album of her career with *Pearls*, a collection of classic song covers, while Blondie, Diana Ross, Rainbow, Showaddywaddy and the long-split Simon & Garfunkel all had big-selling hit singles collections for Christmas.

Clockwise from top left:
Debbie
(later Deborah) Harry,
Bob Marley (without the
Wailers),
Madness and
Adam (without the Ants)

January 1982

2 January 1982

last	this	title	artist
15	1	THE VISITORS	Abba (Epic)
1	2	DARE	Human League (Virgin)
3	3	CHART HITS '81	Various Artists (K-Tel)
4	4	QUEEN'S GREATEST HITS	Queen (EMI)
2	5	PRINCE CHARMING	Adam & the Ants (CBS)
7	6	BEST OF BLONDIE	Blondie (Chrysalis)
8	7	THE SIMON & GARFUNKEL COLLECTION	Simon & Garfunkel (CBS)
5	8	PEARLS	Elkie Brooks (A&M)
6	9	BEGIN THE BEGUINE	Julio Iglesias (CBS)
23	10	WIRED FOR SOUND	Cliff Richard (EMI)
12	11	TONIGHT I'M YOURS	Rod Stewart (Riva)
10	12	GHOST IN THE MACHINE	Police (A&M)
11	13	SHAKY	Shakin' Stevens (Epic)
9	14	FOR THOSE ABOUT TO ROCK	AC/DC (Atlantic)
20	15	ALL THE GREAT HITS	Diana Ross (Motown)
14	16	ARCHITECTURE AND MORALITY	Orchestral Manoeuvres In The Dark (DinDisc)
25	17	PERHAPS LOVE	Placido Domingo & John Denver (CBS)
-	18	IF I SHOULD LOVE AGAIN	Barry Manilow (Arista)
-	19	CHANGESTWOBOWIE	David Bowie (RCA)
22	20	HANSIMANIA	James Last (Polydor)
-	21	CHAS AND DAVE'S CHRISTMAS JAMBOREE BAG	Chas & Dave (Warwick)
18	22	RAISE!	Earth Wind & Fire (CBS)
-	23	DURAN DURAN	Duran Duran (EMI)
-	24	LOVE SONGS	Cliff Richard (EMI)
-	25	REJOICE	St. Paul's Boys Choir (K-Tel)
-	26	HAWAIIAN PARADISE/CHRISTMAS	Woot Steenhuis (Warwick)
-	27	HEDGEHOG SANDWICH	Not The Nine O'Clock News (BBC)
-	28	ISMISM	Godley & Creme (Polydor)
-	29	THE OFFICIAL BBC ALBUM OF THE ROYAL WEDDING	BBC Recording (BBC)
-	30	WE ARE MOST AMUSED – THE VERY BEST OF BRITISH COMEDY	Various Artists (Ronco)

9 January 1982

last	this	title	artist
2	1	DARE	Human League (Virgin)
4	2	QUEEN'S GREATEST HITS	Queen (EMI)
1	3	THE VISITORS	Abba (Epic)
10	4	WIRED FOR SOUND	Cliff Richard (EMI)
3	5	CHART HITS '81	Various Artists (K-Tel)
6	6	BEST OF BLONDIE	Blondie (Chrysalis)
8	7	PEARLS	Elkie Brooks (A&M)
5	8	PRINCE CHARMING	Adam & the Ants (CBS)
12	9	GHOST IN THE MACHINE	Police (A&M)
13	10	SHAKY	Shakin' Stevens (Epic)
16	11	ARCHITECTURE AND MORALITY	Orchestral Manoeuvres In The Dark (DinDisc)
11	12	TONIGHT I'M YOURS	Rod Stewart (Riva)
7	13	THE SIMON & GARFUNKEL COLLECTION	Simon & Garfunkel (CBS)
-	14	HITS HITS HITS	Various Artists (Ronco)
21	15	CHAS AND DAVE'S CHRISTMAS JAMBOREE BAG	Chas & Dave (Warwick)
23	16	DURAN DURAN	Duran Duran (EMI)
9	17	BEGIN THE BEGUINE	Julio Iglesias (CBS)
-	18	HOOKED ON CLASSICS	Louis Clark & the Royal Philharmonic Orchestra (K-Tel)
15	19	ALL THE GREAT HITS	Diana Ross (Motown)
24	20	LOVE SONGS	Cliff Richard (EMI)
19	21	CHANGESTWOBOWIE	David Bowie (RCA)
20	22	HANSIMANIA	James Last (Polydor)
14	23	FOR THOSE ABOUT TO ROCK	AC/DC (Atlantic)
-	24	NON-STOP EROTIC CABARET	Soft Cell (Some Bizzare)
18	25	IF I SHOULD LOVE AGAIN	Barry Manilow (Arista)
-	26	MADNESS 7	Madness (Stiff)
26	27	HAWAIIAN PARADISE/CHRISTMAS	Woot Steenhuis (Warwick)
22	28	RAISE!	Earth Wind & Fire (CBS)
28	29	ISMISM	Godley & Creme (Polydor)
27	30	HEDGEHOG SANDWICH	Not The Nine O'Clock News (BBC)

16 January 1982

last	this	title	artist
1	1	DARE	Human League (Virgin)
2	2	QUEEN'S GREATEST HITS	Queen (EMI)
3	3	THE VISITORS	Abba (Epic)
8	4	PRINCE CHARMING	Adam & the Ants (CBS)
5	5	CHART HITS '81	Various Artists (K-Tel)
14	6	HITS HITS HITS	Various Artists (Ronco)
4	7	WIRED FOR SOUND	Cliff Richard (EMI)
7	8	PEARLS	Elkie Brooks (A&M)
9	9	GHOST IN THE MACHINE	Police (A&M)
11	10	ARCHITECTURE AND MORALITY	Orchestral Manoeuvres In The Dark (DinDisc)
13	11	THE SIMON & GARFUNKEL COLLECTION	Simon & Garfunkel (CBS)
24	12	NON-STOP EROTIC CABARET	Soft Cell (Some Bizzare)
10	13	SHAKY	Shakin' Stevens (Epic)
6	14	BEST OF BLONDIE	Blondie (Chrysalis)
-	15	TIN DRUM	Japan (Virgin)
-	16	ONCE UPON A TIME	Siouxsie & the Banshees (Polydor)
17	17	BEGIN THE BEGUINE	Julio Iglesias (CBS)
28	18	RAISE!	Earth Wind & Fire (CBS)
23	19	FOR THOSE ABOUT TO ROCK	AC/DC (Atlantic)
26	20	MADNESS 7	Madness (Stiff)
12	21	TONIGHT I'M YOURS	Rod Stewart (Riva)
20	22	LOVE SONGS	Cliff Richard (EMI)
-	23	CHRISTOPHER CROSS	Christopher Cross (Warner Bros.)
21	24	CHANGESTWOBOWIE	David Bowie (RCA)
25	25	IF I SHOULD LOVE AGAIN	Barry Manilow (Arista)
-	26	HAPPY BIRTHDAY	Altered Images (Epic)
-	27	THE GEORGE BENSON COLLECTION	George Benson (Warner Bros.)
-	28	BEST OF RAINBOW	Rainbow (Polydor)
19	29	ALL THE GREAT HITS	Diana Ross (Motown)
-	30	4	Foreigner (Atlantic)

23 January 1982

last	this	title	artist
1	1	DARE	Human League (Virgin)
2	2	QUEEN'S GREATEST HITS	Queen (EMI)
3	3	THE VISITORS	Abba (Epic)
6	4	HITS HITS HITS	Various Artists (Ronco)
4	5	PRINCE CHARMING	Adam & the Ants (CBS)
7	6	WIRED FOR SOUND	Cliff Richard (EMI)
8	7	PEARLS	Elkie Brooks (A&M)
9	8	GHOST IN THE MACHINE	Police (A&M)
-	9	LOVE SONGS	Barbra Streisand (CBS)
5	10	CHART HITS '81	Various Artists (K-Tel)
14	11	BEST OF BLONDIE	Blondie (Chrysalis)
10	12	ARCHITECTURE AND MORALITY	Orchestral Manoeuvres In The Dark (DinDisc)
22	13	LOVE SONGS	Cliff Richard (EMI)
13	14	SHAKY	Shakin' Stevens (Epic)
12	15	NON-STOP EROTIC CABARET	Soft Cell (Some Bizzare)
-	16	MODERN DANCE	Various Artists (K-Tel)
30	17	4	Foreigner (Atlantic)
-	18	DURAN DURAN	Duran Duran (EMI)
20	19	MADNESS 7	Madness (Stiff)
11	20	THE SIMON & GARFUNKEL COLLECTION	Simon & Garfunkel (CBS)
15	21	TIN DRUM	Japan (Virgin)
21	22	TONIGHT I'M YOURS	Rod Stewart (Riva)
23	23	CHRISTOPHER CROSS	Christopher Cross (Warner Bros.)
16	24	ONCE UPON A TIME	Siouxsie & the Ba (Polydor)
19	25	FOR THOSE ABOUT TO ROCK	AC/DC (Atlantic)
-	26	ANTHEM	Toyah (Safari)
-	27	SOMETHING SPECIAL	Kool & the Gang (De-Lite)
-	28	TRAVELOGUE	Human League (Virgin)
17	29	BEGIN THE BEGUINE	Julio Iglesias (CBS)
-	30	DEAD RINGER	Meatloaf (Epic)

Abba, as was becoming their habit, celebrated a change of year with a chart-topping album, *The Visitors*. It was the Swedish quartet's seventh Number 1 LP, but with a break-up looming, this would be the last set of original material from them. Human League's *Dare* was to be their biggest-selling album, and the UK's best seller for most of the first two months of 1982. And who could possibly have been buying Chas And Dave's Christmas set during the week after New Year?

30 January 1982

last week	this week	Title / Artist
1	1	DARE — Human League (Virgin)
3	2	THE VISITORS — Abba (Epic)
4	3	HITS HITS HITS — Various Artists (Ronco)
2	4	QUEEN'S GREATEST HITS — Queen (EMI)
9	5	LOVE SONGS — Barbra Streisand (CBS)
16	6	MODERN DANCE — Various Artists (K-Tel)
12	7	ARCHITECTURE AND MORALITY — Orchestral Manoeuvres In The Dark (DinDisc)
8	8	GHOST IN THE MACHINE — Police (A&M)
5	9	PRINCE CHARMING — Adam & the Ants (CBS)
7	10	PEARLS — Elkie Brooks (A&M)
27	11	SOMETHING SPECIAL — Kool & the Gang (De-Lite)
10	12	CHART HITS '81 — Various Artists (K-Tel)
13	13	LOVE SONGS — Cliff Richard (EMI)
30	14	DEAD RINGER — Meatloaf (Epic)
6	15	WIRED FOR SOUND — Cliff Richard (EMI)
28	16	TRAVELOGUE — Human League (Virgin)
14	17	SHAKY — Shakin' Stevens (Epic)
18	18	DURAN DURAN — Duran Duran (EMI)
22	19	TONIGHT I'M YOURS — Rod Stewart (Riva)
11	20	BEST OF BLONDIE — Blondie (Chrysalis)
19	21	MADNESS 7 — Madness (Stiff)
17	22	4 — Foreigner (Atlantic)
23	23	CHRISTOPHER CROSS — Christopher Cross (Warner Bros.)
20	24	THE SIMON & GARFUNKEL COLLECTION — Simon & Garfunkel (CBS)
29	25	BEGIN THE BEGUINE — Julio Iglesias (CBS)
15	26	NON-STOP EROTIC CABARET — Soft Cell (Some Bizzare)
-	27	CHANGESTWOBOWIE — David Bowie (RCA)
-	28	SECRET COMBINATION — Randy Crawford (Warner Bros.)
25	29	FOR THOSE ABOUT TO ROCK — AC/DC (Atlantic)
21	30	TIN DRUM — Japan (Virgin)

6 February 1982

last week	this week	Title / Artist
5	1	LOVE SONGS — Barbra Streisand (CBS)
1	2	DARE — Human League (Virgin)
3	3	HITS HITS HITS — Various Artists (Ronco)
2	4	THE VISITORS — Abba (Epic)
10	5	PEARLS — Elkie Brooks (A&M)
6	6	MODERN DANCE — Various Artists (K-Tel)
7	7	ARCHITECTURE AND MORALITY — Orchestral Manoeuvres In The Dark (DinDisc)
11	8	SOMETHING SPECIAL — Kool & the Gang (De-Lite)
22	9	4 — Foreigner (Atlantic)
4	10	QUEEN'S GREATEST HITS — Queen (EMI)
-	11	THE FRIENDS OF MR CAIRO — Jon & Vangelis (Polydor)
14	12	DEAD RINGER — Meatloaf (Epic)
8	13	GHOST IN THE MACHINE — Police (A&M)
9	14	PRINCE CHARMING — Adam & the Ants (CBS)
23	15	CHRISTOPHER CROSS — Christopher Cross (Warner Bros.)
-	16	IF I SHOULD LOVE AGAIN — Barry Manilow (Arista)
26	17	NON-STOP EROTIC CABARET — Soft Cell (Some Bizzare)
-	18	LA FOLIE — Stranglers (Liberty)
13	19	LOVE SONGS — Cliff Richard (EMI)
30	20	TIN DRUM — Japan (Virgin)
24	21	THE SIMON & GARFUNKEL COLLECTION — Simon & Garfunkel (CBS)
19	22	TONIGHT I'M YOURS — Rod Stewart (Riva)
17	23	SHAKY — Shakin' Stevens (Epic)
-	24	THE MAN MACHINE — Kraftwerk (Capitol)
16	25	TRAVELOGUE — Human League (Virgin)
12	26	CHART HITS '81 — Various Artists (K-Tel)
-	27	PERHAPS LOVE — Placido Domingo & John Denver (CBS)
20	28	BEST OF BLONDIE — Blondie (Chrysalis)
-	29	SEXTET — A Certain Ratio (Factory)
15	30	WIRED FOR SOUND — Cliff Richard (EMI)

13 February 1982

last week	this week	Title / Artist
2	1	DARE — Human League (Virgin)
1	2	LOVE SONGS — Barbra Streisand (CBS)
7	3	ARCHITECTURE AND MORALITY — Orchestral Manoeuvres In The Dark (DinDisc)
5	4	PEARLS — Elkie Brooks (A&M)
12	5	DEAD RINGER — Meatloaf (Epic)
9	6	4 — Foreigner (Atlantic)
8	7	SOMETHING SPECIAL — Kool & the Gang (De-Lite)
15	8	CHRISTOPHER CROSS — Christopher Cross (Warner Bros.)
10	9	QUEEN'S GREATEST HITS — Queen (EMI)
17	10	NON-STOP EROTIC CABARET — Soft Cell (Some Bizzare)
11	11	THE FRIENDS OF MR CAIRO — Jon & Vangelis (Polydor)
6	12	MODERN DANCE — Various Artists (K-Tel)
24	13	THE MAN MACHINE — Kraftwerk (Capitol)
4	14	THE VISITORS — Abba (Epic)
3	15	HITS HITS HITS — Various Artists (Ronco)
-	16	THE GEORGE BENSON COLLECTION — George Benson (Warner Bros.)
-	17	BAT OUT OF HELL — Meatloaf (Epic)
-	18	ALL FOR A SONG — Barbara Dickson (Epic)
18	19	LA FOLIE — Stranglers (Liberty)
16	20	IF I SHOULD LOVE AGAIN — Barry Manilow (Arista)
20	21	TIN DRUM — Japan (Virgin)
-	22	TRANS-EUROPE EXPRESS — Kraftwerk ((Capitol)
19	23	LOVE SONGS — Cliff Richard (EMI)
27	24	PERHAPS LOVE — Placido Domingo & John Denver (CBS)
-	25	PRIVATE EYES — Daryl Hall & John Oates (RCA)
14	26	PRINCE CHARMING — Adam & the Ants (CBS)
23	27	SHAKY — Shakin' Stevens (Epic)
21	28	THE SIMON & GARFUNKEL COLLECTION — Simon & Garfunkel (CBS)
-	29	PENTHOUSE AND PAVEMENT — Heaven 17 (Virgin)
-	30	SPEAK AND SPELL — Depeche Mode (Mute)

20 February 1982

last week	this week	Title / Artist
1	1	DARE — Human League (Virgin)
2	2	LOVE SONGS — Barbra Streisand (CBS)
3	3	ARCHITECTURE AND MORALITY — Orchestral Manoeuvres In The Dark (DinDisc)
4	4	PEARLS — Elkie Brooks (A&M)
10	5	NON-STOP EROTIC CABARET — Soft Cell (Some Bizzare)
13	6	THE MAN MACHINE — Kraftwerk (Capitol)
11	7	THE FRIENDS OF MR CAIRO — Jon & Vangelis (Polydor)
6	8	4 — Foreigner (Atlantic)
5	9	DEAD RINGER — Meatloaf (Epic)
25	10	PRIVATE EYES — Daryl Hall & John Oates (RCA)
14	11	THE VISITORS — Abba (Epic)
12	12	MODERN DANCE — Various Artists (K-Tel)
20	13	IF I SHOULD LOVE AGAIN — Barry Manilow (Arista)
19	14	LA FOLIE — Stranglers (Liberty)
17	15	BAT OUT OF HELL — Meatloaf (Epic)
9	16	QUEEN'S GREATEST HITS — Queen (EMI)
8	17	CHRISTOPHER CROSS — Christopher Cross (Warner Bros.)
18	18	ALL FOR A SONG — Barbara Dickson (Epic)
21	19	TIN DRUM — Japan (Virgin)
27	20	SHAKY — Shakin' Stevens (Epic)
-	21	THE SOUND OF YOUR CRY — Elvis Presley (RCA)
-	22	GHOST IN THE MACHINE — Police (A&M)
-	23	ENGLISH SETTLEMENT — XTC (Virgin)
7	24	SOMETHING SPECIAL — Kool & the Gang (De-Lite)
29	25	PENTHOUSE AND PAVEMENT — Heaven 17 (Virgin)
24	26	PERHAPS LOVE — Placido Domingo & John Denver (CBS)
-	27	PRESENT ARMS — UB40 (DEP International)
15	28	HITS HITS HITS — Various Artists (Ronco)
16	29	THE GEORGE BENSON COLLECTION — George Benson (Warner Bros.)
22	30	TRANS-EUROPE EXPRESS — Kraftwerk ((Capitol)

Although probably unaware of the coincidence, Barbra Streisand emulated Cliff Richard with a compilation of favourite ballads titled *Love Songs*, and sold even more prodigiously with it - this was to be one of 1982's top albums, and a chart fixture for many months. Foreigner, the Anglo-American band led by ex-Spooky Tooth guitarist Mick Jones, had found only minor UK success with their first three albums, but *4* was helped to Top 10 status by their hit single *Waiting For A Girl Like You*.

27 February 1982

last week	this week	Title	Artist
2	1	LOVE SONGS	Barbra Streisand (CBS)
3	2	ARCHITECTURE AND MORALITY	Orchestral Manoeuvres In The Dark (DinDisc)
1	3	DARE	Human League (Virgin)
4	4	PEARLS	Elkie Brooks (A&M)
6	5	THE MAN MACHINE	Kraftwerk (Capitol)
10	6	PRIVATE EYES	Daryl Hall & John Oates (RCA)
5	7	NON-STOP EROTIC CABARET	Soft Cell (Some Bizzare)
23	8	ENGLISH SETTLEMENT	XTC (Virgin)
7	9	THE FRIENDS OF MR CAIRO	Jon & Vangelis (Polydor)
14	10	LA FOLIE	Stranglers (Liberty)
8	11	4	Foreigner (Atlantic)
15	12	BAT OUT OF HELL	Meatloaf (Epic)
-	13	DREAMING	Various Artists (K-Tel)
9	14	DEAD RINGER	Meatloaf (Epic)
-	15	MECHANIX	UFO (Chrysalis)
17	16	CHRISTOPHER CROSS	Christopher Cross (Warner Bros.)
-	17	PHYSICAL	Olivia Newton-John (EMI)
-	18	TRAVELOGUE	Human League (Virgin)
-	19	COMPUTER WORLD	Kraftwerk (EMI)
12	20	MODERN DANCE	Various Artists (K-Tel)
18	21	ALL FOR A SONG	Barbara Dickson (Epic)
13	22	IF I SHOULD LOVE AGAIN	Barry Manilow (Arista)
29	23	THE GEORGE BENSON COLLECTION	George Benson (Warner Bros.)
10	24	THE VISITORS	Abba (Epic)
25	25	PENTHOUSE AND PAVEMENT	Heaven 17 (Virgin)
19	26	TIN DRUM	Japan (Virgin)
-	27	ACTION TRAX	Various Artists (K-Tel)
24	28	SOMETHING SPECIAL	Kool & the Gang (De-Lite)
16	29	QUEEN'S GREATEST HITS	Queen (EMI)
26	30	PERHAPS LOVE	Placido Domingo & John Denver (CBS)

6 March 1982

last week	this week	Title	Artist
1	1	LOVE SONGS	Barbra Streisand (CBS)
3	2	DARE	Human League (Virgin)
4	3	PEARLS	Elkie Brooks (A&M)
13	4	DREAMING	Various Artists (K-Tel)
2	5	ARCHITECTURE AND MORALITY	Orchestral Manoeuvres In The Dark (DinDisc)
8	6	ENGLISH SETTLEMENT	XTC (Virgin)
7	7	NON-STOP EROTIC CABARET	Soft Cell (Some Bizzare)
6	8	PRIVATE EYES	Daryl Hall & John Oates (RCA)
9	9	THE FRIENDS OF MR CAIRO	Jon & Vangelis (Polydor)
21	10	ALL FOR A SONG	Barbara Dickson (Epic)
12	11	BAT OUT OF HELL	Meatloaf (Epic)
14	12	DEAD RINGER	Meatloaf (Epic)
5	13	THE MAN MACHINE	Kraftwerk (Capitol)
29	14	QUEEN'S GREATEST HITS	Queen (EMI)
17	15	PHYSICAL	Olivia Newton-John (EMI)
-	16	MESOPOTAMIA	B52s (Island)
18	17	TRAVELOGUE	Human League (Virgin)
-	18	PELICAN WEST	Haircut 100 (Arista)
11	19	4	Foreigner (Atlantic)
10	20	LA FOLIE	Stranglers (Liberty)
24	21	THE VISITORS	Abba (Epic)
16	22	CHRISTOPHER CROSS	Christopher Cross (Warner Bros.)
30	23	PERHAPS LOVE	Placido Domingo & John Denver (CBS)
-	24	FREEZE FRAME	J Geils Band (EMI America)
23	25	THE GEORGE BENSON COLLECTION	George Benson (Warner Bros.)
-	26	TONIGHT	Four Tops (Casablanca)
25	27	PENTHOUSE AND PAVEMENT	Heaven 17 (Virgin)
-	28	FOR THOSE ABOUT TO ROCK	AC/DC (Atlantic)
-	29	WORD OF MOUTH	Toni Basil (Radialchoice)
28	30	SOMETHING SPECIAL	Kool & the Gang (De-Lite)

13 March 1982

last week	this week	Title	Artist
1	1	LOVE SONGS	Barbra Streisand (CBS)
4	2	DREAMING	Various Artists (K-Tel)
18	3	PELICAN WEST	Haircut 100 (Arista)
-	4	ACTION TRAX	Various Artists (K-Tel)
7	5	NON-STOP EROTIC CABARET	Soft Cell (Some Bizzare)
3	6	PEARLS	Elkie Brooks (A&M)
5	7	ARCHITECTURE AND MORALITY	Orchestral Manoeuvres In The Dark (DinDisc)
10	8	ALL FOR A SONG	Barbara Dickson (Epic)
2	9	DARE	Human League (Virgin)
6	10	ENGLISH SETTLEMENT	XTC (Virgin)
8	11	PRIVATE EYES	Daryl Hall & John Oates (RCA)
29	12	WORD OF MOUTH	Toni Basil (Radialchoice)
9	13	THE FRIENDS OF MR CAIRO	Jon & Vangelis (Polydor)
-	14	CHASE THE DRAGON	Magnum (Jet)
-	15	TWENTY WITH A BULLET	Various Artists (EMI)
12	16	DEAD RINGER	Meatloaf (Epic)
16	17	MESOPOTAMIA	B52s (Island)
11	18	BAT OUT OF HELL	Meatloaf (Epic)
20	19	LA FOLIE	Stranglers (Liberty)
24	20	FREEZE FRAME	J Geils Band (EMI America)
-	21	YOU CAN'T HIDE YOUR LOVE FOREVER	Orange Juice (Polydor)
13	22	THE MAN MACHINE	Kraftwerk (Capitol)
21	23	THE VISITORS	Abba (Epic)
19	24	4	Foreigner (Atlantic)
-	25	SEE JUNGLE! SEE JUNGLE! GO JOIN YOUR GANG YEAH CITY ALL OVER! GO APE CRAZY	Bow Wow Wow (RCA)
-	26	WESTWORLD	Theatre Of Hate (Burning Rome)
-	27	ANTHEM	Toyah (Safari)
25	28	THE GEORGE BENSON COLLECTION	George Benson (Warner Bros.)
-	29	SPEAK AND SPELL	Depeche Mode (Mute)
15	30	PHYSICAL	Olivia Newton-John (EMI)

20 March 1982

last week	this week	Title	Artist
3	1	PELICAN WEST	Haircut 100 (Arista)
1	2	LOVE SONGS	Barbra Streisand (CBS)
4	3	ACTION TRAX	Various Artists (K-Tel)
9	4	DARE	Human League (Virgin)
5	5	NON-STOP EROTIC CABARET	Soft Cell (Some Bizzare)
8	6	ALL FOR A SONG	Barbara Dickson (Epic)
6	7	PEARLS	Elkie Brooks (A&M)
-	8	THE GIFT	Jam (Polydor)
7	9	ARCHITECTURE AND MORALITY	Orchestral Manoeuvres In The Dark (DinDisc)
2	10	DREAMING	Various Artists (K-Tel)
11	11	PRIVATE EYES	Daryl Hall & John Oates (RCA)
10	12	ENGLISH SETTLEMENT	XTC (Virgin)
20	13	FREEZE FRAME	J Geils Band (EMI America)
-	14	ONE NIGHT AT BUDOKAN	Michael Schenker Group (Chrysalis)
26	15	WESTWORLD	Theatre Of Hate (Burning Rome)
18	16	BAT OUT OF HELL	Meatloaf (Epic)
-	17	DIAMOND	Spandau Ballet (Reformation)
16	18	DEAD RINGER	Meatloaf (Epic)
24	19	4	Foreigner (Atlantic)
12	20	WORD OF MOUTH	Toni Basil (Radialchoice)
15	21	TWENTY WITH A BULLET	Various Artists (EMI)
14	22	CHASE THE DRAGON	Magnum (Jet)
19	23	LA FOLIE	Stranglers (Liberty)
13	24	THE FRIENDS OF MR CAIRO	Jon & Vangelis (Polydor)
28	25	THE GEORGE BENSON COLLECTION	George Benson (Warner Bros.)
23	26	THE VISITORS	Abba (Epic)
25	27	SEE JUNGLE! SEE JUNGLE! GO JOIN YOUR GANG YEAH CITY ALL OVER! GO APE CRAZY	Bow Wow Wow (RCA)
-	28	BEGIN THE BEGUINE	Julio Iglesias (CBS)
-	29	DR HECKLE AND MR JIVE	Pigbag (Y)
17	30	MESOPOTAMIA	B52s (Island)

Haircut 100 topped the chart with their debut album *Pelican West* just as their second (and biggest) hit single *Love Plus One* was peaking at Number 3, while another Top 10 album boosted by a current single was Hall & Oates' *Private Eyes* - none of their previous LPs had made the UK Top 20, but this one had the Top-Tenner *I Can't Go For That* batting for it. Malcolm McLaren protegees Bow Wow Wow, meanwhile, had probably the most stupidly-titled chart album ever.

27 March 1982

last week	this week		
8	1	THE GIFT	Jam (Polydor)
1	2	PELICAN WEST	Haircut 100 (Arista)
2	3	LOVE SONGS	Barbra Streisand (CBS)
3	4	ACTION TRAX	Various Artists (K-Tel)
9	5	ARCHITECTURE AND MORALITY	Orchestral Manoeuvres In T Dark (DinDisc)
-	6	FUN BOY THREE	Fun Boy Three (Chrysalis)
7	7	PEARLS	Elkie Brooks (A&M)
5	8	NON-STOP EROTIC CABARET	Soft Cell (Some Bizzare)
4	9	DARE	Human League (Virgin)
6	10	ALL FOR A SONG	Barbara Dickson (Epic)
14	11	ONE NIGHT AT BUDOKAN	Michael Schenker Group (Chrysalis)
17	12	DIAMOND	Spandau Ballet (Reformation)
21	13	TWENTY WITH A BULLET	Various Artists (EMI)
10	14	DREAMING	Various Artists (K-Tel)
28	15	BEGIN THE BEGUINE	Julio Iglesias (CBS)
-	16	SPEAK AND SPELL	Depeche Mode (Mute)
16	17	BAT OUT OF HELL	Meatloaf (Epic)
15	18	WESTWORLD	Theatre Of Hate (Burning Rome)
13	19	FREEZE FRAME	J Geils Band (EMI America)
12	20	ENGLISH SETTLEMENT	XTC (Virgin)
11	21	PRIVATE EYES	Daryl Hall & John Oates (RCA)
20	22	WORD OF MOUTH	Toni Basil (Radialchoice)
29	23	DR HECKLE AND MR JIVE	Pigbag (Y)
-	24	PHYSICAL	Olivia Newton-John (EMI)
27	25	SEE JUNGLE! SEE JUNGLE! GO JOIN YOUR GANG YEAH CITY ALL OVER! GO APE CRAZY	Bow Wow Wow (RCA)
-	26	QUEEN'S GREATEST HITS	Queen (EMI)
26	27	THE VISITORS	Abba (Epic)
30	28	MESOPOTAMIA	B52s (Island)
-	29	FILTH HOUNDS OF HADES	Tank (Kamaflage)
23	30	LA FOLIE	Stranglers (Liberty)

3 April 1982

1	1	THE GIFT	Jam (Polydor)
3	2	LOVE SONGS	Barbra Streisand (CBS)
2	3	PELICAN WEST	Haircut 100 (Arista)
15	4	BEGIN THE BEGUINE	Julio Iglesias (CBS)
10	5	ALL FOR A SONG	Barbara Dickson (Epic)
7	6	PEARLS	Elkie Brooks (A&M)
4	7	ACTION TRAX	Various Artists (K-Tel)
9	8	DARE	Human League (Virgin)
6	9	FUN BOY THREE	Fun Boy Three (Chrysalis)
-	10	FIVE MILES OUT	Mike Oldfield (Virgin)
14	11	DREAMING	Various Artists (K-Tel)
-	12	TIN DRUM	Japan (Virgin)
-	13	THE BEST OF THE FOUR TOPS	Four Tops (K-Tel)
11	14	ONE NIGHT AT BUDOKAN	Michael Schenker Group (Chrysalis)
-	15	KEEP FIT AND DANCE	Peter Powell (K-Tel)
8	16	NON-STOP EROTIC CABARET	Soft Cell (Some Bizzare)
-	17	THE CONCERT IN CENTRAL PARK	Simon & Garfunkel (CBS)
13	18	TWENTY WITH A BULLET	Various Artists (EMI)
12	19	DIAMOND	Spandau Ballet (Reformation)
5	20	ARCHITECTURE AND MORALITY	Orchestral Manoeuvres In The Dark (DinDisc)
17	21	BAT OUT OF HELL	Meatloaf (Epic)
-	22	PORTRAIT	Nolans (Epic)
22	23	WORD OF MOUTH	Toni Basil (Radialchoice)
20	24	ENGLISH SETTLEMENT	XTC (Virgin)
19	25	FREEZE FRAME	J Geils Band (EMI America)
-	26	JAMES BOND"S GREATEST HITS	Various Artists (Liberty)
-	27	THE SECRET POLICEMAN'S OTHER BALL	Various Artists (Springtime)
23	28	DR HECKLE AND MR JIVE	Pigbag (Y)
30	29	LA FOLIE	Stranglers (Liberty)
18	30	WESTWORLD	Theatre Of Hate (Burning Rome)

10 April 1982

3	1	PELICAN WEST	Haircut 100 (Arista)
2	2	LOVE SONGS	Barbra Streisand (CBS)
1	3	THE GIFT	Jam (Polydor)
-	4	THE ANVIL	Visage (Polydor)
4	5	BEGIN THE BEGUINE	Julio Iglesias (CBS)
12	6	TIN DRUM	Japan (Virgin)
6	7	PEARLS	Elkie Brooks (A&M)
5	8	ALL FOR A SONG	Barbara Dickson (Epic)
7	9	ACTION TRAX	Various Artists (K-Tel)
19	10	DIAMOND	Spandau Ballet (Reformation)
26	11	JAMES BOND"S GREATEST HITS	Various Artists (Liberty)
22	12	PORTRAIT	Nolans (Epic)
9	13	FUN BOY THREE	Fun Boy Three (Chrysalis)
10	14	FIVE MILES OUT	Mike Oldfield (Virgin)
21	15	BAT OUT OF HELL	Meatloaf (Epic)
8	16	DARE	Human League (Virgin)
-	17	SKY 4 – FORTHCOMING	Sky (Ariola)
14	18	ONE NIGHT AT BUDOKAN	Michael Schenker Group (Chrysalis)
-	19	BODY TALK	Imagination (R&B)
20	20	ARCHITECTURE AND MORALITY	Orchestral Manoeuvres In The Dark (DinDisc)
28	21	DR HECKLE AND MR JIVE	Pigbag (Y)
23	22	WORD OF MOUTH	Toni Basil (Radialchoice)
11	23	DREAMING	Various Artists (K-Tel)
-	24	MAYBE IT'S LIVE	Robert Palmer (Island)
15	25	KEEP FIT AND DANCE	Peter Powell (K-Tel)
-	26	CHARIOTS OF FIRE	Vangelis (Polydor)
-	27	CHRISTOPHER CROSS	Christopher Cross (Warner Bros.)
17	28	THE CONCERT IN CENTRAL PARK	Simon & Garfunkel (CBS)
13	29	THE BEST OF THE FOUR TOPS	Four Tops (K-Tel)
27	30	THE SECRET POLICEMAN'S OTHER BALL	Various Artists (Springtime)

17 April 1982

-	1	THE NUMBER OF THE BEAST	Iron Maiden (EMI)
2	2	LOVE SONGS	Barbra Streisand (CBS)
8	3	ALL FOR A SONG	Barbara Dickson (Epic)
1	4	PELICAN WEST	Haircut 100 (Arista)
6	5	TIN DRUM	Japan (Virgin)
5	6	BEGIN THE BEGUINE	Julio Iglesias (CBS)
4	7	THE ANVIL	Visage (Polydor)
3	8	THE GIFT	Jam (Polydor)
17	9	SKY 4 – FORTHCOMING	Sky (Ariola)
-	10	BLACKOUT	Scorpions (Harvest)
-	11	THE NAME OF THIS BAND IS TALKING HEADS	Talking Heads (Sire)
7	12	PEARLS	Elkie Brooks (A&M)
19	13	BODY TALK	Imagination (R&B)
14	14	FIVE MILES OUT	Mike Oldfield (Virgin)
9	15	ACTION TRAX	Various Artists (K-Tel)
-	16	FREEZE FRAME	J Geils Band (EMI America)
-	17	IRON FIST	Motorhead (Bronze)
11	18	JAMES BOND"S GREATEST HITS	Various Artists (Liberty)
26	19	CHARIOTS OF FIRE	Vangelis (Polydor)
-	20	ASIA	Asia (Geffen)
10	21	DIAMOND	Spandau Ballet (Reformation)
16	22	DARE	Human League (Virgin)
-	23	100PERCENT COTTON	Jets (EMI)
25	24	KEEP FIT AND DANCE	Peter Powell (K-Tel)
12	25	PORTRAIT	Nolans (Epic)
18	26	ONE NIGHT AT BUDOKAN	Michael Schenker Group (Chrysalis)
28	27	THE CONCERT IN CENTRAL PARK	Simon & Garfunkel (CBS)
-	28	PENTHOUSE AND PAVEMENT	Heaven 17 (Virgin)
15	29	BAT OUT OF HELL	Meatloaf (Epic)
-	30	20 WITH A BULLET	Various Artists (EMI)

Though albums by the Jam, Haircut 100 and Iron Maiden came and went at Number 1 around it, Barbra Streisand's *Love Songs* was overall, the best-selling album through March and April - a demonstration of its continued selling power two months after release. Iron Maiden's *Number Of The Beast* was the band's third album but first chart-topper, and it led a new heavy metal assault onto the chart, which also included German band the Scorpions at No.10, and the UK's Motorhead at 17.

24 April 1982

last week	this week	Title / Artist (Label)
2	1	LOVE SONGS — Barbra Streisand (CBS)
4	2	PELICAN WEST — Haircut 100 (Arista)
17	3	IRON FIST — Motorhead (Bronze)
1	4	THE NUMBER OF THE BEAST — Iron Maiden (EMI)
3	5	ALL FOR A SONG — Barbara Dickson (Epic)
18	6	JAMES BOND"S GREATEST HITS — Various Artists (Liberty)
8	7	THE GIFT — Jam (Polydor)
25	8	PORTRAIT — Nolans (Epic)
6	9	BEGIN THE BEGUINE — Julio Iglesias (CBS)
5	10	TIN DRUM — Japan (Virgin)
9	11	SKY 4 – FORTHCOMING — Sky (Ariola)
14	12	FIVE MILES OUT — Mike Oldfield (Virgin)
7	13	THE ANVIL — Visage (Polydor)
12	14	PEARLS — Elkie Brooks (A&M)
19	15	CHARIOTS OF FIRE — Vangelis (Polydor)
-	16	1982 — Status Quo (Vertigo)
29	17	BAT OUT OF HELL — Meatloaf (Epic)
-	18	SEVEN TEARS — Goombay Dance Band (Epic)
15	19	ACTION TRAX — Various Artists (K-Tel)
20	20	ASIA — Asia (Geffen)
13	21	BODY TALK — Imagination (R&B)
22	22	DARE — Human League (Virgin)
-	23	BRITISH ELECRIC FOUNDATION PRESENTS MUSIC OF QUALITY AND DISTINCTION, VOL.1 — British Electric Foundation (Virgin)
-	24	JUMP UP — Elton John (Rocket)
10	25	BLACKOUT — Scorpions (Harvest)
-	26	FUN BOY THREE — Fun Boy Three (Chrysalis)
11	27	THE NAME OF THIS BAND IS TALKING HEADS — Talking Heads (Sire)
-	28	HEDGEHOG SANDWICH — Not The Nine O'Clock News (BBC)
24	29	KEEP FIT AND DANCE — Peter Powell (K-Tel)
-	30	DR HECKLE AND MR JIVE — Pigbag (Y)

1 May 1982

last week	this week	Title / Artist (Label)
2	1	PELICAN WEST — Haircut 100 (Arista)
4	2	THE NUMBER OF THE BEAST — Iron Maiden (EMI)
16	3	1982 — Status Quo (Vertigo)
1	4	LOVE SONGS — Barbra Streisand (CBS)
-	5	STRAIGHT BETWEEN THE EYES — Rainbow (Polydor)
15	6	CHARIOTS OF FIRE — Vangelis (Polydor)
5	7	ALL FOR A SONG — Barbara Dickson (Epic)
8	8	PORTRAIT — Nolans (Epic)
11	9	SKY 4 – FORTHCOMING — Sky (Ariola)
3	10	IRON FIST — Motorhead (Bronze)
6	11	JAMES BOND"S GREATEST HITS — Various Artists (Liberty)
24	12	JUMP UP — Elton John (Rocket)
20	13	ASIA — Asia (Geffen)
7	14	THE GIFT — Jam (Polydor)
10	15	TIN DRUM — Japan (Virgin)
-	16	BARRY LIVE IN BRITAIN — Barry Manilow (Arista)
17	17	BAT OUT OF HELL — Meatloaf (Epic)
-	18	THE SLIDE AREA — Ry Cooder (Warner Bros.)
23	19	BRITISH ELECRIC FOUNDATION PRESENTS MUSIC OF QUALITY AND DISTINCTION, VOL.1 — British Electric Foundation (Virgin)
-	20	SHOOT THE MOON — Judy Tzuke (Chrysalis)
13	21	THE ANVIL — Visage (Polydor)
-	22	COMPLETE MADNESS — Madness (Stiff)
14	23	PEARLS — Elkie Brooks (A&M)
18	24	SEVEN TEARS — Goombay Dance Band (Epic)
-	25	NON-STOP EROTIC CABARET — Soft Cell (Some Bizzare)
21	26	BODY TALK — Imagination (R&B)
26	27	FUN BOY THREE — Fun Boy Three (Chrysalis)
9	28	BEGIN THE BEGUINE — Julio Iglesias (CBS)
12	29	FIVE MILES OUT — Mike Oldfield (Virgin)
30	30	DR HECKLE AND MR JIVE — Pigbag (Y)

8 May 1982

last week	this week	Title / Artist (Label)
16	1	BARRY LIVE IN BRITAIN — Barry Manilow (Arista)
22	2	COMPLETE MADNESS — Madness (Stiff)
3	3	1982 — Status Quo (Vertigo)
1	4	PELICAN WEST — Haircut 100 (Arista)
2	5	THE NUMBER OF THE BEAST — Iron Maiden (EMI)
4	6	LOVE SONGS — Barbra Streisand (CBS)
-	7	DISCO UK AND DISCO USA — Various Artists (Ronco)
6	8	CHARIOTS OF FIRE — Vangelis (Polydor)
12	9	JUMP UP — Elton John (Rocket)
5	10	STRAIGHT BETWEEN THE EYES — Rainbow (Polydor)
-	11	TUG OF WAR — Paul McCartney (Parlophone)
9	12	SKY 4 – FORTHCOMING — Sky (Ariola)
13	13	ASIA — Asia (Geffen)
15	14	TIN DRUM — Japan (Virgin)
8	15	PORTRAIT — Nolans (Epic)
-	16	MUSTN'T GRUMBLE — Chas & Dave (Rockney)
23	17	PEARLS — Elkie Brooks (A&M)
17	18	BAT OUT OF HELL — Meatloaf (Epic)
-	19	SHAPE UP AND DANCE VOL 2 — Angela Rippon (Lifestyle)
11	20	JAMES BOND"S GREATEST HITS — Various Artists (Liberty)
7	21	ALL FOR A SONG — Barbara Dickson (Epic)
21	22	THE ANVIL — Visage (Polydor)
-	23	DIVER DOWN — Van Halen (Warner Bros.)
30	24	DR HECKLE AND MR JIVE — Pigbag (Y)
10	25	IRON FIST — Motorhead (Bronze)
-	26	TIME PIECES – THE BEST OF ERIC CLAPTON — Eric Clapton (RSO)
29	27	FIVE MILES OUT — Mike Oldfield (Virgin)
19	28	BRITISH ELECRIC FOUNDATION PRESENTS MUSIC OF QUALITY AND DISTINCTION, VOL.1 — British Electric Foundation (Virgin)
-	29	THE BROADSWORD AND THE BEAST — Jethro Tull (Chrysalis)
14	30	THE GIFT — Jam (Polydor)

15 May 1982

last week	this week	Title / Artist (Label)
11	1	TUG OF WAR — Paul McCartney (Parlophone)
1	2	BARRY LIVE IN BRITAIN — Barry Manilow (Arista)
2	3	COMPLETE MADNESS — Madness (Stiff)
3	4	1982 — Status Quo (Vertigo)
4	5	PELICAN WEST — Haircut 100 (Arista)
7	6	DISCO UK AND DISCO USA — Various Artists (Ronco)
8	7	CHARIOTS OF FIRE — Vangelis (Polydor)
6	8	LOVE SONGS — Barbra Streisand (CBS)
-	9	ARE YOU READY? — Bucks Fizz (RCA)
5	10	THE NUMBER OF THE BEAST — Iron Maiden (EMI)
-	11	DIAMOND — Spandau Ballet (Reformation)
19	12	SHAPE UP AND DANCE VOL 2 — Angela Rippon (Lifestyle)
18	13	BAT OUT OF HELL — Meatloaf (Epic)
9	14	JUMP UP — Elton John (Rocket)
10	15	STRAIGHT BETWEEN THE EYES — Rainbow (Polydor)
-	16	REVELATIONS — Killing Joke (Malicious Damage)
12	17	SKY 4 – FORTHCOMING — Sky (Ariola)
21	18	ALL FOR A SONG — Barbara Dickson (Epic)
14	19	TIN DRUM — Japan (Virgin)
17	20	PEARLS — Elkie Brooks (A&M)
-	21	FUN BOY THREE — Fun Boy Three (Chrysalis)
30	22	THE GIFT — Jam (Polydor)
13	23	ASIA — Asia (Geffen)
27	24	FIVE MILES OUT — Mike Oldfield (Virgin)
20	25	JAMES BOND"S GREATEST HITS — Various Artists (Liberty)
24	26	DR HECKLE AND MR JIVE — Pigbag (Y)
25	27	IRON FIST — Motorhead (Bronze)
15	28	PORTRAIT — Nolans (Epic)
16	29	MUSTN'T GRUMBLE — Chas & Dave (Rockney)
26	30	TIME PIECES – THE BEST OF ERIC CLAPTON — Eric Clapton (RSO)

James Bond's Greatest Hits was not a gimmicky attempt to present Roger Moore or Sean Connery singing, but was a TV-advertised compilation which gathered up the themes and some of the incidental musical pieces from all the Bond films (except *Casino Royale*) to date, most of them co-written, played or accompanied by John Barry. Barry Manilow's *Live In Britain* was custom-released for the UK market, and despite topping the chart here, it was not released in his native USA at all.

22 May 1982

Last	This	Album / Artist (Label)
3	1	COMPLETE MADNESS — Madness (Stiff)
1	2	TUG OF WAR — Paul McCartney (Parlophone)
2	3	BARRY LIVE IN BRITAIN — Barry Manilow (Arista)
5	4	PELICAN WEST — Haircut 100 (Arista)
-	5	HOT SPACE — Queen (EMI)
-	6	NIGHT BIRDS — Shakatak (Polydor)
-	7	CHARTBUSTERS '82 — Various Artists (Ronco)
-	8	THE CONCERTS IN CHINA — Jean-Michel Jarre (Polydor)
9	9	ARE YOU READY? — Bucks Fizz (RCA)
7	10	CHARIOTS OF FIRE — Vangelis (Polydor)
6	11	DISCO UK AND DISCO USA — Various Artists (Ronco)
-	12	PINKY BLUE — Altered Images (Epic)
-	13	PORNOGRAPHY — Cure (Fiction)
-	14	SWEETS FROM A STRANGER — Squeeze (A&M)
10	15	THE NUMBER OF THE BEAST — Iron Maiden (EMI)
8	16	LOVE SONGS — Barbra Streisand (CBS)
4	17	1982 — Status Quo (Vertigo)
11	18	DIAMOND — Spandau Ballet (Reformation)
13	19	BAT OUT OF HELL — Meatloaf (Epic)
-	20	I LOVE ROCK 'N' ROLL — Joan Jett & the Blackhearts (Epic)
12	21	SHAPE UP AND DANCE VOL 2 — Angela Rippon (Lifestyle)
15	22	STRAIGHT BETWEEN THE EYES — Rainbow (Polydor)
-	23	COMBAT ROCK — Clash (CBS)
20	24	PEARLS — Elkie Brooks (A&M)
18	25	ALL FOR A SONG — Barbara Dickson (Epic)
-	26	STRAIGHT FROM THE HEART — Patrice Rushen (Elektra)
19	27	TIN DRUM — Japan (Virgin)
14	28	JUMP UP — Elton John (Rocket)
21	29	FUN BOY THREE — Fun Boy Three (Chrysalis)
29	30	MUSTN'T GRUMBLE — Chas & Dave (Rockney)

29 May 1982

Last	This	Album / Artist (Label)
1	1	COMPLETE MADNESS — Madness (Stiff)
2	2	TUG OF WAR — Paul McCartney (Parlophone)
7	3	CHARTBUSTERS '82 — Various Artists (Ronco)
3	4	BARRY LIVE IN BRITAIN — Barry Manilow (Arista)
-	5	RIO — Duran Duran (EMI)
23	6	COMBAT ROCK — Clash (CBS)
5	7	HOT SPACE — Queen (EMI)
4	8	PELICAN WEST — Haircut 100 (Arista)
6	9	NIGHT BIRDS — Shakatak (Polydor)
-	10	THE EAGLE HAS LANDED — Saxon (Carrere)
8	11	THE CONCERTS IN CHINA — Jean-Michel Jarre (Polydor)
16	12	LOVE SONGS — Barbra Streisand (CBS)
17	13	1982 — Status Quo (Vertigo)
15	14	THE NUMBER OF THE BEAST — Iron Maiden (EMI)
12	15	PINKY BLUE — Altered Images (Epic)
19	16	BAT OUT OF HELL — Meatloaf (Epic)
-	17	CHURCH OF HAWKWIND — Hawkwind (RCA)
11	18	DISCO UK AND DISCO USA — Various Artists (Ronco)
9	19	ARE YOU READY? — Bucks Fizz (RCA)
18	20	DIAMOND — Spandau Ballet (Reformation)
-	21	SULK — Associates (Associates)
24	22	PEARLS — Elkie Brooks (A&M)
10	23	CHARIOTS OF FIRE — Vangelis (Polydor)
-	24	STEVIE WONDER'S ORIGINAL MUSIQUARIUM 1 — Stevie Wonder (Motown)
26	25	STRAIGHT FROM THE HEART — Patrice Rushen (Elektra)
-	26	WE ARE ...THE LEAGUE — Anti-Nowhere League (WXYZ)
27	27	TIN DRUM — Japan (Virgin)
-	28	DARE — Human League (Virgin)
13	29	PORNOGRAPHY — Cure (Fiction)
28	30	JUMP UP — Elton John (Rocket)

5 June 1982

Last	This	Album / Artist (Label)
1	1	COMPLETE MADNESS — Madness (Stiff)
5	2	RIO — Duran Duran (EMI)
3	3	CHARTBUSTERS '82 — Various Artists (Ronco)
2	4	TUG OF WAR — Paul McCartney (Parlophone)
4	5	BARRY LIVE IN BRITAIN — Barry Manilow (Arista)
24	6	STEVIE WONDER'S ORIGINAL MUSIQUARIUM 1 — Stevie Wonder (Motown)
7	7	HOT SPACE — Queen (EMI)
10	8	THE EAGLE HAS LANDED — Saxon (Carrere)
14	9	THE NUMBER OF THE BEAST — Iron Maiden (EMI)
6	10	COMBAT ROCK — Clash (CBS)
9	11	NIGHT BIRDS — Shakatak (Polydor)
8	12	PELICAN WEST — Haircut 100 (Arista)
23	13	CHARIOTS OF FIRE — Vangelis (Polydor)
21	14	SULK — Associates (Associates)
-	15	SELECT — Kim Wilde (RAK)
19	16	ARE YOU READY? — Bucks Fizz (RCA)
13	17	1982 — Status Quo (Vertigo)
11	18	THE CONCERTS IN CHINA — Jean-Michel Jarre (Polydor)
25	19	STRAIGHT FROM THE HEART — Patrice Rushen (Elektra)
22	20	PEARLS — Elkie Brooks (A&M)
-	21	TROPICAL GANGSTERS — Kid Creole & the Coconuts (Ze)
-	22	THE HUNTER — Blondie (Chrysalis)
-	23	AVALON — Roxy Music (EG)
12	24	LOVE SONGS — Barbra Streisand (CBS)
15	25	PINKY BLUE — Altered Images (Epic)
16	26	BAT OUT OF HELL — Meatloaf (Epic)
20	27	DIAMOND — Spandau Ballet (Reformation)
18	28	DISCO UK AND DISCO USA — Various Artists (Ronco)
28	29	DARE — Human League (Virgin)
26	30	WE ARE ...THE LEAGUE — Anti-Nowhere League (WXYZ)

12 June 1982

Last	This	Album / Artist (Label)
1	1	COMPLETE MADNESS — Madness (Stiff)
7	2	HOT SPACE — Queen (EMI)
2	3	RIO — Duran Duran (EMI)
23	4	AVALON — Roxy Music (EG)
4	5	TUG OF WAR — Paul McCartney (Parlophone)
5	6	BARRY LIVE IN BRITAIN — Barry Manilow (Arista)
3	7	CHARTBUSTERS '82 — Various Artists (Ronco)
11	8	NIGHT BIRDS — Shakatak (Polydor)
6	9	STEVIE WONDER'S ORIGINAL MUSIQUARIUM 1 — Stevie Wonder (Motown)
9	10	THE NUMBER OF THE BEAST — Iron Maiden (EMI)
22	11	THE HUNTER — Blondie (Chrysalis)
8	12	THE EAGLE HAS LANDED — Saxon (Carrere)
12	13	PELICAN WEST — Haircut 100 (Arista)
19	14	STRAIGHT FROM THE HEART — Patrice Rushen (Elektra)
21	15	TROPICAL GANGSTERS — Kid Creole & the Coconuts (Ze)
25	16	PINKY BLUE — Altered Images (Epic)
13	17	CHARIOTS OF FIRE — Vangelis (Polydor)
18	18	THE CONCERTS IN CHINA — Jean-Michel Jarre (Polydor)
14	19	SULK — Associates (Associates)
26	20	BAT OUT OF HELL — Meatloaf (Epic)
10	21	COMBAT ROCK — Clash (CBS)
24	22	LOVE SONGS — Barbra Streisand (CBS)
-	23	THE GIFT — Jam (Polydor)
-	24	STILL LIFE (AMERICAN CONCERTS 1981) — Rolling Stones (Rolling Stones)
-	25	PhD — PhD (WEA)
30	26	WE ARE ...THE LEAGUE — Anti-Nowhere League (WXYZ)
-	27	NON-STOP EROTIC CABARET — Soft Cell (Some Bizzare)
-	28	ANIMATION — Jon Anderson (Polydor)
15	29	SELECT — Kim Wilde (RAK)
20	30	PEARLS — Elkie Brooks (A&M)

May 22 had an album chart particularly notable for its turnover rate - exactly a third of the Top 30 were new entries, four of them debuting in the Top 10. Oddly, though, the sales of virtually every one of those newcomers dropped away in their second week, the notable exception being the Clash's *Combat Rock*, which started chart life quite modestly before snatching two weeks of Top 10 action. Madness' four-week chart-topper *Complete Madness* was a compilation of their hit singles to date.

June – July 1982

Appearing a full two years after their previous album *Flesh And Blood*, Roxy Music's *Avalon* indicated no loss of commercial appeal for Bryan Ferry and Co, emulating its predecessor's Number 1 status, and holding the top slot for four straight weeks - consigning the Rolling Stones, in the process, to yet another Number 2 album with their live set *Still Life*. The Genesis set *Three Sides Live* was exactly that - a double set consisting of one double-sided LP and one single-sided disc!

224

last week	this week	17 July 1982	
2	1	THE LEXICON OF LOVE	ABC (Neutron)
1	2	AVALON	Roxy Music (EG)
-	3	FAME	Soundtrack (RSO)
14	4	ABRACADABRA	Steve Miller Band (Mercury)
5	5	TROPICAL GANGSTERS	Kid Creole & the Coconuts (Ze)
3	6	COMPLETE MADNESS	Madness (Stiff)
4	6	STILL LIFE (AMERICAN CONCERTS 1981)	Rolling Stones (Rolling Stones)
7	8	RIO	Duran Duran (EMI)
15	9	TURBO TRAX	Various Artists (K-Tel)
-	10	PICTURES AT ELEVEN	Robert Plant (Swansong)
6	11	NON-STOP ECSTATIC DANCING	Soft Cell (Some Bizzare)
-	12	MIRAGE	Fleetwood Mac (Warner Bros.)
-	13	IMPERIAL BEDROOM	Elvis Costello & the Attraction (F-Beat)
11	14	THE CHANGELING	Toyah (Safari)
-	15	LOVE AND DANCE	League Unlimited Orchestra (Virgin)
9	16	THREE SIDES LIVE	Genesis (Charisma)
13	17	TUG OF WAR	Paul McCartney (Parlophone)
21	18	ASIA	Asia (Geffen)
22	19	OVERLOAD	Various Artists (Ronco)
10	20	HOT SPACE	Queen (EMI)
23	21	CHARIOTS OF FIRE	Vangelis (Polydor)
8	22	NIGHT BIRDS	Shakatak (Polydor)
12	23	FABRIQUE	Fashion (Arista)
20	24	PELICAN WEST	Haircut 100 (Arista)
-	25	FRIENDS	Shalamar (Solar)
-	26	ARE YOU READY?	Bucks Fizz (RCA)
18	27	WINDSONG	Randy Crawford (Warner Bros.)
-	28	CHILL OUT	Black Uhuru (Island)
-	29	BARRY LIVE IN BRITAIN	Barry Manilow (Arista)
-	30	1982	Status Quo (Vertigo)

		24 July 1982	
1	1	THE LEXICON OF LOVE	ABC (Neutron)
3	2	FAME	Soundtrack (RSO)
2	3	AVALON	Roxy Music (EG)
15	4	LOVE AND DANCE	League Unlimited Orchestra (Virgin)
10	5	PICTURES AT ELEVEN	Robert Plant (Swansong)
6	6	STILL LIFE (AMERICAN CONCERTS 1981)	Rolling Stones (Rolling Stones)
-	7	SCREAMING FOR VENGEANCE	Judas Priest (CBS)
4	8	ABRACADABRA	Steve Miller Band (Mercury)
6	9	COMPLETE MADNESS	Madness (Stiff)
13	10	IMPERIAL BEDROOM	Elvis Costello & the Attractions (F-Beat)
5	11	TROPICAL GANGSTERS	Kid Creole & the Coconuts (Ze)
-	12	GOOD TROUBLE	REO Speedwagon (Epic)
19	13	OVERLOAD	Various Artists (Ronco)
12	14	MIRAGE	Fleetwood Mac (Warner Bros.)
-	15	THE CONCERT IN CENTRAL PARK	Simon & Garfunkel (CBS)
18	16	ASIA	Asia (Geffen)
8	17	RIO	Duran Duran (EMI)
-	18	HAPPY TOGETHER	Odyssey (RCA)
22	19	NIGHT BIRDS	Shakatak (Polydor)
11	20	NON-STOP ECSTATIC DANCING	Soft Cell (Some Bizzare)
17	21	TUG OF WAR	Paul McCartney (Parlophone)
25	22	FRIENDS	Shalamar (Solar)
20	23	HOT SPACE	Queen (EMI)
16	24	THREE SIDES LIVE	Genesis (Charisma)
9	24	TURBO TRAX	Various Artists (K-Tel)
24	26	PELICAN WEST	Haircut 100 (Arista)
21	27	CHARIOTS OF FIRE	Vangelis (Polydor)
-	28	LOVE SONGS	Barbra Streisand (CBS)
14	29	THE CHANGELING	Toyah (Safari)
23	30	FABRIQUE	Fashion (Arista)

		31 July 1982	
1	1	THE LEXICON OF LOVE	ABC (Neutron)
2	2	FAME	Soundtrack (RSO)
4	3	LOVE AND DANCE	League Unlimited Orchestra (Virgin)
3	4	AVALON	Roxy Music (EG)
8	5	ABRACADABRA	Steve Miller Band (Mercury)
9	6	COMPLETE MADNESS	Madness (Stiff)
11	7	TROPICAL GANGSTERS	Kid Creole & the Coconuts (Ze)
15	8	THE CONCERT IN CENTRAL PARK	Simon & Garfunkel (CBS)
6	9	STILL LIFE (AMERICAN CONCERTS 1981)	Rolling Stones (Rolling Stones)
5	9	PICTURES AT ELEVEN	Robert Plant (Swansong)
14	11	MIRAGE	Fleetwood Mac (Warner Bros.)
16	12	ASIA	Asia (Geffen)
17	13	RIO	Duran Duran (EMI)
-	14	THE KIDS FROM FAME	Kids From Fame (BBC)
13	15	OVERLOAD	Various Artists (Ronco)
18	16	HAPPY TOGETHER	Odyssey (RCA)
22	17	FRIENDS	Shalamar (Solar)
24	18	THREE SIDES LIVE	Genesis (Charisma)
19	19	NIGHT BIRDS	Shakatak (Polydor)
12	19	GOOD TROUBLE	REO Speedwagon (Epic)
20	21	NON-STOP ECSTATIC DANCING	Soft Cell (Some Bizzare)
10	21	IMPERIAL BEDROOM	Elvis Costello & the Attractions (F-Beat)
7	23	SCREAMING FOR VENGEANCE	Judas Priest (CBS)
23	24	HOT SPACE	Queen (EMI)
29	25	THE CHANGELING	Toyah (Safari)
-	26	COMBAT ROCK	Clash (CBS)
-	27	A CONCERT FOR THE PEOPLE (BERLIN)	Barclay James Harvest (Polydor)
21	28	TUG OF WAR	Paul McCartney (Parlophone)
27	29	CHARIOTS OF FIRE	Vangelis (Polydor)
-	30	MUSTN'T GRUMBLE	Chas & Dave (Rockney)

		7 August 1982	
14	1	THE KIDS FROM FAME	Kids From Fame (BBC)
2	2	FAME	Soundtrack (RSO)
1	3	THE LEXICON OF LOVE	ABC (Neutron)
6	4	COMPLETE MADNESS	Madness (Stiff)
4	5	AVALON	Roxy Music (EG)
7	6	TROPICAL GANGSTERS	Kid Creole & the Coconuts (Ze)
9	7	PICTURES AT ELEVEN	Robert Plant (Swansong)
3	8	LOVE AND DANCE	League Unlimited Orchestra (Virgin)
5	9	ABRACADABRA	Steve Miller Band (Mercury)
8	10	THE CONCERT IN CENTRAL PARK	Simon & Garfunkel (CBS)
17	11	FRIENDS	Shalamar (Solar)
28	12	TUG OF WAR	Paul McCartney (Parlophone)
9	13	STILL LIFE (AMERICAN CONCERTS 1981)	Rolling Stones (Rolling Stones)
23	14	SCREAMING FOR VENGEANCE	Judas Priest (CBS)
-	15	DONNA SUMMER	Donna Summer (Warner Bros.)
11	16	MIRAGE	Fleetwood Mac (Warner Bros.)
12	17	ASIA	Asia (Geffen)
-	18	CAN'T STOP THE CLASSICS – HOOKED ON CLASSICS 2	Louis Clark & the Royal Philharmonic Orchestra (K-Tel)
15	19	OVERLOAD	Various Artists (Ronco)
16	20	HAPPY TOGETHER	Odyssey (RCA)
21	21	IMPERIAL BEDROOM	Elvis Costello & the Attractions (F-Beat)
13	22	RIO	Duran Duran (EMI)
-	23	WINDSONG	Randy Crawford (Warner Bros.)
-	24	TOO-RYE-AY	Dexy's Midnight Runners (Mercury)
21	25	NON-STOP ECSTATIC DANCING	Soft Cell (Some Bizzare)
19	26	NIGHT BIRDS	Shakatak (Polydor)
-	27	PELICAN WEST	Haircut 100 (Arista)
-	28	ARE YOU READY?	Bucks Fizz (RCA)
-	29	I WANT CANDY	Bow Wow Wow (EMI)
18	30	THREE SIDES LIVE	Genesis (Charisma)

ABC's debut album, following after two Top 10 singles, was the clear best-seller in July, though closely followed by the two-year-old soundtrack from the film *Fame*. This, together with its title track single performed by Irene Cara (which hit Number 1 on July 24) were sudden if belated British successes due to the success of the spin-off *Fame* TV series. The new BBC album *The Kids From Fame*, containing music from the television series, was an almost instant chart-topper.

August – September 1982

Dexy's Midnight Runners' million-selling single *Come On Eileen* was instrumental in making its parent album *Too-Rye-Ay* (this title being a key phrase from the single's lyric) the group's most successful yet, snatching a two-week stay at Number 1 from *The Kids From Fame*. The Commodores became the third major act with a few months to release a ballads compilation titled *Love Songs* and score a hit with it, though this package was not destined to follow Cliff and Streisand to Number 1.

September – October 1982

11 September 1982

last week	this week	Title
-	1	UPSTAIRS AT ERIC'S — Yazoo (Mute)
1	2	THE KIDS FROM FAME — Kids From Fame (BBC)
2	3	TOO-RYE-AY — Dexy's Midnight Runners (Mercury)
6	4	RIO — Duran Duran (EMI)
4	5	THE LEXICON OF LOVE — ABC (Neutron)
5	6	TROPICAL GANGSTERS — Kid Creole & the Coconuts (Ze)
24	7	NOW YOU SEE ME, NOW YOU DON'T — Cliff Richard (EMI)
15	8	LOVE SONGS — Commodores (K-Tel)
3	9	LOVE AND DANCE — League Unlimited Orch (Virgin)
7	10	COMPLETE MADNESS — Madness (Stiff)
10	11	FAME — Soundtrack (RSO)
12	12	TALKING BACK TO THE NIGHT — Steve Winwood (Island)
9	13	AVALON — Roxy Music (EG)
8	14	EYE OF THE TIGER — Survivor (Scotti Bros.)
16	15	THE SINGLES ALBUM — UB40 (Graduate)
18	16	MIRAGE — Fleetwood Mac (Warner Bros.)
21	17	THE JIMI HENDRIX CONCERTS — Jimi Hendrix (CBS)
23	18	ROUGH DIAMONDS — Bad Company (Swansong)
-	19	DEEP PURPLE LIVE IN LONDON — Deep Purple (Harvest)
-	20	ROCKY III — Soundtrack (Liberty)
22	21	NON-STOP ECSTATIC DANCING — Soft Cell (Some Bizzare)
13	22	CAN'T STOP THE CLASSICS – HOOKED ON CLASSICS 2 — Louis Clark & the Royal Philharmonic Orchestra (K-Tel)
14	23	THE CAGE — Tygers Of Pan Tang (MCA)
-	24	WELL KEPT SECRET — John Martyn (WEA)
-	25	ASIA — Asia (Geffen)
-	26	THE PARTY'S OVER — Talk Talk (EMI)
19	27	THE CONCERT IN CENTRAL PARK — Simon & Garfunkel (CBS)
27	28	NIGHT BIRDS — Shakatak (Polydor)
11	29	DONNA SUMMER — Donna Summer (Warner Bros.)
20	30	CHRIST THE ALBUM — Crass (Crass)

18 September 1982

last week	this week	Title
2	1	THE KIDS FROM FAME — Kids From Fame (BBC)
3	2	TOO-RYE-AY — Dexy's Midnight Runners (Mercury)
1	3	UPSTAIRS AT ERIC'S — Yazoo (Mute)
4	4	RIO — Duran Duran (EMI)
7	5	NOW YOU SEE ME, NOW YOU DON'T — Cliff Richard (EMI)
9	6	LOVE AND DANCE — League Unlimited Orch (Virgin)
5	7	THE LEXICON OF LOVE — ABC (Neutron)
-	8	IN THE HEAT OF THE NIGHT — Imagination (R&B)
-	9	BREAKOUT — Various Artists (Ronco)
10	10	COMPLETE MADNESS — Madness (Stiff)
-	11	IT'S HARD — Who (Polydor)
14	12	EYE OF THE TIGER — Survivor (Scotti Bros.)
8	13	LOVE SONGS — Commodores (K-Tel)
11	14	FAME — Soundtrack (RSO)
6	15	TROPICAL GANGSTERS — Kid Creole & the Coconuts (Ze)
16	16	MIRAGE — Fleetwood Mac (Warner Bros.)
12	17	TALKING BACK TO THE NIGHT — Steve Winwood (Island)
-	18	HIGHWAY SONG – BLACKFOOT LIVE — Blackfoot (Atco)
15	19	THE SINGLES ALBUM — UB40 (Graduate)
13	20	AVALON — Roxy Music (EG)
17	21	THE JIMI HENDRIX CONCERTS — Jimi Hendrix (CBS)
-	22	SIGNALS — Rush (Mercury)
-	23	I, ASSASSIN — Gary Numan (Beggars Banquet)
21	24	NON-STOP ECSTATIC DANCING — Soft Cell (Some Bizzare)
27	25	THE CONCERT IN CENTRAL PARK — Simon & Garfunkel (CBS)
-	26	PETER GABRIEL — Peter Gabriel (Charisma)
20	27	ROCKY III — Soundtrack (Liberty)
-	28	SONGS TO REMEMBER — Scritti Politti (Rough Trade)
26	29	THE PARTY'S OVER — Talk Talk (EMI)
-	30	MAKIN' MOVIES — Dire Straits (Vertigo)

25 September 1982

last week	this week	Title
1	1	THE KIDS FROM FAME — Kids From Fame (BBC)
3	2	UPSTAIRS AT ERIC'S — Yazoo (Mute)
7	3	THE LEXICON OF LOVE — ABC (Neutron)
26	4	PETER GABRIEL — Peter Gabriel (Charisma)
4	5	RIO — Duran Duran (EMI)
8	6	IN THE HEAT OF THE NIGHT — Imagination (R&B)
23	7	I, ASSASSIN — Gary Numan (Beggars Banquet)
9	8	BREAKOUT — Various Artists (Ronco)
22	9	SIGNALS — Rush (Mercury)
5	10	NOW YOU SEE ME, NOW YOU DON'T — Cliff Richard (EMI)
2	11	TOO-RYE-AY — Dexy's Midnight Runners (Mercury)
10	12	COMPLETE MADNESS — Madness (Stiff)
-	13	CHART BEAT, CHART HEAT — Various Artists (K-Tel)
11	14	IT'S HARD — Who (Polydor)
6	15	LOVE AND DANCE — League Unlimited Orch (Virgin)
13	16	LOVE SONGS — Commodores (K-Tel)
-	17	THE DREAMING — Kate Bush (EMI)
-	18	NEW GOLD DREAM (81,82,83,84) — Simple Minds (Virgin)
18	19	HIGHWAY SONG – BLACKFOOT LIVE — Blackfoot (Atco)
15	20	TROPICAL GANGSTERS — Kid Creole & the Coconuts (Ze)
20	21	AVALON — Roxy Music (EG)
14	22	FAME — Soundtrack (RSO)
-	23	ASIA — Asia (Geffen)
-	24	FICTION — Comsat Angels (Polydor)
28	25	SONGS TO REMEMBER — Scritti Politti (Rough Trade)
12	26	EYE OF THE TIGER — Survivor (Scotti Bros.)
-	27	ACTING VERY STRANGE — Mike Rutherford (WEA)
27	28	ROCKY III — Soundtrack (Liberty)
-	29	MYSTERY — Hot Chocolate (RAK)
-	30	THE COLLECTION 1977-1982 — Stranglers (Liberty)

2 October 1982

last week	this week	Title
1	1	THE KIDS FROM FAME — Kids From Fame (BBC)
3	2	THE LEXICON OF LOVE — ABC (Neutron)
2	3	UPSTAIRS AT ERIC'S — Yazoo (Mute)
13	4	CHART BEAT, CHART HEAT — Various Artists (K-Tel)
-	5	LOVE OVER GOLD — Dire Straits (Vertigo)
6	6	IN THE HEAT OF THE NIGHT — Imagination (R&B)
17	7	THE DREAMING — Kate Bush (EMI)
5	8	RIO — Duran Duran (EMI)
18	9	NEW GOLD DREAM (81,82,83,84) — Simple Minds (Virgin)
11	10	TOO-RYE-AY — Dexy's Midnight Runners (Mercury)
30	11	THE COLLECTION 1977-1982 — Stranglers (Liberty)
8	12	BREAKOUT — Various Artists (Ronco)
7	13	I, ASSASSIN — Gary Numan (Beggars Banquet)
4	14	PETER GABRIEL — Peter Gabriel (Charisma)
9	15	SIGNALS — Rush (Mercury)
16	16	LOVE SONGS — Commodores (K-Tel)
29	17	MYSTERY — Hot Chocolate (RAK)
15	18	LOVE AND DANCE — League Unlimited Orch (Virgin)
10	19	NOW YOU SEE ME, NOW YOU DON'T — Cliff Richard (EMI)
-	20	FRIENDS — Shalamar (Solar)
-	21	LIFE IN THE JUNGLE/ LIVE AT ABBEY ROAD — Shadows (Polydor)
-	22	NEBRASKA — Bruce Springsteen (CBS)
20	23	TROPICAL GANGSTERS — Kid Creole & the Coconuts (Ze)
-	24	SOMETHING'S GOING ON — Frida (Epic)
21	25	AVALON — Roxy Music (EG)
-	26	MIRAGE — Fleetwood Mac (Warner Bros.)
27	27	ACTING VERY STRANGE — Mike Rutherford (WEA)
24	28	FICTION — Comsat Angels (Polydor)
26	29	EYE OF THE TIGER — Survivor (Scotti Bros.)
12	30	COMPLETE MADNESS — Madness (Stiff)

Yazoo, the duo formed by ex-Depeche Mode keyboards player Vince Clark and vocalist Alison Moyet became one of only a handful of acts in history to debut in the Number 1 slot with their first album, *Upstairs At Eric's* (the title being a refence to the studio where the LP was recorded). Peter Gabriel charted with his fourth album (and the last, fortunately) to be called just *Peter Gabriel*, while the Shadows' album was a studio set with a free live LP attached.

October 1982

9 October 1982

last	this	title / artist
5	1	LOVE OVER GOLD — Dire Straits (Vertigo)
1	2	THE KIDS FROM FAME — Kids From Fame (BBC)
4	3	CHART BEAT, CHART HEAT — Various Artists (K-Tel)
9	4	NEW GOLD DREAM (81,82,83,84) — Simple Minds (Virgin)
3	5	UPSTAIRS AT ERIC'S — Yazoo (Mute)
6	6	IN THE HEAT OF THE NIGHT — Imagination (R&B)
22	7	NEBRASKA — Bruce Springsteen (CBS)
7	8	THE DREAMING — Kate Bush (EMI)
20	9	FRIENDS — Shalamar (Solar)
2	10	THE LEXICON OF LOVE — ABC (Neutron)
10	11	TOO-RYE-AY — Dexy's Midnight Runners (Mercury)
8	12	RIO — Duran Duran (EMI)
16	13	LOVE SONGS — Commodores (K-Tel)
11	14	THE COLLECTION 1977-1982 — Stranglers (Liberty)
-	15	FOREVER NOW — Psychedlic Furs (CBS)
18	16	LOVE AND DANCE — League Unlimited Orchestra (Virgin)
12	17	BREAKOUT — Various Artists (Ronco)
14	18	PETER GABRIEL — Peter Gabriel (Charisma)
-	19	UB44 — UB40 (DEP International)
-	20	MAGIC — Gillan (Virgin)
17	21	MYSTERY — Hot Chocolate (RAK)
19	22	NOW YOU SEE ME, NOW YOU DON'T — Cliff Richard (EMI)
15	23	SIGNALS — Rush (Mercury)
-	24	A BROKEN FRAME — Depeche Mode (Mute)
-	25	NOW THEN — Stiff Little Fingers (Chrysalis)
-	26	SHALAMAR'S GREATEST HITS — Shalamar (Solar)
29	27	EYE OF THE TIGER — Survivor (Scotti Bros.)
21	28	LIFE IN THE JUNGLE – LIVE AT ABBEY ROAD — Shadows (Polydor)
-	29	AS ONE — Kool & the Gang (De-Lite)
24	30	SOMETHING'S GOING ON — Frida (Epic)

16 October 1982

last	this	title / artist
1	1	LOVE OVER GOLD — Dire Straits (Vertigo)
19	2	UB44 — UB40 (DEP International)
7	3	NEBRASKA — Bruce Springsteen (CBS)
2	4	THE KIDS FROM FAME — Kids From Fame (BBC)
5	5	UPSTAIRS AT ERIC'S — Yazoo (Mute)
4	6	NEW GOLD DREAM (81,82,83,84) — Simple Minds (Virgin)
24	7	A BROKEN FRAME — Depeche Mode (Mute)
10	8	THE LEXICON OF LOVE — ABC (Neutron)
-	9	GIVE ME YOUR HEART TONIGHT — Shakin' Stevens (Epic)
11	10	TOO-RYE-AY — Dexy's Midnight Runners (Mercury)
3	11	CHART BEAT, CHART HEAT — Various Artists (K-Tel)
13	12	LOVE SONGS — Commodores (K-Tel)
-	13	AVALON — Roxy Music (EG)
6	14	IN THE HEAT OF THE NIGHT — Imagination (R&B)
9	15	FRIENDS — Shalamar (Solar)
20	16	MAGIC — Gillan (Virgin)
8	17	THE DREAMING — Kate Bush (EMI)
-	18	SPECIAL BEAT SERVICE — Beat (Go-Feet)
12	19	RIO — Duran Duran (EMI)
18	20	PETER GABRIEL — Peter Gabriel (Charisma)
15	21	FOREVER NOW — Psychedlic Furs (CBS)
-	22	MIRAGE — Fleetwood Mac (Warner Bros.)
-	23	TROPICAL GANGSTERS — Kid Creole & the Coconuts (Ze)
26	24	SHALAMAR'S GREATEST HITS — Shalamar (Solar)
14	25	THE COLLECTION 1977-1982 — Stranglers (Liberty)
23	26	SIGNALS — Rush (Mercury)
-	27	SOUL DAZE, SOUL NITES — Various Artists ((Ronco)
-	28	GET LOOSE — Evelyn King (RCA)
17	29	BREAKOUT — Various Artists (Ronco)
21	30	MYSTERY — Hot Chocolate (RAK)

23 October 1982

last	this	title / artist
1	1	LOVE OVER GOLD — Dire Straits (Vertigo)
-	2	THE KIDS FROM FAME AGAIN — Kids From Fame (RCA)
9	3	GIVE ME YOUR HEART TONIGHT — Shakin' Stevens (Epic)
2	4	UB44 — UB40 (DEP International)
-	5	CHART ATTACK — Various Artists (Telstar)
6	6	NEW GOLD DREAM (81,82,83,84) — Simple Minds (Virgin)
-	7	KISSING TO BE CLEVER — Culture Club (Virgin)
14	8	IN THE HEAT OF THE NIGHT — Imagination (R&B)
5	9	UPSTAIRS AT ERIC'S — Yazoo (Mute)
7	10	A BROKEN FRAME — Depeche Mode (Mute)
10	11	TOO-RYE-AY — Dexy's Midnight Runners (Mercury)
8	12	THE LEXICON OF LOVE — ABC (Neutron)
3	13	NEBRASKA — Bruce Springsteen (CBS)
-	14	FRIEND OR FOE — Adam Ant (CBS)
12	15	LOVE SONGS — Commodores (K-Tel)
23	16	TROPICAL GANGSTERS — Kid Creole & the Coconuts (Ze)
-	17	REFLECTIONS — Various Artists (CBS)
-	18	AMOR — Julio Iglesias (CBS)
11	19	CHART BEAT, CHART HEAT — Various Artists (K-Tel)
15	20	FRIENDS — Shalamar (Solar)
4	21	THE KIDS FROM FAME — Kids From Fame (BBC)
24	22	SHALAMAR'S GREATEST HITS — Shalamar (Solar)
13	23	AVALON — Roxy Music (EG)
30	24	MYSTERY — Hot Chocolate (RAK)
20	25	PETER GABRIEL — Peter Gabriel (Charisma)
18	26	SPECIAL BEAT SERVICE — Beat (Go-Feet)
17	27	THE DREAMING — Kate Bush (EMI)
-	28	HAPPY FAMILIES — Blancmange (London)
19	29	RIO — Duran Duran (EMI)
26	30	SIGNALS — Rush (Mercury)

30 October 1982

last	this	title / artist
2	1	THE KIDS FROM FAME AGAIN — Kids From Fame (RCA)
1	2	LOVE OVER GOLD — Dire Straits (Vertigo)
21	3	THE KIDS FROM FAME — Kids From Fame (BBC)
14	4	FRIEND OR FOE — Adam Ant (CBS)
7	5	KISSING TO BE CLEVER — Culture Club (Virgin)
-	6	QUARTET — Ultravox (Chrysalis)
17	7	REFLECTIONS — Various Artists (CBS)
3	8	GIVE ME YOUR HEART TONIGHT — Shakin' Stevens (Epic)
4	9	UB44 — UB40 (DEP International)
5	10	CHART ATTACK — Various Artists (Telstar)
9	11	UPSTAIRS AT ERIC'S — Yazoo (Mute)
12	12	THE LEXICON OF LOVE — ABC (Neutron)
-	13	THE SKY'S GONE OUT — Bauhaus (Beggars Banquet)
8	14	IN THE HEAT OF THE NIGHT — Imagination (R&B)
10	15	A BROKEN FRAME — Depeche Mode (Mute)
-	16	STRAWBERRIES — Damned (Bronze)
20	17	FRIENDS — Shalamar (Solar)
11	18	TOO-RYE-AY — Dexy's Midnight Runners (Mercury)
15	19	LOVE SONGS — Commodores (K-Tel)
18	20	AMOR — Julio Iglesias (CBS)
13	21	NEBRASKA — Bruce Springsteen (CBS)
6	22	NEW GOLD DREAM (81,82,83,84) — Simple Minds (Virgin)
16	23	TROPICAL GANGSTERS — Kid Creole & the Coconuts (Ze)
-	24	20 GREATEST HITS — Beatles (Parlophone)
-	25	BORROWED TIME — Diamond Head (MCA)
-	26	CHOOSE YOUR MASQUES — Hawkwind (RCA)
29	27	RIO — Duran Duran (EMI)
-	28	SILK ELECTRIC — Diana Ross (Capitol)
-	29	ENDLESS LOVE — Various Artists (TV)
-	30	OLIVIA NEWTON-JOHN'S GREATEST HITS — Olivia Newton-John (EMI)

Love Over Gold was only the fourth album from the not hugely prolific Dire Straits in five years, and became their first to top the chart, hitting Number 1 two weeks after the extracted *Private Investigations* gave them their debut Number 1 single. *The Kids From Fame Again*, the next LP chart-topper, was released by RCA, which did not repeat its (in retrospect) dumb move of declining the first *Kids* album and allowing BBC Records to licence - and sell vast quantities of - it.

6 November 1982

last week	this week		
2	1	LOVE OVER GOLD	Dire Straits (Vertigo)
1	2	THE KIDS FROM FAME AGAIN	Kids From Fame (RCA)
3	3	THE KIDS FROM FAME	Kids From Fame (BBC)
5	4	KISSING TO BE CLEVER	Culture Club (Virgin)
13	5	THE SKY'S GONE OUT	Bauhaus (Beggars Banquet)
23	6	TROPICAL GANGSTERS	Kid Creole & the Coconuts (Ze)
6	7	QUARTET	Ultravox (Chrysalis)
7	8	REFLECTIONS	Various Artists (CBS)
24	9	20 GREATEST HITS	Beatles (Parlophone)
8	10	GIVE ME YOUR HEART TONIGHT	Shakin' Stevens (Epic)
30	11	OLIVIA NEWTON-JOHN'S GREATEST HITS	Olivia Newton-John (EMI)
4	12	FRIEND OR FOE	Adam Ant (CBS)
10	13	CHART ATTACK	Various Artists (Telstar)
20	14	AMOR	Julio Iglesias (CBS)
12	15	THE LEXICON OF LOVE	ABC (Neutron)
11	16	UPSTAIRS AT ERIC'S	Yazoo (Mute)
-	17	THE LOVE SONGS ALBUM	Various Artists (K-Tel)
-	18	THE DOLLAR ALBUM	Dollar (WEA)
15	19	A BROKEN FRAME	Depeche Mode (Mute)
-	20	HEARTBREAKER	Dionne Warwick (Arista)
19	21	LOVE SONGS	Commodores (K-Tel)
29	22	ENDLESS LOVE	Various Artists (TV)
17	23	FRIENDS	Shalamar (Solar)
28	24	SILK ELECTRIC	Diana Ross (Capitol)
9	25	UB44	UB40 (DEP International)
-	26	CHART BEAT, CHART HEAT	Various Artists (K-Tel)
-	27	THE NIGHTFLY	Donald Fagen (Warner Bros.)
22	28	NEW GOLD DREAM (81,82,83,84)	Simple Minds (Virgin)
-	29	ASSAULT ATTACK	Michael Schenker Group (Chrysalis)
16	30	STRAWBERRIES	Damned (Bronze)

13 November 1982

3	1	THE KIDS FROM FAME	Kids From Fame (BBC)
4	2	KISSING TO BE CLEVER	Culture Club (Virgin)
1	3	LOVE OVER GOLD	Dire Straits (Vertigo)
2	4	THE KIDS FROM FAME AGAIN	Kids From Fame (RCA)
-	5	FAMOUS LAST WORDS	Supertramp (A&M)
-	6	SINGLES – 45s AND UNDER	Squeeze (A&M)
6	7	TROPICAL GANGSTERS	Kid Creole & the Coconuts (Ze)
8	8	REFLECTIONS	Various Artists (CBS)
14	9	AMOR	Julio Iglesias (CBS)
5	10	THE SKY'S GONE OUT	Bauhaus (Beggars Banquet)
20	11	HEARTBREAKER	Dionne Warwick (Arista)
9	12	20 GREATEST HITS	Beatles (Parlophone)
11	13	OLIVIA NEWTON-JOHN'S GREATEST HITS	Olivia Newton-John (EMI)
10	14	GIVE ME YOUR HEART TONIGHT	Shakin' Stevens (Epic)
-	15	H2O	Daryl Hall & John Oates (RCA)
7	16	QUARTET	Ultravox (Chrysalis)
15	17	THE LEXICON OF LOVE	ABC (Neutron)
-	18	HELLO, I MUST BE GOING!	Phil Collins (Virgin)
21	19	LOVE SONGS	Commodores (K-Tel)
16	20	UPSTAIRS AT ERIC'S	Yazoo (Mute)
18	21	THE DOLLAR ALBUM	Dollar (WEA)
-	22	IN THE HEAT OF THE NIGHT	Imagination (R&B)
17	23	THE LOVE SONGS ALBUM	Various Artists (K-Tel)
-	24	CREATURES OF THE NIGHT	Kiss (Casablanca)
-	25	FLASH TRACKS	Various Artists (TV)
-	26	HITS OF THE SCREAMING SIXTIES	Various Artists (Warwick)
24	27	SILK ELECTRIC	Diana Ross (Capitol)
-	28	VOICE OF A GENERATION	Blitz (No Future)
12	29	FRIEND OR FOE	Adam Ant (CBS)
25	30	UB44	UB40 (DEP International)

20 November 1982

1	1	THE KIDS FROM FAME	Kids From Fame (BBC)
6	2	SINGLES – 45s AND UNDER	Squeeze (A&M)
-	3	FROM THE MAKERS OF ...	Status Quo (Vertigo)
11	4	HEARTBREAKER	Dionne Warwick (Arista)
4	5	THE KIDS FROM FAME AGAIN	Kids From Fame (RCA)
18	6	HELLO, I MUST BE GOING!	Phil Collins (Virgin)
8	7	REFLECTIONS	Various Artists (CBS)
3	8	LOVE OVER GOLD	Dire Straits (Vertigo)
2	9	KISSING TO BE CLEVER	Culture Club (Virgin)
5	10	FAMOUS LAST WORDS	Supertramp (A&M)
14	11	GIVE ME YOUR HEART TONIGHT	Shakin' Stevens (Epic)
-	12	MADNESS PRESENTS THE RISE AND FALL	Madness (Stiff)
7	13	TROPICAL GANGSTERS	Kid Creole & the Coconuts (Ze)
-	14	A KISS IN THE DREAMHOUSE	Siouxsie & the Banshees (Polydor)
-	15	WARRIOR ROCK – TOYAH ON TOUR	Toyah (Safari)
19	16	LOVE SONGS	Commodores (K-Tel)
12	17	20 GREATEST HITS	Beatles (Parlophone)
10	18	THE SKY'S GONE OUT	Bauhaus (Beggars Banquet)
25	19	FLASH TRACKS	Various Artists (TV)
-	20	PEARLS II	Elkie Brooks (A&M)
27	21	SILK ELECTRIC	Diana Ross (Capitol)
20	22	UPSTAIRS AT ERIC'S	Yazoo (Mute)
13	23	OLIVIA NEWTON-JOHN'S GREATEST HITS	Olivia Newton-John (EMI)
-	24	WAXWORKS – SOME SINGLES (1977-82)	XTC (Virgin)
26	25	HITS OF THE SCREAMING SIXTIES	Various Artists (Warwick)
21	26	THE DOLLAR ALBUM	Dollar (WEA)
15	27	H2O	Daryl Hall & John Oates (RCA)
-	28	GET NERVOUS	Pat Benatar (Chrysalis)
22	29	IN THE HEAT OF THE NIGHT	Imagination (R&B)
-	30	LOVE SONGS	Elton John (TV)

27 November 1982

4	1	HEARTBREAKER	Dionne Warwick (Arista)
6	2	HELLO, I MUST BE GOING!	Phil Collins (Virgin)
-	3	THE SINGLES – THE FIRST TEN YEARS	Abba (Epic)
1	3	THE KIDS FROM FAME	Kids From Fame (BBC)
2	5	SINGLES – 45s AND UNDER	Squeeze (A&M)
3	6	FROM THE MAKERS OF ...	Status Quo (Vertigo)
12	7	MADNESS PRESENTS THE RISE AND FALL	Madness (Stiff)
7	8	REFLECTIONS	Various Artists (CBS)
-	9	THE JOHN LENNON COLLECTION	John Lennon (Parlophone)
20	10	PEARLS II	Elkie Brooks (A&M)
-	11	MIDNIGHT LOVE	Marvin Gaye (CBS)
-	12	CHART HITS '82	Various Artists (K-Tel)
5	13	THE KIDS FROM FAME AGAIN	Kids From Fame (RCA)
10	14	FAMOUS LAST WORDS	Supertramp (A&M)
-	15	LINING MY LIFE	Grace Jones (Island)
9	16	KISSING TO BE CLEVER	Culture Club (Virgin)
11	17	GIVE ME YOUR HEART TONIGHT	Shakin' Stevens (Epic)
8	18	LOVE OVER GOLD	Dire Straits (Vertigo)
-	19	RIO	Duran Duran (EMI)
14	20	A KISS IN THE DREAMHOUSE	Siouxsie & the Banshees (Polydor)
13	21	TROPICAL GANGSTERS	Kid Creole & the Coconuts (Ze)
17	22	20 GREATEST HITS	Beatles (Parlophone)
15	23	WARRIOR ROCK – TOYAH ON TOUR	Toyah (Safari)
-	24	HAPPY FAMILIES	Blancmange (London)
19	25	FLASH TRACKS	Various Artists (TV)
22	26	UPSTAIRS AT ERIC'S	Yazoo (Mute)
-	27	RIP IT UP	Orange Juice (Holden Caulfield Universal)
26	28	THE DOLLAR ALBUM	Dollar (WEA)
-	29	GREATEST LOVE SONGS	Nat 'King' Cole (Capitol)
30	30	LOVE SONGS	Elton John (TV)

Interestingly, the first *Kids From Fame* album resurged to outsell its successor during November, grabbing two further weeks at Number 1 after *Kids From Fame Again* had dropped. The Beatles Top 10 album *20 Greatest Hits* was a new compilation issued to coincide with the 20th anniversary of the release of their first EMI single *Love Me Do* - this track was not only included on the album but also successfully re-promoted on single, reaching Number 3 (24 places higher than the first time around!).

December 1982

4 December 1982

last week	this week	
3	1	THE SINGLES – THE FIRST TEN YEARS Abba (Epic)
1	2	HEARTBREAKER Dionne Warwick (Arista)
-	3	I WANNA DO IT WITH YOU Barry Manilow (Arista)
3	4	THE KIDS FROM FAME Kids From Fame (BBC)
2	5	HELLO, I MUST BE GOING! Phil Collins (Virgin)
6	6	FROM THE MAKERS OF ... Status Quo (Vertigo)
9	7	THE JOHN LENNON COLLECTION John Lennon (Parlophone)
5	8	SINGLES – 45s AND UNDER Squeeze (A&M)
10	9	PEARLS II Elkie Brooks (A&M)
29	10	GREATEST LOVE SONGS Nat 'King' Cole (Capitol)
-	11	SAINTS 'N' SINNERS Whitesnake (Liberty)
19	12	RIO Duran Duran (EMI)
11	13	MIDNIGHT LOVE Marvin Gaye (CBS)
8	14	REFLECTIONS Various Artists (CBS)
-	15	CHART WARS – MAY THE HITS BE WITH YOU Various Artists (Ronco)
13	16	THE KIDS FROM FAME AGAIN Kids From Fame (RCA)
17	17	GIVE ME YOUR HEART TONIGHT Shakin' Stevens (Epic)
26	18	UPSTAIRS AT ERIC'S Yazoo (Mute)
-	19	KILLER ON THE RAMPAGE Eddy Grant (Ice)
7	20	MADNESS PRESENTS THE RISE AND FALL Madness (Stiff)
14	21	FAMOUS LAST WORDS Supertramp (A&M)
16	22	KISSING TO BE CLEVER Culture Club (Virgin)
21	23	TROPICAL GANGSTERS Kid Creole & the Coconuts (Ze)
-	24	INVITATIONS Shakatak (Polydor)
-	25	LIONEL RICHIE Lionel Richie (Motown)
12	26	CHART HITS '82 Various Artists (K-Tel)
18	27	LOVE OVER GOLD Dire Straits (Vertigo)
22	28	20 GREATEST HITS Beatles (Parlophone)
24	29	HAPPY FAMILIES Blancmange (London)
20	30	A KISS IN THE DREAMHOUSE Siouxsie & the Banshees (Polydor)

11 December 1982

1	1	THE SINGLES – THE FIRST TEN YEARS Abba (Epic)
7	2	THE JOHN LENNON COLLECTION John Lennon (Parlophone)
9	3	PEARLS II Elkie Brooks (A&M)
6	4	FROM THE MAKERS OF ... Status Quo (Vertigo)
4	5	THE KIDS FROM FAME Kids From Fame (BBC)
10	6	GREATEST LOVE SONGS Nat 'King' Cole (Capitol)
-	7	CODA Led Zeppelin (Swansong)
2	8	HEARTBREAKER Dionne Warwick (Arista)
12	9	RIO Duran Duran (EMI)
8	10	SINGLES – 45s AND UNDER Squeeze (A&M)
3	11	I WANNA DO IT WITH YOU Barry Manilow (Arista)
5	12	HELLO, I MUST BE GOING! Phil Collins (Virgin)
14	13	REFLECTIONS Various Artists (CBS)
13	14	MIDNIGHT LOVE Marvin Gaye (CBS)
26	15	CHART HITS '82 Various Artists (K-Tel)
-	16	THE YOUTH OF TODAY Musical Youth (MCA)
25	17	LIONEL RICHIE Lionel Richie (Motown)
17	18	GIVE ME YOUR HEART TONIGHT Shakin' Stevens (Epic)
27	19	LOVE OVER GOLD Dire Straits (Vertigo)
15	20	CHART WARS – MAY THE HITS BE WITH YOU Various Artists (Ronco)
11	21	SAINTS 'N' SINNERS Whitesnake (Liberty)
19	22	KILLER ON THE RAMPAGE Eddy Grant (Ice)
-	23	OLIVIA NEWTON-JOHN'S GREATEST HITS Olivia Newton-John (EMI)
20	24	MADNESS PRESENTS THE RISE AND FALL Madness (Stiff)
21	25	FAMOUS LAST WORDS Supertramp (A&M)
22	26	KISSING TO BE CLEVER Culture Club (Virgin)
18	27	UPSTAIRS AT ERIC'S Yazoo (Mute)
16	28	THE KIDS FROM FAME AGAIN Kids From Fame (RCA)
-	29	WILD THINGS RUN FAST Joni Mitchell (Geffen)
-	30	LOVE SONGS Diana Ross (K-Tel)

18 December 1982

1	1	THE SINGLES – THE FIRST TEN YEARS Abba (Epic)
2	2	THE JOHN LENNON COLLECTION John Lennon (Parlophone)
9	3	RIO Duran Duran (EMI)
3	4	PEARLS II Elkie Brooks (A&M)
7	5	CODA Led Zeppelin (Swansong)
30	6	LOVE SONGS Diana Ross (K-Tel)
15	7	CHART HITS '82 Various Artists (K-Tel)
5	8	THE KIDS FROM FAME Kids From Fame (BBC)
8	9	HEARTBREAKER Dionne Warwick (Arista)
6	10	GREATEST LOVE SONGS Nat 'King' Cole (Capitol)
4	11	FROM THE MAKERS OF ... Status Quo (Vertigo)
28	12	THE KIDS FROM FAME AGAIN Kids From Fame (RCA)
-	13	QUARTET Ultravox (Chrysalis)
12	14	HELLO, I MUST BE GOING! Phil Collins (Virgin)
26	15	KISSING TO BE CLEVER Culture Club (Virgin)
24	16	MADNESS PRESENTS THE RISE AND FALL Madness (Stiff)
-	17	THRILLER Michael Jackson (Epic)
11	18	I WANNA DO IT WITH YOU Barry Manilow (Arista)
19	19	LOVE OVER GOLD Dire Straits (Vertigo)
10	20	SINGLES – 45s AND UNDER Squeeze (A&M)
17	21	LIONEL RICHIE Lionel Richie (Motown)
14	22	MIDNIGHT LOVE Marvin Gaye (CBS)
-	23	RICHARD CLAYDERMAN Richard Clayderman (Delphine)
-	24	THE STORY OF THE STONES Rolling Stones (K-Tel)
-	25	BEST OF CLASSIC ROCK London Symphony Orchestra & the Royal Choral Society (K-Tel)
23	26	OLIVIA NEWTON-JOHN'S GREATEST HITS Olivia Newton-John (EMI)
18	27	GIVE ME YOUR HEART TONIGHT Shakin' Stevens (Epic)
16	28	THE YOUTH OF TODAY Musical Youth (MCA)
21	29	SAINTS 'N' SINNERS Whitesnake (Liberty)
13	30	REFLECTIONS Various Artists (CBS)

25 December 1982

2	1	THE JOHN LENNON COLLECTION John Lennon (Parlophone)
1	2	THE SINGLES – THE FIRST TEN YEARS Abba (Epic)
-	3	DIG THE NEW BREED Jam (Polydor)
3	4	RIO Duran Duran (EMI)
9	5	HEARTBREAKER Dionne Warwick (Arista)
10	6	GREATEST LOVE SONGS Nat 'King' Cole (Capitol)
4	7	PEARLS II Elkie Brooks (A&M)
6	8	LOVE SONGS Diana Ross (K-Tel)
11	9	FROM THE MAKERS OF ... Status Quo (Vertigo)
8	10	THE KIDS FROM FAME Kids From Fame (BBC)
23	11	RICHARD CLAYDERMAN Richard Clayderman (Delphine)
15	12	KISSING TO BE CLEVER Culture Club (Virgin)
18	13	I WANNA DO IT WITH YOU Barry Manilow (Arista)
16	14	MADNESS PRESENTS THE RISE AND FALL Madness (Stiff)
-	15	FRIENDS Shalamar (Solar)
5	16	CODA Led Zeppelin (Swansong)
21	17	LIONEL RICHIE Lionel Richie (Motown)
27	18	GIVE ME YOUR HEART TONIGHT Shakin' Stevens (Epic)
20	19	SINGLES – 45s AND UNDER Squeeze (A&M)
7	20	CHART HITS '82 Various Artists (K-Tel)
24	21	THE STORY OF THE STONES Rolling Stones (K-Tel)
-	22	FLOCK OF SEAGULLS Flock Of Seagulls (Jive)
12	23	THE KIDS FROM FAME AGAIN Kids From Fame (RCA)
17	24	THRILLER Michael Jackson (Epic)
-	25	CACHARPAYA (PANPIPES OF THE ANDES) Incantation (Beggars Banquet)
19	26	LOVE OVER GOLD Dire Straits (Vertigo)
30	27	REFLECTIONS Various Artists (CBS)
-	28	RAIDERS OF THE POP CHARTS Various Artists (Ronco)
14	29	HELLO, I MUST BE GOING! Phil Collins (Virgin)
29	30	SAINTS 'N' SINNERS Whitesnake (Liberty)

True to form, the now all-but-defunct Abba had December's biggest-selling album, this time with their third (and biggest) hit singles compilation. The actual Christmas chart-topper, though, was another singles compilation, the TV-promoted *John Lennon Collection*. Meanwhile, the *Love Songs* saga continued, with Diana Ross being the fourth act in close recent memory to use that title. Nat 'King' Cole at least had *Greatest...* added to his similar album with which Diana shared the Top 10.

8 January 1983

last week	this week	
1	1	THE JOHN LENNON COLLECTION — John Lennon (Parlophone)
3	2	DIG THE NEW BREED — Jam (Polydor)
2	3	THE SINGLES - THE FIRST TEN YEARS — Abba (Epic)
15	4	FRIENDS — Shalamar (Solar)
14	5	MADNESS PRESENTS THE RISE AND FALL — Madness (Stiff)
7	6	PEARLS II — Elkie Brooks (A&M)
8	7	LOVE SONGS — Diana Ross (K-Tel)
4	8	RIO — Duran Duran (EMI)
5	9	HEARTBREAKER — Dionne Warwick (Arista)
11	10	RICHARD CLAYDERMAN — Richard Clayderman (Decca/Delphine)
17	11	LIONEL RICHIE — Lionel Richie (Motown)
12	12	KISSING TO BE CLEVER — Culture Club (Virgin)
29	13	HELLO, I MUST BE GOING! — Phil Collins (Virgin)
6	14	GREATEST LOVE SONGS — Nat 'King' Cole (Capitol)
13	15	I WANNA DO IT WITH YOU — Barry Manilow (Arista)
10	16	THE KIDS FROM FAME — Various Artists (BBC)
8	17	FROM THE MAKERS OF .... — Status Quo (Vertigo)
28	18	RAIDERS OF THE POP CHARTS — Various Artists (Ronco)
22	19	FLOCK OF SEAGULLS — Flock of Seagulls (Jive)
18	20	GIVE ME YOUR HEART TONIGHT — Shakin' Stevens (Epic)
21	21	THE STORY OF THE STONES — Rolling Stones (K-Tel)
20	22	CHART HITS '82 — Various Artists (K-Tel)
23	23	THE KIDS FROM FAME AGAIN — Various Artists (K-Tel)
19	24	SINGLES - 45s AND UNDER — Squeeze (A&M)
24	25	THRILLER — Michael Jackson (EPIC)
16	26	CODA — Led Zeppelin (Swansong)
-	27	QUARTET — Ultravox (Chrysalis)
-	28	ET - THE EXTRA-TERRESTRIAL — John Williams (MCA)
-	29	UPSTAIRS AT ERIC'S — Yazoo (Mute)
25	30	CACHARPAYA (PANPIPES OF THE ANDES) — Incantation (Beggars Banquet)

15 January 1983

last week	this week	
1	1	THE JOHN LENNON COLLECTION — John Lennon (Parlophone)
9	2	HEARTBREAKER — Dionne Warwick (Arista)
8	3	RIO — Duran Duran (EMI)
18	4	RAIDERS OF THE POP CHARTS — Various Artists (Ronco)
2	5	DIG THE NEW BREED — Jam (Polydor)
3	6	THE SINGLES - THE FIRST TEN YEARS — Abba (Epic)
4	7	FRIENDS — Shalamar (Solar)
6	8	PEARLS II — Elkie Brooks (A&M)
11	9	LIONEL RICHIE — Lionel Richie (Motown)
13	10	HELLO, I MUST BE GOING! — Phil Collins (Virgin)
12	11	KISSING TO BE CLEVER — Culture Club (Virgin)
7	12	LOVE SONGS — Diana Ross (K-Tel)
5	12	MADNESS PRESENTS THE RISE AND FALL — Madness (Stiff)
10	14	RICHARD CLAYDERMAN — Richard Clayderman (Decca/Delphine)
17	15	FROM THE MAKERS OF .... — Status Quo (Vertigo)
16	16	THE KIDS FROM FAME — Various Artists (BBC)
-	17	OLIVIA NEWTON-JOHN'S GREATEST HITS — Olivia Newton-John (EMI)
-	18	COMPLETE MADNESS — Madness (Stiff)
-	19	20 GREATEST HITS — Beatles (Parlophone)
23	20	THE KIDS FROM FAME AGAIN — Various Artists (K-Tel)
-	21	BUSINESS AS USUAL — Men at Work (Epic)
25	22	THRILLER — Michael Jackson (Epic)
14	23	GREATEST LOVE SONGS — Nat 'King' Cole (Capitol)
27	24	QUARTET — Ultravox (Chrysalis)
-	25	TOO-RYE-AY — Dexy's Midnight Runners (Mercury)
22	26	CHART HITS '82 — Various Artists (K-Tel)
24	27	SINGLES - 45s AND UNDER — Squeeze (A&M)
15	28	I WANNA DO IT WITH YOU — Barry Manilow (Arista)
28	29	ET - THE EXTRA-TERRESTRIAL — John Williams (MCA)
29	30	UPSTAIRS AT ERIC'S — Yazoo (Mute)

22 January 1983

last week	this week	
1	1	THE JOHN LENNON COLLECTION — John Lennon (Parlophone)
21	2	BUSINESS AS USUAL — Men at Work (Epic)
3	3	RIO — Duran Duran (EMI)
10	4	HELLO, I MUST BE GOING! — Phil Collins (Virgin)
2	5	HEARTBREAKER — Dionne Warwick (Arista)
4	6	RAIDERS OF THE POP CHARTS — Various Artists (Ronco)
11	7	KISSING TO BE CLEVER — Culture Club (Virgin)
6	8	THE SINGLES - THE FIRST TEN YEARS — Abba (Epic)
-	9	CACHARPAYA (PANPIPES OF THE ANDES) — Incantation (Beggars Banquet)
7	10	FRIENDS — Shalamar (Solar)
8	11	PEARLS II — Elkie Brooks (A&M)
14	12	RICHARD CLAYDERMAN — Richard Clayderman (Decca/Delphine)
17	13	OLIVIA NEWTON-JOHN'S GREATEST HITS — Olivia Newton-John (EMI)
24	14	QUARTET — Ultravox (Chrysalis)
5	15	DIG THE NEW BREED — Jam (Polydor)
18	16	COMPLETE MADNESS — Madness (Stiff)
-	17	LOVE OVER GOLD — Dire Straits (Vertigo)
22	18	THRILLER — Michael Jackson (Epic)
15	19	FROM THE MAKERS OF .... — Status Quo (Vertigo)
16	20	THE KIDS FROM FAME — Various Artists (BBC)
25	21	TOO-RYE-AY — Dexy's Midnight Runners (Mercury)
12	22	MADNESS PRESENTS THE RISE AND FALL — Madness (Stiff)
9	23	LIONEL RICHIE — Lionel Richie (Motown)
30	24	UPSTAIRS AT ERIC'S — Yazoo (Mute)
27	25	SINGLES - 45s AND UNDER — Squeeze (A&M)
-	26	MIDNIGHT LOVE — Marvin Gaye (CBS)
-	27	FELINE — Stranglers (Epic)
-	28	THE ART OF FALLING APART — Soft Cell (Some Bizzare)
19	29	20 GREATEST HITS — Beatles (Parlophone)
-	30	LIVE EVIL — Black Sabbath (Vertigo)

The Jam's *Dig The New Breed* (a phrase appropriated from James Brown) was their last album prior to splitting, while Lionel Richie's eponymous set was his first solo release since leaving the Commodores. It started slowly on the chart and gradually built to huge sales - as, interestingly, did Michael Jackson's *Thriller*.

January – February 1983

29 January 1983

last week / this week

last	this	
2	1	BUSINESS AS USUAL — Men at Work (Epic)
4	2	HELLO, I MUST BE GOING! — Phil Collins (Virgin)
1	3	THE JOHN LENNON COLLECTION — John Lennon (Parlophone)
6	4	RAIDERS OF THE POP CHARTS — Various Artists (Ronco)
5	5	HEARTBREAKER — Dionne Warwick (Arista)
27	6	FELINE — Stranglers (Epic)
28	7	THE ART OF FALLING APART — Soft Cell (Some Bizzare)
3	8	RIO — Duran Duran (EMI)
10	9	FRIENDS — Shalamar (Solar)
12	10	RICHARD CLAYDERMAN — Richard Clayderman (Decca/Delphine)
30	11	LIVE EVIL — Black Sabbath (Vertigo)
9	12	CACHARPAYA (PANPIPES OF THE ANDES) — Incantation (Beggars Banquet)
7	13	KISSING TO BE CLEVER — Culture Club (Virgin)
-	14	LOVE SONGS — Diana Ross (K-Tel)
8	15	THE SINGLES - THE FIRST TEN YEARS — Abba (Epic)
13	16	OLIVIA NEWTON-JOHN'S GREATEST HITS — Olivia Newton-John (EMI)
16	17	COMPLETE MADNESS — Madness (Stiff)
26	18	MIDNIGHT LOVE — Marvin Gaye (CBS)
17	19	LOVE OVER GOLD — Dire Straits (Vertigo)
-	20	NIGHT AND DAY — Joe Jackson (A&M)
18	21	THRILLER — Michael Jackson (Epic)
14	22	QUARTET — Ultravox (Chrysalis)
-	23	RARE — David Bowie (RCA)
-	24	KILLER ON THE RAMPAGE — Eddy Grant (Ice)
19	25	FROM THE MAKERS OF .... — Status Quo (Vertigo)
11	26	PEARLS II — Elkie Brooks (A&M)
-	27	SKY FIVE LIVE — Sky (Ariola)
15	28	DIG THE NEW BREED — Jam (Polydor)
29	29	20 GREATEST HITS — Beatles (Parlophone)
21	30	TOO-RYE-AY — Dexy's Midnight Runners (Mercury)

5 February 1983

last	this	
1	1	BUSINESS AS USUAL — Men at Work (Epic)
2	2	HELLO, I MUST BE GOING! — Phil Collins (Virgin)
3	3	THE JOHN LENNON COLLECTION — John Lennon (Parlophone)
20	4	NIGHT AND DAY — Joe Jackson (A&M)
6	5	FELINE — Stranglers (Epic)
10	6	RICHARD CLAYDERMAN — Richard Clayderman) (Decca/Delphine)
5	7	HEARTBREAKER — Dionne Warwick (Arista)
7	8	THE ART OF FALLING APART — Soft Cell (Some Bizzare)
24	9	KILLER ON THE RAMPAGE — Eddy Grant (Ice)
8	10	RIO — Duran Duran (EMI)
12	11	CACHARPAYA (PANPIPES OF THE ANDES) — Incantation (Beggars Banquet)
4	12	RAIDERS OF THE POP CHARTS — Various Artists (Ronco)
13	13	KISSING TO BE CLEVER — Culture Club (Virgin)
26	14	PEARLS II — Elkie Brooks (A&M)
9	15	FRIENDS — Shalamar (Solar)
19	16	LOVE OVER GOLD — Dire Straits (Vertigo)
16	17	OLIVIA NEWTON-JOHN'S GREATEST HITS — Olivia Newton-John (EMI)
11	18	LIVE EVIL — Black Sabbath (Vertigo)
21	19	THRILLER — Michael Jackson (Epic)
-	20	LIONEL RICHIE — Lionel Richie (Motown)
15	21	THE SINGLES - THE FIRST TEN YEARS — Abba (Epic)
25	22	FROM THE MAKERS OF .... — Status Quo (Vertigo)
-	23	THE VERY BEST OF CILLA BLACK — Cilla Black (Parlophone)
17	24	COMPLETE MADNESS — Madness (Stiff)
27	25	SKY FIVE LIVE — Sky (Ariola)
22	26	QUARTET — Ultravox (Chrysalis)
28	27	DIG THE NEW BREED — Jam (Polydor)
23	28	RARE — David Bowie (RCA)
18	29	MIDNIGHT LOVE — Marvin Gaye (CBS)
-	30	DIFFICULT SHAPES AND PASSIVE RHYTHMS — China Crisis (Virgin)

12 February 1983

last	this	
1	1	BUSINESS AS USUAL — Men at Work (Epic)
2	2	HELLO, I MUST BE GOING! — Phil Collins (Virgin)
3	3	NIGHT AND DAY — Joe Jackson (A&M)
6	4	RICHARD CLAYDERMAN — Richard Clayderman (Decca/delphine)
5	5	FELINE — Stranglers (Epic)
9	6	KILLER ON THE RAMPAGE — Eddy Grant (Ice)
3	7	THE JOHN LENNON COLLECTION — John Lennon (Parlophone)
12	8	RAIDERS OF THE POP CHARTS — Various Artists (Ronco)
19	9	THRILLER — Michael Jackson (Epic)
-	10	TRANS — Neil Young (Geffen)
11	11	CACHARPAYA (PANPIPES OF THE ANDES) — Incantation (Beggars Banquet)
7	12	HEARTBREAKER — Dionne Warwick (Arista)
8	13	THE ART OF FALLING APART — Soft Cell (Some Bizzare)
14	14	PEARLS II — Elkie Brooks (A&M)
23	15	THE VERY BEST OF CILLA BLACK — Cilla Black (Parlophone)
18	16	LIVE EVIL — Black Sabbath (Vertigo)
10	17	RIO — Duran Duran (EMI)
17	18	OLIVIA NEWTON-JOHN'S GREATEST HITS — Olivia Newton-John (EMI)
30	19	DIFFICULT SHAPES AND PASSIVE RHYTHMS — China Crisis (Virgin)
-	20	THE NIGHTFLY — Donald Fagen (Warner Bros.)
-	21	PORCUPINE — Echo & the Bunnymen (Korova)
25	22	SKY FIVE LIVE — Sky (Ariola)
15	23	FRIENDS — Shalamar (Solar)
22	24	FROM THE MAKERS OF .... — Status Quo (Vertigo)
16	25	LOVE OVER GOLD — Dire Straits (Vertigo)
-	26	THE BELLE STARS — Belle Stars (Stiff)
13	27	KISSING TO BE CLEVER — Culture Club (Virgin)
-	28	VISIONS — Various Artists (K-Tel)
29	29	MIDNIGHT LOVE — Marvin Gaye (CBS)
21	30	THE SINGLES - THE FIRST TEN YEARS — Abba (Epic)

19 February 1983

last	this	
1	1	BUSINESS AS USUAL — Men at Work (Epic)
21	2	PORCUPINE — Echo & the Bunnymen (Korova)
3	3	THE JOHN LENNON COLLECTION — John Lennon (Parlophone)
3	4	NIGHT AND DAY — Joe Jackson (A&M)
9	5	THRILLER — Michael Jackson (Epic)
12	6	HEARTBREAKER — Dionne Warwick (Arista)
2	7	HELLO, I MUST BE GOING! — Phil Collins (Virgin)
6	8	KILLER ON THE RAMPAGE — Eddy Grant (Ice)
5	9	FELINE — Stranglers (Epic)
4	10	RICHARD CLAYDERMAN — Richard Clayderman (Decca/Delphine)
-	11	MAKING CONTACT — UFO (Chrysalis)
8	12	RAIDERS OF THE POP CHARTS — Various Artists (Ronco)
28	13	VISIONS — Various Artists (K-Tel)
-	14	ALL THE BEST — Stiff Little Fingers (Chrysalis)
-	15	GREATEST LOVE SONGS — Nat 'King' Cole (Capitol)
-	16	FRONTIERS — Journey (CBS)
22	17	SKY FIVE LIVE — Sky (Ariola)
14	18	PEARLS II — Elkie Brooks (A&M)
-	19	SWEET DREAMS (ARE MADE OF THIS) — Eurythmics (RCA)
10	20	TRANS — Neil Young (Geffen)
19	21	DIFFICULT SHAPES AND PASSIVE RHYTHMS — China Crisis (Virgin)
26	22	THE BELLE STARS — Belle Stars (Stiff)
11	23	CACHARPAYA (PANPIPES OF THE ANDES) — Incantation (Beggars Banquet)
16	24	LIVE EVIL — Black Sabbath (Vertigo)
17	25	RIO — Duran Duran (EMI)
25	26	LOVE OVER GOLD — Dire Straits (Vertigo)
-	27	OCTOBER — U2 (Island)
13	28	THE ART OF FALLING APART — Soft Cell (Some Bizzare)
-	29	SHAPE UP AND DANCE VOL 1 — Felicity Kendall (Lifestyle)
-	30	MONEY & CIGARETTES — Eric Clapton (Duck)

Australia's Men At Work had already found Number 1 US success in 1982, so the UK was catching up in February 1983 when their *Business As Usual* album topped the chart simultaneously with the single *Down Under*. The album actually outlived the 45 at the top, logging five straight Number 1 weeks, and holding Phil Collins' second solo set *Hello I Must Be Going* (also boosted by a Number 1 single) in second place.

February – March 1983

26 February 1983

last week	this week		
1	1	BUSINESS AS USUAL	Men at Work (Epic)
5	2	THRILLER	Michael Jackson (Epic)
4	3	NIGHT AND DAY	Joe Jackson (A&M)
2	3	PORCUPINE	Echo & the Bunnymen (Korova)
3	5	THE JOHN LENNON COLLECTION	John Lennon (Parlophone)
7	6	HELLO, I MUST BE GOING!	Phil Collins (Virgin)
-	7	WAITING	Fun Boy Three (Chrysalis)
-	8	ANOTHER PAGE	Christopher Cross (Warner Bros.)
10	9	RICHARD CLAYDERMAN	Richard Clayderman (Decca/Delphine)
16	9	FRONTIERS	Journey (CBS)
6	11	HEARTBREAKER	Dionne Warwick (Arista)
18	12	PEARLS II	Elkie Brooks (A&M)
22	13	THE BELLE STARS	Belle Stars (Stiff)
13	14	VISIONS	Various Artists (K-Tel)
21	15	DIFFICULT SHAPES AND PASSIVE RHYTHMS	China Crisis (Virgin)
14	16	ALL THE BEST	Stiff Little Fingers (Chrysalis)
30	17	MONEY & CIGARETTES	Eric Clapton (Duck)
8	18	KILLER ON THE RAMPAGE	Eddy Grant (Ice)
25	19	RIO	Duran Duran (EMI)
-	20	POWERLIGHT	Earth Wind & Fire (CBS)
12	21	RAIDERS OF THE POP CHARTS	Various Artists (Ronco)
15	22	GREATEST LOVE SONGS	Nat 'King' Cole (Capitol)
9	23	FELINE	Stranglers (Epic)
19	24	SWEET DREAMS (ARE MADE OF THIS)	Eurythmics (RCA)
23	25	CACHARPAYA (PANPIPES OF THE ANDES)	Incantation (Beggars Banquet)
-	26	LIONEL RICHIE	Lionel Richie (Motown)
-	27	COMPLETE MADNESS	Madness (Stiff)
11	28	MAKING CONTACT	UFO (Chrysalis)
20	29	TRANS	Neil Young (Geffen)
26	30	LOVE OVER GOLD	Dire Straits (Vertigo)

5 March 1983

2	1	THRILLER	Michael Jackson (Epic)
1	1	BUSINESS AS USUAL	Men at Work (Epic)
8	3	ANOTHER PAGE	Christopher Cross (Warner Bros.)
-	4	QUICK STEP AND SIDE KICK	Thompson Twins (Arista)
3	5	NIGHT AND DAY	Joe Jackson (A&M)
11	6	HEARTBREAKER	Dionne Warwick (Arista)
-	7	TOTO IV	Toto (CBS)
3	8	PORCUPINE	Echo & the Bunnymen (Korova)
5	9	THE JOHN LENNON COLLECTION	John Lennon (Parlophone)
14	10	VISIONS	Various Artists (K-Tel)
9	11	RICHARD CLAYDERMAN	Richard Clayderman (Decca/Delphine)
6	12	HELLO, I MUST BE GOING!	Phil Collins (Virgin)
9	13	FRONTIERS	Journey (CBS)
7	14	WAITING	Fun Boy Three (Chrysalis)
17	15	MONEY & CIGARETTES	Eric Clapton (Duck)
-	16	JANE FONDA'S WORKOUT RECORD	Jane Fonda (CBS)
-	17	WRECKIN' CREW	Meteors (Identity)
13	18	THE BELLE STARS	Belle Stars (Stiff)
19	19	RIO	Duran Duran (EMI)
-	20	SHOW PEOPLE	Mari Wilson (Compact)
26	21	LIONEL RICHIE	Lionel Richie (Motown)
-	22	WHAT'S WORDS WORTH	Motorhead (Big Beat)
16	23	ALL THE BEST	Stiff Little Fingers (Chrysalis)
-	24	UB40 LIVE	UB40 (DEP Int)
15	25	DIFFICULT SHAPES AND PASSIVE RHYTHMS	China Crisis (Virgin)
24	26	SWEET DREAMS (ARE MADE OF THIS)	Eurythmics (RCA)
27	27	COMPLETE MADNESS	Madness (Stiff)
18	28	KILLER ON THE RAMPAGE	Eddy Grant (Ice)
12	29	PEARLS II	Elkie Brooks (A&M)
22	30	GREATEST LOVE SONGS	Nat 'King' Cole (Capitol)

12 March 1983

1	1	THRILLER	Michael Jackson (Epic)
4	2	QUICK STEP AND SIDE KICK	Thompson Twins (Arista)
7	3	TOTO IV	Toto (CBS)
1	4	BUSINESS AS USUAL	Men at Work (Epic)
26	5	SWEET DREAMS (ARE MADE OF THIS)	Eurythmics (RCA)
3	6	ANOTHER PAGE	Christopher Cross (Warner Bros.)
5	7	NIGHT AND DAY	Joe Jackson (A&M)
-	8	WAR	U2 (Island)
11	9	RICHARD CLAYDERMAN	Richard Clayderman (Decca/Delphine)
16	10	JANE FONDA'S WORKOUT RECORD	Jane Fonda (CBS)
18	11	THE BELLE STARS	Belle Stars (Stiff)
6	12	HEARTBREAKER	Dionne Warwick (Arista)
9	13	THE JOHN LENNON COLLECTION	John Lennon (Parlophone)
19	14	RIO	Duran Duran (EMI)
14	15	WAITING	Fun Boy Three (Chrysalis)
-	16	THUNDER AND LIGHTNING	Thin Lizzy (Vertigo)
8	17	PORCUPINE	Echo & the Bunnymen (Korova)
10	18	VISIONS	Various Artists (K-Tel)
12	19	HELLO, I MUST BE GOING!	Phil Collins (Virgin)
21	20	LIONEL RICHIE	Lionel Richie (Motown)
13	21	FRONTIERS	Journey (CBS)
28	22	KILLER ON THE RAMPAGE	Eddy Grant (Ice)
20	23	SHOW PEOPLE	Mari Wilson (Compact)
15	24	MONEY & CIGARETTES	Eric Clapton (Duck)
29	25	PEARLS II	Elkie Brooks (A&M)
-	26	HOTLINE	Various Artists (K-Tel)
-	27	PYROMANIA	Def Leppard (Vertigo)
17	28	WRECKIN' CREW	Meteors (Identity)
-	29	BATTLE HYMNS FOR CHILDREN SINGING	Haysi Fantayzee (Regard)
25	30	DIFFICULT SHAPES AND PASSIVE RHYTHMS	China Crisis (Virgin)

19 March 1983

1	1	THRILLER	Michael Jackson (Epic)
16	2	THUNDER AND LIGHTNING	Thin Lizzy (Vertigo)
8	3	WAR	U2 (Island)
5	4	SWEET DREAMS (ARE MADE OF THIS)	Eurythmics (RCA)
-	5	TRUE	Spandau Ballet (Reformation)
-	6	DAZZLE SHIPS	Orchestral Manoeuvres in the Dark (Telegraph)
26	7	HOTLINE	Various Artists (K-Tel)
3	8	TOTO IV	Toto (CBS)
-	9	THE KEY	Joan Armatrading (A&M)
4	10	BUSINESS AS USUAL	Men at Work (Epic)
2	11	QUICK STEP AND SIDE KICK	Thompson Twins (Arista)
18	12	VISIONS	Various Artists (K-Tel)
10	13	JANE FONDA'S WORKOUT RECORD	Jane Fonda (CBS)
15	14	WAITING	Fun Boy Three (Chrysalis)
6	15	ANOTHER PAGE	Christopher Cross (Warner Bros.)
27	16	PYROMANIA	Def Leppard (Vertigo)
-	17	THE HURTING	Tears for Fears (Mercury)
9	18	RICHARD CLAYDERMAN	Richard Clayderman (Decca/Delphine)
11	19	THE BELLE STARS	Belle Stars (Stiff)
19	20	HELLO, I MUST BE GOING!	Phil Collins (Virgin)
7	21	NIGHT AND DAY	Joe Jackson (A&M)
12	22	HEARTBREAKER	Dionne Warwick (Arista)
17	23	PORCUPINE	Echo & the Bunnymen (Korova)
13	24	THE JOHN LENNON COLLECTION	John Lennon (Parlophone)
23	25	SHOW PEOPLE	Mari Wilson (Compact)
-	26	COMPLETE MADNESS	Madness (Stiff)
-	27	DEEP SEA SKIVING	Bananarama (London)
21	28	FRONTIERS	Journey (CBS)
24	29	MONEY & CIGARETTES	Eric Clapton (Duck)
14	30	RIO	Duran Duran (EMI)

Given a boost by the extracted single *Billie Jean*, which hit Number 1 on March 5, Michael Jackson's *Thriller* album also finally topped the chart on the same day - the beginning of a very long stay at or near Number 1 which would eventually see the album as one of the UK's all-time Top 5 sellers (it would also be, globally, the best-selling album of all time, moving more than 40 million copies by 1985).

March – April 1983

The Eurythmics and Tears For Fears, both now major names on the singles chart, swung confidently into contention with their first successful albums. The Eurythmics snatched a week at Number 1 from *Thriller* with *Sweet Dreams*, but Tears For Fears' *The Hurting* was held at 2 by *The Final Cut*, the first new release since 1979's *The Wall* by Pink Floyd - who had supposedly already irrevocably broken up.

April 1983

last week	this week	23 April 1983	
4	1	THRILLER	Michael Jackson (Epic)
1	2	THE FINAL CUT	Pink Floyd (Harvest)
-	3	FASTER THAN THE SPEED OF NIGHT	Bonnie Tyler (CBS)
5	4	SWEET DREAMS (ARE MADE OF THIS)	Eurythmics (RCA)
2	5	THE HURTING	Tears for Fears (Mercury)
3	6	WAR	U2 (Island)
12	7	TRUE	Spandau Ballet (Reformation)
16	8	QUICK STEP AND SIDE KICK	Thompson Twins (Arista)
-	9	LET'S DANCE	David Bowie (EMI America)
5	10	RIO	Duran Duran (EMI)
11	11	SCRIPT FOR A JESTER'S TEAR	Marillion (EMI)
9	12	THE KEY	Joan Armatrading (A&M)
-	13	LOCAL HERO	Mark Knopfler (Vertigo)
7	14	TOTO IV	Toto (CBS)
10	15	CHARTRUNNERS	Various Artists (Ronco)
15	16	DEEP SEA SKIVING	Bananarama (London)
14	17	DAZZLE SHIPS	Orchestral Manoeuvres in the Dark (Telegraph)
21	18	INARTICULATE SPEECH OF THE HEART	Van Morrison (Mercury)
8	19	HELLO, I MUST BE GOING!	Phil Collins (Virgin)
17	20	BUSINESS AS USUAL	Men at Work (Epic)
30	21	THE KIDS FROM FAME LIVE	Kids From Fame (BBC)
27	22	NIGHT AND DAY	Joe Jackson (A&M)
29	23	KISSING TO BE CLEVER	Culture Club (Virgin)
-	24	HIGH LAND, HARD RAIN	Aztec Camera (Rough Trade)
-	25	HEADHUNTER	Krokus (Arista)
22	26	THE HIGH ROAD	Roxy Music (EG)
-	27	PRIDE	Robert Palmer (Island)
13	28	HAND CUT	Bucks Fizz (RCA)
-	29	A CHILD'S ADVENTURE	Marianne Faithful (Island)
26	30	RARE	David Bowie (RCA)
18	31	POWER AND THE GLORY	Saxon (Carrere)
28	32	LIONEL RICHIE	Lionel Richie (Motown)
-	33	WAITING	Fun Boy Three (Chrysalis)
20	34	SURPRISE, SURPRISE	Mezzoforte (Steinar)
-	35	LAZY WAYS	Marine Girls (Cherry Red)
19	36	THUNDER AND LIGHTNING	Thin Lizzy (Vertigo)
-	37	THE SIN OF PRIDE	Undertones (Ardeck)
-	38	ANOTHER PAGE	Christopher Cross (Warner Bros.)
-	39	WORKOUT	Jane Fonda (CBS)
24	40	HEARTBREAKER	Dionne Warwick (Arista)
25	41	MAGICAL RING	Clannad (RCA)
-	42	MONEY & CIGARETTES	Eric Clapton (Duck)
-	43	LIVING MY LIFE	Grace Jones (Island)
-	44	STREET SOUNDS EDITION 3	Various Artists (Street Sounds)
-	45	SHOW PEOPLE	Mari Wilson (Compact)
-	46	ELIMINATOR	ZZ Top (WEA)
-	47	BAT OUT OF HELL	Meatloaf (Epic)
-	48	JARREAU	Al Jarreau (WEA)
-	49	RIP IT UP	Orange Juice (Polydor)
-	50	JOURNEY THROUGH THE CLASSICS	Louis Clark and the Royal Philharmonic Orchestra (K-Tel)

last week	this week	30 April 1983	
9	1	LET'S DANCE	David Bowie (EMI America)
1	2	THRILLER	Michael Jackson (Epic)
3	3	FASTER THAN THE SPEED OF NIGHT	Bonnie Tyler (CBS)
2	4	THE FINAL CUT	Pink Floyd (Harvest)
4	5	SWEET DREAMS (ARE MADE OF THIS)	Eurythmics (RCA)
7	6	TRUE	Spandau Ballet (Reformation)
6	7	WAR	U2 (Island)
5	8	THE HURTING	Tears for Fears (Mercury)
8	9	QUICK STEP AND SIDE KICK	Thompson Twins (Arista)
13	10	LOCAL HERO	Mark Knopfler (Vertigo)
14	11	TOTO IV	Toto (CBS)
24	12	HIGH LAND, HARD RAIN	Aztec Camera (Rough Trade)
10	13	RIO	Duran Duran (EMI)
20	14	BUSINESS AS USUAL	Men at Work (Epic)
27	15	PRIDE	Robert Palmer (Island)
21	16	THE KIDS FROM FAME LIVE	Kids From Fame (BBC)
-	17	WHITE FEATHERS	Kajagoogoo (EMI)
11	18	SCRIPT FOR A JESTER'S TEAR	Marillion (EMI)
12	19	THE KEY	Joan Armatrading (A&M)
-	20	CARGO	Men At Work (Epic)
19	21	HELLO, I MUST BE GOING!	Phil Collins (Virgin)
23	22	KISSING TO BE CLEVER	Culture Club (Virgin)
-	23	GRAPES OF WRATH	Spear of Destiny (Epic)
15	24	CHARTRUNNERS	Various Artists (Ronco)
16	25	DEEP SEA SKIVING	Bananarama (London)
44	26	STREET SOUNDS EDITION 3	Various Artists (Street Sounds)
17	27	DAZZLE SHIPS	Orchestral Manoeuvres in the Dark (Telegraph)
18	28	INARTICULATE SPEECH OF THE HEART	Van Morrison (Mercury)
-	29	HIGHLY STRUNG	Steve Hackett (Charisma)
48	30	JARREAU	Al Jarreau (WEA)
50	31	JOURNEY THROUGH THE CLASSICS	Louis Clark and the Royal Philharmonic Orchestra (K-Tel)
22	32	NIGHT AND DAY	Joe Jackson (A&M)
32	33	LIONEL RICHIE	Lionel Richie (Motown)
31	34	POWER AND THE GLORY	Saxon (Carrere)
-	35	FASTWAY	Fastway (CBS)
46	36	ELIMINATOR	ZZ Top (WEA)
-	37	SUBTERRANEAN JUNGLE	Ramones (Sire)
49	38	RIP IT UP	Orange Juice (Polydor)
42	39	MONEY & CIGARETTES	Eric Clapton (Duck)
-	40	THE PERFECT BEAT	Various Artists (Polydor)
33	41	WAITING	Fun Boy Three (Chrysalis)
-	42	THE RISE AND FALL OF ZIGGY STARDUST AND THE SPIDERS FROM MARS	David Bowie (RCA)
-	43	YELLOW MOON	Don Williams (MCA)
-	44	PRIMITIVE MAN	Icehouse (Chrysalis)
34	45	SURPRISE, SURPRISE	Mezzoforte (Steinar)
25	46	HEADHUNTER	Krokus (Arista)
26	47	THE HIGH ROAD	Roxy Music (EG)
28	48	HAND CUT	Bucks Fizz (RCA)
-	49	TRICK OF THE LIGHT	Modern Romance (WEA)
-	50	PORCUPINE	Echo & the Bunnymen (Korova)

last week	this week	7 May 1983	
1	1	LET'S DANCE	David Bowie (EMI America)
2	2	THRILLER	Michael Jackson (Epic)
20	3	CARGO	Men At Work (Epic)
6	4	TRUE	Spandau Ballet (Reformation)
5	5	SWEET DREAMS (ARE MADE OF THIS)	Eurythmics (RCA)
3	6	FASTER THAN THE SPEED OF NIGHT	Bonnie Tyler (CBS)
4	7	THE FINAL CUT	Pink Floyd (Harvest)
17	8	WHITE FEATHERS	Kajagoogoo (EMI)
9	9	QUICK STEP AND SIDE KICK	Thompson Twins (Arista)
-	10	THE LUXURY GAP	Heaven 17 (Virgin)
-	11	MIDNIGHT AT THE LOST AND FOUND	Meatloaf (Epic)
11	12	TOTO IV	Toto (CBS)
7	13	WAR	U2 (Island)
8	14	THE HURTING	Tears for Fears (Mercury)
12	15	HIGH LAND, HARD RAIN	Aztec Camera (Rough Trade)
29	16	HIGHLY STRUNG	Steve Hackett (Charisma)
13	17	RIO	Duran Duran (EMI)
10	18	LOCAL HERO	Mark Knopfler (Vertigo)
19	19	THE KEY	Joan Armatrading (A&M)
-	20	YOU CAN'T STOP ROCK 'N' ROLL	Twisted Sister (Atlantic)
15	21	PRIDE	Robert Palmer (Island)
-	22	LISTEN	Flock of Seagulls (Jive)
18	23	SCRIPT FOR A JESTER'S TEAR	Marillion (EMI)
30	24	JARREAU	Al Jarreau (WEA)
22	25	KISSING TO BE CLEVER	Culture Club (Virgin)
23	26	GRAPES OF WRATH	Spear of Destiny (Epic)
16	27	THE KIDS FROM FAME LIVE	Kids From Fame (BBC)
36	28	ELIMINATOR	ZZ Top (WEA)
35	29	FASTWAY	Fastway (CBS)
37	30	SUBTERRANEAN JUNGLE	Ramones (Sire)
21	31	HELLO, I MUST BE GOING!	Phil Collins (Virgin)
24	32	CHARTRUNNERS	Various Artists (Ronco)
26	33	STREET SOUNDS EDITION 3	Various Artists (Street Sounds)
-	34	STONEKILLERS	Prince Charles & the City Band (Virgin)
14	35	BUSINESS AS USUAL	Men at Work (Epic)
34	36	POWER AND THE GLORY	Saxon (Carrere)
-	37	LIVING MY LIFE	Grace Jones (Island)
33	38	LIONEL RICHIE	Lionel Richie (Motown)
27	39	DAZZLE SHIPS	Orchestral Manoeuvres in the Dark (Telegraph)
-	40	TWICE AS KOOL	Kool & the Gang (De-Lite)
-	41	STEVE MILLER BAND LIVE!	Steve Miller Band (Mercury)
31	42	JOURNEY THROUGH THE CLASSICS	Louis Clark and the Royal Philharmonic Orchestra (K-Tel)
45	43	SURPRISE, SURPRISE	Mezzoforte (Steinar)
42	44	THE RISE AND FALL OF ZIGGY STARDUST AND THE SPIDERS FROM MARS	David Bowie (RCA)
-	45	JAILHOUSE ROCK	Elvis Presley (RCA)
40	46	THE PERFECT BEAT	Various Artists (Polydor)
-	47	PHIL EVERLY	Phil Everly (Capitol)
-	48	MAMA AFRICA	Peter Tosh (EMI)
-	49	THE MAN WHO SOLD THE WORLD	David Bowie (RCA)
39	50	MONEY & CIGARETTES	Eric Clapton (Duck)

After its longest-ever period of stable length, the NME Top 30 album chart finally expanded to a Top 50, in reflection of the growth of album sales against those of singles during the 1980s. Michael Jackson returned to the top of the first expanded chart, but was then immediately dislodged by David Bowie's comeback album under his new deal with EMI. Its title track had already been a Number 1 single.

May 1983

14 May 1983

Last	This	Title	Artist (Label)
1	1	LET'S DANCE	David Bowie (EMI America)
2	2	THRILLER	Michael Jackson (Epic)
4	3	TRUE	Spandau Ballet (Reformation)
11	4	MIDNIGHT AT THE LOST AND FOUND	Meatloaf (Epic)
10	5	THE LUXURY GAP	Heaven 17 (Virgin)
6	6	FASTER THAN THE SPEED OF NIGHT	Bonnie Tyler (CBS)
3	7	CARGO	Men At Work (Epic)
5	8	SWEET DREAMS (ARE MADE OF THIS)	Eurythmics (RCA)
9	9	QUICK STEP AND SIDE KICK	Thompson Twins (Arista)
7	10	THE FINAL CUT	Pink Floyd (Harvest)
8	11	WHITE FEATHERS	Kajagoogoo (EMI)
14	12	THE HURTING	Tears for Fears (Mercury)
22	13	LISTEN	Flock of Seagulls (Jive)
12	14	TOTO IV	Toto (CBS)
-	15	POWER, CORRUPTION AND LIES	New Order (Factory)
20	16	YOU CAN'T STOP ROCK 'N' ROLL	Twisted Sister (Atlantic)
-	17	SONGS	Kids from Fame (BBC)
17	18	RIO	Duran Duran (EMI)
15	19	HIGH LAND, HARD RAIN	Aztec Camera (Rough Trade)
13	20	WAR	U2 (Island)
19	21	THE KEY	Joan Armatrading (A&M)
21	22	PRIDE	Robert Palmer (Island)
40	23	TWICE AS KOOL	Kool & the Gang (De-Lite)
28	24	ELIMINATOR	ZZ Top (WEA)
18	25	LOCAL HERO	Mark Knopfler (Vertigo)
32	26	CHARTRUNNERS	Various Artists (Ronco)
16	27	HIGHLY STRUNG	Steve Hackett (Charisma)
23	28	SCRIPT FOR A JESTER'S TEAR	Marillion (EMI)
34	29	STONEKILLERS	Prince Charles and the City Band (Virgin)
38	30	LIONEL RICHIE	Lionel Richie (Motown)
-	31	WE ARE ONE	Maze (Capitol)
27	32	THE KIDS FROM FAME LIVE	Kids From Fame (BBC)
31	33	HELLO, I MUST BE GOING!	Phil Collins (Virgin)
25	34	KISSING TO BE CLEVER	Culture Club (Virgin)
-	35	MAGICAL RING	Clannad (RCA)
30	36	SUBTERRANEAN JUNGLE	Ramones (Sire)
33	37	STREET SOUNDS EDITION 3	Various Art (Street Sounds)
-	38	CHIMERA	Bill Nelson (Mercury)
26	39	GRAPES OF WRATH	Spear of Destiny (Epic)
39	40	DAZZLE SHIPS	Orchestral Manoeuvres in Dark (Telegraph)
24	41	JARREAU	Al Jarreau (WEA)
41	42	STEVE MILLER BAND LIVE!	Steve Miller Ban (Mercury)
-	43	NIGHT DUBBING	Imagination (R&B)
44	44	WAITING	Fun Boy Three (Chrysalis)
35	45	BUSINESS AS USUAL	Men at Work (Epic)
50	46	MONEY & CIGARETTES	Eric Clapton (Duck)
-	47	THE HEIGHT OF BAD MANNERS	Bad Manners (Telstar)
29	48	FASTWAY	Fastway (CBS)
36	49	POWER AND THE GLORY	Saxon (Carrere)
37	50	LIVING MY LIFE	Grace Jones (Island)

21 May 1983

Last	This	Title	Artist (Label)
3	1	TRUE	Spandau Ballet (Reformation)
1	2	LET'S DANCE	David Bowie (EMI America)
5	3	THE LUXURY GAP	Heaven 17 (Virgin)
2	4	THRILLER	Michael Jackson (Epic)
15	5	POWER, CORRUPTION AND LIES	New Order (Factory)
12	6	THE HURTING	Tears for Fears (Mercury)
7	7	CARGO	Men At Work (Epic)
4	8	MIDNIGHT AT THE LOST AND FOUND	Meatloaf (Epic)
8	9	SWEET DREAMS (ARE MADE OF THIS)	Eurythmics (RCA)
6	10	FASTER THAN THE SPEED OF NIGHT	Bonnie Tyler (CBS)
10	11	THE FINAL CUT	Pink Floyd (Harvest)
9	12	QUICK STEP AND SIDE KICK	Thompson Twins (Arista)
38	13	CHIMERA	Bill Nelson (Mercury)
13	14	LISTEN	Flock of Seagulls (Jive)
11	15	WHITE FEATHERS	Kajagoogoo (EMI)
43	16	NIGHT DUBBING	Imagination (R&B)
17	17	SONGS	Kids from Fame (BBC)
23	18	TWICE AS KOOL	Kool & the Gang (De-Lite)
16	19	YOU CAN'T STOP ROCK 'N' ROLL	Twisted Sister (Atlantic)
14	20	TOTO IV	Toto (CBS)
-	21	DRESSED FOR THE OCCASION	Cliff Richard (EMI)
44	22	WAITING	Fun Boy Three (Chrysalis)
18	23	RIO	Duran Duran (EMI)
25	24	LOCAL HERO	Mark Knopfler (Vertigo)
19	25	HIGH LAND, HARD RAIN	Aztec Camera (Rough Trade)
20	26	WAR	U2 (Island)
31	27	WE ARE ONE	Maze (Capitol)
35	28	MAGICAL RING	Clannad (RCA)
-	29	SIAGO	Blackfoot (Atco)
24	30	ELIMINATOR	ZZ Top (WEA)
-	31	HAPPY FAMILIES	Blancmange (London)
47	32	THE HEIGHT OF BAD MANNERS	Bad Manners (Telstar)
-	33	THE LAUGHTER AND TEARS COLLECTION	Various Artists (WEA)
22	34	PRIDE	Robert Palmer (Island)
33	35	HELLO, I MUST BE GOING!	Phil Collins (Virgin)
41	36	JARREAU	Al Jarreau (WEA)
-	37	H2 O	Daryl Hall & John Oates (RCA)
27	38	HIGHLY STRUNG	Steve Hackett (Charisma)
21	39	THE KEY	Joan Armatrading (A&M)
30	40	LIONEL RICHIE	Lionel Richie (Motown)
-	41	THE RISE AND FALL OF ZIGGY STARDUST AND THE SPIDERS FROM MARS	David Bowie (RCA)
28	42	SCRIPT FOR A JESTER'S TEAR	Marillion (EMI)
-	43	TOO-RYE-AY	Dexy's Midnight Runners (Mercury)
42	44	STEVE MILLER BAND LIVE!	Steve Miller Band (Mercury)
-	45	THE FORMER 12 YEAR-OLD GENIUS	Coati Mundi (Virgin)
45	46	BUSINESS AS USUAL	Men at Work (Epic)
34	47	KISSING TO BE CLEVER	Culture Club (Virgin)
37	48	STREET SOUNDS EDITION 3	Various Artists (Street Sounds)
-	49	WORDS	F R David (Carrere)
29	50	STONEKILLERS	Prince Charles and the City Band (Virgin)

28 May 1983

Last	This	Title	Artist (Label)
3	1	THE LUXURY GAP	Heaven 17 (Virgin)
1	2	TRUE	Spandau Ballet (Reformation)
4	3	THRILLER	Michael Jackson (Epic)
2	4	LET'S DANCE	David Bowie (EMI America)
5	5	POWER, CORRUPTION AND LIES	New Or (Factory)
7	6	CARGO	Men At Work (Epic)
6	7	THE HURTING	Tears for Fears (Mercury)
8	8	MIDNIGHT AT THE LOST AND FOUND	Meatloaf (Epic)
16	9	NIGHT DUBBING	Imagination (R&B)
21	10	DRESSED FOR THE OCCASION	Cliff Richard (EMI)
10	11	FASTER THAN THE SPEED OF NIGHT	Bonnie Tyler (CBS)
12	12	QUICK STEP AND SIDE KICK	Thompson Twins (Arista)
9	13	SWEET DREAMS (ARE MADE OF THIS)	Eurythmics (RCA)
-	14	PIECE OF MIND	Iron Maiden (EMI)
-	15	FEAST	Creatures (Polydor)
18	16	TWICE AS KOOL	Kool & the Gang (De-Lite)
-	17	CONFRONTATION	Bob Marley & the Wailers (Island)
11	18	THE FINAL CUT	Pink Floyd (Harvest)
-	19	WHAMMY!	B52s (Island)
20	20	TOTO IV	Toto (CBS)
13	21	CHIMERA	Bill Nelson (Mercury)
-	22	CHART ENCOUNTERS OF THE HIT KIND	Various Artists (Ronco)
29	23	SIAGO	Blackfoot (Atco)
17	24	SONGS	Kids from Fame (BBC)
15	25	WHITE FEATHERS	Kajagoogoo (EMI)
22	26	WAITING	Fun Boy Three (Chrysalis)
37	27	H2 O	Daryl Hall & John Oates (RCA)
19	28	YOU CAN'T STOP ROCK 'N' ROLL	Twisted Sister (Atlantic)
27	29	WE ARE ONE	Maze (Capitol)
14	30	LISTEN	Flock of Seagulls (Jive)
-	31	THE ELEVENTH HOUR	Magnum (Jet)
25	32	HIGH LAND, HARD RAIN	Aztec Camera (Rough Trade)
40	33	LIONEL RICHIE	Lionel Richie (Motown)
23	34	RIO	Duran Duran (EMI)
26	35	WAR	U2 (Island)
-	36	THE COLLECTION	Dionne Warwick (Arista)
-	37	RING OF CHANGES	Barclay James Ha (Polydor)
41	38	THE RISE AND FALL OF ZIGGY STARDUST AND THE SPIDERS FROM MARS	David Bowie (RCA)
35	39	HELLO, I MUST BE GOING!	Phil Collins (Virgin)
36	40	JARREAU	Al Jarreau (WEA)
34	41	PRIDE	Robert Palmer (Island)
-	42	A TRICK OF THE LIGHT	Modern Romance (WEA)
30	43	ELIMINATOR	ZZ Top (WEA)
33	44	THE LAUGHTER AND TEARS COLLECTION	Various Artists (WEA)
24	45	LOCAL HERO	Mark Knopfler (Vertigo)
-	46	LIVING MY LIFE	Grace Jones (Island)
32	47	THE HEIGHT OF BAD MANNERS	Bad Manners (Telstar)
42	48	SCRIPT FOR A JESTER'S TEAR	Marillion (EMI)
-	49	REACH THE BEACH	Fixx (MCA)
46	50	BUSINESS AS USUAL	Men at Work (Epic)

Spandau Ballet had the country's best-selling single and album on May 21 with the same title, *True*. Meatloaf this time failed to reach the Top 3, though Heaven 17, boosted by their Number 2 single *Temptation*, also scored a (one-week) chart-topper. Meanwhile, the appeal of the Kids From Fame had noticeably cooled, as their new album *Songs* stuck at its debut peak of Number 17 before sinking away.

4 June 1983

last week	this week	title	artist (label)
3	1	THRILLER	Michael Jackson (Epic)
2	2	TRUE	Spandau Ballet (Reformation)
17	3	CONFRONTATION	Bob Marley & the Wailers (Island)
1	4	THE LUXURY GAP	Heaven 17 (Virgin)
14	5	PIECE OF MIND	Iron Maiden (EMI)
4	6	LET'S DANCE	David Bowie (EMI America)
5	7	POWER, CORRUPTION AND LIES	New Order (Factory)
15	8	FEAST	Creatures (Polydor)
16	9	TWICE AS KOOL	Kool & the Gang (De-Lite)
10	10	DRESSED FOR THE OCCASION	Cliff Richard (EMI)
7	11	THE HURTING	Tears for Fears (Mercury)
9	12	NIGHT DUBBING	Imagination (R&B)
6	13	CARGO	Men At Work (Epic)
12	14	QUICK STEP AND SIDE KICK	Thompson Twins (Arista)
8	15	MIDNIGHT AT THE LOST AND FOUND	Meatloaf (Epic)
11	16	FASTER THAN THE SPEED OF NIGHT	Bonnie Tyler (CBS)
22	17	CHART ENCOUNTERS OF THE HIT KIND	Various Artists (Ronco)
19	18	WHAMMY!	B52s (Island)
13	19	SWEET DREAMS (ARE MADE OF THIS)	Eurythmics (RCA)
20	20	TOTO IV	Toto (CBS)
-	21	DUCK ROCK	Malcolm McLaren (Charisma)
37	22	RING OF CHANGES	Barclay James Harvest (Polydor)
18	23	THE FINAL CUT	Pink Floyd (Harvest)
24	24	SONGS	Kids from Fame (BBC)
25	25	WHITE FEATHERS	Kajagoogoo (EMI)
-	26	CRISES	Mike Oldfield (Virgin)
36	27	THE COLLECTION	Dionne Warwick (Arista)
-	28	ANOTHER PERFECT DAY	Motorhead (Bronze)
21	29	CHIMERA	Bill Nelson (Mercury)
27	30	H2 O	Daryl Hall & John Oates (RCA)
23	31	SIAGO	Blackfoot (Atco)
32	32	HIGH LAND, HARD RAIN	Aztec Camera (Rough Trade)
40	33	JARREAU	Al Jarreau (WEA)
26	34	WAITING	Fun Boy Three (Chrysalis)
30	35	LISTEN	Flock of Seagulls (Jive)
28	36	YOU CAN'T STOP ROCK 'N' ROLL	Twisted Sister (Atlantic)
41	37	PRIDE	Robert Palmer (Island)
44	38	THE LAUGHTER AND TEARS COLLECTION	Various Artists (WEA)
-	39	OUTSIDE INSIDE	Tubes (Capitol)
-	40	NAKED	Kissing the Pink (Magnet)
29	41	WE ARE ONE	Maze (Capitol)
31	42	THE ELEVENTH HOUR	Magnum (Jet)
39	43	HELLO, I MUST BE GOING!	Phil Collins (Virgin)
-	44	HUNKY DORY	David Bowie (RCA)
38	45	THE RISE AND FALL OF ZIGGY STARDUST AND THE SPIDERS FROM MARS	David Bowie (RCA)
34	46	RIO	Duran Duran (EMI)
48	47	SCRIPT FOR A JESTER'S TEAR	Marillion (EMI)
35	48	WAR	U2 (Island)
45	49	LOCAL HERO	Mark Knopfler (Vertigo)
33	50	LIONEL RICHIE	Lionel Richie (Motown)

11 June 1983

last week	this week	title	artist (label)
1	1	THRILLER	Michael Jackson (Epic)
6	2	LET'S DANCE	David Bowie (EMI America)
2	3	TRUE	Spandau Ballet (Reformation)
3	4	CONFRONTATION	Bob Marley & the Wailers (Island)
5	5	PIECE OF MIND	Iron Maiden (EMI)
4	6	THE LUXURY GAP	Heaven 17 (Virgin)
7	7	POWER, CORRUPTION AND LIES	New Order (Factory)
8	8	FEAST	Creatures (Polydor)
26	9	CRISES	Mike Oldfield (Virgin)
9	10	TWICE AS KOOL	Kool & the Gang (De-Lite)
21	11	DUCK ROCK	Malcolm McLaren (Charisma)
12	12	NIGHT DUBBING	Imagination (R&B)
13	13	CARGO	Men At Work (Epic)
11	14	THE HURTING	Tears for Fears (Mercury)
10	15	DRESSED FOR THE OCCASION	Cliff Richard (EMI)
28	16	ANOTHER PERFECT DAY	Motorhead (Bronze)
15	17	MIDNIGHT AT THE LOST AND FOUND	Meatloaf (Epic)
14	18	QUICK STEP AND SIDE KICK	Thompson Twins (Arista)
20	19	TOTO IV	Toto (CBS)
17	20	CHART ENCOUNTERS OF THE HIT KIND	Various Artists (Ronco)
-	21	TOO LATE FOR ZERO	Elton John (Rocket)
19	22	SWEET DREAMS (ARE MADE OF THIS)	Eurythmics (RCA)
16	23	FASTER THAN THE SPEED OF NIGHT	Bonnie Tyler (CBS)
-	24	IN YOUR EYES	George Benson (WEA)
-	25	WHAT IS BEAT? (THE BEST OF THE BEAT)	Beat (Go Feet)
22	26	RING OF CHANGES	Barclay James Harvest (Polydor)
18	27	WHAMMY!	B52s (Island)
27	28	THE COLLECTION	Dionne Warwick (Arista)
25	29	WHITE FEATHERS	Kajagoogoo (EMI)
23	30	THE FINAL CUT	Pink Floyd (Harvest)
-	31	HOLY DIVER	Dio (Vertigo)
34	32	WAITING	Fun Boy Three (Chrysalis)
24	33	SONGS	Kids from Fame (BBC)
43	34	HELLO, I MUST BE GOING!	Phil Collins (Virgin)
40	35	NAKED	Kissing the Pink (Magnet)
-	36	TUBULAR BELLS	Mike Oldfield (Virgin)
33	37	JARREAU	Al Jarreau (WEA)
32	38	HIGH LAND, HARD RAIN	Aztec Camera (Rough Trade)
30	39	H2 O	Daryl Hall & John Oates (RCA)
39	40	OUTSIDE INSIDE	Tubes (Capitol)
-	41	WRAP YOUR ARMS AROUND ME	Agnetha Faltskog (Epic)
-	42	YES SIR I WILL	Crass (Crass)
44	43	HUNKY DORY	David Bowie (RCA)
37	44	PRIDE	Robert Palmer (Island)
45	45	THE RISE AND FALL OF ZIGGY STARDUST AND THE SPIDERS FROM MARS	David Bowie (RCA)
31	46	SIAGO	Blackfoot (Atco)
29	47	CHIMERA	Bill Nelson (Mercury)
41	48	WE ARE ONE	Maze (Capitol)
38	49	THE LAUGHTER AND TEARS COLLECTION	Various Artists (WEA)
-	50	MARY JANE GIRLS	Mary Jane Girls (Gordy)

18 June 1983

last week	this week	title	artist (label)
2	1	LET'S DANCE	David Bowie (EMI America)
1	2	THRILLER	Michael Jackson (Epic)
3	3	TRUE	Spandau Ballet (Reformation)
4	4	CONFRONTATION	Bob Marley & the Wailers (Island)
9	5	CRISES	Mike Oldfield (Virgin)
21	6	TOO LATE FOR ZERO	Elton John (Rocket)
10	7	TWICE AS KOOL	Kool & the Gang (De-Lite)
6	8	THE LUXURY GAP	Heaven 17 (Virgin)
24	9	IN YOUR EYES	George Benson (WEA)
25	10	WHAT IS BEAT? (THE BEST OF THE BEAT)	Beat (Go Feet)
5	11	PIECE OF MIND	Iron Maiden (EMI)
31	12	HOLY DIVER	Dio (Vertigo)
14	13	THE HURTING	Tears for Fears (Mercury)
-	14	PETER GABRIEL PLAYS LIVE	Peter Gabriel (Charisma)
11	15	DUCK ROCK	Malcolm McLaren (Charisma)
20	16	CHART ENCOUNTERS OF THE HIT KIND	Various Artists (Ronco)
28	17	THE COLLECTION	Dionne Warwick (Arista)
13	18	CARGO	Men At Work (Epic)
-	19	SPEAKING IN TONGUES	Talking Heads (Sire)
29	20	WHITE FEATHERS	Kajagoogoo (EMI)
12	21	NIGHT DUBBING	Imagination (R&B)
7	22	POWER, CORRUPTION AND LIES	New Order (Factory)
-	23	BODY WISHES	Rod Stewart (Warner Bros.)
8	24	FEAST	Creatures (Wonderland)
-	25	OIL ON CANVAS	Japan (Virgin)
16	26	ANOTHER PERFECT DAY	Motorhead (Bronze)
41	27	WRAP YOUR ARMS AROUND ME	Agnetha Faltskog (Epic)
17	28	MIDNIGHT AT THE LOST AND FOUND	Meatloaf (Epic)
22	29	SWEET DREAMS (ARE MADE OF THIS)	Eurythmics (RCA)
27	30	WHAMMY!	B52s (Island)
15	31	DRESSED FOR THE OCCASION	Cliff Richard (EMI)
19	32	TOTO IV	Toto (CBS)
18	33	QUICK STEP AND SIDE KICK	Thompson Twins (Arista)
36	34	TUBULAR BELLS	Mike Oldfield (Virgin)
23	35	FASTER THAN THE SPEED OF NIGHT	Bonnie Tyler (CBS)
-	36	SOUTHERN DEATH CULT	Southern Death Cult (Beggars Banquet)
35	37	NAKED	Kissing the Pink (Magnet)
37	38	JARREAU	Al Jarreau (WEA)
30	39	THE FINAL CUT	Pink Floyd (Harvest)
-	40	WATER SIGN	Chris Rea (Magnet)
39	41	H2 O	Daryl Hall & John Oates (RCA)
-	42	SAMURAI	Grand Prix (Chrysalis)
42	43	YES SIR I WILL	Crass (Crass)
43	44	HUNKY DORY	David Bowie (RCA)
50	45	MARY JANE GIRLS	Mary Jane Girls (Gordy)
-	46	HEAD FIRST	Uriah Heep (Bronze)
33	47	SONGS	Kids from Fame (BBC)
26	48	RING OF CHANGES	Barclay James Harvest (Polydor)
45	49	THE RISE AND FALL OF ZIGGY STARDUST AND THE SPIDERS FROM MARS	David Bowie (RCA)
32	50	WAITING	Fun Boy Three (Chrysalis)

A posthumous set of previous unheard Bob Marley recordings, *Confrontation*, was the major challenge to the ongoing Jackson/Bowie/Spandau stranglehold at the chart-top. *Duck Rock*, the first album by former Sex Pistols manager Malcolm McLaren, now a maverick music-maker in his own right, raised a few eyebrows when it climbed to Number 11. Mike Oldfield's *Tubular Bells* followed his new album in!

June – July 1983

last / this week

25 June 1983

Last	This	Title	Artist
1	1	LET'S DANCE	David Bowie (EMI America)
2	2	THRILLER	Michael Jackson (Epic)
25	3	OIL ON CANVAS	Japan (Virgin)
6	4	TOO LATE FOR ZERO	Elton John (Rocket)
23	5	BODY WISHES	Rod Stewart (Warner Bros.)
9	6	IN YOUR EYES	George Benson (WEA)
5	7	CRISES	Mike Oldfield (Virgin)
14	8	PETER GABRIEL PLAYS LIVE	Peter Gabriel (Charisma)
4	9	CONFRONTATION	Bob Marley & the Wailers (Island)
7	10	TWICE AS KOOL	Kool & the Gang (De-Lite)
10	11	WHAT IS BEAT? (THE BEST OF THE BEAT)	Beat (Go Feet)
3	12	TRUE	Spandau Ballet (Reformation)
19	13	SPEAKING IN TONGUES	Talking Heads (Sire)
-	14	SYNCHRONICITY	Police (A&M)
8	15	THE LUXURY GAP	Heaven 17 (Virgin)
36	16	SOUTHERN DEATH CULT	Southern Death Cult (Beggars Banquet)
12	17	HOLY DIVER	Dio (Vertigo)
11	18	PIECE OF MIND	Iron Maiden (EMI)
13	19	THE HURTING	Tears for Fears (Mercury)
22	20	POWER, CORRUPTION AND LIES	New Order (Factory)
16	21	CHART ENCOUNTERS OF THE HIT KIND	Various Artists (Ronco)
-	22	CHART STARS	Various Artists (K-Tel)
17	23	THE COLLECTION	Dionne Warwick (Arista)
27	24	WRAP YOUR ARMS AROUND ME	Agnetha Faltskog (Epic)
18	25	CARGO	Men At Work (Epic)
15	26	DUCK ROCK	Malcolm McLaren (Charisma)
20	27	WHITE FEATHERS	Kajagoogoo (EMI)
46	28	HEAD FIRST	Uriah Heep (Bronze)
35	29	FASTER THAN THE SPEED OF NIGHT	Bonnie Tyler (CBS)
29	30	SWEET DREAMS (ARE MADE OF THIS)	Eurythmics (RCA)
33	31	QUICK STEP AND SIDE KICK	Thompson Twins (Arista)
-	32	BITE	Altered Images (Epic)
30	33	WHAMMY!	B52s (Island)
42	34	SAMURAI	Grand Prix (Chrysalis)
21	35	NIGHT DUBBING	Imagination (R&B)
-	36	OFF THE BONE	Cramps (Illegal)
28	37	MIDNIGHT AT THE LOST AND FOUND	Meatloaf (Epic)
34	38	TUBULAR BELLS	Mike Oldfield (Virgin)
26	39	ANOTHER PERFECT DAY	Motorhead (Bronze)
-	40	STREET SOUNDS EDITION 4	Various Artists (Street Sounds)
-	41	THE FUGITIVE	Tony Banks (Charisma)
24	42	FEAST	Creatures (Wonderland)
37	43	NAKED	Kissing the Pink (Magnet)
-	44	SYNCHRO SYSTEM	King Sunny Ade (Island)
31	45	DRESSED FOR THE OCCASION	Cliff Richard (EMI)
-	46	ELIMINATOR	ZZ Top (WEA)
44	47	HUNKY DORY	David Bowie (RCA)
40	48	WATER SIGN	Chris Rea (Magnet)
47	49	SONGS	Kids from Fame (BBC)
32	50	TOTO IV	Toto (CBS)

2 July 1983

Last	This	Title	Artist
14	1	SYNCHRONICITY	Police (A&M)
2	2	THRILLER	Michael Jackson (Epic)
1	3	LET'S DANCE	David Bowie (EMI America)
5	4	BODY WISHES	Rod Stewart (Warner Bros.)
6	5	IN YOUR EYES	George Benson (WEA)
4	6	TOO LATE FOR ZERO	Elton John (Rocket)
3	7	OIL ON CANVAS	Japan (Virgin)
7	8	CRISES	Mike Oldfield (Virgin)
10	9	TWICE AS KOOL	Kool & the Gang (De-Lite)
32	10	BITE	Altered Images (Epic)
12	11	TRUE	Spandau Ballet (Reformation)
13	12	SPEAKING IN TONGUES	Talking Heads (Sire)
8	13	PETER GABRIEL PLAYS LIVE	Peter Gabriel (Charisma)
11	14	WHAT IS BEAT? (THE BEST OF THE BEAT)	Beat (Go Feet)
9	15	CONFRONTATION	Bob Marley & Wailers (Island)
15	16	THE LUXURY GAP	Heaven 17 (Virgin)
22	17	CHART STARS	Various Artists (K-Tel)
-	18	SECRET MESSAGES	Electric Light Orchestra (Jet)
18	19	PIECE OF MIND	Iron Maiden (EMI)
40	20	STREET SOUNDS EDITION 4	Various Artists (Street Sounds)
23	21	THE COLLECTION	Dionne Warwick (Arista)
26	22	DUCK ROCK	Malcolm McLaren (Charisma)
36	23	OFF THE BONE	Cramps (Illegal)
17	24	HOLY DIVER	Dio (Vertigo)
16	25	SOUTHERN DEATH CULT	Southern Death Cult (Beggars Banquet)
25	26	CARGO	Men At Work (Epic)
20	27	POWER, CORRUPTION AND LIES	New Order (Factory)
24	28	WRAP YOUR ARMS AROUND ME	Agnetha Faltskog (Epic)
27	29	WHITE FEATHERS	Kajagoogoo (EMI)
19	30	THE HURTING	Tears for Fears (Mercury)
-	31	THE WILD HEART	Stevie Nicks (WEA)
-	32	THE PRIVATE COLLECTION	Jon & Vangelis (Polydor)
-	33	MARY JANE GIRLS	Mary Jane Girls (Gordy)
44	34	SYNCHRO SYSTEM	King Sunny Ade (Island)
29	35	FASTER THAN THE SPEED OF NIGHT	Bonnie Tyler (CBS)
38	36	TUBULAR BELLS	Mike Oldfield (Virgin)
-	37	HAND OF KINDNESS	Richard Thompson (Hannibal)
30	38	SWEET DREAMS (ARE MADE OF THIS)	Eurythmics (RCA)
39	39	ANOTHER PERFECT DAY	Motorhead (Bronze)
-	40	UPSTAIRS AT ERIC'S	Yazoo (Mute)
-	41	JARREAU	Al Jarreau (WEA International)
-	42	XL-1	Pete Shelley (Genetic)
31	43	QUICK STEP AND SIDE KICK	Thompson Twins (Arista)
50	44	TOTO IV	Toto (CBS)
35	45	NIGHT DUBBING	Imagination (R&B)
-	46	GIRL AT HER VOLCANO	Rickie Lee Jones (Warner Bros.)
-	47	H2O	Daryl Hall & John Oates (RCA)
21	48	CHART ENCOUNTERS OF THE HIT KIND	Various Artists (Ronco)
41	49	THE FUGITIVE	Tony Banks (Charisma)
28	50	HEAD FIRST	Uriah Heep (Bronze)

9 July 1983

Last	This	Title	Artist
1	1	SYNCHRONICITY	Police (A&M)
4	2	BODY WISHES	Rod Stewart (Warner Bros.)
2	3	THRILLER	Michael Jackson (Epic)
18	4	SECRET MESSAGES	Electric Light Orchestra (Jet)
3	5	LET'S DANCE	David Bowie (EMI America)
8	6	CRISES	Mike Oldfield (Virgin)
5	7	IN YOUR EYES	George Benson (WEA)
6	8	TOO LATE FOR ZERO	Elton John (Rocket)
7	9	OIL ON CANVAS	Japan (Virgin)
16	10	THE LUXURY GAP	Heaven 17 (Virgin)
11	11	TRUE	Spandau Ballet (Reformation)
9	12	TWICE AS KOOL	Kool & the Gang (De-Lite)
-	13	FANTASTIC	Wham! (Innervision)
10	14	BITE	Altered Images (Epic)
13	15	PETER GABRIEL PLAYS LIVE	Peter Gabriel (Charisma)
32	16	THE PRIVATE COLLECTION	Jon & Vangelis (Polydor)
14	17	WHAT IS BEAT? (THE BEST OF THE BEAT)	Beat (Go Feet)
12	18	SPEAKING IN TONGUES	Talking Heads (Sire)
-	19	FLASHDANCE	Soundtrack (Casablanca)
22	20	DUCK ROCK	Malcolm McLaren (Charisma)
31	21	THE WILD HEART	Stevie Nicks (WEA)
15	22	CONFRONTATION	Bob Marley & the Wailers (Island)
46	23	GIRL AT HER VOLCANO	Rickie Lee Jones (Warner Bros.)
17	24	CHART STARS	Various Artists (K-Tel)
20	25	STREET SOUNDS EDITION 4	Various Artists (Street Sounds)
-	26	JULIO	Julio Iglesias (CBS)
21	27	THE COLLECTION	Dionne Warwick (Arista)
24	28	HOLY DIVER	Dio (Vertigo)
42	29	XL-1	Pete Shelley (Genetic)
41	30	JARREAU	Al Jarreau (WEA International)
23	31	OFF THE BONE	Cramps (Illegal)
19	32	PIECE OF MIND	Iron Maiden (EMI)
34	33	SYNCHRO SYSTEM	King Sunny Ade (Island)
-	34	WAR	U2 (Island)
30	35	THE HURTING	Tears for Fears (Mercury)
27	36	POWER, CORRUPTION AND LIES	New Order (Factory)
28	37	WRAP YOUR ARMS AROUND ME	Agnetha Faltskog (Epic)
-	38	LOVERS ONLY	Various Artists (Ronco)
35	39	FASTER THAN THE SPEED OF NIGHT	Bonnie Tyler (CBS)
36	40	TUBULAR BELLS	Mike Oldfield (Virgin)
40	41	UPSTAIRS AT ERIC'S	Yazoo (Mute)
-	42	DANCE MIX	Various Artists (Epic)
-	43	RIO	Duran Duran (EMI)
38	44	SWEET DREAMS (ARE MADE OF THIS)	Eurythmics (RCA)
29	45	WHITE FEATHERS	Kajagoogoo (EMI)
33	46	MARY JANE GIRLS	Mary Jane Girls (Gordy)
49	47	THE FUGITIVE	Tony Banks (Charisma)
44	48	TOTO IV	Toto (CBS)
-	49	DON'T TAKE MY COCONUTS	Coconuts (EMI-America)
-	50	PAN-ORAMA	Flash and the Pan (Easy Beat)

It took the new Police album *Synchronicity* to convincingly break up the existing chart-top cartel (although Thriller was not finished with the Number 1 slot yet, as later months would reveal). The Police set topped the chart simultaneously with its extracted single, *Every Breath You Take* - though the latter was quite quickly deposed by Rod Stewart's *Baby Jane*, whereas Rod's *Body Wishes* album was held at 2.

16 July 1983

last week	this week	Title	Artist (Label)
13	1	FANTASTIC	Wham! (Innervision)
1	2	SYNCHRONICITY	Police (A&M)
5	3	LET'S DANCE	David Bowie (EMI America)
2	4	BODY WISHES	Rod Stewart (Warner Bros.)
6	5	CRISES	Mike Oldfield (Virgin)
4	6	SECRET MESSAGES	Electric Light Orchestra (Jet)
3	7	THRILLER	Michael Jackson (Epic)
7	8	IN YOUR EYES	George Benson (WEA)
10	9	THE LUXURY GAP	Heaven 17 (Virgin)
8	10	TOO LATE FOR ZERO	Elton John (Rocket)
19	11	FLASHDANCE	Soundtrack (Casablanca)
-	12	YOU AND ME BOTH	Yazoo (Mute)
9	13	OIL ON CANVAS	Japan (Virgin)
26	14	JULIO	Julio Iglesias (CBS)
20	15	DUCK ROCK	Malcolm McLaren (Charisma)
12	16	TWICE AS KOOL	Kool & the Gang (De-Lite)
18	17	SPEAKING IN TONGUES	Talking Heads (Sire)
21	18	THE WILD HEART	Stevie Nicks (WEA)
22	19	CONFRONTATION	Bob Marley & the Wailers (Island)
32	20	PIECE OF MIND	Iron Maiden (EMI)
16	21	THE PRIVATE COLLECTION	Jon & Vangelis (Polydor)
23	22	GIRL AT HER VOLCANO	Rickie Lee Jones (Warner Bros.)
11	23	TRUE	Spandau Ballet (Reformation)
14	24	BITE	Altered Images (Epic)
30	25	JARREAU	Al Jarreau (WEA International)
15	26	PETER GABRIEL PLAYS LIVE	Peter Gabriel (Charisma)
38	27	LOVERS ONLY	Various Artists (Ronco)
17	28	WHAT IS BEAT? (THE BEST OF THE BEAT)	Beat (Go Feet)
28	29	HOLY DIVER	Dio (Vertigo)
25	30	STREET SOUNDS EDITION 4	Various Artists (Street Sounds)
29	31	XL-1	Pete Shelley (Genetic)
34	32	WAR	U2 (Island)
24	33	CHART STARS	Various Artists (K-Tel)
33	34	SYNCHRO SYSTEM	King Sunny Ade (Island)
27	35	THE COLLECTION	Dionne Warwick (Arista)
-	36	MICHAEL JACKSON & THE JACKSONS' 18 GREATEST HITS	Michael Jackson & the Jacksons (Star)
-	37	IN THE GROOVE	Various Artists (Telstar)
43	38	RIO	Duran Duran (EMI)
35	39	THE HURTING	Tears for Fears (Mercury)
31	40	OFF THE BONE	Cramps (Illegal)
-	41	ROSS	Diana Ross (Capitol)
-	42	SHE WORKS HARD FOR THE MONEY	Donna Summer (Mercury)
-	43	CARGO	Men At Work (Epic)
44	44	SWEET DREAMS (ARE MADE OF THIS)	Eurythmics (RCA)
-	45	SCRIPT FOR A JESTER'S TEAR	Marillion (EMI)
-	46	QUICK STEP AND SIDE KICK	Thompson Twins (Arista)
-	47	I-LEVEL	I-Level (Virgin)
40	48	TUBULAR BELLS	Mike Oldfield (Virgin)
-	49	MAGICAL RING	Clannad (RCA)
36	50	POWER, CORRUPTION AND LIES	New Order (Factory)

23 July 1983

last week	this week	Title	Artist (Label)
1	1	FANTASTIC	Wham! (Innervision)
12	2	YOU AND ME BOTH	Yazoo (Mute)
7	3	THRILLER	Michael Jackson (Epic)
2	4	SYNCHRONICITY	Police (A&M)
4	5	BODY WISHES	Rod Stewart (Warner Bros.)
5	6	CRISES	Mike Oldfield (Virgin)
3	7	LET'S DANCE	David Bowie (EMI America)
9	8	THE LUXURY GAP	Heaven 17 (Virgin)
11	9	FLASHDANCE	Soundtrack (Casablanca)
6	10	SECRET MESSAGES	Electric Light Orchestra (Jet)
8	11	IN YOUR EYES	George Benson (WEA)
14	12	JULIO	Julio Iglesias (CBS)
15	13	DUCK ROCK	Malcolm McLaren (Charisma)
20	14	PIECE OF MIND	Iron Maiden (EMI)
10	15	TOO LATE FOR ZERO	Elton John (Rocket)
-	16	BURNING FROM THE INSIDE	Bauhaus (Beggars Banquet)
42	17	SHE WORKS HARD FOR THE MONEY	Donna Summer (Mercury)
13	18	OIL ON CANVAS	Japan (Virgin)
21	19	THE PRIVATE COLLECTION	Jon & Vangelis (Polydor)
23	20	TRUE	Spandau Ballet (Reformation)
16	21	TWICE AS KOOL	Kool & the Gang (De-Lite)
44	22	SWEET DREAMS (ARE MADE OF THIS)	Eurythmics (RCA)
17	23	SPEAKING IN TONGUES	Talking Heads (Sire)
-	24	FIRE DANCES	Killing Joke (EG)
19	25	CONFRONTATION	Bob Marley & Wailers (Island)
41	26	ROSS	Diana Ross (Capitol)
18	27	THE WILD HEART	Stevie Nicks (WEA)
50	28	POWER, CORRUPTION AND LIES	New Order (Factory)
22	29	GIRL AT HER VOLCANO	Rickie Lee Jones (Warner Bros.)
31	30	XL-1	Pete Shelley (Genetic)
24	31	BITE	Altered Images (Epic)
26	32	PETER GABRIEL PLAYS LIVE	Peter Gabriel (Charisma)
27	33	LOVERS ONLY	Various Artists (Ronco)
32	34	WAR	U2 (Island)
34	35	SYNCHRO SYSTEM	King Sunny Ade (Island)
40	36	OFF THE BONE	Cramps (Illegal)
-	37	MARY JANE GIRLS	Mary Jane Girls (Gordy)
25	38	JARREAU	Al Jarreau (WEA International)
39	39	THE HURTING	Tears for Fears (Mercury)
30	40	STREET SOUNDS EDITION 4	Various Artists (Street Sounds)
46	41	QUICK STEP AND SIDE KICK	Thompson Twins (Arista)
-	42	FASTER THAN THE SPEED OF NIGHT	Bonnie Tyler (CBS)
28	43	WHAT IS BEAT? (THE BEST OF THE BEAT)	Beat (Go Feet)
36	44	MICHAEL JACKSON & THE JACKSONS' 18 GREATEST HITS	Michael Jackson & the Jacksons (Star)
-	45	ELIMINATOR	ZZ Top (WEA)
29	46	HOLY DIVER	Dio (Vertigo)
33	47	CHART STARS	Various Artists (K-Tel)
35	48	THE COLLECTION	Dionne Warwick (Arista)
43	49	CARGO	Men At Work (Epic)
-	50	GET IT RIGHT	Aretha Franklin (Arista)

30 July 1983

last week	this week	Title	Artist (Label)
1	1	FANTASTIC	Wham! (Innervision)
2	2	YOU AND ME BOTH	Yazoo (Mute)
4	3	SYNCHRONICITY	Police (A&M)
3	4	THRILLER	Michael Jackson (Epic)
8	5	THE LUXURY GAP	Heaven 17 (Virgin)
6	6	CRISES	Mike Oldfield (Virgin)
16	7	BURNING FROM THE INSIDE	Bauhaus (Beggars Banquet)
-	8	PRINCIPLE OF MOMENTS	Robert Plant (WEA)
11	9	IN YOUR EYES	George Benson (WEA)
7	10	LET'S DANCE	David Bowie (EMI America)
5	11	BODY WISHES	Rod Stewart (Warner Bros.)
12	12	JULIO	Julio Iglesias (CBS)
9	13	FLASHDANCE	Soundtrack (Casablanca)
10	14	SECRET MESSAGES	Electric Light Orchestra (Jet)
15	15	TOO LATE FOR ZERO	Elton John (Rocket)
13	16	DUCK ROCK	Malcolm McLaren (Charisma)
-	17	THE LOOK	Shalamar (Solar)
-	18	NO PARLEZ	Paul Young (CBS)
24	19	FIRE DANCES	Killing Joke (EG)
22	20	SWEET DREAMS (ARE MADE OF THIS)	Eurythmics (RCA)
18	21	OIL ON CANVAS	Japan (Virgin)
23	22	SPEAKING IN TONGUES	Talking Heads (Sire)
34	23	WAR	U2 (Island)
20	24	TRUE	Spandau Ballet (Reformation)
14	25	PIECE OF MIND	Iron Maiden (EMI)
17	26	SHE WORKS HARD FOR THE MONEY	Donna Summer (Mercury)
25	27	CONFRONTATION	Bob Marley & the Wailers (Island)
29	28	GIRL AT HER VOLCANO	Rickie Lee Jones (Warner Bros.)
21	29	TWICE AS KOOL	Kool & the Gang (De-Lite)
27	30	THE WILD HEART	Stevie Nicks (WEA)
-	31	RIO	Duran Duran (EMI)
37	32	MARY JANE GIRLS	Mary Jane Girls (Gordy)
-	33	HITS ON FIRE	Various Artists (Ronco)
19	34	THE PRIVATE COLLECTION	Jon & Vangelis (Polydor)
26	35	ROSS	Diana Ross (Capitol)
49	36	CARGO	Men At Work (Epic)
39	37	THE HURTING	Tears for Fears (Mercury)
44	38	MICHAEL JACKSON & THE JACKSONS' 18 GREATEST HITS	Michael Jackson & the Jacksons (Star)
35	39	SYNCHRO SYSTEM	King Sunny Ade (Island)
33	40	LOVERS ONLY	Various Artists (Ronco)
42	41	FASTER THAN THE SPEED OF NIGHT	Bonnie Tyler (CBS)
30	42	XL-1	Pete Shelley (Genetic)
43	43	WHAT IS BEAT? (THE BEST OF THE BEAT)	Beat (Go Feet)
48	44	THE COLLECTION	Dionne Warwick (Arista)
31	45	BITE	Altered Images (Epic)
32	46	PETER GABRIEL PLAYS LIVE	Peter Gabriel (Charisma)
36	47	OFF THE BONE	Cramps (Illegal)
28	48	POWER, CORRUPTION AND LIES	New Order (Factory)
-	49	MAKIN' MOVIES	Dire Straits (Vertigo)
47	50	CHART STARS	Various Artists (K-Tel)

Highlighted by the inclusion of their first three big hit singles, the reception for Wham!'s first album *Fantastic* was just that, giving it a three-week initial run (it would return later) at the top which would stop Yazoo's second album *You And Me Both* from emulating the chart-topping achievement of their first. A surprise chartmaker was Rickie Lee Jones, whose new album had no hit single and very little radio play.

August 1983

6 August 1983

last week	this week	Title	Artist (Label)
18	1	NO PARLEZ	Paul Young (CBS)
2	2	YOU AND ME BOTH	Yazoo (Mute)
1	3	FANTASTIC	Wham! (Innervision)
3	4	SYNCHRONICITY	Police (A&M)
4	5	THRILLER	Michael Jackson (Epic)
8	6	PRINCIPLE OF MOMENTS	Robert Plant (WEA)
17	7	THE LOOK	Shalamar (Solar)
5	8	THE LUXURY GAP	Heaven 17 (Virgin)
6	9	CRISES	Mike Oldfield (Virgin)
-	10	THE CROSSING	Big Country (Mercury)
11	11	BODY WISHES	Rod Stewart (Warner Bros.)
16	12	DUCK ROCK	Malcolm McLaren (Charisma)
10	13	LET'S DANCE	David Bowie (EMI America)
7	14	BURNING FROM THE INSIDE	Bauhaus (Beggars Banquet)
15	15	TOO LATE FOR ZERO	Elton John (Rocket)
9	16	IN YOUR EYES	George Benson (WEA)
-	17	THE VERY BEST OF THE BEACH BOYS	Beach Boys (Capitol)
13	18	FLASHDANCE	Soundtrack (Casablanca)
38	19	MICHAEL JACKSON & THE JACKSONS' 18 GREATEST HITS	Michael Jackson & the Jacksons (Star)
12	20	JULIO	Julio Iglesias (CBS)
20	21	SWEET DREAMS (ARE MADE OF THIS)	Eurythmics (RCA)
33	22	HITS ON FIRE	Various Artists (Ronco)
14	23	SECRET MESSAGES	Electric Light Orchestra (Jet)
26	24	SHE WORKS HARD FOR THE MONEY	Donna Summer (Mercury)
23	25	WAR	U2 (Island)
24	26	TRUE	Spandau Ballet (Reformation)
36	27	CARGO	Men At Work (Epic)
19	28	FIRE DANCES	Killing Joke (EG)
25	29	PIECE OF MIND	Iron Maiden (EMI)
-	30	JARREAU	Al Jarreau (WEA International)
48	31	POWER, CORRUPTION AND LIES	New Order (Factory)
45	32	BITE	Altered Images (Epic)
29	33	TWICE AS KOOL	Kool & the Gang (De-Lite)
27	34	CONFRONTATION	Bob Marley & the Wailers (Island)
21	35	OIL ON CANVAS	Japan (Virgin)
37	36	THE HURTING	Tears for Fears (Mercury)
32	37	MARY JANE GIRLS	Mary Jane Girls (Gordy)
35	38	ROSS	Diana Ross (Capitol)
44	39	THE COLLECTION	Dionne Warwick (Arista)
-	40	JERKY VERSIONS OF THE DREAM	Howard Devoto (Virgin)
34	41	THE PRIVATE COLLECTION	Jon & Vangelis (Polydor)
30	42	THE WILD HEART	Stevie Nicks (WEA)
22	43	SPEAKING IN TONGUES	Talking Heads (Sire)
39	44	SYNCHRO SYSTEM	King Sunny Ade (Island)
-	45	PORCUPINE	Echo & the Bunnymen (Korova)
28	46	GIRL AT HER VOLCANO	Rickie Lee Jones (Warner Bros.)
41	47	FASTER THAN THE SPEED OF NIGHT	Bonnie Tyler (CBS)
50	48	CHART STARS	Various Artists (K-Tel)
46	49	PETER GABRIEL PLAYS LIVE	Peter Gabriel (Charisma)
-	50	HOLY DIVER	Dio (Vertigo)

13 August 1983

last week	this week	Title	Artist (Label)
1	1	NO PARLEZ	Paul Young (CBS)
10	2	THE CROSSING	Big Country (Mercury)
3	3	FANTASTIC	Wham! (Innervision)
2	4	YOU AND ME BOTH	Yazoo (Mute)
6	5	PRINCIPLE OF MOMENTS	Robert Plant (WEA)
7	6	THE LOOK	Shalamar (Solar)
5	7	THRILLER	Michael Jackson (Epic)
19	8	MICHAEL JACKSON & THE JACKSONS' 18 GREATEST HITS	Michael Jackson & the Jacksons (Star)
4	9	SYNCHRONICITY	Police (A&M)
-	10	PUNCH THE CLOCK	Elvis Costello (F-Beat)
17	11	THE VERY BEST OF THE BEACH BOYS	Beach Boys (Capitol)
13	12	LET'S DANCE	David Bowie (EMI America)
8	13	THE LUXURY GAP	Heaven 17 (Virgin)
9	14	CRISES	Mike Oldfield (Virgin)
16	15	IN YOUR EYES	George Benson (WEA)
15	16	TOO LATE FOR ZERO	Elton John (Rocket)
12	17	DUCK ROCK	Malcolm McLaren (Charisma)
21	18	SWEET DREAMS (ARE MADE OF THIS)	Eurythmics (RCA)
22	19	HITS ON FIRE	Various Artists (Ronco)
40	20	JERKY VERSIONS OF THE DREAM	Howard Devoto (Virgin)
18	21	FLASHDANCE	Soundtrack (Casablanca)
11	22	BODY WISHES	Rod Stewart (Warner Bros.)
14	23	BURNING FROM THE INSIDE	Bauhaus (Beggars Banquet)
20	24	JULIO	Julio Iglesias (CBS)
23	25	SECRET MESSAGES	Electric Light Orchestra (Jet)
26	26	TRUE	Spandau Ballet (Reformation)
-	27	CLOSE TO THE BONE	Tom Tom Club (Island)
25	28	WAR	U2 (Island)
24	29	PIECE OF MIND	Iron Maiden (EMI)
28	30	FIRE DANCES	Killing Joke (EG)
-	31	CRACKDOWN	Cabaret Voltaire (Some Bizzare)
-	32	LAWYERS IN LOVE	Jackson Browne (Elektra)
-	33	THE WATERBOYS	Waterboys (Chicken Jazz)
-	34	APOLLO ATMOSPHERES AND SOUNDTRACKS	Eno (EG)
31	35	POWER, CORRUPTION AND LIES	New Order (Factory)
30	36	JARREAU	Al Jarreau (WEA International)
24	37	SHE WORKS HARD FOR THE MONEY	Donna Summer (Mercury)
35	38	OIL ON CANVAS	Japan (Virgin)
27	39	CARGO	Men At Work (Epic)
-	40	BAT OUT OF HELL	Meatloaf (Epic)
41	41	THE PRIVATE COLLECTION	Jon & Vangelis (Polydor)
-	42	RIO	Duran Duran (EMI)
-	43	QUICK STEP AND SIDE KICK	Thompson Twins (Arista)
-	44	LIVE	Doobie Brothers (Warner Bros.)
38	45	ROSS	Diana Ross (Capitol)
33	46	TWICE AS KOOL	Kool & the Gang (De-Lite)
-	47	XL-1	Pete Shelley (Genetic)
43	48	SPEAKING IN TONGUES	Talking Heads (Sire)
-	49	ALL THE GOOD ONES ARE TAKEN	Ian Hunter (CBS)
-	50	LIVE IN BERLIN	Au Pairs (AKA)

20 August 1983

last week	this week	Title	Artist (Label)
10	1	PUNCH THE CLOCK	Elvis Costello (F-Beat)
2	2	THE CROSSING	Big Country (Mercury)
1	3	NO PARLEZ	Paul Young (CBS)
3	4	FANTASTIC	Wham! (Innervision)
8	5	MICHAEL JACKSON & THE JACKSONS' 18 GREATEST HITS	Michael Jackson & the Jacksons (Star)
5	6	PRINCIPLE OF MOMENTS	Robert Plant (WEA)
11	7	THE VERY BEST OF THE BEACH BOYS	Beach Boys (Capitol)
7	8	THRILLER	Michael Jackson (Epic)
6	9	THE LOOK	Shalamar (Solar)
9	10	SYNCHRONICITY	Police (A&M)
16	11	TOO LATE FOR ZERO	Elton John (Rocket)
4	12	YOU AND ME BOTH	Yazoo (Mute)
13	13	THE LUXURY GAP	Heaven 17 (Virgin)
12	14	LET'S DANCE	David Bowie (EMI America)
32	15	LAWYERS IN LOVE	Jackson Browne (Elektra)
-	16	ALPHA	Asia (Geffen)
14	17	CRISES	Mike Oldfield (Virgin)
31	18	CRACKDOWN	Cabaret Voltaire (Some Bizzare)
-	19	STREET SOUNDS EDITION 5	Various Artists (Street Sounds)
17	20	DUCK ROCK	Malcolm McLaren (Charisma)
15	21	IN YOUR EYES	George Benson (WEA)
26	22	TRUE	Spandau Ballet (Reformation)
21	23	FLASHDANCE	Soundtrack (Casablanca)
22	24	BODY WISHES	Rod Stewart (Warner Bros.)
28	25	WAR	U2 (Island)
19	26	HITS ON FIRE	Various Artists (Ronco)
18	27	SWEET DREAMS (ARE MADE OF THIS)	Eurythmics (RCA)
24	28	JULIO	Julio Iglesias (CBS)
-	29	GOLDEN YEARS	David Bowie (RCA)
23	30	BURNING FROM THE INSIDE	Bauhaus (Beggars Banquet)
27	31	CLOSE TO THE BONE	Tom Tom Club (Island)
44	32	LIVE	Doobie Brothers (Warner Bros.)
45	33	ROSS	Diana Ross (Capitol)
42	34	RIO	Duran Duran (EMI)
25	35	SECRET MESSAGES	Electric Light Orchestra (Jet)
35	36	POWER, CORRUPTION AND LIES	New Order (Factory)
48	37	SPEAKING IN TONGUES	Talking Heads (Sire)
20	38	JERKY VERSIONS OF THE DREAM	Howard Devoto (Virgin)
40	39	BAT OUT OF HELL	Meatloaf (Epic)
43	40	QUICK STEP AND SIDE KICK	Thompson Twins (Arista)
38	41	OIL ON CANVAS	Japan (Virgin)
46	42	TWICE AS KOOL	Kool & the Gang (De-Lite)
30	43	FIRE DANCES	Killing Joke (EG)
-	44	THE WILD HEART	Stevie Nicks (WEA)
29	45	PIECE OF MIND	Iron Maiden (EMI)
-	46	THE PROPHET RIDES AGAIN	Dennis Brown (A&M)
-	47	TORMENT AND TOREROS	Marc and the Mambas (Some Bizzare)
-	48	FEAST	Creatures (Wonderland)
-	49	WRAP YOUR ARMS AROUND ME	Agnetha Faltskog (Epic)
-	50	ALL IN A NIGHT'S WORK	K C and the Sunshine Band (Epic)

After many years of trying as a group vocalist, Paul Young finally made it as a solist with his chart-topping revival of Marvin Gaye's *Wherever I Lay My Hat*, and his follow-up album *No Parlez* would cement this success, eventually becoming one of the year's biggest sellers. The Jacksons' new Top-Tenner was a TV-advertised package of the group's and Michael's early solo hits, licensed from Motown.

27 August 1983

last week	this week	Title	Artist (Label)
4	1	FANTASTIC	Wham! (Innervision)
5	2	MICHAEL JACKSON & THE JACKSONS' 18 GREATEST HITS	Michael Jackson & the Jacksons (Star)
3	3	NO PARLEZ	Paul Young (CBS)
1	4	PUNCH THE CLOCK	Elvis Costello (F-Beat)
6	5	PRINCIPLE OF MOMENTS	Robert Plant (WEA)
16	6	ALPHA	Asia (Geffen)
7	7	THE VERY BEST OF THE BEACH BOYS	Beach Boys (Capitol)
11	8	TOO LATE FOR ZERO	Elton John (Rocket)
8	9	THRILLER	Michael Jackson (Epic)
12	10	YOU AND ME BOTH	Yazoo (Mute)
2	11	THE CROSSING	Big Country (Mercury)
22	12	TRUE	Spandau Ballet (Reformation)
9	13	THE LOOK	Shalamar (Solar)
10	14	SYNCHRONICITY	Police (A&M)
19	15	STREET SOUNDS EDITION 5	Various Artists (Street Sounds)
13	16	THE LUXURY GAP	Heaven 17 (Virgin)
21	17	IN YOUR EYES	George Benson (WEA)
14	18	LET'S DANCE	David Bowie (EMI America)
17	19	CRISES	Mike Oldfield (Virgin)
15	20	LAWYERS IN LOVE	Jackson Browne (Elektra)
18	21	CRACKDOWN	Cabaret Voltaire (Some Bizzare)
20	22	DUCK ROCK	Malcolm McLaren (Charisma)
27	23	SWEET DREAMS (ARE MADE OF THIS)	Eurythmics (RCA)
24	24	BODY WISHES	Rod Stewart (Warner Bros.)
47	25	TORMENT AND TOREROS	Marc and the Mambas (Some Bizzare)
29	26	GOLDEN YEARS	David Bowie (RCA)
26	27	HITS ON FIRE	Various Artists (Ronco)
25	28	WAR	U2 (Island)
23	29	FLASHDANCE	Soundtrack (Casablanca)
34	30	RIO	Duran Duran (EMI)
30	31	BURNING FROM THE INSIDE	Bauhaus (Beggars Banquet)
28	32	JULIO	Julio Iglesias (CBS)
39	33	BAT OUT OF HELL	Meatloaf (Epic)
33	34	ROSS	Diana Ross (Capitol)
31	35	CLOSE TO THE BONE	Tom Tom Club (Island)
36	36	POWER, CORRUPTION AND LIES	New Order (Factory)
-	37	THE PRIVATE COLLECTION	Jon & Vangelis (Polydor)
37	38	SPEAKING IN TONGUES	Talking Heads (Sire)
-	39	OFF THE BONE	Cramps (Illegal)
-	40	FUTURE SHOCK	Herbie Hancock (CBS)
32	41	LIVE	Doobie Brothers (Warner Bros.)
46	42	THE PROPHET RIDES AGAIN	Dennis Brown (A&M)
-	43	LIVE AT RONNIE SCOTT'S	Weekend (Rough Trade)
38	44	JERKY VERSIONS OF THE DREAM	Howard Devoto (Virgin)
40	45	QUICK STEP AND SIDE KICK	Thompson Twins (Arista)
41	46	OIL ON CANVAS	Japan (Virgin)
-	47	SING FOR YOU	Kids from Fame (BBC)
-	48	TOTO IV	Toto (CBS)
-	49	I WAS THE ONE	Elvis Presley (RCA)
-	50	HEROES	David Bowie (RCA)

3 September 1983

this week	this week	Title	Artist (Label)
1	1	FANTASTIC	Wham! (Innervision)
2	2	MICHAEL JACKSON & THE JACKSONS' 18 GREATEST HITS	Michael Jackson & the Jacksons (Star)
7	3	THE VERY BEST OF THE BEACH BOYS	Beach Boys (Capitol)
6	4	ALPHA	Asia (Geffen)
12	5	TRUE	Spandau Ballet (Reformation)
8	6	TOO LATE FOR ZERO	Elton John (Rocket)
5	7	PRINCIPLE OF MOMENTS	Robert Plant (WEA)
9	8	THRILLER	Michael Jackson (Epic)
3	9	NO PARLEZ	Paul Young (CBS)
4	10	PUNCH THE CLOCK	Elvis Costello (F-Beat)
11	11	THE CROSSING	Big Country (Mercury)
-	12	FLICK OF THE SWITCH	AC/DC (Atlantic)
13	13	THE LOOK	Shalamar (Solar)
14	14	SYNCHRONICITY	Police (A&M)
10	15	YOU AND ME BOTH	Yazoo (Mute)
-	16	CONSTRUCTION TIME AGAIN	Depeche Mode (Mute)
-	17	STANDING IN THE LIGHT	Level 42 (Polydor)
40	18	FUTURE SHOCK	Herbie Hancock (CBS)
15	19	STREET SOUNDS EDITION 5	Various Artists (Street Sounds)
24	20	BODY WISHES	Rod Stewart (Warner Bros.)
26	21	GOLDEN YEARS	David Bowie (RCA)
17	22	IN YOUR EYES	George Benson (WEA)
18	23	LET'S DANCE	David Bowie (EMI America)
23	24	SWEET DREAMS (ARE MADE OF THIS)	Eurythmics (RCA)
-	25	EVERYBODY'S ROCKIN'	Neil Young (Geffen)
-	26	ELIMINATOR	ZZ Top (WEA)
19	27	CRISES	Mike Oldfield (Virgin)
16	28	THE LUXURY GAP	Heaven 17 (Virgin)
25	29	TORMENT AND TOREROS	Marc and the Mambas (Some Bizzare)
-	30	HEADSTONE – BEST OF UFO	UFO (Chrysalis)
33	31	BAT OUT OF HELL	Meatloaf (Epic)
36	32	POWER, CORRUPTION AND LIES	New Order (Factory)
28	33	WAR	U2 (Island)
20	34	LAWYERS IN LOVE	Jackson Browne (Elektra)
22	35	DUCK ROCK	Malcolm McLaren (Charisma)
29	36	FLASHDANCE	Soundtrack (Casablanca)
32	37	JULIO	Julio Iglesias (CBS)
21	38	CRACKDOWN	Cabaret Voltaire (Some Bizzare)
-	39	HITS ON FIRE	Various Artists (Ronco)
-	40	ALL IN A NIGHT'S WORK	K C and the Sunshine Band (Epic)
-	41	TWICE AS KOOL	Kool & the Gang (De-Lite)
-	42	SCRIPT OF THE BRIDGE	Chameleons (Statik)
45	43	QUICK STEP AND SIDE KICK	Thompson Twins (Arista)
-	44	HOLY DIVER	Dio (Vertigo)
27	45	HITS ON FIRE	Various Artists (Ronco)
30	46	RIO	Duran Duran (EMI)
39	47	OFF THE BONE	Cramps (Illegal)
31	48	BURNING FROM THE INSIDE	Bauhaus (Beggars Banquet)
-	49	PIECE OF MIND	Iron Maiden (EMI)
44	50	JERKY VERSIONS OF THE DREAM	Howard Devoto (Virgin)

10 September 1983

this week	this week	Title	Artist (Label)
12	1	FLICK OF THE SWITCH	AC/DC (Atlantic)
1	2	FANTASTIC	Wham! (Innervision)
3	3	THE VERY BEST OF THE BEACH BOYS	Beach Boys (Capitol)
16	4	CONSTRUCTION TIME AGAIN	Depeche Mode (Mute)
2	5	MICHAEL JACKSON & THE JACKSONS' 18 GREATEST HITS	Michael Jackson & the Jacksons (Star)
17	6	STANDING IN THE LIGHT	Level 42 (Polydor)
4	7	ALPHA	Asia (Geffen)
11	8	THE CROSSING	Big Country (Mercury)
5	9	TRUE	Spandau Ballet (Reformation)
6	10	TOO LATE FOR ZERO	Elton John (Rocket)
7	11	PRINCIPLE OF MOMENTS	Robert Plant (WEA)
8	12	THRILLER	Michael Jackson (Epic)
9	13	NO PARLEZ	Paul Young (CBS)
10	14	PUNCH THE CLOCK	Elvis Costello (F-Beat)
13	15	THE LOOK	Shalamar (Solar)
15	16	YOU AND ME BOTH	Yazoo (Mute)
14	17	SYNCHRONICITY	Police (A&M)
20	18	BODY WISHES	Rod Stewart (Warner Bros.)
18	19	FUTURE SHOCK	Herbie Hancock (CBS)
19	20	STREET SOUNDS EDITION 5	Various Artists (Street Sounds)
30	21	HEADSTONE – BEST OF UFO	UFO (Chrysalis)
22	22	IN YOUR EYES	George Benson (WEA)
28	23	THE LUXURY GAP	Heaven 17 (Virgin)
25	24	EVERYBODY'S ROCKIN'	Neil Young (Geffen)
-	25	BUILT TO DESTROY	Michael Schenker Group (Chrysalis)
33	26	WAR	U2 (Island)
32	27	POWER, CORRUPTION AND LIES	New Order (Factory)
34	28	LAWYERS IN LOVE	Jackson Browne (Elektra)
-	29	MEAN STREAK	Y & T (A&M)
21	30	GOLDEN YEARS	David Bowie (RCA)
27	31	CRISES	Mike Oldfield (Virgin)
-	32	SUNNY AFTERNOON	Various Artists (Impression)
24	33	SWEET DREAMS (ARE MADE OF THIS)	Eurythmics (RCA)
36	34	FLASHDANCE	Soundtrack (Casablanca)
46	35	RIO	Duran Duran (EMI)
47	36	OFF THE BONE	Cramps (Illegal)
-	37	MUMMER	XTC (Virgin)
26	38	ELIMINATOR	ZZ Top (WEA)
-	39	MERRY CHRISTMAS MR LAWRENCE	Ryuichi Sakamoto (Virgin)
29	40	TORMENT AND TOREROS	Marc and the Mambas (Some Bizzare)
23	41	LET'S DANCE	David Bowie (EMI America)
40	42	ALL IN A NIGHT'S WORK	K C and the Sunshine Band (Epic)
-	43	COME WITH CLUB – CLUB TRACKS VOL 2	Various Artists (Club)
37	44	JULIO	Julio Iglesias (CBS)
41	45	TWICE AS KOOL	Kool & the Gang (De-Lite)
-	46	ROCK SYMPHONIES	London Symphony Orchestra (K-Tel)
31	47	BAT OUT OF HELL	Meatloaf (Epic)
43	48	QUICK STEP AND SIDE KICK	Thompson Twins (Arista)
-	49	THE PRESENT	Moody Blues (Threshold)
-	50	BOYS DON'T CRY	Cure (Fiction)

The Beach Boys' *Very Best Of* compilation was no less than their fifth Top 10 album to recycle their Capitol hits of the 1960s and early '70s, the first having been *Best Of The Beach Boys* way back at the end of 1966, and the biggest the trend-setting *20 Golden Greats*, which had launched EMI's successful TV-advertised series in 1976. The newcomer (a double album) also benefited from a TV ad campaign.

September – October 1983

last week	this week	17 September 1983	
4	1	CONSTRUCTION TIME AGAIN	Depeche Mode (Mute)
13	2	NO PARLEZ	Paul Young (CBS)
3	3	THE VERY BEST OF THE BEACH BOYS	Beach Boys (Capitol)
1	4	FLICK OF THE SWITCH	AC/DC (Atlantic)
8	5	THE CROSSING	Big Country (Mercury)
2	6	FANTASTIC	Wham! (Innervision)
5	7	MICHAEL JACKSON & THE JACKSONS' 18 GREATEST HITS	Michael Jackson & the Jacksons (Star)
6	8	STANDING IN THE LIGHT	Level 42 (Polydor)
9	9	TRUE	Spandau Ballet (Reformation)
12	10	THRILLER	Michael Jackson (Epic)
10	11	TOO LATE FOR ZERO	Elton John (Rocket)
18	12	BODY WISHES	Rod Stewart (Warner Bros.)
49	13	THE PRESENT	Moody Blues (Threshold)
11	14	PRINCIPLE OF MOMENTS	Robert Plant (WEA)
25	15	BUILT TO DESTROY	Michael Schenker Group (Chrysalis)
15	16	THE LOOK	Shalamar (Solar)
23	17	THE LUXURY GAP	Heaven 17 (Virgin)
16	18	YOU AND ME BOTH	Yazoo (Mute)
7	19	ALPHA	Asia (Geffen)
41	20	LET'S DANCE	David Bowie (EMI America)
14	21	PUNCH THE CLOCK	Elvis Costello (F-Beat)
17	22	SYNCHRONICITY	Police (A&M)
19	23	FUTURE SHOCK	Herbie Hancock (CBS)
-	24	BENT OUT OF SHAPE	Rainbow (Polydor)
29	25	MEAN STREAK	Y & T (A&M)
32	26	SUNNY AFTERNOON	Various Artists (Impression)
20	27	STREET SOUNDS EDITION 5	Various Artists (Street Sounds)
37	28	MUMMER	XTC (Virgin)
39	29	MERRY CHRISTMAS MR LAWRENCE	Ryuichi Sakamoto (Virgin)
-	30	AN INNOCENT MAN	Billy Joel (CBS)
22	31	IN YOUR EYES	George Benson (WEA)
21	32	HEADSTONE – BEST OF UFO	UFO (Chrysalis)
31	33	CRISES	Mike Oldfield (Virgin)
-	34	HEADLINE HITS	Various Artists (K-Tel)
27	35	POWER, CORRUPTION AND LIES	New Order (Factory)
34	36	FLASHDANCE	Soundtrack (Casablanca)
26	37	WAR	U2 (Island)
-	38	DOPPELGANGER	Kid Creole & the Coconuts (Island)
28	39	LAWYERS IN LOVE	Jackson Browne (Elektra)
24	40	EVERYBODY'S ROCKIN'	Neil Young (Geffen)
33	41	SWEET DREAMS (ARE MADE OF THIS)	Eurythmics (RCA)
-	42	BLUE SUNSHINE	Glove (Wonderland)
30	43	GOLDEN YEARS	David Bowie (RCA)
47	44	BAT OUT OF HELL	Meatloaf (Epic)
35	45	RIO	Duran Duran (EMI)
36	46	OFF THE BONE	Cramps (Illegal)
-	47	CRACKDOWN	Cabaret Voltaire (Some Bizzare)
-	48	RANT 'N' RAVE WITH THE STRAY CATS	Stray Cats (Arista)
-	49	SECRET MESSAGES	Electric Light Orchestra (Jet)
42	50	ALL IN A NIGHT'S WORK	K C and the Sunshine Band (Epic)

last week	this week	24 September 1983	
2	1	NO PARLEZ	Paul Young (CBS)
5	2	THE CROSSING	Big Country (Mercury)
3	3	THE VERY BEST OF THE BEACH BOYS	Beach Boys (Capitol)
6	4	FANTASTIC	Wham! (Innervision)
8	5	STANDING IN THE LIGHT	Level 42 (Polydor)
7	6	MICHAEL JACKSON & THE JACKSONS' 18 GREATEST HITS	Michael Jackson & the Jacksons (Star)
24	7	BENT OUT OF SHAPE	Rainbow (Polydor)
4	8	FLICK OF THE SWITCH	AC/DC (Atlantic)
1	9	CONSTRUCTION TIME AGAIN	Depeche Mode (Mute)
10	10	THRILLER	Michael Jackson (Epic)
9	11	TRUE	Spandau Ballet (Reformation)
-	12	LABOUR OF LOVE	UB40 (DEP International)
34	13	HEADLINE HITS	Various Artists (K-Tel)
11	14	TOO LATE FOR ZERO	Elton John (Rocket)
38	15	DOPPELGANGER	Kid Creole & the Coconuts (Island)
17	16	THE LUXURY GAP	Heaven 17 (Virgin)
12	17	BODY WISHES	Rod Stewart (Warner Bros.)
14	18	PRINCIPLE OF MOMENTS	Robert Plant (WEA)
20	19	LET'S DANCE	David Bowie (EMI America)
-	20	BORN AGAIN	Black Sabbath (Vertigo)
15	21	BUILT TO DESTROY	Michael Schenker Group (Chrysalis)
13	22	THE PRESENT	Moody Blues (Threshold)
16	23	THE LOOK	Shalamar (Solar)
-	24	WARRIORS	Gary Numan (Beggars Banquet)
21	25	PUNCH THE CLOCK	Elvis Costello (F-Beat)
18	26	YOU AND ME BOTH	Yazoo (Mute)
26	27	SUNNY AFTERNOON	Various Artists (Impression)
-	28	BORN TO LOVE	Peabo Bryson & Roberta Flack (Capitol)
42	29	BLUE SUNSHINE	Glove (Wonderland)
22	30	SYNCHRONICITY	Police (A&M)
19	31	ALPHA	Asia (Geffen)
-	32	THE HIT SQUAD	Various Artists (Ronco)
31	33	IN YOUR EYES	George Benson (WEA)
45	34	RIO	Duran Duran (EMI)
-	35	NO. 8	J J Cale (Mercury)
35	36	POWER, CORRUPTION AND LIES	New Order (Factory)
-	37	UNFORGETTABLE	Johnny Mathis & Natalie Cole (CBS)
37	38	WAR	U2 (Island)
36	39	FLASHDANCE	Soundtrack (Casablanca)
33	40	CRISES	Mike Oldfield (Virgin)
-	41	LIKE GANGBUSTERS	Jo Boxers (RCA)
-	42	CANTERBURY	Diamond Head (MCA)
27	43	STREET SOUNDS EDITION 5	Various Artists (Street Sounds)
30	44	AN INNOCENT MAN	Billy Joel (CBS)
40	45	EVERYBODY'S ROCKIN'	Neil Young (Geffen)
48	46	RANT 'N' RAVE WITH THE STRAY CATS	Stray Cats (Arista)
25	47	MEAN STREAK	Y & T (A&M)
23	48	FUTURE SHOCK	Herbie Hancock (CBS)
-	49	KISSING TO BE CLEVER	Culture Club (Virgin)
29	50	MERRY CHRISTMAS MR LAWRENCE	Ryuichi Sakamoto (Virgin)

last week	this week	1 October 1983	
12	1	LABOUR OF LOVE	UB40 (DEP International)
1	2	NO PARLEZ	Paul Young (CBS)
2	3	THE CROSSING	Big Country (Mercury)
20	4	BORN AGAIN	Black Sabbath (Vertigo)
4	5	FANTASTIC	Wham! (Innervision)
10	6	THRILLER	Michael Jackson (Epic)
11	7	TRUE	Spandau Ballet (Reformation)
3	8	THE VERY BEST OF THE BEACH BOYS	Beach Boys (Capitol)
6	9	MICHAEL JACKSON & THE JACKSONS' 18 GREATEST HITS	Michael Jackson & the Jacksons (Star)
24	10	WARRIORS	Gary Numan (Beggars Banquet)
5	11	STANDING IN THE LIGHT	Level 42 (Polydor)
9	12	CONSTRUCTION TIME AGAIN	Depeche Mode (Mute)
7	13	BENT OUT OF SHAPE	Rainbow (Polydor)
32	14	THE HIT SQUAD	Various Artists (Ronco)
8	15	FLICK OF THE SWITCH	AC/DC (Atlantic)
41	16	LIKE GANGBUSTERS	Jo Boxers (RCA)
15	17	DOPPELGANGER	Kid Creole & the Coconuts (Island)
19	18	LET'S DANCE	David Bowie (EMI America)
16	19	THE LUXURY GAP	Heaven 17 (Virgin)
13	20	HEADLINE HITS	Various Artists (K-Tel)
42	21	CANTERBURY	Diamond Head (MCA)
14	22	TOO LATE FOR ZERO	Elton John (Rocket)
37	23	UNFORGETTABLE	Johnny Mathis & Natalie Cole (CBS)
22	24	THE PRESENT	Moody Blues (Threshold)
18	25	PRINCIPLE OF MOMENTS	Robert Plant (WEA)
23	26	THE LOOK	Shalamar (Solar)
17	27	BODY WISHES	Rod Stewart (Warner Bros.)
27	28	SUNNY AFTERNOON	Various Artists (Impression)
28	29	BORN TO LOVE	Peabo Bryson & Roberta Flack (Capitol)
26	30	YOU AND ME BOTH	Yazoo (Mute)
35	31	NO. 8	J J Cale (Mercury)
21	32	BUILT TO DESTROY	Michael Schenker Group (Chrysalis)
48	33	FUTURE SHOCK	Herbie Hancock (CBS)
31	34	ALPHA	Asia (Geffen)
30	35	SYNCHRONICITY	Police (A&M)
33	36	IN YOUR EYES	George Benson (WEA)
34	37	RIO	Duran Duran (EMI)
38	38	WAR	U2 (Island)
29	39	BLUE SUNSHINE	Glove (Wonderland)
36	40	POWER, CORRUPTION AND LIES	New Order (Factory)
50	41	MERRY CHRISTMAS MR LAWRENCE	Ryuichi Sakamoto (Virgin)
25	42	PUNCH THE CLOCK	Elvis Costello (F-Beat)
40	43	CRISES	Mike Oldfield (Virgin)
-	44	DANCE MIX - DANCE HITS II	Various Artists (Epic)
-	45	RITMO	Judie Tzuke (Chrysalis)
-	46	SWORDFISHTROMBONE	Tom Waits (Island)
44	47	AN INNOCENT MAN	Billy Joel (CBS)
-	48	MIKE'S MURDER	Joe Jackson (A&M)
-	49	HARD	Gang of Four (EMI)
47	50	MEAN STREAK	Y & T (A&M)

Several titles, mostly among the resurgent flurry of Top 10 sellers by heavy metal bands - AC/DC, Rainbow, Black Sabbath - were displaying a sales pattern which would become ever more apparent by the end of the 1980s: making a solid arrival in the upper reaches, having their best sales in their second week, then dropping away ultra-quickly. Eventually, most hard rock would sell strongest in its *first* week.

October 1983

8 October 1983

last week	this week		
1	1	LABOUR OF LOVE	UB40 (DEP International)
2	2	NO PARLEZ	Paul Young (CBS)
3	3	THE CROSSING	Big Country (Mercury)
18	4	LET'S DANCE	David Bowie (EMI America)
4	5	BORN AGAIN	Black Sabbath (Vertigo)
6	6	THRILLER	Michael Jackson (Epic)
5	7	FANTASTIC	Wham! (Innervision)
14	8	THE HIT SQUAD	Various Artists (Ronco)
12	9	CONSTRUCTION TIME AGAIN	Depeche Mode (Mute)
11	10	STANDING IN THE LIGHT	Level 42 (Polydor)
7	11	TRUE	Spandau Ballet (Reformation)
9	12	MICHAEL JACKSON & THE JACKSONS' 18 GREATEST HITS	Michael Jackson & the Jacksons (Star)
8	13	THE VERY BEST OF THE BEACH BOYS	Beach Boys (Capitol)
10	14	WARRIORS	Gary Numan (Beggars Banquet)
19	15	THE LUXURY GAP	Heaven 17 (Virgin)
-	16	LICK IT UP	Kiss (Vertigo)
23	17	UNFORGETTABLE	Johnny Mathis & Natalie Cole (CBS)
45	18	RITMO	Judie Tzuke (Chrysalis)
17	19	DOPPELGANGER	Kid Creole & the Coconuts (Island)
15	20	FLICK OF THE SWITCH	AC/DC (Atlantic)
16	21	LIKE GANGBUSTERS	Jo Boxers (RCA)
-	22	LIVE IN TOKYO	Public Image Ltd (Virgin)
22	23	TOO LATE FOR ZERO	Elton John (Rocket)
13	24	BENT OUT OF SHAPE	Rainbow (Polydor)
29	25	BORN TO LOVE	Peabo Bryson & Roberta Flack (Capitol)
-	26	KISSING TO BE CLEVER	Culture Club (Virgin)
21	27	CANTERBURY	Diamond Head (MCA)
24	28	THE PRESENT	Moody Blues (Threshold)
31	29	NO. 8	J J Cale (Mercury)
36	30	IN YOUR EYES	George Benson (WEA)
-	31	A TOUCH MORE MAGIC	Barry Manilow (Arista)
26	32	THE LOOK	Shalamar (Solar)
28	33	SUNNY AFTERNOON	Various Artists (Impression)
-	34	THE GOLDEN SECTION	John Foxx (Virgin)
46	35	SWORDFISHTROMBONE	Tom Waits (Island)
41	36	MERRY CHRISTMAS MR LAWRENCE	Ryuichi Sakamoto (Virgin)
30	37	YOU AND ME BOTH	Yazoo (Mute)
42	38	PUNCH THE CLOCK	Elvis Costello (F-Beat)
20	39	HEADLINE HITS	Various Artists (K-Tel)
39	40	BLUE SUNSHINE	Glove (Wonderland)
-	41	DANCE IN THE MIDNIGHT	Marc Bolan (Marc on Wax)
40	42	POWER, CORRUPTION AND LIES	New Order (Factory)
32	43	BUILT TO DESTROY	Michael Schenker Group (Chrysalis)
35	44	SYNCHRONICITY	Police (A&M)
25	45	PRINCIPLE OF MOMENTS	Robert Plant (WEA)
27	46	BODY WISHES	Rod Stewart (Warner Bros.)
38	47	WAR	U2 (Island)
-	48	STAYIN' ALIVE	Soundtrack (RSO)
47	49	AN INNOCENT MAN	Billy Joel (CBS)
37	50	RIO	Duran Duran (EMI)

15 October 1983

1	1	LABOUR OF LOVE	UB40 (DEP International)
2	2	NO PARLEZ	Paul Young (CBS)
3	3	THE CROSSING	Big Country (Mercury)
4	4	LET'S DANCE	David Bowie (EMI America)
7	5	FANTASTIC	Wham! (Innervision)
-	6	GENESIS	Genesis (Charisma/Virgin)
6	7	THRILLER	Michael Jackson (Epic)
16	8	LICK IT UP	Kiss (Vertigo)
22	9	LIVE IN TOKYO	Public Image Ltd (Virgin)
9	10	CONSTRUCTION TIME AGAIN	Depeche Mode (Mute)
31	11	A TOUCH MORE MAGIC	Barry Manilow (Arista)
30	12	IN YOUR EYES	George Benson (WEA)
5	13	BORN AGAIN	Black Sabbath (Vertigo)
15	14	THE LUXURY GAP	Heaven 17 (Virgin)
11	15	TRUE	Spandau Ballet (Reformation)
8	16	THE HIT SQUAD	Various Artists (Ronco)
17	17	UNFORGETTABLE	Johnny Mathis & Natalie Coie (CBS)
14	18	WARRIORS	Gary Numan (Beggars Banquet)
12	19	MICHAEL JACKSON & THE JACKSONS' 18 GREATEST HITS	Michael Jackson & the Jacksons (Star)
18	20	RITMO	Judie Tzuke (Chrysalis)
10	21	STANDING IN THE LIGHT	Level 42 (Polydor)
13	22	THE VERY BEST OF THE BEACH BOYS	Beach Boys (Capitol)
25	23	BORN TO LOVE	Peabo Bryson & Roberta Flack (Capitol)
-	24	STREET SOUNDS EDITION 6	Various Artists (Street Sounds)
48	25	STAYIN' ALIVE	Soundtrack (RSO)
34	26	THE GOLDEN SECTION	John Foxx (Virgin)
23	27	TOO LATE FOR ZERO	Elton John (Rocket)
20	28	FLICK OF THE SWITCH	AC/DC (Atlantic)
-	29	SILVER	Cliff Richard (EMI)
-	30	TWO OF US	Various Artists (K-Tel)
-	31	VICES	Waysted (Chrysalis)
19	32	DOPPELGANGER	Kid Creole & the Coconuts (Island)
21	33	LIKE GANGBUSTERS	Jo Boxers (RCA)
47	34	WAR	U2 (Island)
-	35	THE MUSIC OF RICHARD CLAYDERMAN	Richard Clayderman (Decca/Delphine)
-	36	FLIGHTS OF FANCY	Paul Leoni (Nouveau)
-	37	INTRODUCING	Style Council (Polydor Import)
35	38	SWORDFISHTROMBONE	Tom Waits (Island)
24	39	BENT OUT OF SHAPE	Rainbow (Polydor)
26	40	KISSING TO BE CLEVER	Culture Club (Virgin)
37	41	YOU AND ME BOTH	Yazoo (Mute)
42	42	POWER, CORRUPTION AND LIES	New Order (Factory)
-	43	IS NOTHING SACRED?	Lords of the New Church (LNC)
28	44	THE PRESENT	Moody Blues (Threshold)
32	45	THE LOOK	Shalamar (Solar)
27	46	CANTERBURY	Diamond Head (MCA)
-	47	THE WILD HEART	Stevie Nicks (WEA)
40	48	BLUE SUNSHINE	Glove (Wonderland)
38	49	PUNCH THE CLOCK	Elvis Costello (F-Beat)
-	50	LIVE FROM EARTH	Pat Benatar (Chrysalis)

22 October 1983

6	1	GENESIS	Genesis (Charisma/Virgin)
2	2	NO PARLEZ	Paul Young (CBS)
1	3	LABOUR OF LOVE	UB40 (DEP International)
-	4	COLOUR BY NUMBERS	Culture Club (Virgin)
-	5	SNAP!	Jam (Polydor)
3	6	THE CROSSING	Big Country (Mercury)
5	7	FANTASTIC	Wham! (Innervision)
4	8	LET'S DANCE	David Bowie (EMI America)
7	9	THRILLER	Michael Jackson (Epic)
12	10	IN YOUR EYES	George Benson (WEA)
29	11	SILVER	Cliff Richard (EMI)
10	12	CONSTRUCTION TIME AGAIN	Depeche Mode (Mute)
8	13	LICK IT UP	Kiss (Vertigo)
9	14	LIVE IN TOKYO	Public Image Ltd (Virgin)
25	15	STAYIN' ALIVE	Soundtrack (RSO)
11	16	A TOUCH MORE MAGIC	Barry Manilow (Arista)
23	17	BORN TO LOVE	Peabo Bryson & Roberta Flack (Capitol)
16	18	THE HIT SQUAD	Various Artists (Ronco)
27	19	TOO LATE FOR ZERO	Elton John (Rocket)
37	20	INTRODUCING	Style Council (Polydor Import)
-	21	VOICE OF THE HEART	Carpenters (A&M)
20	22	RITMO	Judie Tzuke (Chrysalis)
40	23	KISSING TO BE CLEVER	Culture Club (Virgin)
50	24	LIVE FROM EARTH	Pat Benatar (Chrysalis)
14	25	THE LUXURY GAP	Heaven 17 (Virgin)
38	26	SWORDFISHTROMBONE	Tom Waits (Island)
-	27	MONUMENT (LIVE)	Ultravox (Chrysalis)
21	28	STANDING IN THE LIGHT	Level 42 (Polydor)
-	29	CHAS AND DAVE'S KNEES UP - JAMBOREE BAG NO.2	Chas & Dave (Rockney)
26	30	THE GOLDEN SECTION	John Foxx (Virgin)
15	31	TRUE	Spandau Ballet (Reformation)
19	32	MICHAEL JACKSON & THE JACKSONS' 18 GREATEST HITS	Michael Jackson & the Jacksons (Star)
18	33	WARRIORS	Gary Numan (Beggars Banquet)
-	34	BAT OUT OF HELL	Meatloaf (Epic)
31	35	VICES	Waysted (Chrysalis)
-	36	WINDOW IN THE JUNGLE	10 c.c. (Mercury)
17	37	UNFORGETTABLE	Johnny Mathis & Natalie Cole (CBS)
30	38	TWO OF US	Various Artists (K-Tel)
41	39	YOU AND ME BOTH	Yazoo (Mute)
32	40	DOPPELGANGER	Kid Creole & the Coconuts (Island)
-	41	RESPOND PACKAGE	Various Artists (Respond)
24	42	STREET SOUNDS EDITION 6	Various Artists (Street Sounds)
-	43	MUTINY	David Essex (Mercury)
45	44	THE LOOK	Shalamar (Solar)
36	45	FLIGHTS OF FANCY	Paul Leoni (Nouveau)
42	46	POWER, CORRUPTION AND LIES	New Order (Factory)
28	47	FLICK OF THE SWITCH	AC/DC (Atlantic)
43	48	IS NOTHING SACRED?	Lords of the New Church (LNC)
-	49	BUILT TO DESTROY	Michael Schenker Group (Chrysalis)
35	50	THE MUSIC OF RICHARD CLAYDERMAN	Richard Clayderman (Decca/Delphine)

The return to prominence of David Bowie's *Let's Dance* was down to his Number 2 single *Modern Love*, while Genesis also had a Number 2 single, *Mama*, to kick-start their eponymously-titled new chart-topping album. Kiss' *Lick It Up* was, surprisingly, the 1970s veterans' first UK Top 10 album ever. Cliff Richard's *Silver* was, initially a box set containing a bonus *Rock'n'Roll Silver* oldies set.

October – November 1983

29 October 1983

last week	this week	title	artist
4	1	COLOUR BY NUMBERS	Culture Club (Virgin)
5	2	SNAP!	Jam (Polydor)
1	3	GENESIS	Genesis (Charisma/Virgin)
3	4	LABOUR OF LOVE	UB40 (DEP International)
2	5	NO PARLEZ	Paul Young (CBS)
6	6	THE CROSSING	Big Country (Mercury)
7	7	FANTASTIC	Wham! (Innervision)
11	8	SILVER	Cliff Richard (EMI)
27	9	MONUMENT (LIVE)	Ultravox (Chrysalis)
8	10	LET'S DANCE	David Bowie (EMI America)
21	11	VOICE OF THE HEART	Carpenters (A&M)
9	12	THRILLER	Michael Jackson (Epic)
10	13	IN YOUR EYES	George Benson (WEA)
13	14	LICK IT UP	Kiss (Vertigo)
-	15	OUT OF THIS WORLD	Shakatak (Polydor)
19	16	TOO LATE FOR ZERO	Elton John (Rocket)
-	17	CAN'T SLOW DOWN	Lionel Richie (Motown)
38	18	TWO OF US	Various Artists (K-Tel)
17	19	BORN TO LOVE	Peabo Bryson & Roberta Flack (Capitol)
15	20	STAYIN' ALIVE	Soundtrack (RSO)
14	21	LIVE IN TOKYO	Public Image Ltd (Virgin)
16	22	A TOUCH MORE MAGIC	Barry Manilow (Arista)
-	23	NORTH OF A MIRACLE	Nick Heyward (Arista)
37	24	UNFORGETTABLE	Johnny Mathis & Natalie Cole (CBS)
25	25	THE LUXURY GAP	Heaven 17 (Virgin)
-	26	STREET SOUNDS ELECTRO I	Various Artists (Street Sounds)
-	27	ALIVE, SHE CRIED	Doors (Elektra)
28	28	STANDING IN THE LIGHT	Level 42 (Polydor)
-	29	THE RHYTHM OF LIFE	Paul Haig (Crepuscule)
-	30	COOKIN' ON THE ROOF	Roman Holiday (Jive)
-	31	NIGHTLINE	Randy Crawford (Warner Bros.)
29	32	CHAS AND DAVE'S KNEES UP - JAMBOREE BAG NO.2	Chas & Dave (Rockney)
-	33	BORN AGAIN	Black Sabbath (Vertigo)
45	34	FLIGHTS OF FANCY	Paul Leoni (Nouveau)
-	35	GONNA GET YOU	Freeez (Beggards Banquet)
12	36	CONSTRUCTION TIME AGAIN	Depeche Mode (Mute)
-	37	XXV	Shadows (EMI)
18	38	THE HIT SQUAD	Various Artists (Ronco)
-	39	AN INNOCENT MAN	Billy Joel (CBS)
34	40	BAT OUT OF HELL	Meatloaf (Epic)
32	41	MICHAEL JACKSON & THE JACKSONS' 18 GREATEST HITS	Michael Jackson & the Jacksons (Star)
23	42	KISSING TO BE CLEVER	Culture Club (Virgin)
46	43	POWER, CORRUPTION AND LIES	New Order (Factory)
-	44	THE WILD HEART	Stevie Nicks (WEA)
20	45	INTRODUCING	Style Council (Polydor Import)
42	46	STREET SOUNDS EDITION 6	Various Artists (Street Sounds)
43	47	MUTINY	David Essex (Mercury)
31	48	TRUE	Spandau Ballet (Reformation)
-	49	ROCK 'N' SOUL (PART 1)	Daryl Hall & John Oates (RCA)
-	50	WAR	U2 (Island)

5 November 1983

last week	this week	title	artist
1	1	COLOUR BY NUMBERS	Culture Club (Virgin)
2	2	SNAP!	Jam (Polydor)
17	3	CAN'T SLOW DOWN	Lionel Richie (Motown)
4	4	LABOUR OF LOVE	UB40 (DEP International)
3	5	GENESIS	Genesis (Charisma/Virgin)
23	6	NORTH OF A MIRACLE	Nick Heyward (Arista)
5	7	NO PARLEZ	Paul Young (CBS)
11	8	VOICE OF THE HEART	Carpenters (A&M)
12	9	THRILLER	Michael Jackson (Epic)
9	10	MONUMENT (LIVE)	Ultravox (Chrysalis)
6	11	THE CROSSING	Big Country (Mercury)
10	12	LET'S DANCE	David Bowie (EMI America)
7	13	FANTASTIC	Wham! (Innervision)
13	14	IN YOUR EYES	George Benson (WEA)
49	15	ROCK 'N' SOUL (PART 1)	Daryl Hall & John Oates (RCA)
39	16	AN INNOCENT MAN	Billy Joel (CBS)
16	17	TOO LATE FOR ZERO	Elton John (Rocket)
8	18	SILVER	Cliff Richard (EMI)
-	19	ZIGGY STARDUST - THE MOTION PICTURE	David Bowie (RCA)
18	20	TWO OF US	Various Artists (K-Tel)
-	21	SOUL MINING	The The (Some Bizzare)
27	22	ALIVE, SHE CRIED	Doors (Elektra)
24	23	UNFORGETTABLE	Johnny Mathis & Natalie Cole (CBS)
25	24	THE LUXURY GAP	Heaven 17 (Virgin)
19	25	BORN TO LOVE	Peabo Bryson & Roberta Flack (Capitol)
-	26	HEAD OVER HEELS	Cocteau Twins (4AD)
34	27	FLIGHTS OF FANCY	Paul Leoni (Nouveau)
22	28	A TOUCH MORE MAGIC	Barry Manilow (Arista)
36	29	CONSTRUCTION TIME AGAIN	Depeche Mo (Mute)
-	30	GET OUT AND WALK	Farmers Boys (EMI)
26	31	STREET SOUNDS ELECTRO I	Various Artists (Street Sounds)
20	32	STAYIN' ALIVE	Soundtrack (RSO)
21	33	LIVE IN TOKYO	Public Image Ltd (Virgin)
32	34	CHAS AND DAVE'S KNEES UP - JAMBOREE BAG NO.2	Chas & Dave (Rockney)
41	35	MICHAEL JACKSON & THE JACKSONS' 18 GREATEST HITS	Michael Jackson & the Jacksons (Star)
31	36	NIGHTLINE	Randy Crawford (Warner Bros.)
37	37	XXV	Shadows (EMI)
46	38	STREET SOUNDS EDITION 6	Various Artists (Street Sounds)
15	39	OUT OF THIS WORLD	Shakatak (Polydor)
-	40	THE MUSIC OF RICHARD CLAYDERMAN	Richard Clayderman (Decca/Delphine)
29	41	THE RHYTHM OF LIFE	Paul Haig (Crepuscule)
45	42	INTRODUCING	Style Council (Polydor Import)
-	43	LETTIN' LOOSE	Heavy Pettin' (Polydor)
14	44	LICK IT UP	Kiss (Vertigo)
-	45	IMAGINATIONS	Various Artists (CBS)
28	46	STANDING IN THE LIGHT	Level 42 (Polydor)
-	47	SO AMAZING	Dionne Warwick (Arista)
-	48	THE LOOK	Shalamar (Solar)
48	49	TRUE	Spandau Ballet (Reformation)
44	50	THE WILD HEART	Stevie Nicks (WEA)

12 November 1983

last week	this week	title	artist
1	1	COLOUR BY NUMBERS	Culture Club (Virgin)
3	2	CAN'T SLOW DOWN	Lionel Richie (Motown)
2	3	SNAP!	Jam (Polydor)
4	4	LABOUR OF LOVE	UB40 (DEP International)
5	5	GENESIS	Genesis (Charisma/Virgin)
8	6	VOICE OF THE HEART	Carpenters (A&M)
6	7	NORTH OF A MIRACLE	Nick Heyward (Arista)
7	8	NO PARLEZ	Paul Young (CBS)
-	9	PIPES OF PEACE	Paul McCartney (Parlophone)
19	10	ZIGGY STARDUST - THE MOTION PICTURE	David Bowie (RCA)
13	11	FANTASTIC	Wham! (Innervision)
20	12	TWO OF US	Various Artists (K-Tel)
9	13	THRILLER	Michael Jackson (Epic)
16	14	AN INNOCENT MAN	Billy Joel (CBS)
15	15	ROCK 'N' SOUL (PART 1)	Daryl Hall & John Oates (RCA)
17	16	TOO LATE FOR ZERO	Elton John (Rocket)
14	17	IN YOUR EYES	George Benson (WEA)
10	18	MONUMENT (LIVE)	Ultravox (Chrysalis)
11	19	THE CROSSING	Big Country (Mercury)
-	20	INFIDELS	Bob Dylan (CBS)
22	21	ALIVE, SHE CRIED	Doors (Elektra)
26	22	HEAD OVER HEELS	Cocteau Twins (4AD)
12	23	LET'S DANCE	David Bowie (EMI America)
45	24	IMAGINATIONS	Various Artists (CBS)
-	25	LOVE IS THE LAW	Toyah (Safari)
18	26	SILVER	Cliff Richard (EMI)
21	27	SOUL MINING	The The (Some Bizzare)
-	28	HYPERBOREA	Tangerine Dream (Virgin)
32	29	STAYIN' ALIVE	Soundtrack (RSO)
-	30	WORKING WITH FIRE AND STEEL	China Crisis (Virgin)
-	31	SWORDFISHTROMBONE	Tom Waits (Island)
25	32	BORN TO LOVE	Peabo Bryson & Roberta Flack (Capitol)
39	33	OUT OF THIS WORLD	Shakatak (Polydor)
40	34	THE MUSIC OF RICHARD CLAYDERMAN	Richard Clayderman (Decca/Delphine)
-	35	DAVID GRANT	David Grant (Chrysalis)
-	36	LOVE STORIES	Don Williams (K-Tel)
24	37	THE LUXURY GAP	Heaven 17 (Virgin)
28	38	A TOUCH MORE MAGIC	Barry Manilow (Arista)
35	39	MICHAEL JACKSON & THE JACKSONS' 18 GREATEST HITS	Michael Jackson & the Jacksons (Star)
-	40	LIVE IN YUGOSLAVIA	Anti-Nowhere League (ID)
30	41	GET OUT AND WALK	Farmers Boys (EMI)
-	42	SYNCHRONICITY	Police (A&M)
31	43	STREET SOUNDS ELECTRO I	Various Artists (Street Sounds)
-	44	THE ATLANTIC YEARS 1973-80	Roxy Music (EG)
46	45	STANDING IN THE LIGHT	Level 42 (Polydor)
23	46	UNFORGETTABLE	Johnny Mathis & Natalie Cole (CBS)
33	47	LIVE IN TOKYO	Public Image Ltd (Virgin)
42	48	INTRODUCING	Style Council (Polydor Import)
43	49	LETTIN' LOOSE	Heavy Pettin' (Polydor)
38	50	STREET SOUNDS EDITION 6	Various Artists (Street Sounds)

Culture Club's million-plus-selling *Karma Chameleon* was 1983's biggest single, and hugely boosted the profile of its parent album *Colour By Numbers*, which would dominate the top of the chart for much of the rest of the year. Culture Club's enormous sales meant, that the Jam's retrospective singles collection *Snap!* was held at 2. The Doors' *Alive, She Cried* was a mini-album containing newly-discovered live tracks.

November – December 1983

19 November 1983

last week	this week	Title	Artist (Label)
2	1	CAN'T SLOW DOWN	Lionel Richie (Motown)
1	2	COLOUR BY NUMBERS	Culture Club (Virgin)
20	3	INFIDELS	Bob Dylan (CBS)
9	4	PIPES OF PEACE	Paul McCartney (Parlophone)
4	5	LABOUR OF LOVE	UB40 (DEP International)
5	6	GENESIS	Genesis (Charisma/Virgin)
3	7	SNAP!	Jam (Polydor)
14	8	AN INNOCENT MAN	Billy Joel (CBS)
-	9	UNDERCOVER	Rolling Stones (Rolling Stones)
8	10	NO PARLEZ	Paul Young (CBS)
12	11	TWO OF US	Various Artists (K-Tel)
13	12	THRILLER	Michael Jackson (Epic)
6	13	VOICE OF THE HEART	Carpenters (A&M)
10	14	ZIGGY STARDUST - THE MOTION PICTURE	David Bowie (RCA)
11	15	FANTASTIC	Wham! (Innervision)
44	16	THE ATLANTIC YEARS 1973-80	Roxy Music (EG)
16	17	TOO LATE FOR ZERO	Elton John (Rocket)
15	18	ROCK 'N' SOUL (PART 1)	Daryl Hall & John Oates (RCA)
30	19	WORKING WITH FIRE AND STEEL	China Crisis (Virgin)
-	20	HEARTS AND BONES	Paul Simon (Warner Bros.)
7	21	NORTH OF A MIRACLE	Nick Heyward (Arista)
-	22	STRIP	Adam Ant (CBS)
19	23	THE CROSSING	Big Country (Mercury)
21	24	ALIVE, SHE CRIED	Doors (Elektra)
-	25	STARFLEET PROJECT	Brian May (EMI)
-	26	SCANDALOUS	Imagination (Red Bus)
17	27	IN YOUR EYES	George Benson (WEA)
23	28	LET'S DANCE	David Bowie (EMI America)
26	29	SILVER	Cliff Richard (EMI)
24	30	IMAGINATIONS	Various Artists (CBS)
-	31	STAGES	Elaine Paige (K-Tel)
27	32	SOUL MINING	The The (Some Bizzare)
18	33	MONUMENT (LIVE)	Ultravox (Chrysalis)
22	34	HEAD OVER HEELS	Cocteau Twins (4AD)
39	35	MICHAEL JACKSON & THE JACKSONS' 18 GREATEST HITS	Michael Jackson & the Jacksons (Star)
-	36	THANK YOU FOR THE MUSIC	Abba (Epic)
42	37	SYNCHRONICITY	Police (A&M)
25	38	LOVE IS THE LAW	Toyah (Safari)
-	39	HAVE YOU EVER BEEN IN LOVE	Leo Sayer (Chrysalis)
-	40	THE ESSENTIAL JEAN MICHEL JARRE	Jean Michel Jarre (Polydor)
-	41	SNAKE CHARMER	Jah Wobble (Island)
43	42	STREET SOUNDS ELECTRO I	Various Artists (Street Sounds)
32	43	BORN TO LOVE	Peabo Bryson & Roberta Flack (Capitol)
35	44	DAVID GRANT	David Grant (Chrysalis)
-	45	DADA	Alice Cooper (Warner Bros.)
-	46	PLAY DIRTY	Girlschool (Bronze)
-	47	CHART HITS '83	Various Artists (K-Tel)
36	48	LOVE STORIES	Don Williams (K-Tel)
-	49	THE WILD HEART	Stevie Nicks (WEA)
28	50	HYPERBOREA	Tangerine Dream (Virgin)

26 November 1983

last week	this week	Title	Artist (Label)
2	1	COLOUR BY NUMBERS	Culture Club (Virgin)
1	2	CAN'T SLOW DOWN	Lionel Richie (Motown)
9	3	UNDERCOVER	Rolling Stones (Rolling Stones)
8	4	AN INNOCENT MAN	Billy Joel (CBS)
4	5	PIPES OF PEACE	Paul McCartney (Parlophone)
10	6	NO PARLEZ	Paul Young (CBS)
6	7	GENESIS	Genesis (Charisma/Virgin)
12	8	THRILLER	Michael Jackson (Epic)
5	9	LABOUR OF LOVE	UB40 (DEP International)
3	10	INFIDELS	Bob Dylan (CBS)
7	11	SNAP!	Jam (Polydor)
-	12	BEAUTY STAB	ABC (Neutron)
13	13	VOICE OF THE HEART	Carpenters (A&M)
22	14	STRIP	Adam Ant (CBS)
-	15	TOUCH	Eurythmics (RCA)
31	16	STAGES	Elaine Paige (K-Tel)
16	17	THE ATLANTIC YEARS 1973-80	Roxy Music (EG)
47	18	CHART HITS '83	Various Artists (K-Tel)
15	19	FANTASTIC	Wham! (Innervision)
14	20	ZIGGY STARDUST - THE MOTION PICTURE	David Bowie (RCA)
18	21	ROCK 'N' SOUL (PART 1)	Daryl Hall & John Oates (RCA)
11	22	TWO OF US	Various Artists (K-Tel)
27	23	IN YOUR EYES	George Benson (WEA)
17	24	TOO LATE FOR ZERO	Elton John (Rocket)
21	25	NORTH OF A MIRACLE	Nick Heyward (Arista)
39	26	HAVE YOU EVER BEEN IN LOVE	Leo Sayer (Chrysalis)
36	27	THANK YOU FOR THE MUSIC	Abba (Epic)
25	28	STARFLEET PROJECT	Brian May (EMI)
23	29	THE CROSSING	Big Country (Mercury)
-	30	FADE TO GREY	Visage (Polydor)
-	31	90125	Yes (Atco)
-	32	LIZZY LIFE	Thin Lizzy (Vertigo)
-	33	THE BOP WON'T STOP	Shakin' Stevens (Epic)
-	34	TRACK RECORD	Joan Armatrading (A&M)
-	35	ROOTS REGGAE 'N' REGGAE ROCK	Various Artists (Telstar)
37	36	SYNCHRONICITY	Police (A&M)
-	37	MARVIN GAYE'S GREATEST HITS	Marvin Gaye (Telstar)
-	38	HIT SQUAD - HITS OF '83	Various Artists (Ronco)
19	39	WORKING WITH FIRE AND STEEL	China Crisis (Virgin)
20	40	HEARTS AND BONES	Paul Simon (Warner Bros.)
28	41	LET'S DANCE	David Bowie (EMI America)
-	42	SMELL OF FEMALE	Cramps (Big Beat)
29	43	SILVER	Cliff Richard (EMI)
-	44	SUPERCHART '83	Various Artists (Telstar)
-	45	YENTL	Barbra Streisand (CBS)
34	46	HEAD OVER HEELS	Cocteau Twins (4AD)
-	47	CHAS AND DAVE'S KNEES UP - JAMBOREE BAG NO.2	Chas & Dave (Rockney)
30	48	IMAGINATIONS	Various Artists (CBS)
35	49	MICHAEL JACKSON & THE JACKSONS' 18 GREATEST HITS	Michael Jackson & the Jacksons (Star)
-	50	BAY OF KINGS	Steve Hackett (Lamborghini)

3 December 1983

last week	this week	Title	Artist (Label)
1	1	COLOUR BY NUMBERS	Culture Club (Virgin)
2	2	CAN'T SLOW DOWN	Lionel Richie (Motown)
3	3	UNDERCOVER	Rolling Stones (Rolling Stones)
15	4	TOUCH	Eurythmics (RCA)
4	5	AN INNOCENT MAN	Billy Joel (CBS)
12	6	BEAUTY STAB	ABC (Neutron)
6	7	NO PARLEZ	Paul Young (CBS)
-	8	SEVEN AND THE RAGGED TIGER	Duran Duran (EMI)
-	9	U2 LIVE: UNDER A BLOOD RED SKY	U2 (Island)
18	10	CHART HITS '83	Various Artists (K-Tel)
8	11	THRILLER	Michael Jackson (Epic)
5	12	PIPES OF PEACE	Paul McCartney (Parlophone)
7	13	GENESIS	Genesis (Charisma/Virgin)
31	14	90125	Yes (Atco)
19	15	FANTASTIC	Wham! (Innervision)
9	16	LABOUR OF LOVE	UB40 (DEP International)
33	17	THE BOP WON'T STOP	Shakin' Stevens (Epic)
16	18	STAGES	Elaine Paige (K-Tel)
-	19	BACK TO BACK	Status Quo (Vertigo)
11	20	SNAP!	Jam (Polydor)
13	21	VOICE OF THE HEART	Carpenters (A&M)
32	22	LIZZY LIFE	Thin Lizzy (Vertigo)
14	23	STRIP	Adam Ant (CBS)
23	24	IN YOUR EYES	George Benson (WEA)
10	25	INFIDELS	Bob Dylan (CBS)
38	26	HIT SQUAD - HITS OF '83	Various Artists (Ronco)
37	27	MARVIN GAYE'S GREATEST HITS	Marvin Gaye (Telstar)
-	28	NOCTURNE	Siouxsie and the Banshees (Wonderland)
21	29	ROCK 'N' SOUL (PART 1)	Daryl Hall & John Oates (RCA)
42	30	SMELL OF FEMALE	Cramps (Big Beat)
26	31	HAVE YOU EVER BEEN IN LOVE	Leo Sayer (Chrysalis)
27	32	THANK YOU FOR THE MUSIC	Abba (Epic)
24	33	TOO LATE FOR ZERO	Elton John (Rocket)
44	34	SUPERCHART '83	Various Artists (Telstar)
34	35	TRACK RECORD	Joan Armatrading (A&M)
22	36	TWO OF US	Various Artists (K-Tel)
20	37	ZIGGY STARDUST - THE MOTION PICTURE	David Bowie (RCA)
17	38	THE ATLANTIC YEARS 1973-80	Roxy Music (EG)
46	39	HEAD OVER HEELS	Cocteau Twins (4AD)
48	40	IMAGINATIONS	Various Artists (CBS)
39	41	WORKING WITH FIRE AND STEEL	China Crisis (Virgin)
45	42	YENTL	Barbra Streisand (CBS)
30	43	FADE TO GREY	Visage (Polydor)
28	44	STARFLEET PROJECT	Brian May (EMI)
29	45	THE CROSSING	Big Country (Mercury)
25	46	NORTH OF A MIRACLE	Nick Heyward (Arista)
-	47	WALK INTO LIGHT	Ian Anderson (Chrysalis)
-	48	ELIMINATOR	ZZ Top (WEA)
-	49	THESE ARE 2-TONE	Various Artists (2-Tone)
35	50	ROOTS REGGAE 'N' REGGAE ROCK	Various Artists (Telstar)

Lionel Richie's second solo album *Can't Slow Down* managed a one-week penetration of Culture Club's armour - compensation for Richie's titled-track single just failing to dislodge either Boy George & Co. or Billy Joel's *Uptown Girl* from atop the singles chart. Joel, meanwhile, aided by his new-found singles success, moved into contention with what would be his all-time best-selling UK album, *An Innocent Man*.

December 1983

10 December 1983

last week	this week		
9	1	U2 LIVE: UNDER A BLOOD RED SKY	U2 (Island)
8	2	SEVEN AND THE RAGGED TIGER	Duran Duran (EMI)
1	3	COLOUR BY NUMBERS	Culture Club (Virgin)
2	4	CAN'T SLOW DOWN	Lionel Richie (Motown)
4	5	TOUCH	Eurythmics (RCA)
11	6	THRILLER	Michael Jackson (Epic)
19	7	BACK TO BACK	Status Quo (Vertigo)
7	8	NO PARLEZ	Paul Young (CBS)
3	9	UNDERCOVER	Rolling Stones (Rolling Stones)
5	10	AN INNOCENT MAN	Billy Joel (CBS)
18	11	STAGES	Elaine Paige (K-Tel)
13	12	GENESIS	Genesis (Charisma/Virgin)
28	13	NOCTURNE	Siouxsie and the Banshees (Wonderland)
10	14	CHART HITS '83	Various Artists (K-Tel)
15	15	FANTASTIC	Wham! (Innervision)
12	16	PIPES OF PEACE	Paul McCartney (Parlophone)
14	17	91502	Yes (Atco)
6	18	BEAUTY STAB	ABC (Neutron)
16	19	LABOUR OF LOVE	UB40 (DEP International)
-	20	BARK AT THE MOON	Ozzy Osbourne (Epic)
35	21	TRACK RECORD	Joan Armatrading (A&M)
20	22	SNAP!	Jam (Polydor)
29	23	ROCK 'N' SOUL (PART 1)	Daryl Hall & John Oates (RCA)
-	24	YOU BROKE MY HEART IN 17 PLACES	Tracey Ullman (Stiff)
32	25	THANK YOU FOR THE MUSIC	Abba (Epic)
22	26	LIZZY LIFE	Thin Lizzy (Vertigo)
27	27	MARVIN GAYE'S GREATEST HITS	Marvin Gaye (Telstar)
17	28	THE BOP WON'T STOP	Shakin' Stevens (Epic)
31	29	HAVE YOU EVER BEEN IN LOVE	Leo Sayer (Chrysalis)
42	30	YENTL	Barbra Streisand (CBS)
33	31	TOO LATE FOR ZERO	Elton John (Rocket)
-	32	CHAS AND DAVE'S KNEES UP - JAMBOREE BAG NO.2	Chas & Dave (Rockney)
25	33	INFIDELS	Bob Dylan (CBS)
30	34	SMELL OF FEMALE	Cramps (Big Beat)
26	35	HIT SQUAD - HITS OF '83	Various Artists (Ronco)
34	36	SUPERCHART '83	Various Artists (Telstar)
-	37	BUCKS FIZZ - GREATEST HITS	Bucks Fizz (RCA)
21	38	VOICE OF THE HEART	Carpenters (A&M)
39	39	HEAD OVER HEELS	Cocteau Twins (4AD)
36	40	TWO OF US	Various Artists (K-Tel)
44	41	STARFLEET PROJECT	Brian May (EMI)
37	42	ZIGGY STARDUST - THE MOTION PICTURE	David Bowie (RCA)
48	43	ELIMINATOR	ZZ Top (WEA)
41	44	WORKING WITH FIRE AND STEEL	China Crisis (Virgin)
-	45	FIRE AND WATER	Dave Greenfield & Jean-Jaques Burnel (Epic)
24	46	IN YOUR EYES	George Benson (WEA)
-	47	FORMULA 30	Various Artists (Decca)
23	48	STRIP	Adam Ant (CBS)
38	49	THE ATLANTIC YEARS 1973-80	Roxy Music (EG)
43	50	FADE TO GREY	Visage (Polydor)

17 December 1983

last week	this week		
6	1	THRILLER	Michael Jackson (Epic)
1	2	U2 LIVE: UNDER A BLOOD RED SKY	U2 (Island)
3	3	COLOUR BY NUMBERS	Culture Club (Virgin)
2	4	SEVEN AND THE RAGGED TIGER	Duran Duran (EMI)
8	5	NO PARLEZ	Paul Young (CBS)
4	6	CAN'T SLOW DOWN	Lionel Richie (Motown)
11	7	STAGES	Elaine Paige (K-Tel)
5	8	TOUCH	Eurythmics (RCA)
-	9	NOW THAT'S WHAT I CALL MUSIC	Various Artists (EMI/Virgin)
10	10	AN INNOCENT MAN	Billy Joel (CBS)
12	11	GENESIS	Genesis (Charisma/Virgin)
15	12	FANTASTIC	Wham! (Innervision)
20	13	BARK AT THE MOON	Ozzy Osbourne (Epic)
7	14	BACK TO BACK	Status Quo (Vertigo)
9	15	UNDERCOVER	Rolling Stones (Rolling Stones)
14	16	CHART HITS '83	Various Artists (K-Tel)
16	17	PIPES OF PEACE	Paul McCartney (Parlophone)
19	18	LABOUR OF LOVE	UB40 (DEP International)
13	19	NOCTURNE	Siouxsie and the Banshees (Wonderland)
21	20	TRACK RECORD	Joan Armatrading (A&M)
23	21	ROCK 'N' SOUL (PART 1)	Daryl Hall & John Oates (RCA)
32	22	CHAS AND DAVE'S KNEES UP - JAMBOREE BAG NO.2	Chas & Dave (Rockney)
-	23	ALL WRAPPED UP	Undertones (Ardeck)
27	24	MARVIN GAYE'S GREATEST HITS	Marvin Gaye (Telstar)
24	25	YOU BROKE MY HEART IN 17 PLACES	Tracey Ullman (Stiff)
25	26	THANK YOU FOR THE MUSIC	Abba (Epic)
28	27	THE BOP WON'T STOP	Shakin' Stevens (Epic)
22	28	SNAP!	Jam (Polydor)
17	29	91502	Yes (Atco)
29	30	HAVE YOU EVER BEEN IN LOVE	Leo Sayer (Chrysalis)
47	31	FORMULA 30	Various Artists (Decca)
38	32	VOICE OF THE HEART	Carpenters (A&M)
43	33	ELIMINATOR	ZZ Top (WEA)
33	34	INFIDELS	Bob Dylan (CBS)
31	35	TOO LATE FOR ZERO	Elton John (Rocket)
-	36	SILVER	Cliff Richard (EMI)
-	37	PHIL SPECTOR'S GREATEST HITS	Various Artists (Impression)
-	38	STREET SOUNDS EDITION 7	Various Artists (Street Sounds)
-	39	LIVE AND DIRECT	Aswad (Island)
-	40	THESE ARE 2-TONE	Various Artists (2-Tone)
18	41	BEAUTY STAB	ABC (Neutron)
-	42	OOH WALLAH WALLAH	King Kurt (Stiff)
49	43	THE ATLANTIC YEARS 1973-80	Roxy Music (EG)
-	44	LIFE'S A RIOT WITH SPY VS SPY	Billy Bragg (Go! Discs)
46	45	IN YOUR EYES	George Benson (WEA)
30	46	YENTL	Barbra Streisand (CBS)
48	47	STRIP	Adam Ant (CBS)
40	48	TWO OF US	Various Artists (K-Tel)
26	49	LIZZY LIFE	Thin Lizzy (Vertigo)
34	50	SMELL OF FEMALE	Cramps (Big Beat)

24 December 1983

last week	this week		
1	1	THRILLER	Michael Jackson (Epic)
3	2	COLOUR BY NUMBERS	Culture Club (Virgin)
5	3	NO PARLEZ	Paul Young (CBS)
9	4	NOW THAT'S WHAT I CALL MUSIC	Various Artists (EMI/Virgin)
2	5	U2 LIVE: UNDER A BLOOD RED SKY	U2 (Island)
7	6	STAGES	Elaine Paige (K-Tel)
4	7	SEVEN AND THE RAGGED TIGER	Duran Duran (EMI)
6	8	CAN'T SLOW DOWN	Lionel Richie (Motown)
12	9	FANTASTIC	Wham! (Innervision)
11	10	GENESIS	Genesis (Charisma/Virgin)
10	11	AN INNOCENT MAN	Billy Joel (CBS)
8	12	TOUCH	Eurythmics (RCA)
31	13	FORMULA 30	Various Artists (Decca)
18	14	LABOUR OF LOVE	UB40 (DEP International)
22	15	CHAS AND DAVE'S KNEES UP - JAMBOREE BAG NO.2	Chas & Dave (Rockney)
14	16	BACK TO BACK	Status Quo (Vertigo)
20	17	TRACK RECORD	Joan Armatrading (A&M)
16	18	CHART HITS '83	Various Artists (K-Tel)
24	19	MARVIN GAYE'S GREATEST HITS	Marvin Gaye (Telstar)
25	20	YOU BROKE MY HEART IN 17 PLACES	Tracey Ullman (Stiff)
37	21	PHIL SPECTOR'S GREATEST HITS	Various Artists (Impression)
13	22	BARK AT THE MOON	Ozzy Osbourne (Epic)
17	23	PIPES OF PEACE	Paul McCartney (Parlophone)
15	24	UNDERCOVER	Rolling Stones (Rolling Stones)
32	25	VOICE OF THE HEART	Carpenters (A&M)
-	26	THE ESSENTIAL JEAN MICHEL JARRE	Jean Michel Jarre (Polydor)
21	27	ROCK 'N' SOUL (PART 1)	Daryl Hall & John Oates (RCA)
30	28	HAVE YOU EVER BEEN IN LOVE	Leo Sayer (Chrysalis)
-	29	MICHAEL JACKSON & THE JACKSONS' 18 GREATEST HITS	Michael Jackson & the Jacksons (Star)
29	30	91502	Yes (Atco)
-	31	GREEN VELVET	Various Artists (Ronco)
-	32	JAPANESE WHISPERS	Cure (Fiction)
34	33	INFIDELS	Bob Dylan (CBS)
38	34	STREET SOUNDS EDITION 7	Various Artists (Street Sounds)
28	35	SNAP!	Jam (Polydor)
27	36	THE BOP WON'T STOP	Shakin' Stevens (Epic)
36	37	SILVER	Cliff Richard (EMI)
19	38	NOCTURNE	Siouxsie and the Banshees (Wonderland)
33	39	ELIMINATOR	ZZ Top (WEA)
39	40	LIVE AND DIRECT	Aswad (Island)
41	41	BEAUTY STAB	ABC (Neutron)
26	42	THANK YOU FOR THE MUSIC	Abba (Epic)
-	43	LOVE STORIES	Don Williams (K-Tel)
-	44	IMAGINATIONS	Various Artists (K-Tel)
35	45	TOO LATE FOR ZERO	Elton John (Rocket)
45	46	IN YOUR EYES	George Benson (WEA)
-	47	LIVE AT THE ALBANY	Flying Pickets (AVM)
23	48	ALL WRAPPED UP	Undertones (Ardeck)
-	49	PERVERTED BY LANGUAGE	Fall (Rough Trade)
-	50	THE VERY BEST OF NEIL DIAMOND	Neil Diamond (K-Tel)

U2's *Under A Blood Red Sky* was the band's first chart-topper, bettering *War*'s peak of Number 3 earlier in the year. It was also their first live album, recorded at 1983 tour gigs in the US and Germany.

The joint EMI/Virgin various artists compilation *Now That's What I Call Music* was the opener in what would be the best-selling UK compilation series of all time, with some volumes topping a million sales.

7 January 1984

last week	this week	Title	Artist (Label)
3	1	NO PARLEZ	Paul Young (CBS)
4	2	NOW THAT'S WHAT I CALL MUSIC	Various Artists (EMI/Virgin)
1	3	THRILLER	Michael Jackson (Epic)
2	4	COLOUR BY NUMBERS	Culture Club (Virgin)
6	5	STAGES	Elaine Paige (K-Tel)
8	6	CAN'T SLOW DOWN	Lionel Richie (Motown)
10	7	GENESIS	Genesis (Charisma)
26	8	THE ESSENTIAL JEAN MICHEL JARRE	Jean Michel Jarre (Polydor)
5	9	U2 LIVE: UNDER A BLOOD RED SKY	U2 (Island)
13	10	FORMULA 30	Various Artists (Decca)
7	11	SEVEN AND THE RAGGED TIGER	Duran Duran (EMI)
14	12	LABOUR OF LOVE	UB40 (DEP International)
9	13	FANTASTIC	Wham! (Innervision)
12	14	TOUCH	Eurythmics (RCA)
11	15	AN INNOCENT MAN	Billy Joel (CBS)
20	16	YOU BROKE MY HEART IN 17 PLACES	Tracey Ullman (Stiff)
23	17	PIPES OF PEACE	Paul McCartney (Parlophone)
-	18	PORTRAIT	Diana Ross (Telstar)
19	19	MARVIN GAYE'S GREATEST HITS	Marvin Gaye (Telstar)
31	20	GREEN VELVET	Various Artists (Ronco)
21	21	PHIL SPECTOR'S GREATEST HITS	Various Artists (Impression)
16	22	BACK TO BACK	Status Quo (Vertigo)
18	23	CHART HITS '83	Various Artists (K-Tel)
15	24	CHAS AND DAVE'S KNEES UP - JAMBOREE BAG NO.2	Chas & Dave (Rockney)
17	25	TRACK RECORD	Joan Armatrading (A&M)
29	26	MICHAEL JACKSON & THE JACKSON FIVE'S 18 GREATEST HITS	Michael Jackson & the Jackson Five (Star)
35	27	SNAP!	Jam (Polydor)
27	28	ROCK 'N' SOUL (PART 1)	Daryl Hall & John Oates (RCA)
24	29	UNDERCOVER	Rolling Stones (Rolling Stones)
47	30	LIVE AT THE ALBANY EMPIRE	Flying Pickets (AVM)
50	31	THE VERY BEST OF NEIL DIAMOND	Neil Diamond (K-Tel)
28	32	HAVE YOU EVER BEEN IN LOVE	Leo Sayer (Chrysalis)
33	33	INFIDELS	Bob Dylan (CBS)
37	34	SILVER	Cliff Richard (EMI)
25	35	VOICE OF THE HEART	Carpenters (A&M)
39	36	ELIMINATOR	ZZ Top (WEA)
-	37	ZIGGY STARDUST - THE MOTION PICTURE	David Bowie (RCA)
22	38	BARK AT THE MOON	Ozzy Osbourne (Epic)
32	39	JAPANESE WHISPERS	Cure (Fiction)
40	40	LIVE AND DIRECT	Aswad (Island)
44	41	IMAGINATIONS	Various Artists (CBS)
45	42	TOO LOW FOR ZERO	Elton John (Rocket)
-	43	HIT SQUAD – HITS OF '83	Various (Ronco)
-	44	OUT DEH	Gregory Isaacs (Island)
30	45	90125	Yes (Atco)
46	46	IN YOUR EYES	George Benson (WEA)
-	47	THE MUSIC OF RICHARD CLAYDERMAN	Richard Clayderman (Decca/Delphine)
34	48	STREETSOUNDS EDITION 7	Various Artists (Street Sounds)
36	49	THE BOP WON'T STOP	Shakin' Stevens (Epic)
-	50	CLASSIC TRANQUILITY	Phil Coulter (K-Tel)

14 January 1984

last week	this week	Title	Artist (Label)
3	1	THRILLER	Michael Jackson (Epic)
1	2	NO PARLEZ	Paul Young (CBS)
2	3	NOW THAT'S WHAT I CALL MUSIC	Various Artists (EMI/Virgin)
4	4	COLOUR BY NUMBERS	Culture Club (Virgin)
6	5	CAN'T SLOW DOWN	Lionel Richie (Motown)
5	6	STAGES	Elaine Paige (K-Tel)
17	7	PIPES OF PEACE	Paul McCartney (Parlophone)
15	8	AN INNOCENT MAN	Billy Joel (CBS)
8	9	THE ESSENTIAL JEAN MICHEL JARRE	Jean Michel Jarre (Polydor)
10	10	FORMULA 30	Various Artists (Decca/delphine)
12	11	LABOUR OF LOVE	UB40 (DEP International)
9	12	U2 LIVE: UNDER A BLOOD RED SKY	U2 (Island)
7	13	GENESIS	Genesis (Charisma)
13	14	FANTASTIC	Wham! (Innervision)
20	15	GREEN VELVET	Various Artists (Ronco)
18	16	PORTRAIT	Diana Ross (Telstar)
14	17	TOUCH	Eurythmics (RCA)
11	18	SEVEN AND THE RAGGED TIGER	Duran Duran (EMI)
25	19	TRACK RECORD	Joan Armatrading (A&M)
26	20	MICHAEL JACKSON & THE JACKSON FIVE'S 18 GREATEST HITS	Michael Jackson & the Jackson Five (Star)
19	21	MARVIN GAYE'S GREATEST HITS	Marvin Gaye (Telstar)
24	22	CHAS AND DAVE'S KNEES UP - JAMBOREE BAG NO.2	Chas & Dave (Rockney)
22	23	BACK TO BACK	Status Quo (Vertigo)
39	24	JAPANESE WHISPERS	Cure (Fiction)
16	25	YOU BROKE MY HEART IN 17 PLACES	Tracey Ullman (Stiff)
42	26	TOO LOW FOR ZERO	Elton John (Rocket)
-	27	STREET SOUNDS ELECTRO 2	Various Artists (Street Sounds)
36	28	ELIMINATOR	ZZ Top (WEA)
46	29	IN YOUR EYES	George Benson (WEA)
-	30	CHART TREK VOLUME 1 & 2	Various Artists (Ronco)
28	31	ROCK 'N' SOUL (PART 1)	Daryl Hall & John Oates (RCA)
27	32	SNAP!	Jam (Polydor)
-	33	HEAD OVER HEELS	Cocteau Twins (4AD)
-	34	IN THE HEART	Kool & the Gang (De-Lite)
29	35	UNDERCOVER	Rolling Stones (Rolling Stones)
21	36	PHIL SPECTOR'S GREATEST HITS	Various Artists (Impression)
-	37	YENTL	Barbra Streisand (CBS)
34	38	SILVER	Cliff Richard (EMI)
48	39	STREETSOUNDS EDITION 7	Various Artists (Street Sounds)
-	40	NOCTURNE	Siouxsie & the Banshees (Wonderland)
40	41	LIVE AND DIRECT	Aswad (Island)
23	42	CHART HITS '83	Various Artists (K-Tel)
-	43	QUICK STEP AND SIDE KICK	Thompson Twins (Arista)
30	44	LIVE AT ALBANY EMPIRE	Flying Pickets (AVM)
45	45	90125	Yes (Atco)
-	46	BUCKS FIZZ - GREATEST HITS	Bucks Fizz (RCA)
49	47	THE BOP WON'T STOP	Shakin' Stevens (Epic)
-	48	THE LUXURY GAP	Heaven 17 (BEF/Virgin)
-	49	CADMIUM	Sky (Ariola)
33	50	INFIDELS	Bob Dylan (CBS)

21 January 1984

last week	this week	Title	Artist (Label)
1	1	THRILLER	Michael Jackson (Epic)
2	2	NO PARLEZ	Paul Young (CBS)
4	3	COLOUR BY NUMBERS	Culture Club (Virgin)
3	4	NOW THAT'S WHAT I CALL MUSIC	Various Artists (EMI/Virgin)
12	5	U2 LIVE: UNDER A BLOOD RED SKY	U2 (Island)
7	6	PIPES OF PEACE	Paul McCartney (Parlophone)
8	7	AN INNOCENT MAN	Billy Joel (CBS)
11	8	LABOUR OF LOVE	UB40 (DEP International)
5	9	CAN'T SLOW DOWN	Lionel Richie (Motown)
17	10	TOUCH	Eurythmics (RCA)
16	11	PORTRAIT	Diana Ross (Telstar)
12	12	GENESIS	Genesis (Charisma)
-	13	LEARNING TO CRAWL	Pretenders (WEA)
24	14	JAPANESE WHISPERS	Cure (Fiction)
9	15	THE ESSENTIAL JEAN MICHEL JARRE	Jean Michel Jarre (Polydor)
23	16	BACK TO BACK	Status Quo (Vertigo)
18	17	SEVEN AND THE RAGGED TIGER	Duran Duran (EMI)
25	18	YOU BROKE MY HEART IN 17 PLACES	Tracey Ullman (Stiff)
6	19	STAGES	Elaine Paige (K-Tel)
14	20	FANTASTIC	Wham! (Innervision)
10	21	FORMULA 30	Various Artists (Decca/delphine)
19	22	TRACK RECORD	Joan Armatrading (A&M)
26	23	TOO LOW FOR ZERO	Elton John (Rocket)
15	24	GREEN VELVET	Various Artists (Ronco)
21	25	MARVIN GAYE'S GREATEST HITS	Marvin Gaye (Telstar)
28	26	ELIMINATOR	ZZ Top (WEA)
41	27	LIVE AND DIRECT	Aswad (Island)
30	28	CHART TREK VOL 1 & 2	Various Artists (Ronco)
-	29	WORKING WITH FIRE AND STEEL	China Crisis (Virgin)
32	30	SNAP!	Jam (Polydor)
27	31	STREET SOUNDS ELECTRO 2	Various Artists (Street Sounds)
-	32	THE CROSSING	Big Country (Mercury)
-	33	SYNCHRONICITY	Police (A&M)
31	34	ROCK 'N' SOUL (PART 1)	Daryl Hall & John Oates (RCA)
33	35	HEAD OVER HEELS	Cocteau Twins (4AD)
-	36	BUSY BODY	Luther Vandross (Epic)
20	37	MICHAEL JACKSON & THE JACKSON FIVE'S 18 GREATEST HITS	Michael Jackson & the Jackson Five (Star)
-	38	LIFE'S A RIOT WITH SPY VS SPY	Billy Bragg (Go! Discs)
43	39	QUICK STEP AND SIDE KICK	Thompson Twins (Arista)
35	40	UNDERCOVER	Rolling Stones (Rolling Stones)
39	41	STREETSOUNDS 7	Various (Street Sounds)
34	42	IN THE HEART	Kool & the Gang (De-Lite)
29	43	IN YOUR EYES	George Benson (WEA)
-	44	LET'S DANCE	David Bowie (RCA)
22	45	CHAS AND DAVE'S KNEES UP - JAMBOREE BAG NO.2	Chas & Dave (Rockney)
-	46	OUT DEH	Gregory Isaacs (Island)
-	47	PERVERTED BY LANGUAGE	Fall (Rough Trade)
-	48	WAR	U2 (Island)
-	49	HIGH LAND HARD RAIN	Aztec Camera (Rough Trade)
-	50	TRUE	Spandau Ballet (Chrysalis)

Paul McCartney's *Pipes Of Peace* album, after a comparatively modest start, established itself as a firm Top 10 seller on the back of its namesake single's elevation to Number 1. The arrival of Diana Ross' *Portrait* compilation on Telstar, meanwhile, provided another addition to the ranks of Motown hits packages licensed by TV-marketing labels. Marvin Gaye and the Jacksons were already similarly charted.

January – February 1984

28 January 1984

last week	this week	Title	Artist (Label)
1	1	THRILLER	Michael Jackson (Epic)
2	2	NO PARLEZ	Paul Young (CBS)
6	3	PIPES OF PEACE	Paul McCartney (Parlophone)
13	4	LEARNING TO CRAWL	Pretenders (WEA)
5	5	U2 LIVE: UNDER A BLOOD RED SKY	U2 (Island)
9	6	CAN'T SLOW DOWN	Lionel Richie (Motown)
7	7	AN INNOCENT MAN	Billy Joel (CBS)
4	8	NOW THAT'S WHAT I CALL MUSIC	Various Artists (EMI/Virgin)
10	9	TOUCH	Eurythmics (RCA)
3	10	COLOUR BY NUMBERS	Culture Club (Virgin)
8	11	LABOUR OF LOVE	UB40 (DEP International)
11	12	PORTRAIT	Diana Ross (Telstar)
12	13	GENESIS	Genesis (Charisma)
14	14	JAPANESE WHISPERS	Cure (Fiction)
16	15	BACK TO BACK	Status Quo (Vertigo)
38	16	LIFE'S A RIOT WITH SPY VS SPY	Billy Bragg (Go! Discs)
33	17	SYNCHRONICITY	Police (A&M)
19	18	STAGES	Elaine Paige (K-Tel)
18	19	YOU BROKE MY HEART IN 17 PLACES	Tracey Ullman (Stiff)
23	20	TOO LOW FOR ZERO	Elton John (Rocket)
15	21	THE ESSENTIAL JEAN MICHEL JARRE	Jean Michel Jarre (Polydor)
24	22	GREEN VELVET	Various Artists (Ronco)
32	23	THE CROSSING	Big Country (Mercury)
21	24	FORMULA 30	Various Artists (Decca/delphine)
31	25	STREET SOUNDS ELECTRO 2	Various Artists (Street Sounds)
-	26	DEFENDERS OF THE FAITH	Judas Priest (CBS)
29	27	WORKING WITH FIRE AND STEEL	China Crisis (Virgin)
17	28	SEVEN AND THE RAGGED TIGER	Duran Duran (EMI)
26	29	ELIMINATOR	ZZ Top (WEA)
36	30	BUSY BODY	Luther Vandross (Epic)
27	31	LIVE AND DIRECT	Aswad (Island)
35	32	HEAD OVER HEELS	Cocteau Twins (4AD)
-	33	SOMETIMES WHEN WE TOUCH	Various (Ronco)
20	34	FANTASTIC	Wham! (Innervision)
22	35	TRACK RECORD	Joan Armatrading (A&M)
39	36	QUICK STEP AND SIDE KICK	Thompson Twins (Arista)
-	37	1984	Van Halen (WEA)
40	38	UNDERCOVER	Rolling Stones (Rolling Stones)
34	39	ROCK 'N' SOUL (PART 1)	Daryl Hall & John Oates (RCA)
48	40	WAR	U2 (Island)
49	41	HIGH LAND HARD RAIN	Aztec Camera (Rough Trade)
-	42	WHAT'S NEW?	Linda Ronstadt (Asylum)
28	43	CHART TREK VOLUME 1 & 2	Various (Ronco)
46	44	OUT DEH	Gregory Isaacs (Island)
37	45	MICHAEL JACKSON & THE JACKSON FIVE'S 18 GREATEST HITS	Michael Jackson & the Jackson Five (Star)
47	46	PERVERTED BY LANGUAGE	Fall (Rough Trade)
-	47	BALLS TO THE WALL	Accept (Lark)
25	48	MARVIN GAYE'S GREATEST HITS	Marvin Gaye (Telstar)
43	49	IN YOUR EYES	George Benson (WEA)
42	50	IN THE HEART	Kool & the Gang (De-Lite)

4 February 1984

last week	this week	Title	Artist (Label)
1	1	THRILLER	Michael Jackson (Epic)
3	2	PIPES OF PEACE	Paul McCartney (Parlophone)
4	3	LEARNING TO CRAWL	Pretenders (WEA)
5	4	U2 LIVE: UNDER A BLOOD RED SKY	U2 (Island)
7	5	AN INNOCENT MAN	Billy Joel (CBS)
-	6	MILK AND HONEY	John Lennon & Yoko Ono (Polydor)
6	7	CAN'T SLOW DOWN	Lionel Richie (Motown)
2	8	NO PARLEZ	Paul Young (CBS)
8	9	NOW THAT'S WHAT I CALL MUSIC	Various Artists (EMI/Virgin)
9	10	TOUCH	Eurythmics (RCA)
10	11	COLOUR BY NUMBERS	Culture Club (Virgin)
12	12	PORTRAIT	Diana Ross (Telstar)
23	13	THE CROSSING	Big Country (Mercury)
11	14	LABOUR OF LOVE	UB40 (DEP International)
26	15	DEFENDERS OF THE FAITH	Judas Priest (CBS)
16	16	LIFE'S A RIOT WITH SPY VS SPY	Billy Bragg (Go! Discs)
27	17	WORKING WITH FIRE AND STEEL	China Crisis (Virgin)
15	18	BACK TO BACK	Status Quo (Vertigo)
14	19	JAPANESE WHISPERS	Cure (Fiction)
37	20	1984	Van Halen (WEA)
13	21	GENESIS	Genesis (Charisma)
17	22	SYNCHRONICITY	Police (A&M)
18	23	STAGES	Elaine Paige (K-Tel)
33	24	SOMETIMES WHEN WE TOUCH	Various (Ronco)
42	25	WHAT'S NEW?	Linda Ronstadt (Asylum)
36	26	QUICK STEP AND SIDE KICK	Thompson Twins (Arista)
21	27	THE ESSENTIAL JEAN MICHEL JARRE	Jean Michel Jarre (Polydor)
32	28	HEAD OVER HEELS	Cocteau Twins (4AD)
30	29	BUSY BODY	Luther Vandross (Epic)
28	30	SEVEN AND THE RAGGED TIGER	Duran Duran (EMI)
31	31	LIVE AND DIRECT	Aswad (Island)
19	32	YOU BROKE MY HEART IN 17 PLACES	Tracey Ullman (Stiff)
20	33	TOO LOW FOR ZERO	Elton John (Rocket)
35	34	TRACK RECORD	Joan Armatrading (A&M)
34	35	FANTASTIC	Wham! (Innervision)
39	36	ROCK 'N' SOUL (PART 1)	Daryl Hall & John Oates (RCA)
25	37	STREET SOUNDS ELECTRO 2	Various Artists (Street Sounds)
22	38	GREEN VELVET	Various Artists (Ronco)
40	39	WAR	U2 (Island)
49	40	IN YOUR EYES	George Benson (WEA)
-	41	BEAUTY STAB	ABC (Neutron)
45	42	MICHAEL JACKSON & THE JACKSON FIVE'S 18 GREATEST HITS	Michael Jackson & the Jackson Five (Star)
-	43	NEW GOLD DREAM	Simple Minds (Virgin)
-	44	LET'S DANCE	David Bowie (EMIAmerica)
50	45	IN THE HEART	Kool & the Gang (De-Lite)
-	46	THE MUSIC OF RICHARD CLAYDERMAN	Richard Clayderman (Decca/delphine)
-	47	THE BOP WON'T STOP	Shakin' Stevens (Epic)
44	48	OUT DEH	Gregory Isaacs (Island)
24	49	FORMULA 30	Various Artists (Decca/delphine)
38	50	UNDERCOVER	Rolling Stones (Rolling Stones)

11 February 1984

last week	this week	Title	Artist (Label)
6	1	MILK AND HONEY	John Lennon & Yoko Ono (Polydor)
10	2	TOUCH	Eurythmics (RCA)
1	3	THRILLER	Michael Jackson (Epic)
8	4	NO PARLEZ	Paul Young (CBS)
5	5	AN INNOCENT MAN	Billy Joel (CBS)
7	6	CAN'T SLOW DOWN	Lionel Richie (Motown)
3	7	LEARNING TO CRAWL	Pretenders (WEA)
4	8	U2 LIVE: UNDER A BLOOD RED SKY	U2 (Island)
2	9	PIPES OF PEACE	Paul McCartney (Parlophone)
20	10	1984	Van Halen (WEA)
13	11	THE CROSSING	Big Country (Mercury)
-	12	SLIDE IT IN	Whitesnake (Liberty)
9	13	NOW THAT'S WHAT I CALL MUSIC	Various Artists (EMI/Virgin)
12	14	PORTRAIT	Diana Ross (Telstar)
11	15	COLOUR BY NUMBERS	Culture Club (Virgin)
16	16	LIFE'S A RIOT WITH SPY VS SPY	Billy Bragg (Go! Discs)
17	17	WORKING WITH FIRE AND STEEL	China Crisis (Virgin)
14	18	LABOUR OF LOVE	UB40 (DEP International)
26	19	QUICK STEP AND SIDE KICK	Thompson Twins (Arista)
15	20	DEFENDERS OF THE FAITH	Judas Priest (CBS)
21	21	GENESIS	Genesis (Charisma)
-	22	HEAVEN IS WAITING	Danse Society (Arista)
35	23	FANTASTIC	Wham! (Innervision)
19	24	JAPANESE WHISPERS	Cure (Fiction)
22	25	SYNCHRONICITY	Police (A&M)
-	26	CRUSADER	Saxon (Carrerre)
23	27	BUSY BODY	Luther Vandross (Epic)
23	28	STAGES	Elaine Paige (K-Tel)
31	29	LIVE AND DIRECT	Aswad (Island)
28	30	HEAD OVER HEELS	Cocteau Twins (4AD)
18	31	BACK TO BACK	Status Quo (Vertigo)
37	32	STREET SOUNDS ELECTRO 2	Various Artists (Street Sounds)
24	33	SOMETIMES WHEN WE TOUCH	Various (Ronco)
27	34	THE ESSENTIAL JEAN MICHEL JARRE	Jean Michel Jarre (Polydor)
-	35	WHITE FLAME	Snowy White (Towerbell)
30	36	SEVEN AND THE RAGGED TIGER	Duran Duran (EMI)
-	37	4,000 WEEKS HOLIDAY	Ian Dury (Polydor)
32	38	YOU BROKE MY HEART IN 17 PLACES	Tracey Ullman (Stiff)
39	39	WAR	U2 (Island)
33	40	TOO LOW FOR ZERO	Elton John (Rocket)
-	41	ELIMINATOR	ZZ Top (WEA)
40	42	IN YOUR EYES	George Benson (WEA)
-	43	AUF WIEDERSEHEN PET - TV SOUNDTRACK	Various Artists (Towerbell)
-	44	THE COLLECTION - 20 GREATEST HITS	Gladys Knight & The Pips (Star Blend)
-	45	MARVIN GAYE'S GREATEST HITS	Marvin Gaye (Telstar)
45	46	IN THE HEART	Kool & the Gang (De-Lite)
25	47	WHAT'S NEW?	Linda Ronstadt (Asylum)
-	48	HIGH LAND HARD RAIN	Aztec Camera (Rough Trade)
48	49	OUT DEH	Gregory Isaacs (Island)
34	50	TRACK RECORD	Joan Armatrading (A&M)

John and Yoko's *Milk And Honey* set, released more than three years after Lennon's death, was a selection from the material the pair had been working on during 1980, the initial pick of which had been used in their *Double Fantasy* album. Lennon also had a simultaneous posthumous Number 2 hit single with *Nobody Told Me*, taken from the album. Van Halen had the most obviously topical LP title of the year yet.

18 February 1984

last week	this week	Title	Artist (Label)
2	1	TOUCH	Eurythmics (RCA)
3	2	THRILLER	Michael Jackson (Epic)
1	3	MILK AND HONEY	John Lennon & Yoko Ono (Polydor)
12	4	SLIDE IT IN	Whitesnake (Liberty)
6	5	CAN'T SLOW DOWN	Lionel Richie (Motown)
8	6	U2 LIVE: UNDER A BLOOD RED SKY	U2 (Island)
4	7	NO PARLEZ	Paul Young (CBS)
5	8	AN INNOCENT MAN	Billy Joel (CBS)
-	9	SPARKLE IN THE RAIN	Simple Minds (Virgin)
11	10	THE CROSSING	Big Country (Mercury)
7	11	LEARNING TO CRAWL	Pretenders (WEA)
10	12	1984	Van Halen (WEA)
15	13	COLOUR BY NUMBERS	Culture Club (Virgin)
9	14	PIPES OF PEACE	Paul McCartney (Parlophone)
18	15	LABOUR OF LOVE	UB40 (DEP International)
14	16	PORTRAIT	Diana Ross (Telstar)
13	17	NOW THAT'S WHAT I CALL MUSIC	Various Artists (EMI/Virgin)
26	18	CRUSADER	Saxon (Carrere)
21	19	GENESIS	Genesis (Charisma)
19	20	QUICK STEP AND SIDE KICK	Thompson Twins (Arista)
-	21	THE FLAT EARTH	Thomas Dolby (Parlophone)
22	22	HEAVEN IS WAITING	Danse Society (Arista)
-	23	VICTIMS OF THE FUTURE	Gary Moore (Virgin)
16	24	LIFE'S A RIOT WITH SPY VS SPY	Billy Bragg (Go! Discs)
36	25	SEVEN AND THE RAGGED TIGER	Duran Duran (EMI)
17	26	WORKING WITH FIRE AND STEEL	China Crisis (Virgin)
33	27	SOMETIMES WHEN WE TOUCH	Various (Ronco)
28	28	STAGES	Elaine Paige (K-Tel)
35	29	WHITE FLAME	Snowy White (Towerbell)
31	30	BACK TO BACK	Status Quo (Vertigo)
24	31	JAPANESE WHISPERS	Cure (Fiction)
25	32	SYNCHRONICITY	Police (A&M)
27	33	BUSY BODY	Luther Vandross (Epic)
-	34	YENTL	Barbra Streisand (CBS)
20	35	DEFENDERS OF THE FAITH	Judas Priest (CBS)
40	36	TOO LOW FOR ZERO	Elton John (Rocket)
-	37	THE VERY BEST OF MOTOWN LOVE SONGS	Various Artists (Telstar)
30	38	HEAD OVER HEELS	Cocteau Twins (4AD)
-	39	CHRISTINE McVIE	Christine McVie (Warner Bros.)
50	40	TRACK RECORD	Joan Armatrading (A&M)
-	41	BEAUTY STAB	ABC (Neutron)
34	42	THE ESSENTIAL JEAN MICHEL JARRE	Jean Michel Jarre (Polydor)
23	43	FANTASTIC	Wham! (Innervision)
-	44	ROCK 'N' SOUL (PART 1)	Daryl Hall & John Oates (RCA)
38	45	YOU BROKE MY HEART IN 17 PLACES	Tracey Ullman (Stiff)
-	46	LIVING IN OZ	Rick Springfield (RCA)
44	47	THE COLLECTION - 20 GREATEST HITS	Gladys Knight & The Pips (Star Blend)
-	48	LET'S DANCE	David Bowie (EM Americal)
29	49	LIVE AND DIRECT	Aswad (Island)
32	50	STREET SOUNDS ELECTRO 2	Various Artists (Street Sounds)

25 February 1984

last week	this week	Title	Artist (Label)
9	1	SPARKLE IN THE RAIN	Simple Minds (Virgin)
2	2	THRILLER	Michael Jackson (Epic)
1	3	TOUCH	Eurythmics (RCA)
-	4	INTO THE GAP	Thompson Twins (Arista)
-	5	AN INNOCENT MAN	Billy Joel (CBS)
21	6	THE FLAT EARTH	Thomas Dolby (Parlophone)
5	7	CAN'T SLOW DOWN	Lionel Richie (Motown)
10	8	THE CROSSING	Big Country (Mercury)
6	9	U2 LIVE: UNDER A BLOOD RED SKY	U2 (Island)
7	10	NO PARLEZ	Paul Young (CBS)
23	11	VICTIMS OF THE FUTURE	Gary Moore (Virgin)
4	12	SLIDE IT IN	Whitesnake (Liberty)
3	13	MILK AND HONEY	John Lennon & Yoko Ono (Polydor)
12	14	1984	Van Halen (WEA)
18	15	CRUSADER	Saxon (Carrere)
11	16	LEARNING TO CRAWL	Pretenders (WEA)
14	17	PIPES OF PEACE	Paul McCartney (Parlophone)
37	18	THE VERY BEST OF MOTOWN LOVE SONGS	Various Artists (Telstar)
-	19	DECLARATION	Alarm (Mute)
13	20	COLOUR BY NUMBERS	Culture Club (Virgin)
29	21	WHITE FLAME	Snowy White (Towerbell)
15	22	LABOUR OF LOVE	UB40 (DEP International)
17	23	NOW THAT'S WHAT I CALL MUSIC	Various Artists (EMI/Virgin)
20	24	QUICK STEP AND SIDE KICK	Thompson Twins (Arista)
27	25	SOMETIMES WHEN WE TOUCH	Various Artists (Ronco)
22	26	HEAVEN IS WAITING	Danse Society (Arista)
24	27	LIFE'S A RIOT WITH SPY VS SPY	Billy Bragg (Go! Discs)
19	28	GENESIS	Genesis (Charisma)
34	29	YENTL	Barbra Streisand (CBS)
-	30	SHE'S SO UNUSUAL	Cyndi Lauper (Portrait)
25	31	SEVEN AND THE RAGGED TIGER	Duran Duran (EMI)
30	32	BACK TO BACK	Status Quo (Vertigo)
-	33	MADONNA	Madonna (Sire)
43	34	FANTASTIC	Wham! (Innervision)
49	35	LIVE AND DIRECT	Aswad (Island)
28	36	STAGES	Elaine Paige (K-Tel)
26	37	WORKING WITH FIRE AND STEEL	China Crisis (Virgin)
-	38	SENTINEL	Pallas (Liberty)
46	39	LIVING IN OZ	Rick Springfield (RCA)
16	40	PORTRAIT	Diana Ross (Telstar)
38	41	HEAD OVER HEELS	Cocteau Twins (4AD)
-	42	IT'S MY LIFE	Talk Talk (EMI)
33	43	BUSY BODY	Luther Vandross (Epic)
39	44	CHRISTINE McVIE	Christine McVie (Warner Bros.)
32	45	SYNCHRONICITY	Police (A&M)
42	46	THE ESSENTIAL JEAN MICHEL JARRE	Jean Michel Jarre (Polydor)
47	47	THE COLLECTION - 20 GREATEST HITS	Gladys Knight & The Pips (Star Blend)
45	48	YOU BROKE MY HEART IN 17 PLACES	Tracey Ullman (Stiff)
-	49	BODIES AND SOULS	Manhattan Transfer (Atlantic)
36	50	TOO LOW FOR ZERO	Elton John (Rocket)

3 March 1984

last week	this week	Title	Artist (Label)
4	1	INTO THE GAP	Thompson Twins (Arista)
1	2	SPARKLE IN THE RAIN	Simple Minds (Virgin)
2	3	THRILLER	Michael Jackson (Epic)
3	4	TOUCH	Eurythmics (RCA)
5	5	AN INNOCENT MAN	Billy Joel (CBS)
8	6	THE CROSSING	Big Country (Mercury)
19	7	DECLARATION	Alarm (Mute)
7	8	CAN'T SLOW DOWN	Lionel Richie (Motown)
6	9	THE FLAT EARTH	Thomas Dolby (Parlophone)
-	10	THE SMITHS	Smiths (Rough Trade)
9	11	U2 LIVE: UNDER A BLOOD RED SKY	U2 (Island)
10	12	NO PARLEZ	Paul Young (CBS)
14	13	1984	Van Halen (WEA)
16	14	LEARNING TO CRAWL	Pretenders (WEA)
12	15	SLIDE IT IN	Whitesnake (Liberty)
11	16	VICTIMS OF THE FUTURE	Gary Moore (Virgin)
18	17	THE VERY BEST OF MOTOWN LOVE SONGS	Various Artists (Telstar)
13	18	MILK AND HONEY	John Lennon & Yoko Ono (Polydor)
22	19	LABOUR OF LOVE	UB40 (DEP International)
28	20	GENESIS	Genesis (Charisma)
25	21	SOMETIMES WHEN WE TOUCH	Various Artists (Ronco)
33	22	MADONNA	Madonna (Sire)
42	23	IT'S MY LIFE	Talk Talk (EMI)
-	24	KEEP MOVING	Madness (Stiff)
20	25	COLOUR BY NUMBERS	Culture Club (Virgin)
23	26	NOW THAT'S WHAT I CALL MUSIC	Various Artists (EMI/Virgin)
15	27	CRUSADER	Saxon (Carrere)
-	28	LIVE IN BELFAST	Van Morrison (Mercury)
-	29	THE TUBE	Various Artists (K-Tel)
17	30	PIPES OF PEACE	Paul McCartney (Parlophone)
-	31	IN THE HEART	Kool & the Gang (De-Lite)
-	32	WORLD SHUT YOUR MOUTH	Julian Cope (Mercury)
31	33	SEVEN AND THE RAGGED TIGER	Duran Duran (EMI)
26	34	HEAVEN IS WAITING	Danse Society (Arista)
38	35	SENTINEL	Pallas (Liberty)
36	36	STAGES	Elaine Paige (K-Tel)
27	37	LIFE'S A RIOT WITH SPY VS SPY	Billy Bragg (Go! Discs)
-	38	HAIL TO ENGLAND	Manowar (Music for Nations)
24	39	QUICK STEP AND SIDE KICK	Thompson Twins (Arista)
40	40	PORTRAIT	Diana Ross (Telstar)
21	41	WHITE FLAME	Snowy White (Towerbell)
29	42	YENTL	Barbra Streisand (CBS)
-	43	AMMONIA AVENUE	Alan Parsons Project (Arista)
-	44	PRIVATE PARTY	Bobby Nunn (Motown)
-	45	NEW GOLD DREAM	Simple Minds (Virgin)
43	46	BUSY BODY	Luther Vandross (Epic)
-	47	E.S.P.	Millie Jackson (Sire)
41	48	HEAD OVER HEELS	Cocteau Twins (4AD)
30	49	SHE'S SO UNUSUAL	Cyndi Lauper (Portrait)
32	50	BACK TO BACK	Status Quo (Vertigo)

Thriller continued to be the most consistently-selling album in the country, while several other acts and titles took turns with a brief glory moment at Number 1 above it. *Into The Gap* was to be the all-time biggest-selling album for the Thompson Twins (who were a group with the name of a duo), while *Touch* was the second chart-topping LP by the Eurythmics (who were actually a duo with the name of a group!)

March 1984

10 March 1984

last	this	title	artist (label)
1	1	INTO THE GAP	Thompson Twins (Arista)
10	2	THE SMITHS	Smiths (Rough Trade)
2	3	SPARKLE IN THE RAIN	Simple Minds (Virgin)
4	4	TOUCH	Eurythmics (RCA)
3	5	THRILLER	Michael Jackson (Epic)
24	6	KEEP MOVING	Madness (Stiff)
5	7	AN INNOCENT MAN	Billy Joel (CBS)
8	8	CAN'T SLOW DOWN	Lionel Richie (Motown)
7	9	DECLARATION	Alarm (Mute)
6	10	THE CROSSING	Big Country (Mercury)
12	11	NO PARLEZ	Paul Young (CBS)
-	12	THE WORKS	Queen (EMI)
13	13	1984	Van Halen (WEA)
11	14	U2 LIVE: UNDER A BLOOD RED SKY	U2 (Island)
9	15	THE FLAT EARTH	Thomas Dolby (Parlophone)
17	16	THE VERY BEST OF MOTOWN LOVE SONGS	Various Artists (Telstar)
31	17	IN THE HEART	Kool & the Gang (De-Lite)
32	18	WORLD SHUT YOUR MOUTH	Julian Cope (Mercury)
43	19	AMMONIA AVENUE	Alan Parsons Project (Arista)
25	20	COLOUR BY NUMBERS	Culture Club (Virgin)
21	21	SOMETIMES WHEN WE TOUCH	Various Artists (Ronco)
28	22	LIVE IN BELFAST	Van Morrison (Mercury)
37	23	LIFE'S A RIOT WITH SPY VS SPY	Billy Bragg (Go! Discs)
19	24	LABOUR OF LOVE	UB40 (DEP International)
26	25	NOW THAT'S WHAT I CALL MUSIC	Various Artists (EMI/Virgin)
30	26	PIPES OF PEACE	Paul McCartney (Parlophone)
20	27	GENESIS	Genesis (Charisma)
15	28	SLIDE IT IN	Whitesnake (Liberty)
16	29	VICTIMS OF THE FUTURE	Gary Moore (Virgin)
18	30	MILK AND HONEY	John Lennon & Yoko Ono (Polydor)
-	31	TEXAS FEVER	Orange Juice (Polydor)
-	32	HUMAN RACING	Nik Kershaw (MCA)
33	33	SEVEN AND THE RAGGED TIGER	Duran Duran (EMI)
39	34	QUICK STEP AND SIDE KICK	Thompson Twins (Arista)
14	35	LEARNING TO CRAWL	Pretenders (WEA)
22	36	MADONNA	Madonna (Sire)
34	37	HEAVEN IS WAITING	Danse Society (Arista)
27	38	CRUSADER	Saxon (Carrere)
29	39	THE TUBE	Various Artists (K-Tel)
23	40	IT'S MY LIFE	Talk Talk (EMI)
-	41	STREET SOUNDS EDITION 8	Various Artists (Street Sounds)
48	42	HEAD OVER HEELS	Cocteau Twins (4AD)
-	43	SERENADE	Juan Martin (K-Tel)
40	44	PORTRAIT	Diana Ross (Telstar)
42	45	YENTL	Barbra Streisand (CBS)
-	46	LOVE WARS	Womack & Womack (Elektra)
36	47	STAGES	Elaine Paige (K-Tel)
47	48	E.S.P.	Millie Jackson (Sire)
-	49	FANTASTIC	Wham! (Innervision)
35	50	SENTINEL	Pallas (Liberty)

17 March 1984

last	this	title	artist (label)
1	1	INTO THE GAP	Thompson Twins (Arista)
12	2	THE WORKS	Queen (EMI)
2	3	THE SMITHS	Smiths (Rough Trade)
5	4	THRILLER	Michael Jackson (Epic)
3	5	SPARKLE IN THE RAIN	Simple Minds (Virgin)
8	6	CAN'T SLOW DOWN	Lionel Richie (Motown)
4	7	TOUCH	Eurythmics (RCA)
13	8	1984	Van Halen (WEA)
6	9	KEEP MOVING	Madness (Stiff)
7	10	AN INNOCENT MAN	Billy Joel (CBS)
32	11	HUMAN RACING	Nik Kershaw (MCA)
-	12	HUMAN'S LIB	Howard Jones (WEA)
10	13	THE CROSSING	Big Country (Mercury)
11	14	NO PARLEZ	Paul Young (CBS)
9	15	DECLARATION	Alarm (Mute)
16	16	THE VERY BEST OF MOTOWN LOVE SONGS	Various Artists (Telstar)
14	17	U2 LIVE: UNDER A BLOOD RED SKY	U2 (Island)
17	18	IN THE HEART	Kool & the Gang (De-Lite)
15	19	THE FLAT EARTH	Thomas Dolby (Parlophone)
19	20	AMMONIA AVENUE	Alan Parsons Project (Arista)
31	21	TEXAS FEVER	Orange Juice (Polydor)
41	22	STREET SOUNDS EDITION 8	Various Artists (Street Sounds)
20	23	COLOUR BY NUMBERS	Culture Club (Virgin)
-	24	ABOUT FACE	Dave Gilmour (Harvest)
-	25	OFF THE WALL	Michael Jackson (Epic)
21	26	SOMETIMES WHEN WE TOUCH	Various Artists (Ronco)
22	27	LIVE IN BELFAST	Van Morrison (Mercury)
25	28	NOW THAT'S WHAT I CALL MUSIC	Various Artists (EMI/Virgin)
-	29	STREET SOUNDS CRUCIAL ELECTRO	Various Artists (Street Sounds)
-	30	SWOON	Prefab Sprout (Kitchenware)
35	31	LEARNING TO CRAWL	Pretenders (WEA)
33	32	SEVEN AND THE RAGGED TIGER	Duran Duran (EMI)
23	33	LIFE'S A RIOT WITH SPY VS SPY	Billy Bragg (Go! Discs)
39	34	THE TUBE	Various Artists (K-Tel)
18	35	WORLD SHUT YOUR MOUTH	Julian Cope (Mercury)
-	36	MR HEARTBREAK	Laurie Anderson (Warner Bros.)
29	37	VICTIMS OF THE FUTURE	Gary Moore (Virgin)
-	38	MICHAEL JACKSON & THE JACKSON FIVE'S 18 GREATEST HITS	Michael Jackson & the Jackson Five (Star)
24	39	LABOUR OF LOVE	UB40 (DEP International)
42	40	HEAD OVER HEELS	Cocteau Twins (4AD)
27	41	GENESIS	Genesis (Charisma)
34	42	QUICK STEP AND SIDE KICK	Thompson Twins (Arista)
-	43	SOMEBODY'S WATCHING ME	Rockwell (Motown)
-	44	PACIFIC STREET	Pale Fountains (Virgin)
28	45	SLIDE IT IN	Whitesnake (Liberty)
-	46	IN YOUR EYES	George Benson (WEA)
-	47	MAKING HISTORY	Linton Kwesi Johnson (Island)
-	48	BODIES AND SOULS	Manhattan Transfer (Atlantic)
36	49	MADONNA	Madonna (Sire)
38	50	CRUSADER	Saxon (Carrere)

24 March 1984

last	this	title	artist (label)
12	1	HUMAN'S LIB	Howard Jones (WEA)
1	2	INTO THE GAP	Thompson Twins (Arista)
2	3	THE WORKS	Queen (EMI)
3	4	THE SMITHS	Smiths (Rough Trade)
-	5	CAFE BLEU	Style Council (Polydor)
4	6	THRILLER	Michael Jackson (Epic)
6	7	CAN'T SLOW DOWN	Lionel Richie (Motown)
-	8	FUGAZI	Marillion (EMI)
10	9	AN INNOCENT MAN	Billy Joel (CBS)
5	10	SPARKLE IN THE RAIN	Simple Minds (Virgin)
11	11	HUMAN RACING	Nik Kershaw (MCA)
-	12	ALCHEMY - DIRE STRAITS LIVE	Dire Straits (Vertigo)
7	13	TOUCH	Eurythmics (RCA)
8	14	1984	Van Halen (WEA)
9	15	KEEP MOVING	Madness (Stiff)
13	16	THE CROSSING	Big Country (Mercury)
30	17	SWOON	Prefab Sprout (Kitchenware)
18	18	IN THE HEART	Kool & the Gang (De-Lite)
24	19	ABOUT FACE	Dave Gilmour (Harvest)
16	20	THE VERY BEST OF MOTOWN LOVE SONGS	Various Artists (Telstar)
21	21	TEXAS FEVER	Orange Juice (Polydor)
29	22	STREET SOUNDS CRUCIAL ELECTRO	Various Artists (Street Sounds)
17	23	U2 LIVE: UNDER A BLOOD RED SKY	U2 (Island)
19	24	THE FLAT EARTH	Thomas Dolby (Parlophone)
14	25	NO PARLEZ	Paul Young (CBS)
25	26	OFF THE WALL	Michael Jackson (Epic)
20	27	AMMONIA AVENUE	Alan Parsons Project (Arista)
-	28	LOVE AT FIRST STING	Scorpions (Harvest)
22	29	STREET SOUNDS EDITION 8	Various Artists (Street Sounds)
23	30	COLOUR BY NUMBERS	Culture Club (Virgin)
-	31	THE DRUM IS EVERYTHING	Carmel (London)
15	32	DECLARATION	Alarm (Mute)
42	33	QUICK STEP AND SIDE KICK	Thompson Twins (Arista)
27	34	LIVE IN BELFAST	Van Morrison (Mercury)
26	35	SOMETIMES WHEN WE TOUCH	Various Artists (Ronco)
28	36	NOW THAT'S WHAT I CALL MUSIC	Various Artists (EMI/Virgin)
-	37	THE FISH PEOPLE TAPES	Alexei Sayle (Island)
39	38	LABOUR OF LOVE	UB40 (DEP International)
-	39	LET THE MUSIC PLAY	Shannon (Club)
-	40	E.S.P.	Millie Jackson (Sire)
33	41	LIFE'S A RIOT WITH SPY VS SPY	Billy Bragg (Go! Discs)
34	42	THE TUBE	Various Artists (K-Tel)
41	43	GENESIS	Genesis (Charisma)
-	44	NENA	Nena (Epic)
-	45	YOU BROKE MY HEART IN 17 PLACES	Tracey Ullman (Stiff)
-	46	G FORCE	Kenny G (Arista)
32	47	SEVEN AND THE RAGGED TIGER	Duran Duran (EMI)
35	48	WORLD SHUT YOUR MOUTH	Julian Cope (Mercury)
37	49	VICTIMS OF THE FUTURE	Gary Moore (Virgin)
40	50	HEAD OVER HEELS	Cocteau Twins (4AD)

The Smiths' debut album, boosted by the Mancunian group's growing popularity in the singles chart, became the independent Rough Trade label's biggest-selling LP to date. Though neither it nor Queen's *The Works* were able to push aside the Thompson Twins at the top, *Human's Lib*, the first album by new UK hitmaking singer-songwriter Howard Jones, did, also outselling similarly-marketed Nik Kershaw's debut.

31 March 1984

last week	this week	Title	Artist (Label)
1	1	HUMAN'S LIB	Howard Jones (WEA)
5	2	CAFE BLEU	Style Council (Polydor)
12	3	ALCHEMY - DIRE STRAITS LIVE	Dire Straits (Vertigo)
8	4	FUGAZI	Marillion (EMI)
2	5	INTO THE GAP	Thompson Twins (Arista)
7	6	CAN'T SLOW DOWN	Lionel Richie (Motown)
3	7	THE WORKS	Queen (EMI)
6	8	THRILLER	Michael Jackson (Epic)
9	9	AN INNOCENT MAN	Billy Joel (CBS)
4	10	THE SMITHS	Smiths (Rough Trade)
11	11	HUMAN RACING	Nik Kershaw (MCA)
31	12	THE DRUM IS EVERYTHING	Carmel (London)
10	13	SPARKLE IN THE RAIN	Simple Minds (Virgin)
14	14	1984	Van Halen (WEA)
13	15	TOUCH	Eurythmics (RCA)
16	16	THE CROSSING	Big Country (Mercury)
15	17	KEEP MOVING	Madness (Stiff)
28	18	LOVE AT FIRST STING	Scorpions (Harvest)
18	19	IN THE HEART	Kool & the Gang (De-Lite)
-	20	THIS LAST NIGHT	Soft Cell (Some Bizzare)
26	21	OFF THE WALL	Michael Jackson (Epic)
20	22	THE VERY BEST OF MOTOWN LOVE SONGS	Various Artists (Telstar)
19	23	ABOUT FACE	Dave Gilmour (Harvest)
27	24	AMMONIA AVENUE	Alan Parsons Project (Arista)
44	25	NENA	Nena (Epic)
17	26	SWOON	Prefab Sprout (Kitchenware)
23	27	U2 LIVE - UNDER A BLOOD RED SKY	U2 (Island)
46	28	G FORCE	Kenny G (Arista)
35	29	SOMETIMES WHEN WE TOUCH	Various Artist (Ronco)
38	30	LABOUR OF LOVE	UB40 (DEP International)
25	31	NO PARLEZ	Paul Young (CBS)
-	32	THREE OF A PERFECT PAIR	King Crimson (EG)
21	33	TEXAS FEVER	Orange Juice (Polydor)
30	34	COLOUR BY NUMBERS	Culture Club (Virgin)
24	35	THE FLAT EARTH	Thomas Dolby (Parlophone)
22	36	STREET SOUNDS CRUCIAL ELECTRO	Various Artists (Street Sounds)
-	37	DOMINO THEORY	Weather Report (CBS)
33	38	QUICK STEP AND SIDE KICK	Thompson Twins (Arista)
40	39	E.S.P.	Millie Jackson (Sire)
36	40	NOW THAT'S WHAT I CALL MUSIC	Various Artists (EMI/Virgin)
48	41	WORLD SHUT YOUR MOUTH	Julian Cope (Mercury)
37	42	THE FISH PEOPLE TAPES	Alexei Sayle (Island)
32	43	DECLARATION	Alarm (Mute)
29	44	STREET SOUNDS EDITION 8	Various Artists (Street Sounds)
-	45	THE ICICLE WORKS	Icicle Works (Beggars Banquet)
-	46	SOMEBODY'S WATCHING ME	Rockwell (Motown)
39	47	LET THE MUSIC PLAY	Shannon (Club/Phonogram)
43	48	GENESIS	Genesis (Charisma)
-	49	YENTL	Barbra Streisand (CBS)
34	50	LIVE IN BELFAST	Van Morrison (Mercury)

7 April 1984

last week	this week	Title	Artist (Label)
6	1	CAN'T SLOW DOWN	Lionel Richie (Motown)
1	2	HUMAN'S LIB	Howard Jones (WEA)
2	3	CAFE BLEU	Style Council (Polydor)
3	4	ALCHEMY - DIRE STRAITS LIVE	Dire Straits (Vertigo)
8	5	THRILLER	Michael Jackson (Epic)
5	6	INTO THE GAP	Thompson Twins (Arista)
4	7	FUGAZI	Marillion (EMI)
9	8	AN INNOCENT MAN	Billy Joel (CBS)
10	9	THE SMITHS	Smiths (Rough Trade)
7	10	THE WORKS	Queen (EMI)
20	11	THIS LAST NIGHT	Soft Cell (Some Bizzare)
13	12	SPARKLE IN THE RAIN	Simple Minds (Virgin)
11	13	HUMAN RACING	Nik Kershaw (MCA)
15	14	TOUCH	Eurythmics (RCA)
14	15	1984	Van Halen (WEA)
30	16	LABOUR OF LOVE	UB40 (DEP International)
45	17	THE ICICLE WORKS	Icicle Works (Beggars Banquet)
12	18	THE DRUM IS EVERYTHING	Carmel (London)
21	19	OFF THE WALL	Michael Jackson (Epic)
22	20	THE VERY BEST OF MOTOWN LOVE SONGS	Various Artists (Telstar)
27	21	U2 LIVE - UNDER A BLOOD RED SKY	U2 (Island)
-	22	NOW THAT'S WHAT I CALL MUSIC 2	Various Artists (EMI/Virgin)
18	23	LOVE AT FIRST STING	Scorpions (Harvest)
32	24	THREE OF A PERFECT PAIR	King Crimson (EG)
34	25	COLOUR BY NUMBERS	Culture Club (Virgin)
26	26	SWOON	Prefab Sprout (Kitchenware)
16	27	THE CROSSING	Big Country (Mercury)
25	28	NENA	Nena (Epic)
17	29	KEEP MOVING	Madness (Stiff)
-	30	CLIMATE OF HUNTER	Scott Walker (Virgin)
35	31	THE FLAT EARTH	Thomas Dolby (Parlophone)
28	32	G FORCE	Kenny G (Arista)
23	33	ABOUT FACE	Dave Gilmour (Harvest)
31	34	NO PARLEZ	Paul Young (CBS)
44	35	STREET SOUNDS EDITION 8	Various Artists (Street Sounds)
36	36	STREET SOUNDS CRUCIAL ELECTRO	Various Artists (Street Sounds)
19	37	IN THE HEART	Kool & the Gang (De-Lite)
24	38	AMMONIA AVENUE	Alan Parsons Project (Arista)
-	39	LIONEL RICHIE	Lionel Richie (Motown)
-	40	THE ROSE OF TRALEE	James Last (Polydor)
-	41	BODY AND SOUL	Joe Jackson (A&M)
39	42	E.S.P.	Millie Jackson (Sire)
33	43	TEXAS FEVER	Orange Juice (Polydor)
42	44	THE FISH PEOPLE TAPES	Alexei Sayle (Island)
-	45	STREET SOUNDS ELECTRO 3	Various Artists (Street Sounds)
41	46	WORLD SHUT YOUR MOUTH	Julian Cope (Mercury)
-	47	IT'S YOUR NIGHT	James Ingram (Qwest)
48	48	GENESIS	Genesis (Charisma)
-	49	THE F C'S TREAT US LIKE PRICKS	A Flux of Pink Indians (Mortarhate)
-	50	VENICE IN PERIL	Rondo Veneziano (Ferroway)

14 April 1984

last week	this week	Title	Artist (Label)
1	1	CAN'T SLOW DOWN	Lionel Richie (Motown)
2	2	HUMAN'S LIB	Howard Jones (WEA)
22	3	NOW THAT'S WHAT I CALL MUSIC 2	Various Artists (EMI/Virgin)
4	4	ALCHEMY - DIRE STRAITS LIVE	Dire Straits (Vertigo)
5	5	THRILLER	Michael Jackson (Epic)
6	6	INTO THE GAP	Thompson Twins (Arista)
3	7	CAFE BLEU	Style Council (Polydor)
8	8	AN INNOCENT MAN	Billy Joel (CBS)
9	9	FUGAZI	Marillion (EMI)
10	10	THE SMITHS	Smiths (Rough Trade)
12	11	SPARKLE IN THE RAIN	Simple Minds (Virgin)
41	12	BODY AND SOUL	Joe Jackson (A&M)
13	13	HUMAN RACING	Nik Kershaw (MCA)
25	14	COLOUR BY NUMBERS	Culture Club (Virgin)
10	15	THE WORKS	Queen (EMI)
14	16	TOUCH	Eurythmics (RCA)
21	17	U2 LIVE - UNDER A BLOOD RED SKY	U2 (Island)
-	18	LAMENT	Ultravox (Chrysalis)
16	19	LABOUR OF LOVE	UB40 (DEP International)
45	20	STREET SOUNDS ELECTRO 3	Various Artists (Street Sounds)
20	21	THE VERY BEST OF MOTOWN LOVE SONGS	Various Artists (Telstar)
-	22	GHETTO BLASTER	Crusaders (MCA)
-	23	YENTL	Barbra Streisand (CBS)
18	24	THE DRUM IS EVERYTHING	Carmel (London)
11	25	THIS LAST NIGHT	Soft Cell (Some Bizzare)
24	26	THREE OF A PERFECT PAIR	King Crimson (EG)
15	27	1984	Van Halen (WEA)
17	28	THE ICICLE WORKS	Icicle Works (Beggars Banquet)
27	29	THE CROSSING	Big Country (Mercury)
-	30	VICTIMS OF CIRCUMSTANCE	Barclay James Harvest (Polydor)
31	31	THE FLAT EARTH	Thomas Dolby (Parlophone)
-	32	SILVER	Cliff Richard (EMI)
-	33	STAGES	Elaine Paige (K-Tel)
-	34	I CAN HELP	Elvis Presley (RCA)
37	35	IN THE HEART	Kool & the Gang (De-Lite)
19	36	OFF THE WALL	Michael Jackson (Epic)
23	37	LOVE AT FIRST STIN	Scorpions (Harvest)
35	38	STREET SOUNDS EDITION 8	Various Artists (Street Sounds)
34	39	NO PARLEZ	Paul Young (CBS)
26	40	SWOON	Prefab Sprout (Kitchenware)
47	41	IT'S YOUR NIGHT	James Ingram (Qwest)
32	42	G FORCE	Kenny G (Arista)
33	43	ABOUT FACE	Dave Gilmour (Harvest)
38	44	AMMONIA AVENUE	Alan Parsons Project (Arista)
-	45	INTIMATE CONNECTION	Kleeer (Atlantic)
-	46	ROBERTA FLACK'S GREATEST HITS	Roberta Flack (K-Tel)
28	47	NENA	Nena (Epic)
29	48	KEEP MOVING	Madness (Stiff)
39	49	LIONEL RICHIE	Lionel Richie (Motown)
30	50	CLIMATE OF HUNTER	Scott Walker (Virgin)

Cafe Bleu was the first album by former Jam leader Paul Weller's new (and contrasting) band the Style Council, who had already had a year's success with five Top 20 singles by the time of its release. Lionel Richie's sudden dash to the top after some months of consistent Top 10 service with *Can't Slow Down* was the result of the boost given by the simultaneous 5-week Number 1 run by its extracted single *Hello*.

April – May 1984

21 April 1984

last week	this week	title	artist
1	1	CAN'T SLOW DOWN	Lionel Richie (Motown)
5	2	THRILLER	Michael Jackson (Epic)
3	3	NOW THAT'S WHAT I CALL MUSIC 2	Various Artists (EMI/Virgin)
2	4	HUMAN'S LIB	Howard Jones (WEA)
6	5	INTO THE GAP	Thompson Twins (Arista)
4	6	ALCHEMY - DIRE STRAITS LIVE	Dire Straits (Vertigo)
18	7	LAMENT	Ultravox (Chrysalis)
7	8	CAFE BLEU	Style Council (Polydor)
8	9	AN INNOCENT MAN	Billy Joel (CBS)
10	10	THE SMITHS	Smiths (Rough Trade)
-	11	MARVIN GAYE'S GREATEST HITS	Marvin Gaye (Telstar)
11	12	SPARKLE IN THE RAIN	Simple Minds (Virgin)
15	13	THE WORKS	Queen (EMI)
12	14	BODY AND SOUL	Joe Jackson (A&M)
14	15	COLOUR BY NUMBERS	Culture Club (Virgin)
13	16	HUMAN RACING	Nik Kershaw (MCA)
9	17	FUGAZI	Marillion (EMI)
17	18	U2 LIVE: UNDER A BLOOD RED SKY	U2 (Island)
16	19	TOUCH	Eurythmics (RCA)
19	20	LABOUR OF LOVE	UB40 (DEP International)
21	21	THE VERY BEST OF MOTOWN LOVE SONGS	Various Artists (Telstar)
28	22	THE ICICLE WORKS	Icicle Works (Beggars Banquet)
30	23	VICTIMS OF CIRCUMSTANCE	Barclay James Harvest (Polydor)
41	24	IT'S YOUR NIGHT	James Ingram (Qwest)
29	25	THE CROSSING	Big Country (Mercury)
25	26	THIS LAST NIGHT	Soft Cell (Some Bizzare)
22	27	GHETTO BLASTER	Crusaders (MCA)
20	28	STREET SOUNDS ELECTRO 3	Various Artists (Street Sounds)
39	29	NO PARLEZ	Paul Young (CBS)
-	30	THE BOP WON'T STOP	Shakin' Stevens (Epic)
-	31	AND I LOVE YOU SO	Howard Keel (Warwick)
31	32	THE FLAT EARTH	Thomas Dolby (Parlophone)
35	33	IN THE HEART	Kool & the Gang (De-Lite)
-	34	POINTS ON A CURVE	Wang Chung (Geffin)
-	35	THE ROSE OF TRALEE	James Last (Polydor)
-	36	WIRED TO THE MOON	Chris Rea (Magnet)
34	37	I CAN HELP	Elvis Presley (RCA)
36	38	OFF THE WALL	Michael Jackson (Epic)
24	39	THE DRUM IS EVERYTHING	Carmel (London)
-	40	MADONNA	Madonna (Sire)
27	41	1984	Van Halen (WEA)
40	42	SWOON	Prefab Sprout (Kitchenware)
-	43	SEANCE	Church (Carrere)
26	44	THREE OF A PERFECT PAIR	King Crimson (EG)
-	45	IN YOUR EYES	George Benson (WEA)
47	46	NENA	Nena (Epic)
23	47	YENTL	Barbra Streisand (CBS)
38	48	STREET SOUNDS EDITION 8	Various Artists (Street Sounds)
43	49	ABOUT FACE	Dave Gilmour (Harvest)
-	50	THE POET II	Bobby Womack (Motown)

28 April 1984

last week	this week	title	artist
3	1	NOW THAT'S WHAT I CALL MUSIC 2	Various Artists (EMI/Virgin)
1	2	CAN'T SLOW DOWN	Lionel Richie (Motown)
5	3	INTO THE GAP	Thompson Twins (Arista)
2	4	THRILLER	Michael Jackson (Epic)
4	5	HUMAN'S LIB	Howard Jones (WEA)
6	6	ALCHEMY - DIRE STRAITS LIVE	Dire Straits (Vertigo)
7	7	LAMENT	Ultravox (Chrysalis)
9	8	AN INNOCENT MAN	Billy Joel (CBS)
13	9	THE WORKS	Queen (EMI)
10	10	THE SMITHS	Smiths (Rough Trade)
8	11	CAFE BLEU	Style Council (Polydor)
14	12	BODY AND SOUL	Joe Jackson (A&M)
16	13	HUMAN RACING	Nik Kershaw (MCA)
15	14	COLOUR BY NUMBERS	Culture Club (Virgin)
-	15	GRACE UNDER PRESSURE	Rush (Vertigo)
12	16	SPARKLE IN THE RAIN	Simple Minds (Virgin)
11	17	MARVIN GAYE'S GREATEST HITS	Marvin Gaye (Telstar)
20	18	LABOUR OF LOVE	UB40 (DEP International)
-	19	SOPHISTICATED BOOM BOOM	Dead or Alive (Epic)
19	20	TOUCH	Eurythmics (RCA)
38	21	OFF THE WALL	Michael Jackson (Epic)
31	22	AND I LOVE YOU SO	Howard Keel (Warwick)
23	23	VICTIMS OF CIRCUMSTANCE	Barclay James Harvest (Polydor)
18	24	U2 LIVE: UNDER A BLOOD RED SKY	U2 (Island)
21	25	THE VERY BEST OF MOTOWN LOVE SONGS	Various Artists (Telstar)
-	26	ONE EYED JACKS	Spear of Destiny (Epic)
17	27	FUGAZI	Marillion (EMI)
34	28	POINTS ON A CURVE	Wang Chung (Geffin)
-	29	STOMPIN' AT THE SAVOY	Rufus with Chaka Khan (Warner Bros.)
24	30	IT'S YOUR NIGHT	James Ingram (Qwest)
-	31	BANANARAMA	Bananarama (London)
36	32	WIRED TO THE MOON	Chris Rea (Magnet)
25	33	THE CROSSING	Big Country (Mercury)
41	34	1984	Van Halen (WEA)
30	35	THE BOP WON'T STOP	Shakin' Stevens (Epic)
-	36	AT WAR WITH SATAN	Venom (Neat)
-	37	A LITTLE SPICE	Loose Ends (Virgin)
-	38	NOW THAT'S WHAT I CALL MUSIC	Various Artists (EMI/Virgin)
-	39	AGAINST ALL ODDS	Soundtrack (Virgin)
29	40	NO PARLEZ	Paul Young (CBS)
40	41	MADONNA	Madonna (Sire)
50	42	THE POET II	Bobby Womack (Motown)
-	43	FOOTLOOSE	Soundtrack (CBS)
22	44	THE ICICLE WORKS	Icicle Works (Beggars Banquet)
47	45	YENTL	Barbra Streisand (CBS)
-	46	RECKONING	REM (IRS)
27	47	GHETTO BLASTER	Crusaders (MCA)
-	48	G FORCE	Kenny G (Arista)
49	49	FAME AND FASHION (ALL TIME GREATEST HITS)	David Bowie (RCA)
-	50	LOVE WARS	Womack & Womack (Elektra)

5 May 1984

last week	this week	title	artist
1	1	NOW THAT'S WHAT I CALL MUSIC 2	Various Artists (EMI/Virgin)
2	2	CAN'T SLOW DOWN	Lionel Richie (Motown)
9	3	THE WORKS	Queen (EMI)
4	4	THRILLER	Michael Jackson (Epic)
3	5	INTO THE GAP	Thompson Twins (Arista)
6	6	ALCHEMY - DIRE STRAITS LIVE	Dire Straits (Vertigo)
5	7	HUMAN'S LIB	Howard Jones (WEA)
15	8	GRACE UNDER PRESSURE	Rush (Vertigo)
8	9	AN INNOCENT MAN	Billy Joel (CBS)
7	10	LAMENT	Ultravox (Chrysalis)
13	11	HUMAN RACING	Nik Kershaw (MCA)
22	12	AND I LOVE YOU SO	Howard Keel (Warwick)
17	13	MARVIN GAYE'S GREATEST HITS	Marvin Gaye (Telstar)
12	14	BODY AND SOUL	Joe Jackson (A&M)
19	15	SOPHISTICATED BOOM BOOM	Dead or Alive (Epic)
42	16	THE POET II	Bobby Womack (Motown)
31	17	BANANARAMA	Bananarama (London)
10	18	THE SMITHS	Smiths (Rough Trade)
14	19	COLOUR BY NUMBERS	Culture Club (Virgin)
11	20	CAFE BLEU	Style Council (Polydor)
43	21	FOOTLOOSE	Soundtrack (CBS)
21	22	OFF THE WALL	Michael Jackson (Epic)
18	23	LABOUR OF LOVE	UB40 (DEP International)
16	24	SPARKLE IN THE RAIN	Simple Minds (Virgin)
20	25	TOUCH	Eurythmics (RCA)
49	26	FAME AND FASHION (ALL TIME GREATEST HITS)	David Bowie (RCA)
23	27	VICTIMS OF CIRCUMSTANCE	Barclay James Harvest (Polydor)
29	28	STOMPIN' AT THE SAVOY	Rufus with Chaka Khan (Warner Bros.)
24	29	U2 LIVE: UNDER A BLOOD RED SKY	U2 (Island)
33	30	THE CROSSING	Big Country (Mercury)
32	31	WIRED TO THE MOON	Chris Rea (Magnet)
30	32	IT'S YOUR NIGHT	James Ingram (Qwest)
46	33	RECKONING	REM (IRS)
-	34	IN THE HEART	Kool & the Gang (De-Lite)
-	35	THE FLAT EARTH	Thomas Dolby (Parlophone)
-	36	OASIS	Oasis (WEA)
25	37	THE VERY BEST OF MOTOWN LOVE SONGS	Various Artists (Telstar)
-	38	STREET SOUNDS ELECTRO 3	Various Artists (Street Sounds)
50	39	LOVE WARS	Womack & Womack (Elektra)
48	40	G FORCE	Kenny G (Arista)
-	41	CAUGHT IN THE ACT	Styx (A&M)
-	42	SEVEN AND THE RAGGED TIGER	Duran Duran (EMI)
-	43	BON JOVI	Bon Jovi (Vertigo)
35	44	THE BOP WON'T STOP	Shakin' Stevens (Epic)
38	45	NOW THAT'S WHAT I CALL MUSIC	Various Artists (EMI/Virgin)
27	46	FUGAZI	Marillion (EMI)
45	47	YENTL	Barbra Streisand (CBS)
40	48	NO PARLEZ	Paul Young (CBS)
47	49	GHETTO BLASTER	Crusaders (MCA)
41	50	MADONNA	Madonna (Sire)

The collaborative EMI/Virgin compilation *Now That's What I Call Music 2* proved an even faster seller than its predecessor. The *Now* line, offering an anthology of recent (and often current) big single hits by major names, was to become established through the 1980s as the biggest-selling compilation series ever in the UK. Several would reach triple-platinum status, indicating sales around a million each.

May 1984

12 May 1984

last week	this week	Title	Artist
1	1	NOW THAT'S WHAT I CALL MUSIC 2	Various Artists (EMI/Virgin)
2	2	CAN'T SLOW DOWN	Lionel Richie (Motown)
3	3	THE WORKS	Queen (EMI)
4	4	THRILLER	Michael Jackson (Epic)
5	5	INTO THE GAP	Thompson Twins (Arista)
6	6	ALCHEMY - DIRE STRAITS LIVE	Dire Straits (Vertigo)
8	7	GRACE UNDER PRESSURE	Rush (Vertigo)
7	8	HUMAN'S LIB	Howard Jones (WEA)
21	9	FOOTLOOSE	Soundtrack (CBS)
12	10	AND I LOVE YOU SO	Howard Keel (Warwick)
-	11	OCEAN RAIN	Echo & the Bunnymen (Korova)
9	12	AN INNOCENT MAN	Billy Joel (CBS)
11	13	HUMAN RACING	Nik Kershaw (MCA)
10	14	LAMENT	Ultravox (Chrysalis)
-	15	JUNK CULTURE	Orchestral Manoeuvres In The Dark (Virgin)
14	16	BODY AND SOUL	Joe Jackson (A&M)
18	17	THE SMITHS	Smiths (Rough Trade)
13	18	MARVIN GAYE'S GREATEST HITS	Marvin Gaye (Telstar)
17	19	BANANARAMA	Bananarama (London)
-	20	ONE EYED JACKS	Spear of Destiny (Epic)
-	21	THE TOP	Cure (Fiction)
16	22	THE POET II	Bobby Womack (Motown)
20	23	CAFE BLEU	Style Council (Polydor)
-	24	THE PROS AND CONS OF HITCH HIKING	Roger Waters (Harvest)
19	25	COLOUR BY NUMBERS	Culture Club (Virgin)
15	26	SOPHISTICATED BOOM BOOM	Dead or Alive (Epic)
22	27	OFF THE WALL	Michael Jackson (Epic)
34	28	IN THE HEART	Kool & the Gang (De-Lite)
37	29	THE VERY BEST OF MOTOWN LOVE SONGS	Various Artists (Telstar)
32	30	IT'S YOUR NIGHT	James Ingram (Qwest)
25	31	TOUCH	Eurythmics (RCA)
28	32	STOMPIN' AT THE SAVOY	Rufus with Chaka Khan (Warner Bros.)
24	33	SPARKLE IN THE RAIN	Simple Minds (Virgin)
29	34	U2 LIVE: UNDER A BLOOD RED SKY	U2 (Island)
39	35	LOVE WARS	Womack & Womack (Elektra)
23	36	LABOUR OF LOVE	UB40 (DEP International)
31	37	WIRED TO THE MOON	Chris Rea (Magnet)
42	38	SEVEN AND THE RAGGED TIGER	Duran Duran (EMI)
-	39	LEGEND (MUSIC FROM ROBIN OF SHERWOOD)	Clannad (RCA)
46	40	FUGAZI	Marillion (EMI)
41	41	CAUGHT IN THE ACT	Styx (A&M)
-	42	LIONEL RICHIE	Lionel Richie (Motown)
-	43	AGAINST ALL ODDS	Soundtrack (Virgin)
-	44	HEAD OVER HEELS	Cocteau Twins (4AD)
33	45	RECKONING	REM (IRS)
-	46	QUICK STEP AND SIDE KICK	Thompson Twins (Arista)
-	47	QUEEN'S GREATEST HITS	Queen (EMI)
30	48	THE CROSSING	Big Country (Mercury)
27	49	VICTIMS OF CIRCUMSTANCE	Barclay James Harvest (Polydor)
26	50	FAME AND FASHION (ALL TIME GREATEST HITS)	David Bowie (RCA)

19 May 1984

last week	this week	Title	Artist
1	1	NOW THAT'S WHAT I CALL MUSIC 2	Various Artists (EMI/Virgin)
11	2	OCEAN RAIN	Echo & the Bunnymen (Korova)
2	3	CAN'T SLOW DOWN	Lionel Richie (Motown)
4	4	THRILLER	Michael Jackson (Epic)
3	5	THE WORKS	Queen (EMI)
9	6	FOOTLOOSE	Soundtrack (CBS)
21	7	THE TOP	Cure (Fiction)
15	8	JUNK CULTURE	Orchestral Manoeuvres In The Dark (Virgin)
5	9	INTO THE GAP	Thompson Twins (Arista)
6	10	ALCHEMY - DIRE STRAITS LIVE	Dire Straits (Vertigo)
-	11	HYSTERIA	Human League (Virgin)
7	12	GRACE UNDER PRESSURE	Rush (Vertigo)
24	13	THE PROS AND CONS OF HITCH HIKING	Roger Waters (Harvest)
12	14	AN INNOCENT MAN	Billy Joel (CBS)
-	15	LEGEND	Bob Marley & the Wailers (Island)
-	16	MIRROR MOVES	Psychedlic Furs (CBS)
10	17	AND I LOVE YOU SO	Howard Keel (Warwick)
8	18	HUMAN'S LIB	Howard Jones (WEA)
13	19	HUMAN RACING	Nik Kershaw (MCA)
-	20	STREET SOUNDS EDITION 9	Various Artists (Street Sounds)
18	21	MARVIN GAYE'S GREATEST HITS	Marvin Gaye (Telstar)
38	22	SEVEN AND THE RAGGED TIGER	Duran Duran (EMI)
14	23	LAMENT	Ultravox (Chrysalis)
22	24	THE POET II	Bobby Womack (Motown)
17	25	THE SMITHS	Smiths (Rough Trade)
39	26	LEGEND (MUSIC FROM ROBIN OF SHERWOOD)	Clannad (RCA)
19	27	BANANARAMA	Bananarama (London)
20	28	ONE EYED JACKS	Spear of Destiny (Epic)
34	29	U2 LIVE: UNDER A BLOOD RED SKY	U2 (Island)
-	30	MAN ON THE LINE	Chris DeBurgh (A&M)
25	31	COLOUR BY NUMBERS	Culture Club (Virgin)
28	32	IN THE HEART	Kool & the Gang (De-Lite)
27	33	OFF THE WALL	Michael Jackson (Epic)
31	34	TOUCH	Eurythmics (RCA)
16	35	BODY AND SOUL	Joe Jackson (A&M)
23	36	CAFE BLEU	Style Council (Polydor)
26	37	SOPHISTICATED BOOM BOOM	Dead Or Alive (Epic)
40	38	FUGAZI	Marillion (EMI)
-	39	BREAK OUT	Pointer Sisters (Planet)
43	40	AGAINST ALL ODDS	Soundtrack (Virgin)
36	40	LABOUR OF LOVE	UB40 (DEP International)
29	42	THE VERY BEST OF MOTOWN LOVE SONGS	Various Artists (Telstar)
30	43	IT'S YOUR NIGHT	James Ingram (Qwest)
-	44	OASIS	Oasis (WEA)
33	45	SPARKLE IN THE RAIN	Simple Minds (Virgin)
35	46	LOVE WARS	Womack & Womack (Elektra)
37	47	WIRED TO THE MOON	Chris Rea (Magnet)
32	48	STOMPIN' AT THE SAVOY	Rufus with Chaka Khan (Warner Bros.)
41	49	CAUGHT IN THE ACT	Styx (A&M)
42	50	LIONEL RICHIE	Lionel Richie (Motwn)

26 May 1984

last week	this week	Title	Artist
15	1	LEGEND	Bob Marley & the Wailers (Island)
11	2	HYSTERIA	Human League (Virgin)
2	3	OCEAN RAIN	Echo & the Bunnymen (Korova)
3	4	CAN'T SLOW DOWN	Lionel Richie (Motown)
1	5	NOW THAT'S WHAT I CALL MUSIC 2	Various Artists (EMI/Virgin)
6	6	FOOTLOOSE	Soundtrack (CBS)
5	7	THE WORKS	Queen (EMI)
8	8	JUNK CULTURE	Orchestral Manoeuvres In The Dark (Virgin)
4	9	THRILLER	Michael Jackson (Epic)
7	10	THE TOP	Cure (Fiction)
10	11	ALCHEMY - DIRE STRAITS LIVE	Dire Straits (Vertigo)
30	12	MAN ON THE LINE	Chris DeBurgh (A&M)
16	13	MIRROR MOVES	Psychedlic Furs (CBS)
9	14	INTO THE GAP	Thompson Twins (Arista)
13	15	THE PROS AND CONS OF HITCH HIKING	Roger Waters (Harvest)
17	16	AND I LOVE YOU SO	Howard Keel (Warwick)
14	17	AN INNOCENT MAN	Billy Joel (CBS)
22	18	SEVEN AND THE RAGGED TIGER	Duran Duran (EMI)
18	19	HUMAN'S LIB	Howard Jones (WEA)
-	20	MANGE TOUT	Blancmange (London)
12	21	GRACE UNDER PRESSURE	Rush (Vertigo)
26	22	LEGEND (MUSIC FROM ROBIN OF SHERWOOD)	Clannad (RCA)
19	23	HUMAN RACING	Nik Kershaw (MCA)
21	24	MARVIN GAYE'S GREATEST HITS	Marvin Gaye (Telstar)
20	25	STREET SOUNDS EDITION 9	Various Artists (Street Sounds)
36	26	CAFE BLEU	Style Council (Polydor)
39	27	BREAK OUT	Pointer Sisters (Planet)
24	28	THE POET II	Bobby Womack (Motown)
25	29	THE SMITHS	Smiths (Rough Trade)
44	30	OASIS	Oasis (WEA)
-	31	MASTERPIECES - THE VERY BEST OF SKY	Sky (Telstar)
28	32	ONE EYED JACKS	Spear of Destiny (Epic)
46	33	LOVE WARS	Womack & Womack (Elektra)
31	34	COLOUR BY NUMBERS	Culture Club (Virgin)
35	35	BODY AND SOUL	Joe Jackson (A&M)
23	36	LAMENT	Ultravox (Chrysalis)
33	37	OFF THE WALL	Michael Jackson (Epic)
32	38	IN THE HEART	Kool & the Gang (De-Lite)
40	39	AGAINST ALL ODDS	Soundtrack (Virgin)
40	40	LABOUR OF LOVE	UB40 (DEP International)
27	41	BANANARAMA	Bananarama (London)
-	42	TOUCH SENSITIVE	Bruce Foxton (Arista)
-	43	DYNAMITE	Jermaine Jackson (Arista)
48	44	STOMPIN' AT THE SAVOY	Rufus with Chaka Khan (Warner Bros.)
34	45	TOUCH	Eurythmics (RCA)
38	46	FUGAZI	Marillion (EMI)
29	47	U2 LIVE: UNDER A BLOOD RED SKY	U2 (Island)
-	48	VENGEANCE	New Model Army (Abstract)
-	49	THROUGH THE FIRE	Hagar, Schon, aaronson, Shrieve (Geffin)
-	50	LOVE YOU TILL TUESDAY	David Bowie (London)

Veteran soul singer Bobby Womack's Top 20 success with *The Poet II* (his first-ever UK chart album) is worthy of note because it was due entirely to word-of-mouth, good reviews and strong club play - there was no accompanying hit single to boost it by getting radio airplay. The album was the sequel to an earlier highly-rated set, *The Poet* (hence this one's title), which had only been available here as an US import.

June 1984

2 June 1984

last week	this week	Title	Artist (Label)
1	1	LEGEND	Bob Marley & the Wailers (Island)
2	2	HYSTERIA	Human League (Virgin)
20	3	MANGE TOUT	Blancmange (London)
7	4	THE WORKS	Queen (EMI)
9	5	THRILLER	Michael Jackson (Epic)
5	6	NOW THAT'S WHAT I CALL MUSIC 2	Various Artists (EMI/Virgin)
4	7	CAN'T SLOW DOWN	Lionel Richie (Motown)
6	8	FOOTLOOSE	Soundtrack (CBS)
3	9	OCEAN RAIN	Echo & the Bunnymen (Korova)
12	10	MAN ON THE LINE	Chris DeBurgh (A&M)
11	11	ALCHEMY - DIRE STRAITS LIVE	Dire Straits (Vertigo)
8	12	JUNK CULTURE	Orchestral Manoeuvres In The Dark (Virgin)
14	13	INTO THE GAP	Thompson Twins (Arista)
13	14	MIRROR MOVES	Psychedlic Furs (CBS)
17	15	AN INNOCENT MAN	Billy Joel (CBS)
10	16	THE TOP	Cure (Fiction)
-	17	HUNGRY FOR HITS	Various Artists (K-Tel)
27	18	BREAK OUT	Pointer Sisters (Planet)
19	19	HUMAN'S LIB	Howard Jones (WEA)
22	20	LEGEND (MUSIC FROM ROBIN OF SHERWOOD)	Clannad (RCA)
36	21	LAMENT	Ultravox (Chrysalis)
-	22	DON'T STOP DANCIN'	Various Artists (Telstar)
24	23	MARVIN GAYE'S GREATEST HITS	Marvin Gaye (Telstar)
16	24	AND I LOVE YOU SO	Howard Keel (Warwick)
18	25	SEVEN AND THE RAGGED TIGER	Duran Duran (EMI)
15	26	THE PROS AND CONS OF HITCH HIKING	Roger Waters (Harvest)
31	27	MASTERPIECES - THE VERY BEST OF SKY	Sky (Telstar)
21	28	GRACE UNDER PRESSURE	Rush (Vertigo)
33	29	LOVE WARS	Womack & Womack (Elektra)
-	30	THEN CAME ROCK 'N' ROLL	Various Artists (EMI)
26	31	CAFE BLEU	Style Council (Polydor)
-	32	CHANGE OF HEART	Change (WEA)
23	33	HUMAN RACING	Nik Kershaw (MCA)
25	34	STREET SOUNDS EDITION 9	Various Artists (Street Sounds)
29	35	THE SMITHS	Smiths (Rough Trade)
-	36	FROM HER TO ETERNITY	Nick Cave & the bad seeds (Mute)
46	37	FUGAZI	Marillion (EMI)
-	38	WOULD YA LIKE MORE SCRATCHIN'	Malcolm McLaren (Virgin/Charisma)
39	39	AGAINST ALL ODDS	Soundtrack (Virgin)
-	40	DANCIN' ON THE EDGE	Lita Ford (Vertigo)
28	41	THE POET II	Bobby Womack (Motown)
30	42	OASIS	Oasis (WEA)
32	43	ONE EYED JACKS	Spear of Destiny (Epic)
-	44	LIFE'S A RIOT WITH SPY VS SPY	Billy Bragg (Go! Discs)
-	45	FROM THE PROMISED LAND	Playdead (Clay)
35	46	BODY AND SOUL	Joe Jackson (A&M)
37	47	OFF THE WALL	Michael Jackson (Epic)
-	48	ISLANDS	Kajagoogoo (EMI)
34	49	COLOUR BY NUMBERS	Culture Club (Virgin)
38	50	IN THE HEART	Kool & the Gang (De-Lite)

9 June 1984

last week	this week	Title	Artist (Label)
1	1	LEGEND	Bob Marley & the Wailers (Island)
4	2	THE WORKS	Queen (EMI)
2	3	HYSTERIA	Human League (Virgin)
6	4	NOW THAT'S WHAT I CALL MUSIC 2	Various Artists (EMI/Virgin)
3	5	MANGE TOUT	Blancmange (London)
7	6	CAN'T SLOW DOWN	Lionel Richie (Motown)
5	7	THRILLER	Michael Jackson (Epic)
8	8	FOOTLOOSE	Soundtrack (CBS)
17	9	HUNGRY FOR HITS	Various Artists (K-Tel)
10	10	MAN ON THE LINE	Chris DeBurgh (A&M)
9	11	OCEAN RAIN	Echo & the Bunnymen (Korova)
19	12	HUMAN'S LIB	Howard Jones (WEA)
13	13	INTO THE GAP	Thompson Twins (Arista)
15	14	AN INNOCENT MAN	Billy Joel (CBS)
30	15	THEN CAME ROCK 'N' ROLL	Various Artists (EMI)
20	16	LEGEND (MUSIC FROM ROBIN OF SHERWOOD)	Clannad (RCA)
31	17	CAFE BLEU	Style Council (Polydor)
11	18	ALCHEMY - DIRE STRAITS LIVE	Dire Straits (Vertigo)
21	19	LAMENT	Ultravox (Chrysalis)
22	20	DON'T STOP DANCIN'	Various Artists (Telstar)
35	21	THE SMITHS	Smiths (Rough Trade)
14	22	MIRROR MOVES	Psychedlic Furs (CBS)
16	23	THE TOP	Cure (Fiction)
48	24	BREAK OUT	Pointer Sisters (Planet)
12	25	JUNK CULTURE	Orchestral Manoeuvres In The Dark (Virgin)
25	26	SEVEN AND THE RAGGED TIGER	Duran Duran (EMI)
36	27	FROM HER TO ETERNITY	Nick Cave & the bad seeds (Mute)
33	28	HUMAN RACING	Nik Kershaw (MCA)
24	29	AND I LOVE YOU SO	Howard Keel (Warwick)
48	30	ISLANDS	Kajagoogoo (EMI)
29	31	LOVE WARS	Womack & Womack (Elektra)
32	32	CHANGE OF HEART	Change (WEA)
41	33	THE POET II	Bobby Womack (Motown)
27	34	MASTERPIECES - THE VERY BEST OF SKY	Sky (Telstar)
23	35	MARVIN GAYE'S GREATEST HITS	Marvin Gaye (Telstar)
26	36	THE PROS AND CONS OF HITCH HIKING	Roger Waters (Harvest)
-	37	STREET SOUNDS ELECTRO 4	Various Artists (Street Sounds)
-	38	TOUCH DANCE	Eurythmics (RCA)
43	39	ONE EYED JACKS	Spear of Destiny (Epic)
28	40	GRACE UNDER PRESSURE	Rush (Vertigo)
-	41	LABOUR OF LOVE	UB40 (DEP International)
-	42	VENGEANCE	New Model Army (Abstract)
-	43	LOST BOYS	Flying Pickets (10 Records)
34	44	STREET SOUNDS EDITION 9	Various Artists (Street Sounds)
42	45	OASIS	Oasis (WEA)
49	47	COLOUR BY NUMBERS	Culture Club (Virgin)
-	48	1984	Van Halen (Warner Bros.)
38	49	WOULD YA LIKE MORE SCRATCHIN'	Malcolm McLaren (Virgin/Charisma)
39	50	AGAINST ALL ODDS	Soundtrack (Virgin)

16 June 1984

last week	this week	Title	Artist (Label)
1	1	LEGEND	Bob Marley & the Wailers (Island)
2	2	THE WORKS	Queen (EMI)
4	3	NOW THAT'S WHAT I CALL MUSIC 2	Various Artists (EMI/Virgin)
14	4	AN INNOCENT MAN	Billy Joel (CBS)
7	5	THRILLER	Michael Jackson (Epic)
6	6	CAN'T SLOW DOWN	Lionel Richie (Motown)
12	7	HUMAN'S LIB	Howard Jones (WEA)
17	8	CAFE BLEU	Style Council (Polydor)
9	9	HUNGRY FOR HITS	Various Artists (K-Tel)
-	10	BORN IN THE USA	Bruce Springsteen (CBS)
8	11	FOOTLOOSE	Soundtrack (CBS)
5	12	MANGE TOUT	Blancmange (London)
15	13	THEN CAME ROCK 'N' ROLL	Various Artists (EMI)
-	14	BREAK MACHINE	Break Machine (Record Shack)
16	15	LEGEND (MUSIC FROM ROBIN OF SHERWOOD)	Clannad (RCA)
3	16	HYSTERIA	Human League (Virgin)
-	17	HYENA	Siouxsie and the Banshees (Wonderland)
21	18	THE SMITHS	Smiths (Rough Trade)
26	19	SEVEN AND THE RAGGED TIGER	Duran Duran (EMI)
43	20	LOST BOYS	Flying Pickets (10 Records)
37	21	STREET SOUNDS ELECTRO 4	Various Artists (Street Sounds)
-	22	FAREWELL MY SUMMER LOVE	Michael Jackson (Motown)
34	23	MASTERPIECES - THE VERY BEST OF SKY	Sky (Telstar)
10	24	MAN ON THE LINE	Chris DeBurgh (A&M)
13	25	INTO THE GAP	Thompson Twins (Arista)
-	26	EDEN	Everything but the Girl (Blanco Y Negro)
19	27	LAMENT	Ultravox (Chrysalis)
20	28	DON'T STOP DANCIN'	Various Artists (Telstar)
18	29	ALCHEMY - DIRE STRAITS LIVE	Dire Straits (Vertigo)
32	30	CHANGE OF HEART	Change (WEA)
38	31	TOUCH DANCE	Eurythmics (RCA)
24	32	BREAK OUT	Pointer Sisters (Planet)
28	33	HUMAN RACING	Nik Kershaw (MCA)
-	34	20 FAMILY FAVOURITES	Vera Lynn (EMI)
11	35	OCEAN RAIN	Echo & the Bunnymen (Korova)
33	36	THE POET II	Bobby Womack (Motown)
29	37	AND I LOVE YOU SO	Howard Keel (Warwick)
25	38	JUNK CULTURE	Orchestral Manoeuvres In The Dark (Virgin)
36	39	THE PROS AND CONS OF HITCH HIKING	Roger Waters (Harvest)
22	40	MIRROR MOVES	Psychedlic Furs (CBS)
27	41	FROM HER TO ETERNITY	Nick Cave & the Bad Seeds (Mute)
41	42	LABOUR OF LOVE	UB40 (DEP International)
23	43	THE TOP	Cure (Fiction)
40	44	GRACE UNDER PRESSURE	Rush (Vertigo)
-	45	BREAKDANCE	Soundtrack (Polydor)
30	46	ISLANDS	Kajagoogoo (EMI)
31	47	LOVE WARS	Womack & Womack (Elektra)
-	48	NEW SENSATION	Lou Reed (RCA)
50	49	AGAINST ALL ODDS	Soundtrack (Virgin)
44	50	STREET SOUNDS EDITION 9	Various Artists (Street Sounds)

Legend, a compilation of the hits and the best of the late Bob Marley, was to be not only Marley's biggest seller, but also the biggest-selling reggae album of all time, and a still very hardy perennial in Island's catalogue by the 1990s. Its nine straight weeks at Number 1 were the longest continuous chart-topping run since Adam & The Ants' three-month stay with *Kings Of The Wild Frontier* in 1981.

June – July 1984

23 June 1984

last	this	Title	Artist
1	1	LEGEND	Bob Marley & the Wailers (Island)
10	2	BORN IN THE USA	Bruce Springsteen (CBS)
2	3	THE WORKS	Queen (EMI)
4	4	AN INNOCENT MAN	Billy Joel (CBS)
5	5	THRILLER	Michael Jackson (Epic)
6	6	CAN'T SLOW DOWN	Lionel Richie (Motown)
7	7	HUMAN'S LIB	Howard Jones (WEA)
26	8	EDEN Everything but the Girl (Blanco Y Negro)	
17	9	HYENA Siouxsie & the Banshees (Wonderland)	
3	10	NOW THAT'S WHAT I CALL MUSIC 2 Various Artists (EMI/Virgin)	
9	11	HUNGRY FOR HITS	Various Artists (K-Tel)
20	12	LOST BOYS	Flying Pickets (10 Records)
8	13	CAFE BLEU	Style Council (Polydor)
-	14	CAMOUFLAGE	Rod Stewart (Warner Bros.)
11	15	FOOTLOOSE	Soundtrack (CBS)
13	16	THEN CAME ROCK 'N' ROLL Various Artists (EMI)	
28	17	DON'T STOP DANCIN' Various Artists (Telstar)	
18	18	THE SMITHS	Smiths (Rough Trade)
22	19	FAREWELL MY SUMMER LOVE Michael Jackson (Motown)	
-	20	AMERICAN HEARTBEAT Various Artists (Epic)	
45	21	BREAKDANCE	Soundtrack (Polydor)
12	22	MANGE TOUT	Blancmange (London)
24	23	MAN ON THE LINE	Chris DeBurgh (A&M)
16	24	HYSTERIA	Human League (Virgin)
21	25	STREET SOUNDS ELECTRO 4 Various Artists (Street Sounds)	
-	26	IN THE STUDIO	Special AKA (2-Tone)
-	27	STAY HUNGRY	Twisted Sister (Atlantic)
27	28	LAMENT	Ultravox (Chrysalis)
14	29	BREAK MACHINE Break Machine (Record Shack)	
23	30	MASTERPIECES - THE VERY BEST OF SKY Sky (Telstar)	
-	31	ROCK WILL NEVER DIE Michael Schenker (Chrysalis)	
31	32	TOUCH DANCE	Eurythmics (RCA)
25	33	INTO THE GAP	Thompson Twins (Arista)
33	34	HUMAN RACING	Nik Kershaw (MCA)
41	35	FROM HER TO ETERNITY Nick Cave & the Bad Seeds (Mute)	
47	36	LOVE WARS	Womack & Womack (Elektra)
32	37	BREAK OUT	Pointer Sisters (Planet)
35	38	OCEAN RAIN	Echo & the Bunnymen (Korova)
30	39	CHANGE OF HEART	Change (WEA)
29	40	ALCHEMY - DIRE STRAITS LIVE Dire Straits (Vertigo)	
-	41	VOICE OF AMERICA Little Steven (EMI America)	
36	42	THE POET II	Bobby Womack (Motown)
15	43	LEGEND (MUSIC FROM ROBIN OF SHERWOOD) Clannad (RCA)	
38	44	JUNK CULTURE Orchestral Manoeuvres In The Dark (Virgin)	
19	45	SEVEN AND THE RAGGED TIGER Duran Duran (EMI)	
-	46	BACKTRACKIN'	Eric Clapton (Starblend)
39	47	THE PROS AND CONS OF HITCH HIKING Roger Waters (Harvest)	
-	48	NOW	Patrice Rushen (Elektra)
-	49	FANTASTIC	Wham! (Innervision)
-	50	CREW CUTS	Various Artists (Island)

30 June 1984

last	this	Title	Artist
1	1	LEGEND	Bob Marley & the Wailers (Island)
2	2	BORN IN THE USA	Bruce Springsteen (CBS)
-	3	BREAKING HEARTS	Elton John (Rocket)
4	4	AN INNOCENT MAN	Billy Joel (CBS)
14	5	CAMOUFLAGE	Rod Stewart (Warner Bros.)
6	6	CAN'T SLOW DOWN	Lionel Richie (Motown)
3	7	THE WORKS	Queen (EMI)
20	8	AMERICAN HEARTBEAT Various Artists (Epic)	
8	9	EDEN Everything but the Girl (Blanco Y Negro)	
21	10	BREAKDANCE	Soundtrack (Polydor)
16	11	THEN CAME ROCK 'N' ROLL Various Artists (EMI)	
5	12	THRILLER	Michael Jackson (Epic)
7	13	HUMAN'S LIB	Howard Jones (WEA)
31	14	ROCK WILL NEVER DIE Michael Schenker (Chrysalis)	
19	15	FAREWELL MY SUMMER LOVE Michael Jackson (Motown)	
29	16	BREAK MACHINE Break Machine (Record Shack)	
13	17	CAFE BLEU	Style Council (Polydor)
26	18	IN THE STUDIO	Special AKA (2-Tone)
9	19	HYENA Siouxsie & the Banshees (Wonderland)	
10	20	NOW THAT'S WHAT I CALL MUSIC 2 Various Artists (EMI/Virgin)	
15	21	FOOTLOOSE	Soundtrack (CBS)
24	22	HYSTERIA	Human League (Virgin)
12	23	LOST BOYS	Flying Pickets (10 Records)
-	24	PRIVATE DANCER	Tina Turner (Capitol)
37	25	BREAK OUT	Pointer Sisters (Planet)
34	26	HUMAN RACING	Nik Kershaw (MCA)
18	27	THE SMITHS	Smiths (Rough Trade)
-	28	HEARTBEATS	Barbara Dixon (Epic)
22	29	MANGE TOUT	Blancmange (London)
23	30	MAN ON THE LINE	Chris DeBurgh (A&M)
25	31	STREET SOUNDS ELECTRO 4 Various Artists (Street Sounds)	
39	32	CHANGE OF HEART	Change (WEA)
30	33	MASTERPIECES - THE VERY BEST OF SKY Sky (Telstar)	
47	34	THE PROS AND CONS OF HITCH HIKING Roger Waters (Harvest)	
11	35	HUNGRY FOR HITS	Various Artists (K-Tel)
17	36	DON'T STOP DANCIN' Various Artists (Telstar)	
40	37	ALCHEMY - DIRE STRAITS LIVE Dire Straits (Vertigo)	
45	38	SEVEN AND THE RAGGED TIGER Duran Duran (EMI)	
44	39	JUNK CULTURE Orchestral Manoeuvres In The Dark (Virgin)	
32	40	TOUCH DANCE	Eurythmics (RCA)
35	41	FROM HER TO ETERNITY Nick Cave & the Bad Seeds (Mute)	
43	42	LEGEND (MUSIC FROM ROBIN OF SHERWOOD) Clannad (RCA)	
-	43	BROKEN DREAMS	Various Artists (Starblend)
-	44	MIRROR MOVES	Psychedelic Furs (CBS)
-	45	STREET SOUNDS NUMBER ONES Various Artists (Street Sounds)	
46	46	NYLON CURTAIN	Billy Joel (CBS)
-	47	MADONNA	Madonna (Sire)
-	48	THE THEMES ALBUM	Various Artists (K-Tel)
38	49	OCEAN RAIN Echo & the Bunnymen (Korova)	
48	50	NOW	Patrice Rushen (Elektra)

7 July 1984

last	this	Title	Artist
1	1	LEGEND	Bob Marley & the Wailers (Island)
3	2	BREAKING HEARTS	Elton John (Rocket)
2	3	BORN IN THE USA	Bruce Springsteen (CBS)
4	4	AN INNOCENT MAN	Billy Joel (CBS)
8	5	AMERICAN HEARTBEAT Various Artists (Epic)	
10	6	BREAKDANCE	Soundtrack (Polydor)
-	7	PARADE	Spandau Ballet (Chrysalis)
6	8	CAN'T SLOW DOWN	Lionel Richie (Motown)
5	9	CAMOUFLAGE	Rod Stewart (Warner Bros.)
-	10	BRILLIANT TREES	David Sylvian (Virgin)
24	11	PRIVATE DANCER	Tina Turner (Capitol)
15	12	FAREWELL MY SUMMER LOVE Michael Jackson (Motown)	
-	13	GOODBYE CRUEL WORLD Elvis Costello (F Beat)	
7	14	THE WORKS	Queen (EMI)
13	15	HUMAN'S LIB	Howard Jones (WEA)
12	16	THRILLER	Michael Jackson (Epic)
26	17	HUMAN RACING	Nik Kershaw (MCA)
25	18	BREAK OUT	Pointer Sisters (Planet)
17	19	CAFE BLEU	Style Council (Polydor)
9	20	EDEN Everything but the Girl (Blanco Y Negro)	
-	21	DISCOVERY	Mike Oldfield (Virgin)
11	22	THEN CAME ROCK 'N' ROLL Various Artists (EMI)	
21	23	FOOTLOOSE	Soundtrack (CBS)
19	24	HYENA Siouxsie & the Banshees (Wonderland)	
20	25	NOW THAT'S WHAT I CALL MUSIC 2 Various Artists (EMI/Virgin)	
22	26	HYSTERIA	Human League (Virgin)
-	27	REWIND 1971-1984 (THE BEST OF THE ROLLING STONES) Rolling Stones (Rolling Stones)	
-	28	STRANGE FRONTIER	Roger Taylor (EMI)
46	29	NYLON CURTAIN	Billy Joel (CBS)
14	30	ROCK WILL NEVER DIE Michael Schenker (Chrysalis)	
40	31	TOUCH DANCE	Eurythmics (RCA)
32	32	CHANGE OF HEART	Change (WEA)
39	33	JUNK CULTURE Orchestral Manoeuvres In The Dark (Virgin)	
16	34	BREAK MACHINE Break Machine (Record Shack)	
18	35	IN THE STUDIO	Special AKA (2-Tone)
28	36	HEARTBEATS	Barbara Dixon (Epic)
50	37	NOW	Patrice Rushen (Elektra)
-	38	SHE'S SO UNUSUAL	Cyndi Lauper (Portrait)
-	39	MARCUS MILLER Marcus Miller (Warner Bros.)	
-	40	LOVE LANGUAGE Teddy Pendergrass (Asylum)	
-	41	TOCSIN	X-Mal Deutschland (4AD)
27	42	THE SMITHS	Smiths (Rough Trade)
30	43	MAN ON THE LINE	Chris DeBurgh (A&M)
31	44	STREET SOUNDS ELECTRO 4 Various Artists (Street Sounds)	
29	45	MANGE TOUT	Blancmange (London)
23	46	LOST BOYS	Flying Pickets (10 Records)
-	47	LAMENT	Ultravox (Chrysalis)
-	48	STREET SOUNDS UK ELECTRO Various Artists (Street Sounds)	
35	49	HUNGRY FOR HITS	Various Artists (K-Tel)
-	50	INTO THE GAP	Thompson Twins (Arista)

Bruce Springsteen emerged with what was to be his all-time best-selling (and hit single offloading) album, *Born In The USA*. However, despite US chart-topping success, he was never able to muster enough concentrated sales here initially to dethrone the Bob Marley compilation, and in fact *Born In The USA* would not reach Number 1 in the UK until much later in its prodigious chart run, during February 1985.

July 1984

last week	this week	14 July 1984	
1	1	LEGEND	Bob Marley & the Wailers (Island)
2	2	BREAKING HEARTS	Elton John (Rocket)
7	3	PARADE	Spandau Ballet (Chrysalis)
10	4	BRILLIANT TREES	David Sylvian (Virgin)
13	5	GOODBYE CRUEL WORLD	Elvis Costello (F Beat)
4	6	AN INNOCENT MAN	Billy Joel (CBS)
5	7	AMERICAN HEARTBEAT	Various Artists (Epic)
8	8	CAN'T SLOW DOWN	Lionel Richie (Motown)
6	9	BREAKDANCE	Soundtrack (Polydor)
17	10	HUMAN RACING	Nik Kershaw (MCA)
21	11	DISCOVERY	Mike Oldfield (Virgin)
11	12	PRIVATE DANCER	Tina Turner (Capitol)
3	13	BORN IN THE USA	Bruce Springsteen (CBS)
27	14	REWIND 1971-1984 (THE BEST OF THE ROLLING STONES)	Rolling Stones (Rolling Stones)
14	15	THE WORKS	Queen (EMI)
12	16	FAREWELL MY SUMMER LOVE	Michael Jackson (Motown)
9	17	CAMOUFLAGE	Rod Stewart (Warner Bros.)
18	18	BREAK OUT	Pointer Sisters (Planet)
33	19	JUNK CULTURE	Orchestral Manoeuvres In The Dark (Virgin)
16	20	THRILLER	Michael Jackson (Epic)
28	21	STRANGE FRONTIER	Roger Taylor (EMI)
15	22	HUMAN'S LIB	Howard Jones (WEA)
-	23	BEAT STREET	Soundtrack (Atlantic)
25	24	NOW THAT'S WHAT I CALL MUSIC 2	Various Artists (EMI/Virgin)
38	25	SHE'S SO UNUSUAL	Cyndi Lauper (Portrait)
50	26	INTO THE GAP	Thompson Twins (Arista)
26	27	HYSTERIA	Human League (Virgin)
20	28	EDEN	Everything but the Girl (Blanco Y Negro)
22	29	THEN CAME ROCK 'N' ROLL	Various Artists (EMI)
30	30	ROCK WILL NEVER DIE	Michael Schenker (Chrysalis)
24	31	HYENA	Siouxsie & the Banshees (Wonderland)
35	32	IN THE STUDIO	Special AKA (2-Tone)
32	33	CHANGE OF HEART	Change (WEA)
41	34	TOCSIN	X-Mal Deutschland (4AD)
47	35	LAMENT	Ultravox (Chrysalis)
46	36	LOST BOYS	Flying Pickets (10 Records)
49	37	HUNGRY FOR HITS	Various Artists (K-Tel)
42	38	THE SMITHS	Smiths (Rough Trade)
23	39	FOOTLOOSE	Soundtrack (CBS)
19	40	CAFE BLEU	Style Council (Polydor)
-	41	MASTERPIECES - THE VERY BEST OF SKY	Sky (Telstar)
45	42	MANGE TOUT	Blancmange (London)
-	43	ROCK 'N' SOUL (PART 1)	Daryl Hall & John Oates (RCA)
-	44	ALCHEMY - DIRE STRAITS LIVE	Dire Straits (Vertigo)
29	45	NYLON CURTAIN	Billy Joel (CBS)
34	46	BREAK MACHINE	Break Machine (Record Shack)
36	47	HEARTBEATS	Barbara Dixon (Epic)
44	48	STREET SOUNDS ELECTRO 4	Various Artists (Street Sounds)
48	49	STREET SOUNDS UK ELECTRO	Various Artists (Street Sounds)
-	50	COLOUR BY NUMBERS	Culture Club (Virgin)

last week	this week	21 July 1984	
1	1	LEGEND	Bob Marley & the Wailers (Island)
3	2	PARADE	Spandau Ballet (Chrysalis)
-	3	VICTORY	Jacksons (Epic)
2	4	BREAKING HEARTS	Elton John (Rocket)
8	5	CAN'T SLOW DOWN	Lionel Richie (Motown)
6	6	AN INNOCENT MAN	Billy Joel (CBS)
-	7	THE LAST IN LINE	Dio (Vertigo)
18	8	BREAK OUT	Pointer Sisters (Planet)
9	9	BREAKDANCE	Soundtrack (Polydor)
10	10	HUMAN RACING	Nik Kershaw (MCA)
12	11	PRIVATE DANCER	Tina Turner (Capitol)
5	12	GOODBYE CRUEL WORLD	Elvis Costello (F Beat)
7	13	AMERICAN HEARTBEAT	Various Artists (Epic)
4	14	BRILLIANT TREES	David Sylvian (Virgin)
20	15	THRILLER	Michael Jackson (Epic)
11	16	DISCOVERY	Mike Oldfield (Virgin)
13	17	BORN IN THE USA	Bruce Springsteen (CBS)
15	18	THE WORKS	Queen (EMI)
14	19	REWIND 1971-1984 (THE BEST OF THE ROLLING STONES)	Rolling Stones (Rolling Stones)
22	20	HUMAN'S LIB	Howard Jones (WEA)
25	21	SHE'S SO UNUSUAL	Cyndi Lauper (Portrait)
24	22	NOW THAT'S WHAT I CALL MUSIC 2	Various Artists (EMI/Virgin)
17	23	CAMOUFLAGE	Rod Stewart (Warner Bros.)
16	24	FAREWELL MY SUMMER LOVE	Michael Jackson (Motown)
-	25	PURPLE RAIN	Prince & the Revolution (Warner Bros.)
26	26	INTO THE GAP	Thompson Twins (Arista)
23	27	BEAT STREET	Soundtrack (Atlantic)
-	28	OCEAN RAIN	Echo & the Bunnymen (Korova)
35	29	LAMENT	Ultravox (Chrysalis)
27	30	HYSTERIA	Human League (Virgin)
19	31	JUNK CULTURE	Orchestral Manoeuvres In The Dark (Virgin)
-	32	NOW	Patrice Rushen (Elektra)
39	33	FOOTLOOSE	Soundtrack (CBS)
-	34	20 ORIGINAL GREATS	Cliff Richard & the Shadows (EMI)
-	35	STREET TALK	Steve Perry (CBS)
-	36	THIS IS WHAT YOU WANT	Public Image Ltd (Virgin)
32	37	IN THE STUDIO	Special AKA (2-Tone)
33	38	CHANGE OF HEART	Change (WEA)
34	39	TOCSIN	X-Mal Deutschland (4AD)
28	40	EDEN	Everything but the Girl (Blanco Y Negro)
-	41	MINUTES	Elkie Brooks (A&M)
-	42	CIVILIZED MAN	Joe Cocker (Capitol)
38	43	THE SMITHS	Smiths (Rough Trade)
48	44	STREET SOUNDS ELECTRO 4	Various Artists (Street Sounds)
49	45	STREET SOUNDS UK ELECTRO	Various Artists (Street Sounds)
21	46	STRANGE FRONTIER	Roger Taylor (EMI)
-	47	DIFFORD AND TILBROOK	Difford & Tilbrook (A&M)
-	48	AFTER MIDNIGHT	Eric Clapton (RSO)
-	49	RED OCTOPUS	Jefferson Starship (RCA)
-	50	HALLOWED GROUND	Violent Femmes (London)

last week	this week	28 July 1984	
3	1	VICTORY	Jacksons (Epic)
1	2	LEGEND	Bob Marley & the Wailers (Island)
7	3	THE LAST IN LINE	Dio (Vertigo)
2	4	PARADE	Spandau Ballet (Chrysalis)
11	5	PRIVATE DANCER	Tina Turner (Capitol)
10	6	HUMAN RACING	Nik Kershaw (MCA)
4	7	BREAKING HEARTS	Elton John (Rocket)
8	8	BREAK OUT	Pointer Sisters (Planet)
6	9	AN INNOCENT MAN	Billy Joel (CBS)
25	10	PURPLE RAIN	Prince & the Revolution (Warner Bros.)
-	11	DIAMOND LIFE	Sade (CBS)
5	12	CAN'T SLOW DOWN	Lionel Richie (Motown)
9	13	BREAKDANCE	Soundtrack (Polydor)
14	14	BRILLIANT TREES	David Sylvian (Virgin)
13	15	AMERICAN HEARTBEAT	Various Artists (Epic)
12	16	GOODBYE CRUEL WORLD	Elvis Costello (F Beat)
15	17	THRILLER	Michael Jackson (Epic)
16	18	DISCOVERY	Mike Oldfield (Virgin)
21	19	SHE'S SO UNUSUAL	Cyndi Lauper (Portrait)
18	20	THE WORKS	Queen (EMI)
-	21	PRIMITIVE	Neil Diamond (CBS)
17	22	BORN IN THE USA	Bruce Springsteen (CBS)
27	23	BEAT STREET	Soundtrack (Atlantic)
20	24	HUMAN'S LIB	Howard Jones (WEA)
19	25	REWIND 1971-1984 (THE BEST OF THE ROLLING STONES)	Rolling Stones (Rolling Stones)
28	26	OCEAN RAIN	Echo & the Bunnymen (Korova)
36	27	THIS IS WHAT YOU WANT	Public Image Ltd (Virgin)
26	28	INTO THE GAP	Thompson Twins (Arista)
22	29	NOW THAT'S WHAT I CALL MUSIC 2	Various Artists (EMI/Virgin)
23	30	CAMOUFLAGE	Rod Stewart (Warner Bros.)
31	31	JUNK CULTURE	Orchestral Manoeuvres In The Dark (Virgin)
41	32	MINUTES	Elkie Brooks (A&M)
29	33	LAMENT	Ultravox (Chrysalis)
24	34	FAREWELL MY SUMMER LOVE	Michael Jackson (Motown)
40	35	EDEN	Everything but the Girl (Blanco Y Negro)
38	36	CHANGE OF HEART	Change (WEA)
37	37	IN THE STUDIO	Special AKA (2-Tone)
35	38	STREET TALK	Steve Perry (CBS)
47	39	DIFFORD AND TILBROOK	Difford & Tilbrook (A&M)
30	40	HYSTERIA	Human League (Virgin)
32	41	NOW	Patrice Rushen (Elektra)
33	42	FOOTLOOSE	Soundtrack (CBS)
39	43	TOCSIN	X-Mal Deutschland (4AD)
-	44	SEND ME YOUR LOVE	Kashif (Arista)
-	45	STREET SOUNDS NUMBER ONES	Various Artists (Street Sounds)
-	46	WIPEOUT	Various Artists (Impression)
-	47	INCREASE THE PRESSURE	Conflict (Mortarhate)
-	48	CAFE BLEU	Style Council (Polydor)
43	49	THE SMITHS	Smiths (Rough Trade)
46	50	STRANGE FRONTIER	Roger Taylor (EMI)

The Jacksons' *Victory* album was their first-ever chart-topping LP as a group, and clearly benefitted from the spin-off effect of the continuing enormous sales of Michael Jackson's *Thriller* and its associated singles. An extra boost also came from *Victory*'s own spin-off 45, *State Of Shock*, which owed little to the traditional Jacksons sound, and instead highlighted a vocal duet between Michael and guest Mick Jagger.

4 August 1984

last week	this week	Title	Artist (Label)
2	1	LEGEND	Bob Marley & the Wailers (Island)
5	2	PRIVATE DANCER	Tina Turner (Capitol)
11	3	DIAMOND LIFE	Sade (CBS)
4	4	PARADE	Spandau Ballet (Chrysalis)
1	5	VICTORY	Jacksons (Epic)
3	6	THE LAST IN LINE	Dio (Vertigo)
12	7	CAN'T SLOW DOWN	Lionel Richie (Motown)
21	8	PRIMITIVE	Neil Diamond (CBS)
7	9	BREAKING HEARTS	Elton John (Rocket)
10	10	PURPLE RAIN	Prince & the Revolution (Warner Bros.)
9	11	AN INNOCENT MAN	Billy Joel (CBS)
20	12	THE WORKS	Queen (EMI)
6	13	HUMAN RACING	Nik Kershaw (MCA)
13	14	BREAKDANCE	Soundtrack (Polydor)
17	15	THRILLER	Michael Jackson (Epic)
8	16	BREAK OUT	Pointer Sisters (Planet)
19	17	SHE'S SO UNUSUAL	Cyndi Lauper (Portrait)
25	18	REWIND 1971-1984 (THE BEST OF THE ROLLING STONES)	Rolling Stones (Rolling Stones)
16	19	GOODBYE CRUEL WORLD	Elvis Costello (F Beat)
22	20	BORN IN THE USA	Bruce Springsteen (CBS)
15	21	AMERICAN HEARTBEAT	Various Artists (Epic)
26	22	OCEAN RAIN	Echo & the Bunnymen (Korova)
28	23	INTO THE GAP	Thompson Twins (Arista)
24	24	HUMAN'S LIB	Howard Jones (WEA)
18	25	DISCOVERY	Mike Oldfield (Virgin)
14	26	BRILLIANT TREES	David Sylvian (Virgin)
23	27	BEAT STREET	Soundtrack (Atlantic)
40	28	HYSTERIA	Human League (Virgin)
33	29	LAMENT	Ultravox (Chrysalis)
-	30	A WORD TO THE WISE GUY	Mighty Wah (Beggars Banquet)
31	31	JUNK CULTURE	Orchestral Manoeuvres In The Dark (Virgin)
30	32	CAMOUFLAGE	Rod Stewart (Warner Bros.)
35	33	EDEN	Everything but the Girl (Blanco Y Negro)
42	34	FOOTLOOSE	Soundtrack (CBS)
45	35	STREET SOUNDS NUMBER ONES	Various Artists (Street Sounds)
-	36	BREAKDANCE - YOU CAN DO IT	Various Artists (K-Tel)
32	37	MINUTES	Elkie Brooks (A&M)
34	38	FAREWELL MY SUMMER LOVE	Michael Jackson (Motown)
27	39	THIS IS WHAT YOU WANT	Public Image Ltd (Virgin)
29	40	NOW THAT'S WHAT I CALL MUSIC 2	Various Artists (EMI/Virgin)
36	41	CHANGE OF HEART	Change (WEA)
38	42	STREET TALK	Steve Perry (CBS)
39	43	DIFFORD AND TILBROOK	Difford & Tilbrook (A&M)
48	44	CAFE BLEU	Style Council (Polydor)
-	45	GREATEST MESSAGES	Grandmaster Flash (Sugarhill)
-	46	ANTHEM	Black Uhuru (Island)
-	47	CLUB TRACKS	Various Artists (Club)
-	48	BACKTRACKIN'	Eric Clapton (Starblend)
41	49	NOW	Patrice Rushen (Elektra)
50	50	STRANGE FRONTIER	Roger Taylor (EMI)

11 August 1984

last week	this week	Title	Artist (Label)
3	1	DIAMOND LIFE	Sade (CBS)
2	2	PRIVATE DANCER	Tina Turner (Capitol)
1	3	LEGEND	Bob Marley & the Wailers (Island)
7	4	CAN'T SLOW DOWN	Lionel Richie (Motown)
4	5	PARADE	Spandau Ballet (Chrysalis)
12	6	THE WORKS	Queen (EMI)
15	7	THRILLER	Michael Jackson (Epic)
10	8	PURPLE RAIN	Prince & the Revolution (Warner Bros.)
11	9	AN INNOCENT MAN	Billy Joel (CBS)
16	10	BREAK OUT	Pointer Sisters (Planet)
8	11	PRIMITIVE	Neil Diamond (CBS)
5	12	VICTORY	Jacksons (Epic)
9	13	BREAKING HEARTS	Elton John (Rocket)
14	14	BREAKDANCE	Soundtrack (Polydor)
6	15	THE LAST IN LINE	Dio (Vertigo)
13	16	HUMAN RACING	Nik Kershaw (MCA)
17	17	SHE'S SO UNUSUAL	Cyndi Lauper (Portrait)
-	18	NOW THAT'S WHAT I CALL MUSIC 3	Various Artists (EMI/Virgin)
24	19	HUMAN'S LIB	Howard Jones (WEA)
-	20	STARLIGHT EXPRESS	Various (Starlight/Polydor)
23	21	INTO THE GAP	Thompson Twins (Arista)
25	22	DISCOVERY	Mike Oldfield (Virgin)
30	23	A WORD TO THE WISE GUY	Mighty Wah (Beggars Banquet)
22	24	OCEAN RAIN	Echo & the Bunnymen (Korova)
20	25	BORN IN THE USA	Bruce Springsteen (CBS)
27	26	BEAT STREET	Soundtrack (Atlantic)
21	27	AMERICAN HEARTBEAT	Various Artists (Epic)
26	28	BRILLIANT TREES	David Sylvian (Virgin)
32	29	CAMOUFLAGE	Rod Stewart (Warner Bros.)
38	30	FAREWELL MY SUMMER LOVE	Michael Jackson (Motown)
-	31	STREET SOUNDS CRUCIAL ELECTRO 2	Various Artists (Street Sounds)
-	32	CONDITION CRITICAL	Quiet Riot (Epic)
18	33	REWIND 1971-1984 (THE BEST OF THE ROLLING STONES)	Rolling Stones (Rolling Stones)
19	34	GOODBYE CRUEL WORLD	Elvis Costello (F Beat)
-	35	SISTERS	Bluebells (London)
36	36	BREAKDANCE - YOU CAN DO IT	Various Artists (K-Tel)
-	37	REVOLUTION	Theatre of Hate (Burning Rome)
-	38	ALCHEMY - DIRE STRAITS LIVE	Dire Straits (Vertigo)
34	39	FOOTLOOSE	Soundtrack (CBS)
-	40	MANGE TOUT	Blancmange (London)
-	41	SEVEN AND THE RAGGED TIGER	Duran Duran (EMI)
40	42	NOW THAT'S WHAT I CALL MUSIC 2	Various Artists (EMI/Virgin)
29	43	LAMENT	Ultravox (Chrysalis)
31	44	JUNK CULTURE	Orchestral Manoeuvres In The Dark (Virgin)
-	45	MAN ON THE LINE	Chris DeBurgh (A&M)
-	46	INTOLERANCE	Tik & Tok (Survival)
41	47	CHANGE OF HEART	Change (WEA)
33	48	EDEN	Everything but the Girl (Blanco Y Negro)
37	49	MINUTES	Elkie Brooks (A&M)
35	50	STREET SOUNDS NUMBER ONES	Various Artists (Street Sounds)

18 August 1984

last week	this week	Title	Artist (Label)
18	1	NOW THAT'S WHAT I CALL MUSIC 3	Various Artists (EMI/Virgin)
1	2	DIAMOND LIFE	Sade (CBS)
2	3	PRIVATE DANCER	Tina Turner (Capitol)
3	4	LEGEND	Bob Marley & the Wailers (Island)
6	5	THE WORKS	Queen (EMI)
10	6	BREAK OUT	Pointer Sisters (Planet)
4	7	CAN'T SLOW DOWN	Lionel Richie (Motown)
9	8	AN INNOCENT MAN	Billy Joel (CBS)
8	9	PURPLE RAIN	Prince & the Revolution (Warner Bros.)
7	10	THRILLER	Michael Jackson (Epic)
5	11	PARADE	Spandau Ballet (Chrysalis)
13	12	BREAKING HEARTS	Elton John (Rocket)
14	13	BREAKDANCE	Soundtrack (Polydor)
35	14	SISTERS	Bluebells (London)
11	15	PRIMITIVE	Neil Diamond (CBS)
16	16	HUMAN RACING	Nik Kershaw (MCA)
19	17	HUMAN'S LIB	Howard Jones (WEA)
12	18	VICTORY	Jacksons (Epic)
15	19	THE LAST IN LINE	Dio (Vertigo)
17	20	SHE'S SO UNUSUAL	Cyndi Lauper (Portrait)
24	21	OCEAN RAIN	Echo & the Bunnymen (Korova)
20	22	STARLIGHT EXPRESS	Various (Starlight/Polydor)
21	23	INTO THE GAP	Thompson Twins (Arista)
23	24	A WORD TO THE WISE GUY	Mighty Wah (Beggars Banquet)
25	25	BORN IN THE USA	Bruce Springsteen (CBS)
-	26	THE BEST OF JON AND VANGELIS	Jon & Vangelis (Polydor)
22	27	DISCOVERY	Mike Oldfield (Virgin)
27	28	AMERICAN HEARTBEAT	Various Artists (Epic)
31	29	STREET SOUNDS CRUCIAL ELECTRO 2	Various Artists (Street Sounds)
29	30	CAMOUFLAGE	Rod Stewart (Warner Bros.)
34	31	GOODBYE CRUEL WORLD	Elvis Costello (F Beat)
26	32	BEAT STREET	Soundtrack (Atlantic)
28	33	BRILLIANT TREES	David Sylvian (Virgin)
43	34	LAMENT	Ultravox (Chrysalis)
42	35	NOW THAT'S WHAT I CALL MUSIC 2	Various Artists (EMI/Virgin)
-	36	WELL PLEASED	Chas & Dave (Rockney)
-	37	IN ROCK WE TRUST	Y & T (A&M)
33	38	REWIND 1971-1984 (THE BEST OF THE ROLLING STONES)	Rolling Stones (Rolling Stones)
38	39	ALCHEMY - DIRE STRAITS LIVE	Dire Straits (Vertigo)
47	40	CHANGE OF HEART	Change (WEA)
48	41	EDEN	Everything but the Girl (Blanco Y Negro)
-	42	STREET SOUNDS EDITION 10	Various Artists (Street Sounds)
-	43	CHUNKS OF FUNK	Various Artists (MCA)
37	44	REVOLUTION	Theatre of Hate (Burning Rome)
41	45	SEVEN AND THE RAGGED TIGER	Duran Duran (EMI)
40	46	MANGE TOUT	Blancmange (London)
36	47	BREAKDANCE - YOU CAN DO IT	Various Artists (K-Tel)
-	48	GREATEST MESSAGES	Grandmaster Flash (Sugarhill)
-	49	BACKTRACKIN'	Eric Clapton (Starblend)
39	50	FOOTLOOSE	Soundtrack (CBS)

The Number 1 success of Sade's *Diamond Life* made her only the second female solo singer (after Kate Bush in 1978) to top the UK chart with her debut album - even if its reign at the top was restricted to one week before giving way to the third and best-selling yet of the blockbuster *Now That's What I Call Music* compilations. Tina Turner only just failed to achieve this feat with *Private Dancer*, peaking at 2.

August – September 1984

25 August 1984

last	this	Title	Artist (Label)
1	1	NOW THAT'S WHAT I CALL MUSIC 3	Various Artists (EMI/Virgin)
2	2	DIAMOND LIFE	Sade (CBS)
3	3	PRIVATE DANCER	Tina Turner (Capitol)
4	4	LEGEND	Bob Marley & the Wailers (Island)
9	5	PURPLE RAIN	Prince & the Revolution (Warner Bros.)
5	6	THE WORKS	Queen (EMI)
6	7	BREAK OUT	Pointer Sisters (Planet)
7	8	CAN'T SLOW DOWN	Lionel Richie (Motown)
8	9	AN INNOCENT MAN	Billy Joel (CBS)
10	10	THRILLER	Michael Jackson (Epic)
11	11	PARADE	Spandau Ballet (Chrysalis)
17	12	HUMAN'S LIB	Howard Jones (WEA)
13	13	BREAKDANCE	Soundtrack (Polydor)
12	14	BREAKING HEARTS	Elton John (Rocket)
18	15	VICTORY	Jacksons (Epic)
19	16	THE LAST IN LINE	Dio (Vertigo)
20	17	SHE'S SO UNUSUAL	Cyndi Lauper (Portrait)
23	18	INTO THE GAP	Thompson Twins (Arista)
16	19	HUMAN RACING	Nik Kershaw (MCA)
14	20	SISTERS	Bluebells (London)
37	21	IN ROCK WE TRUST	Y & T (A&M)
21	22	OCEAN RAIN	Echo & the Bunnymen (Korova)
24	23	A WORD TO THE WISE GUY	Mighty Wah (Beggars Banquet)
30	24	CAMOUFLAGE	Rod Stewart (Warner Bros.)
33	25	BRILLIANT TREES	David Sylvian (Virgin)
26	26	THE BEST OF JON AND VANGELIS	Jon & Vangelis (Polydor)
15	27	PRIMITIVE	Neil Diamond (CBS)
27	28	DISCOVERY	Mike Oldfield (Virgin)
25	29	BORN IN THE USA	Bruce Springsteen (CBS)
42	30	STREET SOUNDS EDITION 10	Various Artists (Street Sounds)
44	31	REVOLUTION	Theatre of Hate (Burning Rome)
-	32	SELF CONTROL	Laura Branigan (Atlantic)
28	33	AMERICAN HEARTBEAT	Various Artists (Epic)
36	34	WELL PLEASED	Chas & Dave (Rockney)
22	35	STARLIGHT EXPRESS	Various Artists (Starlight/Polydor)
29	36	SREET SOUNDS CRUCIAL ELECTRO 2	Various Artists (Street Sounds)
39	37	ALCHEMY - DIRE STRAITS LIVE	Dire Straits (Vertigo)
40	38	CHANGE OF HEART	Change (WEA)
47	39	BREAKDANCE - YOU CAN DO IT	Various Artists (K-Tel)
-	40	WINDJAMMER II	Windjammer (MCA)
-	41	JAM SCIENCE	Shreikback (Arista)
32	42	BEAT STREET	Soundtrack (Atlantic)
41	43	EDEN	Everything but the Girl (Blanco Y Negro)
35	44	NOW THAT'S WHAT I CALL MUSIC 2	Various Artists (EMI/Virgin)
-	45	L.A. IS MY LADY	Frank Sinatra (Qwest)
-	46	ELECTRIC DREAMS	Soundtrack (Virgin)
38	47	REWIND 1971-1984 (THE BEST OF THE ROLLING STONES)	Rolling Stones (Rolling Stones)
31	48	GOODBYE CRUEL WORLD	Elvis Costello (F Beat)
34	49	LAMENT	Ultravox (Chrysalis)
43	50	CHUNKS OF FUNK	Various Artists (MCA)

1 September 1984

last	this	Title	Artist (Label)
1	1	NOW THAT'S WHAT I CALL MUSIC 3	Various Artists (EMI/Virgin)
3	2	PRIVATE DANCER	Tina Turner (Capitol)
2	3	DIAMOND LIFE	Sade (CBS)
4	4	LEGEND	Bob Marley & the Wailers (Island)
5	5	PURPLE RAIN	Prince & the Revolution (Warner Bros.)
6	6	THE WORKS	Queen (EMI)
11	7	PARADE	Spandau Ballet (Chrysalis)
8	8	CAN'T SLOW DOWN	Lionel Richie (Motown)
10	9	THRILLER	Michael Jackson (Epic)
7	10	BREAK OUT	Pointer Sisters (Planet)
12	11	HUMAN'S LIB	Howard Jones (WEA)
14	12	BREAKING HEARTS	Elton John (Rocket)
-	13	DOWN ON THE STREET	Shakatak (Polydor)
-	14	PHIL FEARON AND GALAXY	Phil Fearon & Galaxy (Ensign)
9	15	AN INNOCENT MAN	Billy Joel (CBS)
17	16	SHE'S SO UNUSUAL	Cyndi Lauper (Portrait)
13	17	BREAKDANCE	Soundtrack (Polydor)
29	18	BORN IN THE USA	Bruce Springsteen (CBS)
30	19	STREET SOUNDS EDITION 10	Various Artists (Street Sounds)
15	20	VICTORY	Jacksons (Epic)
19	21	HUMAN RACING	Nik Kershaw (MCA)
39	22	BREAKDANCE - YOU CAN DO IT	Various Artists (K-Tel)
20	23	SISTERS	Bluebells (London)
44	24	NOW THAT'S WHAT I CALL MUSIC 2	Various Artists (EMI/Virgin)
22	25	OCEAN RAIN	Echo & the Bunnymen (Korova)
21	26	IN ROCK WE TRUST	Y & T (A&M)
33	27	AMERICAN HEARTBEAT	Various Artists (Epic)
-	28	1984	Van Halen (Warner Bros.)
23	29	A WORD TO THE WISE GUY	Mighty Wah (Beggars Banquet)
27	30	PRIMITIVE	Neil Diamond (CBS)
28	31	DISCOVERY	Mike Oldfield (Virgin)
32	32	SELF CONTROL	Laura Branigan (Atlantic)
35	33	STARLIGHT EXPRESS	Various Artists (Starlight/Polydor)
26	34	THE BEST OF JON AND VANGELIS	Jon & Vangelis (Polydor)
18	35	INTO THE GAP	Thompson Twins (Arista)
24	36	CAMOUFLAGE	Rod Stewart (Warner Bros.)
25	37	BRILLIANT TREES	David Sylvian (Virgin)
40	38	WINDJAMMER II	Windjammer (MCA)
19	39	THE LAST IN LINE	Dio (Vertigo)
46	40	ELECTRIC DREAMS	Soundtrack (Virgin)
-	41	JUST THE WAY YOU LIKE IT	SOS Band (Tabu/Epic)
34	42	WELL PLEASED	Chas & Dave (Rockney)
31	43	REVOLUTION	Theatre of Hate (Burning Rome)
-	44	OUT OF CONTROL	Brothers Johnson (A&M)
-	45	QUEEN'S GREATEST HITS	Queen (EMI)
-	46	THE STORY OF A YOUNG HEART	A Flock of Seagulls (Jive)
-	47	MAN ON THE LINE	Chris DeBurgh (A&M)
-	48	1100 BEL AIR PLACE	Julio Iglesias (CBS)
45	49	L.A. IS MY LADY	Frank Sinatra (Qwest)
36	50	SREET SOUNDS CRUCIAL ELECTRO 2	Various Artists (Street Sounds)

8 September 1984

last	this	Title	Artist (Label)
1	1	NOW THAT'S WHAT I CALL MUSIC 3	Various Artists (EMI/Virgin)
2	2	PRIVATE DANCER	Tina Turner (Capitol)
3	3	DIAMOND LIFE	Sade (CBS)
6	4	THE WORKS	Queen (EMI)
4	5	LEGEND	Bob Marley & the Wailers (Island)
8	6	CAN'T SLOW DOWN	Lionel Richie (Motown)
5	7	PURPLE RAIN	Prince & the Revolution (Warner Bros.)
7	8	PARADE	Spandau Ballet (Chrysalis)
14	9	PHIL FEARON AND GALAXY	Phil Fearon & Galaxy (Ensign)
10	10	BREAK OUT	Pointer Sisters (Planet)
11	11	HUMAN'S LIB	Howard Jones (WEA)
12	12	BREAKING HEARTS	Elton John (Rocket)
9	13	THRILLER	Michael Jackson (Epic)
13	14	DOWN ON THE STREET	Shakatak (Polydor)
18	15	BORN IN THE USA	Bruce Springsteen (CBS)
41	16	JUST THE WAY YOU LIKE IT	SOS Band (Tabu/Epic)
15	17	AN INNOCENT MAN	Billy Joel (CBS)
21	18	HUMAN RACING	Nik Kershaw (MCA)
20	19	VICTORY	Jacksons (Epic)
17	20	BREAKDANCE	Soundtrack (Polydor)
35	21	INTO THE GAP	Thompson Twins (Arista)
32	22	SELF CONTROL	Laura Branigan (Atlantic)
48	23	1100 BEL AIR PLACE	Julio Iglesias (CBS)
19	24	STREET SOUNDS EDITION 10	Various Artists (Street Sounds)
23	25	SISTERS	Bluebells (London)
24	26	NOW THAT'S WHAT I CALL MUSIC 2	Various Artists (EMI/Virgin)
36	27	CAMOUFLAGE	Rod Stewart (Warner Bros.)
16	28	SHE'S SO UNUSUAL	Cyndi Lauper (Portrait)
25	29	OCEAN RAIN	Echo & the Bunnymen (Korova)
30	30	PRIMITIVE	Neil Diamond (CBS)
-	31	ELIMINATOR	ZZ Top (WEA)
-	32	GOODBYE CRUEL WORLD	Elvis Costello (F Beat)
46	33	THE STORY OF A YOUNG HEART	A Flock of Seagulls (Jive)
37	34	BRILLIANT TREES	David Sylvian (Virgin)
22	35	BREAKDANCE - YOU CAN DO IT	Various Artists (K-Tel)
28	36	1984	Van Halen (Warner Bros.)
-	37	DREAMLINE	Cult (Beggars Banquet)
50	38	SREET SOUNDS CRUCIAL ELECTRO 2	Various Artists (Street Sounds)
49	39	L.A. IS MY LADY	Frank Sinatra (Qwest)
-	40	THE CROSSING	Big Country (Mercury)
-	41	BREAK MACHINE	Break Machine (Record Shack)
39	42	THE LAST IN LINE	Dio (Vertigo)
45	43	QUEEN'S GREATEST HITS	Queen (EMI)
26	44	IN ROCK WE TRUST	Y & T (A&M)
38	45	WINDJAMMER II	Windjammer (MCA)
29	46	A WORD TO THE WISE GUY	Mighty Wah (Beggars Banquet)
-	47	BRYAN LOREN	Bryan Loren (Virgin)
34	48	THE BEST OF JON AND VANGELIS	Jon & Vangelis (Polydor)
-	49	ALCHEMY - DIRE STRAITS LIVE	Dire Straits (Vertigo)
-	50	BEAT STREET	Soundtrack (Atlantic)

Prince's *Purple Rain* album, the soundtrack from his film of the same title, was a chart-topper for over 6 months in the US, but did not conquer quite so convincingly in the UK - where it was actually his first album to figure in the chart at all. Its Number 5 placing in August was the highest it would reach, despite a lengthy Top 10 residency and the boosting effect of the Top 3 *When Doves Cry* single.

15 September 1984

last week	this week	Title	Artist
1	1	NOW THAT'S WHAT I CALL MUSIC 3	Various Artists (EMI/Virgin)
3	2	DIAMOND LIFE	Sade (CBS)
2	3	PRIVATE DANCER	Tina Turner (Capitol)
4	4	THE WORKS	Queen (EMI)
5	5	LEGEND	Bob Marley & the Wailers (Island)
6	6	CAN'T SLOW DOWN	Lionel Richie (Motown)
8	7	PARADE	Spandau Ballet (Chrysalis)
7	8	PURPLE RAIN	Prince & the Revolution (Warner Bros.)
11	9	HUMAN'S LIB	Howard Jones (WEA)
31	10	ELIMINATOR	ZZ Top (WEA)
-	11	POWERSLAVE	Iron Maiden (EMI)
12	12	BREAKING HEARTS	Elton John (Rocket)
9	13	PHIL FEARON AND GALAXY	Phil Fearon & Galaxy (Ensign)
37	14	DREAMLINE	Cult (Beggars Banquet)
10	15	BREAK OUT	Pointer Sisters (Planet)
13	16	THRILLER	Michael Jackson (Epic)
23	17	1100 BEL AIR PLACE	Julio Iglesias (CBS)
22	18	SELF CONTROL	Laura Branigan (Atlantic)
-	19	NO REMORSE	Motorhead (Bronze)
15	20	BORN IN THE USA	Bruce Springsteen (CBS)
-	21	UNDER WRAPS	Jethro Tull (Chrysalis)
17	22	AN INNOCENT MAN	Billy Joel (CBS)
18	23	HUMAN RACING	Nik Kershaw (MCA)
14	24	DOWN ON THE STREET	Shakatak (Polydor)
19	25	VICTORY	Jacksons (Epic)
16	26	JUST THE WAY YOU LIKE IT	SOS Band (Tabu/Epic)
-	27	WHOSE SIDE ARE YOU ON	Matt Bianco (WEA)
28	28	SHE'S SO UNUSUAL	Cyndi Lauper (Portrait)
33	29	THE STORY OF A YOUNG HEART	Flock of Seagulls (Jive)
21	30	INTO THE GAP	Thompson Twins (Arista)
26	31	NOW THAT'S WHAT I CALL MUSIC 2	Various Artists (EMI/Virgin)
20	32	BREAKDANCE	Soundtrack (Polydor)
-	33	REFLECTIONS	Rick James (Motown)
46	34	A WORD TO THE WISE GUY	Mighty Wah (Beggars Banquet)
-	35	1999	Prince (Warner Bros.)
43	36	QUEEN'S GREATEST HITS	Queen (EMI)
40	37	THE CROSSING	Big Country (Mercury)
-	38	CHANGE OF HEART	Change (WEA)
25	39	SISTERS	Bluebells (London)
42	40	THE LAST IN LINE	Dio (Vertigo)
50	41	BEAT STREET	Soundtrack (Atlantic)
39	42	L.A. IS MY LADY	Frank Sinatra (Qwest)
34	43	BRILLIANT TREES	David Sylvian (Virgin)
-	44	BURNING OIL	Skeletal Family (Red Rhino)
24	45	STREET SOUNDS EDITION 10	Various Artists (Street Sounds)
27	46	CAMOUFLAGE	Rod Stewart (Warner Bros.)
35	47	BREAKDANCE - YOU CAN DO IT	Various Artists (K-Tel)
-	48	RIDE THE LIGHTNING	Metallica (Music For Nations)
-	49	W.A.S.P.	W.A.S.P. (Capitol)
-	50	THE LAS VEGAS STORY	Gun Club (Animal/Chrysalis)

22 September 1984

last week	this week	Title	Artist
1	1	NOW THAT'S WHAT I CALL MUSIC 3	Various Artists (EMI/Virgin)
11	2	POWERSLAVE	Iron Maiden (EMI)
3	3	PRIVATE DANCER	Tina Turner (Capitol)
2	4	DIAMOND LIFE	Sade (CBS)
8	5	PURPLE RAIN	Prince & the Revolution (Warner Bros.)
10	6	ELIMINATOR	ZZ Top (WEA)
4	7	THE WORKS	Queen (EMI)
19	8	NO REMORSE	Motorhead (Bronze)
5	9	LEGEND	Bob Marley & the Wailers (Island)
7	10	PARADE	Spandau Ballet (Chrysalis)
6	11	CAN'T SLOW DOWN	Lionel Richie (Motown)
9	12	HUMAN'S LIB	Howard Jones (WEA)
-	13	THE WOMAN IN RED - ORIGINAL SOUNDTRACK	Stevie Wonder (Motown)
18	14	SELF CONTROL	Laura Branigan (Atlantic)
15	15	BREAK OUT	Pointer Sisters (Planet)
12	16	BREAKING HEARTS	Elton John (Rocket)
21	17	UNDER WRAPS	Jethro Tull (Chrysalis)
16	18	THRILLER	Michael Jackson (Epic)
17	19	1100 BEL AIR PLACE	Julio Iglesias (CBS)
14	20	DREAMLINE	Cult (Beggars Banquet)
20	21	BORN IN THE USA	Bruce Springsteen (CBS)
13	22	PHIL FEARON AND GALAXY	Phil Fearon & Galaxy (Ensign)
26	23	JUST THE WAY YOU LIKE IT	SOS Band (Tabu/Epic)
22	24	AN INNOCENT MAN	Billy Joel (CBS)
25	25	VICTORY	Jacksons (Epic)
-	26	CRE-OLE	Kid Creole & the Coconuts (Island)
24	27	DOWN ON THE STREET	Shakatak (Polydor)
32	28	BREAKDANCE	Soundtrack (Polydor)
30	29	INTO THE GAP	Thompson Twins (Arista)
28	30	SHE'S SO UNUSUAL	Cyndi Lauper (Portrait)
-	31	A SPECIAL PART OF ME	Johnny Mathis (CBS)
-	32	SWEET SIXTEEN	Sweet (Anagram)
31	33	NOW THAT'S WHAT I CALL MUSIC 2	Various Artists (EMI/Virgin)
36	34	QUEEN'S GREATEST HITS	Queen (EMI)
23	35	HUMAN RACING	Nik Kershaw (MCA)
46	36	CAMOUFLAGE	Rod Stewart (Warner Bros.)
42	37	L.A. IS MY LADY	Frank Sinatra (Qwest)
33	38	REFLECTIONS	Rick James (Motown)
35	39	1999	Prince (Warner Bros.)
29	40	THE STORY OF A YOUNG HEART	Flock of Seagulls (Jive)
-	41	CATS WITHOUT CLAWS	Donna Summer (Warner Bros.)
45	42	STREET SOUNDS EDITION 10	Various Artists (Street Sounds)
-	43	NIGHT MOVES	Various Artists (K-Tel)
-	44	YOU, ME AND HE	M'Tume (Epic)
27	45	WHOSE SIDE ARE YOU ON	Matt Bianco (WEA)
-	46	ALCHEMY - DIRE STRAITS LIVE	Dire Straits (Vertigo)
-	47	ANTHEM	Black Uhuru (Island)
-	48	IF I KISSED HER	400 Blows (Illuminated)
43	49	BRILLIANT TREES	David Sylvian (Virgin)
-	50	WAR	U2 (Island)

29 September 1984

last week	this week	Title	Artist
13	1	THE WOMAN IN RED - ORIGINAL SOUNDTRACK	Stevie Wonder (Motown)
4	2	DIAMOND LIFE	Sade (CBS)
3	3	PRIVATE DANCER	Tina Turner (Capitol)
6	4	ELIMINATOR	ZZ Top (WEA)
2	5	POWERSLAVE	Iron Maiden (EMI)
1	6	NOW THAT'S WHAT I CALL MUSIC 3	Various Artists (EMI/Virgin)
5	7	PURPLE RAIN	Prince & the Revolution (Warner Bros.)
8	8	NO REMORSE	Motorhead (Bronze)
7	9	THE WORKS	Queen (EMI)
9	10	LEGEND	Bob Marley & the Wailers (Island)
10	11	PARADE	Spandau Ballet (Chrysalis)
12	12	HUMAN'S LIB	Howard Jones (WEA)
11	13	CAN'T SLOW DOWN	Lionel Richie (Motown)
14	14	SELF CONTROL	Laura Branigan (Atlantic)
16	15	BREAKING HEARTS	Elton John (Rocket)
18	16	THRILLER	Michael Jackson (Epic)
17	17	UNDER WRAPS	Jethro Tull (Chrysalis)
-	18	KNIFE	Aztec Camera (WEA)
19	19	1100 BEL AIR PLACE	Julio Iglesias (CBS)
15	20	BREAK OUT	Pointer Sisters (Planet)
22	21	PHIL FEARON AND GALAXY	Phil Fearon & Galaxy (Ensign)
20	22	DREAMLINE	Cult (Beggars Banquet)
34	23	QUEEN'S GREATEST HITS	Queen (EMI)
23	24	JUST THE WAY YOU LIKE IT	SOS Band (Tabu/Epic)
21	25	BORN IN THE USA	Bruce Springsteen (CBS)
26	26	CRE-OLE	Kid Creole & the Coconuts (Island)
24	27	AN INNOCENT MAN	Billy Joel (CBS)
27	28	DOWN ON THE STREET	Shakatak (Polydor)
-	29	HOPE AND GLORY	Tom Robinson (Castaway)
-	30	GHOSTBUSTERS	Soundtrack (Arista)
35	31	HUMAN RACING	Nik Kershaw (MCA)
-	32	THE SMITHS	Smiths (Rough Trade)
-	33	WE ARE FAMILY	Sister Sledge (Cotillion)
33	34	NOW THAT'S WHAT I CALL MUSIC 2	Various Artists (EMI/Virgin)
37	35	L.A. IS MY LADY	Frank Sinatra (Qwest)
-	36	THE LAST IN LINE	Dio (Vertigo)
-	37	SISTERS	Bluebells (London)
-	38	AMERICAN HEARTBEAT	Various Artists (Epic)
25	39	VICTORY	Jacksons (Epic)
30	40	SHE'S SO UNUSUAL	Cyndi Lauper (Portrait)
28	41	BREAKDANCE	Soundtrack (Polydor)
41	42	CATS WITHOUT CLAWS	Donna Summer (Warner Bros.)
46	43	ALCHEMY - DIRE STRAITS LIVE	Dire Straits (Vertigo)
-	44	BREAKDANCE - YOU CAN DO IT	Various Artists (K-Tel)
-	45	TILL WE HAVE FACES	Steve Hackett (Lamborghini)
-	46	BURNING OIL	Skeletal Family (Red Rhino)
-	47	SOIL FESTIVITIES	Vangelis (Polydor)
29	48	INTO THE GAP	Thompson Twins (Arista)
36	49	CAMOUFLAGE	Rod Stewart (Warner Bros.)
39	50	1999	Prince (Warner Bros.)

The Woman In Red was Stevie Wonder's soundtrack for the Gene Wilder-starring movie of the same title, and proved a better commercial prospect than Stevie's previous soundtrack experimentation with *The Secret Life Of Plants*. The album contained both vocal and instrumental tracks, plus guest vocals by Dionne Warwick, but the obvious highlight was the million-selling single *I Just Called To Say I Love You*..

6 October 1984

last week	this week	Title	Artist
1	1	THE WOMAN IN RED - ORIGINAL SOUNDTRACK	Stevie Wonder (Motown)
4	2	ELIMINATOR	ZZ Top (WEA)
2	3	DIAMOND LIFE	Sade (CBS)
6	4	NOW THAT'S WHAT I CALL MUSIC 3	Various Artists (EMI/Virgin)
3	5	PRIVATE DANCER	Tina Turner (Capitol)
7	6	PURPLE RAIN	Prince & the Revolution (Warner Bros.)
5	7	POWERSLAVE	Iron Maiden (EMI)
18	8	KNIFE	Aztec Camera (WEA)
-	9	TONIGHT	David Bowie (EMI America)
9	10	THE WORKS	Queen (EMI)
13	11	CAN'T SLOW DOWN	Lionel Richie (Motown)
10	12	LEGEND	Bob Marley & the Wailers (Island)
11	13	PARADE	Spandau Ballet (Chrysalis)
33	14	WE ARE FAMILY	Sister Sledge (Cotillion)
29	15	HOPE AND GLORY	Tom Robinson (Castaway)
16	16	THRILLER	Michael Jackson (Epic)
12	17	HUMAN'S LIB	Howard Jones (WEA)
-	18	SOME GREAT REWARD	Depeche Mode (Mute)
-	19	ANIMALIZE	Kiss (Vertigo)
-	20	HOW MEN ARE	Heaven 17 (Virgin)
25	21	BORN IN THE USA	Bruce Springsteen (CBS)
-	22	U2 LIVE: UNDER A BLOOD RED SKY	U2 (Island)
14	23	SELF CONTROL	Laura Branigan (Atlantic)
15	24	BREAKING HEARTS	Elton John (Rocket)
30	25	GHOSTBUSTERS	Soundtrack (Arista)
20	26	BREAK OUT	Pointer Sisters (Planet)
31	27	HUMAN RACING	Nik Kershaw (MCA)
-	28	VERTICAL SMILES	Blackfoot (Atco)
17	29	UNDER WRAPS	Jethro Tull (Chrysalis)
27	30	AN INNOCENT MAN	Billy Joel (CBS)
22	31	DREAMLINE	Cult (Beggars Banquet)
8	32	NO REMORSE	Motorhead (Bronze)
19	33	1100 BEL AIR PLACE	Julio Iglesias (CBS)
26	34	CRE-OLE	Kid Creole & the Coconuts (Island)
21	35	PHIL FEARON AND GALAXY	Phil Fearon & Galaxy (Ensign)
23	36	QUEEN'S GREATEST HITS	Queen (EMI)
-	37	STREET SOUNDS ELECTRO 5	Various Artists (Street Sounds)
-	38	EDEN	Everything but the Girl (Blanco Y Negro)
39	39	VICTORY	Jacksons (Epic)
40	40	SHE'S SO UNUSUAL	Cyndi Lauper (Portrait)
-	41	ALL BY MYSELF	Various Artists (K-Tel)
-	42	THE STORY OF A YOUNG HEART	A Flock of Seagulls (Jive)
-	43	WAR	U2 (Island)
48	44	INTO THE GAP	Thompson Twins (Arista)
24	45	JUST THE WAY YOU LIKE IT	SOS Band (Tabu/Epic)
28	46	DOWN ON THE STREET	Shakatak (Polydor)
34	47	NOW THAT'S WHAT I CALL MUSIC 2	Various Artists (EMI/Virgin)
35	48	L.A. IS MY LADY	Frank Sinatra (Qwest)
32	49	THE SMITHS	Smiths (Rough Trade)
50	50	1999	Prince (Warner Bros.)

13 October 1984

last week	this week	Title	Artist
9	1	TONIGHT	David Bowie (EMI America)
3	2	DIAMOND LIFE	Sade (CBS)
2	3	ELIMINATOR	ZZ Top (WEA)
1	4	THE WOMAN IN RED - ORIGINAL SOUNDTRACK	Stevie Wonder (Motown)
6	5	PURPLE RAIN	Prince & the Revolution (Warner Bros.)
18	6	SOME GREAT REWARD	Depeche Mode (Mute)
4	7	NOW THAT'S WHAT I CALL MUSIC 3	Various Artists (EMI/Virgin)
20	8	HOW MEN ARE	Heaven 17 (Virgin)
5	9	PRIVATE DANCER	Tina Turner (Capitol)
14	10	WE ARE FAMILY	Sister Sledge (Cotillion)
-	11	THE UNFORGETTABLE FIRE	U2 (Island)
10	12	THE WORKS	Queen (EMI)
8	13	KNIFE	Aztec Camera (WEA)
11	14	CAN'T SLOW DOWN	Lionel Richie (Motown)
13	15	PARADE	Spandau Ballet (Chrysalis)
12	16	LEGEND	Bob Marley & the Wailers (Island)
16	17	THRILLER	Michael Jackson (Epic)
23	18	SELF CONTROL	Laura Branigan (Atlantic)
17	19	HUMAN'S LIB	Howard Jones (WEA)
15	20	HOPE AND GLORY	Tom Robinson (Castaway)
7	21	POWERSLAVE	Iron Maiden (EMI)
19	22	ANIMALIZE	Kiss (Vertigo)
37	23	STREET SOUNDS ELECTRO 5	Various Artists (Street Sounds)
26	24	BREAK OUT	Pointer Sisters (Planet)
30	25	AN INNOCENT MAN	Billy Joel (CBS)
22	26	U2 LIVE: UNDER A BLOOD RED SKY	U2 (Island)
-	27	TRUE COLOURS	Level 42 (Polydor)
24	28	BREAKING HEARTS	Elton John (Rocket)
27	29	HUMAN RACING	Nik Kershaw (MCA)
41	30	ALL BY MYSELF	Various Artists (K-Tel)
31	31	DREAMLINE	Cult (Beggars Banquet)
-	32	SWEPT AWAY	Diana Ross (Capitol)
-	33	THE PLAN	Gary Numan (Beggars Banquet)
21	34	BORN IN THE USA	Bruce Springsteen (CBS)
-	35	THE MAGAZINE	Rickie Lee Jones (Warner Bros.)
25	36	GHOSTBUSTERS	Soundtrack (Arista)
29	37	UNDER WRAPS	Jethro Tull (Chrysalis)
-	38	WE WANT MOORE!	Gary Moore (10/Virgin)
34	39	CRE-OLE	Kid Creole & the Coconuts (Island)
35	40	PHIL FEARON AND GALAXY	Phil Fearon & Galaxy (Ensign)
36	41	QUEEN'S GREATEST HITS	Queen (EMI)
-	42	NIGHT MOVES	Various Artists (K-Tel)
33	43	1100 BEL AIR PLACE	Julio Iglesias (CBS)
32	44	NO REMORSE	Motorhead (Bronze)
40	45	SHE'S SO UNUSUAL	Cyndi Lauper (Portrait)
-	46	YOU, ME AND HE	M'Tume (Epic)
-	47	SIGN OF THE HAMMER	Manowar (10/Virgin)
38	48	EDEN	Everything but the Girl (Blanco Y Negro)
45	49	JUST THE WAY YOU LIKE IT	SOS Band (Tabu/Epic)
-	50	HEARTBEAT CITY	Cars (Elektra)

20 October 1984

last week	this week	Title	Artist
11	1	THE UNFORGETTABLE FIRE	U2 (Island)
2	2	DIAMOND LIFE	Sade (CBS)
1	3	TONIGHT	David Bowie (EMI America)
4	4	THE WOMAN IN RED - ORIGINAL SOUNDTRACK	Stevie Wonder (Motown)
3	5	ELIMINATOR	ZZ Top (WEA)
5	6	PURPLE RAIN	Prince & the Revolution (Warner Bros.)
6	7	SOME GREAT REWARD	Depeche Mode (Mute)
10	8	WE ARE FAMILY	Sister Sledge (Cotillion)
9	9	PRIVATE DANCER	Tina Turner (Capitol)
7	10	NOW THAT'S WHAT I CALL MUSIC 3	Various Artists (EMI/Virgin)
27	11	TRUE COLOURS	Level 42 (Polydor)
-	12	GEFFREY MORGAN	UB40 (DEP International)
12	13	THE WORKS	Queen (EMI)
8	14	HOW MEN ARE	Heaven 17 (Virgin)
14	15	CAN'T SLOW DOWN	Lionel Richie (Motown)
-	16	RATTLESNAKES	Lloyd Cole & the Commotions (Polydor)
15	17	PARADE	Spandau Ballet (Chrysalis)
13	18	KNIFE	Aztec Camera (WEA)
-	19	THE AGE OF CONSENT	Bronski Beat (London)
23	20	STREET SOUNDS ELECTRO 5	Various Artists (Street Sounds)
35	21	THE MAGAZINE	Rickie Lee Jones (Warner Bros.)
20	22	HOPE AND GLORY	Tom Robinson (Castaway)
16	23	LEGEND	Bob Marley & the Wailers (Island)
22	24	ANIMALIZE	Kiss (Vertigo)
18	25	SELF CONTROL	Laura Branigan (Atlantic)
-	26	HITS, HITS, HITS	Various Artists (Telstar)
30	27	ALL BY MYSELF	Various Artists (K-Tel)
17	28	THRILLER	Michael Jackson (Epic)
38	29	WE WANT MOORE!	Gary Moore (10/Virgin)
-	30	RANDY CRAWFORD'S GREATEST HITS	Randy Crawford (K-Tel)
-	31	BREWING UP WITH BILLY BRAGG	Billy Bragg (Go! Discs)
21	32	POWERSLAVE	Iron Maiden (EMI)
26	33	U2 LIVE: UNDER A BLOOD RED SKY	U2 (Island)
-	34	MUSIC MAGIC	Rose Royce (Streetwave)
19	35	HUMAN'S LIB	Howard Jones (WEA)
42	36	NIGHT MOVES	Various Artists (K-Tel)
34	37	BORN IN THE USA	Bruce Springsteen (CBS)
29	38	HUMAN RACING	Nik Kershaw (MCA)
28	39	BREAKING HEARTS	Elton John (Rocket)
50	40	HEARTBEAT CITY	Cars (Elektra)
-	41	TWO STEPS FROM THE MOVE	Hanoi Rocks (CBS)
-	42	DON'T STOP	Jeffrey Osborne (A&M)
24	43	BREAK OUT	Pointer Sisters (Planet)
25	44	AN INNOCENT MAN	Billy Joel (CBS)
49	45	JUST THE WAY YOU LIKE IT	SOS Band (Tabu/Epic)
-	46	JUST LIKE DREAMING	Terri Wells (London)
33	47	THE PLAN	Gary Numan (Beggars Banquet)
32	48	SWEPT AWAY	Diana Ross (Capitol)
41	49	QUEEN'S GREATEST HITS	Queen (EMI)
31	50	DREAMLINE	Cult (Beggars Banquet)

David Bowie scored a second straight chart-topper with his second EMI America album *Tonight*, but the set did not have the longevity either at Number 1 (just one week) or in the Top 50 chart as a whole that its predecessor *Let's Dance* had displayed. *Eliminator* marked Texan hard boogie band ZZ Top's first UK album chart appearace, and thereby guaranteed them final place in the artist index of this book!

27 October 1984

last week	this week	Title	Artist
1	1	THE UNFORGETTABLE FIRE	U2 (Island)
2	2	DIAMOND LIFE	Sade (CBS)
12	3	GEFFREY MORGAN	UB40 (DEP International)
19	4	THE AGE OF CONSENT	Bronski Beat (London)
3	5	TONIGHT	David Bowie (EMI America)
5	6	ELIMINATOR	ZZ Top (WEA)
4	7	THE WOMAN IN RED - ORIGINAL SOUNDTRACK	Stevie Wonder (Motown)
16	8	RATTLESNAKES	Lloyd Cole & the Commotions (Polydor)
6	9	PURPLE RAIN	Prince & the Revolution (Warner Bros.)
31	10	BREWING UP WITH BILLY BRAGG	Billy Bragg (Go! Discs)
-	11	STEELTOWN	Big Country (Mercury)
8	12	WE ARE FAMILY	Sister Sledge (Cotillion)
11	13	TRUE COLOURS	Level 42 (Polydor)
10	14	NOW THAT'S WHAT I CALL MUSIC 3	Various Artists (EMI/Virgin)
26	15	HITS, HITS, HITS	Various Artists (Telstar)
30	16	RANDY CRAWFORD'S GREATEST HITS	Randy Crawford (K-Tel)
7	17	SOME GREAT REWARD	Depeche Mode (Mute)
27	18	ALL BY MYSELF	Various Artists (K-Tel)
9	19	PRIVATE DANCER	Tina Turner (Capitol)
-	20	IT'LL END IN TEARS	This Mortal Coil (4AD)
15	21	CAN'T SLOW DOWN	Lionel Richie (Motown)
14	22	HOW MEN ARE	Heaven 17 (Virgin)
41	23	TWO STEPS FROM THE MOVE	Hanoi Rocks (CBS)
17	24	PARADE	Spandau Ballet (Chrysalis)
37	25	BORN IN THE USA	Bruce Springsteen (CBS)
13	26	THE WORKS	Queen (EMI)
18	27	KNIFE	Aztec Camera (WEA)
21	28	THE MAGAZINE	Rickie Lee Jones (Warner Bros.)
39	29	BREAKING HEARTS	Elton John (Rocket)
23	30	LEGEND	Bob Marley & the Wailers (Island)
36	31	NIGHT MOVES	Various Artists (K-Tel)
-	32	I FEEL FOR YOU	Chaka Khan (WEA)
20	33	STREET SOUNDS ELECTRO 5	Various Artists (Street Sounds)
-	34	EMOTION	Barbra Streisand (CBS)
-	35	SEA OF TRANQUILITY	Phil Coulter (K-Tel)
-	36	THE WONDERFUL AND FRIGHTENING WORLD OF	Fall (Beggars Banquet)
42	37	DON'T STOP	Jeffrey Osborne (A&M)
-	38	MUSIC FROM THE FILM CAL	Mark Knopfler (Vertigo)
22	39	HOPE AND GLORY	Tom Robinson (Castaway)
29	40	WE WANT MOORE!	Gary Moore (10/Virgin)
28	41	THRILLER	Michael Jackson (Epic)
43	42	BREAK OUT	Pointer Sisters (Planet)
38	43	HUMAN RACING	Nik Kershaw (MCA)
40	44	HEARTBEAT CITY	Cars (Elektra)
24	45	ANIMALIZE	Kiss (Vertigo)
33	46	U2 LIVE: UNDER A BLOOD RED SKY	U2 (Island)
-	47	ELECTRIC DREAMS	Soundtrack (Virgin)
45	48	JUST THE WAY YOU LIKE IT	SOS Band (Tabu/Epic)
47	49	THE PLAN	Gary Numan (Beggars Banquet)
34	50	MUSIC MAGIC	Rose Royce (Streetwave)

3 November 1984

last week	this week	Title	Artist
11	1	STEELTOWN	Big Country (Mercury)
2	2	DIAMOND LIFE	Sade (CBS)
1	3	THE UNFORGETTABLE FIRE	U2 (Island)
4	4	THE AGE OF CONSENT	Bronski Beat (London)
6	5	ELIMINATOR	ZZ Top (WEA)
3	6	GEFFREY MORGAN	UB40 (DEP International)
-	7	WAKING UP WITH THE HOUSE ON FIRE	Culture Club (Virgin)
7	8	THE WOMAN IN RED - ORIGINAL SOUNDTRACK	Stevie Wonder (Motown)
-	9	GIVE MY REGARDS TO BROAD STREET	Paul McCartney (EMI)
5	10	TONIGHT	David Bowie (EMI America)
10	11	BREWING UP WITH BILLY BRAGG	Billy Bragg (Go! Discs)
8	12	RATTLESNAKES	Lloyd Cole & the Commotions (Polydor)
34	13	EMOTION	Barbra Streisand (CBS)
15	14	HITS, HITS, HITS	Various Artists (Telstar)
14	15	NOW THAT'S WHAT I CALL MUSIC 3	Various Artists (EMI/Virgin)
9	16	PURPLE RAIN	Prince & the Revolution (Warner Bros.)
18	17	ALL BY MYSELF	Various Artists (K-Tel)
12	18	WE ARE FAMILY	Sister Sledge (Cotillion)
16	19	RANDY CRAWFORD'S GREATEST HITS	Randy Crawford (K-Tel)
32	20	I FEEL FOR YOU	Chaka Khan (WEA)
-	21	BIM BAM BOOM	Hall & Oates (RCA)
21	22	CAN'T SLOW DOWN	Lionel Richie (Motown)
13	23	TRUE COLOURS	Level 42 (Polydor)
26	24	THE WORKS	Queen (EMI)
19	25	PRIVATE DANCER	Tina Turner (Capitol)
-	26	YESTERDAY ONCE MORE	Carpenters (EMI/A&M)
24	27	PARADE	Spandau Ballet (Chrysalis)
-	28	VALOTTE	Julian Lennon (Charisma/Virgin)
41	29	THRILLER	Michael Jackson (Epic)
30	30	LEGEND	Bob Marley & the Wailers (Island)
-	31	CINEMA	Elaine Paige (K-Tel)
29	32	BREAKING HEARTS	Elton John (Rocket)
-	33	GREATEST LOVE CLASSICS	Andy Williams (EMI)
-	34	THEM OR US	Frank Zappa (EMI)
17	35	SOME GREAT REWARD	Depeche Mode (Mute)
-	36	STOP MAKING SENSE	Talking Heads (EMI)
28	37	THE MAGAZINE	Rickie Lee Jones (Warner Bros.)
-	38	THE BIG EXPRESS	XTC (Virgin)
-	39	DES O'CONNOR NOW	Des O'Connor (Telstar)
20	40	IT'LL END IN TEARS	This Mortal Coil (4AD)
25	41	BORN IN THE USA	Bruce Springsteen (CBS)
35	42	SEA OF TRANQUILITY	Phil Coulter (K-Tel)
22	43	HOW MEN ARE	Heaven 17 (Virgin)
44	44	HEARTBEAT CITY	Cars (Elektra)
-	45	CREW CUTS - LESSON 2	Various Artists (Island)
36	46	THE WONDERFUL AND FRIGHTENING WORLD OF	Fall (Beggars Banquet)
47	47	CONCERT - THE CURE LIVE	Cure (Fiction)
46	48	U2 LIVE: UNDER A BLOOD RED SKY	U2 (Island)
47	49	ELECTRIC DREAMS	Soundtrack (Virgin)
37	50	DON'T STOP	Jeffrey Osborne (A&M)

10 November 1984

last week	this week	Title	Artist
-	1	WELCOME TO THE PLEASUREDOME	Frankie Goes To Hollywood (ZTT)
1	2	STEELTOWN	Big Country (Mercury)
9	3	GIVE MY REGARDS TO BROAD STREET	Paul McCartney (EMI)
2	4	DIAMOND LIFE	Sade (CBS)
7	5	WAKING UP WITH THE HOUSE ON FIRE	Culture Club (Virgin)
5	6	ELIMINATOR	ZZ Top (WEA)
3	7	THE UNFORGETTABLE FIRE	U2 (Island)
4	8	THE AGE OF CONSENT	Bronski Beat (London)
6	9	GEFFREY MORGAN	UB40 (DEP International)
19	10	RANDY CRAWFORD'S GREATEST HITS	Randy Crawford (K-Tel)
28	11	VALOTTE	Julian Lennon (Charisma/Virgin)
-	12	PERFECT STRANGERS	Deep Purple (Polydor)
8	13	THE WOMAN IN RED - ORIGINAL SOUNDTRACK	Stevie Wonder (Motown)
20	14	I FEEL FOR YOU	Chaka Khan (WEA)
10	15	TONIGHT	David Bowie (EMI America)
14	16	HITS, HITS, HITS	Various Artists (Telstar)
-	17	THE COLLECTION	Ultravox (Chrysalis)
22	18	CAN'T SLOW DOWN	Lionel Richie (Motown)
15	19	NOW THAT'S WHAT I CALL MUSIC 3	Various Artists (EMI/Virgin)
47	20	CONCERT - THE CURE LIVE	Cure (Fiction)
12	21	RATTLESNAKES	Lloyd Cole & the Commotions (Polydor)
26	22	YESTERDAY ONCE MORE	Carpenters (EMI/A&M)
-	23	BAD ATTITUDE	Meatloaf (Arista)
13	24	EMOTION	Barbra Streisand (CBS)
31	25	CINEMA	Elaine Paige (K-Tel)
25	26	PRIVATE DANCER	Tina Turner (Capitol)
27	27	PARADE	Spandau Ballet (Chrysalis)
11	28	BREWING UP WITH BILLY BRAGG	Billy Bragg (Go! Discs)
36	29	STOP MAKING SENSE	Talking Heads (EMI)
17	30	ALL BY MYSELF	Various Artists (K-Tel)
38	31	THE BIG EXPRESS	XTC (Virgin)
-	32	REBEL SOULS	Aswad (Island)
16	33	PURPLE RAIN	Prince & the Revolution (Warner Bros.)
18	34	WE ARE FAMILY	Sister Sledge (Cotillion)
29	35	THRILLER	Michael Jackson (Epic)
-	36	THE EVERLY BROTHERS	Everly Brothers (Mercury)
21	37	BIM BAM BOOM	Hall & Oates (RCA)
33	38	GREATEST LOVE CLASSICS	Andy Williams (EMI)
41	39	BORN IN THE USA	Bruce Springsteen (CBS)
44	40	HEARTBEAT CITY	Cars (Elektra)
23	41	TRUE COLOURS	Level 42 (Polydor)
24	42	THE WORKS	Queen (EMI)
43	43	HOW MEN ARE	Heaven 17 (Virgin)
-	44	THE FUGITIVE KIND	Swans Way (Balgier)
-	45	RED ROSES FOR ME	Pogues (Stiff)
30	46	LEGEND	Bob Marley & the Wailers (Island)
-	47	VERMIN IN ERMINE	Marc Almond & the Willing Sinners (Some Bizzare)
35	48	SOME GREAT REWARD	Depeche Mode (Mute)
42	49	SEA OF TRANQUILITY	Phil Coulter (K-Tel)
40	50	IT'LL END IN TEARS	This Mortal Coil (4AD)

Paul McCartney's *Give My Regards To Broad Street* was yet another of 1984's big albums based around the artist's soundtrack to a movie - in this case, McCartney's own less-than-blockbuster vehicle of the same title, in which the music, including unexpected revivals of several Beatles oldies, was most definitely the biggest plus factor. (Broad Street, a London rail terminus, has sincebeen obliterated by development!)

November - December 1984

17 November 1984

last week	this week	title	artist
1	1	WELCOME TO THE PLEASUREDOME	Frankie Goes To Hollywood (ZTT)
4	2	DIAMOND LIFE	Sade (CBS)
6	3	ELIMINATOR	ZZ Top (WEA)
17	4	THE COLLECTION	Ultravox (Chrysalis)
3	5	GIVE MY REGARDS TO BROAD STREET	Paul McCartney (EMI)
12	6	PERFECT STRANGERS	Deep Purple (Polydor)
-	7	MAKE IT BIG	Wham! (CBS)
5	8	WAKING UP WITH THE HOUSE ON FIRE	Culture Club (Virgin)
23	9	BAD ATTITUDE	Meatloaf (Arista)
2	10	STEELTOWN	Big Country (Mercury)
7	11	THE UNFORGETTABLE FIRE	U2 (Island)
-	12	ALF	Alison Moyet (CBS)
14	13	I FEEL FOR YOU	Chaka Khan (WEA)
8	14	THE AGE OF CONSENT	Bronski Beat (London)
-	15	AURAL SCULPTURE	Stranglers (Epic)
11	16	VALOTTE	Julian Lennon (Charisma/Virgin)
13	17	THE WOMAN IN RED - ORIGINAL SOUNDTRACK	Stevie Wonder (Motown)
10	18	RANDY CRAWFORD'S GREATEST HITS	Randy Crawford (K-Tel)
24	19	EMOTION	Barbra Streisand (CBS)
22	20	YESTERDAY ONCE MORE	Carpenters (EMI/A&M)
9	21	GEFFREY MORGAN	UB40 (DEP International)
-	22	REAL TO REEL	Marillion (EMI)
18	23	CAN'T SLOW DOWN	Lionel Richie (Motown)
26	24	PRIVATE DANCER	Tina Turner (Capitol)
15	25	TONIGHT	David Bowie (EMI America)
33	26	PURPLE RAIN	Prince & the Revolution (Warner Bros.)
19	27	NOW THAT'S WHAT I CALL MUSIC 3	Various Artists (EMI/Virgin)
16	28	HITS, HITS, HITS	Various Artists (Telstar)
29	29	STOP MAKING SENSE	Talking Heads (EMI)
25	30	CINEMA	Elaine Paige (K-Tel)
21	31	RATTLESNAKES	Lloyd Cole & the Commotions (Polydor)
27	32	PARADE	Spandau Ballet (Chrysalis)
20	33	CONCERT - THE CURE LIVE	Cure (Fiction)
32	34	REBEL SOULS	Aswad (Island)
28	35	BREWING UP WITH BILLY BRAGG	Billy Bragg (Go! Discs)
47	36	VERMIN IN ERMINE	Marc Almond & the Willing Sinners (Some Bizzare)
39	37	BORN IN THE USA	Bruce Springsteen (CBS)
38	38	GREATEST LOVE CLASSICS	Andy Williams (EMI)
30	39	ALL BY MYSELF	Various Artists (K-Tel)
37	40	BIM BAM BOOM	Hall & Oates (RCA)
35	41	THRILLER	Michael Jackson (Epic)
46	42	LEGEND	Bob Marley & the Wailers (Island)
49	43	SEA OF TRANQUILITY	Phil Coulter (K-Tel)
34	44	WE ARE FAMILY	Sister Sledge (Cotillion)
42	45	THE WORKS	Queen (EMI)
41	46	TRUE COLOURS	Level 42 (Polydor)
43	47	HOW MEN ARE	Heaven 17 (Virgin)
40	48	HEARTBEAT CITY	Cars (Elektra)
-	49	NO BRAKES	John Waite (EMI)
31	50	THE BIG EXPRESS	XTC (Virgin)

24 November 1984

last week	this week	title	artist
7	1	MAKE IT BIG	Wham! (CBS)
1	2	WELCOME TO THE PLEASUREDOME	Frankie Goes To Hollywood (ZTT)
12	3	ALF	Alison Moyet (CBS)
4	4	THE COLLECTION	Ultravox (Chrysalis)
2	5	DIAMOND LIFE	Sade (CBS)
3	6	ELIMINATOR	ZZ Top (WEA)
6	7	PERFECT STRANGERS	Deep Purple (Polydor)
22	8	REAL TO REEL	Marillion (EMI)
5	9	GIVE MY REGARDS TO BROAD STREET	Paul McCartney (EMI)
13	10	I FEEL FOR YOU	Chaka Khan (WEA)
15	11	AURAL SCULPTURE	Stranglers (Epic)
11	12	THE UNFORGETTABLE FIRE	U2 (Island)
9	13	BAD ATTITUDE	Meatloaf (Arista)
-	14	ARENA	Duran Duran (EMI)
-	15	HATFUL OF HOLLOW	Smiths (Rough Trade)
8	16	WAKING UP WITH THE HOUSE ON FIRE	Culture Club (Virgin)
10	17	STEELTOWN	Big Country (Mercury)
14	18	THE AGE OF CONSENT	Bronski Beat (London)
18	19	RANDY CRAWFORD'S GREATEST HITS	Randy Crawford (K-Tel)
-	20	WHO'S LAST	Who (MCA)
-	21	SHAKIN' STEVENS GREATEST HITS	Shakin' Stevens (Epic)
-	22	THE ART GARFUNKEL ALBUM	Art Garfunkel (CBS)
20	23	YESTERDAY ONCE MORE	Carpenters (EMI/A&M)
23	24	CAN'T SLOW DOWN	Lionel Richie (Motown)
17	25	THE WOMAN IN RED - ORIGINAL SOUNDTRACK	Stevie Wonder (Motown)
30	26	CINEMA	Elaine Paige (K-Tel)
-	27	GOLDEN DAYS	Fureys with Davey Arthur (K-Tel)
-	28	TREASURE	Cocteau Twins (4AD)
24	29	PRIVATE DANCER	Tina Turner (Capitol)
16	30	VALOTTE	Julian Lennon (Charisma/Virgin)
27	31	NOW THAT'S WHAT I CALL MUSIC 3	Various Artists (EMI/Virgin)
19	32	EMOTION	Barbra Streisand (CBS)
21	33	GEFFREY MORGAN	UB40 (DEP International)
37	34	BORN IN THE USA	Bruce Springsteen (CBS)
-	35	THE VERY BEST OF FOSTER AND ALLEN	Foster & Allen (Ritz)
-	36	ALL BY MYSELF	Various Artists (K-Tel)
41	37	THRILLER	Michael Jackson (Epic)
40	38	BIM BAM BOOM	Hall & Oates (RCA)
-	39	SAPPHIRE	John Martyn (Island)
43	40	SEA OF TRANQUILITY	Phil Coulter (K-Tel)
31	41	RATTLESNAKES	Lloyd Cole & the Commotions (Polydor)
45	42	THE WORKS	Queen (EMI)
-	43	HIGH CRIME	Al Jarreau (WEA)
-	44	ALL THE HITS	Eddy Grant (K-Tel)
-	45	1984 (FOR THE LOVE OF BIG BROTHER)	Eurythmics (Virgin)
28	46	HITS, HITS, HITS	Various Artists (Telstar)
29	47	STOP MAKING SENSE	Talking Heads (EMI)
25	48	TONIGHT	David Bowie (EMI America)
-	49	ORANGE JUICE	Orange Juice (Polydor)
26	50	PURPLE RAIN	Prince & the Revolution (Warner Bros.)

1 December 1984

last week	this week	title	artist
1	1	MAKE IT BIG	Wham! (CBS)
3	2	ALF	Alison Moyet (CBS)
2	3	WELCOME TO THE PLEASUREDOME	Frankie Goes To Hollywood (ZTT)
4	4	THE COLLECTION	Ultravox (Chrysalis)
6	5	ELIMINATOR	ZZ Top (WEA)
14	6	ARENA	Duran Duran (EMI)
5	7	DIAMOND LIFE	Sade (CBS)
15	8	HATFUL OF HOLLOW	Smiths (Rough Trade)
9	9	GIVE MY REGARDS TO BROAD STREET	Paul McCartney (EMI)
8	10	REAL TO REEL	Marillion (EMI)
10	11	I FEEL FOR YOU	Chaka Khan (WEA)
21	12	SHAKIN' STEVENS GREATEST HITS	Shakin' Stevens (Epic)
12	13	THE UNFORGETTABLE FIRE	U2 (Island)
-	14	THE HITS ALBUM	Various Artists (WEA/CBS)
22	15	THE ART GARFUNKEL ALBUM	Art Garfunkel (CBS)
13	16	BAD ATTITUDE	Meatloaf (Arista)
26	17	CINEMA	Elaine Paige (K-Tel)
45	18	1984 (FOR THE LOVE OF BIG BROTHER)	Eurythmics (Virgin)
44	19	ALL THE HITS	Eddy Grant (K-Tel)
-	20	THE RIDDLE	Nik Kershaw (MCA)
23	21	YESTERDAY ONCE MORE	Carpenters (EMI/A&M)
24	22	CAN'T SLOW DOWN	Lionel Richie (Motown)
18	23	THE AGE OF CONSENT	Bronski Beat (London)
7	24	PERFECT STRANGERS	Deep Purple (Polydor)
29	25	PRIVATE DANCER	Tina Turner (Capitol)
11	26	AURAL SCULPTURE	Stranglers (Epic)
17	27	STEELTOWN	Big Country (Mercury)
35	28	THE VERY BEST OF FOSTER AND ALLEN	Foster & Allen (Ritz)
19	29	RANDY CRAWFORD'S GREATEST HITS	Randy Crawford (K-Tel)
27	30	GOLDEN DAYS	Fureys with Davey Arthur (K-Tel)
-	31	ZOOLOOK	Jean Michel Jarre (Polydor)
34	32	BORN IN THE USA	Bruce Springsteen (CBS)
28	33	TREASURE	Cocteau Twins (4AD)
16	34	WAKING UP WITH THE HOUSE ON FIRE	Culture Club (Virgin)
-	35	TWELVE GOLD BARS VOLUMES 1 & 2	Status Quo (Vertigo)
25	36	THE WOMAN IN RED - ORIGINAL SOUNDTRACK	Stevie Wonder (Motown)
-	37	LIKE A VIRGIN	Madonna (Sire)
33	38	GEFFREY MORGAN	UB40 (DEP International)
-	39	BESERKER	Gary Numan (Numa)
30	40	VALOTTE	Julian Lennon (Charisma/Virgin)
31	41	NOW THAT'S WHAT I CALL MUSIC 3	Various Artists (EMI/Virgin)
46	42	HITS, HITS, HITS	Various Artists (Telstar)
-	43	THE LOVE SONGS - 16 CLASSIC HITS	Stevie Wonder (Telstar)
20	44	WHO'S LAST	Who (MCA)
-	45	2 AM PARADISE CAFE	Barry Manilow (Arista)
49	46	ORANGE JUICE	Orange Juice (Polydor)
-	47	THE MUSIC OF LOVE	Richard Clayderman (Decca/Delphine)
-	48	SUDDENLY	Billy Ocean (Jive)
-	49	FRIED	Julian Cope (Mercury)
48	50	TONIGHT	David Bowie (EMI America)

Frankie Goes To Hollywood's *Welcome To The Pleasuredome* album was one of the most eagerly awaited sets of the year, after the group had had two million-selling singles with *Relax* and *Two Tribes*.

Despite huge advance orders and big sales for its first couple of weeks, however, it didn't hog the chart top for the extended period many expected, and quickly surrendered to Wham!'s hit-heavy *Make It Big*.

December 1984

Having seen the EMI/Virgin partnership clean up in the compilation field during 1984 with the *Now* series, major record labels CBS and WEA teamed up to fight back with a similar series of their own, adventurously titled *Hits*. The initial *Hits Album* proved sufficiently strong in recent hit content to outsell the latest volume from the opposition (No.4), and capture the coveted Christmas Number 1 slot.

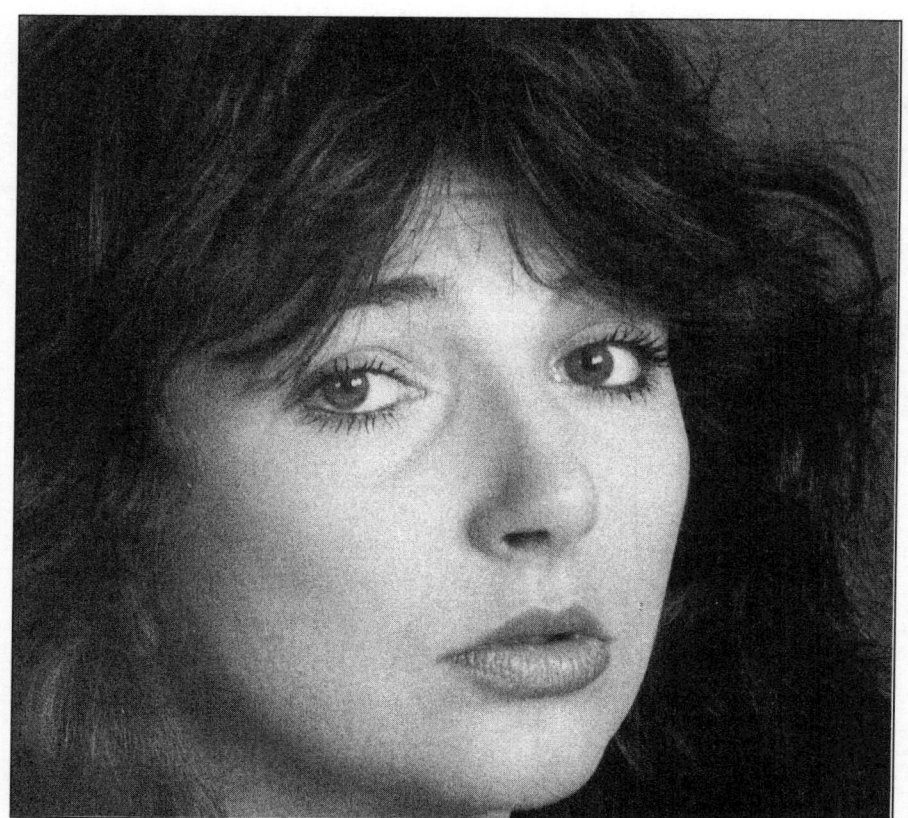

Faces making the album charts in the 80s:
Kate Bush (left)
Boy George (bottom left)
ABC (below)

January 1985

5 January 1985

last this
week

last	this		
1	1	THE HITS ALBUM	Various Artists (WEA/CBS)
2	2	NOW THAT'S WHAT I CALL MUSIC 4	Various Artists (EMI/Virgin)
4	3	MAKE IT BIG	Wham! (CBS)
3	4	ALF	Alison Moyet (CBS)
5	5	THE COLLECTION	Ultravox (Chrysalis)
6	6	WELCOME TO THE PLEASUREDOME	Frankie Goes to Hollywood (ZTT)
13	7	PARTY, PARTY	Black Lace (Flair)
8	8	DIAMOND LIFE	Sade (CBS)
7	9	ELIMINATOR	ZZ Top (Warner Brothers)
11	10	ARENA	Duran Duran (EMI)
10	11	GIVE MY REGARDS TO BROAD STREET	Paul McCartney (EMI)
17	12	THE ART GARFUNKEL ALBUM	Art Garfunkel (CBS)
12	13	12 GOLD BARS VOLUMES 1 & 2	Status Quo (Vertigo)
16	14	CHAS & DAVE'S GREATEST HITS	Chas & Dave (Rockney)
14	15	SHAKIN' STEVENS GREATEST HITS	Shakin' Stevens (Epic)
9	16	THE RIDDLE	Nik Kershaw (MCA)
23	17	GOLDEN DAYS Fureys with Davey Arthur (K-Tel)	
15	18	YESTERDAY ONCE MORE Carpenters (EMI/A&M)	
18	19	THE VERY BEST OF FOSTER & ALLEN	Foster & Allen (Ritz)
22	20	CINEMA	Elaine Paige (K-Tel)
24	21	1984 (FOR THE LOVE OF BIG BROTHER)	Eurythmics (Virgin)
-	22	AGENT PROVOCATEUR	Foreigner (Atlantic)
21	23	PRIVATE DANCER	Tina Turner (Capitol)
42	24	THE UNFORGETTABLE FIRE	U2 (Island)
41	25	ALL THE HITS	Eddy Grant (K-Tel)
-	26	THE COLLECTION	John Denver (Telstar)
25	27	REAL LIVE	Bob Dylan (CBS)
31	28	EMERGENCY	Kool and the Gang (De-Lite)
32	29	LIKE A VIRGIN	Madonna (Sire)
35	30	DES O'CONNOR NOW	Des O'Connor (Telstar)
19	31	THE LOVE SONGS - 16 CLASSIC HITS	Stevie Wonder (Telstar)
50	32	I AM WHAT I AM	Shirley Bassey (Towerbell)
27	33	PARADE	Spandau Ballet (Chrysalis)
49	34	GREEN VELVET	Various Artists (Telstar)
20	35	THE 12-INCH ALBUM	Howard Jones (WEA)
38	36	BAD ATTITUDE	Meatloaf (Arista)
29	37	HATFUL OF HOLLOW	Smiths (Rough Trade)
-	38	THE MUSIC OF LOVE	Richard Clayderman (Decca/Delphine)
-	39	FANS	Malcolm McLaren (Charisma)
34	40	HOOKED ON NUMBER ONES	Various Artists (K-Tel)
-	41	RANDY CRAWFORD'S GREATEST HITS	Randy Crawford (K-Tel)
36	42	CAN'T SLOW DOWN	Lionel Richie (Motown)
37	43	STEELTOWN	Big Country (Mercury)
26	44	I FEEL FOR YOU	Chaka Khan (WEA)
33	45	BORN IN THE USA	Bruce Springsteen (CBS)
29	46	EXORCISING GHOSTS	Japan (Virgin)
39	47	SEA OF TRANQUILITY	Phil Coulter (K-Tel)
47	48	THRILLER	Michael Jackson (Epic)
48	49	LOVE SONGS	Various Artists (Telstar)
43	50	WAKING UP WITH THE HOUSE ON FIRE	Culture Club (Virgin)

12 January 1985

last	this		
1	1	THE HITS ALBUM	Various Artists (WEA/CBS)
2	2	NOW THAT'S WHAT I CALL MUSIC 4	Various Artists (EMI/Virgin)
4	3	ALF	Alison Moyet (CBS)
3	4	MAKE IT BIG	Wham! (CBS)
5	5	THE COLLECTION	Ultravox (Chrysalis)
6	6	WELCOME TO THE PLEASUREDOME	Frankie Goes to Hollywood (ZTT)
8	7	DIAMOND LIFE	Sade (CBS)
7	8	PARTY, PARTY	Black Lace (Flair)
10	9	ARENA	Duran Duran (EMI)
15	10	SHAKIN' STEVENS GREATEST HITS	Shakin' Stevens (Epic)
11	11	GIVE MY REGARDS TO BROAD STREET	Paul McCartney (EMI)
9	12	ELIMINATOR	ZZ Top (Warner Brothers)
23	13	PRIVATE DANCER	Tina Turner (Capitol)
12	14	THE ART GARFUNKEL ALBUM	Art Garfunkel (CBS)
16	15	THE RIDDLE	Nik Kershaw (MCA)
13	16	12 GOLD BARS VOLUMES 1 & 2	Status Quo (Vertigo)
18	17	YESTERDAY ONCE MORE Carpenters (EMI/A&M)	
22	18	AGENT PROVOCATEUR	Foreigner (Atlantic)
39	19	FANS	Malcolm McLaren (Charisma)
-	20	VERY BEST OF CHRIS DE BURGH	Chris De Burgh (Telstar)
-	21	THE AGE OF CONSENT	Bronski Beat (Forbidden Fruit)
47	22	SEA OF TRANQUILITY	Phil Coulter (K-Tel)
-	23	TRULY FOR YOU	Temptations (Motown)
35	24	THE 12-INCH ALBUM	Howard Jones (WEA)
33	25	PARADE	Spandau Ballet (Chrysalis)
28	26	EMERGENCY	Kool and the Gang (De-Lite)
17	27	GOLDEN DAYS Fureys with Davey Arthur (K-Tel)	
21	28	1984 (FOR THE LOVE OF BIG BROTHER)	Eurythmics (Virgin)
20	29	CINEMA	Elaine Paige (K-Tel)
14	30	CHAS & DAVE'S GREATEST HITS	Chas & Dave (Rockney)
31	31	THE LOVE SONGS - 16 CLASSIC HITS	Stevie Wonder (Telstar)
34	32	GREEN VELVET	Various Artists (Telstar)
44	33	I FEEL FOR YOU	Chaka Khan (WEA)
24	34	THE UNFORGETTABLE FIRE	U2 (Island)
19	35	THE VERY BEST OF FOSTER & ALLEN	Foster & Allen (Ritz)
32	36	I AM WHAT I AM	Shirley Bassey (Towerbell)
26	37	THE COLLECTION	John Denver (Telstar)
29	38	LIKE A VIRGIN	Madonna (Sire)
42	39	CAN'T SLOW DOWN	Lionel Richie (Motown)
37	40	HATFUL OF HOLLOW	Smiths (Rough Trade)
45	41	BORN IN THE USA	Bruce Springsteen (CBS)
-	42	EUGENE WILDE	Eugene Wilde (Fourth & Broadway)
-	43	BREAK OUT	Pointer Sisters (Planet)
-	44	RATTLESNAKES	Lloyd Cole & the Commotions (Polydor)
49	45	LOVE SONGS	Various Artists (Telstar)
27	46	REAL LIVE	Bob Dylan (CBS)
48	47	THRILLER	Michael Jackson (Epic)
30	48	NOW	Des O'Connor (Telstar)
46	49	EXORCISING GHOSTS	Japan (Virgin)
25	50	ALL THE HITS	Eddy Grant (K-Tel)

19 January 1985

last	this		
1	1	THE HITS ALBUM	Various Artists (WEA/CBS)
3	2	ALF	Alison Moyet (CBS)
2	3	NOW THAT'S WHAT I CALL MUSIC 4	Various Artists (EMI/Virgin)
4	4	MAKE IT BIG	Wham! (CBS)
7	5	DIAMOND LIFE	Sade (CBS)
6	6	WELCOME TO THE PLEASUREDOME	Frankie Goes to Hollywood (ZTT)
5	7	THE COLLECTION	Ultravox (Chrysalis)
12	8	ELIMINATOR	ZZ Top (Warner Brothers)
18	9	AGENT PROVOCATEUR	Foreigner (Atlantic)
9	10	ARENA	Duran Duran (EMI)
21	11	THE AGE OF CONSENT	Bronski Beat (Forbidden Fruit)
38	12	LIKE A VIRGIN	Madonna (Sire)
25	13	PARADE	Spandau Ballet (Chrysalis)
13	14	PRIVATE DANCER	Tina Turner (Capitol)
8	15	PARTY, PARTY	Black Lace (Flair)
15	16	THE RIDDLE	Nik Kershaw (MCA)
24	17	THE 12-INCH ALBUM	Howard Jones (WEA)
34	18	THE UNFORGETTABLE FIRE	U2 (Island)
19	19	FANS	Malcolm McLaren (Charisma)
40	20	HATFUL OF HOLLOW	Smiths (Rough Trade)
10	21	SHAKIN' STEVENS GREATEST HITS	Shakin' Stevens (Epic)
-	22	STEELTOWN	Big Country (Mercury)
28	23	1984 (FOR THE LOVE OF BIG BROTHER)	Eurythmics (Virgin)
44	24	RATTLESNAKES	Lloyd Cole & the Commotions (Polydor)
11	25	GIVE MY REGARDS TO BROAD STREET	Paul McCartney (EMI)
16	26	12 GOLD BARS VOLUMES 1 & 2	Status Quo (Vertigo)
39	27	CAN'T SLOW DOWN	Lionel Richie (Motown)
20	28	VERY BEST OF CHRIS DE BURGH	Chris De Burgh (Telstar)
26	29	EMERGENCY	Kool and the Gang (De-Lite)
35	30	THE VERY BEST OF FOSTER & ALLEN	Foster & Allen (Ritz)
33	31	I FEEL FOR YOU	Chaka Khan (WEA)
-	32	VALOTTE	Julian Lennon (Chrisma)
17	33	YESTERDAY ONCE MORE Carpenters (EMI/A&M)	
-	34	GEFFERY MORGAN	UB40 (Dep International)
-	35	GHOSTBUSTERS	Soundtrack (Arista)
31	36	THE LOVE SONGS - 16 CLASSIC HITS	Stevie Wonder (Telstar)
-	37	THE ESSENTIAL JEAN MICHEL JARRE	Jean Michel Jarre (Polystar)
23	38	TRULY FOR YOU	Temptations (Motown)
14	39	THE ART GARFUNKEL ALBUM	Art Garfunkel (CBS)
-	40	TREASURE	Cocteau Twins (4AD)
45	41	LOVE SONGS	Various Artists (Telstar)
-	42	BIG BAM BOOM Daryl Hall & John Oates (RCA)	
-	43	WAKING UP WITH THE HOUSE ON FIRE	Culture Club (Virgin)
46	44	REAL LIVE	Bob Dylan (CBS)
43	45	BREAK OUT	Pointer Sisters (Planet)
29	46	CINEMA	Elaine Paige (K-Tel)
22	47	SEA OF TRANQUILITY	Phil Coulter (K-Tel)
47	48	THRILLER	Michael Jackson (Epic)
49	49	EXORCISING GHOSTS	Japan (Virgin)
-	50	PERFECT STRANGERS	Deep Purple (Polydor)

Cabaret group Black Lace, the scourge of the mid-80s singles charts with their irritatingly infectious singalongs like *Agadoo*, made a rare appearance among the big album sellers with their *Party, Party* set - intended, and no doubt bought, for Christmas and New Year party play. Many probably acquired *Chas & Dave's Greatest Hits*, which peaked at 14 in the first week of the year, for the same reason.

January – February 1985

last this
week

26 January 1985

last	this	title	artist
2	1	ALF	Alison Moyet (CBS)
9	2	AGENT PROVOCATEUR	Foreigner (Atlantic)
4	3	MAKE IT BIG	Wham! (CBS)
8	4	ELIMINATOR	ZZ Top (Warner Brothers)
1	5	THE HITS ALBUM	Various Artists (WEA/CBS)
5	6	DIAMOND LIFE	Sade (CBS)
6	7	WELCOME TO THE PLEASUREDOME	Frankie Goes to Hollywood (ZTT)
7	8	THE COLLECTION	Ultravox (Chrysalis)
-	9	BORN IN THE USA	Bruce Springsteen (CBS)
3	10	NOW THAT'S WHAT I CALL MUSIC 4	Various Artists (EMI/Virgin)
12	11	LIKE A VIRGIN	Madonna (Sire)
11	12	THE AGE OF CONSENT	Bronski Beat (Forbidden Fruit)
14	13	PRIVATE DANCER	Tina Turner (Capitol)
10	14	ARENA	Duran Duran (EMI)
18	15	THE UNFORGETTABLE FIRE	U2 (Island)
-	16	20/20	George Benson (Warner Bros.)
-	17	THE BARBARA DICKSON SONGBOOK	Barbara Dickson (K-Tel)
13	18	PARADE	Spandau Ballet (Chrysalis)
28	19	VERY BEST OF CHRIS DE BURGH	Chris De Burgh (Telstar)
16	20	THE RIDDLE	Nik Kershaw (MCA)
23	21	1984 (FOR THE LOVE OF BIG BROTHER)	Eurythmics (Virgin)
17	22	THE 12-INCH ALBUM	Howard Jones (WEA)
21	23	SHAKIN' STEVENS GREATEST HITS	Shakin' Stevens (Epic)
15	24	PARTY, PARTY	Black Lace (Flair)
19	25	FANS	Malcolm McLaren (Charisma)
-	26	BREAKDANCE II	Various Artists (Polydor)
20	27	HATFUL OF HOLLOW	Smiths (Rough Trade)
24	28	RATTLESNAKES	Lloyd Cole & the Commotions (Polydor)
38	29	TRULY FOR YOU	Temptations (Motown)
31	30	I FEEL FOR YOU	Chaka Khan (WEA)
35	31	GHOSTBUSTERS	Soundtrack (Arista)
22	32	STEELTOWN	Big Country (Mercury)
25	33	GIVE MY REGARDS TO BROAD STREET	Paul McCartney (EMI)
26	34	12 GOLD BARS VOLUMES 1 & 2	Status Quo (Vertigo)
29	35	EMERGENCY	Kool and the Gang (De-Lite)
-	36	CHESS	Original Cast (RCA)
-	37	BAD ATTITUDE	Meatloaf (Arista)
40	38	TREASURE	Cocteau Twins (4AD)
-	39	LOVE HURTS	Everly Brothers (K-Tel)
-	40	1999	Prince (Warner Bros.)
27	41	CAN'T SLOW DOWN	Lionel Richie (Motown)
30	42	THE VERY BEST OF FOSTER & ALLEN	Foster & Allen (Ritz)
32	43	VALOTTE	Julian Lennon (Chrisma)
-	44	THE HONEYDRIPPERS VOLUME 1	Honeydrippers (Es Paranza)
43	45	WAKING UP WITH THE HOUSE ON FIRE	Culture Club (Virgin)
44	46	REAL LIVE	Bob Dylan (CBS)
33	47	YESTERDAY ONCE MORE	Carpenters (EMI/A&M)
41	48	LOVE SONGS	Various Artists (Telstar)
-	49	THE COLLECTION	John Denver (Telstar)
-	50	(WHO'S AFRAID OF) THE ART OF NOISE	Art of Noise (ZTT)

2 February 1985

last	this	title	artist
2	1	AGENT PROVOCATEUR	Foreigner (Atlantic)
1	2	ALF	Alison Moyet (CBS)
4	3	ELIMINATOR	ZZ Top (Warner Brothers)
9	4	BORN IN THE USA	Bruce Springsteen (CBS)
12	5	THE AGE OF CONSENT	Bronski Beat (Forbidden Fruit)
-	6	HITS OUT OF HELL	Meatloaf (Epic)
3	7	MAKE IT BIG	Wham! (CBS)
8	8	THE COLLECTION	Ultravox (Chrysalis)
16	9	20/20	George Benson (Warner Bros.)
5	10	THE HITS ALBUM	Various Artists (WEA/CBS)
11	11	LIKE A VIRGIN	Madonna (Sire)
6	12	DIAMOND LIFE	Sade (CBS)
15	13	THE UNFORGETTABLE FIRE	U2 (Island)
7	14	WELCOME TO THE PLEASUREDOME	Frankie Goes to Hollywood (ZTT)
19	15	VERY BEST OF CHRIS DE BURGH	Chris De Burgh (Telstar)
10	16	NOW THAT'S WHAT I CALL MUSIC 4	Various Artists (EMI/Virgin)
17	17	THE BARBARA DICKSON SONGBOOK	Barbara Dickson (K-Tel)
13	18	PRIVATE DANCER	Tina Turner (Capitol)
14	19	ARENA	Duran Duran (EMI)
30	20	I FEEL FOR YOU	Chaka Khan (WEA)
18	21	PARADE	Spandau Ballet (Chrysalis)
21	22	1984 (FOR THE LOVE OF BIG BROTHER)	Eurythmics (Virgin)
40	23	1999	Prince (Warner Bros.)
-	24	TOO TOUGH TO DIE	Ramones (Beggars Banquet)
32	25	STEELTOWN	Big Country (Mercury)
22	26	THE 12-INCH ALBUM	Howard Jones (WEA)
41	27	CAN'T SLOW DOWN	Lionel Richie (Motown)
27	28	HATFUL OF HOLLOW	Smiths (Rough Trade)
25	29	FANS	Malcolm McLaren (Charisma)
28	30	RATTLESNAKES	Lloyd Cole & the Commotions (Polydor)
26	31	BREAKDANCE II	Various Artists (Polydor)
24	32	PARTY, PARTY	Black Lace (Flair)
20	33	THE RIDDLE	Nik Kershaw (MCA)
31	34	GHOSTBUSTERS	Soundtrack (Arista)
-	35	CINEMA	Elaine Paige (K-Tel)
-	36	TROPICO	Pat Benatar (Chrysalis)
39	37	LOVE HURTS	Everly Brothers (K-Tel)
50	38	(WHO'S AFRAID OF) THE ART OF NOISE	Art of Noise (ZTT)
36	39	CHESS	Original Cast (RCA)
-	40	PURPLE RAIN	Prince& The Revolution (Warner Bros.)
35	41	EMERGENCY	Kool and the Gang (De-Lite)
-	42	SCREEN GEMS	Elkie Brooks (EMI)
23	43	SHAKIN' STEVENS GREATEST HITS	Shakin' Stevens (Epic)
33	44	GIVE MY REGARDS TO BROAD STREET	Paul McCartney (EMI)
29	45	TRULY FOR YOU	Temptations (Motown)
44	46	THE HONEYDRIPPERS VOLUME 1	Honeydrippers (Es Paranza)
-	47	THE DEED IS DONE	Molly Hatchet (Epic)
-	48	NO PARLEZ	Paul Young (CBS)
-	49	BREAK OUT	Pointer Sisters (Planet)
38	50	TREASURE	Cocteau Twins (4AD)

9 February 1985

last	this	title	artist
1	1	AGENT PROVOCATEUR	Foreigner (Atlantic)
3	2	ELIMINATOR	ZZ Top (Warner Brothers)
4	3	BORN IN THE USA	Bruce Springsteen (CBS)
2	4	ALF	Alison Moyet (CBS)
9	5	20/20	George Benson (Warner Bros.)
6	6	HITS OUT OF HELL	Meatloaf (Epic)
5	7	THE AGE OF CONSENT	Bronski Beat (Forbidden Fruit)
7	8	MAKE IT BIG	Wham! (CBS)
15	9	VERY BEST OF CHRIS DE BURGH	Chris De Burgh (Telstar)
8	10	THE COLLECTION	Ultravox (Chrysalis)
11	11	LIKE A VIRGIN	Madonna (Sire)
12	12	DIAMOND LIFE	Sade (CBS)
14	13	WELCOME TO THE PLEASUREDOME	Frankie Goes to Hollywood (ZTT)
17	14	THE BARBARA DICKSON SONGBOOK	Barbara Dickson (K-Tel)
13	15	THE UNFORGETTABLE FIRE	U2 (Island)
23	16	1999	Prince (Warner Bros.)
28	17	HATFUL OF HOLLOW	Smiths (Rough Trade)
10	18	THE HITS ALBUM	Various Artists (WEA/CBS)
39	19	CHESS	Original Cast (RCA)
20	20	I FEEL FOR YOU	Chaka Khan (WEA)
35	21	CINEMA	Elaine Paige (K-Tel)
-	22	STEPS IN TIME	King (CBS)
19	23	ARENA	Duran Duran (EMI)
18	24	PRIVATE DANCER	Tina Turner (Capitol)
-	25	A SENSE OF WONDER	Van Morrison (Mercury)
27	26	CAN'T SLOW DOWN	Lionel Richie (Motown)
21	27	PARADE	Spandau Ballet (Chrysalis)
26	28	THE 12-INCH ALBUM	Howard Jones (WEA)
25	29	STEELTOWN	Big Country (Mercury)
16	30	NOW THAT'S WHAT I CALL MUSIC 4	Various Artists (EMI/Virgin)
22	31	1984 (FOR THE LOVE OF BIG BROTHER)	Eurythmics (Virgin)
24	32	TOO TOUGH TO DIE	Ramones (Beggars Banquet)
38	33	(WHO'S AFRAID OF) THE ART OF NOISE	Art of Noise (ZTT)
31	34	BREAKDANCE II	Various Artists (Polydor)
-	35	PLANETARY INVASION	Midnight Star (Solar)
36	36	TROPICO	Pat Benatar (Chrysalis)
-	37	CHICAGO 17	Chicago (Full Moon)
-	38	BREWING UP WITH BILLY BRAGG	Billy Bragg (Go! Discs)
30	39	RATTLESNAKES	Lloyd Cole & the Commotions (Polydor)
-	40	IT'S YOUR NIGHT	James Ingram (Qwest)
-	41	EUGENE WILDE	Eugene Wilde (Fourth & Broadway)
50	42	TREASURE	Cocteau Twins (4AD)
-	43	HEARTBEAT CITY	Cars (Elektra)
34	44	GHOSTBUSTERS	Soundtrack (Arista)
44	45	GIVE MY REGARDS TO BROAD STREET	Paul McCartney (EMI)
49	46	BREAK OUT	Pointer Sisters (Planet)
32	47	PARTY, PARTY	Black Lace (Flair)
-	48	THRILLER	Michael Jackson (Epic)
40	49	PURPLE RAIN	Prince& The Revolution (Warner Bros.)
-	50	SO GOOD	Whispers (Solar)

Alison Moyet's debut solo album *Alf* (the title referred to her nickname) finally topped the chart after nine weeks in the Top 10, only to be eclipsed after a sole week of glory by Foreigner's first UK chart-topping album *Agent Provocateur*. The latter was boosted hugely by the simultaneous Number 1 success of the group's hymnal single *I Want To Know What Love Is*, which the album included.

February – March 1985

16 February 1985

last week	this week	Title	Artist
1	1	AGENT PROVOCATEUR	Foreigner (Atlantic)
3	2	BORN IN THE USA	Bruce Springsteen (CBS)
6	3	HITS OUT OF HELL	Meatloaf (Epic)
2	4	ELIMINATOR	ZZ Top (Warner Brothers)
4	5	ALF	Alison Moyet (CBS)
7	6	THE AGE OF CONSENT	Bronski Beat (Forbidden Fruit)
22	7	STEPS IN TIME	King (CBS)
5	8	20/20	George Benson (Warner Bros.)
9	9	VERY BEST OF CHRIS DE BURGH	Chris De Burgh (Telstar)
12	10	DIAMOND LIFE	Sade (CBS)
8	11	MAKE IT BIG	Wham! (CBS)
14	12	THE BARBARA DICKSON SONGBOOK	Barbara Dickson (K-Tel)
10	13	THE COLLECTION	Ultravox (Chrysalis)
25	14	A SENSE OF WONDER	Van Morrison (Mercury)
28	15	THE 12-INCH ALBUM	Howard Jones (WEA)
11	16	LIKE A VIRGIN	Madonna (Sire)
13	17	WELCOME TO THE PLEASUREDOME	Frankie Goes to Hollywood (ZTT)
19	18	CHESS	Original Cast (RCA)
33	19	(WHO'S AFRAID OF) THE ART OF NOISE	Art of Noise (ZTT)
16	20	1999	Prince (Warner Bros.)
21	21	CINEMA	Elaine Paige (K-Tel)
20	22	I FEEL FOR YOU	Chaka Khan (WEA)
24	23	PRIVATE DANCER	Tina Turner (Capitol)
29	24	STEELTOWN	Big Country (Mercury)
23	25	ARENA	Duran Duran (EMI)
38	26	BREWING UP WITH BILLY BRAGG	Billy Bragg (Go! Discs)
30	27	NOW THAT'S WHAT I CALL MUSIC 4	Various Artists (EMI/Virgin)
-	28	LIFE'S A RIOT WITH SPY VS SPY	Billy Bragg (Go! Discs)
26	29	CAN'T SLOW DOWN	Lionel Richie (Motown)
18	30	THE HITS ALBUM	Various Artists (WEA/CBS)
17	31	HATFUL OF HOLLOW	Smiths (Rough Trade)
-	32	SECRET SECRETS	Joan Armatrading (A&M)
-	33	NO PARLEZ	Paul Young (CBS)
36	34	TROPICO	Pat Benatar (Chrysalis)
15	35	THE UNFORGETTABLE FIRE	U2 (Island)
27	36	PARADE	Spandau Ballet (Chrysalis)
31	37	1984 (FOR THE LOVE OF BIG BROTHER)	Eurythmics (Virgin)
32	38	TOO TOUGH TO DIE	Ramones (Beggars Banquet)
40	39	IT'S YOUR NIGHT	James Ingram (Qwest)
39	40	RATTLESNAKES	Lloyd Cole & the Commotions (Polydor)
-	41	LEGEND	Bob Marley & the Wailers (Island)
-	42	U2 LIVE: UNDER A BLOOD RED SKY	U2 (Island)
-	43	CENTERFIELD	John Fogerty (Warner Bros.)
34	44	BREAKDANCE II	Various Artists (Polydor)
35	45	PLANETARY INVASION	Midnight Star (Solar)
50	46	SO GOOD	Whispers (Solar)
42	47	TREASURE	Cocteau Twins (4AD)
-	48	VARIOUS POSITIONS	Leonard Cohen (CBS)
-	49	PERHAPS	Associates (WEA)
-	50	THE RIDDLE	Nik Kershaw (MCA)

23 February 1985

last week	this week	Title	Artist
2	1	BORN IN THE USA	Bruce Springsteen (CBS)
5	2	ALF	Alison Moyet (CBS)
1	3	AGENT PROVOCATEUR	Foreigner (Atlantic)
4	4	ELIMINATOR	ZZ Top (Warner Brothers)
7	5	STEPS IN TIME	King (CBS)
3	6	HITS OUT OF HELL	Meatloaf (Epic)
10	7	DIAMOND LIFE	Sade (CBS)
8	8	20/20	George Benson (Warner Bros.)
32	9	SECRET SECRETS	Joan Armatrading (A&M)
-	10	MEAT IS MURDER	Smiths (Rough Trade)
18	11	CHESS	Original Cast (RCA)
9	12	VERY BEST OF CHRIS DE BURGH	Chris De Burgh (Telstar)
11	13	MAKE IT BIG	Wham! (CBS)
12	14	THE BARBARA DICKSON SONGBOOK	Barbara Dickson (K-Tel)
13	15	THE COLLECTION	Ultravox (Chrysalis)
6	16	THE AGE OF CONSENT	Bronski Beat (Forbidden Fruit)
49	17	PERHAPS	Associates (WEA)
19	18	(WHO'S AFRAID OF) THE ART OF NOISE	Art of Noise (ZTT)
14	19	A SENSE OF WONDER	Van Morrison (Mercury)
20	20	1999	Prince (Warner Bros.)
-	21	CHICAGO 17	Chicago (Full Moon)
16	22	LIKE A VIRGIN	Madonna (Sire)
-	23	THE BAD AND LOWDOWN WORLD OF THE KANE GANG	Kane Gang (Kitchenware)
17	24	WELCOME TO THE PLEASUREDOME	Frankie Goes to Hollywood (ZTT)
15	25	THE 12-INCH ALBUM	Howard Jones (WEA)
23	26	PRIVATE DANCER	Tina Turner (Capitol)
43	27	CENTERFIELD	John Fogerty (Warner Bros.)
22	28	I FEEL FOR YOU	Chaka Khan (WEA)
21	29	CINEMA	Elaine Paige (K-Tel)
24	30	STEELTOWN	Big Country (Mercury)
31	31	HATFUL OF HOLLOW	Smiths (Rough Trade)
-	32	BEYOND THE ASTRAL SKIES	Uli Jon Roth (EMI)
30	33	THE HITS ALBUM	Various Artists (WEA/CBS)
33	34	NO PARLEZ	Paul Young (CBS)
-	35	FROM ACROSS THE KITCHEN TABLE	Pale Fountains (Virgin)
27	36	NOW THAT'S WHAT I CALL MUSIC 4	Various Artists (EMI/Virgin)
28	37	LIFE'S A RIOT WITH SPY VS SPY	Billy Bragg (Go! Discs)
29	38	CAN'T SLOW DOWN	Lionel Richie (Motown)
-	39	FACE VALUE	Phil Collins (Virgin)
25	40	ARENA	Duran Duran (EMI)
26	41	BREWING UP WITH BILLY BRAGG	Billy Bragg (Go! Discs)
35	42	THE UNFORGETTABLE FIRE	U2 (Island)
48	43	VARIOUS POSITIONS	Leonard Cohen (CBS)
-	44	BEVERLY HILLS COP	Soundtrack (MCA)
-	45	V.U.	Velvet Underground (Polydor)
45	46	PLANETARY INVASION	Midnight Star (Solar)
-	47	SOLID	Ashford & Simpson (Capitol)
34	48	TROPICO	Pat Benatar (Chrysalis)
37	49	1984 (FOR THE LOVE OF BIG BROTHER)	Eurythmics (Virgin)
40	50	RATTLESNAKES	Lloyd Cole & the Commotions (Polydor)

2 March 1985

last week	this week	Title	Artist
10	1	MEAT IS MURDER	Smiths (Rough Trade)
1	2	BORN IN THE USA	Bruce Springsteen (CBS)
2	3	ALF	Alison Moyet (CBS)
-	4	NO JACKET REQUIRED	Phil Collins (Virgin)
5	5	STEPS IN TIME	King (CBS)
3	6	AGENT PROVOCATEUR	Foreigner (Atlantic)
7	7	DIAMOND LIFE	Sade (CBS)
23	8	THE BAD AND LOWDOWN WORLD OF THE KANE GANG	Kane Gang (Kitchenware)
16	9	THE AGE OF CONSENT	Bronski Beat (Forbidden Fruit)
4	10	ELIMINATOR	ZZ Top (Warner Brothers)
6	11	HITS OUT OF HELL	Meatloaf (Epic)
9	12	SECRET SECRETS	Joan Armatrading (A&M)
8	13	20/20	George Benson (Warner Bros.)
11	14	CHESS	Original Cast (RCA)
13	15	MAKE IT BIG	Wham! (CBS)
14	16	THE BARBARA DICKSON SONGBOOK	Barbara Dickson (K-Tel)
12	17	VERY BEST OF CHRIS DE BURGH	Chris De Burgh (Telstar)
24	18	WELCOME TO THE PLEASUREDOME	Frankie Goes to Hollywood (ZTT)
-	19	NIGHTSHIFT	Commodores (Tamla Motown)
15	20	THE COLLECTION	Ultravox (Chrysalis)
-	21	THE FIRM	Firm (Atlantic)
18	22	(WHO'S AFRAID OF) THE ART OF NOISE	Art of Noise (ZTT)
47	23	SOLID	Ashford & Simpson (Capitol)
-	24	RECKLESS	Bryan Adams (A&M)
25	25	THE 12-INCH ALBUM	Howard Jones (WEA)
17	26	PERHAPS	Associates (WEA)
21	27	CHICAGO 17	Chicago (Full Moon)
19	28	A SENSE OF WONDER	Van Morrison (Mercury)
45	29	V.U.	Velvet Underground (Polydor)
20	30	1999	Prince (Warner Bros.)
26	31	PRIVATE DANCER	Tina Turner (Capitol)
31	32	HATFUL OF HOLLOW	Smiths (Rough Trade)
34	33	NO PARLEZ	Paul Young (CBS)
37	34	LIFE'S A RIOT WITH SPY VS SPY	Billy Bragg (Go! Discs)
32	35	BEYOND THE ASTRAL SKIES	Uli Jon Roth (EMI)
-	36	VULTURE CULTURE	Alan Parsons Project (Arista)
27	37	CENTERFIELD	John Fogerty (Warner Bros.)
22	38	LIKE A VIRGIN	Madonna (Sire)
29	39	CINEMA	Elaine Paige (K-Tel)
38	40	CAN'T SLOW DOWN	Lionel Richie (Motown)
-	41	SHAKATAK LIVE!	Shakatak (Polydor)
-	42	SECRETS	Wilton Felder (MCA)
35	43	FROM ACROSS THE KITCHEN TABLE	Pale Fountains (Virgin)
42	44	THE UNFORGETTABLE FIRE	U2 (Island)
-	45	LOST AND FOUND	Jason & the Scorchers (EMI)
-	46	PARIS, TEXAS - SOUNDTRACK	Ry Cooder (Warner Bros.)
33	47	THE HITS ALBUM	Various Artists (WEA/CBS)
40	48	ARENA	Duran Duran (EMI)
28	49	I FEEL FOR YOU	Chaka Khan (WEA)
-	50	STOP MAKING SENSE	Talking Heads (EMI)

Bruce Springsteen's *Born In The USA* had been riding the UK chart for just over eight months when it finally got the extra push to No. 1 on February 23, much of the impetus clearly coming from the success of the extracted single *Dancing In The Dark*, which was now in the Top 5 on its second release, having under-performed in 1984 first time around. Bruce was soon uprooted, though, by the Smiths' first Number 1.

March 1985

9 March 1985

last	this	title	artist
4	1	NO JACKET REQUIRED	Phil Collins (Virgin)
2	2	BORN IN THE USA	Bruce Springsteen (CBS)
1	3	MEAT IS MURDER	Smiths (Rough Trade)
3	4	ALF	Alison Moyet (CBS)
24	5	RECKLESS	Bryan Adams (A&M)
5	6	STEPS IN TIME	King (CBS)
10	7	ELIMINATOR	ZZ Top (Warner Brothers)
21	8	THE FIRM	Firm (Atlantic)
7	9	DIAMOND LIFE	Sade (CBS)
9	10	THE AGE OF CONSENT	Bronski Beat (Forbidden Fruit)
6	11	AGENT PROVOCATEUR	Foreigner (Atlantic)
11	12	HITS OUT OF HELL	Meatloaf (Epic)
8	13	THE BAD AND LOWDOWN WORLD OF THE KANE GANG	Kane Gang (Kitchenware)
14	14	CHESS	Original Cast (RCA)
16	15	THE BARBARA DICKSON SONGBOOK	Barbara Dickson (K-Tel)
17	16	VERY BEST OF CHRIS DE BURGH	Chris De Burgh (Telstar)
13	17	20/20	George Benson (Warner Bros.)
19	18	NIGHTSHIFT	Commodores (Tamla Motown)
12	19	SECRET SECRETS	Joan Armatrading (A&M)
15	20	MAKE IT BIG	Wham! (CBS)
30	21	1999	Prince (Warner Bros.)
-	22	NIGHT TIME	Killing Joke (EG)
-	23	BUILDING THE PERFECT BEAST	Don Henley (Geffen)
18	24	WELCOME TO THE PLEASUREDOME	Frankie Goes to Hollywood (ZTT)
37	25	CENTERFIELD	John Fogerty (Warner Bros.)
-	26	PURPLE RAIN	Prince & the Revolution (Warner Bros.)
-	27	MODERN LOVE	Various Artists (K-Tel)
23	28	SOLID	Ashford & Simpson (Capitol)
-	29	STREET SOUNDS ELECTRO 6	Various Artists (Street Sounds)
38	30	LIKE A VIRGIN	Madonna (Sire)
27	31	CHICAGO 17	Chicago (Full Moon)
25	32	THE 12-INCH ALBUM	Howard Jones (WEA)
-	33	CRAZY FROM THE HEAT	David Lee Roth (Warner Bros.)
31	34	PRIVATE DANCER	Tina Turner (Capitol)
32	35	HATFUL OF HOLLOW	Smiths (Rough Trade)
-	36	DANGEROUS MUSIC	Robin George (Bronze)
29	37	V.U.	Velvet Underground (Polydor)
-	38	BEVERLY HILLS COP	Soundtrack (MCA)
26	39	PERHAPS	Associates (WEA)
20	40	THE COLLECTION	Ultravox (Chrysalis)
47	41	THE HITS ALBUM	Various Artists (WEA/CBS)
-	42	CASHMERE	Cashmere (Fourth & Broadway)
50	43	STOP MAKING SENSE	Talking Heads (EMI)
22	44	(WHO'S AFRAID OF) THE ART OF NOISE	Art of Noise (ZTT)
28	45	A SENSE OF WONDER	Van Morrison (Mercury)
34	46	LIFE'S A RIOT WITH SPY VS SPY	Billy Bragg (Go! Discs)
35	47	BEYOND THE ASTRAL SKIES	Uli Jon Roth (EMI)
40	48	CAN'T SLOW DOWN	Lionel Richie (Motown)
42	49	SECRETS	Wilton Felder (MCA)
45	50	LOST AND FOUND	Jason & the Scorchers (EMI)

16 March 1985

last	this	title	artist
1	1	NO JACKET REQUIRED	Phil Collins (Virgin)
2	2	BORN IN THE USA	Bruce Springsteen (CBS)
-	3	SONGS FROM THE BIG CHAIR	Tears For Fears (Mercury)
3	4	MEAT IS MURDER	Smiths (Rough Trade)
5	5	RECKLESS	Bryan Adams (A&M)
4	6	ALF	Alison Moyet (CBS)
23	7	BUILDING THE PERFECT BEAST	Don Henley (Geffen)
7	8	ELIMINATOR	ZZ Top (Warner Brothers)
22	9	NIGHT TIME	Killing Joke (EG)
12	10	HITS OUT OF HELL	Meatloaf (Epic)
9	11	DIAMOND LIFE	Sade (CBS)
-	12	SHE'S THE BOSS	Mick Jagger (CBS)
21	13	1999	Prince (Warner Bros.)
8	14	THE FIRM	Firm (Atlantic)
10	15	THE AGE OF CONSENT	Bronski Beat (Forbidden Fruit)
14	16	CHESS	Original Cast (RCA)
34	17	PRIVATE DANCER	Tina Turner (Capitol)
20	18	MAKE IT BIG	Wham! (CBS)
11	19	AGENT PROVOCATEUR	Foreigner (Atlantic)
18	20	NIGHTSHIFT	Commodores (Tamla Motown)
6	21	STEPS IN TIME	King (CBS)
30	22	LIKE A VIRGIN	Madonna (Sire)
26	23	PURPLE RAIN	Prince & the Revolution (Warner Bros.)
29	24	STREET SOUNDS ELECTRO 6	Various Artists (Street Sounds)
31	25	CHICAGO 17	Chicago (Full Moon)
13	26	THE BAD AND LOWDOWN WORLD OF THE KANE GANG	Kane Gang (Kitchenware)
15	27	THE BARBARA DICKSON SONGBOOK	Barbara Dickson (K-Tel)
17	28	20/20	George Benson (Warner Bros.)
35	29	HATFUL OF HOLLOW	Smiths (Rough Trade)
27	30	MODERN LOVE	Various Artists (K-Tel)
32	31	THE 12-INCH ALBUM	Howard Jones (WEA)
19	32	SECRET SECRETS	Joan Armatrading (A&M)
-	33	CAN'T STOP THE LOVE	Maze (Capitol)
16	34	VERY BEST OF CHRIS DE BURGH	Chris De Burgh (Telstar)
37	35	V.U.	Velvet Underground (Polydor)
28	36	SOLID	Ashford & Simpson (Capitol)
38	37	BEVERLY HILLS COP	Soundtrack (MCA)
24	38	WELCOME TO THE PLEASUREDOME	Frankie Goes to Hollywood (ZTT)
46	39	LIFE'S A RIOT WITH SPY VS SPY	Billy Bragg (Go! Discs)
40	40	THE COLLECTION	Ultravox (Chrysalis)
25	41	CENTERFIELD	John Fogerty (Warner Bros.)
42	42	CASHMERE	Cashmere (Fourth & Broadway)
44	43	(WHO'S AFRAID OF) THE ART OF NOISE	Art of Noise (ZTT)
45	44	A SENSE OF WONDER	Van Morrison (Mercury)
48	45	CAN'T SLOW DOWN	Lionel Richie (Motown)
50	46	LOST AND FOUND	Jason & the Scorchers (EMI)
-	47	BREWING UP WITH BILLY BRAGG	Billy Bragg (Go! Discs)
-	48	FACE VALUE	Phil Collins (Virgin)
39	49	PERHAPS	Associates (WEA)
41	50	THE HITS ALBUM	Various Artists (WEA/CBS)

23 March 1985

last	this	title	artist
1	1	NO JACKET REQUIRED	Phil Collins (Virgin)
3	2	SONGS FROM THE BIG CHAIR	Tears For Fears (Mercury)
2	3	BORN IN THE USA	Bruce Springsteen (CBS)
12	4	SHE'S THE BOSS	Mick Jagger (CBS)
6	5	ALF	Alison Moyet (CBS)
5	6	RECKLESS	Bryan Adams (A&M)
11	7	DIAMOND LIFE	Sade (CBS)
7	8	BUILDING THE PERFECT BEAST	Don Henley (Geffen)
8	9	ELIMINATOR	ZZ Top (Warner Brothers)
10	10	HITS OUT OF HELL	Meatloaf (Epic)
-	11	DREAM INTO ACTION	Howard Jones (WEA)
9	12	NIGHT TIME	Killing Joke (EG)
22	13	LIKE A VIRGIN	Madonna (Sire)
20	14	NIGHTSHIFT	Commodores (Tamla Motown)
4	15	MEAT IS MURDER	Smiths (Rough Trade)
17	16	PRIVATE DANCER	Tina Turner (Capitol)
23	17	PURPLE RAIN	Prince & the Revolution (Warner Bros.)
-	18	BEHIND THE SUN	Eric Clapton (Duck)
15	19	THE AGE OF CONSENT	Bronski Beat (Forbidden Fruit)
-	20	FIRST AND LAST AND ALWAYS	Sisters of Mercy (Merciful Release)
13	21	1999	Prince (Warner Bros.)
14	22	THE FIRM	Firm (Atlantic)
-	23	WHATEVER HAPPENED TO JUGULA?	Roy Harper & Jimmy Page (Beggars Banquet)
16	24	CHESS	Original Cast (RCA)
18	25	MAKE IT BIG	Wham! (CBS)
24	26	STREET SOUNDS ELECTRO 6	Various Artists (Street Sounds)
39	27	LIFE'S A RIOT WITH SPY VS SPY	Billy Bragg (Go! Discs)
26	28	THE BAD AND LOWDOWN WORLD OF THE KANE GANG	Kane Gang (Kitchenware)
37	29	BEVERLY HILLS COP	Soundtrack (MCA)
21	30	STEPS IN TIME	King (CBS)
33	31	CAN'T STOP THE LOVE	Maze (Capitol)
32	32	SECRET SECRETS	Joan Armatrading (A&M)
-	33	NO PARLEZ	Paul Young (CBS)
31	34	THE 12-INCH ALBUM	Howard Jones (WEA)
36	35	SOLID	Ashford & Simpson (Capitol)
41	36	CENTERFIELD	John Fogerty (Warner Bros.)
38	37	WELCOME TO THE PLEASUREDOME	Frankie Goes to Hollywood (ZTT)
-	38	STOP MAKING SENSE	Talking Heads (EMI)
34	39	VERY BEST OF CHRIS DE BURGH	Chris De Burgh (Telstar)
30	40	MODERN LOVE	Various Artists (K-Tel)
-	41	ALL OVER THE PLACE	Bangles (CBS)
19	42	AGENT PROVOCATEUR	Foreigner (Atlantic)
25	43	CHICAGO 17	Chicago (Full Moon)
29	44	HATFUL OF HOLLOW	Smiths (Rough Trade)
27	45	THE BARBARA DICKSON SONGBOOK	Barbara Dickson (K-Tel)
48	46	FACE VALUE	Phil Collins (Virgin)
28	47	20/20	George Benson (Warner Bros.)
44	48	A SENSE OF WONDER	Van Morrison (Mercury)
50	49	THE HITS ALBUM	Various Artists (WEA/CBS)
40	50	THE COLLECTION	Ultravox (Chrysalis)

Phil Collins' third solo album *No Jacket Required* was to be his biggest seller yet - in fact, it was also to be one of Virgin Records' best sellers yet, and would eventually be the eighth top-selling album of the 1980s. After five consecutive weeks at Number 1, it would remain close to the top of the chart through until the middle of 1985, denying an immediate top place to Tears For Fears' *Songs From The Big Chair*.

30 March 1985

last week	this week	Title	Artist
1	1	NO JACKET REQUIRED	Phil Collins (Virgin)
11	2	DREAM INTO ACTION	Howard Jones (WEA)
2	3	SONGS FROM THE BIG CHAIR	Tears For Fears (Mercury)
5	4	ALF	Alison Moyet (CBS)
3	5	BORN IN THE USA	Bruce Springsteen (CBS)
18	6	BEHIND THE SUN	Eric Clapton (Duck)
8	7	BUILDING THE PERFECT BEAST	Don Henley (Geffen)
13	8	LIKE A VIRGIN	Madonna (Sire)
6	9	RECKLESS	Bryan Adams (A&M)
16	10	PRIVATE DANCER	Tina Turner (Capitol)
4	11	SHE'S THE BOSS	Mick Jagger (CBS)
7	12	DIAMOND LIFE	Sade (CBS)
9	13	ELIMINATOR	ZZ Top (Warner Brothers)
-	14	REQUIEM	Andrew Lloyd Webber & Various Artists (HMV)
10	15	HITS OUT OF HELL	Meatloaf (Epic)
20	16	FIRST AND LAST AND ALWAYS	Sisters of Mercy (Merciful Release)
15	17	MEAT IS MURDER	Smiths (Rough Trade)
14	18	NIGHTSHIFT	Commodores (Tamla Motown)
17	19	PURPLE RAIN	Prince & the Revolution (Warner Bros.)
12	20	NIGHT TIME	Killing Joke (EG)
19	21	THE AGE OF CONSENT	Bronski Beat (Forbidden Fruit)
25	22	MAKE IT BIG	Wham! (CBS)
24	23	CHESS	Original Cast (RCA)
30	24	STEPS IN TIME	King (CBS)
45	25	THE BARBARA DICKSON SONGBOOK	Barbara Dickson (K-Tel)
33	26	NO PARLEZ	Paul Young (CBS)
23	27	WHATEVER HAPPENED TO JUGULA?	Roy Harper & Jimmy Page (Beggars Banquet)
27	28	LIFE'S A RIOT WITH SPY VS SPY	Billy Bragg (Go! Discs)
31	29	CAN'T STOP THE LOVE	Maze (Capitol)
-	30	METAL HEART	Accept (Portrait)
46	31	FACE VALUE	Phil Collins (Virgin)
-	32	BEYOND APPEARANCES	Santana (CBS)
-	33	THE RIDDLE	Nik Kershaw (MCA)
40	34	MODERN LOVE	Various Artists (K-Tel)
-	35	LEGEND	Clannad (RCA)
-	36	THE ARTISTS VOLUME 1	Various Artists (Street Sounds)
29	37	BEVERLY HILLS COP	Soundtrack (MCA)
32	38	SECRET SECRETS	Joan Armatrading (A&M)
36	39	CENTERFIELD	John Fogerty (Warner Bros.)
37	40	WELCOME TO THE PLEASUREDOME	Frankie Goes to Hollywood (ZTT)
26	41	STREET SOUNDS ELECTRO 6	Various Artists (Street Sounds)
41	42	ALL OVER THE PLACE	Bangles (CBS)
-	43	BREWING UP WITH BILLY BRAGG	Billy Bragg (Go! Discs)
47	44	20/20	George Benson (Warner Bros.)
28	45	THE BAD AND LOWDOWN WORLD OF THE KANE GANG	Kane Gang (Kitchenware)
38	46	STOP MAKING SENSE	Talking Heads (EMI)
21	47	1999	Prince (Warner Bros.)
22	48	THE FIRM	Firm (Atlantic)
-	49	CASHMERE	Cashmere (Fourth & Broadway)
-	50	WHOSE SIDE ARE YOU ON	Matt Bianco (WEA)

6 April 1985

last week	this week	Title	Artist
1	1	NO JACKET REQUIRED	Phil Collins (Virgin)
2	2	DREAM INTO ACTION	Howard Jones (WEA)
-	3	THE SECRET OF ASSOCIATION	Paul Young (CBS)
4	4	ALF	Alison Moyet (CBS)
5	5	BORN IN THE USA	Bruce Springsteen (CBS)
3	6	SONGS FROM THE BIG CHAIR	Tears For Fears (Mercury)
14	7	REQUIEM	Andrew Lloyd Webber/Various (HMV)
6	8	BEHIND THE SUN	Eric Clapton (Duck)
10	9	PRIVATE DANCER	Tina Turner (Capitol)
9	10	RECKLESS	Bryan Adams (A&M)
8	11	LIKE A VIRGIN	Madonna (Sire)
12	12	DIAMOND LIFE	Sade (CBS)
7	13	BUILDING THE PERFECT BEAST	Don Henley (Geffen)
11	14	SHE'S THE BOSS	Mick Jagger (CBS)
17	15	MEAT IS MURDER	Smiths (Rough Trade)
13	16	ELIMINATOR	ZZ Top (Warner Brothers)
19	17	PURPLE RAIN	Prince & the Revolution (Warner Bros.)
40	18	WELCOME TO THE PLEASUREDOME	Frankie Goes to Hollywood (ZTT)
15	19	HITS OUT OF HELL	Meatloaf (Epic)
-	20	CHINESE WALL	Philip Bailey (CBS)
16	21	FIRST AND LAST AND ALWAYS	Sisters of Mercy (Merciful Release)
-	22	THE POWER STATION	Power Station (Parlophone)
-	23	WORKING NIGHTS	Working Week (Virgin)
18	24	NIGHTSHIFT	Commodores (Tamla Motown)
-	25	THE NIGHT I FELL IN LOVE	Luther Vandross (Epic)
44	26	20/20	George Benson (Warner Bros.)
28	27	LIFE'S A RIOT WITH SPY VS SPY	Billy Bragg (Go! Discs)
20	28	NIGHT TIME	Killing Joke (EG)
38	29	SECRET SECRETS	Joan Armatrading (A&M)
-	30	VERY BEST OF BRENDA LEE	Brenda Lee (MCA)
22	31	MAKE IT BIG	Wham! (CBS)
24	32	STEPS IN TIME	King (CBS)
21	33	THE AGE OF CONSENT	Bronski Beat (Forbidden Fruit)
-	34	BIRDY – MUSIC FROM THE FILM	Peter Gabriel (Charisma)
29	35	CAN'T STOP THE LOVE	Maze (Capitol)
35	36	LEGEND	Clannad (RCA)
23	37	CHESS	Original Cast (RCA)
26	38	NO PARLEZ	Paul Young (CBS)
37	39	BEVERLY HILLS COP	Soundtrack (MCA)
-	40	REGGAE HITS VOL 1	Various Artists (Jetstar)
45	41	THE BAD AND LOWDOWN WORLD OF THE KANE GANG	Kane Gang (Kitchenware)
25	42	THE BARBARA DICKSON SONGBOOK	Barbara Dickson (K-Tel)
31	43	FACE VALUE	Phil Collins (Virgin)
46	44	STOP MAKING SENSE	Talking Heads (EMI)
32	45	BEYOND APPEARANCES	Santana (CBS)
33	46	THE RIDDLE	Nik Kershaw (MCA)
-	47	POWER AND PASSION	Mama's Boys (Jive)
-	48	HOW WILL THE WOLF SURVIVE?	Los Lobos (Slash)
50	49	WHOSE SIDE ARE YOU ON	Matt Bianco (WEA)
-	50	HIP PRIEST AND KAMERADS	Fall (Situation Two)

13 April 1985

last week	this week	Title	Artist
3	1	THE SECRET OF ASSOCIATION	Paul Young (CBS)
1	2	NO JACKET REQUIRED	Phil Collins (Virgin)
6	3	SONGS FROM THE BIG CHAIR	Tears For Fears (Mercury)
5	4	BORN IN THE USA	Bruce Springsteen (CBS)
2	5	DREAM INTO ACTION	Howard Jones (WEA)
4	6	ALF	Alison Moyet (CBS)
7	7	REQUIEM	Andrew Lloyd Webber/ Various (HMV)
22	8	THE POWER STATION	Power Station (Parlophone)
9	9	PRIVATE DANCER	Tina Turner (Capitol)
10	10	RECKLESS	Bryan Adams (A&M)
8	11	BEHIND THE SUN	Eric Clapton (Duck)
11	12	LIKE A VIRGIN	Madonna (Sire)
18	13	WELCOME TO THE PLEASUREDOME	Frankie Goes to Hollywood (ZTT)
16	14	ELIMINATOR	ZZ Top (Warner Brothers)
19	15	HITS OUT OF HELL	Meatloaf (Epic)
20	16	CHINESE WALL	Philip Bailey (CBS)
17	17	PURPLE RAIN	Prince & the Revolution (Warner Bros.)
25	18	THE NIGHT I FELL IN LOVE	Luther Vandross (Epic)
12	19	DIAMOND LIFE	Sade (CBS)
-	20	HITS 2	Various Artists (CBS/WEA)
23	21	WORKING NIGHTS	Working Week (Virgin)
13	22	BUILDING THE PERFECT BEAST	Don Henley (Geffen)
30	23	VERY BEST OF BRENDA LEE	Brenda Lee (MCA)
14	24	SHE'S THE BOSS	Mick Jagger (CBS)
31	25	MAKE IT BIG	Wham! (CBS)
38	26	NO PARLEZ	Paul Young (CBS)
32	27	STEPS IN TIME	King (CBS)
33	28	THE AGE OF CONSENT	Bronski Beat (Forbidden Fruit)
15	29	MEAT IS MURDER	Smiths (Rough Trade)
21	30	FIRST AND LAST AND ALWAYS	Sisters of Mercy (Merciful Release)
24	31	NIGHTSHIFT	Commodores (Tamla Motown)
47	32	POWER AND PASSION	Mama's Boys (Jive)
-	33	AGENT PROVOCATEUR	Foreigner (Atlantic)
40	34	REGGAE HITS VOL 1	Various Artists (Jetstar)
27	35	LIFE'S A RIOT WITH SPY VS SPY	Billy Bragg (Go! Discs)
49	36	WHOSE SIDE ARE YOU ON	Matt Bianco (WEA)
39	37	BEVERLY HILLS COP	Soundtrack (MCA)
26	38	20/20	George Benson (Warner Bros.)
34	39	BIRDY – MUSIC FROM THE FILM	Peter Gabriel (Charisma)
-	40	DANCIN' IN THE KEY OF LIFE	Steve Arrington (Atlantic)
48	41	HOW WILL THE WOLF SURVIVE?	Los Lobos (Slash)
-	42	GO WEST/BANGS AND CRASHES	Go West (Chrysalis)
35	43	CAN'T STOP THE LOVE	Maze (Capitol)
-	44	MYSTERY	Rah Band (RCA)
-	45	STREET SOUNDS ELECTRO 6	Various Artists (Street Sounds)
43	46	FACE VALUE	Phil Collins (Virgin)
37	47	CHESS	Original Cast (RCA)
28	48	NIGHT TIME	Killing Joke (EG)
36	49	LEGEND	Clannad (RCA)
29	50	SECRET SECRETS	Joan Armatrading (A&M)

Thanks to Phil Collins' extended run at the chart top, Howard Jones second album (excluding the 12" compilation issued at Christmas) *Dream Into Action* just failed to emulate the Number 1 success of his debut, peaking at 2. Paul Young, whose second solo effort *The Secret Of Association* was (strategically?) released two weeks later, had no such problems, and his was the album to finally end the Collins run.

April – May 1985

20 April 1985

last week	this week	Title	Artist (Label)
1	1	THE SECRET OF ASSOCIATION	Paul Young (CBS)
2	2	NO JACKET REQUIRED	Phil Collins (Virgin)
3	3	SONGS FROM THE BIG CHAIR	Tears For Fears (Mercury)
20	4	HITS 2	Various Artists (CBS/WEA)
5	5	DREAM INTO ACTION	Howard Jones (WEA)
4	6	BORN IN THE USA	Bruce Springsteen (CBS)
6	7	ALF	Alison Moyet (CBS)
7	8	REQUIEM	Andrew Lloyd Webber & Various (HMV)
13	9	WELCOME TO THE PLEASUREDOME	Frankie Goes to Hollywood (ZTT)
8	10	THE POWER STATION	Power Station (Parlophone)
9	11	PRIVATE DANCER	Tina Turner (Capitol)
42	12	GO WEST/BANGS AND CRASHES	Go West (Chrysalis)
10	13	RECKLESS	Bryan Adams (A&M)
12	14	LIKE A VIRGIN	Madonna (Sire)
21	15	WORKING NIGHTS	Working Week (Virgin)
14	16	ELIMINATOR	ZZ Top (Warner Brothers)
18	17	THE NIGHT I FELL IN LOVE	Luther Vandross (Epic)
11	18	BEHIND THE SUN	Eric Clapton (Duck)
15	19	HITS OUT OF HELL	Meatloaf (Epic)
23	20	VERY BEST OF BRENDA LEE	Brenda Lee (MCA)
16	21	CHINESE WALL	Philip Bailey (CBS)
-	22	STRAWBERRY SWITCHBLADE	Strawberry Switchblade (Korova)
28	23	THE AGE OF CONSENT	Bronski Beat (Forbidden Fruit)
19	24	DIAMOND LIFE	Sade (CBS)
-	25	SO WHERE ARE YOU?	Loose Ends (Virgin)
25	26	MAKE IT BIG	Wham! (CBS)
17	27	PURPLE RAIN	Prince & the Revolution (Warner Bros.)
22	28	BUILDING THE PERFECT BEAST	Don Henley (Geffen)
-	29	THE BEST OF ELVIS COSTELLO - THE MAN	Elvis Costello (Telstar)
-	30	TOMMY BOY'S GREATEST BEATS	Various Artists (Tommy Boy)
41	31	HOW WILL THE WOLF SURVIVE?	Los Lobos (Slash)
26	32	NO PARLEZ	Paul Young (CBS)
-	33	THE UPS AND DOWNS	Stephen TinTin Duffy (10)
24	34	SHE'S THE BOSS	Mick Jagger (CBS)
-	35	SOUTHERN ACCENTS	Tom Petty & the Heartbreakers (MCA)
27	36	STEPS IN TIME	King (CBS)
29	37	MEAT IS MURDER	Smiths (Rough Trade)
-	38	WHITE NOISE - LIVE	Gary Numan (Numa)
40	39	DANCIN' IN THE KEY OF LIFE	Steve Arrington (Atlantic)
44	40	MYSTERY	Rah Band (RCA)
49	41	LEGEND	Clannad (RCA)
45	42	STREET SOUNDS ELECTRO 6	Various Artists (Street Sounds)
35	43	LIFE'S A RIOT WITH SPY VS SPY	Billy Bragg (Go! Discs)
30	44	FIRST AND LAST AND ALWAYS	Sisters of Mercy (Merciful Release)
32	45	POWER AND PASSION	Mama's Boys (Jive)
33	46	AGENT PROVOCATEUR	Foreigner (Atlantic)
34	47	REGGAE HITS VOL 1	Various Artists (Jetstar)
38	48	20/20	George Benson (Warner Bros.)
39	49	BIRDY – MUSIC FROM THE FILM	Peter Gabriel (Charisma)
48	50	NIGHT TIME	Killing Joke (EG)

27 April 1985

last week	this week	Title	Artist (Label)
4	1	HITS 2	Various Artists (CBS/WEA)
1	2	THE SECRET OF ASSOCIATION	Paul Young (CBS)
2	3	NO JACKET REQUIRED	Phil Collins (Virgin)
3	4	SONGS FROM THE BIG CHAIR	Tears For Fears (Mercury)
6	5	BORN IN THE USA	Bruce Springsteen (CBS)
12	6	GO WEST/BANGS AND CRASHES	Go West (Chrysalis)
8	7	REQUIEM	Andrew Lloyd Webber/ Various (HMV)
5	8	DREAM INTO ACTION	Howard Jones (WEA)
7	9	ALF	Alison Moyet (CBS)
10	10	THE POWER STATION	Power Station (Parlophone)
9	11	WELCOME TO THE PLEASUREDOME	Frankie Goes to Hollywood (ZTT)
35	12	SOUTHERN ACCENTS	Tom Petty & the Heartbreakers (MCA)
13	13	RECKLESS	Bryan Adams (A&M)
25	14	SO WHERE ARE YOU?	Loose Ends (Virgin)
11	15	PRIVATE DANCER	Tina Turner (Capitol)
14	16	LIKE A VIRGIN	Madonna (Sire)
26	17	MAKE IT BIG	Wham! (CBS)
-	18	LOVE NOT MONEY	Everything But The Girl (Blanco y Negro)
18	19	BEHIND THE SUN	Eric Clapton (Duck)
23	20	THE AGE OF CONSENT	Bronski Beat (Forbidden Fruit)
17	21	THE NIGHT I FELL IN LOVE	Luther Vandross (Epic)
16	22	ELIMINATOR	ZZ Top (Warner Brothers)
24	23	DIAMOND LIFE	Sade (CBS)
15	24	WORKING NIGHTS	Working Week (Virgin)
21	25	CHINESE WALL	Philip Bailey (CBS)
27	26	PURPLE RAIN	Prince & the Revolution (Warner Bros.)
38	27	WHITE NOISE - LIVE	Gary Numan (Numa)
36	28	STEPS IN TIME	King (CBS)
41	29	LEGEND	Clannad (RCA)
29	30	THE BEST OF ELVIS COSTELLO - THE MAN	Elvis Costello (Telstar)
34	31	SHE'S THE BOSS	Mick Jagger (CBS)
22	32	STRAWBERRY SWITCHBLADE	Strawberry Switchblade (Korova)
31	33	HOW WILL THE WOLF SURVIVE?	Los Lobos (Slash)
20	34	VERY BEST OF BRENDA LEE	Brenda Lee(MCA)
39	35	DANCIN' IN THE KEY OF LIFE	Steve Arrington (Atlantic)
19	36	HITS OUT OF HELL	Meatloaf (Epic)
-	37	CAN'T STOP THE LOVE	Maze (Capitol)
43	38	LIFE'S A RIOT WITH SPY VS SPY	Billy Bragg (Go! Discs)
32	39	NO PARLEZ	Paul Young (CBS)
30	40	TOMMY BOY'S GREATEST BEATS	Various Artists (Tommy Boy)
46	41	AGENT PROVOCATEUR	Foreigner (Atlantic)
-	42	TURN ON THE RADIO	Change (Cooltempo)
28	43	BUILDING THE PERFECT BEAST	Don Henley (Geffen)
-	44	TROPICO	Pat Benatar (Chrysalis)
44	45	FIRST AND LAST AND ALWAYS	Sisters of Mercy (Merciful Release)
40	46	MYSTERY	Rah Band (RCA)
47	47	REGGAE HITS VOL 1	Various Artists (Jetstar)
-	48	NIGHTSHIFT	Commodores (Tamla Motown)
-	49	FACE VALUE	Phil Collins (Virgin)
-	50	HELLO, I MUST BE GOING	Phil Collins (Virgin)

4 May 1985

last week	this week	Title	Artist (Label)
1	1	HITS 2	Various Artists (CBS/WEA)
3	2	NO JACKET REQUIRED	Phil Collins (Virgin)
4	3	SONGS FROM THE BIG CHAIR	Tears For Fears (Mercury)
2	4	THE SECRET OF ASSOCIATION	Paul Young (CBS)
5	5	BORN IN THE USA	Bruce Springsteen (CBS)
8	6	DREAM INTO ACTION	Howard Jones (WEA)
6	7	GO WEST/BANGS AND CRASHES	Go West (Chrysalis)
-	8	AROUND THE WORLD IN A DAY	Prince & the Revolution (Warner Bros.)
7	9	REQUIEM	Andrew Lloyd Webber & Various (HMV)
11	10	WELCOME TO THE PLEASUREDOME	Frankie Goes to Hollywood (ZTT)
13	11	RECKLESS	Bryan Adams (A&M)
18	12	LOVE NOT MONEY	Everything But The Girl (Blanco y Negro)
9	13	ALF	Alison Moyet (CBS)
14	14	SO WHERE ARE YOU?	Loose Ends (Virgin)
12	15	SOUTHERN ACCENTS	Tom Petty & the Heartbreakers (MCA)
15	16	PRIVATE DANCER	Tina Turner (Capitol)
16	17	LIKE A VIRGIN	Madonna (Sire)
20	18	THE AGE OF CONSENT	Bronski Beat (Forbidden Fruit)
17	19	MAKE IT BIG	Wham! (CBS)
22	20	ELIMINATOR	ZZ Top (Warner Brothers)
10	21	THE POWER STATION	Power Station (Parlophone)
29	22	LEGEND	Clannad (RCA)
23	23	DIAMOND LIFE	Sade (CBS)
30	24	THE BEST OF ELVIS COSTELLO - THE MAN	Elvis Costello (Telstar)
26	25	PURPLE RAIN	Prince & the Revolution (Warner Bros.)
28	26	STEPS IN TIME	King (CBS)
25	27	CHINESE WALL	Philip Bailey (CBS)
-	28	VIRGINS AND PHILISTINES	Colour Field (Chrysalis)
41	29	AGENT PROVOCATEUR	Foreigner (Atlantic)
42	30	TURN ON THE RADIO	Change (Cooltempo)
21	31	THE NIGHT I FELL IN LOVE	Luther Vandross (Epic)
24	32	WORKING NIGHTS	Working Week (Virgin)
35	33	DANCIN' IN THE KEY OF LIFE	Steve Arrington (Atlantic)
-	34	MOVE CLOSER	Phyllis Nelson (Carrere)
49	35	FACE VALUE	Phil Collins (Virgin)
34	36	VERY BEST OF BRENDA LEE	Brenda Lee (MCA)
27	37	WHITE NOISE - LIVE	Gary Numan (Numa)
19	38	BEHIND THE SUN	Eric Clapton (Duck)
47	39	REGGAE HITS VOL 1	Various Artists (Jetstar)
-	40	VOICES FROM THE HOLY LAND	BBC Welsh Chorus (BBC)
-	41	WILDWEED	Jeffrey Lee Pierce (Statik)
-	42	THE UPS AND DOWNS	Stephen 'Tin Tin' Duffy (10)
-	43	ROSE MARIE SINGS JUST FOR YOU	Rose Marie (A1)
-	44	THE HITS ALBUM	Various Artists (CBS/WEA)
31	45	SHE'S THE BOSS	Mick Jagger (CBS)
32	46	STRAWBERRY SWITCHBLADE	Strawberry Switchblade (Korova)
50	47	HELLO, I MUST BE GOING	Phil Collins (Virgin)
46	48	MYSTERY	Rah Band (RCA)
37	49	CAN'T STOP THE LOVE	Maze (Capitol)
-	50	BAD INFLUENCE	Robert Cray Band (Demon)

The Power Station, finding Top 10 success with their eponymous album, were basically a spin-off from Duran Duran, whose Andy and John Taylor teamed on a studio-only basis with vocalist Robert Palmer and former Chic members Bernard Edwards and Tony Thompson. The studio they used was The Power Station in New York, hence the name of the group. *Hits 2*, meanwhile, equalled the success of *Hits*.

May 1985

last / this week

last	this		
1	1	HITS 2	Various Artists (CBS/WEA)
2	2	NO JACKET REQUIRED	Phil Collins (Virgin)
3	3	SONGS FROM THE BIG CHAIR	
			Tears For Fears (Mercury)
4	4	THE SECRET OF ASSOCIATION	Paul Young (CBS)
8	5	AROUND THE WORLD IN A DAY	
			Prince & the Revolution (Warner Bros.)
5	6	BORN IN THE USA	Bruce Springsteen (CBS)
7	7	GO WEST/BANGS AND CRASHES	
			Go West (Chrysalis)
6	8	DREAM INTO ACTION	Howard Jones (WEA)
12	9	LOVE NOT MONEY	
			Everything But The Girl (Blanco y Negro)
13	10	ALF	Alison Moyet (CBS)
-	11	BE YOURSELF TONIGHT	Eurythmics (RCA)
28	12	VIRGINS AND PHILISTINES	Colour Field (Chrysalis)
14	13	SO WHERE ARE YOU?	Loose Ends (Virgin)
18	14	THE AGE OF CONSENT	
			Bronski Beat (Forbidden Fruit)
9	15	REQUIEM	
			Andrew Lloyd Webber & Various Artists (HMV)
16	16	PRIVATE DANCER	Tina Turner (Capitol)
11	17	RECKLESS	Bryan Adams (A&M)
24	18	THE BEST OF ELVIS COSTELLO - THE MAN	
			Elvis Costello (Telstar)
21	19	THE POWER STATION	Power Station (Parlophone)
-	20	MR BAD GUY	Freddie Mercury (CBS)
17	21	LIKE A VIRGIN	Madonna (Sire)
10	22	WELCOME TO THE PLEASUREDOME	
			Frankie Goes to Hollywood (ZTT)
-	23	FLAUNT THE IMPERFECTION	China Crisis (Virgin)
15	24	SOUTHERN ACCENTS	
			Tom Petty & the Heartbreakers (MCA)
34	25	MOVE CLOSER	Phyllis Nelson (Carrere)
40	26	VOICES FROM THE HOLY LAND	
			BBC Welsh Chorus (BBC)
27	27	CHINESE WALL	Philip Bailey (CBS)
-	28	THE UNFORGETTABLE FIRE	U2 (Island)
22	29	LEGEND	Clannad (RCA)
23	30	DIAMOND LIFE	Sade (CBS)
19	31	MAKE IT BIG	Wham! (CBS)
20	32	ELIMINATOR	ZZ Top (Warner Brothers)
33	33	DANCIN' IN THE KEY OF LIFE	
			Steve Arrington (Atlantic)
30	34	TURN ON THE RADIO	Change (Cooltempo)
26	35	STEPS IN TIME	King (CBS)
31	36	THE NIGHT I FELL IN LOVE	Luther Vandross (Epic)
-	37	SO DELICIOUS	Fatback Band (Cotillion)
-	38	7800 DEGREES FAHRENHEIT	Bon Jovi (Vertigo)
35	39	FACE VALUE	Phil Collins (Virgin)
44	40	THE HITS ALBUM	Various Artists (CBS/WEA)
29	41	AGENT PROVOCATEUR	Foreigner (Atlantic)
25	42	PURPLE RAIN	
			Prince & the Revolution (Warner Bros.)
42	43	THE UPS AND DOWNS	
			Stephen 'Tin Tin' Duffy (10)
39	44	REGGAE HITS VOL 1	Various Artists (Jetstar)
-	45	LIVE AND UNCENSORED	
			Millie Jackson (Important)
-	46	TROPICO	Pat Benatar (Chrysalis)
48	47	MYSTERY	Rah Band (RCA)
41	48	WILDWEED	Jeffrey Lee Pierce (Statik)
32	49	WORKING NIGHTS	Working Week (Virgin)
45	50	SHE'S THE BOSS	Mick Jagger (CBS)

1	1	HITS 2	Various Artists (CBS/WEA)
3	2	SONGS FROM THE BIG CHAIR	
			Tears For Fears (Mercury)
2	3	NO JACKET REQUIRED	Phil Collins (Virgin)
4	4	THE SECRET OF ASSOCIATION	Paul Young (CBS)
5	5	AROUND THE WORLD IN A DAY	
			Prince & the Revolution (Warner Bros.)
11	6	BE YOURSELF TONIGHT	Eurythmics (RCA)
6	7	BORN IN THE USA	Bruce Springsteen (CBS)
20	8	MR BAD GUY	Freddie Mercury (CBS)
7	9	GO WEST/BANGS AND CRASHES	
			Go West (Chrysalis)
23	10	FLAUNT THE IMPERFECTION	China Crisis (Virgin)
8	11	DREAM INTO ACTION	Howard Jones (WEA)
10	12	ALF	Alison Moyet (CBS)
18	13	THE BEST OF ELVIS COSTELLO - THE MAN	
			Elvis Costello (Telstar)
12	14	VIRGINS AND PHILISTINES	Colour Field (Chrysalis)
9	15	LOVE NOT MONEY	
			Everything But The Girl (Blanco y Negro)
14	16	THE AGE OF CONSENT	
			Bronski Beat (Forbidden Fruit)
13	17	SO WHERE ARE YOU?	Loose Ends (Virgin)
22	18	WELCOME TO THE PLEASUREDOME	
			Frankie Goes to Hollywood (ZTT)
16	19	PRIVATE DANCER	Tina Turner (Capitol)
19	20	THE POWER STATION	Power Station (Parlophone)
17	21	RECKLESS	Bryan Adams (A&M)
38	22	7800 DEGREES FAHRENHEIT	Bon Jovi (Vertigo)
26	23	VOICES FROM THE HOLY LAND	
			BBC Welsh Chorus (BBC)
31	24	MAKE IT BIG	Wham! (CBS)
33	25	DANCIN' IN THE KEY OF LIFE	
			Steve Arrington (Atlantic)
30	26	DIAMOND LIFE	Sade (CBS)
36	27	THE NIGHT I FELL IN LOVE	Luther Vandross (Epic)
15	28	REQUIEM	
			Andrew Lloyd Webber & Various Artists (HMV)
21	29	LIKE A VIRGIN	Madonna (Sire)
24	30	SOUTHERN ACCENTS	
			Tom Petty & the Heartbreakers (MCA)
25	31	MOVE CLOSER	Phyllis Nelson (Carrere)
32	32	ELIMINATOR	ZZ Top (Warner Brothers)
34	33	TURN ON THE RADIO	Change (Cooltempo)
28	34	THE UNFORGETTABLE FIRE	U2 (Island)
-	35	BEST OF THE EAGLES	Eagles (Asylum)
-	36	YOUTHQUAKE	Dead Or Alive (Epic)
42	37	PURPLE RAIN	
			Prince & the Revolution (Warner Bros.)
35	38	STEPS IN TIME	King (CBS)
-	39	HEARTS OF FORTUNE	Immaculate Fools (A&M)
47	40	MYSTERY	Rah Band (RCA)
46	41	TROPICO	Pat Benatar (Chrysalis)
-	42	CAN'T STOP THE LOVE	Maze (Capitol)
-	43	STREET SOUNDS ELECTRO 7	
			Various Artists (Street Sounds)
-	44	HITS OUT OF HELL	Meatloaf (Epic)
39	45	FACE VALUE	Phil Collins (Virgin)
27	46	CHINESE WALL	Philip Bailey (CBS)
29	47	LEGEND	Clannad (RCA)
-	48	STREET SOUNDS EDITION 12	
			Various Artists (Street Sounds)
37	49	SO DELICIOUS	Fatback Band (Cotillion)
-	50	BEST OF THE 20TH CENTURY BOY	Marc Bolan (K-Tel)

2	1	SONGS FROM THE BIG CHAIR	
			Tears For Fears (Mercury)
3	2	NO JACKET REQUIRED	Phil Collins (Virgin)
6	3	BE YOURSELF TONIGHT	Eurythmics (RCA)
1	4	HITS 2	Various Artists (CBS/WEA)
-	5	BROTHERS IN ARMS	Dire Straits (Vertigo)
8	6	MR BAD GUY	Freddie Mercury (CBS)
4	7	THE SECRET OF ASSOCIATION	Paul Young (CBS)
10	8	FLAUNT THE IMPERFECTION	China Crisis (Virgin)
5	9	AROUND THE WORLD IN A DAY	
			Prince & the Revolution (Warner Bros.)
7	10	BORN IN THE USA	Bruce Springsteen (CBS)
13	11	THE BEST OF ELVIS COSTELLO - THE MAN	
			Elvis Costello (Telstar)
9	12	GO WEST/BANGS AND CRASHES	
			Go West (Chrysalis)
16	13	THE AGE OF CONSENT	
			Bronski Beat (Forbidden Fruit)
36	14	YOUTHQUAKE	Dead Or Alive (Epic)
50	15	BEST OF THE 20TH CENTURY BOY	Marc Bolan (K-Tel)
43	16	STREET SOUNDS ELECTRO 7	
			Various Artists (Street Sounds)
12	17	ALF	Alison Moyet (CBS)
35	18	BEST OF THE EAGLES	Eagles (Asylum)
15	19	LOVE NOT MONEY	
			Everything But The Girl (Blanco y Negro)
11	20	DREAM INTO ACTION	Howard Jones (WEA)
-	21	OUT NOW!	Various Artists (Chrysalis/MCA)
20	22	THE POWER STATION	Power Station (Parlophone)
19	23	PRIVATE DANCER	Tina Turner (Capitol)
21	24	RECKLESS	Bryan Adams (A&M)
-	25	SHAMROCK DIARIES	Chris Rea (Magnet)
17	26	SO WHERE ARE YOU?	Loose Ends (Virgin)
-	27	LOW-LIFE	New Order (Factory)
22	28	7800 DEGREES FAHRENHEIT	Bon Jovi (Vertigo)
18	29	WELCOME TO THE PLEASUREDOME	
			Frankie Goes to Hollywood (ZTT)
31	30	MOVE CLOSER	Phyllis Nelson (Carrere)
23	31	VOICES FROM THE HOLY LAND	
			BBC Welsh Chorus (BBC)
24	32	MAKE IT BIG	Wham! (CBS)
-	33	ROCK ME TONIGHT	Freddie Jackson (Capitol)
-	34	WEST SIDE STORY	Leonard Bernstein
			& Studio Cast (Deutsche Grammophon)
14	35	VIRGINS AND PHILISTINES	Colour Field (Chrysalis)
25	36	DANCIN' IN THE KEY OF LIFE	
			Steve Arrington (Atlantic)
48	37	STREET SOUNDS EDITION 12	
			Various Artists (Street Sounds)
41	38	TROPICO	Pat Benatar (Chrysalis)
32	39	ELIMINATOR	ZZ Top (Warner Brothers)
26	40	DIAMOND LIFE	Sade (CBS)
46	41	CHINESE WALL	Philip Bailey (CBS)
28	42	REQUIEM	
			Andrew Lloyd Webber & Various Artists (HMV)
42	43	CAN'T STOP THE LOVE	Maze (Capitol)
33	44	TURN ON THE RADIO	Change (Cooltempo)
-	45	NO REST FOR THE WICKED	New Model Army (EMI)
-	46	BROTHER WHERE YOU BOUND	Supertramp (A&M)
-	47	WE ARE THE WORLD	USA For Africa (CBS)
29	48	LIKE A VIRGIN	Madonna (Sire)
27	49	THE NIGHT I FELL IN LOVE	Luther Vandross (Epic)
34	50	THE UNFORGETTABLE FIRE	U2 (Island)

Queen vocalist Freddie Mercury, who had signed a separate solo recording deal with CBS, unveiled its first fruits on the solo album *Mr Bad Guy*, and was rewarded with Queen-sized sales as the set bounded into the Top 10. Meanwhile, Tears For Fears' *Songs From The Big Chair* finally snatched a week at Number 1 after 10 weeks of almost making it behind Phil Collins, Paul Young and the *Hits 2* compilation.

June 1985

1 June 1985

last	this		
5	1	BROTHERS IN ARMS	Dire Straits (Vertigo)
1	2	SONGS FROM THE BIG CHAIR	
			Tears For Fears (Mercury)
2	3	NO JACKET REQUIRED	Phil Collins (Virgin)
21	4	OUT NOW!	Various Artists (Chrysalis/MCA)
27	5	LOW-LIFE	New Order (Factory)
3	6	BE YOURSELF TONIGHT	Eurythmics (RCA)
4	7	HITS 2	Various Artists (CBS/WEA)
10	8	BORN IN THE USA	Bruce Springsteen (CBS)
14	9	YOUTHQUAKE	Dead Or Alive (Epic)
18	10	BEST OF THE EAGLES	Eagles (Asylum)
8	11	FLAUNT THE IMPERFECTION	China Crisis (Virgin)
11	12	THE BEST OF ELVIS COSTELLO - THE MAN	
			Elvis Costello (Telstar)
6	13	MR BAD GUY	Freddie Mercury (CBS)
7	14	THE SECRET OF ASSOCIATION	Paul Young (CBS)
25	15	SHAMROCK DIARIES	Chris Rea (Magnet)
15	16	BEST OF THE 20TH CENTURY BOY	
			Marc Bolan (K-Tel)
12	17	GO WEST/BANGS AND CRASHES	
			Go West (Chrysalis)
34	18	WEST SIDE STORY	Leonard Bernstein
			& Studio Cast (Deutsche Grammophon)
-	19	NOW DANCE	Various Artists (EMI/Virgin)
46	20	BROTHER WHERE YOU BOUND	Supertramp (A&M)
45	21	NO REST FOR THE WICKED	New Model Army (EMI)
16	22	STREET SOUNDS ELECTRO 7	
			Various Artists (Street Sounds)
9	23	AROUND THE WORLD IN A DAY	
			Prince & the Revolution (Warner Bros.)
17	24	ALF	Alison Moyet (CBS)
13	25	THE AGE OF CONSENT	
			Bronski Beat (Forbidden Fruit)
-	26	ON A STORYTELLER'S NIGHT	Magnum (FM)
-	27	SHAKEN 'N' STIRRED	Robert Plant (Es Paranza)
26	28	SO WHERE ARE YOU?	Loose Ends (Virgin)
22	29	THE POWER STATION	Power Station (Parlophone)
47	30	WE ARE THE WORLD	USA For Africa (CBS)
23	31	PRIVATE DANCER	Tina Turner (Capitol)
28	32	7800 DEGREES FAHRENHEIT	Bon Jovi (Vertigo)
33	33	ROCK ME TONIGHT	Freddie Jackson (Capitol)
20	34	DREAM INTO ACTION	Howard Jones (WEA)
31	35	VOICES FROM THE HOLY LAND	
			BBC Welsh Chorus (BBC)
19	36	LOVE NOT MONEY	
			Everything But The Girl (Blanco y Negro)
36	37	DANCIN' IN THE KEY OF LIFE	
			Steve Arrington (Atlantic)
37	38	STREET SOUNDS EDITION 12	
			Various Artists (Street Sounds)
50	39	THE UNFORGETTABLE FIRE	U2 (Island)
24	40	RECKLESS	Bryan Adams (A&M)
30	41	MOVE CLOSER	Phyllis Nelson (Carrere)
-	42	WHAT DOES ANYTHING MEAN? BASICALLY	
			Chameleons (Statik)
32	43	MAKE IT BIG	Wham! (CBS)
35	44	VIRGINS AND PHILISTINES	Colour Field (Chrysalis)
29	45	WELCOME TO THE PLEASUREDOME	
			Frankie Goes to Hollywood (ZTT)
39	46	ELIMINATOR	ZZ Top (Warner Brothers)
43	47	CAN'T STOP THE LOVE	Maze (Capitol)
49	48	THE NIGHT I FELL IN LOVE	Luther Vandross (Epic)
48	49	LIKE A VIRGIN	Madonna (Sire)
-	50	STEP BY STEP	Jeff Lorber (Club)

8 June 1985

this		
1	1	BROTHERS IN ARMS	Dire Straits (Vertigo)
3	2	NO JACKET REQUIRED	Phil Collins (Virgin)
5	3	LOW-LIFE	New Order (Factory)
2	4	SONGS FROM THE BIG CHAIR	
			Tears For Fears (Mercury)
4	5	OUT NOW!	Various Artists (Chrysalis/MCA)
7	6	HITS 2	Various Artists (CBS/WEA)
16	7	BEST OF THE 20TH CENTURY BOY	
			Marc Bolan (K-Tel)
10	8	BEST OF THE EAGLES	Eagles (Asylum)
6	9	BE YOURSELF TONIGHT	Eurythmics (RCA)
19	10	NOW DANCE	Various Artists (EMI/Virgin)
8	11	BORN IN THE USA	Bruce Springsteen (CBS)
27	12	SHAKEN 'N' STIRRED	Robert Plant (Es Paranza)
17	13	GO WEST/BANGS AND CRASHES	
			Go West (Chrysalis)
9	14	YOUTHQUAKE	Dead Or Alive (Epic)
15	15	SHAMROCK DIARIES	Chris Rea (Magnet)
-	16	OUR FAVOURITE SHOP	Style Council (Polydor)
12	17	THE BEST OF ELVIS COSTELLO - THE MAN	
			Elvis Costello (Telstar)
14	18	THE SECRET OF ASSOCIATION	Paul Young (CBS)
20	19	BROTHER WHERE YOU BOUND	Supertramp (A&M)
11	20	FLAUNT THE IMPERFECTION	China Crisis (Virgin)
18	21	WEST SIDE STORY	Leonard Bernstein
			& Studio Cast (Deutsche Grammophon)
25	22	THE AGE OF CONSENT	
			Bronski Beat (Forbidden Fruit)
24	23	ALF	Alison Moyet (CBS)
23	24	AROUND THE WORLD IN A DAY	
			Prince & the Revolution (Warner Bros.)
13	25	MR BAD GUY	Freddie Mercury (CBS)
21	26	NO REST FOR THE WICKED	New Model Army (EMI)
29	27	THE POWER STATION	Power Station (Parlophone)
22	28	STREET SOUNDS ELECTRO 7	
			Various Artists (Street Sounds)
28	29	SO WHERE ARE YOU?	Loose Ends (Virgin)
40	30	RECKLESS	Bryan Adams (A&M)
31	31	PRIVATE DANCER	Tina Turner (Capitol)
37	32	DANCIN' IN THE KEY OF LIFE	
			Steve Arrington (Atlantic)
32	33	7800 DEGREES FAHRENHEIT	Bon Jovi (Vertigo)
-	34	ALEXANDER O'NEAL	
			Alexander O'Neal (Tabu/Epic)
42	35	WHAT DOES ANYTHING MEAN? BASICALLY	
			Chameleons (Statik)
30	36	WE ARE THE WORLD	USA For Africa (CBS)
38	37	STREET SOUNDS EDITION 12	
			Various Artists (Street Sounds)
46	38	ELIMINATOR	ZZ Top (Warner Brothers)
35	39	VOICES FROM THE HOLY LAND	
			BBC Welsh Chorus (BBC)
34	40	DREAM INTO ACTION	Howard Jones (WEA)
33	41	ROCK ME TONIGHT	Freddie Jackson (Capitol)
39	42	THE UNFORGETTABLE FIRE	U2 (Island)
-	43	MASSIVE	Various Artists (Virgin)
43	44	MAKE IT BIG	Wham! (CBS)
41	45	MOVE CLOSER	Phyllis Nelson (Carrere)
45	46	WELCOME TO THE PLEASUREDOME	
			Frankie Goes to Hollywood (ZTT)
-	47	CHINESE WALL	Philip Bailey (CBS)
-	48	DIAMOND LIFE	Sade (CBS)
49	49	LIKE A VIRGIN	Madonna (Sire)
-	50	GRAVITY	Kenny G (Arista)

15 June 1985

this		
1	1	BROTHERS IN ARMS	Dire Straits (Vertigo)
16	2	OUR FAVOURITE SHOP	Style Council (Polydor)
5	3	OUT NOW!	Various Artists (Chrysalis/MCA)
11	4	BORN IN THE USA	Bruce Springsteen (CBS)
10	5	NOW DANCE	Various Artists (EMI/Virgin)
3	6	LOW-LIFE	New Order (Factory)
4	7	SONGS FROM THE BIG CHAIR	
			Tears For Fears (Mercury)
2	8	NO JACKET REQUIRED	Phil Collins (Virgin)
7	9	BEST OF THE 20TH CENTURY BOY	
			Marc Bolan (K-Tel)
6	10	HITS 2	Various Artists (CBS/WEA)
-	11	BOYS AND GIRLS	Bryan Ferry (EG)
13	12	GO WEST/BANGS AND CRASHES	
			Go West (Chrysalis)
8	13	BEST OF THE EAGLES	Eagles (Asylum)
15	14	SHAMROCK DIARIES	Chris Rea (Magnet)
9	15	BE YOURSELF TONIGHT	Eurythmics (RCA)
12	16	SHAKEN 'N' STIRRED	Robert Plant (Es Paranza)
20	17	FLAUNT THE IMPERFECTION	China Crisis (Virgin)
14	18	YOUTHQUAKE	Dead Or Alive (Epic)
18	19	THE SECRET OF ASSOCIATION	Paul Young (CBS)
30	20	RECKLESS	Bryan Adams (A&M)
17	21	THE BEST OF ELVIS COSTELLO - THE MAN	
			Elvis Costello (Telstar)
25	22	MR BAD GUY	Freddie Mercury (CBS)
-	23	KATRINA AND THE WAVES	
			Katrina & the Waves (Capitol)
22	24	THE AGE OF CONSENT	
			Bronski Beat (Forbidden Fruit)
21	25	WEST SIDE STORY	Leonard Bernstein
			& Studio Cast (Deutsche Grammophon)
27	26	THE POWER STATION	Power Station (Parlophone)
39	27	VOICES FROM THE HOLY LAND	
			BBC Welsh Chorus (BBC)
24	28	AROUND THE WORLD IN A DAY	
			Prince & the Revolution (Warner Bros.)
-	29	ON A STORYTELLER'S NIGHT	Magnum (FM)
40	30	DREAM INTO ACTION	Howard Jones (WEA)
33	31	7800 DEGREES FAHRENHEIT	Bon Jovi (Vertigo)
19	32	BROTHER WHERE YOU BOUND	
			Supertramp (A&M)
23	33	ALF	Alison Moyet (CBS)
-	34	SUDDENLY	Billy Ocean (Jive)
-	35	ROMANCE	David Cassidy (Arista)
41	36	ROCK ME TONIGHT	Freddie Jackson (Capitol)
-	37	THE RIVER	Bruce Springsteen (CBS)
36	38	WE ARE THE WORLD	USA For Africa (CBS)
-	39	THE FIRST BORN IS DEAD	Nick Cave (Mute)
-	40	GAS, FOOD, LODGING	Green on Red (Zippo)
34	41	ALEXANDER O'NEAL	
			Alexander O'Neal (Tabu/Epic)
42	42	THE UNFORGETTABLE FIRE	U2 (Island)
47	43	CHINESE WALL	Philip Bailey (CBS)
26	44	NO REST FOR THE WICKED	New Model Arm (EMI)
29	45	SO WHERE ARE YOU?	Loose Ends (Virgin)
31	46	PRIVATE DANCER	Tina Turner (Capitol)
46	47	WELCOME TO THE PLEASUREDOME	
			Frankie Goes to Hollywood (ZTT)
28	48	STREET SOUNDS ELECTRO 7	
			Various Artists (Street Sounds)
50	49	GRAVITY	Kenny G (Arista)
48	50	DIAMOND LIFE	Sade (CBS)

Brothers In Arms was only Dire Straits' sixth album in eight years, but it turned out to be just the release the new upwardly-mobile CD buyers of the 80s were looking for, and quickly outsold everything the band had done previously. After its initial run at the chart top in June, it would keep returning to Number 1 throughout the year (and in 1986), and would prove to be the biggest-selling album (and CD) of the 1980s.

22 June 1985

last week	this week	Title	Artist (Label)
11	1	BOYS AND GIRLS	Bryan Ferry (EG)
4	2	BORN IN THE USA	Bruce Springsteen (CBS)
1	3	BROTHERS IN ARMS	Dire Straits (Vertigo)
2	4	OUR FAVOURITE SHOP	Style Council (Polydor)
3	5	OUT NOW!	Various Artists (Chrysalis/MCA)
8	6	NO JACKET REQUIRED	Phil Collins (Virgin)
5	7	NOW DANCE	Various Artists (EMI/Virgin)
9	8	BEST OF THE 20TH CENTURY BOY	Marc Bolan (K-Tel)
6	9	LOW-LIFE	New Order (Factory)
7	10	SONGS FROM THE BIG CHAIR	Tears For Fears (Mercury)
12	11	GO WEST/BANGS AND CRASHES	Go West (Chrysalis)
15	12	BE YOURSELF TONIGHT	Eurythmics (RCA)
13	13	BEST OF THE EAGLES	Eagles (Asylum)
14	14	SHAMROCK DIARIES	Chris Rea (Magnet)
10	15	HITS 2	Various Artists (CBS/WEA)
-	16	CUPID AND PSYCHE '85	Scritti Politti (Virgin)
19	17	THE SECRET OF ASSOCIATION	Paul Young (CBS)
17	18	FLAUNT THE IMPERFECTION	China Crisis (Virgin)
23	19	KATRINA AND THE WAVES	Katrina & the Waves (Capitol)
-	20	STEVE McQUEEN	Prefab Sprout (Kitchenware)
20	21	RECKLESS	Bryan Adams (A&M)
35	22	ROMANCE	David Cassidy (Arista)
26	23	THE POWER STATION	Power Station (Parlophone)
-	24	EMPIRE BURLESQUE	Bob Dylan (CBS)
37	25	THE RIVER	Bruce Springsteen (CBS)
24	26	THE AGE OF CONSENT	Bronski Beat (Forbidden Fruit)
18	27	YOUTHQUAKE	Dead Or Alive (Epic)
16	28	SHAKEN 'N' STIRRED	Robert Plant (Es Paranza)
-	29	BORN TO RUN	Bruce Springsteen (CBS)
-	30	WATCHING YOU WATCHING ME	Bill Withers (CBS)
25	31	WEST SIDE STORY	Leonard Bernstein & Studio Cast (Deutsche Grammophon)
34	32	SUDDENLY	Billy Ocean (Jive)
21	33	THE BEST OF ELVIS COSTELLO - THE MAN	Elvis Costello (Telstar)
28	34	AROUND THE WORLD IN A DAY	Prince & the Revolution (Warner Bros.)
43	35	CHINESE WALL	Philip Bailey (CBS)
22	36	MR BAD GUY	Freddie Mercury (CBS)
27	37	VOICES FROM THE HOLY LAND	BBC Welsh Chorus (BBC)
33	38	ALF	Alison Moyet (CBS)
-	39	AS THE BAND TURNS	Atlantic Starr (A&M)
-	40	THE CAT IS OUT	Judy Tzuke (Legacy)
-	41	LIKE A VIRGIN	Madonna (Sire)
-	42	YOU'RE UNDER ARREST	Miles Davis (CBS)
31	43	7800 DEGREES FAHRENHEIT	Bon Jovi (Vertigo)
32	44	BROTHER WHERE YOU BOUND	Supertramp (A&M)
36	45	ROCK ME TONIGHT	Freddie Jackson (Capitol)
-	46	DARKNESS ON THE EDGE OF TOWN	Bruce Springsteen (CBS)
42	47	THE UNFORGETTABLE FIRE	U2 (Island)
45	48	SO WHERE ARE YOU?	Loose Ends (Virgin)
30	49	DREAM INTO ACTION	Howard Jones (WEA)
-	50	RADIO M.U.S.I.C. MAN	Womack & Womack (Elektra)

29 June 1985

last week	this week	Title	Artist (Label)
2	1	BORN IN THE USA	Bruce Springsteen (CBS)
3	2	BROTHERS IN ARMS	Dire Straits (Vertigo)
1	3	BOYS AND GIRLS	Bryan Ferry (EG)
4	4	OUR FAVOURITE SHOP	Style Council (Polydor)
16	5	CUPID AND PSYCHE '85	Scritti Politti (Virgin)
-	6	MISPLACED CHILDHOOD	Marillion (EMI)
24	7	EMPIRE BURLESQUE	Bob Dylan (CBS)
5	8	OUT NOW!	Various Artists (Chrysalis/MCA)
10	9	SONGS FROM THE BIG CHAIR	Tears For Fears (Mercury)
8	10	BEST OF THE 20TH CENTURY BOY	Marc Bolan (K-Tel)
6	11	NO JACKET REQUIRED	Phil Collins (Virgin)
7	12	NOW DANCE	Various Artists (EMI/Virgin)
-	13	LITTLE CREATURES	Talking Heads (EMI)
20	14	STEVE McQUEEN	Prefab Sprout (Kitchenware)
-	15	THE DREAM OF THE BLUE TURTLES	Sting (A&M)
32	16	SUDDENLY	Billy Ocean (Jive)
18	17	FLAUNT THE IMPERFECTION	China Crisis (Virgin)
13	18	BEST OF THE EAGLES	Eagles (Asylum)
11	19	GO WEST/BANGS AND CRASHES	Go West (Chrysalis)
-	20	WHEN THE BOYS MEET THE GIRLS	Sister Sledge (Atlantic)
17	21	THE SECRET OF ASSOCIATION	Paul Young (CBS)
-	22	CRUSH	Orchestral Manoeuvres in the Dark (Virgin)
15	23	HITS 2	Various Artists (CBS/WEA)
14	24	SHAMROCK DIARIES	Chris Rea (Magnet)
12	25	BE YOURSELF TONIGHT	Eurythmics (RCA)
19	26	KATRINA AND THE WAVES	Katrina & the Waves (Capitol)
25	27	THE RIVER	Bruce Springsteen (CBS)
50	28	RADIO M.U.S.I.C. MAN	Womack & Womack (Elektra)
34	29	AROUND THE WORLD IN A DAY	Prince & the Revolution (Warner Bros.)
9	30	LOW-LIFE	New Order (Factory)
-	31	FABLES OF THE RECONSTRUCTION	REM (IRS)
-	32	WORLD WIDE LIVE	Scorpions (Harvest)
29	33	BORN TO RUN	Bruce Springsteen (CBS)
26	34	THE AGE OF CONSENT	Bronski Beat (Forbidden Fruit)
46	35	DARKNESS ON THE EDGE OF TOWN	Bruce Springsteen (CBS)
-	36	DREAM OF A LIFETIME	Marvin Gaye (CBS)
-	37	MAKE IT BIG	Wham! (CBS)
37	38	VOICES FROM THE HOLY LAND	BBC Welsh Chorus (BBC)
41	39	LIKE A VIRGIN	Madonna (Sire)
21	40	RECKLESS	Bryan Adams (A&M)
31	41	WEST SIDE STORY	Leonard Bernstein & Studio Cast (Deutsche Grammophon)
36	42	MR BAD GUY	Freddie Mercury (CBS)
35	43	CHINESE WALL	Philip Bailey (CBS)
33	44	THE BEST OF ELVIS COSTELLO - THE MAN	Elvis Costello (Telstar)
39	45	AS THE BAND TURNS	Atlantic Starr (A&M)
38	46	ALF	Alison Moyet (CBS)
48	47	SO WHERE ARE YOU?	Loose Ends (Virgin)
-	48	THE BEACH BOYS	Beach Boys (Caribou)
22	49	ROMANCE	David Cassidy (Arista)
23	50	THE POWER STATION	Power Station (Parlophone)

6 July 1985

last week	this week	Title	Artist (Label)
6	1	MISPLACED CHILDHOOD	Marillion (EMI)
1	2	BORN IN THE USA	Bruce Springsteen (CBS)
3	3	BOYS AND GIRLS	Bryan Ferry (EG)
2	4	BROTHERS IN ARMS	Dire Straits (Vertigo)
5	5	CUPID AND PSYCHE '85	Scritti Politti (Virgin)
15	6	THE DREAM OF THE BLUE TURTLES	Sting (A&M)
9	7	SONGS FROM THE BIG CHAIR	Tears For Fears (Mercury)
13	8	LITTLE CREATURES	Talking Heads (EMI)
4	9	OUR FAVOURITE SHOP	Style Council (Polydor)
22	10	CRUSH	Orchestral Manoeuvres in the Dark (Virgin)
32	11	WORLD WIDE LIVE	Scorpions (Harvest)
7	12	EMPIRE BURLESQUE	Bob Dylan (CBS)
10	13	BEST OF THE 20TH CENTURY BOY	Marc Bolan (K-Tel)
8	14	OUT NOW!	Various Artists (Chrysalis/MCA)
11	15	NO JACKET REQUIRED	Phil Collins (Virgin)
16	16	SUDDENLY	Billy Ocean (Jive)
12	17	NOW DANCE	Various Artists (EMI/Virgin)
31	18	FABLES OF THE RECONSTRUCTION	REM (IRS)
27	19	THE RIVER	Bruce Springsteen (CBS)
21	20	THE SECRET OF ASSOCIATION	Paul Young (CBS)
25	21	BE YOURSELF TONIGHT	Eurythmics (RCA)
20	22	WHEN THE BOYS MEET THE GIRLS	Sister Sledge (Atlantic)
-	23	ALL THROUGH THE NIGHT	Aled Jones (BBC)
14	24	STEVE McQUEEN	Prefab Sprout (Kitchenware)
33	25	BORN TO RUN	Bruce Springsteen (CBS)
18	26	BEST OF THE EAGLES	Eagles (Asylum)
35	27	DARKNESS ON THE EDGE OF TOWN	Bruce Springsteen (CBS)
26	28	KATRINA AND THE WAVES	Katrina & the Waves (Capitol)
19	29	GO WEST/BANGS AND CRASHES	Go West (Chrysalis)
38	30	VOICES FROM THE HOLY LAND	BBC Welsh Chorus (BBC)
39	31	LIKE A VIRGIN	Madonna (Sire)
23	32	HITS 2	Various Artists (CBS/WEA)
-	33	THE ANTHOLOGY	Deep Purple (Harvest)
45	34	AS THE BAND TURNS	Atlantic Starr (A&M)
-	35	LONE JUSTICE	Lone Justice (Geffen)
36	36	DREAM OF A LIFETIME	Marvin Gaye (CBS)
-	37	FLIP	Nils Lofgren (Towerbell)
24	38	SHAMROCK DIARIES	Chris Rea (Magnet)
-	39	HISTORY	Mai Tai (Virgin)
30	40	LOW-LIFE	New Order (Factory)
29	41	AROUND THE WORLD IN A DAY	Prince & the Revolution (Warner Bros.)
34	42	THE AGE OF CONSENT	Bronski Beat (Forbidden Fruit)
-	43	BEYOND THE SUNSET	Rain Parade (Island)
-	44	BEVERLY HILLS COP	Soundtrack (MCA)
28	45	RADIO M.U.S.I.C. MAN	Womack & Womack (Elektra)
40	46	RECKLESS	Bryan Adams (A&M)
47	47	SO WHERE ARE YOU?	Loose Ends (Virgin)
50	48	THE POWER STATION	Power Station (Parlophone)
-	49	DREAM INTO ACTION	Howard Jones (WEA)
43	50	CHINESE WALL	Philip Bailey (CBS)

The arrival of Bruce Springsteen's spectacular Born In The USA tour in Britain created a wave of interest which not only propelled the album of the same title back to Number 1, but also boosted sales on Springsteen's earlier albums *Born To Run*, *The River* and *Darkness On The Edge Of Town* sufficiently to pull all of them into the chart again too. Bryan Ferry and Marillion also snatched a Number 1 week apiece.

July 1985

The Dream Of The Blue Turtles was former Police vocalist Sting's first solo album, and like Freddie Mercury's a few months previously, it found success almost on the same level as the group's releases. *Fly On The Wall*, meanwhile, was Aussie hard rockers AC/DC's first album for two years, but its almost immediate Top 5 placing suggested no drop-off in the hard-touring band's record popularity.

3 August 1985

last week	this week	Title	Artist (Label)
1	1	BORN IN THE USA	Bruce Springsteen (CBS)
3	2	BE YOURSELF TONIGHT	Eurythmics (RCA)
2	3	BROTHERS IN ARMS	Dire Straits (Vertigo)
6	4	SONGS FROM THE BIG CHAIR	Tears For Fears (Mercury)
11	5	NO JACKET REQUIRED	Phil Collins (Virgin)
9	6	BILLY JOEL'S GREATEST HITS VOL 1 & VOL 2	Billy Joel (CBS)
16	7	LIKE A VIRGIN	Madonna (Sire)
22	8	PHANTASMAGORIA	Damned (MCA)
4	9	MISPLACED CHILDHOOD	Marillion (EMI)
-	10	THE UNFORGETTABLE FIRE	U2 (Island)
10	11	BOYS AND GIRLS	Bryan Ferry (EG)
7	12	THE DREAM OF THE BLUE TURTLES	Sting (A&M)
18	13	THE SECRET OF ASSOCIATION	Paul Young (CBS)
13	14	THE RIVER	Bruce Springsteen (CBS)
5	15	FLY ON THE WALL	AC/DC (Atlantic)
-	16	U2 LIVE: UNDER A BLOOD RED SKY	U2 (Island)
8	17	ALL THROUGH THE NIGHT	Aled Jones (BBC)
12	18	CUPID AND PSYCHE '85	Scritti Politti (Virgin)
26	19	THEATRE OF PAIN	Motley Crue (Elektra)
-	20	THE KENNY ROGERS STORY	Kenny Rogers (Liberty)
38	21	DIAMOND LIFE	Sade (CBS)
23	22	CONTACT	Pointer Sisters (Planet)
14	23	SUDDENLY	Billy Ocean (Jive)
15	24	WHEN THE BOYS MEET THE GIRLS	Sister Sledge (Atlantic)
19	25	LITTLE CREATURES	Talking Heads (EMI)
24	26	VOICES FROM THE HOLY LAND	BBC Welsh Chorus (BBC)
37	27	OUT NOW!	Various Artists (Chrysalis/MCA)
-	28	QUEEN'S GREATEST HITS	Queen (EMI)
40	29	MAKE IT BIG	Wham! (CBS)
31	30	NIGHT OF A THOUSAND CANDLES	Men They Couldn't Hang (Imp)
-	31	MR BAD GUY	Freddie Mercury (CBS)
20	32	OUR FAVOURITE SHOP	Style Council (Polydor)
21	33	BORN TO RUN	Bruce Springsteen (CBS)
17	34	A SECRET WISH	Propaganda (ZTT)
28	35	PRIVATE DANCER	Tina Turner (Capitol)
-	36	WAR	U2 (Island)
30	37	GO WEST/BANGS AND CRASHES	Go West (Chrysalis)
36	38	ALF	Alison Moyet (CBS)
34	39	STREET SOUNDS ELECTRO 8	Various Artists (Street Sounds)
-	40	BOY	U2 (Island)
-	41	BIG BAM BOOM	Daryll Hall & John Oates (RCA)
-	42	VITAL IDOL	Billy Idol (Chrysalis)
27	43	WORLD WIDE LIVE	Scorpions (Harvest)
-	44	FLIP	Nils Lofgren (Towerbell)
41	45	BEVERLY HILLS COP	Soundtrack (MCA)
44	46	THE ARTISTS VOL II	Various Artists (Street Sounds)
-	47	OPEN FIRE	Y & T (A&M)
-	48	THE WORKS	Queen (EMI)
39	49	HITS 2	Various Artists (CBS/WEA)
33	50	DARKNESS ON THE EDGE OF TOWN	Bruce Springsteen (CBS)

10 August 1985

last week	this week	Title	Artist (Label)
3	1	BROTHERS IN ARMS	Dire Straits (Vertigo)
1	2	BORN IN THE USA	Bruce Springsteen (CBS)
4	3	BE YOURSELF TONIGHT	Eurythmics (RCA)
4	4	SONGS FROM THE BIG CHAIR	Tears For Fears (Mercury)
7	5	LIKE A VIRGIN	Madonna (Sire)
5	6	NO JACKET REQUIRED	Phil Collins (Virgin)
6	7	BILLY JOEL'S GREATEST HITS VOL 1 & VOL 2	Billy Joel (CBS)
10	8	THE UNFORGETTABLE FIRE	U2 (Island)
20	9	THE KENNY ROGERS STORY	Kenny Rogers (Liberty)
13	10	THE SECRET OF ASSOCIATION	Paul Young (CBS)
8	11	PHANTASMAGORIA	Damned (MCA)
9	12	MISPLACED CHILDHOOD	Marillion (EMI)
12	13	THE DREAM OF THE BLUE TURTLES	Sting (A&M)
16	14	U2 LIVE: UNDER A BLOOD RED SKY	U2 (Island)
11	15	BOYS AND GIRLS	Bryan Ferry (EG)
35	16	PRIVATE DANCER	Tina Turner (Capitol)
-	17	MINX	Toyah (Portrait)
17	18	ALL THROUGH THE NIGHT	Aled Jones (BBC)
-	19	LUXURY OF LIFE	Five Star (Tent)
28	20	QUEEN'S GREATEST HITS	Queen (EMI)
18	21	CUPID AND PSYCHE '85	Scritti Politti (Virgin)
14	22	THE RIVER	Bruce Springsteen (CBS)
-	23	MADONNA	Madonna (Sire)
26	24	VOICES FROM THE HOLY LAND	BBC Welsh Chorus (BBC)
22	25	CONTACT	Pointer Sisters (Planet)
25	26	LITTLE CREATURES	Talking Heads (EMI)
34	27	A SECRET WISH	Propaganda (ZTT)
-	28	DRINKING GASOLINE	Cabaret Voltaire (Some Bizzare)
-	29	THE MAGIC OF TORVILL AND DEAN	Various Artists (Stylus)
37	30	GO WEST/BANGS AND CRASHES	Go West (Chrysalis)
30	31	NIGHT OF A THOUSAND CANDLES	Men They Couldn't Hang (Imp)
24	32	WHEN THE BOYS MEET THE GIRLS	Sister Sledge (Atlantic)
33	33	BORN TO RUN	Bruce Springsteen (CBS)
38	34	ALF	Alison Moyet (CBS)
15	35	FLY ON THE WALL	AC/DC (Atlantic)
-	36	PHILIP OAKEY AND GIORGIO MORODER	Philip Oakey & Giorgio Moroder (Virgin)
32	37	OUR FAVOURITE SHOP	Style Council (Polydor)
42	38	VITAL IDOL	Billy Idol (Chrysalis)
-	39	INVASION OF YOUR PRIVACY	Ratt (Island)
-	40	LONE JUSTICE	Lone Justice (Geffen)
36	41	WAR	U2 (Island)
-	42	THE ALLNIGHTER	Glen Frey (MCA)
27	43	OUT NOW!	Various Artists (Chrysalis/MCA)
-	44	CRUSH	Orchestral Manoeuvres in the Dark (Virgin)
-	45	WIDE AWAKE IN AMERICA	U2 (Island)
21	46	DIAMOND LIFE	Sade (CBS)
23	47	SUDDENLY	Billy Ocean (Jive)
19	48	THEATRE OF PAIN	Motley Crue (Elektra)
31	49	MR BAD GUY	Freddie Mercury (CBS)
43	50	WORLD WIDE LIVE	Scorpions (Harvest)

17 August 1985

last week	this week	Title	Artist (Label)
1	1	BROTHERS IN ARMS	Dire Straits (Vertigo)
2	2	BORN IN THE USA	Bruce Springsteen (CBS)
5	3	LIKE A VIRGIN	Madonna (Sire)
3	4	BE YOURSELF TONIGHT	Eurythmics (RCA)
4	5	SONGS FROM THE BIG CHAIR	Tears For Fears (Mercury)
6	6	NO JACKET REQUIRED	Phil Collins (Virgin)
-	7	NOW THAT'S WHAT I CALL MUSIC 5	Various Artists (EMI/Virgin)
8	8	THE UNFORGETTABLE FIRE	U2 (Island)
7	9	BILLY JOEL'S GREATEST HITS VOL 1 & VOL 2	Billy Joel (CBS)
9	10	THE KENNY ROGERS STORY	Kenny Rogers (Liberty)
13	11	THE DREAM OF THE BLUE TURTLES	Sting (A&M)
10	12	THE SECRET OF ASSOCIATION	Paul Young (CBS)
-	13	RUM, SODOMY AND THE LASH	Pogues (Stiff)
23	14	MADONNA	Madonna (Sire)
12	15	MISPLACED CHILDHOOD	Marillion (EMI)
15	16	BOYS AND GIRLS	Bryan Ferry (EG)
20	17	QUEEN'S GREATEST HITS	Queen (EMI)
19	18	LUXURY OF LIFE	Five Star (Tent)
16	19	PRIVATE DANCER	Tina Turner (Capitol)
11	20	PHANTASMAGORIA	Damned (MCA)
14	21	U2 LIVE: UNDER A BLOOD RED SKY	U2 (Island)
21	22	CUPID AND PSYCHE '85	Scritti Politti (Virgin)
37	23	OUR FAVOURITE SHOP	Style Council (Polydor)
18	24	ALL THROUGH THE NIGHT	Aled Jones (BBC)
38	25	VITAL IDOL	Billy Idol (Chrysalis)
45	26	WIDE AWAKE IN AMERICA	U2 (Island)
-	27	FLASH	Jeff Beck (Epic)
31	28	NIGHT OF A THOUSAND CANDLES	Men They Couldn't Hang (Imp)
30	29	GO WEST/BANGS AND CRASHES	Go West (Chrysalis)
36	30	PHILIP OAKEY AND GIORGIO MORODER	Philip Oakey & Giorgio Moroder (Virgin)
-	31	RECKLESS	Bryan Adams (A&M)
39	32	INVASION OF YOUR PRIVACY	Ratt (Island)
28	33	DRINKING GASOLINE	Cabaret Voltaire (Some Bizzare)
43	34	OUT NOW!	Various Artists (Chrysalis/MCA)
17	35	MINX	Toyah (Portrait)
46	36	DIAMOND LIFE	Sade (CBS)
-	37	HEARTBEAT CITY	Cars (Elektra)
41	38	WAR	U2 (Island)
25	39	CONTACT	Pointer Sisters (Planet)
27	40	A SECRET WISH	Propaganda (ZTT)
33	41	BORN TO RUN	Bruce Springsteen (CBS)
29	42	THE MAGIC OF TORVILL AND DEAN	Various Artists (Stylus)
32	43	WHEN THE BOYS MEET THE GIRLS	Sister Sledge (Atlantic)
47	44	SUDDENLY	Billy Ocean (Jive)
24	45	VOICES FROM THE HOLY LAND	BBC Welsh Chorus (BBC)
-	46	STREET SOUNDS EDITION 13	Various Artists (Street Sounds)
22	47	THE RIVER	Bruce Springsteen (CBS)
35	48	FLY ON THE WALL	AC/DC (Atlantic)
42	49	THE ALLNIGHTER	Glen Frey (MCA)
-	50	AROUND THE WORLD IN A DAY	Prince & the Revolution (Warner Bros.)

As Springsteen fever died somewhat and his back-catalogue began to slip out of the chart, that for Dire Straits reasserted itself, and *Brothers In Arms* returned to Number 1 in place of *Born In The USA*. The new Straits sales spurt was at least party generated by the simultaneous Top 5 success of the wry *Money For Nothing*, the most successful of the several singles to be extracted from *Brothers In Arms*.

August – September 1985

Eight months after *Now That's What I Call Music 4* had just failed to top the chart because CBS/WEA's first *Hits* volume pipped it at the post, *Now 5* soared to Number 1 with no such opposition from another mega-hit compilation. Apart from Dire Straits, its biggest challenger was Madonna, whose nine-month-old *Like A Virgin* album was now selling like crazy following her chart-topping *Into The Groove* single.

14 September 1985

last week	this week	Title	Artist (Label)
2	1	BROTHERS IN ARMS	Dire Straits (Vertigo)
3	2	LIKE A VIRGIN	Madonna (Sire)
1	3	NOW THAT'S WHAT I CALL MUSIC 5	Various Artists (EMI/Virgin)
22	4	WORLD SERVICE	Spear Of Destiny (Epic)
12	5	SACRED HEART	Dio (Vertigo)
4	6	BORN IN THE USA	Bruce Springsteen (CBS)
21	7	THE HEAD ON THE DOOR	Cure (Fiction)
5	8	NO JACKET REQUIRED	Phil Collins (Virgin)
8	9	SONGS FROM THE BIG CHAIR	Tears For Fears (Mercury)
6	10	MADONNA	Madonna (Sire)
9	11	THE UNFORGETTABLE FIRE	U2 (Island)
11	12	PRIVATE DANCER	Tina Turner (Capitol)
7	13	BE YOURSELF TONIGHT	Eurythmics (RCA)
13	14	WIDE AWAKE IN AMERICA	U2 (Island)
20	15	BOYS AND GIRLS	Bryan Ferry (EG)
17	16	THE KENNY ROGERS STORY	Kenny Rogers (Liberty)
14	17	VITAL IDOL	Billy Idol (Chrysalis)
24	18	COSI FAN TUTTI FRUTTI	Squeeze (A&M)
10	19	RUM, SODOMY AND THE LASH	Pogues (Stiff)
-	20	BAGGARADDIM	UB40 (Dep International)
-	21	RUN FOR COVER	Gary Moore (10/Virgin)
50	22	RECKLESS	Bryan Adams (A&M)
16	23	THE DREAM OF THE BLUE TURTLES	Sting (A&M)
23	24	QUEEN'S GREATEST HITS	Queen (EMI)
19	25	U2 LIVE: UNDER A BLOOD RED SKY	U2 (Island)
15	26	GO WEST/BANGS AND CRASHES	Go (Chrysalis)
26	27	HEARTBEAT CITY	Cars (Elektra)
29	28	MISPLACED CHILDHOOD	Marillion (EMI)
18	29	NIGHT BEAT	Various Artists (Styles)
-	30	VIVE LE ROCK	Adam Ant (CBS)
-	31	OLD WAYS	Neil Young (Geffen)
25	32	SHANGRI-LA	Animal Nightlife (Island)
49	33	ELIMINATOR	ZZ Top (Warner Bros.)
30	34	BILLY JOEL'S GREATEST HITS VOL 1 & VOL 2	Billy Joel (CBS)
27	35	LUXURY OF LIFE	Five Star (Tent)
31	36	THE SECRET OF ASSOCIATION	Paul Young (CBS)
35	37	SINGLE LIFE	Cameo (Club)
33	38	FACE VALUE	Phil Collins (Virgin)
32	39	DISCO BEACH PARTY	Various Artists (Stylus)
40	40	ALL THROUGH THE NIGHT	Aled Jones (BBC)
-	41	LOVE OVER GOLD	Dire Straits (Vertigo)
42	42	MAKE IT BIG	Wham! (CBS)
47	43	SREET CALLED DESIRE	Renee & Angela (Club)
36	44	CUPID AND PSYCHE '85	Scritti Politti (Virgin)
38	45	SUDDENLY	Billy Ocean (Jive)
-	46	INNOCENCE IS NO EXCUSE	Saxon (Parlophone)
-	47	ALCHEMY - DIRE STRAITS LIVE	Dire Straits (Vertigo)
46	48	CONTACT	Pointer Sisters (Planet)
44	49	FLAUNT THE IMPERFECTION	China Crisis (Virgin)
-	50	ALF	Alison Moyet (CBS)

21 September 1985

last week	this week	Title	Artist (Label)
3	1	NOW THAT'S WHAT I CALL MUSIC 5	Various Artists (EMI/Virgin)
2	2	LIKE A VIRGIN	Madonna (Sire)
7	3	THE HEAD ON THE DOOR	Cure (Fiction)
1	4	BROTHERS IN ARMS	Dire Straits (Vertigo)
5	5	SACRED HEART	Dio (Vertigo)
21	6	RUN FOR COVER	Gary Moore (10/Virgin)
9	7	SONGS FROM THE BIG CHAIR	Tears For Fears (Mercury)
8	8	NO JACKET REQUIRED	Phil Collins (Virgin)
6	9	BORN IN THE USA	Bruce Springsteen (CBS)
16	10	THE KENNY ROGERS STORY	Kenny Rogers (Liberty)
20	11	BAGGARADDIM	UB40 (Dep International)
15	12	BOYS AND GIRLS	Bryan Ferry (EG)
4	13	WORLD SERVICE	Spear Of Destiny (Epic)
28	14	MISPLACED CHILDHOOD	Marillion (EMI)
10	15	MADONNA	Madonna (Sire)
46	16	INNOCENCE IS NO EXCUSE	Saxon (Parlophone)
12	17	PRIVATE DANCER	Tina Turner (Capitol)
31	18	OLD WAYS	Neil Young (Geffen)
27	19	HEARTBEAT CITY	Cars (Elektra)
17	20	VITAL IDOL	Billy Idol (Chrysalis)
11	21	THE UNFORGETTABLE FIRE	U2 (Island)
13	22	BE YOURSELF TONIGHT	Eurythmics (RCA)
25	23	U2 LIVE: UNDER A BLOOD RED SKY	U2 (Island)
-	24	DON'T STAND DOWN	Dexys Midnight Runners (Mercury)
19	25	RUM, SODOMY AND THE LASH	Pogues (Stiff)
18	26	COSI FAN TUTTI FRUTTI	Squeeze (A&M)
30	27	VIVE LE ROCK	Adam Ant (CBS)
-	28	OPEN TOP CARS AND GIRLS IN T-SHIRTS	Various Artists (Telstar)
14	29	WIDE AWAKE IN AMERICA	U2 (Island)
23	30	THE DREAM OF THE BLUE TURTLES	Sting (A&M)
26	31	GO WEST/BANGS AND CRASHES	Go West (Chrysalis)
24	32	QUEEN'S GREATEST HITS	Queen (EMI)
22	33	RECKLESS	Bryan Adams (A&M)
-	34	STREET SOUNDS EDITION 13	Various Artists (Street Sounds)
-	35	SPORTS	Huey Lewis & the News (Chrysalis)
-	36	HUNDREDS AND THOUSANDS	Bronski Beat (Forbidden Fruit)
29	37	NIGHT BEAT	Various Artists (Styles)
-	38	HEAVEN KNOWS	Jaki Graham (EMI)
34	39	BILLY JOEL'S GREATEST HITS VOL 1 & VOL 2	Billy Joel (CBS)
-	40	ALEXANDER O'NEAL	Alexander O'Neal (Tabu/Epic)
35	41	LUXURY OF LIFE	Five Star (Tent)
37	42	SINGLE LIFE	Cameo (Club)
39	43	DISCO BEACH PARTY	Various Artists (Stylus)
-	44	THE RIVER	Bruce Springsteen (CBS)
-	45	HOLD ME	Laura Branigan (Atlantic)
43	46	SREET CALLED DESIRE	Renee & Angela (Club)
32	47	SHANGRI-LA	Animal Nightlife (Island)
36	48	THE SECRET OF ASSOCIATION	Paul Young (CBS)
48	49	CONTACT	Pointer Sisters (Planet)
50	50	ALF	Alison Moyet (CBS)

28 September 1985

last week	this week	Title	Artist (Label)
2	1	LIKE A VIRGIN	Madonna (Sire)
4	2	BROTHERS IN ARMS	Dire Straits (Vertigo)
1	3	NOW THAT'S WHAT I CALL MUSIC 5	Various Artists (EMI/Virgin)
-	4	HOUNDS OF LOVE	Kate Bush (EMI)
10	5	THE KENNY ROGERS STORY	Kenny Rogers (Liberty)
-	6	IN SQUARE CIRCLE	Stevie Wonder (Tamla Motown)
8	7	NO JACKET REQUIRED	Phil Collins (Virgin)
3	8	THE HEAD ON THE DOOR	Cure (Fiction)
14	9	MISPLACED CHILDHOOD	Marillion (EMI)
24	10	DON'T STAND DOWN	Dexys Midnight Runners (Mercury)
6	11	RUN FOR COVER	Gary Moore (10/Virgin)
11	12	BAGGARADDIM	UB40 (Dep International)
15	13	MADONNA	Madonna (Sire)
7	14	SONGS FROM THE BIG CHAIR	Tears For Fears (Mercury)
12	15	BOYS AND GIRLS	Bryan Ferry (EG)
9	16	BORN IN THE USA	Bruce Springsteen (CBS)
-	17	HERE'S TO FUTURE DAYS	Thompson Twins (Arista)
23	18	U2 LIVE: UNDER A BLOOD RED SKY	U2 (Island)
30	19	THE DREAM OF THE BLUE TURTLES	Sting (A&M)
20	20	VITAL IDOL	Billy Idol (Chrysalis)
36	21	HUNDREDS AND THOUSANDS	Bronski Beat (Forbidden Fruit)
5	22	SACRED HEART	Dio (Vertigo)
21	23	THE UNFORGETTABLE FIRE	U2 (Island)
25	24	RUM, SODOMY AND THE LASH	Progues (Stiff)
35	25	SPORTS	Huey Lewis & the News (Chrysalis)
28	26	OPEN TOP CARS AND GIRLS IN T-SHIRTS	Various Artists (Telstar)
26	27	COSI FAN TUTTI FRUTTI	Squeeze (A&M)
-	28	THIS IS THE SEA	Waterboys (Ensign)
13	29	WORLD SERVICE	Spear Of Destiny (Epic)
22	30	BE YOURSELF TONIGHT	Eurythmics (RCA)
18	31	OLD WAYS	Neil Young (Geffen)
-	32	LIVE AT THE APOLLO	Daryll Hall & John Oates (RCA)
33	33	RECKLESS	Bryan Adams (A&M)
32	34	QUEEN'S GREATEST HITS	Queen (EMI)
37	35	NIGHT BEAT	Various Artists (Styles)
19	36	HEARTBEAT CITY	Cars (Elektra)
16	37	INNOCENCE IS NO EXCUSE	Saxon (Parlophone)
38	38	HEAVEN KNOWS	Jaki Graham (EMI)
39	39	BILLY JOEL'S GREATEST HITS VOL 1 & VOL 2	Billy Joel (CBS)
29	40	WIDE AWAKE IN AMERICA	U2 (Island)
48	41	THE SECRET OF ASSOCIATION	Paul Young (CBS)
40	42	ALEXANDER O'NEAL	Alexander O'Neal (Tabu/Epic)
-	43	SO MANY RIVERS	Bobby Womack (MCA)
-	44	SUDDENLY	Billy Ocean (Jive)
-	45	FOUR STAR COUNTRY	Various Artists (K-Tel)
-	46	THE VERSATILE BOBBY DARIN	Bobby Darin (Capitol)
42	47	SINGLE LIFE	Cameo (Club)
-	48	WAITING FOR THE FLOODS	Armoury Show (Parlophone)
-	49	LEAVE THE BEST TO LAST	James Last (Polydor)
17	50	PRIVATE DANCER	Tina Turner (Capitol)

Like A Virgin eventually topped the UK chart for Madonna the best part of a year after its release, as the peroxide singer's star rating grew by leaps and bounds - at the end of August, she had been the first female singer (and only one of a handful of acts altogether) to have held Numbers 1 and 2 on the singles chart simultaneously, with *Into The Groove* and *Holiday*. Her first LP was also still in the Top 10.

October 1985

5 October 1985

last week	this week	title	artist
4	1	HOUNDS OF LOVE	Kate Bush (EMI)
1	2	LIKE A VIRGIN	Madonna (Sire)
6	3	IN SQUARE CIRCLE	Stevie Wonder (Tamla Motown)
2	4	BROTHERS IN ARMS	Dire Straits (Vertigo)
3	5	NOW THAT'S WHAT I CALL MUSIC 5	Various Artists (EMI/Virgin)
17	6	HERE'S TO FUTURE DAYS	Thompson Twins (Arista)
9	7	MISPLACED CHILDHOOD	Marillion (EMI)
7	8	NO JACKET REQUIRED	Phil Collins (Virgin)
20	9	VITAL IDOL	Billy Idol (Chrysalis)
5	10	THE KENNY ROGERS STORY	Kenny Rogers (Liberty)
8	11	THE HEAD ON THE DOOR	Cure (Fiction)
15	12	BOYS AND GIRLS	Bryan Ferry (EG)
12	13	BAGGARADDIM	UB40 (Dep International)
32	14	LIVE AT THE APOLLO	Daryll Hall & John Oates (RCA)
-	15	THE FURY	Gary Numan (Numa)
13	16	MADONNA	Madonna (Sire)
43	17	SO MANY RIVERS	Bobby Womack (MCA)
14	18	SONGS FROM THE BIG CHAIR	Tears For Fears (Mercury)
10	19	DON'T STAND DOWN	Dexys Midnight Runners (Mercury)
11	20	RUN FOR COVER	Gary Moore (10/Virgin)
-	21	STORIES OF JOHNNY	Marc Almond (Some Bizzare)
26	22	OPEN TOP CARS AND GIRLS IN T-SHIRTS	Various Artists (Telstar)
-	23	EATEN ALIVE	Diana Ross (Capitol)
50	24	PRIVATE DANCER	Tina Turner (Capitol)
28	25	THIS IS THE SEA	Waterboys (Ensign)
16	26	BORN IN THE USA	Bruce Springsteen (CBS)
-	27	ASYLUM	Kiss (Vertigo)
24	28	RUM, SODOMY AND THE LASH	Pogues (Stiff)
18	29	U2 LIVE: UNDER A BLOOD RED SKY	U2 (Island)
34	30	QUEEN'S GREATEST HITS	Queen (EMI)
23	31	THE UNFORGETTABLE FIRE	U2 (Island)
39	32	BILLY JOEL'S GREATEST HITS VOL 1 & VOL 2	Billy Joel (CBS)
22	33	SACRED HEART	Dio (Vertigo)
21	34	HUNDREDS AND THOUSANDS	Bronski Beat (Forbidden Fruit)
19	35	THE DREAM OF THE BLUE TURTLES	Sting (A&M)
25	36	SPORTS	Huey Lewis & the News (Chrysalis)
-	37	STREET SOUNDS ELECTRO 9	Various Artists (Street Sounds)
47	38	SINGLE LIFE	Cameo (Club)
30	39	BE YOURSELF TONIGHT	Eurythmics (RCA)
35	40	NIGHT BEAT	Various Artists (Styles)
29	41	WORLD SERVICE	Spear Of Destiny (Epic)
38	42	HEAVEN KNOWS	Jaki Graham (EMI)
36	43	HEARTBEAT CITY	Cars (Elektra)
42	44	ALEXANDER O'NEAL	Alexander O'Neal (Tabu/Epic)
-	45	THE TV HITS ALBUM	Various Artists (Towerbell)
-	46	REBEL YELL	Billy Idol (Chrysalis)
27	47	COSI FAN TUTTI FRUTTI	Squeeze (A&M)
33	48	RECKLESS	Bryan Adams (A&M)
31	49	OLD WAYS	Neil Young (Geffen)
-	50	REGGAE HITS VOL 2	Various Artists (Jetstar)

12 October 1985

last week	this week	title	artist
1	1	HOUNDS OF LOVE	Kate Bush (EMI)
2	2	LIKE A VIRGIN	Madonna (Sire)
4	3	BROTHERS IN ARMS	Dire Straits (Vertigo)
9	4	VITAL IDOL	Billy Idol (Chrysalis)
6	5	HERE'S TO FUTURE DAYS	Thompson Twins (Arista)
7	6	MISPLACED CHILDHOOD	Marillion (EMI)
3	7	IN SQUARE CIRCLE	Stevie Wonder (Tamla Motown)
5	8	NOW THAT'S WHAT I CALL MUSIC 5	Various Artists (EMI/Virgin)
10	9	THE KENNY ROGERS STORY	Kenny Rogers (Liberty)
27	10	ASYLUM	Kiss (Vertigo)
8	11	NO JACKET REQUIRED	Phil Collins (Virgin)
16	12	MADONNA	Madonna (Sire)
37	13	STREET SOUNDS ELECTRO 9	Various Artists (Street Sounds)
11	14	THE HEAD ON THE DOOR	Cure (Fiction)
36	15	SPORTS	Huey Lewis & the News (Chrysalis)
29	16	U2 LIVE: UNDER A BLOOD RED SKY	U2 (Island)
21	17	STORIES OF JOHNNY	Marc Almond (Some Bizzare)
12	18	BOYS AND GIRLS	Bryan Ferry (EG)
26	19	BORN IN THE USA	Bruce Springsteen (CBS)
24	20	PRIVATE DANCER	Tina Turner (Capitol)
-	21	MAD NOT MAD	Madness (Zarjazz)
17	22	SO MANY RIVERS	Bobby Womack (MCA)
14	23	LIVE AT THE APOLLO	Daryll Hall & John Oates (RCA)
34	24	HUNDREDS AND THOUSANDS	Bronski Beat (Forbidden Fruit)
18	25	SONGS FROM THE BIG CHAIR	Tears For Fears (Mercury)
13	26	BAGGARADDIM	UB40 (Dep International)
-	27	EXPRESSIONS	Various Artists (K-Tel)
22	28	OPEN TOP CARS AND GIRLS IN T-SHIRTS	Various Artists (Telstar)
31	29	THE UNFORGETTABLE FIRE	U2 (Island)
28	30	RUM, SODOMY AND THE LASH	Pogues (Stiff)
48	31	RECKLESS	Bryan Adams (A&M)
35	32	THE DREAM OF THE BLUE TURTLES	Sting (A&M)
-	33	LUXURY OF LIFE	Five Star (Tent)
25	34	THIS IS THE SEA	Waterboys (Ensign)
38	35	SINGLE LIFE	Cameo (Club)
30	36	QUEEN'S GREATEST HITS	Queen (EMI)
-	37	RATTLESNAKES	Lloyd Cole and the Commotions (Polydor)
20	38	RUN FOR COVER	Gary Moore (10/Virgin)
-	39	THIS NATION'S SAVING GRACE	Fall (Beggars Banquet)
23	40	EATEN ALIVE	Diana Ross (Capitol)
19	41	DON'T STAND DOWN	Dexys Midnight Runners (Mercury)
39	42	BE YOURSELF TONIGHT	Eurythmics (RCA)
32	43	BILLY JOEL'S GREATEST HITS VOL 1 & VOL 2	Billy Joel (CBS)
15	44	THE FURY	Gary Numan (Numa)
-	45	GO WEST/BANGS AND CRASHES	Go West (Chrysalis)
-	46	LEAVE THE BEST TO LAST	James Last (Polydor)
42	47	HEAVEN KNOWS	Jaki Graham (EMI)
47	48	COSI FAN TUTTI FRUTTI	Squeeze (A&M)
43	49	HEARTBEAT CITY	Cars (Elektra)
45	50	THE TV HITS ALBUM	Various Artists (Towerbell)

19 October 1985

last week	this week	title	artist
1	1	HOUNDS OF LOVE	Kate Bush (EMI)
3	2	BROTHERS IN ARMS	Dire Straits (Vertigo)
2	3	LIKE A VIRGIN	Madonna (Sire)
4	4	VITAL IDOL	Billy Idol (Chrysalis)
6	5	MISPLACED CHILDHOOD	Marillion (EMI)
7	6	IN SQUARE CIRCLE	Stevie Wonder (Tamla Motown)
8	7	NOW THAT'S WHAT I CALL MUSIC 5	Various Artists (EMI/Virgin)
14	8	THE HEAD ON THE DOOR	Cure (Fiction)
21	9	MAD NOT MAD	Madness (Zarjazz)
15	10	SPORTS	Huey Lewis & the News (Chrysalis)
12	11	MADONNA	Madonna (Sire)
-	12	THE GIFT	Midge Ure (Chrysalis)
5	13	HERE'S TO FUTURE DAYS	Thompson Twins (Arista)
9	14	THE KENNY ROGERS STORY	Kenny Rogers (Liberty)
18	15	BOYS AND GIRLS	Bryan Ferry (EG)
11	16	NO JACKET REQUIRED	Phil Collins (Virgin)
20	17	PRIVATE DANCER	Tina Turner (Capitol)
27	18	EXPRESSIONS	Various Artists (K-Tel)
16	19	U2 LIVE: UNDER A BLOOD RED SKY	U2 (Island)
10	20	ASYLUM	Kiss (Vertigo)
17	21	STORIES OF JOHNNY	Marc Almond (Some Bizzare)
19	22	BORN IN THE USA	Bruce Springsteen (CBS)
-	23	RAIN DOGS	Tom Waits (Island)
13	24	STREET SOUNDS ELECTRO 9	Various Artists (Street Sounds)
22	25	SO MANY RIVERS	Bobby Womack (MCA)
25	26	SONGS FROM THE BIG CHAIR	Tears For Fears (Mercury)
26	27	BAGGARADDIM	UB40 (Dep International)
33	28	LUXURY OF LIFE	Five Star (Tent)
-	29	FALSE ACCUSATIONS	Robert Cray (Demon)
-	30	THE DREAM ACADEMY	Dream Academy (Blanco y Negro)
-	31	DIAMOND LIFE	Sade (CBS)
32	32	THE DREAM OF THE BLUE TURTLES	Sting (A&M)
29	33	THE UNFORGETTABLE FIRE	U2 (Island)
39	34	THIS NATION'S SAVING GRACE	Fall (Beggars Banquet)
50	35	THE TV HITS ALBUM	Various Artists (Towerbell)
-	36	ONE POUND NINETY NINE	Various Artists (Beggars Banquet)
34	37	THIS IS THE SEA	Waterboys (Ensign)
-	38	LIBRA	Julio Iglesias (CBS)
-	39	THE LOVE SONGS	George Benson (K-Tel)
38	40	RUN FOR COVER	Gary Moore (10/Virgin)
-	41	ZANG TUMB TUUM SAMPLED	Various Artists (ZTT)
-	42	ROCK ME TONIGHT	Freddy Jackson (Capitol)
23	43	LIVE AT THE APOLLO	Daryll Hall & John Oates (RCA)
35	44	SINGLE LIFE	Cameo (Club)
-	45	REGGAE HITS VOL 2	Various Artists (Jetstar)
46	46	LEAVE THE BEST TO LAST	James Last (Polydor)
-	47	WIDE AWAKE IN AMERICA	U2 (Island)
30	48	RUM, SODOMY AND THE LASH	Pogues (Stiff)
44	49	THE FURY	Gary Numan (Numa)
31	50	RECKLESS	Bryan Adams (A&M)

Despite being her first release since *The Dreaming*, three years earlier, Kate Bush's *Hounds Of Love* easily swept aside the competition to give her another Number 1 album - which it remained for four consecutive weeks. Meanwhile, Ultravox lead vocalist Midge Ure emulated Sting's and Freddie Mercury's recent successes by charting a solo album, *The Gift*, alongside his chart-topping single *If I Was*.

26 October 1985

last week	this week	Title	Artist
1	1	HOUNDS OF LOVE	Kate Bush (EMI)
2	2	BROTHERS IN ARMS	Dire Straits (Vertigo)
3	3	LIKE A VIRGIN	Madonna (Sire)
12	4	THE GIFT	Midge Ure (Chrysalis)
-	5	LIVE AFTER DEATH	Iron Maiden (EMI)
5	6	MISPLACED CHILDHOOD	Marillion (EMI)
-	7	LOVE	Cult (Beggars Banquet)
6	8	IN SQUARE CIRCLE	Stevie Wonder (Tamla Motown)
8	9	THE HEAD ON THE DOOR	Cure (Fiction)
39	10	THE LOVE SONGS	George Benson (K-Tel)
-	11	OUT NOW! 2	Various Artists (Chrysalis)
9	12	MAD NOT MAD	Madness (Zarjazz)
23	13	RAIN DOGS	Tom Waits (Island)
7	14	NOW THAT'S WHAT I CALL MUSIC 5	Various Artists (EMI/Virgin)
13	15	HERE'S TO FUTURE DAYS	Thompson Twins (Arista)
18	16	EXPRESSIONS	Various Artists (K-Tel)
15	17	BOYS AND GIRLS	Bryan Ferry (EG)
16	18	NO JACKET REQUIRED	Phil Collins (Virgin)
19	19	U2 LIVE: UNDER A BLOOD RED SKY	U2 (Island)
14	20	THE KENNY ROGERS STORY	Kenny Rogers (Liberty)
26	21	SONGS FROM THE BIG CHAIR	Tears For Fears (Mercury)
-	22	WORLD MACHINE	Level 42 (Polydor)
32	23	THE DREAM OF THE BLUE TURTLES	Sting (A&M)
11	24	MADONNA	Madonna (Sire)
4	25	VITAL IDOL	Billy Idol (Chrysalis)
31	26	DIAMOND LIFE	Sade (CBS)
10	27	SPORTS	Huey Lewis & the News (Chrysalis)
27	28	BAGGARADDIM	UB40 (Dep International)
22	29	BORN IN THE USA	Bruce Springsteen (CBS)
24	30	STREET SOUNDS ELECTRO 9	Various Artists (Street Sounds)
-	31	THE SINGLES '81-'85	Depeche Mode (Mute)
-	32	STRENGTH	Alarm (IRS)
-	33	PICTURE BOOK	Simply Red (Elektra)
-	34	BELIEVE YOU	Blancmange (London)
-	35	BILLY JOEL'S GREATEST HITS VOL 1 & VOL 2	Billy Joel (CBS)
17	37	PRIVATE DANCER	Tina Turner (Capitol)
-	38	PEACE AND TRANQUILITY	Phil Coulter (Harmac)
-	39	REELIN' IN THE YEARS	Steely Dan (MCA)
25	40	SO MANY RIVERS	Bobby Womack (MCA)
-	41	FLIP YOUR WIG	Husker Du (SST)
-	42	MACALLA	Clannad (RCA)
45	43	REGGAE HITS VOL 2	Various Artists (Jetstar)
48	44	RUM, SODOMY AND THE LASH	Pogues (Stiff)
28	45	LUXURY OF LIFE	Five Star (Tent)
44	46	SINGLE LIFE	Cameo (Club)
-	47	HOW TO BE A ZILLIONAIRE	ABC (Neutron)
21	48	STORIES OF JOHNNY	Marc Almond (Some Bizzare)
50	49	RECKLESS	Bryan Adams (A&M)
20	50	ASYLUM	Kiss (Vertigo)

2 November 1985

last week	this week	Title	Artist
5	1	LIVE AFTER DEATH	Iron Maiden (EMI)
1	2	HOUNDS OF LOVE	Kate Bush (EMI)
7	3	LOVE	Cult (Beggars Banquet)
10	4	THE LOVE SONGS	George Benson (K-Tel)
11	5	OUT NOW! 2	Various Artists (Chrysalis)
4	6	THE GIFT	Midge Ure (Chrysalis)
3	7	LIKE A VIRGIN	Madonna (Sire)
31	8	THE SINGLES '81-'85	Depeche Mode (Mute)
-	9	ONCE UPON A TIME	Simple Minds (Virgin)
25	10	VITAL IDOL	Billy Idol (Chrysalis)
2	11	BROTHERS IN ARMS	Dire Straits (Vertigo)
22	12	WORLD MACHINE	Level 42 (Polydor)
13	13	RAIN DOGS	Tom Waits (Island)
-	14	MUSIC FROM MIAMI VICE	Various Artists (BBC)
-	15	WEST SIDE STORY	Leonard Bernstein & Studio Cast (Deutsche Grammophon)
32	16	STRENGTH	Alarm (IRS)
6	17	MISPLACED CHILDHOOD	Marillion (EMI)
8	18	IN SQUARE CIRCLE	Stevie Wonder (Tamla Motown)
14	19	NOW THAT'S WHAT I CALL MUSIC 5	Various Artists (EMI/Virgin)
45	20	LUXURY OF LIFE	Five Star (Tent)
16	21	EXPRESSIONS	Various Artists (K-Tel)
9	22	THE HEAD ON THE DOOR	Cure (Fiction)
33	23	PICTURE BOOK	Simply Red (Elektra)
35	24	BILLY JOEL'S GREATEST HITS VOL 1 & VOL 2	Billy Joel (CBS)
47	25	HOW TO BE A ZILLIONAIRE	ABC (Neutron)
17	26	BOYS AND GIRLS	Bryan Ferry (EG)
20	27	THE KENNY ROGERS STORY	Kenny Rogers (Liberty)
12	28	MAD NOT MAD	Madness (Zarjazz)
23	29	THE DREAM OF THE BLUE TURTLES	Sting (A&M)
15	30	HERE'S TO FUTURE DAYS	Thompson Twins (Arista)
24	31	MADONNA	Madonna (Sire)
39	32	REELIN' IN THE YEARS	Steely Dan (MCA)
-	33	STREET SOUNDS EDITION 13	Various Artists (Street Sounds)
-	34	HEART	Heart (Capitol)
18	35	NO JACKET REQUIRED	Phil Collins (Virgin)
19	36	U2 LIVE: UNDER A BLOOD RED SKY	U2 (Island)
40	37	SO MANY RIVERS	Bobby Womack (MCA)
30	38	STREET SOUNDS ELECTRO 9	Various Artists (Street Sounds)
21	39	SONGS FROM THE BIG CHAIR	Tears For Fears (Mercury)
46	40	SINGLE LIFE	Cameo (Club)
38	41	PEACE AND TRANQUILITY	Phil Coulter (Harmac)
29	42	BORN IN THE USA	Bruce Springsteen (CBS)
42	43	MACALLA	Clannad (RCA)
41	44	FLIP YOUR WIG	Husker Du (SST)
-	45	THIS IS THE SEA	Waterboys (Ensign)
-	46	LITTLE CREATURES	Talking Heads (EMI)
-	47	BLUE SKIES	Kiri Te Kanawa (London)
-	48	THE COVENANT, THE SWORD AND THE ARM OF THE LAW	Cabaret Voltaire (Some Bizzare)
-	49	YOU MIGHT BE SURPRISED	Roy Ayers (CBS)
-	50	LIBRA	Julio Iglesias (CBS)

9 November 1985

last week	this week	Title	Artist
9	1	ONCE UPON A TIME	Simple Minds (Virgin)
4	2	THE LOVE SONGS	George Benson (K-Tel)
5	3	OUT NOW! 2	Various Artists (Chrysalis)
2	4	HOUNDS OF LOVE	Kate Bush (EMI)
1	5	LIVE AFTER DEATH	Iron Maiden (EMI)
-	6	AFTERBURNER	ZZ Top (Warner Bros.)
7	7	LIKE A VIRGIN	Madonna (Sire)
3	8	LOVE	Cult (Beggars Banquet)
8	9	THE SINGLES '81-'85	Depeche Mode (Mute)
11	10	BROTHERS IN ARMS	Dire Straits (Vertigo)
12	11	WORLD MACHINE	Level 42 (Polydor)
-	12	POWER WINDOWS	Rush (Vertigo)
6	13	THE GIFT	Midge Ure (Chrysalis)
14	14	MUSIC FROM MIAMI VICE	Various Artists (BBC)
10	15	VITAL IDOL	Billy Idol (Chrysalis)
15	16	WEST SIDE STORY	Leonard Bernstein & Studio Cast (Deutsche Grammophon)
-	17	THE CARS' GREATEST HITS	Cars (Elektra)
13	18	RAIN DOGS	Tom Waits (Island)
24	19	BILLY JOEL'S GREATEST HITS VOL 1 & VOL 2	Billy Joel (CBS)
17	20	MISPLACED CHILDHOOD	Marillion (EMI)
21	21	EXPRESSIONS	Various Artists (K-Tel)
39	22	SONGS FROM THE BIG CHAIR	Tears For Fears (Mercury)
-	23	THE LAST COMMAND	W.A.S.P. (Capitol)
20	24	LUXURY OF LIFE	Five Star (Tent)
-	25	DIAMOND LIFE	Sade (CBS)
36	26	U2 LIVE: UNDER A BLOOD RED SKY	U2 (Island)
-	27	SLAVE TO THE RHYTHM	Grace Jones (ZTT)
16	28	STRENGTH	Alarm (IRS)
31	29	MADONNA	Madonna (Sire)
18	30	IN SQUARE CIRCLE	Stevie Wonder (Tamla Motown)
34	31	HEART	Heart (Capitol)
35	32	NO JACKET REQUIRED	Phil Collins (Virgin)
-	33	THE UNFORGETTABLE FIRE	U2 (Island)
19	34	NOW THAT'S WHAT I CALL MUSIC 5	Various Artists (EMI/Virgin)
29	35	THE DREAM OF THE BLUE TURTLES	Sting (A&M)
-	36	PRIVATE DANCER	Tina Turner (Capitol)
37	37	SO MANY RIVERS	Bobby Womack (MCA)
-	38	HAVE A GOOD FOREVER	Cool Notes (Abstract Dance)
-	39	LEAVE THE BEST TO LAST	James Last (Polydor)
-	40	SUZANNE VEGA	Suzanne Vega (A&M)
-	41	THE COMPLETE MIKE OLDFIELD	Mike Oldfield (Virgin)
-	42	JOHN PARR	John Parr (London)
23	43	PICTURE BOOK	Simply Red (Elektra)
30	44	HERE'S TO FUTURE DAYS	Thompson Twins (Arista)
41	45	PEACE AND TRANQUILITY	Phil Coulter (Harmac)
43	46	MACALLA	Clannad (RCA)
45	47	THIS IS THE SEA	Waterboys (Ensign)
46	48	LITTLE CREATURES	Talking Heads (EMI)
40	49	SINGLE LIFE	Cameo (Club)
32	50	REELIN' IN THE YEARS	Steely Dan (MCA)

George Benson's *The Love Songs*, a TV-marketed compilation of former singles and LP tracks, proved even stronger commercially than many of his "official" releases, giving the smooth singer/guitarist his highest-ever UK chart placing. Leonard Bernstein's new studio re-creation of his famed *West Side Story* musical score was an all-star affair with Jose Carreras and Kiri Te Kanawa in the lead roles.

November 1985

16 November 1985

last week	this week	Title	Artist (Label)
1	1	ONCE UPON A TIME	Simple Minds (Virgin)
2	2	THE LOVE SONGS	George Benson (K-Tel)
6	3	AFTERBURNER	ZZ Top (Warner Bros.)
3	4	OUT NOW! 2	Various Artists (Chrysalis)
4	5	HOUNDS OF LOVE	Kate Bush (EMI)
12	6	POWER WINDOWS	Rush (Vertigo)
9	7	THE SINGLES '81-'85	Depeche Mode (Mute)
10	8	BROTHERS IN ARMS	Dire Straits (Vertigo)
-	9	PROMISE	Sade (Epic)
8	10	LOVE	Cult (Beggars Banquet)
11	11	WORLD MACHINE	Level 42 (Polydor)
27	12	SLAVE TO THE RHYTHM	Grace Jones (ZTT)
-	13	JENNIFER RUSH	Jennifer Rush (CBS)
5	14	LIVE AFTER DEATH	Iron Maiden (EMI)
7	15	LIKE A VIRGIN	Madonna (Sire)
-	16	THE SINGLES COLLECTION	Spandau Ballet (Chrysalis)
-	17	ICE ON FIRE	Elton John (Rocket)
-	18	CUT THE CRAP	Clash (CBS)
13	19	THE GIFT	Midge Ure (Chrysalis)
14	20	MUSIC FROM MIAMI VICE	Various Artists (BBC)
17	21	THE CARS' GREATEST HITS	Cars (Elektra)
-	22	HUNTING HIGH AND LOW	A Ha (Warner Bros.)
16	23	WEST SIDE STORY	Leonard Bernstein & Studio Cast (Deutsche Grammophon)
18	24	RAIN DOGS	Tom Waits (Island)
20	25	MISPLACED CHILDHOOD	Marillion (EMI)
15	26	VITAL IDOL	Billy Idol (Chrysalis)
-	27	ROCK ANTHEMS	Various Artists (K-Tel)
32	28	NO JACKET REQUIRED	Phil Collins (Virgin)
19	29	BILLY JOEL'S GREATEST HITS VOL 1 & VOL 2	Billy Joel (CBS)
24	30	LUXURY OF LIFE	Five Star (Tent)
-	31	THE 10-5-60 LP	Long Ryders (PVC)
-	32	UNDER A RAGING SUN	Roger Daltrey (10/Virgin)
-	33	BOYS AND GIRLS	Bryan Ferry (EG)
-	34	EAST ENDERS	Various Artists (BBC)
-	35	LIPSTICK, POWDER AND PAINT	Shakin' Stevens (Epic)
-	36	LOVE HURTS	Elaine Paige (WEA)
-	37	THE HEAD ON THE DOOR	Cure (Fiction)
-	38	THIS IS BIG AUDIO DYNAMITE	Big Audio Dynamite (CBS)
21	39	EXPRESSIONS	Various Artists (K-Tel)
34	40	NOW THAT'S WHAT I CALL MUSIC 5	Various Artists (EMI/Virgin)
-	41	THE POWER OF CLASSIC ROCK	London Symphony Orchestra (Portrait)
28	42	STRENGTH	Alarm (IRS)
35	43	THE DREAM OF THE BLUE TURTLES	Sting (A&M)
41	44	THE COMPLETE MIKE OLDFIELD	Mike Oldfield (Virgin)
43	45	PICTURE BOOK	Simply Red (Elektra)
48	46	LITTLE CREATURES	Talking Heads (EMI)
37	47	SO MANY RIVERS	Bobby Womack (MCA)
25	48	DIAMOND LIFE	Sade (CBS)
26	49	U2 LIVE: UNDER A BLOOD RED SKY	U2 (Island)
23	50	THE LAST COMMAND	W.A.S.P. (Capitol)

23 November 1985

last week	this week	Title	Artist (Label)
9	1	PROMISE	Sade (Epic)
3	2	AFTERBURNER	ZZ Top (Warner Bros.)
2	3	THE LOVE SONGS	George Benson (K-Tel)
1	4	ONCE UPON A TIME	Simple Minds (Virgin)
13	5	JENNIFER RUSH	Jennifer Rush (CBS)
17	6	ICE ON FIRE	Elton John (Rocket)
16	7	THE SINGLES COLLECTION	Spandau Ballet (Chrysalis)
8	8	BROTHERS IN ARMS	Dire Straits (Vertigo)
11	9	WORLD MACHINE	Level 42 (Polydor)
7	10	THE SINGLES '81-'85	Depeche Mode (Mute)
5	11	HOUNDS OF LOVE	Kate Bush (EMI)
18	12	CUT THE CRAP	Clash (CBS)
4	13	OUT NOW! 2	Various Artists (Chrysalis)
12	14	SLAVE TO THE RHYTHM	Grace Jones (ZTT)
15	15	LIKE A VIRGIN	Madonna (Sire)
-	16	SONGS TO LEARN AND SING	Echo & the Bunnymen (Korova)
-	17	BITTER SWEET	King (CBS)
35	18	LIPSTICK, POWDER AND PAINT	Shakin' Stevens (Epic)
27	19	ROCK ANTHEMS	Various Artists (K-Tel)
6	20	POWER WINDOWS	Rush (Vertigo)
-	21	FEARGAL SHARKEY	Feargal Sharkey (Virgin)
41	22	THE POWER OF CLASSIC ROCK	London Symphony Orchestra (Portrait)
14	23	LIVE AFTER DEATH	Iron Maiden (EMI)
-	24	SONGS FROM THE BIG CHAIR	Tears For Fears (Mercury)
36	25	LOVE HURTS	Elaine Paige (WEA)
21	26	THE CARS' GREATEST HITS	Cars (Elektra)
19	27	THE GIFT	Midge Ure (Chrysalis)
-	28	BAGGARADDIM	UB40 (Dep International)
20	29	MUSIC FROM MIAMI VICE	Various Artists (BBC)
22	30	HUNTING HIGH AND LOW	A Ha (Warner Bros.)
29	31	BILLY JOEL'S GREATEST HITS VOL 1 & VOL 2	Billy Joel (CBS)
45	32	PICTURE BOOK	Simply Red (Elektra)
-	33	MANILOW	Barry Manilow (RCA)
-	34	SUZANNE VEGA	Suzanne Vega (A&M)
-	35	STREET SOUNDS EDITION 14	Various Artists (Street Sounds)
26	36	VITAL IDOL	Billy Idol (Chrysalis)
23	37	WEST SIDE STORY	Leonard Bernstein & Studio Cast (Deutsche Grammophon)
24	38	RAIN DOGS	Tom Waits (Island)
31	39	THE 10-5-60 LP	Long Ryders (PVC)
38	40	THIS IS BIG AUDIO DYNAMITE	Big Audio Dynamite (CBS)
34	41	EAST ENDERS	Various Artists (BBC)
46	42	LITTLE CREATURES	Talking Heads (EMI)
-	43	BE YOURSELF TONIGHT	Eurythmics (RCA)
-	44	CHRONICLE OF THE BLACK SWORD	Hawkwind (Flicknife)
-	45	BALLADS	Elvis Presley (Telstar)
-	46	GREATEST HITS OF '85	Various Artists (Telstar)
-	47	JAMBOREE BAG NUMBER THREE	Chas & Dave (Rockney)
42	48	STRENGTH	Alarm (IRS)
47	49	SO MANY RIVERS	Bobby Womack (MCA)
-	50	RIPTIDE	Robert Palmer (Island)

30 November 1985

last week	this week	Title	Artist (Label)
1	1	PROMISE	Sade (Epic)
3	2	THE LOVE SONGS	George Benson (K-Tel)
21	3	FEARGAL SHARKEY	Feargal Sharkey (Virgin)
6	4	ICE ON FIRE	Elton John (Rocket)
16	5	SONGS TO LEARN AND SING	Echo & the Bunnymen (Korova)
4	6	ONCE UPON A TIME	Simple Minds (Virgin)
5	7	JENNIFER RUSH	Jennifer Rush (CBS)
7	8	THE SINGLES COLLECTION	Spandau Ballet (Chrysalis)
8	9	BROTHERS IN ARMS	Dire Straits (Vertigo)
2	10	AFTERBURNER	ZZ Top (Warner Bros.)
17	11	BITTER SWEET	King (CBS)
9	12	WORLD MACHINE	Level 42 (Polydor)
46	13	GREATEST HITS OF '85	Various Artists (Telstar)
-	14	EASY PIECES	Lloyd Cole & the Commotions (Polydor)
15	15	LIKE A VIRGIN	Madonna (Sire)
22	16	THE POWER OF CLASSIC ROCK	London Symphony Orchestra (Portrait)
25	17	LOVE HURTS	Elaine Paige (WEA)
10	18	THE SINGLES '81-'85	Depeche Mode (Mute)
19	19	ROCK ANTHEMS	Various Artists (K-Tel)
11	20	HOUNDS OF LOVE	Kate Bush (EMI)
-	21	PSYCHOCANDY	Jesus & Mary Chain (Blanco y Negro)
-	22	THE LOVE ALBUM	Various Artists (Telstar)
-	23	1979-1983	Bauhaus (Beggars Banquet)
-	24	LOVE	Cult (Beggars Banquet)
-	25	GOLD	Barbara Dickson (K-Tel)
-	26	I LOVE A PARTY	Russ Abbott (K-Tel)
-	27	TELLY HITS - 16 TOP TV THEMES	Various Artists (Stylus)
12	28	CUT THE CRAP	Clash (CBS)
35	29	STREET SOUNDS EDITION 14	Various Artists (Street Sounds)
20	30	POWER WINDOWS	Rush (Vertigo)
13	31	OUT NOW! 2	Various Artists (Chrysalis)
-	32	ALED JONES WITH THE BBC WELSH CHORUS	Aled Jones (10/BBC)
14	33	SLAVE TO THE RHYTHM	Grace Jones (ZTT)
28	34	BAGGARADDIM	UB40 (Dep International)
23	35	LIVE AFTER DEATH	Iron Maiden (EMI)
-	36	PAUL HARDCASTLE	Paul Hardcastle (Chrysalis)
26	37	THE CARS' GREATEST HITS	Cars (Elektra)
32	38	PICTURE BOOK	Simply Red (Elektra)
24	39	SONGS FROM THE BIG CHAIR	Tears For Fears (Mercury)
30	40	HUNTING HIGH AND LOW	A Ha (Warner Bros.)
-	41	WHITE CITY	Pete Townshend (Atco)
-	42	SCARECROW	John Cougar Mellencamp (RCA)
27	43	THE GIFT	Midge Ure (Chrysalis)
-	44	DOG EAT DOG	Joni Mitchell (Geffen)
-	45	NOW - THE CHRISTMAS ALBUM	Various Artists (EMI/Virgin)
-	46	KNEE DEEP IN THE HOOPLA	Starship (Grunt)
-	47	REMINISCING - THE HOWARD KEEL COLLECTION	Howard Keel (Telstar)
50	48	RIPTIDE	Robert Palmer (Island)
41	49	EAST ENDERS	Various Artists (BBC)
47	50	JAMBOREE BAG NUMBER THREE	Chas & Dave (Rockney)

As Simple Minds celebrated their second Number 1 album with *Once Upon A Time*, Sade scored an even more notable double with *Promise*, which gave her two chart-topping albums from two releases. Jennifer Rush's eponymous album found top 10 success on the back of her hit single *The Power Of Love* (the year's biggest-selling single and only million-seller), while ex-Undertone Feargal Sharkey made his solo mark.

December 1985

7 December 1985

last week	this week	Title	Artist
9	1	BROTHERS IN ARMS	Dire Straits (Vertigo)
2	2	THE LOVE SONGS	George Benson (K-Tel)
1	3	PROMISE	Sade (Epic)
14	4	EASY PIECES	Lloyd Cole & the Commotions (Polydor)
-	5	NOW THAT'S WHAT I CALL MUSIC 6	Various Artists (EMI/Virgin)
13	6	GREATEST HITS OF '85	Various Artists (Telstar)
4	7	ICE ON FIRE	Elton John (Rocket)
-	8	HITS 3	Various Artists (CBS/WEA)
8	9	THE SINGLES COLLECTION	Spandau Ballet (Chrysalis)
3	10	FEARGAL SHARKEY	Feargal Sharkey (Virgin)
22	11	THE LOVE ALBUM	Various Artists (Telstar)
45	12	NOW - THE CHRISTMAS ALBUM	Various Artists (EMI/Virgin)
7	13	JENNIFER RUSH	Jennifer Rush (CBS)
5	14	SONGS TO LEARN AND SING	Echo & the Bunnymen (Korova)
17	15	LOVE HURTS	Elaine Paige (WEA)
12	16	WORLD MACHINE	Level 42 (Polydor)
16	17	THE POWER OF CLASSIC ROCK	London Symphony Orchestra (Portrait)
19	18	ROCK ANTHEMS	Various Artists (K-Tel)
6	19	ONCE UPON A TIME	Simple Minds (Virgin)
21	20	PSYCHOCANDY	Jesus & Mary Chain (Blanco y Negro)
15	21	LIKE A VIRGIN	Madonna (Sire)
11	21	BITTER SWEET	King (CBS)
23	23	1979-1983	Bauhaus (Beggars Banquet)
10	24	AFTERBURNER	ZZ Top (Warner Bros.)
44	25	DOG EAT DOG	Joni Mitchell (Geffen)
-	26	GREATEST HITS VOL 1 & VOL 2	Billy Joel (CBS)
25	27	GOLD	Barbara Dickson (K-Tel)
31	28	OUT NOW! 2	Various Artists (Chrysalis)
47	29	REMINISCING - THE HOWARD KEEL COLLECTION	Howard Keel (Telstar)
-	30	SO RED THE ROSE	Arcadia (EMI)
36	31	PAUL HARDCASTLE	Paul Hardcastle (Chrysalis)
20	32	HOUNDS OF LOVE	Kate Bush (EMI)
26	33	I LOVE A PARTY	Russ Abbott (K-Tel)
-	34	THE VERY BEST OF THE COMMODORES	Commodores (Telstar)
29	35	STREET SOUNDS EDITION 14	Various Artists (Street Sounds)
34	36	BAGGARADDIM	UB40 (Dep International)
50	37	JAMBOREE BAG NUMBER THREE	Chas & Dave (Rockney)
27	38	TELLY HITS - 16 TOP TV THEMES	Various Artists (Stylus)
-	39	LEAVE THE BEST TO LAST	James Last (Polydor)
37	40	THE CARS' GREATEST HITS	Cars (Elektra)
49	41	EAST ENDERS	Various Artists (BBC)
24	42	LOVE	Cult (Beggars Banquet)
-	43	SEVEN THE HARD WAY	Pat Benatar (Chrysalis)
-	44	WEST SIDE STORY	Leonard Bernstein & Studio Cast (Deutsche Grammophon)
-	45	JUST A MILLION DREAMS	Alan Vega (Elektra)
-	46	NO JACKET REQUIRED	Phil Collins (Virgin)
39	47	SONGS FROM THE BIG CHAIR	Tears For Fears (Mercury)
43	48	THE GIFT	Midge Ure (Chrysalis)
-	49	NAIL	Scraping Foetus off the Wheel (Some Bizzare)
35	50	LIVE AFTER DEATH	Iron Maiden (EMI)

14 December 1985

last week	this week	Title	Artist
5	1	NOW THAT'S WHAT I CALL MUSIC 6	Various Artists (EMI/Virgin)
8	2	HITS 3	Various Artists (CBS/WEA)
1	3	BROTHERS IN ARMS	Dire Straits (Vertigo)
2	4	THE LOVE SONGS	George Benson (K-Tel)
12	5	NOW - THE CHRISTMAS ALBUM	Various Artists (EMI/Virgin)
4	6	EASY PIECES	Lloyd Cole & the Commotions (Polydor)
3	7	PROMISE	Sade (Epic)
6	8	GREATEST HITS OF '85	Various Artists (Telstar)
9	9	THE SINGLES COLLECTION	Spandau Ballet (Chrysalis)
7	10	ICE ON FIRE	Elton John (Rocket)
11	11	THE LOVE ALBUM	Various Artists (Telstar)
16	12	WORLD MACHINE	Level 42 (Polydor)
15	13	LOVE HURTS	Elaine Paige (WEA)
30	14	SO RED THE ROSE	Arcadia (EMI)
13	15	JENNIFER RUSH	Jennifer Rush (CBS)
27	16	GOLD	Barbara Dickson (K-Tel)
19	17	ONCE UPON A TIME	Simple Minds (Virgin)
21	18	LIKE A VIRGIN	Madonna (Sire)
18	19	ROCK ANTHEMS	Various Artists (K-Tel)
10	20	FEARGAL SHARKEY	Feargal Sharkey (Virgin)
14	21	SONGS TO LEARN AND SING	Echo & the Bunnymen (Korova)
26	22	GREATEST HITS VOL 1 & VOL 2	Billy Joel (CBS)
39	23	LEAVE THE BEST TO LAST	James Last (Polydor)
24	24	AFTERBURNER	ZZ Top (Warner Bros.)
17	25	THE POWER OF CLASSIC ROCK	London Symphony Orchestra (Portrait)
32	26	HOUNDS OF LOVE	Kate Bush (EMI)
-	27	ISLAND LIFE	Grace Jones (Island)
43	28	SEVEN THE HARD WAY	Pat Benatar (Chrysalis)
20	29	PSYCHOCANDY	Jesus & Mary Chain (Blanco y Negro)
33	30	I LOVE A PARTY	Russ Abbott (K-Tel)
-	31	LITTLE CREATURES	Talking Heads (EMI)
34	32	THE VERY BEST OF THE COMMODORES	Commodores (Telstar)
21	33	BITTER SWEET	King (CBS)
-	34	ASTRA	Asia (Geffen)
47	35	SONGS FROM THE BIG CHAIR	Tears For Fears (Mercury)
-	36	PARTY PARTY 2	Black Lace (Telstar)
-	37	WHITNEY HOUSTON	Whitney Houston (Arista)
-	38	COME OUT AND PLAY	Twisted Sister (Atlantic)
25	39	DOG EAT DOG	Joni Mitchell (Geffen)
-	40	ALED JONES WITH THE BBC WELSH CHORUS	Aled Jones (10/BBC)
29	41	REMINISCING - THE HOWARD KEEL COLLECTION	Howard Keel (Telstar)
44	42	WEST SIDE STORY	Leonard Bernstein & Studio Cast (Deutsche Grammophon)
36	43	BAGGARADDIM	UB40 (Dep International)
-	44	RECKLESS	Bryan Adams (A&M)
-	45	DONE WITH MIRRORS	Aerosmith (Geffen)
-	46	BORN IN THE USA	Bruce Springsteen (CBS)
23	47	1979-1983	Bauhaus (Beggars Banquet)
-	48	PACK UP THE PLANTATION	Tom Petty & the Heartbreakers (MCA)
-	49	FRANKENCHRIST	Dead Kennedys (Alternative Tentacles)
-	50	VITAL IDOL	Billy Idol (Chrysalis)

21 December 1985

last week	this week	Title	Artist
1	1	NOW THAT'S WHAT I CALL MUSIC 6	Various Artists (EMI/Virgin)
2	2	HITS 3	Various Artists (CBS/WEA)
5	3	NOW - THE CHRISTMAS ALBUM	Various Artists (EMI/Virgin)
4	4	THE LOVE SONGS	George Benson (K-Tel)
9	5	THE SINGLES COLLECTION	Spandau Ballet (Chrysalis)
3	6	BROTHERS IN ARMS	Dire Straits (Vertigo)
7	7	PROMISE	Sade (Epic)
11	8	THE LOVE ALBUM	Various Artists (Telstar)
8	9	GREATEST HITS OF '85	Various Artists (Telstar)
10	10	ICE ON FIRE	Elton John (Rocket)
6	11	EASY PIECES	Lloyd Cole & the Commotions (Polydor)
18	12	LIKE A VIRGIN	Madonna (Sire)
13	13	LOVE HURTS	Elaine Paige (WEA)
16	14	GOLD	Barbara Dickson (K-Tel)
12	15	WORLD MACHINE	Level 42 (Polydor)
23	16	LEAVE THE BEST TO LAST	James Last (Polydor)
30	17	I LOVE A PARTY	Russ Abbott (K-Tel)
37	18	WHITNEY HOUSTON	Whitney Houston (Arista)
27	19	ISLAND LIFE	Grace Jones (Island)
-	20	JAMBOREE BAG NO.3	Chas & Dave (Rockney)
14	21	SO RED THE ROSE	Arcadia (EMI)
15	22	JENNIFER RUSH	Jennifer Rush (CBS)
41	23	REMINISCING - THE HOWARD KEEL COLLECTION	Howard Keel (Telstar)
36	24	PARTY PARTY 2	Black Lace (Telstar)
22	25	GREATEST HITS VOL 1 & VOL 2	Billy Joel (CBS)
19	26	ROCK ANTHEMS	Various Artists (K-Tel)
24	27	AFTERBURNER	ZZ Top (Warner Bros.)
26	28	HOUNDS OF LOVE	Kate Bush (EMI)
20	29	FEARGAL SHARKEY	Feargal Sharkey (Virgin)
-	30	ROCK A LITTLE	Stevie Nicks (Modern)
-	31	FINE YOUNG CANNIBALS	Fine Young Cannibals (London)
34	32	ASTRA	Asia (Geffen)
40	33	ALED JONES WITH THE BBC WELSH CHORUS	Aled Jones (10/BBC)
35	34	SONGS FROM THE BIG CHAIR	Tears For Fears (Mercury)
-	35	THE CLASSIC TOUCH	Richard Clayderman (Decca)
25	36	THE POWER OF CLASSIC ROCK	LSO (Portrait)
33	37	BITTER SWEET	King (CBS)
48	38	PACK UP THE PLANTATION	Tom Petty & the Heartbreakers (MCA)
38	39	COME OUT AND PLAY	Twisted Sister (Atlantic)
29	40	PSYCHOCANDY	Jesus & Mary Chain (Blanco y Negro)
-	41	THE LEGEND OF BILLIE HOLIDAY	Billie Holiday (MCA)
42	42	WEST SIDE STORY	Leonard Bernstein & Studio Cast (Deutsche Grammophon)
32	43	THE VERY BEST OF THE COMMODORES	Commodores (Telstar)
17	44	ONCE UPON A TIME	Simple Minds (Virgin)
-	45	CLUB NINJA	Blue Oyster Cult (CBS)
49	46	FRANKENCHRIST	Dead Kennedys (Alternative Tentacles)
21	47	SONGS TO LEARN AND SING	Echo & the Bunnymen (Korova)
-	48	THE SINGLES '81-'85	Depeche Mode (Mute)
39	49	DOG EAT DOG	Joni Mitchell (Geffen)
45	50	DONE WITH MIRRORS	Aerosmith (Geffen)

Following yet another *Brothers In Arms* sales spurt at the beginning of December, the major Christmas sales battle was clearly going to be, as in 1984, between the major labels' mega-hits compilations. This time, the honours went the other way, with EMI/Virgin's *Now 6* holding CBS/WEA's *Hits 3* into second place. Moreover, *The Christmas Album* boosted the *Now* partnership's share, locking in behind at Number 3.

January 1986

4 January 1986

last	this		
1	1	NOW THAT'S WHAT I CALL MUSIC 6	Various Artists (EMI/Virgin)
3	2	NOW – THE CHRISTMAS ALBUM	Various Artists (EMI/Virgin)
2	3	HITS 3	Various Artists (CBS/WEA)
6	4	BROTHERS IN ARMS	Dire Straits (Vertigo)
4	5	THE LOVE SONGS	George Benson (K-Tel)
7	6	PROMISE	Sade (Epic)
5	7	THE SINGLES COLLECTION	Spandau Ballet (Chrysalis)
12	8	LIKE A VIRGIN	Madonna (Sire)
8	9	THE LOVE ALBUM	Various Artists (Telstar)
10	10	ICE ON FIRE	Elton John (Rocket)
14	11	GOLD	Barbara Dickson (K-Tel)
22	12	JENNIFER RUSH	Jennifer Rush (CBS)
18	13	WHITNEY HOUSTON	Whitney Houston (Arista)
9	14	GREATEST HITS OF '85	Various Artists (Telstar)
15	15	WORLD MACHINE	Level 42 (Polydor)
16	16	LEAVE THE BEST TO LAST	James Last (Polydor)
13	17	LOVE HURTS	Elaine Paige (WEA)
17	18	I LOVE A PARTY	Russ Abbot (K-Tel)
11	19	EASY PIECES	Lloyd Cole & the Commotions (Polydor)
31	20	FINE YOUNG CANNIBALS	Fine Young Cannibals (London)
20	21	JAMBOREE BAG NO.3	Chas & Dave (Rockneyl)
19	22	ISLAND LIFE	Grace Jones (Island)
-	23	STREET SOUNDS EDITION 15	Various Artists (Street Sounds)
36	24	THE POWER OF CLASSIC ROCK	London Symphony Orchestra (Portrait)
23	25	REMINISCING – THE HOWARD KEEL COLLECTION	Howard Keel (Telstar)
-	26	CRACKERS – THE SLADE CHRISTMAS PARTY ALBUM	Slade (Telstar)
25	27	GREATEST HITS VOL 1 & VOL 2	Billy Joel (CBS)
43	28	THE VERY BEST OF THE COMMODORES	Commodores (Telstar)
-	29	NO JACKET REQUIRED	Phil Collins (Virgin)
29	30	FEARGAL SHARKEY	Feargal Sharkey (Virgin)
33	31	ALED JONES WITH THE BBC WELSH CHORUS	Aled Jones (10/BBC)
24	32	PARTY PARTY 2	Black Lace (Telstar)
28	33	HOUNDS OF LOVE	Kate Bush (EMI)
44	34	ONCE UPON A TIME	Simple Minds (Virgin)
34	35	SONGS FROM THE BIG CHAIR	Tears for Fears (Mercury)
-	36	GO WEST/BANGS AND CRASHES	Go West (Chrysalis)
47	37	SONGS TO LEARN AND SING	Echo & the Bunnymen (Korova)
49	38	DOG EAT DOG	Joni Mitchell (Geffen)
45	39	CLUB NINJA	Blue Oyster Cult (CBS)
-	40	BALLADS	Elvis Presley (Telstar)
-	41	STREETSOUNDS ELECTRO 10	Various Artists (Street Sounds)
35	42	THE CLASSIC TOUCH	Richard Clayderman (Decca/Delphine)
30	43	ROCK A LITTLE	Stevie Nicks (Modern)
40	44	PSYCHOCANDY	Jesus & Mary Chain (Blanco Y Negro)
21	45	SO RED THE ROSE	Arcadia (EMI)
-	46	VELVET WATERS	Various Artists (Stylus)
-	47	THE HEART OF THE MATTER	Kenny Rogers (RCA)
-	48	HEART AND SOUL	Barry White (K-Tel)
-	49	BEST OF THE DOORS	Doors (Elektra)
-	50	AMAZING GRACE	Judy Collins (Telstar)

11 January 1986

last	this		
4	1	BROTHERS IN ARMS	Dire Straits (Vertigo)
1	2	NOW THAT'S WHAT I CALL MUSIC 6	Various Artists (EMI/Virgin)
6	3	PROMISE	Sade (Epic)
3	4	HITS 3	Various Artists (CBS/WEA)
8	5	LIKE A VIRGIN	Madonna (Sire)
5	6	THE LOVE SONGS	George Benson (K-Tel)
13	7	WHITNEY HOUSTON	Whitney Houston (Arista)
2	8	NOW – THE CHRISTMAS ALBUM	Various Artists (EMI/Virgin)
9	9	THE LOVE ALBUM	Various Artists (Telstar)
15	10	WORLD MACHINE	Level 42 (Polydor)
12	11	JENNIFER RUSH	Jennifer Rush (CBS)
31	12	ALED JONES WITH THE BBC WELSH CHORUS	Aled Jones (10/BBC)
7	13	THE SINGLES COLLECTION	Spandau Ballet (Chrysalis)
11	14	GOLD	Barbara Dickson (K-Tel)
21	15	JAMBOREE BAG NO.3	Chas & Dave (Rockney)
16	16	LOVE HURTS	Elaine Paige (WEA)
20	17	FINE YOUNG CANNIBALS	Fine Young Cannibals (London)
22	18	ISLAND LIFE	Grace Jones (Island)
23	19	STREET SOUNDS EDITION 15	Various Artists (Street Sounds)
19	20	EASY PIECES	Lloyd Cole & the Commotions (Polydor)
16	21	LEAVE THE BEST TO LAST	James Last (Polydor)
27	22	GREATEST HITS VOL 1 & VOL 2	Billy Joel (CBS)
14	23	GREATEST HITS OF '85	Various Artists (Telstar)
36	24	GO WEST/BANGS AND CRASHES	Go West (Chrysalis)
30	25	FEARGAL SHARKEY	Feargal Sharkey (Virgin)
37	26	SONGS TO LEARN AND SING	Echo & the Bunnymen (Korova)
41	27	STREETSOUNDS ELECTRO 10	Various Artists (Street Sounds)
10	28	ICE ON FIRE	Elton John (Rocket)
42	29	THE CLASSIC TOUCH	Richard Clayderman (Decca/Delphine)
18	30	I LOVE A PARTY	Russ Abbot (K-Tel)
-	31	BLUE SKIES	Kiri Te Kanawa (London)
-	32	MADONNA	Madonna (Epic)
-	33	LITTLE CREATURES	Talking Heads (EMI)
33	34	HOUNDS OF LOVE	Kate Bush (EMI)
35	35	ONCE UPON A TIME	Simple Minds (Virgin)
29	36	NO JACKET REQUIRED	Phil Collins (Virgin)
24	37	THE POWER OF CLASSIC ROCK	LSO (Portrait)
44	38	PSYCHOCANDY	Jesus & Mary Chain (Blanco Y Negro)
28	39	THE VERY BEST OF THE COMMODORES	Commodores (Telstar)
32	40	PARTY PARTY 2	Black Lace (Telstar)
25	41	REMINISCING – THE HOWARD KEEL COLLECTION	Howard Keel (Telstar)
46	42	VELVET WATERS	Various Artists (Stylus)
35	43	SONGS FROM THE BIG CHAIR	Tears for Fears (Mercury)
-	44	THE COMPLETE MIKE OLDFIELD	Mike Oldfield (Virgin)
-	45	THE DREAM OF THE BLUE TURTLES	Sting (A&M)
26	46	CRACKERS – THE SLADE CHRISTMAS PARTY ALBUM	Slade (Telstar)
47	47	THE HEART OF THE MATTER	Kenny Rogers (RCA)
48	48	HEART AND SOUL	Barry White (K-Tel)
-	49	FRANKENCHRIST	Dead Kennedys (Alternative Tentacles)
-	50	ALCHEMY – DIRE STRAITS LIVE	Dire Straits (Vertigo)

18 January 1986

last	this		
1	1	BROTHERS IN ARMS	Dire Straits (Vertigo)
2	2	NOW THAT'S WHAT I CALL MUSIC 6	Various Artists (EMI/Virgin)
5	3	LIKE A VIRGIN	Madonna (Sire)
3	4	PROMISE	Sade (Epic)
4	5	HITS 3	Various Artists (CBS/WEA)
7	6	WHITNEY HOUSTON	Whitney Houston (Arista)
10	7	WORLD MACHINE	Level 42 (Polydor)
18	8	ISLAND LIFE	Grace Jones (Island)
13	9	THE SINGLES COLLECTION	Spandau Ballet (Chrysalis)
6	10	THE LOVE SONGS	George Benson (K-Tel)
-	11	HUNTING HIGH AND LOW	A-Ha (Warner Bros.)
11	12	JENNIFER RUSH	Jennifer Rush (CBS)
24	13	GO WEST/BANGS AND CRASHES	Go West (Chrysalis)
43	14	SONGS FROM THE BIG CHAIR	Tears for Fears (Mercury)
28	15	ICE ON FIRE	Elton John (Rocket)
20	16	EASY PIECES	Lloyd Cole & the Commotions (Polydor)
23	17	GREATEST HITS OF '85	Various Artists (Telstar)
45	18	THE DREAM OF THE BLUE TURTLES	Sting (A&M)
22	19	GREATEST HITS VOL 1 & VOL 2	Billy Joel (CBS)
35	20	ONCE UPON A TIME	Simple Minds (Virgin)
34	21	HOUNDS OF LOVE	Kate Bush (EMI)
36	22	NO JACKET REQUIRED	Phil Collins (Virgin)
17	23	FINE YOUNG CANNIBALS	Fine Young Cannibals (London)
-	24	THE BROADWAY ALBUM	Barbra Streisand (CBS)
9	25	THE LOVE ALBUM	Various Artists (Telstar)
25	26	FEARGAL SHARKEY	Feargal Sharkey (Virgin)
14	27	GOLD	Barbara Dickson (K-Tel)
29	28	THE CLASSIC TOUCH	Richard Clayderman (Decca/Delphine)
37	29	THE POWER OF CLASSIC ROCK	LSO (Portrait)
19	30	STREET SOUNDS EDITION 15	Various Artists (Street Sounds)
-	31	LUXURY OF LIFE	Five Star (Tent)
-	32	ELIMINATOR	ZZ Top (Warner Bros.)
32	33	MADONNA	Madonna (Epic)
41	34	REMINISCING – THE HOWARD KEEL COLLECTION	Howard Keel (Telstar)
21	35	LEAVE THE BEST TO LAST	James Last (Polydor)
16	36	LOVE HURTS	Elaine Paige (WEA)
15	37	JAMBOREE BAG NO.3	Chas & Dave (Rockney/l)
48	38	HEART AND SOUL	Barry White (K-Tel)
44	39	THE COMPLETE MIKE OLDFIELD	Mike Oldfield (Virgin)
39	40	THE VERY BEST OF THE COMMODORES	Commodores (Telstar)
-	41	BITTER SWEET	King (CBS)
-	42	PRIVATE DANCER	Tina Turner (Capitol)
-	43	BAGGARADDIM	UB40 (DEP Int)
-	44	WHO'S ZOOMIN' WHO	Aretha Franklin (Arista)
47	45	THE HEART OF THE MATTER	Kenny Rogers (RCA)
26	46	SONGS TO LEARN AND SING	Echo & the Bunnymen (Korova)
27	47	STREETSOUNDS ELECTRO 10	Various Artists (Street Sounds)
38	48	PSYCHOCANDY	Jesus & Mary Chain (Blanco Y Negro)
12	49	ALED JONES WITH THE BBC WELSH CHORUS	Aled Jones (10/BBC)
33	50	LITTLE CREATURES	Talking Heads (EMI)

As the hits compilations lost some of their impetus after Christmas, Dire Straits' *Brothers In Arms* reasserted itself at the top of the charts again, helped once more by the Top 5 success of an extracted single - *Walk Of Life*. By the end of the 1980s, this album would have passed three million sales in the UK alone, putting it second only to the Beatles' *Sergeant Pepper* as the country's all-time best-seller.

25 January 1986

last week	this week	Title	Artist (Label)
1	1	BROTHERS IN ARMS	Dire Straits (Vertigo)
11	2	HUNTING HIGH AND LOW	A-Ha (Warner Bros.)
18	3	THE DREAM OF THE BLUE TURTLE	Sting (A&M)
8	4	ISLAND LIFE	Grace Jones (Island)
7	5	WORLD MACHINE	Level 42 (Polydor)
6	6	WHITNEY HOUSTON	Whitney Houston (Arista)
4	7	PROMISE	Sade (Epic)
3	8	LIKE A VIRGIN	Madonna (Sire)
24	9	THE BROADWAY ALBUM	Barbra Streisand (CBS)
2	10	NOW THAT'S WHAT I CALL MUSIC 6	Various Artists (EMI/Virgin)
13	11	GO WEST/BANGS AND CRASHES	Go West (Chrysalis)
26	12	FEARGAL SHARKEY	Feargal Sharkey (Virgin)
23	13	FINE YOUNG CANNIBALS	Fine Young Cannibals (London)
9	14	THE SINGLES COLLECTION	Spandau Ballet (Chrysalis)
16	15	EASY PIECES	Lloyd Cole & the Commotions (Polydor)
15	16	ICE ON FIRE	Elton John (Rocket)
14	17	SONGS FROM THE BIG CHAIR	Tears for Fears (Mercury)
22	18	NO JACKET REQUIRED	Phil Collins (Virgin)
12	19	JENNIFER RUSH	Jennifer Rush (CBS)
5	20	HITS 3	Various Artists (CBS/WEA)
20	21	ONCE UPON A TIME	Simple Minds (Virgin)
-	22	BE YOURSELF TONIGHT	Eurythmics (RCA)
46	23	SONGS TO LEARN AND SING	Echo & the Bunnymen (Korova)
25	24	THE LOVE ALBUM	Various Artists (Telstar)
-	25	HIGH PRIORITY	Cherrelle (Tabu)
31	26	LUXURY OF LIFE	Five Star (Tent)
30	27	STREET SOUNDS EDITION 15	Various Artists (Street Sounds)
21	28	HOUNDS OF LOVE	Kate Bush (EMI)
10	29	THE LOVE SONGS	George Benson (K-Tel)
42	30	PRIVATE DANCER	Tina Turner (Capitol)
19	31	GREATEST HITS VOL 1 & VOL 2	Billy Joel (CBS)
-	32	RECKLESS	Bryan Adams (A&M)
17	33	GREATEST HITS OF '85	Various Artists (Telstar)
36	34	LOVE HURTS	Elaine Paige (WEA)
38	35	HEART AND SOUL	Barry White (K-Tel)
44	36	WHO'S ZOOMIN' WHO	Aretha Franklin (Arista)
50	37	LITTLE CREATURES	Talking Heads (EMI)
27	38	GOLD	Barbara Dickson (K-Tel)
49	39	ALED JONES WITH THE BBC WELSH CHORUS	Aled Jones (10/BBC)
39	40	THE COMPLETE MIKE OLDFIELD	Mike Oldfield (Virgin)
28	41	THE CLASSIC TOUCH	Richard Clayderman (Decca/Delphine))
-	42	BORN IN THE USA	Bruce Springsteen (CBS)
-	43	THE JAZZ SINGER	Neil Diamond (Capitol)
-	44	THE SECRET OF ASSOCIATION	Paul Young (CBS)
-	45	FULL FORCE	Full Force (CBS)
-	46	LISTEN LIKE THIEVES	INXS (Mercury)
41	47	BITTER SWEET	King (CBS)
47	48	STREETSOUNDS ELECTRO 10	Various Artists (Street Sounds)
-	49	THE BEST OF ANDREW LLOYD WEBBER	Various Artists (K-Tel)
-	50	DOUBLE TROUBLE	Molly Hatchet (Epic)

1 February 1986

last week	this week	Title	Artist (Label)
1	1	BROTHERS IN ARMS	Dire Straits (Vertigo)
2	2	HUNTING HIGH AND LOW	A-Ha (Warner Bros.)
5	3	WORLD MACHINE	Level 42 (Polydor)
3	4	THE DREAM OF THE BLUE TURTLES	Sting (A&M)
6	5	WHITNEY HOUSTON	Whitney Houston (Arista)
9	6	THE BROADWAY ALBUM	Barbra Streisand (CBS)
12	7	FEARGAL SHARKEY	Feargal Sharkey (Virgin)
4	8	ISLAND LIFE	Grace Jones (Island)
8	9	LIKE A VIRGIN	Madonna (Sire)
11	10	GO WEST/BANGS AND CRASHES	Go West (Chrysalis)
7	11	PROMISE	Sade (Epic)
13	12	FINE YOUNG CANNIBALS	Fine Young Cannibals (London)
22	13	BE YOURSELF TONIGHT	Eurythmics (RCA)
25	14	HIGH PRIORITY	Cherrelle (Tabu)
10	15	NOW THAT'S WHAT I CALL MUSIC 6	Various Artists (EMI/Virgin)
21	16	ONCE UPON A TIME	Simple Minds (Virgin)
15	17	EASY PIECES	Lloyd Cole & the Commotions (Polydor)
26	18	LUXURY OF LIFE	Five Star (Tent)
19	19	JENNIFER RUSH	Jennifer Rush (CBS)
17	20	SONGS FROM THE BIG CHAIR	Tears for Fears (Mercury)
29	21	THE LOVE SONGS	George Benson (K-Tel)
14	22	THE SINGLES COLLECTION	Spandau Ballet (Chrysalis)
18	23	NO JACKET REQUIRED	Phil Collins (Virgin)
30	24	PRIVATE DANCER	Tina Turner (Capitol)
16	25	ICE ON FIRE	Elton John (Rocket)
27	26	STREET SOUNDS EDITION 15	Various Artists (Street Sounds)
36	27	WHO'S ZOOMIN' WHO	Aretha Franklin (Arista)
-	28	SUZANNE VEGA	Suzanne Vega (A&M)
35	29	HEART AND SOUL	Barry White (K-Tel)
41	30	THE CLASSIC TOUCH	Richard Clayderman (Decca)
43	31	THE JAZZ SINGER	Neil Diamond (Capitol)
-	32	MACALLA	Clannad (RCA)
-	33	ROCK A LITTLE	Stevie Nicks (Modern)
32	34	RECKLESS	Bryan Adams (A&M)
-	35	THE UNFORGETTABLE FIRE	U2 (Island)
20	36	HITS 3	Various Artists (CBS/WEA)
23	37	SONGS TO LEARN AND SING	Echo & the Bunnymen (Korova)
28	38	HOUNDS OF LOVE	Kate Bush (EMI)
24	39	THE LOVE ALBUM	Various Artists (Telstar)
-	40	ALEXANDER O'NEAL	Alexander O'Neal (Tabu/Epic)
-	41	BLACK AND WHITE	Terraplane (Epic)
-	42	ROCK ME TONIGHT	Freddie Jackson (Capitol)
47	43	BITTER SWEET	King (CBS)
46	44	LISTEN LIKE THIEVES	INXS (Mercury)
50	45	DOUBLE TROUBLE	Molly Hatchet (Epic)
34	46	LOVE HURTS	Elaine Paige (WEA)
42	47	BORN IN THE USA	Bruce Springsteen (CBS)
-	48	THE BEST OF INCANTATION	Incantation (West Five)
-	49	ALL THROUGH THE NIGHT	Aled Jones (BBC)
-	50	LEAVE THE BEST TO LAST	James Last (Polydor)

8 February 1986

last week	this week	Title	Artist (Label)
1	1	BROTHERS IN ARMS	Dire Straits (Vertigo)
2	2	HUNTING HIGH AND LOW	A-Ha (Warner Bros.)
4	3	THE DREAM OF THE BLUE TURTLES	Sting (A&M)
3	4	WORLD MACHINE	Level 42 (Polydor)
8	5	ISLAND LIFE	Grace Jones (Island)
5	6	WHITNEY HOUSTON	Whitney Houston (Arista)
6	7	THE BROADWAY ALBUM	Barbra Streisand (CBS)
9	8	LIKE A VIRGIN	Madonna (Sire)
13	9	BE YOURSELF TONIGHT	Eurythmics (RCA)
10	10	GO WEST/BANGS AND CRASHES	Go West (Chrysalis)
7	11	FEARGAL SHARKEY	Feargal Sharkey (Virgin)
12	12	FINE YOUNG CANNIBALS	Fine Young Cannibals (London)
14	13	HIGH PRIORITY	Cherrelle (Tabu)
18	14	LUXURY OF LIFE	Five Star (Tent)
11	15	PROMISE	Sade (Epic)
16	16	ONCE UPON A TIME	Simple Minds (Virgin)
20	17	SONGS FROM THE BIG CHAIR	Tears for Fears (Mercury)
15	18	NOW THAT'S WHAT I CALL MUSIC 6	Various Artists (EMI/Virgin)
17	19	EASY PIECES	Lloyd Cole & the Commotions (Polydor)
32	20	MACALLA	Clannad (RCA)
27	21	WHO'S ZOOMIN' WHO	Aretha Franklin (Arista)
-	22	THIS IS BIG AUDIO DYNAMITE	Big Audio Dynamite (CBS)
-	23	ROCKY IV	Soundtrack (Scotti Brothers)
-	24	LITTLE CREATURES	Talking Heads (EMI)
19	25	JENNIFER RUSH	Jennifer Rush (CBS)
26	26	STREET SOUNDS EDITION 15	Various Artists (Street Sounds)
-	27	BACK IN THE DHSS	Half Man Half Biscuit (Probe Plus)
24	28	PRIVATE DANCER	Tina Turner (Capitol)
34	29	RECKLESS	Bryan Adams (A&M)
25	30	ICE ON FIRE	Elton John (Rocket)
30	31	THE CLASSIC TOUCH	Richard Clayderman (Decca)
28	32	SUZANNE VEGA	Suzanne Vega (A&M)
42	33	ROCK ME TONIGHT	Freddie Jackson (Capitol)
40	34	ALEXANDER O'NEAL	Alexander O'Neal (Tabu/Epic)
21	35	THE LOVE SONGS	George Benson (K-Tel)
47	36	BORN IN THE USA	Bruce Springsteen (CBS)
38	37	HOUNDS OF LOVE	Kate Bush (EMI)
39	38	THE LOVE ALBUM	Various Artists (Telstar)
44	39	LISTEN LIKE THIEVES	INXS (Mercury)
22	40	THE SINGLES COLLECTION	Spandau Ballet (Chrysalis)
29	41	HEART AND SOUL	Barry White (K-Tel)
-	42	DAMNED BUT NOT FORGOTTEN	Damned (Dojo)
31	43	THE JAZZ SINGER	Neil Diamond (Capitol)
37	44	SONGS TO LEARN AND SING	Echo & the Bunnymen (Korova)
23	45	NO JACKET REQUIRED	Phil Collins (Virgin)
-	46	SOUNDTRACK FROM MISTRAL'S DAUGHTER	Vladimir Cosma (Carrere)
45	47	DOUBLE TROUBLE	Molly Hatchet (Epic)
48	48	THE BEST OF INCANTATION - MUSIC FROM THE ANDES	Incantation (West Five)
41	49	BLACK AND WHITE	Terraplane (Epic)
36	50	HITS 3	Various Artists (CBS/WEA)

Sting's resurgence into the Top 3 with the seven-month-old *The Dream Of The Blue Turtles* was largely attributable to extensive airplay for its track *Russians*, which made the Top 10 as a single at the same time. Barbra Streisand made the Top 10 for the first time since her *Love Songs* compilation in 1982 with an album of Broadway show tunes which, stylistically, went back to her early 1960s stage roots.

February – March 1986

15 February 1986

1	1	BROTHERS IN ARMS	Dire Straits (Vertigo)
2	2	HUNTING HIGH AND LOW	A-Ha (Warner Bros.)
4	3	WORLD MACHINE	Level 42 (Polydor)
3	4	THE DREAM OF THE BLUE TURTLES	Sting (A&M)
5	5	ISLAND LIFE	Grace Jones (Island)
6	6	WHITNEY HOUSTON	Whitney Houston (Arista)
9	7	BE YOURSELF TONIGHT	Eurythmics (RCA)
7	8	THE BROADWAY ALBUM	Barbra Streisand (CBS)
16	9	ONCE UPON A TIME	Simple Minds (Virgin)
8	10	LIKE A VIRGIN	Madonna (Sire)
12	11	FINE YOUNG CANNIBALS	Fine Young Cannibals (London)
14	12	LUXURY OF LIFE	Five Star (Tent)
11	13	FEARGAL SHARKEY	Feargal Sharkey (Virgin)
10	14	GO WEST/BANGS AND CRASHES	Go West (Chrysalis)
24	15	LITTLE CREATURES	Talking Heads (EMI)
23	16	ROCKY IV	Soundtrack (Scotti Brothers)
13	17	HIGH PRIORITY	Cherrelle (Tabu)
15	18	PROMISE	Sade (Epic)
19	19	EASY PIECES	Lloyd Cole & the Commotions (Polydor)
-	20	ALBUM/CASSETTE	Public Image Limited (Virgin)
20	21	MACALLA	Clannad (RCA)
21	22	WHO'S ZOOMIN' WHO	Aretha Franklin (Arista)
35	23	THE LOVE SONGS	George Benson (K-Tel)
28	24	PRIVATE DANCER	Tina Turner (Capitol)
18	25	NOW THAT'S WHAT I CALL MUSIC 6	Various Artists (EMI/Virgin)
31	26	THE CLASSIC TOUCH	Richard Clayderman (Decca/Delphine)
17	27	SONGS FROM THE BIG CHAIR	Tears for Fears (Mercury)
30	28	ICE ON FIRE	Elton John (Rocket)
25	29	JENNIFER RUSH	Jennifer Rush (CBS)
-	30	U2 LIVE: UNDER A BLOOD RED SKY	U2 (Island)
27	31	BACK IN THE DHSS	Half Man Half Biscuit (Probe Plus)
45	32	NO JACKET REQUIRED	Phil Collins (Virgin)
39	33	LISTEN LIKE THIEVES	INXS (Mercury)
32	34	SUZANNE VEGA	Suzanne Vega (A&M)
48	35	THE BEST OF INCANTATION - MUSIC FROM THE ANDES	Incantation (West Five)
34	36	ALEXANDER O'NEAL	Alexander O'Neal (Tabu)
-	37	PSYCHOCANDY	Jesus & Mary Chain (Blanco Y Negro)
-	38	STEVE McQUEEN	Prefab Sprout (Kitchenware)
38	39	THE LOVE ALBUM	Various Artists (Telstar)
33	40	ROCK ME TONIGHT	Freddie Jackson (Capitol)
-	41	ALCHEMY – DIRE STRAITS LIVE	Dire Straits (Vertigo)
44	42	SONGS TO LEARN AND SING	Echo & the Bunnymen (Korova)
43	43	THE JAZZ SINGER	Neil Diamond (Capitol)
-	44	ROCK A LITTLE	Stevie Nicks (Modern)
40	45	THE SINGLES COLLECTION	Spandau Ballet (Chrysalis)
-	46	THE POWER OF CLASSIC ROCK	London Symphony Orchestra (Portrait)
-	47	THE FIRST ALBUM	Madonna (Sire)
-	48	MISPLACED CHILDHOOD	Marillion (EMI)
-	49	STRENGTH	Alarm (IRS/MCA)
-	50	THE VERY BEST OF THE COMMODORES	Commodores (Telstar)

22 February 1986

1	1	BROTHERS IN ARMS	Dire Straits (Vertigo)
2	2	HUNTING HIGH AND LOW	A-Ha (Warner Bros.)
20	3	ALBUM/CASSETTE	Public Image Limited (Virgin)
6	4	WHITNEY HOUSTON	Whitney Houston (Arista)
3	5	WORLD MACHINE	Level 42 (Polydor)
5	6	ISLAND LIFE	Grace Jones (Island)
16	7	ROCKY IV	Soundtrack (Scotti Brothers)
7	8	BE YOURSELF TONIGHT	Eurythmics (RCA)
8	9	THE BROADWAY ALBUM	Barbra Streisand (CBS)
12	10	LUXURY OF LIFE	Five Star (Tent)
4	11	THE DREAM OF THE BLUE TURTLES	Sting (A&M)
9	12	ONCE UPON A TIME	Simple Minds (Virgin)
14	13	GO WEST/BANGS AND CRASHES	Go West (Chrysalis)
32	14	NO JACKET REQUIRED	Phil Collins (Virgin)
10	15	LIKE A VIRGIN	Madonna (Sire)
13	16	FEARGAL SHARKEY	Feargal Sharkey (Virgin)
-	17	THE ULTIMATE SUN	Ozzy Osbourne (Epic)
11	18	FINE YOUNG CANNIBALS	Fine Young Cannibals (London)
15	19	LITTLE CREATURES	Talking Heads (EMI)
-	20	WELCOME TO THE REAL WORLD	Mr Mister (RCA)
18	21	PROMISE	Sade (Epic)
-	22	THE DANCE HITS ALBUM	Various Artists (Towerbell)
-	23	JONATHAN KING'S ENTERTAINMENT USA	Various Artists (Stylus)
21	24	MACALLA	Clannad (RCA)
-	25	HOUNDS OF LOVE	Kate Bush (EMI)
24	26	PRIVATE DANCER	Tina Turner (Capitol)
17	27	HIGH PRIORITY	Cherrelle (Tabu)
19	28	EASY PIECES	Lloyd Cole & the Commotions (Polydor)
31	29	BACK IN THE DHSS	Half Man Half Biscuit (Probe Plus)
44	30	ROCK A LITTLE	Stevie Nicks (Modern)
22	31	WHO'S ZOOMIN' WHO	Aretha Franklin (Arista)
27	32	SONGS FROM THE BIG CHAIR	Tears for Fears (Mercury)
26	33	THE CLASSIC TOUCH	Richard Clayderman (Decca/Delphine)
-	34	HITS 3	Various Artists (CBS/WEA)
25	35	NOW THAT'S WHAT I CALL MUSIC 6	Various Artists (EMI/Virgin)
36	36	ALEXANDER O'NEAL	Alexander O'Neal (Tabu)
45	37	THE SINGLES COLLECTION	Spandau Ballet (Chrysalis)
28	38	ICE ON FIRE	Elton John (Rocket)
-	39	THE SECRET OF ASSOCIATION	Paul Young (CBS)
-	40	RECKLESS	Bryan Adams (A&M)
33	41	LISTEN LIKE THIEVES	INXS (Mercury)
38	42	STEVE McQUEEN	Prefab Sprout (Kitchenware)
40	43	ROCK ME TONIGHT	Freddie Jackson (Capitol)
23	44	THE LOVE SONGS	George Benson (K-Tel)
-	45	RADIO	L L Cool J (Def Jam)
41	46	ALCHEMY – DIRE STRAITS LIVE	Dire Straits (Vertigo)
48	47	MISPLACED CHILDHOOD	Marillion (EMI)
-	48	LEGEND	Bob Marley & the Wailers (Island)
46	49	THE POWER OF CLASSIC ROCK	London Symphony Orchestra (Portrait)
47	50	THE FIRST ALBUM	Madonna (Sire)

1 March 1986

1	1	BROTHERS IN ARMS	Dire Straits (Vertigo)
4	2	WHITNEY HOUSTON	Whitney Houston (Arista)
2	3	HUNTING HIGH AND LOW	A-Ha (Warner Bros.)
7	4	ROCKY IV	Soundtrack (Scotti Brothers)
6	5	ISLAND LIFE	Grace Jones (Island)
14	6	NO JACKET REQUIRED	Phil Collins (Virgin)
5	7	WORLD MACHINE	Level 42 (Polydor)
8	8	BE YOURSELF TONIGHT	Eurythmics (RCA)
9	9	THE BROADWAY ALBUM	Barbra Streisand (CBS)
17	10	THE ULTIMATE SUN	Ozzy Osbourne (Epic)
11	11	THE DREAM OF THE BLUE TURTLE	Sting (A&M)
3	12	ALBUM/CASSETTE	Public Image Limited (Virgin)
22	13	THE DANCE HITS ALBUM	Various Artists (Towerbell)
10	14	LUXURY OF LIFE	Five Star (Tent)
12	15	ONCE UPON A TIME	Simple Minds (Virgin)
16	16	LIKE A VIRGIN	Madonna (Sire)
16	17	FEARGAL SHARKEY	Feargal Sharkey (Virgin)
-	18	THE COLOUR OF SPRING	Talk Talk (EMI)
13	19	GO WEST/BANGS AND CRASHES	Go West (Chrysalis)
23	20	JONATHAN KING'S ENTERTAINMENT USA	Various Artists (Stylus)
19	21	LITTLE CREATURES	Talking Heads (EMI)
20	22	WELCOME TO THE REAL WORLD	Mr Mister (RCA)
-	23	KING OF AMERICA	Costello Show (F-Beat)
21	24	PROMISE	Sade (Epic)
43	25	ROCK ME TONIGHT	Freddie Jackson (Capitol)
31	26	WHO'S ZOOMIN' WHO	Aretha Franklin (Arista)
-	27	A DATE WITH ELVIS	Cramps (Big Beat)
27	28	HIGH PRIORITY	Cherrelle (Tabu)
18	29	FINE YOUNG CANNIBALS	Fine Young Cannibals (London)
32	30	SONGS FROM THE BIG CHAIR	Tears for Fears (Mercury)
29	31	BACK IN THE DHSS	Half Man Half Biscuit (Probe Plus)
28	32	EASY PIECES	Lloyd Cole & the Commotions (Polydor)
25	33	HOUNDS OF LOVE	Kate Bush (EMI)
-	34	SEVENTH STAR	Black Sabbath (Vertigo)
-	35	ALONE	Nana Mouskouri (Philips)
33	36	THE CLASSIC TOUCH	Richard Clayderman (Decca/Delphine)
-	37	SUDDENLY	Billy Ocean (Jive)
46	38	ALCHEMY – DIRE STRAITS LIVE	Dire Straits (Vertigo)
24	39	MACALLA	Clannad (RCA)
34	40	HITS 3	Various Artists (CBS/WEA)
44	41	THE LOVE SONGS	George Benson (K-Tel)
42	42	STEVE McQUEEN	Prefab Sprout (Kitchenware)
50	43	THE FIRST ALBUM	Madonna (Sire)
-	44	GREATEST HITS VOL 1 & VOL 2	Billy Joel (CBS)
30	45	ROCK A LITTLE	Stevie Nicks (Modern)
35	46	NOW THAT'S WHAT I CALL MUSIC 6	Various Artists (EMI/Virgin)
-	47	THE LOVE ALBUM	Various Artists (Telstar)
-	48	THE BLIND LEADING THE NAKED	Violent Femmes (Slash)
-	49	THE UNFORGETTABLE FIRE	U2 (Island)
-	50	THE WEDGE	Pallas (Harvest)

Whitney Houston's debut album had first charted in December 1985 when her chart-topping single *Saving All My Love For You* took off. It took its time making the Top 10, however, to finally peak at Number 2 in March after a further boost from Whitney's next hit *How Will I Know?* Public Image Ltd's set had a different title depending on which format you bought - i.e. album or cassette (the later CD was called *CD*).

8 March 1986

last week	this week	Title	Artist (Label)
1	1	BROTHERS IN ARMS	Dire Straits (Vertigo)
6	2	NO JACKET REQUIRED	Phil Collins (Virgin)
2	3	WHITNEY HOUSTON	Whitney Houston (Arista)
4	4	ROCKY IV	Soundtrack (Scotti Brothers)
5	5	ISLAND LIFE	Grace Jones (Island)
3	6	HUNTING HIGH AND LOW	A-Ha (Warner Bros.)
8	7	BE YOURSELF TONIGHT	Eurythmics (RCA)
18	8	THE COLOUR OF SPRING	Talk Talk (EMI)
10	9	THE ULTIMATE SUN	Ozzy Osbourne (Epic)
23	10	KING OF AMERICA	Costello Show (F-Beat)
9	11	THE BROADWAY ALBUM	Barbra Streisand (CBS)
7	12	WORLD MACHINE	Level 42 (Polydor)
15	13	ONCE UPON A TIME	Simple Minds (Virgin)
20	14	JONATHAN KING'S ENTERTAINMENT USA	Various Artists (Stylus)
14	15	LUXURY OF LIFE	Five Star (Tent)
33	16	HOUNDS OF LOVE	Kate Bush (EMI)
11	17	THE DREAM OF THE BLUE TURTLES	Sting (A&M)
21	18	LITTLE CREATURES	Talking Heads (EMI)
12	19	ALBUM/CASSETTE	Public Image Limited (Virgin)
16	20	LIKE A VIRGIN	Madonna (Sire)
19	21	GO WEST/BANGS AND CRASHES	Go West (Chrysalis)
13	22	THE DANCE HITS ALBUM	Various Artists (Towerbell)
22	23	WELCOME TO THE REAL WORLD	Mr Mister (RCA)
30	24	SONGS FROM THE BIG CHAIR	Tears for Fears (Mercury)
35	25	ALONE	Nana Mouskouri (Philips)
-	26	BIG COCK	King Kurt (Stiff)
29	27	FINE YOUNG CANNIBALS	Fine Young Cannibals (London)
37	28	SUDDENLY	Billy Ocean (Jive)
-	29	FINAL VINYL	Rainbow (Polydor)
27	30	A DATE WITH ELVIS	Cramps (Big Beat)
17	31	FEARGAL SHARKEY	Feargal Sharkey (Virgin)
25	32	ROCK ME TONIGHT	Freddie Jackson (Capitol)
28	33	HIGH PRIORITY	Cherrelle (Tabu)
31	34	BACK IN THE DHSS	Half Man Half Biscuit (Probe Plus)
34	35	SEVENTH STAR	Black Sabbath (Vertigo)
48	36	THE BLIND LEADING THE NAKED	Violent Femmes (Slash)
-	37	PIECE BY PIECE	John Martyn (Island)
24	38	PROMISE	Sade (Epic)
26	39	WHO'S ZOOMIN' WHO	Aretha Franklin (Arista)
38	40	ALCHEMY – DIRE STRAITS LIVE	Dire Straits (Vertigo)
-	41	PRECIOUS MEMORIES	Ann Williamson (Emerald)
39	42	MACALLA	Clannad (RCA)
-	43	ALEXANDER O'NEAL	Alexander O'Neal (Tabu)
32	44	EASY PIECES	Lloyd Cole & the Commotions (Polydor)
41	45	THE LOVE SONGS	George Benson (K-Tel)
43	46	THE FIRST ALBUM	Madonna (Sire)
-	47	IT TAKES TWO	Juicy (Epic)
-	48	SEVEN SINGLES DEEP	Icicle Works (Beggars Banquet)
49	49	THE UNFORGETTABLE FIRE	U2 (Island)
46	50	NOW THAT'S WHAT I CALL MUSIC 6	Various Artists (EMI/Virgin)

15 March 1986

last week	this week	Title	Artist (Label)
1	1	BROTHERS IN ARMS	Dire Straits (Vertigo)
3	2	WHITNEY HOUSTON	Whitney Houston (Arista)
2	3	NO JACKET REQUIRED	Phil Collins (Virgin)
4	4	THE COLOUR OF SPRING	Talk Talk (EMI)
4	5	ROCKY IV	Soundtrack (Scotti Brothers)
14	6	JONATHAN KING'S ENTERTAINMENT USA	Various Artists (Stylus)
7	7	BE YOURSELF TONIGHT	Eurythmics (RCA)
10	8	KING OF AMERICA	Costello Show (F-Beat)
16	9	HOUNDS OF LOVE	Kate Bush (EMI)
21	10	GO WEST/BANGS AND CRASHES	Go West (Chrysalis)
17	11	THE DREAM OF THE BLUE TURTLES	Sting (A&M)
-	12	HITS FOR LOVERS	Various Artists (Epic)
6	13	HUNTING HIGH AND LOW	A-Ha (Warner Bros.)
5	14	ISLAND LIFE	Grace Jones (Island)
13	15	ONCE UPON A TIME	Simple Minds (Virgin)
18	16	LITTLE CREATURES	Talking Heads (EMI)
37	17	PIECE BY PIECE	John Martyn (Island)
11	18	THE BROADWAY ALBUM	Barbra Streisand (CBS)
12	19	WORLD MACHINE	Level 42 (Polydor)
-	20	LIVES IN THE BALANCE	Jackson Browne (Asylum)
22	21	THE DANCE HITS ALBUM	Various Artists (Towerbell)
23	22	WELCOME TO THE REAL WORLD	Mr Mister (RCA)
9	23	THE ULTIMATE SUN	Ozzy Osbourne (Epic)
25	24	ALONE	Nana Mouskouri (Philips)
-	25	BALANCE OF POWER	Electric Light Orchestra (Epic)
29	26	FINAL VINYL	Rainbow (Polydor)
26	27	BIG COCK	King Kurt (Stiff)
34	28	BACK IN THE DHSS	Half Man Half Biscuit (Probe Plus)
-	29	LIVE IN NEW YORK CITY	John Lennon (Parlophone)
35	30	SEVENTH STAR	Black Sabbath (Vertigo)
-	31	DIFFERENT LIGHT	Bangles (CBS)
-	32	MASTER OF PUPPETS	Metallica (Music For Nations)
15	33	LUXURY OF LIFE	Five Star (Tent)
19	34	ALBUM/CASSETTE	Public Image Limited (Virgin)
20	35	LIKE A VIRGIN	Madonna (Sire)
43	36	ALEXANDER O'NEAL	Alexander O'Neal (Tabu)
24	37	SONGS FROM THE BIG CHAIR	Tears for Fears (Mercury)
28	38	SUDDENLY	Billy Ocean (Jive)
30	39	A DATE WITH ELVIS	Cramps (Big Beat)
-	40	TOTAL CONTRAST	Total Contrast (London)
-	41	PASSION	William Bell (Wilbe import)
32	42	ROCK ME TONIGHT	Freddie Jackson (Capitol)
33	43	HIGH PRIORITY	Cherrelle (Tabu)
40	44	ALCHEMY – DIRE STRAITS LIVE	Dire Straits (Vertigo)
31	45	FEARGAL SHARKEY	Feargal Sharkey (Virgin)
-	46	MEETS THE MOTHERS OF PREVENTION	Frank Zappa (EMI)
47	47	NIGHT BEAT 2	Various Artists (Stylus)
41	48	PRECIOUS MEMORIES	Ann Williamson (Emerald)
38	49	PROMISE	Sade (Epic)
39	50	WHO'S ZOOMIN' WHO	Aretha Franklin (Arista)

22 March 1986

last week	this week	Title	Artist (Label)
1	1	BROTHERS IN ARMS	Dire Straits (Vertigo)
3	2	NO JACKET REQUIRED	Phil Collins (Virgin)
-	3	HITS FOR LOVERS	Various Artists (Epic)
9	4	HOUNDS OF LOVE	Kate Bush (EMI)
2	5	WHITNEY HOUSTON	Whitney Houston (Arista)
5	6	ROCKY IV	Soundtrack (Scotti Brothers)
7	7	BE YOURSELF TONIGHT	Eurythmics (RCA)
16	8	LITTLE CREATURES	Talking Heads (EMI)
4	9	THE COLOUR OF SPRING	Talk Talk (EMI)
25	10	BALANCE OF POWER	Electric Light Orchestra (Epic)
8	11	KING OF AMERICA	Costello Show (F-Beat)
6	12	JONATHAN KING'S ENTERTAINMENT USA	Various Artists (Stylus)
15	13	ONCE UPON A TIME	Simple Minds (Virgin)
36	14	ALEXANDER O'NEAL	Alexander O'Neal (Tabu/Epic)
10	15	GO WEST/BANGS AND CRASHES	Go West (Chrysalis)
18	16	THE BROADWAY ALBUM	Barbra Streisand (CBS)
13	17	HUNTING HIGH AND LOW	A-Ha (Warner Bros.)
14	18	ISLAND LIFE	Grace Jones (Island)
22	19	WELCOME TO THE REAL WORLD	Mr Mister (RCA)
31	20	DIFFERENT LIGHT	Bangles (CBS)
11	21	THE DREAM OF THE BLUE TURTLES	Sting (A&M)
17	22	PIECE BY PIECE	John Martyn (Island)
19	23	WORLD MACHINE	Level 42 (Polydor)
32	24	MASTER OF PUPPETS	Metallica (Music For Nations)
20	25	LIVES IN THE BALANCE	Jackson Browne (Asylum)
-	26	NEITHER MOSCOW NOR WASHINGTON	Redskins (Decca)
47	27	NIGHT BEAT 2	Various Artists (Stylus)
24	28	ALONE	Nana Mouskouri (Philips)
-	29	MATT BIANCO	Matt Bianco (WEA)
27	30	BIG COCK	King Kurt (Stiff)
-	31	CUTS LIKE A KNIFE	Bryan Adams (Capitol)
48	32	PRECIOUS MEMORIES	Ann Williamson (Emerald)
35	33	LIKE A VIRGIN	Madonna (Sire)
-	34	NEW YORK, NEW YORK (GREATEST HITS)	Frank Sinatra (Reprise)
26	35	FINAL VINYL	Rainbow (Polydor)
42	36	ROCK ME TONIGHT	Freddie Jackson (Capitol)
-	37	HYMNS	Huddersfield Choral Society (HMV)
38	38	SUDDENLY	Billy Ocean (Jive)
45	39	FEARGAL SHARKEY	Feargal Sharkey (Virgin)
34	40	ALBUM/CASSETTE	Public Image Limited (Virgin)
33	41	LUXURY OF LIFE	Five Star (Tent)
30	42	SEVENTH STAR	Black Sabbath (Vertigo)
-	43	THE CINEMA HITS ALBUM	Various Artists (Towerbell)
29	44	LIVE IN NEW YORK CITY	John Lennon (Parlophone)
39	45	A DATE WITH ELVIS	Cramps (Big Beat)
-	46	DAMNED BUT NOT FORGOTTEN	Damned (Dojo)
21	47	THE DANCE HITS ALBUM	Various (Towerbell)
-	48	IT TAKES TWO	Juicy (Epic)
28	49	BACK IN THE DHSS	Half Man Half Biscuit (Probe Plus)
40	50	TOTAL CONTRAST	Total Contrast (London)

Brothers In Arms' early 1986 stretch at the top of the chart lasted for exactly 3 months with no gaps - one of the longest consecutive stays of modern times. Among the albums which just failed to dislodge it in March was Phil Collins' *No Jacket Required*, now a chart resident for just over a year! ELO returned after a three-year recording absence with what would be their last Top 10 album, *Balance Of Power*.

March – April 1986

29 March 1986

last week	this week	Title	Artist
1	1	BROTHERS IN ARMS	Dire Straits (Vertigo)
5	2	WHITNEY HOUSTON	Whitney Houston (Arista)
2	3	NO JACKET REQUIRED	Phil Collins (Virgin)
4	4	HOUNDS OF LOVE	Kate Bush (EMI)
10	5	BALANCE OF POWER	Electric Light Orchestra (Epic)
3	6	HITS FOR LOVERS	Various Artists (Epic)
6	7	ROCKY IV	Soundtrack (Scotti Brothers)
19	8	WELCOME TO THE REAL WORLD	Mr Mister (RCA)
9	9	THE COLOUR OF SPRING	Talk Talk (EMI)
-	10	HITS 4	Various Artists (CBS/WEA)
7	11	BE YOURSELF TONIGHT	Eurythmics (RCA)
14	12	ALEXANDER O'NEAL	Alexander O'Neal (Tabu)
-	13	EATEN ALIVE	Diana Ross (Capitol)
29	14	MATT BIANCO	Matt Bianco (WEA)
8	15	LITTLE CREATURES	Talking Heads (EMI)
12	16	JONATHAN KING'S ENTERTAINMENT USA	Various Artists (Stylus)
18	17	ISLAND LIFE	Grace Jones (Island)
31	18	CUTS LIKE A KNIFE	Bryan Adams (Capitol)
20	19	DIFFERENT LIGHT	Bangles (CBS)
26	20	NEITHER MOSCOW NOR WASHINGTON	Redskins (Decca)
27	21	NIGHT BEAT 2	Various Artists (Stylus)
-	22	BLACK CELEBRATION	Depeche Mode (Mute)
13	23	ONCE UPON A TIME	Simple Minds (Virgin)
17	24	HUNTING HIGH AND LOW	A-Ha (Warner Bros.)
11	25	KING OF AMERICA	Costello Show (F-Beat)
34	26	NEW YORK, NEW YORK (GREATEST HITS)	Frank Sinatra (Reprise)
16	27	THE BROADWAY ALBUM	Barbra Streisand (CBS)
25	28	LIVES IN THE BALANCE	Jackson Browne (Asylum)
49	29	BACK IN THE DHSS	Half Man Half Biscuit (Probe Plus)
-	30	STREET SOUNDS HIP HOP ELECTRO 11	Various Artists (Street Sounds)
37	31	HYMNS	Huddersfield Choral Society (HMV)
36	32	ROCK ME TONIGHT	Freddie Jackson (Capitol)
21	33	THE DREAM OF THE BLUE TURTLES	Sting (A&M)
24	34	MASTER OF PUPPETS	Metallica (Music For Nations)
-	35	9012 LIVE: THESOLOS	Yes (Atlantic)
22	36	PIECE BY PIECE	John Martyn (Island)
38	37	SUDDENLY	Billy Ocean (Jive)
47	38	THE DANCE HITS ALBUM	Various Artists (Towerbell)
23	39	WORLD MACHINE	Level 42 (Polydor)
15	40	GO WEST/BANGS AND CRASHES	Go West (Chrysalis)
45	41	A DATE WITH ELVIS	Cramps (Big Beat)
-	42	CANDY APPLE GREY	Husker Du (Warner Bros.)
48	43	IT TAKES TWO	Juicy (Epic)
50	44	TOTAL CONTRAST	Total Contrast (London)
35	45	FINAL VINYL	Rainbow (Polydor)
41	46	LUXURY OF LIFE	Five Star (Tent)
43	47	THE CINEMA HITS ALBUM	Various (Towerbell)
-	48	PAINT YOUR WAGON	Red Lorry Yellow Lorry (Red Rhino)
46	49	DAMNED BUT NOT FORGOTTEN	Damned (Dojo)
28	50	ALONE	Nana Mouskouri (Philips)

5 April 1986

last	this	Title	Artist
1	1	BROTHERS IN ARMS	Dire Straits (Vertigo)
10	2	HITS 4	Various Artists (CBS/WEA)
2	3	WHITNEY HOUSTON	Whitney Houston (Arista)
11	4	BE YOURSELF TONIGHT	Eurythmics (RCA)
3	5	NO JACKET REQUIRED	Phil Collins (Virgin)
9	6	THE COLOUR OF SPRING	Talk Talk (EMI)
5	7	BALANCE OF POWER	Electric Light Orchestra (Epic)
-	8	DIRTY WORK	Rolling Stones (CBS)
22	9	BLACK CELEBRATION	Depeche Mode (Mute)
6	10	HITS FOR LOVERS	Various Artists (Epic)
8	11	WELCOME TO THE REAL WORLD	Mr Mister (RCA)
13	12	EATEN ALIVE	Diana Ross (Capitol)
4	13	HOUNDS OF LOVE	Kate Bush (EMI)
7	14	ROCKY IV	Soundtrack (Scotti Brothers)
24	15	HUNTING HIGH AND LOW	A-Ha (Warner Bros.)
30	16	STREET SOUNDS HIP HOP ELECTRO 11	Various Artists (Street Sounds)
32	17	ROCK ME TONIGHT	Freddie Jackson (Capitol)
14	18	MATT BIANCO	Matt Bianco (WEA)
31	19	HYMNS	Huddersfield Choral Society (HMV)
15	20	LITTLE CREATURES	Talking Heads (EMI)
26	21	NEW YORK, NEW YORK (GREATEST HITS)	Frank Sinatra (Reprise)
12	22	ALEXANDER O'NEAL	Alexander O'Neal (Tabu)
18	23	CUTS LIKE A KNIFE	Bryan Adams (Capitol)
20	24	NEITHER MOSCOW NOR WASHINGTON	Redskins (Decca)
23	25	ONCE UPON A TIME	Simple Minds (Virgin)
33	26	THE DREAM OF THE BLUE TURTLES	Sting (A&M)
17	27	ISLAND LIFE	Grace Jones (Island)
16	28	JONATHAN KING'S ENTERTAINMENT USA	Various Artists (Stylus)
-	29	5150	Van Halen (Warner Bros.)
-	30	MEAN BUSINESS	Firm (Atlantic)
35	31	9012 LIVE: THESOLOS	Yes (Atlantic)
-	32	PLEASE	Pet Shop Boys (Parlophone)
50	33	ALONE	Nana Mouskouri (Philips)
-	34	THE ALBUM	Mantronix (10)
19	35	DIFFERENT LIGHT	Bangles (CBS)
-	36	THIS IS BIG AUDIO DYNAMITE	Big Audio Dynamite (CBS)
34	37	MASTER OF PUPPETS	Metallica (Music For Nations)
48	38	PAINT YOUR WAGON	Red Lorry Yellow Lorry (Red Rhino)
47	39	THE CINEMA HITS ALBUM	Various Artists (Towerbell)
-	40	PHANTASMAGORIA	Damned (MCA)
28	41	LIVES IN THE BALANCE	Jackson Browne (Asylum)
25	42	KING OF AMERICA	Costello Show (F-Beat)
27	43	THE BROADWAY ALBUM	Barbra Streisand (CBS)
29	44	BACK IN THE DHSS	Half Man Half Biscuit (Probe Plus)
42	45	CANDY APPLE GREY	Husker Du (Warner Bros.)
-	46	SPORTS	Huey Lewis and the News (Chrysalis)
-	47	BIG WORLD	Joe Jackson (A&M)
21	48	NIGHT BEAT 2	Various Artists (Stylus)
-	49	MASTERS OF METAL	Various Artists (Powersaw/K-Tel)
40	50	GO WEST/BANGS AND CRASHES	Go West (Chrysalis)

12 April 1986

last	this	Title	Artist
2	1	HITS 4	Various Artists (CBS/WEA)
1	2	BROTHERS IN ARMS	Dire Straits (Vertigo)
3	3	WHITNEY HOUSTON	Whitney Houston (Arista)
9	4	BLACK CELEBRATION	Depeche Mode (Mute)
11	5	WELCOME TO THE REAL WORLD	Mr Mister (RCA)
8	6	DIRTY WORK	Rolling Stones (CBS)
10	7	HITS FOR LOVERS	Various Artists (Epic)
5	8	NO JACKET REQUIRED	Phil Collins (Virgin)
12	9	EATEN ALIVE	Diana Ross (Capitol)
32	10	PLEASE	Pet Shop Boys (Parlophone)
14	11	ROCKY IV	Soundtrack (Scotti Brothers)
29	12	5150	Van Halen (Warner Bros.)
6	13	THE COLOUR OF SPRING	Talk Talk (EMI)
17	14	ROCK ME TONIGHT	Freddie Jackson (Capitol)
21	15	NEW YORK, NEW YORK (GREATEST HITS)	Frank Sinatra (Reprise)
22	16	ALEXANDER O'NEAL	Alexander O'Neal (Tabu/Epic)
25	17	ONCE UPON A TIME	Simple Minds (Virgin)
4	18	BE YOURSELF TONIGHT	Eurythmics (RCA)
13	19	HOUNDS OF LOVE	Kate Bush (EMI)
7	20	BALANCE OF POWER	Electric Light Orchestra (Epic)
19	21	HYMNS	Huddersfield Choral Society (HMV)
15	22	HUNTING HIGH AND LOW	A-Ha (Warner Bros.)
16	23	STREET SOUNDS HIP HOP ELECTRO 11	Various Artists (Street Sounds)
-	24	PARADE	Prince & the Revolution (Warner Bros.)
27	25	ISLAND LIFE	Grace Jones (Island)
26	26	THE DREAM OF THE BLUE TURTLES	Sting (A&M)
30	27	MEAN BUSINESS	Firm (Atlantic)
18	28	MATT BIANCO	Matt Bianco (WEA)
-	29	SONGS FROM THE BIG CHAIR	Tears for Fears (Mercury)
-	30	ABSOLUTE BEGINNERS	Soundtrack (Virgin)
-	31	STREET SOUNDS EDITION 16	Various Artists (Street Sounds)
40	32	PHANTASMAGORIA	Damned (MCA)
-	33	FROM LUXURY TO HEARTACHE	Culture Club (Virgin)
36	34	THIS IS BIG AUDIO DYNAMITE	Big Audio Dynamite (CBS)
35	35	DIFFERENT LIGHT	Bangles (CBS)
20	36	LITTLE CREATURES	Talking Heads (EMI)
48	37	NIGHT BEAT 2	Various Artists (Stylus)
34	38	THE ALBUM	Mantronix (10)
23	39	CUTS LIKE A KNIFE	Bryan Adams (Capitol)
39	40	THE CINEMA HITS ALBUM	Various Artists (Towerbell)
46	41	SPORTS	Huey Lewis and the News (Chrysalis)
41	42	LIVES IN THE BALANCE	Jackson Browne (Asylum)
24	43	NEITHER MOSCOW NOR WASHINGTON	Redskins (Decca)
28	44	JONATHAN KING'S ENTERTAINMENT USA	Various Artists (Stylus)
43	45	THE BROADWAY ALBUM	Barbra Streisand (CBS)
42	46	KING OF AMERICA	Costello Show (F-Beat)
50	47	GO WEST/BANGS AND CRASHES	Go West (Chrysalis)
31	48	9012 LIVE: THESOLOS	Yes (Atlantic)
47	49	BIG WORLD	Joe Jackson (A&M)
-	50	STREET SOUNDS EDITION 15	Various Artists (Street Sounds)

Acts celebrating their first UK Top 10 albums after finding singles success included Talk Talk with *The Colour Of Spring* and Mr Mister with *Welcome To The Real World*, while Depeche Mode had their sixth Top Tenner in a row with *Black Celebration*. James Brown could also claim his first hit UK album with the *Rocky IV* soundtrack, which was dominated by his hit single from the movie, *Living In America*.

April – May 1986

last week	this week	19 April 1986		
1	1	HITS 4	Various Artists (CBS/WEA)	
2	2	BROTHERS IN ARMS	Dire Straits (Vertigo)	
10	3	PLEASE	Pet Shop Boys (Parlophone)	
3	4	WHITNEY HOUSTON	Whitney Houston (Arista)	
24	5	PARADE	Prince & the Revolution (Warner Bros.)	
6	6	DIRTY WORK	Rolling Stones (CBS)	
5	7	WELCOME TO THE REAL WORLD	Mr Mister (RCA)	
22	8	HUNTING HIGH AND LOW	A-Ha (Warner Bros.)	
33	9	FROM LUXURY TO HEARTACHE	Culture Club (Virgin)	
12	10	5150	Van Halen (Warner Bros.)	
8	11	NO JACKET REQUIRED	Phil Collins (Virgin)	
7	12	HITS FOR LOVERS	Various Artists (Epic)	
15	13	NEW YORK, NEW YORK (GREATEST HITS)	Frank Sinatra (Reprise)	
30	14	ABSOLUTE BEGINNERS	Soundtrack (Virgin)	
18	15	BE YOURSELF TONIGHT	Eurythmics (RCA)	
-	16	RENDEZ-VOUS	Jean Michel Jarre (Polydor)	
31	17	STREET SOUNDS EDITION 16	Various Artists (Street Sounds)	
4	18	BLACK CELEBRATION	Depeche Mode (Mute)	
17	19	ONCE UPON A TIME	Simple Minds (Virgin)	
16	20	ALEXANDER O'NEAL	Alexander O'Neal (Tabu)	
11	21	ROCKY IV	Soundtrack (Scotti Brothers)	
9	22	EATEN ALIVE	Diana Ross (Capitol)	
-	23	ANIMAL MAGIC	Blow Monkeys (RCA)	
34	24	THIS IS BIG AUDIO DYNAMITE	Big Audio Dynamite (CBS)	
13	25	THE COLOUR OF SPRING	Talk Talk (EMI)	
26	26	THE DREAM OF THE BLUE TURTLES	Sting (A&M)	
-	27	LITTLE MISS DANGEROUS	Ted Nugent (WEA)	
49	28	BIG WORLD	Joe Jackson (A&M)	
19	29	HOUNDS OF LOVE	Kate Bush (EMI)	
-	30	HEART TO HEART	Various Artists (K-Tel)	
-	31	SHALAMAR: THE GREATEST HITS	Shalamar (Stylus)	
-	32	WORLD MACHINE	Level 42 (Polydor)	
21	33	HYMNS	Huddersfield Choral Society (HMV)	
32	34	PHANTASMAGORIA	Damned (MCA)	
14	35	ROCK ME TONIGHT	Freddie Jackson (Capitol)	
23	36	STREET SOUNDS HIP HOP ELECTRO 11	Various Artists (Street Sounds)	
27	37	MEAN BUSINESS	Firm (Atlantic)	
-	38	TURBO	Judas Priest (CBS)	
-	39	CONTROL	Janet Jackson (A&M)	
-	40	LIKE A VIRGIN	Madonna (Sire)	
-	41	THE TV ALBUM TWO	Various Artists (Towerbell)	
-	42	AS THE BAND TURNS	Atlantic Star (A&M)	
38	43	THE ALBUM	Mantronix (10)	
20	44	BALANCE OF POWER	Electric Light Orchestra (Epic)	
36	45	LITTLE CREATURES	Talking Heads (EMI)	
-	46	HOME OF THE BRAVE	Laurie Anderson (Warner Bros.)	
37	47	NIGHT BEAT 2	Various Artists (Stylus)	
35	48	DIFFERENT LIGHT	Bangles (CBS)	
-	49	LUXURY OF LIFE	Five Star (Tent)	
-	50	SUZANNE VEGA	Suzanne Vega (A&M)	

		26 April 1986		
1	1	HITS 4	Various Artists (CBS/WEA)	
2	2	BROTHERS IN ARMS	Dire Straits (Vertigo)	
5	3	PARADE	Prince & the Revolution (Warner Bros.)	
4	4	WHITNEY HOUSTON	Whitney Houston (Arista)	
3	5	PLEASE	Pet Shop Boys (Parlophone)	
7	6	WELCOME TO THE REAL WORLD	Mr Mister (RCA)	
11	7	NO JACKET REQUIRED	Phil Collins (Virgin)	
8	8	HUNTING HIGH AND LOW	A-Ha (Warner Bros.)	
10	9	5150	Van Halen (Warner Bros.)	
-	10	STREET LIFE - 20 GREAT HITS	Bryan Ferry & Roxy Music (EG)	
6	11	DIRTY WORK	Rolling Stones (CBS)	
19	12	ONCE UPON A TIME	Simple Minds (Virgin)	
16	13	RENDEZ-VOUS	Jean Michel Jarre (Polydor)	
24	14	THIS IS BIG AUDIO DYNAMITE	Big Audio Dynamite (CBS)	
38	15	TURBO	Judas Priest (CBS)	
-	16	TINDERBOX	Siouxsie & the Banshees (Wonderland)	
12	17	HITS FOR LOVERS	Various Artists (Epic)	
-	18	VICTORIALAND	Cocteau Twins (4AD)	
31	19	SHALAMAR: THE GREATEST HITS	Shalamar (Stylus)	
14	20	ABSOLUTE BEGINNERS	Soundtrack (Virgin)	
23	21	ANIMAL MAGIC	Blow Monkeys (RCA)	
9	22	FROM LUXURY TO HEARTACHE	Culture Club (Virgin)	
30	23	HEART TO HEART	Various Artists (K-Tel)	
17	24	STREET SOUNDS EDITION 16	Various Artists (Street Sounds)	
-	25	ON THE BEACH	Chris Rea (Magnet)	
18	26	BLACK CELEBRATION	Depeche Mode (Mute)	
21	27	ROCKY IV	Soundtrack (Scotti Brothers)	
15	28	BE YOURSELF TONIGHT	Eurythmics (RCA)	
29	29	HOUNDS OF LOVE	Kate Bush (EMI)	
-	30	HIPSWAY	Hipsway (Mercury)	
-	31	THE MAN AND HIS MUSIC	Sam Cooke (RCA)	
-	32	LIKE A ROCK	Bob Seger (Capitol)	
25	33	THE COLOUR OF SPRING	Talk Talk (EMI)	
20	34	ALEXANDER O'NEAL	Alexander O'Neal (Tabu)	
35	35	ROCK ME TONIGHT	Freddie Jackson (Capitol)	
-	36	IN VISIBLE SILENCE	Art Of Noise (China)	
50	37	SUZANNE VEGA	Suzanne Vega (A&M)	
13	38	NEW YORK, NEW YORK (GREATEST HITS)	Frank Sinatra (Reprise)	
39	39	CONTROL	Janet Jackson (A&M)	
28	40	BIG WORLD	Joe Jackson (A&M)	
-	41	ROCK ANTHEMS VOLUME TWO	Various (K-Tel)	
-	42	GO WEST/BANGS AND CRASHES	Go West (Chrysalis)	
22	43	EATEN ALIVE	Diana Ross (Capitol)	
26	44	THE DREAM OF THE BLUE TURTLES	Sting (A&M)	
27	45	LITTLE MISS DANGEROUS	Ted Nugent (WEA)	
40	46	LIKE A VIRGIN	Madonna (Sire)	
-	47	IT TAKES TWO	Juicy (Epic)	
43	48	THE ALBUM	Mantronix (10)	
41	49	THE TV ALBUM TWO	Various Artists (Towerbell)	
-	50	CHILDREN OF THE NIGHT	52nd Street (10/)	

		3 May 1986		
10	1	STREET LIFE - 20 GREAT HITS	Bryan Ferry & Roxy Music (EG)	
1	2	HITS 4	Various Artists (CBS/WEA)	
2	3	BROTHERS IN ARMS	Dire Straits (Vertigo)	
4	4	WHITNEY HOUSTON	Whitney Houston (Arista)	
5	5	PLEASE	Pet Shop Boys (Parlophone)	
16	6	TINDERBOX	Siouxsie & the Banshees (Wonderland)	
8	7	HUNTING HIGH AND LOW	A-Ha (Warner Bros.)	
19	8	SHALAMAR: THE GREATEST HITS	Shalamar (Stylus)	
20	9	ABSOLUTE BEGINNERS	Soundtrack (Virgin)	
3	10	PARADE	Prince & the Revolution (Warner Bros.)	
25	11	ON THE BEACH	Chris Rea (Magnet)	
13	12	RENDEZ-VOUS	Jean Michel Jarre (Polydor)	
6	13	WELCOME TO THE REAL WORLD	Mr Mister (RCA)	
18	14	VICTORIALAND	Cocteau Twins (4AD)	
31	15	THE MAN AND HIS MUSIC	Sam Cooke (RCA)	
12	16	ONCE UPON A TIME	Simple Minds (Virgin)	
23	17	HEART TO HEART	Various Artists (K-Tel)	
7	18	NO JACKET REQUIRED	Phil Collins (Virgin)	
9	19	5150	Van Halen (Warner Bros.)	
14	20	THIS IS BIG AUDIO DYNAMITE	Big Audio Dynamite (CBS)	
36	21	IN VISIBLE SILENCE	Art Of Noise (China)	
37	22	SUZANNE VEGA	Suzanne Vega (A&M)	
11	23	DIRTY WORK	Rolling Stones (CBS)	
17	24	HITS FOR LOVERS	Various Artists (Epic)	
32	25	LIKE A ROCK	Bob Seger (Capitol)	
21	26	ANIMAL MAGIC	Blow Monkeys (RCA)	
49	27	THE TV ALBUM TWO	Various Artists (Towerbell)	
15	28	TURBO	Judas Priest (CBS)	
24	29	STREET SOUNDS EDITION 16	Various Artists (Street Sounds)	
30	30	HIPSWAY	Hipsway (Mercury)	
-	31	WORLD MACHINE	Level 42 (Polydor)	
27	32	ROCKY IV	Soundtrack (Scotti Brothers)	
-	33	BACK TO THE CENTRE	Paul Brady (Mercury)	
-	34	FALCO 3	Falco (A&M)	
41	35	ROCK ANTHEMS VOLUME TWO	Various (K-Tel)	
26	36	BLACK CELEBRATION	Depeche Mode (Mute)	
35	37	ROCK ME TONIGHT	Freddie Jackson (Capitol)	
-	38	DO ME BABY	Meli'sa Morgan (Capitol)	
33	39	THE COLOUR OF SPRING	Talk Talk (EMI)	
28	40	BE YOURSELF TONIGHT	Eurythmics (RCA)	
-	41	LITTLE CREATURES	Talking Heads (EMI)	
22	42	FROM LUXURY TO HEARTACHE	Culture Club (Virgin)	
-	43	QUEEN'S GREATEST HITS	Queen (EMI)	
34	44	ALEXANDER O'NEAL	Alexander O'Neal (Tabu)	
46	45	LIKE A VIRGIN	Madonna (Sire)	
29	46	HOUNDS OF LOVE	Kate Bush (EMI)	
-	47	SONGS FROM THE BIG CHAIR	Tears for Fears (Mercury)	
39	48	CONTROL	Janet Jackson (A&M)	
43	49	EATEN ALIVE	Diana Ross (Capitol)	
-	50	PORTRAIT	Diana Ross (Telstar)	

In the absence of new recordings either by Bryan Ferry or his erstwhile band Roxy Music, the TV-promoted compilation *Street Life* filled the gap effectively by combining for the first time the hit recordings by both band and soloist. Also scoring with hits compilations were Frank Sinatra (his sixth such collection to make the charts) and Shalamar - the latter group's compilation also being TV-advertised.

May 1986

10 May 1986

LW	TW	Title	Artist (Label)
1	1	STREET LIFE - 20 GREAT HITS	Bryan Ferry & Roxy Music (EG)
4	2	WHITNEY HOUSTON	Whitney Houston (Arista)
3	3	BROTHERS IN ARMS	Dire Straits (Vertigo)
2	4	HITS 4	Various Artists (CBS/WEA)
6	5	TINDERBOX	Siouxsie & the Banshees (Wonderland)
8	6	SHALAMAR: THE GREATEST HITS	Shalamar (Stylus)
15	7	THE MAN AND HIS MUSIC	Sam Cooke (RCA)
14	8	VICTORIALAND	Cocteau Twins (4AD)
7	9	HUNTING HIGH AND LOW	A-Ha (Warner Bros.)
5	10	PLEASE	Pet Shop Boys (Parlophone)
11	11	ON THE BEACH	Chris Rea (Magnet)
16	12	ONCE UPON A TIME	Simple Minds (Virgin)
19	13	5150	Van Halen (Warner Bros.)
12	14	RENDEZ-VOUS	Jean Michel Jarre (Polydor)
10	15	PARADE	Prince & the Revolution (Warner Bros.)
18	16	NO JACKET REQUIRED	Phil Collins (Virgin)
22	17	SUZANNE VEGA	Suzanne Vega (A&M)
13	18	WELCOME TO THE REAL WORLD	Mr Mister (RCA)
17	19	HEART TO HEART	Various Artists (K-Tel)
20	20	THIS IS BIG AUDIO DYNAMITE	Big Audio Dynamite (CBS)
31	21	WORLD MACHINE	Level 42 (Polydor)
23	22	DIRTY WORK	Rolling Stones (CBS)
35	23	ROCK ANTHEMS VOLUME TWO	Various (K-Tel)
-	24	TRUTHDARE DOUBLEDARE	Bronski Beat (London)
-	25	RAPTURE	Anita Baker (Elektra)
-	26	LUXURY OF LIFE	Five Star (Tent)
24	27	HITS FOR LOVERS	Various Artists (Epic)
21	28	IN VISIBLE SILENCE	Art Of Noise (China)
36	29	BLACK CELEBRATION	Depeche Mode (Mute)
26	30	ANIMAL MAGIC	Blow Monkeys (RCA)
9	31	ABSOLUTE BEGINNERS	Soundtrack (Virgin)
27	32	THE TV ALBUM TWO	Various Artists (Towerbell)
-	33	SANDS OF TIME	SOS Band (Tabu)
46	34	HOUNDS OF LOVE	Kate Bush (EMI)
32	35	ROCKY IV	Soundtrack (Scotti Brothers)
25	36	LIKE A ROCK	Bob Seger (Capitol)
48	37	CONTROL	Janet Jackson (A&M)
28	38	TURBO	Judas Priest (CBS)
-	39	RUSSIAN ROULETTE	Accept (Portrait)
-	40	GETTING THE HOLY GHOST ACROSS	Bill Nelson (Portrait)
49	41	EATEN ALIVE	Diana Ross (Capitol)
44	42	ALEXANDER O'NEAL	Alexander O'Neal (Tabu)
33	43	BACK TO THE CENTRE	Paul Brady (Mercury)
-	44	THE OTHER SIDE OF LIFE	Moody Blues (Threshold)
-	45	THE COLLECTION	Earth Wind & Fire (K-Tel)
30	46	HIPSWAY	Hipsway (Mercury)
-	47	OUT OF AFRICA	Soundtrack (MCA)
-	48	BACK IN THE DHSS	Half Man Half Biscuit (Probe Plus)
34	49	FALCO 3	Falco (A&M)
-	50	MOVIN'	Jennifer Rush (CBS)

17 May 1986

LW	TW	Title	Artist (Label)
1	1	STREET LIFE - 20 GREAT HITS	Bryan Ferry & Roxy Music (EG)
3	2	BROTHERS IN ARMS	Dire Straits (Vertigo)
6	3	SHALAMAR: THE GREATEST HITS	Shalamar (Stylus)
2	4	WHITNEY HOUSTON	Whitney Houston (Arista)
12	5	ONCE UPON A TIME	Simple Minds (Virgin)
4	6	HITS 4	Various Artists (CBS/WEA)
21	7	WORLD MACHINE	Level 42 (Polydor)
9	8	HUNTING HIGH AND LOW	A-Ha (Warner Bros.)
7	9	THE MAN AND HIS MUSIC	Sam Cooke (RCA)
11	10	ON THE BEACH	Chris Rea (Magnet)
16	11	NO JACKET REQUIRED	Phil Collins (Virgin)
10	12	PLEASE	Pet Shop Boys (Parlophone)
17	13	SUZANNE VEGA	Suzanne Vega (A&M)
-	14	UTTERLY UTTERLY LIVE!	Comic Relief (Comic Relief/WEA)
19	15	HEART TO HEART	Various Artists (K-Tel)
-	16	HOME AND ABROAD	Style Council (Polydor)
45	17	THE COLLECTION	Earth Wind & Fire (K-Tel)
14	18	RENDEZ-VOUS	Jean Michel Jarre (Polydor)
26	19	LUXURY OF LIFE	Five Star (Tent)
24	20	TRUTHDARE DOUBLEDARE	Bronski Beat (London)
13	21	5150	Van Halen (Warner Bros.)
8	22	VICTORIALAND	Cocteau Twins (4AD)
5	23	TINDERBOX	Siouxsie & the Banshees (Wonderland)
15	24	PARADE	Prince & the Revolution (Warner Bros.)
20	25	THIS IS BIG AUDIO DYNAMITE	Big Audio Dynamite (CBS)
25	26	RAPTURE	Anita Baker (Elektra)
-	27	LOVE ZONE	Billy Ocean (Jive)
18	28	WELCOME TO THE REAL WORLD	Mr Mister (RCA)
33	29	SANDS OF TIME	SOS Band (Tabu)
31	30	ABSOLUTE BEGINNERS	Soundtrack (Virgin)
34	31	HOUNDS OF LOVE	Kate Bush (EMI)
30	32	ANIMAL MAGIC	Blow Monkeys (RCA)
36	33	LIKE A ROCK	Bob Seger (Capitol)
-	34	DO ME BABY	Meli'sa Morgan (Capitol)
37	35	CONTROL	Janet Jackson (A&M)
48	36	BACK IN THE DHSS	Half Man Half Biscuit (Probe Plus)
27	37	HITS FOR LOVERS	Various Artists (Epic)
32	38	THE TV ALBUM TWO	Various Artists (Towerbell)
-	39	DIFFERENT LIGHT	Bangles (CBS)
-	40	HEART	Heart (Capitol)
-	41	DAVE CLARK'S TIME	Various Artists (EMI)
28	42	IN VISIBLE SILENCE	Art Of Noise (China)
43	43	BACK TO THE CENTRE	Paul Brady (Mercury)
46	44	HIPSWAY	Hipsway (Mercury)
-	45	QUEEN'S GREATEST HITS	Queen (EMI)
-	46	ROCK ME TONIGHT	Freddie Jackson (Capitol)
49	47	FALCO 3	Falco (A&M)
-	48	LISTEN LIKE THIEVES	INXS (Mercury)
22	49	DIRTY WORK	Rolling Stones (CBS)
29	50	BLACK CELEBRATION	Depeche Mode (Mute)

24 May 1986

LW	TW	Title	Artist (Label)
1	1	STREET LIFE - 20 GREAT HITS	Bryan Ferry & Roxy Music (EG)
2	2	BROTHERS IN ARMS	Dire Straits (Vertigo)
16	3	HOME AND ABROAD	Style Council (Polydor)
27	4	LOVE ZONE	Billy Ocean (Jive)
4	5	WHITNEY HOUSTON	Whitney Houston (Arista)
17	6	THE COLLECTION	Earth Wind & Fire (K-Tel)
3	7	SHALAMAR'S GREATEST HITS	Shalamar (Stylus)
5	8	ONCE UPON A TIME	Simple Minds (Virgin)
29	9	SANDS OF TIME	SOS Band (Tabu)
7	10	WORLD MACHINE	Level 42 (Polydor)
6	11	HITS 4	Various Artists (CBS/WEA)
14	12	UTTERLY UTTERLY LIVE!	Comic Relief (Comic Relief/WEA)
-	13	PRINCESS	Princess (Supreme)
21	14	5150	Van Halen (Warner Bros.)
13	15	SUZANNE VEGA	Suzanne Vega (A&M)
9	16	THE MAN AND HIS MUSIC	Sam Cooke (RCA)
11	17	NO JACKET REQUIRED	Phil Collins (Virgin)
8	18	HUNTING HIGH AND LOW	A-Ha (Warner Bros.)
15	19	HEART TO HEART	Various Artists (K-Tel)
-	20	RAISED ON RADIO	Journey (CBS)
10	21	ON THE BEACH	Chris Rea (Magnet)
12	22	PLEASE	Pet Shop Boys (Parlophone)
-	23	SECRET DREAMS AND FORBIDDEN FIRE	Bonnie Tyler (CBS)
20	24	TRUTHDARE DOUBLEDARE	Bronski Beat (London)
41	25	DAVE CLARK'S TIME	Various Artists (EMI)
28	26	WELCOME TO THE REAL WORLD	Mr Mister (RCA)
22	27	VICTORIALAND	Cocteau Twins (4AD)
18	28	RENDEZ-VOUS	Jean Michel Jarre (Polydor)
19	29	LUXURY OF LIFE	Five Star (Tent)
26	30	RAPTURE	Anita Baker (Elektra)
31	31	HOUNDS OF LOVE	Kate Bush (EMI)
-	32	THE FINAL FRONTIER	Keel (Vertigo)
35	33	CONTROL	Janet Jackson (A&M)
36	34	BACK IN THE DHSS	Half Man Half Biscuit (Probe Plus)
-	35	URBAN BEACHES	Cactus World News (MCA)
-	36	MOONLIGHT SHADOWS	Shadows (Polydor)
32	37	ANIMAL MAGIC	Blow Monkeys (RCA)
-	38	GUN SHY	Screaming Blue Messiahs (WEA)
23	39	TINDERBOX	Siouxsie & the Banshees (Wonderland)
24	40	PARADE	Prince & the Revolution (Warner Bros.)
25	41	THIS IS BIG AUDIO DYNAMITE	Big Audio Dynamite (CBS)
-	42	THE WINNER IN YOU	Patti LaBelle (MCA)
-	43	MANIC POP THRILL	That Petrol Emotion (Demon)
-	44	SPEED KILLS II	Various Artists (Under One Flag)
-	45	BOXED SET	Velvet Underground (Polydor)
30	46	ABSOLUTE BEGINNERS	Soundtrack (Virgin)
34	47	DO ME BABY	Meli'sa Morgan (Capitol)
42	48	IN VISIBLE SILENCE	Art Of Noise (China)
44	49	HIPSWAY	Hipsway (Mercury)
45	50	QUEEN'S GREATEST HITS	Queen (EMI)

Sam Cooke's *The Man And His Music*, its profile boosted by the recent Number 2 single success of the 21-years-dead singer with *Wonderful World* (itself attributable to exposure on a Levi's Jeans TV ad), was a double album anthologising the biggest selection available to date of Cooke's hit recordings from the 1950s and '60s. Ironically, this was his only album ever to make the UK chart, never mind the Top 10!

288

31 May 1986

last week	this week	Title	Artist (Label)
1	1	STREET LIFE - 20 GREAT HITS	Bryan Ferry & Roxy Music (EG)
2	2	BROTHERS IN ARMS	Dire Straits (Vertigo)
4	3	LOVE ZONE	Billy Ocean (Jive)
-	4	SO	Peter Gabriel (Virgin)
3	5	HOME AND ABROAD	Style Council (Polydor)
6	6	THE COLLECTION	Earth Wind & Fire (K-Tel)
10	7	WORLD MACHINE	Level 42 (Polydor)
5	8	WHITNEY HOUSTON	Whitney Houston (Arista)
18	9	HUNTING HIGH AND LOW	A-Ha (Warner Bros.)
11	10	HITS 4	Various Artists (CBS/WEA)
-	11	PICTURE BOOK	Simply Red (Elektra)
20	12	RAISED ON RADIO	Journey (CBS)
16	13	THE MAN AND HIS MUSIC	Sam Cooke (RCA)
8	14	ONCE UPON A TIME	Simple Minds (Virgin)
36	15	MOONLIGHT SHADOWS	Shadows (Polydor)
9	16	SANDS OF TIME	SOS Band (Tabu)
7	17	SHALAMAR: THE GREATEST HITS	Shalamar (Stylus)
21	18	ON THE BEACH	Chris Rea (Magnet)
13	19	PRINCESS	Princess (Supreme)
-	20	STANDING ON THE BEACH - THE SINGLES	Cure (Fiction)
12	21	UTTERLY UTTERLY LIVE!	Comic Relief (Comic Relief/WEA)
29	22	LUXURY OF LIFE	Five Star (Tent)
-	23	BANGS AND CRASHES	Go West (Chrysalis)
-	24	LET'S HEAR IT FROM THE GIRLS	Various Artists (Stylus)
22	25	PLEASE	Pet Shop Boys (Parlophone)
-	26	SLEIGHT OF HAND	Joan Armatrading (A&M)
42	27	THE WINNER IN YOU	Patti LaBelle (MCA)
14	28	5150	Van Halen (Warner Bros.)
-	29	ANIMAL BOY	Ramones (Beggers Banquet)
15	30	SUZANNE VEGA	Suzanne Vega (A&M)
17	31	NO JACKET REQUIRED	Phil Collins (Virgin)
33	32	CONTROL	Janet Jackson (A&M)
26	33	WELCOME TO THE REAL WORLD	Mr Mister (RCA)
25	34	DAVE CLARK'S TIME	Various Artists (EMI)
41	35	THIS IS BIG AUDIO DYNAMITE	Big Audio Dynamite (CBS)
37	36	ANIMAL MAGIC	Blow Monkeys (RCA)
35	37	URBAN BEACHES	Cactus World News (MCA)
-	38	MISTRIAL	Lou Reed (RCA)
27	39	VICTORIALAND	Cocteau Twins (4AD)
39	40	TINDERBOX	Siouxsie & the Banshees (Wonderland)
19	41	HEART TO HEART	Various Artists (K-Tel)
40	42	PARADE	Prince & the Revolution (Warner Bros.)
24	43	TRUTHDARE DOUBLEDARE	Bronski Beat (London)
23	44	SECRET DREAMS AND FORBIDDEN FIRE	Bonnie Tyler (CBS)
-	45	ALCHEMY – DIRE STRAITS LIVE	Dire Straits (Vertigo)
31	46	HOUNDS OF LOVE	Kate Bush (EMI)
43	47	MANIC POP THRILL	That Petrol Emotion (Demon)
48	48	IN VISIBLE SILENCE	Art Of Noise (China)
-	49	HEADED FOR THE FUTURE	Neil Diamond (CBS)
-	50	SISTERS ARE DOIN' IT	Various Artists (Towerbell)

7 June 1986

last week	this week	Title	Artist (Label)
4	1	SO	Peter Gabriel (Virgin)
1	2	STREET LIFE - 20 GREAT HITS	Bryan Ferry & Roxy Music (EG)
20	3	STANDING ON THE BEACH - THE SINGLES	Cure (Fiction)
2	4	BROTHERS IN ARMS	Dire Straits (Vertigo)
11	5	PICTURE BOOK	Simply Red (Elektra)
3	6	LOVE ZONE	Billy Ocean (Jive)
7	7	WORLD MACHINE	Level 42 (Polydor)
6	8	THE COLLECTION	Earth Wind & Fire (K-Tel)
23	9	BANGS AND CRASHES	Go West (Chrysalis)
8	10	WHITNEY HOUSTON	Whitney Houston (Arista)
13	11	THE MAN AND HIS MUSIC	Sam Cooke (RCA)
28	12	5150	Van Halen (Warner Bros.)
14	13	ONCE UPON A TIME	Simple Minds (Virgin)
18	14	ON THE BEACH	Chris Rea (Magnet)
-	15	WHO MADE WHO	AC/DC (Atlantic)
10	16	HITS 4	Various Artists (CBS/WEA)
9	17	HUNTING HIGH AND LOW	A-Ha (Warner Bros.)
25	18	PLEASE	Pet Shop Boys (Parlophone)
5	19	HOME AND ABROAD	Style Council (Polydor)
27	20	THE WINNER IN YOU	Patti LaBelle (MCA)
12	21	RAISED ON RADIO	Journey (CBS)
21	22	UTTERLY UTTERLY LIVE!	Comic Relief (Comic Relief/WEA)
17	23	SHALAMAR: THE GREATEST HITS	Shalamar (Stylus)
29	24	ANIMAL BOY	Ramones (Beggers Banquet)
15	25	MOONLIGHT SHADOWS	Shadows (Polydor)
24	26	LET'S HEAR IT FROM THE GIRLS	Various Artists (Stylus)
38	27	MISTRIAL	Lou Reed (RCA)
33	28	WELCOME TO THE REAL WORLD	Mr Mister (RCA)
16	29	SANDS OF TIME	SOS Band (Tabu)
19	30	PRINCESS	Princess (Supreme)
31	31	NO JACKET REQUIRED	Phil Collins (Virgin)
22	32	LUXURY OF LIFE	Five Star (Tent)
30	33	SUZANNE VEGA	Suzanne Vega (A&M)
-	34	THE COLOUR OF SPRING	Talk Talk (EMI)
26	35	SLEIGHT OF HAND	Joan Armatrading (A&M)
50	36	SISTERS ARE DOIN' IT	Various Artists (Towerbell)
-	37	QUEEN'S GREATEST HITS	Queen (EMI)
46	38	HOUNDS OF LOVE	Kate Bush (EMI)
-	39	INTO THE LIGHT	Chris DeBurgh (A&M)
-	40	WHERE YOU GONNA BE TONIGHT?	Willie Collins (Capitol)
35	41	THIS IS BIG AUDIO DYNAMITE	Big Audio Dynamite (CBS)
49	42	HEADED FOR THE FUTURE	Neil Diamond (CBS)
37	43	URBAN BEACHES	Cactus World News (MCA)
39	44	VICTORIALAND	Cocteau Twins (4AD)
47	45	MANIC POP THRILL	That Petrol Emotion (Demon)
-	46	RIPTIDE	Robert Palmer (Island)
32	47	CONTROL	Janet Jackson (A&M)
34	48	DAVE CLARK'S TIME	Various Artists (EMI)
36	49	ANIMAL MAGIC	Blow Monkeys (RCA)
43	50	TRUTHDARE DOUBLEDARE	Bronski Beat (London)

14 June 1986

last week	this week	Title	Artist (Label)
1	1	SO	Peter Gabriel (Virgin)
5	2	PICTURE BOOK	Simply Red (Elektra)
2	3	STREET LIFE - 20 GREAT HITS	Bryan Ferry & Roxy Music (EG)
3	4	STANDING ON THE BEACH - THE SINGLES	Cure (Fiction)
4	5	BROTHERS IN ARMS	Dire Straits (Vertigo)
7	6	WORLD MACHINE	Level 42 (Polydor)
9	7	BANGS AND CRASHES	Go West (Chrysalis)
39	8	INTO THE LIGHT	Chris DeBurgh (A&M)
6	9	LOVE ZONE	Billy Ocean (Jive)
-	10	A KIND OF MAGIC	Queen (EMI)
15	11	WHO MADE WHO	AC/DC (Atlantic)
10	12	WHITNEY HOUSTON	Whitney Houston (Arista)
8	13	THE COLLECTION	Earth Wind & Fire (K-Tel)
11	14	THE MAN AND HIS MUSIC	Sam Cooke (RCA)
25	15	MOONLIGHT SHADOWS	Shadows (Polydor)
18	16	PLEASE	Pet Shop Boys (Parlophone)
17	17	HUNTING HIGH AND LOW	A-Ha (Warner Bros.)
13	18	ONCE UPON A TIME	Simple Minds (Virgin)
14	19	ON THE BEACH	Chris Rea (Magnet)
33	20	SUZANNE VEGA	Suzanne Vega (A&M)
21	21	RAISED ON RADIO	Journey (CBS)
-	22	UPFRONT1	Various Artists (Serious)
31	23	NO JACKET REQUIRED	Phil Collins (Virgin)
32	24	LUXURY OF LIFE	Five Star (Tent)
23	25	SHALAMAR: THE GREATEST HITS	Shalamar (Stylus)
12	26	5150	Van Halen (Warner Bros.)
20	27	THE WINNER IN YOU	Patti LaBelle (MCA)
30	28	PRINCESS	Princess (Supreme)
24	29	ANIMAL BOY	Ramones (Beggers Banquet)
34	30	THE COLOUR OF SPRING	Talk Talk (EMI)
47	31	CONTROL	Janet Jackson (A&M)
19	32	HOME AND ABROAD	Style Council (Polydor)
29	33	SANDS OF TIME	SOS Band (Tabu)
16	34	HITS 4	Various Artists (CBS/WEA)
22	35	UTTERLY UTTERLY LIVE!	Comic Relief (Comic Relief/WEA)
26	36	LET'S HEAR IT FROM THE GIRLS	Various Artists (Stylus)
-	37	MARVIN GAYE'S GREATEST HITS	Marvin Gaye (Telstar)
41	38	THIS IS BIG AUDIO DYNAMITE	Big Audio Dynamite (CBS)
-	39	RAPTURE	Anita Baker (Elektra)
43	40	URBAN BEACHES	Cactus World News (MCA)
27	41	MISTRIAL	Lou Reed (RCA)
35	42	SLEIGHT OF HAND	Joan Armatrading (A&M)
38	43	HOUNDS OF LOVE	Kate Bush (EMI)
28	44	WELCOME TO THE REAL WORLD	Mr Mister (RCA)
46	45	RIPTIDE	Robert Palmer (Island)
44	46	VICTORIALAND	Cocteau Twins (4AD)
-	47	BE YOURSELF TONIGHT	Eurythmics (RCA)
-	48	SECRET DREAMS AND FORBIDDEN FIRE	Bonnie Tyler (CBS)
-	49	LITTLE CREATURES	Talking Heads (EMI)
-	50	DIRTY WORK	Rolling Stones (CBS)

Seven albums into his solo career (including his soundtrack set for the film *Birdy*), Peter Gabriel scored his all-time biggest seller with *So* (which was only his third album - again including the soundtrack - not to be titled *Peter Gabriel*!) A vital factor in the initial success of this set, which by 1992 would be Virgin Records' eighth best-seller of all time, was the single *Sledgehammer* and its award-winning video.

June – July 1986

Genesis replaced their former lead singer Peter Gabriel at Number 1 in typically swift chart-topping style with *Invisible Touch* (though the title track had failed to get anywhere near Gabriel's *Sledgehammer* in the singles chart). Both acts, in the process of this exchange, kept Queen to another Number 2 album with *A Kind Of Magic*. Meanwhile, almost unnoticed at the foot of the chart, Erasure made a quiet debut.

12 July 1986

last week	this week		
1	1	INVISIBLE TOUCH	Genesis (Charisma)
3	2	SO	Peter Gabriel (Virgin)
2	3	A KIND OF MAGIC	Queen (EMI)
-	4	TRUE BLUE	Madonna (Sire)
10	5	LONDON 0 - HULL 4	Housemartins (Go! Discs)
4	6	THE QUEEN IS DEAD	Smiths (Rough Trade)
5	7	PICTURE BOOK	Simply Red (Elektra)
19	8	EVERY BEAT OF MY HEART	Rod Stewart (Warner Bros.)
-	9	REVENGE	Eurythmics (RCA)
12	10	BRING ON THE NIGHT	Sting (A&M)
16	11	SUZANNE VEGA	Suzanne Vega (A&M)
6	12	BROTHERS IN ARMS	Dire Straits (Vertigo)
-	13	INTERMISSION	Dio (Vertigo)
18	14	INTO THE LIGHT	Chris DeBurgh (A&M)
8	15	HUNTING HIGH AND LOW	A-Ha (Warner Bros.)
-	16	BACK IN THE HIGH LIFE	Stevie Winwood (Island)
11	17	WHITNEY HOUSTON	Whitney Houston (Arista)
13	18	RIPTIDE	Robert Palmer (Island)
7	19	STREET LIFE - 20 GREAT HITS	Bryan Ferry & Roxy Music (EG)
24	20	WORLD MACHINE	Level 42 (Polydor)
22	21	ONCE UPON A TIME	Simple Minds (Virgin)
49	22	STANDING ON THE BEACH - THE SINGLES	Cure (Fiction)
9	23	LOVE ZONE	Billy Ocean (Jive)
17	24	PLEASE	Pet Shop Boys (Parlophone)
14	25	MOONLIGHT SHADOWS	Shadows (Polydor)
15	26	THE MAN AND HIS MUSIC	Sam Cooke (RCA)
21	27	CASHFLOW	Cashflow (Club)
-	28	LABYRINTH - ORIGINAL SOUNDTRACK	David Bowie (EMI America)
23	29	BANGS AND CRASHES	Go West (Chrysalis)
-	30	GIANT	Woodentops (Rough Trade)
35	31	POOLSIDE	Nu Shooz (Atlantic)
28	32	STREET SOUNDS ELECTRO 12	Various Artists (Street Sounds)
41	33	HEADLINES	Midnight Star (MCA)
20	34	UPFRONT1	Various Artists (Serious)
50	35	DANCE HITS 2	Various Artists (Towerbell)
30	36	THE WINNER IN YOU	Patti LaBelle (MCA)
47	37	WHERE YOU GONNA BE TONIGHT?	Willie Collins (Capitol)
-	38	TO THE TOP	Aswad (Simba)
31	39	NO JACKET REQUIRED	Phil Collins (Virgin)
26	40	ON THE BEACH	Chris Rea (Magnet)
-	41	SHALAMAR: THE GREATEST HITS	Shalamar (Stylus)
-	42	PRINCESS	Princess (Supreme)
-	43	BEST OF THE REAL THING	Real Thing (PRT)
32	44	BORN SANDY DEVOTIONAL	Triffids (Hot)
33	45	WHO MADE WHO	AC/DC (Atlantic)
-	46	SHRINE	D C Lee (CBS)
42	47	CONTROL	Janet Jackson (A&M)
44	48	FALCO 3	Falco (A&M)
-	49	MAKE IT BIG	Wham! (Epic)
-	50	OUT OF THE GREY	Dream Syndicate (Chrysalis)

19 July 1986

last week	this week		
4	1	TRUE BLUE	Madonna (Sire)
9	2	REVENGE	Eurythmics (RCA)
1	3	INVISIBLE TOUCH	Genesis (Charisma)
5	4	LONDON 0 - HULL 4	Housemartins (Go! Discs)
3	5	A KIND OF MAGIC	Queen (EMI)
8	6	EVERY BEAT OF MY HEART	Rod Stewart (Warner Bros.)
-	7	THE SEER	Big Country (Mercury)
16	8	BACK IN THE HIGH LIFE	Stevie Winwood (Island)
7	9	PICTURE BOOK	Simply Red (Elektra)
-	10	THE FINAL	Wham! (Epic)
2	11	SO	Peter Gabriel (Virgin)
6	12	THE QUEEN IS DEAD	Smiths (Rough Trade)
14	13	INTO THE LIGHT	Chris DeBurgh (A&M)
12	14	BROTHERS IN ARMS	Dire Straits (Vertigo)
15	15	HUNTING HIGH AND LOW	A-Ha (Warner Bros.)
11	16	SUZANNE VEGA	Suzanne Vega (A&M)
-	17	NOW – THE SUMMER ALBUM	Various Artists (EMI/Virgin)
19	18	STREET LIFE - 20 GREAT HITS	Bryan Ferry & Roxy Music (EG)
-	19	DISCOVER	Gene Love Jezebel (Beggars Banquet)
10	20	BRING ON THE NIGHT	Sting (A&M)
18	21	RIPTIDE	Robert Palmer (Island)
17	22	WHITNEY HOUSTON	Whitney Houston (Arista)
20	23	WORLD MACHINE	Level 42 (Polydor)
22	24	STANDING ON THE BEACH - THE SINGLES	Cure (Fiction)
13	25	INTERMISSION	Dio (Vertigo)
24	26	PLEASE	Pet Shop Boys (Parlophone)
40	27	ON THE BEACH	Chris Rea (Magnet)
30	28	GIANT	Woodentops (Rough Trade)
26	29	THE MAN AND HIS MUSIC	Sam Cooke (RCA)
43	30	BEST OF THE REAL THING	Real Thing (PRT)
-	31	EAT 'EM AND SMILE	David Lee Roth (Warner Bros.)
21	32	ONCE UPON A TIME	Simple Minds (Virgin)
25	33	MOONLIGHT SHADOWS	Shadows (Polydor)
23	34	LOVE ZONE	Billy Ocean (Jive)
29	35	BANGS AND CRASHES	Go West (Chrysalis)
47	36	CONTROL	Janet Jackson (A&M)
27	37	CASHFLOW	Cashflow (Club)
35	38	DANCE HITS 2	Various Artists (Towerbell)
38	39	TO THE TOP	Aswad (Simba)
33	40	HEADLINES	Midnight Star (MCA)
32	41	STREET SOUNDS ELECTRO 12	Various Artists (Street Sounds)
39	42	NO JACKET REQUIRED	Phil Collins (Virgin)
45	43	WHO MADE WHO	AC/DC (Atlantic)
31	44	POOLSIDE	Nu Shooz (Atlantic)
49	45	MAKE IT BIG	Wham! (Epic)
37	46	WHERE YOU GONNA BE TONIGHT?	Willie Collins (Capitol)
-	47	DISCO BEACH PARTY	Various Artists (Stylus)
36	48	THE WINNER IN YOU	Patti LaBelle (MCA)
48	49	FALCO 3	Falco (A&M)
44	50	BORN SANDY DEVOTIONAL	Triffids (Hot)

26 July 1986

last week	this week		
1	1	TRUE BLUE	Madonna (Sire)
2	2	REVENGE	Eurythmics (RCA)
8	3	BACK IN THE HIGH LIFE	Stevie Winwood (Island)
10	4	THE FINAL	Wham! (Epic)
7	5	THE SEER	Big Country (Mercury)
5	6	A KIND OF MAGIC	Queen (EMI)
6	7	EVERY BEAT OF MY HEART	Rod Stewart (Warner Bros)
3	8	INVISIBLE TOUCH	Genesis (Charisma)
17	9	NOW – THE SUMMER ALBUM	Various Artists (EMI/Virgin)
4	10	LONDON 0 - HULL 4	Housemartins (Go! Discs)
13	11	INTO THE LIGHT	Chris DeBurgh (A&M)
14	12	BROTHERS IN ARMS	Dire Straits (Vertigo)
9	13	PICTURE BOOK	Simply Red (Elektra)
11	14	SO	Peter Gabriel (Virgin)
15	15	HUNTING HIGH AND LOW	A-Ha (Warner Bros.)
16	16	SUZANNE VEGA	Suzanne Vega (A&M)
21	17	RIPTIDE	Robert Palmer (Island)
12	18	THE QUEEN IS DEAD	Smiths (Rough Trade)
31	19	EAT 'EM AND SMILE	David Lee Roth (Warner Bros.)
24	20	STANDING ON THE BEACH - THE SINGLES	Cure (Fiction)
18	21	STREET LIFE - 20 GREAT HITS	Bryan Ferry & Roxy Music (EG)
32	22	ONCE UPON A TIME	Simple Minds (Virgin)
22	23	WHITNEY HOUSTON	Whitney Houston (Arista)
19	24	DISCOVER	Gene Love Jezebel (Beggars Banquet)
34	25	LOVE ZONE	Billy Ocean (Jive)
20	26	BRING ON THE NIGHT	Sting (A&M)
28	27	GIANT	Woodentops (Rough Trade)
30	28	BEST OF THE REAL THING	Real Thing (PRT)
38	29	DANCE HITS 2	Various Artists (Towerbell)
42	30	NO JACKET REQUIRED	Phil Collins (Virgin)
27	31	ON THE BEACH	Chris Rea (Magnet)
-	32	STREET SOUNDS EDITION 17	Various Artists (Street Sounds)
-	33	TOUCH ME	Samantha Fox (Jive)
25	34	INTERMISSION	Dio (Vertigo)
23	35	WORLD MACHINE	Level 42 (Polydor)
40	36	HEADLINES	Midnight Star (MCA)
-	37	QUEEN'S GREATEST HITS	Queen (EMI)
29	38	THE MAN AND HIS MUSIC	Sam Cooke (RCA)
26	39	PLEASE	Pet Shop Boys (Parlophone)
-	40	PIE JESU	Aled Jones (10)
-	41	DRIVE TIME USA	Various Artists (K-Tel)
-	42	GIFT	Sisterhood (Merciful Release)
-	43	TRUE CONFESSIONS	Bananarama (London)
35	44	BANGS AND CRASHES	Go West (Chrysalis)
-	45	GTR	GTR (Arista)
-	46	PRINCESS	Princess (Supreme)
41	47	STREET SOUNDS ELECTRO 12	Various Artists (Street Sounds)
43	48	WHO MADE WHO	AC/DC (Atlantic)
-	49	UPFRONT1	Various Artists (Serious)
36	50	CONTROL	Janet Jackson (A&M)

Madonna's third album *True Blue*, eagerly awaited some 18 months after the release of her second, was predictably her biggest seller yet - indeed, the ninth biggest-selling album of the 1980s by the end of the decade. It was obviously not going to have the long, slow climb to the chart top that *Like A Virgin* had displayed, and almost immediately unseated Genesis to stake a five-week residence at the summit.

August 1986

2 August 1986

last	this		
1	1	TRUE BLUE	Madonna (Sire)
4	2	THE FINAL	Wham! (Epic)
11	3	INTO THE LIGHT	Chris DeBurgh (A&M)
3	4	BACK IN THE HIGH LIFE	
			Stevie Winwood (Island)
6	5	A KIND OF MAGIC	Queen (EMI)
7	6	EVERY BEAT OF MY HEART	
			Rod Stewart (Warner Bros.)
2	7	REVENGE	Eurythmics (RCA)
12	8	BROTHERS IN ARMS	Dire Straits (Vertigo)
5	9	THE SEER	Big Country (Mercury)
17	10	RIPTIDE	Robert Palmer (Island)
8	11	NOW – THE SUMMER ALBUM	
			Various Artists (EMI/Virgin)
7	12	INVISIBLE TOUCH	Genesis (Charisma)
14	13	SO	Peter Gabriel (Virgin)
10	14	LONDON O - HULL 4	Housemartins (Go! Discs)
16	15	SUZANNE VEGA	Suzanne Vega (A&M)
19	16	EAT 'EM AND SMILE	
			David Lee Roth (Warner Bros.)
13	17	PICTURE BOOK	Simply Red (Elektra)
15	18	HUNTING HIGH AND LOW	A-Ha (Warner Bros.)
33	19	TOUCH ME	Samantha Fox (Jive)
-	20	NO GURU, NO METHOD, NO TEACHER	
			Van Morrison (Mercury)
-	21	KNOCKED OUT LOADED	Bob Dylan (CBS)
18	22	THE QUEEN IS DEAD	Smiths (Rough Trade)
23	23	WHITNEY HOUSTON	
			Whitney Houston (Arista)
-	24	LANDING ON WATER	Neil Young (Geffen)
21	25	STREET LIFE - 20 GREAT HITS	
			Bryan Ferry & Roxy Music (EG)
22	26	ONCE UPON A TIME	Simple Minds (Virgin)
41	27	DRIVE TIME USA	Various Artists (K-Tel)
35	28	WORLD MACHINE	Level 42 (Polydor)
40	29	PIE JESU	Aled Jones (10)
32	30	STREET SOUNDS EDITION 17	
			Various Artists (Street Sounds)
-	31	COMMUNARDS	Communards (London)
24	32	DISCOVER	
			Gene Love Jezebel (Beggars Banquet)
27	33	GIANT	Woodentops (Rough Trade)
20	34	STANDING ON THE BEACH - THE SINGLES	
			Cure (Fiction)
34	35	INTERMISSION	Dio (Vertigo)
42	36	GIFT	Sisterhood (Merciful Release)
37	37	QUEEN'S GREATEST HITS	Queen (EMI)
31	38	ON THE BEACH	Chris Rea (Magnet)
26	39	BRING ON THE NIGHT	Sting (A&M)
28	40	BEST OF THE REAL THING	
			Real Thing (PRT)
-	41	RAISING HELL	Run DMC (Profile/London)
39	42	PLEASE	Pet Shop Boys (Parlophone)
50	43	CONTROL	Janet Jackson (A&M)
30	44	NO JACKET REQUIRED	Phil Collins (Virgin)
29	45	DANCE HITS 2	Various Artists (Towerbell)
25	46	LOVE ZONE	Billy Ocean (Jive)
38	47	THE MAN AND HIS MUSIC	Sam Cooke (RCA)
-	48	RAGE FOR ORDER	
			Queensryche (EMI America)
-	49	SHOULD THE WORLD FAIL TO FALL APART	
			Peter Murphy (Beggars Banquet)
-	50	THIS IS BIG AUDIO DYNAMITE	
			Big Audio Dynamite (CBS)

9 August 1986

last	this		
1	1	TRUE BLUE	Madonna (Sire)
3	2	INTO THE LIGHT	Chris DeBurgh (A&M)
2	3	THE FINAL	Wham! (Epic)
7	4	REVENGE	Eurythmics (RCA)
5	5	A KIND OF MAGIC	Queen (EMI)
4	6	BACK IN THE HIGH LIFE	
			Stevie Winwood (Island)
10	7	RIPTIDE	Robert Palmer (Island)
6	8	EVERY BEAT OF MY HEART	
			Rod Stewart (Warner Bros.)
8	9	BROTHERS IN ARMS	Dire Straits (Vertigo)
17	10	PICTURE BOOK	Simply Red (Elektra)
13	11	SO	Peter Gabriel (Virgin)
21	12	KNOCKED OUT LOADED	Bob Dylan (CBS)
11	13	NOW – THE SUMMER ALBUM	
			Various Artists (EMI/Virgin)
20	14	NO GURU, NO METHOD, NO TEACHER	
			Van Morrison (Mercury)
9	15	THE SEER	Big Country (Mercury)
-	16	RAT IN THE KITCHEN	UB40 (DEP Int)
16	17	EAT 'EM AND SMILE	
			David Lee Roth (Warner Bros.)
-	18	FLAUNT IT	Sigue Sigue Sputnik (Parlophone)
12	19	INVISIBLE TOUCH	
			Genesis (Charisma)
18	20	HUNTING HIGH AND LOW	A-Ha (Warner Bros.)
19	21	TOUCH ME	Samantha Fox (Jive)
24	22	LANDING ON WATER	Neil Young (Geffen)
31	23	COMMUNARDS	Communards (London)
14	24	LONDON O - HULL 4	Housemartins (Go! Discs)
15	25	SUZANNE VEGA	Suzanne Vega (A&M)
-	26	STUTTER	James (Sire)
22	27	THE QUEEN IS DEAD	Smiths (Rough Trade)
25	28	STREET LIFE - 20 GREAT HITS	
			Bryan Ferry & Roxy Music (EG)
37	29	QUEEN'S GREATEST HITS	Queen (EMI)
27	30	DRIVE TIME USA	Various Artists (K-Tel)
23	31	WHITNEY HOUSTON	
			Whitney Houston (Arista)
34	32	STANDING ON THE BEACH - THE SINGLES	
			Cure (Fiction)
-	33	VACATE	Stan Ridgway (IRS)
40	34	BEST OF THE REAL THING	Real Thing (PRT)
32	35	DISCOVER	
			Gene Love Jezebel (Beggars Banquet)
33	36	GIANT	Woodentops (Rough Trade)
39	37	BRING ON THE NIGHT	Sting (A&M)
41	38	RAISING HELL	Run DMC (Profile/London)
-	39	ORGASMATRON	Motorhead (GWR)
-	40	AT LAST WE GOT SHOES	
			Southside Johnny (RCA)
48	41	RAGE FOR ORDER	
			Queensryche (EMI America)
-	42	DESTINY	Chaka Khan (Warner Bros.)
-	43	ALWAYS IN THE MOOD	Shirley Jones (PIR)
28	44	WORLD MACHINE	Level 42 (Polydor)
26	45	ONCE UPON A TIME	Simple Minds (Virgin)
-	46	JOYRIDE	Pieces of a Dream (Capitol)
30	47	STREET SOUNDS EDITION 17	
			Various Artists (Street Sounds)
46	48	LOVE ZONE	Billy Ocean (Jive)
-	49	DO ME BABY	Meli'sa Morgan (Capitol)
50	50	THIS IS BIG AUDIO DYNAMITE	
			Big Audio Dynamite (CBS)

16 August 1986

last	this		
1	1	TRUE BLUE	Madonna (Sire)
2	2	INTO THE LIGHT	Chris DeBurgh (A&M)
3	3	THE FINAL	Wham! (Epic)
7	4	RIPTIDE	Robert Palmer (Island)
16	5	RAT IN THE KITCHEN	UB40 (DEP Int)
5	6	A KIND OF MAGIC	Queen (EMI)
4	7	REVENGE	Eurythmics (RCA)
9	8	BROTHERS IN ARMS	Dire Straits (Vertigo)
18	9	FLAUNT IT	
			Sigue Sigue Sputnik (Parlophone)
10	10	PICTURE BOOK	Simply Red (Elektra)
6	11	BACK IN THE HIGH LIFE	
			Stevie Winwood (Island)
8	12	EVERY BEAT OF MY HEART	
			Rod Stewart (Warner Bros.)
39	13	ORGASMATRON	Motorhead (GWR)
11	14	SO	Peter Gabriel (Virgin)
19	15	INVISIBLE TOUCH	Genesis (Charisma)
13	16	NOW – THE SUMMER ALBUM	
			Various Artists (EMI/Virgin)
12	17	KNOCKED OUT LOADED	Bob Dylan (CBS)
20	18	HUNTING HIGH AND LOW	
			A-Ha (Warner Bros.)
17	19	EAT 'EM AND SMILE	
			David Lee Roth (Warner Bros.)
15	20	THE SEER	Big Country (Mercury)
24	21	LONDON O - HULL 4	Housemartins (Go! Discs)
22	22	LANDING ON WATER	Neil Young (Geffen)
14	23	NO GURU, NO METHOD, NO TEACHER	
			Van Morrison (Mercury)
-	24	THE BRIDGE	Billy Joel (CBS)
31	25	WHITNEY HOUSTON	
			Whitney Houston (Arista)
23	26	COMMUNARDS	Communards (London)
38	27	RAISING HELL	Run DMC (Profile/London)
28	28	STREET LIFE - 20 GREAT HITS	
			Bryan Ferry & Roxy Music (EG)
29	29	QUEEN'S GREATEST HITS	Queen (EMI)
21	30	TOUCH ME	Samantha Fox (Jive)
27	31	THE QUEEN IS DEAD	Smiths (Rough Trade)
30	32	DRIVE TIME USA	Various Artists (K-Tel)
32	33	STANDING ON THE BEACH - THE SINGLES	
			Cure (Fiction)
40	34	AT LAST WE GOT SHOES	
			Southside Johnny (RCA)
-	35	GIFT	Sisterhood (Merciful Release)
25	36	SUZANNE VEGA	Suzanne Vega (A&M)
26	37	STUTTER	James (Sire)
34	38	BEST OF THE REAL THING	Real Thing (PRT)
33	39	VACATE	Stan Ridgway (IRS)
43	40	ALWAYS IN THE MOOD	Shirley Jones (PIR)
35	41	DISCOVER	
			Gene Love Jezebel (Beggars Banquet)
36	42	GIANT	Woodentops (Rough Trade)
-	43	QR3	Quiet Riot (Epic)
-	44	RAPTURE	Anita Baker (Elektra)
-	45	LISTEN LIKE THIEVES	INXS (Mercury)
-	46	LIKE A VIRGIN	Madonna (Sire)
42	47	DESTINY	Chaka Khan (Warner Bros.)
-	48	THE MAN AND HIS MUSIC	Sam Cooke (RCA)
47	49	STREET SOUNDS EDITION 17	
			Various Artists (Street Sounds)
-	50	BEST OF CHRIS DE BURGH	
			Chris De Burgh (A&M)

Into The Light was Chris De Burgh's best-selling album yet, easily eclipsing his previous Top 10 entry in 1984 with a hits compilation. The key to the new set's success was what would probably prove to be De Burgh's most enduring song, *The Lady In Red*. This topped the singles chart in the week that *Into The Light* reached the Top 3 - and would ironically drop in the very week that the album finally hit Number 1.

23 August 1986

last week	this week	Title	Artist
2	1	INTO THE LIGHT	Chris DeBurgh (A&M)
1	2	TRUE BLUE	Madonna (Sire)
6	3	A KIND OF MAGIC	Queen (EMI)
-	4	NOW THAT'S WHAT I CALL MUSIC 7	Various Artists (EMI Virgin)
4	5	RIPTIDE	Robert Palmer (Island)
7	6	REVENGE	Eurythmics (RCA)
3	7	THE FINAL	Wham! (Epic)
5	8	RAT IN THE KITCHEN	UB40 (DEP Int)
8	9	BROTHERS IN ARMS	Dire Straits (Vertigo)
11	10	BACK IN THE HIGH LIFE	Stevie Winwood (Island)
-	11	DANCING ON THE CEILING	Lionel Richie (Motown)
10	12	PICTURE BOOK	Simply Red (Elektra)
12	13	EVERY BEAT OF MY HEART	Rod Stewart (Warner Bros.)
-	14	THE ORIGINALS	Various Artists (Towerbell)
24	15	THE BRIDGE	Billy Joel (CBS)
15	16	INVISIBLE TOUCH	Genesis (Charisma)
26	17	COMMUNARDS	Communards (London)
16	18	NOW – THE SUMMER ALBUM	Various Artists (EMI/Virgin)
9	19	FLAUNT IT	Sigue Sigue Sputnik (Parlophone)
14	20	SO	Peter Gabriel (Virgin)
18	21	HUNTING HIGH AND LOW	A-Ha (Warner Bros.)
-	22	THREE HEARTS IN THE HAPPY ENDING MACHINE	Daryl Hall (RCA)
-	23	THE PAVAROTTI COLLECTION	Luciano Pavarotti (Stylus)
13	24	ORGASMATRON	Motorhead (GWR)
29	25	QUEEN'S GREATEST HITS	Queen (EMI)
17	26	KNOCKED OUT LOADED	Bob Dylan (CBS)
20	27	THE SEER	Big Country (Mercury)
31	28	THE QUEEN IS DEAD	Smiths (Rough Trade)
19	29	EAT 'EM AND SMILE	David Lee Roth (Warner Bros.)
21	30	LONDON O – HULL 4	Housemartins (Go! Discs)
-	31	PARADE	Prince & the Revolution (Warner Bros.)
23	32	NO GURU, NO METHOD, NO TEACHER	Van Morrison (Mercury)
28	33	STREET LIFE - 20 GREAT HITS	Bryan Ferry & Roxy Music (EG)
-	34	ONCE UPON A TIME	Simple Minds (Virgin)
25	35	WHITNEY HOUSTON	Whitney Houston (Arista)
-	36	RENDEZ-VOUS	Jean Michel Jarre (Polydor)
22	37	LANDING ON WATER	Neil Young (Geffen)
27	38	RAISING HELL	Run DMC (Profile/London)
44	39	RAPTURE	Anita Baker (Elektra)
43	40	QR3	Quiet Riot (Epic)
-	41	UPFRONT1	Various Artists (Serious)
33	42	STANDING ON THE BEACH - THE SINGLES	Cure (Fiction)
45	43	LISTEN LIKE THIEVES	INXS (Mercury)
46	44	LIKE A VIRGIN	Madonna (Sire)
-	45	THE GREATEST STORY EVER TOLD	Balaam & the Angel (Virgin)
-	46	LOVE ZONE	Billy Ocean (Jive)
32	47	DRIVE TIME USA	Various Artists (K-Tel)
36	48	SUZANNE VEGA	Suzanne Vega (A&M)
-	49	THE HEAT IS ON	Various Artists (Portrait)
42	50	GIANT	Woodentops (Rough Trade)

30 August 1986

last week	this week	Title	Artist
4	1	NOW THAT'S WHAT I CALL MUSIC 7	Various Artists (EMI Virgin)
2	2	TRUE BLUE	Madonna (Sire)
11	3	DANCING ON THE CEILING	Lionel Richie (Motown)
1	4	INTO THE LIGHT	Chris DeBurgh (A&M)
3	5	A KIND OF MAGIC	Queen (EMI)
7	6	THE FINAL	Wham! (Epic)
6	7	REVENGE	Eurythmics (RCA)
5	8	RIPTIDE	Robert Palmer (Island)
12	9	PICTURE BOOK	Simply Red (Elektra)
8	10	RAT IN THE KITCHEN	UB40 (DEP Int)
9	11	BROTHERS IN ARMS	Dire Straits (Vertigo)
36	12	RENDEZ-VOUS	Jean Michel Jarre (Polydor)
-	13	SILK AND STEEL	Five Star (Tent/RCA)
22	14	THREE HEARTS IN THE HAPPY ENDING MACHINE	Daryl Hall (RCA)
13	15	EVERY BEAT OF MY HEART	Rod Stewart (Warner Bros.)
49	16	THE HEAT IS ON	Various Artists (Portrait)
10	17	BACK IN THE HIGH LIFE	Stevie Winwood (Island)
28	18	THE QUEEN IS DEAD	Smiths (Rough Trade)
19	19	FLAUNT IT	Sigue Sigue Sputnik (Parlophone)
15	20	THE BRIDGE	Billy Joel (CBS)
29	21	EAT 'EM AND SMILE	David Lee Roth (Warner Bros.)
21	22	HUNTING HIGH AND LOW	A-Ha (Warner Bros.)
20	23	SO	Peter Gabriel (Virgin)
-	24	KICKING AGAINST THE PRICKS	Nick Cave & the Bad Seeds (Mute)
16	25	INVISIBLE TOUCH	Genesis (Charisma)
23	26	THE PAVAROTTI COLLECTION	Luciano Pavarotti (Stylus)
30	27	LONDON O - HULL 4	Housemartins (Go! Discs)
-	28	WORLD MACHINE	Level 42 (Polydor)
25	29	QUEEN'S GREATEST HITS	Queen (EMI)
24	30	ORGASMATRON	Motorhead (GWR)
43	31	LISTEN LIKE THIEVES	INXS (Mercury)
39	32	RAPTURE	Anita Baker (Elektra)
-	33	UPFRONT 2	Various Artists (Serious)
27	34	THE SEER	Big Country (Mercury)
-	35	GOOD TO GO LOVER	Gwen Guthrie (Boiling Point)
32	36	NO GURU, NO METHOD, NO TEACHER	Van Morrison (Mercury)
47	37	DRIVE TIME USA	Various Artists (K-Tel)
31	38	PARADE	Prince & the Revolution (Warner Bros.)
-	39	A LOT OF LOVE	Melba Moore (Capitol)
41	40	UPFRONT1	Various Artists (Serious)
18	41	NOW – THE SUMMER ALBUM	Various Artists (EMI/Virgin)
-	42	ALWAYS IN THE MOOD	Shirley Jones (Philly Int)
-	43	TAKE IT FROM ME	Glenn Jones (RCA)
40	44	QR3	Quiet Riot (Epic)
38	45	RAISING HELL	Run DMC (Profile/London)
35	46	WHITNEY HOUSTON	Whitney Houston (Arista)
33	47	STREET LIFE - 20 GREAT HITS	Bryan Ferry & Roxy Music (EG)
48	48	SUZANNE VEGA	Suzanne Vega (A&M)
-	49	DESTINY	Chaka Khan (Warner Bros.)
14	50	THE ORIGINALS	Various Artists (Towerbell)

6 September 1986

last week	this week	Title	Artist
1	1	NOW THAT'S WHAT I CALL MUSIC 7	Various Artists (EMI Virgin)
2	2	TRUE BLUE	Madonna (Sire)
3	3	DANCING ON THE CEILING	Lionel Richie (Motown)
5	4	A KIND OF MAGIC	Queen (EMI)
4	5	INTO THE LIGHT	Chris DeBurgh (A&M)
13	6	SILK AND STEEL	Five Star (Tent/RCA)
12	7	RENDEZ-VOUS	Jean Michel Jarre (Polydor)
6	8	THE FINAL	Wham! (Epic)
7	9	REVENGE	Eurythmics (RCA)
9	10	PICTURE BOOK	Simply Red (Elektra)
8	11	RIPTIDE	Robert Palmer (Island)
16	12	THE HEAT IS ON	Various Artists (Portrait)
-	13	IN THE ARMY NOW	Status Quo (Vertigo)
10	14	RAT IN THE KITCHEN	UB40 (DEP Int)
-	15	LIFE'S RICH PAGEANT	REM (IRS)
11	16	BROTHERS IN ARMS	Dire Straits (Vertigo)
14	17	THREE HEARTS IN THE HAPPY ENDING MACHINE	Daryl Hall (RCA)
17	18	BACK IN THE HIGH LIFE	Stevie Winwood (Island)
-	19	BABY THE STARS SHINE BRIGHT	Everything But The Girl (Blanco y Negro)
25	20	INVISIBLE TOUCH	Genesis (Charisma)
-	21	COMMUNARDS	Communards (London)
15	22	EVERY BEAT OF MY HEART	Rod Stewart (Warner Bros.)
35	23	GOOD TO GO LOVER	Gwen Guthrie (Boiling Point)
26	24	THE PAVAROTTI COLLECTION	Luciano Pavarotti (Stylus)
20	25	THE BRIDGE	Billy Joel (CBS)
24	26	KICKING AGAINST THE PRICKS	Nick Cave & the Bad Seeds (Mute)
33	27	UPFRONT 2	Various Artists (Serious)
38	28	PARADE	Prince & the Revolution (Warner Bros.)
29	29	QUEEN'S GREATEST HITS	Queen (EMI)
50	30	THE ORIGINALS	Various Artists (Towerbell)
22	31	HUNTING HIGH AND LOW	A-Ha (Warner Bros.)
-	32	WATCH YOUR STEP	Ted Hawkins (Windows of the World)
18	33	THE QUEEN IS DEAD	Smiths (Rough Trade)
23	34	SO	Peter Gabriel (Virgin)
47	35	STREET LIFE - 20 GREAT HITS	Bryan Ferry & Roxy Music (EG)
-	36	CONTROL	Janet Jackson (A&M)
-	37	STREET SOUNDS HIP-HOP ELECTRO 13	Various Artists (Street Sounds)
32	38	RAPTURE	Anita Baker (Elektra)
44	39	QR3	Quiet Riot (Epic)
48	40	SUZANNE VEGA	Suzanne Vega (A&M)
30	41	ORGASMATRON	Motorhead (GWR)
-	42	GUITAR TOWN	Steve Earle (MCA)
46	43	WHITNEY HOUSTON	Whitney Houston (Arista)
19	44	FLAUNT IT	Sigue Sigue Sputnik (Parlophone)
21	45	EAT 'EM AND SMILE	David Lee Roth (Warner Bros.)
-	46	THE BIG LAD IN THE WINDMILL	It Bites (Virgin)
-	47	WHILE THE CITY SLEEPS	George Benson (Warner Bros.)
-	48	NEVER FELT SO GOOD	James Ingram (Qwest)
28	49	WORLD MACHINE	Level 42 (Polydor)
27	50	LONDON O - HULL 4	Housemartins (Go! Discs)

Now That's What I Call Music 7 kept up the remarkable chart success of this series, becoming an easy late summer chart-topper with no sign of opposition from the opposing *Hits* camp (which, in fact, had also had an unopposed chart-topper in April with its fourth volume). With equal ease, Lionel Richie made it three Top 10 albums from as many realeases, with *Dancing On The Ceiling*.

September 1986

last week	this week	13 September 1986	
1	1	NOW THAT'S WHAT I CALL MUSIC 7	
			Various Artists (EMI Virgin)
3	2	DANCING ON THE CEILING	
			Lionel Richie (Motown)
2	3	TRUE BLUE	Madonna (Sire)
4	4	A KIND OF MAGIC	Queen (EMI)
9	5	REVENGE	Eurythmics (RCA)
5	6	INTO THE LIGHT	Chris DeBurgh (A&M)
47	7	WHILE THE CITY SLEEPS	
			George Benson (Warner Bros.)
13	8	IN THE ARMY NOW	Status Quo (Vertigo)
6	9	SILK AND STEEL	Five Star (Tent/RCA)
21	10	COMMUNARDS	Communards (London)
7	11	RENDEZ-VOUS	
			Jean Michel Jarre (Polydor)
10	12	PICTURE BOOK	Simply Red (Elektra)
16	13	BROTHERS IN ARMS	Dire Straits (Vertigo)
12	14	THE HEAT IS ON	Various Artists (Portrait)
8	15	THE FINAL	Wham! (Epic)
19	16	BABY THE STARS SHINE BRIGHT	
			Everything But The Girl (Blanco y Negro)
11	17	RIPTIDE	Robert Palmer (Island)
36	18	CONTROL	Janet Jackson (A&M)
20	19	INVISIBLE TOUCH	Genesis (Charisma)
37	20	STREET SOUNDS HIP-HOP ELECTRO 13	
			Various Artists (Street Sounds)
28	21	PARADE	Prince & the Revolution (Warner Bros.)
46	22	THE BIG LAD IN THE WINDMILL	It Bites (Virgin)
-	23	PRESS TO PLAY	Paul McCartney (EMI)
-	24	GRACELAND	Paul Simon (Warner Bros.)
15	25	LIFE'S RICH PAGEANT	REM (IRS)
24	26	THE PAVAROTTI COLLECTION	
			Luciano Pavarotti (Stylus)
32	27	WATCH YOUR STEP	
			Ted Hawkins (Windows of the World)
18	28	BACK IN THE HIGH LIFE	Stevie Winwood (Island)
17	29	THREE HEARTS IN THE HAPPY ENDING	
		MACHINE	Daryl Hall (RCA)
31	30	HUNTING HIGH AND LOW	A-Ha (Warner Bros.)
-	31	GONE TO EARTH	David Sylvian (Virgin)
-	32	LOVE ZONE	Billy Ocean (Jive)
29	33	QUEEN'S GREATEST HITS	Queen (EMI)
22	34	EVERY BEAT OF MY HEART	
			Rod Stewart (Warner Bros.)
14	35	RAT IN THE KITCHEN	UB40 (DEP Int)
27	36	UPFRONT 2	Various Artists (Serious)
23	37	GOOD TO GO LOVER	
			Gwen Guthrie (Boiling Point)
30	38	THE ORIGINALS	Various Artists (Towerbell)
-	39	THE BEST OF 10 YEARS	Boney M (Stylus)
38	40	RAPTURE	Anita Baker (Elektra)
-	41	RAISING HELL	Run DMC (Profile)
25	42	THE BRIDGE	Billy Joel (CBS)
-	43	ONCE UPON A TIME	Simple Minds (Virgin)
43	44	WHITNEY HOUSTON	Whitney Houston (Arista)
50	45	LONDON O - HULL 4	Housemartins (Go! Discs)
-	46	THE WAY IT IS	
			Bruce Hornsby & the Range (RCA)
26	47	KICKING AGAINST THE PRICKS	
			Nick Cave & the Bad Seeds (Mute)
34	48	SO	Peter Gabriel (Virgin)
35	49	STREET LIFE - 20 GREAT HITS	
			Bryan Ferry & Roxy Music (EG)
42	50	GUITAR TOWN	Steve Earle (MCA)

last week	this week	20 September 1986	
1	1	NOW THAT'S WHAT I CALL MUSIC 7	
			Various Artists (EMI Virgin)
24	2	GRACELAND	Paul Simon (Warner Bros.)
2	3	DANCING ON THE CEILING	
			Lionel Richie (Motown)
9	4	SILK AND STEEL	Five Star (Tent/RCA)
3	5	TRUE BLUE	Madonna (Sire)
5	6	REVENGE	Eurythmics (RCA)
10	7	COMMUNARDS	Communards (London)
23	8	PRESS TO PLAY	Paul McCartney (EMI)
46	9	THE WAY IT IS	
			Bruce Hornsby & the Range (RCA)
8	10	IN THE ARMY NOW	Status Quo (Vertigo)
4	11	A KIND OF MAGIC	Queen (EMI)
7	12	WHILE THE CITY SLEEPS	
			George Benson (Warner Bros.)
6	13	INTO THE LIGHT	Chris DeBurgh (A&M)
-	14	BREAK EVERY RULE	Tina Turner (Capitol)
15	15	CRASH	Human League (Virgin)
-	16	SLIPPERY WHEN WET	Bon Jovi (Vertigo)
18	17	CONTROL	Janet Jackson (A&M)
14	18	THE HEAT IS ON	Various Artists (Portrait)
16	19	BABY THE STARS SHINE BRIGHT	
			Everything But The Girl (Blanco y Negro)
19	20	INVISIBLE TOUCH	Genesis (Charisma)
21	21	PARADE	Prince & the Revolution (Warner Bros.)
20	22	STREET SOUNDS HIP-HOP ELECTRO 13	
			Various Artists (Street Sounds)
12	23	PICTURE BOOK	Simply Red (Elektra)
13	24	BROTHERS IN ARMS	Dire Straits (Vertigo)
31	25	GONE TO EARTH	David Sylvian (Virgin)
11	26	RENDEZ-VOUS	
			Jean Michel Jarre (Polydor)
15	27	THE FINAL	Wham! (Epic)
-	28	FORE!	Huey Lewis & the News (Chrysalis)
17	29	RIPTIDE	Robert Palmer (Island)
35	30	RAT IN THE KITCHEN	UB40 (DEP Int)
22	31	THE BIG LAD IN THE WINDMILL	It Bites (Virgin)
25	32	LIFE'S RICH PAGEANT	REM (IRS)
26	33	THE PAVAROTTI COLLECTION	
			Luciano Pavarotti (Stylus)
42	34	THE BRIDGE	Billy Joel (CBS)
27	35	WATCH YOUR STEP	
			Ted Hawkins (Windows of the World)
-	36	STANDING ON THE BEACH - THE SINGLES	
			Cure (Fiction)
49	37	STREET LIFE - 20 GREAT HITS	
			Bryan Ferry & Roxy Music (EG)
-	38	INDISCREET	FM (Portrait)
28	39	BACK IN THE HIGH LIFE	
			Stevie Winwood (Island)
30	40	HUNTING HIGH AND LOW	A-Ha (Warner Bros.)
40	41	RAPTURE	Anita Baker (Elektra)
43	42	ONCE UPON A TIME	Simple Minds (Virgin)
-	43	BREAKING AWAY	Jaki Graham (EMI)
29	44	THREE HEARTS IN THE HAPPY ENDING	
		MACHINE	Daryl Hall (RCA)
-	45	STRANGE TIMES	Chameleons (Geffen)
-	46	OFF THE BEATEN TRACK	Stranglers (Liberty)
-	47	A LOT OF LOVE	Melba Moore (Capitol)
48	48	SO	Peter Gabriel (Virgin)
44	49	WHITNEY HOUSTON	Whitney Houston (Arista)
47	50	KICKING AGAINST THE PRICKS	
			Nick Cave & the Bad Seeds (Mute)

last week	this week	27 September 1986	
14	1	BREAK EVERY RULE	Tina Turner (Capitol)
2	2	GRACELAND	Paul Simon (Warner Bros.)
1	3	NOW THAT'S WHAT I CALL MUSIC 7	
			Various Artists (EMI Virgin)
16	4	SLIPPERY WHEN WET	Bon Jovi (Vertigo)
28	5	FORE!	Huey Lewis & the News (Chrysalis)
6	6	REVENGE	Eurythmics (RCA)
5	7	TRUE BLUE	Madonna (Sire)
4	8	SILK AND STEEL	Five Star (Tent/RCA)
11	9	A KIND OF MAGIC	Queen (EMI)
3	10	DANCING ON THE CEILING	
			Lionel Richie (Motown)
15	11	CRASH	Human League (Virgin)
13	12	INTO THE LIGHT	Chris DeBurgh (A&M)
7	13	COMMUNARDS	Communards (London)
-	14	TRUE STORIES	Talking Heads (EMI)
-	15	BLOOD AND CHOCOLATE	
			Elvis Costello (Imp)
8	16	PRESS TO PLAY	Paul McCartney (EMI)
9	17	THE WAY IT IS	
			Bruce Hornsby & the Range (RCA)
12	18	WHILE THE CITY SLEEPS	
			George Benson (Warner Bros.)
10	19	IN THE ARMY NOW	Status Quo (Vertigo)
18	20	THE HEAT IS ON	Various Artists (Portrait)
23	21	PICTURE BOOK	Simply Red (Elektra)
24	22	BROTHERS IN ARMS	Dire Straits (Vertigo)
45	23	STRANGE TIMES	Chameleons (Geffen)
17	24	CONTROL	Janet Jackson (A&M)
19	25	BABY THE STARS SHINE BRIGHT	
			Everything But The Girl (Blanco y Negro)
-	26	ROCK THE NATION	Saxon (EMI)
31	27	THE BIG LAD IN THE WINDMILL	It Bites (Virgin)
20	28	INVISIBLE TOUCH	Genesis (Charisma)
32	29	LIFE'S RICH PAGEANT	REM (IRS)
43	30	BREAKING AWAY	Jaki Graham (EMI)
-	31	GOOD TO GO LOVER	
			Gwen Guthrie (Boiling Point)
-	32	COMPANEROS	Working Week (Virgin)
21	33	PARADE	
			Prince & the Revolution (Warner Bros.)
22	34	STREET SOUNDS HIP-HOP ELECTRO 13	
			Various Artists (Street Sounds)
34	35	THE BRIDGE	Billy Joel (CBS)
-	36	L IS FOR LOVER	Al Jarreau (WEA)
26	37	RENDEZ-VOUS	
			Jean Michel Jarre (Polydor)
27	38	THE FINAL	Wham! (Epic)
25	39	GONE TO EARTH	David Sylvian (Virgin)
-	40	EVERY BEAT OF MY HEART	
			Rod Stewart (Warner Bros.)
-	41	ON THE BOARDWALK	Ted Hawkins (Brave)
29	42	RIPTIDE	Robert Palmer (Island)
30	43	RAT IN THE KITCHEN	UB40 (DEP Int)
33	44	THE PAVAROTTI COLLECTION	
			Luciano Pavarotti (Stylus)
39	45	BACK IN THE HIGH LIFE	
			Stevie Winwood (Island)
37	46	STREET LIFE - 20 GREAT HITS	
			Bryan Ferry & Roxy Music (EG)
48	47	SO	Peter Gabriel (Virgin)
49	48	WHITNEY HOUSTON	Whitney Houston (Arista)
42	49	ONCE UPON A TIME	Simple Minds (Virgin)
40	50	HUNTING HIGH AND LOW	A-Ha (Warner Bros.)

Graceland was Paul Simon's first album since 1983's *Hearts And Bones*, which had barely sniffed at chart success. The reception for this one was to be quite different, as its mixture of first and third-world rhythms brought Simon a huge new following. *Graceland* would be the decade's 11th best-selling album - but even so, it was (albeit briefly) beaten to the Number 1 slot by Tina Turner's *Break Every Rule*.

last week	this week	4 October 1986	
2	1	GRACELAND	Paul Simon (Warner Bros.)
8	2	SILK AND STEEL	Five Star (Tent/RCA)
1	3	BREAK EVERY RULE	Tina Turner (Capitol)
14	4	TRUE STORIES	Talking Heads (EMI)
3	5	NOW THAT'S WHAT I CALL MUSIC 7	
			Various Artists (EMI Virgin)
6	6	REVENGE	Eurythmics (RCA)
7	7	TRUE BLUE	Madonna (Sire)
5	8	FORE!	Huey Lewis & the News (Chrysalis)
4	9	SLIPPERY WHEN WET	Bon Jovi (Vertigo)
11	10	CRASH	Human League (Virgin)
13	11	COMMUNARDS	Communards (London)
-	12	TALKING WITH THE TAXMAN ABOUT POETRY	
			Billy Bragg (Go! Discs)
15	13	BLOOD AND CHOCOLATE	
			Elvis Costello (Imp)
9	14	A KIND OF MAGIC	Queen (EMI)
10	15	DANCING ON THE CEILING	
			Lionel Richie (Motown)
12	16	INTO THE LIGHT	Chris DeBurgh (A&M)
17	17	THE WAY IT IS	
			Bruce Hornsby & the Range (RCA)
19	18	IN THE ARMY NOW	Status Quo (Vertigo)
26	19	ROCK THE NATION	Saxon (EMI)
18	20	WHILE THE CITY SLEEPS	
			George Benson (Warner Bros.)
22	21	BROTHERS IN ARMS	Dire Straits (Vertigo)
-	22	HAPPY HEAD	Might Lemon Drops (Chrysalis)
-	23	VIGILANTE	Magnum (Polydor)
21	24	PICTURE BOOK	Simply Red (Elektra)
20	25	THE HEAT IS ON	Various Artists (Portrait)
-	26	EYE OF THE ZOMBIE	
			John Fogerty (Warner Bros.)
16	27	PRESS TO PLAY	Paul McCartney (EMI)
28	28	INVISIBLE TOUCH	
			Genesis (Charisma)
23	29	STRANGE TIMES	Chameleons (Geffen)
32	30	COMPANEROS	Working Week (Virgin)
24	31	CONTROL	Janet Jackson (A&M)
-	32	RAISING HELL	Run DMC (Profile)
-	33	LIVE IN LOS ANGELES	Maze (Capitol)
30	34	BREAKING AWAY	Jaki Graham (EMI)
47	35	SO	Peter Gabriel (Virgin)
38	36	THE FINAL	Wham! (Epic)
25	37	BABY THE STARS SHINE BRIGHT	
			Everything But The Girl (Blanco y Negro)
41	38	ON THE BOARDWALK	Ted Hawkins (Brave)
-	39	LONDON O - HULL 4	
			Housemartins (Go! Discs)
33	40	PARADE	
			Prince & the Revolution (Warner Bros.)
39	41	GONE TO EARTH	David Sylvian (Virgin)
43	42	RAT IN THE KITCHEN	UB40 (DEP Int)
36	43	L IS FOR LOVER	Al Jarreau (WEA)
48	44	WHITNEY HOUSTON	Whitney Houston (Arista)
49	45	ONCE UPON A TIME	Simple Minds (Virgin)
27	46	THE BIG LAD IN THE WINDMILL	
			It Bites (Virgin)
29	47	LIFE'S RICH PAGEANT	REM (IRS)
35	48	THE BRIDGE	Billy Joel (CBS)
31	49	GOOD TO GO LOVER	
			Gwen Guthrie (Boiling Point)
46	50	STREET LIFE - 20 GREAT HITS	
			Bryan Ferry & Roxy Music (EG)

		11 October 1986	
1	1	GRACELAND	Paul Simon (Warner Bros.)
2	2	SILK AND STEEL	Five Star (Tent/RCA)
7	3	TRUE BLUE	Madonna (Sire)
6	4	REVENGE	Eurythmics (RCA)
12	5	TALKING WITH THE TAXMAN ABOUT POETRY	
			Billy Bragg (Go! Discs)
3	6	BREAK EVERY RULE	Tina Turner (Capitol)
4	7	TRUE STORIES	Talking Heads (EMI)
5	8	NOW THAT'S WHAT I CALL MUSIC 7	
			Various Artists (EMI Virgin)
11	9	COMMUNARDS	Communards (London)
8	10	FORE!	Huey Lewis & the News (Chrysalis)
9	11	SLIPPERY WHEN WET	Bon Jovi (Vertigo)
-	12	SOMEWHERE IN TIME	Iron Maiden (EMI)
16	13	INTO THE LIGHT	Chris DeBurgh (A&M)
14	14	A KIND OF MAGIC	Queen (EMI)
15	15	DANCING ON THE CEILING	
			Lionel Richie (Motown)
18	16	IN THE ARMY NOW	Status Quo (Vertigo)
-	17	BROTHERHOOD	New Order (Factory)
23	18	VIGILANTE	Magnum (Polydor)
28	19	INVISIBLE TOUCH	
			Genesis (Charisma)
21	20	BROTHERS IN ARMS	Dire Straits (Vertigo)
24	21	PICTURE BOOK	Simply Red (Elektra)
13	22	BLOOD AND CHOCOLATE	
			Elvis Costello (Imp)
-	23	THE GHOST OF CAIN	
			New Model Army (EMI)
-	24	TRUE COLORS	Cyndi Lauper (CBS)
-	25	HUNTING HIGH AND LOW	A-Ha (Warner Bros.)
17	26	THE WAY IT IS	
			Bruce Hornsby & the Range (RCA)
31	27	CONTROL	Janet Jackson (A&M)
-	28	THE PACIFIC AGE	
			Orchestral Manoeuvres in the Dark (Virgin)
10	29	CRASH	Human League (Virgin)
-	30	FRANTIC ROMANTIC	
			Jermain Stewart (10/Virgin)
-	31	BLAH BLAH BLAH	Iggy Pop (A&M)
-	32	INDISCREET	FM (Portrait)
25	33	THE HEAT IS ON	Various Artists (Portrait)
27	34	PRESS TO PLAY	Paul McCartney (EMI)
20	35	WHILE THE CITY SLEEPS	
			George Benson (Warner Bros.)
33	36	LIVE IN LOS ANGELES	Maze (Capitol)
34	37	BREAKING AWAY	Jaki Graham (EMI)
39	38	LONDON O - HULL 4	
			Housemartins (Go! Discs)
38	39	ON THE BOARDWALK	Ted Hawkins (Brave)
-	40	WHO'S BEEN TALKING	Robert Cray (Charly)
-	41	BLIND BEFORE I STOP	Meat Loaf (Arista)
19	42	ROCK THE NATION	Saxon (EMI)
-	43	BEND SINISTER	Fall (Beggars Banquet)
-	44	STREET SOUNDS HIP-HOP ELECTRO 14	
			Various Artists (Street Sounds)
-	45	RAPTURE	Anita Baker (Elektra)
-	46	DIFFERENT LIGHT	Bangles (CBS)
22	47	HAPPY HEAD	
			Might Lemon Drops (Chrysalis)
35	48	SO	Peter Gabriel (Virgin)
44	49	WHITNEY HOUSTON	
			Whitney Houston (Arista)
45	50	ONCE UPON A TIME	Simple Minds (Virgin)

		18 October 1986	
1	1	GRACELAND	Paul Simon (Warner Bros.)
2	2	SILK AND STEEL	Five Star (Tent/RCA)
12	3	SOMEWHERE IN TIME	Iron Maiden (EMI)
3	4	TRUE BLUE	Madonna (Sire)
4	5	REVENGE	Eurythmics (RCA)
25	6	HUNTING HIGH AND LOW	A-Ha (Warner Bros.)
-	7	SOUTH PACIFIC	Various Artists (CBS)
17	8	BROTHERHOOD	New Order (Factory)
6	9	BREAK EVERY RULE	Tina Turner (Capitol)
9	10	COMMUNARDS	Communards (London)
5	11	TALKING WITH THE TAXMAN ABOUT POETRY	
			Billy Bragg (Go! Discs)
28	12	THE PACIFIC AGE	
			Orchestral Manoeuvres in the Dark (Virgin)
7	13	TRUE STORIES	Talking Heads (EMI)
10	14	FORE!	Huey Lewis & the News (Chrysalis)
13	15	INTO THE LIGHT	Chris DeBurgh (A&M)
-	16	STREET SOUNDS EDITION 18	
			Various Artists (Street Sounds)
8	17	NOW THAT'S WHAT I CALL MUSIC 7	
			Various Artists (EMI Virgin)
-	18	WORD UP	Cameo (Club)
16	19	IN THE ARMY NOW	Status Quo (Vertigo)
14	20	A KIND OF MAGIC	Queen (EMI)
15	21	DANCING ON THE CEILING	
			Lionel Richie (Motown)
20	22	BROTHERS IN ARMS	Dire Straits (Vertigo)
23	23	THE GHOST OF CAIN	New Model Army (EMI)
24	24	TRUE COLORS	Cyndi Lauper (CBS)
38	25	LONDON O - HULL 4	
			Housemartins (Go! Discs)
-	26	THIRD STAGE	Boston (MCA)
19	27	INVISIBLE TOUCH	Genesis (Charisma)
41	28	BLIND BEFORE I STOP	Meat Loaf (Arista)
11	29	SLIPPERY WHEN WET	Bon Jovi (Vertigo)
-	30	ZAGORA	Loose Ends (Virgin)
43	31	BEND SINISTER	Fall (Beggars Banquet)
-	32	FILIGREE AND SHADOW	
			This Mortal Coil (4AD)
18	33	VIGILANTE	Magnum (Polydor)
47	34	HAPPY HEAD	Might Lemon Drops (Chrysalis)
31	35	BLAH BLAH BLAH	Iggy Pop (A&M)
-	36	NASTY, NASTY	Black 'n' Blue (Atlantic)
27	37	CONTROL	Janet Jackson (A&M)
22	38	BLOOD AND CHOCOLATE	
			Elvis Costello (Imp)
44	39	STREET SOUNDS HIP-HOP ELECTRO 14	
			Various Artists (Street Sounds)
26	40	THE WAY IT IS	
			Bruce Hornsby & the Range (RCA)
21	41	PICTURE BOOK	Simply Red (Elektra)
30	42	FRANTIC ROMANTIC	
			Jermain Stewart (10/Virgin)
-	43	GOOD TO GO LOVER	
			Gwen Guthrie (Boiling Point)
29	44	CRASH	Human League (Virgin)
35	45	WHILE THE CITY SLEEPS	
			George Benson (Warner Bros.)
45	46	RAPTURE	Anita Baker (Elektra)
32	47	INDISCREET	FM (Portrait)
36	48	LIVE IN LOS ANGELES	Maze (Capitol)
-	49	THE AUTOBIOGRAPHY OF SUPERTRAMP	
			Supertramp (A&M)
-	50	THE FINAL	Wham! (Epic)

Graceland settled into a six-week straight run at the chart top, which meant that the UK family vocal group Five Star had to be content with three weeks at Number 2 for their biggest-selling album *Silk And Steel* (the title of which was taken from a phrase in the song *Rain Or Shine*, simultaneously a Number 2 single). Meanwhile, Billy Bragg made the Top 10 for the first time with his intriguingly-titled third album.

October – November 1986

last / this week

25 October 1986

last	this	title	artist
1	1	GRACELAND	Paul Simon (Warner Bros.)
-	2	SCOUNDREL DAYS	A-Ha (Warner Bros.)
4	3	TRUE BLUE	Madonna (Sire)
2	4	SILK AND STEEL	Five Star (Tent/RCA)
3	5	SOMEWHERE IN TIME	Iron Maiden (EMI)
5	6	REVENGE	Eurythmics (RCA)
7	7	SOUTH PACIFIC	Various Artists (CBS)
18	8	WORD UP	Cameo (Club)
10	9	COMMUNARDS	Communards (London)
30	10	ZAGORA	Loose Ends (Virgin)
8	11	BROTHERHOOD	New Order (Factory)
14	12	FORE!	Huey Lewis & the News (Chrysalis)
-	13	U-VOX	Ultravox (Chrysalis)
25	14	LONDON O - HULL 4	Housemartins (Go! Discs)
26	15	THIRD STAGE	Boston (MCA)
9	16	BREAK EVERY RULE	Tina Turner (Capitol)
20	17	A KIND OF MAGIC	Queen (EMI)
15	18	INTO THE LIGHT	Chris DeBurgh (A&M)
-	19	THE CHART	Various Artists (Telstar)
-	20	ONE TO ONE	Howard Jones (WEA)
17	21	NOW THAT'S WHAT I CALL MUSIC 7	Various Artists (EMI Virgin)
33	22	VIGILANTE	Magnum (Polydor)
19	23	IN THE ARMY NOW	Status Quo (Vertigo)
11	24	TALKING WITH THE TAXMAN ABOUT POETRY	Billy Bragg (Go! Discs)
12	25	THE PACIFIC AGE	Orchestral Manoeuvres in the Dark (Virgin)
27	26	INVISIBLE TOUCH	Genesis (Charisma)
-	27	POWER OF LOVE	Various Artists (West Five)
6	28	HUNTING HIGH AND LOW	A-Ha (Warner Bros.)
-	29	DANCE UNDERCOVER	Ratt (Atlantic)
13	30	TRUE STORIES	Talking Heads (EMI)
21	31	DANCING ON THE CEILING	Lionel Richie (Motown)
22	32	BROTHERS IN ARMS	Dire Straits (Vertigo)
16	33	STREET SOUNDS EDITION 18	Various Artists (Street Sounds)
-	34	JOURNEY TO THE URGE WITHIN	Courtney Pine (Island)
-	35	TOP GUN	Soundtrack (CBS)
49	36	THE AUTOBIOGRAPHY OF SUPERTRAMP	Supertramp (A&M)
-	37	DARING ADVENTURES	Richard Thompson (Polydor)
24	38	TRUE COLORS	Cyndi Lauper (CBS)
-	39	TUTU	Miles Davis (Warner Bros.)
50	40	THE FINAL	Wham! (Epic)
45	41	WHILE THE CITY SLEEPS	George Benson (Warner Bros.)
-	42	WHO'S BEEN TALKING	Robert Cray (Charly)
32	43	FILIGREE AND SHADOW	This Mortal Coil (4AD)
39	44	STREET SOUNDS HIP-HOP ELECTRO 14	Various Artists (Street Sounds)
29	45	SLIPPERY WHEN WET	Bon Jovi (Vertigo)
23	46	THE GHOST OF CAIN	New Model Army (EMI)
28	47	BLIND BEFORE I STOP	Meat Loaf (Arista)
-	48	SPIT IN YOUR EAR	Spitting Image (Virgin)
-	49	WOMEN HOLD UP HALF THE SKY	Ruby Turner (Jive)
31	50	BEND SINISTER	Fall (Beggars Banquet)

1 November 1986

last	this	title	artist
1	1	GRACELAND	Paul Simon (Warner Bros.)
3	2	TRUE BLUE	Madonna (Sire)
2	3	SCOUNDREL DAYS	A-Ha (Warner Bros.)
5	4	SOMEWHERE IN TIME	Iron Maiden (EMI)
4	5	SILK AND STEEL	Five Star (Tent/RCA)
-	6	GET CLOSE	Pretenders (Real)
-	7	LIVERPOOL	Frankie Goes To Hollywood (ZZT)
19	8	THE CHART	Various Artists (Telstar)
6	9	REVENGE	Eurythmics (RCA)
7	10	SOUTH PACIFIC	Various Artists (CBS)
20	11	ONE TO ONE	Howard Jones (WEA)
8	12	WORD UP	Cameo (Club)
-	13	BETWEEN TWO FIRES	Paul Young (CBS)
13	14	U-VOX	Ultravox (Chrysalis)
14	15	LONDON O - HULL 4	Housemartins (Go! Discs)
9	16	COMMUNARDS	Communards (London)
35	17	TOP GUN	Soundtrack (CBS)
-	18	WHIPLASH SMILE	Billy Idol (Chrysalis)
12	19	FORE!	Huey Lewis & the News (Chrysalis)
16	20	BREAK EVERY RULE	Tina Turner (Capitol)
38	21	TRUE COLORS	Cyndi Lauper (CBS)
32	22	BROTHERS IN ARMS	Dire Straits (Vertigo)
17	23	A KIND OF MAGIC	Queen (EMI)
18	24	INTO THE LIGHT	Chris DeBurgh (A&M)
-	25	PLEASE	Pet Shop Boys (EMI)
30	26	TRUE STORIES	Talking Heads (EMI)
24	27	TALKING WITH THE TAXMAN ABOUT POETRY	Billy Bragg (Go! Discs)
15	28	THIRD STAGE	Boston (MCA)
34	29	JOURNEY TO THE URGE WITHIN	Courtney Pine (Island)
11	30	BROTHERHOOD	New Order (Factory)
10	31	ZAGORA	Loose Ends (Virgin)
36	32	THE AUTOBIOGRAPHY OF SUPERTRAMP	Supertramp (A&M)
23	33	IN THE ARMY NOW	Status Quo (Vertigo)
-	34	CONSTRICTOR	Alice Cooper (WEA)
29	35	DANCE UNDERCOVER	Ratt (Atlantic)
-	36	GIVE ME THE REASON	Luther Vandross (Epic)
21	37	NOW THAT'S WHAT I CALL MUSIC 7	Various Artists (EMI Virgin)
31	38	DANCING ON THE CEILING	Lionel Richie (Motown)
40	39	THE FINAL	Wham! (Epic)
26	40	INVISIBLE TOUCH	Genesis (Charisma)
-	41	ENTERTAINMENT USA II	Various Artists (Priority)
33	42	STREET SOUNDS EDITION 18	Various Artists (Street Sounds)
41	43	WHILE THE CITY SLEEPS	George Benson (Warner Bros.)
25	44	THE PACIFIC AGE	Orchestral Manoeuvres in the Dark (Virgin)
39	45	TUTU	Miles Davis (Warner Bros.)
50	46	BEND SINISTER	Fall (Beggars Banquet)
45	47	SLIPPERY WHEN WET	Bon Jovi (Vertigo)
46	48	THE GHOST OF CAIN	New Model Army (EMI)
-	49	DIESEL RIVER	Weather Prophets (Rough Trade)
-	50	SO	Peter Gabriel (Virgin)

8 November 1986

last	this	title	artist
1	1	GRACELAND	Paul Simon (Warner Bros.)
18	2	WHIPLASH SMILE	Billy Idol (Chrysalis)
6	3	GET CLOSE	Pretenders (Real)
7	4	LIVERPOOL	Frankie Goes To Hollywood (ZZT)
2	5	TRUE BLUE	Madonna (Sire)
3	6	SCOUNDREL DAYS	A-Ha (Warner Bros.)
5	7	SILK AND STEEL	Five Star (Tent/RCA)
13	8	BETWEEN TWO FIRES	Paul Young (CBS)
17	9	TOP GUN	Soundtrack (CBS)
15	10	LONDON O - HULL 4	Housemartins (Go! Discs)
8	11	THE CHART	Various Artists (Telstar)
-	12	EVERY BREATH YOU TAKE - THE SINGLES	Police (A&M)
36	13	GIVE ME THE REASON	Luther Vandross (Epic)
12	14	WORD UP	Cameo (Club)
-	15	NO. 10 UPPING STREET	Big Audio Dynamite (CBS)
21	16	TRUE COLORS	Cyndi Lauper (CBS)
-	17	DREAMTIME	Stranglers (Epic)
9	18	REVENGE	Eurythmics (RCA)
10	19	SOUTH PACIFIC	Various Artists (CBS)
19	20	FORE!	Huey Lewis & the News (Chrysalis)
4	21	SOMEWHERE IN TIME	Iron Maiden (EMI)
34	22	CONSTRICTOR	Alice Cooper (WEA)
28	23	THIRD STAGE	Boston (MCA)
-	24	INSIDE THE ELECTRIC CIRCUS	W.A.S.P. (Capitol)
-	25	NOW DANCE '86	Various Artists (EMI/Virgin)
-	26	JUST LIKE THE FIRST TIME	Freddie Jackson (Capitol)
14	27	U-VOX	Ultravox (Chrysalis)
-	28	UPFRONT 3	Various Artists (Serious)
11	29	ONE TO ONE	Howard Jones (WEA)
22	30	BROTHERS IN ARMS	Dire Straits (Vertigo)
33	31	IN THE ARMY NOW	Status Quo (Vertigo)
32	32	THE AUTOBIOGRAPHY OF SUPERTRAMP	Supertramp (A&M)
38	33	DANCING ON THE CEILING	Lionel Richie (Motown)
47	34	SLIPPERY WHEN WET	Bon Jovi (Vertigo)
20	35	BREAK EVERY RULE	Tina Turner (Capitol)
16	36	COMMUNARDS	Communards (London)
25	37	PLEASE	Pet Shop Boys (EMI)
-	38	REMINISCING	Foster & Allen (Stylus)
-	39	SHELTER	Lone Justice (Geffen)
-	40	HOW GREEN IS THE VALLEY	Men They Couldn't Hang (MCA)
23	41	A KIND OF MAGIC	Queen (EMI)
27	42	TALKING WITH THE TAXMAN ABOUT POETRY	Billy Bragg (Go! Discs)
39	43	THE FINAL	Wham! (Epic)
-	44	THE PAVAROTTI COLLECTION	Luciano Pavarotti (Stylus)
-	45	WHITNEY HOUSTON	Whitney Houston (Arista)
31	46	ZAGORA	Loose Ends (Virgin)
-	47	PICTURE BOOK	Simply Red (Elektra)
24	48	INTO THE LIGHT	Chris DeBurgh (A&M)
-	49	SIMON BATES - OUR TUNE	Various Artists (Polydor)
-	50	AN IMITATION OF LOVE	Millie Jackson (Jive)

New albums by a plethora of major names failed to dislodge Paul Simon from the chart top, with A-Ha and Billy Idol coming closest with Number 2 placings. Frankie Goes To Hollywood's second album *Liverpool* proved not to have the sales stamina of their debut release, peaking at Number 4, while Paul Young's *Between Two Fires*, his follow-up to a duo of chart-toppers, had to be content with Number 7.

15 November 1986

last week	this week	Title	Artist (Label)
12	1	EVERY BREATH YOU TAKE - THE SINGLES	Police (A&M)
1	2	GRACELAND	Paul Simon (Warner Bros.)
9	3	TOP GUN	Soundtrack (CBS)
4	4	LIVERPOOL	Frankie Goes To Hollywood (ZZT)
2	5	WHIPLASH SMILE	Billy Idol (Chrysalis)
15	6	NO. 10 UPPING STREET	Big Audio Dynamite (CBS)
8	7	BETWEEN TWO FIRES	Paul Young (CBS)
7	8	SILK AND STEEL	Five Star (Tent/RCA)
3	9	GET CLOSE	Pretenders (Real)
17	10	DREAMTIME	Stranglers (Epic)
25	11	NOW DANCE '86	Various Artists (EMI/Virgin)
5	12	TRUE BLUE	Madonna (Sire)
6	13	SCOUNDREL DAYS	A-Ha (Warner Bros.)
10	14	LONDON O - HULL 4	Housemartins (Go! Discs)
26	15	JUST LIKE THE FIRST TIME	Freddie Jackson (Capitol)
14	16	WORD UP	Cameo (Club)
11	17	THE CHART	Various Artists (Telstar)
18	18	REVENGE	Eurythmics (RCA)
20	19	FORE!	Huey Lewis & the News (Chrysalis)
34	20	SLIPPERY WHEN WET	Bon Jovi (Vertigo)
19	21	SOUTH PACIFIC	Various Artists (CBS)
13	22	GIVE ME THE REASON	Luther Vandross (Epic)
41	23	A KIND OF MAGIC	Queen (EMI)
33	24	DANCING ON THE CEILING	Lionel Richie (Motown)
32	25	THE AUTOBIOGRAPHY OF SUPERTRAMP	Supertramp (A&M)
-	26	LEATHER JACKET	Elton John (Rocket)
31	27	IN THE ARMY NOW	Status Quo (Vertigo)
46	28	ZAGORA	Loose Ends (Virgin)
24	29	INSIDE THE ELECTRIC CIRCUS	W.A.S.P. (Capitol)
16	30	TRUE COLORS	Cyndi Lauper (CBS)
38	31	REMINISCING	Foster & Allen (Stylus)
30	32	BROTHERS IN ARMS	Dire Straits (Vertigo)
-	33	SO	Peter Gabriel (Virgin)
-	34	THE GREATEST HITS OF 1986	Various Artists (Telstar)
28	35	UPFRONT 3	Various Artists (Serious)
-	36	JOURNEY TO THE URGE WITHIN	Courtney Pine (Island)
21	37	SOMEWHERE IN TIME	Iron Maiden (EMI)
40	38	HOW GREEN IS THE VALLEY	Men They Couldn't Hang (MCA)
-	39	TOGETHER	Various Artists (K-Tel)
35	40	BREAK EVERY RULE	Tina Turner (Capitol)
36	41	COMMUNARDS	Communards (London)
-	42	RADIO MUSICOLA	Nik Kershaw (MCA)
47	43	PICTURE BOOK	Simply Red (Elektra)
27	44	U-VOX	Ultravox (Chrysalis)
42	45	TALKING WITH THE TAXMAN ABOUT POETRY	Billy Bragg (Go! Discs)
23	46	THIRD STAGE	Boston (MCA)
-	47	ULTIMATE TRAX VOL 1	Various Artists (Champion)
-	48	ARETHA	Aretha Franklin (Arista)
39	49	SHELTER	Lone Justice (Geffen)
50	50	AN IMITATION OF LOVE	Millie Jackson (Jive)

22 November 1986

last week	this week	Title	Artist (Label)
1	1	EVERY BREATH YOU TAKE - THE SINGLES	Police (A&M)
2	2	GRACELAND	Paul Simon (Warner Bros.)
3	3	TOP GUN	Soundtrack (CBS)
-	4	LIVE 1975-85	Bruce Springsteen & the E Street Band (CBS)
11	5	NOW DANCE '86	Various Artists (EMI/Virgin)
12	6	TRUE BLUE	Madonna (Sire)
8	7	SILK AND STEEL	Five Star (Tent/RCA)
20	8	SLIPPERY WHEN WET	Bon Jovi (Vertigo)
-	9	THE WHOLE STORY	Kate Bush (EMI)
9	10	GET CLOSE	Pretenders (Real)
34	11	THE GREATEST HITS OF 1986	Various Artists (Telstar)
26	12	LEATHER JACKET	Elton John (Rocket)
-	13	HIT MIX '86	Various Artists (Stylus)
18	14	REVENGE	Eurythmics (RCA)
4	15	LIVERPOOL	Frankie Goes To Hollywood (ZZT)
7	16	BETWEEN TWO FIRES	Paul Young (CBS)
6	17	NO. 10 UPPING STREET	Big Audio Dynamite (CBS)
-	18	HITS 5	Various Artists (CBS/WEA)
5	19	WHIPLASH SMILE	Billy Idol (Chrysalis)
25	20	THE AUTOBIOGRAPHY OF SUPERTRAMP	Supertramp (A&M)
31	21	REMINISCING	Foster & Allen (Stylus)
13	22	SCOUNDREL DAYS	A-Ha (Warner Bros.)
-	23	GOD'S OWN MEDICINE	Mission (Mercury)
10	24	DREAMTIME	Stranglers (Epic)
33	25	SO	Peter Gabriel (Virgin)
14	26	LONDON O - HULL 4	Housemartins (Go! Discs)
-	27	THE FINAL COUNTDOWN	Europe (Epic)
16	28	WORD UP	Cameo (Club)
22	29	GIVE ME THE REASON	Luther Vandross (Epic)
-	30	DIFFERENT LIGHT	Bangles (CBS)
-	31	BRIGHTER THAN A THOUSAND SUNS	Killing Joke (EG)
15	32	JUST LIKE THE FIRST TIME	Freddie Jackson (Capitol)
23	33	A KIND OF MAGIC	Queen (EMI)
36	34	JOURNEY TO THE URGE WITHIN	Courtney Pine (Island)
-	35	STRONG PERSUADER	Robert Cray Band (Mercury)
29	36	INSIDE THE ELECTRIC CIRCUS	W.A.S.P. (Capitol)
-	37	TOGETHER	Various Artists (K-Tel)
32	38	BROTHERS IN ARMS	Dire Straits (Vertigo)
19	39	FORE!	Huey Lewis & the News (Chrysalis)
-	40	ELECTRIC CAFE	Kraftwerk (EMI)
-	41	SAY WHAT	Trouble Funk (Fourth & Broadway)
-	42	YOUR FUNERAL ...... MY TRIAL	Nick Cave & the Bad Seeds (Mute)
17	43	THE CHART	Various Artists (Telstar)
-	44	BLACK MAGIC	Various Artists (Stylus)
27	45	IN THE ARMY NOW	Status Quo (Vertigo)
40	46	BREAK EVERY RULE	Tina Turner (Capitol)
28	47	ZAGORA	Loose Ends (Virgin)
-	48	THE FINAL	Wham! (Epic)
-	49	THEIR VERY BEST BACK-TO-BACK	Various Artists (Priority)
49	50	SHELTER	Lone Justice (Geffen)

29 November 1986

last week	this week	Title	Artist (Label)
1	1	EVERY BREATH YOU TAKE - THE SINGLES	Police (A&M)
18	2	HITS 5	Various Artists (CBS/WEA)
9	3	THE WHOLE STORY	Kate Bush (EMI)
4	4	LIVE 1975-85	Bruce Springsteen & the E Street Band (CBS)
3	5	TOP GUN	Soundtrack (CBS)
2	6	GRACELAND	Paul Simon (Warner Bros.)
8	7	SLIPPERY WHEN WET	Bon Jovi (Vertigo)
6	8	TRUE BLUE	Madonna (Sire)
7	9	SILK AND STEEL	Five Star (Tent/RCA)
13	10	HIT MIX '86	Various Artists (Stylus)
5	11	NOW DANCE '86	Various Artists (EMI/Virgin)
23	12	GOD'S OWN MEDICINE	Mission (Mercury)
11	13	THE GREATEST HITS OF 1986	Various Artists (Telstar)
20	14	THE AUTOBIOGRAPHY OF SUPERTRAMP	Supertramp (A&M)
15	15	LIVERPOOL	Frankie Goes To Hollywood (ZZT)
10	16	GET CLOSE	Pretenders (Real)
25	17	SO	Peter Gabriel (Virgin)
38	18	BROTHERS IN ARMS	Dire Straits (Vertigo)
-	19	SWEET FREEDOM	Michael McDonald (Warner Bros.)
-	20	INFECTED	The The (Some Bizzare)
21	21	REMINISCING	Foster & Allen (Stylus)
-	22	THROUGH THE BARRICADES	Spandau Ballet (Reformation)
17	23	NO. 10 UPPING STREET	Big Audio Dynamite (CBS)
27	24	THE FINAL COUNTDOWN	Europe (Epic)
-	25	WHITNEY HOUSTON	Whitney Houston (Arista)
16	26	BETWEEN TWO FIRES	Paul Young (CBS)
28	27	WORD UP	Cameo (Club)
29	28	GIVE ME THE REASON	Luther Vandross (Epic)
32	29	JUST LIKE THE FIRST TIME	Freddie Jackson (Capitol)
35	30	STRONG PERSUADER	Robert Cray Band (Mercury)
44	31	BLACK MAGIC	Various Artists (Stylus)
26	32	LONDON O - HULL 4	Housemartins (Go! Discs)
14	33	REVENGE	Eurythmics (RCA)
33	34	A KIND OF MAGIC	Queen (EMI)
37	35	TOGETHER	Various Artists (K-Tel)
12	36	LEATHER JACKET	Elton John (Rocket)
22	37	SCOUNDREL DAYS	A-Ha (Warner Bros.)
24	38	DREAMTIME	Stranglers (Epic)
-	39	RAPTURE	Anita Baker (Elektra)
49	40	THEIR VERY BEST BACK-TO-BACK	Various Artists (Priority)
-	41	THE MOON AND THE MELODIES	Harold Budd with the Cocteau Twins (4AD)
47	42	ZAGORA	Loose Ends (Virgin)
-	43	TRILOGY	Yngwie J Malmsteen (Polydor)
30	44	DIFFERENT LIGHT	Bangles (CBS)
40	45	ELECTRIC CAFE	Kraftwerk (EMI)
-	46	INSIDE STORY	Grace Jones (Manhattan)
-	47	ROCKBIRD	Debbie Harry (Chrysalis)
31	48	BRIGHTER THAN A THOUSAND SUNS	Killing Joke (EG)
36	49	INSIDE THE ELECTRIC CIRCUS	W.A.S.P. (Capitol)
34	50	JOURNEY TO THE URGE WITHIN	Courtney Pine (Island)

Although the Police had been disbanded, and the three former members busily embroiled in solo careers, for some years by the end of 1986, their commercial profile was still high, as proved by the success of the belated hits compilation *Every Breath You Take - The Singles*. One unusual highlight of this set was a radically remixed version of the 1980 hit *Don't Stand So Close To Me*, also issued as a single.

December 1986

6 December 1986

last week	this week	Title	Artist (label)
2	1	HITS 5	Various Artists (CBS/WEA)
3	2	THE WHOLE STORY	Kate Bush (EMI)
1	3	EVERY BREATH YOU TAKE - THE SINGLES	Police (A&M)
7	4	SLIPPERY WHEN WET	Bon Jovi (Vertigo)
4	5	LIVE 1975-85	Bruce Springsteen & the E Street Band (CBS)
22	6	THROUGH THE BARRICADES	Spandau Ballet (Reformation)
5	7	TOP GUN	Soundtrack (CBS)
-	8	NOW THAT'S WHAT I CALL MUSIC 8	Various Artists (EMI/Virgin/PolyGram)
6	9	GRACELAND	Paul Simon (Warner Bros.)
20	10	INFECTED	The The (Some Bizzare)
-	11	DISCO	Pet Shop Boys (Parlophone)
9	12	SILK AND STEEL	Five Star (Tent/RCA)
8	13	TRUE BLUE	Madonna (Sire)
10	14	HIT MIX '86	Various Artists (Stylus)
47	15	ROCKBIRD	Debbie Harry (Chrysalis)
24	16	THE FINAL COUNTDOWN	Europe (Epic)
12	17	GOD'S OWN MEDICINE	Mission (Mercury)
46	18	INSIDE STORY	Grace Jones (Manhattan)
-	19	NOTORIOUS	Duran Duran (EMI)
-	20	AUGUST	Eric Clapton (Duck)
17	21	SO	Peter Gabriel (Virgin)
11	22	NOW DANCE '86	Various Artists (EMI/Virgin)
18	23	BROTHERS IN ARMS	Dire Straits (Vertigo)
33	24	REVENGE	Eurythmics (RCA)
14	25	THE AUTOBIOGRAPHY OF SUPERTRAMP	Supertramp (A&M)
21	26	REMINISCING	Foster & Allen (Stylus)
28	27	GIVE ME THE REASON	Luther Vandross (Epic)
19	28	SWEET FREEDOM	Michael McDonald (Warner Bros.)
13	29	THE GREATEST HITS OF 1986	Various Artists (Telstar)
39	30	RAPTURE	Anita Baker (Elektra)
-	31	UTTER MADNESS	Madness (Zarjazz)
-	32	THE VERY BEST OF THE DRIFTERS	Drifters (Telstar)
25	33	WHITNEY HOUSTON	Whitney Houston (Arista)
34	34	A KIND OF MAGIC	Queen (EMI)
16	35	GET CLOSE	Pretenders (Real)
-	36	WHAT PRICE PARADISE	China Crisis (Virgin)
-	37	SHOP ASSISTANTS	Shop Assistants (Blue Guitar)
-	38	THE CIRCLE AND THE SQUARE	Red Box (WEA)
-	39	IN THE ARMY NOW	Status Quo (Vertigo)
-	40	INTENTIONS	Maxi Priest (10)
27	41	WORD UP	Cameo (Club)
29	42	JUST LIKE THE FIRST TIME	Freddie Jackson (Capitol)
15	43	LIVERPOOL	Frankie Goes To Hollywood (ZTT)
26	44	BETWEEN TWO FIRES	Paul Young (CBS)
42	45	ZAGORA	Loose Ends (Virgin)
40	46	THEIR VERY BEST BACK-TO-BACK	Various Artists (Priority)
37	47	SCOUNDREL DAYS	A-Ha (Warner Bros.)
-	48	BROADCAST	Cutting Crew (Siren)
-	49	LOVERS	Various Artists (Telstar)
-	50	TOGETHER	Various Artists (K-Tel)

13 December 1986

last week	this week	Title	Artist (label)
8	1	NOW THAT'S WHAT I CALL MUSIC 8	Various Artists (EMI/Virgin/PolyGram)
2	2	THE WHOLE STORY	Kate Bush (EMI)
1	3	HITS 5	Various Artists (CBS/WEA)
3	4	EVERY BREATH YOU TAKE - THE SINGLES	Police (A&M)
4	5	SLIPPERY WHEN WET	Bon Jovi (Vertigo)
7	6	TOP GUN	Soundtrack (CBS)
9	7	GRACELAND	Paul Simon (Warner Bros.)
6	8	THROUGH THE BARRICADES	Spandau Ballet (Reformation)
5	9	LIVE 1975-85	Bruce Springsteen & the E Street Band (CBS)
13	10	TRUE BLUE	Madonna (Sire)
-	11	LIVE MAGIC	Queen (EMI)
12	12	SILK AND STEEL	Five Star (Tent/RCA)
11	13	DISCO	Pet Shop Boys (Parlophone)
20	14	AUGUST	Eric Clapton (Duck)
14	15	HIT MIX '86	Various Artists (Stylus)
15	16	ROCKBIRD	Debbie Harry (Chrysalis)
-	17	ANYTHING	Damned (MCA)
16	18	THE FINAL COUNTDOWN	Europe (Epic)
22	19	NOW DANCE '86	Various Artists (EMI/Virgin)
29	20	THE GREATEST HITS OF 1986	Various Artists (Telstar)
49	21	LOVERS	Various Artists (Telstar)
23	22	BROTHERS IN ARMS	Dire Straits (Vertigo)
31	23	UTTER MADNESS	Madness (Zarjazz)
10	24	INFECTED	The The (Some Bizzare)
26	25	REMINISCING	Foster & Allen (Stylus)
-	26	DIFFERENT LIGHT	Bangles (CBS)
19	27	NOTORIOUS	Duran Duran (EMI)
21	28	SO	Peter Gabriel (Virgin)
30	29	RAPTURE	Anita Baker (Elektra)
24	30	REVENGE	Eurythmics (RCA)
25	31	THE AUTOBIOGRAPHY OF SUPERTRAMP	Supertramp (A&M)
32	32	THE VERY BEST OF THE DRIFTERS	Drifters (Telstar)
28	33	SWEET FREEDOM	Michael McDonald (Warner Bros.)
-	34	NOW - THE CHRISTMAS ALBUM	Various Artists (EMI/Virgin)
36	35	WHAT PRICE PARADISE	China Crisis (Virgin)
17	36	GOD'S OWN MEDICINE	Mission (Mercury)
-	37	SIXTIES MANIA	Various Artists (Telstar)
-	38	FORE!	Huey Lewis & the News (Chrysalis)
39	39	IN THE ARMY NOW	Status Quo (Vertigo)
46	40	THEIR VERY BEST BACK-TO-BACK	Various Artists (Priority)
-	41	DEEP IN THE HEART OF NOWHERE	Bob Geldof (Mercury)
-	42	MUSIC FROM THE SINGING DETECTIVE	Various Artists (BBC)
33	43	WHITNEY HOUSTON	Whitney Houston (Arista)
47	44	SCOUNDREL DAYS	A-Ha (Warner Bros.)
34	45	A KIND OF MAGIC	Queen (EMI)
-	46	THE FINAL	Wham! (Epic)
18	47	INSIDE STORY	Grace Jones (Manhattan)
-	48	SOUTH PACIFIC	Various Artists (CBS)
-	49	JAZZ FROM HELL	Frank Zappa (EMI)
-	50	STREET SOUNDS EDITION 19	Various Artists (Street Sounds)

20 December 1986

last week	this week	Title	Artist (label)
1	1	NOW THAT'S WHAT I CALL MUSIC 8	Various Artists (EMI/Virgin/PolyGram)
3	2	HITS 5	Various Artists (CBS/WEA)
2	3	THE WHOLE STORY	Kate Bush (EMI)
4	4	EVERY BREATH YOU TAKE - THE SINGLES	Police (A&M)
11	5	LIVE MAGIC	Queen (EMI)
7	6	GRACELAND	Paul Simon (Warner Bros.)
5	7	SLIPPERY WHEN WET	Bon Jovi (Vertigo)
10	8	TRUE BLUE	Madonna (Sire)
6	9	TOP GUN	Soundtrack (CBS)
9	10	LIVE 1975-85	Bruce Springsteen & the E Street Band (CBS)
12	11	SILK AND STEEL	Five Star (Tent/RCA)
26	12	DIFFERENT LIGHT	Bangles (CBS)
30	13	REVENGE	Eurythmics (RCA)
14	14	AUGUST	Eric Clapton (Duck)
21	15	LOVERS	Various Artists (Telstar)
8	16	THROUGH THE BARRICADES	Spandau Ballet (Reformation)
22	17	BROTHERS IN ARMS	Dire Straits (Vertigo)
25	18	REMINISCING	Foster & Allen (Stylus)
48	19	SOUTH PACIFIC	Various Artists (CBS)
17	20	ANYTHING	Damned (MCA)
38	21	FORE!	Huey Lewis & the News (Chrysalis)
34	22	NOW - THE CHRISTMAS ALBUM	Various Artists (EMI/Virgin)
24	23	INFECTED	The The (Some Bizzare)
37	24	SIXTIES MANIA	Various Artists (Telstar)
20	25	THE GREATEST HITS OF 1986	Various Artists (Telstar)
15	26	HIT MIX '86	Various Artists (Stylus)
44	27	SCOUNDREL DAYS	A-Ha (Warner Bros.)
19	28	NOW DANCE '86	Various Artists (EMI/Virgin)
13	29	DISCO	Pet Shop Boys (Parlophone)
18	30	THE FINAL COUNTDOWN	Europe (Epic)
27	31	NOTORIOUS	Duran Duran (EMI)
29	32	RAPTURE	Anita Baker (Elektra)
39	33	IN THE ARMY NOW	Status Quo (Vertigo)
46	34	THE FINAL	Wham! (Epic)
36	35	GOD'S OWN MEDICINE	Mission (Mercury)
-	36	LONDON O - HULL 4	Housemartins (Go! Discs)
33	37	SWEET FREEDOM	Michael McDonald (Warner Bros.)
-	38	MUSIC MADNESS	Mantronix (10/Virgin)
-	39	BOSTIN' STEVE AUSTIN	We've Got A Fuzzbox And We're Gonna Use It (Vindaloo WEA)
16	40	ROCKBIRD	Debbie Harry (Chrysalis)
-	41	MOTOWN CHARTBUSTERS	Various Artists (Telstar)
43	42	WHITNEY HOUSTON	Whitney Houston (Arista)
-	43	COMMUNARDS	Communards (London)
-	44	THE CAROLS ALBUM	Huddersfield Choral Society (EMI)
-	45	WOMAGIC	Bobby Womack (MCA)
28	46	SO	Peter Gabriel (Virgin)
-	47	AN ALBUM OF HYMNS	Aled Jones (EMI)
23	48	UTTER MADNESS	Madness (Zarjazz)
-	49	TOGETHER	Various Artists (K-Tel)
-	50	BEDTIME FOR DEMOCRACY	Dead Kennedys (Alternative Tentacles)

Kate Bush's *The Whole Story*, an anthology of her hit singles and key work to date, narrowly failed to give her another chart-topping album. The inevitable December culprits were the year-end volumes in the *Hits* and *Now* compilation series, which squared their third Christmas scorecard with a draw - this time, both *Hits 5* and *Now Music 8* made Number 1 (though EMI/Virgin might claim the final Yule advantage).

last	this	**3 January 1987**	
week			
1	1	NOW THAT'S WHAT I CALL MUSIC 8	
		Various Artists (EMI/Virgin/PolyGram)	
3	2	THE WHOLE STORY	Kate Bush (EMI)
2	3	HITS 5	Various Artists (CBS/WEA)
5	4	LIVE MAGIC	Queen (EMI)
6	5	GRACELAND	Paul Simon (Warner Bros.)
4	6	EVERY BREATH YOU TAKE - THE SINGLES	
			Police (A&M)
8	7	TRUE BLUE	Madonna (Sire)
7	8	SLIPPERY WHEN WET	Bon Jovi (Vertigo)
21	9	FORE!	Huey Lewis & the News (Chrysalis)
37	10	SWEET FREEDOM	
		Michael McDonald (Warner Bros.)	
11	11	SILK AND STEEL	Five Star (Tent/RCA)
9	12	TOP GUN	Soundtrack (CBS)
13	13	REVENGE	Eurythmics (RCA)
12	14	DIFFERENT LIGHT	Bangles (CBS)
14	15	AUGUST	Eric Clapton (Duck)
22	16	NOW - THE CHRISTMAS ALBUM	
		Various Artists (EMI/Virgin/PolyGram)	
18	17	REMINISCING	Foster & Allen (Stylus)
19	18	SOUTH PACIFIC	Various Artists (CBS)
10	19	LIVE 1975-85	
		Bruce Springsteen & the E Street Band (CBS)	
15	20	LOVERS	Various Artists (Telstar)
16	21	THROUGH THE BARRICADES	
		Spandau Ballet (Reformation)	
30	22	THE FINAL COUNTDOWN	Europe (Epic)
36	23	LONDON O - HULL 4	
		Housemartins (Go! Discs)	
34	24	THE FINAL	Wham! (Epic)
-	25	CHRISTMAS	Elaine Paige (WEA)
-	26	MUSIC FROM THE SINGING DETECTIVE	
		Various Artists (BBC)	
24	27	SIXTIES MANIA	Various Artists (Telstar)
-	28	BONNIE TYLER'S GREATEST HITS	
		Bonnie Tyler (Telstar)	
26	29	HIT MIX '86	Various Artists (Stylus)
-	30	HIGHWAY OF LIFE	Harry Secombe (Telstar)
47	31	AN ALBUM OF HYMNS	Aled Jones (EMI)
44	32	THE CAROLS ALBUM	
		Huddersfield Choral Society (EMI)	
42	33	WHITNEY HOUSTON	Whitney Houston (Arista)
32	34	RAPTURE	Anita Baker (Elektra)
33	35	IN THE ARMY NOW	Status Quo (Vertigo)
17	36	BROTHERS IN ARMS	Dire Straits (Vertigo)
20	37	ANYTHING	Damned (MCA)
27	38	SCOUNDREL DAYS	A-Ha (Warner Bros.)
31	39	NOTORIOUS	Duran Duran (EMI)
35	40	GOD'S OWN MEDICINE	Mission (Mercury)
39	41	BOSTIN' STEVE AUSTIN	We've Got A Fuzzbox
		And We're Gonna Use It (Vindaloo WEA)	
46	42	SO	Peter Gabriel (Virgin)
43	43	COMMUNARDS	Communards (London)
41	44	MOTOWN CHARTBUSTERS	
		Various Artists (Telstar)	
25	45	THE GREATEST HITS OF 1986	
		Various Artists (Telstar)	
-	46	JAZZ FROM HELL	Frank Zappa (EMI)
-	47	CHRISTMAS WITH KIRI	
		Kiri Te Kanawa (Decca)	
-	48	INVISIBLE TOUCH	Genesis (Charisma)
23	49	INFECTED	The The (Some Bizzare)
29	50	DISCO	Pet Shop Boys (Parlophone)

		10 January 1987	
1	1	NOW THAT'S WHAT I CALL MUSIC 8	
		Various Artists (EMI/Virgin/PolyGram)	
5	2	GRACELAND	Paul Simon (Warner Bros.)
3	3	HITS 5	Various Artists (CBS/WEA)
2	4	THE WHOLE STORY	Kate Bush (EMI)
6	5	EVERY BREATH YOU TAKE - THE SINGLES	
			Police (A&M)
8	6	SLIPPERY WHEN WET	Bon Jovi (Vertigo)
7	7	TRUE BLUE	Madonna (Sire)
4	8	LIVE MAGIC	Queen (EMI)
11	9	SILK AND STEEL	Five Star (Tent/RCA)
13	10	REVENGE	Eurythmics (RCA)
9	11	FORE!	Huey Lewis & the News (Chrysalis)
23	12	LONDON O - HULL 4	
		Housemartins (Go! Discs)	
10	13	SWEET FREEDOM	
		Michael McDonald (Warner Bros.)	
26	14	MUSIC FROM THE SINGING DETECTIVE	
		Various Artists (BBC)	
14	15	DIFFERENT LIGHT	Bangles (CBS)
38	16	SCOUNDREL DAYS	A-Ha (Warner Bros.)
12	17	TOP GUN	Soundtrack (CBS)
24	18	THE FINAL	Wham! (Epic)
31	19	AN ALBUM OF HYMNS	Aled Jones (EMI)
36	20	BROTHERS IN ARMS	
			Dire Straits (Vertigo)
20	21	LOVERS	Various Artists (Telstar)
17	22	REMINISCING	Foster & Allen (Stylus)
18	23	SOUTH PACIFIC	Various Artists (CBS)
16	24	NOW - THE CHRISTMAS ALBUM	
		Various Artists (EMI/Virgin/PolyGram)	
-	25	GET CLOSE	Pretenders (WEA)
49	26	INFECTED	The The (Some Bizzare)
43	27	COMMUNARDS	Communards (London)
35	28	IN THE ARMY NOW	Status Quo (Vertigo)
19	29	LIVE 1975-85	
		Bruce Springsteen & the E Street Band (CBS)	
15	30	AUGUST	Eric Clapton (Duck)
27	31	SIXTIES MANIA	Various Artists (Telstar)
44	32	MOTOWN CHARTBUSTERS	
		Various Artists (Telstar)	
-	33	DANCING ON THE CEILING	
		Lionel Ritchie (Motown)	
33	34	WHITNEY HOUSTON	
		Whitney Houston (Arista)	
22	35	THE FINAL COUNTDOWN	Europe (Epic)
-	36	WONDERLAND	Erasure (Mute)
29	37	HIT MIX '86	Various Artists (Stylus)
30	38	HIGHWAY OF LIFE	Harry Secombe (Telstar)
34	39	RAPTURE	Anita Baker (Elektra)
21	40	THROUGH THE BARRICADES	
		Spandau Ballet (Reformation)	
28	41	BONNIE TYLER'S GREATEST HITS	
		Bonnie Tyler (Telstar)	
39	42	NOTORIOUS	Duran Duran (EMI)
25	43	CHRISTMAS	Elaine Paige (WEA)
-	44	JUST GOOD FRIENDS	Paul Nicholas (K-Tel)
42	45	SO	Peter Gabriel (Virgin)
-	46	A KIND OF MAGIC	Queen (EMI)
48	47	INVISIBLE TOUCH	Genesis (Charisma)
50	48	DISCO	Pet Shop Boys (Parlophone)
-	49	NO MORE THE FOOL	Elkie Brooks (Legend)
-	50	HOLLYWOOD AND BROADWAY	
		Richard Clayderman (Decca/Delphine)	

		17 January 1987	
2	1	GRACELAND	Paul Simon (Warner Bros.)
1	2	NOW THAT'S WHAT I CALL MUSIC 8	
		Various Artists (EMI/Virgin/PolyGram)	
4	3	THE WHOLE STORY	Kate Bush (EMI)
7	4	TRUE BLUE	Madonna (Sire)
6	5	SLIPPERY WHEN WET	Bon Jovi (Vertigo)
8	6	LIVE MAGIC	Queen (EMI)
9	7	SILK AND STEEL	Five Star (Tent/RCA)
3	8	HITS 5	Various Artists (CBS/WEA)
5	9	EVERY BREATH YOU TAKE - THE SINGLES	
			Police (A&M)
13	10	SWEET FREEDOM	
		Michael McDonald (Warner Bros.)	
10	11	REVENGE	Eurythmics (RCA)
15	12	DIFFERENT LIGHT	Bangles (CBS)
12	13	LONDON O - HULL 4	
		Housemartins (Go! Discs)	
16	14	SCOUNDREL DAYS	A-Ha (Warner Bros.)
27	15	COMMUNARDS	Communards (London)
14	16	MUSIC FROM THE SINGING DETECTIVE	
		Various Artists (BBC)	
11	17	FORE!	Huey Lewis & the News (Chrysalis)
17	18	TOP GUN	Soundtrack (CBS)
48	19	DISCO	Pet Shop Boys (Parlophone)
49	20	NO MORE THE FOOL	Elkie Brooks (Legend)
20	21	BROTHERS IN ARMS	Dire Straits (Vertigo)
35	22	THE FINAL COUNTDOWN	Europe (Epic)
18	23	THE FINAL	Wham! (Epic)
23	24	SOUTH PACIFIC	Various Artists (CBS)
41	25	BONNIE TYLER'S GREATEST HITS	
		Bonnie Tyler (Telstar)	
25	26	GET CLOSE	Pretenders (WEA)
30	27	AUGUST	Eric Clapton (Duck)
45	28	SO	Peter Gabriel (Virgin)
26	29	INFECTED	The The (Some Bizzare)
-	30	SUZANNE VEGA	Suzanne Vega (A&M)
-	31	GIVE ME THE REASON	
		Luther Vandross (Epic)	
33	32	DANCING ON THE CEILING	
		Lionel Ritchie (Motown)	
31	33	SIXTIES MANIA	Various Artists (Telstar)
37	34	HIT MIX '86	Various Artists (Stylus)
28	35	IN THE ARMY NOW	Status Quo (Vertigo)
39	36	RAPTURE	Anita Baker (Elektra)
-	37	CROOKED MILE	Microdisney (Virgin)
-	38	JUST LIKE THE FIRST TIME	
		Freddie Jackson (Capitol)	
21	39	LOVERS	Various Artists (Telstar)
-	40	WORD UP	Cameo (Club)
32	41	MOTOWN CHARTBUSTERS	
		Various Artists (Telstar)	
-	42	BEDTIME FOR DEMOCRACY	
		Dead Kennedys (Alternative Tentacles)	
-	43	LICENCED TO ILL	
		Beastie Boys (Def Jam)	
22	44	REMINISCING	Foster & Allen (Stylus)
36	45	WONDERLAND	Erasure (Mute)
34	46	WHITNEY HOUSTON	
		Whitney Houston (Arista)	
40	47	THROUGH THE BARRICADES	
		Spandau Ballet (Reformation)	
19	48	AN ALBUM OF HYMNS	Aled Jones (EMI)
-	49	BREAK EVERY RULE	Tina Turner (Capitol)
46	50	A KIND OF MAGIC	Queen (EMI)

Top US vocalist Michael McDonald opened 1987 in the Top 10 with his only significant UK album success, the compilation *Sweet Freedom*, which was titled after his biggest solo success (a hit in 1986), and also included his even better-known duets with James Ingram (*Yah Mo Be There*) and Patti LaBelle (*On My Own*). Springsteen's *Live 1975-85* box set, still huge in the US, dropped rapidly out of the Top 10 here.

last week	this week		

24 January 1987

last	this		
1	1	GRACELAND	Paul Simon (Warner Bros.)
3	2	THE WHOLE STORY	Kate Bush (EMI)
2	3	NOW THAT'S WHAT I CALL MUSIC 8	Various Artists (EMI/Virgin/PolyGram)
4	4	TRUE BLUE	Madonna (Sire)
5	5	SLIPPERY WHEN WET	Bon Jovi (Vertigo)
6	6	LIVE MAGIC	Queen (EMI)
9	7	EVERY BREATH YOU TAKE - THE SINGLES	Police (A&M)
7	8	SILK AND STEEL	Five Star (Tent/RCA)
12	9	DIFFERENT LIGHT	Bangles (CBS)
11	10	REVENGE	Eurythmics (RCA)
10	11	SWEET FREEDOM	Michael McDonald (Warner Bros.)
8	12	HITS 5	Various Artists (CBS/WEA)
26	13	GET CLOSE	Pretenders (WEA)
13	14	LONDON O - HULL 4	Housemartins (Go! Discs)
17	15	FORE!	Huey Lewis & the News (Chrysalis)
-	16	THE HOUSE OF BLUE LIGHT	Deep Purple (Polydor)
27	17	AUGUST	Eric Clapton (Duck)
14	18	SCOUNDREL DAYS	A-Ha (Warner Bros.)
29	19	INFECTED	The The (Some Bizzare)
15	20	COMMUNARDS	Communards (London)
22	21	THE FINAL COUNTDOWN	Europe (Epic)
21	22	BROTHERS IN ARMS	Dire Straits (Vertigo)
-	23	RENDEZ-VOUS	Jean Michel Jarre (Polydor)
28	24	SO	Peter Gabriel (Virgin)
-	25	LIVE ALIVE	Stevie Ray Vaughan (Epic)
16	26	MUSIC FROM THE SINGING DETECTIVE	Various Artists (BBC)
-	27	THE VERY BEST OF ELKIE BROOKS	Elkie Brooks (Telstar)
-	28	GOD'S OWN MEDICINE	Mission (Mercury)
23	29	THE FINAL	Wham! (Epic)
20	30	NO MORE THE FOOL	Elkie Brooks (Legend)
-	31	COUNT THREE AND PRAY	Berlin (Mercury)
-	32	SURFACE	Surface (CBS)
36	33	RAPTURE	Anita Baker (Elektra)
43	34	LICENCED TO ILL	Beastie Boys (Def Jam)
37	35	CROOKED MILE	Microdisney (Virgin)
-	36	WHEN SECONDS COUNT	Survivor (Scotti Bros.)
44	37	REMINISCING	Foster & Allen (Stylus)
25	38	BONNIE TYLER'S GREATEST HITS	Bonnie Tyler (Telstar)
30	39	SUZANNE VEGA	Suzanne Vega (A&M)
32	40	DANCING ON THE CEILING	Lionel Ritchie (Motown)
47	41	THROUGH THE BARRICADES	Spandau Ballet (Reformation)
-	42	THE PHILADELPHIA STORY	Various Artists (Street Sounds)
-	43	SHAKE YOU DOWN	Gregory Abbott (CBS)
-	44	MUSICAL MADNESS	Mantronix (10)
18	45	TOP GUN	Soundtrack (CBS)
19	46	DISCO	Pet Shop Boys (Parlophone)
40	47	WORD UP	Cameo (Club)
31	48	GIVE ME THE REASON	Luther Vandross (Epic)
50	49	A KIND OF MAGIC	Queen (EMI)
42	50	BEDTIME FOR DEMOCRACY	Dead Kennedys (Alternative Tentacles)

31 January 1987

last	this		
1	1	GRACELAND	Paul Simon (Warner Bros.)
2	2	THE WHOLE STORY	Kate Bush (EMI)
16	3	THE HOUSE OF BLUE LIGHT	Deep Purple (Polydor)
6	4	LIVE MAGIC	Queen (EMI)
4	5	TRUE BLUE	Madonna (Sire)
5	6	SLIPPERY WHEN WET	Bon Jovi (Vertigo)
9	7	DIFFERENT LIGHT	Bangles (CBS)
13	8	GET CLOSE	Pretenders (WEA)
3	9	NOW THAT'S WHAT I CALL MUSIC 8	Various Artists (EMI/Virgin/PolyGram)
7	10	EVERY BREATH YOU TAKE - THE SINGLES	Police (A&M)
11	11	SWEET FREEDOM	Michael McDonald (Warner Bros.)
10	12	REVENGE	Eurythmics (RCA)
27	13	THE VERY BEST OF ELKIE BROOKS	Elkie Brooks (Telstar)
30	14	NO MORE THE FOOL	Elkie Brooks (Legend)
17	15	AUGUST	Eric Clapton (Duck)
15	16	FORE!	Huey Lewis & the News (Chrysalis)
14	17	LONDON O - HULL 4	Housemartins (Go! Discs)
22	18	BROTHERS IN ARMS	Dire Straits (Vertigo)
25	19	LIVE ALIVE	Stevie Ray Vaughan (Epic)
28	20	GOD'S OWN MEDICINE	Mission (Mercury)
8	21	SILK AND STEEL	Five Star (Tent/RCA)
20	22	COMMUNARDS	Communards (London)
46	23	DISCO	Pet Shop Boys (Parlophone)
18	24	SCOUNDREL DAYS	A-Ha (Warner Bros.)
-	25	INVISIBLE TOUCH	Genesis (Charisma)
31	26	COUNT THREE AND PRAY	Berlin (Mercury)
40	27	DANCING ON THE CEILING	Lionel Ritchie (Motown)
33	28	RAPTURE	Anita Baker (Elektra)
12	29	HITS 5	Various Artists (CBS/WEA)
32	30	SURFACE	Surface (CBS)
19	31	INFECTED	The The (Some Bizzare)
21	32	THE FINAL COUNTDOWN	Europe (Epic)
50	33	BEDTIME FOR DEMOCRACY	Dead Kennedys (Alternative Tentacles)
39	34	SUZANNE VEGA	Suzanne Vega (A&M)
29	35	THE FINAL	Wham! (Epic)
-	36	BLAH BLAH BLAH	Iggy Pop (A&M)
-	37	STARBRIGHT	Womack & Womack (Manhattan)
-	38	THE HOUSE SOUND OF CHICAGO	Various Artists (D J Int)
-	39	WHITNEY HOUSTON	Whitney Houston (Arista)
-	40	ZAZU	Rosie Vela (A&M)
49	41	A KIND OF MAGIC	Queen (EMI)
-	42	A CHANGE OF HEART	David Sanborn (Warner Bros.)
-	43	STREET SOUNDS CRUCIAL ELECTRO 3	Various Artists (Street Sounds)
26	44	MUSIC FROM THE SINGING DETECTIVE	Various Artists (BBC)
35	45	CROOKED MILE	Microdisney (Virgin)
-	46	THE PLACIDO DOMINGO COLLECTION	Placido Domingo (Stylus)
-	47	BACK IN THE HIGH LIFE	Steve Winwood (Island)
-	48	RAT IN THE KITCHEN	UB40 (DEP International)
48	49	GIVE ME THE REASON	Luther Vandross (Epic)
34	50	LICENCED TO ILL	Beastie Boys (Def Jam)

7 February 1987

last	this		
1	1	GRACELAND	Paul Simon (Warner Bros.)
2	2	THE WHOLE STORY	Kate Bush (EMI)
6	3	SLIPPERY WHEN WET	Bon Jovi (Vertigo)
7	4	DIFFERENT LIGHT	Bangles (CBS)
4	5	LIVE MAGIC	Queen (EMI)
5	6	TRUE BLUE	Madonna (Sire)
3	7	THE HOUSE OF BLUE LIGHT	Deep Purple (Polydor)
8	8	GET CLOSE	Pretenders (WEA)
14	9	NO MORE THE FOOL	Elkie Brooks (Legend)
15	10	AUGUST	Eric Clapton (Duck)
11	11	SWEET FREEDOM	Michael McDonald (Warner Bros.)
13	12	THE VERY BEST OF ELKIE BROOKS	Elkie Brooks (Telstar)
12	13	REVENGE	Eurythmics (RCA)
20	14	GOD'S OWN MEDICINE	Mission (Mercury)
40	15	ZAZU	Rosie Vela (A&M)
10	16	EVERY BREATH YOU TAKE - THE SINGLES	Police (A&M)
21	17	SILK AND STEEL	Five Star (Tent/RCA)
23	18	DISCO	Pet Shop Boys (Parlophone)
32	19	THE FINAL COUNTDOWN	Europe (Epic)
9	20	NOW THAT'S WHAT I CALL MUSIC 8	Various Artists (EMI/Virgin/PolyGram)
22	21	COMMUNARDS	Communards (London)
31	22	INFECTED	The The (Some Bizzare)
-	23	UPFRONT 4	Various Artists (Serious)
17	24	LONDON O - HULL 4	Housemartins (Go! Discs)
27	25	DANCING ON THE CEILING	Lionel Ritchie (Motown)
18	26	BROTHERS IN ARMS	Dire Straits (Vertigo)
28	27	RAPTURE	Anita Baker (Elektra)
-	28	BY THE LIGHT OF THE MOON	Los Lobos (London)
44	29	MUSIC FROM THE SINGING DETECTIVE	Various Artists (BBC)
16	30	FORE!	Huey Lewis & the News (Chrysalis)
25	31	INVISIBLE TOUCH	Genesis (Charisma)
29	32	HITS 5	Various Artists (CBS/WEA)
24	33	SCOUNDREL DAYS	A-Ha (Warner Bros.)
19	34	LIVE ALIVE	Stevie Ray Vaughan (Epic)
35	35	SO	Peter Gabriel (Virgin)
39	36	WHITNEY HOUSTON	Whitney Houston (Arista)
26	37	COUNT THREE AND PRAY	Berlin (Mercury)
43	38	STREET SOUNDS CRUCIAL ELECTRO 3	Various Artists (Street Sounds)
-	39	ONCE UPON A TIME	Simple Minds (Virgin)
48	40	RAT IN THE KITCHEN	UB40 (DEP International)
38	41	THE HOUSE SOUND OF CHICAGO	Various Artists (D J Int)
36	42	BLAH BLAH BLAH	Iggy Pop (A&M)
42	43	A CHANGE OF HEART	David Sanborn (Warner Bros.)
50	44	LICENCED TO ILL	Beastie Boys (Def Jam)
49	45	GIVE ME THE REASON	Luther Vandross (Epic)
-	46	GEORGIA SATELLITES	Georgia Satellites (Elektra)
-	47	THE WEST END STORY	Various Artists (Street Sounds)
34	48	SUZANNE VEGA	Suzanne Vega (A&M)
30	49	SURFACE	Surface (CBS)
35	50	THE FINAL	Wham! (Epic)

Graceland took to the top of the chart again for another extended stay - a further six consecutive weeks. Showing similar longevity was Kate Bush's *The Whole Story* compilation, which saw off the pre-Christmas Various Artists compilations that kept it from Number 1, and held on doggedly for a further month at 2. Elkie Brooks attacked the Top 20 with simultaneous hit albums, one of them a hits package.

14 February 1987

last week	this week	Title	Artist (Label)
1	1	GRACELAND	Paul Simon (Warner Bros.)
2	2	THE WHOLE STORY	Kate Bush (EMI)
4	3	DIFFERENT LIGHT	Bangles (CBS)
5	4	LIVE MAGIC	Queen (EMI)
10	5	AUGUST	Eric Clapton (Duck)
3	6	SLIPPERY WHEN WET	Bon Jovi (Vertigo)
15	7	ZAZU	Rosie Vela (A&M)
6	8	TRUE BLUE	Madonna (Sire)
11	9	SWEET FREEDOM	Michael McDonald (Warner Bros.)
12	10	THE VERY BEST OF ELKIE BROOKS	Elkie Brooks (Telstar)
9	11	NO MORE THE FOOL	Elkie Brooks (Legend)
17	12	SILK AND STEEL	Five Star (Tent/RCA)
19	13	THE FINAL COUNTDOWN	Europe (Epic)
27	14	RAPTURE	Anita Baker (Elektra)
-	15	THE COST OF LOVING	Style Council (Polydor)
8	16	GET CLOSE	Pretenders (WEA)
13	17	REVENGE	Eurythmics (RCA)
26	18	BROTHERS IN ARMS	Dire Straits (Vertigo)
23	19	UPFRONT 4	Various Artists (Serious)
-	20	MIDNIGHT TO MIDNIGHT	Psychedelic Furs (CBS)
20	21	NOW THAT'S WHAT I CALL MUSIC 8	Various Artists (EMI/Virgin/PolyGram)
16	22	EVERY BREATH YOU TAKE - THE SINGLES	Police (A&M)
45	23	GIVE ME THE REASON	Luther Vandross (Epic)
7	24	THE HOUSE OF BLUE LIGHT	Deep Purple (Polydor)
25	25	DANCING ON THE CEILING	Lionel Ritchie (Motown)
-	26	GAP BAND VIII	Gap Band (Total Experience)
46	27	GEORGIA SATELLITES	Georgia Satellites (Elektra)
18	28	DISCO	Pet Shop Boys (Parlophone)
28	29	BY THE LIGHT OF THE MOON	Los Lobos (London)
30	30	FORE!	Huey Lewis & the News (Chrysalis)
-	31	ABSTRACT EMOTIONS	Randy Crawford (Warner Bros.)
-	32	MASTER OF PUPPETS	Metallica (Music for Nations)
42	33	BLAH BLAH BLAH	Iggy Pop (A&M)
14	34	GOD'S OWN MEDICINE	Mission (Mercury)
35	35	SO	Peter Gabriel (Virgin)
-	36	WAREHOUSE: SONGS AND STORIES	Husker Du (Warner Bros.)
33	37	SCOUNDREL DAYS	A-Ha (Warner Bros.)
21	38	COMMUNARDS	Communards (London)
24	39	LONDON O - HULL 4	Housemartins (Go! Discs)
-	40	PICTURE BOOK	Simply Red (Elektra)
41	41	THE HOUSE SOUND OF CHICAGO	Various Artists (D J Int)
40	42	RAT IN THE KITCHEN	UB40 (DEP International)
44	43	LICENCED TO ILL	Beastie Boys (Def Jam)
47	44	THE WEST END STORY	Various Artists (Stre Sounds)
22	45	INFECTED	The The (Some Bizzare)
38	46	STREET SOUNDS CRUCIAL ELECTRO 3	Various Artists (Street Sounds)
29	47	MUSIC FROM THE SINGING DETECTIVE	Various Artists (BBC)
31	48	INVISIBLE TOUCH	Genesis (Charisma)
36	49	WHITNEY HOUSTON	Whitney Houston (Arista)
-	50	IMPRESSIONS	Various Artists (K-Tel)

21 February 1987

last week	this week	Title	Artist (Label)
1	1	GRACELAND	Paul Simon (Warner Bros.)
5	2	AUGUST	Eric Clapton (Duck)
15	3	THE COST OF LOVING	Style Council (Polydor)
2	4	THE WHOLE STORY	Kate Bush (EMI)
3	5	DIFFERENT LIGHT	Bangles (CBS)
-	6	THE PHANTOM OF THE OPERA	Original Cast (Polydor)
20	7	MIDNIGHT TO MIDNIGHT	Psychedelic Furs (CBS)
7	8	ZAZU	Rosie Vela (A&M)
12	9	SILK AND STEEL	Five Star (Tent/RCA)
8	10	TRUE BLUE	Madonna (Sire)
4	11	LIVE MAGIC	Queen (EMI)
9	12	SWEET FREEDOM	Michael McDonald (Warner Bros.)
16	13	GET CLOSE	Pretenders (WEA)
31	14	ABSTRACT EMOTIONS	Randy Crawford (Warner Bros.)
6	15	SLIPPERY WHEN WET	Bon Jovi (Vertigo)
23	16	GIVE ME THE REASON	Luther Vandross (Epic)
14	17	RAPTURE	Anita Baker (Elektra)
17	18	REVENGE	Eurythmics (RCA)
10	19	THE VERY BEST OF ELKIE BROOKS	Elkie Brooks (Telstar)
-	20	MAD, BAD AND DANGEROUS TO KNOW	Dead or Alive (Epic)
11	21	NO MORE THE FOOL	Elkie Brooks (Legend)
28	22	DISCO	Pet Shop Boys (Parlophone)
13	23	THE FINAL COUNTDOWN	Europe (Epic)
22	24	EVERY BREATH YOU TAKE - THE SINGLES	Police (A&M)
-	25	STREET SOUNDS EDITION 20	Various Artists (Street Sounds)
21	26	NOW THAT'S WHAT I CALL MUSIC 8	Various Artists (EMI/Virgin/PolyGram)
35	27	SO	Peter Gabriel (Virgin)
24	28	THE HOUSE OF BLUE LIGHT	Deep Purple (Polydor)
29	29	BY THE LIGHT OF THE MOON	Los Lobos (London)
18	30	BROTHERS IN ARMS	Dire Straits (Vertigo)
40	31	PICTURE BOOK	Simply Red (Elektra)
19	32	UPFRONT 4	Various Artists (Serious)
27	33	GEORGIA SATELLITES	Georgia Satellites (Elektra)
37	34	SCOUNDREL DAYS	A-Ha (Warner Bros.)
30	35	FORE!	Huey Lewis & the News (Chrysalis)
45	36	INFECTED	The The (Some Bizzare)
-	37	CHASIN' A DREAM	Tashan (Def Jam)
39	38	LONDON O - HULL 4	Housemartins (Go! Discs)
49	39	WHITNEY HOUSTON	Whitney Houston (Arista)
-	40	SURFACE	Surface (CBS)
38	41	COMMUNARDS	Communards (London)
-	42	BACK IN THE HIGH LIFE	Steve Winwood (Island)
34	43	GOD'S OWN MEDICINE	Mission (Mercury)
-	44	BACK AGAIN IN THE DHSS	Half Man Half Biscuit (Probe Plus)
32	45	MASTER OF PUPPETS	Metallica (Music for Nations)
-	46	JUST LIKE THE FIRST TIME	Freddie Jackson (Capitol)
43	47	LICENCED TO ILL	Beastie Boys (Def Jam)
25	48	DANCING ON THE CEILING	Lionel Ritchie (Motown)
26	49	GAP BAND VIII	Gap Band (Total Experience)
36	50	WAREHOUSE: SONGS AND STORIES	Husker Du (Warner Bros.)

28 February 1987

last week	this week	Title	Artist (Label)
6	1	THE PHANTOM OF THE OPERA	Original Cast (Polydor)
1	2	GRACELAND	Paul Simon (Warner Bros.)
2	3	AUGUST	Eric Clapton (Duck)
9	4	SILK AND STEEL	Five Star (Tent/RCA)
27	5	SO	Peter Gabriel (Virgin)
5	6	DIFFERENT LIGHT	Bangles (CBS)
4	7	THE WHOLE STORY	Kate Bush (EMI)
16	8	GIVE ME THE REASON	Luther Vandross (Epic)
3	9	THE COST OF LOVING	Style Council (Polydor)
31	10	PICTURE BOOK	Simply Red (Elektra)
-	11	THE VERY BEST OF HOT CHOCOLATE	Hot Chocolate (RAK)
17	12	RAPTURE	Anita Baker (Elektra)
15	13	SLIPPERY WHEN WET	Bon Jovi (Vertigo)
8	14	ZAZU	Rosie Vela (A&M)
12	15	SWEET FREEDOM	Michael McDonald (Warner Bros.)
30	16	BROTHERS IN ARMS	Dire Straits (Vertigo)
14	17	ABSTRACT EMOTIONS	Randy Crawford (Warner Bros.)
18	18	REVENGE	Eurythmics (RCA)
7	19	MIDNIGHT TO MIDNIGHT	Psychedelic Furs (CBS)
10	20	TRUE BLUE	Madonna (Sire)
11	21	LIVE MAGIC	Queen (EMI)
23	22	THE FINAL COUNTDOWN	Europe (Epic)
20	23	MAD, BAD AND DANGEROUS TO KNOW	Dead or Alive (Epic)
47	24	LICENCED TO ILL	Beastie Boys (Def Jam)
50	25	WAREHOUSE: SONGS AND STORIES	Husker Du (Warner Bros.)
39	26	WHITNEY HOUSTON	Whitney Houston (Arista)
22	27	DISCO	Pet Shop Boys (Parlophone)
19	28	THE VERY BEST OF ELKIE BROOKS	Elkie Brooks (Telstar)
44	29	BACK AGAIN IN THE DHSS	Half Man Half Biscuit (Probe Plus)
13	30	GET CLOSE	Pretenders (WEA)
48	31	DANCING ON THE CEILING	Lionel Ritchie (Motown)
41	32	COMMUNARDS	Communards (London)
34	33	SCOUNDREL DAYS	A-Ha (Warner Bros.)
33	34	GEORGIA SATELLITES	Georgia Satellites (Elektra)
37	35	CHASIN' A DREAM	Tashan (Def Jam)
49	36	GAP BAND VIII	Gap Band (Total Experience)
26	37	NOW THAT'S WHAT I CALL MUSIC 8	Various Artists (EMI/Virgin/PolyGram)
29	38	BY THE LIGHT OF THE MOON	Los Lobos (London)
46	39	JUST LIKE THE FIRST TIME	Freddie Jackson (Capitol)
32	40	UPFRONT 4	Various Artists (Serious)
21	41	NO MORE THE FOOL	Elkie Brooks (Legend)
38	42	LONDON O - HULL 4	Housemartins (Go! Discs)
25	43	STREET SOUNDS EDITION 20	Various Artists (Street Sounds)
-	44	ARETHA	Aretha Franklin (Arista)
-	45	ALIVE AND SCREAMING	Krokus (Arista)
24	46	EVERY BREATH YOU TAKE - THE SINGLES	Police (A&M)
35	47	FORE!	Huey Lewis & the News (Chrysalis)
42	48	BACK IN THE HIGH LIFE	Steve Winwood (Island)
43	49	GOD'S OWN MEDICINE	Mission (Mercury)
-	50	COUNT THREE AND PRAY	Berlin (Mercury)

The most successful stage musical on record for many years proved to be Andrew Lloyd Webber's adaptation of a much-filmed chiller, *The Phantom Of The Opera*, starring Michael Crawford and Sarah Brightman. The original cast album was snapped up so readily that it reached Number 1 in its second chart week, while the show itself would still be playing to capacity West End audiences six years later.

March 1987

7 March 1987

last	this			
1	1	THE PHANTOM OF THE OPERA		
			Original Cast (Polydor)	
2	2	GRACELAND	Paul Simon (Warner Bros.)	
3	3	AUGUST	Eric Clapton (Duck)	
11	4	THE VERY BEST OF HOT CHOCOLATE		
		Chocolate (RAK)		
10	5	PICTURE BOOK	Simply Red (Elektra)	
4	6	SILK AND STEEL	Five Star (Tent/RCA)	
8	7	GIVE ME THE REASON	Luther Vandross (Epic)	
22	8	THE FINAL COUNTDOWN	Europe (Epic)	
21	9	LIVE MAGIC	Queen (EMI)	
5	10	SO	Peter Gabriel (Virgin)	
-	11	THE WORLD WON'T LISTEN		
			Smiths (Rough Trade)	
6	12	DIFFERENT LIGHT	Bangles (CBS)	
13	13	REVENGE	Eurythmics (RCA)	
12	14	RAPTURE	Anita Baker (Elektra)	
20	15	TRUE BLUE	Madonna (Sire)	
7	16	THE WHOLE STORY	Kate Bush (EMI)	
16	17	BROTHERS IN ARMS	Dire Straits (Vertigo)	
13	18	SLIPPERY WHEN WET	Bon Jovi (Vertigo)	
24	19	LICENCED TO ILL	Beastie Boys (Def Jam)	
9	20	THE COST OF LOVING	Style Council (Polydor)	
27	21	DISCO	Pet Shop Boys (Parlophone)	
26	22	WHITNEY HOUSTON	Whitney Houston (Arista)	
29	23	BACK AGAIN IN THE DHSS		
			Half Man Half Biscuit (Probe Plus)	
17	24	ABSTRACT EMOTIONS		
			Randy Crawford (Warner Bros.)	
32	25	COMMUNARDS	Communards (London)	
34	26	GEORGIA SATELLITES	Georgia Satellites (Elektra)	
-	27	HAPPY	Surface (CBS)	
37	28	NOW THAT'S WHAT I CALL MUSIC 8		
			Various Artists (EMI/Virgin/PolyGram)	
15	29	SWEET FREEDOM		
			Michael McDonald (Warner Bros.)	
-	30	SHABINI	Bhundu Boys (Discafrique)	
14	31	ZAZU	Rosie Vela (A&M)	
39	32	JUST LIKE THE FIRST TIME		
			Freddie Jackson (Capitol)	
-	33	THE TEXAS CAMPFIRE TAPES		
			Michelle Shocked (Cooking Vinyl)	
28	34	THE VERY BEST OF ELKIE BROOKS		
			Elkie Brooks (Telstar)	
41	35	NO MORE THE FOOL	Elkie Brooks (Legend)	
35	36	CHASIN' A DREAM	Tashan (Def Jam)	
38	37	BY THE LIGHT OF THE MOON		
			Los Lobos (London)	
19	38	MIDNIGHT TO MIDNIGHT	Psychedelic Furs (CBS)	
-	39	MECHANICAL RESONANCE	Tesla (Geffen)	
-	40	A CHANGE OF HEART	David Sanborn (Warner Bros.)	
-	41	THROUGH THE BARRICADES		
			Spandau Ballet (Reformation)	
-	42	VIVA	Xmal Deutschland (X-ile)	
-	43	FLASH LIGHT	Tom Verlaine (Fontana)	
-	44	IMPRESSIONS	Various Artists (K-Tel)	
-	45	ULTIMATE TRAX VOL 2	Various Artists (Champion)	
46	46	EVERY BREATH YOU TAKE - THE SINGLES		
			Police (A&M)	
49	47	GOD'S OWN MEDICINE	Mission (Mercury)	
-	48	ROCK THE HOUSE		
			DJ Jazzy & Fresh Prince (Champion)	
-	49	NAJEE'S THEME	Najee (EMI America)	
-	50	THE HOUSE OF BLUE LIGHT	Deep Purple (Polydor)	

14 March 1987

last	this		
1	1	THE PHANTOM OF THE OPERA	
			Original Cast (Polydor)
2	2	GRACELAND	Paul Simon (Warner Bros.)
11	3	THE WORLD WON'T LISTEN	
			Smiths (Rough Trade)
3	4	AUGUST	Eric Clapton (Duck)
5	5	PICTURE BOOK	Simply Red (Elektra)
4	6	THE VERY BEST OF HOT CHOCOLATE	
			Hot Chocolate (RAK)
6	7	SILK AND STEEL	Five Star (Tent/RCA)
8	8	THE FINAL COUNTDOWN	Europe (Epic)
9	9	LIVE MAGIC	Queen (EMI)
7	10	GIVE ME THE REASON	Luther Vandross (Epic)
10	11	SO	Peter Gabriel (Virgin)
18	12	SLIPPERY WHEN WET	Bon Jovi (Vertigo)
-	13	SAINT JULIAN	Julian Cope (Island)
12	14	DIFFERENT LIGHT	Bangles (CBS)
13	15	REVENGE	Eurythmics (RCA)
-	16	WILD FRONTIER	Gary Moore (10)
25	17	COMMUNARDS	Communards (London)
16	18	THE WHOLE STORY	Kate Bush (EMI)
15	19	TRUE BLUE	Madonna (Sire)
19	20	LICENCED TO ILL	Beastie Boys (Def Jam)
17	21	BROTHERS IN ARMS	Dire Straits (Vertigo)
-	22	THROUGH THE LOOKING GLASS	
			Siouxsie and the Banshees (Wonderland)
14	23	RAPTURE	Anita Baker (Elektra)
-	24	SCOUNDREL DAYS	A-Ha (Warner Bros.)
24	25	ABSTRACT EMOTIONS	
			Randy Crawford (Warner Bros.)
29	26	SWEET FREEDOM	
			Michael McDonald (Warner Bros.)
-	27	PLEASE PLEASE ME	Beatles (Parlophone)
47	28	GOD'S OWN MEDICINE	Mission (Mercury)
-	29	FIGHTING THE WORLD	Manowar (Atco)
-	30	STAND BY ME	Ben E King (Atlantic)
44	31	IMPRESSIONS	Various Artists (K-Tel)
21	32	DISCO	Pet Shop Boys (Parlophone)
22	33	WHITNEY HOUSTON	Whitney Houston (Arista)
34	34	THE VERY BEST OF ELKIE BROOKS	
			Elkie Brooks (Telstar)
32	35	JUST LIKE THE FIRST TIME	
			Freddie Jackson (Capitol)
-	36	WITH THE BEATLES	Beatles (Parlophone)
26	37	GEORGIA SATELLITES	
			Georgia Satellites (Elektra)
-	38	WAREHOUSE: SONGS AND STORIES	Husker Du
		(Warner Bros.)	
20	39	THE COST OF LOVING	Style Council (Polydor)
38	40	MIDNIGHT TO MIDNIGHT	Psychedelic Furs (CBS)
35	41	NO MORE THE FOOL	Elkie Brooks (Legend)
-	42	A HARD DAY'S NIGHT	Beatles (Parlophone)
-	43	BEATLES FOR SALE	Beatles (Parlophone)
-	44	BACK IN THE HIGH LIFE	Steve Winwood (Island)
23	45	BACK AGAIN IN THE DHSS	
			Half Man Half Biscuit (Probe Plus)
42	46	VIVA	Xmal Deutschland (X-ile)
43	47	FLASH LIGHT	Tom Verlaine (Fontana)
-	48	WHEN A MAN LOVES A WOMAN	
			Percy Sledge (Atlantic)
28	49	NOW THAT'S WHAT I CALL MUSIC 8	
			Various Artists (EMI/Virgin/PolyGram)
41	50	THROUGH THE BARRICADES	
			Spandau Ballet (Reformation)

21 March 1987

last	this		
-	1	THE JOSHUA TREE	U2 (Island)
1	2	THE PHANTOM OF THE OPERA	
			Original Cast (Polydor)
3	3	THE WORLD WON'T LISTEN	
			Smiths (Rough Trade)
2	4	GRACELAND	Paul Simon (Warner Bros.)
4	5	AUGUST	Eric Clapton (Duck)
6	6	THE VERY BEST OF HOT CHOCOLATE	
			Hot Chocolate (RAK)
13	7	SAINT JULIAN	Julian Cope (Island)
16	8	WILD FRONTIER	Gary Moore (10)
22	9	THROUGH THE LOOKING GLASS	
			Siouxsie and the Banshees (Wonderland)
8	10	THE FINAL COUNTDOWN	Europe (Epic)
21	11	BROTHERS IN ARMS	Dire Straits (Vertigo)
10	12	GIVE ME THE REASON	Luther Vandross (Epic)
7	13	SILK AND STEEL	Five Star (Tent/RCA)
30	14	STAND BY ME	Ben E King (Atlantic)
20	15	LICENCED TO ILL	Beastie Boys (Def Jam)
9	16	LIVE MAGIC	Queen (EMI)
15	17	REVENGE	Eurythmics (RCA)
18	18	THE WHOLE STORY	Kate Bush (EMI)
5	19	PICTURE BOOK	Simply Red (Elektra)
12	20	SLIPPERY WHEN WET	Bon Jovi (Vertigo)
14	21	DIFFERENT LIGHT	Bangles (CBS)
11	22	SO	Peter Gabriel (Virgin)
19	23	TRUE BLUE	Madonna (Sire)
-	24	MOVE CLOSER	Various Artists (CBS)
17	25	COMMUNARDS	Communards (London)
48	26	WHEN A MAN LOVES A WOMAN	
			Percy Sledge (Atlantic)
31	27	IMPRESSIONS	Various Artists (K-Tel)
24	28	SCOUNDREL DAYS	A-Ha (Warner Bros.)
28	29	GOD'S OWN MEDICINE	Mission (Mercury)
-	30	IF YOU WANT TO DEFEAT YOUR ENEMY, SING	
		HIS SONG	Icicle Works (Beggars Banquet)
-	31	MEN AND WOMEN	Simply Red (WEA)
26	32	SWEET FREEDOM	
			Michael McDonald (Warner Bros.)
23	33	RAPTURE	Anita Baker (Elektra)
34	34	THE VERY BEST OF ELKIE BROOKS	
			Elkie Brooks (Telstar)
42	35	A HARD DAY'S NIGHT	Beatles (Parlophone)
-	36	RUNNING IN THE FAMILY	Level 42 (Polydor)
-	37	ALED	Aled Jones (10)
-	38	SHEILA E	Sheila E (Paisley Park)
-	39	NAJEE'S THEME	Najee (EMI America)
-	40	A CHANGE OF HEART	
			David Sanborn (Warner Bros.)
45	41	BACK AGAIN IN THE DHSS	
			Half Man Half Biscuit (Probe Plus)
-	42	SURFACE	Surface (CBS)
27	43	PLEASE PLEASE ME	Beatles (Parlophone)
44	44	BACK IN THE HIGH LIFE	
			Steve Winwood (Island)
-	45	DANCING ON THE CEILING	
			Lionel Richie (Motown)
32	46	DISCO	Pet Shop Boys (Parlophone)
35	47	JUST LIKE THE FIRST TIME	
			Freddie Jackson (Capitol)
33	48	WHITNEY HOUSTON	Whitney Houston (Arista)
39	49	THE COST OF LOVING	Style Council (Polydor)
49	50	NOW THAT'S WHAT I CALL MUSIC 8	
			Various Artists (EMI/Virgin/PolyGram)

The Beatles' first four albums (*Please Please Me, With The Beatles, A Hard Day's Night* and *Beatles For Sale*) were issued for the first time on CD in March, and such was the interest created that all four jumped back into the chart simultaneously, entirely on their digital format sales - many of these undoubtedly to people who had first bought the same releases on vinyl 23 and 24 years previously!

28 March 1987

last week	this week	Title	Artist (Label)
1	1	THE JOSHUA TREE	U2 (Island)
31	2	MEN AND WOMEN	Simply Red (WEA)
3	3	THE WORLD WON'T LISTEN	Smiths (Rough Trade)
4	4	GRACELAND	Paul Simon (Warner Bros.)
6	5	THE VERY BEST OF HOT CHOCOLATE	Hot Chocolate (RAK)
36	6	RUNNING IN THE FAMILY	Level 42 (Polydor)
19	7	PICTURE BOOK	Simply Red (Elektra)
2	8	THE PHANTOM OF THE OPERA	Original Cast (Polydor)
8	9	WILD FRONTIER	Gary Moore (10)
24	10	MOVE CLOSER	Various Artists (CBS)
13	11	SILK AND STEEL	Five Star (Tent/RCA)
5	12	AUGUST	Eric Clapton (Duck)
14	13	STAND BY ME	Ben E King (Atlantic)
30	14	IF YOU WANT TO DEFEAT YOUR ENEMY, SING HIS SONG	Icicle Works (Beggars Banquet)
10	15	THE FINAL COUNTDOWN	Europe (Epic)
15	16	LICENCED TO ILL	Beastie Boys (Def Jam)
16	17	LIVE MAGIC	Queen (EMI)
12	18	GIVE ME THE REASON	Luther Vandross (Epic)
25	19	COMMUNARDS	Communards (London)
7	20	SAINT JULIAN	Julian Cope (Island)
9	21	THROUGH THE LOOKING GLASS	Siouxsie and the Banshees (Wonderland)
21	22	DIFFERENT LIGHT	Bangles (CBS)
27	23	IMPRESSIONS	Various Artists (K-Tel)
22	24	SO	Peter Gabriel (Virgin)
11	25	BROTHERS IN ARMS	Dire Straits (Vertigo)
23	26	TRUE BLUE	Madonna (Sire)
26	27	WHEN A MAN LOVES A WOMAN	Percy Sledge (Atlantic)
38	28	SHEILA E	Sheila E (Paisley Park)
-	29	CONTROL	Janet Jackson (A&M)
-	30	UPFRONT 5	Various Artists (Serious)
47	31	JUST LIKE THE FIRST TIME	Freddie Jackson (Capitol)
-	32	LICENSED TO KILL	Malice (Atlantic)
-	33	STRONG PERSUADER	Robert Cray Band (Mercury)
18	34	THE WHOLE STORY	Kate Bush (EMI)
-	35	THE FINER THINGS IN LIFE	Chuck Stanley (Def Jam)
20	36	SLIPPERY WHEN WET	Bon Jovi (Vertigo)
-	37	GET CLOSE	Pretenders (WEA)
-	38	ULTIMATE TRAX VOL 2	Various Artists (Champion)
-	39	LOVE ME RIGHT	Millie Scott (Fourth & Broadway)
-	40	TRIO	Parton/Ronstadt/Harris (Warner Bros.)
-	41	RHYTHM OF THE NIGHT	Various Artists (K-Tel)
-	42	INVISIBLE TOUCH	Genesis (Charisma)
-	43	THE DANCE CHART	Various Artists (Telstar)
40	44	A CHANGE OF HEART	David Sanborn (Warner Bros.)
-	45	CLASSIC SONGS	James Taylor (CBS/WEA)
-	46	PRIVATE REVOLUTION	World Party (Chrysalis)
28	47	SCOUNDREL DAYS	A-Ha (Warner Bros.)
45	48	DANCING ON THE CEILING	Lionel Richie (Motown)
49	49	THE COST OF LOVING	Style Council (Polydor)
33	50	RAPTURE	Anita Baker (Elektra)

4 April 1987

last week	this week	Title	Artist (Label)
1	1	THE JOSHUA TREE	U2 (Island)
2	2	MEN AND WOMEN	Simply Red (WEA)
6	3	RUNNING IN THE FAMILY	Level 42 (Polydor)
4	4	GRACELAND	Paul Simon (Warner Bros.)
8	5	THE PHANTOM OF THE OPERA	Original Cast (Polydor)
5	6	THE VERY BEST OF HOT CHOCOLATE	Hot Chocolate (RAK)
-	7	NOW THAT'S WHAT I CALL MUSIC 9	Various Artists (EMI/Virgin/PolyGram)
12	8	AUGUST	Eric Clapton (Duck)
11	9	SILK AND STEEL	Five Star (Tent/RCA)
42	10	INVISIBLE TOUCH	Genesis (Charisma)
9	11	WILD FRONTIER	Gary Moore (10)
10	12	MOVE CLOSER	Various Artists (CBS)
24	13	SO	Peter Gabriel (Virgin)
16	14	LICENCED TO ILL	Beastie Boys (Def Jam)
3	15	THE WORLD WON'T LISTEN	Smiths (Rough Trade)
18	16	GIVE ME THE REASON	Luther Vandross (Epic)
7	17	PICTURE BOOK	Simply Red (Elektra)
17	18	LIVE MAGIC	Queen (EMI)
23	19	IMPRESSIONS	Various Artists (K-Tel)
29	20	CONTROL	Janet Jackson (A&M)
26	21	TRUE BLUE	Madonna (Sire)
19	22	COMMUNARDS	Communards (London)
13	23	STAND BY ME	Ben E King (Atlantic)
14	24	IF YOU WANT TO DEFEAT YOUR ENEMY, SING HIS SONG	Icicle Works (Beggars Banquet)
-	25	REVENGE	Eurythmics (RCA)
15	26	THE FINAL COUNTDOWN	Europe (Epic)
48	27	DANCING ON THE CEILING	Lionel Richie (Motown)
21	28	THROUGH THE LOOKING GLASS	Siouxsie and the Banshees (Wonderland)
20	29	SAINT JULIAN	Julian Cope (Island)
30	30	UPFRONT 5	Various Artists (Serious)
25	31	BROTHERS IN ARMS	Dire Straits (Vertigo)
22	32	DIFFERENT LIGHT	Bangles (CBS)
46	33	PRIVATE REVOLUTION	World Party (Chrysalis)
32	34	LICENSED TO KILL	Malice (Atlantic)
35	35	THE FINER THINGS IN LIFE	Chuck Stanley (Def Jam)
43	36	THE DANCE CHART	Various Artists (Telstar)
50	37	RAPTURE	Anita Baker (Elektra)
36	38	SLIPPERY WHEN WET	Bon Jovi (Vertigo)
34	39	THE WHOLE STORY	Kate Bush (EMI)
47	40	SCOUNDREL DAYS	A-Ha (Warner Bros.)
27	41	WHEN A MAN LOVES A WOMAN	Percy Sledge (Atlantic)
37	42	GET CLOSE	Pretenders (WEA)
39	43	LOVE ME RIGHT	Millie Scott (4th & Broadway)
-	44	THE KILLER INSIDE ME	Green On Red (Mercury)
-	45	GOD'S OWN MEDICINE	Mission (Mercury)
45	46	CLASSIC SONGS	James Taylor (CBS/WEA)
-	47	A HARD DAY'S NIGHT	Beatles (Parlophone)
-	48	OPUS DEI	Laibach (Mute)
-	49	DISCO	Pet Shop Boys (Parlophone)
-	50	SWEET FREEDOM	Michael McDonald (Warner Bros.)

11 April 1987

last week	this week	Title	Artist (Label)
1	1	THE JOSHUA TREE	U2 (Island)
3	2	RUNNING IN THE FAMILY	Level 42 (Polydor)
2	3	MEN AND WOMEN	Simply Red (WEA)
7	4	NOW THAT'S WHAT I CALL MUSIC 9	Various Artists (EMI/Virgin/PolyGram)
4	5	GRACELAND	Paul Simon (Warner Bros.)
5	6	THE PHANTOM OF THE OPERA	Original Cast (Polydor)
13	7	SO	Peter Gabriel (Virgin)
12	8	MOVE CLOSER	Various Artists (CBS)
6	9	THE VERY BEST OF HOT CHOCOLATE	Hot Chocolate (RAK)
-	10	SIGN 'O' THE TIMES	Prince (Paisley Park)
8	11	AUGUST	Eric Clapton (Duck)
-	12	WHITESNAKE 1987	Whitesnake (EMI)
20	13	CONTROL	Janet Jackson (A&M)
14	14	LICENCED TO ILL	Beastie Boys (Def Jam)
-	15	THE CIRCUS	Erasure (Mute)
17	16	PICTURE BOOK	Simply Red (Elektra)
15	17	THE WORLD WON'T LISTEN	Smiths (Rough Trade)
-	18	INTO THE FIRE	Bryan Adams (A&M)
18	19	LIVE MAGIC	Queen (EMI)
10	20	INVISIBLE TOUCH	Genesis (Charisma)
21	21	TRUE BLUE	Madonna (Sire)
11	22	WILD FRONTIER	Gary Moore (10)
9	23	SILK AND STEEL	Five Star (Tent/RCA)
19	24	IMPRESSIONS	Various Artists (K-Tel)
16	25	GIVE ME THE REASON	Luther Vandross (Epic)
31	26	BROTHERS IN ARMS	Dire Straits (Vertigo)
36	27	THE DANCE CHART	Various Artists (Telstar)
22	28	COMMUNARDS	Communards (London)
30	29	UPFRONT 5	Various Artists (Serious)
23	30	STAND BY ME	Ben E King (Atlantic)
26	31	THE FINAL COUNTDOWN	Europe (Epic)
27	32	DANCING ON THE CEILING	Lionel Richie (Motown)
25	33	REVENGE	Eurythmics (RCA)
28	34	THROUGH THE LOOKING GLASS	Siouxsie and the Banshees (Wonderland)
-	35	FIGHTIN' THE WORLD	ManOWar (Atlantic)
-	36	THE PAVAROTTI COLLECTION	Luciano Pavarotti (Stylus)
24	37	IF YOU WANT TO DEFEAT YOUR ENEMY, SING HIS SONG	Icicle Works (Beggars Banquet)
29	38	SAINT JULIAN	Julian Cope (Island)
-	39	REUNION WILDERNESS	Railway Children (Factory)
43	40	LOVE ME RIGHT	Millie Scott (4th & Broadway)
32	41	DIFFERENT LIGHT	Bangles (CBS)
-	42	L IS FOR LOVER	Al Jarreau (WEA)
33	43	PRIVATE REVOLUTION	World Party (Chrysalis)
-	44	SIGNS OF LIFE	Penguin Cafe Orchestra (Editons EG)
39	45	THE WHOLE STORY	Kate Bush (EMI)
-	46	U2 LIVE: UNDER A BLOOD RED SKY	U2 (Island)
37	47	RAPTURE	Anita Baker (Elektra)
38	48	SLIPPERY WHEN WET	Bon Jovi (Vertigo)
49	49	DISCO	Pet Shop Boys (Parlophone)
-	50	ALF	Alison Moyet (CBS)

U2 had allowed a gap of almost two-and-a-half years between their previous album *The Unforgettable Fire* and the new set *The Joshua Tree* - a hiatus which made it all the more eagerly awaited, particularly as their status as international performers had climbed to superstar level in the interim. This album was their first to debut at Number 1(where it stayed for six weeks), and became the 10th-best seller of the 1980s.

April – May 1987

18 April 1987

last week	this week	TITLE	Artist (Label)
1	1	THE JOSHUA TREE	U2 (Island)
4	2	NOW THAT'S WHAT I CALL MUSIC 9	Various Artists (EMI/Virgin/PolyGram)
2	3	RUNNING IN THE FAMILY	Level 42 (Polydor)
3	4	MEN AND WOMEN	Simply Red (WEA)
10	5	SIGN 'O' THE TIMES	Prince (Paisley Park)
18	6	INTO THE FIRE	Bryan Adams (A&M)
12	7	WHITESNAKE 1987	Whitesnake (EMI)
-	8	RAINDANCING	Alison Moyet (CBS)
15	9	THE CIRCUS	Erasure (Mute)
5	10	GRACELAND	Paul Simon (Warner Bros.)
-	11	ELECTRIC	Cult (Beggars Banquet)
6	12	THE PHANTOM OF THE OPERA	Original Cast (Polydor)
13	13	CONTROL	Janet Jackson (A&M)
7	14	SO	Peter Gabriel (Virgin)
8	15	MOVE CLOSER	Various Artists (CBS)
11	16	AUGUST	Eric Clapton (Duck)
9	17	THE VERY BEST OF HOT CHOCOLATE	Hot Chocolate (RAK)
14	18	LICENCED TO ILL	Beastie Boys (Def Jam)
-	19	AMONG THE LIVING	Anthrax (Island)
-	20	THIS TIME	Culture Club (Virgin)
16	21	PICTURE BOOK	Simply Red (Elektra)
21	22	TRUE BLUE	Madonna (Sire)
23	23	SILK AND STEEL	Five Star (Tent/RCA)
25	24	GIVE ME THE REASON	Luther Vandross (Epic)
17	25	THE WORLD WON'T LISTEN	Smiths (Rough Trade)
27	26	THE DANCE CHART	Various Artists (Telstar)
20	27	INVISIBLE TOUCH	Genesis (Charisma)
48	28	SLIPPERY WHEN WET	Bon Jovi (Vertigo)
22	29	WILD FRONTIER	Gary Moore (10)
19	30	LIVE MAGIC	Queen (EMI)
26	31	BROTHERS IN ARMS	Dire Straits (Vertigo)
24	32	IMPRESSIONS	Various Artists (K-Tel)
38	33	SAINT JULIAN	Julian Cope (Island)
-	34	CLASSIC SONGS	James Taylor (CBS/WEA)
28	35	COMMUNARDS	Communards (London)
45	36	THE WHOLE STORY	Kate Bush (EMI)
-	37	THE ENGELBERT HUMPERDINCK COLLECTION	Engelbert Humperdinck (Telstar)
29	38	UPFRONT 5	Various Artists (Serious)
34	39	THROUGH THE LOOKING GLASS	Siouxsie and the Banshees (Wonderland)
-	40	THE HOUSE SOUND OF CHICAGO 2	Various Artists (DJ International)
-	41	STRONG PERSUADER	Robert Cray Band (Mercury)
41	42	DIFFERENT LIGHT	Bangles (CBS)
42	43	L IS FOR LOVER	Al Jarreau (WEA)
39	44	REUNION WILDERNESS	Railway Children (Factory)
-	45	CRUSH ON YOU	Jets (MCA)
31	46	THE FINAL COUNTDOWN	Europe (Epic)
32	47	DANCING ON THE CEILING	Lionel Richie (Motown)
-	48	SHAKA ZULU	Ladysmith Black Mambazo (Warner Bros.)
33	49	REVENGE	Eurythmics (RCA)
36	50	THE PAVAROTTI COLLECTION	Luciano Pavarotti (Stylus)

25 April 1987

last week	this week	TITLE	Artist (Label)
1	1	THE JOSHUA TREE	U2 (Island)
5	2	SIGN 'O' THE TIMES	Prince (Paisley Park)
2	3	NOW THAT'S WHAT I CALL MUSIC 9	Various Artists (EMI/Virgin/PolyGram)
8	4	RAINDANCING	Alison Moyet (CBS)
3	5	RUNNING IN THE FAMILY	Level 42 (Polydor)
11	6	ELECTRIC	Cult (Beggars Banquet)
6	7	INTO THE FIRE	Bryan Adams (A&M)
7	8	WHITESNAKE 1987	Whitesnake (EMI)
4	9	MEN AND WOMEN	Simply Red (WEA)
9	10	THE CIRCUS	Erasure (Mute)
10	11	GRACELAND	Paul Simon (Warner Bros.)
19	12	AMONG THE LIVING	Anthrax (Island)
22	13	TRUE BLUE	Madonna (Sire)
13	14	CONTROL	Janet Jackson (A&M)
14	15	SO	Peter Gabriel (Virgin)
-	16	TANGO IN THE NIGHT	Fleetwood Mac (Warner Bros.)
15	17	MOVE CLOSER	Various Artists (CBS)
20	18	THIS TIME	Culture Club (Virgin)
17	19	THE VERY BEST OF HOT CHOCOLATE	Hot Chocolate (RAK)
-	20	FLM	Mel & Kim (Supreme)
16	21	AUGUST	Eric Clapton (Duck)
12	22	THE PHANTOM OF THE OPERA	Original Cast (Polydor)
18	23	LICENCED TO ILL	Beastie Boys (Def Jam)
23	24	SILK AND STEEL	Five Star (Tent/RCA)
21	25	PICTURE BOOK	Simply Red (Elektra)
30	26	LIVE MAGIC	Queen (EMI)
48	27	SHAKA ZULU	Ladysmith Black Mambazo (Warner Bros.)
27	28	INVISIBLE TOUCH	Genesis (Charisma)
46	29	THE FINAL COUNTDOWN	Europe (Epic)
-	30	THE RETURN OF BRUNO	Bruce Willis ((Motown)
31	31	BROTHERS IN ARMS	Dire Straits (Vertigo)
28	32	SLIPPERY WHEN WET	Bon Jovi (Vertigo)
47	33	DANCING ON THE CEILING	Lionel Richie (Motown)
37	34	THE ENGELBERT HUMPERDINCK COLLECTION	Engelbert Humperdinck (Telstar)
-	35	NICK KAMEN	Nick Kamen (WEA)
49	36	REVENGE	Eurythmics (RCA)
40	37	THE HOUSE SOUND OF CHICAGO 2	Various Artists (DJ International)
-	38	MOTHER FIST AND HER FIVE DAUGHTERS	Marc Almond (Some Bizzare)
-	39	UH! TEARS BABY	Win (London)
-	40	SHE WAS ONLY A GROCER'S DAUGHTER	Blow Monkeys (RCA)
-	41	HYPNO BEAT	Woodentops (Rough Trade)
39	42	THROUGH THE LOOKING GLASS	Siouxsie and the Banshees (Wonderland)
35	43	COMMUNARDS	Communards (London)
42	44	DIFFERENT LIGHT	Bangles (CBS)
24	45	GIVE ME THE REASON	Luther Vandross (Epic)
25	46	THE WORLD WON'T LISTEN	Smiths (Rough Trade)
41	47	STRONG PERSUADER	Robert Cray Band (Mercury)
-	48	HEART OVER MIND	Jennifer Rush (CBS)
26	49	THE DANCE CHART	Various Artists (Telstar)
36	50	THE WHOLE STORY	Kate Bush (EMI)

2 May 1987

last week	this week	TITLE	Artist (Label)
4	1	RAINDANCING	Alison Moyet (CBS)
3	2	NOW THAT'S WHAT I CALL MUSIC 9	Various Artists (EMI/Virgin/PolyGram)
1	3	THE JOSHUA TREE	U2 (Island)
6	4	ELECTRIC	Cult (Beggars Banquet)
16	5	TANGO IN THE NIGHT	Fleetwood Mac (Warner Bros.)
20	6	FLM	Mel & Kim (Supreme)
5	7	RUNNING IN THE FAMILY	Level 42 (Polydor)
2	8	SIGN 'O' THE TIMES	Prince (Paisley Park)
11	9	GRACELAND	Paul Simon (Warner Bros.)
9	10	MEN AND WOMEN	Simply Red (WEA)
18	11	THIS TIME	Culture Club (Virgin)
12	12	AMONG THE LIVING	Anthrax (Island)
-	13	NEVER LET ME DOWN	David Bowie (EMI America)
17	14	MOVE CLOSER	Various Artists (CBS)
28	15	INVISIBLE TOUCH	Genesis (Charisma)
8	16	WHITESNAKE 1987	Whitesnake (EMI)
10	17	THE CIRCUS	Erasure (Mute)
7	18	INTO THE FIRE	Bryan Adams (A&M)
13	19	TRUE BLUE	Madonna (Sire)
24	20	SILK AND STEEL	Five Star (Tent/RCA)
40	21	SHE WAS ONLY A GROCER'S DAUGHTER	Blow Monkeys (RCA)
15	22	SO	Peter Gabriel (Virgin)
14	23	CONTROL	Janet Jackson (A&M)
19	24	THE VERY BEST OF HOT CHOCOLATE	Hot Chocolate (RAK)
-	25	OUTLAND	Spear Of Destiny (10)
-	26	REIGN IN BLOOD	Slayer (Def Jam)
30	27	THE RETURN OF BRUNO	Bruce Willis ((Motown)
45	28	GIVE ME THE REASON	Luther Vandross (Epic)
32	29	SLIPPERY WHEN WET	Bon Jovi (Vertigo)
31	30	BROTHERS IN ARMS	Dire Straits (Vertigo)
46	31	THE WORLD WON'T LISTEN	Smiths (Rough Trade)
27	32	SHAKA ZULU	Ladysmith Black Mambazo (Warner Bros.)
23	33	LICENCED TO ILL	Beastie Boys (Def Jam)
37	34	THE HOUSE SOUND OF CHICAGO 2	Various Artists (London)
-	35	BIG LIFE	Nightranger (MCA)
-	36	CLOSE TO THE BONE	Thompson Twins (Arista)
22	37	THE PHANTOM OF THE OPERA	Original Cast (Polydor)
-	38	FORE!	Huey Lewis & the News (Chrysalis)
21	39	AUGUST	Eric Clapton (Duck)
26	40	LIVE MAGIC	Queen (EMI)
25	41	PICTURE BOOK	Simply Red (Elektra)
35	42	NICK KAMEN	Nick Kamen (WEA)
-	43	HAPPY HOUR	Ted Hawkins (Windows on the World)
29	44	THE FINAL COUNTDOWN	Europe (Epic)
50	45	THE WHOLE STORY	Kate Bush (EMI)
49	46	THE DANCE CHART	Various Artists (Telstar)
34	47	THE ENGELBERT HUMPERDINCK COLLECTION	Engelbert Humperdinck (Telstar)
36	48	REVENGE	Eurythmics (RCA)
-	49	BY REQUEST	James Last (Polydor)
-	50	SWEET FREEDOM	Michael McDonald (Warner Bros.)

Continuing massive sales for U2's *The Joshua Tree* kept the ninth volume of *Now Music* at Number 2 on the chart, while U2 were eventually deposed by Alison Moyet's *Raindancing* - a release which hoisted her into the tiny club of female atists to have had Number 1 sellers with consecutive albums. Actor Bruce Willis from TV's *Moonlighting*, meanwhile, charted his *Return Of Bruno* album - on Motown!

9 May 1987

last week	this week		
3	1	THE JOSHUA TREE	U2 (Island)
5	2	TANGO IN THE NIGHT	Fleetwood Mac (Warner Bros.)
6	3	FLM	Mel & Kim (Supreme)
1	4	RAINDANCING	Alison Moyet (CBS)
13	5	NEVER LET ME DOWN	David Bow America
7	6	RUNNING IN THE FAMILY	Level 42 (Polydor)
2	7	NOW THAT'S WHAT I CALL MUSIC 9	Various Artists (EMI/Virgin/PolyGram)
15	8	INVISIBLE TOUCH	Genesis (Charisma)
8	9	SIGN 'O' THE TIMES	Prince (Paisley Park)
10	10	MEN AND WOMEN	Simply Red (WEA)
4	11	ELECTRIC	Cult (Beggars Banquet)
-	12	KEEP YOUR DISTANCE	Curiosity Killed The Cat (Mercury)
11	13	THIS TIME	Culture Club (Virgin)
25	14	OUTLAND	Spear Of Destiny (10)
9	15	GRACELAND	Paul Simon (Warner Bros.)
17	16	THE CIRCUS	Erasure (Mute)
-	17	SOLITUDE STANDING	Suzanne Vega (A&M)
19	18	TRUE BLUE	Madonna (Sire)
21	19	SHE WAS ONLY A GROCER'S DAUGHTER	Blow Monkeys (RCA)
16	20	WHITESNAKE 1987	Whitesnake (EMI)
12	21	AMONG THE LIVING	Anthrax (Island)
20	22	SILK AND STEEL	Five Star (Tent/RCA)
23	23	CONTROL	Janet Jackson (A&M)
29	24	SLIPPERY WHEN WET	Bon Jovi (Vertigo)
22	25	SO	Peter Gabriel (Virgin)
26	26	REIGN IN BLOOD	Slayer (Def Jam)
14	27	MOVE CLOSER	Various Artists (CBS)
37	28	THE PHANTOM OF THE OPERA	Original Cast (Polydor)
18	29	INTO THE FIRE	Bryan Adams (A&M)
32	30	SHAKA ZULU	Ladysmith Black Mambazo (Warner Bros.)
-	31	LILLO	Lillo Thomas (Capitol)
28	32	GIVE ME THE REASON	Luther Vandross (Epic)
31	33	THE WORLD WON'T LISTEN	Smiths (Rough Trade)
27	34	THE RETURN OF BRUNO	Bruce Willis ((Motown)
-	35	LET ME UP (I'VE HAD ENOUGH)	Tom Pretty & the Heartbreakers (MCA)
36	36	CLOSE TO THE BONE	Thompson Twins (Arista)
24	37	THE VERY BEST OF HOT CHOCOLATE	Hot Chocolate (RAK)
-	38	BOYS' NIGHT OUT	First Circle (EMI America)
50	39	SWEET FREEDOM	Michael McDonald (Warner Bros.)
33	40	LICENCED TO ILL	Beastie Boys (Def Jam)
30	41	BROTHERS IN ARMS	Dire Straits (Vertigo)
44	42	THE FINAL COUNTDOWN	Europe (Epic)
41	43	PICTURE BOOK	Simply Red (Elektra)
38	44	FORE!	Huey Lewis & the News (Chrysalis)
39	45	AUGUST	Eric Clapton (Duck)
40	46	LIVE MAGIC	Queen (EMI)
45	47	THE WHOLE STORY	Kate Bush (EMI)
-	48	BREAK EVERY RULE	Tina Turner (Capitol)
-	49	DANCING ON THE CEILING	Lionel Richie (Motown)
43	50	HAPPY HOUR	Ted Hawkins (Windows on the World)

16 May 1987

last week	this week		
12	1	KEEP YOUR DISTANCE	Curiosity Killed The Cat (Mercury)
2	2	TANGO IN THE NIGHT	Fleetwood Mac (Warner Bros.)
17	3	SOLITUDE STANDING	Suzanne Vega (A&M)
1	4	THE JOSHUA TREE	U2 (Island)
4	5	RAINDANCING	Alison Moyet (CBS)
5	6	NEVER LET ME DOWN	David Bow America
8	7	INVISIBLE TOUCH	Genesis (Charisma)
3	8	FLM	Mel & Kim (Supreme)
7	9	NOW THAT'S WHAT I CALL MUSIC 9	Various Artists (EMI/Virgin/PolyGram)
6	10	RUNNING IN THE FAMILY	Level 42 (Polydor)
14	11	OUTLAND	Spear Of Destiny (10)
15	12	GRACELAND	Paul Simon (Warner Bros.)
11	13	ELECTRIC	Cult (Beggars Banquet)
9	14	SIGN 'O' THE TIMES	Prince (Paisley Park)
18	15	TRUE BLUE	Madonna (Sire)
10	16	MEN AND WOMEN	Simply Red (WEA)
-	17	LIVING IN A BOX	Living in a Box (Chrysalis)
22	18	SILK AND STEEL	Five Star (Tent/RCA)
20	19	WHITESNAKE 1987	Whitesnake (EMI)
23	20	CONTROL	Janet Jackson (A&M)
26	21	REIGN IN BLOOD	Slayer (Def Jam)
13	22	THIS TIME	Culture Club (Virgin)
25	23	SO	Peter Gabriel (Virgin)
29	24	INTO THE FIRE	Bryan Adams (A&M)
19	25	SHE WAS ONLY A GROCER'S DAUGHTER	Blow Monkeys (RCA)
16	26	THE CIRCUS	Erasure (Mute)
-	27	HILLBILLY DELUXE	Dwight Yoakam (Reprise)
21	28	AMONG THE LIVING	Anthrax (Island)
-	29	RHYTHM KILLERS	Sly & Robbie (Fourth & Broadway)
31	30	LILLO	Lillo Thomas (Capitol)
27	31	MOVE CLOSER	Various Artists (CBS)
-	32	COMING ROUND AGAIN	Carly Simon (Arista)
35	33	LET ME UP (I'VE HAD ENOUGH)	Tom Pretty & the Heartbreakers (MCA)
30	34	SHAKA ZULU	Ladysmith Black Mambazo (Warner Bros.)
-	35	JOIN THE ARMY	Suicidal Tendencies (Virgin)
24	36	SLIPPERY WHEN WET	Bon Jovi (Vertigo)
32	37	GIVE ME THE REASON	Luther Vandross (Epic)
28	38	THE PHANTOM OF THE OPERA	Original Cast (Polydor)
39	39	SWEET FREEDOM	Michael McDonald (Warner Bros.)
37	40	THE VERY BEST OF HOT CHOCOLATE	Hot Chocolate (RAK)
38	41	BOYS' NIGHT OUT	First Circle (EMI America)
40	42	LICENCED TO ILL	Beastie Boys (Def Jam)
-	43	THE FINER THINGS IN LIFE	Chuck Stanley (Def Jam)
-	44	MAYFLOWER	Weather Prophets (Elevation)
-	45	THIS IS THE STORY	Proclaimers (Chrysalis)
-	46	CAN'T BE WITH YOU TONIGHT	Judy Boucher (Orbitone)
-	47	S. O. D. – THE EPIC YEARS	Spear Of Destiny (Epic)
33	48	THE WORLD WON'T LISTEN	Smiths (Rough Trade)
41	49	BROTHERS IN ARMS	Dire Straits (Vertigo)
42	50	THE FINAL COUNTDOWN	Europe (Epic)

23 May 1987

last week	this week		
3	1	SOLITUDE STANDING	Suzanne Vega (A&M)
1	2	KEEP YOUR DISTANCE	Curiosity Killed The Cat (Mercury)
2	3	TANGO IN THE NIGHT	Fleetwood Mac (Warner Bros.)
4	4	THE JOSHUA TREE	U2 (Island)
7	5	INVISIBLE TOUCH	Genesis (Charisma)
5	6	RAINDANCING	Alison Moyet (CBS)
10	7	RUNNING IN THE FAMILY	Level 42 (Polydor)
8	8	FLM	Mel & Kim (Supreme)
13	9	ELECTRIC	Cult (Beggars Banquet)
-	10	IT'S BETTER TO TRAVEL	Swing Out Sister (Mercury)
-	11	TRIBUTE	Ozzy Osbourne (Epic)
23	12	SO	Peter Gabriel (Virgin)
11	13	OUTLAND	Spear Of Destiny (10)
6	14	NEVER LET ME DOWN	David Bowie (EMI America)
9	15	NOW THAT'S WHAT I CALL MUSIC 9	Various Artists (EMI/Virgin/PolyGram)
15	16	TRUE BLUE	Madonna (Sire)
12	17	GRACELAND	Paul Simon (Warner Bros.)
16	18	MEN AND WOMEN	Simply Red (WEA)
18	19	SILK AND STEEL	Five Star (Tent/RCA)
26	20	THE CIRCUS	Erasure (Mute)
17	21	LIVING IN A BOX	Living in a Box (Chrysalis)
20	22	CONTROL	Janet Jackson (A&M)
22	23	THIS TIME	Culture Club (Virgin)
14	24	SIGN 'O' THE TIMES	Prince (Paisley Park)
32	25	COMING ROUND AGAIN	Carly Simon (Arista)
35	26	JOIN THE ARMY	Suicidal Tendencies (Virgin)
-	27	UPFRONT 6	Various Artists (Upfront)
29	28	RHYTHM KILLERS	Sly & Robbie (Fourth & Broadway)
25	29	SHE WAS ONLY A GROCER'S DAUGHTER	Blow Monkeys (RCA)
38	30	THE PHANTOM OF THE OPERA	Original Cast (Polydor)
19	31	WHITESNAKE 1987	Whitesnake (EMI)
-	32	TOM JONES' GREATEST HITS	Tom Jones (Telstar)
42	33	LICENCED TO ILL	Beastie Boys (Def Jam)
28	34	AMONG THE LIVING	Anthrax (Island)
27	35	HILLBILLY DELUXE	Dwight Yoakam (Reprise)
21	36	REIGN IN BLOOD	Slayer (Def Jam)
-	37	BY REQUEST	James Last (Polydor)
31	38	MOVE CLOSER	Various Artists (CBS)
36	39	SLIPPERY WHEN WET	Bon Jovi (Vertigo)
50	40	THE FINAL COUNTDOWN	Europe (Epic)
37	41	GIVE ME THE REASON	Luther Vandross (Epic)
30	42	LILLO	Lillo Thomas (Capitol)
24	43	INTO THE FIRE	Bryan Adams (A&M)
33	44	LET ME UP (I'VE HAD ENOUGH)	Tom Pretty & the Heartbreakers (MCA)
-	45	REVOLVER	Beatles (Parlophone)
-	46	PUBLIC ENEMY	Public Enemy (Def Jam)
-	47	WALLS OF JERICHO	Helloween (Noise International)
39	48	SWEET FREEDOM	Michael McDonald (Warner Bros.)
40	49	THE VERY BEST OF HOT CHOCOLATE	Hot Chocolate (RAK)
-	50	DEAD LETTER OFFICE	REM (IRS)

Though it was not, incredibly, to reach Number 1 until November, Fleetwood Mac's *Tango In The Night* was the most consistently high-selling album of May 1987, sitting doggedly at Number 2 in the chart while short-lived Number 1s rose and fell in brief shows of glory around it. Eventually the seventh biggest-selling album of the 1980s, it sales would rival that of Mac's yardstick *Rumours* from 1977.

30 May 1987

last week	this week	title	artist (label)
10	1	IT'S BETTER TO TRAVEL	Swing Out Sister (Mercury)
1	2	SOLITUDE STANDING	Suzanne Vega (A&M)
2	3	KEEP YOUR DISTANCE	Curiosity Killed The Cat (Mercury)
3	4	TANGO IN THE NIGHT	Fleetwood Mac (Warner Bros.)
7	5	RUNNING IN THE FAMILY	Level 42 (Polydor)
4	6	THE JOSHUA TREE	U2 (Island)
12	7	SO	Peter Gabriel (Virgin)
6	8	RAINDANCING	Alison Moyet (CBS)
8	9	FLM	Mel & Kim (Supreme)
11	10	TRIBUTE	Ozzy Osbourne (Epic)
9	11	ELECTRIC	Cult (Beggars Banquet)
5	12	INVISIBLE TOUCH	Genesis (Charisma)
18	13	MEN AND WOMEN	Simply Red (WEA)
13	14	OUTLAND	Spear Of Destiny (10)
-	15	BABBLE	That Petrol Emotion (Polydor)
22	16	CONTROL	Janet Jackson (A&M)
-	17	GIRLS GIRLS GIRLS	Motley Crue (Elektra)
15	18	NOW THAT'S WHAT I CALL MUSIC 9	Various Artists (EMI/Virgin/PolyGram)
17	19	GRACELAND	Paul Simon (Warner Bros.)
19	20	SILK AND STEEL	Five Star (Tent/RCA)
16	21	TRUE BLUE	Madonna (Sire)
21	22	LIVING IN A BOX	Living in a Box (Chrysalis)
40	23	THE FINAL COUNTDOWN	Europe (Epic)
27	24	UPFRONT 6	Various Artists (Upfront)
25	25	COMING ROUND AGAIN	Carly Simon (Arista)
32	26	TOM JONES' GREATEST HITS	Tom Jones (Telstar)
33	27	LICENCED TO ILL	Beastie Boys (Def Jam)
28	28	RHYTHM KILLERS	Sly & Robbie (Fourth & Broadway)
20	29	THE CIRCUS	Erasure (Mute)
-	30	ONE VOICE	Barbra Streisand (CBS)
41	31	GIVE ME THE REASON	Luther Vandross (Epic)
29	32	SHE WAS ONLY A GROCER'S DAUGHTER	Blow Monkeys (RCA)
-	33	THE WORLD WON'T LISTEN	Smiths (Rough Trade)
-	34	S. O. D. – THE EPIC YEARS	Spear of Destiny (Epic)
-	35	THIS IS THE STORY	Proclaimers (Chrysalis)
38	36	MOVE CLOSER	Various Artists (CBS)
30	37	THE PHANTOM OF THE OPERA	Original Cast (Polydor)
-	38	PLEASED TO MEET YOU	Replacements (Sire)
45	39	REVOLVER	Beatles (Parlophone)
50	40	DEAD LETTER OFFICE	REM (IRS)
35	41	HILLBILLY DELUXE	Dwight Yoakam (Reprise)
39	42	SLIPPERY WHEN WET	Bon Jovi (Vertigo)
23	43	THIS TIME	Culture Club (Virgin)
37	44	BY REQUEST	James Last (Polydor)
31	45	WHITESNAKE 1987	Whitesnake (EMI)
24	46	SIGN 'O' THE TIMES	Prince (Paisley Park)
42	47	LILLO	Lillo Thomas (Capitol)
-	48	ROGER WHITTAKER'S FINEST COLLECTION	Roger Whittaker (Tembo)
43	49	INTO THE FIRE	Bryan Adams (A&M)
49	50	THE VERY BEST OF HOT CHOCOLATE	Hot Chocolate (RAK)

6 June 1987

last week	this week	title	artist (label)
2	1	SOLITUDE STANDING	Suzanne Vega (A&M)
1	2	IT'S BETTER TO TRAVEL	Swing Out Sister (Mercury)
-	3	LIVE IN THE CITY OF LIGHT	Simple Minds (Virgin)
3	4	KEEP YOUR DISTANCE	Curiosity Killed The Cat (Mercury)
6	5	THE JOSHUA TREE	U2 (Island)
7	6	SO	Peter Gabriel (Virgin)
4	7	TANGO IN THE NIGHT	Fleetwood Mac (Warner Bros.)
-	8	KISS ME KISS ME KISS ME	Cure (Fiction)
5	9	RUNNING IN THE FAMILY	Level 42 (Polydor)
10	10	TRIBUTE	Ozzy Osbourne (Epic)
9	11	FLM	Mel & Kim (Supreme)
13	12	MEN AND WOMEN	Simply Red (WEA)
17	13	GIRLS GIRLS GIRLS	Motley Crue (Elektra)
8	14	RAINDANCING	Alison Moyet (CBS)
11	15	ELECTRIC	Cult (Beggars Banquet)
19	16	GRACELAND	Paul Simon (Warner Bros.)
27	17	LICENCED TO ILL	Beastie Boys (Def Jam)
22	18	LIVING IN A BOX	Living in a Box (Chrysalis)
12	19	INVISIBLE TOUCH	Genesis (Charisma)
21	20	TRUE BLUE	Madonna (Sire)
14	21	OUTLAND	Spear Of Destiny (10)
-	22	LOUDER THAN BOMBS	Smiths (Rough Trade)
-	23	FREEDOM NO COMPROMISE	Little Steven (Manhattan)
-	24	DANCING ON THE COUCH	Go West (Chrysalis)
26	25	TOM JONES' GREATEST HITS	Tom Jones (Telstar)
-	26	BAD ANIMALS	Heart (Capitol)
28	27	RHYTHM KILLERS	Sly & Robbie (Fourth & Broadway)
15	28	BABBLE	That Petrol Emotion (Polydor)
20	29	SILK AND STEEL	Five Star (Tent/RCA)
18	30	NOW THAT'S WHAT I CALL MUSIC 9	Various Artists (EMI/Virgin/PolyGram)
29	31	THE CIRCUS	Erasure (Mute)
30	32	ONE VOICE	Barbra Streisand (CBS)
25	33	COMING ROUND AGAIN	Carly Simon (Arista)
24	34	UPFRONT 6	Various Artists (Upfront)
-	35	RED HOT RHYTHM 'N' BLUES	Diana Ross (EMI)
-	36	MICK AND CAROLINE	Latin Quarter (Rockin' Horse)
16	37	CONTROL	Janet Jackson (A&M)
36	38	MOVE CLOSER	Various Artists (CBS)
34	39	S. O. D. – THE EPIC YEARS	Spear of Destiny (Epic)
-	40	WHITNEY	Whitney Houston (Arista)
-	41	THUNDER	Andy Taylor (MCA)
23	42	THE FINAL COUNTDOWN	Europe (Epic)
48	43	ROGER WHITTAKER'S FINEST COLLECTION	Roger Whittaker (Tembo)
-	44	NEVER LET ME DOWN	David Bowie (EMI America)
-	45	DAWNRAZOR	Fields of the Nephilim (Situation 2)
47	46	LILLO	Lillo Thomas (Capitol)
45	47	WHITESNAKE 1987	Whitesnake (EMI)
-	48	BLUE MOODS	Keni Stevens (Jam Today)
41	49	HILLBILLY DELUXE	Dwight Yoakam (Reprise)
-	50	ATLANTIC SOUL	Various Artists (Atlantic)

13 June 1987

last week	this week	title	artist (label)
3	1	LIVE IN THE CITY OF LIGHT	Simple Minds (Virgin)
2	2	IT'S BETTER TO TRAVEL	Swing Out Sister (Mercury)
8	3	KISS ME KISS ME KISS ME	Cure (Fiction)
1	4	SOLITUDE STANDING	Suzanne Vega (A&M)
40	5	WHITNEY	Whitney Houston (Arista)
5	6	THE JOSHUA TREE	U2 (Island)
4	7	KEEP YOUR DISTANCE	Curiosity Killed The Cat (Mercury)
7	8	TANGO IN THE NIGHT	Fleetwood Mac (Warner Bros.)
13	9	GIRLS GIRLS GIRLS	Motley Crue (Elektra)
17	10	LICENCED TO ILL	Beastie Boys (Def Jam)
14	11	RAINDANCING	Alison Moyet (CBS)
26	12	BAD ANIMALS	Heart (Capitol)
9	13	RUNNING IN THE FAMILY	Level 42 (Polydor)
11	14	FLM	Mel & Kim (Supreme)
15	15	ELECTRIC	Cult (Beggars Banquet)
19	16	INVISIBLE TOUCH	Genesis (Charisma)
12	17	MEN AND WOMEN	Simply Red (WEA)
-	18	SGT PEPPER'S LONELY HEARTS CLUB BAND	Beatles (Parlophone)
6	19	SO	Peter Gabriel (Virgin)
31	20	THE CIRCUS	Erasure (Mute)
50	21	ATLANTIC SOUL	Various Artists (Atlantic)
22	22	LOUDER THAN BOMBS	Smiths (Rough Trade)
20	23	TRUE BLUE	Madonna (Sire)
29	24	SILK AND STEEL	Five Star (Tent/RCA)
25	25	TOM JONES' GREATEST HITS	Tom Jones (Telstar)
16	26	GRACELAND	Paul Simon (Warner Bros.)
18	27	LIVING IN A BOX	Living in a Box (Chrysalis)
10	28	TRIBUTE	Ozzy Osbourne (Epic)
24	29	DANCING ON THE COUCH	Go West (Chrysalis)
21	30	OUTLAND	Spear Of Destiny (10)
27	31	RHYTHM KILLERS	Sly & Robbie (Fourth & Broadway)
28	32	BABBLE	That Petrol Emotion (Polydor)
-	33	JUST GETS BETTER WITH TIME	Whispers (Solar)
23	34	FREEDOM NO COMPROMISE	Little Steven (Manhattan)
-	35	TALLULAH	Go-Betweens (Beggars Banquet)
-	36	PRIEST LIVE	Judas Priest (CBS)
32	37	ONE VOICE	Barbra Streisand (CBS)
30	38	NOW THAT'S WHAT I CALL MUSIC 9	Various Artists (EMI/Virgin/PolyGram)
-	39	GIVE ME THE REASON	Luther Vandross (Epic)
43	40	ROGER WHITTAKER'S FINEST COLLECTION	Roger Whittaker (Tembo)
34	41	UPFRONT 6	Various Artists (Upfront)
-	42	ANNIVERSARY	Tammy Wynette (Epic)
46	43	LILLO	Lillo Thomas (Capitol)
45	44	DAWNRAZOR	Fields of the Nephilim (Situation 2)
41	45	THUNDER	Andy Taylor (MCA)
-	46	I CAN'T LET YOU GO	Norwood (MCA)
-	47	TWO-FISTED TALES	Long Ryders (Island)
33	48	COMING ROUND AGAIN	Carly Simon (Arista)
36	49	MICK AND CAROLINE	Latin Quarter (Rockin' Horse)
37	50	CONTROL	Janet Jackson (A&M)

Suzanne Vega, the most prominent of a new wave of mid-1980s female singer-songwriters, topped the chart for a week with her second album, while new British group Swing Out Sister went one better by reaching the summit - again, for one week only - with their debut package. Whitney Houston's second album started modestly on the chart, but her concurrent Number 1 single success quickly boosted it.

20 June 1987

last week	this week	title	artist (label)
5	1	WHITNEY	Whitney Houston (Arista)
1	2	LIVE IN THE CITY OF LIGHT	Simple Minds (Virgin)
4	3	SOLITUDE STANDING	Suzanne Vega (A&M)
6	4	THE JOSHUA TREE	U2 (Island)
10	5	LICENCED TO ILL	Beastie Boys (Def Jam)
2	6	IT'S BETTER TO TRAVEL	Swing Out Sister (Mercury)
3	7	KISS ME KISS ME KISS ME	Cure (Fiction)
18	8	SGT PEPPER'S LONELY HEARTS CLUB BAND	Beatles (Parlophone)
7	9	KEEP YOUR DISTANCE	Curiosity Killed The Cat (Mercury)
8	10	TANGO IN THE NIGHT	Fleetwood Mac (Warner Bros.)
11	11	RAINDANCING	Alison Moyet (CBS)
20	12	THE CIRCUS	Erasure (Mute)
12	13	BAD ANIMALS	Heart (Capitol)
21	14	ATLANTIC SOUL	Various Artists (Atlantic)
17	15	MEN AND WOMEN	Simply Red (WEA)
13	16	RUNNING IN THE FAMILY	Level 42 (Polydor)
25	17	TOM JONES' GREATEST HITS	Tom Jones (Telstar)
16	18	INVISIBLE TOUCH	Genesis (Charisma)
26	19	GRACELAND	Paul Simon (Warner Bros.)
15	20	ELECTRIC	Cult (Beggars Banquet)
36	21	PRIEST LIVE	Judas Priest (CBS)
23	22	TRUE BLUE	Madonna (Sire)
9	23	GIRLS GIRLS GIRLS	Motley Crue (Elektra)
-	24	FRIENDS AND LOVERS	Various Artists (K-Tel)
19	25	SO	Peter Gabriel (Virgin)
29	26	DANCING ON THE COUCH	Go West (Chrysalis)
-	27	MATADOR	Various Artists (Epic)
38	28	NOW THAT'S WHAT I CALL MUSIC 9	Various Artists (EMI/Virgin/PolyGram)
24	29	SILK AND STEEL	Five Star (Tent/RCA)
37	30	ONE VOICE	Barbra Streisand (CBS)
-	31	NEVER LET ME DOWN	David Bowie (EMI America)
39	32	GIVE ME THE REASON	Luther Vandross (Epic)
33	33	JUST GETS BETTER WITH TIME	Whispers (Solar)
-	34	CHICAGO JACKBEAT	Various Artists (Rhythm King)
35	35	TALLULAH	Go-Betweens (Beggars Banquet)
-	36	THE PHANTOM OF THE OPERA	Original Cast (Polydor)
-	37	WHITNEY HOUSTON	Whitney Houston (Arista)
-	38	BROTHERS IN ARMS	Dire Straits (Vertigo)
-	39	BACK TO BASICS	Billy Bragg (Go! Discs)
-	40	STRONG PERSUADER	Robert Cray Band (Mercury)
28	41	TRIBUTE	Ozzy Osbourne (Epic)
44	42	DAWNRAZOR	Fields of the Nephilim (Situation 2)
22	43	LOUDER THAN BOMBS	Smiths (Rough Trade)
27	44	LIVING IN A BOX	Living in a Box (Chrysalis)
-	45	STREET SOUNDS HIP-HOP ELECTRO 16	Various Artists (Street Sounds)
47	46	TWO-FISTED TALES	Long Ryders (Island)
43	47	LILLO	Lillo Thomas (Capitol)
30	48	OUTLAND	Spear Of Destiny (10)
-	49	BIGGER AND DEFFER	LL Cool J (Def Jam)
-	50	THE RETURN OF BRUNO	Bruce Willis (Motown)

27 June 1987

last week	this week	title	artist (label)
1	1	WHITNEY	Whitney Houston (Arista)
2	2	LIVE IN THE CITY OF LIGHT	Simple Minds (Virgin)
4	3	THE JOSHUA TREE	U2 (Island)
3	4	SOLITUDE STANDING	Suzanne Vega (A&M)
9	5	KEEP YOUR DISTANCE	Curiosity Killed The Cat (Mercury)
5	6	LICENCED TO ILL	Beastie Boys (Def Jam)
6	7	IT'S BETTER TO TRAVEL	Swing Out Sister (Mercury)
10	8	TANGO IN THE NIGHT	Fleetwood Mac (Warner Bros.)
8	9	SGT PEPPER'S LONELY HEARTS CLUB BAND	Beatles (Parlophone)
14	10	ATLANTIC SOUL	Various Artists (Atlantic)
24	11	FRIENDS AND LOVERS	Various Artists (K-Tel)
12	12	THE CIRCUS	Erasure (Mute)
50	13	THE RETURN OF BRUNO	Bruce Willis (Motown)
11	14	RAINDANCING	Alison Moyet (CBS)
7	15	KISS ME KISS ME KISS ME	Cure (Fiction)
18	16	INVISIBLE TOUCH	Genesis (Charisma)
-	17	FLM	Mel & Kim (Supreme)
15	18	MEN AND WOMEN	Simply Red (WEA)
17	19	TOM JONES' GREATEST HITS	Tom Jones (Telstar)
19	20	GRACELAND	Paul Simon (Warner Bros.)
13	21	BAD ANIMALS	Heart (Capitol)
16	22	RUNNING IN THE FAMILY	Level 42 (Polydor)
-	23	SOLD	Boy George (Virgin)
25	24	SO	Peter Gabriel (Virgin)
28	25	NOW THAT'S WHAT I CALL MUSIC 9	Various Artists (EMI/Virgin/PolyGram)
21	26	PRIEST LIVE	Judas Priest (CBS)
22	27	TRUE BLUE	Madonna (Sire)
29	28	SILK AND STEEL	Five Star (Tent/RCA)
39	29	BACK TO BASICS	Billy Bragg (Go! Discs)
20	30	ELECTRIC	Cult (Beggars Banquet)
-	31	RADIO K.A.O.S.	Roger Waters (EMI)
31	32	NEVER LET ME DOWN	David Bowie (EMI America)
32	33	GIVE ME THE REASON	Luther Vandross (Epic)
23	34	GIRLS GIRLS GIRLS	Motley Crue (Elektra)
27	35	MATADOR	Various Artists (Epic)
26	36	DANCING ON THE COUCH	Go West (Chrysalis)
40	37	STRONG PERSUADER	Robert Cray Band (Mercury)
30	38	ONE VOICE	Barbra Streisand (CBS)
49	39	BIGGER AND DEFFER	LL Cool J (Def Jam)
-	40	ROGER WHITTAKER'S FINEST COLLECTION	Roger Whittaker (Tembo)
-	41	WHITESNAKE 1987	Whitesnake (EMI)
33	42	JUST GETS BETTER WITH TIME	Whispers (Solar)
37	43	WHITNEY HOUSTON	Whitney Houston (Arista)
34	44	CHICAGO JACKBEAT	Various Artists (Rhythm King)
36	45	THE PHANTOM OF THE OPERA	Original Cast (Polydor)
-	46	SIGN 'O' THE TIMES	Prince (Paisley Park)
42	47	DAWNRAZOR	Fields of the Nephilim (Situation 2)
38	48	BROTHERS IN ARMS	Dire Straits (Vertigo)
41	49	TRIBUTE	Ozzy Osbourne (Epic)
45	50	STREET SOUNDS HIP-HOP ELECTRO 16	Various Artists (Street Sounds)

4 July 1987

last week	this week	title	artist (label)
1	1	WHITNEY	Whitney Houston (Arista)
3	2	THE JOSHUA TREE	U2 (Island)
2	3	LIVE IN THE CITY OF LIGHT	Simple Minds (Virgin)
4	4	SOLITUDE STANDING	Suzanne Vega (A&M)
13	5	THE RETURN OF BRUNO	Bruce Willis (Motown)
-	6	CLUTCHING AT STRAWS	Marillion (EMI)
5	7	KEEP YOUR DISTANCE	Curiosity Killed The Cat (Mercury)
7	8	IT'S BETTER TO TRAVEL	Swing Out Sister (Mercury)
10	9	ATLANTIC SOUL	Various Artists (Atlantic)
6	10	LICENCED TO ILL	Beastie Boys (Def Jam)
16	11	INVISIBLE TOUCH	Genesis (Charisma)
11	12	FRIENDS AND LOVERS	Various Artists (K-Tel)
9	13	SGT PEPPER'S LONELY HEARTS CLUB BAND	Beatles (Parlophone)
8	14	TANGO IN THE NIGHT	Fleetwood Mac (Warner Bros.)
31	15	RADIO K.A.O.S.	Roger Waters (EMI)
12	16	THE CIRCUS	Erasure (Mute)
32	17	NEVER LET ME DOWN	David Bowie (EMI America)
40	18	ROGER WHITTAKER'S FINEST COLLECTION	Roger Whittaker (Tembo)
18	19	MEN AND WOMEN	Simply Red (WEA)
14	20	RAINDANCING	Alison Moyet (CBS)
21	21	BAD ANIMALS	Heart (Capitol)
15	22	KISS ME KISS ME KISS ME	Cure (Fiction)
19	23	TOM JONES' GREATEST HITS	Tom Jones (Telstar)
20	24	GRACELAND	Paul Simon (Warner Bros.)
-	25	HITS REVIVAL	Various Artists (K-Tel)
39	26	BIGGER AND DEFFER	LL Cool J (Def Jam)
17	27	FLM	Mel & Kim (Supreme)
41	28	WHITESNAKE 1987	Whitesnake (EMI)
-	29	LIFE	Neil Young (Geffen)
-	30	FIRST CHAPTER	Mission (Mercury)
-	31	EXIT O	Steve Earle (MCA)
22	32	RUNNING IN THE FAMILY	Level 42 (Polydor)
27	33	TRUE BLUE	Madonna (Sire)
28	34	SILK AND STEEL	Five Star (Tent/RCA)
46	35	SIGN 'O' THE TIMES	Prince (Paisley Park)
-	36	BREAK EVERY RULE	Tina Turner (Capitol)
23	37	SOLD	Boy George (Virgin)
37	38	STRONG PERSUADER	Robert Cray Band (Mercury)
30	39	ELECTRIC	Cult (Beggars Banquet)
24	40	SO	Peter Gabriel (Virgin)
43	41	WHITNEY HOUSTON	Whitney Houston (Arista)
35	42	MATADOR	Various Artists (Epic)
33	43	GIVE ME THE REASON	Luther Vandross (Epic)
29	44	BACK TO BASICS	Billy Bragg (Go! Discs)
-	45	THE MARIA CALLAS COLLECTION	Maria Callas (Stylus)
25	46	NOW THAT'S WHAT I CALL MUSIC 9	Various Artists (EMI/Virgin/PolyGram)
-	47	INTERVIEW	Bhundu Boys (Discafrique)
-	48	THE HOLIDAY ALBUM	Various Artists (CBS)
-	49	THE ROCK 'N' ROLL YEARS 1964-67	Various Artists (BBC)
-	50	THE VERY BEST OF HOT CHOCOLATE	Hot Chocolate (RAK)

Once into its stride, there was no holding Whitney Houston's *Whitney*. Her first album had been a long stayer near the top of the chart a year earlier. but had actually peaked at Number 2. The follow-up managed six straight weeks at Number 1, and would eventually become the second biggest-selling album of the 1980s by a female artist, outselling Madonna's *True Blue*, and beaten only by Kylie Minogue's debut.

July 1987

11 July 1987

last	this		
1	1	WHITNEY	Whitney Houston (Arista)
6	2	CLUTCHING AT STRAWS	Marillion (EMI)
2	3	THE JOSHUA TREE	U2 (Island)
5	4	THE RETURN OF BRUNO	Bruce Willis (Motown)
3	5	LIVE IN THE CITY OF LIGHT	
			Simple Minds (Virgin)
7	6	KEEP YOUR DISTANCE	
			Curiosity Killed The Cat (Mercury)
4	7	SOLITUDE STANDING	Suzanne Vega (A&M)
11	8	INVISIBLE TOUCH	Genesis (Charisma)
9	9	ATLANTIC SOUL	Various Artists (Atlantic)
10	10	LICENCED TO ILL	Beastie Boys (Def Jam)
8	11	IT'S BETTER TO TRAVEL	
			Swing Out Sister (Mercury)
16	12	THE CIRCUS	Erasure (Mute)
21	13	BAD ANIMALS	Heart (Capitol)
25	14	HITS REVIVAL	Various Artists (K-Tel)
14	15	TANGO IN THE NIGHT	
			Fleetwood Mac (Warner Bros.)
28	16	WHITESNAKE 1987	Whitesnake (EMI)
17	17	NEVER LET ME DOWN	
			David Bowie (EMI America)
12	18	FRIENDS AND LOVERS	Various Artists (K-Tel)
13	19	SGT PEPPER'S LONELY HEARTS CLUB BAND	
			Beatles (Parlophone)
27	20	FLM	Mel & Kim (Supreme)
24	21	GRACELAND	Paul Simon (Warner Bros.)
15	22	RADIO K.A.O.S.	Roger Waters (EMI)
20	23	RAINDANCING	Alison Moyet (CBS)
30	24	FIRST CHAPTER	Mission (Mercury)
-	25	FOREVER, FOR ALWAYS, FOR LOVE	
			Luther Vandross (Epic)
-	26	GIVE ME CONVENIENCE	
			Dead Kennedys (Alternative Tentacles)
48	27	THE HOLIDAY ALBUM	Various Artists (CBS)
19	28	MEN AND WOMEN	Simply Red (WEA)
35	29	SIGN 'O' THE TIMES	Prince (Paisley Park)
40	30	SO	Peter Gabriel (Virgin)
33	31	TRUE BLUE	Madonna (Sire)
-	32	WHISPERING JACK	John Farnham (RCA)
-	33	LIVE AT THE HOLLYWOOD BOWL	
			Doors (Elektra)
18	34	ROGER WHITTAKER'S FINEST COLLECTION	
			Roger Whittaker (Tembo)
-	35	CONTROL	Janet Jackson (A&M)
23	36	TOM JONES' GREATEST HITS	
			Tom Jones (Telstar)
22	37	KISS ME KISS ME KISS ME	Cure (Fiction)
32	38	RUNNING IN THE FAMILY	Level 42 (Polydor)
-	39	DISCO	Pet Shop Boys (Parlophone)
29	40	LIFE	Neil Young (Geffen)
-	41	ONE SECOND	Yello (Mercury)
31	42	EXIT O	Steve Earle (MCA)
-	43	SAMMY HAGAR	Sammy Hagar (Geffen)
-	44	TALLULAH	Go-Betweens (Beggars Banquet)
-	45	LONELY IS AN EYESORE	Various Artists (4AD)
37	46	SOLD	Boy George (Virgin)
45	47	THE MARIA CALLAS COLLECTION	
			Maria Callas (Stylus)
38	48	STRONG PERSUADER	
			Robert Cray Band (Mercury)
-	49	STREET SOUNDS DANCE MUSIC '87	
			Various Artists (Street Sounds)
26	50	BIGGER AND DEFFER	LL Cool J (Def Jam)

18 July 1987

last	this		
1	1	WHITNEY	Whitney Houston (Arista)
3	2	THE JOSHUA TREE	U2 (Island)
2	3	CLUTCHING AT STRAWS	Marillion (EMI)
8	4	INVISIBLE TOUCH	Genesis (Charisma)
4	5	THE RETURN OF BRUNO	Bruce Willis (Motown)
5	6	LIVE IN THE CITY OF LIGHT	
			Simple Minds (Virgin)
6	7	KEEP YOUR DISTANCE	
			Curiosity Killed The Cat (Mercury)
7	8	SOLITUDE STANDING	Suzanne Vega (A&M)
13	9	BAD ANIMALS	Heart (Capitol)
14	10	HITS REVIVAL	Various Artists (K-Tel)
-	11	ECHO AND THE BUNNYMEN	
			Echo & the Bunnymen (WEA)
9	12	ATLANTIC SOUL	Various Artists (Atlantic)
11	13	IT'S BETTER TO TRAVEL	
			Swing Out Sister (Mercury)
10	14	LICENCED TO ILL	Beastie Boys (Def Jam)
25	15	FOREVER, FOR ALWAYS, FOR LOVE	
			Luther Vandross (Epic)
20	16	FLM	Mel & Kim (Supreme)
27	17	THE HOLIDAY ALBUM	Various Artists (CBS)
16	18	WHITESNAKE 1987	Whitesnake (EMI)
32	19	WHISPERING JACK	John Farnham (RCA)
35	20	CONTROL	Janet Jackson (A&M)
15	21	TANGO IN THE NIGHT	
			Fleetwood Mac (Warner Bros.)
29	22	SIGN 'O' THE TIMES	Prince (Paisley Park)
12	23	THE CIRCUS	Erasure (Mute)
30	24	SO	Peter Gabriel (Virgin)
17	25	NEVER LET ME DOWN	
			David Bowie (EMI America)
37	26	KISS ME KISS ME KISS ME	Cure (Fiction)
24	27	FIRST CHAPTER	Mission (Mercury)
31	28	TRUE BLUE	Madonna (Sire)
23	29	RAINDANCING	Alison Moyet (CBS)
48	30	STRONG PERSUADER	
			Robert Cray Band (Mercury)
-	31	THE ISLAND STORY	Various Artists (Island)
-	32	IN CONCERT - LYON AND HOUSTON	
			Jean Michel Jarre (Polydor)
-	33	NO PROTECTION	Starship (Grunt)
45	34	LONELY IS AN EYESORE	Various Artists (4AD)
33	35	LIVE AT THE HOLLYWOOD BOWL	
			Doors (Elektra)
26	36	GIVE ME CONVENIENCE	
			Dead Kennedys (Alternative Tentacles)
38	37	RUNNING IN THE FAMILY	Level 42 (Polydor)
19	38	SGT PEPPER'S LONELY HEARTS CLUB BAND	
			Beatles (Parlophone)
21	39	GRACELAND	Paul Simon (Warner Bros.)
40	40	ONE SECOND	Yello (Mercury)
40	41	LIFE	Neil Young (Geffen)
28	42	MEN AND WOMEN	Simply Red (WEA)
49	43	STREET SOUNDS DANCE MUSIC '87	
			Various Artists (Street Sounds)
39	44	DISCO	Pet Shop Boys (Parlophone)
-	45	QUEEN'S GREATEST HITS	Queen (EMI)
46	46	SOLD	Boy George (Virgin)
42	47	EXIT O	Steve Earle (MCA)
-	48	THE PLAGUE	Nuclear Assault (Under One Flag)
18	49	FRIENDS AND LOVERS	Various Artists (K-Tel)
34	50	ROGER WHITTAKER'S FINEST COLLECTION	
			Roger Whittaker (Tembo)

25 July 1987

last	this		
1	1	WHITNEY	Whitney Houston (Arista)
2	2	THE JOSHUA TREE	U2 (Island)
11	3	ECHO AND THE BUNNYMEN	
			Echo & the Bunnymen (WEA)
5	4	THE RETURN OF BRUNO	Bruce Willis (Motown)
4	5	INVISIBLE TOUCH	Genesis (Charisma)
3	6	CLUTCHING AT STRAWS	Marillion (EMI)
6	7	LIVE IN THE CITY OF LIGHT	Simple Minds (Virgin)
-	8	INTRODUCING THE HARDLINE ACCORDING TO	
			Terence Trent D'Arby (CBS)
7	9	KEEP YOUR DISTANCE	
			Curiosity Killed The Cat (Mercury)
9	10	BAD ANIMALS	Heart (Capitol)
31	11	THE ISLAND STORY	Various Artists (Island)
8	12	SOLITUDE STANDING	Suzanne Vega (A&M)
20	13	CONTROL	Janet Jackson (A&M)
12	14	ATLANTIC SOUL	Various Artists (Atlantic)
-	15	HITS 6	Various Artists (CBS/WEA/BMG)
32	16	IN CONCERT - LYON AND HOUSTON	
			Jean Michel Jarre (Polydor)
16	17	FLM	Mel & Kim (Supreme)
10	18	HITS REVIVAL	Various Artists (K-Tel)
21	19	TANGO IN THE NIGHT	
			Fleetwood Mac (Warner Bros.)
14	20	LICENCED TO ILL	Beastie Boys (Def Jam)
15	21	FOREVER, FOR ALWAYS, FOR LOVE	
			Luther Vandross (Epic)
-	22	SIXTIES MIX	Various Artists (Stylus)
30	23	STRONG PERSUADER	
			Robert Cray Band (Mercury)
13	24	IT'S BETTER TO TRAVEL	
			Swing Out Sister (Mercury)
23	25	THE CIRCUS	Erasure (Mute)
18	26	WHITESNAKE 1987	Whitesnake (EMI)
33	27	NO PROTECTION	Starship (Grunt)
19	28	WHISPERING JACK	John Farnham (RCA)
-	29	SHABINI	Bhundu Boys (Discafrique)
26	30	KISS ME KISS ME KISS ME	Cure (Fiction)
28	31	TRUE BLUE	Madonna (Sire)
-	32	COLLABORATION	
			George Benson & Earl Klugh (Warner Bros.)
41	33	LIFE	Neil Young (Geffen)
22	34	SIGN 'O' THE TIMES	Prince (Paisley Park)
-	35	FAMOUS BLUE RAINCOAT	Jennifer Warnes (RCA)
42	36	MEN AND WOMEN	Simply Red (WEA)
43	37	STREET SOUNDS DANCE MUSIC '87	
			Various Artists (Street Sounds)
37	38	RUNNING IN THE FAMILY	Level 42 (Polydor)
-	39	ALL IN THE NAME OF LOVE	
			Atlantic Starr (Warner Bros.)
-	40	RADIO K.A.O.S.	Roger Waters (EMI)
24	41	SO	Peter Gabriel (Virgin)
17	42	THE HOLIDAY ALBUM	Various Artists (CBS)
34	43	LONELY IS AN EYESORE	Various Artists (4AD)
44	44	DISCO	Pet Shop Boys (Parlophone)
-	45	U2 LIVE: UNDER A BLOOD RED SKY	U2 (Island)
36	46	GIVE ME CONVENIENCE	
			Dead Kennedys (Alternative Tentacles)
47	47	EXIT O	Steve Earle (MCA)
50	48	ROGER WHITTAKER'S FINEST COLLECTION	
			Roger Whittaker (Tembo)
25	49	NEVER LET ME DOWN	
			David Bowie (EMI America)
29	50	RAINDANCING	Alison Moyet (CBS)

Bruce Willis' *The Return Of Bruno* had seemed an unlikely major album seller at first, notwithstanding the actor's TV popularity. However, the singles taken from it were giving Willis huge success in the singles chart - *Under The Boardwalk* was at Number 2 in the week the album peaked at 4 - and the benefits of the resulting airplay fed back to the parent package. This was, however, his only hit album.

1 August 1987

last	this week	Title	Artist (Label)
8	1	INTRODUCING THE HARDLINE ACCORDING TO	Terence Trent D'Arby (CBS)
15	2	HITS 6	Various Artists (CBS/WEA/BMG)
1	3	WHITNEY	Whitney Houston (Arista)
2	4	THE JOSHUA TREE	U2 (Island)
5	5	INVISIBLE TOUCH	Genesis (Charisma)
10	6	BAD ANIMALS	Heart (Capitol)
4	7	THE RETURN OF BRUNO	Bruce Willis (Motown)
22	8	SIXTIES MIX	Various Artists (Stylus)
3	9	ECHO AND THE BUNNYMEN	Echo & the Bunnymen (WEA)
17	10	FLM	Mel & Kim (Supreme)
11	11	THE ISLAND STORY	Various Artists (Island)
9	12	KEEP YOUR DISTANCE	Curiosity Killed The Cat (Mercury)
-	13	WHO'S THAT GIRL	Soundtrack (Warner Bros.)
7	14	LIVE IN THE CITY OF LIGHT	Simple Minds (Virgin)
12	15	SOLITUDE STANDING	Suzanne Vega (A&M)
20	16	LICENCED TO ILL	Beastie Boys (Def Jam)
13	17	CONTROL	Janet Jackson (A&M)
6	18	CLUTCHING AT STRAWS	Marillion (EMI)
16	19	IN CONCERT - LYON AND HOUSTON	Jean Michel Jarre (Polydor)
24	20	IT'S BETTER TO TRAVEL	Swing Out Sister (Mercury)
31	21	TRUE BLUE	Madonna (Sire)
21	22	FOREVER, FOR ALWAYS, FOR LOVE	Luther Vandross (Epic)
14	23	ATLANTIC SOUL	Various Artists (Atlantic)
35	24	FAMOUS BLUE RAINCOAT	Jennifer Warnes (RCA)
-	25	LOVE IS FOR SUCKERS	Twisted Sister (Atlantic)
25	26	THE CIRCUS	Erasure (Mute)
19	27	TANGO IN THE NIGHT	Fleetwood Mac (Warner Bros.)
18	28	HITS REVIVAL	Various Artists (K-Tel)
26	29	WHITESNAKE 1987	Whitesnake (EMI)
48	30	ROGER WHITTAKER'S FINEST COLLECTION	Roger Whittaker (Tembo)
49	31	NEVER LET ME DOWN	David Bowie (EMI America)
-	32	THE LIVING DAYLIGHTS	Soundtrack (Warner Bros.)
27	33	NO PROTECTION	Starship (Grunt)
32	34	COLLABORATION	George Benson & Earl Klugh (Warner Bros.)
-	35	APPETITE FOR DESTRUCTION	Guns 'N' Roses (Geffen)
42	36	THE HOLIDAY ALBUM	Various Artists (CBS)
-	37	BROTHERS IN ARMS	Dire Straits (Vertigo)
23	38	STRONG PERSUADER	Robert Cray Band (Mercury)
39	39	ALL IN THE NAME OF LOVE	Atlantic Starr (Warner Bros.)
40	40	RADIO K.A.O.S.	Roger Waters (EMI)
37	41	STREET SOUNDS DANCE MUSIC '87	Various Artists (Street Sounds)
-	42	ALL BY MYSELF	Regina Belle (CBS)
-	43	LILLO	Lillo Thomas (Capitol)
28	44	WHISPERING JACK	John Farnham (RCA)
44	45	DISCO	Pet Shop Boys (Parlophone)
38	46	RUNNING IN THE FAMILY	Level 42 (Polydor)
30	47	KISS ME KISS ME KISS ME	Cure (Fiction)
36	48	MEN AND WOMEN	Simply Red (WEA)
50	49	RAINDANCING	Alison Moyet (CBS)
-	50	SGT PEPPER'S LONELY HEARTS CLUB BAND	Beatles (Parlophone)

8 August 1987

last	this week	Title	Artist (Label)
1	1	INTRODUCING THE HARDLINE ACCORDING TO	Terence Trent D'Arby (CBS)
2	2	HITS 6	Various Artists (CBS/WEA/BMG)
3	3	WHITNEY	Whitney Houston (Arista)
4	4	THE JOSHUA TREE	U2 (Island)
13	5	WHO'S THAT GIRL	Soundtrack (Warner Bros.)
6	6	BAD ANIMALS	Heart (Capitol)
7	7	THE RETURN OF BRUNO	Bruce Willis (Motown)
8	8	SIXTIES MIX	Various Artists (Stylus)
14	9	LIVE IN THE CITY OF LIGHT	Simple Minds (Virgin)
5	10	INVISIBLE TOUCH	Genesis (Charisma)
10	11	FLM	Mel & Kim (Supreme)
15	12	SOLITUDE STANDING	Suzanne Vega (A&M)
16	13	LICENCED TO ILL	Beastie Boys (Def Jam)
11	14	THE ISLAND STORY	Various Artists (Island)
12	15	KEEP YOUR DISTANCE	Curiosity Killed The Cat (Mercury)
18	16	CLUTCHING AT STRAWS	Marillion (EMI)
21	17	TRUE BLUE	Madonna (Sire)
20	18	IT'S BETTER TO TRAVEL	Swing Out Sister (Mercury)
22	19	FOREVER, FOR ALWAYS, FOR LOVE	Luther Vandross (Epic)
-	20	SAMANTHA FOX	Samantha Fox (Jive)
35	21	APPETITE FOR DESTRUCTION	Guns 'N' Roses (Geffen)
9	22	ECHO AND THE BUNNYMEN	Echo & the Bunnymen (WEA)
23	23	ATLANTIC SOUL	Various Artists (Atlantic)
17	24	CONTROL	Janet Jackson (A&M)
27	25	TANGO IN THE NIGHT	Fleetwood Mac (Warner Bros.)
-	26	HEARSAY	Alexander O'Neal (Tabu)
24	27	FAMOUS BLUE RAINCOAT	Jennifer Warnes (RCA)
34	28	COLLABORATION	George Benson & Earl Klugh (Warner Bros.)
32	29	THE LIVING DAYLIGHTS	Soundtrack (Warner Bros.)
45	30	DISCO	Pet Shop Boys (Parlophone)
-	31	FASTER PUSSYCAT	Faster Pussycat (Elektra)
19	32	IN CONCERT - LYON AND HOUSTON	Jean Michel Jarre (Polydor)
26	33	THE CIRCUS	Erasure (Mute)
29	34	WHITESNAKE 1987	Whitesnake (EMI)
28	35	HITS REVIVAL	Various Artists (K-Tel)
39	36	ALL IN THE NAME OF LOVE	Atlantic Starr (Warner Bros.)
25	37	LOVE IS FOR SUCKERS	Twisted Sister (Atlantic)
-	38	FIERCE	Various Artists (Cooltempo)
42	39	ALL BY MYSELF	Regina Belle (CBS)
30	40	ROGER WHITTAKER'S FINEST COLLECTION	Roger Whittaker (Tembo)
37	41	BROTHERS IN ARMS	Dire Straits (Vertigo)
44	42	WHISPERING JACK	John Farnham (RCA)
46	43	RUNNING IN THE FAMILY	Level 42 (Polydor)
47	44	KISS ME KISS ME KISS ME	Cure (Fiction)
49	45	RAINDANCING	Alison Moyet (CBS)
-	46	GRACELAND	Paul Simon (Warner Bros.)
-	47	SO	Peter Gabriel (Virgin)
48	48	MEN AND WOMEN	Simply Red (WEA)
-	49	BOUNCING OFF SATELLITES	B-52s (Island)
50	50	SGT PEPPER'S LONELY HEARTS CLUB BAND	Beatles (Parlophone)

15 August 1987

last	this week	Title	Artist (Label)
2	1	HITS 6	Various Artists (CBS/WEA/BMG)
1	2	INTRODUCING THE HARDLINE ACCORDING TO	Terence Trent D'Arby (CBS)
4	3	THE JOSHUA TREE	U2 (Island)
8	4	SIXTIES MIX	Various Artists (Stylus)
6	5	BAD ANIMALS	Heart (Capitol)
3	6	WHITNEY	Whitney Houston (Arista)
5	7	WHO'S THAT GIRL	Soundtrack (Warner Bros.)
10	8	INVISIBLE TOUCH	Genesis (Charisma)
17	9	TRUE BLUE	Madonna (Sire)
11	10	FLM	Mel & Kim (Supreme)
7	11	THE RETURN OF BRUNO	Bruce Willis (Motown)
-	12	KICK IT - THE DEF JAM SAMPLER	Various Artists (Def Jam)
26	13	HEARSAY	Alexander O'Neal (Tabu)
13	14	LICENCED TO ILL	Beastie Boys (Def Jam)
9	15	LIVE IN THE CITY OF LIGHT	Simple Minds (Virgin)
-	16	DUOTONES	Kenny G (Arista)
12	17	SOLITUDE STANDING	Suzanne Vega (A&M)
16	18	CLUTCHING AT STRAWS	Marillion (EMI)
-	19	U2 LIVE: UNDER A BLOOD RED SKY	U2 (Island)
15	20	KEEP YOUR DISTANCE	Curiosity Killed The Cat (Mercury)
21	21	APPETITE FOR DESTRUCTION	Guns 'N' Roses (Geffen)
22	22	ECHO AND THE BUNNYMEN	Echo & the Bunnymen (WEA)
18	23	IT'S BETTER TO TRAVEL	Swing Out Sister (Mercury)
-	24	MIRACLE	Kane Gang (Kitchenware)
14	25	THE ISLAND STORY	Various Artists (Island)
19	26	FOREVER, FOR ALWAYS, FOR LOVE	Luther Vandross (Epic)
36	27	ALL IN THE NAME OF LOVE	Atlantic Starr (Warner Bros.)
39	28	ALL BY MYSELF	Regina Belle (CBS)
-	29	GIRLS GIRLS GIRLS	Motley Crue (Elektra)
-	30	PRIDE	White Lion (Atlantic)
32	31	IN CONCERT - LYON AND HOUSTON	Jean Michel Jarre (Polydor)
20	32	SAMANTHA FOX	Samantha Fox (Jive)
23	33	ATLANTIC SOUL	Various Artists (Atlantic)
25	34	TANGO IN THE NIGHT	Fleetwood Mac (Warner Bros.)
38	35	FIERCE	Various Artists (Cooltempo)
24	36	CONTROL	Janet Jackson (A&M)
27	37	FAMOUS BLUE RAINCOAT	Jennifer Warnes (RCA)
-	38	STRANGE WEATHER	Marianne Faithfull (Island)
-	39	THE UNFORGETTABLE FIRE	U2 (Island)
-	40	DEFENDER	Rory Gallagher (Demon)
-	41	MUSICAL MADNESS	Mantronix (10)
-	42	UNDER THE INFLUENCE	Mary Coughlan (WEA)
29	43	THE LIVING DAYLIGHTS	Soundtrack (Warner Bros.)
34	44	WHITESNAKE 1987	Whitesnake (EMI)
35	45	HITS REVIVAL	Various Artists (K-Tel)
44	46	KISS ME KISS ME KISS ME	Cure (Fiction)
30	47	DISCO	Pet Shop Boys (Parlophone)
49	48	BOUNCING OFF SATELLITES	B-52s (Island)
28	49	COLLABORATION	George Benson & Earl Klugh (Warner Bros.)
31	50	FASTER PUSSYCAT	Faster Pussycat (Elektra)

Terence Trent D'Arby, a startling songwriting and performing talent in a credible R&B idiom, broke from obscurity to mega-success almost overnight, with one of the most highly-praised and successful debut albums of recent years, from which also flowed a number of major hit singles. D'Arby's major flaw was an apparent arrogance based on his appreciation of his own talent, and the critics soon turned on him.

August – September 1987

22 August 1987

		Title	Artist
1	1	HITS 6	Various Artists (CBS/WEA/BMG)
2	2	INTRODUCING THE HARDLINE ACCORDING TO	Terence Trent D'Arby (CBS)
6	3	WHITNEY	Whitney Houston (Arista)
7	4	WHO'S THAT GIRL	Soundtrack (Warner Bros.)
4	5	SIXTIES MIX	Various Artists (Stylus)
3	6	THE JOSHUA TREE	U2 (Island)
5	7	BAD ANIMALS	Heart (Capitol)
13	8	HEARSAY	Alexander O'Neal (Tabu)
9	9	TRUE BLUE	Madonna (Sire)
8	10	INVISIBLE TOUCH	Genesis (Charisma)
12	11	KICK IT - THE DEF JAM SAMPLER	Various Artists (Def Jam)
-	12	DREAM EVIL	Dio (Vertigo)
11	13	THE RETURN OF BRUNO	Bruce Willis (Motown)
20	14	KEEP YOUR DISTANCE	Curiosity Killed The Cat (Mercury)
14	15	LICENCED TO ILL	Beastie Boys (Def Jam)
10	16	FLM	Mel & Kim (Supreme)
15	17	LIVE IN THE CITY OF LIGHT	Simple Minds (Virgin)
17	18	SOLITUDE STANDING	Suzanne Vega (A&M)
18	19	CLUTCHING AT STRAWS	Marillion (EMI)
-	20	LA BAMBA	Soundtrack (London)
34	21	TANGO IN THE NIGHT	Fleetwood Mac (Warner Bros.)
22	22	ECHO AND THE BUNNYMEN	Echo & the Bunnymen (WEA)
26	23	FOREVER, FOR ALWAYS, FOR LOVE	Luther Vandross (Epic)
23	24	IT'S BETTER TO TRAVEL	Swing Out Sister (Mercury)
33	25	ATLANTIC SOUL	Various Artists (Atlantic)
19	26	U2 LIVE: UNDER A BLOOD RED SKY	U2 (Island)
37	27	FAMOUS BLUE RAINCOAT	Jennifer Warnes (RCA)
16	28	DUOTONES	Kenny G (Arista)
24	29	MIRACLE	Kane Gang (Kitchenware)
-	30	UPFRONT 7	Various Artists (Serious)
39	31	THE UNFORGETTABLE FIRE	U2 (Island)
21	32	APPETITE FOR DESTRUCTION	Guns 'N' Roses (Geffen)
30	33	PRIDE	White Lion (Atlantic)
32	34	SAMANTHA FOX	Samantha Fox (Jive)
-	35	BROTHERS IN ARMS	Dire Straits (Vertigo)
44	36	WHITESNAKE 1987	Whitesnake (EMI)
27	37	ALL IN THE NAME OF LOVE	Atlantic Starr (Warner Bros.)
-	38	SLIPPERY WHEN WET	Bon Jovi (Vertigo)
28	39	ALL BY MYSELF	Regina Belle (CBS)
-	40	ELVIS PRESLEY - THE ALL TIME GREATEST HITS	Elvis Presley (RCA)
-	41	LILLO	Lillo Thomas (Capitol)
50	42	FASTER PUSSYCAT	Faster Pussycat (Elektra)
25	43	THE ISLAND STORY	Various Artists (Island)
29	44	GIRLS GIRLS GIRLS	Motley Crue (Elektra)
40	45	DEFENDER	Rory Gallagher (Demon)
-	46	GIVE ME THE REASON	Luther Vandross (Epic)
-	47	JAZZ JUICE 5	Various Artists (Street Sounds)
47	48	DISCO	Pet Shop Boys (Parlophone)
46	49	KISS ME KISS ME KISS ME	Cure (Fiction)
-	50	THE CIRCUS	Erasure (Mute)

29 August 1987

		Title	Artist
1	1	HITS 6	Various Artists (CBS/WEA/BMG)
2	2	INTRODUCING THE HARDLINE ACCORDING TO	Terence Trent D'Arby (CBS)
3	3	WHITNEY	Whitney Houston (Arista)
-	4	HYSTERIA	Def Leppard (Bludgen Riffola)
5	5	SIXTIES MIX	Various Artists (Stylus)
7	6	BAD ANIMALS	Heart (Capitol)
4	7	WHO'S THAT GIRL	Soundtrack (Warner Bros.)
12	8	DREAM EVIL	Dio (Vertigo)
6	9	THE JOSHUA TREE	U2 (Island)
9	10	TRUE BLUE	Madonna (Sire)
10	11	INVISIBLE TOUCH	Genesis (Charisma)
15	12	LICENCED TO ILL	Beastie Boys (Def Jam)
-	13	SUBSTANCE	New Order (Factory)
13	14	THE RETURN OF BRUNO	Bruce Willis (Motown)
14	15	KEEP YOUR DISTANCE	Curiosity Killed The Cat (Mercury)
8	16	HEARSAY	Alexander O'Neal (Tabu)
11	17	KICK IT - THE DEF JAM SAMPLER	Various Artists (Def Jam)
40	18	ELVIS PRESLEY - THE ALL TIME GREATEST HITS	Elvis Presley (RCA)
20	19	LA BAMBA	Soundtrack (London)
16	20	FLM	Mel & Kim (Supreme)
17	21	LIVE IN THE CITY OF LIGHT	Simple Minds (Virgin)
38	22	SLIPPERY WHEN WET	Bon Jovi (Vertigo)
21	23	TANGO IN THE NIGHT	Fleetwood Mac (Warner Bros.)
46	24	GIVE ME THE REASON	Luther Vandross (Epic)
18	25	SOLITUDE STANDING	Suzanne Vega (A&M)
19	26	CLUTCHING AT STRAWS	Marillion (EMI)
26	27	U2 LIVE: UNDER A BLOOD RED SKY	U2 (Island)
23	28	FOREVER, FOR ALWAYS, FOR LOVE	Luther Vandross (Epic)
24	29	IT'S BETTER TO TRAVEL	Swing Out Sister (Mercury)
22	30	ECHO AND THE BUNNYMEN	Echo & the Bunnymen (WEA)
27	31	FAMOUS BLUE RAINCOAT	Jennifer Warnes (RCA)
28	32	DUOTONES	Kenny G (Arista)
29	33	MIRACLE	Kane Gang (Kitchenware)
42	34	FASTER PUSSYCAT	Faster Pussycat (Elektra)
25	35	ATLANTIC SOUL	Various Artists (Atlantic)
34	36	SAMANTHA FOX	Samantha Fox (Jive)
31	37	THE UNFORGETTABLE FIRE	U2 (Island)
-	38	THE PRINCE'S TRUST	Various Artists (A&M)
-	39	LIKE A VIRGIN	Madonna (Sire)
-	40	STRONG PERSUADER	Robert Cray Band (Mercury)
39	41	ALL BY MYSELF	Regina Belle (CBS)
-	42	CHANGING FACES – THE VERY BEST OF 10 c.c. AND GODLEY AND CREME	10 c.c. & Godley & Creme (Phonogram)
32	43	APPETITE FOR DESTRUCTION	Guns 'N' Roses (Geffen)
33	44	PRIDE	White Lion (Atlantic)
-	45	MEN AND WOMEN	Simply Red (WEA)
35	46	BROTHERS IN ARMS	Dire Straits (Vertigo)
-	47	GRACELAND	Paul Simon (Warner Bros.)
43	48	THE ISLAND STORY	Various Artists (Island)
45	49	DEFENDER	Rory Gallagher (Demon)
50	50	THE CIRCUS	Erasure (Mute)

5 September 1987

4	1	HYSTERIA	Def Leppard (Bludgen Riffola)
1	2	HITS 6	Various Artists (CBS/WEA/BMG)
13	3	SUBSTANCE	New Order (Factory)
3	4	WHITNEY	Whitney Houston (Arista)
7	5	WHO'S THAT GIRL	Soundtrack (Warner Bros.)
2	6	INTRODUCING THE HARDLINE ACCORDING TO	Terence Trent D'Arby (CBS)
9	7	THE JOSHUA TREE	U2 (Island)
5	8	SIXTIES MIX	Various Artists (Stylus)
8	9	DREAM EVIL	Dio (Vertigo)
6	10	BAD ANIMALS	Heart (Capitol)
18	11	ELVIS PRESLEY - THE ALL TIME GREATEST HITS	Elvis Presley (RCA)
10	12	TRUE BLUE	Madonna (Sire)
16	13	HEARSAY	Alexander O'Neal (Tabu)
11	14	INVISIBLE TOUCH	Genesis (Charisma)
22	15	SLIPPERY WHEN WET	Bon Jovi (Vertigo)
20	16	FLM	Mel & Kim (Supreme)
42	17	CHANGING FACES – THE VERY BEST OF 10 c.c. AND GODLEY AND CREME	10c.c. & Godley & Creme (Phonogram)
24	18	GIVE ME THE REASON	Luther Vandross (Epic)
-	19	PERMANENT VACATION	Aerosmith (Geffen)
15	20	KEEP YOUR DISTANCE	Curiosity Killed The Cat (Mercury)
-	21	SHERRICK	Sherrick (Warner Bros.)
19	22	LA BAMBA	Soundtrack (London)
28	23	FOREVER, FOR ALWAYS, FOR LOVE	Luther Vandross (Epic)
-	24	FRANK'S WILD YEARS	Tom Waits (Island)
12	25	LICENCED TO ILL	Beastie Boys (Def Jam)
43	26	APPETITE FOR DESTRUCTION	Guns 'N' Roses (Geffen)
-	27	ROCK 'N' ROLL	Motorhead (GWR)
14	28	THE RETURN OF BRUNO	Bruce Willis (Motown)
26	29	CLUTCHING AT STRAWS	Marillion (EMI)
25	30	SOLITUDE STANDING	Suzanne Vega (A&M)
-	31	IF I WERE YOUR WOMAN	Stephanie Mills (MCA)
-	32	THE BIG THROWDOWN	Levert (Atlantic)
17	33	KICK IT - THE DEF JAM SAMPLER	Various Artists (Def Jam)
45	34	MEN AND WOMEN	Simply Red (WEA)
27	35	U2 LIVE: UNDER A BLOOD RED SKY	U2 (Island)
30	36	ECHO AND THE BUNNYMEN	Echo & the Bunnymen (WEA)
23	37	TANGO IN THE NIGHT	Fleetwood Mac (Warner Bros.)
31	38	FAMOUS BLUE RAINCOAT	Jennifer Warnes (RCA)
49	39	DEFENDER	Rory Gallagher (Demon)
29	40	IT'S BETTER TO TRAVEL	Swing Out Sister (Mercury)
35	41	ATLANTIC SOUL	Various Artists (Atlantic)
-	42	NEVER TOO MUCH	Luther Vandross (Epic)
-	43	WHITESNAKE 1987	Whitesnake (EMI)
-	44	JUST GETS BETTER WITH TIME	Whispers (MCA)
32	45	DUOTONES	Kenny G (Arista)
38	46	THE PRINCE'S TRUST	Various Artists (A&M)
-	47	SGT PEPPER'S LONELY HEARTS CLUB BAND	Beatles (Parlophone)
37	48	THE UNFORGETTABLE FIRE	U2 (Island)
21	49	LIVE IN THE CITY OF LIGHT	Simple Minds (Virgin)
39	50	LIKE A VIRGIN	Madonna (Sire)

Elvis Presley's *The All Time Greatest Hits*, his first major chart album for many years despite a constant archive-raiding policy by RCA, was a double-album package of his most familiar chartmakers, compiled to mark the 10th anniversary (August 16) of his death. Def Leppard scored their first UK Number 1 with *Hysteria*, after huge US successes, while Heart had their first ever UK Top-Tenner with *Bad Animals*.

12 September 1987

Last	This	Title	Artist (Label)
1	1	HYSTERIA	Def Leppard (Bludgen Riffola)
-	2	BAD	Michael Jackson (Epic)
2	3	HITS 6	Various Artists (CBS/WEA/BMG)
3	4	SUBSTANCE	New Order (Factory)
4	5	WHITNEY	Whitney Houston (Arista)
11	6	ELVIS PRESLEY - THE ALL TIME GREATEST HITS	Elvis Presley (RCA)
6	7	INTRODUCING THE HARDLINE ACCORDING TO	Terence Trent D'Arby (CBS)
17	8	CHANGING FACES – THE VERY BEST OF 10 c.c. AND GODLEY AND CREME	10c.c. & Godley & Creme (Phonogram)
7	9	THE JOSHUA TREE	U2 (Island)
12	10	TRUE BLUE	Madonna (Sire)
10	11	BAD ANIMALS	Heart (Capitol)
5	12	WHO'S THAT GIRL	Soundtrack (Warner Bros.)
8	13	SIXTIES MIX	Various Artists (Stylus)
-	14	DARKLANDS	Jesus & Mary Chain (Blanco y Negro)
18	15	GIVE ME THE REASON	Luther Vandross (Epic)
24	16	FRANK'S WILD YEARS	Tom Waits (Island)
13	17	HEARSAY	Alexander O'Neal (Tabu)
14	18	INVISIBLE TOUCH	Genesis (Charisma)
28	19	THE RETURN OF BRUNO	Bruce Willis (Motown)
21	20	SHERRICK	Sherrick (Warner Bros.)
19	21	PERMANENT VACATION	Aerosmith (Geffen)
9	22	DREAM EVIL	Dio (Vertigo)
25	23	LICENCED TO ILL	Beastie Boys (Def Jam)
15	24	SLIPPERY WHEN WET	Bon Jovi (Vertigo)
16	25	FLM	Mel & Kim (Supreme)
20	26	KEEP YOUR DISTANCE	Curiosity Killed The Cat (Mercury)
37	27	TANGO IN THE NIGHT	Fleetwood Mac (Warner Bros.)
27	28	ROCK 'N' ROLL	Motorhead (GWR)
49	29	LIVE IN THE CITY OF LIGHT	Simple Minds (Virgin)
-	30	THE BEATLES	Beatles (Parlophone)
30	31	SOLITUDE STANDING	Suzanne Vega (A&M)
-	32	SIGN 'O' THE TIMES	Prince (Paisley Park)
-	33	WHERE THE ACTION IS	Westworld (RCA)
29	34	CLUTCHING AT STRAWS	Marillion (EMI)
-	35	TROUBLE OVER HERE	Trouble Funk (Fourth & Broadway)
22	36	LA BAMBA	Soundtrack (London)
38	37	FAMOUS BLUE RAINCOAT	Jennifer Warnes (RCA)
32	38	THE BIG THROWDOWN	Levert (Atlantic)
-	39	JONATHAN BUTLER	Jonathan Butler (Jive)
23	40	FOREVER, FOR ALWAYS, FOR LOVE	Luther Vandross (Epic)
41	41	ATLANTIC SOUL	Various Artists (Atlantic)
35	42	U2 LIVE: UNDER A BLOOD RED SKY	U2 (Island)
-	43	JODY WATLEY	Jody Watley (MCA)
26	44	APPETITE FOR DESTRUCTION	Guns 'N' Roses (Geffen)
-	45	RARE	Various Artists (RCA)
-	46	DOOR TO DOOR	Cars (Elektra)
40	47	IT'S BETTER TO TRAVEL	Swing Out Sister (Mercury)
47	48	SGT PEPPER'S LONELY HEARTS CLUB BAND	Beatles (Parlophone)
33	49	KICK IT - THE DEF JAM SAMPLER	Various Artists (Def Jam)
31	50	IF I WERE YOUR WOMAN	Stephanie Mills (MCA)

19 September 1987

Last	This	Title	Artist (Label)
2	1	BAD	Michael Jackson (Epic)
1	2	HYSTERIA	Def Leppard (Bludgen Riffola)
4	3	SUBSTANCE	New Order (Factory)
14	4	DARKLANDS	Jesus & Mary Chain (Blanco y Negro)
3	5	HITS 6	Various Artists (CBS/WEA/BMG)
9	6	THE JOSHUA TREE	U2 (Island)
8	7	CHANGING FACES – THE VERY BEST OF 10 c.c. AND GODLEY AND CREME	10c.c. & Godley & Creme (Phonogram)
5	8	WHITNEY	Whitney Houston (Arista)
6	9	ELVIS PRESLEY - THE ALL TIME GREATEST HITS	Elvis Presley (RCA)
-	10	ACTUALLY	Pet Shop Boys (Parlophone)
-	11	A MOMENTARY LAPSE OF REASON	Pink Floyd (EMI)
7	12	INTRODUCING THE HARDLINE ACCORDING TO	Terence Trent D'Arby (CBS)
39	13	JONATHAN BUTLER	Jonathan Butler (Jive)
15	14	GIVE ME THE REASON	Luther Vandross (Epic)
18	15	INVISIBLE TOUCH	Genesis (Charisma)
19	16	THE RETURN OF BRUNO	Bruce Willis (Motown)
12	17	WHO'S THAT GIRL	Soundtrack (Warner Bros.)
11	18	BAD ANIMALS	Heart (Capitol)
10	19	TRUE BLUE	Madonna (Sire)
17	20	HEARSAY	Alexander O'Neal (Tabu)
13	21	SIXTIES MIX	Various Artists (Stylus)
-	22	RUNNING IN THE FAMILY	Level 42 (Polydor)
27	23	TANGO IN THE NIGHT	Fleetwood Mac (Warner Bros.)
16	24	FRANK'S WILD YEARS	Tom Waits (Island)
26	25	KEEP YOUR DISTANCE	Curiosity Killed The Cat (Mercury)
20	26	SHERRICK	Sherrick (Warner Bros.)
-	27	BEST OF HOUSE VOL 2	Various Artists (Serious)
-	28	POETIC CHAMPIONS COMPOSE	Van Morrison (Mercury)
21	29	PERMANENT VACATION	Aerosmith (Geffen)
25	30	FLM	Mel & Kim (Supreme)
29	31	LIVE IN THE CITY OF LIGHT	Simple Minds (Virgin)
-	32	CREST OF A KNAVE	Jethro Tull (Chrysalis)
23	33	LICENCED TO ILL	Beastie Boys (Def Jam)
38	34	THE BIG THROWDOWN	Levert (Atlantic)
22	35	DREAM EVIL	Dio (Vertigo)
-	36	PAID IN FULL	Eric B & Rakim (Fourth & Broadway)
-	37	WHITESNAKE 1987	Whitesnake (EMI)
46	38	DOOR TO DOOR	Cars (Elektra)
31	39	SOLITUDE STANDING	Suzanne Vega (A&M)
24	40	SLIPPERY WHEN WET	Bon Jovi (Vertigo)
40	41	FOREVER, FOR ALWAYS, FOR LOVE	Luther Vandross (Epic)
-	42	THRILLER	Michael Jackson (Epic)
41	43	ATLANTIC SOUL	Various Artists (Atlantic)
-	44	AMERICAN ENGLISH	Wax (RCA)
-	45	IN THE DARK	Grateful Dead (Arista)
28	46	ROCK 'N' ROLL	Motorhead (GWR)
-	47	WELCOME TO MY ROOM	Randy Brown (Threeway)
32	48	SIGN 'O' THE TIMES	Prince (Paisley Park)
33	49	WHERE THE ACTION IS	Westworld (RCA)
35	50	TROUBLE OVER HERE	Trouble Funk (Fourth & Broadway)

26 September 1987

Last	This	Title	Artist (Label)
1	1	BAD	Michael Jackson (Epic)
10	2	ACTUALLY	Pet Shop Boys (Parlophone)
11	3	A MOMENTARY LAPSE OF REASON	Pink Floyd (EMI)
2	4	HYSTERIA	Def Leppard (Bludgen Riffola)
7	5	CHANGING FACES – THE VERY BEST OF 10 c.c. AND GODLEY AND CREME	10c.c. & Godley & Creme (Phonogram)
5	6	HITS 6	Various Artists (CBS/WEA/BMG)
3	7	SUBSTANCE	New Order (Factory)
6	8	THE JOSHUA TREE	U2 (Island)
4	9	DARKLANDS	Jesus & Mary Chain (Blanco y Negro)
-	10	DANCING WITH STRANGERS	Chris Rea (Magnet)
-	11	WONDERFUL LIFE	Black (A&M)
13	12	JONATHAN BUTLER	Jonathan Butler (Jive)
8	13	WHITNEY	Whitney Houston (Arista)
9	14	ELVIS PRESLEY - THE ALL TIME GREATEST HITS	Elvis Presley (RCA)
-	15	ALWAYS GUARANTEED	Cliff Richard (EMI)
-	16	BABYLON AND ON	Squeeze (A&M)
12	17	INTRODUCING THE HARDLINE ACCORDING TO	Terence Trent D'Arby (CBS)
-	18	BETWEEN THE LINES	Five Star (RCA)
28	19	POETIC CHAMPIONS COMPOSE	Van Morrison (Mercury)
-	20	LIFE IN THE RAW	W.A.S.P. (Capitol)
19	21	TRUE BLUE	Madonna (Sire)
32	22	CREST OF A KNAVE	Jethro Tull (Chrysalis)
14	23	GIVE ME THE REASON	Luther Vandross (Epic)
17	24	WHO'S THAT GIRL	Soundtrack (Warner Bros.)
22	25	RUNNING IN THE FAMILY	Level 42 (Polydor)
-	26	DOCUMENT	REM (IRS)
-	27	THE CREAM OF ERIC CLAPTON	Eric Clapton (Polydor)
41	28	FOREVER, FOR ALWAYS, FOR LOVE	Luther Vandross (Epic)
-	29	RAINDANCING	Alison Moyet (CBS)
-	30	INVISIBLE TOUCH	Genesis (Charisma)
31	31	LIVE IN THE CITY OF LIGHT	Simple Minds (Virgin)
21	32	SIXTIES MIX	Various Artists (Stylus)
16	33	THE RETURN OF BRUNO	Bruce Willis (Motown)
45	34	IN THE DARK	Grateful Dead (Arista)
43	35	ATLANTIC SOUL	Various Artists (Atlantic)
42	36	THRILLER	Michael Jackson (Epic)
48	37	SIGN 'O' THE TIMES	Prince (Paisley Park)
30	38	FLM	Mel & Kim (Supreme)
37	39	WHITESNAKE 1987	Whitesnake (EMI)
29	40	PERMANENT VACATION	Aerosmith (Geffen)
23	41	TANGO IN THE NIGHT	Fleetwood Mac (Warner Bros.)
39	42	SOLITUDE STANDING	Suzanne Vega (A&M)
27	43	BEST OF HOUSE VOL 2	Various Artists (Serious)
24	44	FRANK'S WILD YEARS	Tom Waits (Island)
26	45	SHERRICK	Sherrick (Warner Bros.)
20	46	HEARSAY	Alexander O'Neal (Tabu)
44	47	AMERICAN ENGLISH	Wax (RCA)
-	48	HAPPY?	PiL (Virgin)
-	49	WOW!	Bananarama (London)
34	50	THE BIG THROWDOWN	Levert (Atlantic)

Michael Jackson's *Bad* broke all existing UK records for first-week sales by a new album, moving over 340,000 copies in its first seven days, and demolishing the existing record of 230,000 set only a few months previously by U2's *The Joshua Tree*. In its first week at the top, it was estimated to be outselling the Number 1 single (Rick Astley's *Never Gonna Give You Up*) by a factor of four to one.

October 1987

3 October 1987

last	this		
1	1	BAD	Michael Jackson (Epic)
10	2	DANCING WITH STRANGERS	Chris Rea (Magnet)
11	3	WONDERFUL LIFE	Black (A&M)
2	4	ACTUALLY	Pet Shop Boys (Parlophone)
3	5	A MOMENTARY LAPSE OF REASON	Pink Floyd (EMI)
15	6	ALWAYS GUARANTEED	Cliff Richard (EMI)
18	7	BETWEEN THE LINES	Five Star (RCA)
5	8	CHANGING FACES – THE VERY BEST OF 10 c.c. AND GODLEY AND CREME	10c.c. & Godley Creme (Phonogram)
4	9	HYSTERIA	Def Leppard (Bludgen Riffola)
-	10	NOW! SMASH HITS	Various Artists (Virgin/EMI)
27	11	THE CREAM OF ERIC CLAPTON	Eric Clapton (Polydor)
-	12	THE PEOPLE WHO GRINNED THEMSELVES TO DEATH	Housemartins (Go! Discs)
26	13	DOCUMENT	REM (IRS)
8	14	THE JOSHUA TREE	U2 (Island)
20	15	LIFE IN THE RAW	W.A.S.P. (Capitol)
-	16	POPPED IN SOULED OUT	Wet Wet Wet (Precious)
13	17	WHITNEY	Whitney Houston (Arista)
-	18	BRIDGE OF SPIES	T'Pau (Siren)
12	19	JONATHAN BUTLER	Jonathan Butler (Jive)
22	20	CREST OF A KNAVE	Jethro Tull (Chrysalis)
14	21	ELVIS PRESLEY - THE ALL TIME GREATEST HITS	Elvis Presley (RCA)
6	22	HITS 6	Various Artists (CBS/WEA/BMG)
19	23	POETIC CHAMPIONS COMPOSE	Van Morrison (Mercury)
21	24	TRUE BLUE	Madonna (Sire)
16	25	BABYLON AND ON	Squeeze (A&M)
7	26	SUBSTANCE	New Order (Factory)
41	27	TANGO IN THE NIGHT	Fleetwood Mac (Warner Bros.)
23	28	GIVE ME THE REASON	Luther Vandross (Epic)
17	29	INTRODUCING THE HARDLINE ACCORDING TO	Terence Trent D'Arby (CBS)
9	30	DARKLANDS	Jesus & Mary Chain (Blanco y Negro)
25	31	RUNNING IN THE FAMILY	Level 42 (Polydor)
44	32	FRANK'S WILD YEARS	Tom Waits (Island)
-	33	A SAMPLE OF BLUE NOTE	Various Artists (Blue Note)
48	34	HAPPY?	PiL (Virgin)
24	35	WHO'S THAT GIRL	Soundtrack (Warner Bros.)
-	36	EXHIBITION	Gary Numan (Beggars Banquet)
-	37	PRIMITIVE COOL	Mick Jagger (CBS)
-	38	LONESOME JUBILEE	John Cougar Mellencamp (Mercury)
-	39	LINDA'S PARTY	Bolshoi (Beggars Banquet)
45	40	SHERRICK	Sherrick (Warner Bros.)
-	41	ANOTHER STEP	Kim Wilde (MCA)
46	42	HEARSAY	Alexander O'Neal (Tabu)
43	43	BEST OF HOUSE VOL 2	Various Artists (Serious)
33	44	THE RETURN OF BRUNO	Bruce Willis (Motown)
34	45	IN THE DARK	Grateful Dead (Arista)
39	46	WHITESNAKE 1987	Whitesnake (EMI)
49	47	WOW!	Bananarama (London)
47	48	AMERICAN ENGLISH	Wax (RCA)
-	49	PORTRAIT	Andres Segovia (Stylus)
-	50	ODYSSEY - THE GREATEST HITS	Odyssey (Stylus)

10 October 1987

last	this		
1	1	BAD	Michael Jackson (Epic)
2	2	DANCING WITH STRANGERS	Chris Rea (Magnet)
3	3	WONDERFUL LIFE	Black (A&M)
10	4	NOW! SMASH HITS	Various Artists (Virgin/EMI)
4	5	ACTUALLY	Pet Shop Boys (Parlophone)
16	6	POPPED IN SOULED OUT	Wet Wet Wet (Precious)
11	7	THE CREAM OF ERIC CLAPTON	Eric Clapton (Polydor)
	8	STRANGEWAYS HERE WE COME	Smiths (Rough Trade)
6	9	ALWAYS GUARANTEED	Cliff Richard (EMI)
12	10	THE PEOPLE WHO GRINNED THEMSELVES TO DEATH	Housemartins (Go! Discs)
9	11	HYSTERIA	Def Leppard (Bludgen Riffola)
7	12	BETWEEN THE LINES	Five Star (RCA)
5	13	A MOMENTARY LAPSE OF REASON	Pink Floyd (EMI)
14	14	THE JOSHUA TREE	U2 (Island)
8	15	CHANGING FACES – THE VERY BEST OF 10 c.c. AND GODLEY AND CREME	10c.c. & Godley & Creme (Phonogram)
-	16	MUSIC FOR THE MASSES	Depeche Mode (Mute)
17	17	WHITNEY	Whitney Houston (Arista)
-	18	BIG GENERATOR	Yes (Atco)
26	19	SUBSTANCE	New Order (Factory)
13	20	DOCUMENT	REM (IRS)
28	21	GIVE ME THE REASON	Luther Vandross (Epic)
37	22	PRIMITIVE COOL	Mick Jagger (CBS)
19	23	JONATHAN BUTLER	Jonathan Butler (Jive)
-	24	HALFWAY TO SANITY	Ramones (Beggars Banquet)
18	25	BRIDGE OF SPIES	T'Pau (Siren)
15	26	LIFE IN THE RAW	W.A.S.P. (Capitol)
24	27	TRUE BLUE	Madonna (Sire)
22	28	HITS 6	Various Artists (CBS/WEA/BMG)
29	29	INTRODUCING THE HARDLINE ACCORDING TO	Terence Trent D'Arby (CBS)
21	30	ELVIS PRESLEY - THE ALL TIME GREATEST HITS	Elvis Presley (RCA)
30	31	DARKLANDS	Jesus & Mary Chain (Blanco y Negro)
27	32	TANGO IN THE NIGHT	Fleetwood Mac (Warner Bros.)
-	33	FIRST (THE SOUND OF MUSIC)	Then Jerico (London)
23	34	POETIC CHAMPIONS COMPOSE	Van Morrison (Mercury)
-	35	ISLANDS	Mike Oldfield (Virgin)
-	36	ATLANTIC SOUL	Various Artists (Atlantic)
-	37	ESP	Bee Gees (Warner Bros.)
20	38	CREST OF A KNAVE	Jethro Tull (Chrysalis)
31	39	RUNNING IN THE FAMILY	Level 42 (Polydor)
34	40	HAPPY?	PiL (Virgin)
25	41	BABYLON AND ON	Squeeze (A&M)
35	42	WHO'S THAT GIRL	Soundtrack (Warner Bros.)
-	43	BAD ANIMALS	Heart (Capitol)
42	44	HEARSAY	Alexander O'Neal (Tabu)
36	45	EXHIBITION	Gary Numan (Beggars Banquet)
38	46	LONESOME JUBILEE	John Cougar Mellencamp (Mercury)
-	47	TRACKS OF MY TEARS	Various Artists (Telstar)
32	48	FRANK'S WILD YEARS	Tom Waits (Island)
-	49	CRUSHIN'	Fat Boys (Urban)
39	50	LINDA'S PARTY	Bolshoi (Beggars Banquet)

17 October 1987

last	this		
1	1	BAD	Michael Jackson (Epic)
8	2	STRANGEWAYS HERE WE COME	Smiths (Rough Trade)
2	3	DANCING WITH STRANGERS	Chris Rea (Magnet)
-	4	TUNNEL OF LOVE	Bruce Springsteen (CBS)
5	5	ACTUALLY	Pet Shop Boys (Parlophone)
6	6	POPPED IN SOULED OUT	Wet Wet Wet (Precious)
16	7	MUSIC FOR THE MASSES	Depeche Mode (Mute)
7	8	THE CREAM OF ERIC CLAPTON	Eric Clapton (Polydor)
3	9	WONDERFUL LIFE	Black (A&M)
9	10	ALWAYS GUARANTEED	Cliff Richard (EMI)
11	11	HYSTERIA	Def Leppard (Bludgen Riffola)
4	12	NOW! SMASH HITS	Various Artists (Virgin/EMI)
10	13	THE PEOPLE WHO GRINNED THEMSELVES TO DEATH	Housemartins (Go! Discs)
12	14	BETWEEN THE LINES	Five Star (RCA)
14	15	THE JOSHUA TREE	U2 (Island)
18	16	BIG GENERATOR	Yes (Atco)
13	17	A MOMENTARY LAPSE OF REASON	Pink Floyd (EMI)
-	18	RED	Communards (London)
15	19	CHANGING FACES – THE VERY BEST OF 10 c.c. AND GODLEY AND CREME	10c.c. & Godley Creme (Phonogram)
29	20	INTRODUCING THE HARDLINE ACCORDING TO	Terence Trent D'Arby (CBS)
17	21	WHITNEY	Whitney Houston (Arista)
19	22	SUBSTANCE	New Order (Factory)
21	23	GIVE ME THE REASON	Luther Vandross (Epic)
37	24	ESP	Bee Gees (Warner Bros.)
32	25	TANGO IN THE NIGHT	Fleetwood Mac (Warner Bros.)
23	26	JONATHAN BUTLER	Jonathan Butler (Jive)
46	27	LONESOME JUBILEE	John Cougar Mellencamp (Mercury)
39	28	RUNNING IN THE FAMILY	Level 42 (Polydor)
27	29	TRUE BLUE	Madonna (Sire)
-	30	THE CIRCUS	Erasure (Mute)
38	31	CREST OF A KNAVE	Jethro Tull (Chrysalis)
24	32	HALFWAY TO SANITY	Ramones (Beggars Banquet)
-	33	PERMANENT VACATION	Aerosmith (Geffen)
20	34	DOCUMENT	REM (IRS)
25	35	BRIDGE OF SPIES	T'Pau (Siren)
28	36	HITS 6	Various Artists (CBS/WEA/BMG)
30	37	ELVIS PRESLEY - THE ALL TIME GREATEST HITS	Elvis Presley (RCA)
35	38	ISLANDS	Mike Oldfield (Virgin)
-	39	IN NO SENSE/NONSENSE	Art of Noise (China)
22	40	PRIMITIVE COOL	Mick Jagger (CBS)
36	41	ATLANTIC SOUL	Various Artists (Atlantic)
-	42	DO IT AGAIN - THE VERY BEST OF STEELY DAN	Steely Dan (Telstar)
31	43	DARKLANDS	Jesus & Mary Chain (Blanco y Negro)
-	44	BEST OF JAMES BROWN	James Brown (K-Tel)
33	45	FIRST (THE SOUND OF MUSIC)	Then Jerico (London)
26	46	LIFE IN THE RAW	W.A.S.P. (Capitol)
-	47	REFLECTIONS	Foster & Allen (Stylus)
41	48	BABYLON AND ON	Squeeze (A&M)
43	49	BAD ANIMALS	Heart (Capitol)
-	50	ODYSSEY - GREATEST HITS	Odyssey (Stylus)

Chris Rea had by far his biggest-selling album to date (and first Top 5 entry) with *Dancing With Strangers*, even though at Number 2 it was hardly denting the sort of sales which were keeping *Bad* in place at the chart top. The Number 13 placing for *Document* was also the highest UK chart position yet reached by the still somewhat cultish US band REM, whose mega-sales were to arrive during the 1990s.

24 October 1987

last week	this week	title	artist (label)
4	1	TUNNEL OF LOVE	Bruce Springsteen (CBS)
1	2	BAD	Michael Jackson (Epic)
2	3	STRANGEWAYS HERE WE COME	Smiths (Rough Trade)
9	4	WONDERFUL LIFE	Black (A&M)
18	5	RED	Communards (London)
8	6	THE CREAM OF ERIC CLAPTON	Eric Clapton (Polydor)
5	7	ACTUALLY	Pet Shop Boys (Parlophone)
3	8	DANCING WITH STRANGERS	Chris Rea (Magnet)
6	9	POPPED IN SOULED OUT	Wet Wet Wet (Precious)
-	10	NOTHING LIKE THE SUN	Sting (A&M)
12	11	NOW! SMASH HITS	Various Artists (Virgin/EMI)
19	12	CHANGING FACES – THE VERY BEST OF 10 c.c. AND GODLEY AND CREME	10c.c. & Godley & Creme (Phonogram)
24	13	ESP	Bee Gees (Warner Bros.)
-	14	ALPHABET CITY	ABC (Neutron)
25	15	TANGO IN THE NIGHT	Fleetwood Mac (Warner Bros.)
14	16	BETWEEN THE LINES	Five Star (RCA)
10	17	ALWAYS GUARANTEED	Cliff Richard (EMI)
11	18	HYSTERIA	Def Leppard (Bludgen Riffola)
7	19	MUSIC FOR THE MASSES	Depeche Mode (Mute)
15	20	THE JOSHUA TREE	U2 (Island)
21	21	WHITNEY	Whitney Houston (Arista)
20	22	INTRODUCING THE HARDLINE ACCORDING TO	Terence Trent D'Arby (CBS)
17	23	A MOMENTARY LAPSE OF REASON	Pink Floyd (EMI)
16	24	BIG GENERATOR	Yes (Atco)
-	25	HIT FACTORY	Various Artists (Stylus)
-	26	UPFRONT 8	Various Artists (Serious)
13	27	THE PEOPLE WHO GRINNED THEMSELVES TO DEATH	Housemartins (Go! Discs)
44	28	BEST OF JAMES BROWN	James Brown (K-Tel)
23	29	GIVE ME THE REASON	Luther Vandross (Epic)
27	30	LONESOME JUBILEE	John Cougar Mellencamp (Mercury)
38	31	ISLANDS	Mike Oldfield (Virgin)
-	32	AFTER DARK	Ray Parker Jnr (Warner Bros.)
-	33	RARE GROOVES	Various Artists (RCA/Arista)
-	34	CRUSHIN'	Fat Boys (Urban)
28	35	RUNNING IN THE FAMILY	Level 42 (Polydor)
30	36	THE CIRCUS	Erasure (Mute)
49	37	BAD ANIMALS	Heart (Capitol)
-	38	THE RIGHT NIGHT AND BARRY WHITE	Barry White (A&M)
-	39	TRACKS OF MY TEARS	Various Artists (Telstar)
-	40	TRUE LOVE	Various Artists (K-Tel)
22	41	SUBSTANCE	New Order (Factory)
29	42	TRUE BLUE	Madonna (Sire)
26	43	JONATHAN BUTLER	Jonathan Butler (Jive)
-	44	SONIC FLOWER GROOVE	Primal Scream (Elevation)
-	45	MIAMI VICE 2	Various Artists (MCA)
35	46	BRIDGE OF SPIES	T'Pau (Siren)
-	47	THE HOUSE OF DOLLS	Gene Loves Jezebel (Beggars Banquet)
32	48	HALFWAY TO SANITY	Ramones (Beggars Banquet)
40	49	PRIMITIVE COOL	Mick Jagger (CBS)
48	50	BABYLON AND ON	Squeeze (A&M)

31 October 1987

last week	this week	title	artist (label)
1	1	TUNNEL OF LOVE	Bruce Springsteen (CBS)
10	2	NOTHING LIKE THE SUN	Sting (A&M)
2	3	BAD	Michael Jackson (Epic)
13	4	ESP	Bee Gees (Warner Bros.)
14	5	ALPHABET CITY	ABC (Neutron)
6	6	THE CREAM OF ERIC CLAPTON	Eric Clapton (Polydor)
5	7	RED	Communards (London)
15	8	TANGO IN THE NIGHT	Fleetwood Mac (Warner Bros.)
4	9	WONDERFUL LIFE	Black (A&M)
8	10	DANCING WITH STRANGERS	Chris Rea (Magnet)
16	11	BETWEEN THE LINES	Five Star (RCA)
9	12	POPPED IN SOULED OUT	Wet Wet Wet (Precious)
3	13	STRANGEWAYS HERE WE COME	Smiths (Rough Trade)
7	14	ACTUALLY	Pet Shop Boys (Parlophone)
22	15	INTRODUCING THE HARDLINE ACCORDING TO	Terence Trent D'Arby (CBS)
12	16	CHANGING FACES – THE VERY BEST OF 10 c.c. AND GODLEY AND CREME	10c.c. & Godley & Creme (Phonogram)
-	17	SIMPLY SHADOWS	Shadows (Polydor)
-	18	THE CHRISTIANS	Christians (Island)
11	19	NOW! SMASH HITS	Various Artists (Virgin/EMI)
20	20	THE JOSHUA TREE	U2 (Island)
28	21	BEST OF JAMES BROWN	James Brown (K-Tel)
-	22	REFLECTIONS	Foster & Allen (Stylus)
30	23	LONESOME JUBILEE	John Cougar Mellencamp (Mercury)
26	24	UPFRONT 8	Various Artists (Serious)
21	25	WHITNEY	Whitney Houston (Arista)
36	26	THE CIRCUS	Erasure (Mute)
23	27	A MOMENTARY LAPSE OF REASON	Pink Floyd (EMI)
37	28	BAD ANIMALS	Heart (Capitol)
27	29	THE PEOPLE WHO GRINNED THEMSELVES TO DEATH	Housemartins (Go! Discs)
-	30	GEORGE BEST	Wedding Present (Reception)
17	31	ALWAYS GUARANTEED	Cliff Richard (EMI)
18	32	HYSTERIA	Def Leppard (Bludgen Riffola)
24	33	BIG GENERATOR	Yes (Atco)
46	34	BRIDGE OF SPIES	T'Pau (Siren)
25	35	HIT FACTORY	Various Artists (Stylus)
19	36	MUSIC FOR THE MASSES	Depeche Mode (Mute)
32	37	AFTER DARK	Ray Parker Jnr (Warner Bros.)
-	38	PERMANENT VACATION	Aerosmith (Geffen)
-	39	GLENN JONES	Glenn Jones (Jive)
-	40	STREET SOUNDS HIP HOP 18	Various Artists (Street Sounds)
29	41	GIVE ME THE REASON	Luther Vandross (Epic)
-	42	HIT FACTORY	Various Artists (Stylus)
-	43	ODYSSEY - THE GREATEST HITS	Odyssey (Stylus)
35	44	RUNNING IN THE FAMILY	Level 42 (Polydor)
-	45	JUST VISITING THIS PLANET	Jellybean (Chrysalis)
43	46	JONATHAN BUTLER	Jonathan Butler (Jive)
50	47	BABYLON AND ON	Squeeze (A&M)
39	48	TRACKS OF MY TEARS	Various Artists (Telstar)
41	49	SUBSTANCE	New Order (Factory)
-	50	PERFECT TIMING	MSG (EMI)

7 November 1987

last week	this week	title	artist (label)
2	1	NOTHING LIKE THE SUN	Sting (A&M)
4	2	ESP	Bee Gees (Warner Bros.)
8	3	TANGO IN THE NIGHT	Fleetwood Mac (Warner Bros.)
3	4	BAD	Michael Jackson (Epic)
1	5	TUNNEL OF LOVE	Bruce Springsteen (CBS)
18	6	THE CHRISTIANS	Christians (Island)
14	7	ACTUALLY	Pet Shop Boys (Parlophone)
34	8	BRIDGE OF SPIES	T'Pau (Siren)
6	9	THE CREAM OF ERIC CLAPTON	Eric Clapton (Polydor)
-	10	CRAZY NIGHTS	Kiss (Vertigo)
13	11	STRANGEWAYS HERE WE COME	Smiths (Rough Trade)
-	12	BEST OF UB40 VOL 1	UB40 (Virgin)
5	13	ALPHABET CITY	ABC (Neutron)
-	14	MAINSTREAM	Lloyd Cole & the Commotions (Polydor)
20	15	THE JOSHUA TREE	U2 (Island)
15	16	INTRODUCING THE HARDLINE ACCORDING TO	Terence Trent D'Arby (CBS)
17	17	SIMPLY SHADOWS	Shadows (Polydor)
-	18	THE SINGLES	Pretenders (WEA)
-	19	CHRONICLES	Steve Winwood (Island)
20	20	BEST OF JAMES BROWN	James Brown (K-Tel)
9	21	WONDERFUL LIFE	Black (A&M)
10	22	DANCING WITH STRANGERS	Chris Rea (Magnet)
7	23	RED	Communards (London)
11	24	BETWEEN THE LINES	Five Star (RCA)
22	25	REFLECTIONS	Foster & Allen (Stylus)
-	26	BEST SHOTS	Pat Benatar (Chrysalis)
31	27	ALWAYS GUARANTEED	Cliff Richard (EMI)
16	28	CHANGING FACES – THE VERY BEST OF 10 c.c. AND GODLEY AND CREME	10c.c. & Godley & Creme (Phonogram)
27	29	A MOMENTARY LAPSE OF REASON	Pink Floyd (EMI)
12	30	POPPED IN SOULED OUT	Wet Wet Wet (Precious)
-	31	RAISE YOUR FIST AND YELL	Alice Cooper (MCA)
25	32	WHITNEY	Whitney Houston (Arista)
35	33	HIT FACTORY	Various Artists (Stylus)
-	34	SIRIUS	Clannad (RCA)
39	35	GLENN JONES	Glenn Jones (Jive)
26	36	THE CIRCUS	Erasure (Mute)
19	37	NOW! SMASH HITS	Various Artists (Virgin/EMI)
-	38	ABBEY ROAD	Beatles (Parlophone)
24	39	UPFRONT 8	Various Artists (Serious)
23	40	LONESOME JUBILEE	John Cougar Mellencamp (Mercury)
37	41	AFTER DARK	Ray Parker Jnr (Warner Bros.)
-	42	HEARSAY	Alexander O'Neal (Tabu)
45	43	JUST VISITING THIS PLANET	Jellybean (Chrysalis)
30	44	GEORGE BEST	Wedding Present (Reception)
32	45	HYSTERIA	Def Leppard (Bludgen Riffola)
-	46	FROM MOTOWN WITH LOVE	Various Artists (K-Tel)
41	47	GIVE ME THE REASON	Luther Vandross (Epic)
28	48	BAD ANIMALS	Heart (Capitol)
-	49	JACKMASTER VOL 1	Various Artists (DJ International)
43	50	ODYSSEY - THE GREATEST HITS	Odyssey (Stylus)

It took the long-awaited new album by Bruce Springsteen, *Tunnel Of Love*, to muster enough sales to overtake Michael Jackson and snatch Number 1. Also in close contention were the Bee Gees, whose *ESP* was their first UK chart album since their greatest hits set made the Top 10 almost eight years earlier. The trio were simultaneously back at the top of the singles chart, with *You Win Again*.

November 1987

14 November 1987

last	this		
3	1	TANGO IN THE NIGHT	Fleetwood Mac (Warner Bros.)
8	2	BRIDGE OF SPIES	T'Pau (Siren)
18	3	THE SINGLES	Pretenders (WEA)
12	4	BEST OF UB40 VOL 1	UB40 (Virgin)
10	5	CRAZY NIGHTS	Kiss (Vertigo)
-	6	FAITH	George Michael (Epic)
1	7	NOTHING LIKE THE SUN	Sting (A&M)
14	8	MAINSTREAM	Lloyd Cole & the Commotions (Polydor)
19	9	CHRONICLES	Steve Winwood (Island)
6	10	THE CHRISTIANS	Christians (Island)
4	11	BAD	Michael Jackson (Epic)
2	12	ESP	Bee Gees (Warner Bros.)
26	13	BEST SHOTS	Pat Benatar (Chrysalis)
5	14	TUNNEL OF LOVE	Bruce Springsteen (CBS)
-	15	BETE NOIRE	Bryan Ferry (Virgin)
-	16	ALL THE BEST!	Paul McCartney (Parlophone)
7	17	ACTUALLY	Pet Shop Boys (Parlophone)
9	18	THE CREAM OF ERIC CLAPTON	Eric Clapton (Polydor)
17	19	SIMPLY SHADOWS	Shadows (Polydor)
16	20	INTRODUCING THE HARDLINE ACCORDING TO	Terence Trent D'Arby (CBS)
25	21	REFLECTIONS	Foster & Allen (Stylus)
-	22	SEDUCED AND ABANDONED	Hue And Cry (Circa)
31	23	RAISE YOUR FIST AND YELL	Alice Cooper (MCA)
24	24	BETWEEN THE LINES	Five Star (RCA)
-	25	CLOUD NINE	George Harrison (Dark Horse)
22	26	DANCING WITH STRANGERS	Chris Rea (Magnet)
36	27	THE CIRCUS	Erasure (Mute)
15	28	THE JOSHUA TREE	U2 (Island)
-	29	EYE OF THE HURRICANE	Alarm (IRS)
34	30	SIRIUS	Clannad (RCA)
41	31	AFTER DARK	Ray Parker Jnr (Warner Bros.)
11	32	STRANGEWAYS HERE WE COME	Smiths (Rough Trade)
21	33	WONDERFUL LIFE	Black (A&M)
33	34	HIT FACTORY	Various Artists (Stylus)
20	35	BEST OF JAMES BROWN	James Brown (K-Tel)
23	36	RED	Communards (London)
47	37	GIVE ME THE REASON	Luther Vandross (Epic)
46	38	FROM MOTOWN WITH LOVE	Various Artists (K-Tel)
28	39	CHANGING FACES – THE VERY BEST OF 10 c.c. AND GODLEY AND CREME	10c.c. & Godley & Creme (Phonogram)
-	40	RUNNING IN THE FAMILY	Level 42 (Polydor)
-	41	DIRTY DANCING	Soundtrack (RCA)
-	42	DRILL YOUR OWN HOLE	Gaye Bykers On Acid (Virgin)
27	43	ALWAYS GUARANTEED	Cliff Richard (EMI)
13	44	ALPHABET CITY	ABC (Neutron)
-	45	SECRETS OF THE BEEHIVE	David Sylvian (Virgin)
29	46	A MOMENTARY LAPSE OF REASON	Pink Floyd (EMI)
-	47	LIVE AT WEMBLEY	Meat Loaf (RCA)
-	48	CALENTURE	Triffids (Island)
30	49	POPPED IN SOULED OUT	Wet Wet Wet (Precious)
32	50	WHITNEY	Whitney Houston (Arista)

21 November 1987

6	1	FAITH	George Michael (Epic)
2	2	BRIDGE OF SPIES	T'Pau (Siren)
1	3	TANGO IN THE NIGHT	Fleetwood Mac (Warner Bros.)
16	4	ALL THE BEST!	Paul McCartney (Parlophone)
4	5	BEST OF UB40 VOL 1	UB40 (Virgin)
3	6	THE SINGLES	Pretenders (WEA)
15	7	BETE NOIRE	Bryan Ferry (Virgin)
25	8	CLOUD NINE	George Harrison (Dark Horse)
13	9	BEST SHOTS	Pat Benatar (Chrysalis)
12	10	ESP	Bee Gees (Warner Bros.)
10	11	THE CHRISTIANS	Christians (Island)
11	12	BAD	Michael Jackson (Epic)
-	13	SAVAGE	Eurythmics (RCA)
7	14	NOTHING LIKE THE SUN	Sting (A&M)
40	15	RUNNING IN THE FAMILY	Level 42 (Polydor)
-	16	HOLD YOUR FIRE	Rush (Vertigo)
38	17	FROM MOTOWN WITH LOVE	Various Artists (K-Tel)
9	18	CHRONICLES	Steve Winwood (Island)
14	19	TUNNEL OF LOVE	Bruce Springsteen (CBS)
8	20	MAINSTREAM	Lloyd Cole & the Commotions (Polydor)
29	21	EYE OF THE HURRICANE	Alarm (IRS)
-	22	CONTROL - THE REMIXES	Janet Jackson (Breakout)
36	23	RED	Communards (London)
19	24	SIMPLY SHADOWS	Shadows (Polydor)
5	25	CRAZY NIGHTS	Kiss (Vertigo)
17	26	ACTUALLY	Pet Shop Boys (Parlophone)
41	27	DIRTY DANCING	Soundtrack (RCA)
-	28	GET RHYTHM	Ry Cooder (Warner Bros.)
20	29	INTRODUCING THE HARDLINE ACCORDING TO	Terence Trent D'Arby (CBS)
18	30	THE CREAM OF ERIC CLAPTON	Eric Clapton (Polydor)
-	31	HEARSAY	Alexander O'Neal (Tabu)
26	32	DANCING WITH STRANGERS	Chris Rea (Magnet)
30	33	SIRIUS	Clannad (RCA)
31	34	AFTER DARK	Ray Parker Jnr (Warner Bros.)
34	35	HIT FACTORY	Various Artists (Stylus)
32	36	STRANGEWAYS HERE WE COME	Smiths (Rough Trade)
42	37	DRILL YOUR OWN HOLE	Gaye Bykers On Acid (Virgin)
-	38	URBAN CLASSICS	Various Artists (Urban)
-	39	IT'S CALLED LOVE	Aztec Camera (WEA)
48	40	CALENTURE	Triffids (Island)
35	41	BEST OF JAMES BROWN	James Brown (K-Tel)
-	42	THE LOVE SONGS	Randy Crawford (Telstar)
21	43	REFLECTIONS	Foster & Allen (Stylus)
-	44	ROBBIE ROBERTSON	Robbie Robertson (Geffen)
33	45	WONDERFUL LIFE	Black (A&M)
-	46	ESCAPE FROM TV	Jan Hammer (MCA)
-	47	BEST OF HOUSE VOL 3	Various Artists (Serious)
45	48	SECRETS OF THE BEEHIVE	David Sylvian (Virgin)
22	49	SEDUCED AND ABANDONED	Hue And Cry (Circa)
23	50	RAISE YOUR FIST AND YELL	Alice Cooper (MCA)

28 November 1987

2	1	BRIDGE OF SPIES	T'Pau (Siren)
4	2	ALL THE BEST!	Paul McCartney (Parlophone)
5	3	BEST OF UB40 VOL 1	UB40 (Virgin)
3	4	TANGO IN THE NIGHT	Fleetwood Mac (Warner Bros.)
13	5	SAVAGE	Eurythmics (RCA)
1	6	FAITH	George Michael (Epic)
6	7	THE SINGLES	Pretenders (WEA)
8	8	CLOUD NINE	George Harrison (Dark Horse)
9	9	BEST SHOTS	Pat Benatar (Chrysalis)
16	10	HOLD YOUR FIRE	Rush (Vertigo)
-	11	YOU CAN DANCE	Madonna (Sire)
-	12	FLOODLANDS	Sisters of Mercy (WEA)
-	13	WHENEVER YOU NEED SOMEBODY	Rick Astley (RCA)
17	14	FROM MOTOWN WITH LOVE	Various Artists (K-Tel)
10	15	ESP	Bee Gees (Warner Bros.)
12	16	BAD	Michael Jackson (Epic)
-	17	GREATEST HITS OF '87	Various Artists (Telstar)
15	18	RUNNING IN THE FAMILY	Level 42 (Polydor)
26	19	ACTUALLY	Pet Shop Boys (Parlophone)
7	20	BETE NOIRE	Bryan Ferry (Virgin)
35	21	HIT FACTORY	Various Artists (Stylus)
43	22	REFLECTIONS	Foster & Allen (Stylus)
30	23	THE CREAM OF ERIC CLAPTON	Eric Clapton (Polydor)
22	24	CONTROL - THE REMIXES	Janet Jackson (Breakout)
-	25	WHITNEY	Whitney Houston (Arista)
14	26	NOTHING LIKE THE SUN	Sting (A&M)
25	27	CRAZY NIGHTS	Kiss (Vertigo)
-	28	MY BABY JUST CARES FOR ME	Nina Simone (Charly)
21	29	EYE OF THE HURRICANE	Alarm (IRS)
11	30	THE CHRISTIANS	Christians (Island)
18	31	CHRONICLES	Steve Winwood (Island)
19	32	TUNNEL OF LOVE	Bruce Springsteen (CBS)
24	33	SIMPLY SHADOWS	Shadows (Polydor)
-	34	CHARACTERS	Stevie Wonder (Motown)
42	35	THE LOVE SONGS	Randy Crawford (Telstar)
23	36	RED	Communards (London)
36	37	STRANGEWAYS HERE WE COME	Smiths (Rough Trade)
39	38	IT'S CALLED LOVE	Aztec Camera (WEA)
27	39	DIRTY DANCING	Soundtrack (RCA)
28	40	GET RHYTHM	Ry Cooder (Warner Bros.)
-	41	KICK	INXS (Mercury)
20	42	MAINSTREAM	Lloyd Cole & the Commotions (Polydor)
31	43	HEARSAY	Alexander O'Neal (Tabu)
-	44	SIXTIES MIX	Various Artists (Stylus)
-	45	THE LOVE SONGS	Michael Jackson & Diana Ross (Telstar)
-	46	KOHYEP - LIVE IN LENINGRAD	Billy Joel (CBS)
32	47	DANCING WITH STRANGERS	Chris Rea (Magnet)
29	48	INTRODUCING THE HARDLINE ACCORDING TO	Terence Trent D'Arby (CBS)
44	49	ROBBIE ROBERTSON	Robbie Robertson (Geffen)
-	50	MY FAIR LADY	Kiri Te Kanawa (Decca)

After originally peaking at Number 2 shortly after its release in April, Fleetwood Mac's *Tango In The Night* finally made Number 1 six months later, having in the interim descended as low as 41 before reasserting itself. A factor in the resurrection was certainly the Top 5 success of the extracted single *Little Lies*, but *Tango* would now remain a highly-charted album for some months to come.

5 December 1987

last week	this week	Title	Artist (Label)
13	1	WHENEVER YOU NEED SOMEBODY	Rick Astley (RCA)
1	2	BRIDGE OF SPIES	T'Pau (Siren)
3	3	BEST OF UB40 VOL 1	UB40 (Virgin)
2	4	ALL THE BEST!	Paul McCartney (Parlophone)
11	5	YOU CAN DANCE	Madonna (Sire)
6	6	FAITH	George Michael (Epic)
4	7	TANGO IN THE NIGHT	Fleetwood Mac (Warner Bros.)
7	8	THE SINGLES	Pretenders (WEA)
-	9	HITS 7	Various Artists (CBS/WEA/BMG)
-	10	NOW THAT'S WHAT I CALL MUSIC10	Various Artists (EMI/Virgin/PolyGram)
12	11	FLOODLANDS	Sisters of Mercy (WEA)
9	12	BEST SHOTS	Pat Benatar (Chrysalis)
14	13	FROM MOTOWN WITH LOVE	Various Artists (K-Tel)
5	14	SAVAGE	Eurythmics (RCA)
16	15	BAD	Michael Jackson (Epic)
17	16	GREATEST HITS OF '87	Various Artists (Telstar)
8	17	CLOUD NINE	George Harrison (Dark Horse)
19	18	ACTUALLY	Pet Shop Boys (Parlophone)
43	19	HEARSAY	Alexander O'Neal (Tabu)
32	20	TUNNEL OF LOVE	Bruce Springsteen (CBS)
33	21	SIMPLY SHADOWS	Shadows (Polydor)
25	22	WHITNEY	Whitney Houston (Arista)
41	23	KICK	INXS (Mercury)
30	24	THE CHRISTIANS	Christians (Island)
15	25	ESP	Bee Gees (Warner Bros.)
34	26	CHARACTERS	Stevie Wonder (Motown)
42	27	MAINSTREAM	Lloyd Cole & the Commotions (Polydor)
18	28	RUNNING IN THE FAMILY	Level 42 (Polydor)
22	29	REFLECTIONS	Foster & Allen (Stylus)
-	30	SPECIAL OLYMPICS – A VERY SPECIAL CHRISTMAS	Various Artists (A&M)
45	31	THE LOVE SONGS	Michael Jackson & Diana Ross (Telstar)
20	32	BETE NOIRE	Bryan Ferry (Virgin)
26	33	NOTHING LIKE THE SUN	Sting (A&M)
44	34	SIXTIES MIX	Various Artists (Stylus)
36	35	RED	Communards (London)
-	36	ALWAYS GUARANTEED	Cliff Richard (EMI)
39	37	DIRTY DANCING	Soundtrack (RCA)
10	38	HOLD YOUR FIRE	Rush (Vertigo)
-	39	BACK FOR THE ATTACK	Dokken (Elektra)
28	40	MY BABY JUST CARES FOR ME	Nina Simone (Charly)
37	41	STRANGEWAYS HERE WE COME	Smiths (Rough Trade)
21	42	HIT FACTORY	Various Artists (Stylus)
23	43	THE CREAM OF ERIC CLAPTON	Eric Clapton (Polydor)
31	44	CHRONICLES	Steve Winwood (Island)
24	45	CONTROL - THE REMIXES	Janet Jackson (Breakout)
40	46	GET RHYTHM	Ry Cooder (Warner Bros.)
48	47	INTRODUCING THE HARDLINE ACCORDING TO	Terence Trent D'Arby (CBS)
47	48	DANCING WITH STRANGERS	Chris Rea (Magnet)
-	49	LOVE CHANGES	Kashif (Arista)
46	50	KOHYEPT- LIVE IN LENINGRAD	Billy Joel (CBS)

12 December 1987

last week	this week	Title	Artist (Label)
10	1	NOW THAT'S WHAT I CALL MUSIC10	Various Artists (EMI/Virgin/PolyGram)
1	2	WHENEVER YOU NEED SOMEBODY	Rick Astley (RCA)
9	3	HITS 7	Various Artists (CBS/WEA/BMG)
2	4	BRIDGE OF SPIES	T'Pau (Siren)
3	5	BEST OF UB40 VOL 1	UB40 (Virgin)
4	6	ALL THE BEST!	Paul McCartney (Parlophone)
8	7	THE SINGLES	Pretenders (WEA)
7	8	TANGO IN THE NIGHT	Fleetwood Mac (Warner Bros.)
5	9	YOU CAN DANCE	Madonna (Sire)
15	10	BAD	Michael Jackson (Epic)
31	11	THE LOVE SONGS	Michael Jackson & Diana Ross (Telstar)
6	12	FAITH	George Michael (Epic)
21	13	SIMPLY SHADOWS	Shadows (Polydor)
12	14	BEST SHOTS	Pat Benatar (Chrysalis)
18	15	ACTUALLY	Pet Shop Boys (Parlophone)
13	16	FROM MOTOWN WITH LOVE	Various Artists (K-Tel)
19	17	HEARSAY	Alexander O'Neal (Tabu)
22	18	WHITNEY	Whitney Houston (Arista)
36	19	ALWAYS GUARANTEED	Cliff Richard (EMI)
-	20	SONGS FROM STAGE AND SCREEN	Michael Crawford (Telstar)
17	21	CLOUD NINE	George Harrison (Dark Horse)
11	22	FLOODLANDS	Sisters of Mercy (WEA)
14	23	SAVAGE	Eurythmics (RCA)
-	24	MAXI	Maxi Priest (10)
29	25	REFLECTIONS	Foster & Allen (Stylus)
35	26	RED	Communards (London)
28	27	RUNNING IN THE FAMILY	Level 42 (Polydor)
47	28	INTRODUCING THE HARDLINE ACCORDING TO	Terence Trent D'Arby (CBS)
16	29	GREATEST HITS OF '87	Various Artists (Telstar)
-	30	SENTIMENTALLY YOURS	Rose Marie (Telstar)
-	31	THE JOSHUA TREE	U2 (Island)
27	32	MAINSTREAM	Lloyd Cole & the Commotions (Polydor)
-	33	THE LIGHT AT THE END OF THE TUNNEL	Damned (MCA)
34	34	SIXTIES MIX	Various Artists (Stylus)
25	35	ESP	Bee Gees (Warner Bros.)
33	36	NOTHING LIKE THE SUN	Sting (A&M)
45	37	CONTROL - THE REMIXES	Janet Jackson (Breakout)
41	38	STRANGEWAYS HERE WE COME	Smiths (Rough Trade)
-	39	WHITESNAKE 1987	Whitesnake (EMI)
40	40	MY BABY JUST CARES FOR ME	Nina Simone (Charly)
49	41	LOVE CHANGES	Kashif (Arista)
43	42	THE CREAM OF ERIC CLAPTON	Eric Clapton (Polydor)
20	43	TUNNEL OF LOVE	Bruce Springsteen (CBS)
24	44	THE CHRISTIANS	Christians (Island)
30	45	SPECIAL OLYMPICS – A VERY SPECIAL CHRISTMAS	Various Artists (A&M)
37	46	DIRTY DANCING	Soundtrack (RCA)
23	47	KICK	INXS (Mercury)
-	48	MEMORIES	Elaine Paige (Telstar)
26	49	CHARACTERS	Stevie Wonder (Motown)
-	50	ALWAYS AND FOREVER	Various Artists (Telstar)

19 December 1987

last week	this week	Title	Artist (Label)
1	1	NOW THAT'S WHAT I CALL MUSIC10	Various Artists (EMI/Virgin/PolyGram)
3	2	HITS 7	Various Artists (CBS/WEA/BMG)
2	3	WHENEVER YOU NEED SOMEBODY	Rick Astley (RCA)
6	4	ALL THE BEST!	Paul McCartney (Parlophone)
4	5	BRIDGE OF SPIES	T'Pau (Siren)
10	6	BAD	Michael Jackson (Epic)
7	7	THE SINGLES	Pretenders (WEA)
5	8	BEST OF UB40 VOL 1	UB40 (Virgin)
8	9	TANGO IN THE NIGHT	Fleetwood Mac (Warner Bros.)
12	10	FAITH	George Michael (Epic)
9	11	YOU CAN DANCE	Madonna (Sire)
13	12	SIMPLY SHADOWS	Shadows (Polydor)
15	13	ACTUALLY	Pet Shop Boys (Parlophone)
20	14	SONGS FROM STAGE AND SCREEN	Michael Crawford (Telstar)
17	15	HEARSAY	Alexander O'Neal (Tabu)
18	16	WHITNEY	Whitney Houston (Arista)
19	17	ALWAYS GUARANTEED	Cliff Richard (EMI)
34	18	SIXTIES MIX	Various Artists (Stylus)
11	19	THE LOVE SONGS	Michael Jackson & Diana Ross (Telstar)
14	20	BEST SHOTS	Pat Benatar (Chrysalis)
42	21	THE CREAM OF ERIC CLAPTON	Eric Clapton (Polydor)
39	22	WHITESNAKE 1987	Whitesnake (EMI)
-	23	RAINDANCING	Alison Moyet (CBS)
-	24	THIS IS THE STORY	Proclaimers (Chrysalis)
-	25	SONGS OF LOVE	Richard Clayderman (Decca)
25	26	REFLECTIONS	Foster & Allen (Stylus)
23	27	SAVAGE	Eurythmics (RCA)
16	28	FROM MOTOWN WITH LOVE	Various Artists (K-Tel)
48	29	MEMORIES	Elaine Paige (Telstar)
30	30	SENTIMENTALLY YOURS	Rose Marie (Telstar)
21	31	CLOUD NINE	George Harrison (Dark Horse)
-	32	BETWEEN THE LINES	Five Star (RCA)
26	33	RED	Communards (London)
35	34	ESP	Bee Gees (Warner Bros.)
32	35	MAINSTREAM	Lloyd Cole & the Commotions (Polydor)
-	36	A PORTRAIT OF MARIO LANZA	Mario Lanza (Stylus)
24	37	MAXI	Maxi Priest (10)
44	38	THE CHRISTIANS	Christians (Island)
33	39	THE LIGHT AT THE END OF THE TUNNEL	Damned (MCA)
-	40	NO MORE COCOONS	Jello Biafra (Alternative Tentacles)
40	41	MY BABY JUST CARES FOR ME	Nina Simone (Charly)
28	42	INTRODUCING THE HARDLINE ACCORDING TO	Terence Trent D'Arby (CBS)
31	43	THE JOSHUA TREE	U2 (Island)
27	44	RUNNING IN THE FAMILY	Level 42 (Polydor)
36	45	NOTHING LIKE THE SUN	Sting (A&M)
29	46	GREATEST HITS OF '87	Various Artists (Telstar)
-	47	POPPED IN SOULED OUT	Wet Wet Wet (Precious)
45	48	SPECIAL OLYMPICS – A VERY SPECIAL CHRISTMAS	Various Artists (A&M)
-	49	GOOD LOVE	M'lissa Morgan (Capitol)
-	50	THE CIRCUS	Erasure (Mute)

Although Rick Asley's debut album was hotly tipped as the likely biggest seller for the end of the year (and did reach Number 1), the actual battle, with more than a touch of deja vu about it, was between the inevitable *Now* and *Hits* compilations. In a repeat of the previous year's result, the *Now* volume won the contest, settling into its second week at the top as its rival moved up to Number 2 during Christmas week.

Tina Turner's been singing since the 60s, but made it biggest in the late 80s.
Bottom left: Pet Shop Boys
Below: Whitney Houston

9 January 1988

last week	this week	Title	Artist (Label)
1	1	NOW THAT'S WHAT I CALL MUSIC10	Various Artists (EMI/Virgin/PolyGram)
2	2	HITS 7	Various Artists (CBS/WEA/BMG)
3	3	WHENEVER YOU NEED SOMEBODY	Rick Astley (RCA)
4	4	ALL THE BEST!	Paul McCartney (Parlophone)
5	5	BRIDGE OF SPIES	T'Pau (Siren)
6	6	BAD	Michael Jackson (Epic)
9	7	TANGO IN THE NIGHT	Fleetwood Mac (Warner Bros.)
7	8	THE SINGLES	Pretenders (WEA)
8	9	BEST OF UB40 VOL 1	UB40 (Virgin)
23	10	RAINDANCING	Alison Moyet (CBS)
10	11	FAITH	George Michael (Epic)
13	12	ACTUALLY	Pet Shop Boys (Parlophone)
14	13	SONGS FROM STAGE AND SCREEN	Michael Crawford (Telstar)
11	14	YOU CAN DANCE	Madonna (Sire)
17	15	ALWAYS GUARANTEED	Cliff Richard (EMI)
-	16	NOW – THE CHRISTMAS ALBUM	Various Artists (EMI/Virgin/PolyGram)
12	17	SIMPLY SHADOWS	Shadows (Polydor)
15	18	HEARSAY	Alexander O'Neal (Tabu)
29	19	MEMORIES	Elaine Paige (Telstar)
28	20	FROM MOTOWN WITH LOVE	Various Artists (K-Tel)
19	21	THE LOVE SONGS	Michael Jackson & Diana Ross (Telstar)
30	22	SENTIMENTALLY YOURS	Rose Marie (Telstar)
21	23	THE CREAM OF CLAPTON	Eric Clapton (Polydor)
33	24	RED	Communards (London)
22	25	WHITESNAKE 1987	Whitesnake (EMI)
20	26	BEST SHOTS	Pat Benatar (Chrysalis)
16	27	WHITNEY	Whitney Houston (Arista)
18	28	SIXTIES MIX	Various Artists (Stylus)
-	29	INSIDE INFORMATION	Foreigner (Atlantic)
25	30	SONGS OF LOVE	Richard Clayderman (Decca)
47	31	POPPED IN SOULED OUT	Wet Wet Wet (Precious)
27	32	SAVAGE	Eurythmics (RCA)
-	33	THE PHANTOM OF THE OPERA	Original Cast (Polydor)
26	34	REFLECTIONS	Foster & Allen (Stylus)
31	35	CLOUD NINE	George Harrison (Dark Horse)
46	36	GREATEST HITS OF '87	Various Artists (Telstar)
-	37	UPFRONT 9	Various Artists (Serious)
36	38	A PORTRAIT OF MARIO LANZA	Mario Lanza (Stylus)
-	39	CLASSIC ROCK COUNTDOWN	London Symphony Orchestra (CBS)
24	40	THIS IS THE STORY	Proclaimers (Chrysalis)
34	41	ESP	Bee Gees (Warner Bros.)
32	42	BETWEEN THE LINES	Five Star (Tent)
48	43	SPECIAL OLYMPICS – A VERY SPECIAL CHRISTMAS	Various Artists (A&M)
49	44	GOOD LOVE	M'lissa Morgan (Capitol)
38	45	THE CHRISTIANS	Christians (Island)
43	46	THE JOSHUA TREE	U2 (Island)
42	47	INTRODUCING THE HARDLINE ACCORDING TO	Terence Trent D'Arby (CBS)
-	48	ALWAYS AND FOREVER	Various Artists (Telstar)
45	49	NOTHING LIKE THE SUN	Sting (A&M)
-	50	THE PEOPLE WHO GRINNED THEMSELVES TO DEATH	Housemartins (Go! Discs)

16 January 1988

last week	this week	Title	Artist (Label)
1	1	NOW THAT'S WHAT I CALL MUSIC10	Various Artists (EMI/Virgin/PolyGram)
6	2	BAD	Michael Jackson (Epic)
12	3	ACTUALLY	Pet Shop Boys (Parlophone)
2	4	HITS 7	Various Artists (CBS/WEA/BMG)
3	5	WHENEVER YOU NEED SOMEBODY	Rick Astley (RCA)
7	6	TANGO IN THE NIGHT	Fleetwood Mac (Warner Bros.)
5	7	BRIDGE OF SPIES	T'Pau (Siren)
31	8	POPPED IN SOULED OUT	Wet Wet Wet (Precious)
4	9	ALL THE BEST!	Paul McCartney (Parlophone)
8	10	THE SINGLES	Pretenders (WEA)
27	11	WHITNEY	Whitney Houston (Arista)
45	12	THE CHRISTIANS	Christians (Island)
11	13	FAITH	George Michael (Epic)
23	14	THE CREAM OF CLAPTON	Eric Clapton (Polydor)
10	15	RAINDANCING	Alison Moyet (CBS)
9	16	BEST OF UB40 VOL 1	UB40 (Virgin)
46	17	THE JOSHUA TREE	U2 (Island)
25	18	WHITESNAKE 1987	Whitesnake (EMI)
18	19	HEARSAY	Alexander O'Neal (Tabu)
14	20	YOU CAN DANCE	Madonna (Sire)
-	21	KICK	INXS (Mercury)
-	22	LIFE IN THE FAST LANE	Various Artists (Telstar)
-	23	THE MICHAEL JACKSON MIX	Michael Jackson (Stylus)
-	24	HYSTERIA	Def Leppard (Bludgeon Riffola)
-	25	THE BEST OF MIRAGE JACK MIX 88	Mirage (Stylus)
-	26	THE GREATEST LOVE	Various Artists (Telstar)
19	27	MEMORIES	Elaine Paige (Telstar)
-	28	THE CIRCUS	Erasure (Mute)
21	29	THE LOVE SONGS	Michael Jackson & Diana Ross (Telstar)
-	30	RUNNING IN THE FAMILY	Level 42 (Polydor)
20	31	FROM MOTOWN WITH LOVE	Various Artists (K-Tel)
32	32	SAVAGE	Eurythmics (RCA)
-	33	HEAVEN ON EARTH	Belinda Carlisle (Virgin)
-	34	JUST VISITING THIS PLANET	Jellybean (Chrysalis)
-	35	COME INTO MY LIFE	Joyce Sims (London)
15	36	ALWAYS GUARANTEED	Cliff Richard (EMI)
22	37	SENTIMENTALLY YOURS	Rose Marie (Telstar)
-	38	SUBSTANCE	New Order (Factory)
17	39	SIMPLY SHADOWS	Shadows (Polydor)
24	40	RED	Communards (London)
-	41	RUM, SODOMY AND THE LASH	Pogues (Stiff)
26	42	BEST SHOTS	Pat Benatar (Chrysalis)
44	43	GOOD LOVE	M'lissa Morgan (Capitol)
35	44	CLOUD NINE	George Harrison (Dark Horse)
47	45	INTRODUCING THE HARDLINE ACCORDING TO	Terence Trent D'Arby (CBS)
42	46	BETWEEN THE LINES	Five Star (Tent)
28	47	SIXTIES MIX	Various Artists (Stylus)
49	48	NOTHING LIKE THE SUN	Sting (A&M)
-	49	BROTHERS IN ARMS	Dire Straits (Vertigo)
48	50	ALWAYS AND FOREVER	Various Artists (Telstar)

23 January 1988

last week	this week	Title	Artist (Label)
8	1	POPPED IN SOULED OUT	Wet Wet Wet (Precious)
45	2	INTRODUCING THE HARDLINE ACCORDING TO	Terence Trent D'Arby (CBS)
3	3	ACTUALLY	Pet Shop Boys (Parlophone)
2	4	BAD	Michael Jackson (Epic)
5	5	WHENEVER YOU NEED SOMEBODY	Rick Astley (RCA)
6	6	TANGO IN THE NIGHT	Fleetwood Mac (Warner Bros.)
1	7	NOW THAT'S WHAT I CALL MUSIC10	Various Artists (EMI/Virgin/PolyGram)
12	8	THE CHRISTIANS	Christians (Island)
7	9	BRIDGE OF SPIES	T'Pau (Siren)
13	10	FAITH	George Michael (Epic)
33	11	HEAVEN ON EARTH	Belinda Carlisle (Virgin)
17	12	THE JOSHUA TREE	U2 (Island)
4	13	HITS 7	Various Artists (CBS/WEA/BMG)
11	14	WHITNEY	Whitney Houston (Arista)
15	15	RAINDANCING	Alison Moyet (CBS)
-	16	TURN BACK THE CLOCK	Johnny Hates Jazz (Virgin)
10	17	THE SINGLES	Pretenders (WEA)
25	18	THE BEST OF MIRAGE JACK MIX 88	Mirage (Stylus)
35	19	COME INTO MY LIFE	Joyce Sims (London)
9	20	ALL THE BEST!	Paul McCartney (Parlophone)
22	21	LIFE IN THE FAST LANE	Various Artists (Telstar)
18	22	WHITESNAKE 1987	Whitesnake (EMI)
21	23	KICK	INXS (Mercury)
19	24	HEARSAY	Alexander O'Neal (Tabu)
16	25	BEST OF UB40 VOL 1	UB40 (Virgin)
14	26	THE CREAM OF CLAPTON	Eric Clapton (Polydor)
-	27	CHER	Cher (Geffen)
20	28	YOU CAN DANCE	Madonna (Sire)
23	29	THE MICHAEL JACKSON MIX	Michael Jackson (Stylus)
34	30	JUST VISITING THIS PLANET	Jellybean (Chrysalis)
44	31	CLOUD NINE	George Harrison (Dark Horse)
30	32	RUNNING IN THE FAMILY	Level 42 (Polydor)
28	33	THE CIRCUS	Erasure (Mute)
-	34	SINITTA	Sinitta (Fanfare)
-	35	DIRTY DANCING	Soundtrack (RCA)
-	36	GIVE ME THE REASON	Luther Vandross (Epic)
-	37	MAKE IT LAST FOREVER	Keith Sweat (Elektra)
43	38	GOOD LOVE	M'lissa Morgan (Capitol)
26	39	THE GREATEST LOVE	Various Artists (Telstar)
27	40	MEMORIES	Elaine Paige (Telstar)
24	41	HYSTERIA	Def Leppard (Bludgeon Riffola)
29	42	THE LOVE SONGS	Michael Jackson & Diana Ross (Telstar)
-	43	GRACELAND	Paul Simon (Warner Bros.)
42	44	BEST SHOTS	Pat Benatar (Chrysalis)
31	45	FROM MOTOWN WITH LOVE	Various Artists (K-Tel)
32	46	SAVAGE	Eurythmics (RCA)
-	47	MEN AND WOMEN	Simply Red (Elektra)
40	48	RED	Communards (London)
49	49	BROTHERS IN ARMS	Dire Straits (Vertigo)
-	50	DANCING WITH STRANGERS	Chris Rea (Magnet)

The success of current singles seemed to be a factor in many people's New Year album buying as 1988 opened: the Top 10 hit *Angel Eyes* helped Wet Wet Wet's *Popped In Souled Out* to a stronger second chart run than its first in the previous October, this time snatching a week at Number 1. Terence Trent D'Arby also soared upwards again after almost dropping out, boosted by the single *Sign Your Name*.

January – February 1988

last this
week

30 January 1988

last	this		
16	1	TURN BACK THE CLOCK	
		Johnny Hates Jazz (Virgin)	
1	2	POPPED IN SOULED OUT	
		Wet Wet Wet (Precious)	
2	3	INTRODUCING THE HARDLINE ACCORDING TO	
		Terence Trent D'Arby (CBS)	
11	4	HEAVEN ON EARTH	Belinda Carlisle (Virgin)
8	5	THE CHRISTIANS	Christians (Island)
4	6	BAD	Michael Jackson (Epic)
5	7	WHENEVER YOU NEED SOMEBODY	
		Rick Astley (RCA)	
-	8	IF I SHOULD FALL FROM GRACE WITH GOD	
		Pogues (Pogue Mahone)	
6	9	TANGO IN THE NIGHT	
		Fleetwood Mac (Warner Bros.)	
21	10	LIFE IN THE FAST LANE Various Artists (Telstar)	
10	11	FAITH	George Michael (Epic)
18	12	THE BEST OF MIRAGE JACK MIX 88	
		Mirage (Stylus)	
3	13	ACTUALLY	Pet Shop Boys (Parlophone)
23	14	KICK	INXS (Mercury)
9	15	BRIDGE OF SPIES	T'Pau (Siren)
19	16	COME INTO MY LIFE	Joyce Sims (London)
12	17	THE JOSHUA TREE	U2 (Island)
7	18	NOW THAT'S WHAT I CALL MUSIC10	
		Various Artists (EMI/Virgin/PolyGram)	
14	19	WHITNEY	Whitney Houston (Arista)
17	20	THE SINGLES	Pretenders (WEA)
22	21	WHITESNAKE 1987	Whitesnake (EMI)
27	22	CHER	Cher (Geffen)
39	23	THE GREATEST LOVE	Various Artists (Telstar)
15	24	RAINDANCING	Alison Moyet (CBS)
24	25	HEARSAY	Alexander O'Neal (Tabu)
30	26	JUST VISITING THIS PLANET	
		Jellybean (Chrysalis)	
13	27	HITS 7	Various Artists (CBS/WEA/BMG)
35	28	DIRTY DANCING	Soundtrack (RCA)
25	29	BEST OF UB40 VOL 1	UB40 (Virgin)
26	30	THE CREAM OF CLAPTON Eric Clapton (Polydor)	
20	31	ALL THE BEST!	Paul McCartney (Parlophone)
42	32	THE LOVE SONGS	
		Michael Jackson & Diana Ross (Telstar)	
28	33	YOU CAN DANCE	Madonna (Sire)
36	34	GIVE ME THE REASON	Luther Vandross (Epic)
37	35	MAKE IT LAST FOREVER	Keith Sweat (Elektra)
29	36	THE MICHAEL JACKSON MIX	
		Michael Jackson (Stylus)	
32	37	RUNNING IN THE FAMILY	Level 42 (Polydor)
44	38	BEST SHOTS	Pat Benatar (Chrysalis)
33	39	THE CIRCUS	Erasure (Mute)
43	40	GRACELAND	Paul Simon (Warner Bros.)
-	41	MAINSTREAM	
		Lloyd Cole & the Commotions (Polydor)	
34	42	SINITTA	Sinitta (Fanfare)
45	43	FROM MOTOWN WITH LOVE	
		Various Artists (K-Tel)	
41	44	HYSTERIA	Def Leppard (Bludgeon Riffola)
40	45	MEMORIES	Elaine Paige (Telstar)
46	46	SAVAGE	Eurythmics (RCA)
50	47	DANCING WITH STRANGERS Chris Rea (Magnet)	
-	48	THE LION AND THE COBRA	
		Sinead O'Connor (Ensign)	
47	49	MEN AND WOMEN	Simply Red (Elektra)
49	50	BROTHERS IN ARMS	Dire Straits (Vertigo)

6 February 1988

last	this		
3	1	INTRODUCING THE HARDLINE ACCORDING TO	
		Terence Trent D'Arby (CBS)	
1	2	TURN BACK THE CLOCK	
		Johnny Hates Jazz (Virgin)	
8	3	IF I SHOULD FALL FROM GRACE WITH GOD	
		Pogues (Pogue Mahone)	
2	4	POPPED IN SOULED OUT Wet Wet Wet (Precious)	
5	5	THE CHRISTIANS	Christians (Island)
4	6	HEAVEN ON EARTH	Belinda Carlisle (Virgin)
14	7	KICK	INXS (Mercury)
6	8	BAD	Michael Jackson (Epic)
9	9	TANGO IN THE NIGHT	
		Fleetwood Mac (Warner Bros.)	
16	10	COME INTO MY LIFE	Joyce Sims (London)
12	11	THE BEST OF MIRAGE JACK MIX 88	
		Mirage (Stylus)	
15	12	BRIDGE OF SPIES	T'Pau (Siren)
11	13	FAITH	George Michael (Epic)
7	14	WHENEVER YOU NEED SOMEBODY	
		Rick Astley (RCA)	
-	15	SKYSCRAPER	David Lee Roth (Warner Bros.)
36	16	THE MICHAEL JACKSON MIX	
		Michael Jackson (Stylus)	
13	17	ACTUALLY	Pet Shop Boys (Parlophone)
24	18	RAINDANCING	Alison Moyet (CBS)
19	19	WHITNEY	Whitney Houston (Arista)
26	20	JUST VISITING THIS PLANET	
		Jellybean (Chrysalis)	
22	21	CHER	Cher (Geffen)
-	22	DUSTY - THE SILVER COLLECTION	
		Dusty Springfield (Philips)	
48	23	THE LION AND THE COBRA	
		Sinead O'Connor (Ensign)	
23	24	THE GREATEST LOVE	Various Artists (Telstar)
10	25	LIFE IN THE FAST LANE Various Artists (Telstar)	
20	26	THE SINGLES	Pretenders (WEA)
25	27	HEARSAY	Alexander O'Neal (Tabu)
17	28	THE JOSHUA TREE	U2 (Island)
27	29	HITS 7	Various Artists (CBS/WEA/BMG)
18	30	NOW THAT'S WHAT I CALL MUSIC10	
		Various Artists (EMI/Virgin/PolyGram)	
34	31	GIVE ME THE REASON	Luther Vandross (Epic)
21	32	WHITESNAKE 1987	Whitesnake (EMI)
30	33	THE CREAM OF CLAPTON Eric Clapton (Polydor)	
-	34	DESTINY'S SONG	Courtney Pine (Island)
35	35	MAKE IT LAST FOREVER	Keith Sweat (Elektra)
-	36	GOOD LOVE	M'lissa Morgan (Capitol)
28	37	DIRTY DANCING	Soundtrack (RCA)
29	38	BEST OF UB40 VOL 1	UB40 (Virgin)
47	39	DANCING WITH STRANGERS Chris Rea (Magnet)	
42	40	SINITTA	Sinitta (Fanfare)
-	41	THE HOUSE SOUND OF CHICAGO 3	
		Various Artists (DJ International)	
-	42	PENETENTIARY	Soundtrack (RCA)
31	43	ALL THE BEST!	Paul McCartney (Parlophone)
-	44	RADIO K.A.O.S.	Roger Waters (EMI)
32	45	THE LOVE SONGS	
		Michael Jackson & Diana Ross (Telstar)	
33	46	YOU CAN DANCE	Madonna (Sire)
40	47	GRACELAND	Paul Simon (Warner Bros.)
37	48	RUNNING IN THE FAMILY	Level 42 (Polydor)
-	49	CLASSIC ROCK COUNTDOWN	
		London Symphony Orchestra (CBS)	
38	50	BEST SHOTS	Pat Benatar (Chrysalis)

13 February 1988

last	this		
1	1	INTRODUCING THE HARDLINE ACCORDING TO	
		Terence Trent D'Arby (CBS)	
3	2	IF I SHOULD FALL FROM GRACE WITH GOD	
		Pogues (Pogue Mahone)	
5	3	THE CHRISTIANS	Christians (Island)
4	4	POPPED IN SOULED OUT Wet Wet Wet (Precious)	
2	5	TURN BACK THE CLOCK	
		Johnny Hates Jazz (Virgin)	
7	6	KICK	INXS (Mercury)
12	7	BRIDGE OF SPIES	T'Pau (Siren)
15	8	SKYSCRAPER	David Lee Roth (Warner Bros.)
-	9	BLOW UP YOUR VIDEO	AC/DC (Atlantic)
10	10	COME INTO MY LIFE	Joyce Sims (London)
11	11	THE BEST OF MIRAGE JACK MIX 88	
		Mirage (Stylus)	
8	12	BAD	Michael Jackson (Epic)
6	13	HEAVEN ON EARTH	Belinda Carlisle (Virgin)
13	14	FAITH	George Michael (Epic)
20	15	JUST VISITING THIS PLANET	
		Jellybean (Chrysalis)	
9	16	TANGO IN THE NIGHT	
		Fleetwood Mac (Warner Bros.)	
17	17	ACTUALLY	Pet Shop Boys (Parlophone)
14	18	WHENEVER YOU NEED SOMEBODY	
		Rick Astley (RCA)	
23	19	THE LION AND THE COBRA	
		Sinead O'Connor (Ensign)	
16	20	THE MICHAEL JACKSON MIX	
		Michael Jackson (Stylus)	
19	21	WHITNEY	Whitney Houston (Arista)
21	22	CHER	Cher (Geffen)
18	23	RAINDANCING	Alison Moyet (CBS)
22	24	DUSTY - THE SILVER COLLECTION	
		Dusty Springfield (Philips)	
35	25	MAKE IT LAST FOREVER	Keith Sweat (Elektra)
24	26	THE GREATEST LOVE	Various Artists (Telstar)
32	27	WHITESNAKE 1987	Whitesnake (EMI)
34	28	DESTINY'S SONG	Courtney Pine (Island)
25	29	LIFE IN THE FAST LANE Various Artists (Telstar)	
-	30	THE PHANTOM OF THE OPERA	
		Original Cast (Polydor)	
30	31	NOW THAT'S WHAT I CALL MUSIC10	
		Various Artists (EMI/Virgin/PolyGram)	
27	32	HEARSAY	Alexander O'Neal (Tabu)
26	33	THE SINGLES	Pretenders (WEA)
28	34	THE JOSHUA TREE	U2 (Island)
31	35	GIVE ME THE REASON	Luther Vandross (Epic)
-	36	EVERYTHING	Climie Fisher (EMI)
33	37	THE CREAM OF CLAPTON Eric Clapton (Polydor)	
-	38	MAINSTREAM	
		Lloyd Cole & the Commotions (Polydor)	
37	39	DIRTY DANCING	Soundtrack (RCA)
-	40	OUT OF THE BLUE	Debbie Gibson (Atlantic)
46	41	YOU CAN DANCE	Madonna (Sire)
41	42	THE HOUSE SOUND OF CHICAGO 3	
		Various Artists (DJ International)	
29	43	HITS 7	Various Artists (CBS/WEA/BMG)
38	44	BEST OF UB40 VOL 1	UB40 (Virgin)
-	45	SHOVE IT	Cross (Virgin)
39	46	DANCING WITH STRANGERS Chris Rea (Magnet)	
-	47	THE CIRCUS	Erasure (Mute)
43	48	ALL THE BEST!	Paul McCartney (Parlophone)
48	49	RUNNING IN THE FAMILY	Level 42 (Polydor)
47	50	GRACELAND	Paul Simon (Warner Bros.)

Johnny Hates Jazz joined the honour roll of acts to have achieved a Number 1 album with their first release, although they had a brief stay before Terence Trent Darby's *Hardline* re-established itself at the top for a second spell which was to last most of the next month and a half. The Pogues also enjoyed their best-selling album yet with their third release, *If I Should Fall From Grace With God*, which peaked at 2.

February – March 1988

20 February 1988

9	1	BLOW UP YOUR VIDEO	AC/DC (Atlantic)
1	2	INTRODUCING THE HARDLINE ACCORDING TO	Terence Trent D'Arby (CBS)
3	3	THE CHRISTIANS	Christians (Island)
4	4	POPPED IN SOULED OUT	Wet Wet Wet (Precious)
5	5	TURN BACK THE CLOCK	Johnny Hates J (Virgin)
2	6	IF I SHOULD FALL FROM GRACE WITH GOD	Pogues (Pogue Mahone)
7	7	BRIDGE OF SPIES	T'Pau (Siren)
10	8	COME INTO MY LIFE	Joyce Sims (London)
6	9	KICK	INXS (Mercury)
8	10	SKYSCRAPER	David Lee Roth (Warner Bros.)
11	11	THE BEST OF MIRAGE JACK MIX 88	Mirage (Stylus)
16	12	TANGO IN THE NIGHT	Fleetwood Mac (Warn Bros.)
13	13	HEAVEN ON EARTH	Belinda Carlisle (Virgin)
-	14	ALL LIVE AND ALL OF THE NIGHT	Stranglers (Epic)
12	15	BAD	Michael Jackson (Epic)
15	16	JUST VISITING THIS PLANET	Jellybean (Chrysalis)
19	17	THE LION AND THE COBRA	Sinead O'Connor (Ensign)
18	18	WHENEVER YOU NEED SOMEBODY	Rick Astley (RCA)
24	19	DUSTY - THE SILVER COLLECTION	Dusty Springfield (Philips)
14	20	FAITH	George Michael (Epic)
35	21	GIVE ME THE REASON	Luther Vandross (Epic)
36	22	EVERYTHING	Climie Fisher (EMI)
26	23	THE GREATEST LOVE	Various Artists (Telstar)
17	24	ACTUALLY	Pet Shop Boys (Parlophone)
23	25	RAINDANCING	Alison Moyet (CBS)
20	26	THE MICHAEL JACKSON MIX	Michael Jackson (Stylus)
22	27	CHER	Cher (Geffen)
25	28	MAKE IT LAST FOREVER	Keith Sweat (Elektra)
28	29	DESTINY'S SONG	Courtney Pine (Island)
37	30	THE CREAM OF CLAPTON	Eric Clapton (Polydor)
32	31	HEARSAY	Alexander O'Neal (Tabu)
34	32	THE JOSHUA TREE	U2 (Island)
40	33	OUT OF THE BLUE	Debbie Gibson (Atlantic)
-	34	WHO KILLED THE JAMS	Justified Ancients of Mu Mu (Jams)
-	35	SCALLYWAG JAZ	Thomas Lang (Epic)
21	36	WHITNEY	Whitney Houston (Arista)
27	37	WHITESNAKE 1987	Whitesnake (EMI)
29	38	LIFE IN THE FAST LANE	Various Artists (Telstar)
39	39	DIRTY DANCING	Soundtrack (RCA)
-	40	TIME AND TIDE	Basia (Portrait)
42	41	THE HOUSE SOUND OF CHICAGO 3	Various Artists DJ International)
45	42	SHOVE IT	Cross (Virgin)
-	43	GEORGE THOROGOOD	George Thorogood (EMI)
30	44	THE PHANTOM OF THE OPERA	Original Cast (Polydor)
-	45	FATAL ATTRACTION	Lion (Polydor)
31	46	NOW THAT'S WHAT I CALL MUSIC10	Various Artists (EMI/Virgin/PolyGram)
-	47	BIRTH SCHOOL WORK DEATH	Godfathers (Epic)
-	48	ELVIS PRESLEY – THE ALL TIME GREATEST HITS	Elvis Presley (RCA)
33	49	THE SINGLES	Pretenders (WEA)
43	50	HITS 7	Various Artists (CBS/WEA/BMG)

27 February 1988

2	1	INTRODUCING THE HARDLINE ACCORDING TO	Terence Trent D'Arby (CBS)
3	2	THE CHRISTIANS	Christians (Island)
7	3	BRIDGE OF SPIES	T'Pau (Siren)
4	4	POPPED IN SOULED OUT	Wet Wet Wet (Precious)
1	5	BLOW UP YOUR VIDEO	AC/DC (Atlantic)
14	6	ALL LIVE AND ALL OF THE NIGHT	Stranglers (Epic)
9	7	KICK	INXS (Mercury)
5	8	TURN BACK THE CLOCK	Johnny Hates Jazz (Virgin)
15	9	BAD	Michael Jackson (Epic)
24	10	ACTUALLY	Pet Shop Boys (Parlophone)
19	11	DUSTY - THE SILVER COLLECTION	Dusty Springfield (Philips)
18	12	WHENEVER YOU NEED SOMEBODY	Rick Astley (RCA)
8	13	COME INTO MY LIFE	Joyce Sims (London)
32	14	THE JOSHUA TREE	U2 (Island)
10	15	SKYSCRAPER	David Lee Roth (Warner Bros.)
6	16	IF I SHOULD FALL FROM GRACE WITH GOD	Pogues (Pogue Mahone)
17	17	THE LION AND THE COBRA	Sinead O'Connor (Ensign)
-	18	ALL ABOUT EVE	All About Eve (Mercury)
12	19	TANGO IN THE NIGHT	Fleetwood Mac (Warner Bros.)
21	20	GIVE ME THE REASON	Luther Vandross (Epic)
-	21	I'M YOUR MAN	Leonard Cohen (CBS)
16	22	JUST VISITING THIS PLANET	Jellybean (Chrysalis)
23	23	THE GREATEST LOVE	Various Artists (Telstar)
20	24	FAITH	George Michael (Epic)
11	25	THE BEST OF MIRAGE JACK MIX 88	Mirage (Stylus)
25	26	RAINDANCING	Alison Moyet (CBS)
13	27	HEAVEN ON EARTH	Belinda Carlisle (Virgin)
22	28	EVERYTHING	Climie Fisher (EMI)
31	29	HEARSAY	Alexander O'Neal (Tabu)
26	30	THE MICHAEL JACKSON MIX	Michael Jackson (Stylus)
35	31	SCALLYWAG JAZ	Thomas Lang (Epic)
43	32	GEORGE THOROGOOD	George Thorogood (EMI)
-	33	ALL OUR LOVE	Gladys Knight & the Pips (MCA)
-	34	WALTER BEASLEY	Walter Beasley (Urban)
-	35	ESP	Bee Gees (Warner Bros.)
28	36	MAKE IT LAST FOREVER	Keith Sweat (Elektra)
40	37	TIME AND TIDE	Basia (Portrait)
-	38	LIFE PLUS ONE	Frehley's Comet (Atlantic)
-	39	WE CARE A LOT	Faith No More (Mordam)
33	40	OUT OF THE BLUE	Debbie Gibson (Atlantic)
44	41	THE PHANTOM OF THE OPERA	Original Cast (Polydor)
27	42	CHER	Cher (Geffen)
39	43	DIRTY DANCING	Soundtrack (RCA)
47	44	BIRTH SCHOOL WORK DEATH	Godfathers (Epic)
-	45	GLOBE OF FROGS	Robyn Hitchcock (A&M)
-	46	WOW	Bananarama (London)
30	47	THE CREAM OF CLAPTON	Eric Clapton (Polydor)
36	48	WHITNEY	Whitney Houston (Arista)
-	49	VITAL IDOL	Billy Idol (Chrysalis)
49	50	THE SINGLES	Pretenders (WEA)

5 March 1988

1	1	INTRODUCING THE HARDLINE ACCORDING TO	Terence Trent D'Arby (CBS)
2	2	THE CHRISTIANS	Christians (Island)
4	3	POPPED IN SOULED OUT	Wet Wet Wet (Precious)
-	4	TIFFANY	Tiffany (MCA)
3	5	BRIDGE OF SPIES	T'Pau (Siren)
18	6	ALL ABOUT EVE	All About Eve (Mercury)
8	7	TURN BACK THE CLOCK	Johnny Hates Jazz (Virgin)
5	8	BLOW UP YOUR VIDEO	AC/DC (Atlantic)
12	9	WHENEVER YOU NEED SOMEBODY	Rick Astley (RCA)
9	10	BAD	Michael Jackson (Epic)
13	11	COME INTO MY LIFE	Joyce Sims (London)
10	12	ACTUALLY	Pet Shop Boys (Parlophone)
7	13	KICK	INXS (Mercury)
19	14	TANGO IN THE NIGHT	Fleetwood Mac (Warner Bros.)
11	15	DUSTY - THE SILVER COLLECTION	Dusty Springfield (Philips)
6	16	ALL LIVE AND ALL OF THE NIGHT	Stranglers (Epic)
15	17	SKYSCRAPER	David Lee Roth (Warner Bros.)
16	18	IF I SHOULD FALL FROM GRACE WITH GOD	Pogues (Pogue Mahone)
20	19	GIVE ME THE REASON	Luther Vandross (Epic)
-	20	TATTOOED BEAT MESSIAH	Zodiac Mindwarp (Mercury)
-	21	THE WORLD WITHOUT END	Mighty Lemondrops (Blue Guitar)
21	22	I'M YOUR MAN	Leonard Cohen (CBS)
-	23	NOTHING LIKE THE SUN	Sting (A&M)
27	24	HEAVEN ON EARTH	Belinda Carlisle (Virgin)
14	25	THE JOSHUA TREE	U2 (Island)
17	26	THE LION AND THE COBRA	Sinead O'Connor (Ensign)
36	27	MAKE IT LAST FOREVER	Keith Sweat (Elektra)
-	28	WOODEN FOOT COPS ON THE HIGHWAY	Woodentops (Rough Trade)
24	29	FAITH	George Michael (Epic)
-	30	CRY FREEDOM	Soundtrack (MCA)
44	31	BIRTH SCHOOL WORK DEATH	Godfathers (Epic)
-	32	TELL IT TO MY HEART	Taylor Dayne (Arista)
33	33	ALL OUR LOVE	Gladys Knight & the Pips (MCA)
25	34	THE BEST OF MIRAGE JACK MIX 88	Mirage (Stylus)
-	35	LA GUNS	LA Guns (Vertigo)
38	36	LIFE PLUS ONE	Frehley's Comet (Atlantic)
23	37	THE GREATEST LOVE	Various Artists (Telstar)
-	38	FOREVER YOURS	Tony Terry (Epic)
-	39	RAINTOWN	Deacon Blue (CBS)
46	40	WOW	Bananarama (London)
22	41	JUST VISITING THIS PLANET	Jellybean (Chrysalis)
29	42	HEARSAY	Alexander O'Neal (Tabu)
-	43	WHITESNAKE 1987	Whitesnake (EMI)
-	44	IF YOU CAN'T LICK 'EM, LICK 'EM	Ted Nugent (WEA)
34	45	WALTER BEASLEY	Walter Beasley (Urban)
40	46	OUT OF THE BLUE	Debbie Gibson (Atlantic)
-	47	GET HERE	Brenda Russell (A&M)
-	48	MAXI	Maxi Priest (10/Virgin)
-	49	LIVE IN AUSTRALIA	Elton John (Rocket)
-	50	SAY IT AGAIN	Jermaine Stewart (Siren)

Dusty Springfield's *The Silver Collection* was a compilation of most of her 1960s hits, released to mark the 25th anniversary of the start of her solo recording career. It was her first chart album since the mid-60s. By contrast, another female soloist, Sinead O'Connor, was having her first chart entry of any kind with *The Lion And The Cobra*, and teenager Tiffany's eponymous debut was even more spectacular.

March 1988

last week	this week		

12 March 1988

last	this	title	artist
1	1	INTRODUCING THE HARDLINE ACCORDING TO	Terence Trent D'Arby (CBS)
5	2	BRIDGE OF SPIES	T'Pau (Siren)
7	3	TURN BACK THE CLOCK	Johnny Hates Jazz (Virgin)
2	4	THE CHRISTIANS	Christians (Island)
4	5	TIFFANY	Tiffany (MCA)
3	6	POPPED IN SOULED OUT	Wet Wet Wet (Precious)
9	7	WHENEVER YOU NEED SOMEBODY	Rick Astley (RCA)
10	8	BAD	Michael Jackson (Epic)
19	9	GIVE ME THE REASON	Luther Vandross (Epic)
6	10	ALL ABOUT EVE	All About Eve (Mercury)
-	11	LITTLE CHILDREN	Mission (Mercury)
24	12	HEAVEN ON EARTH	Belinda Carlisle (Virgin)
20	13	TATTOOED BEAT MESSIAH	Zodiac Mindwarp (Mercury)
23	14	NOTHING LIKE THE SUN	Sting (A&M)
13	15	KICK	INXS (Mercury)
-	16	NOW AND ZEN	Robert Plant (Ez paranza)
12	17	ACTUALLY	Pet Shop Boys (Parlophone)
42	18	HEARSAY	Alexander O'Neal (Tabu)
26	19	THE LION AND THE COBRA	Sinead O'Connor (Ensign)
37	20	THE GREATEST LOVE	Various Artists (Telstar)
14	21	TANGO IN THE NIGHT	Fleetwood Mac (Warner Bros.)
11	22	COME INTO MY LIFE	Joyce Sims (London)
25	23	THE JOSHUA TREE	U2 (Island)
8	24	BLOW UP YOUR VIDEO	AC/DC (Atlantic)
18	25	IF I SHOULD FALL FROM GRACE WITH GOD	Pogues (Pogue Mahone)
-	26	THE FRENZ EXPERIMENT	Fall (Beggars Banquet)
29	27	FAITH	George Michael (Epic)
15	28	DUSTY - THE SILVER COLLECTION	Dusty Springfield (Philips)
32	29	TELL IT TO MY HEART	Taylor Dayne (Arista)
16	30	ALL LIVE AND ALL OF THE NIGHT	Stranglers (Epic)
-	31	IDLEWILD	Everything But The Girl (Blanco Y Negro)
-	32	THE BEST OF OMD	Orchestral Manoeuvres in the Dark (Virgin)
43	33	WHITESNAKE 1987	Whitesnake (EMI)
50	34	SAY IT AGAIN	Jermaine Stewart (Siren)
39	35	RAINTOWN	Deacon Blue (CBS)
17	36	SKYSCRAPER	David Lee Roth (Warner Bros.)
28	37	WOODEN FOOT COPS ON THE HIGHWAY	Woodentops (Rough Trade)
35	38	LA GUNS	LA Guns (Vertigo)
44	39	IF YOU CAN'T LICK 'EM, LICK 'EM	Ted Nugent (WEA)
-	40	UNFORGETTABLE	Various Artists (EMI)
27	41	MAKE IT LAST FOREVER	Keith Sweat (Elektra)
22	42	I'M YOUR MAN	Leonard Cohen (CBS)
47	43	GET HERE	Brenda Russell (A&M)
21	44	THE WORLD WITHOUT END	Mighty Lemondrops (Blue Guitar)
33	45	ALL OUR LOVE	Gladys Knight & the Pips (MCA)
49	46	LIVE IN AUSTRALIA	Elton John (Rocket)
-	47	THE ISLEY BROTHERS' GREATEST HITS	Isley Brothers (Telstar)
40	48	WOW	Bananarama (London)
46	49	OUT OF THE BLUE	Debbie Gibson (Atlantic)
34	50	THE BEST OF MIRAGE JACK MIX 88	Mirage (Stylus)

19 March 1988

last	this	title	artist
1	1	INTRODUCING THE HARDLINE ACCORDING TO	Terence Trent D'Arby (CBS)
11	2	LITTLE CHILDREN	Mission (Mercury)
2	3	BRIDGE OF SPIES	T'Pau (Siren)
16	4	NOW AND ZEN	Robert Plant (Ez paranza)
32	5	THE BEST OF OMD	Orchestral Manoeuvres in the Dark (Virgin)
9	6	GIVE ME THE REASON	Luther Vandross (Epic)
6	7	POPPED IN SOULED OUT	Wet Wet Wet (Precious)
7	8	WHENEVER YOU NEED SOMEBODY	Rick Astley (RCA)
31	9	IDLEWILD	Everything But The Girl (Blanco Y Negro)
3	10	TURN BACK THE CLOCK	Johnny Hates Jazz (Virgin)
26	11	THE FRENZ EXPERIMENT	Fall (Beggars Banquet)
4	12	THE CHRISTIANS	Christians (Island)
12	13	HEAVEN ON EARTH	Belinda Carlisle (Virgin)
40	14	UNFORGETTABLE	Various Artists (EMI)
5	15	TIFFANY	Tiffany (MCA)
18	16	HEARSAY	Alexander O'Neal (Tabu)
-	17	TEAR DOWN THESE WALLS	Billy Ocean (Jive)
23	18	THE JOSHUA TREE	U2 (Island)
10	19	ALL ABOUT EVE	All About Eve (Mercury)
21	20	TANGO IN THE NIGHT	Fleetwood Mac (Warner Bros.)
15	21	KICK	INXS (Mercury)
-	22	BEST OF HOUSE VOL 4	Various Artists (Serious)
-	23	WHO'S BETTER, WHO'S BEST	Who (Polydor)
29	24	TELL IT TO MY HEART	Taylor Dayne (Arista)
13	25	TATTOOED BEAT MESSIAH	Zodiac Mindwarp (Mercury)
20	26	THE GREATEST LOVE	Various Artists (Telstar)
14	27	NOTHING LIKE THE SUN	Sting (A&M)
17	28	ACTUALLY	Pet Shop Boys (Parlophone)
22	29	COME INTO MY LIFE	Joyce Sims (London)
-	30	WHITNEY	Whitney Houston (Arista)
-	31	FLOODLAND	Sisters of Mercy (Merciful Release)
25	32	IF I SHOULD FALL FROM GRACE WITH GOD	Pogues (Pogue Mahone)
36	33	SKYSCRAPER	David Lee Roth (Warner Bros.)
-	34	BAD ANIMALS	Heart (Capitol)
19	35	THE LION AND THE COBRA	Sinead O'Connor (Ensign)
35	36	RAINTOWN	Deacon Blue (CBS)
37	37	WOODEN FOOT COPS ON THE HIGHWAY	Woodentops (Rough Trade)
24	38	BLOW UP YOUR VIDEO	AC/DC (Atlantic)
28	39	DUSTY - THE SILVER COLLECTION	Dusty Springfield (Philips)
42	40	I'M YOUR MAN	Leonard Cohen (CBS)
45	41	YOU'RE A PART OF ME	Jean Carne (RCA)
45	42	ALL OUR LOVE	Gladys Knight & the Pips (MCA)
-	43	WALTER BEASLEY	Walter Beasley (Urban)
27	44	FAITH	George Michael (Epic)
-	45	THE CIRCUS	Erasure (Mute)
-	46	HORIZONS	Various Artists (K-Tel)
33	47	WHITESNAKE 1987	Whitesnake (EMI)
46	48	LIVE IN AUSTRALIA	Elton John (Rocket)
50	49	THE BEST OF MIRAGE JACK MIX 88	Mirage (Stylus)
44	50	THE WORLD WITHOUT END	Mighty Lemondrops (Blue Guitar)

26 March 1988

last	this	title	artist
5	1	THE BEST OF OMD	Orchestral Manoeuvres in the Dark (Virgin)
1	2	INTRODUCING THE HARDLINE ACCORDING TO	Terence Trent D'Arby (CBS)
2	3	LITTLE CHILDREN	Mission (Mercury)
23	4	WHO'S BETTER, WHO'S BEST	Who (Polydor)
-	5	VIVA HATE	Morrissey (HMV)
17	6	TEAR DOWN THESE WALLS	Billy Ocean (Jive)
7	7	POPPED IN SOULED OUT	Wet Wet Wet (Precious)
14	8	UNFORGETTABLE	Various Artists (EMI)
16	9	HEARSAY	Alexander O'Neal (Tabu)
6	10	GIVE ME THE REASON	Luther Vandross (Epic)
8	11	WHENEVER YOU NEED SOMEBODY	Rick Astley (RCA)
-	12	NAKED	Talking Heads (EMI)
10	13	TURN BACK THE CLOCK	Johnny Hates Jazz (Virgin)
9	14	IDLEWILD	Everything But The Girl (Blanco Y Negro)
13	15	HEAVEN ON EARTH	Belinda Carlisle (Virgin)
4	16	NOW AND ZEN	Robert Plant (Ez paranza)
3	17	BRIDGE OF SPIES	T'Pau (Siren)
-	18	SO FAR SO GOOD...SO WHAT!	Megadeth (Capitol)
30	19	WHITNEY	Whitney Houston (Arista)
20	20	TANGO IN THE NIGHT	Fleetwood Mac (Warner Bros.)
12	21	THE CHRISTIANS	Christians (Island)
-	22	BAD	Michael Jackson (Epic)
15	23	TIFFANY	Tiffany (MCA)
21	24	KICK	INXS (Mercury)
11	25	THE FRENZ EXPERIMENT	Fall (Beggars Banquet)
-	26	KINGDOM COME	Kingdom Come (Polydor)
26	27	THE GREATEST LOVE	Various Artists (Telstar)
33	28	SKYSCRAPER	David Lee Roth (Warner Bros.)
18	29	THE JOSHUA TREE	U2 (Island)
25	30	TATTOOED BEAT MESSIAH	Zodiac Mindwarp (Mercury)
27	31	NOTHING LIKE THE SUN	Sting (A&M)
-	32	ROCK THE NATION	Various Artists (Dover)
19	33	ALL ABOUT EVE	All About Eve (Mercury)
22	34	BEST OF HOUSE VOL 4	Various Artists (Serious)
28	35	ACTUALLY	Pet Shop Boys (Parlophone)
34	36	BAD ANIMALS	Heart (Capitol)
40	37	I'M YOUR MAN	Leonard Cohen (CBS)
-	38	DIRTY DANCING	Soundtrack (RCA)
-	39	STREET SOUNDS HIP HOP 20	Various Artists (Street Sounds)
-	40	PAST MASTERS VOL 1	Beatles (Parlophone)
41	41	YOU'RE A PART OF ME	Jean Carne (RCA)
-	42	PAST MASTERS VOL 2	Beatles (Parlophone)
-	43	LA GUNS	LA Guns (Vertigo)
29	44	COME INTO MY LIFE	Joyce Sims (London)
45	45	THE CIRCUS	Erasure (Mute)
-	46	YOU SEND ME	Roy Ayers (Polydor)
-	47	WILL DOWNING	Will Downing (Fourth & Broadway)
31	48	FLOODLAND	Sisters of Mercy (Merciful Release)
24	49	TELL IT TO MY HEART	Taylor Dayne (Arista)
-	50	STREET SOUNDS 88-1	Various Artists (Street Sounds)

Orchestral Manoeuvres In The Dark (now more commonly known by the snappier acronym OMD) punctuated Terence Trent D'Arby's Number 1 run with just a week of their own at the summit with a compilation of their string of hit singles to date. It was the Liverpudlians' first album release for well over a year, and their highest-placed ever. The Mission also had their best seller to date with *Little Children*.

last this week — 2 April 1988

last	this		
5	1	VIVA HATE	Morrissey (HMV)
12	2	NAKED	Talking Heads (EMI)
1	3	THE BEST OF OMD	Orchestral Manoeuvres in the Dark (Virgin)
-	4	FROM LANGLEY PARK TO MEMPHIS	Prefab Sprout (Kitchenware)
6	5	TEAR DOWN THESE WALLS	Billy Ocean (Jive)
7	6	POPPED IN SOULED OUT	Wet Wet Wet (Precious Organisation)
9	7	HEARSAY	Alexander O'Neal (Tabu)
2	8	INTRODUCING THE HARDLINE ACCORDING TO	Terence Trent D'Arby (CBS)
4	9	WHO'S BETTER, WHO'S BEST	Who (Polydor)
13	10	TURN BACK THE CLOCK	Johnny Hates Jazz (Virgin)
18	11	SO FAR SO GOOD...SO WHAT!	Megadeth (Capitol)
-	12	NOW THAT'S WHAT I CALL MUSIC 11	Various Artists (EMI/Virgin/PolyGram)
8	13	UNFORGETTABLE	Various Artists (EMI)
17	14	BRIDGE OF SPIES	T'Pau (Siren)
-	15	THE STORY OF THE CLASH	Clash (CBS)
11	16	WHENEVER YOU NEED SOMEBODY	Rick Astley (RCA)
24	17	KICK	INXS (Mercury)
32	18	ROCK THE NATION	Various Artists (Dover)
3	19	LITTLE CHILDREN	Mission (Mercury)
-	20	LIVE IN EUROPE	Tina Turner (Capitol)
15	21	HEAVEN ON EARTH	Belinda Carlisle (Virgin)
10	22	GIVE ME THE REASON	Luther Vandross (Epic)
19	23	WHITNEY	Whitney Houston (Arista)
21	24	THE CHRISTIANS	Christians (Island)
23	25	TIFFANY	Tiffany (MCA)
22	26	BAD	Michael Jackson (Epic)
14	27	IDLEWILD	Everything But The Girl (Blanco Y Negro)
-	28	HORIZONS	Various Artists (K-Tel)
26	29	KINGDOM COME	Kingdom Come (Polydor)
47	30	WILL DOWNING	Will Downing (Fourth & Broadway)
-	31	CHALK MARKS IN A RAIN STORM	Joni Mitchell (Geffen)
20	32	TANGO IN THE NIGHT	Fleetwood Mac (Warner Bros.)
35	33	ACTUALLY	Pet Shop Boys (Parlophone)
31	34	NOTHING LIKE THE SUN	Sting (A&M)
38	35	DIRTY DANCING	Soundtrack (RCA)
45	36	THE CIRCUS	Erasure (Mute)
16	37	NOW AND ZEN	Robert Plant (Ez paranza)
27	38	THE GREATEST LOVE	Various Artists (Telstar)
-	39	LITTLE LOVE AFFAIRS	Nanci Griffiths (MCA)
-	40	IN FULL EFFECT	Mantronix (10)
29	41	THE JOSHUA TREE	U2 (Island)
33	42	ALL ABOUT EVE	All About Eve (Mercury)
41	43	YOU'RE A PART OF ME	Jean Carne (RCA)
43	44	LA GUNS	LA Guns (Vertigo)
25	45	THE FRENZ EXPERIMENT	Fall (Beggars Banquet)
-	46	TAJA SEVELLE	Taja Sevelle (Paisley Park)
-	47	ALL OUR LOVE	Gladys Knight & the Pips (MCA)
28	48	SKYSCRAPER	David Lee Roth (Warner Bros.)
36	49	BAD ANIMALS	Heart (Capitol)
-	50	THE WORD VOL 2	Various Artists (Jive)

9 April 1988

12	1	NOW THAT'S WHAT I CALL MUSIC 11	Various Artists (EMI/Virgin/PolyGram)
1	2	VIVA HATE	Morrissey (HMV)
3	3	THE BEST OF OMD	Orchestral Manoeuvres in the Dark (Virgin)
20	4	LIVE IN EUROPE	Tina Turner (Capitol)
2	5	NAKED	Talking Heads (EMI)
15	6	THE STORY OF THE CLASH	Clash (CBS)
6	7	POPPED IN SOULED OUT	Wet Wet Wet (Precious)
4	8	FROM LANGLEY PARK TO MEMPHIS	Prefab Sprout (Kitchenware)
8	9	INTRODUCING THE HARDLINE ACCORDING TO	Terence Trent D'Arby (CBS)
7	10	HEARSAY	Alexander O'Neal (Tabu)
10	11	TURN BACK THE CLOCK	Johnny Hates Jazz (Virgin)
5	12	TEAR DOWN THESE WALLS	Billy Ocean (Jive)
28	13	HORIZONS	Various Artists (K-Tel)
23	14	WHITNEY	Whitney Houston (Arista)
9	15	WHO'S BETTER, WHO'S BEST	Who (Polydor)
-	16	PUSH	Bros (CBS)
31	17	CHALK MARKS IN A RAIN STORM	Joni Mitchell (Geffen)
11	18	SO FAR SO GOOD...SO WHAT!	Megadeth (Capitol)
35	19	DIRTY DANCING	Soundtrack (RCA)
16	20	WHENEVER YOU NEED SOMEBODY	Rick Astley (RCA)
13	21	UNFORGETTABLE	Various Artists (EMI)
17	22	KICK	INXS (Mercury)
21	23	HEAVEN ON EARTH	Belinda Carlisle (Virgin)
32	24	TANGO IN THE NIGHT	Fleetwood Mac (Warner Bros.)
25	25	TIFFANY	Tiffany (MCA)
19	26	LITTLE CHILDREN	Mission (Mercury)
22	27	GIVE ME THE REASON	Luther Vandross (Epic)
18	28	ROCK THE NATION	Various Artists (Dover)
14	29	BRIDGE OF SPIES	T'Pau (Siren)
26	30	BAD	Michael Jackson (Epic)
33	31	ACTUALLY	Pet Shop Boys (Parlophone)
30	32	WILL DOWNING	Will Downing (Fourth & Broadway)
-	33	DISTANT THUNDER	Aswad (Mango)
38	34	THE GREATEST LOVE	Various Artists (Telstar)
29	35	KINGDOM COME	Kingdom Come (Polydor)
24	36	THE CHRISTIANS	Christians (Island)
-	37	HIP HOP AND RAPPING IN THE HOUSE	Various Artists (Stylus)
-	38	EVERYTHING	Cimie Fisher (EMI)
46	39	TAJA SEVELLE	Taja Sevelle (Paisley Park)
37	40	NOW AND ZEN	Robert Plant (Ez paranza)
-	41	PAID IN FULL	Eric & Rakim (4th & Broadway)
40	42	IN FULL EFFECT	Mantronix (10)
-	43	ONCE AROUND THE WORLD	It Bites (Virgin)
27	44	IDLEWILD	Everything But The Girl (Blanco Y Negro)
34	45	NOTHING LIKE THE SUN	Sting (A&M)
-	46	PLIGHT AND PREMONITION	David Sylvian & Holger Czukay (Vertigo)
-	47	A PORTRAIT OF ELLA FITZGERALD	Ella Fitzgerald (Stylus)
49	48	BAD ANIMALS	Heart (Capitol)
-	49	THE ISLEY BROTHERS' GREATEST HITS	Isley Brothers (Telstar)
-	50	TELL IT TO MY HEART	Taylor Dayne (Arista)

16 April 1988

1	1	NOW THAT'S WHAT I CALL MUSIC 11	Various Artists (EMI/Virgin/PolyGram)
3	2	THE BEST OF OMD	Orchestral Manoeuvres in the Dark (Virgin)
16	3	PUSH	Bros (CBS)
4	4	LIVE IN EUROPE	Tina Turner (Capitol)
7	5	POPPED IN SOULED OUT	Wet Wet Wet (Precious Organisation)
2	6	VIVA HATE	Morrissey (HMV)
-	7	LOVELY	Primitives (RCA)
-	8	WINGS OF HEAVEN	Magnum (Polydor)
5	9	NAKED	Talking Heads (EMI)
33	10	DISTANT THUNDER	Aswad (Mango)
24	11	TANGO IN THE NIGHT	Fleetwood Mac (Warner Bros.)
6	12	THE STORY OF THE CLASH	Clash (CBS)
11	13	TURN BACK THE CLOCK	Johnny Hates Jazz (Virgin)
9	14	INTRODUCING THE HARDLINE ACCORDING TO	Terence Trent D'Arby (CBS)
14	15	WHITNEY	Whitney Houston (Arista)
19	16	DIRTY DANCING	Soundtrack (RCA)
8	17	FROM LANGLEY PARK TO MEMPHIS	Prefab Sprout (Kitchenware)
31	18	ACTUALLY	Pet Shop Boys (Parlophone)
25	19	TIFFANY	Tiffany (MCA)
20	20	WHENEVER YOU NEED SOMEBODY	Rick Astley (RCA)
29	21	BRIDGE OF SPIES	T'Pau (Siren)
10	22	HEARSAY	Alexander O'Neal (Tabu)
17	23	CHALK MARKS IN A RAIN STORM	Joni Mitchell (Geffen)
37	24	HIP HOP AND RAPPING IN THE HOUSE	Various Artists (Stylus)
23	25	HEAVEN ON EARTH	Belinda Carlisle (Virgin)
28	26	ROCK THE NATION	Various Artists (Dover)
15	27	WHO'S BETTER, WHO'S BEST	Who (Polydor)
-	28	WHAT'S UP DOG	Was Not Was (Fontana)
12	29	TEAR DOWN THESE WALLS	Billy Ocean (Jive)
18	30	SO FAR SO GOOD...SO WHAT!	Megadeth (Capitol)
-	31	RICHARD MARX	Richard Marx (Manhattan)
-	32	GLADSOME, HUMOUR AND BLUE	Martin Stephenson & the Daintees (Kitchenwear)
32	33	WILL DOWNING	Will Downing (Fourth & Broadway)
-	34	DESTINY	Saxon (EMI)
21	35	UNFORGETTABLE	Various Artists (EMI)
36	36	THE CHRISTIANS	Christians (Island)
22	37	KICK	INXS (Mercury)
48	38	BAD ANIMALS	Heart (Capitol)
-	39	HEART	Heart (Capitol)
26	40	LITTLE CHILDREN	Mission (Mercury)
-	41	FILE UNDER ROCK	Eddy Grant (Parlophone)
13	42	HORIZONS	Various Artists (K-Tel)
27	43	GIVE ME THE REASON	Luther Vandross (Epic)
35	44	KINGDOM COME	Kingdom Come (Polydor)
-	45	SGT PEPPER KNEW MY FATHER	Various Artists (NME/Island)
-	46	IN HEAT	Black 'n' Blue (Geffen)
-	47	PASSION	Norman Connors (Capitol)
-	48	UPFRONT 10	Various Artists (Serious)
30	49	BAD	Michael Jackson (Epic)
38	50	EVERYTHING	Cimie Fisher (EMI)

Previously the lead singer with the Smiths, who had split amid general acrimony between key members himself and Johnny Marr, Morrissey wasted no time launching what would be an equally high-profile solo career, and began it by topping the Smiths' former album chart successes with an immediate Number 1 release, *Viva Hate*. No doubt he was unimpressed to then be deposed almost immediately by *Now 11*!

April – May 1988

Bros had just had two Number 2 singles - *When Will I Be Famous* and *Drop The Boy* - in quick succession, when their *Push* album was released, and were already shaping up as the latest UK teen sensation.

The surprise, then, was not that the album should reach Number 1, but that it should come and go from the summit quite so fast. Possibly, most of the trio's young fans were exclusively singles buyers.

14 May 1988

last week	this week		
2	1	TANGO IN THE NIGHT	Fleetwood Mac (Warner Bros.)
1	2	THE INNOCENTS	Erasure (Mute)
4	3	SEVENTH SON OF A SEVENTH SON	Iron Maiden (EMI)
5	4	DIRTY DANCING	Soundtrack (RCA)
6	5	THE BEST OF OMD	Orchestral Manoeuvres in the Dark (Virgin)
12	6	ACTUALLY	Pet Shop Boys (Parlophone)
3	7	NOW THAT'S WHAT I CALL MUSIC 11	Various Artists (EMI/Virgin/PolyGram)
7	8	PUSH	Bros (CBS)
8	9	HIP HOP AND RAPPING IN THE HOUSE	Various Artists (Stylus)
-	10	STRONGER THAN PRIDE	Sade (Epic)
11	11	POPPED IN SOULED OUT	Wet Wet Wet (Precious)
14	12	BRIDGE OF SPIES	T'Pau (Siren)
18	13	LIFE'S TOO GOOD	Sugarcubes (One Little Indian)
-	14	STAY ON THESE ROADS	A-Ha (WEA)
9	15	BARBED WIRE KISS	Jesus & Mary Chain (Blanco Y Negro)
-	16	MORE DIRTY DANCING	Various Artists (RCA)
23	17	WHITNEY	Whitney Houston (Arista)
20	18	NITE FLITE	Various Artists (CBS)
13	19	THE CHRISTIANS	Christians (Island)
10	20	EVERYTHING	Cimie Fisher (EMI)
17	21	WILL DOWNING	Will Downing (Fourth & Broadway)
-	22	SIXTIES MIX 2	Various Artists (Stylus)
43	23	ALIENS ATE MY BUICK	Thomas Dolby (EMI)
21	24	FAITH	George Michael (Epic)
26	25	FROM LANGLEY PARK TO MEMPHIS	Prefab Sprout (Kitchenware)
15	26	NAKED	Talking Heads (EMI)
16	27	THIS NOTE'S FOR YOU	Neil Young & the Blue Notes (Reprise)
22	28	HEAVEN ON EARTH	Belinda Carlisle (Virgin)
34	29	REMEMBER YOU'RE MINE	Foster & Allen (Stylus)
28	30	INTRODUCING THE HARDLINE ACCORDING TO	Terence Trent D'Arby (CBS)
49	31	BAD	Michael Jackson (Epic)
-	32	BLIND	Icicle Works (Beggars Banquet)
-	33	SCENES FROM THE SOUTHSIDE	Bruce Hornsby and the Range (RCA)
24	34	LOVELY	Primitives (RCA)
29	35	HEARSAY	Alexander O'Neal (Tabu)
19	36	LIVE IN EUROPE	Tina Turner (Capitol)
27	37	DISTANT THUNDER	Aswad (Mango)
50	38	THIS IS OUR ART	Soup Dragons (Sire)
-	39	EVERLASTING	Natalie Cole (Manhattan)
45	40	MAKE IT LAST FOREVER	Keith Sweat (Elektra)
31	41	WINGS OF HEAVEN	Magnum (Polydor)
-	42	PEBBLES	Pebbles (MCA)
-	43	NARADA	Narada Michael Walden (Warner Bros.)
25	44	VIVA-HaTE	Morrissey (HMV)
30	45	TURN BACK THE CLOCK	Johnny Hates Jazz (Virgin)
32	46	LOVE	Aztec Camera (Warner Bros.)
37	47	CHER	Cher (Geffen)
42	47	JOE JACKSON LIVE 1980-86	Joe Jackson (A&M)
35	49	GIVE ME THE REASON	Luther Vandross (Epic)
38	50	RAINTOWN	Deacon Blue (CBS)

21 May 1988

1	1	TANGO IN THE NIGHT	Fleetwood Mac (Warner Bros.)
10	2	STRONGER THAN PRIDE	Sade (Epic)
14	3	STAY ON THESE ROADS	A-Ha (WEA)
2	4	THE INNOCENTS	Erasure (Mute)
4	5	DIRTY DANCING	Soundtrack (RCA)
16	6	MORE DIRTY DANCING	Various Artists (RCA)
-	7	LOVESEXY	Prince (Paisley Park)
11	8	POPPED IN SOULED OUT	Wet Wet Wet (Precious)
19	9	THE CHRISTIANS	Christians (Island)
5	10	THE BEST OF OMD	Orchestral Manoeuvres in the Dark (Virgin)
17	11	WHITNEY	Whitney Houston (Arista)
7	12	NOW THAT'S WHAT I CALL MUSIC 11	Various Artists (EMI/Virgin/PolyGram)
9	13	HIP HOP AND RAPPING IN THE HOUSE	Various Artists (Stylus)
-	14	SAVAGE AMUSEMENT	Scorpions (Harvest)
8	15	PUSH	Bros (CBS)
13	16	LIFE'S TOO GOOD	Sugarcubes (One Little Indian)
6	17	ACTUALLY	Pet Shop Boys (Parlophone)
22	18	SIXTIES MIX 2	Various Artists (Stylus)
3	19	SEVENTH SON OF A SEVENTH SON	Iron Maiden (EMI)
-	20	OPEN UP AND SAY AHH	Poison (Capitol)
18	21	NITE FLITE	Various Artists (CBS)
25	22	FROM LANGLEY PARK TO MEMPHIS	Prefab Sprout (Kitchenware)
-	23	SGT PEPPER KNEW MY FATHER	Various Artists (NME/Island)
20	24	EVERYTHING	Cimie Fisher (EMI)
32	25	BLIND	Icicle Works (Beggars Banquet)
-	26	RUMOURS	Fleetwood Mac (Warner Bros.)
12	27	BRIDGE OF SPIES	T'Pau (Siren)
30	28	INTRODUCING THE HARDLINE ACCORDING TO	Terence Trent D'Arby (CBS)
33	29	SCENES FROM THE SOUTHSIDE	Bruce Hornsby and the Range (RCA)
-	30	NOW THATS WHAT I CALL QUITE GOOD	Housemartins (Go! Discs)
-	31	ODYSSEY	Yngwie Malmstein (Polydor)
28	32	HEAVEN ON EARTH	Belinda Carlisle (Virgin)
43	33	NARADA	Narada Michael Walden (Warner Bros.)
-	34	HOUSE HITS	Various Artists (Needle)
34	35	LOVELY	Primitives (RCA)
24	36	FAITH	George Michael (Epic)
15	37	BARBED WIRE KISS	Jesus & Mary Chain (Blanco Y Negro)
41	38	WINGS OF HEAVEN	Magnum (Polydor)
46	39	LOVE	Aztec Camera (Warner Bros.)
-	40	THE XENON CODE	Hawkwind (GWR)
21	41	WILL DOWNING	Will Downing (Fourth & Broadway)
26	42	NAKED	Talking Heads (EMI)
29	43	REMEMBER YOU'RE MINE	Foster & Allen (Stylus)
31	44	BAD	Michael Jackson (Epic)
-	45	TSOP - THE SOUND OF PHILADELPHIA	Various Artists (K-Tel)
42	46	PEBBLES	Pebbles (MCA)
35	47	HEARSAY	Alexander O'Neal (Tabu)
-	48	WOW	Bananarama (London)
36	49	LIVE IN EUROPE	Tina Turner (Capitol)
50	50	RAINTOWN	Deacon Blue (CBS)

28 May 1988

7	1	LOVESEXY	Prince (Paisley Park)
2	2	STRONGER THAN PRIDE	Sade (Epic)
1	3	TANGO IN THE NIGHT	Fleetwood Mac (Warner Bros.)
9	4	THE CHRISTIANS	Christians (Island)
8	5	POPPED IN SOULED OUT	Wet Wet Wet (Precious)
30	6	NOW THATS WHAT I CALL QUITE GOOD	Housemartins (Go! Discs)
3	7	STAY ON THESE ROADS	A-Ha (WEA)
5	8	DIRTY DANCING	Soundtrack (RCA)
11	9	WHITNEY	Whitney Houston (Arista)
6	10	MORE DIRTY DANCING	Various Artists (RCA)
4	11	THE INNOCENTS	Erasure (Mute)
-	12	MOTOWN DANCE PARTY	Various Artists (Motown)
-	13	BULLET FROM A GUN	Derek B (Tuff Audio)
18	14	SIXTIES MIX 2	Various Artists (Stylus)
32	15	HEAVEN ON EARTH	Belinda Carlisle (Virgin)
29	16	SCENES FROM THE SOUTHSIDE	Bruce Hornsby and the Range (RCA)
10	17	THE BEST OF OMD	Orchestral Manoeuvres in the Dark (Virgin)
-	18	THE SEA OF LOVE	Adventures (Elektra)
20	19	OPEN UP AND SAY AHH	Poison (Capitol)
24	20	EVERYTHING	Cimie Fisher (EMI)
31	21	ODYSSEY	Yngwie Malmstein (Polydor)
22	22	FROM LANGLEY PARK TO MEMPHIS	Prefab Sprout (Kitchenware)
26	23	RUMOURS	Fleetwood Mac (Warner Bros.)
21	24	NITE FLITE	Various Artists (CBS)
19	25	SEVENTH SON OF A SEVENTH SON	Iron Maiden (EMI)
12	26	NOW THAT'S WHAT I CALL MUSIC 11	Various Artists (EMI/Virgin/PolyGram)
-	27	RAM IT DOWN	Judas Priest (CBS)
15	28	PUSH	Bros (CBS)
-	29	THE FIRST OF A MILLION KISSES	Fairground Attraction (RCA)
13	30	HIP HOP AND RAPPING IN THE HOUSE	Various Artists (Stylus)
17	31	ACTUALLY	Pet Shop Boys (Parlophone)
34	32	HOUSE HITS	Various Artists (Needle)
-	33	JOY	Teddy Pendergrass (Elektra)
16	34	LIFE'S TOO GOOD	Sugarcubes (One Little Indian)
-	35	ALL SYSTEMS GO	Vinnie Vincent (Chrysalis)
14	36	SAVAGE AMUSEMENT	Scorpions (Harvest)
23	37	SGT PEPPER KNEW MY FATHER	Various Artists (NME/Island)
27	38	BRIDGE OF SPIES	T'Pau (Siren)
33	39	NARADA	Narada Michael Walden (Warner Bros.)
-	40	THE NEW ORDER	Testament (Atlantic)
36	41	FAITH	George Michael (Epic)
37	42	BARBED WIRE KISS	Jesus & Mary Chain (Blanco Y Negro)
-	43	NORTH AND SOUTH	Gerry Rafferty (London)
47	44	HEARSAY	Alexander O'Neal (Tabu)
28	45	INTRODUCING THE HARDLINE ACCORDING TO	Terence Trent D'Arby (CBS)
25	46	BLIND	Icicle Works (Beggars Banquet)
42	47	NAKED	Talking Heads (EMI)
-	48	HE'S THE DJ, I'M THE RAPPER	DJ Jazzy Jeff & the Fresh Prince (Jive)
-	49	IN EFFECT MODE	Al B Sure (Warner Bros.)
-	50	BROOMFIELD	Broomfield (Vision)

After five previous UK charting albums since his 1984 breakthrough with *Purple Rain*, Prince's *Lovesexy* was the first to take him all the way to Number 1, the previous year's *Sign 'O' The Times* having halted at 2. The album he replaced at Number 1 was none other than Fleetwood Mac's *Tango In The Night*, resurgent once again after more than a year in the chart, and enjoying its second spell at the top.

June 1988

4 June 1988

last week	this week	Title / Artist (Label)
3	1	TANGO IN THE NIGHT — Fleetwood Mac (Warner Bros.)
1	2	LOVESEXY — Prince (Paisley Park)
8	3	DIRTY DANCING — Soundtrack (RCA)
10	4	MORE DIRTY DANCING — Various Artists (RCA)
2	5	STRONGER THAN PRIDE — Sade (Epic)
29	6	THE FIRST OF A MILLION KISSES — Fairground Attraction (RCA)
13	7	BULLET FROM A GUN — Derek B (Tuff Audio)
9	8	WHITNEY — Whitney Houston (Arista)
5	9	POPPED IN SOULED OUT — Wet Wet Wet (Precious)
24	10	NITE FLITE — Various Artists (CBS)
4	11	THE CHRISTIANS — Christians (Island)
12	12	MOTOWN DANCE PARTY — Various Artists (Motown)
6	13	NOW THATS WHAT I CALL QUITE GOOD — Housemartins (Go! Discs)
27	14	RAM IT DOWN — Judas Priest (CBS)
-	15	OU812 — Van Halen (Warner Bros.)
15	16	HEAVEN ON EARTH — Belinda Carlisle (Virgin)
7	17	STAY ON THESE ROADS — A-Ha (WEA)
-	18	LOVE — Aztec Camera (Warner Bros.)
36	19	SAVAGE AMUSEMENT — Scorpions (Harvest)
16	20	SCENES FROM THE SOUTHSIDE — Bruce Hornsby and the Range (RCA)
11	21	THE INNOCENTS — Erasure (Mute)
23	22	RUMOURS — Fleetwood Mac (Warner Bros.)
19	23	OPEN UP AND SAY AHH — Poison (Capitol)
22	24	FROM LANGLEY PARK TO MEMPHIS — Prefab Sprout (Kitchenware)
37	25	SGT PEPPER KNEW MY FATHER — Various Artists (NME/Island)
-	26	OUT OF ORDER — Rod Stewart (Warner Bros.)
40	27	THE NEW ORDER — Testament (Atlantic)
14	28	SIXTIES MIX 2 — Various Artists (Stylus)
26	29	NOW THATS WHAT I CALL MUSIC 11 — Various Artists (EMI/Virgin/PolyGram)
-	30	REMEMBER YOU'RE MINE — Foster & Allen (Stylus)
18	31	THE SEA OF LOVE — Adventures (Elektra)
-	32	TSOP - THE SOUND OF PHILADELPHIA — Various Artists (K-Tel)
35	33	ALL SYSTEMS GO — Vinnie Vincent (Chrysalis)
21	34	ODYSSEY — Yngwie Malmstein (Polydor)
-	35	TOUGHER THAN LEATHER — Run DMC (London)
30	36	HIP HOP AND RAPPING IN THE HOUSE — Various Artists (Stylus)
-	37	OPERATION MINDCRIME — Queensryche (Manhattan)
17	38	THE BEST OF OMD — Orchestral Manoeuvres in the Dark (Virgin)
20	39	EVERYTHING — Cimie Fisher (EMI)
31	40	ACTUALLY — Pet Shop Boys (Parlophone)
44	41	HEARSAY — Alexander O'Neal (Tabu)
34	42	LIFE'S TOO GOOD — Sugarcubes (One Little Indian)
43	43	NORTH AND SOUTH — Gerry Rafferty (London)
33	44	JOY — Teddy Pendergrass (Elektra)
-	45	REGGAE CLASSICS VOL 2 — Various Artists (Trojan)
28	46	PUSH — Bros (CBS)
32	47	HOUSE HITS — Various Artists (Needle)
38	48	BRIDGE OF SPIES — T'Pau (Siren)
-	49	DISTANT THUNDER — Aswad (Mango)
-	50	SLAUGHTERHOUSE — Various Artists (Lambs to the Slaughter)

11 June 1988

last week	this week	Title / Artist (Label)
1	1	TANGO IN THE NIGHT — Fleetwood Mac (Warner Bros.)
10	2	NITE FLITE — Various Artists (CBS)
5	3	STRONGER THAN PRIDE — Sade (Epic)
3	4	DIRTY DANCING — Soundtrack (RCA)
2	5	LOVESEXY — Prince (Paisley Park)
9	6	POPPED IN SOULED OUT — Wet Wet Wet (Precious)
12	7	MOTOWN DANCE PARTY — Various Artists (Motown)
4	8	MORE DIRTY DANCING — Various Artists (RCA)
8	9	WHITNEY — Whitney Houston (Arista)
6	10	THE FIRST OF A MILLION KISSES — Fairground Attraction (RCA)
16	11	HEAVEN ON EARTH — Belinda Carlisle (Virgin)
26	12	OUT OF ORDER — Rod Stewart (Warner Bros.)
35	13	TOUGHER THAN LEATHER — Run DMC (London)
15	14	OU812 — Van Halen (Warner Bros.)
18	15	LOVE — Aztec Camera (Warner Bros.)
7	16	BULLET FROM A GUN — Derek B (Tuff Audio)
11	17	THE CHRISTIANS — Christians (Island)
21	18	THE INNOCENTS — Erasure (Mute)
24	19	FROM LANGLEY PARK TO MEMPHIS — Prefab Sprout (Kitchenware)
20	20	SCENES FROM THE SOUTHSIDE — Bruce Hornsby and the Range (RCA)
30	21	REMEMBER YOU'RE MINE — Foster & Allen (Stylus)
25	22	SGT PEPPER KNEW MY FATHER — Various Artists (NME/Island)
39	23	EVERYTHING — Cimie Fisher (EMI)
28	24	SIXTIES MIX 2 — Various Artists (Stylus)
22	25	RUMOURS — Fleetwood Mac (Warner Bros.)
38	26	THE BEST OF OMD — Orchestral Manoeuvres in the Dark (Virgin)
46	27	PUSH — Bros (CBS)
17	28	STAY ON THESE ROADS — A-Ha (WEA)
32	29	TSOP - THE SOUND OF PHILADELPHIA — Various Artists (K-Tel)
14	30	RAM IT DOWN — Judas Priest (CBS)
34	31	ODYSSEY — Yngwie Malmstein (Polydor)
37	32	OPERATION MINDCRIME — Queensryche (Manhattan)
45	33	REGGAE CLASSICS VOL 2 — Various Artists (Trojan)
-	34	TIME ODYSSEY — Vinny Moore (Phonogram)
13	35	NOW THATS WHAT I CALL QUITE GOOD — Housemartins (Go! Discs)
-	36	OUT OF THE BLUE — Debbie Gibson (Atlantic)
40	37	ACTUALLY — Pet Shop Boys (Parlophone)
-	38	GIVE ME THE REASON — Luther Vandross (Epic)
41	39	HEARSAY — Alexander O'Neal (Tabu)
-	40	SUBSTANCE — New Order (Factory)
27	41	THE NEW ORDER — Testament (Atlantic)
-	42	TRACY CHAPMAN — Tracy Chapman (Elektra)
19	43	SAVAGE AMUSEMENT — Scorpions (Harvest)
29	44	NOW THAT'S WHAT I CALL MUSIC 11 — Various Artists (EMI/Virgin/PolyGram)
33	45	ALL SYSTEMS GO — Vinnie Vincent (Chrysalis)
31	46	THE SEA OF LOVE — Adventures (Elektra)
36	47	HIP HOP AND RAPPING IN THE HOUSE — Various Artists (Stylus)
44	48	JOY — Teddy Pendergrass (Elektra)
-	49	EUREKA — Bible (Chrysalis)
-	50	STREET SOUNDS HIP HOP 21 — Various Artists (Street Sounds)

18 June 1988

last week	this week	Title / Artist (Label)
2	1	NITE FLITE — Various Artists (CBS)
1	2	TANGO IN THE NIGHT — Fleetwood Mac (Warner Bros.)
7	3	MOTOWN DANCE PARTY — Various Artists (Motown)
11	4	HEAVEN ON EARTH — Belinda Carlisle (Virgin)
4	5	DIRTY DANCING — Soundtrack (RCA)
15	6	LOVE — Aztec Camera (Warner Bros.)
-	7	PROVISION — Scritti Politti (Virgin)
27	8	PUSH — Bros (CBS)
-	9	PEOPLE — Hothouse Flowers (London)
3	10	STRONGER THAN PRIDE — Sade (Epic)
6	11	POPPED IN SOULED OUT — Wet Wet Wet (Precious)
8	12	MORE DIRTY DANCING — Various Artists (RCA)
9	13	WHITNEY — Whitney Houston (Arista)
10	14	THE FIRST OF A MILLION KISSES — Fairground Attraction (RCA)
-	15	AIN'T COMPLAINING — Status Quo (Vertigo)
39	16	HEARSAY — Alexander O'Neal (Tabu)
17	17	THE CHRISTIANS — Christians (Island)
-	18	HEART — Heart (Capitol)
12	19	OUT OF ORDER — Rod Stewart (Warner Bros.)
18	20	THE INNOCENTS — Erasure (Mute)
24	21	SIXTIES MIX 2 — Various Artists (Stylus)
-	22	BAD — Michael Jackson (Epic)
26	23	THE BEST OF OMD — Orchestral Manoeuvres in the Dark (Virgin)
5	24	LOVESEXY — Prince (Paisley Park)
19	25	FROM LANGLEY PARK TO MEMPHIS — Prefab Sprout (Kitchenware)
29	26	TSOP - THE SOUND OF PHILADELPHIA — Various Artists (K-Tel)
21	27	REMEMBER YOU'RE MINE — Foster & Allen (Stylus)
37	28	ACTUALLY — Pet Shop Boys (Parlophone)
13	29	TOUGHER THAN LEATHER — Run DMC (London)
20	30	SCENES FROM THE SOUTHSIDE — Bruce Hornsby and the Range (RCA)
28	31	STAY ON THESE ROADS — A-Ha (WEA)
14	32	OU812 — Van Halen (Warner Bros.)
-	33	TIFFANY — Tiffany (MCA)
35	34	NOW THATS WHAT I CALL QUITE GOOD — Housemartins (Go! Discs)
44	35	NOW THAT'S WHAT I CALL MUSIC 11 — Various Artists (EMI/Virgin/PolyGram)
-	36	FAITH — George Michael (Epic)
-	37	DISTANT THUNDER — Aswad (Mango)
36	38	OUT OF THE BLUE — Debbie Gibson (Atlantic)
42	39	TRACY CHAPMAN — Tracy Chapman (Elektra)
23	40	EVERYTHING — Cimie Fisher (EMI)
-	41	BACK ON THE ROAD — Various Artists (Stylus)
-	42	VIVA-HaTE — Morrissey (HMV)
-	43	BRIDGE OF SPIES — T'Pau (Siren)
25	44	RUMOURS — Fleetwood Mac (Warner Bros.)
-	45	THE HITS OF HOUSE ARE HERE — Various Artists (K-Tel)
-	46	INTRODUCING THE HARDLINE ACCORDING TO — Terence Trent D'Arby (CBS)
38	47	GIVE ME THE REASON — Luther Vandross (Epic)
16	48	BULLET FROM A GUN — Derek B (Tuff Audio)
-	49	THE COLLECTION – 20 GREATEST HITS — Frankie Valli & the Four Seasons (Telstar)
-	50	WOLF — Hugh Cornwell (Virgin)

The *Sgt. Pepper Knew My Father* compilation owes its origins to he NME, and was first made available by mail order to the paper's readers, prior to going on general sale through Island Records. A charity project (for Childline), the album featured all the songs from the Beatles' *Sgt.Pepper* album as covered by 1980s acts, and it spun off the chart-topping Wet Wet Wet single *With A Little Help From My Friends*.

25 June 1988

last week	this week		
1	1	NITE FLITE	Various Artists (CBS)
2	2	TANGO IN THE NIGHT	Fleetwood Mac (Warner Bros.)
9	3	PEOPLE	Hothouse Flowers (London)
3	4	MOTOWN DANCE PARTY	Various Artists (Motown)
4	5	HEAVEN ON EARTH	Belinda Carlisle (Virgin)
8	6	PUSH	Bros (CBS)
5	7	DIRTY DANCING	Soundtrack (RCA)
39	8	TRACY CHAPMAN	Tracy Chapman (Elektra)
7	9	PROVISION	Scritti Politti (Virgin)
13	10	WHITNEY	Whitney Houston (Arista)
11	11	POPPED IN SOULED OUT	Wet Wet Wet (Precious)
10	12	STRONGER THAN PRIDE	Sade (Epic)
45	13	THE HITS OF HOUSE ARE HERE	Various Artists (K-Tel)
40	14	EVERYTHING	Cimie Fisher (EMI)
20	15	THE INNOCENTS	Erasure (Mute)
6	16	LOVE	Aztec Camera (Warner Bros.)
12	17	MORE DIRTY DANCING	Various Artists (RCA)
26	18	TSOP - THE SOUND OF PHILADELPHIA	Various Artists (K-Tel)
15	19	AIN'T COMPLAINING	Status Quo (Vertigo)
14	20	THE FIRST OF A MILLION KISSES	Fairground Attraction (RCA)
17	21	THE CHRISTIANS	Christians (Island)
-	22	DOWN IN THE GROOVE	Bob Dylan (CBS)
18	23	HEART	Heart (Capitol)
36	24	FAITH	George Michael (Epic)
16	25	HEARSAY	Alexander O'Neal (Tabu)
22	26	BAD	Michael Jackson (Epic)
31	27	STAY ON THESE ROADS	A-Ha (WEA)
19	28	OUT OF ORDER	Rod Stewart (Warner Bros.)
23	29	THE BEST OF OMD	Orchestral Manoeuvres in the Dark (Virgin)
27	30	REMEMBER YOU'RE MINE	Foster & Allen (Stylus)
21	31	SIXTIES MIX 2	Various Artists (Stylus)
-	32	I'M REAL	James Brown with Full Force (Scotti Brothers)
24	33	LOVESEXY	Prince (Paisley Park)
30	34	SCENES FROM THE SOUTHSIDE	Bruce Hornsby and the Range (RCA)
-	35	BROTHERS IN ARMS	Dire Straits (Vertigo)
42	36	VIVA-HaTE	Morrissey (HMV)
41	37	BACK ON THE ROAD	Various Artists (Stylus)
28	38	ACTUALLY	Pet Shop Boys (Parlophone)
-	39	SAVAGE	Eurythmics (RCA)
-	40	BY ALL MEANS NECESSARY	Boogie Down Productions (Jive)
25	41	FROM LANGLEY PARK TO MEMPHIS	Prefab Sprout (Kitchenware)
38	42	OUT OF THE BLUE	Debbie Gibson (Atlantic)
-	43	SUR LA MER	Moody Blues (Polydor)
44	44	RUMOURS	Fleetwood Mac (Warner Bros.)
35	45	NOW THAT'S WHAT I CALL MUSIC 11	Various Artists (EMI/Virgin/PolyGram)
29	46	TOUGHER THAN LEATHER	Run DMC (London)
43	47	BRIDGE OF SPIES	T'Pau (Siren)
37	48	DISTANT THUNDER	Aswad (Mango)
32	49	OU812	Van Halen (Warner Bros.)
-	50	FACE VALUE	Phil Collins (Virgin)

2 July 1988

8	1	TRACY CHAPMAN	Tracy Chapman (Elektra)
1	2	NITE FLITE	Various Artists (CBS)
2	3	TANGO IN THE NIGHT	Fleetwood Mac (Warner Bros.)
6	4	PUSH	Bros (CBS)
-	5	ROLL WITH IT	Steve Winwood (Virgin)
10	6	WHITNEY	Whitney Houston (Arista)
7	7	DIRTY DANCING	Soundtrack (RCA)
5	8	HEAVEN ON EARTH	Belinda Carlisle (Virgin)
-	9	IDOL SONGS - 11 OF THE BEST	Billy Idol (Chrysalis)
12	10	STRONGER THAN PRIDE	Sade (Epic)
11	11	POPPED IN SOULED OUT	Wet Wet Wet (Precious)
4	12	MOTOWN DANCE PARTY	Various Artists (Motown)
3	13	PEOPLE	Hothouse Flowers (London)
13	14	THE HITS OF HOUSE ARE HERE	Various Artists (K-Tel)
9	15	PROVISION	Scritti Politti (Virgin)
17	16	MORE DIRTY DANCING	Various Artists (RCA)
35	17	BROTHERS IN ARMS	Dire Straits (Vertigo)
38	18	ACTUALLY	Pet Shop Boys (Parlophone)
-	19	LET IT BEE	Voice of the Beehive (London)
15	20	THE INNOCENTS	Erasure (Mute)
16	21	LOVE	Aztec Camera (Warner Bros.)
14	22	EVERYTHING	Cimie Fisher (EMI)
43	23	SUR LA MER	Moody Blues (Polydor)
-	24	JACK MIX IN FULL EFFECT	Mirage (Stylus)
24	25	FAITH	George Michael (Epic)
-	26	CONFESSIONS OF A POP GROUP	Style Council (Polydor)
39	27	SAVAGE	Eurythmics (RCA)
18	28	TSOP - THE SOUND OF PHILADELPHIA	Various Artists (K-Tel)
21	29	THE CHRISTIANS	Christians (Island)
32	30	I'M REAL	James Brown with Full Force (Scotti Brothers)
23	31	HEART	Heart (Capitol)
26	32	BAD	Michael Jackson (Epic)
T'Pau	33	AIN'T COMPLAINING	Status Quo (Vertigo)
30	34	REMEMBER YOU'RE MINE	Foster & Allen (Stylus)
33	35	LOVESEXY	Prince (Paisley Park)
20	36	THE FIRST OF A MILLION KISSES	Fairground Attraction (RCA)
31	37	SIXTIES MIX 2	Various Artists (Stylus)
50	38	FACE VALUE	Phil Collins (Virgin)
22	39	DOWN IN THE GROOVE	Bob Dylan (CBS)
-	40	TUNNEL OF LOVE	Bruce Springsteen (CBS)
29	41	THE BEST OF OMD	Orchestral Manoeuvres in the Dark (Virgin)
-	42	BEST OF HOUSE VOL 5	Various Artists (Serious)
25	43	HEARSAY	Alexander O'Neal (Tabu)
27	44	STAY ON THESE ROADS	A-Ha (WEA)
44	45	RUMOURS	Fleetwood Mac (Warner Bros.)
47	46	BRIDGE OF SPIES	T'Pau (Siren)
37	47	BACK ON THE ROAD	Various Artists (Stylus)
34	48	SCENES FROM THE SOUTHSIDE	Bruce Hornsby and the Range (RCA)
-	49	IRISH HEARTBEAT	Van Morrison with the Chieftains (Mercury)
-	50	THE OUTRIDER	Jimmy Page (Geffen)

9 July 1988

1	1	TRACY CHAPMAN	Tracy Chapman (Elektra)
9	2	IDOL SONGS - 11 OF THE BEST	Billy Idol (Chrysalis)
4	3	PUSH	Bros (CBS)
5	4	ROLL WITH IT	Steve Winwood (Virgin)
3	5	TANGO IN THE NIGHT	Fleetwood Mac (Warner Bros.)
2	6	NITE FLITE	Various Artists (CBS)
7	7	DIRTY DANCING	Soundtrack (RCA)
-	8	HEAVY NOVA	Robert Palmer (EMI)
8	9	HEAVEN ON EARTH	Belinda Carlisle (Virgin)
-	10	THE COLLECTION	Barry White (Mercury)
6	11	WHITNEY	Whitney Houston (Arista)
40	12	TUNNEL OF LOVE	Bruce Springsteen (CBS)
10	13	STRONGER THAN PRIDE	Sade (Epic)
14	14	THE HITS OF HOUSE ARE HERE	Various Artists (K-Tel)
19	15	LET IT BEE	Voice of the Beehive (London)
11	16	POPPED IN SOULED OUT	Wet Wet Wet (Precious Organisation)
13	17	PEOPLE	Hothouse Flowers (London)
-	18	TIGHTEN UP VOL 88	Big Audio Dynamite (CBS)
49	19	IRISH HEARTBEAT	Van Morrison with the Chieftains (Mercury)
24	20	JACK MIX IN FULL EFFECT	Mirage (Stylus)
12	21	MOTOWN DANCE PARTY	Various Artists (Motown)
18	22	ACTUALLY	Pet Shop Boys (Parlophone)
26	23	CONFESSIONS OF A POP GROUP	Style Council (Polydor)
16	24	MORE DIRTY DANCING	Various Artists (RCA)
27	25	SAVAGE	Eurythmics (RCA)
20	26	THE INNOCENTS	Erasure (Mute)
15	27	PROVISION	Scritti Politti (Virgin)
25	28	FAITH	George Michael (Epic)
17	29	BROTHERS IN ARMS	Dire Straits (Vertigo)
32	30	BAD	Michael Jackson (Epic)
22	31	EVERYTHING	Cimie Fisher (EMI)
46	32	BRIDGE OF SPIES	T'Pau (Siren)
23	33	SUR LA MER	Moody Blues (Polydor)
21	34	LOVE	Aztec Camera (Warner Bros.)
29	35	THE CHRISTIANS	Christians (Island)
50	36	THE OUTRIDER	Jimmy Page (Geffen)
47	37	BACK ON THE ROAD	Various Artists (Stylus)
38	38	FACE VALUE	Phil Collins (Virgin)
31	39	HEART	Heart (Capitol)
-	40	INDIGO	Matt Bianco (WEA)
43	41	HEARSAY	Alexander O'Neal (Tabu)
36	42	THE FIRST OF A MILLION KISSES	Fairground Attraction (RCA)
-	43	OPEN ALL NIGHT	Georgia Satellites (Elektra)
37	44	SIXTIES MIX 2	Various Artists (Stylus)
-	45	KICK	INXS (Mercury)
-	46	OUT OF THE BLUE	Debbie Gibson (Atlantic)
-	47	JULIA FORDHAM	Julia Fordham (Virgin)
30	48	I'M REAL	James Brown with Full Force (Scotti Brothers)
-	49	OUTSIDE THE GATE	Killing Joke (EG)
41	50	THE BEST OF OMD	Orchestral Manoeuvres in the Dark (Virgin)

Singer-songwriter Tracy Chapman suddenly found herself atop the album chart with her eponymous debut set after a memorable performance (as a virtual unknown) at the internationally televised Nelson Mandela Birthday Party concert at London's Wembley Stadium. Whitney Houston, another performer at the same concert, also saw her perennial *Whitney* album rebound into the Top 10.

July 1988

16 July 1988

last	this	title	artist
1	1	TRACY CHAPMAN	Tracy Chapman (Elektra)
2	2	IDOL SONGS - 11 OF THE BEST	Billy Idol (Chrysalis)
3	3	PUSH	Bros (CBS)
-	4	KYLIE –	Kylie Minogue (PWL)
5	5	TANGO IN THE NIGHT	Fleetwood Mac (Warner Bros.)
4	6	ROLL WITH IT	Steve Winwood (Virgin)
10	7	THE COLLECTION	Barry White (Mercury)
12	8	TUNNEL OF LOVE	Bruce Springsteen (CBS)
7	9	DIRTY DANCING	Soundtrack (RCA)
-	10	WIDE AWAKE IN DREAMLAND	Pat Benatar (Chrysalis)
6	11	NITE FLITE	Various Artists (CBS)
16	12	POPPED IN SOULED OUT	Wet Wet Wet (Precious)
9	13	HEAVEN ON EARTH	Belinda Carlisle (Virgin)
20	14	JACK MIX IN FULL EFFECT	Mirage (Stylus)
13	15	STRONGER THAN PRIDE	Sade (Epic)
8	16	HEAVY NOVA	Robert Palmer (EMI)
11	17	WHITNEY	Whitney Houston (Arista)
-	18	REG STRIKES BACK	Elton John (Rocket)
24	19	MORE DIRTY DANCING	Various Artists (RCA)
28	20	FAITH	George Michael (Epic)
30	21	BAD	Michael Jackson (Epic)
32	22	BRIDGE OF SPIES	T'Pau (Siren)
14	23	THE HITS OF HOUSE ARE HERE	Various Artists (K-Tel)
40	24	INDIGO	Matt Bianco (WEA)
45	25	KICK	INXS (Mercury)
-	26	THE SHOUTING STAGE	Joan Armatrading (A&M)
17	27	PEOPLE	Hothouse Flowers (London)
-	28	MAXI	Maxi Priest (10)
-	29	NOBODY'S PERFECT	Deep Purple (Polydor)
25	30	SAVAGE	Eurythmics (RCA)
18	31	TIGHTEN UP VOL 88	Big Audio Dynamite (CBS)
-	32	VENICE IN PERIL	Rondo Veneziano (Fanfare)
15	33	LET IT BEE	Voice of the Beehive (London)
29	34	BROTHERS IN ARMS	Dire Straits (Vertigo)
34	35	LOVE	Aztec Camera (Warner Bros.)
21	36	MOTOWN DANCE PARTY	Various Artists (Motown)
22	37	ACTUALLY	Pet Shop Boys (Parlophone)
26	38	THE INNOCENTS	Erasure (Mute)
19	39	IRISH HEARTBEAT	Van Morrison with the Chieftains (Mercury)
35	40	THE CHRISTIANS	Christians (Island)
27	41	PROVISION	Scritti Politti (Virgin)
37	42	BACK ON THE ROAD	Various Artists (Stylus)
23	43	CONFESSIONS OF A POP GROUP	Style Council (Polydor)
50	44	THE BEST OF OMD	Orchestral Manoeuvres in the Dark (Virgin)
39	45	HEART	Heart (Capitol)
31	46	EVERYTHING	Cimie Fisher (EMI)
-	47	UPFRONT 11	Various Artists (Serious)
46	48	OUT OF THE BLUE	Debbie Gibson (Atlantic)
33	49	SUR LA MER	Moody Blues (Polydor)
42	50	THE FIRST OF A MILLION KISSES	Fairground Attraction (RCA)

23 July 1988

last	this	title	artist
-	1	NOW THAT'S WHAT I CALL MUSIC 12	Various Artists (EMI/Virgin/Polygram)
1	2	TRACY CHAPMAN	Tracy Chapman (Elektra)
4	3	KYLIE –	Kylie Minogue (PWL)
21	4	BAD	Michael Jackson (Epic)
2	5	IDOL SONGS - 11 OF THE BEST	Billy Idol (Chrysalis)
7	6	THE COLLECTION	Barry White (Mercury)
5	7	TANGO IN THE NIGHT	Fleetwood Mac (Warner Bros.)
3	8	PUSH	Bros (CBS)
-	9	UB40	UB40 (DEP International)
14	10	JACK MIX IN FULL EFFECT	Mirage (Stylus)
9	11	DIRTY DANCING	Soundtrack (RCA)
8	12	TUNNEL OF LOVE	Bruce Springsteen (CBS)
-	13	SUBSTANCE 1977-1980	Joy Division (Factory)
10	14	WIDE AWAKE IN DREAMLAND	Pat Benatar (Chrysalis)
12	15	POPPED IN SOULED OUT	Wet Wet Wet (Precious)
13	16	HEAVEN ON EARTH	Belinda Carlisle (Virgin)
15	17	STRONGER THAN PRIDE	Sade (Epic)
18	18	FAITH	George Michael (Epic)
11	19	NITE FLITE	Various Artists (CBS)
6	20	ROLL WITH IT	Steve Winwood (Virgin)
17	21	WHITNEY	Whitney Houston (Arista)
18	22	REG STRIKES BACK	Elton John (Rocket)
22	23	BRIDGE OF SPIES	T'Pau (Siren)
25	24	KICK	INXS (Mercury)
-	25	WHAT YOU SEE IS WHAT YOU GET	Glen Goldsmith (Reproduction)
16	26	HEAVY NOVA	Robert Palmer (EMI)
27	27	PEOPLE	Hothouse Flowers (London)
26	28	THE SHOUTING STAGE	Joan Armatrading (A&M)
19	29	MORE DIRTY DANCING	Various Artists (RCA)
35	30	LOVE	Aztec Camera (Warner Bros.)
24	31	INDIGO	Matt Bianco (WEA)
30	32	SAVAGE	Eurythmics (RCA)
28	33	MAXI	Maxi Priest (10)
23	34	THE HITS OF HOUSE ARE HERE	Various Artists (K-Tel)
34	35	BROTHERS IN ARMS	Dire Straits (Vertigo)
-	36	LOVESEXY	Prince (Paisley Park)
42	37	BACK ON THE ROAD	Various Artists (Stylus)
-	38	FEARLESS	Eighth Wonder (CBS)
32	39	VENICE IN PERIL	Rondo Veneziano (Fanfare)
38	40	THE INNOCENTS	Erasure (Mute)
33	41	LET IT BEE	Voice of the Beehive (London)
-	42	SOUTH OF HEAVEN	Slayer (Def Jam)
37	43	ACTUALLY	Pet Shop Boys (Parlophone)
29	44	NOBODY'S PERFECT	Deep Purple (Polydor)
-	45	LONG COLD WINTER	Cinderella (Vertigo)
44	46	THE BEST OF OMD	Orchestral Manoeuvres in the Dark (Virgin)
-	47	HEARSAY	Alexander O'Neal (Tabu)
-	48	THRILLER	Michael Jackson (Epic)
36	49	MOTOWN DANCE PARTY	Various Artists (Motown)
-	50	ROACHFORD	Roachford (CBS)

30 July 1988

last	this	title	artist
1	1	NOW THAT'S WHAT I CALL MUSIC 12	Various Artists (EMI/Virgin/Polygram)
2	2	TRACY CHAPMAN	Tracy Chapman (Elektra)
-	3	THE HITS ALBUM – HITS 8	Various Artists (CBS/WEA/BMG)
4	4	BAD	Michael Jackson (Epic)
3	5	KYLIE –	Kylie Minogue (PWL)
5	6	IDOL SONGS - 11 OF THE BEST	Billy Idol (Chrysalis)
-	7	IT TAKES A NATION OF MILLIONS TO HOLD US BACK	Public Enemy (Def Jam)
13	8	SUBSTANCE 1977-1980	Joy Division (Factory)
7	9	TANGO IN THE NIGHT	Fleetwood Mac (Warner Bros.)
8	10	PUSH	Bros (CBS)
6	11	THE COLLECTION	Barry White (Mercury)
11	12	DIRTY DANCING	Soundtrack (RCA)
12	13	TUNNEL OF LOVE	Bruce Springsteen (CBS)
24	14	KICK	INXS (Mercury)
15	15	POPPED IN SOULED OUT	Wet Wet Wet (Precious)
9	16	UB40	UB40 (DEP International)
18	17	FAITH	George Michael (Epic)
48	18	THRILLER	Michael Jackson (Epic)
25	19	WHAT YOU SEE IS WHAT YOU GET	Glen Goldsmith (Reproduction)
14	20	WIDE AWAKE IN DREAMLAND	Pat Benatar (Chrysalis)
21	21	WHITNEY	Whitney Houston (Arista)
16	22	HEAVEN ON EARTH	Belinda Carlisle (Virgin)
20	23	ROLL WITH IT	Steve Winwood (Virgin)
23	24	BRIDGE OF SPIES	T'Pau (Siren)
17	25	STRONGER THAN PRIDE	Sade (Epic)
42	26	SOUTH OF HEAVEN	Slayer (Def Jam)
30	27	LOVE	Aztec Camera (Warner Bros.)
10	28	JACK MIX IN FULL EFFECT	Mirage (Stylus)
29	29	MORE DIRTY DANCING	Various Artists (RCA)
-	30	DON'T LET LOVE SLIP AWAY	Freddie Jackson (Capitol)
27	31	PEOPLE	Hothouse Flowers (London)
22	32	REG STRIKES BACK	Elton John (Rocket)
35	33	BROTHERS IN ARMS	Dire Straits (Vertigo)
36	34	LOVESEXY	Prince (Paisley Park)
31	35	INDIGO	Matt Bianco (WEA)
28	36	THE SHOUTING STAGE	Joan Armatrading (A&M)
-	37	TOMMY	Wedding Present (Reception)
-	38	THE MICHAEL JACKSON MIX	Michael Jackson (Stylus)
45	39	LONG COLD WINTER	Cinderella (Vertigo)
-	40	OUT OF THE BLUE	Debbie Gibson (Atlantic)
32	41	SAVAGE	Eurythmics (RCA)
19	42	NITE FLITE	Various Artists (CBS)
-	43	HYSTERIA	Def Leppard (Bludgeon Riffola)
47	44	HEARSAY	Alexander O'Neal (Tabu)
34	45	THE HITS OF HOUSE ARE HERE	Various Artists (K-Tel)
-	46	THE FIRST OF A MILLION KISSES	Fairground Attraction (RCA)
26	47	HEAVY NOVA	Robert Palmer (EMI)
38	48	FEARLESS	Eighth Wonder (CBS)
41	49	LET IT BEE	Voice of the Beehive (London)
33	50	MAXI	Maxi Priest (10)

Kylie Minogue's first album was an eagerly awaited item, since the teenage Australian actress had already registered a Number 1 and a Number 2 single with her first two UK releases. Near the top of the chart for the rest of the year, moving over a million copies, it would become the best-selling debut album ever in the UK, the top all-time seller by a female artist, and the fifth biggest UK seller of the 1980s.

6 August 1988

last week	this week		
1	1	NOW THAT'S WHAT I CALL MUSIC 12	Various Artists (EMI/Virgin/Polygram)
3	2	THE HITS ALBUM – HITS 8	Various Artists (CBS/WEA/BMG)
2	3	TRACY CHAPMAN	Tracy Chapman (Elektra)
5	4	KYLIE	Kylie Minogue (PWL)
4	5	BAD	Michael Jackson (Epic)
6	6	IDOL SONGS - 11 OF THE BEST	Billy Idol (Chrysalis)
7	7	IT TAKES A NATION OF MILLIONS TO HOLD US BACK	Public Enemy (Def Jam)
10	8	PUSH	Bros (CBS)
9	9	TANGO IN THE NIGHT	Fleetwood Mac (Warner Bros.)
12	10	DIRTY DANCING	Soundtrack (RCA)
13	11	TUNNEL OF LOVE	Bruce Springsteen (CBS)
-	12	FOLLOW THE LEADER	Eric B & Rakim (MCA)
15	13	POPPED IN SOULED OUT	Wet Wet Wet (Precious)
11	14	THE COLLECTION	Barry White (Mercury)
8	15	SUBSTANCE 1977-1980	Joy Division (Factory)
18	16	THRILLER	Michael Jackson (Epic)
14	17	KICK	INXS (Mercury)
16	18	UB40	UB40 (DEP International)
-	19	A SALT WITH A DEADLY PEPA	Salt 'N' Pepa (London)
27	20	LOVE	Aztec Camera (Warner Bros.)
17	21	FAITH	George Michael (Epic)
22	22	HEAVEN ON EARTH	Belinda Carlisle (Virgin)
43	23	HYSTERIA	Def Leppard (Bludgeon Riffola)
34	24	LOVESEXY	Prince (Paisley Park)
25	25	STRONGER THAN PRIDE	Sade (Epic)
20	26	WIDE AWAKE IN DREAMLAND	Pat Benatar (Chrysalis)
28	27	JACK MIX IN FULL EFFECT	Mirage (Stylus)
46	28	THE FIRST OF A MILLION KISSES	Fairground Attraction (RCA)
-	29	SMALL WORLD	Huey Lewis & the News (Chrysalis)
30	30	DON'T LET LOVE SLIP AWAY	Freddie Jackson (Capitol)
21	31	WHITNEY	Whitney Houston (Arista)
40	32	OUT OF THE BLUE	Debbie Gibson (Atlantic)
29	33	MORE DIRTY DANCING	Various Artists (RCA)
44	34	HEARSAY	Alexander O'Neal (Tabu)
23	35	ROLL WITH IT	Steve Winwood (Virgin)
38	36	THE MICHAEL JACKSON MIX	Michael Jackson (Stylus)
24	37	BRIDGE OF SPIES	T'Pau (Siren)
33	38	BROTHERS IN ARMS	Dire Straits (Vertigo)
19	39	WHAT YOU SEE IS WHAT YOU GET	Glen Goldsmith (Reproduction)
-	40	RAINTOWN	Deacon Blue (CBS)
31	41	PEOPLE	Hothouse Flowers (London)
-	42	THE GREATEST EVER ROCK 'N' ROLL MIX	Various Artists (Stylus)
-	43	OFF THE WALL	Michael Jackson (Epic)
41	44	SAVAGE	Eurythmics (RCA)
35	45	INDIGO	Matt Bianco (WEA)
49	46	LET IT BEE	Voice of the Beehive (London)
-	47	THE CHRISTIANS	Christians (Island)
-	48	IDLEWILD	Everything But The Girl (Blanco Y Negro)
32	49	REG STRIKES BACK	Elton John (Rocket)
-	50	OLD 8 X 10	Randy Travis (Warner Bros.)

13 August 1988

1	1	NOW THAT'S WHAT I CALL MUSIC 12	Various Artists (EMI/Virgin/Polygram)
2	2	THE HITS ALBUM – HITS 8	Various Artists (CBS/WEA/BMG)
3	3	TRACY CHAPMAN	Tracy Chapman (Elektra)
4	4	KYLIE	Kylie Minogue (PWL)
6	5	IDOL SONGS - 11 OF THE BEST	Billy Idol (Chrysalis)
5	6	BAD	Michael Jackson (Epic)
28	7	THE FIRST OF A MILLION KISSES	Fairground Attraction (RCA)
8	8	PUSH	Bros (CBS)
9	9	TANGO IN THE NIGHT	Fleetwood Mac (Warner Bros.)
14	10	THE COLLECTION	Barry White (Mercury)
10	11	DIRTY DANCING	Soundtrack (RCA)
42	12	THE GREATEST EVER ROCK 'N' ROLL MIX	Various Artists (Stylus)
29	13	SMALL WORLD	Huey Lewis and the News (Chrysalis)
24	14	LOVESEXY	Prince (Paisley Park)
15	15	POPPED IN SOULED OUT	Wet Wet Wet (Precious)
16	16	THRILLER	Michael Jackson (Epic)
17	17	KICK	INXS (Mercury)
48	18	IDLEWILD	Everything But The Girl (Blanco Y Negro)
26	19	WIDE AWAKE IN DREAMLAND	Pat Benatar (Chrysalis)
20	20	LOVE	Aztec Camera (Warner Bros.)
19	21	A SALT WITH A DEADLY PEPA	Salt 'N' Pepa (London)
31	22	WHITNEY	Whitney Houston (Arista)
11	23	TUNNEL OF LOVE	Bruce Springsteen (CBS)
34	24	HEARSAY	Alexander O'Neal (Tabu)
22	25	HEAVEN ON EARTH	Belinda Carlisle (Virgin)
7	26	IT TAKES A NATION OF MILLIONS TO HOLD US BACK	Public Enemy (Def Jam)
15	27	SUBSTANCE 1977-1980	Joy Division (Factory)
21	28	FAITH	George Michael (Epic)
12	29	FOLLOW THE LEADER	Eric B & Rakim (MCA)
40	30	RAINTOWN	Deacon Blue (CBS)
23	31	HYSTERIA	Def Leppard (Bludgeon Riffola)
41	32	PEOPLE	Hothouse Flowers (London)
35	33	ROLL WITH IT	Steve Winwood (Virgin)
-	34	JULIA FORDHAM	Julia Fordham (Virgin)
18	35	UB40	UB40 (DEP International)
33	36	MORE DIRTY DANCING	Various Artists (RCA)
27	37	JACK MIX IN FULL EFFECT	Mirage (Stylus)
38	38	BROTHERS IN ARMS	Dire Straits (Vertigo)
25	39	STRONGER THAN PRIDE	Sade (Epic)
47	40	THE CHRISTIANS	Christians (Island)
-	41	ALL OF THIS AND NOTHING	Psychedelic Furs (CBS)
30	42	DON'T LET LOVE SLIP AWAY	Freddie Jackson (Capitol)
44	43	SAVAGE	Eurythmics (RCA)
46	44	LET IT BEE	Voice of the Beehive (London)
37	45	BRIDGE OF SPIES	T'Pau (Siren)
32	46	OUT OF THE BLUE	Debbie Gibson (Atlantic)
45	47	INDIGO	Matt Bianco (WEA)
-	48	BUENOS NOCHES FROM A LONELY ROOM	Dwight Yoakam (Warner Bros.)
39	49	WHAT YOU SEE IS WHAT YOU GET	Glen Goldsmith (Reproduction)
-	50	LONG COLD WINTER	Cinderella (Vertigo)

20 August 1988

1	1	NOW THAT'S WHAT I CALL MUSIC 12	Various Artists (EMI/Virgin/Polygram)
4	2	KYLIE	Kylie Minogue (PWL)
3	3	TRACY CHAPMAN	Tracy Chapman (Elektra)
5	4	IDOL SONGS - 11 OF THE BEST	Billy Idol (Chrysalis)
2	5	THE HITS ALBUM – HITS 8	Various Artists (CBS/WEA/BMG)
7	6	THE FIRST OF A MILLION KISSES	Fairground Attraction (RCA)
6	7	BAD	Michael Jackson (Epic)
12	8	THE GREATEST EVER ROCK 'N' ROLL MIX	Various Artists (Stylus)
9	9	TANGO IN THE NIGHT	Fleetwood Mac (Warner Bros.)
-	10	BEST OF THE EAGLES	Eagles (Asylum)
8	11	PUSH	Bros (CBS)
30	12	RAINTOWN	Deacon Blue (CBS)
11	13	DIRTY DANCING	Soundtrack (RCA)
10	14	THE COLLECTION	Barry White (Mercury)
13	15	SMALL WORLD	Huey Lewis & the News (Chrysalis)
18	16	IDLEWILD	Everything But The Girl (Blanco Y Negro)
14	17	LOVESEXY	Prince (Paisley Park)
15	18	POPPED IN SOULED OUT	Wet Wet Wet (Precious)
20	19	LOVE	Aztec Camera (Warner Bros.)
17	20	KICK	INXS (Mercury)
19	21	WIDE AWAKE IN DREAMLAND	Pat Benatar (Chrysalis)
22	22	WHITNEY	Whitney Houston (Arista)
25	23	HEAVEN ON EARTH	Belinda Carlisle (Virgin)
24	24	HEARSAY	Alexander O'Neal (Tabu)
31	25	HYSTERIA	Def Leppard (Bludgeon Riffola)
34	26	JULIA FORDHAM	Julia Fordham (Virgin)
21	27	A SALT WITH A DEADLY PEPA	Salt 'N' Pepa (London)
16	28	THRILLER	Michael Jackson (Epic)
44	29	LET IT BEE	Voice of the Beehive (London)
33	30	ROLL WITH IT	Steve Winwood (Virgin)
23	31	TUNNEL OF LOVE	Bruce Springsteen (CBS)
32	32	PEOPLE	Hothouse Flowers (London)
35	33	UB40	UB40 (DEP International)
26	34	IT TAKES A NATION OF MILLIONS TO HOLD US BACK	Public Enemy (Def Jam)
36	35	MORE DIRTY DANCING	Various Artists (RCA)
46	36	OUT OF THE BLUE	Debbie Gibson (Atlantic)
28	37	FAITH	George Michael (Epic)
38	38	BROTHERS IN ARMS	Dire Straits (Vertigo)
43	39	SAVAGE	Eurythmics (RCA)
-	40	ON THE BEACH	Chris Rea (WEA)
27	41	SUBSTANCE 1977-1980	Joy Division (Factory)
40	42	THE CHRISTIANS	Christians (Island)
-	43	APPETITE FOR DESTRUCTION	Guns 'N' Roses (Geffen)
29	44	FOLLOW THE LEADER	Eric B & Rakim (MCA)
45	45	BRIDGE OF SPIES	T'Pau (Siren)
-	46	ALL ABOUT EVE	All About Eve (Mercury)
-	47	CLOSE	Kim Wilde (MCA)
42	48	DON'T LET LOVE SLIP AWAY	Freddie Jackson (Capitol)
47	49	INDIGO	Matt Bianco (WEA)
-	50	INTRODUCING THE HARDLINE ACCORDING TO	Terence Trent D'Arby (CBS)

August saw another head-to-head between the *Now* and *Hits* compilation series, with volume 12 of the former series having the sales edge, as was becoming the consistent pattern. Many were surprised to see the militant black rap group Public Enemy riding the UK Top 10; in fact, they never quite managed to replicate the success of *It Takes A Nation Of Millions To Hold Us Back*, either on the single or album charts.

August – September 1988

27 August 1988

Last	This	Title	Artist (Label)
1	1	NOW THAT'S WHAT I CALL MUSIC 12	Various Artists (EMI/Virgin/Polygram)
2	2	KYLIE	Kylie Minogue (PWL)
6	3	THE FIRST OF A MILLION KISSES	Fairground Attraction (RCA)
3	4	TRACY CHAPMAN	Tracy Chapman (Elektra)
4	5	IDOL SONGS - 11 OF THE BEST	Billy Idol (Chrysalis)
10	6	BEST OF THE EAGLES	Eagles (Asylum)
8	7	THE GREATEST EVER ROCK 'N' ROLL MIX	Various Artists (Stylus)
5	8	THE HITS ALBUM – HITS 8	Various Artists (CBS/WEA/BMG)
7	9	BAD	Michael Jackson (Epic)
-	10	TURN BACK THE CLOCK	Johnny Hates Jazz (Virgin)
13	11	DIRTY DANCING	Soundtrack (RCA)
9	12	TANGO IN THE NIGHT	Fleetwood Mac (Warner Bros.)
25	13	HYSTERIA	Def Leppard (Bludgeon Riffola)
-	14	ROCK THE WORLD	Five Star (Tent)
11	15	PUSH	Bros (CBS)
20	16	KICK	INXS (Mercury)
19	17	LOVE	Aztec Camera (Warner Bros.)
12	18	RAINTOWN	Deacon Blue (CBS)
14	19	THE COLLECTION	Barry White (Mercury)
-	20	EIGHT LEGGED GROOVE MACHINE	Wonderstuff (Polydor)
15	21	SMALL WORLD	Huey Lewis & the News (Chrysalis)
22	22	WHITNEY	Whitney Houston (Arista)
23	23	HEAVEN ON EARTH	Belinda Carlisle (Virgin)
18	24	POPPED IN SOULED OUT	Wet Wet Wet (Precious)
30	25	ROLL WITH IT	Steve Winwood (Virgin)
21	26	WIDE AWAKE IN DREAMLAND	Pat Benatar (Chrysalis)
24	27	HEARSAY	Alexander O'Neal (Tabu)
16	28	IDLEWILD	Everything But The Girl (Blanco Y Negro)
27	29	A SALT WITH A DEADLY PEPA	Salt 'N' Pepa (London)
46	30	ALL ABOUT EVE	All About Eve (Mercury)
17	31	LOVESEXY	Prince (Paisley Park)
33	32	UB40	UB40 (DEP International)
29	33	LET IT BEE	Voice of the Beehive (London)
38	34	BROTHERS IN ARMS	Dire Straits (Vertigo)
43	35	APPETITE FOR DESTRUCTION	Guns 'N' Roses (Geffen)
40	36	ON THE BEACH	Chris Rea (WEA)
-	37	A MOMENTARY LAPSE OF REASON	Pink Floyd (EMI)
-	38	HOT CITY NIGHTS	Various Artists (Vertigo)
35	39	MORE DIRTY DANCING	Various Artists (RCA)
26	40	JULIA FORDHAM	Julia Fordham (Virgin)
-	41	ROBBIE ROBERTSON	Robbie Robertson (Geffen)
28	42	THRILLER	Michael Jackson (Epic)
31	43	TUNNEL OF LOVE	Bruce Springsteen (CBS)
47	44	CLOSE	Kim Wilde (MCA)
50	45	INTRODUCING THE HARDLINE ACCORDING TO	Terence Trent D'Arby (CBS)
37	46	FAITH	George Michael (Epic)
34	47	IT TAKES A NATION OF MILLIONS TO HOLD US BACK	Public Enemy (Def Jam)
-	48	SEVENTH SON OF A SEVENTH SON	Iron Maiden (EMI)
42	49	THE CHRISTIANS	Christians (Island)
-	50	EVERLASTING	Natalie Cole (Capitol)

3 September 1988

Last	This	Title	Artist (Label)
3	1	THE FIRST OF A MILLION KISSES	Fairground Attraction (RCA)
2	2	KYLIE	Kylie Minogue (PWL)
4	3	TRACY CHAPMAN	Tracy Chapman (Elektra)
1	4	NOW THAT'S WHAT I CALL MUSIC 12	Various Artists (EMI/Virgin/Polygram)
7	5	THE GREATEST EVER ROCK 'N' ROLL MIX	Various Artists (Stylus)
6	6	BEST OF THE EAGLES	Eagles (Asylum)
5	7	IDOL SONGS - 11 OF THE BEST	Billy Idol (Chrysalis)
10	8	TURN BACK THE CLOCK	Johnny Hates Jazz (Virgin)
9	9	BAD	Michael Jackson (Epic)
11	10	DIRTY DANCING	Soundtrack (RCA)
38	11	HOT CITY NIGHTS	Various Artists (Vertigo)
8	12	THE HITS ALBUM – HITS 8	Various Artists (CBS/WEA/BMG)
13	13	HYSTERIA	Def Leppard (Bludgeon Riffola)
12	14	TANGO IN THE NIGHT	Fleetwood Mac (Warner Bros.)
41	15	ROBBIE ROBERTSON	Robbie Robertson (Geffen)
16	16	KICK	INXS (Mercury)
-	17	SO GOOD	Mica Paris (Fourth & Broadway)
17	18	LOVE	Aztec Camera (Warner Bros.)
19	19	THE COLLECTION	Barry White (Mercury)
14	20	ROCK THE WORLD	Five Star (Tent)
15	21	PUSH	Bros (CBS)
18	22	RAINTOWN	Deacon Blue (CBS)
30	23	ALL ABOUT EVE	All About Eve (Mercury)
36	24	ON THE BEACH	Chris Rea (WEA)
22	25	WHITNEY	Whitney Houston (Arista)
29	26	A SALT WITH A DEADLY PEPA	Salt 'N' Pepa (London)
20	27	EIGHT LEGGED GROOVE MACHINE	Wonderstuff (Polydor)
34	28	BROTHERS IN ARMS	Dire Straits (Vertigo)
24	29	POPPED IN SOULED OUT	Wet Wet Wet (Precious)
23	30	HEAVEN ON EARTH	Belinda Carlisle (Virgin)
39	31	MORE DIRTY DANCING	Various Artists (RCA)
-	32	NON STOP	Julio Iglesias (CBS)
31	33	LOVESEXY	Prince (Paisley Park)
35	34	APPETITE FOR DESTRUCTION	Guns 'N' Roses (Geffen)
-	35	HOUSE SOUND OF LONDON – THE JACKIN' ZONE VOL 4	Various Artists (London)
25	36	ROLL WITH IT	Steve Winwood (Virgin)
21	37	SMALL WORLD	Huey Lewis & the News (Chrysalis)
-	38	CONSCIENCE	Womack & Womack (Fourth & Broadway)
-	39	ROCKS THE HOUSE!	Jellybean (Chrysalis)
26	40	WIDE AWAKE IN DREAMLAND	Pat Benatar (Chrysalis)
46	41	FAITH	George Michael (Epic)
27	42	HEARSAY	Alexander O'Neal (Tabu)
42	43	THRILLER	Michael Jackson (Epic)
44	44	CLOSE	Kim Wilde (MCA)
-	45	DON'T BE AFRAID OF THE DARK	Robert Cray Band (Mercury)
-	46	INDIGO	Matt Bianco (WEA)
-	47	OUT OF THE BLUE	Debbie Gibson (Atlantic)
28	48	IDLEWILD	Everything But The Girl (Blanco Y Negro)
40	49	JULIA FORDHAM	Julia Fordham (Virgin)
32	50	UB40	UB40 (DEP International)

10 September 1988

Last	This	Title	Artist (Label)
2	1	KYLIE	Kylie Minogue (PWL)
1	2	THE FIRST OF A MILLION KISSES	Fairground Attraction (RCA)
3	3	TRACY CHAPMAN	Tracy Chapman (Elektra)
4	4	NOW THAT'S WHAT I CALL MUSIC 12	Various Artists (EMI/Virgin/Polygram)
11	5	HOT CITY NIGHTS	Various Artists (Vertigo)
6	6	BEST OF THE EAGLES	Eagles (Asylum)
17	7	SO GOOD	Mica Paris (Fourth & Broadway)
9	8	BAD	Michael Jackson (Epic)
7	9	IDOL SONGS - 11 OF THE BEST	Billy Idol (Chrysalis)
8	10	TURN BACK THE CLOCK	Johnny Hates Jazz (Virgin)
5	11	THE GREATEST EVER ROCK 'N' ROLL MIX	Various Artists (Stylus)
45	12	DON'T BE AFRAID OF THE DARK	Robert Cray Band (Mercury)
38	13	CONSCIENCE	Womack & Womack (Fourth & Broadway)
12	14	THE HITS ALBUM – HITS 8	Various Artists (CBS/WEA/BMG)
15	15	ROBBIE ROBERTSON	Robbie Robertson (Geffen)
10	16	DIRTY DANCING	Soundtrack (RCA)
18	17	LOVE	Aztec Camera (Warner Bros.)
34	18	APPETITE FOR DESTRUCTION	Guns 'N' Roses (Geffen)
39	19	ROCKS THE HOUSE!	Jellybean (Chrysalis)
13	20	HYSTERIA	Def Leppard (Bludgeon Riffola)
14	21	TANGO IN THE NIGHT	Fleetwood Mac (Warner)
16	22	KICK	INXS (Mercury)
-	23	RAP TRAX	Various Artists (Stylus)
-	24	PURPLE RAIN	Prince & the Revolution (Warner Bros.)
21	25	PUSH	Bros (CBS)
23	26	ALL ABOUT EVE	All About Eve (Mercury)
31	27	MORE DIRTY DANCING	Various Artists (RCA)
33	28	LOVESEXY	Prince (Paisley Park)
22	29	RAINTOWN	Deacon Blue (CBS)
-	30	TWICE THE LOVE	George Benson (Warner Bros.)
29	31	POPPED IN SOULED OUT	Wet Wet Wet (Precious)
24	32	ON THE BEACH	Chris Rea (WEA)
25	33	WHITNEY	Whitney Houston (Arista)
32	34	NON STOP	Julio Iglesias (CBS)
27	35	EIGHT LEGGED GROOVE MACHINE	Wonderstuff (Polydor)
-	36	SHORT SHARP SHOCKED	Michelle Shocked (Cooking Vinyl)
28	37	BROTHERS IN ARMS	Dire Straits (Vertigo)
42	38	HEARSAY	Alexander O'Neal (Tabu)
40	39	WIDE AWAKE IN DREAMLAND	Pat Benatar (Chrysalis)
19	40	THE COLLECTION	Barry White (Mercury)
30	41	HEAVEN ON EARTH	Belinda Carlisle (Virgin)
20	42	ROCK THE WORLD	Five Star (Tent)
43	43	THRILLER	Michael Jackson (Epic)
44	44	CLOSE	Kim Wilde (MCA)
26	45	A SALT WITH A DEADLY PEPA	Salt 'N' Pepa (London)
36	46	ROLL WITH IT	Steve Winwood (Virgin)
46	47	INDIGO	Matt Bianco (WEA)
41	48	FAITH	George Michael (Epic)
37	49	SMALL WORLD	Huey Lewis & the News (Chrysalis)
-	50	PEOPLE	Hothouse Flowers (London)

Fairground Attraction added their name to the several who had scored a chart-topper with their debut albums in 1988. The group got a head start from their singles *Perfect* (which topped the chart in May) and *Find My Love* (Number 6 in August), but the album had initially peaked at only Number 6 in June, before dropping away for a while and then reasserting itself all the way to the top (for the obligatory single week!)

17 September 1988

last week	this week	Title	Artist (Label)
-	1	RANK	Smiths (Rough Trade)
1	2	KYLIE	Kylie Minogue (PWL)
23	3	RAP TRAX	Various Artists (Stylus)
-	4	...AND JUSTICE FOR ALL	Metallica (Vertigo)
3	5	TRACY CHAPMAN	Tracy Chapman (Elektra)
2	6	THE FIRST OF A MILLION KISSES	Fairground Attraction (RCA)
8	7	BAD	Michael Jackson (Epic)
5	8	HOT CITY NIGHTS	Various Artists (Vertigo)
25	9	PUSH	Bros (CBS)
4	10	NOW THAT'S WHAT I CALL MUSIC 12	Various Artists (EMI/Virgin/Polygram)
6	11	BEST OF THE EAGLES	Eagles (Asylum)
-	12	THE NEPHILIM	Fields of the Nephilim (Situation Two)
11	13	THE GREATEST EVER ROCK 'N' ROLL MIX	Various Artists (Stylus)
7	14	SO GOOD	Mica Paris (Fourth & Broadway)
-	15	PEEPSHOW	Siouxsie & the Banshees (Wonderland)
18	16	APPETITE FOR DESTRUCTION	Guns 'N' Roses (Geffen)
9	17	IDOL SONGS - 11 OF THE BEST	Billy Idol (Chrysalis)
20	18	HYSTERIA	Def Leppard (Bludgeon Riffola)
12	19	DON'T BE AFRAID OF THE DARK	Robert Cray Band (Mercury)
41	20	HEAVEN ON EARTH	Belinda Carlisle (Virgin)
30	21	TWICE THE LOVE	George Benson (Warner Bros.)
16	22	DIRTY DANCING	Soundtrack (RCA)
21	23	TANGO IN THE NIGHT	Fleetwood Mac (Warner Bros.)
-	24	OUT OF THIS WORLD	Europe (Epic)
33	25	WHITNEY	Whitney Houston (Arista)
13	26	CONSCIENCE	Womack & Womack (Broadway)
14	27	THE HITS ALBUM – HITS 8	Various Artists (CBS/WEA/BMG)
22	28	KICK	INXS (Mercury)
15	29	ROBBIE ROBERTSON	Robbie Robertson (Geffen)
19	30	ROCKS THE HOUSE!	Jellybean (Chrysalis)
31	31	POPPED IN SOULED OUT	Wet Wet Wet (Precious)
10	32	TURN BACK THE CLOCK	Johnny Hates Jazz (Virgin)
43	33	THRILLER	Michael Jackson (Epic)
24	34	PURPLE RAIN	Prince & the Revolution (Warner Bros.)
17	35	LOVE	Aztec Camera (Warner Bros.)
34	36	NON STOP	Julio Iglesias (CBS)
-	37	ANSWERS TO NOTHING	Midge Ure (Chrysalis)
27	38	MORE DIRTY DANCING	Various Artists (RCA)
37	39	BROTHERS IN ARMS	Dire Straits (Vertigo)
26	40	ALL ABOUT EVE	All About Eve (Mercury)
36	41	SHORT SHARP SHOCKED	Michelle Shocked (Cooking Vinyl)
29	42	RAINTOWN	Deacon Blue (CBS)
45	43	A SALT WITH A DEADLY PEPA	Salt 'N' Pepa (London)
50	44	PEOPLE	Hothouse Flowers (London)
38	45	HEARSAY	Alexander O'Neal (Tabu)
46	46	ROLL WITH IT	Steve Winwood (Virgin)
32	47	ON THE BEACH	Chris Rea (WEA)
-	48	KEEPER OF THE 7 KEYS PT 2	Helloween (Noise)
28	49	LOVESEXY	Prince (Paisley Park)
48	50	FAITH	George Michael (Epic)

24 September 1988

last week	this week	Title	Artist (Label)
2	1	KYLIE	Kylie Minogue (PWL)
8	2	HOT CITY NIGHTS	Various Artists (Vertigo)
3	3	RAP TRAX	Various Artists (Stylus)
1	4	RANK	Smiths (Rough Trade)
5	5	TRACY CHAPMAN	Tracy Chapman (Elektra)
9	6	PUSH	Bros (CBS)
7	7	THE FIRST OF A MILLION KISSES	Fairground Attraction (RCA)
7	8	BAD	Michael Jackson (Epic)
-	9	STATE OF EUPHORIA	Anthrax (Island)
10	10	NOW THAT'S WHAT I CALL MUSIC 12	Various Artists (EMI/Virgin/Polygram)
13	11	THE GREATEST EVER ROCK 'N' ROLL MIX	Various Artists (Stylus)
4	12	...AND JUSTICE FOR ALL	Metallica (Vertigo)
11	13	BEST OF THE EAGLES	Eagles (Asylum)
24	14	OUT OF THIS WORLD	Europe (Epic)
22	15	DIRTY DANCING	Soundtrack (RCA)
17	16	IDOL SONGS - 11 OF THE BEST	Billy Idol (Chrysalis)
-	17	BUSTER	Soundtrack (Virgin)
20	18	HEAVEN ON EARTH	Belinda Carlisle (Virgin)
26	19	CONSCIENCE	Womack & Womack (Broadway)
16	20	APPETITE FOR DESTRUCTION	Guns 'N' Roses (Geffen)
14	21	SO GOOD	Mica Paris (Fourth & Broadway)
-	22	SPIRIT OF EDEN	Talk Talk (Parlophone)
23	23	TANGO IN THE NIGHT	Fleetwood Mac (Warner Bros.)
21	24	TWICE THE LOVE	George Benson (Warner Bros.)
31	25	POPPED IN SOULED OUT	Wet Wet Wet (Precious)
12	26	THE NEPHILIM	Fields of the Nephilim (Situation Two)
25	27	WHITNEY	Whitney Houston (Arista)
18	28	HYSTERIA	Def Leppard (Bludgeon Riffola)
-	29	SUNSHINE ON LEITH	Proclaimers (Chrysalis)
28	30	KICK	INXS (Mercury)
43	31	A SALT WITH A DEADLY PEPA	Salt 'N' Pepa (London)
19	32	DON'T BE AFRAID OF THE DARK	Robert Cray Band (Mercury)
27	33	THE HITS ALBUM – HITS 8	Various Artists (CBS/WEA/BMG)
15	34	PEEPSHOW	Siouxsie & the Banshees (Wonderland)
30	35	ROCKS THE HOUSE!	Jellybean (Chrysalis)
34	36	PURPLE RAIN	Prince & the Revolution (Warner Bros.)
45	37	HEARSAY	Alexander O'Neal (Tabu)
48	38	KEEPER OF THE SEVEN KEYS PART 2	Helloween (Noise)
36	39	NON STOP	Julio Iglesias (CBS)
29	40	ROBBIE ROBERTSON	Robbie Robertson (Geffen)
39	41	BROTHERS IN ARMS	Dire Straits (Vertigo)
-	42	ANCIENT HEART	Tanita Tikaram (WEA)
32	43	TURN BACK THE CLOCK	Johnny Hates Jazz (Virgin)
41	44	SHORT SHARP SHOCKED	Michelle Shocked (Cooking Vinyl)
49	45	LOVESEXY	Prince (Paisley Park)
38	46	MORE DIRTY DANCING	Various Artists (RCA)
-	47	FUR	Jane Wiedlin (EMI Manhattan)
-	48	ALL THE HITS AND MORE	Hollies (EMI)
40	49	ALL ABOUT EVE	All About Eve (Mercury)
-	50	GREATEST HITS	Bill Withers (CBS)

1 October 1988

last week	this week	Title	Artist (Label)
-	1	STARING AT THE SUN	Level 42 (Polydor)
-	2	NEW JERSEY	Bon Jovi (Vertigo)
2	3	HOT CITY NIGHTS	Various Artists (Vertigo)
1	4	KYLIE	Kylie Minogue (PWL)
8	5	BAD	Michael Jackson (Epic)
3	6	RAP TRAX	Various Artists (Stylus)
5	7	TRACY CHAPMAN	Tracy Chapman (Elektra)
17	8	BUSTER	Soundtrack (Virgin)
19	9	CONSCIENCE	Womack & Womack (Fourth & Broadway)
7	10	THE FIRST OF A MILLION KISSES	Fairground Attraction (RCA)
6	11	PUSH	Bros (CBS)
29	12	SUNSHINE ON LEITH	Proclaimers (Chrysalis)
10	13	NOW THAT'S WHAT I CALL MUSIC 12	Various Artists (EMI/Virgin/Polygram)
42	14	ANCIENT HEART	Tanita Tikaram (WEA)
15	15	DIRTY DANCING	Soundtrack (RCA)
4	16	RANK	Smiths (Rough Trade)
-	17	BLUE BELL KNOLL	Cocteau Twins (4AD)
22	18	SPIRIT OF EDEN	Talk Talk (Parlophone)
11	19	THE GREATEST EVER ROCK 'N' ROLL MIX	Various Artists (Stylus)
27	20	WHITNEY	Whitney Houston (Arista)
-	21	WORKER'S PLAYTIME	Billy Bragg (Go! Discs)
18	22	HEAVEN ON EARTH	Belinda Carlisle (Virgin)
9	23	STATE OF EUPHORIA	Anthrax (Island)
16	24	IDOL SONGS - 11 OF THE BEST	Billy Idol (Chrysalis)
23	25	TANGO IN THE NIGHT	Fleetwood Mac (Warner Bros.)
20	26	APPETITE FOR DESTRUCTION	Guns 'N' Roses (Geffen)
37	27	HEARSAY	Alexander O'Neal (Tabu)
13	28	BEST OF THE EAGLES	Eagles (Asylum)
28	29	HYSTERIA	Def Leppard (Bludgeon Riffola)
30	30	KICK	INXS (Mercury)
25	31	POPPED IN SOULED OUT	Wet Wet Wet (Precious)
12	32	...AND JUSTICE FOR ALL	Metallica (Vertigo)
21	33	SO GOOD	Mica Paris (Fourth & Broadway)
14	34	OUT OF THIS WORLD	Europe (Epic)
31	35	A SALT WITH A DEADLY PEPA	Salt 'N' Pepa (London)
24	36	TWICE THE LOVE	George Benson (Warner Bros.)
33	37	THE HITS ALBUM – HITS 8	Various Artists (CBS/WEA/BMG)
41	38	BROTHERS IN ARMS	Dire Straits (Vertigo)
47	39	FUR	Jane Wiedlin (EMI Manhattan)
-	40	THE RARE GROOVE MIX	Various Artists (Stylus)
-	41	EIGHT LEGGED GROOVE MACHINE	Wonderstuff (Polydor)
36	42	PURPLE RAIN	Prince & the Revolution (Warner Bros.)
48	43	ALL THE HITS AND MORE	Hollies (EMI)
-	44	THRILLER	Michael Jackson (Epic)
45	45	LOVESEXY	Prince (Paisley Park)
40	46	ROBBIE ROBERTSON	Robbie Robertson (Geffen)
43	47	TURN BACK THE CLOCK	Johnny Hates Jazz (Virgin)
-	48	THE JOSHUA TREE	U2 (Island)
44	49	SHORT SHARP SHOCKED	Michelle Shocked (Cooking Vinyl)
32	50	DON'T BE AFRAID OF THE DARK	Robert Cray Band (Mercury)

The posthumous release *Rank* by the Smiths demonstrated a sales pattern more frequently displayed by singles in the late 1980s, concentrating all its sales very shortly after release (usually a sign that avid fans are buying, and few others are following up). After debuting at Number 1, it immediately dropped to 4, in its third chart week fell out of the Top 15, and after a month - had vanished!

October 1988

8 October 1988

last	this	title	artist (label)
2	1	NEW JERSEY	Bon Jovi (Vertigo)
1	2	STARING AT THE SUN	Level 42 (Polydor)
9	3	CONSCIENCE	Womack & Womack (Fourth & Broadway)
-	4	MOONLIGHTING	VariousArtists (WEA)
6	5	RAP TRAX	Various Artists (Stylus)
8	6	BUSTER	Soundtrack (Virgin)
-	7	PEACE IN OUR TIME	Big Country (Mercury)
3	8	HOT CITY NIGHTS	Various Artists (Vertigo)
4	9	KYLIE	Kylie Minogue (PWL)
-	10	REVOLUTIONS	Jean Michel Jarre (Polydor)
7	11	TRACY CHAPMAN	Tracy Chapman (Elektra)
12	12	SUNSHINE ON LEITH	Proclaimers (Chrysalis)
5	13	BAD	Michael Jackson (Epic)
14	14	ANCIENT HEART	Tanita Tikaram (WEA)
-	15	...AND THE BEAT GOES ON	Various Artists (Telstar)
11	16	PUSH	Bros (CBS)
10	17	THE FIRST OF A MILLION KISSES	Fairground Attraction (RCA)
22	18	HEAVEN ON EARTH	Belinda Carlisle (Virgin)
-	19	THE STARS WE ARE	Marc Almond (Parlophone)
20	20	WHITNEY	Whitney Houston (Arista)
15	21	DIRTY DANCING	Soundtrack (RCA)
-	22	BIG TIME	Tom Waits (Island)
13	23	NOW THAT'S WHAT I CALL MUSIC 12	Various Artists (EMI/Virgin/Polygram)
17	24	BLUE BELL KNOLL	Cocteau Twins (4AD)
27	25	HEARSAY	Alexander O'Neal (Tabu)
24	26	IDOL SONGS - 11 OF THE BEST	Billy Idol (Chrysalis)
21	27	WORKER'S PLAYTIME	Billy Bragg (Go! Discs)
-	28	THE WORLDS OF FOSTER AND ALLEN	Foster & Allen (Stylus)
25	29	TANGO IN THE NIGHT	Fleetwood Mac (Warner Bros.)
40	30	THE RARE GROOVE MIX	Various Artists (Stylus)
26	31	APPETITE FOR DESTRUCTION	Guns 'N' Rose (Geffen)
18	32	SPIRIT OF EDEN	Talk Talk (Parlophone)
28	33	BEST OF THE EAGLES	Eagles (Asylum)
-	34	METAL RHYTHM	Gary Numan (Illegal)
16	35	RANK	Smiths (Rough Trade)
19	36	THE GREATEST EVER ROCK 'N' ROLL MIX	Various Artists (Stylus)
33	37	SO GOOD	Mica Paris (Fourth & Broadway)
23	38	STATE OF EUPHORIA	Anthrax (Island)
29	39	HYSTERIA	Def Leppard (Bludgeon Riffola)
43	40	ALL THE HITS AND MORE	Hollies (EMI)
-	41	THE INNOCENTS	Erasure (Mute)
30	42	KICK	INXS (Mercury)
-	43	ALL THAT JAZZ	Breathe (Siren)
35	44	A SALT WITH A DEADLY PEPA	Salt 'N' Pepa (London)
-	45	ONES ON 1	Various Artists (BBC)
49	46	SHORT SHARP SHOCKED	Michelle Shocked (Cooking Vinyl)
-	47	NOT ME	Glenn Medeiros (London)
31	48	POPPED IN SOULED OUT	Wet Wet Wet (Precious)
38	49	BROTHERS IN ARMS	Dire Straits (Vertigo)
-	50	VIXEN	Vixen (EMI Manhattan)

15 October 1988

last	this	title	artist (label)
1	1	NEW JERSEY	Bon Jovi (Vertigo)
10	2	REVOLUTIONS	Jean Michel Jarre (Polydor)
4	3	MOONLIGHTING	VariousArtists (WEA)
3	4	CONSCIENCE	Womack & Womack (Fourth & Broadway)
2	5	STARING AT THE SUN	Level 42 (Polydor)
5	6	RAP TRAX	Various Artists (Stylus)
7	7	PEACE IN OUR TIME	Big Country (Mercury)
-	8	FLYING COLOURS	Chris De Burgh (A&M)
8	9	HOT CITY NIGHTS	Various Artists (Vertigo)
-	10	POP ART	Transvision Vamp (MCA)
9	11	KYLIE	Kylie Minogue (PWL)
11	12	TRACY CHAPMAN	Tracy Chapman (Elektra)
45	13	ONES ON 1	Various Artists (BBC)
15	14	...AND THE BEAT GOES ON	Various Artists (Telstar)
6	15	BUSTER	Soundtrack (Virgin)
13	16	BAD	Michael Jackson (Epic)
21	17	DIRTY DANCING	Soundtrack (RCA)
30	18	THE RARE GROOVE MIX	Various Artists (Stylus)
16	19	PUSH	Bros (CBS)
12	20	SUNSHINE ON LEITH	Proclaimers (Chrysalis)
18	21	HEAVEN ON EARTH	Belinda Carlisle (Virgin)
25	22	HEARSAY	Alexander O'Neal (Tabu)
20	23	WHITNEY	Whitney Houston (Arista)
17	24	THE FIRST OF A MILLION KISSES	Fairground Attraction (RCA)
23	25	NOW THAT'S WHAT I CALL MUSIC 12	Various Artists (EMI/Virgin/Polygram)
14	26	ANCIENT HEART	Tanita Tikaram (WEA)
28	27	THE WORLDS OF FOSTER AND ALLEN	Foster & Allen (Stylus)
43	28	ALL THAT JAZZ	Breathe (Siren)
31	29	APPETITE FOR DESTRUCTION	Guns 'N' Roses (Geffen)
42	30	KICK	INXS (Mercury)
29	31	TANGO IN THE NIGHT	Fleetwood Mac (Warner Bros.)
-	32	BROTHERS IN RHYTHM	Various Artists (Ariola)
46	33	SHORT SHARP SHOCKED	Michelle Shocked (Cooking Vinyl)
41	34	THE INNOCENTS	Erasure (Mute)
32	35	SPIRIT OF EDEN	Talk Talk (Parlophone)
26	36	IDOL SONGS - 11 OF THE BEST	Billy Idol (Chrysalis)
-	37	THE MOTOWN SONGBOOK	Ruby Turner (Jive)
-	38	TALK IS CHEAP	Keith Richards (Virgin)
19	39	THE STARS WE ARE	Marc Almond (Parlophone)
44	40	A SALT WITH A DEADLY PEPA	Salt 'N' Pepa (London)
33	41	BEST OF THE EAGLES	Eagles (Asylum)
-	42	BEST OF AL GREEN: HI LIFE	Al Green (K-Tel)
-	43	PURPLE RAIN	Prince & the Revolution (Warner Bros.)
39	44	HYSTERIA	Def Leppard (Bludgeon Riffola)
34	45	METAL RHYTHM	Gary Numan (Illegal)
22	46	BIG TIME	Tom Waits (Island)
-	47	ONE MOMENT IN TIME	Various Artists (Arista)
37	48	SO GOOD	Mica Paris (Fourth & Broadway)
-	49	NO SLEEP AT ALL	Motorhead (GWR)
24	50	BLUE BELL KNOLL	Cocteau Twins (4AD)

22 October 1988

last	this	title	artist (label)
-	1	RATTLE AND HUM	U2 (Island)
2	2	REVOLUTIONS	Jean Michel Jarre (Polydor)
-	3	INTROSPECTIVE	Pet Shop Boys (Parlophone)
8	4	FLYING COLOURS	Chris De Burgh (A&M)
1	5	NEW JERSEY	Bon Jovi (Vertigo)
11	6	KYLIE	Kylie Minogue (PWL)
-	7	TO WHOM IT MAY CONCERN	Pasadenas (CBS)
3	8	MOONLIGHTING	VariousArtists (WEA)
4	9	CONSCIENCE	Womack & Womack (Fourth & Broadway)
13	10	ONES ON 1	Various Artists (BBC)
10	11	POP ART	Transvision Vamp (MCA)
5	12	STARING AT THE SUN	Level 42 (Polydor)
6	13	RAP TRAX	Various Artists (Stylus)
12	14	TRACY CHAPMAN	Tracy Chapman (Elektra)
-	15	THE GREATEST HITS COLLECTION	Bananarama (London)
17	16	DIRTY DANCING	Soundtrack (RCA)
16	17	BAD	Michael Jackson (Epic)
9	18	HOT CITY NIGHTS	Various Artists (Vertigo)
23	19	WHITNEY	Whitney Houston (Arista)
-	20	WATERMARK	Enya (WEA)
14	21	...AND THE BEAT GOES ON	Various Artists (Telstar)
22	22	HEARSAY	Alexander O'Neal (Tabu)
7	23	PEACE IN OUR TIME	Big Country (Mercury)
34	24	THE INNOCENTS	Erasure (Mute)
20	25	SUNSHINE ON LEITH	Proclaimers (Chrysalis)
-	26	NO REST FOR THE WICKED	Ozzy Osbourne (CBS)
15	27	BUSTER	Soundtrack (Virgin)
19	28	PUSH	Bros (CBS)
-	29	INTO THE DRAGON	Bomb the Brass (Rhythm King)
42	30	BEST OF AL GREEN: HI LIFE	Al Green (K-Tel)
37	31	THE MOTOWN SONGBOOK	Ruby Turner (Jive)
18	32	THE RARE GROOVE MIX	Various Artists (Stylus)
24	33	THE FIRST OF A MILLION KISSES	Fairground Attraction (RCA)
32	34	BROTHERS IN RHYTHM	Various Artists (Ariola)
21	35	HEAVEN ON EARTH	Belinda Carlisle (Virgin)
26	36	ANCIENT HEART	Tanita Tikaram (WEA)
30	37	KICK	INXS (Mercury)
31	38	TANGO IN THE NIGHT	Fleetwood Mac (Warner Bros.)
40	39	A SALT WITH A DEADLY PEPA	Salt 'N' Pepa (London)
48	40	SO GOOD	Mica Paris (Fourth & Broadway)
-	41	URBAN ACID	Various Artists (Urban)
25	42	NOW THAT'S WHAT I CALL MUSIC 12	Various Artists (EMI/Virgin/Polygram)
-	43	THE MAGIC OF NANA MOUSKOURI	Nana Mouskouri (Philips)
47	44	ONE MOMENT IN TIME	Various Artists (Arista)
36	45	IDOL SONGS - 11 OF THE BEST	Billy Idol (Chrysalis)
27	46	THE WORLDS OF FOSTER AND ALLEN	Foster & Allen (Stylus)
-	47	THE PRICE YOU PAY	Spear of Destiny (Virgin)
29	48	APPETITE FOR DESTRUCTION	Guns 'N' Roses (Geffen)
-	49	BARCELONA	Freddie Mercury & Montserrat Caballe (Polydor)
38	50	TALK IS CHEAP	Keith Richards (Virgin)

Exactly two years on from their first Top 5 album *Slippery When Wet*, US heavy rockers Bon Jovi - who were indeed from New Jersey - scored their first chart-topper with *New Jersey*. Also enjoying their biggest-ever album were the husband-and-wife soul vocal team Womack & Womack (the "he" being Cecil Womack, brother of chartmaker Bobby), with *Conscience*, their first Fourth & Broadway recording.

29 October 1988

last week	this week		
1	1	RATTLE AND HUM	U2 (Island)
-	2	MONEY FOR NOTHING	Dire Straits (Vertigo)
3	3	INTROSPECTIVE	Pet Shop Boys (Parlophone)
15	4	THE GREATEST HITS COLLECTION	Bananarama (London)
-	5	THE BEST OF CHRIS REA - NEW LIGHT THROUGH OLD WINDOWS	Chris Rea (WEA)
6	6	KYLIE	Kylie Minogue (PWL)
-	7	ANY LOVE	Luther Vandross (Epic)
7	8	TO WHOM IT MAY CONCERN	Pasadenas (CBS)
8	9	MOONLIGHTING	VariousArtists (WEA)
20	10	WATERMARK	Enya (WEA)
2	11	REVOLUTIONS	Jean Michel Jarre (Polydor)
4	12	FLYING COLOURS	Chris De Burgh (A&M)
-	13	GIVING YOU THE BEST THAT I GOT	Anita Baker (Elektra)
9	14	CONSCIENCE	Womack & Womack (Fourth & Broadway)
13	15	RAP TRAX	Various Artists (Stylus)
10	16	ONES ON 1	Various Artists (BBC)
-	17	BIG THING	Duran Duran (EMI)
5	18	NEW JERSEY	Bon Jovi (Vertigo)
-	19	FISHERMAN'S BLUES	Waterboys (Chrysalis)
12	20	STARING AT THE SUN	Level 42 (Polydor)
14	21	TRACY CHAPMAN	Tracy Chapman (Elektra)
29	22	INTO THE DRAGON	Bomb the Brass (Rhythm King)
16	23	DIRTY DANCING	Soundtrack (RCA)
36	24	ANCIENT HEART	Tanita Tikaram (WEA)
11	25	POP ART	Transvision Vamp (MCA)
-	26	MY NATION UNDERGROUND	Julian Cope (Island)
17	27	BAD	Michael Jackson (Epic)
18	28	HOT CITY NIGHTS	Various Artists (Vertigo)
-	29	COMEDY	Black (A&M)
24	30	THE INNOCENTS	Erasure (Mute)
19	31	WHITNEY	Whitney Houston (Arista)
-	32	THE CLASSICAL EXPERIENCE	Various Artists (EMI)
25	33	SUNSHINE ON LEITH	Proclaimers (Chrysalis)
21	34	...AND THE BEAT GOES ON	Various Artists (Telstar)
30	35	BEST OF AL GREEN: HI LIFE	Al Green (K-Tel)
26	36	NO REST FOR THE WICKED	Ozzy Osbourne (CBS)
27	37	BUSTER	Soundtrack (Virgin)
46	38	THE WORLDS OF FOSTER AND ALLEN	Foster & Allen (Stylus)
49	39	BARCELONA	Freddie Mercury & Montserrat Caballe (Polydor)
22	40	HEARSAY	Alexander O'Neal (Tabu)
-	41	THE GREATEST LOVE	Various Artists (Telstar)
23	42	PEACE IN OUR TIME	Big Country (Mercury)
31	43	THE MOTOWN SONGBOOK	Ruby Turner (Jive)
28	44	PUSH	Bros (CBS)
-	45	LOVE	Aztec Camera (Warner Bros.)
41	46	URBAN ACID	Various Artists (Urban)
-	47	MOTOWN IN MOTION	Various Artists (K-Tel)
-	48	RAINTOWN	Deacon Blue (CBS)
-	49	EPONYMOUS	REM (IRS)
40	50	SO GOOD	Mica Paris (Fourth & Broadway)

5 November 1988

last week	this week		
2	1	MONEY FOR NOTHING	Dire Straits (Vertigo)
1	2	RATTLE AND HUM	U2 (Island)
7	3	ANY LOVE	Luther Vandross (Epic)
6	4	KYLIE	Kylie Minogue (PWL)
10	5	WATERMARK	Enya (WEA)
3	6	INTROSPECTIVE	Pet Shop Boys (Parlophone)
5	7	THE BEST OF CHRIS REA - NEW LIGHT THROUGH OLD WINDOWS	Chris Rea (WEA)
-	8	RAGE	T'Pau (Siren)
13	9	GIVING YOU THE BEST THAT I GOT	Anita Baker (Elektra)
4	10	THE GREATEST HITS COLLECTION	Bananarama (London)
-	11	SMASH HITS PARTY '88	Various Artists (Chrysalis)
8	12	TO WHOM IT MAY CONCERN	Pasadenas (CBS)
12	13	FLYING COLOURS	Chris De Burgh (A&M)
41	14	THE GREATEST LOVE	Various Artists (Telstar)
11	15	REVOLUTIONS	Jean Michel Jarre (Polydor)
30	16	THE INNOCENTS	Erasure (Mute)
19	17	FISHERMAN'S BLUES	Waterboys (Chrysalis)
14	18	CONSCIENCE	Womack & Womack (Fourth & Broadway)
24	19	ANCIENT HEART	Tanita Tikaram (WEA)
21	20	TRACY CHAPMAN	Tracy Chapman (Elektra)
20	21	STARING AT THE SUN	Level 42 (Polydor)
17	22	BIG THING	Duran Duran (EMI)
-	23	NEGOTIATIONS AND LOVE SONGS 1971-1986	Paul Simon (Warner Bros.)
31	24	WHITNEY	Whitney Houston (Arista)
23	25	DIRTY DANCING	Soundtrack (RCA)
9	26	MOONLIGHTING	VariousArtists (WEA)
-	27	SOFT METAL	Various Artists (Stylus)
32	28	THE CLASSICAL EXPERIENCE	Various Artists (EMI)
18	29	NEW JERSEY	Bon Jovi (Vertigo)
38	30	THE WORLDS OF FOSTER AND ALLEN	Foster & Allen (Stylus)
25	31	POP ART	Transvision Vamp (MCA)
-	32	THE RARE GROOVE MIX	Various Artists (Stylus)
27	33	BAD	Michael Jackson (Epic)
16	34	ONES ON 1	Various Artists (BBC)
15	35	RAP TRAX	Various Artists (Stylus)
37	36	BUSTER	Soundtrack (Virgin)
-	37	HEAVY NOVA	Robert Palmer (EMI)
29	38	COMEDY	Black (A&M)
47	39	MOTOWN IN MOTION	Various Artists (K-Tel)
33	40	SUNSHINE ON LEITH	Proclaimers (Chrysalis)
-	41	ELECTRIC FOLKLORE	Alarm (IRS)
-	42	THE LEGENDARY ROY ORBISON	Roy Orbison (Telstar)
-	43	THE BEAT THE RHYME THE NOISE	Wee Papa Girl Rappers (Jive)
48	44	RAINTOWN	Deacon Blue (CBS)
50	45	SO GOOD	Mica Paris (Fourth & Broadway)
-	46	THE TRAVELING WILBURYS VOL 1	Traveling Wilburys (Wilbury)
22	47	INTO THE DRAGON	Bomb the Brass (Rhythm King)
44	48	PUSH	Bros (CBS)
-	49	KICK	INXS (Mercury)
26	50	MY NATION UNDERGROUND	Julian Cope (Island)

12 November 1988

last week	this week		
1	1	MONEY FOR NOTHING	Dire Straits (Vertigo)
2	2	RATTLE AND HUM	U2 (Island)
5	3	WATERMARK	Enya (WEA)
4	4	KYLIE	Kylie Minogue (PWL)
11	5	SMASH HITS PARTY '88	Various Artists (Chrysalis)
8	6	RAGE	T'Pau (Siren)
-	7	GREATEST HITS	Human League (Virgin)
13	8	FLYING COLOURS	Chris De Burgh (A&M)
27	9	SOFT METAL	Various Artists (Stylus)
3	10	ANY LOVE	Luther Vandross (Epic)
-	11	UNFORGETTABLE	Various Artists (EMI)
6	12	INTROSPECTIVE	Pet Shop Boys (Parlophone)
10	13	THE GREATEST HITS COLLECTION	Bananarama (London)
7	14	THE BEST OF CHRIS REA - NEW LIGHT THROUGH OLD WINDOWS	Chris Rea (WEA)
14	15	THE GREATEST LOVE	Various Artists (Telstar)
12	16	TO WHOM IT MAY CONCERN	Pasadenas (CBS)
15	17	REVOLUTIONS	Jean Michel Jarre (Polydor)
19	18	ANCIENT HEART	Tanita Tikaram (WEA)
23	19	NEGOTIATIONS AND LOVE SONGS 1971-1986	Paul Simon (Warner Bros.)
9	20	GIVING YOU THE BEST THAT I GOT	Anita Baker (Elektra)
16	21	THE INNOCENTS	Erasure (Mute)
48	22	PUSH	Bros (CBS)
20	23	TRACY CHAPMAN	Tracy Chapman (Elektra)
40	24	SUNSHINE ON LEITH	Proclaimers (Chrysalis)
17	25	FISHERMAN'S BLUES	Waterboys (Chrysalis)
25	26	DIRTY DANCING	Soundtrack (RCA)
37	27	HEAVY NOVA	Robert Palmer (EMI)
30	28	THE WORLDS OF FOSTER AND ALLEN	Foster & Allen (Stylus)
-	29	THE PREMIERE COLLECTION: THE BEST OF ANDREW LLOYD WEBBER	Various Artists (Really Useful)
18	30	CONSCIENCE	Womack & Womack (Fourth & Broadway)
-	31	THE HIT FACTORY: THE BEST OF STOCK AITKEN WATERMAN VOL 2	Various Artists (PWL)
24	32	WHITNEY	Whitney Houston (Arista)
28	33	THE CLASSICAL EXPERIENCE	Various Artists (EMI)
-	34	THE LOVERS	Various Artists (K-Tel)
33	35	BAD	Michael Jackson (Epic)
21	36	STARING AT THE SUN	Level 42 (Polydor)
36	37	BUSTER	Soundtrack (Virgin)
44	38	RAINTOWN	Deacon Blue (CBS)
29	39	NEW JERSEY	Bon Jovi (Vertigo)
32	40	THE RARE GROOVE MIX	Various Artists (Stylus)
49	41	KICK	INXS (Mercury)
39	42	MOTOWN IN MOTION	Various Artists (K-Tel)
-	43	...AND THE BEAT GOES ON	Various Artists (Telstar)
-	44	THE SINGLES COLLECTION	Kool & the Gang (De-Lite)
-	45	A SALT WITH A DEADLY PEPA	Salt 'N' Pepa (London)
-	46	I AM KURIOUS ORANJ	Fall (Beggars Banquet)
31	47	POP ART	Transvision Vamp (MCA)
-	48	THE HEART AND SOUL OF ROCK 'N' ROLL	Various Artists (Telstar)
35	49	RAP TRAX	Various Artists (Stylus)
43	50	THE BEAT THE RHYME THE NOISE	Wee Papa Girl Rappers (Jive)

Hits compilations began to dominate the late autumn charts of 1988, the most successful, predictably, being Dire Straits' *Money For Nothing*, which anthologised the best of the band's material since 1978. Other hits packages selling particularly well were those by Chris Rea, the Human League and Bananarama, all Top 5 items. Enya's New Age-styled *Watermark* followed her Number 1 single *Orinoco Flow* to the heights.

November – December 1988

19 November 1988

last week	this week	Title	Artist
1	1	MONEY FOR NOTHING	Dire Straits (Vertigo)
4	2	KYLIE	Kylie Minogue (PWL)
7	3	GREATEST HITS	Human League (Virgin)
3	4	WATERMARK	Enya (WEA)
2	5	RATTLE AND HUM	U2 (Island)
14	6	THE BEST OF CHRIS REA - NEW LIGHT THROUGH OLD WINDOWS	Chris Rea (WEA)
8	7	FLYING COLOURS	Chris De Burgh (A&M)
13	8	THE GREATEST HITS COLLECTION	Bananarama (London)
-	9	THE MEMPHIS SESSIONS	Wet Wet Wet (Precious)
5	10	SMASH HITS PARTY '88	Various Artists (Chrysalis)
9	11	SOFT METAL	Various Artists (Stylus)
6	12	RAGE	T'Pau (Siren)
11	13	UNFORGETTABLE	Various Artists (EMI)
-	14	THE ULTIMATE COLLECTION	Bryan Ferry with Roxy Music (EG)
12	15	INTROSPECTIVE	Pet Shop Boys (Parlophone)
-	16	THE TRAVELING WILBURYS VOL 1	Traveling Wilburys (Wilbury)
31	17	THE HIT FACTORY: THE BEST OF STOCK AITKEN WATERMAN VOL 2	Various Artists (PWL)
41	18	KICK	INXS (Mercury)
10	19	ANY LOVE	Luther Vandross (Epic)
-	20	PRIVATE COLLECTION (1979-1988)	Cliff Richard (EMI)
15	21	THE GREATEST LOVE	Various Artists (Telstar)
29	22	THE PREMIERE COLLECTION: THE BEST OF ANDREW LLOYD WEBBER	Various Artists (Really Useful)
18	23	ANCIENT HEART	Tanita Tikaram (WEA)
24	24	SUNSHINE ON LEITH	Proclaimers (Chrysalis)
37	25	BUSTER	Soundtrack (Virgin)
19	26	NEGOTIATIONS AND LOVE SONGS 1971-1986	Paul Simon (Warner Bros.)
27	27	HEAVY NOVA	Robert Palmer (EMI)
16	28	TO WHOM IT MAY CONCERN	Pasadenas (CBS)
21	29	THE INNOCENTS	Erasure (Mute)
38	30	RAINTOWN	Deacon Blue (CBS)
26	31	DIRTY DANCING	Soundtrack (RCA)
28	32	THE WORLDS OF FOSTER AND ALLEN	Foster & Allen (Stylus)
34	33	THE LOVERS	Various Artists (K-Tel)
44	34	THE SINGLES COLLECTION	Kool & the Gang (De-Lite)
-	35	SO GOOD	Mica Paris (Fourth & Broadway)
-	36	THE LEGENDARY ROY ORBISON	Roy Orbison (Telstar)
22	37	PUSH	Bros (CBS)
30	38	CONSCIENCE	Womack & Womac (Fourth & Broadway)
-	39	APPETITE FOR DESTRUCTION	Guns 'N' Roses (Geffen)
-	40	GREEN	REM (Warner Bros.)
20	41	GIVING YOU THE BEST THAT I GOT	Anita Baker (Elektra)
23	42	TRACY CHAPMAN	Tracy Chapman (Elektra)
35	43	BAD	Michael Jackson (Epic)
32	44	WHITNEY	Whitney Houston (Arista)
17	45	REVOLUTIONS	Jean Michel Jarre (Polydor)
42	46	MOTOWN IN MOTION	Various Artists (K-Tel)
-	47	COPPERHEAD ROAD	Steve Earle (MCA)
-	48	GOOD MORNING VIETNAM - ORIGINAL SOUNDTRACK	Various Artists (A&M)
-	49	ANYTHING FOR YOU	Gloria Estefan & Miami Sound Machine (Epic)
39	50	NEW JERSEY	Bon Jovi (Vertigo)

26 November 1988

last week	this week	Title	Artist
2	1	KYLIE	Kylie Minogue (PWL)
1	2	MONEY FOR NOTHING	Dire Straits (Vertigo)
3	3	GREATEST HITS	Human League (Virgin)
9	4	THE MEMPHIS SESSIONS	Wet Wet Wet (Precious)
-	5	WANTED	Yazz (Big Life)
20	6	PRIVATE COLLECTION (1979-1988)	Cliff Richard (EMI)
14	7	THE ULTIMATE COLLECTION	Bryan Ferry with Roxy Music (EG)
6	8	THE BEST OF CHRIS REA - NEW LIGHT THROUGH OLD WINDOWS	Chris Rea (WEA)
18	9	KICK	INXS (Mercury)
-	10	THE GREATEST HITS OF '88	Various Artists (Telstar)
5	11	RATTLE AND HUM	U2 (Island)
16	12	THE TRAVELING WILBURYS VOL 1	Traveling Wilburys (Wilbury)
7	13	FLYING COLOURS	Chris De Burgh (A&M)
8	14	THE GREATEST HITS COLLECTION	Bananarama (London)
11	15	SOFT METAL	Various Artists (Stylus)
4	16	WATERMARK	Enya (WEA)
-	17	GET EVEN	Brother Beyond (Parlophone)
22	18	THE PREMIERE COLLECTION: THE BEST OF ANDREW LLOYD WEBBER	Various Artists (Really Useful Records)
17	19	THE HIT FACTORY: THE BEST OF STOCK AITKEN WATERMAN VOL 2	Various Artists (PWL)
15	20	INTROSPECTIVE	Pet Shop Boys (Parlophone)
49	21	ANYTHING FOR YOU	Gloria Estefan & Miami Sound Machine (Epic)
21	22	THE GREATEST LOVE	Various Artists (Telstar)
10	23	SMASH HITS PARTY '88	Various Artists (Chrysalis)
12	24	RAGE	T'Pau (Siren)
19	25	ANY LOVE	Luther Vandross (Epic)
28	26	TO WHOM IT MAY CONCERN	Pasadenas (CBS)
23	27	ANCIENT HEART	Tanita Tikaram (WEA)
-	28	HEARSAY	Alexander O'Neal (Tabu)
35	29	SO GOOD	Mica Paris (Fourth & Broadway)
25	30	BUSTER	Soundtrack (Virgin)
27	31	HEAVY NOVA	Robert Palmer (EMI)
40	32	GREEN	REM (Warner Bros.)
13	33	UNFORGETTABLE	Various Artists (EMI)
24	34	SUNSHINE ON LEITH	Proclaimers (Chrysalis)
43	35	BAD	Michael Jackson (Epic)
26	36	NEGOTIATIONS AND LOVE SONGS 1971-1986	Paul Simon (Warner Bros.)
30	37	RAINTOWN	Deacon Blue (CBS)
37	38	PUSH	Bros (CBS)
33	39	THE LOVERS	Various Artists (K-Tel)
-	40	THE LOVE ALBUM '88	Various Artists (Telstar)
34	41	THE SINGLES COLLECTION	Kool & the Gang (De-Lite)
-	42	NITE FLITE	Various Artists (CBS)
31	43	DIRTY DANCING	Soundtrack (RCA)
-	44	MACHISMO	Cameo (Club)
29	45	THE INNOCENTS	Erasure (Mute)
38	46	CONSCIENCE	Womack & Womack (Fourth & Broadway)
48	47	GOOD MORNING VIETNAM - ORIGINAL SOUNDTRACK	Various Artists (A&M)
32	48	THE WORLDS OF FOSTER AND ALLEN	Foster & Allen (Stylus)
-	49	HIT MIX '88	Various Artists (Stylus)
-	50	A SALT WITH A DEADLY PEPA	Salt 'N' Pepa (London)

3 December 1988

last week	this week	Title	Artist
-	1	NOW THAT'S WHAT I CALL MUSIC 13	Various Artists (EMI/Virgin/Polygram)
1	2	KYLIE	Kylie Minogue (PWL)
6	3	PRIVATE COLLECTION (1979-1988)	Cliff Richard (EMI)
-	4	FLEETWOOD MAC'S GREATEST HITS	Fleetwood Mac (Warner Bros.)
2	5	MONEY FOR NOTHING	Dire Straits (Vertigo)
5	6	WANTED	Yazz (Big Life)
9	7	KICK	INXS (Mercury)
7	8	THE ULTIMATE COLLECTION	Bryan Ferry with Roxy Music (EG)
3	9	GREATEST HITS	Human League (Virgin)
-	10	DELICATE SOUND OF THUNDER	Pink Floyd (EMI)
18	11	THE PREMIERE COLLECTION: THE BEST OF ANDREW LLOYD WEBBER	Various Artists (Really Useful)
4	12	THE MEMPHIS SESSIONS	Wet Wet Wet (Precious)
13	13	FLYING COLOURS	Chris De Burgh (A&M)
8	14	THE BEST OF CHRIS REA - NEW LIGHT THROUGH OLD WINDOWS	Chris Rea (WEA)
23	15	SMASH HITS PARTY '88	Various Artists (Chrysalis)
15	16	SOFT METAL	Various Artists (Stylus)
10	17	THE GREATEST HITS OF '88	Various Artists (Telstar)
28	18	HEARSAY	Alexander O'Neal (Tabu)
19	19	THE HIT FACTORY: THE BEST OF STOCK AITKEN WATERMAN VOL 2	Various Artists (PWL)
14	20	THE GREATEST HITS COLLECTION	Bananarama (London)
11	21	RATTLE AND HUM	U2 (Island)
-	22	TILL I LOVED YOU	Barbra Streisand (CBS)
22	23	THE GREATEST LOVE	Various Artists (Telstar)
24	24	RAGE	T'Pau (Siren)
-	25	BEST OF THE ART OF NOISE	Art of Noise (China)
20	26	INTROSPECTIVE	Pet Shop Boys (Parlophone)
16	27	WATERMARK	Enya (WEA)
12	28	THE TRAVELING WILBURYS VOL 1	Traveling Wilburys (Wilbury)
36	29	NEGOTIATIONS AND LOVE SONGS 1971-1986	Paul Simon (Warner Bros.)
35	30	BAD	Michael Jackson (Epic)
17	31	GET EVEN	Brother Beyond (Parlophone)
43	32	DIRTY DANCING	Soundtrack (RCA)
38	33	PUSH	Bros (CBS)
30	34	BUSTER	Soundtrack (Virgin)
26	35	TO WHOM IT MAY CONCERN	Pasadenas (CBS)
21	36	ANYTHING FOR YOU	Gloria Estefan & Miami Sound Machine (Epic)
49	37	HIT MIX '88	Various Artists (Stylus)
37	38	RAINTOWN	Deacon Blue (CBS)
27	39	ANCIENT HEART	Tanita Tikaram (WEA)
25	40	ANY LOVE	Luther Vandross (Epic)
-	41	HOUSE HITS '88	Various Artists (Telstar)
41	42	THE SINGLES COLLECTION	Kool & the Gang (De-Lite)
29	43	SO GOOD	Mica Paris (Fourth & Broadway)
-	44	RAPPIN' IN THE HOUSE	Various Artists (K-Tel)
31	45	HEAVY NOVA	Robert Palmer (EMI)
-	46	GIVING YOU THE BEST THAT I GOT	Anita Baker (Elektra)
46	47	CONSCIENCE	Womack & Womack (Fourth & Broadway)
34	48	SUNSHINE ON LEITH	Proclaimers (Chrysalis)
48	49	THE WORLDS OF FOSTER AND ALLEN	Foster & Allen (Stylus)
50	50	A SALT WITH A DEADLY PEPA	Salt 'N' Pepa (London)

Kylie made the top of the chart for the second time in November, as the Minogue hit singles continued to roll, and the album began to build to its really major sales in the run-up to Christmas. It was joined by still more hits compilations - Cliff Richard's *Private Collection*, Bryan Ferry & Roxy Music's *Ultimate Collection*, and *Fleetwood Mac's Greatest Hits* - plus the inevitable *Now Music*, currently up to volume 13.

10 December 1988

last	this	Title	Artist (Label)
1	1	NOW THAT'S WHAT I CALL MUSIC 13	Various Artists (EMI/Virgin/Polygram)
3	2	PRIVATE COLLECTION (1979-1988)	Cliff Richard (EMI)
2	3	KYLIE	Kylie Minogue (PWL)
4	4	FLEETWOOD MAC'S GREATEST HITS	Fleetwood Mac (Warner Bros.)
5	5	MONEY FOR NOTHING	Dire Straits (Vertigo)
11	6	THE PREMIERE COLLECTION: THE BEST OF ANDREW LLOYD WEBBER	Various Artists (Really Useful Records)
-	7	THE THIEVING MAGPIE	Marillion (EMI)
8	8	THE ULTIMATE COLLECTION	Bryan Ferry with Roxy Music (EG)
16	9	SOFT METAL	Various Artists (Stylus)
-	10	HOLD ME IN YOUR ARMS	Rick Astley (RCA)
9	11	GREATEST HITS	Human League (Virgin)
7	12	KICK	INXS (Mercury)
17	13	THE GREATEST HITS OF '88	Various Artists (Telstar)
6	14	WANTED	Yazz (Big Life)
33	15	PUSH	Bros (CBS)
10	16	DELICATE SOUND OF THUNDER	Pink Floyd (EMI)
14	17	THE BEST OF CHRIS REA - NEW LIGHT THROUGH OLD WINDOWS	Chris Rea (WEA)
20	18	THE GREATEST HITS COLLECTION	Bananarama (London)
31	19	GET EVEN	Brother Beyond (Parlophone)
13	20	FLYING COLOURS	Chris De Burgh (A&M)
21	21	RATTLE AND HUM	U2 (Island)
19	22	THE HIT FACTORY: THE BEST OF STOCK AITKEN WATERMAN VOL 2	Various Artists (PWL)
12	23	THE MEMPHIS SESSIONS	Wet Wet Wet (Precious)
18	24	HEARSAY	Alexander O'Neal (Tabu)
23	25	THE GREATEST LOVE	Various Artists (Telstar)
42	26	THE SINGLES COLLECTION	Kool & the Gang (De-Lite)
-	27	SMASHES, THRASHES AND HITS	Kiss (Vertigo)
15	28	SMASH HITS PARTY '88	Various Artists (Chrysalis)
34	29	BUSTER	Soundtrack (Virgin)
41	30	HOUSE HITS '88	Various Artists (Telstar)
29	31	NEGOTIATIONS AND LOVE SONGS 1971-1986	Paul Simon (Warner Bros.)
30	32	BAD	Michael Jackson (Epic)
27	33	WATERMARK	Enya (WEA)
44	34	RAPPIN' IN THE HOUSE	Various Artists (K-Tel)
24	35	RAGE	T'Pau (Siren)
26	36	INTROSPECTIVE	Pet Shop Boys (Parlophone)
22	37	TILL I LOVED YOU	Barbra Streisand (CBS)
37	38	HIT MIX '88	Various Artists (Stylus)
-	39	THE INNOCENTS	Erasure (Mute)
-	40	DANCE DANCE DANCE	James Last (Polydor)
25	41	BEST OF THE ART OF NOISE	Art of Noise (China)
-	42	THE FLAG	Yello (Mercury)
35	43	TO WHOM IT MAY CONCERN	Pasadenas (CBS)
50	44	A SALT WITH A DEADLY PEPA	Salt 'N' Pepa (London)
39	45	ANCIENT HEART	Tanita Tikaram (WEA)
-	46	THE CLASSICAL EXPERIENCE	Various Artists (EMI)
-	47	THE QUEEN ALBUM	Elaine Paige (Siren)
-	48	REMOTE	Hue & Cry (Circa)
-	49	EVERYTHING	Bangles (CBS)
32	50	DIRTY DANCING	Soundtrack (RCA)

17 December 1988

last	this	Title	Artist (Label)
1	1	NOW THAT'S WHAT I CALL MUSIC 13	Various Artists (EMI/Virgin/Polygram)
2	2	PRIVATE COLLECTION (1979-1988)	Cliff Richard (EMI)
3	3	KYLIE	Kylie Minogue (PWL)
-	4	THE HITS ALBUM	Various Artists (CBS/WEA/BMG)
5	5	MONEY FOR NOTHING	Dire Straits (Vertigo)
6	6	THE PREMIERE COLLECTION: THE BEST OF ANDREW LLOYD WEBBER	Various Artists (Really Useful)
4	7	FLEETWOOD MAC'S GREATEST HITS	Fleetwood Mac (Warner Bros.)
18	8	THE GREATEST HITS COLLECTION	Bananarama (London)
8	9	THE ULTIMATE COLLECTION	Bryan Ferry with Roxy Music (EG)
10	10	HOLD ME IN YOUR ARMS	Rick Astley (RCA)
9	11	SOFT METAL	Various Artists (Stylus)
15	12	PUSH	Bros (CBS)
36	13	INTROSPECTIVE	Pet Shop Boys (Parlophone)
11	14	GREATEST HITS	Human League (Virgin)
13	15	THE GREATEST HITS OF '88	Various Artists (Telstar)
12	16	KICK	INXS (Mercury)
21	17	RATTLE AND HUM	U2 (Island)
17	18	THE BEST OF CHRIS REA - NEW LIGHT THROUGH OLD WINDOWS	Chris Rea (WEA)
32	19	BAD	Michael Jackson (Epic)
14	20	WANTED	Yazz (Big Life)
20	21	FLYING COLOURS	Chris De Burgh (A&M)
29	22	BUSTER	Soundtrack (Virgin)
19	23	GET EVEN	Brother Beyond (Parlophone)
23	24	THE MEMPHIS SESSIONS	Wet Wet Wet (Precious)
39	25	THE INNOCENTS	Erasure (Mute)
-	26	G N' R LIES	Guns N' Roses (Geffen)
7	27	THE THIEVING MAGPIE	Marillion (EMI)
22	28	THE HIT FACTORY: THE BEST OF STOCK AITKEN WATERMAN VOL 2	Various Artists (PWL)
26	29	THE SINGLES COLLECTION	Kool & the Gang (De-Lite)
-	30	MY GIFT TO YOU	Alexander O'Neal (Tabu)
16	31	DELICATE SOUND OF THUNDER	Pink Floyd (EMI)
28	32	SMASH HITS PARTY '88	Various Artists (Chrysalis)
43	33	TO WHOM IT MAY CONCERN	Pasadenas (CBS)
30	34	HOUSE HITS '88	Various Artists (Telstar)
25	35	THE GREATEST LOVE	Various Artists (Telstar)
44	36	A SALT WITH A DEADLY PEPA	Salt 'N' Pepa (London)
31	37	NEGOTIATIONS AND LOVE SONGS 1971-1986	Paul Simon (Warner Bros.)
37	38	TILL I LOVED YOU	Barbra Streisand (CBS)
-	39	TRACY CHAPMAN	Tracy Chapman (Elektra)
-	40	CHRISTMAS WITH NAT 'KING' COLE	Nat 'King' Cole (Stylus)
-	41	THE LEGENDARY ROY ORBISON	Roy Orbison (Telstar)
24	42	HEARSAY	Alexander O'Neal (Tabu)
-	43	THE TRAVELING WILBURYS VOL 1	Traveling Wilburys (Wilbury)
-	44	NOW - THE CHRISTMAS ALBUM	Various Artists (EMI/Virgin/PolyGram)
-	45	SO GOOD	Mica Paris (Fourth & Broadway)
45	46	ANCIENT HEART	Tanita Tikaram (WEA)
33	47	WATERMARK	Enya (WEA)
-	48	SUNSHINE ON LEITH	Proclaimers (Chrysalis)
50	49	DIRTY DANCING	Soundtrack (RCA)
27	50	SMASHES, THRASHES AND HITS	Kiss (Vertigo)

24 December 1988

last	this	Title	Artist (Label)
2	1	PRIVATE COLLECTION (1979-1988)	Cliff Richard (EMI)
1	2	NOW THAT'S WHAT I CALL MUSIC 13	Various Artists (EMI/Virgin/Polygram)
3	3	KYLIE	Kylie Minogue (PWL)
4	4	THE HITS ALBUM	Various Artists (CBS/WEA/BMG)
5	5	MONEY FOR NOTHING	Dire Straits (Vertigo)
7	6	GREATEST HITS	Fleetwood Mac (Warner Bros.)
41	7	THE LEGENDARY ROY ORBISON	Roy Orbison (Telstar)
6	8	THE PREMIERE COLLECTION: THE BEST OF ANDREW LLOYD WEBBER	Various Artists (Really Useful)
8	9	THE GREATEST HITS COLLECTION	Bananarama (London)
12	10	PUSH	Bros (CBS)
9	11	THE ULTIMATE COLLECTION	Bryan Ferry with Roxy Music (EG)
10	12	HOLD ME IN YOUR ARMS	Rick Astley (RCA)
43	13	THE TRAVELING WILBURYS VOL 1	Traveling Wilburys (Wilbury)
17	14	RATTLE AND HUM	U2 (Island)
14	15	GREATEST HITS	Human League (Virgin)
15	16	THE GREATEST HITS OF '88	Various Artists (Telstar)
11	17	SOFT METAL	Various Artists (Stylus)
13	18	INTROSPECTIVE	Pet Shop Boys (Parlophone)
18	19	THE BEST OF CHRIS REA - NEW LIGHT THROUGH OLD WINDOWS	Chris Rea (WEA)
44	20	NOW - THE CHRISTMAS ALBUM	Various Artists (EMI/Virgin/PolyGram)
19	21	BAD	Michael Jackson (Epic)
16	22	KICK	INXS (Mercury)
-	23	THE JOE LONGTHORNE SONGBOOK	Joe Longthorne (Telstar)
22	24	BUSTER	Soundtrack (Virgin)
25	25	THE INNOCENTS	Erasure (Mute)
20	26	WANTED	Yazz (Big Life)
21	27	FLYING COLOURS	Chris De Burgh (A&M)
23	28	GET EVEN	Brother Beyond (Parlophone)
28	29	THE HIT FACTORY: THE BEST OF STOCK AITKEN WATERMAN VOL 2	Various Artists (PWL)
-	30	THE GREATEST HITS OF HOUSE	Various Artists (Stylus)
24	31	THE MEMPHIS SESSIONS	Wet Wet Wet (Precious)
32	32	SMASH HITS PARTY '88	Various Artists (Chrysalis)
29	33	THE SINGLES COLLECTION	Kool & the Gang (De-Lite)
40	34	CHRISTMAS WITH NAT 'KING' COLE	Nat 'King' Cole (Stylus)
35	35	THE GREATEST LOVE	Various Artists (Telstar)
33	36	TO WHOM IT MAY CONCERN	Pasadenas (CBS)
30	37	MY GIFT TO YOU	Alexander O'Neal (Tabu)
39	38	TRACY CHAPMAN	Tracy Chapman (Elektra)
37	39	NEGOTIATIONS AND LOVE SONGS 1971-1986	Paul Simon (Warner Bros.)
31	40	DELICATE SOUND OF THUNDER	Pink Floyd (EMI)
36	41	A SALT WITH A DEADLY PEPA	Salt 'N' Pepa (London)
26	42	G N' R LIES	Guns N' Roses (Geffen)
47	43	WATERMARK	Enya (WEA)
38	44	TILL I LOVED YOU	Barbra Streisand (CBS)
34	45	HOUSE HITS '88	Various Artists (Telstar)
46	46	ANCIENT HEART	Tanita Tikaram (WEA)
49	47	DIRTY DANCING	Soundtrack (RCA)
-	48	DANCE DANCE DANCE	James Last (Polydor)
-	49	BACK TO THE 60'S	Various Artists (Telstar)
-	50	NEW JERSEY	Bon Jovi (Vertigo)

The *Premiere Collection* of Andrew Lloyd Webber favourites anthologised the original or hit versions of most of the best-known tracks from virtually every Lloyd Webber musical, thereby saving a lot of people the need to buy individual cast albums! *Kylie* emerged as 1988's top-selling album by year's end, but the actual year-end No. 1 went to Cliff Richard, also topping the singles chart with *Mistletoe & Wine*.

January 1989

With her duet with Jason Donovan, *Especially For You*, topping the singles chat, Kylie Minogue picked up the record-token-for-Christmas market to return to the Number 1 slot at the beginning of the New Year, before being dethroned by Erasure's *The Innocents* - which had been in the chart for more than eight months before getting its biggest sales boost from the success of the duo's *Crackers International* EP.

February 1989

4 February 1989

last	this	title	artist (label)
1	1	THE LEGENDARY ROY ORBISON	Roy Orbison (Telstar)
2	2	THE INNOCENTS	Erasure (Mute)
7	3	THE LIVING YEARS	Mike & the Mechanics (WEA)
4	4	GREATEST HITS	Fleetwood Mac (Warner Bros.)
3	5	ANYTHING FOR YOU	Gloria Estefan & the Miami Sound Machine (Epic)
5	6	THE PREMIERE COLLECTION: THE BEST OF ANDREW LLOYD WEBBER	Various Artists (Really Useful)
14	7	WATERMARK	Enya (WEA)
10	8	THE ULTIMATE COLLECTION	Bryan Ferry & Roxy Music (EG)
6	9	KYLIE	Kylie Minogue (PWL)
17	10	CLOSE	Kim Wilde (MCA)
11	11	KICK	INXS (Mercury)
8	12	BAD	Michael Jackson (Epic)
9	13	THE GREATEST HITS COLLECTION	Bananarama (London)
12	14	MONEY FOR NOTHING	Dire Straits (Vertigo)
32	15	ANCIENT HEART	Tanita Tikaram (WEA)
13	16	THE GREATEST LOVE 2	Various Artists (Telstar)
20	17	A SHOW OF HANDS	Rush (Vertigo)
19	18	TRAVELING WILBURYS VOL.1	Traveling Wilburys (Wilbury)
15	19	BUSTER - SOUNDTRACK	Various Artists (Virgin)
22	20	WANTED	Yazz (Big Life)
21	21	PRIVATE COLLECTION (1979-1988)	Cliff Richard (EMI)
16	22	NOW THAT'S WHAT I CALL MUSIC 13	Various Artists (EMI/Virgin/PolyGram)
-	23	THE MARQUEE 30 LEGENDARY YEARS	Various Artists (Polydor)
38	24	FLYING COLOURS	Chris De Burgh (A&M)
18	25	INTROSPECTIVE	Pet Shop Boys (Parlophone)
28	26	SO GOOD	Mica Paris (Fourth & Broadway)
23	27	LOVE SUPREME	Supremes featuring Diana Ross (Motown)
45	28	NEW YORK	Lou Reed (Sire)
26	29	GET EVEN	Brother Beyond (Parlophone)
34	30	HOLD ME IN YOUR ARMS	Rick Astley (RCA)
24	31	THE GREATEST HITS OF HOUSE	Various Artists (Stylus)
25	32	PUSH	Bros (CBS)
33	33	NEW JERSEY	Bon Jovi (Vertigo)
27	34	THE BEST OF CHRIS REA - NEW LIGHT THROUGH OLD WINDOWS	Chris Rea (WEA)
43	35	ALL OR NOTHING	Milli Vanilli (Cooltempo)
31	36	FISHERMAN'S BLUES	Waterboys (Ensign)
29	37	GREATEST HITS	Human League (Virgin)
48	38	REMOTE	Hue & Cry (Circa)
40	39	TRACY CHAPMAN	Tracy Chapman (Elektra)
49	40	WHITNEY	Whitney Houston (Arista)
-	41	THE CREAM OF ERIC CLAPTON	Eric Clapton & Cream (Polydor)
30	42	RATTLE AND HUM	U2 (Island)
-	43	NEW ROOTS	Various Artists (Stylus)
-	44	THE CIRCUS	Erasure (Mute)
-	45	GREEN	R.E.M. (Warner Bros.)
36	46	SOFT METAL	Various Artists (Stylus)
39	47	RAINTOWN	Deacon Blue (CBS)
-	48	MORE THAN FRIENDS	Jonathan Butler (Jive)
-	49	HYSTERIA	Def Leppard (Bludgeon Riffola)
-	50	SHOOTING RUBBERBANDS AT THE STARS	Edie Brickell & New Bohemians (Geffen)

11 February 1989

last	this	title	artist (label)
-	1	TECHNIQUE	New Order (Factory)
-	2	MYSTERY GIRL	Roy Orbison (Virgin)
1	3	THE LEGENDARY ROY ORBISON	Roy Orbison (Telstar)
3	4	THE LIVING YEARS	Mike & the Mechanics (WEA)
23	5	THE MARQUEE 30 LEGENDARY YEARS	Various Artists (Polydor)
15	6	ANCIENT HEART	Tanita Tikaram (WEA)
2	7	THE INNOCENTS	Erasure (Mute)
7	8	WATERMARK	Enya (WEA)
5	9	ANYTHING FOR YOU	Gloria Estefan & the Miami Sound Machine (Epic)
4	10	GREATEST HITS	Fleetwood Mac (Warner Bros.)
6	11	THE PREMIERE COLLECTION: THE BEST OF ANDREW LLOYD WEBBER	Various Artists (Really Useful)
-	12	AFTER THE WAR	Gary Moore (Virgin)
27	13	LOVE SUPREME	Supremes featuring Diana Ross (Motown)
8	14	THE ULTIMATE COLLECTION	Bryan Ferry & Roxy Music (EG)
9	15	KYLIE	Kylie Minogue (PWL)
11	16	KICK	INXS (Mercury)
10	17	CLOSE	Kim Wilde (MCA)
28	18	NEW YORK	Lou Reed (Sire)
19	19	BUSTER - SOUNDTRACK	Various Artists (Virgin)
20	20	WANTED	Yazz (Big Life)
12	21	BAD	Michael Jackson (Epic)
14	22	MONEY FOR NOTHING	Dire Straits (Vertigo)
18	23	TRAVELING WILBURYS VOL.1	Traveling Wilburys (Wilbury)
13	24	THE GREATEST HITS COLLECTION	Bananarama (London)
-	25	COCKTAIL - SOUNDTRACK	Various Artists (Elektra)
24	26	FLYING COLOURS	Chris De Burgh (A&M)
36	27	FISHERMAN'S BLUES	Waterboys (Ensign)
29	28	GET EVEN	Brother Beyond (Parlophone)
16	29	THE GREATEST LOVE 2	Various Artists (Telstar)
-	30	ROACHFORD	Roachford (CBS)
25	31	INTROSPECTIVE	Pet Shop Boys (Parlophone)
38	32	REMOTE	Hue & Cry (Circa)
21	33	PRIVATE COLLECTION (1979-1988)	Cliff Richard (EMI)
41	34	THE CREAM OF ERIC CLAPTON	Eric Clapton & Cream (Polydor)
-	35	HEARSAY	Alexander O'Neal (Tabu)
39	36	TRACY CHAPMAN	Tracy Chapman (Elektra)
30	37	HOLD ME IN YOUR ARMS	Rick Astley (RCA)
42	38	RATTLE AND HUM	U2 (Island)
47	39	RAINTOWN	Deacon Blue (CBS)
26	40	SO GOOD	Mica Paris (Fourth & Broadway)
31	41	THE GREATEST HITS OF HOUSE	Various Artists (Stylus)
22	42	NOW THAT'S WHAT I CALL MUSIC 13	Various Artists (EMI/Virgin/PolyGram)
32	43	PUSH	Bros (CBS)
17	44	A SHOW OF HANDS	Rush (Vertigo)
-	45	ATLANTIC REALM	Clannad (BBC)
48	46	MORE THAN FRIENDS	Jonathan Butler (Jive)
-	47	THE STARS WE ARE	Marc Almond (Parlophone)
-	48	ELECTRIC YOUTH	Debbie Gibson (Atlantic)
-	49	ANY LOVE	Luther Vandross (Epic)
34	50	THE BEST OF CHRIS REA - NEW LIGHT THROUGH OLD WINDOWS	Chris Rea (WEA)

18 February 1989

last	this	title	artist (label)
-	1	THE RAW AND THE COOKED	Fine Young Cannibals (London)
2	2	MYSTERY GIRL	Roy Orbison (Virgin)
1	3	TECHNIQUE	New Order (Factory)
3	4	THE LEGENDARY ...	Roy Orbison (Telstar)
4	5	THE LIVING YEARS	Mike & the Mechanics (WEA)
5	6	THE MARQUEE 30 LEGENDARY YEARS	Various Artists (Polydor)
6	7	ANCIENT HEART	Tanita Tikaram (WEA)
7	8	THE INNOCENTS	Erasure (Mute)
-	9	SPIKE	Elvis Costello (Warner Bros.)
9	10	ANYTHING FOR YOU	Gloria Estefan & the Miami Sound Machine (Epic)
25	11	COCKTAIL - SOUNDTRACK	Various Artists (Elektra)
30	12	ROACHFORD	Roachford (CBS)
8	13	WATERMARK	Enya (WEA)
32	14	REMOTE	Hue & Cry (Circa)
48	15	ELECTRIC YOUTH	Debbie Gibson (Atlantic)
20	16	WANTED	Yazz (Big Life)
13	17	LOVE SUPREME	Supremes featuring Diana Ross (Motown)
15	18	KYLIE	Kylie Minogue (PWL)
16	19	KICK	INXS (Mercury)
10	20	GREATEST HITS	Fleetwood Mac (Warner Bros.)
-	21	THUNDER AND CONSOLATION	New Model Army (EMI)
22	22	MONEY FOR NOTHING	Dire Straits (Vertigo)
11	23	THE PREMIERE COLLECTION: THE BEST OF ANDREW LLOYD WEBBER	Various Artists (Really Useful)
14	24	THE ULTIMATE COLLECTION	Bryan Ferry & Roxy Music (EG)
-	25	POP SAID	Darling Buds (Epic)
24	26	THE GREATEST HITS COLLECTION	Bananarama (London)
17	27	CLOSE	Kim Wilde (MCA)
21	28	BAD	Michael Jackson (Epic)
-	29	FOUNDATION	Ten City (Atlantic)
37	30	HOLD ME IN YOUR ARMS	Rick Astley (RCA)
19	31	BUSTER - SOUNDTRACK	Various Artists (Virgin)
-	32	THE GREAT RADIO CONTROVERSY	Tesla (Geffen)
-	33	DYLAN AND THE DEAD	Bob Dylan & the Grateful Dead (CBS)
23	34	TRAVELING WILBURYS VOL.1	Traveling Wilburys (Wilbury)
12	35	AFTER THE WAR	Gary Moore (Virgin)
18	36	NEW YORK	Lou Reed (Sire)
35	37	HEARSAY	Alexander O'Neal (Tabu)
50	38	THE BEST OF CHRIS REA - NEW LIGHT THROUGH OLD WINDOWS	Chris Rea (WEA)
-	39	SHOOTING RUBBERBANDS AT THE STARS	Edie Brickell & New Bohemians (Geffen)
26	40	FLYING COLOURS	Chris De Burgh (A&M)
29	41	THE GREATEST LOVE 2	Various Artists (Telstar)
-	42	HYSTERIA	Def Leppard (Bludgeon Riffola)
33	43	PRIVATE COLLECTION (1979-1988)	Cliff Richard (EMI)
28	44	GET EVEN	Brother Beyond (Parlophone)
39	45	RAINTOWN	Deacon Blue (CBS)
27	46	FISHERMAN'S BLUES	Waterboys (Ensign)
-	47	THE SINGLES : THE UA YEARS	Stranglers (EMI)
38	48	RATTLE AND HUM	U2 (Island)
-	49	GREEN	R.E.M. (Warner Bros.)
43	50	PUSH	Bros (CBS)

Roy Orbison's sudden death in December 1988, just as he was returning to prominence as a member of the all-star Traveling Wilburys, brought him a posthumous flurry of chart success reminiscent of that which had followed John Lennon's assassination exactly eight years earlier. While the hits compilation went to Number 1, the all-new *Mystery Girl*, the Big O's last recordings, crashed in at 2.

February – March 1989

25 February 1989

		Title	Artist (Label)
-	1	A NEW FLAME	Simply Red (Elektra)
10	2	ANYTHING FOR YOU	Gloria Estefan & the Miami Sound Machine (Epic)
1	3	THE RAW AND THE COOKED	Fine Young Cannibals (London)
2	4	MYSTERY GIRL	Roy Orbison (Virgin)
9	5	SPIKE	Elvis Costello (Warner Bros.)
16	6	WANTED	Yazz (Big Life)
7	7	ANCIENT HEART	Tanita Tikaram (WEA)
4	8	THE LEGENDARY ...	Roy Orbison (Telstar)
5	9	THE LIVING YEARS	Mike & the Mechanics (WEA)
6	10	THE MARQUEE 30 LEGENDARY YEARS	Various Artists (Polydor)
31	11	BUSTER - SOUNDTRACK	Various Artists (Virgin)
8	12	THE INNOCENTS	Erasure (Mute)
3	13	TECHNIQUE	New Order (Factory)
30	14	HOLD ME IN YOUR ARMS	Rick Astley (RCA)
11	15	COCKTAIL - SOUNDTRACK	Various Artists (Elektra)
13	16	WATERMARK	Enya (WEA)
28	17	BAD	Michael Jackson (Epic)
-	18	TRUE LOVE WAYS	Buddy Holly & the Crickets (Telstar)
12	19	ROACHFORD	Roachford (CBS)
42	20	HYSTERIA	Def Leppard (Bludgeon Riffola)
14	21	REMOTE	Hue & Cry (Circa)
19	22	KICK	INXS (Mercury)
29	23	FOUNDATION	Ten City (Atlantic)
18	24	KYLIE	Kylie Minogue (PWL)
22	25	MONEY FOR NOTHING	Dire Straits (Vertigo)
24	26	THE ULTIMATE COLLECTION	Bryan Ferry & Roxy Music (EG)
39	27	SHOOTING RUBBERBANDS AT THE STARS	Edie Brickell & New Bohemians (Geffen)
27	28	CLOSE	Kim Wilde (MCA)
20	29	GREATEST HITS	Fleetwood Mac (Warner Bros.)
38	30	THE BEST OF CHRIS REA - NEW LIGHT THROUGH OLD WINDOWS	Chris Rea (WEA)
-	31	THE FIRST OF A MILLION KISSES	Fairground Attraction (RCA)
23	32	THE PREMIERE COLLECTION: THE BEST OF ANDREW LLOYD WEBBER	Various Artists (Really Useful)
15	33	ELECTRIC YOUTH	Debbie Gibson (Atlantic)
26	34	THE GREATEST HITS	Bananarama (London)
-	35	TRACY CHAPMAN	Tracy Chapman (Elektra)
17	36	LOVE SUPREME	Supremes featuring Diana Ross (Motown)
37	37	HEARSAY	Alexander O'Neal (Tabu)
25	38	POP SAID	Darling Buds (Epic)
36	39	NEW YORK	Lou Reed (Sire)
50	40	PUSH	Bros (CBS)
44	41	GET EVEN	Brother Beyond (Parlophone)
21	42	THUNDER AND CONSOLATION	New Model Army (EMI)
33	43	DYLAN AND THE DEAD	Bob Dylan & the Grateful Dead (CBS)
43	44	PRIVATE COLLECTION (1979-1988)	Cliff Richard (EMI)
45	45	RAINTOWN	Deacon Blue (CBS)
-	46	STOP	Sam Brown (A&M)
40	47	FLYING COLOURS	Chris De Burgh (A&M)
-	48	THE BEST YEARS OF OUR LIVES	Neil Diamond (CBS)
41	49	THE GREATEST LOVE 2	Various Artists (Telstar)
-	50	GIVING YOU THE BEST THAT I GOT	Anita Baker (Elektra)

4 March 1989

		Title	Artist (Label)
1	1	A NEW FLAME	Simply Red (Elektra)
2	2	ANYTHING FOR YOU	Gloria Estefan & the Miami Sound Machine (Epic)
7	3	ANCIENT HEART	Tanita Tikaram (WEA)
3	4	THE RAW AND THE COOKED	Fine Young Cannibals (London)
-	5	THE BIG AREA	Then Jerico (London)
20	6	HYSTERIA	Def Leppard (Bludgeon Riffola)
4	7	MYSTERY GIRL	Roy Orbison (Virgin)
8	8	THE LEGENDARY ROY ORBISON	Roy Orbiso (Telstar)
17	9	BAD	Michael Jackson (Epic)
5	10	SPIKE	Elvis Costello (Warner Bros.)
9	11	THE LIVING YEARS	Mike & the Mechanics (WEA)
6	12	WANTED	Yazz (Big Life)
31	13	THE FIRST OF A MILLION KISSES	Fairground Attraction (RCA)
15	14	COCKTAIL - SOUNDTRACK	Various Artists (Elektra)
29	15	GREATEST HITS	Fleetwood Mac (Warner Bros.)
10	16	THE MARQUEE 30 LEGENDARY YEARS	Various Artists (Polydor)
12	17	THE INNOCENTS	Erasure (Mute)
16	18	WATERMARK	Enya (WEA)
11	19	BUSTER - SOUNDTRACK	Various Artists (Virgin)
24	20	KYLIE	Kylie Minogue (PWL)
30	21	THE BEST OF CHRIS REA - NEW LIGHT THROUGH OLD WINDOWS	Chris Rea (WEA)
18	22	TRUE LOVE WAYS	Buddy Holly & the Crickets (Telstar)
14	23	HOLD ME IN YOUR ARMS	Rick Astley (RCA)
22	24	KICK	INXS (Mercury)
35	25	TRACY CHAPMAN	Tracy Chapman (Elektra)
21	26	REMOTE	Hue & Cry (Circa)
13	27	TECHNIQUE	New Order (Factory)
25	28	MONEY FOR NOTHING	Dire Straits (Vertigo)
19	29	ROACHFORD	Roachford (CBS)
28	30	CLOSE	Kim Wilde (MCA)
26	31	THE ULTIMATE COLLECTION	Bryan Ferry & Roxy Music (EG)
46	32	STOP	Sam Brown (A&M)
23	33	FOUNDATION	Ten City (Atlantic)
32	34	THE PREMIERE COLLECTION: THE BEST OF ANDREW LLOYD WEBBER	Various Artists (Really Useful)
27	35	SHOOTING RUBBERBANDS AT THE STARS	Edie Brickell & New Bohemians (Geffen)
37	36	HEARSAY	Alexander O'Neal (Tabu)
41	37	GET EVEN	Brother Beyond (Parlophone)
-	38	SO GOOD	Mica Paris (Fourth & Broadway)
40	39	PUSH	Bros (CBS)
34	40	THE GREATEST HITS	Bananarama (London)
44	41	PRIVATE COLLECTION (1979-1988)	Cliff Richard (EMI)
-	42	DON'T BE CRUEL	Bobby Brown (MCA)
33	43	ELECTRIC YOUTH	Debbie Gibson (Atlantic)
-	44	THE LOVER IN ME	Sheena Easton (MCA)
-	45	THE AWARDS 1989	Various Artists (Telstar)
36	46	LOVE SUPREME	Supremes featuring Diana Ross (Motown)
-	47	CONSCIENCE	Womack & Womack (Fourth & Broadway)
-	48	TRAVELING WILBURYS VOL.1	Traveling Wilburys (Wilbury)
49	49	THE GREATEST LOVE 2	Various Artists (Telstar)
-	50	AND ALL BECAUSE THE LADY LOVES ...	Various Artists (Dover)

11 March 1989

		Title	Artist (Label)
1	1	A NEW FLAME	Simply Red (Elektra)
2	2	ANYTHING FOR YOU	Gloria Estefan & the Miami Sound Machine (Epic)
3	3	ANCIENT HEART	Tanita Tikaram (WEA)
10	4	SPIKE	Elvis Costello (Warner Bros.)
9	5	BAD	Michael Jackson (Epic)
4	6	THE RAW AND THE COOKED	Fine Young Cannibals (London)
6	7	HYSTERIA	Def Leppard (Bludgeon Riffola)
7	8	MYSTERY GIRL	Roy Orbison (Virgin)
5	9	THE BIG AREA	Then Jerico (London)
-	10	CHEEK TO CHEEK	Various Artists (CBS)
22	11	TRUE LOVE WAYS	Buddy Holly & the Crickets (Telstar)
12	12	WANTED	Yazz (Big Life)
-	13	DEEP HEAT	Various Artists (Telstar)
8	14	THE LEGENDARY ROY ORBISON	Roy Orbison (Telstar)
25	15	TRACY CHAPMAN	Tracy Chapman (Elektra)
11	16	THE LIVING YEARS	Mike & the Mechanics (WEA)
17	17	THE INNOCENTS	Erasure (Mute)
16	18	THE MARQUEE 30 LEGENDARY YEARS	Various Artists (Polydor)
26	19	REMOTE	Hue & Cry (Circa)
32	20	STOP	Sam Brown (A&M)
45	21	THE AWARDS 1989	Various Artists (Telstar)
50	22	AND ALL BECAUSE THE LADY LOVES ...	Various Artists (Dover)
15	23	GREATEST HITS	Fleetwood Mac (Warner Bros.)
18	24	WATERMARK	Enya (WEA)
47	25	CONSCIENCE	Womack & Womack (Fourth & Broadway)
19	26	BUSTER - SOUNDTRACK	Various Artists (Virgin)
13	27	THE FIRST OF A MILLION KISSES	Fairground Attraction (RCA)
35	28	SHOOTING RUBBERBANDS AT THE STARS	Edie Brickell & New Bohemians (Geffen)
44	29	THE LOVER IN ME	Sheena Easton (MCA)
-	30	ORANGES AND LEMONS	XTC (Virgin)
20	31	KYLIE	Kylie Minogue (PWL)
41	32	PRIVATE COLLECTION (1979-1988)	Cliff Richard (EMI)
14	33	COCKTAIL - SOUNDTRACK	Various Artists (Elektra)
21	34	THE BEST OF CHRIS REA - NEW LIGHT THROUGH OLD WINDOWS	Chris Rea (WEA)
24	35	KICK	INXS (Mercury)
-	36	FLYING COLOURS	Chris De Burgh (A&M)
-	37	NEW YORK	Lou Reed (Sire)
23	38	HOLD ME IN YOUR ARMS	Rick Astley (RCA)
42	39	DON'T BE CRUEL	Bobby Brown (MCA)
-	40	RAINTOWN	Deacon Blue (CBS)
30	41	CLOSE	Kim Wilde (MCA)
27	42	TECHNIQUE	New Order (Factory)
39	43	PUSH	Bros (CBS)
28	44	MONEY FOR NOTHING	Dire Straits (Vertigo)
36	45	HEARSAY	Alexander O'Neal (Tabu)
-	46	BEAT THIS - 20 HITS OF RHYTHM KING	Various Artists (Stylus)
38	47	SO GOOD	Mica Paris (Fourth & Broadway)
29	48	ROACHFORD	Roachford (CBS)
48	49	TRAVELING WILBURYS VOL.1	Traveling Wilburys (Wilbury)
-	50	INTROSPECTIVE	Pet Shop Boys (Parlophone)

Simly Red had made the Top 3 with both their previous albums, but *A New Flame* was the release which established the Mick Hucknall-led group as mega-record sellers. After an initial five weeks at Number 1, the album would never be far from the top of the chart for much of the year - and indeed would be 1989's top seller until it was overtaken in the closing days of December (about which more later).

18 March 1989

last week	this week		
1	1	A NEW FLAME	Simply Red (Elektra)
10	2	CHEEK TO CHEEK	Various Artists (CBS)
2	3	ANYTHING FOR YOU	Gloria Estefan & the Miami Sound Machine (Epic)
3	4	ANCIENT HEART	Tanita Tikaram (WEA)
20	5	STOP	Sam Brown (A&M)
-	6	THE SINGULAR ADVENTURES OF THE STYLE COUNCIL - GREATEST HITS VOLUME 1	Style Council (Polydor)
39	7	DON'T BE CRUEL	Bobby Brown (MCA)
4	8	SPIKE	Elvis Costello (Warner Bros.)
6	9	THE RAW AND THE COOKED	Fine Young Cannibals (London)
11	10	TRUE LOVE WAYS	Buddy Holly & the Crickets (Telstar)
13	11	DEEP HEAT	Various Artists (Telstar)
8	12	MYSTERY GIRL	Roy Orbison (Virgin)
22	13	AND ALL BECAUSE THE LADY LOVES ..	Various Artists (Dover)
12	14	WANTED	Yazz (Big Life)
7	15	HYSTERIA	Def Leppard (Bludgeon Riffola)
36	16	FLYING COLOURS	Chris De Burgh (A&M)
5	17	BAD	Michael Jackson (Epic)
32	18	PRIVATE COLLECTION (1979-1988)	Cliff Richard (EMI)
17	19	THE INNOCENTS	Erasure (Mute)
38	20	HOLD ME IN YOUR ARMS	Rick Astley (RCA)
14	21	THE LEGENDARY...	Roy Orbison (Telstar)
9	22	THE BIG AREA	Then Jerico (London)
-	23	OPEN UP AND SAY ... AAH!	Poison (Capitol)
16	24	THE LIVING YEARS	Mike & the Mechanics (WEA)
15	25	TRACY CHAPMAN	Tracy Chapman (Elektra)
23	26	GREATEST HITS	Fleetwood Mac (Warner Bros.)
-	27	JULIA FORDHAM	Julia Fordham (Circa)
19	28	REMOTE	Hue & Cry (Circa)
41	29	CLOSE	Kim Wilde (MCA)
-	30	UNFORGETTABLE 2	Various Artists (EMI)
25	31	CONSCIENCE	Womack & Womack (Fourth & Broadway)
-	32	THE PREMIERE COLLECTION: THE BEST OF ANDREW LLOYD WEBBER	Various Artists (Really Useful)
24	33	WATERMARK	Enya (WEA)
50	34	INTROSPECTIVE	Pet Shop Boys (Parlophone)
18	35	THE MARQUEE 30 LEGENDARY YEARS	Various Artists (Polydor)
-	36	RADIO ONE	Jimi Hendrix Experience (Castle Collectors Series)
34	37	THE BEST OF CHRIS REA - NEW LIGHT THROUGH OLD WINDOWS	Chris Rea (WEA)
49	38	TRAVELING WILBURYS VOL.1	Traveling Wilburys (Wilbury)
31	39	KYLIE	Kylie Minogue (PWL)
21	40	THE AWARDS 1989	Various Artists (Telstar)
-	41	FOUNDATION	Ten City (Atlantic)
26	42	BUSTER - SOUNDTRACK	Various Artists (Virgin)
40	43	RAINTOWN	Deacon Blue (CBS)
-	44	SCANDAL - SOUNDTRACK	Various Artists (Parlophone)
30	45	ORANGES AND LEMONS	XTC (Virgin)
42	46	TECHNIQUE	New Order (Factory)
48	47	ROACHFORD	Roachford (CBS)
44	48	MONEY FOR NOTHING	Dire Straits (Vertigo)
27	49	THE FIRST OF A MILLION KISSES	Fairground Attraction (RCA)
35	50	KICK	INXS (Mercury)

25 March 1989

1	1	A NEW FLAME	Simply Red (Elektra)
3	2	ANYTHING FOR YOU	Gloria Estefan & the Miami Sound Machine (Epic)
-	3	101	Depeche Mode (Mute)
11	4	DEEP HEAT	Various Artists (Telstar)
4	5	ANCIENT HEART	Tanita Tikaram (WEA)
2	6	CHEEK TO CHEEK	Various Artists (CBS)
5	7	STOP	Sam Brown (A&M)
30	8	UNFORGETTABLE 2	Various Artists (EMI)
-	9	SOUTHSIDE	Texas (Mercury)
6	10	THE SINGULAR ADVENTURES OF THE STYLE COUNCIL	Style Council (Polydor)
7	11	DON'T BE CRUEL	Bobby Brown (MCA)
8	12	SPIKE	Elvis Costello (Warner Bros.)
-	13	THE GREATEST HITS	Bananarama (London)
10	14	TRUE LOVE WAYS	Buddy Holly & the Crickets (Telstar)
17	15	BAD	Michael Jackson (Epic)
9	16	THE RAW AND THE COOKED	Fine Young Cannibals (London)
14	17	WANTED	Yazz (Big Life)
12	18	MYSTERY GIRL	Roy Orbison (Virgin)
27	19	JULIA FORDHAM	Julia Fordham (Circa)
46	20	TECHNIQUE	New Order (Factory)
39	21	KYLIE	Kylie Minogue (PWL)
15	22	HYSTERIA	Def Leppard (Bludgeon Riffola)
19	23	THE INNOCENTS	Erasure (Mute)
23	24	OPEN UP AND SAY ... AAH!	Poison (Capitol)
21	25	THE LEGENDARY...	Roy Orbison (Telstar)
-	26	A GRAVEYARD OF EMPTY BOTTLES	Dogs D'Amour (China)
26	27	GREATEST HITS	Fleetwood Mac (Warner Bros.)
22	28	THE BIG AREA	Then Jerico (London)
13	29	AND ALL BECAUSE THE LADY LOVES ...	Various Artists (Dover)
28	30	REMOTE	Hue & Cry (Circa)
43	31	RAINTOWN	Deacon Blue (CBS)
38	32	TRAVELING WILBURYS VOL.1	Traveling Wilburys (Wilbury)
25	33	TRACY CHAPMAN	Tracy Chapman (Elektra)
33	34	WATERMARK	Enya (WEA)
49	35	THE FIRST OF A MILLION KISSES	Fairground Attraction (RCA)
16	36	FLYING COLOURS	Chris De Burgh (A&M)
24	37	THE LIVING YEARS	Mike & the Mechanics (WEA)
-	38	ANOTHER PLACE AND TIME	Donna Summer (Warner Bros.)
31	39	CONSCIENCE	Womack & Womack (Fourth & Broadway)
18	40	PRIVATE COLLECTION (1979-1988)	Cliff Richard (EMI)
-	41	HIP HOUSE - 20 HIP HOUSE HITS	Various Artists (Stylus)
29	42	CLOSE	Kim Wilde (MCA)
20	43	HOLD ME IN YOUR ARMS	Rick Astley (RCA)
47	44	ROACHFORD	Roachford (CBS)
34	45	INTROSPECTIVE	Pet Shop Boys (Parlophone)
-	46	THE LOVER IN ME	Sheena Easton (MCA)
48	47	MONEY FOR NOTHING	Dire Straits (Vertigo)
37	48	THE BEST OF CHRIS REA - NEW LIGHT THROUGH OLD WINDOWS	Chris Rea (WEA)
35	49	THE MARQUEE 30 LEGENDARY YEARS	Various Artists (Polydor)
-	50	BEAT THIS - 20 HITS OF RHYTHM KING	Various Artists (Stylus)

1 April 1989

-	1	LIKE A PRAYER	Madonna (Sire)
2	2	ANYTHING FOR YOU	Gloria Estefan & the Miami Sound Machine (Epic)
-	3	NOW THAT'S WHAT I CALL MUSIC 14	Various Artists (EMI/Virgin/PolyGram)
1	4	A NEW FLAME	Simply Red (Elektra)
9	5	SOUTHSIDE	Texas (Mercury)
8	6	UNFORGETTABLE 2	Various Artists (EMI)
4	7	DEEP HEAT	Various Artists (Telstar)
3	8	101	Depeche Mode (Mute)
7	9	STOP	Sam Brown (A&M)
-	10	ORIGINAL SOUNDTRACK	S'Express (Rhythm King)
5	11	ANCIENT HEART	Tanita Tikaram (WEA)
18	12	MYSTERY GIRL	Roy Orbison (Virgin)
11	13	DON'T BE CRUEL	Bobby Brown (MCA)
6	14	CHEEK TO CHEEK	Various Artists (CBS)
10	15	THE SINGULAR ADVENTURES OF THE STYLE COUNCIL - GREATEST HITS VOLUME 1	Style Council (Polydor)
38	16	ANOTHER PLACE AND TIME	Donna Summer (Warner Bros.)
13	17	THE GREATEST HITS	Bananarama (London)
14	18	TRUE LOVE WAYS	Buddy Holly & the Crickets (Telstar)
41	19	HIP HOUSE - 20 HIP HOUSE HITS	Various Artists (Stylus)
-	20	APPETITE FOR DESTRUCTION	Guns N' Roses (Geffen)
15	21	BAD	Michael Jackson (Epic)
12	22	SPIKE	Elvis Costello (Warner Bros.)
22	23	HYSTERIA	Def Leppard (Bludgeon Riffola)
21	24	KYLIE	Kylie Minogue (PWL)
16	25	THE RAW AND THE COOKED	Fine Young Cannibals (London)
31	26	RAINTOWN	Deacon Blue (CBS)
44	27	ROACHFORD	Roachford (CBS)
23	28	THE INNOCENTS	Erasure (Mute)
25	29	THE LEGENDARY ROY ORBISON	Roy Orbison (Telstar)
17	30	WANTED	Yazz (Big Life)
20	31	TECHNIQUE	New Order (Factory)
-	32	HIP HOUSE	Various Artists (K-Tel)
28	33	THE BIG AREA	Then Jerico (London)
19	34	JULIA FORDHAM	Julia Fordham (Circa)
32	35	TRAVELING WILBURYS VOL.1	Traveling Wilburys (Wilbury)
42	36	CLOSE	Kim Wilde (MCA)
33	37	TRACY CHAPMAN	Tracy Chapman (Elektra)
-	38	3 FEET HIGH AND RISING	De La Soul (Big Life)
27	39	GREATEST HITS	Fleetwood Mac (Warner Bros.)
34	40	WATERMARK	Enya (WEA)
-	41	RAW	Alyson Williams (Def Jam)
-	42	KICK	INXS (Mercury)
-	43	RATTLE AND HUM	U2 (Island)
35	44	THE FIRST OF A MILLION KISSES	Fairground Attraction (RCA)
39	45	CONSCIENCE	Womack & Womack (Fourth & Broadway)
29	46	AND ALL BECAUSE THE LADY LOVES ...	Various Artists (Dover)
24	47	OPEN UP AND SAY ... AAH!	Poison (Capitol)
46	48	THE LOVER IN ME	Sheena Easton (MCA)
30	49	REMOTE	Hue & Cry (Circa)
26	50	A GRAVEYARD OF EMPTY BOTTLES	Dogs D'Amour (China)

The times were proving fruitful for female recording artists, with Gloria Estefan, Sam Brown and Tanita Tikaram (the latter two with their debut albums) all riding the Top 5 (simultaneously, on March 18), and the likes of Yazz, Julia Fordham and a revitalised (by Stock/Aitken/Waterman) Donna Summer selling extremely well. Madonna's immediate Number 1 with *Like A Prayer* was just the icing on the distaff cake.

April 1989

Guns N' Roses, still not the worldwide superstars they would become during the 1990s, made the Top 10 for the first time with their *Appetite For Destruction*, while another Top 10 debutant was Bobby Bown, whose *Don't Be Cruel* was his first solo album sucess, but who had originally been a member of the best selling black vocal group First Edition in the early 1980s, reaching No. 1 with the single *Candy Girl*.

29 April 1989

last week	this week		
2	1	A NEW FLAME	Simply Red (Elektra)
1	2	WHEN THE WORLD KNOWS YOUR NAME	Deacon Blue (CBS)
6	3	CLUB CLASSICS VOL.1	Soul II Soul (10)
3	4	LIKE A PRAYER	Madonna (Sire)
7	5	ANYTHING FOR YOU	Gloria Estefan & the Miami Sound Machine (Epic)
4	6	NOW THAT'S WHAT I CALL MUSIC 14	Various Artists (EMI/Virgin/PolyGram)
5	7	SONIC TEMPLE	Cult (Beggars Banquet)
8	8	THE RAW AND THE COOKED	Fine Young Cannibals (London)
9	9	APPETITE FOR DESTRUCTION	Guns N' Roses (Geffen)
14	10	EVERYTHING	Bangles (CBS)
10	11	FOREVER YOUR GIRL	Paula Abdul (Siren)
48	12	HEY HEY IT'S THE MONKEES - GREATEST HITS	Monkees (K-Tel)
11	13	DON'T BE CRUEL	Bobby Brown (MCA)
24	14	KICK	INXS (Mercury)
15	15	SOUTHSIDE	Texas (Mercury)
22	16	GIPSY KINGS	Gipsy Kings (Telstar)
13	17	MYSTERY GIRL	Roy Orbison (Virgin)
31	18	POP ART	Transvision Vamp (MCA)
-	19	HEADLESS CROSS	Black Sabbath (IRS)
50	20	GOOD DEEDS AND DIRTY RAGS	Goodbye Mr. Mackenzie (Capitol)
21	21	3 FEET HIGH AND RISING	De La Soul (Big Life)
12	22	THE SINGULAR ADVENTURES OF THE STYLE COUNCIL	Style Council (Polydor)
17	23	CHEEK TO CHEEK	Various Artists (CBS)
16	24	ORIGINAL SOUNDTRACK	S'Express (Rhythm King)
-	25	WHAT'S THAT NOISE?	Coldcut (Ahead Of Our Time)
28	26	KYLIE	Kylie Minogue (PWL)
27	27	1984-1989	Lloyd Cole & the Commotions (Polydor)
-	28	UKRAINSKI VISTUPI V JOHNA PEELA	Wedding Present (RCA)
18	29	ANCIENT HEART	Tanita Tikaram (WEA)
-	30	DEEP HEAT - THE SECOND BURN	Various Artists (Telstar)
23	31	BAD	Michael Jackson (Epic)
40	32	RATTLE AND HUM	U2 (Island)
29	33	ANOTHER PLACE AND TIME	Donna Summer (Warner Bros.)
25	34	HYSTERIA	Def Leppard (Bludgeon Riffola)
26	35	STOP	Sam Brown (A&M)
20	36	UNFORGETTABLE 2	Various Artists (EMI)
-	37	ONE	Bee Gees (Warner Bros.)
-	38	BLAZE OF GLORY	Joe Jackson (A&M)
32	39	ROACHFORD	Roachford (CBS)
-	40	DOOLITTLE	Pixies (4AD)
19	41	THE HEADLESS CHILDREN	W.A.S.P. (Capitol)
42	42	DIRTY DANCING - SOUNDTRACK	Various Artists (RCA)
39	43	SPIKE	Elvis Costello (Warner Bros.)
47	44	THE BIG AREA	Then Jerico (London)
35	45	THE INNOCENTS	Erasure (Mute)
34	46	TRAVELING WILBURYS VOL.1	Traveling Wilburys (Wilbury)
33	47	THE GREATEST HITS COLLECTION	Bananarama (London)
38	48	DEEP HEAT	Various Artists (Telstar)
30	49	TECHNIQUE	New Order (Factory)
46	50	THE LEGENDARY...	Roy Orbison (Telstar)

6 May 1989

last week	this week		
-	1	BLAST	Holly Johnson (MCA)
1	2	A NEW FLAME	Simply Red (Elektra)
5	3	ANYTHING FOR YOU	Gloria Estefan & the Miami Sound Machine (Epic)
2	4	WHEN THE WORLD KNOWS YOUR NAME	Deacon Blue (CBS)
8	5	THE RAW AND THE COOKED	Fine Young Cannibals (London)
4	6	LIKE A PRAYER	Madonna (Sire)
3	7	CLUB CLASSICS VOL.1	Soul II Soul (10)
14	8	KICK	INXS (Mercury)
10	9	EVERYTHING	Bangles (CBS)
40	10	DOOLITTLE	Pixies (4AD)
6	11	NOW THAT'S WHAT I CALL MUSIC 14	Various Artists (EMI/Virgin/PolyGram)
9	12	APPETITE FOR DESTRUCTION	Guns N' Roses (Geffen)
18	13	POP ART	Transvision Vamp (MCA)
12	14	HEY HEY IT'S THE MONKEES - GREATEST HITS	Monkees (K-Tel)
30	15	DEEP HEAT - THE SECOND BURN	Various Artists (Telstar)
13	16	DON'T BE CRUEL	Bobby Brown (MCA)
15	17	SOUTHSIDE	Texas (Mercury)
11	18	FOREVER YOUR GIRL	Paula Abdul (Siren)
17	19	MYSTERY GIRL	Roy Orbison (Virgin)
7	20	SONIC TEMPLE	Cult (Beggars Banquet)
16	21	GIPSY KINGS	Gipsy Kings (Telstar)
25	22	WHAT'S THAT NOISE?	Coldcut (Ahead Of Our Time)
22	23	THE SINGULAR ADVENTURES OF THE STYLE COUNCIL	Style Council (Polydor)
-	24	BORN THIS WAY!	Cookie Crew (London)
26	25	KYLIE	Kylie Minogue (PWL)
23	26	CHEEK TO CHEEK	Various Artists (CBS)
37	27	ONE	Bee Gees (Warner Bros.)
29	28	ANCIENT HEART	Tanita Tikaram (WEA)
27	29	1984-1989	Lloyd Cole & the Commotions (Polydor)
-	30	PASTPRESENT	Clannad (RCA)
45	31	THE INNOCENTS	Erasure (Mute)
32	32	RATTLE AND HUM	U2 (Island)
21	33	3 FEET HIGH AND RISING	De La Soul (Big Life)
31	34	BAD	Michael Jackson (Epic)
28	35	UKRAINSKI VISTUPI V JOHNA PEELA	Wedding Present (RCA)
19	36	HEADLESS CROSS	Black Sabbath (IRS)
42	37	DIRTY DANCING - SOUNDTRACK	Various Artists (RCA)
24	38	ORIGINAL SOUNDTRACK	S'Express (Rhythm King)
34	39	HYSTERIA	Def Leppard (Bludgeon Riffola)
-	40	OPEN UP AND SAY ... AAH!	Poison (Capitol)
35	41	STOP	Sam Brown (A&M)
38	42	BLAZE OF GLORY	Joe Jackson (A&M)
46	43	TRAVELING WILBURYS VOL.1	Traveling Wilburys (Wilbury)
39	44	ROACHFORD	Roachford (CBS)
20	45	GOOD DEEDS AND DIRTY RAGS	Goodbye Mr. Mackenzie (Capitol)
47	46	THE GREATEST HITS	Bananarama (London)
33	47	ANOTHER PLACE AND TIME	Donna Summer (Warner Bros.)
-	48	GET EVEN	Brother Beyond (Parlophone)
-	49	DIESEL AND DUST	Midnight Oil (CBS)
-	50	THE SINGER AND THE SONG	Various Artists (Stylus)

13 May 1989

last week	this week		
-	1	STREET FIGHTING YEARS	Simple Minds (Virgin)
-	2	TEN GOOD REASONS	Jason Donovan (PWL)
-	3	DISINTEGRATION	Cure (Fiction)
2	4	A NEW FLAME	Simply Red (Elektra)
1	5	BLAST	Holly Johnson (MCA)
3	6	ANYTHING FOR YOU	Gloria Estefan & the Miami Sound Machine (Epic)
5	7	THE RAW AND THE COOKED	Fine Young Cannibals (London)
9	8	EVERYTHING	Bangles (CBS)
6	9	LIKE A PRAYER	Madonna (Sire)
4	10	WHEN THE WORLD KNOWS YOUR NAME	Deacon Blue (CBS)
7	11	CLUB CLASSICS VOL.1	Soul II Soul (10)
15	12	DEEP HEAT - THE SECOND BURN	Various Artists (Telstar)
30	13	PASTPRESENT	Clannad (RCA)
8	14	KICK	INXS (Mercury)
13	15	POP ART	Transvision Vamp (MCA)
16	16	DON'T BE CRUEL	Bobby Brown (MCA)
12	17	APPETITE FOR DESTRUCTION	Guns N' Roses (Geffen)
11	18	NOW THAT'S WHAT I CALL MUSIC 14	Various Artists (EMI/Virgin/PolyGram)
25	19	KYLIE	Kylie Minogue (PWL)
18	20	FOREVER YOUR GIRL	Paula Abdul (Siren)
14	21	HEY HEY IT'S THE MONKEES - GREATEST HITS	Monkees (K-Tel)
19	22	MYSTERY GIRL	Roy Orbison (Virgin)
-	23	WANTED	Yazz (Big Life)
17	24	SOUTHSIDE	Texas (Mercury)
21	25	GIPSY KINGS	Gipsy Kings (Telstar)
-	26	THIS IS THE DAY, THIS IS THE HOUR	Pop Will Eat Itself (RCA)
23	27	THE SINGULAR ADVENTURES OF THE STYLE COUNCIL	Style Council (Polydor)
34	28	BAD	Michael Jackson (Epic)
10	29	DOOLITTLE	Pixies (4AD)
-	30	IN YOUR FACE	Kingdom Come (Polydor)
20	31	SONIC TEMPLE	Cult (Beggars Banquet)
28	32	ANCIENT HEART	Tanita Tikaram (WEA)
24	33	BORN THIS WAY!	Cookie Crew (London)
40	34	OPEN UP AND SAY ... AAH!	Poison (Capitol)
49	35	DIESEL AND DUST	Midnight Oil (CBS)
22	36	WHAT'S THAT NOISE?	Coldcut (Ahead Of Our Time)
43	37	TRAVELING WILBURYS VOL.1	Traveling Wilburys (Wilbury)
-	38	MONEY FOR NOTHING	Dire Straits (Vertigo)
-	39	SILVERTOWN	Men They Couldn't Hang (Silvertone)
37	40	DIRTY DANCING - SOUNDTRACK	Various Artists (RCA)
31	41	THE INNOCENTS	Erasure (Mute)
50	42	THE SINGER AND THE SONG	Various Artists (Stylus)
-	43	BLUE MURDER	Blue Murder (Geffen)
26	44	CHEEK TO CHEEK	Various Artists (CBS)
32	45	RATTLE AND HUM	U2 (Island)
27	46	ONE	Bee Gees (Warner Bros.)
41	47	STOP	Sam Brown (A&M)
33	48	3 FEET HIGH AND RISING	De La Soul (Big Life)
-	49	GREATEST HITS	Fleetwood Mac (Warner Bros.)
-	50	REMOTE	Hue & Cry (Circa)

Holly Johnson, former lead singer with Frankie Goes To Hollywood, got off to the best possible start with his debut solo album *Blast*, entering the chart at Number 1. He was, however, quickly eclipsed after one week by the rare instance of three new titles debuting simultaneously in the chart's top three places - by Simple Minds, newcomer (and growing teen idol) Jason Donovan, and the Cure.

May – June 1989

last week	this week	20 May 1989	
2	1	TEN GOOD REASONS	Jason Donovan (PWL)
1	2	STREET FIGHTING YEARS	Simple Minds (Virgin)
3	3	DISINTEGRATION	Cure (Fiction)
7	4	THE RAW AND THE COOKED	Fine Young Cannibals (London)
-	5	PARADISE	Inner City (10)
-	6	NITE FLITE 2	Various Artists (CBS)
5	7	BLAST	Holly Johnson (MCA)
4	8	A NEW FLAME	Simply Red (Elektra)
6	9	ANYTHING FOR YOU	Gloria Estefan & the Miami Sound Machine (Epic)
8	10	EVERYTHING	Bangles (CBS)
11	11	CLUB CLASSICS VOL.1	Soul II Soul (10)
10	12	WHEN THE WORLD KNOWS YOUR NAME	Deacon Blue (CBS)
9	13	LIKE A PRAYER	Madonna (Sire)
13	14	PASTPRESENT	Clannad (RCA)
16	15	DON'T BE CRUEL	Bobby Brown (MCA)
-	16	GOOD TO BE BACK	Natalie Cole (EMI Manhattan)
14	17	KICK	INXS (Mercury)
35	18	DIESEL AND DUST	Midnight Oil (CBS)
-	19	KALEIDOSCOPE WORLD	Swing Out Sister (Fontana)
19	20	KYLIE	Kylie Minogue (PWL)
15	21	POP ART	Transvision Vamp (MCA)
17	22	APPETITE FOR DESTRUCTION	Guns N' Roses (Geffen)
20	23	FOREVER YOUR GIRL	Paula Abdul (Siren)
23	24	WANTED	Yazz (Big Life)
12	25	DEEP HEAT - THE SECOND BURN	Various Artists (Telstar)
18	26	NOW THAT'S WHAT I CALL MUSIC 14	Various Artists (EMI/Virgin/PolyGram)
21	27	HEY HEY IT'S THE MONKEES - GREATEST HITS	Monkees (K-Tel)
50	28	REMOTE	Hue & Cry (Circa)
-	29	THE STONE ROSES	Stone Roses (Silvertone)
24	30	SOUTHSIDE	Texas (Mercury)
31	31	SONIC TEMPLE	Cult (Beggars Banquet)
-	32	SONGS TO MAKE THE WHOLE WORLD SING	Barry Manilow (Arista)
25	33	GIPSY KINGS	Gipsy Kings (Telstar)
26	34	THIS IS THE DAY, THIS IS THE HOUR	Pop Will Eat Itself (RCA)
28	35	BAD	Michael Jackson (Epic)
-	36	IN SEARCH OF SANITY	Onslaught (London)
27	37	THE SINGULAR ADVENTURES OF THE STYLE COUNCIL - GREATEST HITS VOLUME 1	Style Council (Polydor)
-	38	STEPPIN' TO THE SHADOWS	Shadows (Polydor)
22	39	MYSTERY GIRL	Roy Orbison (Virgin)
-	40	ROACHFORD	Roachford (CBS)
30	41	IN YOUR FACE	Kingdom Come (Polydor)
34	42	OPEN UP AND SAY ... AAH!	Poison (Capitol)
49	43	GREATEST HITS	Fleetwood Mac (Warner Bros.)
-	44	AT THIS MOMENT	Various Artists (Jive)
47	45	STOP	Sam Brown (A&M)
40	46	DIRTY DANCING - SOUNDTRACK	Various Artists (RCA)
41	47	THE INNOCENTS	Erasure (Mute)
42	48	THE SINGER AND THE SONG	Various Artists (Stylus)
45	49	RATTLE AND HUM	U2 (Island)
32	50	ANCIENT HEART	Tanita Tikaram (WEA)

last week	this week	27 May 1989	
1	1	TEN GOOD REASONS	Jason Donovan (PWL)
2	2	STREET FIGHTING YEARS	Simple Minds (Virgin)
6	3	NITE FLITE 2	Various Artists (CBS)
-	4	MIND BOMB	The The (Epic)
5	5	PARADISE	Inner City (10)
4	6	THE RAW AND THE COOKED	Fine Young Cannibals (London)
12	7	WHEN THE WORLD KNOWS YOUR NAME	Deacon Blue (CBS)
8	8	A NEW FLAME	Simply Red (Elektra)
14	9	PASTPRESENT	Clannad (RCA)
16	10	GOOD TO BE BACK	Natalie Cole (EMI Manhattan)
19	11	KALEIDOSCOPE WORLD	Swing Out Sister (Fontana)
7	12	BLAST	Holly Johnson (MCA)
38	13	STEPPIN' TO THE SHADOWS	Shadows (Polydor)
9	14	ANYTHING FOR YOU	Gloria Estefan & the Miami Sound Machine (Epic)
11	15	CLUB CLASSICS VOL.1	Soul II Soul (10)
-	16	BLIND MAN'S ZOO	10,000 Maniacs (Elektra)
3	17	DISINTEGRATION	Cure (Fiction)
15	18	DON'T BE CRUEL	Bobby Brown (MCA)
13	19	LIKE A PRAYER	Madonna (Sire)
32	20	SONGS TO MAKE THE WHOLE WORLD SING	Barry Manilow (Arista)
10	21	EVERYTHING	Bangles (CBS)
28	22	REMOTE	Hue & Cry (Circa)
17	23	KICK	INXS (Mercury)
21	24	POP ART	Transvision Vamp (MCA)
18	25	DIESEL AND DUST	Midnight Oil (CBS)
-	26	BIG DADDY	John Cougar Mellencamp (Mercury)
20	27	KYLIE	Kylie Minogue (PWL)
23	28	FOREVER YOUR GIRL	Paula Abdul (Siren)
22	29	APPETITE FOR DESTRUCTION	Guns N' Roses (Geffen)
-	30	LARGER THAN LIFE	Jody Watley (MCA)
24	31	WANTED	Yazz (Big Life)
26	32	NOW THAT'S WHAT I CALL MUSIC 14	Various Artists (EMI/Virgin/PolyGram)
33	33	GIPSY KINGS	Gipsy Kings (Telstar)
42	34	OPEN UP AND SAY ... AAH!	Poison (Capitol)
-	35	WORKIN' OVERTIME	Diana Ross (EMI)
35	36	BAD	Michael Jackson (Epic)
30	37	SOUTHSIDE	Texas (Mercury)
27	38	HEY HEY IT'S THE MONKEES - GREATEST HITS	Monkees (K-Tel)
-	39	COMING ALIVE AGAIN	Barbara Dickson (Telstar)
25	40	DEEP HEAT - THE SECOND BURN	Various Artists (Telstar)
45	41	STOP	Sam Brown (A&M)
-	42	PRECIOUS METAL	Various Artists (Stylus)
44	43	AT THIS MOMENT	Various Artists (Jive)
37	44	THE SINGULAR ADVENTURES OF THE STYLE COUNCIL - GREATEST HITS VOLUME 1	Style Council (Polydor)
-	45	WATERMARK	Enya (WEA)
-	46	HYSTERIA	Def Leppard (Bludgeon Riffola)
39	47	MYSTERY GIRL	Roy Orbison (Virgin)
31	48	SONIC TEMPLE	Cult (Beggars Banquet)
-	49	CHART SHOW ROCK THE NATION VOL.II	Various Artists (Dover)
47	50	THE INNOCENTS	Erasure (Mute)

last week	this week	3 June 1989	
-	1	THE MIRACLE	Queen (Parlophone)
1	2	TEN GOOD REASONS	Jason Donovan (PWL)
-	3	TIN MACHINE	Tin Machine (EMI USA)
2	4	STREET FIGHTING YEARS	Simple Minds (Virgin)
3	5	NITE FLITE 2	Various Artists (CBS)
9	6	PASTPRESENT	Clannad (RCA)
-	7	THE HITS ALBUM 10	Various Artists (CBS/WEA/BMG)
18	8	DON'T BE CRUEL	Bobby Brown (MCA)
5	9	PARADISE	Inner City (10)
7	10	WHEN THE WORLD KNOWS YOUR NAME	Deacon Blue (CBS)
4	11	MIND BOMB	The The (Epic)
15	12	CLUB CLASSICS VOL.1	Soul II Soul (10)
6	13	THE RAW AND THE COOKED	Fine Young Cannibals (London)
8	14	A NEW FLAME	Simply Red (Elektra)
29	15	APPETITE FOR DESTRUCTION	Guns N' Roses (Geffen)
22	16	REMOTE	Hue & Cry (Circa)
12	17	BLAST	Holly Johnson (MCA)
14	18	ANYTHING FOR YOU	Gloria Estefan & the Miami Sound Machine (Epic)
10	19	GOOD TO BE BACK	Natalie Cole (EMI Manhattan)
16	20	BLIND MAN'S ZOO	10,000 Maniacs (Elektra)
13	21	STEPPIN' TO THE SHADOWS	Shadows (Polydor)
42	22	PRECIOUS METAL	Various Artists (Stylus)
19	23	LIKE A PRAYER	Madonna (Sire)
11	24	KALEIDOSCOPE WORLD	Swing Out Sister (Fontana)
21	25	EVERYTHING	Bangles (CBS)
-	26	LIFE IS A DANCE (THE REMIX PROJECT)	Chaka Khan (Warner Bros.)
35	27	WORKIN' OVERTIME	Diana Ross (EMI)
17	28	DISINTEGRATION	Cure (Fiction)
23	29	KICK	INXS (Mercury)
27	30	KYLIE	Kylie Minogue (PWL)
28	31	FOREVER YOUR GIRL	Paula Abdul (Siren)
41	32	STOP	Sam Brown (A&M)
24	33	POP ART	Transvision Vamp (MCA)
26	34	BIG DADDY	John Cougar Mellencamp (Mercury)
33	35	GIPSY KINGS	Gipsy Kings (Telstar)
36	36	BAD	Michael Jackson (Epic)
20	37	SONGS TO MAKE THE WHOLE WORLD SING	Barry Manilow (Arista)
32	38	NOW THAT'S WHAT I CALL MUSIC 14	Various Artists (EMI/Virgin/PolyGram)
25	39	DIESEL AND DUST	Midnight Oil (CBS)
-	40	ELECTRIC YOUTH	Debbie Gibson (Atlantic)
37	41	SOUTHSIDE	Texas (Mercury)
31	42	WANTED	Yazz (Big Life)
45	43	WATERMARK	Enya (WEA)
-	44	LOC'ED AFTER DARK	Tone Loc (Delicious)
30	45	LARGER THAN LIFE	Jody Watley (MCA)
-	46	ANOTHER PLACE AND TIME	Donna Summer (Warner Bros.)
34	47	OPEN UP AND SAY ... AAH!	Poison (Capitol)
44	48	THE SINGULAR ADVENTURES OF THE STYLE COUNCIL - GREATEST HITS VOLUME 1	Style Council (Polydor)
40	49	DEEP HEAT - THE SECOND BURN	Various Artists (Telstar)
38	50	HEY HEY IT'S THE MONKEES - GREATEST HITS	Monkees (K-Tel)

Jason Donovan's *Ten Good Reasons* (which actually had eleven tracks - a source of puzzlement to many until it was ascertained that the title was actually a phrase from one of the songs, *Too Many Broken Hearts*) turned the chart tables on Simple Minds' *Street Fighting Years* in their second week of sales, and after two weeks at Number 1 would settle in near the chart top for most of the rest of 1989.

June 1989

10 June 1989

last	this	title	artist
1	1	THE MIRACLE	Queen (Parlophone)
7	2	THE HITS ALBUM 10	Various Artists (CBS/WEA/BMG)
2	3	TEN GOOD REASONS	Jason Donovan (PWL)
3	4	TIN MACHINE	Tin Machine (EMI USA)
-	5	THE OTHER SIDE OF THE MIRROR	Stevie Nicks (EMI)
8	6	DON'T BE CRUEL	Bobby Brown (MCA)
4	7	STREET FIGHTING YEARS	Simple Minds (Virgin)
5	8	NITE FLITE 2	Various Artists (CBS)
12	9	CLUB CLASSICS VOL.1	Soul II Soul (10)
6	10	PASTPRESENT	Clannad (RCA)
19	11	GOOD TO BE BACK	Natalie Cole (EMI Manhattan)
10	12	WHEN THE WORLD KNOWS YOUR NAME	Deacon Blue (CBS)
9	13	PARADISE	Inner City (10)
26	14	LIFE IS A DANCE (THE REMIX PROJECT)	Chaka Khan (Warner Bros.)
15	15	APPETITE FOR DESTRUCTION	Guns N' Roses (Geffen)
13	16	THE RAW AND THE COOKED	Fine Young Cannibals (London)
11	17	MIND BOMB	The The (Epic)
14	18	A NEW FLAME	Simply Red (Elektra)
21	19	STEPPIN' TO THE SHADOWS	Shadows (Polydor)
18	20	ANYTHING FOR YOU	Gloria Estefan & the Miami Sound Machine (Epic)
-	21	AVALON SUNSET	Van Morrison (Polydor)
23	22	LIKE A PRAYER	Madonna (Sire)
30	23	KYLIE	Kylie Minogue (PWL)
22	24	PRECIOUS METAL	Various Artists (Stylus)
17	25	BLAST	Holly Johnson (MCA)
16	26	REMOTE	Hue & Cry (Circa)
-	27	THE CHART SHOW DANCE MASTERS	Various Artists (Dover)
31	28	FOREVER YOUR GIRL	Paula Abdul (Siren)
27	29	WORKIN' OVERTIME	Diana Ross (EMI)
30	30	BLIND MAN'S ZOO	10,000 Maniacs (Elektra)
44	31	LOC'ED AFTER DARK	Tone Loc (Delicious)
24	32	KALEIDOSCOPE WORLD	Swing Out Sister (Fontana)
32	33	STOP	Sam Brown (A&M)
25	34	EVERYTHING	Bangles (CBS)
28	35	DISINTEGRATION	Cure (Fiction)
49	36	DEEP HEAT - THE SECOND BURN	Various Artists (Telstar)
29	37	KICK	INXS (Mercury)
47	38	OPEN UP AND SAY ... AAH!	Poison (Capitol)
46	39	ANOTHER PLACE AND TIME	Donna Summer (Warner Bros.)
-	40	9	Public Image Ltd. (Virgin)
36	41	BAD	Michael Jackson (Epic)
33	42	POP ART	Transvision Vamp (MCA)
34	43	BIG DADDY	John Cougar Mellencamp (Mercury)
35	44	GIPSY KINGS	Gipsy Kings (Telstar)
-	45	THROUGH THE STORM	Aretha Franklin (Arista)
38	46	NOW THAT'S WHAT I CALL MUSIC 14	Various Artists (EMI/Virgin/PolyGram)
-	47	DIRTY DANCING - SOUNDTRACK	Various Artists (RCA)
39	48	DIESEL AND DUST	Midnight Oil (CBS)
-	49	ANCIENT HEART	Tanita Tikaram (WEA)
48	50	THE SINGULAR ADVENTURES OF THE STYLE COUNCIL	Style Council (Polydor)

17 June 1989

last	this	title	artist
2	1	THE HITS ALBUM 10	Various Artists (CBS/WEA/BMG)
3	2	TEN GOOD REASONS	Jason Donovan (PWL)
1	3	THE MIRACLE	Queen (Parlophone)
5	4	THE OTHER SIDE OF THE MIRROR	Stevie Nicks (EMI)
6	5	DON'T BE CRUEL	Bobby Brown (MCA)
4	6	TIN MACHINE	Tin Machine (EMI USA)
15	7	APPETITE FOR DESTRUCTION	Guns N' Roses (Geffen)
9	8	CLUB CLASSICS VOL.1	Soul II Soul (10)
21	9	AVALON SUNSET	Van Morrison (Polydor)
12	10	WHEN THE WORLD KNOWS YOUR NAME	Deacon Blue (CBS)
8	11	NITE FLITE 2	Various Artists (CBS)
-	12	FLOWERS IN THE DIRT	Paul McCartney (Parlophone)
7	13	STREET FIGHTING YEARS	Simple Minds (Virgin)
10	14	PASTPRESENT	Clannad (RCA)
11	15	GOOD TO BE BACK	Natalie Cole (EMI Manhattan)
13	16	PARADISE	Inner City (10)
-	17	RAW LIKE SUSHI	Neneh Cherry (Circa)
16	18	THE RAW AND THE COOKED	Fine Young Cannibals (London)
-	19	WATERMARK	Enya (WEA)
-	20	ffrr - SILVER ON BLACK	Various Artists (ffrr)
22	21	LIKE A PRAYER	Madonna (Sire)
18	22	A NEW FLAME	Simply Red (Elektra)
23	23	KYLIE	Kylie Minogue (PWL)
24	24	PRECIOUS METAL	Various Artists (Stylus)
14	25	LIFE IS A DANCE (THE REMIX PROJECT)	Chaka Khan (Warner Bros.)
20	26	ANYTHING FOR YOU	Gloria Estefan & the Miami Sound Machine (Epic)
17	27	MIND BOMB	The The (Epic)
31	28	LOC'ED AFTER DARK	Tone Loc (Delicious)
27	29	THE CHART SHOW DANCE MASTERS	Various Artists (Dover)
30	30	BLIND MAN'S ZOO	10,000 Maniacs (Elektra)
34	31	EVERYTHING	Bangles (CBS)
33	32	STOP	Sam Brown (A&M)
37	33	KICK	INXS (Mercury)
19	34	STEPPIN' TO THE SHADOWS	Shadows (Polydor)
-	35	STAGE HEROES	Colm Wilkinson (RCA)
-	36	PASSION	Peter Gabriel (Virgin)
28	37	FOREVER YOUR GIRL	Paula Abdul (Siren)
39	38	ANOTHER PLACE AND TIME	Donna Summer (Warner Bros.)
36	39	DEEP HEAT - THE SECOND BURN	Various Artists (Telstar)
46	40	NOW THAT'S WHAT I CALL MUSIC 14	Various Artists (EMI/Virgin/PolyGram)
47	41	DIRTY DANCING - SOUNDTRACK	Various Artists (RCA)
43	42	BIG DADDY	John Cougar Mellencamp (Mercury)
25	43	BLAST	Holly Johnson (MCA)
26	44	REMOTE	Hue & Cry (Circa)
42	45	POP ART	Transvision Vamp (MCA)
-	46	GREEN	R.E.M. (Warner Bros.)
-	47	NEW YORK	Lou Reed (Sire)
49	48	ANCIENT HEART	Tanita Tikaram (WEA)
44	49	GIPSY KINGS	Gipsy Kings (Telstar)
38	50	OPEN UP AND SAY ... AAH!	Poison (Capitol)

24 June 1989

last	this	title	artist
1	1	THE HITS ALBUM 10	Various Artists (CBS/WEA/BMG)
2	2	TEN GOOD REASONS	Jason Donovan (PWL)
17	3	RAW LIKE SUSHI	Neneh Cherry (Circa)
8	4	CLUB CLASSICS VOL.1	Soul II Soul (10)
3	5	THE MIRACLE	Queen (Parlophone)
4	6	THE OTHER SIDE OF THE MIRROR	Stevie Nicks (EMI)
12	7	FLOWERS IN THE DIRT	Paul McCartney (Parlophone)
11	8	NITE FLITE 2	Various Artists (CBS)
-	9	RAINBOW WARRIORS	Various Artists (RCA)
19	10	WATERMARK	Enya (WEA)
5	11	DON'T BE CRUEL	Bobby Brown (MCA)
7	12	APPETITE FOR DESTRUCTION	Guns N' Roses (Geffen)
14	13	PASTPRESENT	Clannad (RCA)
6	14	TIN MACHINE	Tin Machine (EMI USA)
9	15	AVALON SUNSET	Van Morrison (Polydor)
10	16	WHEN THE WORLD KNOWS YOUR NAME	Deacon Blue (CBS)
13	17	STREET FIGHTING YEARS	Simple Minds (Virgin)
15	18	GOOD TO BE BACK	Natalie Cole (EMI Manhattan)
16	19	PARADISE	Inner City (10)
24	20	PRECIOUS METAL	Various Artists (Stylus)
23	21	KYLIE	Kylie Minogue (PWL)
35	22	STAGE HEROES	Colm Wilkinson (RCA)
18	23	THE RAW AND THE COOKED	Fine Young Cannibals (London)
22	24	A NEW FLAME	Simply Red (Elektra)
21	25	LIKE A PRAYER	Madonna (Sire)
31	26	EVERYTHING	Bangles (CBS)
37	27	FOREVER YOUR GIRL	Paula Abdul (Siren)
28	28	LOC'ED AFTER DARK	Tone Loc (Delicious)
26	29	ANYTHING FOR YOU	Gloria Estefan & the Miami Sound Machine (Epic)
25	30	LIFE IS A DANCE (THE REMIX PROJECT)	Chaka Khan (Warner Bros.)
29	31	THE CHART SHOW DANCE MASTERS	Various Artists (Dover)
30	32	BLIND MAN'S ZOO	10,000 Maniacs (Elektra)
27	33	MIND BOMB	The The (Epic)
32	34	STOP	Sam Brown (A&M)
20	35	ffrr - SILVER ON BLACK	Various Artists (ffrr)
46	36	GREEN	R.E.M. (Warner Bros.)
45	37	POP ART	Transvision Vamp (MCA)
33	38	KICK	INXS (Mercury)
40	39	NOW THAT'S WHAT I CALL MUSIC 14	Various Artists (EMI/Virgin/PolyGram)
34	40	STEPPIN' TO THE SHADOWS	Shadows (Polydor)
36	41	PASSION	Peter Gabriel (Virgin)
39	42	DEEP HEAT - THE SECOND BURN	Various Artists (Telstar)
43	43	BLAST	Holly Johnson (MCA)
38	44	ANOTHER PLACE AND TIME	Donna Summer (Warner Bros.)
44	45	REMOTE	Hue & Cry (Circa)
-	46	BAD	Michael Jackson (Epic)
41	47	DIRTY DANCING	Various Artists (RCA)
-	48	THE SONGS THAT GOT AWAY	Sarah Brightman (Really Useful)
-	49	DISINTEGRATION	Cure (Fiction)
-	50	THE ESSENTIAL DOMINGO	Placido Domingo (Deutsche Grammophon)

Queen had released a fair number of albums which had sold strongly but peaked at Number 2 during the 1980s, and so must have been gratified by the instant Number 1 success of *The Miracle*, their first release for over two years, and first studio recording since mid-1986. It was dethroned by the *Hits 10* compilation, notable for restoring the identifying number (abandoned on volume 9) to the title.

July 1989

last this

week

1 July 1989

last	this		
-	1	BATMAN	Prince (Warner Bros.)
4	2	CLUB CLASSICS VOL.1	Soul II Soul (10)
1	3	THE HITS ALBUM 10	
			Various Artists (CBS/WEA/BMG)
7	4	FLOWERS IN THE DIRT	
			Paul McCartney (Parlophone)
9	5	RAINBOW WARRIORS	Various Artists (RCA)
2	6	TEN GOOD REASONS	Jason Donovan (PWL)
3	7	RAW LIKE SUSHI	Neneh Cherry (Circa)
12	8	APPETITE FOR DESTRUCTION	
			Guns N' Roses (Geffen)
5	9	THE MIRACLE	Queen (Parlophone)
13	10	PASTPRESENT	Clannad (RCA)
11	11	DON'T BE CRUEL	Bobby Brown (MCA)
10	12	WATERMARK	Enya (WEA)
8	13	NITE FLITE 2	Various Artists (CBS)
6	14	THE OTHER SIDE OF THE MIRROR	
			Stevie Nicks (EMI)
17	15	STREET FIGHTING YEARS	
			Simple Minds (Virgin)
24	16	A NEW FLAME	Simply Red (Elektra)
-	17	ANYWAYAWANNA	Beatmasters (Rhythm King)
16	18	WHEN THE WORLD KNOWS YOUR NAME	
			Deacon Blue (CBS)
25	19	LIKE A PRAYER	Madonna (Sire)
40	20	STEPPIN' TO THE SHADOWS	
			Shadows (Polydor)
23	21	THE RAW AND THE COOKED	
			Fine Young Cannibals (London)
50	22	THE ESSENTIAL DOMINGO	
			Placido Domingo (Deutsche Grammophon)
-	23	A NIGHT TO REMEMBER	Cyndi Lauper (Epic)
20	24	PRECIOUS METAL	Various Artists (Stylus)
36	25	GREEN	R.E.M. (Warner Bros.)
19	26	PARADISE	Inner City (10)
14	27	TIN MACHINE	Tin Machine (EMI USA)
21	28	KYLIE	Kylie Minogue (PWL)
29	29	ANYTHING FOR YOU	Gloria Estefan
			& the Miami Sound Machine (Epic)
15	30	AVALON SUNSET	Van Morrison (Polydor)
18	31	GOOD TO BE BACK	Natalie Cole (EMI Manhattan)
28	32	LOC'ED AFTER DARK	Tone Loc (Delicious)
22	33	STAGE HEROES	Colm Wilkinson (RCA)
30	34	LIFE IS A DANCE (THE REMIX PROJECT)	
			Chaka Khan (Warner Bros.)
-	35	EAT ME IN ST. LOUIS	It Bites (Virgin)
-	36	KARYN WHITE	Karyn White (Warner Bros)
43	37	BLAST	Holly Johnson (MCA)
31	38	THE CHART SHOW DANCE MASTERS	
			Various Artists (Dover)
26	39	EVERYTHING	Bangles (CBS)
27	40	FOREVER YOUR GIRL	Paula Abdul (Siren)
-	41	PROTEST SONGS	Prefab Sprout (Kitchenware)
-	42	BADLANDS	Badlands (Atlantic)
-	43	RATTLE AND HUM	U2 (Island)
-	44	GIPSY KINGS	Gipsy Kings (Telstar)
-	45	PRIVATE COLLECTION (1979-1988)	
			Cliff Richard (EMI)
46	46	BAD	Michael Jackson (Epic)
-	47	ANCIENT HEART	Tanita Tikaram (WEA)
-	48	HEAVY NOVA	Robert Palmer (EMI)
32	49	BLIND MAN'S ZOO	10,000 Maniacs (Elektra)
44	50	ANOTHER PLACE AND TIME	
			Donna Summer (Warner Bros.)

8 July 1989

1	1	BATMAN	Prince (Warner Bros.)
-	2	VELVETEEN	Transvision Vamp (MCA)
2	3	CLUB CLASSICS VOL.1	Soul II Soul (10)
11	4	DON'T BE CRUEL	Bobby Brown (MCA)
6	5	TEN GOOD REASONS	Jason Donovan (PWL)
10	6	PASTPRESENT	Clannad (RCA)
-	7	FULL MOON FEVER	Tom Petty (MCA)
3	8	THE HITS ALBUM 10	
			Various Artists (CBS/WEA/BMG)
7	9	RAW LIKE SUSHI	Neneh Cherry (Circa)
5	10	RAINBOW WARRIORS	Various Artists (RCA)
23	11	A NIGHT TO REMEMBER	Cyndi Lauper (Epic)
4	12	FLOWERS IN THE DIRT	
			Paul McCartney (Parlophone)
8	13	APPETITE FOR DESTRUCTION	
			Guns N' Roses (Geffen)
18	14	WHEN THE WORLD KNOWS YOUR NAME	
			Deacon Blue (CBS)
41	15	PROTEST SONGS	Prefab Sprout (Kitchenware)
9	16	THE MIRACLE	Queen (Parlophone)
13	17	NITE FLITE 2	Various Artists (CBS)
-	18	WALKING ON SUNSHINE - VERY BEST OF EDDY	
		GRANT	Eddy Grant (Parlophone)
39	19	EVERYTHING	Bangles (CBS)
19	20	LIKE A PRAYER	Madonna (Sire)
12	21	WATERMARK	Enya (WEA)
16	22	A NEW FLAME	Simply Red (Elektra)
21	23	THE RAW AND THE COOKED	
			Fine Young Cannibals (London)
15	24	STREET FIGHTING YEARS	
			Simple Minds (Virgin)
24	25	PRECIOUS METAL	Various Artists (Stylus)
14	26	THE OTHER SIDE OF THE MIRROR	
			Stevie Nicks (EMI)
29	27	ANYTHING FOR YOU	Gloria Estefan
			& the Miami Sound Machine (Epic)
37	28	BLAST	Holly Johnson (MCA)
26	29	PARADISE	Inner City (10)
17	30	ANYWAYAWANNA	Beatmasters (Rhythm King)
30	31	AVALON SUNSET	Van Morrison (Polydor)
28	32	KYLIE	Kylie Minogue (PWL)
-	33	ANDERSON BRUFORD WAKEMAN AND HOWE	
			Anderson Bruford Wakeman & Howe (Arista)
20	34	STEPPIN' TO THE SHADOWS	Shadows (Polydor)
32	35	LOC'ED AFTER DARK	Tone Loc (Delicious)
-	36	G N' R LIES	Guns N' Roses (Geffen)
36	37	KARYN WHITE	Karyn White (Warner Bros)
34	38	LIFE IS A DANCE (THE REMIX PROJECT)	
			Chaka Khan (Warner Bros.)
31	39	GOOD TO BE BACK	
			Natalie Cole (EMI Manhattan)
25	40	GREEN	R.E.M. (Warner Bros.)
22	41	THE ESSENTIAL DOMINGO	
			Placido Domingo (Deutsche Grammophon)
-	42	DON'T STOP THE MUSIC	Various Artists (Stylus)
-	43	GATECRASHING	Living In A Box (Chrysalis)
27	44	TIN MACHINE	Tin Machine (EMI USA)
43	45	RATTLE AND HUM	U2 (Island)
33	46	STAGE HEROES	Colm Wilkinson (RCA)
-	47	BIG GAME	White Lion (Atlantic)
-	48	2300 JACKSON STREET	Jacksons (Epic)
-	49	DOOLITTLE	Pixies (4AD)
50	50	ANOTHER PLACE AND TIME	
			Donna Summer (Warner Bros.)

15 July 1989

3	1	CLUB CLASSICS VOL.1	Soul II Soul (10)
2	2	VELVETEEN	Transvision Vamp (MCA)
4	3	DON'T BE CRUEL	Bobby Brown (MCA)
1	4	BATMAN	Prince (Warner Bros.)
22	5	A NEW FLAME	Simply Red (Elektra)
6	6	PASTPRESENT	Clannad (RCA)
13	7	APPETITE FOR DESTRUCTION	
			Guns N' Roses (Geffen)
5	8	TEN GOOD REASONS	Jason Donovan (PWL)
-	9	NOW DANCE '89	Various Artists (EMI/Virgin)
7	10	FULL MOON FEVER	Tom Petty (MCA)
16	11	THE MIRACLE	Queen (Parlophone)
9	12	RAW LIKE SUSHI	Neneh Cherry (Circa)
19	13	EVERYTHING	Bangles (CBS)
11	14	A NIGHT TO REMEMBER	Cyndi Lauper (Epic)
10	15	RAINBOW WARRIORS	Various Artists (RCA)
8	16	THE HITS ALBUM 10	
			Various Artists (CBS/WEA/BMG)
33	17	ANDERSON BRUFORD WAKEMAN AND HOWE	
			Anderson Bruford Wakeman & Howe (Arista)
12	18	FLOWERS IN THE DIRT	
			Paul McCartney (Parlophone)
20	19	LIKE A PRAYER	Madonna (Sire)
36	20	G N' R LIES	Guns N' Roses (Geffen)
14	21	WHEN THE WORLD KNOWS YOUR NAME	
			Deacon Blue (CBS)
38	22	LIFE IS A DANCE (THE REMIX PROJECT)	
			Chaka Khan (Warner Bros.)
43	23	GATECRASHING	Living In A Box (Chrysalis)
-	24	HIT FACTORY 3	Various Artists (PWL)
21	25	WATERMARK	Enya (WEA)
26	26	THE OTHER SIDE OF THE MIRROR	
			Stevie Nicks (EMI)
23	27	THE RAW AND THE COOKED	
			Fine Young Cannibals (London)
29	28	PARADISE	Inner City (10)
24	29	STREET FIGHTING YEARS	
			Simple Minds (Virgin)
-	30	WALTZ DARLING	Malcolm McLaren & the
			Bootzilla Orchestra (Epic)
37	31	KARYN WHITE	Karyn White (Warner Bros)
44	32	TIN MACHINE	Tin Machine (EMI USA)
39	33	GOOD TO BE BACK	Natalie Cole (EMI Manhattan)
27	34	ANYTHING FOR YOU	Gloria Estefan
			& the Miami Sound Machine (Epic)
17	35	NITE FLITE 2	Various Artists (CBS)
-	36	REMOTE	Hue & Cry (Circa)
-	37	BAD	Michael Jackson (Epic)
18	38	WALKING ON SUNSHINE - VERY BEST OF EDDY	
		GRANT	Eddy Grant (Parlophone)
28	39	BLAST	Holly Johnson (MCA)
15	40	PROTEST SONGS	Prefab Sprout (Kitchenware)
25	41	PRECIOUS METAL	Various Artists (Stylus)
32	42	KYLIE	Kylie Minogue (PWL)
35	43	LOC'ED AFTER DARK	Tone Loc (Delicious)
40	44	GREEN	R.E.M. (Warner Bros.)
31	45	AVALON SUNSET	Van Morrison (Polydor)
-	46	WALKING WITH A PANTHER	
			L.L. Cool J. (Def Jam)
-	47	SEMINAL LIVE	Fall (Beggars Banquet)
34	48	STEPPIN' TO THE SHADOWS	Shadows (Polydor)
41	49	THE ESSENTIAL DOMINGO	
			Placido Domingo (Deutsche Grammophon)
-	50	ROACHFORD	Roachford (CBS)

It might have been his raised profile as a Traveling Wilbury which made the difference, but Tom Petty had by far his highest-charted album yet with the Heartbreakers on *Full Moon Fever* - which actually debuted inside the Top 10 which previous Petty offerings had been unable to climb to. Also riding a new high was Prince, whose LP had some of the best movie promotion ever via the blockbusting *Batman*.

342

22 July 1989

last week	this week		
1	1	CLUB CLASSICS VOL.1	Soul II Soul (10)
5	2	A NEW FLAME	Simply Red (Elektra)
9	3	NOW DANCE '89	Various Artists (EMI/Virgin)
3	4	DON'T BE CRUEL	Bobby Brown (MCA)
2	5	VELVETEEN	Transvision Vamp (MCA)
7	6	APPETITE FOR DESTRUCTION	Guns N' Roses (Geffen)
4	7	BATMAN	Prince (Warner Bros.)
6	8	PASTPRESENT	Clannad (RCA)
8	9	TEN GOOD REASONS	Jason Donovan (PWL)
11	10	THE MIRACLE	Queen (Parlophone)
19	11	LIKE A PRAYER	Madonna (Sire)
12	12	RAW LIKE SUSHI	Neneh Cherry (Circa)
21	13	WHEN THE WORLD KNOWS YOUR NAME	Deacon Blue (CBS)
13	14	EVERYTHING	Bangles (CBS)
27	15	THE RAW AND THE COOKED	Fine Young Cannibals (London)
10	16	FULL MOON FEVER	Tom Petty (MCA)
22	17	LIFE IS A DANCE (THE REMIX PROJECT)	Chaka Khan (Warner Bros.)
18	18	FLOWERS IN THE DIRT	Paul McCartney (Parlophone)
24	19	HIT FACTORY 3	Various Artists (PWL)
15	20	RAINBOW WARRIORS	Various Artists (RCA)
37	21	BAD	Michael Jackson (Epic)
14	22	A NIGHT TO REMEMBER	Cyndi Lauper (Epic)
25	23	WATERMARK	Enya (WEA)
31	24	KARYN WHITE	Karyn White (Warner Bros)
-	25	BEACHES	Soundtrack (Atlantic)
20	26	G N' R LIES	Guns N' Roses (Geffen)
16	27	THE HITS ALBUM 10	Various Artists (CBS/WEA/BMG)
29	28	STREET FIGHTING YEARS	Simple Minds (Virgin)
38	29	WALKING ON SUNSHINE - VERY BEST OF EDDY GRANT	Eddy Grant (Parlophone)
-	30	THEMES	Vangelis (Polydor)
17	31	ANDERSON BRUFORD WAKEMAN AND HOWE	Anderson Bruford Wakeman & Howe (Arista)
28	32	PARADISE	Inner City (10)
34	33	ANYTHING FOR YOU	Gloria Estefan & the Miami Sound Machine (Epic)
26	34	THE OTHER SIDE OF THE MIRROR	Stevie Nicks (EMI)
41	35	PRECIOUS METAL	Various Artists (Stylus)
30	36	WALTZ DARLING	Malcolm McLaren & the Bootzilla Orchestra (Epic)
-	37	RATTLE AND HUM	U2 (Island)
32	38	TIN MACHINE	Tin Machine (EMI USA)
-	39	DEEP HEAT 3 - THE THIRD DEGREE	Various Artists (Telstar)
49	40	THE ESSENTIAL DOMINGO	Placido Domingo (Deutsche Grammophon)
-	41	GIPSY KINGS	Gipsy Kings (Telstar)
23	42	GATECRASHING	Living In A Box (Chrysalis)
33	43	GOOD TO BE BACK	Natalie Cole (EMI Manhattan)
-	44	EARTH MOVING	Mike Oldfield (Virgin)
-	45	PROTECT THE INNOCENT	Various Artists (Telstar)
-	46	FOREVER YOUR GIRL	Paula Abdul (Siren)
-	47	AFTER DARK	Tom Jones (Stylus)
45	48	AVALON SUNSET	Van Morrison (Polydor)
39	49	BLAST	Holly Johnson (MCA)
-	50	KICK	INXS (Mercury)

29 July 1989

last week	this week		
2	1	A NEW FLAME	Simply Red (Elektra)
1	2	CLUB CLASSICS VOL.1	Soul II Soul (10)
3	3	NOW DANCE '89	Various Artists (EMI/Virgin)
4	4	DON'T BE CRUEL	Bobby Brown (MCA)
-	5	PEACE AND LOVE	Pogues (Pogue Mahone)
9	6	TEN GOOD REASONS	Jason Donovan (PWL)
6	7	APPETITE FOR DESTRUCTION	Guns N' Roses (Geffen)
7	8	BATMAN	Prince (Warner Bros.)
33	9	ANYTHING FOR YOU	Gloria Estefan & the Miami Sound Machine (Epic)
5	10	VELVETEEN	Transvision Vamp (MCA)
30	11	THEMES	Vangelis (Polydor)
28	12	STREET FIGHTING YEARS	Simple Minds (Virgin)
8	13	PASTPRESENT	Clannad (RCA)
10	14	THE MIRACLE	Queen (Parlophone)
13	15	WHEN THE WORLD KNOWS YOUR NAME	Deacon Blue (CBS)
12	16	RAW LIKE SUSHI	Neneh Cherry (Circa)
19	17	HIT FACTORY 3	Various Artists (PWL)
39	18	DEEP HEAT 3 - THE THIRD DEGREE	Various Artists (Telstar)
11	19	LIKE A PRAYER	Madonna (Sire)
15	20	THE RAW AND THE COOKED	Fine Young Cannibals (London)
25	21	BEACHES	Soundtrack (Atlantic)
14	22	EVERYTHING	Bangles (CBS)
24	23	KARYN WHITE	Karyn White (Warner Bros)
22	24	A NIGHT TO REMEMBER	Cyndi Lauper (Epic)
18	25	FLOWERS IN THE DIRT	Paul McCartney (Parlophone)
23	26	WATERMARK	Enya (WEA)
16	27	FULL MOON FEVER	Tom Petty (MCA)
21	28	BAD	Michael Jackson (Epic)
17	29	LIFE IS A DANCE (THE REMIX PROJECT)	Chaka Khan (Warner Bros.)
-	30	THE 12 COMMANDMENTS OF DANCE	London Boys (WEA)
32	31	PARADISE	Inner City (10)
44	32	EARTH MOVING	Mike Oldfield (Virgin)
43	33	GOOD TO BE BACK	Natalie Cole (EMI Manhattan)
40	34	THE ESSENTIAL DOMINGO	Placido Domingo (Deutsche Grammophon)
-	35	GHETTO MUSIC	Boogie Down Productions (Jive)
26	36	G N' R LIES	Guns N' Roses (Geffen)
35	37	PRECIOUS METAL	Various Artists (Stylus)
20	38	RAINBOW WARRIORS	Various Artists (RCA)
-	39	3 FEET HIGH AND RISING	De La Soul (Big Life)
-	40	BEEBOP MOPTOP	Danny Wilson (Virgin)
31	41	ANDERSON BRUFORD WAKEMAN AND HOWE	Anderson Bruford Wakeman & Howe (Arista)
29	42	WALKING ON SUNSHINE - VERY BEST OF EDDY GRANT	Eddy Grant (Parlophone)
48	43	AVALON SUNSET	Van Morrison (Polydor)
34	44	THE OTHER SIDE OF THE MIRROR	Stevie Nicks (EMI)
27	45	THE HITS ALBUM 10	Various (CBS/WEA/BMG)
36	46	WALTZ DARLING	Malcolm McLaren & the Bootzilla Orchestra (Epic)
-	47	THE COMPLETE	Glen Campbell (Stylus)
-	48	THE END OF THE INNOCENCE	Don Henley (Geffen)
41	49	GIPSY KINGS	Gipsy Kings (Telstar)
-	50	JUMP - THE BEST OF THE POINTER SISTERS	Pointer Sisters (RCA)

5 August 1989

last week	this week		
-	1	CUTS BOTH WAYS	Gloria Estefan (Epic)
1	2	A NEW FLAME	Simply Red (Elektra)
2	3	CLUB CLASSICS VOL.1	Soul II Soul (10)
3	4	NOW DANCE '89	Various Artists (EMI/Virgin)
30	5	THE 12 COMMANDMENTS OF DANCE	London Boys (WEA)
4	6	DON'T BE CRUEL	Bobby Brown (MCA)
18	7	DEEP HEAT 3 - THE THIRD DEGREE	Various Artists (Telstar)
5	8	PEACE AND LOVE	Pogues (Pogue Mahone)
6	9	TEN GOOD REASONS	Jason Donovan (PWL)
7	10	APPETITE FOR DESTRUCTION	Guns N' Roses (Geffen)
10	11	VELVETEEN	Transvision Vamp (MCA)
8	12	BATMAN	Prince (Warner Bros.)
12	13	STREET FIGHTING YEARS	Simple Minds (Virgin)
11	14	THEMES	Vangelis (Polydor)
14	15	THE MIRACLE	Queen (Parlophone)
16	16	RAW LIKE SUSHI	Neneh Cherry (Circa)
15	17	WHEN THE WORLD KNOWS YOUR NAME	Deacon Blue (CBS)
9	18	ANYTHING FOR YOU	Gloria Estefan & the Miami Sound Machine (Epic)
13	19	PASTPRESENT	Clannad (RCA)
20	20	THE RAW AND THE COOKED	Fine Young Cannibals (London)
19	21	LIKE A PRAYER	Madonna (Sire)
40	22	BEEBOP MOPTOP	Danny Wilson (Virgin)
21	23	BEACHES	Soundtrack (Atlantic)
17	24	HIT FACTORY 3	Various Artists (PWL)
25	25	FLOWERS IN THE DIRT	Paul McCartney (Parlophone)
39	26	3 FEET HIGH AND RISING	De La Soul (Big Life)
24	27	A NIGHT TO REMEMBER	Cyndi Lauper (Epic)
31	28	PARADISE	Inner City (10)
27	29	FULL MOON FEVER	Tom Petty (MCA)
22	30	EVERYTHING	Bangles (CBS)
23	31	KARYN WHITE	Karyn White (Warner Bros)
-	32	ESPECIALLY FOR YOU	Joe Longthorne (Telstar)
26	33	WATERMARK	Enya (WEA)
28	34	BAD	Michael Jackson (Epic)
36	35	G N' R LIES	Guns N' Roses (Geffen)
29	36	LIFE IS A DANCE (THE REMIX PROJECT)	Chaka Khan (Warner Bros.)
48	37	THE END OF THE INNOCENCE	Don Henley (Geffen)
50	38	JUMP - THE BEST OF THE POINTER SISTERS	Pointer Sisters (RCA)
-	39	KYLIE	Kylie Minogue (PWL)
-	40	HOT SUMMER NIGHTS	Various Artists (Stylus)
49	41	GIPSY KINGS	Gipsy Kings (Telstar)
-	42	PAUL'S BOUTIQUE	Beastie Boys (Capitol)
44	43	THE OTHER SIDE OF THE MIRROR	Stevie Nicks (EMI)
-	44	BLAST	Holly Johnson (MCA)
33	45	GOOD TO BE BACK	Natalie Cole (EMI Manhattan)
42	46	WALKING ON SUNSHINE - VERY BEST OF EDDY GRANT	Eddy Grant (Parlophone)
-	47	KICK	INXS (Mercury)
-	48	NITE FLITE 2	Various Artists (CBS)
37	49	PRECIOUS METAL	Various Artists (Stylus)
-	50	THE STONE ROSES	Stone Roses (Silvertone)

With *Cuts Both Ways*, Gloria Estefan, who had begun her recorded career without an identifying credit as part of Miami Sound Machine, then graduated (on *Anything For You*) to promotion up front, finally made it to ostensible solo billing - though in fact there had been no material change, and she still sang fronting the band (which was led by her husband and producer Emilio Estefan).

August 1989

Following Soul II Soul's July Number 1 album with *Club Classics Vol.1*, several dance-oriented acts, whom received record industry wisdom suggested were incapable of "sustaining" hit albums, were making the upper echelons of the chart. WEA's gimmicky dance duo the London Boys actually made the Top 3, while Inner City and club-style girl singers Karyn White and Nena Cherry also sold strongly.

last week	this week		

2 September 1989

last	this		
2	1	NOW THAT'S WHAT I CALL MUSIC 15	Various Artists (EMI/Virgin/PolyGram)
1	2	CUTS BOTH WAYS	Gloria Estefan (Epic)
3	3	TEN GOOD REASONS	Jason Donovan (PWL)
10	4	TRASH	Alice Cooper (Epic)
5	5	HEART AND SOUL - 18 CLASSIC SOUL CUTS	Various Artists (Polydor)
4	6	A NEW FLAME	Simply Red (Elektra)
9	7	BATMAN	Prince (Warner Bros.)
26	8	BIG BANG	Fuzzbox (WEA)
7	9	VELVETEEN	Transvision Vamp (MCA)
30	10	CHOICES - THE SINGLES CONNECTION	Blow Monkeys (RCA)
12	11	RAW LIKE SUSHI	Neneh Cherry (Circa)
8	12	DON'T BE CRUEL	Bobby Brown (MCA)
11	13	CLUB CLASSICS VOL.1	Soul II Soul (10)
6	14	THE 12 COMMANDMENTS OF DANCE	London Boys (WEA)
13	15	JUMP - THE BEST OF THE POINTER SISTERS	Pointer Sisters (RCA)
20	16	THE MIRACLE	Queen (Parlophone)
23	17	ALL THE HITS	Imagination (Stylus)
17	18	ANYTHING FOR YOU	Gloria Estefan & the Miami Sound Machine (Epic)
-	19	SACRED HEART	Shakespear's Sister (London)
15	20	THEMES	Vangelis (Polydor)
16	21	APPETITE FOR DESTRUCTION	Guns N' Roses (Geffen)
14	22	NOW DANCE '89	Various Artists (EMI/Virgin)
21	23	THE RAW AND THE COOKED	Fine Young Cannibals (London)
18	24	STREET FIGHTING YEARS	Simple Minds (Virgin)
24	25	A NIGHT TO REMEMBER	Cyndi Lauper (Epic)
-	26	ROCK ISLAND	Jethro Tull (Chrysalis)
33	27	WHEN THE WORLD KNOWS YOUR NAME	Deacon Blue (CBS)
19	28	PARADISE	Inner City (10)
22	29	DEEP HEAT 3 - THE THIRD DEGREE	Various Artists (Telstar)
28	30	THE END OF THE INNOCENCE	Don Henley (Geffen)
35	31	LIKE A PRAYER	Madonna (Sire)
40	32	WATERMARK	Enya (WEA)
41	33	THE BIG AREA	Then Jerico (London)
-	34	FRENCH KISS: THE COMPLETE MIX COLLECTION (EP)	L'il Louis (ffrr)
36	35	FULL MOON FEVER	Tom Petty (MCA)
25	36	FLOWERS IN THE DIRT	Paul McCartney (Parlophone)
27	37	KYLIE	Kylie Minogue (PWL)
48	38	ELECTRIC YOUTH	Debbie Gibson (Atlantic)
32	39	PASTPRESENT	Clannad (RCA)
29	40	HOT SUMMER NIGHTS	Various Artists (Stylus)
34	41	SOUTHSIDE	Texas (Mercury)
43	42	G N' R LIES	Guns N' Roses (Geffen)
-	43	KICK	INXS (Mercury)
39	44	KARYN WHITE	Karyn White (Warner Bros)
-	45	NEW JERSEY	Bon Jovi (Vertigo)
31	46	ESPECIALLY FOR YOU	Joe Longthorne (Telstar)
44	47	BAD	Michael Jackson (Epic)
-	48	SINGALONGAWARYEARS	Max Bygraves (Parkfield Music)
50	49	DISINTEGRATION	Cure (Fiction)
45	50	WALTZ DARLING	Malcolm McLaren & the Bootzilla Orchestra (Epic)

9 September 1989

last	this		
1	1	NOW THAT'S WHAT I CALL MUSIC 15	Various Artists (EMI/Virgin/PolyGram)
2	2	CUTS BOTH WAYS	Gloria Estefan (Epic)
3	3	TEN GOOD REASONS	Jason Donovan (PWL)
4	4	TRASH	Alice Cooper (Epic)
5	5	HEART AND SOUL - 18 CLASSIC SOUL CUTS	Various Artists (Polydor)
11	6	RAW LIKE SUSHI	Neneh Cherry (Circa)
6	7	A NEW FLAME	Simply Red (Elektra)
7	8	BATMAN	Prince (Warner Bros.)
10	9	CHOICES - THE SINGLES CONNECTION	Blow Monkeys (RCA)
19	10	SACRED HEART	Shakespear's Sister (London)
12	11	DON'T BE CRUEL	Bobby Brown (MCA)
17	12	ALL THE HITS	Imagination (Stylus)
9	13	VELVETEEN	Transvision Vamp (MCA)
14	14	CLUB CLASSICS VOL.1	Soul II Soul (10)
16	15	THE MIRACLE	Queen (Parlophone)
20	16	THEMES	Vangelis (Polydor)
14	17	THE 12 COMMANDMENTS OF DANCE	London Boys (WEA)
8	18	BIG BANG	Fuzzbox (WEA)
26	19	ROCK ISLAND	Jethro Tull (Chrysalis)
18	20	ANYTHING FOR YOU	Gloria Estefan & the Miami Sound Machine (Epic)
23	21	THE RAW AND THE COOKED	Fine Young Cannibals (London)
48	22	SINGALONGAWARYEARS	Max Bygraves (Parkfield Music)
21	23	APPETITE FOR DESTRUCTION	Guns N' Roses (Geffen)
31	24	LIKE A PRAYER	Madonna (Sire)
27	25	WHEN THE WORLD KNOWS YOUR NAME	Deacon Blue (CBS)
-	26	ADEVA	Adeva (Cooltempo)
15	27	JUMP - THE BEST OF	Pointer Sisters (RCA)
24	28	STREET FIGHTING YEARS	Simple Minds (Virgin)
28	29	PARADISE	Inner City (10)
44	30	KARYN WHITE	Karyn White (Warner Bros)
35	31	FULL MOON FEVER	Tom Petty (MCA)
22	32	NOW DANCE '89	Various Artists (EMI/Virgin)
32	33	WATERMARK	Enya (WEA)
37	34	KYLIE	Kylie Minogue (PWL)
30	35	THE END OF THE INNOCENCE	Don Henley (Geffen)
25	36	A NIGHT TO REMEMBER	Cyndi Lauper (Epic)
46	37	ESPECIALLY FOR YOU	Joe Longthorne (Telstar)
38	38	ELECTRIC YOUTH	Debbie Gibson (Atlantic)
33	39	THE BIG AREA	Then Jerico (London)
-	40	REPEAT OFFENDER	Richard Marx (EMI USA)
-	41	DIRTY DANCING - SOUNDTRACK	Various Artists (RCA)
39	42	PASTPRESENT	Clannad (RCA)
29	43	DEEP HEAT 3 - THE THIRD DEGREE	Various Artists (Telstar)
34	44	FRENCH KISS: THE COMPLETE MIX COLLECTION (EP)	L'il Louis (ffrr)
-	45	HYSTERIA	Def Leppard (Bludgeon Riffola)
36	46	FLOWERS IN THE DIRT	Paul McCartney (Parlophone)
41	47	SOUTHSIDE	Texas (Mercury)
43	48	KICK	INXS (Mercury)
-	49	GREATEST EVER ROCK'N'ROLL MIX	Various Artists (Stylus)
-	50	ANYWAYAWANNA	Beatmasters (Rhythm King)

16 September 1989

last	this		
1	1	NOW THAT'S WHAT I CALL MUSIC 15	Various Artists (EMI/Virgin/PolyGram)
2	2	CUTS BOTH WAYS	Gloria Estefan (Epic)
3	3	TEN GOOD REASONS	Jason Donovan (PWL)
21	4	THE RAW AND THE COOKED	Fine Young Cannibals (London)
7	5	A NEW FLAME	Simply Red (Elektra)
4	6	TRASH	Alice Cooper (Epic)
8	7	BATMAN	Prince (Warner Bros.)
-	8	ASPECTS OF LOVE	Various Artists (Really Useful)
26	9	ADEVA	Adeva (Cooltempo)
12	10	ALL THE HITS	Imagination (Stylus)
22	11	SINGALONGAWARYEARS	Max Bygraves (Parkfield Music)
6	12	RAW LIKE SUSHI	Neneh Cherry (Circa)
-	13	DR. FEELGOOD	Motley Crue (Elektra)
9	14	CHOICES - THE SINGLES CONNECTION	Blow Monkeys (RCA)
24	15	LIKE A PRAYER	Madonna (Sire)
11	16	DON'T BE CRUEL	Bobby Brown (MCA)
5	17	HEART AND SOUL - 18 CLASSIC SOUL CUTS	Various Artists (Polydor)
25	18	WHEN THE WORLD KNOWS YOUR NAME	Deacon Blue (CBS)
14	19	CLUB CLASSICS VOL.1	Soul II Soul (10)
40	20	REPEAT OFFENDER	Richard Marx (EMI USA)
15	21	THE MIRACLE	Queen (Parlophone)
17	22	THE 12 COMMANDMENTS OF DANCE	London Boys (WEA)
23	23	APPETITE FOR DESTRUCTION	Guns N' Roses (Geffen)
13	24	VELVETEEN	Transvision Vamp (MCA)
20	25	ANYTHING FOR YOU	Gloria Estefan & the Miami Sound Machine (Epic)
16	26	THEMES	Vangelis (Polydor)
29	27	PARADISE	Inner City (10)
31	28	FULL MOON FEVER	Tom Petty (MCA)
47	29	SOUTHSIDE	Texas (Mercury)
10	30	SACRED HEART	Shakespear's Sister (London)
28	31	STREET FIGHTING YEARS	Simple Minds (Virgin)
18	32	BIG BANG	Fuzzbox (WEA)
41	33	DIRTY DANCING - SOUNDTRACK	Various Artists (RCA)
30	34	KARYN WHITE	Karyn White (Warner Bros)
19	35	ROCK ISLAND	Jethro Tull (Chrysalis)
35	36	THE END OF THE INNOCENCE	Don Henley (Geffen)
-	37	A SHADE OF RED	Redhead Kingpin & the FBI (10)
33	38	WATERMARK	Enya (WEA)
-	39	MEGATOP PHOENIX	Big Audio Dynamite (CBS)
34	40	KYLIE	Kylie Minogue (PWL)
-	41	RAW	Alyson Williams (Def Jam)
38	42	ELECTRIC YOUTH	Debbie Gibson (Atlantic)
-	43	WE'LL MEET AGAIN	Vera Lynn (Telstar)
27	44	JUMP - THE BEST OF THE POINTER SISTERS	Pointer Sisters (RCA)
-	45	MARTIKA	Martika (CBS)
37	46	ESPECIALLY FOR YOU	Joe Longthorne (Telstar)
45	47	HYSTERIA	Def Leppard (Bludgeon Riffola)
50	48	ANYWAYAWANNA	Beatmasters (Rhythm King)
32	49	NOW DANCE '89	Various Artists (EMI/Virgin)
36	50	A NIGHT TO REMEMBER	Cyndi Lauper (Epic)

Trash was Alice Coper's first UK Top 10 album since *Billion Dollar Babies*, over 16 years previously; its success was spurred by Cooper's Top 5 single *Poison* - also his first big hit single since 1973. Meanwhile, hits compilations abounded in the chart much as they had prior to the previous Christmas, with Imagination, the Blow Monkeys, the Pointer Sisters and even Vangelis all finding major hit anthology success.

last week	this week	23 September 1989	
8	1	ASPECTS OF LOVE	Various Artists (Really Useful)
1	2	NOW THAT'S WHAT I CALL MUSIC 15	Various Artists (EMI/Virgin/PolyGram)
-	3	WE TOO ARE ONE	Eurythmics (RCA)
2	4	CUTS BOTH WAYS	Gloria Estefan (Epic)
3	5	TEN GOOD REASONS	Jason Donovan (PWL)
-	6	PUMP	Aerosmith (Geffen)
13	7	DR. FEELGOOD	Motley Crue (Elektra)
5	8	A NEW FLAME	Simply Red (Elektra)
4	9	THE RAW AND THE COOKED	Fine Young Cannibals (London)
20	10	REPEAT OFFENDER	Richard Marx (EMI USA)
7	11	BATMAN	Prince (Warner Bros.)
-	12	STEEL WHEELS	Rolling Stones (CBS)
15	13	LIKE A PRAYER	Madonna (Sire)
6	14	TRASH	Alice Cooper (Epic)
10	15	ALL THE HITS	Imagination (Stylus)
12	16	RAW LIKE SUSHI	Neneh Cherry (Circa)
12	17	SINGALONGAWARYEARS	Max Bygraves (Parkfield Music)
16	18	DON'T BE CRUEL	Bobby Brown (MCA)
-	19	SLEEPING WITH THE PAST	Elton John (Rocket)
26	20	THEMES	Vangelis (Polydor)
41	21	RAW	Alyson Williams (Def Jam)
23	22	APPETITE FOR DESTRUCTION	Guns N' Roses (Geffen)
18	23	WHEN THE WORLD KNOWS YOUR NAME	Deacon Blue (CBS)
9	24	ADEVA	Adeva (Cooltempo)
17	25	HEART AND SOUL - 18 CLASSIC SOUL CUTS	Various Artists (Polydor)
14	26	CHOICES - THE SINGLES CONNECTION	Blow Monkeys (RCA)
45	27	MARTIKA	Martika (CBS)
34	28	KARYN WHITE	Karyn White (Warner Bros)
25	29	ANYTHING FOR YOU	Gloria Estefan & the Miami Sound Machine (Epic)
19	30	CLUB CLASSICS VOL.1	Soul II Soul (10)
24	31	VELVETEEN	Transvision Vamp (MCA)
21	32	THE MIRACLE	Queen (Parlophone)
27	33	PARADISE	Inner City (10)
39	34	MEGATOP PHOENIX	Big Audio Dynamite (CBS)
22	35	THE 12 COMMANDMENTS OF DANCE	London Boys (WEA)
31	36	STREET FIGHTING YEARS	Simple Minds (Virgin)
29	37	SOUTHSIDE	Texas (Mercury)
36	38	THE END OF THE INNOCENCE	Don Henley (Geffen)
40	39	KYLIE	Kylie Minogue (PWL)
28	40	FULL MOON FEVER	Tom Petty (MCA)
-	41	THE ULTIMATE COLLECTION	Kinks (Castle Communications)
30	42	SACRED HEART	Shakespear's Sister (London)
-	43	WAKE ME UP WHEN IT'S OVER	Faster Pussycat (Elektra)
33	44	DIRTY DANCING - SOUNDTRACK	Various Artists (RCA)
32	45	BIG BANG	Fuzzbox (WEA)
35	46	ROCK ISLAND	Jethro Tull (Chrysalis)
42	47	ELECTRIC YOUTH	Debbie Gibson (Atlantic)
-	48	DISINTEGRATION	Cure (Fiction)
37	49	A SHADE OF RED	Redhead Kingpin & the FBI (10)
-	50	STORMS	Nanci Griffith (MCA)

last week	this week	30 September 1989	
3	1	WE TOO ARE ONE	Eurythmics (RCA)
-	2	FOREIGN AFFAIR	Tina Turner (Capitol)
12	3	STEEL WHEELS	Rolling Stones (CBS)
6	4	PUMP	Aerosmith (Geffen)
2	5	NOW THAT'S WHAT I CALL MUSIC 15	Various Artists (EMI/Virgin/PolyGram)
4	6	CUTS BOTH WAYS	Gloria Estefan (Epic)
19	7	SLEEPING WITH THE PAST	Elton John (Rocket)
-	8	JANET JACKSON'S RHYTHM NATION 1814	Janet Jackson (A&M)
1	9	ASPECTS OF LOVE	Various Artists (Really Useful)
10	10	REPEAT OFFENDER	Richard Marx (EMI USA)
-	11	JUST SEVENTEEN - HEARTBEATS	Various Artists (Fanfare)
13	12	LIKE A PRAYER	Madonna (Sire)
5	13	TEN GOOD REASONS	Jason Donovan (PWL)
-	14	DEEP HEAT 4 - PLAY WITH FIRE	Various Artists (Telstar)
8	15	A NEW FLAME	Simply Red (Elektra)
9	16	THE RAW AND THE COOKED	Fine Young Cannibals (London)
11	17	BATMAN	Prince (Warner Bros.)
24	18	ADEVA	Adeva (Cooltempo)
23	19	WHEN THE WORLD KNOWS YOUR NAME	Deacon Blue (CBS)
16	20	RAW LIKE SUSHI	Neneh Cherry (Circa)
7	21	DR. FEELGOOD	Motley Crue (Elektra)
14	22	TRASH	Alice Cooper (Epic)
22	23	APPETITE FOR DESTRUCTION	Guns N' Roses (Geffen)
-	24	ERROL FLYNN	Dogs D'Amour (China)
15	25	ALL THE HITS	Imagination (Stylus)
18	26	DON'T BE CRUEL	Bobby Brown (MCA)
30	27	CLUB CLASSICS VOL.1	Soul II Soul (10)
25	28	HEART AND SOUL	Various Artists (Polydor)
-	29	LOVEHOUSE	Various Artists (K-Tel)
-	30	CHANGE	Alarm (IRS)
29	31	ANYTHING FOR YOU	Gloria Estefan & the Miami Sound Machine (Epic)
-	32	ANOTHER PLACE AND TIME	Donna Summer (Warner Bros.)
21	33	RAW	Alyson Williams (Def Jam)
50	34	STORMS	Nanci Griffith (MCA)
17	35	SINGALONGAWARYEARS	Max Bygraves (Parkfield Music)
26	36	CHOICES	Blow Monkeys (RCA)
35	37	THE 12 COMMANDMENTS OF DANCE	London Boys (WEA)
41	38	THE ULTIMATE COLLECTION	Kinks (Castle Communications)
31	39	VELVETEEN	Transvision Vamp (MCA)
32	40	THE MIRACLE	Queen (Parlophone)
-	41	HEART LIKE A SKY	Spandau Ballet (CBS)
33	42	PARADISE	Inner City (10)
-	43	STRAIGHT OUTTA COMPTON	NWA (Fourth & Broadway)
20	44	THEMES	Vangelis (Polydor)
-	45	LEGENDS AND HEROES	Various Artists (Stylus)
36	46	STREET FIGHTING YEARS	Simple Minds (Virgin)
47	47	IS THIS LOVE	Various Artists (EMI)
-	48	SATURDAY NIGHT SUNDAY MORNING	River Detectives (WEA)
-	49	COCKED AND LOADED	L.A. Guns (Vertigo)
-	50	HOME LOVIN' MAN	Roger Whittaker (Tembo)

last week	this week	7 October 1989	
-	1	THE SEEDS OF LOVE	Tears For Fears (Fontana)
2	2	FOREIGN AFFAIR	Tina Turner (Capitol)
14	3	DEEP HEAT 4 - PLAY WITH FIRE	Various Artists (Telstar)
1	4	WE TOO ARE ONE	Eurythmics (RCA)
6	5	CUTS BOTH WAYS	Gloria Estefan (Epic)
4	6	PUMP	Aerosmith (Geffen)
10	7	REPEAT OFFENDER	Richard Marx (EMI USA)
8	8	JANET JACKSON'S RHYTHM NATION 1814	Janet Jackson (A&M)
12	9	LIKE A PRAYER	Madonna (Sire)
13	10	TEN GOOD REASONS	Jason Donovan (PWL)
11	11	JUST SEVENTEEN - HEARTBEATS	Various Artists (Fanfare)
5	12	NOW THAT'S WHAT I CALL MUSIC 15	Various Artists (EMI/Virgin/PolyGram)
3	13	STEEL WHEELS	Rolling Stones (CBS)
32	14	ANOTHER PLACE AND TIME	Donna Summer (Warner Bros.)
-	15	SEASONS END	Marillion (EMI)
15	16	A NEW FLAME	Simply Red (Elektra)
29	17	LOVEHOUSE	Various Artists (K-Tel)
7	18	SLEEPING WITH THE PAST	Elton John (Rocket)
37	19	THE 12 COMMANDMENTS OF DANCE	London Boys (WEA)
18	20	ADEVA	Adeva (Cooltempo)
47	21	IS THIS LOVE	Various Artists (EMI)
9	22	ASPECTS OF LOVE	Various Artists (Really Useful)
20	23	RAW LIKE SUSHI	Neneh Cherry (Circa)
16	24	THE RAW AND THE COOKED	Fine Young Cannibals (London)
19	25	WHEN THE WORLD KNOWS YOUR NAME	Deacon Blue (CBS)
22	26	TRASH	Alice Cooper (Epic)
17	27	BATMAN	Prince (Warner Bros.)
27	28	CLUB CLASSICS VOL.1	Soul II Soul (10)
26	29	DON'T BE CRUEL	Bobby Brown (MCA)
28	30	HEART AND SOUL - 18 CLASSIC SOUL CUTS	Various Artists (Polydor)
30	31	CHANGE	Alarm (IRS)
-	32	KARYN WHITE	Karyn White (Warner Bros)
31	33	ANYTHING FOR YOU	Gloria Estefan & the Miami Sound Machine (Epic)
50	34	HOME LOVIN' MAN	Roger Whittaker (Tembo)
23	35	APPETITE FOR DESTRUCTION	Guns N' Roses (Geffen)
33	36	RAW	Alyson Williams (Def Jam)
25	37	ALL THE HITS	Imagination (Stylus)
-	38	CANDLELAND	Ian McCulloch (WEA)
41	39	HEART LIKE A SKY	Spandau Ballet (CBS)
21	40	DR. FEELGOOD	Motley Crue (Elektra)
36	41	CHOICES	Blow Monkeys (RCA)
24	42	ERROL FLYNN	Dogs D'Amour (China)
43	43	STRAIGHT OUTTA COMPTON	NWA (Fourth & Broadway)
39	44	VELVETEEN	Transvision Vamp (MCA)
40	45	THE MIRACLE	Queen (Parlophone)
-	46	IT'S A BIG DADDY THING	Big Daddy Kane (Cold Chillin')
42	47	PARADISE	Inner City (10)
-	48	HEART OF STONE	Cher (Geffen)
38	49	THE ULTIMATE COLLECTION	Kinks (Castle Communications)
-	50	FLYING COWBOYS	Rickie Lee Jones (Geffen)

Like *The Phantom Of The Opera* before it, another new hit Andrew Lloyd Webber West End musical, *Aspects Of Love*, managed to place its original cast album at the top of the chart. The show's most popular song was *Love Changes Everything*, which, sung by Michael Ball, had been a major hit single at the beginning of the year. *Aspects*' most unusual aspect was its odd chart moves from 8 to 1, and back to 9.

14 October 1989

last week	this week	Title	Artist (Label)
1	1	THE SEEDS OF LOVE	Tears For Fears (Fontana)
-	2	CROSSROADS	Tracy Chapman (Elektra)
3	3	DEEP HEAT 4 - PLAY WITH FIRE	Various Artists (Telstar)
2	4	FOREIGN AFFAIR	Tina Turner (Capitol)
5	5	CUTS BOTH WAYS	Gloria Estefan (Epic)
9	6	LIKE A PRAYER	Madonna (Sire)
21	7	IS THIS LOVE	Various Artists (EMI)
4	8	WE TOO ARE ONE	Eurythmics (RCA)
8	9	JANET JACKSON'S RHYTHM NATION 1814	Janet Jackson (A&M)
10	10	TEN GOOD REASONS	Jason Donovan (PWL)
6	11	PUMP	Aerosmith (Geffen)
-	12	OH MERCY	Bob Dylan (CBS)
7	13	REPEAT OFFENDER	Richard Marx (EMI USA)
13	14	STEEL WHEELS	Rolling Stones (CBS)
25	15	WHEN THE WORLD KNOWS YOUR NAME	Deacon Blue (CBS)
-	16	HUP	Wonder Stuff (Polydor)
33	17	ANYTHING FOR YOU	Gloria Estefan & the Miami Sound Machine (Epic)
16	18	A NEW FLAME	Simply Red (Elektra)
19	19	THE 12 COMMANDMENTS OF DANCE	London Boys (WEA)
20	20	ADEVA	Adeva (Cooltempo)
12	21	NOW THAT'S WHAT I CALL MUSIC 15	Various Artists (EMI/Virgin/PolyGram)
38	22	CANDLELAND	Ian McCulloch (WEA)
23	23	RAW LIKE SUSHI	Neneh Cherry (Circa)
-	24	SEARCHLIGHT	Runrig (Chrysalis)
15	25	SEASONS END	Marillion (EMI)
22	26	ASPECTS OF LOVE	Various Artists (Really Useful)
14	27	ANOTHER PLACE AND TIME	Donna Summer (Warner Bros.)
17	28	LOVEHOUSE	Various Artists (K-Tel)
24	29	THE RAW AND THE COOKED	Fine Young Cannibals (London)
48	30	HEART OF STONE	Cher (Geffen)
11	31	JUST SEVENTEEN - HEARTBEATS	Various Artists (Fanfare)
18	32	SLEEPING WITH THE PAST	Elton John (Rocket)
28	33	CLUB CLASSICS VOL.1	Soul II Soul (10)
32	34	KARYN WHITE	Karyn White (Warner Bros)
44	35	VELVETEEN	Transvision Vamp (MCA)
30	36	HEART AND SOUL - 18 CLASSIC SOUL CUTS	Various Artists (Polydor)
29	37	DON'T BE CRUEL	Bobby Brown (MCA)
26	38	TRASH	Alice Cooper (Epic)
27	39	BATMAN	Prince (Warner Bros.)
-	40	JARRE LIVE	Jean-Michel Jarre (Polydor)
-	41	SACRED HEART	Shakespear's Sister (London)
-	42	TOUGH IT OUT	FM (Epic)
35	43	APPETITE FOR DESTRUCTION	Guns N' Roses (Geffen)
-	44	ETERNAL LOVE	Various Artists (K-tel)
36	45	RAW	Alyson Williams (Def Jam)
-	46	STREET FIGHTING YEARS	Simple Minds (Virgin)
-	47	VIVALDI: THE FOUR SEASONS	Nigel Kennedy with the English Chamber Orchestra (EMI)
34	48	HOME LOVIN' MAN	Roger Whittaker (Tembo)
-	49	HERE TODAY, TOMORROW, NEXT WEEK	Sugarcubes (One Little Indian)
-	50	LIQUIDIZER	Jesus Jones (Food)

21 October 1989

last week	this week	Title	Artist (Label)
-	1	ENJOY YOURSELF	Kylie Minogue (PWL)
2	2	CROSSROADS	Tracy Chapman (Elektra)
3	3	DEEP HEAT 4 - PLAY WITH FIRE	Various Artists (Telstar)
4	4	FOREIGN AFFAIR	Tina Turner (Capitol)
1	5	THE SEEDS OF LOVE	Tears For Fears (Fontana)
12	6	OH MERCY	Bob Dylan (CBS)
5	7	CUTS BOTH WAYS	Gloria Estefan (Epic)
6	8	LIKE A PRAYER	Madonna (Sire)
7	9	IS THIS LOVE	Various Artists (EMI)
-	10	AUTOMATIC	Jesus & Mary Chain (blanco y negro)
10	11	TEN GOOD REASONS	Jason Donovan (PWL)
8	12	WE TOO ARE ONE	Eurythmics (RCA)
-	13	RESULTS	Liza Minnelli (Epic)
19	14	THE 12 COMMANDMENTS OF DANCE	London Boys (WEA)
16	15	HUP	Wonder Stuff (Polydor)
9	16	JANET JACKSON'S RHYTHM NATION 1814	Janet Jackson (A&M)
49	17	HERE TODAY, TOMORROW, NEXT WEEK	Sugarcubes (One Little Indian)
40	18	JARRE LIVE	Jean-Michel Jarre (Polydor)
18	19	A NEW FLAME	Simply Red (Elektra)
15	20	WHEN THE WORLD KNOWS YOUR NAME	Deacon Blue (CBS)
11	21	PUMP	Aerosmith (Geffen)
29	22	THE RAW AND THE COOKED	Fine Young Cannibals (London)
17	23	ANYTHING FOR YOU	Gloria Estefan & the Miami Sound Machine (Epic)
13	24	REPEAT OFFENDER	Richard Marx (EMI USA)
-	25	ITALIA - DANCE MUSIC FROM ITALY	Various Artists (deConstruction)
14	26	STEEL WHEELS	Rolling Stones (CBS)
20	27	ADEVA	Adeva (Cooltempo)
30	28	HEART OF STONE	Cher (Geffen)
23	29	RAW LIKE SUSHI	Neneh Cherry (Circa)
34	30	KARYN WHITE	Karyn White (Warner Bros)
-	31	RETRO	Lou Reed (RCA)
35	32	VELVETEEN	Transvision Vamp (MCA)
27	33	ANOTHER PLACE AND TIME	Donna Summer (Warner Bros.)
33	34	CLUB CLASSICS VOL.1	Soul II Soul (10)
21	35	NOW THAT'S WHAT I CALL MUSIC 15	Various Artists (EMI/Virgin/PolyGram)
-	36	HATS	Blue Nile (Linn)
50	37	LIQUIDIZER	Jesus Jones (Food)
26	38	ASPECTS OF LOVE	Various Artists (Really Useful)
32	39	SLEEPING WITH THE PAST	Elton John (Rocket)
37	40	DON'T BE CRUEL	Bobby Brown (MCA)
-	41	COMING IN FOR THE KILL	Climie Fisher (EMI)
44	42	ETERNAL LOVE	Various Artists (K-tel)
38	43	TRASH	Alice Cooper (Epic)
25	44	SEASONS END	Marillion (EMI)
39	45	BATMAN	Prince (Warner Bros.)
24	46	SEARCHLIGHT	Runrig (Chrysalis)
-	47	FREEDOM	Neil Young (Reprise)
-	48	PORCELAIN	Julia Fordham (Circa)
43	49	APPETITE FOR DESTRUCTION	Guns N' Roses (Geffen)
42	50	TOUGH IT OUT	FM (Epic)

28 October 1989

last week	this week	Title	Artist (Label)
-	1	WILD!	Erasure (Mute)
-	2	THE SENSUAL WORLD	Kate Bush (EMI)
1	3	ENJOY YOURSELF	Kylie Minogue (PWL)
2	4	CROSSROADS	Tracy Chapman (Elektra)
-	5	THE TIME	Bros (CBS)
3	6	DEEP HEAT 4 - PLAY WITH FIRE	Various Artists (Telstar)
5	7	THE SEEDS OF LOVE	Tears For Fears (Fontana)
4	8	FOREIGN AFFAIR	Tina Turner (Capitol)
7	9	CUTS BOTH WAYS	Gloria Estefan (Epic)
-	10	SCARLET AND OTHER STORIES	All About Eve (Mercury)
14	11	THE 12 COMMANDMENTS OF DANCE	London Boys (WEA)
36	12	HATS	Blue Nile (Linn)
8	13	LIKE A PRAYER	Madonna (Sire)
11	14	TEN GOOD REASONS	Jason Donovan (PWL)
6	15	OH MERCY	Bob Dylan (CBS)
47	16	FREEDOM	Neil Young (Reprise)
9	17	IS THIS LOVE	Various Artists (EMI)
12	18	WE TOO ARE ONE	Eurythmics (RCA)
-	19	PURE	Primitives (RCA)
10	20	AUTOMATIC	Jesus & Mary Chain (blanco y negro)
13	21	RESULTS	Liza Minnelli (Epic)
48	22	PORCELAIN	Julia Fordham (Circa)
-	23	DEF, DUMB AND BLONDE	Deborah Harry (Chrysalis)
28	24	HEART OF STONE	Cher (Geffen)
-	25	THE RIGHT STUFF REMIX '89	Various Artists (Stylus)
19	26	A NEW FLAME	Simply Red (Elektra)
31	27	RETRO	Lou Reed (RCA)
20	28	WHEN THE WORLD KNOWS YOUR NAME	Deacon Blue (CBS)
-	29	2X2	Milli Vanilli (Cooltempo)
-	30	MOTOWN HEARTBREAKERS	Various Artists (Telstar)
49	31	APPETITE FOR DESTRUCTION	Guns N' Roses (Geffen)
23	32	ANYTHING FOR YOU	Gloria Estefan & the Miami Sound Machine (Epic)
16	33	JANET JACKSON'S RHYTHM NATION 1814	Janet Jackson (A&M)
27	34	ADEVA	Adeva (Cooltempo)
21	35	PUMP	Aerosmith (Geffen)
15	36	HUP	Wonder Stuff (Polydor)
22	37	THE RAW AND THE COOKED	Fine Young Cannibals (London)
18	38	JARRE LIVE	Jean-Michel Jarre (Polydor)
26	39	STEEL WHEELS	Rolling Stones (CBS)
34	40	CLUB CLASSICS VOL.1	Soul II Soul (10)
-	41	FEELING FREE	Sydney Youngblood (Circa)
-	42	SMASH HITS PARTY '89	Various Artists (Dover)
33	43	ANOTHER PLACE AND TIME	Donna Summer (Warner Bros.)
17	44	HERE TODAY, TOMORROW, NEXT WEEK	Sugarcubes (One Little Indian)
-	45	3 FEET HIGH AND RISING	De La Soul (Big Life)
40	46	DON'T BE CRUEL	Bobby Brown (MCA)
38	47	ASPECTS OF LOVE	Various Artists (Really Useful)
-	48	GREATEST HITS	Five Star (Tent)
24	49	REPEAT OFFENDER	Richard Marx (EMI USA)
29	50	RAW LIKE SUSHI	Neneh Cherry (Circa)

Another strong chart period for female singers, who occupied all three top places and two more slots in the Top 10 at the end of October. Tracy Chapman's second album just failed to emulate its chart-topping predecessor, but Kylie Minogue's *Enjoy Yourself* equalled her debut's Number 1 status, without having the same chart longevity, while *The Sensual World* just failed to extend Kate Bush's Number 1 tally.

November 1989

last this
week

4 November 1989

last	this		
1	1	WILD!	Erasure (Mute)
3	2	ENJOY YOURSELF	Kylie Minogue (PWL)
2	3	THE SENSUAL WORLD	Kate Bush (EMI)
-	4	WELCOME TO THE BEAUTIFUL SOUTH	Beautiful South (Go! Discs)
-	5	RUNAWAY HORSES	Belinda Carlisle (Virgin)
-	6	NEITHER FISH NOR FLESH	Terence Trent D'Arby (CBS)
29	7	2X2	Milli Vanilli (Cooltempo)
9	8	CUTS BOTH WAYS	Gloria Estefan (Epic)
4	9	CROSSROADS	Tracy Chapman (Elektra)
8	10	FOREIGN AFFAIR	Tina Turner (Capitol)
25	11	THE RIGHT STUFF REMIX '89	Various Artists (Stylus)
34	12	ADEVA	Adeva (Cooltempo)
5	13	THE TIME	Bros (CBS)
-	14	BIZARRO	Wedding Present (RCA)
7	15	THE SEEDS OF LOVE	Tears For Fears (Fontana)
-	16	SPARK TO A FLAME - THE VERY BEST OF CHRIS DE BURGH	Chris De Burgh (A&M)
11	17	THE 12 COMMANDMENTS OF DANCE	London Boys (WEA)
-	18	GREATEST HITS	Billy Ocean (Jive)
-	19	STORM FRONT	Billy Joel (CBS)
26	20	A NEW FLAME	Simply Red (Elektra)
6	21	DEEP HEAT 4 - PLAY WITH FIRE	Various Artists (Telstar)
10	22	SCARLET AND OTHER STORIES	All About Eve (Mercury)
-	23	THE SINGLES ALBUM	Gladys Knight & the Pips (PolyGram TV)
24	24	HEART OF STONE	Cher (Geffen)
42	25	SMASH HITS PARTY '89	Various Artists (Dover)
-	26	HOT IN THE SHADE	Kiss (Fontana)
45	27	3 FEET HIGH AND RISING	De La Soul (Big Life)
14	28	TEN GOOD REASONS	Jason Donovan (PWL)
13	29	LIKE A PRAYER	Madonna (Sire)
18	30	WE TOO ARE ONE	Eurythmics (RCA)
23	31	DEF, DUMB AND BLONDE	Deborah Harry (Chrysalis)
-	32	RAP ATTACK	Various Artists (K-tel)
17	33	IS THIS LOVE	Various Artists (EMI)
41	34	FEELING FREE	Sydney Youngblood (Circa)
21	35	RESULTS	Liza Minnelli (Epic)
32	36	ANYTHING FOR YOU	Gloria Estefan & the Miami Sound Machine (Epic)
12	37	HATS	Blue Nile (Linn)
31	38	APPETITE FOR DESTRUCTION	Guns N' Roses (Geffen)
15	39	OH MERCY	Bob Dylan (CBS)
-	40	GETAHEAD	Curiosity Killed The Cat (Mercury)
16	41	FREEDOM	Neil Young (Reprise)
-	42	VELVETEEN	Transvision Vamp (MCA)
20	43	AUTOMATIC	Jesus & Mary Chain (blanco y negro)
22	44	PORCELAIN	Julia Fordham (Circa)
37	45	THE RAW AND THE COOKED	Fine Young Cannibals (London)
-	46	THE GREATEST LOVE 3	Various Artists (Telstar)
19	47	PURE	Primitives (RCA)
33	48	JANET JACKSON'S RHYTHM NATION 1814	Janet Jackson (A&M)
-	49	THEIR GREATEST HITS	Foster & Allen (Stylus)
35	50	PUMP	Aerosmith (Geffen)

11 November 1989

last	this		
1	1	WILD!	Erasure (Mute)
-	2	THE ROAD TO HELL	Chris Rea (WEA)
-	3	HOLDING BACK THE RIVER	Wet Wet Wet (Precious Organisation)
4	4	WELCOME TO THE BEAUTIFUL SOUTH	Beautiful South (Go! Discs)
2	5	ENJOY YOURSELF	Kylie Minogue (PWL)
5	6	RUNAWAY HORSES	Belinda Carlisle (Virgin)
16	7	SPARK TO A FLAME - THE VERY BEST OF CHRIS DE BURGH	Chris De Burgh (A&M)
19	8	STORM FRONT	Billy Joel (CBS)
7	9	2X2	Milli Vanilli (Cooltempo)
-	10	STRONGER	Cliff Richard (EMI)
18	11	GREATEST HITS	Billy Ocean (Jive)
3	12	THE SENSUAL WORLD	Kate Bush (EMI)
25	13	SMASH HITS PARTY '89	Various Artists (Dover)
-	14	THE BEST OF LUTHER VANDROSS - THE BEST OF LOVE	Luther Vandross (Epic)
23	15	THE SINGLES ALBUM	Gladys Knight & the Pips (PolyGram TV)
8	16	CUTS BOTH WAYS	Gloria Estefan (Epic)
9	17	CROSSROADS	Tracy Chapman (Elektra)
11	18	THE RIGHT STUFF REMIX '89	Various (Stylus)
10	19	FOREIGN AFFAIR	Tina Turner (Capitol)
6	20	NEITHER FISH NOR FLESH	Terence Trent D'Arby (CBS)
20	21	A NEW FLAME	Simply Red (Elektra)
24	22	HEART OF STONE	Cher (Geffen)
30	23	WE TOO ARE ONE	Eurythmics (RCA)
12	24	ADEVA	Adeva (Cooltempo)
-	25	ROCK CITY NIGHTS	Various Artists (Vertigo)
28	26	TEN GOOD REASONS	Jason Donovan (PWL)
27	27	3 FEET HIGH AND RISING	De La Soul (Big Life)
13	28	THE TIME	Bros (CBS)
17	29	THE 12 COMMANDMENTS OF DANCE	London Boys (WEA)
40	30	GETAHEAD	Curiosity Killed The Cat (Mercury)
15	31	THE SEEDS OF LOVE	Tears For Fears (Fontana)
29	32	LIKE A PRAYER	Madonna (Sire)
21	33	DEEP HEAT 4 - PLAY WITH FIRE	Various Artists (Telstar)
14	34	BIZARRO	Wedding Present (RCA)
-	35	GATECRASHING	Living In A Box (Chrysalis)
31	36	DEF, DUMB AND BLONDE	Deborah Harry (Chrysalis)
-	37	MONSTER HITS	Various Artists (CBS/WEA/BMG)
42	38	VELVETEEN	Transvision Vamp (MCA)
-	39	WHEN THE WORLD KNOWS YOUR NAME	Deacon Blue (CBS)
34	40	FEELING FREE	Sydney Youngblood (Circa)
46	41	THE GREATEST LOVE 3	Various Artists (Telstar)
-	42	HUP	Wonder Stuff (Polydor)
45	43	THE RAW AND THE COOKED	Fine Young Cannibals (London)
26	44	HOT IN THE SHADE	Kiss (Fontana)
-	45	"ADDICTIONS" VOLUME ONE	Robert Palmer (Island)
22	46	SCARLET AND OTHER STORIES	All About Eve (Mercury)
36	47	ANYTHING FOR YOU	Gloria Estefan & the Miami Sound Machine (Epic)
-	48	A LITTLE BIT OF THIS A LITTLE BIT OF THAT	D Mob (ffrr)
-	49	THOUGHTS OF HOME	Daniel O'Donnell (Telstar)
38	50	APPETITE FOR DESTRUCTION	Guns N' Roses (Geffen)

18 November 1989

last	this		
2	1	THE ROAD TO HELL	Chris Rea (WEA)
3	2	HOLDING BACK THE RIVER	Wet Wet Wet (Precious Organisation)
-	3	JOURNEYMAN	Eric Clapton (Duck)
5	4	ENJOY YOURSELF	Kylie Minogue (PWL)
-	5	LEVEL BEST	Level 42 (Polydor)
11	6	GREATEST HITS	Billy Ocean (Jive)
1	7	WILD!	Erasure (Mute)
14	8	THE BEST OF LUTHER VANDROSS - THE BEST OF LOVE	Luther Vandross (Epic)
6	9	RUNAWAY HORSES	Belinda Carlisle (Virgin)
18	10	THE RIGHT STUFF REMIX '89	Various (Stylus)
10	11	STRONGER	Cliff Richard (EMI)
9	12	2X2	Milli Vanilli (Cooltempo)
13	13	SMASH HITS PARTY '89	Various Artists (Dover)
7	14	SPARK TO A FLAME - THE VERY BEST OF CHRIS DE BURGH	Chris De Burgh (A&M)
15	15	THE SINGLES ALBUM	Gladys Knight & the Pips (PolyGram TV)
4	16	WELCOME TO THE BEAUTIFUL SOUTH	Beautiful South (Go! Discs)
8	17	STORM FRONT	Billy Joel (CBS)
23	18	WE TOO ARE ONE	Eurythmics (RCA)
45	19	"ADDICTIONS" VOLUME ONE	Robert Palmer (Island)
16	20	CUTS BOTH WAYS	Gloria Estefan (Epic)
41	21	THE GREATEST LOVE 3	Various Artists (Telstar)
12	22	THE SENSUAL WORLD	Kate Bush (EMI)
25	23	ROCK CITY NIGHTS	Various Artists (Vertigo)
17	24	CROSSROADS	Tracy Chapman (Elektra)
-	25	MARTIKA	Martika (CBS)
21	26	A NEW FLAME	Simply Red (Elektra)
26	27	TEN GOOD REASONS	Jason Donovan (PWL)
-	28	JANET JACKSON'S RHYTHM NATION 1814	Janet Jackson (A&M)
22	29	HEART OF STONE	Cher (Geffen)
-	30	CRY LIKE A RAINSTORM - HOWL LIKE THE WIND	Linda Ronstadt (Elektra)
29	31	THE 12 COMMANDMENTS OF DANCE	London Boys (WEA)
19	32	FOREIGN AFFAIR	Tina Turner (Capitol)
31	33	THE SEEDS OF LOVE	Tears For Fears (Fontana)
20	34	NEITHER FISH NOR FLESH	Terence Trent D'Arby (CBS)
38	35	VELVETEEN	Transvision Vamp (MCA)
27	36	3 FEET HIGH AND RISING	De La Soul (Big Life)
35	37	GATECRASHING	Living In A Box (Chrysalis)
24	38	ADEVA	Adeva (Cooltempo)
-	39	THE CLASSIC EXPERIENCE	Various Artists (EMI)
28	40	THE TIME	Bros (CBS)
-	41	CAPTAIN SWING	Michelle Shocked (Cooking Vinyl)
36	42	DEF, DUMB AND BLONDE	Deborah Harry (Chrysalis)
37	43	MONSTER HITS	Various Artists (CBS/WEA/BMG)
-	44	DANCE DECADE - DANCE HITS OF THE 80'S	Various Artists (London)
32	45	LIKE A PRAYER	Madonna (Sire)
43	46	THE RAW AND THE COOKED	Fine Young Cannibals (London)
40	47	FEELING FREE	Sydney Youngblood (Circa)
-	48	THE 80'S - ALBUM OF THE DECADE	Various (EMI)
-	49	MOTOWN HEARTBREAKERS	Various Artists (Telstar)
-	50	QUADRASTATE	808 State (Creed)

Unlike their previous album *The Innocents*, Erasure's *Wild!* was an instant chart-topper, marking the duo's status, after several years of steadily growing popularity, as one of the major pop/rock attractions of the late 80s. The same sort of status, after something of a wilderness period, had now accrued to Chris Rea, whose *The Road To Hell* album and its namesake hit single were his all-time biggest sellers.

last this
week

25 November 1989

last	this	title	artist
1	1	THE ROAD TO HELL	Chris Rea (WEA)
5	2	LEVEL BEST	Level 42 (Polydor)
3	3	JOURNEYMAN	Eric Clapton (Duck)
6	4	GREATEST HITS	Billy Ocean (Jive)
4	5	ENJOY YOURSELF	Kylie Minogue (PWL)
14	6	SPARK TO A FLAME - THE VERY BEST OF CHRIS DE BURGH	Chris De Burgh (A&M)
-	7	SLIP OF THE TONGUE	Whitesnake (EMI)
9	8	RUNAWAY HORSES	Belinda Carlisle (Virgin)
11	9	STRONGER	Cliff Richard (EMI)
12	10	2X2	Milli Vanilli (Cooltempo)
-	11	DECADE	Duran Duran (EMI)
48	12	THE 80'S - ALBUM OF THE DECADE	Various (EMI)
2	13	HOLDING BACK THE RIVER	Wet Wet Wet (Precious Organisation)
7	14	WILD!	Erasure (Mute)
8	15	THE BEST OF LUTHER VANDROSS - THE BEST OF LOVE	Luther Vandross (Epic)
-	16	THE GREATEST HITS OF THE '80S	Various (Telstar)
19	17	"ADDICTIONS" VOLUME ONE	Robert Palm (Island)
13	18	SMASH HITS PARTY '89	Various Artists (Dover)
16	19	WELCOME TO THE BEAUTIFUL SOUTH	Beautiful South (Go! Discs)
15	20	THE SINGLES ALBUM	Gladys Knight & the Pips (PolyGram TV)
18	21	WE TOO ARE ONE	Eurythmics (RCA)
17	22	STORM FRONT	Billy Joel (CBS)
27	23	TEN GOOD REASONS	Jason Donovan (PWL)
33	24	THE SEEDS OF LOVE	Tears For Fears (Fontana)
-	25	THE BEST OF ROD STEWART	Rod Stewart (Warner Bros.)
30	26	CRY LIKE A RAINSTORM - HOWL LIKE THE WIND	Linda Ronstadt (Elektra)
-	27	THE GREATEST HITS OF '89	Various (Telstar)
26	28	A NEW FLAME	Simply Red (Elektra)
20	29	CUTS BOTH WAYS	Gloria Estefan (Epic)
22	30	THE SENSUAL WORLD	Kate Bush (EMI)
10	31	THE RIGHT STUFF REMIX '89	Various (Stylus)
46	32	THE RAW AND THE COOKED	Fine Young Cannibals (London)
21	33	THE GREATEST LOVE 3	Various Artists (Telstar)
24	34	CROSSROADS	Tracy Chapman (Elektra)
29	35	HEART OF STONE	Cher (Geffen)
32	36	FOREIGN AFFAIR	Tina Turner (Capitol)
31	37	THE 12 COMMANDMENTS OF DANCE	London Boys (WEA)
41	38	CAPTAIN SWING	Michelle Shocked (Cooking Vinyl)
-	39	A PORTRAIT OF DORIS DAY	Doris Day (Stylus)
-	40	COME TOGETHER AS ONE	Will Downing (Fourth & Broadway)
-	41	DEEP HEAT '89 - FIGHT THE FLAME	Various Artists (Telstar)
25	42	MARTIKA	Martika (CBS)
36	43	3 FEET HIGH AND RISING	De La Soul (Big Life)
50	44	QUADRASTATE	808 State (Creed)
28	45	JANET JACKSON'S RHYTHM NATION 1814	Janet Jackson (A&M)
-	46	THE WANTED REMIXES	Yazz (Big Life)
-	47	TRUST	Brother Beyond (Parlophone)
38	48	ADEVA	Adeva (Cooltempo)
-	49	THE BEST YEARS OF OUR LIVES	Neil Diamond (CBS)
42	50	DEF, DUMB AND BLONDE	Deborah Harry (Chrysalis)

2 December 1989

last	this	title	artist
1	1	... BUT SERIOUSLY	Phil Collins (Virgin)
1	2	THE ROAD TO HELL	Chris Rea (WEA)
-	3	AFFECTION	Lisa Stansfield (Arista)
-	4	NOW THAT'S WHAT I CALL MUSIC 16	Various Artists (EMI/Virgin/PolyGram)
5	5	ENJOY YOURSELF	Kylie Minogue (PWL)
25	6	THE BEST OF ROD STEWART	Rod Stewart (Warner Bros.)
11	7	DECADE	Duran Duran (EMI)
6	8	SPARK TO A FLAME - THE VERY BEST OF CHRIS DE BURGH	Chris De Burgh (A&M)
9	9	STRONGER	Cliff Richard (EMI)
2	10	LEVEL BEST	Level 42 (Polydor)
16	11	THE GREATEST HITS OF THE '80S	Various (Telstar)
12	12	THE 80'S - ALBUM OF THE DECADE	Various (EMI)
7	13	SLIP OF THE TONGUE	Whitesnake (EMI)
4	14	GREATEST HITS	Billy Ocean (Jive)
20	15	THE SINGLES ALBUM	Gladys Knight & the Pips (PolyGram TV)
23	16	TEN GOOD REASONS	Jason Donovan (PWL)
3	17	JOURNEYMAN	Eric Clapton (Duck)
10	18	2X2	Milli Vanilli (Cooltempo)
-	19	DANCE ... YA KNOW IT	Bobby Brown (MCA)
17	20	"ADDICTIONS" VOLUME ONE	Robert Palm (Island)
8	21	RUNAWAY HORSES	Belinda Carlisle (Virgin)
29	22	CUTS BOTH WAYS	Gloria Estefan (Epic)
-	23	THE HEART OF CHICAGO	Chicago (WEA)
-	24	MONSTER HITS	Various Artists (CBS/WEA/BMG)
24	25	THE SEEDS OF LOVE	Tears For Fears (Fontana)
14	26	WILD!	Erasure (Mute)
19	27	WELCOME TO THE BEAUTIFUL SOUTH	Beautiful South (Go! Discs)
21	28	WE TOO ARE ONE	Eurythmics (RCA)
13	29	HOLDING BACK THE RIVER	Wet Wet Wet (Precious Organisation)
22	30	STORM FRONT	Billy Joel (CBS)
15	31	THE BEST OF LUTHER VANDROSS - THE BEST OF LOVE	Luther Vandross (Epic)
32	32	THE RAW AND THE COOKED	Fine Young Cannibals (London)
41	33	DEEP HEAT '89 - FIGHT THE FLAME	Various (Telstar)
-	34	THEIR GREATEST HITS	Foster & Allen (Stylus)
-	35	AFTER THE LAUGHTER	Freddie Starr (Dover)
26	36	CRY LIKE A RAINSTORM - HOWL LIKE THE WIND	Linda Ronstadt (Elektra)
28	37	A NEW FLAME	Simply Red (Elektra)
-	38	GREATEST HITS LIVE	Diana Ross (EMI)
27	39	THE GREATEST HITS OF '89	Various Artists (Telstar)
30	40	THE SENSUAL WORLD	Kate Bush (EMI)
-	41	A COLLECTION - GREATEST HITS ... AND MORE	Barbra Streisand (CBS)
-	42	THE STONE ROSES	Stone Roses (Silvertone)
18	43	SMASH HITS PARTY '89	Various Artists (Dover)
31	44	THE RIGHT STUFF REMIX '89	Various Artists (Stylus)
34	45	CROSSROADS	Tracy Chapman (Elektra)
36	46	FOREIGN AFFAIR	Tina Turner (Capitol)
-	47	THE LOVE SONGS OF ANDREW LLOYD WEBBER	Richard Clayderman (Decca Delphine)
42	48	MARTIKA	Martika (CBS)
45	49	JANET JACKSON'S RHYTHM NATION 1814	Janet Jackson (A&M)
-	50	JUKE BOX JIVE MIX	Various Artists (Stylus)

9 December 1989

last	this	title	artist
1	1	... BUT SERIOUSLY	Phil Collins (Virgin)
4	2	NOW THAT'S WHAT I CALL MUSIC 16	Various Artists (EMI/Virgin/PolyGram)
24	3	MONSTER HITS	Various Artists (CBS/WEA/BMG)
3	4	AFFECTION	Lisa Stansfield (Arista)
5	5	ENJOY YOURSELF	Kylie Minogue (PWL)
6	6	THE BEST OF ROD STEWART	Rod Stewart (Warner Bros.)
-	7	LABOUR OF LOVE II	UB40 (DEP International)
16	8	TEN GOOD REASONS	Jason Donovan (PWL)
2	9	THE ROAD TO HELL	Chris Rea (WEA)
8	10	SPARK TO A FLAME - THE VERY BEST OF CHRIS DE BURGH	Chris De Burgh (A&M)
20	11	"ADDICTIONS" VOLUME ONE	Robert Palmer (Island)
-	12	HANGIN' TOUGH	New Kids On The Block (CBS)
9	13	STRONGER	Cliff Richard (EMI)
11	14	THE GREATEST HITS OF THE '80S	Various Artists (Telstar)
12	15	THE 80'S - ALBUM OF THE DECADE	Various Artists (EMI)
10	16	LEVEL BEST	Level 42 (Polydor)
47	17	THE LOVE SONGS OF ANDREW LLOYD WEBBER	Richard Clayderman (Decca Delphine)
25	18	THE SEEDS OF LOVE	Tears For Fears (Fontana)
-	19	READ MY LIPS	Jimmy Somerville (London)
14	20	GREATEST HITS	Billy Ocean (Jive)
7	21	DECADE	Duran Duran (EMI)
22	22	CUTS BOTH WAYS	Gloria Estefan (Epic)
-	23	JIVE BUNNY - THE ALBUM	Jive Bunny & the Mastermixers (Telstar)
18	24	2X2	Milli Vanilli (Cooltempo)
46	25	FOREIGN AFFAIR	Tina Turner (Capitol)
17	26	JOURNEYMAN	Eric Clapton (Duck)
35	27	AFTER THE LAUGHTER	Freddie Starr (Dover)
26	28	WILD!	Erasure (Mute)
23	29	THE HEART OF CHICAGO	Chicago (WEA)
19	30	DANCE ... YA KNOW IT	Bobby Brown (MCA)
15	31	THE SINGLES ALBUM	Gladys Knight & the Pips (PolyGram TV)
27	32	WELCOME TO THE BEAUTIFUL SOUTH	Beautiful South (Go! Discs)
33	33	DEEP HEAT '89 - FIGHT THE FLAME	Various Artists (Telstar)
21	34	RUNAWAY HORSES	Belinda Carlisle (Virgin)
28	35	WE TOO ARE ONE	Eurythmics (RCA)
13	36	SLIP OF THE TONGUE	Whitesnake (EMI)
30	37	STORM FRONT	Billy Joel (CBS)
42	38	THE STONE ROSES	Stone Roses (Silvertone)
40	39	THE SENSUAL WORLD	Kate Bush (EMI)
29	40	HOLDING BACK THE RIVER	Wet Wet Wet (Precious Organisation)
34	41	THEIR GREATEST HITS	Foster & Allen (Stylus)
-	42	PRESTO	Rush (Atlantic)
32	43	THE RAW AND THE COOKED	Fine Young Cannibals (London)
36	44	CRY LIKE A RAINSTORM - HOWL LIKE THE WIND	Linda Ronstadt (Elektra)
48	45	MARTIKA	Martika (CBS)
39	46	THE GREATEST HITS OF '89	Various (Telstar)
31	47	THE BEST OF LUTHER VANDROSS - THE BEST OF LOVE	Luther Vandross (Epic)
50	48	JUKE BOX JIVE MIX	Various Artists (Stylus)
37	49	A NEW FLAME	Simply Red (Elektra)
-	50	MOSAIQUE	Gipsy Kings (Telstar)

Phil Collins' ...*But Seriously* was to become his all-time best-seller and also the biggest-ever for Virgin Records, overtaking Mike Oldfield's *Tubular Bells*. Its initial sales were prodigious enough: it went double Platinum (600,000 copies sold) during just its first four weeks in the chart. For once, the customary year-end *Now That's What I Call Music* compilation was to be held from the top by a stronger album.

December 1989

last week	this week	16 December 1989	
1	1	... BUT SERIOUSLY	Phil Collins (Virgin)
2	2	NOW THAT'S WHAT I CALL MUSIC 16	
			Various Artists (EMI/Virgin/PolyGram)
23	3	JIVE BUNNY - THE ALBUM	
			Jive Bunny & the Mastermixers (Telstar)
5	4	ENJOY YOURSELF	Kylie Minogue (PWL)
3	5	MONSTER HITS	Various Artists (CBS/WEA/BMG)
4	6	AFFECTION	Lisa Stansfield (Arista)
12	7	HANGIN' TOUGH	New Kids On The Block (CBS)
9	8	THE ROAD TO HELL	Chris Rea (WEA)
25	9	FOREIGN AFFAIR	Tina Turner (Capitol)
10	10	SPARK TO A FLAME - THE VERY BEST OF	
		CHRIS DE BURGH	Chris De Burgh (A&M)
6	11	THE BEST OF ROD STEWART	
			Rod Stewart (Warner Bros.)
8	12	TEN GOOD REASONS	Jason Donovan (PWL)
7	13	LABOUR OF LOVE II	UB40 (DEP International)
11	14	"ADDICTIONS" VOLUME ONE	
			Robert Palmer (Island)
14	15	THE GREATEST HITS OF THE '80S	Various (Telstar)
13	16	STRONGER	Cliff Richard (EMI)
29	17	THE HEART OF CHICAGO	Chicago (WEA)
16	18	LEVEL BEST	Level 42 (Polydor)
33	19	DEEP HEAT '89 - FIGHT THE FLAME	
			Various Artists (Telstar)
-	20	IT'S CHRISTMAS	Various Artists (EMI)
18	21	THE SEEDS OF LOVE	Tears For Fears (Fontana)
22	22	CUTS BOTH WAYS	Gloria Estefan (Epic)
15	23	THE 80'S - ALBUM OF THE DECADE	
			Various Artists (EMI)
21	24	DECADE	Duran Duran (EMI)
17	25	THE LOVE SONGS OF ANDREW LLOYD	
		WEBBER	Richard Clayderman (Decca Delphine)
50	26	MOSAIQUE	Gipsy Kings (Telstar)
26	27	JOURNEYMAN	Eric Clapton (Duck)
27	28	AFTER THE LAUGHTER	Freddie Starr (Dover)
43	29	THE RAW AND THE COOKED	
			Fine Young Cannibals (London)
20	30	GREATEST HITS	Billy Ocean (Jive)
-	31	ASPECTS OF LOVE	Various Artists (Polydor)
28	32	WILD!	Erasure (Mute)
24	33	2X2	Milli Vanilli (Cooltempo)
34	34	RUNAWAY HORSES	Belinda Carlisle (Virgin)
19	35	READ MY LIPS	Jimmy Somerville (London)
39	36	THE SENSUAL WORLD	Kate Bush (EMI)
49	37	A NEW FLAME	Simply Red (Elektra)
32	38	WELCOME TO THE BEAUTIFUL SOUTH	
			Beautiful South (Go! Discs)
-	39	A PORTRAIT OF DORIS DAY	Doris Day (Stylus)
-	40	NINETY	808 State (ZTT)
35	41	WE TOO ARE ONE	Eurythmics (RCA)
40	42	HOLDING BACK THE RIVER	
			Wet Wet Wet (Precious Organisation)
-	43	WAR OF THE WORLDS	Jeff Wayne (CBS)
-	44	THE JOE LONGTHORNE CHRISTMAS ALBUM	
			Joe Longthorne (Telstar)
30	45	DANCE ... YA KNOW IT	Bobby Brown (MCA)
45	46	MARTIKA	Martika (CBS)
-	47	FOSTER AND ALLEN CHRISTMAS COLLECTION	
			Foster & Allen (Stylus)
31	48	THE SINGLES ALBUM	
			Gladys Knight & the Pips (PolyGram TV)
-	49	QUEEN AT THE BEEB	Queen (Band Of Joy)
37	50	STORM FRONT	Billy Joel (CBS)

last week	this week	23 December 1989	
1	1	... BUT SERIOUSLY	Phil Collins (Virgin)
3	2	JIVE BUNNY - THE ALBUM	
			Jive Bunny & the Mastermixers (Telstar)
9	3	FOREIGN AFFAIR	Tina Turner (Capitol)
4	4	ENJOY YOURSELF	Kylie Minogue (PWL)
2	5	NOW THAT'S WHAT I CALL MUSIC 16	
			Various Artists (EMI/Virgin/PolyGram)
12	6	TEN GOOD REASONS	Jason Donovan (PWL)
20	7	IT'S CHRISTMAS	Various Artists (EMI)
8	8	THE ROAD TO HELL	Chris Rea (WEA)
6	9	AFFECTION	Lisa Stansfield (Arista)
5	10	MONSTER HITS	Various Artists (CBS/WEA/BMG)
10	11	SPARK TO A FLAME - THE VERY BEST OF	
		CHRIS DE BURGH	Chris De Burgh (A&M)
29	12	THE RAW AND THE COOKED	
			Fine Young Cannibals (London)
11	13	THE BEST OF ROD STEWART	
			Rod Stewart (Warner Bros.)
13	14	LABOUR OF LOVE II	UB40 (DEP International)
7	15	HANGIN' TOUGH	New Kids On The Block (CBS)
18	16	LEVEL BEST	Level 42 (Polydor)
16	17	STRONGER	Cliff Richard (EMI)
15	18	THE GREATEST HITS OF THE '80S	Various(Telstar)
14	19	"ADDICTIONS" VOLUME ONE	
			Robert Palmer (Island)
32	20	WILD!	Erasure (Mute)
22	21	CUTS BOTH WAYS	Gloria Estefan (Epic)
42	22	HOLDING BACK THE RIVER	
			Wet Wet Wet (Precious Organisation)
21	23	THE SEEDS OF LOVE	Tears For Fears (Fontana)
24	24	DECADE	Duran Duran (EMI)
27	25	JOURNEYMAN	Eric Clapton (Duck)
25	26	THE LOVE SONGS OF ANDREW LLOYD	
		WEBBER	Richard Clayderman (Decca Delphine)
30	27	GREATEST HITS	Billy Ocean (Jive)
17	28	THE HEART OF CHICAGO	Chicago (WEA)
-	29	AT THEIR VERY BEST	Shadows (Polydor)
26	30	MOSAIQUE	Gipsy Kings (Telstar)
19	31	DEEP HEAT '89 - FIGHT THE FLAME	Various (Telstar)
37	32	A NEW FLAME	Simply Red (Elektra)
28	33	AFTER THE LAUGHTER	Freddie Starr (Dover)
-	34	THE 12 COMMANDMENTS OF DANCE	
			London Boys (WEA)
31	35	ASPECTS OF LOVE	Various Artists (Polydor)
33	36	2X2	Milli Vanilli (Cooltempo)
-	37	THE VERY BEST OF ELECTRIC LIGHT	
		ORCHESTRA	Electric Light Orchestra (CBS)
23	38	THE 80'S - ALBUM OF THE DECADE	Various (EMI)
34	39	RUNAWAY HORSES	Belinda Carlisle (Virgin)
36	40	THE SENSUAL WORLD	Kate Bush (EMI)
47	41	FOSTER AND ALLEN CHRISTMAS COLLECTION	
			Foster & Allen (Stylus)
41	42	WE TOO ARE ONE	Eurythmics (RCA)
-	43	CRY LIKE A RAINSTORM - HOWL LIKE THE	
		WIND	Linda Ronstadt (Elektra)
-	44	WITH LOVE	Michael Crawford (Telstar)
-	45	THE BEST OF LUTHER VANDROSS - THE BEST	
		OF LOVE	Luther Vandross (Epic)
-	46	PUMP UP THE JAM	Technotronic (Swanyard)
38	47	WELCOME TO THE BEAUTIFUL SOUTH	
			Beautiful South (Go! Discs)
50	48	STORM FRONT	Billy Joel (CBS)
-	49	CROSSROADS	Tracy Chapman (Elektra)
-	50	LIKE A PRAYER	Madonna (Sire)

Though Phil Collins ruled the Christmas roost, selling upwards of 20,000 copies a day, the year-end also belonged to Jason Donovan's *Ten Good Reasons*, which, as it went into a Yule sales spurt, topped sales of one-and-a-half million, and just pipped (on Christmas Eve, before the shops closed for the holiday) Simply Red's *A New Flame* as the biggest-selling album of 1989.

*Making it at the end of the
80s, and into the 90s:
Clockwise from top;
Guns N' Roses
Elton John
Nigel Kennedy
REM*

January 1990

13 January 1990

last week	this week	Album	Artist
1	1	... BUT SERIOUSLY	Phil Collins (Vertigo)
4	2	ENJOY YOURSELF	Kylie Minogue (PWL)
3	3	FOREIGN AFFAIR	Tina Turner (Capitol)
5	4	TEN GOOD REASONS	Jason Donovan (PWL)
2	5	JIVE BUNNY - THE ALBUM	Jive Bunny & the Mastermixers (Telstar)
27	6	HANGIN' TOUGH	New Kids On The Block (CBS)
14	7	THE BEST OF ROD STEWART	Rod Stewart (Warner Bros.)
9	8	THE ROAD TO HELL	Chris Rea (WEA)
6	9	NOW THAT'S WHAT I CALL MUSIC 16	Various Artists (EMI/Virgin/PolyGram)
11	10	AFFECTION	Lisa Stansfield (Arista)
41	11	CLUB CLASSICS VOL 1	Soul II Soul (10)
10	12	MONSTER HITS	Various Artists (CBS/WEA/BMG)
7	13	HOLDING BACK THE RIVER	Wet Wet Wet (Precious Organisation)
44	14	LIKE A PRAYER	Madonna (Sire)
12	15	CUTS BOTH WAYS	Gloria Estefan (Epic)
17	16	THE GREATEST HITS OF THE 80S	Various (Telstar)
16	17	LEVEL BEST	Level 42 (Polydor)
18	18	WILD!	Erasure (Mute)
-	19	3 FEET HIGH AND RISING	De La Soul (Big Life)
13	20	SPARK TO A FLAME - THE VERY BESTOF CHRIS DE BURGH	Chris De Burgh (A&M)
24	21	DECADE	Duran Duran (EMI)
20	22	THE RAW AND THE COOKED	Fine Young Cannibals (London)
29	23	A NEW FLAME	Simply Red (Elektra)
21	24	LABOUR OF LOVE II	UB40 (DEP International)
38	25	2X2	Milli Vanilli (Cooltempo)
15	26	STRONGER	Cliff Richard (EMI)
25	27	DEEP HEAT '89 - FIGHT THE FLAME	Various Artists (Telstar)
22	28	"ADDICTIONS" VOLUME 1	Robert Palmer (Island)
28	29	THE SENSUAL WORLD	Kate Bush (EMI)
40	30	STORM FRONT	Billy Joel (CBS)
26	31	THE SEEDS OF LOVE	Tears For Fears (Fontana)
30	32	JOURNEYMAN	Eric Clapton (Duck)
-	33	THE STONE ROSES	Stone Roses (Silvertone)
33	34	THE 12 COMMANDMENTS OF DANCE	London Boys (WEA)
50	35	RUNAWAY HORSES	Belinda Carlisle (Virgin)
-	36	WARE'S THE HOUSE	Various Artists (Stylus)
-	37	MARTIKA	Martika (CBS)
38	38	GREATEST HITS	Billy Ocean (Jive)
45	39	THE TIME	Bros (CBS)
-	40	THE LOVE SONGS	Dionne Warwick (Arista)
43	41	THE BEST OF LUTHER VANDROSS - THE BEST OF LOVE	Luther Vandross (Epic)
19	42	AT THEIR VERY BEST	Shadows (Polydor)
-	43	RAW LIKE SUSHI	Neneh Cherry (Circa)
-	44	WHEN THE WORLD KNOWS YOUR NAME	Deacon Blue (CBS)
31	45	THE LOVE SONGS OF ANDREW LLOYD-WEBBER	Richard Clayderman (Decca Delphine)
39	46	THE '80S: ALBUM OF THE DECADE	Various Artists (EMI)
47	47	WELCOME TO THE BEAUTIFUL SOUTH	Beautiful South (Go! Discs)
-	48	FEELING FREE	Sydney Youngblood (Circa)
32	49	MOSAIQUE	Gipsy Kings (Telstar)
23	50	VERY BEST OF ELO	Electric Light Orchestra (Telstar)

20 January 1990

last week	this week	Album	Artist
1	1	... BUT SERIOUSLY	Phil Collins (Vertigo)
2	2	ENJOY YOURSELF	Kylie Minogue (PWL)
6	3	HANGIN' TOUGH	New Kids On The Block (CBS)
3	4	FOREIGN AFFAIR	Tina Turner (Capitol)
8	5	TEN GOOD REASONS	Jason Donovan (PWL)
8	6	THE ROAD TO HELL	Chris Rea (WEA)
5	7	JIVE BUNNY - THE ALBUM	Jive Bunny & the Mastermixers (Telstar)
10	8	AFFECTION	Lisa Stansfield (Arista)
40	9	THE LOVE SONGS	Dionne Warwick (Arista)
7	10	THE BEST OF ROD STEWART	Rod Stewart (Warner Bros.)
13	11	HOLDING BACK THE RIVER	Wet Wet Wet (Precious Organisation)
14	12	LIKE A PRAYER	Madonna (Sire)
11	13	CLUB CLASSICS VOL 1	Soul II Soul (10)
9	14	NOW THAT'S WHAT I CALL MUSIC 16	Various Artists (EMI/Virgin/PolyGram)
22	15	THE RAW AND THE COOKED	Fine Young Cannibals (London)
36	16	WARE'S THE HOUSE	Various Artists (Stylus)
12	17	MONSTER HITS	Various Artists (CBS/WEA/BMG)
19	18	3 FEET HIGH AND RISING	De La Soul (Big Life)
23	19	A NEW FLAME	Simply Red (Elektra)
18	20	WILD!	Erasure (Mute)
21	21	DECADE	Duran Duran (EMI)
33	22	THE STONE ROSES	Stone Roses (Silvertone)
15	23	CUTS BOTH WAYS	Gloria Estefan (Epic)
20	24	SPARK TO A FLAME - THE VERY BESTOF CHRIS DE BURGH	Chris De Burgh (A&M)
37	25	MARTIKA	Martika (CBS)
17	26	LEVEL BEST	Level 42 (Polydor)
-	27	PURE SOFT METAL	Various Artists (Stylus)
27	28	DEEP HEAT '89 - FIGHT THE FLAME	Various Artists (Telstar)
-	29	THE SINGLES 1969-1973	Carpenters (A&M)
24	30	LABOUR OF LOVE II	UB40 (DEP International)
30	31	STORM FRONT	Billy Joel (CBS)
16	32	THE GREATEST HITS OF THE 80S	Various (Telstar)
47	33	WELCOME TO THE BEAUTIFUL SOUTH	Beautiful South (Go! Discs)
26	34	STRONGER	Cliff Richard (EMI)
28	35	"ADDICTIONS" VOLUME 1	Robert Palmer (Island)
31	36	THE SEEDS OF LOVE	Tears For Fears (Fontana)
25	37	2X2	Milli Vanilli (Cooltempo)
-	38	VIVALDI: THE FOUR SEASONS	Nigel Kennedy with the English Chamber Orchestra
34	39	THE 12 COMMANDMENTS OF DANCE	London Boys (WEA)
50	40	VERY BEST OF ELO	Electric Light Orchestra (Telstar)
29	41	THE SENSUAL WORLD	Kate Bush (EMI)
41	42	THE BEST OF LUTHER VANDROSS - THE BEST OF LOVE	Luther Vandross (Epic)
32	43	JOURNEYMAN	Eric Clapton (Duck)
-	44	THE SINGLES 1974-1978	Carpenters (A&M)
35	45	RUNAWAY HORSES	Belinda Carlisle (Virgin)
44	46	WHEN THE WORLD KNOWS YOUR NAME	Deacon Blue (CBS)
42	47	AT THEIR VERY BEST	Shadows (Polydor)
-	48	READ MY LIPS	Jimmy Somerville (London)
-	49	A COLLECTION - GREATEST HITS ... AND MORE	Barbra Streisand (CBS)
38	50	GREATEST HITS	Billy Ocean (Jive)

27 January 1990

last week	this week	Album	Artist
-	1	COLOUR	Christians (Island)
1	2	... BUT SERIOUSLY	Phil Collins (Vertigo)
3	3	HANGIN' TOUGH	New Kids On The Block (CBS)
2	4	ENJOY YOURSELF	Kylie Minogue (PWL)
4	5	FOREIGN AFFAIR	Tina Turner (Capitol)
6	6	THE ROAD TO HELL	Chris Rea (WEA)
8	7	AFFECTION	Lisa Stansfield (Arista)
27	8	PURE SOFT METAL	Various Artists (Stylus)
10	9	THE BEST OF ROD STEWART	Rod Stewart (Warner Bros.)
5	10	TEN GOOD REASONS	Jason Donovan (PWL)
9	11	THE LOVE SONGS	Dionne Warwick (Arista)
13	12	CLUB CLASSICS VOL 1	Soul II Soul (10)
7	13	JIVE BUNNY - THE ALBUM	Jive Bunny & the Mastermixers (Telstar)
22	14	THE STONE ROSES	Stone Roses (Silvertone)
11	15	HOLDING BACK THE RIVER	Wet Wet Wet (Precious Organisation)
43	16	JOURNEYMAN	Eric Clapton (Duck)
16	17	WARE'S THE HOUSE	Various Artists (Stylus)
12	18	LIKE A PRAYER	Madonna (Sire)
-	19	READING, WRITING AND ARITHMETIC	Sundays (Rough Trade)
25	20	MARTIKA	Martika (CBS)
23	21	CUTS BOTH WAYS	Gloria Estefan (Epic)
15	22	THE RAW AND THE COOKED	Fine Young Cannibals (London)
49	23	A COLLECTION - GREATEST HITS ... AND MORE	Barbra Streisand (CBS)
18	24	3 FEET HIGH AND RISING	De La Soul (Big Life)
19	25	A NEW FLAME	Simply Red (Elektra)
33	26	WELCOME TO THE BEAUTIFUL SOUTH	Beautiful South (Go! Discs)
30	27	LABOUR OF LOVE II	UB40 (DEP International)
17	28	MONSTER HITS	Various Artists (CBS/WEA/BMG)
24	29	SPARK TO A FLAME - THE VERY BESTOF CHRIS DE BURGH	Chris De Burgh (A&M)
20	30	WILD!	Erasure (Mute)
-	31	WE TOO ARE ONE	Eurythmics (RCA)
38	32	VIVALDI: THE FOUR SEASONS	Nigel Kennedy with the English Chamber Orchestra
14	33	NOW THAT'S WHAT I CALL MUSIC 16	Various Artists (EMI/Virgin/PolyGram)
21	34	DECADE	Duran Duran (EMI)
48	35	READ MY LIPS	Jimmy Somerville (London)
29	36	THE SINGLES 1969-1973	Carpenters (A&M)
46	37	WHEN THE WORLD KNOWS YOUR NAME	Deacon Blue (CBS)
-	38	RAW LIKE SUSHI	Neneh Cherry (Circa)
-	39	FLOWERS IN THE DIRT	Paul McCartney (Parlophone)
26	40	LEVEL BEST	Level 42 (Polydor)
28	41	DEEP HEAT '89 - FIGHT THE FLAME	Various Artists (Telstar)
-	42	PUMP UP THE JAM	Technotronic (Swanyard)
47	43	AT THEIR VERY BEST	Shadows (Polydor)
35	44	"ADDICTIONS" VOLUME 1	Robert Palmer (Island)
31	45	STORM FRONT	Billy Joel (CBS)
-	46	BACK ON THE BLOCK	Quincy Jones (Qwest)
-	47	HEART OF STONE	Cher (Geffen)
44	48	THE SINGLES 1974-1978	Carpenters (A&M)
36	49	THE SEEDS OF LOVE	Tears For Fears (Fontana)
34	50	STRONGER	Cliff Richard (EMI)

Apart from the two weeks when the Christians' *Colour* overtook it, Phil Collins' *...But Seriously* was to totally dominate album sales during the early months of 1990, clocking up another two months at Number 1 to add to its tally from the previous year. Its eventual UK sales total would reach about two-and-a-half million, making it one of the half-dozen best-selling albums of all time.

3 February 1990

last week	this week	Title	Artist
1	1	COLOUR	Christians (Island)
2	2	... BUT SERIOUSLY	Phil Collins (Vertigo)
8	3	PURE SOFT METAL	Various Artists (Stylus)
19	4	READING, WRITING AND ARITHMETIC	Sundays (Rough Trade)
3	5	HANGIN' TOUGH	New Kids On The Block (CBS)
16	6	JOURNEYMAN	Eric Clapton (Duck)
11	7	THE LOVE SONGS	Dionne Warwick (Arista)
4	8	ENJOY YOURSELF	Kylie Minogue (PWL)
5	9	FOREIGN AFFAIR	Tina Turner (Capitol)
7	10	AFFECTION	Lisa Stansfield (Arista)
-	11	DEEP HEAT 5 - FEED THE FEVER	Various(Telstar)
6	12	THE ROAD TO HELL	Chris Rea (WEA)
9	13	THE BEST OF ROD STEWART	Rod Stewart (Warner Bros.)
14	14	THE STONE ROSES	Stone Roses (Silvertone)
24	15	3 FEET HIGH AND RISING	De La Soul (Big Life)
12	16	CLUB CLASSICS VOL 1	Soul II Soul (10)
20	17	MARTIKA	Martika (CBS)
15	18	HOLDING BACK THE RIVER	Wet Wet Wet (Precious Organisation)
10	19	TEN GOOD REASONS	Jason Donovan (PWL)
17	20	WARE'S THE HOUSE	Various Artists (Stylus)
42	21	PUMP UP THE JAM	Technotronic (Swanyard)
22	22	THE RAW AND THE COOKED	Fine Young Cannibals (London)
13	23	JIVE BUNNY - THE ALBUM	Jive Bunny & the Mastermixers (Telstar)
47	24	HEART OF STONE	Cher (Geffen)
18	25	LIKE A PRAYER	Madonna (Sire)
32	26	VIVALDI: THE FOUR SEASONS	Nigel Kennedy with the English Chamber Orchestra
21	27	CUTS BOTH WAYS	Gloria Estefan (Epic)
-	28	DONE BY THE FORCES OF NATURE	Jungle Brothers (Eternal)
23	29	A COLLECTION - GREATEST HITS ... AND MORE	Barbra Streisand (CBS)
-	30	THE VERY BEST OF CAT STEVENS	Cat Stevens (Island)
31	31	WE TOO ARE ONE	Eurythmics (RCA)
26	32	WELCOME TO THE BEAUTIFUL SOUTH	Beautiful South (Go! Discs)
25	33	A NEW FLAME	Simply Red (Elektra)
27	34	LABOUR OF LOVE II	UB40 (DEP International)
35	35	READ MY LIPS	Jimmy Somerville (London)
36	36	THE SINGLES 1969-1973	Carpenters (A&M)
30	37	WILD!	Erasure (Mute)
46	38	BACK ON THE BLOCK	Quincy Jones (Qwest)
28	39	MONSTER HITS	Various Artists (CBS/WEA/BMG)
38	40	RAW LIKE SUSHI	Neneh Cherry (Circa)
29	41	SPARK TO A FLAME - THE VERY BESTOF CHRIS DE BURGH	Chris De Burgh (A&M)
-	42	A GILDED ETERNITY	Loop (Situation Two)
37	43	WHEN THE WORLD KNOWS YOUR NAME	Deacon Blue (CBS)
33	44	NOW THAT'S WHAT I CALL MUSIC 16	Various Artists (EMI/Virgin/PolyGram)
34	45	DECADE	Duran Duran (EMI)
-	46	GREATEST HITS	Billy Ocean (Jive)
49	47	THE SEEDS OF LOVE	Tears For Fears (Fontana)
40	48	LEVEL BEST	Level 42 (Polydor)
44	49	"ADDICTIONS" VOLUME 1	Robert Palmer (Island)
39	50	FLOWERS IN THE DIRT	Paul McCartney (Parlophone)

10 February 1990

last week	this week	Title	Artist
2	1	... BUT SERIOUSLY	Phil Collins (Vertigo)
-	2	THE SWEET KEEPER	Tanita Tikaram (East West)
11	3	DEEP HEAT 5 - FEED THE FEVER	Various (Telstar)
-	4	A BIT OF WHAT YOU FANCY	Quireboys (Parlophone)
1	5	COLOUR	Christians (Island)
30	6	THE VERY BEST OF CAT STEVENS	Cat Stevens (Island)
6	7	JOURNEYMAN	Eric Clapton (Duck)
10	8	AFFECTION	Lisa Stansfield (Arista)
12	9	THE ROAD TO HELL	Chris Rea (WEA)
5	10	HANGIN' TOUGH	New Kids On The Block (CBS)
-	11	VIGIL IN A WILDERNESS OF MIRRORS	Fish (EMI)
21	12	PUMP UP THE JAM	Technotronic (Swanyard)
3	13	PURE SOFT METAL	Various Artists (Stylus)
24	14	HEART OF STONE	Cher (Geffen)
8	15	ENJOY YOURSELF	Kylie Minogue (PWL)
9	16	FOREIGN AFFAIR	Tina Turner (Capitol)
7	17	THE LOVE SONGS	Dionne Warwick (Arista)
14	18	THE STONE ROSES	Stone Roses (Silvertone)
4	19	READING, WRITING AND ARITHMETIC	Sundays (Rough Trade)
13	20	THE BEST OF ...	Rod Stewart (Warner Bros.)
16	21	CLUB CLASSICS VOL 1	Soul II Soul (10)
19	22	TEN GOOD REASONS	Jason Donovan (PWL)
22	23	THE RAW AND THE COOKED	Fine Young Cannibals (London)
33	24	A NEW FLAME	Simply Red (Elektra)
20	25	WARE'S THE HOUSE	Various Artists (Stylus)
15	26	3 FEET HIGH AND RISING	De La Soul (Big Life)
35	27	READ MY LIPS	Jimmy Somerville (London)
17	28	MARTIKA	Martika (CBS)
31	29	WE TOO ARE ONE	Eurythmics (RCA)
26	30	VIVALDI: THE FOUR SEASONS	Nigel Kennedy with the English Chamber Orchestra
43	31	WHEN THE WORLD KNOWS YOUR NAME	Deacon Blue (CBS)
18	32	HOLDING BACK THE RIVER	Wet Wet Wet (Precious Organisation)
27	33	CUTS BOTH WAYS	Gloria Estefan (Epic)
-	34	PARADISE REMIXED	Inner City (10)
25	35	LIKE A PRAYER	Madonna (Sire)
28	36	DONE BY THE FORCES OF NATURE	Jungle Brothers (Eternal)
-	37	THE CREAM OF ERIC CLAPTON	Eric Clapton & Cream (Polydor)
23	38	JIVE BUNNY - THE ALBUM	Jive Bunny & the Mastermixers (Telstar)
38	39	BACK ON THE BLOCK	Quincy Jones (Qwest)
29	40	A COLLECTION - GREATEST HITS ... AND MORE	Barbra Streisand (CBS)
32	41	WELCOME TO THE BEAUTIFUL SOUTH	Beautiful South (Go! Discs)
-	42	SKID ROW	Skid Row (Atlntic)
-	43	THE LION AND THE COBRA	Sinead O'Connor (Ensign)
37	44	WILD!	Erasure (Mute)
34	45	LABOUR OF LOVE II	UB40 (DEP International)
-	46	BUMMED	Happy Mondays (Factory)
49	47	"ADDICTIONS" VOLUME 1	Robert Palmer (Island)
40	48	RAW LIKE SUSHI	Neneh Cherry (Circa)
42	49	A GILDED ETERNITY	Loop (Situation Two)
-	50	APPETITE FOR DESTRUCTION	Guns N' Roses (Geffen)

17 February 1990

last week	this week	Title	Artist
1	1	... BUT SERIOUSLY	Phil Collins (Vertigo)
-	2	CARVED IN SAND	Mission (Mercury)
3	3	DEEP HEAT 5 - FEED THE FEVER	Various(Telstar)
7	4	JOURNEYMAN	Eric Clapton (Duck)
4	5	A BIT OF WHAT YOU FANCY	Quireboys (Parlophone)
2	6	THE SWEET KEEPER	Tanita Tikaram (East West)
6	7	THE VERY BEST OF CAT STEVENS	Cat Stevens (Island)
5	8	COLOUR	Christians (Island)
12	9	PUMP UP THE JAM	Technotronic (Swanyard)
11	10	VIGIL IN A WILDERNESS OF MIRRORS	Fish (EMI)
8	11	AFFECTION	Lisa Stansfield (Arista)
-	12	THE LANGUAGE OF LIFE	Everything But The Girl (blanco y negro)
20	13	THE BEST OF ROD STEWART	Rod Stewart (Warner Bros.)
9	14	THE ROAD TO HELL	Chris Rea (WEA)
13	15	PURE SOFT METAL	Various Artists (Stylus)
10	16	HANGIN' TOUGH	New Kids On The Block (CBS)
14	17	HEART OF STONE	Cher (Geffen)
18	18	THE STONE ROSES	Stone Roses (Silvertone)
16	19	FOREIGN AFFAIR	Tina Turner (Capitol)
34	20	PARADISE REMIXED	Inner City (10)
15	21	ENJOY YOURSELF	Kylie Minogue (PWL)
19	22	READING, WRITING AND ARITHMETIC	Sundays (Rough Trade)
28	23	MARTIKA	Martika (CBS)
-	24	THIS SHOULD MOVE YA	Mantronix (Capitol)
29	25	WE TOO ARE ONE	Eurythmics (RCA)
17	26	THE LOVE SONGS	Dionne Warwick (Arista)
39	27	BACK ON THE BLOCK	Quincy Jones (Qwest)
24	28	A NEW FLAME	Simply Red (Elektra)
21	29	CLUB CLASSICS VOL 1	Soul II Soul (10)
-	30	BODY AND SOUL - HEART AND SOUL II	Various Artists (Heart & Soul)
26	31	3 FEET HIGH AND RISING	De La Soul (Big Life)
22	32	TEN GOOD REASONS	Jason Donovan (PWL)
37	33	THE CREAM OF ERIC CLAPTON	Eric Clapton & Cream (Polydor)
40	34	A COLLECTION - GREATEST HITS ... AND MORE	Barbra Streisand (CBS)
30	35	VIVALDI: THE FOUR SEASONS	Nigel Kennedy with the English Chamber Orchestra
23	36	THE RAW AND THE COOKED	Fine Young Cannibals (London)
-	37	DECADE	Duran Duran (EMI)
42	38	SKID ROW	Skid Row (Atlntic)
-	39	ALL BY MYSELF	Various Artists (Dover)
25	40	WARE'S THE HOUSE	Various Artists (Stylus)
31	41	WHEN THE WORLD KNOWS YOUR NAME	Deacon Blue (CBS)
45	42	LABOUR OF LOVE II	UB40 (DEP International)
27	43	READ MY LIPS	Jimmy Somerville (London)
32	44	HOLDING BACK THE RIVER	Wet Wet Wet (Precious Organisation)
35	45	LIKE A PRAYER	Madonna (Sire)
44	46	WILD!	Erasure (Mute)
43	47	THE LION AND THE COBRA	Sinead O'Connor (Ensign)
33	48	CUTS BOTH WAYS	Gloria Estefan (Epic)
41	49	WELCOME TO THE BEAUTIFUL SOUTH	Beautiful South (Go! Discs)
48	50	RAW LIKE SUSHI	Neneh Cherry (Circa)

Despite a curious lack of hit singles after 1988, Tanita Tikaram proved her consistency as an album seller when her second set *The Sweet Keeper* actually bettered its predecessor *Ancient Heart* by one place on the chart, reaching Number 2. The former lead singer with Marillion, Fish, made his solo debut with *Vigil In A Wilderness Of Mirrors*, and achieved something approaching Marillion-like sales with it.

February – March 1990

24 February 1990

last week	this week	Title	Artist
1	1	... BUT SERIOUSLY	Phil Collins (Vertigo)
4	2	JOURNEYMAN	Eric Clapton (Duck)
9	3	PUMP UP THE JAM	Technotronic (Swanyard)
11	4	AFFECTION	Lisa Stansfield (Arista)
6	5	THE SWEET KEEPER	Tanita Tikaram (East West)
14	6	THE ROAD TO HELL	Chris Rea (WEA)
7	7	THE VERY BEST OF CAT STEVENS	Cat Stevens (Island)
17	8	HEART OF STONE	Cher (Geffen)
8	9	COLOUR	Christians (Island)
12	10	THE LANGUAGE OF LIFE	Everything But The Girl (blanco y negro)
13	11	THE BEST OF ROD STEWART	Rod Stewart (Warner Bros.)
15	12	PURE SOFT METAL	Various Artists (Stylus)
19	13	FOREIGN AFFAIR	Tina Turner (Capitol)
2	14	CARVED IN SAND	Mission (Mercury)
23	15	MARTIKA	Martika (CBS)
30	16	BODY AND SOUL - HEART AND SOUL II	Various Artists (Heart & Soul)
18	17	THE STONE ROSES	Stone Roses (Silvertone)
3	18	DEEP HEAT 5 - FEED THE FEVER	Various Artists (Telstar)
16	19	HANGIN' TOUGH	New Kids On The Block (CBS)
22	20	READING, WRITING AND ARITHMETIC	Sundays (Rough Trade)
5	21	A BIT OF WHAT YOU FANCY	Quireboys (Parlophone)
-	22	MISS SAIGON	London Cast (Warner Bros.)
27	23	BACK ON THE BLOCK	Quincy Jones (Qwest)
21	24	ENJOY YOURSELF	Kylie Minogue (PWL)
26	25	THE LOVE SONGS	Dionne Warwick (Arista)
-	26	RUNNING FREE/SANCTUARY	Iron Maiden (EMI)
39	27	ALL BY MYSELF	Various Artists (Dover)
20	28	PARADISE REMIXED	Inner City (10)
-	29	WAKING HOURS	Del Amitri (A&M)
28	30	A NEW FLAME	Simply Red (Elektra)
25	31	WE TOO ARE ONE	Eurythmics (RCA)
24	32	THIS SHOULD MOVE YA	Mantronix (Capitol)
33	33	THE CREAM OF ERIC CLAPTON	Eric Clapton & Cream (Polydor)
34	34	A COLLECTION - GREATEST HITS ... AND MORE	Barbra Streisand (CBS)
35	35	VIVALDI: THE FOUR SEASONS	Nigel Kennedy with the English Chamber Orchestra
10	36	VIGIL IN A WILDERNESS OF MIRRORS	Fish (EMI)
-	37	STAY SICK!	Cramps (Enigma)
38	38	SKID ROW	Skid Row (Atlntic)
29	39	CLUB CLASSICS VOL 1	Soul II Soul (10)
-	40	THE BLUES BROTHERS - SOUNDTRACK	Various Artists (Atlantic)
-	41	MILESTONES - 20 ROCK OPERAS	Various Artists (Telstar)
31	42	3 FEET HIGH AND RISING	De La Soul (Big Life)
36	43	THE RAW AND THE COOKED	Fine Young Cannibals (London)
41	44	WHEN THE WORLD KNOWS YOUR NAME	Deacon Blue (CBS)
32	45	TEN GOOD REASONS	Jason Donovan (PWL)
50	46	RAW LIKE SUSHI	Neneh Cherry (Circa)
45	47	LIKE A PRAYER	Madonna (Sire)
42	48	LABOUR OF LOVE II	UB40 (DEP International)
37	49	DECADE	Duran Duran (EMI)
-	50	THE COMFORTS OF MADNESS	Pale Saints (4AD)

3 March 1990

last week	this week	Title	Artist
1	1	... BUT SERIOUSLY	Phil Collins (Vertigo)
2	2	JOURNEYMAN	Eric Clapton (Duck)
4	3	AFFECTION	Lisa Stansfield (Arista)
22	4	MISS SAIGON	London Cast (Warner Bros.)
6	5	THE ROAD TO HELL	Chris Rea (WEA)
8	6	HEART OF STONE	Cher (Geffen)
13	7	FOREIGN AFFAIR	Tina Turner (Capitol)
29	8	WAKING HOURS	Del Amitri (A&M)
3	9	PUMP UP THE JAM	Technotronic (Swanyard)
-	10	LLOYD COLE	Lloyd Cole (Polydor)
11	11	THE BEST OF ROD STEWART	Rod Stewart (Warner Bros.)
12	12	PURE SOFT METAL	Various Artists (Stylus)
7	13	THE VERY BEST OF CAT STEVENS	Cat Stevens (Island)
39	14	CLUB CLASSICS VOL 1	Soul II Soul (10)
-	15	WOMEN IN UNIFORM/TWILIGHT ZONE	Iron Maiden (EMI)
15	16	MARTIKA	Martika (CBS)
16	17	BODY AND SOUL - HEART AND SOUL II	Various Artists (Heart & Soul)
5	18	THE SWEET KEEPER	Tanita Tikaram (East West)
27	19	ALL BY MYSELF	Various Artists (Dover)
43	20	THE RAW AND THE COOKED	Fine Young Cannibals (London)
-	21	THE AWARDS 1990	Various Artists (Telstar)
35	22	VIVALDI: THE FOUR SEASONS	Nigel Kennedy with the English Chamber Orchestra
26	23	RUNNING FREE/SANCTUARY	Iron Maiden (EMI)
46	24	RAW LIKE SUSHI	Neneh Cherry (Circa)
-	25	WALK ON BY	Sybil (PWL)
-	26	HAPPINESS	Beloved (East West)
9	27	COLOUR	Christians (Island)
17	28	THE STONE ROSES	Stone Roses (Silvertone)
19	29	HANGIN' TOUGH	New Kids On The Block (CBS)
31	30	WE TOO ARE ONE	Eurythmics (RCA)
10	31	THE LANGUAGE OF LIFE	Everything But The Girl (blanco y negro)
-	32	CUTS BOTH WAYS	Gloria Estefan (Epic)
33	33	THE CREAM OF ERIC CLAPTON	Eric Clapton & Cream (Polydor)
24	34	ENJOY YOURSELF	Kylie Minogue (PWL)
14	35	CARVED IN SAND	Mission (Mercury)
30	36	A NEW FLAME	Simply Red (Elektra)
41	37	MILESTONES - 20 ROCK OPERAS	Various (Telstar)
32	38	THIS SHOULD MOVE YA	Mantronix (Capitol)
38	39	SKID ROW	Skid Row (Atlntic)
-	40	THE SEEDS OF LOVE	Tears For Fears (Fontana)
18	41	DEEP HEAT 5 - FEED THE FEVER	Various Artists (Telstar)
20	42	READING, WRITING AND ARITHMETIC	Sundays (Rough Trade)
25	43	THE LOVE SONGS	Dionne Warwick (Arista)
40	44	THE BLUES BROTHERS - SOUNDTRACK	Various Artists (Atlantic)
34	45	A COLLECTION - GREATEST HITS ... AND MORE	Barbra Streisand (CBS)
-	46	EXTRICATE	Fall (Cog Sinister)
21	47	A BIT OF WHAT YOU FANCY	Quireboys (Parlophone)
50	48	THE COMFORTS OF MADNESS	Pale Saints (4AD)
23	49	BACK ON THE BLOCK	Quincy Jones (Qwest)
-	50	HOLDING BACK THE RIVER	Wet Wet Wet (Precious Organisation)

10 March 1990

last week	this week	Title	Artist
1	1	... BUT SERIOUSLY	Phil Collins (Vertigo)
3	2	AFFECTION	Lisa Stansfield (Arista)
2	3	JOURNEYMAN	Eric Clapton (Duck)
9	4	PUMP UP THE JAM	Technotronic (Swanyard)
-	5	THE HOUSE OF LOVE	House Of Love (Fontana)
5	6	THE ROAD TO HELL	Chris Rea (WEA)
11	7	THE BEST OF ROD STEWART	Rod Stewart (Warner Bros.)
7	8	FOREIGN AFFAIR	Tina Turner (Capitol)
6	9	HEART OF STONE	Cher (Geffen)
-	10	NOW DANCE 901	Various Artists (EMI/Virgin/PolyGram)
14	11	CLUB CLASSICS VOL 1	Soul II Soul (10)
20	12	THE RAW AND THE COOKED	Fine Young Cannibals (London)
10	13	LLOYD COLE	Lloyd Cole (Polydor)
-	14	PURGATORY/MAIDEN JAPAN	Iron Maiden (EMI)
26	15	HAPPINESS	Beloved (East West)
13	16	THE VERY BEST OF CAT STEVENS	Cat Stevens (Island)
4	17	MISS SAIGON	London Cast (Warner Bros.)
8	18	WAKING HOURS	Del Amitri (A&M)
24	19	RAW LIKE SUSHI	Neneh Cherry (Circa)
17	20	BODY AND SOUL - HEART AND SOUL II	Various Artists (Heart & Soul)
28	21	THE STONE ROSES	Stone Roses (Silvertone)
18	22	THE SWEET KEEPER	Tanita Tikaram (East West)
12	23	PURE SOFT METAL	Various Artists (Stylus)
32	24	CUTS BOTH WAYS	Gloria Estefan (Epic)
21	25	THE AWARDS 1990	Various Artists (Telstar)
40	26	THE SEEDS OF LOVE	Tears For Fears (Fontana)
16	27	MARTIKA	Martika (CBS)
22	28	VIVALDI: THE FOUR SEASONS	Nigel Kennedy with the English Chamber Orchestra
-	29	3 FEET HIGH AND RISING	De La Soul (Big Life)
43	30	THE LOVE SONGS	Dionne Warwick (Arista)
-	31	THE 49ERS	49ers (Fourth & Broadway)
36	32	A NEW FLAME	Simply Red (Elektra)
-	33	THE SYNTHESIZER ALBUM	Project D (Telstar)
-	34	BLUE SKY MINING	Midnight Oil (CBS)
15	35	WOMEN IN UNIFORM/TWILIGHT ZONE	Iron Maiden (EMI)
19	36	ALL BY MYSELF	Various Artists (Dover)
27	37	COLOUR	Christians (Island)
-	38	THE RIGHT STUFF 2 - NOTHIN' BUT A HOUSE PARTY	Various Artists (Stylus)
-	39	WILD!	Erasure (Mute)
29	40	HANGIN' TOUGH	New Kids On The Block (CBS)
25	41	WALK ON BY	Sybil (PWL)
30	42	WE TOO ARE ONE	Eurythmics (RCA)
34	43	ENJOY YOURSELF	Kylie Minogue (PWL)
-	44	THAT LOVING FEELING VOL. 2	Various Artists (Dino)
44	45	THE BLUES BROTHERS - SOUNDTRACK	Various Artists (Atlantic)
35	46	CARVED IN SAND	Mission (Mercury)
31	47	THE LANGUAGE OF LIFE	Everything But The Girl (blanco y negro)
-	48	MOVE YOUR SKIN	And Why Not (Island)
50	49	HOLDING BACK THE RIVER	Wet Wet Wet (Precious Organisation)
33	50	THE CREAM OF ERIC CLAPTON	Eric Clapton & Cream (Polydor)

Journeyman was a slightly self-deprecating album title for one whom many still considered a god of the electric guitar. But the album in question was to prove one of Eric Clapton's best sellers. Joining it in the Top 10 (albeit briefly) was the original UK cast recording of another hit West End stage musical, *Miss Saigon*. Possibly the most unusual thing about this successful show was its *lack* of Lloyd Webber involvement!

March 1990

last week	this week	17 March 1990	
1	1	... BUT SERIOUSLY	Phil Collins (Vertigo)
10	2	NOW DANCE 901	
		Various Artists (EMI/Virgin/PolyGram)	
4	3	PUMP UP THE JAM	Technotronic (Swanyard)
2	4	AFFECTION	Lisa Stansfield (Arista)
7	5	THE BEST OF ROD STEWART	
		Rod Stewart (Warner Bros.)	
6	6	THE ROAD TO HELL	Chris Rea (WEA)
8	7	FOREIGN AFFAIR	Tina Turner (Capitol)
5	8	THE HOUSE OF LOVE	House Of Love (Fontana)
-	9	RUN TO THE HILLS/THE NUMBER OF THE BEAST	Iron Maiden (EMI)
3	10	JOURNEYMAN	Eric Clapton (Duck)
9	11	HEART OF STONE	Cher (Geffen)
-	12	MISSING ... PRESUMED HAVING A GOOD TIME	Notting Hillbillies (Vertigo)
12	13	THE RAW AND THE COOKED	
		Fine Young Cannibals (London)	
38	14	THE RIGHT STUFF 2 - NOTHIN' BUT A HOUSE PARTY	Various Artists (Stylus)
24	15	CUTS BOTH WAYS	Gloria Estefan (Epic)
16	16	THE VERY BEST OF CAT STEVENS	Cat Stevens (Island)
33	17	THE SYNTHESIZER ALBUM	Project D (Telstar)
18	18	WAKING HOURS	Del Amitri (A&M)
21	19	THE STONE ROSES	Stone Roses (Silvertone)
17	20	MISS SAIGON	London Cast (Warner Bros.)
11	21	CLUB CLASSICS VOL 1	Soul II Soul (10)
39	22	WILD!	Erasure (Mute)
-	23	10	Stranglers (Epic)
28	24	VIVALDI: THE FOUR SEASONS	Nigel Kennedy with the English Chamber Orchestra
13	25	LLOYD COLE	Lloyd Cole (Polydor)
19	26	RAW LIKE SUSHI	Neneh Cherry (Circa)
-	27	SOUL PROVIDER	Michael Bolton (CBS)
48	28	MOVE YOUR SKIN	And Why Not (Island)
-	29	BACK STREET SYMPHONY	Thunder (EMI)
49	30	HOLDING BACK THE RIVER	
		Wet Wet Wet (Precious Organisation)	
15	31	HAPPINESS	Beloved (East West)
22	32	THE SWEET KEEPER	
		Tanita Tikaram (East West)	
30	33	THE LOVE SONGS	Dionne Warwick (Arista)
27	34	MARTIKA	Martika (CBS)
40	35	HANGIN' TOUGH	
		New Kids On The Block (CBS)	
32	36	A NEW FLAME	Simply Red (Elektra)
20	37	BODY AND SOUL - HEART AND SOUL II	
		Various Artists (Heart & Soul)	
34	38	BLUE SKY MINING	Midnight Oil (CBS)
29	39	3 FEET HIGH AND RISING	De La Soul (Big Life)
26	40	THE SEEDS OF LOVE	Tears For Fears (Fontana)
46	41	CARVED IN SAND	Mission (Mercury)
23	42	PURE SOFT METAL	Various Artists (Stylus)
14	43	PURGATORY/MAIDEN JAPAN	
		Iron Maiden (EMI)	
-	44	LIVE ON BROADWAY	Barry Manilow (Arista)
31	45	THE 49ERS	49ers (Fourth & Broadway)
25	46	THE AWARDS 1990	Various Artists (Telstar)
37	47	COLOUR	Christians (Island)
36	48	ALL BY MYSELF	Various Artists (Dover)
-	49	THE ESSENTIAL PAVAROTTI	
		Luciano Pavarotti (Decca)	
-	50	THE GREATEST HITS	Thompson Twins (Stylus)

		24 March 1990	
-	1	I DO NOT WANT WHAT I HAVEN'T GOT	
		Sinead O'Connor (Ensign)	
2	2	NOW DANCE 901	
		Various Artists (EMI/Virgin/PolyGram)	
1	3	... BUT SERIOUSLY	Phil Collins (Vertigo)
12	4	MISSING ... PRESUMED HAVING A GOOD TIME	Notting Hillbillies (Vertigo)
-	5	CHANGESBOWIE	David Bowie (EMI)
24	6	VIVALDI: THE FOUR SEASONS	Nigel Kennedy with the English Chamber Orchestra
-	7	FLIGHT OF ICARUS/THE TROOPER	
		Iron Maiden (EMI)	
27	8	SOUL PROVIDER	Michael Bolton (CBS)
14	9	THE RIGHT STUFF 2 - NOTHIN' BUT A HOUSE PARTY	Various Artists (Stylus)
49	10	THE ESSENTIAL PAVAROTTI	
		Luciano Pavarotti (Decca)	
35	11	HANGIN' TOUGH	
		New Kids On The Block (CBS)	
6	12	THE ROAD TO HELL	Chris Rea (WEA)
7	13	FOREIGN AFFAIR	Tina Turner (Capitol)
3	14	PUMP UP THE JAM	Technotronic (Swanyard)
5	15	THE BEST OF ROD STEWART	
		Rod Stewart (Warner Bros.)	
44	16	LIVE ON BROADWAY	Barry Manilow (Arista)
4	17	AFFECTION	Lisa Stansfield (Arista)
23	18	10	Stranglers (Epic)
11	19	HEART OF STONE	Cher (Geffen)
10	20	JOURNEYMAN	Eric Clapton (Duck)
22	21	WILD!	Erasure (Mute)
50	22	THE GREATEST HITS	
		Thompson Twins (Stylus)	
15	23	CUTS BOTH WAYS	Gloria Estefan (Epic)
8	24	THE HOUSE OF LOVE	House Of Love (Fontana)
19	25	THE STONE ROSES	Stone Roses (Silvertone)
16	26	THE VERY BEST OF CAT STEVENS	Cat Stevens (Island)
13	27	THE RAW AND THE COOKED	
		Fine Young Cannibals (London)	
18	28	WAKING HOURS	Del Amitri (A&M)
40	29	THE SEEDS OF LOVE	Tears For Fears (Fontana)
-	30	MANNERS AND PHYSIQUE	Adam Ant (MCA)
17	31	THE SYNTHESIZER ALBUM	Project D (Telstar)
25	32	LLOYD COLE	Lloyd Cole (Polydor)
21	33	CLUB CLASSICS VOL 1	Soul II Soul (10)
-	34	LABOUR OF LOVE II	UB40 (DEP International)
26	35	RAW LIKE SUSHI	Neneh Cherry (Circa)
36	36	A NEW FLAME	Simply Red (Elektra)
20	37	MISS SAIGON	London Cast (Warner Bros.)
29	38	BACK STREET SYMPHONY	Thunder (EMI)
34	39	MARTIKA	Martika (CBS)
39	40	3 FEET HIGH AND RISING	De La Soul (Big Life)
-	41	JIVE BUNNY - THE ALBUM	
		Jive Bunny & the Mastermixers (Telstar)	
-	42	PENNIES FROM HEAVEN	Various Artists (BBC)
30	43	HOLDING BACK THE RIVER	
		Wet Wet Wet (Precious Organisation)	
-	44	JOIN TOGETHER	Who (Virgin)
28	45	MOVE YOUR SKIN	And Why Not (Island)
-	46	WE TOO ARE ONE	Eurythmics (RCA)
41	47	CARVED IN SAND	Mission (Mercury)
31	48	HAPPINESS	Beloved (East West)
38	49	BLUE SKY MINING	Midnight Oil (CBS)
33	50	THE LOVE SONGS	Dionne Warwick (Arista)

		31 March 1990	
1	1	I DO NOT WANT WHAT I HAVEN'T GOT	
		Sinead O'Connor (Ensign)	
-	2	VIOLATOR	Depeche Mode (Mute)
5	3	CHANGESBOWIE	David Bowie (EMI)
2	4	NOW DANCE 901	
		Various Artists (EMI/Virgin/PolyGram)	
6	5	VIVALDI: THE FOUR SEASONS	Nigel Kennedy with the English Chamber Orchestra
-	6	DEEP HEAT 6 - THE SIXTH SENSE	
		Various Artists (Telstar)	
3	7	... BUT SERIOUSLY	Phil Collins (Vertigo)
-	8	2 MINUTES TO MIDNIGHT/ACES HIGH	
		Iron Maiden (EMI)	
4	9	MISSING ... PRESUMED HAVING A GOOD TIME	Notting Hillbillies (Vertigo)
10	10	THE ESSENTIAL PAVAROTTI	
		Luciano Pavarotti (Decca)	
-	11	COSMIC THING	B-52's (Reprise)
9	12	THE RIGHT STUFF 2 - NOTHIN' BUT A HOUSE PARTY	Various Artists (Stylus)
12	13	THE ROAD TO HELL	Chris Rea (WEA)
28	14	WAKING HOURS	Del Amitri (A&M)
11	15	HANGIN' TOUGH	New Kids On The Block (CBS)
13	16	FOREIGN AFFAIR	Tina Turner (Capitol)
8	17	SOUL PROVIDER	Michael Bolton (CBS)
-	18	MANIC NIRVANA	Robert Plant (Es Paranza)
23	19	CUTS BOTH WAYS	Gloria Estefan (Epic)
17	20	AFFECTION	Lisa Stansfield (Arista)
14	21	PUMP UP THE JAM	Technotronic (Swanyard)
15	22	THE BEST OF ROD STEWART	
		Rod Stewart (Warner Bros.)	
21	23	WILD!	Erasure (Mute)
19	24	HEART OF STONE	Cher (Geffen)
25	25	THE STONE ROSES	Stone Roses (Silvertone)
24	26	THE HOUSE OF LOVE	House Of Love (Fontana)
30	27	MANNERS AND PHYSIQUE	Adam Ant (MCA)
-	28	JUST THE TWO OF US	Various (Columbia)
20	29	JOURNEYMAN	Eric Clapton (Duck)
-	30	ONLY YESTERDAY	Carpenters (A&M)
-	31	THE CAUTION HORSES	Cowboy Junkies (RCA)
34	32	LABOUR OF LOVE II	UB40 (DEP International)
22	33	THE GREATEST HITS	Thompson Twins (Stylus)
26	34	THE VERY BEST OF CAT STEVENS	
		Cat Stevens (Island)	
48	35	HAPPINESS	Beloved (East West)
29	36	THE SEEDS OF LOVE	Tears For Fears (Fontana)
33	37	CLUB CLASSICS VOL 1	Soul II Soul (10)
31	38	THE SYNTHESIZER ALBUM	Project D (Telstar)
7	39	FLIGHT OF ICARUS/THE TROOPER	
		Iron Maiden (EMI)	
18	40	10	Stranglers (Epic)
27	41	THE RAW AND THE COOKED	
		Fine Young Cannibals (London)	
43	42	HOLDING BACK THE RIVER	
		Wet Wet Wet (Precious Organisation)	
-	43	COLLECTION: RAY CHARLES	
		Ray Charles (Arcade)	
35	44	RAW LIKE SUSHI	Neneh Cherry (Circa)
32	45	LLOYD COLE	Lloyd Cole (Polydor)
16	46	LIVE ON BROADWAY	Barry Manilow (Arista)
44	47	JOIN TOGETHER	Who (Virgin)
36	48	A NEW FLAME	Simply Red (Elektra)
-	49	WILD AND LONELY	Associates (Circa)
-	50	SKID ROW	Skid Row (Atlntic)

The somewhat odd Top 10 entries by Iron Maiden in three consecutive charts, each surviving for barely more than a week, were listed, in a sense, by default. Each was a double package of two original Maiden 12-inch singles, released as a limited collectors edition, but their length and number of tracks precluded their inclusion in the singles chart, so with the albums, briefly, they were lumped.

April 1990

7 April 1990

last week	this week	title	artist
3	1	CHANGESBOWIE	David Bowie (EMI)
1	2	I DO NOT WANT WHAT I HAVEN'T GOT	Sinead O'Connor (Ensign)
30	3	ONLY YESTERDAY	Carpenters (A&M)
2	4	VIOLATOR	Depeche Mode (Mute)
6	5	DEEP HEAT 6 - THE SIXTH SENSE	Various (Telstar)
7	6	... BUT SERIOUSLY	Phil Collins (Vertigo)
10	7	THE ESSENTIAL PAVAROTTI	Luciano Pavarotti (Decca)
11	8	COSMIC THING	B-52's (Reprise)
5	9	VIVALDI: THE FOUR SEASONS	Nigel Kennedy with the English Chamber Orchestra
4	10	NOW DANCE 901	Various Artists (EMI/Virgin/PolyGram)
16	11	FOREIGN AFFAIR	Tina Turner (Capitol)
13	12	THE ROAD TO HELL	Chris Rea (WEA)
9	13	MISSING ... PRESUMED HAVING A GOOD TIME	Notting Hillbillies (Vertigo)
-	14	THE BEST OF VAN MORRISON	Van Morrison (Polydor)
-	15	RUNNING FREE (LIVE)/RUN TO THE HILLS (LIVE)	Iron Maiden (EMI)
22	16	THE BEST OF ROD STEWART	Rod Stewart (Warner Bros.)
12	17	THE RIGHT STUFF 2 - NOTHIN' BUT A HOUSE PARTY	Various Artists (Stylus)
17	18	SOUL PROVIDER	Michael Bolton (CBS)
18	19	MANIC NIRVANA	Robert Plant (Es Paranza)
23	20	WILD!	Erasure (Mute)
14	21	WAKING HOURS	Del Amitri (A&M)
19	22	CUTS BOTH WAYS	Gloria Estefan (Epic)
-	23	FLOOD	They Might Be Giants (Elektra)
20	24	AFFECTION	Lisa Stansfield (Arista)
24	25	HEART OF STONE	Cher (Geffen)
15	26	HANGIN' TOUGH	New Kids On The Block (CBS)
32	27	LABOUR OF LOVE II	UB40 (DEP International)
21	28	PUMP UP THE JAM	Technotronic (Swanyard)
25	29	THE STONE ROSES	Stone Roses (Silvertone)
28	30	JUST THE TWO OF US	Various Artists (Columbia)
-	31	MISS SAIGON	London Cast (Warner Bros.)
26	32	THE HOUSE OF LOVE	House Of Love (Fontana)
42	33	HOLDING BACK THE RIVER	Wet Wet Wet (Precious Organisation)
29	34	JOURNEYMAN	Eric Clapton (Duck)
-	35	STILL GOT THE BLUES	Gary Moore (Virgin)
35	36	HAPPINESS	Beloved (East West)
31	37	THE CAUTION HORSES	Cowboy Junkies (RCA)
34	38	THE VERY BEST OF CAT STEVENS	Cat Stevens (Island)
37	39	CLUB CLASSICS VOL 1	Soul II Soul (10)
50	40	SKID ROW	Skid Row (Atlntic)
33	41	THE GREATEST HITS	Thompson Twins (Stylus)
27	42	MANNERS AND PHYSIQUE	Adam Ant (MCA)
38	43	THE SYNTHESIZER ALBUM	Project D (Telstar)
43	44	COLLECTION	Ray Charles (Arcade)
-	45	SKINBEAT - THE FIRST TOUCH	Various (Polydor)
-	46	A COLLECTION - GREATEST HITS ... AND MORE	Barbra Streisand (CBS)
8	47	2 MINUTES TO MIDNIGHT/ACES HIGH	Iron Maiden (EMI)
41	48	THE RAW AND THE COOKED	Fine Young Cannibals (London)
-	49	JANET JACKSON'S RHYTHM NATION 1814	Janet Jackson (A&M)
36	50	THE SEEDS OF LOVE	Tears For Fears (Fontana)

14 April 1990

last week	this week	title	artist
3	1	ONLY YESTERDAY	Carpenters (A&M)
1	2	CHANGESBOWIE	David Bowie (EMI)
14	3	THE BEST OF VAN MORRISON	Van Morrison (Polydor)
2	4	I DO NOT WANT WHAT I HAVEN'T GOT	Sinead O'Connor (Ensign)
6	5	... BUT SERIOUSLY	Phil Collins (Vertigo)
5	6	DEEP HEAT 6 - THE SIXTH SENSE	Various (Telstar)
4	7	VIOLATOR	Depeche Mode (Mute)
-	8	BRIGADE	Heart (Capitol)
-	9	WASTED YEARS/STRANGER IN A STRANGE LAND	Iron Maiden (EMI)
8	10	COSMIC THING	B-52's (Reprise)
9	11	VIVALDI: THE FOUR SEASONS	Nigel Kennedy with the English Chamber Orchestra
7	12	THE ESSENTIAL PAVAROTTI	Luciano Pavarotti (Decca)
23	13	FLOOD	They Might Be Giants (Elektra)
12	14	THE ROAD TO HELL	Chris Rea (WEA)
17	15	THE RIGHT STUFF 2 - NOTHIN' BUT A HOUSE PARTY	Various Artists (Stylus)
13	16	MISSING ... PRESUMED HAVING A GOOD TIME	Notting Hillbillies (Vertigo)
35	17	STILL GOT THE BLUES	Gary Moore (Virgin)
27	18	LABOUR OF LOVE II	UB40 (DEP International)
20	19	WILD!	Erasure (Mute)
-	20	LET THEM EAT BINGO	Beats International (Go Beat)
11	21	FOREIGN AFFAIR	Tina Turner (Capitol)
22	22	CUTS BOTH WAYS	Gloria Estefan (Epic)
16	23	THE BEST OF ROD STEWART	Rod Stewart (Warner Bros.)
28	24	PUMP UP THE JAM	Technotronic (Swanyard)
25	25	HEART OF STONE	Cher (Geffen)
10	26	NOW DANCE 901	Various Artists (EMI/Virgin/PolyGram)
21	27	WAKING HOURS	Del Amitri (A&M)
26	28	HANGIN' TOUGH	New Kids On The Block (CBS)
34	29	JOURNEYMAN	Eric Clapton (Duck)
24	30	AFFECTION	Lisa Stansfield (Arista)
45	31	SKINBEAT - THE FIRST TOUCH	Various Artists (Polydor)
18	32	SOUL PROVIDER	Michael Bolton (CBS)
30	33	JUST THE TWO OF US	Various Artists (Columbia)
32	34	THE HOUSE OF LOVE	House Of Love (Fontana)
29	35	THE STONE ROSES	Stone Roses (Silvertone)
41	36	THE GREATEST HITS	Thompson Twins (Stylus)
-	37	LILY WAS HERE - ORIGINAL SOUNDTRACK	David A. Stewart featuring Candy Dulfer (AnXious)
33	38	HOLDING BACK THE RIVER	Wet Wet Wet (Precious Organisation)
19	39	MANIC NIRVANA	Robert Plant (Es Paranza)
-	40	RAW LIKE SUSHI	Neneh Cherry (Circa)
-	41	BEZERK	Tigertailz (Music For Nations)
36	42	HAPPINESS	Beloved (East West)
-	43	HUNKY DORY	David Bowie (EMI)
-	44	3 FEET HIGH AND RISING	De La Soul (Big Life)
-	45	APRIL MOON	Sam Brown (A&M)
-	46	THE MAN WHO SOLD THE WORLD	David Bowie (EMI)
39	47	CLUB CLASSICS VOL 1	Soul II Soul (10)
-	48	WITNESS	Halo James (Epic)
49	49	JANET JACKSON'S RHYTHM NATION 1814	Janet Jackson (A&M)
-	50	SPACE ODDITY	David Bowie (EMI)

21 April 1990

last week	this week	title	artist
-	1	BEHIND THE MASK	Fleetwood Mac (Warner Bros.)
1	2	ONLY YESTERDAY	Carpenters (A&M)
2	3	CHANGESBOWIE	David Bowie (EMI)
8	4	BRIGADE	Heart (Capitol)
3	5	THE BEST OF VAN MORRISON	Van Morrison (Polydor)
5	6	... BUT SERIOUSLY	Phil Collins (Vertigo)
18	7	LABOUR OF LOVE II	UB40 (DEP International)
4	8	I DO NOT WANT WHAT I HAVEN'T GOT	Sinead O'Connor (Ensign)
-	9	CAN I PLAY WITH MADNESS/THE EVIL THAT MEN DO	Iron Maiden (EMI)
6	10	DEEP HEAT 6 - THE SIXTH SENSE	Various (Telstar)
11	11	VIVALDI: THE FOUR SEASONS	Nigel Kennedy with the English Chamber Orchestra
7	12	VIOLATOR	Depeche Mode (Mute)
10	13	COSMIC THING	B-52's (Reprise)
25	14	HEART OF STONE	Cher (Geffen)
14	15	THE ROAD TO HELL	Chris Rea (WEA)
16	16	MISSING ... PRESUMED HAVING A GOOD TIME	Notting Hillbillies (Vertigo)
-	17	ABSOLUTELY	ABC (Neutron)
24	18	PUMP UP THE JAM	Technotronic (Swanyard)
20	19	LET THEM EAT BINGO	Beats International (Go Beat)
48	20	WITNESS	Halo James (Epic)
12	21	THE ESSENTIAL PAVAROTTI	Luciano Pavarotti (Decca)
15	22	THE RIGHT STUFF 2 - NOTHIN' BUT A HOUSE PARTY	Various Artists (Stylus)
13	23	FLOOD	They Might Be Giants (Elektra)
19	24	WILD!	Erasure (Mute)
33	25	JUST THE TWO OF US	Various Artists (Columbia)
23	26	THE BEST OF ROD STEWART	Rod Stewart (Warner Bros.)
27	27	WAKING HOURS	Del Amitri (A&M)
-	28	CLASSICS BY MOONLIGHT	James Last (Polydor)
21	29	FOREIGN AFFAIR	Tina Turner (Capitol)
-	30	MONTAGE	Kenny G (Arista)
17	31	STILL GOT THE BLUES	Gary Moore (Virgin)
29	32	JOURNEYMAN	Eric Clapton (Duck)
22	33	CUTS BOTH WAYS	Gloria Estefan (Epic)
45	34	APRIL MOON	Sam Brown (A&M)
9	35	WASTED YEARS/STRANGER IN A STRANGE LAND	Iron Maiden (EMI)
28	36	HANGIN' TOUGH	New Kids On The Block (CBS)
-	37	THE VOICE	Brenda Cochrane (Polydor)
26	38	NOW DANCE 901	Various Artists (EMI/Virgin/PolyGram)
30	39	AFFECTION	Lisa Stansfield (Arista)
-	40	MARTIKA	Martika (CBS)
35	41	THE STONE ROSES	Stone Roses (Silvertone)
32	42	SOUL PROVIDER	Michael Bolton (CBS)
34	43	THE HOUSE OF LOVE	House Of Love (Fontana)
38	44	HOLDING BACK THE RIVER	Wet Wet Wet (Precious Organisation)
-	45	THE BLUES BROTHERS - SOUNDTRACK	Various Artists (Atlantic)
31	46	SKINBEAT - THE FIRST TOUCH	Various Artists (Polydor)
43	47	HUNKY DORY	David Bowie (EMI)
36	48	THE GREATEST HITS	Thompson Twins (Stylus)
49	49	JANET JACKSON'S RHYTHM NATION 1814	Janet Jackson (A&M)
-	50	COLOUR	Christians (Island)

Seven years after the death of Karen Carpenter, the timeless appeal of the Carpenters' music proved itself once again as their *Only Yesterday* retrospective package gave the duo their first Number 1 album since the 1970s. It displaced another hits package, David Bowie's *Changesbowie*. Meanwhile, for the first time ever, there were two classical albums, by Pavarotti and Nigel Kennedy, in the Top 10.

28 April 1990

last	this week	Title	Artist
1	1	BEHIND THE MASK	Fleetwood Mac (Warner Bros.)
2	2	ONLY YESTERDAY	Carpenters (A&M)
3	3	CHANGESBOWIE	David Bowie (EMI)
6	4	... BUT SERIOUSLY	Phil Collins (Vertigo)
17	5	ABSOLUTELY	ABC (Neutron)
4	6	BRIGADE	Heart (Capitol)
7	7	LABOUR OF LOVE II	UB40 (DEP International)
-	8	DAYS OF OPEN HAND	Suzanne Vega (A&M)
5	9	THE BEST OF VAN MORRISON	Van Morrison (Polydor)
8	10	I DO NOT WANT WHAT I HAVEN'T GOT	Sinead O'Connor (Ensign)
-	11	FEAR OF A BLACK PLANET	Public Enemy (Def Jam)
11	12	VIVALDI: THE FOUR SEASONS	Nigel Kennedy with the English Chamber Orchestra
-	13	THE CLAIRVOYANT/INFINITE DREAMS (LIVE)	Iron Maiden (EMI)
14	14	HEART OF STONE	Cher (Geffen)
25	15	JUST THE TWO OF US	Various Artists (Columbia)
10	16	DEEP HEAT 6 - THE SIXTH SENSE	Various (Telstar)
18	17	PUMP UP THE JAM	Technotronic (Swanyard)
12	18	VIOLATOR	Depeche Mode (Mute)
-	19	ALANNAH MYLES	Alannah Myles (Atlantic)
15	20	THE ROAD TO HELL	Chris Rea (WEA)
21	21	THE ESSENTIAL PAVAROTTI	Luciano Pavarotti (Decca)
16	22	MISSING ... PRESUMED HAVING A GOOD TIME	Notting Hillbillies (Vertigo)
13	23	COSMIC THING	B-52's (Reprise)
36	24	HANGIN' TOUGH	New Kids On The Block (CBS)
29	25	FOREIGN AFFAIR	Tina Turner (Capitol)
28	26	CLASSICS BY MOONLIGHT	James Last (Polydor)
31	27	STILL GOT THE BLUES	Gary Moore (Virgin)
33	28	CUTS BOTH WAYS	Gloria Estefan (Epic)
-	29	REBEL MUSIC	Rebel MC (Desire)
45	30	THE BLUES BROTHERS - SOUNDTRACK	Various Artists (Atlantic)
24	31	WILD!	Erasure (Mute)
40	32	MARTIKA	Martika (CBS)
30	33	MONTAGE	Kenny G (Arista)
26	34	THE BEST OF ROD STEWART	Rod Stewart (Warner Bros.)
9	35	CAN I PLAY WITH MADNESS/THE EVIL THAT MEN DO	Iron Maiden (EMI)
20	36	WITNESS	Halo James (Epic)
39	37	AFFECTION	Lisa Stansfield (Arista)
19	38	LET THEM EAT BINGO	Beats International (Go Beat)
27	39	WAKING HOURS	Del Amitri (A&M)
41	40	THE STONE ROSES	Stone Roses (Silvertone)
42	41	SOUL PROVIDER	Michael Bolton (CBS)
32	42	JOURNEYMAN	Eric Clapton (Duck)
22	43	THE RIGHT STUFF 2 - NOTHIN' BUT A HOUSE PARTY	Various Artists (Stylus)
-	44	LIKE A PRAYER	Madonna (Sire)
23	45	FLOOD	They Might Be Giants (Elektra)
-	46	A BIT OF WHAT YOU FANCY	Quireboys (Parlophone)
-	47	THE GOOD SON	Nick Cave & the Bad Seeds (Mute)
43	48	THE HOUSE OF LOVE	House Of Love (Fontana)
37	49	THE VOICE	Brenda Cochrane (Polydor)
-	50	A LITTLE BIT OF THIS A LITTLE BIT OF THAT	D Mob (ffrr)

5 May 1990

last	this week	Title	Artist
1	1	BEHIND THE MASK	Fleetwood Mac (Warner Bros.)
2	2	ONLY YESTERDAY	Carpenters (A&M)
4	3	... BUT SERIOUSLY	Phil Collins (Vertigo)
19	4	ALANNAH MYLES	Alannah Myles (Atlantic)
12	5	VIVALDI: THE FOUR SEASONS	Nigel Kennedy with the English Chamber Orchestra
-	6	LIFE	Inspiral Carpets (Cow)
11	7	FEAR OF A BLACK PLANET	Public Enemy (Def Jam)
3	8	CHANGESBOWIE	David Bowie (EMI)
6	9	BRIGADE	Heart (Capitol)
-	10	NOW THAT'S WHAT I CALL MUSIC 17	Various Artists (EMI/Virgin/PolyGram)
8	11	DAYS OF OPEN HAND	Suzanne Vega (A&M)
7	12	LABOUR OF LOVE II	UB40 (DEP International)
5	13	ABSOLUTELY	ABC (Neutron)
10	14	I DO NOT WANT WHAT I HAVEN'T GOT	Sinead O'Connor (Ensign)
9	15	THE BEST OF VAN MORRISON	Van Morrison (Polydor)
15	16	JUST THE TWO OF US	Various Artists (Columbia)
14	17	HEART OF STONE	Cher (Geffen)
16	18	DEEP HEAT 6 - THE SIXTH SENSE	Various Artists (Telstar)
17	19	PUMP UP THE JAM	Technotronic (Swanyard)
-	20	DREAMLAND	Black Box (deConstruction)
20	21	THE ROAD TO HELL	Chris Rea (WEA)
29	22	REBEL MUSIC	Rebel MC (Desire)
24	23	HANGIN' TOUGH	New Kids On The Block (CBS)
25	24	FOREIGN AFFAIR	Tina Turner (Capitol)
22	25	MISSING ... PRESUMED HAVING A GOOD TIME	Notting Hillbillies (Vertigo)
32	26	MARTIKA	Martika (CBS)
30	27	THE BLUES BROTHERS - SOUNDTRACK	Various Artists (Atlantic)
18	28	VIOLATOR	Depeche Mode (Mute)
-	29	SONGS FOR DRELLA	Lou Reed & John Cale (Sire)
23	30	COSMIC THING	B-52's (Reprise)
21	31	THE ESSENTIAL PAVAROTTI	Luciano Pavarotti (Decca)
26	32	CLASSICS BY MOONLIGHT	James Last (Polydor)
49	33	THE VOICE	Brenda Cochrane (Polydor)
31	34	WILD!	Erasure (Mute)
28	35	CUTS BOTH WAYS	Gloria Estefan (Epic)
34	36	THE BEST OF ROD STEWART	Rod Stewart (Warner Bros.)
-	37	THE REAL THING	Faith No More (Slash)
27	38	STILL GOT THE BLUES	Gary Moore (Virgin)
37	39	AFFECTION	Lisa Stansfield (Arista)
-	40	EVERYBODY KNOWS	Sonia (Chrysalis)
13	41	THE CLAIRVOYANT/INFINITE DREAMS (LIVE)	Iron Maiden (EMI)
-	42	MANIC NIRVANA	Robert Plant (Es Paranza)
40	43	THE STONE ROSES	Stone Roses (Silvertone)
33	44	MONTAGE	Kenny G (Arista)
-	45	CLUB CLASSICS VOL 1	Soul II Soul (10)
-	46	NICK OF TIME	Bonnie Raitt (Capitol)
-	47	ECLIPSE	Yngwie J. Malmsteen (Polydor)
39	48	WAKING HOURS	Del Amitri (A&M)
38	49	LET THEM EAT BINGO	Beats International (Go Beat)
42	50	JOURNEYMAN	Eric Clapton (Duck)

12 May 1990

last	this week	Title	Artist
10	1	NOW THAT'S WHAT I CALL MUSIC 17	Various Artists (EMI/Virgin/PolyGram)
3	2	... BUT SERIOUSLY	Phil Collins (Vertigo)
2	3	ONLY YESTERDAY	Carpenters (A&M)
6	4	LIFE	Inspiral Carpets (Cow)
5	5	VIVALDI: THE FOUR SEASONS	Nigel Kennedy with the English Chamber Orchestra
1	6	BEHIND THE MASK	Fleetwood Mac (Warner Bros.)
4	7	ALANNAH MYLES	Alannah Myles (Atlantic)
-	8	CHARMED LIFE	Billy Idol (Chrysalis)
9	9	BRIGADE	Heart (Capitol)
12	10	LABOUR OF LOVE II	UB40 (DEP International)
13	11	ABSOLUTELY	ABC (Neutron)
8	12	CHANGESBOWIE	David Bowie (EMI)
40	13	EVERYBODY KNOWS	Sonia (Chrysalis)
16	14	JUST THE TWO OF US	Various Artists (Columbia)
11	15	DAYS OF OPEN HAND	Suzanne Vega (A&M)
14	16	I DO NOT WANT WHAT I HAVEN'T GOT	Sinead O'Connor (Ensign)
20	17	DREAMLAND	Black Box (deConstruction)
23	18	HANGIN' TOUGH	New Kids On The Block (CBS)
29	19	SONGS FOR DRELLA	Lou Reed & John Cale (Sire)
7	20	FEAR OF A BLACK PLANET	Public Enemy (Def Jam)
-	21	GET ON THIS!!! 30 DANCE HITS VOLUME 1	Various Artists (Telstar)
15	22	THE BEST OF VAN MORRISON	Van Morrison (Polydor)
-	23	SOUL PROVIDER	Michael Bolton (CBS)
-	24	A POCKETFUL OF DREAMS	Big Fun (Jive)
38	25	STILL GOT THE BLUES	Gary Moore (Virgin)
17	26	HEART OF STONE	Cher (Geffen)
22	27	REBEL MUSIC	Rebel MC (Desire)
-	28	FOREVER YOUR GIRL	Paula Abdul (Siren)
21	29	THE ROAD TO HELL	Chris Rea (WEA)
18	30	DEEP HEAT 6 - THE SIXTH SENSE	Various Artists (Telstar)
37	31	THE REAL THING	Faith No More (Slash)
19	32	PUMP UP THE JAM	Technotronic (Swanyard)
27	33	THE BLUES BROTHERS - SOUNDTRACK	Various Artists (Atlantic)
24	34	FOREIGN AFFAIR	Tina Turner (Capitol)
35	35	CUTS BOTH WAYS	Gloria Estefan (Epic)
-	36	DISINTEGRATION	Cure (Fiction)
46	37	NICK OF TIME	Bonnie Raitt (Capitol)
33	38	THE VOICE	Brenda Cochrane (Polydor)
25	39	MISSING ... PRESUMED HAVING A GOOD TIME	Notting Hillbillies (Vertigo)
32	40	CLASSICS BY MOONLIGHT	James Last (Polydor)
-	41	HELLO, I MUST BE GOING!	Phil Collins (Vertigo)
26	42	MARTIKA	Martika (CBS)
30	43	COSMIC THING	B-52's (Reprise)
42	44	MANIC NIRVANA	Robert Plant (Es Paranza)
34	45	WILD!	Erasure (Mute)
-	46	APRIL MOON	Sam Brown (A&M)
-	47	NO JACKET REQUIRED	Phil Collins (Vertigo)
43	48	THE STONE ROSES	Stone Roses (Silvertone)
28	49	VIOLATOR	Depeche Mode (Mute)
36	50	THE BEST OF ROD STEWART	Rod Stewart (Warner Bros.)

The last of the Iron Maiden 12-inch packages hit the Top 20 briefly at the end of April, after which the album charts belonged to the albums again - and notably, at that point in time, to Fleetwood Mac, whose *Behind The Mask* album has never been one of their most highly-regarded releases, but nevertheless at its time of release managed three straight weeks at Number 1 without a hit single.

May – June 1990

19 May 1990

last	this		
1	1	NOW THAT'S WHAT I CALL MUSIC 17	
		Various Artists (EMI/Virgin/PolyGram)	
2	2	... BUT SERIOUSLY	Phil Collins (Vertigo)
3	3	ONLY YESTERDAY	Carpenters (A&M)
28	4	FOREVER YOUR GIRL	Paula Abdul (Siren)
6	5	BEHIND THE MASK	Fleetwood Mac (Warner Bros.)
7	6	ALANNAH MYLES	Alannah Myles (Atlantic)
5	7	VIVALDI: THE FOUR SEASONS	Nigel Kennedy
		with the English Chamber Orchestra	
18	8	HANGIN' TOUGH	New Kids On The Block (CBS)
21	9	GET ON THIS!!! 30 DANCE HITS VOLUME 1	
		Various Artists (Telstar)	
10	10	LABOUR OF LOVE II	UB40 (DEP International)
-	11	TATTOOED MILLIONAIRE	Bruce Dickinson (EMI)
24	12	A POCKETFUL OF DREAMS	Big Fun (Jive)
9	13	BRIGADE	Heart (Capitol)
4	14	LIFE	Inspiral Carpets (Cow)
14	15	JUST THE TWO OF US	Various Artists (Columbia)
23	16	SOUL PROVIDER	Michael Bolton (CBS)
8	17	CHARMED LIFE	Billy Idol (Chrysalis)
11	18	ABSOLUTELY	ABC (Neutron)
12	19	CHANGESBOWIE	David Bowie (EMI)
13	20	EVERYBODY KNOWS	Sonia (Chrysalis)
43	21	COSMIC THING	B-52's (Reprise)
15	22	DAYS OF OPEN HAND	Suzanne Vega (A&M)
-	23	THE EARTHQUAKE ALBUM - ROCK AID	
		ARMENIA Various Artists (Live Aid Armenia)	
26	24	HEART OF STONE	Cher (Geffen)
-	25	JANET JACKSON'S RHYTHM NATION 1814	
		Janet Jackson (A&M)	
16	26	I DO NOT WANT WHAT I HAVEN'T GOT	
		Sinead O'Connor (Ensign)	
-	27	THE ESSENTIAL PAVAROTTI	
		Luciano Pavarotti (Decca)	
17	28	DREAMLAND	Black Box (deConstruction)
25	29	STILL GOT THE BLUES	Gary Moore (Virgin)
-	30	LIVE AND DIRECT	Adamski (MCA)
46	31	APRIL MOON	Sam Brown (A&M)
37	32	NICK OF TIME	Bonnie Raitt (Capitol)
29	33	THE ROAD TO HELL	Chris Rea (WEA)
32	34	PUMP UP THE JAM	Technotronic (Swanyard)
34	35	FOREIGN AFFAIR	Tina Turner (Capitol)
49	36	VIOLATOR	Depeche Mode (Mute)
35	37	CUTS BOTH WAYS	Gloria Estefan (Epic)
22	38	THE BEST OF VAN MORRISON	
		Van Morrison (Polydor)	
33	39	THE BLUES BROTHERS - SOUNDTRACK	
		Various Artists (Atlantic)	
-	40	GOODBYE JUMBO	World Party (Ensign)
-	41	THE INTERNATIONALE	Billy Bragg (Utility)
20	42	FEAR OF A BLACK PLANET	
		Public Enemy (Def Jam)	
-	43	THE GOOD THE BAD AND THE LIVE (THE 6 1/2	
		YEAR ANNIVERSARY 12" COLLECTION)	
		Metallica (Vertigo)	
27	44	REBEL MUSIC	Rebel MC (Desire)
19	45	SONGS FOR DRELLA	
		Lou Reed & John Cale (Sire)	
40	46	CLASSICS BY MOONLIGHT	James Last (Polydor)
38	47	THE VOICE	Brenda Cochrane (Polydor)
31	48	THE REAL THING	Faith No More (Slash)
-	49	ENERGY ORCHARD	Energy Orchard (MCA)
-	50	SALUTATION ROAD	Martin Stephenson
		& the Daintees (Kitchenware)	

26 May 1990

1	1	NOW THAT'S WHAT I CALL MUSIC 17	
		Various Artists (EMI/Virgin/PolyGram)	
3	2	ONLY YESTERDAY	Carpenters (A&M)
2	3	... BUT SERIOUSLY	Phil Collins (Vertigo)
4	4	FOREVER YOUR GIRL	Paula Abdul (Siren)
-	5	THROUGH A BIG COUNTRY - GREATEST HITS	
		Big Country (Mercury)	
10	6	LABOUR OF LOVE II	UB40 (DEP International)
7	7	VIVALDI: THE FOUR SEASONS	Nigel Kennedy
		with the English Chamber Orchestra	
-	8	PACKED!	Pretenders (WEA)
9	9	GET ON THIS!!! 30 DANCE HITS VOLUME 1	
		Various Artists (Telstar)	
8	10	HANGIN' TOUGH	New Kids On The Block (CBS)
6	11	ALANNAH MYLES	Alannah Myles (Atlantic)
12	12	A POCKETFUL OF DREAMS	Big Fun (Jive)
5	13	BEHIND THE MASK	Fleetwood Mac (Warner Bros.)
14	14	LIFE	Inspiral Carpets (Cow)
16	15	SOUL PROVIDER	Michael Bolton (CBS)
21	16	COSMIC THING	B-52's (Reprise)
26	17	I DO NOT WANT WHAT I HAVEN'T GOT	
		Sinead O'Connor (Ensign)	
13	18	BRIGADE	Heart (Capitol)
24	19	HEART OF STONE	Cher (Geffen)
27	20	THE ESSENTIAL PAVAROTTI	
		Luciano Pavarotti (Decca)	
11	21	TATTOOED MILLIONAIRE	Bruce Dickinson (EMI)
18	22	ABSOLUTELY	ABC (Neutron)
29	23	STILL GOT THE BLUES	Gary Moore (Virgin)
15	24	JUST THE TWO OF US	Various Artists (Columbia)
33	25	THE ROAD TO HELL	Chris Rea (WEA)
22	26	DAYS OF OPEN HAND	Suzanne Vega (A&M)
25	27	JANET JACKSON'S RHYTHM NATION 1814	
		Janet Jackson (A&M)	
-	28	LOCK UP THE WOLVES	Dio (Vertigo)
19	29	CHANGESBOWIE	David Bowie (EMI)
17	30	CHARMED LIFE	Billy Idol (Chrysalis)
30	31	LIVE AND DIRECT	Adamski (MCA)
31	32	APRIL MOON	Sam Brown (A&M)
-	33	MENDELSOHN VIOLIN CONCERTO IN E MINOR	
		Nigel Kennedy with Jeffrey Tate	
		& the English Chamber Orchestra	
20	34	EVERYBODY KNOWS	Sonia (Chrysalis)
-	35	LET THEM EAT BINGO	Beats International (Go Beat)
-	36	FREEDOM TO PARTY - FIRST LEGAL RAVE	
		Various Artists (Trax)	
28	37	DREAMLAND	Black Box (deConstruction)
-	38	WORLD POWER	Snap (Arista)
40	39	GOODBYE JUMBO	World Party (Ensign)
36	40	VIOLATOR	Depeche Mode (Mute)
42	41	FEAR OF A BLACK PLANET	
		Public Enemy (Def Jam)	
50	42	SALUTATION ROAD	Martin Stephenson
		& the Daintees (Kitchenware)	
-	43	MISSING ... PRESUMED HAVING A GOOD TIME	
		Notting Hillbillies (Vertigo)	
-	44	TAKE IT TO HEART	Michael McDonald (Reprise)
46	45	CLASSICS BY MOONLIGHT	James Last (Polydor)
-	46	A NIGHT AT THE OPERA	Various Artists (Telstar)
47	47	CIRCLE OF ONE	Oleta Adams (Fontana)
38	48	THE BEST OF VAN MORRISON	
		Van Morrison (Polydor)	
49	49	CLASSIC EXPERIENCE II	Various Artists (EMI)
-	50	AFFECTION	Lisa Stansfield (Arista)

2 June 1990

-	1	I'M BREATHLESS	Madonna (Sire)
-	2	VOLUME II - 1990 A NEW DECADE	
		Soul II Soul (10)	
1	3	NOW THAT'S WHAT I CALL MUSIC 17	
		Various Artists (EMI/Virgin/PolyGram)	
2	4	ONLY YESTERDAY	Carpenters (A&M)
5	5	THROUGH A BIG COUNTRY - GREATEST HITS	
		Big Country (Mercury)	
3	6	... BUT SERIOUSLY	Phil Collins (Vertigo)
6	7	LABOUR OF LOVE II	UB40 (DEP International)
10	8	HANGIN' TOUGH	New Kids On The Block (CBS)
49	9	CLASSIC EXPERIENCE II	Various Artists (EMI)
4	10	FOREVER YOUR GIRL	Paula Abdul (Siren)
16	11	COSMIC THING	B-52's (Reprise)
7	12	VIVALDI: THE FOUR SEASONS	Nigel Kennedy
		with the English Chamber Orchestra	
15	13	SOUL PROVIDER	Michael Bolton (CBS)
20	14	THE ESSENTIAL PAVAROTTI	
		Luciano Pavarotti (Decca)	
9	15	GET ON THIS!!! 30 DANCE HITS VOLUME 1	
		Various Artists (Telstar)	
8	16	PACKED!	Pretenders (WEA)
11	17	ALANNAH MYLES	Alannah Myles (Atlantic)
23	18	STILL GOT THE BLUES	Gary Moore (Virgin)
13	19	BEHIND THE MASK	Fleetwood Mac (Warner Bros.)
17	20	I DO NOT WANT WHAT I HAVEN'T GOT	
		Sinead O'Connor (Ensign)	
19	21	HEART OF STONE	Cher (Geffen)
40	22	VIOLATOR	Depeche Mode (Mute)
18	23	BRIGADE	Heart (Capitol)
12	24	A POCKETFUL OF DREAMS	Big Fun (Jive)
25	25	THE ROAD TO HELL	Chris Rea (WEA)
22	26	ABSOLUTELY	ABC (Neutron)
14	27	LIFE	Inspiral Carpets (Cow)
24	28	JUST THE TWO OF US	Various Artists (Columbia)
37	29	DREAMLAND	Black Box (deConstruction)
-	30	FOREIGN AFFAIR	Tina Turner (Capitol)
44	31	TAKE IT TO HEART	Michael McDonald (Reprise)
29	32	CHANGESBOWIE	David Bowie (EMI)
-	33	SIXTIES MIX 3	Various Artists (Stylus)
32	34	APRIL MOON	Sam Brown (A&M)
39	35	GOODBYE JUMBO	World Party (Ensign)
30	36	CHARMED LIFE	Billy Idol (Chrysalis)
33	37	MENDELSOHN VIOLIN CONCERTO IN E MINOR	
		Nigel Kennedy with Jeffrey Tate & the English	
		Chamber Orchestra	
-	38	LOVE MOVES	Kim Wilde (MCA)
-	39	PASSION AND WARFARE	
		Steve Vai (Food For Thought)	
26	40	DAYS OF OPEN HAND	Suzanne Vega (A&M)
21	41	TATTOOED MILLIONAIRE	Bruce Dickinson (EMI)
47	42	CIRCLE OF ONE	Oleta Adams (Fontana)
27	43	JANET JACKSON'S RHYTHM NATION 1814	
		Janet Jackson (A&M)	
36	44	FREEDOM TO PARTY - FIRST LEGAL RAVE	
		Various Artists (Trax)	
-	45	LET LOVE RULE	Lenny Kravitz (Virgin America)
48	46	THE BEST OF VAN MORRISON	
		Van Morrison (Polydor)	
31	47	LIVE AND DIRECT	Adamski (MCA)
35	48	LET THEM EAT BINGO	Beats International (Go Beat)
28	49	LOCK UP THE WOLVES	Dio (Vertigo)
43	50	MISSING ... PRESUMED HAVING A GOOD TIME	
		Notting Hillbillies (Vertigo)	

Paula Abdul's *Forever Your Girl*, which had originally charted in 1989, swept back in favour alongside the singer's smash hit single *Opposites Attract*. In the US, this had been one of the biggest-selling debut albums ever released, but Abdul's UK singles success was patchier, with the LP reflecting this. Madonna's *I'm Breathless*, meanwhile, drew its inspiration from her role in the film *Dick Tracy*.

9 June 1990

last week	this week	Title	Artist (Label)
2	1	VOLUME II - 1990 A NEW DECADE	Soul II Soul (10)
-	2	BETWEEN THE LINES	Jason Donovan (PWL)
1	3	I'M BREATHLESS	Madonna (Sire)
4	4	ONLY YESTERDAY	Carpenters (A&M)
3	5	NOW THAT'S WHAT I CALL MUSIC 17	Various Artists (EMI/Virgin/PolyGram)
5	6	THROUGH A BIG COUNTRY - GREATEST HITS	Big Country (Mercury)
6	7	... BUT SERIOUSLY	Phil Collins (Vertigo)
9	8	CLASSIC EXPERIENCE II	Various Artists (EMI)
11	9	COSMIC THING	B-52's (Reprise)
13	10	SOUL PROVIDER	Michael Bolton (CBS)
7	11	LABOUR OF LOVE II	UB40 (DEP International)
14	12	THE ESSENTIAL PAVAROTTI	Luciano Pavarotti (Decca)
12	13	VIVALDI: THE FOUR SEASONS	Nigel Kennedy with the English Chamber Orchestra
39	14	PASSION AND WARFARE	Steve Vai (Food For Thought)
10	15	FOREVER YOUR GIRL	Paula Abdul (Siren)
8	16	HANGIN' TOUGH	New Kids On The Block (CBS)
18	17	STILL GOT THE BLUES	Gary Moore (Virgin)
-	18	THE VERY BEST OF TALK TALK - NATURAL HISTORY	Talk Talk (Parlophone)
26	19	ABSOLUTELY	ABC (Neutron)
20	20	I DO NOT WANT WHAT I HAVEN'T GOT	Sinead O'Connor (Ensign)
17	21	ALANNAH MYLES	Alannah Myles (Atlantic)
19	22	BEHIND THE MASK	Fleetwood Mac (Warner Bros.)
22	23	VIOLATOR	Depeche Mode (Mute)
-	24	GREATEST HITS	Bangles (CBS)
15	25	GET ON THIS!!! 30 DANCE HITS VOLUME 1	Various Artists (Telstar)
48	26	LET THEM EAT BINGO	Beats International (Go Beat)
35	27	GOODBYE JUMBO	World Party (Ensign)
33	28	SIXTIES MIX 3	Various Artists (Stylus)
-	29	NITEFLITE 3 - BEING WITH YOU	Various Artists (Columbia)
-	30	BORN TO SING	En Vogue (Atlantic)
23	31	BRIGADE	Heart (Capitol)
21	32	HEART OF STONE	Cher (Geffen)
29	33	DREAMLAND	Black Box (deConstruction)
37	34	MENDELSOHN VIOLIN CONCERTO IN E MINOR	Nigel Kennedy with Jeffrey Tate & the English Chamber Orchestra
46	35	THE BEST OF VAN MORRISON	Van Morrison (Polydor)
30	36	FOREIGN AFFAIR	Tina Turner (Capitol)
25	37	THE ROAD TO HELL	Chris Rea (WEA)
32	38	CHANGESBOWIE	David Bowie (EMI)
24	39	A POCKETFUL OF DREAMS	Big Fun (Jive)
27	40	LIFE	Inspiral Carpets (Cow)
-	41	CUTS BOTH WAYS	Gloria Estefan (Epic)
-	42	AFFECTION	Lisa Stansfield (Arista)
28	43	JUST THE TWO OF US	Various Artists (Columbia)
16	44	PACKED!	Pretenders (WEA)
-	45	POD	Breeders (4AD)
34	46	APRIL MOON	Sam Brown (A&M)
31	47	TAKE IT TO HEART	Michael McDonald (Reprise)
-	48	WILD!	Erasure (Mute)
-	49	PUMP UP THE JAM	Technotronic (Swanyard)
-	50	HELL TO PAY	Jeff Healey Band (Arista)

16 June 1990

last week	this week	Title	Artist (Label)
1	1	VOLUME II - 1990 A NEW DECADE	Soul II Soul (10)
18	2	THE VERY BEST OF TALK TALK - NATURAL HISTORY	Talk Talk (Parlophone)
3	3	I'M BREATHLESS	Madonna (Sire)
2	4	BETWEEN THE LINES	Jason Donovan (PWL)
24	5	GREATEST HITS	Bangles (CBS)
4	6	ONLY YESTERDAY	Carpenters (A&M)
8	7	CLASSIC EXPERIENCE II	Various Artists (EMI)
-	8	HOME	Hothouse Flowers (London)
7	9	... BUT SERIOUSLY	Phil Collins (Vertigo)
6	10	THROUGH A BIG COUNTRY - GREATEST HITS	Big Country (Mercury)
9	11	COSMIC THING	B-52's (Reprise)
12	12	THE ESSENTIAL PAVAROTTI	Luciano Pavarotti (Decca)
11	13	LABOUR OF LOVE II	UB40 (DEP International)
-	14	OTHER VOICES	Paul Young (CBS)
29	15	NITEFLITE 3 - BEING WITH YOU	Various Artists (Columbia)
10	16	SOUL PROVIDER	Michael Bolton (CBS)
-	17	GOLD MOTHER	James (Fontana)
13	18	VIVALDI: THE FOUR SEASONS	Nigel Kennedy with the English Chamber Orchestra
16	19	HANGIN' TOUGH	New Kids On The Block (CBS)
50	20	HELL TO PAY	Jeff Healey Band (Arista)
5	21	NOW THAT'S WHAT I CALL MUSIC 17	Various Artists (EMI/Virgin/PolyGram)
20	22	I DO NOT WANT WHAT I HAVEN'T GOT	Sinead O'Connor (Ensign)
-	23	ONE WORLD ONE VOICE	Various Artists (Virgin)
45	24	POD	Breeders (4AD)
17	25	STILL GOT THE BLUES	Gary Moore (Virgin)
22	26	BEHIND THE MASK	Fleetwood Mac (Warner Bros.)
15	27	FOREVER YOUR GIRL	Paula Abdul (Siren)
34	28	MENDELSOHN VIOLIN CONCERTO IN E MINOR	Nigel Kennedy with Jeffrey Tate & the English Chamber Orchestra
21	29	ALANNAH MYLES	Alannah Myles (Atlantic)
14	30	PASSION AND WARFARE	Steve Vai (Food For Thought)
-	31	ENCHANTED	Marc Almond (Some Bizzare)
32	32	HEART OF STONE	Cher (Geffen)
19	33	ABSOLUTELY	ABC (Neutron)
27	34	GOODBYE JUMBO	World Party (Ensign)
23	35	VIOLATOR	Depeche Mode (Mute)
36	36	FOREIGN AFFAIR	Tina Turner (Capitol)
-	37	STRAY	Aztec Camera (WEA)
26	38	LET THEM EAT BINGO	Beats International (Go Beat)
31	39	BRIGADE	Heart (Capitol)
33	40	DREAMLAND	Black Box (deConstruction)
35	41	THE BEST OF VAN MORRISON	Van Morrison (Polydor)
40	42	LIFE	Inspiral Carpets (Cow)
25	43	GET ON THIS!!! 30 DANCE HITS VOLUME 1	Various Artists (Telstar)
43	44	JUST THE TWO OF US	Various Artists (Columbia)
28	45	SIXTIES MIX 3	Various Artists (Stylus)
-	46	1234	Propaganda (Virgin)
38	47	CHANGESBOWIE	David Bowie (EMI)
37	48	THE ROAD TO HELL	Chris Rea (WEA)
-	49	PRETTY WOMAN - SOUNDTRACK	Various Artists (EMI USA)
-	50	HEARTS AND FLOWERS	Joan Armatrading (A&M)

23 June 1990

last week	this week	Title	Artist (Label)
1	1	VOLUME II - 1990 A NEW DECADE	Soul II Soul (10)
2	2	THE VERY BEST OF TALK TALK - NATURAL HISTORY	Talk Talk (Parlophone)
12	3	THE ESSENTIAL PAVAROTTI	Luciano Pavarotti (Decca)
4	4	BETWEEN THE LINES	Jason Donovan (PWL)
14	5	OTHER VOICES	Paul Young (CBS)
8	6	HOME	Hothouse Flowers (London)
7	7	CLASSIC EXPERIENCE II	Various Artists (EMI)
3	8	I'M BREATHLESS	Madonna (Sire)
-	9	THE CHIMES	Chimes (CBS)
5	10	GREATEST HITS	Bangles (CBS)
6	11	ONLY YESTERDAY	Carpenters (A&M)
9	12	... BUT SERIOUSLY	Phil Collins (Vertigo)
10	13	THROUGH A BIG COUNTRY - GREATEST HITS	Big Country (Mercury)
19	14	HANGIN' TOUGH	New Kids On The Block (CBS)
15	15	NITEFLITE 3 - BEING WITH YOU	Various Artists (Columbia)
13	16	LABOUR OF LOVE II	UB40 (DEP International)
17	17	GOLD MOTHER	James (Fontana)
11	18	COSMIC THING	B-52's (Reprise)
16	19	SOUL PROVIDER	Michael Bolton (CBS)
-	20	WAITING FOR COUSTEAU	Jean-Michel Jarre (Dreyfus)
37	21	STRAY	Aztec Camera (WEA)
18	22	VIVALDI: THE FOUR SEASONS	Nigel Kennedy with the English Chamber Orchestra
-	23	THE RISE AND FALL OF ZIGGY STARDUST AND THE SPIDERS FROM MARS	David Bowie (EMI)
50	24	HEARTS AND FLOWERS	Joan Armatrading (A&M)
25	25	STILL GOT THE BLUES	Gary Moore (Virgin)
22	26	I DO NOT WANT WHAT I HAVEN'T GOT	Sinead O'Connor (Ensign)
27	27	FOREVER YOUR GIRL	Paula Abdul (Siren)
45	28	SIXTIES MIX 3	Various Artists (Stylus)
34	29	GOODBYE JUMBO	World Party (Ensign)
-	30	SUMMER DREAMS	Beach Boys (Capitol)
-	31	CUTS BOTH WAYS	Gloria Estefan (Epic)
26	32	BEHIND THE MASK	Fleetwood Mac (Warner Bros.)
32	33	HEART OF STONE	Cher (Geffen)
33	34	ABSOLUTELY	ABC (Neutron)
36	35	FOREIGN AFFAIR	Tina Turner (Capitol)
28	36	MENDELSOHN VIOLIN CONCERTO IN E MINOR	Nigel Kennedy with Jeffrey Tate & the English Chamber Orchestra
29	37	ALANNAH MYLES	Alannah Myles (Atlantic)
35	38	VIOLATOR	Depeche Mode (Mute)
21	39	NOW THAT'S WHAT I CALL MUSIC 17	Various Artists (EMI/Virgin/PolyGram)
20	40	HELL TO PAY	Jeff Healey Band (Arista)
-	41	WILD!	Erasure (Mute)
-	42	SLEEPING WITH THE PAST	Elton John (Rocket)
41	43	THE BEST OF VAN MORRISON	Van Morrison (Polydor)
39	44	BRIGADE	Heart (Capitol)
24	45	POD	Breeders (4AD)
30	46	PASSION AND WARFARE	Steve Vai (Food For Thought)
-	47	WAKING HOURS	Del Amitri (A&M)
-	48	THE NORTHERN BEAT	Various Artists (London)
23	49	ONE WORLD ONE VOICE	Various Artists (Virgin)
-	50	THE STONE ROSES	Stone Roses (Silvertone)

As their *Volume II - 1990 A New Decade* hit the chart top, Soul II Soul became the first UK dance/R&B act ever to have two consecutive Number 1 albums. It significantly outsold Jason Donovan's second album *Between The Lines*, which could only eventually muster a fraction of the huge sales of its predecessor, failing to reach Number 1 and only spending just over a month in the Top 10.

June – July 1990

30 June 1990

last week	this week	title	artist
3	1	THE ESSENTIAL PAVAROTTI	Luciano Pavarotti (Decca)
30	2	SUMMER DREAMS	Beach Boys (Capitol)
-	3	STEP BY STEP	New Kids On The Block (CBS)
1	4	VOLUME II - 1990 A NEW DECADE	Soul II Soul (10)
10	5	GREATEST HITS	Bangles (CBS)
2	6	THE VERY BEST OF TALK TALK - NATURAL HISTORY	Talk Talk (Parlophone)
4	7	BETWEEN THE LINES	Jason Donovan (PWL)
7	8	CLASSIC EXPERIENCE II	Various Artists (EMI)
-	9	THE SONGS 1975-1990	Barry Manilow (Arista)
11	10	ONLY YESTERDAY	Carpenters (A&M)
12	11	... BUT SERIOUSLY	Phil Collins (Vertigo)
8	12	I'M BREATHLESS	Madonna (Sire)
13	13	THROUGH A BIG COUNTRY - GREATEST HITS	Big Country (Mercury)
16	14	LABOUR OF LOVE II	UB40 (DEP International)
20	15	WAITING FOR COUSTEAU	Jean-Michel Jarre (Dreyfus)
9	16	THE CHIMES	Chimes (CBS)
-	17	A NIGHT AT THE OPERA	Various Artists (Telstar)
5	18	OTHER VOICES	Paul Young (CBS)
6	19	HOME	Hothouse Flowers (London)
22	20	VIVALDI: THE FOUR SEASONS	Nigel Kennedy with the English Chamber Orchestra
-	21	PRETTY WOMAN - SOUNDTRACK	Various Artists (EMI USA)
19	22	SOUL PROVIDER	Michael Bolton (CBS)
25	23	STILL GOT THE BLUES	Gary Moore (Virgin)
18	24	COSMIC THING	B-52's (Reprise)
35	25	FOREIGN AFFAIR	Tina Turner (Capitol)
36	26	MENDELSOHN VIOLIN CONCERTO IN E MINOR	Nigel Kennedy with Jeffrey Tate & the English Chamber Orchestra
26	27	I DO NOT WANT WHAT I HAVEN'T GOT	Sinead O'Connor (Ensign)
-	28	A NIGHT ON THE TOWN	Bruce Hornsby & the Range (RCA)
15	29	NITEFLITE 3 - BEING WITH YOU	Various Artists (Columbia)
23	30	THE RISE AND FALL OF ZIGGY STARDUST AND THE SPIDERS FROM MARS	David Bowie (EMI)
31	31	CUTS BOTH WAYS	Gloria Estefan (Epic)
42	32	SLEEPING WITH THE PAST	Elton John (Rocket)
17	33	GOLD MOTHER	James (Fontana)
37	34	ALANNAH MYLES	Alannah Myles (Atlantic)
14	35	HANGIN' TOUGH	New Kids On The Block (CBS)
21	36	STRAY	Aztec Camera (WEA)
27	37	FOREVER YOUR GIRL	Paula Abdul (Siren)
-	38	WILSON PHILLIPS	Wilson Phillips (SBK)
-	39	LEATHER AND LACE	Various Artists (Dino)
-	40	THE ROAD TO HELL	Chris Rea (WEA)
32	41	BEHIND THE MASK	Fleetwood Mac (Warner Bros.)
28	42	SIXTIES MIX 3	Various Artists (Stylus)
38	43	VIOLATOR	Depeche Mode (Mute)
-	44	CHANGESBOWIE	David Bowie (EMI)
-	45	THE SAME SKY	Horse (Echo Chamber)
33	46	HEART OF STONE	Cher (Geffen)
29	47	GOODBYE JUMBO	World Party (Ensign)
24	48	HEARTS AND FLOWERS	Joan Armatrading (A&M)
-	49	ONE TRUE PASSION	Revenge (Factory)
44	50	BRIGADE	Heart (Capitol)

7 July 1990

last week	this week	title	artist
3	1	STEP BY STEP	New Kids On The Block (CBS)
1	2	THE ESSENTIAL PAVAROTTI	Luciano Pavarotti (Decca)
2	3	SUMMER DREAMS	Beach Boys (Capitol)
4	4	VOLUME II - 1990 A NEW DECADE	Soul II Soul (10)
6	5	THE VERY BEST OF TALK TALK - NATURAL HISTORY	Talk Talk (Parlophone)
5	6	GREATEST HITS	Bangles (CBS)
9	7	THE SONGS 1975-1990	Barry Manilow (Arista)
38	8	WILSON PHILLIPS	Wilson Phillips (SBK)
9	9	BETWEEN THE LINES	Jason Donovan (PWL)
8	10	CLASSIC EXPERIENCE II	Various Artists (EMI)
21	11	PRETTY WOMAN - SOUNDTRACK	Various Artists (EMI USA)
11	12	... BUT SERIOUSLY	Phil Collins (Vertigo)
10	13	ONLY YESTERDAY	Carpenters (A&M)
13	14	THROUGH A BIG COUNTRY - GREATEST HITS	Big Country (Mercury)
14	15	LABOUR OF LOVE II	UB40 (DEP International)
-	16	REPUTATION	Dusty Springfield (Parlophone)
16	17	THE CHIMES	Chimes (CBS)
20	18	VIVALDI: THE FOUR SEASONS	Nigel Kennedy with the English Chamber Orchestra
-	19	HOT ROCKS 1964-1971	Rolling Stones (London)
12	20	I'M BREATHLESS	Madonna (Sire)
28	21	A NIGHT ON THE TOWN	Bruce Hornsby & the Range (RCA)
-	22	DEEP HEAT 7 - SEVENTH HEAVEN	Various Artists (Telstar)
18	23	OTHER VOICES	Paul Young (CBS)
32	24	SLEEPING WITH THE PAST	Elton John (Rocket)
15	25	WAITING FOR COUSTEAU	Jean-Michel Jarre (Dreyfus)
-	26	GOO	Sonic Youth (DGC)
31	27	CUTS BOTH WAYS	Gloria Estefan (Epic)
17	28	A NIGHT AT THE OPERA	Various Artists (Telstar)
25	29	FOREIGN AFFAIR	Tina Turner (Capitol)
19	30	HOME	Hothouse Flowers (London)
22	31	SOUL PROVIDER	Michael Bolton (CBS)
-	32	WILD!	Erasure (Mute)
23	33	STILL GOT THE BLUES	Gary Moore (Virgin)
39	34	LEATHER AND LACE	Various Artists (Dino)
34	35	ALANNAH MYLES	Alannah Myles (Atlantic)
24	36	COSMIC THING	B-52's (Reprise)
27	37	I DO NOT WANT WHAT I HAVEN'T GOT	Sinead O'Connor (Ensign)
40	38	THE ROAD TO HELL	Chris Rea (WEA)
-	39	WORLD POWER	Snap (Arista)
26	40	MENDELSOHN VIOLIN CONCERTO IN E MINOR	Nigel Kennedy with Jeffrey Tate & the English Chamber Orchestra
-	41	THE HARD WAY	Steve Earle & the Dukes (MCA)
30	42	THE RISE AND FALL OF ZIGGY STARDUST AND THE SPIDERS FROM MARS	David Bowie (EMI)
35	43	HANGIN' TOUGH	New Kids On The Block (CBS)
41	44	BEHIND THE MASK	Fleetwood Mac (Warner Bros.)
47	45	GOODBYE JUMBO	World Party (Ensign)
-	46	THE STONE ROSES	Stone Roses (Silvertone)
36	47	STRAY	Aztec Camera (WEA)
29	48	NITEFLITE 3 - BEING WITH YOU	Various Artists (Columbia)
43	49	VIOLATOR	Depeche Mode (Mute)
37	50	FOREVER YOUR GIRL	Paula Abdul (Siren)

14 July 1990

last week	this week	title	artist
2	1	THE ESSENTIAL PAVAROTTI	Luciano Pavarotti (Decca)
19	2	HOT ROCKS 1964-1971	Rolling Stones (London)
24	3	SLEEPING WITH THE PAST	Elton John (Rocket)
3	4	SUMMER DREAMS	Beach Boys (Capitol)
1	5	STEP BY STEP	New Kids On The Block (CBS)
22	6	DEEP HEAT 7 - SEVENTH HEAVEN	Various Artists (Telstar)
4	7	VOLUME II - 1990 A NEW DECADE	Soul II Soul (10)
6	8	GREATEST HITS	Bangles (CBS)
11	9	PRETTY WOMAN - SOUNDTRACK	Various Artists (EMI USA)
-	10	COMPOSITIONS	Anita Baker (Elektra)
8	11	WILSON PHILLIPS	Wilson Phillips (SBK)
5	12	THE VERY BEST OF TALK TALK - NATURAL HISTORY	Talk Talk (Parlophone)
12	13	... BUT SERIOUSLY	Phil Collins (Vertigo)
20	14	I'M BREATHLESS	Madonna (Sire)
9	15	BETWEEN THE LINES	Jason Donovan (PWL)
16	16	REPUTATION	Dusty Springfield (Parlophone)
7	17	THE SONGS 1975-1990	Barry Manilow (Arista)
13	18	ONLY YESTERDAY	Carpenters (A&M)
41	19	THE HARD WAY	Steve Earle & the Dukes (MCA)
14	20	THROUGH A BIG COUNTRY - GREATEST HITS	Big Country (Mercury)
15	21	LABOUR OF LOVE II	UB40 (DEP International)
18	22	VIVALDI: THE FOUR SEASONS	Nigel Kennedy with the English Chamber Orchestra
10	23	CLASSIC EXPERIENCE II	Various Artists (EMI)
17	24	THE CHIMES	Chimes (CBS)
33	25	STILL GOT THE BLUES	Gary Moore (Virgin)
36	26	COSMIC THING	B-52's (Reprise)
23	27	OTHER VOICES	Paul Young (CBS)
26	28	GOO	Sonic Youth (DGC)
27	29	CUTS BOTH WAYS	Gloria Estefan (Epic)
30	30	HOME	Hothouse Flowers (London)
45	31	GOODBYE JUMBO	World Party (Ensign)
21	32	A NIGHT ON THE TOWN	Bruce Hornsby & the Range (RCA)
-	33	WAKING HOURS	Del Amitri (A&M)
31	34	SOUL PROVIDER	Michael Bolton (CBS)
-	35	BONAFIDE	Maxi Priest (10)
37	36	I DO NOT WANT WHAT I HAVEN'T GOT	Sinead O'Connor (Ensign)
-	37	STEEL WHEELS	Rolling Stones (CBS)
25	38	WAITING FOR COUSTEAU	Jean-Michel Jarre (Dreyfus)
32	39	WILD!	Erasure (Mute)
-	40	LIFE	Inspiral Carpets (Cow)
49	41	VIOLATOR	Depeche Mode (Mute)
-	42	THE NORTHERN BEAT	Various Artists (London)
38	43	THE ROAD TO HELL	Chris Rea (WEA)
44	44	BEHIND THE MASK	Fleetwood Mac (Warner Bros.)
29	45	FOREIGN AFFAIR	Tina Turner (Capitol)
35	46	ALANNAH MYLES	Alannah Myles (Atlantic)
-	47	SMASH HITS - RAVE!	Various Artists (Dover)
46	48	THE STONE ROSES	Stone Roses (Silvertone)
-	49	PUMP UP THE JAM	Technotronic (Swanyard)
39	50	WORLD POWER	Snap (Arista)

As World Cup fever hit much of the world, the greatest non-footballing beneficiary was Luciano Pavarotti, one of the world's greatest tenors, whose recording of Puccini's *Nessun Dorma* was chosen as the theme to the BBC's coverage of the tournament from Italy. His compilation album *The Essential Pavarotti*, including the aria, became, historically, the first ever classical album to top the UK chart.

21 July 1990

last week	this week	title	artist
1	1	THE ESSENTIAL PAVAROTTI	Luciano Pavarotti (Decca)
3	2	SLEEPING WITH THE PAST	Elton John (Rocket)
2	3	HOT ROCKS 1964-1971	Rolling Stones (London)
-	4	FLESH AND BLOOD	Poison (Enigma)
10	5	COMPOSITIONS	Anita Baker (Elektra)
9	6	PRETTY WOMAN - SOUNDTRACK	Various Artists (EMI USA)
47	7	SMASH HITS - RAVE!	Various Artists (Dover)
4	8	SUMMER DREAMS	Beach Boys (Capitol)
5	9	STEP BY STEP	New Kids On The Block (CBS)
12	10	THE VERY BEST OF TALK TALK - NATURAL HISTORY	Talk Talk (Parlophone)
8	11	GREATEST HITS	Bangles (CBS)
13	12	... BUT SERIOUSLY	Phil Collins (Vertigo)
35	13	BONAFIDE	Maxi Priest (10)
15	14	BETWEEN THE LINES	Jason Donovan (PWL)
7	15	VOLUME II - 1990 A NEW DECADE	Soul II Soul (10)
14	16	I'M BREATHLESS	Madonna (Sire)
22	17	VIVALDI: THE FOUR SEASONS	Nigel Kennedy with the English Chamber Orchestra
6	18	DEEP HEAT 7 - SEVENTH HEAVEN	Various Artists (Telstar)
17	19	THE SONGS 1975-1990	Barry Manilow (Arista)
37	20	STEEL WHEELS	Rolling Stones (CBS)
11	21	WILSON PHILLIPS	Wilson Phillips (SBK)
-	22	GOODNIGHT L.A.	Magnum (Polydor)
18	23	ONLY YESTERDAY	Carpenters (A&M)
34	24	SOUL PROVIDER	Michael Bolton (CBS)
21	25	LABOUR OF LOVE II	UB40 (DEP International)
36	26	I DO NOT WANT WHAT I HAVEN'T GOT	Sinead O'Connor (Ensign)
-	27	THE ULTIMATE '60S COLLECTION	Various Artists (Castle Communications)
20	28	THROUGH A BIG COUNTRY - GREATEST HITS	Big Country (Mercury)
-	29	DANCE THIS MESS AROUND (BEST OF THE B52'S)	B-52's (Island)
50	30	WORLD POWER	Snap (Arista)
29	31	CUTS BOTH WAYS	Gloria Estefan (Epic)
-	32	ARE YOU OKAY?	Was (Not Was) (Fontana)
16	33	REPUTATION	Dusty Springfield (Parlophone)
45	34	FOREIGN AFFAIR	Tina Turner (Capitol)
26	35	COSMIC THING	B-52's (Reprise)
25	36	STILL GOT THE BLUES	Gary Moore (Virgin)
48	37	THE STONE ROSES	Stone Roses (Silvertone)
19	38	THE HARD WAY	Steve Earle & the Dukes (MCA)
49	39	PUMP UP THE JAM	Technotronic (Swanyard)
39	40	WILD!	Erasure (Mute)
27	41	OTHER VOICES	Paul Young (CBS)
-	42	CRAIG MCLACHLAN AND CHECK 1-2	Craig McLachlan & Check 1-2 (Epic)
33	43	WAKING HOURS	Del Amitri (A&M)
41	44	VIOLATOR	Depeche Mode (Mute)
-	45	CHANGESBOWIE	David Bowie (EMI)
30	46	HOME	Hothouse Flowers (London)
24	47	THE CHIMES	Chimes (CBS)
32	48	A NIGHT ON THE TOWN	Bruce Hornsby & the Range (RCA)
23	49	CLASSIC EXPERIENCE II	Various Artists (EMI)
-	50	BRICK BY BRICK	Iggy Pop (Virgin America)

28 July 1990

2	1	SLEEPING WITH THE PAST	Elton John (Rocket)
1	2	THE ESSENTIAL PAVAROTTI	Luciano Pavarotti (Decca)
3	3	HOT ROCKS 1964-1971	Rolling Stones (London)
4	4	FLESH AND BLOOD	Poison (Enigma)
6	5	PRETTY WOMAN - SOUNDTRACK	Various Artists (EMI USA)
16	6	I'M BREATHLESS	Madonna (Sire)
8	7	SUMMER DREAMS	Beach Boys (Capitol)
7	8	SMASH HITS - RAVE!	Various Artists (Dover)
12	9	... BUT SERIOUSLY	Phil Collins (Vertigo)
-	10	NOW DANCE 902	Various Artists (EMI/Virgin/PolyGram)
5	11	COMPOSITIONS	Anita Baker (Elektra)
9	12	STEP BY STEP	New Kids On The Block (CBS)
22	13	GOODNIGHT L.A.	Magnum (Polydor)
14	14	BETWEEN THE LINES	Jason Donovan (PWL)
11	15	GREATEST HITS	Bangles (CBS)
10	16	THE VERY BEST OF TALK TALK - NATURAL HISTORY	Talk Talk (Parlophone)
18	17	DEEP HEAT 7 - SEVENTH HEAVEN	Various Artists (Telstar)
26	18	I DO NOT WANT WHAT I HAVEN'T GOT	Sinead O'Connor (Ensign)
15	19	VOLUME II - 1990 A NEW DECADE	Soul II Soul (10)
28	20	THROUGH A BIG COUNTRY - GREATEST HITS	Big Country (Mercury)
42	21	CRAIG MCLACHLAN AND CHECK 1-2	Craig McLachlan & Check 1-2 (Epic)
23	22	ONLY YESTERDAY	Carpenters (A&M)
24	23	SOUL PROVIDER	Michael Bolton (CBS)
20	24	STEEL WHEELS	Rolling Stones (CBS)
-	25	PLEASE HAMMER DON'T HURT 'EM	MC Hammer (Capitol)
21	26	WILSON PHILLIPS	Wilson Phillips (SBK)
37	27	THE STONE ROSES	Stone Roses (Silvertone)
33	28	REPUTATION	Dusty Springfield (Parlophone)
13	29	BONAFIDE	Maxi Priest (10)
-	30	TEENAGE NINJA MUTANT TURTLES - SOUNDTRACK	Various Artists (SBK)
17	31	VIVALDI: THE FOUR SEASONS	Nigel Kennedy with the English Chamber Orchestra
-	32	ALADDIN SANE	David Bowie (EMI)
41	33	OTHER VOICES	Paul Young (CBS)
25	34	LABOUR OF LOVE II	UB40 (DEP International)
32	35	ARE YOU OKAY?	Was (Not Was) (Fontana)
19	36	THE SONGS 1975-1990	Barry Manilow (Arista)
30	37	WORLD POWER	Snap (Arista)
34	38	FOREIGN AFFAIR	Tina Turner (Capitol)
46	39	HOME	Hothouse Flowers (London)
27	40	THE ULTIMATE '60S COLLECTION	Various Artists (Castle Communications)
-	41	PIN UPS	David Bowie (EMI)
39	42	PUMP UP THE JAM	Technotronic (Swanyard)
31	43	CUTS BOTH WAYS	Gloria Estefan (Epic)
48	44	A NIGHT ON THE TOWN	Bruce Hornsby & the Range (RCA)
40	45	WILD!	Erasure (Mute)
35	46	COSMIC THING	B-52's (Reprise)
-	47	LIKE A PRAYER	Madonna (Sire)
36	48	STILL GOT THE BLUES	Gary Moore (Virgin)
47	49	THE CHIMES	Chimes (CBS)
38	50	THE HARD WAY	Steve Earle & the Dukes (MCA)

4 August 1990

10	1	NOW DANCE 902	Various Artists (EMI/Virgin/PolyGram)
1	2	SLEEPING WITH THE PAST	Elton John (Rocket)
6	3	I'M BREATHLESS	Madonna (Sire)
2	4	THE ESSENTIAL PAVAROTTI	Luciano Pavarotti (Decca)
7	5	SUMMER DREAMS	Beach Boys (Capitol)
5	6	PRETTY WOMAN - SOUNDTRACK	Various Artists (EMI USA)
3	7	HOT ROCKS 1964-1971	Rolling Stones (London)
9	8	... BUT SERIOUSLY	Phil Collins (Vertigo)
15	9	GREATEST HITS	Bangles (CBS)
4	10	FLESH AND BLOOD	Poison (Enigma)
19	11	VOLUME II - 1990 A NEW DECADE	Soul II Soul (10)
12	12	STEP BY STEP	New Kids On The Block (CBS)
14	13	BETWEEN THE LINES	Jason Donovan (PWL)
21	14	CRAIG MCLACHLAN AND CHECK 1-2	Craig McLachlan & Check 1-2 (Epic)
18	15	I DO NOT WANT WHAT I HAVEN'T GOT	Sinead O'Connor (Ensign)
8	16	SMASH HITS - RAVE!	Various Artists (Dover)
20	17	THROUGH A BIG COUNTRY - GREATEST HITS	Big Country (Mercury)
25	18	PLEASE HAMMER DON'T HURT 'EM	MC Hammer (Capitol)
22	19	ONLY YESTERDAY	Carpenters (A&M)
16	20	THE VERY BEST OF TALK TALK - NATURAL HISTORY	Talk Talk (Parlophone)
30	21	TEENAGE NINJA MUTANT TURTLES - SOUNDTRACK	Various Artists (SBK)
11	22	COMPOSITIONS	Anita Baker (Elektra)
34	23	LABOUR OF LOVE II	UB40 (DEP International)
23	24	SOUL PROVIDER	Michael Bolton (CBS)
-	25	EROICA	Wendy & Lisa (Virgin)
29	26	BONAFIDE	Maxi Priest (10)
-	27	WAKING HOURS	Del Amitri (A&M)
37	28	WORLD POWER	Snap (Arista)
-	29	HEART & SOUL III - HEART FULL OF SOUL	Various Artists (Heart & Soul)
39	30	HOME	Hothouse Flowers (London)
26	31	WILSON PHILLIPS	Wilson Phillips (SBK)
13	32	GOODNIGHT L.A.	Magnum (Polydor)
31	33	VIVALDI: THE FOUR SEASONS	Nigel Kennedy with the English Chamber Orchestra
33	34	OTHER VOICES	Paul Young (CBS)
27	35	THE STONE ROSES	Stone Roses (Silvertone)
36	36	THE SONGS 1975-1990	Barry Manilow (Arista)
-	37	THE VEGETARIANS OF LOVE	Bob Geldof (Mercury)
24	38	STEEL WHEELS	Rolling Stones (CBS)
28	39	REPUTATION	Dusty Springfield (Parlophone)
-	40	ARMCHAIR THEATRE	Jeff Lynne (Reprise)
38	41	FOREIGN AFFAIR	Tina Turner (Capitol)
42	42	PUMP UP THE JAM	Technotronic (Swanyard)
17	43	DEEP HEAT 7 - SEVENTH HEAVEN	Various Artists (Telstar)
40	44	THE ULTIMATE '60S COLLECTION	Various Artists (Castle Communications)
48	45	STILL GOT THE BLUES	Gary Moore (Virgin)
49	46	THE CHIMES	Chimes (CBS)
-	47	THE WILD ONE	Various Artists (EMI)
43	48	CUTS BOTH WAYS	Gloria Estefan (Epic)
-	49	JUST THE TWO OF US	Various Artists (Columbia)
45	50	WILD!	Erasure (Mute)

Elton John, whose single *Sacrifice* prevented Pavarotti's *Nessun Dorma* from giving him an historic double Number 1 in both album and singles charts, coincidentally also removed the Italian from the Number 1 album slot with *Sleeping In The Past* - although this too quickly surrendered the summit, being replaced by the second volume of EMI/Virgin's newly-inaugurated *Now Dance 90* compilation series.

August 1990

The chart-topping Knebworth compilation album consisted of live recordings of some of the biggest names from over 30 years of UK recording history, all captured at the Silver Clef Award Winners Show, in aid of the Music Therapy charity, at Knebworth Park. Participants in the show and album included Phil Collins, Dire Straits, Elton John, Eric Clapton, Paul McCartney, Pink Floyd and Cliff & the Shadows.

1 September 1990

last week	this	Title	Artist (Label)
-	1	MUSIC FROM GRAFFITI BRIDGE	Prince (Paisley Park)
2	2	SLEEPING WITH THE PAST	Elton John (Rocket)
10	3	BLAZE OF GLORY/YOUNG GUNS II	Jon Bon Jovi (Vertigo)
6	4	BOSSANOVA	Pixies (4AD)
1	5	KNEBWORTH - THE ALBUM	Various (Polydor)
3	6	SNAP IT UP - MONSTER HITS 2	Various Artists (CBS/WEA/BMG)
4	7	MEGABASS	Various Artists (Telstar)
9	8	STEP BY STEP	New Kids On The Block (CBS)
-	9	IN CONCERT	Luciano Pavarotti, Placido Domingo & José Carreras (Decca)
8	10	... BUT SERIOUSLY	Phil Collins (Vertigo)
-	11	LIBERTY	Duran Duran (Parlophone)
5	12	THE ESSENTIAL PAVAROTTI	Luciano Pavarotti (Decca)
20	13	WILSON PHILLIPS	Wilson Phillips (SBK)
12	14	SUMMER DREAMS	Beach Boys (Capitol)
16	15	FOREIGN AFFAIR	Tina Turner (Capitol)
36	16	SOUL PROVIDER	Michael Bolton (CBS)
24	17	LOOK SHARP!	Roxette (EMI)
11	18	LOVEGOD	Soup Dragons (Raw TV)
7	19	NOW DANCE 902	Various Artists (EMI/Virgin/PolyGram)
14	20	I'M BREATHLESS	Madonna (Sire)
13	21	PRETTY WOMAN - SOUNDTRACK	Various Artists (EMI USA)
18	22	PLEASE HAMMER DON'T HURT 'EM	MC Hammer (Capitol)
15	23	HOT ROCKS 1964-1971	Rolling Stones (London)
19	24	LABOUR OF LOVE II	UB40 (DEP International)
21	25	GREATEST HITS	Bangles (CBS)
38	26	ONLY YESTERDAY	Carpenters (A&M)
-	27	TYR	Black Sabbath (IRS)
17	28	HOME	Hothouse Flowers (London)
30	29	SAXUALITY	Candy Dulfer (RCA)
27	30	PUMP UP THE JAM	Technotronic (Swanyard)
35	31	GET ON THIS!!! 2	Various Artists (Telstar)
46	32	SAY SOMETHING GOOD	River City People (EMI)
23	33	CRAIG MCLACHLAN AND CHECK 1-2	Craig McLachlan & Check 1-2 (Epic)
28	34	FLESH AND BLOOD	Poison (Enigma)
31	35	VIVALDI: THE FOUR SEASONS	Nigel Kennedy with the English Chamber Orchestra
33	36	VOLUME II - 1990 A NEW DECADE	Soul II Soul (10)
34	37	THE VERY BEST OF TALK TALK - NATURAL HISTORY	Talk Talk (Parlophone)
39	38	CHANGESONEBOWIE	David Bowie (EMI)
43	39	HEART OF STONE	Cher (Geffen)
29	40	TEENAGE NINJA MUTANT TURTLES - SOUNDTRACK	Various Artists (SBK)
47	41	THE STONE ROSES	Stone Roses (Silvertone)
32	42	I DO NOT WANT WHAT I HAVEN'T GOT	Sinead O'Connor (Ensign)
26	43	REV IT UP	Vixen (EMI USA)
40	44	COMPOSITIONS	Anita Baker (Elektra)
37	45	BETWEEN THE LINES	Jason Donovan (PWL)
22	46	HEART & SOUL III - HEART FULL OF SOUL	Various Artists (Heart & Soul)
-	47	THE VEGETARIANS OF LOVE	Bob Geldof (Mercury)
42	48	THE HUNGER	Michael Bolton (CBS)
25	49	BROTHER'S KEEPER	Neville Brothers (A&M)
41	50	THROUGH A BIG COUNTRY - GREATEST HITS	Big Country (Mercury)

8 September 1990

last	this	Title	Artist (Label)
1	1	MUSIC FROM GRAFFITI BRIDGE	Prince (Paisley Park)
9	2	IN CONCERT	Luciano Pavarotti, Placido Domingo & José Carreras (Decca)
2	3	SLEEPING WITH THE PAST	Elton John (Rocket)
7	4	MEGABASS	Various Artists (Telstar)
16	5	SOUL PROVIDER	Michael Bolton (CBS)
3	6	BLAZE OF GLORY/YOUNG GUNS II	Jon Bon Jovi (Vertigo)
17	7	LOOK SHARP!	Roxette (EMI)
-	8	PERSISTENCE OF TIME	Anthrax (Island)
8	9	STEP BY STEP	New Kids On The Block (CBS)
-	10	JORDAN: THE COMEBACK	Prefab Sprout (Kitchenware)
10	11	... BUT SERIOUSLY	Phil Collins (Vertigo)
4	12	BOSSANOVA	Pixies (4AD)
31	13	GET ON THIS!!! 2	Various Artists (Telstar)
11	14	LIBERTY	Duran Duran (Parlophone)
14	15	SUMMER DREAMS	Beach Boys (Capitol)
20	16	I'M BREATHLESS	Madonna (Sire)
13	17	WILSON PHILLIPS	Wilson Phillips (SBK)
12	18	THE ESSENTIAL PAVAROTTI	Luciano Pavarotti (Decca)
6	19	SNAP IT UP - MONSTER HITS 2	Various Artists (CBS/WEA/BMG)
22	20	PLEASE HAMMER DON'T HURT 'EM	MC Hammer (Capitol)
15	21	FOREIGN AFFAIR	Tina Turner (Capitol)
-	22	JUST THE TWO OF US	Various Artists (Columbia)
18	23	LOVEGOD	Soup Dragons (Raw TV)
34	24	FLESH AND BLOOD	Poison (Enigma)
5	25	KNEBWORTH - THE ALBUM	Various Artists (Polydor)
21	26	PRETTY WOMAN - SOUNDTRACK	Various Artists (EMI USA)
25	27	GREATEST HITS	Bangles (CBS)
28	28	HOME	Hothouse Flowers (London)
37	29	THE VERY BEST OF TALK TALK - NATURAL HISTORY	Talk Talk (Parlophone)
24	30	LABOUR OF LOVE II	UB40 (DEP International)
19	31	NOW DANCE 902	Various (EMI/Virgin/PolyGram)
-	32	BONAFIDE	Maxi Priest (10)
23	33	HOT ROCKS 1964-1971	Rolling Stones (London)
26	34	ONLY YESTERDAY	Carpenters (A&M)
29	35	SAXUALITY	Candy Dulfer (RCA)
-	36	WORLD CLIQUE	Deee-Lite (Elektra)
35	37	VIVALDI: THE FOUR SEASONS	Nigel Kennedy with the English Chamber Orchestra
30	38	PUMP UP THE JAM	Technotronic (Swanyard)
33	39	CRAIG MCLACHLAN AND CHECK 1-2	Craig McLachlan & Check 1-2 (Epic)
41	40	THE STONE ROSES	Stone Roses (Silvertone)
-	41	POISON	Bell Biv Devoe (MCA)
45	42	BETWEEN THE LINES	Jason Donovan (PWL)
42	43	I DO NOT WANT WHAT I HAVEN'T GOT	Sinead O'Connor (Ensign)
36	44	VOLUME II - 1990 A NEW DECADE	Soul II Soul (10)
32	45	SAY SOMETHING GOOD	River City People (EMI)
-	46	WHEN THE WORLD KNOWS YOUR NAME	Deacon Blue (CBS)
-	47	BACK STREET SYMPHONY	Thunder (EMI)
39	48	HEART OF STONE	Cher (Geffen)
38	49	CHANGESONEBOWIE	David Bowie (EMI)
-	50	RITUAL DE LO HABITUAL	Jane's Addiction (Warner Bros.)

15 September 1990

last	this	Title	Artist (Label)
-	1	LISTEN WITHOUT PREJUDICE VOLUME 1	George Michael (Epic)
2	2	IN CONCERT	Luciano Pavarotti, Placido Domingo & José Carreras (Decca)
1	3	MUSIC FROM GRAFFITI BRIDGE	Prince (Paisley Park)
5	4	SOUL PROVIDER	Michael Bolton (CBS)
3	5	SLEEPING WITH THE PAST	Elton John (Rocket)
6	6	BLAZE OF GLORY/YOUNG GUNS II	Jon Bon Jovi (Vertigo)
10	7	JORDAN: THE COMEBACK	Prefab Sprout (Kitchenware)
4	8	MEGABASS	Various Artists (Telstar)
7	9	LOOK SHARP!	Roxette (EMI)
9	10	STEP BY STEP	New Kids On The Block (CBS)
11	11	... BUT SERIOUSLY	Phil Collins (Vertigo)
17	12	WILSON PHILLIPS	Wilson Phillips (SBK)
8	13	PERSISTENCE OF TIME	Anthrax (Island)
36	14	WORLD CLIQUE	Deee-Lite (Elektra)
21	15	FOREIGN AFFAIR	Tina Turner (Capitol)
12	16	BOSSANOVA	Pixies (4AD)
15	17	SUMMER DREAMS	Beach Boys (Capitol)
26	18	PRETTY WOMAN - SOUNDTRACK	Various Artists (EMI USA)
-	19	MARIAH CAREY	Mariah Carey (CBS)
13	20	GET ON THIS!!! 2	Various Artists (Telstar)
22	21	JUST THE TWO OF US	Various Artists (Columbia)
16	22	I'M BREATHLESS	Madonna (Sire)
18	23	THE ESSENTIAL PAVAROTTI	Luciano Pavarotti (Decca)
23	24	LOVEGOD	Soup Dragons (Raw TV)
20	25	PLEASE HAMMER DON'T HURT 'EM	MC Hammer (Capitol)
27	26	GREATEST HITS	Bangles (CBS)
29	27	THE VERY BEST OF TALK TALK - NATURAL HISTORY	Talk Talk (Parlophone)
-	28	TIME'S UP	Living Colour (Epic)
34	29	ONLY YESTERDAY	Carpenters (A&M)
28	30	HOME	Hothouse Flowers (London)
30	31	LABOUR OF LOVE II	UB40 (DEP International)
24	32	FLESH AND BLOOD	Poison (Enigma)
14	33	LIBERTY	Duran Duran (Parlophone)
33	34	HOT ROCKS 1964-1971	Rolling Stones (London)
25	35	KNEBWORTH - THE ALBUM	Various (Polydor)
44	36	VOLUME II - 1990 A NEW DECADE	Soul II Soul (10)
35	37	SAXUALITY	Candy Dulfer (RCA)
-	38	THE REAL THING	Faith No More (Slash)
32	39	BONAFIDE	Maxi Priest (10)
19	40	SNAP IT UP - MONSTER HITS 2	Various Artists (CBS/WEA/BMG)
-	41	45 84 89 (A-SIDES)	Fall (Beggars Banquet)
37	42	VIVALDI: THE FOUR SEASONS	Nigel Kennedy with the English Chamber Orchestra
50	43	RITUAL DE LO HABITUAL	Jane's Addiction (Warner Bros.)
31	44	NOW DANCE 902	Various (EMI/Virgin/PolyGram)
-	45	WORLD POWER	Snap (Arista)
-	46	JANET JACKSON'S RHYTHM NATION 1814	Janet Jackson (A&M)
38	47	PUMP UP THE JAM	Technotronic (Swanyard)
43	48	I DO NOT WANT WHAT I HAVEN'T GOT	Sinead O'Connor (Ensign)
-	49	CUTS BOTH WAYS	Gloria Estefan (Epic)
-	50	HARMONY OF CORRUPTION	Napalm Death (Earache)

Prince's fourth soundtrack album from his own movie *Graffiti Bridge*, became his second such release to top the chart, following *Batman* the previous year. Another act whose success was fuelled by a film was Jon Bon Jovi, who worked as a soloist on *Blaze Of Glory*, which contained the soundtrack songs from the western *Young Guns II*. George Michael returned with his first album for three years.

September – October 1990

Listen Without Prejudice Volume 1 was, as its title suggested, designed as the first part of a longer project, and George Michael originally intimated that *Volume 2* would be following hot on its heels. These plans were clearly drastically changed somewhere along the line, since the follow-up is still awaited in 1993, and Michael has turned his attention to suing his record company instead.

13 October 1990

last week	this week	Title / Artist (Label)
-	1	NO PRAYER FOR THE DYING Iron Maiden (EMI)
1	2	X INXS (Mercury)
2	3	IN CONCERT Luciano Pavarotti, Placido Domingo & José Carreras (Decca)
3	4	LISTEN WITHOUT PREJUDICE VOLUME 1 George Michael (Epic)
4	5	THE RAZOR'S EDGE AC/DC (Atco)
14	6	SOUL PROVIDER Michael Bolton (CBS)
9	7	SLEEPING WITH THE PAST Elton John (Rocket)
5	8	OOH LAS VEGAS Deacon Blue (CBS)
-	9	HELL'S DITCH Pogues (Pogue Mahone)
-	10	THAT LOVING FEELING VOL. 3 Various Artists (Dino)
11	11	RUST IN PEACE Megadeth (Capitol)
6	12	ROOM TO ROAM Waterboys (Ensign)
8	13	SLAMMIN' Various Artists (A&M)
12	14	MARIAH CAREY Mariah Carey (CBS)
10	15	BOOMANIA Betty Boo (Rhythm King)
17	16	... BUT SERIOUSLY Phil Collins (Vertigo)
-	17	DOCTOR ADAMSKI'S MUSICAL PHARMACY Adamski (MCA)
13	18	FOREIGN AFFAIR Tina Turner (Capitol)
15	19	LOOK SHARP! Roxette (EMI)
22	20	SEASONS IN THE ABYSS Slayer (Def American)
7	21	HEAVEN OR LAS VEGAS Cocteau Twins (4AD)
-	22	WE ARE IN LOVE Harry Connick Jr. (CBS)
19	23	WILSON PHILLIPS Wilson Phillips (SBK)
23	24	LOOK HOW LONG Loose Ends (10)
20	25	STEPPING OUT - THE VERY BEST OF JOE JACKSON Joe Jackson (A&M)
25	26	JORDAN: THE COMEBACK Prefab Sprout (Kitchenware)
29	27	ELIZIUM Fields Of The Nephilim (Beggars Banquet)
18	28	JUST SEVENTEEN - GET KICKIN' Various Artists (Dover)
16	29	UNDER THE RED SKY Bob Dylan (CBS)
26	30	WORLD CLIQUE Deee-Lite (Elektra)
-	31	THE BEST OF 1968-1973 Steve Miller Band (Capitol)
27	32	STEP BY STEP New Kids On The Block (CBS)
-	33	THE LA'S La's (Go! Discs)
38	34	PLEASE HAMMER DON'T HURT 'EM MC Hammer (Capitol)
30	35	THE VERY BEST OF TALK TALK - NATURAL HISTORY Talk Talk (Parlophone)
24	36	IMPURITY New Model Army (EMI)
-	37	UK BLAK Caron Wheeler (RCA)
21	38	MIDNIGHT STROLL Robert Cray Band (Mercury)
37	39	BLAZE OF GLORY/YOUNG GUNS II Jon Bon Jovi (Vertigo)
31	40	HIGH ON EMOTION - LIVE FROM DUBLIN Chris De Burgh (A&M)
33	41	DAYS OF THUNDER - SOUNDTRACK Various Artists (Epic)
45	42	JUST THE TWO OF US Various Artists (Columbia)
35	43	BETWEEN THE LINES Jason Donovan (PWL)
39	44	ONLY YESTERDAY Carpenters (A&M)
-	45	JANET JACKSON'S RHYTHM NATION 1814 Janet Jackson (A&M)
32	46	RAGGED GLORY Neil Young & Crazy Horse (Reprise)
43	47	LABOUR OF LOVE II UB40 (DEP International)
-	48	PUMP UP THE JAM Technotronic (Swanyard)
40	49	MUSIC FROM GRAFFITI BRIDGE Prince (Paisley Park)
-	50	THE NORTH AT ITS HEIGHTS MC Tunes (ZTT)

20 October 1990

last week	this week	Title / Artist (Label)
3	1	IN CONCERT Luciano Pavarotti Placido Domingo & José Carreras (Decca)
1	2	NO PRAYER FOR THE DYING Iron Maiden (EMI)
-	3	SOME FRIENDLY Charlatans (Situation Two)
2	4	X INXS (Mercury)
4	5	LISTEN WITHOUT PREJUDICE VOLUME 1 George Michael (Epic)
6	6	SOUL PROVIDER Michael Bolton (CBS)
7	7	SLEEPING WITH THE PAST Elton John (Rocket)
17	8	DOCTOR ADAMSKI'S MUSICAL PHARMACY Adamski (MCA)
10	9	THAT LOVING FEELING VOL. 3 Various Artists (Dino)
-	10	ENLIGHTENMENT Van Morrison (Polydor)
8	11	OOH LAS VEGAS Deacon Blue (CBS)
9	12	HELL'S DITCH Pogues (Pogue Mahone)
5	13	THE RAZOR'S EDGE AC/DC (Atco)
34	14	PLEASE HAMMER DON'T HURT 'EM MC Hammer (Capitol)
18	15	FOREIGN AFFAIR Tina Turner (Capitol)
16	16	... BUT SERIOUSLY Phil Collins (Vertigo)
14	17	MARIAH CAREY Mariah Carey (CBS)
-	18	ROCKING ALL OVER THE YEARS Status Quo (Vertigo)
37	19	UK BLAK Caron Wheeler (RCA)
-	20	REFLECTION Shadows (Roll Over)
-	21	SOUL DECADE: THE SIXTIES Various Artists (Motown)
15	22	BOOMANIA Betty Boo (Rhythm King)
22	23	WE ARE IN LOVE Harry Connick Jr. (CBS)
12	24	ROOM TO ROAM Waterboys (Ensign)
45	25	JANET JACKSON'S RHYTHM NATION 1814 Janet Jackson (A&M)
42	26	JUST THE TWO OF US Various Artists (Columbia)
19	27	LOOK SHARP! Roxette (EMI)
23	28	WILSON PHILLIPS Wilson Phillips (SBK)
26	29	JORDAN: THE COMEBACK Prefab Sprout (Kitchenware)
-	30	DOWN TO EARTH Monie Love (Cooltempo)
32	31	STEP BY STEP New Kids On The Block (CBS)
11	32	RUST IN PEACE Megadeth (Capitol)
25	33	STEPPING OUT - THE VERY BEST OF JOE JACKSON Joe Jackson (A&M)
50	34	THE NORTH AT ITS HEIGHTS MC Tunes (ZTT)
41	35	DAYS OF THUNDER - SOUNDTRACK Various Artists (Epic)
-	36	IN THE BLOOD Londonbeat (AnXious)
33	37	THE LA'S La's (Go! Discs)
30	38	WORLD CLIQUE Deee-Lite (Elektra)
39	39	ANAM Clannad (RCA)
39	40	BLAZE OF GLORY/YOUNG GUNS II Jon Bon Jovi (Vertigo)
-	41	MISSING YOU - AN ALBUM OF LOVE Various Artists (EMI)
21	42	HEAVEN OR LAS VEGAS Cocteau Twins (4AD)
-	43	ELECTRIBAL MEMORIES Electribe 101 (Mercury)
35	44	THE VERY BEST OF TALK TALK - NATURAL HISTORY Talk Talk (Parlophone)
24	45	LOOK HOW LONG Loose Ends (10)
31	46	THE BEST OF 1968-1973 Steve Miller Band (Capitol)
13	47	SLAMMIN' Various Artists (A&M)
-	48	ESSENTIAL CLASSICS Various Artists (Deutsche Grammophon)
-	49	SAY SOMETHING GOOD River City People (EMI)
48	50	PUMP UP THE JAM Technotronic (Swanyard)

27 October 1990

last week	this week	Title / Artist (Label)
-	1	RHYTHM OF THE SAINTS Paul Simon (Warner Bros.)
3	2	SOME FRIENDLY Charlatans (Situation Two)
18	3	ROCKING ALL OVER THE YEARS Status Quo (Vertigo)
5	4	LISTEN WITHOUT PREJUDICE VOLUME 1 George Michael (Epic)
1	5	IN CONCERT Luciano Pavarotti, Placido Domingo & José Carreras (Decca)
41	6	MISSING YOU - AN ALBUM OF LOVE Various Artists (EMI)
10	7	ENLIGHTENMENT Van Morrison (Polydor)
4	8	X INXS (Mercury)
-	9	BONA DRAG Morrissey (HMV)
-	10	RECYCLER ZZ Top (Warner Bros.)
6	11	SOUL PROVIDER Michael Bolton (CBS)
7	12	SLEEPING WITH THE PAST Elton John (Rocket)
-	13	NOWHERE Ride (Creation)
2	14	NO PRAYER FOR THE DYING Iron Maiden (EMI)
39	15	ANAM Clannad (RCA)
15	16	FOREIGN AFFAIR Tina Turner (Capitol)
9	17	THAT LOVING FEELING VOL. 3 Various Artists (Dino)
-	18	REMASTERS Led Zeppelin (Atlantic)
8	19	DOCTOR ADAMSKI'S MUSICAL PHARMACY Adamski (MCA)
16	20	... BUT SERIOUSLY Phil Collins (Vertigo)
22	21	BOOMANIA Betty Boo (Rhythm King)
11	22	OOH LAS VEGAS Deacon Blue (CBS)
14	23	PLEASE HAMMER DON'T HURT 'EM MC Hammer (Capitol)
26	24	JUST THE TWO OF US Various Artists (Columbia)
12	25	HELL'S DITCH Pogues (Pogue Mahone)
20	26	REFLECTION Shadows (Roll Over)
17	27	MARIAH CAREY Mariah Carey (CBS)
27	28	LOOK SHARP! Roxette (EMI)
31	29	STEP BY STEP New Kids On The Block (CBS)
-	30	TOP GUN - SOUNDTRACK Various Artists (CBS)
23	31	WE ARE IN LOVE Harry Connick Jr. (CBS)
-	32	CONTRIBUTION Mica Paris (Fourth & Broadway)
43	33	ELECTRIBAL MEMORIES Electribe 101 (Mercury)
19	34	UK BLAK Caron Wheeler (RCA)
13	35	THE RAZOR'S EDGE AC/DC (Atco)
28	36	WILSON PHILLIPS Wilson Phillips (SBK)
25	37	JANET JACKSON'S RHYTHM NATION 1814 Janet Jackson (A&M)
-	38	DEEP HEAT 8 - THE HAND OF FATE Various (Telstar)
29	39	JORDAN: THE COMEBACK Prefab Sprout (Kitchenware)
-	40	THE BEST OF BEN E. KING AND THE DRIFTERS Ben E. King & the Drifters (Telstar)
21	41	SOUL DECADE: THE SIXTIES Various Artists (Motown)
-	42	THE SYNTHESIZER ALBUM Project D (Telstar)
-	43	VERY BEST OF ELO Electric Light Orchestra (Telstar)
30	44	DOWN TO EARTH Monie Love (Cooltempo)
24	45	ROOM TO ROAM Waterboys (Ensign)
36	46	IN THE BLOOD Londonbeat (AnXious)
33	47	STEPPING OUT - THE VERY BEST OF JOE JACKSON Joe Jackson (A&M)
38	48	WORLD CLIQUE Deee-Lite (Elektra)
35	49	DAYS OF THUNDER - SOUNDTRACK Various Artists (Epic)
50	50	PUMP UP THE JAM Technotronic (Swanyard)

For the second time this year, a classical album achieved the previously-thought-impossible by topping the UK chart, and once again Luciano Pavarotti was involved. *In Concert* was a recording of the historic coming together of three of the world's most celebrated tenors - Pavarotti, Placido Domingo and Jose Carreras - at a gala concert staged in Italy as part of the general World Cup extravaganza.

November 1990

3 November 1990

last	this		
1	1	RHYTHM OF THE SAINTS	Paul Simon (Warner Bros.)
-	2	BEHAVIOUR	Pet Shop Boys (Parlophone)
3	3	ROCKING ALL OVER THE YEARS	Status Quo (Vertigo)
5	4	IN CONCERT	Luciano Pavarotti, Placido Domingo & José Carreras (Decca)
4	5	LISTEN WITHOUT PREJUDICE VOLUME 1	George Michael (Epic)
6	6	MISSING YOU - AN ALBUM OF LOVE	Various (EMI)
-	7	VISION THING	Sisters Of Mercy (Merciful Release)
2	8	SOME FRIENDLY	Charlatans (Situation Two)
10	9	RECYCLER	ZZ Top (Warner Bros.)
11	10	SOUL PROVIDER	Michael Bolton (CBS)
38	11	DEEP HEAT 8 - THE HAND OF FATE	Various (Telstar)
12	12	SLEEPING WITH THE PAST	Elton John (Rocket)
13	13	NOWHERE	Ride (Creation)
18	14	REMASTERS	Led Zeppelin (Atlantic)
7	15	ENLIGHTENMENT	Van Morrison (Polydor)
23	16	PLEASE HAMMER DON'T HURT 'EM	MC Hammer (Capitol)
16	17	FOREIGN AFFAIR	Tina Turner (Capitol)
8	18	X	INXS (Mercury)
-	19	GRAINS OF SAND	Mission (Mercury)
20	20	... BUT SERIOUSLY	Phil Collins (Vertigo)
9	21	BONA DRAG	Morrissey (HMV)
40	22	THE BEST OF BEN E. KING AND THE DRIFTERS	Ben E. King & the Drifters (Telstar)
28	23	LOOK SHARP!	Roxette (EMI)
-	24	EAST OF THE SUN, WEST OF THE MOON	A-ha (Warner Bros.)
14	25	NO PRAYER FOR THE DYING	Iron Maiden (EMI)
-	26	CORNERSTONES 1967-1970	Jimi Hendrix (Polydor)
26	27	REFLECTION	Shadows (Roll Over)
15	28	ANAM	Clannad (RCA)
-	29	LLOYD WEBBER PLAYS LLOYD WEBBER	Julian Lloyd Webber (Philips)
43	30	VERY BEST OF ELO	Electric Light Orchestra (Telstar)
-	31	RED HOT + BLUE	Various Artists (Chrysalis)
19	32	DOCTOR ADAMSKI'S MUSICAL PHARMACY	Adamski (MCA)
32	33	CONTRIBUTION	Mica Paris (Fourth & Broadway)
17	34	THAT LOVING FEELING VOL. 3	Various Artists (Dino)
-	35	BACKSTAGE - THE GREATEST HITS AND MORE	Gene Pitney (Polydor)
29	36	STEP BY STEP	New Kids On The Block (CBS)
27	37	MARIAH CAREY	Mariah Carey (CBS)
-	38	THE FINAL COUNTDOWN - THE VERY BEST OF SOFT METAL	Various Artists (Telstar)
22	39	OOH LAS VEGAS	Deacon Blue (CBS)
-	40	SMASH HITS 1990	Various Artists (Dover)
21	41	BOOMANIA	Betty Boo (Rhythm King)
-	42	EN TACT	Shamen (One Little Indian)
31	43	WE ARE IN LOVE	Harry Connick Jr. (CBS)
-	44	CURE FOR SANITY	Pop Will Eat Itself (RCA)
-	45	SYNTHESIZER GREATEST	Ed Starink (Arcade)
-	46	NEW KIDS ON THE BLOCK	New Kids On The Block (CBS)
36	47	WILSON PHILLIPS	Wilson Phillips (SBK)
37	48	JANET JACKSON'S RHYTHM NATION 1814	Janet Jackson (A&M)
-	49	SLAVES AND MASTERS	Deep Purple (RCA)
25	50	HELL'S DITCH	Pogues (Pogue Mahone)

10 November 1990

last	this		
1	1	RHYTHM OF THE SAINTS	Paul Simon (Warner Bros.)
-	2	CHOKE	Beautiful South (Go! Discs)
2	3	BEHAVIOUR	Pet Shop Boys (Parlophone)
-	4	THE VERY BEST OF ELTON JOHN	Elton John (Rocket)
3	5	ROCKING ALL OVER THE YEARS	Status Quo (Vertigo)
4	6	IN CONCERT	Luciano Pavarotti, Placido Domingo & José Carreras (Decca)
26	7	CORNERSTONES 1967-1970	Jimi Hendrix (Polydor)
5	8	LISTEN WITHOUT PREJUDICE VOLUME 1	George Michael (Epic)
6	9	MISSING YOU - AN ALBUM OF LOVE	Various (EMI)
46	10	NEW KIDS ON THE BLOCK	New Kids On The Block (CBS)
7	11	VISION THING	Sisters Of Mercy (Merciful Release)
24	12	EAST OF THE SUN, WEST OF THE MOON	A-ha (Warner Bros.)
10	13	SOUL PROVIDER	Michael Bolton (CBS)
14	14	REMASTERS	Led Zeppelin (Atlantic)
8	15	SOME FRIENDLY	Charlatans (Situation Two)
-	16	TRIP ON THIS - THE REMIXES	Technotronic (Swanyard)
31	17	RED HOT + BLUE	Various Artists (Chrysalis)
34	18	THAT LOVING FEELING VOL. 3	Various (Dino)
9	19	RECYCLER	ZZ Top (Warner Bros.)
-	20	TRAVELING WILBURYS VOLUME 3	Traveling Wilburys (Wilbury)
23	21	LOOK SHARP!	Roxette (EMI)
40	22	SMASH HITS 1990	Various Artists (Dover)
27	23	REFLECTION	Shadows (Roll Over)
12	24	SLEEPING WITH THE PAST	Elton John (Rocket)
-	25	THE VERY BEST OF THE GREATEST LOVE	Various Artists (Telstar)
16	26	PLEASE HAMMER DON'T HURT 'EM	MC Hammer (Capitol)
29	27	LLOYD WEBBER PLAYS LLOYD WEBBER	Julian Lloyd Webber (Philips)
18	28	X	INXS (Mercury)
-	29	BELIEF	Innocence (Cooltempo)
-	30	NOW DANCE 903	Various (EMI/Virgin/PolyGram)
11	31	DEEP HEAT 8 - THE HAND OF FATE	Various (Telstar)
41	32	BOOMANIA	Betty Boo (Rhythm King)
15	33	ENLIGHTENMENT	Van Morrison (Polydor)
-	34	THE GREATEST HITS SO FAR	Public Image Ltd. (Virgin)
42	35	EN TACT	Shamen (One Little Indian)
13	36	NOWHERE	Ride (Creation)
17	37	FOREIGN AFFAIR	Tina Turner (Capitol)
20	38	... BUT SERIOUSLY	Phil Collins (Vertigo)
30	39	VERY BEST OF ELO	Electric Light Orchestra (Telstar)
21	40	BONA DRAG	Morrissey (HMV)
-	41	I DO NOT WANT WHAT I HAVEN'T GOT	Sinead O'Connor (Ensign)
-	42	GHOST	Soundtrack (Milan)
-	43	THE HOUSE OF LOVE	House Of Love (Fontana)
39	44	OOH LAS VEGAS	Deacon Blue (CBS)
19	45	GRAINS OF SAND	Mission (Mercury)
28	46	ANAM	Clannad (RCA)
-	47	THE BEST OF MATT BIANCO	Matt Bianco (East West)
36	48	STEP BY STEP	New Kids On The Block (CBS)
-	49	WORLD CLIQUE	Deee-Lite (Elektra)
-	50	GHOST OF A DOG	Edie Brickell & New Bohemians (Geffen)

17 November 1990

last	this		
4	1	THE VERY BEST OF ELTON JOHN	Elton John (Rocket)
-	2	PILLS 'N' THRILLS AND BELLYACHES	Happy Mondays (Factory)
2	3	CHOKE	Beautiful South (Go! Discs)
-	4	SERIOUS HITS ... LIVE!	Phil Collins (Vertigo)
1	5	RHYTHM OF THE SAINTS	Paul Simon (Warner Bros.)
-	6	MIXED UP	Cure (Fiction)
3	7	BEHAVIOUR	Pet Shop Boys (Parlophone)
-	8	I'M YOUR BABY TONIGHT	Whitney Houston (Arista)
5	9	ROCKING ALL OVER THE YEARS	Status Quo (Vertigo)
-	10	TRIPPING THE LIVE FANTASTIC	Paul McCartney (Parlophone)
8	11	LISTEN WITHOUT PREJUDICE VOLUME 1	George Michael (Epic)
6	12	IN CONCERT	Luciano Pavarotti, Placido Domingo & José Carreras (Decca)
20	13	VOLUME 3	Traveling Wilburys (Wilbury)
-	14	FROM A DISTANCE ... THE EVENT	Cliff Richard (EMI)
30	15	NOW DANCE 903	Various (EMI/Virgin/PolyGram)
14	16	REMASTERS	Led Zeppelin (Atlantic)
7	17	CORNERSTONES 1967-1970	Jimi Hendrix (Polydor)
9	18	MISSING YOU - AN ALBUM OF LOVE	Various (EMI)
13	19	SOUL PROVIDER	Michael Bolton (CBS)
16	20	TRIP ON THIS - THE REMIXES	Technotronic (Swanyard)
12	21	EAST OF THE SUN, WEST OF THE MOON	A-ha (Warner Bros.)
22	22	SMASH HITS 1990	Various Artists (Dover)
11	23	VISION THING	Sisters Of Mercy (Merciful Release)
-	24	THE VERY BEST OF ...	Bee Gees (Polydor)
15	25	SOME FRIENDLY	Charlatans (Situation Two)
34	26	THE GREATEST HITS SO FAR	Public Image Ltd. (Virgin)
21	27	LOOK SHARP!	Roxette (EMI)
10	28	NEW KIDS ON THE BLOCK	New Kids On The Block (CBS)
19	29	RECYCLER	ZZ Top (Warner Bros.)
-	30	REFUGEES OF THE HEART	Steve Winwood (Virgin)
23	31	REFLECTION	Shadows (Roll Over)
42	32	GHOST	Soundtrack (Milan)
25	33	THE VERY BEST OF THE GREATEST LOVE	Various Artists (Telstar)
27	34	LLOYD WEBBER PLAYS LLOYD WEBBER	Julian Lloyd Webber (Philips)
28	35	X	INXS (Mercury)
-	36	DON'T EXPLAIN	Robert Palmer (EMI)
33	37	ENLIGHTENMENT	Van Morrison (Polydor)
-	38	BEST OF...	Ben E. King & the Drifters (Telstar)
29	39	BELIEF	Innocence (Cooltempo)
-	40	SHUT UP AND DANCE (THE DANCE REMIXES)	Paula Abdul (Virgin America)
24	41	SLEEPING WITH THE PAST	Elton John (Rocket)
26	42	PLEASE HAMMER DON'T HURT 'EM	MC Hammer (Capitol)
31	43	DEEP HEAT 8 - THE HAND OF FATE	Various (Telstar)
41	44	I DO NOT WANT WHAT I HAVEN'T GOT	Sinead O'Connor (Ensign)
37	45	FOREIGN AFFAIR	Tina Turner (Capitol)
-	46	PIGEONHOLE	New Fast Automatic Daffodils (Play It Again Sam)
18	47	THAT LOVING FEELING VOL. 3	Various Artists (Dino)
-	48	BALLADS	Roy Orbison (Telstar)
39	49	VERY BEST OF...	Electric Light Orchestra (Telstar)
43	50	THE HOUSE OF LOVE	House Of Love (Fontana)

Though it was not to have quite the mega-success worldwide of his 1986 project *Graceland*, Paul Simon's *Rhythm Of The Saints* shared some of its predecessor's characteristics - notably in influx of World Music influences, particularly this time from South America. *Cornerstones 1967-1970* was a high-profile repackage of Jimi Hendrix tracks - the first of several such compilations dominating late-year sales.

24 November 1990

last week	this week	Title	Artist (label)
1	1	THE VERY BEST OF ELTON JOHN	Elton John (Rocket)
-	2	THE IMMACULATE COLLECTION	Madonna (Sire)
4	3	SERIOUS HITS ... LIVE!	Phil Collins (Vertigo)
-	4	RHYTHM OF LOVE	Kylie Minogue (PWL)
5	5	RHYTHM OF THE SAINTS	Paul Simon (Warner Bros.)
8	6	I'M YOUR BABY TONIGHT	Whitney Houston (Arista)
2	7	PILLS 'N' THRILLS AND BELLYACHES	Happy Mondays (Factory)
3	8	CHOKE	Beautiful South (Go! Discs)
9	9	ROCKING ALL OVER THE YEARS	Status Quo (Vertigo)
15	10	NOW DANCE 903	Various (EMI/Virgin/PolyGram)
24	11	THE VERY BEST OF ...	Bee Gees (Polydor)
6	12	MIXED UP	Cure (Fiction)
12	13	IN CONCERT	Luciano Pavarotti, Placido Domingo & José Carreras (Decca)
-	14	THE SINGLES COLLECTION 1984-1990	Jimmy Somerville (London)
22	15	SMASH HITS 1990	Various Artists (Dover)
18	16	MISSING YOU - AN ALBUM OF LOVE	Various (EMI)
14	17	FROM A DISTANCE ... THE EVENT	Cliff Richard (EMI)
7	18	BEHAVIOUR	Pet Shop Boys (Parlophone)
20	19	TRIP ON THIS - THE REMIXES	Technotronic (Swanyard)
16	20	REMASTERS	Led Zeppelin (Atlantic)
11	21	LISTEN WITHOUT PREJUDICE VOLUME 1	George Michael (Epic)
17	22	CORNERSTONES 1967-1970	Jimi Hendrix (Polydor)
13	23	VOLUME 3	Traveling Wilburys (Wilbury)
19	24	SOUL PROVIDER	Michael Bolton (CBS)
30	25	REFUGEES OF THE HEART	Steve Winwood (Virgin)
10	26	TRIPPING THE LIVE FANTASTIC	Paul McCartney (Parlophone)
27	27	LOOK SHARP!	Roxette (EMI)
28	28	NEW KIDS ON THE BLOCK	New Kids On The Block (CBS)
-	29	TRULY UNFORGETTABLE	Various Artists (EMI)
36	30	DON'T EXPLAIN	Robert Palmer (EMI)
25	31	SOME FRIENDLY	Charlatans (Situation Two)
-	32	THE GREATEST HITS OF 1990	Various(Telstar)
34	33	LLOYD WEBBER PLAYS LLOYD WEBBER	Julian Lloyd Webber (Philips)
31	34	REFLECTION	Shadows (Roll Over)
45	35	FOREIGN AFFAIR	Tina Turner (Capitol)
29	36	RECYCLER	ZZ Top (Warner Bros.)
35	37	X	INXS (Mercury)
44	38	I DO NOT WANT WHAT I HAVEN'T GOT	Sinead O'Connor (Ensign)
32	39	GHOST	Soundtrack (Milan)
33	40	THE VERY BEST OF THE GREATEST LOVE	Various Artists (Telstar)
21	41	EAST OF THE SUN, WEST OF THE MOON	A-ha (Warner Bros.)
26	42	THE GREATEST HITS SO FAR	Public Image Ltd. (Virgin)
42	43	PLEASE HAMMER DON'T HURT 'EM	MC Hammer (Capitol)
-	44	BOOMANIA	Betty Boo (Rhythm King)
38	45	BEST OF ...	Ben E. King & the Drifters (Telstar)
-	46	THE WANDERER	Freddie Starr (Dover)
48	47	BALLADS	Roy Orbison (Telstar)
-	48	DO ME AGAIN	Freddie Jackson (Capitol)
-	49	NECK AND NECK	Chet Atkins & Mark Knopfler (CBS)
-	50	BLAZE OF GLORY/YOUNG GUNS II	Jon Bon Jovi (Vertigo)

1 December 1990

last week	this week	Title	Artist (label)
2	1	THE IMMACULATE COLLECTION	Madonna (Sire)
1	2	THE VERY BEST OF ELTON JOHN	Elton John (Rocket)
3	3	SERIOUS HITS ... LIVE!	Phil Collins (Vertigo)
5	4	RHYTHM OF THE SAINTS	Paul Simon (Warner Bros.)
14	5	THE SINGLES COLLECTION 1984-1990	Jimmy Somerville (London)
-	6	NOW THAT'S WHAT I CALL MUSIC 18	Various Artists (EMI/Virgin/PolyGram)
8	7	CHOKE	Beautiful South (Go! Discs)
13	8	IN CONCERT	Luciano Pavarotti, Placido Domingo & José Carreras (Decca)
9	9	ROCKING ALL OVER THE YEARS	Status Quo (Vertigo)
7	10	PILLS 'N' THRILLS AND BELLYACHES	Happy Mondays (Factory)
6	11	I'M YOUR BABY TONIGHT	Whitney Houston (Arista)
11	12	THE VERY BEST OF ...	Bee Gees (Polydor)
4	13	RHYTHM OF LOVE	Kylie Minogue (PWL)
16	14	MISSING YOU - AN ALBUM OF LOVE	Various (EMI)
-	15	SHAKING THE TREE - GOLDEN GREATS	Peter Gabriel (Virgin)
17	16	FROM A DISTANCE ... THE EVENT	Cliff Richard (EMI)
10	17	NOW DANCE 903	Various (EMI/Virgin/PolyGram)
18	18	BEHAVIOUR	Pet Shop Boys (Parlophone)
21	19	LISTEN WITHOUT PREJUDICE VOLUME 1	George Michael (Epic)
12	20	MIXED UP	Cure (Fiction)
24	21	SOUL PROVIDER	Michael Bolton (CBS)
-	22	DEEP HEAT 90	Various Artists (Telstar)
15	23	SMASH HITS 1990	Various Artists (Dover)
32	24	THE GREATEST HITS OF 1990	Various(Telstar)
-	25	HEARTBREAK STATION	Cinderella (Vertigo)
19	26	TRIP ON THIS - THE REMIXES	Technotronic (Swanyard)
-	27	MUSIC FROM TWIN PEAKS	Angelo Badalamenti (Warner Bros.)
-	28	BE MY LOVE ...	Placido Domingo (EMI)
27	29	LOOK SHARP!	Roxette (EMI)
20	30	REMASTERS	Led Zeppelin (Atlantic)
-	31	THE BEST OF ...	Donna Summer (Warner Bros.)
22	32	CORNERSTONES 1967-1970	Jimi Hendrix (Polydor)
-	33	ROCK'N'ROLL LOVE SONGS	Various Artists (Dino)
37	34	X	INXS (Mercury)
49	35	NECK AND NECK	Chet Atkins & Mark Knopfler (CBS)
-	36	REASON TO BELIEVE	Rita MacNeil (Polydor)
29	37	TRULY UNFORGETTABLE	Various Artists (EMI)
-	38	UNCHAINED MELODY - THE VERY BEST OF ...	Righteous Brothers (Verve)
28	39	NEW KIDS ON THE BLOCK	New Kids On The Block (CBS)
23	40	VOLUME 3	Traveling Wilburys (Wilbury)
33	41	LLOYD WEBBER PLAYS LLOYD WEBBER	Julian Lloyd Webber (Philips)
30	42	DON'T EXPLAIN	Robert Palmer (EMI)
25	43	REFUGEES OF THE HEART	Steve Winwood (Virgin)
44	44	BOOMANIA	Betty Boo (Rhythm King)
38	45	I DO NOT WANT WHAT I HAVEN'T GOT	Sinead O'Connor (Ensign)
31	46	SOME FRIENDLY	Charlatans (Situation Two)
26	47	TRIPPING THE LIVE FANTASTIC	Paul McCartney (Parlophone)
-	48	BLISSED OUT	Beloved (East West)
-	49	SOUVENIRS	Foster & Allen (Telstar)
35	50	FOREIGN AFFAIR	Tina Turner (Capitol)

8 December 1990

last week	this week	Title	Artist (label)
6	1	NOW THAT'S WHAT I CALL MUSIC 18	Various Artists (EMI/Virgin/PolyGram)
1	2	THE IMMACULATE COLLECTION	Madonna (Sire)
2	3	THE VERY BEST OF ELTON JOHN	Elton John (Rocket)
3	4	SERIOUS HITS ... LIVE!	Phil Collins (Vertigo)
5	5	THE SINGLES COLLECTION 1984-1990	Jimmy Somerville (London)
16	6	FROM A DISTANCE ... THE EVENT	Cliff Richard (EMI)
8	7	IN CONCERT	Luciano Pavarotti, Placido Domingo & José Carreras (Decca)
4	8	RHYTHM OF THE SAINTS	Paul Simon (Warner Bros.)
38	9	UNCHAINED MELODY - THE VERY BEST OF ...	Righteous Brothers (Verve)
7	10	CHOKE	Beautiful South (Go! Discs)
9	11	ROCKING ALL OVER THE YEARS	Status Quo (Vertigo)
12	12	THE VERY BEST OF ...	Bee Gees (Polydor)
15	13	SHAKING THE TREE - GOLDEN GREATS	Peter Gabriel (Virgin)
11	14	I'M YOUR BABY TONIGHT	Whitney Houston (Arista)
21	15	SOUL PROVIDER	Michael Bolton (CBS)
10	16	PILLS 'N' THRILLS AND BELLYACHES	Happy Mondays (Factory)
22	17	DEEP HEAT 90	Various Artists (Telstar)
18	18	BEHAVIOUR	Pet Shop Boys (Parlophone)
19	19	LISTEN WITHOUT PREJUDICE VOLUME 1	George Michael (Epic)
28	20	BE MY LOVE ...	Placido Domingo (EMI)
14	21	MISSING YOU - AN ALBUM OF LOVE	Various (EMI)
30	22	REMASTERS	Led Zeppelin (Atlantic)
23	23	SMASH HITS 1990	Various Artists (Dover)
31	24	THE BEST OF ...	Donna Summer (Warner Bros.)
-	25	STARRY NIGHT	Julio Iglesias (CBS)
13	26	RHYTHM OF LOVE	Kylie Minogue (PWL)
27	27	MUSIC FROM TWIN PEAKS	Angelo Badalamenti (Warner Bros.)
-	28	KIM APPLEBY	Kim Appleby (Parlophone)
-	29	MY CLASSIC COLLECTION	Richard Clayderman (Decca Delphine)
44	30	BOOMANIA	Betty Boo (Rhythm King)
-	31	PLEASE HAMMER DON'T HURT 'EM	MC Hammer (Capitol)
17	32	NOW DANCE 903	Various (EMI/Virgin/PolyGram)
20	33	MIXED UP	Cure (Fiction)
26	34	TRIP ON THIS - THE REMIXES	Technotronic (Swanyard)
49	35	SOUVENIRS	Foster & Allen (Telstar)
29	36	LOOK SHARP!	Roxette (EMI)
-	37	THE LA'S	La's (Go! Discs)
24	38	THE GREATEST HITS OF 1990	Various (Telstar)
48	39	BLISSED OUT	Beloved (East West)
34	40	X	INXS (Mercury)
41	41	LLOYD WEBBER PLAYS LLOYD WEBBER	Julian Lloyd Webber (Philips)
-	42	REFLECTION	Shadows (Roll Over)
25	43	HEARTBREAK STATION	Cinderella (Vertigo)
45	44	I DO NOT WANT WHAT I HAVEN'T GOT	Sinead O'Connor (Ensign)
35	45	NECK AND NECK	Chet Atkins & Mark Knopfle (CBS)
32	46	CORNERSTONES 1967-1970	Jimi Hendrix (Polydor)
-	47	GREATEST HITS 1977-1990	Stranglers (Epic)
47	48	TRIPPING THE LIVE FANTASTIC	Paul McCartney (Parlophone)
33	49	ROCK'N'ROLL LOVE SONGS	Various Artists (Dino)
-	50	BEST OF ...	Ben E. King & the Drifters (Telstar)

The flavour of the end of the year was to be greatest hits compilations - no rare thing in the pre-Christmas market, but in 1990 they involved some of the most bankable album sellers around. Elton John was the first to see his anthology top the charts, but it was then quickly eclipsed by Madonna's *Immaculate Collection*, which comprehensively rounded up the material girl's many hit singles to date.

December 1990

15 December 1990

last	this	
2	1	THE IMMACULATE COLLECTION Madonna (Sire)
3	2	THE VERY BEST OF ELTON JOHN Elton John (Rocket)
4	3	SERIOUS HITS ... LIVE! Phil Collins (Vertigo)
7	4	IN CONCERT Luciano Pavarotti, Placido Domingo & José Carreras (Decca)
5	5	THE SINGLES COLLECTION 1984-1990 Jimmy Somerville (London)
6	6	FROM A DISTANCE ... THE EVENT Cliff Richard (EMI)
12	7	THE VERY BEST OF ... Bee Gees (Polydor)
11	8	ROCKING ALL OVER THE YEARS Status Quo (Vertigo)
13	9	SHAKING THE TREE Peter Gabriel (Virgin)
14	10	I'M YOUR BABY TONIGHT Whitney Houston (Arista)
8	11	RHYTHM OF THE SAINTS Paul Simon (Warner Bros.)
10	12	CHOKE Beautiful South (Go! Discs)
9	13	UNCHAINED MELODY - THE VERY BEST OF... Righteous Brothers (Verve)
15	14	SOUL PROVIDER Michael Bolton (CBS)
19	15	LISTEN WITHOUT PREJUDICE VOLUME 1 George Michael (Epic)
-	16	TO THE EXTREME Vanilla Ice (SBK)
20	17	BE MY LOVE ... Placido Domingo (EMI)
40	18	X INXS (Mercury)
16	19	PILLS 'N' THRILLS AND BELLYACHES Happy Mondays (Factory)
-	20	MERRY MERRY CHRISTMAS New Kids On The Block (CBS)
-	21	ONLY YESTERDAY Carpenters (A&M)
28	22	KIM APPLEBY Kim Appleby (Parlophone)
18	23	BEHAVIOUR Pet Shop Boys (Parlophone)
35	24	SOUVENIRS Foster & Allen (Telstar)
22	25	REMASTERS Led Zeppelin (Atlantic)
25	26	STARRY NIGHT Julio Iglesias (CBS)
29	27	MY CLASSIC COLLECTION Richard Clayderman (Decca Delphine)
42	28	REFLECTION Shadows (Roll Over)
26	29	RHYTHM OF LOVE Kylie Minogue (PWL)
30	30	BOOMANIA Betty Boo (Rhythm King)
27	31	MUSIC FROM TWIN PEAKS Angelo Badalamenti (Warner Bros.)
31	32	PLEASE HAMMER DON'T HURT 'EM MC Hammer (Capitol)
-	33	STEP BY STEP New Kids On The Block (CBS)
34	34	TRIP ON THIS - THE REMIXES Technotronic (Swanyard)
41	35	LLOYD WEBBER PLAYS LLOYD WEBBER Julian Lloyd Webber (Philips)
36	36	LOOK SHARP! Roxette (EMI)
-	37	TEENAGE NINJA MUTANT TURTLES Various (SBK)
24	38	THE BEST OF ... Donna Summer (Warner Bros.)
37	39	THE LA'S La's (Go! Discs)
44	40	I DO NOT WANT WHAT I HAVEN'T GOT Sinead O'Connor (Ensign)
33	41	MIXED UP Cure (Fiction)
50	42	BEST OF ... Ben E. King & the Drifters (Telstar)
46	43	CORNERSTONES 1967-1970 Jimi Hendrix (Polydor)
-	44	FOREIGN AFFAIR Tina Turner (Capitol)
48	45	TRIPPING THE LIVE FANTASTIC Paul McCartney (Parlophone)
-	46	... BUT SERIOUSLY Phil Collins (Vertigo)
-	47	RED HOT + BLUE Various Artists (Chrysalis)
-	48	BELIEF Innocence (Cooltempo)
-	49	THE RAW AND THE REMIX Fine Young Cannibals (London)
-	50	VOLUME 3 Traveling Wilburys (Wilbury)

22 December 1990

last	this	
1	1	THE IMMACULATE COLLECTION Madonna (Sire)
2	2	THE VERY BEST OF ELTON JOHN Elton John (Rocket)
3	3	SERIOUS HITS ... LIVE! Phil Collins (Vertigo)
4	4	IN CONCERT Luciano Pavarotti Placido Domingo & José Carreras (Decca)
5	5	THE SINGLES COLLECTION 1984-1990 Jimmy Somerville (London)
7	6	THE VERY BEST OF ... Bee Gees (Polydor)
6	7	FROM A DISTANCE ... THE EVENT Cliff Richard (EMI)
14	8	SOUL PROVIDER Michael Bolton (CBS)
10	9	I'M YOUR BABY TONIGHT Whitney Houston (Arista)
11	10	RHYTHM OF THE SAINTS Paul Simon (Warner Bros.)
15	11	LISTEN WITHOUT PREJUDICE VOLUME 1 George Michael (Epic)
8	12	ROCKING ALL OVER THE YEARS Status Quo (Vertigo)
13	13	UNCHAINED MELODY - THE VERY BEST OF ... Righteous Brothers (Verve)
12	14	CHOKE Beautiful South (Go! Discs)
16	15	TO THE EXTREME Vanilla Ice (SBK)
18	16	X INXS (Mercury)
21	17	ONLY YESTERDAY Carpenters (A&M)
20	18	MERRY MERRY CHRISTMAS New Kids On The Block (CBS)
9	19	SHAKING THE TREE Peter Gabriel (Virgin)
29	20	RHYTHM OF LOVE Kylie Minogue (PWL)
23	21	BEHAVIOUR Pet Shop Boys (Parlophone)
25	22	REMASTERS Led Zeppelin (Atlantic)
19	23	PILLS 'N' THRILLS AND BELLYACHES Happy Mondays (Factory)
17	24	BE MY LOVE ... Placido Domingo (EMI)
31	25	MUSIC FROM TWIN PEAKS Angelo Badalamenti (Warner Bros.)
24	26	SOUVENIRS Foster & Allen (Telstar)
22	27	KIM APPLEBY Kim Appleby (Parlophone)
26	28	STARRY NIGHT Julio Iglesias (CBS)
28	29	REFLECTION Shadows (Roll Over)
30	30	BOOMANIA Betty Boo (Rhythm King)
27	31	MY CLASSIC COLLECTION Richard Clayderman (Decca Delphine)
32	32	PLEASE HAMMER DON'T HURT 'EM MC Hammer (Capitol)
33	33	STEP BY STEP New Kids On The Block (CBS)
36	34	LOOK SHARP! Roxette (EMI)
35	35	LLOYD WEBBER PLAYS LLOYD WEBBER Julian Lloyd Webber (Philips)
-	36	THE ESSENTIAL PAVAROTTI Luciano Pavarotti (Decca)
49	37	THE RAW AND THE REMIX Fine Young Cannibals (London)
44	38	FOREIGN AFFAIR Tina Turner (Capitol)
40	39	I DO NOT WANT WHAT I HAVEN'T GOT Sinead O'Connor (Ensign)
45	40	TRIPPING THE LIVE FANTASTIC Paul McCartney (Parlophone)
34	41	TRIP ON THIS - THE REMIXES Technotronic (Swanyard)
37	42	TEENAGE NINJA MUTANT TURTLES Various (SBK)
38	43	THE BEST OF... Donna Summer (Warner Bros.)
39	44	THE LA'S La's (Go! Discs)
46	45	... BUT SERIOUSLY Phil Collins (Vertigo)
42	46	BEST OF... Ben E. King & the Drifters (Telstar)
-	47	PRETTY WOMAN - SOUNDTRACK Various (EMI USA)
-	48	NECK AND NECK Chet Atkins & Mark Knopfler (CBS)
41	49	MIXED UP Cure (Fiction)
43	50	CORNERSTONES 1967-1970 Jimi Hendrix (Polydor)

The compilations came in thick and fast to see the year out, with Madonna and Elton joined by Jimmy Somerville, The Bee Gees, Status Quo and (spurred by their chart-topping single with the reissued *Unchained Melody*) the Righteous Brothers.

5 January 1991

last week	this week		
1	1	THE IMMACULATE COLLECTION	Madonna (Sire)
2	2	THE VERY BEST OF ELTON JOHN	Elton John (Rocket)
3	3	SERIOUS HITS ... LIVE!	Phil Collins (Virgin)
4	4	IN CONCERT	Luciano Pavarotti, Placido Domingo and José Carreras (Decca)
7	5	FROM A DISTANCE ...THE EVENT	Cliff Richard (EMI)
5	6	THE SINGLES COLLECTION 1984-1990	Jimmy Somerville (London)
9	7	I'M YOUR BABY TONIGHT	Whitney Houston (Arista)
8	8	SOUL PROVIDER	Michael Bolton (CBS)
10	9	THE RHYTHM OF THE SAINTS	Paul Simon (Warner Bros.)
6	10	THE VERY BEST OF...	Bee Gees (Polydor)
11	11	LISTEN WITHOUT PREJUDICE VOLUME 1	George Michael (Epic)
12	12	ROCKING ALL OVER THE YEARS	Status Quo (Vertigo)
19	13	SHAKING THE TREE	Peter Gabriel (Virgin)
15	14	TO THE EXTREME	Vanilla Ice (SBK)
13	15	UNCHAINED MELODY - THE VERY BEST OF	Righteous Brothers (Verve)
16	16	X	INXS (Mercury)
17	17	ONLY YESTERDAY	Carpenters (A&M)
22	18	REMASTERS	Led Zeppelin (Atlantic)
26	19	SOUVENIRS	Foster & Allen (Telstar)
18	20	MERRY MERRY CHRISTMAS	New Kids On The Block (CBS)
14	21	CHOKE	Beautiful South (Go! Discs)
36	22	THE ESSENTIAL ...	Luciano Pavarotti (Decca)
20	23	RHYTHM OF LOVE	Kylie Minogue (PWL)
23	24	PILLS 'N' THRILLS	Happy Mondays (Factory)
30	25	BOOMANIA	Betty Boo (Rhythm King)
24	26	BE MY LOVE ...	Placido Domingo (EMI)
21	27	BEHAVIOUR	Pet Shop Boys (Parlophone)
27	28	KIM APPLEBY	Kim Appleby (Parlophone)
29	29	REFLECTION	Shadows (Roll Over)
32	30	PLEASE HAMMER DON'T HURT 'EM	MC Hammer (Capitol)
31	31	MY CLASSIC COLLECTION	Richard Clayderman (Decca Delphine)
28	32	STARRY NIGHT	Julio Iglesias (CBS)
33	33	STEP BY STEP	New Kids On The Block (CBS)
-	34	TRIPPING THE LIVE FANTASTIC - HIGHLIGHTS	Paul McCartney (Parlophone)
35	35	LLOYD WEBBER PLAYS LLOYD WEBBER	Julian Lloyd Webber (Philips)
25	36	MUSIC FROM TWIN PEAKS	Angelo Badalamenti (Warner Bros.)
38	37	FOREIGN AFFAIR	Tina Turner (Capitol)
-	38	VIVALDI: THE FOUR SEASONS	Nigel Kennedy with the English Chamber Orchestra (EMI)
34	39	LOOK SHARP!	Roxette (EMI)
47	40	PRETTY WOMAN	Various (EMI USA)
45	41	... BUT SERIOUSLY	Phil Collins (Virgin)
41	42	TRIP ON THIS - THE REMIXES	Technotronic (Telstar)
39	43	I DO NOT WANT WHAT I HAVEN'T GOT	Sinead O'Connor (Ensign)
37	44	THE RAW AND THE REMIX	Fine Young Cannibals (London)
42	45	TEENAGE NINJA MUTANT TURTLES	Various (SBK)
-	46	CHRISTMAS COLLECTION	Foster & Allen (Telstar)
49	47	MIXED UP	Cure (Fiction)
40	48	TRIPPING THE LIVE FANTASTIC	Paul McCartney (Parlophone)
-	49	MCMXC AD	Enigma (Virgin International)
48	50	NECK AND NECK	Chet Atkins & Mark Knopfler (CBS)

12 January 1991

1	1	THE IMMACULATE COLLECTION	Madonna (Sire)
2	2	THE VERY BEST OF ELTON JOHN	Elton John (Rocket)
3	3	SERIOUS HITS ... LIVE!	Phil Collins (Virgin)
7	4	I'M YOUR BABY TONIGHT	Whitney Houston (Arista)
13	5	SHAKING THE TREE	Peter Gabriel (Virgin)
11	6	LISTEN WITHOUT PREJUDICE VOLUME 1	George Michael (Epic)
4	7	IN CONCERT	Luciano Pavarotti, Placido Domingo and José Carreras (Decca)
6	8	THE SINGLES COLLECTION 1984-1990	Jimmy Somerville (London)
8	9	SOUL PROVIDER	Michael Bolton (CBS)
5	10	FROM A DISTANCE ... THE EVENT	Cliff Richard (EMI)
9	11	THE RHYTHM OF THE SAINTS	Paul Simon (Warner Bros.)
14	12	TO THE EXTREME	Vanilla Ice (SBK)
10	13	THE VERY BEST OF...	Bee Gees (Polydor)
12	14	ROCKING ALL OVER THE YEARS	Status Quo (Vertigo)
15	15	UNCHAINED MELODY - THE VERY BEST OF ...	Righteous Brothers (Verve)
21	16	CHOKE	Beautiful South (Go! Discs)
16	17	X	INXS (Mercury)
30	18	PLEASE HAMMER DON'T HURT 'EM	MC Hammer (Capitol)
23	19	RHYTHM OF LOVE	Kylie Minogue (PWL)
17	20	ONLY YESTERDAY	Carpenters (A&M)
27	21	BEHAVIOUR	Pet Shop Boys (Parlophone)
18	22	REMASTERS	Led Zeppelin (Atlantic)
24	23	PILLS 'N' THRILLS AND BELLYACHES	Happy Mondays (Factory)
49	24	MCMXC AD	Enigma (Virgin International)
22	25	THE ESSENTIAL PAVAROTTI	Luciano Pavarotti (Decca)
25	26	BOOMANIA	Betty Boo (Rhythm King)
38	27	VIVALDI: THE FOUR SEASONS	Nigel Kennedy with the English Chamber Orchestra (EMI)
-	28	DIRTY DANCING - SOUNDTRACK	Various (RCA)
19	29	SOUVENIRS	Foster & Allen (Telstar)
28	30	KIM APPLEBY	Kim Appleby (Parlophone)
34	31	TRIPPING THE LIVE FANTASTIC - HIGHLIGHTS	Paul McCartney (Parlophone)
-	32	CORNERSTONES 1967-1970	Jimi Hendrix (Polydor)
40	33	PRETTY WOMAN	Various (EMI USA)
26	34	BE MY LOVE ...	Placido Domingo (EMI)
33	35	STEP BY STEP	New Kids On The Block (CBS)
43	36	I DO NOT WANT WHAT I HAVEN'T GOT	Sinead O'Connor (Ensign)
39	37	LOOK SHARP!	Roxette (EMI)
42	38	TRIP ON THIS - THE REMIXES	Technotronic (Telstar)
-	39	DREAMLAND	Black Box (deConstruction)
-	40	NO PRAYER FOR THE DYING	Iron Maiden (EMI)
-	41	WORLD POWER	Snap (Arista)
29	42	REFLECTION	Shadows (Roll Over)
41	43	... BUT SERIOUSLY	Phil Collins (Virgin)
37	44	FOREIGN AFFAIR	Tina Turner (Capitol)
47	45	MIXED UP	Cure (Fiction)
-	46	THE LA'S	La's (Go! Discs)
-	47	BELIEF	Innocence (Cooltempo)
31	48	MY CLASSIC COLLECTION	Richard Clayderman (Decca Delphine)
20	49	MERRY MERRY CHRISTMAS	New Kids On The Block (CBS)
32	50	STARRY NIGHT	Julio Iglesias (CBS)

19 January 1991

1	1	THE IMMACULATE COLLECTION	Madonna (Sire)
2	2	THE VERY BEST OF ELTON JOHN	Elton John (Rocket)
3	3	SERIOUS HITS ... LIVE!	Phil Collins (Virgin)
6	4	LISTEN WITHOUT PREJUDICE VOLUME 1	George Michael (Epic)
4	5	I'M YOUR BABY TONIGHT	Whitney Houston (Arista)
24	6	MCMXC AD	Enigma (Virgin International)
12	7	TO THE EXTREME	Vanilla Ice (SBK)
5	8	SHAKING THE TREE	Peter Gabriel (Virgin)
7	9	IN CONCERT	Luciano Pavarotti Placido Domingo and José Carreras (Decca)
9	10	SOUL PROVIDER	Michael Bolton (CBS)
8	11	THE SINGLES COLLECTION 1984-1990	Jimmy Somerville (London)
17	12	X	INXS (Mercury)
16	13	CHOKE	Beautiful South (Go! Discs)
11	14	THE RHYTHM OF THE SAINTS	Paul Simon (Warner Bros.)
28	15	DIRTY DANCING - SOUNDTRACK	Various (RCA)
14	16	ROCKING ALL OVER THE YEARS	Status Quo (Vertigo)
18	17	PLEASE HAMMER DON'T HURT 'EM	MC Hammer (Capitol)
15	18	UNCHAINED MELODY - THE VERY BEST OF ...	Righteous Brothers (Verve)
13	19	THE VERY BEST OF...	Bee Gees (Polydor)
22	20	REMASTERS	Led Zeppelin (Atlantic)
10	21	FROM A DISTANCE ... THE EVENT	Cliff Richard (EMI)
23	22	PILLS 'N' THRILLS AND BELLYACHES	Happy Mondays (Factory)
20	23	ONLY YESTERDAY	Carpenters (A&M)
21	24	BEHAVIOUR	Pet Shop Boys (Parlophone)
25	25	THE ESSENTIAL PAVAROTTI	Luciano Pavarotti (Decca)
26	26	BOOMANIA	Betty Boo (Rhythm King)
36	27	I DO NOT WANT WHAT I HAVEN'T GOT	Sinead O'Connor (Ensign)
27	28	VIVALDI: THE FOUR SEASONS	Nigel Kennedy with the English Chamber Orchestra (EMI)
40	29	NO PRAYER FOR THE DYING	Iron Maiden (EMI)
33	30	PRETTY WOMAN	Various (EMI USA)
19	31	RHYTHM OF LOVE	Kylie Minogue (PWL)
32	32	CORNERSTONES 1967-1970	Jimi Hendrix (Polydor)
34	33	BE MY LOVE ... AN ALBUM OF LOVE	Placido Domingo (EMI)
30	34	KIM APPLEBY	Kim Appleby (Parlophone)
39	35	DREAMLAND	Black Box (deConstruction)
-	36	THE LOST BOYS - SOUNDTRACK	Various (Atlantic)
46	37	THE LA'S	La's (Go! Discs)
47	38	BELIEF	Innocence (Cooltempo)
41	39	WORLD POWER	Snap (Arista)
31	40	TRIPPING THE LIVE FANTASTIC - HIGHLIGHTS	Paul McCartney (Parlophone)
37	41	LOOK SHARP!	Roxette (EMI)
38	42	TRIP ON THIS - THE REMIXES	Technotronic (Telstar)
45	43	MIXED UP	Cure (Fiction)
35	44	STEP BY STEP	New Kids On The Block (CBS)
-	45	NECK AND NECK	Chet Atkins & Mark Knopfler (CBS)
43	46	... BUT SERIOUSLY	Phil Collins (Virgin)
-	47	SOME FRIENDLY	Charlatans (Situation Two)
-	48	MUSIC FROM TWIN PEAKS	Angelo Badalamenti (Warner Bros.)
-	49	VERY BEST OF	Ben E. King & the Drifters (Telstar)
-	50	THE RAZOR'S EDGE	AC/DC (Atco)

Just prior to the end of 1990, a decision had been taken by MRIB, compiler and supplier of the NME album chart, to henceforth exclude Various Artists compilations from the chart, making it totally artist-orientated (the British record industry's own chart had taken a similar decision a year earlier). Thus, there were no such compilations to be seen in the Top 50 when 1991 began, nor would there be in future charts.

January – February 1991

26 January 1991

last week	this week	title	artist
1	1	THE IMMACULATE COLLECTION	Madonna (Sire)
2	2	THE VERY BEST OF ELTON JOHN	Elton John (Rocket)
6	3	MCMXC AD	Enigma (Virgin International)
4	4	LISTEN WITHOUT PREJUDICE VOLUME 1	George Michael (Epic)
5	5	I'M YOUR BABY TONIGHT	Whitney Houston (Arista)
3	6	SERIOUS HITS ... LIVE!	Phil Collins (Virgin)
8	7	SHAKING THE TREE	Peter Gabriel (Virgin)
11	8	THE SINGLES COLLECTION 1984-1990	Jimmy Somerville (London)
-	9	A LITTLE AIN'T ENOUGH	David Lee Roth (Warner Bros.)
7	10	TO THE EXTREME	Vanilla Ice (SBK)
12	11	X	INXS (Mercury)
9	12	IN CONCERT	Luciano Pavarotti, Placido Domingo and José Carreras (Decca)
10	13	SOUL PROVIDER	Michael Bolton (CBS)
15	14	DIRTY DANCING - SOUNDTRACK	Various (RCA)
13	15	CHOKE	Beautiful South (Go! Discs)
22	16	PILLS 'N' THRILLS AND BELLYACHES	Happy Mondays (Factory)
18	17	UNCHAINED MELODY - THE VERY BEST OF ...	Righteous Brothers (Verve)
-	18	WICKED GAME	Chris Isaak (Reprise)
17	19	PLEASE HAMMER DON'T HURT 'EM	MC Hammer (Capitol)
20	20	REMASTERS	Led Zeppelin (Atlantic)
14	21	THE RHYTHM OF THE SAINTS	Paul Simon (Warner Bros.)
16	22	ROCKING ALL OVER THE YEARS	Status Quo (Vertigo)
21	23	FROM A DISTANCE ... THE EVENT	Cliff Richard (EMI)
19	24	THE VERY BEST OF THE BEE GEES	Bee Gees (Polydor)
27	25	I DO NOT WANT WHAT I HAVEN'T GOT	Sinead O'Connor (Ensign)
36	26	THE LOST BOYS - SOUNDTRACK	Various (Atlantic)
29	27	NO PRAYER FOR THE DYING	Iron Maiden (EMI)
23	28	ONLY YESTERDAY	Carpenters (A&M)
-	29	DON'T EXPLAIN	Robert Palmer (EMI)
24	30	BEHAVIOUR	Pet Shop Boys (Parlophone)
25	31	THE ESSENTIAL PAVAROTTI	Luciano Pavarotti (Decca)
39	32	WORLD POWER	Snap (Arista)
30	33	PRETTY WOMAN	Various (EMI USA)
26	34	BOOMANIA	Betty Boo (Rhythm King)
28	35	VIVALDI: THE FOUR SEASONS	Nigel Kennedy with the English Chamber Orchestra (EMI)
38	36	BELIEF	Innocence (Cooltempo)
35	37	DREAMLAND	Black Box (deConstruction)
32	38	CORNERSTONES 1967-1970	Jimi Hendrix (Polydor)
31	39	RHYTHM OF LOVE	Kylie Minogue (PWL)
43	40	MIXED UP	Cure (Fiction)
-	41	GREATEST HITS 1977-1990	Stranglers (Epic)
41	42	LOOK SHARP!	Roxette (EMI)
-	43	SWEET DREAMS	Patsy Cline (MCA)
33	44	BE MY LOVE ...	Placido Domingo (EMI)
45	45	NECK AND NECK	Chet Atkins & Mark Knopfler (CBS)
50	46	THE RAZOR'S EDGE	AC/DC (Atco)
37	47	THE LA'S	La's (Go! Discs)
-	48	RUNAWAY HORSES	Belinda Carlisle (Virgin)
48	49	MUSIC FROM TWIN PEAKS	Angelo Badalamenti (Warner Bros.)
-	50	JORDAN: THE COMEBACK	Prefab Sprout (Kitchenware)

2 February 1991

last week	this week	title	artist
3	1	MCMXC AD	Enigma (Virgin International)
9	2	A LITTLE AIN'T ENOUGH	David Lee Roth (Warner Bros.)
1	3	THE IMMACULATE COLLECTION	Madonna (Sire)
2	4	THE VERY BEST OF ELTON JOHN	Elton John (Rocket)
-	5	THE SOUL CAGES	Sting (A&M)
18	6	WICKED GAME	Chris Isaak (Reprise)
6	7	SERIOUS HITS ... LIVE!	Phil Collins (Virgin)
-	8	ALL TRUE MAN	Alexander O'Neal (Tabu)
5	9	I'M YOUR BABY TONIGHT	Whitney Houston (Arista)
10	10	TO THE EXTREME	Vanilla Ice (SBK)
4	11	LISTEN WITHOUT PREJUDICE VOLUME 1	George Michael (Epic)
14	12	DIRTY DANCING - SOUNDTRACK	Various (RCA)
13	13	SOUL PROVIDER	Michael Bolton (CBS)
7	14	SHAKING THE TREE	Peter Gabriel (Virgin)
12	15	IN CONCERT	Luciano Pavarotti, Placido Domingo and José Carreras (Decca)
29	16	DON'T EXPLAIN	Robert Palmer (EMI)
8	17	THE SINGLES COLLECTION 1984-1990	Jimmy Somerville (London)
16	18	PILLS 'N' THRILLS AND BELLYACHES	Happy Mondays (Factory)
11	19	X	INXS (Mercury)
26	20	THE LOST BOYS - SOUNDTRACK	Various (Atlantic)
19	21	PLEASE HAMMER DON'T HURT 'EM	MC Hammer (Capitol)
21	22	THE RHYTHM OF THE SAINTS	Paul Simon (Warner Bros.)
15	23	CHOKE	Beautiful South (Go! Discs)
-	24	1916	Motorhead (Epic)
17	25	UNCHAINED MELODY - THE VERY BEST OF ...	Righteous Brothers (Verve)
20	26	REMASTERS	Led Zeppelin (Atlantic)
32	27	WORLD POWER	Snap (Arista)
22	28	ROCKING ALL OVER THE YEARS	Status Quo (Vertigo)
25	29	I DO NOT WANT WHAT I HAVEN'T GOT	Sinead O'Connor (Ensign)
24	30	THE VERY BEST OF...	Bee Gees (Polydor)
28	31	ONLY YESTERDAY	Carpenters (A&M)
43	32	SWEET DREAMS	Patsy Cline (MCA)
41	33	GREATEST HITS 1977-1990	Stranglers (Epic)
39	34	RHYTHM OF LOVE	Kylie Minogue (PWL)
23	35	FROM A DISTANCE ... THE EVENT	Cliff Richard (EMI)
48	36	RUNAWAY HORSES	Belinda Carlisle (Virgin)
31	37	THE ESSENTIAL PAVAROTTI	Luciano Pavarotti (Decca)
37	38	DREAMLAND	Black Box (deConstruction)
36	39	BELIEF	Innocence (Cooltempo)
30	40	BEHAVIOUR	Pet Shop Boys (Parlophone)
27	41	NO PRAYER FOR THE DYING	Iron Maiden (EMI)
38	42	CORNERSTONES 1967-1970	Jimi Hendrix (Polydor)
-	43	STEP IN THE ARENA	Gang Starr (Cooltempo)
34	44	BOOMANIA	Betty Boo (Rhythm King)
49	45	MUSIC FROM TWIN PEAKS	Angelo Badalamenti (Warner Bros.)
35	46	VIVALDI: THE FOUR SEASONS	Nigel Kennedy with the English Chamber Orchestra (EMI)
33	47	PRETTY WOMAN - SOUNDTRACK	Various (EMI USA)
40	48	MIXED UP	Cure (Fiction)
42	49	LOOK SHARP!	Roxette (EMI)
-	50	SHAKE YOUR MONEY MAKER	Black Crowes (Def American)

9 February 1991

last week	this week	title	artist
5	1	THE SOUL CAGES	Sting (A&M)
8	2	ALL TRUE MAN	Alexander O'Neal (Tabu)
1	3	MCMXC AD	Enigma (Virgin International)
3	4	THE IMMACULATE COLLECTION	Madonna (Sire)
-	5	DOUBT	Jesus Jones (Food)
6	6	WICKED GAME	Chris Isaak (Reprise)
4	7	THE VERY BEST OF ELTON JOHN	Elton John (Rocket)
9	8	I'M YOUR BABY TONIGHT	Whitney Houston (Arista)
7	9	SERIOUS HITS ... LIVE!	Phil Collins (Virgin)
2	10	A LITTLE AIN'T ENOUGH	David Lee Roth (Warner Bros.)
11	11	LISTEN WITHOUT PREJUDICE VOLUME 1	George Michael (Epic)
16	12	DON'T EXPLAIN	Robert Palmer (EMI)
17	13	THE SINGLES COLLECTION 1984-1990	Jimmy Somerville (London)
12	14	DIRTY DANCING - SOUNDTRACK	Various (RCA)
10	15	TO THE EXTREME	Vanilla Ice (SBK)
13	16	SOUL PROVIDER	Michael Bolton (CBS)
27	17	WORLD POWER	Snap (Arista)
15	18	IN CONCERT	Luciano Pavarotti, Placido Domingo and José Carreras (Decca)
20	19	THE LOST BOYS - SOUNDTRACK	Various (Atlantic)
14	20	SHAKING THE TREE	Peter Gabriel (Virgin)
24	21	1916	Motorhead (Epic)
19	22	X	INXS (Mercury)
32	23	SWEET DREAMS	Patsy Cline (MCA)
18	24	PILLS 'N' THRILLS AND BELLYACHES	Happy Mondays (Factory)
21	25	PLEASE HAMMER DON'T HURT 'EM	MC Hammer (Capitol)
23	26	CHOKE	Beautiful South (Go! Discs)
25	27	UNCHAINED MELODY - THE VERY BEST OF ...	Righteous Brothers (Verve)
33	28	GREATEST HITS 1977-1990	Stranglers (Epic)
22	29	THE RHYTHM OF THE SAINTS	Paul Simon (Warner Bros.)
36	30	RUNAWAY HORSES	Belinda Carlisle (Virgin)
34	31	RHYTHM OF LOVE	Kylie Minogue (PWL)
28	32	ROCKING ALL OVER THE YEARS	Status Quo (Vertigo)
30	33	THE VERY BEST OF ...	Bee Gees (Polydor)
26	34	REMASTERS	Led Zeppelin (Atlantic)
-	35	ROCKY V - SOUNDTRACK	Various (Capitol)
-	36	STARRY NIGHT	Julio Iglesias (CBS)
31	37	ONLY YESTERDAY	Carpenters (A&M)
-	38	THE SIMPSONS SING THE BLUES	Simpsons (Geffen)
29	39	I DO NOT WANT WHAT I HAVEN'T GOT	Sinead O'Connor (Ensign)
-	40	GONNA MAKE YOU SWEAT	C&C Music Factory (Columbia)
38	41	DREAMLAND	Black Box (deConstruction)
43	42	STEP IN THE ARENA	Gang Starr (Cooltempo)
-	43	BACK FROM RIO	Roger McGuinn (Arista)
45	44	MUSIC FROM TWIN PEAKS	Angelo Badalamenti (Warner Bros.)
39	45	BELIEF	Innocence (Cooltempo)
47	46	PRETTY WOMAN - SOUNDTRACK	Various (EMI USA)
-	47	MARIAH CAREY	Mariah Carey (CBS)
46	48	VIVALDI: THE FOUR SEASONS	Nigel Kennedy with the English Chamber Orchestra (EMI)
-	49	ENLIGHTENMENT	Van Morrison (Polydor)
-	50	SOMEWHERE SOON	High (London)

Enigma's album, with its mysterious Roman numeral title, rose to Number 1 on the back of their haunting hit single *Sadness*, which topped the chart at the same time. Groups were in a comparative minority among the top album sellers at this point, however, as an influx of male solo vocalists virtually took over the Top 10 - Alexander O'Neal, Peter Gabriel, David Lee Roth, Chris Isaak, and Sting, who also hit Number 1.

February – March 1991

16 February 1991

-	1	INNUENDO	Queen (Parlophone)
5	2	DOUBT	Jesus Jones (Food)
1	3	THE SOUL CAGES	Sting (A&M)
3	4	MCMXC AD	Enigma (Virgin International)
6	5	WICKED GAME	Chris Isaak (Reprise)
2	6	ALL TRUE MAN	Alexander O'Neal (Tabu)
4	7	THE IMMACULATE COLLECTION	Madonna (Sire)
7	8	THE VERY BEST OF ELTON JOHN	Elton John (Rocket)
-	9	INTO THE LIGHT	Gloria Estefan (Epic)
8	10	I'M YOUR BABY TONIGHT	Whitney Houston (Arista)
9	11	SERIOUS HITS ... LIVE!	Phil Collins (Virgin)
12	12	DON'T EXPLAIN	Robert Palmer (EMI)
11	13	LISTEN WITHOUT PREJUDICE VOLUME 1	George Michael (Epic)
30	14	RUNAWAY HORSES	Belinda Carlisle (Virgin)
23	15	SWEET DREAMS	Patsy Cline (MCA)
13	16	THE SINGLES COLLECTION 1984-1990	Jimmy Somerville (London)
15	17	TO THE EXTREME	Vanilla Ice (SBK)
19	18	THE LOST BOYS - SOUNDTRACK	Various (Atlantic)
22	19	X	INXS (Mercury)
14	20	DIRTY DANCING - SOUNDTRACK	Various (RCA)
-	21	DEDICATION - THE VERY BEST OF THIN LIZZY	Thin Lizzy (Vertigo)
18	22	IN CONCERT	Luciano Pavarotti, Placido Domingo and José Carreras (Decca)
17	23	WORLD POWER	Snap (Arista)
16	24	SOUL PROVIDER	Michael Bolton (CBS)
10	25	A LITTLE AIN'T ENOUGH	David Lee Roth (Warner Bros.)
20	26	SHAKING THE TREE	Peter Gabriel (Virgin)
25	27	PLEASE HAMMER DON'T HURT 'EM	MC Hammer (Capitol)
38	28	THE SIMPSONS SING THE BLUES	Simpsons (Geffen)
31	29	RHYTHM OF LOVE	Kylie Minogue (PWL)
29	30	THE RHYTHM OF THE SAINTS	Paul Simon (Warner Bros.)
-	31	AND NOW THE LEGACY BEGINS	Dream Warriors (Fourth & Broadway)
28	32	GREATEST HITS 1977-1990	Stranglers (Epic)
-	33	EVERYBODY'S ANGEL	Tanita Tikaram (East West)
24	34	PILLS 'N' THRILLS AND BELLYACHES	Happy Mondays (Factory)
-	35	THE TRACKS OF MY TEARS	Smokey Robinson and Various Artists (Motown)
-	36	LIVE AT THE BRIXTON ACADEMY	Faith No More (Slash)
40	37	GONNA MAKE YOU SWEAT	C&C Music Factory (Columbia)
26	38	CHOKE	Beautiful South (Go! Discs)
36	39	STARRY NIGHT	Julio Iglesias (CBS)
35	40	ROCKY V - SOUNDTRACK	Various (Capitol)
21	41	1916	Motorhead (Epic)
27	42	UNCHAINED MELODY - THE VERY BEST OF ...	Righteous Brothers (Verve)
43	43	BACK FROM RIO	Roger McGuinn (Arista)
33	44	THE VERY BEST OF ...	Bee Gees (Polydor)
44	45	MUSIC FROM TWIN PEAKS	Angelo Badalamenti (Warner Bros.)
41	46	DREAMLAND	Black Box (deConstruction)
45	47	BELIEF	Innocence (Cooltempo)
46	48	PRETTY WOMAN	Various (EMI USA)
-	49	WAKING HOURS	Del Amitri (A&M)
-	50	JORDAN: THE COMEBACK	Prefab Sprout (Kitchenware)

23 February 1991

1	1	INNUENDO	Queen (Parlophone)
9	2	INTO THE LIGHT	Gloria Estefan (Epic)
5	3	WICKED GAME	Chris Isaak (Reprise)
8	4	THE VERY BEST OF ELTON JOHN	Elton John (Rocket)
2	5	DOUBT	Jesus Jones (Food)
21	6	DEDICATION - THE VERY BEST OF THIN LIZZY	Thin Lizzy (Vertigo)
13	7	LISTEN WITHOUT PREJUDICE VOLUME 1	George Michael (Epic)
3	8	THE SOUL CAGES	Sting (A&M)
7	9	THE IMMACULATE COLLECTION	Madonna (Sire)
4	10	MCMXC AD	Enigma (Virgin International)
6	11	ALL TRUE MAN	Alexander O'Neal (Tabu)
14	12	RUNAWAY HORSES	Belinda Carlisle (Virgin)
31	13	AND NOW THE LEGACY BEGINS	Dream Warriors (Fourth & Broadway)
11	14	SERIOUS HITS ... LIVE!	Phil Collins (Virgin)
22	15	IN CONCERT	Luciano Pavarotti, Placido Domingo and José Carreras (Decca)
10	16	I'M YOUR BABY TONIGHT	Whitney Houston (Arista)
19	17	X	INXS (Mercury)
33	18	EVERYBODY'S ANGEL	Tanita Tikaram (East West)
16	19	THE SINGLES COLLECTION 1984-1990	Jimmy Somerville (London)
28	20	THE SIMPSONS SING THE BLUES	Simpsons (Geffen)
18	21	THE LOST BOYS - SOUNDTRACK	Various (Atlantic)
36	22	LIVE AT THE BRIXTON ACADEMY	Faith No More (Slash)
12	23	DON'T EXPLAIN	Robert Palmer (EMI)
15	24	SWEET DREAMS	Patsy Cline (MCA)
17	25	TO THE EXTREME	Vanilla Ice (SBK)
20	26	DIRTY DANCING - SOUNDTRACK	Various (RCA)
30	27	THE RHYTHM OF THE SAINTS	Paul Simon (Warner Bros.)
24	28	SOUL PROVIDER	Michael Bolton (CBS)
38	29	CHOKE	Beautiful South (Go! Discs)
34	30	PILLS 'N' THRILLS AND BELLYACHES	Happy Mondays (Factory)
25	31	A LITTLE AIN'T ENOUGH	David Lee Roth (Warner Bros.)
32	32	GREATEST HITS 1977-1990	Stranglers (Epic)
23	33	WORLD POWER	Snap (Arista)
27	34	PLEASE HAMMER DON'T HURT 'EM	MC Hammer (Capitol)
29	35	RHYTHM OF LOVE	Kylie Minogue (PWL)
35	36	THE TRACKS OF MY TEARS	Smokey Robinson and Various Artists (Motown)
-	37	THE COLLECTION	Barry White (Mercury)
45	38	MUSIC FROM TWIN PEAKS	Angelo Badalamenti (Warner Bros.)
42	39	UNCHAINED MELODY - THE VERY BEST OF ...	Righteous Brothers (Verve)
26	40	SHAKING THE TREE	Peter Gabriel (Virgin)
40	41	ROCKY V - SOUNDTRACK	Various (Capitol)
44	42	THE VERY BEST OF...	Bee Gees (Polydor)
37	43	GONNA MAKE YOU SWEAT	C&C Music Factory (Columbia)
-	44	THE BEST OF THE DOORS	Doors (Elektra)
43	45	BACK FROM RIO	Roger McGuinn (Arista)
39	46	STARRY NIGHT	Julio Iglesias (CBS)
-	47	ROCKING ALL OVER THE YEARS	Status Quo (Vertigo)
-	48	BITE	Ned's Atomic Dustbin (Rough Trade)
-	49	KIM APPLEBY	Kim Appleby (Parlophone)
-	50	SATELLITES	Big Dish (East West)

2 March 1991

1	1	INNUENDO	Queen (Parlophone)
3	2	WICKED GAME	Chris Isaak (Reprise)
2	3	INTO THE LIGHT	Gloria Estefan (Epic)
7	4	LISTEN WITHOUT PREJUDICE VOLUME 1	George Michael (Epic)
-	5	CIRCLE OF ONE	Oleta Adams (Fontana)
4	6	THE VERY BEST OF ELTON JOHN	Elton John (Rocket)
6	7	DEDICATION - THE VERY BEST OF THIN LIZZY	Thin Lizzy (Vertigo)
9	8	THE IMMACULATE COLLECTION	Madonna (Sire)
5	9	DOUBT	Jesus Jones (Food)
12	10	RUNAWAY HORSES	Belinda Carlisle (Virgin)
20	11	THE SIMPSONS SING THE BLUES	Simpsons (Geffen)
16	12	I'M YOUR BABY TONIGHT	Whitney Houston (Arista)
-	13	FREE	Rick Astley (RCA)
-	14	THE BEST OF FREE - ALL RIGHT NOW	Free (Island)
11	15	ALL TRUE MAN	Alexander O'Neal (Tabu)
10	16	MCMXC AD	Enigma (Virgin International)
14	17	SERIOUS HITS ... LIVE!	Phil Collins (Virgin)
8	18	THE SOUL CAGES	Sting (A&M)
17	19	X	INXS (Mercury)
21	20	THE LOST BOYS - SOUNDTRACK	Various (Atlantic)
15	21	IN CONCERT	Luciano Pavarotti, Placido Domingo and José Carreras (Decca)
30	22	PILLS 'N' THRILLS AND BELLYACHES	Happy Mondays (Factory)
-	23	30 SOMETHING	Carter - The Unstoppable Sex Machine (Rough Trade)
19	24	THE SINGLES COLLECTION 1984-1990	Jimmy Somerville (London)
-	25	THE ESSENTIAL JOSE CARRERAS	José Carreras (Philips)
13	26	AND NOW THE LEGACY BEGINS	Dream Warriors (Fourth & Broadway)
29	27	CHOKE	Beautiful South (Go! Discs)
23	28	DON'T EXPLAIN	Robert Palmer (EMI)
24	29	SWEET DREAMS	Patsy Cline (MCA)
-	30	NO MORE GAMES - THE REMIX ALBUM	New Kids On The Block (CBS)
25	31	TO THE EXTREME	Vanilla Ice (SBK)
28	32	SOUL PROVIDER	Michael Bolton (CBS)
34	33	PLEASE HAMMER DON'T HURT 'EM	MC Hammer (Capitol)
26	34	DIRTY DANCING - SOUNDTRACK	Various (RCA)
-	35	YOUNG GODS	Little Angels (Polydor)
37	36	THE COLLECTION	Barry White (Mercury)
22	37	LIVE AT THE BRIXTON ACADEMY	Faith No More (Slash)
18	38	EVERYBODY'S ANGEL	Tanita Tikaram (East West)
32	39	GREATEST HITS 1977-1990	Stranglers (Epic)
-	40	GREEN MIND	DinosaurJr. (blanco y negro)
41	41	ROCKY V - SOUNDTRACK	Various (Capitol)
27	42	THE RHYTHM OF THE SAINTS	Paul Simon (Warner Bros.)
50	43	SATELLITES	Big Dish (East West)
-	44	THE REAL RAMONA	Throwing Muses (4AD)
-	45	THE ROAD TO HELL	Chris Rea (WEA)
35	46	RHYTHM OF LOVE	Kylie Minogue (PWL)
33	47	WORLD POWER	Snap (Arista)
36	48	THE TRACKS OF MY TEARS	Smokey Robinson and Various Artists (Motown)
-	49	RALPH TRESVANT	Ralph Tresvant (MCA)
31	50	A LITTLE AIN'T ENOUGH	David Lee Roth (Warner Bros.)

Queen's *Innuendo* album topped the chart alongside its title track, which made Number 1 as a single; these were the last chart-toppers singer Freedie Mercury would have during his lifetime. Meanwhile, Patsy Cline's *Sweet Dreams* compilation was spurred to big sales by the Top 10 reissue of her 1961 single *Crazy*. These were the biggest chart successes ever for the country vocalist who had died way back in 1963.

March 1991

9 March 1991

last	this	Title	Artist
-	1	AUBERGE	Chris Rea (East West)
5	2	CIRCLE OF ONE	Oleta Adams (Fontana)
1	3	INNUENDO	Queen (Parlophone)
2	4	WICKED GAME	Chris Isaak (Reprise)
14	5	THE BEST OF FREE - ALL RIGHT NOW	Free (Island)
3	6	INTO THE LIGHT	Gloria Estefan (Epic)
4	7	LISTEN WITHOUT PREJUDICE VOLUME 1	George Michael (Epic)
8	8	THE IMMACULATE COLLECTION	Madonna (Sire)
6	9	THE VERY BEST OF ELTON JOHN	Elton John (Rocket)
11	10	THE SIMPSONS SING THE BLUES	Simpsons (Geffen)
13	11	FREE	Rick Astley (RCA)
7	12	DEDICATION - THE VERY BEST OF THIN LIZZY	Thin Lizzy (Vertigo)
23	13	30 SOMETHING	Carter - The Unstoppable Sex Machine (Rough Trade)
17	14	SERIOUS HITS ... LIVE!	Phil Collins (Virgin)
20	15	THE LOST BOYS - SOUNDTRACK	Various (Atlantic)
9	16	DOUBT	Jesus Jones (Food)
16	17	MCMXC AD	Enigma (Virgin International)
12	18	I'M YOUR BABY TONIGHT	Whitney Houston (Arista)
10	19	RUNAWAY HORSES	Belinda Carlisle (Virgin)
22	20	PILLS 'N' THRILLS AND BELLYACHES	Happy Mondays (Factory)
26	21	AND NOW THE LEGACY BEGINS	Dream Warriors (Fourth & Broadway)
19	22	X	INXS (Mercury)
18	23	THE SOUL CAGES	Sting (A&M)
15	24	ALL TRUE MAN	Alexander O'Neal (Tabu)
35	25	YOUNG GODS	Little Angels (Polydor)
33	26	PLEASE HAMMER DON'T HURT 'EM	MC Hammer (Capitol)
21	27	IN CONCERT	Luciano Pavarotti, Placido Domingo and José Carreras (Decca)
28	28	DON'T EXPLAIN	Robert Palmer (EMI)
30	29	NO MORE GAMES - THE REMIX ALBUM	New Kids On The Block (CBS)
-	30	NIGHT RIDE HOME	Joni Mitchell (Geffen)
-	31	THE VERY BEST OF...	Bee Gees (Polydor)
24	32	THE SINGLES COLLECTION 1984-1990	Jimmy Somerville (London)
34	33	DIRTY DANCING - SOUNDTRACK	Various (RCA)
31	34	TO THE EXTREME	Vanilla Ice (SBK)
40	35	GREEN MIND	DinosaurJr. (blanco y negro)
39	36	GREATEST HITS 1977-1990	Stranglers (Epic)
25	37	THE ESSENTIAL	José Carreras (Philips)
32	38	SOUL PROVIDER	Michael Bolton (CBS)
44	39	THE REAL RAMONA	Throwing Muses (4AD)
-	40	MUSIC FROM TWIN PEAKS	Angelo Badalamenti (Warner Bros.)
29	41	SWEET DREAMS	Patsy Cline (MCA)
41	42	ROCKY V - SOUNDTRACK	Various (Capitol)
-	43	BIRDLAND	Birdland (Lazy)
42	44	THE RHYTHM OF THE SAINTS	Paul Simon (Warner Bros.)
45	45	THE ROAD TO HELL	Chris Rea (WEA)
27	46	CHOKE	Beautiful South (Go! Discs)
-	47	GODDESS	Soho (S&M)
36	48	THE COLLECTION	Barry White (Mercury)
-	49	GREASE	Soundtrack (Polydor)
37	50	LIVE AT THE BRIXTON ACADEMY	Faith No More (Slash)

16 March 1991

last	this	Title	Artist
-	1	SPARTACUS	Farm (Produce)
1	2	AUBERGE	Chris Rea (East West)
2	3	CIRCLE OF ONE	Oleta Adams (Fontana)
-	4	EX : EL	808 State (ZTT)
-	5	KILL UNCLE	Morrissey (HMV)
3	6	INNUENDO	Queen (Parlophone)
-	7	THE WHITE ROOM	KLF (KLF Communications)
8	8	THE IMMACULATE COLLECTION	Madonna (Sire)
7	9	LISTEN WITHOUT PREJUDICE VOLUME 1	George Michael (Epic)
4	10	WICKED GAME	Chris Isaak (Reprise)
5	11	THE BEST OF FREE - ALL RIGHT NOW	Free (Island)
6	12	INTO THE LIGHT	Gloria Estefan (Epic)
9	13	THE VERY BEST OF ELTON JOHN	Elton John (Rocket)
10	14	THE SIMPSONS SING THE BLUES	Simpsons (Geffen)
12	15	DEDICATION	Thin Lizzy (Vertigo)
36	16	GREATEST HITS 1977-1990	Stranglers (Epic)
-	17	INSPECTOR MORSE	Barrington Pheloung (Virgin Television)
11	18	FREE	Rick Astley (RCA)
14	19	SERIOUS HITS ... LIVE!	Phil Collins (Virgin)
13	20	30 SOMETHING	Carter - The Unstoppable Sex Machine (Rough Trade)
16	21	DOUBT	Jesus Jones (Food)
17	22	MCMXC AD	Enigma (Virgin International)
-	23	THE COMPLETE PICTURE	Deborah Harry and Blondie (Chrysalis)
18	24	I'M YOUR BABY TONIGHT	Whitney Houston (Arista)
-	25	PEGGY SUICIDE	Julian Cope (Island)
27	26	IN CONCERT	Luciano Pavarotti, Placido Domingo and José Carreras (Decca)
20	27	PILLS 'N' THRILLS AND BELLYACHES	Happy Mondays (Factory)
15	28	THE LOST BOYS - SOUNDTRACK	Various (Atlantic)
37	29	THE ESSENTIAL	José Carreras (Philips)
22	30	X	INXS (Mercury)
31	31	THE VERY BEST OF ...	Bee Gees (Polydor)
26	32	PLEASE HAMMER DON'T HURT 'EM	MC Hammer (Capitol)
19	33	RUNAWAY HORSES	Belinda Carlisle (Virgin)
23	34	THE SOUL CAGES	Sting (A&M)
30	35	NIGHT RIDE HOME	Joni Mitchell (Geffen)
24	36	ALL TRUE MAN	Alexander O'Neal (Tabu)
25	37	YOUNG GODS	Little Angels (Polydor)
40	38	MUSIC FROM TWIN PEAKS	Angelo Badalamenti (Warner Bros.)
21	39	AND NOW THE LEGACY BEGINS	Dream Warriors (Fourth & Broadway)
-	40	THE VERY BEST OF ...	Joan Armatrading (A&M)
32	41	THE SINGLES COLLECTION 1984-1990	Jimmy Somerville (London)
-	42	WORLD POWER	Snap (Arista)
45	43	THE ROAD TO HELL	Chris Rea (WEA)
28	44	DON'T EXPLAIN	Robert Palmer (EMI)
33	45	DIRTY DANCING - SOUNDTRACK	Various Artists (RCA)
-	46	TIME'S UP	Living Colour (Epic)
-	47	EVERYBODY'S ANGEL	Tanita Tikaram (East West)
49	48	GREASE	Soundtrack (Polydor)
42	49	ROCKY V - SOUNDTRACK	Various (Capitol)
34	50	TO THE EXTREME	Vanilla Ice (SBK)

23 March 1991

last	this	Title	Artist
1	1	SPARTACUS	Farm (Produce)
2	2	AUBERGE	Chris Rea (East West)
-	3	OUT OF TIME	R.E.M. (Warner Bros.)
7	4	THE WHITE ROOM	KLF (KLF Communications)
4	5	EX : EL	808 State (ZTT)
23	6	THE COMPLETE PICTURE	Deborah Harry and Blondie (Chrysalis)
3	7	CIRCLE OF ONE	Oleta Adams (Fontana)
10	8	WICKED GAME	Chris Isaak (Reprise)
8	9	THE IMMACULATE COLLECTION	Madonna (Sire)
5	10	KILL UNCLE	Morrissey (HMV)
9	11	LISTEN WITHOUT PREJUDICE VOLUME 1	George Michael (Epic)
6	12	INNUENDO	Queen (Parlophone)
17	13	INSPECTOR MORSE	Barrington Pheloung (Virgin Television)
13	14	THE VERY BEST OF ELTON JOHN	Elton John (Rocket)
40	15	THE VERY BEST OF JOAN ARMATRADING	Joan Armatrading (A&M)
12	16	INTO THE LIGHT	Gloria Estefan (Epic)
46	17	TIME'S UP	Living Colour (Epic)
16	18	GREATEST HITS 1977-1990	Stranglers (Epic)
11	19	THE BEST OF FREE - ALL RIGHT NOW	Free (Island)
15	20	DEDICATION	Thin Lizzy (Vertigo)
26	21	IN CONCERT	Luciano Pavarotti, Placido Domingo and José Carreras (Decca)
14	22	THE SIMPSONS SING THE BLUES	Simpsons (Geffen)
25	23	PEGGY SUICIDE	Julian Cope (Island)
35	24	NIGHT RIDE HOME	Joni Mitchell (Geffen)
21	25	DOUBT	Jesus Jones (Food)
29	26	THE ESSENTIAL	José Carreras (Philips)
18	27	FREE	Rick Astley (RCA)
24	28	I'M YOUR BABY TONIGHT	Whitney Houston (Arista)
19	29	SERIOUS HITS ... LIVE!	Phil Collins (Virgin)
-	30	PINK BUBBLES GO APE	Helloween (EMI)
22	31	MCMXC AD	Enigma (Virgin International)
20	32	30 SOMETHING	Carter - The Unstoppable Sex Machine (Rough Trade)
31	33	THE VERY BEST OF ...	Bee Gees (Polydor)
27	34	PILLS 'N' THRILLS AND BELLYACHES	Happy Mondays (Factory)
41	35	THE SINGLES COLLECTION 1984-1990	Jimmy Somerville (London)
28	36	THE LOST BOYS - SOUNDTRACK	Various (Atlantic)
32	37	PLEASE HAMMER DON'T HURT 'EM	MC Hammer (Capitol)
38	38	MUSIC FROM TWIN PEAKS	Angelo Badalamenti (Warner Bros.)
30	39	X	INXS (Mercury)
33	40	RUNAWAY HORSES	Belinda Carlisle (Virgin)
43	41	THE ROAD TO HELL	Chris Rea (WEA)
37	42	YOUNG GODS	Little Angels (Polydor)
-	43	LLOYD WEBBER PLAYS LLOYD WEBBER	Julian Lloyd Webber & the Royal Philharmonic Orchestra (Philips)
36	44	ALL TRUE MAN	Alexander O'Neal (Tabu)
34	45	THE SOUL CAGES	Sting (A&M)
-	46	CHOKE	Beautiful South (Go! Discs)
45	47	DIRTY DANCING - SOUNDTRACK	Various Artists (RCA)
-	48	LOOK SHARP!	Roxette (EMI)
-	49	THE COLLECTION	Barry White (Mercury)
-	50	SWEET DREAMS	Patsy Cline (MCA)

Auberge gave Chris Rea his second consecutive chart-topper, following *The Road To Hell*, while Morrissey's second solo album, *Kill Uncle*, did not quite scale the same heights as its short-lived predecessor - it did vanish from contention just as rapidly, however, with all its notable sales being packed into two Top 10 weeks and three more much further down the Top 50.

last week	this week	30 March 1991	
3	1	OUT OF TIME	R.E.M. (Warner Bros.)
-	2	GREATEST HITS	Eurythmics (RCA)
2	3	AUBERGE	Chris Rea (East West)
6	4	THE COMPLETE PICTURE	Deborah Harry and Blondie (Chrysalis)
1	5	SPARTACUS	Farm (Produce)
13	6	INSPECTOR MORSE	Barrington Pheloung (Virgin Television)
5	7	EX : EL	808 State (ZTT)
4	8	THE WHITE ROOM KLF	(KLF Communications)
8	9	WICKED GAME	Chris Isaak (Reprise)
15	10	THE VERY BEST OF ...	Joan Armatrading (A&M)
9	11	THE IMMACULATE COLLECTION	Madonna (Sire)
11	12	LISTEN WITHOUT PREJUDICE VOLUME 1	George Michael (Epic)
14	13	THE VERY BEST OF ELTON JOHN	Elton John (Rocket)
7	14	CIRCLE OF ONE	Oleta Adams (Fontana)
12	15	INNUENDO	Queen (Parlophone)
16	16	INTO THE LIGHT	Gloria Estefan (Epic)
19	17	THE BEST OF FREE - ALL RIGHT NOW	Free (Island)
18	18	GREATEST HITS 1977-1990	Stranglers (Epic)
17	19	TIME'S UP	Living Colour (Epic)
-	20	THE STORY OF THE CLASH VOLUME 1	Clash (CBS)
20	21	DEDICATION	Thin Lizzy (Vertigo)
34	22	PILLS 'N' THRILLS AND BELLYACHES	Happy Mondays (Factory)
10	23	KILL UNCLE	Morrissey (HMV)
25	24	DOUBT	Jesus Jones (Food)
28	25	I'M YOUR BABY TONIGHT	Whitney Houston (Arista)
33	26	THE VERY BEST OF ...	Bee Gees (Polydor)
31	27	MCMXC AD	Enigma (Virgin International)
21	28	IN CONCERT	Luciano Pavarotti, Placido Domingo and José Carreras (Decca)
22	29	THE SIMPSONS SING THE BLUES	Simpsons (Geffen)
23	30	PEGGY SUICIDE	Julian Cope (Island)
27	31	FREE	Rick Astley (RCA)
-	32	SLINKY	Milltown Brothers (A&M)
26	33	THE ESSENTIAL	José Carreras (Philips)
39	34	X	INXS (Mercury)
-	35	SOUL DESTRUCTION	Almighty (Polydor)
45	36	THE SOUL CAGES	Sting (A&M)
29	37	SERIOUS HITS ... LIVE!	Phil Collins (Virgin)
44	38	ALL TRUE MAN	Alexander O'Neal (Tabu)
32	39	30 SOMETHING	Carter - The Unstoppable Sex Machine (Rough Trade)
-	40	THE INCREDIBLE SOUND MACHINE	Mantronix (Capitol)
24	41	NIGHT RIDE HOME	Joni Mitchell (Geffen)
36	42	THE LOST BOYS - SOUNDTRACK	Various (Atlantic)
37	43	PLEASE HAMMER DON'T HURT 'EM	MC Hammer (Capitol)
35	44	THE SINGLES COLLECTION 1984-1990	Jimmy Somerville (London)
-	45	SOUL PROVIDER	Michael Bolton (CBS)
48	46	LOOK SHARP!	Roxette (EMI)
40	47	RUNAWAY HORSES	Belinda Carlisle (Virgin)
38	48	MUSIC FROM TWIN PEAKS	Angelo Badalamenti (Warner Bros.)
30	49	PINK BUBBLES GO APE	Helloween (EMI)
46	50	CHOKE	Beautiful South (Go! Discs)

		5 April 1991	
2	1	GREATEST HITS	Eurythmics (RCA)
1	2	OUT OF TIME	R.E.M. (Warner Bros.)
3	3	AUBERGE	Chris Rea (East West)
4	4	THE COMPLETE PICTURE	Deborah Harry and Blondie (Chrysalis)
6	5	INSPECTOR MORSE	Barrington Pheloung (Virgin Television)
5	6	SPARTACUS	Farm (Produce)
12	7	LISTEN WITHOUT PREJUDICE VOLUME 1	George Michael (Epic)
10	8	THE VERY BEST OF ...	Joan Armatrading (A&M)
-	9	VAGABOND HEART	Rod Stewart (Warner Bros.)
11	10	THE IMMACULATE COLLECTION	Madonna (Sire)
-	11	ENTREAT	Cure (Fiction)
20	12	THE STORY OF THE CLASH VOLUME 1	Clash (CBS)
7	13	EX : EL	808 State (ZTT)
9	14	WICKED GAME	Chris Isaak (Reprise)
13	15	THE VERY BEST OF ELTON JOHN	Elton John (Rocket)
14	16	CIRCLE OF ONE	Oleta Adams (Fontana)
8	17	THE WHITE ROOM KLF	(KLF Communications)
15	18	INNUENDO	Queen (Parlophone)
16	19	INTO THE LIGHT	Gloria Estefan (Epic)
17	20	TIME'S UP	Living Colour (Epic)
24	21	DOUBT	Jesus Jones (Food)
18	22	GREATEST HITS 1977-1990	Stranglers (Epic)
22	23	PILLS 'N' THRILLS AND BELLYACHES	Happy Mondays (Factory)
-	24	THE DOORS - SOUNDTRACK	Doors (Elektra)
17	25	THE BEST OF FREE - ALL RIGHT NOW	Free (Island)
28	26	IN CONCERT	Luciano Pavarotti, Placido Domingo and José Carreras (Decca)
34	27	X	INXS (Mercury)
-	28	BRAHMS VIOLIN CONCERTO	Nigel Kennedy (EMI)
29	29	THE SIMPSONS SING THE BLUES	Simpsons (Geffen)
35	30	SOUL DESTRUCTION	Almighty (Polydor)
31	31	FREE	Rick Astley (RCA)
21	32	DEDICATION - THE VERY BEST OF THIN LIZZY	Thin Lizzy (Vertigo)
26	33	THE VERY BEST OF ...	Bee Gees (Polydor)
27	34	MCMXC AD	Enigma (Virgin International)
-	35	HIGH CIVILIZATION	Bee Gees (Warner Bros.)
33	36	THE ESSENTIAL JOSE CARRERAS	José Carreras (Philips)
38	37	ALL TRUE MAN	Alexander O'Neal (Tabu)
25	38	I'M YOUR BABY TONIGHT	Whitney Houston (Arista)
36	39	THE SOUL CAGES	Sting (A&M)
-	40	EARTH INFERNO	Fields Of The Nephilim (Beggars Banquet)
43	41	PLEASE HAMMER DON'T HURT 'EM	MC Hammer (Capitol)
-	42	WHEN YOU'RE A BOY	Susanna Hoffs (Columbia)
23	43	KILL UNCLE	Morrissey (HMV)
45	44	SOUL PROVIDER	Michael Bolton (CBS)
42	45	THE LOST BOYS - SOUNDTRACK	Various (Atlantic)
32	46	SLINKY	Milltown Brothers (A&M)
30	47	PEGGY SUICIDE	Julian Cope (Island)
37	48	SERIOUS HITS ... LIVE!	Phil Collins (Virgin)
50	49	CHOKE	Beautiful South (Go! Discs)
41	50	NIGHT RIDE HOME	Joni Mitchell (Geffen)

		12 April 1991	
1	1	GREATEST HITS	Eurythmics (RCA)
9	2	VAGABOND HEART	Rod Stewart (Warner Bros.)
2	3	OUT OF TIME	R.E.M. (Warner Bros.)
-	4	JOYRIDE	Roxette (EMI)
4	5	THE COMPLETE PICTURE	Deborah Harry and Blondie (Chrysalis)
3	6	AUBERGE	Chris Rea (East West)
5	7	INSPECTOR MORSE	Barrington Pheloung (Virgin Television)
11	8	ENTREAT	Cure (Fiction)
24	9	THE DOORS - SOUNDTRACK	Doors (Elektra)
-	10	GOD FODDER	Ned's Atomic Dustbin (Furtive)
7	11	LISTEN WITHOUT PREJUDICE VOLUME 1	George Michael (Epic)
10	12	THE IMMACULATE COLLECTION	Madonna (Sire)
6	13	SPARTACUS	Farm (Produce)
12	14	THE STORY OF THE CLASH VOLUME 1	Clash (CBS)
14	15	WICKED GAME	Chris Isaak (Reprise)
28	16	BRAHMS VIOLIN CONCERTO	Nigel Kennedy (EMI)
35	17	HIGH CIVILIZATION	Bee Gees (Warner Bros.)
8	18	THE VERY BEST OF JOAN ARMATRADING	Joan Armatrading (A&M)
15	19	THE VERY BEST OF ELTON JOHN	Elton John (Rocket)
-	20	MAMA SAID	Lenny Kravitz (Virgin America)
21	21	DOUBT	Jesus Jones (Food)
18	22	INNUENDO	Queen (Parlophone)
29	23	THE SIMPSONS SING THE BLUES	Simpsons (Geffen)
19	24	INTO THE LIGHT	Gloria Estefan (Epic)
20	25	TIME'S UP	Living Colour (Epic)
16	26	CIRCLE OF ONE	Oleta Adams (Fontana)
13	27	EX : EL	808 State (ZTT)
22	28	GREATEST HITS 1977-1990	Stranglers (Epic)
-	29	HISTORY REVISITED - THE REMIXES	Talk Talk (Parlophone)
17	30	THE WHITE ROOM KLF	(KLF Communications)
26	31	IN CONCERT	Luciano Pavarotti, Placido Domingo and José Carreras (Decca)
27	32	X	INXS (Mercury)
23	33	PILLS 'N' THRILLS AND BELLYACHES	Happy Mondays (Factory)
32	34	DEDICATION	Thin Lizzy (Vertigo)
-	35	THE BEST OF THE DOORS	Doors (Elektra)
40	36	EARTH INFERNO	Fields Of The Nephilim (Beggars Banquet)
42	37	WHEN YOU'RE A BOY	Susanna Hoffs (Columbia)
-	38	THE BOOTLEG SERIES VOLUMES 1-3 (RARE & UNRELEASED) 196-1991	Bob Dylan (CBS)
46	39	SLINKY	Milltown Brothers (A&M)
30	40	SOUL DESTRUCTION	Almighty (Polydor)
33	41	THE VERY BEST OF ...	Bee Gees (Polydor)
34	42	MCMXC AD	Enigma (Virgin International)
25	43	THE BEST OF FREE - ALL RIGHT NOW	Free (Island)
36	44	THE ESSENTIAL JOSE CARRERAS	José Carreras (Philips)
31	45	FREE	Rick Astley (RCA)
48	46	SERIOUS HITS ... LIVE!	Phil Collins (Virgin)
47	47	PEGGY SUICIDE	Julian Cope (Island)
43	48	KILL UNCLE	Morrissey (HMV)
-	49	RIPE	Banderas (London)
-	50	A DREAM FULFILLED	Will Downing (Fourth & Broadway)

The chart-topping success of *Out Of Time*, coupled with the strong showings of the several singles which would be taken from it, confirmed the rise of REM - cult favourites for much of the 1980s - to the position of one of the world's top rock bands. *Out Of Time* remained in the Top 10 for much of the remainder of the year. The unusual spectacle of a TV soundtrack in the Top 10 was provided by *Inspector Morse*.

April – May 1991

20 April 1991

last week	this week	title	artist (label)
-	1	REAL LIFE	Simple Minds (Virgin)
1	2	GREATEST HITS	Eurythmics (RCA)
4	3	JOYRIDE	Roxette (EMI)
2	4	VAGABOND HEART	Rod Stewart (Warner Bros.)
3	5	OUT OF TIME	R.E.M. (Warner Bros.)
10	6	GOD FODDER	Ned's Atomic Dustbin (Furtive)
-	7	FLASHPOINT	Rolling Stones (Rolling Stones)
20	8	MAMA SAID	Lenny Kravitz (Virgin America)
5	9	THE COMPLETE PICTURE	Deborah Harry and Blondie (Chrysalis)
9	10	THE DOORS - SOUNDTRACK	Doors (Elektra)
6	11	AUBERGE	Chris Rea (East West)
12	12	THE IMMACULATE COLLECTION	Madonna (Sire)
7	13	INSPECTOR MORSE (ORIGINAL MUSIC FROM THE ITV SERIES)	Barrington Pheloung (Virgin Television)
23	14	THE SIMPSONS SING THE BLUES	Simpsons (Geffen)
-	15	BLUE LINES	Massive Attack (Wild Bunch)
14	16	THE STORY OF THE CLASH VOLUME 1	Clash (CBS)
24	17	INTO THE LIGHT	Gloria Estefan (Epic)
13	18	SPARTACUS	Farm (Produce)
11	19	LISTEN WITHOUT PREJUDICE VOLUME 1	George Michael (Epic)
26	20	CIRCLE OF ONE	Oleta Adams (Fontana)
8	21	ENTREAT	Cure (Fiction)
15	22	WICKED GAME	Chris Isaak (Reprise)
21	23	DOUBT	Jesus Jones (Food)
16	24	BRAHMS VIOLIN CONCERTO	Nigel Kennedy (EMI)
19	25	THE VERY BEST OF ELTON JOHN	Elton John (Rocket)
35	26	THE BEST OF THE DOORS	Doors (Elektra)
38	27	THE BOOTLEG SERIES VOLUMES 1-3 (RARE & UNRELEASED) 196-1991	Bob Dylan (CBS)
30	28	THE WHITE ROOM	KLF (KLF Communications)
-	29	RAIN TREE CROW	Rain Tree Crow (Virgin)
25	30	TIME'S UP	Living Colour (Epic)
18	31	THE VERY BEST OF...	Joan Armatrading (A&M)
22	32	INNUENDO	Queen (Parlophone)
28	33	GREATEST HITS 1977-1990	Stranglers (Epic)
-	34	BUDDY'S SONG	Chesney Hawkes (Chrysalis)
17	35	HIGH CIVILIZATION	Bee Gees (Warner Bros.)
33	36	PILLS 'N' THRILLS AND BELLYACHES	Happy Mondays (Factory)
27	37	EX : EL	808 State (ZTT)
34	38	DEDICATION	Thin Lizzy (Vertigo)
-	39	MANE ATTRACTION	White Lion (Atlantic)
-	40	PLEASE HAMMER DON'T HURT 'EM	MC Hammer (Capitol)
32	41	X	INXS (Mercury)
42	42	MCMXC AD	Enigma (Virgin International)
31	43	IN CONCERT	Luciano Pavarotti, Placido Domingo and José Carreras (Decca)
47	44	PEGGY SUICIDE	Julian Cope (Island)
43	45	THE BEST OF FREE - ALL RIGHT NOW	Free (Island)
49	46	RIPE	Banderas (London)
40	47	SOUL DESTRUCTION	Almighty (Polydor)
29	48	HISTORY REVISITED - THE REMIXES	Talk Talk (Parlophone)
39	49	SLINKY	Milltown Brothers (A&M)
-	50	LOOK SHARP!	Roxette (EMI)

27 April 1991

last week	this week	title	artist (label)
2	1	GREATEST HITS	Eurythmics (RCA)
1	2	REAL LIFE	Simple Minds (Virgin)
7	3	FLASHPOINT	Rolling Stones (Rolling Stones)
3	4	JOYRIDE	Roxette (EMI)
4	5	VAGABOND HEART	Rod Stewart (Warner Bros.)
5	6	OUT OF TIME	R.E.M. (Warner Bros.)
12	7	THE IMMACULATE COLLECTION	Madonna (Sire)
15	8	BLUE LINES	Massive Attack (Wild Bunch)
9	9	THE COMPLETE PICTURE	Deborah Harry and Blondie (Chrysalis)
8	10	MAMA SAID	Lenny Kravitz (Virgin America)
10	11	THE DOORS - SOUNDTRACK	Doors (Elektra)
11	12	AUBERGE	Chris Rea (East West)
17	13	INTO THE LIGHT	Gloria Estefan (Epic)
14	14	THE SIMPSONS SING THE BLUES	Simpsons (Geffen)
19	15	LISTEN WITHOUT PREJUDICE VOLUME 1	George Michael (Epic)
26	16	THE BEST OF THE DOORS	Doors (Elektra)
16	17	THE STORY OF THE CLASH VOLUME 1	Clash (CBS)
13	18	INSPECTOR MORSE	Barrington Pheloung (Virgin Television)
25	19	THE VERY BEST OF ELTON JOHN	Elton John (Rocket)
22	20	WICKED GAME	Chris Isaak (Reprise)
20	21	CIRCLE OF ONE	Oleta Adams (Fontana)
24	22	BRAHMS VIOLIN CONCERTO	Nigel Kennedy (EMI)
29	23	RAIN TREE CROW	Rain Tree Crow (Virgin)
6	24	GOD FODDER	Ned's Atomic Dustbin (Furtive)
18	25	SPARTACUS	Farm (Produce)
33	26	GREATEST HITS 1977-1990	Stranglers (Epic)
-	27	SONGS FROM THE MARDI GRAS	Feargal Sharkey (Virgin)
31	28	THE VERY BEST OF ...	Joan Armatrading (A&M)
23	29	DOUBT	Jesus Jones (Food)
34	30	BUDDY'S SONG	Chesney Hawkes (Chrysalis)
40	31	PLEASE HAMMER DON'T HURT 'EM	MC Hammer (Capitol)
-	32	WORD OF MOUTH	Mike & the Mechanics (Virgin)
32	33	INNUENDO	Queen (Parlophone)
41	34	X	INXS (Mercury)
43	35	IN CONCERT	Luciano Pavarotti, Placido Domingo and José Carreras (Decca)
28	36	THE WHITE ROOM	KLF (KLF Communications)
27	37	THE BOOTLEG SERIES VOLUMES 1-3 (RARE & UNRELEASED) 196-1991	Bob Dylan (CBS)
21	38	ENTREAT	Cure (Fiction)
36	39	PILLS 'N' THRILLS AND BELLYACHES	Happy Mondays (Factory)
37	40	EX : EL	808 State (ZTT)
42	41	MCMXC AD	Enigma (Virgin International)
35	42	HIGH CIVILIZATION	Bee Gees (Warner Bros.)
38	43	DEDICATION - THE VERY BEST OF THIN LIZZY	Thin Lizzy (Vertigo)
30	44	TIME'S UP	Living Colour (Epic)
-	45	DANCES WITH WOLVES - SOUNDTRACK	John Barry (Epic)
39	46	MANE ATTRACTION	White Lion (Atlantic)
44	47	PEGGY SUICIDE	Julian Cope (Island)
46	48	RIPE	Banderas (London)
50	49	LOOK SHARP!	Roxette (EMI)
-	50	ADVENTURES BEYOND THE ULTRAWORLD	Orb (Big Life)

4 May 1991

last week	this week	title	artist (label)
1	1	GREATEST HITS	Eurythmics (RCA)
2	2	REAL LIFE	Simple Minds (Virgin)
4	3	JOYRIDE	Roxette (EMI)
6	4	OUT OF TIME	R.E.M. (Warner Bros.)
-	5	THE BEAST INSIDE	Inspiral Carpets (Cow)
5	6	VAGABOND HEART	Rod Stewart (Warner Bros.)
11	7	THE DOORS - SOUNDTRACK	Doors (Elektra)
13	8	INTO THE LIGHT	Gloria Estefan (Epic)
-	9	GOLD MOTHER	James (Fontana)
7	10	THE IMMACULATE COLLECTION	Madonna (Sire)
9	11	THE COMPLETE PICTURE	Deborah Harry and Blondie (Chrysalis)
32	12	WORD OF MOUTH	Mike & the Mechanics (Virgin)
3	13	FLASHPOINT	Rolling Stones (Rolling Stones)
12	14	AUBERGE	Chris Rea (East West)
26	15	GREATEST HITS 1977-1990	Stranglers (Epic)
16	16	THE BEST OF THE DOORS	Doors (Elektra)
19	17	THE VERY BEST OF ELTON JOHN	Elton John (Rocket)
-	18	HOODOO	Alison Moyet (Columbia)
14	19	THE SIMPSONS SING THE BLUES	Simpsons (Geffen)
10	20	MAMA SAID	Lenny Kravitz (Virgin America)
15	21	LISTEN WITHOUT PREJUDICE VOLUME 1	George Michael (Epic).
20	22	WICKED GAME	Chris Isaak (Reprise)
8	23	BLUE LINES	Massive Attack (Wild Bunch)
21	24	CIRCLE OF ONE	Oleta Adams (Fontana)
25	25	SPARTACUS	Farm (Produce)
17	26	THE STORY OF THE CLASH VOLUME 1	Clash (CBS)
18	27	INSPECTOR MORSE (ORIGINAL MUSIC FROM THE ITV SERIES)	Barrington Pheloung (Virgin Television)
27	28	SONGS FROM THE MARDI GRAS	Feargal Sharkey (Virgin)
31	29	PLEASE HAMMER DON'T HURT 'EM	MC Hammer (Capitol)
22	30	BRAHMS VIOLIN CONCERTO	Nigel Kennedy (EMI)
-	31	SHIFT-WORK	Fall (Beggars Banquet)
30	32	BUDDY'S SONG	Chesney Hawkes (Chrysalis)
36	33	THE WHITE ROOM	KLF (KLF Communications)
29	34	DOUBT	Jesus Jones (Food)
34	35	X	INXS (Mercury)
35	36	IN CONCERT	Luciano Pavarotti Placido Domingo and José Carreras (Decca)
-	37	THE EMOTIONAL HOOLIGAN	Gary Clail On-U Sound System (Perfecto)
33	38	INNUENDO	Queen (Parlophone)
50	39	ADVENTURES BEYOND THE ULTRAWORLD	Orb (Big Life)
-	40	RAW	Alarm (IRS)
40	41	EX : EL	808 State (ZTT)
39	42	PILLS 'N' THRILLS AND BELLYACHES	Happy Mondays (Factory)
24	43	GOD FODDER	Ned's Atomic Dustbin (Furtive)
28	44	THE VERY BEST OF JOAN ARMATRADING	Joan Armatrading (A&M)
42	45	HIGH CIVILIZATION	Bee Gees (Warner Bros.)
41	46	MCMXC AD	Enigma (Virgin International)
-	47	LOVE CAN DO THAT	Elaine Paige (RCA)
-	48	THE DOORS	Doors (Elektra)
-	49	THE VERY BEST OF ...	Bee Gees (Polydor)
38	50	ENTREAT	Cure (Fiction)

The Eurythmics had eschewed the Christmas 1990 compilation scramble, but cannily released their *Greatest Hits* set at Easter instead, when it got the top of the chart to itself after dethroning Simple Minds. Four weeks at the top and a stay of several months in the Top 10 helped make it the duo's bigest-selling album ever. The *Doors* soundtrack music, by the way, was provided by the band's original records.

last	this		
week		**11 May 1991**	

last	this		
1	1	GREATEST HITS	Eurythmics (RCA)
-	2	THE BEST OF THE WATERBOYS '81-'91	
			Waterboys (Ensign)
9	3	GOLD MOTHER	James (Fontana)
3	4	JOYRIDE	Roxette (EMI)
2	5	REAL LIFE	Simple Minds (Virgin)
5	6	THE BEAST INSIDE	Inspiral Carpets (Cow)
4	7	OUT OF TIME	R.E.M. (Warner Bros.)
8	8	INTO THE LIGHT	Gloria Estefan (Epic)
15	9	GREATEST HITS 1977-1990	Stranglers (Epic)
18	10	HOODOO	Alison Moyet (Columbia)
6	11	VAGABOND HEART	Rod Stewart (Warner Bros.)
10	12	THE IMMACULATE COLLECTION	Madonna (Sire)
7	13	THE DOORS - SOUNDTRACK	Doors (Elektra)
33	14	THE WHITE ROOM	KLF (KLF Communications)
14	15	AUBERGE	Chris Rea (East West)
11	16	THE COMPLETE PICTURE	
			Deborah Harry and Blondie (Chrysalis)
-	17	UNION	Yes (Arista)
16	18	THE BEST OF THE DOORS	Doors (Elektra)
29	19	PLEASE HAMMER DON'T HURT 'EM	
			MC Hammer (Capitol)
31	20	SHIFT-WORK	Fall (Beggars Banquet)
12	21	WORD OF MOUTH	Mike & the Mechanics (Virgin)
25	22	SPARTACUS	Farm (Produce)
19	23	THE SIMPSONS SING THE BLUES	
			Simpsons (Geffen)
17	24	THE VERY BEST OF ELTON JOHN	
			Elton John (Rocket)
24	25	CIRCLE OF ONE	Oleta Adams (Fontana)
22	26	WICKED GAME	Chris Isaak (Reprise)
21	27	LISTEN WITHOUT PREJUDICE VOLUME 1	
			George Michael (Epic)
37	28	THE EMOTIONAL HOOLIGAN	
			Gary Clail On-U Sound System (Perfecto)
20	29	MAMA SAID	Lenny Kravitz (Virgin America)
-	30	TRUE LOVE	Pat Benatar (Chrysalis)
26	31	THE STORY OF THE CLASH VOLUME 1	
			Clash (CBS)
40	32	RAW	Alarm (IRS)
36	33	IN CONCERT	Luciano Pavarotti
			Placido Domingo and José Carreras (Decca)
27	34	INSPECTOR MORSE (ORIGINAL MUSIC FROM	
		THE ITV SERIES)	
			Barrington Pheloung (Virgin Television)
30	35	BRAHMS VIOLIN CONCERTO	Nigel Kennedy (EMI)
32	36	BUDDY'S SONG	Chesney Hawkes (Chrysalis)
13	37	FLASHPOINT	Rolling Stones (Rolling Stones)
-	38	WHIRLPOOL	Chapterhouse (Dedicated)
28	39	SONGS FROM THE MARDI GRAS	
			Feargal Sharkey (Virgin)
-	40	BLOOD	This Mortal Coil (4AD)
23	41	BLUE LINES	Massive Attack (Wild Bunch)
34	42	DOUBT	Jesus Jones (Food)
-	43	SOUL PROVIDER	Michael Bolton (CBS)
42	44	PILLS 'N' THRILLS AND BELLYACHES	
			Happy Mondays (Factory)
38	45	INNUENDO	Queen (Parlophone)
46	46	MCMXC AD	Enigma (Virgin International)
41	47	EX : EL	808 State (ZTT)
49	48	THE VERY BEST OF...	Bee Gees (Polydor)
35	49	X	INXS (Mercury)
-	50	SMOKE & STRONG WHISKEY	
			Christy Moore (Newberry)

last	this		
week		**18 May 1991**	

1	1	GREATEST HITS	Eurythmics (RCA)
-	2	SCHUBERT DIP	EMF (Parlophone)
2	3	THE BEST OF THE WATERBOYS '81-'91	
			Waterboys (Ensign)
-	4	TIME, LOVE & TENDERNESS	
			Michael Bolton (Columbia)
3	5	GOLD MOTHER	James (Fontana)
4	6	JOYRIDE	Roxette (EMI)
14	7	THE WHITE ROOM	KLF (KLF Communications)
7	8	OUT OF TIME	R.E.M. (Warner Bros.)
5	9	REAL LIFE	Simple Minds (Virgin)
-	10	SUGAR TAX	
			Orchestral Manoeuvres In The Dark (Virgin)
17	11	UNION	Yes (Arista)
8	12	INTO THE LIGHT	Gloria Estefan (Epic)
9	13	GREATEST HITS 1977-1990	Stranglers (Epic)
19	14	PLEASE HAMMER DON'T HURT 'EM	
			MC Hammer (Capitol)
12	15	THE IMMACULATE COLLECTION	Madonna (Sire)
11	16	VAGABOND HEART	Rod Stewart (Warner Bros.)
15	17	AUBERGE	Chris Rea (East West)
13	18	THE DOORS - SOUNDTRACK	Doors (Elektra)
6	19	THE BEAST INSIDE	Inspiral Carpets (Cow)
23	20	THE SIMPSONS SING THE BLUES	
			Simpsons (Geffen)
22	21	SPARTACUS	Farm (Produce)
10	22	HOODOO	Alison Moyet (Columbia)
16	23	THE COMPLETE PICTURE	
			Deborah Harry and Blondie (Chrysalis)
-	24	GET READY!	Roachford (Columbia)
18	25	THE BEST OF THE DOORS	Doors (Elektra)
25	26	CIRCLE OF ONE	Oleta Adams (Fontana)
24	27	THE VERY BEST OF ELTON JOHN	
			Elton John (Rocket)
26	28	WICKED GAME	Chris Isaak (Reprise)
27	29	LISTEN WITHOUT PREJUDICE VOLUME 1	
			George Michael (Epic)
-	30	ZUCCHERO	Zucchero (A&M)
29	31	MAMA SAID	Lenny Kravitz (Virgin America)
21	32	WORD OF MOUTH	Mike & the Mechanics (Virgin)
38	33	WHIRLPOOL	Chapterhouse (Dedicated)
43	34	SOUL PROVIDER	Michael Bolton (CBS)
31	35	THE STORY OF THE CLASH VOLUME 1	
			Clash (CBS)
35	36	BRAHMS VIOLIN CONCERTO	Nigel Kennedy (EMI)
33	37	IN CONCERT	Luciano Pavarotti,
			Placido Domingo and José Carreras (Decca)
30	38	TRUE LOVE	Pat Benatar (Chrysalis)
37	39	FLASHPOINT	Rolling Stones (Rolling Stones)
36	40	BUDDY'S SONG	Chesney Hawkes (Chrysalis)
34	41	INSPECTOR MORSE (ORIGINAL MUSIC FROM	
		THE ITV SERIES)	Barrington Pheloung (Virg
		Television)	
48	42	THE VERY BEST OF...	Bee Gees (Polydor)
-	43	LAUGHTER & LUST	Joe Jackson (Virgin America)
45	44	INNUENDO	Queen (Parlophone)
41	45	BLUE LINES	Massive Attack (Wild Bunch)
20	46	SHIFT-WORK	Fall (Beggars Banquet)
44	47	PILLS 'N' THRILLS AND BELLYACHES	
			Happy Mondays (Factory)
46	48	MCMXC AD	Enigma (Virgin International)
-	49	HARD AT PLAY	
			Huey Lewis & the News (Chrysalis)
-	50	HEART OF STONE	Cher (Geffen)

last	this		
week		**25 May 1991**	

4	1	TIME, LOVE & TENDERNESS	
			Michael Bolton (Columbia)
1	2	GREATEST HITS	Eurythmics (RCA)
2	3	SCHUBERT DIP	EMF (Parlophone)
8	4	OUT OF TIME	R.E.M. (Warner Bros.)
-	5	MIGHTY LIKE A ROSE	Elvis Costello (Warner Bros.)
6	6	JOYRIDE	Roxette (EMI)
10	7	SUGAR TAX	
			Orchestral Manoeuvres In The Dark (Virgin)
-	8	DE LA SOUL IS DEAD	De La Soul (Big Life)
3	9	THE BEST OF THE WATERBOYS '81-'91	
			Waterboys (Ensign)
7	10	THE WHITE ROOM	KLF (KLF Communications)
9	11	REAL LIFE	Simple Minds (Virgin)
14	12	PLEASE HAMMER DON'T HURT 'EM	
			MC Hammer (Capitol)
15	13	THE IMMACULATE COLLECTION	Madonna (Sire)
-	14	POWER OF LOVE	Luther Vandross (Epic)
5	15	GOLD MOTHER	James (Fontana)
12	16	INTO THE LIGHT	Gloria Estefan (Epic)
18	17	THE DOORS - SOUNDTRACK	Doors (Elektra)
16	18	VAGABOND HEART	Rod Stewart (Warner Bros.)
13	19	GREATEST HITS 1977-1990	Stranglers (Epic)
11	20	UNION	Yes (Arista)
31	21	MAMA SAID	Lenny Kravitz (Virgin America)
24	22	GET READY!	Roachford (Columbia)
17	23	AUBERGE	Chris Rea (East West)
20	24	THE SIMPSONS SING THE BLUES	
			Simpsons (Geffen)
25	25	THE BEST OF THE DOORS	Doors (Elektra)
23	26	THE COMPLETE PICTURE	
			Deborah Harry and Blondie (Chrysalis)
-	27	LEGEND	Bob Marley & the Wailers (Island)
27	28	THE VERY BEST OF ELTON JOHN	
			Elton John (Rocket)
30	29	ZUCCHERO	Zucchero (A&M)
-	30	KEEP THE MUSIC PLAYING	Shirley Bassey (Dino)
26	31	CIRCLE OF ONE	Oleta Adams (Fontana)
21	32	SPARTACUS	Farm (Produce)
29	33	LISTEN WITHOUT PREJUDICE VOLUME 1	
			George Michael (Epic)
28	34	WICKED GAME	Chris Isaak (Reprise)
36	35	BRAHMS VIOLIN CONCERTO	Nigel Kennedy (EMI)
34	36	SOUL PROVIDER	Michael Bolton (CBS)
35	37	THE STORY OF THE CLASH VOLUME 1	
			Clash (CBS)
-	38	POP LIFE	Bananarama (London)
19	39	THE BEAST INSIDE	Inspiral Carpets (Cow)
37	40	IN CONCERT	Luciano Pavarotti,
			Placido Domingo and José Carreras (Decca)
22	41	HOODOO	Alison Moyet (Columbia)
41	42	INSPECTOR MORSE (ORIGINAL MUSIC FROM	
		THE ITV SERIES)	
			Barrington Pheloung (Virgin Television)
-	43	THE RHYTHM OF THE SAINTS	
			Paul Simon (Warner Bros.)
32	44	WORD OF MOUTH	Mike & the Mechanics (Virgin)
-	45	THE SOUL CAGES	Sting (A&M)
-	46	X	INXS (Mercury)
47	47	5,000,000	Dread Zeppelin (IRS)
-	48	MARIAH CAREY	Mariah Carey (CBS)
49	49	HARD AT PLAY	
			Huey Lewis & the News (Chrysalis)
-	50	TURTLE SOUP	Mock Turtles (Imaginary)

The Waterboys were another group to benefit from a strong-selling springtime compilation of the pick of their oldies, but *The Best Of '81-'91* just failed to unseat the Euythmics from the top. That honour went to US singer Michael Bolton, whose previous *Soul Provider* set had been a solid Top-Tenner in 1990, but whose new *Time, Love And Tenderness* outpaced the more hotly tipped EMF and James albums to the top.

1 June 1991

last week	this week	Title	Artist (Label)
2	1	GREATEST HITS	Eurythmics (RCA)
1	2	TIME, LOVE & TENDERNESS	Michael Bolton (Columbia)
-	3	UNPLUGGED (THE OFFICIAL BOOTLEG)	Paul McCartney (Parlophone)
-	4	SEAL	Seal (ZTT)
5	5	MIGHTY LIKE A ROSE	Elvis Costello (Warner Bros.)
4	6	OUT OF TIME	R.E.M. (Warner Bros.)
3	7	SCHUBERT DIP	EMF (Parlophone)
6	8	JOYRIDE	Roxette (EMI)
8	9	DE LA SOUL IS DEAD	De La Soul (Big Life)
-	10	BEVERLY CRAVEN	Beverly Craven (Columbia)
10	11	THE WHITE ROOM	KLF (KLF Communications)
14	12	POWER OF LOVE	Luther Vandross (Epic)
17	13	THE DOORS - SOUNDTRACK	Doors (Elektra)
7	14	SUGAR TAX	Orchestral Manoeuvres In The Dark (Virgin)
-	15	MEMORABILIA - THE SINGLES	Soft Cell/Marc Almond (Some Bizzare)
9	16	THE BEST OF THE WATERBOYS '81-'91	Waterboys (Ensign)
11	17	REAL LIFE	Simple Minds (Virgin)
12	18	PLEASE HAMMER DON'T HURT 'EM	MC Hammer (Capitol)
27	19	LEGEND	Bob Marley & the Wailers (Island)
13	20	THE IMMACULATE COLLECTION	Madonna (Sire)
19	21	GREATEST HITS 1977-1990	Stranglers (Epic)
25	22	THE BEST OF THE DOORS	Doors (Elektra)
16	23	INTO THE LIGHT	Gloria Estefan (Epic)
15	24	GOLD MOTHER	James (Fontana)
18	25	VAGABOND HEART	Rod Stewart (Warner Bros.)
28	26	THE VERY BEST OF ELTON JOHN	Elton John (Rocket)
30	27	KEEP THE MUSIC PLAYING	Shirley Bassey (Dino)
20	28	UNION	Yes (Arista)
-	29	IN CONCERT	Doors (Elektra)
21	30	MAMA SAID	Lenny Kravitz (Virgin America)
26	31	THE COMPLETE PICTURE	Deborah Harry and Blondie (Chrysalis)
32	32	SPARTACUS	Farm (Produce)
22	33	GET READY!	Roachford (Columbia)
38	34	POP LIFE	Bananarama (London)
24	35	THE SIMPSONS SING THE BLUES	Simpsons (Geffen)
23	36	AUBERGE	Chris Rea (East West)
31	37	CIRCLE OF ONE	Oleta Adams (Fontana)
29	38	ZUCCHERO	Zucchero (A&M)
33	39	LISTEN WITHOUT PREJUDICE VOLUME 1	George Michael (Epic)
40	40	IN CONCERT	Luciano Pavarotti, Placido Domingo and José Carreras (Decca)
-	41	WILSON PHILLIPS	Wilson Phillips (SBK)
43	42	THE RHYTHM OF THE SAINTS	Paul Simon (Warner Bros.)
36	43	SOUL PROVIDER	Michael Bolton (CBS)
-	44	INNUENDO	Queen (Parlophone)
42	45	INSPECTOR MORSE (ORIGINAL MUSIC FROM THE ITV SERIES)	Barrington Pheloung (Virgin Television)
48	46	MARIAH CAREY	Mariah Carey (CBS)
34	47	WICKED GAME	Chris Isaak (Reprise)
35	48	BRAHMS VIOLIN CONCERTO	Nigel Kennedy (EMI)
-	49	O.G.: ORIGINAL GANGSTER	Ice-T (Sire)
46	50	X	INXS (Mercury)

8 June 1991

last week	this week	Title	Artist (Label)
4	1	SEAL	Seal (ZTT)
-	2	NEVER LOVED ELVIS	Wonder Stuff (Polydor)
1	3	GREATEST HITS	Eurythmics (RCA)
-	4	ELECTRONIC	Electronic (Factory)
6	5	OUT OF TIME	R.E.M. (Warner Bros.)
2	6	TIME, LOVE & TENDERNESS	Michael Bolton (Columbia)
3	7	UNPLUGGED (THE OFFICIAL BOOTLEG)	Paul McCartney (Parlophone)
10	8	BEVERLY CRAVEN	Beverly Craven (Columbia)
8	9	JOYRIDE	Roxette (EMI)
15	10	MEMORABILIA - THE SINGLES	Soft Cell/Marc Almond (Some Bizzare)
7	11	SCHUBERT DIP	EMF (Parlophone)
19	12	LEGEND	Bob Marley & the Wailers (Island)
-	13	SEAMONSTERS	Wedding Present (RCA)
22	14	THE BEST OF THE DOORS	Doors (Elektra)
17	15	REAL LIFE	Simple Minds (Virgin)
5	16	MIGHTY LIKE A ROSE	Elvis Costello (Warner Bros.)
11	17	THE WHITE ROOM	KLF (KLF Communications)
13	18	THE DOORS - SOUNDTRACK	Doors (Elektra)
9	19	DE LA SOUL IS DEAD	De La Soul (Big Life)
20	20	THE IMMACULATE COLLECTION	Madonna (Sire)
16	21	THE BEST OF THE WATERBOYS '81-'91	Waterboys (Ensign)
14	22	SUGAR TAX	Orchestral Manoeuvres In The Dark (Virgin)
-	23	WE ARE IN LOVE	Harry Connick Jr. (CBS)
21	24	GREATEST HITS 1977-1990	Stranglers (Epic)
29	25	IN CONCERT	Doors (Elektra)
18	26	PLEASE HAMMER DON'T HURT 'EM	MC Hammer (Capitol)
12	27	POWER OF LOVE	Luther Vandross (Epic)
-	28	THE VERY BEST OF DEXY'S MIDNIGHT RUNNERS	Dexy's Midnight Runners (Mercury)
26	29	THE VERY BEST OF ELTON JOHN	Elton John (Rocket)
25	30	VAGABOND HEART	Rod Stewart (Warner Bros.)
23	31	INTO THE LIGHT	Gloria Estefan (Epic)
24	32	GOLD MOTHER	James (Fontana)
27	33	KEEP THE MUSIC PLAYING	Shirley Bassey (Dino)
-	34	JUNGLE FEVER SOUNDTRACK	Stevie Wonder (Motown)
35	35	THE SIMPSONS SING THE BLUES	Simpsons (Geffen)
28	36	UNION	Yes (Arista)
30	37	MAMA SAID	Lenny Kravitz (Virgin America)
36	38	AUBERGE	Chris Rea (East West)
31	39	THE COMPLETE PICTURE - THE VERY BEST OF DEBORAH HARRY AND BLONDIE	Deborah Harry and Blondie (Chrysalis)
39	40	LISTEN WITHOUT PREJUDICE VOLUME 1	George Michael (Epic)
37	41	CIRCLE OF ONE	Oleta Adams (Fontana)
-	42	ELECTRIC LIGHT ORCHESTRA PART 2	Electric Light Orchestra Part 2 (Telstar)
40	43	IN CONCERT	Luciano Pavarotti, Placido Domingo and José Carreras (Decca)
41	44	WILSON PHILLIPS	Wilson Phillips (SBK)
32	45	SPARTACUS	Farm (Produce)
-	46	BLACK	Black (A&M)
44	47	INNUENDO	Queen (Parlophone)
-	48	MERMAIDS - SOUNDTRACK	Various (Epic)
33	49	GET READY!	Roachford (Columbia)
38	50	ZUCCHERO	Zucchero (A&M)

15 June 1991

last week	this week	Title	Artist (Label)
1	1	SEAL	Seal (ZTT)
4	2	ELECTRONIC	Electronic (Factory)
2	3	NEVER LOVED ELVIS	Wonder Stuff (Polydor)
-	4	FELLOW HOODLUMS	Deacon Blue (Columbia)
3	5	GREATEST HITS	Eurythmics (RCA)
5	6	OUT OF TIME	R.E.M. (Warner Bros.)
8	7	BEVERLY CRAVEN	Beverly Craven (Columbia)
6	8	TIME, LOVE & TENDERNESS	Michael Bolton (Columbia)
12	9	LEGEND	Bob Marley & the Wailers (Island)
28	10	THE VERY BEST OF DEXY'S MIDNIGHT RUNNERS	Dexy's Midnight Runners (Mercury)
18	11	THE DOORS - SOUNDTRACK	Doors (Elektra)
11	12	SCHUBERT DIP	EMF (Parlophone)
-	13	LOVE AND KISSES	Dannii Minogue (MCA)
9	14	JOYRIDE	Roxette (EMI)
10	15	MEMORABILIA - THE SINGLES	Soft Cell/Marc Almond (Some Bizzare)
17	16	THE WHITE ROOM	KLF (KLF Communications)
14	17	THE BEST OF THE DOORS	Doors (Elektra)
20	18	THE IMMACULATE COLLECTION	Madonna (Sire)
26	19	PLEASE HAMMER DON'T HURT 'EM	MC Hammer (Capitol)
24	20	GREATEST HITS 1977-1990	Stranglers (Epic)
15	21	REAL LIFE	Simple Minds (Virgin)
23	22	WE ARE IN LOVE	Harry Connick Jr. (CBS)
22	23	SUGAR TAX	Orchestral Manoeuvres In The Dark (Virgin)
13	24	SEAMONSTERS	Wedding Present (RCA)
21	25	THE BEST OF THE WATERBOYS '81-'91	Waterboys (Ensign)
30	26	VAGABOND HEART	Rod Stewart (Warner Bros.)
16	27	MIGHTY LIKE A ROSE	Elvis Costello (Warner Bros.)
37	28	MAMA SAID	Lenny Kravitz (Virgin America)
29	29	THE VERY BEST OF ELTON JOHN	Elton John (Rocket)
25	30	IN CONCERT	Doors (Elektra)
7	31	UNPLUGGED (THE OFFICIAL BOOTLEG)	Paul McCartney (Parlophone)
19	32	DE LA SOUL IS DEAD	De La Soul (Big Life)
27	33	POWER OF LOVE	Luther Vandross (Epic)
38	34	AUBERGE	Chris Rea (East West)
31	35	INTO THE LIGHT	Gloria Estefan (Epic)
35	36	THE SIMPSONS SING THE BLUES	Simpsons (Geffen)
41	37	CIRCLE OF ONE	Oleta Adams (Fontana)
32	38	GOLD MOTHER	James (Fontana)
-	39	EXTREME II PORNOGRAFFITI	Extreme (A&M)
39	40	THE COMPLETE PICTURE	Deborah Harry and Blondie (Chrysalis)
33	41	KEEP THE MUSIC PLAYING	Shirley Bassey (Dino)
43	42	IN CONCERT	Luciano Pavarotti, Placido Domingo and José Carreras (Decca)
40	43	LISTEN WITHOUT PREJUDICE VOLUME 1	George Michael (Epic)
44	44	WILSON PHILLIPS	Wilson Phillips (SBK)
-	45	EFIL4ZREGGIN	NWA (Fourth & Broadway)
34	46	JUNGLE FEVER SOUNDTRACK	Stevie Wonder (Motown)
45	47	SPARTACUS	Farm (Produce)
48	48	MERMAIDS - SOUNDTRACK	Various (Epic)
-	49	BLUE LINES	Massive Attack (Wild Bunch)
42	50	ELECTRIC LIGHT ORCHESTRA PART 2	Electric Light Orchestra (Telstar)

Paul McCartney's *Unplugged (The Official Bootleg)* was a recording of the unique accoustic live set which McCartney and current band performed on cable TV channel MTV's new showcase programme, also titled *Unplugged*. Over the next couple of years, many acts, from Eric Clapton to Rod Stewart, would also have major chart success by releasing their acoustic sets like this after appearing on the MTV show.

22 June 1991

LW	TW	Title	Artist (Label)
1	1	SEAL	Seal (ZTT)
4	2	FELLOW HOODLUMS	Deacon Blue (Columbia)
6	3	OUT OF TIME	R.E.M. (Warner Bros.)
-	4	SLAVE TO THE GRIND	Skid Row (Atlantic)
5	5	GREATEST HITS	Eurythmics (RCA)
2	6	ELECTRONIC	Electronic (Factory)
3	7	NEVER LOVED ELVIS	Wonder Stuff (Polydor)
7	8	BEVERLY CRAVEN	Beverly Craven (Columbia)
8	9	TIME, LOVE & TENDERNESS	Michael Bolton (Columbia)
-	10	THE MIX	Kraftwerk (EMI)
-	11	SUPERSTITION	Siouxsie & the Banshees (Wonderland)
14	12	JOYRIDE	Roxette (EMI)
13	13	LOVE AND KISSES	Dannii Minogue (MCA)
9	14	LEGEND	Bob Marley & the Wailers (Island)
11	15	THE DOORS - SOUNDTRACK	Doors (Elektra)
10	16	THE VERY BEST OF DEXY'S MIDNIGHT RUNNERS	Dexy's Midnight Runners (Mercury)
12	17	SCHUBERT DIP	EMF (Parlophone)
15	18	MEMORABILIA - THE SINGLES	Soft Cell/Marc Almond (Some Bizzare)
21	19	REAL LIFE	Simple Minds (Virgin)
20	20	GREATEST HITS 1977-1990	Stranglers (Epic)
16	21	THE WHITE ROOM	KLF (KLF Communications)
-	22	THE PROMISE	T'Pau (China)
18	23	THE IMMACULATE COLLECTION	Madonna (Sire)
17	24	THE BEST OF THE DOORS	Doors (Elektra)
26	25	VAGABOND HEART	Rod Stewart (Warner Bros.)
-	26	POP SYMPHONIES	James Last (Polydor)
28	27	MAMA SAID	Lenny Kravitz (Virgin America)
19	28	PLEASE HAMMER DON'T HURT 'EM	MC Hammer (Capitol)
22	29	WE ARE IN LOVE	Harry Connick Jr. (CBS)
-	30	RAW MELODY MEN	New Model Army (EMI)
23	31	SUGAR TAX	Orchestral Manoeuvres In The Dark (Virgin)
35	32	INTO THE LIGHT	Gloria Estefan (Epic)
39	33	EXTREME II PORNOGRAFFITI	Extreme (A&M)
45	34	EFIL4ZREGGIN	NWA (Fourth & Broadway)
25	35	THE BEST OF THE WATERBOYS '81-'91	Waterboys (Ensign)
34	36	AUBERGE	Chris Rea (East West)
-	37	BODY TO BODY	Technotronic (ARS)
37	38	CIRCLE OF ONE	Oleta Adams (Fontana)
29	39	THE VERY BEST OF ELTON JOHN	Elton John (Rocket)
-	40	CHANGING CABINS	Nomad (Rumour)
32	41	DE LA SOUL IS DEAD	De La Soul (Big Life)
24	42	SEAMONSTERS	Wedding Present (RCA)
41	43	KEEP THE MUSIC PLAYING	Shirley Bassey (Dino)
-	44	THE BIG WHEEL	Runrig (Chrysalis)
49	45	BLUE LINES	Massive Attack (Wild Bunch)
-	46	HEART IN MOTION	Amy Grant (A&M)
27	47	MIGHTY LIKE A ROSE	Elvis Costello (Warner Bros.)
30	48	IN CONCERT	Doors (Elektra)
33	49	POWER OF LOVE	Luther Vandross (Epic)
31	50	UNPLUGGED (THE OFFICIAL BOOTLEG)	Paul McCartney (Parlophone)

29 June 1991

LW	TW	Title	Artist (Label)
-	1	LOVE HURTS	Cher (Geffen)
3	2	OUT OF TIME	R.E.M. (Warner Bros.)
1	3	SEAL	Seal (ZTT)
5	4	GREATEST HITS	Eurythmics (RCA)
4	5	SLAVE TO THE GRIND	Skid Row (Atlantic)
20	6	GREATEST HITS 1977-1990	Stranglers (Epic)
2	7	FELLOW HOODLUMS	Deacon Blue (Columbia)
9	8	TIME, LOVE & TENDERNESS	Michael Bolton (Columbia)
6	9	ELECTRONIC	Electronic (Factory)
8	10	BEVERLY CRAVEN	Beverly Craven (Columbia)
26	11	POP SYMPHONIES	James Last (Polydor)
10	12	THE MIX	Kraftwerk (EMI)
29	13	WE ARE IN LOVE	Harry Connick Jr. (CBS)
-	14	FOR UNLAWFUL CARNAL KNOWLEDGE	Van Halen (Warner Bros.)
22	15	THE PROMISE	T'Pau (China)
25	16	VAGABOND HEART	Rod Stewart (Warner Bros.)
27	17	MAMA SAID	Lenny Kravitz (Virgin America)
7	18	NEVER LOVED ELVIS	Wonder Stuff (Polydor)
16	19	THE VERY BEST OF DEXY'S MIDNIGHT RUNNERS	Dexy's Midnight Runners (Mercury)
-	20	CHICKEN RHYTHMS	Northside (Factory)
12	21	JOYRIDE	Roxette (EMI)
19	22	REAL LIFE	Simple Minds (Virgin)
11	23	SUPERSTITION	Siouxsie & the Banshees (Wonderland)
14	24	LEGEND	Bob Marley & the Wailers (Island)
44	25	THE BIG WHEEL	Runrig (Chrysalis)
23	26	THE IMMACULATE COLLECTION	Madonna (Sire)
18	27	MEMORABILIA - THE SINGLES	Soft Cell/Marc Almond (Some Bizzare)
33	28	EXTREME II PORNOGRAFFITI	Extreme (A&M)
15	29	THE DOORS - SOUNDTRACK	Doors (Elektra)
-	30	STARS CRASH DOWN	Hue & Cry (Circa)
13	31	LOVE AND KISSES	Dannii Minogue (MCA)
32	32	INTO THE LIGHT	Gloria Estefan (Epic)
21	33	THE WHITE ROOM	KLF (KLF Communications)
24	34	THE BEST OF THE DOORS	Doors (Elektra)
36	35	AUBERGE	Chris Rea (East West)
46	36	HEART IN MOTION	Amy Grant (A&M)
17	37	SCHUBERT DIP	EMF (Parlophone)
28	38	PLEASE HAMMER DON'T HURT 'EM	MC Hammer (Capitol)
38	39	CIRCLE OF ONE	Oleta Adams (Fontana)
-	40	BABY	Yello (Mercury)
31	41	SUGAR TAX	Orchestral Manoeuvres In The Dark (Virgin)
39	42	THE VERY BEST OF ELTON JOHN	Elton John (Rocket)
-	43	IN CONCERT	Luciano Pavarotti, Placido Domingo and José Carreras (Decca)
-	44	LOVE AND LIFE - A JOURNEY WITH THE CHAMELEONS	Definition Of Sound (Circa)
35	45	THE BEST OF THE WATERBOYS '81-'91	Waterboys (Ensign)
30	46	RAW MELODY MEN	New Model Army (EMI)
43	47	KEEP THE MUSIC PLAYING	Shirley Bassey (Dino)
37	48	BODY TO BODY	Technotronic (ARS)
40	49	CHANGING CABINS	Nomad (Rumour)
45	50	BLUE LINES	Massive Attack (Wild Bunch)

6 July 1991

LW	TW	Title	Artist (Label)
1	1	LOVE HURTS	Cher (Geffen)
2	2	OUT OF TIME	R.E.M. (Warner Bros.)
4	3	GREATEST HITS	Eurythmics (RCA)
3	4	SEAL	Seal (ZTT)
6	5	GREATEST HITS 1977-1990	Stranglers (Epic)
10	6	BEVERLY CRAVEN	Beverly Craven (Columbia)
-	7	HOLIDAYS IN EDEN	Marillion (EMI)
14	8	FOR UNLAWFUL CARNAL KNOWLEDGE	Van Halen (Warner Bros.)
13	9	WE ARE IN LOVE	Harry Connick Jr. (CBS)
7	10	FELLOW HOODLUMS	Deacon Blue (Columbia)
8	11	TIME, LOVE & TENDERNESS	Michael Bolton (Columbia)
17	12	MAMA SAID	Lenny Kravitz (Virgin America)
16	13	VAGABOND HEART	Rod Stewart (Warner Bros.)
5	14	SLAVE TO THE GRIND	Skid Row (Atlantic)
11	15	POP SYMPHONIES	James Last (Polydor)
9	16	ELECTRONIC	Electronic (Factory)
15	17	THE PROMISE	T'Pau (China)
19	18	THE VERY BEST OF DEXY'S MIDNIGHT RUNNERS	Dexy's Midnight Runners (Mercury)
20	19	CHICKEN RHYTHMS	Northside (Factory)
21	20	JOYRIDE	Roxette (EMI)
30	21	STARS CRASH DOWN	Hue & Cry (Circa)
-	22	ELECTRIC LANDLADY	Kirsty MacColl (Virgin)
12	23	THE MIX	Kraftwerk (EMI)
25	24	THE BIG WHEEL	Runrig (Chrysalis)
26	25	THE IMMACULATE COLLECTION	Madonna (Sire)
27	26	MEMORABILIA - THE SINGLES	Soft Cell/Marc Almond (Some Bizzare)
22	27	REAL LIFE	Simple Minds (Virgin)
24	28	LEGEND	Bob Marley & the Wailers (Island)
28	29	EXTREME II PORNOGRAFFITI	Extreme (A&M)
33	30	THE WHITE ROOM	KLF (KLF Communications)
32	31	INTO THE LIGHT	Gloria Estefan (Epic)
-	32	LUCK OF THE DRAW	Bonnie Raitt (Capitol)
18	33	NEVER LOVED ELVIS	Wonder Stuff (Polydor)
34	34	THE BEST OF THE DOORS	Doors (Elektra)
35	35	AUBERGE	Chris Rea (East West)
-	36	EXTREMELY LIVE	Vanilla Ice (SBK)
23	37	SUPERSTITION	Siouxsie & the Banshees (Wonderland)
29	38	THE DOORS - SOUNDTRACK	Doors (Elektra)
38	39	PLEASE HAMMER DON'T HURT 'EM	MC Hammer (Capitol)
39	40	CIRCLE OF ONE	Oleta Adams (Fontana)
31	41	LOVE AND KISSES	Dannii Minogue (MCA)
36	42	HEART IN MOTION	Amy Grant (A&M)
42	43	THE VERY BEST OF ELTON JOHN	Elton John (Rocket)
41	44	SUGAR TAX	Orchestral Manoeuvres In The Dark (Virgin)
37	45	SCHUBERT DIP	EMF (Parlophone)
-	46	UNUSUAL HEAT	Foreigner (Atlantic)
40	47	BABY	Yello (Mercury)
44	48	LOVE AND LIFE - A JOURNEY WITH THE CHAMELEONS	Definition Of Sound (Circa)
50	49	BLUE LINES	Massive Attack (Wild Bunch)
45	50	THE BEST OF THE WATERBOYS '81-'91	Waterboys (Ensign)

When it debuted at the top, Cher's *Love Hurts* gave the singer her first-ever UK Number 1 album - either as a soloist or as half of Sonny & Cher - after 26 years of hitmaking. Its sales were boosted by the inclusion of her revival of the oldie *The Shoop Shoop Song (It's In His Kiss)*, which she also performed in the movie Mermaids; this had already been a Number 1 hit during May as a single.

July 1991

Pavarotti once again proved the pop-sized fervour for his brand of grand opera when a new compilation of his best songs and arias, *Essential Pavarotti II*, gave him another Top 5 hit. Meanwhile, into the Top 5 for the first time came Tom Petty & The Heartbreakers, whose *Into The Great Wide Open* seemed to be benefitting from Petty's hit profile as a Traveling Wilbury, since it had no major hit single to lean on.

3 August 1991

last week	this week		
1	1	GREATEST HITS	Jam (Polydor)
2	2	LOVE HURTS	Cher (Geffen)
9	3	SPELLBOUND	Paula Abdul (Virgin America)
5	4	ESSENTIAL PAVAROTTI II	
			Luciano Pavarotti (Decca)
7	5	SEAL	Seal (ZTT)
4	6	OUT OF TIME	R.E.M. (Warner Bros.)
18	7	UNFORGETTABLE - WITH LOVE	
			Natalie Cole (Elektra)
6	8	GREATEST HITS	Eurythmics (RCA)
3	9	INTO THE GREAT WIDE OPEN	
			Tom Petty & the Heartbreakers (MCA)
25	10	SUGAR TAX	
		Orchestral Manoeuvres In The Dark (Virgin)	
8	11	SOME PEOPLE'S LIVES	Bette Midler (Atlantic)
29	12	EXTREME II PORNOGRAFFITI	Extreme (A&M)
12	13	THE IMMACULATE COLLECTION	Madonna (Sire)
16	14	VAGABOND HEART	
			Rod Stewart (Warner Bros.)
22	15	FELLOW HOODLUMS	Deacon Blue (Columbia)
10	16	BEVERLY CRAVEN	Beverly Craven (Columbia)
14	17	THE HEAT	Dan Reed Network (Mercury)
20	18	TIME, LOVE & TENDERNESS	
			Michael Bolton (Columbia)
13	19	GREATEST HITS 1977-1990	Stranglers (Epic)
17	20	JOYRIDE	Roxette (EMI)
11	21	MAMA SAID	Lenny Kravitz (Virgin America)
-	22	BAT OUT OF HELL	Meatloaf (Epic)
31	23	LEGEND	Bob Marley & the Wailers (Island)
21	24	MEMORABILIA - THE SINGLES	
		Soft Cell/Marc Almond (Some Bizzare)	
30	25	THERE'S NOTHING LIKE THIS	
			Omar (Kongo Dance)
32	26	X	INXS (Mercury)
24	27	THE VERY BEST OF DEXY'S MIDNIGHT	
		RUNNERS Dexy's Midnight Runners (Mercury)	
27	28	WE ARE IN LOVE	Harry Connick Jr. (CBS)
49	29	ROBIN HOOD - PRINCE OF THIEVES	
			Soundtrack (Polydor)
42	30	TWO SIDES	Mock Turtles (Imaginary)
15	31	HEY STOOPID	Alice Cooper (Epic)
38	32	REAL LIFE	Simple Minds (Virgin)
37	33	INTO THE LIGHT	Gloria Estefan (Epic)
35	34	THE WHITE ROOM	KLF (KLF Communications)
26	35	ESTE MUNDO	Gipsy Kings (Columbia)
23	36	AUBERGE	Chris Rea (East West)
36	37	PLEASE HAMMER DON'T HURT 'EM	
			MC Hammer (Capitol)
50	38	LOVE AND KISSES	Dannii Minogue (MCA)
19	39	ATTACK OF THE KILLER B'S	Anthrax (Island)
28	40	ELECTRONIC	Electronic (Factory)
-	41	DOUBT	Jesus Jones (Food)
43	42	THE VERY BEST OF ELTON JOHN	
			Elton John (Rocket)
-	43	CHIC AND ROSE ROYCE - THEIR GREATEST	
		HITS SIDE BY SIDE	Chic/Rose Royce (Dino)
48	44	SCHUBERT DIP	EMF (Parlophone)
46	45	THE BEST OF THE DOORS	Doors (Elektra)
44	46	RECKLESS	Bryan Adams (A&M)
34	47	POP SYMPHONIES	James Last (Polydor)
-	48	FREQUENCIES	LFO (Warp)
-	49	THE BEST OF ROD STEWART	
			Rod Stewart (Warner Bros.)
33	50	THE BIG WHEEL	Runrig (Chrysalis)

10 August 1991

4	1	ESSENTIAL PAVAROTTI II	
			Luciano Pavarotti (Decca)
2	2	LOVE HURTS	Cher (Geffen)
5	3	SEAL	Seal (ZTT)
8	4	GREATEST HITS	Eurythmics (RCA)
6	5	OUT OF TIME	R.E.M. (Warner Bros.)
12	6	EXTREME II PORNOGRAFFITI	Extreme (A&M)
13	7	THE IMMACULATE COLLECTION	Madonna (Sire)
1	8	GREATEST HITS	Jam (Polydor)
3	9	SPELLBOUND	Paula Abdul (Virgin America)
-	10	GONNA MAKE YOU SWEAT	
			C&C Music Factory (Columbia)
15	11	FELLOW HOODLUMS	Deacon Blue (Columbia)
10	12	SUGAR TAX	
		Orchestral Manoeuvres In The Dark (Virgin)	
9	13	INTO THE GREAT WIDE OPEN	
		Tom Petty & the Heartbreakers (MCA)	
16	14	BEVERLY CRAVEN	Beverly Craven (Columbia)
18	15	TIME, LOVE & TENDERNESS	
			Michael Bolton (Columbia)
19	16	GREATEST HITS 1977-1990	Stranglers (Epic)
14	17	VAGABOND HEART	Rod Stewart (Warner Bros.)
7	18	UNFORGETTABLE - WITH LOVE	
			Natalie Cole (Elektra)
-	19	MOVE TO THIS	Cathy Dennis (Polydor)
22	20	BAT OUT OF HELL	Meatloaf (Epic)
11	21	SOME PEOPLE'S LIVES	Bette Midler (Atlantic)
23	22	LEGEND	Bob Marley & the Wailers (Island)
20	23	JOYRIDE	Roxette (EMI)
21	24	MAMA SAID	Lenny Kravitz (Virgin America)
29	25	ROBIN HOOD - PRINCE OF THIEVES	
			Soundtrack (Polydor)
33	26	INTO THE LIGHT	Gloria Estefan (Epic)
28	27	WE ARE IN LOVE	Harry Connick Jr. (CBS)
26	28	X	INXS (Mercury)
34	29	THE WHITE ROOM	KLF (KLF Communications)
38	30	LOVE AND KISSES	Dannii Minogue (MCA)
25	31	THERE'S NOTHING LIKE THIS	Omar (Kongo Dance)
17	32	THE HEAT	Dan Reed Network (Mercury)
-	33	PEACEFUL JOURNEY	Heavy D & the Boyz (MCA)
27	34	THE VERY BEST OF DEXY'S MIDNIGHT	
		RUNNERS Dexy's Midnight Runners (Mercury)	
-	35	IN CONCERT	Luciano Pavarotti,
		Placido Domingo and José Carreras (Decca)	
41	36	DOUBT	Jesus Jones (Food)
48	37	FREQUENCIES	LFO (Warp)
37	38	PLEASE HAMMER DON'T HURT 'EM	
			MC Hammer (Capitol)
46	39	RECKLESS	Bryan Adams (A&M)
24	40	MEMORABILIA - THE SINGLES	
		Soft Cell/Marc Almond (Some Bizzare)	
32	41	REAL LIFE	Simple Minds (Virgin)
-	42	THE ESSENTIAL PAVAROTTI	
			Luciano Pavarotti (Decca)
36	43	AUBERGE	Chris Rea (East West)
35	44	ESTE MUNDO	Gipsy Kings (Columbia)
30	45	TWO SIDES	Mock Turtles (Imaginary)
31	46	HEY STOOPID	Alice Cooper (Epic)
42	47	THE VERY BEST OF...	Elton John (Rocket)
43	48	CHIC AND ROSE ROYCE - THEIR GREATEST	
		HITS SIDE BY SIDE	Chic/Rose Royce (Dino)
49	49	THE BEST OF ROD STEWART	
			Rod Stewart (Warner Bros.)
40	50	ELECTRONIC	Electronic (Factory)

17 August 1991

1	1	ESSENTIAL PAVAROTTI II	
			Luciano Pavarotti (Decca)
2	2	LOVE HURTS	Cher (Geffen)
3	3	SEAL	Seal (ZTT)
19	4	MOVE TO THIS	Cathy Dennis (Polydor)
12	5	SUGAR TAX	
		Orchestral Manoeuvres In The Dark (Virgin)	
4	6	GREATEST HITS	Eurythmics (RCA)
5	7	OUT OF TIME	R.E.M. (Warner Bros.)
11	8	FELLOW HOODLUMS	Deacon Blue (Columbia)
10	9	GONNA MAKE YOU SWEAT	
			C&C Music Factory (Columbia)
6	10	EXTREME II PORNOGRAFFITI	Extreme (A&M)
7	11	THE IMMACULATE COLLECTION	Madonna (Sire)
14	12	BEVERLY CRAVEN	Beverly Craven (Columbia)
8	13	GREATEST HITS	Jam (Polydor)
16	14	GREATEST HITS 1977-1990	Stranglers (Epic)
15	15	TIME, LOVE & TENDERNESS	
			Michael Bolton (Columbia)
13	16	INTO THE GREAT WIDE OPEN	
		Tom Petty & the Heartbreakers (MCA)	
9	17	SPELLBOUND	Paula Abdul (Virgin America)
18	18	UNFORGETTABLE - WITH LOVE	
			Natalie Cole (Elektra)
17	19	VAGABOND HEART	Rod Stewart (Warner Bros.)
42	20	THE ESSENTIAL PAVAROTTI	
			Luciano Pavarotti (Decca)
23	21	JOYRIDE	Roxette (EMI)
20	22	BAT OUT OF HELL	Meatloaf (Epic)
22	23	LEGEND	Bob Marley & the Wailers (Island)
35	24	IN CONCERT	Luciano Pavarotti,
		Placido Domingo and José Carreras (Decca)	
21	25	SOME PEOPLE'S LIVES	Bette Midler (Atlantic)
39	26	RECKLESS	Bryan Adams (A&M)
26	27	INTO THE LIGHT	Gloria Estefan (Epic)
25	28	ROBIN HOOD - PRINCE OF THIEVES	
			Soundtrack (Polydor)
24	29	MAMA SAID	Lenny Kravitz (Virgin America)
29	30	THE WHITE ROOM	KLF (KLF Communications)
27	31	WE ARE IN LOVE	Harry Connick Jr. (CBS)
41	32	REAL LIFE	Simple Minds (Virgin)
28	33	X	INXS (Mercury)
36	34	DOUBT	Jesus Jones (Food)
-	35	DE LA SOUL IS DEAD	De La Soul (Big Life)
30	36	LOVE AND KISSES	Dannii Minogue (MCA)
32	37	THE HEAT	Dan Reed Network (Mercury)
-	38	HEART IN MOTION	Amy Grant (A&M)
49	39	THE BEST OF ROD STEWART	
			Rod Stewart (Warner Bros.)
-	40	SCHUBERT DIP	EMF (Parlophone)
33	41	PEACEFUL JOURNEY	Heavy D & the Boyz (MCA)
43	42	AUBERGE	Chris Rea (East West)
47	43	THE VERY BEST OF ELTON JOHN	
			Elton John (Rocket)
44	44	ESTE MUNDO	Gipsy Kings (Columbia)
38	45	PLEASE HAMMER DON'T HURT 'EM	
			MC Hammer (Capitol)
-	46	HEART OF STONE	Cher (Geffen)
-	47	HOLIDAYS IN EDEN	Marillion (EMI)
-	48	THE BEST OF THE DOORS	Doors (Elektra)
31	49	THERE'S NOTHING LIKE THIS	
			Omar (Kongo Dance)
34	50	THE VERY BEST OF DEXY'S MIDNIGHT	
		RUNNERS Dexy's Midnight Runners (Mercury)	

There could hardly have been two more contrasting compilation albums than the Jam's *Greatest Hits* and the second *Essential Pavarotti* - which did not prevent the latter from succeeding the former at the chart top - amazingly, Pavarotti's third Number 1 album (including the three tenors' *In Concert*). Natalie Cole's *Unforgettable* included a studio-created "duet" with her late father Nat 'King' Cole on the title track.

August – September 1991

24 August 1991

last week	this week	
-	1	METALLICA Metallica (Vertigo)
1	2	ESSENTIAL PAVAROTTI II Luciano Pavarotti (Decca)
2	3	LOVE HURTS Cher (Geffen)
7	4	OUT OF TIME R.E.M. (Warner Bros.)
3	5	SEAL Seal (ZTT)
5	6	SUGAR TAX Orchestral Manoeuvres In The Dark (Virgin)
8	7	FELLOW HOODLUMS Deacon Blue (Columbia)
6	8	GREATEST HITS Eurythmics (RCA)
4	9	MOVE TO THIS Cathy Dennis (Polydor)
10	10	EXTREME II PORNOGRAFFITI Extreme (A&M)
12	11	BEVERLY CRAVEN Beverly Craven (Columbia)
9	12	GONNA MAKE YOU SWEAT C&C Music Factory (Columbia)
15	13	TIME, LOVE & TENDERNESS Michael Bolton (Columbia)
11	14	THE IMMACULATE COLLECTION Madonna (Sire)
13	15	GREATEST HITS Jam (Polydor)
-	16	CMB Color Me Badd (Giant)
14	17	GREATEST HITS 1977-1990 Stranglers (Epic)
17	18	SPELLBOUND Paula Abdul (Virgin America)
20	19	THE ESSENTIAL PAVAROTTI Luciano Pavarotti (Decca)
16	20	INTO THE GREAT WIDE OPEN Tom Petty & the Heartbreakers (MCA)
-	21	HONEY LINGERS Voice Of The Beehive (London)
18	22	UNFORGETTABLE - WITH LOVE Natalie Cole (Elektra)
-	23	MARC COHN Marc Cohn (Atlantic)
22	24	BAT OUT OF HELL Meatloaf (Epic)
19	25	VAGABOND HEART Rod Stewart (Warner Bros.)
21	26	JOYRIDE Roxette (EMI)
23	27	LEGEND Bob Marley & the Wailers (Island)
24	28	IN CONCERT Luciano Pavarotti, Placido Domingo and José Carreras (Decca)
26	29	RECKLESS Bryan Adams (A&M)
27	30	INTO THE LIGHT Gloria Estefan (Epic)
30	31	THE WHITE ROOM KLF (KLF Communications)
25	32	SOME PEOPLE'S LIVES Bette Midler (Atlantic)
-	33	ABRACADABRA ABC (Parlophone)
28	34	ROBIN HOOD - PRINCE OF THIEVES Soundtrack (Polydor)
32	35	REAL LIFE Simple Minds (Virgin)
38	36	HEART IN MOTION Amy Grant (A&M)
35	37	DE LA SOUL IS DEAD De La Soul (Big Life)
29	38	MAMA SAID Lenny Kravitz (Virgin America)
31	39	WE ARE IN LOVE Harry Connick Jr. (CBS)
36	40	LOVE AND KISSES Dannii Minogue (MCA)
42	41	AUBERGE Chris Rea (East West)
47	42	HOLIDAYS IN EDEN Marillion (EMI)
-	43	MCMXC AD Enigma (Virgin International)
33	44	X INXS (Mercury)
-	45	EN-TACT Shamen (One Little Indian)
39	46	THE BEST OF ROD STEWART Rod Stewart (Warner Bros.)
34	47	DOUBT Jesus Jones (Food)
43	48	THE VERY BEST OF ELTON JOHN Elton John (Rocket)
45	49	PLEASE HAMMER DON'T HURT 'EM MC Hammer (Capitol)
-	50	BEATSONGS Blue Aeroplanes (Ensign)

31 August 1991

last week	this week	
1	1	METALLICA Metallica (Vertigo)
2	2	ESSENTIAL PAVAROTTI II Luciano Pavarotti (Decca)
3	3	LOVE HURTS Cher (Geffen)
-	4	JOSEPH AND THE AMAZING TECHNICOLOUR DREAMCOAT Original Cast (Really Useful)
4	5	OUT OF TIME R.E.M. (Warner Bros.)
6	6	SUGAR TAX Orchestral Manoeuvres In The Dark (Virgin)
11	7	BEVERLY CRAVEN Beverly Craven (Columbia)
7	8	FELLOW HOODLUMS Deacon Blue (Columbia)
16	9	CMB Color Me Badd (Giant)
5	10	SEAL Seal (ZTT)
8	11	GREATEST HITS Eurythmics (RCA)
13	12	TIME, LOVE & TENDERNESS Michael Bolton (Columbia)
10	13	EXTREME II PORNOGRAFFITI Extreme (A&M)
21	14	HONEY LINGERS Voice Of The Beehive (London)
14	15	THE IMMACULATE COLLECTION Madonna (Sire)
12	16	GONNA MAKE YOU SWEAT C&C Music Factory (Columbia)
-	17	UNKNOWN TERRITORY Bomb The Bass (Rhythm King)
17	18	GREATEST HITS 1977-1990 Stranglers (Epic)
15	19	GREATEST HITS Jam (Polydor)
9	20	MOVE TO THIS Cathy Dennis (Polydor)
20	21	INTO THE GREAT WIDE OPEN Tom Petty & the Heartbreakers (MCA)
24	22	BAT OUT OF HELL Meatloaf (Epic)
23	23	MARC COHN Marc Cohn (Atlantic)
27	24	LEGEND Bob Marley & the Wailers (Island)
22	25	UNFORGETTABLE - WITH LOVE Natalie Cole (Elektra)
35	26	REAL LIFE Simple Minds (Virgin)
18	27	SPELLBOUND Paula Abdul (Virgin America)
29	28	RECKLESS Bryan Adams (A&M)
25	29	VAGABOND HEART Rod Stewart (Warner Bros.)
-	30	ROAD TO FREEDOM Young Disciples (Talkin' Loud)
31	31	THE WHITE ROOM KLF (KLF Communications)
26	32	JOYRIDE Roxette (EMI)
19	33	THE ESSENTIAL PAVAROTTI Luciano Pavarotti (Decca)
38	34	MAMA SAID Lenny Kravitz (Virgin America)
28	35	IN CONCERT Luciano Pavarotti, Placido Domingo and José Carreras (Decca)
-	36	EVERY GOOD BOY DESERVES FUDGE Mudhoney (Subpop)
34	37	ROBIN HOOD - PRINCE OF THIEVES Soundtrack (Polydor)
36	38	HEART IN MOTION Amy Grant (A&M)
44	39	X INXS (Mercury)
30	40	INTO THE LIGHT Gloria Estefan (Epic)
-	41	SHAKE YOUR MONEY MAKER Black Crowes (Def American)
32	42	SOME PEOPLE'S LIVES Bette Midler (Atlantic)
41	43	AUBERGE Chris Rea (East West)
39	44	WE ARE IN LOVE Harry Connick Jr. (CBS)
43	45	MCMXC AD Enigma (Virgin International)
48	46	THE VERY BEST OF... Elton John (Rocket)
-	47	HEART OF STONE Cher (Geffen)
45	48	EN-TACT Shamen (One Little Indian)
40	49	LOVE AND KISSES Dannii Minogue (MCA)
49	50	PLEASE HAMMER DON'T HURT 'EM MC Hammer (Capitol)

7 September 1991

last week	this week	
4	1	JOSEPH AND THE AMAZING TECHNICOLOUR DREAMCOAT Original Cast (Really Useful)
-	2	LEISURE Blur (Food)
2	3	ESSENTIAL PAVAROTTI II Luciano Pavarotti (Decca)
3	4	LOVE HURTS Cher (Geffen)
5	5	OUT OF TIME R.E.M. (Warner Bros.)
10	6	SEAL Seal (ZTT)
1	7	METALLICA Metallica (Vertigo)
9	8	CMB Color Me Badd (Giant)
7	9	BEVERLY CRAVEN Beverly Craven (Columbia)
8	10	FELLOW HOODLUMS Deacon Blue (Columbia)
12	11	TIME, LOVE & TENDERNESS Michael Bolton (Columbia)
11	12	GREATEST HITS Eurythmics (RCA)
15	13	THE IMMACULATE COLLECTION Madonna (Sire)
6	14	SUGAR TAX Orchestral Manoeuvres In The Dark (Virgin)
13	15	EXTREME II PORNOGRAFFITI Extreme (A&M)
17	16	UNKNOWN TERRITORY Bomb The Bass (Rhythm King)
-	17	TOUCHED BY JESUS All About Eve (Vertigo)
16	18	GONNA MAKE YOU SWEAT C&C Music Factory (Columbia)
19	19	GREATEST HITS Jam (Polydor)
18	20	GREATEST HITS 1977-1990 Stranglers (Epic)
20	21	MOVE TO THIS Cathy Dennis (Polydor)
22	22	BAT OUT OF HELL Meatloaf (Epic)
30	23	ROAD TO FREEDOM Young Disciples (Talkin' Loud)
14	24	HONEY LINGERS Voice Of The Beehive (London)
-	25	A LIFE WITH BRIAN Flowered Up (London)
24	26	LEGEND Bob Marley & the Wailers (Island)
26	27	REAL LIFE Simple Minds (Virgin)
21	28	INTO THE GREAT WIDE OPEN Tom Petty & the Heartbreakers (MCA)
28	29	RECKLESS Bryan Adams (A&M)
29	30	VAGABOND HEART Rod Stewart (Warner Bros.)
23	31	MARC COHN Marc Cohn (Atlantic)
27	32	SPELLBOUND Paula Abdul (Virgin America)
32	33	JOYRIDE Roxette (EMI)
-	34	TERMINATOR 2: JUDGEMENT DAY - ORIGINAL SOUNDTRACK Brad Fiedel (Varese Sarabande)
41	35	SHAKE YOUR MONEY MAKER Black Crowes (Def American)
25	36	UNFORGETTABLE - WITH LOVE Natalie Cole (Elektra)
34	37	MAMA SAID Lenny Kravitz (Virgin America)
35	38	IN CONCERT Luciano Pavarotti Placido Domingo and José Carreras (Decca)
-	39	MARTIKA'S KITCHEN Martika (Columbia)
37	40	ROBIN HOOD - PRINCE OF THIEVES Soundtrack (Polydor)
31	41	THE WHITE ROOM KLF (KLF Communications)
33	42	THE ESSENTIAL PAVAROTTI Luciano Pavarotti (Decca)
-	43	SINGLES Specials (2 Tone)
44	44	WE ARE IN LOVE Harry Connick Jr. (CBS)
-	45	SCHUBERT DIP EMF (Parlophone)
49	46	LOVE AND KISSES Dannii Minogue (MCA)
39	47	X INXS (Mercury)
46	48	THE VERY BEST OF ELTON JOHN Elton John (Rocket)
38	49	HEART IN MOTION Amy Grant (A&M)
-	50	PLAY Squeeze (Reprise)

More dramatic contrasts among the top sellers, as heavy metallurgists Metallica took over the Number 1 slot from Pavarotti, only to then surrender it to a musical cast album, in the shape of another Andrew Lloyd Webber success. *Joseph And The Amazing Technicolour Dreamcoat*, featuring Jason Donovan both on West End stage and record, was a revival of Lloyd Webber and Tim Rice's first-ever collaboration.

14 September 1991

last week	this week	Title	Artist
1	1	JOSEPH AND THE AMAZING TECHNICOLOUR DREAMCOAT	Original Cast (Really Useful)
8	2	CMB	Color Me Badd (Giant)
4	3	LOVE HURTS	Cher (Geffen)
5	4	OUT OF TIME	R.E.M. (Warner Bros.)
6	5	SEAL	Seal (ZTT)
-	6	GUARANTEED	Level 42 (Polydor)
2	7	LEISURE	Blur (Food)
3	8	ESSENTIAL PAVAROTTI II	Luciano Pavarotti (Decca)
12	9	GREATEST HITS	Eurythmics (RCA)
-	10	FROM TIME TO TIME	Paul Young (Columbia)
10	11	FELLOW HOODLUMS	Deacon Blue (Columbia)
13	12	THE IMMACULATE COLLECTION	Madonna (Sire)
-	13	ROLL THE BONES	Rush (Atlantic)
-	14	OF THE HEART, OF THE SOUL AND OF THE CROSS: THE UTOPIAN EXPERIENCE	PM Dawn (Gee Street)
-	15	TIN MACHINE II	Tin Machine (London)
14	16	SUGAR TAX	Orchestral Manoeuvres In The Dark (Virgin)
11	17	TIME, LOVE & TENDERNESS	Michael Bolton (Columbia)
22	18	BAT OUT OF HELL	Meatloaf (Epic)
-	19	TIMESPACE - THE BEST OF...	Stevie Nicks (EMI)
9	20	BEVERLY CRAVEN	Beverly Craven (Columbia)
7	21	METALLICA	Metallica (Vertigo)
15	22	EXTREME II PORNOGRAFFITI	Extreme (A&M)
39	23	MARTIKA'S KITCHEN	Martika (Columbia)
17	24	TOUCHED BY JESUS	All About Eve (Vertigo)
43	25	SINGLES	Specials (2 Tone)
-	26	STRANGER IN THIS TOWN	Richie Sambora (Mercury)
18	27	GONNA MAKE YOU SWEAT	C&C Music Factory (Columbia)
20	28	GREATEST HITS 1977-1990	Stranglers (Epic)
16	29	UNKNOWN TERRITORY	Bomb The Bass (Rhythm King)
27	30	REAL LIFE	Simple Minds (Virgin)
29	31	RECKLESS	Bryan Adams (A&M)
32	32	SPELLBOUND	Paula Abdul (Virgin America)
19	33	GREATEST HITS	Jam (Polydor)
33	34	JOYRIDE	Roxette (EMI)
-	35	CATFISH RISING	Jethro Tull (Chrysalis)
21	36	MOVE TO THIS	Cathy Dennis (Polydor)
24	37	HONEY LINGERS	Voice Of The Beehive (London)
28	38	INTO THE GREAT WIDE OPEN	Tom Petty & the Heartbreakers (MCA)
30	39	VAGABOND HEART	Rod Stewart (Warner Bros.)
26	40	LEGEND	Bob Marley & the Wailers (Island)
23	41	ROAD TO FREEDOM	Young Disciples (Talkin' Loud)
25	42	A LIFE WITH BRIAN	Flowered Up (London)
-	43	APPETITE FOR DESTRUCTION	Guns N' Roses (Geffen)
35	44	SHAKE YOUR MONEY MAKER	Black Crowes (Def American)
36	45	UNFORGETTABLE - WITH LOVE	Natalie Cole (Elektra)
42	46	THE ESSENTIAL PAVAROTTI	Luciano Pavarotti (Decca)
34	47	TERMINATOR 2: JUDGEMENT DAY - ORIGINAL SOUNDTRACK	Brad Fiedel (Varese Sarabande)
49	48	HEART IN MOTION	Amy Grant (A&M)
48	49	THE VERY BEST OF...	Elton John (Rocket)
-	50	THE SPIRIT	Magnum (Polydor)

21 September 1991

last week	this week	Title	Artist
-	1	ON EVERY STREET	Dire Straits (Vertigo)
10	2	FROM TIME TO TIME - THE SINGLES COLLECTION	Paul Young (Columbia)
1	3	JOSEPH AND THE AMAZING TECHNICOLOUR DREAMCOAT	Original Cast (Really Useful)
4	4	OUT OF TIME	R.E.M. (Warner Bros.)
6	5	GUARANTEED	Level 42 (Polydor)
2	6	CMB	Color Me Badd (Giant)
3	7	LOVE HURTS	Cher (Geffen)
14	8	OF THE HEART, OF THE SOUL AND OF THE CROSS: THE UTOPIAN EXPERIENCE	PM Dawn (Gee Street)
5	9	SEAL	Seal (ZTT)
-	10	MR. LUCKY	John Lee Hooker (Silvertone)
13	11	ROLL THE BONES	Rush (Atlantic)
-	12	HYMNS TO THE SILENCE	Van Morrison (Polydor)
17	13	TIME, LOVE & TENDERNESS	Michael Bolton (Columbia)
19	14	TIMESPACE - THE BEST OF...	Stevie Nicks (EMI)
25	15	SINGLES	Specials (2 Tone)
12	16	THE IMMACULATE COLLECTION	Madonna (Sire)
11	17	FELLOW HOODLUMS	Deacon Blue (Columbia)
9	18	GREATEST HITS	Eurythmics (RCA)
18	19	BAT OUT OF HELL	Meatloaf (Epic)
16	20	SUGAR TAX	Orchestral Manoeuvres In The Dark (Virgin)
8	21	ESSENTIAL PAVAROTTI II	Luciano Pavarotti (Decca)
7	22	LEISURE	Blur (Food)
26	23	STRANGER IN THIS TOWN	Richie Sambora (Mercury)
22	24	EXTREME II PORNOGRAFFITI	Extreme (A&M)
23	25	MARTIKA'S KITCHEN	Martika (Columbia)
15	26	TIN MACHINE II	Tin Machine (London)
34	27	JOYRIDE	Roxette (EMI)
28	28	GREATEST HITS 1977-1990	Stranglers (Epic)
20	29	BEVERLY CRAVEN	Beverly Craven (Columbia)
31	30	RECKLESS	Bryan Adams (A&M)
39	31	VAGABOND HEART	Rod Stewart (Warner Bros.)
44	32	SHAKE YOUR MONEY MAKER	Black Crowes (Def American)
27	33	GONNA MAKE YOU SWEAT	C&C Music Factory (Columbia)
21	34	METALLICA	Metallica (Vertigo)
35	35	CATFISH RISING	Jethro Tull (Chrysalis)
33	36	GREATEST HITS	Jam (Polydor)
30	37	REAL LIFE	Simple Minds (Virgin)
36	38	MOVE TO THIS	Cathy Dennis (Polydor)
38	39	INTO THE GREAT WIDE OPEN	Tom Petty & the Heartbreakers (MCA)
43	40	APPETITE FOR DESTRUCTION	Guns N' Roses (Geffen)
24	41	TOUCHED BY JESUS	All About Eve (Vertigo)
40	42	LEGEND	Bob Marley & the Wailers (Island)
48	43	HEART IN MOTION	Amy Grant (A&M)
-	44	PSYCHOTIC SUPPER	Tesla (Geffen)
37	45	HONEY LINGERS	Voice Of The Beehive (London)
45	46	UNFORGETTABLE - WITH LOVE	Natalie Cole (Elektra)
46	47	THE ESSENTIAL PAVAROTTI	Luciano Pavarotti (Decca)
-	48	SCHUBERT DIP	EMF (Parlophone)
-	49	THE BIG WHEEL	Runrig (Chrysalis)
-	50	RITUAL OF LOVE	Karyn White (Warner Bros.)

28 September 1991

last week	this week	Title	Artist
-	1	USE YOUR ILLUSION I	Guns N' Roses (Geffen)
-	2	USE YOUR ILLUSION II	Guns N' Roses (Geffen)
1	3	ON EVERY STREET	Dire Straits (Vertigo)
10	4	MR. LUCKY	John Lee Hooker (Silvertone)
2	5	FROM TIME TO TIME - THE SINGLES COLLECTION	Paul Young (Columbia)
12	6	HYMNS TO THE SILENCE	Van Morrison (Polydor)
-	7	GREATEST HITS	Jason Donovan (PWL)
4	8	OUT OF TIME	R.E.M. (Warner Bros.)
15	9	SINGLES	Specials (2 Tone)
3	10	JOSEPH AND THE AMAZING TECHNICOLOUR DREAMCOAT	Original Cast (Really Useful)
9	11	SEAL	Seal (ZTT)
46	12	UNFORGETTABLE - WITH LOVE	Natalie Cole (Elektra)
-	13	DON'T TRY THIS AT HOME	Billy Bragg (Go! Discs)
14	14	TIMESPACE - THE BEST OF...	Stevie Nicks (EMI)
8	15	OF THE HEART, OF THE SOUL AND OF THE CROSS ...	PM Dawn (Gee Street)
7	16	LOVE HURTS	Cher (Geffen)
6	17	CMB	Color Me Badd (Giant)
-	18	THE ULTIMATE COLLECTION	Marc Bolan & T. Rex (Telstar)
18	19	GREATEST HITS	Eurythmics (RCA)
5	20	GUARANTEED	Level 42 (Polydor)
13	21	TIME, LOVE & TENDERNESS	Michael Bolton (Columbia)
19	22	BAT OUT OF HELL	Meatloaf (Epic)
20	23	SUGAR TAX	Orchestral Manoeuvres In The Dark (Virgin)
25	24	MARTIKA'S KITCHEN	Martika (Columbia)
-	25	PROGENY	Shamen (One Little Indian)
16	26	THE IMMACULATE COLLECTION	Madonna (Sire)
-	27	DON'T GET WEIRD ON ME BABE	Lloyd Cole (Polydor)
-	28	LAUGHING STOCK	Talk Talk (Verve)
24	29	EXTREME II PORNOGRAFFITI	Extreme (A&M)
-	30	NO PLACE LIKE HOME	Big Country (Vertigo)
17	31	FELLOW HOODLUMS	Deacon Blue (Columbia)
27	32	JOYRIDE	Roxette (EMI)
21	33	ESSENTIAL PAVAROTTI II	Luciano Pavarotti (Decca)
28	34	GREATEST HITS 1977-1990	Stranglers (Epic)
29	35	BEVERLY CRAVEN	Beverly Craven (Columbia)
33	36	GONNA MAKE YOU SWEAT	C&C Music Factory (Columbia)
-	37	PURE	Midge Ure (Arista)
30	38	RECKLESS	Bryan Adams (A&M)
-	39	WINGS OF JOY	Cranes (Dedicated)
11	40	ROLL THE BONES	Rush (Atlantic)
22	41	LEISURE	Blur (Food)
-	42	THE BEST OF SPANDAU BALLET	Spandau Ballet (Chrysalis)
34	43	METALLICA	Metallica (Vertigo)
23	44	STRANGER IN THIS TOWN	Richie Sambora (Mercury)
36	45	GREATEST HITS	Jam (Polydor)
26	46	TIN MACHINE II	Tin Machine (London)
50	47	RITUAL OF LOVE	Karyn White (Warner Bros.)
-	48	101 DAMNATIONS	Carter - The Unstoppable Sex Machine (Big Cat)
31	49	VAGABOND HEART	Rod Stewart (Warner Bros.)
32	50	SHAKE YOUR MONEY MAKER	Black Crowes (Def American)

Much was expected of Dire Straits' *On Every Street*, since it was an album many people had never expcted to be made - an official follow-up to 1985's *Brothers In Arms*, now the second-biggest-selling album ever in the UK. In the interim, the group had disbanded, ostensibly for good, then eventually reunited in revised form. The new album sold well, but without the legs to stride the summit for more than a week.

October 1991

5 October 1991

last week	this week	Title	Artist (Label)
-	1	WAKING UP THE NEIGHBOURS	Bryan Adams (A&M)
1	2	USE YOUR ILLUSION I	Guns N' Roses (Geffen)
2	3	USE YOUR ILLUSION II	Guns N' Roses (Geffen)
3	4	ON EVERY STREET	Dire Straits (Vertigo)
18	5	THE ULTIMATE COLLECTION	Marc Bolan & T. Rex (Telstar)
-	6	TROMPE LE MONDE	Pixies (4AD)
5	7	FROM TIME TO TIME - THE SINGLES COLLECTION	Paul Young (Columbia)
-	8	CEREMONY	Cult (Beggars Banquet)
-	9	SCREAMADELICA	Primal Scream (Creation)
4	10	MR. LUCKY	John Lee Hooker (Silvertone)
13	11	DON'T TRY THIS AT HOME	Billy Bragg (Go! Discs)
8	12	OUT OF TIME	R.E.M. (Warner Bros.)
7	13	GREATEST HITS	Jason Donovan (PWL)
-	14	ROCK 'TIL YOU DROP	Status Quo (Vertigo)
16	15	LOVE HURTS	Cher (Geffen)
9	16	SINGLES	Specials (2 Tone)
19	17	GREATEST HITS	Eurythmics (RCA)
6	18	HYMNS TO THE SILENCE	Van Morrison (Polydor)
10	19	JOSEPH AND THE AMAZING TECHNICOLOUR DREAMCOAT	Original Cast (Really Useful)
21	20	TIME, LOVE & TENDERNESS	Michael Bolton (Columbia)
27	21	DON'T GET WEIRD ON ME BABE	Lloyd Cole (Polydor)
11	22	SEAL	Seal (ZTT)
17	23	CMB	Color Me Badd (Giant)
23	24	SUGAR TAX	Orchestral Manoeuvres In The Dark (Virgin)
14	25	TIMESPACE - THE BEST OF STEVIE NICKS	Stevie Nicks (EMI)
26	26	THE IMMACULATE COLLECTION	Madonna (Sire)
31	27	FELLOW HOODLUMS	Deacon Blue (Columbia)
28	28	LAUGHING STOCK	Talk Talk (Verve)
24	29	MARTIKA'S KITCHEN	Martika (Columbia)
22	30	BAT OUT OF HELL	Meatloaf (Epic)
25	31	PROGENY	Shamen (One Little Indian)
-	32	NEVERMIND	Nirvana (DGC)
30	33	NO PLACE LIKE HOME	Big Country (Vertigo)
32	34	JOYRIDE	Roxette (EMI)
12	35	UNFORGETTABLE - WITH LOVE	Natalie Cole (Elektra)
29	36	EXTREME II PORNOGRAFFITI	Extreme (A&M)
15	37	OF THE HEART, OF THE SOUL AND OF THE CROSS: THE UTOPIAN EXPERIENCE	PM Dawn (Gee Street)
35	38	BEVERLY CRAVEN	Beverly Craven (Columbia)
33	39	ESSENTIAL PAVAROTTI II	Luciano Pavarotti (Decca)
34	40	GREATEST HITS 1977-1990	Stranglers (Epic)
20	41	GUARANTEED	Level 42 (Polydor)
-	42	MOTHER'S HEAVEN	Texas (Mercury)
37	43	PURE	Midge Ure (Arista)
38	44	RECKLESS	Bryan Adams (A&M)
41	45	LEISURE	Blur (Food)
42	46	THE BEST OF SPANDAU BALLET	Spandau Ballet (Chrysalis)
47	47	RITUAL OF LOVE	Karyn White (Warner Bros.)
-	48	WORLDWIDE	Everything But The Girl (blanco y negro)
45	49	GREATEST HITS	Jam (Polydor)
43	50	METALLICA	Metallica (Vertigo)

12 October 1991

last week	this week	Title	Artist (Label)
-	1	STARS	Simply Red (East West)
-	2	DIAMONDS AND PEARLS	Prince & the New Power Generation (Paisley Park)
1	3	WAKING UP THE NEIGHBOURS	Bryan Adams (A&M)
4	4	ON EVERY STREET	Dire Straits (Vertigo)
-	5	SIMPLY THE BEST	Tina Turner (Capitol)
6	6	USE YOUR ILLUSION II	Guns N' Roses (Geffen)
7	7	FROM TIME TO TIME - THE SINGLES COLLECTION	Paul Young (Columbia)
2	8	USE YOUR ILLUSION I	Guns N' Roses (Geffen)
-	9	THE BEST OF R.E.M.	R.E.M. (IRS)
5	10	THE ULTIMATE COLLECTION	Marc Bolan & T. Rex (Telstar)
6	11	TROMPE LE MONDE	Pixies (4AD)
12	12	OUT OF TIME	R.E.M. (Warner Bros.)
14	13	ROCK 'TIL YOU DROP	Status Quo (Vertigo)
9	14	SCREAMADELICA	Primal Scream (Creation)
8	15	CEREMONY	Cult (Beggars Banquet)
15	16	LOVE HURTS	Cher (Geffen)
13	17	GREATEST HITS	Jason Donovan (PWL)
10	18	MR. LUCKY	John Lee Hooker (Silvertone)
17	19	GREATEST HITS	Eurythmics (RCA)
-	20	BLOOD SUGAR SEX MAGIK	Red Hot Chili Peppers (Warner Bros.)
-	21	THE BEST OF ...	Pogues (Pogue Mahone)
19	22	JOSEPH AND THE AMAZING TECHNICOLOUR DREAMCOAT	Original Cast (Really Useful)
20	23	TIME, LOVE & TENDERNESS	Michael Bolton (Columbia)
22	24	SEAL	Seal (ZTT)
11	25	DON'T TRY THIS AT HOME	Billy Bragg (Go! Discs)
23	26	CMB	Color Me Badd (Giant)
38	27	BEVERLY CRAVEN	Beverly Craven (Columbia)
-	28	LIVE	Happy Mondays (Factory)
18	29	HYMNS TO THE SILENCE	Van Morrison (Polydor)
24	30	SUGAR TAX	Orchestral Manoeuvres In The Dark (Virgin)
26	31	THE IMMACULATE COLLECTION	Madonna (Sire)
-	32	CHANGING FACES	Bros (Columbia)
16	33	SINGLES	Specials (2 Tone)
30	34	BAT OUT OF HELL	Meatloaf (Epic)
27	35	FELLOW HOODLUMS	Deacon Blue (Columbia)
32	36	NEVERMIND	Nirvana (DGC)
39	37	ESSENTIAL PAVAROTTI II	Luciano Pavarotti (Decca)
-	38	RAISE	Swervedriver (Creation)
34	39	JOYRIDE	Roxette (EMI)
37	40	OF THE HEART, OF THE SOUL AND OF THE CROSS: THE UTOPIAN EXPERIENCE	PM Dawn (Gee Street)
36	41	EXTREME II PORNOGRAFFITI	Extreme (A&M)
-	42	CHOBA B CCCP - THE RUSSIAN ALBUM	Paul McCartney (Parlophone)
25	43	TIMESPACE - THE BEST OF STEVIE NICKS	Stevie Nicks (EMI)
-	44	STORYVILLE	Robbie Robertson (Geffen)
44	45	RECKLESS	Bryan Adams (A&M)
42	46	MOTHER'S HEAVEN	Texas (Mercury)
31	47	PROGENY	Shamen (One Little Indian)
-	48	LATE NIGHT GRANDE HOTEL	Nanci Griffith (MCA)
40	49	GREATEST HITS 1977-1990	Stranglers (Epic)
21	50	DON'T GET WEIRD ON ME BABE	Lloyd Cole (Polydor)

19 October 1991

last week	this week	Title	Artist (Label)
1	1	STARS	Simply Red (East West)
2	2	DIAMONDS AND PEARLS	Prince & the New Power Generation (Paisley Park)
3	3	WAKING UP THE NEIGHBOURS	Bryan Adams (A&M)
5	4	SIMPLY THE BEST	Tina Turner (Capitol)
4	5	ON EVERY STREET	Dire Straits (Vertigo)
7	6	FROM TIME TO TIME - THE SINGLES COLLECTION	Paul Young (Columbia)
6	7	USE YOUR ILLUSION II	Guns N' Roses (Geffen)
9	8	THE BEST OF R.E.M.	R.E.M. (IRS)
8	9	USE YOUR ILLUSION I	Guns N' Roses (Geffen)
-	10	APOCALYPSE '91 ... THE ENEMY STRIKES BLACK	Public Enemy (Def Jam)
10	11	THE ULTIMATE COLLECTION	Marc Bolan & T. Rex (Telstar)
18	12	MR. LUCKY	John Lee Hooker (Silvertone)
11	13	TROMPE LE MONDE	Pixies (4AD)
21	14	THE BEST OF ...	Pogues (Pogue Mahone)
12	15	OUT OF TIME	R.E.M. (Warner Bros.)
-	16	NO MORE TEARS	Ozzy Osbourne (Epic)
14	17	SCREAMADELICA	Primal Scream (Creation)
-	18	THE BEST OF DARYL HALL & JOHN OATES - LOOKING BACK	Daryl Hall & John Oates (RCA)
16	19	LOVE HURTS	Cher (Geffen)
13	20	ROCK 'TIL YOU DROP	Status Quo (Vertigo)
-	21	DECADE OF DECADENCE '81-'91	Motley Crue (Elektra)
15	22	CEREMONY	Cult (Beggars Banquet)
20	23	BLOOD SUGAR SEX MAGIK	Red Hot Chili Peppers (Warner Bros.)
28	24	LIVE	Happy Mondays (Factory)
17	25	GREATEST HITS	Jason Donovan (PWL)
19	26	GREATEST HITS	Eurythmics (RCA)
23	27	TIME, LOVE & TENDERNESS	Michael Bolton (Columbia)
32	28	CHANGING FACES	Bros (Columbia)
34	29	BAT OUT OF HELL	Meatloaf (Epic)
30	30	SUGAR TAX	Orchestral Manoeuvres In The Dark (Virgin)
24	31	SEAL	Seal (ZTT)
27	32	BEVERLY CRAVEN	Beverly Craven (Columbia)
44	33	STORYVILLE	Robbie Robertson (Geffen)
31	34	THE IMMACULATE COLLECTION	Madonna (Sire)
22	35	JOSEPH AND THE AMAZING TECHNICOLOUR DREAMCOAT	Original Cast (Really Useful)
26	36	CMB	Color Me Badd (Giant)
41	37	EXTREME II PORNOGRAFFITI	Extreme (A&M)
40	38	OF THE HEART, OF THE SOUL AND OF THE CROSS:	PM Dawn (Gee Street)
29	39	HYMNS TO THE SILENCE	Van Morrison (Polydor)
25	40	DON'T TRY THIS AT HOME	Billy Bragg (Go! Discs)
35	41	FELLOW HOODLUMS	Deacon Blue (Columbia)
-	42	MOVE TO THIS	Cathy Dennis (Polydor)
38	43	RAISE	Swervedriver (Creation)
36	44	NEVERMIND	Nirvana (DGC)
33	45	SINGLES	Specials (2 Tone)
-	46	HELP YOURSELF	Julian Lennon (Virgin)
-	47	SERIOUSLY ORCHESTRAL ...	Royal Philharmonic Orchestra (Virgin)
37	48	ESSENTIAL PAVAROTTI II	Luciano Pavarotti (Decca)
-	49	LEVELLING THE LAND	Levellers (China)
49	50	GREATEST HITS 1977-1990	Stranglers (Epic)

Many had scoffed at Guns N' Roses' announcement of two simultaneously-released albums, with the suggestion that the idea was little more than a gimmick, and that the heavy rock group could not muster sufficient strong material to satisfy such a pair of releases. Fans and buyers thought differently, and Axl Rose & Co made history by debuting at Numbers 1 and 2 with the two parts of *Use Your Illusion*.

26 October 1991

last week	this week	Title	Artist
1	1	STARS	Simply Red (East West)
4	2	SIMPLY THE BEST	Tina Turner (Capitol)
-	3	CHORUS	Erasure (Mute)
3	4	WAKING UP THE NEIGHBOURS	Bryan Adams (A&M)
-	5	VOICES	Kenny Thomas (Cooltempo)
5	6	ON EVERY STREET	Dire Straits (Vertigo)
6	7	FROM TIME TO TIME	Paul Young (Columbia)
2	8	DIAMONDS AND PEARLS	Prince & the New Power Generation (Paisley Park)
18	9	LOOKING BACK	Daryl Hall & John Oates (RCA)
8	10	THE BEST OF R.E.M.	R.E.M. (IRS)
14	11	THE BEST OF ...	Pogues (Pogue Mahone)
-	12	THE GREATEST HITS	Salt 'n' Pepa (ffrr)
7	13	USE YOUR ILLUSION II	Guns N' Roses (Geffen)
15	14	OUT OF TIME	R.E.M. (Warner Bros.)
-	15	LIVE YOUR LIFE BE FREE	Belinda Carlisle (Virgin)
16	16	USE YOUR ILLUSION I	Guns N' Roses (Geffen)
-	17	HIS GREATEST HITS	David Essex (Mercury)
-	18	TWO ROOMS - CELEBRATING THE SONGS OF ELTON JOHN AND BERNIE TAUPIN	Various (Mercury)
10	19	APOCALYPSE '91 ... THE ENEMY STRIKES BLACK	Public Enemy (Def Jam)
-	20	LET'S GET TO IT	Kylie Minogue (PWL)
11	21	THE ULTIMATE COLLECTION	Marc Bolan & T. Rex (Telstar)
-	22	EMOTIONS	Mariah Carey (Columbia)
49	23	LEVELLING THE LAND	Levellers (China)
-	24	TENEMENT SYMPHONY - GRIT AND GLITTER	Marc Almond (Some Bizzare)
-	25	BLUE LIGHT, RED LIGHT	Harry Connick Jr. (Columbia)
16	26	NO MORE TEARS	Ozzy Osbourne (Epic)
26	27	GREATEST HITS	Eurythmics (RCA)
-	28	24 NIGHTS	Eric Clapton (Duck)
12	29	MR. LUCKY	John Lee Hooker (Silvertone)
-	30	IMAGES	Jean-Michel Jarre (Dreyfus)
19	31	LOVE HURTS	Cher (Geffen)
21	32	DECADE OF DECADENCE '81-'91	Motley Crue (Elektra)
34	33	THE IMMACULATE COLLECTION	Madonna (Sire)
42	34	MOVE TO THIS	Cathy Dennis (Polydor)
-	35	PAUL MCCARTNEY'S LIVERPOOL ORATORIO	Carl Davis & the Royal Liverpool Philharmonic Orchestra (EMI Classics)
13	36	TROMPE LE MONDE	Pixies (4AD)
20	37	ROCK 'TIL YOU DROP	Status Quo (Vertigo)
-	38	SONIA	Sonia (IQ)
25	39	GREATEST HITS	Jason Donovan (PWL)
27	40	TIME, LOVE & TENDERNESS	Michael Bolton (Columbia)
29	41	BAT OUT OF HELL	Meatloaf (Epic)
17	42	SCREAMADELICA	Primal Scream (Creation)
35	43	JOSEPH AND THE AMAZING TECHNICOLOUR DREAMCOAT	Original Cast (Really Useful)
41	44	FELLOW HOODLUMS	Deacon Blue (Columbia)
31	46	SEAL	Seal (ZTT)
45	46	SINGLES	Specials (2 Tone)
36	47	CMB	Color Me Badd (Giant)
-	48	JOYRIDE	Roxette (EMI)
32	49	BEVERLY CRAVEN	Beverly Craven (Columbia)
-	50	MIDNIGHT MOODS - THE LOVE COLLECTION	George Benson (Telstar)

2 November 1991

last week	this week	Title	Artist
3	1	CHORUS	Erasure (Mute)
1	2	STARS	Simply Red (East West)
5	3	VOICES	Kenny Thomas (Cooltempo)
4	4	WAKING UP THE NEIGHBOURS	Bryan Adams (A&M)
2	5	SIMPLY THE BEST	Tina Turner (Capitol)
15	6	LIVE YOUR LIFE BE FREE	Belinda Carlisle (Virgin)
22	7	EMOTIONS	Mariah Carey (Columbia)
18	8	TWO ROOMS - CELEBRATING THE SONGS OF ELTON JOHN AND BERNIE TAUPIN	Various (Mercury)
7	9	FROM TIME TO TIME - THE SINGLES COLLECTION	Paul Young (Columbia)
8	10	DIAMONDS AND PEARLS	Prince & the New Power Generation (Paisley Park)
-	11	THE COMMITMENTS	Commitments (MCA)
9	12	THE BEST OF DARYL HALL & JOHN OATES - LOOKING BACK	Daryl Hall & John Oates (RCA)
-	13	WELD	Neil Young & Crazy Horse (Reprise)
6	14	ON EVERY STREET	Dire Straits (Vertigo)
30	15	IMAGES	Jean-Michel Jarre (Dreyfus)
25	16	BLUE LIGHT, RED LIGHT	Harry Connick Jr. (Columbia)
28	17	24 NIGHTS	Eric Clapton (Duck)
12	18	THE GREATEST HITS	Salt 'n' Pepa (ffrr)
13	19	USE YOUR ILLUSION II	Guns N' Roses (Geffen)
20	20	LET'S GET TO IT	Kylie Minogue (PWL)
21	21	THE ULTIMATE COLLECTION	Marc Bolan & T. Rex (Telstar)
10	22	THE BEST OF R.E.M.	R.E.M. (IRS)
11	23	THE BEST OF	Pogues (Pogue Mahone)
17	24	HIS GREATEST HITS	David Essex (Mercury)
14	25	OUT OF TIME	R.E.M. (Warner Bros.)
31	26	LOVE HURTS	Cher (Geffen)
34	27	MOVE TO THIS	Cathy Dennis (Polydor)
27	28	GREATEST HITS	Eurythmics (RCA)
29	29	MR. LUCKY	John Lee Hooker (Silvertone)
16	30	USE YOUR ILLUSION I	Guns N' Roses (Geffen)
40	31	TIME, LOVE & TENDERNESS	Michael Bolton (Columbia)
33	32	THE IMMACULATE COLLECTION	Madonna (Sire)
49	33	BEVERLY CRAVEN	Beverly Craven (Columbia)
-	34	DECADE OF AGGRESSION LIVE	Slayer (Def American)
19	35	APOCALYPSE '91 ... THE ENEMY STRIKES BLACK	Public Enemy (Def Jam)
-	36	FOXBASE ALPHA	Saint Etienne (Heavenly)
-	37	WORLD IN UNION	Union (Columbia)
-	38	TOO LEGIT TO QUIT	Hammer (Capitol)
-	39	CRAZY WORLD	Scorpions (Vertigo)
24	40	TENEMENT SYMPHONY - GRIT AND GLITTER	Marc Almond (Some Bizzare)
-	41	SWEPT	Julia Fordham (Circa)
23	42	LEVELLING THE LAND	Levellers (China)
41	43	BAT OUT OF HELL	Meatloaf (Epic)
37	44	ROCK 'TIL YOU DROP	Status Quo (Vertigo)
-	45	SUGAR TAX	Orchestral Manoeuvres In The Dark (Virgin)
46	46	SEAL	Seal (ZTT)
26	47	NO MORE TEARS	Ozzy Osbourne (Epic)
-	48	THIS IS THE WORLD	River City People (EMI)
-	49	WATERMARK	Enya (WEA)
44	50	FELLOW HOODLUMS	Deacon Blue (Columbia)

9 November 1991

last week	this week	Title	Artist
-	1	GREATEST HITS II	Queen (Parlophone)
2	2	STARS	Simply Red (East West)
3	3	VOICES	Kenny Thomas (Cooltempo)
5	4	SIMPLY THE BEST	Tina Turner (Capitol)
1	5	CHORUS	Erasure (Mute)
4	6	WAKING UP THE NEIGHBOURS	Bryan Adams (A&M)
11	7	THE COMMITMENTS	Commitments (MCA)
9	8	FROM TIME TO TIME	Paul Young (Columbia)
7	9	EMOTIONS	Mariah Carey (Columbia)
10	10	DIAMONDS AND PEARLS	Prince & the New Power Generation (Paisley Park)
8	11	TWO ROOMS - CELEBRATING THE SONGS OF ELTON JOHN AND BERNIE TAUPIN	Various (Mercury)
-	12	INTERNAL EXILE	Fish (Polydor)
15	13	IMAGES	Jean-Michel Jarre (Dreyfus)
14	14	ON EVERY STREET	Dire Straits (Vertigo)
13	15	WELD	Neil Young & Crazy Horse (Reprise)
6	16	LIVE YOUR LIFE BE FREE	Belinda Carlisle (Virgin)
24	17	HIS GREATEST HITS	David Essex (Mercury)
12	18	THE BEST OF DARYL HALL & JOHN OATES - LOOKING BACK	Daryl Hall & John Oates (RCA)
26	19	LOVE HURTS	Cher (Geffen)
-	20	TIMELESS - THE VERY BEST OF NEIL SEDAKA	Neil Sedaka (Flying Music/Polydor)
31	21	TIME, LOVE & TENDERNESS	Michael Bolton (Columbia)
18	22	THE GREATEST HITS	Salt 'n' Pepa (ffrr)
20	23	LET'S GET TO IT	Kylie Minogue (PWL)
21	24	THE ULTIMATE COLLECTION	Marc Bolan & T. Rex (Telstar)
27	25	MOVE TO THIS	Cathy Dennis (Polydor)
16	26	BLUE LIGHT, RED LIGHT	Harry Connick Jr. (Columbia)
37	27	WORLD IN UNION	Union (Columbia)
19	28	USE YOUR ILLUSION II	Guns N' Roses (Geffen)
22	29	THE BEST OF R.E.M.	R.E.M. (IRS)
39	30	CRAZY WORLD	Scorpions (Vertigo)
33	31	BEVERLY CRAVEN	Beverly Craven (Columbia)
34	32	DECADE OF AGGRESSION LIVE	Slayer (Def American)
28	33	GREATEST HITS	Eurythmics (RCA)
25	34	OUT OF TIME	R.E.M. (Warner Bros.)
17	35	24 NIGHTS	Eric Clapton (Duck)
23	36	THE BEST OF THE POGUES	Pogues (Pogue Mahone)
30	37	USE YOUR ILLUSION I	Guns N' Roses (Geffen)
32	38	THE IMMACULATE COLLECTION	Madonna (Sire)
-	39	BEST OF ME	Maxi Priest (10)
46	40	SEAL	Seal (ZTT)
29	41	MR. LUCKY	John Lee Hooker (Silvertone)
43	42	BAT OUT OF HELL	Meatloaf (Epic)
38	43	TOO LEGIT TO QUIT	Hammer (Capitol)
35	44	APOCALYPSE '91 ... THE ENEMY STRIKES BLACK	Public Enemy (Def Jam)
42	45	LEVELLING THE LAND	Levellers (China)
36	46	FOXBASE ALPHA	Saint Etienne (Heavenly)
45	47	SUGAR TAX	Orchestral Manoeuvres In The Dark (Virgin)
50	48	FELLOW HOODLUMS	Deacon Blue (Columbia)
49	49	WATERMARK	Enya (WEA)
-	50	MIDNIGHT MOODS - THE LOVE COLLECTION	George Benson (Telstar)

Simply Red's *Stars* was destined to outstrip even the group's one-and-a-half million-selling *A New Flame*, to become their most successful recording to date and take up what seemed like almost permanent residence close to the top end of the chart. Meanwhile, the *Two Rooms* compilation, which escaped the "Various Artists" exclusion rule because of its thematic approach, featured Elton John/Bernie Taupin classics.

November 1991

last week	this week	16 November 1991	
-	1	SHEPHERD MOONS	Enya (WEA)
-	2	DISCOGRAPHY - THE COMPLETE SINGLES COLLECTION	Pet Shop Boys (Parlophone)
1	3	GREATEST HITS II	Queen (Parlophone)
2	4	STARS	Simply Red (East West)
4	5	SIMPLY THE BEST	Tina Turner (Capitol)
7	6	THE COMMITMENTS	Commitments (MCA)
-	7	LIVE BABY LIVE	INXS (Mercury)
8	8	FROM TIME TO TIME	Paul Young (Columbia)
3	9	VOICES	Kenny Thomas (Cooltempo)
6	10	WAKING UP THE NEIGHBOURS	Bryan Adams (A&M)
5	11	CHORUS	Erasure (Mute)
9	12	EMOTIONS	Mariah Carey (Columbia)
10	13	DIAMONDS AND PEARLS	Prince & the New Power Generation (Paisley Park)
19	14	LOVE HURTS	Cher (Geffen)
20	15	TIMELESS	Neil Sedaka (Flying Music/Polydor)
13	16	IMAGES	Jean-Michel Jarre (Dreyfus)
14	17	ON EVERY STREET	Dire Straits (Vertigo)
11	18	TWO ROOMS - CELEBRATING THE SONGS OF ELTON JOHN AND BERNIE TAUPIN	Various (Mercury)
-	19	HEADLINES AND DEADLINES - THE HITS OF A-HA	A-ha (Warner Bros.)
18	20	THE BEST OF DARYL HALL & JOHN OATES - LOOKING BACK	Daryl Hall & John Oates (RCA)
27	21	WORLD IN UNION	Union (Columbia)
50	22	MIDNIGHT MOODS - THE LOVE COLLECTION	George Benson (Telstar)
16	23	LIVE YOUR LIFE BE FREE	Belinda Carlisle (Virgin)
22	24	THE GREATEST HITS	Salt 'n' Pepa (ffrr)
17	25	HIS GREATEST HITS	David Essex (Mercury)
21	26	TIME, LOVE & TENDERNESS	Michael Bolton (Columbia)
-	27	I WILL CURE YOU	Vic Reeves (Sense)
12	28	INTERNAL EXILE	Fish (Polydor)
-	29	BANDWAGONESQUE	Teenage Fanclub (Creation)
-	30	CMB	Color Me Badd (Giant)
33	31	GREATEST HITS	Eurythmics (RCA)
34	32	OUT OF TIME	R.E.M. (Warner Bros.)
-	33	MEMORIES	Foster & Allen (Telstar)
40	34	SEAL	Seal (ZTT)
-	35	TOGETHER AT LAST	Richard Clayderman & James Last (Delphine)
23	36	LET'S GET TO IT	Kylie Minogue (PWL)
-	37	THE VERY BEST OF DANIEL O'DONNELL	Daniel O'Donnell (Ritz)
24	38	THE ULTIMATE COLLECTION	Marc Bolan & T. Rex (Telstar)
28	39	USE YOUR ILLUSION II	Guns N' Roses (Geffen)
39	40	BEST OF ME	Maxi Priest (10)
29	41	THE BEST OF R.E.M.	R.E.M. (IRS)
15	42	WELD	Neil Young & Crazy Horse (Reprise)
31	43	BEVERLY CRAVEN	Beverly Craven (Columbia)
25	44	MOVE TO THIS	Cathy Dennis (Polydor)
26	45	BLUE LIGHT, RED LIGHT	Harry Connick Jr. (Columbia)
-	46	THE SINGLES	Clash (Columbia)
36	47	THE BEST OF THE POGUES	Pogues (Pogue Mahone)
30	48	CRAZY WORLD	Scorpions (Vertigo)
37	49	USE YOUR ILLUSION I	Guns N' Roses (Geffen)
35	50	24 NIGHTS	Eric Clapton (Duck)

last week	this week	23 November 1991	
-	1	WE CAN'T DANCE	Genesis (Virgin)
1	2	SHEPHERD MOONS	Enya (WEA)
3	3	GREATEST HITS II	Queen (Parlophone)
2	4	DISCOGRAPHY - THE COMPLETE SINGLES COLLECTION	Pet Shop Boys (Parlophone)
-	5	REAL LOVE	Lisa Stansfield (Arista)
4	6	STARS	Simply Red (East West)
6	7	THE COMMITMENTS	Commitments (MCA)
8	8	FROM TIME TO TIME	Paul Young (Columbia)
5	9	SIMPLY THE BEST	Tina Turner (Capitol)
7	10	LIVE BABY LIVE	INXS (Mercury)
10	11	WAKING UP THE NEIGHBOURS	Bryan Adams (A&M)
9	12	VOICES	Kenny Thomas (Cooltempo)
15	13	TIMELESS	Neil Sedaka (Flying Music/Polydor)
19	14	HEADLINES AND DEADLINES - THE HITS OF A-HA	A-ha (Warner Bros.)
-	15	LOVELESS	My Bloody Valentine (Creation)
11	16	CHORUS	Erasure (Mute)
16	17	IMAGES	Jean-Michel Jarre (Dreyfus)
27	18	I WILL CURE YOU	Vic Reeves (Sense)
13	19	DIAMONDS AND PEARLS	Prince & the New Power Generation (Paisley Park)
26	20	TIME, LOVE & TENDERNESS	Michael Bolton (Columbia)
14	21	LOVE HURTS	Cher (Geffen)
12	22	EMOTIONS	Mariah Carey (Columbia)
33	23	MEMORIES	Foster & Allen (Telstar)
29	24	BANDWAGONESQUE	Teenage Fanclub (Creation)
-	25	SEX MACHINE - THE VERY BEST OF JAMES BROWN	James Brown (Polydor)
22	26	MIDNIGHT MOODS - THE LOVE COLLECTION	George Benson (Telstar)
18	27	TWO ROOMS - CELEBRATING THE SONGS OF ELTON JOHN AND BERNIE TAUPIN	Various (Mercury)
34	28	SEAL	Seal (ZTT)
17	29	ON EVERY STREET	Dire Straits (Vertigo)
-	30	THE CONCERT IN THE PARK - AUGUST 15TH 1991	Paul Simon (Warner Bros.)
23	31	LIVE YOUR LIFE BE FREE	Belinda Carlisle (Virgin)
20	32	THE BEST OF DARYL HALL & JOHN OATES - LOOKING BACK	Daryl Hall & John Oates (RCA)
-	33	WALL OF HITS	Slade (Polydor)
35	34	TOGETHER AT LAST	Richard Clayderman & James Last (Delphine)
43	35	BEVERLY CRAVEN	Beverly Craven (Columbia)
-	36	THEMES AND DREAMS	Shadows (Polydor)
24	37	THE GREATEST HITS	Salt 'n' Pepa (ffrr)
32	38	OUT OF TIME	R.E.M. (Warner Bros.)
30	39	CMB	Color Me Badd (Giant)
25	40	HIS GREATEST HITS	David Essex (Mercury)
31	41	GREATEST HITS	Eurythmics (RCA)
41	42	THE BEST OF R.E.M.	R.E.M. (IRS)
37	43	THE VERY BEST OF DANIEL O'DONNELL	Daniel O'Donnell (Ritz)
40	44	BEST OF ME	Maxi Priest (10)
-	45	LOVESCAPE	Neil Diamond (Columbia)
21	46	WORLD IN UNION	Union (Columbia)
39	47	USE YOUR ILLUSION II	Guns N' Roses (Geffen)
-	48	THE UNFORGETTABLE NAT 'KING' COLE	Nat King Cole (EMI)
-	49	EXTREME II PORNOGRAFFITI	Extreme (A&M)
-	50	THE IMMACULATE COLLECTION	Madonna (Sire)

last week	this week	30 November 1991	
-	1	ACHTUNG BABY	U2 (Island)
1	2	WE CAN'T DANCE	Genesis (Virgin)
2	3	SHEPHERD MOONS	Enya (WEA)
3	4	GREATEST HITS II	Queen (Parlophone)
6	5	STARS	Simply Red (East West)
5	6	REAL LOVE	Lisa Stansfield (Arista)
8	7	FROM TIME TO TIME	Paul Young (Columbia)
4	8	DISCOGRAPHY - THE COMPLETE SINGLES COLLECTION	Pet Shop Boys (Parlophone)
9	9	SIMPLY THE BEST	Tina Turner (Capitol)
7	10	THE COMMITMENTS	Commitments (MCA)
20	11	TIME, LOVE & TENDERNESS	Michael Bolton (Columbia)
11	12	WAKING UP THE NEIGHBOURS	Bryan Adams (A&M)
12	13	VOICES	Kenny Thomas (Cooltempo)
-	14	DANGEROUS	Michael Jackson (Epic)
28	15	SEAL	Seal (ZTT)
-	16	TOGETHER WITH CLIFF RICHARD	Cliff Richard (EMI)
16	17	CHORUS	Erasure (Mute)
13	18	TIMELESS	Neil Sedaka (Flying Music/Polydor)
23	19	MEMORIES	Foster & Allen (Telstar)
10	20	LIVE BABY LIVE	INXS (Mercury)
19	21	DIAMONDS AND PEARLS	Prince & the New Power Generation (Paisley Park)
27	22	TWO ROOMS - CELEBRATING THE SONGS OF ELTON JOHN AND BERNIE TAUPIN	Various (Mercury)
-	23	THE DEFINITIVE SIMON AND GARFUNKEL	Simon & Garfunkel (Columbia)
34	24	TOGETHER AT LAST	Richard Clayderman & James Last (Delphine)
29	25	ON EVERY STREET	Dire Straits (Vertigo)
33	26	WALL OF HITS	Slade (Polydor)
25	27	SEX MACHINE - THE VERY BEST OF JAMES BROWN	James Brown (Polydor)
35	28	BEVERLY CRAVEN	Beverly Craven (Columbia)
14	29	HEADLINES AND DEADLINES - THE HITS OF A-HA	A-ha (Warner Bros.)
37	30	THE GREATEST HITS	Salt 'n' Pepa (ffrr)
21	31	LOVE HURTS	Cher (Geffen)
15	32	LOVELESS	My Bloody Valentine (Creation)
38	33	OUT OF TIME	R.E.M. (Warner Bros.)
32	34	THE BEST OF DARYL HALL & JOHN OATES - LOOKING BACK	Daryl Hall & John Oates (RCA)
41	35	GREATEST HITS	Eurythmics (RCA)
36	36	THEMES AND DREAMS	Shadows (Polydor)
31	37	LIVE YOUR LIFE BE FREE	Belinda Carlisle (Virgin)
40	38	HIS GREATEST HITS	David Essex (Mercury)
49	39	EXTREME II PORNOGRAFFITI	Extreme (A&M)
48	40	THE UNFORGETTABLE..	Nat King Cole (EMI)
17	41	IMAGES	Jean-Michel Jarre (Dreyfus)
22	42	EMOTIONS	Mariah Carey (Columbia)
39	43	CMB	Color Me Badd (Giant)
26	44	MIDNIGHT MOODS - THE LOVE COLLECTION	George Benson (Telstar)
30	45	THE CONCERT IN THE PARK - AUGUST 15TH 1991	Paul Simon (Warner Bros.)
18	46	I WILL CURE YOU	Vic Reeves (Sense)
44	47	BEST OF ME	Maxi Priest (10)
50	48	THE IMMACULATE COLLECTION	Madonna (Sire)
-	49	NEVERMIND	Nirvana (DGC)
47	50	USE YOUR ILLUSION II	Guns N' Roses (Geffen)

Major names weighed in with a vengeance for a share of the lucrative 1991 pre-Christmas market, arriving on the chart at a rate of one or two a week with a new album or compilation, and generally denying each other more than a week's peace at Number 1 before abrupt removal. Hence, Queen, Enya, Genesis, U2 and Michael Jackson all topped the chart in possibly the most rapid star-studded succession ever.

December 1991

7 December 1991

last week	this week	Title	Artist (Label)
14	1	DANGEROUS	Michael Jackson (Epic)
4	2	GREATEST HITS II	Queen (Parlophone)
1	3	ACHTUNG BABY	U2 (Island)
5	4	STARS	Simply Red (East West)
2	5	WE CAN'T DANCE	Genesis (Virgin)
9	6	SIMPLY THE BEST	Tina Turner (Capitol)
11	7	TIME, LOVE & TENDERNESS	Michael Bolton (Columbia)
3	8	SHEPHERD MOONS	Enya (WEA)
7	9	FROM TIME TO TIME	Paul Young (Columbia)
16	10	TOGETHER WITH CLIFF RICHARD	Cliff Richard (EMI)
10	11	THE COMMITMENTS	Commitments (MCA)
6	12	REAL LOVE	Lisa Stansfield (Arista)
8	13	DISCOGRAPHY - THE COMPLETE SINGLES COLLECTION	Pet Shop Boys (Parlophone)
15	14	SEAL	Seal (ZTT)
12	15	WAKING UP THE NEIGHBOURS	Bryan Adams (A&M)
23	16	THE DEFINITIVE SIMON AND GARFUNKEL	Simon & Garfunkel (Columbia)
-	17	GREATEST HITS	Queen (EMI)
17	18	CHORUS	Erasure (Mute)
13	19	VOICES	Kenny Thomas (Cooltempo)
18	20	TIMELESS	Neil Sedaka (Flying Music/Polydor)
22	21	TWO ROOMS - CELEBRATING THE SONGS OF ELTON JOHN AND BERNIE TAUPIN	Various (Mercury)
28	22	BEVERLY CRAVEN	Beverly Craven (Columbia)
19	23	MEMORIES	Foster & Allen (Telstar)
21	24	DIAMONDS AND PEARLS	Prince & the New Power Generation (Paisley Park)
24	25	TOGETHER AT LAST	Richard Clayderman & James Last (Delphine)
25	26	ON EVERY STREET	Dire Straits (Vertigo)
35	27	GREATEST HITS	Eurythmics (RCA)
30	28	THE GREATEST HITS	Salt 'n' Pepa (ffrr)
40	29	THE UNFORGETTABLE ...	Nat King Cole (EMI)
33	30	OUT OF TIME	R.E.M. (Warner Bros.)
31	31	LOVE HURTS	Cher (Geffen)
36	32	THEMES AND DREAMS	Shadows (Polydor)
49	33	NEVERMIND	Nirvana (DGC)
38	34	HIS GREATEST HITS	David Essex (Mercury)
37	35	LIVE YOUR LIFE BE FREE	Belinda Carlisle (Virgin)
20	36	LIVE BABY LIVE	INXS (Mercury)
27	37	SEX MACHINE - THE VERY BEST OF JAMES BROWN	James Brown (Polydor)
39	38	EXTREME II PORNOGRAFFITI	Extreme (A&M)
29	39	HEADLINES AND DEADLINES - THE HITS OF A-HA	A-ha (Warner Bros.)
34	40	THE BEST OF DARYL HALL & JOHN OATES - LOOKING BACK	Daryl Hall & John Oates (RCA)
-	41	MICHAEL CRAWFORD PERFORMS ANDREW LLOYD WEBBER	Michael Crawford (Telstar)
48	42	THE IMMACULATE COLLECTION	Madonna (Sire)
41	43	IMAGES	Jean-Michel Jarre (Dreyfus)
43	44	CMB	Color Me Badd (Giant)
42	45	EMOTIONS	Mariah Carey (Columbia)
44	46	MIDNIGHT MOODS - THE LOVE COLLECTION	George Benson (Telstar)
-	47	INNUENDO	Queen (Parlophone)
46	48	I WILL CURE YOU	Vic Reeves (Sense)
-	49	ESSENTIAL PAVAROTTI II	Luciano Pavarotti (Decca)
50	50	USE YOUR ILLUSION II	Guns N' Roses (Geffen)

14 December 1991

last week	this week	Title	Artist (Label)
2	1	GREATEST HITS II	Queen (Parlophone)
1	2	DANGEROUS	Michael Jackson (Epic)
4	3	STARS	Simply Red (East West)
17	4	GREATEST HITS	Queen (EMI)
3	5	ACHTUNG BABY	U2 (Island)
5	6	WE CAN'T DANCE	Genesis (Virgin)
7	7	TIME, LOVE & TENDERNESS	Michael Bolton (Columbia)
6	8	SIMPLY THE BEST	Tina Turner (Capitol)
9	9	FROM TIME TO TIME	Paul Young (Columbia)
8	10	SHEPHERD MOONS	Enya (WEA)
12	11	REAL LOVE	Lisa Stansfield (Arista)
16	12	THE DEFINITIVE SIMON AND GARFUNKEL	Simon & Garfunkel (Columbia)
10	13	TOGETHER WITH CLIFF RICHARD	Cliff Richard (EMI)
13	14	DISCOGRAPHY - THE COMPLETE SINGLES COLLECTION	Pet Shop Boys (Parlophone)
47	15	INNUENDO	Queen (Parlophone)
21	16	TWO ROOMS - CELEBRATING THE SONGS OF ELTON JOHN AND BERNIE TAUPIN	Various (Mercury)
19	17	VOICES	Kenny Thomas (Cooltempo)
11	18	THE COMMITMENTS	Commitments (MCA)
15	19	WAKING UP THE NEIGHBOURS	Bryan Adams (A&M)
18	20	CHORUS	Erasure (Mute)
33	21	NEVERMIND	Nirvana (DGC)
14	22	SEAL	Seal (ZTT)
30	23	OUT OF TIME	R.E.M. (Warner Bros.)
25	24	TOGETHER AT LAST	Richard Clayderman & James Last (Delphine)
20	25	TIMELESS	Neil Sedaka (Flying Music/Polydor)
24	26	DIAMONDS AND PEARLS	Prince & the New Power Generation (Paisley Park)
26	27	ON EVERY STREET	Dire Straits (Vertigo)
22	28	BEVERLY CRAVEN	Beverly Craven (Columbia)
41	29	MICHAEL CRAWFORD PERFORMS ANDREW LLOYD WEBBER	Michael Crawford (Telstar)
-	30	SWALLOW THIS LIVE	Poison (Capitol)
-	31	THE FORCE BEHIND THE POWER	Diana Ross (EMI)
29	32	THE UNFORGETTABLE...	Nat King Cole (EMI)
27	33	GREATEST HITS	Eurythmics (RCA)
31	34	LOVE HURTS	Cher (Geffen)
23	35	MEMORIES	Foster & Allen (Telstar)
28	36	THE GREATEST HITS	Salt 'n' Pepa (ffrr)
32	37	THEMES AND DREAMS	Shadows (Polydor)
37	38	SEX MACHINE - THE VERY BEST OF JAMES BROWN	James Brown (Polydor)
38	39	EXTREME II PORNOGRAFFITI	Extreme (A&M)
34	40	HIS GREATEST HITS	David Essex (Mercury)
42	41	THE IMMACULATE COLLECTION	Madonna (Sire)
46	42	MIDNIGHT MOODS - THE LOVE COLLECTION	George Benson (Telstar)
-	43	JOSEPH AND THE AMAZING TECHNICOLOUR DREAMCOAT	Original Cast (Really Useful)
-	44	AUBERGE	Chris Rea (East West)
-	45	MOVE TO THIS	Cathy Dennis (Polydor)
35	46	LIVE YOUR LIFE BE FREE	Belinda Carlisle (Virgin)
44	47	CMB	Color Me Badd (Giant)
-	48	THE VERY BEST OF DANIEL O'DONNELL	Daniel O'Donnell (Ritz)
49	49	ESSENTIAL PAVAROTTI II	Luciano Pavarotti (Decca)
36	50	LIVE BABY LIVE	INXS (Mercury)

21 December 1991

last week	this week	Title	Artist (Label)
1	1	GREATEST HITS II	Queen (Parlophone)
3	2	STARS	Simply Red (East West)
4	3	GREATEST HITS	Queen (EMI)
2	4	DANGEROUS	Michael Jackson (Epic)
29	5	MICHAEL CRAWFORD PERFORMS ANDREW LLOYD WEBBER	Michael Crawford (Telstar)
8	6	SIMPLY THE BEST	Tina Turner (Capitol)
7	7	TIME, LOVE & TENDERNESS	Michael Bolton (Columbia)
31	8	THE FORCE BEHIND THE POWER	Diana Ross (EMI)
6	9	WE CAN'T DANCE	Genesis (Virgin)
5	10	ACHTUNG BABY	U2 (Island)
10	11	SHEPHERD MOONS	Enya (WEA)
13	12	TOGETHER WITH CLIFF RICHARD	Cliff Richard (EMI)
12	13	THE DEFINITIVE SIMON AND GARFUNKEL	Simon & Garfunkel (Columbia)
9	14	FROM TIME TO TIME	Paul Young (Columbia)
16	15	TWO ROOMS - CELEBRATING THE SONGS OF ELTON JOHN AND BERNIE TAUPIN	Various (Mercury)
17	16	VOICES	Kenny Thomas (Cooltempo)
11	17	REAL LOVE	Lisa Stansfield (Arista)
18	18	THE COMMITMENTS	Commitments (MCA)
14	19	DISCOGRAPHY - THE COMPLETE SINGLES COLLECTION	Pet Shop Boys (Parlophone)
24	20	TOGETHER AT LAST	Richard Clayderman & James Last (Delphine)
19	21	WAKING UP THE NEIGHBOURS	Bryan Adams (A&M)
23	22	OUT OF TIME	R.E.M. (Warner Bros.)
25	23	TIMELESS	Neil Sedaka (Flying Music/Polydor)
28	24	BEVERLY CRAVEN	Beverly Craven (Columbia)
21	25	NEVERMIND	Nirvana (DGC)
20	26	CHORUS	Erasure (Mute)
34	27	LOVE HURTS	Cher (Geffen)
15	28	INNUENDO	Queen (Parlophone)
27	29	ON EVERY STREET	Dire Straits (Vertigo)
35	30	MEMORIES	Foster & Allen (Telstar)
-	31	H.I.T.S.	New Kids On The Block (CBS)
36	32	THE GREATEST HITS	Salt 'n' Pepa (ffrr)
22	33	SEAL	Seal (ZTT)
43	34	JOSEPH AND THE AMAZING TECHNICOLOUR DREAMCOAT	Original Cast (Really Useful)
33	35	GREATEST HITS	Eurythmics (RCA)
32	36	THE UNFORGETTABLE...	Nat King Cole (EMI)
37	37	THEMES AND DREAMS	Shadows (Polydor)
26	38	DIAMONDS AND PEARLS	Prince & the New Power Generation (Paisley Park)
41	39	THE IMMACULATE COLLECTION	Madonna (Sire)
48	40	THE VERY BEST OF DANIEL O'DONNELL	Daniel O'Donnell (Ritz)
39	41	EXTREME II PORNOGRAFFITI	Extreme (A&M)
46	42	LIVE YOUR LIFE BE FREE	Belinda Carlisle (Virgin)
40	43	HIS GREATEST HITS	David Essex (Mercury)
49	44	ESSENTIAL PAVAROTTI II	Luciano Pavarotti (Decca)
-	45	THE VERY BEST OF...	Elton John (Rocket)
45	46	MOVE TO THIS	Cathy Dennis (Polydor)
-	47	USE YOUR ILLUSION I	Guns N' Roses (Geffen)
-	48	JOYRIDE	Roxette (EMI)
44	49	AUBERGE	Chris Rea (East West)
-	50	THE BEST OF DARYL HALL & JOHN OATES - LOOKING BACK	Daryl Hall & John Oates (RCA)

A significant and tragic event towards the end of the year was the death of Queen's Freddie Mercury. Inevitably, the magnitude of this loss to the music world sent the sales of Queen material into orbit, putting their recently-issued *Greatest Hits II* set back at Number 1, the original *Greatest Hits* (now approaching 3 million sales) close behind it, and the reissued *Bohemian Rhapsody* atop the singles chart.

January 1992

last week	this week	11 January 1992	
2	1	STARS	Simply Red (East West)
1	2	GREATEST HITS II	Queen (Parlophone)
6	3	SIMPLY THE BEST	Tina Turner (Capitol)
4	4	DANGEROUS	Michael Jackson (Epic)
17	5	REAL LOVE	Lisa Stansfield (Arista)
10	6	ACHTUNG BABY	U2 (Island)
7	7	TIME, LOVE & TENDERNESS	Michael Bolton (Columbia)
5	8	MICHAEL CRAWFORD PERFORMS ANDREW LLOYD WEBBER	Michael Crawford (Telstar)
13	9	THE DEFINITIVE SIMON AND GARFUNKEL	Simon & Garfunkel (Columbia)
9	10	WE CAN'T DANCE	Genesis (Virgin)
3	11	GREATEST HITS	Queen (EMI)
11	12	SHEPHERD MOONS	Enya (WEA)
14	13	FROM TIME TO TIME	Paul Young (Columbia)
8	14	THE FORCE BEHIND THE POWER	Diana Ross (EMI)
16	15	VOICES	Kenny Thomas (Cooltempo)
21	16	WAKING UP THE NEIGHBOURS	Bryan Adams (A&M)
38	17	DIAMONDS AND PEARLS	Prince & the New Power Generation (Paisley Park)
15	18	TWO ROOMS - CELEBRATING THE SONGS OF ELTON JOHN AND BERNIE TAUPIN	Various Artists (Mercury)
22	19	OUT OF TIME	R.E.M. (Warner Bros.)
12	20	TOGETHER WITH CLIFF RICHARD	Cliff Richard (EMI)
19	21	DISCOGRAPHY - THE COMPLETE SINGLES COLLECTION	Pet Shop Boys (Parlophone)
26	22	CHORUS	Erasure (Mute)
34	23	JOSEPH AND THE AMAZING TECHNICOLOUR DREAMCOAT	Original Cast (Really Useful)
27	24	LOVE HURTS	Cher (Geffen)
29	25	ON EVERY STREET	Dire Straits (Vertigo)
33	26	SEAL	Seal (ZTT)
32	27	THE GREATEST HITS	Salt 'n' Pepa (ffrr)
25	28	NEVERMIND	Nirvana (DGC)
45	29	THE VERY BEST OF...	Elton John (Rocket)
18	30	THE COMMITMENTS	Commitments (MCA)
24	31	BEVERLEY CRAVEN	Beverley Craven (Epic)
35	32	GREATEST HITS	Eurythmics (RCA)
20	33	TOGETHER AT LAST	Richard Clayderman & James Last (Decca Delphine)
37	34	THEMES AND DREAMS	Shadows (Polydor)
47	35	USE YOUR ILLUSION I	Guns N' Roses (Geffen)
28	36	INNUENDO	Queen (Parlophone)
41	37	EXTREME II PORNOGRAFFITTI	Extreme (A&M)
30	38	MEMORIES	Foster & Allen (Telstar)
44	39	ESSENTIAL PAVAROTTI II	Luciano Pavarotti (Decca)
36	40	THE UNFORGETTABLE...	Nat King Cole (EMI)
-	41	USE YOUR ILLUSION II	Guns N' Roses (Geffen)
39	42	THE IMMACULATE COLLECTION	Madonna (Sire)
46	43	MOVE TO THIS	Cathy Dennis (Polydor)
-	44	IN CONCERT	Luciano Pavarotti, Placido Domingo & José Carreras (Decca)
-	45	GREATEST HITS	Jason Donovan (PWL)
48	46	JOYRIDE	Roxette (EMI)
23	47	TIMELESS	Neil Sedaka (Flying Music/Polydor)
42	48	LIVE YOUR LIFE BE FREE	Belinda Carlisle (Virgin)
40	49	THE VERY BEST OF DANIEL O'DONNELL	Daniel O'Donnell (Ritz)
50	50	THE BEST OF DARYL HALL & JOHN OATES - LOOKING BACK	Daryl Hall & John Oates (RCA)

last week	this week	18 January 1992	
1	1	STARS	Simply Red (East West)
2	2	GREATEST HITS II	Queen (Parlophone)
3	3	SIMPLY THE BEST	Tina Turner (Capitol)
4	4	DANGEROUS	Michael Jackson (Epic)
5	5	REAL LOVE	Lisa Stansfield (Arista)
6	6	ACHTUNG BABY	U2 (Island)
10	7	WE CAN'T DANCE	Genesis (Virgin)
11	8	GREATEST HITS	Queen (EMI)
13	9	FROM TIME TO TIME - THE SINGLES COLLECTION	Paul Young (Columbia)
15	10	VOICES	Kenny Thomas (Cooltempo)
17	11	DIAMONDS AND PEARLS	Prince & the New Power Generation (Paisley Park)
28	12	NEVERMIND	Nirvana (DGC)
9	13	THE DEFINITIVE SIMON AND GARFUNKEL	Simon & Garfunkel (Columbia)
19	14	OUT OF TIME	R.E.M. (Warner Bros.)
12	15	SHEPHERD MOONS	Enya (WEA)
21	16	DISCOGRAPHY - THE COMPLETE SINGLES COLLECTION	Pet Shop Boys (Parlophone)
16	17	WAKING UP THE NEIGHBOURS	Bryan Adams (A&M)
7	18	TIME, LOVE & TENDERNESS	Michael Bolton (Columbia)
24	19	LOVE HURTS	Cher (Geffen)
30	20	THE COMMITMENTS	Commitments (MCA)
8	21	MICHAEL CRAWFORD PERFORMS ANDREW LLOYD WEBBER	Michael Crawford (Telstar)
14	22	THE FORCE BEHIND THE POWER	Diana Ross (EMI)
22	23	CHORUS	Erasure (Mute)
23	24	JOSEPH AND THE AMAZING TECHNICOLOUR DREAMCOAT	Original Cast (Really Useful)
37	25	EXTREME II PORNOGRAFFITTI	Extreme (A&M)
35	26	USE YOUR ILLUSION I	Guns N' Roses (Geffen)
18	27	TWO ROOMS - CELEBRATING THE SONGS OF ELTON JOHN AND BERNIE TAUPIN	Various Artists (Mercury)
26	28	SEAL	Seal (ZTT)
41	29	USE YOUR ILLUSION II	Guns N' Roses (Geffen)
43	30	MOVE TO THIS	Cathy Dennis (Polydor)
27	31	THE GREATEST HITS	Salt 'n' Pepa (ffrr)
36	32	INNUENDO	Queen (Parlophone)
46	33	JOYRIDE	Roxette (EMI)
32	34	GREATEST HITS	Eurythmics (RCA)
42	35	THE IMMACULATE COLLECTION	Madonna (Sire)
-	36	LITTLE EARTHQUAKES	Tori Amos (East West)
25	37	ON EVERY STREET	Dire Straits (Vertigo)
29	38	THE VERY BEST OF ELTON JOHN	Elton John (Rocket)
31	39	BEVERLEY CRAVEN	Beverley Craven (Epic)
-	40	EMOTIONS	Mariah Carey (Columbia)
48	41	LIVE YOUR LIFE BE FREE	Belinda Carlisle (Virgin)
39	42	ESSENTIAL PAVAROTTI II	Luciano Pavarotti (Decca)
-	43	MARTIKA'S KITCHEN	Martika (Columbia)
-	44	THE BEST OF R.E.M.	R.E.M. (IRS)
33	45	TOGETHER AT LAST	Richard Clayderman & James Last (Decca Delphine)
44	46	IN CONCERT	Luciano Pavarotti, Placido Domingo & José Carreras (Decca)
-	47	THE WHITE ROOM	KLF (KLF Communications)
45	48	GREATEST HITS	Jason Donovan (PWL)
50	49	THE BEST OF DARYL HALL & JOHN OATES - LOOKING BACK	Daryl Hall & John Oates (RCA)
-	50	LIVE BABY LIVE	INXS (Mercury)

last week	this week	25 January 1992	
1	1	STARS	Simply Red (East West)
7	2	WE CAN'T DANCE	Genesis (Virgin)
2	3	GREATEST HITS II	Queen (Parlophone)
3	4	SIMPLY THE BEST	Tina Turner (Capitol)
6	5	ACHTUNG BABY	U2 (Island)
5	6	REAL LOVE	Lisa Stansfield (Arista)
4	7	DANGEROUS	Michael Jackson (Epic)
-	8	MAGIC AND LOSS	Lou Reed (Sire)
12	9	NEVERMIND	Nirvana (DGC)
8	10	GREATEST HITS	Queen (EMI)
36	11	LITTLE EARTHQUAKES	Tori Amos (East West)
11	12	DIAMONDS AND PEARLS	Prince & the New Power Generation (Paisley Park)
14	13	OUT OF TIME	R.E.M. (Warner Bros.)
9	14	FROM TIME TO TIME	Paul Young (Columbia)
15	15	SHEPHERD MOONS	Enya (WEA)
10	16	VOICES	Kenny Thomas (Cooltempo)
20	17	THE COMMITMENTS	Commitments (MCA)
21	18	MICHAEL CRAWFORD PERFORMS ANDREW LLOYD WEBBER	Michael Crawford (Telstar)
13	19	THE DEFINITIVE SIMON AND GARFUNKEL	Simon & Garfunkel (Columbia)
16	20	DISCOGRAPHY - THE COMPLETE SINGLES COLLECTION	Pet Shop Boys (Parlophone)
18	21	TIME, LOVE & TENDERNESS	Michael Bolton (Columbia)
17	22	WAKING UP THE NEIGHBOURS	Bryan Adams (A&M)
19	23	LOVE HURTS	Cher (Geffen)
22	24	THE FORCE BEHIND THE POWER	Diana Ross (EMI)
23	25	CHORUS	Erasure (Mute)
24	26	JOSEPH AND THE AMAZING TECHNICOLOUR DREAMCOAT	Original Cast (Really Useful)
28	27	SEAL	Seal (ZTT)
26	28	USE YOUR ILLUSION I	Guns N' Roses (Geffen)
25	29	EXTREME II PORNOGRAFFITTI	Extreme (A&M)
29	30	USE YOUR ILLUSION II	Guns N' Roses (Geffen)
35	31	THE IMMACULATE COLLECTION	Madonna (Sire)
31	32	THE GREATEST HITS	Salt 'n' Pepa (ffrr)
34	33	GREATEST HITS	Eurythmics (RCA)
30	34	MOVE TO THIS	Cathy Dennis (Polydor)
27	35	TWO ROOMS - CELEBRATING THE SONGS OF ELTON JOHN AND BERNIE TAUPIN	Various Artists (Mercury)
43	36	MARTIKA'S KITCHEN	Martika (Columbia)
38	37	THE VERY BEST OF ELTON JOHN	Elton John (Rocket)
32	38	INNUENDO	Queen (Parlophone)
-	39	BILL AND TED'S BOGUS JOURNEY - SOUNDTRACK	Various Artists (Interscope)
44	40	THE BEST OF R.E.M.	R.E.M. (IRS)
47	41	THE WHITE ROOM	KLF (KLF Communications)
37	42	ON EVERY STREET	Dire Straits (Vertigo)
33	43	JOYRIDE	Roxette (EMI)
39	44	BEVERLEY CRAVEN	Beverley Craven (Epic)
41	45	LIVE YOUR LIFE BE FREE	Belinda Carlisle (Virgin)
-	46	NO REGRETS - 1965-1976	Scott Walker & the Walker Brothers (Fontana)
40	47	EMOTIONS	Mariah Carey (Columbia)
49	48	THE BEST OF DARYL HALL & JOHN OATES - LOOKING BACK	Daryl Hall & John Oates (RCA)
46	49	IN CONCERT	Luciano Pavarotti, Placido Domingo & José Carreras (Decca)
-	50	SEX MACHINE - THE VERY BEST OF JAMES BROWN	James Brown (Polydor)

Simply Red's *Stars* took its second turn at the top for the first month of 1992 - it would not be the album's only visit to the summit during the year. Genesis' *We Can't Dance* also rebounded as far as Number 2, with a prod coming from the success of its title track as a Top 10 single. In the Top 10 for the first time were Nirvana, whose *Nevermind* album was the commercial spearhead of the rootsy US grunge style.

1 February 1992

last week	this week	Title	Artist (Label)
1	1	STARS	Simply Red (East West)
2	2	WE CAN'T DANCE	Genesis (Virgin)
3	3	GREATEST HITS II	Queen (Parlophone)
6	4	REAL LOVE	Lisa Stansfield (Arista)
4	5	SIMPLY THE BEST	Tina Turner (Capitol)
8	6	MAGIC AND LOSS	Lou Reed (Sire)
9	7	NEVERMIND	NIrvana (DGC)
5	8	ACHTUNG BABY	U2 (Island)
11	9	LITTLE EARTHQUAKES	Tori Amos (East West)
10	10	GREATEST HITS	Queen (EMI)
12	11	DIAMONDS AND PEARLS	Prince & the New Power Generation (Paisley Park)
7	12	DANGEROUS	Michael Jackson (Epic)
-	13	30 SOMETHING	Carter The Unstoppable Sex Machine (Chrysalis)
46	14	NO REGRETS 1965-1976	Scott Walker & the Walker Brothers (Fontana)
15	15	SHEPHERD MOONS	Enya (WEA)
13	16	OUT OF TIME	R.E.M. (Warner Bros.)
18	17	MICHAEL CRAWFORD PERFORMS ANDREW LLOYD WEBBER	Michael Crawford (Telstar)
17	18	THE COMMITMENTS	Commitments (MCA)
16	19	VOICES	Kenny Thomas (Cooltempo)
14	20	FROM TIME TO TIME - THE SINGLES COLLECTION	Paul Young (Columbia)
19	21	THE DEFINITIVE SIMON AND GARFUNKEL	Simon & Garfunkel (Columbia)
21	22	TIME, LOVE & TENDERNESS	Michael Bolton (Columbia)
24	23	THE FORCE BEHIND THE POWER	Diana Ross (EMI)
23	24	LOVE HURTS	Cher (Geffen)
-	25	BOING	Airhead (Korova)
39	26	BILL AND TED'S BOGUS JOURNEY - SOUNDTRACK	Various Artists (Interscope)
26	27	JOSEPH AND THE AMAZING TECHNICOLOUR DREAMCOAT	Original Cast (Really Useful)
27	28	SEAL	Seal (ZTT)
-	29	WIND OF CHANGE - CLASSIC ROCK	London Symphony Orchestra (Columbia)
22	30	WAKING UP THE NEIGHBOURS	Bryan Adams (A&M)
28	31	USE YOUR ILLUSION I	Guns N' Roses (Geffen)
36	32	MARTIKA'S KITCHEN	Martika (Columbia)
37	33	THE VERY BEST OF ELTON JOHN	Elton John (Rocket)
47	34	EMOTIONS	Mariah Carey (Columbia)
30	35	USE YOUR ILLUSION II	Guns N' Roses (Geffen)
20	36	DISCOGRAPHY - THE COMPLETE SINGLES COLLECTION	Pet Shop Boys (Parlophone)
41	37	THE WHITE ROOM	KLF (KLF Communications)
29	38	EXTREME II PORNOGRAFFITTI	Extreme (A&M)
34	39	MOVE TO THIS	Cathy Dennis (Polydor)
25	40	CHORUS	Erasure (Mute)
33	41	GREATEST HITS	Eurythmics (RCA)
-	42	SCREAMADELICA	Primal Scream (Creation)
32	43	THE GREATEST HITS	Salt 'n' Pepa (ffrr)
38	44	INNUENDO	Queen (Parlophone)
-	45	MCMXC AD	Enigma (Virgin International)
35	46	TWO ROOMS - CELEBRATING THE SONGS OF ELTON JOHN AND BERNIE TAUPIN	Various Artists (Mercury)
31	47	THE IMMACULATE COLLECTION	Madonna (Sire)
44	48	BEVERLEY CRAVEN	Beverley Craven (Epic)
43	49	JOYRIDE	Roxette (EMI)
42	50	ON EVERY STREET	Dire Straits (Vertigo)

8 February 1992

last week	this week	Title	Artist (Label)
-	1	HIGH ON THE HAPPY SIDE	Wet Wet Wet (Precious Organisation)
1	2	STARS	Simply Red (East West)
2	3	WE CAN'T DANCE	Genesis (Virgin)
3	4	GREATEST HITS II	Queen (Parlophone)
4	5	REAL LOVE	Lisa Stansfield (Arista)
7	6	NEVERMIND	NIrvana (DGC)
14	7	NO REGRETS 1965-1976	Scott Walker & the Walker Brothers (Fontana)
5	8	SIMPLY THE BEST	Tina Turner (Capitol)
-	9	SPOOKY	Lush (4AD)
-	10	FINALLY	Ce Ce Peniston (A&M)
11	11	DIAMONDS AND PEARLS	Prince & the New Power Generation (Paisley Park)
34	12	EMOTIONS	Mariah Carey (Columbia)
12	13	DANGEROUS	Michael Jackson (Epic)
8	14	ACHTUNG BABY	U2 (Island)
22	15	TIME, LOVE & TENDERNESS	Michael Bolton (Columbia)
10	16	GREATEST HITS	Queen (EMI)
9	17	LITTLE EARTHQUAKES	Tori Amos (East West)
21	18	THE DEFINITIVE SIMON AND GARFUNKEL	Simon & Garfunkel (Columbia)
15	19	SHEPHERD MOONS	Enya (WEA)
42	20	SCREAMADELICA	Primal Scream (Creation)
16	21	OUT OF TIME	R.E.M. (Warner Bros.)
6	22	MAGIC AND LOSS	Lou Reed (Sire)
18	23	THE COMMITMENTS	Commitments (MCA)
20	24	FROM TIME TO TIME - THE SINGLES COLLECTION	Paul Young (Columbia)
24	25	LOVE HURTS	Cher (Geffen)
17	26	MICHAEL CRAWFORD PERFORMS ANDREW LLOYD WEBBER	Michael Crawford (Telstar)
19	27	VOICES	Kenny Thomas (Cooltempo)
30	28	WAKING UP THE NEIGHBOURS	Bryan Adams (A&M)
13	29	30 SOMETHING	Carter The Unstoppable Sex Machine (Chrysalis)
23	30	THE FORCE BEHIND THE POWER	Diana Ross (EMI)
25	31	BOING	Airhead (Korova)
41	32	GREATEST HITS	Eurythmics (RCA)
27	33	JOSEPH AND THE AMAZING TECHNICOLOUR DREAMCOAT	Original Cast (Really Useful)
29	34	WIND OF CHANGE - CLASSIC ROCK	London Symphony Orchestra (Columbia)
37	35	THE WHITE ROOM	KLF (KLF Communications)
26	36	BILL AND TED'S BOGUS JOURNEY - SOUNDTRACK	Various Artists (Interscope)
28	37	SEAL	Seal (ZTT)
31	38	USE YOUR ILLUSION I	Guns N' Roses (Geffen)
-	39	INTO THE GREAT WIDE OPEN	Tom Petty & the Heartbreakers (MCA)
38	40	EXTREME II PORNOGRAFFITTI	Extreme (A&M)
48	41	BEVERLEY CRAVEN	Beverley Craven (Epic)
47	42	THE IMMACULATE COLLECTION	Madonna (Sire)
44	43	INNUENDO	Queen (Parlophone)
39	44	MOVE TO THIS	Cathy Dennis (Polydor)
36	45	DISCOGRAPHY - THE COMPLETE SINGLES COLLECTION	Pet Shop Boys (Parlophone)
-	46	SWEPT	Julia Fordham (Circa)
33	47	THE VERY BEST OF ELTON JOHN	Elton John (Rocket)
35	48	USE YOUR ILLUSION II	Guns N' Roses (Geffen)
-	49	EAT YOURSELF WHOLE	Kingmaker (Scorch)
40	50	CHORUS	Erasure (Mute)

15 February 1992

last week	this week	Title	Artist (Label)
1	1	HIGH ON THE HAPPY SIDE	Wet Wet Wet (Precious Organisation)
2	2	STARS	Simply Red (East West)
3	3	WE CAN'T DANCE	Genesis (Virgin)
7	4	NO REGRETS 1965-1976	Scott Walker & the Walker Brothers (Fontana)
5	5	REAL LOVE	Lisa Stansfield (Arista)
13	6	DANGEROUS	Michael Jackson (Epic)
4	7	GREATEST HITS II	Queen (Parlophone)
10	8	FINALLY	Ce Ce Peniston (A&M)
6	9	NEVERMIND	NIrvana (DGC)
8	10	SIMPLY THE BEST	Tina Turner (Capitol)
12	11	EMOTIONS	Mariah Carey (Columbia)
9	12	SPOOKY	Lush (4AD)
15	13	TIME, LOVE & TENDERNESS	Michael Bolton (Columbia)
11	14	DIAMONDS AND PEARLS	Prince & the New Power Generation (Paisley Park)
14	15	ACHTUNG BABY	U2 (Island)
20	16	SCREAMADELICA	Primal Scream (Creation)
16	17	GREATEST HITS	Queen (EMI)
23	18	THE COMMITMENTS	Commitments (MCA)
19	19	SHEPHERD MOONS	Enya (WEA)
17	20	LITTLE EARTHQUAKES	Tori Amos (East West)
21	21	OUT OF TIME	R.E.M. (Warner Bros.)
22	22	MAGIC AND LOSS	Lou Reed (Sire)
28	23	WAKING UP THE NEIGHBOURS	Bryan Adams (A&M)
26	24	MICHAEL CRAWFORD PERFORMS ANDREW LLOYD WEBBER	Michael Crawford (Telstar)
25	25	LOVE HURTS	Cher (Geffen)
-	26	BLACK EYED MAN	Cowboy Junkies (RCA)
24	27	FROM TIME TO TIME - THE SINGLES COLLECTION	Paul Young (Columbia)
30	28	THE FORCE BEHIND THE POWER	Diana Ross (EMI)
27	29	VOICES	Kenny Thomas (Cooltempo)
-	30	DECENCY	Diesel Park West (Food)
18	31	THE DEFINITIVE SIMON AND GARFUNKEL	Simon & Garfunkel (Columbia)
33	32	JOSEPH AND THE AMAZING TECHNICOLOUR DREAMCOAT	Original Cast (Really Useful)
-	33	ROPIN' THE WIND	Garth Brooks (Capitol)
35	34	THE WHITE ROOM	KLF (KLF Communications)
-	35	PAVAROTTI IN HYDE PARK	Luciano Pavarotti (Decca)
36	36	BILL AND TED'S BOGUS JOURNEY - SOUNDTRACK	Various Artists (Interscope)
45	37	DISCOGRAPHY - THE COMPLETE SINGLES COLLECTION	Pet Shop Boys (Parlophone)
41	38	BEVERLEY CRAVEN	Beverley Craven (Epic)
37	39	SEAL	Seal (ZTT)
32	40	GREATEST HITS	Eurythmics (RCA)
34	41	WIND OF CHANGE - CLASSIC ROCK	London Symphony Orchestra (Columbia)
43	42	INNUENDO	Queen (Parlophone)
38	43	USE YOUR ILLUSION I	Guns N' Roses (Geffen)
29	44	30 SOMETHING	Carter The Unstoppable Sex Machine (Chrysalis)
49	45	EAT YOURSELF WHOLE	Kingmaker (Scorch)
-	46	THE GREATEST HITS	Salt 'n' Pepa (ffrr)
-	47	BANDWAGONESQUE	Teenage Fanclub (Creation)
40	48	EXTREME II PORNOGRAFFITTI	Extreme (A&M)
42	49	THE IMMACULATE COLLECTION	Madonna (Sire)
-	50	T.V. SKY	Young Gods (Play It Again Sam)

Wet Wet Wet's resurrection to major album sales, which brought their *High On The Happy Side* straight in at Number 1, was initiated by the success of their single *Goodnight Girl*, which was already topping the chart when the album was released. Initial copies of the CD of *High On The Happy side* carried an entire bonus disc, also performed by Wet Wet Wet, but in the spurious guise of "Maggie Pie & The Imposters".

February – March 1992

22 February 1992

2	1	STARS	Simply Red (East West)
1	2	HIGH ON THE HAPPY SIDE	Wet Wet Wet (Precious Organisation)
3	3	WE CAN'T DANCE	Genesis (Virgin)
5	4	REAL LOVE	Lisa Stansfield (Arista)
11	5	EMOTIONS	Mariah Carey (Columbia)
6	6	DANGEROUS	Michael Jackson (Epic)
7	7	GREATEST HITS II	Queen (Parlophone)
4	8	NO REGRETS 1965-1976	Scott Walker & the Walker Brothers (Fontana)
13	9	TIME, LOVE & TENDERNESS	Michael Bolton (Columbia)
14	10	DIAMONDS AND PEARLS	Prince & the New Power Generation (Paisley Park)
39	11	SEAL	Seal (ZTT)
-	12	STICK AROUND FOR JOY	Sugarcubes (One Little Indian)
10	13	SIMPLY THE BEST	Tina Turner (Capitol)
21	14	OUT OF TIME	R.E.M. (Warner Bros.)
9	15	NEVERMIND	Nirvana (DGC)
-	16	GENERATION TERRORISTS	Manic Street Preachers (Columbia)
18	17	THE COMMITMENTS	Commitments (MCA)
-	18	FROM THE HEART - HIS GREATEST LOVE SONGS	Elvis Presley (RCA)
38	19	BEVERLEY CRAVEN	Beverley Craven (Epic)
34	20	THE WHITE ROOM	KLF (KLF Communications)
19	21	SHEPHERD MOONS	Enya (WEA)
28	22	THE FORCE BEHIND THE POWER	Diana Ross (EMI)
35	23	PAVAROTTI IN HYDE PARK	Luciano Pavarotti (Decca)
17	24	GREATEST HITS	Queen (EMI)
23	25	WAKING UP THE NEIGHBOURS	Bryan Adams (A&M)
8	26	FINALLY	Ce Ce Peniston (A&M)
15	27	ACHTUNG BABY	U2 (Island)
24	28	MICHAEL CRAWFORD PERFORMS ANDREW LLOYD WEBBER	Michael Crawford (Telstar)
16	29	SCREAMADELICA	Primal Scream (Creation)
20	30	LITTLE EARTHQUAKES	Tori Amos (East West)
29	31	VOICES	Kenny Thomas (Cooltempo)
27	32	FROM TIME TO TIME	Paul Young (Columbia)
48	33	EXTREME II PORNOGRAFFITTI	Extreme (A&M)
26	34	BLACK EYED MAN	Cowboy Junkies (RCA)
25	35	LOVE HURTS	Cher (Geffen)
40	36	GREATEST HITS	Eurythmics (RCA)
32	37	JOSEPH AND THE AMAZING TECHNICOLOUR DREAMCOAT	Original Cast (Really Useful)
12	38	SPOOKY	Lush (4AD)
-	39	LOVESCAPE	Neil Diamond (Columbia)
37	40	DISCOGRAPHY - THE COMPLETE SINGLES COLLECTION	Pet Shop Boys (Parlophone)
31	41	THE DEFINITIVE SIMON AND GARFUNKEL	Simon & Garfunkel (Columbia)
22	42	MAGIC AND LOSS	Lou Reed (Sire)
-	43	THE VERY BEST OF ELTON JOHN	Elton John (Rocket)
49	44	THE IMMACULATE COLLECTION	Madonna (Sire)
42	45	INNUENDO	Queen (Parlophone)
43	46	USE YOUR ILLUSION I	Guns N' Roses (Geffen)
-	47	NEVER LOVED ELVIS	Wonder Stuff (Polydor)
36	48	BILL AND TED'S BOGUS JOURNEY - SOUNDTRACK	Various Artists (Interscope)
33	49	ROPIN' THE WIND	Garth Brooks (Capitol)
-	50	MOVE TO THIS	Cathy Dennis (Polydor)

29 February 1992

-	1	SEVEN	Jam (Polydor)
1	2	STARS	Simply Red (East West)
2	3	HIGH ON THE HAPPY SIDE	Wet Wet Wet (Precious Organisation)
-	4	HORMONALLY YOURS	Shakespear's Sister (London)
3	5	WE CAN'T DANCE	Genesis (Virgin)
11	6	SEAL	Seal (ZTT)
19	7	BEVERLEY CRAVEN	Beverley Craven (Epic)
4	8	REAL LOVE	Lisa Stansfield (Arista)
6	9	DANGEROUS	Michael Jackson (Epic)
18	10	FROM THE HEART - HIS GREATEST LOVE SONGS	Elvis Presley (RCA)
-	11	CURTIS STIGERS	Curtis Stigers (Arista)
5	12	EMOTIONS	Mariah Carey (Columbia)
7	13	GREATEST HITS II	Queen (Parlophone)
10	14	DIAMONDS AND PEARLS	Prince & the New Power Generation (Paisley Park)
25	15	WAKING UP THE NEIGHBOURS	Bryan Adams (A&M)
9	16	TIME, LOVE & TENDERNESS	Michael Bolton (Columbia)
13	17	SIMPLY THE BEST	Tina Turner (Capitol)
16	18	GENERATION TERRORISTS	Manic Street Preachers (Columbia)
17	19	THE COMMITMENTS	Commitments (MCA)
12	20	STICK AROUND FOR JOY	Sugarcubes (One Little Indian)
8	21	NO REGRETS 1965-1976	Scott Walker & the Walker Brothers (Fontana)
14	22	OUT OF TIME	R.E.M. (Warner Bros.)
15	23	NEVERMIND	Nirvana (DGC)
21	24	SHEPHERD MOONS	Enya (WEA)
20	25	THE WHITE ROOM	KLF (KLF Communications)
24	26	GREATEST HITS	Queen (EMI)
27	27	ACHTUNG BABY	U2 (Island)
33	28	EXTREME II PORNOGRAFFITTI	Extreme (A&M)
28	29	MICHAEL CRAWFORD PERFORMS ANDREW LLOYD WEBBER	Michael Crawford (Telstar)
22	30	THE FORCE BEHIND THE POWER	Diana Ross (EMI)
29	31	SCREAMADELICA	Primal Scream (Creation)
31	32	VOICES	Kenny Thomas (Cooltempo)
35	33	LOVE HURTS	Cher (Geffen)
-	34	MIND ADVENTURES	Des'ree (Dusted Sound)
36	35	GREATEST HITS	Eurythmics (RCA)
32	36	FROM TIME TO TIME	Paul Young (Columbia)
23	37	PAVAROTTI IN HYDE PARK	Luciano Pavarotti (Decca)
-	38	THE ESSENTIAL KIRI	Kiri Te Kanawa (Decca)
26	39	FINALLY	Ce Ce Peniston (A&M)
45	40	INNUENDO	Queen (Parlophone)
37	41	JOSEPH AND THE AMAZING TECHNICOLOUR DREAMCOAT	Original Cast (Really Useful)
41	42	THE DEFINITIVE SIMON AND GARFUNKEL	Simon & Garfunkel (Columbia)
46	43	USE YOUR ILLUSION I	Guns N' Roses (Geffen)
39	44	LOVESCAPE	Neil Diamond (Columbia)
34	45	BLACK EYED MAN	Cowboy Junkies (RCA)
30	46	LITTLE EARTHQUAKES	Tori Amos (East West)
-	47	ON EVERY STREET	Dire Straits (Vertigo)
40	48	DISCOGRAPHY - THE COMPLETE SINGLES COLLECTION	Pet Shop Boys (Parlophone)
43	49	THE VERY BEST OF ELTON JOHN	Elton John (Rocket)
44	50	THE IMMACULATE COLLECTION	Madonna (Sire)

7 March 1992

2	1	STARS	Simply Red (East West)
1	2	SEVEN	Jam (Polydor)
4	3	HORMONALLY YOURS	Shakespear's Sister (London)
-	4	DIVINE MADNESS	Madness (Virgin)
5	5	WE CAN'T DANCE	Genesis (Virgin)
9	6	DANGEROUS	Michael Jackson (Epic)
-	7	TEN	Pearl Jam (Epic)
3	8	HIGH ON THE HAPPY SIDE	Wet Wet Wet (Precious Organisation)
6	9	SEAL	Seal (ZTT)
10	10	FROM THE HEART - HIS GREATEST LOVE SONGS	Elvis Presley (RCA)
11	11	CURTIS STIGERS	Curtis Stigers (Arista)
7	12	BEVERLEY CRAVEN	Beverley Craven (Epic)
-	13	YOURS SINCERELY	Pasadenas (Columbia)
8	14	REAL LOVE	Lisa Stansfield (Arista)
17	15	SIMPLY THE BEST	Tina Turner (Capitol)
12	16	EMOTIONS	Mariah Carey (Columbia)
13	17	GREATEST HITS II	Queen (Parlophone)
-	18	WASTED IN AMERICA	Love/Hate (Columbia)
15	19	WAKING UP THE NEIGHBOURS	Bryan Adams (A&M)
27	20	ACHTUNG BABY	U2 (Island)
-	21	SEBASTOPOL RD	Mega City Four (Big Life)
14	22	DIAMONDS AND PEARLS	Prince & the New Power Generation (Paisley Park)
22	23	OUT OF TIME	R.E.M. (Warner Bros.)
23	24	NEVERMIND	Nirvana (DGC)
16	25	TIME, LOVE & TENDERNESS	Michael Bolton (Columbia)
-	26	BLEACH	Nirvana (Tupelo)
21	27	NO REGRETS - THE BEST OF SCOTT WALKER AND THE WALKER BROTHERS 1965-1976	Scott Walker & the Walker Brothers (Fontana)
-	28	LITTLE VILLAGE	Little Village (Reprise)
25	29	THE WHITE ROOM	KLF (KLF Communications)
24	30	SHEPHERD MOONS	Enya (WEA)
34	31	MIND ADVENTURES	Des'ree (Dusted Sound)
-	32	MIRMAMA	Eddie Reader with the Patron Saints Of Imperfection (RCA)
-	33	THAT WHAT IS NOT	Public Image Ltd. (Virgin)
19	34	THE COMMITMENTS	Commitments (MCA)
43	35	USE YOUR ILLUSION I	Guns N' Roses (Geffen)
26	36	GREATEST HITS	Queen (EMI)
28	37	EXTREME II PORNOGRAFFITTI	Extreme (A&M)
38	38	THE ESSENTIAL KIRI	Kiri Te Kanawa (Decca)
18	39	GENERATION TERRORISTS	Manic Street Preachers (Columbia)
29	40	MICHAEL CRAWFORD PERFORMS ANDREW LLOYD WEBBER	Michael Crawford (Telstar)
-	41	WOODFACE	Crowded House (Capitol)
20	42	STICK AROUND FOR JOY	Sugarcubes (One Little Indian)
-	43	HANDS ON	Thousand Yard Stare (Polydor)
35	44	GREATEST HITS	Eurythmics (RCA)
-	45	FERMENT	Catherine Wheel (Fontana)
-	46	MOTOWN'S GREATEST HITS	Diana Ross (Motown)
48	47	DISCOGRAPHY - THE COMPLETE SINGLES COLLECTION	Pet Shop Boys (Parlophone)
33	48	LOVE HURTS	Cher (Geffen)
30	49	THE FORCE BEHIND THE POWER	Diana Ross (EMI)
32	50	VOICES	Kenny Thomas (Cooltempo)

All at once the album chart was strong with Top 10-registering solo female artists once again: joining Lisa Stansfield's *Real Love* and Tina Turner's hits compilation *Simply The Best*, were albums by Ce Ce Peniston, Mariah Carey, Beverley Craven and girl duo Shakespear's Sister, who were just into a six-week stay at Number 1 on the singles chart with *Stay*. Their LP *Hormonally Yours*, however, peaked at 3.

14 March 1992

last week	this week		
-	1	TEARS ROLL DOWN (GREATEST HITS '82-'92)	Tears For Fears (Fontana)
4	2	DIVINE MADNESS	Madness (Virgin)
1	3	STARS	Simply Red (East West)
3	4	HORMONALLY YOURS	Shakespear's Sister (London)
2	5	SEVEN	Jam (Polydor)
13	6	YOURS SINCERELY	Pasadenas (Columbia)
6	7	DANGEROUS	Michael Jackson (Epic)
8	8	HIGH ON THE HAPPY SIDE	Wet Wet Wet (Precious Organisation)
5	9	WE CAN'T DANCE	Genesis (Virgin)
15	10	SIMPLY THE BEST	Tina Turner (Capitol)
10	11	FROM THE HEART - HIS GREATEST LOVE SONGS	Elvis Presley (RCA)
14	12	REAL LOVE	Lisa Stansfield (Arista)
11	13	CURTIS STIGERS	Curtis Stigers (Arista)
7	14	TEN	Pearl Jam (Epic)
9	15	SEAL	Seal (ZTT)
-	16	THE VERY BEST OF...	Frankie Valli & the Four Seasons (Flying Music/PolyGram TV)
20	17	ACHTUNG BABY	U2 (Island)
24	18	NEVERMIND	Nirvana (DGC)
19	19	WAKING UP THE NEIGHBOURS	Bryan Adams (A&M)
12	20	BEVERLEY CRAVEN	Beverley Craven (Epic)
17	21	GREATEST HITS II	Queen (Parlophone)
22	22	DIAMONDS AND PEARLS	Prince & the New Power Generation (Paisley Park)
25	23	TIME, LOVE & TENDERNESS	Michael Bolton (Columbia)
23	24	OUT OF TIME	R.E.M. (Warner Bros.)
16	25	EMOTIONS	Mariah Carey (Columbia)
-	26	BRAND NEW HEAVIES	Brand New Heavies (Acid Jazz)
29	27	THE WHITE ROOM	KLF (KLF Communications)
26	28	BLEACH	Nirvana (Tupelo)
41	29	WOODFACE	Crowded House (Capitol)
18	30	WASTED IN AMERICA	Love/Hate (Columbia)
35	31	USE YOUR ILLUSION I	Guns N' Roses (Geffen)
27	32	NO REGRETS - THE BEST OF SCOTT WALKER AND THE WALKER BROTHERS 1965-1976	Scott Walker & the Walker Brothers (Fontana)
28	33	LITTLE VILLAGE	Little Village (Reprise)
30	34	SHEPHERD MOONS	Enya (WEA)
-	35	MUSIC FROM THE ITV SERIES INSPECTOR MORSE VOLUME 2	Barrington Pheloung (Virgin Television)
36	36	GREATEST HITS	Queen (EMI)
38	37	THE ESSENTIAL KIRI	Kiri Te Kanawa (Decca)
37	38	EXTREME II PORNOGRAFFITTI	Extreme (A&M)
34	39	THE COMMITMENTS	Commitments (MCA)
-	40	GET READY	2 Unlimited (PWL Continental)
46	41	MOTOWN'S GREATEST HITS	Diana Ross (Motown)
-	42	USE YOUR ILLUSION II	Guns N' Roses (Geffen)
21	43	SEBASTOPOL RD	Mega City Four (Big Life)
44	44	GREATEST HITS	Eurythmics (RCA)
33	45	THAT WHAT IS NOT	Public Image Ltd. (Virgin)
40	46	MICHAEL CRAWFORD PERFORMS ANDREW LLOYD WEBBER	Michael Crawford (Telstar)
48	47	LOVE HURTS	Cher (Geffen)
32	48	MIRMAMA	Eddie Reader with the Patron Saints Of Imperfection (RCA)
31	49	MIND ADVENTURES	Des'ree (Dusted Sound)
-	50	UH-OH	David Byrne (Luaka Bop)

21 March 1992

2	1	DIVINE MADNESS	Madness (Virgin)
1	2	TEARS ROLL DOWN (GREATEST HITS '82-'92)	Tears For Fears (Fontana)
3	3	STARS	Simply Red (East West)
-	4	AFTER HOURS	Gary Moore (Virgin)
-	5	GOING BLANK AGAIN	Ride (Creation)
4	6	HORMONALLY YOURS	Shakespear's Sister (London)
5	7	SEVEN	Jam (Polydor)
-	8	DOPPELGANGER	Curve (AnXious)
8	9	HIGH ON THE HAPPY SIDE	Wet Wet Wet (Precious Organisation)
29	10	WOODFACE	Crowded House (Capitol)
11	11	ACHTUNG BABY	U2 (Island)
12	12	REAL LOVE	Lisa Stansfield (Arista)
11	13	FROM THE HEART - HIS GREATEST LOVE SONGS	Elvis Presley (RCA)
10	14	SIMPLY THE BEST	Tina Turner (Capitol)
18	15	NEVERMIND	Nirvana (DGC)
19	16	WAKING UP THE NEIGHBOURS	Bryan Adams (A&M)
9	17	WE CAN'T DANCE	Genesis (Virgin)
7	18	DANGEROUS	Michael Jackson (Epic)
6	19	YOURS SINCERELY	Pasadenas (Columbia)
13	20	CURTIS STIGERS	Curtis Stigers (Arista)
16	21	THE VERY BEST OF FRANKIE VALLI AND THE FOUR SEASONS	Frankie Valli & the Four Seasons (Flying Music/PolyGram TV)
15	22	SEAL	Seal (ZTT)
21	23	GREATEST HITS II	Queen (Parlophone)
23	24	TIME, LOVE & TENDERNESS	Michael Bolton (Columbia)
27	25	THE WHITE ROOM	KLF (KLF Communications)
24	26	OUT OF TIME	R.E.M. (Warner Bros.)
22	27	DIAMONDS AND PEARLS	Prince & the New Power Generation (Paisley Park)
20	28	BEVERLEY CRAVEN	Beverley Craven (Epic)
14	29	TEN	Pearl Jam (Epic)
50	30	UH-OH	David Byrne (Luaka Bop)
31	31	USE YOUR ILLUSION I	Guns N' Roses (Geffen)
-	32	INNER CHILD	Shanice (Motown)
28	33	BLEACH	Nirvana (Tupelo)
26	34	BRAND NEW HEAVIES	Brand New Heavies (Acid Jazz)
37	35	THE ESSENTIAL KIRI	Kiri Te Kanawa (Decca)
39	36	THE COMMITMENTS	Commitments (MCA)
33	37	LITTLE VILLAGE	Little Village (Reprise)
42	38	USE YOUR ILLUSION II	Guns N' Roses (Geffen)
38	39	EXTREME II PORNOGRAFFITTI	Extreme (A&M)
-	40	COINCIDENCE AND LIKELY STORIES	Buffy Sainte-Marie (Ensign)
25	41	EMOTIONS	Mariah Carey (Columbia)
32	42	NO REGRETS - THE BEST OF SCOTT WALKER AND THE WALKER BROTHERS 1965-1976	Scott Walker & the Walker Brothers (Fontana)
34	43	SHEPHERD MOONS	Enya (WEA)
36	44	GREATEST HITS	Queen (EMI)
35	45	MUSIC FROM THE ITV SERIES INSPECTOR MORSE VOLUME 2	Barrington Pheloung (Virgin Television)
44	46	GREATEST HITS	Eurythmics (RCA)
30	47	WASTED IN AMERICA	Love/Hate (Columbia)
46	48	MICHAEL CRAWFORD PERFORMS ANDREW LLOYD WEBBER	Michael Crawford (Telstar)
-	49	MYSTERIO	Ian McCulloch (East West)
-	50	THE IMMACULATE COLLECTION	Madonna (Sire)

28 March 1992

1	1	DIVINE MADNESS	Madness (Virgin)
2	2	TEARS ROLL DOWN (GREATEST HITS '82-'92)	Tears For Fears (Fontana)
3	3	STARS	Simply Red (East West)
4	4	AFTER HOURS	Gary Moore (Virgin)
6	5	HORMONALLY YOURS	Shakespear's Sister (London)
10	6	WOODFACE	Crowded House (Capitol)
12	7	REAL LOVE	Lisa Stansfield (Arista)
9	8	HIGH ON THE HAPPY SIDE	Wet Wet Wet (Precious Organisation)
15	9	NEVERMIND	Nirvana (DGC)
-	10	UP	Right Said Fred (Tug)
5	11	GOING BLANK AGAIN	Ride (Creation)
16	12	WAKING UP THE NEIGHBOURS	Bryan Adams (A&M)
21	13	THE VERY BEST OF FRANKIE VALLI AND THE FOUR SEASONS	Frankie Valli & the Four Seasons (Flying Music/PolyGram TV)
11	14	ACHTUNG BABY	U2 (Island)
14	15	SIMPLY THE BEST	Tina Turner (Capitol)
13	16	FROM THE HEART - HIS GREATEST LOVE SONGS	Elvis Presley (RCA)
7	17	SEVEN	Jam (Polydor)
8	18	DOPPELGANGER	Curve (AnXious)
18	19	DANGEROUS	Michael Jackson (Epic)
17	20	WE CAN'T DANCE	Genesis (Virgin)
24	21	TIME, LOVE & TENDERNESS	Michael Bolton (Columbia)
20	22	CURTIS STIGERS	Curtis Stigers (Arista)
23	23	GREATEST HITS II	Queen (Parlophone)
27	24	DIAMONDS AND PEARLS	Prince & the New Power Generation (Paisley Park)
22	25	SEAL	Seal (ZTT)
26	26	OUT OF TIME	R.E.M. (Warner Bros.)
32	27	INNER CHILD	Shanice (Motown)
41	28	EMOTIONS	Mariah Carey (Columbia)
-	29	CODE: SELFISH	Fall (Cog Sinister)
19	30	YOURS SINCERELY	Pasadenas (Columbia)
-	31	GREATEST REMIXES VOL.1	Clivilles & Cole (Columbia)
25	32	THE WHITE ROOM	KLF (KLF Communications)
36	33	THE COMMITMENTS	Commitments (MCA)
31	34	USE YOUR ILLUSION I	Guns N' Roses (Geffen)
28	35	BEVERLEY CRAVEN	Beverley Craven (Epic)
35	36	THE ESSENTIAL KIRI	Kiri Te Kanawa (Decca)
29	37	TEN	Pearl Jam (Epic)
33	38	BLEACH	Nirvana (Tupelo)
43	39	SHEPHERD MOONS	Enya (WEA)
-	40	FINALLY	Ce Ce Peniston (A&M)
40	41	COINCIDENCE AND LIKELY STORIES	Buffy Sainte-Marie (Ensign)
38	42	USE YOUR ILLUSION II	Guns N' Roses (Geffen)
34	43	BRAND NEW HEAVIES	Brand New Heavies (Acid Jazz)
39	44	EXTREME II PORNOGRAFFITTI	Extreme (A&M)
46	45	GREATEST HITS	Eurythmics (RCA)
30	46	UH-OH	David Byrne (Luaka Bop)
-	47	KING'S X	King's X (Atlantic)
50	48	THE IMMACULATE COLLECTION	Madonna (Sire)
45	49	MUSIC FROM THE ITV SERIES INSPECTOR MORSE VOLUME 2	Barrington Pheloung (Virgin Television)
-	50	INGENUE	k.d. lang (Sire)

Two established groups from the 1980s looked back on their past successes with Number 1 compilation albums: Tears For Fears with *Tears Roll Down*, and Madness with *Divine Madness*. The latter was the third in a series of compilations which began with *Complete Madness* as far back as 1982, and continued with *Utter Madness* in 1986; the new album effectively anthologised its two predecessors.

April 1992

4 April 1992

last week	this week	title
1	1	DIVINE MADNESS — Madness (Virgin)
10	2	UP — Right Said Fred (Tug)
3	3	STARS — Simply Red (East West)
2	4	TEARS ROLL DOWN (GREATEST HITS '82-'92) — Tears For Fears (Fontana)
4	5	AFTER HOURS — Gary Moore (Virgin)
6	6	WOODFACE — Crowded House (Capitol)
5	7	HORMONALLY YOURS — Shakespear's Sister (London)
9	8	NEVERMIND — Nirvana (DGC)
-	9	HONEY'S DEAD — Jesus & Mary Chain (blanco y negro)
-	10	BETWEEN 10TH AND 11TH — Charlatans (Situation Two)
7	11	REAL LOVE — Lisa Stansfield (Arista)
12	12	WAKING UP THE NEIGHBOURS — Bryan Adams (A&M)
8	13	HIGH ON THE HAPPY SIDE — Wet Wet Wet (Precious Organisation)
14	14	ACHTUNG BABY — U2 (Island)
-	15	"ADDICTIONS" VOLUME 2 Robert Palmer (Island)
15	16	SIMPLY THE BEST — Tina Turner (Capitol)
11	17	GOING BLANK AGAIN — Ride (Creation)
17	18	SEVEN — Jam (Polydor)
13	19	THE VERY BEST OF ... — Frankie Valli & the Four Seasons (Flying Music/PolyGram TV)
18	20	DOPPELGANGER — Curve (AnXious)
19	21	DANGEROUS — Michael Jackson (Epic)
21	22	TIME, LOVE & TENDERNESS — Michael Bolton (Columbia)
16	23	FROM THE HEART - HIS GREATEST LOVE SONGS — Elvis Presley (RCA)
20	24	WE CAN'T DANCE — Genesis (Virgin)
24	25	DIAMONDS AND PEARLS — Prince & the New Power Generation (Paisley Park)
40	26	FINALLY — Ce Ce Peniston (A&M)
22	27	CURTIS STIGERS — Curtis Stigers (Arista)
28	28	EMOTIONS — Mariah Carey (Columbia)
29	29	CODE: SELFISH — Fall (Cog Sinister)
-	30	HISTORY - THE SINGLES '85-'91 — New Model Army (EMI)
26	31	OUT OF TIME — R.E.M. (Warner Bros.)
23	32	GREATEST HITS II — Queen (Parlophone)
33	33	THE COMMITMENTS — Commitments (MCA)
25	34	SEAL — Seal (ZTT)
37	35	TEN — Pearl Jam (Epic)
-	36	EVERYTHING'S ALRIGHT FOREVER — Boo Radleys (Creation)
-	37	BLOOD SUGAR SEX MAGIK — Red Hot Chili Peppers (Warner Bros.)
34	38	USE YOUR ILLUSION I — Guns N' Roses (Geffen)
27	39	INNER CHILD — Shanice (Motown)
49	40	MUSIC FROM INSPECTOR MORSE VOLUME 2 — Barrington Pheloung (Virgin Television)
50	41	INGENUE — k.d. lang (Sire)
32	42	THE WHITE ROOM KLF (KLF Communications)
-	43	IN RIBBONS — Pale Saints (4AD)
30	44	YOURS SINCERELY — Pasadenas (Columbia)
-	45	EVERYBODY'S FREE — Rozalla (Pulse 8)
35	46	BEVERLEY CRAVEN — Beverley Craven (Epic)
31	47	GREATEST REMIXES VOL.1 — Clivilles & Cole (Columbia)
36	48	THE ESSENTIAL KIRI — Kiri Te Kanawa (Decca)
38	49	BLEACH — Nirvana (Tupelo)
-	50	MICHAEL CRAWFORD PERFORMS ANDREW LLOYD WEBBER — Michael Crawford (Telstar)

11 April 1992

last week	this week	title
-	1	ADRENALIZE — Def Leppard (Bludgeon Riffola)
-	2	HUMAN TOUCH — Bruce Springsteen (Columbia)
-	3	LUCKY TOWN — Bruce Springsteen (Columbia)
2	4	UP — Right Said Fred (Tug)
3	5	STARS — Simply Red (East West)
1	6	DIVINE MADNESS — Madness (Virgin)
-	7	0898 — Beautiful South (Go! Discs)
4	8	TEARS ROLL DOWN (GREATEST HITS '82-'92) — Tears For Fears (Fontana)
11	9	REAL LOVE — Lisa Stansfield (Arista)
13	10	HIGH ON THE HAPPY SIDE — Wet Wet Wet (Precious Organisation)
6	11	WOODFACE — Crowded House (Capitol)
7	12	HORMONALLY YOURS — Shakespear's Sister (London)
16	13	SIMPLY THE BEST — Tina Turner (Capitol)
19	14	THE VERY BEST OF FRANKIE VALLI AND THE FOUR SEASONS — Frankie Valli & the Four Seasons (Flying Music/PolyGram TV)
15	15	"ADDICTIONS" VOLUME 2 Robert Palmer (Island)
12	16	WAKING UP THE NEIGHBOURS — Bryan Adams (A&M)
5	17	AFTER HOURS — Gary Moore (Virgin)
-	18	HEAR MY SONG (THE BEST OF JOSEF LOCKE) — Josef Locke (EMI)
8	19	NEVERMIND — Nirvana (DGC)
9	20	HONEY'S DEAD — Jesus & Mary Chain (blanco y negro)
14	21	ACHTUNG BABY — U2 (Island)
27	22	CURTIS STIGERS — Curtis Stigers (Arista)
22	23	TIME, LOVE & TENDERNESS — Michael Bolton (Columbia)
10	24	BETWEEN 10TH AND 11TH — Charlatans (Situation Two)
23	25	FROM THE HEART - HIS GREATEST LOVE SONGS — Elvis Presley (RCA)
25	26	DIAMONDS AND PEARLS — Prince & the New Power Generation (Paisley Park)
18	27	SEVEN — Jam (Polydor)
21	28	DANGEROUS — Michael Jackson (Epic)
-	29	LEAN INTO IT — Mr. Big (Atlantic)
24	30	WE CAN'T DANCE — Genesis (Virgin)
32	31	GREATEST HITS II — Queen (Parlophone)
-	32	DRY — PJ Harvey (Too Pure)
-	33	THE DEFINITIVE SIMON AND GARFUNKEL — Simon & Garfunkel (Columbia)
33	34	THE COMMITMENTS — Commitments (MCA)
-	35	CHORUS — Erasure (Mute)
-	36	LAZER GUIDED MELODIES — Spiritualized (Dedicated)
31	37	OUT OF TIME — R.E.M. (Warner Bros.)
-	38	NIGHT CALLS — Joe Cocker (Capitol)
-	39	ARKANSAS TRAVELER — Michelle Shocked (London)
28	40	EMOTIONS — Mariah Carey (Columbia)
40	41	MUSIC FROM THE ITV SERIES INSPECTOR MORSE VOLUME 2 — Barrington Pheloung (Virgin Television)
45	42	EVERYBODY'S FREE — Rozalla (Pulse 8)
17	43	GOING BLANK AGAIN — Ride (Creation)
44	44	YOURS SINCERELY — Pasadenas (Columbia)
20	45	DOPPELGANGER — Curve (AnXious)
34	47	SEAL — Seal (ZTT)
46	48	BEVERLEY CRAVEN — Beverley Craven (Epic)
48	49	THE ESSENTIAL KIRI — Kiri Te Kanawa (Decca)
26	50	FINALLY — Ce Ce Peniston (A&M)

18 April 1992

last week	this week	title
-	1	DIVA — Annie Lennox (RCA)
1	2	ADRENALIZE — Def Leppard (Bludgeon Riffola)
4	3	UP — Right Said Fred (Tug)
6	4	DIVINE MADNESS — Madness (Virgin)
2	5	HUMAN TOUCH — Bruce Springsteen (Columbia)
7	6	0898 — Beautiful South (Go! Discs)
3	7	LUCKY TOWN — Bruce Springsteen (Columbia)
5	8	STARS — Simply Red (East West)
8	9	TEARS ROLL DOWN (GREATEST HITS '82-'92) — Tears For Fears (Fontana)
18	10	HEAR MY SONG (THE BEST OF JOSEF LOCKE) — Josef Locke (EMI)
12	11	HORMONALLY YOURS — Shakespear's Sister (London)
9	12	REAL LOVE — Lisa Stansfield (Arista)
32	13	DRY — PJ Harvey (Too Pure)
11	14	WOODFACE — Crowded House (Capitol)
-	15	GALLUS — Gun (A&M)
22	16	CURTIS STIGERS — Curtis Stigers (Arista)
16	17	WAKING UP THE NEIGHBOURS — Bryan Adams (A&M)
10	18	HIGH ON THE HAPPY SIDE — Wet Wet Wet (Precious Organisation)
15	19	"ADDICTIONS" VOLUME 2 Robert Palmer (Island)
29	20	LEAN INTO IT — Mr. Big (Atlantic)
19	21	NEVERMIND — Nirvana (DGC)
21	22	ACHTUNG BABY — U2 (Island)
17	23	AFTER HOURS — Gary Moore (Virgin)
30	24	WE CAN'T DANCE — Genesis (Virgin)
14	25	THE VERY BEST OF... — Frankie Valli & the Four Seasons (Flying Music/PolyGram TV)
13	26	SIMPLY THE BEST — Tina Turner (Capitol)
38	27	NIGHT CALLS — Joe Cocker (Capitol)
23	28	TIME, LOVE & TENDERNESS — Michael Bolton (Columbia)
26	29	DIAMONDS AND PEARLS — Prince & the New Power Generation (Paisley Park)
35	30	CHORUS — Erasure (Mute)
28	31	DANGEROUS — Michael Jackson (Epic)
27	32	SEVEN — Jam (Polydor)
-	33	EXTRAS — Jam (Polydor)
-	34	MOTOWN'S GREATEST HITS — Temptations (Motown)
33	35	THE DEFINITIVE SIMON AND GARFUNKEL — Simon & Garfunkel (Columbia)
34	36	THE COMMITMENTS — Commitments (MCA)
-	37	SENSE — Lightning Seeds (Virgin)
36	38	LAZER GUIDED MELODIES — Spiritualized (Dedicated)
37	39	OUT OF TIME — R.E.M. (Warner Bros.)
-	40	JOYRIDE — Roxette (EMI)
-	41	GREATEST HITS — Eurythmics (RCA)
31	42	GREATEST HITS II — Queen (Parlophone)
25	43	FROM THE HEART - HIS GREATEST LOVE SONGS — Elvis Presley (RCA)
44	44	YOURS SINCERELY — Pasadenas (Columbia)
48	45	BEVERLEY CRAVEN — Beverley Craven (Epic)
47	46	SEAL — Seal (ZTT)
40	47	EMOTIONS — Mariah Carey (Columbia)
24	48	BETWEEN 10TH AND 11TH — Charlatans (Situation Two)
41	49	MUSIC FROM THE ITV SERIES INSPECTOR MORSE VOLUME 2 — Barrington Pheloung (Virgin Television)
39	50	ARKANSAS TRAVELER — Michelle Shocked (London)

Following (though for certain not intentionally) in the footsteps of Guns N' Roses a few months earlier, Bruce Springsteen released two new albums simultaneously. Unlike the GN'R set, though, *Human Touch* and *Lucky Town* were not presented as two halves of a single project, but rather two differently-styled projects - one more deliberately commercial, the other more laid back - completed simultaneously.

last week	this week	25 April 1992	
1	1	DIVA	Annie Lennox (RCA)
3	2	UP	Right Said Fred (Tug)
2	3	ADRENALIZE	Def Leppard (Bludgeon Riffola)
-	4	VOLUME III JUST RIGHT	Soul II Soul (10)
4	5	DIVINE MADNESS	Madness (Virgin)
8	6	STARS	Simply Red (East West)
-	7	GREATEST HITS	ZZ Top (Warner Bros.)
9	8	TEARS ROLL DOWN (GREATEST HITS '82-'92) Tears For Fears (Fontana)	
6	9	0898	Beautiful South (Go! Discs)
16	10	CURTIS STIGERS	Curtis Stigers (Arista)
10	11	HEAR MY SONG (THE BEST OF JOSEF LOCKE) Josef Locke (EMI)	
12	12	REAL LOVE	Lisa Stansfield (Arista)
5	13	HUMAN TOUCH	Bruce Springsteen (Columbia)
11	14	HORMONALLY YOURS Shakespear's Sister (London)	
33	15	EXTRAS	Jam (Polydor)
24	16	WE CAN'T DANCE	Genesis (Virgin)
14	17	WOODFACE	Crowded House (Capitol)
7	18	LUCKY TOWN	Bruce Springsteen (Columbia)
15	19	GALLUS	Gun (A&M)
34	20	MOTOWN'S GREATEST HITS Temptations (Motown)	
17	21	WAKING UP THE NEIGHBOURS Bryan Adams (A&M)	
21	22	NEVERMIND	Nirvana (DGC)
19	23	"ADDICTIONS" VOLUME 2 Robert Palmer (Island)	
-	24	THE COMMITMENTS VOL.2 Commitments (MCA)	
29	25	DIAMONDS AND PEARLS Prince & the New Power Generation (Paisley Park)	
18	26	HIGH ON THE HAPPY SIDE Wet Wet Wet (Precious Organisation)	
23	27	AFTER HOURS	Gary Moore (Virgin)
26	28	SIMPLY THE BEST	Tina Turner (Capitol)
27	29	NIGHT CALLS	Joe Cocker (Capitol)
30	30	CHORUS	Erasure (Mute)
25	31	THE VERY BEST OF Frankie Valli & the Four Seasons (Flying Music/PolyGram TV)	
22	32	ACHTUNG BABY	U2 (Island)
31	33	DANGEROUS	Michael Jackson (Epic)
20	34	LEAN INTO IT	Mr. Big (Atlantic)
32	35	SEVEN	Jam (Polydor)
28	36	TIME, LOVE & TENDERNESS Michael Bolton (Columbia)	
47	37	EMOTIONS	Mariah Carey (Columbia)
13	38	DRY	PJ Harvey (Too Pure)
42	39	GREATEST HITS II	Queen (Parlophone)
49	40	MUSIC FROM THE ITV SERIES INSPECTOR MORSE VOLUME 2 Barrington Pheloung (Virgin Television)	
44	41	YOURS SINCERELY	Pasadenas (Columbia)
35	42	THE DEFINITIVE SIMON AND GARFUNKEL Simon & Garfunkel (Columbia)	
37	43	SENSE	Lightning Seeds (Virgin)
-	44	FINALLY	Ce Ce Peniston (A&M)
-	45	THE COMFORT ZONE Vanessa Williams (Polydor)	
-	46	TEN	Pearl Jam (Epic)
39	47	OUT OF TIME	R.E.M. (Warner Bros.)
-	48	TOO BLIND TO SEE IT	Kym Sims (Atco)
36	49	THE COMMITMENTS	Commitments (MCA)
43	50	FROM THE HEART - HIS GREATEST LOVE SONGS Elvis Presley (RCA)	

last week	this week	2 May 1992	
-	1	WISH	Cure (Fiction)
1	2	DIVA	Annie Lennox (RCA)
2	3	UP	Right Said Fred (Tug)
7	4	GREATEST HITS	ZZ Top (Warner Bros.)
5	5	DIVINE MADNESS	Madness (Virgin)
6	6	STARS	Simply Red (East West)
4	7	VOLUME III JUST RIGHT	Soul II Soul (10)
8	8	TEARS ROLL DOWN (GREATEST HITS '82-'92) Tears For Fears (Fontana)	
12	9	REAL LOVE	Lisa Stansfield (Arista)
39	10	GREATEST HITS II	Queen (Parlophone)
3	11	ADRENALIZE	Def Leppard (Bludgeon Riffola)
10	12	CURTIS STIGERS	Curtis Stigers (Arista)
24	13	THE COMMITMENTS VOL.2 Commitments (MCA)	
11	14	HEAR MY SONG (THE BEST OF JOSEF LOCKE) Josef Locke (EMI)	
9	15	0898	Beautiful South (Go! Discs)
16	16	WE CAN'T DANCE	Genesis (Virgin)
14	17	HORMONALLY YOURS Shakespear's Sister (London)	
17	18	WOODFACE	Crowded House (Capitol)
13	19	HUMAN TOUCH	Bruce Springsteen (Columbia)
20	20	MOTOWN'S GREATEST HITS Temptations (Motown)	
28	21	SIMPLY THE BEST	Tina Turner (Capitol)
22	22	NEVERMIND	Nirvana (DGC)
26	23	HIGH ON THE HAPPY SIDE Wet Wet Wet (Precious Organisation)	
21	24	WAKING UP THE NEIGHBOURS Bryan Adams (A&M)	
33	25	DANGEROUS	Michael Jackson (Epic)
25	26	DIAMONDS AND PEARLS Prince & the New Power Generation (Paisley Park)	
-	27	GREATEST HITS	Queen (EMI)
27	28	AFTER HOURS	Gary Moore (Virgin)
18	29	LUCKY TOWN	Bruce Springsteen (Columbia)
-	30	GREATEST HITS	Foreigner (Atlantic)
-	31	USE YOUR ILLUSION I	Guns N' Roses (Geffen)
23	32	"ADDICTIONS" VOLUME 2 Robert Palmer (Island)	
-	33	BRICKS ARE HEAVY	L7 (Slash)
49	34	THE COMMITMENTS	Commitments (MCA)
45	35	THE COMFORT ZONE Vanessa Williams (Polydor)	
32	36	ACHTUNG BABY	U2 (Island)
-	37	LOVE HURTS	Cher (Geffen)
19	38	GALLUS	Gun (A&M)
44	39	FINALLY	Ce Ce Peniston (A&M)
30	40	CHORUS	Erasure (Mute)
-	41	SEAL	Seal (ZTT)
15	42	EXTRAS	Jam (Polydor)
35	43	SEVEN	Jam (Polydor)
-	44	USE YOUR ILLUSION II	Guns N' Roses (Geffen)
34	45	LEAN INTO IT	Mr. Big (Atlantic)
36	46	TIME, LOVE & TENDERNESS Michael Bolton (Columbia)	
31	47	THE VERY BEST OF FRANKIE VALLI AND THE FOUR SEASONS Frankie Valli & the Four Seasons (Flying Music/PolyGram TV)	
29	48	NIGHT CALLS	Joe Cocker (Capitol)
40	49	MUSIC FROM THE ITV SERIES INSPECTOR MORSE VOLUME 2 Barrington Pheloung (Virgin Television)	
-	50	EXTREME II PORNOGRAFFITTI Extreme (A&M)	

last week	this week	9 May 1992	
1	1	WISH	Cure (Fiction)
2	2	DIVA	Annie Lennox (RCA)
3	3	UP	Right Said Fred (Tug)
4	4	GREATEST HITS	ZZ Top (Warner Bros.)
6	5	STARS	Simply Red (East West)
5	6	DIVINE MADNESS	Madness (Virgin)
10	7	GREATEST HITS II	Queen (Parlophone)
-	8	POWER OF TEN	Chris De Burgh (A&M)
8	9	TEARS ROLL DOWN (GREATEST HITS '82-'92) Tears For Fears (Fontana)	
7	10	VOLUME III JUST RIGHT	Soul II Soul (10)
-	11	SOME GIRLS WANDER BY MISTAKE Sisters Of Mercy (Merciful Release)	
11	12	ADRENALIZE	Def Leppard (Bludgeon Riffola)
12	13	CURTIS STIGERS	Curtis Stigers (Arista)
9	14	REAL LOVE	Lisa Stansfield (Arista)
30	15	GREATEST HITS	Foreigner (Atlantic)
13	16	THE COMMITMENTS VOL.2 Commitments (MCA)	
22	17	NEVERMIND	Nirvana (DGC)
16	18	WE CAN'T DANCE	Genesis (Virgin)
17	19	HORMONALLY YOURS Shakespear's Sister (London)	
14	20	HEAR MY SONG (THE BEST OF JOSEF LOCKE) Josef Locke (EMI)	
50	21	EXTREME II PORNOGRAFFITTI Extreme (A&M)	
31	22	USE YOUR ILLUSION I	Guns N' Roses (Geffen)
15	23	0898	Beautiful South (Go! Discs)
27	24	GREATEST HITS	Queen (EMI)
-	25	MATTERS OF THE HEART Tracy Chapman (Elektra)	
25	26	DANGEROUS	Michael Jackson (Epic)
34	27	THE COMMITMENTS	Commitments (MCA)
18	28	WOODFACE	Crowded House (Capitol)
19	29	HUMAN TOUCH	Bruce Springsteen (Columbia)
21	30	SIMPLY THE BEST	Tina Turner (Capitol)
20	31	MOTOWN'S GREATEST HITS Temptations (Motown)	
44	32	USE YOUR ILLUSION II	Guns N' Roses (Geffen)
-	33	NONSUCH	XTC (Virgin)
24	34	WAKING UP THE NEIGHBOURS Bryan Adams (A&M)	
33	35	BRICKS ARE HEAVY	L7 (Slash)
37	36	LOVE HURTS	Cher (Geffen)
-	37	HENRY'S DREAM Nick Cave & the Bad Seeds (Mute)	
23	38	HIGH ON THE HAPPY SIDE Wet Wet Wet (Precious Organisation)	
26	39	DIAMONDS AND PEARLS Prince & the New Power Generation (Paisley Park)	
36	40	ACHTUNG BABY	U2 (Island)
29	41	LUCKY TOWN	Bruce Springsteen (Columbia)
-	42	OUT OF TIME	R.E.M. (Warner Bros.)
35	43	THE COMFORT ZONE Vanessa Williams (Polydor)	
-	44	APPETITE FOR DESTRUCTION Guns N' Roses (Geffen)	
32	45	"ADDICTIONS" VOLUME 2 Robert Palmer (Island)	
38	46	GALLUS	Gun (A&M)
46	47	TIME, LOVE & TENDERNESS Michael Bolton (Columbia)	
28	48	AFTER HOURS	Gary Moore (Virgin)
-	49	UNDER THE WATER-LINE Ten Sharp (Columbia)	
40	50	CHORUS	Erasure (Mute)

The success of Right Said Fred's debut album *Up* coincided with that of their third consecutive hit single, and first Number 1, *Deeply Dippy*, which was engaged on a 4-week chart-topping run. Perhaps surprisingly, the album itself failed to make Number 1, held at bay by the success of Def Leppard's *Adrenalise*, Annie Lennox' first solo set *Diva* and the Cure's equally succinctly-titled *Wish*.

May 1992

16 May 1992

last week	this week		
-	1	1992 THE LOVE ALBUM	Carter The Unstoppable Sex Machine (Chrysalis)
5	2	STARS	Simply Red (East West)
3	3	UP	Right Said Fred (Tug)
2	4	DIVA	Annie Lennox (RCA)
4	5	GREATEST HITS	ZZ Top (Warner Bros.)
8	6	POWER OF TEN	Chris De Burgh (A&M)
1	7	WISH	Cure (Fiction)
11	8	SOME GIRLS WANDER BY MISTAKE	Sisters Of Mercy (Merciful Release)
6	9	DIVINE MADNESS	Madness (Virgin)
13	10	CURTIS STIGERS	Curtis Stigers (Arista)
12	11	ADRENALIZE	Def Leppard (Bludgeon Riffola)
7	12	GREATEST HITS II	Queen (Parlophone)
10	13	VOLUME III JUST RIGHT	Soul II Soul (10)
9	14	TEARS ROLL DOWN (GREATEST HITS '82-'92)	Tears For Fears (Fontana)
19	15	HORMONALLY YOURS	Shakespear's Sister (London)
14	16	REAL LOVE	Lisa Stansfield (Arista)
27	17	THE COMMITMENTS	Commitments (MCA)
17	18	NEVERMIND	Nirvana (DGC)
15	19	GREATEST HITS	Foreigner (Atlantic)
18	20	WE CAN'T DANCE	Genesis (Virgin)
20	21	HEAR MY SONG (THE BEST OF JOSEF LOCKE)	Josef Locke (EMI)
16	22	THE COMMITMENTS VOL.2	Commitments (MCA)
21	23	EXTREME II PORNOGRAFFITTI	Extreme (A&M)
26	24	DANGEROUS	Michael Jackson (Epic)
-	25	EMOTIONS	Mariah Carey (Columbia)
32	26	USE YOUR ILLUSION II	Guns N' Roses (Geffen)
23	27	0898	Beautiful South (Go! Discs)
24	28	GREATEST HITS	Queen (EMI)
30	29	SIMPLY THE BEST	Tina Turner (Capitol)
22	30	USE YOUR ILLUSION I	Guns N' Roses (Geffen)
-	31	GET IN TOUCH WITH YOURSELF	Swing Out Sister (Fontana)
25	32	MATTERS OF THE HEART	Tracy Chapman (Elektra)
36	33	LOVE HURTS	Cher (Geffen)
40	34	ACHTUNG BABY	U2 (Island)
31	35	MOTOWN'S GREATEST HITS	Temptations (Motown)
33	36	NONSUCH	XTC (Virgin)
-	37	METALLICA	Metallica (Vertigo)
47	38	TIME, LOVE & TENDERNESS	Michael Bolton (Columbia)
28	39	WOODFACE	Crowded House (Capitol)
37	40	HENRY'S DREAM	Nick Cave & the Bad Seeds (Mute)
39	41	DIAMONDS AND PEARLS	Prince & the New Power Generation (Paisley Park)
29	42	HUMAN TOUCH	Bruce Springsteen (Columbia)
42	43	OUT OF TIME	R.E.M. (Warner Bros.)
-	44	BRAND NEW HEAVIES	Brand New Heavies (Acid Jazz)
-	45	TENEMENT SYMPHONY	Marc Almond (Some Bizzare)
34	46	WAKING UP THE NEIGHBOURS	Bryan Adams (A&M)
35	47	BRICKS ARE HEAVY	L7 (Slash)
38	48	HIGH ON THE HAPPY SIDE	Wet Wet Wet (Precious Organisation)
49	49	UNDER THE WATER-LINE	Ten Sharp (Columbia)
-	50	NEED FOR NOT	Levitation (Rough Trade)

23 May 1992

last week	this week		
-	1	FEAR OF THE DARK	Iron Maiden (EMI)
1	2	1992 THE LOVE ALBUM	Carter The Unstoppable Sex Machine (Chrysalis)
-	3	THE SOUTHERN HARMONY AND MUSICAL COMPANION	Black Crowes (Def American)
2	4	STARS	Simply Red (East West)
3	5	UP	Right Said Fred (Tug)
5	6	GREATEST HITS	ZZ Top (Warner Bros.)
4	7	DIVA	Annie Lennox (RCA)
6	8	POWER OF TEN	Chris De Burgh (A&M)
20	9	WE CAN'T DANCE	Genesis (Virgin)
-	10	GREATEST HITS	Squeeze (A&M)
9	11	DIVINE MADNESS	Madness (Virgin)
-	12	REVENGE	Kiss (Mercury)
15	13	HORMONALLY YOURS	Shakespear's Sister (London)
7	14	WISH	Cure (Fiction)
11	15	ADRENALIZE	Def Leppard (Bludgeon Riffola)
12	16	GREATEST HITS II	Queen (Parlophone)
17	17	THE COMMITMENTS	Commitments (MCA)
23	18	EXTREME II PORNOGRAFFITTI	Extreme (A&M)
10	19	CURTIS STIGERS	Curtis Stigers (Arista)
19	20	GREATEST HITS	Foreigner (Atlantic)
16	21	REAL LOVE	Lisa Stansfield (Arista)
26	22	USE YOUR ILLUSION II	Guns N' Roses (Geffen)
14	23	TEARS ROLL DOWN (GREATEST HITS '82-'92)	Tears For Fears (Fontana)
13	24	VOLUME III JUST RIGHT	Soul II Soul (10)
24	25	DANGEROUS	Michael Jackson (Epic)
18	26	NEVERMIND	Nirvana (DGC)
33	27	LOVE HURTS	Cher (Geffen)
28	28	GREATEST HITS	Queen (EMI)
22	29	THE COMMITMENTS VOL.2	Commitments (MCA)
34	30	ACHTUNG BABY	U2 (Island)
8	31	SOME GIRLS WANDER BY MISTAKE	Sisters Of Mercy (Merciful Release)
30	32	USE YOUR ILLUSION I	Guns N' Roses (Geffen)
37	33	METALLICA	Metallica (Vertigo)
21	34	HEAR MY SONG (THE BEST OF JOSEF LOCKE)	Josef Locke (EMI)
25	35	EMOTIONS	Mariah Carey (Columbia)
29	36	SIMPLY THE BEST	Tina Turner (Capitol)
42	37	HUMAN TOUCH	Bruce Springsteen (Columbia)
27	38	0898	Beautiful South (Go! Discs)
31	39	GET IN TOUCH WITH YOURSELF	Swing Out Sister (Fontana)
35	40	MOTOWN'S GREATEST HITS	Temptations (Motown)
41	41	DIAMONDS AND PEARLS	Prince & the New Power Generation (Paisley Park)
45	42	TENEMENT SYMPHONY	Marc Almond (Some Bizzare)
39	43	WOODFACE	Crowded House (Capitol)
32	44	MATTERS OF THE HEART	Tracy Chapman (Elektra)
43	45	OUT OF TIME	R.E.M. (Warner Bros.)
46	46	WAKING UP THE NEIGHBOURS	Bryan Adams (A&M)
-	47	LUCKY TOWN	Bruce Springsteen (Columbia)
38	48	TIME, LOVE & TENDERNESS	Michael Bolton (Columbia)
40	49	HENRY'S DREAM	Nick Cave & the Bad Seeds (Mute)
-	50	NIGHT CALLS	Joe Cocker (Capitol)

30 May 1992

last week	this week		
1	1	FEAR OF THE DARK	Iron Maiden (EMI)
3	2	THE SOUTHERN HARMONY AND MUSICAL COMPANION	Black Crowes (Def American)
4	3	STARS	Simply Red (East West)
5	4	UP	Right Said Fred (Tug)
10	5	GREATEST HITS	Squeeze (A&M)
13	6	HORMONALLY YOURS	Shakespear's Sister (London)
2	7	1992 THE LOVE ALBUM	Carter The Unstoppable Sex Machine (Chrysalis)
7	8	DIVA	Annie Lennox (RCA)
6	9	GREATEST HITS	ZZ Top (Warner Bros.)
-	10	THIS THING CALLED LOVE - THE GREATEST HITS OF ALEXANDER O'NEAL	Alexander O'Neal (Tabu)
14	11	WISH	Cure (Fiction)
8	12	POWER OF TEN	Chris De Burgh (A&M)
9	13	WE CAN'T DANCE	Genesis (Virgin)
12	14	REVENGE	Kiss (Mercury)
15	15	ADRENALIZE	Def Leppard (Bludgeon Riffola)
11	16	DIVINE MADNESS	Madness (Virgin)
-	17	MICHAEL BALL	Michael Ball (Polydor)
18	18	EXTREME II PORNOGRAFFITTI	Extreme (A&M)
19	19	CURTIS STIGERS	Curtis Stigers (Arista)
16	20	GREATEST HITS II	Queen (Parlophone)
17	21	THE COMMITMENTS	Commitments (MCA)
22	22	USE YOUR ILLUSION II	Guns N' Roses (Geffen)
21	23	REAL LOVE	Lisa Stansfield (Arista)
26	24	NEVERMIND	Nirvana (DGC)
20	25	GREATEST HITS	Foreigner (Atlantic)
24	26	VOLUME III JUST RIGHT	Soul II Soul (10)
23	27	TEARS ROLL DOWN (GREATEST HITS '82-'92)	Tears For Fears (Fontana)
-	28	UNFORGETTABLE - WITH LOVE	Natalie Cole (Elektra)
29	29	THE COMMITMENTS VOL.2	Commitments (MCA)
27	30	LOVE HURTS	Cher (Geffen)
25	31	DANGEROUS	Michael Jackson (Epic)
28	32	GREATEST HITS	Queen (EMI)
30	33	ACHTUNG BABY	U2 (Island)
32	34	USE YOUR ILLUSION I	Guns N' Roses (Geffen)
-	35	INGENUE	k.d. lang (Sire)
33	36	METALLICA	Metallica (Vertigo)
34	37	HEAR MY SONG (THE BEST OF JOSEF LOCKE)	Josef Locke (EMI)
35	38	EMOTIONS	Mariah Carey (Columbia)
37	39	HUMAN TOUCH	Bruce Springsteen (Columbia)
-	40	LOVE IS	Kim Wilde (MCA)
36	41	SIMPLY THE BEST	Tina Turner (Capitol)
31	42	SOME GIRLS WANDER BY MISTAKE	Sisters Of Mercy (Merciful Release)
45	43	OUT OF TIME	R.E.M. (Warner Bros.)
46	44	WAKING UP THE NEIGHBOURS	Bryan Adams (A&M)
41	45	DIAMONDS AND PEARLS	Prince & the New Power Generation (Paisley Park)
50	46	NIGHT CALLS	Joe Cocker (Capitol)
-	47	APPETITE FOR DESTRUCTION	Guns N' Roses (Geffen)
38	48	0898	Beautiful South (Go! Discs)
47	49	LUCKY TOWN	Bruce Springsteen (Columbia)
43	50	WOODFACE	Crowded House (Capitol)

Carter The Unstoppable Sex Machine (or just Carter to their more celibate friends and fans) became the seventh act already in 1992 to enter the album chart at Number 1. *1992 The Love Album* had but a week there, though, before being ousted by a further chart-topper from heavy mob Iron Maiden, *Fear Of The Dark*. American hard rockers the Black Crowes, meanwhile, made an impressive debut at 3.

6 June 1992

last week	this week	Title	Artist (Label)
-	1	LIVE AT WEMBLEY '86	Queen (Parlophone)
-	2	BACK TO FRONT	Lionel Richie (Motown)
3	3	STARS	Simply Red (East West)
8	4	DIVA	Annie Lennox (RCA)
17	5	MICHAEL BALL	Michael Ball (Polydor)
6	6	HORMONALLY YOURS	Shakespear's Sister (London)
4	7	UP	Right Said Fred (Tug)
10	8	THIS THING CALLED LOVE - THE GREATEST HITS OF ALEXANDER O'NEAL	Alexander O'Neal (Tabu)
5	9	GREATEST HITS	Squeeze (A&M)
2	10	THE SOUTHERN HARMONY AND MUSICAL COMPANION	Black Crowes (Def American)
22	11	USE YOUR ILLUSION II	Guns N' Roses (Geffen)
9	12	GREATEST HITS	ZZ Top (Warner Bros.)
1	13	FEAR OF THE DARK	Iron Maiden (EMI)
11	14	WISH	Cure (Fiction)
21	15	THE COMMITMENTS	Commitments (MCA)
16	16	DIVINE MADNESS	Madness (Virgin)
7	17	1992 THE LOVE ALBUM	Carter The Unstoppable Sex Machine (Chrysalis)
23	18	REAL LOVE	Lisa Stansfield (Arista)
18	19	EXTREME II PORNOGRAFFITTI	Extreme (A&M)
12	20	POWER OF TEN	Chris De Burgh (A&M)
19	21	CURTIS STIGERS	Curtis Stigers (Arista)
34	22	USE YOUR ILLUSION I	Guns N' Roses (Geffen)
15	23	ADRENALIZE	Def Leppard (Bludgeon Riffola)
35	24	INGENUE	k.d. lang (Sire)
24	25	NEVERMIND	Nirvana (DGC)
13	26	WE CAN'T DANCE	Genesis (Virgin)
28	27	UNFORGETTABLE - WITH LOVE	Natalie Cole (Elektra)
20	28	GREATEST HITS II	Queen (Parlophone)
27	29	TEARS ROLL DOWN (GREATEST HITS '82-'92)	Tears For Fears (Fontana)
33	30	ACHTUNG BABY	U2 (Island)
29	31	THE COMMITMENTS VOL.2	Commitments (MCA)
-	32	FINALLY	Ce Ce Peniston (A&M)
26	33	VOLUME III JUST RIGHT	Soul II Soul (10)
38	34	EMOTIONS	Mariah Carey (Columbia)
14	35	REVENGE	Kiss (Mercury)
25	36	GREATEST HITS	Foreigner (Atlantic)
41	37	SIMPLY THE BEST	Tina Turner (Capitol)
40	38	LOVE IS	Kim Wilde (MCA)
31	39	DANGEROUS	Michael Jackson (Epic)
30	40	LOVE HURTS	Cher (Geffen)
39	41	HUMAN TOUCH	Bruce Springsteen (Columbia)
32	42	GREATEST HITS	Queen (EMI)
46	43	NIGHT CALLS	Joe Cocker (Capitol)
47	44	APPETITE FOR DESTRUCTION	Guns N' Roses (Geffen)
-	45	WAYNE'S WORLD - SOUNDTRACK	Various Artists (Warner Bros.)
-	46	GROOVUS MAXIMUS	Electric Boys (Vertigo)
36	47	METALLICA	Metallica (Vertigo)
37	48	HEAR MY SONG (THE BEST OF JOSEF LOCKE)	Josef Locke (EMI)
-	49	VALHALLA AVENUE	Fatima Mansions (Radioactive)
44	50	WAKING UP THE NEIGHBOURS	Bryan Adams (A&M)

13 June 1992

last week	this week	Title	Artist (Label)
2	1	BACK TO FRONT	Lionel Richie (Motown)
-	2	CHANGE EVERYTHING	Del Amitri (A&M)
1	3	LIVE AT WEMBLEY '86	Queen (Parlophone)
3	4	STARS	Simply Red (East West)
5	5	MICHAEL BALL	Michael Ball (Polydor)
4	6	DIVA	Annie Lennox (RCA)
6	7	HORMONALLY YOURS	Shakespear's Sister (London)
-	8	AS UGLY AS THEY WANNA BE	Ugly Kid Joe (Mercury)
7	9	UP	Right Said Fred (Tug)
-	10	SHADOWS AND LIGHT	Wilson Phillips (SBK)
8	11	THIS THING CALLED LOVE - THE GREATEST HITS OF ALEXANDER O'NEAL	Alexander O'Neal (Tabu)
9	12	GREATEST HITS	Squeeze (A&M)
12	13	GREATEST HITS	ZZ Top (Warner Bros.)
11	14	USE YOUR ILLUSION II	Guns N' Roses (Geffen)
14	15	WISH	Cure (Fiction)
18	16	REAL LOVE	Lisa Stansfield (Arista)
15	17	THE COMMITMENTS	Commitments (MCA)
-	18	COMPLETELY HOOKED - THE BEST OF DR. HOOK	Dr. Hook (Capitol)
10	19	THE SOUTHERN HARMONY AND MUSICAL COMPANION	Black Crowes (Def American)
30	20	ACHTUNG BABY	U2 (Island)
16	21	DIVINE MADNESS	Madness (Virgin)
19	22	EXTREME II PORNOGRAFFITTI	Extreme (A&M)
22	23	USE YOUR ILLUSION I	Guns N' Roses (Geffen)
25	24	NEVERMIND	Nirvana (DGC)
45	25	WAYNE'S WORLD - SOUNDTRACK	Various Artists (Warner Bros.)
21	26	CURTIS STIGERS	Curtis Stigers (Arista)
20	27	POWER OF TEN	Chris De Burgh (A&M)
24	28	INGENUE	k.d. lang (Sire)
23	29	ADRENALIZE	Def Leppard (Bludgeon Riffola)
37	30	SIMPLY THE BEST	Tina Turner (Capitol)
28	31	GREATEST HITS II	Queen (Parlophone)
13	32	FEAR OF THE DARK	Iron Maiden (EMI)
26	33	WE CAN'T DANCE	Genesis (Virgin)
-	34	FUNKY DIVAS	En Vogue (East West America)
31	35	THE COMMITMENTS VOL.2	Commitments (MCA)
29	36	TEARS ROLL DOWN (GREATEST HITS '82-'92)	Tears For Fears (Fontana)
27	37	UNFORGETTABLE - WITH LOVE	Natalie Cole (Elektra)
33	38	VOLUME III JUST RIGHT	Soul II Soul (10)
17	39	1992 THE LOVE ALBUM	Carter The Unstoppable Sex Machine (Chrysalis)
39	40	DANGEROUS	Michael Jackson (Epic)
32	41	FINALLY	Ce Ce Peniston (A&M)
-	42	0898	Beautiful South (Go! Discs)
44	43	APPETITE FOR DESTRUCTION	Guns N' Roses (Geffen)
34	44	EMOTIONS	Mariah Carey (Columbia)
43	45	NIGHT CALLS	Joe Cocker (Capitol)
42	46	GREATEST HITS	Queen (EMI)
40	47	LOVE HURTS	Cher (Geffen)
36	48	GREATEST HITS	Foreigner (Atlantic)
47	49	METALLICA	Metallica (Vertigo)
-	50	DIAMONDS AND PEARLS	Prince & the New Power Generation (Paisley Park)

20 June 1992

last week	this week	Title	Artist (Label)
1	1	BACK TO FRONT	Lionel Richie (Motown)
2	2	CHANGE EVERYTHING	Del Amitri (A&M)
-	3	ANGEL DUST	Faith No More (Slash)
3	4	LIVE AT WEMBLEY '86	Queen (Parlophone)
4	5	STARS	Simply Red (East West)
18	6	COMPLETELY HOOKED - THE BEST OF DR. HOOK	Dr. Hook (Capitol)
11	7	THIS THING CALLED LOVE - THE GREATEST HITS OF ALEXANDER O'NEAL	Alexander O'Neal (Tabu)
6	8	DIVA	Annie Lennox (RCA)
8	9	AS UGLY AS THEY WANNA BE	Ugly Kid Joe (Mercury)
10	10	SHADOWS AND LIGHT	Wilson Phillips (SBK)
-	11	RUSH STREET	Richard Marx (Capitol)
7	12	HORMONALLY YOURS	Shakespear's Sister (London)
14	13	USE YOUR ILLUSION II	Guns N' Roses (Geffen)
-	14	THE CRIMSON IDOL	W.A.S.P. (Parlophone)
5	15	MICHAEL BALL	Michael Ball (Polydor)
15	16	WISH	Cure (Fiction)
-	17	HIT PARADE 1	Wedding Present (RCA)
20	18	ACHTUNG BABY	U2 (Island)
9	19	UP	Right Said Fred (Tug)
16	20	REAL LOVE	Lisa Stansfield (Arista)
-	21	A SINGLES COLLECTION 1982-1992	Marillion (EMI)
25	22	WAYNE'S WORLD - SOUNDTRACK	Various Artists (Warner Bros.)
12	23	GREATEST HITS	Squeeze (A&M)
13	24	GREATEST HITS	ZZ Top (Warner Bros.)
23	25	USE YOUR ILLUSION I	Guns N' Roses (Geffen)
17	26	THE COMMITMENTS	Commitments (MCA)
41	27	FINALLY	Ce Ce Peniston (A&M)
21	28	DIVINE MADNESS	Madness (Virgin)
24	29	NEVERMIND	Nirvana (DGC)
22	30	EXTREME II PORNOGRAFFITTI	Extreme (A&M)
31	31	GREATEST HITS II	Queen (Parlophone)
19	32	THE SOUTHERN HARMONY AND MUSICAL COMPANION	Black Crowes (Def American)
44	33	EMOTIONS	Mariah Carey (Columbia)
33	34	WE CAN'T DANCE	Genesis (Virgin)
26	35	CURTIS STIGERS	Curtis Stigers (Arista)
30	36	SIMPLY THE BEST	Tina Turner (Capitol)
34	37	FUNKY DIVAS	En Vogue (East West America)
43	38	APPETITE FOR DESTRUCTION	Guns N' Roses (Geffen)
42	39	0898	Beautiful South (Go! Discs)
-	40	LEVELLING THE LAND	Levellers (China)
-	41	SQUARE THE CIRCLE	Joan Armatrading (A&M)
27	42	POWER OF TEN	Chris De Burgh (A&M)
-	43	WOODFACE	Crowded House (Capitol)
29	44	ADRENALIZE	Def Leppard (Bludgeon Riffola)
40	45	DANGEROUS	Michael Jackson (Epic)
28	46	INGENUE	k.d. lang (Sire)
37	47	UNFORGETTABLE - WITH LOVE	Natalie Cole (Elektra)
32	48	FEAR OF THE DARK	Iron Maiden (EMI)
39	49	1992 THE LOVE ALBUM	Carter The Unstoppable Sex Machine (Chrysalis)
36	50	TEARS ROLL DOWN (GREATEST HITS '82-'92)	Tears For Fears (Fontana)

The release of a vintage live performance by Queen on record reiterated the public's hunger for the now officially disbanded supergroup's material by debuting at the top. An album with more eventual staying power, however, was Lionel Richie's *Back To Front*, with his first solo recordings for nearly 5 years.

June – July 1992

27 June 1992

last	this	Title	Artist (Label)
-	1	THE ONE	Elton John (Rocket)
1	2	BACK TO FRONT	Lionel Richie (Motown)
5	3	STARS	Simply Red (East West)
7	4	THIS THING CALLED LOVE - THE GREATEST HITS OF ALEXANDER O'NEAL	Alexander O'Neal (Tabu)
6	5	COMPLETELY HOOKED - THE BEST OF DR. HOOK	Dr. Hook (Capitol)
2	6	CHANGE EVERYTHING	Del Amitri (A&M)
3	7	ANGEL DUST	Faith No More (Slash)
13	8	USE YOUR ILLUSION II	Guns N' Roses (Geffen)
4	9	LIVE AT WEMBLEY '86	Queen (Parlophone)
11	10	RUSH STREET	Richard Marx (Capitol)
8	11	DIVA	Annie Lennox (RCA)
18	12	ACHTUNG BABY	U2 (Island)
19	13	UP	Right Said Fred (Tug)
10	14	SHADOWS AND LIGHT	Wilson Phillips (SBK)
12	15	HORMONALLY YOURS	Shakespear's Sister (London)
9	16	AS UGLY AS THEY WANNA BE	Ugly Kid Joe (Mercury)
16	17	WISH	Cure (Fiction)
25	18	USE YOUR ILLUSION I	Guns N' Roses (Geffen)
15	19	MICHAEL BALL	Michael Ball (Polydor)
26	20	THE COMMITMENTS	Commitments (MCA)
39	21	0898	Beautiful South (Go! Discs)
-	22	THE COMPLETE TOM JONES	Tom Jones (London/The Hit Label)
-	23	DIAMONDS AND PEARLS	Prince & the New Power Generation (Paisley Park)
21	24	A SINGLES COLLECTION 1982-1992	Marillion (EMI)
22	25	WAYNE'S WORLD - SOUNDTRACK	Various Artists (Warner Bros.)
43	26	WOODFACE	Crowded House (Capitol)
20	27	REAL LOVE	Lisa Stansfield (Arista)
23	28	GREATEST HITS	Squeeze (A&M)
28	29	DIVINE MADNESS	Madness (Virgin)
38	30	APPETITE FOR DESTRUCTION	Guns N' Roses (Geffen)
-	31	THE LEGEND - THE ESSENTIAL COLLECTION	Joe Cocker (PolyGram TV)
29	32	NEVERMIND	Nirvana (DGC)
33	33	EMOTIONS	Mariah Carey (Columbia)
31	34	GREATEST HITS II	Queen (Parlophone)
14	35	THE CRIMSON IDOL	W.A.S.P. (Parlophone)
27	36	FINALLY	Ce Ce Peniston (A&M)
17	37	HIT PARADE 1	Wedding Present (RCA)
44	38	ADRENALIZE	Def Leppard (Bludgeon Riffola)
24	39	GREATEST HITS	ZZ Top (Warner Bros.)
-	40	VOLUME III JUST RIGHT	Soul II Soul (10)
-	41	HEARTBEAT - MUSIC FROM THE YORKSHIRE TV SERIES	Various Artists (Columbia)
40	42	LEVELLING THE LAND	Levellers (China)
-	43	TOTALLY KROSSED OUT	Kris Kross (Columbia)
45	44	DANGEROUS	Michael Jackson (Epic)
32	45	THE SOUTHERN HARMONY AND MUSICAL COMPANION	Black Crowes (Def American)
30	46	EXTREME II PORNOGRAFFITTI	Extreme (A&M)
42	47	POWER OF TEN	Chris De Burgh (A&M)
34	48	WE CAN'T DANCE	Genesis (Virgin)
-	49	DEATH IS NOT THE END	Shut Up And Dance (Shut Up And Dance)
35	50	CURTIS STIGERS	Curtis Stigers (Arista)

4 July 1992

last	this	Title	Artist (Label)
1	1	THE ONE	Elton John (Rocket)
2	2	BACK TO FRONT	Lionel Richie (Motown)
41	3	HEARTBEAT - MUSIC FROM THE YORKSHIRE TV SERIES	Various Artists (Columbia)
5	4	COMPLETELY HOOKED	Dr. Hook (Capitol)
3	5	STARS	Simply Red (East West)
4	6	THIS THING CALLED LOVE - THE GREATEST HITS OF ALEXANDER O'NEAL	Alexander O'Neal (Tabu)
31	7	THE LEGEND - THE ESSENTIAL COLLECTION	Joe Cocker (PolyGram TV)
-	8	SGT PEPPER'S LONELY HEARTS CLUB BAND	Beatles (Parlophone)
9	9	LIVE AT WEMBLEY '86	Queen (Parlophone)
12	10	ACHTUNG BABY	U2 (Island)
10	11	RUSH STREET	Richard Marx (Capitol)
8	12	USE YOUR ILLUSION II	Guns N' Roses (Geffen)
15	13	HORMONALLY YOURS	Shakespear's Sister (London)
22	14	THE COMPLETE TOM JONES	Tom Jones (London/The Hit Label)
-	15	THE GREATEST HITS 1966-1992	Neil Diamond (Columbia)
23	16	DIAMONDS AND PEARLS	Prince & the New Power Generation (Paisley Park)
6	17	CHANGE EVERYTHING	Del Amitri (A&M)
27	18	REAL LOVE	Lisa Stansfield (Arista)
-	19	MASQUE	Mission (Vertigo)
7	20	ANGEL DUST	Faith No More (Slash)
18	21	USE YOUR ILLUSION I	Guns N' Roses (Geffen)
11	22	DIVA	Annie Lennox (RCA)
13	23	UP	Right Said Fred (Tug)
16	24	AS UGLY AS THEY WANNA BE	Ugly Kid Joe (Mercury)
20	25	THE COMMITMENTS	Commitments (MCA)
17	26	WISH	Cure (Fiction)
-	27	DEHUMANIZE	Black Sabbath (IRS)
26	28	WOODFACE	Crowded House (Capitol)
38	29	ADRENALIZE	Def Leppard (Bludgeon Riffola)
33	30	EMOTIONS	Mariah Carey (Columbia)
14	31	SHADOWS AND LIGHT	Wilson Phillips (SBK)
29	32	DIVINE MADNESS	Madness (Virgin)
21	33	0898	Beautiful South (Go! Discs)
39	34	GREATEST HITS	ZZ Top (Warner Bros.)
19	35	MICHAEL BALL	Michael Ball (Polydor)
32	36	NEVERMIND	Nirvana (DGC)
25	37	WAYNE'S WORLD	Various (Warner Bros.)
28	38	GREATEST HITS	Squeeze (A&M)
-	39	INFINITY WITHIN	Deee-Lite (Elektra)
-	40	TRIBES, VIBES AND SCRIBES	Incognito (Talkin' Loud)
30	41	APPETITE FOR DESTRUCTION	Guns N' Roses (Geffen)
34	42	GREATEST HITS II	Queen (Parlophone)
43	43	TOTALLY KROSSED OUT	Kris Kross (Columbia)
44	44	DANGEROUS	Michael Jackson (Epic)
-	45	SIMPLY THE BEST	Tina Turner (Capitol)
49	46	DEATH IS NOT THE END	Shut Up And Dance (Shut Up And Dance)
48	47	WE CAN'T DANCE	Genesis (Virgin)
36	48	FINALLY	Ce Ce Peniston (A&M)
47	49	POWER OF TEN	Chris De Burgh (A&M)
24	50	A SINGLES COLLECTION 1982-1992	Marillion (EMI)

11 July 1992

last	this	Title	Artist (Label)
1	1	THE ONE	Elton John (Rocket)
2	2	BACK TO FRONT	Lionel Richie (Motown)
3	3	HEARTBEAT - MUSIC FROM THE YORKSHIRE TV SERIES	Various Artists (Columbia)
15	4	THE GREATEST HITS 1966-1992	Neil Diamond (Columbia)
5	5	STARS	Simply Red (East West)
7	6	THE LEGEND - THE ESSENTIAL COLLECTION	Joe Cocker (PolyGram TV)
6	7	THIS THING CALLED LOVE - THE GREATEST HITS	Alexander O'Neal (Tabu)
4	8	COMPLETELY HOOKED	Dr. Hook (Capitol)
-	9	GOOD STUFF	B52's (Epic)
10	10	ACHTUNG BABY	U2 (Island)
-	11	THE BEST OF PREFAB SPROUT: A LIFE OF SURPRISES	Prefab Sprout (Kitchenware)
16	12	DIAMONDS AND PEARLS	Prince & the New Power Generation (Paisley Park)
17	13	CHANGE EVERYTHING	Del Amitri (A&M)
11	14	RUSH STREET	Richard Marx (Capitol)
14	15	THE COMPLETE TOM JONES	Tom Jones (London/The Hit Label)
12	16	USE YOUR ILLUSION II	Guns N' Roses (Geffen)
8	17	SGT PEPPER'S LONELY HEARTS CLUB BAND	Beatles (Parlophone)
25	18	THE COMMITMENTS	Commitments (MCA)
29	19	ADRENALIZE	Def Leppard (Bludgeon Riffola)
9	20	LIVE AT WEMBLEY '86	Queen (Parlophone)
18	21	REAL LOVE	Lisa Stansfield (Arista)
22	22	DIVA	Annie Lennox (RCA)
28	23	WOODFACE	Crowded House (Capitol)
20	24	ANGEL DUST	Faith No More (Slash)
19	25	MASQUE	Mission (Vertigo)
23	26	UP	Right Said Fred (Tug)
13	27	HORMONALLY YOURS	Shakespear's Sister (London)
30	28	EMOTIONS	Mariah Carey (Columbia)
36	29	NEVERMIND	Nirvana (DGC)
21	30	USE YOUR ILLUSION I	Guns N' Roses (Geffen)
24	31	AS UGLY AS THEY WANNA BE	Ugly Kid Joe (Mercury)
31	32	SHADOWS AND LIGHT	Wilson Phillips (SBK)
32	33	DIVINE MADNESS	Madness (Virgin)
-	34	ASQUARIUS	Cud (A&M)
37	35	WAYNE'S WORLD - SOUNDTRACK	Various Artists (Warner Bros.)
-	36	LEVELLING THE LAND	Levellers (China)
26	37	WISH	Cure (Fiction)
33	38	0898	Beautiful South (Go! Discs)
-	39	CURTIS STIGERS	Curtis Stigers (Arista)
42	40	GREATEST HITS II	Queen (Parlophone)
39	41	INFINITY WITHIN	Deee-Lite (Elektra)
41	42	APPETITE FOR DESTRUCTION	Guns N' Roses (Geffen)
27	43	DEHUMANIZE	Black Sabbath (IRS)
40	44	TRIBES, VIBES AND SCRIBES	Incognito (Talkin' Loud)
44	45	DANGEROUS	Michael Jackson (Epic)
-	46	1992 THE LOVE ALBUM	Carter The Unstoppable Sex Machine (Chrysalis)
34	47	GREATEST HITS	ZZ Top (Warner Bros.)
38	48	GREATEST HITS	Squeeze (A&M)
-	49	PRAISE	Inner City (10)
47	50	WE CAN'T DANCE	Genesis (Virgin)

Emulating his previous two albums, *Sleeping With The Past* and *The Very Best Of* in 1990, Elton John's *The One* soared easily to a three-week spell at the top.

Meanwhile, the sudden reappearance in the Top 10 of the Beatles' *Sgt Pepper* album was mostly due to wide media coverage of its own 25th anniversary!

18 July 1992

last week	this week	Title	Artist
-	1	U.F. ORB	Orb (Big Life)
2	2	BACK TO FRONT	Lionel Richie (Motown)
3	3	HEARTBEAT - MUSIC FROM THE YORKSHIRE TV SERIES	Various Artists (Columbia)
1	4	THE ONE	Elton John (Rocket)
-	5	COUNTDOWN TO EXTINCTION	Megadeth (Capitol)
4	6	THE GREATEST HITS 1966-1992	Neil Diamond (Columbia)
6	7	THE LEGEND - THE ESSENTIAL COLLECTION	Joe Cocker (PolyGram TV)
-	8	MTV UNPLUGGED (EP)	Mariah Carey (Columbia)
11	9	THE BEST OF PREFAB SPROUT: A LIFE OF SURPRISES	Prefab Sprout (Kitchenware)
9	10	GOOD STUFF	B52's (Epic)
14	11	RUSH STREET	Richard Marx (Capitol)
5	12	STARS	Simply Red (East West)
10	13	ACHTUNG BABY	U2 (Island)
13	14	CHANGE EVERYTHING	Del Amitri (A&M)
8	15	COMPLETELY HOOKED - THE BEST OF DR. HOOK	Dr. Hook (Capitol)
12	16	DIAMONDS AND PEARLS	Prince & the New Power Generation (Paisley Park)
7	17	THIS THING CALLED LOVE - THE GREATEST HITS	Alexander O'Neal (Tabu)
19	18	ADRENALIZE	Def Leppard (Bludgeon Riffola)
27	19	HORMONALLY YOURS	Shakespear's Sister (London)
18	20	THE COMMITMENTS	Commitments (MCA)
-	21	MICHAEL CRAWFORD PERFORMS ANDREW LLOYD WEBBER	Michael Crawford (Telstar)
23	22	WOODFACE	Crowded House (Capitol)
39	23	CURTIS STIGERS	Curtis Stigers (Arista)
16	24	USE YOUR ILLUSION II	Guns N' Roses (Geffen)
22	25	DIVA	Annie Lennox (RCA)
17	26	SGT PEPPER'S LONELY HEARTS CLUB BAND	Beatles (Parlophone)
15	27	THE COMPLETE TOM JONES	Tom Jones (London/The Hit Label)
21	28	REAL LOVE	Lisa Stansfield (Arista)
29	29	NEVERMIND	Nirvana (DGC)
24	30	ANGEL DUST	Faith No More (Slash)
30	31	USE YOUR ILLUSION I	Guns N' Roses (Geffen)
28	32	EMOTIONS	Mariah Carey (Columbia)
20	33	LIVE AT WEMBLEY '86	Queen (Parlophone)
26	34	UP	Right Said Fred (Tug)
-	35	BABE RAINBOW	House Of Love (Fontana)
50	36	WE CAN'T DANCE	Genesis (Virgin)
-	37	THE FORCE BEHIND THE POWER	Diana Ross (EMI)
31	38	AS UGLY AS THEY WANNA BE	Ugly Kid Joe (Mercury)
45	39	DANGEROUS	Michael Jackson (Epic)
-	40	LITTLE EARTHQUAKES	Tori Amos (East West)
34	41	ASQUARIUS	Cud (A&M)
40	42	GREATEST HITS II	Queen (Parlophone)
42	43	APPETITE FOR DESTRUCTION	Guns N' Roses (Geffen)
33	44	DIVINE MADNESS	Madness (Virgin)
38	45	0898	Beautiful South (Go! Discs)
46	46	1992 THE LOVE ALBUM	Carter The Unstoppable Sex Machine (Chrysalis)
36	47	LEVELLING THE LAND	Levellers (China)
35	48	WAYNE'S WORLD	Various Artists (Warner Bros.)
32	49	SHADOWS AND LIGHT	Wilson Phillips (SBK)
47	50	GREATEST HITS	ZZ Top (Warner Bros.)

25 July 1992

last week	this week	Title	Artist
2	1	BACK TO FRONT	Lionel Richie (Motown)
8	2	MTV UNPLUGGED (EP)	Mariah Carey (Columbia)
1	3	U.F. ORB	Orb (Big Life)
6	4	THE GREATEST HITS 1966-1992	Neil Diamond (Columbia)
7	5	THE LEGEND - THE ESSENTIAL COLLECTION	Joe Cocker (PolyGram TV)
3	6	HEARTBEAT - MUSIC FROM THE YORKSHIRE TV SERIES	Various Artists (Columbia)
12	7	STARS	Simply Red (East West)
4	8	THE ONE	Elton John (Rocket)
9	9	THE BEST OF PREFAB SPROUT: A LIFE OF SURPRISES	Prefab Sprout (Kitchenware)
11	10	RUSH STREET	Richard Marx (Capitol)
5	11	COUNTDOWN TO EXTINCTION	Megadeth (Capitol)
14	12	CHANGE EVERYTHING	Del Amitri (A&M)
10	13	GOOD STUFF	B52's (Epic)
17	14	THIS THING CALLED LOVE - THE GREATEST HITS	Alexander O'Neal (Tabu)
15	15	COMPLETELY HOOKED - THE BEST OF DR. HOOK	Dr. Hook (Capitol)
13	16	ACHTUNG BABY	U2 (Island)
16	17	DIAMONDS AND PEARLS	Prince & the New Power Generation (Paisley Park)
-	18	FULL ON ... MASK HYSTERIA	Altern 8 (Network)
19	19	HORMONALLY YOURS	Shakespear's Sister (London)
23	20	CURTIS STIGERS	Curtis Stigers (Arista)
22	21	WOODFACE	Crowded House (Capitol)
20	22	THE COMMITMENTS	Commitments (MCA)
37	23	THE FORCE BEHIND THE POWER	Diana Ross (EMI)
21	24	MICHAEL CRAWFORD PERFORMS ANDREW LLOYD WEBBER	Michael Crawford (Telstar)
24	25	USE YOUR ILLUSION II	Guns N' Roses (Geffen)
18	26	ADRENALIZE	Def Leppard (Bludgeon Riffola)
29	27	NEVERMIND	Nirvana (DGC)
25	28	DIVA	Annie Lennox (RCA)
28	29	REAL LOVE	Lisa Stansfield (Arista)
34	30	UP	Right Said Fred (Tug)
36	31	WE CAN'T DANCE	Genesis (Virgin)
39	32	DANGEROUS	Michael Jackson (Epic)
31	33	USE YOUR ILLUSION I	Guns N' Roses (Geffen)
33	34	LIVE AT WEMBLEY '86	Queen (Parlophone)
27	35	THE COMPLETE TOM JONES	Tom Jones (London/The Hit Label)
26	36	SGT PEPPER'S LONELY HEARTS CLUB BAND	Beatles (Parlophone)
30	37	ANGEL DUST	Faith No More (Slash)
43	38	APPETITE FOR DESTRUCTION	Guns N' Roses (Geffen)
50	39	GREATEST HITS	ZZ Top (Warner Bros.)
-	40	BACK TO BASICS: THE ESSENTIAL COLLECTION 1971-1992	Olivia Newton-John (Mercury)
-	41	PSALM 69: THE WAY TO SUCCEED AND THE WAY TO SUCK EGGS	Ministry (Sire)
-	42	HIGH ON THE HAPPY SIDE	Wet Wet Wet (Precious Organisation)
-	43	OUT OF TIME	R.E.M. (Warner Bros.)
44	44	DIVINE MADNESS	Madness (Virgin)
-	45	LIVE IN JAPAN	George Harrison (Dark Horse)
42	46	GREATEST HITS II	Queen (Parlophone)
-	47	SIMPLY THE BEST	Tina Turner (Capitol)
32	48	EMOTIONS	Mariah Carey (Columbia)
35	49	BABE RAINBOW	House Of Love (Fontana)
40	50	LITTLE EARTHQUAKES	Tori Amos (East West)

1 August 1992

last week	this week	Title	Artist
4	1	THE GREATEST HITS 1966-1992	Neil Diamond (Columbia)
7	2	STARS	Simply Red (East West)
1	3	BACK TO FRONT	Lionel Richie (Motown)
2	4	MTV UNPLUGGED (EP)	Mariah Carey (Columbia)
5	5	THE LEGEND - THE ESSENTIAL COLLECTION	Joe Cocker (PolyGram TV)
9	6	THE BEST OF PREFAB SPROUT: A LIFE OF SURPRISES	Prefab Sprout (Kitchenware)
14	7	THIS THING CALLED LOVE - THE GREATEST HITS	Alexander O'Neal (Tabu)
8	8	THE ONE	Elton John (Rocket)
-	9	DIRTY	Sonic Youth (DGC)
3	10	U.F. ORB	Orb (Big Life)
6	11	HEARTBEAT - MUSIC FROM THE YORKSHIRE TV SERIES	Various Artists (Columbia)
12	12	CHANGE EVERYTHING	Del Amitri (A&M)
27	13	NEVERMIND	Nirvana (DGC)
10	14	RUSH STREET	Richard Marx (Capitol)
32	15	DANGEROUS	Michael Jackson (Epic)
16	16	ACHTUNG BABY	U2 (Island)
19	17	HORMONALLY YOURS	Shakespear's Sister (London)
17	18	DIAMONDS AND PEARLS	Prince & the New Power Generation (Paisley Park)
31	19	WE CAN'T DANCE	Genesis (Virgin)
13	20	GOOD STUFF	B52's (Epic)
18	21	FULL ON ... MASK HYSTERIA	Altern 8 (Network)
40	22	BACK TO BASICS: THE ESSENTIAL COLLECTION 1971-1992	Olivia Newton-John (Mercury)
25	23	USE YOUR ILLUSION II	Guns N' Roses (Geffen)
22	24	THE COMMITMENTS	Commitments (MCA)
-	25	WAKING UP THE NEIGHBOURS	Bryan Adams (A&M)
30	26	UP	Right Said Fred (Tug)
24	27	MICHAEL CRAWFORD PERFORMS ANDREW LLOYD WEBBER	Michael Crawford (Telstar)
21	28	WOODFACE	Crowded House (Capitol)
15	29	COMPLETELY HOOKED	Dr. Hook (Capitol)
28	30	DIVA	Annie Lennox (RCA)
11	31	COUNTDOWN TO EXTINCTION	Megadeth (Capitol)
20	32	CURTIS STIGERS	Curtis Stigers (Arista)
29	33	REAL LOVE	Lisa Stansfield (Arista)
23	34	THE FORCE BEHIND THE POWER	Diana Ross (EMI)
26	35	ADRENALIZE	Def Leppard (Bludgeon Riffola)
33	36	USE YOUR ILLUSION I	Guns N' Roses (Geffen)
34	37	LIVE AT WEMBLEY '86	Queen (Parlophone)
38	38	APPETITE FOR DESTRUCTION	Guns N' Roses (Geffen)
42	39	HIGH ON THE HAPPY SIDE	Wet Wet Wet (Precious Organisation)
-	40	TONGUES AND TAILS	Sophie B. Hawkins (Columbia)
44	41	DIVINE MADNESS	Madness (Virgin)
37	42	ANGEL DUST	Faith No More (Slash)
41	43	PSALM 69: THE WAY TO SUCCEED AND THE WAY TO SUCK EGGS	Ministry (Sire)
-	44	TURNS INTO STONE	Stone Roses (Silvertone)
39	45	GREATEST HITS	ZZ Top (Warner Bros.)
-	46	SHEPHERD MOONS	Enya (WEA)
46	47	GREATEST HITS II	Queen (Parlophone)
47	48	SIMPLY THE BEST	Tina Turner (Capitol)
36	49	SGT PEPPER'S LONELY HEARTS CLUB BAND	Beatles (Parlophone)
43	50	OUT OF TIME	R.E.M. (Warner Bros.)

The soundtrack to the TV series *Heartbeat* was another of the occasional "Various Artists" sets still allowed in the chart, the reason being that it was regarded as a soundtrack *rather* than a compilation. Nevertheless, there was only one new track on board - *Heartbeat*, as sung by the show's star Nick Berry.

August 1992

8 August 1992

last week	this week	Title	Artist (Label)
1	1	THE GREATEST HITS 1966-1992	Neil Diamond (Columbia)
2	2	STARS	Simply Red (East West)
3	3	BACK TO FRONT	Lionel Richie (Motown)
-	4	YOUR ARSENAL	Morrissey (HMV)
5	5	THE LEGEND - THE ESSENTIAL COLLECTION	Joe Cocker (PolyGram TV)
6	6	THE BEST OF PREFAB SPROUT: A LIFE OF SURPRISES	Prefab Sprout (Kitchenware)
13	7	NEVERMIND	Nirvana (DGC)
4	8	MTV UNPLUGGED (EP)	Mariah Carey (Columbia)
7	9	THIS THING CALLED LOVE - THE GREATEST HITS	Alexander O'Neal (Tabu)
15	10	DANGEROUS	Michael Jackson (Epic)
8	11	THE ONE	Elton John (Rocket)
9	12	DIRTY	Sonic Youth (DGC)
-	13	GROWING UP IN PUBLIC	Jimmy Nail (East West)
26	14	UP	Right Said Fred (Tug)
17	15	HORMONALLY YOURS	Shakespear's Sister (London)
14	16	RUSH STREET	Richard Marx (Capitol)
19	17	WE CAN'T DANCE	Genesis (Virgin)
18	18	DIAMONDS AND PEARLS	Prince & the New Power Generation (Paisley Park)
16	19	ACHTUNG BABY	U2 (Island)
24	20	THE COMMITMENTS	Commitments (MCA)
-	21	ASTRONAUTS & HERETICS	Thomas Dolby (Virgin)
23	22	USE YOUR ILLUSION II	Guns N' Roses (Geffen)
-	23	THE MADMAN'S RETURN	Snap (Arista)
30	24	DIVA	Annie Lennox (RCA)
46	25	SHEPHERD MOONS	Enya (WEA)
25	26	WAKING UP THE NEIGHBOURS	Bryan Adams (A&M)
22	27	BACK TO BASICS: THE ESSENTIAL COLLECTION 1971-1992	Olivia Newton-John (Mercury)
12	28	CHANGE EVERYTHING	Del Amitri (A&M)
-	29	OUT OF THE CRADLE	Lindsey Buckingham (Mercury)
36	30	USE YOUR ILLUSION I	Guns N' Roses (Geffen)
28	31	WOODFACE	Crowded House (Capitol)
29	32	COMPLETELY HOOKED - THE BEST OF DR. HOOK	Dr. Hook (Capitol)
11	33	HEARTBEAT - MUSIC FROM THE YORKSHIRE TV SERIES	Various Artists (Columbia)
20	34	GOOD STUFF	B52's (Epic)
27	35	MICHAEL CRAWFORD PERFORMS ANDREW LLOYD WEBBER	Michael Crawford (Telstar)
10	36	U.F. ORB	Orb (Big Life)
33	37	REAL LOVE	Lisa Stansfield (Arista)
41	38	DIVINE MADNESS	Madness (Virgin)
-	39	MARCH OR DIE	Motorhead (Epic)
21	40	FULL ON ... MASK HYSTERIA	Altern 8 (Network)
-	41	THE DEFINITIVE...	Jim Reeves (Arcade)
35	42	ADRENALIZE	Def Leppard (Bludgeon Riffola)
37	43	LIVE AT WEMBLEY '86	Queen (Parlophone)
44	44	TURNS INTO STONE	Stone Roses (Silvertone)
40	45	TONGUES AND TAILS	Sophie B. Hawkins (Columbia)
39	46	HIGH ON THE HAPPY SIDE	Wet Wet Wet (Precious Organisation)
38	47	APPETITE FOR DESTRUCTION	Guns N' Roses (Geffen)
47	48	GREATEST HITS II	Queen (Parlophone)
32	49	CURTIS STIGERS	Curtis Stigers (Arista)
48	50	SIMPLY THE BEST	Tina Turner (Capitol)

15 August 1992

last week	this week	Title	Artist (Label)
-	1	WELCOME TO WHEREVER YOU ARE	INXS (Mercury)
1	2	THE GREATEST HITS 1966-1992	Neil Diamond (Columbia)
13	3	GROWING UP IN PUBLIC	Jimmy Nail (East West)
2	4	STARS	Simply Red (East West)
5	5	THE LEGEND - THE ESSENTIAL COLLECTION	Joe Cocker (PolyGram TV)
10	6	DANGEROUS	Michael Jackson (Epic)
25	7	SHEPHERD MOONS	Enya (WEA)
17	8	WE CAN'T DANCE	Genesis (Virgin)
3	9	BACK TO FRONT	Lionel Richie (Motown)
7	10	NEVERMIND	Nirvana (DGC)
4	11	YOUR ARSENAL	Morrissey (HMV)
8	12	MTV UNPLUGGED (EP)	Mariah Carey (Columbia)
-	13	FLOORED GENIUS - THE BEST OF...	Julian Cope/Teardrop Explodes (Island)
14	14	UP	Right Said Fred (Tug)
41	15	THE DEFINITIVE...	Jim Reeves (Arcade)
9	16	THIS THING CALLED LOVE - THE GREATEST HITS	Alexander O'Neal (Tabu)
38	17	DIVINE MADNESS	Madness (Virgin)
16	18	RUSH STREET	Richard Marx (Capitol)
11	19	THE ONE	Elton John (Rocket)
24	20	DIVA	Annie Lennox (RCA)
20	21	THE COMMITMENTS	Commitments (MCA)
6	22	THE BEST OF PREFAB SPROUT: A LIFE OF SURPRISES	Prefab Sprout (Kitchenware)
15	23	HORMONALLY YOURS	Shakespear's Sister (London)
22	24	USE YOUR ILLUSION II	Guns N' Roses (Geffen)
18	25	DIAMONDS AND PEARLS	Prince & the New Power Generation (Paisley Park)
19	26	ACHTUNG BABY	U2 (Island)
48	27	GREATEST HITS II	Queen (Parlophone)
-	28	BAD	Michael Jackson (Epic)
26	29	WAKING UP THE NEIGHBOURS	Bryan Adams (A&M)
27	30	BACK TO BASICS: THE ESSENTIAL COLLECTION 1971-1992	Olivia Newton-John (Mercury)
-	31	TOUR SOUVENIR PACK	Michael Jackson (Epic)
30	32	USE YOUR ILLUSION I	Guns N' Roses (Geffen)
21	33	ASTRONAUTS & HERETICS	Thomas Dolby (Virgin)
-	34	ANGEL DUST	Faith No More (Slash)
-	35	THRILLER	Michael Jackson (Epic)
23	36	THE MADMAN'S RETURN	Snap (Arista)
37	37	REAL LOVE	Lisa Stansfield (Arista)
12	38	DIRTY	Sonic Youth (DGC)
34	39	GOOD STUFF	B52's (Epic)
31	40	WOODFACE	Crowded House (Capitol)
36	41	U.F. ORB	Orb (Big Life)
-	42	THE EXTREMIST	Joe Satriani (Epic)
29	43	OUT OF THE CRADLE	Lindsey Buckingham (Mercury)
43	44	LIVE AT WEMBLEY '86	Queen (Parlophone)
28	45	CHANGE EVERYTHING	Del Amitri (A&M)
-	46	BARCELONA GAMES	Placido Domingo, Jo Carreras, Montserrat Caballé (RCA Red Seal)
44	47	TURNS INTO STONE	Stone Roses (Silvertone)
32	48	COMPLETELY HOOKED - THE BEST OF DR. HOOK	Dr. Hook (Capitol)
46	49	HIGH ON THE HAPPY SIDE	Wet Wet Wet (Precious Organisation)
47	50	APPETITE FOR DESTRUCTION	Guns N' Roses (Geffen)

22 August 1992

last week	this week	Title	Artist (Label)
1	1	WELCOME TO WHEREVER YOU ARE	INXS (Mercury)
2	2	THE GREATEST HITS 1966-1992	Neil Diamond (Columbia)
8	3	WE CAN'T DANCE	Genesis (Virgin)
-	4	RED HEAVEN	Throwing Muses (4AD)
4	5	STARS	Simply Red (East West)
7	6	SHEPHERD MOONS	Enya (WEA)
6	7	DANGEROUS	Michael Jackson (Epic)
10	8	NEVERMIND	Nirvana (DGC)
3	9	GROWING UP IN PUBLIC	Jimmy Nail (East West)
17	10	DIVINE MADNESS	Madness (Virgin)
5	11	THE LEGEND - THE ESSENTIAL COLLECTION	Joe Cocker (PolyGram TV)
9	12	BACK TO FRONT	Lionel Richie (Motown)
15	13	THE DEFINITIVE...	Jim Reeves (Arcade)
12	14	MTV UNPLUGGED (EP)	Mariah Carey (Columbia)
-	15	BARCELONA	Freddie Mercury & Montserrat Caballé (Polydor)
20	16	DIVA	Annie Lennox (RCA)
14	17	UP	Right Said Fred (Tug)
26	18	ACHTUNG BABY	U2 (Island)
16	19	THIS THING CALLED LOVE - THE GREATEST HITS	Alexander O'Neal (Tabu)
34	20	ANGEL DUST	Faith No More (Slash)
18	21	RUSH STREET	Richard Marx (Capitol)
42	22	THE EXTREMIST	Joe Satriani (Epic)
24	23	USE YOUR ILLUSION II	Guns N' Roses (Geffen)
-	24	THE VERY BEST OF...	Supertramp (A&M)
22	25	THE BEST OF PREFAB SPROUT: A LIFE OF SURPRISES	Prefab Sprout (Kitchenware)
36	26	THE MADMAN'S RETURN	Snap (Arista)
19	27	THE ONE	Elton John (Rocket)
11	28	YOUR ARSENAL	Morrissey (HMV)
13	29	FLOORED GENIUS - THE BEST OF ...	Julian Cope/Teardrop Explodes (Island)
-	30	BRAND NEW HEAVIES	Brand New Heavies (Acid Jazz)
21	31	THE COMMITMENTS	Commitments (MCA)
25	32	DIAMONDS AND PEARLS	Prince & the New Power Generation (Paisley Park)
32	33	USE YOUR ILLUSION I	Guns N' Roses (Geffen)
-	34	CURTIS STIGERS	Curtis Stigers (Arista)
23	35	HORMONALLY YOURS	Shakespear's Sister (London)
-	36	BLOOD SUGAR SEX MAGIK	Red Hot Chili Peppers (Warner Bros.)
27	37	GREATEST HITS II	Queen (Parlophone)
28	38	BAD	Michael Jackson (Epic)
40	39	WOODFACE	Crowded House (Capitol)
-	40	MACHINE + SOUL	Gary Numan (Numan)
-	41	WHIPPED!	Faster Pussycat (Elektra)
31	42	TOUR SOUVENIR PACK	Michael Jackson (Epic)
29	43	WAKING UP THE NEIGHBOURS	Bryan Adams (A&M)
-	44	UNBREAKABLE	Don-E (Fourth & Broadway)
50	45	APPETITE FOR DESTRUCTION	Guns N' Roses (Geffen)
30	46	BACK TO BASICS: THE ESSENTIAL COLLECTION 1971-1992	Olivia Newton-John (Mercury)
37	47	REAL LOVE	Lisa Stansfield (Arista)
-	48	ROUGH AND READY - VOLUME 1	Shabba Ranks (Epic)
38	49	DIRTY	Sonic Youth (DGC)
44	50	LIVE AT WEMBLEY '86	Queen (Parlophone)

Neil Diamond's chart-topping double compilation, featuring the mid-60s hits from the beginning of his career, plus an overview of his 15-odd years with Columbia, was his first major UK album seller since *Primitive* in 1984, but its success demonstrated the amount of silent majority support he clearly still had.

29 August 1992

last week / this week

last	this	Album	Artist (Label)
-	1	BEST ... 1	Smiths (WEA)
3	2	WE CAN'T DANCE	Genesis (Virgin)
2	3	THE GREATEST HITS 1966-1992	Neil Diamond (Columbia)
1	4	WELCOME TO WHEREVER YOU ARE	INXS (Mercury)
7	5	DANGEROUS	Michael Jackson (Epic)
5	6	STARS	Simply Red (East West)
6	7	SHEPHERD MOONS	Enya (WEA)
8	8	NEVERMIND	Nirvana (DGC)
10	9	DIVINE MADNESS	Madness (Virgin)
9	10	GROWING UP IN PUBLIC	Jimmy Nail (East West)
17	11	UP	Right Said Fred (Tug)
-	12	SOME GAVE ALL	Billy Ray Cyrus (Mercury)
16	13	DIVA	Annie Lennox (RCA)
12	14	BACK TO FRONT	Lionel Richie (Motown)
11	15	THE LEGEND - THE ESSENTIAL COLLECTION	Joe Cocker (PolyGram TV)
13	16	THE DEFINITIVE...	Jim Reeves (Arcade)
15	17	BARCELONA	Freddie Mercury & Montserrat Caballé (Polydor)
20	18	ANGEL DUST	Faith No More (Slash)
23	19	USE YOUR ILLUSION II	Guns N' Roses (Geffen)
21	20	RUSH STREET	Richard Marx (Capitol)
26	21	THE MADMAN'S RETURN	Snap (Arista)
31	22	THE COMMITMENTS	Commitments (MCA)
18	23	ACHTUNG BABY	U2 (Island)
19	24	THIS THING CALLED LOVE - THE GREATEST HITS	Alexander O'Neal (Tabu)
22	25	THE EXTREMIST	Joe Satriani (Epic)
24	26	THE VERY BEST OF SUPERTRAMP	Supertramp (A&M)
25	27	THE BEST OF PREFAB SPROUT: A LIFE OF SURPRISES	Prefab Sprout (Kitchenware)
28	28	YOUR ARSENAL	Morrissey (HMV)
4	29	RED HEAVEN	Throwing Muses (4AD)
35	30	HORMONALLY YOURS	Shakespear's Sister (London)
14	31	MTV UNPLUGGED (EP)	Mariah Carey (Columbia)
32	32	DIAMONDS AND PEARLS	Prince & the New Power Generation (Paisley Park)
37	33	GREATEST HITS II	Queen (Parlophone)
27	34	THE ONE	Elton John (Rocket)
33	35	USE YOUR ILLUSION I	Guns N' Roses (Geffen)
34	36	CURTIS STIGERS	Curtis Stigers (Arista)
29	37	FLOORED GENIUS - THE BEST OF...	Julian Cope/Teardrop Explodes (Island)
36	38	BLOOD SUGAR SEX MAGIK	Red Hot Chili Peppers (Warner Bros.)
38	39	BAD	Michael Jackson (Epic)
30	40	BRAND NEW HEAVIES	Brand New Heavies (Acid Jazz)
39	41	WOODFACE	Crowded House (Capitol)
45	42	APPETITE FOR DESTRUCTION	Guns N' Roses (Geffen)
43	43	WAKING UP THE NEIGHBOURS	Bryan Adams (A&M)
50	44	LIVE AT WEMBLEY '86	Queen (Parlophone)
-	45	WATERMARK	Enya (WEA)
47	46	REAL LOVE	Lisa Stansfield (Arista)
42	47	TOUR SOUVENIR PACK	Michael Jackson (Epic)
-	48	SIMPLY THE BEST	Tina Turner (Capitol)
46	49	BACK TO BASICS: THE ESSENTIAL COLLECTION 1971-1992	Olivia Newton-John (Mercury)
-	50	TRUTH AND LOVE	Hue & Cry (Fidelity)

5 September 1992

this	Album	Artist (Label)
1	GREATEST HITS	Kylie Minogue (PWL)
2	LAUGHING ON JUDGEMENT DAY	Thunder (EMI)
3	BEST ... 1	Smiths (WEA)
4	SOME GAVE ALL	Billy Ray Cyrus (Mercury)
5	DANGEROUS	Michael Jackson (Epic)
6	WELCOME TO WHEREVER YOU ARE	INXS (Mercury)
7	WE CAN'T DANCE	Genesis (Virgin)
8	DIVA	Annie Lennox (RCA)
9	NEVERMIND	Nirvana (DGC)
10	THE GREATEST HITS 1966-1992	Neil Diamond (Columbia)
11	BACK TO FRONT	Lionel Richie (Motown)
12	BOBBY	Bobby Brown (MCA)
13	STARS	Simply Red (East West)
14	SHEPHERD MOONS	Enya (WEA)
15	DIVINE MADNESS	Madness (Virgin)
16	GROWING UP IN PUBLIC	Jimmy Nail (East West)
17	TAKE THAT AND PARTY	Take That (RCA)
18	UP	Right Said Fred (Tug)
19	THE LEGEND - THE ESSENTIAL COLLECTION	Joe Cocker (PolyGram TV)
20	THE COMMITMENTS	Commitments (MCA)
21	THE MADMAN'S RETURN	Snap (Arista)
22	ANGEL DUST	Faith No More (Slash)
23	USE YOUR ILLUSION II	Guns N' Roses (Geffen)
24	THE DEFINITIVE JIM REEVES	Jim Reeves (Arcade)
25	RUSH STREET	Richard Marx (Capitol)
26	THE BEST OF PREFAB SPROUT: A LIFE OF SURPRISES	Prefab Sprout (Kitchenware)
27	THIS THING CALLED LOVE - THE GREATEST HITS	Alexander O'Neal (Tabu)
28	ACHTUNG BABY	U2 (Island)
29	FONTANELLE	Babes In Toyland (Southern)
30	HEAVY RHYME EXPERIENCE: VOL. 1	Brand New Heavies (Acid Jazz)
31	THE EXTREMIST	Joe Satriani (Epic)
32	MTV UNPLUGGED (EP)	Mariah Carey (Columbia)
33	THE DEFINITIVE PATSY CLINE	Patsy Cline (Arcade)
34	YOUR ARSENAL	Morrissey (HMV)
35	GREATEST HITS II	Queen (Parlophone)
36	HORMONALLY YOURS	Shakespear's Sister (London)
37	USE YOUR ILLUSION I	Guns N' Roses (Geffen)
38	DIAMONDS AND PEARLS	Prince & the New Power Generation (Paisley Park)
39	BARCELONA	Freddie Mercury & Montserrat Caballé (Polydor)
40	JON SECADA	Jon Secada (SBK)
41	THE ONE	Elton John (Rocket)
42	THE VERY BEST OF SUPERTRAMP	Supertramp (A&M)
43	APPETITE FOR DESTRUCTION	Guns N' Roses (Geffen)
44	BLOOD SUGAR SEX MAGIK	Red Hot Chili Peppers (Warner Bros.)
45	CURTIS STIGERS	Curtis Stigers (Arista)
46	TEN	Pearl Jam (Epic)
47	BAD	Michael Jackson (Epic)
48	WATERMARK	Enya (WEA)
49	DON'T TREAD	Damn Yankees (Warner Bros.)
50	CHANGE EVERYTHING	Del Amitri (A&M)

(last-week positions for 5 September: 1:-, 2:-, 3:1, 4:12, 5:5, 6:4, 7:2, 8:13, 9:8, 10:3, 11:14, 12:-, 13:6, 14:7, 15:9, 16:10, 17:-, 18:11, 19:15, 20:22, 21:21, 22:18, 23:23, 24:16, 25:20, 26:27, 27:24, 28:23, 29:-, 30:-, 31:25, 32:31, 33:-, 34:28, 35:33, 36:30, 37:35, 38:32, 39:17, 40:-, 41:34, 42:26, 43:42, 44:38, 45:36, 46:-, 47:39, 48:45, 49:-, 50:-)

12 September 1992

this	Album	Artist (Label)
1	TUBULAR BELLS II	Mike Oldfield (WEA)
2	GREATEST HITS	Kylie Minogue (PWL)
3	LAUGHING ON JUDGEMENT DAY	Thunder (EMI)
4	UNPLUGGED	Eric Clapton (Duck)
5	TOURISM	Roxette (EMI)
6	BEST ... 1	Smiths (WEA)
7	DANGEROUS	Michael Jackson (Epic)
8	SOME GAVE ALL	Billy Ray Cyrus (Mercury)
9	TAKE THAT AND PARTY	Take That (RCA)
10	DIVA	Annie Lennox (RCA)
11	BACK TO FRONT	Lionel Richie (Motown)
12	THE GREATEST HITS 1966-1992	Neil Diamond (Columbia)
13	WELCOME TO WHEREVER YOU ARE	INXS (Mercury)
14	WE CAN'T DANCE	Genesis (Virgin)
15	BOBBY	Bobby Brown (MCA)
16	PAUL WELLER	Paul Weller (Go! Discs)
17	AMERICA'S LEAST WANTED	Ugly Kid Joe (Vertigo)
18	NEVERMIND	Nirvana (DGC)
19	STARS	Simply Red (East West)
20	THE DEFINITIVE PATSY CLINE	Patsy Cline (Arcade)
21	SHEPHERD MOONS	Enya (WEA)
22	DIVINE MADNESS	Madness (Virgin)
23	GROWING UP IN PUBLIC	Jimmy Nail (East West)
24	ANGEL DUST	Faith No More (Slash)
25	RUSH STREET	Richard Marx (Capitol)
26	I WAS WARNED	Robert Cray Band (Mercury)
27	UP	Right Said Fred (Tug)
28	THE LEGEND - THE ESSENTIAL COLLECTION	Joe Cocker (PolyGram TV)
29	THE COMMITMENTS	Commitments (MCA)
30	JON SECADA	Jon Secada (SBK)
31	USE YOUR ILLUSION II	Guns N' Roses (Geffen)
32	THE MADMAN'S RETURN	Snap (Arista)
33	ACHTUNG BABY	U2 (Island)
34	GREATEST HITS II	Queen (Parlophone)
35	THE BEST OF PREFAB SPROUT: A LIFE OF SURPRISES	Prefab Sprout (Kitchenware)
36	THE DEFINITIVE JIM REEVES	Jim Reeves (Arcade)
37	THIS THING CALLED LOVE - THE GREATEST HITS OF ALEXANDER O'NEAL	Alexander O'Neal (Tabu)
38	MTV UNPLUGGED (EP)	Mariah Carey (Columbia)
39	THE EXTREMIST	Joe Satriani (Epic)
40	USE YOUR ILLUSION I	Guns N' Roses (Geffen)
41	YOUR ARSENAL	Morrissey (HMV)
42	HEAVY RHYME EXPERIENCE: VOL. 1	Brand New Heavies (Acid Jazz)
43	ADRENALIZE	Def Leppard (Bludgeon Riffola)
44	LITTLE EARTHQUAKES	Tori Amos (East West)
45	APPETITE FOR DESTRUCTION	Guns N' Roses (Geffen)
46	DIAMONDS AND PEARLS	Prince & the New Power Generation (Paisley Park)
47	THE ONE	Elton John (Rocket)
48	VIVA ESPANA	James Last (PolyGram TV)
49	CHANGE EVERYTHING	Del Amitri (A&M)
50	BLOOD SUGAR SEX MAGIK	Red Hot Chili Peppers (Warner Bros.)

(last-week positions for 12 September: 1:-, 2:1, 3:2, 4:-, 5:-, 6:3, 7:5, 8:4, 9:17, 10:8, 11:11, 12:10, 13:6, 14:7, 15:12, 16:-, 17:-, 18:9, 19:13, 20:33, 21:14, 22:15, 23:16, 24:22, 25:25, 26:-, 27:18, 28:19, 29:20, 30:40, 31:23, 32:21, 33:28, 34:35, 35:26, 36:24, 37:27, 38:32, 39:31, 40:37, 41:34, 42:30, 43:-, 44:-, 45:43, 46:38, 47:41, 48:-, 49:50, 50:44)

Genesis' *We Can't Dance*, like Simply Red's *Stars* an album which simply would not go away from the Top 10, had its strongest resurgence yet, moving back to Number 2. Billy Ray Cyrus' success with *Some Gave All* was almost unique - he was a new US country artist, a breed woefully short of UK chart recognition.

September – October 1992

19 September 1992

Last week	This week	Title	Artist (Label)
1	1	TUBULAR BELLS II	Mike Oldfield (WEA)
5	2	TOURISM	Roxette (EMI)
2	3	GREATEST HITS	Kylie Minogue (PWL)
4	4	UNPLUGGED	Eric Clapton (Duck)
-	5	THE BEST OF BELINDA CARLISLE VOLUME 1	Belinda Carlisle (Virgin)
10	6	DIVA	Annie Lennox (RCA)
11	7	BACK TO FRONT	Lionel Richie (Motown)
-	8	AMUSED TO DEATH	Roger Waters (Columbia)
6	9	BEST ... 1	Smiths (WEA)
12	10	THE GREATEST HITS 1966-1992	Neil Diamond (Columbia)
8	11	SOME GAVE ALL	Billy Ray Cyrus (Mercury)
16	12	PAUL WELLER	Paul Weller (Go! Discs)
17	13	AMERICA'S LEAST WANTED	Ugly Kid Joe (Vertigo)
7	14	DANGEROUS	Michael Jackson (Epic)
13	15	WELCOME TO WHEREVER YOU ARE	INXS (Mercury)
3	16	LAUGHING ON JUDGEMENT DAY	Thunder (EMI)
18	17	NEVERMIND	Nirvana (DGC)
19	18	STARS	Simply Red (East West)
14	19	WE CAN'T DANCE	Genesis (Virgin)
20	20	THE DEFINITIVE PATSY CLINE	Patsy Cline (Arcade)
21	21	SHEPHERD MOONS	Enya (WEA)
25	22	RUSH STREET	Richard Marx (Capitol)
9	23	TAKE THAT AND PARTY	Take That (RCA)
15	24	BOBBY	Bobby Brown (MCA)
22	25	DIVINE MADNESS	Madness (Virgin)
27	26	UP	Right Said Fred (Tug)
23	27	GROWING UP IN PUBLIC	Jimmy Nail (East West)
26	28	I WAS WARNED	Robert Cray Band (Mercury)
-	29	THE LOOKS OR THE LIFESTYLE	Pop Will Eat Itself (RCA)
24	30	ANGEL DUST	Faith No More (Slash)
29	31	THE COMMITMENTS	Commitments (MCA)
-	32	COPPER BLUE	Sugar (Creation)
48	33	VIVA ESPANA	James Last (PolyGram TV)
32	34	THE MADMAN'S RETURN	Snap (Arista)
-	35	LEGEND	Bob Marley & the Wailers (Island)
34	36	GREATEST HITS II	Queen (Parlophone)
30	37	JON SECADA	Jon Secada (SBK)
35	38	THE BEST OF PREFAB SPROUT: A LIFE OF SURPRISES	Prefab Sprout (Kitchenware)
28	39	THE LEGEND - THE ESSENTIAL COLLECTION	Joe Cocker (PolyGram TV)
31	40	USE YOUR ILLUSION II	Guns N' Roses (Geffen)
-	41	BONE MACHINE	Tom Waits (Island)
49	42	CHANGE EVERYTHING	Del Amitri (A&M)
-	43	99.9F	Suzanne Vega (A&M)
33	44	ACHTUNG BABY	U2 (Island)
-	45	TUBULAR BELLS	Mike Oldfield (Virgin)
43	46	ADRENALIZE	Def Leppard (Bludgeon Riffola)
46	47	DIAMONDS AND PEARLS	Prince & the New Power Generation (Paisley Park)
-	48	THE SINGLES COLLECTION	Four Tops (PolyGram TV)
-	49	IN THE NIGHT	Stranglers (Psycho)
40	50	USE YOUR ILLUSION I	Guns N' Roses (Geffen)

26 September 1992

Last week	This week	Title	Artist (Label)
-	1	III SIDES TO EVERY STORY	Extreme (A&M)
-	2	BOSS DRUM	Shamen (One Little Indian)
1	3	TUBULAR BELLS II	Mike Oldfield (WEA)
5	4	THE BEST OF BELINDA CARLISLE VOLUME 1	Belinda Carlisle (Virgin)
-	5	AM I NOT YOUR GIRL?	Sinead O'Connor (Ensign)
2	6	TOURISM	Roxette (EMI)
7	7	BACK TO FRONT	Lionel Richie (Motown)
4	8	UNPLUGGED	Eric Clapton (Duck)
6	9	DIVA	Annie Lennox (RCA)
3	10	GREATEST HITS	Kylie Minogue (PWL)
9	11	BEST ... 1	Smiths (WEA)
8	12	AMUSED TO DEATH	Roger Waters (Columbia)
18	13	STARS	Simply Red (East West)
17	14	NEVERMIND	Nirvana (DGC)
15	15	WELCOME TO WHEREVER YOU ARE	INXS (Mercury)
19	16	WE CAN'T DANCE	Genesis (Virgin)
20	17	THE DEFINITIVE PATSY CLINE	Patsy Cline (Arcade)
10	18	THE GREATEST HITS 1966-1992	Neil Diamond (Columbia)
11	19	SOME GAVE ALL	Billy Ray Cyrus (Mercury)
14	20	DANGEROUS	Michael Jackson (Epic)
22	21	RUSH STREET	Richard Marx (Capitol)
21	22	SHEPHERD MOONS	Enya (WEA)
32	23	COPPER BLUE	Sugar (Creation)
16	24	LAUGHING ON JUDGEMENT DAY	Thunder (EMI)
43	25	99.9F	Suzanne Vega (A&M)
29	26	THE LOOKS OR THE LIFESTYLE	Pop Will Eat Itself (RCA)
13	27	AMERICA'S LEAST WANTED	Ugly Kid Joe (Vertigo)
12	28	PAUL WELLER	Paul Weller (Go! Discs)
25	29	DIVINE MADNESS	Madness (Virgin)
35	30	LEGEND	Bob Marley & the Wailers (Island)
42	31	CHANGE EVERYTHING	Del Amitri (A&M)
31	32	THE COMMITMENTS	Commitments (MCA)
33	33	VIVA ESPANA	James Last (PolyGram TV)
48	34	THE SINGLES COLLECTION	Four Tops (PolyGram TV)
28	35	I WAS WARNED	Robert Cray Band (Mercury)
41	36	BONE MACHINE	Tom Waits (Island)
24	37	BOBBY	Bobby Brown (MCA)
-	38	A LITTLE LIGHT MUSIC	Jethro Tull (Chrysalis)
44	39	ACHTUNG BABY	U2 (Island)
37	40	JON SECADA	Jon Secada (SBK)
40	41	USE YOUR ILLUSION II	Guns N' Roses (Geffen)
26	42	UP	Right Said Fred (Tug)
27	43	GROWING UP IN PUBLIC	Jimmy Nail (East West)
30	44	ANGEL DUST	Faith No More (Slash)
-	45	NUMBER 10	J.J. Cale (Silvertone)
45	46	TUBULAR BELLS	Mike Oldfield (Virgin)
34	47	THE MADMAN'S RETURN	Snap (Arista)
49	48	IN THE NIGHT	Stranglers (Psycho)
-	49	TEN	Pearl Jam (Epic)
-	50	... XYZ	Moose (Hut)

3 October 1992

Last week	This week	Title	Artist (Label)
-	1	GOLD - GREATEST HITS	Abba (Polydor)
4	2	THE BEST OF BELINDA CARLISLE VOLUME 1	Belinda Carlisle (Virgin)
1	3	III SIDES TO EVERY STORY	Extreme (A&M)
3	4	TUBULAR BELLS II	Mike Oldfield (WEA)
2	5	BOSS DRUM	Shamen (One Little Indian)
7	6	BACK TO FRONT	Lionel Richie (Motown)
5	7	AM I NOT YOUR GIRL?	Sinead O'Connor (Ensign)
8	8	UNPLUGGED	Eric Clapton (Duck)
9	9	DIVA	Annie Lennox (RCA)
6	10	TOURISM	Roxette (EMI)
-	11	SONGS OF FREEDOM	Bob Marley & the Wailers (Tuff Gong)
10	12	GREATEST HITS	Kylie Minogue (PWL)
14	13	NEVERMIND	Nirvana (DGC)
11	14	BEST ... 1	Smiths (WEA)
15	15	WELCOME TO WHEREVER YOU ARE	INXS (Mercury)
13	16	STARS	Simply Red (East West)
20	17	DANGEROUS	Michael Jackson (Epic)
18	18	THE GREATEST HITS 1966-1992	Neil Diamond (Columbia)
16	19	WE CAN'T DANCE	Genesis (Virgin)
-	20	GREATEST MISSES	Public Enemy (Def Jam)
19	21	SOME GAVE ALL	Billy Ray Cyrus (Mercury)
21	22	RUSH STREET	Richard Marx (Capitol)
22	23	SHEPHERD MOONS	Enya (WEA)
17	24	THE DEFINITIVE PATSY CLINE	Patsy Cline (Arcade)
34	25	THE SINGLES COLLECTION	Four Tops (PolyGram TV)
30	26	LEGEND	Bob Marley & the Wailers (Island)
24	27	LAUGHING ON JUDGEMENT DAY	Thunder (EMI)
-	28	JEFF WAYNE'S MUSICAL VERSION OF SPARTACUS	Jeff Wayne (Columbia)
31	29	CHANGE EVERYTHING	Del Amitri (A&M)
12	30	AMUSED TO DEATH	Roger Waters (Columbia)
-	31	WOODFACE	Crowded House (Capitol)
25	32	99.9F	Suzanne Vega (A&M)
32	33	THE COMMITMENTS	Commitments (MCA)
28	34	PAUL WELLER	Paul Weller (Go! Discs)
29	35	DIVINE MADNESS	Madness (Virgin)
23	36	COPPER BLUE	Sugar (Creation)
27	37	AMERICA'S LEAST WANTED	Ugly Kid Joe (Vertigo)
39	38	ACHTUNG BABY	U2 (Island)
-	39	ADRENALIZE	Def Leppard (Bludgeon Riffola)
33	40	VIVA ESPANA	James Last (PolyGram TV)
49	41	TEN	Pearl Jam (Epic)
-	42	BLOOD SUGAR SEX MAGIK	Red Hot Chili Peppers (Warner Bros.)
43	43	GROWING UP IN PUBLIC	Jimmy Nail (East West)
-	44	WAKING UP THE NEIGHBOURS	Bryan Adams (A&M)
37	45	BOBBY	Bobby Brown (MCA)
41	46	USE YOUR ILLUSION II	Guns N' Roses (Geffen)
46	47	TUBULAR BELLS	Mike Oldfield (Virgin)
44	48	ANGEL DUST	Faith No More (Slash)
42	49	UP	Right Said Fred (Tug)
40	50	JON SECADA	Jon Secada (SBK)

Mike Oldfield's *Tubular Bells II* was a virtual re-run of the original piece using the new studio techniques and possibilities not available 20 years before when *Tubular Bells* was cut for release as Virgin's first-ever album. Inevitably, *II* was not to have anything like its predecessor's incredible chart longevity.

last this week

10 October 1992

-	1	AUTOMATIC FOR THE PEOPLE	R.E.M. (Warner Bros.)
-	2	US	Peter Gabriel (Realworld)
1	3	GOLD - GREATEST HITS	Abba (Polydor)
-	4	BACK TO THE LIGHT	Brian May (Parlophone)
-	5	TIMELESS - THE CLASSICS	Michael Bolton (Columbia)
4	6	TUBULAR BELLS II	Mike Oldfield (WEA)
2	7	THE BEST OF BELINDA CARLISLE VOLUME 1	Belinda Carlisle (Virgin)
-	8	... YES PLEASE!	Happy Mondays (Factory)
-	9	GREATEST HITS	Police (A&M)
5	10	BOSS DRUM	Shamen (One Little Indian)
3	11	III SIDES TO EVERY STORY	Extreme (A&M)
6	12	BACK TO FRONT	Lionel Richie (Motown)
11	13	SONGS OF FREEDOM	Bob Marley & the Wailers (Tuff Gong)
-	14	STIGMA	EMF (Parlophone)
8	15	UNPLUGGED	Eric Clapton (Duck)
7	16	AM I NOT YOUR GIRL?	Sinead O'Connor (Ensign)
9	17	DIVA	Annie Lennox (RCA)
10	18	TOURISM	Roxette (EMI)
-	19	HAPPY IN HELL	Christians (Island)
12	20	GREATEST HITS	Kylie Minogue (PWL)
19	21	WE CAN'T DANCE	Genesis (Virgin)
-	22	THE PRODIGY EXPERIENCE	Prodigy (XL Recordings)
17	23	DANGEROUS	Michael Jackson (Epic)
16	24	STARS	Simply Red (East West)
15	25	WELCOME TO WHEREVER YOU ARE	INXS (Mercury)
13	26	NEVERMIND	Nirvana (DGC)
41	27	TEN	Pearl Jam (Epic)
31	28	WOODFACE	Crowded House (Capitol)
26	29	LEGEND	Bob Marley & the Wailers (Island)
14	30	BEST ... 1	Smiths (WEA)
21	31	SOME GAVE ALL	Billy Ray Cyrus (Mercury)
-	32	OUR TIME IN EDEN	10,000 Maniacs (Elektra)
18	33	THE GREATEST HITS 1966-1992	Neil Diamond (Columbia)
20	34	GREATEST MISSES	Public Enemy (Def Jam)
25	35	THE SINGLES COLLECTION	Four Tops (PolyGram TV)
27	36	LAUGHING ON JUDGEMENT DAY	Thunder (EMI)
23	37	SHEPHERD MOONS	Enya (WEA)
22	38	RUSH STREET	Richard Marx (Capitol)
34	39	PAUL WELLER	Paul Weller (Go! Discs)
24	40	THE DEFINITIVE PATSY CLINE	Patsy Cline (Arcade)
28	41	JEFF WAYNE'S MUSICAL VERSION OF SPARTACUS	Jeff Wayne (Columbia)
43	42	GROWING UP IN PUBLIC	Jimmy Nail (East West)
30	43	AMUSED TO DEATH	Roger Waters (Columbia)
29	44	CHANGE EVERYTHING	Del Amitri (A&M)
33	45	THE COMMITMENTS	Commitments (MCA)
32	46	99.9F	Suzanne Vega (A&M)
-	47	GENERATION TERRORISTS	Manic Street Preachers (Columbia)
38	48	ACHTUNG BABY	U2 (Island)
36	49	COPPER BLUE	Sugar (Creation)
35	50	DIVINE MADNESS	Madness (Virgin)

17 October 1992

1	1	AUTOMATIC FOR THE PEOPLE	R.E.M. (Warner Bros.)
-	2	SYMBOL	Prince & the New Power Generation (Paisley Park)
2	3	US	Peter Gabriel (Realworld)
3	4	GOLD - GREATEST HITS	Abba (Polydor)
5	5	TIMELESS - THE CLASSICS	Michael Bolton (Columbia)
6	6	TUBULAR BELLS II	Mike Oldfield (WEA)
4	7	BACK TO THE LIGHT	Brian May (Parlophone)
-	8	KISS THIS	Sex Pistols (Virgin)
7	9	THE BEST OF BELINDA CARLISLE VOLUME 1	Belinda Carlisle (Virgin)
9	10	GREATEST HITS	Police (A&M)
10	11	BOSS DRUM	Shamen (One Little Indian)
12	12	BACK TO FRONT	Lionel Richie (Motown)
-	13	REVENGE OF THE GOLDFISH	Inspiral Carpets (Cow)
8	14	... YES PLEASE!	Happy Mondays (Factory)
-	15	WHAT HITS!?	Red Hot Chili Peppers (EMI USA)
11	16	III SIDES TO EVERY STORY	Extreme (A&M)
15	17	UNPLUGGED	Eric Clapton (Duck)
17	18	DIVA	Annie Lennox (RCA)
14	19	STIGMA	EMF (Parlophone)
13	20	SONGS OF FREEDOM	Bob Marley & the Wailers (Tuff Gong)
-	21	PIECE OF CAKE	Mudhoney (Reprise)
19	22	HAPPY IN HELL	Christians (Island)
-	23	TWICE UPON A TIME - THE SINGLES	Siouxsie & the Banshees (Wonderland)
28	24	WOODFACE	Crowded House (Capitol)
-	25	BROKEN	Nine Inch Nails (Interscope)
16	26	AM I NOT YOUR GIRL?	Sinead O'Connor (Ensign)
23	27	DANGEROUS	Michael Jackson (Epic)
22	28	THE PRODIGY EXPERIENCE	Prodigy (XL Recordings)
24	29	STARS	Simply Red (East West)
18	30	TOURISM	Roxette (EMI)
21	31	WE CAN'T DANCE	Genesis (Virgin)
20	32	GREATEST HITS	Kylie Minogue (PWL)
26	33	NEVERMIND	Nirvana (DGC)
27	34	TEN	Pearl Jam (Epic)
31	35	SOME GAVE ALL	Billy Ray Cyrus (Mercury)
25	36	WELCOME TO WHEREVER YOU ARE	INXS (Mercury)
-	37	IT'S - IT	Sugarcubes (One Little Indian)
29	38	LEGEND	Bob Marley & the Wailers (Island)
32	39	OUR TIME IN EDEN	10,000 Maniacs (Elektra)
36	40	LAUGHING ON JUDGEMENT DAY	Thunder (EMI)
33	41	THE GREATEST HITS 1966-1992	Neil Diamond (Columbia)
37	42	SHEPHERD MOONS	Enya (WEA)
35	43	THE SINGLES COLLECTION	Four Tops (PolyGram TV)
45	44	THE COMMITMENTS	Commitments (MCA)
47	45	GENERATION TERRORISTS	Manic Street Preachers (Columbia)
30	46	BEST ... 1	Smiths (WEA)
34	47	GREATEST MISSES	Public Enemy (Def Jam)
39	48	PAUL WELLER	Paul Weller (Go! Discs)
38	49	RUSH STREET	Richard Marx (Capitol)
40	50	THE DEFINITIVE PATSY CLINE	Patsy Cline (Arcade)

24 October 1992

-	1	GLITTERING PRIZE 81/92	Simple Minds (Virgin)
1	2	AUTOMATIC FOR THE PEOPLE	R.E.M. (Warner Bros.)
2	3	SYMBOL	Prince & the New Power Generation (Paisley Park)
-	4	EROTICA	Madonna (Maverick)
4	5	GOLD - GREATEST HITS	Abba (Polydor)
5	6	TIMELESS - THE CLASSICS	Michael Bolton (Columbia)
6	7	TUBULAR BELLS II	Mike Oldfield (WEA)
3	8	US	Peter Gabriel (Realworld)
8	9	KISS THIS	Sex Pistols (Virgin)
9	10	THE BEST OF BELINDA CARLISLE VOLUME 1	Belinda Carlisle (Virgin)
12	11	BACK TO FRONT	Lionel Richie (Motown)
7	12	BACK TO THE LIGHT	Brian May (Parlophone)
10	13	GREATEST HITS	Police (A&M)
-	14	THE BEST OF - ONCE IN A LIFETIME	Talking Heads (EMI)
11	15	BOSS DRUM	Shamen (One Little Indian)
24	16	WOODFACE	Crowded House (Capitol)
17	17	UNPLUGGED	Eric Clapton (Duck)
18	18	DIVA	Annie Lennox (RCA)
27	19	DANGEROUS	Michael Jackson (Epic)
16	20	III SIDES TO EVERY STORY	Extreme (A&M)
15	21	WHAT HITS!?	Red Hot Chili Peppers (EMI USA)
13	22	REVENGE OF THE GOLDFISH	Inspiral Carpets (Cow)
29	23	STARS	Simply Red (East West)
25	24	BROKEN	Nine Inch Nails (Interscope)
23	25	TWICE UPON A TIME - THE SINGLES	Siouxsie & the Banshees (Wonderland)
33	26	NEVERMIND	Nirvana (DGC)
38	27	LEGEND	Bob Marley & the Wailers (Island)
14	28	... YES PLEASE!	Happy Mondays (Factory)
26	29	AM I NOT YOUR GIRL?	Sinead O'Connor (Ensign)
20	30	SONGS OF FREEDOM	Bob Marley & the Wailers (Tuff Gong)
21	31	PIECE OF CAKE	Mudhoney (Reprise)
22	32	HAPPY IN HELL	Christians (Island)
31	33	WE CAN'T DANCE	Genesis (Virgin)
35	34	SOME GAVE ALL	Billy Ray Cyrus (Mercury)
28	35	THE PRODIGY EXPERIENCE	Prodigy (XL Recordings)
40	36	LAUGHING ON JUDGEMENT DAY	Thunder (EMI)
-	37	IZZY STRADLIN AND THE JU JU HOUNDS	Izzy Stradlin & the Ju Ju Hounds (Geffen)
34	38	TEN	Pearl Jam (Epic)
30	39	TOURISM	Roxette (EMI)
41	40	THE GREATEST HITS 1966-1992	Neil Diamond (Columbia)
-	41	TAKE THAT AND PARTY	Take That (RCA)
42	42	SHEPHERD MOONS	Enya (WEA)
32	43	GREATEST HITS	Kylie Minogue (PWL)
36	44	WELCOME TO WHEREVER YOU ARE	INXS (Mercury)
-	45	GREATEST HITS II	Queen (Parlophone)
46	46	BEST ... 1	Smiths (WEA)
-	47	SAND IN THE VASELINE - POPULAR FAVOURITES 1976-1992	Talking Heads (EMI)
19	48	STIGMA	EMF (Parlophone)
44	49	THE COMMITMENTS	Commitments (MCA)
-	50	CURTIS STIGERS	Curtis Stigers (Arista)

Their previous album had already established them in rock's top echelon, but REM's *Automatic For The People* was their first superstar release, while still gathering critical acclaim from those who might normally be ready by now to shoot the band down. It would still be in the Top 5 by the end of this book....

October – November 1992

31 October 1992

last week	this week	Title	Artist
4	1	EROTICA	Madonna (Maverick)
1	2	GLITTERING PRIZE 81/92	Simple Minds (Virgin)
2	3	AUTOMATIC FOR THE PEOPLE	R.E.M. (Warner Bros.)
3	4	SYMBOL	Prince & the New Power Generation (Paisley Park)
-	5	GREAT EXPECTATIONS	Tasmin Archer (EMI)
5	6	GOLD - GREATEST HITS	Abba (Polydor)
6	7	TIMELESS - THE CLASSICS	Michael Bolton (Columbia)
14	8	THE BEST OF - ONCE IN A LIFETIME	Talking Heads (EMI)
-	9	ARE YOU NORMAL?	Ned's Atomic Dustbin (Furtive)
7	10	TUBULAR BELLS II	Mike Oldfield (WEA)
10	11	THE BEST OF BELINDA CARLISLE VOLUME 1	Belinda Carlisle (Virgin)
-	12	BLIND	Sundays (Parlophone)
11	13	BACK TO FRONT	Lionel Richie (Motown)
13	14	GREATEST HITS	Police (A&M)
18	15	DIVA	Annie Lennox (RCA)
-	16	COOLEYHIGHHARMONY	Boyz II Men (Motown)
8	17	US	Peter Gabriel (Realworld)
15	18	BOSS DRUM	Shamen (One Little Indian)
17	19	UNPLUGGED	Eric Clapton (Duck)
9	20	KISS THIS	Sex Pistols (Virgin)
12	21	BACK TO THE LIGHT	Brian May (Parlophone)
19	22	DANGEROUS	Michael Jackson (Epic)
-	23	JEHOVAH KILL	Julian Cope (Island)
16	24	WOODFACE	Crowded House (Capitol)
50	25	CURTIS STIGERS	Curtis Stigers (Arista)
20	26	III SIDES TO EVERY STORY	Extreme (A&M)
-	27	ALL THE WAY FROM TUAM	Saw Doctors (Solid)
21	28	WHAT HITS!?	Red Hot Chili Peppers (EMI USA)
23	29	STARS	Simply Red (East West)
26	30	NEVERMIND	Nirvana (DGC)
29	31	AM I NOT YOUR GIRL?	Sinead O'Connor (Ensign)
47	32	SAND IN THE VASELINE - POPULAR FAVOURITES 1976-1992	Talking Heads (EMI)
27	33	LEGEND	Bob Marley & the Wailers (Island)
36	34	LAUGHING ON JUDGEMENT DAY	Thunder (EMI)
24	35	BROKEN	Nine Inch Nails (Interscope)
39	36	TOURISM	Roxette (EMI)
38	37	TEN	Pearl Jam (Epic)
-	38	RIDIN' HIGH	Robert Palmer (EMI)
33	39	WE CAN'T DANCE	Genesis (Virgin)
35	40	THE PRODIGY EXPERIENCE	Prodigy (XL Recordings)
25	41	TWICE UPON A TIME - THE SINGLES	Siouxsie & the Banshees (Wonderland)
-	42	THE COLLECTION	Mary Black (Telstar)
22	43	REVENGE OF THE GOLDFISH	Inspiral Carpets (Cow)
-	44	INTO THE LIGHT	Hank Marvin (Polydor)
-	45	ORIGINAL SOUNDTRACK - 1492 CONQUEST OF PARADISE	Vangelis (East West)
34	46	SOME GAVE ALL	Billy Ray Cyrus (Mercury)
31	47	PIECE OF CAKE	Mudhoney (Reprise)
42	48	SHEPHERD MOONS	Enya (WEA)
46	49	BEST ... 1	Smiths (WEA)
-	50	MAIN OFFENDER	Keith Richards (Virgin America)

7 November 1992

last week	this week	Title	Artist
2	1	GLITTERING PRIZE 81/92	Simple Minds (Virgin)
1	2	EROTICA	Madonna (Maverick)
7	3	TIMELESS - THE CLASSICS	Michael Bolton (Columbia)
-	4	LIVE	AC/DC (Atco)
3	5	AUTOMATIC FOR THE PEOPLE	R.E.M. (Warner Bros.)
6	6	GOLD - GREATEST HITS	Abba (Polydor)
4	7	SYMBOL	Prince & the New Power Generation (Paisley Park)
5	8	GREAT EXPECTATIONS	Tasmin Archer (EMI)
8	9	THE BEST OF - ONCE IN A LIFETIME	Talking Heads (EMI)
-	10	BOOM BOOM	John Lee Hooker (Pointblank)
11	11	THE BEST OF BELINDA CARLISLE VOLUME 1	Belinda Carlisle (Virgin)
16	12	COOLEYHIGHHARMONY	Boyz II Men (Motown)
10	13	TUBULAR BELLS II	Mike Oldfield (WEA)
13	14	BACK TO FRONT	Lionel Richie (Motown)
15	15	DIVA	Annie Lennox (RCA)
18	16	BOSS DRUM	Shamen (One Little Indian)
14	17	GREATEST HITS	Police (A&M)
25	18	CURTIS STIGERS	Curtis Stigers (Arista)
-	19	LOVE DELUXE	Sade (Epic)
9	20	ARE YOU NORMAL?	Ned's Atomic Dustbin (Furtive)
17	21	US	Peter Gabriel (Realworld)
19	22	UNPLUGGED	Eric Clapton (Duck)
12	23	BLIND	Sundays (Parlophone)
22	24	DANGEROUS	Michael Jackson (Epic)
-	25	HOMEBREW	Neneh Cherry (Circa)
29	26	STARS	Simply Red (East West)
23	27	JEHOVAH KILL	Julian Cope (Island)
21	28	BACK TO THE LIGHT	Brian May (Parlophone)
30	29	NEVERMIND	Nirvana (DGC)
-	30	3 YEARS, 5 MONTHS AND 2 DAYS IN THE LIFE	Arrested Development (Cooltempo)
27	31	ULTRAVIOLET	All About Eve (MCA)
27	32	ALL THE WAY FROM TUAM	Saw Doctors (Solid)
44	33	INTO THE LIGHT	Hank Marvin (Polydor)
26	34	III SIDES TO EVERY STORY	Extreme (A&M)
24	35	WOODFACE	Crowded House (Capitol)
28	36	WHAT HITS!?	Red Hot Chili Peppers (EMI USA)
36	37	TOURISM	Roxette (EMI)
20	38	KISS THIS	Sex Pistols (Virgin)
33	39	LEGEND	Bob Marley & the Wailers (Island)
-	40	TAKE THAT AND PARTY	Take That (RCA)
39	41	WE CAN'T DANCE	Genesis (Virgin)
32	42	SAND IN THE VASELINE - POPULAR FAVOURITES 1976-1992	Talking Heads (EMI)
38	43	RIDIN' HIGH	Robert Palmer (EMI)
-	44	ENERGIQUE	Bizarre Inc. (Vinyl Solution)
34	45	LAUGHING ON JUDGEMENT DAY	Thunder (EMI)
-	46	TRAINS, BOATS AND PLANES	Frank & Walters (Setanta)
40	47	THE PRODIGY EXPERIENCE	Prodigy (XL Recordings)
45	48	ORIGINAL SOUNDTRACK - 1492 CONQUEST OF PARADISE	Vangelis (East West)
-	49	THE EPIC YEARS	Shaky (Epic)
50	50	MAIN OFFENDER	Keith Richards (Virgin America)

14 November 1992

last week	this week	Title	Artist
1	1	GLITTERING PRIZE 81/92	Simple Minds (Virgin)
-	2	KEEP THE FAITH	Bon Jovi (Jambco)
3	3	TIMELESS - THE CLASSICS	Michael Bolton (Columbia)
2	4	EROTICA	Madonna (Maverick)
-	5	GOD'S GREAT BANANA SKIN	Chris Rea (East West)
4	6	LIVE	AC/DC (Atco)
5	7	AUTOMATIC FOR THE PEOPLE	R.E.M. (Warner Bros.)
6	8	GOLD - GREATEST HITS	Abba (Polydor)
-	9	GREATEST HITS	Gloria Estefan (Epic)
-	10	HARVEST MOON	Neil Young (Reprise)
12	11	COOLEYHIGHHARMONY	Boyz II Men (Motown)
8	12	GREAT EXPECTATIONS	Tasmin Archer (EMI)
16	13	BOSS DRUM	Shamen (One Little Indian)
7	14	SYMBOL	Prince & the New Power Generation (Paisley Park)
11	15	THE BEST OF BELINDA CARLISLE VOLUME 1	Belinda Carlisle (Virgin)
13	16	TUBULAR BELLS II	Mike Oldfield (WEA)
-	17	BEST ... II	Smiths (WEA)
10	18	BOOM BOOM	John Lee Hooker (Pointblank)
9	19	THE BEST OF - ONCE IN A LIFETIME	Talking Heads (EMI)
-	20	GOOD AS I BEEN TO YOU	Bob Dylan (CBS)
14	21	BACK TO FRONT	Lionel Richie (Motown)
19	22	LOVE DELUXE	Sade (Epic)
15	23	DIVA	Annie Lennox (RCA)
24	24	US	Peter Gabriel (Realworld)
30	25	3 YEARS, 5 MONTHS AND 2 DAYS IN THE LIFE	Arrested Development (Cooltempo)
17	26	GREATEST HITS	Police (A&M)
18	27	CURTIS STIGERS	Curtis Stigers (Arista)
26	28	STARS	Simply Red (East West)
25	29	HOMEBREW	Neneh Cherry (Circa)
29	30	NEVERMIND	Nirvana (DGC)
-	31	MADSTOCK	Madness (Go! Discs)
22	32	UNPLUGGED	Eric Clapton (Duck)
40	33	TAKE THAT AND PARTY	Take That (RCA)
24	34	DANGEROUS	Michael Jackson (Epic)
33	35	INTO THE LIGHT	Hank Marvin (Polydor)
35	36	WOODFACE	Crowded House (Capitol)
36	37	WHAT HITS!?	Red Hot Chili Peppers (EMI USA)
38	38	KISS THIS	Sex Pistols (Virgin)
-	39	NURSE	Therapy? (A&M)
41	40	WE CAN'T DANCE	Genesis (Virgin)
39	41	LEGEND	Bob Marley & the Wailers (Island)
-	42	LIVE ALIVE QUO	Status Quo (Polydor)
-	43	LOVE SEE NO COLOUR	Farm (End Product)
28	44	BACK TO THE LIGHT	Brian May (Parlophone)
23	45	BLIND	Sundays (Parlophone)
20	46	ARE YOU NORMAL?	Ned's Atomic Dustbin (Furtive)
34	47	III SIDES TO EVERY STORY	Extreme (A&M)
-	48	HORMONALLY YOURS	Shakespear's Sister (London)
-	49	THE ULTIMATE EXPERIENCE	Jimi Hendrix (PolyGram TV)
-	50	UP	Right Said Fred (Tug)

Madonna's *Erotica* album (available, at least initially, in the equivalent of PG and 18-rated versions) was part of her general multi-media attempt to apparently present herself as the world's most sex-obsessed woman - the other half of the equation being her fantasy-photo book *Sex* (strictly 18-rated only).

21 November 1992

last week	this week	Title	Artist
-	1	CHER'S GREATEST HITS: 1965-1992	Cher (Geffen)
2	2	KEEP THE FAITH	Bon Jovi (Jambco)
1	3	GLITTERING PRIZE 81/92	Simple Minds (Virgin)
3	4	TIMELESS - THE CLASSICS	Michael Bolton (Columbia)
5	5	GOD'S GREAT BANANA SKIN	Chris Rea (East West)
10	6	HARVEST MOON	Neil Young (Reprise)
9	7	GREATEST HITS	Gloria Estefan (Epic)
8	8	GOLD - GREATEST HITS	Abba (Polydor)
7	9	AUTOMATIC FOR THE PEOPLE	R.E.M. (Warner Bros.)
4	10	EROTICA	Madonna (Maverick)
11	11	COOLEYHIGHHARMONY	Boyz II Men (Motown)
13	12	BOSS DRUM	Shamen (One Little Indian)
20	13	GOOD AS I BEEN TO YOU	Bob Dylan (CBS)
14	14	SYMBOL	Prince & the New Power Generation (Paisley Park)
6	15	LIVE	AC/DC (Atco)
17	16	BEST ... II	Smiths (WEA)
15	17	THE BEST OF BELINDA CARLISLE VOLUME 1	Belinda Carlisle (Virgin)
25	18	3 YEARS, 5 MONTHS AND 2 DAYS IN THE LIFE	Arrested Development (Cooltempo)
16	19	TUBULAR BELLS II	Mike Oldfield (WEA)
21	20	BACK TO FRONT	Lionel Richie (Motown)
19	21	THE BEST OF - ONCE IN A LIFETIME	Talking Heads (EMI)
49	22	THE ULTIMATE EXPERIENCE	Jimi Hendrix (PolyGram TV)
12	23	GREAT EXPECTATIONS	Tasmin Archer (EMI)
33	24	TAKE THAT AND PARTY	Take That (RCA)
23	25	DIVA	Annie Lennox (RCA)
27	26	CURTIS STIGERS	Curtis Stigers (Arista)
31	27	MADSTOCK	Madness (Go! Discs)
28	28	STARS	Simply Red (East West)
-	29	INDIAN SUMMER	Go West (Chrysalis)
26	30	GREATEST HITS	Police (A&M)
-	31	FOLLOW YOUR DREAM	Daniel O'Donnell (Ritz)
18	32	BOOM BOOM	John Lee Hooker (Pointblank)
34	33	DANGEROUS	Michael Jackson (Epic)
30	34	NEVERMIND	Nirvana (DGC)
39	35	NURSE	Therapy? (A&M)
32	36	UNPLUGGED	Eric Clapton (Duck)
40	37	WE CAN'T DANCE	Genesis (Virgin)
35	38	INTO THE LIGHT	Hank Marvin (Polydor)
-	39	THE ONE	Elton John (Rocket)
-	40	MANY HAPPY RETURNS - THE HITS	Gary Glitter (EMI)
22	41	LOVE DELUXE	Sade (Epic)
41	42	LEGEND	Bob Marley & the Wailers (Island)
42	43	LIVE ALIVE QUO	Status Quo (Polydor)
24	44	US	Peter Gabriel (Realworld)
36	45	WOODFACE	Crowded House (Capitol)
37	46	WHAT HITS!?	Red Hot Chili Peppers (EMI USA)
-	47	HEART STRINGS	Foster & Allen (Telstar)
-	48	THE VERY BEST OF RICHARD CLAYDERMAN	Richard Clayderman (Decca Delphine)
48	49	HORMONALLY YOURS	Shakespear's Sister (London)
44	50	BACK TO THE LIGHT	Brian May (Parlophone)

28 November 1992

last week	this week	Title	Artist
-	1	POP! - THE FIRST 20 HITS	Erasure (Mute)
1	2	GREATEST HITS: 1965-1992	Cher (Geffen)
-	3	LIVE - THE WAY WE WALK VOL. 1: THE SHORTS	Genesis (Virgin)
3	4	GLITTERING PRIZE 81/92	Simple Minds (Virgin)
4	5	TIMELESS - THE CLASSICS	Michael Bolton (Columbia)
-	6	THE FREDDIE MERCURY ALBUM	Freddie Mercury (Parlophone)
7	7	GREATEST HITS	Gloria Estefan (Epic)
9	8	AUTOMATIC FOR THE PEOPLE	R.E.M. (Warner Bros.)
8	9	GOLD - GREATEST HITS	Abba (Polydor)
2	10	KEEP THE FAITH	Bon Jovi (Jambco)
5	11	GOD'S GREAT BANANA SKIN	Chris Rea (East West)
10	12	EROTICA	Madonna (Maverick)
12	13	BOSS DRUM	Shamen (One Little Indian)
11	14	COOLEYHIGHHARMONY	Boyz II Men (Motown)
20	15	BACK TO FRONT	Lionel Richie (Motown)
17	16	THE BEST OF BELINDA CARLISLE VOLUME 1	Belinda Carlisle (Virgin)
49	17	HORMONALLY YOURS	Shakespear's Sister (London)
24	18	TAKE THAT AND PARTY	Take That (RCA)
31	19	FOLLOW YOUR DREAM	Daniel O'Donnell (Ritz)
19	20	TUBULAR BELLS II	Mike Oldfield (WEA)
18	21	3 YEARS, 5 MONTHS AND 2 DAYS IN THE LIFE	Arrested Development (Cooltempo)
6	22	HARVEST MOON	Neil Young (Reprise)
28	23	STARS	Simply Red (East West)
14	24	SYMBOL	Prince & the New Power Generation (Paisley Park)
25	25	DIVA	Annie Lennox (RCA)
26	26	CURTIS STIGERS	Curtis Stigers (Arista)
-	27	KING OF HEARTS	Roy Orbison (Virgin America)
15	28	LIVE	AC/DC (Atco)
29	29	INDIAN SUMMER	Go West (Chrysalis)
-	30	THE CELTS	Enya (WEA)
27	31	MADSTOCK	Madness (Go! Discs)
22	32	THE ULTIMATE EXPERIENCE	Jimi Hendrix (PolyGram TV)
30	33	GREATEST HITS	Police (A&M)
13	34	GOOD AS I BEEN TO YOU	Bob Dylan (CBS)
16	35	BEST ... II	Smiths (WEA)
23	36	GREAT EXPECTATIONS	Tasmin Archer (EMI)
32	37	BOOM BOOM	John Lee Hooker (Pointblank)
-	38	THE HEART OF ROCK & ROLL: THE BEST OF	Huey Lewis & the News (Chrysalis)
-	39	FEEL THIS	Jeff Healey Band (Arista)
21	40	THE BEST OF - ONCE IN A LIFETIME	Talking Heads (EMI)
41	41	LOVE DELUXE	Sade (Epic)
-	42	PORTRAIT	Des O'Connor (Columbia)
37	43	WE CAN'T DANCE	Genesis (Virgin)
42	44	LEGEND	Bob Marley & the Wailers (Island)
40	45	MANY HAPPY RETURNS - THE HITS	Gary Glitter (EMI)
33	46	DANGEROUS	Michael Jackson (Epic)
34	47	NEVERMIND	Nirvana (DGC)
-	48	SHEPHERD MOONS	Enya (WEA)
-	49	THE BODYGUARD - SOUNDTRACK	Various (Arista)
-	50	BEETHOVEN VIOLIN CONCERTO	Nigel Kennedy/Klaus Tennstedt (EMI Classics)

5 December 1992

last week	this week	Title	Artist
1	1	POP! - THE FIRST 20 HITS	Erasure (Mute)
3	2	LIVE - THE WAY WE WALK VOL. 1: THE SHORTS	Genesis (Virgin)
2	3	GREATEST HITS: 1965-1992	Cher (Geffen)
6	4	THE FREDDIE MERCURY ALBUM	Freddie Mercury (Parlophone)
5	5	TIMELESS - THE CLASSICS	Michael Bolton (Columbia)
4	6	GLITTERING PRIZE 81/92	Simple Minds (Virgin)
7	7	GREATEST HITS	Gloria Estefan (Epic)
8	8	AUTOMATIC FOR THE PEOPLE	R.E.M. (Warner Bros.)
9	9	GOLD - GREATEST HITS	Abba (Polydor)
30	10	THE CELTS	Enya (WEA)
15	11	BACK TO FRONT	Lionel Richie (Motown)
12	12	EROTICA	Madonna (Maverick)
11	13	GOD'S GREAT BANANA SKIN	Chris Rea (East West)
13	14	BOSS DRUM	Shamen (One Little Indian)
10	15	KEEP THE FAITH	Bon Jovi (Jambco)
16	16	THE BEST OF BELINDA CARLISLE VOLUME 1	Belinda Carlisle (Virgin)
18	17	TAKE THAT AND PARTY	Take That (RCA)
17	18	HORMONALLY YOURS	Shakespear's Sister (London)
20	19	TUBULAR BELLS II	Mike Oldfield (WEA)
19	20	FOLLOW YOUR DREAM	Daniel O'Donnell (Ritz)
14	21	COOLEYHIGHHARMONY	Boyz II Men (Motown)
27	22	KING OF HEARTS	Roy Orbison (Virgin America)
23	23	STARS	Simply Red (East West)
24	24	DIVA	Annie Lennox (RCA)
49	25	THE BODYGUARD - SOUNDTRACK	Various (Arista)
24	26	SYMBOL	Prince & the New Power Generation (Paisley Park)
26	27	CURTIS STIGERS	Curtis Stigers (Arista)
21	28	3 YEARS, 5 MONTHS AND 2 DAYS IN THE LIFE	Arrested Development (Cooltempo)
46	29	DANGEROUS	Michael Jackson (Epic)
-	30	INTO THE LIGHT	Hank Marvin (Polydor)
22	31	HARVEST MOON	Neil Young (Reprise)
29	32	INDIAN SUMMER	Go West (Chrysalis)
33	33	GREATEST HITS	Police (A&M)
38	34	THE HEART OF ROCK & ROLL: THE BEST OF	Huey Lewis & the News (Chrysalis)
28	35	LIVE	AC/DC (Atco)
-	36	NICK BERRY	Nick Berry (Columbia)
31	37	MADSTOCK	Madness (Go! Discs)
32	38	THE ULTIMATE EXPERIENCE	Jimi Hendrix (PolyGram TV)
36	39	GREAT EXPECTATIONS	Tasmin Archer (EMI)
44	40	LEGEND	Bob Marley & the Wailers (Island)
-	41	THE FUTURE	Leonard Cohen (Columbia)
-	42	UP	Right Said Fred (Tug)
-	43	CHECK OUT THE GROOVE	Undercover (PWL Continental)
41	44	LOVE DELUXE	Sade (Epic)
45	45	MANY HAPPY RETURNS	Gary Glitter (EMI)
43	46	WE CAN'T DANCE	Genesis (Virgin)
-	47	THE CHRISTMAS ALBUM	Neil Diamond (Columbia)
40	48	THE BEST OF - ONCE IN A LIFETIME	Talking Heads (EMI)
47	49	NEVERMIND	Nirvana (DGC)
-	50	THE PRODIGY EXPERIENCE	Prodigy (XL Recordings)

As at the end of 1991, the major-name compilations vied with each other for year-end chart-topping sales, and it was Cher (with a 27-year career overview stretching back to Sonny & Cher days) and Erasure (rather fewer years to anthologise), who were to toss the Number 1 position back and forth between them.

December 1992

12 December 1992

last	this		
1	1	POP! - THE FIRST 20 HITS	Erasure (Mute)
3	2	GREATEST HITS: 1965-1992	Cher (Geffen)
5	3	TIMELESS - THE CLASSICS	Michael Bolton (Columbia)
4	4	THE FREDDIE MERCURY ALBUM	Freddie Mercury (Parlophone)
2	5	LIVE - THE WAY WE WALK VOL. 1: THE SHORTS	Genesis (Virgin)
7	6	GREATEST HITS	Gloria Estefan (Epic)
8	7	AUTOMATIC FOR THE PEOPLE	R.E.M. (Warner Bros.)
6	8	GLITTERING PRIZE 81/92	Simple Minds (Virgin)
9	9	GOLD - GREATEST HITS	Abba (Polydor)
10	10	THE CELTS	Enya (WEA)
12	11	EROTICA	Madonna (Maverick)
-	12	DUOPHONIC	Charles & Eddie (Capitol)
17	13	TAKE THAT AND PARTY	Take That (RCA)
11	14	BACK TO FRONT	Lionel Richie (Motown)
14	15	BOSS DRUM	Shamen (One Little Indian)
13	16	GOD'S GREAT BANANA SKIN	Chris Rea (East West)
16	17	THE BEST OF BELINDA CARLISLE VOLUME 1	Belinda Carlisle (Virgin)
15	18	KEEP THE FAITH	Bon Jovi (Jambco)
23	19	STARS	Simply Red (East West)
19	20	TUBULAR BELLS II	Mike Oldfield (WEA)
24	21	DIVA	Annie Lennox (RCA)
27	22	CURTIS STIGERS	Curtis Stigers (Arista)
25	23	THE BODYGUARD - SOUNDTRACK	Various (Arista)
20	24	FOLLOW YOUR DREAM	Daniel O'Donnell (Ritz)
29	25	DANGEROUS	Michael Jackson (Epic)
18	26	HORMONALLY YOURS	Shakespear's Sister (London)
43	27	CHECK OUT THE GROOVE	Undercover (PWL Continental)
26	28	SYMBOL	Prince & the New Power Generation (Paisley Park)
30	29	INTO THE LIGHT	Hank Marvin (Polydor)
21	30	COOLEYHIGHHARMONY	Boyz II Men (Motown)
28	31	3 YEARS, 5 MONTHS AND 2 DAYS IN THE LIFE	Arrested Development (Cooltempo)
22	32	KING OF HEARTS	Roy Orbison (Virgin America)
42	33	UP	Right Said Fred (Tug)
-	34	THE BEST OF...	Shirley Bassey (Dino)
36	35	NICK BERRY	Nick Berry (Columbia)
-	36	WELCOME TO WHEREVER YOU ARE	INXS (Mercury)
41	37	THE FUTURE	Leonard Cohen (Columbia)
-	38	THE VERY BEST OF ELAINE PAIGE AND BARBARA DICKSON - TOGETHER	Elaine Paige & Barbara Dickson (Telstar)
38	39	THE ULTIMATE EXPERIENCE	Jimi Hendrix (PolyGram TV)
49	40	NEVERMIND	Nirvana (DGC)
34	41	THE HEART OF ROCK & ROLL: THE BEST OF ...	Huey Lewis & the News (Chrysalis)
40	42	LEGEND	Bob Marley & the Wailers (Island)
33	43	GREATEST HITS	Police (A&M)
31	44	HARVEST MOON	Neil Young (Reprise)
-	45	GREATEST HITS II	Queen (Parlophone)
-	46	ACHTUNG BABY	U2 (Island)
-	47	THE VERY BEST OF	Earth Wind & Fire (Telstar)
46	48	WE CAN'T DANCE	Genesis (Virgin)
50	49	THE PRODIGY EXPERIENCE	Prodigy (XL Recordings)
39	50	GREAT EXPECTATIONS	Tasmin Archer (EMI)

19 December 1992

last	this		
2	1	GREATEST HITS: 1965-1992	Cher (Geffen)
1	2	POP! - THE FIRST 20 HITS	Erasure (Mute)
3	3	TIMELESS - THE CLASSICS	Michael Bolton (Columbia)
6	4	GREATEST HITS	Gloria Estefan (Epic)
5	5	LIVE - THE WAY WE WALK VOL. 1: THE SHORTS	Genesis (Virgin)
8	6	GLITTERING PRIZE 81/92	Simple Minds (Virgin)
4	7	THE FREDDIE MERCURY ALBUM	Freddie Mercury (Parlophone)
9	8	GOLD - GREATEST HITS	Abba (Polydor)
7	9	AUTOMATIC FOR THE PEOPLE	R.E.M. (Warner Bros.)
23	10	THE BODYGUARD - SOUNDTRACK	Various (Arista)
19	11	STARS	Simply Red (East West)
14	12	BACK TO FRONT	Lionel Richie (Motown)
25	13	DANGEROUS	Michael Jackson (Epic)
11	14	EROTICA	Madonna (Maverick)
13	15	TAKE THAT AND PARTY	Take That (RCA)
16	16	GOD'S GREAT BANANA SKIN	Chris Rea (East West)
10	17	THE CELTS	Enya (WEA)
15	18	BOSS DRUM	Shamen (One Little Indian)
-	19	FIXED	Nine Inch Nail (TVT)
12	20	DUOPHONIC	Charles & Eddie (Capitol)
17	21	THE BEST OF BELINDA CARLISLE VOLUME 1	Belinda Carlisle (Virgin)
21	22	DIVA	Annie Lennox (RCA)
24	23	FOLLOW YOUR DREAM	Daniel O'Donnell (Ritz)
18	24	KEEP THE FAITH	Bon Jovi (Jambco)
22	25	CURTIS STIGERS	Curtis Stigers (Arista)
20	26	TUBULAR BELLS II	Mike Oldfield (WEA)
26	27	HORMONALLY YOURS	Shakespear's Sister (London)
38	28	THE VERY BEST – TOGETHER	Elaine Paige & Barbara Dickson (Telstar)
-	29	THE GREATEST HITS 1966-1992	Neil Diamond (Columbia)
45	30	GREATEST HITS II	Queen (Parlophone)
27	31	CHECK OUT THE GROOVE	Undercover (PWL Continental)
34	32	THE BEST OF...	Shirley Bassey (Dino)
33	33	UP	Right Said Fred (Tug)
-	34	ONCE IN A LIFETIME	Talking Heads (EMI)
28	35	SYMBOL	Prince & the New Power Generation (Paisley Park)
29	36	INTO THE LIGHT	Hank Marvin (Polydor)
31	37	3 YEARS, 5 MONTHS AND 2 DAYS IN THE LIFE	Arrested Development (Cooltempo)
-	38	HEART STRINGS	Foster & Allen (Telstar)
46	39	ACHTUNG BABY	U2 (Island)
35	40	NICK BERRY	Nick Berry (Columbia)
36	41	WELCOME TO WHEREVER YOU ARE	INXS (Mercury)
30	42	COOLEYHIGHHARMONY	Boyz II Men (Motown)
40	43	NEVERMIND	Nirvana (DGC)
42	44	LEGEND	Bob Marley & the Wailers (Island)
41	45	THE HEART OF ROCK & ROLL: THE BEST OF	Huey Lewis & the News (Chrysalis)
47	46	THE VERY BEST OF...Earth Wind & Fire (Telstar)	
39	47	THE ULTIMATE EXPERIENCE	Jimi Hendrix (PolyGram TV)
49	48	THE PRODIGY EXPERIENCE	Prodigy (XL Recordings)
-	49	THE CHRISTMAS ALBUM	Neil Diamond (Columbia)
-	50	THE FORCE BEHIND THE POWER	Diana Ross (EMI)

Michael Bolton's Number 3 album was not a set of his own hits (he hadn't yet had enough), but covers of classic pop songs - mainly ballads. Most of the rest of the Top 10 was hits anthologies (or hit album tracks recorded live by Genesis) with only REM raising the contemporary flag.

9 January 1993

last week	this week	Title	Artist (Label)
1	1	GREATEST HITS: 1965-1992	Cher (Geffen)
4	2	GREATEST HITS	Gloria Estefan (Epic)
10	3	THE BODYGUARD - SOUNDTRACK	Various (Arista)
2	4	POP! - THE FIRST 20 HITS	Erasure (Mute)
3	5	TIMELESS - THE CLASSICS	Michael Bolton (Columbia)
5	6	LIVE - THE WAY WE WALK VOLUME ONE: THE SHORTS	Genesis (Virgin)
6	7	GLITTERING PRIZE 81/92	Simple Minds (Virgin)
7	8	THE FREDDIE MERCURY ALBUM	Freddie Mercury (Parlophone)
11	9	STARS	Simply Red (East West)
15	10	TAKE THAT AND PARTY	Take That (RCA)
8	11	GOLD - GREATEST HITS	Abba (Polydor)
12	12	BACK TO FRONT	Lionel Richie (Motown)
13	13	DANGEROUS	Michael Jackson (Epic)
18	14	BOSS DRUM	Shamen (One Little Indian)
9	15	AUTOMATIC FOR THE PEOPLE	R.E.M. (Warner Bros.)
29	16	THE GREATEST HITS 1966-1992	Neil Diamond (Columbia)
14	17	EROTICA	Madonna (Maverick)
50	18	THE FORCE BEHIND THE POWER	Diana Ross (EMI)
-	19	INCESTICIDE	Nirvana (Geffen)
22	20	DIVA	Annie Lennox (RCA)
21	21	THE BEST OF BELINDA CARLISLE VOLUME 1	Belinda Carlisle (Virgin)
28	22	THE BEST OF - TOGETHER	Elaine Paige & Barbara Dickson (Telstar)
20	23	DUOPHONIC	Charles & Eddie (Capitol)
26	24	TUBULAR BELLS II	Mike Oldfield (WEA)
16	25	GOD'S GREAT BANANA SKIN	Chris Rea (East West)
17	26	THE CELTS	Enya (WEA)
23	27	FOLLOW YOUR DREAM	Daniel O'Donnell (Ritz)
24	28	KEEP THE FAITH	Bon Jovi (Jambco)
30	29	GREATEST HITS II	Queen (Parlophone)
34	30	THE BEST OF - ONCE IN A LIFETIME	Talking Heads (EMI)
-	31	SIMPLY THE BEST	Tina Turner (Capitol)
27	32	HORMONALLY YOURS	Shakespear's Sister (London)
25	33	CURTIS STIGERS	Curtis Stigers (Arista)
33	34	UP	Right Said Fred (Tug)
43	35	NEVERMIND	Nirvana (DGC)
37	36	3 YEARS, 5 MONTHS AND 2 DAYS IN THE LIFE	Arrested Development (Cooltempo)
-	37	MICHAEL CRAWFORD PERFORMS ANDREW LLOYD WEBBER	Michael Crawford (Telstar)
38	38	HEART STRINGS	Foster & Allen (Telstar)
32	39	THE BEST OF ...	Shirley Bassey (Dino)
44	40	LEGEND	Bob Marley & the Wailers (Island)
39	41	ACHTUNG BABY	U2 (Island)
36	42	INTO THE LIGHT	Hank Marvin (Polydor)
41	43	WELCOME TO WHEREVER YOU ARE	INXS (Mercury)
-	44	FROM BOTH SIDES NOW	Ian McShane (PolyGram TV)
-	45	GREATEST HITS	Queen (EMI)
35	46	SYMBOL	Prince & the New Power Generation (Paisley Park)
46	47	THE VERY BEST OF	Earth Wind & Fire (Telstar)
-	48	UNPLUGGED	Eric Clapton (Duck)
40	49	NICK BERRY	Nick Berry (Columbia)
42	50	COOLEYHIGHHARMONY	Boyz II Men (Motown)

16 January 1993

last week	this week	Title	Artist (Label)
3	1	THE BODYGUARD - SOUNDTRACK	Various (Arista)
1	2	GREATEST HITS: 1965-1992	Cher (Geffen)
4	3	POP! - THE FIRST 20 HITS	Erasure (Mute)
2	4	GREATEST HITS	Gloria Estefan (Epic)
10	5	TAKE THAT AND PARTY	Take That (RCA)
7	6	GLITTERING PRIZE 81/92	Simple Minds (Virgin)
14	7	BOSS DRUM	Shamen (One Little Indian)
6	8	LIVE - THE WAY WE WALK VOLUME ONE: THE SHORTS	Genesis (Virgin)
15	9	AUTOMATIC FOR THE PEOPLE	R.E.M. (Warner Bros.)
5	10	TIMELESS - THE CLASSICS	Michael Bolton (Columbia)
11	11	GOLD - GREATEST HITS	Abba (Polydor)
9	12	STARS	Simply Red (East West)
12	13	BACK TO FRONT	Lionel Richie (Motown)
13	14	DANGEROUS	Michael Jackson (Epic)
8	15	THE FREDDIE MERCURY ALBUM	Freddie Mercury (Parlophone)
17	16	EROTICA	Madonna (Maverick)
36	17	3 YEARS, 5 MONTHS AND 2 DAYS IN THE LIFE	Arrested Development (Cooltempo)
19	18	INCESTICIDE	Nirvana (Geffen)
35	19	NEVERMIND	Nirvana (DGC)
-	20	HIT PARADE 2	Wedding Present (RCA)
21	21	THE BEST OF - VOL 1	Belinda Carlisle (Virgin)
20	22	DIVA	Annie Lennox (RCA)
28	23	KEEP THE FAITH	Bon Jovi (Jambco)
23	24	DUOPHONIC	Charles & Eddie (Capitol)
32	25	HORMONALLY YOURS	Shakespear's Sister (London)
26	26	THE CELTS	Enya (WEA)
24	27	TUBULAR BELLS II	Mike Oldfield (WEA)
29	28	GREATEST HITS II	Queen (Parlophone)
48	29	UNPLUGGED	Eric Clapton (Duck)
25	30	GOD'S GREAT BANANA SKIN	Chris Rea (East West)
41	31	ACHTUNG BABY	U2 (Island)
33	32	CURTIS STIGERS	Curtis Stigers (Arista)
30	33	THE BEST OF - ONCE IN A LIFETIME	Talking Heads (EMI)
34	34	UP	Right Said Fred (Tug)
-	35	THE PRODIGY EXPERIENCE	Prodigy (XL Recordings)
46	36	SYMBOL	Prince & the New Power Generation (Paisley Park)
18	37	THE FORCE BEHIND THE POWER	Diana Ross (EMI)
16	38	THE GREATEST HITS 1966-1992	Neil Diamond (Columbia)
31	39	SIMPLY THE BEST	Tina Turner (Capitol)
-	40	IT'S A SHAME ABOUT RAY	Lemonheads (Atlantic)
43	41	WELCOME TO WHEREVER YOU ARE	INXS (Mercury)
50	42	COOLEYHIGHHARMONY	Boyz II Men (Motown)
-	43	USE YOUR ILLUSION II	Guns N' Roses (Geffen)
45	44	GREATEST HITS	Queen (EMI)
-	45	TEN	Pearl Jam (Ten)
-	46	USE YOUR ILLUSION I	Guns N' Roses (Geffen)
-	47	THE ULTIMATE EXPERIENCE	Jimi Hendrix (PolyGram TV)
40	48	LEGEND	Bob Marley & the Wailers (Island)
22	49	THE BEST OF - TOGETHER	Elaine Paige & Barbara Dickson (Telstar)
-	50	DIVINE MADNESS	Madness (Virgin)

23 January 1993

last week	this week	Title	Artist (Label)
1	1	THE BODYGUARD - SOUNDTRACK	Various (Arista)
-	2	LIVE - THE WAY WE WALK VOLUME TWO: THE LONGS	Genesis (Virgin)
2	3	GREATEST HITS: 1965-1992	Cher (Geffen)
7	4	BOSS DRUM	Shamen (One Little Indian)
5	5	TAKE THAT AND PARTY	Take That (RCA)
9	6	AUTOMATIC FOR THE PEOPLE	R.E.M. (Warner Bros.)
-	7	CONNECTED	Stereo MCs (Fourth & Broadway)
3	8	POP! - THE FIRST 20 HITS	Erasure (Mute)
6	9	GLITTERING PRIZE 81/92	Simple Minds (Virgin)
4	10	GREATEST HITS	Gloria Estefan (Epic)
11	11	GOLD - GREATEST HITS	Abba (Polydor)
8	12	LIVE - THE WAY WE WALK VOLUME ONE: THE SHORTS	Genesis (Virgin)
18	13	INCESTICIDE	Nirvana (Geffen)
17	14	3 YEARS, 5 MONTHS AND 2 DAYS IN THE LIFE	Arrested Development (Cooltempo)
10	15	TIMELESS - THE CLASSICS	Michael Bolton (Columbia)
13	16	BACK TO FRONT	Lionel Richie (Motown)
12	17	STARS	Simply Red (East West)
14	18	DANGEROUS	Michael Jackson (Epic)
16	19	EROTICA	Madonna (Maverick)
15	20	THE FREDDIE MERCURY ALBUM	Freddie Mercury (Parlophone)
-	21	INTO THE SKYLINE	Cathy Dennis (Polydor)
23	22	KEEP THE FAITH	Bon Jovi (Jambco)
19	23	NEVERMIND	Nirvana (DGC)
20	24	HIT PARADE 2	Wedding Present (RCA)
34	25	UP	Right Said Fred (Tug)
-	26	ONLY YESTERDAY - THE CARPENTER'S GREATEST HITS	Carpenters (A&M)
29	27	UNPLUGGED	Eric Clapton (Duck)
24	28	DUOPHONIC	Charles & Eddie (Capitol)
-	29	LUCKY THIRTEEN	Neil Young (Geffen)
30	30	GOD'S GREAT BANANA SKIN	Chris Rea (East West)
22	31	DIVA	Annie Lennox (RCA)
35	32	THE PRODIGY EXPERIENCE	Prodigy (XL Recordings)
26	33	THE CELTS	Enya (WEA)
-	34	US	Peter Gabriel (Realworld)
21	35	THE BEST OF BELINDA CARLISLE VOLUME 1	Belinda Carlisle (Virgin)
-	36	AGES OF MANN - 22 CLASSIC HITS OF THE '60S	Manfred Mann (PolyGram TV)
25	37	HORMONALLY YOURS	Shakespear's Sister (London)
27	38	TUBULAR BELLS II	Mike Oldfield (WEA)
40	39	IT'S A SHAME ABOUT RAY	Lemonheads (Atlantic)
36	40	SYMBOL	Prince & the New Power Generation (Paisley Park)
28	41	GREATEST HITS II	Queen (Parlophone)
32	42	CURTIS STIGERS	Curtis Stigers (Arista)
31	43	ACHTUNG BABY	U2 (Island)
42	44	COOLEYHIGHHARMONY	Boyz II Men (Motown)
-	45	INSPECTOR MORSE, VOL. 3	Barrington Pheloung (Virgin)
38	46	THE GREATEST HITS 1966-1992	Neil Diamond (Columbia)
39	47	SIMPLY THE BEST	Tina Turner (Capitol)
-	48	ANGEL DUST	Faith No More (Slash)
-	49	SYNTHESIZER GOLD	Ed Starink (Arcade)
33	50	ONCE IN A LIFETIME	Talking Heads (EMI)

The Bodyguard soundtrack album, mostly consisting of songs by the film's leading lady Whitney Houston, was something of a phenomenon. In the US it was estimated to be selling almost a million copies a week at its peak, and the UK release was also to hit the 7-figure sales mark, with two months of consistent Number 1 sales to its credit. It also spawned the million-selling single *I Will Always Love You*.

January – February 1993

30 January 1993

Last	This	Title	Artist
1	1	THE BODYGUARD - SOUNDTRACK	Various (Arista)
2	2	LIVE - THE WAY WE WALK VOLUME TWO: THE LONGS	Genesis (Virgin)
7	3	CONNECTED	Stereo MCs (Fourth & Broadway)
6	4	AUTOMATIC FOR THE PEOPLE	R.E.M. (Warner Bros.)
14	5	3 YEARS, 5 MONTHS AND 2 DAYS IN THE LIFE	Arrested Development (Cooltempo)
3	6	GREATEST HITS: 1965-1992	Cher (Geffen)
4	7	BOSS DRUM	Shamen (One Little Indian)
5	8	TAKE THAT AND PARTY	Take That (RCA)
-	9	SO CLOSE	Dina Carroll (A&M PM)
8	10	POP! - THE FIRST 20 HITS	Erasure (Mute)
21	11	INTO THE SKYLINE	Cathy Dennis (Polydor)
9	12	GLITTERING PRIZE 81/92	Simple Minds (Virgin)
12	13	LIVE - THE WAY WE WALK VOLUME ONE: THE SHORTS	Genesis (Virgin)
13	14	INCESTICIDE	Nirvana (Geffen)
10	15	GREATEST HITS	Gloria Estefan (Epic)
11	16	GOLD - GREATEST HITS	Abba (Polydor)
16	17	BACK TO FRONT	Lionel Richie (Motown)
22	18	KEEP THE FAITH	Bon Jovi (Jambco)
17	19	STARS	Simply Red (East West)
34	20	US	Peter Gabriel (Realworld)
15	21	TIMELESS - THE CLASSICS	Michael Bolton (Columbia)
-	22	SONGS FROM THE MIRROR	Fish (Polydor)
36	23	AGES OF MANN - 22 CLASSIC HITS OF THE '60S	Manfred Mann (PolyGram TV)
23	24	NEVERMIND	Nirvana (DGC)
-	25	THE JULIET LETTERS	Elvis Costello & the Brodsky Quartet (Warner Bros.)
18	26	DANGEROUS	Michael Jackson (Epic)
27	27	UNPLUGGED	Eric Clapton (Duck)
32	28	THE PRODIGY EXPERIENCE	Prodigy (XL Recordings)
19	29	EROTICA	Madonna (Maverick)
31	30	DIVA	Annie Lennox (RCA)
-	31	25	Harry Connick Jr. (Columbia)
20	32	THE FREDDIE MERCURY ALBUM	Freddie Mercury (Parlophone)
28	33	DUOPHONIC	Charles & Eddie (Capitol)
30	34	GOD'S GREAT BANANA SKIN	Chris Rea (East West)
39	35	IT'S A SHAME ABOUT RAY	Lemonheads (Atlantic)
33	36	THE CELTS	Enya (WEA)
26	37	ONLY YESTERDAY - THE CARPENTER'S GREATEST HITS	Carpenters (A&M)
45	38	MUSIC FROM THE ITV SERIES INSPECTOR MORSE, VOL. 3	Barrington Pheloung (Virgin)
35	39	THE BEST OF BELINDA CARLISLE VOLUME 1	Belinda Carlisle (Virgin)
37	40	HORMONALLY YOURS	Shakespear's Sister (London)
-	41	FROM THE HEART - HIS GREATEST HITS	Elvis Presley (RCA)
48	42	ANGEL DUST	Faith No More (Slash)
-	43	COPPER BLUE	Sugar (Creation)
-	44	FUNKY DIVAS	En Vogue (East West)
43	45	ACHTUNG BABY	U2 (Island)
38	46	TUBULAR BELLS II	Mike Oldfield (WEA)
-	47	INDIAN SUMMER	Go West (Chrysalis)
41	48	GREATEST HITS II	Queen (Parlophone)
44	49	COOLEYHIGHHARMONY	Boyz II Men (Motown)
49	50	SYNTHESIZER GOLD	Ed Starink (Arcade)

6 February 1993

Last	This	Title	Artist
1	1	THE BODYGUARD - SOUNDTRACK	Various (Arista)
-	2	JAM	Little Angels (Jam)
2	3	LIVE - THE WAY WE WALK VOLUME TWO: THE LONGS	Genesis (Virgin)
9	4	SO CLOSE	Dina Carroll (A&M PM)
-	5	DUSK	The The (Epic)
4	6	AUTOMATIC FOR THE PEOPLE	R.E.M. (Warner Bros.)
5	7	3 YEARS, 5 MONTHS AND 2 DAYS IN THE LIFE	Arrested Development (Cooltempo)
-	8	PERVERSE	Jesus Jones (Food)
3	9	CONNECTED	Stereo MCs (Fourth & Broadway)
7	10	BOSS DRUM	Shamen (One Little Indian)
8	11	TAKE THAT AND PARTY	Take That (RCA)
6	12	GREATEST HITS: 1965-1992	Cher (Geffen)
18	13	KEEP THE FAITH	Bon Jovi (Jambco)
10	14	POP! - THE FIRST 20 HITS	Erasure (Mute)
20	15	US	Peter Gabriel (Realworld)
13	16	LIVE - THE WAY WE WALK VOLUME ONE: THE SHORTS	Genesis (Virgin)
42	17	ANGEL DUST	Faith No More (Slash)
12	18	GLITTERING PRIZE 81/92	Simple Minds (Virgin)
16	19	GOLD - GREATEST HITS	Abba (Polydor)
11	20	INTO THE SKYLINE	Cathy Dennis (Polydor)
15	21	GREATEST HITS	Gloria Estefan (Epic)
25	22	THE JULIET LETTERS	Elvis Costello & the Brodsky Quartet (Warner Bros.)
19	23	STARS	Simply Red (East West)
17	24	BACK TO FRONT	Lionel Richie (Motown)
14	25	INCESTICIDE	Nirvana (Geffen)
-	26	NO RESERVATIONS	Apache Indian (Island)
21	27	TIMELESS - THE CLASSICS	Michael Bolton (Columbia)
24	28	NEVERMIND	Nirvana (DGC)
27	29	UNPLUGGED	Eric Clapton (Duck)
38	30	MUSIC FROM THE ITV SERIES INSPECTOR MORSE, VOL. 3	Barrington Pheloung (Virgin)
28	31	THE PRODIGY EXPERIENCE	Prodigy (XL Recordings)
30	32	DIVA	Annie Lennox (RCA)
26	33	DANGEROUS	Michael Jackson (Epic)
31	34	25	Harry Connick Jr. (Columbia)
35	35	IT'S A SHAME ABOUT RAY	Lemonheads (Atlantic)
43	36	COPPER BLUE	Sugar (Creation)
33	37	DUOPHONIC	Charles & Eddie (Capitol)
-	38	APPOLONIA	BM-EX (UCR)
22	39	SONGS FROM THE MIRROR	Fish (Polydor)
47	40	INDIAN SUMMER	Go West (Chrysalis)
-	41	DIRT	Alice In Chains (Columbia)
36	42	THE CELTS	Enya (WEA)
34	43	GOD'S GREAT BANANA SKIN	Chris Rea (East West)
37	44	ONLY YESTERDAY - RICHARD AND KAREN CARPENTER'S GREATEST HITS	Carpenters (A&M)
45	45	ACHTUNG BABY	U2 (Island)
32	46	THE FREDDIE MERCURY ALBUM	Freddie Mercury (Parlophone)
29	47	EROTICA	Madonna (Maverick)
23	48	AGES OF MANN - 22 CLASSIC HITS OF THE '60S	Manfred Mann (PolyGram TV)
44	49	FUNKY DIVAS	En Vogue (East West)
48	50	GREATEST HITS II	Queen (Parlophone)

13 February 1993

Last	This	Title	Artist
1	1	THE BODYGUARD - SOUNDTRACK	Various (Arista)
2	2	JAM	Little Angels (Jam)
-	3	OFF THE GROUND	Paul McCartney (Parlophone)
-	4	PURE CULT - FOR ROCKERS, RAVERS, LOVERS AND SINNERS	Cult (Beggars Banquet)
5	5	DUSK	The The (Epic)
-	6	STAR	Belly (4AD)
7	7	3 YEARS, 5 MONTHS AND 2 DAYS IN THE LIFE	Arrested Development (Cooltempo)
4	8	SO CLOSE	Dina Carroll (A&M PM)
3	9	LIVE - THE WAY WE WALK VOLUME TWO: THE LONGS	Genesis (Virgin)
6	10	AUTOMATIC FOR THE PEOPLE	R.E.M. (Warner Bros.)
8	11	PERVERSE	Jesus Jones (Food)
9	12	CONNECTED	Stereo MCs (Fourth & Broadway)
10	13	BOSS DRUM	Shamen (One Little Indian)
11	14	TAKE THAT AND PARTY	Take That (RCA)
40	15	INDIAN SUMMER	Go West (Chrysalis)
12	16	GREATEST HITS: 1965-1992	Cher (Geffen)
-	17	GORECKI: SYMPHONY NO. 3	DaUpshaw/London Sinfonietta/David Zinman (Elektra Nonesuch)
49	18	FUNKY DIVAS	En Vogue (East West)
13	19	KEEP THE FAITH	Bon Jovi (Jambco)
32	20	DIVA	Annie Lennox (RCA)
15	21	US	Peter Gabriel (Realworld)
16	22	LIVE - THE WAY WE WALK VOLUME ONE: THE SHORTS	Genesis (Virgin)
17	23	ANGEL DUST	Faith No More (Slash)
19	24	GOLD - GREATEST HITS	Abba (Polydor)
14	25	POP! - THE FIRST 20 HITS	Erasure (Mute)
-	26	CASUAL SEX IN THE CINEPLEX	Sultans Of Ping FC (Rhythm King)
18	27	GLITTERING PRIZE 81/92	Simple Minds (Virgin)
24	28	BACK TO FRONT	Lionel Richie (Motown)
23	29	STARS	Simply Red (East West)
-	30	THE MADMAN'S RETURN	Snap (Logic)
28	31	NEVERMIND	Nirvana (DGC)
30	32	MUSIC FROM THE ITV SERIES INSPECTOR MORSE, VOL. 3	Barrington Pheloung (Virgin)
21	33	GREATEST HITS	Gloria Estefan (Epic)
35	34	IT'S A SHAME ABOUT RAY	Lemonheads (Atlantic)
-	35	GORGEOUS	808 State (ZTT)
-	36	O3	Sunscreem (Sony Soho Square)
29	37	UNPLUGGED	Eric Clapton (Duck)
31	38	THE PRODIGY EXPERIENCE	Prodigy (XL Recordings)
27	39	TIMELESS - THE CLASSICS	Michael Bolton (Columbia)
25	40	INCESTICIDE	Nirvana (Geffen)
41	41	DIRT	Alice In Chains (Columbia)
33	42	DANGEROUS	Michael Jackson (Epic)
22	43	THE JULIET LETTERS	Elvis Costello & the Brodsky Quartet (Warner Bros.)
26	44	NO RESERVATIONS	Apache Indian (Island)
-	45	ON A WING AND A PRAYER	Gerry Rafferty (A&M)
46	46	THE FREDDIE MERCURY ALBUM	Freddie Mercury (Parlophone)
36	47	COPPER BLUE	Sugar (Creation)
44	48	ONLY YESTERDAY - THE CARPENTER'S GREATEST HITS	Carpenters (A&M)
42	49	THE CELTS	Enya (WEA)
20	50	INTO THE SKYLINE	Cathy Dennis (Polydor)

Genesis' two oddled-titled live albums actually gave straight descriptions of what they contained - *The Shorts* featured the trio's short in-concert numbers, and *The Longs* the extended songs. Elvis Costello's collaboration with the avant-garde classical Brodsky Quartet on *The Juliet Letters* did not bring him universal critical approval, but certainly showed how far Costello had moved on from *My Aim Is True*.

February – March 1993

20 February 1993

1	1	THE BODYGUARD - SOUNDTRACK Various (Arista)
4	2	PURE CULT - FOR ROCKERS, RAVERS, LOVERS AND SINNERS Cult (Beggars Banquet)
-	3	CONSCIENCE Beloved (East West)
-	4	WHERE YOU BEEN Dinosaur Jr. (blanco y negro)
-	5	WANDERING SPIRIT Mick Jagger (Atlantic)
6	6	STAR Belly (4AD)
7	7	3 YEARS, 5 MONTHS AND 2 DAYS IN THE LIFE Arrested Development (Cooltempo)
18	8	FUNKY DIVAS En Vogue (East West)
3	9	OFF THE GROUND Paul McCartney (Parlophone)
10	10	AUTOMATIC FOR THE PEOPLE R.E.M. (Warner Bros.)
12	11	CONNECTED Stereo MCs (Fourth & Broadway)
20	12	DIVA Annie Lennox (RCA)
14	13	TAKE THAT AND PARTY Take That (RCA)
17	14	GORECKI: SYMPHONY NO. 3 Dawn Upshaw/London Sinfonietta/David Zinman (Elektra Nonesuch)
8	15	SO CLOSE Dina Carroll (A&M PM)
2	16	JAM Little Angels (Jam)
30	17	THE MADMAN'S RETURN Snap (Logic)
9	18	LIVE - THE WAY WE WALK VOLUME TWO: THE LONGS Genesis (Virgin)
13	19	BOSS DRUM Shamen (One Little Indian)
-	20	LOVE MAKES NO SENSE Alexander O'Neal (Tabu)
5	21	DUSK The The (Epic)
15	22	INDIAN SUMMER Go West (Chrysalis)
-	23	HEAD OVER HEELS Various Artists (Telstar)
-	24	THE VERY BEST OF SISTER SLEDGE 1973-1993 Sister Sledge (Atlantic)
16	25	GREATEST HITS: 1965-1992 Cher (Geffen)
19	26	KEEP THE FAITH Bon Jovi (Jambco)
35	27	GORGEOUS 808 State (ZTT)
24	28	GOLD - GREATEST HITS Abba (Polydor)
25	29	POP! - THE FIRST 20 HITS Erasure (Mute)
21	30	US Peter Gabriel (Realworld)
-	31	WORDS OF LOVE - 22 CLASSIC HITS Buddy Holly & the Crickets (MCA)
22	32	LIVE - THE WAY WE WALK VOLUME ONE: THE SHORTS Genesis (Virgin)
11	33	PERVERSE Jesus Jones (Food)
23	34	ANGEL DUST Faith No More (Slash)
-	35	SCENES FROM THE SECOND STOREY God Machine (Fiction)
26	36	CASUAL SEX IN THE CINEPLEX Sultans Of Ping FC (Rhythm King)
29	37	STARS Simply Red (East West)
28	38	BACK TO FRONT Lionel Richie (Motown)
27	39	GLITTERING PRIZE 81/92 Simple Minds (Virgin)
36	40	O3 Sunscreem (Sony Soho Square)
31	41	NEVERMIND Nirvana (DGC)
34	42	IT'S A SHAME ABOUT RAY Lemonheads (Atlantic)
37	43	UNPLUGGED Eric Clapton (Duck)
32	44	MUSIC FROM THE ITV SERIES INSPECTOR MORSE, VOL. 3 Barrington Pheloung (Virgin)
38	45	THE PRODIGY EXPERIENCE Prodigy (XL Recordings)
42	46	DANGEROUS Michael Jackson (Epic)
-	47	DUOPHONIC Charles & Eddie (Capitol)
-	48	ACHTUNG BABY U2 (Island)
33	49	GREATEST HITS Gloria Estefan (Epic)
39	50	TIMELESS - THE CLASSICS Michael Bolton (Columbia)

27 February 1993

1	1	THE BODYGUARD - SOUNDTRACK Various (Arista)
10	2	AUTOMATIC FOR THE PEOPLE R.E.M. (Warner Bros.)
31	3	WORDS OF LOVE - 22 CLASSIC HITS Buddy Holly & the Crickets (MCA)
-	4	DURAN DURAN Duran Duran (Parlophone)
-	5	WALTHAMSTOW East 17 (London)
12	6	DIVA Annie Lennox (RCA)
13	7	TAKE THAT AND PARTY Take That (RCA)
2	8	PURE CULT - FOR ROCKERS, RAVERS, LOVERS AND SINNERS Cult (Beggars Banquet)
3	9	CONSCIENCE Beloved (East West)
7	10	3 YEARS, 5 MONTHS AND 2 DAYS IN THE LIFE Arrested Development (Cooltempo)
8	11	FUNKY DIVAS En Vogue (East West)
15	12	SO CLOSE Dina Carroll (A&M PM)
11	13	CONNECTED Stereo MCs (Fourth & Broadway)
14	14	GORECKI: SYMPHONY NO. 3 Dawn Upshaw/London Sinfonietta/David Zinman (Elektra Nonesuch)
37	15	STARS Simply Red (East West)
5	16	WANDERING SPIRIT Mick Jagger (Atlantic)
-	17	THE BEST OF VAN MORRISON VOLUME TWO Van Morrison (Polydor)
20	18	LOVE MAKES NO SENSE Alexander O'Neal (Tabu)
46	19	DANGEROUS Michael Jackson (Epic)
47	20	DUOPHONIC Charles & Eddie (Capitol)
4	21	WHERE YOU BEEN Dinosaur Jr. (blanco y negro)
-	22	GREAT EXPECTATIONS Tasmin Archer (EMI)
6	23	STAR Belly (4AD)
30	24	US Peter Gabriel (Realworld)
48	25	ACHTUNG BABY U2 (Island)
9	26	OFF THE GROUND Paul McCartney (Parlophone)
43	27	UNPLUGGED Eric Clapton (Duck)
41	28	NEVERMIND Nirvana (DGC)
19	29	BOSS DRUM Shamen (One Little Indian)
18	30	LIVE - THE WAY WE WALK VOLUME TWO: THE LONGS Genesis (Virgin)
-	31	HORMONALLY YOURS Shakespear's Sister (London)
29	32	POP! - THE FIRST 20 HITS Erasure (Mute)
25	33	GREATEST HITS: 1965-1992 Cher (Geffen)
22	34	INDIAN SUMMER Go West (Chrysalis)
26	35	KEEP THE FAITH Bon Jovi (Jambco)
17	36	THE MADMAN'S RETURN Snap (Logic)
-	37	WELCOME TO WHEREVER YOU ARE INXS (Mercury)
28	38	GOLD - GREATEST HITS Abba (Polydor)
-	39	HEART AND SOUL T'Pau (Virgin)
32	40	LIVE - THE WAY WE WALK VOLUME ONE: THE SHORTS Genesis (Virgin)
38	41	BACK TO FRONT Lionel Richie (Motown)
39	42	GLITTERING PRIZE 81/92 Simple Minds (Virgin)
-	43	INCESTICIDE Nirvana (Geffen)
-	44	ONLY YESTERDAY - THE CARPENTER'S GREATEST HITS Carpenters (A&M)
23	45	HEAD OVER HEELS Various Artists (Telstar)
16	46	JAM Little Angels (Jam)
21	47	DUSK The The (Epic)
-	48	METALLICA Metallica (Vertigo)
24	49	THE VERY BEST OF SISTER SLEDGE 1973-1993 Sister Sledge (Atlantic)
50	50	TIMELESS - THE CLASSICS Michael Bolton (Columbia)

6 March 1993

1	1	THE BODYGUARD - SOUNDTRACK Various (Arista)
2	2	AUTOMATIC FOR THE PEOPLE R.E.M. (Warner Bros.)
5	3	WALTHAMSTOW East 17 (London)
-	4	LEAD VOCALIST Rod Stewart (Warner Bros.)
-	5	SO TOUGH Saint Etienne (Heavenly)
6	6	DIVA Annie Lennox (RCA)
7	7	TAKE THAT AND PARTY Take That (RCA)
-	8	NATIVE TONGUE Poison (EMI)
4	9	DURAN DURAN Duran Duran (Parlophone)
15	10	STARS Simply Red (East West)
-	11	STAIN Living Colour (Stain)
19	12	DANGEROUS Michael Jackson (Epic)
3	13	WORDS OF LOVE - 22 CLASSIC HITS Buddy Holly & the Crickets (MCA)
8	14	PURE CULT - FOR ROCKERS, RAVERS, LOVERS AND SINNERS Cult (Beggars Banquet)
22	15	GREAT EXPECTATIONS Tasmin Archer (EMI)
11	16	FUNKY DIVAS En Vogue (East West)
-	17	LIVE: RIGHT HERE, RIGHT NOW Van Halen (Warner Bros.)
10	18	3 YEARS, 5 MONTHS AND 2 DAYS IN THE LIFE Arrested Development (Cooltempo)
13	19	CONNECTED Stereo MCs (Fourth & Broadway)
14	20	GORECKI: SYMPHONY NO. 3 Dawn Upshaw/London Sinfonietta/David Zinman (Elektra Nonesuch)
24	21	US Peter Gabriel (Realworld)
12	22	SO CLOSE Dina Carroll (A&M PM)
-	23	IF I WAS: THE VERY BEST OF MIDGE URE AND ULTRAVOX Midge Ure & Ultravox (Chrysalis)
-	24	WEIRD'S BAR & GRILL Pop Will Eat Itself (RCA)
29	25	BOSS DRUM Shamen (One Little Indian)
-	26	INGENUE k.d. lang (Sire)
9	27	CONSCIENCE Beloved (East West)
49	28	THE VERY BEST OF SISTER SLEDGE 1973-1993 Sister Sledge (Atlantic)
28	29	NEVERMIND Nirvana (DGC)
-	30	PABLO HONEY Radiohead (Parlophone)
27	31	UNPLUGGED Eric Clapton (Duck)
31	32	HORMONALLY YOURS Shakespear's Sister (London)
32	33	POP! - THE FIRST 20 HITS Erasure (Mute)
16	34	WANDERING SPIRIT Mick Jagger (Atlantic)
33	35	GREATEST HITS: 1965-1992 Cher (Geffen)
25	36	ACHTUNG BABY U2 (Island)
17	37	THE BEST OF VAN MORRISON VOLUME TWO Van Morrison (Polydor)
23	38	STAR Belly (4AD)
30	39	LIVE - THE WAY WE WALK VOLUME TWO: THE LONGS Genesis (Virgin)
-	40	HARVEST MOON Neil Young (Reprise)
48	41	METALLICA Metallica (Vertigo)
38	42	GOLD - GREATEST HITS Abba (Polydor)
36	43	THE MADMAN'S RETURN Snap (Logic)
35	44	KEEP THE FAITH Bon Jovi (Jambco)
34	45	INDIAN SUMMER Go West (Chrysalis)
37	46	WELCOME TO WHEREVER YOU ARE INXS (Mercury)
42	47	GLITTERING PRIZE 81/92 Simple Minds (Virgin)
18	48	LOVE MAKES NO SENSE Alexander O'Neal (Tabu)
20	49	DUOPHONIC Charles & Eddie (Capitol)
26	50	OFF THE GROUND Paul McCartney (Parlophone)

Though, thanks to the three tenors and Nigel Kennedy, classical albums in the chart were no longer a cause of utter wonder, the success of Polish composer Gorecki's relatively obscure *3rd Symphony* was still extraordinary, and a notable tribute to the widening influence of the new nationwide commercial classic radio station, Classic FM, which playlisted the work recurrently.

March 1993

13 March 1993

last week	this week	Title	Artist (Label)
-	1	ARE YOU GONNA GO MY WAY	Lenny Kravitz (Virgin America)
-	2	TEN SUMMONER'S TALES	Sting (A&M)
-	3	WHATEVER YOU SAY, SAY NOTHING	Deacon Blue (Columbia)
1	4	THE BODYGUARD - SOUNDTRACK	Various (Arista)
6	5	DIVA	Annie Lennox (RCA)
2	6	AUTOMATIC FOR THE PEOPLE	R.E.M. (Warner Bros.)
4	7	LEAD VOCALIST	Rod Stewart (Warner Bros.)
31	8	UNPLUGGED	Eric Clapton (Duck)
12	9	DANGEROUS	Michael Jackson (Epic)
23	10	IF I WAS	Midge Ure & Ultravox (Chrysalis)
7	11	TAKE THAT AND PARTY	Take That (RCA)
13	12	WORDS OF LOVE - 22 CLASSIC HITS	Buddy Holly & the Crickets (MCA)
26	13	INGENUE	k.d. lang (Sire)
5	14	SO TOUGH	Saint Etienne (Heavenly)
10	15	STARS	Simply Red (East West)
19	16	CONNECTED	Stereo MCs (Fourth & Broadway)
3	17	WALTHAMSTOW	East 17 (London)
22	18	SO CLOSE	Dina Carroll (A&M PM)
15	19	GREAT EXPECTATIONS	Tasmin Archer (EMI)
9	20	DURAN DURAN	Duran Duran (Parlophone)
8	21	NATIVE TONGUE	Poison (EMI)
11	22	STAIN	Living Colour (Stain)
18	23	3 YEARS, 5 MONTHS AND 2 DAYS IN THE LIFE	Arrested Development (Cooltempo)
16	24	FUNKY DIVAS	En Vogue (East West)
-	25	EMPIRE OF THE SENSELESS	Senseless Things (Epic)
-	26	RAGE AGAINST THE MACHINE	Rage Against The Machine (Epic)
17	27	LIVE: RIGHT HERE, RIGHT NOW	Van Halen (Warner Bros.)
14	28	PURE CULT - FOR ROCKERS, RAVERS, LOVERS AND SINNERS	Cult (Beggars Banquet)
-	29	LIPSTICK ON YOUR COLLAR	Various Artists (PolyGram TV)
20	30	GORECKI: SYMPHONY NO. 3	Dawn Upshaw /London Sinfonietta/DavidZinman (ElektraNonesuch)
25	31	BOSS DRUM	Shamen (One Little Indian)
21	32	US	Peter Gabriel (Realworld)
-	33	THE LIVING LEGEND	Ray Charles (Arcade)
-	34	ALL THE BEST	Leo Sayer (Chrysalis)
28	35	THE VERY BEST OF SISTER SLEDGE 1973-1993	Sister Sledge (Atlantic)
40	36	HARVEST MOON	Neil Young (Reprise)
29	37	NEVERMIND	Nirvana (DGC)
27	38	CONSCIENCE	Beloved (East West)
34	39	WANDERING SPIRIT	Mick Jagger (Atlantic)
35	40	GREATEST HITS: 1965-1992	Cher (Geffen)
-	41	HEAD OVER HEELS	Various Artists (Telstar)
39	42	LIVE - THE WAY WE WALK VOLUME TWO: THE LONGS	Genesis (Virgin)
32	43	HORMONALLY YOURS	Shakespear's Sister (London)
33	44	POP! - THE FIRST 20 HITS	Erasure (Mute)
30	45	PABLO HONEY	Radiohead (Parlophone)
38	46	STAR	Belly (4AD)
36	47	ACHTUNG BABY	U2 (Island)
37	48	THE BEST OF - VOL TWO	Van Morrison (Polydor)
42	49	GOLD - GREATEST HITS	Abba (Polydor)
43	50	THE MADMAN'S RETURN	Snap (Logic)

20 March 1993

last week	this week	Title	Artist (Label)
1	1	ARE YOU GONNA GO MY WAY	Lenny Kravitz (Virgin America)
2	2	TEN SUMMONER'S TALES	Sting (A&M)
-	3	SONGS FROM THE RAIN	Hothouse Flowers (London)
8	4	UNPLUGGED	Eric Clapton (Duck)
-	5	THE DARK SIDE OF THE MOON - 20TH ANNIVERSARY	Pink Floyd (EMI)
3	6	WHATEVER YOU SAY, SAY NOTHING	Deacon Blue (Columbia)
4	7	THE BODYGUARD - SOUNDTRACK	Various (Arista)
-	8	FRANK BLACK	Frank Black (4AD)
6	9	AUTOMATIC FOR THE PEOPLE	R.E.M. (Warner Bros.)
13	10	INGENUE	k.d. lang (Sire)
5	11	DIVA	Annie Lennox (RCA)
7	12	LEAD VOCALIST	Rod Stewart (Warner Bros.)
-	13	OTHER VOICES, OTHER ROOMS	Nanci Griffith (MCA)
9	14	DANGEROUS	Michael Jackson (Epic)
18	15	SO CLOSE	Dina Carroll (A&M PM)
11	16	TAKE THAT AND PARTY	Take That (RCA)
29	17	LIPSTICK ON YOUR COLLAR	Various Artists (PolyGram TV)
19	18	GREAT EXPECTATIONS	Tasmin Archer (EMI)
10	19	IF I WAS: THE VERY BEST OF MIDGE URE AND ULTRAVOX	Midge Ure & Ultravox (Chrysalis)
15	20	STARS	Simply Red (East West)
16	21	CONNECTED	Stereo MCs (Fourth & Broadway)
17	22	WALTHAMSTOW	East 17 (London)
12	23	WORDS OF LOVE - 22 CLASSIC HITS	Buddy Holly & the Crickets (MCA)
24	24	FUNKY DIVAS	En Vogue (East West)
23	25	3 YEARS, 5 MONTHS AND 2 DAYS IN THE LIFE	Arrested Development (Cooltempo)
26	26	RAGE AGAINST THE MACHINE	Rage Against The Machine (Epic)
20	27	DURAN DURAN	Duran Duran (Parlophone)
28	28	PURE CULT ...	Cult (Beggars Banquet)
-	29	THEIR GREATEST HITS	Hot Chocolate (EMI)
-	30	HIGHER AND HIGHER	Heaven 17 (Virgin)
22	31	STAIN	Living Colour (Stain)
30	32	GORECKI: SYMPHONY NO. 3	Dawn Upshaw/London Sinfonietta/David Zinman (Elektra Nonesuch)
31	33	BOSS DRUM	Shamen (One Little Indian)
14	34	SO TOUGH	Saint Etienne (Heavenly)
37	35	NEVERMIND	Nirvana (DGC)
-	36	ROUND MIDNIGHT	Elkie Brooks (Castle)
32	37	US	Peter Gabriel (Realworld)
34	38	ALL THE BEST	Leo Sayer (Chrysalis)
-	39	NOW AIN'T THE TIME FOR YOUR TEARS	Wendy James (MCA)
38	40	CONSCIENCE	Beloved (East West)
40	41	GREATEST HITS: 1965-1992	Cher (Geffen)
44	42	POP! - THE FIRST 20 HITS	Erasure (Mute)
35	43	THE VERY BEST OF SISTER SLEDGE 1973-1993	Sister Sledge (Atlantic)
36	44	HARVEST MOON	Neil Young (Reprise)
-	45	FEELS LIKE RAIN	Buddy Guy (Silvertone)
-	46	TIMELESS (THE CLASSICS)	Michael Bolton (Columbia)
-	47	THE ULTIMATE ...	Glenn Miller (Telstar)
-	48	OUT OF TIME	R.E.M. (Warner Bros.)
41	49	HEAD OVER HEELS	Various Artists (Telstar)
33	50	THE LIVING LEGEND	Ray Charles (Arcade)

27 March 1993

last week	this week	Title	Artist (Label)
-	1	COVERDALE/PAGE	Coverdale/Page (EMI)
1	2	ARE YOU GONNA GO MY WAY	Lenny Kravitz (Virgin America)
4	3	UNPLUGGED	Eric Clapton (Duck)
5	4	THE DARK SIDE OF THE MOON - 20TH ANNIVERSARY	Pink Floyd (EMI)
10	5	INGENUE	k.d. lang (Sire)
7	6	THE BODYGUARD - SOUNDTRACK	Various (Arista)
2	7	TEN SUMMONER'S TALES	Sting (A&M)
-	8	AMAZING THINGS	Runrig (Chrysalis)
3	9	SONGS FROM THE RAIN	Hothouse Flowers (London)
9	10	AUTOMATIC FOR THE PEOPLE	R.E.M. (Warner Bros.)
11	11	DIVA	Annie Lennox (RCA)
17	12	LIPSTICK ON YOUR COLLAR	Various Artists (PolyGram TV)
14	13	DANGEROUS	Michael Jackson (Epic)
15	14	SO CLOSE	Dina Carroll (A&M PM)
12	15	LEAD VOCALIST	Rod Stewart (Warner Bros.)
29	16	THEIR GREATEST HITS	Hot Chocolate (EMI)
6	17	WHATEVER YOU SAY, SAY NOTHING	Deacon Blue (Columbia)
20	18	STARS	Simply Red (East West)
-	19	BITTER SWEET & TWISTED	Quireboys (Parlophone)
8	20	FRANK BLACK	Frank Black (4AD)
13	21	OTHER VOICES, OTHER ROOMS	Nanci Griffith (MCA)
26	22	RAGE AGAINST THE MACHINE	Rage Against The Machine (Epic)
16	23	TAKE THAT AND PARTY	Take That (RCA)
24	24	FUNKY DIVAS	En Vogue (East West)
21	25	CONNECTED	Stereo MCs (Fourth & Broadway)
25	26	3 YEARS, 5 MONTHS AND 2 DAYS IN THE LIFE	Arrested Development (Cooltempo)
47	27	THE ULTIMATE ...	Glenn Miller (Telstar)
-	28	THE VERY BEST OF ...	Randy Crawford (Dino)
18	29	GREAT EXPECTATIONS	Tasmin Archer (EMI)
22	30	WALTHAMSTOW	East 17 (London)
23	31	WORDS OF LOVE - 22 CLASSIC HITS	Buddy Holly & the Crickets (MCA)
27	32	DURAN DURAN	Duran Duran (Parlophone)
19	33	IF I WAS: THE VERY BEST OF MIDGE URE AND ULTRAVOX	Midge Ure & Ultravox (Chrysalis)
28	34	PURE CULT - FOR ROCKERS, RAVERS, LOVERS AND SINNERS	Cult (Beggars Banquet)
30	35	HIGHER AND HIGHER - THE BEST OF HEAVEN 17	Heaven 17 (Virgin)
-	36	THE GREATEST HITS	Boney M (Telstar)
35	37	NEVERMIND	Nirvana (DGC)
32	38	GORECKI: SYMPHONY NO. 3	Dawn Upshaw/London Sinfonietta/David Zinman (Elektra Nonesuch)
33	39	BOSS DRUM	Shamen (One Little Indian)
34	40	SO TOUGH	Saint Etienne (Heavenly)
-	41	DIRT	Alice In Chains (Columbia)
-	42	MERCURY	American Music Club (Virgin)
48	43	OUT OF TIME	R.E.M. (Warner Bros.)
41	44	GREATEST HITS: 1965-1992	Cher (Geffen)
36	45	ROUND MIDNIGHT	Elkie Brooks (Castle)
46	46	TIMELESS (THE CLASSICS)	Michael Bolton (Columbia)
38	47	ALL THE BEST	Leo Sayer (Chrysalis)
37	48	US	Peter Gabriel (Realworld)
-	49	EROTICA	Madonna (Maverick)
-	50	777	System (Big Life)

Lenny Kravitz, a writer/singer/guitarist whose attitude and mode of dress seemed straight out of 1967, with a firm nod at Jimi Hendrix, nonetheless shaped up in early 1993 as one of the likely bright musical stars of the 90s, his material mixing traditional rock and R&B influences and eschewing modern computer-generations in favour of "real" instruments in a way which gave him an ironically fresh flavour.

3 April 1993

last week	this week	Title	Artist
-	1	SONGS OF FAITH AND DEVOTION	Depeche Mode (Mute)
-	2	A REAL LIVE ONE	Iron Maiden (EMI)
16	3	THEIR GREATEST HITS	Hot Chocolate (EMI)
1	4	COVERDALE/PAGE	Coverdale/Page (EMI)
2	5	ARE YOU GONNA GO MY WAY	Lenny Kravitz (Virgin America)
8	6	AMAZING THINGS	Runrig (Chrysalis)
3	7	UNPLUGGED	Eric Clapton (Duck)
6	8	THE BODYGUARD - SOUNDTRACK	Various (Arista)
5	9	INGENUE	k.d. lang (Sire)
-	10	TAXI	Bryan Ferry (Virgin)
-	11	THE BLISS ALBUM...	PM Dawn (Gee Street)
10	12	AUTOMATIC FOR THE PEOPLE	R.E.M. (Warner Bros.)
12	13	LIPSTICK ON YOUR COLLAR	Various Artists (PolyGram TV)
7	14	TEN SUMMONER'S TALES	Sting (A&M)
4	15	THE DARK SIDE OF THE MOON - 20TH ANNIVERSARY	Pink Floyd (EMI)
11	16	DIVA	Annie Lennox (RCA)
-	17	HOME INVASION	Ice-T (Rhyme Syndicate)
28	18	THE VERY BEST OF...	Randy Crawford (Dino)
27	19	THE ULTIMATE...	Glenn Miller (Telstar)
-	20	THE BUFFALO SKINNERS	Big Country (Compulsion)
14	21	SO CLOSE	Dina Carroll (A&M PM)
13	22	DANGEROUS	Michael Jackson (Epic)
15	23	LEAD VOCALIST	Rod Stewart (Warner Bros.)
9	24	SONGS FROM THE RAIN	Hothouse Flowers (London)
18	25	STARS	Simply Red (East West)
23	26	TAKE THAT AND PARTY	Take That (RCA)
36	27	THE GREATEST HITS	Boney M (Telstar)
22	28	RAGE AGAINST THE MACHINE	Rage Against The Machine (Epic)
17	29	WHATEVER YOU SAY, SAY NOTHING	Deacon Blue (Columbia)
26	30	3 YEARS, 5 MONTHS AND 2 DAYS IN THE LIFE	Arrested Development (Cooltempo)
30	31	WALTHAMSTOW	East 17 (London)
24	32	FUNKY DIVAS	En Vogue (East West)
25	33	CONNECTED	Stereo MCs (Fourth & Broadway)
19	34	BITTER SWEET & TWISTED	Quireboys (Parlophone)
45	35	ROUND MIDNIGHT	Elkie Brooks (Castle)
39	36	BOSS DRUM	Shamen (One Little Indian)
20	37	FRANK BLACK	Frank Black (4AD)
-	38	THE AIR THAT I BREATHE - GREATEST HITS	Hollies (EMI)
29	39	GREAT EXPECTATIONS	Tasmin Archer (EMI)
31	40	WORDS OF LOVE - 22 CLASSIC HITS	Buddy Holly & the Crickets (MCA)
32	41	DURAN DURAN	Duran Duran (Parlophone)
33	42	IF I WAS: THE VERY BEST OF MIDGE URE AND ULTRAVOX	Midge Ure & Ultravox (Chrysalis)
21	43	OTHER VOICES, OTHER ROOMS	Nanci Griffith (MCA)
42	44	MERCURY	American Music Club (Virgin)
38	45	GORECKI: SYMPHONY NO. 3	Dawn Upshaw/London Sinfonietta/David Zinman (Elektra Nonesuch)
-	46	GOLD - GREATEST HITS	Abba (Polydor)
-	47	HIDDEN TREASURES	Barry Manilow (Arista)
-	48	AMERICA'S LEAST WANTED	Ugly Kid Joe (Vertigo)
35	49	HIGHER AND HIGHER	Heaven 17 (Virgin)
41	50	DIRT	Alice In Chains (Columbia)

10 April 1993

last week	this week	Title	Artist
-	1	SUEDE	Suede (Nude)
1	2	SONGS OF FAITH AND DEVOTION	Depeche Mode (Mute)
10	3	TAXI	Bryan Ferry (Virgin)
3	4	THEIR GREATEST HITS	Hot Chocolate (EMI)
5	5	ARE YOU GONNA GO MY WAY	Lenny Kravitz (Virgin America)
8	6	THE BODYGUARD - SOUNDTRACK	Various (Arista)
7	7	UNPLUGGED	Eric Clapton (Duck)
18	8	THE VERY BEST OF...	Randy Crawford (Dino)
12	9	AUTOMATIC FOR THE PEOPLE	R.E.M. (Warner Bros.)
16	10	DIVA	Annie Lennox (RCA)
9	11	INGENUE	k.d. lang (Sire)
13	12	LIPSTICK ON YOUR COLLAR	Various Artists (PolyGram TV)
2	13	A REAL LIVE ONE	Iron Maiden (EMI)
11	14	THE BLISS ALBUM...	PM Dawn (Gee Street)
4	15	COVERDALE/PAGE	Coverdale/Page (EMI)
14	16	TEN SUMMONER'S TALES	Sting (A&M)
21	17	SO CLOSE	Dina Carroll (A&M PM)
-	18	COVER SHOT	David Essex (PolyGram TV)
30	19	3 YEARS, 5 MONTHS AND 2 DAYS IN THE LIFE	Arrested Development (Cooltempo)
-	20	THE LOVE OF HOPELESS CAUSES	New Model Army (Epic)
15	21	THE DARK SIDE OF THE MOON - 20TH ANNIVERSARY	Pink Floyd (EMI)
17	22	HOME INVASION	Ice-T (Rhyme Syndicate)
22	23	DANGEROUS	Michael Jackson (Epic)
6	24	AMAZING THINGS	Runrig (Chrysalis)
25	25	STARS	Simply Red (East West)
-	26	NUMBER ONE	Felix (deConstruction)
27	27	THE GREATEST HITS	Boney M (Telstar)
-	28	LABOURS OF LOVE - THE BEST OF HUE AND CRY	Hue & Cry (Circa)
38	29	THE AIR THAT I BREATHE - GREATEST HITS	Hollies (EMI)
39	30	GREAT EXPECTATIONS	Tasmin Archer (EMI)
28	31	RAGE AGAINST THE MACHINE	Rage Against The Machine (Epic)
41	32	DURAN DURAN	Duran Duran (Parlophone)
31	33	WALTHAMSTOW	East 17 (London)
23	34	LEAD VOCALIST	Rod Stewart (Warner Bros.)
19	35	THE ULTIMATE...	Glenn Miller (Telstar)
20	36	THE BUFFALO SKINNERS	Big Country (Compulsion)
29	37	WHATEVER YOU SAY, SAY NOTHING	Deacon Blue (Columbia)
32	38	FUNKY DIVAS	En Vogue (East West)
-	39	GREATEST HITS	Sheep On Drugs (Transglobal)
-	40	UNPLUGGED	Arrested Development (EMI)
26	41	TAKE THAT AND PARTY	Take That (RCA)
48	42	AMERICA'S LEAST WANTED	Ugly Kid Joe (Vertigo)
33	43	CONNECTED	Stereo MCs (Fourth & Broadway)
24	44	SONGS FROM THE RAIN	Hothouse Flowers (London)
-	45	PLEASE YOURSELF	Bananarama (London)
43	46	OTHER VOICES, OTHER ROOMS	Nanci Griffith (MCA)
47	47	HIDDEN TREASURES	Barry Manilow (Arista)
45	48	GORECKI: SYMPHONY NO. 3	Dawn Upshaw/London Sinfonietta/David Zinman (Elektra Nonesuch)
-	49	NURSE	Therapy? (A&M)
-	50	THE NEW STARLIGHT EXPRESS	Andrew Lloyd Webber (Really Useful)

17 April 1993

last week	this week	Title	Artist
1	1	SUEDE	Suede (Nude)
-	2	BLACK TIE WHITE NOISE	David Bowie (Savage)
2	3	SONGS OF FAITH AND DEVOTION	Depeche Mode (Mute)
-	4	POWERTRIPPIN'	Almighty (Powertrippin')
-	5	BEASTER	Sugar (Creation)
5	6	ARE YOU GONNA GO MY WAY	Lenny Kravitz (Virgin America)
4	7	THEIR GREATEST HITS	Hot Chocolate (EMI)
7	8	UNPLUGGED	Eric Clapton (Duck)
9	9	AUTOMATIC FOR THE PEOPLE	R.E.M. (Warner Bros.)
10	10	DIVA	Annie Lennox (RCA)
17	11	SO CLOSE	Dina Carroll (A&M PM)
18	12	COVER SHOT	David Essex (PolyGram TV)
12	13	LIPSTICK ON YOUR COLLAR	Various (PolyGram TV)
6	14	THE BODYGUARD - SOUNDTRACK	Various (Arista)
8	15	THE VERY BEST OF...	Randy Crawford (Dino)
3	16	TAXI	Bryan Ferry (Virgin)
11	17	INGENUE	k.d. lang (Sire)
16	18	TEN SUMMONER'S TALES	Sting (A&M)
27	19	THE GREATEST HITS	Boney M (Telstar)
19	20	3 YEARS, 5 MONTHS AND 2 DAYS IN THE LIFE	Arrested Development (Cooltempo)
29	21	THE AIR THAT I BREATHE - GREATEST HITS	Hollies (EMI)
23	22	DANGEROUS	Michael Jackson (Epic)
15	23	COVERDALE/PAGE	Coverdale/Page (EMI)
13	24	A REAL LIVE ONE	Iron Maiden (EMI)
14	25	THE BLISS ALBUM...?	PM Dawn (Gee Street)
21	26	THE DARK SIDE OF THE MOON - 20TH ANNIVERSARY	Pink Floyd (EMI)
-	27	GLAD ALL OVER AGAIN	Dave Clark Five (EMI)
41	28	TAKE THAT AND PARTY	Take That (RCA)
-	29	WRESTLEMANIA	WWF Superstars (Arista)
22	30	HOME INVASION	Ice-T (Rhyme Syndicate)
-	31	THE SINGLES COLLECTION	Bluebells (London)
26	32	NUMBER ONE	Felix (deConstruction)
30	33	GREAT EXPECTATIONS	Tasmin Archer (EMI)
31	34	RAGE AGAINST THE MACHINE	Rage Against The Machine (Epic)
25	35	STARS	Simply Red (East West)
-	36	LEONARD BERNSTEIN'S WEST SIDE STORY	Various Artists (IMG)
20	37	THE LOVE OF HOPELESS CAUSES	New Model Army (Epic)
28	38	LABOURS OF LOVE - THE BEST OF HUE AND CRY	Hue & Cry (Circa)
33	39	WALTHAMSTOW	East 17 (London)
32	40	DURAN DURAN	Duran Duran (Parlophone)
38	41	FUNKY DIVAS	En Vogue (East West)
40	42	UNPLUGGED	Arrested Development (EMI)
42	43	AMERICA'S LEAST WANTED	Ugly Kid Joe (Vertigo)
35	44	THE ULTIMATE GLENN MILLER	Glenn Miller (Telstar)
-	45	GREATEST HITS	Gloria Estefan (Epic)
48	46	GORECKI: SYMPHONY NO. 3	Dawn Upshaw/London Sinfonietta/David Zinman (Elektra Nonesuch)
34	47	LEAD VOCALIST	Rod Stewart (Warner Bros.)
37	48	WHATEVER YOU SAY, SAY NOTHING	Deacon Blue (Columbia)
43	49	CONNECTED	Stereo MCs (Fourth & Broadway)
24	50	AMAZING THINGS	Runrig (Chrysalis)

Coverdale/Page were, as their name suggests, a collaboration between David Coverdale, the former lead vocalist of Deep Purple and Whitesnake, and Jimmy Page, once the guitarist with Led Zeppelin and role model to a whole world of heavy-style axe-wielders. Many expected a tired recreation of Zeppelin, with Coverdale in the Robert Plant role, but their album won both critical approval and big sales.

April – May 1993

24 April 1993

last week	this week	Title	Artist
2	1	BLACK TIE WHITE NOISE	David Bowie (Savage)
-	2	IN CONCERT - MTV UNPLUGGED	Bruce Springsteen (Columbia)
1	3	SUEDE	Suede (Nude)
9	4	AUTOMATIC FOR THE PEOPLE	R.E.M. (Warner Bros.)
12	5	COVER SHOT	David Essex (PolyGram TV)
14	6	THE BODYGUARD - SOUNDTRACK	Various (Arista)
20	7	3 YEARS, 5 MONTHS AND 2 DAYS IN THE LIFE	Arrested Development (Cooltempo)
10	8	DIVA	Annie Lennox (RCA)
4	9	POWERTRIPPIN'	Almighty (Powertrippin')
5	10	BEASTER	Sugar (Creation)
8	11	UNPLUGGED	Eric Clapton (Duck)
-	12	SAN FRANCISCO DAYS	Chris Isaak (Reprise)
18	13	TEN SUMMONER'S TALES	Sting (A&M)
6	14	ARE YOU GONNA GO MY WAY	Lenny Kravitz (Virgin America)
3	15	SONGS OF FAITH AND DEVOTION	Depeche Mode (Mute)
11	16	SO CLOSE	Dina Carroll (A&M PM)
7	17	THEIR GREATEST HITS	Hot Chocolate (EMI)
28	18	TAKE THAT AND PARTY	Take That (RCA)
17	19	INGENUE	k.d. lang (Sire)
13	20	LIPSTICK ON YOUR COLLAR	Various (PolyGram TV)
15	21	THE VERY BEST OF...	Randy Crawford (Dino)
19	22	THE GREATEST HITS	Boney M (Telstar)
39	23	WALTHAMSTOW	East 17 (London)
40	24	DURAN DURAN	Duran Duran (Parlophone)
21	25	THE AIR THAT I BREATHE - GREATEST HITS	Hollies (EMI)
46	26	GORECKI: SYMPHONY NO. 3	Dawn Upshaw/London Sinfonietta/David Zinman (Elektra Nonesuch)
22	27	DANGEROUS	Michael Jackson (Epic)
45	28	GREATEST HITS	Gloria Estefan (Epic)
16	29	TAXI	Bryan Ferry (Virgin)
31	30	THE SINGLES COLLECTION	Bluebells (London)
29	31	WRESTLEMANIA	WWF Superstars (Arista)
23	32	COVERDALE/PAGE	Coverdale/Page (EMI)
48	33	WHATEVER YOU SAY, SAY NOTHING	Deacon Blue (Columbia)
26	34	THE DARK SIDE OF THE MOON - 20TH ANNIVERSARY	Pink Floyd (EMI)
27	35	GLAD ALL OVER AGAIN	Dave Clark Five (EMI)
36	36	STARS	Simply Red (East West)
33	37	GREAT EXPECTATIONS	Tasmin Archer (EMI)
34	38	RAGE AGAINST THE MACHINE	Rage Against The Machine (Epic)
-	39	XTRA NAKED	Shabba Ranks (Epic)
-	40	DIANA ROSS LIVE...	Diana Ross (EMI)
24	41	A REAL LIVE ONE	Iron Maiden (EMI)
-	42	THE SINGLES COLLECTION	Connie Francis (PolyGram TV)
43	43	AMERICA'S LEAST WANTED	Ugly Kid Joe (Vertigo)
36	44	LEONARD BERNSTEIN'S WEST SIDE STORY	Various Artists (IMG)
25	45	THE BLISS ALBUM...? (VIBRATIONS AND LOVE AND ANGER AND THE PONDERANCE OF LIFE AND EXISTENCE)	PM Dawn (Gee Street)
30	46	HOME INVASION	Ice-T (Rhyme Syndicate)
41	47	FUNKY DIVAS	En Vogue (East West)
38	48	LABOURS OF LOVE	Hue & Cry (Circa)
-	49	CONSCIENCE	Beloved (East West)
49	50	CONNECTED	Stereo MCs (Fourth & Broadway)

1 May 1993

last week	this week	Title	Artist
-	1	GET A GRIP	Aerosmith (Geffen)
-	2	CLIFF RICHARD - THE ALBUM	Cliff Richard (EMI)
4	3	AUTOMATIC FOR THE PEOPLE	R.E.M. (Warner Bros.)
1	4	BLACK TIE WHITE NOISE	David Bowie (Savage)
5	5	COVER SHOT	David Essex (PolyGram TV)
2	6	IN CONCERT - MTV UNPLUGGED	Bruce Springsteen (Columbia)
6	7	THE BODYGUARD - SOUNDTRACK	Various (Arista)
3	8	SUEDE	Suede (Nude)
7	9	3 YEARS, 5 MONTHS AND 2 DAYS IN THE LIFE	Arrested Development (Cooltempo)
8	10	DIVA	Annie Lennox (RCA)
16	11	SO CLOSE	Dina Carroll (A&M PM)
23	12	WALTHAMSTOW	East 17 (London)
24	13	DURAN DURAN	Duran Duran (Parlophone)
13	14	TEN SUMMONER'S TALES	Sting (A&M)
11	15	UNPLUGGED	Eric Clapton (Duck)
18	16	TAKE THAT AND PARTY	Take That (RCA)
12	17	SAN FRANCISCO DAYS	Chris Isaak (Reprise)
14	18	ARE YOU GONNA GO MY WAY	Lenny Kravitz (Virgin America)
42	19	THE SINGLES COLLECTION	Connie Francis (PolyGram TV)
28	20	GREATEST HITS	Gloria Estefan (Epic)
31	21	WRESTLEMANIA	WWF Superstars (Arista)
19	22	INGENUE	k.d. lang (Sire)
27	23	DANGEROUS	Michael Jackson (Epic)
17	24	THEIR GREATEST HITS	Hot Chocolate (EMI)
-	25	EARTH AND SUN AND MOON	Midnight Oil (Columbia)
22	26	THE GREATEST HITS	Boney M (Telstar)
-	27	JURASSIC SHIFT	Ozric Tentacles (Dovetail)
15	28	SONGS OF FAITH AND DEVOTION	Depeche Mode (Mute)
21	29	THE VERY BEST OF...	Randy Crawford (Dino)
20	30	LIPSTICK ON YOUR COLLAR	Various Artists (PolyGram TV)
25	31	THE AIR THAT I BREATHE - GREATEST HITS	Hollies (EMI)
30	32	THE SINGLES COLLECTION	Bluebells (London)
9	33	POWERTRIPPIN'	Almighty (Powertrippin')
10	34	BEASTER	Sugar (Creation)
35	35	GLAD ALL OVER AGAIN	Dave Clark Five (EMI)
36	36	STARS	Simply Red (East West)
32	37	COVERDALE/PAGE	Coverdale/Page (EMI)
38	38	RAGE AGAINST THE MACHINE	Rage Against The Machine (Epic)
39	39	XTRA NAKED	Shabba Ranks (Epic)
43	40	AMERICA'S LEAST WANTED	Ugly Kid Joe (Vertigo)
-	41	MASTERPIECES - THE ESSENTIAL FLUTE OF JAMES GALWAY	James Galway (RCA Red Seal)
29	42	TAXI	Bryan Ferry (Virgin)
26	43	GORECKI: SYMPHONY NO. 3	Dawn Upshaw/London Sinfonietta/David Zinman (Elektra Nonesuch)
47	44	FUNKY DIVAS	En Vogue (East West)
50	45	CONNECTED	Stereo MCs (Fourth & Broadway)
40	46	DIANA ROSS LIVE...	Diana Ross (EMI)
33	47	WHATEVER YOU SAY, SAY NOTHING	Deacon Blue (Columbia)
37	48	GREAT EXPECTATIONS	Tasmin Archer (EMI)
34	49	THE DARK SIDE OF THE MOON - 20TH ANNIVERSARY	Pink Floyd (EMI)
-	50	OUT OF TIME	R.E.M. (Warner Bros.)

8 May 1993

last week	this week	Title	Artist
-	1	BANG!	World Party (Ensign)
-	2	RID OF ME	PJ Harvey (Island)
2	3	CLIFF RICHARD - THE ALBUM	Cliff Richard (EMI)
1	4	GET A GRIP	Aerosmith (Geffen)
3	5	AUTOMATIC FOR THE PEOPLE	R.E.M. (Warner Bros.)
7	6	THE BODYGUARD - SOUNDTRACK	Various (Arista)
14	7	TEN SUMMONER'S TALES	Sting (A&M)
13	8	DURAN DURAN	Duran Duran (Parlophone)
11	9	SO CLOSE	Dina Carroll (A&M PM)
-	10	THE INFOTAINMENT SCAN	Fall (Cog Sinister)
5	11	COVER SHOT	David Essex (PolyGram TV)
15	12	UNPLUGGED	Eric Clapton (Duck)
4	13	BLACK TIE WHITE NOISE	David Bowie (Savage)
6	14	IN CONCERT - MTV UNPLUGGED	Bruce Springsteen (Columbia)
9	15	3 YEARS, 5 MONTHS AND 2 DAYS IN THE LIFE	Arrested Development (Cooltempo)
-	16	PORNO FOR PYROS	Porno For Pyros (Warner Bros.)
10	17	DIVA	Annie Lennox (RCA)
8	18	SUEDE	Suede (Nude)
19	19	THE SINGLES COLLECTION	Connie Francis (PolyGram TV)
18	20	ARE YOU GONNA GO MY WAY	Lenny Kravitz (Virgin America)
28	21	SONGS OF FAITH AND DEVOTION	Depeche Mode (Mute)
12	22	WALTHAMSTOW	East 17 (London)
20	23	GREATEST HITS	Gloria Estefan (Epic)
-	24	TEN SHORT SONGS ABOUT LOVE	Gary Clark (Circa)
22	25	INGENUE	k.d. lang (Sire)
16	26	TAKE THAT AND PARTY	Take That (RCA)
17	27	SAN FRANCISCO DAYS	Chris Isaak (Reprise)
21	28	WRESTLEMANIA	WWF Superstars (Arista)
29	29	THE VERY BEST OF ...	Randy Crawford (Dino)
35	30	GLAD ALL OVER AGAIN	Dave Clark Five (EMI)
-	31	METAL WORKS 73-93	Judas Priest (Columbia)
47	32	WHATEVER YOU SAY, SAY NOTHING	Deacon Blue (Columbia)
26	33	THE GREATEST HITS	Boney M (Telstar)
-	34	FOREVER	Cranes (Dedicated)
27	35	JURASSIC SHIFT	Ozric Tentacles (Dovetail)
-	36	HARBOR LIGHTS	Bruce Hornsby (RCA)
38	37	RAGE AGAINST THE MACHINE	Rage Against The Machine (Epic)
25	38	EARTH AND SUN AND MOON	Midnight Oil (Columbia)
24	39	THEIR GREATEST HITS	Hot Chocolate (EMI)
36	40	STARS	Simply Red (East West)
-	41	EXPOSED	Vince Neil (Warner Bros.)
23	42	DANGEROUS	Michael Jackson (Epic)
41	43	MASTERPIECES - THE ESSENTIAL FLUTE OF JAMES GALWAY	James Galway (RCA Red Seal)
30	44	LIPSTICK ON YOUR COLLAR	Various Artists (PolyGram TV)
32	45	THE SINGLES COLLECTION	Bluebells (London)
39	46	XTRA NAKED	Shabba Ranks (Epic)
31	47	THE AIR THAT I BREATHE - GREATEST HITS	Hollies (EMI)
40	48	AMERICA'S LEAST WANTED	Ugly Kid Joe (Vertigo)
37	49	COVERDALE/PAGE	Coverdale/Page (EMI)
34	50	BEASTER	Sugar (Creation)

After some years hiding away in the band format of Tin Machine (to most people's continued bemusement), David Bowie emerged once again as a soloist with a new recording deal - although after the release and initial chart success of *Black Tie, White Noise*, this new career move would suffer a setback when the label to which he had signed (in the US), collapsed and went out of business.

May 1993

15 May 1993

last	this	title	artist
-	1	REPUBLIC	New Order (London)
5	2	AUTOMATIC FOR THE PEOPLE	R.E.M. (Warner Bros.)
-	3	SYMPHONY OR DAMN	Terence Trent D'Arby (Columbia)
1	4	BANG!	World Party (Ensign)
7	5	TEN SUMMONER'S TALES	Sting (A&M)
6	6	THE BODYGUARD - SOUNDTRACK	Various (Arista)
3	7	CLIFF RICHARD - THE ALBUM	Cliff Richard (EMI)
2	8	RID OF ME	PJ Harvey (Island)
9	9	SO CLOSE	Dina Carroll (A&M PM)
8	10	DURAN DURAN	Duran Duran (Parlophone)
4	11	GET A GRIP	Aerosmith (Geffen)
12	12	UNPLUGGED	Eric Clapton (Duck)
-	13	BANBA	Clannad (RCA)
21	14	SONGS OF FAITH AND DEVOTION	Depeche Mode (Mute)
15	15	3 YEARS, 5 MONTHS AND 2 DAYS IN THE LIFE	Arrested Development (Cooltempo)
17	16	DIVA	Annie Lennox (RCA)
20	17	ARE YOU GONNA GO MY WAY	Lenny Kravitz (Virgin America)
14	18	IN CONCERT - MTV UNPLUGGED	Bruce Springsteen (Columbia)
26	19	TAKE THAT AND PARTY	Take That (RCA)
25	20	INGENUE	k.d. lang (Sire)
11	21	COVER SHOT	David Essex (PolyGram TV)
37	22	RAGE AGAINST THE MACHINE	Rage Against The Machine (Epic)
18	23	SUEDE	Suede (Nude)
-	24	BREATHLESS	Kenny G (Arista)
13	25	BLACK TIE WHITE NOISE	David Bowie (Savage)
10	26	THE INFOTAINMENT SCAN	Fall (Cog Sinister)
22	27	WALTHAMSTOW	East 17 (London)
23	28	GREATEST HITS	Gloria Estefan (Epic)
16	29	PORNO FOR PYROS	Porno For Pyros (Warner Bros.)
19	30	THE SINGLES COLLECTION	Connie Francis (PolyGram TV)
40	31	STARS	Simply Red (East West)
-	32	TESTAMENT '93	Inner City (Virgin)
30	33	GLAD ALL OVER AGAIN	Dave Clark Five (EMI)
48	34	AMERICA'S LEAST WANTED	Ugly Kid Joe (Vertigo)
24	35	TEN SHORT SONGS ABOUT LOVE	Gary Clark (Circa)
-	36	SHADOWS IN THE NIGHT	Shadows (PolyGram TV)
36	37	HARBOR LIGHTS	Bruce Hornsby (RCA)
29	38	THE VERY BEST OF...	Randy Crawford (Dino)
27	39	SAN FRANCISCO DAYS	Chris Isaak (Reprise)
-	40	I'VE SEEN EVERYTHING	Trash Can Sinatras (Go! Discs)
28	41	WRESTLEMANIA	WWF Superstars (Arista)
33	42	THE GREATEST HITS	Boney M (Telstar)
42	43	DANGEROUS	Michael Jackson (Epic)
46	44	XTRA NAKED	Shabba Ranks (Epic)
-	45	MORE UNCHARTERED HEIGHTS OF DISGRACE	Dogs D'Amour (China)
32	46	WHATEVER YOU SAY, SAY NOTHING	Deacon Blue (Columbia)
31	47	METAL WORKS 73-93	Judas Priest (Columbia)
35	48	JURASSIC SHIFT	Ozric Tentacles (Dovetail)
47	49	THE AIR THAT I BREATHE - GREATEST HITS	Hollies (EMI)
39	50	THEIR GREATEST HITS	Hot Chocolate (EMI)

22 May 1993

last	this	title	artist
-	1	ON THE NIGHT	Dire Straits (Vertigo)
2	2	AUTOMATIC FOR THE PEOPLE	R.E.M. (Warner Bros.)
1	3	REPUBLIC	New Order (London)
-	4	NO LIMITS	2 Unlimited (PWL Continental)
-	5	BEETHOVEN WAS DEAF	Morrissey (HMV)
13	6	BANBA	Clannad (RCA)
3	7	SYMPHONY OR DAMN	Terence Trent D'Arby (Columbia)
5	8	TEN SUMMONER'S TALES	Sting (A&M)
-	9	BLUES ALIVE	Gary Moore (Virgin)
6	10	THE BODYGUARD - SOUNDTRACK	Various Artists (Arista)
9	11	SO CLOSE	Dina Carroll (A&M PM)
4	12	BANG!	World Party (Ensign)
10	13	DURAN DURAN	Duran Duran (Parlophone)
-	14	HOME MOVIES - THE BEST OF...	Everything But The Girl (blanco y negro)
-	15	MODERN LIFE IS RUBBISH	Blur (Food)
24	16	BREATHLESS	Kenny G (Arista)
17	17	ARE YOU GONNA GO MY WAY	Lenny Kravitz (Virgin America)
7	18	CLIFF RICHARD - THE ALBUM	Cliff Richard (EMI)
-	19	SPILT MILK	Jellyfish (Charisma)
12	20	UNPLUGGED	Eric Clapton (Duck)
22	21	RAGE AGAINST THE MACHINE	Rage Against The Machine (Epic)
11	22	GET A GRIP	Aerosmith (Geffen)
14	23	SONGS OF FAITH AND DEVOTION	Depeche Mode (Mute)
16	24	DIVA	Annie Lennox (RCA)
36	25	SHADOWS IN THE NIGHT	Shadows (PolyGram TV)
8	26	RID OF ME	PJ Harvey (Island)
19	27	TAKE THAT AND PARTY	Take That (RCA)
-	28	KEEP THE FAITH	Bon Jovi (Jambco)
15	29	3 YEARS, 5 MONTHS AND 2 DAYS IN THE LIFE	Arrested Development (Cooltempo)
23	30	SUEDE	Suede (Nude)
18	31	IN CONCERT - MTV UNPLUGGED	Bruce Springsteen (Columbia)
20	32	INGENUE	k.d. lang (Sire)
31	33	STARS	Simply Red (East West)
21	34	COVER SHOT	David Essex (PolyGram TV)
25	35	BLACK TIE WHITE NOISE	David Bowie (Savage)
27	36	WALTHAMSTOW	East 17 (London)
28	37	GREATEST HITS	Gloria Estefan (Epic)
42	38	THE GREATEST HITS	Boney M (Telstar)
34	39	AMERICA'S LEAST WANTED	Ugly Kid Joe (Vertigo)
37	40	HARBOR LIGHTS	Bruce Hornsby (RCA)
32	41	TESTAMENT '93	Inner City (Virgin)
45	42	MORE UNCHARTERED HEIGHTS OF DISGRACE	Dogs D'Amour (China)
44	43	XTRA NAKED	Shabba Ranks (Epic)
-	44	CONNECTED	Stereo MCs (Fourth & Broadway)
-	45	SONGS FROM THE RAIN	Hothouse Flowers (London)
38	46	THE VERY BEST OF...	Randy Crawford (Dino)
-	47	OUT OF TIME	R.E.M. (Warner Bros.)
29	48	PORNO FOR PYROS	Porno For Pyros (Warner Bros.)
30	49	THE SINGLES COLLECTION	Connie Francis (PolyGram TV)
43	50	DANGEROUS	Michael Jackson (Epic)

29 May 1993

last	this	title	artist
-	1	JANET	Janet Jackson (Virgin)
2	2	AUTOMATIC FOR THE PEOPLE	R.E.M. (Warner Bros.)
4	3	NO LIMITS	2 Unlimited (PWL Continental)
3	4	REPUBLIC	New Order (London)
1	5	ON THE NIGHT	Dire Straits (Vertigo)
14	6	HOME MOVIES - THE BEST OF EVERYTHING BUT THE GIRL	Everything But The Girl (blanco y negro)
11	7	SO CLOSE	Dina Carroll (A&M PM)
-	8	LIVE AT THE ROYAL ALBERT HALL	Wet Wet Wet with the Wren Orchestra (Precious Organisation)
16	9	BREATHLESS	Kenny G (Arista)
10	10	THE BODYGUARD - SOUNDTRACK	Various Artists (Arista)
6	11	BANBA	Clannad (RCA)
9	12	BLUES ALIVE	Gary Moore (Virgin)
28	13	KEEP THE FAITH	Bon Jovi (Jambco)
8	14	TEN SUMMONER'S TALES	Sting (A&M)
-	15	SLEEPWALKING	Kingmaker (Scorch)
-	16	SOUND OF WHITE NOISE	Anthrax (Elektra)
5	17	BEETHOVEN WAS DEAF	Morrissey (HMV)
13	18	DURAN DURAN	Duran Duran (Parlophone)
17	19	ARE YOU GONNA GO MY WAY	Lenny Kravitz (Virgin America)
12	20	BANG!	World Party (Ensign)
-	21	DREAMLAND	Aztec Camera (WEA)
-	22	ALIVE III	Kiss (Mercury)
7	23	SYMPHONY OR DAMN	Terence Trent D'Arby (Columbia)
21	24	RAGE AGAINST THE MACHINE	Rage Against The Machine (Epic)
20	25	UNPLUGGED	Eric Clapton (Duck)
-	26	POCKET FULL OF KRYPTONITE	Spin Doctors (Epic)
27	27	JIM DIAMOND	Jim Diamond (PolyGram TV)
30	28	SUEDE	Suede (Nude)
15	29	MODERN LIFE IS RUBBISH	Blur (Food)
18	30	CLIFF RICHARD - THE ALBUM	Cliff Richard (EMI)
19	31	SPILT MILK	Jellyfish (Charisma)
24	32	DIVA	Annie Lennox (RCA)
23	33	SONGS OF FAITH AND DEVOTION	Depeche Mode (Mute)
25	34	SHADOWS IN THE NIGHT	Shadows (PolyGram TV)
-	35	BETTER THE DEVIL YOU KNOW	Sonia (Arista)
27	36	TAKE THAT AND PARTY	Take That (RCA)
33	37	STARS	Simply Red (East West)
-	38	THE GOLDEN YEARS OF THE EVERLY BROTHERS	Everly Brothers (Warner Bros.)
44	39	CONNECTED	Stereo MCs (Fourth & Broadway)
31	40	IN CONCERT - MTV UNPLUGGED	Bruce Springsteen (Columbia)
22	41	GET A GRIP	Aerosmith (Geffen)
26	42	RID OF ME	PJ Harvey (Island)
32	43	INGENUE	k.d. lang (Sire)
29	44	3 YEARS, 5 MONTHS AND 2 DAYS IN THE LIFE	Arrested Development (Cooltempo)
34	45	COVER SHOT	David Essex (PolyGram TV)
47	46	OUT OF TIME	R.E.M. (Warner Bros.)
35	47	BLACK TIE WHITE NOISE	David Bowie (Savage)
36	48	WALTHAMSTOW	East 17 (London)
50	49	DANGEROUS	Michael Jackson (Epic)
-	50	JADE TO THE MAX	Jade (Giant)

Label-less for some time since the demise of Factory Records, their home since their days as Joy Division, New Order were signed by London and immediately showed their old commercial muscle (if not universal ability to please the critics) with a convincing Number 1 entry for *Republic*. This was the second of four albums in consecutive weeks which debuted at the top and were then immediately shunted aside!

June 1993

5 June 1993

last	this	title	artist (label)
1	1	JANET	Janet Jackson (Virgin)
-	2	KAMAKIRIAD	Donald Fagen (Reprise)
2	3	AUTOMATIC FOR THE PEOPLE	R.E.M. (Warner Bros.)
-	4	DREAM HARDER	Waterboys (Geffen)
-	5	FATE OF NATIONS	Robert Plant (Es Paranza)
3	6	NO LIMITS	2 Unlimited (PWL Continental)
9	7	BREATHLESS	Kenny G (Arista)
7	8	SO CLOSE	Dina Carroll (A&M PM)
-	9	UNPLUGGED ... AND SEATED	Rod Stewart (Warner Bros.)
4	10	REPUBLIC	New Order (London)
13	11	KEEP THE FAITH	Bon Jovi (Jambco)
26	12	POCKET FULL OF KRYPTONITE	Spin Doctors (Epic)
6	13	HOME MOVIES - THE BEST OF EVERYTHING BUT THE GIRL	Everything But The Girl (blanco y negro)
-	14	MORE ABBA GOLD - MORE ABBA HITS	Abba (Polydor)
-	15	CHRONOLOGIE	Jean-Michel Jarre (Dreyfus)
5	16	ON THE NIGHT	Dire Straits (Vertigo)
10	17	THE BODYGUARD - SOUNDTRACK	Various Artists (Arista)
12	18	BLUES ALIVE	Gary Moore (Virgin)
14	19	TEN SUMMONER'S TALES	Sting (A&M)
8	20	LIVE AT THE ROYAL ALBERT HALL	Wet Wet Wet with the Wren Orchestra (Precious Organisation)
-	21	UTAH SAINTS	Utah Saints (ffrr)
11	22	BANBA	Clannad (RCA)
19	23	ARE YOU GONNA GO MY WAY	Lenny Kravitz (Virgin America)
18	24	DURAN DURAN	Duran Duran (Parlophone)
25	25	UNPLUGGED	Eric Clapton (Duck)
38	26	THE GOLDEN YEARS OF THE EVERLY BROTHERS	Everly Brothers (Warner Bros.)
23	27	SYMPHONY OR DAMN	Terence Trent D'Arby (Columbia)
28	28	SUEDE	Suede (Nude)
24	29	RAGE AGAINST THE MACHINE	Rage Against The Machine (Epic)
20	30	BANG!	World Party (Ensign)
39	31	CONNECTED	Stereo MCs (Fourth & Broadway)
27	32	JIM DIAMOND	Jim Diamond (PolyGram TV)
32	33	DIVA	Annie Lennox (RCA)
16	34	SOUND OF WHITE NOISE	Anthrax (Elektra)
21	35	DREAMLAND	Aztec Camera (WEA)
-	36	TAXI	Bryan Ferry (Virgin)
30	37	CLIFF RICHARD - THE ALBUM	Cliff Richard (EMI)
37	38	STARS	Simply Red (East West)
15	39	SLEEPWALKING	Kingmaker (Scorch)
34	40	SHADOWS IN THE NIGHT	Shadows (PolyGram TV)
33	41	SONGS OF FAITH AND DEVOTION	Depeche Mode (Mute)
35	42	BETTER THE DEVIL YOU KNOW	Sonia (Arista)
36	43	TAKE THAT AND PARTY	Take That (RCA)
-	44	GREAT EXPECTATIONS	Tasmin Archer (EMI)
50	45	JADE TO THE MAX	Jade (Giant)
-	46	BAD TO THE BONE	Inner Circle (Magnet)
-	47	LOVE DELUXE	Sade (Epic)
29	48	MODERN LIFE IS RUBBISH	Blur (Food)
31	49	SPILT MILK	Jellyfish (Charisma)
46	50	OUT OF TIME	R.E.M. (Warner Bros.)

12 June 1993

last	this	title	artist (label)
1	1	JANET	Janet Jackson (Virgin)
3	2	AUTOMATIC FOR THE PEOPLE	R.E.M. (Warner Bros.)
6	3	NO LIMITS	2 Unlimited (PWL Continental)
2	4	KAMAKIRIAD	Donald Fagen (Reprise)
-	5	TOO LONG IN EXILE	Van Morrison (Polydor)
9	6	UNPLUGGED ... AND SEATED	Rod Stewart (Warner Bros.)
12	7	POCKET FULL OF KRYPTONITE	Spin Doctors (Epic)
4	8	DREAM HARDER	Waterboys (Geffen)
5	9	FATE OF NATIONS	Robert Plant (Es Paranza)
8	10	SO CLOSE	Dina Carroll (A&M PM)
7	11	BREATHLESS	Kenny G (Arista)
21	12	UTAH SAINTS	Utah Saints (ffrr)
-	13	NEVER LET ME GO	Luther Vandross (Epic)
11	14	KEEP THE FAITH	Bon Jovi (Jambco)
14	15	MORE ABBA GOLD - MORE ABBA HITS	Abba (Polydor)
-	16	GOOD AND READY	Sybil (PWL International)
15	17	CHRONOLOGIE	Jean-Michel Jarre (Dreyfus)
23	18	ARE YOU GONNA GO MY WAY	Lenny Kravitz (Virgin America)
10	19	REPUBLIC	New Order (London)
31	20	CONNECTED	Stereo MCs (Fourth & Broadway)
17	21	THE BODYGUARD - SOUNDTRACK	Various Artists (Arista)
13	22	HOME MOVIES	Everything But The Girl (blanco y negro)
19	23	TEN SUMMONER'S TALES	Sting (A&M)
43	24	TAKE THAT AND PARTY	Take That (RCA)
25	25	UNPLUGGED	Eric Clapton (Duck)
-	26	THE RAINY SEASON	Marc Cohn (Atlantic)
16	27	ON THE NIGHT	Dire Straits (Vertigo)
37	28	CLIFF RICHARD - THE ALBUM	Cliff Richard (EMI)
18	29	BLUES ALIVE	Gary Moore (Virgin)
28	30	SUEDE	Suede (Nude)
29	31	RAGE AGAINST THE MACHINE	Rage Against The Machine (Epic)
-	32	YOU GOTTA SIN TO BE SAVED	Maria McKee (Geffen)
22	33	BANBA	Clannad (RCA)
36	34	TAXI	Bryan Ferry (Virgin)
33	35	DIVA	Annie Lennox (RCA)
-	36	ORBITAL	Orbital (Internal)
24	37	DURAN DURAN	Duran Duran (Parlophone)
30	38	BANG!	World Party (Ensign)
20	39	LIVE AT THE ROYAL ALBERT HALL	Wet Wet Wet with the Wren Orchestra (Precious Organisation)
26	40	THE GOLDEN YEARS OF THE EVERLY BROTHERS	Everly Brothers (Warner Bros.)
46	41	BAD TO THE BONE	Inner Circle (Magnet)
32	42	JIM DIAMOND	Jim Diamond (PolyGram TV)
44	43	GREAT EXPECTATIONS	Tasmin Archer (EMI)
-	44	THE BEST OF...	Howard Jones (East West)
47	45	LOVE DELUXE	Sade (Epic)
38	46	STARS	Simply Red (East West)
27	47	SYMPHONY OR DAMN	Terence Trent D'Arby (Columbia)
-	48	FOREVER FOR NOW - THE VERY BEST OF ...	Harry Connick Jr. (Columbia)
45	49	JADE TO THE MAX	Jade (Giant)
-	50	SOUVLAKI	Slowdive (Creation)

19 June 1993

last	this	title	artist (label)
-	1	WHAT'S LOVE GOT TO DO WITH IT	Tina Turner (Parlophone)
-	2	ELEMENTAL	Tears For Fears (Mercury)
3	3	NO LIMITS	2 Unlimited (PWL Continental)
1	4	JANET	Janet Jackson (Virgin)
2	5	AUTOMATIC FOR THE PEOPLE	R.E.M. (Warner Bros.)
7	6	POCKET FULL OF KRYPTONITE	Spin Doctors (Epic)
5	7	TOO LONG IN EXILE	Van Morrison (Polydor)
6	8	UNPLUGGED ... AND SEATED	Rod Stewart (Warner Bros.)
10	9	SO CLOSE	Dina Carroll (A&M PM)
20	10	CONNECTED	Stereo MCs (Fourth & Broadway)
4	11	KAMAKIRIAD	Donald Fagen (Reprise)
13	12	NEVER LET ME GO	Luther Vandross (Epic)
8	13	DREAM HARDER	Waterboys (Geffen)
15	14	MORE ABBA GOLD - MORE ABBA HITS	Abba (Polydor)
11	15	BREATHLESS	Kenny G (Arista)
-	16	HAPPY NATION	Ace Of Base (Mega)
16	17	GOOD AND READY	Sybil (PWL International)
14	18	KEEP THE FAITH	Bon Jovi (Jambco)
9	19	FATE OF NATIONS	Robert Plant (Es Paranza)
23	20	TEN SUMMONER'S TALES	Sting (A&M)
18	21	ARE YOU GONNA GO MY WAY	Lenny Kravitz (Virgin America)
12	22	UTAH SAINTS	Utah Saints (ffrr)
25	23	UNPLUGGED	Eric Clapton (Duck)
21	24	THE BODYGUARD - SOUNDTRACK	Various Artists (Arista)
17	25	CHRONOLOGIE	Jean-Michel Jarre (Dreyfus)
28	26	CLIFF RICHARD - THE ALBUM	Cliff Richard (EMI)
26	27	THE RAINY SEASON	Marc Cohn (Atlantic)
-	28	USE YOUR ILLUSION II	Guns N' Roses (Geffen)
24	29	TAKE THAT AND PARTY	Take That (RCA)
19	30	REPUBLIC	New Order (London)
30	31	SUEDE	Suede (Nude)
33	32	BANBA	Clannad (RCA)
43	33	GREAT EXPECTATIONS	Tasmin Archer (EMI)
22	34	HOME MOVIES - THE BEST OF EVERYTHING BUT THE GIRL	Everything But The Girl (blanco y negro)
34	35	TAXI	Bryan Ferry (Virgin)
35	36	DIVA	Annie Lennox (RCA)
32	37	YOU GOTTA SIN TO BE SAVED	Maria McKee (Geffen)
48	38	FOREVER FOR NOW - THE VERY BEST OF HARRY CONNICK JR.	Harry Connick Jr. (Columbia)
-	39	THOUSAND ROADS	David Crosby (Atlantic)
-	40	USE YOUR ILLUSION I	Guns N' Roses (Geffen)
-	41	IN ON THE KILL TAKER	Fugazi (Dischord)
31	42	RAGE AGAINST THE MACHINE	Rage Against The Machine (Epic)
27	43	ON THE NIGHT	Dire Straits (Vertigo)
-	44	GOLD - GREATEST HITS	Abba (Polydor)
37	45	DURAN DURAN	Duran Duran (Parlophone)
46	46	STARS	Simply Red (East West)
-	47	PROVOCATIVE	Johnny Gill (Motown)
29	48	BLUES ALIVE	Gary Moore (Virgin)
45	49	LOVE DELUXE	Sade (Epic)
-	50	AMERICA'S LEAST WANTED	Ugly Kid Joe (Vertigo)

Janet Jackson had failed to make the chart-top in the UK with either of her US mega-selling albums of the 80s, *Control* and *Rhythm Nation 1814*, but it was *Janet*, the first product of her new deal with Virgin, that did the required trick. It was replaced at the top by the doyenne of hard-working female performers, Tina Turner, whose *What's Love Got To Do With It* was the soundtrack to the movie of her life and career.

26 June 1993

last	this		
-	1	EMERGENCY ON PLANET EARTH	Jamiroquai (Orenda)
-	2	UNPLUGGED	Neil Young (Reprise)
1	3	WHAT'S LOVE GOT TO DO WITH IT	Tina Turner (Parlophone)
8	4	UNPLUGGED ... AND SEATED	Rod Stewart (Warner Bros.)
6	5	POCKET FULL OF KRYPTONITE	Spin Doctors (Epic)
5	6	AUTOMATIC FOR THE PEOPLE	R.E.M. (Warner Bros.)
3	7	NO LIMITS	2 Unlimited (PWL Continental)
2	8	ELEMENTAL	Tears For Fears (Mercury)
4	9	JANET	Janet Jackson (Virgin)
-	10	LIBERATOR	Orchestral Manoeuvres In The Dark (Virgin)
10	11	CONNECTED	Stereo MCs (Fourth & Broadway)
9	12	SO CLOSE	Dina Carroll (A&M PM)
20	13	TEN SUMMONER'S TALES	Sting (A&M)
7	14	TOO LONG IN EXILE	Van Morrison (Polydor)
-	15	MEMORIAL BEACH	A-ha (Warner Bros.)
15	16	BREATHLESS	Kenny G (Arista)
-	17	WHISPER A PRAYER	Mica Paris (4th & Broadway)
17	18	GOOD AND READY	Sybil (PWL International)
11	19	KAMAKIRIAD	Donald Fagen (Reprise)
14	20	MORE ABBA GOLD - MORE ABBA HITS	Abba (Polydor)
16	21	HAPPY NATION	Ace Of Base (Mega)
18	22	KEEP THE FAITH	Bon Jovi (Jambco)
23	23	UNPLUGGED	Eric Clapton (Duck)
12	24	NEVER LET ME GO	Luther Vandross (Epic)
13	25	DREAM HARDER	Waterboys (Geffen)
21	26	ARE YOU GONNA GO MY WAY	Lenny Kravitz (Virgin America)
24	27	THE BODYGUARD - SOUNDTRACK	Various Artists (Arista)
19	28	FATE OF NATIONS	Robert Plant (Es Paranza)
22	29	UTAH SAINTS	Utah Saints (ffrr)
26	30	CLIFF RICHARD - THE ALBUM	Cliff Richard (EMI)
25	31	CHRONOLOGIE	Jean-Michel Jarre (Dreyfus)
-	32	TAKE A LOOK	Natalie Cole (Elektra)
38	33	FOREVER FOR NOW - THE VERY BEST OF ...	Harry Connick Jr. (Columbia)
49	34	LOVE DELUXE	Sade (Epic)
32	35	BANBA	Clannad (RCA)
35	36	TAXI	Bryan Ferry (Virgin)
-	37	SYMPHONY OR DAMN	Terence Trent D'Arby (Columbia)
27	38	THE RAINY SEASON	Marc Cohn (Atlantic)
36	39	DIVA	Annie Lennox (RCA)
29	40	TAKE THAT AND PARTY	Take That (RCA)
28	41	USE YOUR ILLUSION II	Guns N' Roses (Geffen)
44	42	GOLD - GREATEST HITS	Abba (Polydor)
30	43	REPUBLIC	New Order (London)
33	44	GREAT EXPECTATIONS	Tasmin Archer (EMI)
34	45	HOME MOVIES	Everything But The Girl (blanco y negro)
31	46	SUEDE	Suede (Nude)
-	47	SIMPLY THE BEST	Tina Turner (Capitol)
-	48	METALLICA	Metallica (Vertigo)
37	49	YOU GOTTA SIN TO BE SAVED	Maria McKee (Geffen)
41	50	IN ON THE KILL TAKER	Fugazi (Dischord)

3 July 1993

1	1	EMERGENCY ON PLANET EARTH	Jamiroquai (Orenda)
4	2	UNPLUGGED ... AND SEATED	Rod Stewart (Warner Bros.)
3	3	WHAT'S LOVE GOT TO DO WITH IT	Tina Turner (Parlophone)
2	4	UNPLUGGED	Neil Young (Reprise)
-	5	GOLD AGAINST THE SOUL	Manic Street Preachers (Columbia)
5	6	POCKET FULL OF KRYPTONITE	Spin Doctors (Epic)
6	7	AUTOMATIC FOR THE PEOPLE	R.E.M. (Warner Bros.)
13	8	TEN SUMMONER'S TALES	Sting (A&M)
7	9	NO LIMITS	2 Unlimited (PWL Continental)
9	10	JANET	Janet Jackson (Virgin)
11	11	CONNECTED	Stereo MCs (Fourth & Broadway)
12	12	SO CLOSE	Dina Carroll (A&M PM)
19	13	KAMAKIRIAD	Donald Fagen (Reprise)
14	14	TOO LONG IN EXILE	Van Morrison (Polydor)
10	15	LIBERATOR	Orchestral Manoeuvres In The Dark (Virgin)
-	16	MUDDY WATERS BLUES - A TRIBUTE TO MUDDY WATERS	Paul Rodgers (Victory)
8	17	ELEMENTAL	Tears For Fears (Mercury)
16	18	BREATHLESS	Kenny G (Arista)
23	19	UNPLUGGED	Eric Clapton (Duck)
32	20	TAKE A LOOK	Natalie Cole (Elektra)
22	21	KEEP THE FAITH	Bon Jovi (Jambco)
27	22	THE BODYGUARD - SOUNDTRACK	Various Artists (Arista)
15	23	MEMORIAL BEACH	A-ha (Warner Bros.)
18	24	GOOD AND READY	Sybil (PWL International)
17	25	WHISPER A PRAYER	Mica Paris (4th & Broadway)
20	26	MORE ABBA GOLD - MORE ABBA HITS	Abba (Polydor)
21	27	HAPPY NATION	Ace Of Base (Mega)
34	28	LOVE DELUXE	Sade (Epic)
28	29	FATE OF NATIONS	Robert Plant (Es Paranza)
25	30	DREAM HARDER	Waterboys (Geffen)
35	31	BANBA	Clannad (RCA)
40	32	TAKE THAT AND PARTY	Take That (RCA)
37	33	SYMPHONY OR DAMN	Terence Trent D'Arby (Columbia)
26	34	ARE YOU GONNA GO MY WAY	Lenny Kravitz (Virgin America)
42	35	GOLD - GREATEST HITS	Abba (Polydor)
31	36	CHRONOLOGIE	Jean-Michel Jarre (Dreyfus)
-	37	A STORM IN HEAVEN	Verve (Hut)
-	38	AUDIENCE WITH THE MIND	House Of Love (Fontana)
29	39	UTAH SAINTS	Utah Saints (ffrr)
36	40	TAXI	Bryan Ferry (Virgin)
24	41	NEVER LET ME GO	Luther Vandross (Epic)
30	42	CLIFF RICHARD - THE ALBUM	Cliff Richard (EMI)
33	43	FOREVER FOR NOW - THE VERY BEST OF ...	Harry Connick Jr. (Columbia)
47	44	SIMPLY THE BEST	Tina Turner (Capitol)
39	45	DIVA	Annie Lennox (RCA)
43	46	REPUBLIC	New Order (London)
-	47	CEREAL KILLER	Green Jelly (Zoo)
41	48	USE YOUR ILLUSION II	Guns N' Roses (Geffen)
38	49	THE RAINY SEASON	Marc Cohn (Atlantic)
-	50	STARS	Simply Red (East West)

10 July 1993

1	1	EMERGENCY ON PLANET EARTH	Jamiroquai (Orenda)
2	2	UNPLUGGED ... AND SEATED	Rod Stewart (Warner Bros.)
6	3	POCKET FULL OF KRYPTONITE	Spin Doctors (Epic)
7	4	AUTOMATIC FOR THE PEOPLE	R.E.M. (Warner Bros.)
3	5	WHAT'S LOVE GOT TO DO WITH IT	Tina Turner (Parlophone)
4	6	UNPLUGGED	Neil Young (Reprise)
8	7	TEN SUMMONER'S TALES	Sting (A&M)
5	8	GOLD AGAINST THE SOUL	Manic Street Preachers (Columbia)
16	9	MUDDY WATERS BLUES - A TRIBUTE TO MUDDY WATERS	Paul Rodgers (Victory)
9	10	NO LIMITS	2 Unlimited (PWL Continental)
-	11	BACK TO BROADWAY	Barbra Streisand (Columbia)
12	12	SO CLOSE	Dina Carroll (A&M PM)
11	13	CONNECTED	Stereo MCs (Fourth & Broadway)
10	14	JANET	Janet Jackson (Virgin)
13	15	KAMAKIRIAD	Donald Fagen (Reprise)
22	16	THE BODYGUARD - SOUNDTRACK	Various Artists (Arista)
-	17	MI TIERRA	Gloria Estefan (Epic)
18	18	BREATHLESS	Kenny G (Arista)
14	19	TOO LONG IN EXILE	Van Morrison (Polydor)
21	20	KEEP THE FAITH	Bon Jovi (Jambco)
19	21	UNPLUGGED	Eric Clapton (Duck)
-	22	CYBERPUNK	Billy Idol (Chrysalis)
-	23	THE BEST OF...	Eric Clapton (Polydor)
15	24	LIBERATOR	Orchestral Manoeuvres In The Dark (Virgin)
47	25	CEREAL KILLER	Green Jelly (Zoo)
20	26	TAKE A LOOK	Natalie Cole (Elektra)
33	27	SYMPHONY OR DAMN	Terence Trent D'Arby (Columbia)
-	28	BEFORE & AFTER	Tim Finn (Capitol)
39	29	UTAH SAINTS	Utah Saints (ffrr)
17	30	ELEMENTAL	Tears For Fears (Mercury)
25	31	WHISPER A PRAYER	Mica Paris (4th & Broadway)
28	32	LOVE DELUXE	Sade (Epic)
27	33	HAPPY NATION	Ace Of Base (Mega)
-	34	LIVE & LOUD	Ozzy Osbourne (Epic)
26	35	MORE ABBA GOLD - MORE ABBA HITS	Abba (Polydor)
35	36	GOLD - GREATEST HITS	Abba (Polydor)
-	37	TEASE ME	Chaka Demus & Pliers (Mango)
30	38	DREAM HARDER	Waterboys (Geffen)
24	39	GOOD AND READY	Sybil (PWL International)
29	40	FATE OF NATIONS	Robert Plant (Es Paranza)
34	41	ARE YOU GONNA GO MY WAY	Lenny Kravitz (Virgin America)
37	42	A STORM IN HEAVEN	Verve (Hut)
-	43	DANGEROUS	Michael Jackson (Epic)
46	44	REPUBLIC	New Order (London)
32	45	TAKE THAT AND PARTY	Take That (RCA)
23	46	MEMORIAL BEACH	A-ha (Warner Bros.)
31	47	BANBA	Clannad (RCA)
-	48	THE MADMAN'S RETURN	Snap (Logic)
-	49	INGENUE	k.d. lang (Sire)
42	50	CLIFF RICHARD - THE ALBUM	Cliff Richard (EMI)

Take note of the Number 50 in the final chart - the ever youthful Cliff who was, of course, at Number 5 in the NME's very first album chart, along with the Shadows, with *The Young Ones*. Cliff has outlasted the George Mitchell Minstrels, and even Elvis and Frank Sinatra from that first chart. Thirty one years on he shows no more sign of retiring than "pop" does of being the passing fad that was so widely predicted.

411

This Title Index is followed by an Artist Index, starting on page 455. The indexes are intended as a guide to locating records in the charts in this book, they are not an exhaustive guide to record titles and artist names. If you have difficulty finding a record in the Title Index, check the correct title under the artist's name in the Artist Index. To make it easy to track songs throughout their chart careers, records are listed in the Title Index every time they enter the chart. In the Artist Index records are only listed once, at their first date of chart entry. Please note that the Artist Index is arranged in order of the first name of the artist, whether they are a person or a group. To find Elvis Presley, therefore, look under 'E'. Records by 'Various Artists', and Cast and Soundtrack albums are not included in the Artist Index. Titles and artists that begin with numerals are placed at the end of each index.

413

COLOURBOX Colourbox	24/08/85	
COMBAT ROCK Clash	22/05/82	
COMBAT ROCK Clash	10/07/82	
COMBAT ROCK Clash	31/07/82	
COMBINE HARVESTER Wurzels	24/07/76	
COMBINE HARVESTER Wurzels	14/08/76	
COME AN' GET IT Whitesnake	18/04/81	
COME INTO MY LIFE Joyce Sims	16/01/88	
COME ON EVERYBODY Elvis Presley	07/08/71	
COME OUT AND PLAY Twisted Sister	14/12/85	
COME TASTE THE BAND Deep Purple	22/11/75	
COME THE DAY Seekers	19/11/66	
COME TO MY PARTY Mrs Mills	17/12/66	
COME TOGETHER AS ONE Will Downing	25/11/89	
COME WITH CLUB – CLUB TRACKS VOL 2 Various Artists	10/09/83	
COMEDY Black	29/10/88	
COMING ALIVE AGAIN Barbara Dickson	27/05/89	
COMING IN FOR THE KILL Climie Fisher	21/10/89	
COMING OUT Manhattan Transfer	19/03/77	
COMING OUT Manhattan Transfer	09/07/77	
COMING OUT Manhattan Transfer	13/08/77	
COMING ROUND AGAIN Carly Simon	16/05/87	
COMMAND PERFORMANCE Various Artists	15/12/73	
COMMODORES' GREATEST HITS Commodores	09/12/78	
COMMODORES' GREATEST HITS Commodores	06/01/79	
COMMODORES' GREATEST HITS Commodores	20/01/79	
COMMODORES' GREATEST HITS Commodores	10/02/79	
COMMONERS CROWN Steeleye Span	22/02/75	
COMMUNARDS Communards	02/08/86	
COMMUNARDS Communards	06/09/86	
COMMUNARDS Communards	20/12/86	
COMMUNIQUE Dire Straits	16/06/79	
COMPANEROS Working Week	27/09/86	
COMPLETE MADNESS Madness	01/05/82	
COMPLETE MADNESS Madness	15/01/83	
COMPLETE MADNESS Madness	26/02/83	
COMPLETE MADNESS Madness	19/03/83	
COMPLETELY HOOKED - THE BEST OF DR. HOOK Dr. Hook	13/06/92	
COMPOSITIONS Anita Baker	14/07/90	
COMPUTER WORLD Kraftwerk	23/05/81	
COMPUTER WORLD Kraftwerk	27/02/82	
CONCERT Cure	03/11/84	
CONCERT FOR BANGLA DESH Various Artists	22/01/72	
CONDITION CRITICAL Quiet Riot	11/08/84	
CONFESSIONS OF A POP GROUP Style Council	02/07/88	
CONFRONTATION Bob Marley & the Wailers	28/05/83	
CONNECTED Stereo MCs	23/01/93	
CONNECTED Stereo MCs	22/05/93	
CONNIE FRANCIS' 20 ALL TIME GREATS Connie Francis	16/07/77	
CONSCIENCE Womack & Womack	03/09/88	
CONSCIENCE Womack & Womack	04/03/89	
CONSCIENCE Beloved	20/02/93	
CONSCIENCE Beloved	24/04/93	
CONSTRICTOR Alice Cooper	01/11/86	
CONSTRUCTION TIME AGAIN Depeche Mode	03/09/83	
CONTACT Pointer Sisters	27/07/85	
CONTACT Pointer Sisters	07/09/85	
CONTENDERS Easterhouse	05/07/86	
CONTRACTUAL OBLIGATION ALBUM Monty Python's Flying Circus	25/10/80	
CONTRIBUTION Mica Paris	27/10/90	
CONTROL Janet Jackson	19/04/86	
CONTROL Janet Jackson	06/09/86	
CONTROL Janet Jackson	28/03/87	
CONTROL Janet Jackson	11/07/87	
CONTROL - THE REMIXES Janet Jackson	21/11/87	
COOKIN' ON THE ROOF Roman Holiday	29/10/83	
COOL FOR CATS Squeeze	12/05/79	
COOL FOR CATS Squeeze	14/07/79	
COOLEYHIGHHARMONY Boyz II Men	31/10/92	
COP YER WACK OF THIS Billy Connolly	04/01/75	
COP YER WHACK OF THIS Billy Connolly	11/01/75	
COP YER WHACK OF THIS Billy Connolly	25/01/75	
COP YER WHACK OF THIS Billy Connolly	29/03/75	
COP YER WHACK OF THIS Billy Connolly	19/04/75	
COPPER BLUE Sugar	19/09/92	
COPPER BLUE Sugar	30/01/93	
COPPERHEAD ROAD Steve Earle	19/11/88	
CORNERSTONES 1967-1970 Jimi Hendrix	03/11/90	
CORNERSTONES 1967-1970 Jimi Hendrix	12/01/91	
COSI FAN TUTTI FRUTTI Squeeze	07/09/85	
COSMIC THING B-52's	31/03/90	
COSMIC THING B-52's	11/08/90	
COSMIC WHEELS Donovan	17/03/73	
COSMIC WHEELS Donovan	31/03/73	
COSMIC WHEELS Donovan	19/05/73	
COSMO'S FACTORY Creedence Clearwater Revival	05/09/70	
COUNT THREE AND PRAY Berlin	24/01/87	
COUNT THREE AND PRAY Berlin	28/02/87	
COUNTDOWN TO EXTINCTION Megadeth	18/07/92	
COUNTRY BOY Don Williams	29/10/77	
COUNTRY COMFORT Various Artists	23/10/76	
COUNTRY GIRL Billy Jo Spears	12/12/81	
COUNTRY GIRL MEETS COUNTRY BOY Various Artists	25/02/78	
COUNTRY LEGENDS Various Artists	22/11/80	
COUNTRY LIFE Roxy Music	23/11/74	
COUNTRY LIFE Roxy Music	15/02/75	
COUNTRY LIFE Various Artists	14/04/79	
COUNTRY NUMBER ONE Don Gibson	19/04/80	
COUNTRY PORTRAITS Various Artists	14/04/79	
COURT AND SPARK Joni Mitchell	16/03/74	
COURT AND SPARK Joni Mitchell	04/05/74	
COVER PLUS Hazel O'Connor	19/09/81	
COVER SHOT David Essex	10/04/93	
COVERDALE/PAGE Coverdale/Page	27/03/93	
CRACKDOWN Cabaret Voltaire	13/08/83	
CRACKDOWN Cabaret Voltaire	17/09/83	
CRACKERS – THE SLADE CHRISTMAS PARTY ALBUM Slade	04/01/86	
CRAIG MCLACHLAN AND CHECK 1-2 Craig McLachlan & Check 1-2	21/07/90	
CRASH Human League	20/09/86	
CRAZY FROM THE HEAT David Lee Roth	09/03/85	
CRAZY HORSES Osmonds	23/12/72	
CRAZY HORSES Osmonds	17/03/73	
CRAZY NIGHTS Kiss	07/11/87	
CRAZY WORLD Scorpions	02/11/91	
CRAZY WORLD OF ARTHUR BROWN Crazy World Of Arthur Brown	29/06/68	
CRE-OLE Kid Creole & the Coconuts	22/09/84	
CREAM OF THE CROP Diana Ross & the Supremes	14/02/70	
CREAM OF THE CROP Diana Ross & the Supremes	28/02/70	
CREATURES OF THE NIGHT Kiss	13/11/82	
CREPES AND DRAPES Showaddywaddy	24/11/79	
CREPES AND DRAPES Showaddywaddy	15/12/79	
CREST OF A KNAVE Jethro Tull	19/09/87	
CREW CUTS Various Artists	23/06/84	
CREW CUTS - LESSON 2 Various Artists	03/11/84	
CRICKLEWOOD GREEN Ten Years After	02/05/70	
CRICKLEWOOD GREEN Ten Years After	01/08/70	
CRIME OF THE CENTURY Supertramp	07/12/74	
CRIME OF THE CENTURY Supertramp	18/01/75	
CRIME OF THE CENTURY Supertramp	17/05/75	
CRIMINAL RECORD Rick Wakeman	10/12/77	
CRISES Mike Oldfield	04/06/83	
CRISIS? WHAT CRISIS? Supertramp	06/12/75	
CRISIS? WHAT CRISIS? Supertramp	20/03/76	
CROCODILES Echo & the Bunnymen	09/08/80	
CROOKED MILE Microdisney	17/01/87	
CROSBY, STILLS & NASH Crosby, Stills & Nash	30/08/69	
CROSBY, STILLS & NASH Crosby, Stills & Nash	13/09/69	
CROSSROADS Tracy Chapman	14/10/89	
CROSSROADS Tracy Chapman	23/12/89	
CRUISIN' Village People	03/02/79	
CRUISIN' Village People	24/02/79	
CRUSADE John Mayall	23/09/67	
CRUSADER Saxon	11/02/84	
CRUSH Orchestral Manoeuvres in the Dark	29/06/85	
CRUSH Orchestral Manoeuvres in the Dark	10/08/85	
CRUSH ON YOU Jets	18/04/87	
CRUSHIN' Fat Boys	10/10/87	
CRUSHIN' Fat Boys	24/10/87	
CRY FREEDOM Soundtrack	05/03/88	
CRY LIKE A RAINSTORM - HOWL LIKE THE WIND Linda Ronstadt	18/11/89	
CRY LIKE A RAINSTORM - HOWL LIKE THE WIND Linda Ronstadt	23/12/89	
CRY OF LOVE Jimi Hendrix	27/03/71	
CRY TOUGH Nils Lofgren	17/04/76	
CRY TOUGH Nils Lofgren	05/06/76	
CSN Crosby Still & Nash	16/07/77	
CULTOSAURUS ERECTUS Blue Oyster Cult	26/07/80	
CUPID AND PSYCHE '85 Scritti Politti	22/06/85	
CURE FOR SANITY Pop Will Eat Itself	03/11/90	
CURED Steve Hackett	29/08/81	
CURTIS STIGERS Curtis Stigers	29/02/92	
CURTIS STIGERS Curtis Stigers	11/07/92	
CURTIS STIGERS Curtis Stigers	22/08/92	
CURTIS STIGERS Curtis Stigers	24/10/92	
CURVED AIR Curved Air	02/10/71	
CUT Slits	29/09/79	
CUT THE CAKE Average White Band	05/07/75	
CUT THE CAKE Average White Band	19/07/75	
CUT THE CRAP Clash	16/11/85	
CUTS BOTH WAYS Gloria Estefan	05/08/89	
CUTS BOTH WAYS Gloria Estefan	03/03/90	
CUTS BOTH WAYS Gloria Estefan	09/06/90	
CUTS BOTH WAYS Gloria Estefan	23/06/90	
CUTS BOTH WAYS Gloria Estefan	15/09/90	
CUTS LIKE A KNIFE Bryan Adams	22/03/86	
CYBERPUNK Billy Idol	10/07/93	
DADA Alice Cooper	19/11/83	
DALTREY Roger Daltrey	19/05/73	
DAMNED BUT NOT FORGOTTEN Damned	08/02/86	
DAMNED BUT NOT FORGOTTEN Damned	22/03/86	
DAMNED DAMNED DAMNED Damned	26/03/77	
DAMNED DAMNED DAMNED Damned	09/04/77	
DANCE Gary Numan	19/09/81	
DANCE CRAZE Soundtrack	21/02/81	
DANCE DANCE DANCE Various Artists	26/09/81	
DANCE DANCE DANCE James Last	10/12/88	
DANCE DANCE DANCE James Last	24/12/88	
DANCE DECADE - DANCE HITS OF THE 80'S Various Artists	18/11/89	
DANCE HITS 2 Various Artists	05/07/86	
DANCE IN THE MIDNIGHT Marc Bolan	08/10/83	
DANCE MIX Various Artists	09/07/83	
DANCE MIX - DANCE HITS II Various Artists	01/10/83	
DANCE THIS MESS AROUND (BEST OF THE B52'S) B-52's	21/07/90	
DANCE TO THE MUSIC Various Artists	12/02/77	
DANCE UNDERCOVER Ratt	25/10/86	
DANCE WITH THE SHADOWS Shadows	09/05/64	
DANCE ... YA KNOW IT Bobby Brown	02/12/89	
DANCES WITH WOLVES - SOUNDTRACK John Barry	27/04/91	
DANCIN' IN THE KEY OF LIFE Steve Arrington	13/04/85	
DANCIN' ON THE EDGE Lita Ford	02/06/84	
DANCING ON THE CEILING Lionel Richie	23/08/86	
DANCING ON THE CEILING Lionel Ritchie	10/01/87	
DANCING ON THE CEILING Lionel Richie	21/03/87	
DANCING ON THE CEILING Lionel Richie	09/05/87	
DANCING ON THE COUCH Go West	06/06/87	
DANCING WITH STRANGERS Chris Rea	26/09/87	
DANCING WITH STRANGERS Chris Rea	23/01/88	
DANDY IN THE UNDERWORLD T Rex	16/04/77	
DANGEROUS Michael Jackson	30/11/91	
DANGEROUS Michael Jackson	10/07/93	
DANGEROUS MUSIC Robin George	09/03/85	
DARE Human League	24/10/81	
DARE Human League	29/05/82	
DARE Human League	03/07/82	
DARE Human League	14/08/82	
DARE Human League	28/08/82	
DARING ADVENTURES Richard Thompson	25/10/86	
DARK SIDE OF THE MOON Pink Floyd	24/03/73	
DARK SIDE OF THE MOON Pink Floyd	20/10/73	
DARK SIDE OF THE MOON Pink Floyd	26/04/75	
DARK SIDE OF THE MOON Pink Floyd	06/12/75	
DARK SIDE OF THE MOON Pink Floyd	14/08/76	
DARKLANDS Jesus & Mary Chain	12/09/87	
DARKNESS ON THE EDGE OF TOWN Bruce Springsteen	24/06/78	
DARKNESS ON THE EDGE OF TOWN Bruce Springsteen	22/06/85	

GOOD AND READY Sybil	12/06/93
GOOD AS I BEEN TO YOU Bob Dylan (CBS)	14/11/92
GOOD BAD BUT BEAUTIFUL Shirley Bassey	25/10/75
GOOD DEEDS AND DIRTY RAGS	
Goodbye Mr. Mackenzie	22/04/89
GOOD LOVE Meli'sa Morgan	19/12/87
GOOD LOVE Meli'sa Morgan	06/02/88
GOOD MORNING AMERICA Various Artists	24/05/80
GOOD MORNING AMERICA Various Artists	14/06/80
GOOD MORNING VIETNAM SOUNDTRACK Various	
Artists	19/11/88
GOOD 'N' COUNTRY Jim Reeves	04/04/64
GOOD 'N' COUNTRY Jim Reeves	29/08/64
GOOD 'N' COUNTRY Jim Reeves	26/09/64
GOOD STUFF B-52's	11/07/92
GOOD TO BE BACK Natalie Cole	20/05/89
GOOD TO GO LOVER Gwen Guthrie	30/08/86
GOOD TO GO LOVER Gwen Guthrie	27/09/86
GOOD TO GO LOVER Gwen Guthrie	18/10/86
GOOD TROUBLE REO Speedwagon	24/07/82
GOOD VIBRATIONS Various Artists	29/09/73
GOODBYE Cream	08/03/69
GOODBYE Cream	26/04/69
GOODBYE CRUEL WORLD Elvis Costello	07/07/84
GOODBYE CRUEL WORLD Elvis Costello	08/09/84
GOODBYE GIRL David Gates	15/07/78
GOODBYE JUMBO World Party	19/05/90
GOODBYE YELLOW BRICK ROAD	
Elton John	20/10/73
GOODBYE YELLOW BRICK ROAD	
Elton John	05/10/74
GOODBYE YELLOW BRICK ROAD	
Elton John	21/12/74
GOODBYE YELLOW BRICK ROAD	
Elton John	25/01/75
GOODNIGHT L.A. Magnum	21/07/90
GOODNIGHT VIENNA Ringo Starr	14/12/74
GOOFY GREATS Various Artists	22/11/75
GOOFY GREATS Various Artists	03/01/76
GORECKI: SYMPHONY NO. 3 Dawn Upshaw/London	
Sinfonietta/David Zinman	13/02/93
GORGEOUS 808 State	13/02/93
GOSH IT'S BAD MANNERS Bad Manners	31/10/81
GRACE UNDER PRESSURE Rush	28/04/84
GRACELAND Paul Simon	13/09/86
GRACELAND Paul Simon	08/08/87
GRACELAND Paul Simon	29/08/87
GRACELAND Paul Simon	23/01/88
GRAINS OF SAND Mission	03/11/90
GRAPES OF WRATH Spear of Destiny	30/04/83
GRAVE NEW WORLD Strawbs	04/03/72
GRAVITY Kenny G	08/06/85
GREASE Soundtrack	15/07/78
GREASE Soundtrack	09/03/91
GREAT EXPECTATIONS Tasmin Archer	31/10/92
GREAT EXPECTATIONS Tasmin Archer	27/02/93
GREAT EXPECTATIONS Tasmin Archer	05/06/93
GREAT LOVE CLASSICS Andy Williams	03/11/84
GREAT WALTZES Roberto Mann	16/12/67
GREATEST EVER ROCK'N'ROLL MIX	
Various Artists	09/09/89
GREATEST HITS Fleetwood Mac	13/05/89
GREATEST HITS Five Star (Tent)	28/10/89
GREATEST HITS Billy Ocean	04/11/89
GREATEST HITS Billy Ocean	03/02/90
GREATEST HITS Bangles	09/06/90
GREATEST HITS Eurythmics	30/03/91
GREATEST HITS Jam	13/07/91
GREATEST HITS Jason Donovan	28/09/91
GREATEST HITS Queen	07/12/91
GREATEST HITS Jason Donovan	11/01/92
GREATEST HITS Eurythmics	18/04/92
GREATEST HITS ZZ Top	25/04/92
GREATEST HITS Foreigner	02/05/92
GREATEST HITS Police	02/05/92
GREATEST HITS Squeeze	23/05/92
GREATEST HITS Kylie Minogue	05/09/92
GREATEST HITS Police	10/10/92
GREATEST HITS Gloria Estefan	14/11/92
GREATEST HITS Queen	09/01/93
GREATEST HITS Sheep On Drugs	10/04/93
GREATEST HITS Gloria Estefan	17/04/93
GREATEST HITS 1972-1978 10 c.c.	13/10/79
GREATEST HITS 1972-1978 10 c.c	26/01/80
GREATEST HITS 1977-1990 Stranglers	08/12/90
GREATEST HITS 1977-1990 Stranglers	26/01/91
GREATEST HITS II Queen	09/11/91
GREATEST HITS II Queen	24/10/92
GREATEST HITS II Queen	12/12/92
GREATEST HITS LIVE Diana Ross	02/12/89
GREATEST HITS OF 10 c.c. 10 c.c.	14/06/75
GREATEST HITS OF 1986 Various Artists	15/11/86
GREATEST HITS OF '85 Various Artists	23/11/85
GREATEST HITS OF '87 Various Artists	28/11/87
GREATEST LOVE SONGS Nat 'King' Cole	27/11/82
GREATEST LOVE SONGS Nat 'King' Cole	19/02/83
GREATEST LOVE SONGS Placido Domingo	30/04/88
GREATEST MESSAGES Grandmaster Flash	04/08/84
GREATEST MESSAGES Grandmaster Flash	18/08/84
GREATEST MISSES Public Enemy	03/10/92
GREATEST REMIXES VOL.1 Clivilles & Cole	28/03/92
GREEN Steve Hillage	29/04/78
GREEN R.E.M.	19/11/88
GREEN R.E.M.	04/02/89
GREEN R.E.M.	18/02/89
GREEN R.E.M.	17/06/89
GREEN R.E.M.	12/08/89
GREEN GREEN GRASS OF HOME Tom Jones	08/04/67
GREEN LIGHT Cliff Richard	21/10/78
GREEN MIND Dinosaur Jr.	02/03/91
GREEN VELVET Various Artists	24/12/83
GREEN VELVET Various Artists	22/12/84
GROOVUS MAXIMUS Electric Boys	06/06/92
GROWING UP IN PUBLIC Jimmy Nail	08/08/92
GTR GTR	26/07/86
GUARANTEED Level 42	14/09/91
GUILTY Barbra Streisand	18/10/80
GUITAR TOWN Steve Earle	06/09/86
GUN SHY Screaming Blue Messiahs	24/05/86
GYPSY Soundtrack	09/02/63
H.I.T.S. New Kids On The Block	21/12/91
H2O Daryl Hall & John Oates	21/05/83
H2O Daryl Hall & John Oates	02/07/83
H20 Daryl Hall & John Oates	13/11/82
HAIL TO ENGLAND Manowar	03/03/84
HAIR London Cast	25/01/69
HAIR London Cast	19/04/69
HAIR London Cast	13/12/69
HAIR London Cast	03/01/70
HAIR London Cast	11/04/70
HALFWAY TO SANITY Ramones	10/10/87
HALL OF FAME Georgie Fame	18/03/67
HALL OF FAME Georgie Fame	06/05/67
HALLOWED GROUND Violent Femmes	21/07/84
HAMBURGER CONCERTO Focus	08/06/74
HAMBURGER CONCERTO Focus	29/06/74
HAND CLAPPIN' - FOOT STOMPIN' - FUNKY BUTT	
- LIVE! Geno Washington	17/12/66
HAND CUT Bucks Fizz	26/03/83
HAND OF KINDNESS Richard Thompson	02/07/83
HANDS ON Thousand Yard Stare	07/03/92
HANDSWORTH REVOLUTION Steel Pulse	05/08/78
HANG ON IN THERE BABY Johnny Bristol	12/10/74
HANGIN' TOUGH New Kids On The Block	09/12/89
HANSIMANIA James Last	05/12/81
HANX Stiff Little Fingers	27/09/80
HAPPINESS Beloved	03/03/90
HAPPY Surface	07/03/87
HAPPY? Public Image Ltd	26/09/87
HAPPY BIRTHDAY Altered Images	26/09/81
HAPPY BIRTHDAY Altered Images	17/10/81
HAPPY BIRTHDAY Altered Images	16/01/82
HAPPY DAYS Various Artists	24/05/80
HAPPY FAMILIES Blancmange	23/10/82
HAPPY FAMILIES Blancmange	27/11/82
HAPPY FAMILIES Blancmange	21/05/83
HAPPY HEAD Might Lemon Drops	04/10/86
HAPPY HOUR Ted Hawkins	02/05/87
HAPPY IN HELL Christians	10/10/92
HAPPY NATION Ace Of Base	19/06/93
HAPPY TO BE Demis Roussos	01/05/76
HAPPY TO BE Demis Roussos	03/07/76
HAPPY TO BE Demis Roussos	25/09/76
HAPPY TOGETHER Odyssey	24/07/82
HARBOR LIGHTS Bruce Hornsby (RCA)	08/05/93
HARBOUR Jack Jones	16/02/74
HARBOUR Jack Jones	06/04/74
HARD Gang of Four	01/10/83
HARD AT PLAY Huey Lewis & the News	18/05/91
HARD NOSE THE HIGHWAY Van Morrison	04/08/73
HARD RAIN Bob Dylan	02/10/76
HAREM HOLIDAY Elvis Presley	08/01/66
HAREM HOLIDAY Elvis Presley	05/02/66
HARMONY OF CORRUPTION Napalm Death	15/09/90
HARMONY ROW Jack Bruce	07/08/71
HARVEST Neil Young	26/02/72
HARVEST Neil Young	19/08/72
HARVEST Neil Young	23/09/72
HARVEST Neil Young	07/04/73
HARVEST MOON Neil Young	14/11/92
HARVEST MOON Neil Young	06/03/93
HASTEN DOWN THE WIND Linda Ronstadt	11/09/76
HATFUL OF HOLLOW Smiths	24/11/84
HATS Blue Nile (Linn)	21/10/89
HATS OFF TO DEL SHANNON Del Shannon	27/04/63
HATS OFF TO DEL SHANNON Del Shannon	01/06/63
HATS OFF TO DEL SHANNON Del Shannon	15/06/63
HAVE A GOOD FOREVER Cool Notes	09/11/85
HAVE I TOLD YOU LATELY THAT I LOVE YOU	
Jim Reeves	10/04/65
HAVE YOU EVER BEEN IN LOVE Leo Sayer	19/11/83
HAWAIIAN PARADISE/CHRISTMAS	
Woot Steenhuis	02/01/82
HE WHO DARES WINS Theatre of Hate	28/03/81
HE WHO DARES WINS Theatre of Hate	18/04/81
HE'LL HAVE TO GO Jim Reeves	29/08/64
HE'S THE DJ, I'M THE RAPPER DJ Jazzy Jeff & the	
Fresh Prince	28/05/88
HEAD OVER HEELS Cocteau Twins	05/11/83
HEAD OVER HEELS Cocteau Twins	14/01/84
HEAD OVER HEELS Cocteau Twins	12/05/84
HEAD OVER HEELS - TELEVISION SOUNDTRACK	
Various Artists	20/02/93
HEAD OVER HEELS - TELEVISION SOUNDTRACK	
Various Artists	13/03/93
HEADED FOR THE FUTURE Neil Diamond	31/05/86
HEADED FOR THE FUTURE Niel Diamond	28/06/86
HEADFIRST Uriah Heep	18/06/83
HEADHUNTER Krokus	23/04/83
HEADLESS CROSS Black Sabbath	29/04/89
HEADLINE HITS Various Artists	17/09/83
HEADLINES Midnight Star	05/07/86
HEADLINES AND DEADLINES - THE HITS OF A-HA	
A-ha	16/11/91
HEADQUARTERS Monkees	08/07/67
HEADSTONE – BEST OF UFO UFO	03/09/83
HEAR MY SONG (THE BEST OF JOSEF LOCKE)	
Josef Locke	11/04/92
HEAR 'N' AID Various Artists	21/06/86
HEARSAY Alexander O'Neal	08/08/87
HEARSAY Alexander O'Neal	07/11/87
HEARSAY Alexander O'Neal	21/11/87
HEARSAY Alexander O'Neal	23/07/88
HEARSAY Alexander O'Neal	26/11/88
HEARSAY Alexander O'Neal	14/01/89
HEARSAY Alexander O'Neal	11/02/89
HEART Heart	02/11/85
HEART Heart	17/05/86
HEART Heart	16/04/88
HEART Heart	18/06/88
HEART AND SOUL Barry White	04/01/86
HEART AND SOUL - 18 CLASSIC SOUL CUTS	
Various Artists	19/08/89
HEART AND SOUL - THE VERY BEST OF T'PAU	
T'Pau	27/02/93
HEART IN MOTION Amy Grant	22/06/91
HEART IN MOTION Amy Grant	17/08/91
HEART LIKE A SKY Spandau Ballet	30/09/89
HEART OF STONE Cher	07/10/89
HEART OF STONE Cher	27/01/90
HEART OF STONE Cher	25/08/90
HEART OF STONE Cher	18/05/91
HEART OF STONE Cher	17/08/91
HEART OF STONE Cher	31/08/91
HEART OVER MIND Jennifer Rush	25/04/87
HEART & SOUL III - HEART FULL OF SOUL	
Various Artists	04/08/90
HEART STRINGS Foster & Allen	21/11/92
HEART STRINGS Foster & Allen	19/12/92
HEART TO HEART Various Artists	19/04/86
HEARTBEAT CITY Cars	13/10/84
HEARTBEAT CITY Cars	09/02/85

MOONMADNESS Camel	24/04/76
MOONTAN Golden Earring	09/02/74
MORE ABBA GOLD - MORE ABBA HITS	
Abba	05/06/93
MORE BOB DYLAN GREATEST HITS	
Bob Dylan	08/01/72
MORE CHUCK BERRY Chuck Berry	06/06/64
MORE DIRTY DANCING Various Artists	14/05/88
MORE GREAT SONG HITS Bachelors	18/09/65
MORE GREAT SONG HITS Bachelors	23/10/65
MORE OF THE HARD STUFF Dubliners	07/10/67
MORE OF THE MONKEES Monkees	15/04/67
MORE SONGS ABOUT BUILDINGS AND FOOD	
Talking Heads	05/08/78
MORE SPECIALS Specials	11/10/80
MORE SPECIALS Specials	15/11/80
MORE THAN FRIENDS Jonathan Butler	04/02/89
MORE TRINI LOPEZ AT PJ'S Trini Lopez	21/03/64
MORE UNCHARTERED HEIGHTS OF DISGRACE	
Dogs D'Amour	15/05/93
MORNING DANCE Spiro Gyra	21/07/79
MOROCCAN ROLL Brand X	28/05/77
MORRISON HOTEL Doors	09/05/70
MOSAIQUE Gipsy Kings	09/12/89
MOST OF THE ANIMALS Animals	07/05/66
MOTHER FIST AND HER FIVE DAUGHTERS	
Marc Almond	25/04/87
MOTHER'S HEAVEN Texas	05/10/91
MOTORVATIN' Chuck Berry	05/02/77
MOTOWN CHARTBUSTERS Various Artists	20/12/86
MOTOWN CHARTBUSTERS VOL 3	
Various Artists	25/10/69
MOTOWN CHARTBUSTERS VOL 3	
Various Artists	01/08/70
MOTOWN CHARTBUSTERS VOL 3	
Various Artists	26/09/70
MOTOWN CHARTBUSTERS VOL 4	
Various Artists	17/10/70
MOTOWN CHARTBUSTERS VOL 5	
Various Artists	10/04/71
MOTOWN CHARTBUSTERS VOL 6	
Various Artists	16/10/71
MOTOWN CHARTBUSTERS VOL 6	
Various Artists	08/04/72
MOTOWN CHARTBUSTERS VOL 7	
Various Artists	02/12/72
MOTOWN CHARTBUSTERS VOL 7	
Various Artists	17/02/73
MOTOWN CHARTBUSTERS VOL 7	
Various Artists	03/03/73
MOTOWN CHARTBUSTERS VOL 8	
Various Artists	10/11/73
MOTOWN CHARTBUSTERS VOL 8	
Various Artists	22/12/73
MOTOWN CHARTBUSTERS VOL 9	
Various Artists	19/10/74
MOTOWN CHARTBUSTERS VOL 9	
Various Artists	23/11/74
MOTOWN CHARTBUSTERS VOL 9	
Various Artists	11/01/75
MOTOWN CHARTBUSTERS VOL 9	
Various Artists	25/01/75
MOTOWN DANCE PARTY Various Artists	28/05/88
MOTOWN GOLD Various Artists	22/11/75
MOTOWN GOLD Various Artists	17/01/76
MOTOWN GOLD Various Artists	31/01/76
MOTOWN HEARTBREAKERS Various Artists	28/10/89
MOTOWN HEARTBREAKERS Various Artists	18/11/89
MOTOWN IN MOTION Various Artists	29/10/88
MOTOWN'S GREATEST HITS Diana Ross	07/03/92
MOTOWN'S GREATEST HITS Temptations	18/04/92
MOTT Mott the Hoople	04/08/73
MOTT Mott the Hoople	18/08/73
MOUNTING EXCITEMENT Various Artists	04/10/80
MOVE Move	06/04/68
MOVE CLOSER Phyllis Nelson	04/05/85
MOVE CLOSER Various Artists	21/03/87
MOVE TO THIS Cathy Dennis	10/08/91
MOVE TO THIS Cathy Dennis	19/10/91
MOVE TO THIS Cathy Dennis	14/12/91
MOVE TO THIS Cathy Dennis	22/02/92
MOVE YOUR SKIN And Why Not	10/03/90
MOVEMENT New Order	05/12/81
MOVEMENT New Order	19/12/81

MOVIN' Jennifer Rush	10/05/86
MOVING PICTURES Rush	21/02/81
MOVING TARGETS Penetration	04/11/78
MOVING WAVES Focus	13/01/73
MR BAD GUY Freddie Mercury	11/05/85
MR BAD GUY Freddie Mercury	03/08/85
MR FANTASY Traffic	06/01/68
MR HEARTBREAK Laurie Anderson	17/03/84
MR. LUCKY John Lee Hooker	21/09/91
MR TAMBOURINE MAN Byrds	21/08/65
MR UNIVERSE Gillan	03/11/79
MR WONDERFUL Fleetwood Mac	31/08/68
MRS ARDIN'S KID Mike Harding	13/09/75
MRS ARDIN'S KID Mike Harding	27/09/75
MTV UNPLUGGED (EP) Mariah Carey	18/07/92
MUD ROCK Mud	28/09/74
MUD ROCK Mud	23/11/74
MUD ROCK Mud	08/03/75
MUD ROCK II Mud	19/07/75
MUD SLIDE SLIM James Taylor	22/05/71
MUD'S GREATEST HITS Mud	08/11/75
MUDDY WATERS BLUES - A TRIBUTE TO MUDDY	
WATERS Paul Rodgers	03/07/93
MUMMER XTC	10/09/83
MUNGO JERRY Mungo Jerry	22/08/70
MUSCLE OF LOVE Alice Cooper	19/01/74
MUSIC Carole King	01/01/72
MUSIC EXPLOSION Various Artists	23/11/74
MUSIC EXPLOSION Various Artists	01/03/75
MUSIC EXPRESS Various Artists	24/01/76
MUSIC FOR THE MASSES Depeche Mode	10/10/87
MUSIC FROM GRAFFITI BRIDGE Prince	01/09/90
MUSIC FROM MIAMI VICE Various Artists	02/11/85
MUSIC FROM THE FILM CAL Mark Knopfler	27/10/84
MUSIC FROM THE ITV SERIES INSPECTOR	
MORSE, VOL. 3 Barrington Pheloung	23/01/93
MUSIC FROM THE ITV SERIES INSPECTOR MORSE	
VOLUME 2 Barrington Pheloung	14/03/92
MUSIC FROM THE SINGING DETECTIVE	
Various Artists	13/12/86
MUSIC FROM THE SINGING DETECTIVE	
Various Artists	03/01/87
MUSIC FROM TWIN PEAKS	
Angelo Badalamenti	01/12/90
MUSIC FROM TWIN PEAKS	
Angelo Badalamenti	19/01/91
MUSIC FROM TWIN PEAKS	
Angelo Badalamenti	09/03/91
MUSIC MAGIC Rose Royce	20/10/84
MUSIC OF AMERICA Various Artists	03/07/76
MUSIC POWER Various Artists	07/06/75
MUSICAL MADNESS Mantronix	20/12/86
MUSICAL MADNESS Mantronix	24/01/87
MUSICAL MADNESS Mantronix	15/08/87
MUSTN'T GRUMBLE Chas & Dave	08/05/82
MUSTN'T GRUMBLE Chas & Dave	31/07/82
MUTINY David Essex	22/10/83
MY AIM IS TRUE Elvis Costello	20/08/77
MY BABY JUST CARES FOR ME	
Nina Simone	28/11/87
MY CHERIE AMOUR Stevie Wonder	20/12/69
MY CHERIE AMOUR Stevie Wonder	10/01/70
MY CLASSIC COLLECTION	
Richard Clayderman	08/12/90
MY FAIR LADY Soundtrack	18/09/65
MY FAIR LADY Soundtrack	20/11/65
MY FAIR LADY Soundtrack	25/12/65
MY FAIR LADY Soundtrack	15/01/66
MY FAIR LADY Kiri Te Kanawa	28/11/87
MY GENERATION Who	18/12/65
MY GENERATION Who	01/11/80
MY GIFT TO YOU Alexander O'Neal	17/12/88
MY LIFE IN THE BUSH OF GHOSTS	
Brian Eno & David Byrne	21/03/81
MY LIFE IN THE BUSH OF GHOSTS	
Brian Eno & David Byrne	04/04/81
MY MERRY GO ROUND Johnny Nash	28/07/73
MY NAME IS BARBRA, TWO	
Barbra Streisand	22/01/66
MY NAME IS BARBRA, TWO	
Barbra Streisand	05/02/66
MY NAME IS BARBRA, TWO	
Barbra Streisand	02/04/66
MY NATION UNDERGROUND Julian Cope	29/10/88

MY WAY Frank Sinatra	07/06/69
MY WAY Frank Sinatra	20/02/71
MYSTERIO Ian McCulloch	21/03/92
MYSTERY Hot Chocolate	25/09/82
MYSTERY Rah Band	13/04/85
MYSTERY GIRL Roy Orbison	11/02/89
NAH POO THE ART OF BLUFF Wah!	18/07/81
NAIL Scraping Foetus off the Wheel	07/12/85
NAJEE'S THEME Najee	07/03/87
NAJEE'S THEME Najee	21/03/87
NAKED Kissing the Pink	04/06/83
NAKED Talking Heads	26/03/88
NANCY & LEE Nancy Sinatra & Lee Hazelwood	
	06/11/71
NARADA Narada Michael Walden	14/05/88
NASHVILLE SKYLINE Bob Dylan	10/05/69
NASHVILLE SKYLINE Bob Dylan	13/09/69
NASTY, NASTY Black 'n' Blue	18/10/86
NAT 'KING' COLE SINGS, THE GEORGE SHEARING	
QUINTET PLAYS Nat 'King' Cole & George	
Shearing	27/10/62
NAT 'KING' COLE SINGS, THE GEORGE SHEARING	
QUINTET PLAYS	
Nat 'King' Cole & George Shearing	10/11/62
NAT 'KING' COLE'S 20 GOLDEN GREATS	
Nat 'King' Cole	01/04/78
NAT 'KING' COLE'S 20 GOLDEN GREATS	
Nat 'King' Cole	15/07/78
NAT 'KING' COLE'S 20 GOLDEN GREATS	
Nat 'King' Cole	23/12/78
NATIVE TONGUE Poison	06/03/93
NATURAL HIGH Commodores	17/06/78
NATURAL HIGH Commodores	29/07/78
NEBRASKA Bruce Springsteen	02/10/82
NECK AND NECK	
Chet Atkins & Mark Knopfler	24/11/90
NECK AND NECK	
Chet Atkins & Mark Knopfler	22/12/90
NECK AND NECK	
Chet Atkins & Mark Knopfler	19/01/91
NEED FOR NOT Levitation	16/05/92
NEGOTIATIONS AND LOVE SONGS 1971-1986	
Paul Simon	05/11/88
NEIL DIAMOND'S 12 GREATEST HITS	
Neil Diamond	25/01/75
NEIL DIAMOND'S 20 GOLDEN GREATS	
Neil Diamond	18/11/78
NEIL DIAMOND'S 20 GOLDEN GREATS	
Neil Diamond	31/03/79
NEIL DIAMOND'S12 GREATEST HITS	
Neil Diamond	06/07/74
NEIL REID Neil Reid	05/02/72
NEIL REID Neil Reid	29/04/72
NEITHER FISH NOR FLESH	
Terence Trent D'Arby	04/11/89
NEITHER MOSCOW NOR WASHINGTON	
Redskins	22/03/86
NENA Nena	24/03/84
NEVER A DULL MOMENT Rod Stewart	29/07/72
NEVER FELT SO GOOD James Ingram	06/09/86
NEVER FOR EVER Kate Bush	20/09/80
NEVER LET ME DOWN David Bowie	02/05/87
NEVER LET ME DOWN David Bowie	06/06/87
NEVER LET ME DOWN David Bowie	20/06/87
NEVER LET ME GO Luther Vandross	12/06/93
NEVER LOVED ELVIS Wonder Stuff	08/06/91
NEVER LOVED ELVIS Wonder Stuff	22/02/92
NEVER MIND THE BOLLOCKS HERE'S THE SEX	
PISTOLS Sex Pistols	05/11/77
NEVER MIND THE BOLLOCKS HERE'S THE SEX	
PISTOLS Sex Pistols	18/03/78
NEVER MIND THE BOLLOCKS HERE'S THE SEX	
PISTOLS Sex Pistols	14/07/79
NEVER NEVER LAND Annihilator	11/08/90
NEVER NEVER NEVER Shirley Bassey	26/05/73
NEVER NEVER NEVER Shirley Bassey	09/06/73
NEVER SAY DIE Black Sabbath	14/10/78
NEVER TOO LATE Status Quo	28/03/81
NEVER TOO MUCH Luther Vandross	05/09/87
NEVERMIND Nirvana	05/10/91
NEVERMIND Nirvana	30/11/91
NEW AGE OF ATLANTIC Various Artists	01/04/72
NEW AGE OF ATLANTIC Various Artists	15/04/72

THE CLASSICAL EXPERIENCE	
Various Artists	29/10/88
THE CLASSICAL EXPERIENCE	
Various Artists	10/12/88
THE COLLECTION Dionne Warwick	28/05/83
THE COLLECTION Gladys Knight & the Pips	11/02/84
THE COLLECTION Ultravox	10/11/84
THE COLLECTION Earth Wind & Fire	10/05/86
THE COLLECTION Barry White	09/07/88
THE COLLECTION Barry White	23/02/91
THE COLLECTION Barry White	23/03/91
THE COLLECTION Mary Black	31/10/92
THE COLLECTION 1977-1982 Stranglers	25/09/82
THE COLLECTION – 20 GREATEST HITS Frankie	
Valli & the Four Seasons	18/06/88
THE COLOUR OF SPRING Talk Talk	01/03/86
THE COLOUR OF SPRING Talk Talk	07/06/86
THE COMFORT ZONE Vanessa Williams	25/04/92
THE COMFORTS OF MADNESS Pale Saints	24/02/90
THE COMMITMENTS Commitments	02/11/91
THE COMMITMENTS VOL.2 Commitments	25/04/92
THE COMPLEAT TOM PAXTON Tom Paxton	01/05/71
THE COMPLETE GLEN CAMPBELL	
Glen Campbell	29/07/89
THE COMPLETE GLEN CAMPBELL	
Glen Campbell	12/08/89
THE COMPLETE MIKE OLDFIELD	
Mike Oldfield	09/11/85
THE COMPLETE MIKE OLDFIELD	
Mike Oldfield	11/01/86
THE COMPLETE PICTURE - THE VERY BEST OF	
DEBORAH HARRY AND BLONDIE	
Deborah Harry and Blondie	16/03/91
THE COMPLETE TOM JONES Tom Jones	27/06/92
THE CONCERT IN CENTRAL PARK	
Simon & Garfunkel	03/04/82
THE CONCERT IN CENTRAL PARK	
Simon & Garfunkel	10/07/82
THE CONCERT IN CENTRAL PARK	
Simon & Garfunkel	24/07/82
THE CONCERT IN THE PARK - AUGUST 15TH 1991	
Paul Simon	23/11/91
THE CONCERT SINATRA Frank Sinatra	27/07/63
THE CONCERTS IN CHINA Jean Michel Jarre	22/05/82
THE CORRECT USE OF SOAP Magazine	17/05/80
THE COST OF LOVING Style Council	14/02/87
THE COUNTRY SIDE OF JIM REEVES	
Jim Reeves	18/10/69
THE COUNTRY SIDE OF JIM REEVES	
Jim Reeves	15/11/69
THE COVENANT, THE SWORD AND THE ARM OF	
THE LAW Cabaret Voltaire	02/11/85
THE CRACK Ruts	27/10/79
THE CREAM OF ERIC CLAPTON	
Eric Clapton & Cream	26/09/87
THE CREAM OF ERIC CLAPTON	
Eric Clapton & Cream	04/02/89
THE CREAM OF ERIC CLAPTON	
Eric Clapton & Cream	10/02/90
THE CRIMSON IDOL W.A.S.P.	20/06/92
THE CROSSING Big Country	06/08/83
THE CROSSING Big Country	21/01/84
THE CROSSING Big Country	08/09/84
THE CRYSTAL GAYLE SINGLES ALBUM	
Crystal Gayle	22/03/80
THE DANCE CHART Various Artists	28/03/87
THE DANCE HITS ALBUM Various Artists	22/02/86
THE DARK SIDE OF THE MOON - 20TH	
ANNIVERSARY Pink Floyd	20/03/93
THE DEED IS DONE Molly Hatchet	02/02/85
THE DEFINITIVE JIM REEVES Jim Reeves	05/09/92
THE DEFINITIVE PATSY CLINE Patsy Cline	05/09/92
THE DEFINITIVE SIMON AND GARFUNKEL	
Simon & Garfunkel	30/11/91
THE DEFINITIVE SIMON AND GARFUNKEL	
Simon & Garfunkel	11/04/92
THE DOLLAR ALBUM Dollar	06/11/82
THE DOORS Doors	04/05/91
THE DOORS - SOUNDTRACK Doors	06/04/91
THE DREAM ACADEMY Dream Academy	19/10/85
THE DREAM OF THE BLUE TURTLES Sting	29/06/85
THE DREAM OF THE BLUE TURTLES Sting	11/01/86
THE DREAM OF THE BLUE TURTLES Sting	28/06/86
THE DREAMING Kate Bush	25/09/82

THE DRIFTERS' GREATEST HITS Drifters	24/06/72
THE DRIFTERS' GREATEST HITS Drifters	22/07/72
THE DRUM IS EVERYTHING Carmel	24/03/84
THE DUDE Quincy Jones	09/05/81
THE DUDE Quincy Jones	30/05/81
THE DUDE Quincy Jones	20/06/81
THE DUDE Quincy Jones	11/07/81
THE EAGLE HAS LANDED Saxon	29/05/82
THE EAGLE HAS LANDED Saxon	10/07/82
THE EARTHQUAKE ALBUM - ROCK AID ARMENIA	
Various Artists	19/05/90
THE EDDIE COCHRAN SINGLES ALBUM	
Eddie Cochran	22/09/79
THE EDWARD WOODWARD ALBUM	
Edward Woodward	26/08/72
THE EDWARD WOODWARD ALBUM	
Edward Woodward	16/09/72
THE ELEVENTH HOUR Magnum	28/05/83
THE ELVIS PRESLEY SUN COLLECTION	
Elvis Presley	13/09/75
THE ELVIS PRESLEY SUN COLLECTION	
Elvis Presley	17/09/77
THE EMOTIONAL HOOLIGAN	
Gary Clail On-U Sound System	04/05/91
THE END OF THE INNOCENCE Don Henley	29/07/89
THE ENGELBERT HUMPERDINCK COLLECTION	
Engelbert Humperdinck	18/04/87
THE EPIC YEARS Shaky	07/11/92
THE ESSENTIAL DOMINGO	
Placido Domingo	24/06/89
THE ESSENTIAL JEAN MICHEL JARRE	
Jean Michel Jarre	19/11/83
THE ESSENTIAL JEAN MICHEL JARRE	
Jean Michel Jarre	24/12/83
THE ESSENTIAL JEAN MICHEL JARRE	
Jean Michel Jarre	19/01/85
THE ESSENTIAL JOSE CARRERAS	
José Carreras	02/03/91
THE ESSENTIAL KIRI Kiri Te Kanawa	29/02/92
THE ESSENTIAL PAVAROTTI	
Luciano Pavarotti	17/03/90
THE ESSENTIAL PAVAROTTI	
Luciano Pavarotti	19/05/90
THE ESSENTIAL PAVAROTTI	
Luciano Pavarotti	22/12/90
THE ESSENTIAL PAVAROTTI	
Luciano Pavarotti	10/08/91
THE ESSENTIALKARAJAN	
Herbert Von Karajan	23/04/88
THE EVERLY BROTHERS Everly Brothers	10/11/84
THE EVERLY BROTHERS' ORIGINAL GREATEST	
HITS Everly Brothers	26/09/70
THE EVERLY BROTHERS' ORIGINAL GREATEST	
HITS Everly Brothers	05/12/70
THE EXTREMIST Joe Satriani	15/08/92
THE F C'S TREAT US LIKE PRICKS	
A Flux of Pink Indians	07/04/84
THE FINAL Wham!	19/07/86
THE FINAL Wham!	18/10/86
THE FINAL Wham!	22/11/86
THE FINAL Wham!	13/12/86
THE FINAL COUNTDOWN Europe	22/11/86
THE FINAL COUNTDOWN - THE VERY BEST OF	
SOFT METAL Various Artists	03/11/90
THE FINAL CUT Pink Floyd	02/04/83
THE FINAL FRONTIER Keel	24/05/86
THE FINE ART OF SURFACING	
Boomtown Rats	10/11/79
THE FINE ART OF SURFACING	
Boomtown Rats	26/01/80
THE FINE ART OF SURFACING	
Boomtown Rats	23/02/80
THE FINER THINGS IN LIFE Chuck Stanley	28/03/87
THE FINER THINGS IN LIFE Chuck Stanley	16/05/87
THE FIRM Firm	02/03/85
THE FIRST ALBUM Madonna	15/02/86
THE FIRST BORN IS DEAD	
Nick Cave & the Bad Seeds	15/06/85
THE FIRST OF A MILLION KISSES	
Fairground Attraction	28/05/88
THE FIRST OF A MILLION KISSES	
Fairground Attraction	30/07/88
THE FIRST OF A MILLION KISSES	
Fairground Attraction	25/02/89

THE FISH PEOPLE TAPES Alexei Sayle	24/03/84
THE FLAG Yello	10/12/88
THE FLAT EARTH Thomas Dolby	18/02/84
THE FLAT EARTH Thomas Dolby	05/05/84
THE FORCE BEHIND THE POWER	
Diana Ross	14/12/91
THE FORCE BEHIND THE POWER	
Diana Ross	18/07/92
THE FORCE BEHIND THE POWER	
Diana Ross	19/12/92
THE FORMER 12 YEAR-OLD GENIUS	
Coati Mundi	21/05/83
THE FOUR & ONLY SEEKERS Seekers	22/03/69
THE FOUR & ONLY SEEKERS Seekers	24/05/69
THE FOUR SEASONS STORY Four Seasons	20/03/76
THE FOUR SEASONS STORY Four Seasons	24/04/76
THE FOUR SIDES OF MELANIE Melanie	14/10/72
THE FOX Elton John	13/06/81
THE FREDDIE MERCURY ALBUM	
Freddie Mercury	28/11/92
THE FREE STORY Free	16/03/74
THE FREEWHEELIN' BOB DYLAN	
Bob Dylan	14/11/64
THE FREEWHEELIN' BOB DYLAN	
Bob Dylan	13/03/65
THE FREEWHEELIN' BOB DYLAN	
Bob Dylan	10/07/65
THE FREEWHEELIN' BOB DYLAN	
Bob Dylan	04/09/65
THE FRENZ EXPERIMENT Fall	12/03/88
THE FRIENDS OF MR CAIRO Jon & Vangelis	06/02/82
THE FUGITIVE Tony Banks	25/06/83
THE FUGITIVE KIND Swans Way	10/11/84
THE FURY Gary Numan	05/10/85
THE FUTURE Leonard Cohen	05/12/92
THE GAME Queen	19/07/80
THE GAME Queen	27/09/80
THE GARDEN John Foxx	03/10/81
THE GEORGE BENSON COLLECTION	
George Benson	21/11/81
THE GEORGE BENSON COLLECTION	
George Benson	16/01/82
THE GEORGE BENSON COLLECTION	
George Benson	13/02/82
THE GHOST OF CAIN New Model Army	11/10/86
THE GIFT Jam	20/03/82
THE GIFT Jam	12/06/82
THE GIFT Midge Ure	19/10/85
THE GLEN CAMPBELL ALBUM	
Glen Campbell	19/12/70
THE GLENN MILLER STORY Glenn Miller	17/01/70
THE GOLDEN SECTION John Foxx	08/10/83
THE GOLDEN YEARS OF THE EVERLY BROTHERS	
Everly Brothers	29/05/93
THE GOOD BOOK Melanie	29/05/71
THE GOOD BOOK Melanie	10/07/71
THE GOOD SON Nick Cave & the Bad Seeds	28/04/90
THE GOOD THE BAD AND THE LIVE (THE 6 1/2	
YEAR ANNIVERSARY 12" COLLECTION)	
Metallica	19/05/90
THE GOOD, THE BAD & THE UGLY	
Soundtrack	02/11/68
THE GOOD, THE BAD & THE UGLY	
Soundtrack	15/02/69
THE GRADUATE Soundtrack	16/11/68
THE GREAT RADIO CONTROVERSY Tesla	18/02/89
THE GREAT ROCK AND ROLL SWINDLE	
Soundtrack	21/06/80
THE GREAT ROCK & ROLL SWINDLE	
Sex Pistols	10/03/79
THE GREAT ROCK & ROLL SWINDLE	
Sex Pistols	28/07/79
THE GREATEST EVER ROCK 'N' ROLL MIX	
Various Artists	06/08/88
THE GREATEST HITS Thompson Twins	17/03/90
THE GREATEST HITS Salt 'n' Pepa	26/10/91
THE GREATEST HITS Salt 'n' Pepa	15/02/92
THE GREATEST HITS Boney M	27/03/93
THE GREATEST HITS 1966-1992	
Neil Diamond	04/07/92
THE GREATEST HITS 1966-1992	
Neil Diamond	19/12/92

445

In the Artist Index records are listed once, at their first date of chart entry. For the full list of chart entry dates for each record see the Title Index. Please note that the Artist Index is arranged in order of the first name of the artist, whether a person or a group. To find Elvis Presley, for example, look under 'E'. Records by 'Various Artists', and Cast and Soundtrack albums are not included in the Artist Index. Artist's names that begin with numerals are placed at the end of the index.

Proclaimers THIS IS THE STORY	16/05/87
Proclaimers SUNSHINE ON LEITH	24/09/88
Prodigy THE PRODIGY EXPERIENCE	10/10/92
Project D THE SYNTHESIZER ALBUM	10/03/90
Propaganda A SECRET WISH	13/07/85
Propaganda 1234	16/06/90
Psychedelic Furs PSYCHEDELIC FURS	29/03/80
Psychedelic Furs TALK TALK TALK	30/05/81
Psychedelic Furs MIDNIGHT TO MIDNIGHT	14/02/87
Psychedelic Furs ALL OF THIS AND NOTHING	13/08/88
Psychedlic Furs FOREVER NOW	09/10/82
Psychedlic Furs MIRROR MOVES	19/05/84
Public Enemy PUBLIC ENEMY	23/05/87
Public Enemy IT TAKES A NATION OF MILLIONS TO HOLD US BACK	30/07/88
Public Enemy FEAR OF A BLACK PLANET	28/04/90
Public Enemy APOCALYPSE '91 ... THE ENEMY STRIKES BLACK	19/10/91
Public Enemy GREATEST MISSES	03/10/92
Public Image Ltd PUBLIC IMAGE	06/01/79
Public Image Ltd METAL BOX	15/12/79
Public Image Ltd FLOWERS OF ROMANCE	18/04/81
Public Image Ltd LIVE IN TOKYO	08/10/83
Public Image Ltd THIS IS WHAT YOU WANT	21/07/84
Public Image Ltd ALBUM/CASSETTE	15/02/86
Public Image Ltd HAPPY?	26/09/87
Public Image Ltd 9	10/06/89
Public Image Ltd THE GREATEST HITS SO FAR	10/11/90
Public Image Ltd THAT WHAT IS NOT	07/03/92
Queen QUEEN II	30/03/74
Queen SHEER HEART ATTACK	16/11/74
Queen A NIGHT AT THE OPERA	06/12/75
Queen A DAY AT THE RACES	18/12/76
Queen NEWS OF THE WORLD	05/11/77
Queen JAZZ	18/11/78
Queen LIVE KILLERS	14/07/79
Queen THE GAME	19/07/80
Queen FLASH GORDON	03/01/81
Queen QUEEN'S GREATEST HITS	14/11/81
Queen HOT SPACE	22/05/82
Queen THE WORKS	10/03/84
Queen A KIND OF MAGIC	14/06/86
Queen LIVE MAGIC	13/12/86
Queen THE MIRACLE	03/06/89
Queen QUEEN AT THE BEEB	16/12/89
Queen INNUENDO	16/02/91
Queen GREATEST HITS II	09/11/91
Queen LIVE AT WEMBLEY '86	06/06/92
Queensryche RAGE FOR ORDER	02/08/86
Queensryche OPERATION MINDCRIME	04/06/88
Queensryche EMPIRE	22/09/90
Quiet Riot CONDITION CRITICAL	11/08/84
Quiet Riot QR3	16/08/86
Quincy Jones THE DUDE	09/05/81
Quincy Jones BACK ON THE BLOCK	27/01/90
Quireboys A BIT OF WHAT YOU FANCY	10/02/90
Quireboys BITTER SWEET & TWISTED	27/03/93
R.E.M. GREEN	04/02/89
R.E.M OUT OF TIME	23/03/91
R.E.M. THE BEST OF R.E.M.	12/10/91
R.E.M. AUTOMATIC FOR THE PEOPLE	10/10/92
Racing Cars DOWNTOWN TONIGHT	26/02/77
Radiohead PABLO HONEY	06/03/93
Rage Against The Machine RAGE AGAINST THE MACHINE	13/03/93
Rah Band MYSTERY	13/04/85
Railway Children REUNION WILDERNESS	11/04/87
Rain Parade BEYOND THE SUNSET	06/07/85
Rain Tree Crow RAIN TREE CROW	20/04/91
Rainbow LONG LIVE ROCK & ROLL	29/04/78
Rainbow DOWN TO EARTH	25/08/79
Rainbow DIFFICULT TO CURE	28/02/81
Rainbow BEST OF RAINBOW	21/11/81
Rainbow STRAIGHT BETWEEN THE EYES	01/05/82
Rainbow BENT OUT OF SHAPE	17/09/83
Rainbow FINAL VINYL	08/03/86
Ralph McTell STREETS	22/02/75
Ralph Tresvant RALPH TRESVANT	02/03/91
Ramones ROAD TO RUIN	07/10/78
Ramones END OF THE CENTURY	16/02/80
Ramones SUBTERRANEAN JUNGLE	30/04/83
Ramones TOO TOUGH TO DIE	02/02/85
Ramones ANIMAL BOY	31/05/86
Ramones HALFWAY TO SANITY	10/10/87

Randy Brown WELCOME TO MY ROOM	19/09/87
Randy Crawford NOW WE MAY BEGIN	20/09/80
Randy Crawford SECRET COMBINATION	06/06/81
Randy Crawford WINDSONG	19/06/82
Randy Crawford NIGHTLINE	29/10/83
Randy Crawford RANDY CRAWFORD'S GREATEST HITS	20/10/84
Randy Crawford ABSTRACT EMOTIONS	14/02/87
Randy Crawford THE LOVE SONGS	21/11/87
Randy Crawford THE VERY BEST OF RANDY CRAWFORD	27/03/93
Randy Travis OLD 8 X 10	06/08/88
Ratt INVASION OF YOUR PRIVACY	13/07/85
Ratt DANCE UNDERCOVER	25/10/86
Ray Charles MODERN SOUNDS IN COUNTRY AND WESTERN	28/07/62
Ray Charles MODERN SOUNDS IN COUNTRY AND WESTERN VOL 2	16/02/63
Ray Charles RAY CHARLES' GREATEST HITS	08/06/63
Ray Charles COLLECTION: RAY CHARLES	31/03/90
Ray Charles THE LIVING LEGEND	13/03/93
Ray Conniff 'S WONDERFUL 'S MARVELLOUS	15/09/62
Ray Conniff RAY CONNIFF HI-FI COMPANION	06/10/62
Ray Conniff RAY CONNIFF, HIS ORCHESTRA, HIS CHORUS, HIS SINGERS, HIS SOUND	21/06/69
Ray Parker Jnr AFTER DARK	24/10/87
Ray Stevens MISTY	04/10/75
Ray Thomas FROM MIGHTY OAKS	16/08/75
Raymond Lefevre RAYMOND LEFEVRE	30/09/67
Real Thing BEST OF THE REAL THING	12/07/86
Rebel MC REBEL MUSIC	28/04/90
Rebel MC BLACK MEANING GOOD	20/07/91
Red Box THE CIRCLE AND THE SQUARE	06/12/86
Red Hot Chili Peppers BLOOD SUGAR SEX MAGIK	12/10/91
Red Hot Chili Peppers WHAT HITS!?	17/10/92
Red Lorry Yellow Lorry PAINT YOUR WAGON	29/03/86
Redhead Kingpin & the FBI A SHADE OF RED	16/09/89
Redskins NEITHER MOSCOW NOR WASHINGTON	22/03/86
Regina Belle ALL BY MYSELF	01/08/87
REM RECKONING	28/04/84
REM FABLES OF THE RECONSTRUCTION	29/06/85
REM LIFE'S RICH PAGEANT	06/09/86
REM DEAD LETTER OFFICE	23/05/87
REM DOCUMENT	26/09/87
REM EPONYMOUS	29/10/88
REM GREEN	19/11/88
Renee & Angela STREET CALLED DESIRE	07/09/85
REO Speedwagon HI INFIDELITY	09/05/81
REO Speedwagon GOOD TROUBLE	24/07/82
Replacements PLEASED TO MEET YOU	30/05/87
Revenge ONE TRUE PASSION	30/06/90
Rezillos CAN'T STAND THE REZILLOS	12/08/78
Rich Kids GHOSTS OF PRINCES IN TOWERS	07/10/78
Richard Chamberlain RICHARD CHAMBERLAIN SINGS	23/03/63
Richard Clayderman RICHARD CLAYDERMAN	18/12/82
Richard Clayderman THE MUSIC OF RICHARD CLAYDERMAN	15/10/83
Richard Clayderman THE MUSIC OF LOVE	01/12/84
Richard Clayderman THE CLASSIC TOUCH	21/12/85
Richard Clayderman HOLLYWOOD AND BROADWAY	10/01/87
Richard Clayderman SONGS OF LOVE	19/12/87
Richard Clayderman THE LOVE SONGS OF ANDREW LLOYD WEBBER	02/12/89
Richard Clayderman MY CLASSIC COLLECTION	08/12/90
Richard Clayderman THE VERY BEST OF RICHARD CLAYDERMAN	21/11/92
Richard Clayderman & James Last TOGETHER AT LAST	16/11/91
Richard Marx RICHARD MARX	16/04/88
Richard Marx REPEAT OFFENDER	09/09/89
Richard Marx RUSH STREET	20/06/92
Richard Thompson HAND OF KINDNESS	02/07/83
Richard Thompson DARING ADVENTURES	25/10/86
Richie Sambora STRANGER IN THIS TOWN	14/09/91
Rick Astley WHENEVER YOU NEED SOMEBODY	28/11/87
Rick Astley HOLD ME IN YOUR ARMS	10/12/88
Rick Astley FREE	02/03/91
Rick James REFLECTIONS	15/09/84

Rick Springfield LIVING IN OZ	18/02/84
Rick Wakeman THE SIX WIVES OF HENRY VIII	17/02/73
Rick Wakeman JOURNEY TO THE CENTRE OF THE EARTH	11/05/74
Rick Wakeman NO EARTHLY CONNECTION	24/04/76
Rick Wakeman WHITE ROCK	05/02/77
Rick Wakeman CRIMINAL RECORD	10/12/77
Rick Wakeman RHAPSODIES	16/06/79
Rick Wakeman & the English Rock Ensemble THE MYTHS AND LEGENDS OF KING ARTHUR AND THE KNIGHTS OF THE ROUND TABLE	05/04/75
Rickie Lee Jones RICKIE LEE JONES	30/06/79
Rickie Lee Jones PIRATES	15/08/81
Rickie Lee Jones GIRL AT HER VOLCANO	02/07/83
Rickie Lee Jones THE MAGAZINE	13/10/84
Rickie Lee Jones FLYING COWBOYS	07/10/89
Ride NOWHERE	27/10/90
Ride GOING BLANK AGAIN	21/03/92
Right Said Fred UP	28/03/92
Righteous Brothers UNCHAINED MELODY - THE VERY BEST OF THE RIGHTEOUS BROTHERS	01/12/90
Ringo Starr SENTIMENTAL JOURNEY	25/04/70
Ringo Starr RINGO	01/12/73
Ringo Starr GOODNIGHT VIENNA	14/12/74
Rita Coolidge ANYTIME, ANYWHERE	22/04/78
Rita Coolidge LOVE ME AGAIN	19/08/78
Rita Coolidge VERY BEST OF RITA COOLIDGE	21/03/81
Rita MacNeil REASON TO BELIEVE	01/12/90
Ritchie Blackmore RAINBOW	06/09/75
Ritchie Blackmore RAINBOW RISING	19/06/76
Ritchie Blackmore's Rainbow ON STAGE	30/07/77
River City People SAY SOMETHING GOOD	25/08/90
River City People THIS IS THE WORLD	02/11/91
River Detectives SATURDAY NIGHT SUNDAY MORNING	30/09/89
Roachford ROACHFORD	23/07/88
Roachford GET READY!	18/05/91
Robbie Robertson ROBBIE ROBERTSON	21/11/87
Robbie Robertson STORYVILLE	12/10/91
Robert Cray Band BAD INFLUENCE	04/05/85
Robert Cray Band FALSE ACCUSATIONS	19/10/85
Robert Cray Band WHO'S BEEN TALKING	11/10/86
Robert Cray Band STRONG PERSUADER	22/11/86
Robert Cray Band DON'T BE AFRAID OF THE DARK	03/09/88
Robert Cray Band MIDNIGHT STROLL	29/09/90
Robert Cray Band I WAS WARNED	12/09/92
Robert Fripp LEAGUE OF GENTLEMEN	04/04/81
Robert Palmer CLUES	13/09/80
Robert Palmer MAYBE IT'S LIVE	10/04/82
Robert Palmer PRIDE	23/04/83
Robert Palmer RIPTIDE	23/11/85
Robert Palmer HEAVY NOVA	09/07/88
Robert Palmer "ADDICTIONS" VOLUME 1	11/11/89
Robert Palmer DON'T EXPLAIN	17/11/90
Robert Palmer "ADDICTIONS" VOLUME 2	04/04/92
Robert Palmer RIDIN' HIGH	31/10/92
Robert Plant PICTURES AT ELEVEN	17/07/82
Robert Plant PRINCIPLE OF MOMENTS	30/07/83
Robert Plant SHAKEN 'N' STIRRED	01/06/85
Robert Plant NOW AND ZEN	12/03/88
Robert Plant MANIC NIRVANA	31/03/90
Robert Plant FATE OF NATIONS	05/06/93
Roberta Flack ROBERTA FLACK'S GREATEST HITS	14/04/84
Roberta Flack & Donny Hathaway ROBERTA FLACK AND DONNY HATHAWAY	28/06/80
Roberto Mann GREAT WALTZES	16/12/67
Robin George DANGEROUS MUSIC	09/03/85
Robin Trower FOR EARTH BELOW	08/03/75
Robin Trower LIVE	20/03/76
Robyn Hitchcock GLOBE OF FROGS	27/02/88
Rock Machine I LOVE YOU	15/03/69
Rockwell SOMEBODY'S WATCHING ME	17/03/84
Rod Stewart EVERY PICTURE TELLS A STORY	24/07/71
Rod Stewart NEVER A DULL MOMENT	29/07/72
Rod Stewart SING IT AGAIN ROD	18/08/73
Rod Stewart SMILER	12/10/74
Rod Stewart ATLANTIC CROSSING	23/08/75
Rod Stewart A NIGHT ON THE TOWN	26/06/76
Rod Stewart BEST OF ROD STEWART	23/07/77
Rod Stewart FOOTLOOSE & FANCY FREE	12/11/77
Rod Stewart BLONDES HAVE MORE FUN	02/12/78

Rod Stewart ROD STEWART'S GREATEST HITS	
	17/11/79
Rod Stewart FOOLISH BEHAVIOUR	29/11/80
Rod Stewart TONIGHT I'M YOURS	21/11/81
Rod Stewart BODY WISHES	18/06/83
Rod Stewart CAMOUFLAGE	23/06/84
Rod Stewart EVERY BEAT OF MY HEART	05/07/86
Rod Stewart OUT OF ORDER	04/06/88
Rod Stewart THE BEST OF ROD STEWART	25/11/89
Rod Stewart VAGABOND HEART	06/04/91
Rod Stewart LEAD VOCALIST	06/03/93
Rod Stewart UNPLUGGED ... AND SEATED	05/06/93
Rod Stewart & the Faces OVERTURE AND BEGINNERS	
	19/01/74
Roger Daltrey DALTREY	19/05/73
Roger Daltrey RIDE A ROCK HORSE	02/08/75
Roger Daltrey McVICAR	27/09/80
Roger Daltrey UNDER A RAGING SUN	16/11/85
Roger McGuinn BACK FROM RIO	09/02/91
Roger Taylor FUN IN SPACE	18/04/81
Roger Taylor STRANGE FRONTIER	07/07/84
Roger Waters THE PROS AND CONS OF HITCH HIKING	
	12/05/84
Roger Waters RADIO K.A.O.S.	27/06/87
Roger Waters THE WALL - LIVE IN BERLIN	29/09/90
Roger Waters AMUSED TO DEATH	19/09/92
Roger Whittaker VERY BEST OF ROGER WHITTAKER	
	06/09/75
Roger Whittaker THE ROGER WHITTAKER ALBUM	
	11/04/81
Roger Whittaker ROGER WHITTAKER'S FINEST	
COLLECTION	30/05/87
Roger Whittaker HOME LOVIN' MAN	30/09/89
Rolling Stones THE ROLLING STONES	25/04/64
Rolling Stones THE ROLLING STONES NO 2	23/01/65
Rolling Stones OUT OF OUR HEADS	02/10/65
Rolling Stones AFTERMATH	23/04/66
Rolling Stones BIG HITS (HIGH TIDE AND GREEN	
GRASS)	12/11/66
Rolling Stones BETWEEN THE BUTTONS	28/01/67
Rolling Stones THEIR SATANIC MAJESTIES REQUEST	
	23/12/67
Rolling Stones BEGGARS BANQUET	14/12/68
Rolling Stones THROUGH THE PAST DARKLY (BIG	
HITS VOL 2)	20/09/69
Rolling Stones LET IT BLEED	13/12/69
Rolling Stones 'GET YOUR YA-YA'S OUT!'	12/09/70
Rolling Stones STONE AGE	13/03/71
Rolling Stones STICKY FINGERS	01/05/71
Rolling Stones GIMME SHELTER	25/09/71
Rolling Stones MILESTONES	11/03/72
Rolling Stones EXILE ON MAIN STREET	03/06/72
Rolling Stones GOATS HEAD SOUP	15/09/73
Rolling Stones IT'S ONLY ROCK 'N' ROLL	26/10/74
Rolling Stones MADE IN THE SHADE	05/07/75
Rolling Stones ROLLED GOLD	06/12/75
Rolling Stones BLACK AND BLUE	01/05/76
Rolling Stones LOVE YOU LIVE	01/10/77
Rolling Stones GET STONED	19/11/77
Rolling Stones SOME GIRLS	17/06/78
Rolling Stones EMOTIONAL RESCUE	05/07/80
Rolling Stones TATTOO YOU	12/09/81
Rolling Stones STILL LIFE (AMERICAN CONCERTS	
1981)	12/06/82
Rolling Stones THE STORY OF THE STONES	18/12/82
Rolling Stones UNDERCOVER	19/11/83
Rolling Stones REWIND 1971-1984	07/07/84
Rolling Stones DIRTY WORK	05/04/86
Rolling Stones STEEL WHEELS	23/09/89
Rolling Stones HOT ROCKS 1964-1971	07/07/90
Rolling Stones FLASHPOINT	20/04/91
Roman Holiday COOKIN' ON THE ROOF	29/10/83
Rondo Veneziano VENICE IN PERIL	07/04/84
Rory Gallagher LIVE IN EUROPE	27/05/72
Rory Gallagher BLUEPRINT	03/03/73
Rory Gallagher TATTOO	01/12/73
Rory Gallagher DEFENDER	15/08/87
Rose Marie ROSE MARIE SINGS JUST FOR YOU	
	04/05/85
Rose Marie SENTIMENTALLY YOURS	12/12/87
Rose Royce IN FULL BLOOM	24/09/77
Rose Royce ROSE ROYCE STRIKES AGAIN	07/10/78
Rose Royce ROSE ROYCE'S GREATEST HITS	15/03/80
Rose Royce MUSIC MAGIC	20/10/84

Rosie Vela ZAZU	31/01/87
Roxette LOOK SHARP!	18/08/90
Roxette JOYRIDE	13/04/91
Roxette TOURISM	12/09/92
Roxy Music ROXY MUSIC	05/08/72
Roxy Music FOR YOUR PLEASURE	31/03/73
Roxy Music STRANDED	24/11/73
Roxy Music COUNTRY LIFE	23/11/74
Roxy Music SIREN	01/11/75
Roxy Music VIVA!	24/07/76
Roxy Music ROXY MUSIC'S GREATEST HITS	26/11/77
Roxy Music MANIFESTO	31/03/79
Roxy Music FLESH AND BLOOD	07/06/80
Roxy Music AVALON	05/06/82
Roxy Music THE HIGH ROAD	26/03/83
Roxy Music THE ATLANTIC YEARS 1973-80	12/11/83
Roy Ayers IN THE DARK	15/12/84
Roy Ayers YOU MIGHT BE SURPRISED	02/11/85
Roy Ayers YOU SEND ME	26/03/88
Roy Harper & Jimmy Page WHATEVER HAPPENED TO	
JUGULA?	23/03/85
Roy Orbison OH, PRETTY WOMAN	05/12/64
Roy Orbison IN DREAMS	29/02/64
Roy Orbison THERE IS ONLY ONE ROY ORBISON	
	18/09/65
Roy Orbison THE CLASSIC ROY ORBISON	24/09/66
Roy Orbison BEST OF ROY ORBISON	17/01/76
Roy Orbison THE LEGENDARY ROY ORBISON	05/11/88
Roy Orbison MYSTERY GIRL	11/02/89
Roy Orbison BALLADS	17/11/90
Roy Orbison KING OF HEARTS	28/11/92
Roy Wood BOULDERS	25/08/73
Royal Philharmonic Orchestra	
SERIOUSLY ORCHESTRAL ...	19/10/91
Royal Philharmonic Orchestra & Mike Oldfield THE	
ORCHESTRAL TUBULAR BELLS	15/02/75
Rozalla EVERYBODY'S FREE	04/04/92
Ruby Turner WOMEN HOLD UP HALF THE SKY	
	15/10/86
Ruby Turner THE MOTOWN SONGBOOK	15/10/88
Rufus with Chaka Khan STOMPIN' AT THE SAVOY	
	28/04/84
Run DMC RAISING HELL	02/08/86
Run DMC TOUGHER THAN LEATHER	04/06/88
Runrig SEARCHLIGHT	14/10/89
Runrig THE BIG WHEEL	22/06/91
Runrig AMAZING THINGS	27/03/93
Rush FAREWELL TO KINGS	15/10/77
Rush HEMISPHERES	25/11/78
Rush PERMANENT WAVES	02/02/80
Rush MOVING PICTURES	21/02/81
Rush EXIT STAGE LEFT	07/11/81
Rush SIGNALS	18/09/82
Rush GRACE UNDER PRESSURE	28/04/84
Rush POWER WINDOWS	09/11/85
Rush HOLD YOUR FIRE	21/11/87
Rush A SHOW OF HANDS	28/01/89
Rush PRESTO	09/12/89
Rush ROLL THE BONES	14/09/91
Russ Abbott I LOVE A PARTY	30/11/85
Rutles THE RUTLES	15/04/78
Ruts THE CRACK	27/10/79
Ry Cooder THE SLIDE AREA	01/05/82
Ry Cooder PARIS, TEXAS - SOUNDTRACK	02/03/85
Ry Cooder GET RHYTHM	21/11/87
Ryuichi Sakamoto MERRY CHRISTMAS MR	
LAWRENCE	10/09/83
S'Express ORIGINAL SOUNDTRACK	01/04/89
Sacha Distel SACHA	09/05/70
Sad Cafe FACADES	05/04/80
Sade DIAMOND LIFE	28/07/84
Sade PROMISE	16/11/85
Sade STRONGER THAN PRIDE	14/05/88
Sade LOVE DELUXE	07/11/92
Saint Etienne FOXBASE ALPHA	02/11/91
Saint Etienne SO TOUGH	06/03/93
Salt 'N' Pepa A SALT WITH A DEADLY PEPA	06/08/88
Salt 'n' Pepa THE GREATEST HITS	26/10/91
Salvation Army BY REQUEST	14/01/78
Sam Brown STOP	25/02/89
Sam Brown APRIL MOON	14/04/90
Sam Cooke THE MAN AND HIS MUSIC	26/04/86
Samantha Fox TOUCH ME	26/07/86

Samantha Fox SAMANTHA FOX	08/08/87
Sammy Davis Jnr AT THE COCOANUT GROVE	25/05/63
Sammy Hagar LOUD AND CLEAR	29/03/80
Sammy Hagar SAMMY HAGAR	11/07/87
Sandie Shaw SANDIE	27/02/65
Santana ABRAXAS	28/11/70
Santana SANTANA 3	06/11/71
Santana CARAVANSERAI	18/11/72
Santana WELCOME	08/12/73
Santana SANTANA'S GREATEST HITS	21/09/74
Santana BARBOLETTA	07/12/74
Santana AMIGOS	17/04/76
Santana FESTIVAL	19/02/77
Santana MOONFLOWER	12/11/77
Santana INNER SECRETS	11/11/78
Santana MARATHON	03/11/79
Santana SHANGO	21/08/82
Santana BEYOND APPEARANCES	30/03/85
Santana & Buddy Miles SANTANA AND BUDDY MILES	
LIVE!	26/08/72
Sarah Brightman THE SONGS THAT GOT AWAY	
	24/06/89
Saw Doctors ALL THE WAY FROM TUAM	31/10/92
Saxon WHEELS OF STEEL	19/04/80
Saxon STRONG ARM OF THE LAW	22/11/80
Saxon DENIM AND LEATHER	03/10/81
Saxon THE EAGLE HAS LANDED	29/05/82
Saxon POWER AND THE GLORY	02/04/83
Saxon CRUSADER	11/02/84
Saxon INNOCENCE IS NO EXCUSE	14/09/85
Saxon ROCK THE NATION	27/09/86
Saxon DESTINY	16/04/88
Scars AUTHOR! AUTHOR!	18/04/81
Scorpions LOVEDRIVE	09/06/79
Scorpions ANIMAL MAGNETISM	17/05/80
Scorpions BLACKOUT	17/04/82
Scorpions LOVE AT FIRST STING	24/03/84
Scorpions WORLD WIDE LIVE	29/06/85
Scorpions SAVAGE AMUSEMENT	21/05/88
Scorpions CRAZY WORLD	02/11/91
Scotland World Cup Squad EASY EASY	01/06/74
Scott Walker SCOTT	09/09/67
Scott Walker SCOTT 2	13/04/68
Scott Walker SCOTT 3	05/04/69
Scott Walker SCOTT WALKER SINGS SONGS FROM	
HIS TV SERIES	05/07/69
Scott Walker CLIMATE OF HUNTER	07/04/84
Scott Walker & the Walker Brothers NO REGRETS - THE	
BEST OF SCOTT WALKER AND THE WALKER	
BROTHERS 1965-1976	25/01/92
Scraping Foetus off the Wheel NAIL	07/12/85
Screaming Blue Messiahs GUN SHY	24/05/86
Scritti Politti SONGS TO REMEMBER	18/09/82
Scritti Politti CUPID AND PSYCHE '85	22/06/85
Scritti Politti PROVISION	18/06/88
Seal SEAL	01/06/91
Searchers MEET THE SEARCHERS	10/08/63
Searchers SUGAR AND SPICE	16/11/63
Searchers IT'S THE SEARCHERS	30/05/64
Searchers SOUNDS LIKE THE SEARCHERS	10/04/65
Secret Affair GLORY BOYS	08/12/79
Seekers THE SEEKERS	12/06/65
Seekers A WORLD OF OUR OWN	03/07/65
Seekers COME THE DAY	19/11/66
Seekers THE SEEKERS AT THE TALK OF THE TOWN	
	14/09/68
Seekers BEST OF THE SEEKERS	16/11/68
Seekers THE FOUR AND ONLY SEEKERS	22/03/69
Selecter TOO MUCH PRESSURE	01/03/80
Sensational Alex Harvey Band THE IMPOSSIBLE DREAM	
	02/11/74
Sensational Alex Harvey Band TOMORROW BELONGS	
TO ME	17/05/75
Sensational Alex Harvey Band NEXT	30/08/75
Sensational Alex Harvey Band LIVE	20/09/75
Sensational Alex Harvey Band PENTHOUSE TAPES	
	10/04/76
Sensational Alex Harvey Band SAHB STORIES	07/08/76
Senseless Things EMPIRE OF THE SENSELESS	13/03/93
Sex Pistols NEVER MIND THE BOLLOCKS HERE'S	
THE SEX PISTOLS	05/11/77
Sex Pistols THE GREAT ROCK & ROLL SWINDLE	
	10/03/79
Sex Pistols SOME PRODUCT	04/08/79